Presented to

_____

By

_____

On

_____

_____

This Certifies that

_____

and

_____

were united in

Holy Matrimony

on _____ the _____

day of _____ , _____ A.D.

at _____

in accordance with the laws of _____

Dated this _____ the _____

day of _____ , _____ A.D.

Officiating _____

Witness _____

Witness _____

Births

Marriages

_____

_____

_____

_____

_____

_____

_____

_____

_____

_____

_____

_____

Deaths

Family Record

_____

_____

_____

_____

_____

_____

_____

_____

_____

_____

Church Record

_____

_____

_____

_____

_____

_____

_____

_____

_____

_____

_____

HARPER STUDY BIBLE

NEW AMERICAN STANDARD BIBLE

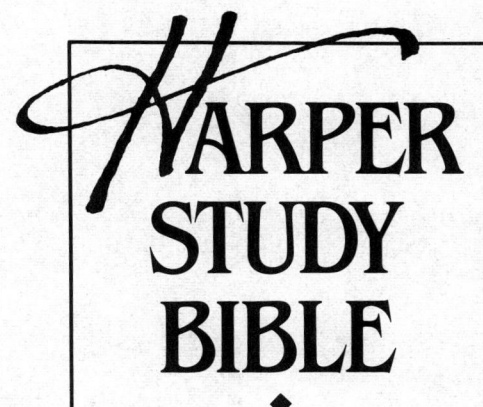

HARPER
STUDY
BIBLE

◆

NEW
AMERICAN
STANDARD
BIBLE

Introductions, Annotations, Topical Headings,
Marginal References, and Index

PREPARED AND EDITED BY

Harold Lindsell. Ph.D., D.D.

adapted to the New American Standard Bible

ZONDERVAN
BIBLE PUBLISHERS
GRAND RAPIDS, MICHIGAN 49506, U.S.A.

Scriptural Promise

"The grass withers, the flower fades,
but the word of our God stands forever."

Isaiah 40:8

Foreword

The New American Standard Bible has been produced with the conviction that the words of Scripture as originally penned in the Hebrew, Aramaic, and Greek were inspired by God. Since they are the eternal Word of God, the Holy Scriptures speak with fresh power to each generation, to give wisdom that leads to salvation, that men may serve Christ to the glory of God.

The Fourfold Aim

OF THE LOCKMAN FOUNDATION

1. These publications shall be true to the original Hebrew, Aramaic, and Greek.

2. They shall be grammatically correct.

3. They shall be understandable to the masses.

4. They shall give the Lord Jesus Christ His proper place, the place which the Word gives Him; therefore, no work will ever be personalized.

PREFACE

TO THE NEW AMERICAN STANDARD BIBLE

In the history of English Bible translations, the King James Version is the most prestigious. This time-honored version of 1611, itself a revision of the Bishops' Bible of 1568, became the basis for the English Revised Version appearing in 1881 (New Testament) and 1885 (Old Testament). The American counterpart of this last work was published in 1901 as the American Standard Version. Recognizing the values of the American Standard Version, the Lockman Foundation felt an urgency to update it by incorporating recent discoveries of Hebrew and Greek textual sources and by rendering it into more current English. Therefore, in 1959 a new translation project was launched, based on the ASV. The result is the New American Standard Bible.

The American Standard Version (1901) has been highly regarded for its scholarship and accuracy. A product of both British and American scholarship, it has frequently been used as a standard for other translations. It is still recognized as a valuable tool for study of the Scriptures. The New American Standard Bible has sought to preserve these and other lasting values of the ASV.

Furthermore, in the preparation of this work numerous other translations have been consulted along with the linguistic tools and literature of biblical scholarship. Decisions about English renderings were made by consensus of a team composed of educators and pastors. Subsequently, review and evaluation by other Hebrew and Greek scholars outside the Editorial Board were sought and carefully considered.

The Editorial Board has continued to function since publication of the complete Bible in 1971. Minor revisions and refinements, recommended over the last several years, are presented in this edition.

Principles of Translation

MODERN ENGLISH USAGE: The attempt has been made to render the grammar and terminology in contemporary English. When it was felt that the word-for-word literalness was unacceptable to the modern reader, a change was made in the direction of a more current English idiom. In the instances where this has been done, the more literal rendering has been indicated in the notes.

ALTERNATIVE READINGS: In addition to the more literal renderings, notations have been made to include alternate translations, readings of variant manuscripts and explanatory equivalents of the text. Only such notations have been used as have been felt justified in assisting the reader's comprehension of the terms used by the original author.

HEBREW TEXT: In the present translation the latest edition of Rudolf Kittel's BIBLIA HEBRAICA has been employed together with the most recent light from lexicography, cognate languages, and the Dead Sea Scrolls.

HEBREW TENSES: Consecution of tenses in Hebrew remains a puzzling factor in translation. The translators have been guided by the requirements of a literal translation, the sequence of tenses, and the immediate and broad contexts.

THE PROPER NAME OF GOD IN THE OLD TESTAMENT: In the Scriptures, the name of God is most significant and understandably so. It is inconceivable to think of spiritual matters without a proper designation for the Supreme Deity. Thus the most common name for the Deity is God, a translation of the original Elohim. One of the titles for God is Lord, a translation of Adonai. There is yet another name which is particularly assigned to God as His special or proper name, that is, the four letters YHWH (Exodus 3:14 and Isaiah 42:8). This name has not been pronounced by the Jews because of reverence for the great sacredness of the divine name. Therefore, it has been consistently translated LORD. The only exception to this translation of YHWH is when it occurs in immediate proximity to the word Lord, that is, Adonai. In that case it is regularly translated GOD in order to avoid confusion. It is known that for many years YHWH has been transliterated as Yahweh, however no complete certainty attaches to this pronunciation.

GREEK TEXT: Consideration was given to the latest available manuscripts with a view to determining the best Greek text. In most instances the 23rd edition of Eberhard Nestle's NOVUM TESTAMENTUM GRAECE was followed.

GREEK TENSES: A careful distinction has been made in the treatment of the Greek aorist tense (usually translated as the English past, "He did") and the Greek imperfect tense (rendered either as English past progressive, "He was doing"; or, if inceptive, as "He *began* to do" or "He started to do"; or else if customary past, as "He used to do"). "Began" is italicized if it renders an imperfect tense, in order to distinguish it from the Greek verb for "begin."

On the other hand, not all aorists have been rendered as English pasts ("He did"), for some of them are clearly to be rendered as English perfects ("He has done"), or even as past perfects ("He had done"), judging from the context in which they occur. Such aorists have been rendered as perfects or past perfects in this translation.

As for the distinction between aorist and present imperatives, the translators have usually rendered these imperatives in the customary manner, rather than attempting any such fine distinction as "Begin to do!" (for the aorist imperative), or, "Continually do!" (for the present imperative).

As for sequence of tenses, the translators took care to follow English rules rather than Greek in translating Greek presents, imperfects and aorists. Thus, where English says, "We knew that he was doing," Greek puts it, "We knew that he does"; similarly, "We knew that he had done" is the Greek, "We knew that he did." Likewise, the English, "When he had come, they met him," is represented in Greek by: "When he came, they met him." In all cases a consistent transfer has been made from the Greek tense in the subordinate clause to the appropriate tense in English.

In the rendering of negative questions introduced by the particle **mē** (which always expects the answer "No") the wording has been altered from a mere, "Will he not do this?" to a more accurate, "He will not do this, will he?"

Editorial Board,
THE LOCKMAN FOUNDATION

Explanation of General Format

FOOTNOTES are used only where the text especially requires them for clarification.

PARAGRAPHS are designated by bold face numbers or letters.

QUOTATION MARKS are used in the text in accordance with modern English usage.

"THOU," "THEE" AND "THY" are not used in this translation except in the language of prayer when addressing Deity.

PERSONAL PRONOUNS are capitalized when pertaining to Deity.

ITALICS are used in the text to indicate words which are not found in the original Hebrew, Aramaic, or Greek but implied by it. Italics are used in the footnotes to signify alternate readings for the text.

SMALL CAPS in the New Testament are used in the text to indicate Old Testament quotations or obvious allusions to Old Testament texts. Variations of Old Testament wording are found in New Testament citations depending on whether the New Testament writer translated from a Hebrew text, used existing Greek or Aramaic translations, or paraphrased the material. It should be noted that modern rules for the indication of direct quotation were not used in biblical times thus allowing freedom for omissions or insertions without specific indication of these.

ASTERISKS are used to mark verbs that are historical presents in the Greek which have been translated with an English past tense in order to conform to modern usage. The translators recognized that in some contexts the present tense seems more unexpected and unjustified to the English reader than a past tense would have been. But Greek authors frequently used the present tense for the sake of heightened vividness, thereby transporting their readers in imagination to the actual scene at the time of occurrence. However, the translators felt that it would be wise to change these historical presents to English past tenses.

ABBREVIATIONS AND SPECIAL MARKINGS:

Aram.	=	Aramaic
Gr.	=	Greek translation of O.T. (Septuagint or LXX) or Greek text of N.T.
Heb.	=	Hebrew text, usually Masoretic
M.T.	=	Masoretic text
Syr.	=	Syriac
Lit.	=	A literal translation
Or	=	An alternate translation justified by the Hebrew, Aramaic, or Greek
[ ]	=	In text, brackets indicate words probably not in the original writings
cf.	=	compare
ms., mss.	=	manuscript, manuscripts
v., vv.	=	verse, verses

[Other abbreviations used in the Annotations, Introductions and marginal references]

f. ff.	=	Indicates that the verse(s) which follow are to be read.
i.e.	=	for example
KJV	=	King James Version
NAS	=	New American Standard
RSV	=	Revised Standard Version
see:	=	Indicates that the verse in the cross reference is the starting point of, or justification for, the verse in the text.

NAS HARPER

CONTENTS

BOOKS OF
The Old Testament

BOOKS OF
The New Testament

FOREWORD

"The Bible can serve its function in the modern world only if it is understood."—from the preface to *The Ancestry of our English Bible,* Ira M. Price (Harper & Row). Such is the purpose of the HARPER STUDY BIBLE.

This work is neither a dictionary of the Bible nor a commentary on the Scriptures, and is not intended as a substitute for such books. A volume of this size, devised for the average reader, cannot deal extensively in involved questions of text and translation differences, important as these are to the world of technical scholarship, and about which there are as many views as there are scholars. To have done this would have focused attention on a subject which would create more problems than could be solved without adding hundreds of pages to an already substantial volume. The HARPER STUDY BIBLE is published primarily for students, clergymen, and laymen who desire the New American Standard version with annotations helpful to an understanding of the text, and useful for personal devotional reading, pulpit exposition, and classroom study. The wide margins will allow for the reader's own notes in ball-point ink or pencil.

The HARPER STUDY BIBLE is made up of seven parts, each having an integral relationship to the others. Serious study of all the parts by the reader is strongly recommended, for only a thorough knowledge of the individual segments will bring the whole Bible into sharper focus, and lead to a greater appreciation and love for the inspired Word of God.

(1) *The Introductions:* Prefacing each book is a substantive introduction—a summation of authorship, background, and proper historical and religious setting and characteristics. A general outline in the introduction capsules the contents, substance, and import of the book.

(2) *The Text:* The text of the New American Standard Bible appears precisely as copyrighted, together with the translators' notes. Single column, wide measure setting provides maximum ease of reading and study.

(3) *The Topical Headings:* Non-theological and non-interpretive, the topical headings provide a reliable guide to the contents and teachings of each book without bringing other books of the Bible to bear upon it. This device, arranged within appropriate verses throughout the text and set by typographers long skilled in Bible production, is an invaluable aid to Bible students and enables the reader to grasp the structure of the book and the meaning of its message quickly.

(4) *The Marginal References:* The cross reference system is unique in that the references, instead of being listed in the order in which they appear in the Bible, are arranged in chronological sequence for immediate association. These appear at the outside of the text, either to the left or right, on facing pages, and as closely adjacent to the related verse as possible. The asterisks (*) next to many of the references indicate an apposite footnote at the bottom of the page, further illustrating the subject under discussion. Parallel names that are spelled differently in the cross references are set in italics here.

(5) *The Annotations:* In addition to the footnotes, the HARPER STUDY BIBLE is amplified by hundreds of interpretive notes written from the standpoint of conservative theological scholarship. These annotations furnish historical, archaeological, biographical, and textual information. Some bear on a given theme or subject, others suggest alternate readings; all bring together related Scripture from various parts of the Bible. Major doctrines of the Christian faith are frankly set forth, obscure passages are brought to light, terms are defined, and parables are clearly explained. The annotations also include specific biblical references, making the material a useful tool for Church schools, Bible classes, and religious workers. Most of this explanatory material appears at the bottom of the relevant pages, thereby eliminating any loss of continuity while reading. It is also an indispensable feature for students who do not have ready access to extensive biblical reference works.

(6) *The Index:* Approximately 1700 entries, appropriately cross-indexed, direct the reader to any subject in the footnote material.

(7) *The Concordance:* This significantly new, practical concordance is a collection of the principal proper nouns and key words in Scripture. Descriptive phrases and references are listed under each proper noun. If the descriptive phrases are numbered, this indicates different individuals or identities. Key words are immediately followed by explanatory words or synonyms.

—HAROLD LINDSELL

Pasadena, California
July, 1985

Old Testament

NEW AMERICAN STANDARD BIBLE

INTRODUCTION TO
THE FIRST BOOK OF MOSES
COMMONLY CALLED
GENESIS

Authorship and Background: Genesis, the title given by the Septuagint translators, means "origin," "beginning." The Hebrew title is *Bereshith*. It means "in the beginning," and is the first word of the Hebrew text. Genesis is the first book of the Pentateuch (a Greek term meaning "five books"), which has been traditionally attributed to Moses. All events recorded in Genesis antedate Moses, so it is likely that he made use of whatever oral and written sources were available to him. One unit source of material, for example, may be 1:1-2:3, where God is called by His generic name *Elohim*, "God." The heading, "This is the account of the heavens and the earth" (2:4) may reflect another unit of source material. In this section (2:4-3:24) God is called *Yahweh*, His personal name; so this part of the book is characterized by the compound title *Yahweh Elohim*, "LORD God."

According to Ex. 17:14; 24:4-8; 34:27; Num. 33:1,2; Deut. 31:9,22,24, Moses was instructed to record certain information. Moreover, other Old Testament books refer to "the law of Moses" (1 Kin. 2:3); "the book of the law of Moses" (2 Kin. 14:6); and "the book of Moses" (Ezra 6:18; Neh. 13:1, etc.). The New Testament also refers to Moses and the Law of Moses (cf. Matt. 19:8; Mark 1:44; 10:4,5; Luke 5:14; 16:31; 20:37; Acts 3:22; 13:39; 15:5ff.; 26:22; Rom. 10:5,19; 1 Cor. 9:9; 2 Cor. 3:15; Rev. 15:3).

The account of the death of Moses (Deut. 34) appears to have been added by a later writer. It is also possible that in the course of time some changes were made in the text, and that notes were added for the purpose of clarifying terms and explaining certain expressions and historical situations. For example, the name of a city in the time of Moses is given as Dan (Gen. 14:14), whereas we are told that prior to the events recorded in Judges 18 this place was known as Laish (v. 29).

During the last two centuries many scholars have objected vigorously to the idea of the Mosaic authorship of the Pentateuch. Among the best-known viewpoints to reject this authorship is the Documentary Hypothesis of Wellhausen, although some eminent liberal scholars of the twentieth century have challenged almost every one of the basic positions represented in this view. Numerous variations of the Documentary Hypothesis and of other theories are current today. It may be said that most of the scholars who adhere to the non-Mosaic school of thought hold to the four documents in the order J, E, D, and P.

Scholars in the conservative tradition, however, regard the Pentateuch as essentially Mosaic and attribute its authorship to Moses, even though minor editorial insertions and changes were obviously made. These same scholars hold that there is not sufficient evidence to categorically undermine the common tradition of Mosaic authorship.

Characteristics: An understanding of the book of Genesis is fundamental to an understanding of the whole Bible. In it is found an account of generation (chs. 1,2), degeneration (chs. 3-11), and regeneration (chs. 12-50). The story of redemption begins after Adam's sin, and is carried forward progressively in the selection of Seth, the saving of the Noahic family, the choice of Abraham, then Isaac (not Ishmael), and Jacob (not Esau). The line of redemption continues through the twelve sons of Jacob (Israel). The favored son, Joseph, is the main character in the closing chapters of Genesis. The account opens with early man in the Garden of Eden and ends with the sons of Israel in Egypt. Much of Genesis is biographical, as the life stories of the leading characters are portrayed. No effort is made to gloss over the sins and shortcomings of the major characters, so that the biographies include stories of trickery, deception, false witness, incest, fornication, and murder. At the same time there are numerous instances of faith and obedience under trying and difficult circumstances. Heroism, sacrifice, devotion, and uprightness of heart may be found in all of its pages. God is revealed by different names, among them *Elohim*, *Yahweh*, and *Yahweh Elohim*. Through the whole book the writer traces the plan and work of God in his specific redemptive program for the world. A leading characteristic of the book is the recurring use of the phrase *'elleh toledoth*, "these are the generations of," which provides the divisions of the general outline.

Genesis begins with a unique view of God that underlies the whole Bible and that marks off the Hebrew-Christian tradition from the other religions of the world as generically different and as springing from a self-revelation of God to man.

Contents:

I. The generations of the heavens and the earth (1:1-4:26): The beginning of the world, followed by the six days of creation, which end with God's Sabbath rest. The creation of Adam and Eve, their temptation in the Garden, and their fall. The consequences of the fall, the promise of a redeemer, and the expulsion of Adam and Eve from the Garden. The birth of Cain and Abel and the murder of Abel by Cain, followed by the birth of Seth and the renewal of the seed of promise.

II. The generations of Adam (5:1-6:8): The descendants of the godly line of Seth and their intermarriage with the sons of Cain, followed by the degeneration of the race.

III. The generations of Noah (6:9-9:29): God's command to Noah to construct the ark. The gathering of the animals and the commencing of the flood. The subsiding of the water and the return of Noah and the animals to the land. The establishment of human government and the promise never to destroy the earth again by water. Noah's drunkenness and later blessing and cursing of his children.

IV. The generations of the sons of Noah (10:1-11:9): The renewal of life on the earth after the flood through the sons of Noah, followed by spiritual degeneration. The confusion of tongues at the tower of Babel.

V. The generations of Shem (11:10-26): The ancestry of Abram, from Shem through Abram's father, Terah.

VI. The generations of Terah (11:27-25:11): Abram's departure from Ur to Haran. His journey to Canaan and then to Egypt. His return to Canaan and the struggle between Lot and himself. Lot's backsliding and deliverance from captivity by Abram. Abram's return from battle and payment of the tithe to Melchizedek. God's covenant with Abram and the promise of a son. Ishmael's birth to Hagar. God's renewal of His promise, the change of Abram's name to Abraham, and the covenant seal of circumcision. God's destruction of Sodom and Gomorrah, and the saving of Lot and his daughters. The birth of Isaac; Ishmael and Hagar cast out. Abraham's offering of Isaac on Mt. Moriah, and God's intervention. Sarah's death and burial. Rebekah the bride of Isaac. Abraham's marriage to Keturah. Abraham's death.

VII. The generations of Ishmael (25:12-18)

VIII. The generations of Isaac (25:19-35:29): Jacob and Esau born; the covenant confirmed to Isaac by God. Jacob's stolen blessing and flight to Laban's home to escape the wrath of Esau. The covenant confirmed to Jacob at Bethel. Jacob's marriages to Leah and Rachel. The birth of sons, the prosperity of Jacob, his trouble with Laban, and his flight. Jacob's wrestling with God at Jabbok; becoming Israel, a prince with God. The meeting with Esau. Dinah's defilement by Shechem; Jacob's sons destroy Shechem and his family. God speaks to Jacob again at Bethel. The birth of Benjamin and Rachel's death. Isaac's death.

IX. The generations of Esau (36:1-43)

X. The generations of Jacob (37:1-50:26): Joseph's vision; his deliverance into slavery. Judah's sin against Tamar and his shame. Joseph's prosperity in Egypt; loss of his position with Potiphar and sentence to prison. Pharaoh's dream and Joseph's interpretation; his elevation to power. The famine; the visit of Joseph's brethren to Egypt. Their bringing of Benjamin. Joseph identifies himself. Jacob's descent to Egypt. His sickness and death: the blessing of his children and Joseph's children prior to his death. Joseph's death, and his body placed in a coffin in Egypt.

THE FIRST BOOK OF MOSES

COMMONLY CALLED

GENESIS

I. *The generations of the heavens and the earth (1:1–4:26)*

A. *The beginning*

1 In the beginning God created the heavens and the earth. 2 And the earth was ¹formless and void, and darkness was over the surface of the deep; and the Spirit of God was ²moving over the surface of the waters.

B. *The seven creative days*

1. *First day: light*

3 Then God said, "Let there be light"; and there was light. 4 And God saw that the light was good; and God separated the light from the darkness. 5 And God called the light day, and the darkness He called night. And there was evening and there was morning, one day.

2. *Second day: expanse*

6 Then God said, "Let there be an expanse in the midst of the waters, and let it separate the waters from the waters." 7 And God made the ³expanse, and separated the waters which were below the expanse from the waters which were above the expanse; and it was so. 8 And God called the expanse heaven. And there was evening and there was morning, a second day.

3. *Third day: dry land and vegetation*

9 Then God said, "Let the waters below the heavens be gathered into one place, and let the dry land appear"; and it was so. 10 And God called the dry land earth, and the gathering of the waters He called seas; and God saw that it was good. 11 Then God said, "Let the earth sprout vegetation, plants yielding seed, *and* fruit trees bearing fruit after their kind, with seed in them, on the earth"; and it was so. 12 And the earth brought forth vegetation, plants yielding seed after their kind,

Cross-references (margin):
*1:1 John 1:1,2; Ps 8:3; Is 44:24; 42:5; 45:18
1:2 Jer 4:23; Ps 104:30
*1:3 Ps 33:6,9; 2 Cor 4:6
1:4 Is 45:7
*1:5 Ps 74:16
1:6 Jer 10:12
1:7 Prov 8:28; Ps 148:4
1:9 Job 26:10; Prov 8:29; Jer 5:22; 2 Pet 3:5
1:10 Ps 33:7
1:11 Luke 6:44

---

¹Or, *a waste and emptiness* ²Or, *hovering* ³Or, *firmament*

1:1 Monotheism, or the belief in one God, has been shown to be a characteristic of the earliest religions. This concept runs counter to the modern notion that the idea of God was gradually evolved from primitive animism to polytheism, and then finally to monotheism. The researches of Schmidt, Langdon, Petrie, and Zwemer strongly support primitive monotheism. The development of polytheism and lower views of God as a retrogression from monotheism may be explained by the advent of sin and the spiritual decline that necessarily ensued. In Rom. 1:19–23 the apostle Paul summarizes this tragic devolution from monotheism.
1:3 The Genesis account of creation is not the only extant record of beginnings, for many of the pagan cultures preserved creation legends. Along with their gross polytheism, the Babylonian and Assyrian creation stories in particular contain certain similarities to the Genesis account. For example, *the deep* (Hebrew *tehom*) of 1:2 refers to the subterranean ocean on which, according to all the peoples of ancient southwestern Asia, the earth rested. Babylonian creation epics mention two primeval monsters (pictured in art as dragons): Apsu, the fresh-water subterranean ocean, and his consort Tiamat (etymologically the same as *tehom*), the salt-water ocean surrounding the earth. The symbol of the sea dragon as a representation of chaos and evil over

which God is victorious is clearly stated in Ps. 74:13,14; Is. 27:1. Another similarity is that the firmament or heavens, like an inverted bowl, separated the waters above from the earth. When *the floodgates of the sky were opened* (7:11), then the waters above descended as rain. In 2:6 the Hebrew word *ed*, translated *mist*, probably derives from Sumerian *id* ("stream," "river"), which the Babylonians personified as the river god Id. Notwithstanding these and many other similarities with ancient sources, there is a vast difference between the exalted monotheism of the Genesis record and the crude polytheism of the pagan myths. Truly the inspired Genesis account gives evidence of the work of the Spirit of God on the mind of the Biblical writer.
1:5 There are differences of opinion as to whether the days of creation were twenty-four-hour solar days or long periods of time marked by a beginning and an ending. The word *day* is used both ways in Scripture. Since this is true, some are of the opinion that it is proper to conclude from a scientific viewpoint that the days were probably periods of time rather than twenty-four-hour days. *Day* in 2:4 cannot possibly mean a twenty-four-hour day, and it may be inferred from 2:7–23 that a considerable period of time was included in the sixth creative day (cf. 1:27, *male and female He created them*).

and trees bearing fruit, with seed in them, after their kind; and God saw that it was good.

13   And there was evening and there was morning, a third day.

4. Fourth day: luminaries

14   Then God said, "Let there be lights in the expanse of the heavens to separate the day from the night, and let them be for signs, and for seasons, and for days and years;

1:14
Ps 74:16;
104:19

15   and let them be for lights in the expanse of the heavens to give light on the earth"; and it was so.

16   And God made the two great lights, the greater light to govern the day, and the lesser light to govern the night; *He made* the stars also.

1:16
Ps 136:8,9;
Job 38:7

17   And God placed them in the expanse of the heavens to give light on the earth,

18   and to govern the day and the night, and to separate the light from the darkness; and God saw that it was good.

1:18
Jer 31:35

19   And there was evening and there was morning, a fourth day.

5. Fifth day: birds and fishes

20   Then God said, "Let the waters teem with swarms of living creatures, and let birds fly above the earth in the open expanse of the heavens."

21   And God created the great sea monsters, and every living creature that moves, with which the waters swarmed after their kind, and every winged bird after its kind; and God saw that it was good.

1:21
Ps 104:25,26

22   And God blessed them, saying, "Be fruitful and multiply, and fill the waters in the seas, and let birds multiply on the earth."

1:22
Gen 8:17

23   And there was evening and there was morning, a fifth day.

6. Sixth day: animals and man

24   Then God said, "Let the earth bring forth living creatures after their kind: cattle and creeping things and beasts of the earth after their kind"; and it was so.

25   And God made the beasts of the earth after their kind, and the cattle after their kind, and everything that creeps on the ground after its kind; and God saw that it was good.

1:25
Jer 27:5

26   Then God said, "Let Us make man in Our image, according to Our likeness; and let them rule over the fish of the sea and over the birds of the sky and over the cattle and over all the earth, and over every creeping thing that creeps on the earth."

*1:26
Ps 100:3;
Acts 17:26,
28,29;
Col 3:10

27   And God created man in His own image, in the image of God He created him; male and female He created them.

1:27
1 Cor 11:7;
Gen 5:2;
Matt 19:4

28   And God blessed them; and God said to them, "Be fruitful and multiply, and fill the earth, and subdue it; and rule over the fish of the sea and over the birds of the sky, and over every living thing that moves on the earth."

1:28
Gen 9:1,7;
Lev 26:9

29   Then God said, "Behold, I have given you every plant yielding seed that is on the surface of all the earth, and every tree which has fruit yielding seed; it shall be food for you;

1:29
Ps 104:14,15;
136:25

30   and to every beast of the earth and to every bird of the sky and to every thing that moves on the earth which has life, *I have given* every green plant for food"; and it was so.

1:30
Ps 145:15;
Job 38:41

31   And God saw all that He had made, and behold, it was very good. And there was evening and there was morning, the sixth day.

1:31
Ps 104:24

7. Seventh day: the Sabbath

2 Thus the heavens and the earth were completed, and all their hosts.

2   And by the seventh day God completed His work which He had done; and He rested on the seventh day from all His work which He had done.

2:1
Ps 33:6
*2:2
Ex 20:11;
Heb 4:4

1:24 *cattle*, a general term referring to domesticated animals, including sheep and goats. *beasts of the earth*, wild animals.
1:26 *Let Us make man.* Many interpret *Us* to mean the Trinity; but early readers probably understood the word as the plural of majesty, just as the plural *Elohim* (Hebrew) is used for God to denote His majesty and attributes. Another possible interpretation is the picture of God consulting with His angelic court, *the host of heaven* (1 Kin. 22:19) or *the sons*

of God (Job 1:6). *Man* is the generic Hebrew term *adam*. The man Adam was a special creation made up of body and spirit. He was made in the moral and spiritual image of God, a free rational being. He possessed something of God's knowledge, righteousness, and holiness (Eph. 4:24; Col. 3:10). All human life derives from Adam and Eve (Acts 17:26; Rom. 5:12; 1 Cor. 15:21,22).
2:2,3a *Rested* is a translation of the Hebrew word *shabath*, "to cease, rest." Thus the seventh day was designated as

3   Then God blessed the seventh day and sanctified it, because in it He rested from all His work which God had created and made.

C. The creation of man

1. Man made: placed in Eden

4   This is the account of the heavens and the earth when they were created, in the day that the LORD God made earth and heaven.

5   Now no shrub of the field was yet in the earth, and no plant of the field had yet sprouted, for the LORD God had not sent rain upon the earth; and there was no man to cultivate the ground.

6   But a mist used to rise from the earth and water the whole surface of the ground.

2:7
Gen 3:19;
Ps 103:14;
Job 33:4;
Acts 17:25;
1 Cor 15:45

7   Then the LORD God formed man of dust from the ground, and breathed into his nostrils the breath of life; and man became a living being.

8   And the LORD God planted a garden toward the east, in Eden; and there He placed the man whom He had formed.

9   And out of the ground the LORD God caused to grow every tree that is pleasing to the sight and good for food; the tree of life also in the midst of the garden, and the tree of the knowledge of good and evil.

10   Now a river flowed out of Eden to water the garden; and from there it divided and became four rivers.

11   The name of the first is Pishon; it flows around the whole land of Havilah, where there is gold.

12   And the gold of that land is good; the bdellium and the onyx stone are there.

13   And the name of the second river is Gihon; it flows around the whole land of Cush.

14   And the name of the third river is Tigris; it flows east of Assyria. And the fourth river is the Euphrates.

2. The forbidden tree

15   Then the LORD God took the man and put him into the garden of Eden to cultivate it and keep it.

16   And the LORD God commanded the man, saying, "From any tree of the garden you may eat freely;

17   but from the tree of the knowledge of good and evil you shall not eat, for in the day that you eat from it you shall surely die."

Shabbath, the holy day of rest, which through the influence of the Septuagint came to be spelled Sabbath.
2:3b   There was a divine order in creation that admits of no other explanation than a divine intelligence at work. To suppose that accident, apart from design, produced all this marvelously adjusted mechanism of the universe is far more difficult to accept than the Biblical account that God devised and constructed it all out of His own marvelous wisdom. "The account of creation is unique in ancient literature. It undoubtedly reflects an advanced monotheistic point of view, with a sequence of creative phases so rational that modern science cannot improve on it, given the same language and the same range of ideas in which to state its conclusions. In fact, modern scientific cosmogonies show a disconcerting tendency to be short-lived and it may be seriously doubted whether science has yet caught up with the biblical story." W. F. Albright, *The Old Testament and Archaeology* (Old Testament Commentary, edited by Alleman and Flack), p. 135.
2:4   The names for God are varied in the Old Testament. Not only are single names given but compound ones as well. Some contend that the use of different names in Genesis presupposes multiple authorship. Others hold that Moses may have drawn his material from different sources that used different names, or he may have used different names himself. (1) *El, Eloah,* and its plural *Elohim* (all of which are translated *God* and imply the Mighty One, the ruler over all the created universe); (2) *Yahweh,* the covenantal name of the God of Israel (often, although erroneously, rendered "Jehovah") meaning "He is" (i.e., He is the covenant-keeping God to His people, according to Ex. 3:14), or "He causes [all things] to be," the theme of the prophets and

psalmists (instead of reading the sacred name *Yahweh,* pious Israelites substituted the word *Adonai,* "Lord," so that *Yahweh* is translated LORD in KJV, RSV, and NAS); (3) *Adonai,* meaning "Lord" (emphasizing God's sovereignty as King); (4) *Elyon,* signifying *the Most High;* and (5) *Shaddai, the Almighty.* Here in 2:4 the compound *Yahweh Elohim* (LORD God) is used, indicating that the mighty Creator of chapter 1 is the One who enters into covenant relationships with mankind.
2:8   The location of the Garden of Eden has never been precisely determined. Scripture locates it generally on the Tigris (designated in KJV by its ancient name Hiddekel) and Euphrates rivers where they were joined by the rivers Pishon and Gihon. The last two have never been identified. Tradition has located Eden south of Ur, at a site known as Eridu. British archaeologists excavated the ruins of Eridu in 1918–19. On the other hand, Albright thinks that Pishon and Gihon may have been the Blue and White Nile.
2:17   "Covenant of works." God made a covenant with Adam in the Garden. It was an agreement between the Creator and man, a free moral agent. Adam was given the privilege of eating of the fruit of the Garden except for the *tree of knowledge.* This prohibition was given to make it clear that Adam's responsibility was to offer God perfect obedience. Moreover he was warned of the consequences of disobedience if he should eat of the forbidden fruit. But Adam disobeyed and thus reaped death for himself and for the human race of which he was the federal head (Rom. 5:12, 18). Every covenant has a seal. The seal of God's covenant with Adam was the tree of life. It was the outward sign. From that tree Adam was separated because of sin. And to that tree believers shall some day be restored because of

3. *The creation of Eve*

18   Then the LORD God said, "It is not good for the man to be alone; I will make him a helper [4]suitable for him."

19   And out of the ground the LORD God formed every beast of the field and every bird of the sky, and brought *them* to the man to see what he would call them; and whatever the man called a living creature, that was its name.

20   And the man gave names to all the cattle, and to the birds of the sky, and to every beast of the field, but for [5]Adam there was not found a helper suitable for him.

21   So the LORD God caused a deep sleep to fall upon the man, and he slept; then He took one of his ribs, and closed up the flesh at that place.

22   And the LORD God [6]fashioned into a woman the rib which He had taken from the man, and brought her to the man.

23   And the man said,
"This is now bone of my bones,
And flesh of my flesh;
She shall be called Woman,
Because she was taken out of Man."

24   For this cause a man shall leave his father and his mother, and shall cleave to his wife; and they shall become one flesh.

25   And the man and his wife were both naked and were not ashamed.

D. *The fall of Adam*

1. *The temptation and sin of Adam and Eve*

3 Now the serpent was more crafty than any beast of the field which the LORD God had made. And he said to the woman, "Indeed, has God said, 'You shall not eat from any tree of the garden' ? "

2   And the woman said to the serpent, "From the fruit of the trees of the garden we may eat;

3   but from the fruit of the tree which is in the middle of the garden, God has said, 'You shall not eat from it or touch it, lest you die.' "

4   And the serpent said to the woman, "You surely shall not die!

5   "For God knows that in the day you eat from it your eyes will be opened, and you will be like God, knowing good and evil."

6   When the woman saw that the tree was good for food, and that it was a

---

Marginal references:

2:18 — 1 Cor 11:9
2:19 — Gen 1:20,24; Ps 8:7
2:21 — 1 Sam 26:12
*2:23 — Eph 5:30; 1 Cor 11:8
*2:24 — Matt 19:5; Mark 10:7,8; 1 Cor 6:16; Eph 5:31
2:25 — Gen 3:7,10,11
*3:1 — 2 Cor 11:3; Rev 12:9; 20:2
*3:3 — 2 Cor 11:3
3:4 — John 8:44
*3:6 — 1 Tim 2:14

---

[4]Lit., *corresponding to*   [5]Or, *man*   [6]Lit., *built*

---

redemption (3:24; Rev. 22:2).

2:23 *Woman* (Eve) was, like Adam, created by God in His own moral and spiritual image (1:27). She was taken from Adam's side (2:21,22), to be a helpmate for him (2:18,20). Woman was made for man (1 Cor. 11:9), was subject to his authority (1 Cor. 11:3), and was to be his glory (1 Cor. 11:7). Sin had its beginnings through Eve, who was first deceived by Satan (3:1–6; 2 Cor. 11:3; 1 Tim. 2:14), although Adam freely chose to sin and thereby merited guilt and death.

2:24 The institution of marriage was established and ordained by God for the welfare and personal fulfillment of man and for the furthering of the human race (1:28; 2:18; 9:1). This is God's plan as given in the Old Testament. The enlargement comes in the New Testament, but this verse was the basis for Jesus' concept of marriage. The New Testament teaching includes the following: (1) marriage is lawful for all (1 Cor. 7:2,28; 1 Tim. 5:14); (2) it is an honorable estate (Heb. 13:4); (3) Christians should marry fellow Christians (1 Cor. 7:39; 2 Cor. 6:14–18); and (4) marriage cannot be dissolved during the life of the partners except for Biblical reasons (Matt. 19:6ff.; Rom. 7:2,3). (See also note to Deut. 24:1 on divorce.)

3:1 Verses 1–6 have in them all of the elements basic to any temptation that is likely to confront man. Doubting God, raising questions, pitting one's will against His, all have theological implications that one is apt to overlook when the story is read casually.

3:3 Adam's probation in the Garden of Eden was conditioned on obedience. God warned Adam of the conse-

quences of eating of the forbidden fruit. The sentence for disobedience was twofold: (1) spiritual death, by which Adam's nature was corrupted and he himself spiritually separated from God by his sin; and (2) physical death, a penalty that was not immediately executed, but which made Adam mortal. According to the New Testament, both physical and spiritual death have been transmitted to the entire human race through Adam (Rom. 5:12–14).

3:6 Adam sinned and fell. This all will admit. The vexing problem is whether the guilt of Adam was imputed to the entire human race. However theologians may differ, they agree that all are sinners and need a Savior. Those who hold that Adam's guilt is imputed believe that infants are born not only sinners by natural inheritance, but are also personally guilty and under condemnation. Infants who die are to be saved only by the free application of Christ's merits. Those who hold that infants are born sinful but without guilt attached also believe that when infants reach the age of accountability they choose to sin and thus need a Savior; but infants who die in infancy are saved by God's grace since they have incurred no personal guilt by overt acts of sin. The former view is known as "federal headship," since by God's *covenant* (Latin, *foedus*) Adam was the covenantal representative of all his descendants.

Adam fell because of his disobedience (3:6–12; Rom. 5:12–19). He was incited by Satan to do so (3:1–5; Rev. 12:9), although he yielded to temptation of his own free will. Adam was banished from Eden, condemned to temporal death, and promised both labor and sorrow (3:14–24). God also imposed penal consequences that passed from Adam to his posterity and thus to all men.

delight to the eyes, and that the tree was desirable to make *one* wise, she took from its fruit and ate; and she gave also to her husband with her, and he ate.

7   Then the eyes of both of them were opened, and they knew that they were naked; and they sewed fig leaves together and made themselves loin coverings.

2. *The judgment of God*

a. *The sin uncovered*

8   And they heard the sound of the LORD God walking in the garden in the cool of the day, and the man and his wife hid themselves from the presence of the LORD God among the trees of the garden.

9   Then the LORD God called to the man, and said to him, "Where are you?"

10   And he said, "I heard the sound of Thee in the garden, and I was afraid because I was naked; so I hid myself."

11   And He said, "Who told you that you were naked? Have you eaten from the tree of which I commanded you not to eat?"

12   And the man said, "The woman whom Thou gavest *to be* with me, she gave me from the tree, and I ate."

13   Then the LORD God said to the woman, "What is this you have done?" And the woman said, "The serpent deceived me, and I ate."

b. *The curse on the serpent*

14   And the LORD God said to the serpent,
"Because you have done this,
Cursed are you more than all cattle,
And more than every beast of the field;
On your belly shall you go,
And dust shall you eat
All the days of your life;

15   And I will put enmity
Between you and the woman,
And between your seed and her seed;
He shall bruise you on the head,
And you shall bruise him on the heel."

c. *The curse on Eve*

16   To the woman He said,
"I will greatly multiply
Your pain in childbirth,
In pain you shall bring forth children;
Yet your desire shall be for your husband,
And he shall rule over you."

d. *The curse on Adam*

17   Then to Adam He said, "Because you have listened to the voice of your wife, and have eaten from the tree about which I commanded you, saying, 'You shall not eat from it';
Cursed is the ground because of you;
In toil you shall eat of it
All the days of your life.

18   "Both thorns and thistles it shall grow for you;
And you shall eat the plants of the field;

19   By the sweat of your face
You shall eat bread,
Till you return to the ground,

Cross-references (margin):

3:8 — Job 31:33; Jer 23:24
3:10 — 1 John 3:20
3:12 — Prov 28:13
3:13 — 2 Cor 11:3; 1 Tim 2:14
*3:14 — Is 65:25; Mic 7:17
*3:15 — John 8:44; Acts 13:10; 1 John 3:8; Is 7:14; Matt 1:23; Rom 16:20; Rev 12:7
3:16 — Is 13:8; Gen 4:7; 1 Cor 11:3; Eph 5:22
3:17 — 1 Sam 15:23; Gen 2:17; Rom 8:20-22
*3:18 — Ps 104:14
3:19 — Gen 2:7; Ps 90:3; 104:29; Eccl 12:7

3:14 Following the fall of Adam, God laid down certain conditions that were to govern the life of man until the end of the age: (1) the serpent, the instrument in the temptation, was cursed; (2) a Redeemer was promised for mankind (v. 15); (3) the condition of womanhood was altered in two respects: (a) multiplied pain in childbirth and (b) a status of subjection to her husband; (4) the ground was cursed to produce thorns and thistles; (5) man was to earn his living by the sweat of his brow; and (6) physical death was to be the lot of all men. (Also read vv. 15–19.)
3:15 This is the first promise of a Redeemer. The conflict

of the ages is predicted—a conflict between the seed of the woman and the seed of the serpent. The Redeemer will finally bring ruin to Satan and his seed, although in the process Satan will bruise the Redeemer (as took place at Calvary). Isaiah 53:10 further reveals that Satan's maltreatment of Christ the Redeemer was in accord with the permissive will and all-wise plan of God the Father.
3:18 It is possible that thorns and thistles, tooth and claw, may have existed already outside of Eden. One need not suppose that death was not present in the animal kingdom long before the sin of man.

Because from it you were taken;
For you are dust,
And to dust you shall return."

e. The expulsion from the garden

20   Now the man called his wife's name [7]Eve, because she was the mother of all *the* living.

21   And the LORD God made garments of skin for Adam and his wife, and clothed them.

22   Then the LORD God said, "Behold, the man has become like one of Us, knowing good and evil; and now, lest he stretch out his hand, and take also from the tree of life, and eat, and live forever"— *3:22
Rev 22:2

23   therefore the LORD God sent him out from the garden of Eden, to cultivate the ground from which he was taken. 3:23
Gen 4:2

24   So He drove the man out; and at the east of the garden of Eden He stationed the cherubim, and the flaming sword which turned every direction, to guard the way to the tree of life. 3:24
Gen 2:8,9

E. Cain and his descendants

1. The offerings of Cain and Abel

4 Now the man had relations with his wife Eve, and she conceived and gave birth to Cain, and she said, "I have gotten a manchild with *the help of* the LORD."

2   And again, she gave birth to his brother Abel. And Abel was a keeper of flocks, but Cain was a tiller of the ground. 4:2
Luke 11:50, 51

3   So it came about in the course of time that Cain brought an offering to the LORD of the fruit of the ground. 4:3
Num 18:12

4   And Abel, on his part also brought of the firstlings of his flock and of their fat portions. And the LORD had regard for Abel and for his offering; *4:4
Num 18:17;
Lev 3:16;
Heb 11:4

5   but for Cain and for his offering He had no regard. So Cain became very angry and his countenance fell. 4:5
Is 3:9;
Jude 11

6   Then the LORD said to Cain, "Why are you angry? And why has your countenance fallen?

7   "If you do well, will not *your countenance* be lifted up? And if you do not do well, sin is crouching at the door; and its desire is for you, but you must master it."

2. Cain kills Abel: God's curse

8   And Cain told Abel his brother. And it came about when they were in the field, that Cain rose up against Abel his brother and killed him. 4:8
Matt 23:35;
1 John 3:12

9   Then the LORD said to Cain, "Where is Abel your brother?" And he said, "I do not know. Am I my brother's keeper?"

10   And He said, "What have you done? The voice of your brother's blood is crying to Me from the ground. 4:10
Heb 12:24;
Rev 6:10

11   "And now you are cursed from the ground, which has opened its mouth to receive your brother's blood from your hand.

12   "When you cultivate the ground, it shall no longer yield its strength to you; you shall be a vagrant and a wanderer on the earth." 4:12
v. 14

13   And Cain said to the LORD, "My punishment is too great to bear!

14   "Behold, Thou hast driven me this day from the face of the ground; and from Thy face I shall be hidden, and I shall be a vagrant and a wanderer on the earth, and it will come about that whoever finds me will kill me." 4:14
Ps 51:11;
Gen 9:6;
Num 35:19,
21,27

15   So the LORD said to him, "Therefore whoever kills Cain, vengeance will be 4:15
Ps 79:12;

[7]I.e., living or life

3:21 Garments in Scripture, when used symbolically, may represent the tattered rags of self-righteousness (Is. 64:6), which make a shabby cloak for our sins; the righteousness and excellencies of Christ are imputed and imparted to the believer (Rev. 3:18; 19:8).

3:22 The implication here is that the *tree of life* was now disallowed only because of knowledge gained through man's sin.

4:4 Abel offered an animal sacrifice; Cain offered the fruit of the ground. From the analogy of Scripture it may be concluded that the difference between the two sacrifices was

not merely one of personal piety and faith. Evidently they had both been told of the necessity for a blood sacrifice as an expression of true faith. Abel therefore offered *a better sacrifice* (Heb. 11:4). He became the first martyr (Matt. 23:35) and is listed as a hero of the faith (Heb. 11:4). His death is compared with that of Christ in Heb. 12:24.

4:7 The same Hebrew word (*chattath*) is used for *sin* and *sin-offering*. In Mosaic usage the offerer placed his hand on the head of the victim, thus identifying himself with his sin offering. Even so *He made Him who knew no sin to be sin on our behalf* (2 Cor. 5:21) so that men could become righteous through faith in Him. (See also note to 1 Pet. 2:24.)

Ezek 9:4,6
taken on him sevenfold." And the LORD appointed a sign for Cain, lest anyone finding him should slay him.

16 Then Cain went out from the presence of the LORD, and settled in the land of Nod, east of Eden.

3. Cain's children

4:17
Ps 49:11
17 And Cain had relations with his wife and she conceived, and gave birth to Enoch; and he built a city, and called the name of the city Enoch, after the name of his son.

4:18
Gen 5:25,28,
30
18 Now to Enoch was born Irad; and Irad became the father of Mehujael; and Mehujael became the father of Methushael; and Methushael became the father of Lamech.

19 And Lamech took to himself two wives: the name of the one was Adah, and the name of the other, Zillah.

20 And Adah gave birth to Jabal; he was the father of those who dwell in tents and *have* livestock.

21 And his brother's name was Jubal; he was the father of all those who play the lyre and pipe.

22 As for Zillah, she also gave birth to Tubal-cain, the forger of all implements of bronze and iron; and the sister of Tubal-cain was Naamah.

4:23
Ex 20:13;
Lev 19:18;
Deut 32:35;
Luke 3:36;
v. 18
23 And Lamech said to his wives,

"Adah and Zillah,
Listen to my voice,
You wives of Lamech,
Give heed to my speech,
For I have killed a man for wounding me;
And a boy for striking me;

4:24
v. 15
24 If Cain is avenged sevenfold,
Then Lamech seventy-sevenfold."

F. The birth of Seth

4:25
Gen 5:3; v. 8
25 And Adam had relations with his wife again; and she gave birth to a son, and named him Seth, for, *she said,* "God has appointed me another offspring in place of Abel; for Cain killed him."

4:26
1 Kin 18:24;
Ps 116:17;
Joel 2:32;
Zeph 3:9;
1 Cor 1:2
26 And to Seth, to him also a son was born; and he called his name Enosh. Then *men* began to call upon the name of the LORD.

II. The generations of Adam (5:1–6:8)

A. Adam and Seth

5:1
Gen 1:26;
Eph 4:24;
Col 3:10
5:2
Gen 1:27
5:3
Gen 4:25
5 This is the book of the generations of Adam. In the day when God created man, He made him in the likeness of God.

2 He created them male and female, and He blessed them and named them [8]Man in the day when they were created.

3 When Adam had lived one hundred and thirty years, he [9]became the father of *a son* in his own likeness, according to his image, and named him Seth.

4 Then the days of Adam after he became the father of Seth were eight hundred years, and he had *other* sons and daughters.

5:5
Gen 3:19;
Heb 9:27
5 So all the days that Adam lived were nine hundred and thirty years, and he died.

B. Seth and Enosh

5:6
Gen 4:26
6 And Seth lived one hundred and five years, and became the father of Enosh.

[8]Lit., *Adam*   [9]Lit., *begot,* and so throughout this context

---

4:22 For nearly three centuries the accepted chronology of the Bible was based on the assumption that Adam commenced his career around 4004 B.C. This chronology was worked out by Archbishop Ussher in the seventeenth century. Recent scientific advances, including the carbon dating method, make the Ussher chronology impossible. Many scholars accept interpretations of the Biblical text that allow for substantial chronological gaps in the genealogical lists of Gen. 5,11, thus allowing for an age of man much greater than that suggested by Ussher. Bronze did not become common until 3300–3000 B.C., and iron did not appear until 1500–1200 B.C. Tubal-cain, the eighth generation from Adam, according to this verse was *the forger of all implements of bronze and iron.* This, along with scientific data, makes it evident that the Biblical chronologies have tremendous gaps in them.

7   Then Seth lived eight hundred and seven years after he became the father of Enosh, and he had *other* sons and daughters.
8   So all the days of Seth were nine hundred and twelve years, and he died.

C. Enosh and Kenan

9   And Enosh lived ninety years, and became the father of Kenan.
10   Then Enosh lived eight hundred and fifteen years after he became the father of Kenan, and he had *other* sons and daughters.
11   So all the days of Enosh were nine hundred and five years, and he died.

D. Kenan and Mahalalel

12   And Kenan lived seventy years, and became the father of Mahalalel.
13   Then Kenan lived eight hundred and forty years after he became the father of Mahalalel, and he had *other* sons and daughters.
14   So all the days of Kenan were nine hundred and ten years, and he died.

E. Mahalalel and Jared

15   And Mahalalel lived sixty-five years, and became the father of Jared.
16   Then Mahalalel lived eight hundred and thirty years after he became the father of Jared, and he had *other* sons and daughters.
17   So all the days of Mahalalel were eight hundred and ninety-five years, and he died.

F. Jared and Enoch

18   And Jared lived one hundred and sixty-two years, and became the father of Enoch.
19   Then Jared lived eight hundred years after he became the father of Enoch, and he had *other* sons and daughters.
20   So all the days of Jared were nine hundred and sixty-two years, and he died.

G. Enoch and Methuselah

21   And Enoch lived sixty-five years, and became the father of Methuselah.
22   Then Enoch walked with God three hundred years after he became the father of Methuselah, and he had *other* sons and daughters.
23   So all the days of Enoch were three hundred and sixty-five years.
24   And Enoch walked with God; and he was not, for God took him.

H. Methuselah and Lamech

25   And Methuselah lived one hundred and eighty-seven years, and became the father of Lamech.
26   Then Methuselah lived seven hundred and eighty-two years after he became the father of Lamech, and he had *other* sons and daughters.
27   So all the days of Methuselah were nine hundred and sixty-nine years, and he died.

I. Lamech and Noah

28   And Lamech lived one hundred and eighty-two years, and became the father of a son.
29   Now he called his name Noah, saying, "This one shall give us rest from our

Cross-references (right margin):
5:7 Luke 3:38
5:11 1 Chr 1:1
5:12 1 Chr 1:2
5:15 1 Chr 1:2
5:18 Jude 14,15
5:21 1 Chr 1:3; Luke 3:37; Jude 14
*5:24 2 Kin 2:11; Heb 11:5
5:26 Luke 3:36
5:29 Gen 3:17-19

5:24 Hebrews 11:5 reveals that Enoch was taken into heaven alive, never tasting physical death. This "translation" was a miracle. The only other instance of this kind in Scripture is that of Elijah (2 Kin. 2:11).
5:27 Methuselah was the oldest person whose life is recorded in Scripture. There has been great debate over the question of longevity and three possible solutions have been proposed. One is that men actually lived nine hundred or more years, because conditions in the antediluvian world were different and thus made longevity possible. Since the flood, the life span of man has been reduced. A second theory is that time must be reduced. There are Babylonian records that speak of men living 30,000 years. The theory of reduction ratio of time hardly appears feasible, however,

and must be rejected. If, for example, one were to divide the ages by ten, then Methuselah's life span was close to one hundred years. But his father (Enoch) would have been six and one-half years of age (Gen. 5:21) when Methuselah was born! The third theory is that the Biblical records deal with the families of the people mentioned and not their chronological ages. Thus it was the family of Methuselah and not the individual about which the author wrote. This view is complicated by the fact that Hebrews 11:5 speaks of Enoch as an individual and records his personal translation, not the translation of his family. Present medical forecasts predict greatly extended life span for men, lending credence to the view that the patriarchal antediluvians may well have lived nine hundred or more years.

work and from the toil of our hands *arising* from the ground which the LORD has cursed."

30   Then Lamech lived five hundred and ninety-five years after he became the father of Noah, and he had *other* sons and daughters.

31   So all the days of Lamech were seven hundred and seventy-seven years, and he died.

J. *Noah and his sons*

5:32
Gen 6:10;
10:21

32   And Noah was five hundred years old, and Noah became the father of Shem, Ham, and Japheth.

K. *The wickedness of men: the judgment of God*

6:1
Gen 1:28

6 Now it came about, when men began to multiply on the face of the land, and daughters were born to them,

6:2
Deut 7:1-4

2   that the sons of God saw that the daughters of men were beautiful; and they took wives for themselves, whomever they chose.

6:3
1 Pet 3:19;
Ps 78:39

3   Then the LORD said, "My Spirit shall not strive with man forever, because he also is flesh; nevertheless his days shall be one hundred and twenty years."

4   The [10]Nephilim were on the earth in those days, and also afterward, when the sons of God came in to the daughters of men, and they bore *children* to them. Those were the mighty men who *were* of old, men of renown.

6:5
Gen 8:21

5   Then the LORD saw that the wickedness of man was great on the earth, and that every intent of the thoughts of his heart was only evil continually.

6:6
1 Sam 15:11,
29;
2 Sam 24:16;
Mal 3:6;
James 1:17;
Is 63:10

6   And the LORD was sorry that He had made man on the earth, and He was grieved in His heart.

7   And the LORD said, "I will blot out man whom I have created from the face of the land, from man to animals to creeping things to birds of the sky; for I am sorry that I have made them."

6:8
Gen 19:19;
Ex 33:12;
Luke 1:30;
Acts 7:46

8   But Noah found favor in the eyes of the LORD.

III. *The generations of Noah (6:9–9:29)*

A. *The command to build the ark*

6:9
Gen 17:1;
Ezek 14:14,
20; Heb 11:7;
2 Pet 2:5;
Gen 5:22

9   These are *the records of* the generations of Noah. Noah was a righteous man, blameless in his time; Noah walked with God.

6:10
Gen 5:32

10   And Noah became the father of three sons: Shem, Ham, and Japheth.

6:11
Rom 2:13;
Ezek 8:17

11   Now the earth was corrupt in the sight of God, and the earth was filled with violence.

6:12
Ps 14:1-3

12   And God looked on the earth, and behold, it was corrupt; for all flesh had corrupted their way upon the earth.

6:13
Ezek 7:2,3;
v. 17

13   Then God said to Noah, "The end of all flesh has come before Me; for the earth is filled with violence because of them; and behold, I am about to destroy them with the earth.

*6:14
Heb 11:7;
1 Pet 3:20

14   "Make for yourself an ark of gopher wood; you shall make the ark with rooms, and shall cover it inside and out with pitch.

15   "And this is how you shall make it: the length of the ark three hundred [11]cubits, its breadth fifty cubits, and its height thirty cubits.

16   "You shall make a window for the ark, and finish it to a cubit from the top;

[10]Or, *giants*   [11]I.e., One cubit equals approx. 18 in.

6:4 The KJV reads: "there were giants in the earth." Many have construed this to mean that angels (the sons of God) were joined in marriage to human beings and spawned a mixed race. The Nephilim were strong, violent, tyrannous men of great wickedness. But it is far more likely that *the sons of God* refers to those descendants of Seth who trusted in the LORD but whose children intermarried with women descended from Cain. The marriage union was not with angels then, but one consummated between the godly and ungodly families of men. Angels neither marry nor are given in marriage, so that the verse hardly applies to them. On the other hand, Peter speaks of angels (2 Pet. 2:4) and apparently refers to the Book of Enoch (20:2) where sons of God is interpreted "angels." It may be then that the explanation of

the original meaning of 6:1–4 has been lost to us.
6:14 Noah's ark probably was about 450 feet long, 75 feet wide and was divided into three stories of about 15 feet each. The task of building the ark, gathering the animals, and storing the food was tremendous. It may well have taken the labors of many more people than the immediate Noahic family. The ark itself was constructed of gopher wood and covered with pitch. How many animals it could have accommodated cannot be determined accurately, although it has been estimated that there was room for 7,000. In the New Testament the ark is regarded as a type of Christ, who serves as a place of refuge for the redeemed (cf. 1 Pet. 3:20,21).

and set the door of the ark in the side of it; you shall make it with lower, second, and third decks.

17 "And behold, I, even I am bringing the flood of water upon the earth, to destroy all flesh in which is the breath of life, from under heaven; everything that is on the earth shall perish.

18 "But I will establish My covenant with you; and you shall enter the ark—you and your sons and your wife, and your sons' wives with you.

19 "And of every living thing of all flesh, you shall bring two of every *kind* into the ark, to keep *them* alive with you; they shall be male and female.

20 "Of the birds after their kind, and of the animals after their kind, of every creeping thing of the ground after its kind, two of every *kind* shall come to you to keep *them* alive.

21 "And as for you, take for yourself some of all food which is edible, and gather *it* to yourself; and it shall be for food for you and for them."

22 Thus Noah did; according to all that God had commanded him, so he did.

B. *The command to fill the ark*

7 Then the LORD said to Noah, "Enter the ark, you and all your household; for you *alone* I have seen *to be* righteous before Me in this time.

2 "You shall take with you of every clean animal by sevens, a male and his female; and of the animals that are not clean two, a male and his female;

3 also of the birds of the sky, by sevens, male and female, to keep offspring alive on the face of all the earth.

4 "For after seven more days, I will send rain on the earth forty days and forty nights; and I will blot out from the face of the land every living thing that I have made."

5 And Noah did according to all that the LORD had commanded him.

C. *The flood*

6 Now Noah was six hundred years old when the flood of water came upon the earth.

7 Then Noah and his sons and his wife and his sons' wives with him entered the ark because of the water of the flood.

8 Of clean animals and animals that are not clean and birds and everything that creeps on the ground,

9 there went into the ark to Noah by twos, male and female, as God had commanded Noah.

10 And it came about after the seven days, that the water of the flood came upon the earth.

11 In the six hundredth year of Noah's life, in the second month, on the seventeenth day of the month, on the same day all the fountains of the great deep burst open, and the floodgates of the sky were opened.

12 And the rain fell upon the earth for forty days and forty nights.

13 On the very same day Noah and Shem and Ham and Japheth, the sons of Noah, and Noah's wife and the three wives of his sons with them, entered the ark,

14 they and every beast after its kind, and all the cattle after their kind, and every creeping thing that creeps on the earth after its kind, and every bird after its kind, all sorts of birds.

15 So they went into the ark to Noah, by twos of all flesh in which was the breath of life.

16 And those that entered, male and female of all flesh, entered as God had commanded him; and the LORD closed *it* behind him.

17 Then the flood came upon the earth for forty days; and the water increased and lifted up the ark, so that it rose above the earth.

18 And the water prevailed and increased greatly upon the earth; and the ark floated on the surface of the water.

*6:17
Gen 7:4,21-23

6:18
Gen 7:1,7,13;
1 Pet 3:20;
2 Pet 2:5
6:19
Gen 7:8,9,15,
16
6:20
Gen 7:9,15

6:22
Heb 11:7;
Gen 7:5

7:1
Matt 24:38;
Luke 17:26
7:2
Lev ch. 11;
10:10;
Ezek 44:23

7:7
Gen 6:22; v. 1

*7:11
Gen 8:2;
Prov 8:28;
Ezek 26:19
7:12
vv. 4,17
7:13
vv. 1,7; 6:18

7:15
Gen 6:20

7:16
vv. 2,3

7:17
vv. 4,12

7:18
Ps 104:26

6:17 There are three views generally held about the extent of the flood: (1) it was geographically and ethnologically universal (all land was covered and all life died); (2) it was geographically local but ethnologically universal (not all land was covered but all life died); and (3) it was geographically and ethnologically local (not all land was covered and not all life died). Extrabiblical evidence appears to be against a universal flood. The genealogies of chapter 10 make no reference to the Negroid and Mongoloid races, which leads one to suppose that these races were not included in the flood.

7:11 *fountains of the great deep.* This is another reference to the subterranean ocean. Thus, the flood is explained as the convergence of the waters below and above the earth.

19   And the water prevailed more and more upon the earth, so that all the high mountains everywhere under the heavens were covered.

20   The water prevailed fifteen cubits higher, and the mountains were covered.

7:21
Gen 6:13,17

21   And all flesh that moved on the earth perished, birds and cattle and beasts and every swarming thing that swarms upon the earth, and all mankind;

7:22
Gen 2:7

22   of all that was on the dry land, all in whose nostrils was the breath of the spirit of life, died.

7:23
1 Pet 3:20;
2 Pet 2:5

23   Thus He blotted out every living thing that was upon the face of the land, from man to animals to creeping things and to birds of the sky, and they were blotted out from the earth; and only Noah was left, together with those that were with him in the ark.

7:24
Gen 8:3

24   And the water prevailed upon the earth one hundred and fifty days.

D. *The subsiding of the waters*

8:1
Gen 19:29;
Ex 2:24;
1 Sam 1:19;
Ex 14:21;
Job 12:15;
Ps 29:10;
Is 44:27;
Nah 1:4

8   But God remembered Noah and all the beasts and all the cattle that were with him in the ark; and God caused a wind to pass over the earth, and the water subsided.

8:2
Gen 7:11;
Job 38:37

2   Also the fountains of the deep and the floodgates of the sky were closed, and the rain from the sky was restrained;

8:3
Gen 7:24
*8:4
Jer 51:27

3   and the water receded steadily from the earth, and at the end of one hundred and fifty days the water decreased.

4   And in the seventh month, on the seventeenth day of the month, the ark rested upon the mountains of Ararat.

5   And the water decreased steadily until the tenth month; in the tenth month, on the first day of the month, the tops of the mountains became visible.

8:6
2 Pet 2:5

6   Then it came about at the end of forty days, that Noah opened the window of the ark which he had made;

8:7
1 Kin 17:4,6

7   and he sent out a raven, and it flew here and there until the water was dried up from the earth.

8   Then he sent out a dove from him, to see if the water was abated from the face of the land;

9   but the dove found no resting place for the sole of her foot, so she returned to him into the ark; for the water was on the surface of all the earth. Then he put out his hand and took her, and brought her into the ark to himself.

10   So he waited yet another seven days; and again he sent out the dove from the ark.

8:11
Matt 10:16

11   And the dove came to him toward evening; and behold, in her beak was a freshly picked olive leaf. So Noah knew that the water was abated from the earth.

12   Then he waited yet another seven days, and sent out the dove; but she did not return to him again.

E. *The return to dry land*

8:13
2 Pet 3:5,6

13   Now it came about in the six hundred and first year, in the first *month,* on the first of the month, the water was dried up from the earth. Then Noah removed the covering of the ark, and looked, and behold, the surface of the ground was dried up.

14   And in the second month, on the twenty-seventh day of the month, the earth was dry.

15   Then God spoke to Noah, saying,

8:16
Gen 7:13

16   "Go out of the ark, you and your wife and your sons and your sons' wives with you.

8:17
Gen 1:22

17   "Bring out with you every living thing of all flesh that is with you, birds and animals and every creeping thing that creeps on the earth, that they may breed abundantly on the earth, and be fruitful and multiply on the earth."

18   So Noah went out, and his sons and his wife and his sons' wives with him.

19   Every beast, every creeping thing, and every bird, everything that moves on the earth, went out by their families from the ark.

8:4 The *mountains of Ararat* constituted a range of mountains, the highest peak of which rose almost 17,000 feet above sea level. The ark hardly could have come to rest on the highest peak. It probably rested on one of the smaller ones far closer to sea level. The Babylonian flood epic has the ark coming to rest on Mt. Nisir, east of the Tigris.

F. *The altar of sacrifice:*
God will never curse the earth again

20   Then Noah built an altar to the LORD, and took of every clean animal and of every clean bird and offered burnt offerings on the altar.
21   And the LORD smelled the soothing aroma; and the LORD said to Himself, "I will never again curse the ground on account of man, for the intent of man's heart is evil from his youth; and I will never again destroy every living thing, as I have done.
22   "While the earth remains,
            Seedtime and harvest,
            And cold and heat,
            And summer and winter,
            And day and night
            Shall not cease."

G. *God allows meat but forbids blood*

9 And God blessed Noah and his sons and said to them, "Be fruitful and multiply, and fill the earth.
2   "And the fear of you and the terror of you shall be on every beast of the earth and on every bird of the sky; with everything that creeps on the ground, and all the fish of the sea, into your hand they are given.
3   "Every moving thing that is alive shall be food for you; I give all to you, as *I gave* the green plant.
4   "Only you shall not eat flesh with its life, *that is*, its blood.
5   "And surely I will require your lifeblood; from every beast I will require it. And from *every* man, from every man's brother I will require the life of man.
6   "Whoever sheds man's blood,
        By man his blood shall be shed,
        For in the image of God
        He made man.
7   "And as for you, be fruitful and multiply;
        Populate the earth abundantly and multiply in it."

H. *The Noahic covenant: the rainbow*

8   Then God spoke to Noah and to his sons with him, saying,
9   "Now behold, I Myself do establish My covenant with you, and with your descendants after you;
10   and with every living creature that is with you, the birds, the cattle, and every beast of the earth with you; of all that comes out of the ark, even every beast of the earth.
11   "And I establish My covenant with you; and all flesh shall never again be cut off by the water of the flood, neither shall there again be a flood to destroy the earth."
12   And God said, "This is the sign of the covenant which I am making between Me and you and every living creature that is with you, for all successive generations;
13   I set My bow in the cloud, and it shall be for a sign of a covenant between Me and the earth.
14   "And it shall come about, when I bring a cloud over the earth, that the bow shall be seen in the cloud,
15   and I will remember My covenant, which is between Me and you and every living creature of all flesh; and never again shall the water become a flood to destroy all flesh.
16   "When the bow is in the cloud, then I will look upon it, to remember the everlasting covenant between God and every living creature of all flesh that is on the earth."

8:20	Gen 12:7,8; 13:18; 22:9; 7:2; 22:2; Ex 10:25
8:21	Lev 1:9; 2 Cor 2:15; Gen 3:17; 6:17; 9:11,15
8:22	Is 54:9; Jer 33:20,25
9:1	v. 7; Gen 1:28
9:3	Deut 12:15; Gen 1:29
9:4	Lev 17:10-16; Deut 12:23; 1 Sam 14:33
9:5	Ex 21:28; Gen 4:9,10
9:6	Ex 21:12,14; Lev 24:17; Matt 26:52; Gen 1:27
9:7	vv. 1,19
9:9	Gen 6:18; Is 54:9
9:10	Ps 149:9
9:11	Is 54:9
9:12	Gen 17:11
9:13	Ezek 1:28; Rev 4:3
9:15	Lev 26:42,45; Deut 7:9
9:16	Gen 17:13,19

8:21 A change of heart (see 3:17).
9:1 After the flood, God made a covenant with Noah. It embraced the following elements: (1) the orderliness and regularity of the seasons and of nature generally were confirmed (8:22); (2) Noah's seed was to be fruitful and replenish the earth (9:1); (3) a system of law and government was begun, together with penalties for crime (9:1–6); (4) the fruit of the earth was given to man for food, and all meat, except for the blood (9:3,4); (5) the seal of the covenant was the rainbow (9:16,17); and (6) the promise of the covenant was that the earth should never again be destroyed by a universal flood such as this (9:15).

17 And God said to Noah, "This is the sign of the covenant which I have established between Me and all flesh that is on the earth."

18 Now the sons of Noah who came out of the ark were Shem and Ham and Japheth; and Ham was the father of Canaan.

19 These three *were* the sons of Noah; and from these the whole earth was populated.

I. *Canaan cursed; Shem blessed*

20 Then Noah began farming and planted a vineyard.

21 And he drank of the wine and became drunk, and uncovered himself inside his tent.

22 And Ham, the father of Canaan, saw the nakedness of his father, and told his two brothers outside.

23 But Shem and Japheth took a garment and laid it upon both their shoulders and walked backward and covered the nakedness of their father; and their faces were turned away, so that they did not see their father's nakedness.

24 When Noah awoke from his wine, he knew what his youngest son had done to him.

25 So he said,
"Cursed be Canaan;
12A servant of servants
He shall be to his brothers."

26 He also said,
"Blessed be the LORD,
The God of Shem;
And let Canaan be his servant.

27 "May God enlarge Japheth,
And let him dwell in the tents of Shem;
And let Canaan be his servant."

28 And Noah lived three hundred and fifty years after the flood.

29 So all the days of Noah were nine hundred and fifty years, and he died.

IV. *The generations of the sons of Noah (10:1–11:9)*

A. *The sons of Japheth*

10 Now these are *the records of* the generations of Shem, Ham, and Japheth, the sons of Noah; and sons were born to them after the flood.

12I.e., The lowest of servants

Marginal references

9:18 Gen 10:6
9:19 Gen 5:32
9:23 Ex 20:12
*9:25 Deut 27:16
9:26 Ps 144:15
9:27 Eph 2:13,14; 3:6

9:17 When God made a covenant between Himself and man He was bound by His own agreement. Seals or signs were given by God as evidence that a covenant had been made. The seal of the Abrahamic covenant was circumcision (see note on 17:9,10). Here (9:17) God covenanted never to destroy life again by a flood. The sign or seal of this covenant was the rainbow across the sky. This was God's guarantee against a similar visitation. Scripture does forecast that the next cataclysmic judgment will take place by means of fire (2 Pet. 3:10,11).
9:21 Noah was never reproved by God for his drunkenness. Fermentation, which turned the juice of the grape into wine, may have become common subsequent to the flood. Scripture affords no evidence of drunkenness prior to this incident.
9:25 Canaan was the son of Ham (10:6), and it is against Canaan that the curse of Noah is directed. The idea that Ham was black and that slavery and other restrictions against blacks are of divine origin is completely untenable. The statement of Noah was prophetically fulfilled when the Canaanites were conquered by the descendants of Shem and later by the Persians, Greeks, and Romans. Ham's descendants, the Canaanites, developed into seven great nations of people in Canaan (Deut. 7:1), but they were idolatrous (Deut. 29:17) and superstitious (Deut. 18:9–11) as well as abominably wicked (Lev. 18:27). Abraham dwelt among them (12:5,6), and the land they occupied was promised to him by God (12:7). Centuries went by before Abraham's posterity entered the land to occupy it; and when they did, God commanded them: (1) to make no covenant with the Canaanites and show no mercy to them (Deut. 7:2); (2) not to follow, but to destroy their idols (Ex. 23:24; Deut. 7:5, 25); (3) not to follow their customs (Lev. 18:26,27); and (4) not to be afraid of them (Deut. 7:17,18; 31:7). Because of Israel's transgression, God permitted a remnant of the Canaanites to remain in the land and to try to chastise Israel (Num. 33:55; Judg. 2:3,21,22; 3:1–4; 4:2).
10:1–32 In this unique genealogy (nothing like it has been found among the nonbiblical sources of the ancient world), the Biblical writer classifies the peoples known to him under the three sons of Noah. In places, however, the alignment is to be understood politically, not racially. For example, the Canaanites, who were Semites (sons of Shem), are listed as sons of Ham (10:6) because for many centuries prior to the invasion by the Israelites the land of Canaan was under the control of the Hamites, the peoples of northeast Africa. If Lud is a reference to the Lydians of Asia Minor, then racially it belongs under Japheth, not Shem (10:22). Many of the names have been found on ancient inscriptions, and positive or very probable identification can be made in a number of cases. For example, *Madai* (10:2) = the Medes; *Javan* = the Ionians (Greeks); *Ashkenaz* (10:3) is probably the Scythians; *Elishah* (10:4) is most likely Alashiya, an ancient designation for the island of Cyprus; *Tarshish* (10:4) is probably southern Spain or Sardinia; *Kittim* (10:4) = people of Cyprus; *Put* (10:6) = Cyrenaica of N. Africa; *Shinar* (10:10) is an ancient name for Babylonia; *Caphtorim* (10:14) = people of Crete; *Heth* (10:15) = the Hittites; and *Sheba* (10:28) = the country in southwest Arabia (approximately present-day Yemen) whose queen visited Solomon.

2   The sons of Japheth *were* Gomer and Magog and Madai and Javan and Tubal and Meshech and Tiras.

3   And the sons of Gomer *were* Ashkenaz and Riphath and Togarmah.

4   And the sons of Javan *were* Elishah and Tarshish, Kittim and Dodanim.

5   From these the coastlands of the nations were separated into their lands, every one according to his language, according to their families, into their nations.

B. *The sons of Ham*

6   And the sons of Ham *were* Cush and Mizraim and Put and Canaan.

7   And the sons of Cush *were* Seba and Havilah and Sabtah and Raamah and Sabteca; and the sons of Raamah *were* Sheba and Dedan.

8   Now Cush became the father of Nimrod; he became a mighty one on the earth.

9   He was a mighty hunter before the LORD; therefore it is said, "Like Nimrod a mighty hunter before the LORD."

10   And the beginning of his kingdom was [13]Babel and Erech and Accad and Calneh, in the land of Shinar.

11   From that land he went forth into Assyria, and built Nineveh and Rehoboth-Ir and Calah,

12   and Resen between Nineveh and Calah; that is the great city.

13   And Mizraim became the father of Ludim and Anamim and Lehabim and Naphtuhim

14   and Pathrusim and Casluhim (from which came the Philistines) and Caphtorim.

15   And Canaan became the father of Sidon, his first-born, and Heth

16   and the Jebusite and the Amorite and the Girgashite

17   and the Hivite and the Arkite and the Sinite

18   and the Arvadite and the Zemarite and the Hamathite; and afterward the families of the Canaanite were spread abroad.

19   And the territory of the Canaanite extended from Sidon as you go toward Gerar, as far as Gaza; as you go toward Sodom and Gomorrah and Admah and Zeboiim, as far as Lasha.

20   These are the sons of Ham, according to their families, according to their languages, by their lands, by their nations.

C. *The sons of Shem*

21   And also to Shem, the father of all the children of Eber, *and* the older brother of Japheth, children were born.

22   The sons of Shem *were* Elam and Asshur and Arpachshad and Lud and Aram.

23   And the sons of Aram *were* Uz and Hul and Gether and Mash.

24   And Arpachshad became the father of Shelah; and Shelah became the father of Eber.

25   And two sons were born to Eber; the name of the one *was* Peleg, for in his days the earth was divided; and his brother's name *was* Joktan.

26   And Joktan became the father of Almodad and Sheleph and Hazarmaveth and Jerah

27   and Hadoram and Uzal and Diklah

28   and Obal and Abimael and Sheba

29   and Ophir and Havilah and Jobab; all these were the sons of Joktan.

30   Now their settlement extended from Mesha as you go toward Sephar, the hill country of the east.

31   These are the sons of Shem, according to their families, according to their languages, by their lands, according to their nations.

32   These are the families of the sons of Noah, according to their genealogies, by their nations; and out of these the nations were separated on the earth after the flood.

[13]Or, *Babylon*

10:2
1 Chr 1:5-7

10:5
Gen 5:32

10:6
1 Chr 1:8-10

10:9
Mic 5:6

10:10
Mic 5:6

10:13
1 Chr 1:8,11

10:15
1 Chr 1:13

10:18
1 Chr 1:16;
18:3
10:19
Num 34:2-12

10:22
1 Chr 1:17;
Gen 14:1,9;
2 Kin 15:29;
Gen 11:10;
Is 66:19
10:23
Job 1:1
10:24
Gen 11:12;
Luke 3:35
10:25
1 Chr 1:19
10:26-29
1 Chr 1:20-23

10:32
v. 1

D. *The tower of Babel: the confusion of tongues*

11 Now the whole earth used the same language and the same words. 2 And it came about as they journeyed east, that they found a plain in the land of Shinar and settled there.

3 And they said to one another, "Come, let us make bricks and burn *them* thoroughly." And they used brick for stone, and they used tar for mortar.

4 And they said, "Come, let us build for ourselves a city, and a tower whose top *will reach* into heaven, and let us make for ourselves a name; lest we be scattered abroad over the face of the whole earth."

5 And the LORD came down to see the city and the tower which the sons of men had built.

6 And the LORD said, "Behold, they are one people, and they all have the same language. And this is what they began to do, and now nothing which they purpose to do will be impossible for them.

7 "Come, let Us go down and there confuse their language, that they may not understand one another's speech."

8 So the LORD scattered them abroad from there over the face of the whole earth; and they stopped building the city.

9 Therefore its name was called [14]Babel, because there the LORD confused the language of the whole earth; and from there the LORD scattered them abroad over the face of the whole earth.

V. *The generations of Shem (11:10–26)*

10 These are *the records of* the generations of Shem. Shem was one hundred years old, and became the father of Arpachshad two years after the flood;

11 and Shem lived five hundred years after he became the father of Arpachshad, and he had *other* sons and daughters.

12 And Arpachshad lived thirty-five years, and became the father of Shelah;

13 and Arpachshad lived four hundred and three years after he became the father of Shelah, and he had *other* sons and daughters.

14 And Shelah lived thirty years, and became the father of Eber;

15 and Shelah lived four hundred and three years after he became the father of Eber, and he had *other* sons and daughters.

16 And Eber lived thirty-four years, and became the father of Peleg;

17 and Eber lived four hundred and thirty years after he became the father of Peleg, and he had *other* sons and daughters.

18 And Peleg lived thirty years, and became the father of Reu;

19 and Peleg lived two hundred and nine years after he became the father of Reu, and he had *other* sons and daughters.

20 And Reu lived thirty-two years, and became the father of Serug;

21 and Reu lived two hundred and seven years after he became the father of Serug, and he had *other* sons and daughters.

22 And Serug lived thirty years, and became the father of Nahor;

23 and Serug lived two hundred years after he became the father of Nahor, and he had *other* sons and daughters.

24 And Nahor lived twenty-nine years, and became the father of Terah;

25 and Nahor lived one hundred and nineteen years after he became the father of Terah, and he had *other* sons and daughters.

[14]Or, *Babylon*

11:1 The languages of men differed at the time of the flood. After the flood, in the area covered, there was now a single language—that which was spoken by Noah and his family. It is true that 10:5,20,31 speak of various languages, but these verses look forward to the history of the Noahic descendants after the incident of the tower of Babel. Subsequent to the flood, the sons of Noah were directed to replenish the earth. This meant geographical dispersion as well as numerical increase. Sin, which was expressed by the building of the tower of Babel, was judged by the confusion of tongues that shall continue until the end of the age.
11:3 Since stone was very scarce in Babylonia (Shinar), it was the custom to build with fired bricks and bitumen mortar.

11:4–9 The Assyrian *Bab-ili* is the native name for the Greek Babylon. It means *Gate of God*. There is no connection between this word and the Hebrew word *balal*, which means "to confound." The story of the tower of Babel has other counterparts, such as the Greek myth of the Titans who tried to climb to heaven. The Biblical account is far older, and from it many of the later tales may have been taken. Various suggestions have been made as to the location of the tower of Babel, e.g., Birs Nimrud (which is seven miles from Babylon), and Amran (which is within the city). In later history Nebuchadnezzar speaks of the Ziggurat Babili (Tower of Babylon), which had been begun by a previous king but had fallen into a ruinous state until Nebuchadnezzar restored and completed it.

Margin references: 11:2 Ex 1:11,14; 5:7-19 | *11:4ff Deut 1:28 | 11:5 Gen 18:21 | 11:6 Acts 17:26; Gen 9:19 | 11:7 Gen 1:26; 42:23; Ex 4:11; 1 Cor 14:2,11 | 11:8 Luke 1:51; Gen 10:25,32 | 11:9 Gen 10:10 | 11:10 Gen 10:22; 1 Chr 1:17 | 11:12 Luke 3:36 | 11:16 1 Chr 1:19 | 11:20 Luke 3:35 | 11:24 Luke 3:34

26 And Terah lived seventy years, and became the father of Abram, Nahor and Haran.

VI. The generations of Terah (11:27–25:11)

A. The genealogy of Abraham

27 Now these are *the records of* the generations of Terah. Terah became the father of Abram, Nahor and Haran; and Haran became the father of Lot.

28 And Haran died in the presence of his father Terah in the land of his birth, in Ur of the Chaldeans.

29 And Abram and Nahor took wives for themselves. The name of Abram's wife was Sarai; and the name of Nahor's wife was Milcah, the daughter of Haran, the father of Milcah and Iscah.

30 And Sarai was barren; she had no child.

31 And Terah took Abram his son, and Lot the son of Haran, his grandson, and Sarai his daughter-in-law, his son Abram's wife; and they went out together from Ur of the Chaldeans in order to enter the land of Canaan; and they went as far as Haran, and settled there.

32 And the days of Terah were two hundred and five years; and Terah died in Haran.

B. The call of Abram

1. The promise to make him a blessing

12 Now the LORD said to Abram,
"Go forth from your country,
And from your relatives
And from your father's house,
To the land which I will show you;

2 And I will make you a great nation,
And I will bless you,
And make your name great;
And so you shall be a blessing;

3 And I will bless those who bless you,
And the one who curses you I will curse.
And in you all the families of the earth shall be blessed."

2. The promise of the land of Canaan

4 So Abram went forth as the LORD had spoken to him; and Lot went with him. Now Abram was seventy-five years old when he departed from Haran.

5 And Abram took Sarai his wife and Lot his nephew, and all their possessions which they had accumulated, and the persons which they had acquired in Haran, and they set out for the land of Canaan; thus they came to the land of Canaan.

6 And Abram passed through the land as far as the site of Shechem, to the oak of Moreh. Now the Canaanite *was* then in the land.

7 And the LORD appeared to Abram and said, "To your descendants I will give this land." So he built an altar there to the LORD who had appeared to him.

8 Then he proceeded from there to the mountain on the east of Bethel, and pitched his tent, with Bethel on the west and Ai on the east; and there he built an altar to the LORD and called upon the name of the LORD.

Marginal references:
11:26 Josh 24:2
11:29 Gen 24:10; 17:15; 20:12; 22:20
11:30 Gen 16:1
*11:31 Gen 15:7; Neh 9:7; Acts 7:4
12:1 Acts 7:3; Heb 11:8
*12:2 Gen 15:5; 17:4,5; 18:18; 22:17; 28:14; 32:12; 35:11; 46:3
12:3 Gen 27:29; Ex 23:22; Num 24:9; Gen 18:18; 22:18; 26:4; Acts 3:25; Gal 3:8
12:4 Gen 11:27,31
12:5 Gen 14:14; 11:31
12:6 Heb 11:9; Deut 11:30; Gen 10:18,19
*12:7 Gen 17:1; 13:15; 17:8; Ps 105:9; Gen 13:4
12:8 Gen 13:4

11:27,28 Abraham has often been thought of as an ignorant nomad, an illiterate and uneducated ancient. This is not so. Archaeological discoveries have shown that Ur of the Chaldeans was a center of advanced culture. There were libraries in the schools and temples. The people used grammars, dictionaries, encyclopedias, and reference works along with textbooks on mathematics, religion, and politics. What was true for Babylonia was also true for Egypt, where, more than a thousand years before Abraham's time, writing was well established. It is quite possible, therefore, that Abraham left written records that were incorporated in the Pentateuch.

11:31 Abraham's ancestors stemmed from this area, because near Haran were towns called Peleg, Serug, Nahor, and Terah, all names of Abraham's ancestors.

12:2 The Abrahamic covenant is mentioned several times in Genesis (12:2,3,7; 13:14–17; chs 15; 17; 18; 21:12; 22:16–18). The covenant was essentially one of promise, the only requirement being Abraham's response in trust and faith to the new God calling him from his family and land. The covenant takes many variations in Genesis, but the two basic features of it are "land" and "descendants." The progeny of Abraham were to be a blessing to all, and Abraham was guaranteed a son through whom his line would be perpetuated.

12:7 Abraham's altar at Shechem implies animal sacrifice, which was common to all Semites.

9   And Abram journeyed on, continuing toward the [15]Negev.

3. The sojourn in Egypt

10   Now there was a famine in the land; so Abram went down to Egypt to sojourn there, for the famine was severe in the land.
11   And it came about when he came near to Egypt, that he said to Sarai his wife, "See now, I know that you are a beautiful woman;
12   and it will come about when the Egyptians see you, that they will say, 'This is his wife'; and they will kill me, but they will let you live.
13   "Please say that you are my sister so that it may go well with me because of you, and that I may live on account of you."
14   And it came about when Abram came into Egypt, the Egyptians saw that the woman was very beautiful.
15   And Pharaoh's officials saw her and praised her to Pharaoh; and the woman was taken into Pharaoh's house.
16   Therefore he treated Abram well for her sake; and gave him sheep and oxen and donkeys and male and female servants and female donkeys and camels.
17   But the LORD struck Pharaoh and his house with great plagues because of Sarai, Abram's wife.
18   Then Pharaoh called Abram and said, "What is this you have done to me? Why did you not tell me that she was your wife?
19   "Why did you say, 'She is my sister,' so that I took her for my wife? Now then, here is your wife, take her and go."
20   And Pharaoh commanded *his* men concerning him; and they escorted him away, with his wife and all that belonged to him.

13 So Abram went up from Egypt to the [15]Negev, he and his wife and all that belonged to him; and Lot with him.

C. The separation of Abram and Lot

1. The strife between the herdsmen of Lot and Abram

2   Now Abram was very rich in livestock, in silver and in gold.
3   And he went on his journeys from the [15]Negev as far as Bethel, to the place where his tent had been at the beginning, between Bethel and Ai,
4   to the place of the altar, which he had made there formerly; and there Abram called on the name of the LORD.
5   Now Lot, who went with Abram, also had flocks and herds and tents.
6   And the land could not sustain them while dwelling together; for their possessions were so great that they were not able to remain together.
7   And there was strife between the herdsmen of Abram's livestock and the herdsmen of Lot's livestock. Now the Canaanite and the Perizzite were dwelling then in the land.

2. Lot chooses Sodom

8   Then Abram said to Lot, "Please let there be no strife between you and me, nor between my herdsmen and your herdsmen, for we are brothers.
9   "Is not the whole land before you? Please separate from me: if *to* the left, then I will go to the right; or if *to* the right, then I will go to the left."
10   And Lot lifted up his eyes and saw all the valley of the Jordan, that it was

[15]I.e., South country

12:9 There are references to the Negev here and elsewhere in Genesis. These take on further significance because of Nelson Glueck's findings, which show that the Negev was occupied from 2100–1800 B.C., the period of Abraham. Thus, when Abraham made his round trip to Egypt he followed a series of water stations from Mamre (Hebron) southwest to Kadesh (later called Kadesh-barnea). Jacob and Moses knew of this route also.
12:10 In times of famine it was customary, according to Egyptian records, for peoples of Palestine and Syria to seek refuge in Egypt.
12:13 God's will, done God's way, never lacks for God's blessing. *Say that you are my sister.* Here Abraham did not

tell the truth. Selfishness overtook this man of faith. Fear for his own life made him forget what consequences his deceit would bring for Sarah and others. Although Abraham was a man of faith he was not a perfect man. This incident serves to illustrate the fact that the end does not justify the means. The means and the end must both be right.
13:7 The strife between the herdsmen of Abraham and Lot represents the first threat to the promise of God that Abraham would possess the land. Abraham lived above this threat in faith, and his gracious attitude toward Lot was rewarded by another confirmation of the promise by God. (Read vv. 14–17 and ch. 15.)

2. The sacrifice offered

7 And He said to him, "I am the LORD who brought you out of Ur of the Chaldeans, to give you this land to possess it."

8 And he said, "O Lord GOD, how may I know that I shall possess it?"

9 So He said to him, "Bring Me a three year old heifer, and a three year old female goat, and a three year old ram, and a turtledove, and a young pigeon."

10 Then he brought all these to Him and cut them in two, and laid each half opposite the other; but he did not cut the birds.

11 And the birds of prey came down upon the carcasses, and Abram drove them away.

12 Now when the sun was going down, a deep sleep fell upon Abram; and behold, terror *and* great darkness fell upon him.

13 And *God* said to Abram, "Know for certain that your descendants will be strangers in a land that is not theirs, where they will be enslaved and oppressed four hundred years.

14 "But I will also judge the nation whom they will serve; and afterward they will come out with many possessions.

15 "And as for you, you shall go to your fathers in peace; you shall be buried at a good old age.

16 "Then in the fourth generation they shall return here, for the iniquity of the Amorite is not yet complete."

3. The promise of a land

17 And it came about when the sun had set, that it was very dark, and behold, *there appeared* a smoking oven and a flaming torch which passed between these pieces.

18 On that day the LORD made a covenant with Abram, saying,
"To your descendants I have given this land,
From the river of Egypt as far as the great river, the river Euphrates:

19 the Kenite and the Kenizzite and the Kadmonite

20 and the Hittite and the Perizzite and the Rephaim

21 and the Amorite and the Canaanite and the Girgashite and the Jebusite."

F. The birth of Ishmael

1. Sarai gives Hagar to Abram

16 Now Sarai, Abram's wife had borne him no *children*, and she had an Egyptian maid whose name was Hagar.

2 So Sarai said to Abram, "Now behold, the LORD has prevented me from bearing *children*. Please go in to my maid; perhaps I shall obtain children through her." And Abram listened to the voice of Sarai.

3 And after Abram had lived ten years in the land of Canaan, Abram's wife

Cross references (margin):
15:7 Gen 11:31; 13:15,17
15:8 Luke 1:18
*15:10 Jer 34:18; Lev 1:17
15:12 Gen 2:21
*15:13 Acts 7:6; Ex 12:40
15:14 Ex 12:36
15:15 Gen 25:8
15:16 1 Kin 21:26
15:17 Jer 34:18,19
15:18 Gen 24:7; 12:7; Ex 23:31; Num 34:3; Deut 11:24; Josh 1:4
16:1 Gen 11:30; 21:9; Gal 4:24
16:2 Gen 30:3,4,9, 10
*16:3 Gen 12:5

---

the apostle Paul uses Abraham as an example of one whose faith, and not his works, justified him. Indeed, he argues that Abraham was justified *before* he was circumcised, a seal that follows faith, not precedes it.

15:10 Cutting the animals in halves may have been part of the normal custom or ritual at a covenant sealing. The Hebrew of 15:18 reads that God "cut a covenant" with Abraham. For a long time Old Testament scholars doubted the accuracy of this expression, but texts have been uncovered in Qatna and Mari informing us that covenants were sealed by some ritual involving the cutting up of donkeys.

15:13 God here revealed to Abraham future history and events in the life of the promised seed. The bondage in Egypt is foretold and its length marked as four hundred years or four generations. The Egyptian bondage, then, was part of the plan of God for the cradling of the Hebrew race. But it also reveals the mercy and kindness of God toward the Amorites, to whom He extended time for repentance before judgment should befall them. (See also note to 12:10.)

16:3 The story of Hagar and Ishmael has real spiritual value and instruction for the believer. Abraham was seventy-five years old when he left Haran and received God's covenantal promise (12:4). Inherent in the covenant was the promise of seed. Now at eighty-five years it appeared quite

impossible of fulfillment. *Abram's wife, Sarai, took Hagar . . . and gave her to her husband Abram as his wife.* Archaeological evidence of Nuzu customs indicates that in some marriage contracts a childless wife was required to furnish a substitute for her husband. In oriental eyes, childlessness was the greatest of tragedies. Nuzu custom stipulated further that the slave wife and her children could not be sent away. Thus the action of Sarah and Abraham was undoubtedly consonant with the customs of that day. When Abraham was eighty-six years of age, Hagar gave birth to Ishmael (16:16). This incident reveals how two genuine believers may seek to fulfill God's will by normally acceptable but spiritually carnal methods. The promise of God was not to Hagar but to Sarah. Sarah suggested the use of Hagar, and Abraham consented to the arrangement. Both were guilty. The birth of Ishmael introduced a people (the nucleus of the later Muslims) who have been a challenge both to the Jews and to the Christian church. It was not until Abraham was a hundred years old that Isaac was born (21:5). From the fulfillment we can draw the lessons that God's ways are not our ways and His thoughts are higher than our thoughts (Is. 55:8,9). Patient waiting would have produced the desired results without the additional problems created by impatience and lack of faith. God always rewards those who have

Sarai took Hagar the Egyptian, her maid, and gave her to her husband Abram as his wife.

4   And he went in to Hagar, and she conceived; and when she saw that she had conceived, her mistress was despised in her sight.

16:5
Gen 31:53

5   And Sarai said to Abram, "May the wrong done me be upon you. I gave my maid into your arms; but when she saw that she had conceived, I was despised in her sight. May the LORD judge between you and me."

6   But Abram said to Sarai, "Behold, your maid is in your power; do to her what is good in your sight." So Sarai treated her harshly, and she fled from her presence.

2. God's promise to Hagar

16:7
Gen 21:17,18;
22:11,15;
31:11; 20:1

7   Now the angel of the LORD found her by a spring of water in the wilderness, by the spring on the way to Shur.

8   And he said, "Hagar, Sarai's maid, where have you come from and where are you going?" And she said, "I am fleeing from the presence of my mistress Sarai."

9   Then the angel of the LORD said to her, "Return to your mistress, and submit yourself to her authority."

16:10
Gen 17:20

10   Moreover, the angel of the LORD said to her, "I will greatly multiply your descendants so that they shall be too many to count."

16:11
Ex 3:7,9

11   The angel of the LORD said to her further,
    "Behold, you are with child,
    And you shall bear a son;
    And you shall call his name [16]Ishmael,
    Because the LORD has given heed to your affliction.

16:12
Gen 25:18

12   "And he will be a wild donkey of a man,
    His hand *will be* against everyone,
    And everyone's hand *will be* against him;
    And he will live to the east of all his brothers."

16:13
Gen 32:30

13   Then she called the name of the LORD who spoke to her, "Thou art a God who sees"; for she said, "Have I even remained alive here after seeing Him?"

14   Therefore the well was called [17]Beer-lahai-roi; behold, it is between Kadesh and Bered.

3. The birth of the baby

16:15
Gal 4:22

15   So Hagar bore Abram a son; and Abram called the name of his son, whom Hagar bore, Ishmael.

16   And Abram was eighty-six years old when Hagar bore Ishmael to him.

G. The circumcision of Abraham

1. The covenant restated

*17:1
Gen 28:3;
Ex 6:3;
Deut 18:13

17
Now when Abram was ninety-nine years old, the LORD appeared to Abram and said to him,
    "I am God Almighty;
    Walk before Me, and be blameless.

17:2
Gen 15:18

2   "And I will establish My covenant between Me and you,
    And I will multiply you exceedingly."

3   And Abram fell on his face, and God talked with him, saying,

17:4
Gen 35:11;
48:19
17:5
Neh 9:7;
Rom 4:17

4   "As for Me, behold, My covenant is with you,
    And you shall be the father of a multitude of nations.

5   "No longer shall your name be called [18]Abram,
    But your name shall be [19]Abraham;

[16]I.e., God hears   [17]I.e., the well of the living one who sees me   [18]I.e., exalted father   [19]I.e., father of a multitude

---

faith to believe His promises.

16:14 The well Beer-lahai-roi, near Kadesh (called Kadesh-barnea in Num. 32:8; 34:4; and in Deuteronomy and Joshua), indicates that Hagar wandered quite a way in the wilderness. 24:62; 25:11 claim that Isaac dwelt in this region.

17:1 *El Shaddai* (Hebrew), meaning *God Almighty*, from the root *shadad* (be violent, irresistibly strong). Some accept another interpretation, "God of the mountain," which is not to be taken as worship of nature (animism) but that God appeared to Abraham on the mountain. El Shaddai appears to Abraham when he is ninety-nine years of age, and when the birth of an heir seems literally impossible. The mighty God steps in and does the impossible. God changes Abram's name to Abraham, *father of a multitude* (17:5), and the following year Isaac is born as the seed of promise. See also note to 2:4 on the names of God.

For I will make you the father of a multitude of nations.

6   "And I will make you exceedingly fruitful, and I will make nations of you, and kings shall come forth from you.

7   "And I will establish My covenant between Me and you and your descendants after you throughout their generations for an everlasting covenant, to be God to you and to your descendants after you.

8   "And I will give to you and to your descendants after you, the land of your sojournings, all the land of Canaan, for an everlasting possession; and I will be their God."

2. *The sign of the covenant*

9   God said further to Abraham, "Now as for you, you shall keep My covenant, you and your descendants after you throughout their generations.

10   "This is My covenant, which you shall keep, between Me and you and your descendants after you: every male among you shall be circumcised.

11   "And you shall be circumcised in the flesh of your foreskin; and it shall be the sign of the covenant between Me and you.

12   "And every male among you who is eight days old shall be circumcised throughout your generations, a *servant* who is born in the house or who is bought with money from any foreigner, who is not of your descendants.

13   "A *servant* who is born in your house or who is bought with your money shall surely be circumcised; thus shall My covenant be in your flesh for an everlasting covenant.

14   "But an uncircumcised male who is not circumcised in the flesh of his foreskin, that person shall be cut off from his people; he has broken My covenant."

15   Then God said to Abraham, "As for Sarai your wife, you shall not call her name Sarai, but 20Sarah *shall be* her name.

3. *The promise of Isaac*

16   "And I will bless her, and indeed I will give you a son by her. Then I will bless her, and she shall be *a mother of* nations; kings of peoples shall come from her."

17   Then Abraham fell on his face and laughed, and said in his heart, "Will a child be born to a man one hundred years old? And will Sarah, who is ninety years old, bear *a child?*"

18   And Abraham said to God, "Oh that Ishmael might live before Thee!"

19   But God said, "No, but Sarah your wife shall bear you a son, and you shall call his name 21Isaac; and I will establish My covenant with him for an everlasting covenant for his descendants after him.

20   "And as for Ishmael, I have heard you; behold, I will bless him, and will make him fruitful, and will multiply him exceedingly. He shall become the father of twelve princes, and I will make him a great nation.

21   "But My covenant I will establish with Isaac, whom Sarah will bear to you at this season next year."

4. *The circumcisions performed*

22   And when He finished talking with him, God went up from Abraham.

23   Then Abraham took Ishmael his son, and all *the servants* who were born in his house and all who were bought with his money, every male among the men of Abraham's household, and circumcised the flesh of their foreskin in the very same day, as God had said to him.

20I.e., princess   21I.e., he laughs

17:6
Gen 35:11;
Matt 1:6
17:7
Gal 3:17;
Gen 26:24;
28:13;
Rom 9:8
17:8
Gen 12:7;
Ps 105:9,11;
Gen 23:4;
28:4; Ex 6:7;
Lev 26:12

17:10
Acts 7:8

17:11
Ex 12:48;
Deut 10:16;
Rom 4:11
17:12
Lev 12:3;
Luke 2:21

17:14
Ex 4:24

17:16
Gen 18:10;
35:11;
Gal 4:31
*17:17
Gen 18:12;
21:6

17:19
Gen 18:10;
21:2; 26:2-5

17:20
Gen 16:10;
25:12,16

17:23
Gen 14:14

17:9,10 Circumcision was covenantal in nature, being the outward sign or seal of the Abrahamic agreement that God made (17:11). The failure to be circumcised separated one from the people of Israel. The command was perpetuated in the Law of Moses (Lev. 12:3; John 7:22,23). In the gospel dispensation, circumcision was abolished (Eph. 2:11–15; Col. 3:11), and to require it now is to revert to legalism. Circumcision in this age is of the heart and not of the flesh, but even when it was binding it had no value unless accompanied by faith and obedience (Rom. 2:25; 3:30; 1 Cor. 7:19; Gal. 5:6).
17:17 After twenty-four years of impatient waiting, the words of God seem an idle fancy to Abraham. All of the

outward circumstances were against him. The biological facts of life stood over against the promise of God. Sight and sense told him the promise was impossible of fulfillment. Yet Abraham was a man of faith who had moments of doubt. How much we can learn from his laugh of disbelief here!
17:18 Abraham still hoped that Ishmael would be recognized, but this plea and God's answer in v. 19 show that man's answers and ways can never be substituted for God's.
17:22–27 Abraham's faith triumphed over his doubts. He responded to the covenant by circumcising himself and all his males. Thus he passed another crucial stage in his walk and experience with the covenant-keeping God.

17:24
Rom 4:11

18:1
Gen 13:18;
14:13
18:2
vv. 16,22;
Gen 32:24;
Josh 5:13;
Judg 13:6-11

18:4
Gen 19:2;
43:24
18:5
Judg 6:18,19;
13:15,16

18:8
Gen 19:3

18:10
Rom 9:9

18:11
Gen 17:17;
Rom 4:19
*18:12ff
1 Pet 3:6

18:14
Jer 32:17,27;
Zech 8:6;
Matt 3:9;
Luke 1:37

18:18
Gal 3:8
18:19
Deut 4:9,10;
6:7;
Josh 24:15;
Eph 6:4
18:20
Gen 19:13;
Ezek 16:49,
50

24 Now Abraham was ninety-nine years old when he was circumcised in the flesh of his foreskin.

25 And Ishmael his son was thirteen years old when he was circumcised in the flesh of his foreskin.

26 In the very same day Abraham was circumcised, and Ishmael his son.

27 And all the men of his household, who were born in the house or bought with money from a foreigner, were circumcised with him.

H. *Sodom and Gomorrah destroyed*

1. *Abraham entertains heavenly visitors*

18 Now the LORD appeared to him by the oaks of Mamre, while he was sitting at the tent door in the heat of the day.

2 And when he lifted up his eyes and looked, behold, three men were standing opposite him; and when he saw *them*, he ran from the tent door to meet them, and bowed himself to the earth,

3 and said, "My lord, if now I have found favor in your sight, please do not pass your servant by.

4 "Please let a little water be brought and wash your feet, and rest yourselves under the tree;

5 and I will bring a piece of bread, that you may refresh yourselves; after that you may go on, since you have visited your servant." And they said, "So do, as you have said."

6 So Abraham hurried into the tent to Sarah, and said, "Quickly, prepare three measures of fine flour, knead *it*, and make bread cakes."

7 Abraham also ran to the herd, and took a tender and choice calf, and gave *it* to the servant; and he hurried to prepare it.

8 And he took curds and milk and the calf which he had prepared, and placed *it* before them; and he was standing by them under the tree as they ate.

2. *Sarah laughs*

9 Then they said to him, "Where is Sarah your wife?" And he said, "Behold, in the tent."

10 And he said, "I will surely return to you at this time next year; and behold, Sarah your wife shall have a son." And Sarah was listening at the tent door, which was behind him.

11 Now Abraham and Sarah were old, advanced in age; Sarah was past child-bearing.

12 And Sarah laughed to herself, saying, "After I have become old, shall I have pleasure, my lord being old also?"

13 And the LORD said to Abraham, "Why did Sarah laugh, saying, 'Shall I indeed bear *a child*, when I am *so* old?'

14 "Is anything too difficult for the LORD? At the appointed time I will return to you, at this time next year, and Sarah shall have a son."

15 Sarah denied *it* however, saying, "I did not laugh"; for she was afraid. And He said, "No, but you did laugh."

3. *God informs Abraham of the end of Sodom and Gomorrah*

16 Then the men rose up from there, and looked down toward Sodom; and Abraham was walking with them to send them off.

17 And the LORD said, "Shall I hide from Abraham what I am about to do,

18 since Abraham will surely become a great and mighty nation, and in him all the nations of the earth will be blessed?

19 "For I have chosen him, in order that he may command his children and his household after him to keep the way of the LORD by doing righteousness and justice; in order that the LORD may bring upon Abraham what He has spoken about him."

20 And the LORD said, "The outcry of Sodom and Gomorrah is indeed great, and their sin is exceedingly grave.

18:12–15 Sarah, like Abraham, passed through periods of doubt and disbelief. It was the laughter of doubt in her heart that caused God to pose the question, *Is anything too difficult for the LORD?* (v. 14). God, who does not change, continues faithful despite the sin of unbelief in His people. In 17:15 the name Sarai, meaning "contentious" or "princely," was changed to Sarah, which means "princess."

21 "I will go down now, and see if they have done entirely according to its outcry, which has come to Me; and if not, I will know."

4. *Abraham intercedes for Sodom*

22   Then the men turned away from there and went toward Sodom, while Abraham was still standing before the LORD.

23   And Abraham came near and said, "Wilt Thou indeed sweep away the righteous with the wicked?

24   "Suppose there are fifty righteous within the city; wilt Thou indeed sweep *it* away and not spare the place for the sake of the fifty righteous who are in it?

25   "Far be it from Thee to do such a thing, to slay the righteous with the wicked, so that the righteous and the wicked are *treated* alike. Far be it from Thee! Shall not the Judge of all the earth deal justly?"

26   So the LORD said, "If I find in Sodom fifty righteous within the city, then I will spare the whole place on their account."

27   And Abraham answered and said, "Now behold, I have ventured to speak to the Lord, although I am *but* dust and ashes.

28   "Suppose the fifty righteous are lacking five, wilt Thou destroy the whole city because of five?" And He said, "I will not destroy *it* if I find forty-five there."

29   And he spoke to Him yet again and said, "Suppose forty are found there?" And He said, "I will not do *it* on account of the forty."

30   Then he said, "Oh may the Lord not be angry, and I shall speak; suppose thirty are found there?" And He said, "I will not do *it* if I find thirty there."

31   And he said, "Now behold, I have ventured to speak to the Lord; suppose twenty are found there?" And He said, "I will not destroy *it* on account of the twenty."

32   Then he said, "Oh may the Lord not be angry, and I shall speak only this once; suppose ten are found there?" And He said, "I will not destroy *it* on account of the ten."

33   And as soon as He had finished speaking to Abraham the LORD departed; and Abraham returned to his place.

5. *Lot entertains two angels*

19   Now the two angels came to Sodom in the evening as Lot was sitting in the gate of Sodom. When Lot saw *them,* he rose to meet them and bowed down *with his* face to the ground.

2   And he said, "Now behold, my lords, please turn aside into your servant's house, and spend the night, and wash your feet; then you may rise early and go on your way." They said however, "No, but we shall spend the night in the square."

3   Yet he urged them strongly, so they turned aside to him and entered his house; and he prepared a feast for them, and baked unleavened bread, and they ate.

4   Before they lay down, the men of the city, the men of Sodom, surrounded the house, both young and old, all the people from every quarter;

5   and they called to Lot and said to him, "Where are the men who came to you tonight? Bring them out to us that we may have relations with them."

6   But Lot went out to them at the doorway, and shut the door behind him,

7   and said, "Please, my brothers, do not act wickedly.

8   "Now behold, I have two daughters who have not had relations with man; please let me bring them out to you, and do to them whatever you like; only do nothing to these men, inasmuch as they have come under the shelter of my roof."

9   But they said, "Stand aside." Furthermore, they said, "This one came in as

Cross-references (right margin):

18:21 Gen 11:5
18:22 Gen 19:1
18:23 Heb 10:22; Num 16:22
18:24 Jer 5:1
*18:25 Job 8:20; Is 3:10,11; Rom 3:6
18:27 Gen 3:19; Job 4:19; 30:19; 42:6; 2 Cor 5:1
*18:32 Judg 6:39; James 5:16
*19:1 Gen 18:22; 18:1ff
19:2 Heb 13:2; Gen 18:4
19:3 Gen 18:8
19:5 Is 3:9; Judg 19:22; Rom 1:24
19:6 Judg 19:23
19:8 see Judg 19:24
19:9 2 Pet 2:7,8; Ex 2:14

18:25 God is love (1 John 4:8), but because He loves holiness and truth, He is also just (Ps. 89:14; 145:17). His judgments are: (1) according to truth (Rev. 19:2); (2) universal and certain (Rom. 2:6); (3) impersonal and impartial (Rom. 2:11); and (4) concerned with motive as well as outward conduct (Luke 12:2,3; Rom. 2:16). Three major judgments are mentioned in Scripture: (1) the judgment of believers' sins, which is past, having been inflicted on the Christ at Calvary (John 5:24; Rom. 8:1); (2) the believers' judgment for rewards (Rom. 14:10; 1 Cor. 3:10–15; 2 Cor. 5:10); and (3) the judgment of unbelievers (Rev. 20:11–15). 18:32 Six times Abraham beseeches God to spare Sodom. Each time God grants his petition. This incident should encourage believers to intercede effectively and to expect responses to prayer. It is a solemn commentary on the awful condition of Sodom that not even ten righteous people could be found within its gates.
19:1 Lot and Abraham both were righteous men (15:6; 2 Pet. 2:7,8), and both enjoyed similar backgrounds and advantages. Abraham, however, looked *for the city which has foundations, whose architect and builder is God* (Heb. 11:10). Lot, on the contrary, looked toward the city without heavenly foundations, choosing for the present time without concern for eternity (13:5–18). Lot's misfortune should be a warning for all.

an alien, and already he is acting like a judge; now we will treat you worse than them." So they pressed hard against Lot and came near to break the door.

10   But the men reached out their hands and brought Lot into the house with them, and shut the door.

11   And they struck the men who were at the doorway of the house with blindness, both small and great, so that they wearied *themselves trying* to find the doorway.

6. *Lot informed of the imminent destruction*

12   Then the men said to Lot, "Whom else have you here? A son-in-law, and your sons, and your daughters, and whomever you have in the city, bring *them* out of the place;

13   for we are about to destroy this place, because their outcry has become so great before the LORD that the LORD has sent us to destroy it."

14   And Lot went out and spoke to his sons-in-law, who were to marry his daughters, and said, "Up, get out of this place, for the LORD will destroy the city." But he appeared to his sons-in-law to be jesting.

7. *The departure of the family of Lot*

15   And when morning dawned, the angels urged Lot, saying, "Up, take your wife and your two daughters, who are here, lest you be swept away in the punishment of the city."

16   But he hesitated. So the men seized his hand and the hand of his wife and the hands of his two daughters, for the compassion of the LORD *was* upon him; and they brought him out, and put him outside the city.

17   And it came about when they had brought them outside, that one said, "Escape for your life! Do not look behind you, and do not stay anywhere in the valley; escape to the mountains, lest you be swept away."

18   But Lot said to them, "Oh no, my lords!

19   "Now behold, your servant has found favor in your sight, and you have magnified your lovingkindness, which you have shown me by saving my life; but I cannot escape to the mountains, lest the disaster overtake me and I die;

20   now behold, this town is near *enough* to flee to, and it is small. Please, let me escape there (is it not small?) that my life may be saved."

21   And he said to him, "Behold, I grant you this request also, not to overthrow the town of which you have spoken.

22   "Hurry, escape there, for I cannot do anything until you arrive there." Therefore the name of the town was called [22]Zoar.

23   The sun had risen over the earth when Lot came to Zoar.

8. *Sodom and Gomorrah destroyed*

24   Then the LORD rained on Sodom and Gomorrah brimstone and fire from the LORD out of heaven,

25   and He overthrew those cities, and all the valley, and all the inhabitants of the cities, and what grew on the ground.

26   But his wife, from behind him, looked *back;* and she became a pillar of salt.

27   Now Abraham arose early in the morning *and went* to the place where he had stood before the LORD;

28   and he looked down toward Sodom and Gomorrah, and toward all the land of the valley, and he saw, and behold, the smoke of the land ascended like the smoke of a furnace.

29   Thus it came about, when God destroyed the cities of the valley, that God remembered Abraham, and sent Lot out of the midst of the overthrow, when He overthrew the cities in which Lot lived.

9. *The sin of Lot's daughters: the origins of the Moabites and Ammonites*

30   And Lot went up from Zoar, and stayed in the mountains, and his two

19:11
see
2 Kin 6:18;
Acts 13:11

19:12
Gen 7:1;
2 Pet 2:7,9

19:13
Gen 18:20;
1 Chr 21:15

19:14
Num 16:21;
Ex 9:21;
Luke 17:28

19:15
Num 16:24,
26; Rev 18:4

19:16
Luke 18:13;
Ps 34:22

19:17
1 Kin 19:3;
Jer 48:6;
v. 26

19:21
Job 42:8,9;
Ps 145:9

*19:24
Deut 29:23;
Is 13:19;
Luke 17:29;
Jude 7

19:25
Ps 107:34

19:26
Luke 17:32

19:27
Gen 18:22

19:28
Rev 9:2; 18:9

19:29
2 Pet 2:7

19:24 Sodom and Gomorrah, in the Valley of Siddim (Dead Sea) filled with *tar pits* (14:3,10), were probably destroyed by lightning and possibly an earthquake (v. 25).

[22]I.e., *small*

daughters with him; for he was afraid to stay in Zoar; and he stayed in a cave, he and his two daughters.

31   Then the first-born said to the younger, "Our father is old, and there is not a man on earth to come in to us after the manner of the earth.

32   "Come, let us make our father drink wine, and let us lie with him, that we may preserve our family through our father."

33   So they made their father drink wine that night, and the first-born went in and lay with her father; and he did not know when she lay down or when she arose.

34   And it came about on the morrow, that the first-born said to the younger, "Behold, I lay last night with my father; let us make him drink wine tonight also; then you go in and lie with him, that we may preserve our family through our father."

35   So they made their father drink wine that night also, and the younger arose and lay with him; and he did not know when she lay down or when she arose.

36   Thus both the daughters of Lot were with child by their father.

37   And the first-born bore a son, and called his name Moab; he is the father of the Moabites to this day.

38   And as for the younger, she also bore a son, and called his name Ben-ammi; he is the father of the sons of Ammon to this day.

I. Abraham and Abimelech

1. Abimelech's sin of ignorance

20 Now Abraham journeyed from there toward the land of the [23]Negev, and settled between Kadesh and Shur; then he sojourned in Gerar.

2   And Abraham said of Sarah his wife, "She is my sister." So Abimelech king of Gerar sent and took Sarah.

3   But God came to Abimelech in a dream of the night, and said to him, "Behold, you are a dead man because of the woman whom you have taken, for she is married."

4   Now Abimelech had not come near her; and he said, "Lord, wilt Thou slay a nation, even *though* blameless?

5   "Did he not himself say to me, 'She is my sister'? And she herself said, 'He is my brother.' In the integrity of my heart and the innocence of my hands I have done this."

6   Then God said to him in the dream, "Yes, I know that in the integrity of your heart you have done this, and I also kept you from sinning against Me; therefore I did not let you touch her.

7   "Now therefore, restore the man's wife, for he is a prophet, and he will pray for you, and you will live. But if you do not restore *her*, know that you shall surely die, you and all who are yours."

2. Abraham's prayer for Abimelech

8   So Abimelech arose early in the morning and called all his servants and told all these things in their hearing; and the men were greatly frightened.

9   Then Abimelech called Abraham and said to him, "What have you done to us? And how have I sinned against you, that you have brought on me and on my kingdom a great sin? You have done to me things that ought not to be done."

10   And Abimelech said to Abraham, "What have you encountered, that you have done this thing?"

11   And Abraham said, "Because I thought, surely there is no fear of God in this place; and they will kill me because of my wife.

12   "Besides, she actually is my sister, the daughter of my father, but not the daughter of my mother, and she became my wife;

13   and it came about, when God caused me to wander from my father's house, that I said to her, 'This is the kindness which you will show to me: everywhere we go, say of me, "He is my brother." '"

14   Abimelech then took sheep and oxen and male and female servants, and gave them to Abraham, and restored his wife Sarah to him.

15   And Abimelech said, "Behold, my land is before you; settle wherever you please."

16   And to Sarah he said, "Behold, I have given your brother a thousand pieces

23I.e., South country

of silver; behold, it is your vindication before all who are with you, and before all men you are cleared.''

20:17
Num 12:13;
Job 42:9
20:18
Gen 12:17

17   And Abraham prayed to God; and God healed Abimelech and his wife and his maids, so that they bore *children*.

18   For the LORD had closed fast all the wombs of the household of Abimelech because of Sarah, Abraham's wife.

J. The birth of Isaac

1. *Birth and circumcision*

21:1
1 Sam 2:21;
Gen 17:16,21;
Gal 4:23
21:2
Acts 7:8;
Gal 4:22;
Heb 11:11;
Gen 17:21
21:3
Gen 17:19
21:4
Gen 17:12;
Acts 7:8
21:5
Gen 17:17
21:6
Ps 126:2;
Is 54:1
21:7
Gen 18:13

21 Then the LORD took note of Sarah as He had said, and the LORD did for Sarah as He had promised.

2   So Sarah conceived and bore a son to Abraham in his old age, at the appointed time of which God had spoken to him.

3   And Abraham called the name of his son who was born to him, whom Sarah bore to him, Isaac.

4   Then Abraham circumcised his son Isaac when he was eight days old, as God had commanded him.

5   Now Abraham was one hundred years old when his son Isaac was born to him.

6   And Sarah said, "God has made laughter for me; everyone who hears will laugh with me."

7   And she said, "Who would have said to Abraham that Sarah would nurse children? Yet I have borne him a son in his old age."

2. *The expulsion of Ishmael*

21:9
Gen 16:15;
Gal 4:29
21:10
Gal 4:30
*21:11
Gen 17:18
21:12
Rom 9:7;
Heb 11:18
21:13
v. 18;
Gen 16:10;
17:20

8   And the child grew and was weaned, and Abraham made a great feast on the day that Isaac was weaned.

9   Now Sarah saw the son of Hagar the Egyptian, whom she had borne to Abraham, mocking.

10   Therefore she said to Abraham, "Drive out this maid and her son, for the son of this maid shall not be an heir with my son Isaac."

11   And the matter distressed Abraham greatly because of his son.

12   But God said to Abraham, "Do not be distressed because of the lad and your maid; whatever Sarah tells you, listen to her, for through Isaac your descendants shall be named.

13   "And of the son of the maid I will make a nation also, because he is your descendant."

14   So Abraham rose early in the morning, and took bread and a skin of water, and gave *them* to Hagar, putting *them* on her shoulder, and *gave her* the boy, and sent her away. And she departed, and wandered about in the wilderness of Beersheba.

3. *The deliverance of Hagar and Ishmael*

15   And the water in the skin was used up, and she left the boy under one of the bushes.

16   Then she went and sat down opposite him, about a bowshot away, for she said, "Do not let me see the boy die." And she sat opposite him, and lifted up her voice and wept.

21:17
Ex 3:7

17   And God heard the lad crying; and the angel of God called to Hagar from heaven, and said to her, "What is the matter with you, Hagar? Do not fear, for God has heard the voice of the lad where he is.

21:18
v. 13

18   "Arise, lift up the lad, and hold him by the hand; for I will make a great nation of him."

21:19
Num 22:31

19   Then God opened her eyes and she saw a well of water; and she went and filled the skin with water, and gave the lad a drink.

21:20
Gen 28:15;
39:2,3,21
21:21
Gen 24:4

20   And God was with the lad, and he grew; and he lived in the wilderness, and became an archer.

21   And he lived in the wilderness of Paran; and his mother took a wife for him from the land of Egypt.

21:11 Abraham's displeasure may well have been a reflection of the fact that customary law of his day forbade the expulsion of a slave wife and her children.

4. The discord between Abraham and Abimelech

22 Now it came about at that time, that Abimelech and Phicol, the commander of his army, spoke to Abraham, saying, "God is with you in all that you do;

23 now therefore, swear to me here by God that you will not deal falsely with me, or with my offspring, or with my posterity; but according to the kindness that I have shown to you, you shall show to me, and to the land in which you have sojourned."

24 And Abraham said, "I swear it."

25 But Abraham complained to Abimelech because of the well of water which the servants of Abimelech had seized.

26 And Abimelech said, "I do not know who has done this thing; neither did you tell me, nor did I hear of it until today."

27 And Abraham took sheep and oxen, and gave them to Abimelech; and the two of them made a covenant.

28 Then Abraham set seven ewe lambs of the flock by themselves.

29 And Abimelech said to Abraham, "What do these seven ewe lambs mean, which you have set by themselves?"

30 And he said, "You shall take these seven ewe lambs from my hand in order that it may be a witness to me, that I dug this well."

31 Therefore he called that place Beersheba; because there the two of them took an oath.

32 So they made a covenant at Beersheba; and Abimelech and Phicol, the commander of his army, arose and returned to the land of the Philistines.

33 And *Abraham* planted a tamarisk tree at Beersheba, and there he called on the name of the LORD, the Everlasting God.

34 And Abraham sojourned in the land of the Philistines for many days.

K. Abraham's sacrifice of Isaac

1. God tests Abraham

22 Now it came about after these things, that God tested Abraham, and said to him, "Abraham!" And he said, "Here I am."

2 And He said, "Take now your son, your only son, whom you love, Isaac, and go to the land of Moriah; and offer him there as a burnt offering on one of the mountains of which I will tell you."

3 So Abraham rose early in the morning and saddled his donkey, and took two of his young men with him and Isaac his son; and he split wood for the burnt offering, and arose and went to the place of which God had told him.

4 On the third day Abraham raised his eyes and saw the place from a distance.

5 And Abraham said to his young men, "Stay here with the donkey, and I and the lad will go yonder; and we will worship and return to you."

6 And Abraham took the wood of the burnt offering and laid it on Isaac his son, and he took in his hand the fire and the knife. So the two of them walked on together.

7 And Isaac spoke to Abraham his father and said, "My father!" And he said, "Here I am, my son." And he said, "Behold, the fire and the wood, but where is the lamb for the burnt offering?"

8 And Abraham said, "God will provide for Himself the lamb for the burnt offering, my son." So the two of them walked on together.

2. God stops obedient Abraham

9 Then they came to the place of which God had told him; and Abraham built

---

Cross references (right margin):

21:22 Gen 20:2; 26:26,28

21:25 Gen 26:15,18, 20-22

21:27 Gen 26:31

21:30 Gen 31:48,52

21:31 Gen 26:33

21:33 Gen 4:26; Deut 33:27

*22:2 Heb 11:17; 2 Chr 3:1

22:6 John 19:17

*22:7 John 1:29,36; Rev 13:8

22:9 Heb 11:17-19

21:32 *land of the Philistines.* This designation for Canaan could be ascribed to a late editor, for the Philistines probably entered the land long after the time of Abraham.
22:2 On the basis of 2 Chr. 3:1 Christian tradition has assumed that Jerusalem was the place where Abraham offered up Isaac. Glueck has called attention to the fact that it would have been odd for Abraham to have carried wood for the offering from Beersheba to the wooded country around Jerusalem, where he could easily have secured all the wood he needed. The *land of Moriah* may have been in Jerusalem or further south. Abraham knew this country well. Moreover, Isaac here may be understood to be a type of Christ.

He was an only son. He was offered up as a sacrifice. It was through Isaac that the descendants of Abraham should be named. And Abraham believed that God was able to raise Isaac from the dead, and, in a manner of speaking, did receive him back from the dead (Heb. 11:17-19). Christ, from whom the type is taken, was an only son; He was offered up as a sacrifice; He was raised from the dead.
22:7 How stunned Abraham must have been when Isaac, carrying the wood, inquired about the missing lamb! Would God require Abraham to carry through with the command of killing his son? Yet with unflinching faith in God he prepared to sacrifice Isaac.

the altar there, and arranged the wood, and bound his son Isaac, and laid him on the altar on top of the wood.

10   And Abraham stretched out his hand, and took the knife to slay his son.

11   But the angel of the LORD called to him from heaven, and said, "Abraham, Abraham!" And he said, "Here I am."

22:12
Gen 26:5;
1 Sam 15:22

12   And he said, "Do not stretch out your hand against the lad, and do nothing to him; for now I know that you fear God, since you have not withheld your son, your only son, from Me."

13   Then Abraham raised his eyes and looked, and behold, behind *him* a ram caught in the thicket by his horns; and Abraham went and took the ram, and offered him up for a burnt offering in the place of his son.

14   And Abraham called the name of that place The LORD Will Provide, as it is said to this day, "In the mount of the LORD it will be provided."

3. *God's blessing repeated*

15   Then the angel of the LORD called to Abraham a second time from heaven,

22:16
Heb 6:13,14

16   and said, "By Myself I have sworn, declares the LORD, because you have done this thing, and have not withheld your son, your only son,

22:17
Gen 15:5;
26:4; 32:12;
24:60

17   indeed I will greatly bless you, and I will greatly multiply your seed as the stars of the heavens, and as the sand which is on the seashore; and your seed shall possess the gate of their enemies.

22:18
Gal 3:8,16;
Acts 3:25;
Gen 18:19

18   "And in your seed all the nations of the earth shall be blessed, because you have obeyed My voice."

19   So Abraham returned to his young men, and they arose and went together to Beersheba; and Abraham lived at Beersheba.

20   Now it came about after these things, that it was told Abraham, saying, "Behold, Milcah also has borne children to your brother Nahor:

21   Uz his first-born and Buz his brother and Kemuel the father of Aram

22   and Chesed and Hazo and Pildash and Jidlaph and Bethuel."

22:23
Gen 24:15

23   And Bethuel became the father of Rebekah: these eight Milcah bore to Nahor, Abraham's brother.

24   And his concubine, whose name was Reumah, also bore Tebah and Gaham and Tahash and Maacah.

L. *The death and burial of Sarah*

23   Now Sarah lived one hundred and twenty-seven years; *these were* the years of the life of Sarah.

23:2
Josh 14:15;
v. 19;
Gen 13:18

2   And Sarah died in Kiriath-arba (that is, Hebron) in the land of Canaan; and Abraham went in to mourn for Sarah and to weep for her.

3   Then Abraham rose from before his dead, and spoke to the sons of Heth, saying,

23:4
1 Chr 29:15;
Ps 105:12;
Heb 11:9,13

4   "I am a stranger and a sojourner among you; give me a burial site among you, that I may bury my dead out of my sight."

5   And the sons of Heth answered Abraham, saying to him,

23:6
Gen 14:14;
24:35

6   "Hear us, my lord, you are a mighty prince among us; bury your dead in the choicest of our graves; none of us will refuse you his grave for burying your dead."

7   So Abraham rose and bowed to the people of the land, the sons of Heth.

23:8
Gen 25:9

8   And he spoke with them, saying, "If it is your wish *for me* to bury my dead out of my sight, hear me, and approach Ephron the son of Zohar for me,

9   that he may give me the cave of Machpelah which he owns, which is at the end of his field; for the full price let him give it to me in your presence for a burial site."

23:10
Gen 24:20,24;
Ruth 4:4

10   Now Ephron was sitting among the sons of Heth; and Ephron the Hittite answered Abraham in the hearing of the sons of Heth; *even* of all who went in at the gate of his city, saying,

---

22:11 *Here I am.* Abraham heard God call him; he was quick to respond. Had he not been listening he *could* not have responded. Had he been disobedient he *would* not have answered yes.

22:13 The ram caught in the thicket was a revelatory event of God to Abraham. When Abraham prepared to offer his only son Isaac in obedience to God's command, his dilemma was this: how could he reconcile the command of God to slay his son with God's previous promise that through this son should come a great posterity? He did not solve the problem by deciding to disobey God's command to offer up Isaac. Rather, by faith he concluded that God Himself could raise Isaac from the dead *after* he had been offered. Spiritually there is a deeper lesson. God, like Abraham, did not spare His own Son (Rom. 8:32). And, as Abraham received back Isaac as though he had been raised from the dead, so Christ has been raised by the Father from the dead.

11 "No, my lord, hear me; I give you the field, and I give you the cave that is in it. In the presence of the sons of my people I give it to you; bury your dead."

12 And Abraham bowed before the people of the land.

13 And he spoke to Ephron in the hearing of the people of the land, saying, "If you will only please listen to me; I will give the price of the field, accept *it* from me, that I may bury my dead there."

14 Then Ephron answered Abraham, saying to him,

15 "My lord, listen to me; a piece of land worth four hundred shekels of silver, what is that between me and you? So bury your dead."

16 And Abraham listened to Ephron; and Abraham weighed out for Ephron the silver which he had named in the hearing of the sons of Heth, four hundred shekels of silver, commercial standard.

17 So Ephron's field, which was in Machpelah, which faced Mamre, the field and cave which was in it, and all the trees which were in the field, that were within all the confines of its border, were deeded over

18 to Abraham for a possession in the presence of the sons of Heth, before all who went in at the gate of his city.

19 And after this, Abraham buried Sarah his wife in the cave of the field at Machpelah facing Mamre (that is, Hebron) in the land of Canaan.

20 So the field, and the cave that is in it, were deeded over to Abraham for a burial site by the sons of Heth.

M. *The marriage of Isaac*

1. *Abraham's instructions to his servant*

24 Now Abraham was old, advanced in age; and the LORD had blessed Abraham in every way.

2 And Abraham said to his servant, the oldest of his household, who had charge of all that he owned, "Please place your hand under my thigh,

3 and I will make you swear by the LORD, the God of heaven and the God of earth, that you shall not take a wife for my son from the daughters of the Canaanites, among whom I live,

4 but you shall go to my country and to my relatives, and take a wife for my son Isaac."

5 And the servant said to him, "Suppose the woman will not be willing to follow me to this land; should I take your son back to the land from where you came?"

6 Then Abraham said to him, "Beware lest you take my son back there!

7 "The LORD, the God of heaven, who took me from my father's house and from the land of my birth, and who spoke to me, and who swore to me, saying, 'To your descendants I will give this land,' He will send His angel before you, and you will take a wife for my son from there.

8 "But if the woman is not willing to follow you, then you will be free from this my oath; only do not take my son back there."

9 So the servant placed his hand under the thigh of Abraham his master, and swore to him concerning this matter.

2. *The servant's prayer for guidance*

10 Then the servant took ten camels from the camels of his master, and set out with a variety of good things of his master's in his hand; and he arose, and went to Mesopotamia, to the city of Nahor.

11 And he made the camels kneel down outside the city by the well of water at evening time, the time when women go out to draw water.

12 And he said, "O LORD, the God of my master Abraham, please grant me success today, and show lovingkindness to my master Abraham.

13 Behold, I am standing by the spring, and the daughters of the men of the city are coming out to draw water;

14 now may it be that the girl to whom I say, 'Please let down your jar so that

---

Cross-references (margin):

23:11 see 2 Sam 24:21-24

23:15 Ex 30:13; Ezek 45:12
23:16 Jer 32:9; Zech 11:12

*23:17 Gen 25:9; 49:30-32; 50:13; Acts 7:16

24:1 v. 35; Gen 13:2
*24:2 Gen 47:29

24:3 Gen 14:22; 10:18,19; 26:34,35; 28:1,2,8
24:4 Gen 28:2; 12:1

24:7 Gen 12:7; 13:15; 15:18; Ex 23:20,23

24:9 v. 2

*24:10 Gen 11:31,32; 27:43

24:11 1 Sam 9:11

24:12 v. 27; Gen 26:24; Ex 3:6
24:13 v. 43

23:17 Hittite real estate transactions made specific reference to the trees on the property.
24:2 *hand under my thigh*, an ancient custom for confirming a solemn oath.
24:10 *Mesopotamia*, Hebrew *Aram-naharaim* (Aram of the Two Rivers), the region also called *Paddan-aram* (25:20; 28:2). *city of Nahor*, a town near Haran, with slightly different spelling in Hebrew from Nahor, Abraham's brother (v. 15).

24:14
see
Judg 6:17,37;
1 Sam 6:7

I may drink,' and who answers, 'Drink, and I will water your camels also';—*may she be the one* whom Thou hast appointed for Thy servant Isaac; and by this I shall know that Thou hast shown lovingkindness to my master."

3. The servant's meeting with Rebekah

24:15
v. 45;
Gen 22:20,23

15   And it came about before he had finished speaking, that behold, Rebekah who was born to Bethuel the son of Milcah, the wife of Abraham's brother Nahor, came out with her jar on her shoulder.

24:16
Gen 26:7

16   And the girl was very beautiful, a virgin, and no man had had relations with her; and she went down to the spring and filled her jar, and came up.

17   Then the servant ran to meet her, and said, "Please let me drink a little water from your jar."

24:18
vv. 14,16

18   And she said, "Drink, my lord"; and she quickly lowered her jar to her hand, and gave him a drink.

24:19
v. 14

19   Now when she had finished giving him a drink, she said, "I will draw also for your camels until they have finished drinking."

20   So she quickly emptied her jar into the trough, and ran back to the well to draw, and she drew for all his camels.

24:21
vv. 12-14; 56

21   Meanwhile, the man was gazing at her in silence, to know whether the LORD had made his journey successful or not.

24:22
v. 47

22   Then it came about, when the camels had finished drinking, that the man took a gold ring weighing a half-shekel and two bracelets for her wrists weighing ten shekels in gold,

23   and said, "Whose daughter are you? Please tell me, is there room for us to lodge in your father's house?"

24:24
v. 15

24   And she said to him, "I am the daughter of Bethuel, the son of Milcah, whom she bore to Nahor."

25   Again she said to him, "We have plenty of both straw and feed, and room to lodge in."

24:26
vv. 48,52
24:27
vv. 42,48,21

26   Then the man bowed low and worshiped the LORD.

27   And he said, "Blessed be the LORD, the God of my master Abraham, who has not forsaken His lovingkindness and His truth toward my master; as for me, the LORD has guided me in the way to the house of my master's brothers."

28   Then the girl ran and told her mother's household about these things.

24:29
Gen 29:5,13

29   Now Rebekah had a brother whose name was Laban; and Laban ran outside to the man at the spring.

30   And it came about that when he saw the ring, and the bracelets on his sister's wrists, and when he heard the words of Rebekah his sister, saying, "This is what the man said to me," he went to the man; and behold, he was standing by the camels at the spring.

24:31
Gen 26:29

31   And he said, "Come in, blessed of the LORD! Why do you stand outside since I have prepared the house, and a place for the camels?"

24:32
Gen 43:24;
Judg 19:21

32   So the man entered the house. Then Laban unloaded the camels, and he gave straw and feed to the camels, and water to wash his feet and the feet of the men who were with him.

33   But when *food* was set before him to eat, he said, "I will not eat until I have told my business." And he said, "Speak on."

4. The servant's request for the hand of Rebekah for Isaac

34   So he said, "I am Abraham's servant.

24:35
v. 1; Gen 13:2

35   "And the LORD has greatly blessed my master, so that he has become rich; and He has given him flocks and herds, and silver and gold, and servants and maids, and camels and donkeys.

24:36
Gen 21:2,10;
25:5
24:37
vv. 2-4

36   "Now Sarah my master's wife bore a son to my master in her old age; and he has given him all that he has.

37   "And my master made me swear, saying, 'You shall not take a wife for my son from the daughters of the Canaanites, in whose land I live;

24:38
v. 4

38   but you shall go to my father's house, and to my relatives, and take a wife for my son.'

24:39
v. 5
24:40
v. 7

39   "And I said to my master, 'Suppose the woman does not follow me.'

40   "And he said to me, 'The LORD, before whom I have walked, will send His angel with you to make your journey successful, and you will take a wife for my son from my relatives, and from my father's house;

41   then you will be free from my oath, when you come to my relatives; and if they do not give her to you, you will be free from my oath.'

24:41
v. 8

42   "So I came today to the spring, and said, 'O Lord, the God of my master Abraham, if now Thou wilt make my journey on which I go successful;

24:42
vv. 11,12

43   behold, I am standing by the spring, and may it be that the maiden who comes out to draw, and to whom I say, "Please let me drink a little water from your jar";

24:43
vv. 13,14

44   and she will say to me, "You drink, and I will draw for your camels also"; let her be the woman whom the Lord has appointed for my master's son.'

45   "Before I had finished speaking in my heart, behold, Rebekah came out with her jar on her shoulder, and went down to the spring and drew; and I said to her, 'Please let me drink.'

24:45
vv. 15,17;
1 Sam 1:13

46   "And she quickly lowered her jar from her *shoulder*, and said, 'Drink, and I will water your camels also'; so I drank, and she watered the camels also.

24:46
v. 18

47   "Then I asked her, and said, 'Whose daughter are you?' And she said, 'The daughter of Bethuel, Nahor's son, whom Milcah bore to him'; and I put the ring on her nose, and the bracelets on her wrists.

24:47
vv. 23,24

48   "And I bowed low and worshiped the Lord, and blessed the Lord, the God of my master Abraham, who had guided me in the right way to take the daughter of my master's kinsman for his son.

24:48
vv. 26,27

49   "So now if you are going to [24]deal kindly and truly with my master, tell me; and if not, let me know, that I may turn to the right hand or the left."

24:49
Gen 47:29;
Josh 2:14

5. Rebekah goes with Abraham's servant

50   Then Laban and Bethuel answered and said, "The matter comes from the Lord; *so* we cannot speak to you bad or good.

24:50
Ps 118:23;
Gen 31:24

51   "Behold, Rebekah is before you, take *her* and go, and let her be the wife of your master's son, as the Lord has spoken."

52   And it came about when Abraham's servant heard their words, that he bowed himself to the ground before the Lord.

24:52
v. 26

53   And the servant brought out articles of silver and articles of gold, and garments, and gave them to Rebekah; he also gave precious things to her brother and to her mother.

24:53
vv. 10,22

54   Then he and the men who were with him ate and drank and spent the night. When they arose in the morning, he said, "Send me away to my master."

24:54
vv. 56,59

55   But her brother and her mother said, "Let the girl stay with us *a few* days, say ten; afterward she may go."

56   And he said to them, "Do not delay me, since the Lord has prospered my way. Send me away that I may go to my master."

57   And they said, "We will call the girl and consult her wishes."

58   Then they called Rebekah and said to her, "Will you go with this man?" And she said, "I will go."

59   Thus they sent away their sister Rebekah and her nurse with Abraham's servant and his men.

24:59
Gen 35:8

60   And they blessed Rebekah and said to her,
"May you, our sister,
Become thousands of ten thousands,
And may your descendants possess
The gate of those who hate them."

24:60
Gen 17:16;
22:17

61   Then Rebekah arose with her maids, and they mounted the camels and followed the man. So the servant took Rebekah and departed.

6. Isaac and Rebekah marry

62   Now Isaac had come from going to Beer-lahai-roi; for he was living in the Negev.

24:62
Gen 16:14;
25:11; 20:1

63   And Isaac went out to meditate in the field toward evening; and he lifted up his eyes and looked, and behold, camels were coming.

24:63
Ps 1:2; 77:12;
119:15;
143:5; 145:5

64   And Rebekah lifted up her eyes, and when she saw Isaac she dismounted from the camel.

65   And she said to the servant, "Who is that man walking in the field to meet

[24]Lit., *show lovingkindness and truth*

us?" And the servant said, "He is my master." Then she took her veil and covered herself.

66 And the servant told Isaac all the things that he had done.

67 Then Isaac brought her into his mother Sarah's tent, and he took Rebekah, and she became his wife; and he loved her; thus Isaac was comforted after his mother's death.

24:67
Gen 29:18;
23:1,2; 25:20

N. Abraham's seed by Keturah

25 Now Abraham took another wife, whose name was Keturah.

2 And she bore to him Zimran and Jokshan and Medan and Midian and Ishbak and Shuah.

25:2
1 Chr 1:32,33

3 And Jokshan became the father of Sheba and Dedan. And the sons of Dedan were Asshurim and Letushim and Leummim.

4 And the sons of Midian *were* Ephah and Epher and Hanoch and Abida and Eldaah. All these *were* the sons of Keturah.

5 Now Abraham gave all that he had to Isaac;

25:5
Gen 24:35,36

6 but to the sons of his concubines, Abraham gave gifts while he was still living, and sent them away from his son Isaac eastward, to the land of the east.

O. The death of Abraham

7 And these are all the years of Abraham's life that he lived, one hundred and seventy-five years.

8 And Abraham breathed his last and died in a ripe old age, an old man and satisfied *with life;* and he was gathered to his people.

25:8
Gen 15:15;
35:29; 49:29,
33

9 Then his sons Isaac and Ishmael buried him in the cave of Machpelah, in the field of Ephron the son of Zohar the Hittite, facing Mamre,

10 the field which Abraham purchased from the sons of Heth; there Abraham was buried with Sarah his wife.

25:10
Gen 23:16

11 And it came about after the death of Abraham, that God blessed his son Isaac; and Isaac lived by Beer-lahai-roi.

25:11
Gen 24:62

VII. The generations of Ishmael (25:12–18)

12 Now these are *the records of* the generations of Ishmael, Abraham's son, whom Hagar the Egyptian, Sarah's maid, bore to Abraham;

25:12
Gen 16:15

13 and these are the names of the sons of Ishmael, by their names, in the order of their birth: Nebaioth, the first-born of Ishmael, and Kedar and Adbeel and Mibsam

25:13
1 Chr 1:29-31

14 and Mishma and Dumah and Massa,

15 Hadad and Tema, Jetur, Naphish and Kedemah.

16 These are the sons of Ishmael and these are their names, by their villages, and by their camps; twelve princes according to their tribes.

25:16
Gen 17:20

17 And these are the years of the life of Ishmael, one hundred and thirty-seven years; and he breathed his last and died, and was gathered to his people.

25:17
v. 8

18 And they settled from Havilah to Shur which is east of Egypt as one goes toward Assyria; he settled in defiance of all his relatives.

25:18
Gen 16:12

VIII. The generations of Isaac (25:19–35:29)

A. The birth of Jacob and Esau

1. The elder shall serve the younger

19 Now these are *the records of* the generations of Isaac, Abraham's son: Abraham became the father of Isaac;

20 and Isaac was forty years old when he took Rebekah, the daughter of Bethuel the Aramean of Paddan-aram, the sister of Laban the Aramean, to be his wife.

25:20
Gen 24:15,29

25:9 *His sons Isaac and Ishmael buried him.* Abraham was one hundred years old when Isaac was born. S. Isaac was seventy-five years old when his father died. Ishmael was fourteen years older than Isaac. Even though some type of friction existed between Isaac and Ishmael they must have been in close contact with each other. Here we find them, at the death of their father Abraham, burying him next to Isaac's mother, Sarah, in the cave of Machpelah. The descendants of Ishmael and Isaac have had almost nothing in common with each other for many centuries despite the fact that both sprang from the loins of a common father, Abraham.

21   And Isaac prayed to the LORD on behalf of his wife, because she was barren; and the LORD answered him and Rebekah his wife conceived.

22   But the children struggled together within her; and she said, "If it is so, why then am I *this way?*" So she went to inquire of the LORD.

23   And the LORD said to her,

     "Two nations are in your womb;

     And two peoples shall be separated from your body;

     And one people shall be stronger than the other;

     And the older shall serve the younger."

24   When her days to be delivered were fulfilled, behold, there were twins in her womb.

25   Now the first came forth red, all over like a hairy garment; and they named him Esau.

26   And afterward his brother came forth with his hand holding on to Esau's heel, so his name was called 25Jacob; and Isaac was sixty years old when she gave birth to them.

2. Esau sells his birthright to Jacob

27   When the boys grew up, Esau became a skillful hunter, a man of the field; but Jacob was a peaceful man, living in tents.

28   Now Isaac loved Esau, because he had a taste for game; but Rebekah loved Jacob.

29   And when Jacob had cooked stew, Esau came in from the field and he was famished;

30   and Esau said to Jacob, "Please let me have a swallow of that red stuff there, for I am famished." Therefore his name was called 26Edom.

31   But Jacob said, "First sell me your birthright."

32   And Esau said, "Behold, I am about to die; so of what *use* then is the birthright to me?"

33   And Jacob said, "First swear to me"; so he swore to him, and sold his birthright to Jacob.

34   Then Jacob gave Esau bread and lentil stew; and he ate and drank, and rose and went on his way. Thus Esau despised his birthright.

B. Isaac and Abimelech

1. The covenant confirmed to Isaac

26 Now there was a famine in the land, besides the previous famine that had occurred in the days of Abraham. So Isaac went to Gerar, to Abimelech king of the Philistines.

2   And the LORD appeared to him and said, "Do not go down to Egypt; stay in the land of which I shall tell you.

3   "Sojourn in this land and I will be with you and bless you, for to you and to your descendants I will give all these lands, and I will establish the oath which I swore to your father Abraham.

4   "And I will multiply your descendants as the stars of heaven, and will give

25I.e., one who takes by the heel, or supplants   26I.e., red

Marginal references:

25:21 1 Sam 1:17; Ps 127:3

25:23 Gen 17:16; Num 20:14; Gen 27:29; Mal 1:3; Rom 9:12

*25:25 Gen 27:11

25:26 Hos 12:3; Gen 27:36

25:27 Gen 27:3,5

25:33 Heb 12:16

26:1 Gen 12:10; 20:1,2

26:2 Gen 12:7; 17:1; 18:1; 19:1

26:3 Gen 20:1; 12:2,7; 13:15; 15:18; 22:16-18

25:25 Esau was the twin brother of Jacob. But he was also the elder twin, with a natal claim to all the rights and privileges of the first-born, including the domestic priesthood, probably a double portion of the inheritance, and the precedence and authority after his father's death. The name *Esau* means "hairy." The name *Edom*, which was given to Esau and which became the name of his descendants the Edomites, means "red." The story of Esau's life may be written in four parts: (1) the sale of his birthright to Jacob for the mess of pottage (25:27–34), which indicated that he despised his birthright and was willing to barter it away for a small consideration; (2) the marriages of Esau, which were consummated with women who were not related to his father's family—except for Mahalath, who was his third wife and whom he married to placate his parents; (3) his failure to secure the patriarchal blessing just prior to the death of his father Isaac; and (4) the re-establishment of brotherly relations with Jacob, and his departure from Canaan for Seir. Esau was careless, motivated by animal appe-

tites, and revengeful after the blessing was stolen from him by Jacob.

25:31 The birthright was of little practical importance when there was an only son. Isaac was Abraham's only true heir, Ishmael not being of the seed of promise. Thus Isaac was the only one in the line of promise and the natural heir of his father's possessions. But Isaac's wife bore him two sons, Esau and Jacob. Now the birthright assumed greater significance. Esau, as the first-born, should have been the one through whom the people of God descended. But he foolishly sold that birthright for carnal considerations and lost it to Jacob. Jacob claimed the privileges of the birthright and from him came the twelve tribes of Israel. The first-born received a double portion of the inheritance (cf. Deut. 21:16–17), and, at least before the establishment of the Aaronic priesthood, the first-born in each family exercised the priestly prerogatives in the home after his father's death.

26:4
Gen 15:5;
22:17;
Ex 32:15;
Gen 12:3;
22:18; Gal 3:8

your descendants all these lands; and by your descendants all the nations of the earth shall be blessed;

5   because Abraham obeyed Me and kept My charge, My commandments, My statutes and My laws."

2. *Isaac deceives Abimelech about Rebekah*

6   So Isaac lived in Gerar.

26:7
Gen 12:13;
20:2,12,13

7   When the men of the place asked about his wife, he said, "She is my sister," for he was afraid to say, "my wife," *thinking*, "the men of the place might kill me on account of Rebekah, for she is beautiful."

8   And it came about, when he had been there a long time, that Abimelech king of the Philistines looked out through a window, and saw, and behold, Isaac was caressing his wife Rebekah.

9   Then Abimelech called Isaac and said, "Behold, certainly she is your wife! How then did you say, 'She is my sister'?" And Isaac said to him, "Because I said, 'Lest I die on account of her.'"

26:10
Gen 20:9

10   And Abimelech said, "What is this you have done to us? One of the people might easily have lain with your wife, and you would have brought guilt upon us."

11   So Abimelech charged all the people, saying, "He who touches this man or his wife shall surely be put to death."

3. *Isaac's riches*

26:12
v. 3

12   Now Isaac sowed in that land, and reaped in the same year a hundredfold. And the LORD blessed him,

13   and the man became rich, and continued to grow richer until he became very wealthy;

26:14
Gen 24:35;
37:11
26:15
Gen 21:25,30

14   for he had possessions of flocks and herds and a great household, so that the Philistines envied him.

15   Now all the wells which his father's servants had dug in the days of Abraham his father, the Philistines stopped up by filling them with earth.

16   Then Abimelech said to Isaac, "Go away from us, for you are too powerful for us."

4. *Isaac's trouble with Abimelech over the wells:* *their covenant*

17   And Isaac departed from there and camped in the valley of Gerar, and settled there.

26:18
Gen 21:31

18   Then Isaac dug again the wells of water which had been dug in the days of his father Abraham, for the Philistines had stopped them up after the death of Abraham; and he gave them the same names which his father had given them.

19   But when Isaac's servants dug in the valley and found there a well of flowing water,

20   the herdsmen of Gerar quarreled with the herdsmen of Isaac, saying, "The water is ours!" So he named the well Esek, because they contended with him.

21   Then they dug another well, and they quarreled over it too, so he named it Sitnah.

26:22
Gen 17:6

22   And he moved away from there and dug another well, and they did not quarrel over it; so he named it Rehoboth, for he said, "At last the LORD has made room for us, and we shall be fruitful in the land."

23   Then he went up from there to Beersheba.

26:24
Gen 17:7;
24:12; Ex 3:6

24   And the LORD appeared to him the same night and said,
"I am the God of your father Abraham;
Do not fear, for I am with you.
I will bless you, and multiply your descendants,
For the sake of My servant Abraham."

26:25
Gen 12:7,8;
13:4,18;
Ps 116:17
26:26
Gen 21:22

25   So he built an altar there, and called upon the name of the LORD, and pitched his tent there; and there Isaac's servants dug a well.

26   Then Abimelech came to him from Gerar with his adviser Ahuzzath, and Phicol the commander of his army.

26:27
v. 16

27   And Isaac said to them, "Why have you come to me, since you hate me, and have sent me away from you?"

28   And they said, "We see plainly that the LORD has been with you; so we said,

'Let there now be an oath between us, *even* between you and us, and let us make a covenant with you,

29   that you will do us no harm, just as we have not touched you and have done to you nothing but good, and have sent you away in peace. You are now the blessed of the LORD.'"

30   Then he made them a feast, and they ate and drank.

31   And in the morning they arose early and exchanged oaths; then Isaac sent them away and they departed from him in peace.

32   Now it came about on the same day, that Isaac's servants came in and told him about the well which they had dug, and said to him, "We have found water."

33   So he called it Shibah; therefore the name of the city is Beersheba to this day.

C. *Esau's marriages: Isaac's sorrow*

34   And when Esau was forty years old he married Judith the daughter of Beeri the Hittite, and Basemath the daughter of Elon the Hittite;

35   and they ²⁷brought grief to Isaac and Rebekah.

D. *The stolen blessing*

1. *Esau hunts for game*

27 Now it came about, when Isaac was old, and his eyes were too dim to see, that he called his older son Esau and said to him, "My son." And he said to him, "Here I am."

2   And Isaac said, "Behold now, I am old *and* I do not know the day of my death.

3   "Now then, please take your gear, your quiver and your bow, and go out to the field and hunt game for me;

4   and prepare a savory dish for me such as I love, and bring it to me that I may eat, so that my soul may bless you before I die."

2. *Rebekah schemes with Jacob*

5   And Rebekah was listening while Isaac spoke to his son Esau. So when Esau went to the field to hunt for game to bring *home,*

6   Rebekah said to her son Jacob, "Behold, I heard your father speak to your brother Esau, saying,

7   'Bring me *some* game and prepare a savory dish for me, that I may eat, and bless you in the presence of the LORD before my death.'

8   "Now therefore, my son, listen to me as I command you.

9   "Go now to the flock and bring me two choice kids from there, that I may prepare them *as* a savory dish for your father, such as he loves.

10   "Then you shall bring *it* to your father, that he may eat, so that he may bless you before his death."

11   And Jacob answered his mother Rebekah, "Behold, Esau my brother is a hairy man and I am a smooth man.

12   "Perhaps my father will feel me, then I shall be as a deceiver in his sight; and I shall bring upon myself a curse and not a blessing."

13   But his mother said to him, "Your curse be on me, my son; only obey my voice, and go, get *them* for me."

14   So he went and got *them,* and brought *them* to his mother; and his mother made savory food such as his father loved.

15   Then Rebekah took the best garments of Esau her elder son, which were with her in the house, and put them on Jacob her younger son.

16   And she put the skins of the kids on his hands and on the smooth part of his neck.

17   She also gave the savory food and the bread, which she had made, to her son Jacob.

3. *Jacob pretends to be Esau: he obtains the blessing*

18   Then he came to his father and said, "My father." And he said, "Here I am. Who are you, my son?"

---

²⁷Lit., *were a bitterness of spirit to*

Margin references:

26:28
Gen 21:22,23

26:31
Gen 21:31

26:33
Gen 21:31

26:34
Gen 28:8;
36:2

26:35
Gen 27:46

27:1
Gen 48:10;
1 Sam 3:2

27:2
Gen 47:29

27:3
Gen 25:27,28

27:4
v. 27;
Gen 48:9,15;
49:28

27:8
v. 13

27:11
Gen 25:25

27:12
vv. 21,22

27:13
v. 8;
Matt 27:25

27:15
v. 27

*27:19
v. 4

19 And Jacob said to his father, "I am Esau your first-born; I have done as you told me. Get up, please, sit and eat of my game, that you may bless me."

20 And Isaac said to his son, "How is it that you have *it* so quickly, my son?" And he said, "Because the LORD your God caused *it* to happen to me."

27:21
v. 12

21 Then Isaac said to Jacob, "Please come close, that I may feel you, my son, whether you are really my son Esau or not."

22 So Jacob came close to Isaac his father, and he felt him and said, "The voice is the voice of Jacob, but the hands are the hands of Esau."

27:23
v. 16

23 And he did not recognize him, because his hands were hairy like his brother Esau's hands; so he blessed him.

24 And he said, "Are you really my son Esau?" And he said, "I am."

27:25
vv. 4,10,19,
31

25 So he said, "Bring *it* to me, and I will eat of my son's game, that I may bless you." And he brought *it* to him, and he ate; he also brought him wine and he drank.

26 Then his father Isaac said to him, "Please come close and kiss me, my son."

27:27
Heb 11:20;
Song 4:11

27 So he came close and kissed him; and when he smelled the smell of his garments, he blessed him and said,

"See, the smell of my son
Is like the smell of a field which the LORD has blessed;

27:28
Deut 33:13,
28; Gen 45:18

28 Now may God give you of the dew of heaven,
And of the fatness of the earth,
And an abundance of grain and new wine;

27:29
Gen 9:25;
25:23; 49:8;
12:3;
Num 24:9;
Zeph 2:8

29 May peoples serve you,
And nations bow down to you;
Be master of your brothers,
And may your mother's sons bow down to you.
Cursed be those who curse you,
And blessed be those who bless you."

4. *Esau learns of the deception*

30 Now it came about, as soon as Isaac had finished blessing Jacob, and Jacob had hardly gone out from the presence of Isaac his father, that Esau his brother came in from his hunting.

27:31
v. 4

31 Then he also made savory food, and brought it to his father; and he said to his father, "Let my father arise, and eat of his son's game, that you may bless me."

27:32
v. 18

32 And Isaac his father said to him, "Who are you?" And he said, "I am your son, your first-born, Esau."

27:33
Gen 28:3,4;
Rom 11:29

33 Then Isaac trembled violently, and said, "Who was he then that hunted game and brought *it* to me, so that I ate of all *of it* before you came, and blessed him? Yes, and he shall be blessed."

27:34
Heb 12:17

34 When Esau heard the words of his father, he cried out with an exceedingly great and bitter cry, and said to his father, "Bless me, *even* me also, O my father!"

35 And he said, "Your brother came deceitfully, and has taken away your blessing."

36 Then he said, "Is he not rightly named Jacob, for he has supplanted me these two times? He took away my birthright, and behold, now he has taken away my blessing." And he said, "Have you not reserved a blessing for me?"

27:37
vv. 28,29

37 But Isaac answered and said to Esau, "Behold, I have made him your master, and all his relatives I have given to him as servants; and with grain and new wine I have sustained him. Now as for you then, what can I do, my son?"

27:38
Heb 12:17

38 And Esau said to his father, "Do you have only one blessing, my father? Bless me, *even* me also, O my father." So Esau lifted his voice and wept.

27:39
v. 28

39 Then Isaac his father answered and said to him,

"Behold, away from the fertility of the earth shall be your dwelling,
And away from the dew of heaven from above.

27:40
Gen 25:23;
2 Kin 8:20-22

40 "And by your sword you shall live,
And your brother you shall serve;
But it shall come about when you become restless,
That you shall break his yoke from your neck."

27:19 Rebekah and Jacob deceived Isaac in order to obtain the blessing. Esau, long before this, had sold the birthright (25:27–34) to his brother. God would undoubtedly have worked out His will for Jacob to obtain the blessing in the end without resort to fraud. This incident is a sad illustration of what happens when believers seek to promote the will of God by dishonest means. Jacob had to pay the price in long years of exile.

5. Rebekah schemes for Jacob to visit Laban

41   So Esau bore a grudge against Jacob because of the blessing with which his father had blessed him; and Esau said to himself, "The days of mourning for my father are near; then I will kill my brother Jacob."

42   Now when the words of her elder son Esau were reported to Rebekah, she sent and called her younger son Jacob, and said to him, "Behold your brother Esau is consoling himself concerning you, *by planning* to kill you.

43   "Now therefore, my son, obey my voice, and arise, flee to Haran, to my brother Laban!

44   "And stay with him a few days, until your brother's fury subsides,

45   until your brother's anger against you subsides, and he forgets what you did to him. Then I shall send and get you from there. Why should I be bereaved of you both in one day?"

46   And Rebekah said to Isaac, "I am tired of living because of the daughters of Heth; if Jacob takes a wife from the daughters of Heth, like these, from the daughters of the land, what good will my life be to me?"

6. Isaac sends Jacob to Laban

28 So Isaac called Jacob and blessed him and charged him, and said to him, "You shall not take a wife from the daughters of Canaan.

2   "Arise, go to Paddan-aram, to the house of Bethuel your mother's father; and from there take to yourself a wife from the daughters of Laban your mother's brother.

3   "And may God Almighty bless you and make you fruitful and multiply you, that you may become a company of peoples.

4   "May He also give you the blessing of Abraham, to you and to your descendants with you; that you may possess the land of your sojournings, which God gave to Abraham."

5   Then Isaac sent Jacob away, and he went to Paddan-aram to Laban, son of Bethuel the Aramean, the brother of Rebekah, the mother of Jacob and Esau.

E. Esau's third wife

6   Now Esau saw that Isaac had blessed Jacob and sent him away to Paddan-aram, to take to himself a wife from there, *and that* when he blessed him he charged him, saying, "You shall not take a wife from the daughters of Canaan,"

7   and that Jacob had obeyed his father and his mother and had gone to Paddan-aram.

8   So Esau saw that the daughters of Canaan displeased his father Isaac;

9   and Esau went to Ishmael, and married, besides the wives that he had, Mahalath the daughter of Ishmael, Abraham's son, the sister of Nebaioth.

F. Jacob's dream at Bethel

10   Then Jacob departed from Beersheba and went toward Haran.

11   And he came to a certain place and spent the night there, because the sun had set; and he took one of the stones of the place and put it under his head, and lay down in that place.

12   And he had a dream, and behold, a ladder was set on the earth with its top reaching to heaven; and behold, the angels of God were ascending and descending on it.

13   And behold, the LORD stood above it and said, "I am the LORD, the God of your father Abraham and the God of Isaac; the land on which you lie, I will give it to you and to your descendants.

14   "Your descendants shall also be like the dust of the earth, and you shall spread out to the west and to the east and to the north and to the south; and in you and in your descendants shall all the families of the earth be blessed.

15   "And behold, I am with you, and will keep you wherever you go, and will bring you back to this land; for I will not leave you until I have done what I have promised you."

16   Then Jacob awoke from his sleep and said, "Surely the LORD is in this place, and I did not know it."

17   And he was afraid and said, "How awesome is this place! This is none other than the house of God, and this is the gate of heaven."

27:41
Gen 32:3-11

27:43
vv. 8,13;
Gen 24:29

27:46
Gen 26:34,35

28:1
Gen 24:3,4

28:2
Gen 25:20

28:3
Gen 17:1,6

28:4
Gen 12:2;
17:8

28:6
v. 1

28:8
Gen 24:3;
26:35
28:9
Gen 36:3

28:12
John 1:51

28:13
Gen 35:1;
48:3; 26:24;
13:15; 35:12
28:14
Gen 13:14-16;
22:17; 12:3;
18:18; 22:18;
26:4
28:15
Gen 26:3;
Num 6:24;
Ps 121:7,8;
Gen 48:21;
Deut 31:6,8
28:16
Ex 3:5;
Josh 5:15

*28:18
Gen 35:14;
Lev 8:10-12
*28:19
Judg 1:23,26;
Hos 4:15
*28:20ff
Gen 31:13;
v. 15;
1 Tim 6:8
28:21
Judg 11:31;
2 Sam 19:24,
30;
Deut 26:17;
2 Sam 15:8
28:22
Gen 35:7,14;
Lev 27:30

18 So Jacob rose early in the morning, and took the stone that he had put under his head and set it up as a pillar, and poured oil on its top.

19 And he called the name of that place [28]Bethel; however, previously the name of the city had been Luz.

20 Then Jacob made a vow, saying, "If God will be with me and will keep me on this journey that I take, and will give me food to eat and garments to wear,

21 and I return to my father's house in safety, then the LORD will be my God.

22 "And this stone, which I have set up as a pillar, will be God's house; and of all that Thou dost give me I will surely give a tenth to Thee."

G. *Jacob and Laban*

1. *Jacob meets Rachel*

29:1
Judg 6:3,33

29 Then Jacob [29]went on his journey, and came to the land of the sons of the east.

2 And he looked, and saw a well in the field, and behold, three flocks of sheep were lying there beside it, for from that well they watered the flocks. Now the stone on the mouth of the well was large.

3 When all the flocks were gathered there, they would then roll the stone from the mouth of the well, and water the sheep, and put the stone back in its place on the mouth of the well.

29:4
Gen 28:10

4 And Jacob said to them, "My brothers, where are you from?" And they said, "We are from Haran."

29:5
Gen 24:24,29

5 And he said to them, "Do you know Laban the son of Nahor?" And they said, "We know *him*."

29:6
Gen 43:27

6 And he said to them, "Is it well with him?" And they said, "It is well, and behold, Rachel his daughter is coming with the sheep."

7 And he said, "Behold, it is still high day; it is not time for the livestock to be gathered. Water the sheep, and go, pasture them."

8 But they said, "We cannot, until all the flocks are gathered, and they roll the stone from the mouth of the well; then we water the sheep."

29:9
Ex 2:16

9 While he was still speaking with them, Rachel came with her father's sheep, for she was a shepherdess.

29:10
Ex 2:17

10 And it came about, when Jacob saw Rachel the daughter of Laban his mother's brother, and the sheep of Laban his mother's brother, that Jacob went up, and rolled the stone from the mouth of the well, and watered the flock of Laban his mother's brother.

11 Then Jacob kissed Rachel, and lifted his voice and wept.

29:12
Gen 13:8;
14:14,16;
24:28
29:13
Gen 24:29,31;
33:4

12 And Jacob told Rachel that he was a relative of her father and that he was Rebekah's son, and she ran and told her father.

13 So it came about, when Laban heard the news of Jacob his sister's son, that he ran to meet him, and embraced him and kissed him, and brought him to his house. Then he related to Laban all these things.

29:14
Judg 9:2

14 And Laban said to him, "Surely you are my bone and my flesh." And he stayed with him a month.

2. *Jacob's marriages to Leah and Rachel*

15 Then Laban said to Jacob, "Because you are my relative, should you therefore serve me for nothing? Tell me, what shall your wages be?"

16 Now Laban had two daughters; the name of the older was Leah, and the name of the younger was Rachel.

17 And Leah's eyes were weak, but Rachel was beautiful of form and face.

---

[28]I.e., the house of God   [29]Lit., *lifted up his feet*

28:18 *pillar*, a memorial stone; *oil*, consecrating the holy place as an altar to God.
28:19 *Luz*, probably meaning "almond-tree," was renamed by Jacob *Bethel*, meaning "house of God," and became a holy place to the children of Israel. It was located on land that later was granted to the tribe of Benjamin and was about twelve miles north of Jerusalem. This sacred place was defiled when Jeroboam erected a golden calf (1 Kin. 12:28–33); therefore God decreed the destruction of the altar (1 Kin. 13:1–5; 2 Kin. 23:15–17; Amos 3:14,15).

28:20–22 Jacob here was not expressing doubt as to whether God would keep His promise of verses 13–15; he used the particle *if* in the sense of "on the basis of the fact that" (cf. Rom. 8:31: *If God is for us*). Nor was he necessarily making a bargain with God, as if he would bribe Him to keep His word. He was simply specifying in the form of a vow the particular expression he would give to his gratitude for God's surprising and wholly undeserved favor. This became a customary type of thanksgiving in Israelite practice and was often solemnized by a votive offering.

18   Now Jacob loved Rachel, so he said, "I will serve you seven years for your younger daughter Rachel."

29:18
Hos 12:12

19   And Laban said, "It is better that I give her to you than that I should give her to another man; stay with me."

20   So Jacob served seven years for Rachel and they seemed to him but a few days because of his love for her.

21   Then Jacob said to Laban, "Give *me* my wife, for my time is completed, that I may go in to her."

29:21
Judg 15:1

22   And Laban gathered all the men of the place, and made a feast.

29:22
Judg 14:10;
John 2:1,2

23   Now it came about in the evening that he took his daughter Leah, and brought her to him; and *Jacob* went in to her.

24   Laban also gave his maid Zilpah to his daughter Leah as a maid.

25   So it came about in the morning that, behold, it was Leah! And he said to Laban, "What is this you have done to me? Was it not for Rachel that I served with you? Why then have you deceived me?"

26   But Laban said, "It is not the practice in our place, to marry off the younger before the first-born.

27   "Complete the week of this one, and we will give you the other also for the service which you shall serve with me for another seven years."

29:27
Judg 14:12

28   And Jacob did so and completed her week, and he gave him his daughter Rachel as his wife.

29   Laban also gave his maid Bilhah to his daughter Rachel as her maid.

30   So *Jacob* went in to Rachel also, and indeed he loved Rachel more than Leah, and he served with Laban for another seven years.

29:30
vv. 17,18

3. *Jacob's children*

a. *Leah's four sons*

31   Now the LORD saw that Leah was unloved, and He opened her womb, but Rachel was barren.

29:31
Ps 127:3;
Gen 30:1

32   And Leah conceived and bore a son and named him Reuben, for she said, "Because the LORD has seen my affliction; surely now my husband will love me."

29:32
Gen 16:11;
31:42

33   Then she conceived again and bore a son and said, "Because the LORD has heard that I am unloved, He has therefore given me this *son* also." So she named him Simeon.

34   And she conceived again and bore a son and said, "Now this time my husband will become attached to me, because I have borne him three sons." Therefore he was named Levi.

29:34
Gen 49:5

35   And she conceived again and bore a son and said, "This time I will praise the LORD." Therefore she named him Judah. Then she stopped bearing.

29:35
Gen 49:8;
Matt 1:2

b. *Bilhah's two sons*

30 Now when Rachel saw that she bore Jacob no children, she became jealous of her sister; and she said to Jacob, "Give me children, or else I die."

30:1
1 Sam 1:5,6

2   Then Jacob's anger burned against Rachel, and he said, "Am I in the place of God, who has withheld from you the fruit of the womb?"

30:2
Gen 20:18;
29:31

3   And she said, "Here is my maid Bilhah, go in to her, that she may bear on my knees, that through her I too may have children."

30:3
Gen 16:2

4   So she gave him her maid Bilhah as a wife, and Jacob went in to her.

30:4
Gen 16:3,4

5   And Bilhah conceived and bore Jacob a son.

6   Then Rachel said, "God has vindicated me, and has indeed heard my voice and has given me a son." Therefore she named him Dan.

30:6
Lam 3:59

7   And Rachel's maid Bilhah conceived again and bore Jacob a second son.

8   So Rachel said, "With mighty wrestlings I have wrestled with my sister, *and* I have indeed prevailed." And she named him Naphtali.

30:8
Matt 4:13

c. *Zilpah's two sons*

9   When Leah saw that she had stopped bearing, she took her maid Zilpah and gave her to Jacob as a wife.

30:9
v. 4

10   And Leah's maid Zilpah bore Jacob a son.

29:25 We have here an illustration of how a man must reap as he has sown. The deceit that Jacob practiced on Esau was returned to him by Laban, who practiced the same kind of deceit. For all of that, however, Jacob was under the cov-enant care of God and did not come out as a loser in the end. Yet in later years Jacob's own sons practiced on him a similar form of deceit in connection with Joseph's abduction (37:32–36).

11   Then Leah said, "How fortunate!" So she named him Gad.

12   And Leah's maid Zilpah bore Jacob a second son.

30:13
Prov 31:28

13   Then Leah said, "Happy am I! For women will call me happy." So she named him Asher.

d. Leah's last two sons: Rachel's first one

30:14
Gen 25:30

14   Now in the days of wheat harvest Reuben went and found mandrakes in the field, and brought them to his mother Leah. Then Rachel said to Leah, "Please give me some of your son's mandrakes."

30:15
Num 16:9,13

15   But she said to her, "Is it a small matter for you to take my husband? And would you take my son's mandrakes also?" So Rachel said, "Therefore he may lie with you tonight in return for your son's mandrakes."

16   When Jacob came in from the field in the evening, then Leah went out to meet him and said, "You must come in to me, for I have surely hired you with my son's mandrakes." So he lay with her that night.

17   And God gave heed to Leah, and she conceived and bore Jacob a fifth son.

18   Then Leah said, "God has given me my wages, because I gave my maid to my husband." So she named him Issachar.

19   And Leah conceived again and bore a sixth son to Jacob.

30:20
Matt 4:13

20   Then Leah said, "God has endowed me with a good gift; now my husband will dwell with me, because I have borne him six sons." So she named him Zebulun.

21   And afterward she bore a daughter and named her Dinah.

30:22
1 Sam 1:19,
20; Gen 29:31
30:23
Is 4:1;
Luke 1:25
30:24
Gen 35:17

22   Then God remembered Rachel, and God gave heed to her and opened her womb.

23   So she conceived and bore a son and said, "God has taken away my reproach."

24   And she named him Joseph, saying, "May the LORD give me another son."

4. Jacob's bargain with Laban

30:25
Gen 24:54,56

25   Now it came about when Rachel had borne Joseph, that Jacob said to Laban, "Send me away, that I may go to my own place and to my own country.

30:26
Gen 29:20,30;
Hos 12:12
30:27
Gen 39:3,5

26   "Give *me* my wives and my children for whom I have served you, and let me depart; for you yourself know my service which I have rendered you."

27   But Laban said to him, "If now [30]it pleases you, *stay with me;* I have divined that the LORD has blessed me on your account."

30:28
Gen 29:15
30:29
Gen 31:38-40

28   And he continued, "Name me your wages, and I will give it."

29   But he said to him, "You yourself know how I have served you and how your cattle have fared with me.

30:30
1 Tim 5:8

30   "For you had little before I came, and it has increased to a multitude; and the LORD has blessed you wherever I turned. But now, when shall I provide for my own household also?"

31   So he said, "What shall I give you?" And Jacob said, "You shall not give me anything. If you will do this *one* thing for me, I will again pasture *and* keep your flock:

30:32
Gen 31:8

32   let me pass through your entire flock today, removing from there every speckled and spotted sheep, and every black one among the lambs, and the spotted and speckled among the goats; and *such* shall be my wages.

30:33
Ps 37:6

33   "So my honesty will answer for me later, when you come concerning my wages. Every one that is not speckled and spotted among the goats and black among the lambs, *if found* with me, will be considered stolen."

34   And Laban said, "Good, let it be according to your word."

35   So he removed on that day the striped and spotted male goats and all the speckled and spotted female goats, every one with white in it, and all the black ones among the sheep, and gave them into the care of his sons.

36   And he put *a distance of* three days' journey between himself and Jacob, and Jacob fed the rest of Laban's flocks.

30:37
Gen 31:9-12

37   Then Jacob took fresh rods of poplar and almond and plane trees, and peeled white stripes in them, exposing the white which *was* in the rods.

38   And he set the rods which he had peeled in front of the flocks in the gutters, *even* in the watering troughs, where the flocks came to drink; and they mated when they came to drink.

[30]Lit., *I have found favor in your eyes*

39 So the flocks mated by the rods, and the flocks brought forth striped, speckled, and spotted.

40 And Jacob separated the lambs, and made the flocks face toward the striped and all the black in the flock of Laban; and he put his own herds apart, and did not put them with Laban's flock.

41 Moreover, it came about whenever the stronger of the flock were mating, that Jacob would place the rods in the sight of the flock in the gutters, so that they might mate by the rods;

42 but when the flock was feeble, he did not put *them* in; so the feebler were Laban's and the stronger Jacob's.

43 So the man became exceedingly prosperous, and had large flocks and female and male servants and camels and donkeys.

5. Jacob plans to return home

31 Now Jacob heard the words of Laban's sons, saying, "Jacob has taken away all that was our father's, and from what belonged to our father he has made all this wealth."

2 And Jacob saw the [31]attitude of Laban, and behold, it was not *friendly* toward him as formerly.

3 Then the LORD said to Jacob, "Return to the land of your fathers and to your relatives, and I will be with you."

4 So Jacob sent and called Rachel and Leah to his flock in the field,

5 and said to them, "I see your father's attitude, that it is not *friendly* toward me as formerly, but the God of my father has been with me.

6 "And you know that I have served your father with all my strength.

7 "Yet your father has cheated me and changed my wages ten times; however, God did not allow him to hurt me.

8 "If he spoke thus, 'The speckled shall be your wages,' then all the flock brought forth speckled; and if he spoke thus, 'The striped shall be your wages,' then all the flock brought forth striped.

9 "Thus God has taken away your father's livestock and given *them* to me.

10 "And it came about at the time when the flock were mating that I lifted up my eyes and saw in a dream, and behold, the male goats which were mating *were* striped, speckled, and mottled.

11 "Then the angel of God said to me in the dream, 'Jacob,' and I said, 'Here I am.'

12 "And he said, 'Lift up, now, your eyes and see *that* all the male goats which are mating are striped, speckled, and mottled; for I have seen all that Laban has been doing to you.

13 'I am the God *of* Bethel, where you anointed a pillar, where you made a vow to Me; now arise, leave this land, and return to the land of your birth.' "

14 And Rachel and Leah answered and said to him, "Do we still have any portion or inheritance in our father's house?

15 "Are we not reckoned by him as foreigners? For he has sold us, and has also entirely consumed our purchase price.

16 "Surely all the wealth which God has taken away from our father belongs to us and our children; now then, do whatever God has said to you."

6. Jacob's flight from Laban

a. Jacob steals away

17 Then Jacob arose and put his children and his wives upon camels;

18 and he drove away all his livestock and all his property which he had gathered, his acquired livestock which he had gathered in Paddan-aram, to go to the land of Canaan to his father Isaac.

19 When Laban had gone to shear his flock, then Rachel stole the household idols that were her father's.

20 And Jacob deceived Laban the Aramean, by not telling him that he was fleeing.

[31]Lit., *face*

31:1 *Laban*, see note to Gen. 29:25.   31:19 *household idols*, idols of clay or metal.

Marginal references:

30:43 Gen 12:16; 13:2; 24:35; 26:13,14

31:3 Gen 28:15,20, 21; 32:9

31:5 vv. 3,42; Gen 48:15

31:7 v. 41; Job 19:3; Ps 37:28; 105:14
31:8 Gen 30:32

31:11 Gen 48:16

31:13 Gen 28:13,18, 20
31:14 Gen 29:15,27

*31:19 vv. 30,34; Judg 17:5; 1 Sam 19:13; Hos 3:4

31:21
Gen 37:25

31:23
Gen 13:8

31:24
Gen 20:3;
Job 33:15;
Gen 24:50

31:26
1 Sam 30:2

31:27
v. 55;
Ruth 1:9,14;
Acts 20:37

31:29
vv. 53,24

31:30
v. 19

31:32
Gen 44:9

*31:35
Ex 20:12;
Lev 19:32

31:39
Ex 22:10-13

31:41
Gen 29:27,30;
v. 7

*31:42
Ps 124:1,2;
v. 53; Is 8:13;
Gen 29:32;
1 Chr 12:17

21   So he fled with all that he had; and he arose and crossed the *Euphrates* River, and set his face toward the hill country of Gilead.

b. Laban overtakes Jacob

22   When it was told Laban on the third day that Jacob had fled,

23   then he took his kinsmen with him, and pursued him *a distance of* seven days' journey; and he overtook him in the hill country of Gilead.

24   And God came to Laban the Aramean in a dream of the night, and said to him, "Be careful that you do not speak to Jacob either good or bad."

25   And Laban caught up with Jacob. Now Jacob had pitched his tent in the hill country, and Laban with his kinsmen camped in the hill country of Gilead.

26   Then Laban said to Jacob, "What have you done by deceiving me and carrying away my daughters like captives of the sword?

27   "Why did you flee secretly and deceive me, and did not tell me, so that I might have sent you away with joy and with songs, with timbrel and with lyre;

28   and did not allow me to kiss my sons and my daughters? Now you have done foolishly.

29   "It is in my power to do you harm, but the God of your father spoke to me last night, saying, 'Be careful not to speak either good or bad to Jacob.'

30   "And now you have indeed gone away because you longed greatly for your father's house; *but* why did you steal my gods?"

31   Then Jacob answered and said to Laban, "Because I was afraid, for I said, 'Lest you would take your daughters from me by force.'

32   "The one with whom you find your gods shall not live; in the presence of our kinsmen point out what is yours among my belongings and take *it* for yourself." For Jacob did not know that Rachel had stolen them.

c. Rachel and Laban's idols

33   So Laban went into Jacob's tent, and into Leah's tent, and into the tent of the two maids, but he did not find *them*. Then he went out of Leah's tent and entered Rachel's tent.

34   Now Rachel had taken the household idols and put them in the camel's saddle, and she sat on them. And Laban felt through all the tent, but did not find *them*.

35   And she said to her father, "Let not my lord be angry that I cannot rise before you, for the manner of women is upon me." So he searched, but did not find the household idols.

36   Then Jacob became angry and contended with Laban; and Jacob answered and said to Laban, "What is my transgression? What is my sin, that you have hotly pursued me?

37   "Though you have felt through all my goods, what have you found of all your household goods? Set *it* here before my kinsmen and your kinsmen, that they may decide between us two.

38   "These twenty years I *have been* with you; your ewes and your female goats have not miscarried, nor have I eaten the rams of your flocks.

39   "That which was torn *of beasts* I did not bring to you; I bore the loss of it myself. You required it of my hand *whether* stolen by day or stolen by night.

40   "*Thus* I was: by day the heat consumed me, and the frost by night, and my sleep fled from my eyes.

41   "These twenty years I have been in your house; I served you fourteen years for your two daughters, and six years for your flock, and you changed my wages ten times.

42   "If the God of my father, the God of Abraham, and the fear of Isaac, had not been for me, surely now you would have sent me away empty-handed. God has seen my affliction and the toil of my hands, so He rendered judgment last night."

d. The covenant between Jacob and Laban: Mizpah

43   Then Laban answered and said to Jacob, "The daughters are my daughters, and the children are my children, and the flocks are my flocks, and all that you see is mine. But what can I do this day to these my daughters or to their children whom they have borne?

31:35 Rachel deceived her father by pretending to be "unclean."

31:42 *fear of Isaac* (a term used for Israel's God), object of Isaac's reverence.

44   "So now come, let us make a covenant, you and I, and let it be a witness between you and me."

45   Then Jacob took a stone and set it up *as* a pillar.

46   And Jacob said to his kinsmen, "Gather stones." So they took stones and made a heap, and they ate there by the heap.

47   Now Laban called it [32]Jegar-sahadutha, but Jacob called it [33] Galeed.

48   And Laban said, "This heap is a witness between you and me this day." Therefore it was named Galeed;

49   and [34]Mizpah, for he said, "May the LORD watch between you and me when we are absent one from the other.

50   "If you mistreat my daughters, or if you take wives besides my daughters, *although* no man is with us, see, God is witness between you and me."

51   And Laban said to Jacob, "Behold this heap and behold the pillar which I have set between you and me.

52   "This heap is a witness, and the pillar is a witness, that I will not pass by this heap to you for harm, and you will not pass by this heap and this pillar to me, for harm.

53   "The God of Abraham and the God of Nahor, the God of their father, judge between us." So Jacob swore by the fear of his father Isaac.

54   Then Jacob offered a sacrifice on the mountain, and called his kinsmen to the meal; and they ate the meal and spent the night on the mountain.

55   And early in the morning Laban arose, and kissed his sons and his daughters and blessed them. Then Laban departed and returned to his place.

H. *Jacob's meeting with Esau*

1. *The preparations*

32 Now as Jacob went on his way, the angels of God met him.

2   And Jacob said when he saw them, "This is God's [35]camp." So he named that place [36]Mahanaim.

3   Then Jacob sent messengers before him to his brother Esau in the land of Seir, the country of Edom.

4   He also commanded them saying, "Thus you shall say to my lord Esau: 'Thus says your servant Jacob, "I have sojourned with Laban, and stayed until now;

5   and I have oxen and donkeys *and* flocks and male and female servants; and I have sent to tell my lord, that I may find favor in your sight."'"

6   And the messengers returned to Jacob, saying, "We came to your brother Esau, and furthermore he is coming to meet you, and four hundred men are with him."

7   Then Jacob was greatly afraid and distressed; and he divided the people who were with him, and the flocks and the herds and the camels, into two companies;

8   for he said, "If Esau comes to the one company and attacks it, then the company which is left will escape."

9   And Jacob said, "O God of my father Abraham and God of my father Isaac, O LORD, who didst say to me, 'Return to your country and to your relatives, and I will prosper you,'

10   I am unworthy of all the lovingkindness and of all the faithfulness which Thou hast shown to Thy servant; for with my staff *only* I crossed this Jordan, and now I have become two companies.

11   "Deliver me, I pray, from the hand of my brother, from the hand of Esau; for I fear him, lest he come and attack me, the mothers with the children.

12   "For Thou didst say, 'I will surely prosper you, and make your descendants as the sand of the sea, which cannot be numbered for multitude.'"

13   So he spent the night there. Then he selected from what he had with him a present for his brother Esau:

Cross-references

31:44 Gen 21:27,32; 26:28; Josh 24:27
31:45 Gen 28:18
31:48 Josh 24:27
***31:49** Judg 11:29; 1 Sam 7:5
31:53 Gen 16:5; 21:23; 28:13; v. 42
31:55 Gen 18:33; 30:25
32:1 Ps 34:7; 91:11; Heb 1:14
32:2 Ps 103:21
32:3 Gen 33:14,16; 25:30; 36:8,9
32:4 Prov 15:1
32:5 Gen 30:43; 33:8,15
32:6 Gen 33:1
32:7 v. 11
***32:9** Gen 31:42; 28:15; 31:13
32:10 Gen 24:27; Job 8:7
32:11 Gen 27:41,42; 33:4
32:12 Gen 28:13-15
32:13 Gen 43:11; Prov 18:16

---

[32]I.e., the heap of witness, in Aramaic   [33]I.e., the heap of witness, in Hebrew   [34]I.e., the watchtower   [35]Or, *company*   [36]I.e., Two Camps, or, Two Companies

---

31:49 God is called as a witness, so that if either Jacob or Laban breaks the agreement the LORD will enforce the covenant.
32:9 Jacob's prayer for deliverance was graciously an-swered. God granted His favor to an undeserving sinner who cast himself wholly on His mercy. Notice, however, that Jacob acted in accord with the proposition that often we should work as though we had never prayed.

14   two hundred female goats and twenty male goats, two hundred ewes and twenty rams,

15   thirty milking camels and their colts, forty cows and ten bulls, twenty female donkeys and ten male donkeys.

16   And he delivered *them* into the hand of his servants, every drove by itself, and said to his servants, "Pass on before me, and put a space between droves."

17   And he commanded the one in front, saying, "When my brother Esau meets you and asks you, saying, 'To whom do you belong, and where are you going, and to whom do these *animals* in front of you belong?'

18   then you shall say, '*These* belong to your servant Jacob; it is a present sent to my lord Esau. And behold, he also is behind us.' "

19   Then he commanded also the second and the third, and all those who followed the droves, saying, "After this manner you shall speak to Esau when you find him;

32:20
Prov 21:14

20   and you shall say, 'Behold, your servant Jacob also is behind us.' " For he said, "I will appease him with the present that goes before me. Then afterward I will see his face; perhaps he will accept me."

21   So the present passed on before him, while he himself spent that night in the camp.

2. Jacob becomes Israel: wrestling at the Jabbok

32:22
Deut 3:16;
Josh 12:2

22   Now he arose that same night and took his two wives and his two maids and his eleven children, and crossed the ford of the Jabbok.

23   And he took them and sent them across the stream. And he sent across whatever he had.

32:24
Josh 12:3,4

24   Then Jacob was left alone, and a man wrestled with him until daybreak.

25   And when he saw that he had not prevailed against him, he touched the socket of his thigh; so the socket of Jacob's thigh was dislocated while he wrestled with him.

32:26
Hos 12:4

26   Then he said, "Let me go, for the dawn is breaking." But he said, "I will not let you go unless you bless me."

27   So he said to him, "What is your name?" And he said, "Jacob."

*32:28
Gen 35:10;
1 Kin 18:31
32:29
Judg 13:17,18

28   And he said, "Your name shall no longer be Jacob, but [37]Israel; for you have striven with God and with men and have prevailed."

29   Then Jacob asked him and said, "Please tell me your name." But he said, "Why is it that you ask my name?" And he blessed him there.

32:30
Gen 16:13;
Ex 24:11;
Num 12:8;
Judg 6:22;
13:22

30   So Jacob named the place [38]Peniel, for *he said*, "I have seen God face to face, yet my life has been preserved."

31   Now the sun rose upon him just as he crossed over Penuel, and he was limping on his thigh.

32   Therefore, to this day the sons of Israel do not eat the sinew of the hip which is on the socket of the thigh, because he touched the socket of Jacob's thigh in the sinew of the hip.

3. Jacob and Esau meet

33:1
Gen 32:6

33   Then Jacob lifted his eyes and looked, and behold, Esau was coming, and four hundred men with him. So he divided the children among Leah and Rachel and the two maids.

2   And he put the maids and their children in front, and Leah and her children next, and Rachel and Joseph last.

33:3
Gen 18:2;
42:6

3   But he himself passed on ahead of them and bowed down to the ground seven times, until he came near to his brother.

*33:4
Gen 45:14,15

4   Then Esau ran to meet him and embraced him, and fell on his neck and kissed him, and they wept.

33:5
Gen 48:9;
Ps 127:3;
Is 8:18

5   And he lifted his eyes and saw the women and the children, and said, "Who are these with you?" So he said, "The children whom God has graciously given your servant."

---

[37]I.e., he who strives with God, or, God strives   [38]I.e., the face of God

---

32:28   Just as God changed Abram's name to Abraham, He now changes Jacob's name to Israel, by which the Hebrews are henceforth to be known. It is a name for the people and for an individual. The normative use of *Israel* in the Bible denotes the people, just as *American* denotes a citizen of the United States.

32:31   *Penuel*, Peniel (v. 30).

33:4   Only God working in the heart of Esau explains the change in him as he greets Jacob in a friendly, not in a hostile, manner.

6   Then the maids came near with their children, and they bowed down.
7   And Leah likewise came near with her children, and they bowed down; and afterward Joseph came near with Rachel, and they bowed down.
8   And he said, "What do you mean by all this company which I have met?" And he said, "To find favor in the sight of my lord."
9   But Esau said, "I have plenty, my brother; let what you have be your own."
10   And Jacob said, "No, please, if now I have found favor in your sight, then take my present from my hand, for I see your face as one sees the face of God, and you have received me favorably.
11   "Please take my gift which has been brought to you, because God has dealt graciously with me, and because I have plenty." Thus he urged him and he took *it.*
12   Then Esau said, "Let us take our journey and go, and I will go before you."
13   But he said to him, "My lord knows that the children are frail and that the flocks and herds which are nursing are a care to me. And if they are driven hard one day, all the flocks will die.
14   "Please let my lord pass on before his servant; and I will proceed at my leisure, according to the pace of the cattle that are before me and according to the pace of the children, until I come to my lord at Seir."

4. Jacob journeys to Shechem

15   And Esau said, "Please let me leave with you some of the people who are with me." But he said, "[39]What need is there? Let me find favor in the sight of my lord."
16   So Esau returned that day on his way to Seir.
17   And Jacob journeyed to [40]Succoth; and built for himself a house, and made booths for his livestock, therefore the place is named Succoth.
18   Now Jacob came safely to the city of Shechem, which is in the land of Canaan, when he came from Paddan-aram, and camped before the city.
19   And he bought the piece of land where he had pitched his tent from the hand of the sons of Hamor, Shechem's father, for one hundred pieces of money.
20   Then he erected there an altar, and called it [41]El-Elohe-Israel.

I. Jacob's later life

1. The rape of Dinah

34 Now Dinah the daughter of Leah, whom she had borne to Jacob, went out to visit the daughters of the land.
2   And when Shechem the son of Hamor the Hivite, the prince of the land, saw her, he took her and lay with her by force.
3   And he was deeply attracted to Dinah the daughter of Jacob, and he loved the girl and spoke tenderly to her.
4   So Shechem spoke to his father Hamor, saying, "Get me this young girl for a wife."
5   Now Jacob heard that he had defiled Dinah his daughter; but his sons were with his livestock in the field, so Jacob kept silent until they came in.
6   Then Hamor the father of Shechem went out to Jacob to speak with him.
7   Now the sons of Jacob came in from the field when they heard *it;* and the men were grieved, and they were very angry because he had done a disgraceful thing in Israel by lying with Jacob's daughter, for such a thing ought not to be done.
8   But Hamor spoke with them, saying, "The soul of my son Shechem longs for your daughter; please give her to him in marriage.
9   "And intermarry with us; give your daughters to us, and take our daughters for yourselves.
10   "Thus you shall live with us, and the land shall be *open* before you; live and trade in it, and acquire property in it."
11   Shechem also said to her father and to her brothers, "If I find favor in your sight, then I will give whatever you say to me.
12   "Ask me ever so much bridal payment and gift, and I will give according as you say to me; but give me the girl in marriage."

[39]Lit., *"Why this?"*   [40]I.e., booths   [41]I.e., God, the God of Israel

33:16 *Seir,* Edom.

33:8 Gen 32:14-16
33:10 Gen 43:3; 2 Sam 3:13
33:11 1 Sam 25:27
33:14 Gen 32:3
33:15 Gen 34:11; 47:25; Ruth 2:13
33:17 Judg 8:5,14
33:18 Josh 24:1; Judg 9:1; Gen 25:20; 28:2
33:19 Josh 24:32; John 4:5
34:1 Gen 30:21
34:4 Judg 14:2
34:7 Deut 22:21; Josh 7:15; Judg 20:6; 2 Sam 13:12
34:10 Gen 13:9; 20:15
34:12 Ex 22:16; Deut 22:29; 1 Sam 18:25

13 But Jacob's sons answered Shechem and his father Hamor, with deceit, and spoke to them, because he had defiled Dinah their sister.

34:14
Gen 17:14

14 And they said to them, "We cannot do this thing, to give our sister to one who is uncircumcised, for that would be a disgrace to us.

15 "Only on this *condition* will we consent to you: if you will become like us, in that every male of you be circumcised,

16 then we will give our daughters to you, and we will take your daughters for ourselves, and we will live with you and become one people.

17 "But if you will not listen to us to be circumcised, then we will take our daughter and go."

2. The revenge for the rape of Dinah

18 Now their words seemed reasonable to Hamor and Shechem, Hamor's son.

34:19
1 Chr 4:9

19 And the young man did not delay to do the thing, because he was delighted with Jacob's daughter. Now he was more respected than all the household of his father.

20 So Hamor and his son Shechem came to the gate of their city, and spoke to the men of their city, saying,

21 "These men are friendly with us; therefore let them live in the land and trade in it, for behold, the land is large enough for them. Let us take their daughters in marriage, and give our daughters to them.

22 "Only on this *condition* will the men consent to us to live with us, to become one people: that every male among us be circumcised as they are circumcised.

23 "Will not their livestock and their property and all their animals be ours? Only let us consent to them, and they will live with us."

34:24
Gen 23:10

24 And all who went out of the gate of his city listened to Hamor and to his son Shechem, and every male was circumcised, all who went out of the gate of his city.

34:25
Gen 49:5-7

25 Now it came about on the third day, when they were in pain, that two of Jacob's sons, Simeon and Levi, Dinah's brothers, each took his sword and came upon the city unawares, and killed every male.

26 And they killed Hamor and his son Shechem with the edge of the sword, and took Dinah from Shechem's house, and went forth.

27 Jacob's sons came upon the slain and looted the city, because they had defiled their sister.

28 They took their flocks and their herds and their donkeys, and that which was in the city and that which was in the field;

29 and they captured and looted all their wealth and all their little ones and their wives, even all that *was* in the houses.

34:30
Gen 49:6;
Ex 5:21;
Gen 36:26,27

30 Then Jacob said to Simeon and Levi, "You have brought trouble on me, by making me odious among the inhabitants of the land, among the Canaanites and the Perizzites; and my men being few in number, they will gather together against me and attack me and I shall be destroyed, I and my household."

31 But they said, "Should he treat our sister as a harlot?"

3. Jacob returns to Bethel: God renews the covenant promises

35:1
Gen 28:19,13;
27:43

35 Then God said to Jacob, "Arise, go up to Bethel, and live there; and make an altar there to God, who appeared to you when you fled from your brother Esau."

35:2
Gen 31:19,30,
34; Ex 19:10,
14

2 So Jacob said to his household and to all who were with him, "Put away the foreign gods which are among you, and purify yourselves, and change your garments;

35:3
Gen 32:7,24;
28:20-22;
28:15

3 and let us arise and go up to Bethel; and I will make an altar there to God, who answered me in the day of my distress, and has been with me wherever I have gone."

35:4
Hos 2:13;
Josh 24:26

4 So they gave to Jacob all the foreign gods which they had, and the rings which were in their ears; and Jacob hid them under the oak which was near Shechem.

5 As they journeyed, there was a great terror upon the cities which were around them, and they did not pursue the sons of Jacob.

35:6
Gen 28:19;
48:3

6 So Jacob came to Luz (that is, Bethel), which is in the land of Canaan, he and all the people who were with him.

35:7
Gen 28:13

7 And he built an altar there, and called the place El-bethel, because there God had revealed Himself to him, when he fled from his brother.

8   Now Deborah, Rebekah's nurse, died, and she was buried below Bethel under the oak; it was named [42]Allon-bacuth.

35:8
Gen 24:59

9   Then God appeared to Jacob again when he came from Paddan-aram, and He blessed him.

35:9
Hos 12:4;
Gen 32:29

10   And God said to him,
  "Your name is Jacob;
  You shall no longer be called Jacob,
  But Israel shall be your name."
Thus He called him Israel.

35:10
Gen 32:28

11   God also said to him,
  "I am God Almighty;
  Be fruitful and multiply;
  A nation and a company of nations shall come from you,
  And kings shall come forth from you.

35:11
Gen 17:1;
28:3; 48:4;
17:6,16;
36:31

12   "And the land which I gave to Abraham and Isaac,
  I will give it to you,
  And I will give the land to your descendants after you."

35:12
Gen 13:15;
26:3; 28:13

13   Then God went up from him in the place where He had spoken with him.
14   And Jacob set up a pillar in the place where He had spoken with him, a pillar of stone, and he poured out a libation on it; he also poured oil on it.

35:13
Gen 17:22
*35:14
Gen 28:18

15   So Jacob named the place where God had spoken with him, [43] Bethel.

*35:15
Gen 28:19

4. Benjamin's birth: Rachel's death

16   Then they journeyed from Bethel; and when there was still some distance to go to Ephrath, Rachel began to give birth and she suffered severe labor.
17   And it came about when she was in severe labor that the midwife said to her, "Do not fear, for now you have *another* son."

35:17
Gen 30:24

18   And it came about as her soul was departing (for she died), that she named him [44]Ben-oni; but his father called him [45]Benjamin.
19   So Rachel died and was buried on the way to Ephrath (that is, Bethlehem).
20   And Jacob set up a pillar over her grave; that is the pillar of Rachel's grave to this day.
21   Then Israel journeyed on and pitched his tent beyond the tower of Eder.

35:19
Gen 48:7;
Ruth 1:2;
Mic 5:2;
Matt 2:6
35:20
1 Sam 10:2;
35:5;
Ex 15:16;
Deut 2:25;
11:25

5. The sin of Reuben

22   And it came about while Israel was dwelling in that land, that Reuben went and lay with Bilhah his father's concubine; and Israel heard *of it*.
  Now there were twelve sons of Jacob—

35:22
Gen 49:2;
1 Chr 5:1;
1 Cor 5:1

6. The sons of Jacob

23   the sons of Leah: Reuben, Jacob's first-born, then Simeon and Levi and Judah and Issachar and Zebulun;
24   the sons of Rachel: Joseph and Benjamin;
25   and the sons of Bilhah, Rachel's maid: Dan and Naphtali;
26   and the sons of Zilpah, Leah's maid: Gad and Asher. These are the sons of Jacob who were born to him in Paddan-aram.

7. The death of Isaac

27   And Jacob came to his father Isaac at Mamre of Kiriath-arba (that is, Hebron), where Abraham and Isaac had sojourned.

35:27
Gen 18:1;
23:9

[42]I.e., oak of weeping   [43]I.e., the house of God   [44]I.e., the son of my sorrow   [45]I.e., the son of the right hand

---

35:14 This is the first mention of the drink offering in the Old Testament. Mosaic sacrifices were often accompanied by drink offerings (Ex. 29:40; Lev. 23:13). In Num. 15:3–10 the quantity is prescribed according to the type of blood sacrifice to be presented. Its use was perverted by those Jews who offered it along with their sacrificial cakes to Ashtoreth, the *queen of heaven* (Jer. 44:17–19). God reproved Israel for offering it to idols (Is. 57:5,6 and 65:11; Jer. 19:13; Ezek. 20:28). The drink offering is symbolic of the outpoured blood of Christ on Calvary (Is. 53:12; Matt. 26:28; Heb. 9:11–14) and of the outpouring of the Holy Spirit on His church (Joel 2:28; Acts 2:17,18; 10:45).
35:15 See here note to 28:19.

35:18 Benjamin was the twelfth and last son of Jacob. He was a full brother to Joseph, being born of Rachel, the favorite wife of Jacob. Benjamin alone was born in Canaan rather than in Paddan-aram, and his mother was buried on the way to Bethlehem in the region later assigned to Benjamin. He and Joseph were special objects of the affection of Jacob because their mother was Rachel. In her dying agonies Rachel gave him the name of *Ben-oni*, 'son my my sorrow," but Jacob named him *Benjamin*, "son of the right hand." The peculiar concern of Joseph for Benjamin during the Egyptian episode may be understood by the fact that they were full brothers, whose half brothers looked on them with envy because of Jacob's special love for them.

28 Now the days of Isaac were one hundred and eighty years.

29 And Isaac breathed his last and died, and was gathered to his people, an old man of ripe age; and his sons Esau and Jacob buried him.

IX. *The generations of Esau (36:1–43)*

36 Now these are *the records of* the generations of Esau (that is, Edom).

2 Esau took his wives from the daughters of Canaan: Adah the daughter of Elon the Hittite, and Oholibamah the daughter of Anah and the granddaughter of Zibeon the Hivite;

3 also Basemath, Ishmael's daughter, the sister of Nebaioth.

4 And Adah bore Eliphaz to Esau, and Basemath bore Reuel,

5 and Oholibamah bore Jeush and Jalam and Korah. These are the sons of Esau who were born to him in the land of Canaan.

6 Then Esau took his wives and his sons and his daughters and all his household, and his livestock and all his cattle and all his goods which he had acquired in the land of Canaan, and went to *another* land away from his brother Jacob.

7 For their property had become too great for them to live together, and the land where they sojourned could not sustain them because of their livestock.

8 So Esau lived in the hill country of Seir; Esau is Edom.

9 These then are *the records of* the generations of Esau the father of the Edomites in the hill country of Seir.

10 These are the names of Esau's sons: Eliphaz the son of Esau's wife Adah, Reuel the son of Esau's wife Basemath.

11 And the sons of Eliphaz were Teman, Omar, Zepho and Gatam and Kenaz.

12 And Timna was a concubine of Esau's son Eliphaz and she bore Amalek to Eliphaz. These are the sons of Esau's wife Adah.

13 And these are the sons of Reuel: Nahath and Zerah, Shammah and Mizzah. These were the sons of Esau's wife Basemath.

14 And these were the sons of Esau's wife Oholibamah, the daughter of Anah and the granddaughter of Zibeon: she bore to Esau, Jeush and Jalam and Korah.

15 These are the chiefs of the sons of Esau. The sons of Eliphaz, the first-born of Esau, are chief Teman, chief Omar, chief Zepho, chief Kenaz,

16 chief Korah, chief Gatam, chief Amalek. These are the chiefs descended from Eliphaz in the land of Edom; these are the sons of Adah.

17 And these are the sons of Reuel, Esau's son: chief Nahath, chief Zerah, chief Shammah, chief Mizzah. These are the chiefs descended from Reuel in the land of Edom; these are the sons of Esau's wife Basemath.

18 And these are the sons of Esau's wife Oholibamah: chief Jeush, chief Jalam, chief Korah. These are the chiefs descended from Esau's wife Oholibamah, the daughter of Anah.

19 These are the sons of Esau (that is, Edom), and these are their chiefs.

20 These are the sons of Seir the Horite, the inhabitants of the land: Lotan and Shobal and Zibeon and Anah,

21 and Dishon and Ezer and Dishan. These are the chiefs descended from the Horites, the sons of Seir in the land of Edom.

22 And the sons of Lotan were Hori and Hemam; and Lotan's sister was Timna.

23 And these are the sons of Shobal: Alvan and Manahath and Ebal, Shepho and Onam.

24 And these are the sons of Zibeon: Aiah and Anah—he is the Anah who found the hot springs in the wilderness when he was pasturing the donkeys of his father Zibeon.

25 And these are the children of Anah: Dishon, and Oholibamah, the daughter of Anah.

26 And these are the sons of Dishon: Hemdan and Eshban and Ithran and Cheran.

27 These are the sons of Ezer: Bilhan and Zaavan and Akan.

Marginal references:
35:29 Gen 25:8; 15:15
36:1 Gen 25:30
36:2 Gen 26:34; 28:9
36:6 Gen 12:5
36:7 Gen 13:6,11; 17:8; 28:4
36:8 Gen 32:3
36:10 1 Chr 1:35
36:12 Ex 17:8,14
36:15 1 Chr 1:34
36:17 1 Chr 1:35,37
36:18 v. 25; 1 Chr 1:52
36:20 Gen 14:6; Deut 2:12,22; 1 Chr 1:38
36:25 v. 18; 1 Chr 1:52
36:27 1 Chr 1:42

36:9 The Edomites sprang from Esau and dwelt in the hill country of Seir. They were inveterate enemies of Israel (Ezek. 35:5), although God forbade His people to hate or to despoil them (Deut. 2:4–6; 23:7; 2 Chr. 20:10). Edom became a symbol of the hardened unbelief and hostility of the world to the people of God, and as such was declared by the prophets to be the object of God's wrath and conquering power in the last days (Is. 11:14; 34:5–6; Obad. 1–4; Amos 9:12).

28   These are the sons of Dishan: Uz and Aran.

29   These are the chiefs descended from the Horites: chief Lotan, chief Shobal, chief Zibeon, chief Anah,

30   chief Dishon, chief Ezer, chief Dishan. These are the chiefs descended from the Horites, according to their *various* chiefs in the land of Seir.

31   Now these are the kings who reigned in the land of Edom before any king reigned over the sons of Israel.

32   Bela the son of Beor reigned in Edom, and the name of his city was Dinhabah.

33   Then Bela died, and Jobab the son of Zerah of Bozrah became king in his place.

34   Then Jobab died, and Husham of the land of the Temanites became king in his place.

35   Then Husham died, and Hadad the son of Bedad, who defeated Midian in the field of Moab, became king in his place; and the name of his city was Avith.

36   Then Hadad died, and Samlah of Masrekah became king in his place.

37   Then Samlah died, and Shaul of Rehoboth on the *Euphrates* River became king in his place.

38   Then Shaul died, and Baal-hanan the son of Achbor became king in his place.

39   Then Baal-hanan the son of Achbor died, and Hadar became king in his place; and the name of his city was Pau; and his wife's name was Mehetabel, the daughter of Matred, daughter of Mezahab.

40   Now these are the names of the chiefs descended from Esau, according to their families *and* their localities, by their names: chief Timna, chief Alvah, chief Jetheth,

41   chief Oholibamah, chief Elah, chief Pinon,

42   chief Kenaz, chief Teman, chief Mibzar,

43   chief Magdiel, chief Iram. These are the chiefs of Edom (that is, Esau, the father of the Edomites), according to their habitations in the land of their possession.

*36:31
1 Chr 1:43

36:39
1 Chr 1:50

36:40
1 Chr 1:51

X. The generations of Jacob (37:1–50:26)

A. Joseph sold into slavery

1. *Joseph's dream: his brothers' hatred*

37 Now Jacob lived in the land where his father had sojourned, in the land of Canaan.

2   These are *the records of* the generations of Jacob.

Joseph, when seventeen years of age, was pasturing the flock with his brothers while he was *still* a youth, along with the sons of Bilhah and the sons of Zilpah, his father's wives. And Joseph brought back a bad report about them to their father.

3   Now Israel loved Joseph more than all his sons, because he was the son of his old age; and he made him a [46]varicolored tunic.

4   And his brothers saw that their father loved him more than all his brothers; and *so* they hated him and could not speak to him [47]on friendly terms.

5   Then Joseph had a dream, and when he told it to his brothers, they hated him even more.

6   And he said to them, "Please listen to this dream which I have had;

7   for behold, we were binding sheaves in the field, and lo, my sheaf rose up and also stood erect; and behold, your sheaves gathered around and bowed down to my sheaf."

8   Then his brothers said to him, "Are you actually going to reign over us? Or are you really going to rule over us?" So they hated him even more for his dreams and for his words.

9   Now he had still another dream, and related it to his brothers, and said, "Lo, I have had still another dream; and behold, the sun and the moon and eleven stars were bowing down to me."

37:1
Gen 17:8;
28:4

37:3
Gen 44:20

37:4
Gen 27:41;
49:22,23

37:7
Gen 42:6,9;
43:26; 44:14

37:8
Gen 49:26

---

[46]Or, *full-length robe*   [47]Lit., *in peace*

36:31 *before any king reigned.* This may be regarded as an indication that this phrase or perhaps the whole list was incorporated after the Israelite monarchy began, or as a prophetic revelation of the kingdoms of Saul and David.

37:10
Gen 27:29

10   And he related *it* to his father and to his brothers; and his father rebuked him and said to him, "What is this dream that you have had? Shall I and your mother and your brothers actually come to bow ourselves down before you to the ground?"

37:11
Acts 7:9

11   And his brothers were jealous of him, but his father kept the saying *in mind*.

2. The conspiracy to kill Joseph

12   Then his brothers went to pasture their father's flock in Shechem.

13   And Israel said to Joseph, "Are not your brothers pasturing *the flock* in Shechem? Come, and I will send you to them." And he said to him, "I will go."

37:14
Gen 35:27

14   Then he said to him, "Go now and see about the welfare of your brothers and the welfare of the flock; and bring word back to me." So he sent him from the valley of Hebron, and he came to Shechem.

15   And a man found him, and behold, he was wandering in the field; and the man asked him, "What are you looking for?"

16   And he said, "I am looking for my brothers; please tell me where they are pasturing *the flock*."

37:17
2 Kin 6:13

17   Then the man said, "They have moved from here; for I heard *them* say, 'Let us go to Dothan.' " So Joseph went after his brothers and found them at Dothan.

37:18
1 Sam 19:1;
Matt 27:1;
Acts 23:12

18   When they saw him from a distance and before he came close to them, they plotted against him to put him to death.

19   And they said to one another, "Here comes this dreamer!

20   "Now then, come and let us kill him and throw him into one of the pits; and we will say, 'A wild beast devoured him.' Then let us see what will become of his dreams!"

37:21
Gen 42:22

21   But Reuben heard *this* and rescued him out of their hands and said, "Let us not take his life."

22   Reuben further said to them, "Shed no blood. Throw him into this pit that is in the wilderness, but do not lay hands on him"—that he might rescue him out of their hands, to restore him to his father.

23   So it came about, when Joseph reached his brothers, that they stripped Joseph of his tunic, the varicolored tunic that was on him;

24   and they took him and threw him into the pit. Now the pit was empty, without any water in it.

3. Joseph sold to traders

37:25
vv. 28,36;
Gen 43:11;
Jer 8:22

25   Then they sat down to eat a meal. And as they raised their eyes and looked, behold, a caravan of Ishmaelites was coming from Gilead, with their camels bearing aromatic gum and balm and myrrh, on their way to bring *them* down to Egypt.

37:26
v. 20;
Gen 4:10;
Job 16:18

26   And Judah said to his brothers, "What profit is it for us to kill our brother and cover up his blood?

37:27
Gen 42:21
*37:28
Judg 6:3;
Gen 45:4,5;
Acts 7:9;
Gen 39:1

27   "Come and let us sell him to the Ishmaelites and not lay our hands on him; for he is our brother, our *own* flesh." And his brothers listened *to him*.

28   Then some Midianite traders passed by, so they pulled *him* up and lifted Joseph out of the pit, and sold him to the Ishmaelites for twenty *shekels* of silver. Thus they brought Joseph into Egypt.

4. Reuben's distress and Jacob's grief

37:29
Gen 44:13

29   Now Reuben returned to the pit, and behold, Joseph was not in the pit; so he tore his garments.

37:30
Gen 42:13,36

30   And he returned to his brothers and said, "The boy is not *there;* as for me, where am I to go?"

37:31
vv. 3,23

31   So they took Joseph's tunic, and slaughtered a male goat, and dipped the tunic in the blood;

32   and they sent the varicolored tunic and brought it to their father and said, "We found this; please examine *it* to *see* whether it is your son's tunic or not."

37:33
v. 20;
Gen 44:28
*37:34
v. 29;
2 Sam 3:31

33   Then he examined it and said, "It is my son's tunic. A wild beast has devoured him; Joseph has surely been torn to pieces!"

34   So Jacob tore his clothes, and put sackcloth on his loins, and mourned for his son many days.

37:28 *Midianite traders.* It is not clear how these descendants of Abraham and Keturah (25:2) were involved in the sale of Joseph to the Ishmaelites, descendants of Abraham and Hagar (16:15). See also 37:36 and 39:2.

37:34 Jacob's experience reflects some fulfillment of the dictum that "whatever a man sows that he will also reap." Himself a deceiver who stole Esau's blessing and bought his birthright, he is now cruelly deceived by his own sons.

35   Then all his sons and all his daughters arose to comfort him, but he refused to be comforted. And he said, "Surely I will go down to Sheol in mourning for my son." So his father wept for him.

36   Meanwhile, the Midianites sold him in Egypt to Potiphar, Pharaoh's officer, the captain of the bodyguard.

B. Judah's adultery

1. The birth of Er and his marriage to Tamar

38 And it came about at that time, that Judah departed from his brothers, and visited a certain Adullamite, whose name was Hirah.

2   And Judah saw there a daughter of a certain Canaanite whose name was Shua; and he took her and went in to her.

3   So she conceived and bore a son and he named him Er.

4   Then she conceived again and bore a son and named him Onan.

5   And she bore still another son and named him Shelah; and it was at Chezib that she bore him.

6   Now Judah took a wife for Er his first-born, and her name *was* Tamar.

7   But Er, Judah's first-born, was evil in the sight of the LORD, so the LORD took his life.

8   Then Judah said to Onan, "Go in to your brother's wife, and perform your duty as a brother-in-law to her, and raise up offspring for your brother."

9   And Onan knew that the offspring would not be his; so it came about that when he went in to his brother's wife, he wasted his seed on the ground, in order not to give offspring to his brother.

10   But what he did was displeasing in the sight of the LORD; so He took his life also.

11   Then Judah said to his daughter-in-law Tamar, "Remain a widow in your father's house until my son Shelah grows up"; for he thought, "*I am afraid* that he too may die like his brothers." So Tamar went and lived in her father's house.

2. Judah goes in to Tamar

12   Now after a considerable time Shua's daughter, the wife of Judah, died; and when the time of mourning was ended, Judah went up to his sheepshearers at Timnah, he and his friend Hirah the Adullamite.

13   And it was told to Tamar, "Behold, your father-in-law is going up to Timnah to shear his sheep."

14   So she removed her widow's garments and covered *herself* with a [48]veil, and wrapped herself, and sat in the gateway of Enaim, which is on the road to Timnah; for she saw that Shelah had grown up, and she had not been given to him as a wife.

15   When Judah saw her, he thought she *was* a harlot, for she had covered her face.

16   So he turned aside to her by the road, and said, "Here now, let me come in to you"; for he did not know that she was his daughter-in-law. And she said, "What will you give me, that you may come in to me?"

17   He said, therefore, "I will send you a kid from the flock." She said, moreover, "Will you give a pledge until you send *it?*"

18   And he said, "What pledge shall I give you?" And she said, "Your seal and your cord, and your staff that is in your hand." So he gave *them* to her, and went in to her, and she conceived by him.

19   Then she arose and departed, and removed her veil and put on her widow's garments.

20   When Judah sent the kid by his friend the Adullamite, to receive the pledge from the woman's hand, he did not find her.

21   And he asked the men of her place, saying, "Where is the temple prostitute who was by the road at Enaim?" But they said, "There has been no temple prostitute here."

[48]Or, *shawl*

Twenty years later the deceiving sons are to experience the anguish of guilty consciences as they see themselves threatened with retribution (see 42:21).

38:8 See note to Deut. 25:5–10.
38:15 *thought . . . harlot.* See Prov. 7:10.

Margin refs: 37:35 2 Sam 12:17; Gen 42:38; 44:29,31 · 37:36 Gen 39:1 · 38:3 Gen 46:12; Num 26:19 · 38:7 1 Chr 2:3 · *38:8 Deut 25:5; Matt 22:24 · 38:9 Deut 25:6 · 38:11 Ruth 1:12,13 · 38:12 Josh 15:10,57 · 38:17 Ezek 16:33; v. 20 · 38:18 v. 25 · 38:19 v. 14

22 So he returned to Judah, and said, "I did not find her; and furthermore, the men of the place said, 'There has been no temple prostitute here.' "

23 Then Judah said, "Let her keep them, lest we become a laughingstock. After all, I sent this kid, but you did not find her."

3. *Tamar justified: Perez and Zerah born*

38:24
Lev 21:9;
Deut 22:21

24 Now it was about three months later that Judah was informed, "Your daughter-in-law Tamar has played the harlot, and behold, she is also with child by harlotry." Then Judah said, "Bring her out and let her be burned!"

38:25
v. 18

25 It was while she was being brought out that she sent to her father-in-law, saying, "I am with child by the man to whom these things belong." And she said, "Please examine and see, whose signet ring and cords and staff are these?"

38:26
1 Sam 24:17;
v. 14

26 And Judah recognized *them,* and said, "She is more righteous than I, inasmuch as I did not give her to my son Shelah." And he did not have relations with her again.

27 And it came about at the time she was giving birth, that behold, there were twins in her womb.

28 Moreover, it took place while she was giving birth, one put out a hand, and the midwife took and tied a scarlet *thread* on his hand, saying, "This one came out first."

38:29
Gen 46:12;
Num 26:20;
Matt 1:3

29 But it came about as he drew back his hand, that behold, his brother came out. Then she said, "What a breach you have made for yourself!" So he was named [49]Perez.

30 And afterward his brother came out who had the scarlet *thread* on his hand; and he was named [50]Zerah.

C. *Joseph, man of integrity*

1. *His prosperity*

39:1
Gen 37:28,36;
Ps 105:17

39 Now Joseph had been taken down to Egypt; and Potiphar, an Egyptian officer of Pharaoh, the captain of the bodyguard, bought him from the Ishmaelites, who had taken him down there.

*39:2
vv. 3,21,23

2 And the LORD was with Joseph, so he became a successful man. And he was in the house of his master, the Egyptian.

39:3
Gen 21:22;
26:28;
Acts 7:9

3 Now his master saw that the LORD was with him and *how* the LORD caused all that he did to prosper in his hand.

39:4
vv. 8,22

4 So Joseph found favor in his sight, and became his personal servant; and he made him overseer over his house, and all that he owned he put in his charge.

39:5
Gen 30:27

5 And it came about that from the time he made him overseer in his house, and over all that he owned, the LORD blessed the Egyptian's house on account of Joseph; thus the LORD's blessing was upon all that he owned, in the house and in the field.

6 So he left everything he owned in Joseph's charge; and with him *there* he did not concern himself with anything except the food which he ate. Now Joseph was handsome in form and appearance.

2. *The solicitation to sin*

39:7
2 Sam 13:11;
Prov 7:15-20

7 And it came about after these events that his master's wife looked with desire at Joseph, and she said, "Lie with me."

8 But he refused and said to his master's wife, "Behold, with me *here,* my master does not concern himself with anything in the house, and he has put all that he owns in my charge.

*39:9
Gen 20:6;
42:18;
2 Sam 12:13

9 "There is no one greater in this house than I, and he has withheld nothing

[49]I.e., a breach   [50]I.e., a dawning or brightness

39:2 When Joseph was sold as a slave he could hardly have known that God was arranging circumstances that would make possible the fulfillment of his dreams (37:5–10). Nor could he have suspected the long years needed before the fulfillment. But of one truth he soon became aware—that God was with him, for no adversity could make him bitter or distrustful of God. Twice we are told *the* LORD *was with Joseph* (39:2,21). Joseph's rich spiritual insight was plainly evidenced when he attributed to God his imprisonment and slavery as well as his rise to power (45:7,8). His brothers

sinned as they wrought their own willful wickedness, but God used it for the accomplishment of the divine purpose (45:7; 50:20; Ps. 76:10).
39:9 Joseph had to choose between his position and his purity. He chose the latter, only to suffer unjust accusation and punishment for a crime he did not commit. Yet his noble stand was not in vain, for it resulted in his meeting with the king's butler and baker; and this contact in turn made possible his becoming premier of Egypt under the pharaoh.

from me except you, because you are his wife. How then could I do this great evil, and sin against God?"

10   And it came about as she spoke to Joseph day after day, that he did not listen to her to lie beside her, *or* be with her.

11   Now it happened one day that he went into the house to do his work, and none of the men of the household was there inside.

12   And she caught him by his garment, saying, "Lie with me!" And he left his garment in her hand and fled, and went outside.

13   When she saw that he had left his garment in her hand, and had fled outside,

14   she called to the men of her household, and said to them, "See, he has brought in a Hebrew to us to make sport of us; he came in to me to lie with me, and I screamed.

15   "And it came about when he heard that I raised my voice and [51] screamed, that he left his garment beside me and fled, and went outside."

16   So she left his garment beside her until his master came home.

17   Then she spoke to him with these words, "The Hebrew slave, whom you brought to us, came in to me to make sport of me;

18   and it happened as I raised my voice and screamed, that he left his garment beside me and fled outside."

3. *Joseph wrongly cast into prison*

19   Now it came about when his master heard the words of his wife, which she spoke to him, saying, "This is what your slave did to me," that his anger burned.

20   So Joseph's master took him and put him into the jail, the place where the king's prisoners were confined; and he was there in the jail.

21   But the LORD was with Joseph and extended kindness to him, and gave him favor in the sight of the chief jailer.

22   And the chief jailer committed to Joseph's charge all the prisoners who were in the jail; so that whatever was done there, he was responsible *for it.*

23   The chief jailer did not supervise anything under Joseph's charge because the LORD was with him; and whatever he did, the LORD made to prosper.

D. *Joseph, interpreter of dreams*

1. *The cupbearer and the baker*

40 Then it came about after these things the cupbearer and the baker for the king of Egypt offended their lord, the king of Egypt.

2   And Pharaoh was furious with his two officials, the chief cupbearer and the chief baker.

3   So he put them in confinement in the house of the captain of the bodyguard, in the jail, the *same* place where Joseph was imprisoned.

4   And the captain of the bodyguard put Joseph in charge of them, and he took care of them; and they were in confinement for some time.

5   Then the cupbearer and the baker for the king of Egypt, who were confined in jail, both had a dream the same night, each man with his *own* dream *and* each dream with its *own* interpretation.

6   When Joseph came to them in the morning and observed them, behold, they were dejected.

7   And he asked Pharaoh's officials who were with him in confinement in his master's house, "Why are your faces so sad today?"

8   Then they said to him, "We have had a dream and there is no one to interpret it." Then Joseph said to them, "Do not interpretations belong to God? Tell *it* to me, please."

2. *The cupbearer's dream and interpretation*

9   So the chief cupbearer told his dream to Joseph, and said to him, "In my dream, behold, *there was* a vine in front of me;

10   and on the vine *were* three branches. And as it was budding, its blossoms came out, *and* its clusters produced ripe grapes.

11   "Now Pharaoh's cup was in my hand; so I took the grapes and squeezed them into Pharaoh's cup, and I put the cup into Pharaoh's hand."

Marginal references:

39:12
Prov 7:13-25

39:17
Ex 23:1;
Ps 120:3

39:19
Prov 6:34,35

39:20
Ps 105:18

39:21
v.21;
Ps 105:19;
Ex 3:21;
Dan 1:9

39:22
v. 4

39:23
vv. 2,3,8

40:1
vv. 11,13

40:3
Gen 39:20,23

40:8
Gen 41:16;
Dan 2:27,28

[51]Lit., *called out*

40:12
Gen 41:12,25;
Dan 2:36;
4:19

40:14
Luke 23:42;
Josh 2:12
40:15
Gen 37:26-28

12 Then Joseph said to him, "This is the interpretation of it: the three branches are three days;

13 within three more days Pharaoh will [52]lift up your head and restore you to your office; and you will put Pharaoh's cup into his hand according to your former custom when you were his cupbearer.

14 "Only keep me in mind when it goes well with you, and please do me a kindness by mentioning me to Pharaoh, and get me out of this house.

15 "For I was in fact kidnapped from the land of the Hebrews, and even here I have done nothing that they should have put me into the dungeon."

3. The baker's dream and interpretation

16 When the chief baker saw that he had interpreted favorably, he said to Joseph, "I also *saw* in my dream, and behold, *there were* three baskets of white bread on my head;

17 and in the top basket *there were* some of all sorts of baked food for Pharaoh, and the birds were eating them out of the basket on my head."

40:18
v. 12

40:19
v. 13

18 Then Joseph answered and said, "This is its interpretation: the three baskets are three days;

19 within three more days Pharaoh will lift up your head from you and will hang you on a tree; and the birds will eat your flesh off you."

4. The fulfillment of the interpretations

40:20
vv. 13,19

20 Thus it came about on the third day, *which was* Pharaoh's birthday, that he made a feast for all his servants; and he lifted up the head of the chief cupbearer and the head of the chief baker among his servants.

40:21
v. 13

21 And he restored the chief cupbearer to his office, and he put the cup into Pharaoh's hand;

40:22
v. 19

22 but he hanged the chief baker, just as Joseph had interpreted to them.

23 Yet the chief cupbearer did not remember Joseph, but forgot him.

E. *Joseph and Pharaoh*

1. *Pharaoh's dream*

41 Now it happened at the end of two full years that Pharaoh had a dream, and behold, he was standing by the Nile.

2 And lo, from the Nile there came up seven cows, sleek and fat; and they grazed in the marsh grass.

3 Then behold, seven other cows came up after them from the Nile, ugly and gaunt, and they stood by the *other* cows on the bank of the Nile.

4 And the ugly and gaunt cows ate up the seven sleek and fat cows. Then Pharaoh awoke.

5 And he fell asleep and dreamed a second time; and behold, seven ears of grain came up on a single stalk, plump and good.

6 Then behold, seven ears, thin and scorched by the east wind, sprouted up after them.

7 And the thin ears swallowed up the seven plump and full ears. Then Pharaoh awoke, and behold, *it was* a dream.

*41:8
Dan 2:1,3;
4:5,19;
Ex 7:11,22;
Dan 2:27; 4:7

8 Now it came about in the morning that his spirit was troubled, so he sent and called for all the magicians of Egypt, and all its wise men. And Pharaoh told them his dreams, but there was no one who could interpret them to Pharaoh.

2. *The cupbearer remembers Joseph*

9 Then the chief cupbearer spoke to Pharaoh, saying, "I would make mention today of my *own* offenses.

41:10
Gen 40:2,3

10 "Pharaoh was furious with his servants, and he put me in confinement in the house of the captain of the bodyguard, *both* me and the chief baker.

41:11
Gen 40:5

11 "And we had a dream on the same night, he and I; each of us dreamed according to the interpretation of his *own* dream.

41:12
Gen 40:12ff

12 "Now a Hebrew youth *was* with us there, a servant of the captain of the

[52]Or possibly, *forgive you*

41:6 *east wind*, the sirocco, a hot wind.   **41:8** Shows the futility of pagan practice.

bodyguard, and we related *them* to him, and he interpreted our dreams for us. To each one he interpreted according to his *own* dream.

13 "And it came about that just as he interpreted for us, so it happened; he restored me in my office, but he hanged him."

3. *Pharaoh tells his dream to Joseph*

14 Then Pharaoh sent and called for Joseph, and they hurriedly brought him out of the dungeon; and when he had shaved himself and changed his clothes, he came to Pharaoh.

15 And Pharaoh said to Joseph, "I have had a dream, but no one can interpret it; and I have heard it said about you, that when you hear a dream you can interpret it."

16 Joseph then answered Pharaoh, saying, "It is not in me; God will give Pharaoh a favorable answer."

17 So Pharaoh spoke to Joseph, "In my dream, behold, I was standing on the bank of the Nile;

18 and behold, seven cows, fat and sleek came up out of the Nile; and they grazed in the marsh grass.

19 "And lo, seven other cows came up after them, poor and very ugly and gaunt, such as I had never seen for ugliness in all the land of Egypt;

20 and the lean and ugly cows ate up the first seven fat cows.

21 "Yet when they had devoured them, it could not be detected that they had devoured them; for they were just as ugly as before. Then I awoke.

22 "I saw also in my dream, and behold, seven ears, full and good, came up on a single stalk;

23 and lo, seven ears, withered, thin, *and* scorched by the east wind, sprouted up after them;

24 and the thin ears swallowed the seven good ears. Then I told it to the magicians, but there was no one who could explain it to me."

4. *Joseph interprets Pharaoh's dream:*
he proposes a solution

25 Now Joseph said to Pharaoh, "Pharaoh's dreams are one *and the same;* God has told to Pharaoh what He is about to do.

26 "The seven good cows are seven years; and the seven good ears are seven years; the dreams are one *and the same.*

27 "And the seven lean and ugly cows that came up after them are seven years, and the seven thin ears scorched by the east wind shall be seven years of famine.

28 "It is as I have spoken to Pharaoh: God has shown to Pharaoh what He is about to do.

29 "Behold, seven years of great abundance are coming in all the land of Egypt;

30 and after them seven years of famine will come, and all the abundance will be forgotten in the land of Egypt; and the famine will ravage the land.

31 "So the abundance will be unknown in the land because of that subsequent famine; for it *will be* very severe.

32 "Now as for the repeating of the dream to Pharaoh twice, *it means* that the matter is determined by God, and God will quickly bring it about.

33 "And now let Pharaoh look for a man discerning and wise, and set him over the land of Egypt.

34 "Let Pharaoh take action to appoint overseers in charge of the land, and let him exact a fifth *of the produce* of the land of Egypt in the seven years of abundance.

35 "Then let them gather all the food of these good years that are coming, and store up the grain for food in the cities under Pharaoh's authority, and let them guard *it.*

36 "And let the food become as a reserve for the land for the seven years of famine which will occur in the land of Egypt, so that the land may not perish during the famine."

5. *Pharaoh makes Joseph a ruler*

37 Now the proposal seemed good to Pharaoh and to all his servants.

38 Then Pharaoh said to his servants, "Can we find a man like this, in whom is a divine spirit?"

41:13
Gen 40:21,22

41:14
Ps 105:20;
Dan 2:25;
Ps 113:7,8

41:15
v. 12

41:16
Dan 2:30;
Acts 3:12;
2 Cor 3:5;
Gen 40:8

41:24
v. 8

41:25
vv. 28,32

41:27
2 Kin 8:1

41:28
vv. 25,32

41:29
v. 47
41:30
vv. 54,56;
Gen 47:13

41:32
Num 23:19;
Is 46:10,11

41:35
v. 48

41:38
Num 27:18;
Dan 4:8,18

39 So Pharaoh said to Joseph, "Since God has informed you of all this, there is no one so discerning and wise as you are.

*41:40
Ps 105:21,22;
Acts 7:10
40 "You shall be over my house, and according to your command all my people shall do homage; only in the throne I will be greater than you."

41:41
Gen 42:6
41 And Pharaoh said to Joseph, "See I have set you over all the land of Egypt."

41:42
Esth 3:10;
Dan 5:7,16,
29
42 Then Pharaoh took off his signet ring from his hand, and put it on Joseph's hand, and clothed him in garments of fine linen, and put the gold necklace around his neck.

41:43
Esth 6:9
43 And he had him ride in his second chariot; and they proclaimed before him, "Bow the knee!" And he set him over all the land of Egypt.

41:44
Ps 105:22
44 Moreover, Pharaoh said to Joseph, "*Though* I am Pharaoh, yet without your permission no one shall raise his hand or foot in all the land of Egypt."

45 Then Pharaoh named Joseph [53]Zaphenath-paneah; and he gave him Asenath, the daughter of Potiphera priest of On, as his wife. And Joseph went forth over the land of Egypt.

6. The fulfillment of the dream

*41:46
Gen 37:2
46 Now Joseph was thirty years old when he [54]stood before Pharaoh, king of Egypt. And Joseph went out from the presence of Pharaoh, and went through all the land of Egypt.

47 And during the seven years of plenty the land brought forth abundantly.

48 So he gathered all the food of *these* seven years which occurred in the land of Egypt, and placed the food in the cities; he placed in every city the food from its own surrounding fields.

49 Thus Joseph stored up grain in great abundance like the sand of the sea, until he stopped measuring *it*, for it was beyond measure.

41:50
Gen 46:20
50 Now before the year of famine came, two sons were born to Joseph, whom Asenath, the daughter of Potiphera priest of [55]On, bore to him.

51 And Joseph named the first-born [56]Manasseh, "For," *he said*, "God has made me forget all my trouble and all my father's household."

41:52
Gen 17:6;
28:3; 49:22
52 And he named the second [57]Ephraim, "For," *he said*, "God has made me fruitful in the land of my affliction."

53 When the seven years of plenty which had been in the land of Egypt came to an end,

41:54
v. 30;
Ps 105:16;
Acts 7:11
54 and the seven years of famine began to come, just as Joseph had said, then there was famine in all the lands; but in all the land of Egypt there was bread.

55 So when all the land of Egypt was famished, the people cried out to Pharaoh for bread; and Pharaoh said to all the Egyptians, "Go to Joseph; whatever he says to you, you shall do."

41:56
Gen 42:6
56 When the famine was *spread* over all the face of the earth, then Joseph opened all the storehouses, and sold to the Egyptians; and the famine was severe in the land of Egypt.

57 And *the people of* all the earth came to Egypt to buy grain from Joseph, because the famine was severe in all the earth.

F. Joseph's brothers in Egypt

1. Jacob sends ten sons

42:1
Acts 7:12
42 Now Jacob saw that there was grain in Egypt, and Jacob said to his sons, "Why are you staring at one another?"

42:2
Gen 43:8
2 And he said, "Behold, I have heard that there is grain in Egypt; go down there and buy *some* for us from that place, so that we may live and not die."

3 Then ten brothers of Joseph went down to buy grain from Egypt.

[53]Probably Egyptian for "God speaks; he lives" [54]Or, *entered the service of* [55]Or, *Heliopolis* [56]I.e., making to forget [57]I.e., fruitfulness

---

41:40 *over my house,* meaning the office of prime minister or vizier.
41:45 *On* was a city in Lower (northern) Egypt noted for its chief temple of the sun god, Re. It was known to the Greeks as Heliopolis, meaning "city of the sun." References are made to it in Is. 19:18 and in Jer. 43:13 (where the NAS translators call it *Heliopolis*). *On* was also the most important seat of learning in the country.

41:46 At least twenty years passed before Joseph's boyhood dreams were fulfilled. He first dreamed when seventeen years of age (37:2). He appeared before Pharaoh thirteen years later (41:46). The seven years of plenty followed. Then came the years of famine. This meant that his brothers had not seen him for at least twenty years. He knew them, but they were unable to recognize him in his new role of splendor and authority.

4   But Jacob did not send Joseph's brother Benjamin with his brothers, for he said, "I am afraid that harm may befall him."

5   So the sons of Israel came to buy grain among those who were coming, for the famine was in the land of Canaan *also*.

2. *Joseph encounters his brothers*

6   Now Joseph was the ruler over the land; he was the one who sold to all the people of the land. And Joseph's brothers came and bowed down to him with *their* faces to the ground.

7   When Joseph saw his brothers he recognized them, but he disguised himself to them and spoke to them harshly. And he said to them, "Where have you come from?" And they said, "From the land of Canaan, to buy food."

8   But Joseph had recognized his brothers, although they did not recognize him.

9   And Joseph remembered the dreams which he had about them, and said to them, "You are spies; you have come to look at the undefended parts of our land."

10   Then they said to him, "No, my lord, but your servants have come to buy food.

11   "We are all sons of one man; we are honest men, your servants are not spies."

12   Yet he said to them, "No, but you have come to look at the undefended parts of our land!"

13   But they said, "Your servants are twelve brothers *in all*, the sons of one man in the land of Canaan; and behold, the youngest is with our father today, and one is no more."

14   And Joseph said to them, "It is as I said to you, you are spies;

15   by this you will be tested: by the life of Pharaoh, you shall not go from this place unless your youngest brother comes here!

16   "Send one of you that he may get your brother, while you remain confined, that your words may be tested, whether there is truth in you. But if not, by the life of Pharaoh, surely you are spies."

17   So he put them all together in prison for three days.

3. *Joseph gives them grain*

18   Now Joseph said to them on the third day, "Do this and live, for I fear God:

19   if you are honest men, let one of your brothers be confined in your prison; but as for *the rest of* you, go, carry grain for the famine of your households,

20   and bring your youngest brother to me, so your words may be verified, and you will not die." And they did so.

21   Then they said to one another, "Truly we are guilty concerning our brother, because we saw the distress of his soul when he pleaded with us, yet we would not listen; therefore this distress has come upon us."

22   And Reuben answered them, saying, "Did I not tell you, 'Do not sin against the boy'; and you would not listen? Now comes the reckoning for his blood."

23   They did not know, however, that Joseph understood, for there was an interpreter between them.

24   And he turned away from them and wept. But when he returned to them and spoke to them, he took Simeon from them and bound him before their eyes.

25   Then Joseph gave orders to fill their bags with grain and to restore every man's money in his sack, and to give them provisions for the journey. And thus it was done for them.

26   So they loaded their donkeys with their grain, and departed from there.

27   And as one *of them* opened his sack to give his donkey fodder at the lodging place, he saw his money; and behold, it was in the mouth of his sack.

28   Then he said to his brothers, "My money has been returned, and behold, it is even in my sack." And their hearts sank, and they *turned* trembling to one another, saying, "What is this that God has done to us?"

4. *The ten sons report to Jacob*

29   When they came to their father Jacob in the land of Canaan, they told him all that had happened to them, saying,

30   "The man, the lord of the land, spoke harshly with us, and took us for spies of the country.

31   "But we said to him, 'We are honest men; we are not spies.

Cross references (right margin)

42:4
Gen 35:24

42:5
Gen 41:57;
Acts 7:11

42:6
Gen 41:41,55;
37:7

42:7
v. 30

42:9
Gen 37:6-9

42:13
Gen 43:7;
37:30

42:18
Lev 25:43

42:20
v. 34

42:21
Hos 5:15;
Prov 21:13

42:22
Gen 37:22;
9:5,6

42:24
Gen 43:30;
45:14,15;
43:14,23

42:25
Gen 44:1;
Rom 12:17,
20,21

42:26
Gen 37:31-35

42:30
v. 7

42:31
v. 11

32   'We are twelve brothers, sons of our father; one is no more, and the youngest is with our father today in the land of Canaan.'

42:33
Gen 15:19,20
33   "And the man, the lord of the land, said to us, 'By this I shall know that you are honest men: leave one of your brothers with me and take *grain for* the famine of your households, and go.

34   'But bring your youngest brother to me that I may know that you are not spies, but honest men. I will give your brother to you, and you may trade in the land.' "

42:35
Gen 43:12,15
35   Now it came about as they were emptying their sacks, that behold, every man's bundle of money *was* in his sack; and when they and their father saw their bundles of money, they were dismayed.

42:36
Gen 43:14
36   And their father Jacob said to them, "You have bereaved me of my children: Joseph is no more, and Simeon is no more, and you would take Benjamin; all these things are against me."

37   Then Reuben spoke to his father, saying, "You may put my two sons to death if I do not bring him *back* to you; put him in my care, and I will return him to you."

42:38
Gen 37:33,35;
44:31
38   But Jacob said, "My son shall not go down with you; for his brother is dead, and he alone is left. If harm should befall him on the journey you are taking, then you will bring my gray hair down to Sheol in sorrow."

G. The second trip to Egypt with Benjamin

1. Jacob unwillingly sends Benjamin

43:1
Gen 41:56,57
43 Now the famine was severe in the land.
2   So it came about when they had finished eating the grain which they had brought from Egypt, that their father said to them, "Go back, buy us a little food."

43:3
Gen 42:20;
44:23
3   Judah spoke to him, however, saying, "The man solemnly warned us, 'You shall not see my face unless your brother is with you.'

4   "If you send our brother with us, we will go down and buy you food.

5   "But if you do not send *him,* we will not go down; for the man said to us, 'You shall not see my face unless your brother is with you.' "

6   Then Israel said, "Why did you treat me so badly by telling the man whether you still had *another* brother?"

43:7
v. 27;
Gen 42:13
7   But they said, "The man questioned particularly about us and our relatives, saying, 'Is your father still alive? Have you *another* brother?' So we answered his questions. Could we possibly know that he would say, 'Bring your brother down'?"

8   And Judah said to his father Israel, "Send the lad with me, and we will arise and go, that we may live and not die, we as well as you and our little ones.

43:9
Gen 42:37;
44:32;
Philem 18,19
9   "I myself will be surety for him; you may hold me responsible for him. If I do not bring him *back* to you and set him before you, then let me bear the blame before you forever.

10   "For if we had not delayed, surely by now we could have returned twice."

43:11
Gen 32:20;
Prov 18:16;
Gen 37:25;
Jer 8:22
11   Then their father Israel said to them, "If *it must be* so, then do this: take some of the best products of the land in your bags, and carry down to the man as a present, a little balm and a little honey, aromatic gum and myrrh, pistachio nuts and almonds.

43:12
Gen 42:35;
vv. 21,22
12   "And take double *the* money in your hand, and take back in your hand the money that was returned in the mouth of your sacks; perhaps it was a mistake.

13   "Take your brother also, and arise, return to the man;

43:14
Gen 17:1;
28:3; 35:11;
Ps 106:46;
Gen 42:24
14   and may God Almighty grant you compassion in the sight of the man, that he may release to you your other brother and Benjamin. And as for me, if I am bereaved of my children, I am bereaved."

15   So the men took this present, and they took double *the* money in their hand, and Benjamin; then they arose and went down to Egypt and stood before Joseph.

2. Joseph dines with his brothers

43:16
Gen 44:1
16   When Joseph saw Benjamin with them, he said to his house steward, "Bring the men into the house, and slay *an animal* and make ready; for the men are to dine with me at noon."

17   So the man did as Joseph said, and brought the men to Joseph's house.

18   Now the men were afraid, because they were brought to Joseph's house; and they said, "*It is* because of the money that was returned in our sacks the first time

that we are being brought in, that he may seek occasion against us and fall upon us, and take us for slaves with our donkeys."

19   So they came near to Joseph's house steward, and spoke to him at the entrance of the house,

20   and said, "Oh, my lord, we indeed came down the first time to buy food, ·
43:20
Gen 42:3,10

21   and it came about when we came to the lodging place, that we opened our sacks, and behold, each man's money was in the mouth of his sack, our money in full. So we have brought it back in our hand.
43:21
Gen 42:35;
vv. 12,15

22   "We have also brought down other money in our hand to buy food; we do not know who put our money in our sacks."

23   And he said, "[58]Be at ease, do not be afraid. Your God and the God of your father has given you treasure in your sacks; I had your money." Then he brought Simeon out to them.
43:23
Gen 42:24

24   Then the man brought the men into Joseph's house and gave them water, and they washed their feet; and he gave their donkeys fodder.
43:24
Gen 18:4;
19:2; 24:32

25   So they prepared the present for Joseph's coming at noon; for they had heard that they were to eat a meal there.

26   When Joseph came home, they brought into the house to him the present which was in their hand and bowed to the ground before him.
43:26
Gen 37:7,10

27   Then he asked them about their welfare, and said, "Is your old father well, of whom you spoke? Is he still alive?"
43:27
v. 7; Gen 45:3

28   And they said, "Your servant our father is well; he is still alive." And they bowed down in homage.
43:28
Gen 37:7,10

29   As he lifted his eyes and saw his brother Benjamin, his mother's son, he said, "Is this your youngest brother, of whom you spoke to me?" And he said, "May God be gracious to you, my son."
43:29
Gen 35:17,18;
42:13;
Num 6:25;
Ps 67:1

30   And Joseph hurried *out* for he was deeply stirred over his brother, and he sought *a place* to weep; and he entered his chamber and wept there.
43:30
Gen 42:24;
45:2,14,15;
46:29

31   Then he washed his face, and came out; and he controlled himself and said, "Serve the meal."
43:31
Gen 45:1

32   So they served him by himself, and them by themselves, and the Egyptians, who ate with him, by themselves; because the Egyptians could not eat bread with the Hebrews, for that is loathsome to the Egyptians.
43:32
Gen 46:34

33   Now they were seated before him, the first-born according to his birthright and the youngest according to his youth, and the men looked at one another in astonishment.

34   And he took portions to them from his own table; but Benjamin's portion was five times as much as any of theirs. So they feasted and drank freely with him.
43:34
Gen 45:22

3. *The seizure of Benjamin*

44 Then he commanded his house steward, saying, "Fill the men's sacks with food, as much as they can carry, and put each man's money in the mouth of his sack.
44:1
Gen 42:25

2   "And put my cup, the silver cup, in the mouth of the sack of the youngest, and his money for the grain." And he did as Joseph had told *him*.

3   As soon as it was light, the men were sent away, they with their donkeys.

4   They had *just* gone out of the city, *and* were not far off, when Joseph said to his house steward, "Up, follow the men; and when you overtake them, say to them, 'Why have you repaid evil for good?

5   'Is not this the one from which my lord drinks, and which he indeed uses for divination? You have done wrong in doing this.' "
44:5
v. 15;
Lev 19:26;
Deut 18:10-14

6   So he overtook them and spoke these words to them.

7   And they said to him, "Why does my lord speak such words as these? Far be it from your servants to do such a thing.

8   "Behold, the money which we found in the mouth of our sacks we have brought back to you from the land of Canaan. How then could we steal silver or gold from your lord's house?
44:8
Gen 43:21

9   "With whomever of your servants it is found, let him die, and we also will be my lord's slaves."
44:9
Gen 31:32

10   So he said, "Now let it also be according to your words; he with whom it is found shall be my slave, and *the rest of* you shall be innocent."

[58]Lit., *Peace be to you*

11 Then they hurried, each man lowered his sack to the ground, and each man opened his sack.

12 And he searched, beginning with the oldest and ending with the youngest, and the cup was found in Benjamin's sack.

44:13
Gen 37:29,34;
Num 14:6

13 Then they tore their clothes, and when each man loaded his donkey, they returned to the city.

4. His brothers bow before Joseph

44:14
Gen 37:7,10

14 When Judah and his brothers came to Joseph's house, he was still there, and they fell to the ground before him.

44:15
v. 5

15 And Joseph said to them, "What is this deed that you have done? Do you not know that such a man as I can indeed practice divination?"

44:16
v. 9

16 So Judah said, "What can we say to my lord? What can we speak? And how can we justify ourselves? God has found out the iniquity of your servants; behold, we are my lord's slaves, both we and the one in whose possession the cup has been found."

17 But he said, "Far be it from me to do this. The man in whose possession the cup has been found, he shall be my slave; but as for you, go up in peace to your father."

44:18
Gen 37:7,8;
41:40-44

18 Then Judah approached him, and said, "Oh my lord, may your servant please speak a word in my lord's ears, and do not be angry with your servant; for you are equal to Pharaoh.

19 "My lord asked his servants, saying, 'Have you a father or a brother?'

44:20
v. 30;
Gen 43:8;
37:33; 42:13,
38

20 "And we said to my lord, 'We have an old father and a little child of *his* old age. Now his brother is dead, so he alone is left of his mother, and his father loves him.'

21 "Then you said to your servants, 'Bring him down to me, that I may set my eyes on him.'

22 "But we said to my lord, 'The lad cannot leave his father, for if he should leave his father, his father would die.'

44:23
Gen 43:3

23 "You said to your servants, however, 'Unless your youngest brother comes down with you, you shall not see my face again.'

24 "Thus it came about when we went up to your servant my father, we told him the words of my lord.

25 "And our father said, 'Go back, buy us a little food.'

26 "But we said, 'We cannot go down. If our youngest brother is with us, then we will go down; for we cannot see the man's face unless our youngest brother is with us.'

27 "And your servant my father said to us, 'You know that my wife bore me two sons;

44:28
Gen 37:31-35

28 and the one went out from me, and I said, "Surely he is torn in pieces," and I have not seen him since.

44:29
Gen 42:36,38

29 'And if you take this one also from me, and harm befalls him, you will bring my gray hair down to Sheol in sorrow.'

30 "Now, therefore, when I come to your servant my father, and the lad is not with us, since his life is bound up in the lad's life,

31 it will come about when he sees that the lad is not *with us*, that he will die. Thus your servants will bring the gray hair of your servant our father down to Sheol in sorrow.

44:32
Gen 43:9

32 "For your servant became surety for the lad to my father, saying, 'If I do not bring him *back* to you, then let me bear the blame before my father forever.'

33 "Now, therefore, please let your servant remain instead of the lad a slave to my lord, and let the lad go up with his brothers.

34 "For how shall I go up to my father if the lad is not with me, lest I see the evil that would overtake my father?"

5. Joseph discloses his identity

45:1
Acts 7:13

45 Then Joseph could not control himself before all those who stood by him, and he cried, "Have everyone go out from me." So there was no man with him when Joseph made himself known to his brothers.

45:2
vv. 14,15;
Gen 46:29

2 And he wept so loudly that the Egyptians heard *it*, and the household of Pharaoh heard *of it*.

3   Then Joseph said to his brothers, "I am Joseph! Is my father still alive?" But his brothers could not answer him, for they were dismayed at his presence.

4   Then Joseph said to his brothers, "Please come closer to me." And they came closer. And he said, "I am your brother Joseph, whom you sold into Egypt.

5   "And now do not be grieved or angry with yourselves, because you sold me here; for God sent me before you to preserve life.

6   "For the famine *has been* in the land these two years, and there are still five years in which there will be neither plowing nor harvesting.

7   "And God sent me before you to preserve for you a remnant in the earth, and to keep you alive by a great deliverance.

8   "Now, therefore, it was not you who sent me here, but God; and He has made me a father to Pharaoh and lord of all his household and ruler over all the land of Egypt.

9   "Hurry and go up to my father, and say to him, 'Thus says your son Joseph, "God has made me lord of all Egypt; come down to me, do not delay.

10   "And you shall live in the land of Goshen, and you shall be near me, you and your children and your children's children and your flocks and your herds and all that you have.

11   "There I will also provide for you, for there are still five years of famine *to come*, lest you and your household and all that you have be impoverished." '

12   "And behold, your eyes see, and the eyes of my brother Benjamin *see*, that it is my mouth which is speaking to you.

13   "Now you must tell my father of all my splendor in Egypt, and all that you have seen; and you must hurry and bring my father down here."

14   Then he fell on his brother Benjamin's neck and wept; and Benjamin wept on his neck.

15   And he kissed all his brothers and wept on them, and afterward his brothers talked with him.

6. Pharaoh invites Joseph's family to Egypt

16   Now when the news was heard in Pharaoh's house that Joseph's brothers had come, it pleased Pharaoh and his servants.

17   Then Pharaoh said to Joseph, "Say to your brothers, 'Do this: load your beasts and go to the land of Canaan,

18   and take your father and your households and come to me, and I will give you the best of the land of Egypt and you shall eat the fat of the land.'

19   "Now you are ordered, 'Do this: take wagons from the land of Egypt for your little ones and for your wives, and bring your father and come.

20   'And do not concern yourselves with your goods, for the best of all the land of Egypt is yours.' "

21   Then the sons of Israel did so; and Joseph gave them wagons according to the command of Pharaoh, and gave them provisions for the journey.

22   To each of them he gave changes of garments, but to Benjamin he gave three hundred *pieces of* silver and five changes of garments.

23   And to his father he sent as follows: ten donkeys loaded with the best things of Egypt, and ten female donkeys loaded with grain and bread and sustenance for his father on the journey.

24   So he sent his brothers away, and as they departed, he said to them, "Do not quarrel on the journey."

25   Then they went up from Egypt, and came to the land of Canaan to their father Jacob.

26   And they told him, saying, "Joseph is still alive, and indeed he is ruler over all the land of Egypt." But he was stunned, for he did not believe them.

27   When they told him all the words of Joseph that he had spoken to them, and when he saw the wagons that Joseph had sent to carry him, the spirit of their father Jacob revived.

28   Then Israel said, "It is enough; my son Joseph is still alive. I will go and see him before I die."

45:3
Gen 43:27

45:4
Gen 37:28

45:5
Is 40:2;
Gen 37:28;
44:20; 50:20

45:8
Gen 41:43

*45:10
Gen 46:28,34;
47:1

45:13
Acts 7:14

45:18
Gen 27:28;
Num 18:12,
29

45:22
Gen 43:34

45:10 *Goshen*, fertile grazing land in the eastern section of the Nile Delta. This verse agrees with 47:6, where Pharaoh tells Joseph to settle his family in Goshen.

H. *Jacob goes to Egypt*

46 So Israel set out with all that he had, and came to Beersheba, and offered sacrifices to the God of his father Isaac.

2   And God spoke to Israel in visions of the night and said, "Jacob, Jacob." And he said, "Here I am."

3   And He said, "I am God, the God of your father; do not be afraid to go down to Egypt, for I will make you a great nation there.

4   "I will go down with you to Egypt, and I will also surely bring you up again; and Joseph will close your eyes."

5   Then Jacob arose from Beersheba; and the sons of Israel carried their father Jacob and their little ones and their wives, in the wagons which Pharaoh had sent to carry him.

6   And they took their livestock and their property, which they had acquired in the land of Canaan, and came to Egypt, Jacob and all his descendants with him:

7   his sons and his grandsons with him, his daughters and his granddaughters and all his descendants he brought with him to Egypt.

I. *The descendants of Jacob*

8   Now these are the names of the sons of Israel, Jacob and his sons, who went to Egypt: Reuben, Jacob's first-born.

9   And the sons of Reuben: Hanoch and Pallu and Hezron and Carmi.

10   And the sons of Simeon: Jemuel and Jamin and Ohad and Jachin and Zohar and Shaul the son of a Canaanite woman.

11   And the sons of Levi: Gershon, Kohath, and Merari.

12   And the sons of Judah: Er and Onan and Shelah and Perez and Zerah (but Er and Onan died in the land of Canaan). And the sons of Perez were Hezron and Hamul.

13   And the sons of Issachar: Tola and Puvvah and Iob and Shimron.

14   And the sons of Zebulun: Sered and Elon and Jahleel.

15   These are the sons of Leah, whom she bore to Jacob in Paddan-aram, with his daughter Dinah; all his sons and his daughters *numbered* thirty-three.

16   And the sons of Gad: Ziphion and Haggi, Shuni and Ezbon, Eri and Arodi and Areli.

17   And the sons of Asher: Imnah and Ishvah and Ishvi and Beriah and their sister Serah. And the sons of Beriah: Heber and Malchiel.

18   These are the sons of Zilpah, whom Laban gave to his daughter Leah; and she bore to Jacob these sixteen persons.

19   The sons of Jacob's wife Rachel: Joseph and Benjamin.

20   Now to Joseph in the land of Egypt were born Manasseh and Ephraim, whom Asenath, the daughter of Potiphera, priest of On, bore to him.

21   And the sons of Benjamin: Bela and Becher and Ashbel, Gera and Naaman, Ehi and Rosh, Muppim and Huppim and Ard.

22   These are the sons of Rachel, who were born to Jacob; *there were* fourteen persons in all.

23   And the sons of Dan: Hushim.

24   And the sons of Naphtali: Jahzeel and Guni and Jezer and Shillem.

25   These are the sons of Bilhah, whom Laban gave to his daughter Rachel, and she bore these to Jacob; *there were* seven persons in all.

26   All the persons belonging to Jacob, who came to Egypt, his direct descendants, not including the wives of Jacob's sons, *were* sixty-six persons in all,

27   and the sons of Joseph, who were born to him in Egypt were two; all the persons of the house of Jacob, who came to Egypt, *were* seventy.

46:3 It has been imagined by some that Jacob was denying the directive will of God when he went down to Egypt and that he was only in the permissive will of God. But this erroneous interpretation is based on the notion that Egypt always symbolizes sin and compromise. It was really God who told Jacob to go to Egypt, for it was in Egypt that God purposed to develop His family into a great nation strong enough to conquer Canaan.
46:12 *Hezron and Hamul,* these grandsons of Judah were most likely born in Egypt but were included to take the places of Er and Onan, who died in Canaan. This is similar to including Manasseh and Ephraim, born in Egypt (v. 20), with those who "came to Egypt."
46:27 Compare with Acts 7:14, where the number *seventy-five* is likely derived from the LXX (Septuagint—Greek translation of the Old Testament Scriptures), which includes two descendants of Manasseh and three descendants of Ephraim in v. 20, making a total of five more than the *seventy* noted in 46:27 of the Masoretic Text (standard Hebrew text of the Old Testament).

J. *The settlement in Egypt*

28 Now he sent Judah before him to Joseph, to point out *the way* before him to Goshen; and they came into the land of Goshen.

29 And Joseph prepared his chariot and went up to Goshen to meet his father Israel; as soon as he appeared before him, he fell on his neck and wept on his neck a long time.

30 Then Israel said to Joseph, "Now let me die, since I have seen your face, that you are still alive."

31 And Joseph said to his brothers and to his father's household, "I will go up and tell Pharaoh, and will say to him, 'My brothers and my father's household, who *were* in the land of Canaan, have come to me;

32 and the men are shepherds, for they have been keepers of livestock; and they have brought their flocks and their herds and all that they have.'

33 "And it shall come about when Pharaoh calls you and says, 'What is your occupation?'

34 that you shall say, 'Your servants have been keepers of livestock from our youth even until now, both we and our fathers,' that you may live in the land of Goshen; for every shepherd is loathsome to the Egyptians."

47 Then Joseph went in and told Pharaoh, and said, "My father and my brothers and their flocks and their herds and all that they have, have come out of the land of Canaan; and behold, they are in the land of Goshen."

2 And he took five men from among his brothers, and presented them to Pharaoh.

3 Then Pharaoh said to his brothers, "What is your occupation?" So they said to Pharaoh, "Your servants are shepherds, both we and our fathers."

4 And they said to Pharaoh, "We have come to sojourn in the land, for there is no pasture for your servants' flocks, for the famine is severe in the land of Canaan. Now, therefore, please let your servants live in the land of Goshen."

5 Then Pharaoh said to Joseph, "Your father and your brothers have come to you.

6 "The land of Egypt is [59]at your disposal; settle your father and your brothers in the best of the land, let them live in the land of Goshen; and if you know any capable men among them, then put them in charge of my livestock."

7 Then Joseph brought his father Jacob and presented him to Pharaoh; and Jacob blessed Pharaoh.

8 And Pharaoh said to Jacob, "How many years have you lived?"

9 So Jacob said to Pharaoh, "The years of my sojourning are one hundred and thirty; few and unpleasant have been the years of my life, nor have they attained the years that my fathers lived during the days of their sojourning."

10 And Jacob blessed Pharaoh, and went out from his presence.

11 So Joseph settled his father and his brothers, and gave them a possession in the land of Egypt, in the best of the land, in the land of Rameses, as Pharaoh had ordered.

12 And Joseph provided his father and his brothers and all his father's household with food, according to their little ones.

K. *The land policies of Joseph*

13 Now there was no food in all the land, because the famine was very severe, so that the land of Egypt and the land of Canaan languished because of the famine.

14 And Joseph gathered all the money that was found in the land of Egypt and in the land of Canaan for the grain which they bought, and Joseph brought the money into Pharaoh's house.

15 And when the money was all spent in the land of Egypt and in the land of

Marginal references

46:28 Gen 47:1

*46:29 Gen 45:14,15

46:31 Gen 47:1

46:33 Gen 47:2,3

46:34 Gen 13:7,8; 26:20; 37:2; 45:10,18; Ex 8:26

47:1 Gen 46:31

47:3 Gen 46:33,34

47:4 Gen 15:13; Deut 26:5; Gen 43:1; 46:34

47:6 v. 11; Gen 45:10,18

47:8 Ps 39:12; Heb 11:9,13; Job 14:1; Gen 25:7; 35:28

47:10 v. 7

*47:11 Ex 1:11; 12:37; 6:27

47:13 Gen 41:30; Acts 7:11

47:14 Gen 41:56

47:15 v. 19

[59]Lit., *before you*

46:29 *Israel.* Another name for Jacob.
47:9 Scripture describes believers of every age as *strangers, pilgrims, sojourners* and *exiles.* Believers are not of this world (John 17:16). Rather they: (1) look for the city whose maker is God (Heb. 11:16); (2) live in the fear of God during the days of their temporary sojourn (1 Pet. 1:17); and (3) constitute a heavenly commonwealth (Phil. 3:20). Exposed to persecution by the world (John 17:14), they are not to be anxious about earthly concerns (Matt. 6:25). They are to lay up their spiritual treasures in heaven (Matt. 6:19), abstaining from the passions of the flesh (1 Pet. 2:11) and shining as lights in the world (Phil. 2:15).
47:11 *land of Rameses,* later called Goshen.

Canaan, all the Egyptians came to Joseph and said, "Give us food, for why should we die in your presence? For *our* money is gone."

16 Then Joseph said, "Give up your livestock, and I will give you *food* for your livestock, since *your* money is gone."

17 So they brought their livestock to Joseph, and Joseph gave them food in exchange for the horses and the flocks and the herds and the donkeys; and he fed them with food in exchange for all their livestock that year.

18 And when that year was ended, they came to him the next year and said to him, "We will not hide from my lord that our money is all spent, and the cattle are my lord's. There is nothing left for my lord except our bodies and our lands.

19 "Why should we die before your eyes, both we and our land? Buy us and our land for food, and we and our land will be slaves to Pharaoh. So give us seed, that we may live and not die, and that the land may not be desolate."

20 So Joseph bought all the land of Egypt for Pharaoh, for every Egyptian sold his field, because the famine was severe upon them. Thus the land became Pharaoh's.

21 And as for the people, he removed them to the cities from one end of Egypt's border to the other.

22 Only the land of the priests he did not buy, for the priests had an allotment from Pharaoh, and they lived off the allotment which Pharaoh gave them. Therefore, they did not sell their land.

23 Then Joseph said to the people, "Behold, I have today bought you and your land for Pharaoh; now, *here* is seed for you, and you may sow the land.

24 "And at the harvest you shall give a fifth to Pharaoh, and four-fifths shall be your own for seed of the field and for your food and for those of your households and as food for your little ones."

25 So they said, "You have saved our lives! Let us find favor in the sight of my lord, and we will be Pharaoh's slaves."

26 And Joseph made it a statute concerning the land of Egypt *valid* to this day, that Pharaoh should have the fifth; only the land of the priests did not become Pharaoh's.

L. *Joseph's promise to Jacob*

27 Now Israel lived in the land of Egypt, in Goshen, and they acquired property in it and were fruitful and became very numerous.

28 And Jacob lived in the land of Egypt seventeen years; so the length of Jacob's life was one hundred and forty-seven years.

29 When the time for Israel to die drew near, he called his son Joseph and said to him, "Please, if I have found favor in your sight, place now your hand under my thigh and deal with me in kindness and [60]faithfulness. Please do not bury me in Egypt,

30 but when I lie down with my fathers, you shall carry me out of Egypt and bury me in their burial place." And he said, "I will do as you have said."

31 And he said, "Swear to me." So he swore to him. Then Israel bowed *in worship* at the head of the bed.

M. *Jacob's last days*

1. *Jacob blesses Joseph's sons: Ephraim preferred over Manasseh*

48 Now it came about after these things that Joseph was told, "Behold, your father is sick." So he took his two sons Manasseh and Ephraim with him.

2 When it was told to Jacob, "Behold, your son Joseph has come to you," Israel collected his strength and sat up in the bed.

3 Then Jacob said to Joseph, "God Almighty appeared to me at Luz in the land of Canaan and blessed me,

4 and He said to me, 'Behold, I will make you fruitful and numerous, and I will make you a company of peoples, and will give this land to your descendants after you for an everlasting possession.'

5 "And now your two sons, who were born to you in the land of Egypt before

[60]Lit., *truth*

24   But his bow remained firm,
      And his arms were agile,
      From the hands of the Mighty One of Jacob
      (From there is the Shepherd, the Stone of Israel),
25   From the God of your father who helps you,
      And by the Almighty who blesses you
      With blessings of heaven above,
      Blessings of the deep that lies beneath,
      Blessings of the breasts and of the womb.
26   "The blessings of your father
      Have surpassed the blessings of my ancestors
      Up to the utmost bound of the everlasting hills;
      May they be on the head of Joseph,
      And on the crown of the head of the one distinguished among his
         brothers.

27   "Benjamin is a ravenous wolf;
      In the morning he devours the prey,
      And in the evening he divides the spoil."

3. The death and burial of Jacob

28   All these are the twelve tribes of Israel, and this is what their father said to
them when he blessed them. He blessed them, every one with the blessing appropriate to him.

29   Then he charged them and said to them, "I am about to be gathered to my
people; bury me with my fathers in the cave that is in the field of Ephron the Hittite,

30   in the cave that is in the field of Machpelah, which is before Mamre, in the
land of Canaan, which Abraham bought along with the field from Ephron the
Hittite for a burial site.

31   "There they buried Abraham and his wife Sarah, there they buried Isaac and
his wife Rebekah, and there I buried Leah—

32   the field and the cave that is in it, purchased from the sons of Heth."

33   When Jacob finished charging his sons, he drew his feet into the bed and
breathed his last, and was gathered to his people.

50 Then Joseph fell on his father's face, and wept over him and kissed him.
    2   And Joseph commanded his servants the physicians to embalm his
father. So the physicians embalmed Israel.

3   Now forty days were required for it, for such is the period required for
embalming. And the Egyptians wept for him seventy days.

4   And when the days of mourning for him were past, Joseph spoke to the
household of Pharaoh, saying, "If now I have found favor in your sight, please
speak to Pharaoh, saying,

5   'My father made me swear, saying, "Behold, I am about to die; in my grave
which I dug for myself in the land of Canaan, there you shall bury me." Now
therefore, please let me go up and bury my father; then I will return.' "

6   And Pharaoh said, "Go up and bury your father, as he made you swear."

7   So Joseph went up to bury his father, and with him went up all the servants
of Pharaoh, the elders of his household and all the elders of the land of Egypt,

8   and all the household of Joseph and his brothers and his father's household;
they left only their little ones and their flocks and their herds in the land of Goshen.

9   There also went up with him both chariots and horsemen; and it was a very
great company.

10   When they came to the threshing floor of Atad, which is beyond the Jordan,
they lamented there with a very great and sorrowful lamentation; and he observed
seven days mourning for his father.

11   Now when the inhabitants of the land, the Canaanites, saw the mourning at
the threshing floor of Atad, they said, "This is a grievous mourning for the
Egyptians." Therefore it was named Abel-mizraim, which is beyond the Jordan.

12   And thus his sons did for him as he had charged them;

13   for his sons carried him to the land of Canaan, and buried him in the cave of

49:24
Ps 18:34;
Is 41:10;
Ps 132:2,5;
Is 1:24;
Ps 23:1;
Is 28:16;
1 Pet 2:6-8
*49:25
Gen 28:3,13;
32:9; 48:3;
27:28

49:26
Deut 33:15,
16

49:28
Gen 23:16-20

49:29
Gen 25:8;
47:30
49:30
Gen 23:16

49:31
Gen 23:19;
25:9; 35:29

49:33
Gen 25:8;
Acts 7:15;
v. 29

50:1
Gen 46:4
*50:2
v. 26

50:3
v. 10;
Num 20:29;
Deut 34:8

50:5
Gen 47:29-31

50:8
Ex 8:22

50:10
2 Sam 1:17;
1 Sam 31:13;
Job 2:13

50:13
Gen 49:29,30;
23:16

49:25 *blessings of heaven,* rain and sunshine; *blessings of the*
deep, rivers and springs.

50:2 *embalm(ed),* Egyptian practice of preparing noted persons for burial.

the field of Machpelah before Mamre, which Abraham had bought along with the field for a burial site from Ephron the Hittite.

14   And after he had buried his father, Joseph returned to Egypt, he and his brothers, and all who had gone up with him to bury his father.

N. *Joseph's kindness to his brethren*

50:15
Gen 37:28;
42:21,22
15   When Joseph's brothers saw that their father was dead, they said, "What if Joseph should bear a grudge against us and pay us back in full for all the wrong which we did to him!"

16   So they sent *a message* to Joseph, saying, "Your father charged before he died, saying,

17   'Thus you shall say to Joseph, "Please forgive, I beg you, the transgression of your brothers and their sin, for they did you wrong." ' And now, please forgive the transgression of the servants of the God of your father." And Joseph wept when they spoke to him.

50:18
Gen 37:7,10;
41:43
18   Then his brothers also came and fell down before him and said, "Behold, we are your servants."

50:19
Gen 45:5;
Deut 32:35;
Rom 12:19;
Heb 10:30
19   But Joseph said to them, "Do not be afraid, for am I in God's place?

20   "And as for you, you meant evil against me, *but* God meant it for good in order to bring about this present result, to preserve many people alive.

50:20
Gen 37:26,27;
45:5,7
50:21
Gen 45:11;
47:12
21   "So therefore, do not be afraid; I will provide for you and your little ones." So he comforted them and spoke kindly to them.

O. *The death and embalming of Joseph*

22   Now Joseph stayed in Egypt, he and his father's household, and Joseph lived one hundred and ten years.

23   And Joseph saw the third generation of Ephraim's sons; also the sons of Machir, the son of Manasseh, were born on Joseph's knees.

50:24
Gen 48:21;
Heb 11:22;
Gen 13:15,17;
15:7,8; 26:3;
28:13; 35:12
24   And Joseph said to his brothers, "I am about to die, but God will surely take care of you, and bring you up from this land to the land which He promised on oath to Abraham, to Isaac and to Jacob."

25   Then Joseph made the sons of Israel swear, saying, "God will surely take care of you, and you shall carry my bones up from here."

26   So Joseph died at the age of one hundred and ten years; and he was embalmed and placed in a coffin in Egypt.

INTRODUCTION TO
THE SECOND BOOK OF MOSES
COMMONLY CALLED

EXODUS

Authorship and Background: Exodus is the second of the five books of the Pentateuch, all ascribed to Moses. The name Exodus, meaning "going out," "departure," is the Greek title given to the book by the Septuagint translators. The Hebrew title, according to ancient custom, is made up of the opening words of the Hebrew text, "And these are the names."

The NAS starts the book with the word "Now," which suggests that it is a continuation of the story begun in Genesis. Without that background the account in Exodus would be puzzling. Moses is the central figure in the book; in fact, no other Old Testament character towers as high as he does. He was a military leader, lawgiver, and key figure in the founding of Israel's religion. The chief event of the book is the crossing of the Red (or Reed) Sea. The prophets and psalmists continually refer back to this mighty act of deliverance. The date of the exodus is still debated. Some scholars hold to a date around 1440 B.C.; others in recent years have supported a date around 1290 B.C.

Characteristics: Exodus is essentially the history of the origin and early years of Israel as God's chosen people of the covenant. The fortunes of this people are traced from Egypt to the wilderness under the leadership of Moses. The rise of the nation Israel as a theocracy, a form of government in which God is king, is unfolded in its pages. Guiding spiritual and moral principles characteristic of the Christian faith for centuries have their foundation in Exodus. There is considerable drama in the events as they unfold, and the effects are heightened by the manner in which they are recounted. The contests of Moses with Pharaoh, the crossing of the Red Sea, the provision of manna, the giving of the Law, and the account of Aaron and the golden calf are samples of events marked by emotion, anger, suspense, and retribution. In it all, however, may be seen the mighty power of the LORD God.

Contents:

I. The deliverance from Egypt (1:1-15:21): Israel is oppressed in Egypt. Moses' birth and education; his flight from Egypt. God calls him to be deliverer of Israel. Moses engages Pharaoh in successive tests marked by miraculous events. Directions for celebrating the Passover. Israel leaves Egypt. The first-born are sanctified, the Red Sea crossed, and the Egyptians drowned. The Song of Moses.

II. The journey to Sinai (15:22-18:27): The bitter waters of Marah made sweet. The people murmur and God provides manna for food. Sabbath instruction. Moses strikes the rock at Horeb to secure water. The battle against Amalek. Jethro becomes advisor to Moses, his son-in-law.

III. The covenant and the Law (19:1-24:18): Israel prepares to receive the covenant. The Ten Commandments given. Various judgments and moral statutes prescribed and the rewards of obedience stated. The people ratify the covenant. Moses returns to Sinai.

IV. The tabernacle in the wilderness (25:1-40:38): The divine plan for the tabernacle, including the furniture, altar, court, and priestly garments, and their consecration. God promises His presence, and adds directions for the tabernacle. The Sabbath, and the tables of testimony. The making of the golden calf, Moses' intercession in behalf of Israel, and the punishment. Moses' further intercession and his vision of the glory of God. The covenant is renewed. The tabernacle is constructed, set up, and the glory of God fills it.

THE SECOND BOOK OF MOSES
COMMONLY CALLED

EXODUS

I. The deliverance from Egypt (1:1–15:21)

A. Introduction

1. The numerical growth of Israel

1 Now these are the names of the sons of Israel who came to Egypt with Jacob; they came each one with his household: **1:1** Gen 46:8-27

2 Reuben, Simeon, Levi and Judah;

3 Issachar, Zebulun and Benjamin;

4 Dan and Naphtali, Gad and Asher.

5 And all the persons who came from the loins of Jacob were seventy in number, but Joseph was *already* in Egypt.   **1:5** Gen 46:27

6 And Joseph died, and all his brothers and all that generation.   **1:6** Gen 50:26

7 But the sons of Israel were fruitful and increased greatly, and multiplied, and became exceedingly mighty, so that the land was filled with them.   *1:7 Gen 46:3; 47:27; Acts 7:17

2. Israel in bondage

8 Now a new king arose over Egypt, who did not know Joseph.   **1:8** Acts 7:18,19

9 And he said to his people, "Behold, the people of the sons of Israel are more and mightier than we.   **1:9** Ps 105:24,25

10 "Come, let us deal wisely with them, lest they multiply and in the event of war, they also join themselves to those who hate us, and fight against us, and depart from the land."

11 So they appointed taskmasters over them to afflict them with hard labor. And they built for Pharaoh storage cities, Pithom and Raamses.   *1:11 Ex 3:7; 5:6

12 But the more they afflicted them, the more they multiplied and the more they spread out, so that they were in dread of the sons of Israel.

13 And the Egyptians compelled the sons of Israel to labor rigorously;

14 and they made their lives bitter with hard labor in mortar and bricks and at all *kinds* of labor in the field, all their labors which they rigorously imposed on them.   **1:14** Ps 81:6

3. The background for Moses

15 Then the king of Egypt spoke to the Hebrew midwives, one of whom was named Shiphrah, and the other was named Puah;

16 and he said, "When you are helping the Hebrew women to give birth and see *them* upon the birthstool, if it is a son, then you shall put him to death; but if it is a daughter, then she shall live."   **1:16** Acts 7:19

17 But the midwives feared God, and did not do as the king of Egypt had commanded them, but let the boys live.   **1:17** v. 21

18 So the king of Egypt called for the midwives, and said to them, "Why have you done this thing, and let the boys live?"

19 And the midwives said to Pharaoh, "Because the Hebrew women are not as the Egyptian women; for they are vigorous, and they give birth before the midwife can get to them."

20 So God was good to the midwives, and the people multiplied, and became very mighty.   **1:20** v. 12; Is 3:10

21 And it came about because the midwives feared God, that He established households for them.   **1:21** 1 Sam 2:35

1:7 *land*, the land of Goshen or Rameses.
1:11 *Pithom and Raamses*, cities in the Nile Delta. If this is a reference to the building operations of the nineteenth-dynasty kings of Egypt, then the exodus took place shortly after 1300 B.C., otherwise it took place in the fifteenth century B.C.

1:22 Acts 7:19	22 Then Pharaoh commanded all his people, saying, "Every son who is born [1]you are to cast into the Nile, and every daughter you are to keep alive."

B. *God's servant Moses*

1. *Moses' birth*

2:1 Ex 6:19,20 2:2 Acts 7:20; Heb 11:23	2 Now a man from the house of Levi went and married a daughter of Levi. 2 And the women conceived and bore a son; and when she saw that he was beautiful, she hid him for three months.
	3 But when she could hide him no longer, she got him a [2]wicker basket and covered it over with tar and pitch. Then she put the child into it, and set *it* among the reeds by the bank of the Nile.
2:4 Ex 15:20; Num 26:59	4 And his sister stood at a distance to find out what would happen to him.
	5 Then the daughter of Pharaoh came down to bathe at the Nile, with her maidens walking alongside the Nile; and she saw the basket among the reeds and sent her maid, and she brought it *to her.*
	6 When she opened *it*, she saw the child, and behold, *the* boy was crying. And she had pity on him and said, "This is one of the Hebrews' children."
	7 Then his sister said to Pharaoh's daughter, "Shall I go and call a nurse for you from the Hebrew women, that she may nurse the child for you?"
	8 And Pharaoh's daughter said to her, "Go *ahead.*" So the girl went and called the child's mother.
	9 Then Pharaoh's daughter said to her, "Take this child away and nurse him for me and I shall give *you* your wages." So the woman took the child and nursed him.
*2:10 Acts 7:21	10 And the child grew, and she brought him to Pharaoh's daughter, and he became her son. And she named him Moses, and said, "Because I drew him out of the water."

2. *Moses' crime and flight*

2:11 Acts 7:23; Heb 11:24-26	11 Now it came about in those days, when Moses had grown up, that he went out to his brethren and looked on their hard labors; and he saw an Egyptian beating a Hebrew, one of his brethren.
2:12 Acts 7:24	12 So he looked this way and that, and when he saw there was no one *around*, he struck down the Egyptian and hid him in the sand.
2:13 Acts 7:26-28	13 And he went out the next day, and behold, two Hebrews were fighting with each other; and he said to the offender, "Why are you striking your companion?"
2:14 Gen 19:9; Acts 7:27	14 But he said, "Who made you a prince or a judge over us? Are you intending to kill me, as you killed the Egyptian?" Then Moses was afraid, and said, "Surely the matter has become known."
*2:15 Acts 7:29; Gen 24:11; 29:2	15 When Pharaoh heard of this matter, he tried to kill Moses. But Moses fled from the presence of Pharaoh and settled in the land of Midian; and he sat down by a well.
2:16 Ex 3:1; 18:12; Gen 24:13,19	16 Now the priest of Midian had seven daughters; and they came to draw water, and filled the troughs to water their father's flock.
2:17 Gen 29:3,10	17 Then the shepherds came and drove them away, but Moses stood up and helped them, and watered their flock.
*2:18 Ex 3:1; Num 10:29	18 When they came to Reuel their father, he said, "Why have you come *back* so soon today?"
	19 So they said, "An Egyptian delivered us from the hand of the shepherds; and what is more, he even drew the water for us and watered the flock."

[1]Some versions insert, *to the Hebrews*   [2]I.e., papyrus reeds

---

2:3 *reeds*, papyrus reeds; *tar*, or asphalt, making the basket watertight.

2:10 Moses was one of the two greatest Old Testament characters—the other being Abraham; and he certainly ranks among the greatest men of all time. He was well educated in Egypt, where his training doubtless included athletics, art, writing, music, geometry, literature, law, astronomy, medicine, and philosophy. Apparently he could have chosen an official life, a literary life, or the life of a soldier. As the leader of Israel he occupied a unique position. He was deliverer, lawgiver, builder, commander-in-chief, judge, author, and intermediary between God and Israel. At forty (according to 2:15; Acts 7:23–29) he fled for

his life from Egypt. At eighty he delivered Israel from Egypt. At one hundred and twenty his ministry was completed. As a member of the tribe of Levi, he consecrated his brother Aaron to the high priesthood and thus, under God, made him the forefather of the priestly line. Faithful and unselfish, Moses was meek before the Lord and courageous before men.

2:15 *land of Midian*, properly speaking, in Arabia, but broadened here to include the Mt. Sinai region.

2:18 *Reuel*, Moses' father-in-law to be, is called Jethro (3:1) and Hobab (Judg. 4:11), although in Num. 10:29 Hobab is called the son of Reuel.

20   And he said to his daughters, "Where is he then? Why is it that you have left the man behind? Invite him to have something to eat."

21   And Moses was willing to dwell with the man, and he gave his daughter Zipporah to Moses.

22   Then she gave birth to a son, and he named him Gershom, for he said, "I have been a sojourner in a foreign land."

3. The call of Moses at the burning bush

a. Moses' conversations with God

23   Now it came about in *the course of* those many days that the king of Egypt died. And the sons of Israel sighed because of the bondage, and they cried out; and their cry for help because of *their* bondage rose up to God.

24   So God heard their groaning; and God remembered His covenant with Abraham, Isaac, and Jacob.

25   And God saw the sons of Israel, and God took notice *of them.*

3 Now Moses was pasturing the flock of Jethro his father-in-law, the priest of Midian; and he led the flock to the west side of the wilderness, and came to Horeb, the mountain of God.

2   And the angel of the LORD appeared to him in a blazing fire from the midst of a bush; and he looked, and behold, the bush was burning with fire, yet the bush was not consumed.

3   So Moses said, "I must turn aside now, and see this marvelous sight, why the bush is not burned up."

4   When the LORD saw that he turned aside to look, God called to him from the midst of the bush, and said, "Moses, Moses!" And he said, "Here I am."

5   Then He said, "Do not come near here; remove your sandals from your feet, for the place on which you are standing is holy ground."

6   He said also, "I am the God of your father, the God of Abraham, the God of Isaac, and the God of Jacob." Then Moses hid his face, for he was afraid to look at God.

7   And the LORD said, "I have surely seen the affliction of My people who are in Egypt, and have given heed to their cry because of their taskmasters, for I am aware of their sufferings.

8   "So I have come down to deliver them from the power of the Egyptians, and to bring them up from that land to a good and spacious land, to a land flowing with milk and honey, to the place of the Canaanite and the Hittite and the Amorite and the Perizzite and the Hivite and the Jebusite.

9   "And now, behold, the cry of the sons of Israel has come to Me; furthermore, I have seen the oppression with which the Egyptians are oppressing them.

10   "Therefore, come now, and I will send you to Pharaoh, so that you may bring My people, the sons of Israel, out of Egypt."

11   But Moses said to God, "Who am I, that I should go to Pharaoh, and that I should bring the sons of Israel out of Egypt?"

12   And He said, "Certainly I will be with you, and this shall be the sign to you that it is I who have sent you: when you have brought the people out of Egypt, you shall worship God at this mountain."

13   Then Moses said to God, "Behold, I am going to the sons of Israel, and I shall say to them, 'The God of your fathers has sent me to you.' Now they may say to me, 'What is His name?' What shall I say to them?"

14   And God said to Moses, "[3]I AM WHO [3]I AM"; and He said, "Thus you shall say to the sons of Israel, '[3]I AM has sent me to you.'"

15   And God, furthermore, said to Moses, "Thus you shall say to the sons of Israel, 'The LORD, the God of your fathers, the God of Abraham, the God of Isaac, and the God of Jacob, has sent me to you.' This is My name forever, and this is My memorial-name to all generations.

16   "Go and gather the elders of Israel together, and say to them, 'The LORD, the God of your fathers, the God of Abraham, Isaac and Jacob, has appeared to me,

[3]Related to the name of God, *YHWH*, rendered LORD, which is derived from the verb *HAYAH, to be*

Cross-references (right margin):

2:20 Gen 31:54
2:21 Acts 7:29; Gen 4:25; 18:2
2:22 Ex 18:3; Heb 11:13,14
2:23 Acts 7:30; Deut 26:7; Ex 3:9; James 5:4
2:24 Ex 6:5; Ps 105:8,42; Gen 22:16-18
2:25 Ex 4:31; 3:7; 4:27; 18:5
3:1 Ex 2:18
*3:2 Deut 33:16; Mark 12:26
3:3 Acts 7:31
3:5 Josh 5:15; Acts 7:33
3:6 Matt 22:31, 32; Mark 12:26; Luke 20:37; Acts 7:32
3:7 Ex 2:25; Neh 9:9; Acts 7:34
3:8 Gen 50:24,25; v. 17; Josh 24:11
3:9 Ex 2:23; 1:13,14
3:10 Mic 6:4
3:12 Gen 31:3; Josh 1:5
3:14 Ex 6:3; John 8:58; Heb 13:8
3:15 Ps 135:13; Hos 12:5

3:2 The phrase *angel of the* LORD may indicate an appearance of the preincarnate Christ in the Old Testament, as, for example, in Judg. 2:1; 6:12–16; 13:3–22, where the texts clearly show that the angel was God Himself.

saying, "I am indeed concerned about you and what has been done to you in Egypt.

3:17
Gen 15:14,16;
Josh 24:11
17 "So I said, I will bring you up out of the affliction of Egypt to the land of the Canaanite and the Hittite and the Amorite and the Perizzite and the Hivite and the Jebusite, to a land flowing with milk and honey."'

3:18
Ex 4:31; 5:1,
3
18 "And they will pay heed to what you say; and you with the elders of Israel will come to the king of Egypt, and you will say to him, 'The LORD, the God of the Hebrews, has met with us. So now, please, let us go a three days' journey into the wilderness, that we may sacrifice to the LORD our God.'

3:19
Ex 5:2; 6:1
19 "But I know that the king of Egypt will not permit you to go, except under compulsion.

3:20
Ex 6:6; 9:15;
Deut 6:22;
Neh 9:10;
Ex 12:31
3:21
Ex 11:3;
12:36
3:22
Ex 11:2,3;
12:35,36
20 "So I will stretch out My hand, and strike Egypt with all My miracles which I shall do in the midst of it; and after that he will let you go.

21 "And I will grant this people favor in the sight of the Egyptians; and it shall be that when you go, you will not go empty-handed.

22 "But every woman shall ask of her neighbor and the woman who lives in her house, articles of silver and articles of gold, and clothing; and you will put them on your sons and daughters. Thus you will plunder the Egyptians."

b. God equips Moses

4:1
Ex 3:18; 6:30
*4:2
vv. 17,20
4 Then Moses answered and said, "What if they will not believe me, or listen to what I say? For they may say, 'The LORD has not appeared to you.'"

2 And the LORD said to him, "What is that in your hand?" And he said, "A staff."

3 Then He said, "Throw it on the ground." So he threw it on the ground, and it became a serpent; and Moses fled from it.

4 But the LORD said to Moses, "Stretch out your hand and grasp *it* by its tail"—so he stretched out his hand and caught it, and it became a staff in his hand—

5 "that they may believe that the LORD, the God of their fathers, the God of Abraham, the God of Isaac, and the God of Jacob, has appeared to you."

4:6
Num 12:10;
2 Kin 5:27
6 And the LORD furthermore said to him, "Now put your hand into your bosom." So he put his hand into his bosom, and when he took it out, behold, his hand was leprous like snow.

4:7
Num 12:13,
14;
Deut 32:39;
2 Kin 5:14;
Matt 8:3
7 Then He said, "Put your hand into your bosom again." So he put his hand into his bosom again; and when he took it out of his bosom, behold, it was restored like *the rest of* his flesh.

8 "And it shall come about that if they will not believe you or heed the witness of the first sign, they may believe the witness of the last sign.

4:9
Ex 7:19
9 "But it shall be that if they will not believe even these two signs or heed what you say, then you shall take some water from the Nile and pour it on the dry ground; and the water which you take from the Nile will become blood on the dry ground."

c. God provides Aaron to speak

4:10
Ex 6:12;
Jer 1:6
4:11
Ps 94:9;
Matt 11:5
4:12
Is 50:4;
Jer 1:9;
Matt 10:19;
Mark 13:11;
Luke 12:11,
12; 21:14,15
4:14
v. 27
4:15
Ex 7:1,2;
Num 23:5,12,
16; Deut 5:31
10 Then Moses said to the LORD, "Please, Lord, I have never been eloquent, neither recently nor in time past, nor since Thou hast spoken to Thy servant; for I am slow of speech and slow of tongue."

11 And the LORD said to him, "Who has made man's mouth? Or who makes *him* dumb or deaf, or seeing or blind? Is it not I, the LORD?

12 "Now then go, and I, even I, will be with your mouth, and teach you what you are to say."

13 But he said, "Please, Lord, now send *the message* by whomever Thou wilt."

14 Then the anger of the LORD burned against Moses, and He said, "Is there not your brother Aaron the Levite? I know that he speaks fluently. And moreover, behold, he is coming out to meet you; when he sees you, he will be glad in his heart.

15 "And you are to speak to him and put the words in his mouth; and I, even I, will be with your mouth and his mouth, and I will teach you what you are to do.

4:2 Moses asked God for some sign by which he might impress Pharaoh that he had come from God. He was given the staff-serpent and the leprous hand (v. 6); however, his credentials served only to prove that unbelief will not be moved by mere signs and wonders. As it turned out, neither sign induced Pharaoh to let Israel go. Another aspect of this incident concerns believers in their walk with God: all God needed was what Moses had in his hand—a staff. When yielded to the Lord in complete surrender and trust, it became a miracle-working instrument. Pebbles and a sling were all David had to oppose Goliath, but God made them enough. So it has always been. Even the smallest and most insignificant object that is wholly dedicated to God in the hands of a willing believer may be used for God's glory and the accomplishment of His will. In this experience of Moses one fact should be carefully noted. Though the signs may not have convinced Pharaoh, they did serve to convince the children of Israel that Moses was truly God's messenger of deliverance (vv. 29–31).

16 "Moreover, he shall speak for you to the people; and it shall come about that he shall be as a mouth for you, and you shall be as God to him.

17 "And you shall take in your hand this staff, with which you shall perform the signs."

d. *Moses starts for Egypt*

18 Then Moses departed and returned to Jethro his father-in-law, and said to him, "Please, let me go, that I may return to my brethren who are in Egypt, and see if they are still alive." And Jethro said to Moses, "Go in peace."

19 Now the LORD said to Moses in Midian, "Go back to Egypt, for all the men who were seeking your life are dead."

20 So Moses took his wife and his sons and mounted them on a donkey, and he returned to the land of Egypt. Moses also took the staff of God in his hand.

21 And the LORD said to Moses, "When you go back to Egypt see that you perform before Pharaoh all the wonders which I have put in your power; but I will harden his heart so that he will not let the people go.

22 "Then you shall say to Pharaoh, 'Thus says the LORD, "Israel is My son, My first-born.

23 "So I said to you, 'Let My son go, that he may serve Me'; but you have refused to let him go. Behold, I will kill your son, your first-born."' ' "

24 Now it came about at the lodging place on the way that the LORD met him and sought to put him to death.

25 Then Zipporah took a flint and cut off her son's foreskin and threw *it* at Moses' feet, and she said, "You are indeed a bridegroom of blood to me."

26 So He let him alone. At that time she said, "*You are* a bridegroom of blood"—because of the circumcision.

27 Now the LORD said to Aaron, "Go to meet Moses in the wilderness." So he went and met him at the mountain of God, and he kissed him.

28 And Moses told Aaron all the words of the LORD with which He had sent him, and all the signs that He had commanded him *to do.*

29 Then Moses and Aaron went and assembled all the elders of the sons of Israel;

30 and Aaron spoke all the words which the LORD had spoken to Moses. He then performed the signs in the sight of the people.

31 So the people believed; and when they heard that the LORD was concerned about the sons of Israel and that He had seen their affliction, then they bowed low and worshiped.

C. *God's method of deliverance*

1. *Moses and Aaron meet with Pharaoh*

a. *Pharaoh refuses to let Israel go*

5 And afterward Moses and Aaron came and said to Pharaoh, "Thus says the LORD, the God of Israel, 'Let My people go that they may celebrate a feast to Me in the wilderness.' "

2 But Pharaoh said, "Who is the LORD that I should obey His voice to let Israel go? I do not know the LORD, and besides, I will not let Israel go."

3 Then they said, "The God of the Hebrews has met with us. Please, let us go a three days' journey into the wilderness that we may sacrifice to the LORD our God, lest He fall upon us with pestilence or with the sword."

4 But the king of Egypt said to them, "Moses and Aaron, why do you draw the people away from their work? Get *back* to your labors!"

5 Again Pharaoh said, "Look, the people of the land are now many, and you would have them cease from their labors!"

4:17	v. 2; Ex 7:9-20
4:19	Ex 2:15,23
4:20	Ex 17:9; Num 20:8
*4:21	Ex 7:3,13; 9:12,35; 10:1; 14:8;
	Deut 2:30; John 12:40; Rom 19:18
4:22	Is 63:16; 64:8; Hos 11:1; Rom 9:4; Jer 31:9
4:23	Ex 5:1; 6:11; 7:16; 12:29
*4:24ff	Num 22:22; Gen 17:14
4:25	Josh 5:2,3
4:27	v. 14; Ex 3:1
4:28	vv. 15,16; 8:9
4:29	Ex 3:16
4:30	v. 16
4:31	v. 8,9; Ex 3:18; 2:25; 3:7; 12:27
5:1	Ex 3:18; 4:23; 10:9
5:2	Job 21:15; Ex 3:19
5:3	Ex 3:18
5:4	Ex 1:11; 2:11; 6:6,7
5:5	Ex 1:7,9

4:21 Moses records not only that God hardened Pharaoh's heart (e.g., 9:12; 10:1), but also that Pharaoh hardened his own heart (e.g., 8:15,32; 9:34). Nowhere are we told that God forced Pharaoh contrary to his own voluntary choice. Rather, it seems that God sent circumstances into Pharaoh's life that hardened his heart and caused him to reject the claims of God. Resisting God must always result in a hardened heart.

4:24–26 The reason that Moses had not circumcised his son is not made clear in the narrative. It may have been that, to please his wife, he had neglected this seal of the Abrahamic covenant. But God made it perfectly evident that he could not effectively serve as God's deliverer until he had fulfilled the covenant condition. Because of Moses' grave illness at the inn, Zipporah, much against her will, had to perform the circumcision. Not to circumcise was tantamount to abrogating the covenant (Gen. 17:14) and meant that the uncircumcised would not be included among the covenant people. Since the advent of Christ, real circumcision has been of the heart and not of the flesh (Rom. 2:29).

5:6
Ex 1:11; 3:7
6   So the same day Pharaoh commanded the taskmasters over the people and their foremen, saying,

7   "You are no longer to give the people straw to make brick as previously; let them go and gather straw for themselves.

5:8
v. 17
8   "But the quota of bricks which they were making previously, you shall impose on them; you are not to reduce any of it. Because they are lazy, therefore they cry out, 'Let us go and sacrifice to our God.'

9   "Let the labor be heavier on the men, and let them work at it that they may pay no attention to false words."

b. *Israel's task made heavier*

5:10
v. 6
10   So the taskmasters of the people and their foremen went out and spoke to the people, saying, "Thus says Pharaoh, 'I am not going to give you *any* straw.

11   'You go *and* get straw for yourselves wherever you can find *it;* but none of your labor will be reduced.' "

12   So the people scattered through all the land of Egypt to gather stubble for straw.

13   And the taskmasters pressed them, saying, "Complete your work quota, *your* daily amount, just as when you had straw."

5:14
v. 6; Is 10:24
14   Moreover, the foremen of the sons of Israel, whom Pharaoh's taskmasters had set over them, were beaten and were asked, "Why have you not completed your required amount either yesterday or today in making brick as previously?"

15   Then the foremen of the sons of Israel came and cried out to Pharaoh, saying, "Why do you deal this way with your servants?

16   "There is no straw given to your servants, yet they keep saying to us, 'Make bricks!' And behold, your servants are being beaten; but it is the fault of your *own* people."

5:17
v. 8
17   But he said, "You are lazy, *very* lazy; therefore you say, 'Let us go *and* sacrifice to the LORD.'

18   "So go now *and* work; for you shall be given no straw, yet you must deliver the quota of bricks."

19   And the foremen of the sons of Israel saw that they were in trouble because they were told, "You must not reduce *your* daily amount of bricks."

20   When they left Pharaoh's presence, they met Moses and Aaron as they were waiting for them.

5:21
Ex 14:11;
15:24;
Gen 16:5;
34:30
21   And they said to them, "May the LORD look upon you and judge *you*, for you have made ⁴us odious in Pharaoh's sight and in the sight of his servants, to put a sword in their hand to kill us."

c. *God's promise of deliverance to Moses*

*5:22
Num 11:11;
Jer 4:10
5:23
Ex 3:8
22   Then Moses returned to the LORD and said, "O Lord, why hast Thou brought harm to this people? Why didst Thou ever send me?

23   "Ever since I came to Pharaoh to speak in Thy name, he has done harm to this people; and Thou hast not delivered Thy people at all."

6:1
Ex 3:19,20;
7:4,5; 12:31,
33,39
6   Then the LORD said to Moses, "Now you shall see what I will do to Pharaoh; for under compulsion he shall let them go, and under compulsion he shall drive them out of his land."

*6:3
Ps 68:4;
83:18;
Is 52:6;
Jer 16:21;
Ezek 37:6,13
2   God spoke further to Moses and said to him, "I am the LORD;

3   and I appeared to Abraham, Isaac, and Jacob, as God Almighty, but *by* My name, ⁵LORD, I did not make Myself known to them.

⁴Lit., *our savor to stink*   ⁵Heb., *YHWH*, usually rendered LORD

5:22 The perplexity of Moses is easy to understand. God had guaranteed to deliver Israel, but their situation seemed to be worsening. Moses did not understand that God's special deliverance is often preceded by great difficulties and apparently unfavorable conditions. Since a believer is to walk by faith and not by sight, he is not to be subject to mere external appearances but to trust God's faithfulness whatever happens. Before Joseph became premier of Egypt he first had become a slave and then was imprisoned for a crime he never committed. Strong faith is challenged, not defeated, by adverse circumstances.

6:3 This verse poses some difficulties because in Gen. 12:8 it states that when Abraham came to the Bethel area *he built an altar . . . to the LORD*. The name "LORD" (with small capital letters) is the common designation in the KJV, RSV, and NAS for *Yahweh*, the personal name for the God of Israel. If the name *Yahweh* was used as early as Gen. 12:8, then 6:3 means that *Yahweh* took on new meaning after God's revelation to Moses. However, if 6:3 is to be interpreted as the origin of the name *Yahweh*, then earlier uses represent a reading back of the name of the God of Israel into earlier patriarchal records.

4 "And I also established My covenant with them, to give them the land of Canaan, the land in which they sojourned.

5 "And furthermore I have heard the groaning of the sons of Israel, because the Egyptians are holding them in bondage; and I have remembered My covenant.

6 "Say, therefore, to the sons of Israel, 'I am the LORD, and I will bring you out from under the burdens of the Egyptians, and I will deliver you from their bondage. I will also redeem you with an outstretched arm and with great judgments.

7 'Then I will take you for My people, and I will be your God; and you shall know that I am the LORD your God, who brought you out from under the burdens of the Egyptians.

8 'And I will bring you to the land which I swore to give to Abraham, Isaac, and Jacob, and I will give it to you *for* a possession; I am the LORD.' "

9 So Moses spoke thus to the sons of Israel, but they did not listen to Moses on account of *their* despondency and cruel bondage.

10 Now the LORD spoke to Moses, saying,

11 "Go, tell Pharaoh king of Egypt to let the sons of Israel go out of his land."

12 But Moses spoke before the LORD, saying, "Behold, the sons of Israel have not listened to me; how then will Pharaoh listen to me, for I am unskilled in speech?"

13 Then the LORD spoke to Moses and to Aaron, and gave them a charge to the sons of Israel and to Pharaoh king of Egypt, to bring the sons of Israel out of the land of Egypt.

d. The genealogy of Israel

14 These are the heads of their fathers' households. The sons of Reuben, Israel's first-born: Hanoch and Pallu, Hezron and Carmi; these are the families of Reuben.

15 And the sons of Simeon: Jemuel and Jamin and Ohad and Jachin and Zohar and Shaul the son of a Canaanite woman; these are the families of Simeon.

16 And these are the names of the sons of Levi according to their generations: Gershon and Kohath and Merari; and the length of Levi's life was one hundred and thirty-seven years.

17 The sons of Gershon: Libni and Shimei, according to their families.

18 And the sons of Kohath: Amram and Izhar and Hebron and Uzziel; and the length of Kohath's life was one hundred and thirty-three years.

19 And the sons of Merari: Mahli and Mushi. These are the families of the Levites according to their generations.

20 And Amram married his father's sister Jochebed, and she bore him Aaron and Moses; and the length of Amram's life was one hundred and thirty-seven years.

21 And the sons of Izhar: Korah and Nepheg and Zichri.

22 And the sons of Uzziel: Mishael and Elzaphan and Sithri.

23 And Aaron married Elisheba, the daughter of Amminadab, the sister of Nahshon, and she bore him Nadab and Abihu, Eleazar and Ithamar.

24 And the sons of Korah: Assir and Elkanah and Abiasaph; these are the families of the Korahites.

25 And Aaron's son Eleazar married one of the daughters of Putiel, and she bore him Phinehas. These are the heads of the fathers' *households* of the Levites according to their families.

26 It was *the same* Aaron and Moses to whom the LORD said, "Bring out the sons of Israel from the land of Egypt according to their hosts."

27 They were the ones who spoke to Pharaoh king of Egypt about bringing out the sons of Israel from Egypt; it was *the same* Moses and Aaron.

e. Moses commanded to speak to Pharaoh again

28 Now it came about on the day when the LORD spoke to Moses in the land of Egypt,

29 that the LORD spoke to Moses, saying, "I am the LORD; speak to Pharaoh king of Egypt all that I speak to you."

30 But Moses said before the LORD, "Behold, I am unskilled in speech; how then will Pharaoh listen to me?"

6:30 *unskilled in speech*, stammering lips.

Margin references:

6:4 Gen 15:18; 28:4
6:5 Ex 2:24
6:6 Deut 26:8
6:7 Deut 4:20; 26:8; Ps 81:6; Ex 16:12; Is 41:20
6:8 Gen 15:18
6:14 Gen 46:9; Num 26:5-11
6:15 Gen 46:10; 1 Chr 4:24
6:16 Gen 46:11; Num 3:17
6:17 1 Chr 6:17
6:18 1 Chr 6:2,18
6:19 1 Chr 6:19
6:20 Ex 2:1,2; Num 26:59
6:21 Num 16:1; 1 Chr 6:37,38
6:22 Lev 10:4; Num 3:30
6:24 Num 26:11
6:25 Josh 24:33; Num 25:7-11; Ps 106:30
6:29 v. 11; Ex 7:2
*6:30 v. 12; Ex 4:10

7:1
Ex 4:16

7:2
Ex 4:15

7:3
Ex 4:21; 11:9

7:4
Ex 3:19,20;
10:1; 11:9;
12:51; 13:3,9;
6:6
7:5
v. 17;
Ex 8:19; 3:20
7:6
v. 2
7:7
Deut 34:7;
Acts 7:23,30

7 Then the LORD said to Moses, "See, I make you *as* God to Pharaoh, and your brother Aaron shall be your prophet.

2 "You shall speak all that I command you, and your brother Aaron shall speak to Pharaoh that he let the sons of Israel go out of his land.

3 "But I will harden Pharaoh's heart that I may multiply My signs and My wonders in the land of Egypt.

4 "When Pharaoh will not listen to you, then I will lay My hand on Egypt, and bring out My hosts, My people the sons of Israel, from the land of Egypt by great judgments.

5 "And the Egyptians shall know that I am the LORD, when I stretch out My hand on Egypt and bring out the sons of Israel from their midst."

6 So Moses and Aaron did *it;* as the LORD commanded them, thus they did.

7 And Moses was eighty years old and Aaron eighty-three, when they spoke to Pharaoh.

2. The miracles of Moses

a. The rod becomes a serpent

7:9
Is 7:11;
John 2:18;
Ex 4:2,17
7:10
v. 9; Ex 4:3

8 Now the LORD spoke to Moses and Aaron, saying,

9 "When Pharaoh speaks to you, saying, 'Work a miracle,' then you shall say to Aaron, 'Take your staff and throw *it* down before Pharaoh, *that* it may become a serpent.'"

10 So Moses and Aaron came to Pharaoh, and thus they did just as the LORD had commanded; and Aaron threw his staff down before Pharaoh and his servants, and it became a serpent.

7:11
Gen 41:8;
v. 22; Ex 8:7,
18

11 Then Pharaoh also called for *the* wise men and *the* sorcerers, and they also, the magicians of Egypt, did the same with their secret arts.

12 For each one threw down his staff and they turned into serpents. But Aaron's staff swallowed up their staffs.

7:13
v. 4; Ex 4:21

13 Yet Pharaoh's heart was hardened, and he did not listen to them, as the LORD had said.

b. The water turned into blood

7:14
Ex 8:15;
10:1,20,27
7:15
v. 10; Ex 4:2,
3

14 Then the LORD said to Moses, "Pharaoh's heart is stubborn; he refuses to let the people go.

15 "Go to Pharaoh in the morning as he is going out to the water, and station yourself to meet him on the bank of the Nile; and you shall take in your hand the staff that was turned into a serpent.

7:16
Ex 3:12,18;
5:1,3

16 "And you will say to him, 'The LORD, the God of the Hebrews, sent me to you, saying, "Let My people go, that they may serve Me in the wilderness. But behold, you have not listened until now."

7:17
v. 5; Ex 5:2;
4:9;
Rev 11:6;
16:4,6
7:18
vv. 21,24

17 'Thus says the LORD, "By this you shall know that I am the LORD: behold, I will strike the water that is in the Nile with the staff that is in my hand, and it shall be turned to blood.

18 "And the fish that are in the Nile will die, and the Nile will become foul; and the Egyptians will find difficulty in drinking water from the Nile." ' "

7:19
Ex 8:5,6,16;
9:22; 10:12;
21; 14:21,26

19 Then the LORD said to Moses, "Say to Aaron, 'Take your staff and stretch out your hand over the waters of Egypt, over their rivers, over their streams, and over their pools, and over all their reservoirs of water, that they may become blood; and there shall be blood throughout all the land of Egypt, both in *vessels of* wood and in *vessels of* stone.'"

7:20
Ps 78:44;
105:29

20 So Moses and Aaron did even as the LORD had commanded. And he lifted up the staff and struck the water that *was* in the Nile, in the sight of Pharaoh and in the sight of his servants, and all the water that *was* in the Nile was turned to blood.

7:21
v. 18

21 And the fish that *were* in the Nile died, and the Nile became foul, so that the Egyptians could not drink water from the Nile. And the blood was through all the land of Egypt.

7:22
v. 11; Ex 8:7

22 But the magicians of Egypt did the same with their secret arts; and Pha-

---

7:3 *will harden,* see note to 4:21.
7:12 Two miracles are recorded here. The first occurred when Aaron's rod became a serpent, only to be challenged by a counter-miracle when the rods of the Egyptians also became serpents. But the supreme power of God was demonstrated when (second miracle) Aaron's serpent swallowed the serpents of the Egyptians.

raoh's heart was hardened, and he did not listen to them, as the LORD had said.

23   Then Pharaoh turned and went into his house with no concern even for this.

24   So all the Egyptians dug around the Nile for water to drink, for they could not drink of the water of the Nile.

c. The plague of frogs

25   And seven days passed after the LORD had struck the Nile.

8 Then the LORD said to Moses, "Go to Pharaoh and say to him, 'Thus says the LORD, "Let My people go, that they may serve Me.

2   "But if you refuse to let *them* go, behold, I will smite your whole territory with frogs.

3   "And the Nile will swarm with frogs, which will come up and go into your house and into your bedroom and on your bed, and into the houses of your servants and on your people, and into your ovens and into your kneading bowls.

4   "So the frogs will come up on you and your people and all your servants." ' "

5   Then the LORD said to Moses, "Say to Aaron, 'Stretch out your hand with your staff over the rivers, over the streams and over the pools, and make frogs come up on the land of Egypt.' "

6   So Aaron stretched out his hand over the waters of Egypt, and the frogs came up and covered the land of Egypt.

7   And the magicians did the same with their secret arts, making frogs come up on the land of Egypt.

8   Then Pharaoh called for Moses and Aaron and said, "Entreat the LORD that He remove the frogs from me and from my people; and I will let the people go, that they may sacrifice to the LORD."

9   And Moses said to Pharaoh, "The honor is yours to tell me: when shall I entreat for you and your servants and your people, that the frogs be destroyed from you and your houses, *that* they may be left only in the Nile?"

10   Then he said, "Tomorrow." So he said, "*May it be* according to your word, that you may know that there is no one like the LORD our God.

11   "And the frogs will depart from you and your houses and your servants and your people; they will be left only in the Nile."

12   Then Moses and Aaron went out from Pharaoh, and Moses cried to the LORD concerning the frogs which He had inflicted upon Pharaoh.

13   And the LORD did according to the word of Moses, and the frogs died out of the houses, the courts, and the fields.

14   So they piled them in heaps, and the land became foul.

15   But when Pharaoh saw that there was relief, he hardened his heart and did not listen to them, as the LORD had said.

d. The plague of gnats

16   Then the LORD said to Moses, "Say to Aaron, 'Stretch out your staff and strike the dust of the earth, that it may become [6]gnats through all the land of Egypt.' "

17   And they did so; and Aaron stretched out his hand with his staff, and struck the dust of the earth, and there were gnats on man and beast. All the dust of the earth became gnats through all the land of Egypt.

18   And the magicians tried with their secret arts to bring forth gnats, but they could not; so there were gnats on man and beast.

19   Then the magicians said to Pharaoh, "This is the finger of God." But Pharaoh's heart was hardened, and he did not listen to them, as the LORD had said.

e. The swarms of flies

20   Now the LORD said to Moses, "Rise early in the morning and present yourself before Pharaoh, as he comes out to the water, and say to him, 'Thus says the LORD, "Let My people go, that they may serve Me.

21   "For if you will not let My people go, behold, I will send swarms of insects on

[6]Or, *lice*

Cross references (margin):

8:1 Ex 3:12,18
8:3 Ps 105:30
8:5 Ex 7:19
8:6 Ps 78:45; 105:30
8:7 Ex 7:11
8:8 vv. 25,28; Ex 9:27,28; 10:17
8:10 Ex 9:14; Deut 33:26; Ps 86:8; Is 46:9; Jer 10:6,7
8:12 v. 30; Ex 9:33; 10:18
8:15 Ex 7:4
8:17 Ps 105:31
8:18 Ex 7:11
*8:19 Ex 7:5; 10:7
8:20 Ex 9:13; 7:15; v. 1

8:19 The magicians of Pharaoh were at last convinced that Moses and Aaron were truly from God, because they themselves could no longer reproduce the miracles of Moses and Aaron. Yet the heart of Pharaoh remained as stone, demonstrating the obstinacy of the rebellious human heart that remains unconvinced of the truth of God's Word, even in the face of overwhelming evidence.

you and on your servants and on your people and into your houses; and the houses of the Egyptians shall be full of swarms of insects, and also the ground on which they *dwell*.

8:22
Ex 9:4,6,26;
10:23; 11:6,7

22 "But on that day I will set apart the land of Goshen, where My people are living, so that no swarms of insects will be there, in order that you may know that I, the LORD, am in the midst of the land.

23 "And I will ⁷put a division between My people and your people. Tomorrow this sign shall occur." ' "

8:24
Ps 78:45;
105:31

24 Then the LORD did so. And there came great swarms of insects into the house of Pharaoh and the houses of his servants and the land was laid waste because of the swarms of insects in all the land of Egypt.

25 And Pharaoh called for Moses and Aaron and said, "Go, sacrifice to your God within the land."

26 But Moses said, "It is not right to do so, for we shall sacrifice to the LORD our God what is an abomination to the Egyptians. If we sacrifice what is an abomination to the Egyptians before their eyes, will they not then stone us?

8:27
Ex 3:18; 5:3

27 "We must go a three days' journey into the wilderness and sacrifice to the LORD our God as He commands us."

8:28
vv. 8,15,29,
32

28 And Pharaoh said, "I will let you go, that you may sacrifice to the LORD your God in the wilderness; only you shall not go very far away. Make supplication for me."

8:29
vv. 8,15

29 Then Moses said, "Behold, I am going out from you, and I shall make supplication to the LORD that the swarms of insects may depart from Pharaoh, from his servants, and from his people tomorrow; only do not let Pharaoh deal deceitfully again in not letting the people go to sacrifice to the LORD."

30 So Moses went out from Pharaoh and made supplication to the LORD.

31 And the LORD did as Moses asked, and removed the swarms of insects from Pharaoh, from his servants and from his people; not one remained.

8:32
vv. 8,15;
Ex 4:21

32 But Pharaoh hardened his heart this time also, and he did not let the people go.

f. The death of the Egyptian cattle

9:1
Ex 8:1

9 Then the LORD said to Moses, "Go to Pharaoh and speak to him, 'Thus says the LORD, the God of the Hebrews, "Let My people go, that they may serve Me.

9:2
Ex 8:2

2 "For if you refuse to let *them* go, and continue to hold them,

3 behold, the hand of the LORD will come *with* a very severe pestilence on your livestock which are in the field, on the horses, on the donkeys, on the camels, on the herds, and on the flocks.

9:4
Ex 8:22

4 "But the LORD will make a distinction between the livestock of Israel and the livestock of Egypt, so that nothing will die of all that belongs to the sons of Israel." ' "

5 And the LORD set a definite time, saying, "Tomorrow the LORD will do this thing in the land."

9:6
Ex 11:5; v. 4

6 So the LORD did this thing on the morrow, and all the livestock of Egypt died; but of the livestock of the sons of Israel, not one died.

9:7
Ex 7:14; 8:32

7 And Pharaoh sent, and behold, there was not even one of the livestock of Israel dead. But the heart of Pharaoh was hardened, and he did not let the people go.

g. The boils and sores

9:9
Rev 16:2

8 Then the LORD said to Moses and Aaron, "Take for yourselves handfuls of soot from a kiln, and let Moses throw it toward the sky in the sight of Pharaoh.

9 "And it will become fine dust over all the land of Egypt, and will become boils breaking out with sores on man and beast through all the land of Egypt."

10 So they took soot from a kiln, and stood before Pharaoh; and Moses threw it toward the sky, and it became boils breaking out with sores on man and beast.

11 And the magicians could not stand before Moses because of the boils, for the boils were on the magicians as well as on all the Egyptians.

9:12
Ex 4:21

12 And the LORD hardened Pharaoh's heart, and he did not listen to them, just as the LORD had spoken to Moses.

⁷Lit., *set a ransom*

h. The hail and fire

13 Then the LORD said to Moses, "Rise up early in the morning and stand before Pharaoh and say to him, 'Thus says the LORD, the God of the Hebrews, "Let My people go, that they may serve Me.

14 "For this time I will send all My plagues on you and your servants and your people, so that you may know that there is no one like Me in all the earth.

15 "For *if by* now I had put forth My hand and struck you and your people with pestilence, you would then have been cut off from the earth.

16 "But, indeed, for this cause I have allowed you to remain, in order to show you My power, and in order to proclaim My name through all the earth.

17 "Still you exalt yourself against My people by not letting them go.

18 "Behold, about this time tomorrow, I will send a very heavy hail, such as has not been *seen* in Egypt from the day it was founded until now.

19 "Now therefore send, bring your livestock and whatever you have in the field to safety. Every man and beast that is found in the field and is not brought home, when the hail comes down on them, will die."' "

20 The one among the servants of Pharaoh who feared the word of the LORD made his servants and his livestock flee into the houses;

21 but he who paid no regard to the word of the LORD left his servants and his livestock in the field.

22 Now the LORD said to Moses, "Stretch out your hand toward the sky, that hail may fall on all the land of Egypt, on man and on beast and on every plant of the field, throughout the land of Egypt."

23 And Moses stretched out his staff toward the sky, and the LORD sent thunder and hail, and fire ran down to the earth. And the LORD rained hail on the land of Egypt.

24 So there was hail, and fire flashing continually in the midst of the hail, very severe, such as had not been in all the land of Egypt since it became a nation.

25 And the hail struck all that was in the field through all the land of Egypt, both man and beast; the hail also struck every plant of the field and shattered every tree of the field.

26 Only in the land of Goshen, where the sons of Israel *were*, there was no hail.

27 Then Pharaoh sent for Moses and Aaron, and said to them, "I have sinned this time; the LORD is the righteous one, and I and my people are the wicked ones.

28 "Make supplication to the LORD, for there has been enough of God's thunder and hail; and I will let you go, and you shall stay no longer."

29 And Moses said to him, "As soon as I go out of the city, I will spread out my hands to the LORD; the thunder will cease, and there will be hail no longer, that you may know that the earth is the LORD'S.

30 "But as for you and your servants, I know that you do not yet fear the LORD God."

31 (Now the flax and the barley were ruined, for the barley was in the ear and the flax was in bud.

32 But the wheat and the spelt were not ruined, for they *ripen* late.)

33 So Moses went out of the city from Pharaoh, and spread out his hands to the LORD; and the thunder and the hail ceased, and rain no longer poured on the earth.

34 But when Pharaoh saw that the rain and the hail and the thunder had ceased, he sinned again and hardened his heart, he and his servants.

35 And Pharaoh's heart was hardened, and he did not let the sons of Israel go, just as the LORD had spoken through Moses.

i. The plague of locusts

10 Then the LORD said to Moses, "Go to Pharaoh, for I have [8]hardened his heart and the heart of his servants, that I may perform these signs of Mine among them,

2 and that you may tell in the hearing of your son, and of your grandson, how I made a mockery of the Egyptians, and how I performed My signs among them; that you may know that I am the LORD."

3 And Moses and Aaron went to Pharaoh and said to him, "Thus says the LORD, the God of the Hebrews, 'How long will you refuse to humble yourself before Me? Let My people go, that they may serve Me.

[8]Lit., *made heavy*

Cross references (margin):

9:13 Ex 8:20
9:14 Ex 8:10
9:15 Ex 3:20
9:16 Rom 9:17
9:18 vv. 23,24
9:20 Prov 13:13
9:22 Rev 16:21
9:23 Gen 19:24; Josh 10:11; Ps 78:47; Is 30:30; Ezek 38:22; Rev 8:7
9:25 v. 19; Ps 78:47; 105:32,33
9:26 Ex 8:22; 9:4, 6; 10:23; 11:7; 12:13
9:27 Ex 8:8; 10:16,17; 2 Chr 12:6; Ps 129:4
9:28 Ex 8:8; 10:17
9:29 1 Kin 8:22; Ps 143:6; Ex 8:22; 19:5; 20:11; Ps 24:1
9:35 Ex 4:21
10:1 Ex 4:21; 7:14
10:2 Ex 12:26,27; 13:8,14,15; Deut 4:9; Ps 44:1; Ex 7:5,15
10:3 James 4:10; 1 Pet 5:6; Ex 4:23

10:4
Rev 9:3
4 'For if you refuse to let My people go, behold, tomorrow I will bring locusts into your territory.

10:5
Ex 9:32;
Joel 1:4; 2:25
5 'And they shall cover the surface of the land, so that no one shall be able to see the land. They shall also eat the rest of what has escaped—what is left to you from the hail—and they shall eat every tree which sprouts for you out of the field.

10:6
Ex 8:3,21
6 'Then your houses shall be filled, and the houses of all your servants and the houses of all the Egyptians, *something* which neither your fathers nor your grandfathers have seen, from the day that they came upon the earth until this day.' " And he turned and went out from Pharaoh.

10:7
Ex 7:5; 8:19;
12:33
7 And Pharaoh's servants said to him, "How long will this man be a snare to us? Let the men go, that they may serve the LORD their God. Do you not realize that Egypt is destroyed?"

10:8
Ex 8:8,25
8 So Moses and Aaron were brought back to Pharaoh, and he said to them, "Go, serve the LORD your God! Who are the ones that are going?"

10:9
Ex 12:37,38;
v. 26; Ex 5:1
9 And Moses said, "We shall go with our young and our old; with our sons and our daughters, with our flocks and our herds we will go, for we must hold a feast to the LORD."

10 Then he said to them, "Thus may the LORD be with you, if ever I let you and your little ones go! Take heed, for evil is in your mind.

10:11
v. 28
11 "Not so! Go now, the men *among you,* and serve the LORD, for that is what you desire." So they were driven out from Pharaoh's presence.

10:12
Ex 7:19;
vv. 4,5
12 Then the LORD said to Moses, "Stretch out your hand over the land of Egypt for the locusts, that they may come up on the land of Egypt, and eat every plant of the land, *even* all that the hail has left."

13 So Moses stretched out his staff over the land of Egypt, and the LORD directed an east wind on the land all that day and all that night; and when it was morning, the east wind brought the locusts.

10:14
Ps 78:46;
105:34;
Joel 2:1-11
14 And the locusts came up over all the land of Egypt and settled in all the territory of Egypt; *they were* very numerous. There had never been so *many* locusts, nor would there be so *many* again.

10:15
v. 5;
Ps 105:35
15 For they covered the surface of the whole land, so that the land was darkened; and they ate every plant of the land and all the fruit of the trees that the hail had left. Thus nothing green was left on tree or plant of the field through all the land of Egypt.

10:16
Ex 9:27
16 Then Pharaoh hurriedly called for Moses and Aaron, and he said, "I have sinned against the LORD your God and against you.

10:17
Ex 8:8,29
17 "Now therefore, please forgive my sin only this once, and make supplication to the LORD your God, that He would only remove this death from me."

18 And he went out from Pharaoh and made supplication to the LORD.

19 So the LORD shifted *the wind* to a very strong west wind which took up the locusts and drove them into the [9]Red Sea; not one locust was left in all the territory of Egypt.

10:20
Ex 4:21;
11:10
20 But the LORD hardened Pharaoh's heart, and he did not let the sons of Israel go.

j. The three days' darkness

10:21
Deut 28:29
21 Then the LORD said to Moses, "Stretch out your hand toward the sky, that there may be darkness over the land of Egypt, even a darkness which may be felt."

10:22
Ps 105:28
22 So Moses stretched out his hand toward the sky, and there was thick darkness in all the land of Egypt for three days.

23 They did not see one another, nor did anyone rise from his place for three days, but all the sons of Israel had light in their dwellings.

10:24
vv. 8,10
24 Then Pharaoh called to Moses, and said, "Go, serve the LORD; only let your flocks and your herds be detained. Even your little ones may go with you."

25 But Moses said, "You must also let us have sacrifices and burnt offerings, that we may sacrifice *them* to the LORD our God.

10:26
v. 9
26 "Therefore, our livestock, too, will go with us; not a hoof will be left behind, for we shall take some of them to serve the LORD our God. And until we arrive there, we ourselves do not know with what we shall serve the LORD."

10:27
v. 20
27 But the LORD hardened Pharaoh's heart, and he was not willing to let them go.

[9]Lit., *Sea of Reeds*

28   Then Pharaoh said to him, "Get away from me! Beware, do not see my face again, for in the day you see my face you shall die!" | 10:28
v. 11

29   And Moses said, "You are right; I shall never see your face again!" | 10:29
Heb 11:27

k. *The death of the first-born*

(1) THE ANNOUNCEMENT BY GOD

11 Now the LORD said to Moses, "One more plague I will bring on Pharaoh and on Egypt; after that he will let you go from here. When he lets you go, he will surely drive you out from here completely. | 11:1
Ex 12:31,33,
39

2   "Speak now in the hearing of the people that each man ask from his neighbor and each woman from her neighbor for articles of silver and articles of gold." | 11:2
Ex 3:22;
12:35,36

3   And the LORD gave the people favor in the sight of the Egyptians. Furthermore, the man Moses *himself* was greatly esteemed in the land of Egypt, *both* in the sight of Pharaoh's servants and in the sight of the people. | 11:3
Ex 3:21;
12:36;
Deut 34:10-12

4   And Moses said, "Thus says the LORD, 'About midnight I am going out into the midst of Egypt, | 11:4
Ex 12:29

5   and all the first-born in the land of Egypt shall die, from the first-born of the Pharaoh who sits on his throne, even to the first-born of the slave girl who is behind the millstones; all the first-born of the cattle as well. | 11:5
Ex 12:12,29;
Ps 78:51;
105:36;
135:8; 136:10

6   'Moreover, there shall be a great cry in all the land of Egypt, such as there has not been *before* and such as shall never be again. | 11:6
Ex 12:30

7   'But against any of the sons of Israel a dog shall not *even* bark, whether against man or beast, that you may understand how the LORD makes a distinction between Egypt and Israel.' | 11:7
Ex 8:22

8   "And all these your servants will come down to me and bow themselves before me, saying, 'Go out, you and all the people who follow you,' and after that I will go out." And he went out from Pharaoh in hot anger. | 11:8
Ex 12:31-33

9   Then the LORD said to Moses, "Pharaoh will not listen to you, so that My wonders will be multiplied in the land of Egypt." | 11:9
Ex 7:3,4

10   And Moses and Aaron performed all these wonders before Pharaoh; yet the LORD hardened Pharaoh's heart, and he did not let the sons of Israel go out of his land. | 11:10
Ex 4:21;
10:20,27

(2) THE INSTITUTION OF THE PASSOVER

12 Now the LORD said to Moses and Aaron in the land of Egypt, |
2   "This month shall be the beginning of months for you; it is to be the first month of the year to you. | *12:2
Ex 13:4;
Deut 16:1

3   "Speak to all the congregation of Israel, saying, 'On the tenth of this month they are each one to take a lamb for themselves, according to their fathers' households, a lamb for each household. |

4   'Now if the household is too small for a lamb, then he and his neighbor nearest to his house are to take one according to the number of persons *in them;* according to what each man should eat, you are to divide the lamb. |

5   'Your lamb shall be an unblemished male a year old; you may take it from the sheep or from the goats. | 12:5
Lev 22:18-20

6   'And you shall keep it until the fourteenth day of the same month, then the whole assembly of the congregation of Israel is to kill it at twilight. | 12:6
Lev 23:5;
Num 9:3;
Deut 16:1,6

7   'Moreover, they shall take some of the blood and put it on the two doorposts and on the lintel of the houses in which they eat it. |

8   'And they shall eat the flesh that *same* night, roasted with fire, and they shall eat it with unleavened bread and bitter herbs. | 12:8
Ex 34:25;
Num 9:11,12;
Deut 16:7

9   'Do not eat any of it raw or boiled at all with water, but rather roasted with fire, *both* its head and its legs along with its entrails. |

10   'And you shall not leave any of it over until morning, but whatever is left of it until morning, you shall burn with fire. | 12:10
Ex 23:18;
34:25

11   'Now you shall eat it in this manner: *with* your loins girded, your sandals on | *12:11
v. 27

12:2 *first month of the year.* Nisan, the latter part of March and the first of April.

12:3 The lamb had to be without blemish. It was to be slain and its blood applied. It was offered as a substitute. Christ met all of these requirements; He was the perfect Lamb of God (John 1:29), who delivered His people from the tyranny of sin, a greater oppressor than Pharaoh.

12:11 On that Passover night the angel of death had respect

only for those households over whose doors the blood had been sprinkled (12:13). The works and characters of the individual believers had nothing to do with its saving benefit. It was the blood alone that authorized the death angel to pass over. So Christ is the perfect sacrifice, slain and offered. When His blood is personally applied by faith, the sinner is declared righteous and his sins are forgiven (Rom. 3:22; 1 Pet. 1:18,19).

your feet, and your staff in your hand; and you shall eat it in haste—it is the LORD's Passover.

12:12
Ex 11:4,5;
Num 33:4

12 'For I will go through the land of Egypt on that night, and will strike down all the first-born in the land of Egypt, both man and beast; and against all the gods of Egypt I will execute judgments—I am the LORD.

13 'And the blood shall be a sign for you on the houses where you live; and when I see the blood I will pass over you, and no plague will befall you to destroy *you* when I strike the land of Egypt.

12:14
v. 6; Ex 13:9;
v. 17;
Ex 13:10

14 'Now this day will be a memorial to you, and you shall celebrate it *as* a feast to the LORD; throughout your generations you are to celebrate it *as* a permanent ordinance.

12:15
Ex 23:15;
34:18;
Lev 23:5,6;
Deut 16:3;
v. 19;
Num 9:13

15 'Seven days you shall eat unleavened bread, but on the first day you shall remove leaven from your houses; for whoever eats anything leavened from the first day until the seventh day, that person shall be cut off from Israel.

12:16
Lev 23:7,8

16 'And on the first day you shall have a holy assembly, and *another* holy assembly on the seventh day; no work at all shall be done on them, except what must be eaten by every person, that alone may be prepared by you.

12:17
v. 41; Ex 13:3

17 'You shall also observe the *Feast of* Unleavened Bread, for on this very day I brought your hosts out of the land of Egypt; therefore you shall observe this day throughout your generations as a permanent ordinance.

12:18
v. 2;
Lev 23:5-8;
Num 28:16-25

18 'In the first *month*, on the fourteenth day of the month at evening, you shall eat unleavened bread, until the twenty-first day of the month at evening.

12:19
v. 15

19 'Seven days there shall be no leaven found in your houses; for whoever eats what is leavened, that person shall be cut off from the congregation of Israel, whether *he is* an alien or a native of the land.

20 'You shall not eat anything leavened; in all your dwellings you shall eat unleavened bread.' "

12:21
Heb 11:28;
v. 11;
Num 9:4

21 Then Moses called for all the elders of Israel, and said to them, "Go and take for yourselves lambs according to your families, and slay the Passover *lamb*.

12:22
v. 7

22 "And you shall take a bunch of hyssop and dip it in the blood which is in the basin, and apply some of the blood that is in the basin to the lintel and the two doorposts; and none of you shall go outside the door of his house until morning.

12:23
vv. 12,13

23 "For the LORD will pass through to smite the Egyptians; and when He sees the blood on the lintel and on the two doorposts, the LORD will pass over the door and will not allow the destroyer to come in to your houses to smite *you*.

12:24
Ex 13:5,10

24 "And you shall observe this event as an ordinance for you and your children forever.

25 "And it will come about when you enter the land which the LORD will give you, as He has promised, that you shall observe this rite.

12:26
Ex 13:14,15;
Josh 4:6

26 "And it will come about when your children will say to you, 'What does this rite mean to you?'

12:27
v. 11; Ex 4:31

27 that you shall say, 'It is a Passover sacrifice to the LORD who passed over the houses of the sons of Israel in Egypt when He smote the Egyptians, but spared our homes.' " And the people bowed low and worshiped.

28 Then the sons of Israel went and did *so;* just as the LORD had commanded Moses and Aaron, so they did.

(3) THE FIRST-BORN KILLED

12:29
Ex 11:4;
4:23; 9:6;
Ps 78:51;
105:36

29 Now it came about at midnight that the LORD struck all the first-born in the land of Egypt, from the first-born of Pharaoh who sat on his throne to the first-born of the captive who was in the dungeon, and all the first-born of cattle.

12:30
Ex 11:6

30 And Pharaoh arose in the night, he and all his servants and all the Egyptians; and there was a great cry in Egypt, for there was no home where there was not someone dead.

12:31
Ex 8:8,25

31 Then he called for Moses and Aaron at night and said, "Rise up, get out from among my people, both you and the sons of Israel; and go, worship the LORD, as you have said.

12:32
Ex 10:9,26

32 "Take both your flocks and your herds, as you have said, and go, and bless me also."

12:33
v. 39;
Ex 10:7;
11:1;
Ps 105:38

33 And the Egyptians urged the people, to send them out of the land in haste, for they said, "We shall all be dead."

34 So the people took their dough before it was leavened, *with* their kneading bowls bound up in the clothes on their shoulders.

35   Now the sons of Israel had done according to the word of Moses, for they had requested from the Egyptians articles of silver and articles of gold, and clothing;

36   and the LORD had given the people favor in the sight of the Egyptians, so that they let them have their request. Thus they plundered the Egyptians.

D. The exodus begun

1. The unleavened bread

37   Now the sons of Israel journeyed from Rameses to Succoth, about six hundred thousand men on foot, aside from children.

38   And a mixed multitude also went up with them, along with flocks and herds, a very large number of livestock.

39   And they baked the dough which they had brought out of Egypt into cakes of unleavened bread. For it had not become leavened, since they were driven out of Egypt and could not delay, nor had they prepared any provisions for themselves.

40   Now the time that the sons of Israel lived in Egypt was four hundred and thirty years.

41   And it came about at the end of four hundred and thirty years, to the very day, that all the hosts of the LORD went out from the land of Egypt.

42   It is a night to be observed for the LORD for having brought them out from the land of Egypt; this night is for the LORD, to be observed by all the sons of Israel throughout their generations.

2. The law of the Passover

43   And the LORD said to Moses and Aaron, "This is the ordinance of the Passover: no [10]foreigner is to eat of it;

44   but every man's slave purchased with money, after you have circumcised him, then he may eat of it.

45   "A sojourner or a hired servant shall not eat of it.

46   "It is to be eaten in a single house; you are not to bring forth any of the flesh outside of the house, nor are you to break any bone of it.

47   "All the congregation of Israel are to celebrate this.

48   "But if a stranger sojourns with you, and celebrates the Passover to the LORD, let all his males be circumcised, and then let him come near to celebrate it; and he shall be like a native of the land. But no uncircumcised person may eat of it.

49   "The same law shall apply to the native as to the stranger who sojourns among you."

50   Then all the sons of Israel did so; they did just as the LORD had commanded Moses and Aaron.

51   And it came about on that same day that the LORD brought the sons of Israel out of the land of Egypt by their hosts.

13   Then the LORD spoke to Moses, saying,
2   "Sanctify to Me every first-born, the first offspring of every womb among the sons of Israel, both of man and beast; it belongs to Me."

3. The speech of Moses

3   And Moses said to the people, "Remember this day in which you went out from Egypt, from the house of slavery; for by a powerful hand the LORD brought you out from this place. And nothing leavened shall be eaten.

4   "On this day in the month of Abib, you are about to go forth.

5   "And it shall be when the LORD brings you to the land of the Canaanite, the Hittite, the Amorite, the Hivite and the Jebusite, which He swore to your fathers to give you, a land flowing with milk and honey, that you shall observe this rite in this month.

6   "For seven days you shall eat unleavened bread, and on the seventh day there shall be a feast to the LORD.

7   "Unleavened bread shall be eaten throughout the seven days; and nothing leavened shall be seen among you, nor shall any leaven be seen among you in all your borders.

[10]Lit., *son of a stranger*

12:35
Ex 3:21,22;
11:2,3

12:36
Ex 3:22

12:37
Num 33:3,4;
Ex 38:26;
Num 1:46;
11:21

12:38
Num 11:4;
Ex 17:3

12:39
vv. 31-33;
Ex 11:1

12:40
Gen 15:13;
Acts 7:6;
Gal 3:17

12:41
v. 17; Ex 3:8,
10; 6:6

12:42
Ex 13:10;
Deut 16:1

12:43
vv. 11,48

12:44
Gen 17:12,13;
Lev 22:11

12:46
Num 9:12;
John 19:33,36

12:47
Num 9:13,14

12:49
Num 15:15,
16; Gal 3:28

12:51
v. 41

13:2
vv. 12,13,15;
Ex 22:29;
Luke 2:23

13:3
Ex 3:20; 6:1;
12:19

13:5
Ex 3:8;
12:25,26

13:6
Ex 12:15-20

13:8
v. 14; Ex 10:2

8 "And you shall tell your son on that day, saying, 'It is because of what the LORD did for me when I came out of Egypt.'

13:9
v. 16;
Ex 12:14;
Deut 6:8;
11:18

9 "And it shall serve as a sign to you on your hand, and as a reminder on your forehead, that the law of the LORD may be in your mouth; for with a powerful hand the LORD brought you out of Egypt.

13:10
Ex 12:24,25

10 "Therefore, you shall keep this ordinance at its appointed time from year to year.

11 "Now it shall come about when the LORD brings you to the land of the Canaanite, as He swore to you and to your fathers, and gives it to you,

13:12
v. 2;
Ex 22:29;
34:19
13:13
Ex 34:20;
Num 18:15,
16

12 that you shall devote to the LORD the first offspring of every womb, and the first offspring of every beast that you own; the males belong to the LORD.

13 "But every first offspring of a donkey you shall redeem with a lamb, but if you do not redeem it, then you shall break its neck; and every first-born of man among your sons you shall redeem.

13:14
Ex 12:26,27;
Deut 6:20;
vv. 3,9

14 "And it shall be when your son asks you in time to come, saying, 'What is this?' then you shall say to him, 'With a powerful hand the LORD brought us out of Egypt, from the house of slavery.

13:15
Ex 12:29

15 'And it came about, when Pharaoh was stubborn about letting us go, that the LORD killed every first-born in the land of Egypt, both the first-born of man and the first-born of beast. Therefore, I sacrifice to the LORD the males, the first offspring of every womb, but every first-born of my sons I redeem.'

13:16
v. 9

16 "So it shall serve as a sign on your hand, and as phylacteries on your forehead, for with a powerful hand the LORD brought us out of Egypt."

4. The pillar of cloud and of fire

13:17
Ex 14:11,12;
Num 14:1-4;
Deut 17:16

17 Now it came about when Pharaoh had let the people go, that God did not lead them by the way of the land of the Philistines, even though it was near; for God said, "Lest the people change their minds when they see war, and they return to Egypt."

18 Hence God led the people around by the way of the wilderness to the Red Sea; and the sons of Israel went up in martial array from the land of Egypt.

13:19
Gen 50:25,26;
Josh 24:32;
Acts 7:16

19 And Moses took the bones of Joseph with him, for he had made the sons of Israel solemnly swear, saying, "God shall surely take care of you; and you shall carry my bones from here with you."

13:20
Num 33:6-8

20 Then they set out from Succoth and camped in Etham on the edge of the wilderness.

*13:21f
Ex 14:19,24;
33:9,10;
Ps 78:14;
105:39;
1 Cor 10:1

21 And the LORD was going before them in a pillar of cloud by day to lead them on the way, and in a pillar of fire by night to give them light, that they might travel by day and by night.

22 He did not take away the pillar of cloud by day, nor the pillar of fire by night, from before the people.

5. Crossing the Red Sea

14:2
Num 33:7,8

14 Now the LORD spoke to Moses, saying, 2 "Tell the sons of Israel to turn back and camp before Pi-hahiroth, between Migdol and the sea; you shall camp in front of Baal-zephon, opposite it, by the sea.

3 "For Pharaoh will say of the sons of Israel, 'They are wandering aimlessly in the land; the wilderness has shut them in.'

14:4
v. 17;
Ex 4:21; 7:5

4 "Thus I will harden Pharaoh's heart, and he will chase after them; and I will be honored through Pharaoh and all his army, and the Egyptians will know that I am the LORD." And they did so.

5 When the king of Egypt was told that the people had fled, Pharaoh and his servants had a change of heart toward the people, and they said, "What is this we have done, that we have let Israel go from serving us?"

6 So he made his chariot ready and took his people with him;

13:21,22 The cloud of glory, which later became known as the *Shekinah* ("abiding," or "dwelling") was called by various names in the Old Testament: *My glory (kabod)* (29:43); *the pillar of cloud* (33:9,10); *the cloud* (34:5); *the cloud of the LORD* (Num. 10:34); *My presence* (Ex. 33:14,15). The purposes of the *Shekinah* were various: (1) to guide Israel (13:21; Neh. 9:19); (2) to control the movements of Israel in the wilderness until they were settled in the land (40:36,37;

Num. 9:17–23); and (3) to defend Israel (14:19; Ps. 105:39). The cloud of glory appeared at other times both in the Old and New Testaments. Of particular significance is its appearance at the transfiguration (Matt. 17:5) and the ascension (Acts 1:9). At His second advent Christ will come *in a cloud with power and great glory* (Luke 21:27; cf. Acts 1:11).
14:5 *had fled*, i.e., permitted to leave.

7   and he took six hundred select chariots, and all the *other* chariots of Egypt with officers over all of them.

8   And the LORD hardened the heart of Pharaoh, king of Egypt, and he chased after the sons of Israel as the sons of Israel were going out boldly.

9   Then the Egyptians chased after them *with* all the horses *and* chariots of Pharaoh, his horsemen and his army, and they overtook them camping by the sea, beside Pi-hahiroth, in front of Baal-zephon.

10   And as Pharaoh drew near, the sons of Israel looked, and behold, the Egyptians were marching after them, and they became very frightened; so the sons of Israel cried out to the LORD.

11   Then they said to Moses, "Is it because there were no graves in Egypt that you have taken us away to die in the wilderness? Why have you dealt with us in this way, bringing us out of Egypt?

12   "Is this not the word that we spoke to you in Egypt, saying, 'Leave us alone that we may serve the Egyptians'? For it would have been better for us to serve the Egyptians than to die in the wilderness."

13   But Moses said to the people, "Do not fear! Stand by and see the salvation of the LORD which He will accomplish for you today; for the Egyptians whom you have seen today, you will never see them again forever.

14   "The LORD will fight for you while you keep silent."

15   Then the LORD said to Moses, "Why are you crying out to Me? Tell the sons of Israel to go forward.

16   "And as for you, lift up your staff and stretch out your hand over the sea and divide it, and the sons of Israel shall go through the midst of the sea on dry land.

17   "And as for Me, behold, I will harden the hearts of the Egyptians so that they will go in after them; and I will be honored through Pharaoh and all his army, through his chariots and his horsemen.

18   "Then the Egyptians will know that I am the LORD, when I am honored through Pharaoh, through his chariots and his horsemen."

19   And the angel of God, who had been going before the camp of Israel, moved and went behind them; and the pillar of cloud moved from before them and stood behind them.

20   So it came between the camp of Egypt and the camp of Israel; and there was the cloud along with the darkness, yet it gave light at night. Thus the one did not come near the other all night.

21   Then Moses stretched out his hand over the sea; and the LORD swept the sea *back* by a strong east wind all night, and turned the sea into dry land, so the waters were divided.

22   And the sons of Israel went through the midst of the sea on the dry land, and the waters *were like* a wall to them on their right hand and on their left.

23   Then the Egyptians took up the pursuit, and all Pharaoh's horses, his chariots and his horsemen went in after them into the midst of the sea.

24   And it came about at the morning watch, that the LORD looked down on the army of the Egyptians through the pillar of fire and cloud and brought the army of the Egyptians into confusion.

25   And He caused their chariot wheels to swerve, and He made them drive with difficulty; so the Egyptians said, "Let us flee from Israel, for the LORD is fighting for them against the Egyptians."

26   Then the LORD said to Moses, "Stretch out your hand over the sea so that the waters may come back over the Egyptians, over their chariots and their horsemen."

27   So Moses stretched out his hand over the sea, and the sea returned to its normal state at daybreak, while the Egyptians were fleeing right into it; then the LORD overthrew the Egyptians in the midst of the sea.

28   And the waters returned and covered the chariots and the horsemen, even

14:8 v. 4; Num 33:3; Acts 13:17 ***14:9** Ex 15:9

14:10 Neh 9:9

14:11 Ps 106:7,8

*14:13 Gen 15:1; v. 30; Ex 15:2

14:14 Ex 15:3; Deut 1:30; 3:22; Is 30:15

14:16 Ex 4:17; Num 20:8,9, 11; Is 10:26 **14:17** v. 4

14:18 v. 25

14:19 Ex 13:21,22

14:21 v. 16; Ps 106:9; 114:3,5; Is 63:12,13 **14:22** Ex 15:19; Neh 9:11; Heb 11:29

14:24 Ex 13:21

14:25 vv. 4,18

14:27 Ex 15:1,7 **14:28** Ps 78:53; 106:11

14:9 *sea.* The fortress towns named indicate that the "Red Sea" that the Israelites crossed was to the north of the Red Sea proper. The name would be more accurately translated "Reed Sea."
14:13 Almost from the beginning of the exodus, the children of Israel manifested a complaining spirit. They allowed circumstances to move them. It is true that the Red Sea was before them and the pharaoh and his soldiers behind them, but they forgot God who was above them. Moses displayed his great faith in the delivering power of God, but even he failed to see how that power would operate. He told Israel to stand still and watch God intervene on their behalf. But then God told them to move forward in faith and against the waters of the sea. Moses used his rod; God parted the waters *by a strong east wind all night* (v. 21); and the children of Israel moved forward dry-shod. God does lead His children forward against apparently impassable barriers, opening doors previously shut fast.

Pharaoh's entire army that had gone into the sea after them; not even one of them remained.

14:29
Ex 15:19;
Neh 9:11;
Heb 11:29

29   But the sons of Israel walked on dry land through the midst of the sea, and the waters *were like* a wall to them on their right hand and on their left.

14:30
Ps 106:8

30   Thus the LORD saved Israel that day from the hand of the Egyptians, and Israel saw the Egyptians dead on the seashore.

14:31
Ps 106:12

31   And when Israel saw the great power which the LORD had used against the Egyptians, the people feared the LORD, and they believed in the LORD and in His servant Moses.

6. *The song of Moses*

*15:1
Ps 106:12;
Rev 15:3

15   Then Moses and the sons of Israel sang this song to the LORD, and said,
"I will sing to the LORD, for He is highly exalted;
The horse and its rider He has hurled into the sea.

15:2
Ps 59:17;
Ex 3:15,16

2   "The LORD is my strength and song,
And He has become my salvation;
This is my God, and I will praise Him;
My father's God, and I will extol Him.

15:3
Ps 24:8;
83:18

3   "The LORD is a warrior;
The LORD is His name.

15:4
Ex 14:6,7,17,
28

4   "Pharaoh's chariots and his army He has cast into the sea;
And the choicest of his officers are drowned in the [11]Red Sea.

15:5
v. 10;
Neh 9:11

5   "The deeps cover them;
They went down into the depths like a stone.

15:6
Ps 118:15

6   "Thy right hand, O LORD, is majestic in power,
Thy right hand, O LORD, shatters the enemy.

15:7
Ex 14:27;
Ps 78:49,50

7   "And in the greatness of Thine excellence Thou dost overthrow those
who rise up against Thee;
Thou dost send forth Thy burning anger, *and* it consumes them as
chaff.

15:8
Ex 14:22,29;
Ps 78:13

8   "And at the blast of Thy nostrils the waters were piled up,
The flowing waters stood up like a heap;
The deeps were congealed in the heart of the sea.

15:9
Ex 14:5

9   "The enemy said, 'I will pursue, I will overtake, I will divide the
spoil;
My desire shall be gratified against them;
I will draw out my sword, my hand shall destroy them.'

15:10
Ex 14:28

10   "Thou didst blow with Thy wind, the sea covered them;
They sank like lead in the mighty waters.

*15:11
Ex 8:10;
Deut 3:24;
Is 6:3;
Rev 4:8;
Ps 22:23;
72:18

11   "Who is like Thee among the gods, O LORD?
Who is like Thee, majestic in holiness,
Awesome in praises, working wonders?

12   "Thou didst stretch out Thy right hand,
The earth swallowed them.

15:13
Neh 9:12;
Ps 77:15;
78:54

13   "In Thy lovingkindness Thou hast led the people whom Thou hast
redeemed;
In Thy strength Thou hast guided *them* to Thy holy habitation.

15:14
Deut 2:25;
Hab 3:7

14   "The peoples have heard, they tremble;
Anguish has gripped the inhabitants of Philistia.

15:15
Gen 36:15;
Num 22:3;
Josh 5:1

15   "Then the chiefs of Edom were dismayed;
The leaders of Moab, trembling grips them;
All the inhabitants of Canaan have melted away.

15:16
Ex 23:27;
1 Sam 25:37;
Ps 74:2

16   "Terror and dread fall upon them;
By the greatness of Thine arm they are motionless as stone;
Until Thy people pass over, O LORD,
Until the people pass over whom Thou hast purchased.

[11]Lit., *Sea of Reeds*

15:1 Singing is an expression of love and thanksgiving, encouraged in Scripture with such phrases as *spiritual songs, singing . . . melody* (Eph. 5:19) and *song of the Lamb* (Rev. 15:3).
15:11 One of the chief attributes of God is His holiness, that is, His complete separation from the finite, from frail-

ty, and from all that is sinful or impure. This holiness of the LORD is incomparable (1 Sam. 2:2). It may be seen in His character (Ps. 22:3), in His name (Is. 57:15), and in His words (Jer. 23:9). We are to praise Him for His holiness (Ps. 30:4) and imitate it (Lev. 11:44; 1 Pet. 1:15,16).

17   "Thou wilt bring them and plant them in the mountain of Thine
            inheritance,
        The place, O LORD, which Thou hast made for Thy dwelling,
        The sanctuary, O Lord, which Thy hands have established."
	15:17
	Ps 44:2;
	78:54

18 "The LORD shall reign forever and ever."	**15:18** Ps 10:16

7. *The song of Miriam*

19 For the horses of Pharaoh with his chariots and his horsemen went into the sea, and the LORD brought back the waters of the sea on them; but the sons of Israel walked on dry land through the midst of the sea.	**15:19** Ex 14:23,28
20 And Miriam the prophetess, Aaron's sister, took the timbrel in her hand, and all the women went out after her with timbrels and with dancing.	**15:20** Judg 4:4; Num 26:59; 1 Sam 18:6;

21   And Miriam answered them,
        "Sing to the LORD, for He is highly exalted;
        The horse and his rider He has hurled into the sea."
	Ps 30:11;
	150:4
	15:21
	v. 1

II. *The journey to Sinai (15:22–18:27)*

A. *The bitter waters of Marah made sweet*

22 Then Moses led Israel from the Red Sea, and they went out into the wilderness of Shur; and they went three days in the wilderness and found no water.	***15:22** Ps 77:20; Num 33:8
23 And when they came to Marah, they could not drink the waters of Marah, for they were bitter; therefore it was named [12]Marah.	***15:23** Num 33:8
24 So the people grumbled at Moses, saying, "What shall we drink?"	**15:24** Ex 14:11;
25 Then he cried out to the LORD, and the LORD showed him a tree; and he threw *it* into the waters, and the waters became sweet. There He made for them a statute and regulation, and there He tested them.	Ps 106:13 **15:25** Ex 14:10; Ps 50:15
26 And He said, "If you will give earnest heed to the voice of the LORD your God, and do what is right in His sight, and give ear to His commandments, and keep all His statutes, I will put none of the diseases on you which I have put on the Egyptians; for I, the LORD, am your healer."	**15:26** Deut 7:12; 28:27
27 Then they came to Elim where there *were* twelve springs of water and seventy date palms, and they camped there beside the waters.	**15:27** Num 33:9,10

B. *The manna and the quail*

1. *The murmuring of the Israelites*

16 Then they set out from Elim, and all the congregation of the sons of Israel came to the wilderness of Sin, which is between Elim and Sinai, on the fifteenth day of the second month after their departure from the land of Egypt.	**16:1** Num 33:11, 12
2 And the whole congregation of the sons of Israel grumbled against Moses and Aaron in the wilderness.	***16:2** Ex 14:11; 1 Cor 10:10
3 And the sons of Israel said to them, "Would that we had died by the LORD's hand in the land of Egypt, when we sat by the pots of meat, when we ate bread to the full; for you have brought us out into this wilderness to kill this whole assembly with hunger."	**16:3** Ex 17:3; Num 11:4,5

2. *God promises bread and meat*

4 Then the LORD said to Moses, "Behold, I will rain bread from heaven for you; and the people shall go out and gather a day's portion every day, that I may test them, whether or not they will walk in My [13]instruction.	**16:4** John 6:31; 1 Cor 10:3; Deut 8:2,16
5 "And it will come about on the sixth day, when they prepare what they bring in, it will be twice as much as they gather daily."	**16:5** v. 22
6 So Moses and Aaron said to all the sons of Israel, "At evening you will know that the LORD has brought you out of the land of Egypt;	
7 and in the morning you will see the glory of the LORD, for He hears your	**16:7** v. 12; Num 14:27; 16:11

[12]I.e., bitterness   [13]Or, *law*

15:22 This was the end of the exodus.
15:23 The bitter waters of Marah provide a spiritual lesson for believers. The pathway of obedience may lead to adversity and trouble that are not of the believer's devising nor a consequence of his disobedience or sin. This was the case at Marah. But here God had an opportunity to show His

mighty power to deliver, and to put His children's faith to the test that it might be strengthened by this experience.
16:2 *congregation . . . grumbled.* This was the recurring sin of the Israelites—complaining against God. It sprang from unbelief, from distrust of God.

grumblings against the LORD; and what are we, that you grumble against us?"

8   And Moses said, *"This will happen* when the LORD gives you meat to eat in the evening, and bread to the full in the morning; for the LORD hears your grumblings which you grumble against Him. And what are we? Your grumblings are not against us but against the LORD."

16:9
Num 16:16

9   Then Moses said to Aaron, "Say to all the congregation of the sons of Israel, 'Come near before the LORD, for He has heard your grumblings.'"

16:10
v. 7;
Num 16:19

10   And it came about as Aaron spoke to the whole congregation of the sons of Israel, that they looked toward the wilderness, and behold, the glory of the LORD appeared in the cloud.

11   And the LORD spoke to Moses, saying,

12   "I have heard the grumblings of the sons of Israel; speak to them, saying, 'At twilight you shall eat meat, and in the morning you shall be filled with bread; and you shall know that I am the LORD your God.'"

3. *God sends quail and gives bread*

16:13
Num 11:31;
Ps 78:27,28;
105:40
16:14
Num 11:7-9;
v. 31
*16:15
v. 4

13   So it came about at evening that the quails came up and covered the camp, and in the morning there was a layer of dew around the camp.

14   When the layer of dew evaporated, behold, on the surface of the wilderness there was a fine flake-like thing, fine as the frost on the ground.

15   When the sons of Israel saw *it*, they said to one another, "What is it?" For they did not know what it was. And Moses said to them, "It is the bread which the LORD has given you to eat.

16   "This is what the LORD has commanded, 'Gather of it every man as much as he should eat; you shall take an omer apiece according to the number of persons each of you has in his tent.'"

17   And the sons of Israel did so, and *some* gathered much and *some* little.

16:18
2 Cor 8:15

18   When they measured it with an omer, he who had gathered much had no excess, and he who had gathered little had no lack; every man gathered as much as he should eat.

16:19
v. 23;
Ex 12:10;
23:18

19   And Moses said to them, "Let no man leave any of it until morning."

20   But they did not listen to Moses, and some left part of it until morning, and it bred worms and became foul; and Moses was angry with them.

21   And they gathered it morning by morning, every man as much as he should eat; but when the sun grew hot, it would melt.

4. *The Sabbath commandment*

16:22
v. 5; Ex 34:31

22   Now it came about on the sixth day they gathered twice as much bread, two omers for each one. When all the leaders of the congregation came and told Moses,

*16:23ff
Ex 20:8;
23:12

23   then he said to them, "This is what the LORD meant: Tomorrow is a sabbath observance, a holy sabbath to the LORD. Bake what you will bake and boil what you will boil, and all that is left over put aside to be kept until morning."

*16:24
v. 20

24   So they put it aside until morning, as Moses had ordered, and it did not become foul, nor was there any worm in it.

25   And Moses said, "Eat it today, for today is a sabbath to the LORD; today you will not find it in the field.

26   "Six days you shall gather it, but on the seventh day, *the* sabbath, there will be none."

27   And it came about on the seventh day that some of the people went out to gather, but they found none.

16:28
Ps 78:10

28   Then the LORD said to Moses, "How long do you refuse to keep My commandments and My [14]instructions?

29   "See, the LORD has given you the sabbath; therefore He gives you bread for two days on the sixth day. Remain every man in his place; let no man go out of his place on the seventh day."

30   So the people rested on the seventh day.

[14]Or, *laws*

16:15 The bread was a free gift from above; it came daily in sufficient quantity for the needs of each day; it was life-giving and sustained the eater; and there was enough of it for all who wished to partake of it by appropriation. Christ (the bread that came down from heaven) is the One from whom the type is taken. The fulfillment far exceeds the type itself. (See John 6:30-41.)

16:23-26 These verses indicate that the idea of the Sabbath existed before the commandment of 20:8-11 and that the Sabbath itself had been observed.

5. An omer of manna kept for a memorial

31 And the house of Israel named it manna, and it was like coriander seed, white; and its taste was like wafers with honey.

32 Then Moses said, "This is what the LORD has commanded, 'Let an omerful of it be kept throughout your generations, that they may see the bread that I fed you in the wilderness, when I brought you out of the land of Egypt.'"

33 And Moses said to Aaron, "Take a jar and put an omerful of manna in it, and place it before the LORD, to be kept throughout your generations."

34 As the LORD commanded Moses, so Aaron placed it before the Testimony, to be kept.

35 And the sons of Israel ate the manna forty years, until they came to an inhabited land; they ate the manna until they came to the border of the land of Canaan.

36 (Now an omer is a tenth of an ephah.)

C. Water from the smitten rock at Rephidim

17 Then all the congregation of the sons of Israel journeyed by stages from the wilderness of Sin, according to the command of the LORD, and camped at Rephidim, and there was no water for the people to drink.

2 Therefore the people quarreled with Moses and said, "Give us water that we may drink." And Moses said to them, "Why do you quarrel with me? Why do you test the LORD?"

3 But the people thirsted there for water; and they grumbled against Moses and said, "Why, now, have you brought us up from Egypt, to kill us and our children and our livestock with thirst?"

4 So Moses cried out to the LORD, saying, "What shall I do to this people? A little more and they will stone me."

5 Then the LORD said to Moses, "Pass before the people and take with you some of the elders of Israel; and take in your hand your staff with which you struck the Nile, and go.

6 "Behold, I will stand before you there on the rock at Horeb; and you shall strike the rock, and water will come out of it, that the people may drink." And Moses did so in the sight of the elders of Israel.

7 And he named the place [15]Massah and [16]Meribah because of the quarrel of the sons of Israel, and because they tested the LORD, saying, "Is the LORD among us, or not?"

D. The defeat of the Amalekites

8 Then Amalek came and fought against Israel at Rephidim.

9 So Moses said to Joshua, "Choose men for us, and go out, fight against Amalek. Tomorrow I will station myself on the top of the hill with the staff of God in my hand."

10 And Joshua did as Moses told him, and fought against Amalek; and Moses, Aaron, and Hur went up to the top of the hill.

11 So it came about when Moses held his hand up, that Israel prevailed, and when he let his hand down, Amalek prevailed.

12 But Moses' hands were heavy. Then they took a stone and put it under him, and he sat on it; and Aaron and Hur supported his hands, one on one side and one on the other. Thus his hands were steady until the sun set.

13 So Joshua overwhelmed Amalek and his people with the edge of the sword.

14 Then the LORD said to Moses, "Write this in a book as a memorial, and recite it to Joshua, that I will utterly blot out the memory of Amalek from under heaven."

15 And Moses built an altar, and named it The LORD is My Banner;

---

[15]I.e., test   [16]I.e., quarrel

16:31 Num 11:6-9
16:33 Heb 9:4
*16:34 Ex 25:16,21
16:35 Josh 5:12; Neh 9:20,21
17:1 Ex 16:1
17:2 Num 20:3; Deut 6:16; 1 Cor 10:9
17:3 Ex 16:2,3
17:4 Ex 14:15; Num 14:10; 1 Sam 30:6
17:5 Ex 3:16,18; 7:20
*17:6 Num 20:10; Ps 114:8; 1 Cor 10:4
17:7 Ps 81:7
*17:8 Num 24:20; Deut 25:17-19
*17:9 Ex 4:20
17:14 Ex 34:27; Num 24:20; Deut 29:19

16:34 *the Testimony,* a name for the ark.
17:6 The rock spoken of here is a type of Christ (1 Cor. 10:4). Just as the life-giving water flowed from the rock, so eternal life flows from the Rock Christ Jesus. And as the water was there for all who appropriated it, so is salvation available for all who lay hold of it by faith (John 1:12). As

thirst is quenched by water, so spiritual thirst is satisfied forever by faith in Christ (John 4:14). (See Num. 20:8.)
17:8 *Amalek,* a nomadic tribe of the Sinai Peninsula and the Negev that resisted the Israelites as intruders.
17:9 *Joshua,* first mentioned here, was probably chosen to assist Moses soon after leaving Egypt.

16   and he said, "The LORD has sworn; the LORD will have war against Amalek from generation to generation."

E. The visit of Jethro, Moses' father-in-law

1. Jethro's advent: the burnt offering and breaking of bread

18 Now Jethro, the priest of Midian, Moses' father-in-law, heard of all that God had done for Moses and for Israel His people, how the LORD had brought Israel out of Egypt.

2   And Jethro, Moses' father-in-law, took Moses' wife Zipporah, after he had sent her away,

3   and her two sons, of whom one was named Gershom, for he said, "I have been a sojourner in a foreign land."

4   And the other was named Eliezer, for *he said*, "The God of my father was my help, and delivered me from the sword of Pharaoh."

5   Then Jethro, Moses' father-in-law, came with his sons and his wife to Moses in the wilderness where he was camped, at the mount of God.

6   And he sent word to Moses, "I, your father-in-law Jethro, am coming to you with your wife and her two sons with her."

7   Then Moses went out to meet his father-in-law, and he bowed down and kissed him; and they asked each other of their welfare, and went into the tent.

8   And Moses told his father-in-law all that the LORD had done to Pharaoh and to the Egyptians for Israel's sake, all the hardship that had befallen them on the journey, and *how* the LORD had delivered them.

9   And Jethro rejoiced over all the goodness which the LORD had done to Israel, in delivering them from the hand of the Egyptians.

10   So Jethro said, "Blessed be the LORD who delivered you from the hand of the Egyptians and from the hand of Pharaoh, *and* who delivered the people from under the hand of the Egyptians.

11   "Now I know that the LORD is greater than all the gods; indeed, it was proven when they dealt proudly against the people."

12   Then Jethro, Moses' father-in-law, took a burnt offering and sacrifices for God, and Aaron came with all the elders of Israel to eat a meal with Moses' father-in-law before God.

2. The selection of judges: the departure of Jethro

13   And it came about the next day that Moses sat to judge the people, and the people stood about Moses from the morning until the evening.

14   Now when Moses' father-in-law saw all that he was doing for the people, he said, "What is this thing that you are doing for the people? Why do you alone sit *as judge* and all the people stand about you from morning until evening?"

15   And Moses said to his father-in-law, "Because the people come to me to inquire of God.

16   "When they have a dispute, it comes to me, and I judge between a man and his neighbor, and make known the statutes of God and His laws."

17   And Moses' father-in-law said to him, "The thing that you are doing is not good.

18   "You will surely wear out, both yourself and these people who are with you, for the task is too heavy for you; you cannot do it alone.

19   "Now listen to me: I shall give you counsel, and God be with you. You be the people's representative before God, and you bring the disputes to God,

20   then teach them the statutes and the laws, and make known to them the way in which they are to walk, and the work they are to do.

21   "Furthermore, you shall select out of all the people able men who fear God, men of truth, those who hate dishonest gain; and you shall place *these* over them, *as* leaders of thousands, of hundreds, of fifties and of tens.

22   "And let them judge the people at all times; and let it be that every major

Marginal references:
- *18:1 Ex 2:16; 3:1
- 18:2 Ex 4:25
- 18:3 Acts 7:29; Ex 2:22
- 18:5 Ex 3:1,12
- 18:7 Gen 43:26-28; Ex 4:27
- 18:8 Ps 81:7
- 18:10 Ps 68:19,20
- 18:11 Ex 12:12; 15:11; 1 Sam 2:3
- 18:15 Num 9:8; Deut 17:8-13
- 18:18 Num 11:14, 17
- 18:19 Ex 3:12; Num 27:5
- 18:20 Deut 1:18
- *18:21ff v. 25; Deut 1:13,15

18:1 Jethro, Moses' father-in-law, is called *the priest of Midian*. In v. 10 he blessed the LORD, in 12 he offered *a burnt offering and sacrifices*, and in 17ff. he advised Moses.
18:21ff. Jethro's sound counsel to Moses was blessed of God. Numbers 11:14–17 makes this evident. God summoned the seventy elders whom Moses had chosen, that they might appear before Him and that He might make His presence known to them (see also 24:9). In imitation of these seventy elders, the number of the New Testament Sanhedrin was fixed at seventy. The same problem of overwork that vexed Moses led the early church to establish the office of deacon in order to free the apostles for their spiritual duties.

dispute they will bring to you, but every minor dispute they themselves will judge. So it will be easier for you, and they will bear *the burden* with you.

23   "If you do this thing and God *so* commands you, then you will be able to endure, and all these people also will go to their place in peace."

24   So Moses listened to his father-in-law, and did all that he had said.

25   And Moses chose able men out of all Israel, and made them heads over the people, leaders of thousands, of hundreds, of fifties and of tens.

26   And they judged the people at all times; the difficult dispute they would bring to Moses, but every minor dispute they themselves would judge.

27   Then Moses bade his father-in-law farewell, and he went his way into his own land.

III. *The covenant and the Law (19:1—24:18)*

A. *The covenant made*

1. *The people at Sinai*

19 In the third month after the sons of Israel had gone out of the land of Egypt, on that very day they came into the wilderness of Sinai.

2   When they set out from Rephidim, they came to the wilderness of Sinai, and camped in the wilderness; and there Israel camped in front of the mountain.

3   And Moses went up to God, and the LORD called to him from the mountain, saying, "Thus you shall say to the house of Jacob and tell the sons of Israel:

4   'You yourselves have seen what I did to the Egyptians, and *how* I bore you on eagles' wings, and brought you to Myself.

5   'Now then, if you will indeed obey My voice and keep My covenant, then you shall be My [17]own possession among all the peoples, for all the earth is Mine;

6   and you shall be to Me a kingdom of priests and a holy nation.' These are the words that you shall speak to the sons of Israel."

7   So Moses came and called the elders of the people, and set before them all these words which the LORD had commanded him.

8   And all the people answered together and said, "All that the LORD has spoken we will do!" And Moses brought back the words of the people to the LORD.

9   And the LORD said to Moses, "Behold, I shall come to you in a thick cloud, in order that the people may hear when I speak with you, and may also believe in you forever." Then Moses told the words of the people to the LORD.

2. *The consecration of the people*

10   The LORD also said to Moses, "Go to the people and consecrate them today and tomorrow, and let them wash their garments;

11   and let them be ready for the third day, for on the third day the LORD will come down on Mount Sinai in the sight of all the people.

12   "And you shall set bounds for the people all around, saying, 'Beware that you do not go up on the mountain or touch the border of it; whoever touches the mountain shall surely be put to death.

13   'No hand shall touch him, but he shall surely be stoned or [18]shot through;

Side references:

18:22 Deut 1:17,18; Num 11:17

18:25 Deut 1:15

18:26 v. 22

18:27 Num 10:29, 30

19:2 Ex 17:1; 18:5

19:3 Ex 20:21; Acts 7:38

19:4 Deut 29:2; Is 63:9

19:5ff Deut 5:2; 7:6; 10:14

19:6 1 Pet 2:5; Rev 1:6; 5:10; Deut 14:21; 26:19

19:8 Ex 24:3,7

19:9 v. 16; Ex 24:15

19:10 Lev 11:44,45; Heb 10:22; Gen 35:2; Num 8:7; 19:19

19:11 v. 16

19:12 Heb 12:20

19:13 v. 17

17Or, *special treasure*   18I.e., with arrows

19:4 Israel was governed as a theocracy (immediate government by God). Israel's movements were directed by God (40:36,37), war was proclaimed by God (Num. 31:1,2), leaders were appointed by Him (Num. 27:18,20), and land in Canaan was distributed by Him (Josh. 13:1–7). God used Moses, Joshua, and later the prophets (e.g., Samuel) as the intermediaries through whom He governed. Saul proved unworthy to continue as God's representative, so David was chosen by the LORD to serve as His theocratic king—an authority conditioned on covenant-obedience, but granted to David's posterity forever (2 Sam. 7:12–16).

19:5–8 Israel here accepts the covenant proposed by God. This relationship has often been designated as God's theocratic rule over Israel. Two things are quite clear: (1) this covenant may be regarded as a fulfillment of the promise made to Abraham; and (2) this covenant was similar in form to a suzerainty treaty in which fealty is acknowledged to a superior lord. The covenant was conditioned on two things: (1) faith, and (2) obedience. The terms clearly stated that unbelief and disobedience would break the covenant, and, as a result, the promised blessings flowing from faith and obedience would be withdrawn. The melancholy history of Israel is a clear example of failure to believe God and to obey Him. Judgment, dispersion among the nations, and the withdrawal of the blessing of God inevitably followed.

19:9 *believe in you forever.* One of the recurring sins of Israel was to doubt and disbelieve Moses despite the fact that God gave Israel evident tokens that he was God's representative, who enjoyed divine approval.

19:10 Moses was commanded to *consecrate* (separate or set apart) the people and to have them wash their clothes. Since they were to come into the presence of a holy God these preparatory measures were essential.

whether beast or man, he shall not live.' When the ram's horn sounds a long blast, they shall come up to the mountain."

14   So Moses went down from the mountain to the people and consecrated the people, and they washed their garments.

15   And he said to the people, "Be ready for the third day; do not go near a woman."

3. Moses meets God on Mount Sinai

19:16
Heb 12:18,
19; Ex 40:34

16   So it came about on the third day, when it was morning, that there were thunder and lightning flashes and a thick cloud upon the mountain and a very loud trumpet sound, so that all the people who *were* in the camp trembled.

17   And Moses brought the people out of the camp to meet God, and they stood at the foot of the mountain.

*19:18
Ps 104:32;
Heb 12:18;
Gen 19:28;
Ps 68:7,8
19:19
Heb 12:21;
Ps 81:7

18   Now Mount Sinai *was* all in smoke because the LORD descended upon it in fire; and its smoke ascended like the smoke of a furnace, and the whole mountain quaked violently.

19   When the sound of the trumpet grew louder and louder, Moses spoke and God answered him with thunder.

20   And the LORD came down on Mount Sinai, to the top of the mountain; and the LORD called Moses to the top of the mountain, and Moses went up.

19:21
Ex 3:5

21   Then the LORD spoke to Moses, "Go down, warn the people, lest they break through to the LORD to gaze, and many of them perish.

19:22
Lev 10:3;
2 Sam 6:7

22   "And also let the priests who come near to the LORD consecrate themselves, lest the LORD break out against them."

19:23
v. 12

23   And Moses said to the LORD, "The people cannot come up to Mount Sinai, for Thou didst warn us, saying, 'Set bounds about the mountain and consecrate it.' "

24   Then the LORD said to him, "Go down and come up *again*, you and Aaron with you; but do not let the priests and the people break through to come up to the LORD, lest He break forth upon them."

25   So Moses went down to the people and told them.

B. The Law given

*20:1
Deut 5:22
20:2
Deut 5:6; 7:8
*20:3
Jer 35:15
20:4
Lev 26:1;
Deut 4:15-19;
Ps 97:7
20:5
Is 44:15,19;

20 Then God spoke all these words, saying,

2   "I am the LORD your God, who brought you out of the land of Egypt, out of the house of slavery.

3   "You shall have no other gods [19]before Me.

4   "You shall not make for yourself [20]an idol, or any likeness of what is in heaven above or on the earth beneath or in the water under the earth.

5   "You shall not worship them or serve them; for I, the LORD your God, am a

[19]Or, *besides Me*   [20]Or, *a graven image*

19:18 *the LORD descended . . . in fire.* As a symbol of holiness, fire is mentioned often in Scripture. Examples may be found in 3:2; 2 Kin. 2:11; 2 Thess. 1:7.

20:1 The Ten Commandments of chapter 20 follow Israel's acceptance of God's theocratic rule over them. The commandments are an expression of the eternal moral nature of God. They embody the basic principles that govern a life of faith, that is, loyalty and reverence toward God and moral responsibility toward man. They were never intended to serve as a basis for man's self-justification (as the legalists of Christ's day supposed), but only as a guide for those already saved, who love God and seek to please their divine Redeemer and carry out His will. Scripture states that these commandments were spoken by God (Deut. 5:4,22), and were written by Him (32:16; Deut. 4:13; 10:4). Christ summed up the two tables of the Law by asserting that people are to love the Lord their God with all their hearts, and souls, and minds, and their neighbors as themselves (Matt. 22:35-40). The commandments contain an indictment against all human righteousness and convey the sentence of death on all who would misuse them for purposes of merit-earning or self-justification. But the same God who promulgated the Ten Commandments also made ample provision for the cleansing of sinners who transgressed these commandments and who in repentance cast them-

selves on His grace. This forgiveness was symbolized through the shedding of the blood of the innocent victim at the altar of sacrifice. Contrary to what most people think, the Law means more than external conformity to rules; it is spiritual, for Christ states that the true locus of sin is in the heart (Matt. 5:28; 12:34; Luke 12:34). The tenth commandment, against coveting, refers explicitly to the motives of man and shows the spiritual nature of the Law. Thus the overt act is only a revelation of what is in the heart; even if the overt act is not performed, a person is already guilty of having broken the Law by the inward condition of the heart (Matt. 5:28; Rom. 7:14).

20:3 Idolatry is strictly and sternly forbidden in Scripture. Everywhere it is regarded as an abomination. The objects of idol worship are called "foreign gods," "gods of wood and stone," "wooden idols." Idolatry consists in : (1) worshiping or bowing down to images whether of God or of man (20:5; Is. 44:17; Dan. 3:5,10,15); (2) sacrificing to other gods or images (22:20; Ps. 106:38; Acts 7:41); (3) worshiping of angels (Col. 2:18); (4) covetousness (Eph. 5:5); and (5) sensuality (Phil. 3:19). (Compare the note at 32:1.) In a general fashion it may be said that idolatry occurs when we place anything before God as the first object of our affection and obedience.

jealous God, visiting the iniquity of the fathers on the children, on the third and the fourth generations of those who hate Me,

6   but showing lovingkindness to thousands, to those who love Me and keep My commandments.

7   "You shall not take the name of the LORD your God in vain, for the LORD will not leave him unpunished who takes His name in vain.

8   "Remember the sabbath day, to keep it holy.

9   "Six days you shall labor and do all your work,

10   but the seventh day is a sabbath of the LORD your God; *in it* you shall not do any work, you or your son or your daughter, your male or your female servant or your cattle or your sojourner who stays with you.

11   "For in six days the LORD made the heavens and the earth, the sea and all that is in them, and rested on the seventh day; therefore the LORD blessed the sabbath day and made it holy.

12   "Honor your father and your mother, that your days may be prolonged in the land which the LORD your God gives you.

13   "You shall not murder.

14   "You shall not commit adultery.

15   "You shall not steal.

16   "You shall not bear false witness against your neighbor.

17   "You shall not covet your neighbor's house; you shall not covet your neighbor's wife or his male servant or his female servant or his ox or his donkey or anything that belongs to your neighbor."

C. *The people afraid*

18   And all the people perceived the thunder and the lightning flashes and the sound of the trumpet and the mountain smoking; and when the people saw *it*, they trembled and stood at a distance.

19   Then they said to Moses, "Speak to us yourself and we will listen; but let not God speak to us, lest we die."

20   And Moses said to the people, "Do not be afraid; for God has come in order to test you, and in order that the fear of Him may remain with you, so that you may not sin."

D. *The laws of the covenant*

1. *The law of the altar*

21   So the people stood at a distance, while Moses approached the thick cloud where God *was*.

22   Then the LORD said to Moses, "Thus you shall say to the sons of Israel, 'You yourselves have seen that I have spoken to you from heaven.

23   'You shall not make *other gods* besides Me; gods of silver or gods of gold, you shall not make for yourselves.

24   'You shall make an altar of earth for Me, and you shall sacrifice on it your burnt offerings and your peace offerings, your sheep and your oxen; in every place where I cause My name to be remembered, I will come to you and bless you.

25   'And if you make an altar of stone for Me, you shall not build it of cut stones, for if you wield your tool on it, you will profane it.

26   'And you shall not go up by steps to My altar, that your nakedness may not be exposed on it.'

2. *Laws concerning slaves*

21 "Now these are the ordinances which you are to set before them.

2   "If you buy a Hebrew slave, he shall serve for six years; but on the seventh he shall go out as a free man without payment.

Marginal references:
Deut 4:24; Jer 32:18
20:6 Deut 7:9
20:7 Lev 19:12; Matt 5:33
20:8 Ex 23:12; 31:15
20:9 Ex 34:21; Luke 13:14
*20:11 Gen 2:2,3
20:12 Lev 19:3; Matt 15:4; Mark 7:10; Eph 6:2
20:13 Rom 13:9
20:14 Matt 19:18
20:15 Matt 19:18
20:16 Ex 23:1; Matt 19:18
20:17 Rom 7:7; 13:9
20:18 Heb 12:18; Ex 19:18
20:19 Deut 5:23-27
20:20 Ex 14:13; 15:25; Deut 4:10
20:21 Deut 5:22
20:22 Neh 9:13
20:23 v. 3; Ex 32:1, 2,4
20:24 Lev 1:2; Deut 12:5; Gen 12:2
20:25 Deut 27:5,6
*21:1 Deut 4:14
21:2 Lev 25:39-41; Deut 15:12-18

20:11 See here Deut. 5:15, where another reason for keeping the Sabbath is given.
20:26 See here Ezek. 43:17, where the altar has steps.
21:1 Under the theocracy (see note to 19:4) God legislated civil statutes or laws that were to govern such a society under the cultural conditions that prevailed in that day. The unit of ordinances found in 21:1–23:33, apparently called *the book of the covenant* in 24:7, is characterized by case law,

"if . . . , then . . . " A number of laws have parallels or similar features to the law codes of Sumer and Babylonia that date some centuries before Moses. But the apodictic form of the Ten Commandments, "Thou shalt not . . . ," is unique to Israel. In the era of the Christian church many of the Pentateuchal regulations are inapplicable. Yet the underlying principles of justice and fairness and equality remain ever valid and foundational for sound jurisprudence.

3 "If he comes alone, he shall go out alone; if he is the husband of a wife, then his wife shall go out with him.

4 "If his master gives him a wife, and she bears him sons or daughters, the wife and her children shall belong to her master, and he shall go out alone.

5 "But if the slave plainly says, 'I love my master, my wife and my children; I will not go out as a free man,'

6 then his master shall bring him to [21]God, then he shall bring him to the door or the doorpost. And his master shall pierce his ear with an awl; and he shall serve him permanently.

7 "And if a man sells his daughter as a female slave, she is not to go free as the male slaves do.

8 "If she is displeasing in the eyes of her master who designated her for himself, then he shall let her be redeemed. He does not have authority to sell her to a foreign people because of his unfairness to her.

9 "And if he designates her for his son, he shall deal with her according to the custom of daughters.

10 "If he takes to himself another woman, he may not reduce her food, her clothing, or her conjugal rights.

11 "And if he will not do these three *things* for her, then she shall go out for nothing, without *payment of* money.

3. Laws relating to murder

12 "He who strikes a man so that he dies shall surely be put to death.

13 "But if he did not lie in wait *for him,* but God let *him* fall into his hand, then I will appoint *him* a place to which he may flee.

14 "If, however, a man acts presumptuously toward his neighbor, so as to kill him craftily, you are to take him *even* from My altar, that he may die.

15 "And he who strikes his father or his mother shall surely be put to death.

16 "And he who kidnaps a man, whether he sells him or he is found in his possession, shall surely be put to death.

17 "And he who curses his father or his mother shall surely be put to death.

4. Laws relating to noncapital offenses

18 "And if men have a quarrel and one strikes the other with a stone or with *his* fist, and he does not die but remains in bed;

19 if he gets up and walks around outside on his staff, then he who struck him shall go unpunished; he shall only pay for his loss of time, and shall take care of him until he is completely healed.

20 "And if a man strikes his male or female slave with a rod and he dies at his hand, he shall be punished.

21 "If, however, he survives a day or two, no vengeance shall be taken; for he is his property.

22 "And *if* men struggle with each other and strike a woman with child so that she has a miscarriage, yet there is no *further* injury, he shall surely be fined as the woman's husband may demand of him; and he shall pay as the judges *decide.*

23 "But if there is *any further* injury, then you shall appoint *as a penalty* life for life,

24 eye for eye, tooth for tooth, hand for hand, foot for foot,

25 burn for burn, wound for wound, bruise for bruise.

26 "And if a man strikes the eye of his male or female slave, and destroys it, he shall let him go free on account of his eye.

27 "And if he knocks out a tooth of his male or female slave, he shall let him go free on account of his tooth.

28 "And if an ox gores a man or a woman to death, the ox shall surely be stoned and its flesh shall not be eaten; but the owner of the ox shall go unpunished.

29 "If, however, an ox was previously in the habit of goring, and its owner has

---

21:6
Ex 22:8,9,28

21:7
Neh 5:5;
vv. 2,3

21:10
1 Cor 7:3,5

21:12
Gen 9:6;
Lev 24:17
21:13
Num 35:22;
Deut 19:4,5
21:14
Deut 19:11,
12;
Heb 10:26;
1 Kin 2:28-34
21:16
Deut 24:7
21:17
Lev 20:9;
Matt 15:4;
Mark 7:10

21:21
Lev 25:45,46

*21:23ff
Lev 24:19

*21:24
Matt 5:38

21:28
Gen 9:5

---

[21]Or, *the judges who acted in God's name*

21:23-25 The concept of punishment equal to the crime was a tremendous advance over the law of revenge illustrated by Gen. 4:24: *If Cain is avenged sevenfold, then Lamech seventy-sevenfold.* The New Testament principle of forgiveness until "seventy times seven times" makes very clear what the attitude of the individual to his fellowman must be.

been warned, yet he does not confine it, and it kills a man or a woman, the ox shall be stoned and its owner also shall be put to death.

30 "If a ransom is demanded of him, then he shall give for the redemption of his life whatever is demanded of him.

31 "Whether it gores a son or a daughter, it shall be done to him according to the same rule.

32 "If the ox gores a male or female slave, the owner shall give his *or her* master thirty shekels of silver, and the ox shall be stoned.

5. *Laws relating to property rights*

33 "And if a man opens a pit, or digs a pit and does not cover it over, and an ox or a donkey falls into it,

34 the owner of the pit shall make restitution; he shall give money to its owner, and the dead *animal* shall become his.

35 "And if one man's ox hurts another's so that it dies, then they shall sell the live ox and divide its price equally; and also they shall divide the dead *ox*.

36 "Or *if* it is known that the ox was previously in the habit of goring, yet its owner has not confined it, he shall surely pay ox for ox, and the dead *animal* shall become his.

22 "If a man steals an ox or a sheep, and slaughters it or sells it, he shall pay five oxen for the ox and four sheep for the sheep.

2 "If the thief is caught while breaking in, and is struck so that he dies, there will be no bloodguiltiness on his account.

3 "*But* if the sun has risen on him, there will be bloodguiltiness on his account. He shall surely make restitution; if he owns nothing, then he shall be sold for his theft.

4 "If what he stole is actually found alive in his possession, whether an ox or a donkey or a sheep, he shall pay double.

5 "If a man lets a field or vineyard be grazed *bare* and lets his animal loose so that it grazes in another man's field, he shall make restitution from the best of his own field and the best of his own vineyard.

6 "If a fire breaks out and spreads to thorn bushes, so that stacked grain or the standing grain or the field *itself* is consumed, he who started the fire shall surely make restitution.

7 "If a man gives his neighbor money or goods to keep *for him*, and it is stolen from the man's house, if the thief is caught, he shall pay double.

8 "If the thief is not caught, then the owner of the house shall appear before the judges, *to* determine whether he laid his hands on his neighbor's property.

9 "For every breach of trust, *whether it is* for ox, for donkey, for sheep, for clothing, *or* for any lost thing about which one says, 'This is it,' the case of both parties shall come before the judges; he whom the judges condemn shall pay double to his neighbor.

10 "If a man gives his neighbor a donkey, an ox, a sheep, or any animal to keep *for him*, and it dies or is hurt or is driven away while no one is looking,

11 an oath before the LORD shall be made by the two of them, that he has not laid hands on his neighbor's property; and its owner shall accept *it*, and he shall not make restitution.

12 "But if it is actually stolen from him, he shall make restitution to its owner.

13 "If it is all torn to pieces, let him bring it as evidence; he shall not make restitution for what has been torn to pieces.

14 "And if a man borrows *anything* from his neighbor, and it is injured or dies while its owner is not with it, he shall make full restitution.

15 "If its owner is with it, he shall not make restitution; if it is hired, it came for its hire.

16 "And if a man seduces a virgin who is not engaged, and lies with her, he must pay a dowry for her *to be* his wife.

17 "If her father absolutely refuses to give her to him, he shall pay money equal to the dowry for virgins.

Marginal references: 21:30 v. 22 | 21:32 see Zech 11:12,13; Matt 26:15 | 21:33 Luke 14:5 | 22:1 2 Sam 12:6 | 22:2 Matt 24:43; Num 35:27 | 22:3 Ex 21:2 | 22:7 v. 4 | 22:8 v. 28; Ex 21:6; Deut 17:8,9; 19:17 | 22:9 vv. 8,28 | 22:11 Heb 6:16 | 22:12 Gen 31:39 | 22:16 Deut 22:28,29 | 22:17 Deut 22:29

6. Other laws

a. Crimes punishable by death

22:18
Lev 20:27;
Deut 18:10

18 "You shall not allow a sorceress to live.

22:19
Lev 18:23;
Deut 27:21

19 "Whoever lies with an animal shall surely be put to death.

22:20
Deut 17:2,3,5

20 "He who sacrifices to any god, other than to the LORD alone, shall be utterly destroyed.

b. Sundry duties

22:21
Lev 19:33;
Deut 10:19

21 "And you shall not wrong a stranger or oppress him, for you were strangers in the land of Egypt.

22:22
Deut 24:17,
18

22 "You shall not afflict any widow or orphan.

22:23
Deut 15:9;
Luke 18:7;
Ps 18:6

23 "If you afflict him at all, *and* if he does cry out to Me, I will surely hear his cry;

22:24
Ps 69:24;
109:9

24 and My anger will be kindled, and I will kill you with the sword; and your wives shall become widows and your children fatherless.

22:25
Lev 25:35-37;
Deut 23:19,
20

25 "If you lend money to My people, to the poor among you, you are not to act as a creditor to him; you shall not charge him interest.

26 "If you ever take your neighbor's cloak as a pledge, you are to return it to him before the sun sets,

27 for that is his only covering; it is his cloak for his body. What else shall he sleep in? And it shall come about that when he cries out to Me, I will hear *him*, for I am gracious.

22:28
Lev 24:15,16;
Acts 23:5

28 "You shall not curse God, nor curse a ruler of your people.

22:29
Ex 23:16;
13:2,12

29 "You shall not delay *the offering from* your harvest and your vintage. The first-born of your sons you shall give to Me.

22:30
Deut 15:19;
Lev 22:27

30 "You shall do the same with your oxen *and* with your sheep. It shall be with its mother seven days; on the eighth day you shall give it to Me.

22:31
Lev 19:6;
22:8

31 "And you shall be holy men to Me, therefore you shall not eat *any* flesh torn to pieces in the field; you shall throw it to the dogs.

c. Ethical instructions

*23:1
Ex 20:16;
Ps 35:11

23 "You shall not bear a false report; do not join your hand with a wicked man to be a malicious witness.

23:2
Deut 16:19

2 "You shall not follow a multitude in doing evil, nor shall you testify in a dispute so as to turn aside after a multitude in order to pervert *justice;*

3 nor shall you be partial to a poor man in his dispute.

23:4
Deut 22:1

4 "If you meet your enemy's ox or his donkey wandering away, you shall surely return it to him.

23:5
Deut 22:4

5 "If you see the donkey of one who hates you lying *helpless* under its load, you shall refrain from leaving it to him, you shall surely release *it* with him.

23:6
vv. 2,3

6 "You shall not pervert the justice *due* to your needy *brother* in his dispute.

23:7
Rom 1:18

7 "Keep far from a false charge, and do not kill the innocent or the righteous, for I will not acquit the guilty.

23:8
Deut 10:17;
16:19

8 "And you shall not take a bribe, for a bribe blinds the clear-sighted and subverts the cause of the just.

23:9
Ex 22:21

9 "And you shall not oppress a stranger, since you yourselves know the feelings of a stranger, for you *also* were strangers in the land of Egypt.

7. Laws of festivals and holidays

23:10
Lev 25:3

10 "And you shall sow your land for six years and gather in its yield,

11 but *on* the seventh year you shall let it rest and lie fallow, so that the needy of your people may eat; and whatever they leave the beast of the field may eat. You are to do the same with your vineyard *and* your olive grove.

23:12
Ex 20:8-11

12 "Six days you are to do your work, but on the seventh day you shall cease *from*

23:1 Slander is a gross sin that is strictly forbidden by God (Prov. 6:16,19; Eph. 4:31; James 4:11). Included within this general category are such sins as: (1) gossip (Rom. 1:29; 2 Cor. 12:20); (2) tattling (1Tim. 5:13); (3) defaming (Jer. 20:10); and (4) base suspicion (1Tim. 6:4). Life in the Spirit enables believers to gain even more victories over this sin; by God's grace they are led to love their neighbors (even the less lovable ones) as themselves.
23:11 The Feast of the Sabbatical Year was kept every seventh year. Its purpose was to provide a Sabbath or fallow year for the land (Lev. 25:2). The people were to live on the fruits of their labor for the sixth year (Lev. 25:20–22). Special commandments governed this year. Field labor was to cease, the fruits of the earth were to be common property, debts were to be remitted, Hebrew servants manumitted, and the Law was to be publicly read (see Lev. 25:4ff.; Deut. 15:1–3,12; 31:10–13; Neh. 10:31). Strangers or non-Israelites were not necessarily to be freed from debts in the sabbatical year (Deut. 15:3). The Babylonian captivity centuries later was partly a consequence of failure to observe these sabbatical years (2 Chr. 36:20,21).

labor in order that your ox and your donkey may rest, and the son of your female slave, as well as your stranger, may refresh themselves.

13 "Now concerning everything which I have said to you, be on your guard; and do not mention the name of other gods, nor let *them* be heard from your mouth.

14 "Three times a year you shall celebrate a feast to Me.

15 "You shall observe the Feast of Unleavened Bread; for seven days you are to eat unleavened bread, as I commanded you, at the appointed time in the month Abib, for in it you came out of Egypt. And none shall appear before Me empty-handed.

16 "Also *you shall observe* the Feast of the Harvest *of* the first fruits of your labors *from* what you sow in the field; also the Feast of the Ingathering at the end of the year when you gather in *the fruit of* your labors from the field.

17 "Three times a year all your males shall appear before the Lord GOD.

18 "You shall not offer the blood of My sacrifice with leavened bread; nor is the fat of My feast to remain overnight until morning.

19 "You shall bring the choice first fruits of your soil into the house of the LORD your God. You are not to boil a kid in the milk of its mother.

8. *God's final injunctions*

20 "Behold, I am going to send an angel before you to guard you along the way, and to bring you into the place which I have prepared.

21 "Be on your guard before him and obey his voice; do not be rebellious toward him, for he will not pardon your transgression, since My name is in him.

22 "But if you will truly obey his voice and do all that I say, then I will be an enemy to your enemies and an adversary to your adversaries.

23 "For My angel will go before you and bring you in to *the land of* the Amorites, the Hittites, the Perizzites, the Canaanites, the Hivites and the Jebusites; and I will completely destroy them.

24 "You shall not worship their gods, nor serve them, nor do according to their deeds; but you shall utterly overthrow them, and break their *sacred* pillars in pieces.

25 "But you shall serve the LORD your God, and He will bless your bread and your water; and I will remove sickness from your midst.

26 "There shall be no one miscarrying or barren in your land; I will fulfill the number of your days.

27 "I will send My terror ahead of you, and throw into confusion all the people among whom you come, and I will make all your enemies turn *their* backs to you.

28 "And I will send hornets ahead of you, that they may drive out the Hivites, the Canaanites, and the Hittites before you.

29 "I will not drive them out before you in a single year, that the land may not become desolate, and the beasts of the field become too numerous for you.

30 "I will drive them out before you little by little, until you become fruitful and take possession of the land.

31 "And I will fix your boundary from the Red Sea to the sea of the Philistines, and from the wilderness to the River *Euphrates;* for I will deliver the inhabitants of the land into your hand, and you will drive them out before you.

32 "You shall make no covenant with them or with their gods.

33 "They shall not live in your land, lest they make you sin against Me; for *if* you serve their gods, it will surely be a snare to you."

23:13 Ps 39:1; Eph 5:15
*23:14 Ex 34:23
23:15 Ex 12:15; 34:20
*23:16 Ex 34:22; Deut 16:13
23:17 Deut 16:16
23:18 Ex 34:25
23:19 Ex 22:29; Deut 14:21
23:20 Ex 32:34; 15:16,17
23:21 Num 14:11; Ps 78:40,56; Num 14:35
23:22 Gen 12:2
23:23 Josh 24:8,11
23:24 Ex 20:5; Lev 18:3; Ex 34:13
23:25 Deut 6:13; Matt 4:10; Deut 28:5; Ex 15:26
23:26 Deut 7:14; Mal 3:11; Job 5:26
23:27 Ex 15:14,16; Deut 7:23
23:28 Deut 7:20; Josh 24:12
23:29 Deut 7:22
23:31 Gen 15:18; Josh 21:44; 24:12,18
23:32 Deut 7:2; vv. 13,24
23:33 Deut 7:1-5,16

23:14 Three times a year all of the male Israelites were to appear before God at the tabernacle: *the Feast of Unleavened Bread* (v. 15), *the Feast of the Harvest* (v. 16), and *the Feast of the Ingathering* (v. 16). Elsewhere they were spoken of as the feasts of Passover, Pentecost, and Tabernacles. (See notes to 12:11; 23:16; Lev. 23:15; Mark 14:1.)

23:16 The Feast of Tabernacles was one of the three national feasts of the Jews (the other two being Passover and Pentecost). It was also called the *Feast of Ingathering* (34:22) and was begun on the fifteenth day of Tishri, the seventh month (Lev. 23:34,39). It was celebrated after the harvest and vintage had been gathered in (Deut. 16:13) and lasted for seven days (Lev. 23:34,41; Deut. 16:13,15). All males were obligated to attend the feast (23:16,17), the first and last days of which were to be celebrated by holy convocations (Lev. 23:35,39; Num. 29:12,35). During the period of the observance the people camped out in booths, family by family (Lev. 23:42). This feast was to be observed perpetually and with thanksgiving (Lev. 23:41; Deut. 16:14,15). It was also called the *Feast of Booths*, and it memorialized the redemption of Israel out of Egypt (Lev. 23:34–44). Zechariah prophetically declares that this feast will ultimately become a memorial feast for all nations (Zech. 14:16–21).

23:30 It was not the intention of God for Israel to subjugate Palestine quickly. The conquest was to be accomplished over a period of time. God commanded Israel to drive out the inhabitants as they went. It was the failure to do this that became a stumbling block to Israel.

9. *Israel's acceptance of the covenant*

a. *The covenant sealed by blood*

24:1
Lev 10:1,2;
Num 11:16

24 Then He said to Moses, "Come up to the LORD, you and Aaron, Nadab and Abihu and seventy of the elders of Israel, and you shall worship at a distance.

2   "Moses alone, however, shall come near to the LORD, but they shall not come near, nor shall the people come up with him."

24:3
v. 7; Ex 19:8

3   Then Moses came and recounted to the people all the words of the LORD and all the ordinances; and all the people answered with one voice, and said, "All the words which the LORD has spoken we will do!"

24:4
Deut 31:9;
Gen 28:18

4   And Moses wrote down all the words of the LORD. Then he arose early in the morning, and built an altar at the foot of the mountain with twelve pillars for the twelve tribes of Israel.

5   And he sent young men of the sons of Israel, and they offered burnt offerings and sacrificed young bulls as peace offerings to the LORD.

24:6
Heb 9:18

6   And Moses took half of the blood and put *it* in basins, and the *other* half of the blood he sprinkled on the altar.

24:7
Heb 9:19;
v. 3

7   Then he took the book of the covenant and read *it* in the hearing of the people; and they said, "All that the LORD has spoken we will do, and we will be obedient!"

24:8
Heb 9:20;
1 Pet 1:2

8   So Moses took the blood and sprinkled *it* on the people, and said, "Behold the blood of the covenant, which the LORD has made with you in accordance with all these words."

24:9
v. 1

9   Then Moses went up with Aaron, Nadab and Abihu, and seventy of the elders of Israel,

*24:10
Ezek 1:26;
Rev 4:3;
Matt 17:2
24:11
Ex 19:21;
Gen 32:30;
31:54

10   and they saw the God of Israel; and under His feet there appeared to be a pavement of sapphire, as clear as the sky itself.

11   Yet He did not stretch out His hand against the nobles of the sons of Israel; and they beheld God, and they ate and drank.

b. *Moses on the mount for forty days*

24:12
vv. 2,15;
Ex 32:15,16

12   Now the LORD said to Moses, "Come up to Me on the mountain and remain there, and I will give you the stone tablets with the law and the commandment which I have written for their instruction."

24:13
Ex 17:9-14;
3:1

13   So Moses arose with Joshua his servant, and Moses went up to the mountain of God.

14   But to the elders he said, "Wait here for us until we return to you. And behold, Aaron and Hur are with you; whoever has a legal matter, let him approach them."

24:15
Ex 19:9
24:16
Ex 16:10

15   Then Moses went up to the mountain, and the cloud covered the mountain.

16   And the glory of the LORD rested on Mount Sinai, and the cloud covered it for six days; and on the seventh day He called to Moses from the midst of the cloud.

24:17
Ex 3:2;
Deut 4:36;
Heb 12:18,29
24:18
Ex 34:28;
Deut 9:9

17   And to the eyes of the sons of Israel the appearance of the glory of the LORD was like a consuming fire on the mountain top.

18   And Moses entered the midst of the cloud as he went up to the mountain; and Moses was on the mountain forty days and forty nights.

IV. *The tabernacle in the wilderness (25:1–40:38)*

A. *The offering for the tabernacle*

25:2
Ex 35:5,21;
2 Cor 8:12;
9:7

25 Then the LORD spoke to Moses, saying, 2 "Tell the sons of Israel to raise a contribution for Me; from every man whose heart moves him you shall raise My contribution.

3   "And this is the contribution which you are to raise from them: gold, silver and bronze,

---

24:10 A theophany is a visible appearance of God to men. This appearance might take place in different ways and under different circumstances. Among the appearances recorded in Scripture the following may be cited: (1) Here in 24:10, where Moses, Aaron, Nadab, Abihu, and the seventy elders saw a manifestation of the glory and person of God without any suggestion that it was by other than ordinary vision; (2) in 33:11, where God spoke to Moses *face to face*, which must be understood in the context of vv. 17–23;

(3) in Is. 6, Ezek. 1, and Dan. 7:9, where God was seen in a vision or a dream; (4) in Gen. 16:7, where the angel of the LORD appeared to Hagar (although the angel of the LORD does not always mean the appearance of God or Christ); (5) in 14:19, where God appeared in the pillar of cloud; and (6) in Deut. 5:24 and elsewhere, where Scripture speaks of men beholding the LORD's glory and greatness. The supreme revelation of God to man is found in the incarnation of Jesus Christ, who *became flesh, and dwelt among us* (John 1:14).

4   blue, purple and scarlet *material*, fine linen, goat *hair*,

5   rams' skins dyed red, porpoise skins, acacia wood,

6   oil for lighting, spices for the anointing oil and for the fragrant incense,

7   onyx stones and setting stones, for the ephod and for the breastpiece.

8   "And let them construct a sanctuary for Me, that I may dwell among them.

9   "According to all that I am going to show you, *as* the pattern of the tabernacle and the pattern of all its furniture, just so you shall construct *it*.

B. *The ark*

10   "And they shall construct an ark of acacia wood two and a half cubits long, and one and a half cubits wide, and one and a half cubits high.

11   "And you shall overlay it with pure gold, inside and out you shall overlay it, and you shall make a gold molding around it.

12   "And you shall cast four gold rings for it, and fasten them on its four feet, and two rings shall be on one side of it and two rings on the other side of it.

13   "And you shall make poles of acacia wood and overlay them with gold.

14   "And you shall put the poles into the rings on the sides of the ark, to carry the ark with them.

15   "The poles shall remain in the rings of the ark; they shall not be removed from it.

16   "And you shall put into the ark the testimony which I shall give you.

17   "And you shall make a [22]mercy seat of pure gold, two and a half cubits long and one and a half cubits wide.

18   "And you shall make two cherubim of gold, make them of hammered work at the two ends of the mercy seat.

19   "And make one cherub at one end and one cherub at the other end; you shall make the cherubim *of one piece* with the mercy seat at its two ends.

20   "And the cherubim shall have *their* wings spread upward, covering the mercy seat with their wings and facing one another; the faces of the cherubim are to be *turned* toward the mercy seat.

21   "And you shall put the mercy seat on top of the ark, and in the ark you shall put the testimony which I shall give to you.

22   "And there I will meet with you; and from above the mercy seat, from between the two cherubim which are upon the ark of the testimony, I will speak to you about all that I will give you in commandment for the sons of Israel.

C. *The table*

23   "And you shall make a table of acacia wood, two cubits long and one cubit wide and one and a half cubits high.

24   "And you shall overlay it with pure gold and make a gold border around it.

25   "And you shall make for it a rim of a handbreadth around *it;* and you shall make a gold border for the rim around it.

26   "And you shall make four gold rings for it and put rings on the four corners which are on its four feet.

27   "The rings shall be close to the rim as holders for the poles to carry the table.

---

[22]Lit., *propitiatory;* and so through v. 22

Cross references (right margin):

25:6
Ex 27:20;
30:23,34
25:7
Ex 28:4,6,15
25:8
Ex 36:1,3,4;
Heb 9:1,2;
Ex 29:45;
Rev 21:3
*25:9
v. 40;
Acts 7:44;
Heb 8:2,5
*25:10
Ex 37:1-9

25:16
Deut 31:26;
Heb 9:4
*25:17
Ex 37:6;
Rom 3:25;
Heb 9:5

25:20
1 Kin 8:7;
Heb 9:5

25:21
Ex 26:34;
v. 16
*25:22
Ex 29:42,43;
30:6,36;
Num 7:89;
Ps 80:1

25:23
Ex 37:10-16;
Heb 9:2

25:9 God commanded Moses to make the tabernacle. It was a movable tent appropriate to the unsettled life of the people (2 Sam. 7:6,7). The Levites were appointed to have charge over it (Num. 1:50; 18:2–4). God's presence or cloud of glory filled the holy place and remained over the ark of the covenant (25:22; Lev. 16:2; Num. 7:89). During the wilderness wanderings of Israel the cloud of glory rested over the tabernacle both day and night, and the movements of the people were guided by the movement of the cloud (40:36–38; Num. 9:15,16).

25:10 The ark was a chest made of acacia wood overlaid with gold. Figuring the cubit at 18 inches, this chest was 3.75 feet long, 2.25 feet wide, and 2.25 feet deep. See also notes to 25:17; 26:33.

25:17 The *mercy seat* was the lid of the ark; the Hebrew term means "propitiatory" and comes from the verb *kippēr*, "to atone." It was made of solid gold, beaten out into the form of two cherubs (winged lions with human heads) that

faced each other at either end. Their wings were outspread in front of them as they looked down at the mercy seat. Within the ark itself (or in front of it) were Aaron's rod, a pot of manna, and the two tables of the Law. The symbolism of the mercy seat surmounting the tables of the Law is representative of the covering of law by mercy. Thus it speaks of Christ and His perfect atonement that met the demands of the Law, making possible divine mercy. The mercy seat is a type of Christ. Once a year the high priest came with blood to make atonement for his sins and the sins of the people (Lev. 16:29–34; Heb. 9:5–7). At the mercy seat God met and communed with those who came through blood (25:22). All believers now have access to the mercy seat through Christ, their high priest (Rom. 3:25; Heb. 4:14–16).

25:22 *the two cherubim.* The concept that the LORD of hosts was enthroned on the cherubim is noted explicitly in 1 Sam. 4:4; 2 Sam. 6:2; 2 Kin. 19:15; 1 Chr. 13:6; Is. 37:16.

28 "And you shall make the poles of acacia wood and overlay them with gold, so that with them the table may be carried.

25:29
Ex 37:16;
Num 4:7

29 "And you shall make its dishes and its pans and its jars and its bowls, with which to pour libations; you shall make them of pure gold.

25:30
Lev 24:5-9

30 "And you shall set the bread of the Presence on the table before Me at all times.

D. *The lampstand*

25:31
Ex 37:17;
Heb 9:2;
Rev 1:12

31 "Then you shall make a lampstand of pure gold. The lampstand *and* its base and its shaft are to be made of hammered work; its cups, its bulbs and its flowers shall be *of one piece* with it.

25:32
Ex 38:18

32 "And six branches shall go out from its sides; three branches of the lampstand from its one side, and three branches of the lampstand from its other side.

33 "Three cups *shall be* shaped like almond *blossoms* in the one branch, a [23] bulb and a flower, and three cups shaped like almond *blossoms* in the other branch, a bulb and a flower—so for six branches going out from the lampstand;

25:34
Ex 37:20

34 and in the lampstand four cups shaped like almond *blossoms*, its bulbs and its flowers.

35 "And a bulb shall be under the *first* pair of branches *coming* out of it, and a bulb under the *second* pair of branches *coming* out of it, and a bulb under the *third* pair of branches *coming* out of it, for the six branches coming out of the lampstand.

36 "Their bulbs and their branches *shall be of one piece* with it; all of it shall be one piece of hammered work of pure gold.

25:37
Ex 27:21;
Lev 24:3,4

37 "Then you shall make its lamps seven *in number;* and they shall mount its lamps so as to shed light on the space in front of it.

38 "And its snuffers and their trays *shall be* of pure gold.

39 "It shall be made from a talent of pure gold, with all these utensils.

25:40
Ex 26:30;
Acts 7:44;
Heb 8:5

40 "And see that you make *them* after the pattern for them, which was shown to you on the mountain.

E. *The tabernacle*

26:1
Ex 36:8

26 "Moreover you shall make the tabernacle with ten curtains of fine twisted linen and [24]blue and purple and scarlet *material;* you shall make them with cherubim, the work of a skillful workman.

2 "The length of each curtain shall be twenty-eight cubits, and the width of each curtain four cubits; all the curtains shall have the same measurements.

26:3
Ex 36:10

3 "Five curtains shall be joined to one another; and *the other* five curtains *shall be* joined to one another.

4 "And you shall make loops of blue on the edge of the outermost curtain in the *first* set, and likewise you shall make *them* on the edge of the curtain that is outermost in the second set.

26:5
Ex 36:12

5 "You shall make fifty loops in the one curtain, and you shall make fifty loops on the edge of the curtain that is in the second set; the loops shall be opposite each other.

6 "And you shall make fifty clasps of gold, and join the curtains to one another with the clasps, that the [25]tabernacle may be a unit.

26:7
Ex 36:14

7 "Then you shall make curtains of goats' *hair* for a tent over the tabernacle; you shall make eleven curtains in all.

8 "The length of each curtain *shall be* thirty cubits, and the width of each curtain four cubits; the eleven curtains shall have the same measurements.

9 "And you shall join five curtains by themselves, and the *other* six curtains by themselves, and you shall double over the sixth curtain at the front of the tent.

10 "And you shall make fifty loops on the edge of the curtain that is outermost in the *first* set, and fifty loops on the edge of the curtain *that is outermost in* the second set.

26:11
Ex 36:18

11 "And you shall make fifty clasps of [26]bronze, and you shall put the clasps into the loops and join the tent together, that it may be a unit.

12 "And the overlapping part that is left over in the curtains of the tent, the half curtain that is left over, shall lap over the back of the tabernacle.

13 "And the cubit on one side and the cubit on the other, of what is left over in

---

[23]Or, *calyx*   [24]Or, *violet,* and so throughout this context   [25]Or, *dwelling place,* and so throughout the ch.   [26]Or, *copper*

the length of the curtains of the tent, shall lap over the sides of the tabernacle on one side and on the other, to cover it.

14 "And you shall make a covering for the tent of rams' skins dyed red, and a covering of porpoise skins above.

26:14
Ex 36:19

15 "Then you shall make the boards for the tabernacle of acacia wood, standing upright.

26:15
Ex 36:20

16 "Ten cubits *shall be* the length of each board, and one and a half cubits the width of each board.

17 "There *shall be* two tenons for each board, fitted to one another; thus you shall do for all the boards of the tabernacle.

18 "And you shall make the boards for the tabernacle: twenty boards for the south side.

19 "And you shall make forty [27]sockets of silver under the twenty boards, two sockets under one board for its two tenons and two sockets under another board for its two tenons;

20 and for the second side of the tabernacle, on the north side, twenty boards,

21 and their forty sockets of silver; two sockets under one board and two sockets under another board.

26:20
Ex 36:23

22 "And for the rear of the tabernacle, to the west, you shall make six boards.

23 "And you shall make two boards for the corners of the tabernacle at the rear.

24 "And they shall be double beneath, and together they shall be complete to its top to the first ring; thus it shall be with both of them: they shall form the two corners.

25 "And there shall be eight boards with their sockets of silver, sixteen sockets; two sockets under one board and two sockets under another board.

26:25
Ex 36:30

26 "Then you shall make bars of acacia wood, five for the boards of one side of the tabernacle,

27 and five bars for the boards of the other side of the tabernacle, and five bars for the boards of the side of the tabernacle for the rear *side* to the west.

28 "And the middle bar in the center of the boards shall pass through from end to end.

29 "And you shall overlay the boards with gold and make their rings of gold *as* holders for the bars; and you shall overlay the bars with gold.

30 "Then you shall erect the tabernacle according to its plan which you have been shown in the mountain.

26:30
Ex 25:9,40;
27:8;
Acts 7:44;
Heb 8:5

F. The veil

31 "And you shall make a veil of blue and purple and scarlet *material* and fine twisted linen; it shall be made with cherubim, the work of a skillful workman.

*26:31
Ex 36:35;
Matt 27:51;
Heb 9:3

32 "And you shall hang it on four pillars of acacia overlaid with gold, their hooks *also being of* gold, on four sockets of silver.

33 "And you shall hang up the veil under the clasps, and shall bring in the ark of the testimony there within the veil; and the veil shall serve for you as a partition between the holy place and the holy of holies.

*26:33
Ex 25:16;
40:21;
Lev 16:2;
Heb 9:2,3
26:34
Ex 25:21;
40:20;
Heb 9:5

34 "And you shall put the mercy seat on the ark of the testimony in the holy of holies.

35 "And you shall set the table outside the veil, and the lampstand opposite the table on the side of the tabernacle toward the south; and you shall put the table on the north side.

26:35
Ex 40:22,24;
Heb 9:2

[27]Or, *bases,* and so throughout this context

26:31 The veil in the tabernacle separated the Holy of Holies from all men, even the priests. It was entered but once a year by the high priest and then only with an offering of blood both for his own sins and for the sins of the people. The figure is plain: man was separated from God by his sin and an approach could be made only by blood and through the priesthood. (See note on Matt. 27:51.)
26:33 The veil here described shut off the Holy of Holies from the outer holy place of the tabernacle. This innermost chamber, called the Holy of Holies, was variously designated as *the sanctuary* (Lev. 4:6); *the holy place* (Lev. 16:2), which is literally in Hebrew "Holy of Holies." In this innermost sanctum was the ark of the covenant. The mercy seat was the lid, made of solid gold. The cherubim were on top

of the lid and were of one piece with it. Inside the ark were the golden jar holding manna from the wilderness (16:33), Aaron's rod (Num. 17:10), and a copy of the Law (Deut. 31:26; 2 Kin. 22:8). Because the golden altar of incense was placed right in front of the inner veil (which curtained off the innermost sanctum from the holy place), and because the smoke of its incense wafted through the veil to cover over the mercy seat, the golden altar itself is spoken of in Heb. 9:3,4 as pertaining to the *Holy of Holies,* even though it was actually placed on the other side of the veil. The Holy of Holies typified the heavenly sanctuary into which Christ was to enter once and for all with His own blood as a sacrifice for the sins of men (Heb. 9:23–26).

26:36
Ex 36:37

36 "And you shall make a screen for the doorway of the tent of blue and purple and scarlet *material* and fine twisted linen, the work of a weaver.

26:37
Ex 36:38

37 "And you shall make five pillars of acacia for the screen, and overlay them with gold, their hooks *also being of* gold; and you shall cast five sockets of bronze for them.

G. *The altar*

27:1
Ex 38:1;
Ezek 43:13

27 "And you shall make the altar of acacia wood, five cubits long and five cubits wide; the altar shall be square, and its height shall be three cubits.

2 "And you shall make its horns on its four corners; its horns shall be of one piece with it, and you shall overlay it with bronze.

27:3
Num 4:14

3 "And you shall make its pails for removing its ashes, and its shovels and its basins and its forks and its firepans; you shall make all its utensils of bronze.

4 "And you shall make for it a grating of network of bronze, and on the net you shall make four bronze rings at its four corners.

5 "And you shall put it beneath, under the ledge of the altar, that the net may reach halfway up the altar.

6 "And you shall make poles for the altar, poles of acacia wood, and overlay them with bronze.

7 "And its poles shall be inserted into the rings, so that the poles shall be on the two sides of the altar when it is carried.

27:8
Ex 25:40;
26:30

8 "You shall make it hollow with planks; as it was shown to you in the mountain, so they shall make *it*.

H. *The court of the tabernacle*

27:9
Ex 38:9

9 "And you shall make the court of the tabernacle. On the south side *there shall be* hangings for the court of fine twisted linen one hundred cubits long for one side;

27:10
Ex 38:17

10 and its pillars *shall be* twenty, with their twenty sockets of bronze; the hooks of the pillars and their bands *shall be* of silver.

11 "And likewise for the north side in length *there shall be* hangings one hundred *cubits* long, and its twenty pillars with their twenty sockets of bronze; the hooks of the pillars and their bands *shall be* of silver.

12 "And *for* the width of the court on the west side *shall be* hangings of fifty cubits *with* their ten pillars and their ten sockets.

13 "And the width of the court on the east side *shall be* fifty cubits.

27:14
Ex 38:15

14 "The hangings for the *one* side *of the gate shall be* fifteen cubits *with* their three pillars and their three sockets.

15 "And for the other side *shall be* hangings of fifteen cubits *with* their three pillars and their three sockets.

27:16
Ex 36:37

16 "And for the gate of the court there *shall be* a screen of twenty cubits, of blue and purple and scarlet *material* and fine twisted linen, the work of a weaver, *with* their four pillars and their four sockets.

17 "All the pillars around the court shall be furnished with silver bands *with* their hooks of silver and their sockets of bronze.

18 "The length of the court *shall be* one hundred cubits, and the width fifty throughout, and the height five cubits of fine twisted linen, and their sockets of bronze.

19 "All the utensils of the tabernacle *used* in all its service, and all its pegs, and all the pegs of the court, *shall be* of bronze.

I. *The service and ritual*

1. *Oil for the lamp*

27:20
Lev 24:2
*27:21
Ex 26:31,33;
30:8; 28:43;
Lev 3:17;
16:34

20 "And you shall charge the sons of Israel, that they bring you clear oil of beaten olives for the light, to make a lamp burn continually.

21 "In the tent of meeting, outside the veil which is before the testimony, Aaron and his sons shall keep it in order from evening to morning before the LORD; *it shall be* a perpetual statute throughout their generations for the sons of Israel.

27:21 *tent of meeting,* clearly another designation for the tabernacle that was the meeting place between God and   His people.

2. The garments for the priesthood

28 "Then bring near to yourself Aaron your brother, and his sons with him, from among the sons of Israel, to minister as priest to Me—Aaron, Nadab and Abihu, Eleazar and Ithamar, Aaron's sons.

2 "And you shall make holy garments for Aaron your brother, for glory and for beauty.

3 "And you shall speak to all the skillful persons whom I have endowed with the spirit of wisdom, that they make Aaron's garments to consecrate him, that he may minister as priest to Me.

4 "And these are the garments which they shall make: a [28]breastpiece and an ephod and a robe and a tunic of checkered work, a turban and a sash, and they shall make holy garments for Aaron your brother and his sons, that he may minister as priest to Me.

5 "And they shall take the gold and the blue and the purple and the scarlet *material* and the fine linen.

6 "They shall also make the ephod of gold, of blue and purple *and* scarlet *material* and fine twisted linen, the work of the skillful workman.

7 "It shall have two shoulder pieces joined to its two ends, that it may be joined.

8 "And the skillfully woven band, which is on it, shall be like its workmanship, of the same material: of gold, of blue and purple and scarlet *material* and fine twisted linen.

9 "And you shall take two onyx stones and engrave on them the names of the sons of Israel,

10 six of their names on the one stone, and the names of the remaining six on the other stone, according to their birth.

11 "As a jeweler engraves a signet, you shall engrave the two stones according to the names of the sons of Israel; you shall set them in filigree *settings* of gold.

12 "And you shall put the two stones on the shoulder pieces of the ephod, *as* stones of memorial for the sons of Israel, and Aaron shall bear their names before the LORD on his two shoulders for a memorial.

13 "And you shall make filigree *settings* of gold,

14 and two chains of pure gold; you shall make them of twisted cordage work, and you shall put the corded chains on the filigree *settings*.

15 "And you shall make a breastpiece of judgment, the work of a skillful workman; like the work of the ephod you shall make it: of gold, of blue and purple and scarlet *material* and fine twisted linen you shall make it.

16 "It shall be square *and* folded double, a span in length and a span in width.

17 "And you shall mount on it four rows of stones; the first row *shall be* a row of ruby, topaz and emerald;

18 and the second row a turquoise, a sapphire and a diamond;

19 and the third row a jacinth, an agate and an amethyst;

20 and the fourth row a beryl and an onyx and a jasper; they shall be set in gold filigree.

21 "And the stones shall be according to the names of the sons of Israel: twelve, according to their names; they shall be *like* the engravings of a seal, each according to his name for the twelve tribes.

22 "And you shall make on the breastpiece chains of twisted cordage work in pure gold.

23 "And you shall make on the breastpiece two rings of gold, and shall put the two rings on the two ends of the breastpiece.

24 "And you shall put the two cords of gold on the two rings at the ends of the breastpiece.

25 "And you shall put the *other* two ends of the two cords on the two filigree *settings*, and put them on the shoulder pieces of the ephod, at the front of it.

26 "And you shall make two rings of gold and shall place them on the two ends of the breastpiece, on the edge of it, which is toward the inner side of the ephod.

27 "And you shall make two rings of gold and put them on the bottom of the two shoulder pieces of the ephod, on the front of it close to the place where it is joined, above the skillfully woven band of the ephod.

[28]Or, *pouch*

28:1 *Aaron*, the high priest, represents Christ, our high priest. In Heb. 5:6ff. the priesthood of Christ (*according to*

the order of Melchizedek) is contrasted with that of Aaron and is shown to surpass it in efficacy.

Marginal references:

28:1 Num 18:7; Heb 5:1,4

28:2 Ex 29:5,29; 31:10

28:3 Ex 31:3,6

28:4 see vv. 6,15, 31,39

28:6 Ex 39:2

28:9 1 Cor 9:22

28:12 v. 29; Ex 39:7

28:15 Ex 39:8

28:17 Ex 39:10ff

28:21 Ex 39:14

28:24 Ex 39:17

28:26 Ex 39:17

28 "And they shall bind the breastpiece by its rings to the rings of the ephod with a blue cord, that it may be on the skillfully woven band of the ephod, and that the breastpiece may not come loose from the ephod.

28:29
v. 12

29 "And Aaron shall carry the names of the sons of Israel in the breastpiece of judgment over his heart when he enters the holy place, for a memorial before the LORD continually.

*28:30
Lev 8:8;
Num 27:21

30 "And you shall put in the breastpiece of judgment the [29]Urim and the Thummim, and they shall be over Aaron's heart when he goes in before the LORD; and Aaron shall carry the judgment of the sons of Israel over his heart before the LORD continually.

28:31
Ex 39:22

31 "And you shall make the robe of the ephod all of blue.

32 "And there shall be an opening at its top in the middle of it; around its opening there shall be a binding of woven work, as it were the opening of a coat of mail, that it may not be torn.

33 "And you shall make on its hem pomegranates of blue and purple and scarlet material, all around on its hem, and bells of gold between them all around:

34 a golden bell and a pomegranate, a golden bell and a pomegranate, all around on the hem of the robe.

35 "And it shall be on Aaron when he ministers; and its tinkling may be heard when he enters and leaves the holy place before the LORD, that he may not die.

28:36
Ex 39:30,31

36 "You shall also make a plate of pure gold and shall engrave on it, like the engravings of a seal, 'Holy to the LORD.'

37 "And you shall fasten it on a blue cord, and it shall be on the turban; it shall be at the front of the turban.

28:38
v. 43;
Lev 10:17;
Num 18:1;
Heb 9:28;
1 Pet 2:24

38 "And it shall be on Aaron's forehead, and Aaron shall take away the iniquity of the holy things which the sons of Israel consecrate, with regard to all their holy gifts; and it shall always be on his forehead, that they may be accepted before the LORD.

39 "And you shall weave the tunic of checkered work of fine linen, and shall make a turban of fine linen, and you shall make a sash, the work of a weaver.

28:40
v. 4;
Ex 39:27-29
28:41
Ex 29:7-9;
30:30;
Lev ch. 8;
Heb 7:28
28:42
Ex 39:28

40 "And for Aaron's sons you shall make tunics; you shall also make sashes for them, and you shall make caps for them, for glory and for beauty.

41 "And you shall put them on Aaron your brother and on his sons with him; and you shall anoint them and ordain them and consecrate them, that they may serve Me as priests.

42 "And you shall make for them linen breeches to cover their bare flesh; they shall reach from the loins even to the thighs.

28:43
Ex 20:26;
Lev 20:19,20;
Ex 27:21;
Lev 17:7

43 "And they shall be on Aaron and on his sons when they enter the tent of meeting, or when they approach the altar to minister in the holy place, so that they do not incur guilt and die. It shall be a statute forever to him and to his descendants after him.

3. The ordination of the priests

a. The ordination ritual

29:1
Lev 8:2

29 "Now this is what you shall do to them to consecrate them to minister as priests to Me: take one young bull and two rams without blemish,

29:2
Lev 6:19-23

2 and unleavened bread and unleavened cakes mixed with oil, and unleavened wafers spread with oil; you shall make them of fine wheat flour.

3 "And you shall put them in one basket, and present them in the basket along with the bull and the two rams.

29:4
Ex 40:12;
Heb 10:22
29:5
Ex 28:2,8

4 "Then you shall bring Aaron and his sons to the doorway of the tent of meeting, and wash them with water.

5 "And you shall take the garments, and put on Aaron the tunic and the robe of

[29]I.e., lights and perfections

28:30 Urim and Thummim signify literally "lights" and "perfections." The precise nature of these is still unclear. They were perhaps two gem-stones that were laid in a receptacle in the breastplate of the high priest. Num. 27:21; 1 Sam. 14:37–42; and 28:6 are passages construed by some to show that these two stones could be cast as lots in determining God's reply to questions of national interest to Israel. There are difficulties with this view, but no other

seems to be better. Whatever the correct explanation, Scripture does indicate that the use of them was a medium whereby guilt or innocence of suspected persons might be ascertained and the will of God discovered (1 Sam. 14). The use of the Urim and Thummim is not mentioned during the reign of David. Ezra 2:63 and Neh. 7:65 note that after the Babylonian exile Israel had no priest with Urim and Thummim. There is no Biblical reference to them thereafter.

the ephod and the ephod and the breastpiece, and gird him with the skillfully woven band of the ephod;

6 and you shall set the turban on his head, and put the holy crown on the turban.

7 "Then you shall take the anointing oil, and pour it on his head and anoint him.

8 "And you shall bring his sons and put tunics on them.

9 "And you shall gird them with sashes, Aaron and his sons, and bind caps on them, and they shall have the priesthood by a perpetual statute. So you shall ordain Aaron and his sons.

b. The sin offering

10 "Then you shall bring the bull before the tent of meeting, and Aaron and his sons shall lay their hands on the head of the bull.

11 "And you shall slaughter the bull before the LORD at the doorway of the tent of meeting.

12 "And you shall take some of the blood of the bull and put it on the horns of the altar with your finger; and you shall pour out all the blood at the base of the altar.

13 "And you shall take all the fat that covers the entrails and the lobe of the liver, and the two kidneys and the fat that is on them, and offer them up in smoke on the altar.

14 "But the flesh of the bull and its hide and its refuse, you shall burn with fire outside the camp; it is a sin offering.

c. The burnt offering

15 "You shall also take the one ram, and Aaron and his sons shall lay their hands on the head of the ram;

16 and you shall slaughter the ram and shall take its blood and sprinkle it around on the altar.

17 "Then you shall cut the ram into its pieces, and wash its entrails and its legs, and put them with its pieces and its head.

18 "And you shall offer up in smoke the whole ram on the altar; it is a burnt offering to the LORD: it is a soothing aroma, an offering by fire to the LORD.

d. The sacrifice on ordination

19 "Then you shall take the other ram, and Aaron and his sons shall lay their hands on the head of the ram.

20 "And you shall slaughter the ram, and take some of its blood and put it on the lobe of Aaron's right ear and on the lobes of his sons' right ears and on the thumbs of their right hands and on the big toes of their right feet, and sprinkle the rest of the blood around on the altar.

21 "Then you shall take some of the blood that is on the altar and some of the anointing oil, and sprinkle it on Aaron and on his garments, and on his sons and on his sons' garments with him; so he and his garments shall be consecrated, as well as his sons and his sons' garments with him.

22 "You shall also take the fat from the ram and the fat tail, and the fat that covers the entrails and the lobe of the liver, and the two kidneys and the fat that is on them and the right thigh (for it is a ram of ordination),

23 and one cake of bread and one cake of bread mixed with oil and one wafer from the basket of unleavened bread which is set before the LORD;

24 and you shall put all these in the hands of Aaron and in the hands of his sons, and shall wave them as a wave offering before the LORD.

25 "And you shall take them from their hands, and offer them up in smoke on the altar on the burnt offering for a soothing aroma before the LORD; it is an offering by fire to the LORD.

26 "Then you shall take the breast of Aaron's ram of ordination, and wave it as a wave offering before the LORD; and it shall be your portion.

27 "And you shall consecrate the breast of the wave offering and the thigh of the heave offering which was waved and which was offered from the ram of ordination, from the one which was for Aaron and from the one which was for his sons.

28 "And it shall be for Aaron and his sons as their portion forever from the sons of Israel, for it is a heave offering; and it shall be a heave offering from the sons of Israel from the sacrifices of their peace offerings, even their heave offering to the LORD.

29:6 Lev 8:9
29:7 Lev 8:12
29:8 Lev 8:13
29:9 Num 18:7; Ex 28:41
29:10 Lev 1:4; 8:14
29:12 Lev 8:15; Ex 27:2
29:13 Lev 3:3
29:14 Lev 4:11,12, 21
29:18 Gen 8:21
29:21 Ex 30:25,31; v. 1; Heb 9:22
29:23 Lev 8:26
29:24 Lev 7:30
29:25 Lev 8:28
29:26 Lev 8:29
29:27 Lev 7:31,34; Deut 18:3
29:28 Lev 10:15

29:29
Num 20:26,
28; 18:8
29:30
Num 20:28;
Lev 8:35;
9:1,8
29:31
Lev 8:31
29:32
Matt 12:4
29:33
Lev 10:14,15,
17; 22:10
29:34
Lev 8:32

29 "And the holy garments of Aaron shall be for his sons after him, that in them they may be anointed and ordained.

30 "For seven days the one of his sons who is priest in his stead shall put them on when he enters the tent of meeting to minister in the holy place.

31 "And you shall take the ram of ordination and boil its flesh in a holy place.

32 "And Aaron and his sons shall eat the flesh of the ram, and the bread that is in the basket, at the doorway of the tent of meeting.

33 "Thus they shall eat those things by which atonement was made at their ordination *and* consecration; but a layman shall not eat *them*, because they are holy.

34 "And if any of the flesh of ordination or any of the bread remains until morning, then you shall burn the remainder with fire; it shall not be eaten, because it is holy.

29:35
Lev 8:33

35 "And thus you shall do to Aaron and to his sons, according to all that I have commanded you; you shall ordain them through seven days.

29:36
Heb 10:11;
Ex 40:10

36 "And each day you shall offer a bull as a sin offering for atonement, and you shall purify the altar when you make atonement for it; and you shall anoint it to consecrate it.

29:37
Ex 40:10;
Matt 23:19

37 "For seven days you shall make atonement for the altar and consecrate it; then the altar shall be most holy, *and* whatever touches the altar shall be holy.

e. The altar of burnt offering

29:38
Num 28:3

38 "Now this is what you shall offer on the altar: two one year old lambs each day, continuously.

39 "The one lamb you shall offer in the morning, and the other lamb you shall offer at twilight;

40 and there *shall be* one-tenth *of an ephah* of fine flour mixed with one-fourth of a hin of beaten oil, and one-fourth of a hin of wine for a libation with one lamb.

41 "And the other lamb you shall offer at twilight, and shall offer with it the same grain offering as the morning and the same libation, for a soothing aroma, an offering by fire to the LORD.

29:42
Ex 30:8

42 "It shall be a continual burnt offering throughout your generations at the doorway of the tent of meeting before the LORD, where I will meet with you, to speak to you there.

29:43
1 Kin 8:11

43 "And I will meet there with the sons of Israel, and it shall be consecrated by My glory.

29:44
Lev 21:15

44 "And I will consecrate the tent of meeting and the altar; I will also consecrate Aaron and his sons to minister as priests to Me.

29:45
Ex 25:8;
Lev 26:12;
Rev 21:3
29:46
Ex 20:2

45 "And I will dwell among the sons of Israel and will be their God.

46 "And they shall know that I am the LORD their God who brought them out of the land of Egypt, that I might dwell among them; I am the LORD their God.

4. The altar of incense

30:1
Ex 37:25

30 "Moreover, you shall make an altar as a place for burning incense; you shall make it of acacia wood.

2 "Its length *shall be* a cubit, and its width a cubit, it shall be square, and its height *shall be* two cubits; its horns *shall be* of one piece with it.

3 "And you shall overlay it with pure gold, its top and its sides all around, and its horns; and you shall make a gold molding all around for it.

4 "And you shall make two gold rings for it under its molding; you shall make *them* on its two side walls—on opposite sides—and they shall be holders for poles with which to carry it.

5 "And you shall make the poles of acacia wood and overlay them with gold.

30:6
Ex 25:21,22

6 "And you shall put this altar in front of the veil that is near the ark of the testimony, in front of the mercy seat that is over *the ark of* the testimony, where I will meet with you.

30:7
vv. 34,35;
Ex 27:21

7 "And Aaron shall burn fragrant incense on it; he shall burn it every morning when he trims the lamps.

8 "And when Aaron trims the lamps at twilight, he shall burn incense. *There shall be* perpetual incense before the LORD throughout your generations.

30:9
Lev 10:1
*30:10
Lev 16:18

9 "You shall not offer any strange incense on this altar, or burnt offering or meal offering; and you shall not pour out a libation on it.

10 "And Aaron shall make atonement on its horns once a year; he shall make

---

30:10 *once a year.* This is a reference to the Day of Atonement. (See note to Lev. 16:6.)

atonement on it with the blood of the sin offering of atonement once a year throughout your generations. It is most holy to the LORD."

5. The offerings for the tabernacle

11 The LORD also spoke to Moses, saying,

12 "When you take a census of the sons of Israel to number them, then each one of them shall give a ransom for himself to the LORD, when you number them, that there may be no plague among them when you number them.

13 "This is what everyone who is numbered shall give: half a shekel according to the shekel of the sanctuary (the shekel is twenty gerahs), half a shekel as a contribution to the LORD.

14 "Everyone who is numbered, from twenty years old and over, shall give the contribution to the LORD.

15 "The rich shall not pay more, and the poor shall not pay less than the half shekel, when you give the contribution to the LORD to make atonement for yourselves.

16 "And you shall take the atonement money from the sons of Israel, and shall give it for the service of the tent of meeting, that it may be a memorial for the sons of Israel before the LORD, to make atonement for yourselves."

6. The bronze laver

17 And the LORD spoke to Moses, saying,

18 "You shall also make a laver of bronze, with its base of bronze, for washing; and you shall put it between the tent of meeting and the altar, and you shall put water in it.

19 "And Aaron and his sons shall wash their hands and their feet from it;

20 when they enter the tent of meeting, they shall wash with water, that they may not die; or when they approach the altar to minister, by offering up in smoke a fire *sacrifice* to the LORD.

21 "So they shall wash their hands and their feet, that they may not die; and it shall be a perpetual statute for them, for Aaron and his descendants throughout their generations."

7. The anointing oil

22 Moreover, the LORD spoke to Moses, saying,

23 "Take also for yourself the finest of spices: of flowing myrrh five hundred *shekels*, and of fragrant cinnamon half as much, two hundred and fifty, and of fragrant cane two hundred and fifty,

24 and of cassia five hundred, according to the shekel of the sanctuary, and of olive oil a hin.

25 "And you shall make of these a holy anointing oil, a perfume mixture, the work of a perfumer; it shall be a holy anointing oil.

26 "And with it you shall anoint the tent of meeting and the ark of the testimony,

27 and the table and all its utensils, and the lampstand and its utensils, and the altar of incense,

28 and the altar of burnt offering and all its utensils, and the laver and its stand.

29 "You shall also consecrate them, that they may be most holy; whatever touches them shall be holy.

30 "And you shall anoint Aaron and his sons, and consecrate them, that they may minister as priests to Me.

31 "And you shall speak to the sons of Israel, saying, 'This shall be a holy anointing oil to Me throughout your generations.

32 'It shall not be poured on anyone's body, nor shall you make *any* like it, in the same proportions; it is holy, *and* it shall be holy to you.

33 'Whoever shall mix *any* like it, or whoever puts any of it on a layman, shall be cut off from his people.' "

8. The incense

34 Then the LORD said to Moses, "Take for yourself spices, stacte and onycha and galbanum, spices with pure frankincense; there shall be an equal part of each.

Cross references: *30:12 Num 1:2,5; 31:50; Matt 20:28; 2 Sam 24:15; 30:13 Matt 17:24; 30:15 Prov 22:2; 30:16 Ex 38:25; Num 16:40; 30:18 Ex 38:8; 40:7,30; 30:19 Ex 40:31,32; 30:21 Ex 28:43; 30:25 Ex 37:29; 40:9; 30:26 Lev 8:10; 30:29 Ex 29:37; 30:30 Lev 8:12,30; 30:32 vv. 25,37; 30:33 v. 38; Ex 12:15

30:12 *a ransom for himself.* The half-shekel sanctuary (later, temple) tax that was to stay the plague the ancients associated with a census.

30:35
v. 25

35 "And with it you shall make incense, a perfume, the work of a perfumer, salted, pure, *and* holy.

30:36
Ex 29:42;
Lev 16:2;
v. 32;
Ex 29:37;
Lev 2:3

36 "And you shall beat some of it very fine, and put part of it before the testimony in the tent of meeting, where I shall meet with you; it shall be most holy to you.

37 "And the incense which you shall make, you shall not make in the same proportions for yourselves; it shall be holy to you for the LORD.

38 "Whoever shall make *any* like it, to use as perfume, shall be cut off from his people."

J. *The appointment of the workmen*

31 Now the LORD spoke to Moses, saying,

31:2
Ex 35:30-36:1

2 "See, I have called by name Bezalel, the son of Uri, the son of Hur, of the tribe of Judah.

3 "And I have filled him with the Spirit of God in wisdom, in understanding, in knowledge, and in all *kinds of* craftsmanship,

4 to make artistic designs for work in gold, in silver, and in bronze,

5 and in the cutting of stones for settings, and in the carving of wood, that he may work in all *kinds of* craftsmanship.

31:6
Ex 35:34

6 "And behold, I Myself have appointed with him Oholiab, the son of Ahisamach, of the tribe of Dan; and in the hearts of all who are skillful I have put skill, that they may make all that I have commanded you:

31:7
Ex 36:8;
37:1,6
31:8
Ex 37:10,17

7 the tent of meeting, and the ark of testimony, and the mercy seat upon it, and all the furniture of the tent,

8 the table also and its utensils, and the pure *gold* lampstand with all its utensils, and the altar of incense,

9 the altar of burnt offering also with all its utensils, and the laver and its stand,

10 the woven garments as well, and the holy garments for Aaron the priest, and the garments of his sons, *with which* to carry on their priesthood;

31:11
Ex 30:25,31;
37:29; 30:34

11 the anointing oil also, and the fragrant incense for the holy place, they are to make *them* according to all that I have commanded you."

K. *The observance of the Sabbath*

12 And the LORD spoke to Moses, saying,

31:13
Lev 19:3,30;
Ezek 20:12,
20

13 "But as for you, speak to the sons of Israel, saying, 'You shall surely observe My sabbaths; for *this* is a sign between Me and you throughout your generations, that you may know that I am the LORD who sanctifies you.

31:14
Ex 35:2;
Num 15:32,
35

14 'Therefore you are to observe the sabbath, for it is holy to you. Everyone who profanes it shall surely be put to death; for whoever does any work on it, that person shall be cut off from among his people.

31:15
Ex 16:23;
20:9,10

15 'For six days work may be done, but on the seventh day there is a sabbath of complete rest, holy to the LORD; whoever does any work on the sabbath day shall surely be put to death.

16 'So the sons of Israel shall observe the sabbath, to celebrate the sabbath throughout their generations as a perpetual covenant.'

31:17
v. 13;
Gen 2:2,3

17 "It is a sign between Me and the sons of Israel forever; for in six days the LORD made heaven and earth, but on the seventh day He ceased *from labor*, and was refreshed."

31:18
Ex 24:12;
32:15,16;
34:1,28

18 And when He had finished speaking with him upon Mount Sinai, He gave Moses the two tablets of the testimony, tablets of stone, written by the finger of God.

L. *Israel breaks the covenant by idolatry*

1. *Aaron makes a golden calf*

*32:1
Ex 24:18;
Deut 9:9;
Acts 7:40;
Ex 13:21

32 Now when the people saw that Moses delayed to come down from the mountain, the people assembled about Aaron, and said to him, "Come,

---

32:1 The making of the golden calf with Aaron's consent was flagrant idolatry. God had delivered His people from Egypt and had worked miracles. They were fed with manna and enjoyed the fire and the cloud for guidance. Yet they turned away from God. This act is called: (1) great sin

(32:21,30,31); (2) disobedience (Deut. 9:12,16); and (3) a forgetting of God (Ps. 106:21). Paul warns against this kind of wickedness (1 Cor. 10:5–7). It is important to observe that the golden calf in this case was intended as a representation of the LORD Himself (or at least of the pedestal on

make us a god who will go before us; as for this Moses, the man who brought us up from the land of Egypt, we do not know what has become of him."

2   And Aaron said to them, "Tear off the gold rings which are in the ears of your wives, your sons, and your daughters, and bring *them* to me."

3   Then all the people tore off the gold rings which were in their ears, and brought *them* to Aaron.

4   And he took *this* from their hand, and fashioned it with a graving tool, and made it into a molten calf; and they said, "This is your god, O Israel, who brought you up from the land of Egypt."

5   Now when Aaron saw *this*, he built an altar before it; and Aaron made a proclamation and said, "Tomorrow *shall be* a feast to the LORD."

6   So the next day they rose early and offered burnt offerings, and brought peace offerings; and the people sat down to eat and to drink, and rose up to play.

2. *Moses intercedes for sinful Israel*

7   Then the LORD spoke to Moses, "Go down at once, for your people, whom you brought up from the land of Egypt, have corrupted *themselves*.

8   "They have quickly turned aside from the way which I commanded them. They have made for themselves a molten calf, and have worshiped it, and have sacrificed to it, and said, 'This is your god, O Israel, who brought you up from the land of Egypt!' "

9   And the LORD said to Moses, "I have seen this people, and behold, they are an obstinate people.

10   "Now then let Me alone, that My anger may burn against them, and that I may destroy them; and I will make of you a great nation."

11   Then Moses entreated the LORD his God, and said, "O LORD, why doth Thine anger burn against Thy people whom Thou hast brought out from the land of Egypt with great power and with a mighty hand?

12   "Why should the Egyptians speak, saying, 'With evil *intent* He brought them out to kill them in the mountains and to destroy them from the face of the earth'? Turn from Thy burning anger and change Thy mind about *doing* harm to Thy people.

13   "Remember Abraham, Isaac, and Israel, Thy servants to whom Thou didst swear by Thyself, and didst say to them, 'I will multiply your descendants as the stars of the heavens, and all this land of which I have spoken I will give to your descendants, and they shall inherit *it* forever.' "

14   So the LORD changed His mind about the harm which He said He would do to His people.

3. *Moses destroys the calf and breaks*
the tables of the law

15   Then Moses turned and went down from the mountain with the two tablets of the testimony in his hand, tablets which were written on both sides; they were written on one *side* and the other.

16   And the tablets were God's work, and the writing was God's writing engraved on the tablets.

17   Now when Joshua heard the sound of the people as they shouted, he said to Moses, "There is a sound of war in the camp."

18   But he said,
"It is not the sound of the cry of triumph,
Nor is it the sound of the cry of defeat;
But the sound of singing I hear."

19   And it came about, as soon as Moses came near the camp, that he saw the calf and *the* dancing; and Moses' anger burned, and he threw the tablets from his hands and shattered them at the foot of the mountain.

20   And he took the calf which they had made and burned *it* with fire, and

Marginal references:
32:2 Ex 35:22
32:4 Deut 9:16; Acts 7:41
32:6 1 Cor 10:7
32:7 Deut 9:12; Dan 9:24; Gen 6:11,12
32:8 Ex 20:3,4,23; 1 Kin 12:28
32:9 Num 14:11-20; Ex 33:3,5; 34:9; Acts 7:31
32:10 Deut 9:14; Num 14:12
32:11 Deut 9:18
32:12 Num 14:13; Deut 9:28; v. 14
32:13 Gen 22:16; Heb 6:13; Gen 12:7; 13:15; Ex 13:5
32:14 Ps 106:45
32:15 Deut 9:15
32:16 Ex 31:18
32:19 Deut 9:16,17
32:20 Deut 9:21

---

which He invisibly stood). Aaron inaugurated its worship by proclaiming a *feast to the LORD* (v. 5). Thus God's hot anger was directed against a worship of Himself that was accompanied by the use of images contrary to His command. Certainly any pictorial representation of God is included in the prohibition of the second commandment:

"You shall not make for yourself an idol, or any likeness of what is in heaven above . . . " By the same token this would forbid bowing before any image of angel or saint dwelling in heaven above. Israel should have known this and was sternly punished for violating God's command.

ground it to powder, and scattered it over the surface of the water, and made the sons of Israel drink *it.*

21 Then Moses said to Aaron, "What did this people do to you, that you have brought *such* great sin upon them?"

22 And Aaron said, "Do not let the anger of my lord burn; you know the people yourself, that they are prone to evil.

23 "For they said to me, 'Make a god for us who will go before us; for this Moses, the man who brought us up from the land of Egypt, we do not know what has become of him.'

24 "And I said to them, 'Whoever has any gold, let them tear it off.' So they gave *it* to me, and I threw it into the fire, and out came this calf."

4. *The slaughter by the Levites*

25 Now when Moses saw that the people were out of control—for Aaron had let them get out of control to be a derision among their enemies—

26 then Moses stood in the gate of the camp, and said, "Whoever is for the LORD, *come* to me!" And all the sons of Levi gathered together to him.

27 And he said to them, "Thus says the LORD, the God of Israel, 'Every man *of you* put his sword upon his thigh, and go back and forth from gate to gate in the camp, and kill every man his brother, and every man his friend, and every man his neighbor.'"

28 So the sons of Levi did as Moses instructed, and about three thousand men of the people fell that day.

29 Then Moses said, "Dedicate yourselves today to the LORD—for every man has been against his son and against his brother—in order that He may bestow a blessing upon you today."

5. *The second intercession of Moses*

30 And it came about on the next day that Moses said to the people, "You yourselves have committed a great sin; and now I am going up to the LORD, perhaps I can make atonement for your sin."

31 Then Moses returned to the LORD, and said, "Alas, this people has committed a great sin, and they have made a god of gold for themselves.

32 "But now, if Thou wilt, forgive their sin—and if not, please blot me out from Thy book which Thou hast written!"

33 And the LORD said to Moses, "Whoever has sinned against Me, I will blot him out of My book.

34 "But go now, lead the people where I told you. Behold, My angel shall go before you; nevertheless in the day when I punish, I will punish them for their sin."

35 Then the LORD smote the people, because of what they did with the calf which Aaron had made.

6. *The renewal of the covenant*

a. *God's command to depart*

33 Then the LORD spoke to Moses, "Depart, go up from here, you and the people whom you have brought up from the land of Egypt, to the land of which I swore to Abraham, Isaac, and Jacob, saying, 'To your descendants I will give it.'

2 "And I will send an angel before you and I will drive out the Canaanite, the Amorite, the Hittite, the Perizzite, the Hivite and the Jebusite.

3 "*Go up* to a land flowing with milk and honey; for I will not go up in your midst, because you are an obstinate people, lest I destroy you on the way."

4 When the people heard this sad word, they went into mourning, and none of them put on his ornaments.

5 For the LORD had said to Moses, "Say to the sons of Israel, 'You are an obstinate people; should I go up in your midst for one moment, I would destroy

32:31 Moses confessed to God the sin of Israel in the making of the golden calf. He prayed for forgiveness as an intercessor for the people. God freely forgave them, but there were consequences of the sin that were unavoidable (see v. 35). The Biblical principle established here is that guilt and penalty may be set aside in response to repentance and confession, but the temporal consequences of the sin may continue all the days of this life. An example of this is Moses arrogantly striking the rock to which he was only supposed to speak (Num. 20:12). His sin was forgiven and the guilt and penalty removed, but the temporal consequence endured—he could not enter the promised land.

you. Now therefore, put off your ornaments from you, that I may know what I will do with you.' "

6   So the sons of Israel stripped themselves of their ornaments from Mount Horeb *onward.*

b. *The tent of meeting*

7   Now Moses used to take the tent and pitch it outside the camp, a good distance from the camp, and he called it the tent of meeting. And it came about, that everyone who sought the Lord would go out to the tent of meeting which was outside the camp.

8   And it came about, whenever Moses went out to the tent, that all the people would arise and stand, each at the entrance of his tent, and gaze after Moses until he entered the tent.

9   And it came about, whenever Moses entered the tent, the pillar of cloud would descend and stand at the entrance of the tent; and the Lord would speak with Moses.

10   When all the people saw the pillar of cloud standing at the entrance of the tent, all the people would arise and worship, each at the entrance of his tent.

11   Thus the Lord used to speak to Moses face to face, just as a man speaks to his friend. When Moses returned to the camp, his servant Joshua, the son of Nun, a young man, would not depart from the tent.

c. *The promise of God's presence*

12   Then Moses said to the Lord, "See, Thou dost say to me, 'Bring up this people!' But Thou Thyself hast not let me know whom Thou wilt send with me. Moreover, Thou hast said, 'I have known you by name, and you have also found favor in My sight.'

13   "Now therefore, I pray Thee, if I have found favor in Thy sight, let me know Thy ways, that I may know Thee, so that I may find favor in Thy sight. Consider too, that this nation is Thy people."

14   And He said, "My presence shall go *with you,* and I will give you rest."

15   Then he said to Him, "If Thy presence does not go *with us,* do not lead us up from here.

16   "For how then can it be known that I have found favor in Thy sight, I and Thy people? Is it not by Thy going with us, so that we, I and Thy people, may be distinguished from all the *other* people who are upon the face of the earth?"

d. *Moses beholds God's glory*

17   And the Lord said to Moses, "I will also do this thing of which you have spoken; for you have found favor in My sight, and I have known you by name."

18   Then Moses said, "I pray Thee, show me Thy glory!"

19   And He said, "I Myself will make all My goodness pass before you, and will proclaim the name of the Lord before you; and I will be gracious to whom I will be gracious, and will show compassion on whom I will show compassion."

20   But He said, "You cannot see My face, for no man can see Me and live!"

21   Then the Lord said, "Behold, there is a place by Me, and you shall stand *there* on the rock;

22   and it will come about, while My glory is passing by, that I will put you in the cleft of the rock and cover you with My hand until I have passed by.

23   "Then I will take My hand away and you shall see My back, but My face shall not be seen."

e. *The second tables of stone: the covenant promise repeated*

34   Now the Lord said to Moses, "Cut out for yourself two stone tablets like the former ones, and I will write on the tablets the words that were on the former tablets which you shattered.

2   "So be ready by morning, and come up in the morning to Mount Sinai, and present yourself there to Me on the top of the mountain.

3   "And no man is to come up with you, nor let any man be seen anywhere on the mountain; even the flocks and the herds may not graze in front of that mountain."

4   So he cut out two stone tablets like the former ones, and Moses rose up early in the morning and went up to Mount Sinai, as the Lord had commanded him, and he took two stone tablets in his hand.

33:7
Ex 29:42,43;
Deut 4:29

33:8
Num 16:27

33:9
Ex 25:22;
31:18;
Ps 99:7

33:11
Num 12:8;
Deut 34:10;
Ex 24:13

33:12
Ex 32:34;
v. 17; Jer 1:5;
John 10:14,
15;
2 Tim 2:19
33:13
Ex 34:9;
Ps 25:4;
Deut 9:26,29

33:14
Is 63:9;
Josh 22:4

33:16
Num 14:14;
Ex 34:10

33:17
v. 12

33:18
vv. 20,23
33:19
Rom 9:15,16,
18

33:20
Gen 32:20;
Is 6:5

33:23
John 1:18

34:1
Ex 32:16,19;
v. 28

34:2
Ex 19:20

34:3
Ex 19:12,13,
21

34:5
Ex 33:19

5   And the LORD descended in the cloud and stood there with him as he called upon the name of the LORD.

34:6
Num 14:18;
Neh 9:17;
Ps 86:15;
103:8

6   Then the LORD passed by in front of him and proclaimed, "The LORD, the LORD God, compassionate and gracious, slow to anger, and abounding in lovingkindness and truth;

34:7
Ex 20:6,7;
Ps 103:3;
Dan 9:9;
Eph 4:32

7   who keeps lovingkindness for thousands, who forgives iniquity, transgression and sin; yet He will by no means leave *the guilty* unpunished, visiting the iniquity of fathers on the children and on the grandchildren to the third and fourth generations."

34:8
Ex 4:31

8   And Moses made haste to bow low toward the earth and worship.

34:9
Ex 33:3,15,16

9   And he said, "If now I have found favor in Thy sight, O Lord, I pray, let the Lord go along in our midst, even though the people are so obstinate; and do Thou pardon our iniquity and our sin, and take us as Thine own possession."

34:10
Deut 5:2;
4:32

10   Then God said, "Behold, I am going to make a covenant. Before all your people I will perform miracles which have not been produced in all the earth, nor among any of the nations; and all the people among whom you live will see the working of the LORD, for it is a fearful thing that I am going to perform with you.

f. *Warning against heathen idolatry*

34:11
Deut 6:3;
Ex 33:2

11   "Be sure to observe what I am commanding you this day: behold, I am going to drive out the Amorite before you, and the Canaanite, the Hittite, the Perizzite, the Hivite and the Jebusite.

34:12
Ex 23:32,33

12   "Watch yourself that you make no covenant with the inhabitants of the land into which you are going, lest it become a snare in your midst.

*34:13
Ex 23:24;
2 Kin 18:4

13   "But *rather*, you are to tear down their altars and smash their *sacred* pillars and cut down their [30]Asherim

*34:14
Ex 20:3,5;
Deut 4:24

14   —for you shall not worship any other god, for the LORD, whose name is Jealous, is a jealous God—

34:15
Judg 2:17;
Num 25:2;
1 Cor 8:4,7,
10

15   lest you make a covenant with the inhabitants of the land and they play the harlot with their gods, and sacrifice to their gods, and someone invite you to eat of his sacrifice;

34:16
Deut 7:3;
Num 25:1

16   and you take some of his daughters for your sons, and his daughters play the harlot with their gods, and cause your sons *also* to play the harlot with their gods.

g. *Diverse commands*

34:17
Ex 32:8

17   "You shall make for yourself no molten gods.

34:18
Ex 12:2,
15-17; 13:4

18   "You shall observe the Feast of Unleavened Bread. For seven days you are to eat unleavened bread, as I commanded you, at the appointed time in the month of Abib, for in the month of Abib you came out of Egypt.

34:19
Ex 13:2;
22:29

19   "The first offspring from every womb belongs to Me, and all your male livestock, the first offspring from cattle and sheep.

34:20
Ex 13:13;
23:15

20   "And you shall redeem with a lamb the first offspring from a donkey; and if you do not redeem *it*, then you shall break its neck. You shall redeem all the first-born of your sons. And none shall appear before Me empty-handed.

34:21
Ex 20:9;
Luke 13:14

21   "You shall work six days, but on the seventh day you shall rest; *even* during plowing time and harvest you shall rest.

34:22
Ex 23:16

22   "And you shall celebrate the Feast of Weeks, *that is*, the first fruits of the wheat harvest, and the Feast of Ingathering at the turn of the year.

34:23
Ex 23:14-17

23   "Three times a year all your males are to appear before the Lord GOD, the God of Israel.

24   "For I will drive out nations before you and enlarge your borders, and no man shall covet your land when you go up three times a year to appear before the LORD your God.

[30]I.e., wooden symbols of a female deity

34:13 *Asherim*, symbols of Asherah, the Canaanite mother-goddess, who figured prominently in the fertility cult of the Canaanites. These objects were certainly of wood because they are referred to as a tree, or a pole; and they could be cut down, burned, plucked up, or broken in pieces (34:13; Deut. 16:21; 2 Chr. 34:4; Mic. 5:14). Some scholars suggest that all the Asherim were images of the goddess. In any case, they were associated with an idolatry of the most

immoral character, and they became a snare to Israel, causing them to disobey the second commandment (20:3–5; Deut. 5:8,9).
34:14 *Jealous . . . God* is a very appropriate way to describe God. When God's just and righteous claim on His creatures is rejected, He is warranted in being angry. In fact, His anger springs from man's refusal to respond to His love and is in full accord with His justice.

25 "You shall not offer the blood of My sacrifice with leavened bread, nor is the sacrifice of the Feast of the Passover to be left over until morning.

26 "You shall bring the very first of the first fruits of your soil into the house of the LORD your God. You shall not boil a kid in its mother's milk."

27 Then the LORD said to Moses, "Write down these words, for in accordance with these words I have made a covenant with you and with Israel."

28 So he was there with the LORD forty days and forty nights; he did not eat bread or drink water. And he wrote on the tablets the words of the covenant, the Ten Commandments.

h. *Moses' shining face: the veil*

29 And it came about when Moses was coming down from Mount Sinai (and the two tablets of the testimony *were* in Moses' hand as he was coming down from the mountain), that Moses did not know that the skin of his face shone because of his speaking with Him.

30 So when Aaron and all the sons of Israel saw Moses, behold, the skin of his face shone, and they were afraid to come near him.

31 Then Moses called to them, and Aaron and all the rulers in the congregation returned to him; and Moses spoke to them.

32 And afterward all the sons of Israel came near, and he commanded them *to do* everything that the LORD had spoken to him on Mount Sinai.

33 When Moses had finished speaking with them, he put a veil over his face.

34 But whenever Moses went in before the LORD to speak with Him, he would take off the veil until he came out; and whenever he came out and spoke to the sons of Israel what he had been commanded,

35 the sons of Israel would see the face of Moses, that the skin of Moses' face shone. So Moses would replace the veil over his face until he went in to speak with Him.

M. *The building of the tabernacle*

1. *The gathering of the materials*

35 Then Moses assembled all the congregation of the sons of Israel, and said to them, "These are the things that the LORD has commanded *you* to do.

2 "For six days work may be done, but on the seventh day you shall have a holy *day*, a sabbath of complete rest to the LORD; whoever does any work on it shall be put to death.

3 "You shall not kindle a fire in any of your dwellings on the sabbath day."

4 And Moses spoke to all the congregation of the sons of Israel, saying, "This is the thing which the LORD has commanded, saying,

5 'Take from among you a contribution to the LORD; whoever is of a willing heart, let him bring it as the LORD's contribution: gold, silver, and bronze,

6 and blue, purple and scarlet *material*, fine linen, goats' *hair*,

7 and rams' skins dyed red, and porpoise skins, and acacia wood,

8 and oil for lighting, and spices for the anointing oil, and for the fragrant incense,

9 and onyx stones and setting stones, for the ephod and for the breastpiece.

10 'And let every skillful man among you come, and make all that the LORD has commanded:

11 the tabernacle, its tent and its covering, its hooks and its boards, its bars, its pillars, and its sockets;

12 the ark and its poles, the mercy seat, and the curtain of the screen;

13 the table and its poles, and all its utensils, and the bread of the [31] Presence;

14 the lampstand also for the light and its utensils and its lamps and the oil for the light;

15 and the altar of incense and its poles, and the anointing oil and the fragrant incense, and the screen for the doorway at the entrance of the tabernacle;

16 the altar of burnt offering with its bronze grating, its poles, and all its utensils, the basin and its stand;

17 the hangings of the court, its pillars and its sockets, and the screen for the gate of the court;

18 the pegs of the tabernacle and the pegs of the court and their cords;

[31]Lit., *Face*

34:25
Ex 23:18;
12:10
34:26
Ex 23:19
34:27
Ex 17:14;
24:4
34:28
Ex 24:18;
31:18; 34:1;
Deut 4:13;
10:4

34:29
Ex 32:15;
Matt 17:2;
2 Cor 3:7,13

34:32
Ex 24:3
34:33
2 Cor 3:13
34:34
2 Cor 3:16

35:1
Ex 34:32
35:2
Ex 31:15
35:3
Ex 16:23
35:4
Ex 25:1-9

35:10
Ex 31:6
35:11
Ex 26:1ff
35:13
Ex 25:23,30;
Lev 24:5,6
35:15
Ex 30:1

35:19
Ex 31:10

19   the woven garments, for ministering in the holy place, the holy garments for Aaron the priest, and the garments of his sons, to minister as priests.'"

20   Then all the congregation of the sons of Israel departed from Moses' presence.

35:21
Ex 25:2

21   And everyone whose heart stirred him and everyone whose spirit moved him came *and* brought the LORD'S contribution for the work of the tent of meeting and for all its service and for the holy garments.

22   Then all whose hearts moved them, both men and women, came *and* brought brooches and earrings and signet rings and bracelets, all articles of gold; so *did* every man who presented an offering of gold to the LORD.

35:23
1 Chr 29:8

23   And every man, who had in his possession blue and purple and scarlet *material* and fine linen and goats' *hair* and rams' skins dyed red and porpoise skins, brought them.

24   Everyone who could make a contribution of silver and bronze brought the LORD'S contribution; and every man, who had in his possession acacia wood for any work of the service, brought it.

35:25
Ex 28:3

25   And all the skilled women spun with their hands, and brought what they had spun, *in* blue and purple *and* scarlet *material* and *in* fine linen.

26   And all the women whose heart stirred with a skill spun the goats' *hair*.

35:27
1 Chr 29:6;
Ezra 2:68

27   And the rulers brought the onyx stones and the stones for setting for the ephod and for the breastpiece;

35:28
Ex 30:23

28   and the spice and the oil for the light and for the anointing oil and for the fragrant incense.

35:29
v. 21

29   The Israelites, all the men and women, whose heart moved them to bring *material* for all the work, which the LORD had commanded through Moses to be done, brought a freewill offering to the LORD.

2. The workmen gathered

35:30
Ex 31:1-6

30   Then Moses said to the sons of Israel, "See, the LORD has called by name Bezalel the son of Uri, the son of Hur, of the tribe of Judah.

31   "And He has filled him with the Spirit of God, in wisdom, in understanding and in knowledge and in all craftsmanship;

32   to make designs for working in gold and in silver and in bronze,

33   and in the cutting of stones for settings, and in the carving of wood, so as to perform in every inventive work.

34   "He also has put in his heart to teach, both he and Oholiab, the son of Ahisamach, of the tribe of Dan.

35:35
v. 31

35   "He has filled them with skill to perform every work of an engraver and of a designer and of an embroiderer, in blue and in purple *and* in scarlet *material*, and in fine linen, and of a weaver, as performers of every work and makers of designs.

36:1
Ex 25:8

36 "Now Bezalel and Oholiab, and every skillful person in whom the LORD has put skill and understanding to know how to perform all the work in the construction of the sanctuary, shall perform in accordance with all that the LORD has commanded."

36:2
Ex 35:21,26;
1 Chr 29:5

2   Then Moses called Bezalel and Oholiab and every skillful person in whom the LORD had put skill, everyone whose heart stirred him, to come to the work to perform it.

36:3
Ex 35:27

3   And they received from Moses all the contributions which the sons of Israel had brought to perform the work in the construction of the sanctuary. And they still *continued* bringing to him freewill offerings every morning.

4   And all the skillful men who were performing all the work of the sanctuary came, each from the work which he was performing,

36:5
2 Chr 24:14;
31:6-10;
2 Cor 8:23

5   and they said to Moses, "The people are bringing much more than enough for the construction work which the LORD commanded *us* to perform."

6   So Moses issued a command, and a proclamation was circulated throughout the camp, saying, "Let neither man nor woman any longer perform work for the contributions of the sanctuary." Thus the people were restrained from bringing *any more*.

7   For the material they had was sufficient and more than enough for all the work, to perform it.

3. *The curtain and coverings made*

8   And all the skillful men among those who were performing the work made the tabernacle with ten curtains; of fine twisted linen and blue and purple and scarlet *material*, with cherubim, the work of a skillful workman, Bezalel made them.

9   The length of each curtain was twenty-eight cubits, and the width of each curtain four cubits; all the curtains had the same measurements.

10   And he joined five curtains to one another, and *the other* five curtains he joined to one another.

11   And he made loops of blue on the edge of the outermost curtain in the first set; he did likewise on the edge of the curtain that was outermost in the second set.

12   He made fifty loops in the one curtain and he made fifty loops on the edge of the curtain that was in the second set; the loops were opposite each other.

13   And he made fifty clasps of gold, and joined the curtains to one another with the clasps, so the tabernacle was a unit.

14   Then he made curtains of goats' *hair* for a tent over the tabernacle; he made eleven curtains in all.

15   The length of each curtain was thirty cubits, and four cubits the width of each curtain; the eleven curtains had the same measurements.

16   And he joined five curtains by themselves, and *the other* six curtains by themselves.

17   Moreover, he made fifty loops on the edge of the curtain that was outermost in the *first* set, and he made fifty loops on the edge of the curtain *that was outermost in* the second set.

18   And he made fifty clasps of bronze to join the tent together, that it might be a unit.

19   And he made a covering for the tent of rams' skins dyed red, and a covering of porpoise skins above.

4. *The framework of the tabernacle constructed*

20   Then he made the boards for the tabernacle of acacia wood, standing upright.

21   Ten cubits was the length of each board, and one and a half cubits the width of each board.

22   There were two tenons for each board, fitted to one another; thus he did for all the boards of the tabernacle.

23   And he made the boards for the tabernacle: twenty boards for the south side;

24   and he made forty sockets of silver under the twenty boards; two sockets under one board for its two tenons and two sockets under another board for its two tenons.

25   Then for the second side of the tabernacle, on the north side, he made twenty boards,

26   and their forty sockets of silver; two sockets under one board and two sockets under another board.

27   And for the rear of the tabernacle, to the west, he made six boards.

28   And he made two boards for the corners of the tabernacle at the rear.

29   And they were double beneath, and together they were complete to its top to the first ring; thus he did with both of them for the two corners.

30   And there were eight boards with their sockets of silver, sixteen sockets, two under every board.

31   Then he made bars of acacia wood, five for the boards of one side of the tabernacle,

32   and five bars for the boards of the other side of the tabernacle, and five bars for the boards of the tabernacle for the rear *side* to the west.

33   And he made the middle bar to pass through in the center of the boards from end to end.

34   And he overlaid the boards with gold and made their rings of gold *as* holders for the bars, and overlaid the bars with gold.

5. *The making of the veil*

35   Moreover, he made the veil of blue and purple and scarlet *material*, and fine twisted linen; he made it with cherubim, the work of a skillful workman.

36:8
Ex 26:1-14

36:12
Ex 26:5

36:14
Ex 26:7

36:19
Ex 26:14

36:20
Ex 26:15-29

36:24
Ex 26:21

36:27
Ex 26:22

36:31
Ex 26:26

36:35
Ex 26:31-37

36   And he made four pillars of acacia for it, and overlaid them with gold, with their hooks of gold; and he cast four sockets of silver for them.

37   And he made a screen for the doorway of the tent, of blue and purple and scarlet *material*, and fine twisted linen, the work of a weaver;

38   and *he made* its five pillars with their hooks, and he overlaid their tops and their bands with gold; but their five sockets were of bronze.

6. *The construction of the ark*

37:1
Ex 25:10-20

37 Now Bezalel made the ark of acacia wood; its length was two and a half cubits, and its width one and a half cubits, and its height one and a half cubits;

2   and he overlaid it with pure gold inside and out, and made a gold molding for it all around.

37:3
Ex 25:12

3   And he cast four rings of gold for it on its four feet; even two rings on one side of it, and two rings on the other side of it.

4   And he made poles of acacia wood and overlaid them with gold.

5   And he put the poles into the rings on the sides of the ark, to carry it.

37:6
Ex 25:17

6   And he made a mercy seat of pure gold, two and a half cubits long, and one and a half cubits wide.

7   And he made two cherubim of gold; he made them of hammered work, at the two ends of the mercy seat;

8   one cherub at the one end, and one cherub at the other end; he made the cherubim *of one piece* with the mercy seat at the two ends.

9   And the cherubim had *their* wings spread upward, covering the mercy seat with their wings, with their faces toward each other; the faces of the cherubim were toward the mercy seat.

7. *The building of the table*

10   Then he made the table of acacia wood, two cubits long and a cubit wide and one and a half cubits high.

11   And he overlaid it with pure gold, and made a gold molding for it all around.

12   And he made a rim for it of a handbreadth all around, and made a gold molding for its rim all around.

13   And he cast four gold rings for it and put the rings on the four corners that were on its four feet.

14   Close by the rim were the rings, the holders for the poles to carry the table.

15   And he made the poles of acacia wood and overlaid them with gold, to carry the table.

37:16
Ex 25:29

16   And he made the utensils which were on the table, its dishes and its pans and its bowls and its jars, with which to pour out libations, of pure gold.

8. *The making of the lampstand*

37:17
Ex 25:31-39

17   Then he made the lampstand of pure gold. He made the lampstand of hammered work, its base and its shaft; its cups, its bulbs and its flowers were *of one piece* with it.

18   And there were six branches going out of its sides; three branches of the lampstand from the one side of it, and three branches of the lampstand from the other side of it;

37:19
Ex 25:33

19   three cups shaped like almond *blossoms,* a bulb and a flower in one branch, and three cups shaped like almond *blossoms,* a bulb and a flower in the other branch—so for the six branches going out of the lampstand.

20   And in the lampstand *there were* four cups shaped like almond *blossoms,* its bulbs and its flowers;

37:21
Ex 25:35

21   and a bulb was under the *first* pair of branches *coming* out of it, and a bulb under the *second* pair of branches *coming* out of it, and a bulb under the *third* pair of branches *coming* out of it, for the six branches coming out of the lampstand.

22   Their bulbs and their branches were *of one piece* with it; the whole of it *was* a single hammered work of pure gold.

23   And he made its seven lamps with its snuffers and its trays of pure gold.

24   He made it and all its utensils from a talent of pure gold.

9. The construction of the altar of incense

25 Then he made the altar of incense of acacia wood: a cubit long and a cubit wide, square, and two cubits high; its horns were *of one piece* with it.

26 And he overlaid it with pure gold, its top and its sides all around, and its horns; and he made a gold molding for it all around.

27 And he made two golden rings for it under its molding, on its two sides—on opposite sides—as holders for poles with which to carry it.

28 And he made the poles of acacia wood and overlaid them with gold.

10. The oil and incense

29 And he made the holy anointing oil and the pure, fragrant incense of spices, the work of a perfumer.

11. The making of the altar of burnt offering

38 Then he made the altar of burnt offering of acacia wood, five cubits long, and five cubits wide, square, and three cubits high.

2 And he made its horns on its four corners, its horns being *of one piece* with it, and he overlaid it with bronze.

3 And he made all the utensils of the altar, the pails and the shovels and the basins, the flesh hooks and the firepans; he made all its utensils of bronze.

4 And he made for the altar a grating of bronze network beneath, under its ledge, reaching halfway up.

5 And he cast four rings on the four ends of the bronze grating *as* holders for the poles.

6 And he made the poles of acacia wood and overlaid them with bronze.

7 And he inserted the poles into the rings on the sides of the altar, with which to carry it. He made it hollow with planks.

8 Moreover, he made the laver of bronze with its base of bronze, from the mirrors of the serving women who served at the doorway of the tent of meeting.

12. The construction of the court

9 Then he made the court: for the south side the hangings of the court were of fine twisted linen, one hundred cubits;

10 their twenty pillars, and their twenty sockets, *made* of bronze; the hooks of the pillars and their bands *were* of silver.

11 And for the north side *there were* one hundred cubits; their twenty pillars and their twenty sockets *were* of bronze, the hooks of the pillars and their bands *were* of silver.

12 And for the west side *there were* hangings of fifty cubits *with* their ten pillars and their ten sockets; the hooks of the pillars and their bands *were* of silver.

13 And for the east side fifty cubits.

14 The hangings for the *one* side *of the gate were* fifteen cubits, *with* their three pillars and their three sockets,

15 and so for the other side. On both sides of the gate of the court *were* hangings of fifteen cubits, *with* their three pillars and their three sockets.

16 All the hangings of the court all around *were* of fine twisted linen.

17 And the sockets for the pillars *were* of bronze, the hooks of the pillars and their bands, of silver; and the overlaying of their tops, of silver, and all the pillars of the court were furnished with silver bands.

18 And the screen of the gate of the court was the work of the weaver, of blue and purple and scarlet *material*, and fine twisted linen. And the length was twenty cubits and the height was five cubits, corresponding to the hangings of the court.

19 And their four pillars and their four sockets *were* of bronze; their hooks *were* of silver, and the overlaying of their tops and their bands *were* of silver.

20 And all the pegs of the tabernacle and of the court all around *were* of bronze.

13. The sum of the metals used

21 This is the number of *the things for* the tabernacle, the tabernacle of the testimony, as they were numbered according to the command of Moses, for the service of the Levites, by the hand of Ithamar, the son of Aaron the priest.

22 Now Bezalel, the son of Uri the son of Hur, of the tribe of Judah, made all that the Lord had commanded Moses.

37:25
Ex 30:1-5

37:29
Ex 30:23,34

38:1
Ex 27:1-8

38:8
Ex 30:18

38:9
Ex 27:9-19

38:11
Ex 27:11

38:14
Ex 27:14

38:18
Ex 27:16

38:21
Num 4:28,33

38:22
Ex 31:2,6

23   And with him was Oholiab, the son of Ahisamach, of the tribe of Dan, an engraver and a skillful workman and a weaver in blue and in purple and in scarlet *material,* and fine linen.

38:24
Ex 30:13

24   All the gold that was used for the work, in all the work of the sanctuary, even the gold of the wave offering, was 29 talents and 730 shekels, according to the shekel of the sanctuary.

38:25
Ex 30:11-16

25   And the silver of those of the congregation who were numbered was 100 talents and 1,775 shekels, according to the shekel of the sanctuary;

38:26
Ex 30:13,15;
Num 1:46

26   a beka a head (*that is,* half a shekel according to the shekel of the sanctuary), for each one who passed over to those who were numbered, from twenty years old and upward, for 603,550 men.

38:27
Ex 26:19,21,
25,32

27   And the hundred talents of silver were for casting the sockets of the sanctuary and the sockets of the veil; one hundred sockets for the hundred talents, a talent for a socket.

28   And of the 1,775 *shekels,* he made hooks for the pillars and overlaid their tops and made bands for them.

29   And the bronze of the wave offering was 70 talents, and 2,400 shekels.

30   And with it he made the sockets to the doorway of the tent of meeting, and the bronze altar and its bronze grating, and all the utensils of the altar,

31   and the sockets of the court all around and the sockets of the gate of the court, and all the pegs of the tabernacle and all the pegs of the court all around.

14. *The making of the dress of the priesthood*

a. *The materials*

39:1
Ex 35:23;
28:4

39 Moreover, from the blue and purple and scarlet *material,* they made finely woven garments for ministering in the holy place, as well as the holy garments which were for Aaron, just as the LORD had commanded Moses.

b. *The making of the ephod*

39:2
Ex 28:6-12

2   And he made the ephod of gold, *and* of blue and purple and scarlet *material,* and fine twisted linen.

3   Then they hammered out gold sheets and cut *them* into threads to be woven in *with* the blue and the purple and the scarlet *material,* and the fine linen, the work of a skillful workman.

4   They made attaching shoulder pieces for the ephod; it was attached at its two *upper* ends.

5   And the skillfully woven band which was on it was like its workmanship, of the same material: of gold *and* of blue and purple and scarlet *material,* and fine twisted linen, just as the LORD had commanded Moses.

39:6
Ex 28:9

6   And they made the onyx stones, set in gold filigree *settings;* they were engraved *like* the engravings of a signet, according to the names of the sons of Israel.

39:7
Ex 28:12

7   And he placed them on the shoulder pieces of the ephod, *as* memorial stones for the sons of Israel, just as the LORD had commanded Moses.

c. *The making of the breastpiece*

39:8
Ex 28:15-28

8   And he made the breastpiece, the work of a skillful workman, like the workmanship of the ephod: of gold *and* of blue and purple and scarlet *material* and fine twisted linen.

9   It was square; they made the breastpiece folded double, a span long and a span wide when folded double.

10   And they mounted four rows of stones on it. The first row *was* a row of ruby, topaz, and emerald;

39:11
Ex 28:18

11   and the second row, a turquoise, a sapphire and a diamond;

12   and the third row, a jacinth, an agate, and an amethyst;

13   and the fourth row, a beryl, an onyx, and a jasper. They were set in gold filigree *settings* when they were mounted.

39:14
Ex 28:21

14   And the stones were corresponding to the names of the sons of Israel; they were twelve, corresponding to their names, *engraved with* the engravings of a signet, each with its name for the twelve tribes.

15   And they made on the breastpiece chains like cords, of twisted cordage work in pure gold.

39:16
Ex 28:24

16   And they made two gold filigree *settings* and two gold rings, and put the two rings on the two ends of the breastpiece.

17   Then they put the two gold cords in the two rings at the ends of the breastpiece.

18   And they put the *other* two ends of the two cords on the two filigree *settings*, and put them on the shoulder pieces of the ephod at the front of it.

19   And they made two gold rings and placed *them* on the two ends of the breastpiece, on its inner edge which was next to the ephod.

20   Furthermore, they made two gold rings and placed them on the bottom of the two shoulder pieces of the ephod, on the front of it, close to the place where it joined, above the woven band of the ephod.

21   And they bound the breastpiece by its rings to the rings of the ephod with a blue cord, that it might be on the woven band of the ephod, and that the breastpiece might not come loose from the ephod, just as the LORD had commanded Moses.

d. *The robe of the ephod*

22   Then he made the robe of the ephod of woven work, all of blue;

23   and the opening of the robe was *at the top* in the center, as the opening of a coat of mail, with a binding all around its opening, that it might not be torn.

24   And they made pomegranates of blue and purple and scarlet *material and* twisted *linen* on the hem of the robe.

25   They also made bells of pure gold, and put the bells between the pomegranates all around on the hem of the robe,

26   alternating a bell and a pomegranate all around on the hem of the robe, for the service, just as the LORD had commanded Moses.

e. *The remainder of the garments*

27   And they made the tunics of finely woven linen for Aaron and his sons,

28   and the turban of fine linen, and the decorated caps of fine linen, and the linen breeches of fine twisted linen,

29   and the sash of fine twisted linen, and blue and purple and scarlet *material,* the work of the weaver, just as the LORD had commanded Moses.

30   And they made the plate of the holy crown of pure gold, and inscribed it like the engravings of a signet, "Holy to the LORD."

31   And they fastened a blue cord to it, to fasten it on the turban above, just as the LORD had commanded Moses.

15. *Moses inspects and blesses the completed work*

32   Thus all the work of the tabernacle of the tent of meeting was completed; and the sons of Israel did according to all that the LORD had commanded Moses; so they did.

33   And they brought the tabernacle to Moses, the tent and all its [32] furnishings: its clasps, its boards, its bars, and its pillars and its sockets;

34   and the covering of rams' skins dyed red, and the covering of porpoise skins, and the screening veil;

35   the ark of the testimony and its poles and the mercy seat;

36   the table, all its utensils, and the bread of the Presence;

37   the pure *gold* lampstand, with its arrangement of lamps and all its utensils, and the oil for the light;

38   and the gold altar, and the anointing oil and the fragrant incense, and the veil for the doorway of the tent;

39   the bronze altar and its bronze grating, its poles and all its utensils, the laver and its stand;

40   the hangings for the court, its pillars and its sockets, and the screen for the gate of the court, its cords and its pegs and all the equipment for the service of the tabernacle, for the tent of meeting;

41   the woven garments for ministering in the holy place and the holy garments for Aaron the priest and the garments of his sons, to minister as priests.

42   So the sons of Israel did all the work according to all that the LORD had commanded Moses.

43   And Moses examined all the work and behold, they had done it; just as the LORD had commanded, this they had done. So Moses blessed them.

[32]Or, *utensils,* and so throughout this context

Marginal references:

39:19 Ex 28:26

39:22 Ex 28:31-34

39:27 Ex 28:39,40, 42

39:30 Ex 28:36,37

39:32 vv. 42,43; Ex 25:40

39:35 Ex 25:16; 30:6

39:41 Ex 26:33

39:43 Lev 9:22,23

16. *The assembling and dedication of the tabernacle*

a. *The command of God to assemble the tabernacle*

40 Then the LORD spoke to Moses, saying,
2 "On the first day of the first month you shall set up the tabernacle of the tent of meeting.
3 "And you shall place the ark of the testimony there, and you shall screen the ark with the veil.
4 "And you shall bring in the table and arrange what belongs on it; and you shall bring in the lampstand and mount its lamps.
5 "Moreover, you shall set the gold altar of incense before the ark of the testimony, and set up the veil for the doorway to the tabernacle.
6 "And you shall set the altar of burnt offering in front of the doorway of the tabernacle of the tent of meeting.
7 "And you shall set the laver between the tent of meeting and the altar, and put water in it.
8 "And you shall set up the court all around and hang up the veil for the gateway of the court.
9 "Then you shall take the anointing oil and anoint the tabernacle and all that is in it, and shall consecrate it and all its furnishings; and it shall be holy.
10 "And you shall anoint the altar of burnt offering and all its utensils, and consecrate the altar; and the altar shall be most holy.
11 "And you shall anoint the laver and its stand, and consecrate it.
12 "Then you shall bring Aaron and his sons to the doorway of the tent of meeting and wash them with water.
13 "And you shall put the holy garments on Aaron and anoint him and consecrate him, that he may minister as a priest to Me.
14 "And you shall bring his sons and put tunics on them;
15 and you shall anoint them even as you have anointed their father, that they may minister as priests to Me; and their anointing shall qualify them for a perpetual priesthood throughout their generations."

b. *The obedience of Moses*

16 Thus Moses did; according to all that the LORD had commanded him, so he did.
17 Now it came about in the first month of the second year, on the first day of the month, that the tabernacle was erected.
18 And Moses erected the tabernacle and laid its sockets, and set up its boards, and inserted its bars and erected its pillars.
19 And he spread the tent over the tabernacle and put the covering of the tent on top of it, just as the LORD had commanded Moses.
20 Then he took the testimony and put *it* into the ark, and attached the poles to the ark, and put the mercy seat on top of the ark.
21 And he brought the ark into the tabernacle, and set up a veil for the screen, and screened off the ark of the testimony, just as the LORD had commanded Moses.
22 Then he put the table in the tent of meeting, on the north side of the tabernacle, outside the veil.
23 And he set the arrangement of bread in order on it before the LORD, just as the LORD had commanded Moses.
24 Then he placed the lampstand in the tent of meeting, opposite the table, on the south side of the tabernacle.
25 And he lighted the lamps before the LORD, just as the LORD had commanded Moses.
26 Then he placed the gold altar in the tent of meeting in front of the veil;
27 and he burned fragrant incense on it, just as the LORD had commanded Moses.
28 Then he set up the veil for the doorway of the tabernacle.
29 And he set the altar of burnt offering *before* the doorway of the tabernacle of the tent of meeting, and offered on it the burnt offering and the meal offering, just as the LORD had commanded Moses.
30 And he placed the laver between the tent of meeting and the altar, and put water in it for washing.
31 And from it Moses and Aaron and his sons washed their hands and their feet.

40:2
Ex 12:2;
13:4; v. 17
40:3
vv. 21-30

40:9
Ex 30:26

40:10
Ex 29:36,37

40:12
Lev 8:1-13

40:13
Ex 28:41

40:15
Num 25:13

40:20
Ex 25:16

40:21
Ex 26:33;
35:12
40:22
Ex 26:35

40:23
v. 4

40:25
Ex 25:37

40:26
v. 5

40:28
Ex 26:36

40:30
v. 7

32   When they entered the tent of meeting, and when they approached the altar, they washed, just as the LORD had commanded Moses.

40:32
Ex 30:19,20

33   And he erected the court all around the tabernacle and the altar, and hung up the veil for the gateway of the court. Thus Moses finished the work.

c. *The glory of the LORD fills the tabernacle*

34   Then the cloud covered the tent of meeting, and the glory of the LORD filled the tabernacle.

*40:34
Num 9:15-23

35   And Moses was not able to enter the tent of meeting because the cloud had settled on it, and the glory of the LORD filled the tabernacle.

36   And throughout all their journeys whenever the cloud was taken up from over the tabernacle, the sons of Israel would set out;

40:36
Num 9:17;
10:11;
Neh 9:19

37   but if the cloud was not taken up, then they did not set out until the day when it was taken up.

38   For throughout all their journeys, the cloud of the LORD was on the tabernacle by day, and there was fire in it by night, in the sight of all the house of Israel.

40:38
Ex 13:21;
Num 9:15

40:34 See also note to 13:21. *The glory of the LORD filled the tabernacle* as it later filled the Solomonic temple (2 Chr. 5:13,14). But at the apostasy of Zedekiah's reign that glory departed (cf. Ezek. 43:1–4) and never returned in visible splendor when the temple was rebuilt in 516 B.C.. Nevertheless the LORD promised the builders of the second temple that the splendor (KJV, "glory") of that later sanctuary would someday surpass that of the former (Hag. 2:9). This came to pass when our Savior came to cleanse the temple and to teach in it five centuries later. When He was afterward rejected and crucified, that spiritual glory departed from the temple forever, and God decreed its destruction within forty years thereafter (A.D. 70). He no longer had any use for it, for now His temple consisted of the New Testament church, the mystical body of Christ.

INTRODUCTION TO
THE THIRD BOOK OF MOSES
COMMONLY CALLED
LEVITICUS

Authorship and Background: The name Leviticus, meaning "pertaining to the Levites," is the Septuagint title of the book. The Israelite priesthood was drawn from the tribe of Levi, and the title suggests that the book discusses the ministry of the levitical priesthood. The Hebrew title is the first phrase of the Hebrew text, "And he called." The key idea of the book is embodied in the command, " . . . you shall be holy for I am holy" (11:45). In Exodus the people covenanted to be the LORD'S holy nation. It was fitting, therefore, that specific ways by which priest and people alike might manifest holiness should be introduced in Leviticus. It is reiterated again and again that these laws were given through Moses, who evidently either wrote them down himself, or had them written under his direction and supervision (4:1; 6:1; 8:1; 11:1; 12:1; 13:1, etc). Leviticus is the third of the five books known as the "Law" of Moses.

Characteristics: In Leviticus there is a blending together of two apparently incompatible concepts, i.e., of law and grace. The book is probably the most legalistic of all the Old Testament Scriptures, demanding of God's people that they render perfect obedience to all His moral laws. At the same time, it clearly states that such obedience of the people is required as their response to the grace and mercy of God, who makes communion with Himself possible by forgiving the sins of the penitent believer. Thus the New Testament gospel is found at the heart of the ritual of sacrifice, and particularly in the rites of the Day of Atonement. The laws laid down are both general and specific; they are moral and ceremonial. Some are forever binding, while others were of value only for the Mosaic dispensation. There is a striking progression of revealed truth that, commencing in Genesis, the book of beginnings, and continuing in Exodus, the book of redemption, culminates in Leviticus, which may be termed the book of communion and religious worship.

Contents:

I. The way of approach to a holy God (1:1-16:34): The law of sacrifice enunciated with particular reference to the burnt offerings, the meal offering, the peace offering, the sin offering, the guilt offering, and various sacrifices. The law of the consecration of the priests, including washing and anointing, and the ceremony of sacrifice and induction into the office. Aaron and his sons are consecrated. Nadab and Abihu offer strange fire and judgment falls upon them. Instructions given to the priests concerning abstinence from wine and the eating of holy things. Clean and unclean animals. The laws governing purification of women after childbirth. The laws of leprosy relating to persons, clothing, houses, and purifications. Rules given for diseases that cause secretions. The rites for the day of atonement, in which expiation is made by the high priest for his own sins and the sins of the people.

II. The maintaining of fellowship with a holy God (17:1-27:34): The place of sacrifice and the sanctity of blood as the sacrificial element. Religious and ethical laws that involve incest and sexual sins; sundry warnings. Laws of conduct toward a neighbor and punishments for violations of the statutes. The priests, who are holy, are forbidden to defile themselves by contact with the dead. Marriage of the priesthood and physical impediments; also sacred oblations. The laws of holy convocations, including the

Sabbath, the annual feasts, first fruits, harvest, pentecost, the Day of Atonement, and the Feast of Tabernacles. The oil and the bread. The penalty for blasphemy. The laws of the sabbatic and jubilee years, together with laws regarding property and personal freedom for servants. God commands obedience and promises blessings on the obedient, and cursings with strong warnings of the consequences of disobedience. The dispersion predicted. The laws concerning vows relative to persons, animals, houses, land, firstlings, devoted things, and the tithe of the land.

LEVITICUS

I. The way of approach to a holy God (1:1–16:34)

A. The laws and rituals of worship

1. The law of burnt offering

1:1
Num 7:89

1 Then the LORD called to Moses and spoke to him from the tent of meeting, saying,

*1:2f
Lev 22:18,19

2 "Speak to the sons of Israel and say to them, 'When any man of you brings an offering to the LORD, you shall bring your offering of animals from the herd or the flock.

1:3
Deut 15:21;
Heb 9:14;
1 Pet 1:19

3 'If his offering is a burnt offering from the herd, he shall offer it, a male without defect; he shall offer it at the doorway of the tent of meeting, that he may be accepted before the LORD.

*1:4f
Ex 29:10;
Lev 9:7;
Num 15:25

4 'And he shall lay his hand on the head of the burnt offering, that it may be accepted for him to make atonement on his behalf.

1:5
Ex 29:11;
Heb 10:11;
12:24;
1 Pet 1:2

5 'And he shall slay the young bull before the LORD; and Aaron's sons, the priests, shall offer up the blood and sprinkle the blood around on the altar that is at the doorway of the tent of meeting.

1:7
Lev 6:8-13

6 'He shall then skin the burnt offering and cut it into its pieces.

7 'And the sons of Aaron the priest shall put fire on the altar and arrange wood on the fire.

8 'Then Aaron's sons, the priests, shall arrange the pieces, the head, and the suet over the wood which is on the fire that is on the altar.

1:9
Num 15:8-10;
Eph 5:2

9 'Its entrails, however, and its legs he shall wash with water. And the priest shall offer up in smoke all of it on the altar for a burnt offering, an offering by fire of a soothing aroma to the LORD.

10 'But if his offering is from the flock, of the sheep or of the goats, for a burnt offering, he shall offer it a male without defect.

1:11
v. 5

11 'And he shall slay it on the side of the altar northward before the LORD, and Aaron's sons, the priests, shall sprinkle its blood around on the altar.

12 'He shall then cut it into its pieces with its head and its suet, and the priest shall arrange them on the wood which is on the fire that is on the altar.

13 'The entrails, however, and the legs he shall wash with water. And the priest shall offer all of it, and offer it up in smoke on the altar; it is a burnt offering, an offering by fire of a soothing aroma to the LORD.

1:14
Lev 5:7

14 'But if his offering to the LORD is a burnt offering of birds, then he shall bring his offering from the turtledoves or from young pigeons.

1:15
Lev 5:9

15 'And the priest shall bring it to the altar and wring off its head, and offer it up in smoke on the altar; and its blood is to be drained out on the side of the altar.

1:16
Lev 6:10

16 'He shall also take away its crop with its feathers, and cast it beside the altar eastward, to the place of the ashes.

17 'Then he shall tear it by its wings, *but* shall not sever *it*. And the priest shall

---

1:2,3 The burnt offering is a type of Christ as the One who offered Himself in atonement for sin (Heb. 10:10). This offering was intended as a substitute for the sinner himself. By laying his hand on the animal's head, the offerer symbolically identified himself with it (v. 4). This act of faith, of which the outward evidence was the laying of the hand on the animal, had validity in view of the sacrifice of Christ. It was then that the animal was to be slain and its blood sprinkled on the altar. So also Christ atoned for our sin and Himself stood in the sinner's place as his representative (1 Pet. 1:18–20). Different animals could be offered, depending on the financial resources of the one who brought the sacrifice. Acceptable sacrifices included an unblemished bull, a sheep, a goat, a turtledove, or pigeon. As distinct from all other sacrifices, the burnt offering was to be wholly consumed by fire on the altar; no part could be eaten by priest or worshiper. It pointed forward to the efficacy of the cross in providing atonement for the totality of sin of fallen man.

1:4,5 In the Old Testament the principle of life is declared to be in the blood (Gen. 9:4). As a basic principle, Scripture also insists that no atonement for sin is possible without the sacrifice of life, the visible representation being the blood (17:11). When the blood was presented, it was evidence in God's sight that life had been given. While Jesus Christ did not die from the loss of blood (for He voluntarily yielded up His spirit, Matt. 27:50), the blood from His crown, nail wounds, and pierced side attested to the sacrifice of His life, the condition for the atonement for our sins.

offer it up in smoke on the altar on the wood which is on the fire; it is a burnt offering, an offering by fire of a soothing aroma to the LORD.

1:17
Lev 5:8;
Gen 15:10

2. The law of the grain offerings

a. Flour, oil, and frankincense

2 'Now when anyone presents a grain offering as an offering to the LORD, his offering shall be of fine flour, and he shall pour oil on it and put frankincense on it.

*2:1
Lev 6:14

2 'He shall then bring it to Aaron's sons, the priests; and shall take from it his handful of its fine flour and of its oil with all of its frankincense. And the priest shall offer *it* up in smoke *as* its memorial portion on the altar, an offering by fire of a soothing aroma to the LORD.

2:2
vv. 9,16;
Lev 5:12;
6:15;
Acts 10:4

3 'And the remainder of the grain offering belongs to Aaron and his sons: a thing most holy, of the offerings to the LORD by fire.

2:3
Lev 6:16;
10:12,13

4 'Now when you bring an offering of a grain offering baked in an oven, *it shall be* unleavened cakes of fine flour mixed with oil, or unleavened wafers spread with oil.

5 'And if your offering is a grain offering *made* on the griddle, *it shall be* of fine flour, unleavened, mixed with oil;

6 you shall break it into bits, and pour oil on it; it is a grain offering.

7 'Now if your offering is a grain offering *made* in a pan, it shall be made of fine flour with oil.

8 'When you bring in the grain offering which is made of these things to the LORD, it shall be presented to the priest and he shall bring it to the altar.

9 'The priest then shall take up from the grain offering its memorial portion, and shall offer *it* up in smoke on the altar *as* an offering by fire of a soothing aroma to the LORD.

2:9
v. 2; Ex 29:18

10 'And the remainder of the grain offering belongs to Aaron and his sons: a thing most holy, of the offerings to the LORD by fire.

2:10
v. 3

b. Leaven and salt

11 'No grain offering, which you bring to the LORD, shall be made with leaven, for you shall not offer up in smoke any leaven or any honey as an offering by fire to the LORD.

2:11
Lev 6:16,17;
Ex 23:18;
34:25

12 'As an offering of first fruits, you shall bring them to the LORD, but they shall not ascend for a soothing aroma on the altar.

2:12
Lev 7:13;
23:10,11
*2:13
Mark 9:49;
Num 18:19

13 'Every grain offering of yours, moreover, you shall season with salt, so that the salt of the covenant of your God shall not be lacking from your grain offering; with all your offerings you shall offer salt.

14 'Also if you bring a grain offering of early ripened things to the LORD, you shall bring fresh heads of grain roasted in the fire, grits of new growth, for the grain offering of your early ripened things.

2:14
Lev 23:10,14

15 'You shall then put oil on it and lay incense on it; it is a grain offering.

16 'And the priest shall offer up in smoke its memorial portion, part of its grits and its oil with all its incense as an offering by fire to the LORD.

2:16
v. 2

3. The law of the peace offerings

3 'Now if his offering is a sacrifice of peace offerings, if he is going to offer out of the herd, whether male or female, he shall offer it without defect before the LORD.

*3:1
Lev 7:11,19;
22:21

2 'And he shall lay his hand on the head of his offering and slay it at the doorway of the tent of meeting, and Aaron's sons, the priests, shall sprinkle the blood around on the altar.

3:2
Lev 1:4;
Ex 29:11,16,
20

3 'And from the sacrifice of the peace offerings, he shall present an offering by fire to the LORD, the fat that covers the entrails and all the fat that is on the entrails,

3:3
Ex 29:13,22

2:1 The *grain* (or meal) *offering* ("meat" in KJV) was made of fine flour, unleavened, seasoned with salt, and presented with oil and incense (2:1,4,5,7,13–15). This sacrifice was not to be offered on the altar of incense (Ex. 30:9) but only on the altar of burnt offering (Ex. 40:29). When offered by a priest it was to be wholly consumed by fire (6:23). When offered by others the priesthood kept the remainder of it for their own food, after the memorial handful had been consigned to the altar flames (6:15,17).

2:13 *salt of the covenant.* This represents the fact that ancient covenants were ratified by meals of food seasoned with salt. Apparently salt became a symbol for the covenant between God and Israel (see Num. 18:19; 2 Chr. 13:5).
3:1 The *peace offerings*, with the exception of the fat and kidneys, were eaten by the priests and worshipers. As such it was a fellowship meal signifying the peace that existed in the covenant relation between God and man and also between men.

4   and the two kidneys with the fat that is on them, which is on the loins, and the lobe of the liver, which he shall remove with the kidneys.

3:5
Lev 7:28-34;
Ex 29:13

5   'Then Aaron's sons shall offer *it* up in smoke on the altar on the burnt offering, which is on the wood that is on the fire; it is an offering by fire of a soothing aroma to the LORD.

3:6
v. 1

6   'But if his offering for a sacrifice of peace offerings to the LORD is from the flock, he shall offer it, male or female, without defect.

3:7
Lev 17:8,9

7   'If he is going to offer a lamb for his offering, then he shall offer it before the LORD,

3:8
Lev 1:4,5;
v. 2

8   and he shall lay his hand on the head of his offering, and slay it before the tent of meeting; and Aaron's sons shall sprinkle its blood around on the altar.

9   'And from the sacrifice of peace offerings he shall bring as an offering by fire to the LORD, its fat, the entire fat tail which he shall remove close to the backbone, and the fat that covers the entrails and all the fat that is on the entrails,

3:10
v. 4

10   and the two kidneys with the fat that is on them, which is on the loins, and the lobe of the liver, which he shall remove with the kidneys.

3:11
vv. 5,16;
Lev 21:6,8,17

11   'Then the priest shall offer *it* up in smoke on the altar, *as* food, an offering by fire to the LORD.

12   'Moreover, if his offering is a goat, then he shall offer it before the LORD,

13   and he shall lay his hand on its head and slay it before the tent of meeting; and the sons of Aaron shall sprinkle its blood around on the altar.

14   'And from it he shall present his offering as an offering by fire to the LORD, the fat that covers the entrails and all the fat that is on the entrails,

15   and the two kidneys with the fat that is on them, which is on the loins, and the lobe of the liver, which he shall remove with the kidneys.

3:16
Lev 7:23-25

16   'And the priest shall offer them up in smoke on the altar *as* food, an offering by fire for a soothing aroma; all fat is the LORD'S.

3:17
Gen 9:4;
Lev 17:10,14;
Deut 12:16

17   'It is a perpetual statute throughout your generations in all your dwellings: you shall not eat any fat or any blood.' "

4. *The law of the sin offerings*

a. *The offering for the priest*

4   Then the LORD spoke to Moses, saying,

*4:2
Lev 5:15-18;
Ps 19:12

2   "Speak to the sons of Israel, saying, 'If a person sins unintentionally in any of the things which the LORD has commanded not to be done, and commits any of them,

*4:3ff
vv. 14,23,28

3   if the anointed priest sins so as to bring guilt on the people, then let him offer to the LORD a bull without defect as a sin offering for the sin he has committed.

4:4
Lev 1:4

4   'And he shall bring the bull to the doorway of the tent of meeting before the LORD, and he shall lay his hand on the head of the bull, and slay the bull before the LORD.

4:5
Lev 16:14

5   'Then the anointed priest is to take some of the blood of the bull and bring it to the tent of meeting,

6   and the priest shall dip his finger in the blood, and sprinkle some of the blood seven times before the LORD, in front of the veil of the sanctuary.

4:7
Lev 8:15;
9:9; Lev 5:9

7   'The priest shall also put some of the blood on the horns of the altar of fragrant incense which is before the LORD in the tent of meeting; and all the blood of the bull he shall pour out at the base of the altar of burnt offering which is at the doorway of the tent of meeting.

4:8
Lev 3:3-5

8   'And he shall remove from it all the fat of the bull of the sin offering: the fat that covers the entrails, and all the fat which is on the entrails,

---

4:2 Sins of ignorance were sins wrongfully committed by an Israelite out of weakness or waywardness without any intent to renounce the sovereignty of God. Sins committed with the intention of rejecting God's sovereignty were to be punished by cutting off their perpetrators from among the people (Num. 15:30-31). That atonement should be required for sins of ignorance demonstrates that ignorance is no adequate excuse for failure to keep the laws of God. Believers are enjoined to study the Scriptures (2 Tim. 2:15), and failure to acquaint themselves with the commandments of God affords no excuse. This kind of sin must also be confessed and forgiven (1 John 1:9). Even in the case of unbelievers, ignorance is basically willful, according to Rom. 1:21,28.

4:3ff. What was prefigured in the Old Testament sacrifices was fulfilled by Christ at Calvary. The sin offering: (1) met the demands of the law (justice was satisfied and vindicated—Heb. 10:10-12); (2) was to be perfect (Christ was the sinless servant—Heb. 4:15); (3) was a substitute offered in the stead of the offerer (Christ was the substitute who bore our sins—2 Cor. 5:2l; 1 Pet. 2:24); and (4) removed the guilt and the penalty of the sin. In contradistinction to the burnt offering (which was not related to particular transgressions but which symbolized an approach to a holy God and gave standing in His sight), the sin offering made an atonement for specific sins for which the offering provided a "covering," and the sin was forgiven.

9   and the two kidneys with the fat that is on them, which is on the loins, and the lobe of the liver, which he shall remove with the kidneys

10   (just as it is removed from the ox of the sacrifice of peace offerings), and the priest is to offer them up in smoke on the altar of burnt offering.

11   'But the hide of the bull and all its flesh with its head and its legs and its entrails and its refuse,

12   that is, all *the rest of* the bull, he is to bring out to a clean place outside the camp where the ashes are poured out, and burn it on wood with fire; where the ashes are poured out it shall be burned.

4:12
Lev 6:11;
Heb 13:11

b. *The offering for the whole congregation*

13   'Now if the whole congregation of Israel commits error, and the matter escapes the notice of the assembly, and they commit any of the things which the LORD has commanded not to be done, and they become guilty;

4:13
Num 15:24-26;
Lev 5:2-4,17

14   when the sin which they have committed becomes known, then the assembly shall offer a bull of the herd for a sin offering, and bring it before the tent of meeting.

4:14
vv. 3,23,28

15   'Then the elders of the congregation shall lay their hands on the head of the bull before the LORD, and the bull shall be slain before the LORD.

4:15
Lev 1:4

16   'Then the anointed priest is to bring some of the blood of the bull to the tent of meeting;

17   and the priest shall dip his finger in the blood, and sprinkle *it* seven times before the LORD, in front of the veil.

4:17
v. 6

18   'And he shall put some of the blood on the horns of the altar which is before the LORD in the tent of meeting; and all the blood he shall pour out at the base of the altar of burnt offering which is at the doorway of the tent of meeting.

19   'And he shall remove all its fat from it and offer it up in smoke on the altar.

20   'He shall also do with the bull just as he did with the bull of the sin offering; thus he shall do with it. So the priest shall make atonement for them, and they shall be forgiven.

4:20
Rom 5:11;
Heb 2:17;
10:10-12

21   'Then he is to bring out the bull to *a place* outside the camp, and burn it as he burned the first bull; it is the sin offering for the assembly.

c. *The offering for a ruler*

22   'When a leader sins and unintentionally does any one of all the things which the LORD God has commanded not to be done, and he becomes guilty,

4:22
vv. 2,13

23   if his sin which he has committed is made known to him, he shall bring for his offering a goat, a male without defect.

4:23
v. 14

24   'And he shall lay his hand on the head of the male goat, and slay it in the place where they slay the burnt offering before the LORD; it is a sin offering.

25   'Then the priest is to take some of the blood of the sin offering with his finger, and put it on the horns of the altar of burnt offering; and *the rest of* its blood he shall pour out at the base of the altar of burnt offering.

4:25
vv. 7,18,30,
34

26   'And all its fat he shall offer up in smoke on the altar as *in the case of* the fat of the sacrifice of peace offerings. Thus the priest shall make atonement for him in regard to his sin, and he shall be forgiven.

4:26
vv. 19,20

d. *The offering for the common man*

27   'Now if anyone of the common people sins unintentionally in doing any of the things which the LORD has commanded not to be done, and becomes guilty,

4:27
v. 2

28   if his sin, which he has committed is made known to him, then he shall bring for his offering a goat, a female without defect, for his sin which he has committed.

4:28
v. 23

29   'And he shall lay his hand on the head of the sin offering, and slay the sin offering at the place of the burnt offering.

4:29
Lev 1:4,5

30   'And the priest shall take some of its blood with his finger and put it on the horns of the altar of burnt offering; and all *the rest of* its blood he shall pour out at the base of the altar.

31   'Then he shall remove all its fat, just as the fat was removed from the sacrifice of peace offerings; and the priest shall offer it up in smoke on the altar for a soothing aroma to the LORD. Thus the priest shall make atonement for him, and he shall be forgiven.

32   'But if he brings a lamb as his offering for a sin offering, he shall bring it, a female without defect.

4:32
v. 28

33 'And he shall lay his hand on the head of the sin offering, and slay it for a sin offering in the place where they slay the burnt offering.

34 'And the priest is to take some of the blood of the sin offering with his finger and put it on the horns of the altar of burnt offering; and all *the rest of* its blood he shall pour out at the base of the altar.

4:35
Lev 3:5;
vv. 26,31

35 'Then he shall remove all its fat, just as the fat of the lamb is removed from the sacrifice of the peace offerings, and the priest shall offer them up in smoke on the altar, on the offerings by fire to the LORD. Thus the priest shall make atonement for him in regard to his sin which he has committed, and he shall be forgiven.

e. Acts requiring a sin offering

5:1
Prov 29:24;
v. 17

5 'Now if a person sins, after he hears a public adjuration to *testify*, when he is a witness, whether he has seen or *otherwise* known, if he does not tell *it*, then he will bear his guilt.

5:2
Lev 11:24-39;
Num 19:11-16

2 'Or if a person touches any unclean thing, whether a carcass of an unclean beast, or the carcass of unclean cattle, or a carcass of unclean swarming things, though it is hidden from him, and he is unclean, then he will be guilty.

3 'Or if he touches human uncleanness, of whatever *sort* his uncleanness *may* be with which he becomes unclean, and it is hidden from him, and then he comes to know *it*, he will be guilty.

4 'Or if a person swears thoughtlessly with his lips to do evil or to do good, in whatever matter a man may speak thoughtlessly with an oath, and it is hidden from him, and then he comes to know *it*, he will be guilty in one of these.

*5:5
Lev 16:21;
26:40;
Num 5:7;
Prov 28:13

5 'So it shall be when he becomes guilty in one of these, that he shall confess that in which he has sinned.

6 'He shall also bring his guilt offering to the LORD for his sin which he has committed, a female from the flock, a lamb or a goat as a sin offering. So the priest shall make atonement on his behalf for his sin.

f. Different sin offerings allowed for the poor

5:7
Lev 12:8;
14:21

7 'But if he cannot afford a lamb, then he shall bring to the LORD his guilt offering for that in which he has sinned, two turtledoves or two young pigeons, one for a sin offering and the other for a burnt offering.

5:8
Lev 1:15,17

8 'And he shall bring them to the priest, who shall offer first that which is for the sin offering and shall nip its head at the front of its neck, but he shall not sever *it*.

5:9
Lev 4:7,18,
30,34

9 'He shall also sprinkle some of the blood of the sin offering on the side of the altar, while the rest of the blood shall be drained out at the base of the altar: it is a sin offering.

5:10
Lev 1:14-17

10 'The second he shall then prepare as a burnt offering according to the ordinance. So the priest shall make atonement on his behalf for his sin which he has committed, and it shall be forgiven him.

5:11
Lev 2:1,2

11 'But if his means are insufficient for two turtledoves or two young pigeons, then for his offering for that which he has sinned, he shall bring the tenth of an [1]ephah of fine flour for a sin offering; he shall not put oil on it or place incense on it, for it is a sin offering.

12 'And he shall bring it to the priest, and the priest shall take his handful of it as its memorial portion and offer *it* up in smoke on the altar, with the offerings of the LORD by fire: it is a sin offering.

5:13
Lev 4:26; 2:3

13 'So the priest shall make atonement for him concerning his sin which he has committed from one of these, and it shall be forgiven him; then *the rest* shall become the priest's, like the grain offering.' "

5. The law of the guilt offering

5:14
Lev 22:14;
7:1-10;
Ex 30:13

14 Then the LORD spoke to Moses, saying,

15 "If a person acts unfaithfully and sins unintentionally against the LORD's holy

[1]I.e., Approx. one bushel

5:5 Confession of sin is essential to a godly walk and life. It is required by God of those who have sinned (5:5; Hos. 5:15), for without repentance and confession it is vain to appeal to the blood sacrifice. The New Testament also bids people to confess their sins (James 5:16), with the assurance that there is pardon and cleansing (1 John 1:9; cf. Ps. 32:5). True confession includes: (1) godly sorrow for sin (Ps. 38:18); (2) self-abasement (Jer. 3:25); (3) a prayer for forgiveness (Ps. 51:1); (4) a willingness to make restitution (Num. 5:6,7); (5) a humble acceptance of the correcting hand of God in punishment (Ezra 9:13; Neh. 9:33); and (6) a turning away from that sin (Prov. 28:13). Two of the finest examples of people who confessed their sins are the prodigal son and the tax collector.

things, then he shall bring his guilt offering to the LORD: a ram without defect from the flock, according to your valuation in silver by shekels, in *terms of* the shekel of the sanctuary, for a guilt offering.

16 "And he shall make restitution for that which he has sinned against the holy thing, and shall add to it a fifth part of it, and give it to the priest. The priest shall then make atonement for him with the ram of the guilt offering, and it shall be forgiven him.

17 "Now if a person sins and does any of the things which the LORD has commanded not to be done, though he was unaware, still he is guilty, and shall bear his punishment.

18 "He is then to bring to the priest a ram without defect from the flock, according to your valuation, for a guilt offering. So the priest shall make atonement for him concerning his error in which he sinned unintentionally and did not know *it*, and it shall be forgiven him.

19 "It is a guilt offering; he was certainly guilty before the LORD."

6 Then the LORD spoke to Moses, saying,

2 "When a person sins and acts unfaithfully against the LORD, and deceives his companion in regard to a deposit or a security entrusted *to him*, or through robbery, or *if* he has extorted from his companion,

3 or has found what was lost and lied about it and sworn falsely, so that he sins in regard to any one of the things a man may do;

4 then it shall be, when he sins and becomes guilty, that he shall restore what he took by robbery, or what he got by extortion, or the deposit which was entrusted to him, or the lost thing which he found,

5 or anything about which he swore falsely; he shall make restitution for it in full, and add to it one-fifth more. He shall give it to the one to whom it belongs on the day *he presents* his guilt offering.

6 "Then he shall bring to the priest his guilt offering to the LORD, a ram without defect from the flock, according to your valuation, for a guilt offering,

7 and the priest shall make atonement for him before the LORD; and he shall be forgiven for any one of the things which he may have done to incur guilt."

6. Instructions for the priests

a. On burnt offerings

8 Then the LORD spoke to Moses, saying,

9 "Command Aaron and his sons, saying, 'This is the law for the burnt offering: the burnt offering itself *shall remain* on the hearth on the altar all night until the morning, and the fire on the altar is to be kept burning on it.

10 'And the priest is to put on his linen robe, and he shall put on undergarments next to his flesh; and he shall take up the ashes *to* which the fire reduces the burnt offering on the altar, and place them beside the altar.

11 'Then he shall take off his garments and put on other garments, and carry the ashes outside the camp to a clean place.

12 'And the fire on the altar shall be kept burning on it. It shall not go out, but the priest shall burn wood on it every morning; and he shall lay out the burnt offering on it, and offer up in smoke the fat portions of the peace offerings on it.

13 'Fire shall be kept burning continually on the altar; it is not to go out.

Marginal references:

*5:16
Lev 6:5;
22:14;
Num 5:7,8;
Lev 4:26

5:17
v. 15; 4:2,13,
22,27

5:18
vv. 15-17

6:2
Num 5:6;
Acts 5:4;
Col 3:9;
Ex 22:7,10;
Prov 24:28
6:3
Deut 22:1-3

6:5
Lev 5:16;
Num 5:7,8

6:6
Lev 5:16

6:7
Lev 4:26

6:10
Ex 28:39-41,
43; 39:27,28

5:16 The *guilt offering* (or, trespass offering) provided for overt sins or offenses that could be assessed as to the amount of damages; otherwise it resembled the sin offering in all of its requirements. Explicit in the guilt offering are: (1) the principle of the shed blood that provides atonement (6:7); (2) the principle of restitution over and above the damage inflicted (six-fifths compensation) to the brother who has suffered loss (6:5); (3) the principle of confession of sin, of which the very act of bringing the offering is outward proof (6:6); (4) the principle of faith, evidenced by the erring believer's acceptance of God's atoning provision for his trespass (6:6); and (5) the principle of forgiveness, by which the sinner, having met the divine conditions, can be assured that his sin is cared for (6:7). In Is. 53:10 the word translated *a guilt offering* is really this term: (*asham*).
6:13 The first fire that enkindled the wood of the sacrifice after the formal consecration of Aaron was kindled by God (9:24). This supernatural origin of the altar fire indicated that only by God's grace could man's sacrifice be acceptable for purposes of atonement. No man-made fire could be used on the altar of the LORD, and it was most important that once the fire was kindled the priests keep it burning. It was the sin of bringing *strange fire* (i.e., fire that they had enkindled themselves) that resulted in the death of Nadab and Abihu (10:1,2).

b. On grain offerings

6:14
Lev 2:1,2

14 'Now this is the law of the grain offering: the sons of Aaron shall present it before the LORD in front of the altar.

15 'Then one *of them* shall lift up from it a handful of the fine flour of the grain offering, with its oil and all the incense that is on the grain offering, and he shall offer *it* up in smoke on the altar, a soothing aroma, as its memorial offering to the LORD.

6:16
Lev 2:3

16 'And what is left of it Aaron and his sons are to eat. It shall be eaten as unleavened cakes in a holy place; they are to eat it in the court of the tent of meeting.

6:17
Lev 2:11;
vv. 26,29,30

17 'It shall not be baked with leaven. I have given it as their share from My offerings by fire; it is most holy, like the sin offering and the guilt offering.

6:18
v. 29;
Num 18:10;
v. 27

18 'Every male among the sons of Aaron may eat it; it is a permanent ordinance throughout your generations, from the offerings by fire to the LORD. Whoever touches them shall become consecrated.' "

19 Then the LORD spoke to Moses, saying,

6:20
Ex 29:1,2

20 "This is the offering which Aaron and his sons are to present to the LORD on the day when he is anointed; the tenth of an ephah of fine flour as a regular grain offering, half of it in the morning and half of it in the evening.

6:21
Lev 2:5

21 "It shall be prepared with oil on a griddle. When it is *well* stirred, you shall bring it. You shall present the grain offering in baked pieces as a soothing aroma to the LORD.

22 "And the anointed priest who will be in his place among his sons shall offer it. By a permanent ordinance it shall be entirely offered up in smoke to the LORD.

23 "So every grain offering of the priest shall be burned entirely. It shall not be eaten."

c. On sin offerings

24 Then the LORD spoke to Moses, saying,

6:25
Lev 4:2,24,
29,33; 1:3,5,
11

25 "Speak to Aaron and to his sons, saying, 'This is the law of the sin offering: in the place where the burnt offering is slain the sin offering shall be slain before the LORD; it is most holy.

6:26
Lev 10:17,18;
v. 16

26 'The priest who offers it for sin shall eat it. It shall be eaten in a holy place, in the court of the tent of meeting.

6:27
Ex 29:37

27 'Anyone who touches its flesh shall become consecrated; and when any of its blood splashes on a garment, in a holy place you shall wash what was splashed on.

6:28
Ex 11:33;
15:12

28 'Also the earthenware vessel in which it was boiled shall be broken; and if it was boiled in a bronze vessel, then it shall be scoured and rinsed in water.

6:29
vv. 18,25

29 'Every male among the priests may eat of it; it is most holy.

6:30
Lev 4:1,7,11,
12,18,21

30 'But no sin offering of which any of the blood is brought into the tent of meeting to make atonement in the holy place shall be eaten; it shall be burned with fire.

d. On guilt offerings

7:1
Lev 5:14-6:7

7 'Now this is the law of the guilt offering; it is most holy.

7:2
Lev 1:11

2 'In the place where they slay the burnt offering they are to slay the guilt offering, and he shall sprinkle its blood around on the altar.

3 'Then he shall offer from it all its fat: the fat tail and the fat that covers the entrails,

7:4
Lev 3:4

4 and the two kidneys with the fat that is on them, which is on the loins, and the lobe on the liver he shall remove with the kidneys.

5 'And the priest shall offer them up in smoke on the altar as an offering by fire to the LORD; it is a guilt offering.

7:6
Lev 6:16-18;
2:3

6 'Every male among the priests may eat of it. It shall be eaten in a holy place; it is most holy.

7:7
Lev 6:25,26

7 'The guilt offering is like the sin offering, there is one law for them; the priest who makes atonement with it shall have it.

8 'Also the priest who presents any man's burnt offering, that priest shall have for himself the skin of the burnt offering which he has presented.

7:9
Lev 2:3,10

9 'Likewise, every grain offering that is baked in the oven, and everything prepared in a pan or on a griddle, shall belong to the priest who presents it.

10 'And every grain offering mixed with oil, or dry, shall belong to all the sons of Aaron, to all alike.

e. On peace offerings

11 'Now this is the law of the sacrifice of peace offerings which shall be presented to the LORD.

12 'If he offers it by way of thanksgiving, then along with the sacrifice of thanksgiving he shall offer unleavened cakes mixed with oil, and unleavened wafers spread with oil, and cakes *of well* stirred fine flour mixed with oil.

13 'With the sacrifice of his peace offerings for thanksgiving, he shall present his offering with cakes of leavened bread.

14 'And of this he shall present one of every offering as a contribution to the LORD; it shall belong to the priest who sprinkles the blood of the peace offerings.

15 'Now *as for* the flesh of the sacrifice of his thanksgiving peace offerings, it shall be eaten on the day of his offering; he shall not leave any of it over until morning.

16 'But if the sacrifice of his offering is a votive or a freewill offering, it shall be eaten on the day that he offers his sacrifice; and on the next day what is left of it may be eaten;

17 but what is left over from the flesh of the sacrifice on the third day shall be burned with fire.

18 'So if any of the flesh of the sacrifice of his peace offerings should *ever* be eaten on the third day, he who offers it shall not be accepted, *and* it shall not be reckoned to his *benefit*. It shall be an offensive thing, and the person who eats of it shall bear his *own* iniquity.

19 'Also the flesh that touches anything unclean shall not be eaten; it shall be burned with fire. As for *other* flesh, anyone who is clean may eat *such* flesh.

20 'But the person who eats the flesh of the sacrifice of peace offerings which belong to the LORD, in his uncleanness, that person shall be cut off from his people.

21 'And when anyone touches anything unclean, whether human uncleanness, or an unclean animal, or any unclean [2]detestable thing, and eats of the flesh of the sacrifice of peace offerings which belong to the LORD, that person shall be cut off from his people.' "

f. Forbidden portions

22 Then the LORD spoke to Moses, saying,

23 "Speak to the sons of Israel, saying, 'You shall not eat any fat *from* an ox, a sheep, or a goat.

24 'Also the fat of *an animal* which dies, and the fat of an animal torn *by beasts*, may be put to any other use, but you must certainly not eat it.

25 'For whoever eats the fat of the animal from which an offering by fire is offered to the LORD, even the person who eats shall be cut off from his people.

26 'And you are not to eat any blood, either of bird or animal, in any of your dwellings.

27 'Any person who eats any blood, even that person shall be cut off from his people.' "

g. The portion for the priesthood

28 Then the LORD spoke to Moses, saying,

29 "Speak to the sons of Israel, saying, 'He who offers the sacrifice of his peace offerings to the LORD shall bring his offering to the LORD from the sacrifice of his peace offerings.

30 'His own hands are to bring offerings by fire to the LORD. He shall bring the fat with the breast, that the breast may be presented as a wave offering before the LORD.

31 'And the priest shall offer up the fat in smoke on the altar; but the breast shall belong to Aaron and his sons.

32 'And you shall give the right thigh to the priest as a contribution from the sacrifices of your peace offerings.

33 'The one among the sons of Aaron who offers the blood of the peace offerings and the fat, the right thigh shall be his as *his* portion.

7:14
Num 18:8,11, 19
7:15
Lev 22:30

7:16
Lev 19:6-8

7:18
Lev 19:7;
Num 18:27

7:20
Lev 22:3

7:21
Lev 11:24,28

7:23
Lev 3:17

*7:26
Lev 17:10-14

7:29
Lev 3:1

7:31
v. 34

---

[2]Some mss. read *swarming thing*

7:26 *eat any blood.* Since shed blood represented the loss of life (Gen. 9:4) and was to be used solely for atonement, it was never to be eaten or drunk. This prohibition refers to the eating or drinking of blood as an item of food; it has nothing to do with the medical use of blood transfusion, as some cultists have claimed. If anything, blood transfusion serves as a beautiful illustration of the life-giving efficacy of Christ's atoning blood for us.

7:34
Num 18:18,
19
34 'For I have taken the breast of the wave offering and the thigh of the contribution from the sons of Israel from the sacrifices of their peace offerings, and have given them to Aaron the priest and to his sons as *their* due forever from the sons of Israel.

35 'This is that which is consecrated to Aaron and that which is consecrated to his sons from the offerings by fire to the LORD, in that day when he presented them to serve as priests to the LORD.

36 'These the LORD had commanded to be given them from the sons of Israel in the day that He anointed them. It is *their* due forever throughout their generations.' "

h. *Summary*

7:37
Lev 6:9,14,
20,25; vv. 1,
11
7:38
Lev 1:1,2
37 This is the law of the burnt offering, the grain offering and the sin offering and the guilt offering and the ordination offering and the sacrifice of peace offerings,

38 which the LORD commanded Moses at Mount Sinai in the day that He commanded the sons of Israel to present their offerings to the LORD in the wilderness of Sinai.

B. *The priestly regulations*

1. *The consecration of the priesthood*

a. *Their anointing*

*8:2
Ex 29:1-3;
28:2,4; 30:24,
25
8 Then the LORD spoke to Moses, saying,
2 "Take Aaron and his sons with him, and the garments and the annointing oil and the bull of the sin offering, and the two rams and the basket of unleavened bread;

3 and assemble all the congregation at the doorway of the tent of meeting."

4 So Moses did just as the LORD commanded him. When the congregation was assembled at the doorway of the tent of meeting,

5 Moses said to the congregation, "This is the thing which the LORD has commanded to do."

8:6
Ex 29:4-6
6 Then Moses had Aaron and his sons come near, and washed them with water.

7 And he put the tunic on him and girded him with the sash, and clothed him with the robe, and put the ephod on him; and he girded him with the artistic band of the ephod, with which he tied *it* to him.

*8:8
Ex 28:30
8 He then placed the breastpiece on him, and in the breastpiece he put [3]the Urim and the Thummim.

8:9
Ex 28:36,37
9 He also placed the turban on his head, and on the turban, at its front, he placed the golden plate, the holy crown, just as the LORD had commanded Moses.

8:10
v. 2
10 Moses then took the anointing oil and anointed the tabernacle and all that was in it, and consecrated them.

11 And he sprinkled some of it on the altar seven times and anointed the altar and all its utensils, and the basin and its stand, to consecrate them.

8:12
Ex 30:30;
Ps 133:2
8:13
Ex 29:8,9
12 Then he poured some of the anointing oil on Aaron's head and anointed him, to consecrate him.

13 Next Moses had Aaron's sons come near and clothed them with tunics, and girded them with sashes, and bound caps on them, just as the LORD had commanded Moses.

b. *The sin offering*

8:14
Ex 29:10;
Lev 4:4
8:15
Lev 4:7;
Heb 9:22
14 Then he brought the bull of the sin offering, and Aaron and his sons laid their hands on the head of the bull of the sin offering.

15 Next Moses slaughtered *it* and took the blood and with his finger put *some of it* around on the horns of the altar, and purified the altar. Then he poured out *the rest of* the blood at the base of the altar and consecrated it, to make atonement for it.

8:16
Lev 4:8
16 He also took all the fat that was on the entrails and the lobe of the liver, and the two kidneys and their fat; and Moses offered it up in smoke on the altar.

[3]I.e., the lights and perfections

8:2 *Aaron and his sons*, set aside as priests of God, had duties distinct from those religious services that were performed by the Levites as a whole.

8:8 *Urim and the Thummim*, see note to Ex. 28:30 for explanation.

17   But the bull and its hide and its flesh and its refuse, he burned in the fire outside the camp, just as the LORD had commanded Moses.

8:17
Lev 4:11,12

c. *The burnt offering*

18   Then he presented the ram of the burnt offering, and Aaron and his sons laid their hands on the head of the ram.

8:18
Ex 29:15

19   And Moses slaughtered *it* and sprinkled the blood around on the altar.
20   When he had cut the ram into its pieces, Moses offered up the head and the pieces and the suet in smoke.
21   After he had washed the entrails and the legs with water, Moses offered up the whole ram in smoke on the altar. It was a burnt offering for a soothing aroma; it was an offering by fire to the LORD, just as the LORD had commanded Moses.

8:21
Ex 29:18

d. *The ram of ordination*

22   Then he presented the second ram, the ram of [4]ordination; and Aaron and his sons laid their hands on the head of the ram.

8:22
Ex 29:19,31

23   And Moses slaughtered *it* and took some of its blood and put it on the lobe of Aaron's right ear, and on the thumb of his right hand, and on the big toe of his right foot.
24   He also had Aaron's sons come near; and Moses put some of the blood on the lobe of their right ear, and on the thumb of their right hand, and on the big toe of their right foot. Moses then sprinkled *the rest of* the blood around on the altar.
25   And he took the fat, and the fat tail, and all the fat that was on the entrails, and the lobe of the liver and the two kidneys and their fat and the right thigh.

8:25
Ex 29:22

26   And from the basket of unleavened bread that was before the LORD, he took one unleavened cake and one cake of bread *mixed with* oil and one wafer, and placed *them* on the portions of fat and on the right thigh.

8:26
Ex 29:23

27   He then put all *these* on the hands of Aaron and on the hands of his sons, and presented them as a wave offering before the LORD.
28   Then Moses took them from their hands and offered them up in smoke on the altar with the burnt offering. They were an ordination offering for a soothing aroma; it was an offering by fire to the LORD.

8:28
Ex 29:25

29   Moses also took the breast and presented it for a wave offering before the LORD; it was Moses' portion of the ram of ordination, just as the LORD had commanded Moses.

8:29
Ex 29:26

30   So Moses took some of the anointing oil and some of the blood which was on the altar, and sprinkled it on Aaron, on his garments, on his sons, and on the garments of his sons with him; and he consecrated Aaron, his garments, and his sons, and the garments of his sons with him.

8:30
Ex 30:30;
Num 3:3

e. *The seven days of the ordination*

31   Then Moses said to Aaron and to his sons, "Boil the flesh at the doorway of the tent of meeting, and eat it there together with the bread which is in the basket of the ordination offering, just as I commanded, saying, 'Aaron and his sons shall eat it.'

8:31
Ex 29:31,32

32   "And the remainder of the flesh and of the bread you shall burn in the fire.
33   "And you shall not go outside the doorway of the tent of meeting for seven days, until the day that the period of your ordination is fulfilled; for he will ordain you through seven days.

8:32
Ex 29:34
8:33
Ex 29:30,35

34   "The LORD has commanded to do as has been done this day, to make atonement on your behalf.

8:34
Heb 7:16

35   "At the doorway of the tent of meeting, moreover, you shall remain day and night for seven days, and keep the charge of the LORD, that you may not die, for so I have been commanded."
36   Thus Aaron and his sons did all the things which the LORD had commanded through Moses.

2. *The sacrifices*

a. *The offering for the priesthood*

9 Now it came about on the eighth day that Moses called Aaron and his sons and the elders of Israel;
2   and he said to Aaron, "Take for yourself a calf, a bull, for a sin offering and

9:2
Lev 8:18;
Ex 29:1

---

[4]Lit., *filling,* and so throughout this context

a ram for a burnt offering, *both* without defect, and offer *them* before the LORD.

9:3
Lev 4:23

3 "Then to the sons of Israel you shall speak, saying, 'Take a male goat for a sin offering, and a calf and a lamb, both one year old, without defect, for a burnt offering,

4 and an ox and a ram for peace offerings, to sacrifice before the LORD, and a grain offering mixed with oil; for today the LORD shall appear to you.' "

5 So they took what Moses had commanded to the front of the tent of meeting, and the whole congregation came near and stood before the LORD.

9:6
v. 23

6 And Moses said, "This is the thing which the LORD has commanded you to do, that the glory of the LORD may appear to you."

9:7
Heb 5:1,3

7 Moses then said to Aaron, "Come near to the altar and offer your sin offering and your burnt offering, that you may make atonement for yourself and for the people; then make the offering for the people, that you may make atonement for them, just as the LORD has commanded."

9:8
Lev 4:1-12

8 So Aaron came near to the altar and slaughtered the calf of the sin offering which was for himself.

9:9
vv. 12,18

9 And Aaron's sons presented the blood to him; and he dipped his finger in the blood, and put *some* on the horns of the altar, and poured out *the rest of* the blood at the base of the altar.

10 The fat and the kidneys and the lobe of the liver of the sin offering, he then offered up in smoke on the altar just as the LORD had commanded Moses.

9:11
Lev 4:11;
8:17

11 The flesh and the skin, however, he burned with fire outside the camp.

12 Then he slaughtered the burnt offering; and Aaron's sons handed the blood to him and he sprinkled it around on the altar.

13 And they handed the burnt offering to him in pieces with the head, and he offered *them* up in smoke on the altar.

14 He also washed the entrails and the legs, and offered *them* up in smoke with the burnt offering on the altar.

b. *The offering for the people*

9:15
Lev 4:27-31

15 Then he presented the people's offering, and took the goat of the sin offering which was for the people, and slaughtered it and offered it for sin, like the first.

9:16
Lev 1:3,10

16 He also presented the burnt offering, and offered it according to the ordinance.

9:17
Lev 2:1,2;
3:5

17 Next he presented the grain offering, and filled his hand with some of it and offered *it* up in smoke on the altar, besides the burnt offering of the morning.

9:18
Lev 3:1-11

18 Then he slaughtered the ox and the ram, the sacrifice of peace offerings which was for the people; and Aaron's sons handed the blood to him and he sprinkled it around on the altar.

19 As for the portions of fat from the ox and from the ram, the fat tail, and the *fat* covering, and the kidneys and the lobe of the liver,

20 they now placed the portions of fat on the breasts; and he offered them up in smoke on the altar.

9:21
Lev 7:30-34

21 But the breasts and the right thigh Aaron presented as a wave offering before the LORD, just as Moses had commanded.

22 Then Aaron lifted up his hands toward the people and blessed them, and he stepped down after making the sin offering and the burnt offering and the peace offerings.

9:23
v. 6;
Num 14:10

23 And Moses and Aaron went into the tent of meeting. When they came out and blessed the people, the glory of the LORD appeared to all the people.

*9:24
1 Kin 18:38,
39

24 Then fire came out from before the LORD and consumed the burnt offering and the portions of fat on the altar; and when all the people saw *it*, they shouted and fell on their faces.

9:24 Fire has been regarded as a sacred symbol by almost all peoples and in almost all religions. As a symbol it illustrates many Biblical truths. Fire was employed to provide God's protection (Num. 9:16); as a weapon of divine vengeance (Deut. 4:24; Heb. 12:29); and as a symbol of the Holy Spirit (Is. 4:4; Acts 2:3). In this verse fire came down from God to enkindle the sacrifice on His altar. All burnt offerings were to be consumed by fire (6:9,12). As a symbol it was used supernaturally in Scripture in many instances: the burning bush (Ex. 3:2); at the giving of the Law on Mt. Sinai (Deut. 4:11,36); and again on Mt. Carmel when Elijah overcame the prophets of Baal (1 Kin. 18:38). On some occasions God Himself appeared in fire (Ex. 3:2 and 19:18). We are told that at the end of the age Christ will return to earth *in flaming fire* (2 Thess. 1:7). It may be thought of as a consuming, purifying, and melting agency, and it certainly connotes the holiness of God (*our God is a consuming fire*, Heb. 12:29; cf. Deut. 9:3).

3. The death of Nadab and Abihu: their strange fire

10 Now Nadab and Abihu, the sons of Aaron, took their respective firepans, and after putting fire in them, placed incense on it and offered strange fire before the LORD, which He had not commanded them.

2   And fire came out from the presence of the LORD and consumed them, and they died before the LORD.

3   Then Moses said to Aaron, "It is what the LORD spoke, saying,
'By those who come near Me I will be treated as holy,
And before all the people I will be honored.' "
So Aaron, therefore, kept silent.

4   Moses called also to Mishael and Elzaphan, the sons of Aaron's uncle Uzziel, and said to them, "Come forward, carry your relatives away from the front of the sanctuary to the outside of the camp."

5   So they came forward and carried them still in their tunics to the outside of the camp, as Moses had said.

6   Then Moses said to Aaron and to his sons Eleazar and Ithamar, "Do not [5]uncover your heads nor tear your clothes, so that you may not die, and that He may not become wrathful against all the congregation. But your kinsmen, the whole house of Israel, shall bewail the burning which the LORD has brought about.

7   "You shall not even go out from the doorway of the tent of meeting, lest you die; for the LORD's anointing oil is upon you." So they did according to the word of Moses.

4. The command against wine for the performing priesthood

8   The LORD then spoke to Aaron, saying,

9   "Do not drink wine or strong drink, neither you nor your sons with you, when you come into the tent of meeting, so that you may not die—it is a perpetual statute throughout your generations—

10   and so as to make a distinction between the holy and the profane, and between the unclean and the clean,

11   and so as to teach the sons of Israel all the statutes which the LORD has spoken to them through Moses."

5. The law of the eating of holy things

12   Then Moses spoke to Aaron, and to his surviving sons, Eleazar and Ithamar, "Take the grain offering that is left over from the LORD's offerings by fire and eat it unleavened beside the altar, for it is most holy.

13   "You shall eat it, moreover, in a holy place, because it is your due and your sons' due out of the LORD's offerings by fire; for thus I have been commanded.

14   "The breast of the wave offering, however, and the thigh of the offering you may eat in a clean place, you and your sons and your daughters with you; for they have been given as your due and your sons' due out of the sacrifices of the peace offerings of the sons of Israel.

15   "The thigh offered by lifting up and the breast offered by waving, they shall bring along with the offerings by fire of the portions of fat, to present as a wave offering before the LORD; so it shall be a thing perpetually due you and your sons with you, just as the LORD has commanded."

16   But Moses searched carefully for the goat of the sin offering, and behold, it had been burned up! So he was angry with Aaron's surviving sons Eleazar and Ithamar, saying,

17   "Why did you not eat the sin offering at the holy place? For it is most holy, and He gave it to you to bear away the guilt of the congregation, to make atonement for them before the LORD.

18   "Behold, since its blood had not been brought inside, into the sanctuary, you should certainly have eaten it in the sanctuary, just as I commanded."

19   But Aaron spoke to Moses, "Behold, this very day they presented their sin

[5]Lit., *unbind*

*10:1
Num 3:3,4;
Lev 16:12;
Ex 30:9

10:2
Num 3:4;
26:61

10:3
Ex 19:22;
30:30;
Lev 21:6

10:4
Ex 6:18,22;
Acts 5:6,9,10

10:6
Lev 21:1,10;
Num 16:22,
46; Josh 7:1;
22:18-20

10:7
Lev 21:12

*10:9
Ezek 44:21

*10:10
Lev 11:47;
20:25;
Ezek 22:26
10:11
Deut 24:8;
Mal 2:7

10:12
Lev 6:14-18;
21:22

10:14
Ex 29:24,26,
27

10:15
Lev 7:29,30,
34

10:17
Lev 6:24-30

*10:19
Lev 9:8,12

10:1 See note on 6:13. It has been inferred from v. 9 of this chapter that Nadab and Abihu had committed their fatal offense while under the influence of intoxicating drink. Hence the appropriateness of the regulation forbidding descendants of Aaron from ever touching fermented drinks before entering on their sacred duties.
10:9 *Strong drink* was probably beer, for the ancients did not have distilled liquors.
10:10 *Unclean* does not mean *dirty*, but ceremonially unclean.

offering and their burnt offering before the LORD. When things like these happened to me, if I had eaten a sin offering today, would it have been good in the sight of the LORD?"

20   And when Moses heard *that*, it seemed good in his sight.

C. The laws of purification

1. Clean and unclean animals

11 The LORD spoke again to Moses and to Aaron, saying to them, 2 "Speak to the sons of Israel, saying, 'These are the creatures which you may eat from all the animals that are on the earth.

3   'Whatever divides a hoof, thus making split hoofs, *and* chews the cud, among the animals, that you may eat.

4   'Nevertheless, you are not to eat of these, among those which chew the cud, or among those which divide the hoof: the camel, for though it chews cud, it does not divide the hoof, it is unclean to you.

5   'Likewise, the rock badger, for though it chews cud, it does not divide the hoof, it is unclean to you;

6   the rabbit also, for though it chews cud, it does not divide the hoof, it is unclean to you;

7   and the pig, for though it divides the hoof, thus making a split hoof, it does not chew cud, it is unclean to you.

8   'You shall not eat of their flesh nor touch their carcasses; they are unclean to you.

9   'These you may eat, whatever is in the water: all that have fins and scales, those in the water, in the seas or in the rivers, you may eat.

10   'But whatever is in the seas and in the rivers, that do not have fins and scales among all the teeming life of the water, and among all the living creatures that are in the water, they are detestable things to you,

11   and they shall be [6]abhorrent to you; you may not eat of their flesh, and their carcasses you shall detest.

12   'Whatever in the water does not have fins and scales is abhorrent to you.

13   'These, moreover, you shall detest among the birds; they are abhorrent, not to be eaten: the eagle and the vulture and the buzzard,

14   and the kite and the falcon in its kind,

15   every raven in its kind,

16   and the ostrich and the owl and the sea gull and the hawk in its kind,

17   and the little owl and the cormorant and the great owl,

18   and the white owl and the pelican and the carrion vulture,

19   and the stork, the heron in its kinds, and the hoopoe, and the bat.

20   'All the winged insects that walk on *all* fours are detestable to you.

21   'Yet these you may eat among all the winged insects which walk on *all* fours: those which have above their feet jointed legs with which to jump on the earth.

22   'These of them you may eat: the locust in its kinds, and the devastating locust in its kinds, and the cricket in its kinds, and the grasshopper in its kinds.

23   'But all other winged insects which are four-footed are detestable to you.

24   'By these, moreover, you will be made unclean: whoever touches their carcasses becomes unclean until evening,

25   and whoever picks up any of their carcasses shall wash his clothes and be unclean until evening.

26   'Concerning all the animals which divide the hoof, but do not make a split *hoof*, or which do not chew cud, they are unclean to you: whoever touches them becomes unclean.

27   'Also whatever walks on its paws, among all the creatures that walk on *all*

[6]Lit., *detestable things*

*11:2
Deut 14:3-21

11:7
Is 65:4; 66:3,
17
11:8
Is 52:11;
Heb 9:10
11:9
Deut 14:9
11:10
Lev 7:18;
Deut 14:3

11:13
Deut 14:12

11:22
Matt 3:4;
Mark 1:6

11:25
v. 40

10:19 *things like these*, the death of Nadab and Abihu.
11:2 The dietary restrictions under the Hebrew theocracy have been rendered obsolete by the atoning work of Christ, who fulfilled all the symbolism of the ceremonial law (cf. Acts 10:14,15; Col. 2:16; 1Tim. 4:3,4). The distinction between clean and unclean foods seems to have been based on the following considerations: (1) the flesh of unclean animals or birds was unwholesome or unsuitable for sanitary reasons, usually because they fed on carrion or that

which had putrified; (2) the animal in question was especially associated with depraved heathen worship (such as the pig, which was offered to the gods of the nether world); and (3) their habits of life or behavior had an objectionable association, such as "creeping things" that were serpentlike in their movements, or bats, which were at home in dark, dank caves and hated the light. The New Testament teaches that these pre-Christian regulations are not binding on believers today.

fours, are unclean to you; whoever touches their carcasses becomes unclean until evening,

28   and the one who picks up their carcasses shall wash his clothes and be unclean until evening; they are unclean to you.

29   'Now these are to you the unclean among the swarming things which swarm on the earth: the mole, and the mouse, and the great lizard in its kinds,

30   and the gecko, and the crocodile, and the lizard, and the sand reptile, and the chameleon.

31   'These are to you the unclean among all the swarming things; whoever touches them when they are dead becomes unclean until evening.

32   'Also anything on which one of them may fall when they are dead, becomes unclean, including any wooden article, or clothing, or a skin, or a sack—any article of which use is made—it shall be put in the water and be unclean until evening, then it becomes clean.

33   'As for any earthenware vessel into which one of them may fall, whatever is in it becomes unclean and you shall break the vessel.

34   'Any of the food which may be eaten, on which water comes, shall become unclean; and any liquid which may be drunk in every vessel shall become unclean.

35   'Everything, moreover, on which part of their carcass may fall becomes unclean; an oven or a [7]stove shall be smashed; they are unclean and shall continue as unclean to you.

36   'Nevertheless a spring or a cistern collecting water shall be clean, though the one who touches their carcass shall be unclean.

37   'And if a part of their carcass falls on any seed for sowing which is to be sown, it is clean.

38   'Though if water is put on the seed, and a part of their carcass falls on it, it is unclean to you.

39   'Also if one of the animals dies which you have for food, the one who touches its carcass becomes unclean until evening.

40   'He too, who eats some of its carcass shall wash his clothes and be unclean until evening; and the one who picks up its carcass shall wash his clothes and be unclean until evening.

41   'Now every swarming thing that swarms on the earth is detestable, not to be eaten.

42   'Whatever crawls on its belly, and whatever walks on *all* fours, whatever has many feet, in respect to every swarming thing that swarms on the earth, you shall not eat them, for they are detestable.

43   'Do not render yourselves detestable through any of the swarming things that swarm; and you shall not make yourselves unclean with them so that you become unclean.

44   'For I am the LORD your God. Consecrate yourselves therefore, and be holy; for I am holy. And you shall not make yourselves unclean with any of the swarming things that swarm on the earth.

45   'For I am the LORD, who brought you up from the land of Egypt, to be your God; thus you shall be holy for I am holy.' "

46   This is the law regarding the animal, and the bird, and every living thing that moves in the waters, and everything that swarms on the earth,

47   to make a distinction between the unclean and the clean, and between the edible creature and the creature which is not to be eaten.

2. Purification of a woman after childbirth

12 Then the LORD spoke to Moses, saying,

2 "Speak to the sons of Israel, saying, 'When a woman gives birth and bears a male *child*, then she shall be unclean for seven days, as in the days of her menstruation she shall be unclean.

3   'And on the eighth day the flesh of his foreskin shall be circumcised.

4   'Then she shall remain in the blood of *her* purification for thirty-three days;

[7]Lit., *hearth for supporting (two) pots*

11:29	Is 66:17
11:32	Lev 15:12
11:33	Lev 6:28; 15:12
11:40	Lev 17:15; 22:8
***11:41**	v. 29
11:43	Lev 20:25
11:44	Ex 6:7; 19:6; Lev 19:2; 1 Pet 1:15,16
11:45	Ex 6:7
11:47	Lev 10:10
12:2	Lev 15:19; 18:19
12:3	Gen 17:12

11:41 *detestable*, "whatever is offensive to God and His plan for man's righteous way of life, whether 'unclean' items of tabooed food, worship of idols, harlotry, or dis-honesty" (*Harper's Bible Dictionary*, p. 3). (See also note to Dan. 9:27 on abomination of desolation.)

she shall not touch any consecrated thing, nor enter the sanctuary, until the days of her purification are completed.

5 'But if she bears a female *child*, then she shall be unclean for two weeks, as in her menstruation; and she shall remain in the blood of *her* purification for sixty-six days.

6 'And when the days of her purification are completed, for a son or for a daughter, she shall bring to the priest at the doorway of the tent of meeting, a one year old lamb for a burnt offering, and a young pigeon or a turtledove for a sin offering.

7 'Then he shall offer it before the LORD and make atonement for her; and she shall be cleansed from the flow of her blood. This is the law for her who bears *a child, whether* a male or a female.

8 'But if she cannot afford a lamb, then she shall take two turtledoves or two young pigeons, the one for a burnt offering and the other for a sin offering; and the priest shall make atonement for her, and she shall be clean.' "

3. The laws of leprosy
a. Diagnosis and treatment of leprosy in man

13 Then the LORD spoke to Moses and to Aaron, saying,
2 "When a man has on the skin of his body a swelling or a scab or a bright spot, and it becomes [8]an infection of leprosy on the skin of his body, then he shall be brought to Aaron the priest, or to one of his sons the priests.

3 "And the priest shall look at the mark on the skin of the body, and if the hair in the infection has turned white and the infection appears to be deeper than the skin of his body, it is an infection of leprosy; when the priest has looked at him, he shall pronounce him unclean.

4 "But if the bright spot is white on the skin of his body, and it does not appear to be deeper than the skin, and the hair on it has not turned white, then the priest shall isolate *him who has* the infection for seven days.

5 "And the priest shall look at him on the seventh day, and if in his eyes the infection has not changed, *and* the infection has not spread on the skin, then the priest shall isolate him for seven more days.

6 "And the priest shall look at him again on the seventh day; and if the infection has faded, and the mark has not spread on the skin, then the priest shall pronounce him clean; it is *only* a scab. And he shall wash his clothes and be clean.

7 "But if the scab spreads farther on the skin, after he has shown himself to the priest for his cleansing, he shall appear again to the priest.

8 "And the priest shall look, and if the scab has spread on the skin, then the priest shall pronounce him unclean; it is leprosy.

9 "When the infection of leprosy is on a man, then he shall be brought to the priest.

10 "The priest shall then look, and if there is a white swelling in the skin, and it has turned the hair white, and there is quick raw flesh in the swelling,

11 it is a chronic leprosy on the skin of his body, and the priest shall pronounce him unclean; he shall not isolate him, for he is unclean.

12 "And if the leprosy breaks out farther on the skin, and the leprosy covers all the skin of *him who has* the infection from his head even to his feet, as far as the priest can see,

13 then the priest shall look, and behold, *if* the leprosy has covered all his body, he shall pronounce clean *him who has* the infection; it has all turned white *and* he is clean.

14 "But whenever raw flesh appears on him, he shall be unclean.

15 "And the priest shall look at the raw flesh, and he shall pronounce him unclean; the raw flesh is unclean, it is leprosy.

16 "Or if the raw flesh turns again and is changed to white, then he shall come to the priest,

17 and the priest shall look at him, and behold, *if* the infection has turned to white, then the priest shall pronounce clean *him who has* the infection; he is clean.

[8]Lit., *a mark, stroke,* and so throughout this context

13:2 *leprosy*, a term that was used to cover a variety of skin diseases. It was extended to include molds or defects in garments (13:47–59) and in houses (14:34–53). Sometimes eczema (see 13:39), a cutaneous disease, was mistaken for leprosy.

18 "And when the body has a boil on its skin, and it is healed,

19   and in the place of the boil there is a white swelling or a reddish-white, bright spot, then it shall be shown to the priest;

20   and the priest shall look, and behold, *if* it appears to be lower than the skin, and the hair on it has turned white, then the priest shall pronounce him unclean; it is the infection of leprosy, it has broken out in the boil.

21   "But if the priest looks at it, and behold, there are no white hairs in it and it is not lower than the skin and is faded, then the priest shall isolate him for seven days;

22   and if it spreads farther on the skin, then the priest shall pronounce him unclean; it is an infection.

23   "But if the bright spot remains in its place, and does not spread, it is *only* the scar of the boil; and the priest shall pronounce him clean.

24 "Or if the body sustains in its skin a burn by fire, and the raw *flesh* of the burn becomes a bright spot, reddish-white, or white,

25   then the priest shall look at it. And if the hair in the bright spot has turned white, and it appears to be deeper than the skin, it is leprosy; it has broken out in the burn. Therefore, the priest shall pronounce him unclean; it is an infection of leprosy.

26   "But if the priest looks at it, and indeed, there is no white hair in the bright spot, and it is no deeper than the skin, but is dim, then the priest shall isolate him for seven days;

27   and the priest shall look at him on the seventh day. If it spreads farther in the skin, then the priest shall pronounce him unclean; it is an infection of leprosy.

28   "But if the bright spot remains in its place, and has not spread in the skin, but is dim, it is the swelling from the burn; and the priest shall pronounce him clean, for it is *only* the scar of the burn.

29 "Now if a man or woman has an infection on the head or on the beard,

30   then the priest shall look at the infection, and if it appears to be deeper than the skin, and there is thin yellowish hair in it, then the priest shall pronounce him unclean; it is a scale, it is leprosy of the head or of the beard.

31   "But if the priest looks at the infection of the scale, and indeed, it appears to be no deeper than the skin, and there is no black hair in it, then the priest shall isolate *the person* with the scaly infection for seven days.

32   "And on the seventh day the priest shall look at the infection, and if the scale has not spread, and no yellowish hair has grown in it, and the appearance of the scale is no deeper than the skin,

33   then he shall shave himself, but he shall not shave the scale; and the priest shall isolate *the person* with the scale seven more days.

34   "Then on the seventh day the priest shall look at the scale, and if the scale has not spread in the skin, and it appears to be no deeper than the skin, the priest shall pronounce him clean; and he shall wash his clothes and be clean.

35   "But if the scale spreads farther in the skin after his cleansing,

36   then the priest shall look at him, and if the scale has spread in the skin, the priest need not seek for the yellowish hair; he is unclean.

37   "If in his sight the scale has remained, however, and black hair has grown in it, the scale has healed, he is clean; and the priest shall pronounce him clean.

38 "And when a man or a woman has bright spots on the skin of the body, *even* white bright spots,

39   then the priest shall look, and if the bright spots on the skin of their bodies are a faint white, it is eczema that has broken out on the skin; he is clean.

40 "Now if a man loses the hair of his head, he is bald; he is clean.

41   "And if his head becomes bald at the front and sides, he is bald on the forehead; he is clean.

42   "But if on the bald head or the bald forehead, there occurs a reddish-white infection, it is leprosy breaking out on his bald head or on his bald forehead.

43   "Then the priest shall look at him; and if the swelling of the infection is reddish-white on his bald head or on his bald forehead, like the appearance of leprosy in the skin of the body,

44   he is a leprous man, he is unclean. The priest shall surely pronounce him unclean; his infection is on his head.

45 "As for the leper who has the infection, his clothes shall be torn, and the hair

---

13:18
Ex 9:9
13:19
v. 43

13:21
Num 12:14, 15

13:25
v. 15

13:27
v. 5

13:29
v. 44

13:32
v. 5

13:34
Lev 14:8

13:36
v. 30

13:40
Ezek 29:18

13:44
v. 29
13:45
Ezek 24:17, 22; Mic 3:7; Lam 4:15

of his head shall be uncovered, and he shall cover his mustache and cry, 'Unclean! Unclean!'

13:46
Num 5:2;
12:14;
2 Kin 7:3;
15:5;
Luke 17:12

46 "He shall remain unclean all the days during which he has the infection; he is unclean. He shall live alone; his dwelling shall be outside the camp.

b. *Diagnosis and treatment of leprosy in garments*

47 "When a garment has a mark of leprosy in it, whether it is a wool garment or a linen garment,

48 whether in warp or woof, of linen or of wool, whether in leather or in any article made of leather,

49 if the mark is greenish or reddish in the garment or in the leather, or in the warp or in the woof, or in any article of leather, it is a leprous mark and shall be shown to the priest.

50 "Then the priest shall look at the mark, and shall quarantine the article with the mark for seven days.

13:51
Lev 14:44

51 "He shall then look at the mark on the seventh day; if the mark has spread in the garment, whether in the warp or in the woof, or in the leather, whatever the purpose for which the leather is used, the mark is a leprous malignancy, it is unclean.

13:52
Lev 14:44

52 "So he shall burn the garment, whether the warp or the woof, in wool or in linen, or any article of leather in which the mark occurs, for it is a leprous malignancy; it shall be burned in the fire.

53 "But if the priest shall look, and indeed, the mark has not spread in the garment, either in the warp or in the woof, or in any article of leather,

13:54
v. 4

54 then the priest shall order them to wash the thing in which the mark occurs, and he shall quarantine it for seven more days.

55 "After the article with the mark has been washed, the priest shall again look, and if the mark has not changed its appearance, even though the mark has not spread, it is unclean; you shall burn it in the fire, whether an eating away has produced bareness on the top or on the front of it.

13:56
Lev 14:8

56 "Then if the priest shall look, and if the mark has faded after it has been washed, then he shall tear it out of the garment or out of the leather, whether from the warp or from the woof;

57 and if it appears again in the garment, whether in the warp or in the woof, or in any article of leather, it is an outbreak; the article with the mark shall be burned in the fire.

58 "And the garment, whether the warp or the woof, or any article of leather from which the mark has departed when you washed it, it shall then be washed a second time and shall be clean."

59 This is the law for the mark of leprosy in a garment of wool or linen, whether in the warp or in the woof, or in any article of leather, for pronouncing it clean or unclean.

c. *The laws of purification for leprosy*

14 Then the LORD spoke to Moses, saying,

14:2
Matt 8:2,4;
Mark 1:40,
44;
Luke 5:12,
14; 17:14

2 "This shall be the law of the leper in the day of his cleansing. Now he shall be brought to the priest,

3 and the priest shall go out to the outside of the camp. Thus the priest shall look, and if the infection of leprosy has been healed in the leper,

14:4
vv. 6,49,51,
52; Num 19:6

4 then the priest shall give orders to take two live clean birds and cedar wood and a scarlet string and hyssop for the one who is to be cleansed.

5 "The priest shall also give orders to slay the one bird in an earthenware vessel over running water.

6 "*As for* the live bird, he shall take it, together with the cedar wood and the scarlet string and the hyssop, and shall dip them and the live bird in the blood of the bird that was slain over the running water.

14:7
2 Kin 5:10,14

7 "He shall then sprinkle seven times the one who is to be cleansed from the leprosy, and shall pronounce him clean, and shall let the live bird go free over the open field.

14:8
Lev 13:6;
Num 8:7

8 "The one to be cleansed shall then wash his clothes and shave off all his hair, and bathe in water and be clean. Now afterward, he may enter the camp, but he shall stay outside his tent for seven days.

9 "And it will be on the seventh day that he shall shave off all his hair: he shall

shave his head and his beard and his eyebrows, even all his hair. He shall then wash his clothes and bathe his body in water and be clean.

10 "Now on the eighth day he is to take two male lambs without defect, and a yearling ewe lamb without defect, and three-tenths *of an ephah* of fine flour mixed with oil for a grain offering, and one [9]log of oil;

11 and the priest who pronounces him clean shall present the man to be cleansed and the aforesaid before the LORD at the doorway of the tent of meeting.

12 "Then the priest shall take the one male lamb and bring it for a guilt offering, with the log of oil, and present them as a wave offering before the LORD.

13 "Next he shall slaughter the male lamb in the place where they slaughter the sin offering and the burnt offering, at the place of the sanctuary—for the guilt offering, like the sin offering, belongs to the priest; it is most holy.

14 "The priest shall then take some of the blood of the guilt offering, and the priest shall put *it* on the lobe of the right ear of the one to be cleansed, and on the thumb of his right hand, and on the big toe of his right foot.

15 "The priest shall also take some of the log of oil, and pour *it* into his left palm;

16 the priest shall then dip his right-hand finger into the oil that is in his left palm, and with his finger sprinkle some of the oil seven times before the LORD.

17 "And of the remaining oil which is in his palm, the priest shall put some on the right ear lobe of the one to be cleansed, and on the thumb of his right hand, and on the big toe of his right foot, on the blood of the guilt offering;

18 while the rest of the oil that is in the priest's palm, he shall put on the head of the one to be cleansed. So the priest shall make atonement on his behalf before the LORD.

19 "The priest shall next offer the sin offering and make atonement for the one to be cleansed from his uncleanness. Then afterward, he shall slaughter the burnt offering.

20 "And the priest shall offer up the burnt offering and the grain offering on the altar. Thus the priest shall make atonement for him, and he shall be clean.

21 "But if he is poor, and his means are insufficient, then he is to take one male lamb for a guilt offering as a wave offering to make atonement for him, and one-tenth *of an ephah* of fine flour mixed with oil for a grain offering, and a log of oil,

22 and two turtledoves or two young pigeons which are within his means, the one shall be a sin offering and the other a burnt offering.

23 "Then the eighth day he shall bring them for his cleansing to the priest, at the doorway of the tent of meeting, before the LORD.

24 "And the priest shall take the lamb of the guilt offering, and the log of oil, and the priest shall offer them for a wave offering before the LORD.

25 "Next he shall slaughter the lamb of the guilt offering; and the priest is to take some of the blood of the guilt offering and put *it* on the lobe of the right ear of the one to be cleansed and on the thumb of his right hand, and on the big toe of his right foot.

26 "The priest shall also pour some of the oil into his left palm;

27 and with his right-hand finger the priest shall sprinkle some of the oil that is in his left palm seven times before the LORD.

28 "The priest shall then put some of the oil that is in his palm on the lobe of the right ear of the one to be cleansed, and on the thumb of his right hand, and on the big toe of his right foot, on the place of the blood of the guilt offering.

29 "Moreover, the rest of the oil that is in the priest's palm he shall put on the head of the one to be cleansed, to make atonement on his behalf before the LORD.

30 "He shall then offer one of the turtledoves or young pigeons, which are within his means.

31 "*He shall offer* what he can afford, the one for a sin offering, and the other for a burnt offering, together with the grain offering. So the priest shall make atonement before the LORD on behalf of the one to be cleansed.

32 "This is the law *for him* in whom there is an infection of leprosy, whose means are limited for his cleansing."

d. Diagnosis and treatment of leprosy in houses

33 The LORD further spoke to Moses and to Aaron, saying,

34 "When you enter the land of Canaan, which I give you for a possession, and I put a mark of leprosy on a house in the land of your possession,

---

14:10
Matt 8:4;
Mark 1:44;
Luke 5:14

14:12
Lev 5:2,8;
6:6,7;
Ex 29:24
14:13
Lev 1:5,11;
6:24-30; 2:3;
7:6
14:14
Lev 8:23

14:18
Lev 4:26

14:19
v. 12

14:21
Lev 5:7,11;
12:8; v. 22
14:22
Lev 12:8;
15:14,15
14:23
vv. 10,11
14:24
v. 12
14:25
v. 14

14:28
Lev 5:6

14:30
v. 22;
Lev 15:15
14:31
Lev 5:7

14:34
Gen 17:8;
Num 32:22;
Deut 7:1

---

[9]I.e., Approx. one pint, and so through v. 24

14:35
Ps 91:10;
Prov 3:33

35 then the one who owns the house shall come and tell the priest, saying, '*Something* like a mark *of leprosy* has become visible to me in the house.'

36 "The priest shall then order that they empty the house before the priest goes in to look at the mark, so that everything in the house need not become unclean; and afterward the priest shall go in to look at the house.

37 "So he shall look at the mark, and if the mark on the walls of the house has greenish or reddish depressions, and appears deeper than the surface;

14:38
Num 12:15

38 then the priest shall come out of the house, to the doorway, and quarantine the house for seven days.

39 "And the priest shall return on the seventh day and make an inspection. If the mark has indeed spread in the walls of the house,

14:40
v. 45

40 then the priest shall order them to tear out the stones with the mark in them and throw them away at an unclean place outside the city.

41 "And he shall have the house scraped all around inside, and they shall dump the plaster that they scrape off at an unclean place outside the city.

42 "Then they shall take other stones and replace *those* stones; and he shall take other plaster and replaster the house.

43 "If, however, the mark breaks out again in the house, after he has torn out the stones and scraped the house, and after it has been replastered,

14:44
Lev 13:51

44 then the priest shall come in and make an inspection. If he sees that the mark has indeed spread in the house, it is a malignant mark in the house; it is unclean.

45 "He shall therefore tear down the house, its stones, and its timbers, and all the plaster of the house, and he shall take *them* outside the city to an unclean place.

46 "Moreover, whoever goes into the house during the time that he has quarantined it, becomes unclean until evening.

47 "Likewise, whoever lies down in the house shall wash his clothes, and whoever eats in the house shall wash his clothes.

48 "If, on the other hand, the priest comes in and makes an inspection, and the mark has not indeed spread in the house after the house has been replastered, then the priest shall pronounce the house clean because the mark has not reappeared.

14:49
v. 4

49 "To cleanse the house then, he shall take two birds and cedar wood and a scarlet string and hyssop,

50 and he shall slaughter the one bird in an earthenware vessel over running water.

14:51
Ps 51:7

51 "Then he shall take the cedar wood and the hyssop and the scarlet string, with the live bird, and dip them in the blood of the slain bird, as well as in the running water, and sprinkle the house seven times.

52 "He shall thus cleanse the house with the blood of the bird and with the running water, along with the live bird and with the cedar wood and with the hyssop and with the scarlet string.

14:53
v. 20

53 "However, he shall let the live bird go free outside the city into the open field. So he shall make atonement for the house, and it shall be clean."

14:54
Lev 13:30

54 This is the law for any mark of leprosy—even for a scale,

55 and for the leprous garment or house,

14:56
Lev 13:2

56 and for a swelling, and for a scab, and for a bright spot—

57 to teach when they are unclean, and when they are clean. This is the law of leprosy.

4. Unclean secretions and cleansing

a. Uncleanness in man: purification

15:2
Lev 22:4;
Num 5:2;
2 Sam 3:29;
Matt 9:20

15 The LORD also spoke to Moses and to Aaron, saying,
2 "Speak to the sons of Israel, and say to them, 'When any man has a discharge from his body, his discharge is unclean.

3 'This, moreover, shall be his uncleanness in his discharge: it is his uncleanness whether his body allows its discharge to flow, or whether his body obstructs its discharge.

4 'Every bed on which the person with the discharge lies becomes unclean, and everything on which he sits becomes unclean.

5 'Anyone, moreover, who touches his bed shall wash his clothes and bathe in water and be unclean until evening;

6 and whoever sits on the thing on which the man with the discharge has been sitting, shall wash his clothes and bathe in water and be unclean until evening.

7 'Also whoever touches the person with the discharge shall wash his clothes and bathe in water and be unclean until evening.

8 'Or if the man with the discharge spits on one who is clean, he too shall wash his clothes and bathe in water and be unclean until evening.

9 'And every saddle on which the person with the discharge rides becomes unclean.

10 'Whoever then touches any of the things which were under him shall be unclean until evening, and he who carries them shall wash his clothes and bathe in water and be unclean until evening.

11 'Likewise, whomever the one with the discharge touches without having rinsed his hands in water shall wash his clothes and bathe in water and be unclean until evening.

12 'However, an earthenware vessel which the person with the discharge touches shall be broken, and every wooden vessel shall be rinsed in water.

13 'Now when the man with the discharge becomes cleansed from his discharge, then he shall count off for himself seven days for his cleansing; he shall then wash his clothes and bathe his body in running water and shall become clean.

14 'Then on the eighth day he shall take for himself two turtledoves or two young pigeons, and come before the LORD to the doorway of the tent of meeting, and give them to the priest;

15 and the priest shall offer them, one for a sin offering, and the other for a burnt offering. So the priest shall make atonement on his behalf before the LORD because of his discharge.

16 'Now if a man has a seminal emission, he shall bathe all his body in water and be unclean until evening.

17 'As for any garment or any leather on which there is seminal emission, it shall be washed with water and be unclean until evening.

18 'If a man lies with a woman so that there is a seminal emission, they shall both bathe in water and be unclean until evening.

b. Uncleanness in woman: purification

19 'When a woman has a discharge, if her discharge in her body is blood, she shall continue in her menstrual impurity for seven days; and whoever touches her shall be unclean until evening.

20 'Everything also on which she lies during her menstrual impurity shall be unclean, and everything on which she sits shall be unclean.

21 'And anyone who touches her bed shall wash his clothes and bathe in water and be unclean until evening.

22 'And whoever touches any thing on which she sits shall wash his clothes and bathe in water and be unclean until evening.

23 'Whether it be on the bed or on the thing on which she is sitting, when he touches it, he shall be unclean until evening.

24 'And if a man actually lies with her, so that her menstrual impurity is on him, he shall be unclean seven days, and every bed on which he lies shall be unclean.

25 'Now if a woman has a discharge of her blood many days, not at the period of her menstrual impurity, or if she has a discharge beyond that period, all the days of her impure discharge she shall continue as though in her menstrual impurity; she is unclean.

26 'Any bed on which she lies all the days of her discharge shall be to her like her bed at menstruation; and every thing on which she sits shall be unclean, like her uncleanness at that time.

27 'Likewise, whoever touches them shall be unclean and shall wash his clothes and bathe in water and be unclean until evening.

28 'When she becomes clean from her discharge, she shall count off for herself seven days; and afterward she shall be clean.

29 'Then on the eighth day she shall take for herself two turtledoves or two young pigeons, and bring them in to the priest, to the doorway of the tent of meeting.

30 'And the priest shall offer the one for a sin offering and the other for a burnt offering. So the priest shall make atonement on her behalf before the LORD because of her impure discharge.'

31 "Thus you shall keep the sons of Israel separated from their uncleanness, lest they die in their uncleanness by their defiling My tabernacle that is among them."

15:7
Num 19:19

15:10
Num 19:10

15:12
Lev 6:28;
11:32,33
15:13
v. 28

15:14
Lev 14:22,23

15:15
Lev 14:30,31

15:16
Lev 22:4;
Deut 23:10

15:18
1 Sam 21:4

15:19
Lev 12:2

15:21
v. 27

15:24
Lev 20:18

15:25
Matt 9:20;
Mark 5:25;
Luke 8:43

15:27
v. 21

15:29
Gen 15:9

15:31
Ezek 44:23;
Num 5:3;
19:13,20;
Ezek 5:11;
23:38

15:32
vv. 2,16

15:33
vv. 19,24,25

32 This is the law for the one with a discharge, and for the man who has a seminal emission so that he is unclean by it,

33 and for the woman who is ill because of menstrual impurity, and for the one who has a discharge, whether a male or a female, or a man who lies with an unclean woman.

D. *The Day of Atonement*

1. *The institution of the ceremony*

16:1
Lev 10:1,2

16:2
Ex 30:10;
Heb 9:7;
10:19;
Ex 25:21,22
16:3
Heb 9:7,12,
24,25;
Lev 4:3
16:4
Ex 28:39,42,
43; v. 24

16:5
Lev 4:13-21

*16:6
Lev 9:7;
Heb 5:2;
7:27,28; 9:7

16 Now the LORD spoke to Moses after the death of the two sons of Aaron, when they had approached the presence of the LORD and died.

2 And the LORD said to Moses, "Tell your brother Aaron that he shall not enter at any time into the holy place inside the veil, before the [10]mercy seat which is on the ark, lest he die; for I will appear in the cloud over the mercy seat.

3 "Aaron shall enter the holy place with this: with a bull for a sin offering and a ram for a burnt offering.

4 "He shall put on the holy linen tunic, and the linen undergarments shall be next to his body, and he shall be girded with the linen sash, and attired with the linen turban (these are holy garments). Then he shall bathe his body in water and put them on.

5 "And he shall take from the congregation of the sons of Israel two male goats for a sin offering and one ram for a burnt offering.

6 "Then Aaron shall offer the bull for the sin offering which is for himself, that he may make atonement for himself and for his household.

7 "And he shall take the two goats and present them before the LORD at the doorway of the tent of meeting.

8 "And Aaron shall cast lots for the two goats, one lot for the LORD and the other lot for the [11]scapegoat.

9 "Then Aaron shall offer the goat on which the lot for the LORD fell, and make it a sin offering.

10 "But the goat on which the lot for the scapegoat fell, shall be presented alive before the LORD, to make atonement upon it, to send it into the wilderness as the scapegoat.

2. *The sin offering for the high priest*

16:11
Heb 7:27; 9:7

16:12
Lev 10:1;
Ex 30:34

11 "Then Aaron shall offer the bull of the sin offering which is for himself, and make atonement for himself and for his household, and he shall slaughter the bull of the sin offering which is for himself.

12 "And he shall take a firepan full of coals of fire from upon the altar before the LORD, and two handfuls of finely ground sweet incense, and bring *it* inside the veil.

[10]Lit., *propitiatory* [11]Lit., *goat of removal*, or else a name: *Azazel*

16:6a The nature of Christ's offering of Himself on the cross is comprehended under the word *atonement* (*kippūr*). This word (derived from the Hebrew *kippēr*, "to atone") means to cover over by an expiatory sacrifice. It includes Christ's payment of the penalty for sin and His rendering to God a life of perfect obedience. He suffered vicariously, i.e., as a substitute, the just for the unjust, dying in our place and stead (2 Cor. 5:21; 1 Pet. 2:24). In the New Testament the word *reconciliation* (from the Greek *katallage*) is used, which means to effect reparation legally and morally for injury done (Rom. 5:11) and thus to bring about a restored relationship between those who were at enmity with each other. Man had broken the law, and God's justice required the penalty of death from the sinner. This penalty Christ paid in the atonement. The effect of the atonement is to provide righteousness and eternal life for those who accept it by faith in Christ (Eph. 2:8–10).
16:6b Day of Atonement. The sacrifice of bulls and goats did not remove sin (Heb. 10:4), for only the death of Christ on Calvary could do that. But redemption before Calvary was possible. The Old Testament sacrificial system enabled men to manifest their faith so that their sins were "covered," looking forward to the death of Christ. Thus, in a sense, each sacrifice was like a check drawn against a bank deposit; in and of itself a check is but a scrap of paper, but it effects true payment nevertheless, because eventually the money itself is transmitted to honor the check. Every faith-

supported sacrifice of pre-Christian times was drawn against the account of Christ's atoning merit on Calvary. In the New Testament era the sacrifice of the Day of Atonement was repeated annually when the high priest entered the Holy of Holies (and not without blood) to atone for himself and for his people (Heb. 9:7). Since the sacrifices were a type of Christ's perfect and final sacrifice, the old dispensation ended with Christ's death; and there was and is no further need for animal sacrifices (Heb. 9:12–28).
16:8 *scapegoat*. The word means literally "goat of removal." Some translations also give it the name, "Azazel." That word appears in the noncanonical book of Enoch as a name given to a certain fallen angel who misled mankind. Outside of the few Biblical references, and that in Enoch, there is nothing further mentioned. We do know that the ceremony spoken of in chapter 16 symbolized the fact that guilt had been removed both from land and people. In some sense it is typical of Christ (Is. 53:6,11,12). (The theory that Azazel is a name for Satan is as old as the third century A.D., but has little to commend it; the notion of a sacrifice to Satan is altogether pagan and contrary to Scripture.) Some understand the Hebrew word as a reduplicated root from *azal* ("depart" or "remove"), signifying "removal" or "that which is removed." Others, like the early translators Aquila and Jerome, construe it as a compound word: "goat of departure or removal." This seems to have been the basis of the rendering "scapegoat."

13 "And he shall put the incense on the fire before the LORD, that the cloud of incense may cover the mercy seat that is on *the ark of* the testimony, lest he die.

14 "Moreover, he shall take some of the blood of the bull and sprinkle *it* with his finger on the mercy seat on the east *side*; also in front of the mercy seat he shall sprinkle some of the blood with his finger seven times.

3. *The sin offering for the people*

15 "Then he shall slaughter the goat of the sin offering which is for the people, and bring its blood inside the veil, and do with its blood as he did with the blood of the bull, and sprinkle it on the mercy seat and in front of the mercy seat.

16 "And he shall make atonement for the holy place, because of the impurities of the sons of Israel, and because of their transgressions, in regard to all their sins; and thus he shall do for the tent of meeting which abides with them in the midst of their impurities.

17 "When he goes in to make atonement in the holy place, no one shall be in the tent of meeting until he comes out, that he may make atonement for himself and for his household and for all the assembly of Israel.

18 "Then he shall go out to the altar that is before the LORD and make atonement for it, and shall take some of the blood of the bull and of the blood of the goat, and put it on the horns of the altar on all sides.

19 "And with his finger he shall sprinkle some of the blood on it seven times, and cleanse it, and from the impurities of the sons of Israel consecrate it.

4. *The scapegoat*

20 "When he finishes atoning for the holy place, and the tent of meeting and the altar, he shall offer the live goat.

21 "Then Aaron shall lay both of his hands on the head of the live goat, and confess over it all the iniquities of the sons of Israel, and all their transgressions in regard to all their sins; and he shall lay them on the head of the goat and send *it* away into the wilderness by the hand of a man who *stands* in readiness.

22 "And the goat shall bear on itself all their iniquities to a solitary land; and he shall release the goat in the wilderness.

23 "Then Aaron shall come into the tent of meeting, and take off the linen garments which he put on when he went into the holy place, and shall leave them there.

24 "And he shall bathe his body with water in a holy place and put on his clothes, and come forth and offer his burnt offering and the burnt offering of the people, and make atonement for himself and for the people.

25 "Then he shall offer up in smoke the fat of the sin offering on the altar.

26 "And the one who released the goat as the scapegoat shall wash his clothes and bathe his body with water; then afterward he shall come into the camp.

27 "But the bull of the sin offering and the goat of the sin offering, whose blood was brought in to make atonement in the holy place, shall be taken outside the camp, and they shall burn their hides, their flesh, and their refuse in the fire.

28 "Then the one who burns them shall wash his clothes and bathe his body with water, then afterward he shall come into the camp.

5. *The Day of Atonement a perpetual statute*

29 "And *this* shall be a permanent statute for you: in the seventh month, on the tenth day of the month, you shall humble your souls, and not do any work, whether the native, or the alien who sojourns among you;

30 for it is on this day that atonement shall be made for you to cleanse you; you shall be clean from all your sins before the LORD.

31 "It is to be a sabbath of solemn rest for you, that you may humble your souls; it is a permanent statute.

32 "So the priest who is anointed and ordained to serve as priest in his father's

---

16:13
Lev 22:9

16:14
Heb 9:13,25;
Lev 4:6,17

16:15
Heb 9:3,7,12

16:16
Ex 29:36;
Heb 2:17

16:18
Lev 4:25;
Ezek 43:20,
22

16:19
v. 14

16:21
Is 53:6

16:22
Is 53:11,12

16:23
v. 4;
Ezek 42:14;
44:19

16:24
vv. 3-5

16:27
Lev 4:12,21;
6:30;
Heb 13:11

*16:29
Lev 23:27;
Num 29:7

16:31
Lev 23:32;
Is 58:3,5

16:32
v. 4;

16:29 Fasting, which is here referred to by the phrase *humble your souls,* was a practice common to both the Old and New Testaments. It involved not only abstinence from food but also self-abasement and mourning (Deut. 9:18; Neh. 9:1; Joel 2:12), confession of sin (1 Sam. 7:6; Neh. 9:1,2), and supplicatory prayer (Ezra 8:23; Dan. 9:3). Fasting was intended to provide self-chastening and humility, of which the fasting was an outward sign (Ps. 35:13; 69:10). It was resorted to in the face of calamities, afflictions, misfortune, and approaching danger. Individuals and nations employed it. Hypocrites used it to gain a reputation for godliness before men, even though they could not impose upon a God who knew how to read the heart. Noteworthy examples of those who fasted are: David (2 Sam. 12:16); Daniel (Dan. 9:3); Cornelius (Acts 10:30); and Paul (2 Cor. 11:27).

Num 20:26, 28
16:33
vv. 6,16-18, 24
16:34
Heb 9:7,25
*17:4
Deut 12:5-21;
Rom 5:13
17:6
Lev 3:2;
Num 18:17
17:7
Ex 22:20;
32:8; 34:15;
Deut 32:17;
2 Chr 11:15
17:9
v. 4
17:10
Lev 3:17;
Deut 12:16, 23
*17:11
v. 14;
Gen 9:4;
Heb 9:22
17:13
Lev 7:26;
Deut 12:16
17:14
v. 11
17:15
Ex 22:31;
Deut 14:21

place shall make atonement: he shall thus put on the linen garments, the holy garments,

33 and make atonement for the holy sanctuary; and he shall make atonement for the tent of meeting and for the altar. He shall also make atonement for the priests and for all the people of the assembly.

34 "Now you shall have this as a permanent statute, to make atonement for the sons of Israel for all their sins once every year." And just as the LORD had commanded Moses, so he did.

II. The maintaining of fellowship with a holy God
(17:1–27:34)

A. Rules for killing of animals

17 Then the LORD spoke to Moses, saying,

2 "Speak to Aaron and to his sons, and to all the sons of Israel, and say to them, 'This is what the LORD has commanded, saying,

3 "Any man from the house of Israel who slaughters an ox, or a lamb, or a goat in the camp, or who slaughters it outside the camp,

4 and has not brought it to the doorway of the tent of meeting to present it as an offering to the LORD before the tabernacle of the LORD, bloodguiltiness is to be reckoned to that man. He has shed blood and that man shall be cut off from among his people.

5 "The reason is so that the sons of Israel may bring their sacrifices which they were sacrificing in the open field, that they may bring them in to the LORD, at the doorway of the tent of meeting to the priest, and sacrifice them as sacrifices of peace offerings to the LORD.

6 "And the priest shall sprinkle the blood on the altar of the LORD at the doorway of the tent of meeting, and offer up the fat in smoke as a soothing aroma to the LORD.

7 "And they shall no longer sacrifice their sacrifices to the goat demons with which they play the harlot. This shall be a permanent statute to them throughout their generations." '

8 "Then you shall say to them, 'Any man from the house of Israel, or from the aliens who sojourn among them, who offers a burnt offering or sacrifice,

9 and does not bring it to the doorway of the tent of meeting to offer it to the LORD, that man also shall be cut off from his people.

B. The eating of blood prohibited

10 'And any man from the house of Israel, or from the aliens who sojourn among them, who eats any blood, I will set My face against that person who eats blood, and will cut him off from among his people.

11 'For the life of the flesh is in the blood, and I have given it to you on the altar to make atonement for your souls; for it is the blood by reason of the life that makes atonement.'

12 "Therefore I said to the sons of Israel, 'No person among you may eat blood, nor may any alien who sojourns among you eat blood.'

13 "So when any man from the sons of Israel, or from the aliens who sojourn among them, in hunting catches a beast or a bird which may be eaten, he shall pour out its blood and cover it with earth.

14 "For as for the life of all flesh, its blood is identified with its life. Therefore I said to the sons of Israel, 'You are not to eat the blood of any flesh, for the life of all flesh is its blood; whoever eats it shall be cut off.'

15 "And when any person eats an animal which dies, or is torn by beasts, whether he is a native or an alien, he shall wash his clothes and bathe in water, and remain unclean until evening; then he will become clean.

16 "But if he does not wash them or bathe his body, then he shall bear his guilt."

17:1ff. The section of laws (17:1–26:45), given by Moses at Sinai (26:46), is commonly called "The Holiness Code" because it sets forth the conditions required of Israel if they were to be a holy people.
17:4 God commanded that all blood sacrifices be made at the tabernacle rather than at shrines of man's own choosing. Otherwise bloodguilt, not forgiveness, would be the result. The right sacrifice made in the wrong way or place availed nothing.
17:11 See note to 1:4,5 on atonement.

C. *Laws on sexual relations*

1. *Introduction*

18 Then the LORD spoke to Moses, saying,

2 "Speak to the sons of Israel and say to them, 'I am the LORD your God.

3 'You shall not do what is done in the land of Egypt where you lived, nor are you to do what is done in the land of Canaan where I am bringing you; you shall not walk in their statutes.

4 'You are to perform My judgments and keep My statutes, to live in accord with them; I am the LORD your God.

5 'So you shall keep My statutes and My judgments, by which a man may live if he does them; I am the LORD.

2. *Incest forbidden*

6 'None of you shall approach any blood relative of his to uncover nakedness; I am the LORD.

7 'You shall not uncover the nakedness of your father, that is, the nakedness of your mother. She is your mother; you are not to uncover her nakedness.

8 'You shall not uncover the nakedness of your father's wife; it is your father's nakedness.

9 'The nakedness of your sister, *either* your father's daughter or your mother's daughter, whether born at home or born outside, their nakedness you shall not uncover.

10 'The nakedness of your son's daughter or your daughter's daughter, their nakedness you shall not uncover; for their nakedness is yours.

11 'The nakedness of your father's wife's daughter, born to your father, she is your sister, you shall not uncover her nakedness.

12 'You shall not uncover the nakedness of your father's sister; she is your father's blood relative.

13 'You shall not uncover the nakedness of your mother's sister, for she is your mother's blood relative.

14 'You shall not uncover the nakedness of your father's brother; you shall not approach his wife, she is your aunt.

15 'You shall not uncover the nakedness of your daughter-in-law; she is your son's wife, you shall not uncover her nakedness.

16 'You shall not uncover the nakedness of your brother's wife; it is your brother's nakedness.

17 'You shall not uncover the nakedness of a woman and of her daughter, nor shall you take her son's daughter or her daughter's daughter, to uncover her nakedness; they are blood relatives. It is lewdness.

18 'And you shall not marry a woman in addition to her sister as a rival while she is alive, to uncover her nakedness.

3. *Other sins of the flesh forbidden*

19 'Also you shall not approach a woman to uncover her nakedness during her menstrual impurity.

20 'And you shall not have intercourse with your neighbor's wife, to be defiled with her.

21 'Neither shall you give any of your offspring to offer them to Molech, nor shall you profane the name of your God; I am the LORD.

22 'You shall not lie with a male as one lies with a female; it is an abomination.

23 'Also you shall not have intercourse with any animal to be defiled with it, nor shall any woman stand before an animal to mate with it; it is a perversion.

4. *Warnings*

24 'Do not defile yourselves by any of these things; for by all these the nations which I am casting out before you have become defiled.

18:6 God laid down laws relative to marriage. It is true that in the first days of the human race, brother married sister, since there was no one else to marry. With the firm establishment of the race, God forbade marriages between people who were closely related by blood. For example, under the Law of Moses a man could not marry his sister or his mother's sister or his daughter-in-law. These same prohibitions for the most part prevail in our modern world, even in non-Christian societies.

18:21 See note to Zeph. 1:5 for *Molech*, or *Milcom*.

18:25
Lev 20:23;
Deut 9:5;
18:12; v. 28

25 'For the land has become defiled, therefore I have visited its punishment upon it, so the land has spewed out its inhabitants.

26 'But as for you, you are to keep My statutes and My judgments, and shall not do any of these abominations, *neither* the native, nor the alien who sojourns among you

27 (for the men of the land who have been before you have done all these abominations, and the land has become defiled);

28 so that the land may not spew you out, should you defile it, as it has spewed out the nation which has been before you.

29 'For whoever does any of these abominations, those persons who do *so* shall be cut off from among their people.

18:30
Lev 22:9;
Deut 11:1;
v. 2

30 'Thus you are to keep My charge, that you do not practice any of the abominable customs which have been practiced before you, so as not to defile yourselves with them; I am the LORD your God.'"

D. Holiness and personal conduct: the law of love

19 Then the LORD spoke to Moses, saying,

19:2
1 Pet 1:16

2 "Speak to all the congregation of the sons of Israel and say to them, 'You shall be holy, for I the LORD your God am holy.

19:3
Ex 20:8,12;
Lev 11:44

3 'Every one of you shall reverence his mother and his father, and you shall keep My sabbaths; I am the LORD your God.

19:4
Lev 26:1;
Ps 96:5;
Ex 20:23;
34:17

4 'Do not turn to idols or make for yourselves molten gods; I am the LORD your God.

5 'Now when you offer a sacrifice of peace offerings to the LORD, you shall offer it so that you may be accepted.

6 'It shall be eaten the same day you offer *it*, and the next day; but what remains until the third day shall be burned with fire.

7 'So if it is eaten at all on the third day, it is an offense; it will not be accepted.

8 'And everyone who eats it will bear his iniquity, for he has profaned the holy thing of the LORD; and that person shall be cut off from his people.

*19:9
Lev 23:22;
Deut 24:20-22

9 'Now when you reap the harvest of your land, you shall not reap to the very corners of your field, neither shall you gather the gleanings of your harvest.

10 'Nor shall you glean your vineyard, nor shall you gather the fallen fruit of your vineyard; you shall leave them for the needy and for the stranger. I am the LORD your God.

19:11
Ex 20:15;
Lev 6:2;
Eph 4:25;
Col 3:9

11 'You shall not steal, nor deal falsely, nor lie to one another.

19:12
Ex 20:7;
Lev 18:21

12 'And you shall not swear falsely by My name, so as to profane the name of your God; I am the LORD.

19:13
Ex 22:7-15;
21-27;
Deut 24:15;
James 5:4

13 'You shall not oppress your neighbor, nor rob *him*. The wages of a hired man are not to remain with you all night until morning.

14 'You shall not curse a deaf man, nor place a stumbling block before the blind, but you shall revere your God; I am the LORD.

19:14
Deut 27:18

15 'You shall do no injustice in judgment; you shall not be partial to the poor nor defer to the great, but you are to judge your neighbor fairly.

19:15
Ex 23:6;
Deut 1:17

16 'You shall not go about as a slanderer among your people, and you are not to act against the life of your neighbor; I am the LORD.

19:16
Ps 15:3;
Ezek 22:9;
Ex 23:7

17 'You shall not hate your fellow countryman in your heart; you may surely reprove your neighbor, but shall not incur sin because of him.

19:17
1 John 2:9,
11; 3:15;
Luke 17:3;
Gal 6:1

18 'You shall not take vengeance, nor bear any grudge against the sons of your people, but you shall love your neighbor as yourself; I am the LORD.

*19:18
Rom 12:19;
Ps 103:9;
Matt 19:19;
Mark 12:31;
Rom 13:9

19 'You are to keep My statutes. You shall not breed together two kinds of your cattle; you shall not sow your field with two kinds of seed, nor wear a garment upon you of two kinds of material mixed together.

19:19
Deut 22:9,11

20 'Now if a man lies carnally with a woman who is a slave acquired for *another* man, but who has in no way been redeemed, nor given her freedom, there shall be punishment; they shall not, *however*, be put to death, because she was not free.

19:21
Lev 5:15

21 'And he shall bring his guilt offering to the LORD to the doorway of the tent of meeting, a ram for a guilt offering.

22 'The priest shall also make atonement for him with the ram of the guilt

---

19:9 See the book of Ruth for a beautiful fulfillment of this law.
19:18 *love your neighbor.* This indicates that the moral aspect is not neglected even in laws chiefly concerned with priests and ritual. Jesus considered this law and Deut. 6:4 as the essence of the moral law. (See, for example, Matt. 19:19 and Luke 10:27.)

offering before the LORD for his sin which he has committed, and the sin which he has committed shall be forgiven him.

23 'And when you enter the land and plant all kinds of trees for food, then you shall count their fruit as forbidden. Three years it shall be forbidden to you; *it* shall not be eaten.

24 'But in the fourth year all its fruit shall be holy, an offering of praise to the LORD.

25 'And in the fifth year you are to eat of its fruit, that its yield may increase for you; I am the LORD your God.

26 'You shall not eat *anything* with the blood, nor practice divination or soothsaying.

27 'You shall not round off the side-growth of your heads, nor harm the edges of your beard.

28 'You shall not make any cuts in your body for the dead, nor make any tattoo marks on yourselves: I am the LORD.

29 'Do not profane your daughter by making her a harlot, so that the land may not fall to harlotry, and the land become full of lewdness.

30 'You shall keep My sabbaths and revere My sanctuary; I am the LORD.

31 'Do not turn to mediums or spiritists; do not seek them out to be defiled by them. I am the LORD your God.

32 'You shall rise up before the grayheaded, and honor the aged, and you shall revere your God; I am the LORD.

33 'When a stranger resides with you in your land, you shall not do him wrong.

34 'The stranger who resides with you shall be to you as the native among you, and you shall love him as yourself; for you were aliens in the land of Egypt: I am the LORD your God.

35 'You shall do no wrong in judgment, in measurement of weight, or capacity.

36 'You shall have just balances, just weights, a just [12]ephah, and a just [13] hin: I am the LORD your God, who brought you out from the land of Egypt.

37 'You shall thus observe all My statutes, and all My ordinances, and do them: I am the LORD.' "

E. Punishments for sin

1. Giving children to Molech

20 Then the LORD spoke to Moses, saying,
2 "You shall also say to the sons of Israel, 'Any man from the sons of Israel or from the aliens sojourning in Israel, who gives any of his offspring to Molech, shall surely be put to death; the people of the land shall stone him with stones.

3 'I will also set My face against that man and will cut him off from among his people, because he has given some of his offspring to Molech, so as to defile My sanctuary and to profane My holy name.

4 'If the people of the land, however, should ever disregard that man when he gives any of his offspring to Molech, so as not to put him to death,

5 then I Myself will set My face against that man and against his family; and I will cut off from among their people both him and all those who play the harlot after him, by playing the harlot after Molech.

2. Consulting mediums and wizards

6 'As for the person who turns to mediums and to spiritists, to play the harlot after them, I will also set My face against that person and will cut him off from among his people.

7 'You shall consecrate yourselves therefore and be holy, for I am the LORD your God.

8 'And you shall keep My statutes and practice them; I am the LORD who sanctifies you.

9 'If *there is* anyone who curses his father or his mother, he shall surely be put to death; he has cursed his father or his mother, his bloodguiltiness is upon him.

3. Adultery

10 'If *there is* a man who commits adultery with another man's wife, one who

Cross references (right margin):
19:24 / Deut 12:17, 18; Prov 3:9
19:26 / Lev 17:10; Deut 18:10
19:27 / Lev 21:5
19:28 / Lev 21:5
19:29 / Deut 23:17
19:30 / v. 3; Lev 26:2
19:31 / Lev 20:6,27; Deut 18:10, 11
19:33 / Ex 22:21
19:34 / Ex 12:48,49; Deut 10:19
20:2 / Lev 18:21
20:3 / Lev 15:31; 18:21
20:4 / Deut 17:2,3,5
20:6 / Lev 19:31
20:7 / 1 Pet 1:16
20:8 / Lev 19:37; Ex 31:13
20:9 / Ex 21:17; Deut 27:16
20:10 / Lev 18:20; Deut 22:22

[12]I.e., Approx. one bushel [13]I.e., Approx. one gallon

commits adultery with his friend's wife, the adulterer and the adulteress shall surely be put to death.

20:11
Lev 18:7,8
11 'If *there is* a man who lies with his father's wife, he has uncovered his father's nakedness; both of them shall surely be put to death, their bloodguiltiness is upon them.

20:12
Lev 18:15
12 'If *there is* a man who lies with his daughter-in-law, both of them shall surely be put to death; they have committed incest, their bloodguiltiness is upon them.

20:13
Lev 18:22
13 'If *there is* a man who lies with a male as those who lie with a woman, both of them have committed a detestable act; they shall surely be put to death. Their bloodguiltiness is upon them.

20:14
Deut 27:23
14 'If *there is* a man who marries a woman and her mother, it is immorality; both he and they shall be burned with fire, that there may be no immorality in your midst.

20:15
Lev 18:23
15 'If *there is* a man who lies with an animal, he shall surely be put to death; you shall also kill the animal.

16 'If *there is* a woman who approaches any animal to mate with it, you shall kill the woman and the animal; they shall surely be put to death. Their bloodguiltiness is upon them.

4. *Other sins of the flesh*

20:17
Lev 18:9
17 'If *there is* a man who takes his sister, his father's daughter or his mother's daughter, so that he sees her nakedness and she sees his nakedness, it is a disgrace; and they shall be cut off in the sight of the sons of their people. He has uncovered his sister's nakedness; he bears his guilt.

20:18
Lev 18:19
18 'If *there is* a man who lies with a menstruous woman and uncovers her nakedness, he has laid bare her flow, and she has exposed the flow of her blood; thus both of them shall be cut off from among their people.

20:19
Lev 18:12,13
19 'You shall also not uncover the nakedness of your mother's sister or of your father's sister, for such a one has made naked his blood relative; they shall bear their guilt.

20:20
Lev 18:14
20 'If *there is* a man who lies with his uncle's wife he has uncovered his uncle's nakedness; they shall bear their sin. They shall die childless.

20:21
Lev 18:16
21 'If *there is* a man who takes his brother's wife, it is abhorrent; he has uncovered his brother's nakedness. They shall be childless.

5. *Command to be holy*

20:22
Lev 18:25,26,
28
20:23
Lev 18:3,24,
27,30
20:24
Ex 13:5;
33:3,16; v. 26
22 'You are therefore to keep all My statutes and all My ordinances and do them, so that the land to which I am bringing you to live will not spew you out.

23 'Moreover, you shall not follow the customs of the nation which I shall drive out before you, for they did all these things, and therefore I have abhorred them.

24 'Hence I have said to you, "You are to possess their land, and I Myself will give it to you to possess it, a land flowing with milk and honey." I am the LORD your God, who has separated you from the peoples.

20:25
Lev 11:1-47;
Deut 14:3-21
25 'You are therefore to make a distinction between the clean animal and the unclean, and between the unclean bird and the clean; and you shall not make yourselves detestable by animal or by bird or by anything that creeps on the ground, which I have separated for you as unclean.

20:26
v. 24
26 'Thus you are to be holy to Me, for I the LORD am holy; and I have set you apart from the peoples to be Mine.

6. *Penalty for being a medium or wizard*

20:27
Lev 19:31
27 'Now a man or a woman who is a medium or a spiritist shall surely be put to death. They shall be stoned with stones, their bloodguiltiness is upon them.' "

F. *Rules for the priesthood*

1. *The sanctity of the priesthood*

21:1
Lev 19:28;
Ezek 44:25
21 Then the LORD said to Moses, "Speak to the priests, the sons of Aaron, and say to them, 'No one shall defile himself for a *dead* person among his people, 2 except for his relatives who are nearest to him, his mother and his father and his son and his daughter and his brother,

3 also for his virgin sister, who is near to him because she has had no husband; for her he may defile himself.

4 'He shall not defile himself as a relative by marriage among his people, and so profane himself.

5 'They shall not make any baldness on their heads, nor shave off the edges of their beards, nor make any cuts in their flesh.

6 'They shall be holy to their God and not profane the name of their God, for they present the offerings by fire to the LORD, the bread of their God; so they shall be holy.

7 'They shall not take a woman who is profaned by harlotry, nor shall they take a woman divorced from her husband; for he is holy to his God.

8 'You shall consecrate him, therefore, for he offers the bread of your God; he shall be holy to you; for I the LORD, who sanctifies you, am holy.

9 'Also the daughter of any priest, if she profanes herself by harlotry, she profanes her father; she shall be burned with fire.

10 'And the priest who is the highest among his brothers, on whose head the anointing oil has been poured, and who has been consecrated to wear the garments, shall not uncover his head, nor tear his clothes;

11 nor shall he approach any dead person, nor defile himself *even* for his father or his mother;

12 nor shall he go out of the sanctuary, nor profane the sanctuary of his God; for the consecration of the anointing oil of his God is on him: I am the LORD.

13 'And he shall take a wife in her virginity.

14 'A widow, or a divorced woman, or one who is profaned by harlotry, these he may not take; but rather he is to marry a virgin of his own people;

15 that he may not profane his offspring among his people: for I am the LORD who sanctifies him.' "

16 Then the LORD spoke to Moses, saying,

17 "Speak to Aaron, saying, 'No man of your offspring throughout their generations who has a defect shall approach to offer the bread of his God.

18 'For no one who has a defect shall approach: a blind man, or a lame man, or he who has a disfigured *face*, or any deformed *limb*,

19 or a man who has a broken foot or broken hand,

20 or a hunchback or a dwarf, or *one who has* a defect in his eye or eczema or scabs or crushed testicles.

21 'No man among the descendants of Aaron the priest, who has a defect, is to come near to offer the LORD's offerings by fire; *since* he has a defect, he shall not come near to offer the bread of his God.

22 'He may eat the bread of his God, *both* of the most holy and of the holy,

23 only he shall not go in to the veil or come near the altar because he has a defect, that he may not profane My sanctuaries. For I am the LORD who sanctifies them.' "

24 So Moses spoke to Aaron and to his sons and to all the sons of Israel.

22 Then the LORD spoke to Moses, saying,

2 "Tell Aaron and his sons to be careful with the holy *gifts* of the sons of Israel, which they dedicate to Me, so as not to profane My holy name; I am the LORD.

3 "Say to them, 'If any man among all your descendants throughout your generations approaches the holy *gifts* which the sons of Israel dedicate to the LORD, while he has an uncleanness, that person shall be cut off from before Me. I am the LORD.

4 'No man, of the descendants of Aaron, who is a leper or who has a discharge, may eat of the holy *gifts* until he is clean. And if one touches anything made unclean by a corpse or if a man has a seminal emission,

5 or if a man touches any teeming things, by which he is made unclean, or any man by whom he is made unclean, whatever his uncleanness;

21:5
Deut 14:1;
Ezek 44:20;
Lev 19:27
21:6
Lev 18:21;
3:11
21:7
vv. 13,14

21:10
Lev 16:32;
10:6,7

21:11
Lev 19:28

21:12
Lev 10:7;
Ex 29:6,7
21:13
v. 7;
Ezek 44:22

*21:17ff
v. 6

21:18
Lev 22:23

21:20
Deut 23:1
21:21
v. 6

21:23
v. 12

*22:3
Lev 7:20

22:4
Lev 14:1-32;
Num 19:11,
12; 15:16,17
22:5
Lev 11:24,43,
44; 15:7,19

21:17ff. Scripture distinguishes between a man's person and the office he occupies. Thus no one of the seed of Aaron could occupy the office of the priesthood if he suffered from certain physical imperfections and disabilities (vv. 18–20). While a descendant of Aaron might be physically disqualified from exercising the priestly function, he was not debarred from receiving his share of the offerings for his personal support (v. 22). (So in the ministry of the church there may be things that would disqualify a man from holding its various offices but that would not bar him from its worship and fellowship.) Thus both the priest and the sacrificial animal itself had to be without blemish in order to be satisfactory. Christ met both of these demands. He was without blemish in Himself, and His sacrifice of His own body was a perfect one (2 Cor. 5:21; 1 Pet. 1:19).
22:3 *Holy gifts* were the portions of the sacrifice given to the priest.

6 a person who touches any such shall be unclean until evening, and shall not eat of the holy *gifts*, unless he has bathed his body in water.

7 'But when the sun sets, he shall be clean, and afterward he shall eat of the holy *gifts*, for it is his food.

8 'He shall not eat *an animal* which dies or is torn *by beasts*, becoming unclean by it; I am the LORD.

9 'They shall therefore keep My charge, so that they may not bear sin because of it, and die thereby because they profane it; I am the LORD who sanctifies them.

10 'No ¹⁴layman, however, is to eat the holy *gift*; a sojourner with the priest or a hired man shall not eat of the holy *gift*.

11 'But if a priest buys a slave as *his* property with his money, that one may eat of it, and those who are born in his house may eat of his food.

12 'And if a priest's daughter is married to a layman, she shall not eat of the offering of the *gifts*.

13 'But if a priest's daughter becomes a widow or divorced, and has no child and returns to her father's house as in her youth, she shall eat of her father's food; but no layman shall eat of it.

14 'But if a man eats a holy *gift* unintentionally, then he shall add to it a fifth of it and shall give the holy *gift* to the priest.

15 'And they shall not profane the holy *gifts* of the sons of Israel which they offer to the LORD,

16 and *so* cause them to bear punishment for guilt by eating their holy *gifts*; for I am the LORD who sanctifies them.' "

2. Acceptable and unacceptable offerings

17 Then the LORD spoke to Moses, saying,

18 "Speak to Aaron and to his sons and to all the sons of Israel, and say to them, 'Any man of the house of Israel or of the aliens in Israel who presents his offering, whether it is any of their votive or any of their freewill offerings, which they present to the LORD for a burnt offering—

19 for you to be accepted—*it must be* a male without defect from the cattle, the sheep, or the goats.

20 'Whatever has a defect, you shall not offer, for it will not be accepted for you.

21 'And when a man offers a sacrifice of peace offerings to the LORD to fulfill a special vow, or for a freewill offering, of the herd or of the flock, it must be perfect to be accepted; there shall be no defect in it.

22 'Those *that are* blind or fractured or maimed or having a running sore or eczema or scabs, you shall not offer to the LORD, nor make of them an offering by fire on the altar to the LORD.

23 'In respect to an ox or a lamb which has an overgrown or stunted *member*, you may present it for a freewill offering, but for a vow it shall not be accepted.

24 'Also anything *with its testicles* bruised or crushed or torn or cut, you shall not offer to the LORD, or sacrifice in your land,

25 nor shall you accept any such from the hand of a foreigner for offering as the food of your God; for their corruption is in them, they have a defect, they shall not be accepted for you.' "

26 Then the LORD spoke to Moses, saying,

27 "When an ox or a sheep or a goat is born, it shall remain seven days with its mother, and from the eighth day on it shall be accepted as a sacrifice of an offering by fire to the LORD.

28 "But, *whether* it is an ox or a sheep, you shall not kill *both* it and its young in one day.

29 "And when you sacrifice a sacrifice of thanksgiving to the LORD, you shall sacrifice it so that you may be accepted.

30 "It shall be eaten on the same day, you shall leave none of it until morning: I am the LORD.

31 "So you shall keep My commandments, and do them: I am the LORD.

32 "And you shall not profane My holy name, but I will be sanctified among the sons of Israel: I am the LORD who sanctifies you,

33 who brought you out from the land of Egypt, to be your God: I am the LORD."

¹⁴Lit., *stranger*

Margin references:

22:8
Ex 22:31;
Lev 17:15
22:9
Lev 18:30;
v. 16
22:10
v. 13

22:13
v. 10

22:14
Lev 5:15,16

22:16
v. 9

22:19
Lev 1:3

22:20
Deut 15:21;
17:1;
Heb 9:14;
1 Pet 1:19
22:21
Lev 3:1,6

22:25
Lev 21:6,17

22:27
Ex 22:30

22:28
Deut 22:6,7

22:29
Lev 7:12

22:30
Lev 7:15

22:31
Lev 19:37
22:32
Lev 18:21;
10:3
22:33
Ex 6:7;
Lev 11:45

G. Laws concerning festivals

1. The Sabbath

23 The LORD spoke again to Moses, saying, 2 "Speak to the sons of Israel, and say to them, 'The LORD's appointed times which you shall proclaim as holy convocations—My appointed times are these:

23:2
vv. 4,37,44;
Num 29:39

3 'For six days work may be done; but on the seventh day there is a sabbath of complete rest, a holy convocation. You shall not do any work; it is a sabbath to the LORD in all your dwellings.

23:3
Lev 19:3;
Ex 31:13-17;
Deut 5:13

2. The Passover and Unleavened Bread

4 'These are the appointed times of the LORD, holy convocations which you shall proclaim at the times appointed for them.

23:4
v. 2

5 'In the first month, on the fourteenth day of the month at twilight is the LORD's Passover.

*23:5
Ex 12:18,19;
Num 28:16,
17

6 'Then on the fifteenth day of the same month there is the Feast of Unleavened Bread to the LORD; for seven days you shall eat unleavened bread.

7 'On the first day you shall have a holy convocation; you shall not do any laborious work.

8 'But for seven days you shall present an offering by fire to the LORD. On the seventh day is a holy convocation; you shall not do any laborious work.' "

23:8
vv. 8,21,25,
35,36

3. The Feast of First Fruits

9 Then the LORD spoke to Moses, saying, 10 "Speak to the sons of Israel, and say to them, 'When you enter the land which I am going to give to you and reap its harvest, then you shall bring in the sheaf of the first fruits of your harvest to the priest.

23:10
Ex 23:16,19;
34:22,26

11 'And he shall wave the sheaf before the LORD for you to be accepted; on the day after the sabbath the priest shall wave it.

12 'Now on the day when you wave the sheaf, you shall offer a male lamb one year old without defect for a burnt offering to the LORD.

13 'Its grain offering shall then be two-tenths *of an ephah* of fine flour mixed with oil, an offering by fire to the LORD *for* a soothing aroma, with its libation, a fourth of a [15]hin of wine.

23:13
Lev 2:14-16

14 'Until this same day, until you have brought in the offering of your God, you shall eat neither bread nor roasted grain nor new growth. It is to be a perpetual statute throughout your generations in all your dwelling places.

4. Pentecost

15 'You shall also count for yourselves from the day after the sabbath, from the day when you brought in the sheaf of the wave offering; there shall be seven complete sabbaths.

*23:15
Deut 16:9

16 'You shall count fifty days to the day after the seventh sabbath; then you shall present a new grain offering to the LORD.

23:16
Num 28:26

17 'You shall bring in from your dwelling places two *loaves* of bread for a wave offering, made of two-tenths *of an ephah*; they shall be of a fine flour, baked with leaven as first fruits to the LORD.

23:17
Lev 2:12;
7:13

18 'Along with the bread, you shall present seven one year old male lambs

---

[15]I.e., Approx. one gallon

23:5 *Passover,* see notes to Ex. 12:11; Mark 14:1.
23:6 *the Feast of Unleavened Bread.* This feast is to be kept distinct from the Passover, although they have a close connection with each other. The Passover was celebrated on the fourteenth day (v. 5), whereas the Feast of Unleavened Bread began on the fifteenth day and continued for seven days. Together they formed a double festival, just as the Feast of Tabernacles and the Day of Atonement formed a double celebration. In Mark 14:1,12 and Luke 22:1 the two feasts (Passover and Unleavened Bread) are spoken of as virtually one. This was due, no doubt, to the fact that the two feasts were not separated by any interval of time. The regulations for the Feast of Unleavened Bread are detailed in vv. 6-8.
23:15 In Old Testament times this event was known as the

Feast of Weeks, or the *Feast of Harvest.* Its New Testament name derives from the Greek word "fiftieth," which, in turn, derives from the fact that the feast took place on the fiftieth day after the feast of Unleavened Bread had been celebrated. (According to our reckoning it would be forty-nine days.) The feast was a prophetic type pointing forward to the descent of the Holy Spirit, who came upon the apostolic church with power on the fiftieth day after the resurrection of Christ from the dead (Acts 2:1ff.). In Old Testament times this feast celebrated the harvest of fruits of the earth; in New Testament times the 120 in the apostolic band constituted the first fruits of Christ's harvest, even as the gift of the Holy Spirit is the first fruit of the believer's heavenly inheritance (see Rom. 8:23; 11:16; James 1:18).

without defect, and a bull of the herd, and two rams; they are to be a burnt offering to the LORD, with their grain offering and their libations, an offering by fire of a soothing aroma to the LORD.

23:19
Num 28:30;
Lev 3:1

19 'You shall also offer one male goat for a sin offering and two male lambs one year old for a sacrifice of peace offerings.

20 'The priest shall then wave them with the bread of the first fruits for a wave offering with two lambs before the LORD; they are to be holy to the LORD for the priest.

23:21
v. 7

21 'On this same day you shall make a proclamation as well; you are to have a holy convocation. You shall do no laborious work. It is to be a perpetual statute in all your dwelling places throughout your generations.

23:22
Lev 19:9

22 'When you reap the harvest of your land, moreover, you shall not reap to the very corners of your field, nor gather the gleaning of your harvest; you are to leave them for the needy and the alien. I am the LORD your God.' "

5. The Feast of Trumpets

23 Again the LORD spoke to Moses, saying,

*23:24
Num 29:1;
Lev 25:9

24 "Speak to the sons of Israel, saying, 'In the seventh month on the first of the month, you shall have a rest, a reminder by blowing *of trumpets*, a holy convocation.

25 'You shall not do any laborious work, but you shall present an offering by fire to the LORD.' "

6. The Day of Atonement

26 And the LORD spoke to Moses, saying,

*23:27
Lev 16:29,30

27 "On exactly the tenth day of this seventh month is the day of atonement; it shall be a holy convocation for you, and you shall humble your souls and present an offering by fire to the LORD.

28 "Neither shall you do any work on this same day, for it is a day of atonement, to make atonement on your behalf before the LORD your God.

23:29
Gen 17:14

29 "If there is any person who will not humble himself on this same day, he shall be cut off from his people.

23:30
Lev 20:3,5,6

30 "As for any person who does any work on this same day, that person I will destroy from among his people.

31 "You shall do no work at all. It is to be a perpetual statute throughout your generations in all your dwelling places.

32 "It is to be a sabbath of complete rest to you, and you shall humble your souls; on the ninth of the month at evening, from evening until evening you shall keep your sabbath."

7. The Feast of Tabernacles

33 Again the LORD spoke to Moses, saying,

*23:34
Ex 23:16;
Num 29:12;
vv. 42,43

34 "Speak to the sons of Israel, saying, 'On the fifteenth of this seventh month is the Feast of Booths for seven days to the LORD.

35 'On the first day is a holy convocation; you shall do no laborious work of any kind.

23:36
Num 29:12-38

36 'For seven days you shall present an offering by fire to the LORD. On the eighth day you shall have a holy convocation and present an offering by fire to the LORD; it is an assembly. You shall do no laborious work.

23:37
vv. 2,4

37 'These are the appointed times of the LORD which you shall proclaim as holy convocations, to present offerings by fire to the LORD—burnt offerings and grain offerings, sacrifices and libations, *each* day's matter on its own day—

38 besides *those of* the sabbaths of the LORD, and besides your gifts, and besides all your votive and freewill offerings, which you give to the LORD.

23:39
Ex 23:16;
Deut 16:13

39 'On exactly the fifteenth day of the seventh month, when you have gathered in the crops of the land, you shall celebrate the feast of the LORD for seven days, with a rest on the first day and a rest on the eighth day.

40 'Now on the first day you shall take for yourselves the foliage of beautiful

---

23:24 "The Feast of Trumpets" was celebrated on the first day of Tishri, the seventh month. Trumpets were blown and sacrifices offered (Num. 29:1–6). It was a day of holy convocation and rest (23:24,25). Since it inaugurated the seventh month of the religious calendar, the feast was connected with the institution of the Sabbath and is mentioned again in Neh. 8:9,10. It constituted the New Year's Day of the civil calendar, and as such is celebrated to this day by the Jews as Rosh Hashanah.
23:27 *day of atonement*, see note to 16:6.
23:34 *Feast of Booths* (also known as the "Feast of Tabernacles" and "Feast of Ingathering"), see note to Ex. 23:16.

trees, palm branches and boughs of leafy trees and willows of the brook; and you shall rejoice before the LORD your God for seven days.

41 'You shall thus celebrate it *as* a feast to the LORD for seven days in the year. It *shall be* a perpetual statute throughout your generations; you shall celebrate it in the seventh month.

42 'You shall live in booths for seven days; all the native-born in Israel shall live in booths,

43 so that your generations may know that I had the sons of Israel live in booths when I brought them out from the land of Egypt. I am the LORD your God.'"

44 So Moses declared to the sons of Israel the appointed times of the LORD.

H. *Laws of ritual and ethics*

1. *The oil and the showbread*

24 Then the LORD spoke to Moses, saying,

2 "Command the sons of Israel that they bring to you clear oil from beaten olives for the light, to make a lamp burn continually.

3 "Outside the veil of testimony in the tent of meeting, Aaron shall keep it in order from evening to morning before the LORD continually; *it shall be* a perpetual statute throughout your generations.

4 "He shall keep the lamps in order on the pure *gold* lampstand before the LORD continually.

5 "Then you shall take fine flour and bake twelve cakes with it; two-tenths *of an ephah* shall be *in* each cake.

6 "And you shall set them *in* two rows, six *to* a row, on the pure *gold* table before the LORD.

7 "And you shall put pure frankincense on each row, that it may be a memorial portion for the bread, *even* an offering by fire to the LORD.

8 "Every sabbath day he shall set it in order before the LORD continually; it is an everlasting covenant for the sons of Israel.

9 "And it shall be for Aaron and his sons, and they shall eat it in a holy place; for it is most holy to him from the LORD'S offerings by fire, *his* portion forever."

2. *Death for blasphemy*

10 Now the son of an Israelite woman, whose father was an Egyptian, went out among the sons of Israel; and the Israelite woman's son and a man of Israel struggled with each other in the camp.

11 And the son of the Israelite woman blasphemed the Name and cursed. So they brought him to Moses. (Now his mother's name was Shelomith, the daughter of Dibri, of the tribe of Dan.)

12 And they put him in custody so that the command of the LORD might be made clear to them.

13 Then the LORD spoke to Moses, saying,

14 "Bring the one who has cursed outside the camp, and let all who heard him lay their hands on his head; then let all the congregation stone him.

15 "And you shall speak to the sons of Israel, saying, 'If anyone curses his God, then he shall bear his sin.

16 'Moreover, the one who blasphemes the name of the LORD shall surely be put to death; all the congregation shall certainly stone him. The alien as well as the native, when he blasphemes the Name, shall be put to death.

17 'And if a man takes the life of any human being, he shall surely be put to death.

18 'And the one who takes the life of an animal shall make it good, life for life.

19 'And if a man injures his neighbor, just as he has done, so it shall be done to him:

Cross references:
23:40 Neh 8:15; Deut 16:14, 15
23:42 Neh 8:14-16
23:44 vv. 2,37
24:2 Ex 27:20,21
24:4 Ex 31:8; 39:37
24:5 Ex 25:30
24:6 Ex 25:24; 1 Kin 7:48
24:8 Num 4:7; 1 Chr 9:32; 2 Chr 2:4
24:9 Matt 12:4; Mark 2:26; Luke 6:4; Lev 8:31
24:11 v. 16
24:12 Num 15:34; Ex 18:15,16
24:14 Deut 13:9; 17:7; Lev 20:2,27; Deut 21:21
*24:16 1 Kin 21:10; Matt 12:31; Mark 3:28
24:17 Ex 21:12; Num 35:30, 31; Deut 19:11, 12
24:18 v. 21

24:16 To blaspheme is to scoff at or revile the name of God, and the Old Testament penalty was death. Ungodly men are peculiarly addicted to blasphemy (Ps. 74:18; Is. 52:5). Idolatry in the Old Testament was also regarded as blasphemy (Is. 65:7), because it implied a contempt for His name as the one true God. Examples of blasphemers include the profane Danite of this chapter (v. 11); King Sennacherib of Assyria (2 Kin. 19:4,10,22); and Hymenaeus, a heretic of the early church (1Tim. 1:20). Unbelievers take delight in accusing the saints of the very sin of which they themselves are guilty. Christ was accused of this crime on the ground that He, being a man, made Himself out to be God (Matt. 26:65; Luke 22:66–71). Members of the early church were also charged with the offense because they affirmed His deity (Acts 6:11–14).

20 fracture for fracture, eye for eye, tooth for tooth; just as he has injured a man, so it shall be inflicted on him.

21 'Thus the one who kills an animal shall make it good, but the one who kills a man shall be put to death.

22 'There shall be one standard for you; it shall be for the stranger as well as the native, for I am the LORD your God.' "

23 Then Moses spoke to the sons of Israel, and they brought the one who had cursed outside the camp and stoned him with stones. Thus the sons of Israel did, just as the LORD had commanded Moses.

I. Laws for the sabbatical and jubilee years

1. The sabbatical year

25 The LORD then spoke to Moses at Mount Sinai, saying,

2 "Speak to the sons of Israel, and say to them, 'When you come into the land which I shall give you, then the land shall have a sabbath to the LORD.

3 'Six years you shall sow your field, and six years you shall prune your vineyard and gather in its crop,

4 but during the seventh year the land shall have a sabbath rest, a sabbath to the LORD; you shall not sow your field nor prune your vineyard.

5 'Your harvest's [16]aftergrowth you shall not reap, and your grapes of untrimmed vines you shall not gather; the land shall have a sabbatical year.

6 'And all of you shall have the sabbath *products* of the land for food; yourself, and your male and female slaves, and your hired man and your foreign resident, those who live as aliens with you.

7 'Even your cattle and the animals that are in your land shall have all its crops to eat.

2. The year of Jubilee

8 'You are also to count off seven sabbaths of years for yourself, seven times seven years, so that you have the time of the seven sabbaths of years, *namely*, forty-nine years.

9 'You shall then sound a ram's horn abroad on the tenth day of the seventh month; on the day of atonement you shall sound a horn all through your land.

10 'You shall thus consecrate the fiftieth year and proclaim [17]a release through the land to all its inhabitants. It shall be a jubilee for you, and each of you shall return to his own property, and each of you shall return to his family.

11 'You shall have the fiftieth year as a jubilee; you shall not sow, nor reap its aftergrowth, nor gather in *from* its untrimmed vines.

12 'For it is a jubilee; it shall be holy to you. You shall eat its crops out of the field.

13 'On this year of jubilee each of you shall return to his own property.

14 'If you make a sale, moreover, to your friend, or buy from your friend's hand, you shall not wrong one another.

15 'Corresponding to the number of years after the jubilee, you shall buy from your friend; he is to sell to you according to the number of years of crops.

16 'In proportion to the extent of the years you shall increase its price, and in proportion to the fewness of the years, you shall diminish its price; for *it is* a number of crops he is selling to you.

17 'So you shall not wrong one another, but you shall fear your God; for I am the LORD your God.

18 'You shall thus observe My statutes, and keep My judgments, so as to carry them out, that you may live securely on the land.

Cross references (left margin)

24:20
Ex 21:23,24;
Deut 19:21;
Matt 5:38
24:21
vv. 17,18
24:22
Ex 12:49;
Num 15:16

25:2
Ex 23:10,11

25:6
vv. 20,21

25:9
Lev 23:24,27

*25:10
vv. 13,28,54

25:13
v. 10
25:14
Lev 19:13;
1 Sam 12:3,4;
1 Cor 6:8
25:15
Lev 27:18,23

25:17
v. 14;
Lev 19:14,32
25:18
Lev 19:37;
26:4,5

---

[16]Lit., *growth from spilled kernels* [17]Or, *liberty*

25:8-10 The observance of the Jubilee was held every fiftieth year. It began on the Day of Atonement. It was called by various names, such as the *year of liberty* (Ezek. 46:17), the *year of redemption* (Is. 63:4), and even in the expression *favorable year of the LORD* (Is. 61:2) there are Jubilee overtones. It was a holy year (v. 12) and was ushered in by the blowing of trumpets (v. 9; Ps. 89:15). During this fiftieth year all field labor was to cease, and the people were to eat of what they had stored up from the previous year. Nonurban property that had been sold could be redeemed, inheritances restored, and slaves set free from their servitude. The Year of Jubilee is spoken of as fulfilled in the gospel (Luke 4:18,19), which sets men free from their bondage and brings them into the glorious liberty of the sons of God.

19 'Then the land will yield its produce, so that you can eat your fill and live securely on it.

20 'But if you say, "What are we going to eat on the seventh year if we do not sow or gather in our crops?"

21   then I will so order My blessing for you in the sixth year that it will bring forth the crop for three years.

22 'When you are sowing the eighth year, you can still eat old things from the crop, eating *the old* until the ninth year when its crop comes in.

23 'The land, moreover, shall not be sold permanently, for the land is Mine; for you are *but* aliens and sojourners with Me.

24 'Thus for every piece of your property, you are to provide for the redemption of the land.

3. *Redemption of property*

25 'If a fellow countryman of yours becomes so poor he has to sell part of his property, then his nearest kinsman is to come and buy back what his relative has sold.

26 'Or in case a man has no kinsman, but so recovers his means as to find sufficient for its redemption,

27   then he shall calculate the years since its sale and refund the balance to the man to whom he sold it, and so return to his property.

28 'But if he has not found sufficient means to get it back for himself, then what he has sold shall remain in the hands of its purchaser until the year of jubilee; but at the jubilee it shall revert, that he may return to his property.

29 'Likewise, if a man sells a dwelling house in a walled city, then his redemption right remains valid until a full year from its sale; his right of redemption lasts a full year.

30 'But if it is not bought back for him within the space of a full year, then the house that is in the walled city passes permanently to its purchaser throughout his generations; it does not revert in the jubilee.

31 'The houses of the villages, however, which have no surrounding wall shall be considered as open fields; they have redemption rights and revert in the jubilee.

32 'As for cities of the Levites, the Levites have a permanent right of redemption for the houses of the cities which are their possession.

33 'What, therefore, belongs to the Levites may be redeemed and a house sale in the city of this possession reverts in the jubilee, for the houses of the cities of the Levites are their possession among the sons of Israel.

34 'But pasture fields of their cities shall not be sold, for that is their perpetual possession.

4. *The law of usury*

35 'Now in case a countryman of yours becomes poor and his means with regard to you falter, then you are to sustain him, like a stranger or a sojourner, that he may live with you.

36 'Do not take usurious interest from him, but revere your God, that your countryman may live with you.

37 'You shall not give him your silver at interest, nor your food for gain.

38 'I am the LORD your God, who brought you out of the land of Egypt to give you the land of Canaan *and* to be your God.

5. *The redemption of servants*

39 'And if a countryman of yours becomes so poor with regard to you that he sells himself to you, you shall not subject him to a slave's service.

40 'He shall be with you as a hired man, as if he were a sojourner; he shall serve with you until the year of jubilee.

41 'He shall then go out from you, he and his sons with him, and shall go back to his family, that he may return to the property of his forefathers.

42 'For they are My servants whom I brought out from the land of Egypt; they are not to be sold *in* a slave sale.

43 'You shall not rule over him with severity, but are to revere your God.

44 'As for your male and female slaves whom you may have—you may acquire male and female slaves from the pagan nations that are around you.

45 'Then, too, *it is* out of the sons of the sojourners who live as aliens among you

25:20
vv. 4,5

25:22
Lev 26:10

25:23
Ex 19:5;
Gen 23:4;
1 Chr 29:15;
Ps 39:12

25:25
Ruth 2:20;
4:4,6

25:27
vv. 50-52

25:28
v. 13

25:32
Num 35:1-8

25:35
Deut 15:7-11;
Ps 37:26;
Luke 6:35

25:36
Ex 22:25;
Deut 23:19,
20

25:38
Lev 11:45

25:39
Ex 21:2;
Deut 15:12;
1 Kin 9:22

25:41
Ex 21:3; v. 28

25:43
vv. 46,53;
Ex 1:13,14

25:45
Is 56:3,6

that you may gain acquisition, and out of their families who are with you, whom they will have produced in your land; they also may become your possession.

25:46
v. 43

46 'You may even bequeath them to your sons after you, to receive as a possession; you can use them as permanent slaves. But in respect to your countrymen, the sons of Israel, you shall not rule with severity over one another.

47 'Now if the means of a stranger or of a sojourner with you becomes sufficient, and a countryman of yours becomes so poor with regard to him as to sell himself to a stranger who is sojourning with you, or to the descendants of a stranger's family,

25:48
Neh 5:5

48 then he shall have redemption right after he has been sold. One of his brothers may redeem him,

25:49
v. 26

49 or his uncle, or his uncle's son, may redeem him, or one of his blood relatives from his family may redeem him; or if he prospers, he may redeem himself.

25:50
Job 7:1;
Is 16:14;
21:16

50 'He then with his purchaser shall calculate from the year when he sold himself to him up to the year of jubilee; and the price of his sale shall correspond to the number of years. *It is* like the days of a hired man *that* he shall be with him.

25:51
Jer 32:7

51 'If there are still many years, he shall refund part of his purchase price in proportion to them for his own redemption;

52 and if few years remain until the year of jubilee, he shall so calculate with him. In proportion to his years he is to refund *the amount for* his redemption.

53 'Like a man hired year by year he shall be with him; he shall not rule over him with severity in your sight.

25:54
vv. 10,13,28

54 'Even if he is not redeemed by these *means,* he shall still go out in the year of jubilee, he and his sons with him.

55 'For the sons of Israel are My servants; they are My servants whom I brought out from the land of Egypt. I am the LORD your God.

J. Promises and warnings

1. *The blessings for obedience*

26:1
Ex 20:4,5;
Lev 19:4;
Deut 5:8

26 'You shall not make for yourselves idols, nor shall you set up for yourselves an image or a *sacred* pillar, nor shall you place a figured stone in your land to bow down to it; for I am the LORD your God.

26:2
Lev 19:30
26:3
Deut 28:1

2 'You shall keep My sabbaths and reverence My sanctuary; I am the LORD.

3 'If you walk in My statutes and keep My commandments so as to carry them out,

4 then I shall give you rains in their season, so that the land will yield its produce and the trees of the field will bear their fruit.

26:5
Amos 9:13;
Lev 25:18,19

5 'Indeed, your threshing will last for you until grape gathering, and grape gathering will last until sowing time. You will thus eat your food to the full and live securely in your land.

26:6
Ps 29:11;
147:14;
Zeph 3:13;
vv. 22,25

6 'I shall also grant peace in the land, so that you may lie down with no one making *you* tremble. I shall also eliminate harmful beasts from the land, and no sword will pass through your land.

7 'But you will chase your enemies, and they will fall before you by the sword;

*26:8
Deut 32:30;
Josh 23:10

8 five of you will chase a hundred, and a hundred of you will chase ten thousand, and your enemies will fall before you by the sword.

26:9
Gen 17:6,7;
22:17;
Neh 9:23

9 'So I will turn toward you and make you fruitful and multiply you, and I will confirm My covenant with you.

26:10
Lev 25:22
26:11
Ex 25:8;
Ps 76:2

10 'And you will eat the old supply and clear out the old because of the new.

11 'Moreover, I will make My dwelling among you, and My soul will not reject you.

26:12
2 Cor 6:16

12 'I will also walk among you and be your God, and you shall be My people.

13 'I am the LORD your God, who brought you out of the land of Egypt so that *you* should not be their slaves, and I broke the bars of your yoke and made you walk erect.

2. *The punishments for disobedience*

26:14
Deut 28:15;
Mal 2:2

14 'But if you do not obey Me and do not carry out all these commandments,

---

26:8 In spiritual things the law that governs is not that of arithmetic progression but of an accumulative effect as the numbers rise. Symbolically, five will chase one hundred but one hundred will chase ten thousand. Especially in prayer may it be said that the power generated will be proportionately greater as more people pray. Thus the more of God's people who work and pray together, the more significant will be the results.

15   if, instead, you reject My statutes, and if your soul abhors My ordinances so as not to carry out all My commandments, *and* so break My covenant,

16   I, in turn, will do this to you: I will appoint over you a sudden terror, consumption and fever that shall waste away the eyes and cause the soul to pine away; also, you shall sow your seed uselessly, for your enemies shall eat it up.

17   'And I will set My face against you so that you shall be struck down before your enemies; and those who hate you shall rule over you, and you shall flee when no one is pursuing you.

18   'If also after these things, you do not obey Me, then I will punish you seven times more for your sins.

19   'And I will also break down your pride of power; I will also make your sky like iron and your earth like bronze.

20   'And your strength shall be spent uselessly, for your land shall not yield its produce and the trees of the land shall not yield their fruit.

21   'If then, you act with hostility against Me and are unwilling to obey Me, I will increase the plague on you seven times according to your sins.

22   'And I will let loose among you the beasts of the field, which shall bereave you of your children and destroy your cattle and reduce your number so that your roads lie deserted.

23   'And if by these things you are not turned to Me, but act with hostility against Me,

24   then I will act with hostility against you; and I, even I, will strike you seven times for your sins.

25   'I will also bring upon you a sword which will execute vengeance for the covenant; and when you gather together into your cities, I will send pestilence among you, so that you shall be delivered into enemy hands.

26   'When I break your staff of bread, ten women will bake your bread in one oven, and they will bring back your bread [18]in rationed amounts, so that you will eat and not be satisfied.

27   'Yet if in spite of this, you do not obey Me, but act with hostility against Me,

28   then I will act with wrathful hostility against you; and I, even I, will punish you seven times for your sins.

29   'Further, you shall eat the flesh of your sons and the flesh of your daughters you shall eat.

30   'I then will destroy your high places, and cut down your incense altars, and heap your remains on the remains of your idols; for My soul shall abhor you.

31   'I will lay waste your cities as well, and will make your sanctuaries desolate; and I will not smell your soothing aromas.

32   'And I will make the land desolate so that your enemies who settle in it shall be appalled over it.

33   'You, however, I will scatter among the nations and will draw out a sword after you, as your land becomes desolate and your cities become waste.

34   'Then the land will enjoy its sabbaths all the days of the desolation, while you are in your enemies' land; then the land will rest and enjoy its sabbaths.

35   'All the days of *its* desolation it will observe the rest which it did not observe on your sabbaths, while you were living on it.

36   'As for those of you who may be left, I will also bring weakness into their hearts in the lands of their enemies. And the sound of a driven leaf will chase them and even when no one is pursuing, they will flee as though from the sword, and they will fall.

37   'They will therefore stumble over each other as if *running* from the sword, although no one is pursuing; and you will have *no strength* to stand up before your enemies.

38   'But you will perish among the nations, and your enemies' land will consume you.

39   'So those of you who may be left will rot away because of their iniquity in the lands of your enemies; and also because of the iniquities of their forefathers they will rot away with them.

---

[18]Lit., *by weight*

26:16
Deut 28:22;
1 Sam 2:33;
Deut 28:35, 51
26:17
Lev 17:10;
Deut 28:25;
Ps 106:41;
53:5; vv. 36, 37
26:18
vv. 21,24,28
26:19
Is 25:11;
Deut 28:23
26:20
Is 17:10,11;
Deut 11:17
26:21
vv. 18,24,27, 40
26:22
Deut 32:24

26:23
Jer 2:30; 5:3

26:24
vv. 21,28,41

26:25
Ezek 5:17;
Num 14:12

*26:26
Ps 105:16;
Is 3:1;
Mic 6:14

26:28
vv. 24,41

26:29
Deut 28:53

26:30
2 Chr 34:3;
Ezek 6:3-6,13
26:31
Ps 74:7;
Is 63:18
*26:32
Jer 9:11;
19:18
26:33
Deut 4:27;
Ezek 12:15
26:34
v. 43;
2 Chr 36:21

26:36
Ezek 21:7

26:37
Josh 7:12,13

26:38
Deut 4:26

26:39
Deut 4:27;
Ezek 4:17

26:26 *staff* in this sense, "sustenance."
26:32 God here lays down the punishment that will be meted out to His people for persistent disobedience and

disregard of the covenant. The warning is amplified in Deut. 28:58–67. The punishment was meted out in the Babylonian captivity of 587 B.C.

*26:40ff
Jer 3:12-15;
Luke 15:18;
1 John 1:9

26:41
Ezek 44:9;
2 Chr 12:6,7

26:42
Gen 28:13-15;
26:2-5;
22:15-18

26:43
vv. 34,35,15

26:44
Deut 4:31;
Rom 11:2

26:45
Ex 6:6-8;
Lev 25:38;
Gen 17:7

*26:46
Lev 7:38;
27:34; 25:1

27:3
Ex 30:13

27:6
Num 18:16

27:8
v. 12

40 'If they confess their iniquity and the iniquity of their forefathers, in their unfaithfulness which they committed against Me, and also in their acting with hostility against Me—

41 I also was acting with hostility against them, to bring them into the land of their enemies—or if their uncircumcised heart becomes humbled so that they then make amends for their iniquity,

42 then I will remember My covenant with Jacob, and I will remember also My covenant with Isaac, and My covenant with Abraham as well, and I will remember the land.

43 'For the land shall be abandoned by them, and shall make up for its sabbaths while it is made desolate without them. They, meanwhile, shall be making amends for their iniquity, because they rejected My ordinances and their soul abhorred My statutes.

44 'Yet in spite of this, when they are in the land of their enemies, I will not reject them, nor will I so abhor them as to destroy them, breaking My covenant with them; for I am the Lord their God.

45 'But I will remember for them the covenant with their ancestors, whom I brought out of the land of Egypt in the sight of the nations, that I might be their God. I am the Lord.' "

46 These are the statutes and ordinances and laws which the Lord established between Himself and the sons of Israel through Moses at Mount Sinai.

K. Appendix: the making of vows

1. Vows involving persons

27 Again, the Lord spoke to Moses, saying, **2** "Speak to the sons of Israel, and say to them, 'When a man makes a difficult vow, he *shall be valued* according to your valuation of persons belonging to the Lord.

3 'If your valuation is of the male from twenty years even to sixty years old, then your valuation shall be fifty shekels of silver, after the shekel of the sanctuary.

4 'Or if it is a female, then your valuation shall be thirty shekels.

5 'And if it be from five years even to twenty years old then your valuation for the male shall be twenty shekels, and for the female ten shekels.

6 'But if *they are* from a month even up to five years old, then your valuation shall be five shekels of silver for the male, and for the female your valuation shall be three shekels of silver.

7 'And if *they are* from sixty years old and upward, if it is a male, then your valuation shall be fifteen shekels, and for the female ten shekels.

8 'But if he is poorer than your valuation, then he shall be placed before the priest, and the priest shall value him; according to the means of the one who vowed, the priest shall value him.

2. Vows involving animals

9 'Now if it is an animal of the kind which men can present as an offering to the Lord, any such that one gives to the Lord shall be holy.

10 'He shall not replace it or exchange it, a good for a bad, or a bad for a good; or if he does exchange animal for animal, then both it and its substitute shall become holy.

11 'If, however, it is any unclean animal of the kind which men do not present as an offering to the Lord, then he shall place the animal before the priest.

26:40ff. The Abrahamic covenant was not to be abrogated by Israel's future disobedience. It would continue in accord with the conditions that governed it. When and if Israel repented of her sins and turned to God, the land would be returned to Israel. This was fulfilled after the Babylon in 539 B.C., and a remnant returned to Palestine under Zerubbabel.
26:46 The Law of Moses is used to describe the Old Testament economy under which the people of Israel lived in relation to God. The Law can be divided into three categories: (1) the moral law, or the Ten Commandments (Deut. 5:22; 10:4); (2) the ceremonial law setting forth the proper approach to God in worship (7:37,38); and (3) the civil law under which the people were to live and be governed (Deut.

17:9–11). The ceremonial law has been completely fulfilled by the Lord Jesus Christ and is therefore not binding on New Testament believers. The civil law was designed especially for the pre-Christian Jewish theocracy, and other nations living under different cultural conditions need not be subject to it. But the basic moral law applies to all people of all ages and serves to: (1) demonstrate to all men that they are sinners in need of a Savior; (2) reveal what is the rule of godly conduct by which believers who love the Lord may know how they can please Him; and (3) exercise a certain restraining influence on mankind as a whole so that a law-governed society is rendered possible. Technically (1) is known as the pedagogic use of the Law; (2) is the normative use; and (3) is the political use.

12 'And the priest shall value it as either good or bad; as you, the priest, value it, so it shall be.

27:12
v. 8

13 'But if he should ever *wish to* redeem it, then he shall add one-fifth of it to your valuation.

27:13
vv. 15,19

3. *Vows involving a house*

14 'Now if a man consecrates his house as holy to the LORD, then the priest shall value it as either good or bad; as the priest values it, so it shall stand.

15 'Yet if the one who consecrates it should *wish to* redeem his house, then he shall add one-fifth of your valuation price to it, so that it may be his.

27:15
v. 20

4. *Vows involving land*

16 'Again, if a man consecrates to the LORD part of the fields of his own property, then your valuation shall be proportionate to the seed needed for it: a homer of barley seed at fifty shekels of silver.

17 'If he consecrates his field as of the year of jubilee, according to your valuation it shall stand.

18 'If he consecrates his field after the jubilee, however, then the priest shall calculate the price for him proportionate to the years that are left until the year of jubilee; and it shall be deducted from your valuation.

27:18
Lev 25:15,16

19 'And if the one who consecrates it should ever wish to redeem the field, then he shall add one-fifth of your valuation price to it, so that it may pass to him.

20 'Yet if he will not redeem the field, but has sold the field to another man, it may no longer be redeemed;

21 and when it reverts in the jubilee, the field shall be holy to the LORD, like a field set apart; it shall be for the priest as his property.

27:21
Lev 25:10,28,
31;
Num 18:14

22 'Or if he consecrates to the LORD a field which he has bought, which is not a part of the field of his own property,

23 then the priest shall calculate for him the amount of your valuation up to the year of jubilee; and he shall on that day give your valuation as holy to the LORD.

27:23
v. 18

24 'In the year of jubilee the field shall return to the one from whom he bought it, to whom the possession of the land belongs.

27:24
Lev 25:28

25 'Every valuation of yours, moreover, shall be after the shekel of the sanctuary. The shekel shall be twenty gerahs.

27:25
Ex 30:13

5. *Vows involving firstlings*

26 'However, a first-born among animals, which as a first-born belongs to the LORD, no man may consecrate it; whether ox or sheep, it is the LORD's.

27:26
Ex 13:2,12

27 'But if *it is* among the unclean animals, then he shall redeem it according to your valuation, and add to it one-fifth of it; and if it is not redeemed, then it shall be sold according to your valuation.

27:27
vv. 11,12

6. *Vows involving devoted things*

28 'Nevertheless, anything which a man [19]sets apart to the LORD out of all that he has, of man or animal or of the fields of his own property, shall not be sold or redeemed. Anything devoted to destruction is most holy to the LORD.

27:28
Josh 6:17-19

29 'No one who may have been set apart among men shall be ransomed; he shall surely be put to death.

7. *Redeeming the tithe*

30 'Thus all the tithe of the land, of the seed of the land or of the fruit of the tree, is the LORD's; it is holy to the LORD.

27:30
Gen 28:22;
Mal 3:8,10

31 'If, therefore, a man wishes to redeem part of his tithe, he shall add to it one-fifth of it.

27:31
v. 13

32 'And for every tenth part of herd or flock, whatever passes under the rod, the tenth one shall be holy to the LORD.

33 'He is not to be concerned whether *it is* good or bad, nor shall he exchange it; or if he does exchange it, then both it and its substitute shall become holy. It shall not be redeemed.' "

27:33
v. 10

34 These are the commandments which the LORD commanded Moses for the sons of Israel at Mount Sinai.

27:34
Lev 26:46;
Deut 4:5

[19]Or, *puts under the ban*

INTRODUCTION TO

THE FOURTH BOOK OF MOSES

COMMONLY CALLED

NUMBERS

Authorship and Background: The fourth book of the Pentateuch is called Numbers in the Septuagint because of the numberings described in chapters 1 and 26. Far more appropriate is the Hebrew title, "in the wilderness," the fifth word in the first line of the Hebrew text. The story traces the journey of the Israelites from Sinai to the plains of Moab. Moses is the key figure, and according to 33:2 he kept a log of the journey.

In Exodus the covenant is made, the Law given, and the tabernacle completed. In Leviticus the priests and people alike receive religious instruction, and then in Numbers the Israelites are prepared for their ultimate goal—the entrance into, and the conquest of, Canaan. Most of the events in Numbers occur in the second and fortieth years of the forty-year period between the exodus and the entering of Canaan. Aside from two events, the thirty-eight weary years in the wilderness are passed over in silence.

Characteristics: There is more to the book of Numbers than the history of the wilderness wanderings. The account manifests the guiding, delivering, sustaining, and protecting hand of God among His people. Disobedience receives its due reward. Repentance results in pardon and restoration. By type and figure the principles underlying this relationship between God and His people may be carried over into the New Testament and even applied to the church today. God indeed is with His people, and these things "were written for our instruction" (1 Cor. 10:11). Rich spiritual lessons may be learned from a study of this book. The narrative sections of Numbers are made more difficult to read by the statistical and geographical summaries (chs. 1, 33, etc.). Some segments of the book appear in poetic form.

Contents:

I. The preparations for leaving Sinai (1:1-10:10): The tribes are numbered and their positions assigned. The Levites are numbered and their duties outlined. Miscellaneous laws and regulations for the removal of uncleanness and defilement; ordeal of jealousy. Nazirite regulations. The arrangements for the religious life of the camp given: the golden lampstand, rules for the Levites, the Passover, the fiery cloud, and the silver trumpets.

II. The journey from Sinai to Moab (10:11-21:35): The departure from Sinai. The people's complaint about the manna and the demand for flesh. Miriam and Aaron complain against Moses; God vindicates him; Moses intercedes for leprosy-stricken Miriam. Israel sojourns in Paran; spies are sent out. Their reports are received and Israel accepts the report of the ten spies and rejects the counsel of Joshua and Caleb. Judgment is about to fall and Moses intercedes with God for the people. Miscellaneous legislation enacted. Korah, Dathan, and Abiram rebel and are punished. Aaron's rod sprouts. The duties and dues of the Levites. Israel marches from Kadesh to Moab. Miriam dies. The miracle of Meribah. Israel clashes with Edom. Aaron dies. Israel wars with the Amorites and the people of Bashan, and both of these enemies are defeated. The bronze serpent.

III. Events in Moab (22:1-36:13): The story of Balaam: Balak, Moab, the ass, and Balaam's oracles. Various laws and incidents: marriage with women of Moab and Midian, the second census, the laws of female inheritance, the appointment of Joshua, the laws of worship relating to daily sacrifices, Sabbath, new moon, unleavened bread, Feast of Weeks and Trumpets, Day of Atonement, and the Feast of Booths. Vows made by women. Israel destroys the Midianites and begins settlements in Trans-Jordan. Gad and Reuben build cities and Manasseh makes settlements in Gilead. The journey from Egypt to Moab summarized and plans formulated for the division of Canaan. The levitical cities and the laws for murder. Laws concerning the marriage of heiresses.

THE FOURTH BOOK OF MOSES
COMMONLY CALLED
NUMBERS

I. The preparations for leaving Sinai (1:1–10:10)

A. The census

1. Selection of the census takers

*1:1
Ex 19:1;
40:2,17

1 Then the LORD spoke to Moses in the wilderness of Sinai, in the tent of meeting, on the first of the second month, in the second year after they had come out of the land of Egypt, saying,

1:2
Ex 38:26;
Num 26:2

2 "Take a ¹census of all the congregation of the sons of Israel, by their families, by their fathers' households, according to the number of names, every male, head by head

3 from twenty years old and upward, whoever *is able to* go out to war in Israel, you and Aaron shall ²number them by their armies.

1:4
v. 16

4 "With you, moreover, there shall be a man of each tribe, each one head of his father's household.

5 "These then are the names of the men who shall stand with you: of Reuben, Elizur the son of Shedeur;

6 of Simeon, Shelumiel the son of Zurishaddai;

7 of Judah, Nahshon the son of Amminadab;

8 of Issachar, Nethanel the son of Zuar;

9 of Zebulun, Eliab the son of Helon;

10 of the sons of Joseph: of Ephraim, Elishama the son of Ammihud; of Manasseh, Gamaliel the son of Pedahzur;

11 of Benjamin, Abidan the son of Gideoni;

12 of Dan, Ahiezer the son of Ammishaddai;

13 of Asher, Pagiel the son of Ochran;

1:14
Num 2:14

14 of Gad, Eliasaph the son of Deuel;

15 of Naphtali, Ahira the son of Enan.

1:16
Num 16:2;
26:9

16 "These are they who were called of the congregation, the leaders of their fathers' tribes; they were the heads of ³divisions of Israel."

2. The numbering of Israel

17 So Moses and Aaron took these men who had been designated by name,

18 and they assembled all the congregation together on the first of the second month. Then they registered by ancestry in their families, by their fathers' households, according to the number of names, from twenty years old and upward, head by head,

19 just as the LORD had commanded Moses. So he numbered them in the wilderness of Sinai.

1:20
Num 26:5-11

20 Now the sons of Reuben, Israel's first-born, their genealogical registration by their families, by their fathers' households, according to the number of names, head by head, every male from twenty years old and upward, whoever *was able to* go out to war,

21 their numbered men, of the tribe of Reuben, *were* 46,500.

1:22
Num 26:12-14

22 Of the sons of Simeon, their genealogical registration by their families, by their fathers' households, their numbered men, according to the number of names, head by head, every male from twenty years old and upward, whoever *was able to* go out to war,

23 their numbered men, of the tribe of Simeon, *were* 59,300.

1:24
Num 26:15-18

24 Of the sons of Gad, their genealogical registration by their families, by their

¹Lit., *sum* ²Lit., *muster*, and so throughout this context ³Lit., *thousands*, or, *clans*

1:1 *second month,* just a month after the erection of the tabernacle (Ex. 40:17). The events described in 1:1–10:10 occurred in just nineteen days (10:11).

fathers' households, according to the number of names, from twenty years old and upward, whoever *was able to* go out to war,
25   their numbered men, of the tribe of Gad, *were* 45,650.
26   Of the sons of Judah, their genealogical registration by their families, by their fathers' households, according to the number of names, from twenty years old and upward, whoever *was able to* go out to war,
27   their numbered men, of the tribe of Judah, *were* 74,600.
28   Of the sons of Issachar, their genealogical registration by their families, by their fathers' households, according to the number of names, from twenty years old and upward, whoever *was able to* go out to war,
29   their numbered men, of the tribe of Issachar, *were* 54,400.
30   Of the sons of Zebulun, their genealogical registration by their families, by their fathers' households, according to the number of names, from twenty years old and upward, whoever *was able to* go out to war,
31   their numbered men, of the tribe of Zebulun, *were* 57,400.
32   Of the sons of Joseph, *namely*, of the sons of Ephraim, their genealogical registration by their families, by their fathers' households, according to the number of names, from twenty years old and upward, whoever *was able to* go out to war,
33   their numbered men, of the tribe of Ephraim, *were* 40,500.
34   Of the sons of Manasseh, their genealogical registration by their families, by their fathers' households, according to the number of names, from twenty years old and upward, whoever *was able to* go out to war,
35   their numbered men, of the tribe of Manasseh, *were* 32,200.
36   Of the sons of Benjamin, their genealogical registration by their families, by their fathers' households, according to the number of names, from twenty years old and upward, whoever *was able to* go out to war,
37   their numbered men, of the tribe of Benjamin, *were* 35,400.
38   Of the sons of Dan, their genealogical registration by their families, by their fathers' households, according to the number of names, from twenty years old and upward, whoever *was able to* go out to war,
39   their numbered men, of the tribe of Dan, *were* 62,700.
40   Of the sons of Asher, their genealogical registration by their families, by their fathers' households, according to the number of names, from twenty years old and upward, whoever *was able to* go out to war,
41   their numbered men, of the tribe of Asher, *were* 41,500.
42   Of the sons of Naphtali, their genealogical registration by their families, by their fathers' households, according to the number of names, from twenty years old and upward, whoever *was able to* go out to war,
43   their numbered men, of the tribe of Naphtali, *were* 53,400.
44   These are the ones who were numbered, whom Moses and Aaron numbered, with the leaders of Israel, twelve men, each of whom was of his father's household.
45   So all the numbered men of the sons of Israel by their fathers' households, from twenty years old and upward, whoever *was able to* go out to war in Israel,
46   even all the numbered men were 603,550.

3. The Levites not numbered: their duties

47   The Levites, however, were not numbered among them by their fathers' tribe.
48   For the LORD had spoken to Moses, saying,
49   "Only the tribe of Levi you shall not number, nor shall you take their census among the sons of Israel.
50   "But you shall appoint the Levites over the [4]tabernacle of the testimony, and over all its furnishings and over all that belongs to it. They shall carry the tabernacle and all its furnishings, and they shall take care of it; they shall also camp around the tabernacle.
51   "So when the tabernacle is to set out, the Levites shall take it down; and when the tabernacle encamps, the Levites shall set it up. But the [5]layman who comes near shall be put to death.

[4]Lit., *dwelling place*, and so throughout this context   [5]Lit., *stranger*

1:49 *you shall not number.* This simply means that the Levites were not to be numbered along with the twelve tribes. They were numbered separately later (3:15).

52 "And the sons of Israel shall camp, each man by his own camp, and each man by his own standard, according to their armies.

53 "But the Levites shall camp around the tabernacle of the testimony, that there may be no wrath on the congregation of the sons of Israel. So the Levites shall keep charge of the tabernacle of the testimony."

54 Thus the sons of Israel did; according to all which the LORD had commanded Moses, so they did.

B. *The camps and leaders of the tribes*

2 Now the LORD spoke to Moses and to Aaron, saying,

2 "The sons of Israel shall camp, each by his own standard, with the banners of their fathers' households; they shall camp around the tent of meeting at a distance.

3 "Now those who camp on the east side toward the sunrise *shall be* of the standard of the camp of Judah, by their armies, and the leader of the sons of Judah: Nahshon the son of Amminadab,

4   and his army, even their numbered men, 74,600.

5 "And those who camp next to him *shall be* the tribe of Issachar, and the leader of the sons of Issachar: Nethanel the son of Zuar,

6   and his army, even their numbered men, 54,400.

7 "Then *comes* the tribe of Zebulun, and the leader of the sons of Zebulun: Eliab the son of Helon,

8   and his army, even his numbered men, 57,400.

9 "The total of the numbered men of the camp of Judah: 186,400, by their armies. They shall set out first.

10 "On the south side *shall be* the standard of the camp of Reuben by their armies, and the leader of the sons of Reuben: Elizur the son of Shedeur,

11   and his army, even their numbered men, 46,500.

12 "And those who camp next to him *shall be* the tribe of Simeon, and the leader of the sons of Simeon: Shelumiel the son of Zurishaddai,

13   and his army, even their numbered men, 59,300.

14 "Then *comes* the tribe of Gad, and the leader of the sons of Gad: Eliasaph the son of Deuel,

15   and his army, even their numbered men, 45,650.

16 "The total of the numbered men of the camp of Reuben: 151,450 by their armies. And they shall set out second.

17 "Then the tent of meeting shall set out *with* the camp of the Levites in the midst of the camps; just as they camp, so they shall set out, every man in his place, by their standards.

18 "On the west side *shall be* the standard of the camp of Ephraim by their armies, and the leader of the sons of Ephraim *shall be* Elishama the son of Ammihud,

19   and his army, even their numbered men, 40,500.

20 "And next to him *shall be* the tribe of Manasseh, and the leader of the sons of Manasseh: Gamaliel the son of Pedahzur,

21   and his army, even their numbered men, 32,200.

22 "Then *comes* the tribe of Benjamin, and the leader of the sons of Benjamin: Abidan the son of Gideoni,

23   and his army, even their numbered men, 35,400.

24 "The total of the numbered men of the camp of Ephraim: 108,100, by their armies. And they shall set out third.

25 "On the north side *shall be* the standard of the camp of Dan by their armies, and the leader of the sons of Dan: Ahiezer the son of Ammishaddai,

26   and his army, even their numbered men, 62,700.

27 "And those who camp next to him *shall be* the tribe of Asher, and the leader of the sons of Asher: Pagiel the son of Ochran,

28   and his army, even their numbered men, 41,500.

29 "Then *comes* the tribe of Naphtali, and the leader of the sons of Naphtali: Ahira the son of Enan,

30   and his army, even their numbered men, 53,400.

31 "The total of the numbered men of the camp of Dan, *was* 157,600. They shall set out last by their standards."

32 These are the numbered men of the sons of Israel by their fathers'

households; the total of the numbered men of the camps by their armies, 603,550.

33   The Levites, however, were not numbered among the sons of Israel, just as the LORD had commanded Moses.

34   Thus the sons of Israel did; according to all that the LORD commanded Moses, so they camped by their standards, and so they set out, every one by his family, according to his father's household.

C. The Levites

1. The sons of Aaron

3 Now these are *the records of* the generations of Aaron and Moses at the time when the LORD spoke with Moses on Mount Sinai.

2   These then are the names of the sons of Aaron: Nadab the first-born, and Abihu, Eleazar and Ithamar.

3   These are the names of the sons of Aaron, the anointed priests, whom he ordained to serve as priests.

4   But Nadab and Abihu died before the LORD when they offered strange fire before the LORD in the wilderness of Sinai; and they had no children. So Eleazar and Ithamar served as priests in the lifetime of their father Aaron.

2. The responsibilities of the Levites

5   Then the LORD spoke to Moses, saying,

6   "Bring the tribe of Levi near and set them before Aaron the priest, that they may serve him.

7   "And they shall perform the duties for him and for the whole congregation before the tent of meeting, to do the service of the tabernacle.

8   "They shall also keep all the furnishings of the tent of meeting, along with the duties of the sons of Israel, to do the service of the tabernacle.

9   "You shall thus give the Levites to Aaron and to his sons; they are wholly given to him from among the sons of Israel.

10   "So you shall appoint Aaron and his sons that they may keep their priesthood, but the layman who comes near shall be put to death."

3. God chooses the Levites instead of every first-born

11   Again the LORD spoke to Moses, saying,

12   "Now, behold, I have taken the Levites from among the sons of Israel instead of every first-born, the first issue of the womb among the sons of Israel. So the Levites shall be Mine.

13   "For all the first-born are Mine; on the day that I struck down all the first-born in the land of Egypt, I sanctified to Myself all the first-born in Israel, from man to beast. They shall be Mine; I am the LORD."

4. The Levites numbered: duties assigned

14   Then the LORD spoke to Moses in the wilderness of Sinai, saying,

15   "Number the sons of Levi by their fathers' households, by their families; every male from a month old and upward you shall number."

16   So Moses numbered them according to the word of the LORD, just as he had been commanded.

17   These then are the sons of Levi by their names: Gershon and Kohath and Merari.

18   And these are the names of the sons of Gershon by their families: Libni and Shimei;

19   and the sons of Kohath by their families: Amram and Izhar, Hebron and Uzziel;

20   and the sons of Merari by their families: Mahli and Mushi. These are the families of the Levites according to their fathers' households.

21   Of Gershon *was* the family of the Libnites and the family of the Shimeites; these *were* the families of the Gershonites.

22   Their numbered men, in the numbering of every male from a month old and upward, *even* their numbered men *were* 7,500.

23   The families of the Gershonites were to camp behind the tabernacle westward,

2:33 Num 1:47

3:2 Num 26:60

3:4 Num 26:61

3:6 Num 8:6-22; 18:1-7

3:9 Num 18:6

3:10 Ex 29:9; Num 1:51

3:12 v. 41; Num 8:16; 18:6

3:13 Ex 13:2,12, 15; Num 8:17

3:15 v. 39

3:17 Ex 6:16-22

3:20 Gen 46:11

3:21 Ex 6:17

3:25
Num 4:24-26;
Ex 25:9

3:27
1 Chr 26:23

3:29
Ex 6:18

3:33
Ex 6:19

3:36
Num 4:29-32

3:38
Num 18:5;
vv. 7,8,10

*3:39
Num 26:62

3:41
vv. 12,45

3:43
v. 39

3:45
vv. 12,41

3:46
Ex 13:13;
Num 18:15
3:47
Ex 30:13

24   and the leader of the fathers' households of the Gershonites *was* Eliasaph the son of Lael.

25   Now the duties of the sons of Gershon in the tent of meeting *involved* the tabernacle and the tent, its covering, and the screen for the doorway of the tent of meeting,

26   and the hangings of the court, and the screen for the doorway of the court, which is around the tabernacle and the altar, and its cords, according to all the service concerning them.

27   And of Kohath *was* the family of the Amramites and the family of the Izharites and the family of the Hebronites and the family of the Uzzielites; these were the families of the Kohathites.

28   In the numbering of every male from a month old and upward, *there were* 8,600, performing the duties of the sanctuary.

29   The families of the sons of Kohath were to camp on the southward side of the tabernacle,

30   and the leader of the fathers' households of the Kohathite families was Elizaphan the son of Uzziel.

31   Now their duties *involved* the ark, the table, the lampstand, the altars, and the utensils of the sanctuary with which they minister, and the screen, and all the service concerning them;

32   and Eleazar the son of Aaron the priest *was* the chief of the leaders of Levi, *and had* the oversight of those who perform the duties of the sanctuary.

33   Of Merari *was* the family of the Mahlites and the family of the Mushites; these *were* the families of Merari.

34   Their numbered men in the numbering of every male from a month old and upward, *were* 6,200.

35   And the leader of the fathers' households of the families of Merari *was* Zuriel the son of Abihail. They *were* to camp on the northward side of the tabernacle.

36   Now the appointed duties of the sons of Merari *involved* the frames of the tabernacle, its bars, its pillars, its sockets, all its equipment, and the service concerning them,

37   and the pillars around the court with their sockets and their pegs and their cords.

38   Now those who were to camp before the tabernacle eastward, before the tent of meeting toward the sunrise, are Moses and Aaron and his sons, performing the duties of the sanctuary for the obligation of the sons of Israel; but the layman coming near was to be put to death.

39   All the numbered men of the Levites, whom Moses and Aaron numbered at the command of the LORD by their families, every male from a month old and upward, *were* 22,000.

5. *The numbering of first-born males*

40   Then the LORD said to Moses, "Number every first-born male of the sons of Israel from a month old and upward, and make a list of their names.

41   "And you shall take the Levites for Me, I am the LORD, instead of all the first-born among the sons of Israel, and the cattle of the Levites instead of all the first-born among the cattle of the sons of Israel."

42   So Moses numbered all the first-born among the sons of Israel, just as the LORD had commanded him;

43   and all the first-born males by the number of names from a month old and upward, for their numbered men were 22,273.

44   Then the LORD spoke to Moses, saying,

45   "Take the Levites instead of all the first-born among the sons of Israel and the cattle of the Levites. And the Levites shall be Mine; I am the LORD.

46   "And for the ransom of the 273 of the first-born of the sons of Israel who are in excess beyond the Levites,

47   you shall take five shekels apiece, per head; you shall take *them* in terms of the shekel of the sanctuary (the shekel is twenty [6]gerahs),

[6]I.e., A gerah equals approx. one-fortieth ounce

3:39 Compare this with 26:62. In the latter account there are one thousand more. Evidently between the time of the first and the second mention the number of Levites from one month of age and over had increased by this number. Round figures are used, a common practice in history at all times.

48   and give the money, the ransom of those who are in excess among them, to Aaron and to his sons."

49   So Moses took the ransom money from those who were in excess, beyond those ransomed by the Levites;

50   from the first-born of the sons of Israel he took the money in terms of the shekel of the sanctuary, 1,365.

3:50
vv. 46-48

51   Then Moses gave the ransom money to Aaron and to his sons, at the command of the LORD, just as the LORD had commanded Moses.

6. *Numbering and service of the Levites*

a. *The sons of Kohath*

4 Then the LORD spoke to Moses and to Aaron, saying,

2   "Take a census of the descendants of Kohath from among the sons of Levi, by their families, by their fathers' households,

3   from thirty years and upward, even to fifty years old, all who enter the service to do the work in the tent of meeting.

4:3
Num 8:24;
vv. 23,30,35

4   "This is the work of the descendants of Kohath in the tent of meeting, *concerning* the most holy things.

5   "When the camp sets out, Aaron and his sons shall go in and they shall take down the veil of the screen and cover the ark of the testimony with it;

6   and they shall lay a covering of porpoise skin on it, and shall spread over *it* a cloth of pure blue, and shall insert its poles.

4:6
v. 25

7   "Over the table of the bread of the Presence they shall also spread a cloth of blue and put on it the dishes and the pans and the sacrificial bowls and the jars for the libation, and the continual bread shall be on it.

4:7
Ex 25:23,29,
30;
Lev 24:5-9

8   "And they shall spread over them a cloth of scarlet *material,* and cover the same with a covering of porpoise skin, and they shall insert its poles.

9   "Then they shall take a blue cloth and cover the lampstand for the light, along with its lamps and its snuffers, and its trays and all its oil vessels, by which they serve it;

4:9
Ex 25:31,37,
38

10   and they shall put it and all its utensils in a covering of porpoise skin, and shall put it on the carrying bars.

11   "And over the golden altar they shall spread a blue cloth and cover it with a covering of porpoise skin, and shall insert its poles;

4:11
Ex 30:1,3

12   and they shall take all the utensils of service, with which they serve in the sanctuary, and put them in a blue cloth and cover them with a covering of porpoise skin, and put them on the carrying bars.

13   "Then they shall take away the ashes from the altar, and spread a purple cloth over it.

14   "They shall also put on it all its utensils by which they serve in connection with it: the firepans, the forks and shovels and the basins, all the utensils of the altar; and they shall spread a cover of porpoise skin over it and insert its poles.

15   "And when Aaron and his sons have finished covering the holy *objects* and all the furnishings of the sanctuary, when the camp is to set out, after that the sons of Kohath shall come to carry *them,* so that they may not touch the holy *objects* and die. These are the things in the tent of meeting which the sons of Kohath are to carry.

4:15
Num 7:9;
2 Sam 6:6,7

16   "And the responsibility of Eleazar the son of Aaron the priest is the oil for the light and the fragrant incense and the continual grain offering and the anointing oil—the responsibility of all the tabernacle and of all that is in it, with the sanctuary and its furnishings."

4:16
Lev 24:1-3;
Ex 30:34;
29:40; 30:23

17   Then the LORD spoke to Moses and to Aaron, saying,

18   "Do not let the tribe of the families of the Kohathites be cut off from among the Levites.

19   "But do this to them that they may live and not die when they approach the most holy *objects:* Aaron and his sons shall go in and assign each of them to his work and to his load;

4:19
vv. 4,15

20   but they shall not go in to see the holy *objects* even for a moment, lest they die."

b. *The sons of Gershon*

21   Then the LORD spoke to Moses, saying,

22   "Take a census of the sons of Gershon also, by their fathers' households, by their families;

23   from thirty years and upward to fifty years old, you shall number them; all who enter to perform the service to do the work in the tent of meeting.

24   "This is the service of the families of the Gershonites, in serving and in carrying:

25   they shall carry the curtains of the tabernacle and the tent of meeting *with* its covering and the covering of porpoise skin that is on top of it, and the screen for the doorway of the tent of meeting,

26   and the hangings of the court, and the screen for the doorway of the gate of the court which is around the tabernacle and the altar, and their cords and all the equipment for their service; and all that is to be done, they shall perform.

27   "All the service of the sons of the Gershonites, in all their loads and in all their work, shall be *performed* at the command of Aaron and his sons; and you shall assign to them as a duty all their loads.

28   "This is the service of the families of the sons of the Gershonites in the tent of meeting, and their duties *shall be* under the direction of Ithamar the son of Aaron the priest.

c. The sons of Merari

29   "*As for* the sons of Merari, you shall number them by their families, by their fathers' households;

30   from thirty years and upward even to fifty years old, you shall number them, everyone who enters the service to do the work of the tent of meeting.

31   "Now this is the duty of their loads, for all their service in the tent of meeting: the boards of the tabernacle and its bars and its pillars and its sockets,

32   and the pillars around the court and their sockets and their pegs and their cords, with all their equipment and with all their service; and you shall assign *each man* by name the items he is to carry.

33   "This is the service of the families of the sons of Merari, according to all their service in the tent of meeting, under the direction of Ithamar the son of Aaron the priest."

d. The results of the census

34   So Moses and Aaron and the leaders of the congregation numbered the sons of the Kohathites by their families, and by their fathers' households,

35   from thirty years and upward even to fifty years old, everyone who entered the service for work in the tent of meeting.

36   And their numbered men by their families were 2,750.

37   These are the numbered men of the Kohathite families, everyone who was serving in the tent of meeting, whom Moses and Aaron numbered according to the commandment of the LORD through Moses.

38   And the numbered men of the sons of Gershon by their families, and by their fathers' households,

39   from thirty years and upward even to fifty years old, everyone who entered the service for work in the tent of meeting.

40   And their numbered men by their families, by their fathers' households, were 2,630.

41   These are the numbered men of the families of the sons of Gershon, everyone who was serving in the tent of meeting, whom Moses and Aaron numbered according to the commandment of the LORD.

42   And the numbered men of the families of the sons of Merari by their families, by their fathers' households,

43   from thirty years and upward even to fifty years old, everyone who entered the service for work in the tent of meeting.

44   And their numbered men by their families were 3,200.

45   These are the numbered men of the families of the sons of Merari, whom Moses and Aaron numbered according to the commandment of the LORD through Moses.

46   All the numbered men of the Levites, whom Moses and Aaron and the leaders of Israel numbered, by their families and by their fathers' households,

47   from thirty years and upward even to fifty years old, everyone who could enter to do the work of service and the work of carrying in the tent of meeting.

48   And their numbered men were 8,580.

49   According to the commandment of the LORD through Moses, they were

numbered, everyone by his serving or carrying; thus these were his numbered men, just as the LORD had commanded Moses.

D. Camp laws and regulations

1. The unclean to be put out of the camp

5 Then the LORD spoke to Moses, saying,

2 "Command the sons of Israel that they send away from the camp every leper and everyone having a discharge and everyone who is unclean because of a *dead* person.

3 "You shall send away both male and female; you shall send them outside the camp so that they will not defile their camp where I dwell in their midst."

4 And the sons of Israel did so and sent them outside the camp; just as the LORD had spoken to Moses, thus the sons of Israel did.

2. The law of restitution

5 Then the LORD spoke to Moses, saying,

6 "Speak to the sons of Israel, 'When a man or woman commits any of the sins of mankind, acting unfaithfully against the LORD, and that person is guilty,

7 then he shall confess his sins which he has committed, and he shall make restitution in full for his wrong, and add to it one-fifth of it, and give *it* to him whom he has wronged.

8 'But if the man has no [7]relative to whom restitution may be made for the wrong, the restitution which is made for the wrong *must go* to the LORD for the priest, besides the ram of atonement, by which atonement is made for him.

9 'Also every contribution pertaining to all the holy *gifts* of the sons of Israel, which they offer to the priest, shall be his.

10 'So every man's holy *gifts* shall be his; whatever any man gives to the priest, it becomes his.' "

3. The law concerning jealousy

11 Then the LORD spoke to Moses, saying,

12 "Speak to the sons of Israel, and say to them, 'If any man's wife goes astray and is unfaithful to him,

13 and a man has intercourse with her and it is hidden from the eyes of her husband and she is undetected, although she has defiled herself, and there is no witness against her and she has not been caught in the act,

14 if a spirit of jealousy comes over him and he is jealous of his wife when she has defiled herself, or if a spirit of jealousy comes over him and he is jealous of his wife when she has not defiled herself,

15 the man shall then bring his wife to the priest, and shall bring *as* an offering for her one-tenth of an ephah of barley meal; he shall not pour oil on it, nor put frankincense on it, for it is a grain offering of jealousy, a grain offering of memorial, a reminder of iniquity.

16 'Then the priest shall bring her near and have her stand before the LORD,

17 and the priest shall take holy water in an earthenware vessel; and he shall take some of the dust that is on the floor of the tabernacle and put *it* into the water.

18 'The priest shall then have the woman stand before the LORD and let *the hair of* the woman's head go loose, and place the grain offering of memorial in her hands, which is the grain offering of jealousy, and in the hand of the priest is to be the water of bitterness that brings a curse.

19 'And the priest shall have her take an oath and shall say to the woman, "If no man has lain with you and if you have not gone astray into uncleanness, *being* under *the authority of* your husband, be immune to this water of bitterness that brings a curse;

20 if you, however, have gone astray, *being* under *the authority of* your husband,

[7]Lit., *redeemer*

5:2ff. Addenda to the laws in Leviticus.
5:11ff. Moses outlines here (vv. 11–31) the law of jealousy by which suspicion of marital unfaithfulness could be cleared or confirmed. The rite prescribed was, in effect, an appeal to God to determine the guilt or innocence of the suspected party. Specific examples of the use of this rite do not exist in Scripture. The custom was not practiced in post-Biblical times, although during the history of the church ordeals were resorted to that bore some affinities to the law of jealousy.

and if you have defiled yourself and a man other than your husband has had intercourse with you"

5:21
Josh 6:26;
1 Sam 14:24;
Neh 10:29

21 (then the priest shall have the woman swear with the oath of the curse, and the priest shall say to the woman), "the LORD make you a curse and an oath among your people by the LORD's making your thigh waste away and your abdomen swell;

5:22
Deut 27:15;
Ps 109:18

22 and this water that brings a curse shall go into your stomach, and make your abdomen swell and your thigh waste away." And the woman shall say, "Amen. Amen."

23 'The priest shall then write these curses on a scroll, and he shall wash them off into the water of bitterness.

24 'Then he shall make the woman drink the water of bitterness that brings a curse, so that the water which brings a curse will go into her and *cause* bitterness.

5:25
Lev 8:27

25 'And the priest shall take the grain offering of jealousy from the woman's hand, and he shall wave the grain offering before the LORD and bring it to the altar;

26 and the priest shall take a handful of the grain offering as its memorial offering and offer *it* up in smoke on the altar, and afterward he shall make the woman drink the water.

5:27
Jer 29:18;
42:18;
Zech 8:13

27 'When he has made her drink the water, then it shall come about, if she has defiled herself and has been unfaithful to her husband, that the water which brings a curse shall go into her and *cause* bitterness, and her abdomen will swell and her thigh will waste away, and the woman will become a curse among her people.

28 'But if the woman has not defiled herself and is clean, she will then be free and conceive children.

5:29
vv. 12,19

29 'This is the law of jealousy: when a wife, *being* under *the authority of* her husband, goes astray and defiles herself,

30 or when a spirit of jealousy comes over a man and he is jealous of his wife, he shall then make the woman stand before the LORD, and the priest shall apply all this law to her.

31 'Moreover, the man shall be free from guilt, but that woman shall bear her guilt.' "

4. The law for a Nazirite

*6:2
Judg 13:5;
16:17;
Amos 2:11,12

6 Again the LORD spoke to Moses, saying, 2 "Speak to the sons of Israel, and say to them, 'When a man or woman makes a special vow, the vow of a ⁸Nazirite, to dedicate himself to the LORD,

3 he shall abstain from wine and strong drink; he shall drink no vinegar, whether made from wine or strong drink, neither shall he drink any grape juice, nor eat fresh or dried grapes.

4 'All the days of his ⁹separation he shall not eat anything that is produced by the grape vine, from *the* seeds even to *the* skin.

6:5
1 Sam 1:11

5 'All the days of his vow of separation no razor shall pass over his head. He shall be holy until the days are fulfilled for which he separated himself to the LORD; he shall let the locks of hair on his head grow long.

6:6
Lev 19:11-22;
21:1-3

6 'All the days of his separation to the LORD he shall not go near to a dead person.

7 'He shall not make himself unclean for his father or for his mother, for his brother or for his sister, when they die, because his separation to God is on his head.

8 'All the days of his separation he is holy to the LORD.

9 'But if a man dies very suddenly beside him and he defiles his dedicated head *of hair*, then he shall shave his head on the day when he becomes clean; he shall shave it on the seventh day.

6:10
Lev 5:7

10 'Then on the eighth day he shall bring two turtledoves or two young pigeons to the priest, to the doorway of the tent of meeting.

11 'And the priest shall offer one for a sin offering and *the* other for a burnt

⁸I.e., one separated   ⁹Or, *living as a Nazirite*, and so through v. 21

6:2 Scripture warns against making vows lightly (Prov. 20:25), but once made they are regarded as binding. Indeed Scripture insists on performance even though the vower may have changed his preference (30:2), and it urges prompt discharge of one's vows (Deut. 23:21,23). There is nothing in Scripture that would require a person to fulfill a vow made in good faith but which later is discovered to be wrong or sinful. To refrain from making a vow is not sinful (Deut. 23:22). Certain restrictions were laid down to pre- vent misuse of the vow: (1) vows of children required the consent of their parents (30:3–5); (2) vows of wives required the consent of their husbands (30:6–8,10–13); and (3) vows of widows and divorced women were binding on them (30:9). Illustrations of those who made vows include: (1) Jephthah (Judg. 11:30,31); (2) Hannah (1 Sam. 1:11); (3) David (Ps. 132:2–5); (4) Paul (Acts 18:18); and (5) the Jews whom Paul sponsored (Acts 21:23,24,26).

offering, and make atonement for him concerning his sin because of the *dead* person. And that same day he shall consecrate his head,

12   and shall dedicate to the LORD his days as a Nazirite, and shall bring a male lamb a year old for a guilt offering; but the former days shall be void because his separation was defiled.

13   'Now this is the law of the Nazirite when the days of his separation are fulfilled, he shall bring the offering to the doorway of the tent of meeting.

14   'And he shall present his offering to the LORD: one male lamb a year old without defect for a burnt offering and one ewe-lamb a year old without defect for a sin offering and one ram without defect for a peace offering,

15   and a basket of unleavened cakes of fine flour mixed with oil and unleavened wafers spread with oil, along with their grain offering and their libations.

16   'Then the priest shall present *them* before the LORD and shall offer his sin offering and his burnt offering.

17   'He shall also offer the ram for a sacrifice of peace offerings to the LORD, together with the basket of unleavened cakes; the priest shall likewise offer its grain offering and its libation.

18   'The Nazirite shall then shave his dedicated head *of hair* at the doorway of the tent of meeting, and take the dedicated hair of his head and put *it* on the fire which is under the sacrifice of peace offerings.

19   'And the priest shall take the ram's shoulder *when it has been* boiled, and one unleavened cake out of the basket, and one unleavened wafer, and shall put *them* on the hands of the Nazirite after he has shaved his dedicated *hair*.

20   'Then the priest shall wave them for a wave offering before the LORD. It is holy for the priest, together with the breast offered by waving and the thigh offered by lifting up; and afterward the Nazirite may drink wine.'

21   "This is the law of the Nazirite who vows his offering to the LORD according to his separation, in addition to what *else* he can afford; according to his vow which he takes, so he shall do according to the law of his separation."

5. *The Aaronic benediction*

22   Then the LORD spoke to Moses, saying,

23   "Speak to Aaron and to his sons, saying, 'Thus you shall bless the sons of Israel. You shall say to them:

24   The LORD bless you, and keep you;
25   The LORD make His face shine on you,
           And be gracious to you;
26   The LORD lift up His countenance on you,
           And give you peace.'

27   "So they shall invoke My name on the sons of Israel, and I then will bless them."

E. *The offerings for the tabernacle*

1. *The dedication of the altar*

7 Now it came about on the day that Moses had finished setting up the tabernacle, he anointed it and consecrated it with all its furnishings and the altar and all its utensils; he anointed them and consecrated them also.

2   Then the leaders of Israel, the heads of their fathers' households, made an offering (they were the leaders of the tribes; they were the ones who were over the numbered men).

3   When they brought their offering before the LORD, six covered carts and twelve oxen, a cart for *every* two of the leaders and an ox for each one, then they presented them before the tabernacle.

4   Then the LORD spoke to Moses, saying,

5   "Accept *these things* from them, that they may be used in the service of the tent of meeting, and you shall give them to the Levites, *to* each man according to his service."

6   So Moses took the carts and the oxen, and gave them to the Levites.

7   Two carts and four oxen he gave to the sons of Gershon, according to their service,

8   and four carts and eight oxen he gave to the sons of Merari, according to their service, under the direction of Ithamar the son of Aaron the priest.

Marginal references:

6:12 Lev 5:6
6:13 Acts 21:26
6:14 Num 15:27; Lev 14:10
6:15 Num 15:1-7
6:18 v. 9; Acts 21:24
6:23 1 Chr 23:13
6:24 Deut 28:3-6
6:25 Ps 80:3,7,19; 119:135; Gen 43:29
6:26 Ps 4:6; 44:3; John 14:27
6:27 Deut 28:10; 2 Chr 7:14
7:1 Ex 40:18
7:2 Num 1:5-16
7:7 Num 4:25
7:8 Num 4:28,31, 33

7:9
Num 4:5-15
7:10
2 Chr 7:9
7:13
Num 3:47
7:14
Ex 30:34
7:17
Lev 3:1
7:18
Num 1:8
7:23
v. 18
7:24
Num 1:9
7:29
Lev 7:32
7:30
Num 1:5
7:34
Heb 10:4
7:36
Num 1:6

9 But he did not give *any* to the sons of Kohath because theirs *was* the service of the holy *objects*, *which* they carried on the shoulder.

10 And the leaders offered the dedication *offering* for the altar when it was anointed, so the leaders offered their offering before the altar.

11 Then the LORD said to Moses, "Let them present their offering, one leader each day, for the dedication of the altar."

2. Nahshon of Judah

12 Now the one who presented his offering on the first day *was* Nahshon the son of Amminadab, of the tribe of Judah;

13 and his offering *was* one silver [10]dish whose weight *was* one hundred and thirty *shekels*, one silver bowl of seventy shekels, according to [11]the shekel of the sanctuary, both of them full of fine flour mixed with oil for a grain offering;

14 one gold pan of ten *shekels*, full of incense;

15 one bull, one ram, one male lamb one year old, for a burnt offering;

16 one male goat for a sin offering;

17 and for the sacrifice of peace offerings, two oxen, five rams, five male goats, five male lambs one year old. This *was* the offering of Nahshon the son of Amminadab.

3. Nethanel of Issachar

18 On the second day Nethanel the son of Zuar, leader of Issachar, presented *an offering;*

19 he presented as his offering one silver dish whose weight *was* one hundred and thirty *shekels*, one silver bowl of seventy shekels, according to the shekel of the sanctuary, both of them full of fine flour mixed with oil for a grain offering;

20 one gold pan of ten *shekels*, full of incense;

21 one bull, one ram, one male lamb one year old, for a burnt offering;

22 one male goat for a sin offering;

23 and for the sacrifice of peace offerings, two oxen, five rams, five male goats, five male lambs one year old. This *was* the offering of Nethanel the son of Zuar.

4. Eliab of Zebulun

24 On the third day *it was* Eliab the son of Helon, leader of the sons of Zebulun;

25 his offering *was* one silver dish whose weight *was* one hundred and thirty *shekels*, one silver bowl of seventy shekels, according to the shekel of the sanctuary, both of them full of fine flour mixed with oil for a grain offering;

26 one gold pan of ten *shekels*, full of incense;

27 one young bull, one ram, one male lamb one year old, for a burnt offering;

28 one male goat for a sin offering;

29 and for the sacrifice of peace offerings, two oxen, five rams, five male goats, five male lambs one year old. This *was* the offering of Eliab the son of Helon.

5. Elizur of Reuben

30 On the fourth day *it was* Elizur the son of Shedeur, leader of the sons of Reuben;

31 his offering *was* one silver dish whose weight *was* one hundred and thirty *shekels*, one silver bowl of seventy shekels, according to the shekel of the sanctuary, both of them full of fine flour mixed with oil for a grain offering;

32 one gold pan of ten *shekels*, full of incense;

33 one bull, one ram, one male lamb one year old, for a burnt offering;

34 one male goat for a sin offering;

35 and for the sacrifice of peace offerings, two oxen, five rams, five male goats, five male lambs one year old. This *was* the offering of Elizur the son of Shedeur.

6. Shelumiel of Simeon

36 On the fifth day *it was* Shelumiel the son of Zurishaddai, leader of the children of Simeon;

37 his offering *was* one silver dish whose weight *was* one hundred and thirty *shekels*, one silver bowl of seventy shekels, according to the shekel of the sanctuary, both of them full of fine flour mixed with oil for a grain offering;

[10]Or, *platter*, and so through v. 85   [11]I.e., Approx. one-half ounce, and so through v. 86

38　one gold pan of ten *shekels*, full of incense;
39　one bull, one ram, one male lamb one year old, for a burnt offering;
40　one male goat for a sin offering;
41　and for the sacrifice of peace offerings, two oxen, five rams, five male goats, five male lambs one year old. This *was* the offering of Shelumiel the son of Zurishaddai.

7. *Eliasaph of Gad*

42　On the sixth day *it was* Eliasaph the son of Deuel, leader of the sons of Gad;
43　his offering *was* one silver dish whose weight *was* one hundred and thirty *shekels*, one silver bowl of seventy shekels, according to the shekel of the sanctuary, both of them full of fine flour mixed with oil for a grain offering;
44　one gold pan of ten *shekels*, full of incense;
45　one bull, one ram, one male lamb one year old, for a burnt offering;
46　one male goat for a sin offering;
47　and for the sacrifice of peace offerings, two oxen, five rams, five male goats, five male lambs one year old. This *was* the offering of Eliasaph the son of Deuel.

8. *Elishama of Ephraim*

48　On the seventh day *it was* Elishama the son of Ammihud, leader of the sons of Ephraim;
49　his offering *was* one silver dish whose weight *was* one hundred and thirty *shekels*, one silver bowl of seventy shekels, according to the shekel of the sanctuary, both of them full of fine flour mixed with oil for a grain offering;
50　one gold pan of ten *shekels*, full of incense;
51　one bull, one ram, one male lamb one year old, for a burnt offering;
52　one male goat for a sin offering;
53　and for the sacrifice of peace offerings, two oxen, five rams, five male goats, five male lambs one year old. This *was* the offering of Elishama the son of Ammihud.

9. *Gamaliel of Manasseh*

54　On the eighth day *it was* Gamaliel the son of Pedahzur, leader of the sons of Manasseh;
55　his offering *was* one silver dish whose weight *was* one hundred and thirty *shekels*, one silver bowl of seventy shekels, according to the shekel of the sanctuary, both of them full of fine flour mixed with oil for a grain offering;
56　one gold pan of ten *shekels*, full of incense;
57　one bull, one ram, one male lamb one year old, for a burnt offering;
58　one male goat for a sin offering;
59　and for the sacrifice of peace offerings, two oxen, five rams, five male goats, five male lambs one year old. This *was* the offering of Gamaliel the son of Pedahzur.

10. *Abidan of Benjamin*

60　On the ninth day *it was* Abidan the son of Gideoni, leader of the sons of Benjamin;
61　his offering *was* one silver dish whose weight *was* one hundred and thirty *shekels*, one silver bowl of seventy shekels, according to the shekel of the sanctuary, both of them full of fine flour mixed with oil for a grain offering;
62　one gold pan of ten *shekels*, full of incense;
63　one bull, one ram, one male lamb one year old, for a burnt offering;
64　one male goat for a sin offering;
65　and for the sacrifice of peace offerings, two oxen, five rams, five male goats, five male lambs one year old. This *was* the offering of Abidan the son of Gideoni.

11. *Ahiezer of Dan*

66　On the tenth day *it was* Ahiezer the son of Ammishaddai, leader of the sons of Dan;
67　his offering *was* one silver dish whose weight *was* one hundred and thirty *shekels*, one silver bowl of seventy shekels, according to the shekel of the sanctuary, both of them full of fine flour mixed with oil for a grain offering;
68　one gold pan of ten *shekels*, full of incense;
69　one bull, one ram, one male lamb one year old, for a burnt offering;

7:40
v. 34

7:42
Num 1:14
[Reuel]

7:46
v. 34

7:48
Num 1:10

7:52
Heb 10:4

7:54
Num 1:10

7:58
v. 52

7:60
Num 1:11

7:64
v. 52

7:66
Num 1:12

7:70
Heb 10:4

70   one male goat for a sin offering;

71   and for the sacrifice of peace offerings, two oxen, five rams, five male goats, five male lambs one year old. This *was* the offering of Ahiezer the son of Ammishaddai.

12. *Pagiel of Asher*

7:72
Num 1:13

72   On the eleventh day *it was* Pagiel the son of Ochran, leader of the sons of Asher;

73   his offering *was* one silver dish whose weight *was* one hundred and thirty *shekels*, one silver bowl of seventy shekels, according to the shekel of the sanctuary, both of them full of fine flour mixed with oil for a grain offering;

74   one gold pan of ten *shekels*, full of incense;

75   one bull, one ram, one male lamb one year old, for a burnt offering;

7:76
v. 70

76   one male goat for a sin offering;

77   and for the sacrifice of peace offerings, two oxen, five rams, five male goats, five male lambs one year old. This *was* the offering of Pagiel the son of Ochran.

13. *Ahira of Naphtali*

7:78
Num 1:15

78   On the twelfth day *it was* Ahira the son of Enan, leader of the sons of Naphtali;

79   his offering *was* one silver dish whose weight *was* one hundred and thirty *shekels*, one silver bowl of seventy shekels, according to the shekel of the sanctuary, both of them full of fine flour mixed with oil for a grain offering;

80   one gold pan of ten *shekels*, full of incense;

81   one bull, one ram, one male lamb one year old, for a burnt offering;

7:82
v. 70

82   one male goat for a sin offering;

83   and for the sacrifice of peace offerings, two oxen, five rams, five male goats, five male lambs one year old. This *was* the offering of Ahira the son of Enan.

7:84
vv. 1,10

84   This *was* the dedication *offering* for the altar from the leaders of Israel when it was anointed: twelve silver dishes, twelve silver bowls, twelve gold pans,

85   each silver dish *weighing* one hundred and thirty *shekels* and each bowl seventy; all the silver of the utensils *was* 2,400 *shekels*, according to the shekel of the sanctuary;

86   the twelve gold pans, full of incense, *weighing* ten *shekels* apiece, according to the shekel of the sanctuary, all the gold of the pans 120 *shekels;*

7:87
Gen 8:20

87   all the oxen for the burnt offering twelve bulls, *all* the rams twelve, the male lambs one year old with their grain offering twelve, and the male goats for a sin offering twelve;

88   and all the oxen for the sacrifice of peace offerings 24 bulls, *all* the rams 60, the male goats 60, the male lambs one year old 60. This *was* the dedication *offering* for the altar after it was anointed.

14. *The voice from above the mercy seat*

*7:89
Ex 33:9,11;
25:21,22

89   Now when Moses went into the tent of meeting to speak with Him, he heard the voice speaking to him from above the mercy seat that was on the ark of the testimony, from between the two cherubim, so He spoke to him.

F. *Final details before the march*

1. *The lampstand*

8:2
Ex 25:37;
Lev 24:2,4

8 Then the LORD spoke to Moses, saying,

2   "Speak to Aaron and say to him, 'When you mount the lamps, the seven lamps will give light in the front of the lampstand.' "

3   Aaron therefore did so; he mounted its lamps at the front of the lampstand, just as the LORD had commanded Moses.

8:4
Ex 25:31-40;
25:18

4   Now this was the workmanship of the lampstand, hammered work of gold; from its base to its flowers, it was hammered work; according to the pattern which the LORD had showed Moses, so he made the lampstand.

2. *Purification of the Levites*

5   Again the LORD spoke to Moses, saying,

7:89 *heard the voice*, see note to Ex. 25:22.

6 "Take the Levites from among the sons of Israel and cleanse them.

7 "And thus you shall do to them, for their cleansing: *sprinkle* purifying water on them, and let them use a razor over their whole body, and wash their clothes, and they shall be clean.

8 "Then let them take a bull with its grain offering, fine flour mixed with oil; and a second bull you shall take for a sin offering.

9 "So you shall present the Levites before the tent of meeting. You shall also assemble the whole congregation of the sons of Israel,

10 and present the Levites before the LORD; and the sons of Israel shall lay their hands on the Levites.

11 "Aaron then shall present the Levites before the LORD as a wave offering from the sons of Israel, that they may qualify to perform the service of the LORD.

12 "Now the Levites shall lay their hands on the heads of the bulls; then offer the one for a sin offering and the other for a burnt offering to the LORD, to make atonement for the Levites.

13 "And you shall have the Levites stand before Aaron and before his sons so as to present them as a wave offering to the LORD.

14 "Thus you shall separate the Levites from among the sons of Israel, and the Levites shall be Mine.

15 "Then after that the Levites may go in to serve the tent of meeting. But you shall cleanse them and present them as a wave offering;

16 for they are wholly given to Me from among the sons of Israel. I have taken them for Myself instead of every first issue of the womb, the first-born of all the sons of Israel.

17 "For every first-born among the sons of Israel is Mine, among the men and among the animals; on the day that I struck down all the first-born in the land of Egypt I sanctified them for Myself.

18 "But I have taken the Levites instead of every first-born among the sons of Israel.

19 "And I have given the Levites as a gift to Aaron and to his sons from among the sons of Israel, to perform the service of the sons of Israel at the tent of meeting, and to make atonement on behalf of the sons of Israel, that there may be no plague among the sons of Israel by their coming near to the sanctuary."

20 Thus did Moses and Aaron and all the congregation of the sons of Israel to the Levites; according to all that the LORD had commanded Moses concerning the Levites, so the sons of Israel did to them.

21 The Levites, too, purified themselves from sin and washed their clothes; and Aaron presented them as a wave offering before the LORD. Aaron also made atonement for them to cleanse them.

22 Then after that the Levites went in to perform their service in the tent of meeting before Aaron and before his sons; just as the LORD had commanded Moses concerning the Levites, so they did to them.

3. Age of service for the Levites

23 Now the LORD spoke to Moses, saying,

24 "This is what *applies* to the Levites: from twenty-five years old and upward they shall enter to perform service in the work of the tent of meeting.

25 "But at the age of fifty years they shall retire from service in the work and not work any more.

26 "They may, however, assist their brothers in the tent of meeting, to keep an obligation; but they *themselves* shall do no work. Thus you shall deal with the Levites concerning their obligations."

4. The Passover command

9 Thus the LORD spoke to Moses in the wilderness of Sinai, in the first month of the second year after they had come out of the land of Egypt, saying,

2 "Now, let the sons of Israel observe the Passover at its appointed time.

3 "On the fourteenth day of this month, at twilight, you shall observe it at its appointed time; you shall observe it according to all its statutes and according to all its ordinances."

4 So Moses told the sons of Israel to observe the Passover.

8:9 See note to Ex. 27:21.

Marginal references:

8:7 Num 19:9,17, 18; Lev 14:8, 9; v. 21

8:8 Lev 2:1

*8:9 Lev 8:3

8:12 Ex 29:10

8:14 Num 3:12,45

8:15 vv. 11,13

8:16 Num 3:12,45

8:19 Num 1:53

8:21 vv. 7,11,12

8:24 Num 4:3

9:1 Num 1:1

9:2 Ex 12:6

5   And they observed the Passover in the first *month,* on the fourteenth day of the month, at twilight, in the wilderness of Sinai; according to all that the LORD had commanded Moses, so the sons of Israel did.

6   But there were *some* men who were unclean because of *the* dead person, so that they could not observe Passover on that day; so they came before Moses and Aaron on that day.

7   And those men said to him, "*Though* we are unclean because of *the* dead person, why are we restrained from presenting the offering of the LORD at its appointed time among the sons of Israel?"

8   Moses therefore said to them, "Wait, and I will listen to what the LORD will command concerning you."

9   Then the LORD spoke to Moses, saying,

10   "Speak to the sons of Israel, saying, 'If any one of you or of your generations becomes unclean because of a *dead* person, or is on a distant journey, he may, however, observe the Passover to the LORD.

11   'In the second month on the fourteenth day at twilight, they shall observe it; they shall eat it with unleavened bread and bitter herbs.

12   'They shall leave none of it until morning, nor break a bone of it; according to all the statute of the Passover they shall observe it.

13   'But the man who is clean and is not on a journey, and yet neglects to observe the Passover, that person shall then be cut off from his people, for he did not present the offering of the LORD at its appointed time. That man shall bear his sin.

14   'And if an alien sojourns among you and observes the Passover to the LORD, according to the statute of the Passover and according to its ordinance, so he shall do; you shall have one statute, both for the alien and for the native of the land.' "

5. *The cloud of guidance*

15   Now on the day that the tabernacle was erected the cloud covered the tabernacle, the tent of the testimony, and in the evening it was like the appearance of fire over the tabernacle, until morning.

16   So it was continuously; the cloud would cover it *by day,* and the appearance of fire by night.

17   And whenever the cloud was lifted from over the tent, afterward the sons of Israel would then set out; and in the place where the cloud settled down, there the sons of Israel would camp.

18   At the command of the LORD the sons of Israel would set out, and at the command of the LORD they would camp; as long as the cloud settled over the tabernacle, they remained camped.

19   Even when the cloud lingered over the tabernacle for many days, the sons of Israel would keep the LORD's charge and not set out.

20   If sometimes the cloud remained a few days over the tabernacle, according to the command of the LORD they remained camped. Then according to the command of the LORD they set out.

21   If sometimes the cloud remained from evening until morning, when the cloud was lifted in the morning, they would move out; or *if it remained* in the daytime and at night, whenever the cloud was lifted, they would set out.

22   Whether it was two days or a month or a year that the cloud lingered over the tabernacle, staying above it, the sons of Israel remained camped and did not set out; but when it was lifted, they did set out.

23   At the command of the LORD they camped, and at the command of the LORD they set out; they kept the LORD's charge, according to the command of the LORD through Moses.

6. *The two silver trumpets*

10   The LORD spoke further to Moses, saying,
2   "Make yourself two trumpets of silver, of hammered work you shall make them; and you shall use them for summoning the congregation and for having the camps set out.

3   "And when both are blown, all the congregation shall gather themselves to you at the doorway of the tent of meeting.

9:5
Josh 5:10

9:6
Num 19:11-22

9:8
Ex 18:15;
Num 27:5

9:11
Ex 12:8

9:12
Ex 12:10,43,
46;
John 19:36

9:13
v. 7; Ex 12:15

9:14
Ex 12:48,49

9:15
Ex 40:34;
Neh 9:12,19;
Ps 78:4;
Ex 13:21;
40:38

9:17
Num 10:11,
12;
Ex 40:36-38

9:18
1 Cor 10:1

9:19
Num 1:53;
3:8

9:22
Ex 40:36,37

10:3
Jer 4:5

9:10,11 Special provision was made for those who, for some reason, did not observe the regular Passover so that they could keep it a month later.

4 "Yet if *only* one is blown, then the leaders, the heads of the divisions of Israel, shall assemble before you.

5 "But when you blow an alarm, the camps that are pitched on the east side shall set out.

6 "And when you blow an alarm the second time, the camps that are pitched on the south side shall set out; an alarm is to be blown for them to set out.

7 "When convening the assembly, however, you shall blow without sounding an alarm.

8 "The priestly sons of Aaron, moreover, shall blow the trumpets; and this shall be for you a perpetual statute throughout your generations.

9 "And when you go to war in your land against the adversary who attacks you, then you shall sound an alarm with the trumpets, that you may be remembered before the LORD your God, and be saved from your enemies.

10 "Also in the day of your gladness and in your appointed feasts, and on the first *days* of your months, you shall blow the trumpets over your burnt offerings, and over the sacrifices of your peace offerings; and they shall be as a reminder of you before your God. I am the LORD your God."

II. The journey from Sinai to Moab (10:11–21:35)

A. The departure

1. The order of march

11 Now it came about in the second year, in the second month, on the twentieth of the month, that the cloud was lifted from over the tabernacle of the testimony;

12 and the sons of Israel set out on their journeys from the wilderness of Sinai. Then the cloud settled down in the wilderness of Paran.

13 So they moved out for the first time according to the commandment of the LORD through Moses.

14 And the standard of the camp of the sons of Judah, according to their armies, set out first, with Nahshon the son of Amminadab, over its army,

15 and Nethanel the son of Zuar, over the tribal army of the sons of Issachar;

16 and Eliab the son of Helon over the tribal army of the sons of Zebulun.

17 Then the tabernacle was taken down; and the sons of Gershon and the sons of Merari, who were carrying the tabernacle, set out.

18 Next the standard of the camp of Reuben, according to their armies, set out with Elizur the son of Shedeur, over its army,

19 and Shelumiel the son of Zurishaddai over the tribal army of the sons of Simeon,

20 and Eliasaph the son of Deuel was over the tribal army of the sons of Gad.

21 Then the Kohathites set out, carrying the holy *objects;* and the tabernacle was set up before their arrival.

22 Next the standard of the camp of the sons of Ephraim, according to their armies, was set out, with Elishama the son of Ammihud over its army,

23 and Gamaliel the son of Pedahzur over the tribal army of the sons of Manasseh;

24 and Abidan the son of Gideoni over the tribal army of the sons of Benjamin.

25 Then the standard of the camp of the sons of Dan, according to their armies, *which formed* the rear guard for all the camps, set out, with Ahiezer the son of Ammishaddai over its army,

26 and Pagiel the son of Ochran over the tribal army of the sons of Asher;

27 and Ahira the son of Enan over the tribal army of the sons of Naphtali.

28 This was the order of march of the sons of Israel by their armies as they set out.

2. The appeal to Hobab

29 Then Moses said to Hobab the son of Reuel the Midianite, Moses'

10:5
v. 14

10:6
v. 18

10:8
Num 31:6

10:9
Num 31:6;
Judg 2:18;
Ps 106:4

***10:10**
Num 29:1;
Lev 23:24;
Ps 81:3-5

10:11
Num 9:17

10:13
Deut 1:6

10:14
Num 2:3-9

10:17
Num 4:21-32

10:18
Num 2:10-16

10:21
Num 4:4-20

10:22
Num 2:18-24

10:25
Num 2:25-31;
Josh 6:9,13

10:29
Judg 4:11;

10:10 The Feast of the New Moon was held on the first day of the month. In celebration of it, sacrifices were to be offered (28:11–15), and the priestly trumpets were to be blown (10:10; Ps. 81:3,4). God condemned the keeping of this feast (as well as all the others) when it was simply an insincere, formal observance (Is. 1:13,14). The feast re- quired a cessation from all business and work, which made it irksome to the ungodly (Amos 8:5). New Testament believers, of course, are not expected to keep feasts that have been abolished by the perfect sacrifice of Christ (Gal. 4:10,11; Col. 2:16).

Ex 2:18;
Gen 12:7;
32:12; Ex 3:8
father-in-law, "We are setting out to the place of which the LORD said, 'I will give it to you'; come with us and we will do you good, for the LORD has promised good concerning Israel."

30 But he said to him, "I will not come, but rather will go to my *own* land and relatives."

31 Then he said, "Please do not leave us, inasmuch as you know where we should camp in the wilderness, and you will be as eyes for us.

10:32
Ps 22:27-31;
Lev 19:34
32 "So it will be, if you go with us, it will come about that whatever good the LORD does for us, we will do for you."

3. *The ark and the cloud of guidance*

10:33
v. 11;
Deut 1:33;
Is 11:10
33 Thus they set out from the mount of the LORD three days' journey, with the ark of the covenant of the LORD journeying in front of them for the three days, to seek out a resting place for them.

10:34
Num 9:15-23
34 And the cloud of the LORD was over them by day, when they set out from the camp.

10:35
Ps 68:1,2;
Deut 7:10;
32:41
35 Then it came about when the ark set out that Moses said,
"Rise up, O LORD!
And let Thine enemies be scattered,
And let those who hate Thee flee [12]before Thee."

36 And when it came to rest, he said,
"Return Thou, O LORD,
To the myriad thousands of Israel."

B. *The sins of Israel*

1. *Complaining at Taberah*

11:1
Num 14:2;
16:11; 17:5;
16:35;
Lev 10:2
11:2
Num 21:7
11 Now the people became like those who complain of adversity in the hearing of the LORD; and when the LORD heard *it*, His anger was kindled, and the fire of the LORD burned among them and consumed *some* of the outskirts of the camp.

2 The people therefore cried out to Moses, and Moses prayed to the LORD, and the fire died out.

3 So the name of that place was called [13]Taberah, because the fire of the LORD burned among them.

2. *The cry for meat*

*11:4
Ex 12:38;
Ps 78:18;
1 Cor 10:6
11:5
Ex 16:3
11:6
Lev 21:5
4 And the rabble who were among them had greedy desires; and also the sons of Israel wept again and said, "Who will give us meat to eat?

5 "We remember the fish which we used to eat free in Egypt, the cucumbers and the melons and the leeks and the onions and the garlic,

6 but now our [14]appetite is gone. There is nothing at all to look at except this manna."

11:7
Ex 16:14,31
7 Now the manna was like coriander seed, and its appearance like that of bdellium.

8 The people would go about and gather *it* and grind *it* between two millstones or beat *it* in the mortar, and boil *it* in the pot and make cakes with it; and its taste was as the taste of cakes baked with oil.

11:9
Ex 16:13,14
9 And when the dew fell on the camp at night, the manna would fall with it.

3. *Moses' prayer for help*

11:10
Ps 78:21
10 Now Moses heard the people weeping throughout their families, each man at the doorway of his tent; and the anger of the LORD was kindled greatly, and Moses was displeased.

11 So Moses said to the LORD, "Why hast Thou [15]been so hard on Thy servant? And why have I not found favor in Thy sight, that Thou hast laid the burden of all this people on me?

11:12
Is 40:11;
49:23;
Gen 26:3;
Ex 13:5
12 "Was it I who conceived all this people? Was it I who brought them forth, that Thou shouldest say to me, 'Carry them in your bosom as a nurse carries a nursing infant, to the land which Thou didst swear to their fathers'?

---

[12]Or, *from Thy presence* [13]I.e., *burning* [14]Lit., *soul is dried up* [15]Lit., *dealt ill with*

10:31 *will be as eyes for us.* Hobab, Moses' brother-in-law, knew the region well and could serve as guide.

11:4 *rabble,* probably the non-Israelites referred to in Ex. 12:38 as the *mixed multitude.*

13 "Where am I to get meat to give to all this people? For they weep before me, saying, 'Give us meat that we may eat!'

14 "I alone am not able to carry all this people, because it is too burdensome for me.

15 "So if Thou art going to deal thus with me, please kill me at once, if I have found favor in Thy sight, and do not let me see my wretchedness."

4. God's reply to Moses:
the appointment of the seventy elders

16 The LORD therefore said to Moses, "Gather for Me seventy men from the elders of Israel, whom you know to be the elders of the people and their officers and bring them to the tent of meeting, and let them take their stand there with you.

17 "Then I will come down and speak with you there, and I will take of the Spirit who is upon you, and will put *Him* upon them; and they shall bear the burden of the people with you, so that you shall not bear *it* all alone.

18 "And say to the people, 'Consecrate yourselves for tomorrow, and you shall eat meat; for you have wept in the ears of the LORD, saying, "Oh that someone would give us meat to eat! For we were well-off in Egypt." Therefore the LORD will give you meat and you shall eat.

19 'You shall eat, not one day, nor two days, nor five days, nor ten days, nor twenty days,

20 but a whole month, until it comes out of your nostrils and becomes loathsome to you; because you have rejected the LORD who is among you and have wept before Him, saying, "Why did we ever leave Egypt?" ' "

21 But Moses said, "The people, among whom I am, are 600,000 on foot; yet Thou hast said, 'I will give them meat in order that they may eat for a whole month.'

22 "Should flocks and herds be slaughtered for them, to be sufficient for them? Or should all the fish of the sea be gathered together for them, to be sufficient for them?"

23 And the LORD said to Moses, "Is the LORD's power limited? Now you shall see whether My word will come true for you or not."

24 So Moses went out and told the people the words of the LORD. Also, he gathered seventy men of the elders of the people, and stationed them around the tent.

25 Then the LORD came down in the cloud and spoke to him; and He took of the Spirit who was upon him and placed *Him* upon the seventy elders. And it came about that when the Spirit rested upon them, they prophesied. But they did not do *it* again.

26 But two men had remained in the camp; the name of one was Eldad and the name of the other Medad. And the Spirit rested upon them (now they were among those who had been registered, but had not gone out to the tent), and they prophesied in the camp.

27 So a young man ran and told Moses and said, "Eldad and Medad are prophesying in the camp."

28 Then Joshua the son of Nun, the attendant of Moses from his youth, answered and said, "Moses, my lord, restrain them."

29 But Moses said to him, "Are you jealous for my sake? Would that all the LORD's people were prophets, that the LORD would put His Spirit upon them!"

30 Then Moses returned to the camp, *both* he and the elders of Israel.

5. God sends quail for meat

31 Now there went forth a wind from the LORD, and it brought quail from the sea, and let *them* fall beside the camp, about a day's journey on this side and a day's journey on the other side, all around the camp, and about two cubits *deep* on the surface of the ground.

32 And the people spent all day and all night and all the next day, and gathered the quail (he who gathered least gathered ten homers) and they spread *them* out for themselves all around the camp.

11:13
vv. 21,22;
John 6:5-9
11:14
Ex 18:18
11:15
1 Kin 19:4;
Jon 4:3
11:16
Ex 24:1,9;
Deut 16:18
11:17
v. 25;
Ex 19:20;
1 Sam 10:6;
2 Kin 2:15
11:18
Ex 19:10;
16:7; v. 5;
Acts 7:39
11:19
Ps 78:29;
106:15;
Num 21:5
11:22
Matt 15:33
11:23
Is 50:2; 59:1;
Num 23:19
11:24
v. 16
11:25
v. 17;
Num 12:5;
1 Sam 10:5,6,
10; Acts 2:17,
18
*11:26
1 Sam 10:6;
20:26
11:28
Mark 9:38-40
11:29
1 Cor 14:5
11:31
Ex 16:13;
Ps 78:26-28;
105:40

11:26 This display of sectarian spirit (for one Israelite conveyed to Moses the news that others were prophesying when he thought only Moses should do so) is suggestive of the incident recorded in Mark 9:38–41. There the disciples requested Jesus to forbid anyone to cast out demons in His name unless he belonged to the same group as the disciples. Sectarianism was an attitude condemned both by Moses and Jesus, and this condemnation should serve as a warning to believers today.

11:33
Ps 78:30,31;
106:15

11:34
Deut 9:22

11:35
Num 33:17

33   While the meat was still between their teeth, before it was chewed, the anger of the LORD was kindled against the people, and the LORD struck the people with a very severe plague.

34   So the name of that place was called [16]Kibroth-hattaavah, because there they buried the people who had been greedy.

35   From Kibroth-hattaavah the people set out for Hazeroth, and they remained at Hazeroth.

C. Miriam and Aaron oppose Moses

1. God vindicates Moses

*12:1
Ex 2:21

12:2
Num 16:3

*12:3
Matt 11:29

12:5
Num 11:25;
16:19

12:6
Gen 46:2;
31:10,11;
1 Kin 3:5

*12:7
Ps 105:26;
Heb 3:2,5

12:8
Ex 33:11;
Deut 34:10;
Ex 33:19

12 Then Miriam and Aaron spoke against Moses because of the Cushite woman whom he had married (for he had married a Cushite woman);

2   and they said, "Has the LORD indeed spoken only through Moses? Has He not spoken through us as well?" And the LORD heard it.

3   (Now the man Moses was very humble, more than any man who was on the face of the earth.)

4   And suddenly the LORD said to Moses and Aaron and to Miriam, "You three come out to the tent of meeting." So the three of them came out.

5   Then the LORD came down in a pillar of cloud and stood at the doorway of the tent, and He called Aaron and Miriam. When they had both come forward,

6   He said,
"Hear now My words:
If there is a prophet among you,
I, the LORD, shall make Myself known to him in a vision.
I shall speak with him in a dream.

7   "Not so, with My servant Moses,
He is faithful in all My household;

8   With him I speak mouth to mouth,
Even openly, and not in dark sayings,
And he beholds the form of the LORD.
Why then were you not afraid
To speak against My servant, against Moses?"

2. Miriam becomes a leper; Moses prays for her healing

12:10
Deut 24:9;
2 Kin 5:27;
15:5

12:11
2 Sam 19:19;
24:10

12:14
Lev 13:46;
Num 5:2,3

9   So the anger of the LORD burned against them and He departed.

10   But when the cloud had withdrawn from over the tent, behold, Miriam *was* leprous, as *white as* snow. As Aaron turned toward Miriam, behold, she *was* leprous.

11   Then Aaron said to Moses, "Oh, my lord, I beg you, do not account *this* sin to us, in which we have acted foolishly and in which we have sinned.

12   "Oh, do not let her be like one dead, whose flesh is half eaten away when he comes from his mother's womb!"

13   And Moses cried out to the LORD, saying, "O God, heal her, I pray!"

14   But the LORD said to Moses, "If her father had but spit in her face, would she not bear her shame for seven days? Let her be shut up for seven days outside the camp, and afterward she may be received again."

15   So Miriam was shut up outside the camp for seven days, and the people did not move on until Miriam was received again.

16   Afterward, however, the people moved out from Hazeroth and camped in the wilderness of Paran.

[16]i.e., the graves of greediness

12:1 *Cushite woman*, generally considered to be an Ethiopian. Whether she was black is debatable. In any case, it was the authority of Moses, not his wife, that was at stake in this incident.
12:3 Some believe that this verse was the work of a later editor.
12:7 Moses was in many respects a type of Christ. (1) He was God's chosen deliverer (Ex. 3:1–10; Acts 7:25); (2) he was a prophet (Deut. 18:15; Acts 3:20–22); (3) he was a faithful servant in God's spiritual house (12:7; Heb. 3:2–6), although Christ had status as the divine Son, whereas Moses was but a human servant; and (4) Moses was an earnest advocate and intercessor for Israel even as Christ is for His church (Ex. 17:1–7; 32:30–35; Heb. 7:25; 1 John 2:1,2).

D. *The twelve spies*

1. *The spies chosen*

13 Then the LORD spoke to Moses saying,
2 "Send out for yourself men so that they may spy out the land of Canaan, which I am going to give to the sons of Israel; you shall send a man from each of their fathers' tribes, every one a leader among them."
3 So Moses sent them from the wilderness of Paran at the command of the LORD, all of them men who were heads of the sons of Israel.
4 These then *were* their names: from the tribe of Reuben, Shammua the son of Zaccur;
5 from the tribe of Simeon, Shaphat the son of Hori;
6 from the tribe of Judah, Caleb the son of Jephunneh;
7 from the tribe of Issachar, Igal the son of Joseph;
8 from the tribe of Ephraim, Hoshea the son of Nun;
9 from the tribe of Benjamin, Palti the son of Raphu;
10 from the tribe of Zebulun, Gaddiel the son of Sodi;
11 from the tribe of Joseph, from the tribe of Manasseh, Gaddi the son of Susi;
12 from the tribe of Dan, Ammiel the son of Gemalli;
13 from the tribe of Asher, Sethur the son of Michael;
14 from the tribe of Naphtali, Nahbi the son of Vophsi;
15 from the tribe of Gad, Geuel the son of Machi.
16 These are the names of the men whom Moses sent to spy out the land; but Moses called Hoshea the son of Nun, Joshua.

2. *The spies sent out*

17 When Moses sent them to spy out the land of Canaan, he said to them, "Go up there into the ¹⁷Negev; then go up into the hill country.
18 "And see what the land is like, and whether the people who live in it are strong *or* weak, whether they are few or many.
19 "And how is the land in which they live, is it good or bad? And how are the cities in which they live, are *they* like *open* camps or with fortifications?
20 "And how is the land, is it fat or lean? Are there trees in it or not? Make an effort then to get some of the fruit of the land." Now the time was the time of the first ripe grapes.
21 So they went up and spied out the land from the wilderness of Zin as far as Rehob, at Lebo-hamath.
22 When they had gone up into the Negev, they came to Hebron where Ahiman, Sheshai and Talmai, the descendants of Anak were. (Now Hebron was built seven years before Zoan in Egypt.)
23 Then they came to the valley of ¹⁸Eshcol and from there cut down a branch with a single cluster of grapes; and they carried it on a pole between two *men*, with some of the pomegranates and the figs.
24 That place was called the valley of Eshcol, because of the cluster which the sons of Israel cut down from there.

3. *The adverse report of the majority*

25 When they returned from spying out the land, at the end of forty days,
26 they proceeded to come to Moses and Aaron and to all the congregation of

Side references:
*13:2 Deut 1:22
13:8 v. 16
13:16 v. 8
*13:17 v. 21
13:20 Deut 1:24,25; 31:6,23
*13:22 Josh 15:13,14; vv. 28,33; Ps 78:12
*13:26 v. 3; Num 20:1,16; 32:8

---

¹⁷I.e., South country, and so throughout this context   ¹⁸I.e., cluster

13:2 *men.* These were the "secret scouts."
13:17 *Negev . . . hill country.* The direct route to Canaan led northeast from Kadesh along some water stations in the Negev (meaning "parched") up to Hebron in the hill country. Abraham and Jacob probably used this route going down to Egypt.
13:22 *Zoan,* also known as "Avaris" or "Tanis," was built about 1700 B.C. in the Nile delta by the Hyksos. Just seven years previously, Hebron was built at the place known to Abraham as Kiriath-arba or Mamre (Gen. 23:2,19). The *field of Zoan* (Ps. 78:12,43) refers to Goshen, where the Israelites dwelt.
13:26 All during the exodus journey, Israel constantly fell into discontent, rebellion, and unbelief. Here at Kadesh this rebelliousness came to a head. God had miraculously

delivered Israel from Egypt, preserved them from the attack of the pharaoh, opened the passage across the sea, fed them with manna and protected them against their foes. And now, after all these demonstrations of God's faithfulness, Israel proved ready to lend credence to the adverse report of the ten spies more than to the God-honoring testimony of Joshua and Caleb. They walked by sight rather than by faith. Hence the report that magnified the difficulties in the way of conquest plunged them into despair and disbelief in the promises of God. Outward circumstances rather than a trust in God's faithfulness resulted in their shameful failure to enter the land by faith. Such unbelief could only be dealt with by discipline, if the nation was ever to be educated for its task of conquest and of possessing the promised land in the name of the Lord. The forty years of

the sons of Israel in the wilderness of Paran, at Kadesh; and they brought back word to them and to all the congregation and showed them the fruit of the land.

27   Thus they told him, and said, "We went in to the land where you sent us; and it certainly does flow with milk and honey, and this is its fruit.

28   "Nevertheless, the people who live in the land are strong, and the cities are fortified *and* very large; and moreover, we saw the descendants of Anak there.

29   "Amalek is living in the land of the Negev and the Hittites and the Jebusites and the Amorites are living in the hill country, and the Canaanites are living by the sea and by the side of the Jordan."

30   Then Caleb quieted the people before Moses, and said, "We should by all means go up and take possession of it, for we shall surely overcome it."

31   But the men who had gone up with him said, "We are not able to go up against the people, for they are too strong for us."

32   So they gave out to the sons of Israel a bad report of the land which they had spied out, saying, "The land through which we have gone, in spying it out, is a land that devours its inhabitants; and all the people whom we saw in it are men of *great* size.

33   "There also we saw the Nephilim (the sons of Anak are part of the Nephilim); and we became like grasshoppers in our own sight, and so we were in their sight."

4. The rebellion of Israel

a. *Their murmuring*

14 Then all the congregation lifted up their voices and cried, and the people wept that night.

2   And all the sons of Israel grumbled against Moses and Aaron; and the whole congregation said to them, "Would that we had died in the land of Egypt! Or would that we had died in this wilderness!

3   "And why is the LORD bringing us into this land, to fall by the sword? Our wives and our little ones will become plunder; would it not be better for us to return to Egypt?"

b. *The plea of Joshua and Caleb*

4   So they said to one another, "Let us appoint a leader and return to Egypt."

5   Then Moses and Aaron fell on their faces in the presence of all the assembly of the congregation of the sons of Israel.

6   And Joshua the son of Nun and Caleb the son of Jephunneh, of those who had spied out the land, tore their clothes;

7   and they spoke to all the congregation of the sons of Israel, saying, "The land which we passed through to spy out is an exceedingly good land.

8   "If the LORD is pleased with us, then He will bring us into this land, and give it to us—a land which flows with milk and honey.

9   "Only do not rebel against the LORD; and do not fear the people of the land, for they shall be our prey. Their protection has been removed from them, and the LORD is with us; do not fear them."

10   But all the congregation said to stone them with stones. Then the glory of the LORD appeared in the tent of meeting to all the sons of Israel.

c. *The anger of God*

11   And the LORD said to Moses, "How long will this people spurn Me? And how long will they not believe in Me, despite all the signs which I have performed in their midst?

12   "I will smite them with pestilence and dispossess them, and I will make you into a nation greater and mightier than they."

d. *Moses intercedes for the people*

13   But Moses said to the LORD, "Then the Egyptians will hear of it, for by Thy strength Thou didst bring up this people from their midst,

14   and they will tell *it* to the inhabitants of this land. They have heard that Thou, O LORD, art in the midst of this people, for Thou, O LORD, art seen eye to

---

13:27
Ex 3:8;
Deut 1:25
*13:28
Deut 1:28

13:29
Num 14:43

13:30
Num 14:6,24

13:31
Deut 1:28

13:32
Num 14:36;
Ps 106:24;
Amos 2:9

13:33
Deut 1:28;
9:2

14:2
Num 11:1,5

14:5
Num 16:4,22

14:7
Num 13:27;
Deut 1:25
14:8
Deut 10:15;
Num 13:27
14:9
Deut 9:7,23,
24; 7:18;
20:1,3,4

14:10
Ex 17:4;
16:10;
Lev 9:23

14:11
Deut 9:7,8;
Ps 78:22;
106:24
14:12
Ex 32:10

14:13
Ps 106:23

14:14
Ex 15:14;

---

wandering in the wilderness would give time for the old, craven-hearted generation to die off and for a new generation, reared in freedom rather than slavery, to fulfill Israel's destiny. Only Caleb and Joshua would remain to lead them in and to serve as a testimony of God's faithfulness to those who sincerely trust Him.
13:28 *fortified.* Some Canaanite cities had walls 12 to 15 feet thick and 30 to 50 feet high.

eye, while Thy cloud stands over them; and Thou dost go before them in a pillar of cloud by day and in a pillar of fire by night.

15 "Now if Thou dost slay this people as one man, then the nations who have heard of Thy fame will say,

16 'Because the LORD could not bring this people into the land which He promised them by oath, therefore He slaughtered them in the wilderness.'

17 "But now, I pray, let the power of the Lord be great, just as Thou hast declared,

18 'The LORD is slow to anger and abundant in lovingkindness, forgiving iniquity and transgression; but He will by no means clear *the guilty,* visiting the iniquity of the fathers on the children to the third and the fourth *generations.'*

19 "Pardon, I pray, the iniquity of this people according to the greatness of Thy lovingkindness, just as Thou also hast forgiven this people, from Egypt even until now."

e. God pronounces judgment on Israel for unbelief

20 So the LORD said, "I have pardoned *them* according to your word;

21 but indeed, as I live, all the earth will be filled with the glory of the LORD.

22 "Surely all the men who have seen My glory and My signs, which I performed in Egypt and in the wilderness, yet have put Me to the test these ten times and have not listened to My voice,

23 shall by no means see the land which I swore to their fathers, nor shall any of those who spurned Me see it.

24 "But My servant Caleb, because he has had a different spirit and has followed Me fully, I will bring into the land which he entered, and his descendants shall take possession of it.

25 "Now the Amalekites and the Canaanites live in the valleys; turn tomorrow and set out to the wilderness by the way of the Red Sea."

26 And the LORD spoke to Moses and Aaron, saying,

27 "How long *shall I bear* with this evil congregation who are grumbling against Me? I have heard the complaints of the sons of Israel, which they are making against Me.

28 "Say to them, 'As I live,' says the LORD, 'just as you have spoken in My hearing, so I will surely do to you;

29 your corpses shall fall in this wilderness, even all your numbered men, according to your complete number from twenty years old and upward, who have grumbled against Me.

30 'Surely you shall not come into the land in which I swore to settle you, except Caleb the son of Jephunneh and Joshua the son of Nun.

31 'Your children, however, whom you said would become a prey—I will bring them in, and they shall know the land which you have rejected.

32 'But as for you, your corpses shall fall in this wilderness.

33 'And your sons shall be shepherds for forty years in the wilderness, and they shall suffer *for* your unfaithfulness, until your corpses lie in the wilderness.

34 'According to the number of days which you spied out the land, forty days, for every day you shall bear your guilt a year, *even* forty years, and you shall know My opposition.

35 'I, the LORD, have spoken, surely this I will do to all this evil congregation who are gathered together against Me. In this wilderness they shall be destroyed, and there they shall die.' "

36 As for the men whom Moses sent to spy out the land and who returned and made all the congregation grumble against him by bringing out a bad report concerning the land,

37 even those men who brought out the very bad report of the land died by a plague before the LORD.

38 But Joshua the son of Nun and Caleb the son of Jephunneh remained alive out of those men who went to spy out the land.

f. Israel's defeat by the Amalekites and Canaanites

39 And when Moses spoke these words to all the sons of Israel, the people mourned greatly.

40 In the morning, however, they rose up early and went up to the ridge of the hill country, saying, "Here we are; we have indeed sinned, but we will go up to the place which the LORD has promised."

Josh 2:9,10;
Ex 13:21

14:16
Deut 9:28

14:18
Ex 34:6,7;
Ps 103:8;
Ex 20:5

14:19
Ex 34:9;
Ps 106:45;
78:38

14:20
Ps 106:23
14:21
Ps 72:19

14:24
vv. 7-9;
Num 32:12;
Josh 14:6-15

14:25
Deut 1:40

14:27
Num 11:1;
Ex 16:12

14:28
v. 21;
Deut 1:35;
see v. 2
14:29
Num 1:45;
26:64

14:30
v. 24;
Deut 1:36
14:31
Deut 1:39;
Ps 106:24
14:32
1 Cor 10:5
14:33
Num 32:13;
Ps 107:40
14:34
Num 13:25;
Ps 95:10

14:35
Num 23:19;
26:65

14:36
Num 13:4-16,
32

14:38
Josh 14:6

14:39
Ex 33:4

14:40
Deut 1:41

41 But Moses said, "Why then are you transgressing the commandment of the LORD, when it will not succeed?

42 "Do not go up, lest you be struck down before your enemies, for the LORD is not among you.

43 "For the Amalekites and the Canaanites will be there in front of you, and you will fall by the sword, inasmuch as you have turned back from following the LORD. And the LORD will not be with you."

44 But they went up heedlessly to the ridge of the hill country; neither the ark of the covenant of the LORD nor Moses left the camp.

45 Then the Amalekites and the Canaanites who lived in that hill country came down, and struck them and beat them down as far as Hormah.

E. Additional laws and regulations

1. Grain offerings

15 Now the LORD spoke to Moses, saying,
2 "Speak to the sons of Israel, and say to them, 'When you enter the land where you are to live, which I am giving you,

3 then make an offering by fire to the LORD, a burnt offering or a sacrifice to fulfill a special vow, or as a freewill offering or in your appointed times, to make a soothing aroma to the LORD, from the herd or from the flock.

4 'And the one who presents his offering shall present to the LORD a grain offering of one-tenth *of an ephah* of fine flour mixed with one-fourth of a [19]hin of oil,

5 and you shall prepare wine for the libation, one-fourth of a hin, with the burnt offering or for the sacrifice, for each lamb.

6 'Or for a ram you shall prepare as a grain offering two-tenths *of an ephah* of fine flour mixed with one-third of a hin of oil;

7 and for the libation you shall offer one-third of a hin of wine as a soothing aroma to the LORD.

8 'And when you prepare a bull as a burnt offering or a sacrifice, to fulfill a special vow, or for peace offerings to the LORD,

9 then you shall offer with the bull a grain offering of three-tenths *of an ephah* of fine flour mixed with one-half a hin of oil;

10 and you shall offer as the libation one-half a hin of wine as an offering by fire, as a soothing aroma to the LORD.

11 'Thus it shall be done for each ox, or for each ram, or for each of the male lambs, or of the goats.

12 'According to the number that you prepare, so you shall do for everyone according to their number.

13 'All who are native shall do these things in this manner, in presenting an offering by fire, as a soothing aroma to the LORD.

14 'And if an alien sojourns with you, or one who may be among you throughout your generations, and he *wishes to* make an offering by fire, as a soothing aroma to the LORD, just as you do, so he shall do.

15 'As for the assembly, there shall be one statute for you and for the alien who sojourns *with you*, a perpetual statute throughout your generations; as you are, so shall the alien be before the LORD.

16 'There is to be one law and one ordinance for you and for the alien who sojourns with you.' "

2. The coarse meal offering

17 Then the LORD spoke to Moses, saying,

18 "Speak to the sons of Israel, and say to them, 'When you enter the land where I bring you,

19 then it shall be, that when you eat of the food of the land, you shall lift up an offering to the LORD.

[19]I.e., Approx. one gallon, and so through v. 10

15:2 Unbelief at Kadesh did not result in a permanent denial of entrance into the promised land but only a delay. The instructions given by God for offerings in the land were intended to reassure Israel that they would enter the land despite the punishment for their disobedience. For the believer, this incident is illustrative of the truth that sin breaks fellowship and results in chastening but God stands ready to forgive.

20 'Of the first of your [20]dough you shall lift up a cake as an offering; as the offering of the threshing floor, so you shall lift it up.

21 'From the first of your [20]dough you shall give to the LORD an offering throughout your generations.

3. Offering for sins done ignorantly

22 'But when you unwittingly fail and do not observe all these commandments, which the LORD has spoken to Moses,

23 even all that the LORD has commanded you through Moses, from the day when the LORD gave commandment and onward throughout your generations,

24 then it shall be, if it is done unintentionally, without the knowledge of the congregation, that all the congregation shall offer one bull for a burnt offering, as a soothing aroma to the LORD, with its grain offering, and its libation, according to the ordinance, and one male goat for a sin offering.

25 'Then the priest shall make atonement for all the congregation of the sons of Israel, and they shall be forgiven; for it was an error, and they have brought their offering, an offering by fire to the LORD, and their sin offering before the LORD, for their error.

26 'So all the congregation of the sons of Israel will be forgiven, with the alien who sojourns among them, for it happened to all the people through error.

27 'Also if one person sins unintentionally, then he shall offer a one year old female goat for a sin offering.

28 'And the priest shall make atonement before the LORD for the person who goes astray when he sins unintentionally, making atonement for him that he may be forgiven.

29 'You shall have one law for him who does anything unintentionally, for him who is native among the sons of Israel and for the alien who sojourns among them.

30 'But the person who does anything defiantly, whether he is native or an alien, that one is blaspheming the LORD; and that person shall be cut off from among his people.

31 'Because he has despised the word of the LORD and has broken His commandment, that person shall be completely cut off; his guilt shall be on him.' "

4. Stoning of Sabbath breakers

32 Now while the sons of Israel were in the wilderness, they found a man gathering wood on the sabbath day.

33 And those who found him gathering wood brought him to Moses and Aaron, and to all the congregation;

34 and they put him in custody because it had not been declared what should be done to him.

35 Then the LORD said to Moses, "The man shall surely be put to death; all the congregation shall stone him with stones outside the camp."

36 So all the congregation brought him outside the camp, and stoned him to death with stones, just as the LORD had commanded Moses.

5. The tassels of remembrance

37 The LORD also spoke to Moses, saying,

38 "Speak to the sons of Israel, and tell them that they shall make for themselves tassels on the corners of their garments throughout their generations, and that they shall put on the tassel of each corner a cord of blue.

39 "And it shall be a tassel for you to look at and remember all the commandments of the LORD, so as to do them and not follow after your own heart and your own eyes, after which you played the harlot,

40 in order that you may remember to do all My commandments, and be holy to your God.

41 "I am the LORD your God who brought you out from the land of Egypt to be your God; I am the LORD your God."

[20]Or, coarse meal

15:30 defiantly, see note to Lev. 4:2.   15:38 tassels, part of the praying mantle.

Cross references (right margin):

15:20 Deut 26:2,10; Lev 2:14

15:22 Lev 4:2

15:24 Lev 4:13; vv. 8-10

15:25 Lev 4:20

15:27 Lev 4:27,28

15:28 Lev 4:35

15:29 v. 15

15:31 2 Sam 12:9; Lev 5:1; Ezek 18:20

15:32 Ex 31:14,15; 35:2,3

15:34 Lev 24:12

15:35 Ex 31:14,15; Lev 24:14; Acts 7:58

*15:38 Deut 22:12; Matt 23:5

15:39 Deut 4:23; Ps 73:27

15:40 Lev 11:44; Rom 12:1; Col 1:22; 1 Pet 1:15,16

F. *The rebellion and death of Korah, Dathan, and Abiram*

1. *Korah's revolt*

*16:1
Ex 6:21;
Jude 11

16 Now Korah the son of Izhar, the son of Kohath, the son of Levi, with Dathan and Abiram, the sons of Eliab, and On the son of Peleth, sons of Reuben, took *action,*

16:2
Num 26:9

2   and they rose up before Moses, together with some of the sons of Israel, two hundred and fifty leaders of the congregation, chosen in the assembly, men of renown.

16:3
Ps 106:16;
Ex 19:6;
Num 14:14

3   And they assembled together against Moses and Aaron, and said to them, "You have gone far enough, for all the congregation are holy, every one of them, and the LORD is in their midst; so why do you exalt yourselves above the assembly of the LORD?"

16:4
Num 14:5
16:5
Lev 10:3;
Ps 65:4;
Num 17:5,8

4   When Moses heard *this,* he fell on his face;

5   and he spoke to Korah and all his company, saying, "Tomorrow morning the LORD will show who is His, and who is holy, and will bring *him* near to Himself; even the one whom He will choose, He will bring near to Himself.

6   "Do this: take censers for yourselves, Korah and all your company,

7   and put fire in them, and lay incense upon them in the presence of the LORD tomorrow; and the man whom the LORD chooses *shall be* the one who is holy. You have gone far enough, you sons of Levi!"

8   Then Moses said to Korah, "Hear now, you sons of Levi,

16:9
Num 3:6,9;
8:14;
Deut 10:8

9   is it not enough for you that the God of Israel has separated you from the *rest of* the congregation of Israel, to bring you near to Himself, to do the service of the tabernacle of the LORD, and to stand before the congregation to minister to them;

10   and that He has brought you near, *Korah,* and all your brothers, sons of Levi, with you? And are you seeking for the priesthood also?

16:11
Ex 16:7,8;
1 Cor 10:10

11   "Therefore you and all your company are gathered together against the LORD; but as for Aaron, who is he that you grumble against him?"

2. *The rebellion of Dathan and Abiram*

12   Then Moses sent a summons to Dathan and Abiram, the sons of Eliab; but they said, "We will not come up.

16:13
Num 11:4-6;
Ex 2:14;
Acts 7:27,35
16:14
Lev 20:24

13   "Is it not enough that you have brought us up out of a land flowing with milk and honey to have us die in the wilderness, but you would also lord it over us?

14   "Indeed, you have not brought us into a land flowing with milk and honey, nor have you given us an inheritance of fields and vineyards. Would you put out the eyes of these men? We will not come up!"

3. *The punishment of the rebels*

16:15
Gen 4:4,5;
1 Sam 12:3

15   Then Moses became very angry and said to the LORD, "Do not regard their offering! I have not taken a single donkey from them, nor have I done harm to any of them."

16:16
vv. 6,7

16   And Moses said to Korah, "You and all your company be present before the LORD tomorrow, both you and they along with Aaron.

17   "And each of you take his firepan and put incense on it, and each of you bring his censer before the LORD, two hundred and fifty firepans; also you and Aaron *shall* each *bring* his firepan."

18   So they each took his *own* censer and put fire on it, and laid incense on it; and they stood at the doorway of the tent of meeting, with Moses and Aaron.

16:19
v. 42;
Num 14:10;
Ex 16:7,10;
Lev 9:6,23
16:21
v. 45;
Ex 32:10,12
16:22
v. 45;
Num 14:5

19   Thus Korah assembled all the congregation against them at the doorway of the tent of meeting. And the glory of the LORD appeared to all the congregation.

20   Then the LORD spoke to Moses and Aaron, saying,

21   "Separate yourselves from among this congregation, that I may consume them instantly."

22   But they fell on their faces, and said, "O God, Thou God of the spirits of all flesh, when one man sins, wilt Thou be angry with the entire congregation?"

16:1 Korah's sin consisted in rebellion against God's authority to appoint as leaders men of His own choosing. It was a sizable revolt both in numbers and in the position of those who joined him. Specifically named with Korah are Dathan and Abiram, who were descendants of Reuben. Thus it involved an intrusion by non-Levites into the office for the Levites alone, although Korah himself was of the priestly tribe. God destroyed the guilty men and their families (except for the descendants of Korah—cf. 26:11), but the congregation of Israel accused Moses and Aaron of having killed the people of the Lord (v. 41). As a consequence God slew 14,700 more by a sudden plague (v. 49).

giving you the priesthood as a bestowed service, but the outsider who comes near shall be put to death."

2. The offerings that belong to the priests

8 Then the LORD spoke to Aaron, "Now behold, I Myself have given you charge of My offerings, even all the holy gifts of the sons of Israel, I have given them to you as a portion, and to your sons as a perpetual allotment.

9 "This shall be yours from the most holy *gifts, reserved* from the fire; every offering of theirs, even every grain offering and every sin offering and every guilt offering, which they shall render to Me, shall be most holy for you and for your sons.

10 "As the most holy *gifts* you shall eat it; every male shall eat it. It shall be holy to you.

11 "This also is yours, the offering of their gift, even all the wave offerings of the sons of Israel; I have given them to you and to your sons and daughters with you, as a perpetual allotment. Everyone of your household who is clean may eat it.

12 "All the best of the fresh oil and all the best of the fresh wine and of the grain, the first fruits of those which they give to the LORD, I give them to you.

13 "The first ripe fruits of all that is in their land, which they bring to the LORD, shall be yours; everyone of your household who is clean may eat it.

14 "Every devoted thing in Israel shall be yours.

15 "Every first issue of the womb of all flesh, whether man or animal, which they offer to the LORD, shall be yours; nevertheless the first-born of man you shall surely redeem, and the first-born of unclean animals you shall redeem.

16 "And as to their redemption price, from a month old you shall redeem them, by your valuation, five [21]shekels in silver, according to the shekel of the sanctuary, which is twenty gerahs.

17 "But the first-born of an ox or the first-born of a sheep or the first-born of a goat, you shall not redeem; they are holy. You shall sprinkle their blood on the altar and shall offer up their fat in smoke *as* an offering by fire, for a soothing aroma to the LORD.

18 "And their meat shall be yours; it shall be yours like the breast of a wave offering and like the right thigh.

19 "All the offerings of the holy *gifts,* which the sons of Israel offer to the LORD, I have given to you and your sons and your daughters with you, as a perpetual allotment. It is an everlasting covenant of salt before the LORD to you and your descendants with you."

20 Then the LORD said to Aaron, "You shall have no inheritance in their land, nor own any portion among them; I am your portion and your inheritance among the sons of Israel.

3. The tithe for the Levites

21 "And to the sons of Levi, behold, I have given all the tithe in Israel for an inheritance, in return for their service which they perform, the service of the tent of meeting.

22 "And the sons of Israel shall not come near the tent of meeting again, lest they bear sin and die.

23 "Only the Levites shall perform the service of the tent of meeting, and they shall bear their iniquity; it shall be a perpetual statute throughout your generations, and among the sons of Israel they shall have no inheritance.

24 "For the tithe of the sons of Israel, which they offer as an offering to the LORD, I have given to the Levites for an inheritance; therefore I have said concerning them, 'They shall have no inheritance among the sons of Israel.'"

4. The Levites' tithe of the tithe

25 Then the LORD spoke to Moses, saying,

26 "Moreover, you shall speak to the Levites and say to them, 'When you take from the sons of Israel the tithe which I have given you from them for your inheritance, then you shall present an offering from it to the LORD, a tithe of the tithe.

Heb 9:3,6

18:8
Lev 6:16,18;
7:6,32;
Ex 29:29;
40:13,15
18:9
Lev 2:2,3;
10:12,13;
6:25,26; 7:7

18:10
Lev 6:16,26

18:11
Ex 29:27,28;
Lev 22:1-16

18:12
Ex 23:19;
Deut 18:4;
Neh 10:35;
Ex 22:29
18:13
Ex 22:29;
23:19; 34:26
18:14
Lev 27:28
18:15
Ex 13:2;
Lev 27:26;
Ex 13:13
18:16
Lev 27:6

18:17
Lev 3:2,5

18:19
v. 11;
2 Chr 13:5

18:20
Deut 10:9;
12:12; 14:27,
29; 18:1,2;
Josh 13:33;
Ezek 44:28

18:21
Lev 27:30-33

18:22
Num 1:51

18:23
Num 3:7;
vv. 1,20

18:26
Neh 10:38

---

[21]I.e., A shekel equals approx. one-half ounce.

27 'And your offering shall be reckoned to you as the grain from the threshing floor or the full produce from the wine vat.

18:28
Ex 29:27

28 'So you shall also present an offering to the LORD from your tithes, which you receive from the sons of Israel; and from it you shall give the LORD's offering to Aaron the priest.

29 'Out of all your gifts you shall present every offering due to the LORD, from all the best of them, the sacred part from them.'

30 "And you shall say to them, 'When you have offered from it the best of it, then *the rest* shall be reckoned to the Levites as the product of the threshing floor, and as the product of the wine vat.

31 'And you may eat it anywhere, you and your households, for it is your compensation in return for your service in the tent of meeting.

18:32
Lev 19:8;
22:2,15,16

32 'And you shall bear no sin by reason of it, when you have offered the best of it. But you shall not profane the sacred gifts of the sons of Israel, lest you die.' "

H. *Purification of the unclean*

1. *The red heifer*

19:2
Deut 21:3

19 Then the LORD spoke to Moses and Aaron, saying,
2 "This is the statute of the law which the LORD has commanded, saying, 'Speak to the sons of Israel that they bring you an unblemished red heifer in which is no defect, *and* on which a yoke has never been placed.

19:3
Lev 4:12,21;
16:27
19:4
Lev 4:6;
Heb 9:13

3 'And you shall give it to Eleazar the priest, and it shall be brought outside the camp and be slaughtered in his presence.

4 'Next Eleazar the priest shall take some of its blood with his finger, and sprinkle some of its blood toward the front of the tent of meeting seven times.

5 'Then the heifer shall be burned in his sight; its hide and its flesh and its blood, with its refuse, shall be burned.

19:6
Lev 15:4,6,49

6 'And the priest shall take cedar wood and hyssop and scarlet *material*, and cast it into the midst of the burning heifer.

19:7
Lev 11:25;
16:26,28;
22:6

7 'The priest shall then wash his clothes and bathe his body in water, and afterward come into the camp, but the priest shall be unclean until evening.

8 'The one who burns it shall also wash his clothes in water and bathe his body in water, and shall be unclean until evening.

19:9
Heb 9:13;
vv. 13,20,21

9 'Now a man who is clean shall gather up the ashes of the heifer and deposit them outside the camp in a clean place, and the congregation of the sons of Israel shall keep it as water to remove impurity; it is purification from sin.

10 'And the one who gathers the ashes of the heifer shall wash his clothes and be unclean until evening; and it shall be a perpetual statute to the sons of Israel and to the alien who sojourns among them.

2. *Purification of uncleanness with water*

19:11
Num 5:2;
Lev 21:1;
Acts 21:26,27
19:12
v. 19;
Num 31:19

11 'The one who touches the corpse of any person shall be unclean for seven days.

12 'That one shall purify himself from uncleanness with the water on the third day and on the seventh day, *and then* he shall be clean; but if he does not purify himself on the third day and on the seventh day, he shall not be clean.

19:13
v. 20;
Lev 15:31;
v. 9;
Num 8:7;
Lev 7:20;
22:3

13 'Anyone who touches a corpse, the body of a man who has died, and does not purify himself, defiles the tabernacle of the LORD; and that person shall be cut off from Israel. Because the water for impurity was not sprinkled on him, he shall be unclean; his uncleanness is still on him.

14 'This is the law when a man dies in a tent: everyone who comes into the tent and everyone who is in the tent shall be unclean for seven days.

15 'And every open vessel, which has no covering tied down on it, shall be unclean.

19:16
v. 11

16 'Also, anyone who in the open field touches one who has been slain with a sword or who has died *naturally*, or a human bone or a grave, shall be unclean for seven days.

19:17
v. 9

17 'Then for the unclean *person* they shall take some of the ashes of the burnt purification from sin and flowing water shall be added to them in a vessel.

18 'And a clean person shall take hyssop and dip *it* in the water, and sprinkle *it* on the tent and on all the furnishings and on the persons who were there, and on the one who touched the bone or the one slain or the one dying *naturally* or the grave.

19 'Then the clean *person* shall sprinkle on the unclean on the third day and on the seventh day; and on the seventh day he shall purify him from uncleanness, and he shall wash his clothes and bathe *himself* in water and shall be clean by evening.

20 'But the man who is unclean and does not purify himself from uncleanness, that person shall be cut off from the midst of the assembly, because he has defiled the sanctuary of the LORD; the water for impurity has not been sprinkled on him, he is unclean.

21 'So it shall be a perpetual statute for them. And he who sprinkles the water for impurity shall wash his clothes, and he who touches the water for impurity shall be unclean until evening.

22 'Furthermore, anything that the unclean *person* touches shall be unclean; and the person who touches *it* shall be unclean until evening.' "

I. Incidents at Kadesh

1. The death of Miriam

20 Then the sons of Israel, the whole congregation, came to the wilderness of Zin in the first month; and the people stayed at Kadesh. Now Miriam died there and was buried there.

2. Water from the rock (Meribah)

2 And there was no water for the congregation; and they assembled themselves against Moses and Aaron.

3 The people thus contended with Moses and spoke, saying, "If only we had perished when our brothers perished before the LORD!

4 "Why then have you brought the LORD's assembly into this wilderness, for us and our beasts to die here?

5 "And why have you made us come up from Egypt, to bring us in to this wretched place? It is not a place of grain or figs or vines or pomegranates, nor is there water to drink."

6 Then Moses and Aaron came in from the presence of the assembly to the doorway of the tent of meeting, and fell on their faces. Then the glory of the LORD appeared to them;

7 and the LORD spoke to Moses, saying,

8 "Take the rod; and you and your brother Aaron assemble the congregation and speak to the rock before their eyes, that it may yield its water. You shall thus bring forth water for them out of the rock and let the congregation and their beasts drink."

9 So Moses took the rod from before the LORD, just as He had commanded him;

3. The sin of Moses: his exclusion from Canaan

10 and Moses and Aaron gathered the assembly before the rock. And he said to them, "Listen now, you rebels; shall we bring forth water for you out of this rock?"

11 Then Moses lifted up his hand and struck the rock twice with his rod; and water came forth abundantly, and the congregation and their beasts drank.

12 But the LORD said to Moses and Aaron, "Because you have not believed Me, to treat Me as holy in the sight of the sons of Israel, therefore you shall not bring this assembly into the land which I have given them."

13 Those *were* the waters of ²²Meribah, because the sons of Israel contended with the LORD, and He proved Himself holy among them.

4. Israel refused passage through Edom

14 From Kadesh Moses then sent messengers to the king of Edom: "Thus your brother Israel has said, 'You know all the hardship that has befallen us;

---

²²I.e., contention

Margin references:

19:19 Ezek 36:25; Heb 10:22

19:20 v. 13

19:22 Hag 2:13,14

*20:1 Num 33:36

20:2 Ex 17:1

20:3 Ex 17:2; Num 14:2,3; 16:31-35

20:4 Ex 17:3

20:6 Num 14:5,10

*20:8 Ex 17:5; Neh 9:15; Is 43:20; 48:21

20:10 Ps 106:32,33

20:11 Ps 78:16; Is 48:21; 1 Cor 10:14

20:12 Num 27:14; Deut 1:37; 3:26,27; Lev 10:3

20:13 Deut 33:8; Ps 95:8

20:14 Deut 2:4

20:1 *first month,* apparently in a year near the end of the wilderness sojourn. Thus this summary verse covers a period of about 37 years, the Israelites having arrived at Kadesh (13:26) not long after leaving Sinai. See Deut. 2:14.

20:8 Moses was commanded to smite a rock at Horeb in Ex. 17:6. Here he is commanded to speak to the rock at Kadesh (later known as Kadesh-barnea), but angrily he struck it twice. There was a note of carnal self-importance and pride in his query, "Listen now, you rebels; shall we bring forth water for you out of this rock?" (20:10). He was punished for his unbelief and disobedience.

15 that our fathers went down to Egypt, and we stayed in Egypt a long time, and the Egyptians treated us and our fathers badly.

16 'But when we cried out to the LORD, He heard our voice and sent an angel and brought us out from Egypt; now behold, we are at Kadesh, a town on the edge of your territory.

17 'Please let us pass through your land. We shall not pass through field or through vineyard; we shall not even drink water from a well. We shall go along the king's highway, not turning to the right or left, until we pass through your territory.' "

18 Edom, however, said to him, "You shall not pass through us, lest I come out with the sword against you."

19 Again, the sons of Israel said to him, "We shall go up by the highway, and if I and my livestock do drink any of your water, then I will pay its price. Let me only pass through on my feet, nothing *else*."

20 But he said, "You shall not pass through." And Edom came out against him with a heavy force, and with a strong hand.

21 Thus Edom refused to allow Israel to pass through his territory; so Israel turned away from him.

J. *Events from Kadesh to Moab*

1. *The death of Aaron*

22 Now when they set out from Kadesh, the sons of Israel, the whole congregation, came to Mount Hor.

23 Then the LORD spoke to Moses and Aaron at Mount Hor by the border of the land of Edom, saying,

24 "Aaron shall be gathered to his people; for he shall not enter the land which I have given to the sons of Israel, because you rebelled against My command at the waters of Meribah.

25 "Take Aaron and his son Eleazar, and bring them up to Mount Hor;

26 and strip Aaron of his garments and put them on his son Eleazar. So Aaron will be gathered *to his people*, and will die there."

27 So Moses did just as the LORD had commanded, and they went up to Mount Hor in the sight of all the congregation.

28 And after Moses had stripped Aaron of his garments and put them on his son Eleazar, Aaron died there on the mountain top. Then Moses and Eleazar came down from the mountain.

29 And when all the congregation saw that Aaron had died, all the house of Israel wept for Aaron thirty days.

2. *The victory over Arad at Hormah*

21 When the Canaanite, the king of Arad, who lived in the [23]Negev, heard that Israel was coming by the way of [24]Atharim, then he fought against Israel, and took some of them captive.

2 So Israel made a vow to the LORD, and said, "If Thou wilt indeed deliver this people into my hand, then I will utterly destroy their cities."

3 And the LORD heard the voice of Israel, and delivered up the Canaanites; then they utterly destroyed them and their cities. Thus the name of the place was called [25]Hormah.

3. *The fiery serpents: the murmuring of Israel*

4 Then they set out from Mount Hor by the way of the Red Sea, to go around the land of Edom; and the people became impatient because of the journey.

5 And the people spoke against God and Moses, "Why have you brought us up out of Egypt to die in the wilderness? For there is no food and no water, and we loathe this miserable food."

6 And the LORD sent fiery serpents among the people and they bit the people, so that many people of Israel died.

7 So the people came to Moses and said, "We have sinned, because we have

[23]I.e., South country [24]Or, *the spies* [25]I.e., a devoted thing; or, Destruction

---

20:17 *king's highway*, meaning the ancient route through Trans-Jordan. Note that passage was refused. (Incidentally, today the route is a paved thoroughfare.)

spoken against the LORD and you; intercede with the LORD, that He may remove the serpents from us." And Moses interceded for the people.

8   Then the LORD said to Moses, "Make a fiery *serpent,* and set it on a standard; and it shall come about, that everyone who is bitten, when he looks at it, he shall live."

9   And Moses made a bronze serpent and set it on the standard; and it came about, that if a serpent bit any man, when he looked to the bronze serpent, he lived.

4. *Israel on the march*

10   Now the sons of Israel moved out and camped in Oboth.

11   And they journeyed from Oboth, and camped at Iyeabarim, in the wilderness which is opposite Moab, to the east.

12   From there they set out and camped in [26]Wadi Zered.

13   From there they journeyed and camped on the other side of the Arnon, which is in the wilderness that comes out of the border of the Amorites, for the Arnon is the border of Moab, between Moab and the Amorites.

14   Therefore it is said in the Book of the Wars of the LORD,
"Waheb in Suphah,
And the wadis of the Arnon,

15   And the slope of the wadis
That extends to the site of Ar,
And leans to the border of Moab."

16   And from there *they continued* to Beer, that is the well where the LORD said to Moses, "Assemble the people, that I may give them water."

17   Then Israel sang this song:
"Spring up, O well! Sing to it!

18   "The well, which the leaders sank,
Which the nobles of the people dug,
With the scepter *and* with their staffs."
And from the wilderness *they continued* to Mattanah,

19   and from Mattanah to Nahaliel, and from Nahaliel to Bamoth,

20   and from Bamoth to the valley that is in the land of Moab, at the top of Pisgah which overlooks the wasteland.

5. *Defeat of Sihon, king of the Amorites*

21   Then Israel sent messengers to Sihon, king of the Amorites, saying,

22   "Let me pass through your land. We will not turn off into field or vineyard; we will not drink water from wells. We will go by the king's highway until we have passed through your border."

23   But Sihon would not permit Israel to pass through his border. So Sihon gathered all his people and went out against Israel in the wilderness, and came to Jahaz and fought against Israel.

24   Then Israel struck him with the edge of the sword, and took possession of his land from the Arnon to the Jabbok, as far as the sons of Ammon; for the border of the sons of Ammon *was* Jazer.

25   And Israel took all these cities and Israel lived in all the cities of the Amorites, in Heshbon, and in all her villages.

26   For Heshbon was the city of Sihon, king of the Amorites, who had fought against the former king of Moab and had taken all his land out of his hand, as far as the Arnon.

27   Therefore those who use proverbs say,
"Come to Heshbon! Let it be built!
So let the city of Sihon be established.

28   "For a fire went forth from Heshbon,
A flame from the town of Sihon;
It devoured Ar of Moab,
The dominant heights of the Arnon.

[26]I.e., a dry ravine except during rainy season

Marginal references:

*21:9 2 Kin 18:4; John 3:14,15
21:10 Num 33:43
21:11 Num 33:44
21:12 Deut 2:13
21:15 v. 28; Deut 2:18,29
21:21 Deut 2:26,27
21:22 Num 20:16, 17
21:23 Num 20:21; Deut 2:32
21:24 Deut 2:33; Josh 12:1,2; Ps 135:10,11
21:28 Jer 48:45,46; Deut 2:9,18; Is 15:1*

Handwritten margin note: The people had to face their afflictions in order to be healed. Did some refuse to do so? God did not remove the serpents, but he made healing possible.

21:9 The bronze serpent was a type of Christ (John 3:14,-15). As men bitten by the fiery serpents died, so men bitten by the satanic serpent of sin must suffer spiritual death. As the bronze serpent was lifted up in the wilderness, so Christ was lifted up to bear the sins of many (John 12:32). Men who had been bitten needed only to look at the bronze serpent that Moses had erected, and they were instantly healed. So, in type, sinners need only look to Him who has been lifted up on the cross, and they will be saved from the guilt, the penalty, and the power of sin (John 1:12; 3:16).

29   "Woe to you, O Moab!
You are ruined, O people of Chemosh!
He has given his sons as fugitives,
And his daughters into captivity,
To an Amorite king, Sihon.

30   "But we have cast them down,
Heshbon is ruined as far as Dibon,
Then we have laid waste even to Nophah,
Which *reaches* to Medeba."

6. Defeat of Og, king of Bashan

31   Thus Israel lived in the land of the Amorites.

32   And Moses sent to spy out Jazer, and they captured its villages and dispossessed the Amorites who *were* there.

33   Then they turned and went up by the way of Bashan, and Og the king of Bashan went out with all his people, for battle at Edrei.

34   But the LORD said to Moses, "Do not fear him, for I have given him into your hand, and all his people and his land; and you shall do to him as you did to Sihon, king of the Amorites, who lived at Heshbon."

35   So they killed him and his sons and all his people, until there was no remnant left him; and they possessed his land.

III. Events in Moab (22:1–36:13)

A. Balak and Balaam

1. Balak sends for Balaam

22 Then the sons of Israel journeyed, and camped in the plains of Moab beyond the Jordan *opposite* Jericho.

2   Now Balak the son of Zippor saw all that Israel had done to the Amorites.

3   So Moab was in great fear because of the people, for they were numerous; and Moab was in dread of the sons of Israel.

4   And Moab said to the elders of Midian, "Now this horde will lick up all that is around us, as the ox licks up the grass of the field." And Balak the son of Zippor was king of Moab at that time.

5   So he sent messengers to Balaam the son of Beor, at Pethor, which is near the [27]River, *in* the land of the sons of his people, to call him, saying, "Behold, a people came out of Egypt; behold, they cover the surface of the land, and they are living opposite me.

6   "Now, therefore, please come, curse this people for me since they are too mighty for me; perhaps I may be able to defeat them and drive them out of the land. For I know that he whom you bless is blessed, and he whom you curse is cursed."

2. God forbids Balaam to go to Balak

7   So the elders of Moab and the elders of Midian departed with the *fees for divination* in their hand; and they came to Balaam and repeated Balak's words to him.

8   And he said to them, "Spend the night here, and I will bring word back to you as the LORD may speak to me." And the leaders of Moab stayed with Balaam.

9   Then God came to Balaam and said, "Who are these men with you?"

10   And Balaam said to God, "Balak the son of Zippor, king of Moab, has sent *word* to me,

11   'Behold, there is a people who came out of Egypt and they cover the surface

[27]I.e., Euphrates

22:1 *beyond the Jordan*, see note to Deut. 1:1 for clarification.
22:5a The importance of this incident involving Balaam may be seen from the fact that it is referred to by three different New Testament writers (see 2 Pet. 2:15; Jude 11; Rev. 2:14). Balaam began as a conscientious prophet of the Lord, but through love of money he became a hireling. In each instance God thwarted the purpose of Balak to harm Israel, for Balaam never did curse the people of God as Balak desired him to do. But Balak did succeed by another device—craftily suggested to him by Balaam, for he corrupted Israel by the allurement of sexual license. This is what might be termed *the teaching of Balaam* (25:1ff.; Rev. 2:14).
22:5b *land of the sons of his people* along the upper Euphrates near Carchemish. This area was noted for its diviners.

of the land; now come, curse them for me; perhaps I may be able to fight against them, and drive them out.' "

12   And God said to Balaam, "Do not go with them; you shall not curse the people; for they are blessed." 22:12 Num 23:20

13   So Balaam arose in the morning and said to Balak's leaders, "Go back to your land, for the Lord has refused to let me go with you."

14   And the leaders of Moab arose and went to Balak, and said, "Balaam refused to come with us."

3. God lets Balaam go

15   Then Balak again sent leaders, more numerous and more distinguished than the former.

16   And they came to Balaam and said to him, "Thus says Balak the son of Zippor, 'Let nothing, I beg you, hinder you from coming to me;

17   for I will indeed honor you richly, and I will do whatever you say to me. Please come then, curse this people for me.' " 22:17 v. 6

18   And Balaam answered and said to the servants of Balak, "Though Balak were to give me his house full of silver and gold, I could not do anything, either small or great, contrary to the command of the Lord my God. 22:18 Num 24:13; 1 Kin 22:14; 2 Chr 18:13

19   "And now please, you also stay here tonight, and I will find out what else the Lord will speak to me."

20   And God came to Balaam at night and said to him, "If the men have come to call you, rise up *and* go with them; but only the word which I speak to you shall you do." 22:20 v. 35; Num 23:12, 26; 24:13

4. Balaam's donkey: God's anger at Balaam's disobedience

21   So Balaam arose in the morning, and saddled his donkey, and went with the leaders of Moab. 22:21 2 Pet 2:15

22   But God was angry because he was going, and the angel of the Lord took his stand in the way as an adversary against him. Now he was riding on his donkey and his two servants were with him.

23   When the donkey saw the angel of the Lord standing in the way with his drawn sword in his hand, the donkey turned off from the way and went into the field; but Balaam struck the donkey to turn her back into the way. 22:23 2 Pet 2:16

24   Then the angel of the Lord stood in a narrow path of the vineyards, *with* a wall on this side and a wall on that side. 22:24 Judg 6:12

25   When the donkey saw the angel of the Lord, she pressed herself to the wall and pressed Balaam's foot against the wall, so he struck her again.

26   And the angel of the Lord went further, and stood in a narrow place where there was no way to turn to the right hand or the left.

27   When the donkey saw the angel of the Lord, she lay down under Balaam; so Balaam was angry and struck the donkey with his stick.

28   And the Lord opened the mouth of the donkey, and she said to Balaam, "What have I done to you, that you have struck me these three times?" 22:28 2 Pet 2:16

29   Then Balaam said to the donkey, "Because you have made a mockery of me! If there had been a sword in my hand, I would have killed you by now." 22:29 Prov 12:10

30   And the donkey said to Balaam, "Am I not your donkey on which you have ridden all your life to this day? Have I ever been accustomed to do so to you?" And he said, "No." 22:30 2 Pet 2:16

31   Then the Lord opened the eyes of Balaam, and he saw the angel of the Lord standing in the way with his drawn sword in his hand; and he bowed all the way to the ground. 22:31 Josh 5:13-15

32   And the angel of the Lord said to him, "Why have you struck your donkey these three times? Behold, I have come out as an adversary, because your way was contrary to me.

33   "But the donkey saw me and turned aside from me these three times. If she

---

22:19   This is one of the clearest Biblical instances of the *permissive* will of God. Balaam knew perfectly well that it was not the will of God for him to go at the bidding of Balak. He needed no further instruction about God's will. He merely needed to obey it. Instead he trifled with the known will of God, and then it was that God's permissive will came into action. God let him go, with the stipulation that the outcome of his disobedience would do no harm to the people of God.

22:22   *adversary*, in Hebrew *satan*. In the book of Job "the satan" or "adversary" accuses Job of serving God for material considerations. After the exile, the term, as the name Satan, was applied to the arch enemy of God. See Zech. 3:1, where the *angel of the* Lord and *Satan* are clearly distinguished.

had not turned aside from me, I would surely have killed you just now, and let her live.''

34   And Balaam said to the angel of the LORD, "I have sinned, for I did not know that you were standing in the way against me. Now then, if it is displeasing to you, I will turn back."

35   But the angel of the LORD said to Balaam, "Go with the men, but you shall speak only the word which I shall tell you." So Balaam went along with the leaders of Balak.

5. *Balaam visits Balak*

36   When Balak heard that Balaam was coming, he went out to meet him at the city of Moab, which is on the Arnon border, at the extreme end of the border.

37   Then Balak said to Balaam, "Did I not urgently send to you to call you? Why did you not come to me? Am I really unable to honor you?"

38   So Balaam said to Balak, "Behold, I have come now to you! Am I able to speak anything at all? The word that God puts in my mouth, that I shall speak."

39   And Balaam went with Balak, and they came to Kiriath-huzoth.

40   And Balak sacrificed oxen and sheep, and sent *some* to Balaam and the leaders who were with him.

6. *Balaam's first blessing*

41   Then it came about in the morning that Balak took Balaam, and brought him up to the high places of Baal; and he saw from there a portion of the people.

23   Then Balaam said to Balak, "Build seven altars for me here, and prepare seven bulls and seven rams for me here."

2   And Balak did just as Balaam had spoken, and Balak and Balaam offered up a bull and a ram on each altar.

3   Then Balaam said to Balak, "Stand beside your burnt offering, and I will go; perhaps the LORD will come to meet me, and whatever He shows me I will tell you." So he went to a bare hill.

4   Now God met Balaam, and he said to Him, "I have set up the seven altars, and I have offered up a bull and a ram on each altar."

5   Then the LORD put a word in Balaam's mouth and said, "Return to Balak, and you shall speak thus."

6   So he returned to him, and behold, he was standing beside his burnt offering, he and all the leaders of Moab.

7   And he took up his [28]discourse and said,

"From Aram Balak has brought me,
Moab's king from the mountains of the East,
'Come curse Jacob for me,
And come, denounce Israel!'

8   "How shall I curse, whom God has not cursed?
And how can I denounce, whom the LORD has not denounced?

9   "As I see him from the top of the rocks,
And I look at him from the hills,
Behold, a people *who* dwells apart,
And shall not be reckoned among the nations.

10   "Who can count the dust of Jacob,
Or number the fourth part of Israel?
Let me die the death of the upright,
And let my end be like his!"

11   Then Balak said to Balaam, "What have you done to me? I took you to curse my enemies, but behold, you have actually blessed them!"

12   And he answered and said, "Must I not be careful to speak what the LORD puts in my mouth?"

7. *Balaam's second blessing*

13   Then Balak said to him, "Please come with me to another place from where you may see them, although you will only see the extreme end of them, and will not see all of them; and curse them for me from there."

[28]Lit., *parable*, and so throughout this context

22:34
Num 14:40;
1 Sam 15:24,
30;
2 Sam 12:13
22:35
v. 20

22:37
v. 17;
Num 24:11
22:38
v. 18;
Num 23:26;
24:13

22:41
Deut 12:2

23:1
v. 29
23:2
vv. 14,30
23:3
v. 15
23:4
v. 16
23:5
v. 16;
Num 22:35;
Deut 18:18;
Jer 1:9
23:7
v. 18;
Num 24:3,15,
23; Job 27:1;
29:1; Ps 78:2;
Num 22:6
23:8
Num 22:12
23:9
Ex 33:16;
Deut 32:8;
33:28
23:10
Gen 13:16;
Ps 116:15
23:11
Num 24:10
23:12
Num 22:20,
38

14   So he took him to the field of Zophim, to the top of Pisgah, and built seven
altars and offered a bull and a ram on *each* altar.

15   And he said to Balak, "Stand here beside your burnt offering, while I myself
meet *the* Lᴏʀᴅ yonder."

16   Then the Lᴏʀᴅ met Balaam and put a word in his mouth and said, "Return
to Balak, and thus you shall speak."

17   And he came to him, and behold, he was standing beside his burnt offering,
and the leaders of Moab with him. And Balak said to him, "What has the Lᴏʀᴅ
spoken?"

18   Then he took up his ²⁹discourse and said,
    "Arise, O Balak, and hear;
    Give ear to me, O son of Zippor!

19   "God is not a man, that He should lie,
    Nor a son of man, that He should repent;
    Has He said, and will He not do it?
    Or has He spoken, and will He not make it good?

20   "Behold, I have received *a command* to bless;
    When He has blessed, then I cannot revoke it.

21   "He has not observed misfortune in Jacob;
    Nor has He seen trouble in Israel;
    The Lᴏʀᴅ his God is with him,
    And the shout of a king is among them.

22   "God brings them out of Egypt,
    He is for them like the horns of the wild ox.

23   "For there is no omen against Jacob,
    Nor is there any divination against Israel;
    At the proper time it shall be said to Jacob
    And to Israel, what God has done.

24   "Behold, a people rises like a lioness,
    And as a lion it lifts itself;
    It shall not lie down until it devours the prey,
    And drinks the blood of the slain."

8. Balaam's third blessing

25   Then Balak said to Balaam, "Do not curse them at all nor bless them at all!"

26   But Balaam answered and said to Balak, "Did I not tell you, 'Whatever the
Lᴏʀᴅ speaks, that I must do'?"

27   Then Balak said to Balaam, "Please come, I will take you to another place;
perhaps it will be agreeable with God that you curse them for me from there."

28   So Balak took Balaam to the top of Peor which overlooks the wasteland.

29   And Balaam said to Balak, "Build seven altars for me here and prepare seven
bulls and seven rams for me here."

30   And Balak did just as Balaam had said, and offered up a bull and a ram on
each altar.

24   When Balaam saw that it pleased the Lᴏʀᴅ to bless Israel, he did not go as at
other times to seek omens but he set his face toward the wilderness.

2   And Balaam lifted up his eyes and saw Israel camping tribe by tribe; and the
Spirit of God came upon him.

3   And he took up his discourse and said,
    "The oracle of Balaam the son of Beor,
    And the oracle of the man whose eye is opened;

4   The oracle of him who hears the words of God,
    Who sees the vision of the Almighty,
    Falling down, yet having his eyes uncovered,

5   How fair are your tents, O Jacob,
    Your dwellings, O Israel!

6   "Like valleys that stretch out,
    Like gardens beside the river,

²⁹Lit., *parable*, and so throughout this context

23:14   These rites were used by Babylonian diviners (see
also vv. 2,30). Note that these were the pagan offerings of
Balak and as such could not commend him toward God.

*23:14
vv. 1,2

23:16
Num 22:20

23:19
1 Sam 15:29;
Mal 3:6;
Rom 11:29;
Titus 1:2;
James 1:17

23:20
Is 43:13

23:21
Ps 32:2,5;
Rom 4:7,8;
Is 40:2;
Ex 29:45,46;
Ps 89:15

23:22
Num 24:8

23:24
Gen 49:9,27

23:26
v. 12;
Num 22:38

23:27
v. 13

23:29
v. 1

24:1
Num 23:3,15

24:2
Num 11:25,
26;
1 Sam 10:10;
2 Chr 15:1

24:3
Num 23:7,18

24:4
Num 22:20;
12:6

24:6
Ps 1:3;
104:16

24:7
v. 20;
1 Sam 15:8,9;
2 Sam 5:12;
1 Chr 14:2

24:8
Num 23:22,
24; Ps 2:9;
45:5;
Jer 50:9,17

24:9
Gen 49:9;
12:3; 27:29

24:11
Num 22:17,
37

24:13
Num 22:18,
20

24:14
Gen 49:1;
Dan 2:28;
Mic 6:5

*24:17
Rev 1:7;
Matt 2:2;
Gen 49:10

24:18
2 Sam 8:14

24:19
Gen 49:10;
Mic 5:2

24:20
Ex 17:8,14,16

Like aloes planted by the LORD,
Like cedars beside the waters.

7 "Water shall flow from his buckets,
And his seed *shall be* by many waters,
And his king shall be higher than Agag,
And his kingdom shall be exalted.

8 "God brings him out of Egypt,
He is for him like the horns of the wild ox.
He shall devour the nations *who are* his adversaries,
And shall crush their bones in pieces,
And shatter *them* with his arrows.

9 "He couches, he lies down as a lion,
And as a lion, who dares rouse him?
Blessed is everyone who blesses you,
And cursed is everyone who curses you."

9. *Balaam's fourth blessing and prophecy*

10 Then Balak's anger burned against Balaam, and he struck his hands together; and Balak said to Balaam, "I called you to curse my enemies, but behold, you have persisted in blessing them these three times!

11 "Therefore, flee to your place now. I said I would honor you greatly, but behold, the LORD has held you back from honor."

12 And Balaam said to Balak, "Did I not tell your messengers whom you had sent to me, saying,

13 'Though Balak were to give me his house full of silver and gold, I could not do anything contrary to the command of the LORD, either good or bad, of my own accord. What the LORD speaks, that I will speak'?

14 "And now behold, I am going to my people; come, *and* I will advise you what this people will do to your people in the days to come."

15 And he took up his discourse and said,
"The oracle of Balaam the son of Beor,
And the oracle of the man whose eye is opened,

16 The oracle of him who hears the words of God,
And knows the knowledge of the Most High,
Who sees the vision of the Almighty,
Falling down, yet having his eyes uncovered.

17 "I see him, but not now;
I behold him, but not near;
A star shall come forth from Jacob,
And a scepter shall rise from Israel,
And shall crush through the forehead of Moab,
And tear down all the sons of [30]Sheth.

18 "And Edom shall be a possession,
Seir, its enemies, also shall be a possession,
While Israel performs valiantly.

19 "One from Jacob shall have dominion,
And shall destroy the remnant from the city."

20 And he looked at Amalek and took up his discourse and said,
"Amalek was the first of the nations,
But his end *shall be* destruction."

21 And he looked at the Kenite, and took up his discourse and said,
"Your dwelling place is enduring,
And your nest is set in the cliff.

22 "Nevertheless Kain shall be consumed;

---

[30]I.e., tumult

24:17 This prophecy of Israel's supremacy over Moab and Edom came true in David's reign, but it extends beyond that to David's greater Son. Balaam did not understand the implications of his prophetic words, for ultimately Jesus Christ is the *star . . . from Jacob* and in His hands is the scepter of kingship. As the Messianic descendant of Jacob He will exercise dominion over all the earth. Christ's kingdom has been established as a spiritual reign. Some Chris-

tians look forward to a literal and earthly manifestation when, during the millennial age, He will rule over the nations with a rod of iron (Rev. 19:15).

Sheth, an ancient name for Moab that has been found in nonbiblical texts.

24:21 *Kenite*, meaning a smith, is probably a reference to those who mined and smelted copper from Edomite mines.

How long shall Asshur keep you captive?"

23   And he took up his discourse and said,
     "Alas, who can live except God has ordained it?
24   "But ships *shall come* from the coast of Kittim,
     And they shall afflict Asshur and shall afflict Eber;
     So they also *shall come* to destruction."

25   Then Balaam arose and departed and returned to his place, and Balak also
went his way.

B. *Israel's idolatry in Shittim*

1. *Israelites yoked to Baal of Peor*

25 While Israel remained at Shittim, the people began to play the harlot with
     the daughters of Moab.
2   For they invited the people to the sacrifices of their gods, and the people ate
and bowed down to their gods.
3   So Israel joined themselves to Baal of Peor, and the LORD was angry against
Israel.
4   And the LORD said to Moses, "Take all the leaders of the people and execute
them in broad daylight before the LORD, so that the fierce anger of the LORD may
turn away from Israel."
5   So Moses said to the judges of Israel, "Each of you slay his men who have
joined themselves to Baal of Peor."

2. *Phinehas slays the Midianite woman*

6   Then behold, one of the sons of Israel came and brought to his relatives a
Midianite woman, in the sight of Moses and in the sight of all the congregation of
the sons of Israel, while they were weeping at the doorway of the tent of meeting.
7   When Phinehas the son of Eleazar, the son of Aaron the priest, saw it, he
arose from the midst of the congregation, and took a spear in his hand;
8   and he went after the man of Israel into the tent, and pierced both of them
through, the man of Israel and the woman, through the body. So the plague on the
sons of Israel was checked.
9   And those who died by the plague were 24,000.
10   Then the LORD spoke to Moses, saying,
11   "Phinehas the son of Eleazar, the son of Aaron the priest, has turned away
My wrath from the sons of Israel, in that he was jealous with My jealousy among
them, so that I did not destroy the sons of Israel in My jealousy.
12   "Therefore say, 'Behold, I give him My covenant of peace;
13   and it shall be for him and his descendants after him, a covenant of a
perpetual priesthood, because he was jealous for his God, and made atonement for
the sons of Israel.' "
14   Now the name of the slain man of Israel who was slain with the Midianite
woman, was Zimri the son of Salu, a leader of a father's household among the
Simeonites.
15   And the name of the Midianite woman who was slain was Cozbi the daughter of Zur, who was head of the people of a father's household in Midian.
16   Then the LORD spoke to Moses, saying,
17   "Be hostile to the Midianites and strike them;
18   for they have been hostile to you with their tricks, with which they have
deceived you in the affair of Peor, and in the affair of Cozbi, the daughter of the
leader of Midian, their sister who was slain on the day of the plague because of
Peor."

C. *Israel's second census*

1. *The command to take the census*

26 Then it came about after the plague, that the LORD spoke to Moses and to
     Eleazar the son of Aaron the priest, saying,
2   "Take a census of all the congregation of the sons of Israel from twenty years
old and upward, by their fathers' households, whoever is able to go out to war in
Israel."

Marginal references:

24:24
Gen 10:4,21;
v. 20

24:25
Num 31:8

25:1
Mic 6:5;
Num 31:16;
1 Cor 10:8;
Rev 2:14
25:2
Ex 34:15;
20:5;
1 Cor 10:20
25:3
Ps 106:28,29;
Hos 9:10
25:4
Deut 4:3

25:7
Ps 106:30

25:9

25:9
Deut 4:3;
1 Cor 10:8
25:11
Ps 106:30;
Ex 20:5;
Deut 32:16,
21
25:12
Is 54:10;
Mal 2:4,5
25:13
Ex 40:15;
Num 16:46;
Heb 2:17

25:15
Num 31:8

25:17
Num 31:2
25:18
Num 31:16

26:2
Ex 30:12;
38:25,26;
Num 1:2

3   So Moses and Eleazar the priest spoke with them in the plains of Moab by the Jordan at Jericho, saying,
4   "Take a census of the people from twenty years old and upward, as the LORD has commanded Moses."
   Now the sons of Israel who came out of the land of Egypt were:

2. The numbering of the tribes

5   Reuben, Israel's first-born, the sons of Reuben: of Hanoch, the family of the Hanochites; of Pallu, the family of the Palluites;
6   of Hezron, the family of the Hezronites; of Carmi, the family of the Carmites.
7   These are the families of the Reubenites, and those who were numbered of them were 43,730.
8   And the son of Pallu: Eliab.
9   And the sons of Eliab: Nemuel and Dathan and Abiram. These are the Dathan and Abiram who were called by the congregation, who contended against Moses and against Aaron in the company of Korah, when they contended against the LORD,
10   and the earth opened its mouth and swallowed them up along with Korah, when that company died, when the fire devoured 250 men, so that they became a warning.
11   The sons of Korah, however, did not die.
12   The sons of Simeon according to their families: of Nemuel, the family of the Nemuelites; of Jamin, the family of the Jaminites; of Jachin, the family of the Jachinites;
13   of Zerah, the family of the Zerahites; of Shaul, the family of the Shaulites.
14   These are the families of the Simeonites, 22,200.
15   The sons of Gad according to their families: of Zephon, the family of the Zephonites; of Haggi, the family of the Haggites; of Shuni, the family of the Shunites;
16   of Ozni, the family of the Oznites; of Eri, the family of the Erites;
17   of Arod, the family of the Arodites; of Areli, the family of the Arelites.
18   These are the families of the sons of Gad according to those who were numbered of them, 40,500.
19   The sons of Judah were Er and Onan, but Er and Onan died in the land of Canaan.
20   And the sons of Judah according to their families were: of Shelah, the family of the Shelanites; of Perez, the family of the Perezites; of Zerah, the family of the Zerahites.
21   And the sons of Perez were: of Hezron, the family of the Hezronites; of Hamul, the family of the Hamulites.
22   These are the families of Judah according to those who were numbered of them, 76,500.
23   The sons of Issachar according to their families: of Tola, the family of the Tolaites; of Puvah, the family of the Punites;
24   of Jashub, the family of the Jashubites; of Shimron, the family of the Shimronites.
25   These are the families of Issachar according to those who were numbered of them, 64,300.
26   The sons of Zebulun according to their families: of Sered, the family of the Seredites; of Elon, the family of the Elonites; of Jahleel, the family of the Jahleelites.
27   These are the families of the Zebulunites according to those who were numbered of them, 60,500.
28   The sons of Joseph according to their families: Manasseh and Ephraim.
29   The sons of Manasseh: of Machir, the family of the Machirites; and Machir became the father of Gilead: of Gilead, the family of the Gileadites.
30   These are the sons of Gilead: of Iezer, the family of the Iezerites; of Helek, the family of the Helekites;
31   and of Asriel, the family of the Asrielites; and of Shechem, the family of the Shechemites;
32   and of Shemida, the family of the Shemidaites; and of Hepher, the family of the Hepherites.

26:5
Ex 6:14

26:9
Num 16:1,2

26:10
Num 16:32,
35,38

26:11
Deut 24:16
26:12
Ex 6:15
Jemuel;
1 Chr 4:24
Jarib
26:13
Gen 46:10
Zohar
26:15
Gen 46:16
Ziphion
26:16
Gen 46:16
Ezbon
26:17
Gen 46:16
Arodi
26:18
Num 1:25

26:22
Num 1:27

26:24
Gen 46:13
Iob
26:25
Num 1:29

26:27
Num 1:31

26:30
see Josh 17:2
Abiezer

33   Now Zelophehad the son of Hepher had no sons, but only daughters; and the names of the daughters of Zelophehad were Mahlah, Noah, Hoglah, Milcah and Tirzah.

34   These are the families of Manasseh; and those who were numbered of them were 52,700.

35   These are the sons of Ephraim according to their families: of Shuthelah, the family of the Shuthelahites; of Becher, the family of the Becherites; of Tahan, the family of the Tahanites.

36   And these are the sons of Shuthelah: of Eran, the family of the Eranites.

37   These are the families of the sons of Ephraim according to those who were numbered of them, 32,500. These are the sons of Joseph according to their families.

38   The sons of Benjamin according to their families: of Bela, the family of the Belaites; of Ashbel, the family of the Ashbelites; of Ahiram, the family of the Ahiramites;

39   of Shephupham, the family of the Shuphamites; of Hupham, the family of the Huphamites.

40   And the sons of Bela were Ard and Naaman: *of Ard*, the family of the Ardites; of Naaman, the family of the Naamites.

41   These are the sons of Benjamin according to their families; and those who were numbered of them were 45,600.

42   These are the sons of Dan according to their families: of Shuham, the family of the Shuhamites. These are the families of Dan according to their families.

43   All the families of the Shuhamites, according to those who were numbered of them, were 64,400.

44   The sons of Asher according to their families: of Imnah, the family of the Imnites; of Ishvi, the family of the Ishvites; of Beriah, the family of the Beriites.

45   Of the sons of Beriah: of Heber, the family of the Heberites; of Malchiel, the family of the Malchielites.

46   And the name of the daughter of Asher *was* Serah.

47   These are the families of the sons of Asher according to those who were numbered of them, 53,400.

48   The sons of Naphtali according to their families: of Jahzeel, the family of the Jahzeelites; of Guni, the family of the Gunites;

49   of Jezer, the family of the Jezerites; of Shillem, the family of the Shillemites.

50   These are the families of Naphtali according to their families; and those who were numbered of them were 45,400.

51   These are those who were numbered of the sons of Israel, 601,730.

3. *The division of the land*

52   Then the LORD spoke to Moses, saying,

53   "Among these the land shall be divided for an inheritance according to the number of names.

54   "To the larger *group* you shall increase their inheritance, and to the smaller *group* you shall diminish their inheritance; each shall be given their inheritance according to those who were numbered of them.

55   "But the land shall be divided by lot. They shall receive their inheritance according to the names of the tribes of their fathers.

56   "According to the selection by lot, their inheritance shall be divided between the larger and the smaller *groups*."

4. *The numbering of the Levites*

57   And these are those who were numbered of the Levites according to their families: of Gershon, the family of the Gershonites; of Kohath, the family of the Kohathites; of Merari, the family of the Merarites.

58   These are the families of Levi: the family of the Libnites, the family of the Hebronites, the family of the Mahlites, the family of the Mushites, the family of the Korahites. And Kohath became the father of Amram.

59   And the name of Amram's wife was Jochebed, the daughter of Levi, who was born to Levi in Egypt; and she bore to Amram: Aaron and Moses and their sister Miriam.

60   And to Aaron were born Nadab and Abihu, Eleazar and Ithamar.

61   But Nadab and Abihu died when they offered strange fire before the LORD.

62   And those who were numbered of them were 23,000, every male from a

26:35
1 Chr 7:20
Bered

26:37
Num 1:33

26:38
Gen 46:21
Ehi

26:39
Gen 46:21
Muppim
Huppim
26:40
1 Chr 8:3
Addar
26:41
Num 1:37
26:42
Gen 46:23
Hushim
26:43
Num 1:39

26:47
Num 1:41

26:50
Num 1:43

26:53
Josh 11:23;
14:1
26:54
Num 33:54

26:55
Num 33:54;
34:13

26:59
Ex 6:20

26:60
Num 3:2
26:61
Lev 10:1,2;
Num 3:4

26:62
Num 1:47;
18:20,23,24
month old and upward, for they were not numbered among the sons of Israel since no inheritance was given to them among the sons of Israel.

5. Summary

63 These are those who were numbered by Moses and Eleazar the priest, who numbered the sons of Israel in the plains of Moab by the Jordan at Jericho.
26:64
Deut 2:14,15
64 But among these there was not a man of those who were numbered by Moses and Aaron the priest, who numbered the sons of Israel in the wilderness of Sinai.
26:65
Num 14:28,
29;
1 Cor 10:5,6;
Num 14:30
65 For the LORD had said of them, "They shall surely die in the wilderness." And not a man was left of them, except Caleb the son of Jephunneh, and Joshua the son of Nun.

D. The case of Zelophehad's daughters

1. Zelophehad's death without sons

*27:1ff
Num 26:33;
36:1
27 Then the daughters of Zelophehad, the son of Hepher, the son of Gilead, the son of Machir, the son of Manasseh, of the families of Manasseh the son of Joseph, came near; and these are the names of his daughters: Mahlah, Noah and Hoglah and Milcah and Tirzah.

2 And they stood before Moses and before Eleazar the priest and before the leaders and all the congregation, at the doorway of the tent of meeting, saying,
27:3
Num 26:64,
65; 26:33;
16:1,2
3 "Our father died in the wilderness, yet he was not among the company of those who gathered themselves together against the LORD in the company of Korah; but he died in his own sin, and he had no sons.
27:4
Josh 17:4
4 "Why should the name of our father be withdrawn from among his family because he had no son? Give us a possession among our father's brothers."

2. The inheritance to pass through the daughters

27:5
Num 9:8
27:6
Num 36:2
5 And Moses brought their case before the LORD.
6 Then the LORD spoke to Moses, saying,
7 "The daughters of Zelophehad are right in *their* statements. You shall surely give them a hereditary possession among their father's brothers, and you shall transfer the inheritance of their father to them.
8 "Further, you shall speak to the sons of Israel, saying, 'If a man dies and has no son, then you shall transfer his inheritance to his daughter.
9 'And if he has no daughter, then you shall give his inheritance to his brothers.
10 'And if he has no brothers, then you shall give his inheritance to his father's brothers.
11 'And if his father has no brothers, then you shall give his inheritance to his nearest relative in his own family, and he shall possess it; and it shall be a statutory ordinance to the sons of Israel, just as the LORD commanded Moses.'"

E. The selection of Joshua to succeed Moses

*27:12
Num 33:47;
Deut 32:49
27:13
Num 31:2
12 Then the LORD said to Moses, "Go up to this mountain of Abarim, and see the land which I have given to the sons of Israel.
13 "And when you have seen it, you too shall be gathered to your people, as Aaron your brother was;
27:14
Num 20:12;
Ex 17:7
14 for in the wilderness of Zin, during the strife of the congregation, you rebelled against My command to treat Me as holy before their eyes at the water." (These are the waters of Meribah of Kadesh in the wilderness of Zin.)
27:16
Num 16:22
15 Then Moses spoke to the LORD, saying,
16 "May the LORD, the God of the spirits of all flesh, appoint a man over the congregation,
27:17
Deut 31:2;
Matt 9:36;
Mark 6:34
17 who will go out and come in before them, and who will lead them out and bring them in, that the congregation of the LORD may not be like sheep which have no shepherd."
27:18
Num 11:25-29;
Deut 34:9
18 So the LORD said to Moses, "Take Joshua the son of Nun, a man in whom is the Spirit, and lay your hand on him;

27:1–10 Provision for inheritance by daughters and others was necessary; otherwise the lack of a son would mean the loss of inheritance of the land allotted. See 36:6,7.
27:11 See note to 27:1–10.

27:12 *mountain of Abarim*, probably another designation for the hill country of Mt. Nebo.
27:15 In answer to Moses' request for a new leader over the people, the Lord tells him to take Joshua (v. 18).

19   and have him stand before Eleazar the priest and before all the congregation; and commission him in their sight.

20   "And you shall put some of your authority on him, in order that all the congregation of the sons of Israel may obey *him.*

21   "Moreover, he shall stand before Eleazar the priest, who shall inquire for him by the judgment of the Urim before the LORD. At his command they shall go out and at his command they shall come in, *both* he and the sons of Israel with him, even all the congregation."

22   And Moses did just as the LORD commanded him; and he took Joshua and set him before Eleazar the priest, and before all the congregation.

23   Then he laid his hands on him and commissioned him, just as the LORD had spoken through Moses.

F. The laws of offerings repeated and explained

1. The daily burnt offering

28 Then the LORD spoke to Moses, saying,

2   "Command the sons of Israel and say to them, 'You shall be careful to present My offering, My food for My offerings by fire, of a soothing aroma to Me, at their appointed time.'

3   "And you shall say to them, 'This is the offering by fire which you shall offer to the LORD; two male lambs one year old without defect *as* a continual burnt offering every day.

4   'You shall offer the one lamb in the morning, and the other lamb you shall offer at twilight;

5   also a tenth of an ephah of fine flour for a grain offering, mixed with a fourth of a hin of beaten oil.

6   'It is a continual burnt offering which was ordained in Mount Sinai as a soothing aroma, an offering by fire to the LORD.

7   'Then the libation with it *shall be* a fourth of a hin for each lamb, in the holy place you shall pour out a libation of strong drink to the LORD.

8   'And the other lamb you shall offer at twilight; as the grain offering of the morning and as its libation, you shall offer it, an offering by fire, a soothing aroma to the LORD.

2. The offering on the Sabbath

9   'Then on the sabbath day two male lambs one year old without defect, and two-tenths *of an ephah* of fine flour mixed with oil as a grain offering, and its libation:

10   '*This is* the burnt offering of every sabbath in addition to the continual burnt offering and its libation.

3. The offering on the new moon

11   'Then at the beginning of each of your months you shall present a burnt offering to the LORD; two bulls and one ram, seven male lambs one year old without defect,

12   and three-tenths *of an ephah* of fine flour for a grain offering, mixed with oil, for each bull; and two-tenths of fine flour for a grain offering, mixed with oil, for the one ram;

13   and a tenth *of an ephah* of fine flour mixed with oil for a grain offering for each lamb, for a burnt offering of a soothing aroma, an offering by fire to the LORD.

14   'And their libations shall be half a hin of wine for a bull and a third of a hin for the ram and a fourth of a hin for a lamb; this is the burnt offering of each month throughout the months of the year.

15   'And one male goat for a sin offering to the LORD; it shall be offered with its libation in addition to the continual burnt offering.

4. The offerings on the Feast of Unleavened Bread

16   'Then on the fourteenth day of the first month shall be the LORD's Passover.

17   'And on the fifteenth day of this month *shall be* a feast, unleavened bread *shall be* eaten for seven days.

18   'On the first day *shall be* a holy convocation; you shall do no laborious work.

19   'And you shall present an offering by fire, a burnt offering to the LORD: two

---

27:19
Deut 31:3,7, 8,23
27:20
Josh 1:16,17

27:21
Ex 28:30

28:2
Lev 3:11

28:3
Ex 29:38

28:7
Ex 29:42

28:10
v. 3

28:11
Num 10:10;
Ezek 45:17;
46:6
28:12
Num 15:4-12

28:15
v. 3

28:16
Ex 12:6,18;
Lev 23:5;
Deut 16:1
28:17
Lev 23:6
28:18
Ex 12:16;
Lev 23:7

bulls and one ram and seven male lambs one year old, having them without defect.

20 'And for their grain offering, you shall offer fine flour mixed with oil: three-tenths *of an ephah* for a bull and two-tenths for the ram.

21 'A tenth *of an ephah* you shall offer for each of the seven lambs,

22 and one male goat for a sin offering, to make atonement for you.

28:23
v. 3
23 'You shall present these besides the burnt offering of the morning, which is for a continual burnt offering.

24 'After this manner you shall present daily, for seven days, the food of the offering by fire, of a soothing aroma to the LORD; it shall be presented with its libation in addition to the continual burnt offering.

28:25
Ex 12:16
25 'And on the seventh day you shall have a holy convocation; you shall do no laborious work.

5. *First fruits (Pentecost) offerings*

28:26
Ex 23:16;
34:22;
Lev 23:10,15;
Deut 16:10
26 'Also on the day of the first fruits, when you present a new grain offering to the LORD in your *Feast of* Weeks, you shall have a holy convocation; you shall do no laborious work.

27 'And you shall offer a burnt offering for a soothing aroma to the LORD, two young bulls, one ram, seven male lambs one year old,

28 and their grain offering, fine flour mixed with oil, three-tenths *of an ephah* for each bull, two-tenths for the one ram,

29 a tenth for each of the seven lambs,

30 one male goat to make atonement for you.

28:31
vv. 3,19
31 'Besides the continual burnt offering and its grain offering, you shall present *them* with their libations. They shall be without defect.

6. *Feast of Trumpets*

29:1
Ex 23:16;
34:22;
Lev 23:24
29 'Now in the seventh month, on the first day of the month, you shall also have a holy convocation; you shall do no laborious work. It will be to you a day for blowing trumpets.

2 'And you shall offer a burnt offering as a soothing aroma to the LORD: one bull, one ram, *and* seven male lambs one year old without defect;

3 also their grain offering, fine flour mixed with oil, three-tenths *of an ephah* for the bull, two-tenths for the ram,

4 and one-tenth for each of the seven lambs.

5 'And *offer* one male goat for a sin offering, to make atonement for you,

29:6
Num 28:3,11
6 besides the burnt offering of the new moon, and its grain offering, and the continual burnt offering and its grain offering, and their libations, according to their ordinance, for a soothing aroma, an offering by fire to the LORD.

7. *The offering on the Day of Atonement*

29:7
Lev 16:29-34;
23:26-32
7 'Then on the tenth day of this seventh month you shall have a holy convocation, and you shall humble yourselves; you shall not do any work.

8 'And you shall present a burnt offering to the LORD *as* a soothing aroma: one bull, one ram, seven male lambs one year old, having them without defect;

9 and their grain offering, fine flour mixed with oil, three-tenths *of an ephah* for the bull, two-tenths for the one ram,

10 a tenth for each of the seven lambs;

29:11
Lev 16:3,5;
Num 28:3
11 one male goat for a sin offering, besides the sin offering of atonement and the continual burnt offering and its grain offering, and their libations.

8. *Offerings at the Feast of Tabernacles*

29:12
Lev 23:33-35
12 'Then on the fifteenth day of the seventh month you shall have a holy convocation; you shall do no laborious work, and you shall observe a feast to the LORD for seven days.

13 'And you shall present a burnt offering, an offering by fire as a soothing aroma to the LORD: thirteen bulls, two rams, fourteen male lambs one year old, which are without defect,

14 and their grain offering, fine flour mixed with oil, three-tenths *of an ephah* for each of the thirteen bulls, two-tenths for each of the two rams,

15 and a tenth for each of the fourteen lambs;

29:16
v. 11
16 and one male goat for a sin offering, besides the continual burnt offering, its grain offering and its libation.

17 'Then on the second day: twelve bulls, two rams, fourteen male lambs one year old without defect;

18   and their grain offering and their libations for the bulls, for the rams and for the lambs, by their number according to the ordinance;

19   and one male goat for a sin offering, besides the continual burnt offering and its grain offering, and their libations.

20   'Then on the third day: eleven bulls, two rams, fourteen male lambs one year old without defect;

21   and their grain offering and their libations for the bulls, for the rams and for the lambs, by their number according to the ordinance;

22   and one male goat for a sin offering, besides the continual burnt offering and its grain offering and its libation.

23   'Then on the fourth day: ten bulls, two rams, fourteen male lambs one year old without defect;

24   their grain offering and their libations for the bulls, for the rams and for the lambs, by their number according to the ordinance;

25   and one male goat for a sin offering, besides the continual burnt offering, its grain offering and its libation.

26   'Then on the fifth day: nine bulls, two rams, fourteen male lambs one year old without defect;

27   and their grain offering and their libations for the bulls, for the rams and for the lambs, by their number according to the ordinance;

28   and one male goat for a sin offering, besides the continual burnt offering and its grain offering and its libation.

29   'Then on the sixth day: eight bulls, two rams, fourteen male lambs one year old without defect;

30   and their grain offering and their libations for the bulls, for the rams and for the lambs, by their number according to the ordinance;

31   and one male goat for a sin offering, besides the continual burnt offering, its grain offering and its libations.

32   'Then on the seventh day: seven bulls, two rams, fourteen male lambs one year old without defect;

33   and their grain offering and their libations for the bulls, for the rams and for the lambs, by their number according to the ordinance;

34   and one male goat for a sin offering, besides the continual burnt offering, its grain offering and its libation.

35   'On the eighth day you shall have a solemn assembly; you shall do no laborious work.

36   'But you shall present a burnt offering, an offering by fire, as a soothing aroma to the LORD: one bull, one ram, seven male lambs one year old without defect;

37   their grain offering and their libations for the bull, for the ram and for the lambs, by their number according to the ordinance;

38   and one male goat for a sin offering, besides the continual burnt offering and its grain offering and its libation.

39   'You shall present these to the LORD at your appointed times, besides your votive offerings and your freewill offerings, for your burnt offerings and for your grain offerings and for your libations and for your peace offerings.' "

40   And Moses spoke to the sons of Israel in accordance with all that the LORD had commanded Moses.

G. The laws of vows

30 Then Moses spoke to the heads of the tribes of the sons of Israel, saying, "This is the word which the LORD has commanded.

2   "If a man makes a vow to the LORD, or takes an oath to bind himself with a binding obligation, he shall not violate his word; he shall do according to all that proceeds out of his mouth.

3   "Also if a woman makes a vow to the LORD, and binds herself by an obligation in her father's house in her youth,

4   and her father hears her vow and her obligation by which she has bound

---

29:18
vv. 3,4,9,10;
Num 15:12;
28:7,14

29:22
Num 28:15

29:28
Num 15:24

29:31
v. 22;
Gen 8:20

29:35
Lev 23:36

29:39
Lev 23:2;
1 Chr 23:31;
2 Chr 31:3;
Lev 7:11,16

*30:2
Deut 23:21;
Matt 5:23

30:2 See note to Num. 6:2 for a detailed explanation on the meaning of vows. It is also interesting to compare Matt. 5:33–37, where Jesus says, "You shall not make false vows . . ."

herself, and her father says nothing to her, then all her vows shall stand, and every obligation by which she has bound herself shall stand.

30:5
Eccl 5:4

5 "But if her father should forbid her on the day he hears *of it*, none of her vows or her obligations by which she has bound herself shall stand; and the LORD will forgive her because her father had forbidden her.

30:6
Ps 56:12

6 "However, if she should marry while under her vows or the rash statement of her lips by which she has bound herself,

7 and her husband hears of it and says nothing to her on the day he hears *it*, then her vows shall stand and her obligations by which she has bound herself shall stand.

30:8
Gen 3:16

8 "But if on the day her husband hears *of it*, he forbids her, then he shall annul her vow which she is under and the rash statement of her lips by which she has bound herself; and the LORD will forgive her.

9 "But the vow of a widow or of a divorced woman, everything by which she has bound herself, shall stand against her.

10 "However, if she vowed in her husband's house, or bound herself by an obligation with an oath,

11 and her husband heard *it*, but said nothing to her *and* did not forbid her, then all her vows shall stand, and every obligation by which she bound herself shall stand.

30:12
Eph 5:22

12 "But if her husband indeed annuls them on the day he hears *them*, then whatever proceeds out of her lips concerning her vows or concerning the obligation of herself, shall not stand; her husband has annulled them, and the LORD will forgive her.

13 "Every vow and every binding oath to humble herself, her husband may confirm it or her husband may annul it.

14 "But if her husband indeed says nothing to her from day to day, then he confirms all her vows or all her obligations which are on her; he has confirmed them, because he said nothing to her on the day he heard them.

30:15
Col 3:18

15 "But if he indeed annuls them after he has heard them, then he shall bear her guilt."

30:16
Ex 15:26

16 These are the statutes which the LORD commanded Moses, *as* between a man and his wife, *and as* between a father and his daughter, *while she is* in her youth in her father's house.

H. *The destruction of the Midianites*

1. *The slaying of the Midianites*

31:2
Num 25:1,16,
17; 27:13

31 Then the LORD spoke to Moses, saying,
2 "Take full vengeance for the sons of Israel on the Midianites; afterward you will be gathered to your people."

3 And Moses spoke to the people, saying, "Arm men from among you for the war, that they may go against Midian, to execute the LORD'S vengeance on Midian.

4 "A thousand from each tribe of all the tribes of Israel you shall send to the war."

5 So there were furnished from the thousands of Israel, a thousand from each tribe, twelve thousand armed for war.

31:6
Num 10:9

6 And Moses sent them, a thousand from each tribe, to the war, and Phinehas the son of Eleazar the priest, to the war with them, and the holy vessels and the trumpets for the alarm in his hand.

7 So they made war against Midian, just as the LORD had commanded Moses, and they killed every male.

31:8
Josh 13:21,
22; v. 16

8 And they killed the kings of Midian along with the *rest of* their slain: Evi and Rekem and Zur and Hur and Reba, the five kings of Midian; they also killed Balaam the son of Beor with the sword.

9 And the sons of Israel captured the women of Midian and their little ones; and all their cattle and all their flocks and all their goods, they plundered.

10 Then they burned all their cities where they lived and all their camps with fire.

31:11
Deut 20:14

11 And they took all the spoil and all the prey, both of man and of beast.

12 And they brought the captives and the prey and the spoil to Moses, and to Eleazar the priest and to the congregation of the sons of Israel, to the camp at the plains of Moab, which are by the Jordan opposite Jericho.

2. *The command to exterminate: rite of purification*

13   And Moses and Eleazar the priest and all the leaders of the congregation went out to meet them outside the camp.

14   And Moses was angry with the officers of the army, the captains of thousands and the captains of hundreds, who had come from service in the war.

15   And Moses said to them, "Have you spared all the women?

16   "Behold, these caused the sons of Israel, through the counsel of Balaam, to trespass against the LORD in the matter of Peor, so the plague was among the congregation of the LORD.

17   "Now therefore, kill every male among the little ones, and kill every woman who has known man intimately.

18   "But all the girls who have not known man intimately, spare for yourselves.

19   "And you, camp outside the camp seven days; whoever has killed any person, and whoever has touched any slain, purify yourselves, you and your captives, on the third day and on the seventh day.

20   "And you shall purify for yourselves every garment and every article of leather and all the work of goats' *hair,* and all articles of wood."

21   Then Eleazar the priest said to the men of war who had gone to battle, "This is the statute of the law which the LORD has commanded Moses:

22   only the gold and the silver, the bronze, the iron, the tin and the lead,

23   everything that can stand the fire, you shall pass through the fire, and it shall be clean, but it shall be purified with water for impurity. But whatever cannot stand the fire you shall pass through the water.

24   "And you shall wash your clothes on the seventh day and be clean, and afterward you may enter the camp."

3. *The division of the booty*

25   Then the LORD spoke to Moses, saying,

26   "You and Eleazar the priest and the heads of the fathers' *households* of the congregation, take a count of the booty that was captured, both of man and of animal;

27   and divide the booty between the warriors who went out to battle and all the congregation.

28   "And levy a tax for the LORD from the men of war who went out to battle, one in five hundred of the persons and of the cattle and of the donkeys and of the sheep;

29   take it from their half and give it to Eleazar the priest, as an offering to the LORD.

30   "And from the sons of Israel's half, you shall take one drawn out of every fifty of the persons, of the cattle, of the donkeys and of the sheep, from all the animals, and give them to the Levites who keep charge of the tabernacle of the LORD."

31   And Moses and Eleazar the priest did just as the LORD had commanded Moses.

32   Now the booty that remained from the spoil which the men of war had plundered was 675,000 sheep,

33   and 72,000 cattle,

34   and 61,000 donkeys,

35   and of human beings, of the women who had not known man intimately, all the persons were 32,000.

36   And the half, the portion of those who went out to war, was *as follows:* the number of sheep was 337,500,

37   and the LORD's levy of the sheep was 675,

38   and the cattle were 36,000, from which the LORD's levy was 72.

39   And the donkeys were 30,500, from which the LORD's levy was 61.

40   And the human beings were 16,000, from whom the LORD's levy was 32 persons.

41   And Moses gave the levy *which was* the LORD's offering to Eleazar the priest, just as the LORD had commanded Moses.

42   As for the sons of Israel's half, which Moses separated from the men who had gone to war—

Marginal references: 31:16 Num 25:1-9; 24:14; 2 Pet 2:15; Rev 2:14 *31:17 Judg 21:11 | 31:19 Num 19:11-22 | 31:23 Num 19:9,17 | 31:24 Lev 11:25 | 31:28 Num 18:21-30 | 31:30 Num 3:7,8, 25; 18:3,4 | 31:32 Gen 49:27; Ex 15:9 | 31:37 vv. 38,41 | 31:41 see Num 18:8,9

31:17 However, the Midianites were not exterminated, for they oppressed the Israelites later on in Canaan. See Judg. 6:1,2.

31:26ff. The *booty* (all that had been seized) was counted and equally divided among everyone, whether soldier or civilian.

43   now the congregation's half was 337,500 sheep,

44   and 36,000 cattle,

45   and 30,500 donkeys,

46   and the human beings were 16,000—

31:47
v. 30

47   and from the sons of Israel's half, Moses took one drawn out of every fifty, both of man and of animals, and gave them to the Levites, who kept charge of the tabernacle of the LORD, just as the LORD had commanded Moses.

4. The offerings of the officers and captains

48   Then the officers who were over the thousands of the army, the captains of thousands and the captains of hundreds, approached Moses;

49   and they said to Moses, "Your servants have taken a census of men of war who are in our charge, and no man of us is missing.

31:50
Ex 30:12,16

50   "So we have brought as an offering to the LORD what each man found, articles of gold, armlets and bracelets, signet rings, earrings and necklaces, to make atonement for ourselves before the LORD."

51   And Moses and Eleazar the priest took the gold from them, all kinds of wrought articles.

52   And all the gold of the offering which they offered up to the LORD, from the captains of thousands and the captains of hundreds, was 16,750 shekels.

31:53
v. 32;
Deut 20:14
31:54
Ex 30:16

53   The men of war had taken booty, every man for himself.

54   So Moses and Eleazar the priest took the gold from the captains of thousands and of hundreds, and brought it to the tent of meeting as a memorial for the sons of Israel before the LORD.

I. The beginning of the settlements: Reuben and Gad in Gilead

1. Their desire to settle east of Jordan

32:1
Ex 12:38;
Num 21:32

32 Now the sons of Reuben and the sons of Gad had an exceedingly large number of livestock. So when they saw the land of Jazer and the land of Gilead, that it was indeed a place suitable for livestock,

2   the sons of Gad and the sons of Reuben came and spoke to Moses and to Eleazar the priest and to the leaders of the congregation, saying,

32:3
v. 36
Bethnimrah;
v. 38 Sibmah;
v. 38
Baal-meon

3   "Ataroth, Dibon, Jazer, Nimrah, Heshbon, Elealeh, Sebam, Nebo and Beon,

4   the land which the LORD conquered before the congregation of Israel, is a land for livestock; and your servants have livestock."

5   And they said, "If we have found favor in your sight, let this land be given to your servants as a possession; do not take us across the Jordan."

6   But Moses said to the sons of Gad and to the sons of Reuben, "Shall your brothers go to war while you yourselves sit here?

32:7
Num 13:27-
14:4
32:8
Num 13:3,26

7   "Now why are you discouraging the sons of Israel from crossing over into the land which the LORD has given them?

8   "This is what your fathers did when I sent them from Kadesh-barnea to see the land.

9   "For when they went up to the valley of Eshcol and saw the land, they discouraged the sons of Israel so that they did not go into the land which the LORD had given them.

32:10
Num 14:11,
21; Deut 1:34
32:11
Num 14:28-30;
Deut 1:35

10   "So the LORD's anger burned in that day, and He swore, saying,

11   'None of the men who came up from Egypt, from twenty years old and upward, shall see the land which I swore to Abraham, to Isaac and to Jacob; for they did not follow Me fully,

32:12
Num 14:24;
Deut 1:36

12   except Caleb the son of Jephunneh the Kenizzite and Joshua the son of Nun, for they have followed the LORD fully.'

32:13
Num 14:33-35;
26:64,65

13   "So the LORD's anger burned against Israel, and He made them wander in the wilderness forty years, until the entire generation of those who had done evil in the sight of the LORD was destroyed.

14   "Now behold, you have risen up in your fathers' place, a brood of sinful men, to add still more to the burning anger of the LORD against Israel.

32:15
Deut 30:17,
18

15   "For if you turn away from following Him, He will once more abandon them in the wilderness; and you will destroy all these people."

2. The agreement to help the others settle west of Jordan

16 Then they came near to him and said, "We will build here sheepfolds for our livestock and cities for our little ones;

17 but we ourselves will be armed ready *to go* before the sons of Israel, until we have brought them to their place, while our little ones live in the fortified cities because of the inhabitants of the land.

18 "We will not return to our homes until every one of the sons of Israel has possessed his inheritance.

19 "For we will not have an inheritance with them on the other side of the Jordan and beyond, because our inheritance has fallen to us on this side of the Jordan toward the east."

20 So Moses said to them, "If you will do this, if you will arm yourselves before the LORD for the war,

21 and all of you armed men cross over the Jordan before the LORD until He has driven His enemies out from before Him,

22 and the land is subdued before the LORD, then afterward you shall return and be free of obligation toward the LORD and toward Israel, and this land shall be yours for a possession before the LORD.

23 "But if you will not do so, behold, you have sinned against the LORD, and be sure your sin will find you out.

24 "Build yourselves cities for your little ones, and sheepfolds for your sheep; and do what you have promised."

25 And the sons of Gad and the sons of Reuben spoke to Moses, saying, "Your servants will do just as my lord commands.

26 "Our little ones, our wives, our livestock and all our cattle shall remain there in the cities of Gilead;

27 while your servants, everyone who is armed for war, will cross over in the presence of the LORD to battle, just as my lord says."

3. Moses' decision

28 So Moses gave command concerning them to Eleazar the priest, and to Joshua the son of Nun, and to the heads of the fathers' *households* of the tribes of the sons of Israel.

29 And Moses said to them, "If the sons of Gad and the sons of Reuben, everyone who is armed for battle, will cross with you over the Jordan in the presence of the LORD, and the land will be subdued before you, then you shall give them the land of Gilead for a possession;

30 but if they will not cross over with you armed, they shall have possessions among you in the land of Canaan."

31 And the sons of Gad and the sons of Reuben answered, saying, "As the LORD has said to your servants, so we will do.

32 "We ourselves will cross over armed in the presence of the LORD into the land of Canaan, and the possession of our inheritance *shall remain* with us across the Jordan."

4. The half-tribe of Manasseh settles in Gilead

33 So Moses gave to them, to the sons of Gad and to the sons of Reuben and to the half-tribe of Joseph's son Manasseh, the kingdom of Sihon, king of the Amorites and the kingdom of Og, the king of Bashan, the land with its cities with *their* territories, the cities of the surrounding land.

34 And the sons of Gad built Dibon and Ataroth and Aroer,

35 and Atroth-shophan and Jazer and Jogbehah,

36 and Beth-nimrah and Beth-haran as fortified cities, and sheepfolds for sheep.

37 And the sons of Reuben built Heshbon and Elealeh and Kiriathaim,

38 and Nebo and Baal-meon—*their* names being changed—and Sibmah, and they gave *other* names to the cities which they built.

39 And the sons of Machir the son of Manasseh went to Gilead and took it, and dispossessed the Amorites who were in it.

40 So Moses gave Gilead to Machir the son of Manasseh, and he lived in it.

41 And Jair the son of Manasseh went and took its towns, and called them Havvoth-jair.

Marginal references:

32:17 Josh 4:12,13
32:18 Josh 22:1-4
32:19 v. 33
32:20 Deut 3:18
32:22 Deut 3:12-20
32:24 vv. 16,34
32:26 Josh 1:14
32:27 Josh 4:12
32:28 Josh 1:13
32:29 v. 1
32:33 Deut 3:12-17; Josh 12:1-6; Num 21:24, 33,35
32:41 Judg 10:4

42   And Nobah went and took Kenath and its villages, and called it Nobah after his own name.

J. The stages of Israel's journey from Egypt to Canaan

33:1
Ps 77:20;
Mic 6:4

33 These are the journeys of the sons of Israel, by which they came out from the land of Egypt by their armies, under the leadership of Moses and Aaron.
2   And Moses recorded their starting places according to their journeys by the command of the LORD, and these are their journeys according to their starting places.

33:3
Ex 12:37;
14:8

3   And they journeyed from Rameses in the first month, on the fifteenth day of the first month; on the next day after the Passover the sons of Israel started out boldly in the sight of all the Egyptians,

33:4
Ex 12:12

4   while the Egyptians were burying all their first-born whom the LORD had struck down among them. The LORD had also executed judgments on their gods.
5   Then the sons of Israel journeyed from Rameses, and camped in Succoth.

33:6
Ex 13:20

6   And they journeyed from Succoth, and camped in Etham, which is on the edge of the wilderness.

33:7
Ex 14:2,9

7   And they journeyed from Etham, and turned back to Pi-hahiroth, which faces Baal-zephon; and they camped before Migdol.

33:8
Ex 14:22

8   And they journeyed from before Hahiroth, and passed through the midst of the sea into the wilderness; and they went three days' journey in the wilderness of Etham, and camped at Marah.

33:9
Ex 15:27

9   And they journeyed from Marah, and came to Elim; and in Elim there were twelve springs of water and seventy palm trees; and they camped there.
10   And they journeyed from Elim, and camped by the Red Sea.

33:11
Ex 16:1

11   And they journeyed from the Red Sea, and camped in the wilderness of Sin.
12   And they journeyed from the wilderness of Sin, and camped at Dophkah.
13   And they journeyed from Dophkah, and camped at Alush.

33:14
Ex 17:1

14   And they journeyed from Alush, and camped at Rephidim; now it was there that the people had no water to drink.

33:15
Ex 19:1
33:16
Num 11:34

15   And they journeyed from Rephidim, and camped in the wilderness of Sinai.
16   And they journeyed from the wilderness of Sinai, and camped at Kibroth-hattaavah.

33:17
Num 11:35

17   And they journeyed from Kibroth-hattaavah, and camped at Hazeroth.
18   And they journeyed from Hazeroth, and camped at Rithmah.
19   And they journeyed from Rithmah, and camped at Rimmon-perez.

33:20
see
Josh 10:29

20   And they journeyed from Rimmon-perez, and camped at Libnah.
21   And they journeyed from Libnah, and camped at Rissah.
22   And they journeyed from Rissah, and camped in Kehelathah.
23   And they journeyed from Kehelathah, and camped at Mount Shepher.
24   And they journeyed from Mount Shepher, and camped at Haradah.
25   And they journeyed from Haradah, and camped at Makheloth.
26   And they journeyed from Makheloth, and camped at Tahath.
27   And they journeyed from Tahath, and camped at Terah.
28   And they journeyed from Terah, and camped at Mithkah.
29   And they journeyed from Mithkah, and camped at Hashmonah.

33:30
Deut 10:6

30   And they journeyed from Hashmonah, and camped at Moseroth.
31   And they journeyed from Moseroth, and camped at Bene-jaakan.
32   And they journeyed from Bene-jaakan, and camped at Hor-haggidgad.

33:33
Deut 10:7

33   And they journeyed from Hor-haggidgad, and camped at Jotbathah.
34   And they journeyed from Jotbathah, and camped at Abronah.

33:35
Deut 2:8
*33:36
Num 20:1

35   And they journeyed from Abronah, and camped at Ezion-geber.
36   And they journeyed from Ezion-geber, and camped in the wilderness of Zin, that is, Kadesh.

33:37
Num 20:16,
22; 21:4

37   And they journeyed from Kadesh, and camped at Mount Hor, at the edge of the land of Edom.

33:38
Num 20:25,
28; Deut 10:6

38   Then Aaron the priest went up to Mount Hor at the command of the LORD, and died there, in the fortieth year after the sons of Israel had come from the land of Egypt on the first *day* in the fifth month.
39   And Aaron was one hundred twenty-three years old when he died on Mount Hor.

33:36 *Ezion-geber*, see note to 1 Kin. 9:26.

40 Now the Canaanite, the king of Arad who lived in the Negev in the land of Canaan, heard of the coming of the sons of Israel.

41 Then they journeyed from Mount Hor, and camped at Zalmonah.

42 And they journeyed from Zalmonah, and camped at Punon.

43 And they journeyed from Punon, and camped at Oboth.

44 And they journeyed from Oboth, and camped at Iye-abarim, at the border of Moab.

45 And they journeyed from Iyim, and camped at Dibon-gad.

46 And they journeyed from Dibon-gad, and camped at Almon-diblathaim.

47 And they journeyed from Almon-diblathaim, and camped in the mountains of Abarim, before Nebo.

48 And they journeyed from the mountains of Abarim, and camped in the plains of Moab by the Jordan *opposite* Jericho.

49 And they camped by the Jordan, from Beth-jeshimoth as far as Abel-shittim in the plains of Moab.

K. God's commands concerning Canaan

1. The command to drive out the inhabitants

50 Then the LORD spoke to Moses in the plains of Moab by the Jordan *opposite* Jericho, saying,

51 "Speak to the sons of Israel and say to them, 'When you cross over the Jordan into the land of Canaan,

52 then you shall drive out all the inhabitants of the land from before you, and destroy all their figured stones, and destroy all their molten images and demolish all their high places;

53 and you shall take possession of the land and live in it, for I have given the land to you to possess it.

54 'And you shall inherit the land by lot according to your families; to the larger you shall give more inheritance, and to the smaller you shall give less inheritance. Wherever the lot falls to anyone, that shall be his. You shall inherit according to the tribes of your fathers.

55 'But if you do not drive out the inhabitants of the land from before you, then it shall come about that those whom you let remain of them *will become* as pricks in your eyes and as thorns in your sides, and they shall trouble you in the land in which you live.

56 'And it shall come about that as I plan to do to them, so I will do to you.' "

2. The boundaries of the land

34 Then the LORD spoke to Moses, saying,

2 "Command the sons of Israel and say to them, 'When you enter the land of Canaan, this is the land that shall fall to you as an inheritance, *even the* land of Canaan according to its borders.

3 'Your southern sector shall extend from the wilderness of Zin along the side of Edom, and your southern border shall extend from the end of the Salt Sea eastward.

4 'Then your border shall turn *direction* from the south to the ascent of Akrabbim, and continue to Zin, and its [31]termination shall be to the south of Kadesh-barnea; and it shall reach Hazaraddar, and continue to Azmon.

5 'And the border shall turn *direction* from Azmon to the brook of Egypt, and its termination shall be at the sea.

6 'As for the western border, you shall have the Great Sea, that is, *its* coastline; this shall be your west border.

7 'And this shall be your north border: you shall draw your *border* line from the Great Sea to Mount Hor.

8 'You shall draw a line from Mount Hor to the Lebo-hamath, and the termination of the border shall be at Zedad;

[Marginal references:]
33:40 Num 21:1
33:43 Num 21:10
33:44 Num 21:11
33:47 Num 27:12
33:48 Num 22:1
33:49 Num 25:1
33:52 Ex 23:24,33; 34:13; Deut 7:2,5; 12:3; Josh 11:12
33:54 Num 26:53-55
*33:55 Josh 23:13; Ps 106:34,36
34:2 Gen 17:8; Deut 1:7; Ps 78:55; Ezek 47:15
34:3 Josh 15:1-3
34:5 Gen 15:18; Josh 15:4,47
34:7 Ezek 47:15-17
*34:8 Num 13:21

---

[31]Lit., *goings out,* and so throughout this context

9　and the border shall proceed to Ziphron, and its termination shall be at Hazar-enan. This shall be your north border.

10　'For your eastern border you shall also draw a line from Hazar-enan to Shepham,

34:11
2 Kin 23:33;
Deut 3:17;
Josh 11:2

11　and the border shall go down from Shepham to Riblah on the east side of Ain; and the border shall go down and reach to the [32]slope on the east side of the Sea of Chinnereth.

12　'And the border shall go down to the Jordan and its termination shall be at the Salt Sea. This shall be your land according to its borders all around.' ''

34:13
Josh 14:1,2

13　So Moses commanded the sons of Israel, saying, "This is the land that you are to apportion by lot among you as a possession, which the LORD has commanded to give to the nine and a half tribes.

34:14
Num 32:33;
Josh 14:2,3

14　"For the tribe of the sons of Reuben have received *theirs* according to their fathers' households, and the tribe of the sons of Gad according to their fathers' households, and the half-tribe of Manasseh have received their possession.

15　"The two and a half tribes have received their possession across the Jordan opposite Jericho, eastward toward the sunrising."

3. The men chosen to divide the land

16　Then the LORD spoke to Moses, saying,

34:17
Josh 14:1

17　"These are the names of the men who shall apportion the land to you for inheritance: Eleazar the priest and Joshua the son of Nun.

34:18
Num 1:4,16

18　"And you shall take one leader of every tribe to apportion the land for inheritance.

19　"And these are the names of the men: of the tribe of Judah, Caleb the son of Jephunneh.

20　"And of the tribe of the sons of Simeon, Samuel the son of Ammihud.

21　"Of the tribe of Benjamin, Elidad the son of Chislon.

22　"And of the tribe of the sons of Dan a leader, Bukki the son of Jogli.

23　"Of the sons of Joseph: of the tribe of the sons of Manasseh a leader, Hanniel the son of Ephod.

24　"And of the tribe of the sons of Ephraim a leader, Kemuel the son of Shiphtan.

25　"And of the tribe of the sons of Zebulun a leader, Elizaphan the son of Parnach.

26　"And of the tribe of the sons of Issachar a leader, Paltiel the son of Azzan.

27　"And of the tribe of the sons of Asher a leader, Ahihud the son of Shelomi.

28　"And of the tribe of the sons of Naphtali a leader, Pedahel the son of Ammihud."

29　These are those whom the LORD commanded to apportion the inheritance to the sons of Israel in the land of Canaan.

4. The Levitical cities

a. The forty-eight cities and pasture land

35　Now the LORD spoke to Moses in the plains of Moab by the Jordan opposite Jericho, saying,

35:2
Lev 25:32-34;
Josh 14:3,4

2　"Command the sons of Israel that they give to the Levites from the inheritance of their possession, cities to live in; and you shall give to the Levites pasture lands around the cities.

3　"And the cities shall be theirs to live in; and their pasture lands shall be for their cattle and for their herds and for all their beasts.

4　"And the pasture lands of the cities which you shall give to the Levites *shall extend* from the wall of the city outward a thousand cubits around.

5　"You shall also measure outside the city on the east side two thousand cubits, and on the south side two thousand cubits, and on the west side two thousand cubits, and on the north side two thousand cubits, with the city in the center. This shall become theirs as pasture lands for the cities.

35:6
Josh 20:7-9;
21:3,13,21,
27,32,36,38

6　"And the cities which you shall give to the Levites *shall be* the six cities of

[32]Lit., *shoulder*

refuge, which you shall give for the manslayer to flee to; and in addition to them you shall give forty-two cities.

7   "All the cities which you shall give to the Levites *shall be* forty-eight cities, together with their pasture lands.

8   "As for the cities which you shall give from the possession of the sons of Israel, you shall take more from the larger and you shall take less from the smaller; each shall give some of his cities to the Levites in proportion to his possession which he inherits."

b. *The cities of refuge*

9   Then the LORD spoke to Moses, saying,

10   "Speak to the sons of Israel and say to them, 'When you cross the Jordan into the land of Canaan,

11   then you shall select for yourselves cities to be your cities of refuge, that the manslayer who has killed any person unintentionally may flee there.

12   'And the cities shall be to you as a refuge from the avenger, so that the manslayer may not die until he stands before the congregation for trial.

13   'And the cities which you are to give shall be your six cities of refuge.

14   'You shall give three cities across the Jordan and three cities in the land of Canaan; they are to be cities of refuge.

15   'These six cities shall be for refuge for the sons of Israel, and for the alien and for the sojourner among them; that anyone who kills a person unintentionally may flee there.

16   'But if he struck him down with an iron object, so that he died, he is a murderer; the murderer shall surely be put to death.

17   'And if he struck him down with a stone in the hand, by which he may die, and *as a result* he died, he is a murderer; the murderer shall surely be put to death.

18   'Or if he struck him with a wooden object in the hand, by which he may die, and *as a result* he died, he is a murderer; the murderer shall surely be put to death.

19   'The blood avenger himself shall put the murderer to death; he shall put him to death when he meets him.

20   'And if he pushed him of hatred, or threw something at him lying in wait and *as a result* he died,

21   or if he struck him down with his hand in enmity, and *as a result* he died, the one who struck him shall surely be put to death, he is a murderer; the blood avenger shall put the murderer to death when he meets him.

22   'But if he pushed him suddenly without enmity, or threw something at him without lying in wait,

23   or with any deadly object of stone, and without seeing it dropped on him so that he died, while he was not his enemy nor seeking his injury,

24   then the congregation shall judge between the slayer and the blood avenger according to these ordinances.

25   'And the congregation shall deliver the manslayer from the hand of the blood avenger, and the congregation shall restore him to his city of refuge to which he fled; and he shall live in it until the death of the high priest who was anointed with the holy oil.

26   'But if the manslayer shall at any time go beyond the border of his city of refuge to which he may flee,

27   and the blood avenger finds him outside the border of his city of refuge, and the blood avenger kills the manslayer, he shall not be guilty of blood

28   because he should have remained in his city of refuge until the death of the high priest. But after the death of the high priest the manslayer shall return to the land of his possession.

29   'And these things shall be for a statutory ordinance to you throughout your generations in all your dwellings.

30   'If anyone kills a person, the murderer shall be put to death at the evidence of witnesses, but no person shall be put to death on the testimony of one witness.

31   'Moreover, you shall not take ransom for the life of a murderer who is guilty of death, but he shall surely be put to death.

32   'And you shall not take ransom for him who has fled to his city of refuge, that he may return to live in the land before the death of the priest.

35:8
Num 26:54;
Lev 25:32-34;
Josh 21:1-42

35:11
Deut 19:1-13;
Ex 21:13
*35:12
Josh 20:2-6

35:15
v. 11

35:16
Ex 21:12,14;
Lev 24:17

35:19
vv. 21,24,27

35:22
v. 11;
Ex 21:13

35:24
v. 12

35:30
v. 16;
Deut 17:6;
19:15;
Matt 18:16;
2 Cor 13:1;
Heb 10:28

35:12 *from the avenger.* The cities of refuge implemented the new law, "an eye for an eye," by protecting the man-slayer from the kinsman who, under the ancient custom of vendetta, was to avenge the death of the deceased.

35:33
Ps 106:38;
Gen 9:6

35:34
Lev 18:25;
Ex 29:45,46

36:1
Num 26:29;
27:1

36:2
Num 26:55;
33:54; 27:1,7

36:4
Lev 25:10

36:6
v. 12

36:8
1 Chr 23:22

36:11
Num 27:1

36:13
Num 22:1;
Lev 26:46;
27:34

33 'So you shall not pollute the land in which you are; for blood pollutes the land and no expiation can be made for the land for the blood that is shed on it, except by the blood of him who shed it.

34 'And you shall not defile the land in which you live, in the midst of which I dwell; for I the Lord am dwelling in the midst of the sons of Israel.' "

5. *Laws concerning the marriage of heiresses*

36 And the heads of the fathers' *households* of the family of the sons of Gilead, the son of Machir, the son of Manasseh, of the families of the sons of Joseph, came near and spoke before Moses and before the leaders, the heads of the fathers' *households* of the sons of Israel,

2 and they said, "The Lord commanded my lord to give the land by lot to the sons of Israel as an inheritance, and my lord was commanded by the Lord to give the inheritance of Zelophehad our brother to his daughters.

3 "But if they marry one of the sons of the *other* tribes of the sons of Israel, their inheritance will be withdrawn from the inheritance of our fathers and will be added to the inheritance of the tribe to which they belong; thus it will be withdrawn from our allotted inheritance.

4 "And when the jubilee of the sons of Israel comes, then their inheritance will be added to the inheritance of the tribe to which they belong; so their inheritance will be withdrawn from the inheritance of the tribe of our fathers."

5 Then Moses commanded the sons of Israel according to the word of the Lord, saying, "The tribe of the sons of Joseph are right in *their* statements.

6 "This is what the Lord has commanded concerning the daughters of Zelophehad, saying, 'Let them marry whom they wish; only they must marry within the family of the tribe of their father.'

7 "Thus no inheritance of the sons of Israel shall be transferred from tribe to tribe, for the sons of Israel shall each hold to the inheritance of the tribe of his fathers.

8 "And every daughter who comes into possession of an inheritance of any tribe of the sons of Israel, shall be wife to one of the family of the tribe of her father, so that the sons of Israel each may possess the inheritance of his fathers.

9 "Thus no inheritance shall be transferred from one tribe to another tribe, for the tribes of the sons of Israel shall each hold to his own inheritance."

10 Just as the Lord had commanded Moses, so the daughters of Zelophehad did:

11 Mahlah, Tirzah, Hoglah, Milcah and Noah, the daughters of Zelophehad married their uncles' sons.

12 They married *those* from the families of the sons of Manasseh the son of Joseph, and their inheritance remained with the tribe of the family of their father.

13 These are the commandments and the ordinances which the Lord commanded to the sons of Israel through Moses in the plains of Moab by the Jordan *opposite* Jericho.

INTRODUCTION TO

THE FIFTH BOOK OF MOSES

COMMONLY CALLED

DEUTERONOMY

Authorship and Background: The title of this book is the English form of the Greek word *deuteronomion*, "second law," or "repetition of the law," which is the Septuagint title for this fifth book of the Pentateuch. The Hebrew title, "These are the words," is simply the first two Hebrew words in the text. Jewish and Samaritan traditions represent Moses as the author. In modern times Mosaic authorship has been disputed by some critical scholars. Many acknowledge, however, that the contents of the book are generally of Mosaic origin. The death of Moses is clearly an addition after his time. The book itself claims Mosaic authority, asserting that "Moses undertook to expound this law, saying" (1:5) and "Moses wrote this law" (31:9) and commanded the Levites, "Take this book of the law and place it beside the ark of the covenant" (31:26).

Deuteronomy presupposes what is found in Exodus and Leviticus. Israel had wandered in the wilderness for almost two decades and now camped outside the promised land, ready to go in. But Moses, because of his sin, had been refused permission to enter Canaan. He was to be replaced by Joshua. Before taking his departure from the people, Moses oriented the new generation to the covenantal relationship that they bore to God and explained the terms of that covenant and its indispensable condition of obedience.

Characteristics: Deuteronomy is hortatory in the sense that Moses warns the people of the consequences of disobedience, and urges on them the necessity of walking according to the will of God. In some measure the book is an inspired account of reminiscences of the prayers, inner life, and thoughts of Moses. Written in prose and poetry, the material is imaginative yet didactic. Moses evidences outbursts of human passion in indignation and personal appeal (9:13-21; 10:10-21). He addresses all of the people in language easily comprehended, specifying what God requires of them. The substance of his discourses is summed up in the words, "What does the LORD your God require from you, but to fear the LORD your God, to walk in all His ways and love Him, and to serve the LORD your God with all your heart and with all your soul" (10:12).

Contents:

I. Moses' first discourse (1:1-4:43): Moses recounts in retrospect what God has done for Israel: the journey, the successes, and God's gift of the land to the people. How Moses bore with the sins of the people. God having acted, Israel must listen and obey. Idolatry is a peril. The LORD is God. The three cities of refuge designated.

II. Moses' second address (4:44-26:19): An extended review of the Ten Commandments. God on the mountain; the purpose of the Law; the greatest commandment; what children are to be taught. The command to wipe out idolatry by exterminating the Canaanites. Illustrations of past discipline because of sins like the making of the golden calf. An exhortation to obedience with blessing. Moses' exposition of principal laws. The one central place of worship. Idolatry to be punished. The law of unclean food and the tithe of fruit. Directions about slaves and the poor; manumission. The Feasts of the Passover, Harvest, and Tabernacles. The duties of officials in the administration of justice: courts, the king, priests, and the prophet. Moses' word on criminal law: homicide, theft, and perjury. The laws concerning wars in the future. Sundry laws: unsolved murder, women taken in war, inheritance, wicked sons, sex, divorce, corporal punishment. Thanksgiving.

III. The covenant renewed (27:1-30:20): Stones to be erected when the Jordan is crossed. The Law to be ratified. Blessings for obedience and cursing for disobedience. The covenant renewed; the choice of life and death set before the people.

IV. Moses' final words and death (31:1-34:12): Moses' last words: Joshua appointed and commissioned; the Law to be placed in the ark. The son of Moses. The blessing of Moses. The command to prepare for death. The death and burial of Moses.

THE FIFTH BOOK OF MOSES

COMMONLY CALLED

DEUTERONOMY

I. *Moses' first address (1.1–4:43)*

A. *The introduction*

1 These are the words which Moses spoke to all Israel across the Jordan in the wilderness, in the Arabah opposite Suph, between Paran and Tophel and Laban and Hazeroth and Dizahab.

2 It is eleven days' *journey* from Horeb by the way of Mount Seir to Kadesh-barnea.

3 And it came about in the fortieth year, on the first day of the eleventh month, that Moses spoke to the children of Israel, according to all that the LORD had commanded him *to give* to them, **1:3 Num 33:38*

4 after he had defeated Sihon the king of the Amorites, who lived in Heshbon, and Og the king of Bashan, who lived in Ashtaroth and Edrei. *1:4 Num 21:24, 33*

5 Across the Jordan in the land of Moab, Moses undertook to expound this law, saying,

B. *The guidance of God from Horeb to Kadesh*

1. *The command to enter the land*

6 "The LORD our God spoke to us at Horeb, saying, 'You have stayed long enough at this mountain. *1:6 Ex 3:1; Num 10:11-13*

7 'Turn and set your journey, and go to the hill country of the Amorites, and to all their neighbors in the Arabah, in the hill country and in the lowland and in the ¹Negev and by the seacoast, the land of the Canaanites, and Lebanon, as far as the great river, the river Euphrates.

8 'See, I have placed the land before you; go in and possess the land which the LORD swore to give to your fathers, to Abraham, to Isaac, and to Jacob, to them and their descendants after them.' *1:8 Gen 12:7; 15:18; 17:7,8; 26:4; 28:13*

2. *The choice of leaders*

9 "And I spoke to you at that time, saying, 'I am not able to bear *the burden* of you alone. *1:9 Ex 18:18*

10 'The LORD your God has multiplied you, and behold, you are this day as the stars of heaven for multitude. *1:10 Gen 15:5; Deut 10:22*

11 'May the LORD, the God of your fathers, increase you a thousand-fold more than you are, and bless you, just as He has promised you! *1:11 Gen 22:17; Ex 32:13*

12 'How can I alone bear the load and burden of you and your strife?

13 'Choose wise and discerning and experienced men from your tribes, and I will appoint them as your heads.' *1:13 Ex 18:21*

14 "And you answered me and said, 'The thing which you have said to do is good.'

15 "So I took the heads of your tribes, wise and experienced men, and appointed *1:15 Ex 18:25*

¹I.e., South country

1:1 *across the Jordan.* This expression has been interpreted to be equivalent to our name "Trans-Jordan," but in 3:20, 25; 11:30 it is not used in this technical sense and clearly means "Canaan." Some believe that the expression is used relative to the speaker or writer. Since Moses never got beyond Moab, *across the Jordan* in vv. 1,5 implies that the writer of the introduction is in Canaan.
1:2 *eleven days' journey.* This interesting note, confirmed by modern travelers, highlights the thirty-eight lost years resulting from Israel's disobedience at Kadesh-barnea.
Horeb, an alternate designation for Sinai. The name occurs only twelve times in the Pentateuch, and nine of

these are in Deuteronomy. The name Sinai occurs thirty-one times in the Pentateuch, but it appears only once in Deuteronomy (33:2).

1:3 *fortieth year,* after the exodus from Egypt. The Israelites crossed the Jordan in the first month of the next year (Josh. 4:19); and of this period of about forty days, thirty were spent in mourning for Moses (34:8). Therefore, the events in this book took place within a week or so.

1:5 *undertook to expound.* This clearly indicates that Deuteronomy is an interpretation, not a mere repetition, of the law.

them heads over you, leaders of thousands, and of hundreds, of fifties and of tens, and officers for your tribes.

1:16
Deut 16:18;
Lev 24:22

16 "Then I charged your judges at that time, saying, 'Hear *the cases* between your fellow countrymen, and judge righteously between a man and his fellow countryman, or the alien who is with him.

1:17
Lev 19:15;
James 2:1;
Ex 18:19-26

17 'You shall not show partiality in judgment; you shall hear the small and the great alike. You shall not fear man, for the judgment is God's. And the case that is too hard for you, you shall bring to me, and I will hear it.'

18 "And I commanded you at that time all the things that you should do.

3. *The episode at Kadesh-barnea: the report of the spies*

1:19
v. 2;
Deut 8:15;
Num 13:26

19 "Then we set out from Horeb, and went through all that great and terrible wilderness which you saw, on the way to the hill country of the Amorites, just as the LORD our God had commanded us; and we came to Kadesh-barnea.

20 "And I said to you, 'You have come to the hill country of the Amorites which the LORD our God is about to give us.

1:21
Josh 1:9

21 'See, the LORD your God has placed the land before you; go up, take possession, as the LORD, the God of your fathers, has spoken to you. Do not fear or be dismayed.'

22 "Then all of you approached me and said, 'Let us send men before us, that they may search out the land for us, and bring back to us word of the way by which we should go up, and the cities which we shall enter.'

1:23
Num 13:1-3

23 "And the thing pleased me and I took twelve of your men, one man for each tribe.

1:24
Num 13:22-24

24 "And they turned and went up into the hill country, and came to the valley of Eshcol, and spied it out.

1:25
Num 13:27

25 "Then they took *some* of the fruit of the land in their hands and brought it down to us; and they brought us back a report and said, 'It is a good land which the LORD our God is about to give us.'

1:26
Num 14:1-4

26 "Yet you were not willing to go up, but rebelled against the command of the LORD your God;

1:27
Deut 9:28;
Ps 106:25

27 and you grumbled in your tents and said, 'Because the LORD hates us, He has brought us out of the land of Egypt to deliver us into the hand of the Amorites to destroy us.

*1:28
Num 13:28,
31-33;
Deut 9:1,2

28 'Where can we go up? Our brethren have made our hearts melt, saying, "The people are bigger and taller than we; the cities are large and fortified to heaven. And besides, we saw the sons of the Anakim there." '

29 "Then I said to you, 'Do not be shocked, nor fear them.

1:30
Ex 14:14;
Deut 3:22

30 'The LORD your God who goes before you will Himself fight on your behalf, just as He did for you in Egypt before your eyes,

1:31
Deut 32:11,
12;
Acts 13:18

31 and in the wilderness where you saw how the LORD your God carried you, just as a man carries his son, in all the way which you have walked, until you came to this place.'

1:32
Ps 106:24
1:33
Ex 13:21;
Num 10:33

32 "But for all this, you did not trust the LORD your God,

33 who goes before you on *your* way, to seek out a place for you to encamp, in fire by night and cloud by day, to show you the way in which you should go.

1:34
Num 14:22-30

34 "Then the LORD heard the sound of your words, and He was angry and took an oath, saying,

35 'Not one of these men, this evil generation, shall see the good land which I swore to give your fathers,

36 except Caleb the son of Jephunneh; he shall see it, and to him and to his sons I will give the land on which he has set foot, because he has followed the LORD fully.'

1:37
Num 20:12;
Deut 3:26;
Ps 106:32

37 "The LORD was angry with me also on your account, saying, 'Not even you shall enter there.

1:38
Num 14:30;
Deut 3:28;
31:7

38 'Joshua the son of Nun, who stands before you, he shall enter there; encourage him, for he shall cause Israel to inherit it.

39 'Moreover, your little ones who you said would become a prey, and your

---

1:28 *fortified to heaven.* The walls of the large Canaanite cities ranged from thirty to fifty feet high.
1:36 Caleb and Joshua are both commended as men who *followed the LORD fully* (see Num. 32:12; Josh. 14:8,9,14). They were not perfect in the sense that they were sinless.

Rather they were blameless in that they walked in obedience to what God commanded them with respect to entering the promised land. No higher commendation can be given a man.

sons, who this day have no knowledge of good or evil, shall enter there, and I will give it to them, and they shall possess it.

40   'But as for you, turn around and set out for the wilderness by the way to the Red Sea.'

41   "Then you answered and said to me, 'We have sinned against the LORD; we will indeed go up and fight, just as the LORD our God commanded us.' And every man of you girded on his weapons of war, and regarded it as easy to go up into the hill country.

42   "And the LORD said to me, 'Say to them, "Do not go up, nor fight, for I am not among you; lest you be defeated before your enemies." '

43   "So I spoke to you, but you would not listen. Instead you rebelled against the command of the LORD, and acted presumptuously and went up into the hill country.

44   "And the Amorites who lived in that hill country came out against you, and chased you as bees do, and crushed you from Seir to Hormah.

45   "Then you returned and wept before the LORD; but the LORD did not listen to your voice, nor give ear to you.

46   "So you remained in Kadesh many days, the days that you spent *there*.

C. *The years in the wilderness*

1. *The command to leave the Edomites alone*

2   "Then we turned and set out for the wilderness by the way to the Red Sea, as the LORD spoke to me, and circled Mount Seir for many days.

2   "And the LORD spoke to me, saying,

3   'You have circled this mountain long enough. *Now* turn north,

4   and command the people, saying, "You will pass through the territory of your brothers the sons of Esau who live in Seir; and they will be afraid of you. So be very careful;

5   do not provoke them, for I will not give you any of their land, even *as little as* a footstep because I have given Mount Seir to Esau as a possession.

6   "You shall buy food from them with money so that you may eat, and you shall also purchase water from them with money so that you may drink.

7   "For the LORD your God has blessed you in all that you have done; He has known your wanderings through this great wilderness. These forty years the LORD your God has been with you; you have not lacked a thing." '

8   "So we passed beyond our brothers the sons of Esau, who live in Seir, away from the Arabah road, away from Elath and from Ezion-geber. And we turned and passed through by the way of the wilderness of Moab.

2. *The command to leave the Moabites alone*

9   "Then the LORD said to me, 'Do not harass Moab, nor provoke them to war, for I will not give you any of their land as a possession, because I have given Ar to the sons of Lot as a possession.

10   (The Emim lived there formerly, a people as great, numerous, and tall as the Anakim.

11   Like the Anakim, they are also regarded as Rephaim, but the Moabites call them Emim.

12   The Horites formerly lived in Seir, but the sons of Esau dispossessed them and destroyed them from before them and settled in their place, just as Israel did to the land of their possession which the LORD gave to them.)

13   'Now arise and cross over the brook Zered yourselves.' So we crossed over the brook Zered.

14   "Now the time that it took for us to come from Kadesh-barnea, until we crossed over the brook Zered, was thirty-eight years; until all the generation of the men of war perished from within the camp, as the LORD had sworn to them.

15   "Moreover the hand of the LORD was against them, to destroy them from within the camp, until they all perished.

2:10–12   Some regard these verses as a scribal insertion;   similarly 2:20–23; 3:9,11,13,14.

Marginal references:

1:39 Num 14:3,31
1:40 Num 14:25
1:41 Num 14:40
1:42 Num 14:42
1:43 Num 14:44, 45
1:44 Ps 118:12
2:1 Num 21:4
2:4 Num 20:14
2:5 Josh 24:4
2:7 Deut 8:2-4
2:8 Judg 11:18
2:9 v. 18; Num 21:28; Gen 19:36,37
*2:10ff Gen 14:5; Num 13:22, 33
2:12 v. 22
2:14 Num 13:26; 14:29-35; 26:64; Deut 1:34,35
2:15 Ps 106:26

3. *The command to leave the Ammonites alone*

16 "So it came about when all the men of war had finally perished from among the people,

17   that the LORD spoke to me, saying,

18   'You shall cross over Ar, the border of Moab, today.

19   'And when you come opposite the sons of Ammon, do not harass them nor provoke them, for I will not give you any of the land of the sons of Ammon as a possession, because I have given it to the sons of Lot as a possession.'

20   (It is also regarded as the land of the Rephaim, *for* Rephaim formerly lived in it, but the Ammonites call them Zamzummin,

21   a people as great, numerous, and tall as the Anakim, but the LORD destroyed them before them. And they dispossessed them and settled in their place,

22   just as He did for the sons of Esau, who live in Seir, when He destroyed the Horites from before them; and they dispossessed them, and settled in their place even to this day.

23   And the Avvim, who lived in villages as far as Gaza, the ²Caphtorim who came from ³Caphtor, destroyed them and lived in their place.)

24   'Arise, set out, and pass through the valley of Arnon. Look! I have given Sihon the Amorite, king of Heshbon, and his land into your hand; begin to take possession and contend with him in battle.

25   'This day I will begin to put the dread and fear of you upon the peoples everywhere under the heavens, who, when they hear the report of you, shall tremble and be in anguish because of you.'

D. *The victories over the Amorites*

1. *Over Sihon, king of Heshbon*

26 "So I sent messengers from the wilderness of Kedemoth to Sihon king of Heshbon with words of peace, saying,

27   'Let me pass through your land, I will travel only on the highway; I will not turn aside to the right or to the left.

28   'You will sell me food for money so that I may eat, and give me water for money so that I may drink, only let me pass through on foot,

29   just as the sons of Esau who live in Seir and the Moabites who live in Ar did for me, until I cross over the Jordan into the land which the LORD our God is giving to us.'

30   "But Sihon king of Heshbon was not willing for us to pass through his land; for the LORD your God hardened his spirit and made his heart obstinate, in order to deliver him into your hand, as *he is* today.

31   "And the LORD said to me, 'See, I have begun to deliver Sihon and his land over to you. Begin to occupy, that you may possess his land.'

32   "Then Sihon with all his people came out to meet us in battle at Jahaz.

33   "And the LORD our God delivered him over to us; and we defeated him with his sons and all his people.

34   "So we captured all his cities at that time, and utterly destroyed the men, women and children of every city. We left no survivor.

35   "We took only the animals as our booty and the spoil of the cities which we had captured.

36   "From Aroer which is on the edge of the valley of Arnon and *from* the city which is in the valley, even to Gilead, there was no city that was too high for us; the LORD our God delivered all over to us.

37   "Only you did not go near to the land of the sons of Ammon, all along the river Jabbok and the cities of the hill country, and wherever the LORD our God had commanded us.

²I.e., Philistines   ³I.e., Crete

2:19
v. 9

2:21
see v. 10

*2:22
Gen 36:8;
v. 12

*2:23
Josh 13:3;
Gen 10:14;
Amos 9:7
2:24
Judg 11:18

2:25
Ex 15:14,15;
Deut 11:25;
Josh 2:9,10

2:26
Deut 20:10

2:27
Num 21:21,
22
2:28
Num 20:19

*2:30
Num 21:23

2:31
Deut 1:8

2:32
Num 21:23,
24; Deut 7:2;
20:16

*2:34
Deut 3:6

2:36
Deut 3:12;
4:48; Ps 44:3

2:37
Num 21:24

2:22 *to this day*, that is, the time of the writing of the note. This is a very common expression in the historical books. See especially Gen. 22:14; 32:32; 35:20; Deut. 3:14; 34:6; Josh. 4:9; 7:26; Judg. 1:21; 10:4; 1 Sam. 6:18; 2 Sam. 4:3; 1 Kin. 9:13; 2 Kin. 8:22.
2:23 *Caphtor*, the island of Crete.
2:30 *hardened his spirit*. See note to Ex. 4:21.

2:34 *left no survivor*. This ancient practice was called *herem*, "devotion to destruction." The enemy and its possessions were devoted to Yahweh. Thus, in this holy war the males, and in some cases women and children (20:16), were slain and the cities destroyed. The booty was divided among the victors.

2. Over Og, king of Bashan

3 "Then we turned and went up the road to Bashan, and Og, king of Bashan, with all his people came out to meet us in battle at Edrei.

2 "But the LORD said to me, 'Do not fear him, for I have delivered him and all his people and his land into your hand; and you shall do to him just as you did to Sihon king of the Amorites, who lived at Heshbon.'

3 "So the LORD our God delivered Og also, king of Bashan, with all his people into our hand, and we smote them until no survivor was left.

4 "And we captured all his cities at that time; there was not a city which we did not take from them: sixty cities, all the region of Argob, the kingdom of Og in Bashan.

5 "All these were cities fortified with high walls, gates and bars, besides a great many unwalled towns.

6 "And we utterly destroyed them, as we did to Sihon king of Heshbon, utterly destroying the men, women and children of every city.

7 "But all the animals and the spoil of the cities we took as our booty.

8 "Thus we took the land at that time from the hand of the two kings of the Amorites who were beyond the Jordan, from the valley of Arnon to Mount Hermon

9 (Sidonians call Hermon Sirion, and the Amorites call it Senir):

10 all the cities of the tableland and all Gilead and all Bashan, as far as Salecah and Edrei, cities of the kingdom of Og in Bashan.

11 (For only Og king of Bashan was left of the remnant of the Rephaim. Behold, his bedstead was an iron bedstead; it is in Rabbah of the sons of Ammon. Its length was nine cubits and its width four cubits by ordinary cubit.)

3. The distribution of the land

12 "So we took possession of this land at that time. From Aroer, which is by the valley of Arnon, and half the hill country of Gilead and its cities, I gave to the Reubenites and to the Gadites.

13 "And the rest of Gilead, and all Bashan, the kingdom of Og, I gave to the half-tribe of Manasseh, all the region of Argob (concerning all Bashan, it is called the land of Rephaim.

14 Jair the son of Manasseh took all the region of Argob as far as the border of the Geshurites and the Maacathites, and called it, *that is*, Bashan, after his own name, Havvoth-jair, *as it is* to this day.)

15 "And to Machir I gave Gilead.

16 "And to the Reubenites and to the Gadites, I gave from Gilead even as far as the valley of Arnon, the middle of the valley as a border and as far as the river Jabbok, the border of the sons of Ammon;

17 the Arabah also, with the Jordan as *a* border, from ⁴Chinnereth even as far as the sea of the Arabah, the Salt Sea, at the foot of the slopes of Pisgah on the east.

18 "Then I commanded you at that time, saying, 'The LORD your God has given you this land to possess it; all you valiant men shall cross over armed before your brothers, the sons of Israel.

19 'But your wives and your little ones and your livestock (I know that you have much livestock), shall remain in your cities which I have given you,

20 until the LORD gives rest to your fellow countrymen as to you, and they also possess the land which the LORD your God will give them beyond the Jordan. Then you may return every man to his possession, which I have given you.'

21 "And I commanded Joshua at that time, saying, 'Your eyes have seen all that the LORD your God has done to these two kings; so the LORD shall do to all the kingdoms into which you are about to cross.

22 'Do not fear them, for the LORD your God is the one fighting for you.'

4. Moses forbidden to cross the Jordan

23 "I also pleaded with the LORD at that time, saying,

24 'O Lord GOD, Thou hast begun to show Thy servant Thy greatness and Thy strong hand; for what god is there in heaven or on earth who can do such works and mighty acts as Thine?

---

⁴I.e., the Sea of Galilee

3:17 *Chinnereth*, Lake Gennesaret, or the Sea of Galilee.

Marginal references:

3:1 Num 21:33-35
3:2 Num 21:34
3:3 Num 21:35
3:4 1 Kin 4:13
3:6 Deut 2:24,34
3:9 Ps 29:6
3:11 Amos 2:9; Gen 14:5; 2 Sam 12:26; Jer 49:2
3:12 Deut 2:36; Num 32:32-38; Josh 13:8-13
3:14 Num 32:41; 1 Chr 2:22
3:15 Num 32:39, 40
*3:17 Num 34:11; Josh 13:27
3:18 Num 32:20
3:20 Josh 22:4
3:22 Deut 1:30
3:24 Ex 15:11; Ps 86:8

3:26
Deut 1:37;
31:2
3:27
Num 27:12
3:28
Num 27:18,
23;
Deut 31:3,7
*3:29
Deut 4:46;
34:6

4:1
Deut 5:33;
8:1; 16:20;
30:16,19
4:2
Deut 12:32;
Josh 1:7;
Rev 22:18,19
4:3
Num 25:4;
Ps 106:28,29

4:6
Deut 30:19,
20; 32:46,47
4:7
2 Sam 7:23;
Ps 46:1;
Is 55:6
4:9
Prov 4:23;
Gen 18:19
Deut 6:7;
11:19;
Ps 78:5,6;
Eph 6:4
4:10
Ex 19:9,16

4:11
Ex 19:18;
Heb 12:18,19
4:12
Deut 5:4,22;
Ex 20:22
4:13
Deut 9:9,11;
Ex 34:28;
24:12; 31:18

4:16
Ex 32:7;
20:4,5;
Deut 5:8

25 'Let me, I pray, cross over and see the fair land that is beyond the Jordan, that good hill country and Lebanon.'

26 "But the LORD was angry with me on your account, and would not listen to me; and the LORD said to me, 'Enough! Speak to Me no more of this matter.

27 'Go up to the top of Pisgah and lift up your eyes to the west and north and south and east, and see *it* with your eyes, for you shall not cross over this Jordan.

28 'But charge Joshua and encourage him and strengthen him; for he shall go across at the head of this people, and he shall give them as an inheritance the land which you will see.'

29 "So we remained in the valley opposite Beth-peor.

E. *The exhortation of Moses*

1. *The command to obedience*

4 "And now, O Israel, listen to the statutes and the judgments which I am teaching you to perform, in order that you may live and go in and take possession of the land which the LORD, the God of your fathers, is giving you.

2 "You shall not add to the word which I am commanding you, nor take away from it, that you may keep the commandments of the LORD your God which I command you.

3 "Your eyes have seen what the LORD has done in the case of Baal-peor, for all the men who followed Baal-peor, the LORD your God has destroyed them from among you.

4 "But you who held fast to the LORD your God are alive today, every one of you.

5 "See, I have taught you statutes and judgments just as the LORD my God commanded me, that you should do thus in the land where you are entering to possess it.

6 "So keep and do *them*, for that is your wisdom and your understanding in the sight of the peoples who will hear all these statutes and say, 'Surely this great nation is a wise and understanding people.'

7 "For what great nation is there that has a god so near to it as is the LORD our God whenever we call on Him?

8 "Or what great nation is there that has statutes and judgments as righteous as this whole law which I am setting before you today?

9 "Only give heed to yourself and keep your soul diligently, lest you forget the things which your eyes have seen, and lest they depart from your heart all the days of your life; but make them known to your sons and your grandsons.

10 "*Remember* the day you stood before the LORD your God at Horeb, when the LORD said to me, 'Assemble the people to Me, that I may let them hear My words so they may learn to [5]fear Me all the days they live on the earth, and that they may teach their children.'

11 "And you came near and stood at the foot of the mountain, and the mountain burned with fire to the *very* heart of the heavens: darkness, cloud and thick gloom.

12 "Then the LORD spoke to you from the midst of the fire; you heard the sound of words, but you saw no form—only a voice.

13 "So He declared to you His covenant which He commanded you to perform, *that is,* the ten commandments; and He wrote them on two tablets of stone.

14 "And the LORD commanded me at that time to teach you statutes and judgments, that you might perform them in the land where you are going over to possess it.

2. *Idolatry forbidden*

15 "So watch yourselves carefully, since you did not see any form on the day the LORD spoke to you at Horeb from the midst of the fire,

16 lest you act corruptly and make a graven image for yourselves in the form of any figure, the likeness of male or female,

17 the likeness of any animal that is on the earth, the likeness of any winged bird that flies in the sky,

[5]Or, *reverence*

3:29 *Beth-peor,* an elevated area close to the burial place of Moses.

4:15 *did not see any form.* God is a spirit and thus is non-material.

18   the likeness of anything that creeps on the ground, the likeness of any fish that is in the water below the earth.

19   "And *beware*, lest you lift up your eyes to heaven and see the sun and the moon and the stars, all the host of heaven, and be drawn away and worship them and serve them, those which the LORD your God has allotted to all the peoples under the whole heaven.

20   "But the LORD has taken you and brought you out of the iron furnace, from Egypt, to be a people for His own possession, as today.

21   "Now the LORD was angry with me on your account, and swore that I should not cross the Jordan, and that I should not enter the good land which the LORD your God is giving you as an inheritance.

22   "For I shall die in this land, I shall not cross the Jordan, but you shall cross and take possession of this good land.

23   "So watch yourselves, lest you forget the covenant of the LORD your God, which He made with you, and make for yourselves a graven image in the form of anything *against* which the LORD your God has commanded you.

24   "For the LORD your God is a consuming fire, a jealous God.

25   "When you become the father of children and children's children and have remained long in the land, and act corruptly, and make an idol in the form of anything, and do that which is evil in the sight of the LORD your God *so as* to provoke Him to anger,

26   I call heaven and earth to witness against you today, that you shall surely perish quickly from the land where you are going over the Jordan to possess it. You shall not live long on it, but shall be utterly destroyed.

27   "And the LORD will scatter you among the peoples, and you shall be left few in number among the nations, where the LORD shall drive you.

28   "And there you will serve gods, the work of man's hands, wood and stone, which neither see nor hear nor eat nor smell.

29   "But from there you will seek the LORD your God, and you will find *Him* if you search for Him with all your heart and all your soul.

30   "When you are in distress and all these things have come upon you, in the latter days, you will return to the LORD your God and listen to His voice.

31   "For the LORD your God is a compassionate God; He will not fail you nor destroy you nor forget the covenant with your fathers which He swore to them.

3. *The peculiar relation of Israel as a chosen nation*

32   "Indeed, ask now concerning the former days which were before you, since the day that God created man on the earth, and *inquire* from one end of the heavens to the other. Has *anything* been done like this great thing, or has *anything* been heard like it?

33   "Has *any* people heard the voice of God speaking from the midst of the fire, as you have heard *it*, and survived?

34   "Or has a god tried to go to take for himself a nation from within *another* nation by trials, by signs and wonders and by war and by a mighty hand and by an outstretched arm and by great terrors, as the LORD your God did for you in Egypt before your eyes?

35   "To you it was shown that you might know that the LORD, He is God; there is no other besides Him.

36   "Out of the heavens He let you hear His voice to discipline you; and on earth He let you see His great fire, and you heard His words from the midst of the fire.

37   "Because He loved your fathers, therefore He chose their descendants after them. And He personally brought you from Egypt by His great power,

38   driving out from before you nations greater and mightier than you, to bring you in *and* to give you their land for an inheritance, as it is today.

39   "Know therefore today, and take it to your heart, that the LORD, He is God in heaven above and on the earth below; there is no other.

40   "So you shall keep His statutes and His commandments which I am giving you today, that it may go well with you and with your children after you, and that you may live long on the land which the LORD your God is giving you for all time."

4:20 *iron furnace.* This designation for Egypt also occurs in Jer. 11:4.

Cross-references (right margin):

4:19
Deut 17:3;
2 Kin 17:16;
Rom 1:25

*4:20
1 Kin 8:51;
Jer 11:4;
Deut 9:29
4:21
Deut 1:37

4:22
Deut 3:25,27

4:23
vv. 9,16;
Ex 20:4,5

4:24
Ex 24:17;
Deut 9:3;
Heb 12:29;
Deut 6:15
4:25
vv. 16,23;
2 Kin 17:17
4:26
Deut 30:18,
19

4:27
Deut 28:62,
64

4:28
Deut 28:64;
1 Sam 26:19;
Ps 115:4,5
4:29
Deut 30:1-3;
2 Chr 15:4;
Is 55:6,7;
Jer 29:12-14
4:31
2 Chr 30:9;
Ps 116:5

4:32
Deut 32:7;
Gen 1:27;
Deut 28:64

4:33
Ex 20:22;
Deut 5:24,26
4:34
Deut 7:19;
Ex 7:3; 13:3;
6:6;
Deut 26:8;
34:12
4:35
Deut 32:39;
Is 45:5,18;
Mark 12:29
4:36
Ex 19:9,19;
Heb 12:18
4:37
Deut 10:15;
Ex 13:3,9,14
4:38
Deut 7:1;
9:1,4,5
4:39
v. 35;
Josh 2:11
4:40
Lev 22:31;
Deut 5:16,29,
33; Eph 6:2,3

F. The cities of refuge

41 Then Moses set apart three cities across the Jordan to the east,

42 that a manslayer might flee there, who unintentionally slew his neighbor without having enmity toward him in time past; and by fleeing to one of these cities he might live:

43 Bezer in the wilderness on the plateau for the Reubenites, and Ramoth in Gilead for the Gadites, and Golan in Bashan for the Manassites.

II. *Moses' second address (4:44–26:19)*

A. *Introduction*

44 Now this is the law which Moses set before the sons of Israel;

45 these are the testimonies and the statutes and the ordinances which Moses spoke to the sons of Israel, when they came out from Egypt,

46 across the Jordan, in the valley opposite Beth-peor, in the land of Sihon king of the Amorites who lived at Heshbon, whom Moses and the sons of Israel defeated when they came out from Egypt.

47 And they took possession of his land and the land of Og king of Bashan, the two kings of the Amorites, *who were* across the Jordan to the east,

48 from Aroer, which is on the edge of the valley of Arnon, even as far as Mount Sion (that is, Hermon),

49 with all the Arabah across the Jordan to the east, even as far as the sea of the Arabah, at the foot of the slopes of Pisgah.

B. *The covenant: the Ten Commandments*

1. *The Commandments stated*

5 Then Moses summoned all Israel, and said to them, "Hear, O Israel, the statutes and the ordinances which I am speaking today in your hearing, that you may learn them and observe them carefully.

2 "The LORD our God made a covenant with us at Horeb.

3 "The LORD did not make this covenant with our fathers, but with us, *with* all those of us alive here today.

4 "The LORD spoke to you face to face at the mountain from the midst of the fire,

5 *while* I was standing between the LORD and you at that time, to declare to you the word of the LORD; for you were afraid because of the fire and did not go up the mountain. He said,

6 'I am the LORD your God, who brought you out of the land of Egypt, out of the house of slavery.

7 'You shall have no other gods before Me.

8 'You shall not make for yourself an idol, *or* any likeness *of* what is in heaven above or on the earth beneath or in the water under the earth.

9 'You shall not worship them or serve them; for I, the LORD your God, am a jealous God, visiting the iniquity of the fathers on the children, and on the third and the fourth *generations* of those who hate Me,

10 but showing lovingkindness to thousands, to those who love Me and keep My commandments.

11 'You shall not take the name of the LORD your God in vain, for the LORD will not leave him unpunished who takes His name in vain.

12 'Observe the sabbath day to keep it holy, as the LORD your God commanded you.

13 'Six days you shall labor and do all your work,

14 but the seventh day is a sabbath of the LORD your God; *in it* you shall not do any work, you or your son or your daughter or your male servant or your female servant or your ox or your donkey or any of your cattle or your sojourner who stays with you, so that your male servant and your female servant may rest as well as you.

15 'And you shall remember that you were a slave in the land of Egypt, and the LORD your God brought you out of there by a mighty hand and by an outstretched arm; therefore the LORD your God commanded you to observe the sabbath day.

Marginal references:
4:41 Num 35:6
4:46 Deut 3:29; Num 21:21-25
4:48 Deut 2:36; 3:12
5:2 Ex 19:5
5:4 Ex 19:9,19; Deut 4:33,36
5:5 Ex 20:18,21
5:6 Ex 20:2-17
*5:9 Ex 34:7
5:10 Jer 32:18
5:14 Gen 2:2; Ex 16:29,30
*5:15 Deut 15:16; 4:34,37

5:9 *jealous God,* see note to Ex. 34:14.
5:12 *Observe.* Ex. 20:8 has *remember.*

5:15 See Ex. 20:11, where another reason is given for keeping the Sabbath.

16 'Honor your father and your mother, as the LORD your God has commanded you, that your days may be prolonged, and that it may go well with you on the land which the LORD your God gives you.

17 'You shall not murder.

18 'You shall not commit adultery.

19 'You shall not steal.

20 'You shall not bear false witness against your neighbor.

21 'You shall not covet your neighbor's wife, and you shall not desire your neighbor's house, his field or his male servant or his female servant, his ox or his donkey or anything that belongs to your neighbor.'

5:21
Rom 7:7;
13:9

2. God and Moses at Sinai

22 "These words the LORD spoke to all your assembly at the mountain from the midst of the fire, of the cloud and of the thick gloom, with a great voice, and He added no more. And He wrote them on two tablets of stone and gave them to me.

5:22
Ex 31:18;
Deut 4:13

23 "And it came about, when you heard the voice from the midst of the darkness, while the mountain was burning with fire, that you came near to me, all the heads of your tribes and your elders.

24 "And you said, 'Behold, the LORD our God has shown us His glory and His greatness, and we have heard His voice from the midst of the fire; we have seen today that God speaks with man, yet he lives.

5:24
Ex 19:19

25 'Now then why should we die? For this great fire will consume us; if we hear the voice of the LORD our God any longer, then we shall die.

5:25
Deut 18:16

26 'For who is there of all flesh, who has heard the voice of the living God speaking from the midst of the fire, as we *have*, and lived?

5:26
Deut 4:33

27 'Go near and hear all that the LORD our God says; then speak to us all that the LORD our God will speak to you, and we will hear and do *it*.'

28 "And the LORD heard the voice of your words when you spoke to me, and the LORD said to me, 'I have heard the voice of the words of this people which they have spoken to you. They have done well in all that they have spoken.

5:28
Deut 18:17

29 'Oh that they had such a heart in them, that they would fear Me, and keep all My commandments always, that it may be well with them and with their sons forever!

5:29
Ps 81:13;
Is 48:18;
Deut 4:40

30 'Go, say to them, "Return to your tents."

31 'But as for you, stand here by Me, that I may speak to you all the commandments and the statutes and the judgments which you shall teach them, that they may observe *them* in the land which I give them to possess.'

5:31
Ex 24:12

32 "So you shall observe to do just as the LORD your God has commanded you; you shall not turn aside to the right or to the left.

5:32
Deut 17:20;
28:14;
Josh 1:7; 23:6

33 "You shall walk in all the way which the LORD your God has commanded you, that you may live, and that it may be well with you, and that you may prolong *your* days in the land which you shall possess.

5:33
Deut 4:40

3. The purpose of the Law

6 "Now this is the commandment, the statutes and the judgments which the LORD your God has commanded *me* to teach you, that you might do *them* in the land where you are going over to possess it,

2 so that you and your son and your grandson might fear the LORD your God, to keep all His statutes and His commandments, which I command you, all the days of your life, and that your days may be prolonged.

6:2
Ex 20:20;
Deut 10:12,
13

3 "O Israel, you should listen and be careful to do *it*, that it may be well with you and that you may multiply greatly, just as the LORD, the God of your fathers, has promised you, *in* a land flowing with milk and honey.

6:3
Deut 5:33;
Gen 15:5;
Ex 3:8

4. The law of love

4 "Hear, O Israel! The LORD is our God, the LORD is one!

*6:4ff
Mark 12:29;
John 17:3;
1 Cor 8:4,6

5:16 *as the LORD your God has commanded you.* This expression also occurs in v. 12 and, with slight variations, is used throughout Deuteronomy.

6:4–9 Later in Israel there arose the practice of reciting these basic verses, called the *Shema* ("Hear"), twice daily. The great teaching of the Scripture about God is that there is a unity in a trinity—three Persons make up the Godhead, yet they constitute but one essence. It is, therefore, a tri-unity, for God is one yet three. This is a great mystery, but it is the only way of reconciling all that the Bible says about God. (See also note to Matt. 28:19 on the Trinity.)

5 "And you shall love the LORD your God with all your heart and with all your soul and with all your might.

6 "And these words, which I am commanding you today, shall be on your heart;

7 and you shall teach them diligently to your sons and shall talk of them when you sit in your house and when you walk by the way and when you lie down and when you rise up.

8 "And you shall bind them as a sign on your hand and they shall be as frontals on your forehead.

9 "And you shall write them on the doorposts of your house and on your gates.

10 "Then it shall come about when the LORD your God brings you into the land which He swore to your fathers, Abraham, Isaac and Jacob, to give you, great and splendid cities which you did not build,

11 and houses full of all good things which you did not fill, and hewn cisterns which you did not dig, vineyards and olive trees which you did not plant, and you shall eat and be satisfied,

12 then watch yourself, lest you forget the LORD who brought you from the land of Egypt, out of the house of slavery.

13 "You shall [6]fear only the LORD your God; and you shall worship Him, and swear by His name.

14 "You shall not follow other gods, any of the gods of the peoples who surround you,

15 for the LORD your God in the midst of you is a jealous God; otherwise the anger of the LORD your God will be kindled against you, and He will wipe you off the face of the earth.

16 "You shall not put the LORD your God to the test, as you tested Him at Massah.

17 "You should diligently keep the commandments of the LORD your God, and His testimonies and His statutes which He has commanded you.

18 "And you shall do what is right and good in the sight of the LORD, that it may be well with you and that you may go in and possess the good land which the LORD swore to give your fathers,

19 by driving out all your enemies from before you, as the LORD has spoken.

5. Explaining the Law to their children

20 "When your son asks you in time to come, saying, 'What do the testimonies and the statutes and the judgments mean which the LORD our God commanded you?'

21 then you shall say to your son, 'We were slaves to Pharaoh in Egypt; and the LORD brought us from Egypt with a mighty hand.

22 'Moreover, the LORD showed great and distressing signs and wonders before our eyes against Egypt, Pharaoh and all his household;

23 and He brought us out from there in order to bring us in, to give us the land which He had sworn to our fathers.'

24 "So the LORD commanded us to observe all these statutes, to fear the LORD our God for our good always and for our survival, as it is today.

25 "And it will be righteousness for us if we are careful to observe all this commandment before the LORD our God, just as He commanded us.

6. Extermination of the Canaanites
a. The evils of idolatry

7 'When the LORD your God shall bring you into the land where you are entering to possess it, and shall clear away many nations before you, the Hittites and the Girgashites and the Amorites and the Canaanites and the Perizzites and the Hivites and the Jebusites, seven nations greater and stronger than you,

2 and when the LORD your God shall deliver them before you, and you shall

[6]Or, reverence

6:5 This verse, according to Jesus, is the first and great commandment. Since heart in Hebrew thought was also considered the seat of intelligence, Jesus was warranted in adding a fourth item, mind (Mark 12:30; Luke 10:27).
6:13 fear, that is, reverence, obedience, submissiveness.
7:2 God at times commanded Israel to annihilate certain peoples. This aspect of God's character has occasioned difficult questions concerning His love, righteousness, and mercy. Because of these problems, some scholars have attempted to distinguish between the God of wrath of the Old Testament and the God of love of the New Testament. This distinction is false. God is the one and same God, both in the

defeat them, then you shall utterly destroy them. You shall make no covenant with them and show no favor to them.

3 "Furthermore, you shall not intermarry with them; you shall not give your daughters to their sons, nor shall you take their daughters for your sons.

4 "For they will turn your sons away from following Me to serve other gods; then the anger of the LORD will be kindled against you, and He will quickly destroy you.

5 "But thus you shall do to them: you shall tear down their altars, and smash their *sacred* pillars, and hew down their [7]Asherim, and burn their graven images with fire.

b. *The peculiar status of Israel*

6 "For you are a holy people to the LORD your God; the LORD your God has chosen you to be a people for His own possession out of all the peoples who are on the face of the earth.

7 "The LORD did not set His love on you nor choose you because you were more in number than any of the peoples, for you were the fewest of all peoples,

8 but because the LORD loved you and kept the oath which He swore to your forefathers, the LORD brought you out by a mighty hand, and redeemed you from the house of slavery, from the hand of Pharaoh king of Egypt.

9 "Know therefore that the LORD your God, He is God, the faithful God, who keeps His covenant and His lovingkindness to a thousandth generation with those who love Him and keep His commandments;

10 but repays those who hate Him to their faces, to destroy them; He will not delay with him who hates Him, He will repay him to his face.

11 "Therefore, you shall keep the commandment and the statutes and the judgments which I am commanding you today, to do them.

12 "Then it shall come about, because you listen to these judgments and keep and do them, that the LORD your God will keep with you His covenant and His lovingkindness which He swore to your forefathers.

13 "And He will love you and bless you and multiply you; He will also bless the fruit of your womb and the fruit of your ground, your grain and your new wine and your oil, the increase of your herd and the young of your flock, in the land which He swore to your forefathers to give you.

14 "You shall be blessed above all peoples; there shall be no male or female barren among you or among your cattle.

15 "And the LORD will remove from you all sickness; and He will not put on you any of the harmful diseases of Egypt which you have known, but He will lay them on all who hate you.

16 "And you shall consume all the peoples whom the LORD your God will deliver to you; your eye shall not pity them, neither shall you serve their gods, for that *would be* a snare to you.

c. *God is greater than the Canaanites: Israel need not fear*

17 "If you should say in your heart, 'These nations are greater than I; how can I dispossess them?'

18 you shall not be afraid of them; you shall well remember what the LORD your God did to Pharaoh and to all Egypt:

19 the great trials which your eyes saw and the signs and the wonders and the mighty hand and the outstretched arm by which the LORD your God brought you out. So shall the LORD your God do to all the peoples of whom you are afraid.

---

[7] i.e., wooden symbols of a female deity

7:3 Ex 34:15,16
7:4 Deut 6:15
7:5 Ex 23:24
*7:6 Ex 19:5,6; Deut 14:2
7:7 Deut 10:22
7:8 Deut 10:15; Ex 32:13; 13:3,14
7:9 Deut 4:35,39; Neh 1:5
7:12 Lev 26:3; Deut 28:1; Ps 105:8,9
7:13 Deut 28:4
7:14 Ex 23:26
7:15 Ex 15:26
7:16 v. 2; Ex 23:33
7:18 Deut 31:6
7:19 Deut 4:34

Old Testament and the New Testament. That He did execute wrath against certain nations admits of no doubt; that He promises to do so again in the end time is clear from the Revelation to John. God's love is a holy and righteous love; He will not show an unfeeling disregard toward the victims of crime by sparing the unrepentant criminal who has injured them. In decreeing their punishment, God shows love toward His moral order and those principles of justice and retribution without which life makes no sense. (Justice and retribution were at work even when Christ, God's love-gift for sinners, bore the sinners' guilt and paid their penalty for them.) The proposition that God is love cannot mean that

God loves evil or protects wickedness. Even so, in these ancient times the wickedness of the people to be destroyed was so great, the patience of God toward them so long-suffering, and the opportunities for repentance so many, that when judgment did fall it came as a just recompense for awful sinfulness. It might be added that judgment in time is no worse than judgment in eternity, and to deny one is just as fallacious as to deny the other.

7:6 *a holy people to the LORD.* Because the people of Israel were God's *own possession*, they were to *utterly destroy* (v. 2) the peoples in Canaan.

7:20
Ex 23:28;
Josh 24:12
7:21
Deut 10:17

7:22
Ex 23:29,30

7:24
v. 16

7:25
1 Chr 14:12;
Josh 7:1,21;
Judg 8:27

20 "Moreover, the LORD your God will send the hornet against them, until those who are left and hide themselves from you perish.

21 "You shall not dread them, for the LORD your God is in your midst, a great and awesome God.

22 "And the LORD your God will clear away these nations before you little by little; you will not be able to put an end to them quickly, lest the wild beasts grow too numerous for you.

23 "But the LORD your God shall deliver them before you, and will throw them into great confusion until they are destroyed.

24 "And He will deliver their kings into your hand so that you shall make their name perish from under heaven; no man will be able to stand before you until you have destroyed them.

25 "The graven images of their gods you are to burn with fire; you shall not covet the silver or the gold that is on them, nor take it for yourselves, lest you be snared by it, for it is an abomination to the LORD your God.

26 "And you shall not bring an abomination into your house, and like it come under the ban; you shall utterly detest it and you shall utterly abhor it, for it is something banned.

7. Moses' reminder of God's past mercies

a. Wilderness mercies

8:1
Deut 4:1

8 "All the commandments that I am commanding you today you shall be careful to do, that you may live and multiply, and go in and possess the land which the LORD swore *to give* to your forefathers.

8:2
Deut 29:5;
13:3

2 "And you shall remember all the way which the LORD your God has led you in the wilderness these forty years, that He might humble you, testing you, to know what was in your heart, whether you would keep His commandments or not.

8:3
Ex 16:2,3,12,
14,35;
Matt 4:4;
Luke 4:7

3 "And He humbled you and let you be hungry, and fed you with manna which you did not know, nor did your fathers know, that He might make you understand that man does not live by bread alone, but man lives by everything that proceeds out of the mouth of the LORD.

8:4
Deut 29:5

4 "Your clothing did not wear out on you, nor did your foot swell these forty years.

8:5
Prov 3:12;
Heb 12:5,6
8:6
Deut 5:33

5 "Thus you are to know in your heart that the LORD your God was disciplining you just as a man disciplines his son.

6 "Therefore, you shall keep the commandments of the LORD your God, to walk in His ways and to fear Him.

8:7
Deut 11:10-12

7 "For the LORD your God is bringing you into a good land, a land of brooks of water, of fountains and springs, flowing forth in valleys and hills;

8 a land of wheat and barley, of vines and fig trees and pomegranates, a land of olive oil and honey;

9 a land where you shall eat food without scarcity, in which you shall not lack anything; a land whose stones are iron, and out of whose hills you can dig copper.

8:10
Deut 6:11,12

10 "When you have eaten and are satisfied, you shall bless the LORD your God for the good land which He has given you.

b. Admonition against pride

11 "Beware lest you forget the LORD your God by not keeping His commandments and His ordinances and His statutes which I am commanding you today;

12 lest, when you have eaten and are satisfied, and have built good houses and lived *in them,*

13 and when your herds and your flocks multiply, and your silver and gold multiply, and all that you have multiplies,

8:14
Ps 106:21
8:15
Num 21:6;
20:11;
Ps 78:15;
114:8
8:16
vv. 2,3;
Ex 16:15

14 then your heart becomes proud, and you forget the LORD your God who brought you out from the land of Egypt, out of the house of slavery.

15 "He led you through the great and terrible wilderness, *with its* fiery serpents and scorpions and thirsty ground where there was no water; He brought water for you out of the rock of flint.

16 "In the wilderness He fed you manna which your fathers did not know, that He might humble you and that He might test you, to do good for you in the end.

8:9 *a land whose stones are iron, and out of whose hills you can dig copper.* Modern explorations have confirmed this to be true in the great rift of the Arabah south of the Dead Sea.

17 "Otherwise, you may say in your heart, 'My power and the strength of my hand made me this wealth.'

18 "But you shall remember the LORD your God, for it is He who is giving you power to make wealth, that He may confirm His covenant which He swore to your fathers, as *it is* this day.

19 "And it shall come about if you ever forget the LORD your God, and go after other gods and serve them and worship them, I testify against you today that you shall surely perish.

20 "Like the nations that the LORD makes to perish before you, so you shall perish; because you would not listen to the voice of the LORD your God.

c. God will give Israel the land:
not because of their righteousness

9 "Hear, O Israel! You are crossing over the Jordan today to go in to dispossess nations greater and mightier than you, great cities fortified to heaven,

2   a people great and tall, the sons of the Anakim, whom you know and of whom you have heard *it said*, 'Who can stand before the sons of Anak?'

3 "Know therefore today that it is the LORD your God who is crossing over before you as a consuming fire. He will destroy them and He will subdue them before you, so that you may drive them out and destroy them quickly, just as the LORD has spoken to you.

4 "Do not say in your heart when the LORD your God has driven them out before you, 'Because of my righteousness the LORD has brought me in to possess this land,' but *it is* because of the wickedness of these nations *that* the LORD is dispossessing them before you.

5 "It is not for your righteousness or for the uprightness of your heart that you are going to possess their land, but *it is* because of the wickedness of these nations *that* the LORD your God is driving them out before you, in order to confirm the oath which the LORD swore to your fathers, to Abraham, Isaac and Jacob.

d. Israel's own sin: the golden calf

6 "Know, then, *it is* not because of your righteousness *that* the LORD your God is giving you this good land to possess, for you are a stubborn people.

7 "Remember, do not forget how you provoked the LORD your God to wrath in the wilderness; from the day that you left the land of Egypt until you arrived at this place, you have been rebellious against the LORD.

8 "Even at Horeb you provoked the LORD to wrath, and the LORD was so angry with you that He would have destroyed you.

9 "When I went up to the mountain to receive the tablets of stone, the tablets of the covenant which the LORD had made with you, then I remained on the mountain forty days and nights; I neither ate bread nor drank water.

10 "And the LORD gave me the two tablets of stone written by the finger of God; and on them *were* all the words which the LORD had spoken with you at the mountain from the midst of the fire on the day of the assembly.

11 "And it came about at the end of forty days and nights that the LORD gave me the two tablets of stone, the tablets of the covenant.

12 "Then the LORD said to me, 'Arise, go down from here quickly, for your people whom you brought out of Egypt have acted corruptly. They have quickly turned aside from the way which I commanded them; they have made a molten image for themselves.'

13 "The LORD spoke further to me, saying, 'I have seen this people, and indeed, it is a stubborn people.

14 'Let Me alone, that I may destroy them and blot out their name from under heaven; and I will make of you a nation mightier and greater than they.'

15 "So I turned and came down from the mountain while the mountain was burning with fire, and the two tablets of the covenant were in my two hands.

16 "And I saw that you had indeed sinned against the LORD your God. You had made for yourselves a molten calf; you had turned aside quickly from the way which the LORD had commanded you.

17 "And I took hold of the two tablets and threw them from my hands, and smashed them before your eyes.

18 "And I fell down before the LORD, as at the first, forty days and nights; I neither ate bread nor drank water, because of all your sin which you had committed in doing what was evil in the sight of the LORD to provoke Him to anger.

8:18
Prov 10:22;
Hos 2:8

8:19
Deut 4:26;
30:18

9:1
Deut 11:31

9:2
Num 13:22,
28,32,33
9:3
Deut 31:3;
4:24; 7:23,24

9:4
Deut 8:17;
18:12;
Lev 18:24,25

9:5
Gen 12:7

9:6
v. 13;
Ex 32:9;
Deut 31:27

9:8
Ex 32:7-10

9:9
Ex 24:12,15,
18

9:10
Ex 31:18;
Deut 4:13

9:12
Ex 32:7,8;
Deut 31:29

9:13
Ex 32:9; v. 6

9:14
Ex 32:10;
Deut 29:20;
Num 14:12
9:15
Ex 32:15-19;
19:18
9:16
Ex 32:19

9:18
Ex 34:28

9:19
Ex 32:10-14

19 "For I was afraid of the anger and hot displeasure with which the LORD was wrathful against you in order to destroy you, but the LORD listened to me that time also.

20 "And the LORD was angry enough with Aaron to destroy him; so I also prayed for Aaron at the same time.

9:21
Ex 32:20

21 "And I took your sinful *thing*, the calf which you had made, and burned it with fire and crushed it, grinding it very small until it was as fine as dust; and I threw its dust into the brook that came down from the mountain.

e. Israel's other sins

9:22
Num 11:3,34;
Ex 17:7

22 "Again at Taberah and at Massah and at Kibroth-hattaavah you provoked the LORD to wrath.

23 "And when the LORD sent you from Kadesh-barnea, saying, 'Go up and possess the land which I have given you,' then you rebelled against the command of the LORD your God; you neither believed Him nor listened to His voice.

9:24
v. 7;
Deut 31:27

24 "You have been rebellious against the LORD from the day I knew you.

f. Moses intercedes for Israel

9:25
v. 18

25 "So I fell down before the LORD the forty days and nights, which I did because the LORD had said He would destroy you.

9:26
Ex 32:11-13

26 "And I prayed to the LORD, and said, 'O Lord GOD, do not destroy Thy people, even Thine inheritance, whom Thou hast redeemed through Thy greatness, whom Thou hast brought out of Egypt with a mighty hand.

27 'Remember Thy servants, Abraham, Isaac, and Jacob; do not look at the stubbornness of this people or at their wickedness or their sin.

28 'Otherwise the land from which Thou didst bring us may say, "Because the LORD was not able to bring them into the land which He had promised them and because He hated them He has brought them out to slay them in the wilderness."

9:29
Deut 4:20,34

29 'Yet they are Thy people, even Thine inheritance, whom Thou hast brought out by Thy great power and Thine outstretched arm.'

g. The two tablets of stone

10:1
Ex 34:1,2;
25:10

10 "At that time the LORD said to me, 'Cut out for yourself two tablets of stone like the former ones, and come up to Me on the mountain, and make an ark of wood for yourself.

10:2
Deut 4:13;
Ex 25:16,21
10:3
Ex 37:1; 34:4

2 'And I will write on the tablets the words that were on the former tablets which you shattered, and you shall put them in the ark.'

3 "So I made an ark of acacia wood and cut out two tablets of stone like the former ones, and went up on the mountain with the two tablets in my hand.

10:4
Ex 20:1

4 "And He wrote on the tablets, like the former writing, the Ten Commandments which the LORD had spoken to you on the mountain from the midst of the fire on the day of the assembly; and the LORD gave them to me.

*10:5
Ex 40:20

5 "Then I turned and came down from the mountain, and put the tablets in the ark which I had made; and there they are, as the LORD commanded me."

10:6
Num 33:30,
31,38

6 (Now the sons of Israel set out from Beeroth Bene-jaakan to Moserah. There Aaron died and there he was buried and Eleazar his son ministered as priest in his place.

10:7
Num 33:32-34

7 From there they set out to Gudgodah; and from Gudgodah to Jotbathah, a land of brooks of water.

*10:8
Num 3:6;
4:15;
Deut 18:5;
21:5
10:9
Num 18:20,
24
10:10
Deut 9:18,25;
Ex 33:17

8 At that time the LORD set apart the tribe of Levi to carry the ark of the covenant of the LORD, to stand before the LORD to serve Him and to bless in His name until this day.

9 Therefore, Levi does not have a portion or inheritance with his brothers; the LORD is his inheritance, just as the LORD your God spoke to him.)

10 "I, moreover, stayed on the mountain forty days and forty nights like the first time, and the LORD listened to me that time also; the LORD was not willing to destroy you.

11 "Then the LORD said to me, 'Arise, proceed on your journey ahead of the people, that they may go in and possess the land which I swore to their fathers to give them.'

10:5 Compare this to 1 Kin. 8:9.   **10:8** *to bless*, as in Num. 6:24–26.

8. God's great requirement

12 "And now, Israel, what does the LORD your God require from you, but to fear the LORD your God, to walk in all His ways and love Him, and to serve the LORD your God with all your heart and with all your soul,

13 *and* to keep the LORD's commandments and His statutes which I am commanding you today for your good?

14 "Behold, to the LORD your God belong heaven and the highest heavens, the earth and all that is in it.

15 "Yet on your fathers did the LORD set His affection to love them, and He chose their descendants after them, *even* you above all peoples, as *it is* this day.

16 "Circumcise then your heart, and stiffen your neck no more.

17 "For the LORD your God is the God of gods and the Lord of lords, the great, the mighty, and the awesome God who does not show partiality, nor take a bribe.

18 "He executes justice for the orphan and the widow, and shows His love for the alien by giving him food and clothing.

19 "So show your love for the alien, for you were aliens in the land of Egypt.

20 "You shall fear the LORD your God; you shall serve Him and cling to Him, and you shall swear by His name.

21 "He is your praise and He is your God, who has done these great and awesome things for you which your eyes have seen.

22 "Your fathers went down to Egypt seventy persons *in all*, and now the LORD your God has made you as numerous as the stars of heaven.

9. Moses' concluding exhortation

a. The command to love God

11 "You shall therefore love the LORD your God, and always keep His charge, His statutes, His ordinances, and His commandments.

2 "And know this day that I *am* not *speaking* with your sons who have not known and who have not seen the [8]discipline of the LORD your God—His greatness, His mighty hand, and His outstretched arm,

3 and His signs and His works which He did in the midst of Egypt to Pharaoh the king of Egypt and to all his land;

4 and what He did to Egypt's army, to its horses and its chariots, when He made the water of the Red Sea to engulf them while they were pursuing you, and the LORD completely destroyed them;

5 and what He did to you in the wilderness until you came to this place;

6 and what He did to Dathan and Abiram, the sons of Eliab, the son of Reuben, when the earth opened its mouth and swallowed them, their households, their tents, and every living thing that followed them, among all Israel—

7 but your own eyes have seen all the great work of the LORD which He did.

b. The order to keep God's commandments

8 "You shall therefore keep every commandment which I am commanding you today, so that you may be strong and go in and possess the land into which you are about to cross to possess it;

9 so that you may prolong *your* days on the land which the LORD swore to your fathers to give to them and to their descendants, a land flowing with milk and honey.

10 "For the land, into which you are entering to possess it, is not like the land of Egypt from which you came, where you used to sow your seed and water it with your [9]foot like a vegetable garden.

11 "But the land into which you are about to cross to possess it, a land of hills and valleys, drinks water from the rain of heaven,

12 a land for which the LORD your God cares; the eyes of the LORD your God are always on it, from the beginning even to the end of the year.

c. The consequences of obedience and disobedience

13 "And it shall come about, if you listen obediently to my commandments which I am commanding you today, to love the LORD your God and to serve Him with all your heart and all your soul,

---

10:12; Mic 6:8; Deut 6:13; 5:33; 6:5
10:14 1 Kin 8:27; Ex 19:5
10:15 Deut 4:37
10:16 Jer 4:4; Deut 9:6
10:17 Josh 22:22; Rev 19:16; Acts 10:34
10:18 Ps 68:5
10:19 Lev 19:34
10:20 Matt 4:10; Deut 11:22; Ps 63:11
10:21 Ex 15:2; Ps 106:21,22
10:22 Gen 46:27; Deut 1:10
11:1 Deut 10:12; Zech 3:7
11:2 Deut 8:5; 5:24
11:4 Ex 14:27,28
11:6 Num 16:31-33
11:8 Josh 1:6,7
11:9 Deut 4:40; 9:5; Ex 3:8
11:11 Deut 8:7
11:13 v. 22; Deut 6:17; 10:12

[8]Or, *instruction*   [9]I.e., probably a treadmill

11:14
Deut 28:12;
Joel 2:23
11:15
Deut 6:11
11:16
Deut 29:18;
8:19
11:17
Deut 6:15;
1 Kin 8:35;
Deut 4:26

14   that He will give the rain for your land in its season, the [10]early and late rain, that you may gather in your grain and your new wine and your oil.

15 "And He will give grass in your fields for your cattle, and you shall eat and be satisfied.

16 "Beware, lest your hearts be deceived and you turn away and serve other gods and worship them.

17 "Or the anger of the LORD will be kindled against you, and He will shut up the heavens so that there will be no rain and the ground will not yield its fruit; and you will perish quickly from the good land which the LORD is giving you.

d. The command to lay up God's Law and to teach it to children

11:18
Deut 6:6,8

18 "You shall therefore impress these words of mine on your heart and on your soul; and you shall bind them as a sign on your hand, and they shall be as frontals on your forehead.

11:19
Deut 4:9,10;
6:7

19 "And you shall teach them to your sons, talking of them when you sit in your house and when you walk along the road and when you lie down and when you rise up.

11:20
Deut 6:9

20 "And you shall write them on the doorposts of your house and on your gates,

21   so that your days and the days of your sons may be multiplied on the land which the LORD swore to your fathers to give them, as long as the heavens remain above the earth.

11:22
Deut 6:17;
10:20

22 "For if you are careful to keep all this commandment which I am commanding you, to do it, to love the LORD your God, to walk in all His ways and hold fast to Him;

11:23
Deut 9:1,5

23   then the LORD will drive out all these nations from before you, and you will dispossess nations greater and mightier than you.

11:24
Josh 1:3;
Gen 15:18;
Ex 23:31

24 "Every place on which the sole of your foot shall tread shall be yours; your border shall be from the wilderness to Lebanon, and from the river, the river Euphrates, as far as [11]the western sea.

11:25
Deut 7:24;
Ex 23:27

25 "There shall no man be able to stand before you; the LORD your God shall lay the dread of you and the fear of you on all the land on which you set foot, as He has spoken to you.

e. A blessing and a curse: Israel must choose for herself

11:26
Deut 30:1,19
11:27
Deut 28:2

26 "See, I am setting before you today a blessing and a curse:

27   the blessing, if you listen to the commandments of the LORD your God, which I am commanding you today;

11:28
Deut 28:15

28   and the curse, if you do not listen to the commandments of the LORD your God, but turn aside from the way which I am commanding you today, by following other gods which you have not known.

11:29
Deut 27:12;
Josh 8:33

29 "And it shall come about, when the LORD your God brings you into the land where you are entering to possess it, that you shall place the blessing on Mount Gerizim and the curse on Mount Ebal.

11:30
Josh 4:19;
Gen 12:6

30 "Are they not across the Jordan, west of the way toward the sunset, in the land of the Canaanites who live in the Arabah, opposite Gilgal, beside the oaks of Moreh?

11:31
Deut 9:1;
Josh 1:11

31 "For you are about to cross the Jordan to go in to possess the land which the LORD your God is giving you, and you shall possess it and live in it,

32   and you shall be careful to do all the statutes and the judgments which I am setting before you today.

C. Moses' exposition of the principal laws

1. Israel shall erect an altar: the place that the LORD will choose

12:1
Deut 4:9,10

12 "These are the statutes and the judgments which you shall carefully observe in the land which the LORD, the God of your fathers, has given you to possess as long as you live on the earth.

2 "You shall utterly destroy all the places where the nations whom you shall dispossess serve their gods, on the high mountains and on the hills and under every green tree.

[10]I.e., autumn and spring rain   [11]I.e., the Mediterranean

3 "And you shall tear down their altars and smash their *sacred* pillars and burn their [12]Asherim with fire, and you shall cut down the engraved images of their gods, and you shall obliterate their name from that place.

4 "You shall not act like this toward the LORD your God.

5 "But you shall seek *the* LORD at the place which the LORD your God shall choose from all your tribes, to establish His name there for His dwelling, and there you shall come.

6 "And there you shall bring your burnt offerings, your sacrifices, your tithes, the contribution of your hand, your votive offerings, your freewill offerings, and the first-born of your herd and of your flock.

7 "There also you and your households shall eat before the LORD your God, and rejoice in all your undertakings in which the LORD your God has blessed you.

8 "You shall not do at all what we are doing here today, every man *doing* whatever is right in his own eyes;

9 for you have not as yet come to the resting place and the inheritance which the LORD your God is giving you.

10 "When you cross the Jordan and live in the land which the LORD your God is giving you to inherit, and He gives you rest from all your enemies around *you* so that you live in security,

11 then it shall come about that the place in which the LORD your God shall choose for His name to dwell, there you shall bring all that I command you: your burnt offerings and your sacrifices, your tithes and the contribution of your hand, and all your choice votive offerings which you will vow to the LORD.

12 "And you shall rejoice before the LORD your God, you and your sons and daughters, your male and female servants, and the Levite who is within your gates, since he has no portion or inheritance with you.

13 "Be careful that you do not offer your burnt offerings in every *cultic* place you see,

14 but in the place which the LORD chooses in one of your tribes, there you shall offer your burnt offerings, and there you shall do all that I command you.

15 "However, you may slaughter and eat meat within any of your gates, whatever you desire, according to the blessing of the LORD your God which He has given you; the unclean and the clean may eat of it, as of the gazelle and the deer.

16 "Only you shall not eat the blood; you are to pour it out on the ground like water.

17 "You are not allowed to eat within your gates the tithe of your grain, or new wine, or oil, or the first-born of your herd or flock, or any of your votive offerings which you vow, or your freewill offerings, or the contribution of your hand.

18 "But you shall eat them before the LORD your God in the place which the LORD your God will choose, you and your son and daughter, and your male and female servants, and the Levite who is within your gates; and you shall rejoice before the LORD your God in all your undertakings.

19 "Be careful that you do not forsake the Levite as long as you live in your land.

20 "When the LORD your God extends your border as He has promised you, and you say, 'I will eat meat,' because you desire to eat meat, *then* you may eat meat, whatever you desire.

21 "If the place which the LORD your God chooses to put His name is too far from you, then you may slaughter of your herd and flock which the LORD has given you, as I have commanded you; and you may eat within your gates whatever you desire.

22 "Just as a gazelle or a deer is eaten, so you shall eat it; the unclean and the clean alike may eat of it.

23 "Only be sure not to eat the blood, for the blood is the life, and you shall not eat the life with the flesh.

24 "You shall not eat it; you shall pour it out on the ground like water.

25 "You shall not eat it, in order that it may be well with you and your sons after you, for you will be doing what is right in the sight of the LORD.

[12]I.e., wooden symbols of a female deity

Cross-references (margin):

*12:3 Deut 7:5

*12:5 v. 11

12:7 Deut 14:26; vv. 12,18

12:10 Deut 11:31

12:11 v. 5

12:12 v. 7; Deut 10:9

12:14 v. 11

12:15 vv. 20-23; Deut 14:5

12:16 Lev 17:10-12

12:18 vv. 5,7,12

12:19 Deut 14:27
12:20 Gen 15:18

12:22 v. 15

12:23 v. 16; Lev 17:11,14

12:25 Deut 4:40; 13:18

12:3 *pillars*, large upright stones at Canaanite sanctuaries. Some suggest that they may have been symbols of Baal, the Canaanite fertility god. *Asherim*, see note to Ex. 34:13.

12:5 *the place.* As a safeguard against idolatry, Israel was to have only one legitimate sanctuary. It was originally at Shiloh, but David moved the sanctuary to Jerusalem.

12:26
v. 17

26 "Only your holy things which you may have and your votive offerings, you shall take and go to the place which the LORD chooses.

27 "And you shall offer your burnt offerings, the flesh and the blood, on the altar of the LORD your God; and the blood of your sacrifices shall be poured out on the altar of the LORD your God, and you shall eat the flesh.

12:28
v. 25;
Deut 4:40

28 "Be careful to listen to all these words which I command you, in order that it may be well with you and your sons after you forever, for you will be doing what is good and right in the sight of the LORD your God.

29 "When the LORD your God cuts off before you the nations which you are going in to dispossess, and you dispossess them and dwell in their land,

30 beware that you are not ensnared to follow them, after they are destroyed before you, and that you do not inquire after their gods, saying, 'How do these nations serve their gods, that I also may do likewise?'

12:31
Deut 9:5;
18:10

31 "You shall not behave thus toward the LORD your God, for every abominable act which the LORD hates they have done for their gods; for they even burn their sons and daughters in the fire to their gods.

12:32
Deut 4:2

32 "Whatever I command you, you shall be careful to do; you shall not add to nor take away from it.

2. The second commandment

a. False prophets to die

13:1
Matt 24:24;
Mark 13:22

13 "If a prophet or a dreamer of dreams arises among you and gives you a sign or a wonder,

13:2
vv. 6,13

2 and the sign or the wonder comes true, concerning which he spoke to you, saying, 'Let us go after other gods (whom you have not known) and let us serve them,'

13:3
Deut 8:2,16

3 you shall not listen to the words of that prophet or that dreamer of dreams; for the LORD your God is testing you to find out if you love the LORD your God with all your heart and with all your soul.

*13:4
2 Kin 23:3;
Deut 10:20

4 "You shall follow the LORD your God and fear Him; and you shall keep His commandments, listen to His voice, serve Him, and cling to Him.

13:5
Deut 18:20;
17:7

5 "But that prophet or that dreamer of dreams shall be put to death, because he has counseled rebellion against the LORD your God who brought you from the land of Egypt and redeemed you from the house of slavery, to seduce you from the way in which the LORD your God commanded you to walk. So you shall purge the evil from among you.

b. Secret idolaters to be cut off

13:6
Deut 17:2-7;
29:18

6 "If your brother, your mother's son, or your son or daughter, or the wife you cherish, or your friend who is as your own soul, entice you secretly, saying, 'Let us go and serve other gods' (whom neither you nor your fathers have known,

7 of the gods of the peoples who are around you, near you or far from you, from one end of the earth to the other end),

8 you shall not yield to him or listen to him; and your eye shall not pity him, nor shall you spare or conceal him.

13:9
Deut 17:5,7

9 "But you shall surely kill him; your hand shall be first against him to put him to death, and afterwards the hand of all the people.

10 "So you shall stone him to death because he has sought to seduce you from the LORD your God who brought you out from the land of Egypt, out of the house of slavery.

13:11
Deut 19:20

11 "Then all Israel will hear and be afraid, and will never again do such a wicked thing among you.

c. Idolatrous cities to be destroyed

12 "If you hear in one of your cities, which the LORD your God is giving you to live in, anyone saying that

13 some worthless men have gone out from among you and have seduced the

13:4 In all ages the indispensable test of one's faith toward God has been grounded in obedience. Obedience must spring from the heart (Rom. 6:17); it must be willing and without reservation (Is. 1:19; Josh. 22:2,3); and it must be constant in its intention (Phil. 2:12). It springs from faith (Heb. 11:6) and consists of the following: (1) obedience to the law of God (11:27; Is. 42:24); (2) obedience to the voice of God (Ex. 19:5; Jer. 7:23); (3) obedience to Christ (2 Cor. 10:5); (4) obedience to the gospel (Rom. 1:5; 6:17; 10:16, 17); and (5) obedience to governing authorities (Rom. 13:1). Punishments are threatened for those who disobey, just as blessings are promised those who obey. Scripture abounds with illustrations of individuals who were obedient and followed God.

inhabitants of their city, saying, 'Let us go and serve other gods' (whom you have not known),

14   then you shall investigate and search out and inquire thoroughly. And if it is true *and* the matter established that this abomination has been done among you,

15   you shall surely strike the inhabitants of that city with the edge of the sword, utterly destroying it and all that is in it and its cattle with the edge of the sword.

16   "Then you shall gather all its booty into the middle of its open square and burn the city and all its booty with fire as a whole burnt offering to the LORD your God; and it shall be a ruin forever. It shall never be rebuilt.

17   "And nothing from that which is put under the ban shall cling to your hand, in order that the LORD may turn from His burning anger and show mercy to you, and have compassion on you and make you increase, just as He has sworn to your fathers,

18   if you will listen to the voice of the LORD your God, keeping all His commandments which I am commanding you today, and doing what is right in the sight of the LORD your God.

3. *Clean and unclean animals*

14   "You are the sons of the LORD your God; you shall not cut yourselves nor shave your forehead for the sake of the dead.

2   "For you are a holy people to the LORD your God; and the LORD has chosen you to be a people for His own possession out of all the peoples who are on the face of the earth.

3   "You shall not eat any detestable thing.

4   "These are the animals which you may eat: the ox, the sheep, the goat,

5   the deer, the gazelle, the roebuck, the wild goat, the ibex, the antelope and the mountain sheep.

6   "And any animal that divides the hoof and has the hoof split in two *and* chews the cud, among the animals, that you may eat.

7   "Nevertheless, you are not to eat of these among those which chew the cud, or among those that divide the hoof in two: the camel and the rabbit and the rock-badger, for though they chew the cud, they do not divide the hoof; they are unclean for you.

8   "And the pig, because it divides the hoof but *does* not *chew* the cud, it is unclean for you. You shall not eat any of their flesh nor touch their carcasses.

9   "These you may eat of all that are in water: anything that has fins and scales you may eat,

10   but anything that does not have fins and scales you shall not eat; it is unclean for you.

11   "You may eat any clean bird.

12   "But these are the ones which you shall not eat: the eagle and the vulture and the buzzard,

13   and the red kite, the falcon, and the kite in their kinds,

14   and every raven in its kind,

15   and the ostrich, the owl, the sea gull, and the hawk in their kinds,

16   the little owl, the great owl, the white owl,

17   the pelican, the carrion vulture, the cormorant,

18   the stork, and the heron in their kinds, and the hoopoe and the bat.

19   "And all the teeming life with wings are unclean to you; they shall not be eaten.

20   "You may eat any clean bird.

21   "You shall not eat anything which dies *of itself*. You may give it to the alien who is in your town, so that he may eat it, or you may sell it to a foreigner, for you are a holy people to the LORD your God. You shall not boil a kid in its mother's milk.

4. *The tithe of fruits*

22   "You shall surely tithe all the produce from what you sow, which comes out of the field every year.

23   "And you shall eat in the presence of the LORD your God, at the place where He chooses to establish His name, the tithe of your grain, your new wine, your oil,

---

13:13
vv. 2,6; see
1 John 2:19

13:15
Ex 22:20

13:16
Josh 6:24;
8:28

13:17
Num 25:4;
Deut 30:3;
7:13

13:18
Deut 12:28

14:1
Rom 8:16;
Lev 21:5
14:2
Deut 7:6

14:4
Lev 11:2-45;
Acts 10:14

14:8
Lev 11:26,27
14:9
Lev 11:9

14:12
Lev 11:3

14:19
Lev 11:20

14:21
Lev 17:15;
v. 2;
Ex 29:19;
34:26

*****14:22ff**
Lev 27:30
14:23
Deut 12:5-7;
4:10

14:22–27 This law of the tithe is different from the law of the tithe found in Num. 18:21–24. The one apparently   superseded the other.

and the first-born of your herd and your flock, in order that you may learn to fear the LORD your God always.

14:24
Deut 12:5,21

24 "And if the distance is so great for you that you are not able to bring *the tithe*, since the place where the LORD your God chooses to set His name is too far away from you when the LORD your God blesses you,

25 then you shall exchange *it* for money, and bind the money in your hand and go to the place which the LORD your God chooses.

*14:26
Deut 12:7,18

26 "And you may spend the money for whatever your heart desires, for oxen, or sheep, or wine, or strong drink, or whatever your heart desires; and there you shall eat in the presence of the LORD your God and rejoice, you and your household.

14:27
Deut 12:12;
Num 18:20

27 "Also you shall not neglect the Levite who is in your town, for he has no portion or inheritance among you.

14:28
Deut 26:12

28 "At the end of every third year you shall bring out all the tithe of your produce in that year, and shall deposit *it* in your town.

14:29
Deut 26:12;
v. 27;
Deut 15:10

29 "And the Levite, because he has no portion or inheritance among you, and the alien, the orphan and the widow who are in your town, shall come and eat and be satisfied, in order that the LORD your God may bless you in all the work of your hand which you do.

5. *Laws relating to slaves and the poor*

a. *The year of release*

15:1
Deut 31:10

15 "At the end of *every* seven years you shall [13]grant a remission *of debts.*
2 "And this is the manner of remission: every creditor shall release what he has loaned to his neighbor; he shall not exact it of his neighbor and his brother, because the LORD's remission has been proclaimed.

3 "From a foreigner you may exact *it,* but your hand shall release whatever of yours is with your brother.

4 "However, there shall be no poor among you, since the LORD will surely bless you in the land which the LORD your God is giving you as an inheritance to possess,

15:5
Deut 28:1

5 if only you listen obediently to the voice of the LORD your God, to observe carefully all this commandment which I am commanding you today.

15:6
Deut 28:12,
13

6 "For the LORD your God shall bless you as He has promised you, and you will lend to many nations, but you will not borrow; and you will rule over many nations, but they will not rule over you.

15:7
1 John 3:17

7 "If there is a poor man with you, one of your brothers, in any of your towns in your land which the LORD your God is giving you, you shall not harden your heart, nor close your hand from your poor brother;

15:8
Lev 25:35

8 but you shall freely open your hand to him, and shall generously lend him sufficient for his need *in* whatever he lacks.

15:9
v. 1;
Deut 24:15

9 "Beware, lest there is a base thought in your heart, saying, 'The seventh year, the year of remission, is near,' and your eye is hostile toward your poor brother, and you give him nothing; then he may cry to the LORD against you, and it will be a sin in you.

15:10
2 Cor 9:5,7;
Deut 24:19

10 "You shall generously give to him, and your heart shall not be grieved when you give to him, because for this thing the LORD your God will bless you in all your work and in all your undertakings.

15:11
Matt 26:11;
Mark 14:7;
John 12:8

11 "For the poor will never cease *to be* in the land; therefore I command you, saying, 'You shall freely open your hand to your brother, to your needy and poor in your land.'

b. *Manumission of slaves*

15:12
Ex 21:2;
Lev 25:39

12 "If your kinsman, a Hebrew man or woman, is sold to you, then he shall serve you six years, but in the seventh year you shall set him free.

13 "And when you set him free, you shall not send him away empty-handed.

14 "You shall furnish him liberally from your flock and from your threshing floor and from your wine vat; you shall give to him as the LORD your God has blessed you.

15:15
Deut 5:15;
16:12

15 "And you shall remember that you were a slave in the land of Egypt, and the LORD your God redeemed you; therefore I command you this today.

[13]Lit., *make a release*

14:26 wine, Hebrew *yayin*, fermented grape juice. *strong drink*, Hebrew *shekar*, probably beer, since the Israelites did not have distilled liquors. The Hebrew word for *strong drink* comes from the verb meaning "to be drunk."

16 "And it shall come about if he says to you, 'I will not go out from you,' because he loves you and your household, since he fares well with you;

17 then you shall take an awl and pierce it through his ear into the door, and he shall be your servant forever. And also you shall do likewise to your maidservant.

18 "It shall not seem hard to you when you set him free, for he has given you six years *with* double the service of a hired man; so the LORD your God will bless you in whatever you do.

c. *Sacrifice of firstling males*

19 "You shall consecrate to the LORD your God all the first-born males that are born of your herd and of your flock; you shall not work with the first-born of your herd, nor shear the first-born of your flock.

20 "You and your household shall eat it every year before the LORD your God in the place which the LORD chooses.

21 "But if it has any defect, *such as* lameness or blindness, *or* any serious defect, you shall not sacrifice it to the LORD your God.

22 "You shall eat it within your gates; the unclean and the clean alike *may eat it*, as a gazelle or a deer.

23 "Only you shall not eat its blood; you are to pour it out on the ground like water.

6. *The Passover*

16 "Observe the month of Abib and celebrate the Passover to the LORD your God, for in the month of Abib the LORD your God brought you out of Egypt by night.

2 "And you shall sacrifice the Passover to the LORD your God from the flock and the herd, in the place where the LORD chooses to establish His name.

3 "You shall not eat leavened bread with it; seven days you shall eat with it unleavened bread, the bread of affliction (for you came out of the land of Egypt in haste), in order that you may remember all the days of your life the day when you came out of the land of Egypt.

4 "For seven days no leaven shall be seen with you in all your territory, and none of the flesh which you sacrifice on the evening of the first day shall remain overnight until morning.

5 "You are not allowed to sacrifice the Passover in any of your towns which the LORD your God is giving you;

6 but at the place where the LORD your God chooses to establish His name, you shall sacrifice the Passover in the evening at sunset, at the time that you came out of Egypt.

7 "And you shall cook and eat *it* in the place which the LORD your God chooses. And in the morning you are to return to your tents.

8 "Six days you shall eat unleavened bread, and on the seventh day there shall be a solemn assembly to the LORD your God; you shall do no work *on it*.

7. *The Feast of Weeks*

9 "You shall count seven weeks for yourself; you shall begin to count seven weeks from the time you begin to put the sickle to the standing grain.

10 "Then you shall celebrate the Feast of Weeks to the LORD your God with a tribute of a freewill offering of your hand, which you shall give just as the LORD your God blesses you;

11 and you shall rejoice before the LORD your God, you and your son and your daughter and your male and female servants and the Levite who is in your town, and the stranger and the orphan and the widow who are in your midst, in the place where the LORD your God chooses to establish His name.

12 "And you shall remember that you were a slave in Egypt, and you shall be careful to observe these statutes.

8. *The Feast of Tabernacles*

13 "You shall celebrate the Feast of Booths seven days after you have gathered in from your threshing floor and your wine vat;

*15:16
Ex 21:5,6

15:19
Ex 13:2

15:20
Deut 12:5-7, 17
15:21
Lev 22:19-25
15:22
Deut 12:15, 22
15:23
Deut 12:16, 23

16:1
Ex 12:2,29, 42; 13:4

16:2
Deut 12:5,26

16:3
Ex 12:8,15

16:4
Ex 13:7; 12:10

16:6
Deut 12:5; Ex 12:6

16:7
Ex 12:8,9

16:8
Ex 12:16

16:9
Ex 23:16; 34:22;
Lev 23:15;
Num 28:26

16:11
Deut 12:7,12

16:12
Deut 15:15

16:13
Ex 23:16;
Lev 23:34

15:16 God had redeemed Israel from slavery in Egypt, therefore no Israelite could be held in slavery perpetually without the consent of the person. In some cases slavery offered more security and better conditions than individual freedom could give.

16:14
v. 11

14 and you shall rejoice in your feast, you and your son and your daughter and your male and female servants and the Levite and the stranger and the orphan and the widow who are in your towns.

16:15
Lev 23:39

15 "Seven days you shall celebrate a feast to the LORD your God in the place which the LORD your God chooses, because the LORD your God will bless you in all your produce and in all the work of your hands, so that you shall be altogether joyful.

16:16
Ex 23:14-17;
34:20,23

16 "Three times in a year all your males shall appear before the LORD your God in the place which He chooses, at the Feast of Unleavened Bread and at the Feast of Weeks and at the Feast of Booths, and they shall not appear before the LORD empty-handed.

17 "Every man shall give as he is able, according to the blessing of the LORD your God which He has given you.

9. The administration of justice

a. Judges

16:18
Deut 1:16

18 "You shall appoint for yourself judges and officers in all your towns which the LORD your God is giving you, according to your tribes, and they shall judge the people with righteous judgment.

16:19
Deut 1:17;
Ex 23:8

19 "You shall not distort justice; you shall not be partial, and you shall not take a bribe, for a bribe blinds the eyes of the wise and perverts the words of the righteous.

20 "Justice, and only justice, you shall pursue, that you may live and possess the land which the LORD your God is giving you.

b. Prohibitions: idolatry and blemished sacrifices

16:21
Ex 34:13;
Deut 7:5

21 "You shall not plant for yourself an Asherah of any kind of tree beside the altar of the LORD your God, which you shall make for yourself.

22 "Neither shall you set up for yourself a sacred pillar which the LORD your God hates.

17:1
Deut 15:21;
Mal 1:8,13
17:2
Deut 13:6

17 "You shall not sacrifice to the LORD your God an ox or a sheep which has a blemish or any defect, for that is a detestable thing to the LORD your God.

2 "If there is found in your midst, in any of your towns, which the LORD your God is giving you, a man or a woman who does what is evil in the sight of the LORD your God, by transgressing His covenant,

3 and has gone and served other gods and worshiped them, or the sun or the moon or any of the heavenly host, which I have not commanded,

17:4
Deut 13:12,
14

4 and if it is told you and you have heard of it, then you shall inquire thoroughly. And behold, if it is true and the thing certain that this detestable thing has been done in Israel,

5 then you shall bring out that man or that woman who has done this evil deed, to your gates, that is, the man or the woman, and you shall stone them to death.

17:6
Num 35:30;
Deut 19:15;
Matt 18:16
17:7
Deut 13:5,9

6 "On the evidence of two witnesses or three witnesses, he who is to die shall be put to death; he shall not be put to death on the evidence of one witness.

7 "The hand of the witnesses shall be first against him to put him to death, and afterward the hand of all the people. So you shall purge the evil from your midst.

c. The court of appeal

17:8
Deut 12:5

8 "If any case is too difficult for you to decide, between one kind of homicide or another, between one kind of lawsuit or another, and between one kind of assault or another, being cases of dispute in your courts, then you shall arise and go up to the place which the LORD your God chooses.

17:9
Deut 19:17;
Ezek 44:24

9 "So you shall come to the Levitical priest or the judge who is in office in those days, and you shall inquire of them, and they will declare to you the verdict in the case.

10 "And you shall do according to the terms of the verdict which they declare to you from that place which the LORD chooses; and you shall be careful to observe according to all that they teach you.

17:11
Deut 25:1

11 "According to the terms of the law which they teach you, and according to the verdict which they tell you, you shall do; you shall not turn aside from the word which they declare to you, to the right or the left.

12 "And the man who acts presumptuously by not listening to the priest who

stands there to serve the LORD your God, nor to the judge, that man shall die; thus you shall purge the evil from Israel.

13 "Then all the people will hear and be afraid, and will not act presumptuously again.

17:13
Deut 13:11;
19:20

10. *The choice of a king*

14 "When you enter the land which the LORD your God gives you, and you possess it and live in it, and you say, 'I will set a king over me like all the nations who are around me,'

*17:14
Deut 11:31;
1 Sam 8:5,19,
20

15 you shall surely set a king over you whom the LORD your God chooses, *one* from among your countrymen you shall set as king over yourselves; you may not put a foreigner over yourselves who is not your countryman.

17:15
Jer 30:21

16 "Moreover, he shall not multiply horses for himself, nor shall he cause the people to return to Egypt to multiply horses, since the LORD has said to you, 'You shall never again return that way.'

*17:16ff
1 Kin 4:26;
10:26,28;
Is 31:1;
Ezek 17:15

17 "Neither shall he multiply wives for himself, lest his heart turn away; nor shall he greatly increase silver and gold for himself.

17:17
cf.
1 Kin 11:3,4

18 "Now it shall come about when he sits on the throne of his kingdom, he shall write for himself a copy of this law on a scroll in the presence of the Levitical priests.

17:18
Deut 31:24-26

19 "And it shall be with him, and he shall read it all the days of his life, that he may learn to fear the LORD his God, by carefully observing all the words of this law and these statutes,

17:19
Josh 1:8

20 that his heart may not be lifted up above his countrymen and that he may not turn aside from the commandment, to the right or the left; in order that he and his sons may continue long in his kingdom in the midst of Israel.

17:20
Deut 5:32

11. *The portion of the priests and Levites*

18 "The Levitical priests, the whole tribe of Levi, shall have no portion or inheritance with Israel; they shall eat the LORD'S offerings by fire and His portion.

18:1
Deut 10:9;
1 Cor 9:13

2 "And they shall have no inheritance among their countrymen; the LORD is their inheritance, as He promised them.

3 "Now this shall be the priests' due from the people, from those who offer a sacrifice, either an ox or a sheep, of which they shall give to the priest the shoulder and the two cheeks and the stomach.

18:3
Lev 7:30-34

4 "You shall give him the first fruits of your grain, your new wine, and your oil, and the first shearing of your sheep.

18:4
Ex 22:29;
Num 18:12

5 "For the LORD your God has chosen him and his sons from all your tribes, to stand and serve in the name of the LORD forever.

18:5
Ex 28:1;
Deut 10:8

6 "Now if a Levite comes from any of your towns throughout Israel where he resides, and comes whenever he desires to the place which the LORD chooses,

7 then he shall serve in the name of the LORD his God, like all his fellow Levites who stand there before the LORD.

8 "They shall eat equal portions, except *what they receive* from the sale of their fathers' *estates*.

18:8
Neh 12:44,47

12. *The law of the prophet*

a. *Canaanitish abominations forbidden*

9 "When you enter the land which the LORD your God gives you, you shall not learn to imitate the detestable things of those nations.

18:9
Deut 12:29-31
*18:10
Deut 12:31;
Lev 19:26,31

10 "There shall not be found among you anyone who makes his son or his

---

17:14 Moses predicted that Israel would ask for a king. Although the people's motive would be offensive to God, He had included all this in His plan and had decreed the eventual establishment of the Davidic throne in anticipation of the reign of Christ.

17:16-20 In the historical books we frequently read of otherwise godly people multiplying horses, wives, silver, and gold contrary to these regulations. David and Solomon had God's blessing in spite of their violating these precepts.

18:10 Divination as practiced by the heathen is sternly forbidden by Scripture. The following classes or categories of diviners are included: diviner, soothsayer, augur, sorcerer, charmer, medium, necromancer (18:10,11), magician

(Gen. 41:8; Dan. 4:7), astrologer (Is. 47:13; Dan. 4:7). According to the Mari tablets, divination flourished in upper Mesopotamia and Syria. One of its chief functions was to determine the proper move. Every army had a diviner, whose task it was to decide, for example, which route to take at the fork of the road. Israel had Yahweh to lead them, therefore such heathen practices were inconsistent with true faith. In the Old Testament, those who practiced these forbidden arts were subject to the death penalty (Ex. 22:18; Lev. 20:27). In the New Testament, it is stated that sorcerers shall not inherit the kingdom of God (Gal. 5:20; Rev. 22:15), although there is no injunction that such profane people should be killed today.

daughter pass through the fire, one who uses divination, one who practices witch-craft, or one who interprets omens, or a sorcerer,

11   or one who casts a spell, or a medium, or a spiritist, or one who calls up the dead.

18:12
Deut 9:4
12   "For whoever does these things is detestable to the LORD; and because of these detestable things the LORD your God will drive them out before you.

13   "You shall be blameless before the LORD your God.

14   "For those nations, which you shall dispossess, listen to those who practice witchcraft and to diviners, but as for you, the LORD your God has not allowed you *to do* so.

b. The predicted coming of the prophet Messiah: the test of a false prophet

*18:15ff
John 1:21;
Acts 3:22;
7:37
15   "The LORD your God will raise up for you a prophet like me from among you, from your countrymen, you shall listen to him.

18:16
Deut 5:23-27;
Ex 20:19
16   "This is according to all that you asked of the LORD your God in Horeb on the day of the assembly, saying, 'Let me not hear again the voice of the LORD my God, let me not see this great fire anymore, lest I die.'

18:17
Deut 5:28
17   "And the LORD said to me, 'They have spoken well.

18:18
v. 15;
Is 51:16;
John 4:25,26
18   'I will raise up a prophet from among their countrymen like you, and I will put My words in his mouth, and he shall speak to them all that I command him.

18:19
Acts 3:23
19   'And it shall come about that whoever will not listen to My words which he shall speak in My name, I Myself will require *it* of him.

18:20
Deut 13:1,2,5
20   'But the prophet who shall speak a word presumptuously in My name which I have not commanded him to speak, or which he shall speak in the name of other gods, that prophet shall die.'

21   "And you may say in your heart, 'How shall we know the word which the LORD has not spoken?'

18:22
Jer 28:9;
v. 20
22   "When a prophet speaks in the name of the LORD, if the thing does not come about or come true, that is the thing which the LORD has not spoken. The prophet has spoken it presumptuously; you shall not be afraid of him.

13. Criminal laws

a. Cities of refuge for accidental manslaughter

19:1
Deut 12:29
19 "When the LORD your God cuts off the nations, whose land the LORD your God gives you, and you dispossess them and settle in their cities and in their houses,

19:2
Num 35:10,
14
2   you shall set aside three cities for yourself in the midst of your land, which the LORD your God gives you to possess.

3   "You shall prepare the roads for yourself, and divide into three parts the territory of your land, which the LORD your God will give you as a possession, so that any manslayer may flee there.

19:4
Num 35:15
4   "Now this is the case of the manslayer who may flee there and live: when he kills his friend unintentionally, not hating him previously—

5   as when *a man* goes into the forest with his friend to cut wood, and his hand swings the axe to cut down the tree, and the iron *head* slips off the handle and strikes his friend so that he dies—he may flee to one of these cities and live;

19:6
Num 35:12
6   lest the avenger of blood pursue the manslayer in the heat of his anger, and overtake him, because the way is long, and take his life, though he was not deserving of death, since he had not hated him previously.

7   "Therefore, I command you, saying, 'You shall set aside three cities for yourself.'

8   "And if the LORD your God enlarges your territory, just as He has sworn to your fathers, and gives you all the land which He promised to give your fathers—

19:9
Josh 20:7,8
9   if you carefully observe all this commandment, which I command you today, to love the LORD your God, and to walk in His ways always—then you shall add three more cities for yourself, besides these three.

19:10
Deut 21:1-9;
Num 35:33
10   "So innocent blood will not be shed in the midst of your land which the LORD your God gives you as an inheritance, and bloodguiltiness be on you.

18:15–22 Since divination of all sorts is outlawed, God promises to raise up a prophet like Moses in succeeding generations. The false prophet will speak God's words, and instruct the people in the way they should go, but he will be proven wrong and he will die for his presumption. The ultimate prophet like Moses was to be Jesus Christ. To see and hear him was to see and hear God.

b. *Punishment for murderers*

11 "But if there is a man who hates his neighbor and lies in wait for him and rises up against him and strikes him so that he dies, and he flees to one of these cities,

12 then the elders of his city shall send and take him from there and deliver him into the hand of the avenger of blood, that he may die.

13 "You shall not pity him, but you shall purge the blood of the innocent from Israel, that it may go well with you.

c. *Removing landmarks*

14 "You shall not move your neighbor's boundary mark, which the ancestors have set, in your inheritance which you shall inherit in the land that the LORD your God gives you to possess.

d. *The law of witnesses*

15 "A single witness shall not rise up against a man on account of any iniquity or any sin which he has committed; on the evidence of two or three witnesses a matter shall be confirmed.

16 "If a malicious witness rises up against a man to accuse him of wrongdoing,

17 then both the men who have the dispute shall stand before the LORD, before the priests and the judges who will be *in office* in those days.

18 "And the judges shall investigate thoroughly; and if the witness is a false witness *and* he has accused his brother falsely,

19 then you shall do to him just as he had intended to do to his brother. Thus you shall purge the evil from among you.

20 "And the rest will hear and be afraid, and will never again do such an evil thing among you.

21 "Thus you shall not show pity: life for life, eye for eye, tooth for tooth, hand for hand, foot for foot.

14. *Laws of war*

a. *Military service*

20 "When you go out to battle against your enemies and see horses and chariots *and* people more numerous than you, do not be afraid of them; for the LORD your God, who brought you up from the land of Egypt, is with you.

2 "Now it shall come about that when you are approaching the battle, the priest shall come near and speak to the people.

3 "And he shall say to them, 'Hear, O Israel, you are approaching the battle against your enemies today. Do not be fainthearted. Do not be afraid, or panic, or tremble before them,

4 for the LORD your God is the one who goes with you, to fight for you against your enemies, to save you.'

5 "The officers also shall speak to the people, saying, 'Who is the man that has built a new house and has not dedicated it? Let him depart and return to his house, lest he die in the battle and another man dedicate it.

6 'And who is the man that has planted a vineyard and has not begun to use its fruit? Let him depart and return to his house, lest he die in the battle and another man begin to use its fruit.

7 'And who is the man that is engaged to a woman and has not married her? Let him depart and return to his house, lest he die in the battle and another man marry her.'

8 "Then the officers shall speak further to the people, and they shall say, 'Who is the man that is afraid and fainthearted? Let him depart and return to his house, so that he might not make his brothers' hearts melt like his heart.'

9 "And it shall come about that when the officers have finished speaking to the people, they shall appoint commanders of armies at the head of the people.

b. *Sieges*

10 "When you approach a city to fight against it, you shall offer it terms of peace.

11 "And it shall come about, if it agrees to make peace with you and opens to you, then it shall be that all the people who are found in it shall become your forced labor and shall serve you.

19:13 Deut 7:2
*19:14 Deut 27:17
19:15 Num 35:30; Deut 17:6; Matt 18:16; 2 Cor 13:1
19:16 Ex 23:1; Ps 27:12
19:17 Deut 17:9
19:19 Prov 19:5,9
19:21 v. 13; Ex 21:23; Lev 24:20; Matt 5:38
20:1 Deut 31:6,8
20:3 v. 1; Josh 23:10
20:4 Deut 1:30
20:6 1 Cor 9:7
20:7 Deut 24:5
20:8 Judg 7:3
*20:10ff Luke 14:31

19:14 *boundary mark.* Evidently it was a common practice to move the boundary stones, thereby encroaching upon and eventually robbing the poor neighbor of some property. **20:10–18** See note to 2:34.

20:14
Josh 8:2; 22:8

12 "However, if it does not make peace with you, but makes war against you, then you shall besiege it.

13 "When the LORD your God gives it into your hand, you shall strike all the men in it with the edge of the sword.

14 "Only the women and the children and the animals and all that is in the city, all its spoil, you shall take as booty for yourself; and you shall use the spoil of your enemies which the LORD your God has given you.

15 "Thus you shall do to all the cities that are very far from you, which are not of the cities of these nations nearby.

20:16
Deut 7:1,2;
Josh 11:14

16 "Only in the cities of these peoples that the LORD your God is giving you as an inheritance, you shall not leave alive anything that breathes.

17 "But you shall utterly destroy them, the Hittite and the Amorite, the Canaanite and the Perizzite, the Hivite and the Jebusite, as the LORD your God has commanded you,

20:18
Ex 23:33

18 in order that they may not teach you to do according to all their detestable things which they have done for their gods, so that you would sin against the LORD your God.

19 "When you besiege a city a long time, to make war against it in order to capture it, you shall not destroy its trees by swinging an axe against them; for you may eat from them, and you shall not cut them down. For is the tree of the field a man, that it should be besieged by you?

20 "Only the trees which you know are not fruit trees you shall destroy and cut down, that you may construct siegeworks against the city that is making war with you until it falls.

15. Sundry laws

a. Sacrifice for unknown murderer's crime

21:1
Josh 1:6

21 "If a slain person is found lying in the open country in the land which the LORD your God gives you to possess, *and* it is not known who has struck him,

2 then your elders and your judges shall go out and measure *the distance* to the cities which are around the slain one.

3 "And it shall be that the city which is nearest to the slain man, that is, the elders of that city, shall take a heifer of the herd, which has not been worked and which has not pulled in a yoke;

4 and the elders of that city shall bring the heifer down to a valley with running water, which has not been plowed or sown, and shall break the heifer's neck there in the valley.

21:5
Deut 17:8-11

5 "Then the priests, the sons of Levi, shall come near, for the LORD your God has chosen them to serve Him and to bless in the name of the LORD; and every dispute and every assault shall be settled by them.

6 "And all the elders of that city which is nearest to the slain man shall wash their hands over the heifer whose neck was broken in the valley;

7 and they shall answer and say, 'Our hands have not shed this blood, nor did our eyes see *it*.

21:8
Jon 1:8

8 '[14]Forgive Thy people Israel whom Thou hast redeemed, O LORD, and do not place the guilt of innocent blood in the midst of Thy people Israel.' And the bloodguiltiness shall be forgiven them.

21:9
Deut 19:13

9 "So you shall remove the guilt of innocent blood from your midst, when you do what is right in the eyes of the LORD.

b. Marrying a captive woman

10 "When you go out to battle against your enemies, and the LORD your God delivers them into your hands, and you take them away captive,

11 and see among the captives a beautiful woman, and have a desire for her and would take her as a wife for yourself,

21:12
Lev 14:8,9;
Num 6:9

12 then you shall bring her home to your house, and she shall shave her head and trim her nails.

13 "She shall also remove the clothes of her captivity and shall remain in your house, and mourn her father and mother a full month; and after that you may go in to her and be her husband and she shall be your wife.

[14]Lit., *Cover over, atone for*

21:7 This verse shows that crime and sin have corporate, as well as individual, implications. (See also v. 9.)

14 "And it shall be, if you are not pleased with her, then you shall let her go wherever she wishes; but you shall certainly not sell her for money, you shall not mistreat her, because you have humbled her.

c. *The law of the first-born*

15 "If a man has two wives, the one loved and the other unloved, and *both* the loved and the unloved have borne him sons, if the first-born son belongs to the unloved,

16 then it shall be in the day he wills what he has to his sons, he cannot make the son of the loved the first-born before the son of the unloved, who is the first-born.

21:16
1 Chr 26:10

17 "But he shall acknowledge the first-born, the son of the unloved, by giving him a double portion of all that he has, for he is the beginning of his strength; to him belongs the right of the first-born.

21:17
Gen 49:3

d. *Stoning of a rebellious son*

18 "If any man has a stubborn and rebellious son who will not obey his father or his mother, and when they chastise him, he will not even listen to them,

21:18
Is 30:1

19 then his father and his mother shall seize him, and bring him out to the elders of his city at the gateway of his home town.

20 "And they shall say to the elders of his city, 'This son of ours is stubborn and rebellious, he will not obey us, he is a glutton and a drunkard.'

21 "Then all the men of his city shall stone him to death; so you shall remove the evil from your midst, and all Israel shall hear *of it* and fear.

21:21
Deut 13:5,11

e. *Burying a hanged criminal*

22 "And if a man has committed a sin worthy of death, and he is put to death, and you hang him on a tree,

23 his corpse shall not hang all night on the tree, but you shall surely bury him on the same day (for he who is hanged is accursed of God), so that you do not defile your land which the LORD your God gives you as an inheritance.

21:23
Josh 8:29;
10:26,27;
John 19:31;
Gal 3:13

f. *The law of neighborliness*

22 "You shall not see your countryman's ox or his sheep straying away, and pay no attention to them; you shall certainly bring them back to your country-man.

22:1
Ex 23:4

2 "And if your countryman is not near you, or if you do not know him, then you shall bring it home to your house, and it shall remain with you until your country-man looks for it; then you shall restore it to him.

3 "And thus you shall do with his donkey, and you shall do the same with his garment, and you shall do likewise with anything lost by your countryman, which he has lost and you have found. You are not allowed to neglect *them*.

4 "You shall not see your countryman's donkey or his ox fallen down on the way, and pay no attention to them; you shall certainly help him to raise *them* up.

22:4
Ex 23:5

g. *Incidental laws*

5 "A woman shall not wear man's clothing, nor shall a man put on a woman's clothing; for whoever does these things is an abomination to the LORD your God.

6 "If you happen to come upon a bird's nest along the way, in any tree or on the ground, with young ones or eggs, and the mother sitting on the young or on the eggs, you shall not take the mother with the young;

22:6
Lev 22:28

7 you shall certainly let the mother go, but the young you may take for yourself, in order that it may be well with you, and that you may prolong your days.

22:7
Deut 4:40

8 "When you build a new house, you shall make a parapet for your roof, that you may not bring bloodguilt on your house if anyone falls from it.

9 "You shall not sow your vineyard with two kinds of seed, lest all the produce of the seed which you have sown, and the increase of the vineyard become defiled.

22:9
Lev 19:19

10 "You shall not plow with an ox and a donkey together.

11 "You shall not wear a material mixed of wool and linen together.

22:11
Lev 19:19
22:12
Num 15:37-41;
Matt 23:5

12 "You shall make yourself tassels on the four corners of your garment with which you cover yourself.

h. *The laws of sexual relationships*

13 "If any man takes a wife and goes in to her and *then* turns against her,

22:13
Deut 24:1

14   and charges her with shameful deeds and publicly defames her, and says, 'I took this woman, *but* when I came near her, I did not find her a virgin,'

22:15
v. 23ff

15   then the girl's father and her mother shall take and bring out the *evidence* of the girl's virginity to the elders of the city at the gate.

16   "And the girl's father shall say to the elders, 'I gave my daughter to this man for a wife, but he turned against her;

17   and behold, he has charged her with shameful deeds, saying, "I did not find your daughter a virgin." But this is the *evidence* of my daughter's virginity.' And they shall spread the garment before the elders of the city.

18   "So the elders of that city shall take the man and chastise him,

19   and they shall fine him a hundred *shekels* of silver and give it to the girl's father, because he publicly defamed a virgin of Israel. And she shall remain his wife; he cannot divorce her all his days.

20   "But if this charge is true, that the girl was not found a virgin,

22:21
Deut 23:17,
18; 13:5

21   then they shall bring out the girl to the doorway of her father's house, and the men of her city shall stone her to death because she has committed an act of folly in Israel, by playing the harlot in her father's house; thus you shall purge the evil from among you.

22:22
Lev 20:10;
John 8:5

22   "If a man is found lying with a married woman, then both of them shall die, the man who lay with the woman, and the woman; thus you shall purge the evil from Israel.

23   "If there is a girl who is a virgin engaged to a man, and *another* man finds her in the city and lies with her,

22:24
vv. 21,22

24   then you shall bring them both out to the gate of that city and you shall stone them to death; the girl, because she did not cry out in the city, and the man, because he has violated his neighbor's wife. Thus you shall purge the evil from among you.

22:25
John 8:1-11

25   "But if in the field the man finds the girl who is engaged, and the man forces her and lies with her, then only the man who lies with her shall die.

26   "But you shall do nothing to the girl; there is no sin in the girl worthy of death, for just as a man rises against his neighbor and murders him, so is this case.

27   "When he found her in the field, the engaged girl cried out, but there was no one to save her.

22:28
Ex 22:16,17

28   "If a man finds a girl who is a virgin, who is not engaged, and seizes her and lies with her and they are discovered,

29   then the man who lay with her shall give to the girl's father fifty *shekels* of silver, and she shall become his wife because he has violated her; he cannot divorce her all his days.

22:30
Deut 27:20

30   "A man shall not take his father's wife so that he shall not uncover his father's skirt.

i. *Those excluded from the congregation of Israel*

23 "No one who is emasculated, or has his male organ cut off, shall enter the assembly of the LORD.

2   "No one of illegitimate birth shall enter the assembly of the LORD; none of his *descendants*, even to the tenth generation, shall enter the assembly of the LORD.

23:3
Neh 13:1,2

3   "No Ammonite or Moabite shall enter the assembly of the LORD; none of their *descendants*, even to the tenth generation, shall ever enter the assembly of the LORD,

23:4
Num 22:5,6

4   because they did not meet you with food and water on the way when you came out of Egypt, and because they hired against you Balaam the son of Beor from Pethor of Mesopotamia, to curse you.

5   "Nevertheless, the LORD your God was not willing to listen to Balaam, but the LORD your God turned the curse into a blessing for you because the LORD your God loves you.

6   "You shall never seek their peace or their prosperity all your days.

23:7
Gen 25:24-26

7   "You shall not detest an Edomite, for he is your brother; you shall not detest an Egyptian, because you were an alien in his land.

8   "The sons of the third generation who are born to them may enter the assembly of the LORD.

9   "When you go out as an army against your enemies, then you shall keep yourself from every evil thing.

j. Camp sanitation in wartime

10 "If there is among you any man who is unclean because of a nocturnal emission, then he must go outside the camp; he may not reenter the camp.

11 "But it shall be when evening approaches, he shall bathe himself with water, and at sundown he may reenter the camp.

12 "You shall also have a place outside the camp and go out there,

13 and you shall have a spade among your tools, and it shall be when you sit down outside, you shall dig with it and shall turn to cover up your excrement.

14 "Since the LORD your God walks in the midst of your camp to deliver you and to defeat your enemies before you, therefore your camp must be holy; and He must not see anything indecent among you lest He turn away from you.

k. Incidental laws

15 "You shall not hand over to his master a slave who has escaped from his master to you.

16 "He shall live with you in your midst, in the place which he shall choose in one of your towns where it pleases him; you shall not mistreat him.

17 "None of the daughters of Israel shall be a cult prostitute, nor shall any of the sons of Israel be a cult prostitute.

18 "You shall not bring the hire of a harlot or the wages of a [15]dog into the house of the LORD your God for any votive offering, for both of these are an abomination to the LORD your God.

19 "You shall not charge interest to your countrymen: interest on money, food, or anything that may be loaned at interest.

20 "You may charge interest to a foreigner, but to your countryman you shall not charge interest, so that the LORD your God may bless you in all that you undertake in the land which you are about to enter to possess.

21 "When you make a vow to the LORD your God, you shall not delay to pay it, for it would be sin in you, and the LORD your God will surely require it of you.

22 "However, if you refrain from vowing, it would not be sin in you.

23 "You shall be careful to perform what goes out from your lips, just as you have voluntarily vowed to the LORD your God, what you have promised.

24 "When you enter your neighbor's vineyard, then you may eat grapes until you are fully satisfied, but you shall not put any in your basket.

25 "When you enter your neighbor's standing grain, then you may pluck the heads with your hand, but you shall not wield a sickle in your neighbor's standing grain.

l. Additional incidental laws

24 "When a man takes a wife and marries her, and it happens that she finds no favor in his eyes because he has found some indecency in her, and he writes her a certificate of divorce and puts it in her hand and sends her out from his house,

2 and she leaves his house and goes and becomes another man's *wife*,

3 and if the latter husband turns against her and writes her a certificate of divorce and puts it in her hand and sends her out of his house, or if the latter husband dies who took her to be his wife,

4 *then* her former husband who sent her away is not allowed to take her again to be his wife, since she has been defiled; for that is an abomination before the LORD, and you shall not bring sin on the land which the LORD your God gives you as an inheritance.

5 "When a man takes a new wife, he shall not go out with the army, nor be

---

Marginal references:

23:10 Lev 15:16
23:14 Lev 26:12
*23:17 Deut 22:21
23:19 Ex 22:25; Lev 25:36,37
23:20 Deut 28:12
23:21 Num 30:2; Matt 5:33
23:25 Matt 12:1; Mark 2:23; Luke 6:1
*24:1 Deut 22:13-21; Matt 5:31; 19:7; Mark 10:4
24:4 Jer 3:1
24:5 Deut 20:7

---

[15]I.e., male prostitute, sodomite

23:17 Sacred prostitution, both male and female, was part of the idolatrous Canaanite worship. In fact, the designations for these prostitutes derives from the word meaning "to be holy."

24:1 This provision was designed to protect the property rights of a divorced woman; this "certificate of divorce" compelled the husband to surrender his claim on her dowry. Christ made it clear that divorce was permitted in Old Testament times because of hardness of heart (Matt. 19:8); it did not imply divine endorsement of divorce, for God's purpose in the institution of marriage was set forth clearly in Gen. 2:24. But for Christians, as citizens of the kingdom of heaven, Christ forbade divorce except on the grounds of adultery (Matt. 5:32 and 19:9). Since the adulterous act, like death, breaks the marriage bond, most Christians feel that Jesus implied the right of the innocent party to remarry. Some have suggested that willful desertion is also grounds for divorce and remarriage, although there is no clear Scripture to support this. Beyond these two reasons there seem to be no others that are acceptable grounds for breaking the marriage relationship. A Christian who marries the innocent party to a divorce is not guilty of sin; but for a Christian to marry a divorced person who was the guilty partner or who was divorced for no Biblical reason is to commit adultery in the eyes of heaven. Some argue that marriage may be dissolved only by death.

charged with any duty; he shall be free at home one year and shall give happiness to his wife whom he has taken.

6 "No one shall take a handmill or an upper millstone in pledge, for he would be taking a life in pledge.

7 "If a man is caught kidnapping any of his countrymen of the sons of Israel, and he deals with him violently, or sells him, then that thief shall die; so you shall purge the evil from among you.

8 "Be careful against an infection of leprosy, that you diligently observe and do according to all that the Levitical priests shall teach you; as I have commanded them, so you shall be careful to do.

9 "Remember what the LORD your God did to Miriam on the way as you came out of Egypt.

10 "When you make your neighbor a loan of any sort, you shall not enter his house to take his pledge.

11 "You shall remain outside, and the man to whom you make the loan shall bring the pledge out to you.

12 "And if he is a poor man, you shall not sleep with his pledge.

13 "When the sun goes down you shall surely return the pledge to him, that he may sleep in his cloak and bless you; and it will be righteousness for you before the LORD your God.

24:14
Lev 25:35-43;
Deut 15:7-18
24:15
Lev 19:13;
James 5:4;
Deut 15:9

14 "You shall not oppress a hired servant *who is* poor and needy, whether *he is* one of your countrymen or one of your aliens who is in your land in your towns.

15 "You shall give him his wages on his day before the sun sets, for he is poor and sets his heart on it; so that he may not cry against you to the LORD and it become sin in you.

24:16
2 Kin 14:6;
2 Chr 25:4;
Jer 31:29,30;
Ezek 18:20
24:17
Deut 1:17;
10:17; 16:19
24:18
Deut 16:12

16 "Fathers shall not be put to death for *their* sons, nor shall sons be put to death for *their* fathers; everyone shall be put to death for his own sin.

17 "You shall not pervert the justice due an alien *or* [16]an orphan, nor take a widow's garment in pledge.

18 "But you shall remember that you were a slave in Egypt, and that the LORD your God redeemed you from there; therefore I am commanding you to do this thing.

19 "When you reap your harvest in your field and have forgotten a sheaf in the field, you shall not go back to get it; it shall be for the alien, for the orphan, and for the widow, in order that the LORD your God may bless you in all the work of your hands.

20 "When you beat your olive tree, you shall not go over the boughs again; it shall be for the alien, for the orphan, and for the widow.

21 "When you gather the grapes of your vineyard, you shall not go over it again; it shall be for the alien, for the orphan, and for the widow.

22 "And you shall remember that you were a slave in the land of Egypt; therefore I am commanding you to do this thing.

25 "If there is a dispute between men and they go to court, and the judges decide their case, and they justify the righteous and condemn the wicked,

2 then it shall be if the wicked man deserves to be beaten, the judge shall then make him lie down and be beaten in his presence with the number of stripes according to his guilt.

3 "He may beat him forty times *but* no more, lest he beat him with many more stripes than these, and your brother be degraded in your eyes.

25:4
1 Cor 9:9;
1 Tim 5:18
*25:5ff
Matt 22:24;
Mark 12:19;

4 "You shall not muzzle the ox while he is threshing.

5 "When brothers live together and one of them dies and has no son, the wife of the deceased shall not be *married* outside *the family* to a strange man. Her

16Or, *the fatherless,* and so throughout this context

25:5–10 The Deuteronomic code provided that when a man died childless his brother, if unmarried, was supposed to raise up seed by the widow. This is known as levirate (Latin *levir,* husband's brother) marriage. The reason for this command is not explicitly stated, but it has been supposed that it was formulated to protect the land rights of the dead man through the continuation of his seed. The first son of a levirate marriage enjoyed the same rights as if he had been begotten by his mother's dead husband. All children

after that were regarded as legal heirs of the father and not of the dead man. The custom is pre-Mosaic, being mentioned in the Nuzi tablets (fourteenth century B.C.). Tamar, in Gen. 38, insisted upon this right against her father-in-law, Judah, and maneuvered him into compliance before the custom was written into the Mosaic Law. This regulation furnished the basis of a Sadducean argument against bodily resurrection in Matt. 22:23–33.

husband's brother shall go in to her and take her to himself as wife and perform the duty of a husband's brother to her.

6 "And it shall be that the first-born whom she bears shall assume the name of his dead brother, that his name may not be blotted out from Israel.

7 "But if the man does not desire to take his brother's wife, then his brother's wife shall go up to the gate to the elders and say, 'My husband's brother refuses to establish a name for his brother in Israel; he is not willing to perform the duty of a husband's brother to me.'

8 "Then the elders of his city shall summon him and speak to him. And *if* he persists and says, 'I do not desire to take her,'

9 then his brother's wife shall come to him in the sight of the elders, and pull his sandal off his foot and spit in his face; and she shall declare, 'Thus it is done to the man who does not build up his brother's house.'

10 "And in Israel his name shall be called, 'The house of him whose sandal is removed.'

11 "If *two* men, a man and his countryman, are struggling together, and the wife of one comes near to deliver her husband from the hand of the one who is striking him, and puts out her hand and seizes his genitals,

12 then you shall cut off her hand; you shall not show pity.

13 "You shall not have in your bag differing weights, a large and a small.

14 "You shall not have in your house differing measures, a large and a small.

15 "You shall have a full and just weight; you shall have a full and just measure, that your days may be prolonged in the land which the LORD your God gives you.

16 "For everyone who does these things, everyone who acts unjustly is an abomination to the LORD your God.

17 "Remember what Amalek did to you along the way when you came out from Egypt,

18 how he met you along the way and attacked among you all the stragglers at your rear when you were faint and weary; and he did not [17]fear God.

19 "Therefore it shall come about when the LORD your God has given you rest from all your surrounding enemies, in the land which the LORD your God gives you as an inheritance to possess, you shall blot out the memory of Amalek from under heaven; you must not forget.

m. Offerings and thanksgiving

26 "Then it shall be, when you enter the land which the LORD your God gives you as an inheritance, and you possess it and live in it,

2 that you shall take some of the first of all the produce of the ground which you shall bring in from your land that the LORD your God gives you, and you shall put *it* in a basket and go to the place where the LORD your God chooses to establish His name.

3 "And you shall go to the priest who is in office at that time, and say to him, 'I declare this day to the LORD my God that I have entered the land which the LORD swore to our fathers to give us.'

4 "Then the priest shall take the basket from your hand and set it down before the altar of the LORD your God.

5 "And you shall answer and say before the LORD your God, 'My father was a wandering Aramean, and he went down to Egypt and sojourned there, few in number; but there he became a great, mighty and populous nation.

6 'And the Egyptians treated us harshly and afflicted us, and imposed hard labor on us.

7 'Then we cried to the LORD, the God of our fathers, and the LORD heard our voice and saw our affliction and our toil and our oppression;

8 and the LORD brought us out of Egypt with a mighty hand and an outstretched arm and with great terror and with signs and wonders;

9 and He has brought us to this place, and has given us this land, a land flowing with milk and honey.

10 'And now behold, I have brought the first of the produce of the ground

---

Luke 20:28

25:6
Gen 38:9;
Ruth 4:10
25:7
Ruth 4:1,2

25:8
Ruth 4:6

*25:9f
Ruth 4:7,11

25:13
Lev 19:35-37

25:16
Prov 11:1

*25:17
Ex 17:8

25:19
1 Sam 15:2,3

26:2
Ex 22:29;
23:16,19;
Num 18:13

*26:5
Hos 12:12;
Gen 43:1,2;
45:7,11;
46:27;
Deut 10:22
26:6
Ex 1:11,14
26:7
Ex 2:23-25
26:8
Deut 4:34
26:9
Ex 3:8

---

[17]Or, *reverence*

25:9,10 Compare the custom described in Ruth 4:7,8. **25:17** *Remember what Amalek did.* The Amalekites were inveterate enemies of early Israel.   **26:5** *Wandering Aramean* is a reference to Jacob. This accords with his close ties to Paddan-aram or Aram-naharaim.

which Thou, O LORD hast given me.' And you shall set it down before the LORD your God, and worship before the LORD your God;

26:11
Deut 12:7

11   and you and the Levite and the alien who is among you shall rejoice in all the good which the LORD your God has given you and your household.

26:12
Deut 14:28, 29; Heb 7:5, 9,10

12   "When you have finished paying all the tithe of your increase in the third year, the year of tithing, then you shall give it to the Levite, to the stranger, to the orphan and to the widow, that they may eat in your towns, and be satisfied.

26:13
Ps 119:141, 153,176

13   "And you shall say before the LORD your God, 'I have removed the sacred *portion* from *my* house, and also have given it to the Levite and the alien, the orphan and the widow, according to all Thy commandments which Thou hast commanded me; I have not transgressed or forgotten any of Thy commandments.

***26:14**
Lev 7:20;
Hos 9:4

14   'I have not eaten of it while mourning, nor have I removed any of it while I was unclean, nor offered any of it to the dead. I have listened to the voice of the LORD my God; I have done according to all that Thou hast commanded me.

15   'Look down from Thy holy habitation, from heaven, and bless Thy people Israel, and the ground which Thou hast given us, a land flowing with milk and honey, as Thou didst swear to our fathers.'

16. *Moses' command to obey God*

26:16
Deut 4:29

16   "This day the LORD your God commands you to do these statutes and ordinances. You shall therefore be careful to do them with all your heart and with all your soul.

17   "You have today declared the LORD to be your God, and that you would walk in His ways and keep His statutes, His commandments and His ordinances, and listen to His voice.

26:18
Deut 7:6

18   "And the LORD has today declared you to be His people, a treasured possession, as He promised you, and that you should keep all His commandments;

26:19
Deut 28:1;
Ps 148:14;
Deut 7:6

19   and that He shall set you high above all nations which He has made, for praise, fame, and honor; and that you shall be a consecrated people to the LORD your God, as He has spoken."

III. *The covenant renewed (27:1–30:20)*

A. *The altar at Mount Ebal*

27 Then Moses and the elders of Israel charged the people, saying, "Keep all the commandments which I command you today.

27:2
Josh 8:30-32

2   "So it shall be on the day when you shall cross the Jordan to the land which the LORD your God gives you, that you shall set up for yourself large stones, and coat them with lime.

27:3
Deut 26:9

3   and write on them all the words of this law, when you cross over, in order that you may enter the land which the LORD your God gives you, a land flowing with milk and honey, as the LORD, the God of your fathers, promised you.

4   "So it shall be when you cross the Jordan, you shall set up on Mount Ebal, these stones, as I am commanding you today, and you shall coat them with lime.

27:5
Ex 20:25;
Josh 8:31

5   "Moreover, you shall build there an altar to the LORD your God, an altar of stones; you shall not wield an iron *tool* on them.

6   "You shall build the altar of the LORD your God of uncut stones; and you shall offer on it burnt offerings to the LORD your God;

7   and you shall sacrifice peace offerings and eat there, and you shall rejoice before the LORD your God.

8   "And you shall write on the stones all the words of this law very distinctly."

27:9
Deut 26:18

9   Then Moses and the Levitical priests spoke to all Israel, saying, "Be silent and listen, O Israel! This day you have become a people for the LORD your God.

10   "You shall therefore obey the LORD your God, and do His commandments and His statutes which I command you today."

11   Moses also charged the people on that day, saying,

27:12
Josh 8:33-35

12   "When you cross the Jordan, these shall stand on Mount Gerizim to bless the people: Simeon, Levi, Judah, Issachar, Joseph, and Benjamin.

26:14 *offered any of it to the dead.* This refers to the use of some of the tithe as an offering placed in or near the tomb. There is no indication that the Israelites sacrificed to the spirits of the dead.
27:1 Chapter 27, which speaks of Moses in the third person, is thought by some to be out of place here because it interrupts the smooth flow of Moses' address. This would be remedied if 28:1 were connected directly to 26:19, without the interference of ch. 27.

13 "And for the curse, these shall stand on Mount Ebal: Reuben, Gad, Asher, Zebulun, Dan, and Naphtali.

14 "The Levites shall then answer and say to all the men of Israel with a loud voice,

B. *The twelve curses at Mount Ebal*

15 'Cursed is the man who makes an idol or a molten image, an abomination to the LORD, the work of the hands of the craftsman, and sets *it* up in secret.' And all the people shall answer and say, 'Amen.'

16 'Cursed is he who dishonors his father or mother.' And all the people shall say, 'Amen.'

17 'Cursed is he who moves his neighbor's boundary mark.' And all the people shall say, 'Amen.'

18 'Cursed is he who misleads a blind *person* on the road.' And all the people shall say, 'Amen.'

19 'Cursed is he who distorts the justice due an alien, orphan, and widow.' And all the people shall say, 'Amen.'

20 'Cursed is he who lies with his father's wife, because he has uncovered his father's skirt.' And all the people shall say, 'Amen.'

21 'Cursed is he who lies with any animal.' And all the people shall say, 'Amen.'

22 'Cursed is he who lies with his sister, the daughter of his father or of his mother.' And all the people shall say, 'Amen.'

23 'Cursed is he who lies with his mother-in-law.' And all the people shall say, 'Amen.'

24 'Cursed is he who strikes his neighbor in secret.' And all the people shall say, 'Amen.'

25 'Cursed is he who accepts a bribe to strike down an innocent person.' And all the people shall say, 'Amen.'

26 'Cursed is he who does not confirm the words of this law by doing them.' And all the people shall say, 'Amen.'

C. *The blessings of obedience*

28 "Now it shall be, if you will diligently obey the LORD your God, being careful to do all His commandments which I command you today, the LORD your God will set you high above all the nations of the earth.

2 "And all these blessings shall come upon you and overtake you, if you will obey the LORD your God.

3 "Blessed *shall* you *be* in the city, and blessed *shall* you *be* in the country.

4 "Blessed *shall be* the offspring of your body and the produce of your ground and the offspring of your beasts, the increase of your herd and the young of your flock.

5 "Blessed *shall be* your basket and your kneading bowl.

6 "Blessed *shall* you *be* when you come in, and blessed *shall* you *be* when you go out.

7 "The LORD will cause your enemies who rise up against you to be defeated before you; they shall come out against you one way and shall flee before you seven ways.

8 "The LORD will command the blessing upon you in your barns and in all that you put your hand to, and He will bless you in the land which the LORD your God gives you.

9 "The LORD will establish you as a holy people to Himself, as He swore to you, if you will keep the commandments of the LORD your God, and walk in His ways.

10 "So all the peoples of the earth shall see that you are called by the name of the LORD; and they shall be afraid of you.

11 "And the LORD will make you abound in prosperity, in the offspring of your body and in the offspring of your beast and in the produce of your ground, in the land which the LORD swore to your fathers to give you.

12 "The LORD will open for you His good storehouse, the heavens, to give rain to your land in its season and to bless all the work of your hand; and you shall lend to many nations, but you shall not borrow.

13 "And the LORD shall make you the head and not the tail, and you only shall be above, and you shall not be underneath, if you will listen to the commandments

---

27:15
Ex 20:4,23;
34:17
27:16
Ex 21:17;
Lev 20:9
27:17
Lev 19:14
27:18
Lev 19:14
27:19
Deut 10:18;
24:17
27:20
Lev 18:8;
Deut 22:30
27:21
Lev 18:23
27:22
Lev 18:9;
20:17
27:23
Lev 20:14
27:24
Lev 24:17;
Num 35:31
27:25
Ex 23:7,8
27:26
Deut 28:15;
Gal 3:10

28:1
Deut 7:12-26;
26:19

28:3
Gen 39:5;
Ps 128:14
28:4
Gen 49:25;
Ps 107:38;
Prov 10:22

28:7
Lev 26:7,8

28:9
Deut 7:6
28:10
2 Chr 7:14
28:11
Deut 30:9

28:12
Lev 26:4;
Deut 15:6

of the LORD your God, which I charge you today, to observe *them* carefully,

14   and do not turn aside from any of the words which I command you today, to the right or to the left, to go after other gods to serve them.

D. The curses of disobedience

15   "But it shall come about, if you will not obey the LORD your God, to observe to do all His commandments and His statutes with which I charge you today, that all these curses shall come upon you and overtake you.

16   "Cursed *shall* you *be* in the city, and cursed *shall* you *be* in the country.

17   "Cursed *shall be* your basket and your kneading bowl.

18   "Cursed *shall be* the offspring of your body and the produce of your ground, the increase of your herd and the young of your flock.

19   "Cursed *shall* you *be* when you come in, and cursed *shall* you *be* when you go out.

20   "The LORD will send upon you curses, confusion, and rebuke, in all you undertake to do, until you are destroyed and until you perish quickly, on account of the evil of your deeds, because you have forsaken Me.

21   "The LORD will make the pestilence cling to you until He has consumed you from the land, where you are entering to possess it.

22   "The LORD will smite you with consumption and with fever and with inflammation and with fiery heat and with [18]the sword and with blight and with mildew, and they shall pursue you until you perish.

23   "And the heaven which is over your head shall be bronze, and the earth which is under you, iron.

24   "The LORD will make the rain of your land powder and dust; from heaven it shall come down on you until you are destroyed.

25   "The LORD will cause you to be defeated before your enemies; you shall go out one way against them, but you shall flee seven ways before them, and you shall be *an example of* terror to all the kingdoms of the earth.

26   "And your carcasses shall be food to all birds of the sky and to the beasts of the earth, and there shall be no one to frighten *them* away.

27   "The LORD will smite you with the boils of Egypt and with tumors and with the scab and with the itch, from which you cannot be healed.

28   "The LORD will smite you with madness and with blindness and with bewilderment of heart;

29   and you shall grope at noon, as the blind man gropes in darkness, and you shall not prosper in your ways; but you shall only be oppressed and robbed continually, with none to save you.

30   "You shall betroth a wife, but another man shall violate her; you shall build a house, but you shall not live in it; you shall plant a vineyard, but you shall not use its fruit.

31   "Your ox shall be slaughtered before your eyes, but you shall not eat of it; your donkey shall be torn away from you, and shall not be restored to you; your sheep shall be given to your enemies, and you shall have none to save you.

32   "Your sons and your daughters shall be given to another people, while your eyes shall look on and yearn for them continually; but there shall be nothing you can do.

33   "A people whom you do not know shall eat up the produce of your ground and all your labors, and you shall never be anything but oppressed and crushed continually.

34   "And you shall be driven mad by the sight of what you see.

35   "The LORD will strike you on the knees and legs with sore boils, from which you cannot be healed, from the sole of your foot to the crown of your head.

36   "The LORD will bring you and your king, whom you shall set over you, to a nation which neither you nor your fathers have known, and there you shall serve other gods, wood and stone.

37   "And you shall become a horror, a proverb, and a taunt among all the people where the LORD will drive you.

38   "You shall bring out much seed to the field but you shall gather in little, for the locust shall consume it.

---

[18]Another reading is *drought*

Marginal references:

28:14 Deut 5:32

28:15 Lev 26:14; Josh 23:15; Mal 2:2

28:20 Deut 4:26

28:21 Lev 26:25; Jer 24:10

28:22 Lev 26:16; Amos 4:9

28:23 Lev 26:19

28:25 Lev 26:17,37; Jer 15:4

28:26 Jer 7:33; 16:4; 34:20

28:27 vv. 60,61

28:29 Job 5:14; Is 59:10

28:30 Jer 8:10; 12:13; Amos 5:11

28:32 v. 41

28:33 Jer 5:17

28:35 v. 27

28:36 2 Kin 17:4,6; 24:12,14; 25:7,11; Deut 4:28

28:37 Jer 24:9; Ps 44:14

28:38 Mic 6:15

39 "You shall plant and cultivate vineyards, but you shall neither drink of the wine nor gather *the grapes,* for the worm shall devour them.

40 "You shall have olive trees throughout your territory but you shall not anoint yourself with the oil, for your olives shall drop off.

41 "You shall have sons and daughters but they shall not be yours, for they shall go into captivity. | 28:41 v. 32

42 "The cricket shall possess all your trees and the produce of your ground. | 28:42 v. 38

43 "The alien who is among you shall rise above you higher and higher, but you shall go down lower and lower. | 28:43 v. 13

44 "He shall lend to you, but you shall not lend to him; he shall be the head, and you shall be the tail. | 28:44 vv. 12,13

45 "So all these curses shall come on you and pursue you and overtake you until you are destroyed, because you would not obey the LORD your God by keeping His commandments and His statutes which He commanded you. | 28:45 v. 15

46 "And they shall become a sign and a wonder on you and your descendants forever.

47 "Because you did not serve the LORD your God with joy and a glad heart, for the abundance of all things; | 28:47 Deut 32:15

48 therefore you shall serve your enemies whom the LORD shall send against you, in hunger, in thirst, in nakedness, and in the lack of all things; and He will put an iron yoke on your neck until He has destroyed you. | 28:48 Jer 28:13,14

49 "The LORD will bring a nation against you from afar, from the end of the earth, as the eagle swoops down, a nation whose language you shall not understand, | 28:49 Jer 5:15

50 a nation of fierce countenance who shall have no respect for the old, nor show favor to the young.

51 "Moreover, it shall eat the offspring of your herd and the produce of your ground until you are destroyed, who also leaves you no grain, new wine, or oil, nor the increase of your herd or the young of your flock until they have caused you to perish. | 28:51 v. 33

52 "And it shall besiege you in all your towns until your high and fortified walls in which you trusted come down throughout your land, and it shall besiege you in all your towns throughout your land which the LORD your God has given you. | 28:52 Jer 10:17,18; Zeph 1:15,16; Josh 1:4

53 "Then you shall eat the offspring of your own body, the flesh of your sons and of your daughters whom the LORD your God has given you, during the siege and the distress by which your enemy shall oppress you. | 28:53 Lev 26:29; Jer 19:9; Lam 2:20

54 "The man who is refined and very delicate among you shall be hostile toward his brother and toward the wife he cherishes and toward the rest of his children who remain,

55 so that he will not give *even* one of them any of the flesh of his children which he shall eat, since he has nothing *else* left, during the siege and the distress by which your enemy shall oppress you in all your towns.

56 "The refined and delicate woman among you, who would not venture to set the sole of her foot on the ground for delicateness and refinement, shall be hostile toward the husband she cherishes and toward her son and daughter, | 28:56 v. 54

57 and toward her afterbirth which issues from between her legs and toward her children whom she bears; for she shall eat them secretly for lack of anything *else,* during the siege and the distress by which your enemy shall oppress you in your towns.

58 "If you are not careful to observe all the words of this law which are written in this book, to fear this honored and awesome name, the LORD your God, | 28:58 Ex 6:3

59 then the LORD will bring extraordinary plagues on you and your descendants, even severe and lasting plagues, and miserable and chronic sicknesses.

60 "And He will bring back on you all the diseases of Egypt of which you were afraid, and they shall cling to you. | 28:60 v. 27

61 "Also every sickness and every plague which, not written in the book of this law, the LORD will bring on you until you are destroyed. | 28:61 Deut 4:25,26

62 "Then you shall be left few in number, whereas you were as the stars of heaven for multitude, because you did not obey the LORD your God. | 28:62 Deut 4:27; 10:22

63 "And it shall come about that as the LORD delighted over you to prosper you, | *28:63 Jer 12:14; 45:4

28:63 This prophetic Scripture was literally fulfilled in the Babylonian captivity and in the dispersion of the Jews by the Roman government, and also by the indignities and hardships suffered by them over many centuries. The present persecutions are part of this prophecy (vv. 63–68), and they will continue until the Jews turn to God in repentance and faith. Yet, Gen. 12:3 makes clear God's displeasure with those who unjustly oppress these people, and His

and multiply you, so the LORD will delight over you to make you perish and destroy you; and you shall be torn from the land where you are entering to possess it.

28:64
Deut 4:27,28

64 "Moreover, the LORD will scatter you among all peoples, from one end of the earth to the other end of the earth; and there you shall serve other gods, wood and stone, which you or your fathers have not known.

28:65
Lev 26:16,36

65 "And among those nations you shall find no rest, and there shall be no resting place for the sole of your foot; but there the LORD will give you a trembling heart, failing of eyes, and despair of soul.

66 "So your life shall hang in doubt before you; and you shall be in dread night and day, and shall have no assurance of your life.

28:67
v. 34

67 "In the morning you shall say, 'Would that it were evening!' And at evening you shall say, 'Would that it were morning!' because of the dread of your heart which you dread, and for the sight of your eyes which you shall see.

68 "And the LORD will bring you back to Egypt in ships, by the way about which I spoke to you, 'You will never see it again!' And there you shall offer yourselves for sale to your enemies as male and female slaves, but there will be no buyer."

E. The exhortation to keep the covenant

*29:1
Deut 5:2,3

29 These are the words of the covenant which the LORD commanded Moses to make with the sons of Israel in the land of Moab, besides the covenant which He had made with them at Horeb.

29:2
Ex 19:4

2 And Moses summoned all Israel and said to them, "You have seen all that the LORD did before your eyes in the land of Egypt to Pharaoh and all his servants and all his land;

3 the great trials which your eyes have seen, those great signs and wonders.

29:4
Is 6:9,10;
Acts 28:26,
27; Eph 4:18
29:5
Deut 8:4
29:6
Deut 8:3

4 "Yet to this day the LORD has not given you a heart to know, nor eyes to see, nor ears to hear.

5 "And I have led you forty years in the wilderness; your clothes have not worn out on you, and your sandal has not worn out on your foot.

6 "You have not eaten bread, nor have you drunk wine or strong drink, in order that you might know that I am the LORD your God.

29:7
Num 21:21-24,
33-35;
Deut 2:32;
3:1
29:8
Num 32:33;
Deut 3:12,13
29:9
Deut 4:6;
Josh 1:7

7 "When you reached this place, Sihon the king of Heshbon and Og the king of Bashan came out to meet us for battle, but we defeated them;

8 and we took their land and gave it as an inheritance to the Reubenites, the Gadites, and the half-tribe of the Manassites.

9 "So keep the words of this covenant to do them, that you may prosper in all that you do.

10 "You stand today, all of you, before the LORD your God: your chiefs, your tribes, your elders and your officers, *even* all the men of Israel,

29:11
Josh 9:21,23,
27

11 your little ones, your wives, and the alien who is within your camps, from the one who chops your wood to the one who draws your water,

12 that you may enter into the covenant with the LORD your God, and into His oath which the LORD your God is making with you today,

29:13
Deut 28:9;
Ex 6:7;
Gen 17:7

13 in order that He may establish you today as His people and that He may be your God, just as He spoke to you and as He swore to your fathers, to Abraham, Isaac, and Jacob.

14 "Now not with you alone am I making this covenant and this oath,

15 but both with those who stand here with us today in the presence of the LORD our God and with those who are not with us here today

F. The punishment for forsaking the covenant

16 (for you know how we lived in the land of Egypt, and how we came through the midst of the nations through which you passed.

29:17
Deut 28:26

17 "Moreover, you have seen their abominations and their idols *of* wood, stone, silver, and gold, which *they had* with them);

29:18
Deut 11:16;
Heb 12:15

18 lest there shall be among you a man or woman, or family or tribe, whose heart turns away today from the LORD our God, to go and serve the gods of those

---

blessing on those who grant them toleration and kindness.
29:1 This covenant (actually only a phase of the Abrahamic covenant) made in Moab governed the entrance of Israel into the land of promise. The conditions were as follows: (1) obedience to God's commands as the indispensable condition of blessing (28:1ff.); (2) chastisement promised for

disobedience (28:15ff.); (3) dispersion promised as a judgment on apostasy (28:63ff.); (4) regathering of Israel promised when they repent (30:1ff.); (5) repossession of the land promised (30:5); (6) judgment of Israel's enemies (30:7); and (7) future prosperity assured (30:9).

nations; lest there shall be among you a root bearing poisonous fruit and worm-wood.

19 "And it shall be when he hears the words of this curse, that he will boast, saying, 'I have peace though I walk in the stubbornness of my heart in order to destroy the watered *land* with the dry.'

20 "The LORD shall never be willing to forgive him, but rather the anger of the LORD and His jealousy will burn against that man, and every curse which is written in this book will rest on him, and the LORD will blot out his name from under heaven.

29:20
Ps 74:1; 79:5;
Deut 9:14;
Ex 32:33

21 "Then the LORD will single him out for adversity from all the tribes of Israel, according to all the curses of the covenant which are written in this book of the law.

29:21
Matt 24:51

22 "Now the generation to come, your sons who rise up after you and the foreigner who comes from a distant land, when they see the plagues of the land and the diseases with which the LORD has afflicted it, will say,

29:22
Jer 19:8

23 'All its land is brimstone and salt, a burning waste, unsown and unproductive, and no grass grows in it, like the overthrow of Sodom and Gomorrah, Admah and Zeboiim, which the LORD overthrew in His anger and in His wrath.'

29:23
Gen 19:24;
Is 34:9;
Jer 20:16

24 "And all the nations shall say, 'Why has the LORD done thus to this land? Why this great outburst of anger?'

29:24
Jer 22:8,9

25 "Then *men* shall say, 'Because they forsook the covenant of the LORD, the God of their fathers, which He made with them when He brought them out of the land of Egypt.

26 'And they went and served other gods and worshiped them, gods whom they have not known and whom He had not allotted to them.

27 'Therefore, the anger of the LORD burned against that land, to bring upon it every curse which is written in this book;

28 and the LORD uprooted them from their land in anger and in fury and in great wrath, and cast them into another land, as *it is* this day.'

29:28
1 Kin 14:15;
2 Chr 7:20

29 "The secret things belong to the LORD our God, but the things revealed belong to us and to our sons forever, that we may observe all the words of this law.

G. Repentance to be followed by forgiveness and blessing

30 "So it shall be when all of these things have come upon you, the blessing and the curse which I have set before you, and you call *them* to mind in all nations where the LORD your God has banished you,

30:1
vv. 15,19;
Deut 11:26;
28:64; 29:28

2 and you return to the LORD your God and obey Him with all your heart and soul according to all that I command you today, you and your sons,

30:2
Deut 4:29,30

3 then the LORD your God will restore you from captivity, and have compassion on you, and will gather you again from all the peoples where the LORD your God has scattered you.

30:3
Jer 29:14;
32:37

4 "If your outcasts are at the ends of the earth, from there the LORD your God will gather you, and from there He will bring you back.

30:4
Neh 1:9;
Is 43:6

5 "And the LORD your God will bring you into the land which your fathers possessed, and you shall possess it; and He will prosper you and multiply you more than your fathers.

6 "Moreover the LORD your God will circumcise your heart and the heart of your descendants, to love the LORD your God with all your heart and with all your soul, in order that you may live.

30:6
Jer 32:39

7 "And the LORD your God will inflict all these curses on your enemies and on those who hate you, who persecuted you.

8 "And you shall again obey the LORD, and observe all His commandments which I command you today.

9 "Then the LORD your God will prosper you abundantly in all the work of your hand, in the offspring of your body and in the offspring of your cattle and in the produce of your ground, for the LORD will again rejoice over you for good, just as He rejoiced over your fathers;

30:9
Deut 28:11;
Jer 32:41

10 if you obey the LORD your God to keep His commandments and His statutes which are written in this book of the law, if you turn to the LORD your God with all your heart and soul.

29:29 This exceptional verse foresees what 30:11–14 un-equivocally tells: the clarity and feasibility of God's revela-tion. Generally speaking, therefore, disobedience indicates a lack of will or proper motivation, not knowledge.

H. *Closing admonition*

1. *The nearness of God's word*

30:11
Is 45:19

11 "For this commandment which I command you today is not too difficult for you, nor is it out of reach.

30:12
Rom 10:6-8

12 "It is not in heaven, that you should say, 'Who will go up to heaven for us to get it for us and make us hear it, that we may observe it?'

13 "Nor is it beyond the sea, that you should say, 'Who will cross the sea for us to get it for us and make us hear it, that we may observe it?'

14 "But the word is very near you, in your mouth and in your heart, that you may observe it.

2. *The choice of life versus death*

30:15
vv. 1, 19

15 "See, I have set before you today life and prosperity, and death and adversity;

16 in that I command you today to love the LORD your God, to walk in His ways and to keep His commandments and His statutes and His judgments, that you may live and multiply, and that the LORD your God may bless you in the land where you are entering to possess it.

17 "But if your heart turns away and you will not obey, but are drawn away and worship other gods and serve them,

30:18
Deut 4:26

18 I declare to you today that you shall surely perish. You shall not prolong *your* days in the land where you are crossing the Jordan to enter and possess it.

30:19
Deut 4:26;
v. 1

19 "I call heaven and earth to witness against you today, that I have set before you life and death, the blessing and the curse. So choose life in order that you may live, you and your descendants,

30:20
Deut 6:5;
10:20;
Ps 27:1;
John 11:25

20 by loving the LORD your God, by obeying His voice, and by holding fast to Him; for this is your life and the length of your days, that you may live in the land which the LORD swore to your fathers, to Abraham, Isaac, and Jacob, to give them."

IV. *Moses' final words and death (31:1–34:12)*

A. *Moses' final arrangements*

1. *The appointment of Joshua*

31 So Moses went and spoke these words to all Israel.

31:2
Deut 34:7;
3:27

2 And he said to them, "I am a hundred and twenty years old today; I am no longer able to come and go, and the LORD has said to me, 'You shall not cross this Jordan.'

31:3
Deut 9:3;
3:28

3 "It is the LORD your God who will cross ahead of you; He will destroy these nations before you, and you shall dispossess them. Joshua is the one who will cross ahead of you, just as the LORD has spoken.

4 "And the LORD will do to them just as He did to Sihon and Og, the kings of the Amorites, and to their land, when He destroyed them.

31:5
Deut 7:2

5 "And the LORD will deliver them up before you, and you shall do to them according to all the commandments which I have commanded you.

31:6
Josh 10:25;
Deut 1:29;
20:4;
Heb 13:5
31:7
Deut 1:38;
3:28

6 "Be strong and courageous, do not be afraid or tremble at them, for the LORD your God is the one who goes with you. He will not fail you or forsake you."

7 Then Moses called to Joshua and said to him in the sight of all Israel, "Be strong and courageous, for you shall go with this people into the land which the LORD has sworn to their fathers to give them, and you shall give it to them as an inheritance.

31:8
v. 6

8 "And the LORD is the one who goes ahead of you; He will be with you. He will not fail you or forsake you. Do not fear, or be dismayed."

2. *The teaching of the Law*

31:9
v. 25;
Num 4:15
31:10
Deut 15:1;
Lev 23:34
31:11
Deut 16:16;
Josh 8:34,35

9 So Moses wrote this law and gave it to the priests, the sons of Levi who carried the ark of the covenant of the LORD, and to all the elders of Israel.

10 Then Moses commanded them, saying, "At the end of *every* seven years, at the time of the year of remission of debts, at the Feast of Booths,

11 when all Israel comes to appear before the LORD your God at the place which He will choose, you shall read this law in front of all Israel in their hearing.

12 "Assemble the people, the men and the women and children and the alien who is in your town, in order that they may hear and learn and fear the LORD your God, and be careful to observe all the words of this law.

13 "And their children, who have not known, will hear and learn to fear the LORD your God, as long as you live on the land which you are about to cross the Jordan to possess."

3. God appears to Moses and Joshua

14 Then the LORD said to Moses, "Behold, the time for you to die is near; call Joshua, and present yourselves at the tent of meeting, that I may commission him." So Moses and Joshua went and presented themselves at the tent of meeting.

15 And the LORD appeared in the tent in a pillar of cloud, and the pillar of cloud stood at the doorway of the tent.

16 And the LORD said to Moses, "Behold, you are about to lie down with your fathers; and this people will arise and play the harlot with the strange gods of the land, into the midst of which they are going, and will forsake Me and break My covenant which I have made with them.

17 "Then My anger will be kindled against them in that day, and I will forsake them and hide My face from them, and they shall be consumed, and many evils and troubles shall come upon them; so that they will say in that day, 'Is it not because our God is not among us that these evils have come upon us?'

18 "But I will surely hide My face in that day because of all the evil which they will do, for they will turn to other gods.

19 "Now therefore, write this song for yourselves, and teach it to the sons of Israel; put it on their lips, in order that this song may be a witness for Me against the sons of Israel.

20 "For when I bring them into the land flowing with milk and honey, which I swore to their fathers, and they have eaten and are satisfied and become prosperous, then they will turn to other gods and serve them, and spurn Me and break My covenant.

21 "Then it shall come about, when many evils and troubles have come upon them, that this song will testify before them as a witness (for it shall not be forgotten from the lips of their descendants); for I know their intent which they are developing today, before I have brought them into the land which I swore."

22 So Moses wrote this song the same day, and taught it to the sons of Israel.

23 Then He commissioned Joshua the son of Nun, and said, "Be strong and courageous, for you shall bring the sons of Israel into the land which I swore to them, and I will be with you."

4. Moses' counsel to the Levites

24 And it came about, when Moses finished writing the words of this law in a book until they were complete,

25 that Moses commanded the Levites who carried the ark of the covenant of the LORD, saying,

26 "Take this book of the law and place it beside the ark of the covenant of the LORD your God, that it may remain there as a witness against you.

27 "For I know your rebellion and your stubbornness; behold, while I am still alive with you today, you have been rebellious against the LORD; how much more, then, after my death?

28 "Assemble to me all the elders of your tribes and your officers, that I may speak these words in their hearing and call the heavens and the earth to witness against them.

29 "For I know that after my death you will act corruptly and turn from the way which I have commanded you; and evil will befall you in the latter days, for you will do that which is evil in the sight of the LORD, provoking Him to anger with the work of your hands."

31:12	Deut 4:10
31:13	Deut 11:2; Ps 78:6,7
31:14	Deut 32:49, 50; v. 23
31:15	Ex 33:9
31:16	Judg 2:11,12; 10:6,13
31:17	Judg 2:14; 6:13; Deut 32:20; Num 14:42
31:20	Deut 6:10-12; 32:15-17; v. 16
31:21	v. 17; Hos 5:3
*31:22	v. 19
31:23	v. 7; Josh 1:6
31:25	v. 9
31:26	v. 19
31:27	Deut 9:6,24
31:28	Deut 4:26
31:29	Deut 32:5; 28:15

31:22 *this song*, that is, the song recorded in 32:1-43.   Deuteronomic law.
31:24 *This law* (also in v. 9) refers explicitly to the

B. *The song of Moses*

1. *Introduction*

30 Then Moses spoke in the hearing of all the assembly of Israel the words of this song, until they were complete:

32:1
Is 1:2

32
"Give ear, O heavens, and let me speak;
And let the earth hear the words of my mouth.

32:2
Is 55:10,11

2 "Let my teaching drop as the rain,
My speech distill as the dew,
As the droplets on the fresh grass
And as the showers on the herb.

32:3
Ex 34:5;
Deut 3:24

3 "For I proclaim the name of the LORD;
Ascribe greatness to our God!

2. *Faithfulness of God contrasted with
the faithlessness of Israel*

32:4
vv. 15,18,30;
Deut 7:9;
Ps 92:15

4 "The Rock! His work is perfect,
For all His ways are just;
A God of faithfulness and without injustice,
Righteous and upright is He.

32:5
Deut 31:29;
Luke 9:41

5 "They have acted corruptly toward Him,
They are not His children, because of their defect;
But are a perverse and crooked generation.

32:6
Deut 1:31

6 "Do you thus repay the LORD,
O foolish and unwise people?
Is not He your Father who has bought you?
He has made you and established you.

32:7
Ex 13:14

7 "Remember the days of old,
Consider the years of all generations.
Ask your father, and he will inform you,
Your elders, and they will tell you.

32:8
Gen 11:8;
Acts 17:26

8 "When the Most High gave the nations their inheritance,
When He separated the sons of man,
He set the boundaries of the peoples
According to the number of the sons of Israel.

32:9
1 Kin 8:51,
53; Jer 10:16
32:10
Jer 2:6;
Zech 2:8

9 "For the LORD's portion is His people;
Jacob is the allotment of His inheritance.

10 "He found him in a desert land,
And in the howling waste of a wilderness;
He encircled him, He cared for him,
He guarded him as the pupil of His eye.

32:11
Ex 19:4;
Is 31:5

11 "Like an eagle that stirs up its nest,
That hovers over its young,
He spread His wings and caught them,
He carried them on His pinions.

32:12
v. 39

12 "The LORD alone guided him,
And there was no foreign god with him.

32:13
Is 58:14;
Job 29:6

13 "He made him ride on the high places of the earth,
And he ate the produce of the field;
And He made him suck honey from the rock,
And oil from the flinty rock,

32:14
Ps 147:14

14 Curds of cows, and milk of the flock,
With fat of lambs,
And rams, the breed of Bashan, and goats,
With the finest of the wheat—
And of the blood of grapes you drank wine.

*32:15
Deut 33:5,26;
Is 1:4; vv. 6,4

15 "But [19]Jeshurun grew fat and kicked—
You are grown fat, thick, and sleek—

[19]I.e., Israel

32:15 *Jeshurun*, meaning "Upright One," may be an ironical title for Israel. See 33:5.

Then he forsook God who made him,
And scorned the Rock of his salvation.

16 "They made Him jealous with strange *gods;*
With abominations they provoked Him to anger.

32:16
Ps 78:58;
1 Cor 10:22

17 "They sacrificed to demons who were not God,
To gods whom they have not known,
New *gods* who came lately,
Whom your fathers did not dread.

32:17
Ps 106:37;
Deut 28:64;
Judg 5:8

18 "You neglected the Rock who begot you,
And forgot the God who gave you birth.

32:18
Is 17:10;
Ps 106:21

3. Why God punished Israel

19 "And the LORD saw *this*, and spurned *them*
Because of the provocation of His sons and daughters.

32:19
Ps 106:40;
Jer 44:21-23

20 "Then He said, 'I will hide My face from them,
I will see what their end *shall be;*
For they are a perverse generation,
Sons in whom is no faithfulness.

32:20
Deut 31:17,
29; v. 5

21 'They have made Me jealous with *what* is not God;
They have provoked Me to anger with their idols.
So I will make them jealous with *those who* are not a people;
I will provoke them to anger with a foolish nation,

32:21
v. 16;
Rom 10:19

22 For a fire is kindled in My anger,
And burns to the lowest part of Sheol,
And consumes the earth with its yield,
And sets on fire the foundations of the mountains.

*32:22
Jer 15:14

23 'I will heap misfortunes on them;
I will use My arrows on them.

32:23
Deut 29:21;
Ezek 5:16

24 '*They shall be* wasted by famine, and consumed by plague
And bitter destruction;
And the teeth of beasts I will send upon them,
With the venom of crawling things of the dust.

32:24
Deut 28:22;
Lev 26:22;
v. 33

25 'Outside the sword shall bereave,
And inside terror—
Both young man and virgin,
The nursling with the man of gray hair.

32:25
Ezek 7:15;
2 Chr 36:17

26 'I would have said; "I will cut them to pieces,
I will remove the memory of them from men,"

32:26
Deut 4:27;
Ps 34:16

27 Had I not feared the provocation by the enemy,
Lest their adversaries should misjudge,
Lest they should say, "Our hand is triumphant,
And the LORD has not done all this." '

32:27
Deut 9:26-28;
Is 10:13

28 "For they are a nation lacking in counsel,
And there is no understanding in them.

29 "Would that they were wise, that they understood this,
That they would discern their future!

32:29
Ps 81:13

30 "How could one chase a thousand,
And two put ten thousand to flight,
Unless their Rock had sold them,
And the LORD had given them up?

32:30
Lev 26:7,8;
v. 4

31 "Indeed their rock is not like our Rock,
Even our enemies themselves judge this.

32:31
1 Sam 2:2;
4:8

32 "For their vine is from the vine of Sodom,
And from the fields of Gomorrah;
Their grapes are grapes of poison,
Their clusters, bitter.

32:22 *Sheol*, translated *hades* in the Septuagint, was the underworld abode of the departed spirits of the dead, both righteous and evil. God's spirit was there (Ps. 139:8); His anger extended there (32:22); it was a gloomy place with worms (Job 17:13–15), and a pit where God could not be praised (Ps. 6:5; Is. 38:18). This concept was carried over into the New Testament as *hades*, the abode of the wicked (see note to Luke 10:15), and associated with the concept of Gehenna. The whole idea of *sheol* was very complex in the Old Testament. The basic idea was delimited in some cases to the wicked (Ps. 9:17), but this emphasis was a clear development in the intertestamental period.

32:33
Ps 58:4

33   "Their wine is the venom of serpents,
      And the deadly poison of cobras.

4. God will show mercy to Israel
and vengeance to her enemies

32:34
Hos 13:12

34   'Is it not laid up in store with Me,
      Sealed up in My treasuries?

32:35
Rom 12:19;
Heb 10:30

35   'Vengeance is Mine, and retribution,
      In due time their foot will slip;
      For the day of their calamity is near,
      And the impending things are hastening upon them.'

32:36
Ps 135:14;
106:45;
Judg 2:18;
Joel 2:14

36   "For the LORD will vindicate His people,
      And will have compassion on His servants;
      When He sees that *their* strength is gone,
      And there is none *remaining,* bond or free.

32:37
Jer 2:28

37   "And He will say, 'Where are their gods,
      The rock in which they sought refuge?

38   'Who ate the fat of their sacrifices,
      And drank the wine of their libation?
      Let them rise up and help you,
      Let them be your hiding place!

32:39
Is 41:4;
Ps 50:22

39   'See now that I, I am He,
      And there is no god besides Me;
      It is I who put to death and give life.
      I have wounded, and it is I who heal;
      And there is no one who can deliver from My hand.

40   'Indeed, I lift up My hand to heaven,
      And say, as I live forever,

32:41
Ezek 21:9,10

41   If I sharpen My flashing sword,
      And My hand takes hold on justice,
      I will render vengeance on My adversaries,
      And I will repay those who hate Me.

32:42
Jer 46:10

42   'I will make My arrows drunk with blood,
      And My sword shall devour flesh,
      With the blood of the slain and the captives,
      From the long-haired leaders of the enemy.'

32:43
Rom 15:10;
Rev 19:2;
Ps 85:1

43   "Rejoice, O nations, *with* His people;
      For He will avenge the blood of His servants,
      And will render vengeance on His adversaries,
      And will atone for His land *and* His people."

44   Then Moses came and spoke all the words of this song in the hearing of the people, he, with Joshua the son of Nun.

45   When Moses had finished speaking all these words to all Israel,

32:46
Deut 6:6;
Ezek 40:4

46   he said to them, "Take to your heart all the words with which I am warning you today, which you shall command your sons to observe carefully, *even* all the words of this law.

32:47
Deut 30:20

47   "For it is not an idle word for you; indeed it is your life. And by this word you shall prolong your days in the land, which you are about to cross the Jordan to possess."

C. God summons Moses to die

48   And the LORD spoke to Moses that very same day, saying,

32:49
Num 27:12-14

49   "Go up to this mountain of the Abarim, Mount Nebo, which is in the land of Moab opposite Jericho, and look at the land of Canaan, which I am giving to the sons of Israel for a possession.

50   "Then die on the mountain where you ascend, and be gathered to your people, as Aaron your brother died on Mount Hor and was gathered to his people,

32:51
Num 20:11-13;
27:14

51   because you broke faith with Me in the midst of the sons of Israel at the waters of Meribah-kadesh, in the wilderness of Zin, because you did not treat Me as holy in the midst of the sons of Israel.

32:52
Deut 34:1-3;
1:37

52   "For you shall see the land at a distance, but you shall not go there, into the land which I am giving the sons of Israel."

D. Moses blesses the people of Israel

33 Now this is the blessing with which Moses the man of God blessed the sons
of Israel before his death.

  2 And he said,
    "The LORD came from Sinai,
    And dawned on them from Seir;
    He shone forth from Mount Paran,
    And He came from the midst of ten thousand holy ones;
    At His right hand there was flashing lightning for them.
  3 "Indeed, He loves the people;
    All Thy holy ones are in Thy hand,
    And they followed in Thy steps;
    Everyone receives of Thy words.
  4 "Moses charged us with a law,
    A possession for the assembly of Jacob.
  5 "And He was king in Jeshurun,
    When the heads of the people were gathered,
    The tribes of Israel together.

  6 "May Reuben live and not die,
    Nor his men be few."

  7 And this regarding Judah; so he said,
    "Hear, O LORD, the voice of Judah,
    And bring him to his people.
    With his hands he contended for them;
    And mayest Thou be a help against his adversaries."

  8 And of Levi he said,
    "*Let* Thy Thummim and Thy Urim *belong* to Thy godly man,
    Whom Thou didst prove at Massah,
    With whom Thou didst contend at the waters of Meribah;
  9 Who said of his father and his mother,
    'I did not consider them';
    And he did not acknowledge his brothers,
    Nor did he regard his own sons,
    For they observed Thy word,
    And kept Thy covenant.
  10 "They shall teach Thine ordinances to Jacob,
    And Thy law to Israel.
    They shall put incense before Thee,
    And whole burnt offerings on Thine altar.
  11 "O LORD, bless his substance,
    And accept the work of his hands;
    Shatter the loins of those who rise up against him,
    And those who hate him, so that they may not rise *again*."

  12 Of Benjamin he said,
    "May the beloved of the LORD dwell in security by Him,
    Who shields him all the day,
    And he dwells between His shoulders."

  13 And of Joseph he said,
    "Blessed of the LORD *be* his land,
    With the choice things of heaven, with the dew,
    And from the deep lying beneath,
  14 And with the choice yield of the sun,
    And with the choice produce of the months.
  15 "And with the best things of the ancient mountains,
    And with the choice things of the everlasting hills,
  16 And with the choice things of the earth and its fulness,
    And the favor of Him who dwelt in the bush.
    Let it come to the head of Joseph,

Cross references (margin):

33:1 Josh 14:6

33:2 Hab 3:3; Dan 7:10; Acts 7:53; Gal 3:19; Rev 5:11

33:3 Hos 11:1; Deut 14:2

33:4 John 1:17; Ps 119:111

*33:7 Gen 49:8-12

33:8 Ex 28:30; 17:7

33:9 Ex 32:26-29

33:10 Deut 31:9-13; Ex 30:7,8; Ps 51:19

33:11 2 Sam 24:23; Ps 20:3

33:13 Gen 49:25; 27:28

33:15 Gen 49:26

33:16 Ex 3:2,4; Acts 7:30,35

33:7 The tribe of Simeon, missing from the blessing, whose borders it dwelt.
may have been implicitly associated with Judah, within

And to the crown of the head of the one distinguished among his
    brothers.

33:17
Num 23:22;
Ps 44:5

17 "As the first-born of his ox, majesty is his,
    And his horns are the horns of the wild ox;
    With them he shall push the peoples,
    All at once, *to* the ends of the earth.
    And those are the ten thousands of Ephraim,
    And those are the thousands of Manasseh."

33:18
Gen 49:13-15

18 And of Zebulun he said,
    "Rejoice, Zebulun, in your going forth,
    And, Issachar, in your tents.

33:19
Is 2:3; Ps 4:5

19 "They shall call peoples *to* the mountain;
    There they shall offer righteous sacrifices;
    For they shall draw out the abundance of the seas,
    And the hidden treasures of the sand."

33:20
Gen 49:19

20 And of Gad he said,
    "Blessed is the one who enlarges Gad;
    He lies down as a lion,
    And tears the arm, also the crown of the head.

33:21
Num 32:1-5,
31,32;
Josh 4:12;
22:1-3

21 "Then he provided the first *part* for himself,
    For there the ruler's portion was reserved;
    And he came *with* the leaders of the people;
    He executed the justice of the LORD,
    And His ordinances with Israel."

33:22
Gen 49:16

22 And of Dan he said,
    "Dan is a lion's whelp,
    That leaps forth from Bashan."

33:23
Gen 49:21

23 And of Naphtali he said,
    "O Naphtali, satisfied with favor,
    And full of the blessing of the LORD,
    Take possession of the sea and the south."

33:24
Gen 49:20;
Job 29;6

24 And of Asher he said,
    "More blessed than sons is Asher;
    May he be favored by his brothers,
    And may he dip his foot in oil.

33:25
Deut 4:40;
32:49

25 "Your locks shall be iron and bronze,
    And according to your days, so shall your leisurely walk be.

33:26
Ex 15:11;
Ps 68:33,34

26 "There is none like the God of [20]Jeshurun,
    Who rides the heavens to your help,
    And through the skies in His majesty.

33:27
Ps 90:1,2;
Josh 24:18

27 "The eternal God is a dwelling place,
    And underneath are the everlasting arms;
    And He drove out the enemy from before you,
    And said, 'Destroy!'

33:28
Num 23:9;
Gen 27:28

28 "So Israel dwells in security,
    The fountain of Jacob secluded,
    In a land of grain and new wine;
    His heavens also drop down dew.

33:29
Ps 144:15;
2 Sam 7:23;
Ps 18:14;
Deut 32:13

29 "Blessed are you, O Israel;
    Who is like you, a people saved by the LORD,
    Who is the shield of your help,
    And the sword of your majesty!
    So your enemies shall cringe before you,
    And you shall tread upon their high places."

[20]I.e., Israel

E. *The death and burial of Moses*

34 Now Moses went up from the plains of Moab to Mount Nebo, to the top of Pisgah, which is opposite Jericho. And the LORD showed him all the land, Gilead as far as Dan,

2 and all Naphtali and the land of Ephraim and Manasseh, and all the land of Judah as far as the [21]western sea,

3 and the Negev and the plain in the valley of Jericho, the city of palm trees, as far as Zoar.

4 Then the LORD said to him, "This is the land which I swore to Abraham, Isaac, and Jacob, saying, 'I will give it to your descendants'; I have let you see *it* with your eyes, but you shall not go over there."

5 So Moses the servant of the LORD died there in the land of Moab, according to the word of the LORD.

6 And He buried him in the valley in the land of Moab, opposite Beth-peor; but no man knows his burial place to this day.

7 Although Moses was one hundred and twenty years old when he died, his eye was not dim, nor his vigor abated.

8 So the sons of Israel wept for Moses in the plains of Moab thirty days; then the days of weeping *and* mourning for Moses came to an end.

9 Now Joshua the son of Nun was filled with the spirit of wisdom, for Moses had laid his hands on him; and the sons of Israel listened to him and did as the LORD had commanded Moses.

10 Since then no prophet has risen in Israel like Moses, whom the LORD knew face to face,

11 for all the signs and wonders which the LORD sent him to perform in the land of Egypt against Pharaoh, all his servants, and all his land,

12 and for all the mighty power and for all the great terror which Moses performed in the sight of all Israel.

[21]I.e., Mediterranean Sea

34:1 Deut 32:49, 52

34:4 Gen 12:7; 28:13

34:5 Deut 32:50; Josh 1:1,2

34:7 Deut 31:2

34:9 Is 11:2; Num 27:18, 23

34:10 Num 12:6,8

34:11 Deut 4:34

INTRODUCTION TO
THE BOOK OF
JOSHUA

Authorship and Background: This book is named after its chief character, Joshua, who was of the tribe of Ephraim. His name was originally Hoshea, "salvation" (Num. 13:8), but Moses changed it to Joshua (Jehoshua), "Yahweh is salvation" (Num. 13:16). Jesus, the Septuagint spelling of Joshua, was the name given the Christ at His birth. The authorship of the book cannot be determined definitely. Jewish tradition attributed it to Joshua, but also held that Eleazar appended the account of Joshua's death, after which Phinehas noted the death of Eleazar. The recurring expression "to this day" implies that the unknown author compiled the book some time after the events occurred, although the sources from which the book is derived were contemporary with the historical incidents. In the Hebrew Bible the historical books of Joshua through 2 Kings (with the exception of Ruth) are listed as "The Former Prophets" because ancient Jewish rabbis considered the traditional authors (Joshua, Samuel, Nathan, Gad, and others) as prophets.

Characteristics: The book of Joshua is both history and biography, for the story of Joshua's life is intermingled with the history of Israel during the time of the conquest of Canaan. The book commences with the call and commission of Joshua; it ends with his death. Joshua is pictured as a man of courage and faith. He is a consecrated leader, a military strategist, and a wise governor of men. Together with Caleb he had earlier submitted a minority report contrary to the discouraging account of the other ten spies. The book of Joshua recounts the success of Israel in the conquest of Canaan. This success is a token of God's faithfulness in the fulfillment of the divine promise made years before. The destruction of the Amorites is an example of divine judgment against national iniquity. Joshua has often been pictured as a type of Christ, the leader of his people. The style of the work is similar to that of the other historical writings.

Contents:

I. The conquest of Canaan (1:1-12:24): Joshua commissioned; the army mobilized; the spies sent. The Jordan crossed; the twelve stones of memorial erected. Israel circumcised; the Passover celebrated; the unseen Captain present. Jericho captured. The fall of Ai. The monument erected on Mt. Ebal. The deception of the Gibeonites. Victory over the five kings. Conquest of southern and northern Canaan; summary of conquests. List of the conquered kings.

II. The partition of the promised land (13:1-21:45): The command to divide the land. East Canaan given to Reuben, Gad, and the half-tribe of Manasseh. West Canaan partitioned: Caleb's portion; Judah's portion; Ephraim's and Manasseh's portions. The erection of the tabernacle at Shiloh. The division of the remaining land among the tribes of Benjamin, Simeon, Zebulun, Issachar, Asher, Naphtali, and Dan. The six cities of refuge; the forty-eight cities apportioned to the priests and Levites.

III. The farewell addresses of Joshua (22:1-24:33): His last words to the two-and-one-half tribes of east Canaan. Their altar at the Jordan; the protest by the other tribes; the apology of the two-and-one-half tribes for erecting the altar. Joshua's last words to the tribes of west Canaan; a rehearsal of the benefits, the promised blessings, and warnings. Joshua's message to the twelve tribes: his own covenant, " . . . for me and my house, we will serve the LORD" (24:15). The death and burial of Joshua; the burial of Joseph's bones; the death and burial of Eleazar.

THE BOOK OF

JOSHUA

I. The conquest of Canaan (1:1–12:24)

A. Introduction: God's instructions to Joshua

1 Now it came about after the death of Moses the servant of the LORD that the LORD spoke to Joshua the son of Nun, Moses' [1]servant, saying,

2 "Moses My servant is dead; now therefore arise, cross this Jordan, you and all this people, to the land which I am giving to them, to the sons of Israel.

3 "Every place on which the sole of your foot treads, I have given it to you, just as I spoke to Moses.

4 "From the wilderness and this Lebanon, even as far as the great river, the river Euphrates, all the land of the Hittites, and as far as the Great Sea toward the setting of the sun, will be your territory.

5 "No man will *be able to* stand before you all the days of your life. Just as I have been with Moses, I will be with you; I will not fail you or forsake you.

6 "Be strong and courageous, for you shall give this people possession of the land which I swore to their fathers to give them.

7 "Only be strong and very courageous; be careful to do according to all the law which Moses My servant commanded you; do not turn from it to the right or to the left, so that you may have success wherever you go.

8 "This book of the law shall not depart from your mouth, but you shall meditate on it day and night, so that you may be careful to do according to all that is written in it; for then you will make your way prosperous, and then you will have success.

9 "Have I not commanded you? Be strong and courageous! Do not tremble or be dismayed, for the LORD your God is with you wherever you go."

B. Preparations for crossing the Jordan

1. The order issued

10 Then Joshua commanded the officers of the people, saying,

11 "Pass through the midst of the camp and command the people, saying, 'Prepare provisions for yourselves, for within three days you are to cross this Jordan, to go in to possess the land which the LORD your God is giving you, to possess it.'"

2. The reminder to Reubenites, Gadites, and the half-tribe of Manasseh

12 And to the Reubenites and to the Gadites and to the half-tribe of Manasseh, Joshua said,

13 "Remember the word which Moses the servant of the LORD commanded you, saying, 'The LORD your God gives you rest, and will give you this land.'

14 "Your wives, your little ones, and your cattle shall remain in the land which Moses gave you beyond the Jordan, but you shall cross before your brothers in battle array, all your valiant warriors, and shall help them,

15 until the LORD gives your brothers rest, as *He gives* you, and they also possess the land which the LORD your God is giving them. Then you shall return to

[1]Or, minister

1:2 Num 12:7; Deut 34:5; v. 11
1:3 Deut 11:24
*1:4 Gen 15:18
*1:5 Deut 7:24; 31:6-8
1:7 Deut 5:32; 28:14
1:8 Deut 17:8,9; Ps 1:1-3
1:9 Deut 31:7,8, 23; Jer 1:8
1:11 Joel 3:2
1:12 Num 32:20-22
1:13 Deut 3:18-20
1:15 Josh 22:1-4

1:4 *Great Sea*, the Mediterranean.
1:5 Joshua (shortened from Jehoshua, "Yahweh is salvation") was a type of Christ. In fact, his name becomes "Jesus" in Greek. He led the people of God into the promised land. He interceded for them when they went astray. He led them to victory over the forces of evil. Likewise Jesus is the captain of our salvation who intercedes for His people, brings them into the promised rest, gives them an inheritance, and makes victory over sin possible. (See Josh. 7:5–9; Acts 20:32; Rom. 1:10; 2 Cor. 1:10; 2:14; Heb. 2:10,11; 4:8,9; 1 John 2:1.)

your own land, and possess that which Moses the servant of the LORD gave you beyond the Jordan toward the sunrise."

16   And they answered Joshua, saying, "All that you have commanded us we will do, and wherever you send us we will go.

1:17
vv. 5,9

17   "Just as we obeyed Moses in all things, so we will obey you; only may the LORD your God be with you, as He was with Moses.

18   "Anyone who rebels against your command and does not obey your words in all that you command him, shall be put to death; only be strong and courageous."

3. Two spies sent to Jericho

a. Rahab hides the spies

2:1
Num 25:1;
Heb 11:31;
James 2:25

2 Then Joshua the son of Nun sent two men as spies secretly from Shittim, saying, "Go, view the land, especially Jericho." So they went and came into the house of a harlot whose name was Rahab, and lodged there.

2   And it was told the king of Jericho, saying, "Behold, men from the sons of Israel have come here tonight to search out the land."

3   And the king of Jericho sent *word* to Rahab, saying, "Bring out the men who have come to you, who have entered your house, for they have come to search out all the land."

4   But the woman had taken the two men and hidden them, and she said, "Yes, the men came to me, but I did not know where they were from.

5   "And it came about when *it was time* to shut the gate, at dark, that the men went out; I do not know where the men went. Pursue them quickly, for you will overtake them."

2:6
James 2:25

6   But she had brought them up to the roof and hidden them in the stalks of flax which she had laid in order on the roof.

7   So the men pursued them on the road to the Jordan to the fords; and as soon as those who were pursuing them had gone out, they shut the gate.

b. Rahab secures a promise of safety from the spies

8   Now before they lay down, she came up to them on the roof,

2:9
Ex 23:27;
Deut 2:25

9   and said to the men, "I know that the LORD has given you the land, and that the terror of you has fallen on us, and that all the inhabitants of the land have melted away before you.

2:10
Ex 14:21;
Num 21:24,
34,35

10   "For we have heard how the LORD dried up the water of the Red Sea before you when you came out of Egypt, and what you did to the two kings of the Amorites who were beyond the Jordan, to Sihon and Og, whom you utterly destroyed.

2:11
Ex 15:14,15;
Josh 5:1;
Deut 4:39

11   "And when we heard *it*, our hearts melted and no courage remained in any man any longer because of you; for the LORD your God, He is God in heaven above and on earth beneath.

2:12
v. 18

12   "Now therefore, please swear to me by the LORD, since I have dealt kindly with you, that you also will deal kindly with my father's household, and give me a pledge of truth,

13   and spare my father and my mother and my brothers and my sisters, with all who belong to them, and deliver our ²lives from death."

2:14
Judg 1:24

14   So the men said to her, "Our life for yours if you do not tell this business of ours; and it shall come about when the LORD gives us the land that we will deal kindly and faithfully with you."

c. The promise of the scarlet cord

15   Then she let them down by a rope through the window, for her house was on the city wall, so that she was living on the wall.

2:16
James 2:25

16   And she said to them, "Go to the hill country, lest the pursuers happen upon

²Lit., *souls*

2:4 Rahab deliberately told a falsehood to protect the Hebrew spies. Some have argued that her act makes it permissible to lie on certain occasions. Calvin said, "As to the falsehood, we must admit that though it was done for a good purpose, it was not free from fault." In the New Testament Rahab is commended for her faith in God (for she risked her life to save the two spies from death), but nothing is said to suggest that her lie was commended (Heb. 11:31; James 2:25). God would have been able to save the spies from

death without the aid of man's (or woman's) sin. Scripture nowhere supports the position that it is justifiable to lie (Ex. 20:16; Deut. 5:20; Matt. 19:18).
2:15 *on the city wall*, literally means "in the wall of the wall." Jericho, like other Canaanite cities, had two walls about 12 to 15 feet apart. Crowded conditions resulted in houses (such as Rahab's) being built on timbers extended across the walls. Escape was facilitated because the window was over the outer wall.

you, and hide yourselves there for three days, until the pursuers return. Then afterward you may go on your way."

17 And the men said to her, "We *shall be* free from this oath to you which you have made us swear,

18 unless, when we come into the land, you tie this cord of scarlet thread in the window through which you let us down, and gather to yourself into the house your father and your mother and your brothers and all your father's household.

19 "And it shall come about that anyone who goes out of the doors of your house into the street, his blood *shall be* on his own head, and we *shall be* free; but anyone who is with you in the house, his blood *shall be* on our head, if a hand is *laid* on him.

20 "But if you tell this business of ours, then we shall be free from the oath which you have made us swear."

21 And she said, "According to your words, so be it." So she sent them away, and they departed; and she tied the scarlet cord in the window.

d. *The return of the spies*

22 And they departed and came to the hill country, and remained there for three days until the pursuers returned. Now the pursuers had sought *them* all along the road, but had not found *them*.

23 Then the two men returned and came down from the hill country and crossed over and came to Joshua the son of Nun, and they related to him all that had happened to them.

24 And they said to Joshua, "Surely the LORD has given all the land into our hands, and all the inhabitants of the land, moreover, have melted away before us."

C. *Israel crossing the Jordan*

1. *The final preparations*

3 Then Joshua rose early in the morning; and he and all the sons of Israel set out from Shittim and came to the Jordan, and they lodged there before they crossed.

2 And it came about at the end of three days that the officers went through the midst of the camp;

3 and they commanded the people, saying, "When you see the ark of the covenant of the LORD your God with the Levitical priests carrying it, then you shall set out from your place and go after it.

4 "However, there shall be between you and it a distance of about 2,000 cubits by measure. Do not come near it, that you may know the way by which you shall go, for you have not passed this way before."

5 Then Joshua said to the people, "Consecrate yourselves, for tomorrow the LORD will do wonders among you."

6 And Joshua spoke to the priests, saying, "Take up the ark of the covenant and cross over ahead of the people." So they took up the ark of the covenant and went ahead of the people.

2. *The promise of God*

7 Now the LORD said to Joshua, "This day I will begin to exalt you in the sight of all Israel, that they may know that just as I have been with Moses, I will be with you.

8 "You shall, moreover, command the priests who are carrying the ark of the covenant, saying, 'When you come to the edge of the waters of the Jordan, you shall stand *still* in the Jordan.'"

9 Then Joshua said to the sons of Israel, "Come here, and hear the words of the LORD your God."

10 And Joshua said, "By this you shall know that the living God is among you, and that He will assuredly dispossess from before you the Canaanite, the Hittite, the Hivite, the Perizzite, the Girgashite, the Amorite, and the Jebusite.

11 "Behold, the ark of the covenant of the Lord of all the earth is crossing over ahead of you into the Jordan.

12 "Now then, take for yourselves twelve men from the tribes of Israel, one man for each tribe.

13 "And it shall come about when the soles of the feet of the priests who carry the ark of the LORD, the Lord of all the earth, shall rest in the waters of the Jordan, the

2:17 Gen 24:8

2:18 v. 12; Josh 6:23

2:19 Ezek 33:4

2:24 v. 9; Josh 6:2

3:1 Josh 2:1

3:2 Josh 1:11

3:3 Deut 31:9

3:5 Ex 19:10,14; Josh 7:13

3:7 Josh 4:7; 1:5

3:8 vv. 3,17

3:10 Deut 7:1

3:12 Josh 4:2

3:13 Ex 15:8; Ps 78:13

waters of the Jordan shall be cut off, *and* the waters which are flowing down from above shall stand in one heap."

3. The crossing begun: the Jordan parted

14 So it came about when the people set out from their tents to cross the Jordan with the priests carrying the ark of the covenant before the people,

15 and when those who carried the ark came into the Jordan, and the feet of the priests carrying the ark were dipped in the edge of the water (for the Jordan overflows all its banks all the days of harvest),

16 that the waters which were flowing down from above stood *and* rose up in one heap, a great distance away at Adam, the city that is beside Zarethan; and those which were flowing down toward the sea of the Arabah, the Salt Sea, were completely cut off. So the people crossed opposite Jericho.

17 And the priests who carried the ark of the covenant of the LORD stood firm on dry ground in the middle of the Jordan while all Israel crossed on dry ground, until all the nation had finished crossing the Jordan.

4. The twelve stones of memorial

4 Now it came about when all the nation had finished crossing the Jordan, that the LORD spoke to Joshua, saying,

2 "Take for yourselves twelve men from the people, one man from each tribe,

3 and command them, saying, 'Take up for yourselves twelve stones from here out of the middle of the Jordan, from the place where the priests' feet are standing firm, and carry them over with you, and lay them down in the lodging place where you will lodge tonight.'"

4 So Joshua called the twelve men whom he had appointed from the sons of Israel, one man from each tribe;

5 and Joshua said to them, "Cross again to the ark of the LORD your God into the middle of the Jordan, and each of you take up a stone on his shoulder, according to the number of the tribes of the sons of Israel.

6 "Let this be a sign among you, so that when your children ask later, saying, 'What do these stones mean to you?'

7 then you shall say to them, 'Because the waters of the Jordan were cut off before the ark of the covenant of the LORD; when it crossed the Jordan, the waters of the Jordan were cut off.' So these stones shall become a memorial to the sons of Israel forever."

8 And thus the sons of Israel did, as Joshua commanded, and took up twelve stones from the middle of the Jordan, just as the LORD spoke to Joshua, according to the number of the tribes of the sons of Israel; and they carried them over with them to the lodging place, and put them down there.

9 Then Joshua set up twelve stones in the middle of the Jordan at the place where the feet of the priests who carried the ark of the covenant were standing, and they are there to this day.

10 For the priests who carried the ark were standing in the middle of the Jordan until everything was completed that the LORD had commanded Joshua to speak to the people, according to all that Moses had commanded Joshua. And the people hurried and crossed;

11 and it came about when all the people had finished crossing, that the ark of the LORD and the priests crossed before the people.

12 And the sons of Reuben and the sons of Gad and the half-tribe of Manasseh crossed over in battle array before the sons of Israel, just as Moses had spoken to them;

13 about 40,000, equipped for war, crossed for battle before the LORD to the desert plains of Jericho.

3:16 This miracle (or special providential act) may have been one of timing, in which an earthquake blocked the river. As recently as 1927 a tremor dislodged some of the cliffs overlooking the river, completely blocking the Jordan for over 21 hours.
4:7 The stones of memorial were to be set up not simply to commemorate the crossing of the Jordan, but as a testimony to the people of God concerning His miraculous and delivering power. The stones would recall what God had done in the past, so that in future difficulties Israel could look to the God who had formerly delivered them. Believers today should erect some stones of remembrance in their own experience that will stand them in good stead when facing great difficulties. Then they will be able to say, "Thus far the Lord has led."
4:9 *there to this day.* Apparently the pile of stones could be seen when the river level was low.

11   So he had the ark of the LORD taken around the city, circling *it* once; then they came into the camp and spent the night in the camp.

12   Now Joshua rose early in the morning, and the priests took up the ark of the LORD.

13   And the seven priests carrying the seven trumpets of rams' horns before the ark of the LORD went on continually, and blew the trumpets; and the armed men went before them, and the rear guard came after the ark of the LORD, while they continued to blow the trumpets.

14   Thus the second day they marched around the city once and returned to the camp; they did so for six days.

2. *The fall of the city*

15   Then it came about on the seventh day that they rose early at the dawning of the day and marched around the city in the same manner seven times; only on that day they marched around the city seven times.

16   And it came about at the seventh time, when the priests blew the trumpets, Joshua said to the people, "Shout! For the LORD has given you the city.

17   "And the city shall be under the ban, it and all that is in it belongs to the LORD; only Rahab the harlot and all who are with her in the house shall live, because she hid the messengers whom we sent.

18   "But as for you, only keep yourselves from the things under the ban, lest you covet *them* and take some of the things under the ban, so you would make the camp of Israel accursed and bring trouble on it.

19   "But all the silver and gold and articles of bronze and iron are holy to the LORD; they shall go into the treasury of the LORD."

20   So the people shouted, and *priests* blew the trumpets; and it came about, when the people heard the sound of the trumpet, that the people shouted with a great shout and the wall fell down flat, so that the people went up into the city, every man straight ahead, and they took the city.

21   And they utterly destroyed everything in the city, both man and woman, young and old, and ox and sheep and donkey, with the edge of the sword.

3. *The rescue of Rahab*

22   And Joshua said to the two men who had spied out the land, "Go into the harlot's house and bring the woman and all she has out of there, as you have sworn to her."

23   So the young men who were spies went in and brought out Rahab and her father and her mother and her brothers and all she had; they also brought out all her relatives, and placed them outside the camp of Israel.

24   And they burned the city with fire, and all that was in it. Only the silver and gold and articles of bronze and iron, they put into the treasury of the [6]house of the LORD.

25   However, Rahab the harlot and her father's household and all she had, Joshua spared; and she has lived in the midst of Israel to this day, for she hid the messengers whom Joshua sent to spy out Jericho.

4. *The curse on Jericho*

26   Then Joshua made them take an oath at that time, saying, "Cursed before the LORD is the man who rises up and builds this city Jericho; with *the loss of* his first-born he shall lay its foundation, and with *the loss of* his youngest son he shall set up its gates."

27   So the LORD was with Joshua, and his fame was in all the land.

[6]I.e., tabernacle

6:17a *belongs to the LORD*, see note to Deut. 2:34 for an explanation.
6:17b *harlot*. Some, like Josephus, have tried to soften this to "innkeeper," but the Hebrew word and the Septuagint translation make this impossible to do.
6:20 *the wall fell down flat*. For six days the soldiers marched around the city once a day. On the seventh day they went around seven times. Whether the collapse was a result of this, or a providential coincidence, or a miracle, the text does not say.
6:25 *However, Rahab ... and all she had*. Because of her coalition with Joshua he saw to it that Rahab and her entire family escaped when Jericho was destroyed.

F. The conquest of Ai

1. Israel flees from Ai

*7:1
Josh 6:17-19

7 But the sons of Israel acted unfaithfully in regard to the things under the ban, for Achan, the son of Carmi, the son of Zabdi, the son of Zerah, from the tribe of Judah, took some of the things under the ban, therefore the anger of the LORD burned against the sons of Israel.

2 Now Joshua sent men from Jericho to Ai, which is near Beth-aven, east of Bethel, and said to them, "Go up and spy out the land." So the men went up and spied out Ai.

3 And they returned to Joshua and said to him, "Do not let all the people go up; *only* about two or three thousand men need go up to Ai; do not make all the people toil up there, for they are few."

7:4
Lev 26:17;
28:25

4 So about three thousand men from the people went up there, but they fled from the men of Ai.

5 And the men of Ai struck down about thirty-six of their men, and pursued them from the gate as far as Shebarim, and struck them down on the descent, so the hearts of the people melted and became as water.

2. Joshua's grief

7:6
Job 2:12;
Rev 18:19

6 Then Joshua tore his clothes and fell to the earth on his face before the ark of the LORD until the evening, *both* he and the elders of Israel; and they put dust on their heads.

7:7
Ex 5:22

7 And Joshua said, "Alas, O Lord GOD, why didst Thou ever bring this people over the Jordan, *only* to deliver us into the hand of the Amorites, to destroy us? If only we had been willing to dwell beyond the Jordan!

8 "O Lord, what can I say since Israel has turned *their* back before their enemies?

7:9
Ex 32:12;
Deut 9:28

9 "For the Canaanites and all the inhabitants of the land will hear of it, and they will surround us and cut off our name from the earth. And what wilt Thou do for Thy great name?"

3. God's way of uncovering sin

10 So the LORD said to Joshua, "Rise up! Why is it that you have fallen on your face?

7:11
v. 1;
Josh 6:18,19;
See Acts 5:1,
2

11 "Israel has sinned, and they have also transgressed My covenant which I commanded them. And they have even taken some of the things under the ban and have both stolen and deceived. Moreover, they have also put *them* among their own things.

12 "Therefore the sons of Israel cannot stand before their enemies; they turn *their* backs before their enemies, for they have become accursed. I will not be with you anymore unless you destroy the things under the ban from your midst.

7:13
Josh 3:5; 6:18

13 "Rise up! Consecrate the people and say, 'Consecrate yourselves for tomorrow, for thus the LORD, the God of Israel, has said, "There are things under the ban in your midst, O Israel. You cannot stand before your enemies until you have removed the things under the ban from your midst."

14 'In the morning then you shall come near by your tribes. And it shall be that the tribe which the LORD takes *by lot* shall come near by families, and the family which the LORD takes shall come near by households, and the household which the LORD takes shall come near man by man.

7:15
v. 11

15 'And it shall be that the one who is taken with the things under the ban shall be burned with fire, he and all that belongs to him, because he has transgressed the covenant of the LORD, and because he has committed a disgraceful thing in Israel.' "

7:1 Valuable lessons may be learned from the sin of Achan. God looked on Israel as an entity, so that the sin of one brought punishment on all. The essential unity of the people of God is thus evident. Since man neither lives nor dies for himself, his activities inevitably affect the lives of many people. Israel's first attack on Ai, which was repulsed, shows this to be true. Achan's sin did not consist in the seizure of the enemy's goods, nor was covetousness the worst of his offenses. His chief sin was flagrant disobedience of God's express command. Israel was released from her own involvement in guilt only after Achan and his family had been dealt with. The terrible punishment meted out to him was a warning to all never to allow greed to lure them into disregard of God's will.

4. *The sin of Achan uncovered*

16 So Joshua arose early in the morning and brought Israel near by tribes, and the tribe of Judah was taken.

17 And he brought the family of Judah near, and he took the family of the Zerahites; and he brought the family of the Zerahites near man by man, and Zabdi was taken.

18 And he brought his household near man by man; and Achan, son of Carmi, son of Zabdi, son of Zerah, from the tribe of Judah, was taken.

19 Then Joshua said to Achan, "My son, I implore you, give glory to the LORD, the God of Israel, and give praise to Him; and tell me now what you have done. Do not hide it from me."

20 So Achan answered Joshua and said, "Truly, I have sinned against the LORD, the God of Israel, and this is what I did:

21 when I saw among the spoil a beautiful mantle from Shinar and two hundred shekels of silver and a bar of gold fifty shekels in weight, then I coveted them and took them; and behold, they are concealed in the earth inside my tent with the silver underneath it."

5. *The stoning of Achan and his family*

22 So Joshua sent messengers, and they ran to the tent; and behold, it was concealed in his tent with the silver underneath it.

23 And they took them from inside the tent and brought them to Joshua and to all the sons of Israel, and they poured them out before the LORD.

24 Then Joshua and all Israel with him, took Achan the son of Zerah, the silver, the mantle, the bar of gold, his sons, his daughters, his oxen, his donkeys, his sheep, his tent and all that belonged to him; and they brought them up to the valley of [7]Achor.

25 And Joshua said, "Why have you troubled us? The LORD will trouble you this day." And all Israel stoned them with stones; and they burned them with fire after they had stoned them with stones.

26 And they raised over him a great heap of stones that stands to this day, and the LORD turned from the fierceness of His anger. Therefore the name of that place has been called the valley of [7]Achor to this day.

6. *The battle for Ai*

a. *The plan of battle*

8 Now the LORD said to Joshua, "Do not fear or be dismayed. Take all the people of war with you and arise, go up to Ai; see, I have given into your hand the king of Ai, his people, his city, and his land.

2 "And you shall do to Ai and its king just as you did to Jericho and its king; you shall take only its spoil and its cattle as plunder for yourselves. Set an ambush for the city behind it."

3 So Joshua rose with all the people of war to go up to Ai; and Joshua chose 30,000 men, valiant warriors, and sent them out at night.

4 And he commanded them, saying, "See, you are going to ambush the city from behind it. Do not go very far from the city, but all of you be ready.

5 "Then I and all the people who are with me will approach the city. And it will come about when they come out to meet us as at the first, that we will flee before them.

6 "And they will come out after us until we have drawn them away from the city, for they will say, '*They* are fleeing before us as at the first.' So we will flee before them.

7 "And you shall rise from *your* ambush and take possession of the city, for the LORD your God will deliver it into your hand.

8 "Then it will be when you have seized the city, that you shall set the city on fire. You shall do *it* according to the word of the LORD. See, I have commanded you."

9 So Joshua sent them away, and they went to the place of ambush and remained between Bethel and Ai, on the west side of Ai; but Joshua spent that night among the people.

---
[7]I.e., trouble

7:17 Num 26:20

7:19 Jer 13:16; John 9:24; Num 5:6,7; 1 Sam 14:43
7:20 Josh 22:20; 1 Chr 2:7

7:24 Josh 15:7

7:25 Josh 6:18; Deut 17:5

7:26 Deut 13:17; Is 65:10; Hos 2:15

8:1 Deut 1:21; 7:18; Josh 1:9; 6:2

8:2 v. 27; Deut 20:14

8:4 see Judg 20:29-32

8:8 v. 2

b. The seizure of the city

8:10
v. 33

10 Now Joshua rose early in the morning and mustered the people, and he went up with the elders of Israel before the people to Ai.

11 Then all the people of war who *were* with him went up and drew near and arrived in front of the city, and camped on the north side of Ai. Now *there was* a valley between him and Ai.

12 And he took about 5,000 men and set them in ambush between Bethel and Ai, on the west side of the city.

13 So they stationed the people, all the army that was on the north side of the city, and its rear guard on the west side of the city, and Joshua spent that night in the midst of the valley.

8:14
Josh 3:16;
Judg 20:34

14 And it came about when the king of Ai saw *it*, that the men of the city hurried and rose up early and went out to meet Israel in battle, he and all his people at the appointed place before the desert plain. But he did not know that *there was* an ambush against him behind the city.

15 And Joshua and all Israel pretended to be beaten before them, and fled by the way of the wilderness.

16 And all the people who were in the city were called together to pursue them, and they pursued Joshua, and were drawn away from the city.

17 So not a man was left in Ai or Bethel who had not gone out after Israel, and they left the city unguarded and pursued Israel.

8:18
v. 26;
Ex 14:16;
17:9-13

18 Then the LORD said to Joshua, "Stretch out the javelin that is in your hand toward Ai, for I will give it into your hand." So Joshua stretched out the javelin that was in his hand toward the city.

8:19
v. 8

19 And the *men in* ambush rose quickly from their place, and when he had stretched out his hand, they ran and entered the city and captured it; and they quickly set the city on fire.

20 When the men of Ai turned back and looked, behold, the smoke of the city ascended to the sky, and they had no place to flee this way or that, for the people who had been fleeing to the wilderness turned against the pursuers.

21 When Joshua and all Israel saw that the *men in* ambush had captured the city and that the smoke of the city ascended, they turned back and slew the men of Ai.

8:22
Deut 7:2

22 And the others came out from the city to encounter them, so that they were *trapped* in the midst of Israel, some on this side and some on that side; and they slew them until no one was left of those who survived or escaped.

23 But they took alive the king of Ai and brought him to Joshua.

c. The slaughter of the inhabitants

24 Now it came about when Israel had finished killing all the inhabitants of Ai in the field in the wilderness where they pursued them, and all of them were fallen by the edge of the sword until they were destroyed, then all Israel returned to Ai and struck it with the edge of the sword.

8:25
Deut 20:16-18

25 And all who fell that day, both men and women, were 12,000—all the people of Ai.

8:26
Ex 17:11,12

26 For Joshua did not withdraw his hand with which he stretched out the javelin until he had utterly destroyed all the inhabitants of Ai.

8:27
v. 2;
Num 31:22
*8:28
Deut 13:16
8:29
Deut 21:22,
23

27 Israel took only the cattle and the spoil of that city as plunder for themselves, according to the word of the LORD which He had commanded Joshua.

28 So Joshua burned Ai and made it a heap forever, a desolation until this day.

29 And he hanged the king of Ai on a tree until evening; and at sunset Joshua gave command and they took his body down from the tree, and threw it at the entrance of the city gate, and raised over it a great heap of stones *that stands* to this day.

7. An altar erected in Mount Ebal

8:30
Deut 27:2-8
8:31
Ex 20:24,25;
Deut 27:5,6

30 Then Joshua built an altar to the LORD, the God of Israel, in Mount Ebal, **31** just as Moses the servant of the LORD had commanded the sons of Israel, as it is written in the book of the law of Moses, an altar of uncut stones, on which no man had wielded an iron *tool;* and they offered burnt offerings on it to the LORD, and sacrificed peace offerings.

8:28 *Ai*, meaning "ruins," was destroyed about 2200 B.C. and was not occupied at all during the Israelite conquest. A probable explanation is that Joshua took Bethel, which was a mile from Ai (see Judg. 1:22–26). Ai may have been a military outpost of Bethel.

32   And he wrote there on the stones a copy of the law of Moses, which he had written, in the presence of the sons of Israel.

33   And all Israel with their elders and officers and their judges were standing on both sides of the ark before the Levitical priests who carried the ark of the covenant of the LORD, the stranger as well as the native. Half of them *stood* in front of Mount Gerizim and half of them in front of Mount Ebal, just as Moses the servant of the LORD had given command at first to bless the people of Israel.

34   Then afterward he read all the words of the law, the blessing and the curse, according to all that is written in the book of the law.

35   There was not a word of all that Moses had commanded which Joshua did not read before all the assembly of Israel with the women and the little ones and the strangers who were living among them.

G. The stratagem of Gibeon

1. The coalition of kings

9 Now it came about when all the kings who were beyond the Jordan, in the hill country and in the lowland and on all the coast of the Great Sea toward Lebanon, the Hittite and the Amorite, the Canaanite, the Perizzite, the Hivite and the Jebusite, heard of it,

2   that they gathered themselves together with one accord to fight with Joshua and with Israel.

2. The treaty with Gibeon

3   When the inhabitants of Gibeon heard what Joshua had done to Jericho and to Ai,

4   they also acted craftily and set out as envoys, and took worn-out sacks on their donkeys, and wineskins, worn-out and torn and mended,

5   and worn-out and patched sandals on their feet, and worn-out clothes on themselves; and all the bread of their provision was dry *and* had become crumbled.

6   And they went to Joshua to the camp at Gilgal, and said to him and to the men of Israel, "We have come from a far country; now therefore, make a covenant with us."

7   And the men of Israel said to the Hivites, "Perhaps you are living within our land; how then shall we make a covenant with you?"

8   But they said to Joshua, "We are your servants." Then Joshua said to them, "Who are you, and where do you come from?"

9   And they said to him, "Your servants have come from a very far country because of the fame of the LORD your God; for we have heard the report of Him and all that He did in Egypt,

10   and all that He did to the two kings of the Amorites who were beyond the Jordan, to Sihon king of Heshbon and to Og king of Bashan who was at Ashtaroth.

11   "So our elders and all the inhabitants of our country spoke to us, saying, 'Take provisions in your hand for the journey, and go to meet them and say to them, "We are your servants; now then, make a covenant with us." '

12   "This our bread *was* warm *when* we took it for our provisions out of our houses on the day that we left to come to you; but now behold, it is dry and has become crumbled.

13   "And these wineskins which we filled were new, and behold, they are torn; and these our clothes and our sandals are worn out because of the very long journey."

14   So the men *of Israel* took some of their provisions, and did not ask for the counsel of the LORD.

15   And Joshua made peace with them and made a covenant with them, to let them live; and the leaders of the congregation swore *an oath* to them.

Marginal references:
- *8:32 — Deut 27:2,8
- 8:33 — Deut 31:9,12; 27:11-14
- *8:34f — Deut 31:11; Josh 1:8
- 8:35 — Deut 31:12
- 9:1 — Josh 3:10
- 9:3 — Josh 10:2; 6:27
- 9:6 — Josh 5:10
- 9:7 — v. 2; Josh 11:19; Ex 23:32
- 9:8 — Deut 20:11
- 9:9 — Deut 20:15; vv. 16,17,24; Josh 2:9,10
- 9:10 — Num 21:24, 33
- *9:14 — Num 27:21
- 9:15 — Ex 23:32

8:32,34,35 Besides the "blessing" and the "curse" (see Deut. 27:3,8,12–26), it is impossible to determine how much of the Law of Moses was inscribed on the stones and read to the people. At the covenant ceremony at Sinai, Moses read *the book of the covenant*, probably Ex. 21–23 (see Ex. 24:7). The limitations of space and time indicate that the reading of the law at Ebal and Gerizim was not much, if any, longer.

9:14 The Gibeonites obtained a treaty of friendship by deception. Yet Israel was not without guilt, nor was it necessary for them to be deceived. They *did not ask for the counsel of the LORD.* Had they done so they would have been delivered from this error in judgment. No matter how favorable the external appearances, we must never rely on our own good judgment or common sense when making a covenantal commitment; we must wait on God and ascertain His will in the matter.

3. *The punishment of the Gibeonites for their deceit*

16   And it came about at the end of three days after they had made a covenant with them, that they heard that they were neighbors and that they were living within their land.

9:17
Josh 18:25-28;
Ezra 2:25
9:18
Ps 15:4;
Eccl 5:2

17   Then the sons of Israel set out and came to their cities on the third day. Now their cities *were* Gibeon and Chephirah and Beeroth and Kiriath-jearim.

18   And the sons of Israel did not strike them because the leaders of the congregation had sworn to them by the Lord the God of Israel. And the whole congregation grumbled against the leaders.

19   But all the leaders said to the whole congregation, "We have sworn to them by the Lord, the God of Israel, and now we cannot touch them.

20   "This we will do to them, even let them live, lest wrath be upon us for the oath which we swore to them."

9:21
v. 15

21   And the leaders said to them, "Let them live." So they became hewers of wood and drawers of water for the whole congregation, just as the leaders had spoken to them.

9:22
vv. 6,9,16,17

22   Then Joshua called for them and spoke to them, saying, "Why have you deceived us, saying, 'We are very far from you,' when you are living within our land?

9:23
Gen 9:25;
vv. 21,27
9:24
Deut 7:1,2

23   "Now therefore, you are cursed, and you shall never cease being slaves, both hewers of wood and drawers of water for the house of my God."

24   So they answered Joshua and said, "Because it was certainly told your servants that the Lord your God had commanded His servant Moses to give you all the land, and to destroy all the inhabitants of the land before you; therefore we feared greatly for our lives because of you, and have done this thing.

9:25
Gen 16:6

25   "And now behold, we are in your hands; do as it seems good and right in your sight to do to us."

26   Thus he did to them, and delivered them from the hands of the sons of Israel, and they did not kill them.

9:27
vv. 21,23;
Deut 12:5

27   But Joshua made them that day hewers of wood and drawers of water for the congregation and for the altar of the Lord, to this day, in the place which He would choose.

H. *The conquest of southern Canaan*

1. *The victory over the Amorites*

a. *The confederation*

10:1
Josh 6:21;
8:22,26,28;
9:15

10   Now it came about when Adoni-zedek king of Jerusalem heard that Joshua had captured Ai, and had utterly destroyed it (just as he had done to Jericho and its king, so he had done to Ai and its king), and that the inhabitants of Gibeon had made peace with Israel and were within their land,

2   that he feared greatly, because Gibeon *was* a great city, like one of the royal cities, and because it was greater than Ai, and all its men *were* mighty.

3   Therefore Adoni-zedek king of Jerusalem sent *word* to Hoham king of Hebron and to Piram king of Jarmuth and to Japhia king of Lachish and to Debir king of Eglon, saying,

10:4
v. 1

4   "Come up to me and help me, and let us attack Gibeon, for it has made peace with Joshua and with the sons of Israel."

10:5
Josh 9:2

5   So the five kings of the Amorites, the king of Jerusalem, the king of Hebron, the king of Jarmuth, the king of Lachish, *and* the king of Eglon, gathered together and went up, they with all their armies, and camped by Gibeon and fought against it.

b. *The battle: God sends hailstones*

6   Then the men of Gibeon sent *word* to Joshua to the camp at Gilgal, saying, "Do not abandon your servants; come up to us quickly and save us and help us, for all the kings of the Amorites that live in the hill country have assembled against us."

7   So Joshua went up from Gilgal, he and all the people of war with him and all the valiant warriors.

10:8
Josh 1:5,9;
11:6

8   And the Lord said to Joshua, "Do not fear them, for I have given them into your hands; not one of them shall stand before you."

10:10
Deut 7:23

9   So Joshua came upon them suddenly by marching all night from Gilgal.

10   And the Lord confounded them before Israel, and He slew them with a great slaughter at Gibeon, and pursued them by the way of the ascent of Beth-horon, and struck them as far as Azekah and Makkedah.

11   And it came about as they fled from before Israel, *while* they were at the descent of Beth-horon, that the LORD threw large stones from heaven on them as far as Azekah, and they died; *there were* more who died from the hailstones than those whom the sons of Israel killed with the sword.

10:11
Ps 18:13,14;
Is 30:30

c. The sun stands still

12   Then Joshua spoke to the LORD in the day when the LORD delivered up the Amorites before the sons of Israel, and he said in the sight of Israel,
    "O sun, stand still at Gibeon,
    And O moon in the valley of Aijalon."

10:12
Hab 3:11

13   So the sun stood still, and the moon stopped,
    Until the nation avenged themselves of their enemies.
Is it not written in the book of Jashar? And the sun stopped in the middle of the sky, and did not hasten to go *down* for about a whole day.

*10:13
2 Sam 1:18;
Is 38:8

14   And there was no day like that before it or after it, when the LORD listened to the voice of a man; for the LORD fought for Israel.

10:14
v. 42

15   Then Joshua and all Israel with him returned to the camp to Gilgal.

*10:15
v. 43

d. The slaughter of the five kings

16   Now these five kings had fled and hidden themselves in the cave at Makkedah.

10:16
v. 5

17   And it was told Joshua, saying, "The five kings have been found hidden in the cave at Makkedah."

18   And Joshua said, "Roll large stones against the mouth of the cave, and assign men by it to guard them,

19   but do not stay *there* yourselves; pursue your enemies and attack them in the rear. Do not allow them to enter their cities, for the LORD your God has delivered them into your hand."

20   And it came about when Joshua and the sons of Israel had finished slaying them with a very great slaughter, until they were destroyed, and the survivors *who* remained of them had entered the fortified cities,

10:20
Deut 20:16

21   that all the people returned to the camp to Joshua at Makkedah in peace. No one uttered a word against any of the sons of Israel.

10:21
Ex 11:7

22   Then Joshua said, "Open the mouth of the cave and bring these five kings out to me from the cave."

10:22
Deut 7:24

23   And they did so, and brought these five kings out to him from the cave: the king of Jerusalem, the king of Hebron, the king of Jarmuth, the king of Lachish, *and* the king of Eglon.

24   And it came about when they brought these kings out to Joshua, that Joshua called for all the men of Israel, and said to the chiefs of the men of war who had gone with him, "Come near, put your feet on the necks of these kings." So they came near and put their feet on their necks.

*10:24
Ps 110:5;
Is 26:5,6;
Mal 4:3

25   Joshua then said to them, "Do not fear or be dismayed! Be strong and courageous, for thus the LORD will do to all your enemies with whom you fight."

10:25
v. 8

26   So afterward Joshua struck them and put them to death, and he hanged them on five trees; and they hung on the trees until evening.

10:26
Josh 8:29

27   And it came about at sunset that Joshua commanded, and they took them down from the trees and threw them into the cave where they had hidden themselves, and put large stones over the mouth of the cave, to this very day.

10:27
Deut 21:23;
Josh 8:9

2. The conquest completed

28   Now Joshua captured Makkedah on that day, and struck it and its king with the edge of the sword; he utterly destroyed it and every [8]person who was in it. He

10:28
Deut 20:16;
Josh 6:21

[8]Lit., *soul*, and so throughout this context

10:13 *the sun stood still.* This has been understood by some to be a figure of speech, by others as evidence of a miracle. It is not a case of whether God could have performed a miracle, but rather whether Scripture teaches that He did so on this occasion. Some hold that vv. 7–18 give the historical happenings, and vv. 12–14 the poetic interpretation from the book of Jasher. Others hold that vv. 12–14 must be

taken literally.
10:15 This verse, identical with 10:43, is out of place here. A return to Gilgal is incongruous because v. 16 continues the story about the five kings. Had Joshua returned, the kings would not have had to hide in a cave.
10:24 *feet on the necks.* This action, symbolic of victory, is illustrated many times in Egyptian and Assyrian sculptures.

left no survivor. Thus he did to the king of Makkedah just as he had done to the king of Jericho.

29 Then Joshua and all Israel with him passed on from Makkedah to Libnah, and fought against Libnah.

30 And the LORD gave it also with its king into the hands of Israel, and he struck it and every person who *was* in it with the edge of the sword. He left no survivor in it. Thus he did to its king just as he had done to the king of Jericho.

31 And Joshua and all Israel with him passed on from Libnah to Lachish, and they camped by it and fought against it.

32 And the LORD gave Lachish into the hands of Israel; and he captured it on the second day, and struck it and every person who *was* in it with the edge of the sword, according to all that he had done to Libnah.

33 Then Horam king of Gezer came up to help Lachish, and Joshua defeated him and his people until he had left him no survivor.

34 And Joshua and all Israel with him passed on from Lachish to Eglon, and they camped by it and fought against it.

35 And they captured it on that day and struck it with the edge of the sword; and he utterly destroyed that day every person who *was* in it, according to all that he had done to Lachish.

36 Then Joshua and all Israel with him went up from Eglon to Hebron, and they fought against it.

37 And they captured it and struck it and its king and all its cities and all the persons who *were* in it with the edge of the sword. He left no survivor, according to all that he had done to Eglon. And he utterly destroyed it and every person who *was* in it.

38 Then Joshua and all Israel with him returned to Debir, and they fought against it.

39 And he captured it and its king and all its cities, and they struck them with the edge of the sword, and utterly destroyed every person *who was* in it. He left no survivor. Just as he had done to Hebron, so he did to Debir and its king, as he had also done to Libnah and its king.

40 Thus Joshua struck all the land, the hill country and the ⁹Negev and the lowland and the slopes and all their kings. He left no survivor, but he utterly destroyed all who breathed, just as the LORD, the God of Israel, had commanded.

41 And Joshua struck them from Kadesh-barnea even as far as Gaza, and all the country of Goshen even as far as Gibeon.

42 And Joshua captured all these kings and their lands at one time, because the LORD, the God of Israel, fought for Israel.

43 So Joshua and all Israel with him returned to the camp at Gilgal.

I. The conquest of northern Canaan

11 Then it came about, when Jabin king of Hazor heard *of it*, that he sent to Jobab king of Madon and to the king of Shimron and to the king of Achshaph,

2 and to the kings who were of the north in the hill country, and in the Arabah—south of ¹⁰Chinneroth and in the lowland and on the heights of Dor on the west—

3 to the Canaanite on the east and on the west, and the Amorite and the Hittite and the Perizzite and the Jebusite in the hill country, and the Hivite at the foot of Hermon in the land of Mizpeh.

4 And they came out, they and all their armies with them, *as* many people *as* the sand that is on the seashore, with very many horses and chariots.

5 So all of these kings having agreed to meet, came and encamped together at the waters of Merom, to fight against Israel.

6 Then the LORD said to Joshua, "Do not be afraid because of them, for

⁹I.e., South country   ¹⁰I.e., Sea of Galilee

Marginal references (left column):

10:29
1 Chr 6:57

10:31
2 Kin 14:19

10:36
Josh 14:13;
15:13;
Judg 1:10

10:38
Josh 15:15;
Judg 1:11

*10:40
Deut 1:7;
7:24; 20:16,
17

*10:41
Josh 11:16;
15:51
10:42
v. 14

11:1
v. 10

11:2
Josh 12:3ff

11:4
Judg 7:12

11:6
Josh 10:8;
2 Sam 8:4

10:37 *its king,* the king of Hebron. He must have been a recent claimant or successor to the throne because the king of Hebron was one of the five kings slain by Joshua (10:26). **10:40** This all-inclusive statement, like those in 11:16–19; 21:44–45, applies only to the enemies whom Joshua defeated in certain areas. Judg. 1:27–33 states that there were a number of Canaanite cities that the Israelites did not capture and destroy. In fact, some did not fall until the time of David and Solomon. These statements must be understood in terms of extent. Joshua had general control over the whole land, even though there were islands of resistance. **10:41** *Goshen,* not the Goshen in Egypt.

tomorrow at this time I will deliver all of them slain before Israel; you shall hamstring their horses and burn their chariots with fire."

7   So Joshua and all the people of war with him came upon them suddenly by the waters of Merom, and attacked them.

8   And the LORD delivered them into the hand of Israel, so that they defeated them, and pursued them as far as Great Sidon and Misrephoth-maim and the valley of Mizpeh to the east; and they struck them until no survivor was left to them.

9   And Joshua did to them as the LORD had told him; he hamstrung their horses, and burned their chariots with fire.

10   Then Joshua turned back at that time, and captured Hazor and struck its king with the sword; for Hazor formerly was the head of all these kingdoms.

11   And they struck every person who was in it with the edge of the sword, utterly destroying *them;* there was no one left who breathed. And he burned Hazor with fire.

12   And Joshua captured all the cities of these kings, and all their kings, and he struck them with the edge of the sword, *and* utterly destroyed them; just as Moses the servant of the LORD had commanded.

13   However, Israel did not burn any cities that stood on their mounds, except Hazor alone, *which* Joshua burned.

14   And all the spoil of these cities and the cattle, the sons of Israel took as their plunder; but they struck every man with the edge of the sword, until they had destroyed them. They left no one who breathed.

15   Just as the LORD had commanded Moses his servant, so Moses commanded Joshua, and so Joshua did; he left nothing undone of all that the LORD had commanded Moses.

J. Summary of the conquests

16   Thus Joshua took all that land: the hill country and all the Negev, all that land of Goshen, the lowland, the Arabah, the hill country of Israel and its lowland

17   from Mount Halak, that rises toward Seir, even as far as Baal-gad in the valley of Lebanon at the foot of Mount Hermon. And he captured all their kings and struck them down and put them to death.

18   Joshua waged war a long time with all these kings.

19   There was not a city which made peace with the sons of Israel except the Hivites living in Gibeon; they took them all in battle.

20   For it was of the LORD to harden their hearts, to meet Israel in battle in order that he might utterly destroy them, that they might receive no mercy, but that he might destroy them, just as the LORD had commanded Moses.

21   Then Joshua came at that time and cut off the Anakim from the hill country, from Hebron, from Debir, from Anab and from all the hill country of Judah and from all the hill country of Israel. Joshua utterly destroyed them with their cities.

22   There were no Anakim left in the land of the sons of Israel; only in Gaza, in Gath, and in Ashdod some remained.

23   So Joshua took the whole land, according to all that the LORD had spoken to Moses, and Joshua gave it for an inheritance to Israel according to their divisions by their tribes. Thus the land had rest from war.

K. The list of conquered kings

1. *The kings of east Canaan*

12 Now these are the kings of the land whom the sons of Israel defeated, and whose land they possessed beyond the Jordan toward the sunrise, from the valley of the Arnon as far as Mount Hermon, and all the Arabah to the east:

2   Sihon king of the Amorites, who lived in Heshbon, *and* ruled from Aroer, which is on the edge of the valley of the Arnon, both the middle of the valley and half of Gilead, even as far as the brook Jabbok, the border of the sons of Ammon;

3   and the Arabah as far as the Sea of [11]Chinneroth toward the east, and as far as the sea of the Arabah, *even* the Salt Sea, eastward toward Beth-jeshimoth, and on the south, at the foot of the slopes of Pisgah;

4   and the territory of Og king of Bashan, one of the remnant of Rephaim, who lived at Ashtaroth and at Edrei,

Marginal references:

11:8 — Josh 13:6

11:9 — v. 6

11:11 — Deut 20:16, 17

11:14 — Num 31:11, 12

11:15 — Ex 34:11,12; Deut 7:2; Josh 1:7

11:16 — Josh 10:40, 41; v. 2

11:17 — Josh 12:7; Deut 7:24

11:19 — Josh 9:3,7

11:20 — Deut 2:30; Rom 9:18; Deut 20:16, 17

11:21 — Num 13:33; Deut 9:2

11:23 — Num 34:2ff

12:1 — Deut 3:8,9

12:2 — Deut 2:33,36

12:3 — Josh 11:2; 13:20

12:4 — Deut 3:11

[11]I.e., Galilee

12:5
Deut 3:8ff

5 and ruled over Mount Hermon and Salecah and all Bashan, as far as the border of the Geshurites and the Maacathites, and half of Gilead, *as far as* the border of Sihon king of Heshbon.

12:6
Num 21:24,
33; 32:29,33

6 Moses the servant of the LORD and the sons of Israel defeated them; and Moses the servant of the LORD gave it to the Reubenites and the Gadites, and the half-tribe of Manasseh as a possession.

2. The kings of west Canaan

12:7
Josh 11:17,23

7 Now these are the kings of the land whom Joshua and the sons of Israel defeated beyond the Jordan toward the west, from Baal-gad in the valley of Lebanon even as far as Mount Halak, which rises toward Seir; and Joshua gave it to the tribes of Israel as a possession according to their divisions,

12:8
Josh 11:16

8 in the hill country, in the lowland, in the Arabah, on the slopes, and in the wilderness, and in the Negev; the Hittite, the Amorite and the Canaanite, the Perizzite, the Hivite and the Jebusite:

*12:9ff
Josh 6:2; 8:29

9 the king of Jericho, one; the king of Ai, which is beside Bethel, one;
10 the king of Jerusalem, one; the king of Hebron, one;
11 the king of Jarmuth, one; the king of Lachish, one;

12:12
Josh 10:33
12:13
Josh 10:38

12 the king of Eglon, one; the king of Gezer, one;
13 the king of Debir, one; the king of Geder, one;
14 the king of Hormah, one; the king of Arad, one;
15 the king of Libnah, one; the king of Adullam, one;
16 the king of Makkedah, one; the king of Bethel, one;
17 the king of Tappuah, one; the king of Hepher, one;
18 the king of Aphek, one; the king of Lasharon, one;
19 the king of Madon, one; the king of Hazor, one;
20 the king of Shimron-meron, one; the king of Achshaph, one;
21 the king of Taanach, one; the king of Megiddo, one;
22 the king of Kedesh, one; the king of Jokneam in Carmel, one;
23 the king of Dor in the heights of Dor, one; the king of Goiim in Gilgal, one;

12:24
Deut 7:24

24 the king of Tirzah, one: in all, thirty-one kings.

II. The partition of the Promised Land (13:1–21:45)

A. The command to divide the land

*13:1
Josh 14:10

13 Now Joshua was old *and* advanced in years when the LORD said to him, "You are old *and* advanced in years, and very much of the land remains to be possessed.
2 "This is the land that remains: all the regions *of* the Philistines and all *those of* the Geshurites;

13:3
Judg 3:3;
Deut 2:23

3 from the Shihor which is east of Egypt, even as far as the border of Ekron to the north (it is counted as Canaanite); the five lords of the Philistines: the Gazite, the Ashdodite, the Ashkelonite, the Gittite, the Ekronite; and the Avvite
4 to the south, all the land of the Canaanite, and Mearah that belongs to the Sidonians, as far as Aphek, to the border of the Amorite;
5 and the land of the Gebalite, and all of Lebanon, toward the east, from Baal-gad below Mount Hermon as far as Lebo-hamath.

13:6
Josh 11:8

6 "All the inhabitants of the hill country from Lebanon as far as Misrephoth-maim, all the Sidonians, I will drive them out from before the sons of Israel; only allot it to Israel for an inheritance as I have commanded you.
7 "Now therefore, apportion this land for an inheritance to the nine tribes, and the half-tribe of Manasseh."

B. The division of east Canaan

1. The boundaries

13:8
Josh 12:1-6

8 With the other half-tribe, the Reubenites and the Gadites received their inheritance which Moses gave them beyond the Jordan to the east, just as Moses the servant of the LORD gave to them;

13:9
v. 16

9 from Aroer, which is on the edge of the valley of the Arnon, with the city which is in the middle of the valley, and all the plain of Medeba, as far as Dibon;

12:9–24 Compare this with Judg. 1:27–29.   **13:1** Beginning the second half of Joshua.

10   and all the cities of Sihon king of the Amorites, who reigned in Heshbon, as far as the border of the sons of Ammon;

11   and Gilead, and the territory of the Geshurites and Maacathites, and all Mount Hermon, and all Bashan as far as Salecah;

12   all the kingdom of Og in Bashan, who reigned in Ashtaroth and in Edrei (he alone was left of the remnant of the Rephaim); for Moses struck them and dispossessed them.

13   But the sons of Israel did not dispossess the Geshurites or the Maacathites; for Geshur and Maacath live among Israel until this day.

14   Only to the tribe of Levi he did not give an inheritance; the offerings by fire to the LORD, the God of Israel, are their inheritance, as He spoke to him.

2. Inheritance of the Reubenites

15   So Moses gave an inheritance to the tribe of the sons of Reuben according to their families.

16   And their territory was from Aroer, which is on the edge of the valley of the Arnon, with the city which is in the middle of the valley and all the plain by Medeba;

17   Heshbon, and all its cities which are on the plain: Dibon and Bamoth-baal and Beth-baal-meon,

18   and Jahaz and Kedemoth and Mephaath,

19   and Kiriathaim and Sibmah and Zereth-shahar on the hill of the valley,

20   and Beth-peor and the slopes of Pisgah and Beth-jeshimoth,

21   even all the cities of the plain and all the kingdom of Sihon king of the Amorites who reigned in Heshbon, whom Moses struck with the chiefs of Midian, Evi and Rekem and Zur and Hur and Reba, the princes of Sihon, who lived in the land.

22   The sons of Israel also killed Balaam the son of Beor, the diviner, with the sword among the rest of their slain.

23   And the border of the sons of Reuben was the Jordan. This was the inheritance of the sons of Reuben according to their families, the cities and their villages.

3. Inheritance of the Gadites

24   Moses also gave an inheritance to the tribe of Gad, to the sons of Gad, according to their families.

25   And their territory was Jazer, and all the cities of Gilead, and half the land of the sons of Ammon, as far as Aroer which is before Rabbah;

26   and from Heshbon as far as Ramath-mizpeh and Betonim, and from Mahanaim as far as the border of Debir;

27   and in the valley, Beth-haram and Beth-nimrah and Succoth and Zaphon, the rest of the kingdom of Sihon king of Heshbon, with the Jordan as a border, as far as the lower end of the Sea of Chinnereth beyond the Jordan to the east.

28   This is the inheritance of the sons of Gad according to their families, the cities and their villages.

4. Inheritance of the half-tribe of Manasseh

29   Moses also gave an inheritance to the half-tribe of Manasseh; and it was for the half-tribe of the sons of Manasseh according to their families.

30   And their territory was from Mahanaim, all Bashan, all the kingdom of Og king of Bashan, and all the towns of Jair, which are in Bashan, sixty cities;

31   also half of Gilead, with Ashtaroth and Edrei, the cities of the kingdom of Og in Bashan, were for the sons of Machir the son of Manasseh, for half of the sons of Machir according to their families.

32   These are the territories which Moses apportioned for an inheritance in the plains of Moab, beyond the Jordan at Jericho to the east.

33   But to the tribe of Levi, Moses did not give an inheritance; the LORD, the God of Israel, is their inheritance, as He had promised to them.

C. The division of west Canaan

1. *Introduction*

14:1
Num 34:17,
18

14 Now these are *the territories* which the sons of Israel inherited in the land of Canaan, which Eleazar the priest, and Joshua the son of Nun, and the heads of the households of the tribes of the sons of Israel apportioned to them for an inheritance,

14:2
Num 26:55

2 by the lot of their inheritance, as the LORD commanded through Moses, for the nine tribes and the half-tribe.

14:3
Num 32:33;
Josh 13:14
14:4
Gen 48:5

3 For Moses had given the inheritance of the two tribes and the half-tribe beyond the Jordan; but he did not give an inheritance to the Levites among them.

4 For the sons of Joseph were two tribes, Manasseh and Ephraim, and they did not give a portion to the Levites in the land, except cities to live in, with their pasture lands for their livestock and for their property.

5 Thus the sons of Israel did just as the LORD had commanded Moses, and they divided the land.

2. *Caleb receives Hebron*

14:6
Num 13:6,26,
30; 14:6,24,
30

6 Then the sons of Judah drew near to Joshua in Gilgal, and Caleb the son of Jephunneh the Kenizzite said to him, "You know the word which the LORD spoke to Moses the man of God concerning you and me in Kadesh-barnea.

14:7
Num 13:6;
14:6

7 "I was forty years old when Moses the servant of the LORD sent me from Kadesh-barnea to spy out the land, and I brought word back to him as *it was* in my heart.

14:8
Num 13:31,
32; 14:24
14:9
Deut 1:36

8 "Nevertheless my brethren who went up with me made the heart of the people melt with fear; but I followed the LORD my God fully.

9 "So Moses swore on that day, saying, 'Surely the land on which your foot has trodden shall be an inheritance to you and to your children forever, because you have followed the LORD my God fully.'

14:10
Num 14:30

10 "And now behold, the LORD has let me live, just as He spoke, these forty-five years, from the time that the LORD spoke this word to Moses, when Israel walked in the wilderness; and now behold, I am eighty-five years old today.

11 "I am still as strong today as I was in the day Moses sent me; as my strength was then, so my strength is now, for war and for going out and coming in.

14:12
Num 13:33

12 "Now then, give me this hill country about which the LORD spoke on that day, for you heard on that day that Anakim *were* there, with great fortified cities; perhaps the LORD will be with me, and I shall drive them out as the LORD has spoken."

13 So Joshua blessed him, and gave Hebron to Caleb the son of Jephunneh for an inheritance.

14:14
Josh 22:6;
vv. 8,9
14:15
Josh 11:23

14 Therefore, Hebron became the inheritance of Caleb the son of Jephunneh the Kenizzite until this day, because he followed the LORD God of Israel fully.

15 Now the name of Hebron was formerly Kiriath-arba; *for Arba* was the greatest man among the Anakim. Then the land had rest from war.

3. *The inheritance of Judah*

a. *The boundaries of Judah*

15:1
Num 34:3,4;
33:36

15 Now the lot for the tribe of the sons of Judah according to their families reached the border of Edom, southward to the wilderness of Zin at the extreme south.

2 And their south border was from the lower end of the Salt Sea, from the bay that turns to the south.

15:3
Num 34:4

3 Then it proceeded southward to the ascent of Akrabbim and continued to Zin, then went up by the south of Kadesh-barnea and continued to Hezron, and went up to Addar and turned about to Karka.

15:4
Num 34:5

4 And it continued to Azmon and proceeded to the brook of Egypt; and the border ended at the sea. This shall be your south border.

5 And the east border *was* the Salt Sea, as far as the mouth of the Jordan. And the border of the north side was from the bay of the sea at the mouth of the Jordan.

15:6
Josh 18:17,19
15:7
Josh 7:24

6 Then the border went up to Beth-hoglah, and continued on the north of Beth-arabah, and the border went up to the stone of Bohan the son of Reuben.

7 And the border went up to Debir from the valley of Achor, and turned

northward toward Gilgal which is opposite the ascent of Adummim, which is on the south of the valley; and the border continued to the waters of En-shemesh, and it ended at En-rogel.

8   Then the border went up the valley of Ben-hinnom to the slope of the Jebusite on the south (that is, Jerusalem); and the border went up to the top of the mountain which is before the valley of Hinnom to the west, which is at the end of the valley of Rephaim toward the north.   `15:8 v. 63`

9   And from the top of the mountain the border curved to the spring of the waters of Nephtoah and proceeded to the cities of Mount Ephron, then the border curved to Baalah (that is, Kiriath-jearim).   `15:9 Josh 18:15`

10   And the border turned about from Baalah westward to Mount Seir, and continued to the slope of Mount Jearim on the north (that is, Chesalon), and went down to Beth-shemesh and continued through Timnah.   `15:10 Judg 14:1`

11   And the border proceeded to the side of Ekron northward. Then the border curved to Shikkeron and continued to Mount Baalah and proceeded to Jabneel, and the border ended at the sea.

12   And the west border *was* at the Great Sea, even *its* coastline. This is the border around the sons of Judah according to their families.   `15:12 v. 47`

b. Caleb's inheritance

13   Now he gave to Caleb the son of Jephunneh a portion among the sons of Judah, according to the command of the LORD to Joshua, *namely*, Kiriath-arba, *Arba being* the father of Anak (that is, Hebron).   `15:13 John 14:13-15`

14   And Caleb drove out from there the three sons of Anak: Sheshai and Ahiman and Talmai, the children of Anak.   `15:14 Josh 11:21, 22; Num 13:22`

15   Then he went up from there against the inhabitants of Debir; now the name of Debir formerly was Kiriath-sepher.   `15:15 Josh 10:38`

16   And Caleb said, "The one who attacks Kiriath-sepher and captures it, I will give him Achsah my daughter as a wife."   `15:16 Judg 1:12,13; 3:9`

17   And Othniel the son of Kenaz, the brother of Caleb, captured it; so he gave him Achsah his daughter as a wife.

18   And it came about that when she came *to him*, she persuaded him to ask her father for a field. So she alighted from the donkey, and Caleb said to her, "What do you want?"   `15:18 Judg 1:14`

19   Then she said, "Give me a blessing; since you have given me the land of the Negev, give me also springs of water." So he gave her the upper springs and the lower springs.

c. The cities of Judah

20   This is the inheritance of the tribe of the sons of Judah according to their families.

21   Now the cities at the extremity of the tribe of the sons of Judah toward the border of Edom in the south were Kabzeel and Eder and Jagur,

22   and Kinah and Dimonah and Adadah,

23   and Kedesh and Hazor and Ithnan,

24   Ziph and Telem and Bealoth,

25   and Hazor-hadattah and Kerioth-hezron (that is, Hazor),

26   Amam and Shema and Moladah,

27   and Hazar-gaddah and Heshmon and Beth-pelet,

28   and Hazar-shual and Beersheba and Biziothiah,   `15:28 Gen 21:31`

29   Baalah and Iim and Ezem,

30   and Eltolad and Chesil and Hormah,

31   and Ziklag and Madmannah and Sansannah,   `15:31 1 Sam 27:6`

32   and Lebaoth and Shilhim and Ain and Rimmon; in all, twenty-nine cities with their villages.

33   In the lowland: Eshtaol and Zorah and Ashnah,   `15:33 Judg 13:25; 16:31`

34   and Zanoah and En-gannim, Tappuah and Enam,

35   Jarmuth and Adullam, Socoh and Azekah,   `15:35 1 Sam 22:1`

36   and Shaaraim and Adithaim and Gederah and Gederothaim; fourteen cities with their villages.

15:32 *twenty-nine cities with their villages.* Thirty-six are listed in vv. 21–32. Presumably, names were added sometime in the process of transmission. Similarly, v. 36 says *fourteen cities with their villages,* whereas fifteen are recorded in vv. 33–36.

15:38
2 Kin 14:7
15:39
Josh 10:3;
2 Kin 14:19

37 Zenan and Hadashah and Migdal-gad,
38 and Dilean and Mizpeh and Joktheel,
39 Lachish and Bozkath and Eglon,
40 and Cabbon and Lahmas and Chitlish,
41 and Gederoth, Beth-dagon and Naamah and Makkedah; sixteen cities with their villages.
42 Libnah and Ether and Ashan,
43 and Iphtah and Ashnah and Nezib,
44 and Keilah and Achzib and Mareshah; nine cities with their villages.
45 Ekron, with its towns and its villages;
46 from Ekron even to the sea, all that were by the side of Ashdod, with their villages.

15:47
v. 4;
Num 34:6

47 Ashdod, its towns and its villages; Gaza, its towns and its villages; as far as the brook of Egypt and the Great Sea, even *its* coastline.
48 And in the hill country: Shamir and Jattir and Socoh,
49 and Dannah and Kiriath-sannah (that is, Debir),
50 and Anab and Eshtemoh and Anim,
51 and Goshen and Holon and Giloh; eleven cities with their villages.

15:51
Josh 10:41;
11:16

52 Arab and Dumah and Eshan,
53 and Janum and Beth-tappuah and Aphekah,
54 and Humtah and Kiriath-arba (that is, Hebron), and Zior; nine cities with their villages.
55 Maon, Carmel and Ziph and Juttah,
56 and Jezreel and Jokdeam and Zanoah,
57 Kain, Gibeah and Timnah; ten cities with their villages.
58 Halhul, Beth-zur and Gedor,
59 and Maarath and Beth-anoth and Eltekon; six cities with their villages.

15:60
Josh 18:14

60 Kiriath-baal (that is, Kiriath-jearim), and Rabbah; two cities with their villages.
61 In the wilderness: Beth-arabah, Middin and Secacah,
62 and Nibshan and the City of Salt and Engedi; six cities with their villages.

15:63
Judg 1:21;
2 Sam 5:6

63 Now as for the Jebusites, the inhabitants of Jerusalem, the sons of Judah could not drive them out; so the Jebusites live with the sons of Judah at Jerusalem until this day.

4. *The inheritance of Joseph*

a. *The general boundaries*

16:1
Josh 18:12

16 Then the lot for the sons of Joseph went from the Jordan at Jericho to the waters of Jericho on the east into the wilderness, going up from Jericho through the hill country to Bethel.

16:2
Josh 18:13

2 And it went from Bethel to Luz, and continued to the border of the Archites at Ataroth.

16:3
Josh 18:13;
2 Chr 8:5

3 And it went down westward to the territory of the Japhletites, as far as the territory of lower Beth-horon even to Gezer, and it ended at the sea.
4 And the sons of Joseph, Manasseh and Ephraim, received their inheritance.

b. *The territory of the Ephraimites*

16:5
Josh 18:13

5 Now *this* was the territory of the sons of Ephraim according to their families: the border of their inheritance eastward was Ataroth-addar, as far as upper Beth-horon.

16:6
Josh 17:7

6 Then the border went westward at Michmethath on the north, and the border turned about eastward to Taanath-shiloh, and continued *beyond* it to the east of Janoah.

16:7
1 Chr 7:28

7 And it went down from Janoah to Ataroth and to Naarah, then reached Jericho and came out at the Jordan.

16:8
Josh 17:8,9

8 From Tappuah the border continued westward to the brook of Kanah, and it ended at the sea. This is the inheritance of the tribe of the sons of Ephraim according to their families,
9 *together* with the cities which were set apart for the sons of Ephraim in the midst of the inheritance of the sons of Manasseh, all the cities with their villages.

15:62 *City of Salt*, probably the ancient name for Qumran, where the Dead Sea Scrolls were found. These scrolls are   also known as the Qumran manuscripts.

10   But they did not drive out the Canaanites who lived in Gezer, so the Canaanites live in the midst of Ephraim to this day, and they became forced laborers.

c. The allotment to the half-tribe of Manasseh

17 Now *this* was the lot for the tribe of Manasseh, for he was the first-born of Joseph. To Machir the first-born of Manasseh, the father of Gilead, was allotted Gilead and Bashan, because he was a man of war.

2   So *the lot* was *made* for the rest of the sons of Manasseh according to their families: for the sons of Abiezer and for the sons of Helek and for the sons of Asriel and for the sons of Shechem and for the sons of Hepher and for the sons of Shemida; these *were* the male *descendants* of Manasseh the son of Joseph according to their families.

3   However, Zelophehad, the son of Hepher, the son of Gilead, the son of Machir, the son of Manasseh, had no sons, only daughters; and these are the names of his daughters: Mahlah and Noah, Hoglah, Milcah and Tirzah.

4   And they came near before Eleazar the priest and before Joshua the son of Nun and before the leaders, saying, "The LORD commanded Moses to give us an inheritance among our brothers." So according to the command of the LORD he gave them an inheritance among their father's brothers.

5   Thus there fell ten portions to Manasseh, besides the land of Gilead and Bashan, which is beyond the Jordan,

6   because the daughters of Manasseh received an inheritance among his sons. And the land of Gilead belonged to the rest of the sons of Manasseh.

7   And the border of Manasseh ran from Asher to Michmethath which was east of Shechem; then the border went southward to the inhabitants of En-tappuah.

8   The land of Tappuah belonged to Manasseh, but Tappuah on the border of Manasseh *belonged* to the sons of Ephraim.

9   And the border went down to the brook of Kanah, southward of the brook (these cities *belonged* to Ephraim among the cities of Manasseh), and the border of Manasseh *was* on the north side of the brook, and it ended at the sea.

10   The south side *belonged* to Ephraim and the north side to Manasseh, and the sea was their border; and they reached to Asher on the north and to Issachar on the east.

11   And in Issachar and in Asher, Manasseh had Beth-shean and its towns and Ibleam and its towns, and the inhabitants of Dor and its towns, and the inhabitants of En-dor and its towns, and the inhabitants of Taanach and its towns, and the inhabitants of Megiddo and its towns, the third is Napheth.

12   But the sons of Manasseh could not take possession of these cities, because the Canaanites persisted in living in that land.

13   And it came about when the sons of Israel became strong, they put the Canaanites to forced labor, but they did not drive them out completely.

d. The complaint of the tribe of Joseph

14   Then the sons of Joseph spoke to Joshua, saying, "Why have you given me only one lot and one portion for an inheritance, since I am a numerous people whom the LORD has thus far blessed?"

15   And Joshua said to them, "If you are a numerous people, go up to the forest and clear a place for yourself there in the land of the Perizzites and of the Rephaim, since the hill country of Ephraim is too narrow for you."

16   And the sons of Joseph said, "The hill country is not enough for us, and all the Canaanites who live in the valley land have chariots of iron, both those who are in Beth-shean and its towns, and those who are in the valley of Jezreel."

17   And Joshua spoke to the house of Joseph, to Ephraim and Manasseh, saying, "You are a numerous people and have great power; you shall not have one lot *only,*

18   but the hill country shall be yours. For though it is a forest, you shall clear it, and to its farthest borders it shall be yours; for you shall drive out the Canaanites, even though they have chariots of iron *and* though they are strong."

16:10
Judg 1:29;
1 Kin 9:16;
Josh 17:12,13

17:1
Gen 41:41;
50:23;
Deut 3:15

17:2
Num 26:29-32

17:3
Num 26:33;
27:1-7

17:4
Num 27:5-7

17:6
Josh 13:30,31

17:7
Josh 16:6

17:8
Josh 16:8

17:9
Josh 16:8,9

17:11
1 Chr 7:29

17:12
Judg 1:27,28

17:13
Josh 16:10

17:14
Num 26:34,
37

17:16
Judg 1:19;
4:3

5. *The division of the remaining land*

a. *The land survey: casting the lot*

18 Then the whole congregation of the sons of Israel assembled themselves at Shiloh, and set up the tent of meeting there; and the land was subdued before them.

2   And there remained among the sons of Israel seven tribes who had not divided their inheritance.

3   So Joshua said to the sons of Israel, "How long will you put off entering to take possession of the land which the LORD, the God of your fathers, has given you?

4   "Provide for yourselves three men from each tribe that I may send them, and that they may arise and walk through the land and write a description of it according to their inheritance; then they shall return to me.

5   "And they shall divide it into seven portions; Judah shall stay in its territory on the south, and the house of Joseph shall stay in their territory on the north.

6   "And you shall describe the land in seven divisions, and bring *the description* here to me. And I will cast lots for you here before the LORD our God.

7   "For the Levites have no portion among you, because the priesthood of the LORD is their inheritance. Gad and Reuben and the half-tribe of Manasseh also have received their inheritance eastward beyond the Jordan, which Moses the servant of the LORD gave them."

8   Then the men arose and went, and Joshua commanded those who went to describe the land, saying, "Go and walk through the land and describe it, and return to me; then I will cast lots for you here before the LORD in Shiloh."

9   So the men went and passed through the land, and described it by cities in seven divisions in a book; and they came to Joshua to the camp at Shiloh.

10   And Joshua cast lots for them in Shiloh before the LORD, and there Joshua divided the land to the sons of Israel according to their divisions.

b. *The inheritance of Benjamin*

11   Now the lot of the tribe of the sons of Benjamin came up according to their families, and the territory of their lot lay between the sons of Judah and the sons of Joseph.

12   And their border on the north side was from the Jordan, then the border went up to the side of Jericho on the north, and went up through the hill country westward; and [12]it ended at the wilderness of Beth-aven.

13   And from there the border continued to Luz, to the side of Luz (that is, Bethel) southward; and the border went down to Ataroth-addar, near the hill which *lies* on the south of lower Beth-horon.

14   And the border extended *from there,* and turned round on the west side southward, from the hill which *lies* before Beth-horon southward; and [12]it ended at Kiriath-baal (that is, Kiriath-jearim), a city of the sons of Judah. This *was* the west side.

15   Then the south side *was* from the edge of Kiriath-jearim, and the border went westward and went to the fountain of the waters of Nephtoah.

16   And the border went down to the edge of the hill which is in the valley of Ben-hinnom, which is in the valley of Rephaim northward; and it went down to the valley of Hinnom, to the slope of the Jebusite southward, and went down to En-rogel.

17   And it extended northward and went to En-shemesh and went to Geliloth, which is opposite the ascent of Adummim, and it went down to the stone of Bohan the son of Reuben.

18   And it continued to the side in front of the Arabah northward, and went down to the Arabah.

19   And the border continued to the side of Beth-hoglah northward; and the [12]border ended at the north bay of the Salt Sea, at the south end of the Jordan. This *was* the south border.

20   Moreover, the Jordan was its border on the east side. This *was* the inheri-

[12]Lit., *goings out of it were*

18:1 The allotment of Canaan, begun in Gilgal, is continued at Shiloh. It is not apparent why Judah, Ephraim, and half of Manasseh should get such a large portion of the land before the remaining seven tribes were given their share.

tance of the sons of Benjamin, according to their families *and* according to its borders all around.

21   Now the cities of the tribe of the sons of Benjamin according to their families were Jericho and Beth-hoglah and Emek-keziz,

22   and Beth-arabah and Zemaraim and Bethel,

23   and Avvim and Parah and Ophrah,

24   and Chephar-ammoni and Ophni and Geba; twelve cities with their villages.

25   Gibeon and Ramah and Beeroth,

26   and Mizpeh and Chephirah and Mozah,

27   and Rekem and Irpeel and Taralah,

28   and Zelah, Haeleph and the Jebusite (that is, Jerusalem), Gibeah, Kiriath; fourteen cities with their villages. This is the inheritance of the sons of Benjamin according to their families.

18:28
Josh 15:8

c. *The inheritance of Simeon*

19 Then the second lot fell to Simeon, to the tribe of the sons of Simeon according to their families, and their inheritance was in the midst of the inheritance of the sons of Judah.

19:1
v. 9

2   So they had as their inheritance Beersheba or Sheba and Moladah,

3   and Hazar-shual and Balah and Ezem,

4   and Eltolad and Bethul and Hormah,

5   and Ziklag and Beth-marcaboth and Hazar-susah,

6   and Beth-lebaoth and Sharuhen, thirteen cities with their villages;

7   Ain, Rimmon and Ether and Ashan, four cities with their villages;

8   and all the villages which *were* around these cities as far as Baalath-beer, Ramah of the Negev. This *was* the inheritance of the tribe of the sons of Simeon according to their families.

19:5
1 Sam 30:1

9   The inheritance of the sons of Simeon *was taken* from the portion of the sons of Judah, for the share of the sons of Judah was too large for them; so the sons of Simeon received *an* inheritance in the midst of Judah's inheritance.

*19:9
v. 1

d. *The inheritance of Zebulun*

10   Now the third lot came up for the sons of Zebulun according to their families. And the territory of their inheritance was as far as Sarid.

11   Then their border went up to the west and to Maralah, it then touched Dabbesheth, and reached to the brook that is before Jokneam.

19:11
Josh 21:34

12   Then it turned from Sarid to the east toward the sunrise as far as the border of Chisloth-tabor, and it proceeded to Daberath and up to Japhia.

13   And from there it continued eastward toward the sunrise to Gath-hepher, to Eth-kazin, and it proceeded to Rimmon which stretches to Neah.

14   And the border circled around it on the north to Hannathon, and it ended at the valley of Iphtahel.

15   *Included* also *were* Kattah and Nahalal and Shimron and Idalah and Beth-lehem; twelve cities with their villages.

19:15
Mic 5:2

16   This *was* the inheritance of the sons of Zebulun according to their families, these cities with their villages.

e. *The inheritance of Issachar*

17   The fourth lot fell to Issachar, to the sons of Issachar according to their families.

19:17
2 Sam 2:9

18   And their territory was to Jezreel and *included* Chesulloth and Shunem,

19   and Hapharaim and Shion and Anaharath,

20   and Rabbith and Kishion and Ebez,

21   and Remeth and En-gannim and En-haddah and Beth-pazzez.

22   And the border reached to Tabor and Shahazumah and Beth-shemesh, and their border ended at the Jordan; sixteen cities with their villages.

23   This *was* the inheritance of the tribe of the sons of Issachar according to their families, the cities with their villages.

f. *The inheritance of Asher*

24   Now the fifth lot fell to the tribe of the sons of Asher according to their families.

19:6 The total is fourteen. (In v. 7, three.)   seldom mentioned thereafter. See note to Deut. 33:7.
19:9 The tribe of Simeon was absorbed into Judah and

25   And their territory was Helkath and Hali and Beten and Achshaph,
26   and Allammelech and Amad and Mishal; and it reached to Carmel on the west and to Shihor-libnath.
27   And it turned toward the east to Beth-dagon, and reached to Zebulun, and to the valley of Iphtahel northward to Beth-emek and Neiel; then it proceeded on north to Cabul,
19:28
Josh 11:8
28   and Ebron and Rehob and Hammon and Kanah, as far as Great Sidon.
29   And the border turned to Ramah, and to the fortified city of Tyre; then the border turned to Hosah, and it ended at the sea by the region of Achzib.
19:30
Josh 21:31
30   *Included* also *were* Ummah, and Aphek and Rehob; twenty-two cities with their villages.
31   This *was* the inheritance of the tribe of the sons of Asher according to their families, these cities with their villages.

g. *The inheritance of Naphtali*

32   The sixth lot fell to the sons of Naphtali; to the sons of Naphtali according to their families.
33   And their border was from Heleph, from the oak in Zaanannim and Adami-nekeb and Jabneel, as far as Lakkum; and it ended at the Jordan.
19:34
Deut 33:23
34   Then the border turned westward to Aznoth-tabor, and proceeded from there to Hukkok; and it reached to Zebulun on the south and touched Asher on the west, and to Judah at the Jordan toward the east.
35   And the fortified cities *were* Ziddim, Zer and Hammath, Rakkath and Chinnereth,
36   and Adamah and Ramah and Hazor,
37   and Kedesh and Edrei and En-hazor,
38   and Yiron and Migdal-el, Horem and Beth-anath and Beth-shemesh; nineteen cities with their villages.
39   This *was* the inheritance of the tribe of the sons of Naphtali according to their families, the cities with their villages.

h. *The inheritance of Dan*

40   The seventh lot fell to the tribe of the sons of Dan according to their families.
41   And the territory of their inheritance was Zorah and Eshtaol and Ir-shemesh,
19:42
Judg 1:35
42   and Shaalabbin and Aijalon and Ithlah,
43   and Elon and Timnah and Ekron,
44   and Eltekeh and Gibbethon and Baalath,
45   and Jehud and Bene-berak and Gath-rimmon,
46   and Me-jarkon and Rakkon, with the territory over against Joppa.
19:47
Judg 18:27-31
47   And the territory of the sons of Dan proceeded beyond them; for the sons of Dan went up and fought with Leshem and captured it. Then they struck it with the edge of the sword and possessed it and settled in it; and they called Leshem Dan after the name of Dan their father.
48   This *was* the inheritance of the tribe of the sons of Dan according to their families, these cities with their villages.

i. *Summary*

49   When they finished apportioning the land for inheritance by its borders, the sons of Israel gave an inheritance in their midst to Joshua the son of Nun.
19:50
Josh 24:30
50   In accordance with the command of the LORD they gave him the city for which he asked, Timnath-serah in the hill country of Ephraim. So he built the city and settled in it.
19:51
Josh 14:1;
18:1,10
51   These are the inheritances which Eleazar the priest and Joshua the son of Nun and the heads of the households of the tribes of the sons of Israel distributed by lot in Shiloh before the LORD, at the doorway of the tent of meeting. So they finished dividing the land.

6. *The six cities of refuge*

20 Then the LORD spoke to Joshua, saying,
20:2
Num 35:6-34;
Deut 4:41;
19:2
2   "Speak to the sons of Israel, saying, 'Designate the cities of refuge, of which I spoke to you through Moses,
3   that the manslayer who kills any person unintentionally, without premeditation, may flee there, and they shall become your refuge from the avenger of blood.

4 'And he shall flee to one of these cities, and shall stand at the entrance of the gate of the city and state his case in the hearing of the elders of that city; and they shall take him into the city to them and give him a place, so that he may dwell among them.

5 'Now if the avenger of blood pursues him, then they shall not deliver the manslayer into his hand, because he struck his neighbor without premeditation and did not hate him beforehand.

6 'And he shall dwell in that city until he stands before the congregation for judgment, until the death of the one who is high priest in those days. Then the manslayer shall return to his own city and to his own house, to the city from which he fled.' "

7 So they set apart Kedesh in Galilee in the hill country of Naphtali and Shechem in the hill country of Ephraim, and Kiriath-arba (that is, Hebron) in the hill country of Judah.

8 And beyond the Jordan east of Jericho, they designated Bezer in the wilderness on the plain from the tribe of Reuben, and Ramoth in Gilead from the tribe of Gad, and Golan in Bashan from the tribe of Manasseh.

9 These were the appointed cities for all the sons of Israel and for the stranger who sojourns among them, that whoever kills any person unintentionally may flee there, and not die by the hand of the avenger of blood until he stands before the congregation.

7. The Levitical cities

a. The method of distribution

21 Then the heads of households of the Levites approached Eleazar the priest and Joshua the son of Nun and the heads of households of the tribes of the sons of Israel.

2 And they spoke to them at Shiloh in the land of Canaan, saying, "The LORD commanded through Moses to give us cities to live in, with their pasture lands for our cattle."

3 So the sons of Israel gave the Levites from their inheritance these cities with their pasture lands, according to the command of the LORD.

4 Then the lot came out for the families of the Kohathites. And the sons of Aaron the priest, who were of the Levites, received thirteen cities by lot from the tribe of Judah and from the tribe of the Simeonites and from the tribe of Benjamin.

5 And the rest of the sons of Kohath received ten cities by lot from the families of the tribe of Ephraim and from the tribe of Dan and from the half-tribe of Manasseh.

6 And the sons of Gershon received thirteen cities by lot from the families of the tribe of Issachar and from the tribe of Asher and from the tribe of Naphtali and from the half-tribe of Manasseh in Bashan.

7 The sons of Merari according to their families received twelve cities from the tribe of Reuben and from the tribe of Gad and from the tribe of Zebulun.

b. The assignment of the cities

8 Now the sons of Israel gave by lot to the Levites these cities with their pasture lands, as the LORD had commanded through Moses.

9 And they gave these cities which are *here* mentioned by name from the tribe of the sons of Judah and from the tribe of the sons of Simeon;

10 and they were for the sons of Aaron, one of the families of the Kohathites, of the sons of Levi, for the lot was theirs first.

11 Thus they gave them Kiriath-arba, *Arba being* the father of Anak (that is, Hebron), in the hill country of Judah, with its surrounding pasture lands.

12 But the fields of the city and its villages, they gave to Caleb the son of Jephunneh as his possession.

13 So to the sons of Aaron the priest they gave Hebron, the city of refuge for the manslayer, with its pasture lands, and Libnah with its pasture lands,

14 and Jattir with its pasture lands and Eshtemoa with its pasture lands,

15 and Holon with its pasture lands and Debir with its pasture lands,

16 and Ain with its pasture lands and Juttah with its pasture lands *and* Beth-shemesh with its pasture lands; nine cities from these two tribes.

17 And from the tribe of Benjamin, Gibeon with its pasture lands, Geba with its pasture lands,

---

20:4
Ruth 4:1,2

20:5
Num 35:12

20:6
Num 35:25

20:7
Josh 21:32;
1 Chr 6:76;
Josh 21:11;
Luke 1:39
20:8
Josh 21:27,
36,38

20:9
Num 35:15;
v. 6

21:1
Num 35:1-8

21:2
Num 35:2

21:4
vv. 8,19

21:5
v. 20ff

21:6
v. 27ff

21:7
v. 34ff

21:8
v. 3

21:11
Josh 15:13,
14;
1 Chr 6:55

21:13
Josh 15:42,
54; 20:7;
1 Chr 6:57
21:15
Josh 15:49,
51;
1 Chr 6:58
21:16
Josh 15:10,
15;
1 Chr 6:59

21:18
1 Chr 6:60

18   Anathoth with its pasture lands and Almon with its pasture lands; four cities.

19   All the cities of the sons of Aaron, the priests, were thirteen cities with their pasture lands.

20   Then the cities from the tribe of Ephraim were allotted to the families of the sons of Kohath, the Levites, *even to* the rest of the sons of Kohath.

21:21
Josh 20:7

21   And they gave them Shechem, the city of refuge for the manslayer, with its pasture lands, in the hill country of Ephraim, and Gezer with its pasture lands,

22   and Kibzaim with its pasture lands and Beth-horon with its pasture lands; four cities.

23   And from the tribe of Dan, Elteke with its pasture lands, Gibbethon with its pasture lands,

24   Aijalon with its pasture lands, Gath-rimmon with its pasture lands; four cities.

25   And from the half-tribe of Manasseh, *they allotted* Taanach with its pasture lands and Gath-rimmon with its pasture lands; two cities.

26   All the cities with their pasture lands for the families of the rest of the sons of Kohath were ten.

21:27
v. 6

27   And to the sons of Gershon, one of the families of the Levites, from the half-tribe of Manasseh, *they gave* Golan in Bashan, the city of refuge for the manslayer, with its pasture lands, and Be-eshterah with its pasture lands; two cities.

28   And from the tribe of Issachar, *they gave* Kishion with its pasture lands, Daberath with its pasture lands,

29   Jarmuth with its pasture lands, En-gannim with its pasture lands; four cities.

30   And from the tribe of Asher, *they gave* Mishal with its pasture lands, Abdon with its pasture lands,

31   Helkath with its pasture lands and Rehob with its pasture lands; four cities.

21:32
Josh 20:7

32   And from the tribe of Naphtali, *they gave* Kedesh in Galilee, the city of refuge for the manslayer, with its pasture lands and Hammoth-dor with its pasture lands and Kartan with its pasture lands; three cities.

33   All the cities of the Gershonites according to their families were thirteen cities with their pasture lands.

21:34
v. 7

34   And to the families of the sons of Merari, the rest of the Levites, *they gave* from the tribe of Zebulun, Jokneam with its pasture lands and Kartah with its pasture lands.

35   Dimnah with its pasture lands, Nahalal with its pasture lands; four cities.

21:36
Josh 20:8

36   And from the tribe of Reuben, *they gave* Bezer with its pasture lands and Jahaz with its pasture lands,

37   Kedemoth with its pasture lands and Mephaath with its pasture lands; four cities.

38   And from the tribe of Gad, *they gave* Ramoth in Gilead, the city of refuge for the manslayer, with its pasture lands and Mahanaim with its pasture lands,

39   Heshbon with its pasture lands, Jazer with its pasture lands; four cities in all.

40   All *these were* the cities of the sons of Merari according to their families, the rest of the families of the Levites; and their lot was twelve cities.

21:41
Num 35:7

41   All the cities of the Levites in the midst of the possession of the sons of Israel were forty-eight cities with their pasture lands.

42   These cities each had its surrounding pasture lands; thus *it was* with all these cities.

8. *The fulfillment of the divine promise*

*21:43ff
Gen 13:15;
Deut 11:31
21:44
Josh 1:13;
11:23;
Deut 7:24

43   So the LORD gave Israel all the land which He had sworn to give to their fathers, and they possessed it and lived in it.

44   And the LORD gave them rest on every side, according to all that He had sworn to their fathers, and no one of all their enemies stood before them; the LORD gave all their enemies into their hand.

21:39 Heshbon, originally assigned to Reuben (13:17), is included here under Gad. This is an indication that the Reubenites, like Simeon, gradually were absorbed and lost their identity. The allotment was made, although territories remained to be possessed by individual tribes.
21:43-45 The intent of this sweeping statement is to show how the promise of 1:5 was essentially fulfilled.

45   Not one of the good promises which the LORD had made to the house of
Israel failed; all came to pass.

III. *The farewell addresses of Joshua (22:1–24:33)*

A. *The message to the two-and-one-half tribes*

1. *Joshua's blessing*

22 Then Joshua summoned the Reubenites and the Gadites and the half-tribe of
Manasseh,

2   and said to them, "You have kept all that Moses the servant of the LORD
commanded you, and have listened to my voice in all that I commanded you.

3   "You have not forsaken your brothers these many days to this day, but have
kept the charge of the commandment of the LORD your God.

4   "And now the LORD your God has given rest to your brothers, as He spoke to
them; therefore turn now and go to your tents, to the land of your possession, which
Moses the servant of the LORD gave you beyond the Jordan.

5   "Only be very careful to observe the commandment and the law which Moses
the servant of the LORD commanded you, to love the LORD your God and walk in all
His ways and keep His commandments and hold fast to Him and serve Him with all
your heart and with all your soul."

6   So Joshua blessed them and sent them away, and they went to their tents.

7   Now to the one half-tribe of Manasseh Moses had given *a possession* in
Bashan, but to the other half Joshua gave *a possession* among their brothers westward beyond the Jordan. So when Joshua sent them away to their tents, he blessed
them,

8   and said to them, "Return to your tents with great riches and with very
much livestock, with silver, gold, bronze, iron, and with very many clothes; divide
the spoil of your enemies with your brothers."

9   And the sons of Reuben and the sons of Gad and the half-tribe of Manasseh
returned *home* and departed from the sons of Israel at Shiloh which is in the land of
Canaan, to go to the land of Gilead, to the land of their possession which they had
possessed, according to the command of the LORD through Moses.

2. *The altar by the Jordan*

10   And when they came to the region of the Jordan which is in the land of
Canaan, the sons of Reuben and the sons of Gad and the half-tribe of Manasseh built
an altar there by the Jordan, a large altar in appearance.

11   And the sons of Israel heard *it* said, "Behold, the sons of Reuben and the
sons of Gad and the half-tribe of Manasseh have built an altar at the frontier of the
land of Canaan, in the region of the Jordan, on the side *belonging to* the sons of
Israel."

12   And when the sons of Israel heard *of it*, the whole congregation of the sons
of Israel gathered themselves at Shiloh, to go up against them in war.

13   Then the sons of Israel sent to the sons of Reuben and to the sons of Gad and
to the half-tribe of Manasseh, into the land of Gilead, Phinehas the son of Eleazar
the priest,

14   and with him ten chiefs, one chief for each father's household from each of
the tribes of Israel; and each one of them *was* the head of his father's household
among the thousands of Israel.

15   And they came to the sons of Reuben and to the sons of Gad and to the
half-tribe of Manasseh, to the land of Gilead, and they spoke with them saying,

16   "Thus says the whole congregation of the LORD, 'What is this unfaithful act
which you have committed against the God of Israel, turning away from following
the LORD this day, by building yourselves an altar, to rebel against the LORD this
day?

17   'Is not the iniquity of Peor enough for us, from which we have not cleansed
ourselves to this day, although a plague came on the congregation of the LORD,

18   that you must turn away this day from following the LORD? And it will come
about if you rebel against the LORD today, that He will be angry with the whole
congregation of Israel tomorrow.

19   'If, however, the land of your possession is unclean, then cross into the land
of the possession of the LORD, where the LORD's tabernacle stands, and take

---

21:45
Josh 23:14

22:2
Num 32:20

22:4
Num 32:18;
Deut 3:20

22:5
Deut 6:6,17;
10:12

22:7
Num 32:33;
Josh 17:5

22:9
Num 32:1,26,
29

22:11
v. 19

22:12
Josh 18:1

22:13
Deut 13:14;
Num 25:7

22:16
v. 11;
Deut 12:13,
14

22:17
Num 25:1-9

22:19
v. 11

possession among us. Only do not rebel against the LORD, or rebel against us by building an altar for yourselves, besides the altar of the LORD our God.

20 'Did not Achan the son of Zerah act unfaithfully in the things under the ban, and wrath fall on all the congregation of Israel? And that man did not perish alone in his iniquity.' "

21 Then the sons of Reuben and the sons of Gad and the half-tribe of Manasseh answered, and spoke to the heads of the families of Israel.

22 "The Mighty One, God, the LORD, the Mighty One, God, the LORD! He knows, and may Israel itself know. If it was in rebellion, or if in an unfaithful act against the LORD do not Thou save us this day!

23 "If we have built us an altar to turn away from following the LORD, or if to offer a burnt offering or grain offering on it, or if to offer sacrifices of peace offerings on it, may the LORD Himself require it.

24 "But truly we have done this out of concern, for a reason, saying, 'In time to come your sons may say to our sons, "What have you to do with the LORD, the God of Israel?

25 "For the LORD has made the Jordan a border between us and you, you sons of Reuben and sons of Gad; you have no portion in the LORD." So your sons may make our sons stop fearing the LORD.

26 "Therefore we said, 'Let us build an altar, not for burnt offering or for sacrifice;

27 rather it shall be a witness between us and you and between our generations after us, that we are to perform the service of the LORD before Him with our burnt offerings, and with our sacrifices and with our peace offerings, that your sons may not say to our sons in time to come, "You have no portion in the LORD." '

28 "Therefore we said, 'It shall also come about if they say this to us or to our generations in time to come, then we shall say, "See the copy of the altar of the LORD which our fathers made, not for burnt offering or for sacrifice; rather it is a witness between us and you." '

29 "Far be it from us that we should rebel against the LORD and turn away from following the LORD this day, by building an altar for burnt offering, for grain offering or for sacrifice, besides the altar of the LORD our God which is before His [13]tabernacle."

30 So when Phinehas the priest and the leaders of the congregation, even the heads of the families of Israel who were with him, heard the words which the sons of Reuben and the sons of Gad and the sons of Manasseh spoke, it pleased them.

31 And Phinehas the son of Eleazar the priest said to the sons of Reuben and to the sons of Gad and to the sons of Manasseh, "Today we know that the LORD is in our midst, because you have not committed this unfaithful act against the LORD; now you have delivered the sons of Israel from the hand of the LORD."

32 Then Phinehas the son of Eleazar the priest and the leaders returned from the sons of Reuben and from the sons of Gad, from the land of Gilead, to the land of Canaan, to the sons of Israel, and brought back word to them.

33 And the word pleased the sons of Israel, and the sons of Israel blessed God; and they did not speak of going up against them in war, to destroy the land in which the sons of Reuben and the sons of Gad were living.

34 And the sons of Reuben and the sons of Gad called the altar Witness; "For," they said, "it is a witness between us that the LORD is God."

B. Joshua's address to the nine-and-one-half tribes

23 Now it came about after many days, when the LORD had given rest to Israel from all their enemies on every side, and Joshua was old, advanced in years,

2 that Joshua called for all Israel, for their elders and their heads and their judges and their officers, and said to them, "I am old, advanced in years.

3 "And you have seen all that the LORD your God has done to all these nations because of you, for the LORD your God is He who has been fighting for you.

4 "See, I have apportioned to you these nations which remain as an inheritance for your tribes, with all the nations which I have cut off, from the Jordan even to the Great Sea toward the setting of the sun.

5 "And the LORD your God, He shall thrust them out from before you and drive

[13]Lit., dwelling place

Margin references:
22:20 Josh 7:1-26
22:22 Deut 10:17; 1 Kin 8:39
22:23 Deut 18:19; 1 Sam 20:16
22:27 Josh 24:27
22:29 Deut 12:13,14
22:31 Lev 26:11,12; 2 Chr 15:2
22:33 1 Chr 29:20
22:34 Josh 24:27
23:1 Josh 21:44; 13:1
23:2 Josh 24:1
23:3 Josh 10:14,42
23:5 Num 33:53

E. *The burial of Joseph*

32 Now they buried the bones of Joseph, which the sons of Israel brought up from Egypt, at Shechem, in the piece of ground which Jacob had bought from the sons of Hamor the father of Shechem for one hundred pieces of money; and they became the inheritance of Joseph's sons.

24:32
Gen 50:24,25;
Ex 13:19;
Gen 33:19

F. *The death and burial of Eleazar*

33 And Eleazar the son of Aaron died; and they buried him at Gibeah of Phinehas his son, which was given him in the hill country of Ephraim.

24:33
Josh 22:13

INTRODUCTION TO
THE BOOK OF
JUDGES

Authorship and Background: The title of the book in Hebrew, the Septuagint, and English derives from the Hebrew word *shophetim*, "judges," which designated the rulers who figured prominently in this period. Rabbinic tradition assigned the authorship of the book to Samuel, but there are internal indications of a later date. In any event, the author obtained his material from diverse sources, oral and written. Some of the material is ancient, such as the Song of Deborah (5:1-31), which may be dated around 1125 B.C. The statement "all the time that the house of God was at Shiloh" (18:31) implies a date after the destruction of Shiloh by the Philistines (1 Sam. 4:10-12; Jer. 7:12). A later date, somewhere during the time of the monarchy, is indicated by the notice "In those days there was no king in Israel" (17:6; 18:1; 19:1; 21:25).

The period of Judges lasted for several centuries. The chronology is related to the date chosen for the exodus. It is clear that although the various judges are discussed consecutively, few of them were supported by more than half of the tribes. In all likelihood, therefore, some of the judges ruled concurrently in different geographical areas.

Characteristics: The author of Judges reflects a philosophy of history often identified as the Deuteronomic philosophy of history, for in that book it finds its finest expression. Prosperity is due to obedience to the will of God; adversity is due to disobedience and rebellion against God. The history of Israel during the period of the Judges bears this out. When the twelve tribes are obedient to God and the covenant requirements, they have a strength and a unity that protects them from their enemies. When their loyalty to the central sanctuary at Shechem or Shiloh is dissipated by Baal worship, the tribes become isolated, disorganized units that fall easy prey to their alert foes. The book is cyclical. Apostasy leads to oppression by Israel's enemies. The oppression leads to renewal and repentance, followed by deliverance through a judge. Then apostasy sets in, followed by oppression, repentance, and again deliverance by another judge.

Contents:

I. Introduction (1:1-2:5): Efforts to finish the conquest of Canaan by Judah and Simeon. The efforts by the tribes of Benjamin and Joseph. The failure to complete the conquest in Ephraim, Zebulun, Asher, Naphtali, and Dan. A review of Israel's blessings, apostasies, disasters, and deliverances.

II. The judges of Israel (2:6-16:31): The first apostasy: servitude under Cushan-rishathaim of Mesopotamia; deliverance by Othniel of Judah. The second apostasy: servitude under Eglon of Moab; deliverance by Ehud; Shamgar. The third apostasy: servitude under Jabin the Canaanite; deliverance by Deborah and Barak. The fourth apostasy: servitude under the Midianites; deliverance by Gideon of Manasseh, to whom God grants miraculous signs and who refuses to be made king. The fifth apostasy: servitude under Abimelech, who is made king over Shechem; deliverance by Tola of Issachar and Jair of Gilead. The sixth apostasy: servitude under the Philistines; deliverance by Jephthah; Ibzan, Elon, and Abdon. The seventh apostasy: servitude under the Philistines; deliverance by Samson, a Nazirite who marries a Philistine, sins at Gaza, and reveals his strength to Delilah.

III. The appendixes (17:1-21:25): Micah sets up his own sanctuary; he secures his own priest. Some Danites remove his priest and rob his sanctuary. The expedition against Laish, which is captured and renamed Dan. Micah's idols and priests. The Levite seeks his concubine. The men of Gibeah abuse the concubine. The Levite calls for help to all Israel. Israel defeats her own tribe of Benjamin, which is nearly extinguished. The remnant of Benjamin preserved from extinction by taking wives from among the virgins of Jabesh-gilead and from dancers at one of the feasts at Shiloh.

303

THE BOOK OF

JUDGES

I. *Introduction (1:1–2:5)*

A. *Conquests by the men of Judah and Simeon*

1 Now it came about after the death of Joshua that the sons of Israel inquired of the LORD, saying, "Who shall go up first for us against the Canaanites, to fight against them?"

2 And the LORD said, "Judah shall go up; behold, I have given the land into his hand."

3 Then Judah said to Simeon his brother, "Come up with me into the territory allotted me, that we may fight against the Canaanites; and I in turn will go with you into the territory allotted you." So Simeon went with him.

4 And Judah went up, and the LORD gave the Canaanites and the Perizzites into their hands; and they defeated ten thousand men at Bezek.

5 And they found Adoni-bezek in Bezek and fought against him and they defeated the Canaanites and the Perizzites.

6 But Adoni-bezek fled; and they pursued him and caught him and cut off his thumbs and big toes.

7 And Adoni-bezek said, "Seventy kings with their thumbs and their big toes cut off used to gather up *scraps* under my table; as I have done, so God has repaid me." So they brought him to Jerusalem and he died there.

8 Then the sons of Judah fought against Jerusalem and captured it and struck it with the edge of the sword and set the city on fire.

9 And afterward the sons of Judah went down to fight against the Canaanites living in the hill country and in the ¹Negev and in the lowland.

10 So Judah went against the Canaanites who lived in Hebron (now the name of Hebron formerly *was* Kiriath-arba); and they struck Sheshai and Ahiman and Talmai.

11 Then from there he went against the inhabitants of Debir (now the name of Debir formerly *was* Kiriath-sepher).

12 And Caleb said, "The one who attacks Kiriath-sepher and captures it, I will even give him my daughter Achsah for a wife."

13 And Othniel the son of Kenaz, Caleb's younger brother, captured it; so he gave him his daughter Achsah for a wife.

14 Then it came about when she came *to him*, that she persuaded him to ask her father for a field. Then she alighted from her donkey, and Caleb said to her, "What do you want?"

15 And she said to him, "Give me a blessing, since you have given me the land of the ¹Negev, give me also springs of water." So Caleb gave her the upper springs and the lower springs.

16 And the descendants of the Kenite, Moses' father-in-law, went up from the city of palms with the sons of Judah, to the wilderness of Judah which is in the south of Arad; and they went and lived with the people.

17 Then Judah went with Simeon his brother, and they struck the Canaanites living in Zephath, and utterly destroyed it. So the name of the city was called Hormah.

18 And Judah took Gaza with its territory and Ashkelon with its territory and Ekron with its territory.

¹I.e., South country

1:1 *after the death of Joshua.* Some have felt that the accounts of the conquest of Canaan as given in Joshua and Judges are at variance since Joshua implies that Israel has achieved full possession of the promised land, while Judges describes the process as gradual and lengthy. The two accounts are supplementary rather than contradictory. Joshua did defeat strong Canaanite forces, but he did not *occupy* all of Palestine. The book of Judges fills in the picture painted in Joshua, but both books depict the conquest of Canaan as incomplete. It was left to each tribe to occupy the territories allocated to it.

19   Now the LORD was with Judah, and they took possession of the hill country; but they could not drive out the inhabitants of the valley because they had iron chariots.

20   Then they gave Hebron to Caleb, as Moses had promised; and he drove out from there the three sons of Anak.

21   But the sons of Benjamin did not drive out the Jebusites who lived in Jerusalem; so the Jebusites have lived with the sons of Benjamin in Jerusalem to this day.

B. *The incomplete conquests of Israel*

22   Likewise the house of Joseph went up against Bethel, and the LORD was with them.

23   And the house of Joseph spied out Bethel (now the name of the city was formerly Luz).

24   And the spies saw a man coming out of the city, and they said to him, "Please show us the entrance to the city and we will treat you kindly."

25   So he showed them the entrance to the city, and they struck the city with the edge of the sword, but they let the man and all his family go free.

26   And the man went into the land of the Hittites and built a city and named it Luz which is its name to this day.

27   But Manasseh did not take possession of Beth-shean and its villages, or Taanach and its villages, or the inhabitants of Dor and its villages, or the inhabitants of Ibleam and its villages, or the inhabitants of Megiddo and its villages; so the Canaanites persisted in living in that land.

28   And it came about when Israel became strong, that they put the Canaanites to forced labor, but they did not drive them out completely.

29   Neither did Ephraim drive out the Canaanites who were living in Gezer; so the Canaanites lived in Gezer among them.

30   Zebulun did not drive out the inhabitants of Kitron, or the inhabitants of Nahalol; so the Canaanites lived among them and became subject to forced labor.

31   Asher did not drive out the inhabitants of Acco, or the inhabitants of Sidon, or of Ahlab, or of Achzib, or of Helbah, or of Aphik, or of Rehob.

32   So the Asherites lived among the Canaanites, the inhabitants of the land; for they did not drive them out.

33   Naphtali did not drive out the inhabitants of Beth-shemesh, or the inhabitants of Beth-anath, but lived among the Canaanites, the inhabitants of the land; and the inhabitants of Beth-shemesh and Beth-anath became forced labor for them.

34   Then the Amorites forced the sons of Dan into the hill country, for they did not allow them to come down to the valley;

35   yet the Amorites persisted in living in Mount Heres, in Aijalon and in Shaalbim; but when the power of the house of Joseph grew strong, they became forced labor.

36   And the border of the Amorites ran from the ascent of Akrabbim, from Sela and upward.

C. *The failure of Israel to keep the covenant*

2 Now the angel of the LORD came up from Gilgal to Bochim. And he said, "I brought you up out of Egypt and led you into the land which I have sworn to your fathers; and I said, 'I will never break My covenant with you,

2   and as for you, you shall make no covenant with the inhabitants of this land; you shall tear down their altars.' But you have not obeyed Me; what is this you have done?

3   "Therefore I also said, 'I will not drive them out before you; but they shall ²become *as thorns* in your sides, and their gods shall be a snare to you.'"

²Some ancient mss. read *be adversaries, and*

Marginal references:

*1:19 v. 2; Josh 17:16,18
1:20 Josh 14:9; 15:13,14; v. 10
1:21 Josh 15:63
1:23 Gen 28:19
1:25 Josh 6:25
*1:27 Josh 17:11-13
1:29 Josh 16:10
1:31 Judg 10:6
1:34 Ex 3:17
1:36 Josh 15:3
*2:1 v. 5; Judg 6:11; Ex 20:2; Gen 17:7; Deut 7:9
2:2 Ex 23:32; 34:12,13
2:3 Josh 23:13; Judg 3:6; Deut 7:16; Ps 106:36

1:19 The Israelites, good hand-to-hand fighters, were successful against their enemies in the hill country, but they were no match for the chariots of iron in the plains, even though the LORD was with them (see 1 Kin. 20:23). Scripture sometimes describes history in terms of God's power and sometimes in terms of man's power, but God is always behind history. God is always the ultimate source of power; man is the proximate, or secondary source. In this particular case the superior military power of the enemy prevailed. **1:27** See notes to Josh. 10:40; 12:9–24. **2:1** This is obviously the Abrahamic covenant as renewed in Ex. 34:10ff. It was not completely unconditional but was dependent on personal obedience to the voice of God. The failure of Israel to drive all of the inhabitants out of the land led to disaster (vv. 2,3).

4   And it came about when the angel of the LORD spoke these words to all the sons of Israel, that the people lifted up their voices and wept.

5   So they named that place ³Bochim; and there they sacrificed to the LORD.

II. The judges of Israel (2:6–16:31)

A. The death and burial of Joshua

2:6
Josh 24:28-31

6   When Joshua had dismissed the people, the sons of Israel went each to his inheritance to possess the land.

7   And the people served the LORD all the days of Joshua, and all the days of the elders who survived Joshua, who had seen all the great work of the LORD which He had done for Israel.

8   Then Joshua the son of Nun, the servant of the LORD, died at the age of one hundred and ten.

9   And they buried him in the territory of his inheritance in Timnath-heres, in the hill country of Ephraim, north of Mount Gaash.

2:10
1 Sam 2:12;
1 Chr 28:9;
Gal 4:8

10   And all that generation also were gathered to their fathers; and there arose another generation after them who did not know the LORD, nor yet the work which He had done for Israel.

B. The apostasy of Israel

2:11
Judg 3:7,12;
4:1; 6:1,25;
8:33; 10:6
2:12
Deut 31:16

11   Then the sons of Israel did evil in the sight of the LORD, and ⁴served   the Baals,

12   and they forsook the LORD, the God of their fathers, who had brought them out of the land of Egypt, and followed other gods from *among* the gods of the peoples who were around them, and bowed themselves down to them; thus they provoked the LORD to anger.

*2:13
Judg 10:6
2:14
Judg 3:8;
Ps 106:40-42;
Deut 28:25

13   So they forsook the LORD and served Baal and the Ashtaroth.

14   And the anger of the LORD burned against Israel, and He gave them into the hands of plunderers who plundered them; and He sold them into the hands of their enemies around *them*, so that they could no longer stand before their enemies.

15   Wherever they went, the hand of the LORD was against them for evil, as the LORD had spoken and as the LORD had sworn to them, so that they were severely distressed.

C. Deliverance through judges and repeated apostasy

*2:16
Ps 106:43-45;
Acts 13:20
2:17
v. 7

16   Then the LORD raised up judges who delivered them from the hands of those who plundered them.

17   And yet they did not listen to their judges, for they played the harlot after other gods and bowed themselves down to them. They turned aside quickly from the way in which their fathers had walked in obeying the commandments of the LORD; they did not do as *their fathers*.

18   And when the LORD raised up judges for them, the LORD was with the judge and delivered them from the hand of their enemies all the days of the judge; for the LORD was moved to pity by their groaning because of those who oppressed and afflicted them.

2:19
Judg 3:12;
4:1; 8:33

19   But it came about when the judge died, that they would turn back and act more corruptly than their fathers, in following other gods to serve them and bow down to them; they did not abandon their practices or their stubborn ways.

2:20
v. 14;
Josh 23:16

20   So the anger of the LORD burned against Israel, and He said, "Because this nation has transgressed My covenant which I commanded their fathers, and has not listened to My voice,

---

³I.e., *weepers*   ⁴Or, *worshiped*

2:13 *Baal*, the singular use of the word refers to local representations of Baal, the lord of the Canaanite pantheon. *Ashtaroth* is the plural of Astarte, the Canaanite goddess of fertility and war.
2:16 After the death of Joshua, the power of Israel began to decline due to religious apostasy. The history of God's people was from that time on characterized by recurring eras of subjugation by, and deliverance from, the peoples of the land. In this period before the appointment of the prophets, when Israel went from apostasy to repentance and

back to apostasy, God provided deliverers such as Othniel, Ehud, Deborah, and Samson. These leaders were called "judges" (a term that in Hebrew implied leadership in government and war as well as in legal cases), and were raised up by God under His theocratic government. None of these judges was of a stature comparable to Moses or Joshua before them, or Samuel and David after them, and none of them had the unified support of all twelve tribes. It was a time of confusion. The description *every man did what was right in his own eyes* (17:6; 21:25) was all too true.

21 I also will no longer drive out before them any of the nations which Joshua left when he died,

22 in order to test Israel by them, whether they will keep the way of the LORD to walk in it as their fathers did, or not.''

23 So the LORD allowed those nations to remain, not driving them out quickly; and He did not give them into the hand of Joshua.

D. *The nations left to test Israel*

3 Now these are the nations which the LORD left, to test Israel by them (*that is*, all who had not experienced any of the wars of Canaan;

2 only in order that the generations of the sons of Israel might be taught war, those who had not experienced it formerly).

3 *These nations are:* the five lords of the Philistines and all the Canaanites and the Sidonians and the Hivites who lived in Mount Lebanon, from Mount Baal-hermon as far as Lebo-hamath.

4 And they were for testing Israel, to find out if they would obey the commandments of the LORD, which He had commanded their fathers through Moses.

5 And the sons of Israel lived among the Canaanites, the Hittites, the Amorites, the Perizzites, the Hivites, and the Jebusites;

6 and they took their daughters for themselves as wives, and gave their own daughters to their sons, and served their gods.

E. *The judgeship of Othniel*

7 And the sons of Israel did what was evil in the sight of the LORD, and forgot the LORD their God, and served the Baals and the [5]Asheroth.

8 Then the anger of the LORD was kindled against Israel, so that He sold them into the hands of Cushan-rishathaim king of Mesopotamia; and the sons of Israel served Cushan-rishathaim eight years.

9 And when the sons of Israel cried to the LORD, the LORD raised up a deliverer for the sons of Israel to deliver them, Othniel the son of Kenaz, Caleb's younger brother.

10 And the Spirit of the LORD came upon him, and he judged Israel. When he went out to war, the LORD gave Cushan-rishathaim king of Mesopotamia into his hand, so that he prevailed over Cushan-rishathaim.

11 Then the land had rest forty years. And Othniel the son of Kenaz died.

F. *The judgeship of Ehud*
1. *The sin of Israel: oppression by Moab*

12 Now the sons of Israel again did evil in the sight of the LORD. So the LORD strengthened Eglon the king of Moab against Israel, because they had done evil in the sight of the LORD.

13 And he gathered to himself the sons of Ammon and Amalek; and he went and defeated Israel, and they possessed the city of the palm trees.

14 And the sons of Israel served Eglon the king of Moab eighteen years.

2. *Ehud murders Eglon*

15 But when the sons of Israel cried to the LORD, the LORD raised up a deliverer for them, Ehud the son of Gera, the Benjamite, a left-handed man. And the sons of Israel sent tribute by him to Eglon the king of Moab.

16 And Ehud made himself a sword which had two edges, a cubit in length; and he bound it on his right thigh under his cloak.

17 And he presented the tribute to Eglon king of Moab. Now Eglon was a very fat man.

---

[5]I.e., wooden symbol of a female deity

2:23 *Joshua* is apparently a reference to Israel, the people led into Canaan by Joshua.
3:7 *Asheroth*, the plural of Asherah, the Canaanite mother-goddess. She, like Ashtaroth in 2:13, was prominent in the fertility rites of the Canaanites.
3:8 *Mesopotamia*, Hebrew *Aram-naharaim*, the region around Haran. Evidently Cushan-rishathaim was an Aramean prince.
3:12 After the death of Othniel, Israel reverted to apostasy. It was only after eighteen years of oppression by Eglon that Israel came to her senses and sought the help of the LORD. Then the LORD heard and delivered Israel.

Marginal references: 2:21 Josh 23:13; 2:22 Judg 3:1,4; 3:1 Judg 2:21,22; 3:3 Josh 13:3; 3:4 Deut 8:2; Judg 2:22; 3:6 Ex 34:16; Deut 7:3,4; *3:7 Judg 2:11,13; Deut 4:9; 3:9 v.15; Judg 1:13; 3:10 Num 11:25,29; 24:2; Judg 6:34; *3:12 Judg 2:11,14; 3:13 Judg 1:16; 3:15 Ps 107:13; 3:17 v.12

18   And it came about when he had finished presenting the tribute, that he sent away the people who had carried the tribute.

19   But he himself turned back from the idols which were at Gilgal, and said, "I have a secret message for you, O king." And he said, "Keep silence." And all who attended him left him.

20   And Ehud came to him while he was sitting alone in his cool roof chamber. And Ehud said, "I have a message from God for you." And he arose from his seat.

21   And Ehud stretched out his left hand, took the sword from his right thigh and thrust it into his belly.

22   The handle also went in after the blade, and the fat closed over the blade, for he did not draw the sword out of his belly; and the refuse came out.

23   Then Ehud went out into the vestibule and shut the doors of the roof chamber behind him, and locked *them*.

3. *The discovery of the murder*

3:24
1 Sam 24:3

24   When he had gone out, his servants came and looked, and behold, the doors of the roof chamber were locked; and they said, "He is only relieving himself in the cool room."

3:25
2 Kin 2:17;
8:11

25   And they waited until they became anxious; but behold, he did not open the doors of the roof chamber. Therefore they took the key and opened them, and behold, their master had fallen to the floor dead.

4. *The defeat of the Moabites*

26   Now Ehud escaped while they were delaying, and he passed by the idols and escaped to Seirah.

27   And it came about when he had arrived, that he blew the trumpet in the hill country of Ephraim; and the sons of Israel went down with him from the hill country, and he *was* in front of them.

3:28
Judg 7:9,15;
24; 12:5

28   And he said to them, "Pursue *them*, for the LORD has given your enemies the Moabites into your hands." So they went down after him and seized the fords of the Jordan opposite Moab, and did not allow anyone to cross.

29   And they struck down at that time about ten thousand Moabites, all robust and valiant men; and no one escaped.

3:30
v. 11

30   So Moab was subdued that day under the hand of Israel. And the land was undisturbed for eighty years.

G. *Delivery by Shamgar*

3:31
Judg 5:6

31   And after him came Shamgar the son of Anath, who struck down six hundred Philistines with an oxgoad; and he also saved Israel.

H. *The judgeships of Deborah and Barak*

1. *The oppression by the Canaanites*

4:1
Judg 2:19
4:2
Josh 11:1,10;
vv. 13,16;
Ps 83:9

4   Then the sons of Israel again did evil in the sight of the LORD, after Ehud died.
2   And the LORD sold them into the hand of Jabin king of Canaan, who reigned in Hazor; and the commander of his army was Sisera, who lived in Harosheth-hagoyim.

4:3
Judg 1:19

3   And the sons of Israel cried to the LORD; for he had nine hundred iron chariots, and he oppressed the sons of Israel severely for twenty years.

2. *Deborah summons Barak*

4   Now Deborah, a prophetess, the wife of Lappidoth, was judging Israel at that time.

5   And she used to sit under the palm tree of Deborah between Ramah and Bethel in the hill country of Ephraim; and the sons of Israel came up to her for judgment.

4:6
Heb 11:32

6   Now she sent and summoned Barak the son of Abinoam from Kedesh-naphtali, and said to him, "Behold, the LORD, the God of Israel, has commanded, 'Go and march to Mount Tabor, and take with you ten thousand men from the sons of Naphtali and from the sons of Zebulun.

4:7
Ps 83:9

7   'And I will draw out to you Sisera, the commander of Jabin's army, with his

chariots and his many *troops* to the river Kishon; and I will give him into your hand.'"

8   Then Barak said to her, "If you will go with me, then I will go; but if you will not go with me, I will not go."

9   And she said, "I will surely go with you; nevertheless, the honor shall not be yours on the journey that you are about to take, for the LORD will sell Sisera into the hands of a woman." Then Deborah arose and went with Barak to Kedesh.

10   And Barak called Zebulun and Naphtali together to Kedesh, and ten thousand men went up with him; Deborah also went up with him.

3. *The victory over the Canaanites*

11   Now Heber the Kenite had separated himself from the Kenites, from the sons of Hobab the father-in-law of Moses, and had pitched his tent as far away as the oak in Zaanannim, which is near Kedesh.

12   Then they told Sisera that Barak the son of Abinoam had gone up to Mount Tabor.

13   And Sisera called together all his chariots, nine hundred iron chariots, and all the people who *were* with him, from Harosheth-hagoyim to the river Kishon.

14   And Deborah said to Barak, "Arise! For this is the day in which the LORD has given Sisera into your hands; [6]behold, the LORD has gone out before you." So Barak went down from Mount Tabor with ten thousand men following him.

15   And the LORD routed Sisera and all *his* chariots and all *his* army, with the edge of the sword before Barak; and Sisera alighted from *his* chariot and fled away on foot.

16   But Barak pursued the chariots and the army as far as Harosheth-hagoyim, and all the army of Sisera fell by the edge of the sword; not even one was left.

4. *Jael slays Sisera*

17   Now Sisera fled away on foot to the tent of Jael the wife of Heber the Kenite, for *there was* peace between Jabin the king of Hazor and the house of Heber the Kenite.

18   And Jael went out to meet Sisera, and said to him, "Turn aside, my master, turn aside to me! Do not be afraid." And he turned aside to her into the tent, and she covered him with a rug.

19   And he said to her, "Please give me a little water to drink, for I am thirsty." So she opened a [7]bottle of milk and gave him a drink; then she covered him.

20   And he said to her, "Stand in the doorway of the tent, and it shall be if anyone comes and inquires of you, and says, 'Is there anyone here?' that you shall say, 'No.'"

21   But Jael, Heber's wife, took a tent peg and seized a hammer in her hand, and went secretly to him and drove the peg into his temple, and it went through into the ground; for he was sound asleep and exhausted. So he died.

22   And behold, as Barak pursued Sisera, Jael came out to meet him and said to him, "Come, and I will show you the man whom you are seeking." And he entered with her, and behold Sisera was lying dead with the tent peg in his temple.

5. *Jabin destroyed*

23   So God subdued on that day Jabin the king of Canaan before the sons of Israel.

24   And the hand of the sons of Israel pressed heavier and heavier upon Jabin the king of Canaan, until they had destroyed Jabin the king of Canaan.

6. *The song of Deborah*

5 Then Deborah and Barak the son of Abinoam sang on that day, saying,
2   "That the leaders led in Israel,
         That the people volunteered,
         Bless the LORD!
3   "Hear, O kings; give ear, O rulers!
         I—to the LORD, I will sing,
         I will sing praise to the LORD, the God of Israel.

---

[6]Or, *has not the LORD gone . . . ?*   [7]I.e., skin container

---

4:11 *Hobab.* See note to Ex. 2:18.   5:1 The war song in poetic form.

Marginal references:

4:9 v. 21

4:10 Judg 5:18; v. 14; Judg 5:15

*4:11 Judg 1:16; v. 6

4:13 v. 3

4:14 Deut 9:3

4:15 Josh 10:10

4:16 Ps 83:9

4:19 Judg 5:25

4:21 Judg 5:26

*5:1 Ex 15:1 5:2 Deut 32:41

5:3 Ps 27:6

5:4
Deut 33:2;
Ps 68:7-9
4   "Lord, when Thou didst go out from Seir,
      When Thou didst march from the field of Edom,
      The earth quaked, the heavens also dripped,
      Even the clouds dripped water.

5:5
Ps 97:5;
Is 64:1,3;
Ps 68:8
5   "The mountains quaked at the presence of the Lord,
      This Sinai, at the presence of the Lord, the God of Israel.

5:6
Judg 3:31;
4:17
6   "In the days of Shamgar the son of Anath,
      In the days of Jael, the highways were deserted,
      And travelers went by roundabout ways.

7   "The peasantry ceased, they ceased in Israel,
      Until I, Deborah, arose,
      Until I arose, a mother in Israel.

5:8
Deut 32:17
8   "New gods were chosen;
      Then war *was* in the gates.
      Not a shield or a spear was seen
      Among forty thousand in Israel.

9   "My heart *goes out* to the commanders of Israel,
      The volunteers among the people;
      Bless the Lord!

10   "You who ride on white donkeys,
      You who sit on *rich* carpets,
      And you who travel on the road—sing!

5:11
1 Sam 12:7;
Mic 6:5
11   "At the sound of those who divide *flocks* among the watering places,
      There they shall recount the righteous deeds of the Lord,
      The righteous deeds for His peasantry in Israel.
      Then the people of the Lord went down to the gates.

5:12
Ps 57:8;
68:18
12   "Awake, awake, Deborah;
      Awake, awake, sing a song!
      Arise, Barak, and take away your captives, O son of Abinoam.

13   "Then survivors came down to the nobles;
      The people of the Lord came down to me as warriors.

5:14
Judg 3:13,27;
Num 32:39
14   "From Ephraim those whose root is in Amalek *came down*,
      Following you, Benjamin, with your peoples;
      From Machir commanders came down,
      And from Zebulun those who wield the staff of office.

5:15
Judg 4:10
15   "And the princes of Issachar *were* with Deborah;
      As *was* Issachar, so *was* Barak;
      Into the valley they rushed at his heels;
      Among the divisions of Reuben
      There were great resolves of heart.

5:16
Num 32:1
16   "Why did you sit among the [8]sheepfolds,
      To hear the piping for the flocks?
      Among the divisions of Reuben
      There were great searchings of heart.

5:17
Josh 13:24-28;
19:29,46
17   "Gilead remained across the Jordan;
      And why did Dan stay in ships?
      Asher sat at the seashore,
      And remained by its landings.

5:18
Judg 4:6,10
18   "Zebulun *was* a people who despised their lives *even* to death,
      And Naphtali also, on the high places of the field.

*5:19ff
Josh 11:1,2;
Judg 1:27
19   "The kings came *and* fought;
      Then fought the kings of Canaan
      At Taanach near the waters of Megiddo;
      They took no plunder in silver.

5:20
Josh 10:11-14
20   "The stars fought from heaven,
      From their courses they fought against Sisera.

5:21
Judg 4:7
21   "The torrent of Kishon swept them away,
      The ancient torrent, the torrent Kishon.

[8]Or, *saddlebags*

5:19–22 A dramatic account of the raging battle at Taanach.

O my soul, march on with strength.

22   "Then the horses' hoofs beat
     From the dashing, the dashing of his valiant steeds.

23   'Curse Meroz,' said the angel of the LORD,
     'Utterly curse its inhabitants;
     Because they did not come to the help of the LORD,
     To the help of the LORD against the warriors.'

24   "Most blessed of women is Jael,
     The wife of Heber the Kenite;
     Most blessed is she of women in the tent.

5:24
Judg 4:17,
19-21

25   "He asked for water *and* she gave him milk;
     In a magnificent bowl she brought him curds.

5:25
Judg 4:19

26   "She reached out her hand for the tent peg,
     And her right hand for the workmen's hammer.
     Then she struck Sisera, she smashed his head;
     And she shattered and pierced his temple.

5:26
Judg 4:21

27   "Between her feet he bowed, he fell, he lay;
     Between her feet he bowed, he fell;
     Where he bowed, there he fell dead.

28   "Out of the window she looked and lamented,
     The mother of Sisera through the lattice,
     'Why does his chariot delay in coming?
     Why do the hoofbeats of his chariots tarry?'

5:28
Prov 7:6

29   "Her wise princesses would answer her,
     Indeed she repeats her words to herself,

30   'Are they not finding, are they not dividing the spoil?
     A maiden, two maidens for every warrior;
     To Sisera a spoil of dyed work,
     A spoil of dyed work embroidered,
     Dyed work of double embroidery on the neck of the spoiler?'

5:30
Ex 15:9

31   "Thus let all Thine enemies perish, O LORD;
     But let those who love Him be like the rising of the sun in its
     might."
And the land was undisturbed for forty years.

5:31
Ps 68:2; 92:9;
19:4,5;
Judg 3:11

I. *The judgeship of Gideon*

1. *Apostasy and servitude*

6   Then the sons of Israel did what was evil in the sight of the LORD; and the LORD
gave them into the hands of Midian seven years.
2   And the power of Midian prevailed against Israel. Because of Midian the
sons of Israel made for themselves the dens which were in the mountains and the
caves and the strongholds.
3   For it was when Israel had sown, that the Midianites would come up with
the Amalekites and the sons of the east and go against them.
4   So they would camp against them and destroy the produce of the earth as far
as Gaza, and leave no sustenance in Israel as well as no sheep, ox, or donkey.
5   For they would come up with their livestock and their tents, they would
come in like locusts for number, both they and their camels were innumerable; and
they came into the land to devastate it.
6   So Israel was brought very low because of Midian, and the sons of Israel
cried to the LORD.

*6:1
Judg 2:11,19;
Num 25:15-18;
31:1-3

6:3
Judg 3:13

6:4
Lev 26:16;
Deut 28:30,
33,51

*6:5
Judg 7:12

6:6
Judg 3:15

2. *The advent of a prophet*

7   Now it came about when the sons of Israel cried to the LORD on account of
Midian,
8   that the LORD sent a prophet to the sons of Israel, and he said to them,
"Thus says the LORD, the God of Israel, 'It was I who brought you up from Egypt,
and brought you out from the house of slavery.

6:8
Judg 2:1,2

5:27 This verse is apparently a poetic description of the
incident in 4:21.
6:1 Cf. with 3:14 where it took eighteen years for Israel to
come to her senses.
6:5 *camels.* This is the first known use of domesticated
camels in warfare.

9 'And I delivered you from the hands of the Egyptians and from the hands of all your oppressors, and dispossessed them before you and gave you their land,

10 and I said to you, "I am the LORD your God; you shall not fear the gods of the Amorites in whose land you live. But you have not obeyed Me."' "

3. Gideon called of the LORD

11 Then the angel of the LORD came and sat under the oak that was in Ophrah, which belonged to Joash the Abiezrite as his son Gideon was beating out wheat in the wine press in order to save *it* from the Midianites.

12 And the angel of the LORD appeared to him and said to him, "The LORD is with you, O valiant warrior."

13 Then Gideon said to him, "O my lord, if the LORD is with us, why then has all this happened to us? And where are all His miracles which our fathers told us about, saying, 'Did not the LORD bring us up from Egypt?' But now the LORD has abandoned us and given us into the hand of Midian."

14 And the LORD looked at him and said, "Go in this your strength and deliver Israel from the hand of Midian. Have I not sent you?"

15 And he said to Him, "O Lord, how shall I deliver Israel? Behold, my family is the least in Manasseh, and I am the youngest in my father's house."

16 But the LORD said to him, "Surely I will be with you, and you shall defeat Midian as one man."

17 So Gideon said to Him, "If now I have found favor in Thy sight, then show me a sign that it is Thou who speakest with me.

18 "Please do not depart from here, until I come *back* to Thee, and bring out my offering and lay it before Thee." And He said, "I will remain until you return."

19 Then Gideon went in and prepared a kid and unleavened bread from an ⁹ephah of flour; he put the meat in a basket and the broth in a pot, and brought *them* out to him under the oak, and presented *them*.

20 And the angel of God said to him, "Take the meat and the unleavened bread and lay them on this rock, and pour out the broth." And he did so.

21 Then the angel of the LORD put out the end of the staff that was in his hand and touched the meat and the unleavened bread; and fire sprang up from the rock and consumed the meat and the unleavened bread. Then the angel of the LORD vanished from his sight.

22 When Gideon saw that he was the angel of the LORD, he said, "Alas, O Lord GOD! For now I have seen the angel of the LORD face to face."

23 And the LORD said to him, "Peace to you, do not fear; you shall not die."

24 Then Gideon built an altar there to the LORD and named it The LORD is Peace. To this day it is still in Ophrah of the Abiezrites.

4. Gideon destroys the altar to Baal

25 Now the same night it came about that the LORD said to him, "Take your father's bull and a second bull seven years old, and pull down the altar of Baal which belongs to your father, and cut down the ¹⁰Asherah that is beside it;

26 and build an altar to the LORD your God on the top of this stronghold in an orderly manner, and take a second bull and offer a burnt offering with the wood of the Asherah which you shall cut down."

27 Then Gideon took ten men of his servants and did as the LORD had spoken to him; and it came about, because he was too afraid of his father's household and the men of the city to do it by day, that he did it by night.

28 When the men of the city arose early in the morning, behold, the altar of Baal was torn down, and the Asherah which was beside it was cut down, and the second bull was offered on the altar which had been built.

29 And they said to one another, "Who did this thing?" And when they searched about and inquired, they said, "Gideon the son of Joash did this thing."

30 Then the men of the city said to Joash, "Bring out your son, that he may die, for he has torn down the altar of Baal, and indeed, he has cut down the Asherah which was beside it."

31 But Joash said to all who stood against him, "Will you contend for Baal, or will you deliver him? Whoever will plead for him shall be put to death by morning.

⁹I.e., Approx. one bushel ¹⁰I.e., wooden symbol of a female deity

If he is a god, let him contend for himself, because someone has torn down his altar."

32   Therefore on that day he named him Jerubbaal, that is to say, "Let Baal contend against him," because he had torn down his altar.

33   Then all the Midianites and the Amalekites and the sons of the east assembled themselves; and they crossed over and camped in the valley of Jezreel.

34   So the Spirit of the LORD came upon Gideon; and he blew a trumpet, and the Abiezrites were called together to follow him.

35   And he sent messengers throughout Manasseh, and they also were called together to follow him; and he sent messengers to Asher, Zebulun, and Naphtali, and they came up to meet them.

5. *Gideon puts out the fleece*

36   Then Gideon said to God, "If Thou wilt deliver Israel through me, as Thou hast spoken,

37   behold, I will put a fleece of wool on the threshing floor. If there is dew on the fleece only, and it is dry on all the ground, then I will know that Thou wilt deliver Israel through me, as Thou hast spoken."

38   And it was so. When he arose early the next morning and squeezed the fleece, he drained the dew from the fleece, a bowl full of water.

39   Then Gideon said to God, "Do not let Thine anger burn against me that I may speak once more; please let me make a test once more with the fleece, let it now be dry only on the fleece, and let there be dew on all the ground."

40   And God did so that night; for it was dry only on the fleece, and dew was on all the ground.

6. *The defeat of the Midianites*
a. *The selection of the three hundred*

7 Then Jerubbaal (that is, Gideon) and all the people who were with him, rose early and camped beside the spring of Harod; and the camp of Midian was on the north side of them by the hill of Moreh in the valley.

2   And the LORD said to Gideon, "The people who are with you are too many for Me to give Midian into their hands, lest Israel become boastful, saying, 'My own power has delivered me.'

3   "Now therefore come, proclaim in the hearing of the people, saying, 'Whoever is afraid and trembling, let him return and depart from Mount Gilead.' " So 22,000 people returned, but 10,000 remained.

4   Then the LORD said to Gideon, "The people are still too many; bring them down to the water and I will test them for you there. Therefore it shall be that he of whom I say to you, 'This one shall go with you,' he shall go with you; but everyone of whom I say to you, 'This one shall not go with you,' he shall not go."

5   So he brought the people down to the water. And the LORD said to Gideon, "You shall separate everyone who laps the water with his tongue, as a dog laps, as well as everyone who kneels to drink."

6   Now the number of those who lapped, putting their hand to their mouth, was 300 men; but all the rest of the people kneeled to drink water.

7   And the LORD said to Gideon, "I will deliver you with the 300 men who lapped and will give the Midianites into your hands; so let all the *other* people go, each man to his home."

8   So the 300 men took the people's provisions and their trumpets into their hands. And Gideon sent all the *other* men of Israel, each to his tent, but retained the 300 men; and the camp of Midian was below him in the valley.

b. *The prophecy against Midian*

9   Now the same night it came about that the LORD said to him, "Arise, go down against the camp, for I have given it into your hands.

10   "But if you are afraid to go down, go with Purah your servant down to the camp,

11   and you will hear what they say; and afterward your hands will be

---

Cross-references (right margin):

6:32 Judg 7:1; 1 Sam 12:11
6:33 v. 3; Josh 17:16
6:34 Judg 3:10,27; 1 Chr 12:18; 2 Chr 24:20

*6:37 see Ex 4:3-7

6:39 Gen 18:32

7:1 Judg 6:32

7:2 Deut 8:17; Is 10:13; 2 Cor 4:7

7:3 Deut 20:8

7:4 1 Sam 14:6

7:7 1 Sam 14:6

7:9 Josh 2:24; 10:8; 11:6

7:11 vv. 13-15

6:37 Gideon and the fleece (vv. 37–40) illustrates one method by which God may guide His children in the decisions of life. However illusory the test of Gideon might appear to modern thinking, the results of the putting out of the fleece confirmed to him the will of God and led him to very definite victory over the Midianites.

strengthened that you may go down against the camp." So he went with Purah his servant down to the outposts of the army that was in the camp.

7:12
Judg 6:5;
8:10;
Josh 11:4

12 Now the Midianites and the Amalekites and all the sons of the east were lying in the valley as numerous as locusts; and their camels were without number, as numerous as the sand on the seashore.

13 When Gideon came, behold, a man was relating a dream to his friend. And he said, "Behold, I had a dream; a loaf of barley bread was tumbling into the camp of Midian, and it came to the tent and struck it so that it fell, and turned it upside down so that the tent lay flat."

7:14
v. 20

14 And his friend answered and said, "This is nothing less than the sword of Gideon the son of Joash, a man of Israel; God has given Midian and all the camp into his hand."

c. Battle orders

7:15
1 Sam 15:31

15 And it came about when Gideon heard the account of the dream and its interpretation, that he bowed in worship. He returned to the camp of Israel and said, "Arise, for the LORD has given the camp of Midian into your hands."

16 And he divided the 300 men into three companies, and he put trumpets and empty pitchers into the hands of all of them, with torches inside the pitchers.

17 And he said to them, "Look at me, and do likewise. And behold, when I come to the outskirts of the camp, do as I do.

7:18
vv. 14,20

18 "When I and all who are with me blow the trumpet, then you also blow the trumpets all around the camp, and say, 'For the LORD and for Gideon.'"

d. The flight of the Midianites

19 So Gideon and the hundred men who were with him came to the outskirts of the camp at the beginning of the middle watch, when they had just posted the watch; and they blew the trumpets and smashed the pitchers that were in their hands.

7:20
v. 14

20 When the three companies blew the trumpets and broke the pitchers, they held the torches in their left hands and the trumpets in their right hands for blowing, and cried, "A sword for the LORD and for Gideon!"

7:21
2 Kin 7:7

21 And each stood in his place around the camp; and all the [11]army ran, crying out as they fled.

7:22
Josh 6:4;
16:20;
1 Sam 14:20

22 And when they blew 300 trumpets, the LORD set the sword of one against another even throughout the whole army; and the army fled as far as Beth-shittah toward Zererah, as far as the edge of Abel-meholah, by Tabbath.

7:23
Judg 6:35

23 And the men of Israel were summoned from Naphtali and Asher and all Manasseh, and they pursued Midian.

7:24
Judg 3:27,28

24 And Gideon sent messengers throughout all the hill country of Ephraim, saying, "Come down against Midian and take the waters before them, as far as Beth-barah and the Jordan." So all the men of Ephraim were summoned, and they took the waters as far as Beth-barah and the Jordan.

7:25
Judg 8:3,4;
Ps 83:11;
Is 10:26

25 And they captured the two leaders of Midian, Oreb and Zeeb, and they killed Oreb at the rock of Oreb, and they killed Zeeb at the wine press of Zeeb, while they pursued Midian; and they brought the heads of Oreb and Zeeb to Gideon from across the Jordan.

e. Gideon's trouble with Ephraim

8:1
Judg 12:1

8 Then the men of Ephraim said to him, "What is this thing you have done to us, not calling us when you went to fight against Midian?" And they contended with him vigorously.

2 But he said to them, "What have I done now in comparison with you? Is not the gleaning of the grapes of Ephraim better than the vintage of Abiezer?

8:3
Judg 7:24,25

3 "God has given the leaders of Midian, Oreb and Zeeb, into your hands; and what was I able to do in comparison with you?" Then their anger toward him subsided when he said that.

f. Succoth and Penuel refuse Gideon supplies

4 Then Gideon and the 300 men who were with him came to the Jordan and crossed over, weary yet pursuing.

8:5
Gen 33:17

5 And he said to the men of Succoth, "Please give loaves of bread to the people

[11]Or, camp

who are following me, for they are weary, and I am pursuing Zebah and Zalmunna, the kings of Midian.''

6   And the leaders of Succoth said, "Are the hands of Zebah and Zalmunna already in your hands, that we should give bread to your army?''

7   And Gideon said, "All right, when the LORD has given Zebah and Zalmunna into my hand, then I will thrash your bodies with the thorns of the wilderness and with briers.''

8   And he went up from there to Penuel, and spoke similarly to them; and the men of Penuel answered him just as the men of Succoth had answered.

9   So he spoke also to the men of Penuel, saying, "When I return safely, I will tear down this tower.''

g. The capture of Zebah and Zalmunna

10   Now Zebah and Zalmunna were in Karkor, and their armies with them, about 15,000 men, all who were left of the entire army of the sons of the east; for the fallen were 120,000 swordsmen.

11   And Gideon went up by the way of those who lived in tents on the east of Nobah and Jogbehah, and attacked the camp, when the camp was unsuspecting.

12   When Zebah and Zalmunna fled, he pursued them and captured the two kings of Midian, Zebah and Zalmunna, and routed the whole army.

h. The punishment of Succoth and Penuel

13   Then Gideon the son of Joash returned from the battle by the ascent of Heres.

14   And he captured a youth from Succoth and questioned him. Then *the youth* wrote down for him the princes of Succoth and its elders, seventy-seven men.

15   And he came to the men of Succoth and said, "Behold Zebah and Zalmunna, concerning whom you taunted me, saying, 'Are the hands of Zebah and Zalmunna already in your hand, that we should give bread to your men who are weary?' ''

16   And he took the elders of the city, and thorns of the wilderness and briers, and he disciplined the men of Succoth with them.

17   And he tore down the tower of Penuel and killed the men of the city.

i. The death of Zebah and Zalmunna

18   Then he said to Zebah and Zalmunna, "What kind of men *were* they whom you killed at Tabor?'' And they said, "They were like you, each one resembling the son of a king.''

19   And he said, "They *were* my brothers, the sons of my mother. *As* the LORD lives, if only you had let them live, I would not kill you.''

20   So he said to Jether his first-born, "Rise, kill them.'' But the youth did not draw his sword, for he was afraid, because he was still a youth.

21   Then Zebah and Zalmunna said, "Rise up yourself, and fall on us; for as the man, so is his strength.'' So Gideon arose and killed Zebah and Zalmunna, and took the crescent ornaments which were on their camels' necks.

7. Gideon refuses the kingship and makes an ephod

22   Then the men of Israel said to Gideon, "Rule over us, both you and your son, also your son's son, for you have delivered us from the hand of Midian.''

23   But Gideon said to them, "I will not rule over you, nor shall my son rule over you; the LORD shall rule over you.''

24   Yet Gideon said to them, "I would request of you, that each of you give me an earring from his spoil.'' (For they had gold earrings, because they were Ishmaelites.)

25   And they said, "We will surely give *them*.'' So they spread out a garment, and every one of them threw an earring there from his spoil.

26   And the weight of the gold earrings that he requested was 1,700 *shekels* of gold, besides the crescent ornaments and the pendants and the purple robes which *were* on the kings of Midian, and besides the neck bands that *were* on their camels' necks.

27   And Gideon made it into an ephod, and placed it in his city, Ophrah, and all

---

8:27 *Ephod* here does not seem to be the usual priestly garment of white linen, but rather some kind of image or idol made out of the spoil of battle. This ephod was "set up" in the city and became a center of idolatrous worship. It

Israel played the harlot with it there, so that it became a snare to Gideon and his household.

8:28
Judg 5:31

28   So Midian was subdued before the sons of Israel, and they did not lift up their heads anymore. And the land was undisturbed for forty years in the days of Gideon.

8. Gideon's death

8:29
Judg 7:1
8:30
Judg 9:2,5

29   Then Jerubbaal the son of Joash went and lived in his own house.
30   Now Gideon had seventy sons who were his direct descendants, for he had many wives.

8:31
Judg 9:1

31   And his concubine who was in Shechem also bore him a son, and he named him Abimelech.
32   And Gideon the son of Joash died at a ripe old age and was buried in the tomb of his father Joash, in Ophrah of the Abiezrites.

9. Israel's apostasy after Gideon's death

*8:33
Judg 2:17,19;
9:4,46
8:34
Judg 3:7;
Deut 4:9

33   Then it came about, as soon as Gideon was dead, that the sons of Israel again played the harlot with the Baals, and made Baal-berith their god.
34   Thus the sons of Israel did not remember the LORD their God, who had delivered them from the hands of all their enemies on every side;
35   nor did they show kindness to the household of Jerubbaal (that is, Gideon), in accord with all the good that he had done to Israel.

J. Abimelech the son of Gideon

1. He murders seventy of his brothers and becomes king of Shechem

9:1
Judg 8:31

9 And Abimelech the son of Jerubbaal went to Shechem to his mother's relatives, and spoke to them and to the whole clan of the household of his mother's father, saying,

9:2
Judg 8:30;
Gen 29:14

2   "Speak, now, in the hearing of all the leaders of Shechem, 'Which is better for you, that seventy men, all the sons of Jerubbaal, rule over you, or that one man rule over you?' Also, remember that I am your bone and your flesh."
3   And his mother's relatives spoke all these words on his behalf in the hearing of all the leaders of Shechem; and they were inclined to follow Abimelech, for they said, "He is our relative."

9:4
Judg 8:33

4   And they gave him seventy pieces of silver from the house of Baal-berith with which Abimelech hired worthless and reckless fellows, and they followed him.

9:5
v. 2

5   Then he went to his father's house at Ophrah, and killed his brothers the sons of Jerubbaal, seventy men, on one stone. But Jotham the youngest son of Jerubbaal was left, for he hid himself.
6   And all the men of Shechem and all [12]Beth-millo assembled together, and they went and made Abimelech king, by the oak of the pillar which was in Shechem.

2. Jotham's parable of the bramble

9:7
Deut 11:29;
27:12;
John 4:20

7   Now when they told Jotham, he went and stood on the top of Mount Gerizim, and lifted his voice and called out. Thus he said to them, "Listen to me, O men of Shechem, that God may listen to you.
8   "Once the trees went forth to anoint a king over them, and they said to the olive tree, 'Reign over us!'
9   "But the olive tree said to them, 'Shall I leave my fatness with which God and men are honored, and go to wave over the trees?'
10   "Then the trees said to the fig tree, 'You come, reign over us!'
11   "But the fig tree said to them, 'Shall I leave my sweetness and my good fruit, and go to wave over the trees?'
12   "Then the trees said to the vine, 'You come, reign over us!'
13   "But the vine said to them, 'Shall I leave my new wine, which cheers God and men, and go to wave over the trees?'

[12]Or, the house of Millo

---

became a snare to Gideon and his household.
8:33 Baal-berith, "Baal (Lord) of the Covenant," was the god worshiped by the Canaanites at Shechem and

elsewhere. In 9:46 he is called El-berith, "God of the Covenant." Excavators have found ruins of a temple to this god (see 9:4).

14 "Finally all the trees said to the bramble, 'You come, reign over us!'

15 "And the bramble said to the trees, 'If in truth you are anointing me as king over you, come and take refuge in my shade; but if not, may fire come out from the bramble and consume the cedars of Lebanon.'

3. The application of the parable

16 "Now therefore, if you have dealt in truth and integrity in making Abimelech king, and if you have dealt well with Jerubbaal and his house, and have dealt with him as he deserved—

17 for my father fought for you and risked his life and delivered you from the hand of Midian;

18 but you have risen against my father's house today and have killed his sons, seventy men, on one stone, and have made Abimelech, the son of his maidservant, king over the men of Shechem, because he is your relative—

19 if then you have dealt in truth and integrity with Jerubbaal and his house this day, rejoice in Abimelech, and let him also rejoice in you.

20 "But if not, let fire come out from Abimelech and consume the men of Shechem and Beth-millo; and let fire come out from the men of Shechem and from Beth-millo, and consume Abimelech."

21 Then Jotham escaped and fled, and went to Beer and remained there because of Abimelech his brother.

4. Discord between Abimelech and Shechem

22 Now Abimelech ruled over Israel three years.

23 Then God sent an evil spirit between Abimelech and the men of Shechem; and the men of Shechem dealt treacherously with Abimelech,

24 in order that the violence done to the seventy sons of Jerubbaal might come, and their blood might be laid on Abimelech their brother, who killed them, and on the men of Shechem, who strengthened his hands to kill his brothers.

25 And the men of Shechem set men in ambush against him on the tops of the mountains, and they robbed all who might pass by them along the road; and it was told to Abimelech.

5. The revolt of Gaal

26 Now Gaal the son of Ebed came with his relatives, and crossed over into Shechem; and the men of Shechem put their trust in him.

27 And they went out into the field and gathered the grapes of their vineyards and trod them, and held a festival; and they went into the house of their god, and ate and drank and cursed Abimelech.

28 Then Gaal the son of Ebed said, "Who is Abimelech, and who is Shechem, that we should serve him? Is he not the son of Jerubbaal, and is Zebul not his lieutenant? Serve the men of Hamor the father of Shechem; but why should we serve him?

29 "Would, therefore, that this people were under my authority! Then I would remove Abimelech." And he said to Abimelech, "Increase your army, and come out."

6. Abimelech informed of Gaal's treachery

30 And when Zebul the ruler of the city heard the words of Gaal the son of Ebed, his anger burned.

31 And he sent messengers to Abimelech deceitfully, saying, "Behold, Gaal the son of Ebed and his relatives have come to Shechem; and behold, they are stirring up the city against you.

32 "Now therefore, arise by night, you and the people who are with you, and lie in wait in the field.

33 "And it shall come about in the morning, as soon as the sun is up, that you shall rise early and rush upon the city; and behold, when he and the people who are with him come out against you, you shall do to them whatever you can."

7. Abimelech quells Gaal's revolt

34 So Abimelech and all the people who were with him arose by night and lay in wait against Shechem in four companies.

35 Now Gaal the son of Ebed went out and stood in the entrance of the city

9:15
Is 30:2; v. 20

9:16
Judg 8:35

9:18
vv. 5,6;
Judg 8:31

9:19
Judg 8:35

9:23
1 Sam 16:14;
18:9,10
9:24
vv. 56,57;
Deut 27:25;
Num 35:33

9:27
Judg 8:33

9:28
Gen 34:2,6

9:29
2 Sam 15:4

9:33
1 Sam 10:7

gate; and Abimelech and the people who *were* with him arose from the ambush.

36   And when Gaal saw the people, he said to Zebul, "Look, people are coming down from the tops of the mountains." But Zebul said to him, "You are seeing the shadow of the mountains as *if they were* men."

9:37
Ezek 38:12

37   And Gaal spoke again and said, "Behold, people are coming down from the highest part of the land, and one company comes by the way of the diviners' oak."

9:38
vv. 28,29

38   Then Zebul said to him, "Where is your boasting now with which you said, 'Who is Abimelech that we should serve him?' Is this not the people whom you despised? Go out now and fight with them!"

9:39
Gen 35:4

39   So Gaal went out before the leaders of Shechem and fought with Abimelech.

40   And Abimelech chased him, and he fled before him; and many fell wounded up to the entrance of the gate.

41   Then Abimelech remained at Arumah, but Zebul drove out Gaal and his relatives so that they could not remain in Shechem.

8. *Abimelech razes Shechem*

42   Now it came about the next day, that the people went out to the field, and it was told to Abimelech.

43   So he took his people and divided them into three companies, and lay in wait in the field; when he looked and saw the people coming out from the city, he arose against them and slew them.

44   Then Abimelech and the company who was with him dashed forward and stood in the entrance of the city gate; the other two companies then dashed against all who *were* in the field and slew them.

9:45
v. 20;
Deut 29:23

45   And Abimelech fought against the city all that day, and he captured the city and killed the people who *were* in it; then he razed the city and sowed it with salt.

9. *The Tower of Shechem burned*

9:46
Judg 8:33

46   When all the leaders of the tower of Shechem heard of *it*, they entered the inner chamber of the temple of El-berith.

47   And it was told Abimelech that all the leaders of the tower of Shechem were gathered together.

9:48
Ps 68:14

48   So Abimelech went up to Mount Zalmon, he and all the people who *were* with him; and Abimelech took an axe in his hand and cut down a branch from the trees, and lifted it and laid *it* on his shoulder. Then he said to the people who *were* with him, "What you have seen me do, hurry *and* do likewise."

49   And all the people also cut down each one his branch and followed Abimelech, and put *them* on the inner chamber and set the inner chamber on fire over those *inside*, so that all the men of the tower of Shechem also died, about a thousand men and women.

10. *Abimelech's death*

9:50
2 Sam 11:21

50   Then Abimelech went to Thebez, and he camped against Thebez and captured it.

51   But there was a strong tower in the center of the city, and all the men and women with all the leaders of the city fled there and shut themselves in; and they went up on the roof of the tower.

52   So Abimelech came to the tower and fought against it, and approached the entrance of the tower to burn it with fire.

9:53
v. 50

53   But a certain woman threw an upper millstone on Abimelech's head, crushing his skull.

54   Then he called quickly to the young man, his armor bearer, and said to him, "Draw your sword and kill me, lest it be said of me, 'A woman slew him.'" So the young man pierced him through, and he died.

55   And when the men of Israel saw that Abimelech was dead, each departed to his home.

9:56
v. 24;
Ps 94:23

56   Thus God repaid the wickedness of Abimelech, which he had done to his father, in killing his seventy brothers.

9:57
v. 20

57   Also God returned all the wickedness of the men of Shechem on their heads, and the curse of Jotham the son of Jerubbaal came upon them.

K. *The judgeship of Tola*

10 Now after Abimelech died, Tola the son of Puah, the son of Dodo, a man of Issachar, arose to save Israel; and he lived in Shamir in the hill country of Ephraim.

2 And he judged Israel twenty-three years. Then he died and was buried in Shamir.

L. *The judgeship of Jair*

3 And after him, Jair the Gileadite arose, and judged Israel twenty-two years.

4 And he had thirty sons who rode on thirty donkeys, and they had thirty cities in the land of Gilead that are called Havvoth-jair to this day.

5 And Jair died and was buried in Kamon.

M. *The judgeship of Jephthah*

1. *The apostasy and oppression*

6 Then the sons of Israel again did evil in the sight of the LORD, served the Baals and the Ashtaroth, the gods of Aram, the gods of Sidon, the gods of Moab, the gods of the sons of Ammon, and the gods of the Philistines; thus they forsook the LORD and did not serve Him.

7 And the anger of the LORD burned against Israel, and He sold them into the hands of the Philistines, and into the hands of the sons of Ammon.

8 And they afflicted and crushed the sons of Israel that year; for eighteen years they *afflicted* all the sons of Israel who were beyond the Jordan in Gilead in the land of the Amorites.

9 And the sons of Ammon crossed the Jordan to fight also against Judah, Benjamin, and the house of Ephraim, so that Israel was greatly distressed.

2. *Israel cries to the LORD for deliverance*

10 Then the sons of Israel cried out to the LORD, saying, "We have sinned against Thee, for indeed, we have forsaken our God and served the Baals."

11 And the LORD said to the sons of Israel, "*Did I* not *deliver you* from the Egyptians, the Amorites, the sons of Ammon, and the Philistines?

12 "Also when the Sidonians, the Amalekites and the Maonites oppressed you, you cried out to Me, and I delivered you from their hands.

13 "Yet you have forsaken Me and served other gods; therefore I will deliver you no more.

14 "Go and cry out to the gods which you have chosen; let them deliver you in the time of your distress."

15 And the sons of Israel said to the LORD, "We have sinned, do to us whatever seems good to Thee; only please deliver us this day."

16 So they put away the foreign gods from among them, and served the LORD; and He could bear the misery of Israel no longer.

17 Then the sons of Ammon were summoned, and they camped in Gilead. And the sons of Israel gathered together, and camped in Mizpah.

18 And the people, the leaders of Gilead, said to one another, "Who is the man who will begin to fight against the sons of Ammon? He shall become head over all the inhabitants of Gilead."

3. *Jephthah's background*

11 Now Jephthah the Gileadite was a valiant warrior, but he was the son of a harlot. And Gilead was the father of Jephthah.

2 And Gilead's wife bore him sons; and when his wife's sons grew up, they drove Jephthah out and said to him, "You shall not have an inheritance in our father's house, for you are the son of another woman."

3 So Jephthah fled from his brothers and lived in the land of Tob; and worthless fellows gathered themselves about Jephthah, and they went out with him.

4. *Israel appeals to Jephthah for deliverance*

4 And it came about after a while that the sons of Ammon fought against Israel.

Marginal references:

10:1 Judg 2:16

10:4 Num 32:41

10:6 Judg 2:11-13; Deut 31:16, 17; 32:15

10:7 Judg 2:14

10:10 1 Sam 12:10

10:11 Ex 14:30; Num 21:21; 24:25; Judg 3:12,13, 31

10:12 Judg 5:19; Ps 106:42,43

10:14 Deut 32:37

10:15 1 Sam 3:18

10:16 Josh 24:23; Jer 18:7,8; Deut 32:36; Ps 106:44,45

10:17 Judg 11:29

10:18 Judg 11:8,11

11:1 Heb 11:32

11:3 2 Sam 10:6,8

11:4 Judg 10:9,17

5   And it happened when the sons of Ammon fought against Israel that the elders of Gilead went to get Jephthah from the land of Tob;

6   and they said to Jephthah, "Come and be our chief that we may fight against the sons of Ammon."

7   Then Jephthah said to the elders of Gilead, "Did you not hate me and drive me from my father's house? So why have you come to me now when you are in trouble?"

8   And the elders of Gilead said to Jephthah, "For this reason we have now returned to you, that you may go with us and fight with the sons of Ammon and become head over all the inhabitants of Gilead."

9   So Jephthah said to the elders of Gilead, "If you take me back to fight against the sons of Ammon and the LORD gives them up to me, will I become your head?"

10   And the elders of Gilead said to Jephthah, "The LORD is witness between us; surely we will do as you have said."

11   Then Jephthah went with the elders of Gilead, and the people made him head and chief over them; and Jephthah spoke all his words before the LORD at Mizpah.

5. *The Ammonites want East Canaan*

12   Now Jephthah sent messengers to the king of the sons of Ammon, saying, "What is between you and me, that you have come to me to fight against my land?"

13   And the king of the sons of Ammon said to the messengers of Jephthah, "Because Israel took away my land when they came up from Egypt, from the Arnon as far as the Jabbok and the Jordan; therefore, return them peaceably now."

14   But Jephthah sent messengers again to the king of the sons of Ammon,

15   and they said to him, "Thus says Jephthah, 'Israel did not take away the land of Moab, nor the land of the sons of Ammon.

16   'For when they came up from Egypt, and Israel went through the wilderness to the Red Sea and came to Kadesh,

17   then Israel sent messengers to the king of Edom, saying, "Please let us pass through your land," but the king of Edom would not listen. And they also sent to the king of Moab, but he would not consent. So Israel remained at Kadesh.

18   'Then they went through the wilderness and around the land of Edom and the land of Moab, and came to the east side of the land of Moab, and they camped beyond the Arnon; but they did not enter the territory of Moab, for the Arnon *was* the border of Moab.

19   'And Israel sent messengers to Sihon king of the Amorites, the king of Heshbon, and Israel said to him, "Please let us pass through your land to our place."

20   'But Sihon did not trust Israel to pass through his territory; so Sihon gathered all his people and camped in Jahaz, and fought with Israel.

21   'And the LORD, the God of Israel, gave Sihon and all his people into the hand of Israel, and they defeated them; so Israel possessed all the land of the Amorites, the inhabitants of that country.

22   'So they possessed all the territory of the Amorites, from the Arnon as far as the Jabbok, and from the wilderness as far as the Jordan.

23   'Since now the LORD, the God of Israel, drove out the Amorites from before His people Israel, are you then to possess it?

24   'Do you not possess what Chemosh your god gives you to possess? So whatever the LORD our God has driven out before us, we will possess it.

25   'And now are you any better than Balak the son of Zippor, king of Moab? Did he ever strive with Israel, or did he ever fight against them?

26   'While Israel lived in Heshbon and its villages, and in Aroer and its villages, and in all the cities that are on the banks of the Arnon, three hundred years, why did you not recover them within that time?

27   'I therefore have not sinned against you, but you are doing me wrong by making war against me; may the LORD, the Judge, judge today between the sons of Israel and the sons of Ammon.' "

28   But the king of the sons of Ammon disregarded the message which Jephthah sent him.

Cross references (margin)

11:8   Judg 10:18
11:10   Jer 42:5
11:11   v. 8; Judg 10:17
11:13   Num 21:24-26
11:15   Deut 2:9,19
11:16   Num 14:25; 20:1,14-21
11:18   Num 21:4; Deut 2:1-9, 18,19
11:19   Num 21:21, 22; Deut 2:26,27
11:20   Num 21:23; Deut 2:32
11:21   Num 21:24, 25; Deut 2:33,34
11:22   Deut 2:36
11:24   Num 21:29; 1 Kin 11:7; Josh 3:10
11:25   Num 22:2; Josh 24:9
*11:26   Num 21:25; Deut 2:36
11:27   Gen 16:5; 18:25; 31:53; 1 Sam 24:12, 15

11:26 *three hundred years.* Probably a round number for the 319 years noted thus far in the period of the judges. However, it may be that some of these judges were ruling concurrently.

6. Jephthah's vow: defeat of the Ammonites

29   Now the Spirit of the LORD came upon Jephthah, so that he passed through Gilead and Manasseh; then he passed through Mizpah of Gilead, and from Mizpah of Gilead he went on to the sons of Ammon.

30   And Jephthah made a vow to the LORD and said, "If Thou wilt indeed give the sons of Ammon into my hand,

31   then it shall be that whatever comes out of the doors of my house to meet me when I return in peace from the sons of Ammon, it shall be the LORD's, and I will offer it up as a burnt offering."

32   So Jephthah crossed over to the sons of Ammon to fight against them; and the LORD gave them into his hand.

33   And he struck them with a very great slaughter from Aroer to the entrance of Minnith, twenty cities, and as far as Abel-keramim. So the sons of Ammon were subdued before the sons of Israel.

7. Jephthah fulfills his vow

34   When Jephthah came to his house at Mizpah, behold, his daughter was coming out to meet him with tambourines and with dancing. Now she was his one *and* only child; besides her he had neither son nor daughter.

35   And it came about when he saw her, that he tore his clothes and said, "Alas, my daughter! You have brought me very low, and you are among those who trouble me; for I have given my word to the LORD, and I cannot take *it* back."

36   So she said to him, "My father, you have given your word to the LORD; do to me as you have said, since the LORD has avenged you of your enemies, the sons of Ammon."

37   And she said to her father, "Let this thing be done for me; let me alone two months, that I may go to the mountains and weep because of my virginity, I and my companions."

38   Then he said, "Go." So he sent her away for two months; and she left with her companions, and wept on the mountains because of her virginity.

39   And it came about at the end of two months that she returned to her father, who did to her according to the vow which he had made; and she had no relations with a man. Thus it became a custom in Israel,

40   that the daughters of Israel went yearly to commemorate the daughter of Jephthah the Gileadite four days in the year.

8. Jephthah's quarrel with Ephraim: Shibboleth or Sibboleth

12   Then the men of Ephraim were summoned, and they crossed to Zaphon and said to Jephthah, "Why did you cross over to fight against the sons of Ammon without calling us to go with you? We will burn your house down on you."

2   And Jephthah said to them, "I and my people were at great strife with the sons of Ammon; when I called you, you did not deliver me from their hand.

3   "And when I saw that you would not deliver *me,* I took my life in my hands and crossed over against the sons of Ammon, and the LORD gave them into my hand. Why then have you come up to me this day, to fight against me?"

4   Then Jephthah gathered all the men of Gilead and fought Ephraim; and the men of Gilead defeated Ephraim, because they said, "You are fugitives of Ephraim, O Gileadites, in the midst of Ephraim *and* in the midst of Manasseh."

5   And the Gileadites captured the fords of the Jordan opposite Ephraim. And it happened when *any of* the fugitives of Ephraim said, "Let me cross over," the men of Gilead would say to him, "Are you an Ephraimite?" If he said, "No,"

6   then they would say to him, "Say now, 'Shibboleth.' " But he said, "Sibboleth," for he could not pronounce it correctly. Then they seized him and slew him at the fords of the Jordan. Thus there fell at that time 42,000 of Ephraim.

7   And Jephthah judged Israel six years. Then Jephthah the Gileadite died and was buried in *one of* the cities of Gilead.

11:29
Judg 3:10

11:33
Ezek 27:17

11:34
Judg 10:17;
Ex 15:20;
1 Sam 18:6;
Jer 31:4
11:35
Num 30:2;
Eccl 5:2,4,5

11:36
Num 30:2;
2 Sam 18:19,
31; Luke 1:38

12:1
Judg 8:1

12:3
1 Sam 19:5;
28:21;
Job 13:14

12:4
Judg 3:28;
7:24

12:5
Judg 3:28;
7:24;
Josh 22:11

12:7
Heb 11:32

11:30,31 Jephthah vowed that if God delivered the children of Ammon into his hands he would offer up a sacrifice. Whether he meant by this a human sacrifice or a living and unbloody sacrifice has been the subject of much discussion. The term *'olah* used here means "whole burnt offering." Unless the meaning of the word is changed, Jephthah likely offered his daughter as a human sacrifice. If this is true, it

does not mean that it was right for him to do so, but Jephthah's rough background may account for his lack of spiritual discernment (cf. 11:1–3).
11:39 *custom in Israel.* This annual four-day feast of lamentation is never mentioned again in Scripture. Apparently it was observed only in Gilead.

N. *The judgeship of Ibzan*

8 Now Ibzan of Bethlehem judged Israel after him.

9 And he had thirty sons, and thirty daughters *whom* he gave in marriage outside *the family*, and he brought in thirty daughters from outside for his sons. And he judged Israel seven years.

10 Then Ibzan died and was buried in Bethlehem.

O. *The judgeship of Elon*

11 Now Elon the Zebulunite judged Israel after him; and he judged Israel ten years.

12 Then Elon the Zebulunite died and was buried at Aijalon in the land of Zebulun.

P. *The judgeship of Abdon*

13 Now Abdon the son of Hillel the Pirathonite judged Israel after him.

12:14
Judg 5:10;
10:4

14 And he had forty sons and thirty grandsons who rode on seventy donkeys; and he judged Israel eight years.

15 Then Abdon the son of Hillel the Pirathonite died and was buried at Pirathon in the land of Ephraim, in the hill country of the Amalekites.

Q. *The judgeship of Samson*

1. *Israel's apostasy and servitude*

*13:1
Judg 2:11;
I Sam 12:9

13 Now the sons of Israel again did evil in the sight of the LORD, so that the LORD gave them into the hands of the Philistines forty years.

2. *The background of Samson*

a. *The promise to Manoah and his wife*

13:2
Josh 19:41

2 And there was a certain man of Zorah, of the family of the Danites, whose name was Manoah; and his wife was barren and had borne no *children*.

13:3
vv. 6,8,10;
Judg 6:12

3 Then the angel of the LORD appeared to the woman, and said to her, "Behold now, you are barren and have borne no *children*, but you shall conceive and give birth to a son.

13:4
v. 14;
Num 6:2,3

4 "Now therefore, be careful not to drink wine or strong drink, nor eat any unclean thing.

*13:5
Luke 1:15;
Num 6:2,5

5 "For behold, you shall conceive and give birth to a son, and no razor shall come upon his head, for the boy shall be a Nazirite to God from the womb; and he shall begin to deliver Israel from the hands of the Philistines."

*13:6
1 Sam 2:27;
Matt 28:3;
vv. 17,18

6 Then the woman came and told her husband, saying, "A man of God came to me and his appearance was like the appearance of the angel of God, very awesome. And I did not ask him where he *came* from, nor did he tell me his name.

7 "But he said to me, 'Behold, you shall conceive and give birth to a son, and now you shall not drink wine or strong drink nor eat any unclean thing, for the boy shall be a Nazirite to God from the womb to the day of his death.' "

b. *Manoah and the angel of the LORD*

13:8
vv. 3,7

8 Then Manoah entreated the LORD and said, "O Lord, please let the man of God whom Thou hast sent come to us again that he may teach us what to do for the boy who is to be born."

9 And God listened to the voice of Manoah; and the angel of God came again

---

13:1 *Philistines*. According to Deut. 2:23; Jer. 47:4 and Amos 9:7, the Philistines came from Caphtor, the island of Crete. They were part of the sea peoples who, having been repulsed by Egypt, settled along the coast of Canaan about 1200 B.C. At that time they began to infiltrate the foothills of Dan and Judah. Deliverance under Samson was far from permanent, because the Philistines plagued the Israelites until David's time. (See also note to 14:4 describing Israel's deliverance under Samson.)
13:5 A Nazirite was a person consecrated to God by a special vow and could be either male or female (Num. 6:2). In the cases of Samson and John the Baptist, they were Nazirites from the womb or before birth (13:5; Luke 1:15).

Certain prohibitions governed those who were Nazirites and among them were: (1) avoidance of wine or strong drink (Num. 6:3; Luke 1:15); (2) avoidance of contact with the dead (Num. 6:6,7); (3) no shaving of the head (Num. 6:5; Judg. 13:5; 16:17); and (4) no contact with grapes or any product of the vine (Num. 6:3,4; Judg. 13:14). These prohibitions lasted as long as the vow was in force. When the term of the vow ended, the individual was brought to the tabernacle door, his head was shaved, sacrifices were offered, and the left shoulder of a ram was presented by the priest as a wave offering (Lev. 7:32; Num. 6:13–20; Acts 18:18; 21:24).
13:6 *awesome*, that is, inspiring awe and reverence.

to the woman as she was sitting in the field, but Manoah her husband was not with her.

10   So the woman ran quickly and told her husband, "Behold, the man who came the *other* day has appeared to me."

11   Then Manoah arose and followed his wife, and when he came to the man he said to him, "Are you the man who spoke to the woman?" And he said, "I am."

12   And Manoah said, "Now when your words come *to pass*, what shall be the boy's mode of life and his vocation?"

13   So the angel of the LORD said to Manoah, "Let the woman pay attention to all that I said. | **13:13** vv. 4,11

14   "She should not eat anything that comes from the vine nor drink wine or strong drink, nor eat any unclean thing; let her observe all that I commanded." | **13:14** Num 6:4

15   Then Manoah said to the angel of the LORD, "Please let us detain you so that we may prepare a kid for you." | **13:15** v. 3

16   And the angel of the LORD said to Manoah, "Though you detain me, I will not eat your food, but if you prepare a burnt offering, *then* offer it to the LORD." For Manoah did not know that he was the angel of the LORD. | **13:16** Judg 6:20

17   And Manoah said to the angel of the LORD, "What is your name, so that when your words come *to pass*, we may honor you?" | **13:17** Gen 32:29

18   But the angel of the LORD said to him, "Why do you ask my name, seeing it is 13wonderful?" | ***13:18** Is 9:6

19   So Manoah took the kid with the grain offering and offered it on the rock to the LORD, and He performed wonders while Manoah and his wife looked on. | **13:19** Judg 6:20,21

20   For it came about when the flame went up from the altar toward heaven, that the angel of the LORD ascended in the flame of the altar. When Manoah and his wife saw *this*, they fell on their faces to the ground. | **13:20** Lev 9:24

c. The birth of Samson

21   Now the angel of the LORD appeared no more to Manoah or his wife. Then Manoah knew that he was the angel of the LORD. | **13:21** v. 16

22   So Manoah said to his wife, "We shall surely die, for we have seen God." | **13:22** Judg 6:22; Deut 5:26

23   But his wife said to him, "If the LORD had desired to kill us, He would not have accepted a burnt offering and a grain offering from our hands, nor would He have shown us all these things, nor would He have let us hear *things* like this at this time."

24   Then the woman gave birth to a son and named him Samson; and the child grew up and the LORD blessed him. | ***13:24** Heb 11:32; 1 Sam 3:19

25   And the Spirit of the LORD began to stir him in 14Mahaneh-dan, between Zorah and Eshtaol. | **13:25** Judg 3:10; 18:11

3. Samson's marriage to the woman of Timnah

a. Samson falls in love

14   Then Samson went down to Timnah and saw a woman in Timnah, *one* of the daughters of the Philistines.

2   So he came back and told his father and mother, "I saw a woman in Timnah, *one* of the daughters of the Philistines; now therefore, get her for me as a wife." | **14:2** Gen 21:21; 34:4

3   Then his father and his mother said to him, "Is there no woman among the daughters of your relatives, or among all our people, that you go to take a wife from the uncircumcised Philistines?" But Samson said to his father, "Get her for me, for she looks good to me."

4   However, his father and mother did not know that it was of the LORD, for | ***14:4** Josh 11:20; Judg 13:1

13I.e., incomprehensible   14I.e., the camp of Dan

13:18 *wonderful*, that is, beyond knowledge, ineffable (see Ps. 139:6).

13:24 Samson succumbed to various carnal desires. Beginning with everything in his favor (he was a Nazirite, his birth was foretold by an angel, and he was separated from sin), he backslid until he was captured and rendered sightless. His life illustrates the truth that small sins lead to big ones and that a stubborn insistence upon one's own will (cf. 14:3) leads ultimately to a ruined life. One of the most pathetic verses of Scripture is Judg. 16:20. However, Samson repented before he died (16:28), and his name is mentioned in Heb. 11:32 as one who gave his life to vindicate

God before the blasphemous heathen. Despite his carnal life he had great faith in God and this faith justified him.

14:4 Scripture here illustrates the truth that even the mistaken decisions of those who profess God may be used to accomplish the purposes of God. Samson was out of the will of God when he insisted that his parents arrange for his marriage to the Philistine woman from Timnah. It was altogether Samson's own choice. But God used it indirectly to deliver Israel from the Philistines. In no sense, however, did this excuse Samson from his responsibility for his decision.

He was seeking an occasion against the Philistines. Now at that time the Philistines were ruling over Israel.

b. The slaying of the lion

5 Then Samson went down to Timnah with his father and mother, and came as far as the vineyards of Timnah; and behold, a young lion *came* roaring toward him.

14:6
Judg 3:10;
13:25

6 And the Spirit of the Lord came upon him mightily, so that he tore him as one tears a kid though he had nothing in his hand; but he did not tell his father or mother what he had done.

14:7
v. 3

7 So he went down and talked to the woman; and she looked good to Samson.

8 When he returned later to take her, he turned aside to look at the carcass of the lion; and behold, a swarm of bees and honey were in the body of the lion.

9 So he scraped the honey into his hands and went on, eating as he went. When he came to his father and mother, he gave *some* to them and they ate *it;* but he did not tell them that he had scraped the honey out of the body of the lion.

c. Samson's riddle at the wedding feast

10 Then his father went down to the woman; and Samson made a feast there, for the young men customarily did this.

11 And it came about when they saw him that they brought thirty companions to be with him.

14:12
1 Kin 10:2;
Ezek 17:2;
Gen 29:27

12 Then Samson said to them, "Let me now propound a riddle to you; if you will indeed tell it to me within the seven days of the feast, and find it out, then I will give you thirty linen wraps and thirty changes of clothes.

13 "But if you are unable to tell me, then you shall give me thirty linen wraps and thirty changes of clothes." And they said to him, "Propound your riddle, that we may hear it."

14 So he said to them,

"Out of the eater came something to eat,
And out of the strong came something sweet."

But they could not tell the riddle in three days.

d. The solution of the riddle: the treachery of Samson's wife

14:15
Judg 16:5;
15:6

15 Then it came about on the fourth day that they said to Samson's wife, "Entice your husband, that he may tell us the riddle, lest we burn you and your father's house with fire. Have you invited us to impoverish us? Is this not *so?* "

16 And Samson's wife wept before him and said, "You only hate me, and you do not love me; you have propounded a riddle to the sons of my people, and have not told *it* to me." And he said to her, "Behold, I have not told *it* to my father or mother; so should I tell you?"

17 However she wept before him seven days while their feast lasted. And it came about on the seventh day that he told her because she pressed him so hard. She then told the riddle to the sons of her people.

14:18
v. 14

18 So the men of the city said to him on the seventh day before the sun went down,

"What is sweeter than honey?
And what is stronger than a lion?"

And he said to them,

"If you had not plowed with my heifer,
You would not have found out my riddle."

14:19
Judg 3:10

19 Then the Spirit of the Lord came upon him mightily, and he went down to Ashkelon and killed thirty of them and took their spoil, and gave the changes *of clothes* to those who told the riddle. And his anger burned, and he went up to his father's house.

14:20
Judg 15:2;
John 3:29

20 But Samson's wife was *given* to his companion who had been his friend.

4. The Philistines slay Samson's wife and father-in-law

15 But after a while, in the time of wheat harvest, it came about that Samson visited his wife with a young goat, and said, "I will go in to my wife in *her* room." But her father did not let him enter.

15:2
Judg 14:20

2 And her father said, "I really thought that you hated her intensely; so I gave her to your companion. Is not her younger sister more beautiful than she? Please let her be yours instead."

3   Samson then said to them, "This time I shall be blameless in regard to the Philistines when I do them harm."

4   And Samson went and caught three hundred foxes, and took torches, and turned *the foxes* tail to tail, and put one torch in the middle between two tails.

5   When he had set fire to the torches, he released the foxes into the standing grain of the Philistines, thus burning up both the shocks and the standing grain, along with the vineyards *and* groves.

6   Then the Philistines said, "Who did this?" And they said, "Samson, the son-in-law of the Timnite, because he took his wife and gave her to his companion." So the Philistines came up and burned her and her father with fire.

7   And Samson said to them, "Since you act like this, I will surely take revenge on you, but after that I will quit."

8   And he struck them ruthlessly with a great slaughter; and he went down and lived in the cleft of the rock of Etam.

5. *Samson in the hands of the Philistines*

a. *Judah delivers him*

9   Then the Philistines went up and camped in Judah, and spread out in Lehi.

10   And the men of Judah said, "Why have you come up against us?" And they said, "We have come up to bind Samson in order to do to him as he did to us."

11   Then 3,000 men of Judah went down to the cleft of the rock of Etam and said to Samson, "Do you not know that the Philistines are rulers over us? What then is this that you have done to us?" And he said to them, "As they did to me, so I have done to them."

12   And they said to him, "We have come down to bind you so that we may give you into the hands of the Philistines." And Samson said to them, "Swear to me that you will not kill me."

13   So they said to him, "No, but we will bind you fast and give you into their hands; yet surely we will not kill you." Then they bound him with two new ropes and brought him up from the rock.

b. *Samson's vengeance on the Philistines*

14   When he came to Lehi, the Philistines shouted as they met him. And the Spirit of the LORD came upon him mightily so that the ropes that were on his arms were as flax that is burned with fire, and his bonds dropped from his hands.

15   And he found a fresh jawbone of a donkey, so he reached out and took it and killed a thousand men with it.

16   Then Samson said,
"With the jawbone of a donkey,
    Heaps upon heaps,
    With the jawbone of a donkey
    I have killed a thousand men."

17   And it came about when he had finished speaking, that he threw the jawbone from his hand; and he named that place [15]Ramath-lehi.

18   Then he became very thirsty, and he called to the LORD and said, "Thou hast given this great deliverance by the hand of Thy servant, and now shall I die of thirst and fall into the hands of the uncircumcised?"

19   But God split the hollow place that is in Lehi so that water came out of it. When he drank, his strength returned and he revived. Therefore, he named it En-hakkore, which is in Lehi to this day.

20   So he judged Israel twenty years in the days of the Philistines.

6. *Samson and the harlot at Gaza*

16   Now Samson went to Gaza and saw a harlot there, and went in to her.
2   *When it was told* to the Gazites, saying, "Samson has come here," they surrounded *the place* and lay in wait for him all night at the gate of the city. And they

15I.e., the high place of the jawbone

15:15 The secret of Samson's strength did not lie in his pledge to refrain from touching strong drink and cutting his hair. Rather it lay in his inner relationship to God, the outward symbols of which were the vows of abstinence to which he solemnly adhered until Delilah tricked him. Samson himself realized that God was the source of his superior strength (v. 18).

Marginal references:

15:6
Judg 14:15

15:9
v. 19

15:11
Judg 13:1;
14:4

15:14
Judg 14:19;
1 Sam 11:6

*15:15
Lev 26:8;
Josh 23:10;
Judg 3:31

15:18
Judg 16:28

15:19
Gen 45:27;
Is 40:29

15:20
Heb 11:32;
Judg 13:1;
16:31

16:2
Ps 118:10-12

kept silent all night, saying, "*Let us wait* until the morning light, then we will kill him."

3   Now Samson lay until midnight, and at midnight he arose and took hold of the doors of the city gate and the two posts and pulled them up along with the bars; then he put them on his shoulders and carried them up to the top of the mountain which is opposite Hebron.

7. Samson and Delilah

a. Delilah seeks the source of Samson's strength

4   After this it came about that he loved a woman in the valley of Sorek, whose name was Delilah.

16:5
Judg 14:15
5   And the lords of the Philistines came up to her, and said to her, "Entice him, and see where his great strength *lies* and how we may overpower him that we may bind him to afflict him. Then we will each give you eleven hundred *pieces* of silver."

6   So Delilah said to Samson, "Please tell me where your great strength is and how you may be bound to afflict you."

7   And Samson said to her, "If they bind me with seven fresh cords that have not been dried, then I shall become weak and be like any *other* man."

8   Then the lords of the Philistines brought up to her seven fresh cords that had not been dried, and she bound him with them.

9   Now she had *men* lying in wait in an inner room. And she said to him, "The Philistines are upon you, Samson!" But he snapped the cords as a string of tow snaps when it touches fire. So his strength was not discovered.

b. Delilah's second attempt

16:10
vv. 13,15
10   Then Delilah said to Samson, "Behold, you have deceived me and told me lies; now please tell me, how you may be bound."

11   And he said to her, "If they bind me tightly with new ropes which have not been used, then I shall become weak and be like any *other* man."

12   So Delilah took new ropes and bound him with them and said to him, "The Philistines are upon you, Samson!" For the *men* were lying in wait in the inner room. But he snapped the ropes from his arms like a thread.

c. Delilah's third attempt

16:13
vv. 10,15
13   Then Delilah said to Samson, "Up to now you have deceived me and told me lies; tell me how you may be bound." And he said to her, "If you weave the seven locks of my hair with the web ¹⁶[and fasten it with a pin, then I shall become weak and be like any other man."]

14   So while he slept, Delilah took the seven locks of his hair and wove them into the web?. And she fastened *it* with the pin, and said to him, "The Philistines are upon you, Samson!" But he awoke from his sleep and pulled out the pin of the loom and the web.

d. Samson succumbs to Delilah's wiles

16:15
Judg 14:16
15   Then she said to him, "How can you say, 'I love you,' when your heart is not with me? You have deceived me these three times and have not told me where your great strength is."

16   And it came about when she pressed him daily with her words and urged him, that his soul was annoyed to death.

16:17
Mic 7:5;
Num 6:5;
Judg 13:5
17   So he told her all *that was* in his heart and said to her, "A razor has never come on my head, for I have been a Nazirite to God from my mother's womb. If I am shaved, then my strength will leave me and I shall become weak and be like any *other* man."

e. The Philistines seize Samson

18   When Delilah saw that he had told her all *that was* in his heart, she sent and called the lords of the Philistines, saying, "Come up once more, for he has told me all *that is* in his heart." Then the lords of the Philistines came up to her, and brought the money in their hands.

16:19
Prov 7:26,27
19   And she made him sleep on her knees, and called for a man and had him shave off the seven locks of his hair. Then she began to afflict him, and his strength left him.

---

¹⁶The passage in brackets is found in Gr. but not in any Heb. mss.

20   And she said, "The Philistines are upon you, Samson!" And he awoke from his sleep and said, "I will go out as at other times and shake myself free." But he did not know that the LORD had departed from him.

21   Then the Philistines seized him and gouged out his eyes; and they brought him down to Gaza and bound him with bronze chains, and he was a grinder in the prison.

22   However, the hair of his head began to grow again after it was shaved off.

f. Samson's final revenge and death

23   Now the lords of the Philistines assembled to offer a great sacrifice to Dagon their god, and to rejoice, for they said,
  "Our god has given Samson our enemy into our hands."

24   When the people saw him, they praised their god, for they said,
  "Our god has given our enemy into our hands,
  Even the destroyer of our country,
  Who has slain many of us."

25   It so happened when they were in high spirits, that they said, "Call for Samson, that he may amuse us." So they called for Samson from the prison, and he entertained them. And they made him stand between the pillars.

26   Then Samson said to the boy who was holding his hand, "Let me feel the pillars on which the house rests, that I may lean against them."

27   Now the house was full of men and women, and all the lords of the Philistines were there. And about 3,000 men and women were on the roof looking on while Samson was amusing *them*.

28   Then Samson called to the LORD and said, "O Lord GOD, please remember me and please strengthen me just this time, O God, that I may at once be avenged of the Philistines for my two eyes."

29   And Samson grasped the two middle pillars on which the house rested, and braced himself against them, the one with his right hand and the other with his left.

30   And Samson said, "Let me die with the Philistines!" And he bent with all his might so that the house fell on the lords and all the people who were in it. So the dead whom he killed at his death were more than those whom he killed in his life.

31   Then his brothers and all his father's household came down, took him, brought him up, and buried him between Zorah and Eshtaol in the tomb of Manoah his father. Thus he had judged Israel twenty years.

III. The appendixes (17:1–21:25)

A. Micah the Ephraimite and his priest

1. Micah makes his own idols

17 Now there was a man of the hill country of Ephraim whose name was Micah. 2   And he said to his mother, "The eleven hundred *pieces* of silver which were taken from you, about which you uttered a curse in my hearing, behold, the silver is with me; I took it." And his mother said, "Blessed be my son by the LORD."

3   He then returned the eleven hundred *pieces* of silver to his mother, and his mother said, "I wholly dedicate the silver from my hand to the LORD for my son to make a graven image and a molten image; now therefore, I will return them to you."

4   So when he returned the silver to his mother, his mother took two hundred *pieces* of silver and gave them to the silversmith who made them into a graven image and a molten image, and they were in the house of Micah.

5   And the man Micah had a [17]shrine and he made an ephod and household idols and consecrated one of his sons, that he might become his priest.

6   In those days there was no king in Israel; every man did what was right in his own eyes.

2. Micah hires a Levite as priest

7   Now there was a young man from Bethlehem in Judah, of the family of Judah, who was a Levite; and he was staying there.

[17]Lit., *house of gods*

17:6 *no king in Israel*. This statement (repeated in 18:1; 19:1; 21:25) is clear indication that the book of Judges was put in its present form sometime during the monarchy.

8   Then the man departed from the city, from Bethlehem in Judah, to stay wherever he might find *a place;* and as he made his journey, he came to the hill country of Ephraim to the house of Micah.

9   And Micah said to him, "Where do you come from?" And he said to him, "I am a Levite from Bethlehem in Judah, and I am going to stay wherever I may find *a place.*"

17:10
Judg 18:19

10   Micah then said to him, "Dwell with me and be a father and a priest to me, and I will give you ten *pieces* of silver a year, a suit of clothes, and your maintenance." So the Levite went *in.*

11   And the Levite agreed to live with the man; and the young man became to him like one of his sons.

17:12
v. 5;
Judg 13:25

12   So Micah consecrated the Levite, and the young man became his priest and lived in the house of Micah.

13   Then Micah said, "Now I know that the LORD will prosper me, seeing I have a Levite as priest."

3. The Danite spies: their report

*18:1
Judg 17:6;
19:1;
Josh 19:47

18 In those days there was no king of Israel; and in those days the tribe of the Danites was seeking an inheritance for themselves to live in, for until that day an inheritance had not been allotted to them as a possession among the tribes of Israel.

18:2
Judg 13:25;
Josh 2:1;
Judg 17:1

2   So the sons of Dan sent from their family five men out of their whole number, valiant men from Zorah and Eshtaol, to spy out the land and to search it; and they said to them, "Go, search the land." And they came to the hill country of Ephraim, to the house of Micah, and lodged there.

3   When they were near the house of Micah, they recognized the voice of the young man, the Levite; and they turned aside there, and said to him, "Who brought you here? And what are you doing in this *place?* And what do you have here?"

18:4
Judg 17:10,12

4   And he said to them, "Thus and so has Micah done to me, and he has hired me, and I have become his priest."

18:5
1 Kin 22:5

5   And they said to him, "Inquire of God, please, that we may know whether our way on which we are going will be prosperous."

18:6
1 Kin 22:6

6   And the priest said to them, "Go in peace; your way in which you are going has the LORD's approval."

18:7
vv. 27,28;
Josh 19:47

7   Then the five men departed and came to Laish and saw the people who were in it living in security, after the manner of the Sidonians, quiet and secure; for there was no ruler humiliating *them* for anything in the land, and they were far from the Sidonians and had no dealings with anyone.

18:8
v. 2

8   When they came back to their brothers at Zorah and Eshtaol, their brothers said to them, "What *do* you *report?*"

18:9
Num 13:30;
1 Kin 22:3

9   And they said, "Arise, and let us go up against them; for we have seen the land, and behold, it is very good. And will you sit still? Do not delay to go, to enter, to possess the land.

18:10
vv. 7,27;
Deut 8:9

10   "When you enter, you shall come to a secure people with a spacious land; for God has given it into your hand, a place where there is no lack of anything that is on the earth."

11   Then from the family of the Danites, from Zorah and from Eshtaol, six hundred men armed with weapons of war set out.

18:12
Judg 13:25

12   And they went up and camped at Kiriath-jearim in Judah. Therefore they called that place [18]Mahaneh-dan to this day; behold, it is west of Kiriath-jearim.

18:13
v. 2

13   And they passed from there to the hill country of Ephraim and came to the house of Micah.

4. The Danites take Micah's idols and priest

18:14
Judg 17:5

14   Then the five men who went to spy out the country of Laish answered and said to their kinsmen, "Do you know that there are in these houses an ephod and

[18]I.e., the camp of Dan

18:1 *an inheritance had not been allotted to them,* that is, they had not been able to conquer the territory assigned (see Josh. 19:47 for the Danites' capture of Lesham). In the lowlands assigned to Dan were fertile plains occupied by the Amorites, who had iron chariots. The tribe of Dan was wanting an all-conquering faith in God. Even if they had had such faith in *any* measure it would have enabled them to overcome their enemies.

¹⁹household idols and a graven image and a molten image? Now therefore, consider what you should do."

15   And they turned aside there and came to the house of the young man, the Levite, to the house of Micah, and asked him of his welfare.

16   And the six hundred men armed with their weapons of war, who were of the sons of Dan, stood by the entrance of the gate.

17   Now the five men who went to spy out the land went up *and* entered there, *and* took the graven image and the ephod and household idols and the molten image, while the priest stood by the entrance of the gate with the six hundred men armed with weapons of war.

18   And when these went into Micah's house and took the graven image, the ephod and household idols and the molten image, the priest said to them, "What are you doing?"

19   And they said to him, "Be silent, put your hand over your mouth and come with us, and be to us a father and a priest. Is it better for you to be a priest to the house of one man, or to be priest to a tribe and a family in Israel?"

20   And the priest's heart was glad, and he took the ephod and household idols and the graven image, and went among the people.

5. *Micah's failure to recover his idols*

21   Then they turned and departed, and put the little ones and the livestock and the valuables in front of them.

22   When they had gone some distance from the house of Micah, the men who *were* in the houses near Micah's house assembled and overtook the sons of Dan.

23   And they cried to the sons of Dan, who turned around and said to Micah, "What is *the matter* with you, that you have assembled together?"

24   And he said, "You have taken away my gods which I made, and the priest, and have gone away, and what do I have besides? So how can you say to me, 'What is *the matter* with you?'"

25   And the sons of Dan said to him, "Do not let your voice be heard among us, lest fierce men fall upon you and you lose your life, with the lives of your household."

26   So the sons of Dan went on their way; and when Micah saw that they were too strong for him, he turned and went back to his house.

6. *The Danites burn Laish and rebuild it*

27   Then they took what Micah had made and the priest who had belonged to him, and came to Laish, to a people quiet and secure, and struck them with the edge of the sword; and they burned the city with fire.

28   And there was no one to deliver *them*, because it was far from Sidon and they had no dealings with anyone, and it was in the valley which is near Beth-rehob. And they rebuilt the city and lived in it.

29   And they called the name of the city Dan, after the name of Dan their father who was born in Israel; however, the name of the city formerly was Laish.

30   And the sons of Dan set up for themselves the graven image; and Jonathan, the son of Gershom, the son of ²⁰Manasseh, he and his sons were priests to the tribe of the Danites until the day of the captivity of the land.

31   So they set up for themselves Micah's graven image which he had made, all the time that the house of God was at Shiloh.

B. *The Levite and his concubine*

1. *The Levite recovers his concubine*

19 Now it came about in those days, when there was no king in Israel, that there was a certain Levite staying in the remote part of the hill country of Ephraim, who took a concubine for himself from Bethlehem in Judah.

2   But his concubine played the harlot against him, and she went away from

---

Margin references:
18:16 v. 11
18:17 vv. 2,14
18:19 Job 21:5; Judg 17:10
18:24 Judg 17:5
18:27 vv. 7,10; Josh 19:47
18:28 v. 7; 2 Sam 10:6
*18:29 Josh 19:47
*18:30 Judg 17:3,5; Ex 2:22
*18:31 Josh 18:1
19:1 Judg 18:1

---

¹⁹Heb., *teraphim*, and so throughout this context   ²⁰Some ancient versions read *Moses*

18:29 *Laish. Leshem* in Josh. 19:47.
18:30 *captivity of the land.* This refers to the captivity of northern Palestine by the Assyrian king Tiglath-pileser III. Reference to this event, which took place about 732 B.C., indicates that the compilation of the book was quite late in the monarchy. Others believe that it refers to the captivity of the ark under Eli.
18:31 The Philistines captured the ark and destroyed Shiloh about 1050 B.C.

him to her father's house in Bethlehem in Judah, and was there for a period of four months.

19:3
Gen 34:3;
50:21

3   Then her husband arose and went after her to speak tenderly to her in order to bring her back, taking with him his servant and a pair of donkeys. So she brought him into her father's house, and when the girl's father saw him, he was glad to meet him.

4   And his father-in-law, the girl's father, detained him; and he remained with him three days. So they ate and drank and lodged there.

19:5
v. 8; Gen 18:5

5   Now it came about on the fourth day that they got up early in the morning, and he prepared to go; and the girl's father said to his son-in-law, "Sustain yourself with a piece of bread, and afterward you may go."

19:6
vv. 9,22

6   So both of them sat down and ate and drank together; and the girl's father said to the man, "Please be willing to spend the night, and let your heart be merry."

7   Then the man arose to go, but his father-in-law urged him so that he spent the night there again.

8   And on the fifth day he arose to go early in the morning, and the girl's father said, "Please sustain yourself, and wait until afternoon"; so both of them ate.

9   When the man arose to go along with his concubine and servant, his father-in-law, the girl's father, said to him, "Behold now, the day has drawn to a close; please spend the night. Lo, the day is coming to an end; spend the night here that your heart may be merry. Then tomorrow you may arise early for your journey so that you may go home."

2. They spend the night at Gibeah

19:10
1 Chr 11:4,5

10   But the man was not willing to spend the night, so he arose and departed and came to *a place* opposite Jebus (that is, Jerusalem). And there were with him a pair of saddled donkeys; his concubine also was with him.

19:11
Judg 1:21

11   When they *were* near Jebus, the day was almost gone; and the servant said to his master, "Please come, and let us turn aside into this city of the Jebusites and spend the night in it."

19:12
Heb 11:13

12   However, his master said to him, "We will not turn aside into the city of foreigners who are not of the sons of Israel; but we will go on as far as Gibeah."

13   And he said to his servant, "Come and let us approach one of these places; and we will spend the night in Gibeah or Ramah."

14   So they passed along and went their way, and the sun set on them near Gibeah which belongs to Benjamin.

19:15
Heb 13:2

15   And they turned aside there in order to enter *and* lodge in Gibeah. When they entered, they sat down in the open square of the city, for no one took them into *his* house to spend the night.

3. The Ephraimite's hospitality

19:16
Ps 104:23;
v. 14

16   Then behold, an old man was coming out of the field from his work at evening. Now the man was from the hill country of Ephraim, and he was staying in Gibeah, but the men of the place were Benjamites.

17   And he lifted up his eyes and saw the traveler in the open square of the city; and the old man said, "Where are you going, and where do you come from?"

19:18
Judg 18:31;
20:18

18   And he said to him, "We are passing from Bethlehem in Judah to the remote part of the hill country of Ephraim, *for* I am from there, and I went to Bethlehem in Judah. But I am *now* going to my house, and no man will take me into his house.

19   "Yet there is both straw and fodder for our donkeys, and also bread and wine for me, your maidservant, and the young man who is with your servants; there is no lack of anything."

20   And the old man said, "Peace to you. Only let me *take care of* all your needs; however, do not spend the night in the open square."

19:21
Gen 24:32,33

21   So he took him into his house and gave the donkeys fodder, and they washed their feet and ate and drank.

4. The abuse of the concubine

19:22
Gen 19:4;
Deut 13:13;
Rom 1:26,27

22   While they were making merry, behold, the men of the city, certain worthless fellows, surrounded the house, pounding the door; and they spoke to the owner of the house, the old man, saying, "Bring out the man who came into your house that we may have relations with him."

19:23
Gen 34:7;

23   Then the man, the owner of the house, went out to them and said to them,

"No, my fellows, please do not act so wickedly; since this man has come into my house, do not commit this act of folly.

24 "Here is my virgin daughter and his concubine. Please let me bring them out that you may ravish them and do to them whatever you wish. But do not commit such an act of folly against this man."

25 But the men would not listen to him, so the man seized his concubine and brought *her* out to them. And they raped her and abused her all night until morning, then let her go at the approach of dawn.

26 As the day began to dawn, the woman came and fell down at the doorway of the man's house where her master was, until *full* daylight.

5. *The Levite's anger*

27 When her master arose in the morning and opened the doors of the house and went out to go on his way, then behold, his concubine was lying at the doorway of the house, with her hands on the threshold.

28 And he said to her, "Get up and let us go," but there was no answer. Then he placed her on the donkey; and the man arose and went to his home.

29 When he entered his house, he took a knife and laid hold of his concubine and cut her in twelve pieces, limb by limb, and sent her throughout the territory of Israel.

30 And it came about that all who saw *it* said, "Nothing like this has *ever* happened or been seen from the day when the sons of Israel came up from the land of Egypt to this day. Consider it, take counsel and speak up!"

6. *War between Israel and Benjamin*

a. *Israel gathers at Mizpah: the Levite tells his tale*

20 Then all the sons of Israel from Dan to Beersheba, including the land of Gilead, came out, and the congregation assembled as one man to the LORD at Mizpah.

2 And the chiefs of all the people, *even* of all the tribes of Israel, took their stand in the assembly of the people of God, 400,000 foot soldiers who drew the sword.

3 (Now the sons of Benjamin heard that the sons of Israel had gone up to Mizpah.) And the sons of Israel said, "Tell *us*, how did this wickedness take place?"

4 So the Levite, the husband of the woman who was murdered, answered and said, "I came with my concubine to spend the night at Gibeah which belongs to Benjamin.

5 "But the men of Gibeah rose up against me and surrounded the house at night because of me. They intended to kill me; instead, they ravished my concubine so that she died.

6 "And I took hold of my concubine and cut her in pieces and sent her throughout the land of Israel's inheritance; for they have committed a lewd and disgraceful act in Israel.

7 "Behold, all you sons of Israel, give your advice and counsel here."

8 Then all the people arose as one man, saying, "Not one of us will go to his tent, nor will any of us return to his house.

9 "But now this is the thing which we will do to Gibeah; *we will go up* against it by lot.

10 "And we will take 10 men out of 100 throughout the tribes of Israel, and 100 out of 1,000, and 1,000 out of 10,000 to supply food for the people, that when they come to Gibeah of Benjamin, they may punish *them* for all the disgraceful acts that they have committed in Israel."

11 Thus all the men of Israel were gathered against the city, united as one man.

b. *The Benjamites refuse to repent*

12 Then the tribes of Israel sent men through the entire tribe of Benjamin, saying, "What is this wickedness that has taken place among you?

13 "Now then, deliver up the men, the [21]worthless fellows in Gibeah, that we may put them to death and remove *this* wickedness from Israel." But the sons of Benjamin would not listen to the voice of their brothers, the sons of Israel.

[21]Lit., *sons of Belial*

Marginal references:

Deut 22:21; 2 Sam 13:12

19:24
Gen 19:8; Deut 21:14

19:28
Judg 20:5

19:29
1 Sam 11:7

19:30
Judg 20:7

20:1
Judg 21:5; 1 Sam 7:5

20:4
Judg 19:15

20:5
Judg 19:22, 25,26

20:6
Judg 19:29; Josh 7:15

20:7
Judg 19:30

20:12
Deut 13:14, 15

20:13
Judg 19:22

14 And the sons of Benjamin gathered from the cities to Gibeah, to go out to battle against the sons of Israel.
15 And from the cities on that day the sons of Benjamin were numbered, 26,000 men who draw the sword, besides the inhabitants of Gibeah who were numbered, 700 choice men.

20:16
Judg 3:15;
1 Chr 12:2

16 Out of all these people 700 choice men were left-handed; each one could sling a stone at a hair and not miss.
17 Then the men of Israel besides Benjamin were numbered, 400,000 men who draw the sword; all these were men of war.

c. Israel seeks the will of God

20:18
vv. 23,26,27;
Num 27:21

18 Now the sons of Israel arose, went up to Bethel, and inquired of God, and said, "Who shall go up first for us to battle against the sons of Benjamin?" Then the LORD said, "Judah *shall go up* first."

d. The initial victory of Benjamin

19 So the sons of Israel arose in the morning and camped against Gibeah.
20 And the men of Israel went out to battle against Benjamin, and the men of Israel arrayed for battle against them at Gibeah.

20:21
v. 25

21 Then the sons of Benjamin came out of Gibeah and felled to the ground on that day 22,000 men of Israel.
22 But the people, the men of Israel, encouraged themselves and arrayed for battle again in the place where they had arrayed themselves the first day.

20:23
v. 18

23 And the sons of Israel went up and wept before the LORD until evening, and inquired of the LORD, saying, "Shall we again draw near for battle against the sons of my brother Benjamin?" And the LORD said, "Go up against him."

e. Benjamin's second victory

24 Then the sons of Israel came against the sons of Benjamin the second day.

20:25
v. 21

25 And Benjamin went out against them from Gibeah the second day and felled to the ground again 18,000 men of the sons of Israel; all these drew the sword.

20:26
v. 23;
Judg 21:2

26 Then all the sons of Israel and all the people went up and came to Bethel and wept; thus they remained there before the LORD and fasted that day until evening. And they offered burnt offerings and peace offerings before the LORD.

20:27
Josh 18:1

27 And the sons of Israel inquired of the LORD (for the ark of the covenant of God *was* there in those days,

*20:28
Josh 24:33;
Deut 18:5;
Judg 7:9

28 and Phinehas the son of Eleazar, Aaron's son, stood before it to *minister* in those days), saying, "Shall I yet again go out to battle against the sons of my brother Benjamin, or shall I cease?" And the LORD said, "Go up, for tomorrow I will deliver them into your hand."

f. The rout of Benjamin

20:29
Josh 8:4

29 So Israel set men in ambush around Gibeah.
30 And the sons of Israel went up against the sons of Benjamin on the third day and arrayed themselves against Gibeah, as at other times.

20:31
Josh 8:16

31 And the sons of Benjamin went out against the people and were drawn away from the city, and they began to strike and kill some of the people, as at other times, on the highways, one of which goes up to Bethel and the other to Gibeah, *and* in the field, about thirty men of Israel.
32 And the sons of Benjamin said, "They are struck down before us, as at the first." But the sons of Israel said, "Let us flee that we may draw them away from the city to the highways."

20:33
Josh 8:19

33 Then all the men of Israel arose from their place and arrayed themselves at Baal-tamar; and the men of Israel in ambush broke out of their place, even out of Maareh-geba.

20:34
Josh 8:14

34 When ten thousand choice men from all Israel came against Gibeah, the battle became fierce; but Benjamin did not know that disaster was close to them.
35 And the LORD struck Benjamin before Israel, so that the sons of Israel destroyed 25,100 men of Benjamin that day, all who draw the sword.

20:36
Josh 8:15

36 So the sons of Benjamin saw that they were defeated. When the men of Israel gave ground to Benjamin because they relied on the men in ambush whom they had set against Gibeah,

---

20:28 Initial defeat did not mean ultimate defeat. Victory came after the first disaster.

37   the men in ambush hurried and rushed against Gibeah; the men in ambush also deployed and struck all the city with the edge of the sword.

38   Now the appointed sign between the men of Israel and the men in ambush was that they should make a great cloud of smoke rise from the city.

39   Then the men of Israel turned in the battle, and Benjamin began to strike and kill about thirty men of Israel, for they said, "Surely they are defeated before us, as in the first battle."

40   But when the cloud began to rise from the city in a column of smoke, Benjamin looked behind them; and behold, the whole city was going up *in smoke* to heaven.

41   Then the men of Israel turned, and the men of Benjamin were terrified; for they saw that disaster was close to them.

42   Therefore, they turned their backs before the men of Israel toward the direction of the wilderness, but the battle overtook them while those who came out of the cities destroyed them in the midst of them.

43   They surrounded Benjamin, pursued them without rest *and* trod them down opposite Gibeah toward the east.

44   Thus 18,000 men of Benjamin fell; all these were valiant warriors.

45   The rest turned and fled toward the wilderness to the rock of Rimmon, but they caught 5,000 of them on the highways and overtook them at Gidom and killed 2,000 of them.

46   So all of Benjamin who fell that day were 25,000 men who draw the sword; all these were valiant warriors.

47   But 600 men turned and fled toward the wilderness to the rock of Rimmon, and they remained at the rock of Rimmon four months.

48   The men of Israel then turned back against the sons of Benjamin and struck them with the edge of the sword, both the entire city with the cattle and all that they found; they also set on fire all the cities which they found.

7. The preservation of the tribe of Benjamin

a. Israel weeps for Benjamin

21 Now the men of Israel had sworn in Mizpah, saying, "None of us shall give his daughter to Benjamin in marriage."

2   So the people came to Bethel and sat there before God until evening, and lifted up their voices and wept bitterly.

3   And they said, "Why, O LORD, God of Israel, has this come about in Israel, so that one tribe should be *missing* today in Israel?"

4   And it came about the next day that the people arose early and built an altar there, and offered burnt offerings and peace offerings.

5   Then the sons of Israel said, "Who is there among all the tribes of Israel who did not come up in the assembly to the LORD?" For they had taken a great oath concerning him who did not come up to the LORD at Mizpah, saying, "He shall surely be put to death."

6   And the sons of Israel were sorry for their brother Benjamin and said, "One tribe is cut off from Israel today.

7   "What shall we do for wives for those who are left, since we have sworn by the LORD not to give them any of our daughters in marriage?"

b. Wives for the Benjamites

(1) THE VIRGINS OF JABESH-GILEAD

8   And they said, "What one is there of the tribes of Israel who did not come up to the LORD at Mizpah?" And behold, no one had come to the camp from Jabesh-gilead to the assembly.

9   For when the people were numbered, behold, not one of the inhabitants of Jabesh-gilead was there.

10   And the congregation sent 12,000 of the valiant warriors there, and commanded them, saying, "Go and strike the inhabitants of Jabesh-gilead with the edge of the sword, with the women and the little ones.

---

*20:37
Josh 8:19

20:38
Josh 8:20

20:39
v. 32

*20:40
Josh 8:20

20:45
Judg 21:13

20:47
Judg 21:13

21:1
vv. 7,18

21:2
Judg 20:18,26

21:4
2 Sam 24:25

21:7
v. 1

20:37,40 Evidences of this destruction have been found by excavators at Gibeah.
21:8 Apparently the old marriage ties between the Benja-mites and Machir (Gilead) (see 1 Chr. 7:14,15) explain why no inhabitants of Jabesh-gilead came up to fight Benjamin.

<table>
<tr><td>

21:11
Num 31:17

</td><td>

11 "And this is the thing that you shall do: you shall utterly destroy every man and every woman who has lain with a man."

12 And they found among the inhabitants of Jabesh-gilead 400 young virgins who had not known a man by lying with him; and they brought them to the camp at Shiloh, which is in the land of Canaan.

</td></tr>
<tr><td>

21:13
Judg 20:47;
Deut 20:10

</td><td>

13 Then the whole congregation sent *word* and spoke to the sons of Benjamin who were at the rock of Rimmon, and proclaimed peace to them.

14 And Benjamin returned at that time, and they gave them the women whom they had kept alive from the women of Jabesh-gilead; yet they were not enough for them.

</td></tr>
<tr><td>

21:15
v. 6

</td><td>

15 And the people were sorry for Benjamin because the LORD had made a breach in the tribes of Israel.

</td></tr>
</table>

(2) THE DAUGHTERS OF SHILOH

<table>
<tr><td></td><td>

16 Then the elders of the congregation said, "What shall we do for wives for those who are left, since the women are destroyed out of Benjamin?"

17 And they said, "*There must be* an inheritance for the survivors of Benjamin, that a tribe may not be blotted out from Israel.

</td></tr>
<tr><td>

21:18
v. 18

</td><td>

18 "But we cannot give them wives of our daughters." For the sons of Israel had sworn, saying, "Cursed is he who gives a wife to Benjamin."

</td></tr>
<tr><td>

21:19
Judg 18:31;
1 Sam 1:3

</td><td>

19 So they said, "Behold, there is a feast of the LORD from year to year in Shiloh, which is on the north side of Bethel, on the east side of the highway that goes up from Bethel to Shechem, and on the south side of Lebonah."

20 And they commanded the sons of Benjamin, saying, "Go and lie in wait in the vineyards,

</td></tr>
<tr><td>

21:21
Ex 15:20;
Judg 11:34

</td><td>

21 and watch; and behold, if the daughters of Shiloh come out to take part in the dances, then you shall come out of the vineyards and each of you shall catch his wife from the daughters of Shiloh, and go to the land of Benjamin.

</td></tr>
<tr><td>

*21:22
vv. 1, 18

</td><td>

22 "And it shall come about, when their fathers or their brothers come to complain to us, that we shall say to them, 'Give them to us voluntarily, because we did not take for each man *of Benjamin* a wife in battle, nor did you give *them* to them, *else* you would now be guilty.' "

</td></tr>
<tr><td>

21:23
Judg 20:48

</td><td>

23 And the sons of Benjamin did so, and took wives according to their number from those who danced, whom they carried away. And they went and returned to their inheritance, and rebuilt the cities and lived in them.

24 And the sons of Israel departed from there at that time, every man to his tribe and family, and each one of them went out from there to his inheritance.

</td></tr>
</table>

8. *Summary of the age of the judges*

<table>
<tr><td>

21:25
Judg 17:6;
18:1; 19:1

</td><td>

25 In those days there was no king in Israel; everyone did what was right in his own eyes.

</td></tr>
</table>

21:22 *nor did you give them.* Israel circumvented its vow, and any guilt from breaking it, by allowing Benjamin to *take* wives from the girls who danced during the feast at Shiloh. This prosperous town had become Israel's headquarters.

RUTH

Authorship and Background: Jewish tradition attributed this book to Samuel, but the reference to David (4:17,21) suggests a later period. The story was most likely transmitted orally around Bethlehem until the reign of David, when it came into prominence. The book names Boaz as the great-grandfather of David, which would place the time of the story around 1100 B.C. This beautiful story, sometimes referred to as the second appendix to the book of Judges, shines brilliantly against the dark background of the anarchy pictured in Judges 17-21. In the Hebrew Bible, however, the book of Ruth is placed in the third, and last, division (*kethubim*, "writings") following Psalms, Job, and Proverbs, and is established as part of the Rolls, along with the Song of Solomon, Ecclesiastes, Lamentations, and Esther. The order in the English Bible stems from the Septuagint. Ruth was a Moabitess, and apparently in her day marriages among the people of Moab and Israel were contracted (see Deut. 23:3-6). Ruth, a non-Israelite, became an ancestress of Jesus, the greater David, who came to break down the dividing wall of hostility between Jews and Gentiles. The author of Ruth is unknown, and the date it was written cannot be determined conclusively.

Relating a story from the period of Judges, a period characterized by savagery, lust, strife, and lawlessness, the book of Ruth presents a strange contrast. Instead of war, bloodshed, cruelty, politics, and intrigue, there is love and marriage, simple faith, and the tilling of the land—the common customs of ordinary people as they lived and died amid the turbulence of their age.

Characteristics: Ruth is the record of tragedy and love in the lives of average people. In it we see the fortunes of Elimelech of Bethlehem, who, with his wife Naomi and his two sons, goes to Moab in a time of famine. He and his sons die there. Naomi yearns for her homeland and returns with Ruth, a young Moabitess who had been married to her deceased son. The story is told in simple language, with the customs of the people being unfolded. The attractiveness of the story derives from the suspense factor, as faithful Ruth, still young and marriageable, is rewarded for her faithfulness when she meets and marries Boaz, a near kinsman. Boaz's preliminary reaction to his kinsman's role, and the refusal of a nearer kinsman to marry Ruth add further suspense to the story. The happy ending and the sequel that marks David as a descendant of Ruth and Boaz add luster to the narrative.

Contents:

IV. **Boaz and Ruth marry (4:1-22):** The nearest kinsman refuses to marry Ruth lest he impair his own inheritance. The transaction is completed with witnesses. Ruth becomes the wife of Boaz. Obed is born and Naomi cares for the child. Obed becomes the father of Jesse, the father of David.

THE BOOK OF

RUTH

I. Ruth returns with Naomi (1:1–22)

A. Naomi's afflictions

1 Now it came about in the days when the judges governed, that there was a famine in the land. And a certain man of Bethlehem in Judah went to sojourn in the land of Moab with his wife and his two sons.

2   And the name of the man *was* Elimelech, and the name of his wife, Naomi; and the names of his two sons *were* Mahlon and Chilion, Ephrathites of Bethlehem in Judah. Now they entered the land of Moab and remained there.

3   Then Elimelech, Naomi's husband, died; and she was left with her two sons.

4   And they took for themselves Moabite women *as* wives; the name of the one was Orpah and the name of the other Ruth. And they lived there about ten years.

5   Then both Mahlon and Chilion also died; and the woman was bereft of her two children and her husband.

B. Naomi decides to return to Bethlehem

6   Then she arose with her daughters-in-law that she might return from the land of Moab, for she had heard in the land of Moab that the LORD had visited His people in giving them food.

7   So she departed from the place where she was, and her two daughters-in-law with her; and they went on the way to return to the land of Judah.

8   And Naomi said to her two daughters-in-law, "Go, return each of you to her mother's house. May the LORD deal kindly with you as you have dealt with the dead and with me.

9   "May the LORD grant that you may find rest, each in the house of her husband." Then she kissed them, and they lifted up their voices and wept.

10   And they said to her, "*No*, but we will surely return with you to your people."

11   But Naomi said, "Return, my daughters. Why should you go with me? Have I yet sons in my womb, that they may be your husbands?

12   "Return, my daughters! Go, for I am too old to have a husband. If I said I have hope, if I should even have a husband tonight and also bear sons,

13   would you therefore wait until they were grown? Would you therefore refrain from marrying? No, my daughters; for it is harder for me than for you, for the hand of the LORD has gone forth against me."

14   And they lifted up their voices and wept again; and Orpah kissed her mother-in-law, but Ruth clung to her.

C. Ruth refuses to leave Naomi

15   Then she said, "Behold, your sister-in-law has gone back to her people and her gods; return after your sister-in-law."

16   But Ruth said, "Do not urge me to leave you *or* turn back from following

*1:1
Judg 2:16

1:2
Gen 35:19;
Judg 3:30

1:6
Ex 4:31

1:8
v. 5;
Ruth 2:20

1:9
Ruth 3:1

*1:11
Deut 25:5

1:13
Judg 2:15;
Ps 32:4

*1:16
2 Kin 2:2,4,6;
Ruth 2:11,12

1:1 *when the judges governed.* The order, peace, and love of the God-honoring society described in this beautiful story are in marked contrast to the dark, chaotic days that characterized Canaan when "there was no king in Israel" and it was every man for himself.
1:4 Ruth was a Moabitess. The Moabites were descended from Moab, who was the son of Lot and his daughter (Gen. 19:36,37). Eventually Ruth the Moabitess, as the wife of Boaz, became an ancestress of Jesus Christ. Matthew lists the names of four women in the Messianic line, and three of them were Gentiles after the flesh: *Rahab, Ruth,* and *the wife of Uriah,* or "Bathsheba" (Matt. 1:5,6).

1:11 Back of Naomi's questions is the concept of levirate marriage, whereby the brother of a deceased husband marries the widow. This is specifically stated in Deut. 25:5,6. (Also see note to Deut. 25:5–10 for a complete survey of this custom.)
1:16 This beautiful passage has been widely acclaimed, and many brides have used it as part of the wedding ceremony. No woman should make the God of her husband her God unless: (1) her husband's God is the true God and not a false one; and (2) her choice is rooted in her own faith in God: for, however good her intention, her choice has no validity if it is not accompanied by saving faith.

you; for where you go, I will go, and where you lodge, I will lodge. Your people *shall be* my people, and your God, my God.

17   "Where you die, I will die, and there I will be buried. Thus may the LORD do to me, and worse, if *anything but* death parts you and me."

1:18
Acts 21:14

18   When she saw that she was determined to go with her, she said no more to her.

D. *Ruth and Naomi return together*

19   So they both went until they came to Bethlehem. And it came about when they had come to Bethlehem, that all the city was stirred because of them, and the women said, "Is this Naomi?"

1:20
Ex 6:3;
Job 6:4
1:21
Job 1:21

20   And she said to them, "Do not call me ¹Naomi; call me ²Mara, for the Almighty has dealt very bitterly with me.

21   "I went out full, but the LORD has brought me back empty. Why do you call me Naomi, since the LORD has witnessed against me and the Almighty has afflicted me?"

1:22
Ex 9:31,32;
Ruth 2:23

22   So Naomi returned, and with her Ruth the Moabitess, her daughter-in-law, who returned from the land of Moab. And they came to Bethlehem at the beginning of barley harvest.

II. *Ruth meets Boaz (2:1–23)*

A. *Ruth gleans in Boaz's field*

2:1
Ruth 1:2;
3:2,12
*2:2
v. 7;
Lev 19:9;
Deut 24:19

2 Now Naomi had a kinsman of her husband, a man of great wealth, of the family of Elimelech, whose name was Boaz.

2   And Ruth the Moabitess said to Naomi, "Please let me go to the field and glean among the ears of grain after one in whose sight I may find favor." And she said to her, "Go, my daughter."

3   So she departed and went and gleaned in the field after the reapers; and she happened to come to the portion of the field belonging to Boaz, who was of the family of Elimelech.

2:4
Ps 129:7,8;
Luke 1:28

4   Now behold, Boaz came from Bethlehem and said to the reapers, "May the LORD be with you." And they said to him, "May the LORD bless you."

5   Then Boaz said to his servant who was in charge of the reapers, "Whose young woman is this?"

2:6
Ruth 1:22

6   And the servant in charge of the reapers answered and said, "She is the young Moabite woman who returned with Naomi from the land of Moab.

7   "And she said, 'Please let me glean and gather after the reapers among the sheaves.' Thus she came and has remained from the morning until now; she has been sitting in the house for a little while."

B. *Boaz commends faithful Ruth*

8   Then Boaz said to Ruth, "Listen carefully, my daughter. Do not go to glean in another field; furthermore, do not go on from this one, but stay here with my maids.

9   "Let your eyes be on the field which they reap, and go after them. Indeed, I have commanded the servants not to touch you. When you are thirsty, go to the water jars and drink from what the servants draw."

2:10
1 Sam 25:23

10   Then she fell on her face, bowing to the ground and said to him, "Why have I found favor in your sight that you should take notice of me, since I am a foreigner?"

*2:11
Ruth 1:14,
16,17

11   And Boaz answered and said to her, "All that you have done for your mother-in-law after the death of your husband has been fully reported to me, and how you left your father and your mother and the land of your birth, and came to a people that you did not previously know.

2:12
1 Sam 24:19;
Ps 17:8;
Ruth 1:16

12   "May the LORD reward your work, and your wages be full from the LORD, the God of Israel, under whose wings you have come to seek refuge."

¹I.e., pleasant ²I.e., bitter

2:2 This custom is in accord with Deut. 24:19.
2:11 Refer back to v. 5 where it is evident that Boaz does not know who Ruth is, but evidently he is fully aware of

Ruth's good reputation and character without any knowledge of her identity.

13   Then she said, "I have found favor in your sight, my lord, for you have comforted me and indeed have spoken kindly to your maidservant, though I am not like one of your maidservants."

14   And at mealtime Boaz said to her, "Come here, that you may eat of the bread and dip your piece of bread in the vinegar." So she sat beside the reapers; and he served her roasted grain, and she ate and was satisfied and had some left.

15   When she rose to glean, Boaz commanded his servants, saying, "Let her glean even among the sheaves, and do not insult her.

16   "And also you shall purposely pull out for her *some grain* from the bundles and leave *it* that she may glean, and do not rebuke her."

2:14
v. 18

C. Ruth confides in Naomi

17   So she gleaned in the field until evening. Then she beat out what she had gleaned, and it was about an ephah of barley.

18   And she took *it* up and went into the city, and her mother-in-law saw what she had gleaned. She also took *it* out and gave Naomi what she had left after she was satisfied.

2:18
v. 14

19   Her mother-in-law then said to her, "Where did you glean today and where did you work? May he who took notice of you be blessed." So she told her mother-in-law with whom she had worked and said, "The name of the man with whom I worked today is Boaz."

2:19
v. 10

20   And Naomi said to her daughter-in-law, "May he be blessed of the LORD who has not withdrawn his kindness to the living and to the dead." Again Naomi said to her, "The man is our relative, he is one of our closest relatives."

2:20
Ruth 3:10;
Prov 17:17;
Ruth 3:9; 4:6

21   Then Ruth the Moabitess said, "Furthermore, he said to me, 'You should stay close to my servants until they have finished all my harvest.' "

22   And Naomi said to Ruth her daughter-in-law, "It is good, my daughter, that you go out with his maids, lest *others* fall upon you in another field."

23   So she stayed close by the maids of Boaz in order to glean until the end of the barley harvest and the wheat harvest. And she lived with her mother-in-law.

*2:23
Deut 16:9

III. *Boaz decides (3:1–18)*

A. Naomi counsels Ruth

3 Then Naomi her mother-in-law said to her, "My daughter, shall I not seek security for you, that it may be well with you?

*3:1
Ruth 1:9

2   "And now is not Boaz our kinsman, with whose maids you were? Behold, he winnows barley at the threshing floor tonight.

3:2
Deut 25:5-10;
Ruth 2:8

3   "Wash yourself therefore, and anoint yourself and put on your *best* clothes, and go down to the threshing floor; *but* do not make yourself known to the man until he has finished eating and drinking.

3:3
2 Sam 14:2

4   "And it shall be when he lies down, that you shall notice the place where he lies, and you shall go and uncover his feet and lie down; then he will tell you what you shall do."

5   And she said to her, "All that you say I will do."

B. Ruth follows Naomi's counsel: Boaz determines to act

6   So she went down to the threshing floor and did according to all that her mother-in-law had commanded her.

7   When Boaz had eaten and drunk and his heart was merry, he went to lie down at the end of the heap of grain; and she came secretly, and uncovered his feet and lay down.

3:7
Judg 19:6,9,
22;
2 Sam 13:28

8   And it happened in the middle of the night that the man was startled and bent forward; and behold, a woman was lying at his feet.

9   And he said, "Who are you?" And she answered, "I am Ruth your maid. So spread your covering over your maid, for you are a ³close relative."

*3:9
v. 12;
Ruth 2:20

³Or, *redeemer*, and so throughout this context

2:23 This verse further illustrates Ruth's compliance, obedience, and moral goodness—qualities that attracted Boaz to her.
3:1 Naomi suggests a course of action consonant with the intention of Israel's levirate custom (see note to 1:11). When

this custom was followed, the first-born was thought of as the son of the woman's deceased husband, but all subsequent children were recognized as those of her second husband. By such action the family ownership of land could be perpetuated.

3:11
Prov 12:4

*3:12
v. 9; Ruth 4:1

3:13
Ruth 4:5

3:18
Ps 37:3-5

4:1
Ruth 3:12

4:3
Lev 25:25

4:4
Jer 32:7,8;
Lev 25:25

*4:5ff
Deut 25:5,6

4:6
Ruth 3:12,13

4:7
Deut 25:7,9

10   Then he said, "May you be blessed of the LORD, my daughter. You have shown your last kindness to be better than the first by not going after young men, whether poor or rich.

11   "And now, my daughter, do not fear. I will do for you whatever you ask, for all my people in the city know that you are a woman of excellence.

12   "And now it is true I am a close relative; however, there is a relative closer than I.

13   "Remain this night, and when morning comes, if he will redeem you, good; let him redeem you. But if he does not wish to redeem you, then I will redeem you, as the LORD lives. Lie down until morning."

C. Ruth returns to Naomi

14   So she lay at his feet until morning and rose before one could recognize another; and he said, "Let it not be known that the woman came to the threshing floor."

15   Again he said, "Give me the cloak that is on you and hold it." So she held it, and he measured six *measures* of barley and laid *it* on her. Then she went into the city.

16   And when she came to her mother-in-law, she said, "How did it go, my daughter?" And she told her all that the man had done for her.

17   And she said, "These six *measures* of barley he gave to me, for he said, 'Do not go to your mother-in-law empty-handed.'"

18   Then she said, "Wait, my daughter, until you know how the matter turns out; for the man will not rest until he has settled it today."

IV. *Boaz and Ruth marry (4:1–22)*

A. *Boaz seeks out the nearest kinsman: the kinsman declines*

4   Now Boaz went up to the gate and sat down there, and behold, the close relative of whom Boaz spoke was passing by, so he said, "Turn aside, friend, sit down here." And he turned aside and sat down.

2   And he took ten men of the elders of the city and said, "Sit down here." So they sat down.

3   Then he said to the closest relative, "Naomi, who has come back from the land of Moab, has to sell the piece of land which belonged to our brother Elimelech.

4   "So I thought to inform you, saying, 'Buy *it* before those who are sitting *here,* and before the elders of my people. If you will redeem *it,* redeem *it;* but if not, tell me that I may know; for there is no one but you to redeem *it,* and I am after you.'" And I said, "I will redeem *it.*"

5   Then Boaz said, "On the day you buy the field from the hand of Naomi, you must also acquire Ruth the Moabitess, the widow of the deceased, in order to raise up the name of the deceased on his inheritance."

6   And the closest relative said, "I cannot redeem *it* for myself, lest I jeopardize my own inheritance. Redeem *it* for yourself; you *may have* my right of redemption, for I cannot redeem *it.*"

B. *Boaz fulfills the legal requirements*

7   Now this was *the custom* in former times in Israel concerning the redemption and the exchange *of land* to confirm any matter: a man removed his sandal and gave it to another; and this was the *manner of* attestation in Israel.

8   So the closest relative said to Boaz, "Buy *it* for yourself." And he removed his sandal.

9   Then Boaz said to the elders and all the people, "You are witnesses today

---

3:9 Ruth's action invited Boaz to perform the function of nearest kinsman and as such was both proper and devoid of any immorality. The custom was common to Israelitish society; however, no Biblical sanction exists for its use today.
3:12 The propriety of Boaz's conduct bespeaks the worth of his character and life.
4:5a Boaz carefully ties the purchase of the land to the marriage of Ruth, and evidently he was aware of the fact

that the nearer kinsman would decline to buy the land if he had to take Ruth with it. (Read Deut. 25:5,6 in this connection.)
4:5b–10 The right of redemption exercised by Boaz involved property (Lev. 25:25) and marriage (Deut. 25:5–10), but the precise details are not exactly in accord with the regulations; for example, while Boaz was a near kinsman, he was not the brother of Mahlon.

that I have bought from the hand of Naomi all that belonged to Elimelech and all that belonged to Chilion and Mahlon.

10 "Moreover, I have acquired Ruth the Moabitess, the widow of Mahlon, to be my wife in order to raise up the name of the deceased on his inheritance, so that the name of the deceased may not be cut off from his brothers or from the court of his *birth* place; you are witnesses today."

4:10
Deut 25:6

11 And all the people who were in the court, and the elders, said, "*We are* witnesses. May the LORD make the woman who is coming into your home like Rachel and Leah, both of whom built the house of Israel; and may you achieve wealth in Ephrathah and become famous in Bethlehem.

4:11
Ps 127:3

12 "Moreover, may your house be like the house of Perez whom Tamar bore to Judah, through the offspring which the LORD shall give you by this young woman."

*4:12
v. 18;
Gen 38:29

C. Boaz and Ruth marry: Obed is born

13 So Boaz took Ruth, and she became his wife, and he went in to her. And the LORD enabled her to conceive, and she gave birth to a son.

4:13
Ruth 3:11;
Gen 29:31;
33:5

14 Then the women said to Naomi, "Blessed is the LORD who has not left you without a redeemer today, and may his name become famous in Israel.

4:14
Luke 1:58

15 "May he also be to you a restorer of life and a sustainer of your old age; for your daughter-in-law, who loves you and is better to you than seven sons, has given birth to him."

4:15
Ruth 1:16,17;
2:11,12

16 Then Naomi took the child and laid him in her lap, and became his nurse.

17 And the neighbor women gave him a name, saying, "A son has been born to Naomi!" So they named him Obed. He is the father of Jesse, the father of David.

D. Ruth enters the Davidic line

18 Now these are the generations of Perez: to Perez was born Hezron,
19 and to Hezron was born Ram, and to Ram, Amminadab,
20 and to Amminadab was born Nahshon, and to Nahshon, Salmon,
21 and to Salmon was born Boaz, and to Boaz, Obed,
22 and to Obed was born Jesse, and to Jesse, David.

*4:18
Matt 1:3-6

4:12 Tamar determined to play the role of a harlot in order to force Judah to perform the part of the near kinsman, since Judah had refused to allow Tamar's brother-in-law to perform this function. However, Tamar protected her pu-

rity and any odium belonged to Judah alone in this instance.
4:18 The genealogy is traced from Perez, who was born to Tamar, rather than from the birth of Obed.

INTRODUCTION TO
THE FIRST BOOK OF
SAMUEL

Authorship and Background: 1 and 2 Samuel, like the two books of Kings, were originally a single book. The Septuagint translators considered these two larger books a complete history of the kingdoms of Israel and Judah, and, after dividing them into four books, they named them "Books of Kingdoms" instead of the Hebrew titles "Samuel" and "Kings." Jerome followed the same division in his Latin Vulgate, but he changed the title to "Books of Kings." The various English Bibles have retained the Hebrew titles, while following the Septuagint-Vulgate divisions. In some instances the four books are subtitled "The First, Second, Third, and Fourth Book of the Kings," as in the Vulgate.

A late Jewish tradition attributed the two books of Samuel to the prophet Samuel, but internal evidence shows that the writer lived later than the events he recorded and that he made use of early source materials such as the Chronicles of Samuel, Nathan, and Gad referred to in 1 Chr. 29:29. For example, 2 Sam. 9-20 may well be based on an old historical record from the royal court of David. The fact that the books were named for Samuel indicates the high regard in which he was held. He was ordained of God to deliver Israel when its national situation appeared hopeless. He was probably the founder of the schools of the prophets. He lived and ministered during the changeover from the judges to the monarchy, and was privileged to train David, who became Israel's great shepherd-king.

Characteristics: The books of Samuel cover the history of Israel from the period of the judges to the close of the reign of David. There are three main characters: Samuel, Saul, and David. Samuel the prophet was, like Moses, a man of destiny. As the last of the judges, he anointed both Saul and David to be king. Thus he was a crucial link in the transition from the dark and forbidding days of the judges to the establishment of the Davidic monarchy. The books of Samuel are both history and biography. No effort is made to gloss over the defects and sins of the chief characters. The stories of their lives reveal them to have been both good and bad, having high ideals at times and falling into disobedience and sin on others occasions. In devotion and obedience to God, Samuel stands out as one of the great Old Testament characters. Yet his sons, like those of Eli, were wicked.

Contents:

I. The judgeship of Samuel (1:1-7:17): Samuel's birth and consecration. His ministry before God in the house of Eli. His prophecy concerning the sons of Eli and of God's new and faithful priest. Eli's house judged. Israel overcome by the Philistines; the ark seized. The death of Eli and the birth of Ichabod. God punishes the Philistines for taking the ark. It is sent to Kiriath-jearim. Israel repents and is victorious at Mizpah; the Ebenezer stone. Samuel is circuit judge at Bethel, Gilgal, Mizpah, and Ramah.

II. The reign of Saul (8:1-31:13): The evil of Samuel's sons. Israel asks for a king. God's description of what the king will be like. God assents to a king and Saul of Benjamin is selected. Saul is secretly anointed and later crowned publicly. Saul wars against Ammon victoriously. Samuel defends his record, and reproves Israel; the people confess their sins. Samuel exhorts to obedience, and offers hope to the repentant and wrath against the disobedient. Saul wars against the Philistines. Geba attacked by Jonathan. Saul offers sacrifice; Samuel reproves him. Saul's army unprepared. Jonathan's victory at Michmash. Saul orders the army not to eat. Jonathan transgresses the order, is found

20   And it came about in due time, after Hannah had conceived, that she gave birth to a son; and she named him Samuel, *saying*, "Because I have asked him of the LORD."

| | 1:20 Gen 41:51,52; Ex 2:10,22 |

2. Samuel dedicated

21   Then the man Elkanah went up with all his household to offer to the LORD the yearly sacrifice and *pay* his vow.

| | 1:21 v. 3 |

22   But Hannah did not go up, for she said to her husband, "*I will not go up* until the child is weaned; then I will bring him, that he may appear before the LORD and stay there forever."

| | 1:22 Luke 2:22; 1 Sam 2:11,18 |

23   And Elkanah her husband said to her, "Do what seems best to you. Remain until you have weaned him; only may the LORD confirm His word." So the woman remained and nursed her son until she weaned him.

| | 1:23 Num 30:7; v. 17 |

24   Now when she had weaned him, she took him up with her, with a three-year-old bull and one ephah of flour and a jug of wine, and brought him to the house of the LORD in Shiloh, although the child was young.

| | 1:24 Deut 12:5; Josh 18:1 |

25   Then they slaughtered the bull, and brought the boy to Eli.

| | *1:25 Lev 1:5; Luke 2:22 |

26   And she said, "Oh, my lord! As your soul lives, my lord, I am the woman who stood here beside you, praying to the LORD.

| | 1:26 2 Kin 2:2 |

27   "For this boy I prayed, and the LORD has given me my petition which I asked of Him.

| | 1:27 vv. 11-13 |

28   "So I have also ¹dedicated him to the LORD; as long as he lives he is ¹dedicated to the LORD." And he worshiped the LORD there.

| | 1:28 vv. 11,22 |

3. Hannah's song of praise

2   Then Hannah prayed and said,
    "My heart exults in the LORD;
    My horn is exalted in the LORD,
    My mouth speaks boldly against my enemies,
    Because I rejoice in Thy salvation.

| | 2:1 Luke 1:46-55; Ps 89:17; Is 12:2,3 |

2   "There is no one holy like the LORD,
    Indeed, there is no one besides Thee,
    Nor is there any rock like our God.

| | 2:2 Lev 19:2; 2 Sam 22:32; Deut 32:30, 31 |

3   "Boast no more so very proudly,
    Do not let arrogance come out of your mouth;
    For the LORD is a God of knowledge,
    And with Him actions are weighed.

| | 2:3 Prov 8:13; 1 Sam 16:7; 1 Kin 8:39; Prov 16:2; 24:12 |

4   "The bows of the mighty are shattered,
    But the feeble gird on strength.

| | 2:4 Ps 76:3 |

5   "Those who were full hire themselves out for bread,
    But those who were hungry cease *to hunger*.
    Even the barren gives birth to seven,
    But she who has many children languishes.

| | 2:5 Ps 113:9; Jer 15:9 |

6   "The LORD kills and makes alive;
    He brings down to Sheol and raises up.

| | 2:6 Deut 32:39; Is 26:19 |

7   "The LORD makes poor and rich;
    He brings low, He also exalts.

| | 2:7 Deut 8:17,18; Job 5:11; Ps 75:6,7 |

8   "He raises the poor from the dust,
    He lifts the needy from the ash heap
    To make them sit with nobles,
    And inherit a seat of honor;
    For the pillars of the earth are the LORD's,
    And He set the world on them.

| | 2:8 Ps 113:7,8; Job 36:7; 38:4,5 |

9   "He keeps the feet of His godly ones,
    But the wicked ones are silenced in darkness;
    For not by might shall a man prevail.

| | 2:9 Ps 91:11,12; Matt 8:12; Ps 33:16,17 |

10 "Those who contend with the LORD will be shattered;
    Against them He will thunder in the heavens,
    The LORD will judge the ends of the earth;

| | 2:10 Ps 2:9; 18:13; 96:13; 21:1,7; 89:24 |

¹Lit., *lent*

1:25 *they slaughtered.* Evidently Elkanah was with Hannah. A text of Samuel found at Qumran indicates this. Moreover, Elkanah returned home after Hannah's prayer at Shiloh (2:11).

> And He will give strength to His king,
> And will exalt the horn of His anointed.''

4. *Samuel ministers before the LORD*

11 Then Elkanah went to his home at Ramah. But the boy ministered to the LORD before Eli the priest.

12 Now the sons of Eli were [2]worthless men; they did not know the LORD **13** and the custom of the priests with the people. When any man was offering a sacrifice, the priest's servant would come while the meat was boiling, with a three-pronged fork in his hand.

14 Then he would thrust it into the pan, or kettle, or caldron, or pot; all that the fork brought up the priest would take for himself. Thus they did in Shiloh to all the Israelites who came there.

15 Also, before they burned the fat, the priest's servant would come and say to the man who was sacrificing, ''Give the priest meat for roasting, as he will not take boiled meat from you, only raw.''

16 And if the man said to him, ''They must surely burn the fat first, and then take as much as you desire,'' then he would say, ''No, but you shall give *it to me* now; and if not, I will take it by force.''

17 Thus the sin of the young men was very great before the LORD, for the men despised the offering of the LORD.

18 Now Samuel was ministering before the LORD, *as* a boy wearing a linen ephod.

19 And his mother would make him a little robe and bring it to him from year to year when she would come up with her husband to offer the yearly sacrifice.

20 Then Eli would bless Elkanah and his wife and say, ''May the LORD give you children from this woman in place of the one she dedicated to the LORD.'' And they went to their own home.

21 And the LORD visited Hannah; and she conceived and gave birth to three sons and two daughters. And the boy Samuel grew before the LORD.

22 Now Eli was very old; and he heard all that his sons were doing to all Israel, and how they lay with the women who served at the doorway of the tent of meeting.

23 And he said to them, ''Why do you do such things, the evil things that I hear from all these people?

24 ''No, my sons; for the report is not good which I hear the LORD's people circulating.

25 ''If one man sins against another, God will mediate for him; but if a man sins against the LORD, who can intercede for him?'' But they would not listen to the voice of their father, for the LORD desired to put them to death.

26 Now the boy Samuel was growing in stature and in favor both with the LORD and with men.

5. *The prophet announces the doom of Eli's house*

27 Then a man of God came to Eli and said to him, ''Thus says the LORD, 'Did I *not* indeed reveal Myself to the house of your father when they were in Egypt *in bondage* to Pharaoh's house?

28 'And did I *not* choose them from all the tribes of Israel to be My priests, to go up to My altar, to burn incense, to carry an ephod before Me; and did I *not* give to the house of your father all the fire *offerings* of the sons of Israel?

29 'Why do you kick at My sacrifice and at My offering which I have commanded *in My* dwelling, and honor your sons above Me, by making yourselves fat with the choicest of every offering of My people Israel?'

30 ''Therefore the LORD God of Israel declares, 'I did indeed say that your house and the house of your father should walk before Me forever'; but now the LORD declares, 'Far be it from Me—for those who honor Me I will honor, and those who despise Me will be lightly esteemed.

31 'Behold, the days are coming when I will break your strength and the strength of your father's house so that there will not be an old man in your house.

32 'And you will see the distress of *My* dwelling, in *spite of* all that I do good for Israel; and an old man will not be in your house forever.

33 'Yet I will not cut off every man of yours from My altar that your eyes may

---

Cross-references (margin):

2:11 1 Sam 3:1
2:12 Jer 2:8; 9:3,6
2:13 Lev 7:29-34
2:15 Lev 3:3,4
2:17 Mal 2:7-9
2:18 vv. 11,28; 1 Sam 3:1
2:19 1 Sam 1:3
2:20 Luke 2:34; 1 Sam 1:11, 27,28
2:21 Gen 21:1; v. 26; 1 Sam 3:19; Luke 2:40
2:22 Ex 38:8
2:24 1 Kin 15:26
2:25 Deut 1:17; Num 15:30; Josh 11:20
2:26 v. 21; Luke 2:52
2:27 1 Kin 13:1; Ex 4:14-16
2:28 Ex 28:1-4; Lev 8:7,8
2:29 vv. 13-17; Deut 12:5; Matt 10:37
2:30 Ex 29:9; Ps 91:14; Mal 2:9
2:31 1 Sam 4:11-18; 22:17-20
2:32 1 Kin 2:26, 27; Zech 8:4

---

[2]Lit., *sons of Belial*

fail *from weeping* and your soul grieve, and all the increase of your house will die in the prime of life.

34 'And this will be the sign to you which shall come concerning your two sons, Hophni and Phinehas: on the same day both of them shall die.

35 'But I will raise up for Myself a faithful priest who will do according to what is in My heart and in My soul; and I will build him an enduring house, and he will walk before My anointed always.

36 'And it shall come about that everyone who is left in your house shall come and bow down to him for a piece of silver or a loaf of bread, and say, "Please assign me to one of the priest's offices so that I may eat a piece of bread.""'"

6. *Samuel announces the doom of Eli's house*

a. *Samuel before the LORD*

3 Now the boy Samuel was ministering to the LORD before Eli. And word from the LORD was rare in those days, visions were infrequent.

b. *The call of God to Samuel*

2 And it happened at that time as Eli was lying down in his place (now his eyesight had begun to grow dim *and* he could not see well),

3 and the lamp of God had not yet gone out, and Samuel was lying down in the temple of the LORD where the ark of God *was*,

4 that the LORD called Samuel; and he said, "Here I am."

5 Then he ran to Eli and said, "Here I am, for you called me." But he said, "I did not call, lie down again." So he went and lay down.

6 And the LORD called yet again, "Samuel!" So Samuel arose and went to Eli, and said, "Here I am, for you called me." But he answered, "I did not call, my son, lie down again."

7 Now Samuel did not yet know the LORD, nor had the word of the LORD yet been revealed to him.

8 So the LORD called Samuel again for the third time. And he arose and went to Eli, and said, "Here I am, for you called me." Then Eli discerned that the LORD was calling the boy.

9 And Eli said to Samuel, "Go lie down, and it shall be if He calls you, that you shall say, 'Speak, LORD, for Thy servant is listening.'" So Samuel went and lay down in his place.

c. *God pronounces judgment of Eli's house*

10 Then the LORD came and stood and called as at other times, "Samuel! Samuel!" And Samuel said, "Speak, for Thy servant is listening."

11 And the LORD said to Samuel, "Behold, I am about to do a thing in Israel at which both ears of everyone who hears it will tingle.

12 "In that day I will carry out against Eli all that I have spoken concerning his house, from beginning to end.

13 "For I have told him that I am about to judge his house forever for the iniquity which he knew, because his sons brought a curse on themselves and he did not rebuke them.

14 "And therefore I have sworn to the house of Eli that the iniquity of Eli's house shall not be atoned for by sacrifice or offering forever."

d. *Samuel tells Eli of the judgment of God*

15 So Samuel lay down until morning. Then he opened the doors of the house of the LORD. But Samuel was afraid to tell the vision to Eli.

16 Then Eli called Samuel and said, "Samuel, my son." And he said, "Here I am."

17 And he said, "What is the word that He spoke to you? Please do not hide it from me. May God do so to you, and more also, if you hide anything from me of all the words that He spoke to you."

18 So Samuel told him everything and hid nothing from him. And he said, "It is the LORD; let Him do what seems good to Him."

2:34
1 Kin 13:3;
1 Sam 4:11
***2:35**
1 Kin 2:35;
2 Sam 7:11,
27;
1 Kin 11:38;
1 Sam 12:3;
16:13
2:36
1 Kin 2:27

3:1
1 Sam 2:11,
18; Ps 74:9;
Amos 8:11

3:2
1 Sam 4:15

3:3
Lev 24:2-4

3:4
Is 6:8

3:7
Acts 19:2

3:11
2 Kin 21:12;
Jer 19:3
3:12
1 Sam 2:30-36

3:13
1 Sam 2:12,
17,22,29-31

3:14
Lev 15:30,31;
Is 22:14

3:17
Ruth 1:17;
2 Sam 3:35

3:18
Job 2:10;
Is 39:8

2:35 *a faithful priest.* According to 1 Kin. 2:27,35 this verse was a prediction of Zadok, the priest appointed by Solomon in place of Abiathar, Eli's great-grandson.

*3:19
1 Sam 2:21;
Gen 21:22;
39:2;
1 Sam 9:6
3:20
Judg 20:1
3:21
v. 10

*4:1
1 Sam 7:12

4:3
Josh 7:7,8;
Num 10:35

*4:4
2 Sam 6:2;
Ex 25:18,22

4:5
Josh 6:5,20

4:6
Ex 15:14

4:9
1 Cor 16:13;
Judg 13:1
4:10
v. 2;
Deut 28:25;
2 Sam 18:17;
2 Kin 14:12
4:11
1 Sam 2:34;
Ps 78:56-64

*4:12
Josh 7:6;
2 Sam 1:2;
Neh 9:1
4:13
v. 18;
1 Sam 1:9

4:15
1 Sam 3:2

4:16
2Sa 1:4

e. Samuel established as a prophet

19 Thus Samuel grew and the LORD was with him and let none of his words fail.
20 And all Israel from Dan even to Beersheba knew that Samuel was confirmed as a prophet of the LORD.
21 And the LORD appeared again at Shiloh, because the LORD revealed Himself to Samuel at Shiloh by the word of the LORD.

4 Thus the word of Samuel came to all Israel. Now Israel went out to meet the Philistines in battle and camped beside Ebenezer while the Philistines camped in Aphek.

B. Samuel welds the theocracy together

1. The defeat of Israel; the capture of the ark

2 And the Philistines drew up in battle array to meet Israel. When the battle spread, Israel was defeated before the Philistines who killed about four thousand men on the battlefield.
3 When the people came into the camp, the elders of Israel said, "Why has the LORD defeated us today before the Philistines? Let us take to ourselves from Shiloh the ark of the covenant of the LORD, that it may come among us and deliver us from the power of our enemies."
4 So the people sent to Shiloh, and from there they carried the ark of the covenant of the LORD of hosts who sits *above* the cherubim; and the two sons of Eli, Hophni and Phinehas, *were* there with the ark of the covenant of God.
5 And it happened as the ark of the covenant of the LORD came into the camp, that all Israel shouted with a great shout, so that the earth resounded.
6 And when the Philistines heard the noise of the shout, they said, "What *does* the noise of this great shout in the camp of the Hebrews *mean?*" Then they understood that the ark of the LORD had come into the camp.
7 And the Philistines were afraid, for they said, "God has come into the camp." And they said, "Woe to us! For nothing like this has happened before.
8 "Woe to us! Who shall deliver us from the hand of these mighty gods? These are the gods who smote the Egyptians with all *kinds of* plagues in the wilderness.
9 "Take courage and be men, O Philistines, lest you become slaves to the Hebrews, as they have been slaves to you; therefore, be men and fight."
10 So the Philistines fought and Israel was defeated, and every man fled to his tent, and the slaughter was very great; for there fell of Israel thirty thousand foot soldiers.
11 And the ark of God was taken; and the two sons of Eli, Hophni and Phinehas, died.

2. The death of Eli

a. His accident

12 Now a man of Benjamin ran from the battle line and came to Shiloh the same day with his clothes torn and dust on his head.
13 When he came, behold, Eli was sitting on *his* seat by the road eagerly watching, because his heart was trembling for the ark of God. So the man came to tell *it* in the city, and all the city cried out.
14 When Eli heard the noise of the outcry, he said, "What *does* the noise of this commotion *mean?*" Then the man came hurriedly and told Eli.
15 Now Eli was ninety-eight years old, and his eyes were set so that he could not see.
16 And the man said to Eli, "I am the one who came from the battle line. Indeed, I escaped from the battle line today." And he said, "How did things go, my son?"
17 Then the one who brought the news answered and said, "Israel has fled before the Philistines and there has also been a great slaughter among the people, and your two sons also, Hophni and Phinehas, are dead, and the ark of God has been taken."

3:19 This verse confirms Samuel's prophetic powers.
4:1 *Philistines*, see note to Judg. 13:1 for background.
4:4 *above the cherubim*, see note to Ex. 25:22.

4:12 *Shiloh.* The story does not tell of the destruction of Shiloh, but archaeological evidence confirms the fact reported in Jer. 7:12; 26:6.

18   And it came about when he mentioned the ark of God that Eli fell off the seat backward beside the gate, and his neck was broken and he died, for he was old and heavy. Thus he judged Israel forty years.

b. The birth of Ichabod

19   Now his daughter-in-law, Phinehas' wife, was pregnant and about to give birth; and when she heard the news that the ark of God was taken and that her father-in-law and her husband had died, she kneeled down and gave birth, for her pains came upon her.
20   And about the time of her death the women who stood by her said to her, "Do not be afraid, for you have given birth to a son." But she did not answer or pay attention.
21   And she called the boy ³Ichabod, saying, "The glory has departed from Israel," because the ark of God was taken and because of her father-in-law and her husband.
22   And she said, "The glory has departed from Israel, for the ark of God was taken."

3. The ark in the hands of the Philistines

a. The ark at Ashdod in the house of Dagon

5 Now the Philistines took the ark of God and brought it from Ebenezer to Ashdod.
2   Then the Philistines took the ark of God and brought it to the house of Dagon, and set it by Dagon.
3   When the Ashdodites arose early the next morning, behold, Dagon had fallen on his face to the ground before the ark of the LORD. So they took Dagon and set him in his place again.
4   But when they arose early the next morning, behold, Dagon had fallen on his face to the ground before the ark of the LORD. And the head of Dagon and both the palms of his hands *were* cut off on the threshold; only the trunk of Dagon was left to him.
5   Therefore neither the priests of Dagon nor all who enter Dagon's house tread on the threshold of Dagon in Ashdod to this day.

b. The ark at Gath and Ekron

6   Now the hand of the LORD was heavy on the Ashdodites, and He ravaged them and smote them with tumors, both Ashdod and its territories.
7   When the men of Ashdod saw that it was so, they said, "The ark of the God of Israel must not remain with us, for His hand is severe on us and on Dagon our god."
8   So they sent and gathered all the lords of the Philistines to them and said, "What shall we do with the ark of the God of Israel?" And they said, "Let the ark of the God of Israel be brought around to Gath." And they brought the ark of the God of Israel *around*.
9   And it came about that after they had brought it around, the hand of the LORD was against the city with very great confusion; and He smote the men of the city, both young and old, so that tumors broke out on them.
10   So they sent the ark of God to Ekron. And it happened as the ark of God came to Ekron that the Ekronites cried out, saying, "They have brought the ark of the God of Israel around to us, to kill us and our people."
11   They sent therefore and gathered all the lords of the Philistines and said, "Send away the ark of the God of Israel, and let it return to its own place, that it may not kill us and our people." For there was a deadly confusion throughout the city; the hand of God was very heavy there.
12   And the men who did not die were smitten with tumors and the cry of the city went up to heaven.

³I.e., no glory

4:21 *Ichabod*, that is, "without glory." So named because of his ill-timed birth.

5:2 *house of Dagon*, the temple containing the image of Dagon (the grain god).

Margin references:

4:18 v. 13

4:20 Gen 35:16-19

4:22 Jer 2:11; v. 11

5:1 1 Sam 4:1; 7:12
*5:2 Judg 16:23

5:3 Is 19:1; 46:1, 2,7

5:4 Ezek 6:4,6

5:6 vv. 7,11; Ex 9:3; 1 Sam 6:5; Deut 28:27; Ps 78:66

5:8 v. 11

5:9 vv. 6,11; 1 Sam 7:13; Ps 78:66

5:11 vv. 6,8,9

4. *The return of the ark*

a. *The ark sent away with sacrifices*

6 Now the ark of the LORD had been in the country of the Philistines seven months.

2   And the Philistines called for the priests and the diviners, saying, "What shall we do with the ark of the LORD? Tell us how we shall send it to its place."

3   And they said, "If you send away the ark of the God of Israel, do not send it empty; but you shall surely return to Him a guilt offering. Then you shall be healed and it shall be known to you why His hand is not removed from you."

4   Then they said, "What shall be the guilt offering which we shall return to Him?" And they said, "Five golden tumors and five golden mice *according to* the number of the lords of the Philistines, for one plague was on all of you and on your lords.

5   "So you shall make likenesses of your tumors and likenesses of your mice that ravage the land, and you shall give glory to the God of Israel; perhaps He will ease His hand from you, your gods, and your land.

6   "Why then do you harden your hearts as the Egyptians and Pharaoh hardened their hearts? When He had severely dealt with them, did they not allow the people to go, and they departed?

7   "Now therefore take and prepare a new cart and two milch cows on which there has never been a yoke; and hitch the cows to the cart and take their calves home, away from them.

8   "And take the ark of the LORD and place it on the cart; and put the articles of gold which you return to Him as a guilt offering in a box by its side. Then send it away that it may go.

9   "And watch, if it goes up by the way of its own territory to Beth-shemesh, then He has done us this great evil. But if not, then we shall know that it was not His hand that struck us; it happened to us by chance."

10   Then the men did so, and took two milch cows and hitched them to the cart, and shut up their calves at home.

11   And they put the ark of the LORD on the cart, and the box with the golden mice and the likenesses of their tumors.

12   And the cows took the straight way in the direction of Beth-shemesh; they went along the highway, lowing as they went, and did not turn aside to the right or to the left. And the lords of the Philistines followed them to the border of Beth-shemesh.

13   Now *the people of* Beth-shemesh were reaping their wheat harvest in the valley, and they raised their eyes and saw the ark and were glad to see *it.*

14   And the cart came into the field of Joshua the Beth-shemite and stood there where *there was* a large stone; and they split the wood of the cart and offered the cows as a burnt offering to the LORD.

15   And the Levites took down the ark of the LORD and the box that was with it, in which were the articles of gold, and put them on the large stone; and the men of Beth-shemesh offered burnt offerings and sacrificed sacrifices that day to the LORD.

16   And when the five lords of the Philistines saw it, they returned to Ekron that day.

b. *The ark sent from Beth-shemesh to Kiriath-jearim*

17   And these are the golden tumors which the Philistines returned for a guilt offering to the LORD: one for Ashdod, one for Gaza, one for Ashkelon, one for Gath, one for Ekron;

18   and the golden mice, *according* to the number of all the cities of the Philistines belonging to the five lords, both of fortified cities and of country villages. The large stone on which they set the ark of the LORD *is a witness* to this day in the field of Joshua the Beth-shemite.

19   And He struck down some of the men of Beth-shemesh because they had looked into the ark of the LORD. He struck down of all the people, 50,070 men, and the people mourned because the LORD had struck the people with a great slaughter.

20   And the men of Beth-shemesh said, "Who is able to stand before the LORD, this holy God? And to whom shall He go up from us?"

21   So they sent messengers to the inhabitants of Kiriath-jearim, saying, "The Philistines have brought back the ark of the LORD; come down and take it up to you."

Marginal cross-references:

6:2
Gen 41:8;
Ex 7:11;
Is 2:6

6:3
Ex 23:15;
Deut 16:16;
Lev 5:15,16

6:4
vv. 17,18;
Josh 13:3;
Judg 3:3

6:5
1 Sam 5:3-11;
Josh 7:19;
Is 42:12

6:6
Ex 8:15;
9:34; 12:31

6:7
2 Sam 6:3;
Num 19:2

6:8
vv. 3-5

6:9
Josh 15:10;
v. 3

6:12
v. 9;
Num 20:19

6:14
2 Sam 24:22;
1 Kin 19:21

6:16
Josh 13:3

6:17
v. 4

6:18
vv. 14,15

6:19
Num 4:5,15,
20; 2 Sam 6:7

6:20
Lev 11:44,45;
2 Sam 6:9

6:21
Josh 9:17;
15:9,60

7 And the men of Kiriath-jearim came and took the ark of the LORD and brought it into the house of Abinadab on the hill, and consecrated Eleazar his son to keep the ark of the LORD.

7:1
2 Sam 6:3,4

2   And it came about from the day that the ark remained at Kiriath-jearim that the time was long, for it was twenty years; and all the house of Israel lamented after the LORD.

5. Samuel overcomes the Philistines

a. The call to repentance

3   Then Samuel spoke to all the house of Israel, saying, "If you return to the LORD with all your heart, remove the foreign gods and the Ashtaroth from among you and direct your hearts to the LORD and serve Him alone; and He will deliver you from the hand of the Philistines."

7:3
Joel 2:2;
Josh 24:14;
Judg 2:13;
Deut 6:13;
Matt 4:10

4   So the sons of Israel removed the Baals and the Ashtaroth and served the LORD alone.

b. The defeat of the Philistines

5   Then Samuel said, "Gather all Israel to Mizpah, and I will pray to the LORD for you."

6   And they gathered to Mizpah, and drew water and poured it out before the LORD, and fasted on that day, and said there, "We have sinned against the LORD." And Samuel judged the sons of Israel at Mizpah.

7:6
Ps 62:8;
Neh 9:1;
Judg 10:10

7   Now when the Philistines heard that the sons of Israel had gathered to Mizpah, the lords of the Philistines went up against Israel. And when the sons of Israel heard it, they were afraid of the Philistines.

7:7
1 Sam 17:11

8   Then the sons of Israel said to Samuel, "Do not cease to cry to the LORD our God for us, that He may save us from the hand of the Philistines."

7:8
Is 37:4

9   And Samuel took a suckling lamb and offered it for a whole burnt offering to the LORD; and Samuel cried to the LORD for Israel and the LORD answered him.

7:9
Ps 99:6;
Jer 15:1

10   Now Samuel was offering up the burnt offering, and the Philistines drew near to battle against Israel. But the LORD thundered with a great thunder on that day against the Philistines and confused them, so that they were routed before Israel.

7:10
Josh 10:10;
1 Sam 2:10;
2 Sam 22:14,
15

11   And the men of Israel went out of Mizpah and pursued the Philistines, and struck them down as far as below Beth-car.

c. The Ebenezer

12   Then Samuel took a stone and set it between Mizpah and Shen, and named it [4]Ebenezer, saying, "Thus far the LORD has helped us."

7:12
Gen 35:14;
Josh 4:9

13   So the Philistines were subdued and they did not come anymore within the border of Israel. And the hand of the LORD was against the Philistines all the days of Samuel.

7:13
Judg 13:1;
1 Sam 13:5

14   And the cities which the Philistines had taken from Israel were restored to Israel, from Ekron even to Gath; and Israel delivered their territory from the hand of the Philistines. So there was peace between Israel and the Amorites.

d. Samuel's circuit

15   Now Samuel judged Israel all the days of his life.

7:15
v. 6;
1 Sam 12:11

16   And he used to go annually on circuit to Bethel and Gilgal and Mizpah, and he judged Israel in all these places.

17   Then his return was to Ramah, for his house was there, and there he judged Israel; and he built there an altar to the LORD.

*7:17
1 Sam 1:19;
7:5;
Judg 20:1;
1 Sam 8:6

[4]I.e., the stone of help

7:17 return . . . to Ramah. Shiloh was in ruins, so Samuel made his headquarters at Ramah, his hometown, where he built an altar. Ramah is also known as Ramathaim-zophim (1 Sam. 1:1).

II. *The reign of Saul (8:1–31:13)*

A. *The appointment of Saul as king*

1. *Israel demands a king*

8:1
Deut 16:18,
19

8 And it came about when Samuel was old that he appointed his sons judges over Israel.

2   Now the name of his first-born was Joel, and the name of his second, Abijah; *they* were judging in Beersheba.

8:3
Ex 23:6,8;
Deut 16:19;
Ps 15:5

3   His sons, however, did not walk in his ways, but turned aside after dishonest gain and took bribes and perverted justice.

8:4
1 Sam 7:17

4   Then all the elders of Israel gathered together and came to Samuel at Ramah;

*8:5ff
Deut 17:14,
15

5   and they said to him, "Behold, you have grown old, and your sons do not walk in your ways. Now appoint a king for us to judge us like all the nations."

8:6
1 Sam 15:11

6   But the thing was displeasing in the sight of Samuel when they said, "Give us a king to judge us." And Samuel prayed to the Lord.

8:7
1 Sam 10:19;
Ex 16:8

7   And the Lord said to Samuel, "Listen to the voice of the people in regard to all that they say to you, for they have not rejected you, but they have rejected Me from being king over them.

8   "Like all the deeds which they have done since the day that I brought them up from Egypt even to this day—in that they have forsaken Me and served other gods—so they are doing to you also.

8:9
v. 11

9   "Now then, listen to their voice; however, you shall solemnly warn them and tell them of the ⁵procedure of the king who will reign over them."

10   So Samuel spoke all the words of the Lord to the people who had asked of him a king.

8:11
1 Sam 14:52;
2 Sam 15:1

11   And he said, "This will be the procedure of the king who will reign over you: he will take your sons and place *them* for himself in his chariots and among his horsemen and they will run before his chariots.

8:12
1 Sam 22:7

12   "And he will appoint for himself commanders of thousands and of fifties, and *some* to do his plowing and to reap his harvest and to make his weapons of war and equipment for his chariots.

13   "He will also take your daughters for perfumers and cooks and bakers.

8:14
1 Kin 21:7;
Ezek 46:18

14   "And he will take the best of your fields and your vineyards and your olive groves, and give *them* to his servants.

15   "And he will take a tenth of your seed and of your vineyards, and give to his officers and to his servants.

16   "He will also take your male servants and your female servants and your best young men and your donkeys, and use *them* for his work.

17   "He will take a tenth of your flocks, and you yourselves will become his servants.

8:18
Prov 1:25-28;
Mic 3:4

18   "Then you will cry out in that day because of your king whom you have chosen for yourselves, but the Lord will not answer you in that day."

19   Nevertheless, the people refused to listen to the voice of Samuel, and they said, "No, but there shall be a king over us,

8:20
v. 5

20   that we also may be like all the nations, that our king may judge us and go out before us and fight our battles."

21   Now after Samuel had heard all the words of the people, he repeated them in the Lord's hearing.

8:22
v. 7

22   And the Lord said to Samuel, "Listen to their voice, and appoint them a king." So Samuel said to the men of Israel, "Go every man to his city."

⁵Lit., *custom*

8:5–7 At Sinai the Israelites ratified a covenant in which God would rule (theocracy) directly through Moses (Ex. 19:8). The theocracy was continued through Joshua and Judges. Samuel functioned as prophet, judge, and priest; but when his sons perverted justice, the people demanded a king. The request greatly displeased Samuel; nevertheless the Lord informed him to comply. Theoretically a monarchy with an obedient king could have been more theocratic than rule by Samuel's wicked sons, but the people were warned of what was in store. They refused to heed the warning, however, and Samuel prepared to anoint Saul as the new king. While this was unquestionably within the plan of God (as a step toward the Davidic kingdom), the sin of Israel's rejection of the theocracy was nonetheless heinous. God predicted that certain unpleasant results would ensue from the establishment of the kingship, and this prophecy was fulfilled to the letter under the rule of the more ungodly kings of Judah and Israel. At the end of the age God once again will govern immediately through Christ His Son, and His theocratic rule shall endure forever (Luke 1:32,33; 1 Tim. 1:17; 6:14–16).

2. *God selects Saul*

a. *The family of Saul*

9 Now there was a man of Benjamin whose name was Kish the son of Abiel, the son of Zeror, the son of Becorath, the son of Aphiah, the son of a Benjamite, a mighty man of valor.

2   And he had a son whose name was Saul, a choice and handsome *man*, and there was not a more handsome person than he among the sons of Israel; from his shoulders and up he was taller than any of the people.

b. *The search for his father's donkeys*

3   Now the donkeys of Kish, Saul's father, were lost. So Kish said to his son Saul, "Take now with you one of the servants, and arise, go search for the donkeys."

4   And he passed through the hill country of Ephraim and passed through the land of Shalishah, but they did not find *them*. Then they passed through the land of Shaalim, but *they were* not *there*. Then he passed through the land of the Benjamites, but they did not find *them*.

5   When they came to the land of Zuph, Saul said to his servant who was with him, "Come, and let us return, lest my father cease *to be concerned* about the donkeys and become anxious for us."

6   And he said to him, "Behold now, there is a man of God in this city, and the man is held in honor; all that he says surely comes true. Now let us go there, perhaps he can tell us about our journey on which we have set out."

7   Then Saul said to his servant, "But behold, if we go, what shall we bring the man? For the bread is gone from our sack and there is no present to bring to the man of God. What do we have?"

8   And the servant answered Saul again and said, "Behold, I have in my hand a fourth of a shekel of silver; I will give *it* to the man of God and he will tell us our way."

9   (Formerly in Israel, when a man went to inquire of God, he used to say, "Come, and let us go to the seer"; for *he who is called* a prophet now was formerly called a seer.)

10   Then Saul said to his servant, "Well said; come, let us go." So they went to the city where the man of God was.

c. *God reveals His choice to Samuel: He and Saul talk and eat together*

11   As they went up the slope to the city, they found young women going out to draw water, and said to them, "Is the seer here?"

12   And they answered them and said, "He is; see, *he is* ahead of you. Hurry now, for he has come into the city today, for the people have a sacrifice on the high place today.

13   "As soon as you enter the city you will find him before he goes up to the high place to eat, for the people will not eat until he comes, because he must bless the sacrifice; afterward those who are invited will eat. Now therefore, go up for you will find him at once."

14   So they went up to the city. As they came into the city, behold, Samuel was coming out toward them to go up to the high place.

15   Now a day before Saul's coming, the LORD had revealed *this* to Samuel saying,

16   "About this time tomorrow I will send you a man from the land of Benjamin, and you shall anoint him to be prince over My people Israel; and he shall deliver My people from the hand of the Philistines. For I have regarded My people, because their cry has come to Me."

17   When Samuel saw Saul, the LORD said to him, "Behold, the man of whom I spoke to you! This one shall rule over My people."

9:1 1 Sam 14:51; 1 Chr 9:36-39

9:2 1 Sam 10:23, 24

9:4 Josh 24:33; 2 Kin 4:42; Josh 19:42

9:5 1 Sam 10:2

*****9:6** Deut 33:1; 1 Sam 3:19

9:7 1 Kin 14:3; 2 Kin 8:8

*****9:9** 2 Sam 24:11; 1 Chr 26:28; Is 30:10

9:11 Gen 24:15

*****9:12** Num 28:11-15; 1 Sam 7:17; 10:5

9:16 1 Sam 10:1; Ex 3:7,9

9:17 1 Sam 16:12

9:6 *this city*, presumably Ramah, Samuel's headquarters. *all that he says surely comes true*. This test of a true prophet is set forth in Deut. 18:21,22.
9:9 This explanatory note of the compiler would seem to be more appropriate after v. 11, where the word *seer* appears for the first time. Many prophets of Samuel's day were

ecstatics, who tended to rove around the country in bands (10:5,6); but Samuel the seer, like the prophets of the compiler's day, spoke the clear word of the LORD.
9:12 *the high place*. With Shiloh in ruins, the altar Samuel built on a hilltop became the center of worship. This was according to custom. (See note to 7:17.)

18   Then Saul approached Samuel in the gate, and said, "Please tell me where the seer's house is."

19   And Samuel answered Saul and said, "I am the seer. Go up before me to the high place, for you shall eat with me today; and in the morning I will let you go, and will tell you all that is on your mind.

20   "And as for your donkeys which were lost three days ago, do not set your mind on them, for they have been found. And for whom is all that is desirable in Israel? Is it not for you and for all your father's household?"

21   And Saul answered and said, "Am I not a Benjamite, of the smallest of the tribes of Israel, and my family the least of all the families of the tribe of Benjamin? Why then do you speak to me in this way?"

22   Then Samuel took Saul and his servant and brought them into the hall, and gave them a place at the head of those who were invited, who were about thirty men.

23   And Samuel said to the cook, "Bring the portion that I gave you, concerning which I said to you, 'Set it aside.'"

24   Then the cook took up the leg with what was on it and set *it* before Saul. And *Samuel* said, "Here is what has been reserved! Set *it* before you *and* eat, because it has been kept for you until the appointed time, since I said I have invited the people." So Saul ate with Samuel that day.

25   When they came down from the high place into the city, *Samuel* spoke with Saul on the roof.[6]

26   And they arose early; and it came about at daybreak that Samuel called to Saul on the roof, saying, "Get up, that I may send you away." So Saul arose, and both he and Samuel went out into the street.

27   As they were going down to the edge of the city, Samuel said to Saul, "Say to the servant that he might go ahead of us and pass on, but you remain standing now, that I may proclaim the word of God to you."

3. Saul's coronation

a. Saul anointed by Samuel; his father's donkeys found

10 Then Samuel took the flask of oil, poured it on his head, kissed him and said, "Has not the LORD anointed you a ruler over His inheritance?

2   "When you go from me today, then you will find two men close to Rachel's tomb in the territory of Benjamin at Zelzah; and they will say to you, 'The donkeys which you went to look for have been found. Now behold, your father has ceased to be concerned about the donkeys and is anxious for you, saying, "What shall I do about my son?"'

3   "Then you will go on further from there, and you will come as far as the oak of Tabor, and there three men going up to God at Bethel will meet you, one carrying three kids, another carrying three loaves of bread, and another carrying a jug of wine;

4   and they will greet you and give you two *loaves* of bread, which you will accept from their hand.

5   "Afterward you will come to the hill of God where the Philistine garrison is; and it shall be as soon as you have come there to the city, that you will meet a group of prophets coming down from the high place with harp, tambourine, flute, and a lyre before them, and they will be prophesying.

6   "Then the Spirit of the LORD will come upon you mightily, and you shall prophesy with them and be changed into another man.

7   "And it shall be when these signs come to you, do for yourself what the occasion requires; for God is with you.

8   "And you shall go down before me to Gilgal; and behold, I will come down to you to offer burnt offerings and sacrifice peace offerings. You shall wait seven days until I come to you and show you what you should do."

9   Then it happened when he turned his back to leave Samuel, God changed his heart; and all those signs came about on that day.

10   When they came to the hill there, behold, a group of prophets met him; and the Spirit of God came upon him mightily, so that he prophesied among them.

---

[6]Gr. adds *and they spread a bed for Saul on the roof and he slept.*

Marginal references

9:20 v. 3; 1 Sam 8:5; 12:13
9:21 1 Sam 15:17; Judg 20:46,48
9:24 Lev 7:32,33; Num 18:18
9:25 Deut 22:8; Acts 10:9
*10:1 1 Sam 16:13; 2 Kin 9:3,6; Ps 2:12; Deut 32:9; Ps 78:71
10:2 Gen 35:19,20; 1 Sam 9:3-5
10:3 Gen 28:22; 35:1,3,7,8
10:5 1 Sam 13:3; 9:12; 19:20; 2 Kin 3:15
10:6 Num 11:25, 29; v. 10; 1 Sam 19:23, 24
10:7 Josh 1:5; Judg 6:12
10:8 1 Sam 11:15; 13:8
*10:9 v. 6
10:10 vv. 5,6; 1 Sam 19:20

10:1 *the* LORD *anointed you.* Two signs are given Saul to assure him that he is the LORD's choice: he will be given two loaves of bread, and he will prophesy.

10:9 *God changed his heart.* This was apparently an experience that prepared Saul to rule Israel.

11   And it came about, when all who knew him previously saw that he prophesied now with the prophets, that the people said to one another, "What has happened to the son of Kish? Is Saul also among the prophets?"

12   And a man there answered and said, "Now, who is their father?" Therefore it became a proverb: "Is Saul also among the prophets?"

13   When he had finished prophesying, he came to the high place.

14   Now Saul's uncle said to him and his servant, "Where did you go?" And he said, "To look for the donkeys. When we saw that they could not be found, we went to Samuel."

15   And Saul's uncle said, "Please tell me what Samuel said to you."

16   So Saul said to his uncle, "He told us plainly that the donkeys had been found." But he did not tell him about the matter of the kingdom which Samuel had mentioned.

b. *Saul accepted and crowned by Israel*

17   Thereafter Samuel called the people together to the LORD at Mizpah;

18   and he said to the sons of Israel, "Thus says the LORD, the God of Israel, 'I brought Israel up from Egypt, and I delivered you from the hand of the Egyptians, and from the power of all the kingdoms that were oppressing you.'

19   "But you today rejected your God, who delivers you from all your calamities and your distresses; yet you have said, 'No, but set a king over us!' Now therefore, present yourselves before the LORD by your tribes and by your clans."

20   Thus Samuel brought all the tribes of Israel near, and the tribe of Benjamin was taken by lot.

21   Then he brought the tribe of Benjamin near by its families, and the Matrite family was taken. And Saul the son of Kish was taken; but when they looked for him, he could not be found.

22   Therefore they inquired further of the LORD, "Has the man come here yet?" So the LORD said, "Behold, he is hiding himself by the baggage."

23   So they ran and took him from there, and when he stood among the people, he was taller than any of the people from his shoulders upward.

24   And Samuel said to all the people, "Do you see him whom the LORD has chosen? Surely there is no one like him among all the people." So all the people shouted and said, "*Long* live the king!"

25   Then Samuel told the people the ordinances of the kingdom, and wrote *them* in the book and placed *it* before the LORD. And Samuel sent all the people away, each one to his house.

26   And Saul also went to his house at Gibeah; and the valiant *men* whose hearts God had touched went with him.

27   But certain worthless men said, "How can this one deliver us?" And they despised him and did not bring him any present. But he kept silent.

B. *The early kingship of Saul*

1. *The Ammonites defeated*

11   Now Nahash the Ammonite came up and besieged Jabesh-gilead; and all the men of Jabesh said to Nahash, "Make a covenant with us and we will serve you."

2   But Nahash the Ammonite said to them, "I will make *it* with you on this condition, that I will gouge out the right eye of every one of you, thus I will make it a reproach on all Israel."

3   And the elders of Jabesh said to him, "Let us alone for seven days, that we may send messengers throughout the territory of Israel. Then, if there is no one to deliver us, we will come out to you."

4   Then the messengers came to Gibeah of Saul and spoke these words in the hearing of the people, and all the people lifted up their voices and wept.

5   Now behold, Saul was coming from the field behind the oxen; and he said,

---

10:11
1 Sam 19:24;
Matt 13:54,
55; John 7:15

10:16
1 Sam 9:20

10:17
1 Sam 7:5,6
10:18
Judg 6:8,9

10:19
1 Sam 8:6,7;
Josh 24:1

10:20
Josh 7:14,16,
17

10:22
1 Sam 23:2,4,
9-11
10:23
1 Sam 9:2

*10:24
2 Sam 21:6;
1 Kin 1:25,39

10:25
1 Sam 8:11-18;
Deut 17:14-20

10:26
1 Sam 11:4

10:27
1 Kin 10:25;
2 Chr 17:5

11:1
1 Sam 12:12;
Judg 21:8;
1 Kin 20:34;
Ezek 17:13
11:2
Num 16:14;
1 Sam 17:26

11:4
1 Sam 10:26;
15:34; 30:4;
Judg 2:4

10:14 *Saul's uncle.* This may have been Ner.
10:24 The choice of Saul, a Benjamite, as king presents something of a problem, since Jacob's blessing had designated Judah as the kingly tribe (Gen. 49:10). Why then was Saul chosen to be king? While one cannot be dogmatic, the following observations may be helpful: (1) Just as God used Samson and the other judges in a period of temporary distress, so he used Saul until David was old enough to serve as theocratic king; and (2) Saul's reign paved the way for David's conquest of the full territory promised to Abraham in Gen. 15:18 and his consolidation of the kingdom on a permanent basis.

"What is *the matter* with the people that they weep?" So they related to him the words of the men of Jabesh.

6 Then the Spirit of God came upon Saul mightily when he heard these words, and he became very angry.

7 And he took a yoke of oxen and cut them in pieces, and sent *them* throughout the territory of Israel by the hand of messengers, saying, "Whoever does not come out after Saul and after Samuel, so shall it be done to his oxen." Then the dread of the LORD fell on the people, and they came out as one man.

8 And he numbered them in Bezek; and the sons of Israel were 300,000, and the men of Judah 30,000.

9 And they said to the messengers who had come, "Thus you shall say to the men of Jabesh-gilead, 'Tomorrow, by the time the sun is hot, you shall have deliverance.' " So the messengers went and told the men of Jabesh; and they were glad.

10 Then the men of Jabesh said, "Tomorrow we will come out to you, and you may do to us whatever seems good to you."

11 And it happened the next morning that Saul put the people in three companies; and they came into the midst of the camp at the morning watch, and struck down the Ammonites until the heat of the day. And it came about that those who survived were scattered, so that no two of them were left together.

12 Then the people said to Samuel, "Who is he that said, 'Shall Saul reign over us?' Bring the men, that we may put them to death."

13 But Saul said, "Not a man shall be put to death this day, for today the LORD has accomplished deliverance in Israel."

14 Then Samuel said to the people, "Come and let us go to Gilgal and renew the kingdom there."

15 So all the people went to Gilgal, and there they made Saul king before the LORD in Gilgal. There they also offered sacrifices of peace offerings before the LORD; and there Saul and all the men of Israel rejoiced greatly.

2. Samuel lays down his office as judge

12 Then Samuel said to all Israel, "Behold, I have listened to your voice in all that you said to me, and I have appointed a king over you.

2 "And now, here is the king walking before you, but I am old and gray, and behold my sons are with you. And I have walked before you from my youth even to this day.

3 "Here I am; bear witness against me before the LORD and His anointed. Whose ox have I taken, or whose donkey have I taken, or whom have I defrauded? Whom have I oppressed, or from whose hand have I taken a bribe to blind my eyes with it? I will restore *it* to you."

4 And they said, "You have not defrauded us, or oppressed us, or taken anything from any man's hand."

5 And he said to them, "The LORD is witness against you, and His anointed is witness this day that you have found nothing in my hand." And they said, "*He is* witness."

6 Then Samuel said to the people, "It is the LORD who appointed Moses and Aaron and who brought your fathers up from the land of Egypt.

7 "So now, take your stand, that I may plead with you before the LORD concerning all the righteous acts of the LORD which He did for you and your fathers.

8 "When Jacob went into Egypt and your fathers cried out to the LORD, then the LORD sent Moses and Aaron who brought your fathers out of Egypt and settled them in this place.

9 "But they forgot the LORD their God, so He sold them into the hand of Sisera, captain of the army of Hazor, and into the hand of the Philistines and into the hand of the king of Moab, and they fought against them.

10 "And they cried out to the LORD and said, 'We have sinned because we have forsaken the LORD and have served the Baals and the Ashtaroth; but now deliver us from the hands of our enemies, and we will serve Thee.'

11 "Then the LORD sent Jerubbaal and [7]Bedan and Jephthah and Samuel, and

[7]Gr. and Syr. read *Barak*

delivered you from the hands of your enemies all around, so that you lived in security.

12 "When you saw that Nahash the king of the sons of Ammon came against you, you said to me, 'No, but a king shall reign over us,' although the LORD your God *was* your king.

13 "Now therefore, here is the king whom you have chosen, whom you have asked for, and behold, the LORD has set a king over you.

14 "If you will fear the LORD and serve Him, and listen to His voice and not rebel against the command of the LORD, then both you and also the king who reigns over you will follow the LORD your God.

15 "And if you will not listen to the voice of the LORD, but rebel against the command of the LORD, then the hand of the LORD will be against you, *as it was* against your fathers.

16 "Even now, take your stand and see this great thing which the LORD will do before your eyes.

17 "Is it not the wheat harvest today? I will call to the LORD, that He may send thunder and rain. Then you will know and see that your wickedness is great which you have done in the sight of the LORD by asking for yourselves a king."

18 So Samuel called to the LORD, and the LORD sent thunder and rain that day; and all the people greatly feared the LORD and Samuel.

19 Then all the people said to Samuel, "Pray for your servants to the LORD your God, so that we may not die, for we have added to all our sins *this* evil by asking for ourselves a king."

20 And Samuel said to the people, "Do not fear. You have committed all this evil, yet do not turn aside from following the LORD, but serve the LORD with all your heart.

21 "And you must not turn aside, for *then you would go* after futile things which can not profit or deliver, because they are futile.

22 "For the LORD will not abandon His people on account of His great name, because the LORD has been pleased to make you a people for Himself.

23 "Moreover, as for me, far be it from me that I should sin against the LORD by ceasing to pray for you; but I will instruct you in the good and right way.

24 "Only [8]fear the LORD and serve Him in truth with all your heart; for consider what great things He has done for you.

25 "But if you still do wickedly, both you and your king shall be swept away."

3. Saul's war against the Philistines

a. Opening battles against the Philistines

13 Saul was *forty* years old when he began to reign, and he reigned *thirty*-two years over Israel.

2 Now Saul chose for himself 3,000 men of Israel, of which 2,000 were with Saul in Michmash and in the hill country of Bethel, while 1,000 were with Jonathan at Gibeah of Benjamin. But he sent away the rest of the people, each to his tent.

3 And Jonathan smote the garrison of the Philistines that was in Geba, and the Philistines heard of *it*. Then Saul blew the trumpet throughout the land, saying, "Let the Hebrews hear."

4 And all Israel heard the news that Saul had smitten the garrison of the Philistines, and also that Israel had become odious to the Philistines. The people were then summoned to Saul at Gilgal.

5 Now the Philistines assembled to fight with Israel, 30,000 chariots and 6,000 horsemen, and people like the sand which is on the seashore in abundance; and they came up and camped in Michmash, east of Beth-aven.

6 When the men of Israel saw that they were in a strait (for the people were hard-pressed), then the people hid themselves in caves, in thickets, in cliffs, in cellars, and in pits.

7 Also *some of* the Hebrews crossed the Jordan into the land of Gad and Gilead. But as for Saul, he *was* still in Gilgal, and all the people followed him trembling.

[8]Or, *reverence*

Marginal references:

12:12
1 Sam 11:1;
8:6,19;
Judg 8:23
12:13
1 Sam 10:24;
8:5;
Hos 13:11
*12:14
Josh 24:14
12:15
Josh 24:20
12:16
Ex 14:13,31
12:17
Prov 26:1;
1 Sam 7:9,10;
8:7
12:18
Ex 14:31
12:19
v. 23;
Ex 9:28;
James 5:15
12:21
Deut 11:16;
Jer 16:19;
Hab 2:18
12:22
1 Kin 6:13;
Josh 7:9;
Deut 7:7,8
12:23
Rom 1:9;
Col 1:9;
2 Tim 1:3;
1 Kin 8:36
12:24
Eccl 12:13;
Deut 10:21
12:25
Josh 24:20;
1 Sam 31:1-5
13:2
1 Sam 10:26
*13:3
1 Sam 10:5
13:5
Josh 11:4
13:6
Judg 6:2

12:14 The monarchy was an acceptable form of rule as long as the king and the people followed the precepts of the LORD, their real King.

13:3 The Israelites were subjugated by Philistine garrisons throughout the country.

b. *Saul intrudes into the priest's office*

13:8
1 Sam 10:8

13:9
2 Sam 24:25

13:10
1 Sam 15:13

13:11
vv. 2,5,16,23

*13:13
2 Chr 16:9;
1 Sam 15:11,
22

13:14
1 Sam 15:28;
Acts 13:22

13:15
1 Sam 14:2

13:17
1 Sam 14:15

13:18
Josh 18:13,
14;
Neh 11:34

*13:19
2 Kin 24:14

13:22
Judg 5:8

14:2
1 Sam 13:15

14:3
1 Sam 22:9-12,
20; 4:21; 2:28

14:4
1 Sam 13:23

14:6
Judg 7:4,7;
1 Sam 17:46,
47

8   Now he waited seven days, according to the appointed time set by Samuel, but Samuel did not come to Gilgal; and the people were scattering from him.

9   So Saul said, "Bring to me the burnt offering and the peace offerings." And he offered the burnt offering.

10   And it came about as soon as he finished offering the burnt offering, that behold, Samuel came; and Saul went out to meet him *and* to greet him.

11   But Samuel said, "What have you done?" And Saul said, "Because I saw that the people were scattering from me, and that you did not come within the appointed days, and that the Philistines were assembling at Michmash,

12   therefore I said, 'Now the Philistines will come down against me at Gilgal, and I have not asked the favor of the LORD.' So I forced myself and offered the burnt offering."

13   And Samuel said to Saul, "You have acted foolishly; you have not kept the commandment of the LORD your God, which He commanded you, for now the LORD would have established your kingdom over Israel forever.

14   "But now your kingdom shall not endure. The LORD has sought out for Himself a man after His own heart, and the LORD has appointed him as ruler over His people, because you have not kept what the LORD commanded you."

15   Then Samuel arose and went up from Gilgal to Gibeah of Benjamin. And Saul numbered the people who were present with him, about six hundred men.

c. *Saul's nondescript army*

16   Now Saul and his son Jonathan and the people who were present with them were staying in Geba of Benjamin while the Philistines camped at Michmash.

17   And the raiders came from the camp of the Philistines in three companies: one company turned toward Ophrah, to the land of Shual,

18   and another company turned toward Beth-horon, and another company turned toward the border which overlooks the valley of Zeboim toward the wilderness.

19   Now no blacksmith could be found in all the land of Israel, for the Philistines said, "Lest the Hebrews make swords or spears."

20   So all Israel went down to the Philistines, each to sharpen his plowshare, his mattock, his axe, and his hoe.

21   And the charge was two-thirds of a shekel for the plowshares, the mattocks, the forks, and the axes, and to fix the hoes.

22   So it came about on the day of battle that neither sword nor spear was found in the hands of any of the people who *were* with Saul and Jonathan, but they were found with Saul and his son Jonathan.

23   And the garrison of the Philistines went out to the pass of Michmash.

d. *Jonathan's exploit at Michmash*

(1) JONATHAN ATTACKS

14   Now the day came that Jonathan, the son of Saul, said to the young man who was carrying his armor, "Come and let us cross over to the Philistines' garrison that is on yonder side." But he did not tell his father.

2   And Saul was staying in the outskirts of Gibeah under the pomegranate tree which is in Migron. And the people who *were* with him *were* about six hundred men,

3   and Ahijah, the son of Ahitub, Ichabod's brother, the son of Phinehas, the son of Eli, the priest of the LORD at Shiloh, was wearing an ephod. And the people did not know that Jonathan had gone.

4   And between the passes by which Jonathan sought to cross over to the Philistines' garrison, there was a sharp crag on the one side, and a sharp crag on the other side, and the name of the one was Bozez, and the name of the other Seneh.

5   The one crag rose on the north opposite Michmash, and the other on the south opposite Geba.

6   Then Jonathan said to the young man who was carrying his armor, "Come and let us cross over to the garrison of these uncircumcised; perhaps the LORD will work for us, for the LORD is not restrained to save by many or by few."

13:13 *You have acted foolishly.* To forestall corruption, the rights and duties of the kingship prohibited the king from acting as the religious leader as well. Even though the people were beginning to desert him, Saul had no right to function as a priest.

13:19 *no blacksmith.* A basic reason for Philistine supremacy over Israel was their monopoly over the smelting and working of iron. The Israelites were helpless without arms.

7   And his armor bearer said to him, "Do all that is in your heart; turn yourself, *and* here I am with you according to your desire."

8   Then Jonathan said, "Behold, we will cross over to the men and reveal ourselves to them.

9   "If they say to us, 'Wait until we come to you'; then we will stand in our place and not go up to them.

10   "But if they say, 'Come up to us,' then we will go up, for the LORD has given them into our hands; and this shall be the sign to us."

11   And when both of them revealed themselves to the garrison of the Philistines, the Philistines said, "Behold, Hebrews are coming out of the holes where they have hidden themselves."

12   So the men of the garrison hailed Jonathan and his armor bearer and said, "Come up to us and we will tell you something." And Jonathan said to his armor bearer, "Come up after me, for the LORD has given them into the hands of Israel."

13   Then Jonathan climbed up on his hands and feet, with his armor bearer behind him; and they fell before Jonathan, and his armor bearer put some to death after him.

14   And that first slaughter which Jonathan and his armor bearer made was about twenty men within about half a furrow in an acre of land.

15   And there was a trembling in the camp, in the field, and among all the people. Even the garrison and the raiders trembled, and the earth quaked so that it became a [9]great trembling.

(2) THE PHILISTINES FLEE

16   Now Saul's watchmen in Gibeah of Benjamin looked, and behold, the multitude melted away; and they went here and *there*.

17   And Saul said to the people who *were* with him, "Number now and see who has gone from us." And when they had numbered, behold, Jonathan and his armor bearer were not *there*.

18   Then Saul said to Ahijah, "Bring the ark of God here." For the ark of God was at that time with the sons of Israel.

19   And it happened while Saul talked to the priest, that the commotion in the camp of the Philistines continued and increased; so Saul said to the priest, "Withdraw your hand."

20   Then Saul and all the people who *were* with him rallied and came to the battle; and behold, every man's sword was against his fellow, *and there was* very great confusion.

21   Now the Hebrews *who* were with the Philistines previously, who went up with them all around in the camp, even they also *turned* to be with the Israelites who *were* with Saul and Jonathan.

22   When all the men of Israel who had hidden themselves in the hill country of Ephraim heard that the Philistines had fled, even they also pursued them closely in the battle.

23   So the LORD delivered Israel that day, and the battle spread beyond Bethaven.

(3) JONATHAN UNWITTINGLY TRANSGRESSES SAUL'S OATH

24   Now the men of Israel were hard-pressed on that day, for Saul had put the people under oath, saying, "Cursed be the man who eats food before evening, and until I have avenged myself on my enemies." So none of the people tasted food.

25   And all *the people* of the land entered the forest, and there was honey on the ground.

26   When the people entered the forest, behold, *there was* a flow of honey; but no man put his hand to his mouth, for the people feared the oath.

27   But Jonathan had not heard when his father put the people under oath; therefore, he put out the end of the staff that *was* in his hand and dipped it in the honeycomb, and put his hand to his mouth, and his eyes brightened.

28   Then one of the people answered and said, "Your father strictly put the people under oath, saying, 'Cursed be the man who eats food today.' " And the people were weary.

29   Then Jonathan said, "My father has troubled the land. See now, how my eyes have brightened because I tasted a little of this honey.

[9]Lit., *trembling of God*

14:10
Gen 24:14;
Judg 6:36,37
14:11
1 Sam 13:6

14:12
1 Sam 17:43, 44;
2 Sam 5:24

14:15
2 Kin 7:6,7;
1 Sam 13:17

14:16
2 Sam 18:24

14:19
Num 27:21

14:20
Judg 7:22;
2 Chr 20:23

14:22
1 Sam 13:6

14:23
Ex 14:30;
Ps 44:6,7;
1 Sam 13:5

14:24
Josh 6:26

14:27
1 Sam 30:12

14:29
1 Kin 18:18

30　"How much more, if only the people had eaten freely today of the spoil of their enemies which they found! For now the slaughter among the Philistines has not been great."

31　And they struck among the Philistines that day from Michmash to Aijalon. And the people were very weary.

14:32
1 Sam 15:19;
Lev 17:10-14

32　And the people rushed greedily upon the spoil, and took sheep and oxen and calves, and slew *them* on the ground; and the people ate *them* with the blood.

33　Then they told Saul, saying, "Behold, the people are sinning against the LORD by eating with the blood." And he said, "You have acted treacherously; roll a great stone to me today."

34　And Saul said, "Disperse yourselves among the people and say to them, 'Each one of you bring me his ox or his sheep, and slaughter *it* here and eat; and do not sin against the LORD by eating with the blood.'" So all the people that night brought each one his ox with him, and slaughtered *it* there.

14:35
1 Sam 7:17

35　And Saul built an altar to the LORD; it was the first altar that he built to the LORD.

(4) JONATHAN'S GUILT DISCOVERED

36　Then Saul said, "Let us go down after the Philistines by night and take spoil among them until the morning light, and let us not leave a man of them." And they said, "Do whatever seems good to you." So the priest said, "Let us draw near to God here."

14:37
1 Sam 10:22;
28:6
14:38
Josh 7:14;
1 Sam 10:19
14:39
2 Sam 12:5

37　And Saul inquired of God, "Shall I go down after the Philistines? Wilt Thou give them into the hand of Israel?" But He did not answer him on that day.

38　And Saul said, "Draw near here, all you chiefs of the people, and investigate and see how this sin has happened today.

39　For as the LORD lives, who delivers Israel, though it is in Jonathan my son, he shall surely die." But not one of all the people answered him.

40　Then he said to all Israel, "You shall be on one side and I and Jonathan my son will be on the other side." And the people said to Saul, "Do what seems good to you."

*14:41
Prov 16:33;
Acts 1:24

41　Therefore, Saul said to the LORD, the God of Israel, "Give a perfect *lot.*" And Jonathan and Saul were taken, but the people escaped.

42　And Saul said, "Cast *lots* between me and Jonathan my son." And Jonathan was taken.

(5) JONATHAN SAVED BY THE PEOPLE

14:43
Josh 7:19;
v. 23

43　Then Saul said to Jonathan, "Tell me what you have done." So Jonathan told him and said, "I indeed tasted a little honey with the end of the staff that was in my hand. Here I am, I must die!"

14:44
Ruth 1:17;
v. 39
14:45
2 Sam 14:11;
1 Kin 1:52;
Acts 27:34

44　And Saul said, "May God do this *to me* and more also, for you shall surely die, Jonathan."

45　But the people said to Saul, "Must Jonathan die, who has brought about this great deliverance in Israel? Far from it! As the LORD lives, there shall not one hair of his head fall to the ground, for he has worked with God this day." So the people rescued Jonathan and he did not die.

46　Then Saul went up from pursuing the Philistines, and the Philistines went to their own place.

e. Saul wars against other nations

14:47
1 Sam 11:1-13;
2 Sam 10:6;
v. 52

47　Now when Saul had taken the kingdom over Israel, he fought against all his enemies on every side, against Moab, the sons of Ammon, Edom, the kings of Zobah, and the Philistines; and wherever he turned, he inflicted punishment.

14:48
1 Sam 15:3,7

48　And he acted valiantly and defeated the Amalekites, and delivered Israel from the hands of those who plundered them.

f. Saul's family and army

14:49
1 Sam 31:2;
1 Chr 8:33;
1 Sam 18:17-20

49　Now the sons of Saul were Jonathan and Ishvi and Malchi-shua; and the names of his two daughters *were these:* the name of the first-born Merab and the name of the younger Michal.

14:50
2 Sam 2:8

50　And the name of Saul's wife was Ahinoam the daughter of Ahimaaz. And the name of the captain of his army was Abner the son of Ner, Saul's uncle.

14:34,35 To protect the people from the sin of eating blood (Lev. 7:26,27; 17:12), Saul built the first of his altars to the LORD and supervised the sacrifices. **14:41** *lot.* See note to Ex. 28:30.

51   And Kish *was* the father of Saul, and Ner the father of Abner *was* the son of Abiel.

52   Now the war against the Philistines was severe all the days of Saul; and when Saul saw any mighty man or any valiant man, he attached him to his staff.

14:51
1 Sam 9:1

14:52
1 Sam 8:11

C. *God rejects Saul*

1. *The war with the Amalekites*

a. *God's command to destroy*

15 Then Samuel said to Saul, "The LORD sent me to anoint you as king over His people, over Israel; now therefore, listen to the words of the LORD.

2   "Thus says the LORD of hosts, 'I will punish Amalek *for* what he did to Israel, how he set himself against him on the way while he was coming up from Egypt.

3   'Now go and strike Amalek and utterly destroy all that he has, and do not spare him; but put to death both man and woman, child and infant, ox and sheep, camel and donkey.' "

15:1
1 Sam 9:16

15:2
Ex 17:8-14;
Num 24:20;
Deut 25:17-19
*15:3
Num 24:20;
Deut 20:16-18;
1 Sam 22:19

b. *Saul's disobedience*

4   Then Saul summoned the people and numbered them in Telaim, 200,000 foot soldiers and 10,000 men of Judah.

5   And Saul came to the city of Amalek, and set an ambush in the valley.

6   And Saul said to the Kenites, "Go, depart, go down from among the Amalekites, lest I destroy you with them; for you showed kindness to all the sons of Israel when they came up from Egypt." So the Kenites departed from among the Amalekites.

7   So Saul defeated the Amalekites, from Havilah as you go to Shur, which is east of Egypt.

8   And he captured Agag the king of the Amalekites alive, and utterly destroyed all the people with the edge of the sword.

9   But Saul and the people spared Agag and the best of the sheep, the oxen, the fatlings, the lambs, and all that was good, and were not willing to destroy them utterly; but everything despised and worthless, that they utterly destroyed.

15:6
Judg 1:16;
4:11;
Ex 18:10,19;
Num 10:29-32

15:7
1 Sam 14:48;
Gen 16:7;
25:17,18;
Ex 15:22
*15:8
1 Kin 20:34ff;
1 Sam 30:1
15:9
vv. 3,15

c. *Samuel delivers God's sentence*

10   Then the word of the LORD came to Samuel, saying,

11   "I regret that I have made Saul king, for he has turned back from following Me, and has not carried out My commands." And Samuel was distressed and cried out to the LORD all night.

12   And Samuel rose early in the morning to meet Saul; and it was told Samuel, saying, "Saul came to Carmel, and behold, he set up a monument for himself, then turned and proceeded on down to Gilgal."

13   And Samuel came to Saul, and Saul said to him, "Blessed are you of the LORD! I have carried out the command of the LORD."

14   But Samuel said, "What then is this bleating of the sheep in my ears, and the lowing of the oxen which I hear?"

15   And Saul said, "They have brought them from the Amalekites, for the people spared the best of the sheep and oxen, to sacrifice to the LORD your God; but the rest we have utterly destroyed."

16   Then Samuel said to Saul, "Wait, and let me tell you what the LORD said to me last night." And he said to him, "Speak!"

17   And Samuel said, "Is it not true, though you were little in your own eyes, you were *made* the head of the tribes of Israel? And the LORD anointed you king over Israel,

18   and the LORD sent you on a mission, and said, 'Go and utterly destroy the sinners, the Amalekites, and fight against them until they are exterminated.'

19   "Why then did you not obey the voice of the LORD, but rushed upon the spoil and did what was evil in the sight of the LORD?"

20   Then Saul said to Samuel, "I did obey the voice of the LORD, and went on

15:11
Gen 6:6,7;
2 Sam 24:16;
1 Kin 9:6,7;
1 Sam 16:1
15:12
Josh 15:55

15:13
Gen 14:19;
Judg 17:2

15:15
vv. 9,21;
Gen 3:12

15:17
1 Sam 9:21

15:18
v. 3

15:19
1 Sam 14:32
15:20
v. 13

15:3 *utterly destroy.* The Amalekites were devoted to the LORD; see note to Deut. 2:34.
15:8 *all the people.* This cannot mean all of the Amalekites because they were a strong group in David's reign (27:8;

30:1,18; 2 Sam. 1:1). There were undoubtedly other Amalekites not included in this account. Also see note to Esth. 3:1 on Amalekites.

the mission on which the LORD sent me, and have brought back Agag the king of Amalek, and have utterly destroyed the Amalekites.

*15:21
v. 15

21 "But the people took *some* of the spoil, sheep and oxen, the choicest of the things devoted to destruction, to sacrifice to the LORD your God at Gilgal."

15:22
Is 1:11-13;
Mic 6:6-8;
Heb 10:6-9;
Hos 6:6;
Mark 12:33

22   And Samuel said,
"Has the LORD as much delight in burnt offerings and sacrifices
As in obeying the voice of the LORD?
Behold, to obey is better than sacrifice,
And to heed than the fat of rams.

*15:23
1 Sam 13:14

23   "For rebellion is as the sin of divination,
And insubordination is as iniquity and idolatry.
Because you have rejected the word of the LORD,
He has also rejected you from *being* king."

d. Saul appears penitent

15:24
2 Sam 12:13;
Prov 29:25;
Is 51:12,13

24   Then Saul said to Samuel, "I have sinned; I have indeed transgressed the command of the LORD and your words, because I feared the people and listened to their voice.

25   "Now therefore, please pardon my sin and return with me, that I may worship the LORD."

15:26
1 Sam 13:14

26   But Samuel said to Saul, "I will not return with you; for you have rejected the word of the LORD, and the LORD has rejected you from being king over Israel."

15:27
1 Kin 11:30, 31
15:28
1 Sam 28:17
*15:29
1 Chr 29:11;
Num 23:19;
Ezek 24:14
15:30
John 12:43;
Is 29:13

27   And as Samuel turned to go, *Saul* seized the edge of his robe, and it tore.

28   So Samuel said to him, "The LORD has torn the kingdom of Israel from you today, and has given it to your neighbor who is better than you.

29   "And also the Glory of Israel will not lie or change His mind; for He is not a man that He should change His mind."

30   Then he said, "I have sinned; *but* please honor me now before the elders of my people and before Israel, and go back with me, that I may worship the LORD your God."

31   So Samuel went back following Saul, and Saul worshiped the LORD.

e. Samuel slays Agag and sees Saul no more

32   Then Samuel said, "Bring me Agag, the king of the Amalekites." And Agag came to him cheerfully. And Agag said, "Surely the bitterness of death is past."

15:33
Gen 9:6;
Judg 1:7

33   But Samuel said, "As your sword has made women childless, so shall your mother be childless among women." And Samuel hewed Agag to pieces before the LORD at Gilgal.

15:34
1 Sam 7:17;
11:4
15:35
1 Sam 19:24;
16:1

34   Then Samuel went to Ramah, but Saul went up to his house at Gibeah of Saul.

35   And Samuel did not see Saul again until the day of his death; for Samuel grieved over Saul. And the LORD regretted that He had made Saul king over Israel.

2. David chosen to be king

a. God sends Samuel to Jesse's house

16:1
1 Sam 15:23, 35; 9:16;
2 Kin 9:1;
Ps 78:70;
Acts 13:22
16:2
1 Sam 20:29

16 Now the LORD said to Samuel, "How long will you grieve over Saul, since I have rejected him from being king over Israel? Fill your horn with oil, and go; I will send you to Jesse the Bethlehemite, for I have selected a king for Myself among his sons."

2   But Samuel said, "How can I go? When Saul hears *of it*, he will kill me." And the LORD said, "Take a heifer with you, and say, 'I have come to sacrifice to the LORD.'

16:3
Ex 4:15;
1 Sam 9:16
16:4
Luke 2:4;
1 Kin 2:13;
2 Kin 9:22
16:5
Ex 19:10

3   "And you shall invite Jesse to the sacrifice, and I will show you what you shall do; and you shall anoint for Me the one whom I designate to you."

4   So Samuel did what the LORD said, and came to Bethlehem. And the elders of the city came trembling to meet him and said, "Do you come in peace?"

5   And he said, "In peace; I have come to sacrifice to the LORD. Consecrate yourselves and come with me to the sacrifice." He also consecrated Jesse and his sons, and invited them to the sacrifice.

15:21 *the people took.* Saul, like Aaron (Ex. 32:22–24), blamed the people; but back of his act was covetousness.
15:23 *divination.* See notes to Deut. 18:10 and

Ezek. 21:21.
15:29 *Glory of Israel,* another name for God.
15:32 See note to Esth. 3:1 on Amalekites.

b. *David selected and anointed king*

6 Then it came about when they entered, that he looked at Eliab and thought, "Surely the LORD's anointed is before Him."

7 But the LORD said to Samuel, "Do not look at his appearance or at the height of his stature, because I have rejected him; for God *sees* not as man sees, for man looks at the outward appearance, but the LORD looks at the heart."

8 Then Jesse called Abinadab, and made him pass before Samuel. And he said, "Neither has the LORD chosen this one."

9 Next Jesse made Shammah pass by. And he said, "Neither has the LORD chosen this one."

10 Thus Jesse made seven of his sons pass before Samuel. But Samuel said to Jesse, "The LORD has not chosen these."

11 And Samuel said to Jesse, "Are these all the children?" And he said, "There remains yet the youngest, and behold, he is tending the sheep." Then Samuel said to Jesse, "Send and bring him; for we will not sit down until he comes here."

12 So he sent and brought him in. Now he was ruddy, with beautiful eyes and a handsome appearance. And the LORD said, "Arise, anoint him; for this is he."

13 Then Samuel took the horn of oil and anointed him in the midst of his brothers; and the Spirit of the LORD came mightily upon David from that day forward. And Samuel arose and went to Ramah.

3. *Saul overtaken by an evil spirit; David joins his court*

14 Now the Spirit of the LORD departed from Saul, and an evil spirit from the LORD terrorized him.

15 Saul's servants then said to him, "Behold now, an evil spirit from God is terrorizing you.

16 "Let our lord now command your servants who are before you. Let them seek a man who is a skillful player on the harp; and it shall come about when the evil spirit from God is on you, that he shall play *the harp* with his hand, and you will be well."

17 So Saul said to his servants, "Provide for me now a man who can play well, and bring *him* to me."

18 Then one of the young men answered and said, "Behold, I have seen a son of Jesse the Bethlehemite who is a skillful musician, a mighty man of valor, a warrior, one prudent in speech, and a handsome man; and the LORD is with him."

19 So Saul sent messengers to Jesse, and said, "Send me your son David who is with the flock."

20 And Jesse took a donkey *loaded with* bread and a jug of wine and a young goat, and sent *them* to Saul by David his son.

21 Then David came to Saul and attended him, and Saul loved him greatly; and he became his armor bearer.

22 And Saul sent to Jesse, saying, "Let David now stand before me; for he has found favor in my sight."

23 So it came about whenever the *evil* spirit from God came to Saul, David would take the harp and play *it* with his hand; and Saul would be refreshed and be well, and the evil spirit would depart from him.

D. The rise of David and his persecutions by Saul

1. *Goliath the Philistine*

17 Now the Philistines gathered their armies for battle; and they were gathered at Socoh which belongs to Judah, and they camped between Socoh and Azekah, in Ephes-dammim.

2 And Saul and the men of Israel were gathered, and camped in the valley of Elah, and drew up in battle array to encounter the Philistines.

Marginal references:

16:6 — 1 Sam 17:13
16:7 — Is 55:8; 1 Kin 8:39; 1 Chr 28:9
16:8 — 1 Sam 17:13
16:9 — 1 Sam 17:13
16:11 — 1 Sam 17:12
16:12 — 1 Sam 17:42; 9:17
*16:13 — 1 Sam 10:1,6, 9,10; Judg 11:29
*16:14 — Judg 16:20; 1 Sam 18:10
16:16 — v. 23; 1 Sam 18:10; 19:9; 2 Kin 3:15
16:18 — 1 Sam 17:32-36; 3:19
16:20 — 1 Sam 10:27; Prov 18:16
*16:21f — Gen 41:46; Prov 22:29
16:23 — vv. 14-16
17:1 — 1 Sam 13:5; 2 Chr 28:18
17:2 — 1 Sam 21:9

16:13 David, the shepherd-king, is a type of Christ. David was taken from responsibility over sheep to become king over Israel. Christ came as the good shepherd who gives His life for the sheep (John 10:11). This shepherd has been raised from the dead for us (Heb. 13:20) and is now exalted at the right hand of the Father (Acts 5:31). Like David, who was made king, so Christ the shepherd is now King of kings, sitting on the heavenly counterpart of the throne of His father David. He is indeed great David's greater Son (Luke 1:32; Acts 2:30). (See also 2 Sam. 8:15; 1 Chr. 17:7; Ps. 89:19,20; Ezek. 37:24; Phil. 2:9.)

16:14 *evil spirit from the LORD.* Saul's disorder is described as punishment initiated by God.

16:21,22 This close relationship between Saul and David does not make impossible the apparent unfamiliarity noted in 17:55–58.

3   And the Philistines stood on the mountain on one side while Israel stood on the mountain on the other side, with the valley between them.

17:4
2 Sam 21:19;
Josh 11:21,22

4   Then a champion came out from the armies of the Philistines named Goliath, from Gath, whose height was six [10]cubits and a span.

5   And *he had* a bronze helmet on his head, and he was clothed with scale-armor which weighed five thousand shekels of bronze.

17:6
v. 45

6   *He* also *had* bronze [11]greaves on his legs and a bronze javelin *slung* between his shoulders.

17:7
2 Sam 21:19;
v. 41
17:8
1 Sam 8:17

7   And the shaft of his spear was like a weaver's beam, and the head of his spear *weighed* six hundred shekels of iron; his shield-carrier also walked before him.

8   And he stood and shouted to the ranks of Israel, and said to them, "Why do you come out to draw up in battle array? Am I not the Philistine and you servants of Saul? Choose a man for yourselves and let him come down to me.

9   "If he is able to fight with me and kill me, then we will become your servants; but if I prevail against him and kill him, then you shall become our servants and serve us."

17:10
vv. 26,36,45

10   Again the Philistine said, "I defy the ranks of Israel this day; give me a man that we may fight together."

11   When Saul and all Israel heard these words of the Philistine, they were dismayed and greatly afraid.

2. David slays Goliath

17:12
Ruth 4:22;
1 Sam 16:18;
Gen 35:19;
1 Sam 16:10,
11;
1 Chr 2:13-15
17:13
1 Sam 16:6,8,
9

12   Now David was the son of the Ephrathite of Bethlehem in Judah, whose name was Jesse, and he had eight sons. And Jesse was old in the days of Saul, advanced *in years* among men.

13   And the three older sons of Jesse had gone after Saul to the battle. And the names of his three sons who went to the battle were Eliab the first-born, and the second to him Abinadab, and the third Shammah.

14   And David was the youngest. Now the three oldest followed Saul,

17:15
1 Sam 16:19

15   but David went back and forth from Saul to tend his father's flock at Bethlehem.

16   And the Philistine came forward morning and evening for forty days, and took his stand.

17   Then Jesse said to David his son, "Take now for your brothers an ephah of this roasted grain and these ten loaves, and run to the camp to your brothers.

17:18
Gen 37:14

18   "Bring also these ten cuts of cheese to the commander of *their* thousand, and look into the welfare of your brothers, and bring back news of them.

19   "For Saul and they and all the men of Israel are in the valley of Elah, fighting with the Philistines."

20   So David arose early in the morning and left the flock with a keeper and took *the supplies* and went as Jesse had commanded him. And he came to the circle of the camp while the army was going out in battle array shouting the war cry.

21   And Israel and the Philistines drew up in battle array, army against army.

22   Then David left his baggage in the care of the baggage keeper, and ran to the battle line and entered in order to greet his brothers.

17:23
vv. 8-10

23   As he was talking with them, behold, the champion, the Philistine from Gath named Goliath, was coming up from the army of the Philistines, and he spoke these same words; and David heard *them*.

24   When all the men of Israel saw the man, they fled from him and were greatly afraid.

17:25
Josh 15:16

25   And the men of Israel said, "Have you seen this man who is coming up? Surely he is coming up to defy Israel. And it will be that the king will enrich the man who kills him with great riches and will give him his daughter and make his father's house [12]free in Israel."

17:26
1 Sam 11:2;
14:6; v. 10;
Deut 5:26

26   Then David spoke to the men who were standing by him, saying, "What will be done for the man who kills this Philistine, and takes away the reproach from Israel? For who is this uncircumcised Philistine, that he should taunt the armies of the living God?"

17:27
v. 25

27   And the people answered him in accord with this word, saying, "Thus it will be done for the man who kills him."

17:28
Gen 37:4ff

28   Now Eliab his oldest brother heard when he spoke to the men; and Eliab's anger burned against David and he said, "Why have you come down? And with

[10]I.e., One cubit equals approx. 18 in.   [11]Or, *shin guards*   [12]I.e., free from taxes and public service

whom have you left those few sheep in the wilderness? I know your insolence and the wickedness of your heart; for you have come down in order to see the battle."

29   But David said, "What have I done now? Was it not just a question?"

30   Then he turned away from him to another and said the same thing; and the people answered the same thing as before.

31   When the words which David spoke were heard, they told *them* to Saul, and he sent for him.

32   And David said to Saul, "Let no man's heart fail on account of him; your servant will go and fight with this Philistine."

33   Then Saul said to David, "You are not able to go against this Philistine to fight with him; for you are *but* a youth while he has been a warrior from his youth."

34   But David said to Saul, "Your servant was tending his father's sheep. When a lion or a bear came and took a lamb from the flock,

35   I went out after him and attacked him, and rescued *it* from his mouth; and when he rose up against me, I seized *him* by his beard and struck him and killed him.

36   "Your servant has killed both the lion and the bear; and this uncircumcised Philistine will be like one of them, since he has taunted the armies of the living God."

37   And David said, "The LORD who delivered me from the paw of the lion and from the paw of the bear, He will deliver me from the hand of this Philistine." And Saul said to David, "Go, and may the LORD be with you."

38   Then Saul clothed David with his garments and put a bronze helmet on his head, and he clothed him with armor.

39   And David girded his sword over his armor and tried to walk, for he had not tested *them*. So David said to Saul, "I cannot go with these, for I have not tested *them*." And David took them off.

40   And he took his stick in his hand and chose for himself five smooth stones from the brook, and put them in the shepherd's bag which he had, even in *his* pouch, and his sling was in his hand; and he approached the Philistine.

41   Then the Philistine came on and approached David, with the shield-bearer in front of him.

42   When the Philistine looked and saw David, he disdained him; for he was *but* a youth, and ruddy, with a handsome appearance.

43   And the Philistine said to David, "Am I a dog, that you come to me with sticks?" And the Philistine cursed David by his gods.

44   The Philistine also said to David, "Come to me, and I will give your flesh to the birds of the sky and the beasts of the field."

45   Then David said to the Philistine, "You come to me with a sword, a spear, and a javelin, but I come to you in the name of the LORD of hosts, the God of the armies of Israel, whom you have taunted.

46   "This day the LORD will deliver you up into my hands, and I will strike you down and remove your head from you. And I will give the dead bodies of the army of the Philistines this day to the birds of the sky and the wild beasts of the earth, that all the earth may know that there is a God in Israel,

47   and that all this assembly may know that the LORD does not deliver by sword or by spear; for the battle is the LORD's and He will give you into our hands."

48   Then it happened when the Philistine rose and came and drew near to meet David, that David ran quickly toward the battle line to meet the Philistine.

49   And David put his hand into his bag and took from it a stone and slung *it*, and struck the Philistine on his forehead. And the stone sank into his forehead, so that he fell on his face to the ground.

50   Thus David prevailed over the Philistine with a sling and a stone, and he struck the Philistine and killed him; but there was no sword in David's hand.

51   Then David ran and stood over the Philistine and took his sword and drew it out of its sheath and killed him, and cut off his head with it. When the Philistines saw that their champion was dead, they fled.

52   And the men of Israel and Judah arose and shouted and pursued the Philistines as far as the valley, and to the gates of Ekron. And the slain Philistines lay along the way to Shaaraim, even to Gath and Ekron.

53   And the sons of Israel returned from chasing the Philistines and plundered their camps.

17:29
v. 17
17:30
vv. 26,27

17:32
Deut 20:1-4;
1 Sam 16:18

17:37
2 Tim 4:17;
1 Sam 20:13;
1 Chr 22:11,
16

17:42
Prov 16:18;
Ps 123:3,4;
1 Sam 16:12
17:43
1 Sam 24:14;
2 Sam 3:8
17:44
1 Kin 20:10
17:45
2 Chr 32:8;
Ps 124:8;
Heb 11:34

17:46
1 Kin 18:36;
2 Kin 19:19;
Is 52:10

17:47
1 Sam 14:6;
2 Chr 14:11;
Ps 44:6,7

17:51
1 Sam 21:9;
Heb 11:34

17:52
Josh 15:36

54   Then David took the Philistine's head and brought it to Jerusalem, but he put his weapons in his tent.

17:55
1 Sam 16:21,
22

55   Now when Saul saw David going out against the Philistine, he said to Abner the commander of the army, "Abner, whose son is this young man?" And Abner said, "By your life, O king, I do not know."

56   And the king said, "You inquire whose son the youth is."

17:57
v. 54

57   So when David returned from killing the Philistine, Abner took him and brought him before Saul with the Philistine's head in his hand.

17:58
v. 12

58   And Saul said to him, "Whose son are you, young man?" And David answered, "*I am* the son of your servant Jesse the Bethlehemite."

3. *The friendship of David and Jonathan*

18:1
Gen 44:30;
Deut 13:6;
1 Sam 20:17;
2 Sam 1:26
18:2
1 Sam 17:15

18 Now it came about when he had finished speaking to Saul, that the soul of Jonathan was knit to the soul of David, and Jonathan loved him as himself.

2   And Saul took him that day and did not let him return to his father's house.

3   Then Jonathan made a covenant with David because he loved him as himself.

4   And Jonathan stripped himself of the robe that was on him and gave it to David, with his armor, including his sword and his bow and his belt.

5   So David went out wherever Saul sent him, *and* prospered; and Saul set him over the men of war. And it was pleasing in the sight of all the people and also in the sight of Saul's servants.

4. *The hatred of Saul*

18:6
Ex 15:20;
Judg 11:34;
Ps 68:25
18:7
Ex 15:21;
1 Sam 21:11

6   And it happened as they were coming, when David returned from killing the Philistine, that the women came out of all the cities of Israel, singing and dancing, to meet King Saul, with tambourines, with joy and with [13]musical instruments.

7   And the women sang as they played, and said,

"Saul has slain his thousands,
And David his ten thousands."

18:8
1 Sam 15:8

8   Then Saul became very angry, for this saying displeased him; and he said, "They have ascribed to David ten thousands, but to me they have ascribed thousands. Now what more can he have but the kingdom?"

9   And Saul looked at David with suspicion from that day on.

18:10
1 Sam 16:14,
23; 19:9,23,
24

10   Now it came about on the next day that an evil spirit from God came mightily upon Saul, and he raved in the midst of the house, while David was playing *the harp* with his hand, as usual; and a spear *was* in Saul's hand.

18:11
1 Sam 19:10;
20:33
18:12
vv. 15,29;
1 Sam 16:13,
14,18
18:13
v. 16;
2 Sam 5:2
18:14
1 Sam 16:18;
Gen 39:2,3,23
18:16
v. 5

11   And Saul hurled the spear for he thought, "I will pin David to the wall." But David escaped from his presence twice.

12   Now Saul was afraid of David, for the LORD was with him but had departed from Saul.

13   Therefore Saul removed him from his presence, and appointed him as his commander of a thousand; and he went out and came in before the people.

14   And David was prospering in all his ways for the LORD *was* with him.

15   When Saul saw that he was prospering greatly, he dreaded him.

16   But all Israel and Judah loved David, and he went out and came in before them.

5. *David loses Merab but marries Michal*

18:17
1 Sam 17:25;
25:28; vv. 21,
25

17   Then Saul said to David, "Here is my older daughter Merab; I will give her to you as a wife, only be a valiant man for me and fight the LORD's battles." For Saul thought, "My hand shall not be against him, but let the hand of the Philistines be against him."

18:18
v. 23;
1 Sam 9:21;
2 Sam 7:18
18:19
2 Sam 21:8;
Judg 7:22
18:20
v. 28
18:21
vv. 17,26

18   But David said to Saul, "Who am I, and what is my life *or* my father's family in Israel, that I should be the king's son-in-law?"

19   So it came about at the time when Merab, Saul's daughter, should have been given to David, that she was given to Adriel the Meholathite for a wife.

20   Now Michal, Saul's daughter, loved David. When they told Saul, the thing was agreeable to him.

21   And Saul thought, "I will give her to him that she may become a snare to

[13]I.e., triangles, or three-stringed instruments

him, and that the hand of the Philistines may be against him." Therefore Saul said to David, "For a second time you may be my son-in-law today."

22   Then Saul commanded his servants, "Speak to David secretly, saying, 'Behold, the king delights in you, and all his servants love you; now therefore, become the king's son-in-law.'"

23   So Saul's servants spoke these words to David. But David said, "Is it trivial in your sight to become the king's son-in-law, since I am a poor man and lightly esteemed?"

24   And the servants of Saul reported to him according to these words *which* David spoke.

25   Saul then said, "Thus you shall say to David, 'The king does not desire any dowry except a hundred foreskins of the Philistines, to take vengeance on the king's enemies.'" Now Saul planned to make David fall by the hand of the Philistines.

26   When his servants told David these words, it pleased David to become the king's son-in-law. Before the days had expired

27   David rose up and went, he and his men, and struck down two hundred men among the Philistines. Then David brought their foreskins, and they gave them in full number to the king, that he might become the king's son-in-law. So Saul gave him Michal his daughter for a wife.

28   When Saul saw and knew that the LORD was with David, and *that* Michal, Saul's daughter, loved him,

29   then Saul was even more afraid of David. Thus Saul was David's enemy continually.

30   Then the commanders of the Philistines went out *to battle*, and it happened as often as they went out, that David behaved himself more wisely than all the servants of Saul. So his name was highly esteemed.

6. *Saul seeks to kill David*

a. *Jonathan's effort to placate Saul*

19 Now Saul told Jonathan his son and all his servants to put David to death. But Jonathan, Saul's son, greatly delighted in David.

2   So Jonathan told David saying, "Saul my father is seeking to put you to death. Now therefore, please be on guard in the morning, and stay in a secret place and hide yourself.

3   "And I will go out and stand beside my father in the field where you are, and I will speak with my father about you; if I find out anything, then I shall tell you."

4   Then Jonathan spoke well of David to Saul his father, and said to him, "Do not let the king sin against his servant David, since he has not sinned against you, and since his deeds *have been* very beneficial to you.

5   "For he took his life in his hand and struck the Philistine, and the LORD brought about a great deliverance for all Israel; you saw *it* and rejoiced. Why then will you sin against innocent blood, by putting David to death without a cause?"

6   And Saul listened to the voice of Jonathan, and Saul vowed, "As the LORD lives, he shall not be put to death."

7   Then Jonathan called David, and Jonathan told him all these words. And Jonathan brought David to Saul, and he was in his presence as formerly.

b. *Saul tries to kill David*

8   When there was war again, David went out and fought with the Philistines, and defeated them with great slaughter, so that they fled before him.

9   Now there was an evil spirit from the LORD on Saul as he was sitting in his house with his spear in his hand, and David was playing *the harp* with *his* hand.

10   And Saul tried to pin David to the wall with the spear, but he slipped away out of Saul's presence, so that he stuck the spear into the wall. And David fled and escaped that night.

c. *Michal helps David escape*

11   Then Saul sent messengers to David's house to watch him, in order to put

---

Margin references:

*18:25
Ex 22:17;
1 Sam 14:24;
v. 17

18:26
v. 21

18:27
v. 13;
2 Sam 3:14

18:30
v. 5

19:1
1 Sam 18:1-3,
8,9

19:3
1 Sam 20:9,13

19:4
1 Sam 20:32;
Gen 42:22

19:5
1 Sam 17:49,
50; 11:13;
20:32

19:7
1 Sam 16:21;
18:2,13

19:9
1 Sam 16:14;
18:10,11
19:10
1 Sam 18:11

18:25 Here the figure one hundred is used. David brought back two hundred, according to v. 27. In 2 Sam. 3:14 it is stated in David's own words " . . . *I was betrothed for a hundred foreskins* . . . " This appears to be a discrepancy. Two possibilities exist. Either some scribe in the course of textual transmission miscopied his original at v. 27, or else David brought back twice as many as were required of him. When indicating in 2 Sam. 3:14 what he had done, he simply stated the price originally demanded by Saul.

him to death in the morning. But Michal, David's wife, told him, saying, "If you do not save your life tonight, tomorrow you will be put to death."

12   So Michal let David down through a window, and he went out and fled and escaped.

13   And Michal took the household idol and laid *it* on the bed, and put a quilt of goats' *hair* at its head, and covered *it* with clothes.

14   When Saul sent messengers to take David, she said, "He is sick."

15   Then Saul sent messengers to see David, saying, "Bring him up to me on his bed, that I may put him to death."

16   When the messengers entered, behold, the household idol *was* on the bed with the quilt of goats' *hair* at its head.

17   So Saul said to Michal, "Why have you deceived me like this and let my enemy go, so that he has escaped?" And Michal said to Saul, "He said to me, 'Let me go! Why should I put you to death?'"

d. *Saul goes to Naioth and prophesies*

18   Now David fled and escaped and came to Samuel at Ramah, and told him all that Saul had done to him. And he and Samuel went and stayed in Naioth.

19   And it was told Saul, saying, "Behold, David is at Naioth in Ramah."

20   Then Saul sent messengers to take David, but when they saw the company of the prophets prophesying, with Samuel standing *and* presiding over them, the Spirit of God came upon the messengers of Saul; and they also prophesied.

21   And when it was told Saul, he sent other messengers, and they also prophesied. So Saul sent messengers again the third time, and they also prophesied.

22   Then he himself went to Ramah, and came as far as the large well that is in Secu; and he asked and said, "Where are Samuel and David?" And *someone* said, "Behold, they are at Naioth in Ramah."

23   And he proceeded there to Naioth in Ramah; and the Spirit of God came upon him also, so that he went along prophesying continually until he came to Naioth in Ramah.

24   And he also stripped off his clothes, and he too prophesied before Samuel and lay down naked all that day and all that night. Therefore they say, "Is Saul also among the prophets?"

7. *Jonathan delivers David*

a. *The discussion of the problem*

20 Then David fled from Naioth in Ramah, and came and said to Jonathan, "What have I done? What is my iniquity? And what is my sin before your father, that he is seeking my life?"

2   And he said to him, "Far from it, you shall not die. Behold, my father does nothing either great or small without disclosing it to me. So why should my father hide this thing from me? It is not so!"

3   Yet David vowed again, saying, "Your father knows well that I have found favor in your sight, and he has said, 'Do not let Jonathan know this, lest he be grieved.' But truly as the LORD lives and as your soul lives, there is hardly a step between me and death."

4   Then Jonathan said to David, "Whatever you say, I will do for you."

5   So David said to Jonathan, "Behold, tomorrow is the new moon, and I ought to sit down to eat with the king. But let me go, that I may hide myself in the field until the third evening.

6   "If your father misses me at all, then say, 'David earnestly asked *leave* of me to run to Bethlehem his city, because it is the yearly sacrifice there for the whole family.'

7   "If he says, 'It is good,' your servant *shall be* safe; but if he is very angry, know that he has decided on evil.

8   "Therefore deal kindly with your servant, for you have brought your servant into a covenant of the LORD with you. But if there is iniquity in me, put me to death yourself; for why then should you bring me to your father?"

9   And Jonathan said, "Far be it from you! For if I should indeed learn that evil has been decided by my father to come upon you, then would I not tell you about it?"

20:5 *new moon.* The first day of the lunar month was a feast day with work suspended.

10   Then David said to Jonathan, "Who will tell me if your father answers you harshly?"

11   And Jonathan said to David, "Come, and let us go out into the field." So both of them went out to the field.

b. The covenant of David and Jonathan

12   Then Jonathan said to David, "The LORD, the God of Israel, *be witness!* When I have sounded out my father about this time tomorrow, *or* the third day, behold, if there is good *feeling* toward David, shall I not then send to you and make it known to you?

13   "If it please my father *to do* you harm, may the LORD do so to Jonathan and more also, if I do not make it known to you and send you away, that you may go in safety. And may the LORD be with you as He has been with my father.

14   "And if I am still alive, will you not show me the lovingkindness of the LORD, that I may not die?

15   "And you shall not cut off your lovingkindness from my house forever, not even when the LORD cuts off every one of the enemies of David from the face of the earth."

16   So Jonathan made a *covenant* with the house of David, *saying,* "May the LORD require *it* at the hands of David's enemies."

17   And Jonathan made David vow again because of his love for him, because he loved him as he loved his own life.

c. The signal arranged

18   Then Jonathan said to him, "Tomorrow is the new moon, and you will be missed because your seat will be empty.

19   "When you have stayed for three days, you shall go down quickly and come to the place where you hid yourself on that eventful day, and you shall remain by the stone Ezel.

20   "And I will shoot three arrows to the side, as though I shot at a target.

21   "And behold, I will send the lad, *saying,* 'Go, find the arrows.' If I specifically say to the lad, 'Behold, the arrows are on this side of you, get them,' then come; for there is safety for you and no harm, as the LORD lives.

22   "But if I say to the youth, 'Behold, the arrows are beyond you,' go, for the LORD has sent you away.

23   "As for the agreement of which you and I have spoken, behold, the LORD is between you and me forever."

d. Jonathan's plea to Saul for David

24   So David hid in the field; and when the new moon came, the king sat down to eat food.

25   And the king sat on his seat as usual, the seat by the wall; then Jonathan rose up and Abner sat down by Saul's side, but David's place was empty.

26   Nevertheless Saul did not speak anything that day, for he thought, "It is an accident, he is not clean, surely *he is* not clean."

27   And it came about the next day, the second *day* of the new moon, that David's place was empty; so Saul said to Jonathan his son, "Why has the son of Jesse not come to the meal, either yesterday or today?"

28   Jonathan then answered Saul, "David earnestly asked leave of me *to go* to Bethlehem,

29   for he said, 'Please let me go, since our family has a sacrifice in the city, and my brother has commanded me to attend. And now, if I have found favor in your sight, please let me get away that I may see my brothers.' For this reason he has not come to the king's table."

e. Saul's anger at Jonathan

30   Then Saul's anger burned against Jonathan and he said to him, "You son of a perverse, rebellious woman! Do I not know that you are choosing the son of Jesse to your own shame and to the shame of your mother's nakedness?

31   "For as long as the son of Jesse lives on the earth, neither you nor your kingdom will be established. Therefore now, send and bring him to me, for he must surely die."

20:15 David did what Jonathan asked by showing kindness to his son Mephibosheth.

Marginal references:

20:13
1 Sam 3:17;
Ruth 1:17;
1 Sam 17:37

*20:15
2 Sam 9:1

20:17
1 Sam 18:1

20:18
vv. 5,25

20:19
1 Sam 19:2

20:22
v. 37

20:23
vv. 14,15;
Gen 31:49,53

20:25
v. 18

20:26
1 Sam 16:5;
Lev 7:20,21

20:28
v. 6

20:30
Deut 21:20

20:32
1 Sam 19:5;
Matt 27:23;
Luke 23:22
20:33
v. 7

32   But Jonathan answered Saul his father and said to him, "Why should he be put to death? What has he done?"

33   Then Saul hurled his spear at him to strike him down; so Jonathan knew that his father had decided to put David to death.

34   Then Jonathan arose from the table in fierce anger, and did not eat food on the second day of the new moon, for he was grieved over David because his father had dishonored him.

f. Jonathan warns David

20:36
vv. 20,21
20:37
v. 22

35   Now it came about in the morning that Jonathan went out into the field for the appointment with David, and a little lad *was* with him.

36   And he said to his lad, "Run, find now the arrows which I am about to shoot." As the lad was running, he shot an arrow past him.

37   When the lad reached the place of the arrow which Jonathan had shot, Jonathan called after the lad, and said, "Is not the arrow beyond you?"

38   And Jonathan called after the lad, "Hurry, be quick, do not stay!" And Jonathan's lad picked up the arrow and came to his master.

39   But the lad was not aware of anything; only Jonathan and David knew about the matter.

40   Then Jonathan gave his weapons to his lad and said to him, "Go, bring *them* to the city."

41   When the lad was gone, David rose from the south side and fell on his face to the ground, and bowed three times. And they kissed each other and wept together, but David more.

20:42
1 Sam 1:17;
v. 22

42   And Jonathan said to David, "Go in safety, inasmuch as we have sworn to each other in the name of the LORD, saying, 'The LORD will be between me and you, and between my descendants and your descendants forever.'" Then he rose and departed, while Jonathan went into the city.

8. David's flight from Saul

a. Ahimelech the priest and the holy bread

21:1
1 Sam 22:19;
14:3; 16:4

21 Then David came to Nob to Ahimelech the priest; and Ahimelech came trembling to meet David, and said to him, "Why are you alone and no one with you?"

2   And David said to Ahimelech the priest, "The king has commissioned me with a matter, and has said to me, 'Let no one know anything about the matter on which I am sending you and with which I have commissioned you; and I have directed the young men to a certain place.'

3   "Now therefore, what do you have on hand? Give me five loaves of bread, or whatever can be found."

21:4
Lev 24:5-9;
Matt 12:4

4   And the priest answered David and said, "There is no ordinary bread on hand, but there is consecrated bread; if only the young men have kept themselves from women."

21:5
Ex 19:14,15

5   And David answered the priest and said to him, "Surely women have been kept from us as previously when I set out and the vessels of the young men were holy, though it was an ordinary journey; how much more then today will their vessels *be holy*?"

21:6
Matt 12:3,4;
Mark 2:25,
26; Lev 24:8,
9
21:7
1 Sam 22:9

6   So the priest gave him consecrated *bread*; for there was no bread there but the bread of the Presence which was removed from before the LORD, in order to put hot bread *in its place* when it was taken away.

7   Now one of the servants of Saul was there that day, detained before the LORD; and his name was Doeg the Edomite, the chief of Saul's shepherds.

b. David takes Goliath's sword

8   And David said to Ahimelech, "Now is there not a spear or a sword on hand? For I brought neither my sword nor my weapons with me, because the king's matter was urgent."

21:9
1 Sam 17:2,51

9   Then the priest said, "The sword of Goliath the Philistine, whom you killed in the valley of Elah, behold, it is wrapped in a cloth behind the ephod; if you would take it for yourself, take *it*. For there is no other except it here." And David said, "There is none like it; give it to me."

c. David goes to Achish, king of Gath

10 Then David arose and fled that day from Saul, and went to Achish king of Gath.

11 But the servants of Achish said to him, "Is this not David the king of the land? Did they not sing of this one as they danced, saying,

    'Saul has slain his thousands,
    And David his ten thousands'?"

12 And David took these words to heart, and greatly feared Achish king of Gath.

13 So he disguised his sanity before them, and acted insanely in their hands, and scribbled on the doors of the gate, and let his saliva run down into his beard.

14 Then Achish said to his servants, "Behold, you see the man behaving as a madman. Why do you bring him to me?

15 "Do I lack madmen, that you have brought this one to act the madman in my presence? Shall this one come into my house?"

d. David in the cave of Adullam

22 So David departed from there and escaped to the cave of Adullam; and when his brothers and all his father's household heard *of it*, they went down there to him.

2 And everyone who was in distress, and everyone who was in debt, and everyone who was discontented, gathered to him; and he became captain over them. Now there were about four hundred men with him.

e. David flees to Mizpah in Moab

3 And David went from there to Mizpah of Moab; and he said to the king of Moab, "Please let my father and my mother come *and stay* with you until I know what God will do for me."

4 Then he left them with the king of Moab; and they stayed with him all the time that David was in the stronghold.

5 And the prophet Gad said to David, "Do not stay in the stronghold; depart, and go into the land of Judah." So David departed and went into the forest of Hereth.

f. Doeg the Edomite betrays Ahimelech to Saul

6 Then Saul heard that David and the men who were with him had been discovered. Now Saul was sitting in Gibeah, under the tamarisk tree on the height with his spear in his hand, and all his servants were standing around him.

7 And Saul said to his servants who stood around him, "Hear now, O Benjamites! Will the son of Jesse also give to all of you fields and vineyards? Will he make you all commanders of thousands and commanders of hundreds?

8 "For all of you have conspired against me so that there is no one who discloses to me when my son makes *a covenant* with the son of Jesse, and there is none of you who is sorry for me or discloses to me that my son has stirred up my servant against me to lie in ambush, as *it is* this day."

9 Then Doeg the Edomite, who was standing by the servants of Saul, answered and said, "I saw the son of Jesse coming to Nob, to Ahimelech the son of Ahitub.

10 "And he inquired of the LORD for him, gave him provisions, and gave him the sword of Goliath the Philistine."

g. Saul slays Ahimelech and the priests

11 Then the king sent someone to summon Ahimelech the priest, the son of Ahitub, and all his father's household, the priests who were in Nob; and all of them came to the king.

12 And Saul said, "Listen now, son of Ahitub." And he answered, "Here I am, my lord."

13 Saul then said to him, "Why have you and the son of Jesse conspired against me, in that you have given him bread and a sword and have inquired of God for him, that he should rise up against me by lying in ambush as *it is* this day?"

14 Then Ahimelech answered the king and said, "And who among all your servants is as faithful as David, even the king's son-in-law, who is captain over your guard, and is honored in your house?

15 "Did I *just* begin to inquire of God for him today? Far be it from me! Do not

21:11
1 Sam 18:7;
29:5

21:12
1 Sam 2:19

22:1
2 Sam 23:13

22:2
1 Sam 23:13;
25:13

22:5
2 Sam 24:11;
1 Chr 29:29;
2 Chr 29:25

22:7
1 Sam 8:14

22:8
1 Sam 18:3;
20:16

22:9
1 Sam 21:1;
14:3

22:10
1 Sam 10:22;
21:6,9

22:14
1 Sam 19:4,5

let the king impute anything to his servant *or* to any of the household of my father, for your servant knows nothing at all of this whole affair.''

16   But the king said, "You shall surely die, Ahimelech, you and all your father's household!"

17   And the king said to the guards who were attending him, "Turn around and put the priests of the LORD to death, because their hand also is with David and because they knew that he was fleeing and did not reveal it to me." But the servants of the king were not willing to put forth their hands to attack the priests of the LORD.

18   Then the king said to Doeg, "You turn around and attack the priests." And Doeg the Edomite turned around and attacked the priests, and he killed that day eighty-five men who wore the linen ephod.

19   And he struck Nob the city of the priests with the edge of the sword, both men and women, children and infants; also oxen, donkeys, and sheep, *he struck* with the edge of the sword.

h. *Abiathar escapes to David*

20   But one son of Ahimelech the son of Ahitub, named Abiathar, escaped and fled after David.

21   And Abiathar told David that Saul had killed the priests of the LORD.

22   Then David said to Abiathar, "I knew on that day, when Doeg the Edomite was there, that he would surely tell Saul. I have brought about *the death* of every person in your father's household.

23   "Stay with me, do not be afraid, for he who seeks my life seeks your life; for you are safe with me."

i. *David at Keilah*

23 Then they told David, saying, "Behold, the Philistines are fighting against Keilah, and are plundering the threshing floors."

2   So David inquired of the LORD, saying, "Shall I go and attack these Philistines?" And the LORD said to David, "Go and attack the Philistines, and deliver Keilah."

3   But David's men said to him, "Behold, we are afraid here in Judah. How much more then if we go to Keilah against the ranks of the Philistines?"

4   Then David inquired of the LORD once more. And the LORD answered him and said, "Arise, go down to Keilah, for I will give the Philistines into your hand."

5   So David and his men went to Keilah and fought with the Philistines; and he led away their livestock and struck them with a great slaughter. Thus David delivered the inhabitants of Keilah.

6   Now it came about, when Abiathar the son of Ahimelech fled to David at Keilah, *that* he came down *with* an ephod in his hand.

7   When it was told Saul that David had come to Keilah, Saul said, "God has delivered him into my hand, for he shut himself in by entering a city with double gates and bars."

8   So Saul summoned all the people for war, to go down to Keilah to besiege David and his men.

9   Now David knew that Saul was plotting evil against him; so he said to Abiathar the priest, "Bring the ephod here."

10   Then David said, "O LORD God of Israel, Thy servant has heard for certain that Saul is seeking to come to Keilah to destroy the city on my account.

11   "Will the men of Keilah surrender me into his hand? Will Saul come down just as Thy servant has heard? O LORD God of Israel, I pray, tell Thy servant." And the LORD said, "He will come down."

12   Then David said, "Will the men of Keilah surrender me and my men into the hand of Saul?" And the LORD said, "They will surrender you."

13   Then David and his men, about six hundred, arose and departed from Keilah, and they went wherever they could go. When it was told Saul that David had escaped from Keilah, he gave up the pursuit.

14   And David stayed in the wilderness in the strongholds, and remained in the

---

23:7 It is easily possible for men to be mistaken about providences that seem to be from God. Thus Saul falsely supposed that God had providentially delivered David into his hands. Righteous David, in turn, was there only because it was the will of God. However, God brings to nought the counsels and designs of men that run counter to His divine will. 2 Samuel 17:14; Neh. 4:15; and Job 5:12 are eloquent illustrations.

hill country in the wilderness of Ziph. And Saul sought him every day, but God did not deliver him into his hand.

j. The treachery of the Ziphites

15 Now David became aware that Saul had come out to seek his life while David was in the wilderness of Ziph at Horesh.

16 And Jonathan, Saul's son, arose and went to David at Horesh, and [14]encouraged him in God.

17 Thus he said to him, "Do not be afraid, because the hand of Saul my father shall not find you, and you will be king over Israel and I will be next to you; and Saul my father knows that also."

18 So the two of them made a covenant before the LORD; and David stayed at Horesh while Jonathan went to his house.

19 Then Ziphites came up to Saul at Gibeah, saying, "Is David not hiding with us in the strongholds at Horesh, on the hill of Hachilah, which is on the south of [15]Jeshimon?

20 "Now then, O king, come down according to all the desire of your soul to do so; and our part *shall be* to surrender him into the king's hand."

21 And Saul said, "May you be blessed of the LORD; for you have had compassion on me.

22 "Go now, make more sure, and investigate and see his place where his haunt is, *and* who has seen him there; for I am told that he is very cunning.

23 "So look, and learn about all the hiding places where he hides himself, and return to me with certainty, and I will go with you; and it shall come about if he is in the land that I will search him out among all the thousands of Judah."

24 Then they arose and went to Ziph before Saul. Now David and his men were in the wilderness of Maon, in the Arabah to the south of Jeshimon.

25 When Saul and his men went to seek *him*, they told David, and he came down to the rock and stayed in the wilderness of Maon. And when Saul heard *it*, he pursued David in the wilderness of Maon.

26 And Saul went on one side of the mountain, and David and his men on the other side of the mountain; and David was hurrying to get away from Saul, for Saul and his men were surrounding David and his men to seize them.

27 But a messenger came to Saul, saying, "Hurry and come, for the Philistines have made a raid on the land."

28 So Saul returned from pursuing David, and went to meet the Philistines; therefore they called that place the Rock of Escape.

29 And David went up from there and stayed in the strongholds of Engedi.

k. David cuts off Saul's skirt at Engedi

24 Now it came about when Saul returned from pursuing the Philistines, he was told, saying, "Behold, David is in the wilderness of Engedi."

2 Then Saul took three thousand chosen men from all Israel, and went to seek David and his men in front of the Rocks of the Wild Goats.

3 And he came to the sheepfolds on the way, where there *was* a cave; and Saul went in to relieve himself. Now David and his men were sitting in the inner recesses of the cave.

4 And the men of David said to him, "Behold, *this is* the day of which the LORD said to you, 'Behold; I am about to give your enemy into your hand, and you shall do to him as it seems good to you.' " Then David arose and cut off the edge of Saul's robe secretly.

5 And it came about afterward that David's conscience bothered him because he had cut off the edge of Saul's *robe.*

6 So he said to his men, "Far be it from me because of the LORD that I should do this thing to my lord, the LORD's anointed, to stretch out my hand against him, since he is the LORD's anointed."

---

[14]Lit., *strengthened his hand* [15]Or, *the desert*

23:14
Josh 15:15;
Ps 54:3,4

23:16
1 Sam 30:6

23:17
1 Sam 20:31;
24:20

23:18
1 Sam 18:3;
20:16,42;
2 Sam 9:1;
21:7
23:19
1 Sam 26:1

23:20
v. 12

23:21
1 Sam 22:8

23:24
Josh 15:55;
1 Sam 25:2

23:26
Ps 17:9

23:29
2 Chr 20:2

24:1
1 Sam 23:28,
29
24:2
1 Sam 26:2

24:3
Judg 3:24

*24:4
1 Sam 23:17;
25:28-30

24:5
2 Sam 24:10

24:6
1 Sam 26:11

24:4 David had several opportunities to kill Saul. On each occasion he refrained from taking his life on the ground that Saul had been anointed king by God's command. He was willing to wait for the fulfillment of God's will in God's way. He did not practice the kind of ethics that supposes that "the end justifies the means." Good ends must be attained by good means. David preferred to wait on God rather than to seize the reins of government by murder. Every believer should learn this valuable lesson: it is God's will done in God's way that leads to God's blessing.

7   And David persuaded his men with *these* words and did not allow them to rise up against Saul. And Saul arose, left the cave, and went on *his* way.

l. *David rebukes Saul*

8   Now afterward David arose and went out of the cave and called after Saul, saying, "My lord the king!" And when Saul looked behind him, David bowed with his face to the ground and prostrated himself.

9   And David said to Saul, "Why do you listen to the words of men, saying, 'Behold, David seeks to harm you'?

10   "Behold, this day your eyes have seen that the LORD had given you today into my hand in the cave, and some said to kill you, but *my eye* had pity on you; and I said, 'I will not stretch out my hand against my lord, for he is the LORD's anointed.'

11   "Now, my father, see! Indeed, see the edge of your robe in my hand! For in that I cut off the edge of your robe and did not kill you, know and perceive that there is no evil or rebellion in my hands, and I have not sinned against you, though you are lying in wait for my life to take it.

12   "May the LORD judge between you and me, and may the LORD avenge me on you; but my hand shall not be against you.

13   "As the proverb of the ancients says, 'Out of the wicked comes forth wickedness'; but my hand shall not be against you.

14   "After whom has the king of Israel come out? Whom are you pursuing? A dead dog, a single flea?

15   "The LORD therefore be judge and decide between you and me; and may He see and plead my cause, and deliver me from your hand."

m. *Saul's seeming repentance*

16   Now it came about when David had finished speaking these words to Saul, that Saul said, "Is this your voice, my son David?" Then Saul lifted up his voice and wept.

17   And he said to David, "You are more righteous than I; for you have dealt well with me, while I have dealt wickedly with you.

18   "And you have declared today that you have done good to me, that the LORD delivered me into your hand and *yet* you did not kill me.

19   "For if a man finds his enemy, will he let him go away safely? May the LORD therefore reward you with good in return for what you have done to me this day.

20   "And now, behold, I know that you shall surely be king, and that the kingdom of Israel shall be established in your hand.

21   "So now swear to me by the LORD that you will not cut off my descendants after me, and that you will not destroy my name from my father's household."

22   And David swore to Saul. And Saul went to his home, but David and his men went up to the stronghold.

n. *David and Abigail*

(1) NABAL'S REFUSAL OF HELP

25   Then Samuel died; and all Israel gathered together and mourned for him, and buried him at his house in Ramah. And David arose and went down to the wilderness of Paran.

2   Now *there was* a man in Maon whose business was in Carmel; and the man was very rich, and he had three thousand sheep and a thousand goats. And it came about while he was shearing his sheep in Carmel

3   (now the man's name was Nabal, and his wife's name was Abigail. And the woman was intelligent and beautiful in appearance, but the man was harsh and evil in *his* dealings, and he was a Calebite),

4   that David heard in the wilderness that Nabal was shearing his sheep.

5   So David sent ten young men, and David said to the young men, "Go up to Carmel, visit Nabal and greet him in my name;

6   and thus you shall say, 'Have a long life, peace be to you, and peace be to your house, and peace be to all that you have.

7   'And now I have heard that you have shearers; now your shepherds have been with us and we have not insulted them, nor have they missed anything all the days they were in Carmel.

8   'Ask your young men and they will tell you. Therefore let *my* young men find favor in your eyes, for we have come on a festive day. Please give whatever you find at hand to your servants and to your son David.' "

9 When David's young men came, they spoke to Nabal according to all these words in David's name; then they waited.

10 But Nabal answered David's servants, and said, "Who is David? And who is the son of Jesse? There are many servants today who are each breaking away from his master.

11 "Shall I then take my bread and my water and my meat that I have slaughtered for my shearers, and give it to men whose origin I do not know?"

12 So David's young men retraced their way and went back; and they came and told him according to all these words.

13 And David said to his men, "Each *of you* gird on his sword." So each man girded on his sword. And David also girded on his sword, and about four hundred men went up behind David while two hundred stayed with the baggage.

(2) ABIGAIL PLACATES DAVID

14 But one of the young men told Abigail, Nabal's wife, saying, "Behold, David sent messengers from the wilderness to greet our master, and he scorned them.

15 "Yet the men were very good to us, and we were not insulted, nor did we miss anything as long as we went about with them, while we were in the fields.

16 "They were a wall to us both by night and by day, all the time we were with them tending the sheep.

17 "Now therefore, know and consider what you should do, for evil is plotted against our master and against all his household; and he is such a worthless man that no one can speak to him."

18 Then Abigail hurried and took two hundred *loaves* of bread and two jugs of wine and five sheep already prepared and five measures of roasted grain and a hundred clusters of raisins and two hundred cakes of figs, and loaded *them* on donkeys.

19 And she said to her young men, "Go on before me; behold, I am coming after you." But she did not tell her husband Nabal.

20 And it came about as she was riding on her donkey and coming down by the hidden part of the mountain, that behold, David and his men were coming down toward her; so she met them.

21 Now David had said, "Surely in vain I have guarded all that this *man* has in the wilderness, so that nothing was missed of all that belonged to him; and he has returned me evil for good.

22 "May God do so to the enemies of David, and more also, if by morning I leave *as much as* one male of any who belong to him."

23 When Abigail saw David, she hurried and dismounted from her donkey, and fell on her face before David, and bowed herself to the ground.

24 And she fell at his feet and said, "On me alone, my lord, be the blame. And please let your maidservant speak to you, and listen to the words of your maidservant.

25 "Please do not let my lord pay attention to this worthless man, Nabal, for as his name is, so is he. Nabal is his name and folly is with him; but I your maidservant did not see the young men of my lord whom you sent.

26 "Now therefore, my lord, as the LORD lives, and as your soul lives, since the LORD has restrained you from shedding blood, and from avenging yourself by your own hand, now then let your enemies, and those who seek evil against my lord, be as Nabal.

27 "And now let this gift which your maidservant has brought to my lord be given to the young men who accompany my lord.

28 "Please forgive the transgression of your maidservant; for the LORD will certainly make for my lord an enduring house, because my lord is fighting the battles of the LORD, and evil shall not be found in you all your days.

29 "And should anyone rise up to pursue you and to seek your life, then the life of my lord shall be bound in the bundle of the living with the LORD your God; but the lives of your enemies He will sling out as from the hollow of a sling.

30 "And it shall come about when the LORD shall do for my lord according to all the good that He has spoken concerning you, and shall appoint you ruler over Israel,

31 that this will not cause grief or a troubled heart to my lord, both by having

---

25:10
Judg 9:28

25:13
1 Sam 23:13;
30:24

25:15
v. 7

25:16
Ex 14:22

25:18
2 Sam 16:1;
1 Chr 12:40

25:19
Gen 32:16,20

25:21
Ps 109:5

25:22
1 Sam 3:17;
20:13;
1 Kin 14:10
25:23
1 Sam 20:41

25:26
Heb 10:30;
2 Sam 18:32

25:27
Gen 33:11;
1 Sam 30:26
25:28
2 Sam 7:11,
27; 18:17;
24:11

25:29
Jer 10:18

25:30
1 Sam 13:14

shed blood without cause and by my lord having avenged himself. When the LORD shall deal well with my lord, then remember your maidservant."

25:32
Ex 18:10

32 Then David said to Abigail, "Blessed be the LORD God of Israel, who sent you this day to meet me,

25:33
v. 26

33 and blessed be your discernment, and blessed be you, who have kept me this day from bloodshed, and from avenging myself by my own hand.

25:34
v. 26

34 "Nevertheless, as the LORD God of Israel lives, who has restrained me from harming you, unless you had come quickly to meet me, surely there would not have been left to Nabal until the morning light *as much as* one male."

25:35
1 Sam 20:42;
2 Kin 5:19;
Gen 19:21

35 So David received from her hand what she had brought him, and he said to her, "Go up to your house in peace. See, I have listened to you and granted your request."

(3) NABAL'S DEATH

25:36
2 Sam 13:23

36 Then Abigail came to Nabal, and behold, he was holding a feast in his house, like the feast of a king. And Nabal's heart was merry within him, for he was very drunk; so she did not tell him anything at all until the morning light.

37 But it came about in the morning, when the wine had gone out of Nabal, that his wife told him these things, and his heart died within him so that he became *as* a stone.

38 And about ten days later, it happened that the LORD struck Nabal, and he died.

25:39
1 Sam 24:15;
vv. 26,34;
1 Kin 2:44

39 When David heard that Nabal was dead, he said, "Blessed be the LORD, who has pleaded the cause of my reproach from the hand of Nabal, and has kept back His servant from evil. The LORD has also returned the evildoing of Nabal on his own head." Then David sent a proposal to Abigail, to take her as his wife.

40 When the servants of David came to Abigail at Carmel, they spoke to her, saying, "David has sent us to you, to take you as his wife."

25:41
Ruth 2:10,13;
Mark 1:7
25:42
Gen 24:61-67

41 And she arose and bowed with her face to the ground and said, "Behold, your maidservant is a maid to wash the feet of my lord's servants."

42 Then Abigail quickly arose, and rode on a donkey, with her five maidens who attended her; and she followed the messengers of David, and became his wife.

25:43
Josh 15:56;
1 Sam 27:3
25:44
2 Sam 3:14;
Is 10:30

43 David had also taken Ahinoam of Jezreel, and they both became his wives.

44 Now Saul had given Michal his daughter, David's wife, to Palti the son of Laish, who was from Gallim.

o. *David spares Saul again*

26:1
1 Sam 23:19

26 Then the Ziphites came to Saul at Gibeah, saying, "Is not David hiding on the hill of Hachilah, *which is* before [16]Jeshimon?"

26:2
1 Sam 13:2;
24:2

2 So Saul arose and went down to the wilderness of Ziph, having with him three thousand chosen men of Israel, to search for David in the wilderness of Ziph.

3 And Saul camped in the hill of Hachilah, which is before [16]Jeshimon, beside the road, and David was staying in the wilderness. When he saw that Saul came after him into the wilderness,

4 David sent out spies, and he knew that Saul was definitely coming.

26:5
1 Sam 14:50;
17:55

5 David then arose and came to the place where Saul had camped. And David saw the place where Saul lay, and Abner the son of Ner, the commander of his army; and Saul was lying in the circle of the camp, and the people were camped around him.

26:6
1 Chr 2:16;
Judg 7:10,11

6 Then David answered and said to Ahimelech the Hittite and to Abishai the son of Zeruiah, Joab's brother, saying, "Who will go down with me to Saul in the camp?" And Abishai said, "I will go down with you."

7 So David and Abishai came to the people by night, and behold, Saul lay sleeping inside the circle of the camp, with his spear stuck in the ground at his head; and Abner and the people were lying around him.

8 Then Abishai said to David, "Today God has delivered your enemy into your hand; now therefore, please let me strike him with the spear to the ground with one stroke, and I will not strike him the second time."

26:9
1 Sam 24:6,7;
2 Sam 1:16
26:10
1 Sam 25:38;
Deut 31:14;
1 Sam 31:6

9 But David said to Abishai, "Do not destroy him, for who can stretch out his hand against the LORD's anointed and be without guilt?"

10 David also said, "As the LORD lives, surely the LORD will strike him, or his day will come that he dies, or he will go down into battle and perish.

[16]Or, *the desert*

11 "The LORD forbid that I should stretch out my hand against the LORD's anointed; but now please take the spear that is at his head and the jug of water, and let us go."

12 So David took the spear and the jug of water from *beside* Saul's head, and they went away, but no one saw or knew *it,* nor did any awake, for they were all asleep, because a sound sleep from the LORD had fallen on them.

13 Then David crossed over to the other side, and stood on top of the mountain at a distance *with* a large area between them.

14 And David called to the people and to Abner the son of Ner, saying, "Will you not answer, Abner?" Then Abner answered and said, "Who are you who calls to the king?"

15 So David said to Abner, "Are you not a man? And who is like you in Israel? Why then have you not guarded your lord the king? For one of the people came to destroy the king your lord.

16 "This thing that you have done is not good. As the LORD lives, *all* of you must surely die, because you did not guard your lord, the LORD's anointed. And now, see where the king's spear is, and the jug of water that was at his head."

17 Then Saul recognized David's voice and said, "Is this your voice, my son David?" And David said, "It is my voice, my lord the king."

18 He also said, "Why then is my lord pursuing his servant? For what have I done? Or what evil is in my hand?

19 "Now therefore, please let my lord the king listen to the words of his servant. If the LORD has stirred you up against me, let Him accept an offering; but if it is men, cursed are they before the LORD, for they have driven me out today that I should have no attachment with the inheritance of the LORD, saying, 'Go, serve other gods.'

20 "Now then, do not let my blood fall to the ground away from the presence of the LORD; for the king of Israel has come out to search for a single flea, just as one hunts a partridge in the mountains."

21 Then Saul said, "I have sinned. Return, my son David, for I will not harm you again because my life was precious in your sight this day. Behold, I have played the fool and have committed a serious error."

22 And David answered and said, "Behold the spear of the king! Now let one of the young men come over and take it.

23 "And the LORD will repay each man *for* his righteousness and his faithfulness; for the LORD delivered you into *my* hand today, but I refused to stretch out my hand against the LORD's anointed.

24 "Now behold, as your life was highly valued in my sight this day, so may my life be highly valued in the sight of the LORD, and may He deliver me from all distress."

25 Then Saul said to David, "Blessed are you, my son David; you will both accomplish much and surely prevail." So David went on his way, and Saul returned to his place.

E. Saul's death in the Philistine war

1. David's flight to the Philistines

a. David joins Achish

27 Then David said to himself, "Now I will perish one day by the hand of Saul. There is nothing better for me than to escape into the land of the Philistines. Saul then will despair of searching for me anymore in all the territory of Israel, and I will escape from his hand."

2 So David arose and crossed over, he and the six hundred men who were with him, to Achish the son of Maoch, king of Gath.

3 And David lived with Achish at Gath, he and his men, each with his household, *even* David with his two wives, Ahinoam the Jezreelitess, and Abigail the Carmelitess, Nabal's widow.

4 Now it was told Saul that David had fled to Gath, so he no longer searched for him.

b. Achish gives David Ziklag

5 Then David said to Achish, "If now I have found favor in your sight, let

26:11
1 Sam 24:6,12

26:12
Gen 2:21;
16:12

26:17
1 Sam 24:16

26:18
1 Sam 24:9,
11-14
26:19
2 Sam 16:11

26:20
1 Sam 24:14

26:21
1 Sam 15:24;
24:17

26:22
1 Sam 24:12,
19

26:24
Ps 54:7

27:2
1 Sam 25:13;
21:10
27:3
1 Sam 30:3;
25:42,43

them give me a place in one of the cities in the country, that I may live there; for why should your servant live in the royal city with you?"

6 So Achish gave him Ziklag that day; therefore Ziklag has belonged to the kings of Judah to this day.

7 And the number of days that David lived in the country of the Philistines was a year and four months.

2. *David's raids*

8 Now David and his men went up and raided the Geshurites and the Girzites and the Amalekites; for they were the inhabitants of the land from ancient times, as you come to Shur even as far as the land of Egypt.

9 And David attacked the land and did not leave a man or a woman alive, and he took away the sheep, the cattle, the donkeys, the camels, and the clothing. Then he returned and came to Achish.

10 Now Achish said, "Where have you made a raid today?" And David said, "Against the [17]Negev of Judah and against the Negev of the Jerahmeelites and against the Negev of the Kenites."

11 And David did not leave a man or a woman alive, to bring to Gath, saying, "Lest they should tell about us, saying, 'So has David done and so *has been* his practice all the time he has lived in the country of the Philistines.'"

12 So Achish believed David, saying, "He has surely made himself odious among his people Israel; therefore he will become my servant forever."

3. *The Philistine plan to battle Israel*

28 Now it came about in those days that the Philistines gathered their armed camps for war, to fight against Israel. And Achish said to David, "Know assuredly that you will go out with me in the camp, you and your men."

2 And David said to Achish, "Very well, you shall know what your servant can do." So Achish said to David, "Very well, I will make you my bodyguard for life."

4. *Saul and the medium at Endor*
a. *God does not answer Saul*

3 Now Samuel was dead, and all Israel had lamented him and buried him in Ramah his own city. And Saul had removed from the land those who were mediums and spiritists.

4 So the Philistines gathered together and came and camped in Shunem; and Saul gathered all Israel together and they camped in Gilboa.

5 When Saul saw the camp of the Philistines, he was afraid and his heart trembled greatly.

6 When Saul inquired of the LORD, the LORD did not answer him, either by dreams or by Urim or by prophets.

7 Then Saul said to his servants, "Seek for me a woman who is a medium, that I may go to her and inquire of her." And his servants said to him, "Behold, there is a woman who is a medium at En-dor."

b. *Saul visits the medium*

8 Then Saul disguised himself by putting on other clothes, and went, he and two men with him, and they came to the woman by night; and he said, "Conjure up for me, please, and bring up for me whom I shall name to you."

9 But the woman said to him, "Behold, you know what Saul has done, how he

[17]I.e., South country

Cross references (left margin):

27:6 Josh 15:31; 19:5
27:7 1 Sam 29:3
27:8 Josh 13:2,13; Ex 17:8; 1 Sam 15:7,8; Ex 15:22
27:9 1 Sam 15:3
27:10 1 Chr 2:9,25; Judg 1:16
*28:1f 1 Sam 29:1
28:3 1 Sam 25:1; 7:17; 15:23; Lev 19:31; Deut 18:10, 11
28:4 2 Kin 4:8; 1 Sam 31:1
28:6 1 Chr 10:13, 14; Prov 1:28; Ex 28:30
*28:7 Acts 16:16; Josh 17:11
28:8 Is 8:19; Deut 18:10, 11
28:9 v. 3

28:1,2 When David first went to Achish (21:10), he apparently wanted to enlist under this leader; but his reception made him fearful, and thus he pretended madness. Later Achish came to trust David, and in these verses he commands him to join him in battle against Israel. David agrees to do so. However, the lords of the Philistines object to his presence (29:3ff.), and Achish is forced to dismiss David. So David does not fight against Saul and his army.
28:7 Even though Saul had tried to root out divination (28:9), in accordance with Deut. 18:10,11, he finally resorted to this illegal means of discerning God's will. Surely

Samuel would have given him instructions, even though God had refused to answer by a private dream, the priestly lot, or the prophetic word. But the spirit of Samuel has only words of doom. Due to the many regulations, both Old and New Testament, against divination of all sorts, some doubt that the medium actually brought up the spirit of Samuel. But the text makes it clear that Saul had no doubts as to the reality of the apparition. In any case, this episode is no justification for modern attempts to contact the spirits of the dead.

379

who are mediums and spiritists from the land. Why are you then
... my life to bring about my death?"
... vowed to her by the LORD, saying, "As the LORD lives, there shall
... come upon you for this thing."
... woman said, "Whom shall I bring up for you?" And he said,
... for me."
... the woman saw Samuel, she cried out with a loud voice; and the
... to Saul, saying, "Why have you deceived me? For you are Saul."
... the king said to her, "Do not be afraid; but what do you see?" And the
... to Saul, "I see a divine being coming up out of the earth."
... he said to her, "What is his form?" And she said, "An old man is
... and he is wrapped with a robe." And Saul knew that it was Samuel, and
with his face to the ground and did homage.

c. The medium calls up Samuel

15 Then Samuel said to Saul, "Why have you disturbed me by bringing me
up?" And Saul answered, "I am greatly distressed; for the Philistines are waging
war against me, and God has departed from me and answers me no more, either
through prophets or by dreams; therefore I have called you, that you may make
known to me what I should do."

16 And Samuel said, "Why then do you ask me, since the LORD has departed
from you and has become your adversary?

17 "And the LORD has done accordingly as He spoke through me; for the LORD
has torn the kingdom out of your hand and given it to your neighbor, to David.

18 "As you did not obey the LORD and did not execute His fierce wrath on
Amalek, so the LORD has done this thing to you this day.

19 "Moreover the LORD will also give over Israel along with you into the hands
of the Philistines, therefore tomorrow you and your sons will be with me. Indeed
the LORD will give over the army of Israel into the hands of the Philistines!"

d. The medium feeds Saul

20 Then Saul immediately fell full length upon the ground and was very afraid
because of the words of Samuel; also there was no strength in him, for he had eaten
no food all day and all night.

21 And the woman came to Saul and saw that he was terrified, and said to him,
"Behold, your maidservant has obeyed you, and I have taken my life in my hand,
and have listened to your words which you spoke to me.

22 "So now also, please listen to the voice of your maidservant, and let me set a
piece of bread before you that *you may* eat and have strength when you go on *your*
way."

23 But he refused and said, "I will not eat." However, his servants together
with the woman urged him, and he listened to them. So he arose from the ground
and sat on the bed.

24 And the woman had a fattened calf in the house, and she quickly slaughtered
it; and she took flour, kneaded it, and baked unleavened bread from it.

25 And she brought *it* before Saul and his servants, and they ate. Then they
arose and went away that night.

5. The Philistines dismiss David

a. The question raised

29 Now the Philistines gathered together all their armies to Aphek, while the
Israelites were camping by the spring which is in Jezreel.

2 And the lords of the Philistines were proceeding on by hundreds and by
thousands, and David and his men were proceeding on in the rear with Achish.

3 Then the commanders of the Philistines said, "What *are* these Hebrews
doing here?" And Achish said to the commanders of the Philistines, "Is this not
David, the servant of Saul the king of Israel, who has been with me these days, or
rather these years, and I have found no fault in him from the day he deserted *to me*
to this day?"

4 But the commanders of the Philistines were angry with him, and the commanders of the Philistines said to him, "Make the man go back, that he may return
to his place where you have assigned him, and do not let him go down to battle with
us, lest in the battle he become an adversary to us. For with what could this *man*

28:14
1 Sam 15:27;
24:8

28:15
1 Sam 18:12;
v. 6

28:17
1 Sam 15:28

28:18
1 Sam 15:9,
20,26
28:19
1 Sam 31:2

28:21
1 Sam 19:5;
Judg 12:3

28:23
2 Kin 5:13

29:1
1 Sam 28:1;
4:1;
Josh 12:18
29:2
1 Sam 28:1,2
29:3
1 Sam 27:7;
Dan 6:5

29:4
1 Chr 12:19;
1 Sam 14:21

make himself acceptable to his lord? *Would it* not *be* with the heads o

29:5
1 Sam 18:7;
21:11

5 "Is this not David, of whom they sing in the dances, saying,

'Saul has slain his thousands,

And David his ten thousands'?"

b. *Achish sends David away*

29:6
v. 3

6 Then Achish called David and said to him, "*As* the LORD lives, yo been upright, and your going out and your coming in with me in the arm pleasing in my sight; for I have not found evil in you from the day of your con to me to this day. Nevertheless, you are not pleasing in the sight of the lor

7 "Now therefore return, and go in peace, that you may not displease the lord of the Philistines."

8 And David said to Achish, "But what have I done? And what have you found in your servant from the day when I came before you to this day, that I may not go and fight against the enemies of my lord the king?"

29:9
2 Sam 14:17,
20; 19:27;
v. 4

9 But Achish answered and said to David, "I know that you are pleasing in my sight, like an angel of God; nevertheless the commanders of the Philistines have said, 'He must not go up with us to the battle.'

29:10
1 Chr 12:19,
22

10 "Now then arise early in the morning with the servants of your lord who have come with you, and as soon as you have arisen early in the morning and have light, depart."

11 So David arose early, he and his men, to depart in the morning, to return to the land of the Philistines. And the Philistines went up to Jezreel.

6. *David destroys Amalek*

a. *Amalekites raid Ziklag*

30:1
1 Sam 29:4,
11; 15:7; 27:8

30 Then it happened when David and his men came to Ziklag on the third day, that the Amalekites had made a raid on the Negev and on Ziklag, and had overthrown Ziklag and burned it with fire;

2 and they took captive the women *and all* who were in it, both small and great, without killing anyone, and carried *them* off and went their way.

3 And when David and his men came to the city, behold, it was burned with fire, and their wives and their sons and their daughters had been taken captive.

4 Then David and the people who were with him lifted their voices and wept until there was no strength in them to weep.

30:5
1 Sam 25:42,
43

5 Now David's two wives had been taken captive, Ahinoam the Jezreelitess and Abigail the widow of Nabal the Carmelite.

30:6
Ex 17:4;
Ps 27:14;
56:3,4,11

6 Moreover David was greatly distressed because the people spoke of stoning him, for all the people were embittered, each one because of his sons and his daughters. But David strengthened himself in the LORD his God.

b. *God orders David to pursue the Amalekites*

30:7
1 Sam 23:9

7 Then David said to Abiathar the priest, the son of Ahimelech, "Please bring me the ephod." So Abiathar brought the ephod to David.

30:8
1 Sam 23:2,4;
v. 18

8 And David inquired of the LORD, saying, "Shall I pursue this band? Shall I overtake them?" And He said to him, "Pursue, for you shall surely overtake them, and you shall surely rescue *all*."

30:9
1 Sam 27:2

9 So David went, he and the six hundred men who were with him, and came to the brook Besor, *where* those left behind remained.

30:10
vv. 9,21

10 But David pursued, he and four hundred men, for two hundred who were too exhausted to cross the brook Besor, remained *behind*.

c. *An Egyptian leads David to the Amalekites*

11 Now they found an Egyptian in the field and brought him to David, and gave him bread and he ate, and they provided him water to drink.

30:12
Judg 15:19

12 And they gave him a piece of fig cake and two clusters of raisins, and he ate; then his spirit revived. For he had not eaten bread or drunk water for three days and three nights.

13 And David said to him, "To whom do you belong? And where are you from?" And he said, "I am a young man of Egypt, a servant of an Amalekite; and my master left me behind when I fell sick three days ago.

*30:14
vv. 1,16;
2 Sam 8:18;
Ezek 25:16;
Josh 14:13

14 "We made a raid on the Negev of the Cherethites, and on that which belongs to Judah, and on the Negev of Caleb, and we burned Ziklag with fire."

15   Then David said to him, "Will you bring me down to this band?" And he said, "Swear to me by God that you will not kill me or deliver me into the hands of my master, and I will bring you down to this band."

d. David smites the Amalekites

16   And when he had brought him down, behold, they were spread over all the land, eating and drinking and dancing because of all the great spoil that they had taken from the land of the Philistines and from the land of Judah.

17   And David slaughtered them from the twilight until the evening of the next day; and not a man of them escaped, except four hundred young men who rode on camels and fled.

18   So David recovered all that the Amalekites had taken, and rescued his two wives.

19   But nothing of theirs was missing, whether small or great, sons or daughters, spoil or anything that they had taken for themselves; David brought *it* all back.

20   So David had captured all the sheep and the cattle *which the people* drove ahead of the *other* livestock, and they said, "This is David's spoil."

e. David divides the spoil

21   When David came to the two hundred men who were too exhausted to follow David, who had also been left at the brook Besor, and they went out to meet David and to meet the people who were with him, then David approached the people and greeted them.

22   Then all the wicked and worthless men among those who went with David answered and said, "Because they did not go with us, we will not give them any of the spoil that we have recovered, except to every man his wife and his children, that they may lead *them* away and depart."

23   Then David said, "You must not do so, my brothers, with what the LORD has given us, who has kept us and delivered into our hand the band that came against us.

24   "And who will listen to you in this matter? For as his share is who goes down to the battle, so shall his share be who stays by the baggage; they shall share alike."

25   And so it has been from that day forward, that he made it a statute and an ordinance for Israel to this day.

f. David sends spoil to Judah

26   Now when David came to Ziklag, he sent *some* of the spoil to the elders of Judah, to his friends, saying, "Behold, a gift for you from the spoil of the enemies of the LORD:

27   to those who were in Bethel, and to those who were in Ramoth of the Negev, and to those who were in Jattir,

28   and to those who were in Aroer, and to those who were in Siphmoth, and to those who were in Eshtemoa,

29   and to those who were in Racal, and to those who were in the cities of the Jerahmeelites, and to those who were in the cities of the Kenites,

30   and to those who were in Hormah, and to those who were in Bor-ashan, and to those who were in Athach,

31   and to those who were in Hebron, and to all the places where David himself and his men were accustomed to go."

7. The death of Saul

31 Now the Philistines were fighting against Israel, and the men of Israel fled from before the Philistines and fell slain on Mount Gilboa.

2   And the Philistines overtook Saul and his sons; and the Philistines killed Jonathan and Abinadab and Malchi-shua the sons of Saul.

3   And the battle went heavily against Saul, and the archers hit him; and he was badly wounded by the archers.

4   Then Saul said to his armor bearer, "Draw your sword and pierce me through with it, lest these uncircumcised come and pierce me through and make

---

Margin references:
30:16 v. 14
30:17 1 Sam 15:3
30:19 v. 8
30:20 vv. 26-31
30:21 v. 10
30:24 Num 31:27; Josh 22:8
30:27 Josh 15:30; 19:8; 15:48
30:28 Josh 13:16; 15:50
30:29 1 Sam 27:10; 15:16
30:30 Judg 1:17
30:31 Josh 14:13
31:1 1 Chr 10:1-12; 1 Sam 28:4
31:3 2 Sam 1:6
*31:4 Judg 9:54; 2 Sam 1:6,10

30:14 *Negev of Caleb.* In David's time the Negev, parched land of southern Canaan, was apparently divided into five sections (see also 27:10). One of these belonged to the Cherethites, a people related to the Philistines and possibly another group of the sea peoples who settled along the seacoast of Canaan.

31:4 *took his sword and fell* . . . Compare this with the report of Saul's death brought by an Amalekite (2 Sam. 1:9–10).

sport of me." But his armor bearer would not, for he was greatly afraid. So Saul took his sword and fell on it.

5   And when his armor bearer saw that Saul was dead, he also fell on his sword and died with him.

6   Thus Saul died with his three sons, his armor bearer, and all his men on that day together.

7   And when the men of Israel who were on the other side of the valley, with those who were beyond the Jordan, saw that the men of Israel had fled and that Saul and his sons were dead, they abandoned the cities and fled; then the Philistines came and lived in them.

8. *Saul decapitated*

8   And it came about on the next day when the Philistines came to strip the slain, that they found Saul and his three sons fallen on Mount Gilboa.

9   And they cut off his head, and stripped off his weapons, and sent *them* throughout the land of the Philistines, to carry the good news to the house of their idols and to the people.

10   And they put his weapons in the temple of Ashtaroth, and they fastened his body to the wall of Beth-shan.

11   Now when the inhabitants of Jabesh-gilead heard what the Philistines had done to Saul,

12   all the valiant men rose and walked all night, and took the body of Saul and the bodies of his sons from the wall of Beth-shan, and they came to Jabesh, and burned them there.

13   And they took their bones and buried them under the tamarisk tree at Jabesh, and fasted seven days.

31.6 Jonathan left a son, Mephibosheth.

31:9
2 Sam 1:20
31:10
1 Sam 7:3;
Judg 2:13;
2 Sam 21:12;
Josh 17:11
31:11
1 Sam 11:3,9,
11
31:12
2 Sam 2:4-7;
2 Chr 16:14
31:13
2 Sam 21:12-14;
1 Sam 22:6;
2 Sam 1:12

INTRODUCTION TO
THE SECOND BOOK OF
SAMUEL

Authorship and Background: See 1 Samuel

Characteristics: See 1 Samuel

Contents:

THE SECOND BOOK OF
SAMUEL

I. *David enters into his kingship (1:1–4:12)*

A. *The news of Saul's death*

1:1
1 Sam 31:6;
30:17,26

1 Now it came about after the death of Saul, when David had returned from the slaughter of the Amalekites, that David remained two days in Ziklag.

1:2
1 Sam 4:10,12

2 And it happened on the third day, that behold, a man came out of the camp from Saul, with his clothes torn and dust on his head. And it came about when he came to David that he fell to the ground and prostrated himself.

3 Then David said to him, "From where do you come?" And he said to him, "I have escaped from the camp of Israel."

4 And David said to him, "How did things go? Please tell me." And he said, "The people have fled from the battle, and also many of the people have fallen and are dead; and Saul and Jonathan his son are dead also."

5 So David said to the young man who told him, "How do you know that Saul and his son Jonathan are dead?"

1:6
1 Sam 31:2-4

6 And the young man who told him said, "By chance I happened to be on Mount Gilboa, and behold, Saul was leaning on his spear. And behold, the chariots and the horsemen pursued him closely.

7 "And when he looked behind him, he saw me and called to me. And I said, 'Here I am.'

1:8
1 Sam 15:3

8 "And he said to me, 'Who are you?' And I answered him, 'I am an Amalekite.'

9 "Then he said to me, 'Please stand beside me and kill me; for agony has seized me because my life still lingers in me.'

1:10
Judg 9:54

10 "So I stood beside him and killed him, because I knew that he could not live after he had fallen. And I took the crown which *was* on his head and the bracelet which *was* on his arm, and I have brought them here to my lord."

1:11
2 Sam 3:31;
13:31
1:12
2 Sam 3:35

11 Then David took hold of his clothes and tore them, and *so* also *did* all the men who *were* with him.

12 And they mourned and wept and fasted until evening for Saul and his son Jonathan and for the people of the LORD and the house of Israel, because they had fallen by the sword.

1:13
v. 8

13 And David said to the young man who told him, "Where are you from?" And he answered, "I am the son of an alien, an Amalekite."

1:14
1 Sam 24:6;
26:9

14 Then David said to him, "How is it you were not afraid to stretch out your hand to destroy the LORD's anointed?"

1:15
2 Sam 4:10,12

15 And David called one of the young men and said, "Go, cut him down." So he struck him and he died.

1:16
2 Sam 3:28,
29; v. 10

16 And David said to him, "Your blood is on your head, for your mouth has testified against you, saying, 'I have killed the LORD's anointed.' "

B. *David's lamentation over Saul and Jonathan*

1:17
2 Chr 35:25
*1:18
1 Sam 31:3;
Josh 10:13
1:19
v. 27
1:20
1 Sam 31:9;
Mic 1:10;
Ex 15:20;
1 Sam 18:6;
31:4

17 Then David chanted with this lament over Saul and Jonathan his son,

18 and he told *them* to teach the sons of Judah *the song of* the bow; behold, it is written in the book of Jashar.

19 "Your beauty, O Israel, is slain on your high places!
How have the mighty fallen!

20 "Tell *it* not in Gath,
Proclaim it not in the streets of Ashkelon;
Lest the daughters of the Philistines rejoice,
Lest the daughters of the uncircumcised exult.

1:18 *book of Jashar*, an old source that is said to be a collection of poems. Other quotations attributed to it may be found in Josh. 10:12,13 and Judg. 5.

385

21

ntains of Gilboa,
.t dew or rain be on you, nor fields of offerings;
.ere the shield of the mighty was defiled,
hield of Saul, not anointed with oil.
1 the blood of the slain, from the fat of the mighty,
bow of Jonathan did not turn back,
1 the sword of Saul did not return empty.
.l and Jonathan, beloved and pleasant in their life,
d in their death they were not parted;
iey were swifter than eagles,
ney were stronger than lions.
/ daughters of Israel, weep over Saul,
Vho clothed you luxuriously in scarlet,
Who put ornaments of gold on your apparel.

"How have the mighty fallen in the midst of the battle!
Jonathan is slain on your high places.

26 "I am distressed for you, my brother Jonathan;
You have been very pleasant to me.
Your love to me was more wonderful
Than the love of women.

27 "How have the mighty fallen,
And the weapons of war perished!"

C. David anointed king over Judah

2 Then it came about afterwards that David inquired of the LORD, saying, "Shall I go up to one of the cities of Judah?" And the LORD said to him, "Go up." So David said, "Where shall I go up?" And He said, "To Hebron."

2 So David went up there, and his two wives also, Ahinoam the Jezreelitess and Abigail the widow of Nabal the Carmelite.

3 And David brought up his men who were with him, each with his household; and they lived in the cities of Hebron.

4 Then the men of Judah came and there anointed David king over the house of Judah.
And they told David, saying, "It was the men of Jabesh-gilead who buried Saul."

5 And David sent messengers to the men of Jabesh-gilead, and said to them, "May you be blessed of the LORD because you have shown this kindness to Saul your lord, and have buried him.

6 "And now may the LORD show lovingkindness and truth to you; and I also will show this goodness to you, because you have done this thing.

7 "Now therefore, let your hands be strong, and be valiant; for Saul your lord is dead, and also the house of Judah has anointed me king over them."

D. The civil war with Israel

1. Abner makes Ish-bosheth king of Israel

8 But Abner the son of Ner, commander of Saul's army, had taken ¹Ish-bosheth the son of Saul, and brought him over to Mahanaim.

9 And he made him king over Gilead, over the Ashurites, over Jezreel, over Ephraim, and over Benjamin, even over all Israel.

10 Ish-bosheth, Saul's son, was forty years old when he became king over Israel, and he was king for two years. The house of Judah, however, followed David.

11 And the time that David was king in Hebron over the house of Judah was seven years and six months.

¹I.e., man of shame

Cross references (right margin):

1:21 1 Sam 31:1; Job 3:3,4; Is 21:5
1:22 Is 34:6; 1 Sam 18:4
1:23 Jer 4:13; Judg 14:18
1:25 vv. 19,27
1:26 1 Sam 18:1-4
1:27 vv. 19,25; 1 Sam 2:4
*2:1 1 Sam 23:2,4, 9-12; 30:31
2:2 1 Sam 30:5
2:3 1 Sam 30:9; 1 Chr 12:1
2:4 2 Sam 5:3,5; 1 Sam 31:11-13
2:5 1 Sam 23:21
*2:8 2 Sam 14:50
2:9 Judg 1:32; 1 Sam 29:1
2:11 2 Sam 5:5

2:1 *Shall I go up . . . ?* David seeks guidance from the LORD as he contemplates conquering the kingdom over which he was secretly anointed to rule (1 Sam. 16:1–13). 2:8 *Ish-bosheth,* that is, "Man of Shame." This may not have been his original name. According to 1 Chr. 8:33 his name was *Eshbaal* (Ishbaal), "Man of Baal"; but the use of Baal in the proper name of an Israelite was so revolting that someone may have substituted *bosheth* (shame) in place of *baal.*

2. Abner defeated

2:12
Josh 18:25

12 Now Abner the son of Ner, went out from Mahanaim to Gibe\ servants of Ish-bosheth the son of Saul.

*2:13
1 Chr 2:16

13 And Joab the son of Zeruiah and the servants of David went out them by the pool of Gibeon; and they sat down, one on the one side of the p the other on the other side of the pool.

14 Then Abner said to Joab, "Now let the young men arise and ²ho contest before us." And Joab said, "Let them arise."

15 So they arose and went over by count, twelve for Benjamin and Ish-bosh\ the son of Saul, and twelve of the servants of David.

16 And each one of them seized his opponent by the head, and *thrust* his sword in his opponent's side; so they fell down together. Therefore that place was called ³Helkath-hazzurim, which is in Gibeon.

2:17
2 Sam 3:1

17 And that day the battle was very severe, and Abner and the men of Israel were beaten before the servants of David.

3. Abner slays Asahel

2:18
1 Chr 2:16;
12:8

18 Now the three sons of Zeruiah were there, Joab and Abishai and Asahel; and Asahel *was as* swift-footed as one of the gazelles which is in the field.

19 And Asahel pursued Abner and did not turn to the right or to the left from following Abner.

20 Then Abner looked behind him and said, "Is that you, Asahel?" And he answered, "It is I."

21 So Abner said to him, "Turn to your right or to your left, and take hold of one of the young men for yourself, and take for yourself his spoil." But Asahel was not willing to turn aside from following him.

2:22
2 Sam 3:27

22 And Abner repeated again to Asahel, "Turn aside from following me. Why should I strike you to the ground? How then could I lift up my face to your brother Joab?"

2:23
2 Sam 3:27;
4:6; 20:10

23 However, he refused to turn aside; therefore Abner struck him in the belly with the butt end of the spear, so that the spear came out at his back. And he fell there and died on the spot. And it came about that all who came to the place where Asahel had fallen and died, stood still.

4. Abner and Joab declare a truce

2:24
Josh 10:41

24 But Joab and Abishai pursued Abner, and when the sun was going down, they came to the hill of Ammah, which is in front of Giah by the way of the wilderness of Gibeon.

25 And the sons of Benjamin gathered together behind Abner and became one band, and they stood on the top of a certain hill.

26 Then Abner called to Joab and said, "Shall the sword devour forever? Do you not know that it will be bitter in the end? How long will you refrain from telling the people to turn back from following their brothers?"

2:27
v. 14

27 And Joab said, "As God lives, if you had not spoken, surely then the people would have gone away in the morning, each from following his brother."

28 So Joab blew the trumpet; and all the people halted and pursued Israel no longer, nor did they continue to fight anymore.

2:29
v. 8

29 Abner and his men then went through the Arabah all that night; so they crossed the Jordan, walked all morning, and came to Mahanaim.

30 Then Joab returned from following Abner; when he had gathered all the people together, nineteen of David's servants besides Asahel were missing.

31 But the servants of David had struck down many of Benjamin and Abner's men, *so that* three hundred and sixty men died.

32 And they took up Asahel and buried him in his father's tomb which was in Bethlehem. Then Joab and his men went all night until the day dawned at Hebron.

²Lit., *make sport* ³I.e., the field of sword-edges

2:13 *pool of Gibeon.* This pool was found in 1956 by ex- cavators at El-jib, the site of ancient Gibeon.

5. Abner and Ish-bosheth quarrel

3 Now there was a long war between the house of Saul and the house of David; and David grew steadily stronger, but the house of Saul grew weaker continually.

2 Sons were born to David at Hebron: his first-born was Amnon, by Ahinoam the Jezreelitess;

3 and his second, Chileab, by Abigail the widow of Nabal the Carmelite; and the third, Absalom the son of Maacah, the daughter of Talmai, king of Geshur;

4 and the fourth, Adonijah the son of Haggith; and the fifth, Shephatiah the son of Abital;

5 and the sixth, Ithream, by David's wife Eglah. These were born to David at Hebron.

6 And it came about while there was war between the house of Saul and the house of David that Abner was making himself strong in the house of Saul.

7 Now Saul had a concubine whose name was Rizpah, the daughter of Aiah; and Ish-bosheth said to Abner, "Why have you gone in to my father's concubine?"

8 Then Abner was very angry over the words of Ish-bosheth and said, "Am I a dog's head that belongs to Judah? Today I show kindness to the house of Saul your father, to his brothers and to his friends, and have not delivered you into the hands of David; and yet today you charge me with a guilt concerning the woman.

9 "May God do so to Abner, and more also, if as the LORD has sworn to David, I do not accomplish this for him,

10 to transfer the kingdom from the house of Saul, and to establish the throne of David over Israel and over Judah, from Dan even to Beersheba."

11 And he could no longer answer Abner a word, because he was afraid of him.

12 Then Abner sent messengers to David in his place, saying, "Whose is the land? Make your covenant with me, and behold, my hand shall be with you to bring all Israel over to you."

13 And he said, "Good! I will make a covenant with you, but I demand one thing of you, namely, you shall not see my face unless you first bring Michal, Saul's daughter, when you come to see me."

14 So David sent messengers to Ish-bosheth, Saul's son, saying, "Give me my wife Michal, to whom I was betrothed for a hundred foreskins of the Philistines."

15 And Ish-bosheth sent and took her from *her* husband, from Paltiel the son of Laish.

16 But her husband went with her, weeping as he went, and followed her as far as Bahurim. Then Abner said to him, "Go, return." So he returned.

6. Joab murders Abner

a. Abner visits David

17 Now Abner had consultation with the elders of Israel, saying, "In times past you were seeking for David to be king over you.

18 "Now then, do *it*! For the LORD has spoken of David, saying, 'By the hand of My servant David I will save My people Israel from the hand of the Philistines and from the hand of all their enemies.'"

19 And Abner also spoke in the hearing of Benjamin; and in addition Abner went to speak in the hearing of David in Hebron all that seemed good to Israel and to the whole house of Benjamin.

20 Then Abner and twenty men with him came to David at Hebron. And David made a feast for Abner and the men who were with him.

21 And Abner said to David, "Let me arise and go, and gather all Israel to my lord the king that they may make a covenant with you, and that you may be king over all that your soul desires." So David sent Abner away, and he went in peace.

b. Joab learns of Abner's visit

22 And behold, the servants of David and Joab came from a raid and brought much spoil with them; but Abner was not with David in Hebron, for he had sent him away, and he had gone in peace.

23 When Joab and all the army that was with him arrived, they told Joab,

---

3:13 Undoubtedly David thought that the restoration of Michal, his former wife, would enhance his chances for unity with the house of Saul. According to Deut. 24:4 a man was not to take back his former wife after she had had another husband.

saying, "Abner the son of Ner came to the king, and he has sent him away, and he has gone in peace."

24 Then Joab came to the king and said, "What have you done? Behold, Abner came to you; why then have you sent him away and he is already gone?

3:25
1 Sam 29:6;
Is 37:28

25 "You know Abner the son of Ner, that he came to deceive you and to learn of your going out and coming in, and to find out all that you are doing."

c. *The slaying of Abner*

26 When Joab came out from David, he sent messengers after Abner, and they brought him back from the well of Sirah; but David did not know *it*.

3:27
2 Sam 2:23;
4:6; 20:9,10;
1 Kin 2:5

27 So when Abner returned to Hebron, Joab took him aside into the middle of the gate to speak with him privately, and there he struck him in the belly so that he died on account of the blood of Asahel his brother.

28 And afterward when David heard it, he said, "I and my kingdom are innocent before the LORD forever of the blood of Abner the son of Ner.

3:29
1 Kin 2:32,
33; Lev 15:2

29 "May it fall on the head of Joab and on all his father's house; and may there not fail from the house of Joab one who has a discharge, or who is a leper, or who takes hold of a distaff, or who falls by the sword, or who lacks bread."

3:30
2 Sam 2:23

30 So Joab and Abishai his brother killed Abner because he had put their brother Asahel to death in the battle at Gibeon.

d. *David's grief over Abner's death*

3:31
Gen 37:34;
2 Sam 1:2,11

31 Then David said to Joab and to all the people who were with him, "Tear your clothes and gird on sackcloth and lament before Abner." And King David walked behind the bier.

32 Thus they buried Abner in Hebron; and the king lifted up his voice and wept at the grave of Abner, and all the people wept.

3:33
2 Sam 1:17

33 And the king chanted a *lament* for Abner and said,
    "Should Abner die as a fool dies?

34 "Your hands were not bound, nor your feet put in fetters;
    As one falls before the wicked, you have fallen."
And all the people wept again over him.

3:35
2 Sam 12:17;
1 Sam 3:17;
2 Sam 1:12

35 Then all the people came to persuade David to eat bread while it was still day; but David vowed, saying, "May God do so to me, and more also, if I taste bread or anything else before the sun goes down."

36 Now all the people took note *of it*, and it pleased them, just as everything the king did pleased all the people.

37 So all the people and all Israel understood that day that it had not been *the will* of the king to put Abner the son of Ner to death.

38 Then the king said to his servants, "Do you not know that a prince and a great man has fallen this day in Israel?

3:39
2 Sam 19:5-7;
1 Kin 2:5,6,
33,34

39 "And I am weak today, though anointed king; and these men the sons of Zeruiah are too difficult for me. May the LORD repay the evildoer according to his evil."

7. *The murder of Ish-bosheth*

4:1
2 Sam 3:27;
Ezra 4:4

4 Now when Ish-bosheth, Saul's son, heard that Abner had died in Hebron, he lost courage, and all Israel was disturbed.

4:2
Josh 18:25

2 And Saul's son *had* two men who were commanders of bands: the name of the one was Baanah and the name of the other Rechab, sons of Rimmon the Beerothite, of the sons of Benjamin (for Beeroth is also considered *part* of Benjamin,

4:3
Neh 11:33

3 and the Beerothites fled to Gittaim, and have been aliens there until this day).

*4:4
2 Sam 9:3,6;
1 Sam 31:1-4

4 Now Jonathan, Saul's son, had a son crippled in his feet. He was five years old when the report of Saul and Jonathan came from Jezreel, and his nurse took him up and fled. And it happened that in her hurry to flee, he fell and became lame. And his name was Mephibosheth.

4:5
2 Sam 2:8

5 So the sons of Rimmon the Beerothite, Rechab and Baanah, departed and came to the house of Ish-bosheth in the heat of the day while he was taking his midday rest.

4:4 *Mephibosheth.* This name, like Ish-bosheth, has been changed. According to 1 Chr. 8:34 his name was *Meribbaal,*   which means "my lord is Baal."

6   And they came to the middle of the house as if to get wheat, and they struck him in the belly; and Rechab and Baanah his brother escaped.

7   Now when they came into the house, as he was lying on his bed in his bedroom, they struck him and killed him and beheaded him. And they took his head and traveled by way of the Arabah all night.

8   Then they brought the head of Ish-bosheth to David at Hebron, and said to the king, "Behold, the head of Ish-bosheth, the son of Saul, your enemy, who sought your life; thus the LORD has given my lord the king vengeance this day on Saul and his descendants."

9   And David answered Rechab and Baanah his brother, sons of Rimmon the Beerothite, and said to them, "As the LORD lives, who has redeemed my life from all distress,

10   when one told me, saying, 'Behold, Saul is dead,' and thought he was bringing good news, I seized him and killed him in Ziklag, which was the reward I gave him for *his* news.

11   "How much more, when wicked men have killed a righteous man in his own house on his bed, shall I not now require his blood from your hand, and destroy you from the earth?"

12   Then David commanded the young men, and they killed them and cut off their hands and feet, and hung them up beside the pool in Hebron. But they took the head of Ish-bosheth and buried it in the grave of Abner in Hebron.

II. *The consolidation of David's kingship (5:1–10:19)*

A. *David made king over all Israel*

5   Then all the tribes of Israel came to David at Hebron and said, "Behold, we are your bone and your flesh.

2   "Previously, when Saul was king over us, you were the one who led Israel out and in. And the LORD said to you, 'You will shepherd My people Israel, and you will be a ruler over Israel.'"

3   So all the elders of Israel came to the king at Hebron, and King David made a covenant with them before the LORD at Hebron; then they anointed David king over Israel.

4   David was thirty years old when he became king, *and* he reigned forty years.

5   At Hebron he reigned over Judah seven years and six months, and in Jerusalem he reigned thirty-three years over all Israel and Judah.

B. *The capture of Jerusalem*

6   Now the king and his men went to Jerusalem against the Jebusites, the inhabitants of the land, and they said to David, "You shall not come in here, but the blind and lame shall turn you away"; thinking, "David cannot enter here."

7   Nevertheless, David captured the stronghold of Zion, that is the city of David.

8   And David said on that day, "Whoever would strike the Jebusites, let him reach the lame and the blind, who are hated by David's soul, through the water tunnel." Therefore they say, "The blind or the lame shall not come into the house."

9   So David lived in the stronghold, and called it the city of David. And David built all around from the ⁴Millo and inward.

10   And David became greater and greater, for the LORD God of hosts was with him.

11   Then Hiram king of Tyre sent messengers to David with cedar trees and carpenters and stonemasons; and they built a house for David.

12   And David realized that the LORD had established him as king over Israel, and that He had exalted his kingdom for the sake of His people Israel.

13   Meanwhile David took more concubines and wives from Jerusalem, after he came from Hebron; and more sons and daughters were born to David.

14   Now these are the names of those who were born to him in Jerusalem: Shammua, Shobab, Nathan, Solomon,

⁴I.e., citadel

5:6 *Jebusites*, read also Judg. 1:21.
5:9 *the Millo*, that is, "the Filling." The nature of this structure is unknown. Apparently it was part of the defenses of the Jebusite city. Solomon rebuilt the Millo (1 Kin. 11:27).

15   Ibhar, Elishua, Nepheg, Japhia,
16   Elishama, Eliada and Eliphelet.

C. David defeats the Philistines

5:17
2 Sam 23:14

17   When the Philistines heard that they had anointed David king over Israel, all the Philistines went up to seek out David; and when David heard *of it*, he went down to the stronghold.

5:18
Josh 15:18;
17:15; 18:16
5:19
1 Sam 23:2;
2 Sam 2:1

18   Now the Philistines came and spread themselves out in the valley of Rephaim.

19   Then David inquired of the LORD, saying, "Shall I go up against the Philistines? Wilt Thou give them into my hand?" And the LORD said to David, "Go up, for I will certainly give the Philistines into your hand."

5:20
Is 28:21

20   So David came to Baal-perazim, and defeated them there; and he said, "The LORD has broken through my enemies before me like the breakthrough of waters." Therefore he named that place ⁵Baal-perazim.

5:21
1 Chr 14:12

21   And they abandoned their idols there, so David and his men carried them away.

5:22
v. 18

22   Now the Philistines came up once again and spread themselves out in the valley of Rephaim.

5:23
v. 19

23   And when David inquired of the LORD, He said, "You shall not go *directly* up; circle around behind them and come at them in front of the ⁶balsam   trees.

*5:24
2 Kin 7:6;
Judg 4:14

24   "And it shall be, when you hear the sound of marching in the tops of the ⁶balsam trees, then you shall act promptly, for then the LORD will have gone out before you to strike the army of the Philistines."

5:25
Josh 12:12;
see
1 Chr 14:16

25   Then David did so, just as the LORD had commanded him, and struck down the Philistines from Geba as far as Gezer.

D. Bringing the ark to Jerusalem

1. The journey begun

*6:2
1 Chr 13:5,6;
Lev 24:16;
1 Sam 4:4

6 Now David again gathered all the chosen men of Israel, thirty thousand.
2   And David arose and went with all the people who were with him to Baale-judah, to bring up from there the ark of God which is called by the Name, the very name of the LORD of hosts who is enthroned *above* the cherubim.

*6:3
1 Sam 6:7

3   And they placed the ark of God on a new cart that they might bring it from the house of Abinadab which was on the hill; and Uzzah and Ahio, the sons of Abinadab, were leading the new cart.

6:4
1 Sam 7:1

4   So they brought it with the ark of God from the house of Abinadab, which was on the hill; and Ahio was walking ahead of the ark.

6:5
1 Sam 18:6,7;
1 Chr 13:8

5   Meanwhile, David and all the house of Israel were celebrating before the LORD with all kinds of *instruments made of* fir wood, and with lyres, harps, tambourines, castanets and cymbals.

2. The sin of Uzzah

6:6
1 Chr 13:9;
Num 4:15,19,
20
6:7
1 Sam 6:19

6   But when they came to the threshing floor of Nacon, Uzzah reached out toward the ark of God and took hold of it, for the oxen nearly upset *it*.

7   And the anger of the LORD burned against Uzzah, and God struck him down there for his irreverence; and he died there by the ark of God.

8   And David became angry because of the LORD's outburst against Uzzah, and that place is called ⁷Perez-uzzah to this day.

9   So David was afraid of the LORD that day; and he said, "How can the ark of the LORD come to me?"

6:10
1 Chr 13:13

10   And David was unwilling to move the ark of the LORD into the city of David with him; but David took it aside to the house of Obed-edom the Gittite.

6:11
1 Chr 13:14

11   Thus the ark of the LORD remained in the house of Obed-edom the Gittite three months, and the LORD blessed Obed-edom and all his household.

---

⁵I.e., the master of breakthrough   ⁶Or, *baka-shrubs*   ⁷I.e., the breakthrough of Uzzah

---

5:24   Here is an instance of guidance by outward circumstances.
6:2   *Baale-judah*, that is, *Kiriath-jearim* (Josh. 15:9; 1 Chr. 13:6). *above the cherubim*. See note to Ex. 25:22.
6:3   God had given specific instructions to Israel about how to carry the ark of God (Num. 4:15). It was to be carried by

four priests, placing the carrying poles on their shoulders; it was not to be transported by any vehicle. David failed to obey God's express instructions in carrying out His pious purpose. Disaster followed, as it always does when God's will is disregarded.

3. The ark brought to Jerusalem

12 Now it was told King David, saying, "The Lord has blessed the house of Obed-edom and all that belongs to him, on account of the ark of God." And David went and brought up the ark of God from the house of Obed-edom into the city of David with gladness.

13 And so it was, that when the bearers of the ark of the Lord had gone six paces, he sacrificed an ox and a fatling.

14 And David was dancing before the Lord with all *his* might, and David was wearing a linen ephod.

15 So David and all the house of Israel were bringing up the ark of the Lord with shouting and the sound of the trumpet.

16 Then it happened *as* the ark of the Lord came into the city of David that Michal the daughter of Saul looked out of the window and saw King David leaping and dancing before the Lord; and she despised him in her heart.

17 So they brought in the ark of the Lord and set it in its place inside the tent which David had pitched for it; and David offered burnt offerings and peace offerings before the Lord.

18 And when David had finished offering the burnt offering and the peace offering, he blessed the people in the name of the Lord of hosts.

19 Further, he distributed to all the people, to all the multitude of Israel, both to men and women, a cake of bread and one of dates and one of raisins to each one. Then all the people departed each to his house.

4. Michal's sin

20 But when David returned to bless his household, Michal the daughter of Saul came out to meet David and said, "How the king of Israel distinguished himself today! He uncovered himself today in the eyes of his servants' maids as one of the foolish ones shamelessly uncovers himself!"

21 So David said to Michal, "*It was* before the Lord, who chose me above your father and above all his house, to appoint me ruler over the people of the Lord, over Israel; therefore I will celebrate before the Lord.

22 "And I will be more lightly esteemed than this and will be humble in my own eyes, but with the maids of whom you have spoken, with them I will be distinguished."

23 And Michal the daughter of Saul had no child to the day of her death.

E. David's desire to build the temple

1. Nathan's approval

7 Now it came about when the king lived in his house, and the Lord had given him rest on every side from all his enemies,

2 that the king said to Nathan the prophet, "See now, I dwell in a house of cedar, but the ark of God dwells within tent curtains."

3 And Nathan said to the king, "Go, do all that is in your mind, for the Lord is with you."

2. God's intervention and disapproval

4 But it came about in the same night that the word of the Lord came to Nathan, saying,

5 "Go and say to My servant David, 'Thus says the Lord, "Are you the one who should build Me a house to dwell in?

6 "For I have not dwelt in a house since the day I brought up the sons of Israel

---

6:12
1 Chr 15:25;
1 Kin 8:1

6:14
Ex 15:20;
1 Sam 2:18
6:15
1 Chr 15:28

*6:16
1 Chr 15:29

6:17
1 Chr 15:1;
16:1;
1 Kin 8:62-65

6:18
1 Kin 8:14,15

6:20
vv. 14,16;
1 Sam 19:24

6:21
1 Sam 13:14;
15:28

7:1
1 Chr 17:1ff

7:2
2 Sam 5:11;
Acts 7:46;
Ex 26:1
7:3
1 Kin 8:17,18

7:5
1 Kin 5:3,4;
8:19
7:6
1 Kin 8:16;
Ex 40:18,34

6:16 *she despised him.* Michal's contempt can hardly be completely explained by David's unbecoming dance. Evidently she resented him for taking her from Paltiel (3:16). **7:4ff.** The Davidic covenant (vv. 4–16) was a phase of the original Abrahamic covenant (Gen. 17:6). It was made between God and David in anticipation of the kingly rule of Christ. It was both conditional and unconditional: conditional in the sense that disobedience would result in punishment; unconditional in the sense that even if there were disobedience, the covenant itself would not be abolished. Four elements made up this agreement: (1) the promise of a

dynasty; (2) the promise of a kingdom to rule over, including land and people; (3) the promise of regal authority; and (4) the promise that this house, ruling over this kingdom, would endure forever. Christ, of course, was the goal of this covenant, and He was to be the lineal descendant of the house of David. Note that the fulfillment of this covenant was announced to His mother in Luke 1:31ff. The spiritual fulfillment of the Davidic promise is referred to in Acts 2:25ff., for Christ has been, since the resurrection, exalted to supreme rule over the kingdom of God.

from Egypt, even to this day; but I have been moving about in a tent, even in a tabernacle.

7 "Wherever I have gone with all the sons of Israel, did I speak a word with one of the tribes of Israel, which I commanded to shepherd My people Israel, saying, 'Why have you not built Me a house of cedar?' " '

8 "Now therefore, thus you shall say to My servant David, 'Thus says the LORD of hosts, "I took you from the pasture, from following the sheep, that you should be ruler over My people Israel.

9 "And I have been with you wherever you have gone and have cut off all your enemies from before you; and I will make you a great name, like the names of the great men who are on the earth.

10 "I will also appoint a place for My people Israel and will plant them, that they may live in their own place and not be disturbed again, nor will the wicked afflict them any more as formerly,

11 even from the day that I commanded judges to be over My people Israel; and I will give you rest from all your enemies. The LORD also declares to you that the LORD will make a house for you.

12 "When your days are complete and you lie down with your fathers, I will raise up your descendant after you, who will come forth from you, and I will establish his kingdom.

13 "He shall build a house for My name, and I will establish the throne of his kingdom forever.

14 "I will be a father to him and he will be a son to Me; when he commits iniquity, I will correct him with the rod of men and the strokes of the sons of men,

15 but My lovingkindness shall not depart from him, as I took it away from Saul, whom I removed from before you.

16 "And your house and your kingdom shall endure before Me forever; your throne shall be established forever." ' " '

17 In accordance with all these words and all this vision, so Nathan spoke to David.

3. David's prayer of yieldingness

18 Then David the king went in and sat before the LORD, and he said, "Who am I, O Lord GOD, and what is my house, that Thou hast brought me this far?

19 "And yet this was insignificant in Thine eyes, O Lord GOD, for Thou hast spoken also of the house of Thy servant concerning the distant future. And this is the custom of man, O Lord GOD.

20 "And again what more can David say to Thee? For Thou knowest Thy servant, O Lord GOD!

21 "For the sake of Thy word, and according to Thine own heart, Thou hast done all this greatness to let Thy servant know.

22 "For this reason Thou art great, O Lord GOD; for there is none like Thee, and there is no God besides Thee, according to all that we have heard with our ears.

23 "And what one nation on the earth is like Thy people Israel, whom God went to redeem for Himself as a people and to make a name for Himself, and to do a great thing for Thee and awesome things for Thy land, before Thy people whom Thou hast redeemed for Thyself from Egypt, from nations and their gods?

24 "For Thou hast established for Thyself Thy people Israel as Thine own people forever, and Thou, O LORD, hast become their God.

25 "Now therefore, O LORD God, the word that Thou hast spoken concerning Thy servant and his house, confirm it forever, and do as Thou hast spoken.

26 that Thy name may be magnified forever, by saying, 'The LORD of hosts is God over Israel'; and may the house of Thy servant David be established before Thee.

27 "For Thou, O LORD of hosts, the God of Israel, hast made a revelation to Thy servant, saying, 'I will build you a house'; therefore Thy servant has found courage to pray this prayer to Thee.

28 "And now, O Lord GOD, Thou art God, and Thy words are truth, and Thou hast promised this good thing to Thy servant.

29 "Now therefore, may it please Thee to bless the house of Thy servant, that it may continue forever before Thee. For Thou, O Lord GOD, hast spoken; and with Thy blessing may the house of Thy servant be blessed forever."

7:7
Lev 26:11,12;
Deut 23:14;
2 Sam 5:2

7:8
1 Sam 16:11,
12; Ps 78:70;
2 Sam 6:21

7:9
1 Sam 18:14;
2 Sam 5:10;
Ps 18:37-42

7:10
Ex 15:17;
Is 5:2,7;
Ps 89:22;
Is 60:18

7:11
Judg 2:16;
1 Sam 12:9-11;
vv. 1,27;
1 Sam 25:28

7:12
1 Kin 2:1

7:13
1 Kin 5:5;
Ps 89:4,29;
36:37; Is 9:7

7:14
Ps 89:26,27;
Heb 1:5;
Ps 89:30-33

7:15
1 Sam 15:23,
28

7:16
Ps 89:36,37

7:18
Ex 3:11;
1 Sam 18:18

7:19
Is 55:8

7:20
1 Sam 16:7;
John 21:17

7:22
Ps 48:1;
86:10;
Ex 15:11;
Deut 3:24;
Ps 44:1

7:23
Deut 4:7,
32-38; 10:21;
15:15; 9:26

7:24
Deut 26:18;
Ps 48:14

7:26
Ps 72:18,19

7:27
v. 13

7:28
John 17:17

7:29
Num 6:24-26

F. David's military victories: Philistines, Moabites, Zobah, Syrians, Edomites, and Ammonites (ch 10)

8 Now after this it came about that David defeated the Philistines and subdued them; and David took control of the chief city from the hand of the Philistines.

2   And he defeated Moab, and measured them with the line, making them lie down on the ground; and he measured two lines to put to death and one full line to keep alive. And the Moabites became servants to David, bringing tribute.

3   Then David defeated Hadadezer, the son of Rehob king of Zobah, as he went to restore his rule at the [8]River.

4   And David captured from him 1,700 horsemen and 20,000 foot soldiers; and David hamstrung the chariot horses, but reserved *enough* of them for 100 chariots.

5   And when the Arameans of Damascus came to help Hadadezer, king of Zobah, David killed 22,000 Arameans.

6   Then David put garrisons among the Arameans of Damascus, and the Arameans became servants to David, bringing tribute. And the LORD helped David wherever he went.

7   And David took the shields of gold which were carried by the servants of Hadadezer, and brought them to Jerusalem.

8   And from Betah and from Berothai, cities of Hadadezer, King David took a very large amount of bronze.

9   Now when Toi king of Hamath heard that David had defeated all the army of Hadadezer,

10 Toi sent Joram his son to King David to greet him and bless him, because he had fought against Hadadezer and defeated him; for Hadadezer had been at war with Toi. And *Joram* brought with him articles of silver, of gold and of bronze.

11 King David also dedicated these to the LORD, with the silver and gold that he had dedicated from all the nations which he had subdued:

12 from [9]Aram and Moab and the sons of Ammon and the Philistines and Amalek, and from the spoil of Hadadezer, son of Rehob, king of Zobah.

13 So David made a name *for himself* when he returned from killing 18,000 [9]Arameans in the Valley of Salt.

14 And he put garrisons in Edom. In all Edom he put garrisons, and all the Edomites became servants to David. And the LORD helped David wherever he went.

15 So David reigned over all Israel; and David administered justice and righteousness for all his people.

16 And Joab the son of Zeruiah *was* over the army, and Jehoshaphat the son of Ahilud *was* recorder.

17 And Zadok the son of Ahitub and Ahimelech the son of Abiathar *were* priests, and Seraiah *was* secretary.

---

[8]I.e., Euphrates   [9]Some mss. read *Edom(ites)*

Cross references (right margin):

8:2 Num 24:17
*8:3 2 Sam 10:15-19
*8:4 Josh 11:6,9
8:5 1 Kin 11:23-25
8:6 v. 14; 2 Sam 7:9
8:7 1 Kin 10:16
8:10 1 Chr 18:10
8:11 1 Kin 7:51; 1 Chr 18:11; 26:25
*8:13 2 Ki 14:7
8:14 Gen 27:29,37, 40; Num 24:17, 18; v. 6
8:16 2 Sam 19:13; 1 Kin 4:3; 2 Kin 18:18, 37
*8:17 1 Chr 24:3

8:3 Ironically, David's victory over Hadadezer made it easier for Assyria, the future enemy of Israel and Judah, to rise to power.

8:4 Compare this with 1 Chr. 18:4, where it is stated that David took *1,000 chariots and 7,000 horsemen and 20,000 foot soldiers*. For this reason the KJV in 2 Sam. 8:4 inserts the word *chariots* after *thousand* so as to bring it into closer harmony with the parallel passage in Chronicles. Since quite a few words have been dropped out of the Hebrew text of Samuel here and there (cf. 1 Sam. 13:1, where the entire number has been lost), it is more than likely that *chariots* dropped out here, although it was preserved in 1 Chr. 18:4. Of course the number of horsemen in Chronicles is much larger also (7,000, rather than the 1,700 here). The number must originally have been written in tallies of some sort, and it may be that here again Samuel was indistinct and the copyist could only see 1,700, rather than 7,000.

8:13 The parallel account in 1 Chr. 18:12 names the Edomites as those defeated in this engagement (the difference between the Hebrew spelling of "Edom" and of "Syria," or "Aram," consist of but one letter—a letter *d*, which closely resembles the Hebrew *r*) and hence the reading here ("Edomites," rather than the KJV's "Syrians") seems well founded. Since the Valley of Salt was located at the southern extremity of the Dead Sea, it is more likely that Edomites were the enemies fought there rather than the Syrians, who dwelt to the north of Israel. 1 Chronicles 18:12 contributes the detail that Abishai was in immediate command of the victorious Israelite army, although he was acting under David's authority. The heading of Ps. 60 indicates that Joab, as chief of staff, masterminded the campaign and therefore deserved credit for the victory.

8:17 The Hebrew word for *secretary* is *sophēr*, meaning "one who numbers" or "who writes." Here the word *secretary* is used. At other times the word *scribe* is used: 2 Kin. 12:10; 18:18; 1 Chr. 2:55; 27:32; 2 Chr. 34:13. In Old Testament times they were (1) usually men of great wisdom (1 Chr. 27:32); (2) able and facile writers (Ps. 45:1); (3) learned in the law (Ezra 7:6); (4) secretaries to kings (20:25; 2 Kin. 12:10); (5) notaries (Jer. 32:11,12); (6) writers of state records (1 Chr. 24:6); (7) secretaries to prophets (Jer. 36:4,26); and (8) secretaries who kept the army rolls for the commanders (2 Kin. 25:19; 2 Chr. 26:11; Jer. 52:25).

Zadok. This is the first mention of the priest who was to become the progenitor of the recognized priesthood (1 Kin. 2:35). In 1 Chr. 6:8 he is in the priestly line of Aaron, Eleazar, and Phinehas, but aside from this genealogical data there is nothing in Biblical history to show where his father Ahitub and previous ancestors served as priests.

*8:18
1 Sam 30:14

*9:1
1 Sam 20:14-17,
42
9:2
2 Sam 16:1-4;
19:17,29

9:3
1 Sam 20:14;
2 Sam 4:4

9:4
2 Sam 17:27

9:6
2 Sam 16:4;
19:24-30

9:7
vv. 1,3;
2 Sam 12:8;
19:28
9:8
2 Sam 16:9

9:9
2 Sam 16:4;
19:29
9:10
vv. 7,11,13;
2 Sam 19:28

9:12
1 Chr 8:34

9:13
vv. 3,7,10

*10:1
1 Chr 19:1ff

10:4
Is 15:2; 20:4

10:6
Gen 34:30;
2 Sam 8:3,5;
Judg 18:28

18   And Benaiah the son of Jehoiada was over the Cherethites and the Pele-thites; and David's sons were chief ministers.

G. David's kindness to Mephibosheth

9 Then David said, "Is there yet anyone left of the house of Saul, that I may show him kindness for Jonathan's sake?"

2   Now there was a servant of the house of Saul whose name was Ziba, and they called him to David; and the king said to him, "Are you Ziba?" And he said, "*I am* your servant."

3   And the king said, "Is there not yet anyone of the house of Saul to whom I may show the kindness of God?" And Ziba said to the king, "There is still a son of Jonathan who is crippled in both feet."

4   So the king said to him, "Where is he?" And Ziba said to the king, "Behold, he is in the house of Machir the son of Ammiel in Lo-debar."

5   Then King David sent and brought him from the house of Machir the son of Ammiel, from Lo-debar.

6   And Mephibosheth, the son of Jonathan the son of Saul, came to David and fell on his face and prostrated himself. And David said, "Mephibosheth." And he said, "Here is your servant!"

7   And David said to him, "Do not fear, for I will surely show kindness to you for the sake of your father Jonathan, and will restore to you all the land of your grandfather Saul; and you shall eat at my table regularly."

8   Again he prostrated himself and said, "What is your servant, that you should regard a dead dog like me?"

9   Then the king called Saul's servant Ziba, and said to him, "All that belonged to Saul and to all his house I have given to your master's grandson.

10   "And you and your sons and your servants shall cultivate the land for him, and you shall bring in *the produce* so that your master's grandson may have food; nevertheless Mephibosheth your master's grandson shall eat at my table regularly." Now Ziba had fifteen sons and twenty servants.

11   Then Ziba said to the king, "According to all that my lord the king commands his servant so your servant will do." So Mephibosheth ate at David's table as one of the king's sons.

12   And Mephibosheth had a young son whose name was Mica. And all who lived in the house of Ziba were servants to Mephibosheth.

13   So Mephibosheth lived in Jerusalem, for he ate at the king's table regularly. Now he was lame in both feet.

H. David's victory over the Ammonites

1. The mistreatment of David's ambassadors

10 Now it happened afterwards that the king of the Ammonites died, and Hanun his son became king in his place.

2   Then David said, "I will show kindness to Hanun the son of Nahash, just as his father showed kindness to me." So David sent some of his servants to console him concerning his father. But when David's servants came to the land of the Ammonites,

3   the princes of the Ammonites said to Hanun their lord, "Do you think that David is honoring your father because he has sent consolers to you? Has David not sent his servants to you in order to search the city, to spy it out and overthrow it?"

4   So Hanun took David's servants and shaved off half of their beards, and cut off their garments in the middle as far as their hips, and sent them away.

5   When they told *it* to David, he sent to meet them, for the men were greatly humiliated. And the king said, "Stay at Jericho until your beards grow, and *then* return."

2. The flight of the Syrians and the Ammonites

6   Now when the sons of Ammon saw that they had become odious to David,

---

8:18 *David's sons were chief ministers.* If David's nonlevitical sons actually served as priests, there is no other passage to bear it out. There is reason to question the text here, because 20:26 has: *Ira the Jairite was also a priest to David,* while 1 Chr. 18:17 reads: *and the sons of David were chiefs at*

the king's side.

9:1 *for Jonathan's sake.* David did not forget his covenant with Jonathan (compare this with 1 Sam. 20:14-17).

10:1 *king of the Ammonites,* that is, Nahash.

the sons of Ammon sent and hired the Arameans of Beth-rehob and the Arameans of Zobah, 20,000 foot soldiers, and the king of Maacah with 1,000 men, and the men of Tob with 12,000 men.

7   When David heard *of it,* he sent Joab and all the army, the mighty men.

8   And the sons of Ammon came out and drew up in battle array at the entrance of the city, while the Arameans of Zobah and of Rehob and the men of Tob and Maacah *were* by themselves in the field.

9   Now when Joab saw that the battle was set against him in front and in the rear, he selected from all the choice men of Israel, and arrayed *them* against the Arameans.

10   But the remainder of the people he placed in the hand of Abishai his brother, and he arrayed *them* against the sons of Ammon.

11   And he said, "If the Arameans are too strong for me, then you shall help me, but if the sons of Ammon are too strong for you, then I will come to help you.

12   "Be strong, and let us show ourselves courageous for the sake of our people and for the cities of our God; and may the LORD do what is good in His sight."

13   So Joab and the people who were with him drew near to the battle against the Arameans, and they fled before him.

14   When the sons of Ammon saw that the Arameans fled, they *also* fled before Abishai and entered the city. Then Joab returned from *fighting* against the sons of Ammon and came to Jerusalem.

3. *The defeat of the Ammonites and Syrians at Helam*

15   When the Arameans saw that they had been defeated by Israel, they gathered themselves together.

16   And Hadadezer sent and brought out the Arameans who were beyond the [10]River, and they came to Helam; and Shobach the commander of the army of Hadadezer led them.

17   Now when it was told David, he gathered all Israel together and crossed the Jordan, and came to Helam. And the Arameans arrayed themselves to meet David and fought against him.

18   But the Arameans fled before Israel, and David killed 700 charioteers of the Arameans and 40,000 horsemen and struck down Shobach the commander of their army, and he died there.

19   When all the kings, servants of Hadadezer, saw that they were defeated by Israel, they made peace with Israel and served them. So the Arameans feared to help the sons of Ammon anymore.

III. *The sin of David (11:1–12:31)*

A. *David commits adultery with Bathsheba*

11   Then it happened in the spring, at the time when kings go out *to battle,* that David sent Joab and his servants with him and all Israel, and they destroyed the sons of Ammon and besieged Rabbah. But David stayed at Jerusalem.

2   Now when evening came David arose from his bed and walked around on the roof of the king's house, and from the roof he saw a woman bathing; and the woman was very beautiful in appearance.

3   So David sent and inquired about the woman. And one said, "Is this not Bathsheba, the daughter of Eliam, the wife of Uriah the Hittite?"

4   And David sent messengers and took her, and when she came to him, he lay with her; and when she had purified herself from her uncleanness, she returned to her house.

5   And the woman conceived; and she sent and told David, and said, "I am pregnant."

Marginal references

10:8 1 Chr 19:9; Judg 11:3,5

10:12 Deut 31:6; 1 Cor 16:13; 1 Sam 3:18
10:13 1 Kin 20:13-21

*10:16 2 Sam 8:3; 1 Chr 19:16

*10:18 1 Chr 19:18; 2 Sam 8:6

11:1 1 Chr 20:1; 1 Kin 20:22, 26; 2 Sam 12:26-28
11:2 Deut 22:8; Matt 5:28

11:3 2 Sam 23:39

11:4 Lev 15:19,28; 18:19

11:5 Lev 20:10

---

[10]I.e., Euphrates

10:16 See note to 8:3.
10:18 The number *700* chariots here appears as *7,000* in the parallel account in 1 Chr. 19:18; but the larger figure seems less likely (in view of the resources of the armies engaged), and was probably derived from a confusion in one of the digits in the decimal system originally used for com-

putation. A second copyist's error appears, for the account states 40,000 *horsemen* in this verse as against 40,000 *foot soldiers* in 1 Chr. 19:18. Most scribal errors derive from two basic faults: (1) illegibility of worn or torn manuscripts, and (2) inaccurate copying due either to weariness or carelessness.

B. *David sends for Uriah; his plan fails*

6   Then David sent to Joab, *saying,* "Send me Uriah the Hittite." So Joab sent Uriah to David.

7   When Uriah came to him, David asked concerning the welfare of Joab and the people and the state of the war.

8   Then David said to Uriah, "Go down to your house, and wash your feet." And Uriah went out of the king's house, and a present from the king was sent out after him.

9   But Uriah slept at the door of the king's house with all the servants of his lord, and did not go down to his house.

10   Now when they told David, saying, "Uriah did not go down to his house," David said to Uriah, "Have you not come from a journey? Why did you not go down to your house?"

11   And Uriah said to David, "The ark and Israel and Judah are staying in temporary shelters, and my lord Joab and the servants of my lord are camping in the open field. Shall I then go to my house to eat and to drink and to lie with my wife? By your life and the life of your soul, I will not do this thing."

12   Then David said to Uriah, "Stay here today also, and tomorrow I will let you go." So Uriah remained in Jerusalem that day and the next.

13   Now David called him, and he ate and drank before him, and he made him drunk; and in the evening he went out to lie on his bed with his lord's servants, but he did not go down to his house.

C. *David has Uriah slain*

14   Now it came about in the morning that David wrote a letter to Joab, and sent *it* by the hand of Uriah.

15   And he had written in the letter, saying, "Place Uriah in the front line of the fiercest battle and withdraw from him, so that he may be struck down and die."

16   So it was as Joab kept watch on the city, that he put Uriah at the place where he knew there *were* valiant men.

17   And the men of the city went out and fought against Joab, and some of the people among David's servants fell; and Uriah the Hittite also died.

18   Then Joab sent and reported to David all the events of the war.

19   And he charged the messenger, saying, "When you have finished telling all the events of the war to the king,

20   and if it happens that the king's wrath rises and he says to you, 'Why did you go so near to the city to fight? Did you not know that they would shoot from the wall?

21   'Who struck down Abimelech the son of Jerubbesheth? Did not a woman throw an upper millstone on him from the wall so that he died at Thebez? Why did you go so near the wall?'—then you shall say, 'Your servant Uriah the Hittite is dead also.'"

22   So the messenger departed and came and reported to David all that Joab had sent him *to tell.*

23   And the messenger said to David, "The men prevailed against us and came out against us in the field, but we pressed them as far as the entrance of the gate.

24   "Moreover, the archers shot at your servants from the wall; so some of the king's servants are dead, and your servant Uriah the Hittite is also dead."

25   Then David said to the messenger, "Thus you shall say to Joab, 'Do not let this thing displease you, for the sword devours one as well as another; make your battle against the city stronger and overthrow it'; and *so* encourage him."

D. *David marries Bathsheba*

26   Now when the wife of Uriah heard that Uriah her husband was dead, she mourned for her husband.

27   When the *time of* mourning was over, David sent and brought her to his house and she became his wife; then she bore him a son. But the thing that David had done was evil in the sight of the LORD.

11:8
Gen 43:24;
Luke 7:44

11:10
2 Sam 7:2,6;
20:6

11:13
v. 9

11:14
1 Kin 21:8-10

11:15
2 Sam 12:9

11:17
v. 21

*11:21
Judg 9:50-54

11:26
Deut 34:8;
1 Sam 31:13
11:27
2 Sam 12:9;
Ps 51:4,5

11:21 *Jerubbesheth,* a reference to Gideon. Even though Gideon was named Jerubbaal because he opposed Baal worship (Judg. 6:32), some scribe probably substituted *baal* for *besheth (bosheth),* "shame"; hence Gideon is sometimes called Jerubbesheth.

E. *Nathan and David*

1. *Nathan's parable*

12 Then the Lord sent Nathan to David. And he came to him, and said, "There were two men in one city, the one rich and the other poor.

2 "The rich man had a great many flocks and herds.

3 "But the poor man had nothing except one little ewe lamb
Which he bought and nourished;
And it grew up together with him and his children.
It would eat of his bread and drink of his cup and lie in his bosom,
And was like a daughter to him.

4 "Now a traveler came to the rich man,
And he was unwilling to take from his own flock or his own herd,
To prepare for the wayfarer who had come to him;
Rather he took the poor man's ewe lamb and prepared it for the man
who had come to him."

5 Then David's anger burned greatly against the man, and he said to Nathan, "As the Lord lives, surely the man who has done this deserves to die.

6 "And he must make restitution for the lamb fourfold, because he did this thing and had no compassion."

2. *The parable applied to David who repents*

7 Nathan then said to David, "You are the man! Thus says the Lord God of Israel, 'It is I who anointed you king over Israel and it is I who delivered you from the hand of Saul.

8 'I also gave you your master's house and your master's wives into your care, and I gave you the house of Israel and Judah; and if *that had been* too little, I would have added to you many more things like these!

9 'Why have you despised the word of the Lord by doing evil in His sight? You have struck down Uriah the Hittite with the sword, have taken his wife to be your wife, and have killed him with the sword of the sons of Ammon.

10 'Now therefore, the sword shall never depart from your house, because you have despised Me and have taken the wife of Uriah the Hittite to be your wife.'

11 "Thus says the Lord, 'Behold, I will raise up evil against you from your own household; I will even take your wives before your eyes, and give *them* to your companion, and he shall lie with your wives in broad daylight.

12 'Indeed you did it secretly, but I will do this thing before all Israel, and under the sun.'"

13 Then David said to Nathan, "I have sinned against the Lord." And Nathan said to David, "The Lord also has taken away your sin; you shall not die.

14 "However, because by this deed you have given occasion to the enemies of the Lord to blaspheme, the child also that is born to you shall surely die."

3. *The death of the child*

15 So Nathan went to his house.

Then the Lord struck the child that Uriah's widow bore to David, so that he was *very* sick.

16 David therefore inquired of God for the child; and David fasted and went and lay all night on the ground.

17 And the elders of his household stood beside him in order to raise him up from the ground, but he was unwilling and would not eat food with them.

18 Then it happened on the seventh day that the child died. And the servants of David were afraid to tell him that the child was dead, for they said, "Behold, while the child was *still* alive, we spoke to him and he did not listen to our voice. How then can we tell him that the child is dead, since he might do *himself* harm!"

19 But when David saw that his servants were whispering together, David perceived that the child was dead; so David said to his servants, "Is the child dead?" And they said, "He is dead."

20 So David arose from the ground, washed, anointed *himself*, and changed his clothes; and he came into the house of the Lord and worshiped. Then he came to his own house, and when he requested, they set food before him and he ate.

21 Then his servants said to him, "What is this thing that you have done?

12:1
2 Sam 14:4-7;
1 Kin 20:35-40

12:5
1 Kin 20:39,
41
12:6
Ex 22:1;
Luke 19:8

12:7
1 Kin 20:42;
1 Sam 16:13

12:9
1 Sam 15:19;
2 Sam 11:15-17,
27
12:10
2 Sam 13:28;
18:14;
1 Kin 2:25
12:11
Deut 28:30;
2 Sam 16:22

12:12
2 Sam 11:4-15;
16:22
12:13
1 Sam 15:24;
2 Sam 24:10;
Prov 28:13;
Mic 7:18
12:14
Is 52:5;
Rom 2:24

12:15
1 Sam 25:38

12:16
2 Sam 13:31

12:20
Job 1:20

While the child was alive, you fasted and wept; but when the child died, you arose and ate food."

12:22
Is 38:1,5;
Jon 3:9
12:23
Gen 37:35;
Job 7:8-10

22   And he said, "While the child was *still* alive, I fasted and wept; for I said, 'Who knows, the LORD may be gracious to me, that the child may live.'

23   "But now he has died; why should I fast? Can I bring him back again? I shall go to him, but he will not return to me."

4. *The birth of Solomon*

12:24
Matt 1:6;
1 Chr 22:9

24   Then David comforted his wife Bathsheba, and went in to her and lay with her; and she gave birth to a son, and he named him Solomon. Now the LORD loved him

25   and sent *word* through Nathan the prophet, and he named him [11] Jedidiah for the LORD's sake.

5. *The victory over the Ammonites*

12:26
1 Chr 20:1-3

26   Now Joab fought against Rabbah of the sons of Ammon, and captured the royal city.

27   And Joab sent messengers to David and said, "I have fought against Rabbah, I have even captured the city of waters.

28   "Now therefore, gather the rest of the people together and camp against the city and capture it, lest I capture the city myself and it be named after me."

29   So David gathered all the people and went to Rabbah, fought against it, and captured it.

12:30
1 Chr 20:2

30   Then he took the crown of their king from his head; and its weight *was* a talent of gold, and *in it was* a precious stone; and it was *placed* on David's head. And he brought out the spoil of the city in great amounts.

31   He also brought out the people who were in it, and set *them* under saws, sharp iron instruments, and iron axes, and made them pass through the brickkiln. And thus he did to all the cities of the sons of Ammon. Then David and all the people returned *to* Jerusalem.

IV. *David's troubles (13:1–18:33)*

A. *Amnon and Tamar*

1. *The incest of Amnon*

13:1
2 Sam 3:2,3;
1 Chr 3:9

13 Now it was after this that Absalom the son of David had a beautiful sister whose name was Tamar, and Amnon the son of David loved her.

2   And Amnon was so frustrated because of his sister Tamar that he made himself ill, for she was a virgin, and it seemed hard to Amnon to do anything to her.

13:3
1 Sam 16:9

3   But Amnon had a friend whose name was Jonadab, the son of Shimeah, David's brother; and Jonadab was a very shrewd man.

4   And he said to him, "O son of the king, why are you so depressed morning after morning? Will you not tell me?" Then Amnon said to him, "I am in love with Tamar, the sister of my brother Absalom."

5   Jonadab then said to him, "Lie down on your bed and pretend to be ill; when your father comes to see you, say to him, 'Please let my sister Tamar come and give me *some* food to eat, and let her prepare the food in my sight, that I may see *it* and eat from her hand.'"

13:6
Gen 18:6

6   So Amnon lay down and pretended to be ill; when the king came to see him, Amnon said to the king, "Please let my sister Tamar come and make me a couple of cakes in my sight, that I may eat from her hand."

7   Then David sent to the house for Tamar, saying, "Go now to your brother Amnon's house, and prepare food for him."

8   So Tamar went to her brother Amnon's house, and he was lying down. And she took dough, kneaded *it,* made cakes in his sight, and baked the cakes.

13:9
Gen 45:1

9   And she took the pan and dished *them* out before him, but he refused to eat. And Amnon said, "Have everyone go out from me." So everyone went out from him.

10   Then Amnon said to Tamar, "Bring the food into the bedroom, that I may

[11]I.e., beloved of the LORD

eat from your hand." So Tamar took the cakes which she had made and brought them into the bedroom to her brother Amnon.

11   When she brought *them* to him to eat, he took hold of her and said to her, "Come, lie with me, my sister."

12   But she answered him, "No, my brother, do not violate me, for such a thing is not done in Israel; do not do this disgraceful thing!

13   "As for me, where could I get rid of my reproach? And as for you, you will be like one of the fools in Israel. Now therefore, please speak to the king, for he will not withhold me from you."

14   However, he would not listen to her; since he was stronger than she, he violated her and lay with her.

15   Then Amnon hated her with a very great hatred; for the hatred with which he hated her was greater than the love with which he had loved her. And Amnon said to her, "Get up, go away!"

16   But she said to him, "No, because this wrong in sending me away is greater than the other that you have done to me!" Yet he would not listen to her.

17   Then he called his young man who attended him and said, "Now throw this woman out of my *presence*, and lock the door behind her."

18   Now she had on a long-sleeved garment; for in this manner the virgin daughters of the king dressed themselves in robes. Then his attendant took her out and locked the door behind her.

19   And Tamar put ashes on her head, and tore her long-sleeved garment which *was* on her; and she put her hand on her head and went away, crying aloud as she went.

2. *Absalom murders Amnon*

20   Then Absalom her brother said to her, "Has Amnon your brother been with you? But now keep silent, my sister, he is your brother; do not take this matter to heart." So Tamar remained and was desolate in her brother Absalom's house.

21   Now when King David heard of all these matters, he was very angry.

22   But Absalom did not speak to Amnon either good or bad; for Absalom hated Amnon because he had violated his sister Tamar.

23   Now it came about after two full years that Absalom had sheepshearers in Baal-hazor, which is near Ephraim, and Absalom invited all the king's sons.

24   And Absalom came to the king and said, "Behold now, your servant has sheepshearers; please let the king and his servants go with your servant."

25   But the king said to Absalom, "No, my son, we should not all go, lest we be burdensome to you." Although he urged him, he would not go, but blessed him.

26   Then Absalom said, "If not, please let my brother Amnon go with us." And the king said to him, "Why should he go with you?"

27   But when Absalom urged him, he let Amnon and all the king's sons go with him.

28   And Absalom commanded his servants, saying, "See now, when Amnon's heart is merry with wine, and when I say to you, 'Strike Amnon,' then put him to death. Do not fear; have not I myself commanded you? Be courageous and be valiant."

29   And the servants of Absalom did to Amnon just as Absalom had commanded. Then all the king's sons arose and each mounted his mule and fled.

30   Now it was while they were on the way that the report came to David, saying, "Absalom has struck down all the king's sons, and not one of them is left."

31   Then the king arose, tore his clothes and lay on the ground; and all his servants were standing by with clothes torn.

32   And Jonadab, the son of Shimeah, David's brother, responded, "Do not let my lord suppose they have put to death all the young men, the king's sons, for Amnon alone is dead; because by the intent of Absalom this has been determined since the day that he violated his sister Tamar.

33   "Now therefore, do not let my lord the king take the report to heart, namely, 'all the king's sons are dead,' for only Amnon is dead."

3. *Absalom flees to Geshur*

34   Now Absalom had fled. And the young man who was the watchman raised his eyes and looked, and behold, many people were coming from the road behind him by the side of the mountain.

13:11
Gen 39:12

13:12
Lev 20:17;
Judg 19:23;
20:6

13:13
Gen 20:12;
Lev 18:9,11

13:14
Deut 22:25

13:18
Gen 37:3;
Judg 5:30

13:19
1 Sam 4:12;
2 Sam 1:2;
Jer 2:37

13:20
2 Sam 14:24

13:22
Gen 31:24;
Lev 19:17,18

13:28
Judg 19:6,9,
22;
1 Sam 25:36

13:29
2 Sam 18:9;
1 Kin 1:33,38

13:31
2 Sam 1:11;
12:16
13:32
v. 3

13:33
2 Sam 19:19

13:34
vv. 37,38;
2 Sam 18:24

35   And Jonadab said to the king, "Behold, the king's sons have come; according to your servant's word, so it happened."

36   And it came about as soon as he had finished speaking, that behold, the king's sons came and lifted their voices and wept; and also the king and all his servants wept very bitterly.

13:37
v. 34;
2 Sam 3:3;
14:23,32

37   Now Absalom fled and went to Talmai the son of Ammihud, the king of Geshur. And *David* mourned for his son every day.

38   So Absalom had fled and gone to Geshur, and was there three years.

13:39
2 Sam 12:19-23

39   And *the heart of* King David longed to go out to Absalom; for he was comforted concerning Amnon, since he was dead.

B. *Joab secures Absalom's return*

1. *The woman of Tekoa*

14:1
2 Sam 13:39

14   Now Joab the son of Zeruiah perceived that the king's heart *was inclined* toward Absalom.

14:2
2 Chr 11:6;
1 Kin 20:35-43;
2 Sam 12:20

2   So Joab sent to Tekoa and brought a wise woman from there and said to her, "Please pretend to be a mourner, and put on mourning garments now, and do not anoint yourself with oil, but be like a woman who has been mourning for the dead many days;

14:3
v. 19

3   then go to the king and speak to him in this manner." So Joab put the words in her mouth.

14:4
2 Sam 1:2;
2 Kin 6:26-28

4   Now when the woman of Tekoa [12]spoke to the king, she fell on her face to the ground and prostrated herself and said, "Help, O king."

14:5
2 Sam 12:1-7

5   And the king said to her, "What is your trouble?" And she answered, "Truly I am a widow, for my husband is dead.

6   "And your maidservant had two sons, but the two of them struggled together in the field, and there was no [13]one to separate them, so one struck the other and killed him.

14:7
Num 35:19;
Deut 19:12;
Matt 21:38

7   "Now behold, the whole family has risen against your maidservant, and they say, 'Hand over the one who struck his brother, that we may put him to death for the life of his brother whom he killed, and destroy the heir also.' Thus they will extinguish my coal which is left, so as to leave my husband neither name nor remnant on the face of the earth."

8   Then the king said to the woman, "Go to your house, and I will give orders concerning you."

14:9
1 Sam 25:24;
Matt 27:25;
1 Kin 2:33

9   And the woman of Tekoa said to the king, "O my lord, the king, the iniquity is on me and my father's house, but the king and his throne are guiltless."

10   So the king said, "Whoever speaks to you, bring him to me, and he will not touch you anymore."

14:11
Num 35:19;
1 Sam 14:45

11   Then she said, "Please let the king remember the LORD your God, *so that* the avenger of blood may not continue to destroy, lest they destroy my son." And he said, "As the LORD lives, not one hair of your son shall fall to the ground."

2. *The plea for Absalom*

12   Then the woman said, "Please let your maidservant speak a word to my lord the king." And he said, "Speak."

14:13
2 Sam 12:7;
1 Kin 20:40-42;
2 Sam 13:37,
38

13   And the woman said, "Why then have you planned such a thing against the people of God? For in speaking this word the king is as one who is guilty, *in that* the king does not bring back his banished one.

14:14
Job 34:15;
Heb 9:27;
Num 35:15,
25,28

14   "For we shall surely die and are like water spilled on the ground which cannot be gathered up again. Yet God does not take away life, but plans ways so that the banished one may not be cast out from him.

15   "Now the reason I have come to speak this word to my lord the king is

[12]Many mss. and ancient versions read *came* [13]Lit., *deliverer between*

13:37 The story of Absalom has a threefold lesson for the Christian. First, it demonstrates the truth that men reap as they have sown, not only in their own lives but also in the lives of their children. David could behold in Absalom the very defects of character that God had mastered in him, but which ran wild in his son. Secondly, the life of Absalom was a fulfillment of the word spoken by Nathan the prophet at the time of David's sin with Bathsheba, that God would raise up evil against David out of his own house (12:11). David's intense grief at the death of Absalom was more than sorrow for the sins of his son; it expressed in part his own sense of guilt. The third lesson derived from the life of Absalom is that repentance does not necessarily imply that the temporal consequences of sin can be avoided. David repented of his sin with Bathsheba, but Absalom was the instrument of God for the chastisement of David, his father.

because the people have made me afraid; so your maidservant said, 'Let me now speak to the king, perhaps the king will perform the request of his maidservant.

16 'For the king will hear and deliver his maidservant from the hand of the man who would destroy both me and my son from the inheritance of God.'

17 "Then your maidservant said, 'Please let the word of my lord the king be comforting, for as the angel of God, so is my lord the king to discern good and evil. And may the LORD your God be with you.' "

3. *David implicates Joab*

18 Then the king answered and said to the woman, "Please do not hide anything from me that I am about to ask you." And the woman said, "Let my lord the king please speak."

19 So the king said, "Is the hand of Joab with you in all this?" And the woman answered and said, "As your soul lives, my lord the king, no one can turn to the right or to the left from anything that my lord the king has spoken. Indeed, it was your servant Joab who commanded me, and it was he who put all these words in the mouth of your maidservant;

20 in order to change the appearance of things your servant Joab has done this thing. But my lord is wise, like the wisdom of the angel of God, to know all that is in the earth."

4. *David brings Absalom back*

21 Then the king said to Joab, "Behold now, I will surely do this thing; go therefore, bring back the young man Absalom."

22 And Joab fell on his face to the ground, prostrated himself and blessed the king; then Joab said, "Today your servant knows that I have found favor in your sight, O my lord, the king, in that the king has performed the request of his servant."

23 So Joab arose and went to Geshur, and brought Absalom to Jerusalem.

24 However the king said, "Let him turn to his own house, and let him not see my face." So Absalom turned to his own house and did not see the king's face.

C. *Absalom's revolt*

1. *Absalom's beauty; his children*

25 Now in all Israel was no one as handsome as Absalom, so highly praised; from the sole of his foot to the crown of his head there was no defect in him.

26 And when he cut the hair of his head (and it was at the end of every year that he cut *it*, for it was heavy on him so he cut it), he weighed the hair of his head at 200 shekels by the king's weight.

27 And to Absalom there were born three sons, and one daughter whose name was Tamar; she was a woman of beautiful appearance.

2. *Absalom's haughtiness*

28 Now Absalom lived two full years in Jerusalem, and did not see the king's face.

29 Then Absalom sent for Joab, to send him to the king, but he would not come to him. So he sent again a second time, but he would not come.

30 Therefore he said to his servants, "See, Joab's [14]field is next to mine, and he has barley there; go and set it on fire." So Absalom's servants set the field on fire.

31 Then Joab arose, came to Absalom at his house and said to him, "Why have your servants set my [14]field on fire?"

32 And Absalom answered Joab, "Behold, I sent for you, saying, 'Come here, that I may send you to the king, to say, "Why have I come from Geshur? It would be better for me still to be there." ' Now therefore, let me see the king's face; and if there is iniquity in me, let him put me to death."

33 So when Joab came to the king and told him, he called for Absalom. Thus he

[14]Lit., *portion*

14:27 Compare this account with 18:18. A discrepancy has been imagined. One of two possibilities exists. Either the setting up of the pillar took place *before* his three sons were born, or it took place *after* the premature death of all three of his sons. In either event, Absalom was left without male heirs, and no mention of them is made in the genealogies.

14:17
v. 20;
2 Sam 19:27

14:19
v. 3

14:20
v. 17;
2 Sam 19:27

14:23
2 Sam 13:37,
38
14:24
2 Sam 3:13

14:25
Is 1:6

14:26
Ezek 44:20

*14:27
2 Sam 18:18

14:28
v. 24

14:32
1 Sam 20:8

14:33
Gen 33:4;
Luke 15:20

came to the king and prostrated himself on his face to the ground before the king, and the king kissed Absalom.

3. Absalom's revolt

15 Now it came about after this that Absalom provided for himself a chariot and horses, and fifty men as runners before him.

2   And Absalom used to rise early and stand beside the way to the gate; and it happened that when any man had a suit to come to the king for judgment, Absalom would call to him and say, "From what city are you?" And he would say, "Your servant is from one of the tribes of Israel."

3   Then Absalom would say to him, "See, your claims are good and right, but no man listens to you on the part of the king."

4   Moreover, Absalom would say, "Oh that one would appoint me judge in the land, then every man who has any suit or cause could come to me, and I would give him justice."

5   And it happened that when a man came near to prostrate himself before him, he would put out his hand and take hold of him and kiss him.

6   And in this manner Absalom dealt with all Israel who came to the king for judgment; so Absalom stole away the hearts of the men of Israel.

7   Now it came about at the end of [15]forty years that Absalom said to the king, "Please let me go and pay my vow which I have vowed to the LORD, in Hebron.

8   "For your servant vowed a vow while I was living at Geshur in Aram, saying, 'If the LORD shall indeed bring me back to Jerusalem, then I will serve the LORD.' "

9   And the king said to him, "Go in peace." So he arose and went to Hebron.

10   But Absalom sent spies throughout all the tribes of Israel, saying, "As soon as you hear the sound of the trumpet, then you shall say, 'Absalom is king in Hebron.' "

11   Then two hundred men went with Absalom from Jerusalem, who were invited and went innocently, and they did not know anything.

12   And Absalom sent for Ahithophel the Gilonite, David's counselor, from his city Giloh, while he was offering the sacrifices. And the conspiracy was strong, for the people increased continually with Absalom.

4. The flight of David

13   Then a messenger came to David, saying, "The hearts of the men of Israel are with Absalom."

14   And David said to all his servants who were with him at Jerusalem, "Arise and let us flee, for otherwise none of us shall escape from Absalom. Go in haste, lest he overtake us quickly and bring down calamity on us and strike the city with the edge of the sword."

15   Then the king's servants said to the king, "Behold, your servants are ready to do whatever my lord the king chooses."

16   So the king went out and all his household with him. But the king left ten concubines to keep the house.

17   And the king went out and all the people with him, and they stopped at the last house.

18   Now all his servants passed on beside him, all the Cherethites, all the Pelethites, and all the Gittites, six hundred men who had come with him from Gath, passed on before the king.

5. The faithfulness of Ittai the Gittite

19   Then the king said to Ittai the Gittite, "Why will you also go with us? Return and remain with the king, for you are a foreigner and also an exile; return to your own place.

20   "You came only yesterday, and shall I today make you wander with us, while I go where I will? Return and take back your brothers; mercy and truth be with you."

21   But Ittai answered the king and said, "As the LORD lives, and as my lord the

[15]Some ancient versions render four

15:1
2 Sam 12:11;
1 Kin 1:5
15:2
2 Sam 19:8

15:4
Judg 9:29

15:6
Rom 16:18

***15:7ff**
2 Sam 3:2,3

15:8
2 Sam 13:37,
38;
Gen 28:20,21

15:11
1 Sam 9:13;
22:15
15:12
v. 31;
Josh 15:51;
Ps 3:1

15:13
v. 6; Judg 9:3

15:14
2 Sam 12:11;
19:9

15:16
2 Sam 16:21,
22

***15:18**
2 Sam 8:18

15:19
2 Sam 18:2

15:20
1 Sam 23:13

15:21
Ruth 1:16,17

15:7ff. Absalom used deceit and treachery to steal the hearts of the people away from his father. Yet David continued to love him.

15:18 Cherethites . . . Pelethites . . . Gittites, constituted David's personal bodyguard. See 8:18 in this connection.

king lives, surely wherever my lord the king may be, whether for death or for life, there also your servant will be."

22   Therefore David said to Ittai, "Go and pass over." So Ittai the Gittite passed over with all his men and all the little ones who *were* with him.

23   While all the country was weeping with a loud voice, all the people passed over. The king also passed over the brook Kidron, and all the people passed over toward the way of the wilderness.

6. *The return of the ark*

24   Now behold, Zadok also *came*, and all the Levites with him carrying the ark of the covenant of God. And they set down the ark of God, and Abiathar came up until all the people had finished passing from the city.

25   And the king said to Zadok, "Return the ark of God to the city. If I find favor in the sight of the LORD, then He will bring me back again, and show me both it and His habitation.

26   "But if He should say thus, 'I have no delight in you,' behold, here I am, let Him do to me as seems good to Him."

27   The king said also to Zadok the priest, "Are you *not* a seer? Return to the city in peace and your two sons with you, your son Ahimaaz and Jonathan the son of Abiathar.

28   "See, I am going to wait at the fords of the wilderness until word comes from you to inform me."

29   Therefore Zadok and Abiathar returned the ark of God to Jerusalem and remained there.

7. *The treachery of Ahithophel*

30   And David went up the ascent of the *Mount of* Olives, and wept as he went, and his head was covered and he walked barefoot. Then all the people who were with him each covered his head and went up weeping as they went.

31   Now someone told David, saying, "Ahithophel is among the conspirators with Absalom." And David said, "O LORD, I pray, make the counsel of Ahithophel foolishness."

8. *Hushai returns to Jerusalem*

32   It happened as David was coming to the summit, where God was worshiped, that behold, Hushai the Archite met him with his coat torn, and dust on his head.

33   And David said to him, "If you pass over with me, then you will be a burden to me.

34   "But if you return to the city, and say to Absalom, 'I will be your servant, O king; as I have been your father's servant in time past, so I will now be your servant,' then you can thwart the counsel of Ahithophel for me.

35   "And are not Zadok and Abiathar the priests with you there? So it shall be that whatever you hear from the king's house, you shall report to Zadok and Abiathar the priests.

36   "Behold their two sons are with them there, Ahimaaz, Zadok's son and Jonathan, Abiathar's son; and by them you shall send me everything that you hear."

37   So Hushai, David's friend, came into the city, and Absalom came into Jerusalem.

9. *Ziba's lie against Mephibosheth*

16 Now when David had passed a little beyond the summit, behold, Ziba the servant of Mephibosheth met him with a couple of saddled donkeys, and on them *were* two hundred loaves of bread, a hundred clusters of raisins, a hundred summer fruits, and a jug of wine.

2   And the king said to Ziba, "Why do you have these?" And Ziba said, "The donkeys are for the king's household to ride, and the bread and summer fruit for the young men to eat, and the wine, for whoever is faint in the wilderness to drink."

3   Then the king said, "And where is your master's son?" And Ziba said to the king, "Behold, he is staying in Jerusalem, for he said, 'Today the house of Israel will restore the kingdom of my father to me.' "

4   So the king said to Ziba, "Behold, all that belongs to Mephibosheth is

15:24
2 Sam 8:17;
Num 4:15;
1 Sam 22:20
15:25
Ps 43:3;
Jer 25:30

15:26
2 Sam 22:20;
1 Kin 10:9;
1 Sam 3:18
15:27
1 Sam 9:6-9;
2 Sam 17:17
15:28
2 Sam 17:16

15:30
Esth 6:12;
2 Sam 19:4;
Is 20:2-4;
Ps 126:6
15:31
v. 12;
2 Sam 16:23;
17:14,23

15:32
Josh 16:2;
2 Sam 1:2
15:33
2 Sam 19:35

15:34
2 Sam 16:19

15:35
2 Sam 17:15,
16

15:36
v. 27;
2 Sam 17:17

15:37
2 Sam 16:16,
17;
1 Chr 27:33

16:1
2 Sam 15:32;
9:2-13

16:2
2 Sam 17:29

16:3
2 Sam 9:9,10;
19:26,27

yours." And Ziba said, "I prostrate myself; let me find favor in your sight, O my lord, the king!"

10. *Shimei curses David*

16:5
2 Sam 3:16-18;
19:16-23;
1 Kin 2:8

5   When King David came to Bahurim, behold, there came out from there a man of the family of the house of Saul whose name was Shimei, the son of Gera; he came out cursing continually as he came.

6   And he threw stones at David and at all the servants of King David; and all the people and all the mighty men were at his right hand and at his left.

16:7
2 Sam 12:9

7   And thus Shimei said when he cursed, "Get out, get out, you man of bloodshed, and worthless fellow!

16:8
2 Sam 21:1-9

8   "The LORD has returned upon you all the bloodshed of the house of Saul, in whose place you have reigned; and the LORD has given the kingdom into the hand of your son Absalom. And behold, you are *taken* in your own evil, for you are a man of bloodshed!"

16:9
2 Sam 19:21;
9:8; Ex 22:28
16:10
2 Sam 19:22;
1 Pet 2:23;
2 Kin 18:25;
Rom 9:20
16:11
2 Sam 12:11;
Gen 45:5

9   Then Abishai the son of Zeruiah said to the king, "Why should this dead dog curse my lord the king? Let me go over now, and cut off his head."

10   But the king said, "What have I to do with you, O sons of Zeruiah? If he curses, and if the LORD has told him, 'Curse David,' then who shall say, 'Why have you done so?' "

11   Then David said to Abishai and to all his servants, "Behold, my son who came out from me seeks my life; how much more now this Benjamite? Let him alone and let him curse, for the LORD has told him.

16:12
Rom 8:28

12   "Perhaps the LORD will look on my affliction and return good to me instead of his cursing this day."

13   So David and his men went on the way; and Shimei went along on the hillside parallel with him and as he went he cursed, and cast stones and threw dust at him.

14   And the king and all the people who were with him arrived weary and he refreshed himself there.

11. *The rule of Absalom in Jerusalem*

a. *Hushai pretends to serve Absalom*

16:15
2 Sam 15:37

15   Then Absalom and all the people, the men of Israel, entered Jerusalem, and Ahithophel with him.

16:16
2 Sam 15:37

16   Now it came about when Hushai the Archite, David's friend, came to Absalom, that Hushai said to Absalom, "*Long* live the king! *Long* live the king!"

16:17
2 Sam 19:25

17   And Absalom said to Hushai, "Is this your loyalty to your friend? Why did you not go with your friend?"

18   Then Hushai said to Absalom, "No! For whom the LORD, this people, and all the men of Israel have chosen, his will I be, and with him I will remain.

16:19
2 Sam 15:34

19   "And besides, whom should I serve? *Should I* not *serve* in the presence of his son? As I have served in your father's presence, so I will be in your presence."

b. *Ahithophel's counsel about the concubines*

16:21
2 Sam 15:16;
1 Sam 13:4;
2 Sam 2:7

20   Then Absalom said to Ahithophel, "Give your advice. What shall we do?"

21   And Ahithophel said to Absalom, "Go in to your father's concubines, whom he has left to keep the house; then all Israel will hear that you have made yourself odious to your father. The hands of all who are with you will also be strengthened."

16:22
2 Sam 12:11,
12

22   So they pitched a tent for Absalom on the roof, and Absalom went in to his father's concubines in the sight of all Israel.

16:23
2 Sam 15:12

23   And the advice of Ahithophel, which he gave in those days, *was* as if one inquired of the word of God; so was all the advice of Ahithophel *regarded* by both David and Absalom.

c. *Ahithophel's counsel to pursue David*

17 Furthermore, Ahithophel said to Absalom, "Please let me choose 12,000 men that I may arise and pursue David tonight.

17:2
2 Sam 16:14;
1 Kin 22:31

2   "And I will come upon him while he is weary and exhausted and will terrify him so that all the people who are with him will flee. Then I will strike down the king alone,

3   and I will bring back all the people to you. The return of everyone depends on the man you seek; *then* all the people shall be at peace."

4   So the plan pleased Absalom and all the elders of Israel.

d. *Hushai's diverse counsel*

5   Then Absalom said, "Now call Hushai the Archite also, and let us hear what he has to say."

6   When Hushai had come to Absalom, Absalom said to him, "Ahithophel has spoken thus. Shall we carry out his plan? If not, you speak."

7   So Hushai said to Absalom, "This time the advice that Ahithophel has given is not good."

8   Moreover, Hushai said, "You know your father and his men, that they are mighty men and they are fierce, like a bear robbed of her cubs in the field. And your father is an expert in warfare, and will not spend the night with the people.

9   "Behold, he has now hidden himself in one of the caves or in another place; and it will be when he falls on them at the first attack, that whoever hears *it* will say, 'There has been a slaughter among the people who follow Absalom.'

10   "And even the one who is valiant, whose heart is like the heart of a lion, will completely lose heart; for all Israel knows that your father is a mighty man and those who are with him are valiant men.

11   "But I counsel that all Israel be surely gathered to you, from Dan even to Beersheba, as the sand that is by the sea in abundance, and that you personally go into battle.

12   "So we shall come to him in one of the places where he can be found, and we will fall on him as the dew falls on the ground; and of him and of all the men who are with him, not even one will be left.

13   "And if he withdraws into a city, then all Israel shall bring ropes to that city, and we will drag it into the valley until not even a small stone is found there."

14   Then Absalom and all the men of Israel said, "The counsel of Hushai the Archite is better than the counsel of Ahithophel." For the LORD had ordained to thwart the good counsel of Ahithophel, in order that the LORD might bring calamity on Absalom.

e. *Hushai reports to David*

15   Then Hushai said to Zadok and to Abiathar the priests, "This is what Ahithophel counseled Absalom and the elders of Israel, and this is what I have counseled.

16   "Now therefore, send quickly and tell David, saying, 'Do not spend the night at the fords of the wilderness, but by all means cross over, lest the king and all the people who are with him be destroyed.'"

17   Now Jonathan and Ahimaaz were staying at En-rogel, and a maidservant would go and tell them, and they would go and tell King David, for they could not be seen entering the city.

18   But a lad did see them, and told Absalom; so the two of them departed quickly and came to the house of a man in Bahurim, who had a well in his courtyard, and they went down into it.

19   And the woman took a covering and spread it over the well's mouth and scattered grain on it, so that nothing was known.

20   Then Absalom's servants came to the woman at the house and said, "Where are Ahimaaz and Jonathan?" And the woman said to them, "They have crossed the brook of water." And when they searched and could not find *them*, they returned to Jerusalem.

21   And it came about after they had departed that they came up out of the well and went and told King David; and they said to David, "Arise and cross over the water quickly for thus Ahithophel has counseled against you."

22   Then David and all the people who *were* with him arose and crossed the Jordan; and by dawn not even one remained who had not crossed the Jordan.

f. *Ahithophel commits suicide*

23   Now when Ahithophel saw that his counsel was not followed, he saddled *his* donkey and arose and went to his home, to his city, and set his house in order, and strangled himself; thus he died and was buried in the grave of his father.

17:5
2 Sam 15:32-34

17:8
Hos 13:8;
1 Sam 16:18

17:10
Josh 2:11

17:14
2 Sam 15:31,
34

17:15
2 Sam 15:35

17:16
2 Sam 15:28

17:17
2 Sam 15:27,
36; Josh 15:7;
18:16

17:18
2 Sam 16:5

17:19
Josh 2:4-6

17:20
Josh 2:3-5;
1 Sam 19:12-17

17:21
vv. 15,16

17:23
2 Sam 15:12;
2 Kin 20:1;
Matt 27:5

D. *The war between David and Absalom*

1. *The background*

17:24
Gen 32:2;
2 Sam 2:8
17:25
2 Sam 19:13;
20:9-12

24   Then David came to Mahanaim. And Absalom crossed the Jordan, he and all the men of Israel with him.

25   And Absalom set Amasa over the army in place of Joab. Now Amasa was the son of a man whose name was Ithra the Israelite, who went in to Abigail the daughter of Nahash, sister of Zeruiah, Joab's mother.

26   And Israel and Absalom camped in the land of Gilead.

17:27
2 Sam 10:1,2;
12:26,29;
19:31,32;
1 Kin 2:7

27   Now when David had come to Mahanaim, Shobi the son of Nahash from Rabbah of the sons of Ammon, Machir the son of Ammiel from Lo-debar, and Barzillai the Gileadite from Rogelim,

28   brought beds, basins, pottery, wheat, barley, flour, parched *grain*, beans, lentils, parched *seeds*,

17:29
2 Sam 16:2

29   honey, curds, sheep, and cheese of the herd, for David and for the people who *were* with him, to eat; for they said, "The people are hungry and weary and thirsty in the wilderness."

2. *The battle in the forest of Ephraim*

18:1
Ex 18:25;
1 Sam 22:7
18:2
1 Sam 11:11;
2 Sam 15:19

18 Then David numbered the people who were with him and set over them commanders of thousands and commanders of hundreds.

2   And David sent the people out, one third under the command of Joab, one third under the command of Abishai the son of Zeruiah, Joab's brother, and one third under the command of Ittai the Gittite. And the king said to the people, "I myself will surely go out with you also."

18:3
2 Sam 21:17

3   But the people said, "You should not go out; for if we indeed flee, they will not care about us, even if half of us die, they will not care about us. But you are worth ten thousand of us; therefore now it is better that you *be ready* to help us from the city."

18:4
v. 24

4   Then the king said to them, "Whatever seems best to you I will do." So the king stood beside the gate, and all the people went out by hundreds and thousands.

18:5
v. 12

5   And the king charged Joab and Abishai and Ittai, saying, "*Deal* gently for my sake with the young man Absalom." And all the people heard when the king charged all the commanders concerning Absalom.

18:6
Josh 17:15,18

6   Then the people went out into the field against Israel, and the battle took place in the forest of Ephraim.

7   And the people of Israel were defeated there before the servants of David, and the slaughter there that day was great, 20,000 men.

8   For the battle there was spread over the whole countryside, and the forest devoured more people that day than the sword devoured.

3. *Absalom slain by Joab*

18:9
2 Sam 14:26

9   Now Absalom happened to meet the servants of David. For Absalom was riding on *his* mule, and the mule went under the thick branches of a great oak. And his head caught fast in the oak, so he was left hanging between heaven and earth, while the mule that was under him kept going.

10   When a certain man saw *it*, he told Joab and said, "Behold, I saw Absalom hanging in an oak."

11   Then Joab said to the man who had told him, "Now behold, you saw *him!* Why then did you not strike him there to the ground? And I would have given you ten *pieces* of silver and a belt."

18:12
v. 5

12   And the man said to Joab, "Even if I should receive a thousand *pieces of* silver in my hand, I would not put out my hand against the king's son; for in our hearing the king charged you and Abishai and Ittai, saying, 'Protect for me the young man Absalom!'

13   "Otherwise, if I had dealt treacherously against his life (and there is nothing hidden from the king), then you yourself would have stood aloof."

18:14
2 Sam 14:30

14   Then Joab said, "I will not waste time here with you." So he took three spears in his hand and thrust them through the heart of Absalom while he was yet alive in the midst of the oak.

15   And ten young men who carried Joab's armor gathered around and struck Absalom and killed him.

16 Then Joab blew the trumpet, and the people returned from pursuing Israel, for Joab restrained the people.

17 And they took Absalom and cast him into a deep pit in the forest and erected over him a very great heap of stones. And all Israel fled, each to his tent.

18 Now Absalom in his lifetime had taken and set up for himself a pillar which is in the King's Valley, for he said, "I have no son to preserve my name." So he named the pillar after his own name, and it is called Absalom's monument to this day.

4. Ahimaaz brings the tidings to David

19 Then Ahimaaz the son of Zadok said, "Please let me run and bring the king news that the LORD has freed him from the hand of his enemies."

20 But Joab said to him, "You are not the man to carry news this day, but you shall carry news another day; however, you shall carry no news today because the king's son is dead."

21 So Joab said to the Cushite, "Go, tell the king what you have seen." So the Cushite bowed to Joab and ran.

22 Now Ahimaaz the son of Zadok said once more to Joab, "But whatever happens, please let me also run after the Cushite." And Joab said, "Why would you run, my son, since you will have no reward for going?"

23 "But whatever happens," *he said,* "I will run." So he said to him, "Run." Then Ahimaaz ran by way of the plain and passed up the Cushite.

24 Now David was sitting between the two gates; and the watchman went up to the roof of the gate by the wall, and raised his eyes and looked, and behold, a man running by himself.

25 And the watchman called and told the king. And the king said, "If he is by himself there is good news in his mouth." And he came nearer and nearer.

26 Then the watchman saw another man running; and the watchman called to the gatekeeper and said, "Behold, *another* man running by himself." And the king said, "This one also is bringing good news."

27 And the watchman said, "I think the running of the first one is like the running of Ahimaaz the son of Zadok." And the king said, "This is a good man and comes with good news."

28 And Ahimaaz called and said to the king, "[16]All is well." And he prostrated himself before the king with his face to the ground. And he said, "Blessed is the LORD your God, who has delivered up the men who lifted their hands against my lord the king."

29 And the king said, "Is it well with the young man Absalom?" And Ahimaaz answered, "When Joab sent the king's servant, and your servant, I saw a great tumult, but I did not know what *it was.*"

30 Then the king said, "Turn aside and stand here." So he turned aside and stood still.

31 And behold, the Cushite arrived, and the Cushite said, "Let my lord the king receive good news, for the LORD has freed you this day from the hand of all those who rose up against you."

32 Then the king said to the Cushite, "Is it well with the young man Absalom?" And the Cushite answered, "Let the enemies of my lord the king, and all who rise up against you for evil, be as that young man!"

33 And the king was deeply moved and went up to the chamber over the gate and wept. And thus he said as he walked, "O my son Absalom, my son, my son Absalom! Would I had died instead of you, O Absalom, my son, my son!"

V. David restored to his kingdom (19:1—20:26)

A. Joab rebukes David

19 Then it was told Joab, "Behold, the king is weeping and mourns for Absalom."

2 And the victory that day was turned to mourning for all the people, for the people heard *it* said that day, "The king is grieved for his son."

3 So the people went by stealth into the city that day, as people who are humiliated steal away when they flee in battle.

---

[16]Lit., *Peace.*

Marginal references (right column):

18:16 — 2 Sam 2:28; 20:22
18:17 — Josh 7:26; 8:29; 2 Sam 19:8
18:18 — 1 Sam 15:12; Gen 14:17; 2 Sam 14:27

18:19 — 2 Sam 15:36; v. 31

18:24 — 2 Sam 19:8; 13:34; 2 Kin 9:17

18:28 — 2 Sam 14:4; 1 Sam 25:23; 17:46

18:29 — v. 22

18:31 — v. 19; Judg 5:31

18:32 — 1 Sam 25:26

18:33 — 2 Sam 19:4; Ex 32:32; Rom 9:3

19:1 — 2 Sam 18:33

19:4
2 Sam 15:30;
18:33
4   And the king covered his face and cried out with a loud voice, "O my son Absalom, O Absalom, my son, my son!"

5   Then Joab came into the house to the king and said, "Today you have covered with shame the faces of all your servants, who today have saved your life and the lives of your sons and daughters, the lives of your wives, and the lives of your concubines,

19:6
Matt 5:46
6   by loving those who hate you, and by hating those who love you. For you have shown today that princes and servants are nothing to you; for I know this day that if Absalom were alive and all of us were dead today, then you would be pleased.

7   "Now therefore arise, go out and speak kindly to your servants, for I swear by the Lord, if you do not go out, surely not a man will pass the night with you, and this will be worse for you than all the evil that has come upon you from your youth until now."

19:8
2 Sam 15:2;
18:4
8   So the king arose and sat in the gate. When they told all the people, saying, "Behold, the king is sitting in the gate," then all the people came before the king. Now Israel had fled, each to his tent.

B. David's return to Jerusalem

1. The elders invite David back

19:9
2 Sam 8:1-14;
5:20; 15:14
9   And all the people were quarreling throughout all the tribes of Israel, saying, "The king delivered us from the hand of our enemies and saved us from the hand of the Philistines, but now he has fled out of the land from Absalom.

10   "However, Absalom, whom we anointed over us, has died in battle. Now then, why are you silent about bringing the king back?"

11   Then King David sent to Zadok and Abiathar the priests, saying, "Speak to the elders of Judah, saying, 'Why are you the last to bring the king back to his house, since the word of all Israel has come to the king, *even* to his house?

19:12
2 Sam 5:1
12   'You are my brothers; you are my bone and my flesh. Why then should you be the last to bring back the king?'

*19:13
2 Sam 17:25;
1 Kin 19:2;
8:16; vv. 5-7
13   "And say to Amasa, 'Are you not my bone and my flesh? May God do so to me, and more also, if you will not be commander of the army before me continually in place of Joab.' "

19:14
Judg 20:1
14   Thus he turned the hearts of all the men of Judah as one man, so that they sent *word* to the king, *saying*, "Return, you and all your servants."

19:15
Josh 5:9
15   The king then returned and came as far as the Jordan. And Judah came to Gilgal in order to go to meet the king, to bring the king across the Jordan.

2. The repentance and forgiveness of Shimei

19:16
2 Sam 16:5;
1 Kin 2:8
16   Then Shimei the son of Gera, the Benjamite who was from Bahurim, hurried and came down with the men of Judah to meet King David.

19:17
2 Sam 16:1,2
17   And there were a thousand men of Benjamin with him, with Ziba the servant of the house of Saul, and his fifteen sons and his twenty servants with him; and they rushed to the Jordan before the king.

18   Then they kept crossing the ford to bring over the king's household, and to do what was good in his sight. And Shimei the son of Gera fell down before the king as he was about to cross the Jordan.

19:19
1 Sam 22:15;
2 Sam 16:6-8;
13:33
19   So he said to the king, "Let not my lord consider me guilty, nor remember what your servant did wrong on the day when my lord the king came out from Jerusalem, so that the king should take *it* to heart.

19:20
2 Sam 16:5
20   "For your servant knows that I have sinned; therefore behold, I have come today, the first of all the house of Joseph to go down to meet my lord the king."

19:21
2 Sam 16:7,8;
Ex 22:28
21   But Abishai the son of Zeruiah answered and said, "Should not Shimei be put to death for this, because he cursed the Lord's anointed?"

19:22
2 Sam 16:10;
1 Sam 11:13
22   David then said, "What have I to do with you, O sons of Zeruiah, that you should this day be an adversary to me? Should any man be put to death in Israel today? For do I not know that I am king over Israel today?"

19:23
1 Kin 2:8
23   And the king said to Shimei, "You shall not die." Thus the king swore to him.

19:13 Joab had fought faithfully over the years for David's best interests. He ignored David's sentimental request to protect Absalom because he knew the kingdom was at stake. Yet for this one act of disobedience David rashly promised to elevate Amasa, chief of Absalom's army, as commander of the army in place of Joab.

3. The explanation of Mephibosheth

24 Then Mephibosheth the [17]son of Saul came down to meet the king; and he had neither cared for his feet, nor trimmed his mustache, nor washed his clothes, from the day the king departed until the day he came *home* in peace.

25 And it was when he came from Jerusalem to meet the king, that the king said to him, "Why did you not go with me, Mephibosheth?"

26 So he answered, "O my lord, the king, my servant deceived me; for your servant said, 'I will saddle a donkey for myself that I may ride on it and go with the king,' because your servant is lame.

27 "Moreover, he has slandered your servant to my lord the king; but my lord the king is like the angel of God, therefore do what is good in your sight.

28 "For all my father's household was nothing but dead men before my lord the king; yet you set your servant among those who ate at your own table. What right do I have yet that I should complain anymore to the king?"

29 So the king said to him, "Why do you still speak of your affairs? I have decided, 'You and Ziba shall divide the land.'"

30 And Mephibosheth said to the king, "Let him even take it all, since my lord the king has come safely to his own house."

4. The blessing by Barzillai

31 Now Barzillai the Gileadite had come down from Rogelim; and he went on to the Jordan with the king to escort him over the Jordan.

32 Now Barzillai was very old, being eighty years old; and he had sustained the king while he stayed at Mahanaim, for he was a very great man.

33 And the king said to Barzillai, "You cross over with me and I will sustain you in Jerusalem with me."

34 But Barzillai said to the king, "How long have I yet to live, that I should go up with the king to Jerusalem?

35 "I am now eighty years old. Can I distinguish between good and bad? Or can your servant taste what I eat or what I drink? Or can I hear anymore the voice of singing men and women? Why then should your servant be an added burden to my lord the king?

36 "Your servant would merely cross over the Jordan with the king. Why should the king compensate me *with* this reward?

37 "Please let your servant return, that I may die in my own city near the grave of my father and my mother. However, here is your servant Chimham, let him cross over with my lord the king, and do for him what is good in your sight."

38 And the king answered, "Chimham shall cross over with me, and I will do for him what is good in your sight; and whatever you require of me, I will do for you."

39 All the people crossed over the Jordan and the king crossed too. The king then kissed Barzillai and blessed him, and he returned to his place.

40 Now the king went on to Gilgal, and Chimham went on with him; and all the people of Judah and also half the people of Israel accompanied the king.

5. Israel's jealousy

41 And behold, all the men of Israel came to the king and said to the king, "Why had our brothers the men of Judah stolen you away, and brought the king and his household and all David's men with him over the Jordan?"

42 Then all the men of Judah answered the men of Israel, "Because the king is a close relative to us. Why then are you angry about this matter? Have we eaten at all at the king's *expense*, or has anything been taken for us?"

43 But the men of Israel answered the men of Judah and said, "We have ten parts in the king, therefore we also have more *claim* on David than you. Why then did you treat us with contempt? Was it not our advice first to bring back our king?" Yet the words of the men of Judah were harsher than the words of the men of Israel.

[17]I.e., grandson

19:24
2 Sam 9:6-10

19:25
2 Sam 16:17

19:26
2 Sam 9:3

19:27
2 Sam 16:3;
14:17,20
19:28
2 Sam 21:6-9;
9:7,10,13

19:31
1 Kin 2:7

19:32
1 Sam 17:27

19:35
Ps 90:10;
Is 5:11,12

19:37
v. 40;
1 Kin 2:7;
Jer 41:17

19:39
Gen 31:55

19:41
v. 15

19:42
v. 12

19:43
1 Kin 11:30,
31

C. Sheba's revolt

1. Sheba calls for rebellion

20 Now a worthless fellow happened to be there whose name was Sheba, the son of Bichri, a Benjamite; and he blew the trumpet and said,
"We have no portion in David,
Nor do we have inheritance in the son of Jesse;
Every man to his tents, O Israel!"

2 So all the men of Israel withdrew from following David, *and* followed Sheba the son of Bichri; but the men of Judah remained steadfast to their king, from the Jordan even to Jerusalem.

3 Then David came to his house at Jerusalem, and the king took the ten women, the concubines whom he had left to keep the house, and placed them under guard and provided them with sustenance, but did not go in to them. So they were shut up until the day of their death, living as widows.

2. Amasa slain by Joab

4 Then the king said to Amasa, "Call out the men of Judah for me within three days, and be present here yourself."

5 So Amasa went to call out *the men of* Judah, but he delayed longer than the set time which he had appointed him.

6 And David said to Abishai, "Now Sheba the son of Bichri will do us more harm than Absalom; take your lord's servants and pursue him, lest he find for himself fortified cities and escape from our sight."

7 So Joab's men went out after him, along with the Cherethites and the Pelethites and all the mighty men; and they went out from Jerusalem to pursue Sheba the son of Bichri.

8 When they were at the large stone which is in Gibeon, Amasa came to meet them. Now Joab was dressed in his military attire, and over it was a belt with a sword in its sheath fastened at his waist; and as he went forward, it fell out.

9 And Joab said to Amasa, "Is it well with you, my brother?" And Joab took Amasa by the beard with his right hand to kiss him.

10 But Amasa was not on guard against the sword which was in Joab's hand so he struck him in the belly with it and poured out his inward parts on the ground, and did not *strike* him again; and he died. Then Joab and Abishai his brother pursued Sheba the son of Bichri.

3. Joab pursues Sheba

11 Now there stood by him one of Joab's young men, and said, "Whoever favors Joab and whoever is for David, *let him* follow Joab."

12 But Amasa lay wallowing in *his* blood in the middle of the highway. And when the man saw that all the people stood still, he removed Amasa from the highway into the field and threw a garment over him when he saw that everyone who came by him stood still.

13 As soon as he was removed from the highway, all the men passed on after Joab to pursue Sheba the son of Bichri.

4. The slaying of Sheba

14 Now he went through all the tribes of Israel to Abel even to Beth-maacah and all the Berites; and they were gathered together and also went after him.

15 And they came and besieged him in Abel Beth-maacah, and they cast up a mound against the city, and it stood by the rampart; and all the people who were with Joab were wreaking destruction in order to topple the wall.

16 Then a wise woman called from the city, "Hear, hear! Please tell Joab, 'Come here that I may speak with you.'"

17 So he approached her, and the woman said, "Are you Joab?" And he answered, "I am." Then she said to him, "Listen to the words of your maidservant." And he answered, "I am listening."

20:1 Sheba took advantage of old hatreds between north and south to rally the northern tribes against David and the tribe of Judah.

20:5 *Amasa*, a poor successor to Joab.
20:15 *Abel Beth-maacah*, in the northernmost part of what is now Palestine, was held by the people of Naphtali.

18   Then she spoke, saying, "Formerly they used to say, 'They will surely ask *advice* at Abel,' and thus they ended *the dispute.*

19   "I am of those who are peaceable *and* faithful in Israel. You are seeking to destroy a city even a mother in Israel. Why would you swallow up the inheritance of the LORD?"

20   And Joab answered and said, "Far be it, far be it from me that I should swallow up or destroy!

21   "Such is not the case. But a man from the hill country of Ephraim, Sheba the son of Bichri by name, has lifted up his hand against King David. Only hand him over, and I will depart from the city." And the woman said to Joab, "Behold, his head will be thrown to you over the wall."

22   Then the woman wisely came to all the people. And they cut off the head of Sheba the son of Bichri and threw it to Joab. So he blew the trumpet, and they were dispersed from the city, each to his tent. Joab also returned to the king at Jerusalem.

23   Now Joab was over the whole army of Israel, and Benaiah the son of Jehoiada was over the Cherethites and the Pelethites;

24   and Adoram was over the forced labor, and Jehoshaphat the son of Ahilud was the recorder;

25   and Sheva was scribe, and Zadok and Abiathar were priests;

26   and Ira the Jairite was also a priest to David.

VI. *The later years of David's kingdom (21:1–24:25)*

A. *The famine*

1. *The bloodguilt of Saul*

21   Now there was a famine in the days of David for three years, year after year; and David sought the presence of the LORD. And the LORD said, "It is for Saul and his bloody house, because he put the Gibeonites to death."

2   So the king called the Gibeonites and spoke to them (now the Gibeonites were not of the sons of Israel but of the remnant of the Amorites, and the sons of Israel made a covenant with them, but Saul had sought to kill them in his zeal for the sons of Israel and Judah).

3   Thus David said to the Gibeonites, "What should I do for you? And how can I make atonement that you may bless the inheritance of the LORD?"

4   Then the Gibeonites said to him, "We have no *concern* of silver or gold with Saul or his house, nor is it for us to put any man to death in Israel." And he said, "I will do for you whatever you say."

5   So they said to the king, "The man who consumed us, and who planned to exterminate us from remaining within any border of Israel,

6   let seven men from his sons be given to us, and we will hang them before the LORD in Gibeah of Saul, the chosen of the LORD." And the king said, "I will give *them.*"

2. *The hanging of seven of Saul's kin*

7   But the king spared Mephibosheth, the son of Jonathan the son of Saul, because of the oath of the LORD which was between them, between David and Saul's son Jonathan.

8   So the king took the two sons of Rizpah the daughter of Aiah, Armoni and Mephibosheth whom she had born to Saul, and the five sons of Merab the daughter of Saul, whom she had born to Adriel the son of Barzillai the Meholathite.

9   Then he gave them into the hands of the Gibeonites, and they hanged them in the mountain before the LORD, so that the seven of them fell together; and they were put to death in the first days of harvest at the beginning of barley harvest.

3. *David's burial of Saul and Jonathan and the seven*

10   And Rizpah the daughter of Aiah took sackcloth and spread it for herself on the rock, from the beginning of harvest until it rained on them from the sky; and she allowed neither the birds of the sky to rest on them by day nor the beasts of the field by night.

20:19
1 Sam 26:19;
2 Sam 21:3

20:21
v. 2

20:22
Eccl 9:13-16;
v. 1

20:23
2 Sam 8:16-18

20:25
2 Sam 8:17
20:26
2 Sam 23:38

21:2
Josh 9:3,
15-17

21:3
2 Sam 20:19

21:4
Num 35:31,
32

21:5
1 Sam 10:24,
26

21:7
2 Sam 4:4;
9:10;
1 Sam 18:3;
20:8,15;
23:18
21:8
2 Sam 3:7

21:10
v. 8;
Deut 21:23;
1 Sam 17:44,
46

20:19 *a mother in Israel.* Abel was a fortress city with dependent villages, known as daughters, about the country side.

11   When it was told David what Rizpah the daughter of Aiah, the concubine of Saul, had done,

21:12
1 Sam 31:10-13

12   then David went and took the bones of Saul and the bones of Jonathan his son from the men of Jabesh-gilead, who had stolen them from the open square of Beth-shan, where the Philistines had hanged them on the day the Philistines struck down Saul in Gilboa.

13   And he brought up the bones of Saul and the bones of Jonathan his son from there, and they gathered the bones of those who had been hanged.

21:14
Josh 18:28;
7:26;
2 Sam 24:25

14   And they buried the bones of Saul and Jonathan his son in the country of Benjamin in Zela, in the grave of Kish his father; thus they did all that the king commanded, and after that God was moved by entreaty for the land.

B. Victories over the Philistines

15   Now when the Philistines were at war again with Israel, David went down and his servants with him; and as they fought against the Philistines, David became weary.

16   Then Ishbi-benob, who was among the descendants of the giant, the weight of whose spear was three hundred *shekels* of bronze in weight, was girded with a new *sword*, and he intended to kill David.

21:17
2 Sam 18:3;
6:17

17   But Abishai the son of Zeruiah helped him, and struck the Philistine and killed him. Then the men of David swore to him, saying, "You shall not go out again with us to battle, that you may not extinguish the lamp of Israel."

21:18
1 Chr 20:4;
11:29

18   Now it came about after this that there was war again with the Philistines at Gob; then Sibbecai the Hushathite struck down Saph, who was among the descendants of the giant.

*21:19
1 Chr 20:5

19   And there was war with the Philistines again at Gob, and Elhanan the son of Jaare-oregim the Bethlehemite killed Goliath the Gittite, the shaft of whose spear was like a weaver's beam.

21:20
1 Chr 20:6

20   And there was war at Gath again, where there was a man of *great* stature who had six fingers on each hand and six toes on each foot, twenty-four in number; and he also had been born to the giant.

21:21
see
1 Sam 16:9
21:22
1 Chr 20:8

21   And when he defied Israel, Jonathan the son of Shimei, David's brother, struck him down.

22   These four were born to the giant in Gath, and they fell by the hand of David and by the hand of his servants.

C. David's psalm of praise

22:1
Ex 15:1;
Judg 5:1;
Ps 18:2-50
22:2
Deut 32:4;
Ps 31:3; 71:3;
91:2; 144:2
22:3
Heb 2:13;
Gen 15:1;
Luke 1:69;
Ps 9:9; 14:6;
Jer 16:19
22:4
Ps 48:1
22:5
Ps 93:4;
Jon 2:3;
Ps 69:14,15
22:6
Ps 116:3
22:7
Ps 116:4;
120:1; 34:6,
15
22:8
Judg 5:4;
Ps 77:18;
Job 26:11

22   And David spoke the words of this song to the LORD in the day that the LORD delivered him from the hand of all his enemies and from the hand of Saul.
2   And he said,
     "The LORD is my rock and my fortress and my deliverer;
3   My God, my rock, in whom I take refuge;
       My shield and the horn of my salvation, my stronghold and my
          refuge;
       My savior, Thou dost save me from violence.
4   "I call upon the LORD, who is worthy to be praised;
       And I am saved from my enemies.
5   "For the waves of death encompassed me;
       The torrents of destruction overwhelmed me;
6   The cords of Sheol surrounded me;
       The snares of death confronted me.
7   "In my distress I called upon the LORD,
       Yes, I cried to my God;
       And from His temple He heard my voice,
       And my cry for help *came* into His ears.
8   "Then the earth shook and quaked,
       The foundations of heaven were trembling
       And were shaken, because He was angry.
9   "Smoke went up out of His nostrils,

21:19 *Elhanan . . . killed Goliath.* The Hebrew text of this verse presents some difficulties. The parallel passage in 1 Chr. 20:5 says that Elhanan *killed Lahmi the brother of Goliath.* In 1 Sam. 17:4; 21:9 the death of Goliath himself is attributed to David, and it would appear that this tradition is to be preferred.

And fire from His mouth devoured;
Coals were kindled by it.

10 "He bowed the heavens also, and came down
With thick darkness under His feet.

11 "And He rode on a cherub and flew;
And He appeared on the wings of the wind.

12 "And He made darkness canopies around Him,
A mass of waters, thick clouds of the sky.

13 "From the brightness before Him
Coals of fire were kindled.

14 "The LORD thundered from heaven,
And the Most High uttered His voice.

15 "And He sent out arrows, and scattered them,
Lightning, and routed them.

16 "Then the channels of the sea appeared,
The foundations of the world were laid bare,
By the rebuke of the LORD,
At the blast of the breath of His nostrils.

17 "He sent from on high, He took me;
He drew me out of many waters.

18 "He delivered me from my strong enemy,
From those who hated me, for they were too strong for me.

19 "They confronted me in the day of my calamity,
But the LORD was my support.

20 "He also brought me forth into a broad place;
He rescued me, because He delighted in me.

21 "The LORD has rewarded me according to my righteousness;
According to the cleanness of my hands He has recompensed me.

22 "For I have kept the ways of the LORD,
And have not acted wickedly against my God.

23 "For all His ordinances *were* before me;
And *as for* His statutes, I did not depart from them.

24 "I was also blameless toward Him,
And I kept myself from my iniquity.

25 "Therefore the LORD has recompensed me according to my
righteousness,
According to my cleanness before His eyes.

26 "With the kind Thou dost show Thyself kind,
With the blameless Thou dost show Thyself blameless;

27 "With the pure Thou dost show Thyself pure,
And with the perverted Thou dost show Thyself astute.

28 "And Thou dost save an afflicted people;
But Thine eyes are on the haughty *whom* Thou dost abase.

29 "For Thou art my lamp, O LORD;
And the LORD illumines my darkness.

30 "For by Thee I can [18]run upon a troop;
By my God I can leap over a wall.

31 "As for God, His way is blameless;
The word of the LORD is tested;
He is a shield to all who take refuge in Him.

32 "For who is God, besides the LORD?
And who is a rock, besides our God?

33 "God is my strong fortress;
And He sets the blameless in His way.

34 "He makes my feet like hinds' *feet*,
And sets me on my high places.

35 "He trains my hands for battle,
So that my arms can bend a bow of bronze.

36 "Thou hast also given me the shield of Thy salvation,
And Thy help makes me great.

37 "Thou dost enlarge my steps under me,
And my feet have not slipped.

[18]Or, *crush a troop*

22:9
Ps 97:3;
Heb 12:29
22:10
Ex 19:16;
1 Kin 8:12;
Ps 97:2
22:11
Ps 104:3
22:12
Ps 97:2

22:13
v. 9

22:14
1 Sam 2:10

22:16
Hab 3:11

22:17
Ps 144:7;
32:6

22:19
Ps 23:4

22:20
Ps 31:8; 22:8

22:21
1 Kin 8:32;
Ps 24:4
22:22
Gen 18:19;
Ps 128:1
22:23
Deut 6:6-9

22:24
Gen 7:1;
17:1; Eph 1:4
22:25
v. 21

22:26
Matt 5:7

22:27
Lev 26:23

22:28
Ps 72:12;
Is 2:11,12,17
22:29
Ps 27:1

22:31
Deut 32:4;
Matt 5:48;
Ps 12:6; v. 3
22:32
1 Sam 2:2;
v. 2
22:33
Ps 27:1;
Ps 101:2,6
22:34
Hab 3:19;
Deut 32:13
22:35
Ps 144:1

22:37
Prov 4:12

38 “I pursued my enemies and destroyed them,
And I did not turn back until they were consumed.

22:39
Mal 4:3
39 “And I have devoured them and shattered them, so that they did not rise;
And they fell under my feet.

22:40
Ps 44:5
40 “For Thou hast girded me with strength for battle;
Thou hast subdued under me those who rose up against me.

22:41
Ex 23:27;
Josh 10:24
41 “Thou hast also made my enemies turn *their* backs to me,
And I destroyed those who hated me.

22:42
Ps 50:22;
1 Sam 28:6
42 “They looked, but there was none to save;
Even to the Lᴏᴿᴅ, but He did not answer them.

22:43
Ps 18:42;
Is 10:6
43 “Then I pulverized them as the dust of the earth,
I crushed *and* stamped them as the mire of the streets.

22:44
2 Sam 3:1;
Deut 28:13;
Is 55:5
44 “Thou hast also delivered me from the contentions of my people;
Thou hast kept me as head of the nations;
A people whom I have not known serve me.

22:45
Ps 66:3
45 “Foreigners pretend obedience to me;
As soon as they hear, they obey me.

22:46
Mic 7:17
46 “Foreigners lose heart,
And come trembling out of their fortresses.

22:47
Ps 89:26
47 “The Lᴏᴿᴅ lives, and blessed be my rock;
And exalted be God, the rock of my salvation,

22:48
Ps 94:1;
144:2
48 The God who executes vengeance for me,
And brings down peoples under me,

22:49
Ps 44:5;
140:1
49 Who also brings me out from my enemies;
Thou dost even lift me above those who rise up against me;
Thou dost rescue me from the violent man.

22:50
Rom 15:9
50 “Therefore I will give thanks to Thee, O Lᴏᴿᴅ, among the nations,
And I will sing praises to Thy name.

22:51
Ps 144:10;
89:20,29;
2 Sam 7:12-16
51 “*He* is a tower of [19]deliverance to His king,
And shows lovingkindness to His anointed,
To David and his descendants forever.”

D. *David's testament*

23:1
2 Sam 7:8,9;
Ps 78:70;
89:27;
1 Sam 16:12,
13; Ps 89:20
23 Now these are the last words of David.
David the son of Jesse declares,
And the man who was raised on high declares,
The anointed of the God of Jacob,
And the sweet psalmist of Israel,

23:2
2 Pet 1:21
2 “The Spirit of the Lᴏᴿᴅ spoke by me,
And His word was on my tongue.

23:3
Deut 32:4;
2 Sam 22:2,
32; Ex 18:21;
2 Chr 19:7,9
3 “The God of Israel said,
The Rock of Israel spoke to me,
'He who rules over men righteously,
Who rules in the fear of God,

23:4
Judg 5:31;
Ps 89:36
4 Is as the light of the morning *when* the sun rises,
A morning without clouds,
When the tender grass *springs* out of the earth,
Through sunshine after rain.'

23:5
Ps 89:29;
Is 55:3
5 “Truly is not my house so with God?
For He has made an everlasting covenant with me,
Ordered in all things, and secured;
For all my salvation and all *my* desire,
Will He not indeed make *it* grow?

23:6
Matt 13:42
6 “But the worthless, every one of them will be thrust away like thorns,
Because they cannot be taken in hand;

7 But the man who touches them
Must be armed with iron and the shaft of a spear,
And they will be completely burned with fire in *their* place.”

[19]I.e., victories

E. *The deeds of David's mighty men*

8 These are the names of the mighty men whom David had: Josheb-bas-shebeth a Tahchemonite, chief of the captains, he was *called* Adino the Eznite, because of eight hundred slain *by him* at one time;

9 and after him was Eleazar the son of Dodo the Ahohite, one of the three mighty men with David when they defied the Philistines who were gathered there to battle and the men of Israel had withdrawn.

10 He arose and struck the Philistines until his hand was weary and clung to the sword, and the LORD brought about a great victory that day; and the people returned after him only to strip *the slain.*

11 Now after him was Shammah the son of Agee a Hararite. And the Philistines were gathered into a troop, where there was a plot of ground full of lentils, and the people fled from the Philistines.

12 But he took his stand in the midst of the plot, defended it and struck the Philistines; and the LORD brought about a great victory.

13 Then three of the thirty chief men went down and came to David in the harvest time to the cave of Adullam, while the troop of the Philistines was camping in the valley of Rephaim.

14 And David was then in the stronghold, while the garrison of the Philistines was then in Bethlehem.

15 And David had a craving and said, "Oh that someone would give me water to drink from the well of Bethlehem which is by the gate!"

16 So the three mighty men broke through the camp of the Philistines, and drew water from the well of Bethlehem which was by the gate, and took *it* and brought *it* to David. Nevertheless he would not drink it, but poured it out to the LORD;

17 and he said, "Be it far from me, O LORD, that I should do this. *Shall I drink* the blood of the men who went in *jeopardy* of their lives?" Therefore he would not drink it. These things the three mighty men did.

18 And Abishai, the brother of Joab, the son of Zeruiah, was chief of the thirty. And he swung his spear against three hundred and killed *them*, and had a name as well as the three.

19 He was most honored of the thirty, therefore he became their commander; however, he did not attain to the three.

20 Then Benaiah the son of Jehoiada, the son of a valiant man of Kabzeel, who had done mighty deeds, killed the two *sons of* Ariel of Moab. He also went down and killed a lion in the middle of a pit on a snowy day.

21 And he killed an Egyptian, an impressive man. Now the Egyptian *had* a spear in his hand, but he went down to him with a club and snatched the spear from the Egyptian's hand, and killed him with his own spear.

22 These *things* Benaiah the son of Jehoiada did, and had a name as well as the three mighty men.

23 He was honored among the thirty, but he did not attain to the three. And David appointed him over his guard.

24 Asahel the brother of Joab was among the thirty; Elhanan the son of Dodo of Bethlehem,

25 Shammah the Harodite, Elika the Harodite,

26 Helez the Paltite, Ira the son of Ikkesh the Tekoite,

27 Abiezer the Anathothite, Mebunnai the Hushathite,

28 Zalmon the Ahohite, Maharai the Netophathite,

29 Heleb the son of Baanah the Netophathite, Ittai the son of Ribai of Gibeah of the sons of Benjamin,

30 Benaiah a Pirathonite, Hiddai of the brooks of Gaash,

31 Abi-albon the Arbathite, Azmaveth the Barhumite,

32 Eliahba the Shaalbonite, the sons of Jashen, Jonathan,

33 Shammah the Hararite, Ahiam the son of Sharar the Ararite,

34 Eliphelet the son of Ahasbai, the son of the Maacathite, Eliam the son of Ahithophel the Gilonite,

35 Hezro the Carmelite, Paarai the Arbite,

23:9
1 Chr 27:4

23:10
1 Chr 11:12-14

23:11
1 Chr 11:27

23:13
1 Sam 22:1;
2 Sam 5:18

23:14
1 Sam 22:4,5

23:17
Lev 17:10

23:18
2 Sam 10:10, 14;
1 Chr 11:20

23:20
2 Sam 8:18;
20:33;
Josh 15:21

23:23
2 Sam 8:18;
20:23
23:24
2 Sam 2:18

23:25
1 Chr 11:27

23:8 Compare this verse with 1 Chr. 11:11, where the figure used is *three hundred.* The first letter of the Hebrew words for three and eight is the same, and in a marred original might have been read incorrectly. Since the two preceding words in the extant Hebrew text of v. 8 are unintelligible, it is possible that the obscurity in the original continued on through the number itself. The 1 Chronicles reference is more likely to be the correct one.

36   Igal the son of Nathan of Zobah, Bani the Gadite,

37   Zelek the Ammonite, Naharai the Beerothite, armor bearers of Joab the son of Zeruiah,

38   Ira the Ithrite, Gareb the Ithrite,

39   Uriah the Hittite; thirty-seven in all.

23:38
2 Sam 20:26
23:39
2 Sam 11:3,6

F. *David's census and punishment*

1. *The numbering of the people*

*24:1
2 Sam 20:1,2;
1 Chr 27:23,
24
24:2
2 Sam 3:10;
Judg 20:1

24 Now again the anger of the LORD burned against Israel, and it incited David against them to say, "Go, number Israel and Judah."

2   And the king said to Joab the commander of the army who was with him, "Go about now through all the tribes of Israel, from Dan to Beersheba, and register the people, that I may know the number of the people."

3   But Joab said to the king, "Now may the LORD your God add to the people a hundred times as many as they are, while the eyes of my lord the king *still* see; but why does my lord the king delight in this thing?"

4   Nevertheless, the king's word prevailed against Joab and against the commanders of the army. So Joab and the commanders of the army went out from the presence of the king, to register the people of Israel.

24:5
Deut 2:36;
Josh 13:9,16;
Num 32:1,3
24:6
Josh 19:28
24:7
Josh 11:3;
Gen 21:22-33

5   And they crossed the Jordan and camped in Aroer, on the right side of the city that is in the middle of the valley of Gad, and toward Jazer.

6   Then they came to Gilead and to [20]the land of Tahtim-hodshi, and they came to Dan-jaan and around to Sidon,

7   and came to the fortress of Tyre and to all the cities of the Hivites and of the Canaanites, and they went out to the south of Judah, *to* Beersheba.

8   So when they had gone about through the whole land, they came to Jerusalem at the end of nine months and twenty days.

*24:9
1 Chr 21:5

9   And Joab gave the number of the registration of the people to the king; and there were in Israel eight hundred thousand valiant men who drew the sword, and the men of Judah were five hundred thousand men.

2. *David's choice of punishment*

24:10
1 Sam 24:5;
2 Sam 12:13;
1 Sam 13:13
24:11
1 Sam 22:5;
9:9;
1 Chr 29:29
24:12
1 Chr 21:12

10   Now David's heart troubled him after he had numbered the people. So David said to the LORD, "I have sinned greatly in what I have done. But now, O LORD, please take away the iniquity of Thy servant, for I have acted very foolishly."

11   When David arose in the morning, the word of the LORD came to the prophet Gad, David's seer, saying,

12   "Go and speak to David, 'Thus the LORD says, "I am offering you three things; choose for yourself one of them, which I may do to you."'"

13   So Gad came to David and told him, and said to him, "Shall seven years of famine come to you in your land? Or will you flee three months before your foes while they pursue you? Or shall there be three days' pestilence in your land? Now consider and see what answer I shall return to Him who sent me."

24:14
Ps 103:8,13,
14

14   Then David said to Gad, "I am in great distress. Let us now fall into the hand of the LORD for His mercies are great, but do not let me fall into the hand of man."

3. *The pestilence*

24:15
1 Chr 21:14;
27:24

15   So the LORD sent a pestilence upon Israel from the morning until the appointed time; and seventy thousand men of the people from Dan to Beersheba died.

24:16
Ex 12:23;
Gen 6:6;
1 Sam 15:11

16   When the angel stretched out his hand toward Jerusalem to destroy it, the LORD relented from the calamity, and said to the angel who destroyed the people,

[20]Or, *Kadesh in the land of the Hittite*

24:1 *the anger of the LORD . . . incited David.* The census had fearful consequences, perhaps because it was an indication of David's trust in men rather than in God. Here the anger of the LORD is said to have incited David. In 1 Chr. 21:1 Satan incited him. Both are true. God was the ultimate cause in the sense that he permitted Satan to incite David. **24:9** Cf. 1 Chr. 21:5. The numbers given in the two ac-

counts vary. Three possible explanations have been given for the discrepancy: (1) that the statements were taken from oral tradition and not from written records; (2) that there have been copyists' errors in either one or both accounts; and (3) that the difference is due to the exclusion or inclusion of the men in the standing army. Either (2) or (3) is preferred.

"It is enough! Now relax your hand!" And the angel of the LORD was by the threshing floor of Araunah the Jebusite.

17   Then David spoke to the LORD when he saw the angel who was striking down the people, and said, "Behold, it is I who have sinned, and it is I who have done wrong; but these sheep, what have they done? Please let Thy hand be against me and against my father's house."

4. *The altar of the threshing floor of Araunah*

18   So Gad came to David that day and said to him, "Go up, erect an altar to the LORD on the threshing floor of Araunah the Jebusite."

19   And David went up according to the word of Gad, just as the LORD had commanded.

20   And Araunah looked down and saw the king and his servants crossing over toward him; and Araunah went out and bowed his face to the ground before the king.

21   Then Araunah said, "Why has my lord the king come to his servant?" And David said, "To buy the threshing floor from you, in order to build an altar to the LORD, that the plague may be held back from the people."

22   And Araunah said to David, "Let my lord the king take and offer up what is good in his sight. Look, the oxen for the burnt offering, the threshing sledges and the yokes of the oxen for the wood.

23   "Everything, O king, Araunah gives to the king." And Araunah said to the king, "May the LORD your God accept you."

24   However, the king said to Araunah, "No, but I will surely buy *it* from you for a price, for I will not offer burnt offerings to the LORD my God which cost me nothing." So David bought the threshing floor and the oxen for fifty shekels of silver.

25   And David built there an altar to the LORD, and offered burnt offerings and peace offerings. Thus the LORD was moved by entreaty for the land, and the plague was held back from Israel.

24:17
v. 10;
1 Chr 21:17

24:18
1 Chr 21:18ff

24:21
Num 16:48,
50

24:22
1 Kin 19:21

24:23
Ezek 20:40,
41
24:24
1 Chr 21:24,
25

24:25
2 Sam 21:14;
v. 21

INTRODUCTION TO
THE FIRST BOOK OF THE
KINGS

Authorship and Background: 1 and 2 Kings, like the two books of Samuel, were originally a single book. The Septuagint translators considered these two larger books a complete history of the kingdoms of Israel and Judah, and after dividing them into four books they named them "Books of Kingdoms," instead of the Hebrew titles "Samuel" and "Kings." Jerome followed the same division in his Latin Vulgate, but he changed the title to "Books of Kings." The various English Bibles have retained the Hebrew titles, while following the divisions of the Septuagint and Vulgate. In some instances the four books are subtitled "First, Second, Third, and Fourth Book of Kings," as in the Vulgate.

1 and 2 Kings cover the period from Adonijah's revolt against David to the release of Jehoiachin from prison in Babylonia about 561 B.C. Jewish tradition attributed the books to Jeremiah. While this cannot be verified, the evidence indicates that the author, whoever he was, did most of his work after Josiah's reform in 621 B.C., with subsequent events being added at various times later on. The fact that David's reign closes in 1 and 2 Kings indicates that Samuel-Kings were probably a consecutive history composed by the same individual. As in the case of Samuel, the writer of Kings used early source materials: for example, the court records of Solomon and of the various kings of Israel and Judah, as well as oral or written narratives concerning Elijah and Elisha.

Characteristics: The author of 1 and 2 Kings gives no chronological data as he covers the last days of the reign of David and the reign of Solomon. After Solomon's day, when the kingdom is divided, he presents in a chronological framework the king or kings of one kingdom and then of the other. Even though each successive king is mentioned in order, chronological problems are numerous because the two kingdoms figured their dates differently: part of a year was considered as a full year in some instances; and sons shared the throne with their fathers in co-regencies.

The author's primary aim is not to chronicle all events of national significance during Solomon's reign and in the divided kingdom. He selects incidents from this era for the purpose of showing that the chosen people can endure only as bearers of God's promise and, therefore, only in the measure that they remain faithful to the covenant and keep its commandments. He reinforces the idea that Jerusalem is the only place of worship, and he does not hesitate to criticize the kings who erected other shrines or who engaged in idolatrous worship. He approves every reform that tended to stamp out idolatry. His work is sweeping and panoramic, for he deals with the history of the people of God generally and as a whole. Only two of the kings are given his unqualified endorsement, Hezekiah and Josiah (2 Kin. 18:3; 22:2). For those who are criticized, the recurring phrase, "did evil in the sight of the LORD" appears.

Contents:

I. The end of David's reign (1:1-2:46): Solomon crowned as king. Adonijah's plot. The anointing of Solomon and the death of David. Adonijah executed; Abiathar removed from the priesthood. Joab and Shimei executed.

II. The Solomonic reign (3:1-11:43): Solomon's marriage to Pharaoh's daughter. His prayer for wisdom and his first wise decision. The internal administration of his kingdom. The building of the temple. The temple dedication. Hiram's dissatisfaction. Solomon's slaves. His material opulence and magnificence. Solomon's sin and failure to repent. His death.

III. The divided kingdom (12:1-22:53): The revolt of the ten tribes under Jeroboam; the division of the kingdom. Ahijah's prophecy under Jeroboam. The two tribes under Rehoboam, Abijam, and Asa. The ten tribes under Nadab, Baasha, Elah, Zimri, and Omri. The ten tribes under Ahab; Elijah the prophet; Elisha his successor. Ahab's first and second Syrian campaigns; Micaiah's prophecy and Ahab's death. The two tribes under Jehoshaphat. The ten tribes under Ahaziah.

THE FIRST BOOK OF THE
KINGS

I. *The end of David's reign (1:1–2:46)*

A. *The struggle for the succession*

1. *David's declining strength*

1 Now King David was old, advanced in age; and they covered him with clothes, but he could not keep warm.
2 So his servants said to him, "Let them seek a young virgin for my lord the king, and let her attend the king and become his nurse; and let her lie in your bosom, that my lord the king may keep warm."
3 So they searched for a beautiful girl throughout all the territory of Israel, and found Abishag the Shunammite, and brought her to the king.
4 And the girl was very beautiful; and she became the king's nurse and served him, but the king did not cohabit with her.

2. *Adonijah seeks to be king*

5 Now Adonijah the son of Haggith exalted himself, saying, "I will be king." So he prepared for himself chariots and horsemen with fifty men to run before him.
6 And his father had never crossed him at any time by asking, "Why have you done so?" And he was also a very handsome man; and he was born after Absalom.
7 And he had conferred with Joab the son of Zeruiah and with Abiathar the priest; and following Adonijah they helped him.
8 But Zadok the priest, Benaiah the son of Jehoiada, Nathan the prophet, Shimei, Rei, and the mighty men who belonged to David, were not with Adonijah.
9 And Adonijah sacrificed sheep and oxen and fatlings by the ¹stone of Zoheleth, which is beside En-rogel; and he invited all his brothers, the king's sons, and all the men of Judah, the king's servants.
10 But he did not invite Nathan the prophet, Benaiah, the mighty men, and Solomon his brother.

3. *Nathan advises Bathsheba*

11 Then Nathan spoke to Bathsheba the mother of Solomon, saying, "Have you not heard that Adonijah the son of Haggith has become king, and David our lord does not know *it?*
12 "So now come, please let me give you counsel and save your life and the life of your son Solomon.
13 "Go at once to King David and say to him, 'Have you not, my lord, O king, sworn to your maidservant, saying, "Surely Solomon your son shall be king after me, and he shall sit on my throne"? Why then has Adonijah become king?'
14 "Behold, while you are still there speaking with the king, I will come in after you and confirm your words."

4. *Bathsheba talks to David*

15 So Bathsheba went in to the king in the bedroom. Now the king was very old, and Abishag the Shunammite was ministering to the king.
16 Then Bathsheba bowed and prostrated herself before the king. And the king said, "What do you wish?"
17 And she said to him, "My lord, you swore to your maidservant by the LORD

¹Or, *Gliding or Serpent Stone*

1:3 Josh 19:18

*1:5 2 Sam 3:4; 15:1
1:6 2 Sam 3:3,4
1:7 1 Chr 11:6; 2 Sam 20:25; 1 Kin 2:22,28
1:8 2 Sam 20:25; 8:18; 12:1; 23:8
*1:9 2 Sam 17:17
1:10 2 Sam 12:24

1:11 2 Sam 3:4

*1:13 v. 30; 1 Chr 22:9-13

1:15 v. 1

1:17 vv. 13,30

1:5 With the death of Absalom, the right of succession, according to ancient custom, fell on Adonijah, the next eldest. But David did not inform him that the custom (see 2:15) was to be ignored. Thus Adonijah was not totally at fault in seeking the throne.

1:9 Adonijah was celebrating his anticipated seizure of the throne.
1:13 Secretly David had promised Bathsheba that Solomon was to reign next.

your God, *saying,* 'Surely your son Solomon shall be king after me and he shall sit on my throne.'

18 "And now, behold, Adonijah is king; and now, my lord the king, you do not know *it.*

19 "And he has sacrificed oxen and fatlings and sheep in abundance, and has invited all the sons of the king and Abiathar the priest and Joab the commander of the army; but he has not invited Solomon your servant.

20 "And as for you now, my lord the king, the eyes of all Israel are on you, to tell them who shall sit on the throne of my lord the king after him.

21 "Otherwise it will come about, as soon as my lord the king sleeps with his fathers, that I and my son Solomon will be considered offenders."

5. *Nathan speaks for Solomon*

22 And behold, while she was still speaking with the king, Nathan the prophet came in.

23 And they told the king, saying, "Here is Nathan the prophet." And when he came in before the king, he prostrated himself before the king with his face to the ground.

24 Then Nathan said, "My lord the king, have you said, 'Adonijah shall be king after me, and he shall sit on my throne'?

25 "For he has gone down today and has sacrificed oxen and fatlings and sheep in abundance, and has invited all the king's sons and the commanders of the army and Abiathar the priest, and behold, they are eating and drinking before him; and they say, '*Long* live King Adonijah!'

26 "But me, *even* me your servant, and Zadok the priest and Benaiah the son of Jehoiada and your servant Solomon, he has not invited.

27 "Has this thing been done by my lord the king, and you have not shown to your servants who should sit on the throne of my lord the king after him?"

6. *David decides for Solomon*

a. *Bathsheba informed*

28 Then King David answered and said, "Call Bathsheba to me." And she came into the king's presence and stood before the king.

29 And the king vowed and said, "As the LORD lives, who has redeemed my life from all distress,

30 surely as I vowed to you by the LORD the God of Israel, saying, 'Your son Solomon shall be king after me, and he shall sit on my throne in my place'; I will indeed do so this day."

31 Then Bathsheba bowed with her face to the ground, and prostrated herself before the king and said, "May my lord King David live forever."

b. *Zadok and Nathan instructed*

32 Then King David said, "Call to me Zadok the priest, Nathan the prophet, and Benaiah the son of Jehoiada." And they came into the king's presence.

33 And the king said to them, "Take with you the servants of your lord, and have my son Solomon ride on my own mule, and bring him down to Gihon.

34 "And let Zadok the priest and Nathan the prophet anoint him there as king over Israel, and blow the trumpet and say, '*Long* live King Solomon!'

35 "Then you shall come up after him, and he shall come and sit on my throne and be king in my place; for I have appointed him to be ruler over Israel and Judah."

36 And Benaiah the son of Jehoiada answered the king and said, "Amen! Thus may the LORD, the God of my lord the king, say.

37 "As the LORD has been with my lord the king, so may He be with Solomon, and make his throne greater than the throne of my lord King David!"

c. *Solomon anointed*

38 So Zadok the priest, Nathan the prophet, Benaiah the son of Jehoiada, the Cherethites, and the Pelethites went down and had Solomon ride on King David's mule, and brought him to Gihon.

39 Zadok the priest then took the horn of oil from the tent and anointed Solomon. Then they blew the trumpet, and all the people said, "*Long* live King Solomon!"

Margin references:

1:19
v. 9

1:21
Deut 31:16;
1 Kin 2:10

1:25
v. 9;
1 Sam 10:24

1:26
vv. 8,10

1:29
2 Sam 4:9

1:30
vv. 13,17

1:31
Neh 2:3;
Dan 2:4

1:33
2 Sam 20:6,7

1:34
1 Sam 10:1;
16:3,12;
2 Sam 15:10;
v. 25

1:37
Josh 1:5,17;
1 Sam 20:13;
v. 47

1:38
vv. 8,33;
2 Sam 8:18

1:39
Ex 30:23-32;
Ps 89:20;
1 Chr 29:22;
v. 34

40 And all the people went up after him, and the people were playing on flutes and rejoicing with great joy, so that the earth shook at their noise.

7. *The submission of Adonijah*

41 Now Adonijah and all the guests who were with him heard *it*, as they finished eating. When Joab heard the sound of the trumpet, he said, "Why is the city making such an uproar?"

42 While he was still speaking, behold, Jonathan the son of Abiathar the priest came. Then Adonijah said, "Come in, for you are a valiant man and bring good news."

43 But Jonathan answered and said to Adonijah, "No! Our lord King David has made Solomon king.

44 "The king has also sent with him Zadok the priest, Nathan the prophet, Benaiah the son of Jehoiada, the Cherethites, and the Pelethites; and they have made him ride on the king's mule.

45 "And Zadok the priest and Nathan the prophet have anointed him king in Gihon, and they have come up from there rejoicing, so that the city is in an uproar. This is the noise which you have heard.

46 "Besides, Solomon has even taken his seat on the throne of the kingdom.

47 "And moreover, the king's servants came to bless our lord King David, saying, 'May your God make the name of Solomon better than your name and his throne greater than your throne!' And the king bowed himself on the bed.

48 "The king has also said thus, 'Blessed be the LORD, the God of Israel, who has granted one to sit on my throne today while my own eyes see *it*.'"

49 Then all the guests of Adonijah were terrified; and they arose and each went on his way.

50 And Adonijah was afraid of Solomon, and he arose, went and took hold of the horns of the altar.

51 Now it was told Solomon, saying, "Behold, Adonijah is afraid of King Solomon, for behold, he has taken hold of the horns of the altar, saying, 'Let King Solomon swear to me today that he will not put his servant to death with the sword.'"

52 And Solomon said, "If he will be a worthy man, not one of his hairs will fall to the ground; but if wickedness is found in him, he will die."

53 So King Solomon sent, and they brought him down from the altar. And he came and prostrated himself before King Solomon, and Solomon said to him, "Go to your house."

B. *David's last words and death*

1. *The charge to Solomon*

2 As David's time to die drew near, he charged Solomon his son, saying,

2 "I am going the way of all the earth. Be strong, therefore, and show yourself a man.

3 "And keep the charge of the LORD your God, to walk in His ways, to keep His statutes, His commandments, His ordinances, and His testimonies, according to what is written in the law of Moses, that you may succeed in all that you do and wherever you turn,

4 so that the LORD may carry out His promise which He spoke concerning me, saying, 'If your sons are careful of their way, to walk before Me in [2]truth with all their heart and with all their soul, you shall not lack a man on the throne of Israel.'

2. *David's last orders*

5 "Now you also know what Joab the son of Zeruiah did to me, what he did to the two commanders of the armies of Israel, to Abner the son of Ner, and to Amasa the son of Jether, whom he killed; he also shed the blood of war in peace. And he put the blood of war on his belt about his waist, and on his sandals on his feet.

6 "So act according to your wisdom, and do not let his gray hair go down to Sheol in peace.

[2]Or, *faithfulness*

1:50 *horns of the altar*, attached to the corners of the altar. By this act Adonijah was appealing for sanctuary until his cause could be heard in court.

7 "But show kindness to the sons of Barzillai the Gileadite, and let them be among those who eat at your table; for they assisted me when I fled from Absalom your brother.

8 "And behold, there is with you Shimei the son of Gera the Benjamite, of Bahurim; now it was he who cursed me with a violent curse on the day I went to Mahanaim. But when he came down to me at the Jordan, I swore to him by the LORD, saying, 'I will not put you to death with the sword.'

9 "Now therefore, do not let him go unpunished, for you are a wise man; and you will know what you ought to do to him, and you will bring his gray hair down to Sheol with blood."

3. *David's death*

10 Then David slept with his fathers and was buried in the city of David.

11 And the days that David reigned over Israel *were* forty years: seven years he reigned in Hebron, and thirty-three years he reigned in Jerusalem.

12 And Solomon sat on the throne of David his father, and his kingdom was firmly established.

C. *Solomon executes David's orders*

1. *Adonijah put to death*

13 Now Adonijah the son of Haggith came to Bathsheba the mother of Solomon. And she said, "Do you come peacefully?" And he said, "Peacefully."

14 Then he said, "I have something *to say* to you." And she said, "Speak."

15 So he said, "You know that the kingdom was mine and that all Israel expected me to be king; however, the kingdom has turned about and become my brother's, for it was his from the LORD.

16 "And now I am making one request of you; do not ³refuse me." And she said to him, "Speak."

17 Then he said, "Please speak to Solomon the king, for he will not refuse you, that he may give me Abishag the Shunammite as a wife."

18 And Bathsheba said, "Very well; I will speak to the king for you."

19 So Bathsheba went to King Solomon to speak to him for Adonijah. And the king arose to meet her, bowed before her, and sat on his throne; then he had a throne set for the king's mother, and she sat on his right.

20 Then she said, "I am making one small request of you; do not refuse me." And the king said to her, "Ask, my mother, for I will not refuse you."

21 So she said, "Let Abishag the Shunammite be given to Adonijah your brother as a wife."

22 And King Solomon answered and said to his mother, "And why are you asking Abishag the Shunammite for Adonijah? Ask for him also the kingdom—for he is my older brother—even for him, for Abiathar the priest, and for Joab the son of Zeruiah!"

23 Then King Solomon swore by the LORD, saying, "May God do so to me and more also, if Adonijah has not spoken this word against his own life.

24 "Now therefore, as the LORD lives, who has established me and set me on the throne of David my father, and who has made me a house as He promised, surely Adonijah will be put to death today."

25 So King Solomon sent Benaiah the son of Jehoiada; and he fell upon him so that he died.

2. *Abiathar banished*

26 Then to Abiathar the priest the king said, "Go to Anathoth to your own field, for you deserve to die; but I will not put you to death at this time, because you carried the ark of the Lord GOD before my father David, and because you were afflicted in everything with which my father was afflicted."

27 So Solomon dismissed Abiathar from being priest to the LORD, in order to

---

³Lit., *turn away my (your) face,* and so in vv. 17, 20

Marginal references:

2:7
2 Sam 19:31, 38; 9:7,10; 17:27

2:8
2 Sam 16:5-8; 19:18-23

2:9
v. 6

2:10
Acts 2:29; 2 Sam 5:7
2:11
2 Sam 5:4; 1 Chr 29:26, 27
2:12
1 Chr 29:23; 2 Chr 1:1

2:13
1 Sam 16:4

2:15
1 Kin 1:5; 1 Chr 22:9, 10; 28:5-7

2:17
1 Kin 1:3,4

2:19
Ps 45:9

2:20
v. 16

*2:21
1 Kin 1:3,4

2:22
2 Sam 12:8; 1 Kin 1:6,7

2:23
Ruth 1:17

2:24
2 Sam 7:11, 13; 1 Chr 22:10

2:26
Josh 21:18; 1 Sam 23:6; 2 Sam 15:24-29; 1 Sam 22:20-23

*2:27
1 Sam 2:31-35

2:21 The request that Abishag the Shunammite be given to Adonijah, the older brother of Solomon, to be his wife had sinister implications. Adonijah might later renew his claim for the throne of David (in preference to Solomon) on the ground that he had married David's last wife. Solomon sensed these dangerous potentialities, saying ironically to Bathsheba, ". . . *Ask for him also the kingdom* . . ." (v. 22). Naturally he refused the request and took energetic measures against his treasonous brother.

2:27 Because Abiathar, the great-grandson of Eli, had

fulfill the word of the LORD, which He had spoken concerning the house of Eli in Shiloh.

3. Joab slain

28 Now the news came to Joab, for Joab had followed Adonijah, although he had not followed Absalom. And Joab fled to the tent of the LORD and took hold of the horns of the altar.

29 And it was told King Solomon that Joab had fled to the tent of the LORD, and behold, he is beside the altar. Then Solomon sent Benaiah the son of Jehoiada, saying, "Go, fall upon him."

30 So Benaiah came to the tent of the LORD, and said to him, "Thus the king has said, 'Come out.'" But he said, "No, for I will die here." And Benaiah brought the king word again, saying, "Thus spoke Joab, and thus he answered me."

31 And the king said to him, "Do as he has spoken and fall upon him and bury him, that you may remove from me and from my father's house the blood which Joab shed without cause.

32 "And the LORD will return his blood on his own head, because he fell upon two men more righteous and better than he and killed them with the sword, while my father David did not know it: Abner the son of Ner, commander of the army of Israel, and Amasa the son of Jether, commander of the army of Judah.

33 "So shall their blood return on the head of Joab and on the head of his descendants forever; but to David and his descendants and his house and his throne, may there be peace from the LORD forever."

34 Then Benaiah the son of Jehoiada went up and fell upon him and put him to death, and he was buried at his own house in the wilderness.

35 And the king appointed Benaiah the son of Jehoiada over the army in his place, and the king appointed Zadok the priest in the place of Abiathar.

4. Shimei's broken oath and death

36 Now the king sent and called for Shimei and said to him, "Build for yourself a house in Jerusalem and live there, and do not go out from there to any place.

37 "For it will happen on the day you go out and cross over the brook Kidron, you will know for certain that you shall surely die; your blood shall be on your own head."

38 Shimei then said to the king, "The word is good. As my lord the king has said, so your servant will do." So Shimei lived in Jerusalem many days.

39 But it came about at the end of three years, that two of the servants of Shimei ran away to Achish son of Maacah, king of Gath. And they told Shimei, saying, "Behold, your servants are in Gath."

40 Then Shimei arose and saddled his donkey, and went to Gath to Achish to look for his servants. And Shimei went and brought his servants from Gath.

41 And it was told Solomon that Shimei had gone from Jerusalem to Gath, and had returned.

42 So the king sent and called for Shimei and said to him, "Did I not make you swear by the LORD and solemnly warn you, saying, 'You will know for certain that on the day you depart and go anywhere, you shall surely die'? And you said to me, 'The word which I have heard is good.'

43 "Why then have you not kept the oath of the LORD, and the command which I have laid on you?"

44 The king also said to Shimei, "You know all the evil which you acknowledge in your heart, which you did to my father David; therefore the LORD shall return your evil on your own head.

45 "But King Solomon shall be blessed, and the throne of David shall be established before the LORD forever."

46 So the king commanded Benaiah the son of Jehoiada, and he went out and fell upon him so that he died. Thus the kingdom was established in the hands of Solomon.

---

defended the right of Adonijah to the throne, Solomon expelled him to Anathoth. This was interpreted as the fulfillment of 1 Sam. 2:31–36. The prophet Jeremiah was a descendant of the priests at Anathoth (Jer. 1:1).
2:28 Joab's appeal for sanctuary was rejected by Solomon because he was a murderer.
2:35 *Zadok . . . in the place of Abiathar.* From this point on, Zadok and his descendants constitute the legitimate priestly line.

II. *The Solomonic reign (3:1–11:43)*

A. *Solomon's early years: marriage to Pharaoh's daughter*

3 Then Solomon formed a marriage alliance with Pharaoh king of Egypt, and took Pharaoh's daughter and brought her to the city of David, until he had finished building his own house and the house of the LORD and the wall around Jerusalem.

2   The people were still sacrificing on the high places, because there was no house built for the name of the LORD until those days.

B. *Prayer for wisdom granted*

3   Now Solomon loved the LORD, walking in the statutes of his father David, except he sacrificed and burned incense on the high places.

4   And the king went to Gibeon to sacrifice there, for that was the great high place; Solomon offered a thousand burnt offerings on that altar.

5   In Gibeon the LORD appeared to Solomon in a dream at night; and God said, "Ask what *you wish* me to give you."

6   Then Solomon said, "Thou hast shown great lovingkindness to Thy servant David my father, according as he walked before Thee in [4]truth and righteousness and uprightness of heart toward Thee; and Thou hast reserved for him this great lovingkindness, that Thou hast given him a son to sit on his throne, as *it is* this day.

7   "And now, O LORD my God, Thou hast made Thy servant king in place of my father David, yet I am but a little child; I do not know how to go out or come in.

8   "And Thy servant is in the midst of Thy people which Thou hast chosen, a great people who cannot be numbered or counted for multitude.

9   "So give Thy servant an understanding heart to judge Thy people to discern between good and evil. For who is able to judge this great people of Thine?"

10   And it was pleasing in the sight of the Lord that Solomon had asked this thing.

11   And God said to him, "Because you have asked this thing and have not asked for yourself long life, nor have asked riches for yourself, nor have you asked for the life of your enemies, but have asked for yourself discernment to understand justice,

12   behold, I have done according to your words. Behold, I have given you a wise and discerning heart, so that there has been no one like you before you, nor shall one like you arise after you.

13   "And I have also given you what you have not asked, both riches and honor, so that there will not be any among the kings like you all your days.

14   "And if you walk in My ways, keeping My statutes and commandments, as your father David walked, then I will prolong your days."

15   Then Solomon awoke, and behold, it was a dream. And he came to Jerusalem and stood before the ark of the covenant of the Lord, and offered burnt offerings and made peace offerings, and made a feast for all his servants.

C. *Solomon's wise decision*

16   Then two women who were harlots came to the king and stood before him.

17   And the one woman said, "Oh, my lord, this woman and I live in the same house; and I gave birth to a child while she *was* in the house.

18   "And it happened on the third day after I gave birth, that this woman also gave birth to a child, and we were together. There was no stranger with us in the house, only the two of us in the house.

19   "And this woman's son died in the night, because she lay on it.

20   "So she arose in the middle of the night and took my son from beside me while your maidservant slept, and laid him in her bosom, and laid her dead son in my bosom.

21   "And when I rose in the morning to nurse my son, behold, he was dead; but

[4]Or, *faithfulness*

3:1   marriage alliance with Pharaoh. This political marriage secured peace with Egypt. It was the first of many such marriages whereby Solomon attempted to ensure a peaceful reign.
3:3,4   high places . . . great high place. Clearly, Solomon did not recognize Jerusalem as the central shrine, even though David brought the ark there. He preferred to sacrifice at various shrines around Jerusalem, in direct violation of Deut. 12:13,14.

Cross references (margin):

*3:1
1 Kin 7:8;
9:24;
2 Sam 5:7;
1 Kin 7:1; ch.
6; 9:15,19
3:2
Lev 17:3-5;
Deut 12:2,4,5

*3:3f
Deut 6:5;
Ps 31:23;
1 Kin 2:3;
9:4; 11:4,6,38
3:4
2 Chr 1:3;
1 Chr 16:39
3:5
1 Kin 9:2;
2 Chr 1:7;
Num 12:6;
Matt 1:20
3:6
2 Chr 1:8ff;
1 Kin 2:4;
9:4; 1:48
3:7
1 Chr 2:9-13;
29:1;
Num 27:17
3:8
Deut 7:6;
Gen 13:16;
15:5
3:9
2 Chr 1:10;
Prov 2:3-9;
James 1:5;
Ps 72:1,2
3:11
James 4:3
3:12
1 John 5:14,
15;
1 Kin 4:29-31
3:13
Matt 6:33;
1 Kin 4:21-24
3:14
v. 6
3:15
Gen 41:7;
1 Kin 8:65;
Esth 1:3;
Dan 5:1;
Mark 6:21
3:17
Num 27:2
3:20
Ruth 4:16

when I looked at him carefully in the morning, behold, he was not my son, whom I had borne."

22   Then the other woman said, "No! For the living one is my son, and the dead one is your son." But the first woman said, "No! For the dead one is your son, and the living one is my son." Thus they spoke before the king.

23   Then the king said, "The one says, 'This is my son who is living, and your son is the dead one'; and the other says, 'No! For your son is the dead one, and my son is the living one.'"

24   And the king said, "Get me a sword." So they brought a sword before the king.

25   And the king said, "Divide the living child in two, and give half to the one and half to the other."

26   Then the woman whose child *was* the living one spoke to the king, for she was deeply stirred over her son and said, "Oh, my lord, give her the living child, and by no means kill him." But the other said, "He shall be neither mine nor yours; divide *him!*"

27   Then the king answered and said, "Give the first woman the living child, and by no means kill him. She is his mother."

28   When all Israel heard of the judgment which the king had handed down, they feared the king; for they saw that the wisdom of God was in him to administer justice.

D. *The appointment of court officials*

4   Now King Solomon was king over all Israel.

2   And these were his officials: Azariah the son of Zadok *was* the priest;

3   Elihoreph and Ahijah, the sons of Shisha *were* secretaries; Jehoshaphat the son of Ahilud *was* the recorder;

4   and Benaiah the son of Jehoiada *was* over the army; and Zadok and Abiathar *were* priests;

5   and Azariah the son of Nathan *was* over the deputies; and Zabud the son of Nathan, a priest, *was* the king's friend;

6   and Ahishar was over the household; and Adoniram the son of Abda *was* over the men subject to forced labor.

7   And Solomon had twelve deputies over all Israel, who provided for the king and his household; each man had to provide for a month in the year.

8   And these are their names: Ben-hur, in the hill country of Ephraim;

9   Ben-deker in Makaz and Shaalbim and Beth-shemesh and Elonbeth-hanan;

10   Ben-hesed, in Arubboth (Socoh *was* his and all the land of Hepher);

11   Ben-abinadab, *in* all the height of Dor (Taphath the daughter of Solomon was his wife);

12   Baana the son of Ahilud, *in* Taanach and Megiddo, and all Beth-shean which is beside Zarethan below Jezreel, from Beth-shean to Abel-meholah as far as the other side of Jokmeam;

13   Ben-geber, in Ramoth-gilead (the towns of Jair, the son of Manasseh, which are in Gilead were his: the region of Argob, which is in Bashan, sixty great cities with walls and bronze bars *were* his);

14   Ahinadab the son of Iddo, *in* Mahanaim;

15   Ahimaaz, in Naphtali (he also married Basemath the daughter of Solomon);

16   Baana the son of Hushai, in Asher and Bealoth;

17   Jehoshaphat the son of Paruah, in Issachar;

18   Shimei the son of Ela, in Benjamin;

19   Geber the son of Uri, in the land of Gilead, the country of Sihon king of the Amorites and of Og king of Bashan; and *he was* the only deputy who *was* in the land.

E. *The household provisions*

20   Judah and Israel *were* as numerous as the sand that is on the seashore in abundance; *they* were eating and drinking and rejoicing.

Margin references

3:26
Gen 43:30;
Is 49:15;
Jer 31:20

*3:28
vv. 9,11,12

4:5
v. 7

4:8
Josh 24:33
4:9
Josh 1:35;
21:16
4:10
Josh 15:35;
12:17
4:11
Josh 11:1,2
4:12
Josh 5:19;
17:11; 3:16;
1 Kin 19:16;
1 Chr 6:68
4:13
Num 32:41;
Deut 3:4
4:14
Josh 13:26
4:15
4:16
2 Sam 15:27
4:18
2 Sam 15:32
4:18
1 Kin 1:8
4:19
Deut 3:8-10

*4:20
Gen 32:12;
1 Kin 3:8

3:28 Fulfillment of vv. 9,11,12.
4:7 *twelve deputies.* It has been inferred that Solomon divided Israel into twelve administrative districts, varying somewhat from the old tribal boundaries, in order to sup-port his elaborate building and military programs.
4:20 *were . . . rejoicing.* This happiness was short-lived because, as 12:10 indicates, Solomon put a heavy yoke on the people.

21   Now Solomon ruled over all the kingdoms from the [5]River *to* the land of the Philistines and to the border of Egypt; *they* brought tribute and served Solomon all the days of his life.

22   And Solomon's provision for one day was thirty [6]kors of fine flour and sixty kors of meal,

23   ten fat oxen, twenty pasture-fed oxen, a hundred sheep besides deer, gazelles, roebucks, and fattened fowl.

24   For he had dominion over everything west of the River, from Tiphsah even to Gaza, over all the kings west of the River; and he had peace on all sides around about him.

25   So Judah and Israel lived in safety, every man under his vine and his fig tree, from Dan even to Beersheba, all the days of Solomon.

26   And Solomon had [7]40,000 stalls of horses for his chariots, and 12,000 horsemen.

27   And those deputies provided for King Solomon and all who came to King Solomon's table, each in his month; they left nothing lacking.

28   They also brought barley and straw for the horses and swift steeds to the place where it should be, each according to his charge.

F. *Solomon's great wisdom*

29   Now God gave Solomon wisdom and very great discernment and breadth of mind, like the sand that is on the seashore.

30   And Solomon's wisdom surpassed the wisdom of all the sons of the east and all the wisdom of Egypt.

31   For he was wiser than all men, than Ethan the Ezrahite, Heman, Calcol and Darda, the sons of Mahol; and his fame was *known* in all the surrounding nations.

32   He also spoke 3,000 proverbs, and his songs were 1,005.

33   And he spoke of trees, from the cedar that is in Lebanon even to the hyssop that grows on the wall; he spoke also of animals and birds and creeping things and fish.

34   And men came from all peoples to hear the wisdom of Solomon, from all the kings of the earth who had heard of his wisdom.

G. *The building of the temple*

1. *Preparations for building*

5 Now Hiram king of Tyre sent his servants to Solomon, when he heard that they had anointed him king in place of his father, for Hiram had always been a friend of David.

2   Then Solomon sent *word* to Hiram, saying,

3   "You know that David my father was unable to build a house for the name of the LORD his God because of the wars which surrounded him, until the LORD put them under the soles of his feet.

4   "But now the LORD my God has given me rest on every side; there is neither adversary nor misfortune.

5   "And behold, I intend to build a house for the name of the LORD my God, as the LORD spoke to David my father, saying, 'Your son, whom I will set on your throne in your place, he will build the house for My name.'

6   "Now therefore, command that they cut for me cedars from Lebanon, and my servants will be with your servants; and I will give you wages for your servants according to all that you say, for you know that there is no one among us who knows how to cut timber like the Sidonians."

7   And it came about when Hiram heard the words of Solomon, that he rejoiced greatly and said, "Blessed be the LORD today, who has given to David a wise son over this great people."

8   So Hiram sent *word* to Solomon, saying, "I have heard *the message* which you have sent me; I will do what you desire concerning the cedar and cypress timber.

4:21
2 Chr 9:26;
Gen 15:18;
Ps 68:29;
72:10,11

4:24
Ps 72:11;
1 Chr 22:9

4:25
Jer 23:6;
Mic 4:4;
Zech 3:10;
Judg 20:1
*4:26
1 Kin 10:26;
2 Chr 1:14
4:27
v. 7

4:29
1 Kin 3:12

4:30
Gen 25:6;
Acts 7:22
4:31
1 Kin 3:12;
1 Chr 15:19;
2:6; 6:33
4:32
Prov 1:1;
Eccl 12:9;
Song 1:1

4:34
1 Kin 10:1;
2 Chr 9:23

5:1
vv. 10,18;
2 Chr 2:3;
2 Sam 5:11;
1 Chr 14:1

*5:3
1 Chr 22:8;
28:3

5:4
1 Kin 4:24;
1 Chr 22:9
5:5
2 Sam 7:12,
13;
1 Chr 17:12;
22:10

---

[5]I.e., Euphrates, and so through v. 24   [6]I.e., One kor equals approx. 10 bushels   [7]One ms. reads 4,000, cf. 2 Chr. 9:25

4:26 Compare this figure with the parallel account in 2 Chr. 9:25, where it is given as *4,000* rather than *40,000.* The copyist misread the Hebrew cipher for *4* as the Hebrew cipher for *40.* The lower number was probably the right one, especially in view of the modest total of 1,400 chariots

mentioned in 10:26. Some of these stalls have been found at Megiddo.
5:3 *under the soles of his feet,* a reference to the symbolic act of putting a foot on the neck of the defeated king. See note to Josh. 10:24.

5:9
2 Chr 2:16;
Ezra 3:7;
Ezek 27:17;
Acts 12:20

5:11
cf. 2 Chr 2:10

5:12
1 Kin 3:12

5:14
1 Kin 4:6

5:15
1 Kin 9:20-22;
2 Chr 2:17,18

5:17
1 Chr 22:2

*6:1
2 Chr 3:1,2;
Acts 7:47

6:2
cf.
Ezek 41:1ff

6:4
Ezek 40:16;
41:16
6:5
Ezek 41:6;
vv. 16,19-21,
31

6:7
Deut 27:5,6

6:9
vv. 14,38

6:12
1 Kin 2:4; 9:4

9 "My servants will bring *them* down from Lebanon to the sea; and I will make them into rafts *to go* by sea to the place where you direct me, and I will have them broken up there, and you shall carry *them* away. Then you shall accomplish my desire by giving food to my household."

10 So Hiram gave Solomon as much as he desired of the cedar and cypress timber.

11 Solomon then gave Hiram 20,000 kors of wheat as food for his household, and twenty kors of beaten oil; thus Solomon would give Hiram year by year.

12 And the LORD gave wisdom to Solomon, just as He promised him; and there was peace between Hiram and Solomon, and the two of them made a covenant.

13 Now King Solomon levied forced laborers from all Israel; and the forced laborers numbered 30,000 men.

14 And he sent them to Lebanon, 10,000 a month in relays; they were in Lebanon a month *and* two months at home. And Adoniram *was* over the forced laborers.

15 Now Solomon had 70,000 transporters, and 80,000 hewers *of stone* in the mountains,

16 besides Solomon's 3,300 chief deputies who *were* over the project *and* who ruled over the people who were doing the work.

17 Then the king commanded, and they quarried great stones, costly stones, to lay the foundation of the house with cut stones.

18 So Solomon's builders and Hiram's builders and the Gebalites cut them, and prepared the timbers and the stones to build the house.

2. *The description of the temple*

6 Now it came about in the four hundred and eightieth year after the sons of Israel came out of the land of Egypt, in the fourth year of Solomon's reign over Israel, in the month of Ziv which is the second month, that he began to build the house of the LORD.

2 As for the house which King Solomon built for the LORD, its length *was* sixty [8]cubits and its width twenty *cubits* and its height thirty cubits.

3 And the porch in front of the nave of the house *was* twenty cubits in length, corresponding to the width of the house, *and* its depth along the front of the house *was* ten cubits.

4 Also for the house he made windows with *artistic* frames.

5 And against the wall of the house he built stories encompassing the walls of the house around both the nave and the inner sanctuary; thus he made side chambers all around.

6 The lowest story *was* five cubits wide, and the middle *was* six cubits wide, and the third *was* seven cubits wide; for on the outside he made offsets *in the wall* of the house all around in order that *the beams* should not be inserted in the walls of the house.

7 And the house, while it was being built, was built of stone prepared at the quarry, and there was neither hammer nor axe nor any iron tool heard in the house while it was being built.

8 The doorway for the [9]lowest side chamber *was* on the right side of the house; and they would go up by winding stairs to the middle *story*, and from the middle to the third.

9 So he built the house and finished it; and he covered the house with beams and planks of cedar.

10 He also built the stories against the whole house, each five cubits high; and they were fastened to the house with timbers of cedar.

11 Now the word of the LORD came to Solomon saying,

12 "Concerning this house which you are building, if you will walk in My statutes and execute My ordinances and keep all My commandments by walking in them,

[8]I.e., One cubit equals approx. 18 in. [9]So with Gr. and versions; M.T., *middle*

6:1 *four hundred and eightieth year*. If literally true, then the exodus occurred about 1440 B.C. But other evidence (see note to Ex. 1:11, for example) points to a later date. The figure 480 may represent the 12 generations between the exodus and Solomon, figured at the round number of 40 years a generation, or it may have derived from adding the reigns of the judges plus the other periods involved.

6:3 The Solomonic temple was built about four hundred years after the "tent" or "tabernacle," and was to stand for about four hundred years. It took 30,000 Israelites and 150,000 Canaanites seven years at forced labor to complete the temple. Materials were prepared at a distance and quietly assembled. It was destroyed by the Babylonians in 586 B.C.

then I will carry out My word with you which I spoke to David your father.

13 "And I will dwell among the sons of Israel, and will not forsake My people Israel."

6:13
Ex 25:8;
Deut 31:6
6:14
vv. 9,38

14 So Solomon built the house and finished it.

15 Then he built the walls of the house on the inside with boards of cedar; from the floor of the house to the ceiling he overlaid *the walls* on the inside with wood, and he overlaid the floor of the house with boards of cypress.

16 And he built twenty cubits on the rear part of the house with boards of cedar from the floor to the ceiling; he built *them* for it on the inside as an inner sanctuary, *even* as the most holy place.

6:16
Ex 26:33;
Lev 16:2;
1 Kin 8:6;
2 Chr 3:8

17 And the house, that is, the nave in front of *the inner sanctuary*, was forty cubits *long.*

18 And there was cedar on the house within, carved *in the shape* of gourds and open flowers; all was cedar, there was no stone seen.

6:18
1 Kin 7:24

19 Then he prepared an inner sanctuary within the house in order to place there the ark of the covenant of the LORD.

20 And the inner sanctuary *was* twenty cubits in length, twenty cubits in width, and twenty cubits in height, and he overlaid it with pure gold. He also overlaid the altar with cedar.

21 So Solomon overlaid the inside of the house with pure gold. And he drew chains of gold across the front of the inner sanctuary; and he overlaid it with gold.

22 And he overlaid the whole house with gold, until all the house was finished. Also the whole altar which was by the inner sanctuary he overlaid with gold.

6:22
Ex 30:1,3,6

23 Also in the inner sanctuary he made two cherubim of olive wood, each ten cubits high.

*6:23
2 Chr 3:10-12

24 And five cubits *was* the one wing of the cherub and five cubits the other wing of the cherub; from the end of one wing to the end of the other wing *were* ten cubits.

25 And the other cherub *was* ten cubits; both the cherubim were of the same measure and the same form.

26 The height of the one cherub *was* ten cubits, and so *was* the other cherub.

27 And he placed the cherubim in the midst of the inner house, and the wings of the cherubim were spread out, so that the wing of the one was touching the *one* wall, and the wing of the other cherub was touching the other wall. So their wings were touching each other in the center of the house.

6:27
Ex 25:20;
37:9;
1 Kin 8:7;
2 Chr 5:8

28 He also overlaid the cherubim with gold.

29 Then he carved all the walls of the house round about with carved engravings of cherubim, palm trees, and open flowers, inner and outer *sanctuaries.*

30 And he overlaid the floor of the house with gold, inner and outer *sanctuaries.*

31 And for the entrance of the inner sanctuary he made doors of olive wood, the lintel *and* five-sided doorposts.

32 So *he made* two doors of olive wood, and he carved on them carvings of cherubim, palm trees, and open flowers, and overlaid them with gold; and he spread the gold on the cherubim and on the palm trees.

33 So also he made for the entrance of the nave four-sided doorposts of olive wood

34 and two doors of cypress wood; the two leaves of the one door turned on pivots, and the two leaves of the other door turned on pivots.

6:34
Ezek 41:23-25

35 And he carved *on it* cherubim, palm trees, and open flowers, and he overlaid *them* with gold evenly applied on the engraved work.

36 And he built the inner court with three rows of cut stone and a row of cedar beams.

6:36
1 Kin 7:12

37 In the fourth year the foundation of the house of the LORD was laid, in the month of Ziv.

6:37
v. 1

38 And in the eleventh year, in the month of Bul, which is the eighth month, the house was finished throughout all its parts and according to all its plans. So he was seven years in building it.

6:23 *two cherubim.* These composite representations, winged lions with human heads, had a wingspread of 15 feet. God was considered as invisibly enthroned on the cherubim (see note to Ex. 25:22). This concept led the people in Jeremiah's time to trust in the deceptive words, *This is the temple of the LORD* (Jer. 7:4); that is, God resides there, and He will never permit the temple to be destroyed.

3. The description of the palace buildings

7:1
1 Kin 9:10;
2 Chr 8:1
7:2
1 Kin 10:17,
21

7 Now Solomon was building his own house thirteen years, and he finished all his house.

2 And he built the house of the forest of Lebanon; its length was 100 [10] cubits and its width 50 cubits and its height 30 cubits, on four rows of cedar pillars with cedar beams on the pillars.

3 And it was paneled with cedar above the side chambers which were on the 45 pillars, 15 in each row.

4 And *there were artistic window* frames in three rows, and window was opposite window in three ranks.

5 And all the doorways and doorposts *had* squared *artistic* frames, and window was opposite window in three ranks.

6 Then he made the hall of pillars; its length was 50 cubits and its width 30 cubits, and a porch *was* in front of them and pillars and a threshold in front of them.

7:7
1 Kin 6:15,16

7 And he made the hall of the throne where he was to judge, the hall of judgment, and it was paneled with cedar from floor to floor.

7:8
1 Kin 3:1;
2 Chr 8:11

8 And his house where he was to live, the other court inward from the hall, was of the same workmanship. He also made a house like this hall for Pharaoh's daughter, whom Solomon had married.

9 All these were of costly stones, of stone cut according to measure, sawed with saws, inside and outside; even from the foundation to the coping, and so on the outside to the great court.

10 And the foundation was of costly stones, *even* large stones, stones of ten cubits and stones of eight cubits.

11 And above were costly stones, stone cut according to measure, and cedar.

7:12
1 Kin 6:36;
v. 6

12 So the great court all around *had* three rows of cut stone and a row of cedar beams even as the inner court of the house of the LORD, and the porch of the house.

4. The employment of Hiram

*7:13
2 Chr 4:11
*7:14
2 Chr 2:14;
4:16;
Ex 31:3-5;
35:31

13 Now King Solomon sent and brought Hiram from Tyre.

14 He was a widow's son from the tribe of Naphtali, and his father was a man of Tyre, a worker in bronze; and he was filled with wisdom and understanding and skill for doing any work in bronze. So he came to King Solomon and performed all his work.

5. The casting of the bronze pillars

7:15
2 Kin 25:17;
2 Chr 3:15

15 And he fashioned the two pillars of bronze; eighteen cubits was the height of one pillar, and a line of twelve cubits measured the circumference of both.

16 He also made two capitals of molten bronze to set on the tops of the pillars; the height of the one capital was five cubits and the height of the other capital was five cubits.

17 *There were* nets of network and twisted threads of chainwork for the capitals which were on the top of the pillars; seven for the one capital and seven for the other capital.

18 So he made the pillars, and two rows around on the one network to cover the capitals which were on the top of the pomegranates; and so he did for the other capital.

19 And the capitals which *were* on the top of the pillars in the porch were of lily design, four cubits.

7:20
2 Chr 3:16;
4:13;
Jer 52:23

20 And *there were* capitals on the two pillars, even above *and* close to the rounded projection which was beside the network; and the pomegranates *numbered* two hundred in rows around both capitals.

*7:21
2 Chr 3:17;
1 Kin 6:3

21 Thus he set up the pillars at the porch of the nave; and he set up the right pillar and named it [11]Jachin, and he set up the left pillar and named it [12] Boaz.

22 And on the top of the pillars was lily design. So the work of the pillars was finished.

[10]I.e., One cubit equals approx. 18 in.   [11]I.e., he shall establish   [12]I.e., in it is strength

7:13 *Hiram*, not the king noted in 5:1, but the architect and chief craftsman for Solomon.
7:14 *Naphtali*. See 2 Chr. 2:14, where Hiram's mother is assigned to the daughters of Dan.

7:21 Apparently these pillars were freestanding, as in Phoenician architecture, and not a structural part of the temple. The names *Jachin* and *Boaz* may represent the first words of inscriptions placed on the pillars.

6. *The molten sea*

23 Now he made the sea of cast *metal* ten cubits from brim to brim, circular in form, and its height was five cubits, and thirty cubits in circumference.

24 And under its brim gourds went around encircling it ten to a cubit, completely surrounding the sea; the gourds were in two rows, cast with the rest.

25 It stood on twelve oxen, three facing north, three facing west, three facing south, and three facing east; and the sea *was set* on top of them, and all their rear parts *turned* inward.

26 And it was a handbreadth thick, and its brim was made like the brim of a cup, *as* a lily blossom; it could hold two thousand baths.

7. *The ten brass lavers*

27 Then he made the ten stands of bronze; the length of each stand was four cubits and its width four cubits and its height three cubits.

28 And this was the design of the stands: they had borders, even borders between the [13]frames,

29 and on the borders which were between the [13]frames *were* lions, oxen and cherubim; and on the [13]frames there *was* a pedestal above, and beneath the lions and oxen *were* wreaths of hanging work.

30 Now each stand had four bronze wheels with bronze axles, and its four feet had supports; beneath the basin *were* cast supports with wreaths at each side.

31 And its opening inside the crown at the top *was* a cubit, and its opening *was* round like the design of a pedestal, a cubit and a half; and also on its opening *there were* engravings, and their borders were square, not round.

32 And the four wheels *were* underneath the borders, and the axles of the wheels *were* on the stand. And the height of a wheel *was* a cubit and a half.

33 And the workmanship of the wheels *was* like the workmanship of a chariot wheel. Their axles, their rims, their spokes, and their hubs *were* all cast.

34 Now *there were* four supports at the four corners of each stand; its supports *were* part of the stand itself.

35 And on the top of the stand *there was* a circular form half a cubit high, and on the top of the stand its stays and its borders *were* part of it.

36 And he engraved on the plates of its stays and on its borders, cherubim, lions and palm trees, according to the clear space on each, with wreaths *all* around.

37 He made the ten stands like this: all of them had one casting, one measure and one form.

38 And he made ten basins of bronze, one basin held forty baths; each basin *was* four cubits, *and* on each of the ten stands *was* one basin.

39 Then he set the stands, five on the right side of the house and five on the left side of the house; and he set the sea *of cast metal* on the right side of the house eastward toward the south.

8. *Other castings*

40 Now Hiram made the basins and the shovels and the bowls. So Hiram finished doing all the work which he performed for King Solomon *in* the house of the LORD:

41 the two pillars and the *two* bowls of the capitals which *were* on the top of the two pillars, and the two networks to cover the two bowls of the capitals which *were* on the top of the pillars;

42 and the four hundred pomegranates for the two networks, two rows of pomegranates for each network to cover the two bowls of the capitals which *were* on the tops of the pillars;

43 and the ten stands with the ten basins on the stands;

44 and the one sea and the twelve oxen under the sea;

45 and the pails and the shovels and the bowls; even all these utensils which

[13]Or, *crossbars*

Cross references (right margin)

*7:23
2 Kin 25:13;
2 Chr 4:2;
Jer 52:17
7:24
1 Kin 6:18;
2 Chr 4:3
7:25
2 Chr 4:4,5;
Jer 52:20

7:27
v. 38;
2 Chr 4:14

7:30
2 Kin 16:17;
25:13,16

7:37
2 Chr 4:14
7:38
2 Chr 4:6

7:41
vv. 17,18

7:42
v. 20

7:44
vv. 23,25
7:45
2 Chr 4:16

7:23 The filling of the molten sea with water was the work of the Gibeonites or Nethinim, who were responsible for drawing water for the house of God.
7:26 Compare 2 Chr. 4:5, where it is stated that the molten sea held 3,000 baths as against 2,000 in Kings. Different Hebrew verbs are used, and the probable answer is that the molten sea normally contained 2,000 baths, but if it was filled to the brim it would hold 3,000. Others have held that the similarity between the figures in the Hebrew indicates a transmissional error by copyists. Calculations based on the dimensions suggest a capacity of about ten thousand gallons.

Hiram made for King Solomon *in* the house of the LORD *were* of polished bronze.

46   In the plain of the Jordan the king cast them, in the clay ground between Succoth and Zarethan.

47   And Solomon left all the utensils *unweighed*, because *they were* too many; the weight of the bronze could not be ascertained.

9. *The golden vessels*

48   And Solomon made all the furniture which *was in* the house of the LORD: the golden altar and the golden table on which *was* the bread of the Presence;

49   and the lampstands, five on the right side and five on the left, in front of the inner sanctuary, of pure gold; and the flowers and the lamps and the tongs, of gold;

50   and the cups and the snuffers and the bowls and the spoons and the firepans, of pure gold; and the hinges both for the doors of the inner house, the most holy place, *and* for the doors of the house, *that is,* of the nave, of gold.

51   Thus all the work that King Solomon performed *in* the house of the LORD was finished. And Solomon brought in the things dedicated by his father David, the silver and the gold and the utensils, *and* he put them in the treasuries of the house of the LORD.

H. *The dedication of the temple*

1. *The ark brought to the temple*

8 Then Solomon assembled the elders of Israel and all the heads of the tribes, the leaders of the fathers' *households* of the sons of Israel, to King Solomon in Jerusalem, to bring up the ark of the covenant of the LORD from the city of David, which is Zion.

2   And all the men of Israel assembled themselves to King Solomon at the feast, in the month Ethanim, which is the seventh month.

3   Then all the elders of Israel came, and the priests took up the ark.

4   And they brought up the ark of the LORD and the tent of meeting and all the holy utensils, which were in the tent, and the priests and the Levites brought them up.

5   And King Solomon and all the congregation of Israel, who were assembled to him, were with him before the ark, sacrificing so many sheep and oxen they could not be counted or numbered.

6   Then the priests brought the ark of the covenant of the LORD to its place, into the inner sanctuary of the house, to the most holy place, under the wings of the cherubim.

7   For the cherubim spread *their* wings over the place of the ark, and the cherubim made a covering over the ark and its poles from above.

8   But the poles were so long that the ends of the poles could be seen from the holy place before the inner sanctuary, but they could not be seen outside; they are there to this day.

9   There was nothing in the ark except the two tablets of stone which Moses put there at Horeb, where the LORD made a covenant with the sons of Israel, when they came out of the land of Egypt.

10   And it came about when the priests came from the holy place, that the cloud filled the house of the LORD,

11   so that the priests could not stand to minister because of the cloud, for the glory of the LORD filled the house of the LORD.

12   Then Solomon said,

"The LORD has said that He would dwell in the thick cloud.

13   "I have surely built Thee a lofty house,
A place for Thy dwelling forever."

2. *Solomon's speech*

14   Then the king faced about and blessed all the assembly of Israel, while all the assembly of Israel was standing.

15   And he said, "Blessed be the LORD, the God of Israel, who spoke with His mouth to my father David and has fulfilled *it* with His hand, saying,

16   'Since the day that I brought My people Israel from Egypt, I did not choose a city out of all the tribes of Israel *in which* to build a house that My name might be there, but I chose David to be over My people Israel.'

7:46
2 Chr 4:17;
Josh 13:27;
3:16

7:48
Ex 37:10ff

7:49
Ex 31-38

7:51
2 Sam 8:11;
2 Chr 5:1

8:1
2 Chr 5:2;
2 Sam 6:17;
5:7,9

8:2
Lev 23:34;
2 Chr 7:8
8:3
Num 7:9
8:4
1 Kin 3:4;
2 Chr 1:3

8:5
2 Sam 6:13

8:6
2 Sam 6:17;
1 Kin 6:19,27

8:8
Ex 25:14

8:9
Ex 25:21;
Deut 10:2-5;
Heb 9:4;
Ex 24:8
8:10
Ex 40:34,35;
2 Chr 7:1,2

8:12
2 Chr 6:1;
Ps 97:2
8:13
2 Sam 7:13;
Ps 132:14

8:14
2 Sam 6:18
8:15
1 Chr 29:10,
20; Neh 9:5;
2 Sam 7:12,13
8:16
2 Sam 7:4-6;
Deut 12:11;
1 Sam 16:1;
2 Sam 7:8

17 "Now it was in the heart of my father David to build a house for the name of the LORD, the God of Israel.

18 "But the LORD said to my father David, 'Because it was in your heart to build a house for My name, you did well that it was in your heart.

19 'Nevertheless you shall not build the house, but your son who shall be born to you, he shall build the house for My name.'

20 "Now the LORD has fulfilled His word which He spoke; for I have risen in place of my father David and sit on the throne of Israel, as the LORD promised, and have built the house for the name of the LORD, the God of Israel.

21 "And there I have set a place for the ark, in which is the covenant of the LORD, which He made with our fathers when He brought them from the land of Egypt."

3. Solomon's prayer

22 Then Solomon stood before the altar of the LORD in the presence of all the assembly of Israel and spread out his hands toward heaven.

23 And he said, "O LORD, the God of Israel, there is no God like Thee in heaven above or on earth beneath, who art keeping covenant and *showing* loving-kindness to Thy servants who walk before Thee with all their heart,

24 who hast kept with Thy servant, my father David, that which Thou hast promised him; indeed, Thou hast spoken with Thy mouth and hast fulfilled it with Thy hand as it is this day.

25 "Now therefore, O LORD, the God of Israel, keep with Thy servant David my father that which Thou hast promised him, saying, 'You shall not lack a man to sit on the throne of Israel, if only your sons take heed to their way to walk before Me as you have walked.'

26 "Now therefore, O God of Israel, let Thy word, I pray Thee, be confirmed which Thou hast spoken to Thy servant, my father David.

27 "But will God indeed dwell on the earth? Behold, heaven and the highest heaven cannot contain Thee, how much less this house which I have built!

28 "Yet have regard to the prayer of Thy servant and to his supplication, O LORD my God, to listen to the cry and to the prayer which Thy servant prays before Thee today;

29 that Thine eyes may be open toward this house night and day, toward the place of which Thou hast said, 'My name shall be there,' to listen to the prayer which Thy servant shall pray toward this place.

30 "And listen to the supplication of Thy servant and of Thy people Israel, when they pray toward this place; hear Thou in heaven Thy dwelling place; hear and forgive.

31 "If a man sins against his neighbor and is made to take an oath, and he comes *and* takes an oath before Thine altar in this house,

32 then hear Thou in heaven and act and judge Thy servants, condemning the wicked by bringing his way on his own head and justifying the righteous by giving him according to his righteousness.

33 "When Thy people Israel are defeated before an enemy, because they have sinned against Thee, if they turn to Thee again and confess Thy name and pray and make supplication to Thee in this house,

34 then hear Thou in heaven, and forgive the sin of Thy people Israel, and bring them back to the land which Thou didst give to their fathers.

35 "When the heavens are shut up and there is no rain, because they have sinned against Thee, and they pray toward this place and confess Thy name and turn from their sin when Thou dost afflict them,

36 then hear Thou in heaven and forgive the sin of Thy servants and of Thy people Israel, indeed, teach them the good way in which they should walk. And send rain on Thy land, which Thou hast given Thy people for an inheritance.

37 "If there is famine in the land, if there is pestilence, if there is blight *or* mildew, locust *or* grasshopper, if their enemy besieges them in the land of their cities, whatever plague, whatever sickness there is,

38 whatever prayer or supplication is made by any man *or* by all Thy people Israel, each knowing the affliction of his own heart, and spreading his hands toward this house;

39 then hear Thou in heaven Thy dwelling place, and forgive and act and

8:17
2 Sam 7:2;
1 Chr 17:1

8:19
2 Sam 7:5;
12:13;
1 Kin 5:3,5
8:20
1 Chr 28:5,6

8:21
v. 9

8:22
2 Chr 6:12ff;
Ex 9:33;
Ezra 9:5
8:23
1 Sam 2:2;
2 Sam 7:22;
Deut 7:9;
Neh 1:5,9,32

8:25
2 Sam 7:12,
16; 1 Kin 2:4

8:26
2 Sam 7:25

8:27
2 Chr 2:6;
Is 66:1;
Jer 23:24;
Acts 7:49

8:29
Deut 12:11;
Dan 6:10

8:30
Neh 1:6

8:31
Ex 22:11

8:32
Deut 25:1

8:33
Lev 26:17;
Deut 28:25;
Lev 26:39

8:35
Lev 26:19;
Deut 28:23

8:36
1 Sam 12:23;
Ps 27:11;
94:12

8:37
Lev 26:16,25,
26;
Deut 28:21-23,
38-42

8:39
1 Sam 16:7;
1 Chr 28:9;

Ps 11:4;
Jer 17:10

8:40
Ps 130:4

8:42
Deut 3:24

8:43
1 Sam 17:46;
2 Kin 19:19;
Ps 102:15

8:46
2 Chr 6:36;
Prov 20:9;
1 John
1:8-10;
Lev 26:34-39;
Deut 28:36,
64
8:47
Lev 26:40;
Neh 1:6;
Ps 106:6;
Dan 9:5
8:48
Jer 29:12-14;
Dan 6:10

8:50
2 Chr 30:9;
Ps 106:46

8:51
Deut 9:29;
Neh 1:10;
Deut 4:20;
Jer 11:4

8:53
Ex 19:5;
Deut 9:26-29

8:55
v. 14
8:56
Josh 21:45;
23:14

8:57
Josh 1:5;
Rom 8:28;
Heb 13:5
8:58
Ps 119:36

8:60
1 Kin 18:39;
Jer 10:10-12
8:61
1 Kin 11:4;
15:3,14;
2 Kin 20:3

render to each according to all his ways, whose heart Thou knowest, for Thou alone dost know the hearts of all the sons of men,

40 that they may [14]fear Thee all the days that they live in the land which Thou hast given to our fathers.

41 "Also concerning the foreigner who is not of Thy people Israel, when he comes from a far country for Thy name's sake

42 (for they will hear of Thy great name and of Thine mighty hand, and of Thine outstretched arm); when he comes and prays toward this house,

43 hear Thou in heaven Thy dwelling place, and do according to all for which the foreigner calls to Thee, in order that all the peoples of the earth may know Thy name, to [14]fear Thee, as *do* Thy people Israel, and that they may know that this house which I have built is called by Thy name.

44 "When Thy people go out to battle against their enemy, by whatever way Thou shalt send them, and they pray to the LORD toward the city which Thou hast chosen and the house which I have built for Thy name,

45 then hear in heaven their prayer and their supplication, and maintain their cause.

46 "When they sin against Thee (for there is no man who does not sin) and Thou art angry with them and dost deliver them to an enemy, so that they take them away captive to the land of the enemy, far off or near;

47 if they take thought in the land where they have been taken captive, and repent and make supplication to Thee in the land of those who have taken them captive, saying, 'We have sinned and have committed iniquity, we have acted wickedly';

48 if they return to Thee with all their heart and with all their soul in the land of their enemies who have taken them captive, and pray to Thee toward their land which Thou hast given to their fathers, the city which Thou hast chosen, and the house which I have built for Thy name;

49 then hear their prayer and their supplication in heaven Thy dwelling place, and maintain their cause,

50 and forgive Thy people who have sinned against Thee and all their transgressions which they have transgressed against Thee, and make them *objects of compassion* before those who have taken them captive, that they may have compassion on them

51 (for they are Thy people and Thine inheritance which Thou hast brought forth from Egypt, from the midst of the iron furnace),

52 that Thine eyes may be open to the supplication of Thy servant and to the supplication of Thy people Israel, to listen to them whenever they call to Thee.

53 "For Thou hast separated them from all the peoples of the earth as Thine inheritance, as Thou didst speak through Moses Thy servant, when Thou didst bring our fathers forth from Egypt, O Lord GOD."

4. *Solomon's benediction*

54 And it came about that when Solomon had finished praying this entire prayer and supplication to the LORD, he arose from before the altar of the LORD, from kneeling on his knees with his hands spread toward heaven.

55 And he stood and blessed all the assembly of Israel with a loud voice, saying,

56 "Blessed be the LORD, who has given rest to His people Israel, according to all that He promised; not one word has failed of all His good promise, which He promised through Moses His servant.

57 "May the LORD our God be with us, as He was with our fathers; may He not leave us or forsake us,

58 that He may incline our hearts to Himself, to walk in all His ways and to keep His commandments and His statutes and His ordinances, which He commanded our fathers.

59 "And may these words of mine, with which I have made supplication before the LORD, be near to the LORD our God day and night, that He may maintain the cause of His servant and the cause of His people Israel, as each day requires,

60 so that all the peoples of the earth may know that the LORD is God; there is no one else.

61 "Let your heart therefore be wholly devoted to the LORD our God, to walk in His statutes and to keep His commandments, as at this day."

[14]Or, *revere*

5. *The offerings and feast*

62 Now the king and all Israel with him offered sacrifice before the LORD. | 8:62
                                                                                      2 Chr 7:4ff

63 And Solomon offered for the sacrifice of peace offerings, which he offered to the LORD, 22,000 oxen and 120,000 sheep. So the king and all the sons of Israel dedicated the house of the LORD.

64 On the same day the king consecrated the middle of the court that *was* before the house of the LORD, because there he offered the burnt offering and the grain offering and the fat of the peace offerings; for the bronze altar that *was* before the LORD *was* too small to hold the burnt offering and the grain offering and the fat of the peace offerings. | 8:64
                                                                                      2 Chr 7:7; 4:1

65 So Solomon observed the feast at that time, and all Israel with him, a great assembly from the entrance of Hamath to the brook of Egypt, before the LORD our God, for seven days and seven *more* days, *even* fourteen days. | 8:65
                                                                                      v. 2;
                                                                                      Lev 23:34;
                                                                                      Num 34:8;
                                                                                      Josh 13:5;
                                                                                      Gen 15:18;
                                                                                      2 Chr 7:8

66 On the eighth day he sent the people away and they blessed the king. Then they went to their tents joyful and glad of heart for all the goodness that the LORD had shown to David His servant and to Israel His people.

I. *God's conditional covenant with Solomon*

9 Now it came about when Solomon had finished building the house of the LORD, and the king's house, and all that Solomon desired to do, | 9:1
                                                                                          2 Chr 7:11ff;
                                                                                          1 Kin 7:1;
                                                                                          2 Chr 8:6

2 that the LORD appeared to Solomon a second time, as He had appeared to him at Gibeon. | 9:2
                                                                                                 1 Kin 3:5

3 And the LORD said to him, "I have heard your prayer and your supplication, which you have made before Me; I have consecrated this house which you have built by putting My name there forever, and My eyes and My heart will be there perpetually. | 9:3
                                                                                                           2 Kin 20:5;
                                                                                                           1 Kin 8:29;
                                                                                                           Deut 11:12

4 "And as for you, if you will walk before Me as your father David walked, in integrity of heart and uprightness, doing according to all that I have commanded you *and* will keep My statutes and My ordinances, | 9:4
                                                                                                                 Gen 17:1;
                                                                                                                 1 Kin 15:5

5 then I will establish the throne of your kingdom over Israel forever, just as I promised to your father David, saying, 'You shall not lack a man on the throne of Israel.' | 9:5
                                                                                                  2 Sam 7:12,
                                                                                                  16; 1 Kin 2:4;
                                                                                                  1 Chr 22:10

6 "But if you or your sons shall indeed turn away from following Me, and shall not keep My commandments and My statutes which I have set before you and shall go and serve other gods and worship them, | 9:6
                                                                                                                      2 Sam 7:14;
                                                                                                                      2 Chr 7:19,20

7 then I will cut off Israel from the land which I have given them, and the house which I have consecrated for My name, I will cast out of My sight. So Israel will become a proverb and a byword among all peoples. | 9:7
                                                                                                            2 Kin 17:23;
                                                                                                            25:21;
                                                                                                            Jer 7:14;
                                                                                                            Deut 28:37;
                                                                                                            Ps 44:14

8 "And this house will become a heap of ruins; everyone who passes by will be astonished and hiss and say, 'Why has the LORD done thus to this land and to this house?' | 9:8
                                                                                                        2 Chr 7:21;
                                                                                                        Deut 29:24-26;
                                                                                                        Jer 22:8,9

9 "And they will say, 'Because they forsook the LORD their God, who brought their fathers out of the land of Egypt, and adopted other gods and worshiped them and served them, therefore the LORD has brought all this adversity on them.'"

J. *Incidental details about Solomon*

10 And it came about at the end of twenty years in which Solomon had built the two houses, the house of the LORD and the king's house | 9:10
                                                                                               1 Kin 6:37,
                                                                                               38; 7:1;
                                                                                               2 Chr 8:1

11 (Hiram king of Tyre had supplied Solomon with cedar and cypress timber and gold according to all his desire), then King Solomon gave Hiram twenty cities in the land of Galilee. | *9:11
                                                                                                   2 Chr 8:2

12 So Hiram came out from Tyre to see the cities which Solomon had given him, and they did not please him.

13 And he said, "What are these cities which you have given me, my brother?" So they were called the land of [15]Cabul to this day. | 9:13
                                                                                                            Josh 19:27

14 And Hiram sent to the king 120 talents of gold.

---

[15] I.e., as good as nothing

8:63 *22,000 oxen and 120,000 sheep.* These figures seem high. If Solomon spread the sacrifices out over fourteen days—seven days to dedicate the altar and seven days of feasting (2 Chr. 7:9), it would have meant a daily sacrifice of 1,571 oxen and 8,571 sheep, an amazing feat for the priests in the middle court of the temple.

9:11 In 2 Chr. 8:2 Hiram gives the cities to Solomon, who then settles the people of Israel in them. (Hiram is spelled *Huram* in 2 Chr. 8:2.)

15 Now this is the account of the forced labor which King Solomon levied to build the house of the LORD, his own house, the 16Millo, the wall of Jerusalem, Hazor, Megiddo, and Gezer.

16 For Pharaoh king of Egypt had gone up and captured Gezer, and burned it with fire, and killed the Canaanites who lived in the city, and had given it as a dowry to his daughter, Solomon's wife.

17 So Solomon rebuilt Gezer and the lower Beth-horon

18 and Baalath and Tamar in the wilderness, in the land of Judah,

19 and all the storage cities which Solomon had, even the cities for his chariots and the cities for his horsemen, and all that it pleased Solomon to build in Jerusalem, in Lebanon, and in all the land under his rule.

20 As for all the people who were left of the Amorites, the Hittites, the Perizzites, the Hivites and the Jebusites, who were not of the sons of Israel,

21 their descendants who were left after them in the land whom the sons of Israel were unable to destroy utterly, from them Solomon levied forced laborers, even to this day.

22 But Solomon did not make slaves of the sons of Israel; for they were men of war, his servants, his princes, his captains, his chariot commanders, and his horsemen.

23 These were the chief officers who were over Solomon's work, five hundred and fifty, who ruled over the people doing the work.

24 As soon as Pharaoh's daughter came up from the city of David to her house which Solomon had built for her, then he built the Millo.

25 Now three times in a year Solomon offered burnt offerings and peace offerings on the altar which he built to the LORD, burning incense with them on the altar which was before the LORD. So he finished the house.

26 King Solomon also built a fleet of ships in Ezion-geber, which is near Eloth on the shore of the Red Sea, in the land of Edom.

27 And Hiram sent his servants with the fleet, sailors who knew the sea, along with the servants of Solomon.

28 And they went to Ophir, and took four hundred and twenty talents of gold from there, and brought it to King Solomon.

K. The visit of the queen of Sheba

10 Now when the queen of Sheba heard about the fame of Solomon concerning the name of the LORD, she came to test him with difficult questions.

2 So she came to Jerusalem with a very large retinue, with camels carrying spices and very much gold and precious stones. When she came to Solomon, she spoke with him about all that was in her heart.

3 And Solomon answered all her questions; nothing was hidden from the king which he did not explain to her.

4 When the queen of Sheba perceived all the wisdom of Solomon, the house that he had built,

5 the food of his table, the seating of his servants, the attendance of his waiters and their attire, his cupbearers, and his stairway by which he went up to the house of the LORD, there was no more spirit in her.

6 Then she said to the king, "It was a true report which I heard in my own land about your words and your wisdom.

7 "Nevertheless I did not believe the reports, until I came and my eyes had seen it. And behold, the half was not told me. You exceed in wisdom and prosperity the report which I heard.

8 "How blessed are your men, how blessed are these your servants who stand before you continually and hear your wisdom.

16I.e., citadel

9:15 the Millo, that is, "the Filling"; but its exact nature is not known. Hazor, Megiddo, and Gezer. Solomonic construction has been found in each of these Canaanite fortresses.

9:26 Ezion-geber. Evidences of the port have not been found; but an extensive copper-smelting refinery, almost certainly the work of Solomon, has been unearthed there.

9:28 Ophir. Some locate it in southern Arabia, but more likely it was along the African coast somewhere near modern Somalia.

10:1 Sheba, that is, the land of the Sabeans in southwestern Arabia. This region, the eastern part of modern Yemen, controlled the caravan routes via which incense and spice were brought from southern Arabia to Palestine.

10:5 there was no more spirit in her. This simply means that she was so overwhelmed by all the opulence and wisdom that there was no energy left in her to cope with it.

9 "Blessed be the LORD your God who delighted in you to set you on the throne of Israel; because the LORD loved Israel forever, therefore He made you king, to do justice and righteousness."

10 And she gave the king a hundred and twenty talents of gold, and a very great *amount* of spices and precious stones. Never again did such abundance of spices come in as that which the queen of Sheba gave King Solomon.

11 And also the ships of Hiram, which brought gold from Ophir, brought in from Ophir a very great *number of* almug trees and precious stones.

12 And the king made of the almug trees supports for the house of the LORD and for the king's house, also lyres and harps for the singers; such almug trees have not come in *again*, nor have they been seen to this day.

13 And King Solomon gave to the queen of Sheba all her desire which she requested, besides what he gave her according to his royal bounty. Then she turned and went to her own land together with her servants.

L. *The material splendor of Solomon*

14 Now the weight of gold which came in to Solomon in one year *was* 666 talents of gold,

15 besides *that* from the traders and the [17]wares of the merchants and all the kings of the Arabs and the governors of the country.

16 And King Solomon made 200 large shields of beaten gold, using 600 *shekels of* gold on each large shield.

17 And *he made* 300 shields of beaten gold, using three minas of gold on each shield, and the king put them in the house of the forest of Lebanon.

18 Moreover, the king made a great throne of ivory and overlaid it with refined gold.

19 There *were* six steps to the throne and a round top to the throne at its rear, and arms on each side of the seat, and two lions standing beside the arms.

20 And twelve lions were standing there on the six steps on the one side and on the other; nothing like *it* was made for any other kingdom.

21 And all King Solomon's drinking vessels *were* of gold, and all the vessels of the house of the forest of Lebanon *were* of pure gold. None was of silver; it was not considered [18]valuable in the days of Solomon.

22 For the king had at sea the ships of Tarshish with the ships of Hiram; once every three years the ships of Tarshish came bringing gold and silver, ivory and apes and peacocks.

23 So King Solomon became greater than all the kings of the earth in riches and in wisdom.

24 And all the earth was seeking the presence of Solomon, to hear his wisdom which God had put in his heart.

25 And they brought every man his gift, articles of silver and gold, garments, weapons, spices, horses, and mules, so much year by year.

26 Now Solomon gathered chariots and horsemen; and he had 1,400 chariots and 12,000 horsemen, and he stationed them in the chariot cities and with the king in Jerusalem.

27 And the king made silver *as common* as stones in Jerusalem, and he made cedars as plentiful as sycamore trees that are in the [19]lowland.

28 Also Solomon's import of horses was from Egypt and Kue, and the king's merchants procured *them* from Kue for a price.

29 And a chariot was imported from Egypt for 600 *shekels* of silver, and a horse for 150; and by the same means they exported them to all the kings of the Hittites and to the kings of the Arameans.

[17]Or, *traffic* [18]Lit., *anything* [19]Or, *Shephelah*

10:22 *ships of Tarshish.* Apparently this expression was used of large ships such as those employed in trade with Tarshish, a colony somewhere in Sardinia or southern Spain. However, W. F. Albright holds that *Tarshish* may mean "refinery." The Phoenicians controlled the Mediterranean commerce. Solomon's fleets operated in the Red Sea. Then *ships of Tarshish* would mean that the port of origin was the "refinery" at Ezion-geber. **10:28** *Kue,* that is, Cilicia in Asia Minor.

M. *Solomon breaks God's covenant*

1. *He takes strange wives*

11 Now King Solomon loved many foreign women along with the daughter of Pharaoh: Moabite, Ammonite, Edomite, Sidonian, and Hittite women,
2   from the nations concerning which the LORD had said to the sons of Israel, "You shall not associate with them, neither shall they associate with you, *for* they will surely turn your heart away after their gods." Solomon held fast to these in love.
3   And he had seven hundred wives, princesses, and three hundred concubines, and his wives turned his heart away.
4   For it came about when Solomon was old, his wives turned his heart away after other gods; and his heart was not [20]wholly devoted to the LORD his God, as the heart of David his father *had been.*
5   For Solomon went after Ashtoreth the goddess of the Sidonians and after Milcom the detestable idol of the Ammonites.
6   And Solomon did what was evil in the sight of the LORD, and did not follow the LORD fully, as David his father *had done.*
7   Then Solomon built a high place for Chemosh the detestable idol of Moab, on the mountain which is east of Jerusalem, and for Molech the detestable idol of the sons of Ammon.
8   Thus also he did for all his foreign wives, who burned incense and sacrificed to their gods.

2. *God warns Solomon*

9   Now the LORD was angry with Solomon because his heart was turned away from the LORD, the God of Israel, who had appeared to him twice,
10   and had commanded him concerning this thing, that he should not go after other gods; but he did not observe what the LORD had commanded.
11   So the LORD said to Solomon, "Because you have done this, and you have not kept My covenant and My statutes, which I have commanded you, I will surely tear the kingdom from you, and will give it to your servant.
12   "Nevertheless I will not do it in your days for the sake of your father David, *but* I will tear it out of the hand of your son.
13   "However, I will not tear away all the kingdom, *but* I will give one tribe to your son for the sake of My servant David and for the sake of Jerusalem which I have chosen."

3. *God raises up adversaries against Solomon*

a. *Hadad*

14   Then the LORD raised up an adversary to Solomon, Hadad the Edomite; he was of the royal line in Edom.
15   For it came about, when David was in Edom, and Joab the commander of the army had gone up to bury the slain, and had struck down every male in Edom
16   (for Joab and all Israel stayed there six months, until he had cut off every male in Edom),
17   that Hadad fled to Egypt, he and certain Edomites of his father's servants with him, while Hadad *was* a young boy.
18   And they arose from Midian and came to Paran; and they took men with them from Paran and came to Egypt, to Pharaoh king of Egypt, who gave him a house and assigned him food and gave him land.
19   Now Hadad found great favor before Pharaoh, so that he gave him in marriage the sister of his own wife, the sister of Tahpenes the queen.

[20]Lit., *complete with*

11:1 Solomon's many wives and his multiplying of horses, silver, and gold were flagrant violations of Deut. 17:16–17.
11:5 *Ashtoreth*, that is, Astarte, the Canaanite goddess of fertility. *Milcom.* Another designation for Molech, noted in v. 7, the god to whom children were sacrificed (Lev. 20:1–5). See also note to Zeph. 1:5.
11:9 "Backsliding" is a turning away from God that prevents any genuine fellowship. It is spoken of as leaving one's first love (Rev. 2:4). Backsliding may take many forms. It may involve an overt breach of the moral law, as in the case

of David, who committed adultery and murder (2 Sam. 11). It may involve a verbal denial of Christ, as in the case of Peter (Matt. 26:70–74). It may be disobedience to a command of God, as in the case of Saul (1 Sam. 15:11). Backsliding is not irremediable. Repentance, confession, and restitution will bring a true believer back into fellowship with God. Thus Samson repented before his death (Judg. 16:28); David repented of his sin with Bathsheba (2 Sam. 12:13); and Peter repented and became a transformed man after Pentecost (Acts 2:14ff.).

Marginal references:

11:1 Neh 13:26; Deut 17:17
11:2 Ex 34:16; Deut 7:3,4
11:4 1 Kin 8:61; 9:4
*11:5 v. 33; Judg 2:13; 2 Kin 23:13
11:7 Num 21:29; Judg 11:24; 2 Kin 23:13
*11:9 vv. 2,3; 1 Kin 3:5; 9:2
11:10 1 Kin 6:12; 9:6,7
11:11 v. 31; 1 Kin 12:15,16
11:13 2 Sam 7:15; 1 Kin 12:20; Deut 12:11
11:15 2 Sam 8:14; 1 Chr 18:12,13

20   And the sister of Tahpenes bore his son Genubath, whom Tahpenes weaned in Pharaoh's house; and Genubath was in Pharaoh's house among the sons of Pharaoh.

21   But when Hadad heard in Egypt that David slept with his fathers, and that Joab the commander of the army was dead, Hadad said to Pharaoh, "Send me away, that I may go to my own country."

22   Then Pharaoh said to him, "But what have you lacked with me, that behold, you are seeking to go to your own country?" And he answered, "Nothing; nevertheless you must surely let me go."

b. Rezon

23   God also raised up *another* adversary to him, Rezon the son of Eliada, who had fled from his lord Hadadezer king of Zobah.

24   And he gathered men to himself and became leader of a marauding band, after David slew them of *Zobah;* and they went to Damascus and stayed there, and reigned in Damascus.

25   So he was an adversary to Israel all the days of Solomon, along with the evil that Hadad *did;* and he abhorred Israel and reigned over Aram.

c. Jeroboam

26   Then Jeroboam the son of Nebat, an Ephraimite of Zeredah, Solomon's servant, whose mother's name was Zeruah, a widow, also rebelled against the king.

27   Now this was the reason why he rebelled against the king: Solomon built the Millo, *and* closed up the breach of the city of his father David.

28   Now the man Jeroboam was a valiant warrior, and when Solomon saw that the young man was industrious, he appointed him over all the forced labor of the house of Joseph.

29   And it came about at that time, when Jeroboam went out of Jerusalem, that the prophet Ahijah the Shilonite found him on the road. Now Ahijah had clothed himself with a new cloak; and both of them were alone in the field.

30   Then Ahijah took hold of the new cloak which was on him, and tore it into twelve pieces.

31   And he said to Jeroboam, "Take for yourself ten pieces; for thus says the LORD, the God of Israel, 'Behold, I will tear the kingdom out of the hand of Solomon and give you ten tribes

32   (but he will have one tribe, for the sake of My servant David and for the sake of Jerusalem, the city which I have chosen from all the tribes of Israel),

33   because they have forsaken Me, and have worshiped Ashtoreth the goddess of the Sidonians, Chemosh the god of Moab, and Milcom the god of the sons of Ammon; and they have not walked in My ways, doing what is right in My sight and *observing* My statutes and My ordinances, as his father David *did.*

34   'Nevertheless I will not take the whole kingdom out of his hand, but I will make him ruler all the days of his life, for the sake of My servant David whom I chose, who observed My commandments and My statutes;

35   but I will take the kingdom from his son's hand and give it to you, *even* ten tribes.

36   'But to his son I will give one tribe, that My servant David may have a lamp always before Me in Jerusalem, the city where I have chosen for Myself to put My name.

37   'And I will take you, and you shall reign over whatever you desire, and you shall be king over Israel.

38   'Then it will be, that if you listen to all that I command you and walk in My ways, and do what is right in My sight by observing My statutes and My commandments, as My servant David did, then I will be with you and build you an enduring house as I built for David, and I will give Israel to you.

39   'Thus I will afflict the descendants of David for this, but not always.' "

40   Solomon sought therefore to put Jeroboam to death; but Jeroboam arose and fled to Egypt to Shishak king of Egypt, and he was in Egypt until the death of Solomon.

11:32 *one tribe,* a reference to Judah. But inasmuch as Benjamin had been assimilated by its more numerous and powerful neighbor, two tribes were involved. *Jerusalem* . . . *which I have chosen.* This identifies the place referred to in Deut. 12:5–14.

Cross references: 11:21 1 Kin 2:10 | 11:23 v. 14; 2 Sam 8:3 | 11:24 2 Sam 8:3; 10:8,18 | 11:26 1 Kin 12:2; 2 Chr 13:6; 2 Sam 20:21 | 11:27 1 Kin 9:24 | 11:29 1 Kin 14:2 | 11:30 1 Sam 15:27,28 | 11:31 vv. 11-13 | 11:33 vv. 5-7 | 11:35 1 Kin 12:16,17 | 11:36 v. 13; 1 Kin 15:4; 2 Kin 8:19 | 11:38 Josh 1:5; 2 Sam 7:11,27

N. *The death of Solomon*

11:41
2 Chr 9:29

41   Now the rest of the acts of Solomon and whatever he did, and his wisdom, are they not written in the book of the acts of Solomon?

11:42
2Ch9:30

42   Thus the time that Solomon reigned in Jerusalem over all Israel was forty years.

11:43
2 Chr 9:31;
1 Kin 14:21

43   And Solomon slept with his fathers and was buried in the city of his father David, and his son Rehoboam reigned in his place.

III. *The divided kingdom (12:1–22:53)*

A. *The division of the kingdom*

1. *The revolt of the ten tribes*

*12:1
2 Chr 10:1ff

12 Then Rehoboam went to Shechem, for all Israel had come to Shechem to make him king.

12:2
1 Kin 11:26,
40

2   Now it came about when Jeroboam the son of Nebat heard *of it,* that he was living in Egypt (for he was yet in Egypt, where he had fled from the presence of King Solomon).

3   Then they sent and called him, and Jeroboam and all the assembly of Israel came and spoke to Rehoboam, saying,

12:4
1 Sam 8:11-18;
1 Kin 4:7
12:5
v. 12

4   "Your father made our yoke hard; now therefore lighten the hard service of your father and his heavy yoke which he put on us, and we will serve you."

5   Then he said to them, "Depart for three days, then return to me." So the people departed.

6   And King Rehoboam consulted with the elders who had served his father Solomon while he was still alive, saying, "How do you counsel *me* to answer this people?"

12:7
2 Chr 10:7

7   Then they spoke to him, saying, "If you will be a servant to this people today, will serve them, grant them their petition, and speak good words to them, then they will be your servants forever."

12:8
Lev 19:32

8   But he forsook the counsel of the elders which they had given him, and consulted with the young men who grew up with him and served him.

9   So he said to them, "What counsel do you give that we may answer this people who have spoken to me, saying, 'Lighten the yoke which your father put on us'?"

10   And the young men who grew up with him spoke to him, saying, "Thus you shall say to this people who spoke to you, saying, 'Your father made our yoke heavy, now you make it lighter for us!' But you shall speak to them, 'My little finger is thicker than my father's loins!

11   'Whereas my father loaded you with a heavy yoke, I will add to your yoke; my father disciplined you with whips, but I will discipline you with scorpions.' "

12:12
v. 5

12   Then Jeroboam and all the people came to Rehoboam on the third day as the king had directed, saying, "Return to me on the third day."

13   And the king answered the people harshly, for he forsook the advice of the elders which they had given him,

12:14
Ex 1:13,14;
5:5-9,16-18

14   and he spoke to them according to the advice of the young men, saying, "My father made your yoke heavy, but I will add to your yoke; my father disciplined you with whips, but I will discipline you with scorpions."

12:15
v. 24;
Judg 14:4;
2 Chr 10:15;
22:7; 25:20;
1 Kin 11:11,
31
12:16
2 Sam 20:1

15   So the king did not listen to the people; for it was a turn *of events* from the LORD, that He might establish His word, which the LORD spoke through Ahijah the Shilonite to Jeroboam the son of Nebat.

16   When all Israel *saw* that the king did not listen to them, the people answered the king, saying,

"What portion do we have in David?
We have no inheritance in the son of Jesse;
To your tents, O Israel!
Now look after your own house, David!"
So Israel departed to their tents.

12:17
1 Kin 11:13,
36

17   But as for the sons of Israel who lived in the cities of Judah, Rehoboam reigned over them.

12:1   To conciliate the northern tribes Rehoboam went to Shechem, but his haughty attitude and harsh words   alienated them all the more (v. 16).

18 Then King Rehoboam sent Adoram, who was over the forced labor, and all Israel stoned him to death. And King Rehoboam made haste to mount his chariot to flee to Jerusalem.

19 So Israel has been in rebellion against the house of David to this day.

20 And it came about when all Israel heard that Jeroboam had returned, that they sent and called him to the assembly and made him king over all Israel. None but the tribe of Judah followed the house of David.

2. God forbids Rehoboam to war against Jeroboam

21 Now when Rehoboam had come to Jerusalem, he assembled all the house of Judah and the tribe of Benjamin, 180,000 chosen men who were warriors, to fight against the house of Israel to restore the kingdom to Rehoboam the son of Solomon.

22 But the word of God came to Shemaiah the man of God, saying,

23 "Speak to Rehoboam the son of Solomon, king of Judah, and to all the house of Judah and Benjamin and to the rest of the people, saying,

24 'Thus says the LORD, "You must not go up and fight against your relatives the sons of Israel; return every man to his house, for this thing has come from Me." ' " So they listened to the word of the LORD, and returned and went *their way* according to the word of the LORD.

3. The institution of calf worship at Bethel and Dan

25 Then Jeroboam built Shechem in the hill country of Ephraim, and lived there. And he went out from there and built Penuel.

26 And Jeroboam said in his heart, "Now the kingdom will return to the house of David.

27 "If this people go up to offer sacrifices in the house of the LORD at Jerusalem, then the heart of this people will return to their lord, *even* to Rehoboam king of Judah; and they will kill me and return to Rehoboam king of Judah."

28 So the king consulted, and made two golden calves, and he said to them, "It is too much for you to go up to Jerusalem; behold your gods, O Israel, that brought you up from the land of Egypt."

29 And he set one in Bethel, and the other he put in Dan.

30 Now this thing became a sin, for the people went *to worship* before the one as far as Dan.

31 And he made houses on high places, and made priests from among all the people who were not of the sons of Levi.

32 And Jeroboam instituted a feast in the eighth month on the fifteenth day of the month, like the feast which is in Judah, and he went up to the altar; thus he did in Bethel, sacrificing to the calves which he had made. And he stationed in Bethel the priests of the high places which he had made.

33 Then he went up to the altar which he had made in Bethel on the fifteenth day in the eighth month, even in the month which he had devised in his own heart; and he instituted a feast for the sons of Israel, and went up to the altar to burn incense.

B. A man of God from Judah

1. The prophecy about Josiah

13 Now behold, there came a man of God from Judah to Bethel by the word of the LORD, while Jeroboam was standing by the altar to burn incense.

2 And he cried against the altar by the word of the LORD, and said, "O altar, altar, thus says the LORD, 'Behold, a son shall be born to the house of David, Josiah by name; and on you he shall sacrifice the priests of the high places who burn incense on you, and human bones shall be burned on you.' "

3 Then he gave a sign the same day, saying, "This is the sign which the LORD has spoken, 'Behold, the altar shall be split apart and the ashes which are on it shall be poured out.' "

12:25 *built,* that is, fortified and rebuilt.
12:28 In order to have places of worship so the people would not have to go to Jerusalem, Jeroboam set up a calf in Bethel, not far from Jerusalem, and another one in Dan, far to the north. The statement, *"behold your gods . . ."* is a quotation from Ex. 32:4, implying that these calves were the same as the golden calf made by Aaron. Some, however, contend that Jeroboam intended the calves only as pedestals, much like the cherubim, over which the invisible God was enthroned. Later on, of course, the people transferred their worship to the visible objects. In any case, this form of worship resulted in the vilest form of apostasy and set the tone for the ten tribes until their melancholy end in 722 B.C.

4   Now it came about when the king heard the saying of the man of God, which he cried against the altar in Bethel, that Jeroboam stretched out his hand from the altar, saying, "Seize him." But his hand which he stretched out against him dried up, so that he could not draw it back to himself.

5   The altar also was split apart and the ashes were poured out from the altar, according to the sign which the man of God had given by the word of the LORD.

13:6
Ex 8:8; 9:28;
Acts 8:24;
Luke 6:27,28

6   And the king answered and said to the man of God, "Please ²¹entreat the LORD your God, and pray for me, that my hand may be restored to me." So the man of God ²¹entreated the LORD, and the king's hand was restored to him, and it became as it was before.

13:7
1 Sam 9:7,8;
2 Kin 5:15
13:8
vv. 16,17;
Num 22:18;
24:13

7   Then the king said to the man of God, "Come home with me and refresh yourself, and I will give you a reward."

8   But the man of God said to the king, "If you were to give me half your house I would not go with you, nor would I eat bread or drink water in this place.

9   "For so it was commanded me by the word of the LORD, saying, 'You shall eat no bread, nor drink water, nor return by the way which you came.' "

10   So he went another way, and did not return by the way which he came to Bethel.

2. The lying prophet

13:11
v. 25

11   Now an old prophet was living in Bethel; and his sons came and told him all the deeds which the man of God had done that day in Bethel; the words which he had spoken to the king, these also they related to their father.

12   And their father said to them, "Which way did he go?" Now his sons had seen the way which the man of God who came from Judah had gone.

13   Then he said to his sons, "Saddle the donkey for me." So they saddled the donkey for him and he rode away on it.

14   So he went after the man of God and found him sitting under an oak; and he said to him, "Are you the man of God who came from Judah?" And he said, "I am."

15   Then he said to him, "Come home with me and eat bread."

13:16
vv. 8,9
13:17
1 Kin 20:35

16   And he said, "I cannot return with you, nor go with you, nor will I eat bread or drink water with you in this place.

17   "For a command *came* to me by the word of the LORD, 'You shall eat no bread, nor drink water there; do not return by going the way which you came.' "

18   And he said to him, "I also am a prophet like you, and an angel spoke to me by the word of the LORD, saying, 'Bring him back with you to your house, that he may eat bread and drink water.' " *But* he lied to him.

19   So he went back with him, and ate bread in his house and drank water.

3. The man of God killed by a lion for disobedience

20   Now it came about, as they were sitting down at the table, that the word of the LORD came to the prophet who had brought him back;

13:21
1 Sam 15:26

21   and he cried to the man of God who came from Judah, saying, "Thus says the LORD, 'Because you have disobeyed the command of the LORD, and have not observed the commandment which the LORD your God commanded you,

22   but have returned and eaten bread and drunk water in the place of which He said to you, "Eat no bread and drink no water"; your body shall not come to the grave of your fathers.' "

23   And it came about after he had eaten bread and after he had drunk, that he saddled the donkey for him, for the prophet whom he had brought back.

13:24
1 Kin 20:36

24   Now when he had gone, a lion met him on the way and killed him, and his body was thrown on the road, with the donkey standing beside it; the lion also was standing beside the body.

13:25
v. 11

25   And behold, men passed by and saw the body thrown on the road, and the lion standing beside the body; so they came and told *it* in the city where the old prophet lived.

13:26
v. 21

26   Now when the prophet who brought him back from the way heard *it*, he said, "It is the man of God, who disobeyed the command of the LORD; therefore the LORD has given him to the lion, which has torn him and killed him, according to the word of the LORD which He spoke to him."

²¹Lit., *soften(ed) the face of*

27   Then he spoke to his sons, saying, "Saddle the donkey for me." And they saddled *it*.

28   And he went and found his body thrown on the road with the donkey and the lion standing beside the body; the lion had not eaten the body nor torn the donkey.

29   So the prophet took up the body of the man of God and laid it on the donkey, and brought it back and he came to the city of the old prophet to mourn and to bury him.

30   And he laid his body in his own grave, and they mourned over him, *saying*, "Alas, my brother!"

31   And it came about after he had buried him, that he spoke to his sons, saying, "When I die, bury me in the grave in which the man of God is buried; lay my bones beside his bones.

32   "For the thing shall surely come to pass which he cried by the word of the LORD against the altar in Bethel and against all the houses of the high places which are in the cities of Samaria."

4. The continuing apostasy of Jeroboam

33   After this event Jeroboam did not return from his evil way, but again he made priests of the high places from among all the people; any who would, he ordained, to be priests of the high places.

34   And this event became sin to the house of Jeroboam, even to blot *it* out and destroy *it* from off the face of the earth.

C. The house of Jeroboam

1. Ahijah prophesies the death of Jeroboam's son

14 At that time Abijah the son of Jeroboam became sick.
2   And Jeroboam said to his wife, "Arise now, and disguise yourself so that they may not know that you are the wife of Jeroboam, and go to Shiloh; behold, Ahijah the prophet is there, who spoke concerning me *that I would be* king over this people.

3   "And take ten loaves with you, *some* cakes and a jar of honey, and go to him. He will tell you what will happen to the boy."

4   And Jeroboam's wife did so, and arose and went to Shiloh, and came to the house of Ahijah. Now Ahijah could not see, for his eyes were dim because of his age.

5   Now the LORD had said to Ahijah, "Behold, the wife of Jeroboam is coming to inquire of you concerning her son, for he is sick. You shall say thus and thus to her, for it will be when she arrives that she will pretend to be another woman."

6   And it came about when Ahijah heard the sound of her feet coming in the doorway, that he said, "Come in, wife of Jeroboam, why do you pretend to be another woman? For I am sent to you *with* a harsh *message*.

7   "Go, say to Jeroboam, 'Thus says the LORD God of Israel, "Because I exalted you from among the people and made you leader over My people Israel,

8   and tore the kingdom away from the house of David and gave it to you—yet you have not been like My servant David, who kept My commandments and who followed Me with all his heart, to do only that which was right in My sight;

9   you also have done more evil than all who were before you, and have gone and made for yourself other gods and molten images to provoke Me to anger, and have cast Me behind your back—

10   therefore behold, I am bringing calamity on the house of Jeroboam, and will cut off from Jeroboam every male person, both bond and free in Israel, and I will make a clean sweep of the house of Jeroboam, as one sweeps away dung until it is all gone.

11   "Anyone belonging to Jeroboam who dies in the city the dogs will eat. And he who dies in the field the birds of the heavens will eat; for the LORD has spoken *it*." '

12   "Now you arise, go to your house. When your feet enter the city the child will die.

13   "And all Israel shall mourn for him and bury him, for he alone of Jeroboam's *family* shall come to the grave, because in him something good was found toward the LORD God of Israel in the house of Jeroboam.

13:30 Jer 22:18
13:31 2 Kin 23:17, 18
***13:32** v. 2; 2 Kin 23:16, 17,19; see 1 Kin 16:24
13:33 1 Kin 12:31, 32; 2 Chr 11:15; 13:9
13:34 1 Kin 12:30; 14:10
14:2 1 Sam 28:8; 2 Sam 14:2; 1 Kin 11:29-31
14:3 1 Sam 9:7,8
14:4 1 Kin 11:29; 1 Sam 3:2; 4:15
14:5 2 Sam 14:2
14:7 1 Kin 11:28-31; 16:2
14:8 1 Kin 11:31ff
14:9 1 Kin 12:28; 2 Chr 11:15; Ps 50:17; Ex 34:17; Ezek 23:35
14:10 1 Kin 15:29; 21:21; 2 Kin 9:8; Deut 32:36; 2 Kin 14:26
14:11 1 Kin 16:4; 21:24
14:12 v. 17
14:13 2 Chr 12:12

(handwritten: See II kings 12:13 David was...)
(handwritten: completely; forgive)

13:32 *cities of Samaria.* The northern kingdom is designated by the name of the capital city subsequently built *and named the city . . . Samaria* (16:24).

14 "Moreover, the LORD will raise up for Himself a king over Israel who shall cut off the house of Jeroboam this day and from now on.

15 "For the LORD will strike Israel, as a reed is shaken in the water; and He will uproot Israel from this good land which He gave to their fathers, and will scatter them beyond the *Euphrates* River, because they have made their [22]Asherim, provoking the LORD to anger.

16 "And He will give up Israel on account of the sins of Jeroboam, which he committed and with which he made Israel to sin."

2. *The death of Jeroboam*

17 Then Jeroboam's wife arose and departed and came to Tirzah. As she was entering the threshold of the house, the child died.

18 And all Israel buried him and mourned for him, according to the word of the LORD which He spoke through His servant Ahijah the prophet.

19 Now the rest of the acts of Jeroboam, how he made war and how he reigned, behold, they are written in the Book of the Chronicles of the Kings of Israel.

20 And the time that Jeroboam reigned *was* twenty-two years; and he slept with his fathers, and Nadab his son reigned in his place.

D. *The kingdom of Judah*

1. *Rehoboam, son of Solomon*

a. *Judah's apostasy*

21 Now Rehoboam the son of Solomon reigned in Judah. Rehoboam was forty-one years old when he became king, and he reigned seventeen years in Jerusalem, the city which the LORD had chosen from all the tribes of Israel to put His name there. And his mother's name was Naamah the Ammonitess.

22 And Judah did evil in the sight of the LORD, and they provoked Him to jealousy more than all that their fathers had done, with the sins which they committed.

23 For they also built for themselves high places and *sacred* pillars and Asherim on every high hill and beneath every luxuriant tree.

24 And there were also male cult prostitutes in the land. They did according to all the abominations of the nations which the LORD dispossessed before the sons of Israel.

b. *Defeat by Shishak of Egypt*

25 Now it came about in the fifth year of King Rehoboam, that Shishak the king of Egypt came up against Jerusalem.

26 And he took away the treasures of the house of the LORD and the treasures of the king's house, and he took everything, even taking all the shields of gold which Solomon had made.

27 So King Rehoboam made shields of bronze in their place, and committed them to the care of the commanders of the [23]guard who guarded the doorway of the king's house.

28 Then it happened as often as the king entered the house of the LORD, that the [23]guards would carry them and would bring them back into the guards' room.

c. *Death of Rehoboam*

29 Now the rest of the acts of Rehoboam and all that he did, are they not written in the Book of the Chronicles of the Kings of Judah?

30 And there was war between Rehoboam and Jeroboam continually.

31 And Rehoboam slept with his fathers, and was buried with his fathers in the city of David; and his mother's name was Naamah the Ammonitess. And Abijam his son became king in his place.

[22]I.e., wooden symbols of a female deity. Also v. 23   [23]Lit., *runner(s)*

14:15 *Asherim*, see note to Ex. 34:13.
14:17 *Tirzah*. The first capital of northern Israel.
14:19 *Book of the Chronicles*, court records of the northern

kingdom. Similar annals were kept in Judah (v. 29). These records constituted the main sources for our books of Kings and Chronicles.

Marginal references
14:14   1 Kin 15:27-29
*14:15   2 Kin 17:6; Josh 23:15, 16; 2 Kin 15:29; Ex 34:13; Deut 12:3,4
14:16   1 Kin 12:30; 13:34; 15:30, 34
*14:17   1 Kin 16:6-9
14:18   v. 13
*14:19   2 Chr 13:2-20
14:21   2 Chr 12:13; 1 Kin 11:32, 36; v. 31
14:22   2 Chr 12:1; Deut 32:21
14:23   Deut 12:2; Ezek 16:24, 25; 2 Kin 17:9, 10; Is 57:5
14:24   Deut 23:17; 1 Kin 15:12; 2 Kin 23:7
14:25   1 Kin 11:40; 2 Chr 12:2, 9-11
14:26   1 Kin 15:18; 10:17
14:29   2 Chr 12:15
14:30   1 Kin 12:21-24; 15:6
14:31   2 Chr 12:16; v. 21

2. Abijam, king of Judah

15 Now in the eighteenth year of King Jeroboam, the son of Nebat, Abijam became king over Judah.

2 He reigned three years in Jerusalem; and his mother's name was Maacah the daughter of Abishalom.

3 And he walked in all the sins of his father which he had committed before him; and his heart was not wholly devoted to the LORD his God, like the heart of his father David.

4 But for David's sake the LORD his God gave him a lamp in Jerusalem, to raise up his son after him and to establish Jerusalem;

5 because David did what was right in the sight of the LORD, and had not turned aside from anything that He commanded him all the days of his life, except in the case of Uriah the Hittite.

6 And there was war between Rehoboam and Jeroboam all the days of his life.

7 Now the rest of the acts of Abijam and all that he did, are they not written in the Book of the Chronicles of the Kings of Judah? And there was war between Abijam and Jeroboam.

8 And Abijam slept with his fathers and they buried him in the city of David; and Asa his son became king in his place.

3. Asa, king of Judah

a. The reforms of Asa

9 So in the twentieth year of Jeroboam the king of Israel, Asa began to reign as king of Judah.

10 And he reigned forty-one years in Jerusalem; and his mother's name was Maacah the daughter of Abishalom.

11 And Asa did what was right in the sight of the LORD, like David his father.

12 He also put away the male cult prostitutes from the land, and removed all the idols which his fathers had made.

13 And he also removed Maacah his mother from being queen mother, because she had made a horrid image as an Asherah; and Asa cut down her horrid image and burned it at the brook Kidron.

14 But the high places were not taken away; nevertheless the heart of Asa was wholly devoted to the LORD all his days.

15 And he brought into the house of the LORD the dedicated things of his father and his own dedicated things: silver and gold and utensils.

b. War between Asa and Baasha; death of Asa

16 Now there was war between Asa and Baasha king of Israel all their days.

17 And Baasha king of Israel went up against Judah and fortified Ramah in order to prevent anyone from going out or coming in to Asa king of Judah.

18 Then Asa took all the silver and the gold which were left in the treasuries of the house of the LORD and the treasuries of the king's house, and delivered them into the hand of his servants. And King Asa sent them to Ben-hadad the son of Tabrimmon, the son of Hezion, king of Aram, who lived in Damascus, saying,

19 "Let there be a treaty between you and me, as between my father and your father. Behold, I have sent you a present of silver and gold; go, break your treaty with Baasha king of Israel so that he will withdraw from me."

20 So Ben-hadad listened to King Asa and sent the commanders of his armies against the cities of Israel, and conquered Ijon, Dan, Abel-beth-maacah and all Chinneroth, besides all the land of Naphtali.

21 And it came about when Baasha heard of it that he ceased fortifying Ramah, and remained in Tirzah.

22 Then King Asa made a proclamation to all Judah—none was exempt—and they carried away the stones of Ramah and its timber with which Baasha had built. And King Asa built with them Geba of Benjamin and Mizpah.

23 Now the rest of all the acts of Asa and all his might and all that he did and the

Marginal references:
15:1 2 Chr 13:1,2
15:3 1 Kin 11:4
15:4 1 Kin 11:36; 2 Chr 21:7
15:5 1 Kin 14:8; 2 Sam 11:4, 15-17; 12:9
15:6 1 Kin 14:30
15:7 2 Chr 13:2,3, 22
15:8 2 Chr 14:1
15:10 v. 2
15:11 2 Chr 14:2
15:12 1 Kin 14:24; 22:46
15:13 2 Chr 15:16-18; Ex 32:20
15:14 1 Kin 22:43; 2 Chr 15:17, 18; v. 3
15:15 1 Kin 7:51
15:16 v. 32
15:17 2 Chr 16:1ff; Josh 18:25; 1 Kin 12:27
*15:18 v. 15; 2 Chr 16:2; 1 Kin 11:23, 24
15:20 2 Kin 15:29; Judg 18:29; 2 Sam 20:14
15:22 2 Chr 16:6; Josh 21:17
15:23 2 Chr 16:11-14

15:18 Scripture mentions three kings of Damascus, all of whose names were Ben-hadad. The first Ben-hadad is mentioned here. The second one was his son, Ben-hadad II, who warred against Ahab and unsuccessfully besieged Samaria. He was defeated by Ahab at Aphek, and was smothered by Hazael, who seized the crown. Accounts of his life may be found in 1 Kin. 20 and 2 Kin. 7,8. The third Ben-hadad was the son of Hazael, and is mentioned in 2 Kin. 13:24. It was this last Ben-hadad who lost his father's Israelite conquests.

cities which he built, are they not written in the Book of the Chronicles of the Kings of Judah? But in the time of his old age he was diseased in his feet.

15:24
2 Chr 17:1

24 And Asa slept with his fathers and was buried with his fathers in the city of David his father; and Jehoshaphat his son reigned in his place.

E. *The immediate successors to Jeroboam in the northern kingdom*

1. *Nadab*

15:25
1 Kin 14:20

25 Now Nadab the son of Jeroboam became king over Israel in the second year of Asa king of Judah, and he reigned over Israel two years.

15:26
1 Kin 12:30;
14:16

26 And he did evil in the sight of the Lord, and walked in the way of his father and in his sin which he made Israel sin.

15:27
1 Kin 14:14;
Josh 19:44;
21:23

27 Then Baasha the son of Ahijah of the house of Issachar conspired against him, and Baasha struck him down at Gibbethon, which belonged to the Philistines, while Nadab and all Israel were laying siege to Gibbethon.

28 So Baasha killed him in the third year of Asa king of Judah, and reigned in his place.

15:29
1 Kin 14:10,
14

29 And it came about, as soon as he was king, he struck down all the household of Jeroboam. He did not leave to Jeroboam any persons alive, until he had destroyed them, according to the word of the Lord, which He spoke by His servant Ahijah the Shilonite,

15:30
1 Kin 14:9,16

30 *and* because of the sins of Jeroboam which he sinned, and which he made Israel sin, because of his provocation with which he provoked the Lord God of Israel to anger.

15:31
v. 16

31 Now the rest of the acts of Nadab and all that he did, are they not written in the Book of the Chronicles of the Kings of Israel?

32 And there was war between Asa and Baasha king of Israel all their days.

2. *Baasha*

15:34
1 Kin 12:28,
29; 13:33;
14:16

33 In the third year of Asa king of Judah, Baasha the son of Ahijah became king over all Israel at Tirzah, *and reigned* twenty-four years.

34 And he did evil in the sight of the Lord, and walked in the way of Jeroboam and in his sin which he made Israel sin.

16:1
v. 7;
2 Chr 19:2;
20:34
16:2
1 Kin 14:7;
15:34

16 Now the word of the Lord came to Jehu the son of Hanani against Baasha, saying,

2 "Inasmuch as I exalted you from the dust and made you leader over My people Israel, and you have walked in the way of Jeroboam and have made My people Israel sin, provoking Me to anger with their sins,

16:3
v. 11;
1 Kin 14:10;
15:29

3 behold, I will consume Baasha and his house, and I will make your house like the house of Jeroboam the son of Nebat.

16:4
1 Kin 14:11

4 "Anyone of Baasha who dies in the city the dogs shall eat, and anyone of his who dies in the field the birds of the heavens will eat."

16:5
1 Kin 14:19;
15:31

5 Now the rest of the acts of Baasha and what he did, and his might, are they not written in the Book of the Chronicles of the Kings of Israel?

16:6
1 Kin 14:17;
15:21

6 And Baasha slept with his fathers and was buried in Tirzah, and Elah his son became king in his place.

16:7
v. 1;
1 Kin 15:27,
29

7 Moreover, the word of the Lord through the prophet Jehu the son of Hanani also came against Baasha and his household, both because of all the evil which he did in the sight of the Lord, provoking Him to anger with the work of his hands, in being like the house of Jeroboam, and because he struck it.

3. *Elah*

8 In the twenty-sixth year of Asa king of Judah, Elah the son of Baasha became king over Israel at Tirzah, *and reigned* two years.

16:9
2 Kin 9:30-33

9 And his servant Zimri, commander of half his chariots, conspired against him. Now he *was* at Tirzah drinking himself drunk in the house of Arza, who *was* over the household at Tirzah.

10 Then Zimri went in and struck him and put him to death, in the twenty-seventh year of Asa king of Judah, and became king in his place.

4. Zimri

11   And it came about, when he became king, as soon as he sat on his throne, that he killed all the household of Baasha; he did not leave a single male, neither of his relatives nor of his friends.

12   Thus Zimri destroyed all the household of Baasha, according to the word of the Lord, which He spoke against Baasha through Jehu the prophet,

13   for all the sins of Baasha and the sins of Elah his son, which they sinned and which they made Israel sin, provoking the Lord God of Israel to anger with their idols.

14   Now the rest of the acts of Elah and all that he did, are they not written in the Book of the Chronicles of the Kings of Israel?

15   In the twenty-seventh year of Asa king of Judah, Zimri reigned seven days at Tirzah. Now the people were camped against Gibbethon, which belonged to the Philistines.

16   And the people who were camped heard it said, "Zimri has conspired and has also struck down the king." Therefore all Israel made Omri, the commander of the army, king over Israel that day in the camp.

17   Then Omri and all Israel with him went up from Gibbethon, and they besieged Tirzah.

18   And it came about, when Zimri saw that the city was taken, that he went into the citadel of the king's house and burned the king's house over him with fire, and died,

19   because of his sins which he sinned, doing evil in the sight of the Lord, walking in the way of Jeroboam, and in his sin which he did, making Israel sin.

20   Now the rest of the acts of Zimri and his conspiracy which he carried out, are they not written in the Book of the Chronicles of the Kings of Israel?

5. Omri

21   Then the people of Israel were divided into two parts: half of the people followed Tibni the son of Ginath, to make him king; the *other* half followed Omri.

22   But the people who followed Omri prevailed over the people who followed Tibni the son of Ginath. And Tibni died and Omri became king.

23   In the thirty-first year of Asa king of Judah, Omri became king over Israel, *and reigned* twelve years; he reigned six years at Tirzah.

24   And he bought the hill Samaria from Shemer for two talents of silver; and he built on the hill, and named the city which he built Samaria, after the name of Shemer, the owner of the hill.

25   And Omri did evil in the sight of the Lord, and acted more wickedly than all who *were* before him.

26   For he walked in all the way of Jeroboam the son of Nebat, and in his sins which he made Israel sin, provoking the Lord God of Israel with their idols.

27   Now the rest of the acts of Omri which he did and his might which he showed, are they not written in the Book of the Chronicles of the Kings of Israel?

28   So Omri slept with his fathers, and was buried in Samaria; and Ahab his son became king in his place.

F. Ahab of Israel and Elijah the prophet

1. Ahab of Israel and Jezebel his wife

29   Now Ahab the son of Omri became king over Israel in the thirty-eighth year of Asa king of Judah, and Ahab the son of Omri reigned over Israel in Samaria twenty-two years.

30   And Ahab the son of Omri did evil in the sight of the Lord more than all who were before him.

31   And it came about, as though it had been a trivial thing for him to walk in the sins of Jeroboam the son of Nebat, that he married Jezebel the daughter of Ethbaal king of the Sidonians, and went to serve Baal and worshiped him.

Marginal references:

16:12 v. 3; 2 Chr 19:2; 20:34
16:13 Deut 32:21; 1 Sam 12:21; Is 41:29
16:14 v. 5
16:15 1 Kin 15:27
16:18 1 Sam 31:4,5; 2 Sam 17:23
16:19 1 Kin 12:28; 15:26,34
16:20 vv. 5,14,27
16:23 1 Kin 15:21
*16:24 1 Kin 13:32; John 4:4
16:26 Mic 6:16; v. 19
16:30 v. 25; 1 Kin 14:9
*16:31 Deut 7:3; 2 Kin 10:18; 17:16

16:24 *Samaria.* The new capital was remarkably well built. While Omri was very wicked and his activities are mentioned in just six verses (23–28), he was a very important person from the secular point of view; and for about a century the Assyrians designated the land of Israel as the House of Omri. (See Mic. 6:16 for testimony to his importance.)
16:31 Ahab's marriage alliance with Jezebel led to official support for the immoral Baal worship fanatically practiced by his wife.

16:32
2 Kin 10:21,
26,27
16:33
2 Kin 13:6;
vv. 29,30
*16:34
Josh 6:26

32 So he erected an altar for Baal in the house of Baal, which he built in Samaria.

33 And Ahab also made the [24]Asherah. Thus Ahab did more to provoke the LORD God of Israel than all the kings of Israel who were before him.

34 In his days Hiel the Bethelite built Jericho; he laid its foundations with the *loss of* Abiram his first-born, and set up its gates with the *loss of* his youngest son Segub, according to the word of the LORD, which He spoke by Joshua the son of Nun.

2. Elijah fed

a. The ravens at Cherith

17:1
2 Kin 3:14;
Deut 10:8;
1 Kin 18:1;
James 5:17;
Luke 4:25

17 Now Elijah the Tishbite, who was of the settlers of Gilead, said to Ahab, "As the LORD, the God of Israel lives, before whom I stand, surely there shall be neither dew nor rain these years, except by my word."

2 And the word of the LORD came to him, saying,

3 "Go away from here and turn eastward, and hide yourself by the brook Cherith, which is east of the Jordan.

4 "And it shall be that you shall drink of the brook, and I have commanded the ravens to provide for you there."

5 So he went and did according to the word of the LORD, for he went and lived by the brook Cherith, which is east of the Jordan.

6 And the ravens brought him bread and meat in the morning and bread and meat in the evening, and he would drink from the brook.

7 And it happened after a while, that the brook dried up, because there was no rain in the land.

b. The widow at Zarephath

17:9
Obad 20;
Luke 4:26

8 Then the word of the LORD came to him, saying,

9 "Arise, go to Zarephath, which belongs to Sidon, and stay there; behold, I have commanded a widow there to provide for you."

10 So he arose and went to Zarephath, and when he came to the gate of the city, behold, a widow was there gathering sticks; and he called to her and said, "Please get me a little water in a jar, that I may drink."

11 And as she was going to get *it*, he called to her and said, "Please bring me a piece of bread in your hand."

17:12
v. 1;
2 Kin 4:2-7

12 But she said, "As the LORD your God lives, I have no bread, only a handful of flour in the bowl and a little oil in the jar; and behold, I am gathering a few sticks that I may go in and prepare for me and my son, that we may eat it and die."

13 Then Elijah said to her, "Do not fear; go, do as you have said, but make me a little bread cake from it first, and bring *it* out to me, and afterward you may make *one* for yourself and for your son.

17:14
Luke 4:25,26

14 "For thus says the LORD God of Israel, 'The bowl of flour shall not be exhausted, nor shall the jar of oil be empty, until the day that the LORD sends rain on the face of the earth.'"

15 So she went and did according to the word of Elijah, and she and he and her household ate for *many* days.

16 The bowl of flour was not exhausted nor did the jar of oil become empty, according to the word of the LORD which He spoke through Elijah.

c. The widow's dead son brought to life

17 Now it came about after these things, that the son of the woman, the mistress of the house, became sick; and his sickness was so severe, that there was no breath left in him.

17:18
2 Kin 3:13

18 So she said to Elijah, "What do I have to do with you, O man of God? You have come to me to bring my iniquity to remembrance, and to put my son to death!"

[24]I.e., wooden symbol of a female deity

16:34 This was the curse of Joshua (6:26).
17:16 More miracles were performed by Elijah and Elisha than by any other two men after Israel came into the land. According to the Scriptural record, Elijah performed five, and Elisha no fewer than twelve miracles. The total number of miracles recorded in the Old Testament is small when balanced against the number of years over which they were performed. It is to be observed that they were granted by God only at times of major national crisis, especially: (1) at the time of Israel's deliverance from Egypt and their establishment in the promised land (Ex. 7:10–12; 7:20; 8:6; 14:21; Josh. 3:15–17); (2) about the middle of the ninth century, when the kingdom of Israel was at the crossroads of decision (18:25ff.; 2 Kin. 5:1ff.; 7:1ff.); (3) during the Babylonian exile, when the survival of the nation was at stake (Dan. 3:19–27; 6:16–23).

19   And he said to her, "Give me your son." Then he took him from her bosom and carried him up to the upper room where he was living, and laid him on his own bed.

20   And he called to the LORD and said, "O LORD my God, hast Thou also brought calamity to the widow with whom I am staying, by causing her son to die?"

21   Then he stretched himself upon the child three times, and called to the LORD, and said, "O LORD my God, I pray Thee, let this child's life return to him."

22   And the LORD heard the voice of Elijah, and the life of the child returned to him and he revived.

23   And Elijah took the child, and brought him down from the upper room into the house and gave him to his mother; and Elijah said, "See, your son is alive."

24   Then the woman said to Elijah, "Now I know that you are a man of God, and that the word of the LORD in your mouth is truth."

3. Elijah at Mount Carmel

a. Obadiah seeks water

18 Now it came about *after* many days, that the word of the LORD came to Elijah in the third year, saying, "Go, show yourself to Ahab, and I will send rain on the face of the earth."

2   So Elijah went to show himself to Ahab. Now the famine *was* severe in Samaria.

3   And Ahab called Obadiah who *was* over the household. (Now Obadiah [25]feared the LORD greatly;

4   for it came about, when Jezebel destroyed the prophets of the LORD, that Obadiah took a hundred prophets and hid them by fifties in a cave, and provided them with bread and water.)

5   Then Ahab said to Obadiah, "Go through the land to all the springs of water and to all the valleys; perhaps we will find grass and keep the horses and mules alive, and not have to kill some of the cattle."

6   So they divided the land between them to survey it; Ahab went one way by himself and Obadiah went another way by himself.

b. Elijah and Obadiah meet

7   Now as Obadiah was on the way, behold, Elijah met him, and he recognized him and fell on his face and said, "Is this you, Elijah my master?"

8   And he said to him, "It is I. Go, say to your master, 'Behold, Elijah *is* here.'"

9   And he said, "What sin have I committed, that you are giving your servant into the hand of Ahab, to put me to death?

10   "As the LORD your God lives, there is no nation or kingdom where my master has not sent to search for you; and when they said, 'He is not *here*,' he made the kingdom or nation swear that they could not find you.

11   "And now you are saying, 'Go, say to your master, "Behold, Elijah *is* here."'

12   "And it will come about when I leave you that the Spirit of the LORD will carry you where I do not know; so when I come and tell Ahab and he cannot find you, he will kill me, although *I* your servant have feared the LORD from my youth.

13   "Has it not been told to my master what I did when Jezebel killed the prophets of the LORD, that I hid a hundred prophets of the LORD by fifties in a cave, and provided them with bread and water?

14   "And now you are saying, 'Go, say to your master, "Behold, Elijah *is* here"'; he will then kill me."

15   And Elijah said, "As the LORD of hosts lives, before whom I stand, I will surely show myself to him today."

16   So Obadiah went to meet Ahab, and told him; and Ahab went to meet Elijah.

c. Ahab and Elijah meet

17   And it came about, when Ahab saw Elijah that Ahab said to him, "Is this you, you troubler of Israel?"

18   And he said, "I have not troubled Israel, but you and your father's house *have*, because you have forsaken the commandments of the LORD, and you have followed the Baals.

[25] Or, *revered*

*18:19
Josh 19:26;
1 Kin 16:33

19 "Now then send *and* gather to me all Israel at Mount Carmel, *together* with 450 prophets of Baal and 400 prophets of the Asherah, who eat at Jezebel's table."

d. The priests of Baal fail

20 So Ahab sent *a message* among all the sons of Israel, and brought the prophets together at Mount Carmel.

18:21
2 Kin 17:41;
Matt 6:24;
Josh 24:15

21 And Elijah came near to all the people and said, "How long *will* you hesitate between two opinions? If the Lord is God, follow Him; but if Baal, follow him." But the people did not answer him a word.

18:22
1 Kin 19:10,
14; v. 19

22 Then Elijah said to the people, "I alone am left a prophet of the Lord, but Baal's prophets are 450 men.

23 "Now let them give us two oxen; and let them choose one ox for themselves and cut it up, and place it on the wood, but put no fire *under it*; and I will prepare the other ox, and lay it on the wood, and I will not put a fire *under it*.

18:24
v. 38; see
1 Chr 21:26;
Acts 20:10

24 "Then you call on the name of your god, and I will call on the name of the Lord, and the God who answers by fire, He is God." And all the people answered and said, "²⁶That is a good idea."

25 So Elijah said to the prophets of Baal, "Choose one ox for yourselves and prepare it first for you are many, and call on the name of your god, but put no fire *under it*."

18:26
Ps 115:5;
Jer 10:5;
1 Cor 8:4;
12:2

26 Then they took the ox which was given them and they prepared it and called on the name of Baal from morning until noon saying, "O Baal, answer us." But there was no voice and no one answered. And they leaped about the altar which they made.

27 And it came about at noon, that Elijah mocked them and said, "Call out with a loud voice, for he is a god; either he is occupied or gone aside, or is on a journey, or perhaps he is asleep and needs to be awakened."

18:28
Lev 19:28;
Deut 14:1
18:29
v. 26

28 So they cried with a loud voice and cut themselves according to their custom with swords and lances until the blood gushed out on them.

29 And it came about when midday was past, that they raved until the time of the offering of the *evening* sacrifice; but there was no voice, no one answered, and no one paid attention.

e. Elijah's sacrifice burns: fire from heaven

18:30
1 Kin 19:10,
14

30 Then Elijah said to all the people, "Come near to me." So all the people came near to him. And he repaired the altar of the Lord which had been torn down.

18:31
Gen 32:28;
35:10;
2 Kin 17:34

31 And Elijah took twelve stones according to the number of the tribes of the sons of Jacob, to whom the word of the Lord had come, saying, "Israel shall be your name."

18:32
Col 3:17

32 So with the stones he built an altar in the name of the Lord, and he made a trench around the altar, large enough to hold two measures of seed.

18:33
Gen 22:9;
Lev 1:6-8

33 Then he arranged the wood and cut the ox in pieces and laid *it* on the wood. And he said, "Fill four pitchers with water and pour *it* on the burnt offering and on the wood."

34 And he said, "Do it a second time," and they did it a second time. And he said, "Do it a third time," and they did it a third time.

35 And the water flowed around the altar, and he also filled the trench with water.

18:36
Ex 3:6;
1 Kin 8:43;
2 Kin 19:19;
Num 16:28

36 Then it came about at the time of the offering of the *evening* sacrifice, that Elijah the prophet came near and said, "O Lord, the God of Abraham, Isaac and Israel, today let it be known that Thou art God in Israel, and that I am Thy servant, and that I have done all these things at Thy word.

37 "Answer me, O Lord, answer me, that this people may know that Thou, O Lord, art God, and *that* Thou hast turned their heart back again."

18:38
Lev 9:24;
1 Chr 21:26;
2 Chr 7:1
18:39
vv. 21,24

38 Then the fire of the Lord fell, and consumed the burnt offering and the wood and the stones and the dust, and licked up the water that was in the trench.

39 And when all the people saw it, they fell on their faces; and they said, "The Lord, He is God; the Lord, He is God."

18:40
Deut 13:5;
18:20;

40 Then Elijah said to them, "Seize the prophets of Baal; do not let one of them

²⁶Lit., *The matter is good*

18:19 The *400 prophets of the Asherah* do not appear in the rest of the story. (For more information on Asherah, see note to Ex. 34:13 on *Asherim*.)

escape." So they seized them; and Elijah brought them down to the brook Kishon, and slew them there.

2 Kin 10:24, 25

f. *The coming of the rain*

41   Now Elijah said to Ahab, "Go up, eat and drink; for there is the sound of the roar of a *heavy* shower."

42   So Ahab went up to eat and drink. But Elijah went up to the top of Carmel; and he crouched down on the earth, and put his face between his knees.

18:42 vv. 19,20; James 5:17,18

43   And he said to his servant, "Go up now, look toward the sea." So he went up and looked and said, "There is nothing." And he said, "Go back" seven times.

44   And it came about at the seventh *time*, that he said, "Behold, a cloud as small as a man's hand is coming up from the sea." And he said, "Go up, say to Ahab, 'Prepare *your chariot* and go down, so that the *heavy* shower does not stop you.'"

45   So it came about in a little while, that the sky grew black with clouds and wind, and there was a heavy shower. And Ahab rode and went to Jezreel.

46   Then the hand of the LORD was on Elijah, and he girded up his loins and outran Ahab to Jezreel.

18:46 2 Kin 3:15; 4:29

4. *Elijah goes to Horeb*

a. *Jezebel's intention*

19 Now Ahab told Jezebel all that Elijah had done, and how he had killed all the prophets with the sword.

19:1 1 Kin 18:40

2   Then Jezebel sent a messenger to Elijah, saying, "So may the gods do to me and even more, if I do not make your [27]life as the life of one of them by tomorrow about this time."

19:2 1 Kin 20:10; 2 Kin 6:31

3   And he was afraid and arose and ran for his [27]life and came to Beersheba, which belongs to Judah, and left his servant there.

b. *Elijah's flight*

4   But he himself went a day's journey into the wilderness, and came and sat down under a juniper tree; and he requested for himself that he might die, and said, "It is enough; now, O LORD, take my [27]life, for I am not better than my fathers."

19:4 Num 11:15; Jon 4:3,8

5   And he lay down and slept under a juniper tree; and behold, there was an angel touching him, and he said to him, "Arise, eat."

6   Then he looked and behold, there was at his head a bread cake *baked on* hot stones, and a jar of water. So he ate and drank and lay down again.

7   And the angel of the LORD came again a second time and touched him and said, "Arise, eat, because the journey is too great for you."

8   So he arose and ate and drank, and went in the strength of that food forty days and forty nights to Horeb, the mountain of God. (Mt Sinai)

*19:8 Ex 34:28; Deut 9:9-11, 18; Matt 4:2; Ex 3:1

c. *God meets with Elijah*

9   Then he came there to a cave, and lodged there; and behold, the word of the LORD *came* to him, and He said to him, "What are you doing here, Elijah?"

10   And he said, "I have been very zealous for the LORD, the God of hosts; for the sons of Israel have forsaken Thy covenant, torn down Thine altars and killed Thy prophets with the sword. And I alone am left; and they seek my life, to take it away."

19:10 Rom 11:3; 1 Kin 18:4,22

11   So He said, "Go forth, and stand on the mountain before the LORD." And behold, the LORD was passing by! And a great and strong wind was rending the mountains and breaking in pieces the rocks before the LORD; *but* the LORD *was* not in the wind. And after the wind an earthquake, *but* the LORD *was* not in the earthquake.

19:11 Ex 24:12; Ezek 1:4; 37:7

12   And after the earthquake a fire, *but* the LORD *was* not in the fire; and after the fire a sound of a gentle blowing.

13   And it came about when Elijah heard *it*, that he wrapped his face in his mantle, and went out and stood in the entrance of the cave. And behold, a voice *came* to him and said, "What are you doing here, Elijah?"

19:13 Ex 3:6; v. 9

14   Then he said, "I have been very zealous for the LORD, the God of hosts; for

19:14 v. 10

---

[27] Lit., *soul*

19:8 *Horeb*, Mt. Sinai. Apparently Elijah went to this sacred spot in his despondency in order to be renewed by the God of Israel who spoke to Moses.

the sons of Israel have forsaken Thy covenant, torn down Thine altars and killed Thy prophets with the sword. And I alone am left; and they seek my life, to take it away."

19:15
2 Kin 8:12,13

15 And the LORD said to him, "Go, return on your way to the wilderness of Damascus, and when you have arrived, you shall anoint Hazael king over Aram;

19:16
2 Kin 9:1-3;
vv. 19-21;
2 Kin 2:9,15

16 and Jehu the son of Nimshi you shall anoint king over Israel; and Elisha the son of Shaphat of Abel-meholah you shall anoint as prophet in your place.

19:17
2 Kin 8:12;
9:14ff; 13:3,
22

17 "And it shall come about, the one who escapes from the sword of Hazael, Jehu shall put to death, and the one who escapes from the sword of Jehu, Elisha shall put to death.

*19:18
Rom 11:4;
Hos 13:2

18 "Yet I will leave 7,000 in Israel, all the knees that have not bowed to Baal and every mouth that has not kissed him."

d. *Elijah casts his mantle on Elisha*

19:19
2 Kin 2:8,13

19 So he departed from there and found Elisha the son of Shaphat, while he was plowing with twelve pairs *of oxen* before him, and he with the twelfth. And Elijah passed over to him and threw his mantle on him.

19:20
Matt 8:21,22;
Luke 9:61,62

20 And he left the oxen and ran after Elijah and said, "Please let me kiss my father and my mother, then I will follow you." And he said to him, "Go back again, for what have I done to you?"

19:21
2 Sam 24:22

21 So he returned from following him, and took the pair of oxen and sacrificed them and boiled their flesh with the implements of the oxen, and gave *it* to the people and they ate. Then he arose and followed Elijah and ministered to him.

5. *Ahab's first Syrian campaign*

a. *Ben-hadad's demands*

20:1
1 Kin 15:18,
20;
2 Kin 6:24;
1 Kin 22:31;
2 Kin 6:24-29

20 Now Ben-hadad king of Aram gathered all his army, and there *were* thirty-two kings with him, and horses and chariots. And he went up and besieged Samaria, and fought against it.

2 Then he sent messengers to the city to Ahab king of Israel, and said to him, "Thus says Ben-hadad,

3 'Your silver and your gold are mine; your most beautiful wives and children are also mine.' "

4 And the king of Israel answered and said, "It is according to your word, my lord, O king; I am yours, and all that I have."

5 Then the messengers returned and said, "Thus says Ben-hadad, 'Surely, I sent to you saying, "You shall give me your silver and your gold and your wives and your children,"

6 but about this time tomorrow I will send my servants to you, and they will search your house and the houses of your servants; and it shall come about, whatever is desirable in your eyes, they will take in their hand and carry away.' "

b. *Ahab's reply*

20:7
2 Kin 5:7

7 Then the king of Israel called all the elders of the land and said, "Please observe and see how this man is looking for trouble; for he sent to me for my wives and my children and my silver and my gold, and I did not refuse him."

8 And all the elders and all the people said to him, "Do not listen or consent."

9 So he said to the messengers of Ben-hadad, "Tell my lord the king, 'All that you sent for to your servant at the first I will do, but this thing I cannot do.' " And the messengers departed and brought him word again.

20:10
1 Kin 19:2

10 And Ben-hadad sent to him and said, "May the gods do so to me and more also, if the dust of Samaria shall suffice for handfuls for all the people who follow me."

20:11
Prov 27:1

11 Then the king of Israel answered and said, "Tell *him*, 'Let not him who girds on *his armor* boast like him who takes *it* off.' "

20:12
v. 16

12 And it came about when *Ben-hadad* heard this message, as he was drinking with the kings in the temporary shelters, that he said to his servants, "Station *yourselves*." So they stationed *themselves* against the city.

c. *God's promise of victory*

20:13
v. 28

13 Now behold, a prophet approached Ahab king of Israel and said, "Thus says

---

19:18 *7,000 in Israel.* Notwithstanding Elijah's pessimism "... *I alone am left* ..." (18:22), God has His   remnant in Israel.

the LORD, 'Have you seen all this great multitude? Behold, I will deliver them into your hand today, and you shall know that I am the LORD.'"

14 And Ahab said, "By whom?" So he said, "Thus says the LORD, 'By the young men of the rulers of the provinces.'" Then he said, "Who shall begin the battle?" And he answered, "You."

15 Then he mustered the young men of the rulers of the provinces, and there were 232; and after them he mustered all the people, *even* all the sons of Israel, 7,000.

d. Ahab's victory

16 And they went out at noon, while Ben-hadad was drinking himself drunk in the temporary shelters with the thirty-two kings who helped him.

17 And the young men of the rulers of the provinces went out first; and Ben-hadad sent out and they told him, saying, "Men have come out from Samaria."

18 Then he said, "If they have come out for peace, take them alive; or if they have come out for war, take them alive."

19 So these went out from the city, the young men of the rulers of the provinces, and the army which followed them.

20 And they killed each his man; and the Arameans fled, and Israel pursued them, and Ben-hadad king of Aram escaped on a horse with horsemen.

21 And the king of Israel went out and struck the horses and chariots, and killed the Arameans with a great slaughter.

e. A second invasion prophesied

22 Then the prophet came near to the king of Israel, and said to him, "Go, strengthen yourself and observe and see what you have to do; for at the turn of the year the king of Aram will come up against you."

6. Ahab's second Syrian campaign

a. Ben-hadad defeated

23 Now the servants of the king of Aram said to him, "Their gods are gods of the mountains, therefore they were stronger than we; but rather let us fight against them in the plain, *and* surely we shall be stronger than they.

24 "And do this thing: remove the kings, each from his place, and put captains in their place,

25 and muster an army like the army that you have lost, horse for horse, and chariot for chariot. Then we will fight against them in the plain, and surely we shall be stronger than they." And he listened to their voice and did so.

26 So it came about at the turn of the year, that Ben-hadad mustered the Arameans and went up to Aphek to fight against Israel.

27 And the sons of Israel were mustered and were provisioned and went to meet them; and the sons of Israel camped before them like two little flocks of goats, but the Arameans filled the country.

28 Then a man of God came near and spoke to the king of Israel and said, "Thus says the LORD, 'Because the Arameans have said, "The LORD is a god of *the* mountains, but He is not a god of *the* valleys"; therefore I will give all this great multitude into your hand, and you shall know that I am the LORD.'"

29 So they camped one over against the other seven days. And it came about that on the seventh day, the battle was joined, and the sons of Israel killed *of* the Arameans 100,000 foot soldiers in one day.

30 But the rest fled to Aphek into the city, and the wall fell on 27,000 men who were left. And Ben-hadad fled and came into the city into an inner chamber.

b. Ahab spares Ben-hadad

31 And his servants said to him, "Behold now, we have heard that the kings of the house of Israel are merciful kings, please let us put sackcloth on our loins and ropes on our heads, and go out to the king of Israel; perhaps he will save your life."

32 So they girded sackcloth on their loins and *put* ropes on their heads, and came to the king of Israel and said, "Your servant Ben-hadad says, 'Please let me live.'" And he said, "Is he still alive? He is my brother."

33 Now the men took this as an omen, and quickly catching his word said,

Marginal references: 20:16 v. 12; 20:18 2 Kin 14:8-12; 20:22 vv. 13,26; 2 Sam 11:1; *20:23 1 Kin 14:23; *20:26 v. 22; 2 Kin 13:7; 20:28 v. 13; 20:30 v. 26; 1 Kin 22:25; 2 Chr 18:24; 20:31 Gen 37:34; 20:32 vv. 3-6

"Your brother Ben-hadad." Then he said, "Go, bring him." Then Ben-hadad came out to him, and he took him up into the chariot.

20:34
1 Kin 15:20

34   And *Ben-hadad* said to him, "The cities which my father took from your father I will restore, and you shall make streets for yourself in Damascus, as my father made in Samaria." *Ahab said*, "And I will let you go with this covenant." So he made a covenant with him and let him go.

c. *The judgment of God against Ahab*
for sparing Ben-hadad

20:35
2 Kin 2:3-7;
1 Kin 13:17,
18
20:36
1 Kin 13:24

35   Now a certain man of the sons of the prophets said to another by the word of the LORD, "Please strike me." But the man refused to strike him.

36   Then he said to him, "Because you have not listened to the voice of the LORD, behold, as soon as you have departed from me, a lion will kill you." And as soon as he had departed from him a lion found him, and killed him.

37   Then he found another man and said, "Please strike me." And the man struck him, wounding him.

38   So the prophet departed and waited for the king by the way, and disguised himself with a bandage over his eyes.

20:39
2 Kin 10:24

39   And as the king passed by, he cried to the king and said, "Your servant went out into the midst of the battle; and behold, a man turned aside and brought a man to me and said, 'Guard this man; if for any reason he is missing, then your life shall be for his life, or else you shall pay a talent of silver.'

40   "And while your servant was busy here and there, he was gone." And the king of Israel said to him, "So shall your judgment be; you yourself have decided *it.*"

41   Then he hastily took the bandage away from his eyes, and the king of Israel recognized him that he was of the prophets.

20:42
v. 39;
1 Kin 22:31-37

42   And he said to him, "Thus says the LORD, 'Because you have let go out of *your* hand the man whom I had devoted to destruction, therefore your life shall go for his life, and your people for his people.' "

20:43
1 Kin 21:4

43   So the king of Israel went to his house sullen and vexed, and came to Samaria.

7. *Naboth's vineyard*

a. *Ahab covets the vineyard*

21:1
1 Kin 18:45,
46
21:2
1 Sam 8:14

21 Now it came about after these things, that Naboth the Jezreelite had a vineyard which *was* in Jezreel beside the palace of Ahab king of Samaria.

2   And Ahab spoke to Naboth, saying, "Give me your vineyard, that I may have it for a vegetable garden because it is close beside my house, and I will give you a better vineyard than it in its place; if you like, I will give you the price of it in money."

21:3
Lev 25:23;
Num 36:7;
Ezek 46:18
21:4
1 Kin 20:43

3   But Naboth said to Ahab, "The LORD forbid me that I should give you the inheritance of my fathers."

4   So Ahab came into his house sullen and vexed because of the word which Naboth the Jezreelite had spoken to him; for he said, "I will not give you the inheritance of my fathers." And he lay down on his bed and turned away his face and ate no food.

b. *Jezebel seizes the vineyard*

5   But Jezebel his wife came to him and said to him, "How is it that your spirit is so sullen that you are not eating food?"

6   So he said to her, "Because I spoke to Naboth the Jezreelite, and said to him, 'Give me your vineyard for money; or else, if it pleases you, I will give you a vineyard in its place.' But he said, 'I will not give you my vineyard.' "

21:7
1 Sam 8:14

7   And Jezebel his wife said to him, "Do you now reign over Israel? Arise, eat bread, and let your heart be joyful; I will give you the vineyard of Naboth the Jezreelite."

21:8
Esth 3:12;
8:8,10

8   So she wrote letters in Ahab's name and sealed them with his seal, and sent letters to the elders and to the nobles who were living with Naboth in his city.

20:40 God's prophet, who rebuked Ahab for his sin of sparing Ben-hadad, used an illustration that has a spiritual relevance for every believer. Busyness is by itself no virtue; it may involve choosing the good in preference to the best.

Believers are to be busy at work for God, but they are to seek His guidance in all things and to put first things first (Deut. 28:1ff.; Ps. 25:9; Jer. 32:6–8; Matt. 6:10,33; Acts 21:14; Rom. 1:10; 15:32; James 4:15).

9   Now she wrote in the letters, saying, "Proclaim a fast, and seat Naboth at the head of the people;

10   and seat two worthless men before him, and let them testify against him, saying, 'You cursed God and the king.' Then take him out and stone him to death."

11   So the men of his city, the elders and the nobles who lived in his city, did as Jezebel had sent *word* to them, just as it was written in the letters which she had sent them.

12   They proclaimed a fast and seated Naboth at the head of the people.

13   Then the two worthless men came in and sat before him; and the worthless men testified against him, even against Naboth, before the people, saying, "Naboth cursed God and the king." So they took him outside the city and stoned him to death with stones.

14   Then they sent *word* to Jezebel, saying, "Naboth has been stoned, and is dead."

15   And it came about when Jezebel heard that Naboth had been stoned and was dead, that Jezebel said to Ahab, "Arise, take possession of the vineyard of Naboth, the Jezreelite, which he refused to give you for money; for Naboth is not alive, but dead."

16   And it came about when Ahab heard that Naboth was dead, that Ahab arose to go down to the vineyard of Naboth the Jezreelite, to take possession of it.

c. Elijah pronounces doom on Ahab and Jezebel

17   Then the word of the LORD came to Elijah the Tishbite, saying,

18   "Arise, go down to meet Ahab king of Israel, who is in Samaria; behold, he is in the vineyard of Naboth where he has gone down to take possession of it.

19   "And you shall speak to him, saying, 'Thus says the LORD, "Have you murdered, and also taken possession?"' And you shall speak to him, saying, 'Thus says the LORD, "In the place where the dogs licked up the blood of Naboth the dogs shall lick up your blood, even yours."'"

20   And Ahab said to Elijah, "Have you found me, O my enemy?" And he answered, "I have found *you*, because you have sold yourself to do evil in the sight of the LORD.

21   "Behold, I will bring evil upon you, and will utterly sweep you away, and will cut off from Ahab every male, both bond and free in Israel;

22   and I will make your house like the house of Jeroboam the son of Nebat, and like the house of Baasha the son of Ahijah, because of the provocation with which you have provoked *Me* to anger, and *because* you have made Israel sin.

23   "And of Jezebel also has the LORD spoken, saying, 'The dogs shall eat Jezebel in the district of Jezreel.'

24   "The one belonging to Ahab, who dies in the city, the dogs shall eat, and the one who dies in the field the birds of heaven shall eat."

25   Surely there was no one like Ahab who sold himself to do evil in the sight of the LORD, because Jezebel his wife incited him.

26   And he acted very abominably in following idols, according to all that the Amorites had done, whom the LORD cast out before the sons of Israel.

d. Ahab's repentance

27   And it came about when Ahab heard these words, that he tore his clothes and put on sackcloth and fasted, and he lay in sackcloth and went about despondently.

28   Then the word of the LORD came to Elijah the Tishbite, saying,

29   "Do you see how Ahab has humbled himself before Me? Because he has humbled himself before Me, I will not bring the evil in his days, *but* I will bring the evil upon his house in his son's days."

8. Ahab's third Syrian campaign

a. Ahab's agreement with Jehoshaphat of Judah

22   And three years passed without war between Aram and Israel.
   2   And it came about in the third year, that Jehoshaphat the king of Judah came down to the king of Israel.

3   Now the king of Israel said to his servants, "Do you know that Ramoth-gilead belongs to us, and we are still doing nothing to take it out of the hand of the king of Aram?"

21:10
Ex 22:28;
Lev 24:15,16;
Acts 6:11

21:13
2 Kin 9:26

21:17
Ps 9:12
21:18
1 Kin 16:29
21:19
1 Kin 22:38;
2 Kin 9:8

21:20
1 Kin 18:17;
v. 25
21:21
1 Kin 14:10;
2 Kin 9:8
21:22
1 Kin 15:29

21:23
2 Kin 9:10,
30-37
21:24
1 Kin 14:11;
16:4
21:25
v. 20;
1 Kin 16:30-33
21:26
Gen 15:16;
Lev 18:25-30

21:27
2 Sam 3:31;
2 Kin 6:30

21:29
2 Kin 9:25

22:2
2 Chr 18:2ff;
1 Kin 15:24
22:3
Deut 4:43;
Josh 21:38

22:4
2 Kin 3:7

4   And he said to Jehoshaphat, "Will you go with me to battle at Ramoth-gilead?" And Jehoshaphat said to the king of Israel, "I am as you are, my people as your people, my horses as your horses."

b. The lying prophets prophesy victory

5   Moreover, Jehoshaphat said to the king of Israel, "Please inquire first for the word of the LORD."

22:6
1 Kin 18:19

6   Then the king of Israel gathered the prophets together, about four hundred men, and said to them, "Shall I go against Ramoth-gilead to battle or shall I refrain?" And they said, "Go up, for the Lord will give it into the hand of the king."

22:7
2 Kin 3:11

7   But Jehoshaphat said, "Is there not yet a prophet of the LORD here, that we may inquire of him?"

8   And the king of Israel said to Jehoshaphat, "There is yet one man by whom we may inquire of the LORD, but I hate him, because he does not prophesy good concerning me, but evil. He is Micaiah son of Imlah." But Jehoshaphat said, "Let not the king say so."

9   Then the king of Israel called an officer and said, "Bring quickly Micaiah son of Imlah."

22:10
v. 6

10   Now the king of Israel and Jehoshaphat king of Judah were sitting each on his throne, arrayed in their robes, at the threshing floor at the entrance of the gate of Samaria; and all the prophets were prophesying before them.

22:11
Zech 1:18-21;
Deut 33:17

11   Then Zedekiah the son of Chenaanah made horns of iron for himself and said, "Thus says the LORD, 'With these you shall gore the Arameans until they are consumed.' "

12   And all the prophets were prophesying thus, saying, "Go up to Ramoth-gilead and prosper, for the LORD will give it into the hand of the king."

c. Micaiah's true prophecy

13   Then the messenger who went to summon Micaiah spoke to him saying, "Behold now, the words of the prophets are uniformly favorable to the king. Please let your word be like the word of one of them, and speak favorably."

22:14
1 Kin 18:10,
15;
Num 22:18;
24:13
22:15
v. 12

14   But Micaiah said, "As the LORD lives, what the LORD says to me, that I will speak."

15   When he came to the king, the king said to him, "Micaiah, shall we go to Ramoth-gilead to battle, or shall we refrain?" And he answered him, "Go up and succeed, and the LORD will give it into the hand of the king."

16   Then the king said to him, "How many times must I adjure you to speak to me nothing but the truth in the name of the LORD?"

22:17
vv. 34-36

17   So he said,
"I saw all Israel
   Scattered on the mountains,
   Like sheep which have no shepherd.
   And the LORD said, 'These have no master.
   Let each of them return to his house in peace.' "

22:18
v. 8

18   Then the king of Israel said to Jehoshaphat, "Did I not tell you that he would not prophesy good concerning me, but evil?"

22:19
Is 6:1;
Dan 7:9,10

19   And Micaiah said, "Therefore, hear the word of the LORD. I saw the LORD sitting on His throne, and all the host of heaven standing by Him on His right and on His left.

20   "And the LORD said, 'Who will entice Ahab to go up and fall at Ramoth-gilead?' And one said this while another said that.

21   "Then a spirit came forward and stood before the LORD and said, 'I will entice him.'

22:22
Judg 9:23;
1 Sam 16:14;
18:10; 19:9;
2 Thess 2:11
22:23
Ezek 14:9

22   "And the LORD said to him, 'How?' And he said, 'I will go out and be a deceiving spirit in the mouth of all his prophets.' Then He said, 'You are to entice him and also prevail. Go and do so.'

23   "Now therefore, behold, the LORD has put a deceiving spirit in the mouth of all these your prophets; and the LORD has proclaimed disaster against you."

22:24
2 Chr 18:23

24   Then Zedekiah the son of Chenaanah came near and struck Micaiah on the cheek and said, "How did the Spirit of the LORD pass from me to speak to you?"

22:25
1 Kin 20:30

25   And Micaiah said, "Behold, you shall see on that day when you enter an inner room to hide yourself."

26   Then the king of Israel said, "Take Micaiah and return him to Amon the governor of the city and to Joash the king's son;

27 and say, 'Thus says the king, "Put this man in prison, and feed him sparingly with bread and water until I return safely." ' "

28 And Micaiah said, "If you indeed return safely the LORD has not spoken by me." And he said, "Listen, all you people."

d. *Ahab's defeat and death*

29 So the king of Israel and Jehoshaphat king of Judah went up against Ramoth-gilead.

30 And the king of Israel said to Jehoshaphat, "I will disguise myself and go into the battle, but you put on your robes." So the king of Israel disguised himself and went into the battle.

31 Now the king of Aram had commanded the thirty-two captains of his chariots, saying, "Do not fight with small or great, but with the king of Israel alone."

32 So it came about, when the captains of the chariots saw Jehoshaphat, that they said, "Surely it is the king of Israel," and they turned aside to fight against him, and Jehoshaphat cried out.

33 Then it happened, when the captains of the chariots saw that it was not the king of Israel, that they turned back from pursuing him.

34 Now a certain man drew his bow at random and struck the king of Israel in a joint of the armor. So he said to the driver of his chariot, "Turn around, and take me out of the fight; for I am severely wounded."

35 And the battle raged that day, and the king was propped up in his chariot in front of the Arameans, and died at evening, and the blood from the wound ran into the bottom of the chariot.

36 Then a cry passed throughout the army close to sunset, saying, "Every man to his city and every man to his country."

37 So the king died and was brought to Samaria, and they buried the king in Samaria.

38 And they washed the chariot by the pool of Samaria, and the dogs licked up his blood (now the harlots bathed themselves *there*), according to the word of the LORD which He spoke.

39 Now the rest of the acts of Ahab and all that he did and the ivory house which he built and all the cities which he built, are they not written in the Book of the Chronicles of the Kings of Israel?

40 So Ahab slept with his fathers, and Ahaziah his son became king in his place.

9. *Judah under Jehoshaphat*

41 Now Jehoshaphat the son of Asa became king over Judah in the fourth year of Ahab king of Israel.

42 Jehoshaphat was thirty-five years old when he became king, and he reigned twenty-five years in Jerusalem. And his mother's name was Azubah the daughter of Shilhi.

43 And he walked in all the way of Asa his father; he did not turn aside from it, doing right in the sight of the LORD. However, the high places were not taken away; the people still sacrificed and burnt incense on the high places.

44 Jehoshaphat also made peace with the king of Israel.

45 Now the rest of the acts of Jehoshaphat, and his might which he showed and how he warred, are they not written in the Book of the Chronicles of the Kings of Judah?

46 And the remnant of the sodomites who remained in the days of his father Asa, he expelled from the land.

47 Now there was no king in Edom; a deputy was king.

48 Jehoshaphat made ships of Tarshish to go to Ophir for gold, but they did not go for the ships were broken at Ezion-geber.

49 Then Ahaziah the son of Ahab said to Jehoshaphat, "Let my servants go with your servants in the ships." But Jehoshaphat was not willing.

22:27	2 Chr 18:25-27
22:28	Deut 18:22
22:29	vv. 3,4
22:30	2 Chr 25:32
22:31	2 Chr 18:30
22:32	2 Chr 18:31
22:38	1 Kin 21:19
22:39	Amos 3:15
22:41	2 Chr 20:31
22:43	2 Chr 17:3; 1 Kin 15:14; 2 Kin 12:3
22:44	2 Chr 19:2
22:45	2 Chr 20:34
22:46	1 Kin 14:24; 15:12
22:47	2 Sam 8:14; 2 Kin 3:9
*22:48	2 Chr 20:35ff; 1 Kin 10:22

22:34 *bow at random.* Ahab sought to secure himself against the Syrians by assuming the garb of a common soldier, and was shot by a Syrian soldier who was not aiming at anyone in particular. But God directed the arrow so that it hit the man who was marked for destruction. Moreover, Ahab was hit in the abdomen, the place where his armor was no shield against the dart of divine vengeance. Man cannot hide himself from the judgment of God; what appears to be casual and accidental bespeaks the finger of God.
22:48 Jehoshaphat was not successful in these operations as was Solomon (1 Kin. 9:26–28).

22:50
2 Chr 21:1

50   And Jehoshaphat slept with his fathers and was buried with his fathers in the city of his father David, and Jehoram his son became king in his place.

10. *The northern kingdom under Ahaziah*

*22:51
v. 40

51   Ahaziah the son of Ahab became king over Israel in Samaria in the seventeenth year of Jehoshaphat king of Judah, and he reigned two years over Israel.

22:52
1 Kin 15:26;
21:25

52   And he did evil in the sight of the LORD and walked in the way of his father and in the way of his mother and in the way of Jeroboam the son of Nebat, who caused Israel to sin.

22:53
1 Kin 16:30-32

53   So he served Baal and worshiped him and provoked the LORD God of Israel to anger according to all that his father had done.

22:51 Ahaziah followed his father, who was the worst of all the kings of Israel. All nineteen kings of Israel served either the calf or Baal. Baal worship continued for some thirty years and was finally exterminated through the efforts of Elijah, Elisha, and Jehu. Jezebel, of course, was the person responsible for its introduction into Israel, and her daughter Athaliah, who married Jehoram, king of Judah, followed in her mother's footsteps, propagating Baalism among the people of Judah. The wicked influence of Jezebel and Athaliah on both kingdoms staggers the imagination.

INTRODUCTION TO
THE SECOND BOOK OF THE
KINGS

Authorship and Background: See 1 Kings

Characteristics: See 1 Kings

Contents:

III. The divided kingdom (continued from 1 Kings) (1:1-17:41): Ahaziah's sickness. Efforts to seize Elijah. The ten tribes under Jehoram (Joram); Elisha the prophet. The campaign against Moab. Elisha's miracles: the healing of Naaman and further miracles. The two tribes under Jehoram (Joram) and Ahaziah. The ten tribes under Jehu. The two tribes under Athaliah and Joash (Jehoash). The ten tribes under Jehoaz and Jehoash. The two tribes under Amaziah. The ten tribes under Jeroboam II. The two tribes under Uzziah (Azariah). The ten tribes under Zechariah, Shallum, Menahem, Pekahiah, and Pekah. The two tribes under Jotham and Ahaz. The ten tribes under Hoshea; the end of the kingdom.

IV. The kingdom of Judah to the captivity (18:1-25:30): The two tribes under Hezekiah, Manasseh, Amon, Josiah, Jehoahaz, Jehoiakim, Jehoiachin, and Zedekiah. The Babylonian captivity.

III. *The divided kingdom continued (1:1–17:41)*

G. *The ending of Elijah's ministry*

1. *Ahaziah's (Israel) embassy to Baal-zebub*

1 Now Moab rebelled against Israel after the death of Ahab.

2 And Ahaziah fell through the lattice in his upper chamber which *was* in Samaria, and became ill. So he sent messengers and said to them, "Go, inquire of Baal-zebub, the god of Ekron, whether I shall recover from this sickness."

3 But the angel of the LORD said to Elijah the Tishbite, "Arise, go up to meet the messengers of the king of Samaria and say to them, 'Is it because there is no God in Israel *that* you are going to inquire of Baal-zebub, the god of Ekron?'

4 "Now therefore thus says the LORD, 'You shall not come down from the bed where you have gone up, but you shall surely die.'" Then Elijah departed.

5 When the messengers returned to him he said to them, "Why have you returned?"

6 And they said to him, "A man came up to meet us and said to us, 'Go, return to the king who sent you and say to him, "Thus says the LORD, 'Is it because there is no God in Israel *that* you are sending to inquire of Baal-zebub, the god of Ekron? Therefore you shall not come down from the bed where you have gone up, but shall surely die.'"'"

7 And he said to them, "What kind of man was he who came up to meet you and spoke these words to you?"

8 And they answered him, "*He was* a hairy man with a leather girdle bound about his loins." And he said, "It is Elijah the Tishbite."

2. *The attempts to seize Elijah*

9 Then *the king* sent to him a captain of fifty with his fifty. And he went up to him, and behold, he was sitting on the top of the hill. And he said to him, "O man of God, the king says, 'Come down.'"

10 And Elijah answered and said to the captain of fifty, "If I am a man of God, let fire come down from heaven and consume you and your fifty." Then fire came down from heaven and consumed him and his fifty.

11 So he again sent to him another captain of fifty with his fifty. And he answered and said to him, "O man of God, thus says the king, 'Come down quickly.'"

12 And Elijah answered and said to them, "If I am a man of God, let fire come down from heaven and consume you and your fifty." Then the fire of God came down from heaven and consumed him and his fifty.

13 So he again sent the captain of a third fifty with his fifty. When the third captain of fifty went up, he came and bowed down on his knees before Elijah, and begged him and said to him, "O man of God, please let my life and the lives of these fifty servants of yours be precious in your sight.

14 "Behold fire came down from heaven, and consumed the first two captains of fifty with their fifties; but now let my life be precious in your sight."

15 And the angel of the LORD said to Elijah, "Go down with him; do not be afraid of him." So he arose and went down with him to the king.

16 Then he said to him, "Thus says the LORD, 'Because you have sent messengers to inquire of Baal-zebub, the god of Ekron—is it because there is no God in

Marginal references

1:1
2 Sam 8:2;
2 Kin 3:5
*1:2
vv. 3,6;
Matt 10:25;
see
2 Kin 8:7-10

1:4
vv. 6,16

1:8
Zech 13:4;
Matt 3:4

1:10
1 Kin 18:36-38;
Luke 9:54

1:13
1 Sam 26:21;
Ps 72:14

1:15
v. 3

1:16
v. 3

1:2 *Baal-zebub,* "Lord of flies," is probably a scribal change intended to ridicule the original name, Baal-zebul, "Lord Prince." One of the Canaanite titles for Baal was "Prince (Zabul), Lord of the Earth." This name occurs in the New Testament as Beelzebul (or, Beelzebub in KJV), but it has the specific meaning, *the ruler of the demons* (Matt. 12:24).

Israel to inquire of His word?—therefore you shall not come down from the bed where you have gone up, but shall surely die.' "

3. Jehoram, successor to Ahaziah

17 So Ahaziah died according to the word of the LORD which Elijah had spoken. And because he had no son, Jehoram became king in his place in the second year of Jehoram the son of Jehoshaphat, king of Judah.

18 Now the rest of the acts of Ahaziah which he did, are they not written in the Book of the Chronicles of the Kings of Israel?

H. *The reign of Jehoram (Israel)*

1. Elijah's translation

2 And it came about when the LORD was about to take up Elijah by a whirlwind to heaven, that Elijah went with Elisha from Gilgal.

2 And Elijah said to Elisha, "Stay here please, for the LORD has sent me as far as Bethel." But Elisha said, "As the LORD lives and as you yourself live, I will not leave you." So they went down to Bethel.

3 Then the sons of the prophets who *were at* Bethel came out to Elisha and said to him, "Do you know that the LORD will take away your master from over you today?" And he said, "Yes, I know; be still."

4 And Elijah said to him, "Elisha, please stay here, for the LORD has sent me to Jericho." But he said, "As the LORD lives, and as you yourself live, I will not leave you." So they came to Jericho.

5 And the sons of the prophets who *were* at Jericho approached Elisha and said to him, "Do you know that the LORD will take away your master from over you today?" And he answered, "Yes, I know; be still."

6 Then Elijah said to him, "Please stay here, for the LORD has sent me to the Jordan." And he said, "As the LORD lives, and as you yourself live, I will not leave you." So the two of them went on.

7 Now fifty men of the sons of the prophets went and stood opposite *them* at a distance, while the two of them stood by the Jordan.

8 And Elijah took his mantle and folded it together and struck the waters, and they were divided here and there, so that the two of them crossed over on dry ground.

9 Now it came about when they had crossed over, that Elijah said to Elisha, "Ask what I shall do for you before I am taken from you." And Elisha said, "Please, let a double portion of your spirit be upon me."

10 And he said, "You have asked a hard thing. *Nevertheless,* if you see me when I am taken from you, it shall be so for you; but if not, it shall not be *so.*"

11 Then it came about as they were going along and talking, that behold, *there appeared* a chariot of fire and horses of fire which separated the two of them. And Elijah went up by a whirlwind to heaven.

12 And Elisha saw *it* and cried out, "My father, my father, the chariots of Israel and its horsemen!" And he saw him no more. Then he took hold of his own clothes and tore them in two pieces.

2. The beginning of Elisha's ministry

13 He also took up the mantle of Elijah that fell from him, and returned and stood by the bank of the Jordan.

14 And he took the mantle of Elijah that fell from him, and struck the waters and said, "Where is the LORD, the God of Elijah?" And when he also had struck the waters, they were divided here and there; and Elisha crossed over.

15 Now when the sons of the prophets who *were* at Jericho opposite *him* saw him, they said, "The spirit of Elijah rests on Elisha." And they came to meet him and bowed themselves to the ground before him.

16 And they said to him, "Behold now, there are with your servants fifty strong men, please let them go and search for your master; perhaps the Spirit of the LORD

Marginal references

1:17
2 Kin 3:1;
8:16

*2:1
Gen 5:24;
Heb 11:5;
1 Kin 19:21
2:2
Ruth 1:15,16;
vv. 4,6;
1 Sam 1:26;
2 Kin 4:30
*2:3
vv. 5,7,15;
2 Kin 4:1,38
2:4
v. 2;
Josh 6:26

2:5
v. 3

2:6
v. 3; Josh 3:8,
15-17

2:7
vv. 15,16

2:8
1 Kin 19:13,
19; v. 14;
Ex 14:21,22

2:11
2 Kin 6:17;
Ps 104:4

2:12
2 Kin 13:14

2:14
v. 8

2:15
v. 7

2:16
1 Kin 18:12;
Acts 8:39

2:1 *Gilgal,* possibly the one in southwest Samaria.
2:3 *sons of the prophets.* The bands or guilds of prophets that were active at this time.
2:9 *let a double portion of your spirit be upon me.* This is not

a request to be twice as spiritual as Elijah. Rather, a double share was the portion of the first-born, the heir. Thus, Elisha is asking to be Elijah's heir.

has taken him up and cast him on some mountain or into some valley." And he said, "You shall not send."

17   But when they urged him until he was ashamed, he said, "Send." They sent therefore fifty men; and they searched three days, but did not find him.

18   And they returned to him while he was staying at Jericho; and he said to them, "Did I not say to you, 'Do not go'?"

19   Then the men of the city said to Elisha, "Behold now, the situation of this city is pleasant, as my lord sees; but the water is bad, and the land is unfruitful."

20   And he said, "Bring me a new jar, and put salt in it." So they brought *it* to him.

21   And he went out to the spring of water, and threw salt in it and said, "Thus says the LORD, 'I have purified these waters; there shall not be from there death or unfruitfulness any longer.' "

22   So the waters have been purified to this day, according to the word of Elisha which he spoke.

23   Then he went up from there to Bethel; and as he was going up by the way, young lads came out from the city and mocked him and said to him, "Go up, you baldhead; go up, you baldhead!"

24   When he looked behind him and saw them, he cursed them in the name of the LORD. Then two female bears came out of the woods and tore up forty-two lads of their number.

25   And he went from there to Mount Carmel, and from there he returned to Samaria.

3. *Jehoram's campaign against Moab*

3   Now Jehoram the son of Ahab became king over Israel at Samaria in the eighteenth year of Jehoshaphat king of Judah, and reigned twelve years.

2   And he did evil in the sight of the LORD, though not like his father and his mother; for he put away the *sacred* pillar of Baal which his father had made.

3   Nevertheless, he clung to the sins of Jeroboam the son of Nebat, which he made Israel sin; he did not depart from them.

4   Now Mesha king of Moab was a sheep breeder, and used to pay the king of Israel 100,000 lambs and the wool of 100,000 rams.

5   But it came about, when Ahab died, the king of Moab rebelled against the king of Israel.

6   And King Jehoram went out of Samaria at that time and mustered all Israel.

7   Then he went and sent *word* to Jehoshaphat the king of Judah, saying, "The king of Moab has rebelled against me. Will you go with me to fight against Moab?" And he said, "I will go up; I am as you are, my people as your people, my horses as your horses."

8   And he said, "Which way shall we go up?" And he answered, "The way of the wilderness of Edom."

9   So the king of Israel went with the king of Judah and the king of Edom; and they made a circuit of seven days' journey, and there was no water for the army or for the cattle that followed them.

10   Then the king of Israel said, "Alas! For the LORD has called these three kings to give them into the hand of Moab."

11   But Jehoshaphat said, "Is there not a prophet of the LORD here, that we may inquire of the LORD by him?" And one of the king of Israel's servants answered and said, "Elisha the son of Shaphat is here, who used to pour water on the hands of Elijah."

12   And Jehoshaphat said, "The word of the LORD is with him." So the king of Israel and Jehoshaphat and the king of Edom went down to him.

13   Now Elisha said to the king of Israel, "What do I have to do with you? Go to the prophets of your father and to the prophets of your mother." And the king of Israel said to him, "No, for the LORD has called these three kings *together* to give them into the hand of Moab."

14   And Elisha said, "As the LORD of hosts lives, before whom I stand, were it not that I regard the presence of Jehoshaphat the king of Judah, I would not look at you nor see you.

2:17
2 Kin 8:11

2:21
Ex 15:25;
2 Kin 4:41;
6:6

2:24
see
Neh 13:25-27

2:25
2 Kin 4:25;
1 Kin 18:19,
20

3:1
2 Kin 1:17

3:2
2 Kin 10:18,
26-28;
1 Kin 16:31,
32

3:3
1 Kin 12:28-32;
14:9,16

3:4
2 Sam 8:2;
Is 16:1

*3:5
2 Kin 1:1

3:7
1 Kin 22:4

3:9
vv. 1,7;
1 Kin 22:47

3:11
1 Kin 22:7;
19:21

3:13
Ezek 14:3-5;
1 Kin 18:19

3:14
1 Kin 17:1;
2 Kin 5:16

3:5 A stone inscription describing Mesha's revolt against Israel has been found. It was discovered by a Prussian missionary about a century ago and is known as the Moabite Stone.

15 "But now bring me a minstrel." And it came about, when the minstrel played, that the hand of the LORD came upon him.

16 And he said, "Thus says the LORD, 'Make this valley full of trenches.'

17 "For thus says the LORD, 'You shall not see wind nor shall you see rain; yet that valley shall be filled with water, so that you shall drink, both you and your cattle and your beasts.

18 'And this is but a slight thing in the sight of the LORD; He shall also give the Moabites into your hand.

19 'Then you shall strike every fortified city and every choice city, and fell every good tree and stop all springs of water, and mar every good piece of land with stones.'"

20 And it happened in the morning about the time of offering the sacrifice, that behold, water came by the way of Edom, and the country was filled with water.

21 Now all the Moabites heard that the kings had come up to fight against them. And all who were able to put on armor and older were summoned, and stood on the border.

22 And they rose early in the morning, and the sun shone on the water, and the Moabites saw the water opposite *them* as red as blood.

23 Then they said, "This is blood; the kings have surely fought together, and they have slain one another. Now therefore, Moab, to the spoil!"

24 But when they came to the camp of Israel, the Israelites arose and struck the Moabites, so that they fled before them; and they went forward into the land, slaughtering the Moabites.

25 Thus they destroyed the cities; and each one threw a stone on every piece of good land and filled it. So they stopped all the springs of water and felled all the good trees, until in Kir-haraseth *only* they left its stones; however, the slingers went about *it* and struck it.

26 When the king of Moab saw that the battle was too fierce for him, he took with him 700 men who drew swords, to break through to the king of Edom; but they could not.

27 Then he took his oldest son who was to reign in his place, and offered him as a burnt offering on the wall. And there came great wrath against Israel, and they departed from him and returned to their own land.

4. *Some of Elisha's miracles*

a. *The increase of the widow's oil*

4 Now a certain woman of the wives of the sons of the prophets cried out to Elisha, "Your servant my husband is dead, and you know that your servant feared the LORD; and the creditor has come to take my two children to be his slaves."

2 And Elisha said to her, "What shall I do for you? Tell me, what do you have in the house?" And she said, "Your maidservant has nothing in the house except a jar of oil."

3 Then he said, "Go, borrow vessels at large for yourself from all your neighbors, *even* empty vessels; do not get a few.

4 "And you shall go in and shut the door behind you and your sons, and pour out into all these vessels; and you shall set aside what is full."

5 So she went from him and shut the door behind her and her sons; they were bringing *the vessels* to her and she poured.

6 And it came about when the vessels were full, that she said to her son, "Bring me another vessel." And he said to her, "There is not one vessel more." And the oil stopped.

7 Then she came and told the man of God. And he said, "Go, sell the oil and pay your debt, and you *and* your sons can live on the rest."

b. *The promise of a son to the Shunammite woman*

8 Now there came a day when Elisha passed over to Shunem, where there was a prominent woman, and she persuaded him to eat food. And so it was, as often as he passed by, he turned in there to eat food.

3:15
1 Sam 16:23;
Ezek 1:3

3:19
v. 25

3:20
Ex 29:39,40

3:21
Gen 19:37

3:25
v. 19; Is 16:7,
11; Jer 48:31,
36

*3:27
Amos 2:1;
Mic 6:7

4:1
2 Kin 2:3;
Lev 25:39;
Matt 18:25

*4:7
1 Kin 12:22

4:8
Josh 19:18

3:27 Mesha's sacrifice of his eldest son to Molech was revolting to the Israelites.

4:7 The *man of God* was Shemaiah, a prophet. (See 1 Kin. 12:22.)

9　And she said to her husband, "Behold now, I perceive that this is a holy man of God passing by us continually.

10　"Please, let us make a little walled upper chamber and let us set a bed for him there, and a table and a chair and a lampstand; and it shall be, when he comes to us, *that* he can turn in there."

11　One day he came there and turned in to the upper chamber and rested.

12　Then he said to Gehazi his servant, "Call this Shunammite." And when he had called her, she stood before him.

13　And he said to him, "Say now to her, 'Behold, you have been careful for us with all this care; what can I do for you? Would you be spoken for to the king or to the captain of the army?' " And she answered, "I live among my own people."

14　So he said, "What then is to be done for her?" And Gehazi answered, "Truly she has no son and her husband is old."

15　And he said, "Call her." When he had called her, she stood in the doorway.

16　Then he said, "At this season next year you shall embrace a son." And she said, "No, my lord, O man of God, do not lie to your maidservant."

17　And the woman conceived and bore a son at that season the next year, as Elisha had said to her.

c. Elisha raises the dead son of the Shunammite

18　When the child was grown, the day came that he went out to his father to the reapers.

19　And he said to his father, "My head, my head." And he said to his servant, "Carry him to his mother."

20　When he had taken him and brought him to his mother, he sat on her lap until noon, and *then* died.

21　And she went up and laid him on the bed of the man of God, and shut *the door* behind him, and went out.

22　Then she called to her husband and said, "Please send me one of the servants and one of the donkeys, that I may run to the man of God and return."

23　And he said, "Why will you go to him today? It is neither new moon nor sabbath." And she said, "*It will be* well."

24　Then she saddled a donkey and said to her servant, "Drive and go forward; do not slow down the pace for me unless I tell you."

25　So she went and came to the man of God to Mount Carmel. And it came about when the man of God saw her at a distance, that he said to Gehazi his servant, "Behold, yonder is the Shunammite.

26　"Please run now to meet her and say to her, 'Is it well with you? Is it well with your husband? Is it well with the child?' " And she answered, "It is well."

27　When she came to the man of God to the hill, she caught hold of his feet. And Gehazi came near to push her away; but the man of God said, "Let her alone, for her soul is troubled within her; and the LORD has hidden it from me and has not told me."

28　Then she said, "Did I ask for a son from my lord? Did I not say, 'Do not deceive me'?"

29　Then he said to Gehazi, "Gird up your loins and take my staff in your hand, and go your way; if you meet any man, do not salute him, and if anyone salutes you, do not answer him; and lay my staff on the lad's face."

30　And the mother of the lad said, "As the LORD lives and as you yourself live, I will not leave you." And he arose and followed her.

31　Then Gehazi passed on before them and laid the staff on the lad's face, but there was neither sound nor response. So he returned to meet him and told him, "The lad has not awakened."

32　When Elisha came into the house, behold the lad was dead and laid on his bed.

33　So he entered and shut the door behind them both, and prayed to the LORD.

34　And he went up and lay on the child, and put his mouth on his mouth and his eyes on his eyes and his hands on his hands, and he stretched himself on him; and the flesh of the child became warm.

35　Then he returned and walked in the house once back and forth, and went up and stretched himself on him; and the lad sneezed seven times and the lad opened his eyes.

36   And he called Gehazi and said, "Call this Shunammite." So he called her. And when she came in to him, he said, "Take up your son."

37   Then she went in and fell at his feet and bowed herself to the ground, and she took up her son and went out.

d. The poisonous stew made harmless

38   When Elisha returned to Gilgal, *there was* a famine in the land. As the sons of the prophets were sitting before him, he said to his servant, "Put on the large pot and boil stew for the sons of the prophets."

39   Then one went out into the field to gather herbs, and found a wild vine and gathered from it his lap full of wild gourds, and came and sliced them into the pot of stew, for they did not know *what they were*.

40   So they poured *it* out for the men to eat. And it came about as they were eating of the stew, that they cried out and said, "O man of God, there is death in the pot." And they were unable to eat.

41   But he said, "Now bring meal." And he threw it into the pot, and he said, "Pour *it* out for the people that they may eat." Then there was no harm in the pot.

e. The miraculous feeding of the hundred men

42   Now a man came from Baal-shalishah, and brought the man of God bread of the first fruits, twenty loaves of barley and fresh ears of grain in his sack. And he said, "Give *them* to the people that they may eat."

43   And his attendant said, "What, shall I set this before a hundred men?" But he said, "Give *them* to the people that they may eat, for thus says the LORD, 'They shall eat and have *some* left over.' "

44   So he set *it* before them, and they ate and had *some* left over, according to the word of the LORD.

5. Naaman the leper and Elisha

a. The testimony of the Israelitish girl

5 Now Naaman, captain of the army of the king of Aram, was a great man with his master, and highly respected, because by him the LORD had given victory to Aram. The man was also a valiant warrior, *but he was* a leper.

2   Now the Arameans had gone out in bands, and had taken captive a little girl from the land of Israel; and she waited on Naaman's wife.

3   And she said to her mistress, "I wish that my master were with the prophet who is in Samaria! Then he would cure him of his leprosy."

4   And Naaman went in and told his master, saying, "Thus and thus spoke the girl who is from the land of Israel."

5   Then the king of Aram said, "Go now, and I will send a letter to the king of Israel." And he departed and took with him ten talents of silver and six thousand *shekels* of gold and ten changes of clothes.

b. The message of the Syrian king to Jehoram

6   And he brought the letter to the king of Israel, saying, "And now as this letter comes to you, behold, I have sent Naaman my servant to you, that you may cure him of his leprosy."

7   And it came about when the king of Israel read the letter, that he tore his clothes and said, "Am I God, to kill and to make alive, that this man is sending *word* to me to cure a man of his leprosy? But consider now, and see how he is seeking a quarrel against me."

c. Elisha gives orders to Naaman, who is healed

8   And it happened when Elisha the man of God heard that the king of Israel had torn his clothes, that he sent *word* to the king, saying, "Why have you torn your clothes? Now let him come to me, and he shall know that there is a prophet in Israel."

9   So Naaman came with his horses and his chariots, and stood at the doorway of the house of Elisha.

10   And Elisha sent a messenger to him, saying, "Go and wash in the Jordan seven times, and your flesh shall be restored to you and *you shall* be clean."

11   But Naaman was furious and went away and said, "Behold, I thought, 'He will surely come out to me, and stand and call on the name of the LORD his God, and wave his hand over the place, and cure the leper.'

4:37
1 Kin 17:23;
Heb 11:35

4:38
2 Kin 2:1,3;
8:1;
Luke 10:39;
Acts 22:3

4:41
Ex 15:25;
2 Kin 2:21

4:42
1 Sam 9:4,7

4:44
Matt 14:16-21;
15:32-38

5:1
Luke 4:27

5:5
1 Sam 9:8;
2 Kin 8:8,9

5:7
Gen 37:29;
30:2;
Deut 32:39;
1 Sam 2:6;
1 Kin 20:7

5:8
1 Kin 12:22

5:10
John 9:7

v11- quiet miracles are harder to accept than ones with holy histrionics

12　"Are not Abanah and Pharpar, the rivers of Damascus, better than all the waters of Israel? Could I not wash in them and be clean?" So he turned and went away in a rage.

13　Then his servants came near and spoke to him and said, "My father, had the prophet told you *to do some* great thing, would you not have done *it?* How much more *then,* when he says to you, 'Wash, and be clean'?"

14　So he went down and dipped *himself* seven times in the Jordan, according to the word of the man of God; and his flesh was restored like the flesh of a little child, and he was clean.

d. *Elisha refuses a reward*

15　When he returned to the man of God with all his company, and came and stood before him, he said, "Behold now, I know that there is no God in all the earth, but in Israel; so please take a present from your servant now."

16　But he said, "As the LORD lives, before whom I stand, I will take nothing." And he urged him to take *it,* but he refused.

17　And Naaman said, "If not, please let your servant at least be given two mules' load of earth; for your servant will no more offer burnt offering nor will he sacrifice to other gods, but to the LORD.

18　"In this matter may the LORD pardon your servant: when my master goes into the house of Rimmon to worship there, and he leans on my hand and I bow myself in the house of Rimmon, when I bow myself in the house of Rimmon, the LORD pardon your servant in this matter."

19　And he said to him, "Go in peace." So he departed from him some distance.

e. *Gehazi's covetousness and punishment*

20　But Gehazi, the servant of Elisha the man of God, thought, "Behold, my master has spared this Naaman the Aramean, by not receiving from his hands what he brought. As the LORD lives, I will run after him and take something from him."

21　So Gehazi pursued Naaman. When Naaman saw one running after him, he came down from the chariot to meet him and said, "Is all well?"

22　And he said, "All is well. My master has sent me, saying, 'Behold, just now two young men of the sons of the prophets have come to me from the hill country of Ephraim. Please give them a talent of silver and two changes of clothes.' "

23　And Naaman said, "Be pleased to take two talents." And he urged him, and bound two talents of silver in two bags with two changes of clothes, and gave them to two of his servants; and they carried *them* before him.

24　When he came to the hill, he took them from their hand and deposited them in the house, and he sent the men away, and they departed.

25　But he went in and stood before his master. And Elisha said to him, "Where have you been, Gehazi?" And he said, "Your servant went nowhere."

26　Then he said to him, "Did not my heart go *with you,* when the man turned from his chariot to meet you? Is it a time to receive money and to receive clothes and olive groves and vineyards and sheep and oxen and male and female servants?

27　"Therefore, the leprosy of Naaman shall cleave to you and to your descendants forever." So he went out from his presence a leper *as white* as snow.

6. *The further ministry of Elisha*

a. *The recovery of the lost axe head*

6　Now the sons of the prophets said to Elisha, "Behold now, the place before you where we are living is too limited for us.

2　"Please let us go to the Jordan, and each of us take from there a beam, and let us make a place there for ourselves where we may live." So he said, "Go."

3　Then one said, "Please be willing to go with your servants." And he answered, "I shall go."

4　So he went with them; and when they came to the Jordan, they cut down trees.

5　But as one was felling a beam, the axe head fell into the water; and he cried out and said, "Alas, my master! For it was borrowed."

6　Then the man of God said, "Where did it fall?" And when he showed him the place, he cut off a stick, and threw *it* in there, and made the iron float.

7　And he said, "Take it up for yourself." So he put out his hand and took it.

Marginal references (left column):

5:13　2 Kin 6:21; 8:9; 1 Sam 28:23

5:14　v. 10; Job 33:25; Luke 4:27

5:15　1 Sam 15:46, 47; Dan 2:47; 3:29; 1 Sam 25:27

5:16　2 Kin 3:14; vv. 20,26; Gen 14:22,23

5:18　2 Kin 7:2,17

5:20　2 Kin 4:12, 31,36

5:22　2 Kin 4:26; Josh 24:33

5:25　v. 22

5:26　v. 16

5:27　Ex 4:6; Num 12:10; 2 Kin 15:5

6:1　2 Kin 4:38

6:6　2 Kin 2:21

b. Elisha discloses Ben-hadad's plans to Jehoram

8 Now the king of Aram was warring against Israel; and he counseled with his servants saying, "In such and such a place shall be my camp."

9 And the man of God sent *word* to the king of Israel saying, "Beware that you do not pass this place, for the Arameans are coming down there."

10 And the king of Israel sent to the place about which the man of God had told him; thus he warned him, so that he guarded himself there, more than once or twice.

c. Elisha strikes the Syrians blind

11 Now the heart of the king of Aram was enraged over this thing; and he called his servants and said to them, "Will you tell me which of us is for the king of Israel?"

12 And one of his servants said, "No, my lord, O king; but Elisha, the prophet who is in Israel, tells the king of Israel the words that you speak in your bedroom."

13 So he said, "Go and see where he is, that I may send and take him." And it was told him, saying, "Behold, he is in Dothan."

14 And he sent horses and chariots and a great army there, and they came by night and surrounded the city.

15 Now when the attendant of the man of God had risen early and gone out, behold, an army with horses and chariots was circling the city. And his servant said to him, "Alas, my master! What shall we do?"

16 So he answered, "Do not fear, for those who are with us are more than those who are with them."

17 Then Elisha prayed and said, "O Lord, I pray, open his eyes that he may see." And the Lord opened the servant's eyes, and he saw; and behold, the mountain was full of horses and chariots of fire all around Elisha.

18 And when they came down to him, Elisha prayed to the Lord and said, "Strike this people with blindness, I pray." So He struck them with blindness according to the word of Elisha.

19 Then Elisha said to them, "This is not the way, nor is this the city; follow me and I will bring you to the man whom you seek." And he brought them to Samaria.

d. The blind Syrians led to Samaria

20 And it came about when they had come into Samaria, that Elisha said, "O Lord, open the eyes of these *men*, that they may see." So the Lord opened their eyes, and they saw; and behold, they were in the midst of Samaria.

21 Then the king of Israel when he saw them, said to Elisha, "My father, shall I kill them? Shall I kill them?"

22 And he answered, "You shall not kill *them*. Would you kill those you have taken captive with your sword and with your bow? Set bread and water before them, that they may eat and drink and go to their master."

23 So he prepared a great feast for them; and when they had eaten and drunk he sent them away, and they went to their master. And the marauding bands of Arameans did not come again into the land of Israel.

e. Elisha and the siege of Samaria

24 Now it came about after this, that Ben-hadad king of Aram gathered all his army and went up and besieged Samaria.

25 And there was a great famine in Samaria; and behold, they besieged it, until a donkey's head was sold for eighty *shekels* of silver, and a fourth of a ¹kab of dove's dung for five *shekels* of silver.

26 And as the king of Israel was passing by on the wall a woman cried out to him, saying, "Help, my lord, O king!"

27 And he said, "If the Lord does not help you, from where shall I help you? From the threshing floor, or from the wine press?"

28 And the king said to her, "What is the matter with you?" And she answered, "This woman said to me, 'Give your son that we may eat him today, and we will eat my son tomorrow.'

29 "So we boiled my son and ate him; and I said to her on the next day, 'Give your son, that we may eat him'; but she has hidden her son."

¹I.e., One kab equals approx. 2 quarts

6:9
v. 12

6:13
Gen 37:17

6:16
2 Chr 32:7,8;
Ps 55:18;
Rom 8:31
6:17
2 Kin 2:11;
Ps 68:17;
Zech 6:1-7
6:18
Gen 19:11

6:20
v. 17

6:21
2 Kin 2:12;
5:13; 8:9
6:22
Deut 20:11-16;
Rom 12:20

6:23
vv. 8,9;
2 Kin 5:2

6:24
1 Kin 20:1

6:29
Lev 26:27-29;
Deut 28:52,
53,57

6:30
1 Kin 21:27
30   And it came about when the king heard the words of the woman, that he tore his clothes—now he was passing by on the wall—and the people looked, and behold, he had sackcloth beneath on his body.

6:31
Ruth 1:17;
1 Kin 19:2
31   Then he said, "May God do so to me and more also, if the head of Elisha the son of Shaphat remains on him today."

6:32
Ezek 8:1;
20:1;
1 Kin 18:4,
13,14
32   Now Elisha was sitting in his house, and the elders were sitting with him. And *the king* sent a man from his presence; but before the messenger came to him, he said to the elders, "Do you see how this son of a murderer has sent to take away my head? Look, when the messenger comes, shut the door and hold the door shut against him. Is not the sound of his master's feet behind him?"

6:33
Job 2:9
33   And while he was still talking with them, behold, the messenger came down to him, and he said, "Behold, this evil is from the LORD; why should I wait for the LORD any longer?"

7:1
v. 18
7 Then Elisha said, "Listen to the word of the LORD; thus says the LORD, 'Tomorrow about this time a measure of fine flour shall be *sold* for a shekel, and two measures of barley for a shekel, in the gate of Samaria.' "

7:2
vv. 17,19,20;
Mal 3:10
2   And the royal officer on whose hand the king was leaning answered the man of God and said, "Behold, if the LORD should make windows in heaven, could this thing be?" Then he said, "Behold you shall see it with your own eyes, but you shall not eat of it."

7:3
Lev 13:46
3   Now there were four leprous men at the entrance of the gate; and they said to one another, "Why do we sit here until we die?

7:4
2 Kin 6:24
4   "If we say, 'We will enter the city,' then the famine is in the city and we shall die there; and if we sit here, we die also. Now therefore come, and let us go over to the camp of the Arameans. If they spare us, we shall live; and if they kill us, we shall but die."

5   And they arose at twilight to go to the camp of the Arameans; when they came to the outskirts of the camp of the Arameans, behold, there was no one there.

*7:6
2 Sam 5:24;
19:7;
1 Kin 10:29
6   For the Lord had caused the army of the Arameans to hear a sound of chariots and a sound of horses, *even* the sound of a great army, so that they said to one another, "Behold, the king of Israel has hired against us the kings of the Hittites and the kings of the Egyptians, to come upon us."

7:7
Ps 48:4-6
7   Therefore they arose and fled in the twilight, and left their tents and their horses and their donkeys, even the camp just as it was, and fled for their life.

8   When these lepers came to the outskirts of the camp, they entered one tent and ate and drank, and carried from there silver and gold and clothes, and went and hid *them*; and they returned and entered another tent and carried from there *also*, and went and hid *them*.

7:9
2 Sam 18:27
9   Then they said to one another, "We are not doing right. This day is a day of good news, but we are keeping silent; if we wait until morning light, punishment will overtake us. Now therefore come, let us go and tell the king's household."

10   So they came and called to the gatekeepers of the city, and they told them, saying, "We came to the camp of the Arameans, and behold, there was no one there, nor the voice of man, only the horses tied and the donkeys tied, and the tents just as they were."

11   And the gatekeepers called, and told *it* within the king's household.

7:12
2 Kin 6:25-29
12   Then the king arose in the night and said to his servants, "I will now tell you what the Arameans have done to us. They know that we are hungry; therefore they have gone from the camp to hide themselves in the field, saying, 'When they come out of the city, we shall capture them alive and get into the city.' "

13   And one of his servants answered and said, "Please, let some *men* take five of the horses which remain, which are left in the city. Behold, they *will be in any case* like all the multitude of Israel who are left in it; behold, they *will be in any case* like all the multitude of Israel who have already perished, so let us send and see."

14   They took therefore two chariots with horses, and the king sent after the army of the Arameans, saying, "Go and see."

15   And they went after them to the Jordan, and behold, all the way was full of clothes and equipment, which the Arameans had thrown away in their haste. Then the messengers returned and told the king.

7:6 *Egyptians* (Hebrew *misraim*) may be a confusion with *muzrim*, a district in Asia Minor. Kings of this region, not the kings of Egypt, would most likely have been hired along with the Hittites in Asia Minor to attack the Syrians.

16 So the people went out and plundered the camp of the Arameans. Then a measure of fine flour *was sold* for a shekel and two measures of barley for a shekel, according to the word of the LORD.

17 Now the king appointed the royal officer on whose hand he leaned to have charge of the gate; but the people trampled on him at the gate, and he died just as the man of God had said, who spoke when the king came down to him.

18 And it came about just as the man of God had spoken to the king, saying, "Two measures of barley for a shekel and a measure of fine flour for a shekel, shall be *sold* tomorrow about this time at the gate of Samaria."

19 Then the royal officer answered the man of God and said, "Now behold, if the LORD should make windows in heaven, could such a thing be?" And he said, "Behold, you shall see it with your own eyes, but you shall not eat of it."

20 And so it happened to him, for the people trampled on him at the gate, and he died.

7. The Shunammite woman comes home

8 Now Elisha spoke to the woman whose son he had restored to life, saying, "Arise and go with your household, and sojourn wherever you can sojourn; for the LORD has called for a famine, and it shall even come on the land for seven years."

2 So the woman arose and did according to the word of the man of God, and she went with her household and sojourned in the land of the Philistines seven years.

3 And it came about at the end of seven years, that the woman returned from the land of the Philistines; and she went out to appeal to the king for her house and for her field.

4 Now the king was talking with Gehazi, the servant of the man of God, saying, "Please relate to me all the great things that Elisha has done."

5 And it came about, as he was relating to the king how he had restored to life the one who was dead, that behold, the woman whose son he had restored to life, appealed to the king for her house and for her field. And Gehazi said, "My lord, O king, this is the woman and this is her son, whom Elisha restored to life."

6 When the king asked the woman, she related *it* to him. So the king appointed for her a certain officer, saying, "Restore all that was hers and all the produce of the field from the day that she left the land even until now."

8. Elisha anoints Hazael king of Syria

7 Then Elisha came to Damascus. Now Ben-hadad king of Aram was sick, and it was told him, saying, "The man of God has come here."

8 And the king said to Hazael, "Take a gift in your hand and go to meet the man of God, and inquire of the LORD by him, saying, 'Will I recover from this sickness?'"

9 So Hazael went to meet him and took a gift in his hand, even every kind of good thing of Damascus, forty camels' loads; and he came and stood before him and said, "Your son Ben-hadad king of Aram has sent me to you, saying, 'Will I recover from this sickness?'"

10 Then Elisha said to him, "Go, say to him, 'You shall surely recover,' but the LORD has shown me that he will certainly die."

11 And he fixed his gaze steadily *on him* until he was ashamed, and the man of God wept.

12 And Hazael said, "Why does my lord weep?" Then he answered, "Because I know the evil that you will do to the sons of Israel: their strongholds you will set on fire, and their young men you will kill with the sword, and their little ones you will dash in pieces, and their women with child you will rip up."

13 Then Hazael said, "But what is your servant, *who is but* a dog, that he should do this great thing?" And Elisha answered, "The LORD has shown me that you will be king over Aram."

14 So he departed from Elisha and returned to his master, who said to him, "What did Elisha say to you?" And he answered, "He told me that you would surely recover."

15 And it came about on the morrow, that he took the cover and dipped it in water and spread it on his face, so that he died. And Hazael became king in his place.

7:16
v. 1

7:17
v. 2;
2 Kin 6:32

7:18
v. 1

7:19
v. 2

8:1
2 Kin 4:35;
Ps 105:16;
Hag 1:11

8:4
2 Kin 4:12;
5:20-27
8:5
2 Kin 4:35

8:7
1 Kin 11:24;
2 Kin 6:24
8:8
1 Kin 19:15;
14:3;
2 Kin 1:2

8:10
vv. 14,15

8:12
2 Kin 10:32;
12:17; 13:3,7;
15:16;
Hos 13:16;
Amos 1:13
8:13
1 Sam 17:43;
1 Kin 19:15

8:15
v. 10

I. The reign of Jehoram (Judah) (cf. 2 Chr. 21:2–20)

16 Now in the fifth year of Joram the son of Ahab king of Israel, Jehoshaphat being then the king of Judah, Jehoram the son of Jehoshaphat king of Judah became king.

17 He was thirty-two years old when he became king, and he reigned eight years in Jerusalem.

18 And he walked in the way of the kings of Israel, just as the house of Ahab had done, for the daughter of Ahab became his wife; and he did evil in the sight of the LORD.

19 However, the LORD was not willing to destroy Judah, for the sake of David His servant, since He had promised him to give a lamp to him through his sons always.

20 In his days Edom revolted from under the hand of Judah, and made a king over themselves.

21 Then Joram crossed over to Zair, and all his chariots with him. And it came about that he arose by night and struck the Edomites who had surrounded him and the captains of the chariots; but *his* army fled to their tents.

22 So Edom revolted against Judah to this day. Then Libnah revolted at the same time.

23 And the rest of the acts of Joram and all that he did, are they not written in the Book of the Chronicles of the Kings of Judah?

24 So Joram slept with his fathers, and was buried with his fathers in the city of David; and Ahaziah his son became king in his place.

J. The reign of Ahaziah (Judah)

25 In the twelfth year of Joram the son of Ahab king of Israel, Ahaziah the son of Jehoram king of Judah began to reign.

26 Ahaziah *was* twenty-two years old when he became king, and he reigned one year in Jerusalem. And his mother's name *was* Athaliah the granddaughter of Omri king of Israel.

27 And he walked in the way of the house of Ahab, and did evil in the sight of the LORD, like the house of Ahab *had done*, because he was a son-in-law of the house of Ahab.

28 Then he went with Joram the son of Ahab to war against Hazael king of Aram at Ramoth-gilead, and the Arameans wounded Joram.

29 So King Joram returned to be healed in Jezreel of the wounds which the Arameans had inflicted on him at Ramah, when he fought against Hazael king of Aram. Then Ahaziah the son of Jehoram king of Judah went down to see Joram the son of Ahab in Jezreel because he was sick.

K. The reign of Jehu (Israel)

1. Jehu anointed king

9 Now Elisha the prophet called one of the sons of the prophets, and said to him, "Gird up your loins, and take this flask of oil in your hand, and go to Ramoth-gilead.

2 "When you arrive there, search out Jehu the son of Jehoshaphat the son of Nimshi, and go in and bid him arise from among his brothers, and bring him to an inner room.

3 "Then take the flask of oil and pour it on his head and say, 'Thus says the LORD, "I have anointed you king over Israel." ' Then open the door and flee and do not wait."

4 So the young man, the servant of the prophet, went to Ramoth-gilead.

5 When he came, behold, the captains of the army were sitting, and he said, "I have a word for you, O captain." And Jehu said, "For which *one* of us?" And he said, "For you, O captain."

6 And he arose and went into the house, and he poured the oil on his head and said to him, "Thus says the LORD, the God of Israel, 'I have anointed you king over the people of the LORD, *even* over Israel.

8:16
2 Kin 1:17;
3:1;
2 Chr 3:3,4
8:17
2 Chr 21:5-10
8:18
v. 27
8:19
2 Sam 7:13;
1 Kin 11:36;
2 Chr 21:7
8:20
1 Kin 22:4;
2 Kin 3:27;
2 Chr 21:8-10
8:21
2 Sam 18:17;
19:8
8:22
2 Chr 21:10
8:24
2 Chr 21:20;
22:1
8:25
2 Chr 22:1-6
8:28
v. 15;
1 Kin 22:3,29
8:29
2 Kin 9:15;
2 Chr 22:6,7
9:1
2 Kin 2:3;
4:29; 8:28,29
9:2
vv. 5,11
9:3
2 Chr 22:7
9:6
v. 3;
1 Kin 19:16;
2 Chr 22:7

8:26 It was through Athaliah, daughter of Ahab and Jezebel and granddaughter of Omri, that the idolatrous worship of Israel was carried to Judah. As the wife of King Jehoram of Judah, she exercised great influence in the religious realm.

7   'And you shall strike the house of Ahab your master, that I may avenge the blood of My servants the prophets, and the blood of all the servants of the LORD, at the hand of Jezebel.

8   'For the whole house of Ahab shall perish, and I will cut off from Ahab every male person both bond and free in Israel.

9   'And I will make the house of Ahab like the house of Jeroboam the son of Nebat, and like the house of Baasha the son of Ahijah.

10   'And the dogs shall eat Jezebel in the territory of Jezreel, and none shall bury her.' " Then he opened the door and fled.

11   Now Jehu came out to the servants of his master, and one said to him, "Is all well? Why did this mad fellow come to you?" And he said to them, "You know *very well* the man and his talk."

12   And they said, "It is a lie, tell us now." And he said, "Thus and thus he said to me, 'Thus says the LORD, "I have anointed you king over Israel." ' "

13   Then they hurried and each man took his garment and placed it under him on the bare steps, and blew the trumpet, saying, "Jehu is king!"

2. Jehoram (Joram of Israel) defeated and slain

14   So Jehu the son of Jehoshaphat the son of Nimshi conspired against Joram. Now Joram with all Israel was defending Ramoth-gilead against Hazael king of Aram,

15   but King [2]Joram had returned to Jezreel to be healed of the wounds which the Arameans had inflicted on him when he fought with Hazael king of Aram. So Jehu said, "If this is your mind, *then* let no one escape *or* leave the city to go tell *it* in Jezreel."

16   Then Jehu rode in a chariot and went to Jezreel, for Joram was lying there. And Ahaziah king of Judah had come down to see Joram.

17   Now the watchman was standing on the tower in Jezreel and he saw the company of Jehu as he came, and said, "I see a company." And Joram said, "Take a horseman and send him to meet them and let him say, 'Is it peace?' "

18   So a horseman went to meet him and said, "Thus says the king, 'Is it peace?' " And Jehu said, "What have you to do with peace? Turn behind me." And the watchman reported, "The messenger came to them, but he did not return."

19   Then he sent out a second horseman, who came to them and said, "Thus says the king, 'Is it peace?' " And Jehu answered, "What have you to do with peace? Turn behind me."

20   And the watchman reported, "He came even to them, and he did not return; and the driving is like the driving of Jehu the son of Nimshi, for he drives furiously."

21   Then Joram said, "Get ready." And they made his chariot ready. And Joram king of Israel and Ahaziah king of Judah went out, each in his chariot, and they went out to meet Jehu and found him in the property of Naboth the Jezreelite.

22   And it came about, when Joram saw Jehu, that he said, "Is it peace, Jehu?" And he answered, "What peace, so long as the harlotries of your mother Jezebel and her witchcrafts are so many?"

23   So Joram reined about and fled and said to Ahaziah, "*There is* treachery, O Ahaziah!"

24   And Jehu drew his bow with his full strength and shot Joram between his arms; and the arrow went through his heart, and he sank in his chariot.

25   Then *Jehu* said to Bidkar his officer, "Take *him* up and cast him into the [3]property of the field of Naboth the Jezreelite, for I remember when you and I were riding together after Ahab his father, that the LORD laid this oracle against him:

26   'Surely I have seen yesterday the blood of Naboth and the blood of his sons,' says the LORD, 'and I will repay you in this [3]property,' says the LORD. Now then, take and cast him into the property, according to the word of the LORD."

3. Ahaziah (Judah) defeated and slain

27   When Ahaziah the king of Judah saw *this*, he fled by the way of the garden house. And Jehu pursued him and said, "Shoot him too, in the chariot." *So they shot him* at the ascent of Gur, which is at Ibleam. But he fled to Megiddo and died there.

[2]Heb., *Jehoram*, and so throughout this context   [3]Lit., *portion*, and so throughout this context

---

9:7
Deut 32:35;
1 Kin 18:4;
21:15; vv. 32,
37
9:8
2 Kin 10:17;
1 Kin 21:21;
1 Sam 25:22;
Deut 32:36;
2 Kin 14:26
9:9
1 Kin 14:10;
15:29; 16:3-5,
11,12
9:10
vv. 35,36;
1 Kin 21:23
9:11
Jer 29:26;
John 10:20;
Acts 26:24
9:13
Matt 21:7;
2 Sam 15:10;
1 Kin 1:34,39
9:14
2 Kin 8:28
9:15
2 Kin 8:29
9:16
2 Kin 8:29
9:18
vv. 19,22
9:20
2 Sam 18:27;
1 Kin 19:17
9:21
2 Chr 22:7;
v. 26;
1 Kin 21:1-7,
15-19
9:22
1 Kin 16:30-33;
18:19;
2 Chr 21:13
9:23
2 Kin 11:24
9:24
1 Kin 22:34
9:25
1 Kin 21:1,
19,24-29
9:26
1 Kin 21:19
9:27
2 Chr 22:9

28 Then his servants carried him in a chariot to Jerusalem, and buried him in his grave with his fathers in the city of David.

9:28
2 Kin 23:30

29 Now in the eleventh year of Joram, the son of Ahab, Ahaziah became king over Judah.

4. *Jehu's massacre of the house of Ahab*

a. *Jezebel slain*

9:30
Jer 4:30;
Ezek 23:40
9:31
1 Kin 16:9-20

30 When Jehu came to Jezreel, Jezebel heard *of it*, and she painted her eyes and adorned her head, and looked out the window.

31 And as Jehu entered the gate, she said, "Is it well, Zimri, your master's murderer?"

32 Then he lifted up his face to the window and said, "Who is on my side? Who?" And two or three officials looked down at him.

33 And he said, "Throw her down." So they threw her down, and some of her blood was sprinkled on the wall and on the horses, and he trampled her under foot.

9:34
1 Kin 21:25;
16:31

34 When he came in, he ate and drank; and he said, "See now to this cursed woman and bury her, for she is a king's daughter."

35 And they went to bury her, but they found no more of her than the skull and the feet and the palms of her hands.

9:36
1 Kin 21:23

36 Therefore they returned and told him. And he said, "This is the word of the LORD, which He spoke by His servant Elijah the Tishbite, saying, 'In the property of Jezreel the dogs shall eat the flesh of Jezebel;

9:37
Jer 8:1-3

37 and the corpse of Jezebel shall be as dung on the face of the field in the property of Jezreel, so they cannot say, "This is Jezebel." ' "

b. *Ahab's seventy sons beheaded*

10:1
1 Kin 16:24-29

10 Now Ahab had seventy sons in Samaria. And Jehu wrote letters and sent *them* to Samaria, to the rulers of Jezreel, the elders, and to the guardians of *the children of* Ahab, saying,

2 "And now, when this letter comes to you, since your master's sons are with you, as well as the chariots and horses and a fortified city and the weapons,

3 select the best and [4]fittest of your master's sons, and set *him* on his father's throne, and fight for your master's house."

4 But they feared greatly and said, "Behold, the two kings did not stand before him; how then can we stand?"

10:5
see
1 Kin 20:4,32

5 And the one who *was* over the household, and he who *was* over the city, the elders, and the guardians of *the children*, sent *word* to Jehu, saying, "We are your servants, all that you say to us we will do, we will not make any man king; do what is good in your sight."

6 Then he wrote a letter to them a second time saying, "If you are on my side, and you will listen to my voice, take the heads of the men, your master's sons, and come to me at Jezreel tomorrow about this time." Now the king's sons, seventy persons, *were* with the great men of the city, *who* were rearing them.

10:7
1 Kin 21:21

7 And it came about when the letter came to them, that they took the king's sons, and slaughtered *them*, seventy persons, and put their heads in baskets, and sent *them* to him at Jezreel.

8 When the messenger came and told him, saying, "They have brought the heads of the king's sons," he said, "Put them in two heaps at the entrance of the gate until morning."

10:9
2 Kin 9:14-24;
v. 6

9 Now it came about in the morning, that he went out and stood, and said to all the people, "You are innocent; behold, I conspired against my master and killed him, but who killed all these?

10:10
2 Kin 9:7-10;
1 Kin 21:19-29

10 "Know then that there shall fall to the earth nothing of the word of the LORD, which the LORD spoke concerning the house of Ahab, for the LORD has done what He spoke through His servant Elijah."

11 So Jehu killed all who remained of the house of Ahab in Jezreel, and all his great men and his acquaintances and his priests, until he left him without a survivor.

c. *Forty-two princes of Ahaziah slain*

12 Then he arose and departed, and went to Samaria. On the way while he was at [5]Beth-eked of the shepherds,

---

[4]Lit., *most upright*   [5]I.e., house of binding

13   Jehu met the relatives of Ahaziah king of Judah and said, "Who are you?" And they answered, "We are the relatives of Ahaziah; and we have come down to greet the sons of the king and the sons of the queen mother."

14   And he said, "Take them alive." So they took them alive, and killed them at the pit of Beth-eked, forty-two men; and he left none of them.

d. Jehonadab slays the rest of the house of Ahab

15   Now when he had departed from there, he met Jehonadab the son of Rechab coming to meet him; and he greeted him and said to him, "Is your heart right, as my heart is with your heart?" And Jehonadab answered, "It is." Jehu said, "If it is, give me your hand." And he gave him his hand, and he took him up to him into the chariot.

16   And he said, "Come with me and see my zeal for the LORD." So he made him ride in his chariot.

17   And when he came to Samaria, he killed all who remained to Ahab in Samaria, until he had destroyed him, according to the word of the LORD, which He spoke to Elijah.

e. The massacre of the Baal worshipers

18   Then Jehu gathered all the people and said to them, "Ahab served Baal a little; Jehu will serve him much.

19   "And now, summon all the prophets of Baal, all his worshipers and all his priests; let no one be missing, for I have a great sacrifice for Baal; whoever is missing shall not live." But Jehu did it in cunning, in order that he might destroy the worshipers of Baal.

20   And Jehu said, "Sanctify a solemn assembly for Baal." And they proclaimed it.

21   Then Jehu sent throughout Israel and all the worshipers of Baal came, so that there was not a man left who did not come. And when they went into the house of Baal, the house of Baal was filled from one end to the other.

22   And he said to the one who was in charge of the wardrobe, "Bring out garments for all the worshipers of Baal." So he brought out garments for them.

23   And Jehu went into the house of Baal with Jehonadab the son of Rechab; and he said to the worshipers of Baal, "Search and see that there may be here with you none of the servants of the LORD, but only the worshipers of Baal."

24   Then they went in to offer sacrifices and burnt offerings. Now Jehu had stationed for himself eighty men outside, and he had said, "The one who permits any of the men whom I bring into your hands to escape, shall give up his life in exchange."

25   Then it came about, as soon as he had finished offering the burnt offering, that Jehu said to the guard and to the royal officers, "Go in, kill them; let none come out." And they killed them with the edge of the sword; and the guard and the royal officers threw them out, and went to the inner room of the house of Baal.

26   And they brought out the sacred pillars of the house of Baal, and burned them.

27   They also broke down the sacred pillar of Baal and broke down the house of Baal, and made it a latrine to this day.

f. Resumé of Jehu's reign

28   Thus Jehu eradicated Baal out of Israel.

29   However, as for the sins of Jeroboam the son of Nebat, which he made Israel sin, from these Jehu did not depart, even the golden calves that were at Bethel and that were at Dan.

30   And the LORD said to Jehu, "Because you have done well in executing what is right in My eyes, and have done to the house of Ahab according to all that was in My heart, your sons of the fourth generation shall sit on the throne of Israel."

31   But Jehu was not careful to walk in the law of the LORD, the God of Israel, with all his heart; he did not depart from the sins of Jeroboam, which he made Israel sin.

32   In those days the LORD began to cut off portions from Israel; and Hazael defeated them throughout the territory of Israel:

10:13
2 Kin 8:24, 29;
2 Chr 22:8

*10:15
Jer 35:6ff;
1 Chr 2:55;
Ezra 10:19

10:16
1 Kin 19:10

10:17
2 Kin 9:8;
2 Chr 22:8;
v. 10

10:18
1 Kin 16:31, 32

10:19
1 Kin 22:6

10:20
Joel 1:14;
Ex 32:4-6

10:21
1 Kin 16:32;
2 Kin 11:18

10:24
1 Kin 20:39

10:25
1 Kin 18:40

10:26
1 Kin 14:23

10:27
Ezra 6:11;
Dan 2:5; 3:29

10:29
1 Kin 12:28, 29

10:30
v. 35;
2 Kin 15:8,12

10:31
v. 29

10:32
2 Kin 8:12

10:15 Jehonadab. This ascetic is mentioned in Jer. 35:6, where his descendants, the Rechabites, are put to the test by   Jeremiah. Jehu accepted Jehonadab as an honorable man.

33   from the Jordan eastward, all the land of Gilead, the Gadites and the Reubenites and the Manassites, from Aroer, which is by the valley of the Arnon, even Gilead and Bashan.

10:34
Amos 1:3-5

34   Now the rest of the acts of Jehu and all that he did and all his might, are they not written in the Book of the Chronicles of the Kings of Israel?

35   And Jehu slept with his fathers, and they buried him in Samaria. And Jehoahaz his son became king in his place.

36   Now the time which Jehu reigned over Israel in Samaria *was* twenty-eight years.

L. *The reign of Athaliah (Judah)*

1. *Athaliah seizes control*

11:1
2 Chr 22:10-12

11 When Athaliah the mother of Ahaziah saw that her son was dead, she rose and destroyed all the royal offspring.

2   But Jehosheba, the daughter of King Joram, sister of Ahaziah, took Joash the son of Ahaziah and stole him from among the king's sons who were being put to death, and placed him and his nurse in the bedroom. So they hid him from Athaliah, and he was not put to death.

3   So he was hidden with her in the house of the LORD six years, while Athaliah was reigning over the land.

2. *Jehoiada the priest overthrows Athaliah*

*11:4
2 Chr 23:1ff;
v. 19

4   Now in the seventh year Jehoiada sent and brought the captains of hundreds of the Carites and of the ⁶guard, and brought them to him in the house of the LORD. Then he made a covenant with them and put them under oath in the house of the LORD, and showed them the king's son.

11:5
1 Chr 9:25

5   And he commanded them, saying, "This is the thing that you shall do: one third of you, who come in on the sabbath and keep watch over the king's house

6   (one third also *shall be* at the gate Sur, and one third at the gate behind the ⁶guards), shall keep watch over the house for defense.

7   "And two parts of you, *even* all who go out on the sabbath, shall also keep watch over the house of the LORD for the king.

8   "Then you shall surround the king, each with his weapons in his hand; and whoever comes within the ranks shall be put to death. And be with the king when he goes out and when he comes in."

11:9
2 Chr 23:8

9   So the captains of hundreds did according to all that Jehoiada the priest commanded. And each one of them took his men who were to come in on the sabbath, with those who were to go out on the sabbath, and came to Jehoiada the priest.

11:10
2 Sam 8:7;
1 Chr 18:7

10   And the priest gave to the captains of hundreds the spears and shields that had been King David's, which *were* in the house of the LORD.

11   And the guards stood each with his weapons in his hand, from the right side of the house to the left side of the house, by the altar and by the house, around the king.

11:12
1 Sam 10:24

12   Then he brought the king's son out and put the crown on him, and *gave him* the testimony; and they made him king and anointed him, and they clapped their hands and said, "*Long* live the king!"

11:13
2 Chr 23:12ff

13   When Athaliah heard the noise of the guard *and of* the people, she came to the people in the house of the LORD.

11:14
2 Kin 23:3;
2 Chr 34:31;
1 Kin 1:39,
40;
2 Kin 9:23

14   And she looked and behold, the king was standing by the pillar, according to the custom, with the captains and the trumpeters beside the king; and all the people of the land rejoiced and blew trumpets. Then Athaliah tore her clothes and cried, "Treason! Treason!"

15   And Jehoiada the priest commanded the captains of hundreds who were appointed over the army, and said to them, "Bring her out between the ranks, and whoever follows her put to death with the sword." For the priest said, "Let her not be put to death in the house of the LORD."

⁶Lit., *runners*

11:4 *Carites,* another designation for the Cherethites, the foreign mercenaries hired as the royal bodyguard. Note to

2 Sam. 15:18 also explains this.

16   So they seized her, and when she arrived at the horses' entrance of the king's house, she was put to death there.

17   Then Jehoiada made a covenant between the LORD and the king and the people, that they should be the LORD's people, also between the king and the people.

18   And all the people of the land went to the house of Baal, and tore it down; his altars and his images they broke in pieces thoroughly, and killed Mattan the priest of Baal before the altars. And the priest appointed officers over the house of the LORD.

19   And he took the captains of hundreds and the Carites and the guards and all the people of the land; and they brought the king down from the house of the LORD, and came by the way of the gate of the guards to the king's house. And he sat on the throne of the kings.

20   So all the people of the land rejoiced and the city was quiet. For they had put Athaliah to death with the sword at the king's house.

21   Jehoash was seven years old when he became king.

M. *The reign of Jehoash (Joash: Judah)*

1. *Faithful Jehoash*

12   In the seventh year of Jehu, Jehoash became king, and he reigned forty years in Jerusalem; and his mother's name was Zibiah of Beersheba.

2   And Jehoash did right in the sight of the LORD all his days in which Jehoiada the priest instructed him.

3   Only the high places were not taken away; the people still sacrificed and burned incense on the high places.

2. *Jehoash repairs the temple*

4   Then Jehoash said to the priests, "All the money of the sacred things which is brought into the house of the LORD, in current money, *both* the money of each man's assessment *and* all the money which any man's heart prompts him to bring into the house of the LORD,

5   let the priests take it for themselves, each from his acquaintance; and they shall repair the [7]damages of the house wherever any damage may be found.

6   But it came about that in the twenty-third year of King Jehoash the priests had not repaired the damages of the house.

7   Then King Jehoash called for Jehoiada the priest, and for the *other* priests and said to them, "Why do you not repair the damages of the house? Now therefore take no *more* money from your acquaintances, but pay it for the damages of the house."

8   So the priests agreed that they should take no *more* money from the people, nor repair the damages of the house.

9   But Jehoiada the priest took a chest and bored a hole in its lid, and put it beside the altar, on the right side as one comes into the house of the LORD; and the priests who guarded the threshold put in it all the money which was brought into the house of the LORD.

10   And when they saw that there was much money in the chest, the king's scribe and the high priest came up and tied *it* in bags and counted the money which was found in the house of the LORD.

11   And they gave the money which was weighed out into the hands of those who did the work, who had the oversight of the house of the LORD; and they paid it out to the carpenters and the builders, who worked on the house of the LORD;

12   and to the masons and the stonecutters, and for buying timber and hewn stone to repair the damages to the house of the LORD, and for all that was laid out for the house to repair it.

13   But there were not made for the house of the LORD silver cups, snuffers, bowls, trumpets, any vessels of gold, or vessels of silver from the money which was brought into the house of the LORD;

[7]Lit., *breaches,* and so through v. 12

Cross references (right column):

11:17
2 Chr 23:16;
15:12-14;
2 Sam 5:3

11:18
2 Kin 10:26;
Deut 12:3;
2 Chr 23:17ff

11:19
vv. 4,6

11:21
2 Chr 24:1

12:3
2 Kin 14:4;
15:35

12:4
2 Kin 22:4;
Ex 35:5;
1 Chr 29:3-9

12:6
2 Chr 24:5

12:7
2 Chr 24:6

12:9
2 Chr 24:8;
Mark 12:41;
Luke 21:1

12:10
2 Kin 19:2

12:12
2 Kin 22:5,6

12:13
2 Chr 24:14;
1 Kin 7:48,50

11:16   The tragic end of Athaliah was the logical consequence of her hybrid background. Born of Ahab, a nominal Yahweh worshiper, and Jezebel, an outright Baal worshiper, she followed in the footsteps of her idolatrous mother. Just as Jezebel had done before her, Athaliah also evilly influenced a spiritually spineless husband (king of Judah).

14 for they gave that to those who did the work, and with it they repaired the house of the LORD.

15 Moreover, they did not require an accounting from the men into whose hand they gave the money to pay to those who did the work, for they dealt faithfully.

16 The money from the guilt offerings and the money from the sin offerings, was not brought into the house of the LORD; it was for the priests.

3. Jehoash pays off Hazael with temple money

17 Then Hazael king of Aram went up and fought against Gath and captured it, and Hazael set his face to go up to Jerusalem.

18 And Jehoash king of Judah took all the sacred things that Jehoshaphat and Jehoram and Ahaziah, his fathers, kings of Judah, had dedicated, and his own sacred things and all the gold that was found among the treasuries of the house of the LORD and of the king's house, and sent them to Hazael king of Aram. Then he went away from Jerusalem.

4. Jehoash succeeded by Amaziah

19 Now the rest of the acts of Joash and all that he did, are they not written in the Book of the Chronicles of the Kings of Judah?

20 And his servants arose and made a conspiracy, and struck down Joash at the house of Millo as he was going down to Silla.

21 For Jozacar the son of Shimeath, and Jehozabad the son of Shomer, his servants, struck him, and he died; and they buried him with his fathers in the city of David, and Amaziah his son became king in his place.

N. Jehoahaz, king of Israel

13 In the twenty-third year of Joash the son of Ahaziah, king of Judah, Jehoahaz the son of Jehu became king over Israel at Samaria, and he reigned seventeen years.

2 And he did evil in the sight of the LORD, and followed the sins of Jeroboam the son of Nebat, with which he made Israel sin; he did not turn from them.

3 So the anger of the LORD was kindled against Israel, and He gave them continually into the hand of Hazael king of Aram, and into the hand of Ben-hadad the son of Hazael.

4 Then Jehoahaz entreated the favor of the LORD, and the LORD listened to him; for He saw the oppression of Israel, how the king of Aram oppressed them.

5 And the LORD gave Israel a [8]deliverer, so that they escaped from under the hand of the Arameans; and the sons of Israel lived in their tents as formerly.

6 Nevertheless they did not turn away from the sins of the house of Jeroboam, with which he made Israel sin, but walked in them; and the Asherah also remained standing in Samaria.

7 For he left to Jehoahaz of the army not more than fifty horsemen and ten chariots and 10,000 footmen, for the king of Aram had destroyed them and made them like the dust at threshing.

8 Now the rest of the acts of Jehoahaz, and all that he did and his might, are they not written in the Book of the Chronicles of the Kings of Israel?

9 And Jehoahaz slept with his fathers, and they buried him in Samaria; and Joash his son became king in his place.

O. Jehoash (Joash), king of Israel

1. The wickedness of Jehoash

10 In the thirty-seventh year of Joash king of Judah, Jehoash the son of Jehoahaz, became king over Israel in Samaria, and reigned sixteen years.

11 And he did evil in the sight of the LORD; he did not turn away from all the sins of Jeroboam the son of Nebat, with which he made Israel sin, but he walked in them.

12 Now the rest of the acts of Joash and all that he did and his might with which

Cross references (margin):

12:15 2 Kin 22:7
12:16 Lev 5:15-18; 4:24,29; Num 18:9,19
12:17 2 Kin 8:12; 2 Chr 24:23
12:18 1 Kin 15:18; 2 Kin 18:15, 16
12:20 2 Kin 14:5; 2 Chr 24:25; 1 Kin 11:27
*12:21 2 Chr 24:26, 27; 2 Kin 14:1
13:2 1 Kin 12:26-33
13:3 Judg 2:14; 2 Kin 8:12; 12:17
13:4 Num 21:7-9; Ps 78:34; Ex 3:7; 2 Kin 14:26
*13:5 v. 25; 2 Kin 14:25, 27
13:6 v. 2; 1 Kin 16:33
13:7 Amos 1:3
13:9 2 Kin 10:35
13:12 vv. 14-19; 2 Kin 14:8-15; 2 Chr 25:17ff

[8]Or, savior

12:21 Read 2 Chr. 24:25–27.
13:5 A deliverer may be a reference to the Assyrians, who were threatening the Syrians, thereby giving Israel a respite.

he fought against Amaziah king of Judah, are they not written in the Book of the Chronicles of the Kings of Israel?

13   So Joash slept with his fathers, and Jeroboam sat on his throne; and Joash was buried in Samaria with the kings of Israel.

2. Elisha and the LORD's arrow of victory

14   When Elisha became sick with the illness of which he was to die, Joash the king of Israel came down to him and wept over him and said, "My father, my father, the chariots of Israel and its horsemen!"

15   And Elisha said to him, "Take a bow and arrows." So he took a bow and arrows.

16   Then he said to the king of Israel, "Put your hand on the bow." And he put his hand *on it,* then Elisha laid his hands on the king's hands.

17   And he said, "Open the window toward the east," and he opened *it.* Then Elisha said, "Shoot!" And he shot. And he said, "The LORD's arrow of victory, even the arrow of victory over Aram; for you shall defeat the Arameans at Aphek until you have destroyed *them.*"

18   Then he said, "Take the arrows," and he took them. And he said to the king of Israel, "Strike the ground," and he struck *it* three times and stopped.

19   So the man of God was angry with him and said, "You should have struck five or six times, then you would have struck Aram until you would have destroyed *it.* But now you shall strike Aram *only* three times."

3. The miracle at Elisha's tomb

20   And Elisha died, and they buried him. Now the bands of the Moabites would invade the land in the spring of the year.

21   And as they were burying a man, behold, they saw a marauding band; and they cast the man into the grave of Elisha. And when the man touched the bones of Elisha he revived and stood up on his feet.

4. The victories of Israel

22   Now Hazael king of Aram had oppressed Israel all the days of Jehoahaz.

23   But the LORD was gracious to them and had compassion on them and turned to them because of His covenant with Abraham, Isaac, and Jacob, and would not destroy them or cast them from His presence until now.

24   When Hazael king of Aram died, Ben-hadad his son became king in his place.

25   Then Jehoash the son of Jehoahaz took again from the hand of Ben-hadad the son of Hazael the cities which he had taken in war from the hand of Jehoahaz his father. Three times Joash defeated him and recovered the cities of Israel.

P. Amaziah, king of Judah

1. Events of Amaziah's reign

14   In the second year of Joash son of Joahaz king of Israel, Amaziah the son of Joash king of Judah became king.

2   He was twenty-five years old when he became king, and he reigned twenty-nine years in Jerusalem. And his mother's name was Jehoaddin of Jerusalem.

3   And he did right in the sight of the LORD, yet not like David his father; he did according to all that Joash his father had done.

4   Only the high places were not taken away; the people still sacrificed and burned incense on the high places.

5   Now it came about, as soon as the kingdom was firmly in his hand, that he killed his servants who had slain the king his father.

6   But the sons of the slayers he did not put to death, according to what is written in the book of the law of Moses, as the LORD commanded, saying, "The fathers shall not be put to death for the sons, nor the sons be put to death for the fathers; but each shall be put to death for his own sin."

7   He killed *of* Edom in the Valley of Salt 10,000 and took Sela by war, and named it Joktheel to this day.

13:14
2 Kin 2:12

13:17
1 Kin 20:26

13:19
v. 25

13:20
see 2 Kin 3:7;
24:2

13:22
2 Kin 8:12
13:23
2 Kin 14:27;
Ex 2:24,25;
Gen 13:16,17

13:25
2 Kin 10:32,
33; 14:25;
vv. 18,19

14:1
2 Kin 13:10;
2 Chr 25:1

14:4
2 Kin 12:3;
16:4
14:5
2 Kin 12:20

14:6
Deut 24:16;
Ezek 18:4,20

*14:7
2 Chr 25:11;
2 Sam 8:13;
Josh 15:38

14:7 *Sela,* "Rock," the capital city of Edom.

2. Amaziah wars against Israel (Jehoash)

14:8
2 Chr 25:17-24

8   Then Amaziah sent messengers to Jehoash, the son of Jehoahaz son of Jehu, king of Israel, saying, "Come, let us face each other."

14:9
Judg 9:8-15

9   And Jehoash king of Israel sent to Amaziah king of Judah, saying, "The thorn bush which was in Lebanon sent to the cedar which was in Lebanon, saying, 'Give your daughter to my son in marriage.' But there passed by a wild beast that was in Lebanon, and trampled the thorn bush.

14:10
v. 7;
Deut 8:14;
2 Chr 26:16;
32:25
14:11
Josh 19:38

10   "You have indeed defeated Edom, and your heart has become proud. Enjoy your glory and stay at home; for why should you provoke trouble so that you, even you, should fall, and Judah with you?"

11   But Amaziah would not listen. So Jehoash king of Israel went up; and he and Amaziah king of Judah faced each other at Beth-shemesh, which belongs to Judah.

2 Sam 18:17
14:13
Neh 8:16;
12:39;
2 Chr 25:23

12   And Judah was defeated by Israel, and they fled each to his tent.

13   Then Jehoash king of Israel captured Amaziah king of Judah, the son of Jehoash the son of Ahaziah, at Beth-shemesh, and came to Jerusalem and tore down the wall of Jerusalem from the Gate of Ephraim to the Corner Gate, 400 cubits.

14:14
2 Kin 12:18

14   And he took all the gold and silver and all the utensils which were found in the house of the LORD, and in the treasuries of the king's house, the hostages also, and returned to Samaria.

3. Death of Jehoash

14:15
2 Kin 13:12

15   Now the rest of the acts of Jehoash which he did, and his might and how he fought with Amaziah king of Judah, are they not written in the Book of the Chronicles of the Kings of Israel?

16   So Jehoash slept with his fathers and was buried in Samaria with the kings of Israel; and Jeroboam his son became king in his place.

4. Amaziah replaced by Azariah (Uzziah)

14:17
2 Chr 25:25-28

17   And Amaziah the son of Joash king of Judah lived fifteen years after the death of Jehoash son of Jehoahaz king of Israel.

18   Now the rest of the acts of Amaziah, are they not written in the Book of the Chronicles of the Kings of Judah?

14:19
Josh 10:31;
2 Kin 18:14,
17

19   And they conspired against him in Jerusalem, and he fled to Lachish; but they sent after him to Lachish and killed him there.

20   Then they brought him on horses and he was buried at Jerusalem with his fathers in the city of David.

21   And all the people of Judah took Azariah, who *was* sixteen years old, and made him king in the place of his father Amaziah.

14:22
2 Kin 16:6;
2 Chr 26:2

22   He built Elath and restored it to Judah, after the king slept with his fathers.

Q. Reign of Jeroboam II (Israel)

23   In the fifteenth year of Amaziah the son of Joash king of Judah, Jeroboam the son of Joash king of Israel became king in Samaria, *and reigned* forty-one years.

24   And he did evil in the sight of the LORD; he did not depart from all the sins of Jeroboam the son of Nebat, which he made Israel sin.

14:25
2 Kin 10:32;
1 Kin 8:65;
Deut 3:17;
Jon 1:1;
Matt 12:39,
40;
Josh 19:13
14:26
2 Kin 13:4;
Deut 32:36
14:27
2 Kin 13:5,23

25   He restored the border of Israel from the entrance of Hamath as far as the Sea of the Arabah, according to the word of the LORD, the God of Israel, which He spoke through His servant Jonah the son of Amittai, the prophet, who was of Gath-hepher.

26   For the LORD saw the affliction of Israel, *which was* very bitter; for there was neither bond nor free, nor was there any helper for Israel.

27   And the LORD did not say that He would blot out the name of Israel from under heaven, but He saved them by the hand of Jeroboam the son of Joash.

14:28
2 Sam 8:6;
1 Kin 11:24;
2 Chr 8:3

28   Now the rest of the acts of Jeroboam and all that he did and his might, how he fought and how he recovered for Israel, Damascus and Hamath, *which had belonged* to Judah, are they not written in the Book of the Chronicles of the Kings of Israel?

14:29
2 Kin 15:8

29   And Jeroboam slept with his fathers, even with the kings of Israel, and Zechariah his son became king in his place.

14:21 *Azariah*, known also as *Uzziah*.

R. *Judah under Azariah (Uzziah)*

15 In the twenty-seventh year of Jeroboam king of Israel, Azariah son of Amaziah king of Judah became king.

2 He was sixteen years old when he became king, and he reigned fifty-two years in Jerusalem; and his mother's name was Jecoliah of Jerusalem.

3 And he did right in the sight of the LORD, according to all that his father Amaziah had done.

4 Only the high places were not taken away; the people still sacrificed and burned incense on the high places.

5 And the LORD struck the king, so that he was a leper to the day of his death. And he lived in a separate house, while Jotham the king's son was over the household, judging the people of the land.

6 Now the rest of the acts of Azariah and all that he did, are they not written in the Book of the Chronicles of the Kings of Judah?

7 And Azariah slept with his fathers, and they buried him with his fathers in the city of David, and Jotham his son became king in his place.

S. *Reign of Zechariah (Israel)*

8 In the thirty-eighth year of Azariah king of Judah, Zechariah the son of Jeroboam became king over Israel in Samaria *for* six months.

9 And he did evil in the sight of the LORD, as his fathers had done; he did not depart from the sins of Jeroboam the son of Nebat, which he made Israel sin.

10 Then Shallum the son of Jabesh conspired against him and struck him before the people and killed him, and reigned in his place.

11 Now the rest of the acts of Zechariah, behold they are written in the Book of the Chronicles of the Kings of Israel.

12 This is the word of the LORD which He spoke to Jehu, saying, "Your sons to the fourth generation shall sit on the throne of Israel." And so it was.

T. *Reign of Shallum (Israel)*

13 Shallum son of Jabesh became king in the thirty-ninth year of Uzziah king of Judah, and he reigned one month in Samaria.

14 Then Menahem son of Gadi went up from Tirzah and came to Samaria, and struck Shallum son of Jabesh in Samaria, and killed him and became king in his place.

15 Now the rest of the acts of Shallum and his conspiracy which he made, behold they are written in the Book of the Chronicles of the Kings of Israel.

16 Then Menahem struck Tiphsah and all who were in it and its borders from Tirzah, because they did not open *to him*, therefore he struck *it;* and he ripped up all its women who were with child.

U. *Reign of Menahem (Israel)*

17 In the thirty-ninth year of Azariah king of Judah, Menahem son of Gadi became king over Israel *and reigned* ten years in Samaria.

18 And he did evil in the sight of the LORD; he did not depart all his days from the sins of Jeroboam the son of Nebat, which he made Israel sin.

19 Pul, king of Assyria, came against the land, and Menahem gave Pul a thousand talents of silver so that his hand might be with him to strengthen the kingdom under his rule.

20 Then Menahem exacted the money from Israel, even from all the mighty men of wealth, from each man fifty shekels of silver to pay the king of Assyria. So the king of Assyria returned and did not remain there in the land.

21 Now the rest of the acts of Menahem and all that he did, are they not written in the Book of the Chronicles of the Kings of Israel?

22 And Menahem slept with his fathers, and Pekahiah his son became king in his place.

Cross references (right margin):

15:1
2 Kin 14:21;
2 Chr 26:1,3,
4 *Uzziah*
15:2
2 Chr 26:3,4

15:4
2 Kin 12:3;
14:4
15:5
2 Chr 26:19-21

15:7
2 Chr 26:23

15:10
Amos 7:9

15:12
2 Kin 10:30

15:13
vv. 1,8

15:14
1 Kin 14:17

15:16
1 Kin 4:24;
2 Kin 8:12

15:17
vv. 1,8,13

*15:19
1 Chr 5:26

15:19 *Pul,* another name for *Tiglath-pileser III* (744–727 B.C.). His inscriptions mention Menahem's payment of tribute.

V. *Reign of Pekahiah (Israel)*

15:23
vv. 1,8,13,17

23 In the fiftieth year of Azariah king of Judah, Pekahiah son of Menahem became king over Israel in Samaria, *and reigned* two years.

24 And he did evil in the sight of the LORD; he did not depart from the sins of Jeroboam son of Nebat, which he made Israel sin.

15:25
1 Kin 16:18

25 Then Pekah son of Remaliah, his officer, conspired against him and struck him in Samaria, in the castle of the king's house with Argob and Arieh; and with him were fifty men of the Gileadites, and he killed him and became king in his place.

26 Now the rest of the acts of Pekahiah and all that he did, behold they are written in the Book of the Chronicles of the Kings of Israel.

W. *Reign of Pekah (Israel)*

*15:27
v. 23; Is 7:1

27 In the fifty-second year of Azariah king of Judah, Pekah son of Remaliah became king over Israel in Samaria, *and reigned* twenty years.

28 And he did evil in the sight of the LORD; he did not depart from the sins of Jeroboam son of Nebat, which he made Israel sin.

*15:29
v. 19;
2 Kin 17:6;
1 Chr 5:26

29 In the days of Pekah king of Israel, Tiglath-pileser king of Assyria came and captured Ijon and Abel-beth-maacah and Janoah and Kedesh and Hazor and Gilead and Galilee, all the land of Naphtali; and he carried them captive to Assyria.

30 And Hoshea the son of Elah made a conspiracy against Pekah the son of Remaliah, and struck him and put him to death and became king in his place, in the twentieth year of Jotham the son of Uzziah.

31 Now the rest of the acts of Pekah and all that he did, behold, they are written in the Book of the Chronicles of the Kings of Israel.

X. *Reign of Jotham (Judah)*

15:32
2 Chr 27:1ff

32 In the second year of Pekah the son of Remaliah king of Israel, Jotham the son of Uzziah king of Judah became king.

33 He was twenty-five years old when he became king, and he reigned sixteen years in Jerusalem; and his mother's name *was* Jerusha the daughter of Zadok.

15:34
v. 3;
2 Chr 26:4,5
15:35
v. 4;
2 Chr 27:3

34 And he did what was right in the sight of the LORD; he did according to all that his father Uzziah had done.

35 Only the high places were not taken away; the people still sacrificed and burned incense on the high places. He built the upper gate of the house of the LORD.

36 Now the rest of the acts of Jotham and all that he did, are they not written in the Book of the Chronicles of the Kings of Judah?

15:37
2 Kin 16:5;
Is 7:1; v. 27

37 In those days the LORD began to send Rezin king of Aram and Pekah the son of Remaliah against Judah.

38 And Jotham slept with his fathers, and he was buried with his fathers in the city of David his father; and Ahaz his son became king in his place.

Y. *Reign of Ahaz (Judah)*

1. *Description of Ahaz's reign*

16:1
2 Chr 28:1ff

16 In the seventeenth year of Pekah the son of Remaliah, Ahaz the son of Jotham, king of Judah, became king.

2 Ahaz *was* twenty years old when he became king, and he reigned sixteen years in Jerusalem; and he did not do what was right in the sight of the LORD his God, as his father David *had done*.

16:3
Lev 18:21;
2 Kin 17:17;
21:6;
Deut 12:31;
2 Kin 21:2,11
16:4
Deut 12:2;
2 Kin 14:4
16:5
2 Kin 15:37;
Is 7:1;

3 But he walked in the way of the kings of Israel, and even made his son pass through the fire, according to the abominations of the nations whom the LORD had driven out from before the sons of Israel.

4 And he sacrificed and burned incense on the high places and on the hills and under every green tree.

2. *Ahaz delivered from Syria and Israel by Tiglath-pileser*

5 Then Rezin king of Aram and Pekah son of Remaliah, king of Israel, came

---

15:27 *twenty years.* Pekah actually reigned only eight years, but he evidently had the court records include the twelve years he had assisted Pekahiah and Menahem, the two previous kings. See note to 18:1 for further discussion.

15:29 Read 16:5–9 for more details.
15:33 *sixteen years.* Four years of co-regency with Azariah have not been included as was done in v. 30.

up to Jerusalem to *wage* war; and they besieged Ahaz, but could not overcome him. | 2 Chr 28:5,6

6   At that time Rezin king of Aram recovered Elath for Aram, and cleared the Judeans out of Elath entirely; and the Arameans came to Elath, and have lived there to this day. | **16:6**
2 Kin 14:22;
2 Chr 26:2

7   So Ahaz sent messengers to Tiglath-pileser king of Assyria, saying, "I am your servant and your son; come up and deliver me from the hand of the king of Aram, and from the hand of the king of Israel, who are rising up against me." | **16:7**
2 Chr 28:16ff;
2 Kin 15:29

8   And Ahaz took the silver and gold that was found in the house of the LORD and in the treasuries of the king's house, and sent a present to the king of Assyria. | **16:8**
2 Kin 12:17,
18

9   So the king of Assyria listened to him; and the king of Assyria went up against Damascus and captured it, and carried *the people of* it away into exile to Kir, and put Rezin to death. | **16:9**
2 Chr 28:21;
Amos 1:3-5

3. *Ahaz and the strange altar*

10   Now King Ahaz went to Damascus to meet Tiglath-pileser king of Assyria, and saw the altar which *was* at Damascus; and King Ahaz sent to Urijah the priest the pattern of the altar and its model, according to all its workmanship. | **16:10**
2 Kin 15:29;
Is 8:2

11   So Urijah the priest built an altar; according to all that King Ahaz had sent from Damascus, thus Urijah the priest made *it*, before the coming of King Ahaz from Damascus.

12   And when the king came from Damascus, the king saw the altar; then the king approached the altar and went up to it,

13   and burned his burnt offering and his meal offering, and poured his libation and sprinkled the blood of his peace offerings on the altar.

14   And the bronze altar, which *was* before the LORD, he brought from the front of the house, from between *his* altar and the house of the LORD, and he put it on the north side of *his* altar. | **16:14**
2 Chr 4:1

15   Then King Ahaz commanded Urijah the priest, saying, "Upon the great altar burn the morning burnt offering and the evening meal offering and the king's burnt offering and his meal offering, with the burnt offering of all the people of the land and their meal offering and their libations; and sprinkle on it all the blood of the burnt offering and all the blood of the sacrifice. But the bronze altar shall be for me to inquire *by*." | **16:15**
Ex 29:39-41

16   So Urijah the priest did according to all that King Ahaz commanded.

17   Then King Ahaz cut off the borders of the stands, and removed the laver from them; he also took down the sea from the bronze oxen which were under it, and put it on a pavement of stone. | **16:17**
1 Kin 7:23-28

18   And the covered way for the sabbath which they had built in the house, and the outer entry of the king, he removed from the house of the LORD because of the king of Assyria.

4. *Ahaz's death and the succession*

19   Now the rest of the acts of Ahaz which he did, are they not written in the Book of the Chronicles of the Kings of Judah?

20   So Ahaz slept with his fathers, and was buried with his fathers in the city of David; and his son Hezekiah reigned in his place. | **16:20**
2 Chr 28:27

Z. The end of Israel

1. *Samaria captured by Assyria*

17 In the twelfth year of Ahaz king of Judah, Hoshea the son of Elah became king over Israel in Samaria, *and reigned* nine years. | **17:1**
2 Kin 15:30

2   And he did evil in the sight of the LORD, only not as the kings of Israel who were before him.

3   Shalmaneser king of Assyria came up against him, and Hoshea became his servant and paid him tribute. | **17:3**
2 Kin 18:9-12

4   But the king of Assyria found conspiracy in Hoshea, who had sent messengers to So king of Egypt and had offered no tribute to the king of Assyria, as *he had done* year by year; so the king of Assyria shut him up and bound him in prison.

5   Then the king of Assyria invaded the whole land and went up to Samaria and besieged it three years. | **17:5**
Hos 13:16

6   In the ninth year of Hoshea, the king of Assyria captured Samaria and | ***17:6**
Hos 13:16;

carried Israel away into exile to Assyria, and settled them in Halah and Habor, *on* the river of Gozan, and in the cities of the Medes.

2. *The sins of Israel that brought judgment*

7 Now *this* came about, because the sons of Israel had sinned against the LORD their God, who had brought them up from the land of Egypt from under the hand of Pharaoh, king of Egypt, and they had [9]feared other gods

8 and walked in the customs of the nations whom the LORD had driven out before the sons of Israel, and *in the customs* of the kings of Israel which they had introduced.

9 And the sons of Israel did things secretly which were not right, against the LORD their God. Moreover, they built for themselves high places in all their towns, from watchtower to fortified city.

10 And they set for themselves *sacred* pillars and [10]Asherim on every high hill and under every green tree,

11 and there they burned incense on all the high places as the nations *did* which the LORD had carried away to exile before them; and they did evil things provoking the LORD.

12 And they served idols, concerning which the LORD had said to them, "You shall not do this thing."

13 Yet the LORD warned Israel and Judah, through all His prophets *and* every seer, saying, "Turn from your evil ways and keep My commandments, My statutes according to all the law which I commanded your fathers, and which I sent to you through My servants the prophets."

14 However, they did not listen, but stiffened their neck like their fathers, who did not believe in the LORD their God.

15 And they rejected His statutes and His covenant which He made with their fathers, and His warnings with which He warned them. And they followed vanity and became vain, and *went* after the nations which surrounded them, concerning which the LORD had commanded them not to do like them.

16 And they forsook all the commandments of the LORD their God and made for themselves molten images, *even* two calves, and made an Asherah and worshiped all the host of heaven and served Baal.

17 Then they made their sons and their daughters pass through the fire, and practiced divination and enchantments, and sold themselves to do evil in the sight of the LORD, provoking Him.

18 So the LORD was very angry with Israel, and removed them from His sight; none was left except the tribe of Judah.

19 Also Judah did not keep the commandments of the LORD their God, but walked in the customs which Israel had introduced.

20 And the LORD rejected all the descendants of Israel and afflicted them and gave them into the hand of plunderers, until He had cast them out of His sight.

21 When He had torn Israel from the house of David, they made Jeroboam the son of Nebat king. Then Jeroboam drove Israel away from following the LORD, and made them commit a great sin.

22 And the sons of Israel walked in all the sins of Jeroboam which he did; they did not depart from them,

23 until the LORD removed Israel from His sight, as He spoke through all His servants the prophets. So Israel was carried away into exile from their own land to Assyria until this day.

3. *Israel resettled: the origin of the Samaritans*

24 And the king of Assyria brought *men* from Babylon and from Cuthah and

[9]Lit., *revered*, and so throughout this context   [10]I.e., wooden symbols of a female deity

---

17:6 *king of Assyria.* Shalmaneser (727–722 B.C.) initiated the siege of Samaria, but he died before the city capitulated. His successor, Sargon II (722–705 B.C.), claimed to have captured Samaria and taken the people captive. Thus, the northern kingdom ceased late in 722 or early in 721 B.C. **17:7** The captivity of Israel (the ten tribes) was an inevitable penalty for their wickedness. That captivity has never been ended. When some of the people of God returned from the seventy years' captivity, they were largely descendants of the southern tribes of the kingdom of Judah, although

there were also individuals from Israel who returned with them. Hosea predicted that the northern tribes would never return as a nation and set up their kingdom again in the promised land (Hos. 1:6,9). Apparently (judging from the way Paul quotes and interprets Hos. 2:23 in Rom. 9:22–26), their ranks were to be filled by Gentile converts in the church of Christ. **17:24** This policy of interchanging minority groups was carried on by Sargon's grandson, Esarhaddon (681–669 B.C.; see Ezra 4:2), and great-grandson, Ashurbanipal

from Avva and from Hamath and Sephar-vaim, and settled *them* in the cities of Samaria in place of the sons of Israel. So they possessed Samaria and lived in its cities.

25   And it came about at the beginning of their living there, that they did not fear the LORD; therefore the LORD sent lions among them which killed some of them.

26   So they spoke to the king of Assyria, saying, "The nations whom you have carried away into exile in the cities of Samaria do not know the custom of the god of the land; so he has sent lions among them, and behold, they kill them because they do not know the custom of the god of the land."

27   Then the king of Assyria commanded, saying, "Take there one of the priests whom you carried away into exile, and let him go and live there; and let him teach them the custom of the god of the land."   **17:27** Mic 3:11

28   So one of the priests whom they had carried away into exile from Samaria came and lived at Bethel, and taught them how they should fear the LORD.

29   But every nation still made gods of its own and put them in the houses of the high places which the people of Samaria had made, every nation in their cities in which they lived.

30   And the men of Babylon made Succoth-benoth, the men of Cuth made Nergal, the men of Hamath made Ashima,   **17:30** v. 24

31   and the Avvites made Nibhaz and Tartak; and the Sepharvites burned their children in the fire to Adrammelech and Anammelech the gods of Sepharvaim.   **17:31** vv. 17,24

32   They also feared the LORD and appointed from among themselves priests of the high places, who acted for them in the houses of the high places.   **17:32** 1 Kin 12:31

33   They feared the LORD and served their own gods according to the custom of the nations from among whom they had been carried away into exile.   **17:33** Zeph 1:5

34   To this day they do according to the earlier customs: they do not fear the LORD, nor do they follow their statutes or their ordinances or the law, or the commandments which the LORD commanded the sons of Jacob, whom He named Israel;   **17:34** Gen 32:28; 35:10

35   with whom the LORD made a covenant and commanded them, saying, "You shall not fear other gods, nor bow down yourselves to them nor serve them nor sacrifice to them.   **17:35** Judg 6:10; Ex 20:5

36   "But the LORD, who brought you up from the land of Egypt with great power and with an outstretched arm, Him you shall fear, and to Him you shall bow yourselves down, and to Him you shall sacrifice.   **17:36** Ex 6:6; Deut 10:20

37   "And the statutes and the ordinances and the law and the commandment, which He wrote for you, you shall observe to do forever; and you shall not fear other gods.   **17:37** Deut 5:32

38   "And the covenant that I have made with you, you shall not forget, nor shall you fear other gods.   **17:38** Deut 4:23

39   "But the LORD your God you shall fear; and He will deliver you from the hand of all your enemies."

40   However, they did not listen, but they did according to their earlier custom.

41   So while these nations feared the LORD, they also served their idols; their children likewise and their grandchildren, as their fathers did, so they do to this day.   **17:41** vv. 32,33

VI. *The kingdom of Judah to the captivity (18:1–25:30)*

A. *The reign of Hezekiah*

1. *Summary of the acts of Hezekiah*

18   Now it came about in the third year of Hoshea, the son of Elah king of Israel, that Hezekiah the son of Ahaz king of Judah became king.   ***18:1** 2 Kin 17:1; 2 Chr 28:27

(669–633 B.C.), called *Osnappar* in Ezra 4:10.
17:29 *people of Samaria.* Later in the Bible these people are called Samaritans. They were the mixed peoples found in central and northern Palestine, and their name was given to them by the people of Judah. While they served the LORD in name so as to insure their safety, they persisted in worshiping their own gods. See note to John 4:5.
18:1 *Hoshea . . . Hezekiah.* Here and in vv. 9,10 the reigns of these two kings are synchronized. According to v. 13 the

Assyrian king Sennacherib invaded Judah in the fourteenth year of Hezekiah. Since this invasion can be dated accurately at 701 B.C., Hezekiah should have begun his reign in 715 B.C. But Hoshea, the last king of the northern kingdom, ceased to reign in 722 B.C. Several explanations are possible. One is that Hezekiah began a twelve-year co-regency in the third year of Hoshea. A second is that the scribe allowed Pekah the twenty years assigned him (2 Kin. 15:27), thus pushing Hoshea down twelve years later.

*18:2
2 Chr 29:1,2
2   He was twenty-five years old when he became king, and he reigned twenty-nine years in Jerusalem; and his mother's name was Abi the daughter of Zechariah.

3   And he did right in the sight of the LORD, according to all that his father David had done.

18:4
2 Chr 31:1;
Num 21:8,9
4   He removed the high places and broke down the *sacred* pillars and cut down the [11]Asherah. He also broke in pieces the bronze serpent that Moses had made, for until those days the sons of Israel burned incense to it; and it was called [12] Nehushtan.

18:5
2 Kin 19:10;
23:25
18:6
Deut 10:20
5   He trusted in the LORD, the God of Israel; so that after him there was none like him among all the kings of Judah, nor *among those* who were before him.

6   For he clung to the LORD; he did not depart from following Him, but kept His commandments, which the LORD had commanded Moses.

18:7
Gen 39:2,3;
1 Sam 18:14;
2 Kin 16:7
18:8
1 Chr 4:41;
Is 14:29;
2 Kin 17:9
7   And the LORD was with him; wherever he went he prospered. And he rebelled against the king of Assyria and did not serve him.

8   He defeated the Philistines as far as Gaza and its territory, from watchtower to fortified city.

2. The end of the northern kingdom (Israel)

18:9
2 Kin 17:3
9   Now it came about in the fourth year of King Hezekiah, which was the seventh year of Hoshea son of Elah king of Israel, that Shalmaneser king of Assyria came up against Samaria and besieged it.

18:10
2 Kin 17:6
10   And at the end of three years they captured it; in the sixth year of Hezekiah, which was the ninth year of Hoshea king of Israel, Samaria was captured.

18:11
2 Kin 17:6
11   Then the king of Assyria carried Israel away into exile to Assyria, and put them in Halah and on the Habor, the river of Gozan, and in the cities of the Medes,

12   because they did not obey the voice of the LORD their God, but transgressed His covenant, even all that Moses the servant of the LORD commanded; they would neither listen, nor do *it.*

3. Sennacherib's invasion

a. Hezekiah pays tribute

18:13
2 Chr 32:1ff;
Is 36:1ff
13   Now in the fourteenth year of King Hezekiah, Sennacherib king of Assyria came up against all the fortified cities of Judah and seized them.

14   Then Hezekiah king of Judah sent to the king of Assyria at Lachish, saying, "I have done wrong. Withdraw from me; whatever you impose on me I will bear." So the king of Assyria required of Hezekiah king of Judah three hundred talents of silver and thirty talents of gold.

18:15
2 Kin 16:8
15   And Hezekiah gave *him* all the silver which was found in the house of the LORD, and in the treasuries of the king's house.

16   At that time Hezekiah cut off *the gold from* the doors of the temple of the LORD, and *from* the doorposts which Hezekiah king of Judah had overlaid, and gave it to the king of Assyria.

*18:17
Is 20:1; 7:3
17   Then the king of Assyria sent Tartan and Rab-saris and Rabshakeh from Lachish to King Hezekiah with a large army to Jerusalem. So they went up and came to Jerusalem. And when they went up, they came and stood by the conduit of the upper pool, which is on the highway of the [13]fuller's field.

18:18
2 Kin 19:2;
Is 22:15,20
18   When they called to the king, Eliakim the son of Hilkiah, who was over the household, and Shebnah the scribe and Joah the son of Asaph the recorder, came out to them.

b. The Assyrian threats

18:19
2 Chr 32:10ff
19   Then Rabshakeh said to them, "Say now to Hezekiah, 'Thus says the great king, the king of Assyria, "What is this confidence that you have?

20   "You say (but *they are* only empty words), '*I have* counsel and strength for the war.' Now on whom do you rely, that you have rebelled against me?

18:21
Ezek 29:6,7
21   "Now behold, you rely on the staff of this crushed reed, *even* on Egypt; on which if a man leans, it will go into his hand and pierce it. So is Pharaoh king of Egypt to all who rely on him.

---

[11]I.e., wooden symbol of a female deity   [12]I.e., a piece of bronze   [13]I.e., launderer's

18:2 *Abi* is *Abijah* in 2 Chr. 29:1.
18:17a *Tartan and Rab-saris* and *Rabshakeh* are titles of Assyrian officers.

18:17b *conduit of the upper pool.* Read Is. 7:3, where it is also mentioned.

22   "But if you say to me, 'We trust in the LORD our God,' is it not He whose high places and whose altars Hezekiah has taken away, and has said to Judah and to Jerusalem, 'You shall worship before this altar in Jerusalem'?

23   "Now therefore, come, make a bargain with my master the king of Assyria, and I will give you two thousand horses, if you are able on your part to set riders on them.

24   "How then can you repulse one official of the least of my master's servants, and rely on Egypt for chariots and for horsemen?

25   "Have I now come up without the LORD's approval against this place to destroy it? The LORD said to me, 'Go up against this land and destroy it.' " ' "

26   Then Eliakim the son of Hilkiah, and Shebnah and Joah, said to Rabshakeh, "Speak now to your servants in Aramaic, for we understand *it;* and do not speak with us in Judean, in the hearing of the people who are on the wall."

27   But Rabshakeh said to them, "Has my master sent me only to your master and to you to speak these words, *and* not to the men who sit on the wall, *doomed* to eat their own dung and drink their own urine with you?"

28   Then Rabshakeh stood and cried with a loud voice in Judean, saying, "Hear the word of the great king, the king of Assyria.

29   "Thus says the king, 'Do not let Hezekiah deceive you, for he will not be able to deliver you from my hand;

30   nor let Hezekiah make you trust in the LORD, saying, "The LORD will surely deliver us, and this city shall not be given into the hand of the king of Assyria."

31   'Do not listen to Hezekiah, for thus says the king of Assyria, "Make your peace with me and come out to me, and eat each of his vine and each of his fig tree and drink each of the waters of his own cistern,

32   until I come and take you away to a land like your own land, a land of grain and new wine, a land of bread and vineyards, a land of olive trees and honey, that you may live and not die." But do not listen to Hezekiah, when he misleads you, saying, "The LORD will deliver us."

33   'Has any one of the gods of the nations delivered his land from the hand of the king of Assyria?

34   'Where are the gods of Hamath and Arpad? Where are the gods of Sepharvaim, Hena and Ivvah? Have they delivered Samaria from my hand?

35   'Who among all the gods of the lands have delivered their land from my hand, that the LORD should deliver Jerusalem from my hand?' "

36   But the people were silent and answered him not a word, for the king's commandment was, "Do not answer him."

37   Then Eliakim the son of Hilkiah, who was over the household, and Shebna the scribe and Joah the son of Asaph, the recorder, came to Hezekiah with their clothes torn and told him the words of Rabshakeh.

c. Hezekiah sends to Isaiah for a word from God

19 And when King Hezekiah heard *it,* he tore his clothes, covered himself with sackcloth and entered the house of the LORD.

2   Then he sent Eliakim who was over the household with Shebna the scribe and the elders of the priests, covered with sackcloth, to Isaiah the prophet the son of Amoz.

3   And they said to him, "Thus says Hezekiah, 'This day is a day of distress, rebuke, and rejection; for children have come to birth, and there is no strength to *deliver.*

4   'Perhaps the LORD your God will hear all the words of Rabshakeh, whom his master the king of Assyria has sent to reproach the living God, and will rebuke the words which the LORD your God has heard. Therefore, offer a prayer for the remnant that is left.' "

5   So the servants of King Hezekiah came to Isaiah.

6   And Isaiah said to them, "Thus you shall say to your master, 'Thus says the LORD, "Do not be afraid because of the words that you have heard, with which the servants of the king of Assyria have blasphemed Me.

7   "Behold, I will put a spirit in him so that he shall hear a rumor and return to his own land. And I will make him fall by the sword in his own land." ' "

8   Then Rabshakeh returned and found the king of Assyria fighting against Libnah, for he had heard that the king had left Lachish.

9   When he heard *them* say concerning Tirhakah king of Cush, "Behold, he has

18:22
v. 4;
2 Chr 31:1;
32:12

18:24
Is 31:1

18:26
Ezra 4:7

18:29
2 Chr 32:15

18:31
1 Kin 4:20,25

18:32
Deut 8:7-9

18:33
2 Kin 19:12;
2 Chr 32:14;
Is 10:10,11
18:34
2 Kin 19:13;
17:24

18:37
vv. 18,26;
2 Kin 6:30

19:1
2 Chr 32:20-22;
Is 37:1-38;
2 Kin 18:37;
1 Kin 21:27
19:2
Is 1:1; 2:1

19:4
2 Sam 16:12;
2 Kin 18:35;
1:9

19:6
Is 37:6ff;
2 Kin 18:17ff

19:7
vv. 35-37

19:8
Josh 10:29;
2 Kin 18:14

come out to fight against you," he sent messengers again to Hezekiah saying,

19:10
2 Kin 18:5,30

10 "Thus you shall say to Hezekiah king of Judah, 'Do not let your God in whom you trust deceive you saying, "Jerusalem shall not be given into the hand of the king of Assyria."

11 'Behold, you have heard what the kings of Assyria have done to all the lands, destroying them completely. So will you be spared?

19:12
2 Kin 18:33

12 'Did the gods of those nations which my fathers destroyed deliver them, *even* Gozan and Haran and Rezeph and the sons of Eden who *were* in Telassar?

19:13
2 Kin 18:34

13 'Where is the king of Hamath, the king of Arpad, the king of the city of Sepharvaim, and *of* Hena and Ivvah?' "

d. *Hezekiah at prayer*

*19:14
Is 37:14

14 Then Hezekiah took the letter from the hand of the messengers and read it, and he went up to the house of the Lord and spread it out before the Lord.

19:15
1 Sam 4:4;
1 Kin 18:39

15 And Hezekiah prayed before the Lord and said, "O Lord, the God of Israel, who art enthroned *above* the cherubim, Thou art the God, Thou alone, of all the kingdoms of the earth. Thou hast made heaven and earth.

19:16
Ps 31:2;
2 Chr 6:40;
v. 4

16 "Incline Thine ear, O Lord, and hear; open Thine eyes, O Lord, and see; and listen to the words of Sennacherib, which he has sent to reproach the living God.

17 "Truly, O Lord, the kings of Assyria have devastated the nations and their lands

19:18
Ps 115:4;
Jer 10:3

18 and have cast their gods into the fire, for they were not gods but the work of men's hands, wood and stone. So they have destroyed them.

19:19
Ps 83:18;
v. 15

19 "And now, O Lord our God, I pray, deliver us from his hand that all the kingdoms of the earth may know that Thou alone, O Lord, art God."

e. *Isaiah brings an answer to Hezekiah's prayer*

19:20
2 Kin 20:5;
Is 37:21

20 Then Isaiah the son of Amoz sent to Hezekiah saying, "Thus says the Lord, the God of Israel, 'Because you have prayed to Me about Sennacherib king of Assyria, I have heard *you*.'

19:21
Lam 2:13;
Job 16:4;
Ps 22:7,8

21 "This is the word that the Lord has spoken against him:
'She has despised you and mocked you,
  The virgin daughter of Zion;
She has shaken *her* head behind you,
  The daughter of Jerusalem!

19:22
vv. 4,6;
Ps 71:22;
Is 5:24

22 'Whom have you reproached and blasphemed?
  And against whom have you raised *your* voice,
And haughtily lifted up your eyes?
  Against the Holy One of Israel!

19:23
2 Kin 18:17;
Ps 20:7;
Is 10:18

23 'Through your messengers you have reproached the Lord,
  And you have said, "With my many chariots
I came up to the heights of the mountains,
  To the remotest parts of Lebanon;
And I cut down its tall cedars *and* its choice cypresses.
  And I entered its farthest lodging place, its thickest forest.

19:24
Is 19:6

24 "I dug *wells* and drank foreign waters,
  And with the sole of my feet I dried up
All the rivers of Egypt."

19:25
Is 45:7; 10:5

25 'Have you not heard?
  Long ago I did it;
From ancient times I planned it.
  Now I have brought it to pass,
That you should turn fortified cities into ruinous heaps.

19:26
Ps 129:6

26 'Therefore their inhabitants were short of strength,
  They were dismayed and put to shame;
They were as the vegetation of the field and as the green herb,
  As grass on the housetops is scorched before it is grown up.

19:14 See 1 Sam. 1:10. The same principles that were illustrated in the prayer of Hannah are also involved in this petition. A sincere believer who was prepared to trust God implicitly in the face of impossible odds and whose ardent desire was for the glory of God made a specific request of Him. No matter how adverse the circumstances, he believed that God was able and willing to display His redeeming grace; and he embraced the promise as though it had already been fulfilled.

27 'But I know your sitting down,
And your going out and your coming in,
And your raging against Me,
28 'Because of your raging against Me,
And because your arrogance has come up to My ears,
Therefore I will put My hook in your nose,
And My bridle in your lips,
And I will turn you back by the way which you came.

29 'Then this shall be the sign for you: you shall eat this year what grows of itself, in the second year what springs from the same, and in the third year sow, reap, plant vineyards, and eat their fruit.

30 'And the surviving remnant of the house of Judah shall again take root downward and bear fruit upward.

31 'For out of Jerusalem shall go forth a remnant, and out of Mount Zion survivors. The zeal of ¹⁴the LORD shall perform this.

32 'Therefore thus says the LORD concerning the king of Assyria, "He shall not come to this city or shoot an arrow there; neither shall he come before it with a shield, nor throw up a mound against it.

33 "By the way that he came, by the same he shall return, and he shall not come to this city," ' declares the LORD.

34 'For I will defend this city to save it for My own sake and for My servant David's sake.' ' "

f. The divine deliverance

35 Then it happened that night that the angel of the LORD went out, and struck 185,000 in the camp of the Assyrians; and when men rose early in the morning, behold, all of them were dead.

36 So Sennacherib king of Assyria departed and returned *home*, and lived at Nineveh.

37 And it came about as he was worshiping in the house of Nisroch his god, that Adrammelech and Sharezer killed him with the sword; and they escaped into the land of Ararat. And Esarhaddon his son became king in his place.

4. The sickness of Hezekiah

a. His prayer and Isaiah's answer

20 In those days Hezekiah became mortally ill. And Isaiah the prophet the son of Amoz came to him and said to him, "Thus says the LORD, 'Set your house in order, for you shall die and not live.' "

2 Then he turned his face to the wall, and prayed to the LORD, saying,

3 "Remember now, O LORD, I beseech Thee, how I have walked before Thee in truth and with a whole heart, and have done what is good in Thy sight." And Hezekiah wept bitterly.

4 And it came about before Isaiah had gone out of the middle court, that the word of the LORD came to him, saying,

5 "Return and say to Hezekiah the leader of My people, 'Thus says the LORD, the God of your father David, "I have heard your prayer, I have seen your tears; behold, I will heal you. On the third day you shall go up to the house of the LORD.

6 "And I will add fifteen years to your life, and I will deliver you and this city from the hand of the king of Assyria; and I will defend this city for My own sake and for My servant David's sake." ' "

7 Then Isaiah said, "Take a cake of figs." And they took and laid *it* on the boil, and he recovered.

b. The sign of the shadow

8 Now Hezekiah said to Isaiah, "What will be the sign that the LORD will heal me, and that I shall go up to the house of the LORD the third day?"

9 And Isaiah said, "This shall be the sign to you from the LORD, that the LORD

---

¹⁴Some ancient mss. read *the LORD of hosts*

19:35 The account does not say whether the soldiers died of plague or by the exercise of divine wrath, although the latter is suggested by the phrase, *the angel . . . struck.*

19:37 Sennacherib, like David, bypassed his eldest son, and chose Esarhaddon, his favorite, to succeed him. Esarhaddon's reign lasted twelve years.

Marginal references: 19:28 Job 41:2; Ezek 29:4; vv. 33,36 / 19:29 1 Sam 2:34; 2 Kin 20:8,9; Luke 2:12 / 19:30 2 Chr 32:22,23 / 19:31 Is 9:7 / 19:33 v. 28 / 19:34 2 Kin 20:6; 1 Kin 11:12,13 / *19:35 2 Chr 32:21; Is 37:36 / 19:36 vv. 7,28,33; Jon 1:2 / *19:37 2 Chr 32:21; v. 7; Ezra 4:2 / 20:1 2 Chr 32:24; Is 38:1; see 2 Sam 17:23 / 20:3 Neh 13:22; 2 Kin 18:3-6 / 20:5 1 Sam 9:16; 10:1; 2 Kin 19:20; Ps 39:12 / 20:6 2 Kin 19:34 / 20:7 Is 38:21

will do the thing that He has spoken: shall the shadow go forward ten steps or go back ten steps?"

10   So Hezekiah answered, "It is easy for the shadow to decline ten steps; no, but let the shadow turn backward ten steps."

20:11
Josh 10:12-14

11   And Isaiah the prophet cried to the LORD, and He brought the shadow on the stairway back ten steps by which it had gone down on the stairway of Ahaz.

5. Hezekiah's foolishness before Merodach-baladan

20:12
Is 39:1ff

12   At that time Berodach-baladan a son of Baladan, king of Babylon, sent letters and a present to Hezekiah, for he heard that Hezekiah had been sick.

20:13
2 Chr 32:27

13   And Hezekiah listened to them, and showed them all his treasure house, the silver and the gold and the spices and the precious oil and the house of his armor and all that was found in his treasuries. There was nothing in his house, nor in all his dominion, that Hezekiah did not show them.

14   Then Isaiah the prophet came to King Hezekiah and said to him, "What did these men say, and from where have they come to you?" And Hezekiah said, "They have come from a far country, from Babylon."

20:15
v. 13

15   And he said, "What have they seen in your house?" So Hezekiah answered, "They have seen all that is in my house; there is nothing among my treasuries that I have not shown them."

16   Then Isaiah said to Hezekiah, "Hear the word of the LORD.

20:17
2 Kin 24:13;
25:13;
Jer 52:17

17   'Behold, the days are coming when all that is in your house, and all that your fathers have laid up in store to this day shall be carried to Babylon; nothing shall be left,' says the LORD.

20:18
2 Kin 24:12;
2 Chr 33:1;
Dan 1:3-7

18   'And some of your sons who shall issue from you, whom you shall beget, shall be taken away; and they shall become officials in the palace of the king of Babylon.' "

20:19
1 Sam 3:18

19   Then Hezekiah said to Isaiah, "The word of the LORD which you have spoken is good." For he thought, "Is it not so, if there shall be peace and truth in my days?"

*20:20
2 Chr 32:32;
Neh 3:16

20   Now the rest of the acts of Hezekiah and all his might, and how he made the pool and the conduit, and brought water into the city, are they not written in the Book of the Chronicles of the Kings of Judah?

20:21
2 Chr 32:33

21   So Hezekiah slept with his fathers, and Manasseh his son became king in his place.

B. The reign of Manasseh

1. His wickedness

*21:1
2 Chr 33:1ff

21 Manasseh was twelve years old when he became king, and he reigned fifty-five years in Jerusalem; and his mother's name was Hephzibah.

21:2
2 Kin 16:3

2   And he did evil in the sight of the LORD, according to the abominations of the nations whom the LORD dispossessed before the sons of Israel.

21:3
2 Kin 18:4;
1 Kin 16:32,
33;
2 Kin 17:16;
Deut 17:3

3   For he rebuilt the high places which Hezekiah his father had destroyed; and he erected altars for Baal and made an Asherah, as Ahab king of Israel had done, and worshiped all the host of heaven and served them.

21:4
Jer 32:34;
2 Sam 7:13;
1 Kin 8:29

4   And he built altars in the house of the LORD, of which the LORD had said, "In Jerusalem I will put My name."

5   For he built altars for all the host of heaven in the two courts of the house of the LORD.

21:6
Lev 18:21;
2 Kin 16:3;
17:17;
Lev 19:26,31;
Deut 18:20,
11

6   And he made his son pass through the fire, practiced witchcraft and used divination, and dealt with mediums and spiritists. He did much evil in the sight of the LORD provoking *Him* to anger.

21:7
1 Kin 8:29;
9:3;
2 Kin 23:27;
Jer 32:34

7   Then he set the carved image of Asherah that he had made, in the house of which the LORD said to David and to his son Solomon, "In this house and in Jerusalem, which I have chosen from all the tribes of Israel, I will put My name forever.

8   "And I will not make the feet of Israel wander anymore from the land which I gave their fathers, if only they will observe to do according to all that I have

---

20:20 Hezekiah's tunnel was dug through solid rock by two crews, one working from the spring Gihon, and the other from the pool of Siloam. An inscription found in the tunnel near the Siloam end tells of the tense moment when the two crews met.

21:1 Ten years of Manasseh's fifty-five-year reign were in co-regency with Hezekiah.

commanded them, and according to all the law that My servant Moses commanded them."

9   But they did not listen, and Manasseh seduced them to do evil more than the nations whom the LORD destroyed before the sons of Israel.

2. The fall of Jerusalem predicted

10   Now the LORD spoke through His servants the prophets, saying,

11   "Because Manasseh king of Judah has done these abominations, having done wickedly more than all the Amorites did who *were* before him, and has also made Judah sin with his idols;

12   therefore thus says the LORD, the God of Israel, 'Behold, I am bringing *such* calamity on Jerusalem and Judah, that whoever hears of it, both his ears shall tingle.

13   'And I will stretch over Jerusalem the line of Samaria and the plummet of the house of Ahab, and I will wipe Jerusalem as one wipes a dish, wiping it and turning it upside down.

14   'And I will abandon the remnant of My inheritance and deliver them into the hand of their enemies, and they shall become as plunder and spoil to all their enemies;

15   because they have done evil in My sight, and have been provoking Me to anger, since the day their fathers came from Egypt, even to this day.'"

3. Summary of Manasseh's reign

16   Moreover, Manasseh shed very much innocent blood until he had filled Jerusalem from one end to another; besides his sin with which he made Judah sin, in doing evil in the sight of the LORD.

17   Now the rest of the acts of Manasseh and all that he did, and his sin which he committed, are they not written in the Book of the Chronicles of the Kings of Judah?

18   And Manasseh slept with his fathers and was buried in the garden of his own house, in the garden of Uzza, and Amon his son became king in his place.

C. The reign of Amon

19   Amon was twenty-two years old when he became king, and he reigned two years in Jerusalem; and his mother's name *was* Meshullemeth the daughter of Haruz of Jotbah.

20   And he did evil in the sight of the LORD, as Manasseh his father had done.

21   For he walked in all the way that his father had walked, and served the idols that his father had served and worshiped them.

22   So he forsook the LORD, the God of his fathers, and did not walk in the way of the LORD.

23   And the servants of Amon conspired against him and killed the king in his own house.

24   Then the people of the land killed all those who had conspired against King Amon, and the people of the land made Josiah his son king in his place.

25   Now the rest of the acts of Amon which he did, are they not written in the Book of the Chronicles of the Kings of Judah?

26   And he was buried in his grave in the garden of Uzza, and Josiah his son became king in his place.

D. The reign of Josiah

1. Faithful Josiah

22 Josiah was eight years old when he became king, and he reigned thirty-one years in Jerusalem; and his mother's name *was* Jedidah the daughter of Adaiah of Bozkath.

2   And he did right in the sight of the LORD and walked in all the way of his father David, nor did he turn aside to the right or to the left.

2. The repair of the temple

3   Now it came about in the eighteenth year of King Josiah that the king sent Shaphan, the son of Azaliah the son of Meshullam the scribe, to the house of the LORD saying,

---

21:8
2 Sam 7:10

21:9
Prov 29:12

21:11
2 Kin 24:3,4;
1 Kin 21:26;
v. 16

21:12
1 Sam 3:11;
Jer 19:3
21:13
Is 34:11;
Amos 7:7,8

21:16
2 Kin 24:4

21:17
2 Chr 33:11-19

21:18
2 Chr 33:20

21:19
2 Chr 33:21-23

21:20
vv. 2-6,11,16

21:22
1 Kin 11:33

21:23
2 Chr 33:24,
25

21:26
v. 18

22:1
2 Chr 34:1;
Josh 15:39

22:2
Deut 5:32

22:3
2 Chr 34:8ff

22:4
2 Kin 12:4,9,
10
22:5
2 Kin 12:11-14

22:7
2 Kin 12:15

*22:8
Deut 31:24-26;
2 Chr 34:14,
15

22:12
2 Kin 25:22;
2 Chr 34:20

22:13
Deut 29:27

*22:14
2 Chr 34:22

22:17
Deut 29:25-27

22:19
Ps 51:17;
Is 57:15;
1 Kin 21:29;
Lev 26:31;
Jer 26:6

23:1
2 Chr 34:29-32

4 "Go up to Hilkiah the high priest that he may count the money brought in to the house of the LORD which the doorkeepers have gathered from the people.

5 "And let them deliver it into the hand of the workmen who have the oversight of the house of the LORD, and let them give it to the workmen who are in the house of the LORD to repair the damages of the house,

6 to the carpenters and the builders and the masons and for buying timber and hewn stone to repair the house.

7 "Only no accounting shall be made with them for the money delivered into their hands, for they deal faithfully."

3. The finding of the book of the law

8 Then Hilkiah the high priest said to Shaphan the scribe, "I have found the book of the law in the house of the LORD." And Hilkiah gave the book to Shaphan who read it.

9 And Shaphan the scribe came to the king and brought back word to the king and said, "Your servants have emptied out the money that was found in the house, and have delivered it into the hand of the workmen who have the oversight of the house of the LORD."

10 Moreover, Shaphan the scribe told the king saying, "Hilkiah the priest has given me a book." And Shaphan read it in the presence of the king.

4. The reaction of Josiah

11 And it came about when the king heard the words of the book of the law, that he tore his clothes.

12 Then the king commanded Hilkiah the priest, Ahikam the son of Shaphan, Achbor the son of Micaiah, Shaphan the scribe, and Asaiah the king's servant saying,

13 "Go, inquire of the LORD for me and the people and all Judah concerning the words of this book that has been found, for great is the wrath of the LORD that burns against us, because our fathers have not listened to the words of this book, to do according to all that is written concerning us."

5. The words of Huldah the prophetess

14 So Hilkiah the priest, Ahikam, Achbor, Shaphan, and Asaiah went to Huldah the prophetess, the wife of Shallum the son of Tikvah, the son of Harhas, keeper of the wardrobe (now she lived in Jerusalem in the Second Quarter); and they spoke to her.

15 And she said to them, "Thus says the LORD God of Israel, 'Tell the man who sent you to me,

16 thus says the LORD, "Behold, I bring evil on this place and on its inhabitants, even all the words of the book which the king of Judah has read.

17 "Because they have forsaken Me and have burned incense to other gods that they might provoke Me to anger with all the work of their hands, therefore My wrath burns against this place, and it shall not be quenched."'

18 "But to the king of Judah who sent you to inquire of the LORD thus shall you say to him, 'Thus says the LORD God of Israel, "Regarding the words which you have heard,

19 because your heart was tender and you humbled yourself before the LORD when you heard what I spoke against this place and against its inhabitants that they should become a desolation and a curse, and you have torn your clothes and wept before Me, I truly have heard you," declares the LORD.

20 "Therefore, behold, I will gather you to your fathers, and you shall be gathered to your grave in peace, neither shall your eyes see all the evil which I will bring on this place."'" So they brought back word to the king.

6. The renewal of the covenant

23 Then the king sent, and they gathered to him all the elders of Judah and of Jerusalem.

2 And the king went up to the house of the LORD and all the men of Judah and

---

22:8 *book of the law.* On the basis of details noted in Josiah's reform and also some of the material in Jeremiah, it is evident that the Book of the Law constituted much of the material contained in Deuteronomy.

22:14 Hilkiah the priest went to Huldah the prophetess, although the LORD had called Jeremiah in 626 B.C., five years previously.

F. *The reign of Jehoiakim: first capture of Jerusalem by Nebuchadnezzar*

36 Jehoiakim was twenty-five years old when he became king, and he reigned eleven years in Jerusalem; and his mother's name *was* Zebidah the daughter of Pedaiah of Rumah.

37 And he did evil in the sight of the LORD, according to all that his fathers had done.

24 In his days Nebuchadnezzar king of Babylon came up, and Jehoiakim became his servant *for* three years; then he turned and rebelled against him.

2 And the LORD sent against him bands of Chaldeans, bands of Arameans, bands of Moabites, and bands of Ammonites. So He sent them against Judah to destroy it, according to the word of the LORD, which He had spoken through His servants the prophets.

3 Surely at the command of the LORD it came upon Judah, to remove *them* from His sight because of the sins of Manasseh, according to all that he had done,

4 and also for the innocent blood which he shed, for he filled Jerusalem with innocent blood; and the LORD would not forgive.

5 Now the rest of the acts of Jehoiakim and all that he did, are they not written in the Book of the Chronicles of the Kings of Judah?

6 So Jehoiakim slept with his fathers, and Jehoiachin his son became king in his place.

7 And the king of Egypt did not come out of his land again, for the king of Babylon had taken all that belonged to the king of Egypt from the brook of Egypt to the river Euphrates.

G. *The reign of Jehoiachin: the second capture of Jerusalem*

8 Jehoiachin was eighteen years old when he became king, and he reigned three months in Jerusalem; and his mother's name *was* Nehushta the daughter of Elnathan of Jerusalem.

9 And he did evil in the sight of the LORD, according to all that his father had done.

10 At that time the servants of Nebuchadnezzar king of Babylon went up to Jerusalem, and the city came under siege.

11 And Nebuchadnezzar the king of Babylon came to the city, while his servants were besieging it.

12 And Jehoiachin the king of Judah went out to the king of Babylon, he and his mother and his servants and his captains and his officials. So the king of Babylon took him captive in the eighth year of his reign.

13 And he carried out from there all the treasures of the house of the LORD, and the treasures of the king's house, and cut in pieces all the vessels of gold which Solomon king of Israel had made in the temple of the LORD, just as the LORD had said.

14 Then he led away into exile all Jerusalem and all the captains and all the mighty men of valor, ten thousand captives, and all the craftsmen and the smiths. None remained except the poorest people of the land.

15 So he led Jehoiachin away into exile to Babylon; also the king's mother and the king's wives and his officials and the leading men of the land, he led away into exile from Jerusalem to Babylon.

16 And all the men of valor, seven thousand, and the craftsmen and the smiths, one thousand, all strong and fit for war, and these the king of Babylon brought into exile to Babylon.

17 Then the king of Babylon made his uncle Mattaniah, king in his place, and changed his name to Zedekiah.

H. *The reign of Zedekiah*

1. *The rebellion against Babylon*

18 Zedekiah was twenty-one years old when he became king, and he reigned

Cross-references: 23:36 / 2 Chr 36:5 · 24:1 / 2 Chr 36:6; Jer 25:1 · *24:2 / Jer 25:9; 35:11; 2 Kin 23:27 · 24:3 / 2 Kin 18:25; 23:26 · 24:4 / 2 Kin 21:16 · 24:6 / Jer 22:18,19 · 24:7 / Jer 37:5-7; 46:2 · 24:8 / 1 Chr 3:16; 2 Chr 36:9 · 24:10 / Dan 1:1 · 24:12 / Jer 24:1; 29:1,2; 25:1; 2 Kin 25:27; Jer 52:28 · 24:13 / 2 Kin 20:17; Is 39:6; 2 Kin 25:13-15; Jer 20:5 · 24:14 / Jer 24:1; 52:28; 2 Kin 25:12; Jer 40:7 · 24:15 / 2 Chr 36:10; Jer 22:24-28 · 24:16 / Jer 52:28 · 24:17 / Jer 37:1; 1 Chr 3:15; 2 Chr 36:4,10 · 24:18 / 2 Chr 36:11; Jer 52:1; 2 Kin 23:31

24:2 *Chaldeans*, that is, Babylonians.

eleven years in Jerusalem; and his mother's name *was* Hamutal the daughter of Jeremiah of Libnah.

19   And he did evil in the sight of the LORD, according to all that Jehoiakim had done.

20   For through the anger of the LORD *this* came about in Jerusalem and Judah until He cast them out from His presence. And Zedekiah rebelled against the king of Babylon.

25 Now it came about in the ninth year of his reign, on the tenth day of the tenth month, that Nebuchadnezzar king of Babylon came, he and all his army, against Jerusalem, camped against it, and built a siege wall all around it.

2   So the city was under siege until the eleventh year of King Zedekiah.

3   On the ninth day of the *fourth* month the famine was so severe in the city that there was no food for the people of the land.

4   Then the city was broken into, and all the men of war *fled* by night by way of the gate between the two walls beside the king's garden, though the Chaldeans were all around the city. And they went by way of the Arabah.

5   But the army of the Chaldeans pursued the king and overtook him in the plains of Jericho and all his army was scattered from him.

6   Then they captured the king and brought him to the king of Babylon at Riblah, and he passed sentence on him.

7   And they slaughtered the sons of Zedekiah before his eyes, then put out the eyes of Zedekiah and bound him with bronze fetters and brought him to Babylon.

2. The destruction of Jerusalem and the temple

8   Now on the seventh day of the fifth month, which was the nineteenth year of King Nebuchadnezzar, king of Babylon, Nebuzaradan the captain of the guard, a servant of the king of Babylon, came to Jerusalem.

9   And he burned the house of the LORD, the king's house, and all the houses of Jerusalem; even every great house he burned with fire.

10   So all the army of the Chaldeans who *were with* the captain of the guard broke down the walls around Jerusalem.

11   Then the rest of the people who were left in the city and the deserters who had deserted to the king of Babylon and the rest of the multitude, Nebuzaradan the captain of the guard carried away into exile.

12   But the captain of the guard left some of the poorest of the land to be vinedressers and plowmen.

13   Now the bronze pillars which were in the house of the LORD, and the stands and the bronze sea which were in the house of the LORD, the Chaldeans broke in pieces and carried the bronze to Babylon.

14   And they took away the pots, the shovels, the snuffers, the spoons, and all the bronze vessels which were used in *temple* service.

15   The captain of the guard also took away the firepans and the basins, what was fine gold and what was fine silver.

16   The two pillars, the one sea, and the stands which Solomon had made for the house of the LORD—the bronze of all these vessels was beyond weight.

17   The height of the one pillar was eighteen cubits, and a bronze capital was on it; the height of the capital was three cubits, with a network and pomegranates on the capital all around, all of bronze. And the second pillar was like these with network.

3. The killing of the leaders

18   Then the captain of the guard took Seraiah the chief priest and Zephaniah the second priest, with the three officers of the temple.

19   And from the city he took one official who was overseer of the men of war, and five of the king's advisers who were found in the city; and the scribe of the captain of the army, who mustered the people of the land; and sixty men of the people of the land who were found in the city.

20   And Nebuzaradan the captain of the guard took them and brought them to the king of Babylon at Riblah.

21   Then the king of Babylon struck them down and put them to death at Riblah in the land of Hamath. So Judah was led away into exile from its land.

Marginal cross-references:

24:19 / 2 Chr 36:12

24:20 / 2 Chr 36:13

25:1 / 2 Chr 36:13, 17-20; Jer 39:1-7; Ezek 24:1,2

25:3 / Jer 39:1,2

25:4 / Jer 39:4-7

25:6 / Jer 34:21,22; 2 Kin 23:33

25:7 / Jer 39:6,7; Ezek 12:13

25:8 / Jer 52:12-14; 39:9

25:9 / 2 Chr 36:19; Ps 74:3-7; Amos 2:5

25:10 / Neh 1:3; Jer 52:14

25:11 / 2 Chr 36:20; Jer 39:9; 52:15

25:12 / 2 Kin 24:14; Jer 40:7

25:13 / 2 Chr 36:18

25:14 / 1 Kin 7:47-50

25:16 / 1 Kin 7:47

25:17 / 1 Kin 7:15-22

25:18 / 1 Chr 6:14; Ezra 7:1; Jer 21:1; 29:25

25:21 / Deut 28:64; 2 Kin 23:27

4. *The appointment of Gedaliah as governor: his murder*

22   Now *as for* the people who were left in the land of Judah, whom Nebu-chadnezzar king of Babylon had left, he appointed Gedaliah the son of Ahikam, the son of Shaphan over them.

23   When all the captains of the forces, they and *their* men, heard that the king of Babylon had appointed Gedaliah *governor*, they came to Gedaliah to Mizpah, namely, Ishmael the son of Nethaniah, and Johanan the son of Kareah, and Seraiah the son of Tanhumeth the Netophathite, and Jaazaniah the son of the Maacathite, they and their men.

24   And Gedaliah swore to them and their men and said to them, "Do not be afraid of the servants of the Chaldeans; live in the land and serve the king of Babylon, and it will be well with you."

25   But it came about in the seventh month, that Ishmael the son of Nethaniah, the son of Elishama, of the royal family, came with ten men and struck Gedaliah down so that he died along with the Jews and the Chaldeans who were with him at Mizpah.

26   Then all the people, both small and great, and the captains of the forces arose and went to Egypt; for they were afraid of the Chaldeans.

5. *Jehoiachin set free in Babylon*

27   Now it came about in the thirty-seventh year of the exile of Jehoiachin king of Judah, in the twelfth month, on the twenty-seventh *day* of the month, that Evil-merodach king of Babylon, in the year that he became king, released Jehoia-chin king of Judah from prison;

28   and he spoke kindly to him and set his throne above the throne of the kings who *were* with him in Babylon.

29   And Jehoiachin changed his prison clothes, and had his meals in the king's presence regularly all the days of his life;

30   and for his allowance, a regular allowance was given him by the king, a portion for each day, all the days of his life.

25:22
Jer 40:5

25:23
Jer 40:7-9

25:25
Jer 41:1,2

25:26
Jer 43:4-7

*25:27
Jer 52:31-34;
Gen 40:13,20

25:29
2 Sam 9:7

25:27 *Evil-merodach*, the son of Nebuchadnezzar, reigned 561–560 B.C. His Babylonian name was Amel-Marduk, "Man of Marduk"; but a variant form was Awel-Marduk, the source of the Hebrew form Evil-merodach. Thus, the segment "Evil" is an accident of transliteration, and it has no relation in meaning to the adjective "evil." *released*

Jehoiachin. The Babylonians always considered Jehoiachin as the legitimate king of Judah, so they took good care of him and his family. Some clay tablets found in Babylon mention Jehoiachin and five of his sons in connection with rations supplied the captives.

INTRODUCTION TO
THE FIRST BOOK OF THE
CHRONICLES

Authorship and Background: While the English title "Chronicles" derives from Jerome's suggestion, it is fairly close in meaning to the Hebrew title, "Words (events) of the Days." The Septuagint title, "Things Passed Over," indicates that the translators thought of Chronicles primarily as a supplement that included materials neglected by Samuel-Kings. 1 and 2 Chronicles were originally one book, but it was separated into two units by the Septuagint translators. The book of Ezra was also a part of this history (Ezra 1:1-3a is a repetition of 2 Chr. 36:22,23). In the Hebrew Bible, Chronicles appears as the last book, while in the Septuagint and the Vulgate it was placed after Kings.

Some scholars date the Chronicler's work about 300 B.C. on the basis of the genealogies in 1 Chr. 3:17-24 and Neh. 12:10,11,22, but these lists permit a different interpretation. The remarkable similarity in language between Chronicles and the memoirs of Ezra (7:27-9:15) suggests that Ezra was the Chronicler. This view, held by tradition, has the further support of the Aramaic letters from Elephantine (modern Aswan) in Egypt. These date from the fifth century B.C. and mention persons named in Ezra and Nehemiah. Although some material may have been added to the Chronicles later, a date somewhere between 425 and 400 B.C. is most probable for the compilation of this history. Many old sources were employed, such as genealogies, court records of Israel and Judah, and writings of the prophets Samuel, Nathan, Gad, Ahijah, Shemaiah, Iddo, Jehu, and Isaiah.

Characteristics: The Chronicler uses some material in common with Samuel and Kings, but there are also basic differences: (1) Israel, the northern kingdom, is virtually ignored; (2) most of the references to the defects and the sins of David and Solomon are omitted; and (3) the numbers generally are in round figures and larger than those in the other books. The author records events from the vantage point of religious concern and pays particular attention to the temple and the Davidic line. Apparently he wishes the postexilic Jews to understand that their community was a continuation of the former Davidic kingdom. Undoubtedly that is why the first nine chapters consist almost entirely of genealogies, which trace the progenitors of the Israelites back to the first man, Adam. He wishes the people to know that God is with those who are faithful to the covenant. His history is a warning and an encouragement both for the people of his day and for every generation since then. Following the genealogies the writer commences his history with the death of Saul and continues through the accession of David, his preparations for building the temple, the arrangements concerning the Levites, his conduct of the government, and his last instructions to Solomon before his death.

Contents:

I. The genealogies (1:1-9:44): The genealogy from Adam to Noah. Noah's sons. From Noah to Abraham and Isaac. The line of Ishmael and Keturah's sons. From Abraham to Jacob. The sons of Esau and Jacob. The line from Judah to David. The line from David to Anani. The sons of Jacob and their descendants: Judah, Simeon, Reuben, Gad, the half-tribe of Manasseh (west), Ephraim, Asher, Benjamin. The inhabitants of Jerusalem before the exile: the chief priests, Levites, the porters, and the singers.

II. The reign of King David (10:1-29:30): The kingship of Saul: his defeat, death, and burial; his unfaithfulness. The coronation of David over all Israel. The names and exploits of David's chief heroes. The names and numbers of those who supported David.

The removal of the ark from Kiriath-jearim to Obed-edom. The prosperity of David. The bringing of the ark to Jerusalem: the priests, the singers, the march, the offerings, the psalm of thanksgiving, and the appointment of the services. David's desire to build the temple. God's disapproval of David's desire and David's prayer. David's wars and his census; the plague. David's preparations for the temple: the site, the materials, the charge to Solomon, his crowning, the arrangements for the temple service, and the internal organization of the kingdom. David's final temple directions to Solomon, his thanksgiving and prayer, and his death.

The removal of the ... om. The prosperity of David. The belonging of the ... to Jerusalem; the priests; the singers; the march, the offerings; the psalm of thanksgiving. ... services. David's desire to build the temple. God's ... to David's desire. and David's prayer. David's war and his census; the plague. David's preparations for the temple; the site; the materials; the charge to Solomon. His crowning. the arrangements for the temple service; and the internal organisation of the kingdom. David's final temple directions to Solomon, his thanksgiving and prayer, and his death.

THE FIRST BOOK OF THE
CHRONICLES

I. *The genealogies (1:1–9:44)*

A. *The ancestral lines in the patriarchal period*

1:1
Gen 4:25;
5:32

1 Adam, Seth, Enosh,
2 Kenan, Mahalalel, Jared,
3 Enoch, Methuselah, Lamech,
4 Noah, Shem, Ham and Japheth.

1:5
Gen 10:2-4

5 The sons of Japheth *were* Gomer, Magog, Madai, Javan, Tubal, Meshech, and Tiras.
6 And the sons of Gomer *were* Ashkenaz, Diphath, and Togarmah.
7 And the sons of Javan *were* Elishah, Tarshish, Kittim, and Rodanim.

1:8
Gen 10:6ff

8 The sons of Ham *were* Cush, Mizraim, Put, and Canaan.
9 And the sons of Cush *were* Seba, Havilah, Sabta, Raama, and Sabteca; and the sons of Raamah *were* Sheba and Dedan.

1:10
Gen 10:8,13ff

10 And Cush became the father of Nimrod; he began to be a mighty one in the earth.
11 And Mizraim became the father of the people of Lud, Anam, Lehab, Naphtuh,
12 Pathrus, Casluh, from which the Philistines came, and Caphtor.
13 And Canaan became the father of Sidon, his first-born, Heth,
14 and the Jebusites, the Amorites, the Girgashites,
15 the Hivites, the Arkites, the Sinites,
16 the Arvadites, the Zemarites, and the Hamathites.

1:17
Gen 10:22ff

17 The sons of Shem *were* Elam, Asshur, Arpachshad, Lud, Aram, Uz, Hul, Gether, and Meshech.
18 And Arpachshad became the father of Shelah and Shelah became the father of Eber.
19 And two sons were born to Eber, the name of the one was Peleg, for in his days the earth was divided, and his brother's name was Joktan.
20 And Joktan became the father of Almodad, Sheleph, Hazarmaveth, Jerah,
21 Hadoram, Uzal, Diklah,
22 Ebal, Abimael, Sheba,
23 Ophir, Havilah, and Jobab; all these *were* the sons of Joktan.

1:24
Gen 11:10ff

24 Shem, Arpachshad, Shelah,
25 Eber, Peleg, Reu,
26 Serug, Nahor, Terah,
27 Abram, that is Abraham.
28 The sons of Abraham *were* Isaac and Ishmael.

1:29
Gen 25:13-16

29 These are their genealogies: the first-born of Ishmael *was* Nebaioth, then Kedar, Adbeel, Mibsam,
30 Mishma, Dumah, Massa, Hadad, Tema,
31 Jetur, Naphish and Kedemah; these *were* the sons of Ishmael.

1:32
Gen 25:1-4

32 And the sons of Keturah, Abraham's concubine, *whom* she bore, *were* Zimran, Jokshan, Medan, Midian, Ishbak, and Shuah. And the sons of Jokshan *were* Sheba and Dedan.
33 And the sons of Midian *were* Ephah, Epher, Hanoch, Abida, and Eldaah. All these were the sons of Keturah.

1:34
Gen 21:2,3;
25:25,26

34 And Abraham became the father of Isaac. The sons of Isaac *were* Esau and Israel.

1:35
Gen 36:9,10

35 The sons of Esau *were* Eliphaz, Reuel, Jeush, Jalam, and Korah.
36 The sons of Eliphaz *were* Teman, Omar, Zephi, Gatam, Kenaz, Timna, and Amalek.
37 The sons of Reuel *were* Nahath, Zerah, Shammah, and Mizzah.

38   And the sons of Seir *were* Lotan, Shobal, Zibeon, Anah, Dishon, Ezer, and Dishan.

1:38
Gen 36:20-28

39   And the sons of Lotan *were* Hori and Homam; and Lotan's sister *was* Timna.

40   The sons of Shobal *were* Alian, Manahath, Ebal, Shephi, and Onam. And the sons of Zibeon *were* Aiah and Anah.

41   The son of Anah *was* Dishon. And the sons of Dishon *were* Hamran, Eshban, Ithran, and Cheran.

42   The sons of Ezer *were* Bilhan, Zaavan and Jaakan. The sons of Dishan *were* Uz and Aran.

43   Now these are the kings who reigned in the land of Edom before any king of the sons of Israel reigned. Bela *was* the son of Beor, and the name of his city was Dinhabah.

1:43
Gen 36:31-43

44   When Bela died, Jobab the son of Zerah of Bozrah became king in his place.

45   When Jobab died, Husham of the land of the Temanites became king in his place.

46   When Husham died, Hadad the son of Bedad, who defeated Midian in the field of Moab, became king in his place; and the name of his city *was* Avith.

47   When Hadad died, Samlah of Masrekah became king in his place.

48   When Samlah died, Shaul of Rehoboth by the River became king in his place.

49   When Shaul died, Baal-hanan the son of Achbor became king in his place.

50   When Baal-hanan died, Hadad became king in his place; and the name of his city was Pai, and his wife's name was Mehetabel, the daughter of Matred, the daughter of Mezahab.

51   Then Hadad died. Now the chiefs of Edom were: chief Timna, chief Aliah, chief Jetheth,

52   chief Oholibamah, chief Elah, chief Pinon,

53   chief Kenaz, chief Teman, chief Mibzar,

54   chief Magdiel, chief Iram. These *were* the chiefs of Edom.

B. *The descendants of Judah to David*

2   These are the sons of Israel: Reuben, Simeon, Levi, Judah, Issachar, Zebulun,

2:1
Gen 35:23-26;
46:8-25
2:2
Gen 38:2-10

2   Dan, Joseph, Benjamin, Naphtali, Gad, and Asher.

3   The sons of Judah *were* Er, Onan, and Shelah; *these* three were born to him by Bath-shua the Canaanitess. And Er, Judah's first-born, was wicked in the sight of the LORD, so He put him to death.

4   And Tamar his daughter-in-law bore him Perez and Zerah. Judah had five sons in all.

2:4
Gen 38:29,30

5   The sons of Perez *were* Hezron and Hamul.

2:5
Gen 46:12
2:6
Josh 7:1;
1 Kin 4:31
2:7
Josh 6:18; 7:1

6   And the sons of Zerah *were* Zimri, Ethan, Heman, Calcol, and Dara; five of them in all.

7   And the son of Carmi *was* Achar, the troubler of Israel, who violated the ban.

8   And the son of Ethan *was* Azariah.

9   Now the sons of Hezron, who were born to him *were* Jerahmeel, Ram, and Chelubai.

10   And Ram became the father of Amminadab, and Amminadab became the father of Nahshon, leader of the sons of Judah;

2:10
Ruth 4:19,20;
Matt 1:4

11   Nahshon became the father of Salma, Salma became the father of Boaz,

12   Boaz became the father of Obed, and Obed became the father of Jesse;

13   and Jesse became the father of Eliab his first-born, then Abinadab the second, Shimea the third,

2:13
1 Sam 16:6,9

14   Nethanel the fourth, Raddai the fifth,

15   Ozem the sixth, David the seventh;

16   and their sisters *were* Zeruiah and Abigail. And the three sons of Zeruiah *were* Abshai, Joab, and Asahel.

2:16
2 Sam 2:18

17   And Abigail bore Amasa, and the father of Amasa was Jether the Ishmaelite.

2:17
2 Sam 17:25

18   Now Caleb the son of Hezron had sons by Azubah *his* wife, and by Jerioth; and these were her sons: Jesher, Shobab, and Ardon.

2:19
v. 50
2:20
Ex 31:2

19   When Azubah died, Caleb married Ephrath, who bore him Hur.

20   And Hur became the father of Uri, and Uri became the father of Bezalel.

2:21
Num 27:1
21 Afterward Hezron went in to the daughter of Machir the father of Gilead, whom he married when he was sixty years old; and she bore him Segub.

22 And Segub became the father of Jair, who had twenty-three cities in the land of Gilead.

2:23
Num 32:41;
Deut 3:14;
Josh 13:30
2:24
1 Chr 4:5
23 But Geshur and Aram took the towns of Jair from them, with Kenath and its villages, *even* sixty cities. All these were the sons of Machir, the father of Gilead.

24 And after the death of Hezron in Caleb-ephrathah, Abijah, Hezron's wife, bore him Ashhur the father of Tekoa.

25 Now the sons of Jerahmeel the first-born of Hezron *were* Ram the first-born, then Bunah, Oren, Ozem, *and* Ahijah.

26 And Jerahmeel had another wife, whose name was Atarah; she was the mother of Onam.

27 And the sons of Ram, the first-born of Jerahmeel, were Maaz, Jamin, and Eker.

28 And the sons of Onam were Shammai and Jada. And the sons of Shammai *were* Nadab and Abishur.

29 And the name of Abishur's wife *was* Abihail, and she bore him Ahban and Molid.

30 And the sons of Nadab *were* Seled and Appaim, and Seled died without sons.

2:31
vv. 34,35
31 And the son of Appaim *was* Ishi. And the son of Ishi *was* Sheshan. And the son of Sheshan *was* Ahlai.

32 And the sons of Jada the brother of Shammai *were* Jether and Jonathan, and Jether died without sons.

33 And the sons of Jonathan *were* Peleth and Zaza. These were the sons of Jerahmeel.

34 Now Sheshan had no sons, only daughters. And Sheshan had an Egyptian servant whose name was Jarha.

35 And Sheshan gave his daughter to Jarha his servant in marriage, and she bore him Attai.

2:36
1 Chr 11:41
36 And Attai became the father of Nathan, and Nathan became the father of Zabad,

37 and Zabad became the father of Ephlal, and Ephlal became the father of Obed,

38 and Obed became the father of Jehu, and Jehu became the father of Azariah,

39 and Azariah became the father of Helez, and Helez became the father of Eleasah,

40 and Eleasah became the father of Sismai, and Sismai became the father of Shallum,

41 and Shallum became the father of Jekamiah, and Jekamiah became the father of Elishama.

2:42
see
1 Chr 2:18,19
42 Now the sons of Caleb, the brother of Jerahmeel, *were* Mesha his first-born, who was the father of Ziph; and his son was Mareshah, the father of Hebron.

43 And the sons of Hebron *were* Korah and Tappuah and Rekem and Shema.

44 And Shema became the father of Raham, the father of Jorkeam; and Rekem became the father of Shammai.

45 And the son of Shammai was Maon, and Maon *was* the father of Bethzur.

46 And Ephah, Caleb's concubine, bore Haran, Moza, and Gazez; and Haran became the father of Gazez.

47 And the sons of Jahdai *were* Regem, Jotham, Geshan, Pelet, Ephah, and Shaaph.

48 Maacah, Caleb's concubine, bore Sheber and Tirhanah.

49 She also bore Shaaph the father of Madmannah, Sheva the father of Machbena and the father of Gibea; and the daughter of Caleb *was* Achsah.

2:50
1 Chr 4:4
50 These were the sons of Caleb.

The sons of Hur, the first-born of Ephrathah, *were* Shobal the father of Kiriath-jearim,

51 Salma the father of Bethlehem *and* Hareph the father of Beth-gader.

52 And Shobal the father of Kiriath-jearim had sons: Haroeh, half of the Manahathites,

53 and the families of Kiriath-jearim: the Ithrites, the Puthites, the Shumath-

---

2:25 *Jerahmeel* means "may God have compassion." Some non-Israelites, subjects of David, called themselves Jerah- meelites. They are mentioned in 1 Sam. 27:10; 30:29.

ites, and the Mishraites; from these came the Zorathites and the Eshtaolites.

54   The sons of Salma *were* Bethlehem and the Netophathites, Atroth-beth-joab and half of the Manahathites, the Zorites.

55   And the families of scribes who lived at Jabez *were* the Tirathites, the Shimeathites, *and* the Sucathites. Those are the Kenites who came from Hammath, the father of the house of Rechab.

*2:55
Judg 1:16;
Jer 35:2

C. *The descendants of David*

3 Now these were the sons of David who were born to him in Hebron: the first-born *was* Amnon, by Ahinoam the Jezreelitess; the second *was* Daniel, by Abigail the Carmelitess;

3:1
2 Sam 3:2,3;
Josh 15:56

2   the third *was* Absalom the son of Maacah, the daughter of Talmai king of Geshur; the fourth *was* Adonijah the son of Haggith;

3   the fifth *was* Shephatiah, by Abital; the sixth *was* Ithream, by his wife Eglah.

3:3
2 Sam 3:5

4   Six were born to him in Hebron, and there he reigned seven years and six months. And in Jerusalem he reigned thirty-three years.

3:4
2 Sam 2:11;
5:5

5   And these were born to him in Jerusalem: Shimea, Shobab, Nathan, and Solomon, four, by Bath-shua the daughter of Ammiel;

*3:5
2 Sam 5:14-16;
2 Sam 12:24;
11:3

6   and Ibhar, Elishama, Eliphelet,

7   Nogah, Nepheg, and Japhia,

8   Elishama, Eliada, and Eliphelet, nine.

9   All *these were* the sons of David, besides the sons of the concubines; and Tamar *was* their sister.

3:9
2 Sam 13:1

10   Now Solomon's son *was* Rehoboam, Abijah *was* his son, Asa his son, Jehoshaphat his son,

3:10
1 Kin 11:43

11   Joram his son, Ahaziah his son, Joash his son,

12   Amaziah his son, Azariah his son, Jotham his son,

13   Ahaz his son, Hezekiah his son, Manasseh his son,

14   Amon his son, Josiah his son.

15   And the sons of Josiah *were* Johanan the first-born, and the second *was* Jehoiakim, the third Zedekiah, the fourth Shallum.

16   And the sons of Jehoiakim *were* Jeconiah his son, Zedekiah his son.

17   And the sons of Jeconiah, the prisoner, *were* Shealtiel his son,

*3:16
Matt 1:11

18   and Malchiram, Pedaiah, Shenazzar, Jekamiah, Hoshama, and Nedabiah.

19   And the sons of Pedaiah *were* Zerubbabel and Shimei. And the sons of Zerubbabel *were* Meshullam and Hananiah, and Shelomith *was* their sister;

20   and Hashubah, Ohel, Berechiah, Hasadiah, and Jushab-hesed, five.

21   And the sons of Hananiah *were* Pelatiah and Jeshaiah, the sons of Rephaiah, the sons of Arnan, the sons of Obadiah, the sons of Shecaniah.

22   And the ¹son of Shecaniah *was* Shemaiah, and the sons of Shemaiah *were* Hattush, Igal, Bariah, Neariah, and Shaphat, six.

3:22
Ezek 8:2

23   And the sons of Neariah *were* Elioenai, Hizkiah, and Azrikam, three.

24   And the sons of Elioenai *were* Hodaviah, Eliashib, Pelaiah, Akkub, Johanan, Delaiah, and Anani, seven.

D. *The family of Judah*

4 The sons of Judah *were* Perez, Hezron, Carmi, Hur, and Shobal.

2   And Reaiah the son of Shobal became the father of Jahath, and Jahath became the father of Ahumai and Lahad. These *were* the families of the Zorathites.

4:1
Gen 46:12

3   And these *were* the sons of Etam: Jezreel, Ishma, and Idbash; and the name of their sister *was* Hazzelelponi.

¹Lit., *sons*

2:55 *scribes.* These were nonlevitical scribes, although some of the Levites were scribes as well (2 Chr. 34:13 specifically states this).
3:5 *Bath-shua,* that is, Bath-sheba.
3:15 *Johanan.* Apparently he died as a youth. He never reigned and is never mentioned in the historical accounts. *Shallum,* that is, Jehoahaz. See Jer. 22:11.
3:16 *Jeconiah,* that is, Jehoiachin. He is also called Coniah in Jer. 22:24.

3:17 *the prisoner.* The KJV took this word as a proper name, listing it as Assir.
3:19 *Zerubbabel.* The Zerubbabel who led the captives back to Palestine was called *the son of Shealtiel* (Ezra 3:2; Neh. 12:1). Evidently both Shealtiel and Pedaiah had sons named Zerubbabel. Thus, the descendants listed after Zerubbabel here are most likely from the line of Shealtiel, not Pedaiah.

4:4
1 Chr 2:50
4   And Penuel *was* the father of Gedor, and Ezer the father of Hushah. These *were* the sons of Hur, the first-born of Ephrathah, the father of Bethlehem.

4:5
1 Chr 2:24
5   And Ashhur, the father of Tekoa, had two wives, Helah and Naarah.

6   And Naarah bore him Ahuzzam, Hepher, Temeni, and Haahashtari. These were the sons of Naarah.

7   And the sons of Helah *were* Zereth, Izhar and Ethnan.

8   And Koz became the father of Anub and Zobebah, and the families of Aharhel the son of Harum.

*4:9
Gen 34:19
9   And Jabez was more honorable than his brothers, and his mother named him Jabez saying, "Because I bore *him* with pain."

10   Now Jabez called on the God of Israel, saying, "Oh that Thou wouldst bless me indeed, and enlarge my border, and that Thy hand might be with me, and that Thou wouldst keep *me* from harm, that *it* may not pain me!" And God granted him what he requested.

11   And Chelub the brother of Shuhah became the father of Mehir, who was the father of Eshton.

12   And Eshton became the father of Beth-rapha and Paseah, and Tehinnah the father of Ir-nahash. These are the men of Recah.

4:13
Josh 15:17
13   Now the sons of Kenaz *were* Othniel and Seraiah. And the son of Othniel *was* Hathath.

4:14
Neh 11:35
14   And Meonothai became the father of Ophrah, and Seraiah became the father of Joab the father of Ge-harashim, for they were craftsmen.

15   And the sons of Caleb the son of Jephunneh *were* Iru, Elah and Naam; and the son of Elah *was* Kenaz.

16   And the sons of Jehallelel *were* Ziph and Ziphah, Tiria and Asarel.

17   And the sons of Ezrah *were* Jether, Mered, Epher, and Jalon. (And these are the sons of Bithia the daughter of Pharaoh, whom Mered took) and she conceived *and bore* Miriam, Shammai, and Ishbah the father of Eshtemoa.

18   And his Jewish wife bore Jered the father of Gedor, and Heber the father of Soco, and Jekuthiel the father of Zanoah.

19   And the sons of the wife of Hodiah, the sister of Naham, *were* the fathers of Keilah the Garmite and Eshtemoa the Maacathite.

20   And the sons of Shimon *were* Amnon and Rinnah, Benhanan and Tilon. And the sons of Ishi *were* Zoheth and Ben-zoheth.

4:21
Gen 38:1,5
21   The sons of Shelah the son of Judah *were* Er the father of Lecah and Laadah the father of Mareshah, and the families of the house of the linen workers at Beth-ashbea;

22   and Jokim, the men of Cozeba, Joash, Saraph, who ruled in Moab, and Jashubi-lehem. And the records are ancient.

23   These were the potters and the inhabitants of Netaim and Gederah; they lived there with the king for his work.

E. *The family of Simeon*

4:24
Gen 29:33
24   The sons of Simeon *were* Nemuel and Jamin, Jarib, Zerah, Shaul;

25   Shallum his son, Mibsam his son, Mishma his son.

26   And the sons of Mishma *were* Hammuel his son, Zaccur his son, Shimei his son.

27   Now Shimei had sixteen sons and six daughters; but his brothers did not have many sons, nor did all their family multiply like the sons of Judah.

4:28
Josh 19:2
28   And they lived at Beersheba, Moladah, and Hazar-shual,

29   at Bilhah, Ezem, Tolad,

4:30
1 Chr 12:1
30   Bethuel, Hormah, Ziklag,

31   Beth-marcaboth, Hazar-susim, Beth-biri, and Shaaraim. These *were* their cities until the reign of David.

32   And their villages *were* Etam, Ain, Rimmon, Tochen, and Ashan, five cities;

33   and all their villages that *were* around the same cities as far as Baal. These *were* their settlements, and they have their genealogy.

34   And Meshobab and Jamlech and Joshah the son of Amaziah,

35   and Joel and Jehu the son of Joshibiah, the son of Seraiah, the son of Asiel,

---

4:9 *Jabez . . . pain.* If "pain" was the basis for naming the child, then his name should have been *Jazeb;* so it is possible the last two consonants have been interchanged.

4:23 *potters.* Stamped jar handles found in excavations by archaeologists have verified that there were royal potters who worked for the king.

36   and Elioenai, Jaakobah, Jeshohaiah, Asaiah, Adiel, Jesimiel, Benaiah,

37   Ziza the son of Shiphi, the son of Allon, the son of Jedaiah, the son of Shimri, the son of Shemaiah;

38   these mentioned by name *were* leaders in their families; and their fathers' houses increased greatly.

39   And they went to the entrance of Gedor, even to the east side of the valley, to seek pasture for their flocks.

40   And they found rich and good pasture, and the land was broad and quiet and peaceful; for those who lived there formerly *were* Hamites.

41   And these, recorded by name, came in the days of Hezekiah king of Judah, and attacked their tents, and the Meunites who were found there, and destroyed them utterly to this day, and lived in their place; because there was pasture there for their flocks.

42   And from them, from the sons of Simeon, five hundred men went to Mount Seir, with Pelatiah, Neariah, Rephaiah, and Uzziel, the sons of Ishi, as their leaders.

43   And they destroyed the remnant of the Amalekites who escaped, and have lived there to this day.

F. The family of Reuben

5   Now the sons of Reuben the first-born of Israel (for he was the first-born, but because he defiled his father's bed, his birthright was given to the sons of Joseph the son of Israel; so that he is not enrolled in the genealogy according to the birthright.

2   Though Judah prevailed over his brothers, and from him *came* the leader, yet the birthright belonged to Joseph),

3   the sons of Reuben the first-born of Israel *were* Hanoch and Pallu, Hezron and Carmi.

4   The sons of Joel *were* Shemaiah his son, Gog his son, Shimei his son,

5   Micah his son, Reaiah his son, Baal his son,

6   Beerah his son, whom Tilgath-pilneser king of Assyria carried away into exile; he was leader of the Reubenites.

7   And his kinsmen by their families, in the genealogy of their generations, *were* Jeiel the chief, then Zechariah

8   and Bela the son of Azaz, the son of Shema, the son of Joel, who lived in Aroer, even to Nebo and Baal-meon.

9   And to the east he settled as far as the entrance of the wilderness from the river Euphrates, because their cattle had increased in the land of Gilead.

10   And in the days of Saul they made war with the Hagrites, who fell by their hand, so that they occupied their tents throughout all the land east of Gilead.

G. The family of Gad

11   Now the sons of Gad lived opposite them in the land of Bashan as far as Salecah.

12   Joel *was* the chief, and Shapham the second, then Janai and Shaphat in Bashan.

13   And their kinsmen of their fathers' households *were* Michael, Meshullam, Sheba, Jorai, Jacan, Zia, and Eber, seven.

14   These *were* the sons of Abihail, the son of Huri, the son of Jaroah, the son of Gilead, the son of Michael, the son of Jeshishai, the son of Jahdo, the son of Buz;

15   Ahi the son of Abdiel, the son of Guni, *was* head of their fathers' households.

16   And they lived in Gilead, in Bashan and in its towns, and in all the pasture lands of Sharon, as far as their borders.

17   All of these were enrolled in the genealogies in the days of Jotham king of Judah and in the days of Jeroboam king of Israel.

18   The sons of Reuben and the Gadites and the half-tribe of Manasseh, *consisting* of valiant men, men who bore shield and sword and shot with bow, and *were* skillful in battle, *were* 44,760, who went to war.

4:40 *were* Hamites, that is, Canaanites, who were listed under Ham (Gen. 10:6).
5:1,2 While the birthright was passed on to Ephraim and

Manasseh, leadership was placed in the hands of Judah, the most powerful tribe.

Marginal references:

*4:40 Judg 18:7-10
4:41 2 Kin 18:8
4:43 1 Sam 15:8; 30:17; 2 Sam 8:12
*5:1f Gen 29:32; 35:22; 49:4; 48:15,22
5:2 Gen 49:8,10; Mic 5:2; Matt 2:6
5:3 Gen 46:9; Num 26:5
5:7 v. 17
5:8 Josh 13:15,16
5:9 Josh 22:9
5:10 vv. 18-21
5:11 Josh 13:11,24
5:16 1 Chr 27:29
5:17 2 Kin 15:5, 32; 14:16,23

5:19
v. 10;
1 Chr 1:31
5:20
2 Chr 4:11-13;
Ps 22:4,5

5:22
2 Kin 15:29;
17:6

5:25
2 Kin 17:7

*5:26
2 Kin 15:19,
29; 17:6;
18:11

6:1
Ex 6:16;
Num 26:57;
1 Chr 23:6
6:3
Lev 10:1

6:8
2 Sam 8:17;
15:27

6:14
Neh 11:11

6:15
2 Kin 25:18

6:16
Ex 6:16

6:20
v. 42

19 And they made war against the Hagrites, Jetur, Naphish, and Nodab.
20 And they were helped against them, and the Hagrites and all who *were* with them were given into their hand; for they cried out to God in the battle, and He was entreated for them, because they trusted in Him.
21 And they took away their cattle: their 50,000 camels, 250,000 sheep, 2,000 donkeys, and 100,000 men.
22 For many fell slain, because the war *was* of God. And they settled in their place until the exile.

H. *The half-tribe of Manasseh*

23 Now the sons of the half-tribe of Manasseh lived in the land; from Bashan to Baal-hermon and Senir and Mount Hermon they were numerous.
24 And these were the heads of their fathers' households, even Epher, Ishi, Eliel, Azriel, Jeremiah, Hodaviah, and Jahdiel, mighty men of valor, famous men, heads of their fathers' households.
25 But they acted treacherously against the God of their fathers, and played the harlot after the gods of the peoples of the land, whom God had destroyed before them.
26 So the God of Israel stirred up the spirit of Pul, king of Assyria, even the spirit of Tilgath-pilneser king of Assyria, and he carried them away into exile, namely the Reubenites, the Gadites, and the half-tribe of Manasseh, and brought them to Halah, Habor, Hara, and to the river of Gozan, to this day.

I. *The family of Levi*

 6 The sons of Levi *were* Gershon, Kohath and Merari.
2 And the sons of Kohath *were* Amram, Izhar, Hebron, and Uzziel.
3 And the children of Amram *were* Aaron, Moses, and Miriam. And the sons of Aaron *were* Nadab, Abihu, Eleazar, and Ithamar.
4 Eleazar became the father of Phinehas, *and* Phinehas became the father of Abishua,
5 and Abishua became the father of Bukki, and Bukki became the father of Uzzi,
6 and Uzzi became the father of Zerahiah, and Zerahiah became the father of Meraioth,
7 Meraioth became the father of Amariah, and Amariah became the father of Ahitub,
8 and Ahitub became the father of Zadok, and Zadok became the father of Ahimaaz,
9 and Ahimaaz became the father of Azariah, and Azariah became the father of Johanan,
10 and Johanan became the father of Azariah (it was he who served as the priest in the house which Solomon built in Jerusalem),
11 and Azariah became the father of Amariah, and Amariah became the father of Ahitub,
12 and Ahitub became the father of Zadok, and Zadok became the father of Shallum,
13 and Shallum became the father of Hilkiah, and Hilkiah became the father of Azariah,
14 and Azariah became the father of Seraiah, and Seraiah became the father of Jehozadak;
15 and Jehozadak went *along* when the LORD carried Judah and Jerusalem away into exile by Nebuchadnezzar.
16 The sons of Levi *were* Gershom, Kohath, and Merari.
17 And these are the names of the sons of Gershom: Libni and Shimei.
18 And the sons of Kohath *were* Amram, Izhar, Hebron, and Uzziel.
19 The sons of Merari *were* Mahli and Mushi. And these are the families of the Levites according to their fathers' *households.*
20 Of Gershom: Libni his son, Jahath his son, Zimmah his son,
21 Joah his son, Iddo his son, Zerah his son, Jeatherai his son.

5:23 *Mount Hermon* is probably a scribal explanation of Senir, which was the Amorite name for Mt. Hermon (Deut. 3:9).

5:26 *Pul* and *Tilgath-pilneser* (Tiglath-pileser) were different names for the same Assyrian king. See note to 2 Kin. 15:19.

22   The sons of Kohath *were* Amminadab his son, Korah his son, Assir his son,
23   Elkanah his son, Ebiasaph his son, and Assir his son,
24   Tahath his son, Uriel his son, Uzziah his son, and Shaul his son.
25   And the sons of Elkanah *were* Amasai and Ahimoth.
26   *As for* Elkanah, the sons of Elkanah *were* Zophai his son and Nahath his son,
27   Eliab his son, Jeroham his son, Elkanah his son.
28   And the sons of Samuel *were* Joel, the first-born and Abijah, the second.
29   The sons of Merari *were* Mahli, Libni his son, Shimei his son, Uzzah his son,
30   Shimea his son, Haggiah his son, Asaiah his son.
31   Now these are those whom David appointed over the service of song in the house of the Lord, after the ark rested *there*.
32   And they ministered with song before the tabernacle of the tent of meeting, until Solomon had built the house of the Lord in Jerusalem; and they served in their office according to their order.
33   And these are those who served with their sons. From the sons of the Kohathites *were* Heman the singer, the son of Joel, the son of Samuel,
34   the son of Elkanah, the son of Jeroham, the son of Eliel, the son of Toah,
35   the son of Zuph, the son of Elkanah, the son of Mahath, the son of Amasai,
36   the son of Elkanah, the son of Joel, the son of Azariah, the son of Zephaniah,
37   the son of Tahath, the son of Assir, the son of Ebiasaph, the son of Korah,
38   the son of Izhar, the son of Kohath, the son of Levi, the son of Israel.
39   And *Heman's* brother Asaph stood at his right hand, even Asaph the son of Berechiah, the son of Shimea,
40   the son of Michael, the son of Baaseiah, the son of Malchijah,
41   the son of Ethni, the son of Zerah, the son of Adaiah,
42   the son of Ethan, the son of Zimmah, the son of Shimei,
43   the son of Jahath, the son of Gershom, the son of Levi.
44   And on the left hand *were* their kinsmen the sons of Merari: Ethan the son of Kishi, the son of Abdi, the son of Malluch,
45   the son of Hashabiah, the son of Amaziah, the son of Hilkiah,
46   the son of Amzi, the son of Bani, the son of Shemer,
47   the son of Mahli, the son of Mushi, the son of Merari, the son of Levi.
48   And their kinsmen the Levites were appointed for all the service of the tabernacle of the house of God.
49   But Aaron and his sons offered on the altar of burnt offering and on the altar of incense, for all the work of the most holy place, and to make atonement for Israel, according to all that Moses the servant of God had commanded.
50   And these are the sons of Aaron: Eleazar his son, Phinehas his son, Abishua his son,
51   Bukki his son, Uzzi his son, Zerahiah his son,
52   Meraioth his son, Amariah his son, Ahitub his son,
53   Zadok his son, Ahimaaz his son.
54   Now these are their settlements according to their camps within their borders. To the sons of Aaron of the families of the Kohathites (for theirs was the *first* lot),
55   to them they gave Hebron in the land of Judah, and its pasture lands around it;
56   but the fields of the city and its villages, they gave to Caleb the son of Jephunneh.
57   And to the sons of Aaron they gave the *following* cities of refuge: Hebron, Libnah also with its pasture lands, Jattir, Eshtemoa with its pasture lands,
58   Hilen with its pasture lands, Debir with its pasture lands,
59   Ashan with its pasture lands, and Beth-shemesh with its pasture lands;
60   and from the tribe of Benjamin: Geba with its pasture lands, Allemeth with its pasture lands, and Anathoth with its pasture lands. All their cities throughout their families were thirteen cities.
61   Then to the rest of the sons of Kohath *were given* by lot, from the family of the tribe, from the half-tribe, the half of Manasseh, ten cities.

6:25
vv. 35,36
6:26
v. 34

*6:31
1 Chr 15:16-16:6

6:37
Ex 6:24

6:41
v. 21

*6:49
Ex 27:1-8;
30:1-7,10

6:50
vv. 4-8

6:54
Josh 21:4,10

6:55
Josh 21:11,12

6:56
Josh 14:13;
15:13
*6:57
Josh 21:13

6:61
vv. 66-70;
Josh 21:5

6:31 In the realm of song and temple ritual David has an authority equal to that of Moses in the realm of law. The names of some of the singers and musicians are Canaanite in form, causing some to suggest that outwardly the temple ritual, as well as the architecture, was of Canaanite origin.
6:49 They were entirely within their rights.

6:57 *cities of refuge.* Of the cities listed, only Hebron was a city of refuge. Two letters of the Hebrew text have been interchanged and need to be inverted. Then the passage would read, as in Josh. 21:13, *city of refuge*, which explains the apparent discrepancy.

6:63
Josh 21:7,34

6:64
Josh 21:3,41,
42
6:65
vv. 57-60

6:66
v. 61

6:67
Josh 21:21

6:68
see
Josh 21:22-35
where some
names are
differently
given

6:73
see
Josh 21:29;
19:21

6:76
v. 62

6:77
v. 63

62   And to the sons of Gershom, according to their families, *were given* from the tribe of Issachar and from the tribe of Asher, the tribe of Naphtali, and the tribe of Manasseh, thirteen cities in Bashan.

63   To the sons of Merari *were given* by lot, according to their families, from the tribe of Reuben, the tribe of Gad, and the tribe of Zebulun, twelve cities.

64   So the sons of Israel gave to the Levites the cities with their pasture lands.

65   And they gave by lot from the tribe of the sons of Judah, the tribe of the sons of Simeon, and the tribe of the sons of Benjamin, these cities which are mentioned by name.

66   Now some of the families of the sons of Kohath had cities of their territory from the tribe of Ephraim.

67   And they gave to them the *following* cities of refuge: Shechem in the hill country of Ephraim with its pasture lands, Gezer also with its pasture lands,

68   Jokmeam with its pasture lands, Beth-horon with its pasture lands,

69   Aijalon with its pasture lands, and Gath-rimmon with its pasture lands;

70   and from the half-tribe of Manasseh: Aner with its pasture lands and Bileam with its pasture lands, for the rest of the family of the sons of Kohath.

71   To the sons of Gershom *were given*, from the family of the half-tribe of Manasseh: Golan in Bashan with its pasture lands and Ashtaroth with its pasture lands;

72   and from the tribe of Issachar: Kedesh with its pasture lands, Daberath with its pasture lands,

73   and Ramoth with its pasture lands, Anem with its pasture lands;

74   and from the tribe of Asher: Mashal with its pasture lands, Abdon with its pasture lands,

75   Hukok with its pasture lands, and Rehob with its pasture lands;

76   and from the tribe of Naphtali: Kedesh in Galilee with its pasture lands, Hammon with its pasture lands, and Kiriathaim with its pasture lands.

77   To the rest of *the Levites*, the sons of Merari, *were given*, from the tribe of Zebulun: Rimmono with its pasture lands, Tabor with its pasture lands;

78   and beyond the Jordan at Jericho, on the east side of the Jordan, *were given them*, from the tribe of Reuben: Bezer in the wilderness with its pasture lands, Jahzah with its pasture lands,

79   Kedemoth with its pasture lands, and Mephaath with its pasture lands;

80   and from the tribe of Gad: Ramoth in Gilead with its pasture lands, Mahanaim with its pasture lands,

81   Heshbon with its pasture lands, and Jazer with its pasture lands.

J. The family of Issachar

7:1
Gen 46:13;
Num 26:23
7:2
2 Sam 24:1,2

7 Now the sons of Issachar *were* four: Tola, Puah, Jashub, and Shimron.

2   And the sons of Tola *were* Uzzi, Rephaiah, Jeriel, Jahmai, Ibsam, and Samuel, heads of their fathers' households. *The sons* of Tola *were* mighty men of valor in their generations; their number in the days of David was 22,600.

3   And the son of Uzzi *was* Izrahiah. And the sons of Izrahiah *were* Michael, Obadiah, Joel, Isshiah; all five of them *were* chief men.

4   And with them by their generations according to their fathers' households were 36,000 troops of the army for war, for they had many wives and sons.

7:5
1 Chr 6:62,72

5   And their relatives among all the families of Issachar *were* mighty men of valor, enrolled by genealogy, in all 87,000.

K. The family of Benjamin

*7:6
Gen 46:21;
Num 26:38;
1 Chr 8:1-40

6   *The sons of* Benjamin *were* three: Bela and Becher and Jediael.

7   And the sons of Bela were five: Ezbon, Uzzi, Uzziel, Jerimoth, and Iri. They *were* heads of fathers' households, mighty men of valor, and were 22,034 enrolled by genealogy.

8   And the sons of Becher *were* Zemirah, Joash, Eliezer, Elioenai, Omri, Jeremoth, Abijah, Anathoth, and Alemeth. All these *were* the sons of Becher.

9   And they were enrolled by genealogy, according to their generations, heads of their fathers' households, 20,200 mighty men of valor.

7:6 *sons of Benjamin*. It is most likely that Benjamin was a very early scribal mistake for Zebulun. In Hebrew the similarity of names is much closer. Further evidence for this conclusion is that the genealogy for Zebulun is missing, whereas the legitimate genealogy of Benjamin occurs in 8:1–40.

10   And the son of Jediael *was* Bilhan. And the sons of Bilhan *were* Jeush, Benjamin, Ehud, Chenaanah, Zethan, Tarshish, and Ahishahar.

11   All these *were* sons of Jediael, according to the heads of their fathers' households, 17,200 mighty men of valor, who were ready to go out with the army to war.

12   And Shuppim and Huppim *were* the sons of Ir; Hushim *was* the son of Aher.

L. *The family of Naphtali*

13   The sons of Naphtali *were* Jahziel, Guni, Jezer, and Shallum, the sons of Bilhah.

14   The sons of Manasseh *were* Asriel, whom his Aramean concubine bore; she bore Machir the father of Gilead.

15   And Machir took a wife for Huppim and Shuppim, whose sister's name was Maacah. And the name of the second was Zelophehad, and Zelophehad had daughters.

16   And Maacah the wife of Machir bore a son, and she named him Peresh; and the name of his brother *was* Sheresh, and his sons *were* Ulam and Rakem.

17   And the son of Ulam *was* Bedan. These *were* the sons of Gilead the son of Machir, the son of Manasseh.

18   And his sister Hammolecheth bore Ishhod and Abiezer and Mahlah.

19   And the sons of Shemida were Ahian and Shechem and Likhi and Aniam.

M. *The family of Ephraim*

20   And the sons of Ephraim *were* Shuthelah and Bered his son, Tahath his son, Eleadah his son, Tahath his son,

21   Zabad his son, Shuthelah his son, and Ezer and Elead whom the men of Gath who were born in the land killed, because they came down to take their livestock.

22   And their father Ephraim mourned many days, and his relatives came to comfort him.

23   Then he went in to his wife, and she conceived and bore a son, and he named him Beriah, because misfortune had come upon his house.

24   And his daughter was Sheerah, who built lower and upper Beth-horon, also Uzzen-sheerah.

25   And Rephah was his son *along* with Resheph, Telah his son, Tahan his son,

26   Ladan his son, Ammihud his son, Elishama his son,

27   Non his son, and Joshua his son.

28   And their possessions and settlements *were* Bethel with its towns, and to the east Naaran, and to the west Gezer with its towns, and Shechem with its towns as far as Ayyah with its towns,

29   and along the borders of the sons of Manasseh, Beth-shean with its towns, Taanach with its towns, Megiddo with its towns, Dor with its towns. In these lived the sons of Joseph the son of Israel.

N. *The family of Asher*

30   The sons of Asher *were* Imnah, Ishvah, Ishvi and Beriah, and Serah their sister.

31   And the sons of Beriah *were* Heber and Malchiel, who was the father of Birzaith.

32   And Heber became the father of Japhlet, Shomer and Hotham, and Shua their sister.

33   And the sons of Japhlet *were* Pasach, Bimhal, and Ashvath. These were the sons of Japhlet.

34   And the sons of Shemer *were* Ahi and Rohgah, Jehubbah and Aram.

35   And the sons of his brother Helem *were* Zophah, Imna, Shelesh, and Amal.

36   The sons of Zophah *were* Suah, Harnepher, Shual, Beri, and Imrah,

37   Bezer, Hod, Shamma, Shilshah, Ithran, and Beera.

38   And the sons of Jether *were* Jephunneh, Pispa, and Ara.

39   And the sons of Ulla *were* Arah, Hanniel, and Rizia.

---

*7:12
Num 26:39

7:13
Gen 46:24

7:17
1 Sam 12:11

7:20
Num 26:35

7:24
Josh 16:3,5

7:27
Ex 17:9-14;
24:13
7:28
Josh 16:7

7:30
Gen 46:17;
Num 26:44

7:12 *the sons of Ir; Hushim was the son of Aher.* Inasmuch as the genealogy of Dan is completely missing, some scholars think the Hebrew text originally read: "the sons of Dan, Hushim his one son." This is in accord with Gen. 46:23 (*the sons of Dan: Hushim*). Both Chronicles have a number of textual problems.

40   All these *were* the sons of Asher, heads of the fathers' houses, choice and mighty men of valor, heads of the princes. And the number of them enrolled by genealogy for service in war was 26,000 men.

O. *The family of Benjamin*

8 And Benjamin became the father of Bela his first-born, Ashbel the second, Aharah the third,

2   Nohah the fourth, and Rapha the fifth.

3   And Bela had sons: Addar, Gera, Abihud,

4   Abishua, Naaman, Ahoah,

5   Gera, Shephuphan, and Huram.

6   And these are the sons of Ehud: these are the heads of fathers' *households* of the inhabitants of Geba, and they carried them into exile to Manahath,

7   namely, Naaman, Ahijah, and Gera—he carried them into exile; and he became the father of Uzza and Ahihud.

8   And Shaharaim became the father of children in the country of Moab, after he had sent away Hushim and Baara his wives.

9   And by Hodesh his wife he became the father of Jobab, Zibia, Mesha, Malcam,

10   Jeuz, Sachia, Mirmah. These were his sons, heads of fathers' *households*.

11   And by Hushim he became the father of Abitub and Elpaal.

12   And the sons of Elpaal *were* Eber, Misham, and Shemed, who built Ono and Lod, with its towns;

13   and Beriah and Shema, who were heads of fathers' *households* of the inhabitants of Aijalon, who put to flight the inhabitants of Gath;

14   and Ahio, Shashak, and Jeremoth,

15   And Zebadiah, Arad, Eder,

16   Michael, Ishpah, and Joha *were* the sons of Beriah.

17   And Zebadiah, Meshullam, Hizki, Heber,

18   Ishmerai, Izliah, and Jobab *were* the sons of Elpaal.

19   And Jakim, Zichri, Zabdi,

20   Elienai, Zillethai, Eliel,

21   Adaiah, Beraiah, and Shimrath *were* the sons of Shimei.

22   And Ishpan, Eber, Eliel,

23   Abdon, Zichri, Hanan,

24   Hananiah, Elam, Anthothijah,

25   Iphdeiah, and Penuel *were* the sons of Shashak.

26   And Shamsherai, Shehariah, Athaliah,

27   Jaareshiah, Elijah, and Zichri *were* the sons of Jeroham.

28   These were heads of the fathers' *households* according to their generations, chief men, who lived in Jerusalem.

29   Now in Gibeon, *Jeiel*, the father of Gibeon lived, and his wife's name was Maacah;

30   and his first-born son *was* Abdon, then Zur, Kish, Baal, Nadab,

31   Gedor, Ahio, and Zecher.

32   And Mikloth became the father of Shimeah. And they also lived with their relatives in Jerusalem opposite their *other* relatives.

33   And Ner became the father of Kish, and Kish became the father of Saul, and Saul became the father of Jonathan, Malchi-shua, Abinadab, and Eshbaal.

34   And the son of Jonathan *was* Merib-baal, and Merib-baal became the father of Micah.

35   And the sons of Micah *were* Pithon, Melech, Tarea, and Ahaz.

36   And Ahaz became the father of Jehoaddah, and Jehoaddah became the father of Alemeth, Azmaveth, and Zimri; and Zimri became the father of Moza.

37   And Moza became the father of Binea; Raphah *was* his son, Eleasah his son, Azel his son.

38   And Azel had six sons, and these *were* their names: Azrikam, Bocheru, Ishmael, Sheariah, Obadiah and Hanan. All these *were* the sons of Azel.

39   And the sons of Eshek his brother *were* Ulam his first-born, Jeush the second, and Eliphelet the third.

Marginal references

7:40
v. 30

8:1
Gen 46:21;
1 Chr 7:6

8:6
1 Chr 2:52

8:13
v. 21

8:21
v. 13

8:29
1 Chr 9:35

*8:33
1 Chr 9:35-38

*8:34
2 Sam 9:12

8:33 *Eshbaal*, see note to 2 Sam. 2:8.   8:34 *Merib-baal*, see note to 2 Sam. 4:4.

40 And the sons of Ulam were mighty men of valor, archers, and had many sons and grandsons, 150 *of them*. All these *were* of the sons of Benjamin.

P. *The families in Jerusalem*

9 So all Israel was enrolled by genealogies; and behold, they are written in the Book of the Kings of Israel. And Judah was carried away into exile to Babylon for their unfaithfulness.

2 Now the first who lived in their possessions in their cities *were* Israel, the priests, the Levites and the temple servants.

3 And some of the sons of Judah, of the sons of Benjamin, and of the sons of Ephraim and Manasseh lived in Jerusalem:

4 Uthai the son of Ammihud, the son of Omri, the son of Imri, the son of Bani, from the sons of Perez the son of Judah.

5 And from the Shilonites *were* Asaiah the first-born and his sons.

6 And from the sons of Zerah *were* Jeuel and their relatives, 690 *of them*.

7 And from the sons of Benjamin *were* Sallu the son of Meshullam, the son of Hodaviah, the son of Hassenuah,

8 and Ibneiah the son of Jeroham, and Elah the son of Uzzi, the son of Michri, and Meshullam the son of Shephatiah, the son of Reuel, the son of Ibnijah;

9 and their relatives according to their generations, 956 All these *were* heads of fathers' *households* according to their fathers' houses.

10 And from the priests *were* Jedaiah, Jehoiarib, Jachin,

11 and Azariah the son of Hilkiah, the son of Meshullam, the son of Zadok, the son of Meraioth, the son of Ahitub, the chief officer of the house of God;

12 and Adaiah the son of Jeroham, the son of Pashhur, the son of Malchijah, and Maasai the son of Adiel, the son of Jahzerah, the son of Meshullam, the son of Meshillemith, the son of Immer;

13 and their relatives, heads of their fathers' households, 1,760 very able men for the work of the service of the house of God.

14 And of the Levites *were* Shemaiah the son of Hasshub, the son of Azrikam, the son of Hashabiah, of the sons of Merari;

15 and Bakbakkar, Heresh and Galal and Mattaniah the son of Mica, the son of Zichri, the son of Asaph,

16 and Obadiah the son of Shemaiah, the son of Galal, the son of Jeduthun, and Berechiah the son of Asa, the son of Elkanah, who lived in the villages of the Netophathites.

17 Now the gatekeepers *were* Shallum and Akkub and Talmon and Ahiman and their relatives (Shallum the chief

18 *being stationed* until now at the king's gate to the east). These the gatekeepers for the camp of the sons of Levi.

19 And Shallum the son of Kore, the son of Ebiasaph, the son of Korah, his relatives, of his father's house, the Korahites, *were* over the work of the service, keepers of the thresholds of the tent; and their fathers had been over the camp of the LORD, keepers of the entrance.

20 And Phinehas the son of Eleazar was ruler over them previously, *an*d the LORD was with him.

21 Zechariah the son of Meshelemiah was gatekeeper of the entrance of the tent of meeting.

22 All these who were chosen to be gatekeepers in the thresholds were 2 These were enrolled by genealogy in their villages, whom David and Samuel the seer appointed in their office of trust.

23 So they and their sons had charge of the gates of the house of the LORD, even the house of the tent, as guards.

24 The gatekeepers were on the four sides, to the east, west, north, and south.

25 And their relatives in their villages *were* to come in every seven days from time to time *to be* with them;

26 for the four chief gatekeepers who *were* Levites, were in an office of trust, and were over the chambers and over the treasuries in the house of God.

27 And they spent the night around the house of God, because the watch was committed to them; and they *were* in charge of opening *it* morning by morning.

28 Now some of them had charge of the utensils of service, for they counted them when they brought them in and when they took them out.

29 Some of them also were appointed over the furniture and over all the utensils

9:1
1 Chr 5:25,26

9:2
Neh 11:3-22;
Ezra 2:43;
8:20
9:3
Neh 11:1

9:10
Neh 11:10-14

9:14
Neh 11:15-19

9:18
Ezek 46:1,2

9:20
Num 25:7-13
9:21
1 Chr 26:2,14
9:22
Chr 26:1,2;
Chr 31:15;

21:5,7;
1:8

9:27
1 Chr 0-32

9:29
1 Chr 23:2

of the sanctuary and over the fine flour and the wine and the oil and the frankincense and the spices.

9:30
Ex 30:23-25

30   And some of the sons of the priests prepared the mixing of the spices.

31   And Mattithiah, one of the Levites, who was the first-born of Shallum the Korahite, had the responsibility over the things which were baked in pans.

9:32
Lev 24:8

32   And some of their relatives of the sons of the Kohathites *were* over the showbread to prepare it every sabbath.

9:33
1 Chr 6:31;
25:1;
Ps 134:1

33   Now these are the singers, heads of fathers' *households* of the Levites, *who lived in the chambers of the temple* free *from other service;* for they were engaged in their work day and night.

34   These were heads of fathers' *households* of the Levites according to their generations, chief men, who lived in Jerusalem.

Q. The family of Saul

9:35
1 Chr 8:29

35   And in Gibeon Jeiel the father of Gibeon lived, and his wife's name was Maacah,

36   and his first-born son *was* Abdon, then Zur, Kish, Baal, Ner, Nadab,

37   Gedor, Ahio, Zechariah, and Mikloth.

38   And Mikloth became the father of Shimeam. And they also lived with their relatives in Jerusalem opposite their *other* relatives.

*9:39
1 Chr 8:33

39   And Ner became the father of Kish, and Kish became the father of Saul, and Saul became the father of Jonathan, Malchi-shua, Abinadab, and Eshbaal.

40   And the son of Jonathan *was* Merib-baal; and Merib-baal became the father of Micah.

9:41
1 Chr 8:35

41   And the sons of Micah *were* Pithon, Melech, Tahrea, *and Ahaz.*

42   And Ahaz became the father of Jarah, and Jarah became the father of Alemeth, Azmaveth, and Zimri; and Zimri became the father of Moza,

43   and Moza became the father of Binea and Rephaiah his son, Eleasah his son, Azel his son.

44   And Azel had six sons whose names are these: Azrikam, Bocheru and Ishmael and Sheariah and Obadiah and Hanan. These were the sons of Azel.

II. The reign of King David (10:1—29:30)

A. Saul's closing days and death

10:1
1 Sam 31:1,2

Now the Philistines fought against Israel; and the men of Israel fled before the Philistines, and fell slain on Mount Gilboa.

2   And the Philistines closely pursued Saul and his sons, and the Philistines struck down Jonathan, Abinadab and Malchi-shua, the sons of Saul.

3   And the battle became heavy against Saul, and the archers overtook him; and he was wounded by the archers.

4   Then Saul said to his armor bearer, "Draw your sword and thrust me through with it, lest these uncircumcised come and abuse me." But his armor

10:4
cf.
1 Sam 31:4

bearer would not, for he was greatly afraid. Therefore Saul took his sword and fell on it.

5   And when his armor bearer saw that Saul was dead, he likewise fell on his sword and died.

6   Thus Saul died with his three sons, and all *those* of his house died together.

7   When all the men of Israel who were in the valley saw that they had fled, and that Saul and his sons were dead, they forsook their cities and fled; and the Philistines came and lived in them.

8   And it came about the next day, when the Philistines came to strip the slain, that they found Saul and his sons fallen on Mount Gilboa.

9   So they stripped him and took his head and his armor and sent *messengers* around the land of the Philistines, to carry the good news to their idols and to the people.

10:10
1 Sam 31:10

10   And they put his armor in the house of their gods and fastened his head in the house of Dagon.

11   When all Jabesh-gilead heard all that the Philistines had done to Saul,

---

9   Ner's relationship to Saul is not always made clear.

:10   In 1 Sam.:10 we read that Saul's body was fastened to the wall Bethshan and his armor was placed in the temple of Ashtaroth. Here Saul's head was put in the temple of Dagon. All this is quite possible. Excavations at Bethshan have revealed four Canaanite temples.

12   all the valiant men arose and took away the body of Saul and the bodies of his sons, and brought them to Jabesh and buried their bones under the oak in Jabesh, and fasted seven days.

13   So Saul died for his trespass which he committed against the LORD, because of the word of the LORD which he did not keep; and also because he asked counsel of a medium, making inquiry *of it*,

14   and did not inquire of the LORD. Therefore He killed him, and turned the kingdom to David the son of Jesse.

B. *David made king of all Israel*

1. *The capture of Jerusalem*

11 Then all Israel gathered to David at Hebron and said, "Behold, we are your bone and your flesh.

2   "In times past, even when Saul was king, you *were* the one who led out and brought in Israel; and the LORD your God said to you, 'You shall shepherd My people Israel, and you shall be prince over My people Israel.' "

3   So all the elders of Israel came to the king at Hebron, and David made a covenant with them in Hebron before the LORD; and they anointed David king over Israel, according to the word of the LORD through Samuel.

4   Then David and all Israel went to Jerusalem (that is, Jebus); and the Jebusites, the inhabitants of the land, *were* there.

5   And the inhabitants of Jebus said to David, "You shall not enter here." Nevertheless David captured the stronghold of Zion (that is, the city of David).

6   Now David had said, "Whoever strikes down a Jebusite first shall be chief and commander." And Joab the son of Zeruiah went up first, so he became chief.

7   Then David dwelt in the stronghold; therefore it was called the city of David.

8   And he built the city all around, from the ²Millo even to the surrounding area; and Joab repaired the rest of the city.

9   And David became greater and greater, for the LORD of hosts *was* with him.

2. *David's mighty heroes*

10   Now these are the heads of the mighty men whom David had, who gave him strong support in his kingdom, together with all Israel, to make him king, according to the word of the LORD concerning Israel.

11   And these *constitute* the list of the mighty men whom David had: Jashobeam, the son of a Hachmonite, the chief of the thirty; he lifted up his spear against three hundred whom he killed at one time.

12   And after him was Eleazar the son of Dodo, the Ahohite, who *was* one of the three mighty men.

13   He was with David at Pasdammim when the Philistines were gathered together there to battle, and there was a plot of ground full of barley; and the people fled before the Philistines.

14   And they took their stand in the midst of the plot, and defended it, and struck down the Philistines; and the LORD saved them by a great victory.

15   Now three of the thirty chief men went down to the rock to David, into the cave of Adullam, while the army of the Philistines was camping in the valley of Rephaim.

16   And David was then in the stronghold, while the garrison of the Philistines *was* then in Bethlehem.

17   And David had a craving and said, "Oh that someone would give me water to drink from the well of Bethlehem, which is by the gate!"

18   So the three broke through the camp of the Philistines, and drew water from the well of Bethlehem which *was* by the gate, and took *it* and brought *it* to David; nevertheless David would not drink it, but poured it out to the LORD;

19   and he said, "Be it far from me before my God that I should do this. Shall I drink the blood of these men *who went* at the risk of their lives? For at the risk of their lives they brought it." Therefore he would not drink it. These things the three mighty men did.

20   As for Abshai the brother of Joab, he was chief of the thirty, and he swung

²I.e., citadel

Cross references

10:13 — 1 Sam 13:13; 15:23; 28:7

10:14 — 1 Sam 15:28; 1 Chr 12:23

11:1 — 2 Sam 5:1

11:2 — 2 Sam 5:2; Ps 78:71

11:3 — 2 Sam 5:3; 1 Sam 16:1, 12,13

11:4 — Judg 1:21; 19:10

11:6 — 2 Sam 8:16

11:9 — 2 Sam 3:1

11:10 — 2 Sam 23:8-39; v. 3

11:11 — 2 Sam 23:8

11:13 — 2 Sam 23:11, 12

11:15 — 2 Sam 23:13; 1 Chr 14:9

11:20 — 2 Sam 23:18

his spear against three hundred and killed them; and he had a name as well as the thirty.

11:21
2 Sam 23:19
21   Of the three in the second *rank* he was the most honored, and became their commander; however, he did not attain to the *first* three.

11:22
2 Sam 23:20
22   Benaiah the son of Jehoiada, the son of a valiant man of Kabzeel, mighty in deeds, struck down the two *sons of* Ariel of Moab. He also went down and killed a lion inside a pit on a snowy day.

11:23
1 Sam 17:7
23   And he killed an Egyptian, a man of *great* stature five cubits tall. Now in the Egyptian's hand *was* a spear like a weaver's beam, but he went down to him with a club and snatched the spear from the Egyptian's hand, and killed him with his own spear.

24   These *things* Benaiah the son of Jehoiada did, and had a name as well as the three mighty men.

25   Behold, he was honored among the thirty, but he did not attain to the three; and David appointed him over his guard.

11:26
2 Sam 23:24
26   Now the mighty men of the armies *were* Asahel the brother of Joab, Elhanan the son of Dodo of Bethlehem,

27   Shammoth the Harorite, Helez the Pelonite,

28   Ira the son of Ikkesh the Tekoite, Abiezer the Anathothite,

29   Sibbecai the Hushathite, Ilai the Ahohite,

30   Maharai the Netophathite, Heled the son of Baanah the Netophathite,

31   Ithai the son of Ribai of Gibeah of the sons of Benjamin, Benaiah the Pirathonite,

32   Hurai of the brooks of Gaash, Abiel the Arbathite,

33   Azmaveth the Baharumite, Eliahba the Shaalbonite,

34   the sons of Hashem the Gizonite, Jonathan the son of Shagee the Hararite,

35   Ahiam the son of Sacar the Hararite, Eliphal the son of Ur,

36   Hepher the Mecherathite, Ahijah the Pelonite,

37   Hezro the Carmelite, Naarai the son of Ezbai,

38   Joel the brother of Nathan, Mibhar the son of Hagri,

11:39
1 Chr 18:15
39   Zelek the Ammonite, Naharai the Berothite, the armor bearer of Joab the son of Zeruiah,

40   Ira the Ithrite, Gareb the Ithrite,

41   Uriah the Hittite, Zabad the son of Ahlai,

42   Adina the son of Shiza the Reubenite, a chief of the Reubenites, and thirty with him,

43   Hanan the son of Maacah and Joshaphat the Mithnite,

44   Uzzia the Ashterathite, Shama and Jeiel the sons of Hotham the Aroerite,

45   Jediael the son of Shimri and Joha his brother, the Tizite,

46   Eliel the Mahavite and Jeribai and Joshaviah, the sons of Elnaam, and Ithmah the Moabite,

47   Eliel and Obed and Jaasiel the Mezobaite.

3. *The names and numbers of David's supporters*

12:1
1 Sam 27:2-6
12 Now these are the ones who came to David at Ziklag, while he was still restricted because of Saul the son of Kish; and they were among the mighty men who helped *him* in war.

12:2
Judg 20:16
2   They were equipped with bows, using both the right hand and the left *to sling* stones and *to shoot* arrows from the bow; *they were* Saul's kinsmen from Benjamin.

3   The chief was Ahiezer, then Joash, the sons of Shemaah the Gibeathite; and Jeziel and Pelet, the sons of Azmaveth, and Beracah and Jehu the Anathothite,

4   and Ishmaiah the Gibeonite, a mighty man among the thirty, and over the thirty. Then Jeremiah, Jahaziel, Johanan, Jozabad the Gederathite,

5   Eluzai, Jerimoth, Bealiah, Shemariah, Shephatiah the Haruphite,

6   Elkanah, Isshiah, Azarel, Joezer, Jashobeam, the Korahites,

7   and Joelah and Zebadiah, the sons of Jeroham of Gedor.

12:8
2 Sam 2:18
8   And from the Gadites there came over to David in the stronghold in the wilderness, mighty men of valor, men trained for war, who could handle shield and spear, and whose faces were like the faces of lions, and *they were* as swift as the gazelles on the mountains.

9   Ezer *was* the first, Obadiah the second, Eliab the third,

10   Mishmannah the fourth, Jeremiah the fifth,

11   Attai the sixth, Eliel the seventh,
12   Johanan the eighth, Elzabad the ninth,
13   Jeremiah the tenth, Machbannai the eleventh.
14   These of the sons of Gad were captains of the army; he who was least was equal to a hundred and the greatest to a thousand.
15   These are the ones who crossed the Jordan in the first month when it was overflowing all its banks and they put to flight all those in the valleys, both to the east and to the west.

12:15
Josh 3:15

16   Then some of the sons of Benjamin and Judah came to the stronghold to David.
17   And David went out to meet them, and answered and said to them, "If you come peacefully to me to help me, my heart shall be united with you; but if to betray me to my adversaries, since there is no wrong in my hands, may the God of our fathers look on *it* and decide."
18   Then the Spirit came upon Amasai, who was the chief of the thirty, *and he said,*

12:18
Judg 6:34;
2 Sam 17:25

> "*We* are yours, O David,
> And with you, O son of Jesse!
> Peace, peace to you,
> And peace to him who helps you;
> Indeed, your God helps you!"

Then David received them and made them captains of the band.
19   From Manasseh also some defected to David, when he was about to go to battle with the Philistines against Saul. But they did not help them, for the lords of the Philistines after consultation sent him away, saying, "At *the cost of* our heads he may defect to his master Saul."

12:19
1 Sam 29:2,4

20   As he went to Ziklag, there defected to him from Manasseh: Adnah, Jozabad, Jediael, Michael, Jozabad, Elihu, and Zillethai, captains of thousands who belonged to Manasseh.
21   And they helped David against the band of raiders, for they were all mighty men of valor, and were captains in the army.

12:21
1 Sam 30:1,9,
10

22   For day by day *men* came to David to help him, until there was a great army like the army of God.
23   Now these are the numbers of the divisions equipped for war, who came to David at Hebron, to turn the kingdom of Saul to him, according to the word of the LORD.

12:23
2 Sam 2:3,4;
1 Chr 11:1;
10:14;
1 Sam 16:1,3

24   The sons of Judah who bore shield and spear *were* 6,800, equipped for war.
25   Of the sons of Simeon, mighty men of valor for war, 7,100.
26   Of the sons of Levi 4,600.
27   Now Jehoiada was the leader of *the house of* Aaron, and with him were 3,700,
28   also Zadok, a young man mighty of valor, and of his father's house twenty-two captains.

12:28
2 Sam 8:17

29   And of the sons of Benjamin, Saul's kinsmen, 3,000; for until now the greatest part of them had kept their allegiance to the house of Saul.

12:29
2 Sam 2:8,9

30   And of the sons of Ephraim 20,800, mighty men of valor, famous men in their fathers' households.
31   And of the half-tribe of Manasseh 18,000, who were designated by name to come and make David king.
32   And of the sons of Issachar, men who understood the times, with knowledge of what Israel should do, their chiefs were two hundred; and all their kinsmen were at their command.

12:32
Esth 1:13

33   Of Zebulun, there were 50,000 who went out in the army, who could draw up in battle formation with all kinds of weapons of war and helped *David* with an undivided heart.

12:33
Ps 12:2

34   And of Naphtali *there were* 1,000 captains, and with them 37,000 with shield and spear.
35   And of the Danites who could draw up in battle formation, *there were* 28,600.
36   And of Asher *there were* 40,000 who went out in the army to draw up in battle formation.
37   And from the other side of the Jordan, of the Reubenites and the Gadites and of the half-tribe of Manasseh, *there were* 120,000 with all *kinds* of weapons of war for the battle.

12:38
2 Sam 5:1-3

38 All these, being men of war, who could draw up in battle formation, came to Hebron with a perfect heart, to make David king over all Israel; and all the rest also of Israel were of one mind to make David king.

39 And they were there with David three days, eating and drinking; for their kinsmen had prepared for them.

12:40
1 Sam 25:18

40 Moreover those who were near to them, *even* as far as Issachar and Zebulun and Naphtali, brought food on donkeys, camels, mules, and on oxen, great quantities of flour cakes, fig cakes and bunches of raisins, wine, oil, oxen and sheep. There was joy indeed in Israel.

C. David and the ark of the covenant

1. The removal of the ark from Kiriath-jearim to Obed-edom

13 Then David consulted with the captains of the thousands and the hundreds, even with every leader.

13:2
1 Sam 31:1;
Is 37:4

2 And David said to all the assembly of Israel, "If it seems good to you, and if it is from the LORD our God, let us send everywhere to our kinsmen who remain in all the land of Israel, also to the priests and Levites who are with them in their cities with pasture lands, that they may meet with us;

13:3
1 Sam 7:1,2

3 and let us bring back the ark of our God to us, for we did not seek it in the days of Saul."

4 Then all the assembly said that they would do so, for the thing was right in the eyes of all the people.

13:5
2 Sam 6:1;
1 Chr 15:3;
1 Sam 6:21;
7:1
13:6
Josh 15:9;
2 Kin 19:15
13:7
1 Sam 7:1

5 So David assembled all Israel together, from the Shihor of Egypt even to the entrance of Hamath, to bring the ark of God from Kiriath-jearim.

6 And David and all Israel went up to Baalah, *that is,* to Kiriath-jearim, which belongs to Judah, to bring up from there the ark of God, the LORD who is enthroned *above* the cherubim, where His name is called.

7 And they carried the ark of God on a new cart from the house of Abinadab, and Uzza and Ahio drove the cart.

13:8
2 Sam 6:5

8 And David and all Israel were celebrating before God with all *their* might, even with songs and with lyres, harps, tambourines, cymbals, and with trumpets.

13:9
2 Sam 6:6

9 When they came to the threshing floor of Chidon, Uzza put out his hand to hold the ark, because the oxen nearly upset *it.*

13:10
1 Chr 15:13,
15

10 And the anger of the LORD burned against Uzza, so He struck him down because he put out his hand to the ark; and he died there before God.

11 Then David became angry because of the LORD's outburst against Uzza; and he called that place [3]Perez-uzza to this day.

12 And David was afraid of God that day, saying, "How can I bring the ark of God *home* to me?"

13 So David did not take the ark with him to the city of David, but took it aside to the house of Obed-edom the Gittite.

13:14
1 Chr 26:4,5

14 Thus the ark of God remained with the family of Obed-edom in his house three months; and the LORD blessed the family of Obed-edom with all that he had.

2. The prosperity of David

a. His palace and family

*14:1
2 Sam 5:11

14 Now Hiram king of Tyre sent messengers to David with cedar trees, masons, and carpenters, to build a house for him.

2 And David realized that the LORD had established him as king over Israel, *and* that his kingdom was highly exalted, for the sake of His people Israel.

3 Then David took more wives at Jerusalem, and David became the father of more sons and daughters.

14:4
1 Chr 3:5

4 And these are the names of the children born *to him* in Jerusalem: Shammua, Shobab, Nathan, Solomon,

5 Ibhar, Elishua, Elpelet,

6 Nogah, Nepheg, Japhia,

7 Elishama, Beeliada and Eliphelet.

[3]I.e., the breakthrough of Uzza

13:13 *Obed-edom.* His home was blessed because of the ark David placed there.

14:1 Hiram was devoted to David, hence the generosity mentioned here.

b. His defeats of the Philistines

8 When the Philistines heard that David had been anointed king over all Israel, all the Philistines went up in search of David; and David heard of it and went out against them.

9 Now the Philistines had come and made a raid in the valley of Rephaim.

10 And David inquired of God, saying, "Shall I go up against the Philistines? And wilt Thou give them into my hand?" Then the LORD said to him, "Go up, for I will give them into your hand."

11 So they came up to Baal-perazim, and David defeated them there; and David said, "God has broken through my enemies by my hand, like the breakthrough of waters." Therefore they named that place ⁴Baal-perazim.

12 And they abandoned their gods there; so David gave the order and they were burned with fire.

13 And the Philistines made yet another raid in the valley.

14 And David inquired again of God, and God said to him, "You shall not go up after them; circle around behind them, and come at them in front of the balsam trees.

15 "And it shall be when you hear the sound of marching in the tops of the balsam trees, then you shall go out to battle, for God will have gone out before you to strike the army of the Philistines."

16 And David did just as God had commanded him, and they struck down the army of the Philistines from Gibeon even as far as Gezer.

17 Then the fame of David went out into all the lands; and the LORD brought the fear of him on all the nations.

3. The bringing of the ark to Jerusalem

a. The preparations

15 Now *David* built houses for himself in the city of David; and he prepared a place for the ark of God, and pitched a tent for it.

2 Then David said, "No one is to carry the ark of God but the Levites; for the LORD chose them to carry the ark of God, and to minister to Him forever."

3 And David assembled all Israel at Jerusalem, to bring up the ark of the LORD to its place, which he had prepared for it.

4 And David gathered together the sons of Aaron, and the Levites:

5 of the sons of Kohath, Uriel the chief, and 120 of his relatives;

6 of the sons of Merari, Asaiah the chief, and 220 of his relatives;

7 of the sons of Gershom, Joel the chief, and 130 of his relatives;

8 of the sons of Elizaphan, Shemaiah the chief, and 200 of his relatives;

9 of the sons of Hebron, Eliel the chief, and 80 of his relatives;

10 of the sons of Uzziel, Amminadab the chief, and 112 of his relatives.

11 Then David called for Zadok and Abiathar the priests, and for the Levites, for Uriel, Asaiah, Joel, Shemaiah, Eliel, and Amminadab,

12 and said to them, "You are the heads of the fathers' *households* of the Levites; consecrate yourselves both you and your relatives, that you may bring up the ark of the LORD God of Israel, to *the place* that I have prepared for it.

13 "Because you did not *carry it* at the first, the LORD our God made an outburst on us, for we did not seek Him according to the ordinance."

14 So the priests and the Levites consecrated themselves to bring up the ark of the LORD God of Israel.

15 And the sons of the Levites carried the ark of God on their shoulders, with the poles thereon as Moses had commanded according to the word of the LORD.

b. The appointment of the singers and musicians

16 Then David spoke to the chiefs of the Levites to appoint their relatives the singers, with instruments of music, harps, lyres, loud-sounding cymbals, to raise sounds of joy.

17 So the Levites appointed Heman the son of Joel, and from his relatives, Asaph the son of Berechiah; and from the sons of Merari their relatives, Ethan the son of Kushaiah,

⁴I.e., the master of breakthrough

15:16 David's provision for singers and musical accompaniment began with the historic event of bringing the ark to Jerusalem. Note the further instructions in 16:4,7.

Marginal references:

14:8 / 2 Sam 5:17
14:9 / 1 Chr 11:15
14:13 / v. 9; / 2 Sam 5:22 / 14:14 / 2 Sam 5:23
14:16 / 2 Sam 5:25
14:17 / Josh 6:27; / 2 Chr 26:8; / Deut 2:25
15:1 / 1 Chr 16:1
15:2 / Num 4:15; / Deut 10:8; / 31:9 / 15:3 / 1 Kin 8:1; / 1 Chr 13:5
15:8 / Ex 6:22 / 15:9 / Ex 6:18
15:11 / 1 Chr 12:28; / 1 Sam 22:20-23 / 15:12 / Ex 19:14,15; / 2 Chr 35:6
15:13 / 2 Sam 6:3; / 1 Chr 13:7, / 10,11 / 15:14 / v. 12 / 15:15 / Ex 25:14; / Num 4:5
*15:16 / 1 Chr 25:1
15:17 / 1 Chr 6:33, / 39,44

18 and with them their relatives of the second rank, Zechariah, Ben, Jaaziel, Shemiramoth, Jehiel, Unni, Eliab, Benaiah, Maaseiah, Mattithiah, Eliphelehu, Mikneiah, Obed-edom, and Jeiel, the gatekeepers.

19 So the singers, Heman, Asaph, and Ethan *were appointed* to sound aloud cymbals of bronze;

20 and Zechariah, Aziel, Shemiramoth, Jehiel, Unni, Eliab, Maaseiah, and Benaiah, with harps *tuned* to alamoth;

21 and Mattithiah, Eliphelehu, Mikneiah, Obed-edom, Jeiel, and Azaziah, to lead with lyres tuned to the sheminith.

22 And Chenaniah, chief of the Levites, was *in charge of* the singing; he gave instruction in singing because he was skillful.

23 And Berechiah and Elkanah were gatekeepers for the ark.

15:24
v. 28;
1 Chr 16:6

24 And Shebaniah, Joshaphat, Nethanel, Amasai, Zechariah, Benaiah, and Eliezer, the priests, blew the trumpets before the ark of God. Obed-edom and Jehiah also *were* gatekeepers for the ark.

c. David dancing before the ark

15:25
2 Sam 6:12,
15;
1 Chr 13:13

25 So *it was* David, with the elders of Israel and the captains over thousands, who went to bring up the ark of the covenant of the LORD from the house of Obed-edom with joy.

26 And it came about because God was helping the Levites who were carrying the ark of the covenant of the LORD, that they sacrificed seven bulls and seven rams.

27 Now David was clothed with a robe of fine linen with all the Levites who were carrying the ark, and the singers and Chenaniah the leader of the singing *with* the singers. David also wore an ephod of linen.

15:28
1 Chr 13:8

28 Thus all Israel brought up the ark of the covenant of the LORD with shouting, and with sound of the horn, with trumpets, with loud-sounding cymbals, with harps and lyres.

15:29
2 Sam 6:16

29 And it happened when the ark of the covenant of the LORD came to the city of David, that Michal the daughter of Saul looked out of the window, and saw King David leaping and making merry; and she despised him in her heart.

d. The offerings and the music

16:1
2 Sam 6:17-19

16 And they brought in the ark of God and placed it inside the tent which David had pitched for it, and they offered burnt offerings and peace offerings before God.

2 When David had finished offering the burnt offering and the peace offerings, he blessed the people in the name of the LORD.

3 And he distributed to everyone of Israel, both man and woman, to everyone a loaf of bread and a portion *of meat* and a raisin cake.

4 And he appointed some of the Levites *as* ministers before the ark of the LORD, even to celebrate and to thank and praise the LORD God of Israel:

16:5
Ps ch. 50; 73

5 Asaph the chief, and second to him Zechariah, *then* Jeiel, Shemiramoth, Jehiel, Mattithiah, Eliab, Benaiah, Obed-edom, and Jeiel, with musical instruments, harps, lyres; also Asaph *played* loud-sounding cymbals,

6 and Benaiah and Jahaziel the priests *blew* trumpets continually before the ark of the covenant of God.

e. David's psalm of gratitude

16:7
2 Sam 23:1

7 Then on that day David first assigned Asaph and his relatives to give thanks to the LORD.

16:8
Ps 105:1-15

8 Oh give thanks to the LORD, call upon His name;
Make known His deeds among the peoples.

9 Sing to Him, sing praises to Him;
[5]Speak of all His wonders.

10 Glory in His holy name;
Let the heart of those who seek the LORD be glad.

16:11
Ps 24:6

11 Seek the LORD and His strength;
Seek His face continually.

16:12
Ps 77:11;
78:43-68

12 Remember His wonderful deeds which He has done,
His marvels and the judgments from His mouth,

[5]Or, *Meditate on*

15:21 *sheminith*, a musical term, the meaning of which is obscure. See heading of Ps. 6.

13   O seed of Israel His servant,
       Sons of Jacob, His chosen ones!

14   He is the LORD our God;
       His judgments are in all the earth.

16:14
Is 26:9

15   Remember His covenant forever,
       The word which He commanded to a thousand generations,

16   *The covenant* which He made with Abraham,
       And His oath to Isaac.

16:16
Gen 17:2;
26:3; 28:13;
35:11

17   He also confirmed it to Jacob for a statute,
       To Israel as an everlasting covenant,

16:17
Gen 35:11,12

18   Saying, "To you I will give the land of Canaan,
       As the portion of your inheritance."

19   When they were only a few in number,
       Very few, and strangers in it,

16:19
Gen 34:30

20   And they wandered about from nation to nation,
       And from *one* kingdom to another people,

21   He permitted no man to oppress them,
       And He reproved kings for their sakes, *saying,*

16:21
Gen 12:17;
20:3;
Ex 7:15-18

22   "Do not touch My anointed ones,
       And do My prophets no harm."

23   Sing to the LORD, all the earth;
       Proclaim good tidings of His salvation from day to day.

16:23
Ps 96:1-13

24   Tell of His glory among the nations,
       His wonderful deeds among all the peoples.

25   For great is the LORD, and greatly to be praised;
       He also is to be feared above all gods.

16:25
Ps 48:1; 89:7

26   For all the gods of the peoples are idols,
       But the LORD made the heavens.

16:26
Ps 96:5

27   Splendor and majesty are before Him,
       Strength and joy are in His place.

28   Ascribe to the LORD, O families of the peoples,
       Ascribe to the LORD glory and strength.

16:28
Ps 29:1,2

29   Ascribe to the LORD the glory due His name;
       Bring an offering, and come before Him;
       Worship the LORD in holy array.

30   Tremble before Him, all the earth;
       Indeed, the world is firmly established, it will not be moved.

31   Let the heavens be glad, and let the earth rejoice;
       And let them say among the nations, "The LORD reigns."

16:31
Is 49:13;
Ps 93:1

32   Let the sea roar, and all it contains;
       Let the field exult, and all that is in it.

16:32
Ps 98:7

33   Then the trees of the forest will sing for joy before
       the LORD;
       For He is coming to judge the earth.

34   O give thanks to the LORD, for *He is* good;
       For His lovingkindness is everlasting.

16:34
Ps 106:1

35   Then say, "Save us, O God of our salvation,
       And gather us and deliver us from the nations,
       To give thanks to Thy holy name,
       And glory in Thy praise."

16:35
Ps 106:47,48

36   Blessed be the LORD, the God of Israel,
       From everlasting even to everlasting.

16:36
1 Kin 8:15;
Deut 27:15

Then all the people said, "Amen," and praised the LORD.

37   So he left Asaph and his relatives there before the ark of the covenant of the LORD, to minister before the ark continually, as every day's work required;

16:37
vv. 4,5;
2 Chr 8:14

38   and Obed-edom with his 68 relatives; Obed-edom, also the son of Jeduthun, and Hosah as gatekeepers.

16:38
1 Chr 13:14;
26:10

39   And *he left* Zadok the priest and his relatives the priests before the tabernacle of the LORD in the high place which *was* at Gibeon,

*16:39
1 Chr 15:11;
1 Kin 3:4

40   to offer burnt offerings to the LORD on the altar of burnt offering continually

16:39 *tabernacle . . . at Gibeon.* According to this verse (and 21:29) there is every reason to believe that there were two sanctuaries in David's time: one at Jerusalem with the ark, and the other at Gibeon with the tabernacle and its furniture.

morning and evening, even according to all that is written in the law of the LORD, which He commanded Israel.

16:40
Ex 29:38;
Num 28:3

41   And with them *were* Heman and Jeduthun, and the rest who were chosen, who were designated by name, to give thanks to the LORD, because His lovingkindness is everlasting.

16:41
1 Chr 6:33;
25:1-6;
2 Chr 5:13

42   And with them *were* Heman and Jeduthun *with* trumpets and cymbals for those who should sound aloud, and *with* instruments *for* the songs of God, and the sons of Jeduthun for the gate.

43   Then all the people departed each to his house, and David returned to bless his household.

D. *David's desire to build the temple*

1. *David's wish*

17 And it came about, when David dwelt in his house, that David said to Nathan the prophet, "Behold, I am dwelling in a house of cedar, but the ark of the covenant of the LORD is under curtains."

17:1
2 Sam 7:1-29

2   Then Nathan said to David, "Do all that is in your heart, for God is with you."

2. *God's disapproval and covenant*

3   And it came about the same night, that the word of God came to Nathan, saying,

4   "Go and tell David My servant, 'Thus says the LORD, "You shall not build a house for Me to dwell in;

17:4
1 Chr 28:2,3

5   for I have not dwelt in a house since the day that I brought up Israel to this day, but I have gone from tent to tent and from *one* dwelling place *to another*.

17:5
2 Sam 7:6

6   "In all places where I have walked with all Israel, have I spoken a word with any of the judges of Israel, whom I commanded to shepherd My people, saying, 'Why have you not built for Me a house of cedar?' " '

17:6
2 Sam 7:7

7   "Now, therefore, thus shall you say to My servant David, 'Thus says the LORD of hosts, "I took you from the pasture, from following the sheep, that you should be leader over My people Israel.

8   "And I have been with you wherever you have gone, and have cut off all your enemies from before you; and I will make you a name like the name of the great ones who are in the earth.

9   "And I will appoint a place for My people Israel, and will plant them, that they may dwell in their own place and be moved no more; neither shall the wicked waste them anymore as formerly,

10   even from the day that I commanded judges *to be* over My people Israel. And I will subdue all your enemies. Moreover, I tell you that the LORD will build a house for you.

17:10
Judg 2:16

11   "And it shall come about when your days are fulfilled that you must go *to be* with your fathers, that I will set up *one of* your descendants after you, who shall be of your sons; and I will establish his kingdom.

12   "He shall build for Me a house, and I will establish his throne forever.

13   "I will be his father, and he shall be My son; and I will not take My lovingkindness away from him, as I took it from him who was before you.

17:13
2 Sam 7:14,
15; Heb 1:5
17:14
Luke 1:33

14   "But I will settle him in My house and in My kingdom forever, and his throne shall be established forever." ' "

15   According to all these words and according to all this vision, so Nathan spoke to David.

3. *David's prayer*

16   Then David the king went in and sat before the LORD and said, "Who am I, O LORD God, and what is my house that Thou hast brought me this far?

17:16
2 Sam 7:18

17   "And this was a small thing in Thine eyes, O God; but Thou hast spoken of Thy servant's house for a great while to come, and hast regarded me according to the standard of a man of high degree, O LORD God.

18   "What more can David still *say* to Thee concerning the honor *bestowed* on Thy servant? For Thou knowest Thy servant.

19   "O LORD, for Thy servant's sake, and according to Thine own heart, Thou hast wrought all this greatness, to make known all these great things.

17:19
Is 37:35

20 "O Lord, there is none like Thee, neither is there any God besides Thee, according to all that we have heard with our ears.

21 "And what one nation in the earth is like Thy people Israel, whom God went to redeem for Himself *as* a people, to make Thee a name by great and terrible things, in driving out nations from before Thy people, whom Thou didst redeem out of Egypt?

22 "For Thy people Israel Thou didst make Thine own people forever, and Thou, O Lord, didst become their God.

23 "And now, O Lord, let the word that Thou hast spoken concerning Thy servant and concerning his house, be established forever, and do as Thou hast spoken.

24 "And let Thy name be established and magnified forever, saying, 'The Lord of hosts is the God of Israel, *even* a God to Israel; and the house of David Thy servant is established before Thee.'

25 "For Thou, O my God, hast revealed to Thy servant that Thou wilt build for him a house; therefore Thy servant hath found *courage* to pray before Thee.

26 "And now, O Lord, Thou art God, and hast promised this good thing to Thy servant.

27 "And now it hath pleased Thee to bless the house of Thy servant, that it may continue forever before Thee; for Thou, O Lord, hast blessed, and it is blessed forever."

E. *The account of David's victories*

18 Now after this it came about that David defeated the Philistines and subdued them and took Gath and its towns from the hand of the Philistines.

2 And he defeated Moab, and the Moabites became servants to David, bringing tribute.

3 David also defeated Hadadezer king of Zobah *as far as* Hamath, as he went to establish his rule to the Euphrates River.

4 And David took from him 1,000 chariots and 7,000 horsemen and 20,000 foot soldiers, and David hamstrung all the chariot horses, but reserved *enough* of them for 100 chariots.

5 When the Arameans of Damascus came to help Hadadezer king of Zobah, David killed 22,000 men of the Arameans.

6 Then David put *garrisons* among the Arameans of Damascus; and the Arameans became servants to David, bringing tribute. And the Lord helped David wherever he went.

7 And David took the shields of gold which were carried by the servants of Hadadezer, and brought them to Jerusalem.

8 Also from Tibhath and from Cun, cities of Hadadezer, David took a very large amount of bronze, with which Solomon made the bronze sea and the pillars and the bronze utensils.

9 Now when Tou king of Hamath heard that David had defeated all the army of Hadadezer king of Zobah,

10 he sent Hadoram his son to King David, to greet him and to bless him, because he had fought against Hadadezer and had defeated him; for Hadadezer had been at war with Tou. And *Hadoram brought* all kinds of articles of gold and silver and bronze.

11 King David also dedicated these to the Lord with the silver and the gold which he had carried away from all the nations: from Edom, Moab, the sons of Ammon, the Philistines, and from Amalek.

12 Moreover Abishai the son of Zeruiah defeated 18,000 Edomites in the Valley of Salt.

13 Then he put garrisons in Edom, and all the Edomites became servants to David. And the Lord helped David wherever he went.

14 So David reigned over all Israel; and he administered justice and righteousness for all his people.

15 And Joab the son of Zeruiah *was* over the army, and Jehoshaphat the son of Ahilud *was* recorder;

16 and Zadok the son of Ahitub and Abimelech the son of Abiathar *were* priests, and Shavsha *was* secretary;

17 and Benaiah the son of Jehoiada *was* over the Cherethites and the Pelethites, and the sons of David *were* chiefs at the king's side.

19:1
2 Sam 10:1

19:3
2 Sam 10:3

19:4
2 Sam 10:4

19:6
1 Chr 18:5,9

19:7
Num 21:30;
Josh 13:9,16

19:8
2 Sam 10:7

19:11
2 Sam 10:10

19:12
2 Sam 10:11

19:14
2 Sam 10:13

19:16
2 Sam 10:15

19:17
2 Sam 10:17

19:18
2 Sam 10:18

19:19
2 Sam 10:19

*20:1ff
2 Sam 11:1;
12:26

19 Now it came about after this, that Nahash the king of the sons of Ammon died, and his son became king in his place.

2 Then David said, "I will show kindness to Hanun the son of Nahash, because his father showed kindness to me." So David sent messengers to console him concerning his father. And David's servants came into the land of the sons of Ammon to Hanun, to console him.

3 But the princes of the sons of Ammon said to Hanun, "Do you think that David is honoring your father, in that he has sent comforters to you? Have not his servants come to you to search and to overthrow and to spy out the land?"

4 So Hanun took David's servants and shaved them, and cut off their garments in the middle as far as their hips, and sent them away.

5 Then *certain persons* went and told David about the men. And he sent to meet them, for the men were greatly humiliated. And the king said, "Stay at Jericho until your beards grow, and *then* return."

6 When the sons of Ammon saw that they had made themselves odious to David, Hanun and the sons of Ammon sent 1,000 talents of silver to hire for themselves chariots and horsemen from Mesopotamia, from Aram-maacah, and from Zobah.

7 So they hired for themselves 32,000 chariots, and the king of Maacah and his people, who came and camped before Medeba. And the sons of Ammon gathered together from their cities and came to battle.

8 When David heard *of it*, he sent Joab and all the army, the mighty men.

9 And the sons of Ammon came out and drew up in battle array at the entrance of the city, and the kings who had come were by themselves in the field.

10 Now when Joab saw that the battle was set against him in front and in the rear, he selected from all the choice men of Israel and they arrayed themselves against the Arameans.

11 But the remainder of the people he placed in the hand of Abshai his brother; and they arrayed themselves against the sons of Ammon.

12 And he said, "If the Arameans are too strong for me, then you shall help me; but if the sons of Ammon are too strong for you, then I will help you.

13 "Be strong, and let us show ourselves courageous for the sake of our people and for the cities of our God; and may the LORD do what is good in His sight."

14 So Joab and the people who were with him drew near to the battle against the Arameans, and they fled before him.

15 When the sons of Ammon saw that the Arameans fled, they also fled before Abshai his brother, and entered the city. Then Joab came to Jerusalem.

16 When the Arameans saw that they had been defeated by Israel, they sent messengers, and brought out the Arameans who were beyond the ⁶River, with Shophach the commander of the army of Hadadezer leading them.

17 When it was told David, he gathered all Israel together and crossed the Jordan, and came upon them and drew up in formation against them. And when David drew up in battle array against the Arameans, they fought against him.

18 And the Arameans fled before Israel, and David killed of the Arameans 7,000 charioteers and 40,000 foot soldiers, and put to death Shophach the commander of the army.

19 So when the servants of Hadadezer saw that they were defeated by Israel, they made peace with David and served him. Thus the Arameans were not willing to help the sons of Ammon anymore.

20 Then it happened in the spring, at the time when kings go out *to battle*, that Joab led out the army and ravaged the land of the sons of Ammon, and came

⁶I.e., Euphrates

20:1–3 This unit covers the same period of time as 2 Sam. 11:1–12:31. The difference in length occurs because the Chronicler left out the account of David's sin against Bathsheba and Uriah (2 Sam. 11:2–12:25). This story occurred between: *David stayed at Jerusalem*, and *Joab struck Rabbah*. The Chronicler's interest lay in the temple (its rituals, personnel, and importance) and in the law (obedience means blessing; disobedience, cursing). David's difficulties with Saul and his seven years at Hebron fighting for the kingdom are hardly mentioned. The one sin that is clearly depicted is David's census of the people (21:1–29), and this is attributed to the instigation of Satan. Solomon also receives special consideration. The account of his idolatry and punishment (1 Kin. 11:1–40), which would appear between 2 Chr. 9:28,29, has been left out. Israel, considered apostate from the beginning, is mentioned only where it is entwined with some aspect of Judah's history that the Chronicler wants to stress. Along with David and Solomon, the good

and besieged Rabbah. But David stayed at Jerusalem. And Joab struck Rabbah and overthrew it.

2   And David took the crown of their king from his head, and he found it to weigh a talent of gold, and there was a precious stone in it; and it was placed on David's head. And he brought out the spoil of the city, a very great amount.

3   And he brought out the people who *were* in it, and cut *them* with saws and with sharp instruments and with axes. And thus David did to all the cities of the sons of Ammon. Then David and all the people returned *to* Jerusalem.

4   Now it came about after this, that war broke out at Gezer with the Philistines; then Sibbecai the Hushathite killed Sippai, one of the descendants of the giants, and they were subdued.

5   And there was war with the Philistines again, and Elhanan the son of Jair killed Lahmi the brother of Goliath the Gittite, the shaft of whose spear *was* like a weaver's beam.

6   And again there was war at Gath, where there was a man of *great* stature who had twenty-four fingers and toes, six *fingers on each hand* and six *toes on each foot*; and he also was descended from the giants.

7   And when he taunted Israel, Jonathan the son of Shimea, David's brother, killed him.

8   These were descended from the giants in Gath, and they fell by the hand of David and by the hand of his servants.

F. *David's numbering of the people*

1. *The census*

21 Then Satan stood up against Israel and moved David to number Israel.
2   So David said to Joab and to the princes of the people, "Go, number Israel from Beersheba even to Dan, and bring me *word* that I may know their number."

3   And Joab said, "May the LORD add to His people a hundred times as many as they are! But, my lord the king, are they not all my lord's servants? Why does my lord seek this thing? Why should he be a cause of guilt to Israel?"

4   Nevertheless, the king's word prevailed against Joab. Therefore, Joab departed and went throughout all Israel, and came to Jerusalem.

5   And Joab gave the number of the census of *all* the people to David. And all Israel were 1,100,000 men who drew the sword; and Judah *was* 470,000 men who drew the sword.

6   But he did not number Levi and Benjamin among them, for the king's command was abhorrent to Joab.

2. *The plague as a punishment*

7   And God was displeased with this thing, so He struck Israel.

8   And David said to God, "I have sinned greatly, in that I have done this thing. But now, please take away the iniquity of Thy servant, for I have done very foolishly."

9   And the LORD spoke to Gad, David's seer, saying,

10   "Go and speak to David, saying, 'Thus says the LORD, "I offer you three things; choose for yourself one of them, that I may do *it* to you." ' "

11   So Gad came to David and said to him, "Thus says the LORD, 'Take for yourself

12   either three years of famine, or three months to be swept away before your foes, while the sword of your enemies overtakes *you*, or else three days of the sword of the LORD, even pestilence in the land, and the angel of the LORD destroying throughout all the territory of Israel.' Now, therefore, consider what answer I shall return to Him who sent me."

13   And David said to Gad, "I am in great distress; please let me fall into the

20:2 2 Sam 12:30, 31
20:3 2 Sam 12:31
20:4 2 Sam 21:18
*20:5 2 Sam 21:19; 1 Sam 17:7
20:6 2 Sam 21:20
*21:1 2 Sam 24:1-25
21:2 1 Chr 27:23
21:3 Deut 1:11
21:5 cf. 2 Sam 24:9
21:6 1 Chr 27:24
21:8 2 Sam 24:10; 12:13
21:10 1 Chr 29:29; 1 Sam 9:9
21:12 2 Sam 24:13
21:13 Ps 51:1; 130:4,7

kings Asa, Jehoshaphat, Uzziah, Hezekiah, and Josiah are featured, with much material not found in the books of Kings. But from Rehoboam on, most of the kings' sins and difficulties are noted; and usually there is a seer, prophet, or man of God to confront the wayward king.
20:5 See note to 2 Sam. 21:19.
21:1 *Satan* (the Adversary), whose name is specifically given here, is referred to by more than thirty different names and titles in Scripture. Each of these designations brings out some particular phase of his work. Among the most significant are: (1) the *serpent* (Gen. 3:4); (2) *ruler of the world* (John 14:30); (3) *ruler of the demons* (Matt. 12:24); (4) *god of this world* (2 Cor. 4:4); and (5) the *tempter* (1 Thess. 3:5).

hand of the LORD, for His mercies are very great. But do not let me fall into the hand of man.''

*21:14
1 Chr 27:24
21:15
2 Sam 24:16
14   So the LORD sent a pestilence on Israel; 70,000 men of Israel fell.

15   And God sent an angel to Jerusalem to destroy it; but as he was about to destroy it, the LORD saw and was sorry over the calamity, and said to the destroying angel, ''It is enough; now relax your hand.'' And the angel of the LORD was standing by the threshing floor of Ornan the Jebusite.

21:16
2 Chr 3:1
16   Then David lifted up his eyes and saw the angel of the LORD standing between earth and heaven, with his drawn sword in his hand stretched out over Jerusalem. Then David and the elders, covered with sackcloth, fell on their faces.

21:17
2 Sam 7:8;
Ps 74:1
17   And David said to God, ''Is it not I who commanded to count the people? Indeed, I am the one who has sinned and done very wickedly, but these sheep, what have they done? O LORD my God, please let Thy hand be against me and my father's household, but not against Thy people that they should be plagued.''

21:18
2 Chr 3:1
18   Then the angel of the LORD commanded Gad to say to David, that David should go up and build an altar to the LORD on the threshing floor of Ornan the Jebusite.

19   So David went up at the word of Gad, which he spoke in the name of the LORD.

20   Now Ornan turned back and saw the angel, and his four sons who were with him hid themselves. And Ornan was threshing wheat.

21:21
2 Chr 3:1
21   And as David came to Ornan, Ornan looked and saw David, and went out from the threshing floor, and prostrated himself before David with his face to the ground.

22   Then David said to Ornan, ''Give me the site of this threshing floor, that I may build on it an altar to the LORD; for the full price you shall give it to me, that the plague may be restrained from the people.''

23   And Ornan said to David, ''Take it for yourself; and let my lord the king do what is good in his sight. See, I will give the oxen for burnt offerings and the threshing sledges for wood and the wheat for the grain offering; I will give it all.''

24   But King David said to Ornan, ''No, but I will surely buy it for the full price; for I will not take what is yours for the LORD, or offer a burnt offering which costs me nothing.''

*21:25
2 Sam 24:24
21:26
Lev 9:24;
Judg 6:21
25   So David gave Ornan 600 shekels of gold by weight for the site.

26   Then David built an altar to the LORD there, and offered burnt offerings and peace offerings. And he called to the LORD and He answered him with fire from heaven on the altar of burnt offering.

27   And the LORD commanded the angel, and he put his sword back in its sheath.

28   At that time, when David saw that the LORD had answered him on the threshing floor of Ornan the Jebusite, he offered sacrifice there.

21:29
1 Chr 16:39;
1 Kin 3:4
29   For the tabernacle of the LORD, which Moses had made in the wilderness, and the altar of burnt offering were in the high place at Gibeon at that time.

30   But David could not go before it to inquire of God, for he was terrified by the sword of the angel of the LORD.

22:1
1 Chr 21:18-29;
2 Chr 3:1
22 Then David said, ''This is the house of the LORD God, and this is the altar of burnt offering for Israel.''

21:14 Here is an illustration of how punishment sometimes affects also those who, so far as the record shows, had no part in the sin. (Of course it is possible that David's pride in numbers only reflected a similar attitude on the part of his prosperous and successful nation as a whole. But the Scripture does not make that explicit here.) David chose to number the people in disregard of the will of God. Seventy thousand perished as a result of one man's decision. This illustrates one of the inscrutable mysteries of life. Often many suffer because of the sins of the few. In war, for example, devastation comes to those who want no war but who suffer with those who desire it and bring it to pass.
21:25 Compare 2 Sam. 24:24, where it is stated that David paid fifty shekels of silver for the threshing floor and the sacrificial oxen. The explanation of the apparent discrepancy seems to be that he paid six hundred shekels of gold for

Ornan's entire property (Heb. māqōm or ''place''), although the goren or ''threshing floor'' was purchased for only fifty shekels of silver. We know that David purchased more than the threshing floor before he was through with Ornan, because it was on this site (2 Chr. 3:1) that not only the temple itself but also several palace buildings were later erected. This entire Mt. Moriah tract must have included much more than the mere threshing floor, and with the development of the nearby city its real estate value might easily have risen to six hundred shekels of gold. Note that Ornan's name in 2 Sam. 24 is given as Araunah. (Actually it is spelled Avarnah, in the MT in 24:16, Aravnah in v. 18, and Araunah in the rest of the chapter. There was apparently some uncertainty as to the exact pronunciation of this foreign name; but Araunah, which differs from Ornan by only one or two secondary letters in the Hebrew consonants, probably represents the earlier form.)

G. Preparations for the building of the temple

1. Materials gathered

2   So David gave orders to gather the foreigners who were in the land of Israel, and he set stonecutters to hew out stones to build the house of God.

3   And David prepared large quantities of iron to make the nails for the doors of the gates and for the clamps, and more bronze than could be weighed;

4   and timbers of cedar logs beyond number, for the Sidonians and Tyrians brought large quantities of cedar timber to David.

5   And David said, "My son Solomon is young and inexperienced, and the house that is to be built for the LORD shall be exceedingly magnificent, famous and glorious throughout all lands. *Therefore* now I will make preparation for it." So David made ample preparations before his death.

2. Solomon instructed

6   Then he called for his son Solomon, and charged him to build a house for the LORD God of Israel.

7   And David said to Solomon, "My son, I had intended to build a house to the name of the LORD my God.

8   "But the word of the LORD came to me, saying, 'You have shed much blood, and have waged great wars; you shall not build a house to My name, because you have shed *so* much blood on the earth before Me.

9   'Behold, a son shall be born to you, who shall be a man of rest; and I will give him rest from all his enemies on every side; for his name shall be [7]Solomon, and I will give peace and quiet to Israel in his days.

10   'He shall build a house for My name, and he shall be My son, and I will be his father; and I will establish the throne of his kingdom over Israel forever.'

11   "Now, my son, the LORD be with you that you may be successful, and build the house of the LORD your God just as He has spoken concerning you.

12   "Only the LORD give you discretion and understanding, and give you charge over Israel, so that you may keep the law of the LORD your God.

13   "Then you shall prosper, if you are careful to observe the statutes and the ordinances which the LORD commanded Moses concerning Israel. Be strong and courageous, do not fear nor be dismayed.

14   "Now behold, with great pains I have prepared for the house of the LORD 100,000 talents of gold and 1,000,000 talents of silver, and bronze and iron beyond weight, for they are in great quantity; also timber and stone I have prepared, and you may add to them.

15   "Moreover, there are many workmen with you, stonecutters and masons of stone and carpenters, and all men who are skillful in every kind of work.

16   "Of the gold, the silver and the bronze and the iron, there is no limit. Arise and work, and may the LORD be with you."

3. The leaders charged to help

17   David also commanded all the leaders of Israel to help his son Solomon, *saying,*

18   "Is not the LORD your God with you? And has He not given you rest on every side? For He has given the inhabitants of the land into my hand, and the land is subdued before the LORD and before His people.

19   "Now set your heart and your soul to seek the LORD your God; arise, therefore, and build the sanctuary of the LORD God, so that you may bring the ark of the covenant of the LORD, and the holy vessels of God into the house that is to be built for the name of the LORD."

7I.e., peaceful

22:2
1 Kin 9:21;
5:17,18
22:3
1 Chr 29:2,7;
v. 14
22:4
1 Kin 5:6
22:5
1 Chr 29:1
22:7
2 Sam 7:2;
1 Chr 17:1;
Deut 12:5,11
22:8
1 Kin 5:3;
1 Chr 28:3
22:9
1 Kin 4:20,
25;
2 Sam 12:24,
25
22:10
2 Sam 7:13;
1 Chr 17:12,
13
22:11
v. 16
22:12
1 Kin 3:9-12;
2 Chr 1:10
22:13
1 Chr 28:7;
Josh 1:6-9;
1 Chr 28:20
*22:14
v. 3
22:16
v. 11
22:17
1 Chr 28:1-6
*22:18
2 Sam 7:1;
1 Chr 23:25
22:19
1 Chr 28:9;
1 Kin 8:6;
2 Chr 5:7;
v. 7

22:14 *100,000 talents of gold.* This is a good example of the exceedingly large figures that characterize the books of Chronicles. The most gold that came to Solomon in one of his prosperous years was *666 talents* (1 Kin. 10:14; 2 Chr. 9:13). That David, a man devoted primarily to war and expansion of the kingdom, could have accumulated 100,000 talents of gold (today's equivalent in the billions of dollars) is highly improbable. Somewhere in transmission the original figures were greatly expanded.

22:18 *the land is subdued before the LORD and before His people.* Under David and Solomon the kingdom of Israel reached its greatest heights. Starting from slavery in Egypt, Israel now had a territory, a people, and a stable government. The favor of God is revealed. But in a few short years this great kingdom sank into an oblivion from which it never recovered.

H. *The arrangements for the temple service*

1. *The Levites*

23 Now when David reached old age, he made his son Solomon king over Israel.
2   And he gathered together all the leaders of Israel with the priests and the Levites.

3   And the Levites were numbered from thirty years old and upward, and their number by census of men was 38,000.

4   Of these, 24,000 were to oversee the work of the house of the LORD; and 6,000 *were* officers and judges,

5   and 4,000 *were* gatekeepers, and 4,000 *were* praising the LORD with the instruments which David made for giving praise.

6   And David divided them into divisions according to the sons of Levi: Gershon, Kohath, and Merari.

7   Of the Gershonites *were* Ladan and Shimei.

8   The sons of Ladan *were* Jehiel the first and Zetham and Joel, three.

9   The sons of Shimei *were* Shelomoth and Haziel and Haran, three. These were the heads of the fathers' *households* of Ladan.

10   And the sons of Shimei *were* Jahath, Zina, Jeush, and Beriah. These four *were* the sons of Shimei.

11   And Jahath was the first, and Zizah the second; but Jeush and Beriah did not have many sons, so they became a father's household, one class.

12   The sons of Kohath were four: Amram, Izhar, Hebron and Uzziel.

13   The sons of Amram were Aaron and Moses. And Aaron was set apart to sanctify him as most holy, he and his sons forever, to burn incense before the LORD, to minister to Him and to bless in His name forever.

14   But *as for* Moses the man of God, his sons were named among the tribe of Levi.

15   The sons of Moses *were* Gershom and Eliezer.

16   The son of Gershom *was* Shebuel the chief.

17   And the son of Eliezer was Rehabiah the chief; and Eliezer had no other sons, but the sons of Rehabiah were very many.

18   The son of Izhar was Shelomith the chief.

19   The sons of Hebron *were* Jeriah the first, Amariah the second, Jahaziel the third and Jekameam the fourth.

20   The sons of Uzziel *were* Micah the first and Isshiah the second.

21   The sons of Merari were Mahli and Mushi. The sons of Mahli *were* Eleazar and Kish.

22   And Eleazar died and had no sons, but daughters only, so their brothers, the sons of Kish, took them *as wives*.

23   The sons of Mushi *were* three: Mahli, Eder, and Jeremoth.

2. *Their duties*

24   These were the sons of Levi according to their fathers' households, *even* the heads of the fathers' *households* of those of them who were counted, in the number of names by their census, doing the work for the service of the house of the LORD, from twenty years old and upward.

25   For David said, "The LORD God of Israel has given rest to His people, and He dwells in Jerusalem forever.

26   "And also, the Levites will no longer need to carry the tabernacle and all its utensils for its service."

27   For by the last words of David the sons of Levi *were* numbered, from twenty years old and upward.

28   For their office is to assist the sons of Aaron with the service of the house of the LORD, in the courts and in the chambers and in the purifying of all holy things, even the work of the service of the house of God,

29   and with the showbread, and the fine flour for a grain offering, and unleavened wafers, or *what is baked in* the pan, or what is well-mixed, and all measures of volume and size.

Cross-references: 23:1 1 Kin 1:33-39; 1 Chr 29:28; 28:5 · 23:3 Num 4:3-49; v. 24 · 23:4 2 Chr 19:8 · 23:5 1 Chr 15:16 · 23:6 2 Chr 8:14; 29:25 · 23:12 Ex 6:18 · 23:13 Ex 6:20; 28:1; 30:6-10; Deut 21:5 · 23:16 1 Chr 26:24ff · 23:21 1 Chr 24:26ff · *23:24 Num 10:17, 21; v. 3 · 23:25 1 Chr 22:18 · 23:26 Num 4:5 · 23:29 Lev 23:5-9; Ex 25:30; Lev 6:20; 2:4-7; 19:35

23:24 Numbers 4:30 and 1 Chr. 23:3 give the active years of the Levites as *thirty* to *fifty*. Presumably the reason for lowering it here was a need for more Levites to assist the priests.

30   And they are to stand every morning to thank and to praise the LORD, and likewise at evening,

31   and to offer all burnt offerings to the LORD, on the sabbaths, the new moons and the fixed festivals in the number *set* by the ordinance concerning them, continually before the LORD.

23:31
Is 1:13,14;
Lev 23:24

32   Thus they are to keep charge of the tent of meeting, and charge of the holy place, and charge of the sons of Aaron their relatives, for the service of the house of the LORD.

23:32
Num 1:53;
1 Chr 9:27;
Num 3:6

3. *The division of the priests*

24   Now the divisions of the descendants of Aaron *were these:* the sons of Aaron *were* Nadab, Abihu, Eleazar, and Ithamar.

24:1
Ex 6:23

2   But Nadab and Abihu died before their father and had no sons. So Eleazar and Ithamar served as priests.

24:2
Lev 10:2;
Num 3:4

3   And David, with Zadok of the sons of Eleazar and Ahimelech of the sons of Ithamar, divided them according to their offices for their ministry.

4   Since more chief men were found from the descendants of Eleazar than the descendants of Ithamar, they divided them thus: *there were* sixteen heads of fathers' households of the descendants of Eleazar, and eight of the descendants of Ithamar according to their fathers' households.

5   Thus they were divided by lot, the one as the other; for they were officers of the sanctuary and officers of God, both from the descendants of Eleazar and the descendants of Ithamar.

24:5
v. 31

6   And Shemaiah, the son of Nethanel the scribe, from the Levites, recorded them in the presence of the king, the princes, Zadok the priest, Ahimelech the son of Abiathar, and the heads of the fathers' *households* of the priests and of the Levites; one father's household taken for Eleazar and one taken for Ithamar.

7   Now the first lot came out for Jehoiarib, the second for Jedaiah,

8   the third for Harim, the fourth for Seorim,

9   the fifth for Malchijah, the sixth for Mijamin,

10   the seventh for Hakkoz, the eighth for Abijah,

24:10
Neh 12:4,17;
Luke 1:5

11   the ninth for Jeshua, the tenth for Shecaniah,

12   the eleventh for Eliashib, the twelfth for Jakim,

13   the thirteenth for Huppah, the fourteenth for Jeshebeab,

14   the fifteenth for Bilgah, the sixteenth for Immer,

15   the seventeenth for Hezir, the eighteenth for Happizzez,

16   the nineteenth for Pethahiah, the twentieth for Jehezkel,

17   the twenty-first for Jachin, the twenty-second for Gamul,

18   the twenty-third for Delaiah, the twenty-fourth for Maaziah.

19   These were their offices for their ministry, when *they* came in to the house of the LORD according to the ordinance *given* to them through Aaron their father, just as the LORD God of Israel had commanded him.

24:19
1 Chr 9:25

20   Now for the rest of the sons of Levi: of the sons of Amram, Shubael; of the sons of Shubael, Jehdeiah.

21   Of Rehabiah: of the sons of Rehabiah, Isshiah the first.

22   Of the Izharites, Shelomoth; of the sons of Shelomoth, Jahath.

24:21
1 Chr 23:17

23   And the sons *of Hebron:* Jeriah *the first,* Amariah the second, Jahaziel the third, Jekameam the fourth.

24:23
1 Chr 23:19

24   *Of* the sons of Uzziel, Micah; of the sons of Micah, Shamir.

25   The brother of Micah, Isshiah; of the sons of Isshiah, Zechariah.

26   The sons of Merari, Mahli and Mushi; the sons of Jaaziah, Beno.

24:26
1 Chr 23:21

27   The sons of Merari: by Jaaziah *were* Beno, Shoham, Zaccur, and Ibri.

28   By Mahli: Eleazar, who had no sons.

29   By Kish: the sons of Kish, Jerahmeel.

30   And the sons of Mushi: Mahli, Eder, and Jerimoth. These *were* the sons of the Levites according to their fathers' households.

31   These also cast lots just as their relatives the sons of Aaron in the presence of David the king, Zadok, Ahimelech, and the heads of the fathers' *households* of the priests and of the Levites—the head of fathers' *households* as well as those of his younger brother.

24:31
vv. 5,6

4. The arrangements for music

25:1
1 Chr 6:33,
39; 15:16

25 Moreover, David and the commanders of the army set apart for the service *some* of the sons of Asaph and of Heman and of Jeduthun, who *were* to prophesy with lyres, harps, and cymbals; and the number of those who performed their service was:

2 Of the sons of Asaph: Zaccur, Joseph, Nethaniah, and Asharelah; the sons of Asaph *were* under the direction of Asaph, who prophesied under the direction of the king.

25:3
1 Chr 16:41, 42

3 Of Jeduthun, the sons of Jeduthun: Gedaliah, Zeri, Jeshaiah, Shimei, Hashabiah, and Mattithiah, six, under the direction of their father Jeduthun with the harp, who prophesied in giving thanks and praising the LORD.

*25:4
1 Chr 6:33;
v. 25

4 Of Heman, the sons of Heman: Bukkiah, Mattaniah, Uzziel, Shebuel and Jerimoth, Hananiah, Hanani, Eliathah, Giddalti and Romamti-ezer, Joshbeka-shah, Mallothi, Hothir, Mahazioth.

5 All these *were* the sons of Heman the king's seer to exalt him according to the words of God, for God gave fourteen sons and three daughters to Heman.

25:6
1 Chr 15:16, 19

6 All these were under the direction of their father to sing in the house of the LORD, with cymbals, harps and lyres, for the service of the house of God. Asaph, Jeduthun and Heman *were* under the direction of the king.

7 And their number who were trained in singing to the LORD, with their [8]relatives, all who were skillful, *was* 288.

25:8
1 Chr 26:13

8 And they cast lots for their duties, all alike, the small as well as the great, the teacher *as well* as the pupil.

25:9
1 Chr 6:39

9 Now the first lot came out for Asaph to Joseph, the second for Gedaliah, he with his relatives and sons *were* twelve;

10 the third to Zaccur, his sons and his relatives, twelve;

11 the fourth to Izri, his sons and his relatives, twelve;

12 the fifth to Nethaniah, his sons and his relatives, twelve;

13 the sixth to Bukkiah, his sons and his relatives, twelve;

14 the seventh to Jesharelah, his sons and his relatives, twelve;

15 the eighth to Jeshaiah, his sons and his relatives, twelve;

25:16
v. 4

16 the ninth to Mattaniah, his sons and his relatives, twelve;

17 the tenth to Shimei, his sons and his relatives, twelve;

18 the eleventh to Azarel, his sons and his relatives, twelve;

19 the twelfth to Hashabiah, his sons and his relatives, twelve;

20 for the thirteenth, Shubael, his sons and his relatives, twelve;

21 for the fourteenth, Mattithiah, his sons and his relatives, twelve;

22 for the fifteenth to Jeremoth, his sons and his relatives, twelve;

25:23
v. 4

23 for the sixteenth to Hananiah, his sons and his relatives, twelve;

24 for the seventeenth to Joshbekashah, his sons and his relatives, twelve;

25:25
v. 4

25 for the eighteenth to Hanani, his sons and his relatives, twelve;

26 for the nineteenth to Mallothi, his sons and his relatives, twelve;

27 for the twentieth to Eliathah, his sons and his relatives, twelve;

28 for the twenty-first to Hothir, his sons and his relatives, twelve;

29 for the twenty-second to Giddalti, his sons and his relatives, twelve;

30 for the twenty-third to Mahazioth, his sons and his relatives, twelve;

31 for the twenty-fourth to Romamti-ezer, his sons and his relatives, twelve.

5. The arrangements for gatekeepers

26:1
v. 19

26 For the divisions of the gatekeepers *there were* of the Korahites, Meshelemiah the son of Kore, of the sons of Asaph.

2 And Meshelemiah had sons: Zechariah the first-born, Jediael the second, Zebadiah the third, Jathniel the fourth,

3 Elam the fifth, Johanan the sixth, Eliehoenai the seventh.

26:4
1 Chr 15:18

4 And Obed-edom had sons: Shemaiah the first-born, Jehozabad the second, Joah the third, Sacar the fourth, Nethanel the fifth,

---

[8]Lit., *brothers*, and so throughout this context

25:4 *Hananiah . . . Mahazioth.* While the first two of the nine names appear as valid proper names elsewhere, the other forms are impossible as individual names. With slight change of vowels and division of consonants the list becomes a fragment of an old poem or prayer. No one knows how it was interpreted as a list of names and incorporated here.

5 Ammiel the sixth, Issachar the seventh, *and* Peullethai the eighth; God had indeed blessed him.

6 Also to his son Shemaiah sons were born who ruled over the house of their father, for they were mighty men of valor.

7 The sons of Shemaiah *were* Othni, Rephael, Obed, and Elzabad, whose brothers, Elihu and Semachiah, were valiant men.

8 All these *were* of the sons of Obed-edom; they and their sons and their relatives *were* able men with strength for the service, 62 from Obed-edom.

9 And Meshelemiah had sons and relatives, 18 valiant men.

10 Also Hosah, *one* of the sons of Merari had sons: Shimri the first (although he was not the first-born, his father made him first),

11 Hilkiah the second, Tebaliah the third, Zechariah the fourth; all the sons and relatives of Hosah *were* 13.

12 To these divisions of the gatekeepers, the chief men, *were given* duties like their relatives to minister in the house of the LORD.

13 And they cast lots, the small and the great alike, according to their fathers' households, for every gate.

14 And the lot to the east fell to Shelemiah. Then they cast lots *for* his son Zechariah, a counselor with insight, and his lot came out to the north.

15 For Obed-edom *it fell* to the south, and to his sons went the storehouse.

16 For Shuppim and Hosah *it was* to the west, by the gate of Shallecheth, on the ascending highway. Guard corresponded to guard.

17 On the east there were six Levites, on the north four daily, on the south four daily, and at the storehouse two by two.

18 At the [9]Parbar on the west *there were* four at the highway and two at the Parbar.

19 These were the divisions of the gatekeepers of the sons of Korah and of the sons of Merari.

6. *The arrangements for the treasuries*

20 [10]And the Levites, their relatives, had charge of the treasures of the house of God, and of the treasures of the dedicated gifts.

21 The sons of Ladan, the sons of the Gershonites belonging to Ladan, *namely,* the Jehielites, *were* the heads of the fathers' *households,* belonging to Ladan the Gershonite.

22 The sons of Jehieli, Zetham and Joel his brother, had charge of the treasures of the house of the LORD.

23 As for the Amramites, the Izharites, the Hebronites, and the Uzzielites,

24 Shebuel the son of Gershom, the son of Moses, was officer over the treasures.

25 And his relatives by Eliezer *were* Rehabiah his son, Jeshaiah his son, Joram his son, Zichri his son, and Shelomoth his son.

26 This Shelomoth and his relatives had charge of all the treasures of the dedicated gifts, which King David and the heads of the fathers' *households,* the commanders of thousands and hundreds, and commanders of the army, had dedicated.

27 They dedicated part of the spoil won in battles to repair the house of the LORD.

28 And all that Samuel the seer had dedicated and Saul the son of Kish, Abner the son of Ner and Joab the son of Zeruiah, everyone who had dedicated *anything,* *all of this* was in the care of Shelomoth and his relatives.

7. *The arrangements for officers and judges*

29 As for the Izharites, Chenaniah and his sons were *assigned* to outside duties for Israel, as officers and judges.

30 As for the Hebronites, Hashabiah and his relatives, 1,700 capable men, had charge of the affairs of Israel west of the Jordan, for all the work of the LORD and the service of the king.

31 As for the Hebronites, Jerijah the chief (these Hebronites were investigated according to their genealogies and fathers' *households,* in the fortieth year of David's reign, and men of outstanding capability were found among them at Jazer of Gilead)

---

[9]Possibly *court* or *colonnade*   [10]So Gr.; Heb., *As for the Levites, Ahijah had*

26:10
1 Chr 16:38

26:12
v. 1

26:13
1 Chr 24:5,
31; 25:8

26:20
1 Chr 28:12

26:24
1 Chr 23:16

26:25
1 Chr 23:18

26:26
2 Sam 8:11

26:28
1 Sam 9:9

26:29
Neh 11:16;
1 Chr 23:4
26:30
1 Chr 27:17

26:31
1 Chr 23:19

26:32
2 Chr 19:11

32   and his relatives, capable men, *were* 2,700 in number, heads of fathers' *households*. And King David made them overseers of the Reubenites, the Gadites and the half-tribe of the Manassites concerning all the affairs of God and of the king.

I. *The appointment of the military and civil officials*

27 Now *this is* the enumeration of the sons of Israel, the heads of fathers' *households*, the commanders of thousands and of hundreds, and their officers who served the king in all the affairs of the divisions which came in and went out month by month throughout all the months of the year, each division *numbering* 24,000.

27:2
2 Sam 23:8-30;
1 Chr 11:11-31

2   Jashobeam the son of Zabdiel [11]had charge of the first division for the first month; and in his division *were* 24,000.

3   *He was* from the sons of Perez, *and was* chief of all the commanders of the army for the first month.

4   Dodai the Ahohite and his division had charge of the division for the second month, Mikloth *being* the chief officer; and in his division *were* 24,000.

5   The third commander of the army for the third month *was* Benaiah, the son of Jehoiada the priest, *as* chief; and in his division *were* 24,000.

27:6
1 Chr 11:22ff

6   This Benaiah *was* the mighty man of the thirty, and had charge of thirty; and over his division was Ammizabad his son.

27:7
1 Chr 11:26

7   The fourth for the fourth month *was* Asahel the brother of Joab, and Zebadiah his son after him; and in his division *were* 24,000.

8   The fifth for the fifth month *was* the commander Shamhuth the Izrahite; and in his division *were* 24,000.

27:9
1 Chr 11:28

9   The sixth for the sixth month *was* Ira the son of Ikkesh the Tekoite; and in his division *were* 24,000.

27:10
1 Chr 11:27

10   The seventh for the seventh month *was* Helez the Pelonite of the sons of Ephraim; and in his division *were* 24,000.

27:11
1 Chr 11:29

11   The eighth for the eighth month *was* Sibbecai the Hushathite of the Zerahites; and in his division *were* 24,000.

27:12
1 Chr 11:28

12   The ninth for the ninth month *was* Abiezer the Anathothite of the Benjamites; and in his division *were* 24,000.

27:13
1 Chr 11:30

13   The tenth for the tenth month *was* Maharai the Netophathite of the Zerahites; and in his division *were* 24,000.

27:14
1 Chr 11:31

14   The eleventh for the eleventh month *was* Benaiah the Pirathonite of the sons of Ephraim; and in his division *were* 24,000.

15   The twelfth for the twelfth month *was* Heldai the Netophathite of Othniel; and in his division *were* 24,000.

16   Now in charge of the tribes of Israel: chief officer for the Reubenites was Eliezer the son of Zichri; for the Simeonites, Shephatiah the son of Maacah;

17   for Levi, Hashabiah the son of Kemuel; for Aaron, Zadok;

18   for Judah, Elihu, *one* of David's brothers; for Issachar, Omri the son of Michael;

19   for Zebulun, Ishmaiah the son of Obadiah; for Naphtali, Jeremoth the son of Azriel;

20   for the sons of Ephraim, Hoshea the son of Azaziah; for the half-tribe of Manasseh, Joel the son of Pedaiah;

21   for the half-tribe of Manasseh in Gilead, Iddo the son of Zechariah; for Benjamin, Jaasiel the son of Abner;

27:22
1 Chr 28:1

22   for Dan, Azarel the son of Jeroham. These *were* the princes of the tribes of Israel.

27:23
Gen 15:5

23   But David did not count those twenty years of age and under, because the LORD had said He would multiply Israel as the stars of heaven.

27:24
2 Sam 24:15;
1 Chr 21:7

24   Joab the son of Zeruiah had begun to count *them*, but did not finish; and because of this, wrath came upon Israel, and the number was not included in the account of the chronicles of King David.

25   Now Azmaveth the son of Adiel had charge of the king's storehouses. And Jonathan the son of Uzziah had charge of the storehouses in the country, in the cities, in the villages, and in the towers.

26   And Ezri the son of Chelub had charge of the agricultural workers who tilled the soil.

[11]Lit., *was over*, and so throughout the ch.

27   And Shimei the Ramathite had charge of the vineyards; and Zabdi the Shiphmite had charge of the produce of the vineyards *stored* in the wine cellars.
28   And Baal-hanan the Gederite had charge of the olive and sycamore trees in the [12]Shephelah; and Joash had charge of the stores of oil.
29   And Shitrai the Sharonite had charge of the cattle which were grazing in Sharon; and Shaphat the son of Adlai had charge of the cattle in the valleys.
30   And Obil the Ishmaelite had charge of the camels; and Jehdeiah the Meronothite had charge of the donkeys.
31   And Jaziz the Hagrite had charge of the flocks. All these were overseers of the property which belonged to King David.
32   Also Jonathan, David's uncle, *was* a counselor, a man of understanding, and a scribe; and Jehiel the son of Hachmoni tutored the king's sons.
33   And Ahithophel was counselor to the king; and Hushai the Archite was the king's friend.
34   And Jehoiada the son of Benaiah, and Abiathar succeeded Ahithophel; and Joab was the commander of the king's army.

J. David's last words and death

1. The people instructed to assist Solomon

28   Now David assembled at Jerusalem all the officials of Israel, the princes of the tribes, and the commanders of the divisions that served the king, and the commanders of thousands, and the commanders of hundreds, and the overseers of all the property and livestock belonging to the king and his sons, with the officials and the mighty men, even all the valiant men.
2   Then King David rose to his feet and said, "Listen to me, my brethren and my people; I *had* [13]intended to build a [14]permanent home for the ark of the covenant of the LORD and for the footstool of our God. So I had made preparations to build *it*.
3   "But God said to me, 'You shall not build a house for My name because you are a man of war and have shed blood.'
4   "Yet, the LORD, the God of Israel, chose me from all the house of my father to be king over Israel forever. For He has chosen Judah to be a leader; and in the house of Judah, my father's house, and among the sons of my father He took pleasure in me to make *me* king over all Israel.
5   "And of all my sons (for the LORD has given me many sons), He has chosen my son Solomon to sit on the throne of the kingdom of the LORD over Israel.
6   "And He said to me, 'Your son Solomon is the one who shall build My house and My courts; for I have chosen him to be a son to Me, and I will be a father to him.
7   'And I will establish his kingdom forever, if he resolutely performs My commandments and My ordinances, as is done now.'
8   "So now, in the sight of all Israel, the assembly of the LORD, and in the hearing of our God, observe and seek after all the commandments of the LORD your God in order that you may possess the good land and bequeath *it* to your sons after you forever.

2. David's instructions to Solomon

9   "As for you, my son Solomon, know the God of your father, and serve Him with a whole heart and a willing mind; for the LORD searches all hearts, and understands every intent of the thoughts. If you seek Him, He will let you find Him; but if you forsake Him, He will reject you forever.
10   "Consider now, for the LORD has chosen you to build a house for the sanctuary; be courageous and act."
11   Then David gave to his son Solomon the plan of the porch *of the temple*, its buildings, its storehouses, its upper rooms, its inner rooms, and the room for the mercy seat;
12   and the plan of all that he had in mind, for the courts of the house of the LORD, and for all the surrounding rooms, for the storehouses of the house of God, and for the storehouses of the dedicated things;
13   also for the divisions of the priests and the Levites and for all the work of the service of the house of the LORD and for all the utensils of service in the house of the LORD;

---

[12]Or, *lowlands*   [13]Lit., *in my heart*   [14]Lit., *house of rest*

Cross references (right margin):

27:28
1 Kin 10:27;
2 Chr 1:15

27:33
2 Sam 15:12,
32,37
27:34
1 Kin 1:7;
1 Chr 11:6

28:1
1 Chr 27:1-31;
11:10-47

28:2
2 Sam 7:2;
1 Chr 17:1,2;
Ps 132:7

28:3
2 Sam 7:5,13;
1 Chr 22:8
28:4
1 Sam 16:6-13;
1 Chr 17:23,
27; 5:2;
Gen 49:8-10

28:5
1 Chr 3:1-9;
22:9,10
28:6
2 Sam 7:13,
14;
1 Chr 22:9,10
28:7
1 Chr 22:13

28:9
Jer 9:24;
1 Chr 29:17-19;
1 Sam 16:7;
2 Chr 15:2;
Jer 29:13
28:10
1 Chr 22:13

28:11
vv. 12,19;
Ex 25:40

28:12
1 Chr 26:20

28:13
1 Chr 24:1;
23:6

14 for the golden *utensils,* the weight of gold for all utensils for every kind of service; for the silver utensils, the weight *of silver* for all utensils for every kind of service;

28:15
Ex 25:31-39

15 and the weight *of gold* for the golden lampstands and their golden lamps, with the weight of each lampstand and its lamps; and *the weight of silver* for the silver lampstands, with the weight of each lampstand and its lamps according to the use of each lampstand;

16 and the gold by weight for the tables of showbread, for each table; and silver for the silver tables;

17 and the forks, the basins, and the pitchers of pure gold; and for the golden bowls with the weight for each bowl; and for the silver bowls with the weight for each bowl;

28:18
Ex 30:1-10;
25:18-22

18 and for the altar of incense refined gold by weight; and gold for the model of the chariot, *even* the cherubim, that spread out *their wings,* and covered the ark of the covenant of the LORD.

28:19
vv. 11,12

19 "All *this,*" *said David,* "the LORD made me understand in writing by His hand upon me, all the details of this pattern."

28:20
Josh 1:6,7,9;
1 Chr 22:13;
Josh 1:5

20 Then David said to his son Solomon, "Be strong and courageous, and act; do not fear nor be dismayed, for the LORD God, my God, is with you. He will not fail you nor forsake you until all the work for the service of the house of the LORD is finished.

28:21
v. 13;
Ex 35:25-35;
36:1,2

21 "Now behold, *there are* the divisions of the priests and the Levites for all the service of the house of God, and every willing man of any skill will be with you in all the work for all kinds of service. The officials also and all the people will be entirely at your command."

3. David invites the people to give

29:1
1 Chr 22:5;
v. 19

29 Then King David said to the entire assembly, "My son Solomon, whom alone God has chosen, is still young and inexperienced and the work is great; for the temple is not for man, but for the LORD God.

29:2
1 Chr 22:3-5

2 "Now with all my ability I have provided for the house of my God the gold for the *things of* gold, and the silver for the *things of* silver, and the bronze for the *things of* bronze, the iron for the *things of* iron, and wood for the *things of* wood, onyx stones and inlaid *stones,* stones of antimony, and stones of various colors, and all kinds of precious stones, and alabaster in abundance.

3 "And moreover, in my delight in the house of my God, the treasure I have of gold and silver, I give to the house of my God, over and above all that I have already provided for the holy [15]temple,

29:4
1 Chr 22:14;
1 Kin 9:28

4 *namely,* 3,000 talents of gold, of the gold of Ophir, and 7,000 talents of refined silver, to overlay the walls of the buildings;

5 of gold for the *things of* gold, and of silver for the *things of* silver, that is, for all the work done by the craftsmen. Who then is willing to consecrate himself this day to the LORD?"

29:6
1 Chr 27:1;
28:1; 27:25ff

6 Then the rulers of the fathers' *households,* and the princes of the tribes of Israel, and the commanders of thousands and of hundreds, with the overseers over the king's work, offered willingly;

*29:7
Ezra 2:69;
Neh 7:70

7 and for the service for the house of God they gave 5,000 talents and 10,000 darics of gold, and 10,000 talents of silver, and 18,000 talents of brass, and 100,000 talents of iron.

29:8
1 Chr 26:21

8 And whoever possessed *precious* stones gave them to the treasury of the house of the LORD, in care of Jehiel the Gershonite.

29:9
1 Kin 8:61;
2 Cor 9:7

9 Then the people rejoiced because they had offered so willingly, for they made their offering to the LORD with a whole heart, and King David also rejoiced greatly.

4. David's prayer

29:11
Matt 6:13;
1 Tim 1:17;
Rev 5:13

10 So David blessed the LORD in the sight of all the assembly; and David said, "Blessed art Thou, O LORD God of Israel our father, forever and ever.

11 "Thine, O LORD, is the greatness and the power and the glory and the victory

[15]Lit., *house*

29:7 *darics.* The Chronicler has indicated the amount of the freewill offering to David by enumerating part of the gold in terms of darics, Persian coins used in his day.

and the majesty, indeed everything that is in the heavens and the earth; Thine is the dominion, O LORD, and Thou dost exalt Thyself as head over all.

12 "Both riches and honor *come* from Thee, and Thou dost rule over all, and in Thy hand is power and might; and it lies in Thy hand to make great, and to strengthen everyone.

13 "Now therefore, our God, we thank Thee, and praise Thy glorious name.

14 "But who am I and who are my people that we should be able to offer as generously as this? For all things come from Thee, and from Thy hand we have given Thee.

15 "For we are sojourners before Thee, and tenants, as all our fathers were; our days on the earth are like a shadow, and there is no hope.

16 "O LORD our God, all this abundance that we have provided to build Thee a house for Thy holy name, it is from Thy hand, and all is Thine.

17 "Since I know, O my God, that Thou triest the heart and delightest in uprightness, I, in the integrity of my heart, have willingly offered all these *things;* so now with joy I have seen Thy people, who are present here, make *their* offerings willingly to Thee.

18 "O LORD, the God of Abraham, Isaac, and Israel, our fathers, preserve this forever in the intentions of the heart of Thy people, and direct their heart to Thee;

19 "and give to my son Solomon a perfect heart to keep Thy commandments, Thy testimonies, and Thy statutes, and to do *them* all, and to build the temple, for which I have made provision."

20 Then David said to all the assembly, "Now bless the LORD your God." And all the assembly blessed the LORD, the God of their fathers, and bowed low and did homage to the LORD and to the king.

21 And on the next day they made sacrifices to the LORD and offered burnt offerings to the LORD, 1,000 bulls, 1,000 rams *and* 1,000 lambs, with their libations and sacrifices in abundance for all Israel.

22 So they ate and drank that day before the LORD with great gladness.
And they made Solomon the son of David king a second time, and they anointed *him* as ruler for the LORD and Zadok as priest.

5. *Solomon made king*

23 Then Solomon sat on the throne of the LORD as king instead of David his father; and he prospered, and all Israel obeyed him.

24 And all the officials, the mighty men, and also all the sons of King David pledged allegiance to King Solomon.

25 And the LORD highly exalted Solomon in the sight of all Israel, and bestowed on him royal majesty which had not been on any king before him in Israel.

6. *The death of David*

26 Now David the son of Jesse reigned over all Israel.

27 And the period which he reigned over Israel *was* forty years; he reigned in Hebron seven years and in Jerusalem thirty-three *years.*

28 Then he died in a ripe old age, full of days, riches and honor; and his son Solomon reigned in his place.

29 Now the acts of King David, from first to last, are written in the chronicles of Samuel the seer, in the chronicles of Nathan the prophet, and in the chronicles of Gad the seer,

30 with all his reign, his power, and the circumstances which came on him, on Israel, and on all the kingdoms of the lands.

29:12
2 Chr 1:12;
Rom 11:36

29:15
Lev 25:23;
Ps 39:12;
Heb 11:13;
1 Pet 2:11;
Job 14:2
29:17
1 Chr 28:9;
Prov 11:20

29:19
1 Chr 28:9;
Ps 72:1; v. 2;
1 Chr 22:14

29:21
1 Kin 8:62,63

29:22
1 Chr 23:1;
1 Kin 1:33-39

29:25
2 Chr 1:1,12;
1 Kin 3:13

29:26
1 Chr 18:14
29:27
2 Sam 5:4,5;
1 Kin 2:11
29:28
Gen 15:15;
25:8;
1 Chr 23:1

29:30
Dan 2:21;
4:23,25

29:14 David recognized that God is the source of all wealth and the giver of every good gift. Anything we give to God is simply a returning of what He has entrusted to us. In that sense any gifts we bring to Him indicate that we are but stewards of the remainder, which is loaned to us for the balance of our earthly existence.

INTRODUCTION TO
THE SECOND BOOK OF THE
CHRONICLES

Authorship and Background: See 1 Chronicles

Characteristics: The Chronicler's selection of events from history for his purpose, which was begun with the reign of David, is continued through the reign of his son. All references to the idolatry and punishment of Solomon are omitted (whereas they may be found in 1 Kings). But Rehoboam and his successors are evaluated according to a definite standard. A good king is approved if he keeps the law of God, destroys the Asherim, removes the places of idolatrous Baal worship, and refrains from making alliances with other powers, Israel included. Evil kings, and even good kings who make a false move, have to reckon sooner or later with a prophet or man of God: King Rehoboam is confronted by Shemaiah the prophet (12:5); good King Asa by Hanani the seer (16:7); good King Jehoshaphat by Jehu the son of Hanani (19:2) and Eliezer (20:37); Jehoram by a letter from Elijah (21:12); Joash by Zechariah the priest (24:20); Amaziah by a man of God (25:7) and a prophet (25:15); good King Uzziah by Azariah the priest (26:17); Manasseh by the LORD (33:10) and a number of seers (33:18); and Zedekiah by Jeremiah the prophet (36:12).

The normal pattern of the Chronicler is to summarize the reigns of the evil kings as quickly as possible, pausing only to point out their sins, and to go into some detail about the reigns of the good kings. The religious reforms of Asa, Jehoshaphat, Hezekiah, and Josiah are described quite fully, and it is in these sections that much of the material unique to Chronicles appears.

Contents:

I. The reign of Solomon (1:1-9:31): Solomon succeeds to the throne. He builds the temple: preparations for building, selection of the site, the dimensions, and the furniture. The dedication of the temple: bringing in the treasures and the ark; Solomon's address and prayer; God's confirmation of the dedication. Solomon's prosperity and fame: his house, victories, sacrifices, the visit of the Queen of Sheba; his wealth and wisdom; his death.

II. The history of Judah from Solomon's death to the captivity (10:1-36:23): The division of the kingdom—Israel and Judah. The apostasy under Rehoboam and Abijah: Rehoboam's wicked life; his defeat by Shishak of Egypt; his death and the succession of Abijah; Abijah's war with Jeroboam. Reform period under Asa and Jehoshaphat: Asa's victory over Zerah of Egypt; the attempt at reform; the war with Baasha of Israel; Asa's wickedness and death; Jehoshaphat's early reforms; his prosperity; his alliance with Ahab; the reproof of Jehu; Jehoshaphat's later reforms; his victories over his enemies; his alliance with Ahaziah. Apostasy under Jehoram (Joram), Ahaziah, and Athaliah. The reformation under Joash: the restoration of the temple; his backsliding; his defeat by the Syrians; his death. Apostasy under Amaziah, Uzziah, Jotham, and Ahaz: Amaziah's victory over the Edomites, his idolatry, war with Joash, and his death. Uzziah's godly beginning, his sin and punishment by leprosy, the co-regency of Jotham his son; Jotham's godly heart, his wars and periods of peace, his death and successor; Ahaz's idolatry, his military defeats by the Syrians, Israelites, Edomites, and Assyrians; his death and successor. The reformation under Hezekiah: his godly start; the cleansing and reconsecration of the temple; celebration of the Passover; destruction of the heathen altars; his deliverance from Sennacherib; his sickness and new lease on life; his last years and death. The period of apostasy under Manasseh and Amon: Manasseh's ungodly life, his captivity in Babylon, his death and successor; Amon's short and wicked reign. The reformation under Josiah: his good start; the recovery of the Book of the Law; the celebration of the Passover; his struggle with Neco. The final years of apostasy: Jehoahaz's vassalage to Neco; his captivity in Egypt; Jehoiakim's wickedness and captivity in Babylon; Jehoiachin's wickedness and captivity in Babylon; Zedekiah's ungodliness, his rebellion against Nebuchadnezzar; the capture and destruction of Jerusalem and the temple. The proclamation of Cyrus allowing the Jews to return to Jerusalem and to rebuild the temple.

THE SECOND BOOK OF THE
CHRONICLES

I. *The reign of Solomon (1:1—9:31)*

A. *The wisdom and wealth of Solomon*

1:1
1 Kin 2:12,
46; Gen 39:2;
1 Chr 29:25

1 Now Solomon the son of David established himself securely over his kingdom, and the LORD his God *was* with him and exalted him greatly.

1:2
1 Chr 28:1

2 And Solomon spoke to all Israel, to the commanders of thousands and of hundreds and to the judges and to every leader in all Israel, the heads of the fathers' *households*.

*1:3ff
1 Kin 3:4;
Ex 36:8

3 Then Solomon, and all the assembly with him, went to the high place which was at Gibeon; for God's tent of meeting was there, which Moses the servant of the LORD had made in the wilderness.

1:4
2 Sam 6:2,17;
1 Chr 15:1

4 However, David had brought up the ark of God from Kiriath-jearim to the place he had prepared for it; for he had pitched a tent for it in Jerusalem.

1:5
Ex 38:1,2

5 Now the bronze altar, which Bezalel the son of Uri, the son of Hur, had made, was there before the tabernacle of the LORD, and Solomon and the assembly sought it out.

1:6
1 Kin 3:4

6 And Solomon went up there before the LORD to the bronze altar which *was* at the tent of meeting, and offered a thousand burnt offerings on it.

1:7
1 Kin 3:5,6

7 In that night God appeared to Solomon and said to him, "Ask what I shall give you."

1:8
1 Chr 28:5

8 And Solomon said to God, "Thou hast dealt with my father David with great lovingkindness, and hast made me king in his place.

1:9
1 Kin 3:7,8

9 "Now, O LORD God, Thy promise to my father David is fulfilled; for Thou hast made me king over a people as numerous as the dust of the earth.

1:10
1 Kin 3:9

10 "Give me now wisdom and knowledge, that I may go out and come in before this people; for who can rule this great people of Thine?"

1:11
1 Kin 3:11-13

11 And God said to Solomon, "Because you had this in mind, and did not ask for riches, wealth, or honor, or the life of those who hate you, nor have you even asked for long life, but you have asked for yourself wisdom and knowledge, that you may rule My people, over whom I have made you king,

1:12
1 Chr 29:25;
2 Chr 9:22

12 wisdom and knowledge have been granted to you. And I will give you riches and wealth and honor, such as none of the kings who were before you has possessed, nor those who will come after you."

13 So Solomon went from the high place which was at Gibeon, from the tent of meeting, to Jerusalem, and he reigned over Israel.

*1:14ff
1 Kin 4:26;
10:26-29;
2 Chr 9:25

14 And Solomon amassed chariots and horsemen. He had 1,400 chariots, and 12,000 horsemen, and he stationed them in the chariot cities and with the king at Jerusalem.

1:15
1 Kin 10:27;
2 Chr 9:27

15 And the king made silver and gold as plentiful in Jerusalem as stones, and he made cedars as plentiful as sycamores in the lowland.

*1:16
1 Kin 10:28,
29;
2 Chr 9:28

16 And Solomon's horses were imported from Egypt and from Kue; the king's traders procured them from Kue for a price.

17 And they imported chariots from Egypt for 600 *shekels* of silver apiece, and horses for 150 apiece, and by the same means they exported them to all the kings of the Hittites and the kings of Aram.

1:3–6 Apparently the Chronicler knew of the regulation in Deut. 12:13,14 that prohibited burnt offerings except in Jerusalem. Therefore he explained why Solomon offered a thousand burnt offerings at Gibeon: the tent of meeting (tabernacle) and bronze altar were there.
1:14–17 Of Solomon's multiplying of horses, silver, and gold, see note to 1 Kin. 11:3.
1:16 *Kue.* Cilicia in Asia Minor.

B. *The building of the temple*

1. *The preparations for building*

2 Now Solomon decided to build a house for the name of the LORD, and a royal palace for himself.

2 So Solomon assigned 70,000 men to carry loads, and 80,000 men to quarry *stone* in the mountains, and 3,600 to supervise them.

3 Then Solomon sent *word* to Huram the king of Tyre, saying, "As you dealt with David my father, and sent him cedars to build him a house to dwell in, so do for me.

4 "Behold, I am about to build a house for the name of the LORD my God, dedicating it to Him, to burn fragrant incense before Him, and *to set out* the showbread continually, and to offer burnt offerings morning and evening, on sabbaths and on new moons and on the appointed feasts of the LORD our God, this *being required* forever in Israel.

5 "And the house which I am about to build *will be* great; for greater is our God than all the gods.

6 "But who is able to build a house for Him, for the heavens and the highest heavens cannot contain Him? So who am I, that I should build a house for Him, except to ¹burn *incense* before Him?

7 "And now send me a skilled man to work in gold, silver, brass and iron, and in purple, crimson and violet *fabrics,* and who knows how to make engravings, to *work* with the skilled men whom I have in Judah and Jerusalem, whom David my father provided.

8 "Send me also cedar, cypress and algum timber from Lebanon, for I know that your servants know how to cut timber of Lebanon; and indeed, my servants *will work* with your servants,

9 to prepare timber in abundance for me, for the house which I am about to build *will be* great and wonderful.

10 "Now behold, I will give to your servants, the woodsmen who cut the timber, 20,000 ²kors of crushed wheat, and 20,000 kors of barley, and 20,000 baths of wine, and 20,000 baths of oil."

11 Then Huram, king of Tyre, answered in a letter sent to Solomon: "Because the LORD loves His people, He has made you king over them."

12 Then Huram continued, "Blessed be the LORD, the God of Israel, who has made heaven and earth, who has given King David a wise son, endowed with discretion and understanding, who will build a house for the LORD and a royal palace for himself.

13 "And now I am sending a skilled man, endowed with understanding, Huram-abi,

14 the son of a Danite woman and a Tyrian father, who knows how to work in gold, silver, bronze, iron, stone and wood, *and* in purple, violet, linen and crimson fabrics, and *who knows how* to make all kinds of engravings and to execute any design which may be assigned to him, *to work* with your skilled men, and with those of my lord David your father.

15 "Now then, let my lord send to his servants wheat and barley, oil and wine, of which he has spoken.

16 "And we will cut whatever timber you need from Lebanon, and bring it to you on rafts by sea to Joppa, so that you may carry it up to Jerusalem."

17 And Solomon numbered all the aliens who *were* in the land of Israel, following the census which his father David had taken; and 153,600 were found.

¹Lit., *offer up in smoke* ²I.e., A kor equals approx. 10 bushels

Cross references: *2:1 1 Kin 5:5; 2:2 v. 18; 1 Kin 5:15,16; 2:3 1 Kin 5:2-11; 1 Chr 14:1; 2:4 v. 1; Ex 30:7; 25:30; Num 28:9,10; 2:5 1 Chr 16:25; Ps 135:5; 2:6 1 Kin 8:27; 2 Chr 6:18; 2:7 vv. 13,14; 1 Chr 22:15; 2:8 2 Chr 9:10,11; 2:10 1 Kin 5:11; 2:11 1 Kin 10:9; 2 Chr 9:8; 2:12 1 Kin 5:7; Ps 33:6; 102:25; *2:14 1 Kin 7:13,14; 2:15 v. 10; 2:16 1 Kin 5:8,9; 2:17 1 Chr 22:2

2:1 Israel had three major places of worship during its long history. The first was the tabernacle in the wilderness; the second was the temple built by Solomon; the third was the second temple built after the captivity. This latter temple was greatly renovated and adorned by Herod the Great over a forty-six-year period (John 2:20). David had originally hoped to build the first temple himself, but God would not allow him to do it (1 Chr. 22:8). He did, however, gather costly and choice materials from which his son would be able to construct it (1 Chr. 22:2–5,14–16; 29:2–5). It took Solomon seven years to complete the temple (1 Kin. 6:38), and he employed 30,000 Israelites in the work (1 Kin. 5:13, 14). The temple was referred to variously as *the house of the God of Jacob* (Is. 2:3), *Mount Zion* (Ps. 74:2), and *Zion* (Ps. 84:1–7). When Solomon dedicated it, fire from heaven came down on its altar and the shekinah cloud of glory filled it (1 Kin. 8:10,11; 2 Chr. 5:13; 7:2,3). The destruction of the temple by invaders was clearly predicted (Jer. 26:18; Mic. 3:12), and this prophecy was fulfilled by the Chaldeans under Nebuchadnezzar (2 Kin. 25:9,13–17; 2 Chr. 36:18, 19).

2:14 In 1 Kin. 7:14 Hiram (the Huram-abi of v. 13) is said to have been the son of a widow of the tribe of Naphtali. He was an artist and an architect.

2:18
v. 2

18   And he appointed 70,000 of them to carry loads, and 80,000 to quarry *stones* in the mountains, and 3,600 supervisors to make the people work.

2. *The construction of the temple*

a. *The site, dimensions, and materials*

3:1
1 Kin 6:1ff;
1 Chr 21:18

3 Then Solomon began to build the house of the LORD in Jerusalem on Mount Moriah, where *the* LORD had appeared to his father David, at the place that David had prepared, on the threshing floor of Ornan the Jebusite.

2   And he began to build on the second *day* in the second month of the fourth year of his reign.

3   Now these are the foundations which Solomon laid for building the house of God. The length in ³cubits, according to the old standard *was* sixty cubits, and the width twenty cubits.

4   And the porch which was in front of the house was as long as the width of the house, twenty cubits, and the height 120; and inside he overlaid it with pure gold.

3:5
1 Kin 6:17

5   And he overlaid the main room with cypress wood and overlaid it with fine gold, and ornamented it with palm trees and chains.

6   Further, he adorned the house with precious stones; and the gold was gold from Parvaim.

3:7
1 Kin 6:20-22,
29-35
3:8
1 Kin 6:16

7   He also overlaid the house with gold—the beams, the thresholds, and its walls, and its doors; and he carved cherubim on the walls.

8   Now he made the room of the holy of holies: its length, across the width of the house, *was* twenty cubits, and its width *was* twenty cubits; and he overlaid it with fine gold, *amounting* to 600 talents.

9   And the weight of the nails was fifty shekels of gold. He also overlaid the upper rooms with gold.

3:10
1 Kin 6:23-28

10   Then he made two sculptured cherubim in the room of the holy of holies and overlaid them with gold.

11   And the wingspan of the cherubim *was* twenty cubits; the wing of one, of five cubits, touched the wall of the house, and *its* other wing, of five cubits, touched the wing of the other cherub.

12   And the wing of the other cherub, of five cubits, touched the wall of the house; and *its* other wing of five cubits, was attached to the wing of the first cherub.

13   The wings of these cherubim extended twenty cubits, and they stood on their feet facing the *main* room.

3:14
Ex 26:31;
Heb 9:3
*3:15
1 Kin 7:15-20

14   And he made the veil of violet, purple, crimson and fine linen, and he worked cherubim on it.

15   He also made two pillars for the front of the house, thirty-five cubits high, and the capital on the top of each *was* five cubits.

16   And he made chains in the inner sanctuary, and placed *them* on the tops of the pillars; and he made one hundred pomegranates and placed *them* on the chains.

3:17
1 Kin 7:21

17   And he erected the pillars in front of the temple, one on the right and the other on the left, and named the one on the right Jachin and the one on the left Boaz.

b. *The furnishings of the temple*

4:1
Ex 27:1,2;
2 Kin 16:14
4:2
1 Kin 7:23

4 Then he made a bronze altar, twenty cubits in length and twenty cubits in width and ten cubits in height.

2   Also he made the cast *metal* sea, ten cubits from brim to brim, circular in form, and its height *was* five cubits and its circumference thirty cubits.

4:3
1 Kin 7:24-26

3   Now figures like oxen *were* under it *and* all around it, ten cubits, entirely encircling the sea. The oxen *were* in two rows, cast in one piece.

4   It stood on twelve oxen, three facing the north, three facing west, three facing south, and three facing east; and the sea *was set* on top of them, and all their hindquarters turned inwards.

*4:5
1 Kin 7:26

5   And it was a handbreadth thick, and its brim was made like the brim of a cup, *like* a lily blossom; it could hold 3,000 baths.

4:6
1 Kin 7:38

6   He also made ten basins in which to wash, and he set five on the right side and five on the left, to rinse things for the burnt offering; but the sea *was* for the priests to wash in.

---

³I.e., One cubit equals approx. 18 in.

3:15 *thirty-five cubits high.* See 1 Kin. 7:15.   **4:5** *3,000.* See note to 1 Kin. 7:26.

7 Then he made the ten golden lampstands in the way prescribed for them, and he set them in the temple, five on the right side and five on the left.

8 He also made ten tables and placed them in the temple, five on the right side and five on the left. And he made one hundred golden bowls.

9 Then he made the court of the priests and the great court and doors for the court, and overlaid their doors with bronze.

10 And he set the sea on the right side *of the house* toward the southeast.

11 Huram also made the pails, the shovels, and the bowls. So Huram finished doing the work which he performed for King Solomon in the house of God:

12 the two pillars, the bowls and the two capitals on top of the pillars, and the two networks to cover the two bowls of the capitals which were on top of the pillars,

13 and the four hundred pomegranates for the two networks, two rows of pomegranates for each network to cover the two bowls of the capitals which were on the pillars.

14 He also made the stands and he made the basins on the stands,

15 *and* the one sea with the twelve oxen under it.

16 And the pails, the shovels, the forks, and all its utensils, Huram-abi made of polished bronze for King Solomon for the house of the Lord.

17 On the plain of the Jordan the king cast them, in the clay ground between Succoth and Zeredah.

18 Thus Solomon made all these utensils in great quantities, for the weight of the bronze could not be found out.

19 Solomon also made all the things that *were* in the house of God: even the golden altar, the tables with the bread of the Presence on them,

20 the lampstands with their lamps of pure gold, to burn in front of the inner sanctuary in the way prescribed;

21 the flowers, the lamps, and the tongs of gold, of purest gold;

22 and the snuffers, the bowls, the spoons, and the firepans of pure gold; and the entrance of the house, its inner doors for the holy of holies, and the doors of the house, *that is*, of the nave, of gold.

5 Thus all the work that Solomon performed for the house of the Lord was finished. And Solomon brought in the things that David his father had dedicated, even the silver and the gold and all the utensils, *and* put *them* in the treasuries of the house of God.

C. The dedication of the temple

1. The bringing of the ark to the temple

2 Then Solomon assembled to Jerusalem the elders of Israel and all the heads of the tribes, the leaders of the fathers' *households* of the sons of Israel, to bring up the ark of the covenant of the Lord out of the city of David, which is Zion.

3 And all the men of Israel assembled themselves to the king at the feast, that is *in* the seventh month.

4 Then all the elders of Israel came, and the Levites took up the ark.

5 And they brought up the ark and the tent of meeting and all the holy utensils which *were* in the tent; the Levitical priests brought them up.

6 And King Solomon and all the congregation of Israel who were assembled with him before the ark were sacrificing so many sheep and oxen, that they could not be counted or numbered.

7 Then the priests brought the ark of the covenant of the Lord to its place, into the inner sanctuary of the house, to the holy of holies, under the wings of the cherubim.

8 For the cherubim spread their wings over the place of the ark, so that the cherubim made a covering over the ark and its poles.

9 And the poles were so long that the ends of the poles of the ark could be seen in front of the inner sanctuary, but they could not be seen outside; and they are there to this day.

10 There was nothing in the ark except the two tablets which Moses put *there* at

Cross-references (right margin):
- 4:7 — 1 Kin 7:49; Ex 25:31,40
- 4:8 — 1 Kin 7:48
- 4:9 — 1 Kin 6:36; 2 Kin 21:5
- 4:10 — 1 Kin 7:39
- 4:11 — 1 Kin 7:40
- 4:12 — 1 Kin 7:41
- 4:13 — 1 Kin 7:20
- 4:14 — 1 Kin 7:27
- 4:16 — 1 Kin 7:14
- 4:17 — 1 Kin 7:46
- 4:18 — 1 Kin 7:47
- 4:19 — 1 Kin 7:48-50; Ex 25:30
- 4:20 — Ex 25:31-37
- 5:1 — 1 Kin 7:51
- 5:2 — 1 Kin 8:1-9; 2 Sam 6:12
- 5:4 — v. 7
- *5:9 — 1 Kin 8:8,9
- 5:10 — Deut 10:2-5; Heb 9:4

5:9 *to this day.* The poles were not in the temple at the time of the Chronicler because they were destroyed in 586 B.C. This verse was probably taken from a source compiled by the writer of Kings; thus, *this day* refers to the time of that compilation.

Horeb, where the LORD made a covenant with the sons of Israel, when they came out of Egypt.

11 And when the priests came forth from the holy place (for all the priests who were present had sanctified themselves, without regard to divisions),

12 and all the Levitical singers, Asaph, Heman, Jeduthun, and their sons and kinsmen, clothed in fine linen, with cymbals, harps, and lyres, standing east of the altar, and with them one hundred and twenty priests blowing trumpets

13 in unison when the trumpeters and the singers were to make themselves heard with one voice to praise and to glorify the LORD, and when they lifted up their voice accompanied by trumpets and cymbals and instruments of music, and when they praised the LORD *saying*, "*He* indeed is good for His lovingkindness is everlasting," then the house, the house of the LORD, was filled with a cloud,

14 so that the priests could not stand to minister because of the cloud, for the glory of the LORD filled the house of God.

2. The address by Solomon

6 Then Solomon said,
"The LORD has said that He would dwell in the thick cloud.

2 "I have built Thee a lofty house,
And a place for Thy dwelling forever."

3 Then the king faced about and blessed all the assembly of Israel, while all the assembly of Israel was standing.

4 And he said, "Blessed be the LORD, the God of Israel, who spoke with His mouth to my father David and has fulfilled *it* with His hands, saying,

5 'Since the day that I brought My people from the land of Egypt, I did not choose a city out of all the tribes of Israel *in which* to build a house that My name might be there, nor did I choose any man for a leader over My people Israel;

6 but I have chosen Jerusalem that My name might be there, and I have chosen David to be over My people Israel.'

7 "Now it was in the heart of my father David to build a house for the name of the LORD, the God of Israel.

8 "But the LORD said to my father David, 'Because it was in your heart to build a house for My name, you did well that it was in your heart.

9 'Nevertheless you shall not build the house, but your son who shall be born to you, he shall build the house for My name.'

10 "Now the LORD has fulfilled His word which He spoke; for I have risen in the place of my father David and sit on the throne of Israel, as the LORD promised, and have built the house for the name of the LORD, the God of Israel.

11 "And there I have set the ark, in which is the covenant of the LORD, which He made with the sons of Israel."

3. Solomon's prayer of dedication

12 Then he stood before the altar of the LORD in the presence of all the assembly of Israel and spread out his hands.

13 Now Solomon had made a bronze platform, five cubits long, five cubits wide, and three cubits high, and had set it in the midst of the court; and he stood on it, knelt on his knees in the presence of all the assembly of Israel, and spread out his hands toward heaven.

14 And he said, "O LORD, the God of Israel, there is no god like Thee in heaven or on earth, keeping covenant and *showing* lovingkindness to Thy servants who walk before Thee with all their heart;

15 who has kept with Thy servant David, my father, that which Thou hast promised him; indeed, Thou hast spoken with Thy mouth, and hast fulfilled it with Thy hand, as it is this day.

16 "Now therefore, O LORD, the God of Israel, keep with Thy servant David, my father, that which Thou hast promised him, saying, 'You shall not lack a man to sit on the throne of Israel, if only your sons take heed to their way, to walk in My law as you have walked before Me.'

17 "Now therefore, O LORD, the God of Israel, let Thy word be confirmed which Thou hast spoken to Thy servant David.

18 "But will God indeed dwell with mankind on the earth? Behold, heaven and the highest heaven cannot contain Thee; how much less this house which I have built.

Marginal cross-references:

5:11 1 Chr 24:1-5
5:12 1 Chr 25:1-4; 15:24
5:13 2 Chr 7:3; 1 Chr 16:34, 42
5:14 1 Kin 8:11; 2 Chr 7:2
6:1 1 Kin 8:12-50
6:6 2 Chr 12:13; 1 Chr 28:4
6:7 1 Chr 28:2
6:11 2 Chr 5:10
6:12 1 Kin 8:22
6:13 1 Kin 8:54
6:14 Ex 15:11; Deut 7:9
6:15 1 Chr 22:9,10
6:16 2 Sam 7:12, 16; 1 Kin 2:4; 2 Chr 7:18
6:18 2 Chr 2:6

19 "Yet have regard to the prayer of Thy servant and to his supplication, O LORD my God, to listen to the cry and to the prayer which Thy servant prays before Thee;

20   that Thine eyes may be open toward this house day and night, toward the place of which Thou hast said that *Thou wouldst* put Thy name there, to listen to the prayer which Thy servant shall pray toward this place.

21 "And listen to the supplications of Thy servant and of Thy people Israel, when they pray toward this place; hear Thou from Thy dwelling place, from heaven; hear Thou and forgive. *[6:21 Mic 7:18]*

22 "If a man sins against his neighbor, and is made to take an oath, and he comes *and* takes an oath before Thine altar in this house, *[6:22 Matt 5:33]*

23   then hear Thou from heaven and act and judge Thy servants, punishing the wicked by bringing his way on his own head and justifying the righteous by giving him according to his righteousness.

24 "And if Thy people Israel are defeated before an enemy, because they have sinned against Thee, and they return *to Thee* and confess Thy name, and pray and make supplication before Thee in this house, *[6:24 2 Chr 7:14]*

25   then hear Thou from heaven and forgive the sin of Thy people Israel, and bring them back to the land which Thou hast given to them and to their fathers.

26 "When the heavens are shut up and there is no rain because they have sinned against Thee, and they pray toward this place and confess Thy name, and turn from their sin when Thou dost afflict them; *[6:26 1 Kin 17:1]*

27   then hear Thou in heaven and forgive the sin of Thy servants and Thy people Israel, indeed, teach them the good way in which they should walk. And send rain on Thy land, which Thou hast given to Thy people for an inheritance.

28 "If there is famine in the land, if there is pestilence, if there is blight or mildew, if there is locust or grasshopper, if their enemies besiege them in the land of their cities, whatever plague or whatever sickness *there is*, *[6:28 2 Chr 20:9]*

29   whatever prayer or supplication is made by any man or by all Thy people Israel, each knowing his own affliction and his own pain, and spreading his hands toward this house,

30   then hear Thou from heaven Thy dwelling place, and forgive, and render to each according to all his ways, whose heart Thou knowest for Thou alone dost know the hearts of the sons of men, *[6:30 1 Sam 16:7; 1 Chr 28:9]*

31   that they may [4]fear Thee, to walk in Thy ways as long as they live in the land which Thou hast given to our fathers.

32 "Also concerning the foreigner who is not from Thy people Israel, when he comes from a far country for Thy great name's sake and Thy mighty hand and Thine outstretched arm, when they come and pray toward this house, *[6:32 Josh 12:20; Acts 8:27]*

33   then hear Thou from heaven, from Thy dwelling place, and do according to all for which the foreigner calls to Thee, in order that all the peoples of the earth may know Thy name, and [4]fear Thee, as *do* Thy people Israel, and that they may know that this house which I have built is called by Thy name. *[6:33 2 Chr 7:14]*

34 "When Thy people go out to battle against their enemies, by whatever way Thou shalt send them, and they pray to Thee toward this city which Thou hast chosen, and the house which I have built for Thy name,

35   then hear Thou from heaven their prayer and their supplication, and maintain their cause.

36 "When they sin against Thee (for there is no man who does not sin) and Thou art angry with them and dost deliver them to an enemy, so that they take them away captive to a land far off or near, *[6:36 Job 15:14-16; James 3:2; 1 John 1:8-10]*

37   if they take thought in the land where they are taken captive, and repent and make supplication to Thee in the land of their captivity, saying, 'We have sinned, we have committed iniquity, and have acted wickedly'; *[6:37 2 Chr 7:14]*

38   if they return to Thee with all their heart and with all their soul in the land of their captivity, where they have been taken captive, and pray toward their land which Thou hast given to their fathers, and the city which Thou hast chosen, and toward the house which I have built for Thy name,

39   then hear from heaven, from Thy dwelling place, their prayer and supplications, and maintain their cause, and forgive Thy people who have sinned against Thee.

[4]Or, *reverence*

6:40
2 Chr 7:15;
Ps 17:1
6:41
Ps 132:8-10;
1 Chr 28:2

40 "Now, O my God, I pray Thee, let Thine eyes be open, and Thine ears attentive to the prayer *offered* in this place.

41 "Now therefore arise, O LORD God, to Thy resting place, Thou and the ark of Thy might; let Thy priests, O LORD God, be clothed with salvation, and let Thy godly ones rejoice in what is good.

42 "O LORD God, do not turn away the face of Thine anointed; remember *Thy* lovingkindness to Thy servant David."

4. *God's answer to Solomon's prayer*

a. *Fire from heaven*

*7:1
1 Kin 8:54;
18:24,38;
2 Chr 5:13,14

7 Now when Solomon had finished praying, fire came down from heaven and consumed the burnt offering and the sacrifices; and the glory of the LORD filled the house.

7:2
Deut 12:5,11

2 And the priests could not enter into the house of the LORD, because the glory of the LORD filled the LORD's house.

7:3
2 Chr 5:13;
Ps 136:1;
1 Chr 16:41

3 And all the sons of Israel, seeing the fire come down and the glory of the LORD upon the house, bowed down on the pavement with their faces to the ground, and they worshiped and gave praise to the LORD, *saying,* "Truly He is good, truly His lovingkindness is everlasting."

7:4
1 Kin 8:62,63

4 Then the king and all the people offered sacrifice before the LORD.

5 And King Solomon offered a sacrifice of 22,000 oxen, and 120,000 sheep. Thus the king and all the people dedicated the house of God.

7:6
1 Chr 15:16-21;
2 Chr 5:12

6 And the priests stood at their posts and the Levites, with the instruments of music to the LORD, which King David had made for giving praise to the LORD—"for His lovingkindness is everlasting"—whenever he gave praise by their means, while the priests on the other side blew trumpets; and all Israel was standing.

7:7
1 Kin 8:64-66

7 Then Solomon consecrated the middle of the court that *was* before the house of the LORD, for there he offered the burnt offerings and the fat of the peace offerings, because the bronze altar which Solomon had made was not able to contain the burnt offering, the grain offering, and the fat.

7:8
1 Kin 8:65

8 So Solomon observed the feast at that time for seven days, and all Israel with him, a very great assembly, *who came* from the entrance of Hamath to the brook of Egypt.

7:9
Lev 23:36

9 And on the eighth day they held a solemn assembly, for the dedication of the altar they observed seven days, and the feast seven days.

7:10
1 Kin 8:66

10 Then on the twenty-third day of the seventh month he sent the people to their tents, rejoicing and happy of heart because of the goodness that the LORD had shown to David and to Solomon and to His people Israel.

b. *God's appearance and promise*

7:11
1 Kin 9:1-9

11 Thus Solomon finished the house of the LORD and the king's palace, and successfully completed all that he had planned on doing in the house of the LORD and in his palace.

12 Then the LORD appeared to Solomon at night and said to him, "I have heard your prayer, and have chosen this place for Myself as a house of sacrifice.

7:13
2 Chr 6:26-28

13 "If I shut up the heavens so that there is no rain, or if I command the locust to devour the land, or if I send pestilence among My people,

7:14
2 Chr 6:27,
30,37-39

14 and My people who are called by My name humble themselves and pray, and seek My face and turn from their wicked ways, then I will hear from heaven, will forgive their sin, and will heal their land.

7:15
2 Chr 6:40

15 "Now My eyes shall be open and My ears attentive to the prayer *offered* in this place.

7:16
1 Kin 9:3;
2 Chr 6:6;
v. 12

16 "For now I have chosen and consecrated this house that My name may be there forever, and My eyes and My heart will be there perpetually.

7:17
1 Kin 9:4ff

17 "And as for you, if you walk before Me as your father David walked even to do according to all that I have commanded you and will keep My statutes and My ordinances,

7:18
2 Chr 6:16

18 then I will establish your royal throne as I covenanted with your father David, saying, 'You shall not lack a man *to be* ruler in Israel.'

7:1 The *glory* did not fill Ezra's temple.   7:5 *sacrifice,* see note to 1 Kin. 8:63.

c. God's warning against disobedience

19 "But if you turn away and forsake My statutes and My commandments which I have set before you and shall go and serve other gods and worship them,

20   then I will uproot you from My land which I have given you, and this house which I have consecrated for My name I will cast out of My sight, and I will make it a proverb and a byword among all peoples.

21 "As for this house, which was exalted, everyone who passes by it will be astonished and say, 'Why has the LORD done thus to this land and to this house?'

22 "And they will say, 'Because they forsook the LORD, the God of their fathers, who brought them from the land of Egypt, and they adopted other gods and worshiped them and served them, therefore He has brought all this adversity on them.'"

D. Solomon's prosperity and fame

1. His buildings, cities, and victories

8 Now it came about at the end of the twenty years in which Solomon had built the house of the LORD and his own house

2   that he built the cities which Huram had given to him, and settled the sons of Israel there.

3   Then Solomon went to Hamath-zobah and captured it.

4   And he built Tadmor in the wilderness and all the storage cities which he had built in Hamath.

5   He also built upper Beth-horon and lower Beth-horon, fortified cities *with* walls, gates, and bars;

6   and Baalath and all the storage cities that Solomon had, and all the cities for his chariots and cities for his horsemen, and all that it pleased Solomon to build in Jerusalem, in Lebanon, and in all the land under his rule.

7   All of the people who were left of the Hittites, the Amorites, the Perizzites, the Hivites, and the Jebusites, who were not of Israel,

8   namely, from their descendants who were left after them in the land whom the sons of Israel had not destroyed, them Solomon raised as forced laborers to this day.

9   But Solomon did not make slaves for his work from the sons of Israel; they were men of war, his chief captains, and commanders of his chariots and his horsemen.

10   And these were the chief officers of King Solomon, two hundred and fifty who ruled over the people.

2. The house of his Egyptian wife

11   Then Solomon brought Pharaoh's daughter up from the city of David to the house which he had built for her; for he said, "My wife shall not dwell in the house of David king of Israel, because the places are holy where the ark of the LORD has entered."

3. The sacrifices

12   Then Solomon offered burnt offerings to the LORD on the altar of the LORD which he had built before the porch;

13   and *did so* according to the daily rule, offering *them* up according to the commandment of Moses, for the sabbaths, the new moons, and the three annual feasts—the Feast of Unleavened Bread, the Feast of Weeks, and the Feast of Booths.

14   Now according to the ordinance of his father David, he appointed the divisions of the priests for their service, and the Levites for their duties of praise and ministering before the priests according to the daily rule, and the gatekeepers by their divisions at every gate; for David the man of God had so commanded.

15   And they did not depart from the commandment of the king to the priests and Levites in any manner or concerning the storehouses.

16   Thus all the work of Solomon was carried out from the day of the foundation

Cross-references (right margin)

7:19
Lev 26:14,33;
Deut 28:15
7:20
Deut 29:28

7:21
Deut 29:24

8:1
1 Kin 9:1-28

8:5
1 Chr 7:24;
2 Chr 14:7

8:8
1 Kin 4:6;
9:21

8:11
1 Kin 3:1; 7:8

8:12
2 Chr 4:1

8:13
Ex 29:38;
Num 28:3;
Ex 23:14-17

8:14
1 Chr 24:1;
25:1; 26:1;
Neh 12:24,36

8:2 See note to 1 Kin. 9:11, where Solomon gives twenty cities to Hiram.
8:4 *Tadmor*, another name for the oasis Palmyra in the Syrian desert, would hardly have been under the jurisdiction of Solomon. The correct name was Tamar (as in 1 Kin. 9:18), a caravan station in the wilderness southwest of the Dead Sea.

of the house of the LORD, and until it was finished. So the house of the LORD was completed.

*8:17
1 Kin 9:26

17   Then Solomon went to Ezion-geber and to Eloth on the seashore in the land of Edom.

8:18
1 Kin 9:27;
2 Chr 9:10,13

18   And Huram by his servants sent him ships and servants who knew the sea; and they went with Solomon's servants to Ophir, and took from there four hundred and fifty talents of gold, and brought them to King Solomon.

4. *The visit of the Queen of Sheba*

*9:1
1 Kin 10:1-13;
Matt 12:42;
Luke 11:31

9 Now when the queen of Sheba heard of the fame of Solomon, she came to Jerusalem to test Solomon with difficult questions. She had a very large retinue, with camels carrying spices, and a large amount of gold and precious stones; and when she came to Solomon, she spoke with him about all that was on her heart.

2   And Solomon answered all her questions; nothing was hidden from Solomon which he did not explain to her.

9:3
1 Kin 5:12

3   And when the queen of Sheba had seen the wisdom of Solomon, the house which he had built,

4   the food at his table, the seating of his servants, the attendance of his ministers and their attire, his cupbearers and their attire, and his stairway by which he went up to the house of the LORD, she was breathless.

9:5
1 Kin 10:6

5   Then she said to the king, "It was a true report which I heard in my own land about your words and your wisdom.

6   "Nevertheless I did not believe their reports until I came and my eyes had seen it. And behold, the half of the greatness of your wisdom was not told me. You surpass the report that I heard.

7   "How blessed are your men, how blessed are these your servants who stand before you continually and hear your wisdom.

9:8
1 Chr 28:5;
29:23;
2 Chr 2:11

8   "Blessed be the LORD your God who delighted in you, setting you on His throne as king for the LORD your God; because your God loved Israel establishing them forever, therefore He made you king over them, to do justice and righteousness."

9:9
1 Kin 10:10

9   Then she gave the king one hundred and twenty talents of gold, and a very great *amount of* spices and precious stones; there had never been spice like that which the queen of Sheba gave to King Solomon.

9:10
2 Chr 8:18

10   And the servants of Huram and the servants of Solomon who brought gold from Ophir, also brought algum trees and precious stones.

11   And from the algum the king made steps for the house of the LORD and for the king's palace, and lyres and harps for the singers; and none like that was seen before in the land of Judah.

12   And King Solomon gave to the queen of Sheba all her desire which she requested besides *a return for* what she had brought to the king. Then she turned and went to her own land with her servants.

5. *The wealth and wisdom of Solomon*

9:13
1 Kin 10:14-28

13   Now the weight of gold which came to Solomon in one year was 666 talents of gold,

14   besides that which the traders and merchants brought; and all the kings of Arabia and the governors of the country brought gold and silver to Solomon.

15   And King Solomon made 200 large shields of beaten gold, using 600 *shekels of* beaten gold on each large shield.

16   And *he* made 300 shields of beaten gold, using three hundred shekels of gold on each shield, and the king put them in the house of the forest of Lebanon.

17   Moreover, the king made a great throne of ivory and overlaid it with pure gold.

9:18
1 Kin 10:18

18   And *there were* six steps to the throne and a footstool in gold attached to the throne, and arms on each side of the seat, and two lions standing beside the arms.

9:19
1 Kin 10:20

19   And twelve lions were standing there on the six steps on the one side and on the other; nothing like *it* was made for any *other* kingdom.

20   And all King Solomon's drinking vessels *were* of gold, and all the vessels of

---

8:17 *Ezion-geber*, see note to 1 Kin. 9:26 for information.

9:1 *Sheba*, the land of the Sabaeans. See note to 1 Kin. 10:1.

the house of the forest of Lebanon *were* of pure gold; silver was not considered valuable in the days of Solomon.

21   For the king had ships which went to Tarshish with the servants of Huram; once every three years the ships of Tarshish came bringing gold and silver, ivory and apes and peacocks.

22   So King Solomon became greater than all the kings of the earth in riches and wisdom.

23   And all the kings of the earth were seeking the presence of Solomon, to hear his wisdom which God had put in his heart.

24   And they brought every man his gift, articles of silver and gold, garments, weapons, spices, horses, and mules, so much year by year.

25   Now Solomon had 4,000 stalls for horses and chariots and 12,000 horsemen, and he stationed them in the chariot cities and with the king in Jerusalem.

26   And he was the ruler over all the kings from the Euphrates River even to the land of the Philistines, and as far as the border of Egypt.

27   And the king made silver *as common* as stones in Jerusalem, and he made cedars as plentiful as sycamore trees that are in the lowland.

28   And they were bringing horses for Solomon from Egypt and from all countries.

6. *Solomon's death and the succession*

29   Now the rest of the acts of Solomon, from first to last, are they not written in the records of Nathan the prophet, and in the prophecy of Ahijah the Shilonite, and in the visions of Iddo the seer concerning Jeroboam the son of Nebat?

30   And Solomon reigned forty years in Jerusalem over all Israel.

31   And Solomon slept with his fathers and was buried in the city of his father David; and his son Rehoboam reigned in his place.

II. *The history of Judah from Solomon's death to the captivity (10:1–36:23)*

A. *The division of the kingdom*

1. *Rehoboam's ill-chosen words to the ten tribes*

10   Then Rehoboam went to Shechem, for all Israel had come to Shechem to make him king.

2   And it came about when Jeroboam the son of Nebat heard *of it* (for he was in Egypt where he had fled from the presence of King Solomon), that Jeroboam returned from Egypt.

3   So they sent and summoned him. When Jeroboam and all Israel came, they spoke to Rehoboam, saying,

4   "Your father made our yoke hard; now therefore lighten the hard service of your father and his heavy yoke which he put on us, and we will serve you."

5   And he said to them, "Return to me again in three days." So the people departed.

6   Then King Rehoboam consulted with the elders who had served his father Solomon while he was still alive, saying, "How do you counsel *me* to answer this people?"

7   And they spoke to him, saying, "If you will be kind to this people and please them and speak good words to them, then they will be your servants forever."

8   But he forsook the counsel of the elders which they had given him, and consulted with the young men who grew up with him and served him.

9   So he said to them, "What counsel do you give that we may answer this people, who have spoken to me, saying, 'Lighten the yoke which your father put on us'?"

10   And the young men who grew up with him spoke to him, saying, "Thus you shall say to the people who spoke to you, saying, 'Your father made our yoke heavy, but you make it lighter for us.' Thus you shall say to them, 'My little finger is thicker than my father's loins!

11   'Whereas my father loaded you with a heavy yoke, I will add to your yoke;

9:21
2 Chr 20:36, 37

9:22
2 Chr 1:12;
1 Kin 3:13

*9:25
1 Kin 4:26;
10:26;
2 Chr 1:14
9:26
1 Kin 4:21;
Ps 72:8
9:27
1 Kin 10:27;
2 Chr 1:15
*9:28
1 Kin 10:28;
2 Chr 1:16

9:29
1 Kin 11:41;
1 Chr 29:29

9:30
1 Kin 11:42,
43
9:31
1 Kin 2:10

10:1
1 Kin 12:1-20

10:2
1 Kin 11:40

10:6
1 Kin 12:6

10:9
1 Kin 12:9

9:25 1 Kings 4:26 says *40,000 stalls*. There is a copyist's error in one or the other.

9:28 Chronologically, the material contained in 1 Kin. 11:1–40 fits here.

my father disciplined you with whips, but I *will discipline you* with scorpions.' "

2. *The revolt of the ten tribes*

12 So Jeroboam and all the people came to Rehoboam on the third day as the king had directed, saying, "Return to me on the third day."

13 And the king answered them harshly, and King Rehoboam forsook the counsel of the elders.

14 And he spoke to them according to the advice of the young men, saying, "My father made your yoke heavy, but I will add to it; my father disciplined you with whips, but I *will discipline you* with scorpions."

15 So the king did not listen to the people, for it was a turn *of events* from God that the LORD might establish His word, which He spoke through Ahijah the Shilonite to Jeroboam the son of Nebat.

16 And when all Israel *saw* that the king did not listen to them the people answered the king, saying,

"What portion do we have in David?
We have no inheritance in the son of Jesse.
Every man to your tents, O Israel;
Now look after your own house, David."

So all Israel departed to their tents.

17 But as for the sons of Israel who lived in the cities of Judah, Rehoboam reigned over them.

18 Then King Rehoboam sent Hadoram, who was over the forced labor, and the sons of Israel stoned him to death. And King Rehoboam made haste to mount his chariot to flee to Jerusalem.

19 So Israel has been in rebellion against the house of David to this day.

3. *The LORD forbids Judah to war against Israel*

11 Now when Rehoboam had come to Jerusalem, he assembled the house of Judah and Benjamin, 180,000 chosen men who were warriors, to fight against Israel to restore the kingdom to Rehoboam.

2 But the word of the LORD came to Shemaiah the man of God, saying,

3 "Speak to Rehoboam the son of Solomon, king of Judah, and to all Israel in Judah and Benjamin, saying,

4 'Thus says the LORD, "You shall not go up or fight against your relatives; return every man to his house, for this thing is from Me." ' " So they listened to the words of the LORD and returned from going against Jeroboam.

4. *Rehoboam erects fortresses*

5 Rehoboam lived in Jerusalem and built cities for defense in Judah.
6 Thus he built Bethlehem, Etam, Tekoa,
7 Beth-zur, Soco, Adullam,
8 Gath, Mareshah, Ziph,
9 Adoraim, Lachish, Azekah,
10 Zorah, Aijalon, and Hebron, which are fortified cities in Judah and in Benjamin.
11 He also strengthened the fortresses and put officers in them and stores of food, oil and wine.
12 And *he put* shields and spears in every city and strengthened them greatly. So he held Judah and Benjamin.

5. *The Levites remain with Judah*

13 Moreover, the priests and the Levites who were in all Israel stood with him from all their districts.
14 For the Levites left their pasture lands and their property and came to Judah and Jerusalem, for Jeroboam and his sons had excluded them from serving as priests to the LORD.

10:12 Following the death of Solomon, his kingdom was broken up into two divisions: Israel (northern kingdom) and Judah (southern kingdom). Jeroboam founded the northern kingdom. Calf worship and Baal worship characterized the religion of his people. Approximately two hundred years later the northern kingdom was destroyed by Assyria. During this period of two hundred years, there was not a single good king on the throne of Israel, although Judah was blessed by several godly rulers in the Davidic line.

15   And he set up priests of his own for the high places, for the satyrs, and for the calves which he had made.

16   And those from all the tribes of Israel who set their hearts on seeking the LORD God of Israel, followed them to Jerusalem to sacrifice to the LORD God of their fathers.

17   And they strengthened the kingdom of Judah and supported Rehoboam the son of Solomon for three years, for they walked in the way of David and Solomon for three years.

6. *The polygamy of Rehoboam*

18   Then Rehoboam took as a wife Mahalath the daughter of Jerimoth the son of David *and of* Abihail the daughter of Eliab the son of Jesse,

19   and she bore him sons: Jeush, Shemariah, and Zaham.

20   And after her he took Maacah the daughter of Absalom, and she bore him Abijah, Attai, Ziza, and Shelomith.

21   And Rehoboam loved Maacah the daughter of Absalom more than all his *other* wives and concubines. For he had taken eighteen wives and sixty concubines and fathered twenty-eight sons and sixty daughters.

22   And Rehoboam appointed Abijah the son of Maacah as head and leader among his brothers, for he *intended* to make him king.

23   And he acted wisely and distributed some of his sons through all the territories of Judah and Benjamin to all the fortified cities, and he gave them food in abundance. And he sought many wives *for them.*

7. *Shishak defeats Rehoboam*

12 It took place when the kingdom of Rehoboam was established and strong that he and all Israel with him forsook the law of the LORD.

2   And it came about in King Rehoboam's fifth year, because they had been unfaithful to the LORD, that Shishak king of Egypt came up against Jerusalem

3   with 1,200 chariots and 60,000 horsemen. And the people who came with him from Egypt were without number: the Lubim, the Sukkiim, and the Ethiopians.

4   And he captured the fortified cities of Judah and came as far as Jerusalem.

5   Then Shemaiah the prophet came to Rehoboam and the princes of Judah who had gathered at Jerusalem because of Shishak, and he said to them, "Thus says the LORD, 'You have forsaken Me, so I also have forsaken you to Shishak.'"

6   So the princes of Israel and the king humbled themselves and said, "The LORD is righteous."

7   And when the LORD saw that they humbled themselves, the word of the LORD came to Shemaiah, saying, "They have humbled themselves so I will not destroy them, but I will grant them some *measure* of deliverance, and My wrath shall not be poured out on Jerusalem by means of Shishak.

8   "But they will become his slaves so that they may learn *the difference between* My service and the service of the kingdoms of the countries."

9   So Shishak king of Egypt came up against Jerusalem, and took the treasures of the house of the LORD and the treasures of the king's palace. He took everything; he even took the golden shields which Solomon had made.

10   Then King Rehoboam made shields of bronze in their place, and committed them to the care of the commanders of the guard who guarded the door of the king's house.

11   And it happened as often as the king entered the house of the LORD, the guards came and carried them and *then* brought them back into the guards' room.

12   And when he humbled himself, the anger of the LORD turned away from him, so as not to destroy *him* completely; and also conditions were good in Judah.

8. *Summary of Rehoboam's reign*

13   So King Rehoboam strengthened himself in Jerusalem, and reigned. Now Rehoboam was forty-one years old when he began to reign, and he reigned seventeen years in Jerusalem, the city which the LORD had chosen from all the tribes of

Cross references: 11:15 1 Kin 12:28-33; 13:33; 2 Chr 13:9; 11:16 2 Chr 15:9; 11:17 2 Chr 12:1; 11:18 1 Sam 16:6; 11:21 Deut 17:17; 11:22 Deut 21:15-17; *12:1 2 Chr 11:17; 1 Kin 14:22-24; 12:2 1 Kin 14:24, 25; 11:40; 12:3 2 Chr 16:8; 12:5 2 Chr 11:2; 15:2; Deut 28:15; 12:6 Ex 9:27; Dan 9:14; 12:7 1 Kin 21:29; 12:8 Deut 28:47, 48; 12:9 1 Kin 14:25, 26; 2 Chr 9:15,16; 12:12 2 Chr 19:3; 12:13 1 Kin 14:21; 2 Chr 6:6

12:1 Rehoboam inherited the throne from his father Solomon. Due to his folly the kingdom was divided. He turned from the LORD and suffered judgment as a consequence (2 Chr. 12:2). He was followed on the throne by nineteen successors, some of whom were good and some evil. The southern kingdom lasted slightly more than three hundred years, and then was destroyed by Babylon.

Israel, to put His name there. And his mother's name was Naamah the Ammonitess.

12:14
2 Chr 19:3
12:15
1 Kin 14:29,
30;
2 Chr 9:29
12:16
1 Kin 14:31;
2 Chr 11:20

14 And he did evil because he did not set his heart to seek the LORD.

15 Now the acts of Rehoboam, from first to last, are they not written in the records of Shemaiah the prophet and of Iddo the seer, according to genealogical enrollment? And *there were* wars between Rehoboam and Jeroboam continually.

16 And Rehoboam slept with his fathers, and was buried in the city of David; and his son Abijah became king in his place.

B. *The reign of Abijah*

1. *War between Abijah and Jeroboam*

13:1
1 Kin 15:1,2
13:2
2 Chr 11:20;
1 Kin 15:7

13 In the eighteenth year of King Jeroboam, Abijah became king over Judah. 2 He reigned three years in Jerusalem; and his mother's name was Micaiah the daughter of Uriel of Gibeah. And there was war between Abijah and Jeroboam.

3 And Abijah began the battle with an army of valiant warriors, 400,000 chosen men, while Jeroboam drew up in battle formation against him with 800,000 chosen men *who were* valiant warriors.

13:4
Josh 18:22

4 Then Abijah stood on Mount Zemaraim, which is in the hill country of Ephraim, and said, "Listen to me, Jeroboam and all Israel:

13:5
2 Sam 7:12,
13,16;
Num 18:19
13:6
1 Kin 11:26

5 "Do you not know that the LORD God of Israel gave the rule over Israel forever to David and his sons by a covenant of salt?

6 "Yet Jeroboam the son of Nebat, the servant of Solomon the son of David, rose up and rebelled against his master,

7 and worthless men gathered about him, scoundrels, who proved too strong for Rehoboam, the son of Solomon, when he was young and timid and could not hold his own against them.

13:8
1 Kin 12:28;
2 Chr 11:15

8 "So now you intend to resist the kingdom of the LORD through the sons of David, being a great multitude and *having* with you the golden calves which Jeroboam made for gods for you.

13:9
2 Chr 11:14;
Ex 29:35;
Jer 2:11; 5:7

9 "Have you not driven out the priests of the LORD, the sons of Aaron and the Levites, and made for yourselves priests like the peoples of *other* lands? Whoever comes to consecrate himself with a young bull and seven rams, even he may become a priest of *what are* no gods.

10 "But as for us, the LORD is our God, and we have not forsaken Him; and the sons of Aaron are ministering to the LORD as priests, and the Levites attend to their work.

13:11
2 Chr 2:4;
Lev 24:5-9

11 "And every morning and evening they burn to the LORD burnt offerings and fragrant incense, and the showbread is *set* on the clean table, and the golden lampstand with its lamps is *ready* to light every evening; for we keep the charge of the LORD our God, but you have forsaken Him.

13:12
Num 10:8,9;
Acts 5:39

12 "Now behold, God is with us at *our* head and His priests with the signal trumpets to sound the alarm against you. O sons of Israel, do not fight against the LORD God of your fathers, for you will not succeed."

2. *Defeat of Jeroboam*

13 But Jeroboam had set an ambush to come from the rear, so that *Israel* was in front of Judah, and the ambush was behind them.

13:14
2 Chr 14:11

14 When Judah turned around, behold, they were attacked both front and rear; so they cried to the LORD, and the priests blew the trumpets.

13:15
2 Chr 14:12

15 Then the men of Judah raised a war cry, and when the men of Judah raised the war cry, then it was that God routed Jeroboam and all Israel before Abijah and Judah.

13:16
2 Chr 16:8

16 And when the sons of Israel fled before Judah, God gave them into their hand.

17 And Abijah and his people defeated them with a great slaughter, so that 500,000 chosen men of Israel fell slain.

13:18
1 Chr 5:20;
2 Chr 14:11;
Ps 22:5

18 Thus the sons of Israel were subdued at that time, and the sons of Judah conquered because they trusted in the LORD, the God of their fathers.

19 And Abijah pursued Jeroboam, and captured from him *several* cities, Bethel with its villages, Jeshanah with its villages, and Ephron with its villages.

13:20
1 Sam 25:38;
1 Kin 14:20

20 And Jeroboam did not again recover strength in the days of Abijah; and the LORD struck him and he died.

21 But Abijah became powerful, and took fourteen wives to himself; and became the father of twenty-two sons and sixteen daughters.

22 Now the rest of the acts of Abijah, and his ways and his words are written in the treatise of the prophet Iddo.

13:22
2 Chr 12:15

C. *The reign of Asa*

1. *Faithful Asa blessed of God*

14 So Abijah slept with his fathers, and they buried him in the city of David, and his son Asa became king in his place. The land was undisturbed for ten years during his days.

14:1
1 Kin 15:8

2 And Asa did good and right in the sight of the LORD his God,

3 for he removed the foreign altars and high places, tore down the *sacred* pillars, cut down the [5]Asherim,

14:3
Deut 7:5;
1 Kin 15:12-14;
Ex 34:13

4 and commanded Judah to seek the LORD God of their fathers and to observe the law and the commandment.

5 He also removed the high places and the incense altars from all the cities of Judah. And the kingdom was undisturbed under him.

14:5
2 Chr 34:4,7

6 And he built fortified cities in Judah, since the land was undisturbed, and there was no one at war with him during those years, because the LORD had given him rest.

14:6
2 Chr 15:15

7 For he said to Judah, "Let us build these cities and surround *them* with walls and towers, gates and bars. The land is still ours, because we have sought the LORD our God; we have sought Him, and He has given us rest on every side." So they built and prospered.

8 Now Asa had an army of 300,000 from Judah, bearing large shields and spears, and 280,000 from Benjamin, bearing shields and wielding bows; all of them were valiant warriors.

2. *Asa defeats Zerah of Ethiopia*

9 Now Zerah the Ethiopian came out against them with an army of a million men and 300 chariots, and he came to Mareshah.

*14:9
2 Chr 16:8;
11:8

10 So Asa went out to meet him, and they drew up in battle formation in the valley of Zephathah at Mareshah.

11 Then Asa called to the LORD his God, and said, "LORD, there is no one besides Thee to help *in the battle* between the powerful and those who have no strength; so help us, O LORD our God, for we trust in Thee, and in Thy name have come against this multitude. O LORD, Thou art our God; let not man prevail against Thee."

14:11
2 Chr 13:14,
18;
1 Sam 14:6;
17:45

12 So the LORD routed the Ethiopians before Asa and before Judah, and the Ethiopians fled.

14:12
2 Chr 13:15

13 And Asa and the people who *were* with him pursued them as far as Gerar; and so many Ethiopians fell that they could not recover, for they were shattered before the LORD, and before His army. And they carried away very much plunder.

*14:13
Gen 10:19

14 And they destroyed all the cities around Gerar, for the dread of the LORD had fallen on them; and they despoiled all the cities, for there was much plunder in them.

14:14
Gen 35:5;
2 Chr 17:10

15 They also struck down those who owned livestock, and they carried away large numbers of sheep and camels. Then they returned to Jerusalem.

3. *Asa's reform movement*

15 Now the Spirit of God came on Azariah the son of Oded,

2 and he went out to meet Asa and said to him, "Listen to me, Asa, and all Judah and Benjamin: the LORD is with you when you are with Him. And if you seek Him, He will let you find Him; but if you forsake Him, He will forsake you.

15:1
Num 24:2;
2 Chr 20:14;
24:20
15:2
James 4:8;
vv. 4,15;
2 Chr 24:20

3 "And for many days Israel *was* without the true God and without a teaching priest and without law.

*15:3
Hos 3:4;
Lev 10:11;
2 Chr 17:9

---

[5]I.e., wooden symbols of a female deity

14:9 *A million men* is a figure that is either hyperbole or a copyist's error.
14:13 *they could not recover*. The rout of the Ethiopians is pictured with this generalization.
15:3 Indicates how scarce written portions of the law were during much of Judah's history.

15:4
Deut 4:29

15:5
Judg 5:6

15:6
Matt 24:7

15:7
Josh 1:7,9

15:8
2 Chr 13:19

15:9
2 Chr 11:16

15:11
2 Chr 14:13-15

15:12
2 Chr 23:16;
34:31
15:13
Ex 22:20;
Deut 13:5,9,
15

15:15
v. 2;
2 Chr 14:7

*15:16
1 Kin 15:13-15;
Ex 34:13;
2 Chr 14:2-5

16:1
1 Kin 15:17-22

16:4
1 Kin 15:18,
20

16:7
2 Chr 19:2;
14:11; 32:7,8

4 "But in their distress they turned to the LORD God of Israel, and they sought Him, and He let them find Him.

5 "And in those times there was no peace to him who went out or to him who came in, for many disturbances afflicted all the inhabitants of the lands.

6 "And nation was crushed by nation, and city by city, for God troubled them with every kind of distress.

7 "But you, be strong and do not lose courage, for there is reward for your work."

8 Now when Asa heard these words and the prophecy which Azariah the son of Oded the prophet spoke, he took courage and removed the abominable idols from all the land of Judah and Benjamin and from the cities which he had captured in the hill country of Ephraim. He then restored the altar of the LORD which was in front of the porch of the LORD.

9 And he gathered all Judah and Benjamin and those from Ephraim, Manasseh, and Simeon who resided with them, for many defected to him from Israel when they saw that the LORD his God was with him.

10 So they assembled at Jerusalem in the third month of the fifteenth year of Asa's reign.

11 And they sacrificed to the LORD that day 700 oxen and 7,000 sheep from the spoil they had brought.

12 And they entered into the covenant to seek the LORD God of their fathers with all their heart and soul;

13 and whoever would not seek the LORD God of Israel should be put to death, whether small or great, man or woman.

14 Moreover, they made an oath to the LORD with a loud voice, with shouting, with trumpets, and with horns.

15 And all Judah rejoiced concerning the oath, for they had sworn with their whole heart and had sought Him earnestly, and He let them find Him. So the LORD gave them rest on every side.

16 And he also removed Maacah, the mother of King Asa, from the *position of* queen mother, because she had made a horrid image as an Asherah, and Asa cut down her horrid image, crushed *it* and burned *it* at the brook Kidron.

17 But the high places were not removed from Israel; nevertheless Asa's heart was blameless all his days.

18 And he brought into the house of God the dedicated things of his father and his own dedicated things: silver and gold and utensils.

19 And there was no more war until the thirty-fifth year of Asa's reign.

4. Asa's sinful alliance with Ben-hadad

16 In the thirty-sixth year of Asa's reign Baasha king of Israel came up against Judah and fortified Ramah in order to prevent *anyone* from going out or coming in to Asa king of Judah.

2 Then Asa brought out silver and gold from the treasuries of the house of the LORD and the king's house, and sent them to Ben-hadad king of Aram, who lived in Damascus, saying,

3 "*Let there be* a treaty between you and me, *as* between my father and your father. Behold, I have sent you silver and gold; go, break your treaty with Baasha king of Israel so that he will withdraw from me."

4 So Ben-hadad listened to King Asa and sent the commanders of his armies against the cities of Israel, and they conquered Ijon, Dan, Abel-maim, and all the store cities of Naphtali.

5 And it came about when Baasha heard *of it* that he ceased fortifying Ramah and stopped his work.

6 Then King Asa brought all Judah, and they carried away the stones of Ramah and its timber with which Baasha had been building, and with them he fortified Geba and Mizpah.

5. Hanani pronounces God's judgment

7 At that time Hanani the seer came to Asa king of Judah and said to him, "Because you have relied on the king of Aram and have not relied on the LORD your God, therefore the army of the king of Aram has escaped out of your hand.

8 "Were not the Ethiopians and the Lubim an immense army with very many chariots and horsemen? Yet, because you relied on the LORD, He delivered them into your hand.

9 "For the eyes of the LORD move to and fro throughout the earth that He may strongly support those whose heart is completely His. You have acted foolishly in this. Indeed, from now on you will surely have wars."

10 Then Asa was angry with the seer and put him in prison, for he was enraged at him for this. And Asa oppressed some of the people at the same time.

6. Asa's sickness and death

11 And now, the acts of Asa from first to last, behold, they are written in the Book of the Kings of Judah and Israel.

12 And in the thirty-ninth year of his reign Asa became diseased in his feet. His disease was severe, yet even in his disease he did not seek the LORD, but the physicians.

13 So Asa slept with his fathers, having died in the forty-first year of his reign.

14 And they buried him in his own tomb which he had cut out for himself in the city of David, and they laid him in the resting place which he had filled with spices of various kinds blended by the perfumers' art; and they made a very great fire for him.

D. The reign of Jehoshaphat

1. Godly Jehoshaphat

17 Jehoshaphat his son then became king in his place, and made his position over Israel firm.

2 He placed troops in all the fortified cities of Judah, and set garrisons in the land of Judah, and in the cities of Ephraim which Asa his father had captured.

3 And the LORD was with Jehoshaphat because he followed the example of his father David's earlier days and did not seek the Baals,

4 but sought the God of his father, followed His commandments, and did not act as Israel did.

5 So the LORD established the kingdom in his control, and all Judah brought tribute to Jehoshaphat, and he had great riches and honor.

6 And he took great pride in the ways of the LORD and again removed the high places and the Asherim from Judah.

2. The book of the law taught

7 Then in the third year of his reign he sent his officials, Ben-hail, Obadiah, Zechariah, Nethanel, and Micaiah, to teach in the cities of Judah;

8 and with them the Levites, Shemaiah, Nethaniah, Zebadiah, Asahel, Shemiramoth, Jehonathan, Adonijah, Tobijah, and Tobadonijah, the Levites; and with them Elishama and Jehoram, the priests.

9 And they taught in Judah, *having* the book of the law of the LORD with them; and they went throughout all the cities of Judah and taught among the people.

3. Jehoshaphat's prosperity

10 Now the dread of the LORD was on all the kingdoms of the lands which *were* around Judah, so that they did not make war against Jehoshaphat.

11 And some of the Philistines brought gifts and silver as tribute to Jehoshaphat; the Arabians also brought him flocks, 7,700 rams and 7,700 male goats.

12 So Jehoshaphat grew greater and greater, and he built fortresses and store cities in Judah.

13 And he had large supplies in the cities of Judah, and warriors, valiant men, in Jerusalem.

14 And this was their muster according to their fathers' households: of Judah,

16:8 2 Chr 14:9; 12:3
16:9 Prov 15:3; Zech 4:10; 1 Sam 13:13
16:11 1 Kin 15:23
16:12 Jer 17:5
16:13 1 Kin 15:24
16:14 Gen 50:2; John 19:39, 40; 2 Chr 21:19; Jer 34:5
17:1 1 Kin 15:24
17:2 2 Chr 15:8
17:4 1 Kin 12:28
17:5 2 Chr 18:1
17:6 2 Chr 15:17
17:7 2 Chr 15:3
17:8 2 Chr 19:8
*17:9 Deut 6:4-9
17:10 2 Chr 14:14
17:11 2 Chr 9:14; 26:8

17:9 Jehoshaphat's reform, like all other reforms, was based essentially on the rediscovery and teaching of God's law. The priests were charged with the teaching ministry, but here they are aided considerably by the princes and the Levites.

17:14-19 Besides the soldiers stationed in fortified cities, the standing army of Jehoshaphat (drawn from Judah and Benjamin) totals 1,160,000. This is exactly double the 580,000 of Asa's army (14:8)—a very substantial increase in the few years following Asa's reign.

commanders of thousands, Adnah *was* the commander, and with him 300,000 valiant warriors;

15   and next to him *was* Johanan the commander, and with him 280,000;

17:16
Judg 5:2,9;
1 Chr 29:9

16   and next to him Amasiah the son of Zichri, who volunteered for the LORD, and with him 200,000 valiant warriors;

17   and of Benjamin, Eliada a valiant warrior, and with him 200,000 armed with bow and shield;

18   and next to him Jehozabad, and with him 180,000 equipped for war.

19   These are they who served the king, apart from those whom the king put in the fortified cities through all Judah.

4. *Jehoshaphat's alliances with Ahab*

a. *Ahab's proposition*

18:1
2 Chr 17:5

18 Now Jehoshaphat had great riches and honor; and he allied himself by marriage with Ahab.

18:2
1 Kin 22:2-35

2   And some years later he went down to *visit* Ahab at Samaria. And Ahab slaughtered many sheep and oxen for him and the people who were with him, and induced him to go up against Ramoth-gilead.

3   And Ahab king of Israel said to Jehoshaphat king of Judah, "Will you go with me *against* Ramoth-gilead?" And he said to him, "I am as you are, and my people as your people, and *we will be* with you in the battle."

b. *The advice of the false prophets*

18:4
1 Sam 23:2,4;
9; 2 Sam 2:1

4   Moreover, Jehoshaphat said to the king of Israel, "Please inquire first for the word of the LORD."

5   Then the king of Israel assembled the prophets, four hundred men, and said to them, "Shall we go against Ramoth-gilead to battle, or shall I refrain?" And they said, "Go up, for God will give *it* into the hand of the king."

6   But Jehoshaphat said, "Is there not yet a prophet of the LORD here that we may inquire of him?"

18:7
1 Kin 22:8

7   And the king of Israel said to Jehoshaphat, "There is yet one man by whom we may inquire of the LORD, but I hate him, for he never prophesies good concerning me but always evil. He is Micaiah, son of Imla." But Jehoshaphat said, "Let not the king say so."

8   Then the king of Israel called an officer and said, "Bring quickly Micaiah, Imla's son."

18:9
Ruth 4:1

9   Now the king of Israel and Jehoshaphat the king of Judah were sitting each on his throne, arrayed in *their* robes, and *they* were sitting at the threshing floor at the entrance of the gate of Samaria; and all the prophets were prophesying before them.

10   And Zedekiah the son of Chenaanah made horns of iron for himself and said, "Thus says the LORD, 'With these you shall gore the Arameans, until they are consumed.' "

18:11
2 Chr 22:5

11   And all the prophets were prophesying thus, saying, "Go up to Ramoth-gilead and succeed, for the LORD will give *it* into the hand of the king."

c. *Micaiah's true prophecy*

12   Then the messenger who went to summon Micaiah spoke to him saying, "Behold, the words of the prophets are uniformly favorable to the king. So please let your word be like one of them and speak favorably."

18:13
Num 22:18-20,
35

13   But Micaiah said, "As the LORD lives, what my God says, that I will speak."

14   And when he came to the king, the king said to him, "Micaiah, shall we go to Ramoth-gilead to battle, or shall I refrain?" He said, "Go up and succeed, for they will be given into your hand."

15   Then the king said to him, "How many times must I adjure you to speak to me nothing but the truth in the name of the LORD?"

18:16
Num 27:17;
Ezek 34:5-8

16   So he said,

"I saw all Israel
Scattered on the mountains,
Like sheep which have no shepherd;
And the LORD said,
'These have no master.
Let each of them return to his house in peace.' "

17   Then the king of Israel said to Jehoshaphat, "Did I not tell you that he would not prophesy good concerning me, but evil?"

18   And Micaiah said, "Therefore, hear the word of the LORD. I saw the LORD sitting on His throne, and all the host of heaven standing on His right and on His left.

19   "And the LORD said, 'Who will entice Ahab king of Israel to go up and fall at Ramoth-gilead?' And one said this while another said that.

20   "Then a spirit came forward and stood before the LORD and said, 'I will entice him.' And the LORD said to him, 'How?'

21   "And he said, 'I will go and be a deceiving spirit in the mouth of all his prophets.' Then He said, 'You are to entice *him* and prevail also. Go and do so.'

22   "Now therefore, behold, the LORD has put a deceiving spirit in the mouth of these your prophets; for the LORD has proclaimed disaster against you."

23   Then Zedekiah the son of Chenaanah came near and struck Micaiah on the cheek and said, "How did the Spirit of the LORD pass from me to speak to you?"

24   And Micaiah said, "Behold, you shall see on that day, when you enter an inner room to hide yourself."

25   Then the king of Israel said, "Take Micaiah and return him to Amon the governor of the city, and to Joash the king's son;

26   and say, 'Thus says the king, "Put this *man* in prison, and feed him sparingly with bread and water until I return safely." ' "

27   And Micaiah said, "If you indeed return safely, the LORD has not spoken by me." And he said, "Listen, all you people."

d. *The defeat and death of Ahab*

28   So the king of Israel and Jehoshaphat king of Judah went up against Ramoth-gilead.

29   And the king of Israel said to Jehoshaphat, "I will disguise myself and go into battle, but you put on your robes." So the king of Israel disguised himself, and they went into battle.

30   Now the king of Aram had commanded the captains of his chariots, saying, "Do not fight with small or great, but with the king of Israel alone."

31   So it came about when the captains of the chariots saw Jehoshaphat, that they said, "It is the king of Israel," and they turned aside to fight against him. But Jehoshaphat cried out, and the LORD helped him, and God diverted them from him.

32   Then it happened when the captains of the chariots saw that it was not the king of Israel, that they turned back from pursuing him.

33   And a certain man drew his bow at random and struck the king of Israel in a joint of the armor. So he said to the driver of the chariot, "Turn around, and take me out of the fight; for I am severely wounded."

34   And the battle raged that day, and the king of Israel propped himself up in his chariot in front of the Arameans until the evening; and at sunset he died.

e. *Jehu reproves Jehoshaphat*

19 Then Jehoshaphat the king of Judah returned in safety to his house in Jerusalem.

2   And Jehu the son of Hanani the seer went out to meet him and said to King Jehoshaphat, "Should you help the wicked and love those who hate the LORD and so *bring* wrath on yourself from the LORD?

3   "But there is *some* good in you, for you have removed the Asheroth from the land and you have set your heart to seek God."

5. *Additional reforms by Jehoshaphat*

4   So Jehoshaphat lived in Jerusalem and went out again among the people from Beersheba to the hill country of Ephraim and brought them back to the LORD, the God of their fathers.

5   And he appointed judges in the land in all the fortified cities of Judah, city by city.

6   And he said to the judges, "Consider what you are doing, for you do not judge for man but for the LORD who is with you when you render judgment.

7   "Now then let the fear of the LORD be upon you; be very careful what you do, for the LORD our God will have no part in unrighteousness, or partiality, or the taking of a bribe."

18:20
Job 1:6

18:22
Job 12:16;
Ezek 14:9
18:23
Jer 20:2;
Mark 14:65;
Acts 23:2

18:25
v. 8

18:26
2 Chr 16:10

18:27
Mic 1:9

18:31
2 Chr 13:14,
15

18:33
1 Kin 22:34

19:2
1 Kin 16:1;
Ps 139:21;
2 Chr 32:25
19:3
2 Chr 12:12,
14; 17:6;
Ezra 7:10

19:4
2 Chr 15:8-13

19:6
Deut 1:17
19:7
Gen 18:25;
Deut 32:4;
10:17,18;
Rom 2:11;
Col 3:25

8 And in Jerusalem also Jehoshaphat appointed some of the Levites and priests, and some of the heads of the fathers' *households* of Israel, for the judgment of the LORD and to judge disputes among the inhabitants of Jerusalem.

9 Then he charged them saying, "Thus you shall do in the fear of the LORD, faithfully and wholeheartedly.

10 "And whenever any dispute comes to you from your brethren who live in their cities, between blood and blood, between law and commandment, statutes and ordinances, you shall warn them that they may not be guilty before the LORD, and wrath may *not* come on you and your brethren. Thus you shall do and you will not be guilty.

11 "And behold, Amariah the chief priest will be over you in all that pertains to the LORD; and Zebadiah the son of Ishmael, the ruler of the house of Judah, in all that pertains to the king. Also the Levites shall be officers before you. Act resolutely, and the LORD be with the upright."

6. *Jehoshaphat's victory over the Moabites, Ammonites, and Syrians*

a. *Jehoshaphat seeking the LORD*

20 Now it came about after this that the sons of Moab and the sons of Ammon, together with some of the Meunites, came to make war against Jehoshaphat.

2 Then some came and reported to Jehoshaphat, saying, "A great multitude is coming against you from beyond the sea, out of Aram and behold, they are in Hazazon-tamar (that is Engedi)."

3 And Jehoshaphat was afraid and turned his attention to seek the LORD; and proclaimed a fast throughout all Judah.

4 So Judah gathered together to seek help from the LORD; they even came from all the cities of Judah to seek the LORD.

b. *The prayer of Jehoshaphat for help*

5 Then Jehoshaphat stood in the assembly of Judah and Jerusalem, in the house of the LORD before the new court,

6 and he said, "O LORD, the God of our fathers, art Thou not God in the heavens? And art Thou not ruler over all the kingdoms of the nations? Power and might are in Thy hand so that no one can stand against Thee.

7 "Didst Thou not, O our God, drive out the inhabitants of this land before Thy people Israel, and give it to the descendants of Abraham Thy friend forever?

8 "And they lived in it, and have built Thee a sanctuary there for Thy name, saying,

9 'Should evil come upon us, the sword, *or* judgment, or pestilence, or famine, we will stand before this house and before Thee (for Thy name is in this house) and cry to Thee in our distress, and Thou wilt hear and deliver *us*.'

10 "And now behold, the sons of Ammon and Moab and Mount Seir, whom Thou didst not let Israel invade when they came out of the land of Egypt (they turned aside from them and did not destroy them),

11 behold *how* they are rewarding us, by coming to drive us out from Thy possession which Thou hast given us as an inheritance.

12 "O our God, wilt Thou not judge them? For we are powerless before this great multitude who are coming against us; nor do we know what to do, but our eyes are on Thee."

c. *The message of deliverance by Jahaziel the prophet*

13 And all Judah was standing before the LORD, with their infants, their wives, and their children.

14 Then in the midst of the assembly the Spirit of the LORD came upon Jahaziel the son of Zechariah, the son of Benaiah, the son of Jeiel, the son of Mattaniah, the Levite of the sons of Asaph;

15 and he said, "Listen, all Judah and the inhabitants of Jerusalem and King Jehoshaphat: thus says the LORD to you, 'Do not fear or be dismayed because of this great multitude, for the battle is not yours but God's.

20:6 Jehoshaphat's prayer is instructive as a model for us. He begins with adoration of God and acknowledgment of His divine power (v. 6). He draws attention to the promises God has made to His people. Then he sets forth the problem itself (v. 10), confessing that he does not know what to do and asking God specifically for divine help (v. 12). His sublime confidence that the LORD has heard his prayer and intends to deliver His people is eloquently expressed in his exhortation in v. 20. He thus encouraged the faithful to praise God as exultantly for His answer as if they had already received it (v. 21). (See note to Luke 11:1, which lists conditions for effectual prayer.)

16 'Tomorrow go down against them. Behold, they will come up by the ascent of Ziz, and you will find them at the end of the valley in front of the wilderness of Jeruel.

17 'You *need* not fight in this *battle;* station yourselves, stand and see the salvation of the LORD on your behalf, O Judah and Jerusalem.' Do not fear or be dismayed; tomorrow go out to face them, for the LORD is with you."

18 And Jehoshaphat bowed his head with *his* face to the ground, and all Judah and the inhabitants of Jerusalem fell down before the LORD, worshiping the LORD.

19 And the Levites, from the sons of the Kohathites and of the sons of the Korahites, stood up to praise the LORD God of Israel, with a very loud voice.

d. God's deliverance

20 And they rose early in the morning and went out to the wilderness of Tekoa; and when they went out, Jehoshaphat stood and said, "Listen to me, O Judah and inhabitants of Jerusalem, put your trust in the LORD your God, and you will be established. Put your trust in His prophets and succeed."

21 And when he had consulted with the people, he appointed those who sang to the LORD and those who praised *Him* in holy attire, as they went out before the army and said, "Give thanks to the LORD, for His lovingkindness is everlasting."

22 And when they began singing and praising, the LORD set ambushes against the sons of Ammon, Moab, and Mount Seir, who had come against Judah; so they were routed.

23 For the sons of Ammon and Moab rose up against the inhabitants of Mount Seir destroying *them* completely, and when they had finished with the inhabitants of Seir, they helped to destroy one another.

24 When Judah came to the lookout of the wilderness, they looked toward the multitude; and behold, they *were* corpses lying on the ground, and no one had escaped.

25 And when Jehoshaphat and his people came to take their spoil, they found much among them, *including* goods, garments, and valuable things which they took for themselves, more than they could carry. And they were three days taking the spoil because there was so much.

26 Then on the fourth day they assembled in the valley of Beracah, for there they blessed the LORD. Therefore they have named that place "The Valley of ⁶Beracah" until today.

27 And every man of Judah and Jerusalem returned with Jehoshaphat at their head, returning to Jerusalem with joy, for the LORD had made them to rejoice over their enemies.

28 And they came to Jerusalem with harps, lyres, and trumpets to the house of the LORD.

29 And the dread of God was on all the kingdoms of the lands when they heard that the LORD had fought against the enemies of Israel.

30 So the kingdom of Jehoshaphat was at peace, for his God gave him rest on all sides.

7. Summary of Jehoshaphat's reign

31 Now Jehoshaphat reigned over Judah. He *was* thirty-five years old when he became king, and he reigned in Jerusalem twenty-five years. And his mother's name *was* Azubah the daughter of Shilhi.

32 And he walked in the way of his father Asa and did not depart from it, doing right in the sight of the LORD.

33 The high places, however, were not removed; the people had not yet directed their hearts to the God of their fathers.

34 Now the rest of the acts of Jehoshaphat, first to last, behold, they are written in the annals of Jehu the son of Hanani, which is recorded in the Book of the Kings of Israel.

35 And after this Jehoshaphat king of Judah allied himself with Ahaziah king of Israel. He acted wickedly in so doing.

⁶I.e., blessing

Cross references (right margin):

20:17 Ex 14:13,14; 2 Chr 15:2
20:18 Ex 4:31; 2 Chr 7:3
20:20 Is 7:9
20:21 1 Chr 16:29, 34,41; Ps 29:2
20:22 Judg 7:22; 2 Chr 13:13
20:23 1 Sam 14:20
20:27 Neh 12:43
20:29 2 Chr 14:14; 17:10
20:30 2 Chr 14:6,7; 15:15
20:31 1 Kin 22:41-43
*20:33 2 Chr 17:6; 19:3
20:34 1 Kin 16:1,7
20:35 1 Kin 22:48, 49

20:33 Whereas 1 Kin. 22:43 notes that the people continued sacrificing and burning incense at the high places, the Chronicler tries to explain why Jehoshaphat, a king who did *right in the sight of the LORD* (v. 32), did not remove them. Jehoshaphat could not be blamed, because the hearts of the people were not yet ready.

36   So he allied himself with him to make ships to go to Tarshish, and they made the ships in Ezion-geber.

20:37
2 Chr 9:21

37   Then Eliezer the son of Dodavahu of Mareshah prophesied against Jehoshaphat saying, "Because you have allied yourself with Ahaziah, the LORD has destroyed your works." So the ships were broken and could not go to Tarshish.

E. *The reign of Jehoram (Joram)*

1. *The wickedness of Jehoram*

21:1
1 Kin 22:50

21 Then Jehoshaphat slept with his fathers and was buried with his fathers in the city of David, and Jehoram his son became king in his place.

2   And he had brothers, the sons of Jehoshaphat: Azariah, Jehiel, Zechariah, Azaryahu, Michael, and Shephatiah. All these *were* the sons of Jehoshaphat king of Israel.

21:3
2 Chr 11:5

3   And their father gave them many gifts of silver, gold and precious things, with fortified cities in Judah, but he gave the kingdom to Jehoram because he was the first-born.

4   Now when Jehoram had taken over the kingdom of his father and made himself secure, he killed all his brothers with the sword, and some of the rulers of Israel also.

21:5
2 Kin 8:17-22

5   Jehoram *was* thirty-two years old when he became king, and he reigned eight years in Jerusalem.

6   And he walked in the way of the kings of Israel, just as the house of Ahab did (for Ahab's daughter was his wife), and he did evil in the sight of the LORD.

21:7
2 Sam 7:12,
13;
1 Kin 11:36

7   Yet the LORD was not willing to destroy the house of David because of the covenant which He had made with David, and since He had promised to give a lamp to him and his sons forever.

2. *The loss of Edom and Libnah*

21:8
2 Kin 8:20-24

8   In his days Edom revolted [7]against the rule of Judah, and set up a king over themselves.

9   Then Jehoram crossed over with his commanders and all his chariots with him. And it came about that he arose by night and struck down the Edomites who were surrounding him and the commanders of the chariots.

10   So Edom revolted [7]against Judah to this day. Then Libnah revolted at the same time against his rule, because he had forsaken the LORD God of his fathers.

3. *Elijah's pronouncement of judgment*

21:11
Lev 20:5

11   Moreover, he made high places in the mountains of Judah, and caused the inhabitants of Jerusalem to play the harlot and led Judah astray.

*21:12
2 Chr 17:3,4;
14:2-5

12   Then a letter came to him from Elijah the prophet saying, "Thus says the LORD God of your father David, 'Because you have not walked in the ways of Jehoshaphat your father and the ways of Asa king of Judah,

21:13
vv. 6,11;
1 Kin 16:31-33;
v. 4

13   but have walked in the way of the kings of Israel, and have caused Judah and the inhabitants of Jerusalem to play the harlot as the house of Ahab played the harlot, and you have also killed your brothers, your own family, who were better than you,

14   behold, the LORD is going to strike your people, your sons, your wives, and all your possessions with a great calamity;

21:15
vv. 18,19

15   and you will suffer severe sickness, a disease of your bowels, until your bowels come out because of the sickness, day by day.' "

4. *The evil end of Jehoram*

21:16
2 Chr 33:11

16   Then the LORD stirred up against Jehoram the spirit of the Philistines and the Arabs who bordered the Ethiopians;

*21:17
2 Chr 25:23

17   and they came against Judah and invaded it, and carried away all the

[7]Lit., *from under the hand of*

21:6 *Ahab's daughter*, that is, Athaliah, who was like her wicked mother, Jezebel.
21:12 From the context, the *letter* came to Jehoram, the son of Jehoshaphat; but from 2 Kin. 3:11 it is clear that Elijah was dead at the time of Jehoshaphat's reign. Elijah's words were probably adapted by some other man of God.

21:17 This incident is not mentioned in Kings, although such a raid most likely occurred. Either some of the wives of Jehoram were recovered or the writer did not mean that every wife was taken captive, because Athaliah is very much alive and in charge of affairs after her husband's death.

possessions found in the king's house together with his sons and his wives, so that no son was left to him except Jehoahaz, the youngest of his sons.

18 So after all this the LORD smote him in his bowels with an incurable sickness.

19 Now it came about in the course of time, at the end of two years, that his bowels came out because of his sickness and he died in great pain. And his people made no fire for him like the fire for his fathers.

20 He was thirty-two years old when he became king, and he reigned in Jerusalem eight years; and he departed with no one's regret, and they buried him in the city of David, but not in the tombs of the kings.

F. *The reign of Ahaziah and Athaliah*

1. *The wickedness of Ahaziah*

22 Then the inhabitants of Jerusalem made Ahaziah, his youngest son, king in his place, for the band of men who came with the Arabs to the camp had slain all the older *sons*. So Ahaziah the son of Jehoram king of Judah began to reign.

2 Ahaziah *was* twenty-two years old when he became king, and he reigned one year in Jerusalem. And his mother's name was Athaliah, the granddaughter of Omri.

3 He also walked in the ways of the house of Ahab, for his mother was his counselor to do wickedly.

4 And he did evil in the sight of the LORD like the house of Ahab, for they were his counselors after the death of his father, to his destruction.

5 He also walked according to their counsel, and went with Jehoram the son of Ahab king of Israel to wage war against Hazael king of Aram at Ramoth-gilead. But the Arameans wounded Joram.

6 So he returned to be healed in Jezreel of the wounds which they had inflicted on him at Ramah, when he fought against Hazael king of Aram. And Ahaziah, the son of Jehoram king of Judah, went down to see Jehoram the son of Ahab in Jezreel, because he was sick.

2. *Jehu murders Ahaziah*

7 Now the destruction of Ahaziah was from God, in that he went to Joram. For when he came, he went out with Jehoram against Jehu the son of Nimshi, whom the LORD had anointed to cut off the house of Ahab.

8 And it came about when Jehu was executing judgment on the house of Ahab, he found the princes of Judah and the sons of Ahaziah's brothers, ministering to Ahaziah, and slew them.

9 He also sought Ahaziah, and they caught him while he was hiding in Samaria; they brought him to Jehu, put him to death, and buried him. For they said, "He is the son of Jehoshaphat, who sought the LORD with all his heart." So there was no one of the house of Ahaziah to retain the power of the kingdom.

3. *Athaliah seizes the throne*

a. *The murder of the royal princes except Joash*

10 Now when Athaliah the mother of Ahaziah saw that her son was dead, she rose and destroyed all the royal offspring of the house of Judah.

11 But Jehoshabeath the king's daughter took Joash the son of Ahaziah, and stole him from among the king's sons who were being put to death, and placed him and his nurse in the bedroom. So Jehoshabeath, the daughter of King Jehoram, the wife of Jehoiada the priest (for she was the sister of Ahaziah), hid him from Athaliah so that she would not put him to death.

12 And he was hidden with them in the house of God six years while Athaliah reigned over the land.

b. *The revolt fostered by Jehoiada*

23 Now in the seventh year Jehoiada strengthened himself, and took captains of hundreds: Azariah the son of Jeroham, Ishmael the son of Johanan, Azariah the son of Obed, Maaseiah the son of Adaiah, and Elishaphat the son of Zichri, *and they entered* into a covenant with him.

22:1 *Ahaziah*, an inverted form of the name Jehoahaz (21:17).

Cross references:
21:18 v. 15
21:19 2 Chr 16:14
21:20 Jer 22:18,28; 2 Chr 24:25; 28:27
*22:1 2 Kin 8:24-29; 2 Chr 21:16, 17
22:2 2 Chr 21:6
22:5 2 Kin 8:28ff
22:6 2 Kin 9:15
22:7 2 Chr 10:15; 2 Kin 9:6,7, 21
22:8 2 Kin 10:10-14
22:9 2 Kin 9:27, 28; 2 Chr 17:4
22:10 2 Kin 11:1-3
23:1 2 Kin 11:4-20

2   And they went throughout Judah and gathered the Levites from all the cities of Judah, and the heads of the fathers' *households* of Israel, and they came to Jerusalem.

23:3
2 Sam 7:12;
1 Kin 2:4;
2 Chr 6:16;
7:18; 21:7
23:4
1 Chr 9:25

3   Then all the assembly made a covenant with the king in the house of God. And Jehoiada said to them, "Behold, the king's son shall reign, as the LORD has spoken concerning the sons of David.

4   "This is the thing which you shall do: one third of you, of the priests and Levites who come in on the sabbath, *shall be* gatekeepers,

5   and one third *shall be* at the king's house, and a third at the Gate of the Foundation; and all the people *shall be* in the courts of the house of the LORD.

6   "But let no one enter the house of the LORD except the priests and the ministering Levites; they may enter, for they are holy. And let all the people keep the charge of the LORD.

23:7
1 Chr 23:28-32

7   "And the Levites will surround the king, each man with his weapons in his hand; and whoever enters the house, let him be killed. Thus be with the king when he comes in and when he goes out."

23:8
1 Chr 24:1

8   So the Levites and all Judah did according to all that Jehoiada the priest commanded. And each one of them took his men who were to come in on the sabbath, with those who were to go out on the sabbath, for Jehoiada the priest did not dismiss *any of* the divisions.

23:9
v. 1

9   Then Jehoiada the priest gave to the captains of hundreds the spears and the large and small shields which had been King David's, which *were* in the house of God.

10   And he stationed all the people, each man with his weapon in his hand, from the right side of the house to the left side of the house, by the altar and by the house, around the king.

23:11
Ex 25:16;
1 Sam 10:24

11   Then they brought out the king's son and put the crown on him, and *gave him* the testimony, and made him king. And Jehoiada and his sons anointed him and said, "*Long* live the king!"

23:12
2 Kin 11:13

12   When Athaliah heard the noise of the people running and praising the king, she came into the house of the LORD to the people.

13   And she looked, and behold, the king was standing by his pillar at the entrance, and the captains and the trumpeters *were* beside the king. And all the people of the land rejoiced and blew trumpets, the singers with *their* musical instruments leading the praise. Then Athaliah tore her clothes and said, "Treason! Treason!"

14   And Jehoiada the priest brought out the captains of hundreds who were appointed over the army, and said to them, "Bring her out between the ranks; and whoever follows her, put to death with the sword." For the priest said, "Let her not be put to death in the house of the LORD."

23:15
Neh 3:28;
Jer 31:40

15   So they seized her, and when she arrived at the entrance of the Horse Gate of the king's house, they put her to death there.

16   Then Jehoiada made a covenant between himself and all the people and the king, that they should be the LORD'S people.

23:17
Deut 13:9

17   And all the people went to the house of Baal, and tore it down, and they broke in pieces his altars and his images, and killed Mattan the priest of Baal before the altars.

23:18
2 Chr 5:5;
1 Chr 23:6,
30,31; 25:1,2,
6

18   Moreover, Jehoiada placed the offices of the house of the LORD under the authority of the Levitical priests, whom David had assigned over the house of the LORD, to offer the burnt offerings of the LORD, as it is written in the law of Moses—with rejoicing and singing according to the order of David.

23:19
1 Chr 9:22

19   And he stationed the gatekeepers of the house of the LORD, so that no one should enter *who was* in any way unclean.

23:20
2 Kin 11:19

20   And he took the captains of hundreds, the nobles, the rulers of the people, and all the people of the land, and brought the king down from the house of the LORD, and came through the upper gate to the king's house. And they placed the king upon the royal throne.

21   So all of the people of the land rejoiced and the city was quiet. For they had put Athaliah to death with the sword.

G. *The reign of Joash*

1. *The faithfulness of Joash*

24 Joash *was* seven years old when he became king, and he reigned forty years in Jerusalem; and his mother's name *was* Zibiah from Beersheba.

2   And Joash did what was right in the sight of the LORD all the days of Jehoiada the priest.

3   And Jehoiada took two wives for him, and he became the father of sons and daughters.

2. *The repair of the temple*

4   Now it came about after this that Joash decided to restore the house of the LORD.

5   And he gathered the priests and Levites, and said to them, "Go out to the cities of Judah, and collect money from all Israel to repair the house of your God annually, and you shall do the matter quickly." But the Levites did not act quickly.

6   So the king summoned Jehoiada the chief *priest* and said to him, "Why have you not required the Levites to bring in from Judah and from Jerusalem the levy *fixed by* Moses the servant of the LORD on the congregation of Israel for the tent of the testimony?"

7   For the sons of the wicked Athaliah had broken into the house of God and even used the holy things of the house of the LORD for the Baals.

8   So the king commanded, and they made a chest and set it outside by the gate of the house of the LORD.

9   And they made a proclamation in Judah and Jerusalem to bring to the LORD the levy *fixed by* Moses the servant of God on Israel in the wilderness.

10   And all the officers and all the people rejoiced and brought in their levies and dropped *them* into the chest until they had finished.

11   And it came about whenever the chest was brought in to the king's officer by the Levites, and when they saw that there was much money, then the king's scribe and the chief priest's officer would come, empty the chest, take it, and return it to its place. Thus they did daily and collected much money.

12   And the king and Jehoiada gave it to those who did the work of the service of the house of the LORD; and they hired masons and carpenters to restore the house of the LORD, and also workers in iron and bronze to repair the house of the LORD.

13   So the workmen labored, and the repair work progressed in their hands, and they restored the house of God according to its specifications, and strengthened it.

14   And when they had finished, they brought the rest of the money before the king and Jehoiada; and it was made into utensils for the house of the LORD, utensils for the service and the burnt offering, and pans and utensils of gold and silver. And they offered burnt offerings in the house of the LORD continually all the days of Jehoiada.

3. *The death of Jehoiada*

15   Now when Jehoiada reached a ripe old age he died; he was one hundred and thirty years old at his death.

16   And they buried him in the city of David among the kings, because he had done well in Israel and to God and His house.

4. *The apostasy of Joash and Judah*

17   But after the death of Jehoiada the officials of Judah came and bowed down to the king, and the king listened to them.

18   And they abandoned the house of the LORD, the God of their fathers, and served the [8]Asherim and the idols; so wrath came upon Judah and Jerusalem for this their guilt.

19   Yet He sent prophets to them to bring them back to the LORD; though they testified against them, they would not listen.

5. *Joash kills Zechariah the son of Jehoiada*

20   Then the Spirit of God came on Zechariah the son of Jehoiada the priest; and he stood above the people and said to them, "Thus God has said, 'Why do you

[8]I.e., wooden symbols of a female deity

24:1
2 Kin 11:21;
12:1-15
24:2
2 Chr 26:5

24:4
v. 7

24:6
Ex 30:12-16

24:7
2 Chr 21:17

24:9
v. 6

24:11
2 Kin 12:10

24:13
Neh 10:39

24:16
2 Chr 21:2,20

24:18
v. 4;
Ex 34:12-14;
1 Kin 14:23;
Josh 22:20;
2 Chr 19:2
24:19
Jer 7:25

24:20
2 Chr 20:14;
Num 14:41;
2 Chr 15:2

transgress the commandments of the LORD and do not prosper? Because you have forsaken the LORD, He has also forsaken you.' "

24:21
Neh 9:26;
Matt 23:35;
Acts 7:58,59
24:22
Gen 9:5

21   So they conspired against him and at the command of the king they stoned him to death in the court of the house of the LORD.

22   Thus Joash the king did not remember the kindness which his father Jehoiada had shown him, but he murdered his son. And as he died he said, "May the LORD see and avenge!"

6. *The defeat and death of Joash*

24:23
2 Kin 12:17

23   Now it came about at the turn of the year that the army of the Arameans came up against him; and they came to Judah and Jerusalem, destroyed all the officials of the people from among the people, and sent all their spoil to the king of Damascus.

24:24
Lev 26:25;
Deut 28:25;
2 Chr 22:8;
Is 10:5
24:25
2 Kin 12:20;
v. 21

24   Indeed the army of the Arameans came with a small number of men; yet the LORD delivered a very great army into their hands, because they had forsaken the LORD, the God of their fathers. Thus they executed judgment on Joash.

25   And when they had departed from him (for they left him very sick), his own servants conspired against him because of the blood of the son of Jehoiada the priest, and murdered him on his bed. So he died, and they buried him in the city of David, but they did not bury him in the tombs of the kings.

26   Now these are those who conspired against him: Zabad the son of Shimeath the Ammonitess, and Jehozabad the son of Shimrith the Moabitess.

24:27
2 Kin 12:18,
21

27   As to his sons and the many oracles against him and the rebuilding of the house of God, behold, they are written in the treatise of the Book of the Kings. Then Amaziah his son became king in his place.

H. *The reign of Amaziah*

1. *Amaziah's early acts*

25:1
2 Kin 14:1-6

25 Amaziah was twenty-five years old when he became king, and he reigned twenty-nine years in Jerusalem. And his mother's name was Jehoaddan of Jerusalem.

25:2
v. 14

2   And he did right in the sight of the LORD, yet not with a whole heart.

3   Now it came about as soon as the kingdom was firmly in his grasp, that he killed his servants who had slain his father the king.

25:4
Deut 24:16;
2 Kin 14:6

4   However, he did not put their children to death, but *did* as it is written in the law in the book of Moses, which the LORD commanded, saying, "Fathers shall not be put to death for sons, nor sons be put to death for fathers, but each shall be put to death for his own sin."

2. *The defeat of the Edomites in the Valley of Salt*

25:5
Num 1:3

5   Moreover, Amaziah assembled Judah and appointed them according to *their* fathers' households under commanders of thousands and commanders of hundreds throughout Judah and Benjamin; and he took a census of those from twenty years old and upward, and found them to be 300,000 choice men, *able* to go to war *and* handle spear and shield.

6   He hired also 100,000 valiant warriors out of Israel for one hundred talents of silver.

7   But a man of God came to him saying, "O king, do not let the army of Israel go with you, for the LORD is not with Israel *nor with* any of the sons of Ephraim.

25:8
2 Chr 14:11;
20:6

8   "But if you do go, do *it*, be strong for the battle; *yet* God will bring you down before the enemy, for God has power to help and to bring down."

9   And Amaziah said to the man of God, "But what *shall we* do for the hundred talents which I have given to the troops of Israel?" And the man of God answered, "The LORD has much more to give you than this."

10   Then Amaziah dismissed them, the troops which came to him from Ephraim, to go home; so their anger burned against Judah and they returned home in fierce anger.

25:11
2 Kin 14:7

11   Now Amaziah strengthened himself, and led his people forth, and went to the Valley of Salt, and struck down 10,000 of the sons of Seir.

12   The sons of Judah also captured 10,000 alive and brought them to the top of the cliff, and threw them down from the top of the cliff so that they were all dashed to pieces.

13   But the troops whom Amaziah sent back from going with him to battle, raided the cities of Judah, from Samaria to Beth-horon, and struck down 3,000 of them, and plundered much spoil.

3. *Amaziah's idolatry*

14   Now it came about after Amaziah came from slaughtering the Edomites that he brought the gods of the sons of Seir, set them up as his gods, bowed down before them, and burned incense to them.

25:14
2 Chr 28:23;
Ex 20:3,5

15   Then the anger of the LORD burned against Amaziah, and He sent him a prophet who said to him, "Why have you sought the gods of the people who have not delivered their own people from your hand?"

25:15
Ps 96:5;
vv. 11,12

16   And it came about as he was talking with him that the king said to him, "Have we appointed you a royal counselor? Stop! Why should you be struck down?" Then the prophet stopped and said, "I know that God has planned to destroy you, because you have done this, and have not listened to my counsel."

4. *Amaziah's defeat by Joash of Israel*

17   Then Amaziah king of Judah took counsel and sent to Joash the son of Jehoahaz the son of Jehu, the king of Israel, saying, "Come, let us face each other."

25:17
2 Kin 14:8-14

18   And Joash the king of Israel sent to Amaziah king of Judah, saying, "The thorn bush which was in Lebanon sent to the cedar which was in Lebanon, saying, 'Give your daughter to my son in marriage.' But there passed by a wild beast that was in Lebanon, and trampled the thorn bush.

25:18
Judg 9:8-15

19   "You said, 'Behold, you have defeated Edom.' And your heart has become proud in boasting. Now stay at home; for why should you provoke trouble that you, even you, should fall and Judah with you?"

25:19
2 Chr 26:16;
32:25

20   But Amaziah would not listen, for it was from God, that He might deliver them into the hand *of Joash* because they had sought the gods of Edom.

25:20
1 Kin 12:15;
2 Chr 22:7

21   So Joash king of Israel went up, and he and Amaziah king of Judah faced each other at Beth-shemesh, which belonged to Judah.

22   And Judah was defeated by Israel, and they fled each to his tent.

23   Then Joash king of Israel captured Amaziah king of Judah, the son of Joash the son of Jehoahaz, at Beth-shemesh, and brought him to Jerusalem, and tore down the wall of Jerusalem from the Gate of Ephraim to the Corner Gate, 400 cubits.

25:23
2 Chr 21:17;
22:1

24   And *he took* all the gold and silver, and all the utensils which were found in the house of God with Obed-edom, and the treasures of the king's house, the hostages also, and returned to Samaria.

5. *The murder of Amaziah*

25   And Amaziah, the son of Joash king of Judah, lived fifteen years after the death of Joash, son of Jehoahaz, king of Israel.

25:25
2 Kin 14:17-22

26   Now the rest of the acts of Amaziah, from first to last, behold, are they not written in the Book of the Kings of Judah and Israel?

27   And from the time that Amaziah turned away from following the LORD they conspired against him in Jerusalem, and he fled to Lachish; but they sent after him to Lachish and killed him there.

28   Then they brought him on horses and buried him with his fathers in the city of Judah.

I. *The reign of Uzziah (Azariah)*

1. *His godly start*

26   And all the people of Judah took Uzziah, who *was* sixteen years old, and made him king in the place of his father Amaziah.

*26:1
2 Kin 14:21,
22; 15:2,3

2   He built Eloth and restored it to Judah after the king slept with his fathers.

3   Uzziah was sixteen years old when he became king, and he reigned fifty-two years in Jerusalem; and his mother's name was Jechiliah of Jerusalem.

4   And he did right in the sight of the LORD according to all that his father Amaziah had done.

5   And he continued to seek God in the days of Zechariah, who had

*26:5
2 Chr 24:2;

understanding through the vision of God; and as long as he sought the LORD, God prospered him.

2. *His success*

6 Now he went out and warred against the Philistines, and broke down the wall of Gath and the wall of Jabneh and the wall of Ashdod; and he built cities in *the area of* Ashdod and among the Philistines.

7 And God helped him against the Philistines, and against the Arabians who lived in Gur-baal, and the Meunites.

8 The Ammonites also gave tribute to Uzziah, and his fame extended to the border of Egypt, for he became very strong.

9 Moreover, Uzziah built towers in Jerusalem at the Corner Gate and at the Valley Gate and at the corner buttress and fortified them.

10 And he built towers in the wilderness and hewed many cisterns, for he had much livestock, both in the lowland and in the plain. *He also had* plowmen and vinedressers in the hill country and the fertile fields, for he loved the soil.

11 Moreover, Uzziah had an army ready for battle, which entered combat by divisions, according to the number of their muster, prepared by Jeiel the scribe and Maaseiah the official, under the direction of Hananiah, one of the king's officers.

12 The total number of the heads of the households, of valiant warriors, was 2,600.

13 And under their direction was an elite army of 307,500, who could wage war with great power, to help the king against the enemy.

14 Moreover, Uzziah prepared for all the army shields, spears, helmets, body armor, bows and sling stones.

15 And in Jerusalem he made engines *of war* invented by skillful men to be on the towers and on the corners, for the purpose of shooting arrows and great stones. Hence his fame spread afar, for he was marvelously helped until he *was* strong.

3. *His sin and punishment*

16 But when he became strong, his heart was so proud that he acted corruptly, and he was unfaithful to the LORD his God, for he entered the temple of the LORD to burn incense on the altar of incense.

17 Then Azariah the priest entered after him and with him eighty priests of the LORD, valiant men.

18 And they opposed Uzziah the king and said to him, "It is not for you, Uzziah, to burn incense to the LORD, but for the priests, the sons of Aaron who are consecrated to burn incense. Get out of the sanctuary, for you have been unfaithful, and will have no honor from the LORD God."

19 But Uzziah, with a censer in his hand for burning incense, was enraged; and while he was enraged with the priests, the leprosy broke out on his forehead before the priests in the house of the LORD, beside the altar of incense.

20 And Azariah the chief priest and all the priests looked at him, and behold, he *was* leprous on his forehead; and they hurried him out of there, and he himself also hastened to get out because the LORD had smitten him.

21 And King Uzziah was a leper to the day of his death; and he lived in a separate house, being a leper, for he was cut off from the house of the LORD. And Jotham his son *was* over the king's house judging the people of the land.

4. *His death and the succession*

22 Now the rest of the acts of Uzziah, first to last, the prophet Isaiah, the son of Amoz, has written.

23 So Uzziah slept with his fathers, and they buried him with his fathers in the field of the grave which belonged to the kings, for they said, "He is a leper." And Jotham his son became king in his place.

Dan 1:17;
2:19;
2 Chr 15:2

26:6
Is 14:29

26:7
2 Chr 21:16

26:8
2 Chr 17:11

26:9
2 Chr 25:23;
Neh 3:13

26:13
2 Chr 25:5

26:16
Deut 32:15;
2 Chr 25:19;
2 Kin 16:12,
13

26:17
1 Chr 6:10

26:18
Num 16:39,
40; Ex 30:7,8

26:19
2 Kin 5:25-27

26:21
2 Kin 15:5-7;
Lev 13:46;
Num 5:2

26:22
Is 1:1

26:23
2 Kin 15:7;
Is 6:1

26:1 *Uzziah*, the Azariah of 2 Kin. 15:1.
26:5 Uzziah's experience illustrates a lesson for the believer: obedience brings blessing; pride at God-given suc-cess leads to disregard of God's will and tragic failure and loss (vv. 19–21).

J. *The reign of Jotham*

27 Jotham was twenty-five years old when he became king, and he reigned sixteen years in Jerusalem. And his mother's name was Jerushah the daughter of Zadok.

2   And he did right in the sight of the LORD, according to all that his father Uzziah had done; however he did not enter the temple of the LORD. But the people continued acting corruptly.

3   He built the upper gate of the house of the LORD, and he built extensively the wall of Ophel.

4   Moreover, he built cities in the hill country of Judah, and he built fortresses and towers on the wooded *hills*.

5   He fought also with the king of the Ammonites and prevailed over them so that the Ammonites gave him during that year one hundred talents of silver, ten thousand [9]kors of wheat and ten thousand of barley. The Ammonites also paid him this *amount* in the second and in the third year.

6   So Jotham became mighty because he ordered his ways before the LORD his God.

7   Now the rest of the acts of Jotham, even all his wars and his acts, behold, they are written in the Book of the Kings of Israel and Judah.

8   He was twenty-five years old when he became king, and he reigned sixteen years in Jerusalem.

9   And Jotham slept with his fathers, and they buried him in the city of David; and Ahaz his son became king in his place.

K. *The reign of Ahaz*

1. *His evil ways*

28 Ahaz *was* twenty years old when he became king, and he reigned sixteen years in Jerusalem; and he did not do right in the sight of the LORD as David his father *had done*.

2   But he walked in the ways of the kings of Israel; he also made molten images for the Baals.

3   Moreover, he burned incense in the valley of Ben-hinnom, and burned his sons in fire, according to the abominations of the nations whom the LORD had driven out before the sons of Israel.

4   And he sacrificed and burned incense on the high places, on the hills, and under every green tree.

2. *His defeats by Syria and Israel*

5   Wherefore, the LORD his God delivered him into the hand of the king of Aram; and they defeated him and carried away from him a great number of captives, and brought *them* to Damascus. And he was also delivered into the hand of the king of Israel, who inflicted him with heavy casualties.

6   For Pekah the son of Remaliah slew in Judah 120,000 in one day, all valiant men, because they had forsaken the LORD God of their fathers.

7   And Zichri, a mighty man of Ephraim, slew Maaseiah the king's son, and Azrikam the ruler of the house and Elkanah the second to the king.

8   And the sons of Israel carried away captive of their brethren 200,000 women, sons, and daughters; and took also a great deal of spoil from them, and they brought the spoil to Samaria.

9   But a prophet of the LORD was there, whose name *was* Oded; and he went out to meet the army which came to Samaria and said to them, "Behold, because the LORD, the God of your fathers, was angry with Judah, He has delivered them into your hand, and you have slain them in a rage *which* has even reached heaven.

10   "And now you are proposing to subjugate for yourselves the people of Judah and Jerusalem for male and female slaves. Surely, *do* you not *have* transgressions of your own against the LORD your God?

11   "Now therefore, listen to me and return the captives whom you captured from your brothers, for the burning anger of the LORD is against you."

[9]I.e., A kor equals approx. 10 bushels

27:3   *Ophel*, eastern promontory on which Jerusalem of   also refer to Ophel.
Old Testament times was situated; 33:14 and Nehemiah

Cross references (right margin):

27:1 — 2 Kin 15:33-35
27:2 — 2 Chr 26:16
*27:3 — 2 Chr 33:14; Neh 3:26
27:6 — 2 Chr 26:5
27:7 — 2 Kin 15:36
27:8 — v. 1
28:1 — 2 Kin 16:2-4
28:2 — 2 Chr 22:3; Ex 34:17
28:3 — 2 Kin 23:10; Lev 18:21; 2 Kin 16:3; 2 Chr 33:6
28:4 — v. 25
28:5 — Is 7:1; 2 Kin 16:5,6
28:6 — 2 Kin 15:27
28:8 — 2 Chr 11:4
28:9 — 2 Chr 25:15; Is 10:5; 47:6; Ezra 9:6; Rev 18:5
28:10 — Lev 25:39,42, 43,46
28:11 — v. 8

12   Then some of the heads of the sons of Ephraim—Azariah the son of Johanan, Berechiah the son of Meshillemoth, Jehizkiah the son of Shallum, and Amasa the son of Hadlai—arose against those who were coming from the battle,

13   and said to them, "You must not bring the captives in here, for you are proposing *to bring* upon us guilt against the LORD adding to our sins and our guilt; for our guilt is great so that *His* burning anger is against Israel."

14   So the armed men left the captives and the spoil before the officers and all the assembly.

28:15
v. 12;
2 Kin 6:22;
Prov 25:21,
22;
Deut 34:3;
Judg 1:16

15   Then the men who were designated by name arose, took the captives, and they clothed all their naked ones from the spoil; and they gave them clothes and sandals, fed them and gave them drink, anointed them *with oil*, led all their feeble ones on donkeys, and brought them to Jericho, the city of palm trees, to their brothers; then they returned to Samaria.

3. *His defeats by the Edomites and Assyrians, and his death*

28:16
2 Kin 16:7

16   At that time King Ahaz sent to the [10]kings of Assyria for help.

17   For again the Edomites had come and attacked Judah, and carried away captives.

28:18
Ezek 16:57

18   The Philistines also had invaded the cities of the lowland and of the Negev of Judah, and had taken Beth-shemesh, Aijalon, Gederoth, and Soco with its villages, Timnah with its villages, and Gimzo with its villages, and they settled there.

28:19
2 Chr 21:2

19   For the LORD humbled Judah because of Ahaz king of Israel, for he had brought about a lack of restraint in Judah and was very unfaithful to the LORD.

28:20
1 Chr 5:26;
2 Kin 16:8,9

20   So Tilgath-pilneser king of Assyria came against him and afflicted him instead of strengthening him.

21   Although Ahaz took a portion out of the house of the LORD and out of the palace of the king and of the princes, and gave *it* to the king of Assyria, it did not help him.

22   Now in the time of his distress this same King Ahaz became yet more unfaithful to the LORD.

28:23
2 Chr 25:14;
Jer 44:17,18

23   For he sacrificed to the gods of Damascus which had defeated him, and said, "Because the gods of the kings of Aram helped them, I will sacrifice to them that they may help me." But they became the downfall of him and all Israel.

28:24
2 Kin 16:17;
2 Chr 29:7;
30:14; 33:3-5

24   Moreover, when Ahaz gathered together the utensils of the house of God, he cut the utensils of the house of God in pieces; and he closed the doors of the house of the LORD, and made altars for himself in every corner of Jerusalem.

25   And in every city of Judah he made high places to burn incense to other gods, and provoked the LORD, the God of his fathers, to anger.

28:26
2 Kin 16:19,
20
28:27
2 Chr 24:25

26   Now the rest of his acts and all his ways, from first to last, behold, they are written in the Book of the Kings of Judah and Israel.

27   So Ahaz slept with his fathers, and they buried him in the city, in Jerusalem, for they did not bring him into the tombs of the kings of Israel; and Hezekiah his son reigned in his place.

L. *The reign of Hezekiah*

1. *The cleansing of the temple*

a. *The announcement of his intentions*

29:1
2 Kin 18:1-3

29   Hezekiah became king *when he was* twenty-five years old; and he reigned twenty-nine years in Jerusalem. And his mother's name *was* Abijah, the daughter of Zechariah.

29:2
2 Chr 28:1

2   And he did right in the sight of the LORD, according to all that his father David had done.

29:3
v. 7;
2 Chr 28:24

3   In the first year of his reign, in the first month, he opened the doors of the house of the LORD and repaired them.

4   And he brought in the priests and the Levites, and gathered them into the square on the east.

29:5
vv. 15,34;
2 Chr 35:6

5   Then he said to them, "Listen to me, O Levites. Consecrate yourselves now, and consecrate the house of the LORD, the God of your fathers, and carry the uncleanness out from the holy place.

[10]Ancient versions read *king*

6 "For our fathers have been unfaithful and have done evil in the sight of the LORD our God, and have forsaken Him and turned their faces away from the dwelling place of the LORD, and have turned *their* backs.

7 "They have also shut the doors of the porch and put out the lamps, and have not burned incense or offered burnt offerings in the holy place to the God of Israel.

8 "Therefore the wrath of the LORD was against Judah and Jerusalem, and He has made them an object of terror, of horror, and of hissing, as you see with your own eyes.

9 "For behold, our fathers have fallen by the sword, and our sons and our daughters and our wives are in captivity for this.

10 "Now it is in my heart to make a covenant with the LORD God of Israel, that His burning anger may turn away from us.

11 "My sons, do not be negligent now, for the LORD has chosen you to stand before Him, to minister to Him, and to be His ministers and burn incense."

b. The sanctifying of the Levites and the cleansing of the temple

12 Then the Levites arose: Mahath, the son of Amasai and Joel the son of Azariah, from the sons of the Kohathites; and from the sons of Merari, Kish the son of Abdi and Azariah the son of Jehallelel; and from the Gershonites, Joah the son of Zimmah and Eden the son of Joah;

13 and from the sons of Elizaphan, Shimri and Jeiel; and from the sons of Asaph, Zechariah and Mattaniah;

14 and from the sons of Heman, Jehiel and Shimei; and from the sons of Jeduthun, Shemaiah and Uzziel.

15 And they assembled their brothers, consecrated themselves, and went in to cleanse the house of the LORD, according to the commandment of the king by the words of the LORD.

16 So the priests went in to the inner part of the house of the LORD to cleanse *it*, and every unclean thing which they found in the temple of the LORD they brought out to the court of the house of the LORD. Then the Levites received *it* to carry out to the Kidron valley.

17 Now they began the consecration on the first *day* of the first month, and on the eighth day of the month they entered the porch of the LORD. Then they consecrated the house of the LORD in eight days, and finished on the sixteenth day of the first month.

18 Then they went in to King Hezekiah and said, "We have cleansed the whole house of the LORD, the altar of burnt offering with all of its utensils, and the table of showbread with all of its utensils.

19 "Moreover, all the utensils which King Ahaz had discarded during his reign in his unfaithfulness, we have prepared and consecrated; and behold, they are before the altar of the LORD."

c. The consecration of the temple

20 Then King Hezekiah arose early and assembled the princes of the city and went up to the house of the LORD.

21 And they brought seven bulls, seven rams, seven lambs, and seven male goats for a sin offering for the kingdom, the sanctuary, and Judah. And he ordered the priests, the sons of Aaron, to offer *them* on the altar of the LORD.

22 So they slaughtered the bulls, and the priests took the blood and sprinkled it on the altar. They also slaughtered the rams and sprinkled the blood on the altar; they slaughtered the lambs also and sprinkled the blood on the altar.

23 Then they brought the male goats of the sin offering before the king and the assembly, and they laid their hands on them.

24 And the priests slaughtered them and purged the altar with their blood to atone for all Israel, for the king ordered the burnt offering and the sin offering for all Israel.

25 He then stationed the Levites in the house of the LORD with cymbals, with harps, and with lyres, according to the command of David and of Gad the king's seer, and of Nathan the prophet; for the command was from the LORD through His prophets.

26 And the Levites stood with the *musical* instruments of David, and the priests with the trumpets.

27 Then Hezekiah gave the order to offer the burnt offering on the altar. When

the burnt offering began, the song to the LORD also began with the trumpets, *accompanied* by the instruments of David, king of Israel.

28   While the whole assembly worshiped, the singers also sang and the trumpets sounded; all this *continued* until the burnt offering was finished.

29   Now at the completion of the burnt offerings, the king and all who were present with him bowed down and worshiped.

30   Moreover, King Hezekiah and the officials ordered the Levites to sing praises to the LORD with the words of David and Asaph the seer. So they sang praises with joy, and bowed down and worshiped.

d. The sacrifices at the temple

31   Then Hezekiah answered and said, "Now *that* you have consecrated yourselves to the LORD, come near and bring sacrifices and thank offerings to the house of the LORD." And the assembly brought sacrifices and thank offerings, and all those who were willing *brought* burnt offerings.

32   And the number of the burnt offerings which the assembly brought was 70 bulls, 100 rams, and 200 lambs; all these were for a burnt offering to the LORD.

33   And the consecrated things were 600 bulls and 3,000 sheep.

34   But the priests were too few, so that they were unable to skin all the burnt offerings; therefore their brothers the Levites helped them until the work was completed, and until the *other* priests had consecrated themselves. For the Levites were more conscientious to consecrate themselves than the priests.

35   And there *were* also many burnt offerings with the fat of the peace offerings and with the libations for the burnt offerings. Thus the service of the house of the LORD was established *again*.

36   Then Hezekiah and all the people rejoiced over what God had prepared for the people, because the thing came about suddenly.

2. The celebration of the Passover

a. The invitation to all Israel and Judah

30 Now Hezekiah sent to all Israel and Judah and wrote letters also to Ephraim and Manasseh, that they should come to the house of the LORD at Jerusalem to celebrate the Passover to the LORD God of Israel.

2   For the king and his princes and all the assembly in Jerusalem had decided to celebrate the Passover in the second month,

3   since they could not celebrate it at that time, because the priests had not consecrated themselves in sufficient numbers, nor had the people been gathered to Jerusalem.

4   Thus the thing was right in the sight of the king and all the assembly.

5   So they established a decree to circulate a proclamation throughout all Israel from Beersheba even to Dan, that they should come to celebrate the Passover to the LORD God of Israel at Jerusalem. For they had not celebrated *it* in great numbers as it was prescribed.

6   And the couriers went throughout all Israel and Judah with the letters from the hand of the king and his princes, even according to the command of the king, saying, "O sons of Israel, return to the LORD God of Abraham, Isaac, and Israel, that He may return to those of you who escaped *and* are left from the hand of the kings of Assyria.

7   "And do not be like your fathers and your brothers, who were unfaithful to the LORD God of their fathers, so that He made them a horror, as you see.

8   "Now do not stiffen your neck like your fathers, but yield to the LORD and enter His sanctuary which He has consecrated forever, and serve the LORD your God, that His burning anger may turn away from you.

9   "For if you return to the LORD, your brothers and your sons *will find* compassion before those who led them captive, and will return to this land. For the LORD your God is gracious and compassionate, and will not turn *His* face away from you if you return to Him."

10   So the couriers passed from city to city through the country of Ephraim and

Cross-references (margin):

29:29
2 Chr 20:18

29:31
2 Chr 13:9;
Ex 35:5,22

29:34
2 Chr 35:11;
30:3

29:35
v. 32;
Lev 3:16;
Num 15:5-10

30:2
vv. 13,15;
Num 9:10,11
30:3
Ex 12:6,18;
2 Chr 29:34

*30:5
Judg 20:1

30:6
Esth 8:14;
Job 9:25;
Jer 51:31;
2 Chr 20:8

30:7
Ezek 20:18;
2 Chr 29:8
30:8
Ex 32:9;
2 Chr 29:10

30:9
Deut 30:2;
Ex 34:6,7;
Mic 7:18;
Is 55:7
30:10
2 Chr 36:16

30:5 *from Beersheba even to Dan.* The fact that Hezekiah's invitation covered all of Palestine and that his couriers could go from city to city throughout Ephraim, Manasseh, and Zebulun (30:10) is an indication that the northern kingdom had fallen. Jehoshaphat's reform extended only from Beersheba to the hill country of Ephraim (19:4), because the officials of the northern kingdom were a threat to his activities.

Manasseh, and as far as Zebulun, but they laughed them to scorn, and mocked them.

11   Nevertheless some men of Asher, Manasseh, and Zebulun humbled themselves and came to Jerusalem.

12   The hand of God was also on Judah to give them one heart to do what the king and the princes commanded by the word of the LORD.

b. *The keeping of the Passover*

13   Now many people were gathered at Jerusalem to celebrate the Feast of Unleavened Bread in the second month, a very large assembly.

14   And they arose and removed the altars which *were* in Jerusalem; they also removed all the incense altars and cast *them* into the brook Kidron.

15   Then they slaughtered the Passover *lambs* on the fourteenth of the second month. And the priests and Levites were ashamed of themselves and consecrated themselves, and brought burnt offerings to the house of the LORD.

16   And they stood at their stations after their custom, according to the law of Moses the man of God; the priests sprinkled the blood *which they received* from the hand of the Levites.

17   For *there were* many in the assembly who had not consecrated themselves; therefore, the Levites *were* over the slaughter of the Passover *lambs* for everyone who *was* unclean, in order to consecrate *them* to the LORD.

18   For a multitude of the people, *even* many from Ephraim and Manasseh, Issachar and Zebulun, had not purified themselves, yet they ate the Passover otherwise than prescribed. For Hezekiah prayed for them, saying, "May the good LORD pardon

19   everyone who prepares his heart to seek God, the LORD God of his fathers, though not according to the purification *rules* of the sanctuary."

20   So the LORD heard Hezekiah and healed the people.

21   And the sons of Israel present in Jerusalem celebrated the Feast of Unleavened Bread *for* seven days with great joy, and the Levites and the priests praised the LORD day after day with loud instruments to the LORD.

22   Then Hezekiah spoke encouragingly to all the Levites who showed good insight *in the things* of the LORD. So they ate for the appointed seven days, sacrificing peace offerings and giving thanks to the LORD God of their fathers.

c. *The feast continued for seven days*

23   Then the whole assembly decided to celebrate *the feast* another seven days, so they celebrated the seven days with joy.

24   For Hezekiah king of Judah had contributed to the assembly 1,000 bulls and 7,000 sheep, and the princes had contributed to the assembly 1,000 bulls and 10,000 sheep; and a large number of priests consecrated themselves.

25   And all the assembly of Judah rejoiced, with the priests and the Levites, and all the assembly that came from Israel, both the sojourners who came from the land of Israel and those living in Judah.

26   So there was great joy in Jerusalem, because there was nothing like this in Jerusalem since the days of Solomon the son of David, king of Israel.

27   Then the Levitical priests arose and blessed the people; and their voice was heard and their prayer came to His holy dwelling place, to heaven.

3. *Further reforms of Hezekiah*
a. *The high places destroyed*

31   Now when all this was finished, all Israel who were present went out to the cities of Judah, broke the pillars in pieces, cut down the [11]Asherim, and pulled down the high places and the altars throughout all Judah and Benjamin, as well as in Ephraim and Manasseh, until they had destroyed them all. Then all the sons of Israel returned to their cities, each to his possession.

b. *The levitical service reformed*

2   And Hezekiah appointed the divisions of the priests and the Levites by their divisions, each according to his service, *both* the priests and the Levites, for burnt offerings and for peace offerings, to minister and to give thanks and to praise in the gates of the camp of the LORD.

[11]I.e., wooden symbols of a female deity

Marginal references:

30:11 vv. 18,21,25

30:13 v. 2

30:14 2 Chr 28:24

30:15 vv. 2,3; 2 Chr 29:34

30:16 2 Chr 35:10, 15

30:17 2 Chr 29:34

30:18 vv. 11,25; Ex 12:43-49

30:19 2 Chr 19:3

30:21 Ex 12:15; 13:6

30:22 2 Chr 32:6; Ezra 10:11

30:23 1 Kin 8:65

30:24 2 Chr 35:7,8; 29:34

30:27 2 Chr 23:18; Num 6:23; Deut 26:15; Ps 68:5

31:1 2 Kin 18:4

31:2 1 Chr 24:1; 23:28-31

31:3
Num 28:29

3   *He* also *appointed* the king's portion of his goods for the burnt offerings, *namely*, for the morning and evening burnt offerings, and the burnt offerings for the sabbaths and for the new moons and for the fixed festivals, as it is written in the law of the LORD.

31:4
Num 18:8;
Neh 13:10

4   Also he commanded the people who lived in Jerusalem to give the portion due to the priests and the Levites, that they might devote themselves to the law of the LORD.

31:5
Neh 13:12

5   And as soon as the order spread, the sons of Israel provided in abundance the first fruits of grain, new wine, oil, honey, and of all the produce of the field; and they brought in abundantly the tithe of all.

31:6
Lev 27:30;
Deut 14:28

6   And the sons of Israel and Judah who lived in the cities of Judah, also brought in the tithe of oxen and sheep, and the tithe of sacred gifts which were consecrated to the LORD their God, and placed *them* in heaps.

7   In the third month they began to make the heaps, and finished *them* by the seventh month.

8   And when Hezekiah and the rulers came and saw the heaps, they blessed the LORD and His people Israel.

9   Then Hezekiah questioned the priests and the Levites concerning the heaps.

31:10
Mal 3:10

10   And Azariah the chief priest of the house of Zadok said to him, "Since the contributions began to be brought into the house of the LORD, we have had enough to eat with plenty left over, for the LORD has blessed His people, and this great quantity is left over."

11   Then Hezekiah commanded *them* to prepare rooms in the house of the LORD, and they prepared *them*.

12   And they faithfully brought in the contributions and the tithes and the consecrated things; and Conaniah the Levite *was* the officer in charge of them and his brother Shimei *was* second.

31:13
2 Chr 35:9

13   And Jehiel, Azaziah, Nahath, Asahel, Jerimoth, Jozabad, Eliel, Ismachiah, Mahath, and Benaiah *were* overseers under the authority of Conaniah and Shimei his brother by the appointment of King Hezekiah, and Azariah *was* the *chief* officer of the house of God.

14   And Kore the son of Imnah the Levite, the keeper of the eastern *gate, was* over the freewill offerings of God, to apportion the contributions for the LORD and the most holy things.

31:15
2 Chr 29:12;
Josh 21:9-19

15   And under his authority *were* Eden, Miniamin, Jeshua, Shemaiah, Amariah, and Shecaniah in the cities of the priests, to distribute faithfully *their portions* to their brothers by divisions, whether great or small,

31:16
Ezra 3:4

16   without regard to their genealogical enrollment, to the males from thirty years old and upward—everyone who entered the house of the LORD for his daily obligations—for their work in their duties according to their divisions;

31:17
1 Chr 23:24

17   as well as the priests who were enrolled genealogically according to their fathers' households, and the Levites from twenty years old and upwards, by their duties *and* their divisions.

18   And the genealogical enrollment *included* all their little children, their wives, their sons, and their daughters, for the whole assembly, for they consecrated themselves faithfully in holiness.

31:19
Lev 25:34;
Num 35:2;
vv. 12-15

19   Also for the sons of Aaron the priests *who were* in the pasture lands of their cities, or in each and every city, *there were* men who were designated by name to distribute portions to every male among the priests and to everyone genealogically enrolled among the Levites.

c. The personal faithfulness of Hezekiah

31:20
2 Kin 20:3;
22:2

20   And thus Hezekiah did throughout all Judah; and he did what *was* good, right, and true before the LORD his God.

21   And every work which he began in the service of the house of God in law and in commandment, seeking his God, he did with all his heart and prospered.

4. The defeat of Sennacherib

a. The defense against Sennacherib

32:1
2 Kin 18:13-19;
Is 36:1ff

32   After these acts of faithfulness Sennacherib king of Assyria came and invaded Judah and besieged the fortified cities, and thought to break into them for himself.

2   Now when Hezekiah saw that Sennacherib had come, and that he intended to make war on Jerusalem,

3   he decided with his officers and his warriors to cut off the *supply of* water from the springs which *were* outside the city, and they helped him.

4   So many people assembled and stopped up all the springs and the stream which flowed through the region, saying, "Why should the kings of Assyria come and find abundant water?"

5   And he took courage and rebuilt all the wall that had been broken down, and erected towers on it, and *built* another outside wall, and strengthened the Millo *in* the city of David, and made weapons and shields in great number.

6   And he appointed military officers over the people, and gathered them to him in the square at the city gate, and spoke encouragingly to them, saying,

7   "Be strong and courageous, do not fear or be dismayed because of the king of Assyria, nor because of all the multitude which is with him; for the one with us is greater than the one with him.

8   "With him is *only* an arm of flesh, but with us is the LORD our God to help us and to fight our battles." And the people relied on the words of Hezekiah king of Judah.

b. The message of Sennacherib

9   After this Sennacherib king of Assyria sent his servants to Jerusalem while he *was* besieging Lachish with all his forces with him, against Hezekiah king of Judah and against all Judah who *were* at Jerusalem, saying,

10   "Thus says Sennacherib king of Assyria, 'On what are you trusting that you are remaining in Jerusalem under siege?

11   'Is not Hezekiah misleading you to give yourselves over to die by hunger and by thirst, saying, "The LORD our God will deliver us from the hand of the king of Assyria"?

12   'Has not the same Hezekiah taken away His high places and His altars, and said to Judah and Jerusalem, "You shall worship before one altar, and on it you shall burn incense"?

13   'Do you not know what I and my fathers have done to all the peoples of the lands? Were the gods of the nations of the lands able at all to deliver their land from my hand?

14   'Who *was there* among all the gods of those nations which my fathers utterly destroyed who could deliver his people out of my hand, that your God should be able to deliver you from my hand?

15   'Now therefore, do not let Hezekiah deceive you or mislead you like this, and do not believe him, for no god of any nation or kingdom was able to deliver his people from my hand or from the hand of my fathers. How much less shall your God deliver you from my hand?' "

c. Sennacherib's blasphemy against God

16   And his servants spoke further against the LORD God and against His servant Hezekiah.

17   He also wrote letters to insult the LORD God of Israel, and to speak against Him, saying, "As the gods of the nations of the lands have not delivered their people from my hand, so the God of Hezekiah shall not deliver His people from my hand."

18   And they called this out with a loud voice in the language of Judah to the people of Jerusalem who were on the wall, to frighten and terrify them, so that they might take the city.

19   And they spoke of the God of Jerusalem as of the gods of the peoples of the earth, the work of men's hands.

d. Sennacherib turned back by the angel

20   But King Hezekiah and Isaiah the prophet, the son of Amoz, prayed about this and cried out to heaven.

21   And the LORD sent an angel who destroyed every mighty warrior, commander and officer in the camp of the king of Assyria. So he returned in shame to his own land. And when he had entered the temple of his god, some of his own children killed him there with the sword.

22   So the LORD saved Hezekiah and the inhabitants of Jerusalem from the hand of Sennacherib the king of Assyria, and from the hand of all *others*, and guided them on every side.

32:4
2 Kin 20:20;
v. 30

32:5
2 Chr 25:23;
1 Kin 9:24

32:6
2 Chr 30:22

32:7
1 Chr 22:13;
2 Kin 6:16

32:8
Jer 17:5;
2 Chr 13:12;
20:17

32:11
2 Kin 18:30

32:12
2 Kin 18:22;
2 Chr 31:1

32:13
2 Kin 18:33-35

32:14
Is 10:9-11

32:15
2 Kin 18:29

32:17
2 Kin 19:9,12

32:18
2 Kin 18:26-28

32:19
2 Kin 19:18

32:20
2 Kin 19:2,4,
15
32:21
2 Kin 19:35ff

32:23
2 Chr 17:5
23   And many were bringing gifts to the LORD at Jerusalem and choice presents to Hezekiah king of Judah, so that he was exalted in the sight of all nations thereafter.

5. *The extension of life granted to Hezekiah*

32:24
2 Kin 20:1-11;
Is 38:1-8
32:25
Ps 116:12;
2 Chr 26:16;
24:18
32:26
Jer 26:18,19
24   In those days Hezekiah became mortally ill; and he prayed to the LORD, and the LORD spoke to him and gave him a sign.
25   But Hezekiah gave no return for the benefit he received, because his heart was proud; therefore wrath came on him and on Judah and Jerusalem.
26   However, Hezekiah humbled the pride of his heart, both he and the inhabitants of Jerusalem, so that the wrath of the LORD did not come on them in the days of Hezekiah.

6. *The greatness of Hezekiah*

27   Now Hezekiah had immense riches and honor; and he made for himself treasuries for silver, gold, precious stones, spices, shields and all kinds of valuable articles,
28   storehouses also for the produce of grain, wine and oil, pens for all kinds of cattle and sheepfolds for the flocks.
32:29
1 Chr 29:12
29   And he made cities for himself, and acquired flocks and herds in abundance; for God had given him very great wealth.
32:30
2 Kin 20:20;
1 Kin 1:33
30   It was Hezekiah who stopped the upper outlet of the waters of Gihon and directed them to the west side of the city of David. And Hezekiah prospered in all that he did.
32:31
2 Kin 20:12;
Is 39:1;
Deut 8:2,16
31   And even *in the matter of* the envoys of the rulers of Babylon, who sent to him to inquire of the wonder that had happened in the land, God left him *alone only* to test him, that He might know all that was in his heart.

7. *Hezekiah's death and the succession*

32   Now the rest of the acts of Hezekiah and his deeds of devotion, behold, they are written in the vision of Isaiah the prophet, the son of Amoz, in the Book of the Kings of Judah and Israel.
32:33
2 Kin 20:21;
Prov 10:7
33   So Hezekiah slept with his fathers, and they buried him in the upper section of the tombs of the sons of David; and all Judah and the inhabitants of Jerusalem honored him at his death. And his son Manasseh became king in his place.

M. *The reigns of Manasseh and Amon*

1. *The wickedness of Manasseh*

*33:1
2 Kin 21:1-9
33 Manasseh was twelve years old when he became king, and he reigned fifty-five years in Jerusalem.
33:2
Deut 18:9;
2 Chr 28:3
2   And he did evil in the sight of the LORD according to the abominations of the nations whom the LORD dispossessed before the sons of Israel.
33:3
2 Chr 31:1;
Deut 16:21;
2 Kin 23:5,6;
Deut 17:3
3   For he rebuilt the high places which Hezekiah his father had broken down; he also erected altars for the Baals and made [12]Asherim, and worshiped all the host of heaven and served them.
33:4
2 Chr 28:24;
7:16
4   And he built altars in the house of the LORD of which the LORD had said, "My name shall be in Jerusalem forever."
33:5
2 Chr 4:9
5   For he built altars for all the host of heaven in the two courts of the house of the LORD.
33:6
Lev 18:21;
2 Chr 28:3;
Deut 18:10,
11;
2 Kin 21:6
6   And he made his sons pass through the fire in the valley of Ben-hinnom; and he practiced witchcraft, used divination, practiced sorcery, and dealt with mediums and spiritists. He did much evil in the sight of the LORD, provoking Him *to anger*.
33:7
2 Kin 21:7;
vv. 4,15
7   Then he put the carved image of the idol which he had made in the house of God, of which God had said to David and to Solomon his son, "In this house and in Jerusalem, which I have chosen from all the tribes of Israel, I will put My name forever;
33:8
2 Sam 7:10
8   and I will not again remove the foot of Israel from the land which I have appointed for your fathers, if only they will observe to do all that I have commanded

[12]I.e., wooden symbols of a female deity

33:1 *fifty-five years.* Ten years were a co-regency with Hezekiah.

them according to all the law, the statutes, and the ordinances *given* through Moses."

9   Thus Manasseh misled Judah and the inhabitants of Jerusalem to do more evil than the nations whom the LORD destroyed before the sons of Israel.

2. *His imprisonment and release*

10   And the LORD spoke to Manasseh and his people, but they paid no attention.

11   Therefore the LORD brought the commanders of the army of the king of Assyria against them, and they captured Manasseh with [13]hooks, bound him with bronze *chains*, and took him to Babylon.

12   And when he was in distress, he entreated the LORD his God and humbled himself greatly before the God of his fathers.

13   When he prayed to Him, He was moved by his entreaty and heard his supplication, and brought him again to Jerusalem to his kingdom. Then Manasseh knew that the LORD *was* God.

3. *The removal of the heathen altars*

14   Now after this he built the outer wall of the city of David on the west side of Gihon, in the valley, even to the entrance of the Fish Gate; and he encircled the Ophel *with it* and made it very high. Then he put army commanders in all the fortified cities of Judah.

15   He also removed the foreign gods and the idol from the house of the LORD, as well as all the altars which he had built on the mountain of the house of the LORD and in Jerusalem, and he threw *them* outside the city.

16   And he set up the altar of the LORD and sacrificed peace offerings and thank offerings on it; and he ordered Judah to serve the LORD God of Israel.

17   Nevertheless the people still sacrificed in the high places, *although* only to the LORD their God.

4. *The summary of Manasseh's reign and death*

18   Now the rest of the acts of Manasseh even his prayer to his God, and the words of the seers who spoke to him in the name of the LORD God of Israel, behold, they are among the records of the kings of Israel.

19   His prayer also and *how God* was entreated by him, and all his sin, his unfaithfulness, and the sites on which he built high places and erected the Asherim and the carved images, before he humbled himself, behold, they are written in the records of the Hozai.

20   So Manasseh slept with his fathers, and they buried him in his own house. And Amon his son became king in his place.

5. *The reign of Amon*

21   Amon *was* twenty-two years old when he became king, and he reigned two years in Jerusalem.

22   And he did evil in the sight of the LORD as Manasseh his father had done, and Amon sacrificed to all the carved images which his father Manasseh had made, and he served them.

23   Moreover, he did not humble himself before the LORD as his father Manasseh had done, but Amon multiplied guilt.

24   Finally his servants conspired against him and put him to death in his own house.

25   But the people of the land killed all the conspirators against King Amon, and the people of the land made Josiah his son king in his place.

N. *The reign of Josiah*

1. *His removal of the idols and high places*

34
Josiah *was* eight years old when he became king, and he reigned thirty-one years in Jerusalem.

[13]I.e., thong put through the nose

33:10 Because wicked Manasseh would not heed God, judgment fell until he was humbled.

Cross-references (margin):

33:11 Deut 28:36; Ps 107:10,11
33:12 2 Chr 32:26; 1 Pet 5:6
33:13 1 Chr 5:20; Ezra 8:23; Dan 4:25,32
33:14 1 Kin 1:33; Neh 3:3; 2 Chr 27:3
33:15 vv. 3-7
33:17 2 Chr 32:12
33:18 vv. 10,12,18
33:19 vv. 3,13
33:20 2 Kin 21:18
33:21 2 Kin 21:19-24
33:22 vv. 2-7
33:23 v. 12
33:24 see 2 Chr 25:27
34:1 2 Kin 22:1,2

2   And he did right in the sight of the LORD, and walked in the ways of his father David and did not turn aside to the right or to the left.

34:3
2 Chr 15:2;
1 Kin 13:2;
2 Chr 33:17,
22

3   For in the eighth year of his reign while he was still a youth, he began to seek the God of his father David; and in the twelfth year he began to purge Judah and Jerusalem of the high places, the Asherim, the carved images, and the molten images.

34:4
Lev 26:30;
2 Kin 23:4;
Ex 32:20

4   And they tore down the altars of the Baals in his presence, and the incense altars that were high above them he chopped down; also the Asherim, the carved images, and the molten images he broke in pieces and ground to powder and scattered it on the graves of those who had sacrificed to them.

34:5
1 Kin 13:2;
2 Kin 23:20

5   Then he burned the bones of the priests on their altars, and purged Judah and Jerusalem.

34:6
2 Kin 23:15,
19

6   And in the cities of Manasseh, Ephraim, Simeon, even as far as Naphtali, in their surrounding ruins,

34:7
2 Chr 31:1

7   he also tore down the altars and beat the Asherim and the carved images into powder, and chopped down all the incense altars throughout the land of Israel. Then he returned to Jerusalem.

2. His repair of the house of the LORD

34:8
2 Kin 22:3-20

8   Now in the eighteenth year of his reign, when he had purged the land and the house, he sent Shaphan the son of Azaliah, and Maaseiah an official of the city, and Joah the son of Joahaz the recorder, to repair the house of the LORD his God.

34:9
2 Chr 35:8

9   And they came to Hilkiah the high priest and delivered the money that was brought into the house of God, which the Levites, the doorkeepers, had collected from Manasseh and Ephraim, and from all the remnant of Israel, and from all Judah and Benjamin and the inhabitants of Jerusalem.

10   Then they gave it into the hands of the workmen who had the oversight of the house of the LORD, and the workmen who were working in the house of the LORD used it to restore and repair the house.

34:11
2 Chr 33:4-7

11   They in turn gave it to the carpenters and to the builders to buy quarried stone and timber for couplings and to make beams for the houses which the kings of Judah had let go to ruin.

34:12
1 Chr 25:1

12   And the men did the work faithfully with foremen over them to supervise: Jahath and Obadiah, the Levites of the sons of Merari, Zechariah and Meshullam of the sons of the Kohathites, and the Levites, all who were skillful with musical instruments.

34:13
1 Chr 23:4,5

13   They were also over the burden bearers, and supervised all the workmen from job to job; and some of the Levites were scribes and officials and gatekeepers.

3. The discovery of the book of the law

34:14
v. 9

14   When they were bringing out the money which had been brought into the house of the LORD, Hilkiah the priest found the book of the law of the LORD given by Moses.

15   And Hilkiah responded and said to Shaphan the scribe, "I have found the book of the law in the house of the LORD." And Hilkiah gave the book to Shaphan.

34:16
v. 8

16   Then Shaphan brought the book to the king and reported further word to the king, saying, "Everything that was entrusted to your servants they are doing.

17   "They have also emptied out the money which was found in the house of the LORD, and have delivered it into the hands of the supervisors and the workmen."

18   Moreover, Shaphan the scribe told the king saying, "Hilkiah the priest gave me a book." And Shaphan read from it in the presence of the king.

34:19
Josh 7:6

19   And it came about when the king heard the words of the law that he tore his clothes.

20   Then the king commanded Hilkiah, Ahikam the son of Shaphan, Abdon the son of Micah, Shaphan the scribe, and Asaiah the king's servant, saying,

34:21
2 Chr 29:8

21   "Go, inquire of the LORD for me and for those who are left in Israel and in Judah, concerning the words of the book which has been found; for great is the wrath of the LORD which is poured out on us because our fathers have not observed the word of the LORD, to do according to all that is written in this book."

34:22
2 Kin 22:14

22   So Hilkiah and those whom the king had told went to Huldah the prophetess, the wife of Shallum the son of Tokhath, the son of Hasrah, the keeper of the wardrobe (now she lived in Jerusalem in the Second Quarter); and they spoke to her regarding this.

23   And she said to them, "Thus says the LORD, the God of Israel, 'Tell the man who sent you to Me,

24   thus says the LORD, "Behold, I am bringing evil on this place and on its inhabitants, *even* all the curses written in the book which they have read in the presence of the king of Judah.

25   "Because they have forsaken Me and have burned incense to other gods, that they might provoke Me to anger with all the works of their hands, therefore My wrath will be poured out on this place, and it shall not be quenched." '

26   "But to the king of Judah who sent you to inquire of the LORD, thus you will say to him, 'Thus says the LORD God of Israel *regarding* the words which you have heard,

27   "Because your heart was tender and you humbled yourself before God, when you heard His words against this place and against its inhabitants, and *because* you humbled yourself before Me, tore your clothes, and wept before Me, I truly have heard you," declares the LORD.

28   "Behold, I will gather you to your fathers and you shall be gathered to your grave in peace, so your eyes shall not see all the evil which I will bring on this place and on its inhabitants." ' " And they brought back word to the king.

4. *The reading of the Law and the renewal of the covenant*

29   Then the king sent and gathered all the elders of Judah and Jerusalem.

30   And the king went up to the house of the LORD and all the men of Judah, the inhabitants of Jerusalem, the priests, the Levites, and all the people, from the greatest to the least; and he read in their hearing all the words of the book of the covenant which was found in the house of the LORD.

31   Then the king stood in his place and made a covenant before the LORD to walk after the LORD, and to keep His commandments and His testimonies and His statutes with all his heart and with all his soul, to perform the words of the covenant written in this book.

32   Moreover, he made all who were present in Jerusalem and Benjamin to stand *with him*. So the inhabitants of Jerusalem did according to the covenant of God, the God of their fathers.

33   And Josiah removed all the abominations from all the lands belonging to the sons of Israel, and made all who were present in Israel to serve the LORD their God. Throughout his lifetime they did not turn from following the LORD God of their fathers.

5. *The keeping of the Passover*

35   Then Josiah celebrated the Passover to the LORD in Jerusalem, and they slaughtered the Passover *animals* on the fourteenth *day* of the first month.

2   And he set the priests in their offices and encouraged them in the service of the house of the LORD.

3   He also said to the Levites who taught all Israel *and* who were holy to the LORD, "Put the holy ark in the house which Solomon the son of David king of Israel built; it will be a burden on *your* shoulders no longer. Now serve the LORD your God and His people Israel.

4   "And prepare *yourselves* by your fathers' households in your divisions, according to the writing of David king of Israel and according to the writing of his son Solomon.

5   "Moreover, stand in the holy place according to the sections of the fathers' households of your brethren the lay people, and according to the Levites, by division of a father's household.

6   "Now slaughter the Passover *animals*, sanctify yourselves, and prepare for your brethren to do according to the word of the LORD by Moses."

7   And Josiah contributed to the lay people, to all who were present, flocks of lambs and kids, all for the Passover offerings, numbering 30,000 plus 3,000 bulls; these were from the king's possessions.

8   His officers also contributed a freewill offering to the people, the priests, and the Levites. Hilkiah and Zechariah and Jehiel, the officials of the house of God, gave to the priests for the Passover offerings 2,600 *from the flocks* and 300 bulls.

9   Conaniah also, and Shemaiah and Nethanel, his brothers, and Hashabiah and Jeiel and Jozabad, the officers of the Levites, contributed to the Levites for the Passover offerings 5,000 *from the flocks* and 500 bulls.

34:24
2 Chr 36:14-20;
Deut 28:15-68

34:25
2 Chr 33:3

34:27
2 Chr 12:7;
32:26

34:29
2 Kin 23:1-3
34:30
Neh 8:1-3

34:31
2 Kin 11:14;
23:3;
2 Chr 23:3,
16; 29:10

34:33
vv. 3-7;
2 Chr 33:2-7

35:1
2 Kin 23:21,
22; Ex 12:6;
Num 9:3
35:2
2 Chr 23:18;
29:11
35:3
Deut 33:10;
2 Chr 5:7;
1 Chr 23:26
35:4
1 Chr 9:10-13;
2 Chr 8:14

35:5
Ps 134:1

35:6
v. 1;
2 Chr 29:5,
15; Ezra 6:20
35:7
2 Chr 30:24

35:9
2 Chr 31:12

35:10
v. 5;
Ezra 6:18

10 So the service was prepared, and the priests stood at their stations and the Levites by their divisions according to the king's command.

35:11
vv. 1,6;
2 Chr 29:22,
34

11 And they slaughtered the Passover *animals*, and while the priests sprinkled the blood *received* from their hand, the Levites skinned *them*.

12 Then they removed the burnt offerings that *they* might give them to the sections of the fathers' households of the lay people to present to the LORD, as it is written in the book of Moses. *They did* this also with the bulls.

35:13
Ex 12:8,9;
Lev 6:25;
1 Sam 2:13-15

13 So they roasted the Passover *animals* on the fire according to the ordinance, and they boiled the holy things in pots, in kettles, in pans, and carried *them* speedily to all the lay people.

14 And afterwards they prepared for themselves and for the priests, because the priests, the sons of Aaron, *were* offering the burnt offerings and the fat until night; therefore the Levites prepared for themselves and for the priests, the sons of Aaron.

35:15
1 Chr 25:1;
26:12-19

15 The singers, the sons of Asaph, *were* also at their stations according to the command of David, Asaph, Heman, and Jeduthun the king's seer; and the gate-keepers at each gate did not have to depart from their service, because the Levites their brethren prepared for them.

16 So all the service of the LORD was prepared on that day to celebrate the Passover, and to offer burnt offerings on the altar of the LORD according to the command of King Josiah.

35:17
Ex 12:15;
2 Chr 30:21

17 Thus the sons of Israel who were present celebrated the Passover at that time, and the Feast of Unleavened Bread seven days.

*35:18
2 Kin 23:21-23

18 And there had not been celebrated a Passover like it in Israel since the days of Samuel the prophet; nor had any of the kings of Israel celebrated such a Passover as Josiah did with the priests, the Levites, all Judah and Israel who were present, and the inhabitants of Jerusalem.

19 In the eighteenth year of Josiah's reign this Passover was celebrated.

6. Josiah's battle against Neco of Egypt, and his death

35:20
2 Kin 23:29,
30; Is 10:9;
Jer 46:2

20 After all this, when Josiah had set the temple in order, Neco king of Egypt came up to make war at Carchemish on the Euphrates, and Josiah went out to engage him.

21 But Neco sent messengers to him, saying, "What have we to do with each other, O King of Judah? *I am* not *coming* against you today but against the house with which I am at war, and God has ordered me to hurry. Stop for your own sake from *interfering with* God who is with me, that He may not destroy you."

*35:22
2 Chr 18:29;
Judg 5:19

22 However, Josiah would not turn away from him, but disguised himself in order to make war with him; nor did he listen to the words of Neco from the mouth of God, but came to make war on the plain of Megiddo.

23 And the archers shot King Josiah, and the king said to his servants, "Take me away, for I am badly wounded."

35:24
2 Kin 23:30;
Zech 12:11

24 So his servants took him out of the chariot and carried him in the second chariot which he had, and brought him to Jerusalem where he died and was buried in the tombs of his fathers. And all Judah and Jerusalem mourned for Josiah.

35:25
Lam 4:20;
Jer 22:20

25 Then Jeremiah chanted a lament for Josiah. And all the male and female singers speak about Josiah in their lamentations to this day. And they made them an ordinance in Israel; behold, they are also written in the Lamentations.

26 Now the rest of the acts of Josiah and his deeds of devotion as written in the law of the LORD,

27 and his acts, first to last, behold, they are written in the Book of the Kings of Israel and Judah.

35:18 While there was nothing like Hezekiah's celebration of the Passover in Jerusalem since the time of Solomon (30:26), Josiah's Passover was greater still. There had been nothing like it since the days of Samuel or *from the days of the judges* (2 Kin. 23:22).
35:22 *plain of Megiddo.* The fortress of Megiddo, rising above the plain in the southern reaches of the Esdraelon or Jezreel Valley, acquired the name *Har-megiddo,* "The Hill of Megiddo." It guarded the pass on the best north-south

route in Canaan; and it was here that many of the great battles of ancient history were fought, even from the fifteenth century B.C. during the campaigns of Thutmose III of Egypt. It is also here that the Har-Magedon (Armageddon), the climactic battle between good and evil forces, is ultimately to take place (Rev. 16:16).
35:23 During his lifetime Josiah was to see many religious reforms take place as a result of his efforts.

O. *From Josiah to the captivity*

1. *Jehoahaz captive in Egypt*

36 Then the people of the land took [14]Joahaz the son of Josiah, and made him king in place of his father in Jerusalem.

2   Joahaz was twenty-three years old when he became king, and he reigned three months in Jerusalem.

3   Then the king of Egypt deposed him at Jerusalem, and imposed on the land a fine of one hundred talents of silver and one talent of gold.

4   And the king of Egypt made Eliakim his brother king over Judah and Jerusalem, and changed his name to Jehoiakim. But Neco took Joahaz his brother and brought him to Egypt.

2. *Jehoiakim captive in Babylon*

5   Jehoiakim was twenty-five years old when he became king, and he reigned eleven years in Jerusalem; and he did evil in the sight of the LORD his God.

6   Nebuchadnezzar king of Babylon came up against him and bound him with bronze *chains* to take him to Babylon.

7   Nebuchadnezzar also brought *some* of the articles of the house of the LORD to Babylon and put them in his temple at Babylon.

8   Now the rest of the acts of Jehoiakim and the abominations which he did, and what was found against him, behold, they are written in the Book of the Kings of Israel and Judah. And Jehoiachin his son became king in his place.

3. *Jehoiachin captive in Babylon*

9   Jehoiachin was eight years old when he became king, and he reigned three months and ten days in Jerusalem, and he did evil in the sight of the LORD.

10   And at the turn of the year King Nebuchadnezzar sent and brought him to Babylon with the valuable articles of the house of the LORD, and he made his kinsman Zedekiah king over Judah and Jerusalem.

4. *Wicked Zedekiah*

a. *His rebellion against Nebuchadnezzar*

11   Zedekiah was twenty-one years old when he became king, and he reigned eleven years in Jerusalem.

12   And he did evil in the sight of the LORD his God; he did not humble himself before Jeremiah the prophet who spoke for the LORD.

13   And he also rebelled against King Nebuchadnezzar who had made him swear *allegiance* by God. But he stiffened his neck and hardened his heart against turning to the LORD God of Israel.

14   Furthermore, all the officials of the priests and the people were very unfaithful *following* all the abominations of the nations; and they defiled the house of the LORD which He had sanctified in Jerusalem.

b. *The mocking of God's messengers*

15   And the LORD, the God of their fathers, sent *word* to them again and again by His messengers, because He had compassion on His people and on His dwelling place;

16   but they *continually* mocked the messengers of God, despised His words and scoffed at His prophets, until the wrath of the LORD arose against His people, until there was no remedy.

c. *The destruction of the temple and Jerusalem: the captivity*

17   Therefore He brought up against them the king of the Chaldeans who slew their young men with the sword in the house of their sanctuary, and had no compassion on young man or virgin, old man or infirm; He gave *them* all into his hand.

18   And all the articles of the house of God, great and small, and the treasures of

---

14 I.e., short form of Jehoahaz

36:9 *Eight* is an error for *eighteen*. (2 Kin. 24:8 gives the latter figure, which we can assume to be the more   reliable one.)

Marginal references:

36:1 2 Kin 23:30-34; Jer 22:11

36:5 2 Kin 23:36, 37
36:6 2 Kin 24:1; 2 Chr 33:11
36:7 2 Kin 24:13

36:8 2 Kin 24:5; see 1 Chr 3:16

*36:9 2 Kin 24:8-17

36:10 2 Sam 11:1; Jer 37:1

36:11 2 Kin 24:18-20; Jer 52:1
36:12 2 Chr 33:23; Jer 21:3-7
36:13 Jer 52:3; Ezek 17:15; 2 Kin 17:14; 2 Chr 30:8

36:15 Jer 25:3,4; 35:15; 44:4

36:16 2 Chr 30:10; Jer 5:12,13; Prov 1:25; Ezra 5:12

36:17 2 Kin 25:1-7

36:18 2 Kin 25:13ff

the house of the LORD, and the treasures of the king and of his officers, he brought *them* all to Babylon.

19 Then they burned the house of God, and broke down the wall of Jerusalem and burned all its fortified buildings with fire, and destroyed all its valuable articles.

20 And those who had escaped from the sword he carried away to Babylon; and they were servants to him and to his sons until the rule of the kingdom of Persia,

21 to fulfill the word of the LORD by the mouth of Jeremiah, until the land had enjoyed its sabbaths. All the days of its desolation it kept sabbath until seventy years were complete.

5. *The return from the captivity prophesied*

22 Now in the first year of Cyrus king of Persia—in order to fulfill the word of the LORD by the mouth of Jeremiah—the LORD stirred up the spirit of Cyrus king of Persia, so that he sent a proclamation throughout his kingdom, and also *put it* in writing, saying,

23 "Thus says Cyrus king of Persia, 'The LORD, the God of heaven, has given me all the kingdoms of the earth, and He has appointed me to build Him a house in Jerusalem, which is in Judah. Whoever there is among you of all His people, may the LORD his God be with him, and let him go up!'"

36:19 2 Kin 25:9; Jer 52:13
36:20 2 Kin 25:11; Jer 27:7 *36:21 Jer 29:10; Lev 26:34; 25:4
*36:22 Ezra 1:1; Jer 25:12; Is 44:28
36:23 Ezra 1:2,3

36:21 *mouth of Jeremiah*, a reference to Jer. 25:11,12; 29:10, where the seventy years' service to Babylon is mentioned.
36:22 Cyrus was the founder of the Persian empire, which became the largest empire the world had yet seen.

INTRODUCTION TO

THE BOOK OF

EZRA

Authorship and Background: See 1 Chronicles for a discussion of authorship. The book is named for its principal character, Ezra, the priest and scribe. The compilation includes a number of different sources: documents in Hebrew relating to Zerubbabel's return and subsequent difficulties in Jerusalem (1:1-4:7); extracts from Aramaic records (4:8-6:18); and personal writings of Ezra (7:27-9:15). Two different periods of history are considered: the return of the exiles under Zerubbabel (1-6), and the return under Ezra (7-10). The first return and its results are treated in two phases: the decree of Cyrus to the cessation of temple construction (539-535 B.C.), and the resumption of construction until the completion of the temple (520-515 B.C.).

Ezra's return is dated in the seventh year of Artaxerxes (7:7). Some take this to mean Artaxerxes I (465-424 B.C.), in which event Ezra returned in 458 B.C.; others take it to mean Artaxerxes II (404-358 B.C.), which would indicate that Ezra returned in 397 B.C. The traditional fifth-century date for Ezra, however, has been reinforced in the writings of W. F. Albright. The Elephantine letter #30, dated 408 B.C., was addressed to Bigvai (Bagoas), governor of Judea, who was apparently Nehemiah's successor. The same letter noted that Johanan (or Jehohanan), the person mentioned in Ezra 10:6 and Neh. 12:22,23, was priest in Jerusalem in 411 B.C. In fact, nothing in the genealogical lists or the narrative of the Chronicler's history is dated after about 400 B.C. A third view dates Ezra's return to Jerusalem in 428 B.C., on the assumption that a scribal error changed the thirty-seventh year to the seventh year of Artaxerxes, something that could easily have occurred because in the Hebrew the words "thirty," "seven," and "year" all begin with the same letter.

Characteristics: A portion of Ezra is personal, being written in the first person; other parts are in the third person. It is a historical book in the Hagiographa (the *holy writings*, together with the *Law* and the *Prophets*, made up the Old Testament canon of Scripture), which emphasizes Israel's obligation as a people of holiness, i.e., chosen and separated by God from other nations for His express purposes. The Jews are to be kept "pure" by dissolving and avoiding foreign contacts. The book describes how Ezra gets the people to bind themselves to the Law of God, and how he successfully completes the mission given by his king when he is allowed to return to Palestine.

Contents:

   I. The first return to the land (1:1-2:70): Cyrus issues an edict permitting return to Jerusalem. Preparations are made for the return. The returning Israelites are listed. Summaries, and gathering of money for the temple.

  II. The restoration of worship and dedication of the temple (3:1-6:22): The altar rebuilt and the sacrifices commenced. Work on the temple begun. The Samaritans seek to stop the work. The temple completed under Darius after an official investigation. The feasts of the Passover and Unleavened Bread celebrated.

 III. The return of Ezra and the reform that followed (7:1-10:44): The genealogy of Ezra and his career depicted. His commission to return; funds secured. Accompanied by others, he acquires temple servants, puts a guard over the treasure, and comes to Jerusalem. Upon hearing of the mixed marriages, Ezra mourns and prays. The people repent and meet in public assembly. They separate themselves from their foreign spouses; those with foreign wives are listed.

THE BOOK OF

EZRA

I. *The first return to the land (1:1–2:70)*

A. *The edict of Cyrus*

1 Now in the first year of Cyrus king of Persia, in order to fulfill the word of the LORD by the mouth of Jeremiah, the LORD stirred up the spirit of Cyrus king of Persia, so that he sent a proclamation throughout all his kingdom, and also *put it* in writing, saying,

2 "Thus says Cyrus king of Persia, 'The LORD, the God of heaven, has given me all the kingdoms of the earth, and He has appointed me to build Him a house in Jerusalem, which is in Judah.

3 'Whoever there is among you of all His people, may his God be with him! Let him go up to Jerusalem which is in Judah, and rebuild the house of the LORD, the God of Israel; He is the God who is in Jerusalem.

4 'And every survivor, at whatever place he may live, let the men of that place support him with silver and gold, with goods and cattle, together with a freewill offering for the house of God which is in Jerusalem.'"

B. *Preparation for the return*

5 Then the heads of fathers' *households* of Judah and Benjamin and the priests and the Levites arose, even everyone whose spirit God had stirred to go up and rebuild the house of the LORD which is in Jerusalem.

6 And all those about them encouraged them with articles of silver, with gold, with goods, with cattle, and with valuables, aside from all that was given as a freewill offering.

7 Also King Cyrus brought out the articles of the house of the LORD, which Nebuchadnezzar had carried away from Jerusalem and put in the house of his gods;

8 and Cyrus, king of Persia, had them brought out by the hand of Mithredath the treasurer, and he counted them out to Sheshbazzar, the prince of Judah.

9 Now this *was* their number: 30 gold dishes, 1,000 silver dishes, 29 duplicates;

10 30 gold bowls, 410 silver bowls of a second *kind, and* 1,000 other articles.

11 All the articles of gold and silver *numbered* 5,400. Sheshbazzar brought them all up with the exiles who went up from Babylon to Jerusalem.

C. *The first return under Zerubbabel*

2 Now these are the people of the province who came up out of the captivity of the exiles whom Nebuchadnezzar the king of Babylon had carried away to Babylon, and returned to Jerusalem and Judah, each to his city.

2 These came with Zerubbabel, Jeshua, Nehemiah, Seraiah, Reelaiah, Mordecai, Bilshan, Mispar, Bigvai, Rehum, and Baanah.

The number of the men of the people of Israel:

3 the sons of Parosh, 2,172;

4 the sons of Shephatiah, 372;

5 the sons of Arah, 775;

Marginal references:

1:1ff 2 Chr 36:22, 23; Jer 25:12; 29:10; Ezra 5:13,14

1:2 Is 44:28; 45:1,12,13

1:3 Dan 6:26

1:5 Phil 2:13

1:7 Ezra 5:14; 6:5; 2 Kin 24:13; 2 Chr 36:7
1:8 Ezra 5:14

2:1 Neh 7:6-73; 2 Kin 24:14-16; 25:11; 2 Chr 36:20

2:5 cf. Neh 7:10

1:1 *first year*, being 539 B.C. Cyrus reigned 559–530 B.C., but his control over Babylon began in 539 B.C.
1:1–3 These verses, a repetition of 2 Chr. 36:22,23, indicate (along with the style, language, and interests of the book) that Ezra may well have been an integral part of the Chronicler's history. See here the Introductions to 1 and 2 Chronicles.
1:8 *Sheshbazzar*, perhaps the Shenazzar of 1 Chr. 3:18. (Some have even considered that Sheshbazzar was the pseudonym for Zerubbabel.) Being a son of Jehoiachin, he

would have been the one entrusted with the priceless vessels of the temple. In fact, this "prince of Judah" was so well thought of that Cyrus later appointed him governor over the people. (See Ezra 5:14.)
2:5 Nehemiah 7:10 states that Arah had *652* children instead of *775*. This is undoubtedly a copyist's error. A comparison of 2:6–65 with Neh. 7:11–67 will show other differences in numbers. The fact that Jewish letters were used to represent numbers made this confusion almost unavoidable.

6　the sons of Pahath-moab of the sons of Jeshua *and* Joab, 2,812;
7　the sons of Elam, 1,254;
8　the sons of Zattu, 945;
9　the sons of Zaccai, 760;
10　the sons of Bani, 642;
11　the sons of Bebai, 623;
12　the sons of Azgad, 1,222;
13　the sons of Adonikam, 666;
14　the sons of Bigvai, 2,056;
15　the sons of Adin, 454;
16　the sons of Ater of Hezekiah, 98;
17　the sons of Bezai, 323;
18　the sons of Jorah, 112;
19　the sons of Hashum, 223;
20　the sons of Gibbar, 95;
21　the men of Bethlehem, 123;
22　the men of Netophah, 56;
23　the men of Anathoth, 128;
24　the sons of Azmaveth, 42;
25　the sons of Kiriath-arim, Chephirah, and Beeroth, 743;
26　the sons of Ramah and Geba, 621;
27　the men of Michmas, 122;
28　the men of Bethel and Ai, 223;
29　the sons of Nebo, 52;
30　the sons of Magbish, 156;
31　the sons of the other Elam, 1,254;
32　the sons of Harim, 320;
33　the sons of Lod, Hadid, and Ono, 725;
34　the men of Jericho, 345;
35　the sons of Senaah, 3,630.
36　The priests: the sons of Jedaiah of the house of Jeshua, 973;
37　the sons of Immer, 1,052;
38　the sons of Pashhur, 1,247;
39　the sons of Harim, 1,017.
40　The Levites: the sons of Jeshua and Kadmiel, of the sons of Hodaviah, 74.
41　The singers: the sons of Asaph, 128.
42　The sons of the gatekeepers: the sons of Shallum, the sons of Ater, the sons of Talmon, the sons of Akkub, the sons of Hatita, the sons of Shobai, in all 139.
43　The temple servants: the sons of Ziha, the sons of Hasupha, the sons of Tabbaoth,
44　the sons of Keros, the sons of Siaha, the sons of Padon,
45　the sons of Lebanah, the sons of Hagabah, the sons of Akkub,
46　the sons of Hagab, the sons of Shalmai, the sons of Hanan,
47　the sons of Giddel, the sons of Gahar, the sons of Reaiah,
48　the sons of Rezin, the sons of Nekoda, the sons of Gazzam,
49　the sons of Uzza, the sons of Paseah, the sons of Besai,
50　the sons of Asnah, the sons of Meunim, the sons of Nephisim,
51　the sons of Bakbuk, the sons of Hakupha, the sons of Harhur,
52　the sons of Bazluth, the sons of Mehida, the sons of Harsha,
53　the sons of Barkos, the sons of Sisera, the sons of Temah,
54　the sons of Neziah, the sons of Hatipha.
55　The sons of Solomon's servants: the sons of Sotai, the sons of Hassophereth, the sons of Peruda,
56　the sons of Jaalah, the sons of Darkon, the sons of Giddel,
57　the sons of Shephatiah, the sons of Hattil, the sons of Pochereth-hazzebaim, the sons of Ami.
58　All the temple servants, and the sons of Solomon's servants, were 392.
59　Now these are those who came up from Tel-melah, Tel-harsha, Cherub, Addan, *and* Immer, but they were not able to give evidence of their fathers' households, and their descendants, whether they were of Israel:
60　the sons of Delaiah, the sons of Tobiah, the sons of Nekoda, 652.
61　And of the sons of the priests: the sons of Habaiah, the sons of Hakkoz, the

2:6
cf. Neh 7:11

2:16
Neh 7:21

2:21
Neh 7:26

2:31
see v. 7

2:36
1 Chr 24:7-18
2:38
1 Chr 9:12
2:39
1 Chr 24:8

2:43
1 Chr 9:2

2:48
Neh 7:50

2:55
Neh 7:57,60;
11:3

2:58
v. 55

2:61
2 Sam 17:27

2:62
Num 3:10;
16:39,40
*2:63
Lev 2:3,10;
Ex 28:30
2:64
Neh 7:66ff

*2:69
Ezra 8:25-34

3:1
Neh 7:73; 8:1

*3:2
Neh 12:1,8;
Ezra 2:2;
1 Chr 3:17;
Deut 12:5,6
3:3
Ezra 4:4;
Num 28:2-4

3:4
Neh 8:14;
Ex 23:16;
Num 29:12

3:5
Num 28:3,11,
19,26; 29:39

3:7
2 Chr 2:10,
16; Ezra 1:2;
6:3

3:8
v. 2;
Ezra 4:3;
1 Chr 23:24,
27

3:9
Ezra 2:40

3:10
1 Chr 16:5,6,
42; 6:31; 25:1

sons of Barzillai, who took a wife from the daughters of Barzillai the Gileadite, and he was called by their name.

62 These searched *among* their ancestral registration, but they could not be located; therefore they were considered unclean *and excluded* from the priesthood.

63 And the governor said to them that they should not eat from the most holy things until a priest stood up with Urim and Thummim.

64 The whole assembly numbered 42,360,

65 besides their male and female servants, who numbered 7,337; and they had 200 singing men and women.

66 Their horses were 736; their mules, 245;

67 their camels, 435; *their* donkeys, 6,720.

68 And some of the heads of fathers' *households*, when they arrived at the house of the LORD which is in Jerusalem, offered willingly for the house of God to restore it on its foundation.

69 According to their ability they gave to the treasury for the work 61,000 gold drachmas, and 5,000 silver minas, and 100 priestly garments.

70 Now the priests and the Levites, some of the people, the singers, the gatekeepers, and the temple servants lived in their cities, and all Israel in their cities.

II. *The restoration of worship and dedication of the temple (3:1–6:22)*

A. *The altar rebuilt: sacrifices offered*

3 Now when the seventh month came, and the sons of Israel *were* in the cities, the people gathered together as one man to Jerusalem.

2 Then Jeshua the son of Jozadak and his brothers the priests, and Zerubbabel the son of Shealtiel, and his brothers arose and built the altar of the God of Israel, to offer burnt offerings on it, as it is written in the law of Moses, the man of God.

3 So they set up the altar on its foundation, for they were terrified because of the peoples of the lands; and they offered burnt offerings on it to the LORD, burnt offerings morning and evening.

4 And they celebrated the Feast of [1]Booths, as it is written, and *offered* the fixed number of burnt offerings daily, according to the ordinance, as each day required;

5 and afterward *there was* a continual burnt offering, also for the new moons and for all the fixed festivals of the LORD that were consecrated, and from everyone who offered a freewill offering to the LORD.

6 From the first day of the seventh month they began to offer burnt offerings to the LORD, but the foundation of the temple of the LORD had not been laid.

7 Then they gave money to the masons and carpenters, and food, drink, and oil to the Sidonians and to the Tyrians, to bring cedar wood from Lebanon to the sea at Joppa, according to the permission they had from Cyrus king of Persia.

B. *Rebuilding of the temple begun*

8 Now in the second year of their coming to the house of God at Jerusalem in the second month, Zerubbabel the son of Shealtiel and Jeshua the son of Jozadak and the rest of their brothers the priests and the Levites, and all who came from the captivity to Jerusalem, began *the work* and appointed the Levites from twenty years and older to oversee the work of the house of the LORD.

9 Then Jeshua *with* his sons and brothers stood united *with* Kadmiel and his sons, the sons of Judah *and* the sons of Henadad *with* their sons and brothers the Levites, to oversee the workmen in the temple of God.

10 Now when the builders had laid the foundation of the temple of the LORD, the priests stood in their apparel with trumpets, and the Levites, the sons of Asaph, with cymbals, to praise the LORD according to the directions of King David of Israel.

[1]Or, *Tabernacles*

2:63 *Urim and Thummim*, see note to Ex. 28:30. The last mention of these is in Neh. 7:65.
2:69 *drachmas*, probably Greek coins used in the Persian empire.

3:2 *son of Shealtiel*. Zerubbabel was the legitimate heir, since his father was the eldest son of Jehoiachin. (See 1 Chr. 3:17 and note to 1 Chr. 3:19.)

11   And they sang, praising and giving thanks to the LORD, *saying*, "For He is good, for His lovingkindness is upon Israel forever." And all the people shouted with a great shout when they praised the LORD because the foundation of the house of the LORD was laid.

12   Yet many of the priests and Levites and heads of fathers' *households*, the old men who had seen the first temple, wept with a loud voice when the foundation of this house was laid before their eyes, while many shouted aloud for joy;

13   so that the people could not distinguish the sound of the shout of joy from the sound of the weeping of the people, for the people shouted with a loud shout, and the sound was heard far away.

C. *Opposition to the rebuilding*

1. *Help offered and refused*

4   Now when the enemies of Judah and Benjamin heard that the people of the exile were building a temple to the LORD God of Israel,

2   they approached Zerubbabel and the heads of fathers' *households*, and said to them, "Let us build with you, for we, like you, seek your God; and we have been sacrificing to Him since the days of Esarhaddon king of Assyria, who brought us up here."

3   But Zerubbabel and Jeshua and the rest of the heads of fathers' *households* of Israel said to them, "You have nothing in common with us in building a house to our God; but we ourselves will together build to the LORD God of Israel, as King Cyrus, the king of Persia has commanded us."

4   Then the people of the land discouraged the people of Judah, and frightened them from building,

5   and hired counselors against them to frustrate their counsel all the days of Cyrus king of Persia, even until the reign of Darius king of Persia.

2. *The letter to Artaxerxes: the work stopped*

6   Now in the reign of [2]Ahasuerus, in the beginning of his reign, they wrote an accusation against the inhabitants of Judah and Jerusalem.

7   And in the days of Artaxerxes, Bishlam, Mithredath, Tabeel, and the rest of his colleagues, wrote to Artaxerxes king of Persia; and the text of the letter was written in Aramaic and translated *from* Aramaic.

8   Rehum the commander and Shimshai the scribe wrote a letter against Jerusalem to King Artaxerxes, as follows—

9   then *wrote* Rehum the commander and Shimshai the scribe and the rest of their colleagues, the judges and the lesser governors, the officials, the secretaries, the men of Erech, the Babylonians, the men of Susa, that is, the Elamites,

10   and the rest of the nations which the great and honorable Osnappar deported and settled in the city of Samaria, and in the rest of the region beyond the [3] River. And now

11   this is the copy of the letter which they sent to him: "To King Artaxerxes: Your servants, the men in the region beyond the River, and now

12   let it be known to the king, that the Jews who came up from you have come to us at Jerusalem; they are rebuilding the rebellious and evil city, and are finishing the walls and repairing the foundations.

13   "Now let it be known to the king, that if that city is rebuilt and the walls are finished, they will not pay tribute, custom, or toll, and it will damage the revenue of the kings.

14   "Now because we are in the service of the palace, and it is not fitting for us to see the king's dishonor, therefore we have sent and informed the king,

15   so that a search may be made in the record books of your fathers. And you will discover in the record books, and learn that that city is a rebellious city and damaging to kings and provinces, and that they have incited revolt within it in past days; therefore that city was laid waste.

Cross references (margin):

3:11 Ex 15:21; 2 Chr 7:3; Neh 12:24; 1 Chr 16:34, 41

4:1 vv. 7-10

*4:2 2 Kin 17:24, 32,33; 19:37

4:3 Neh 2:20; Ezra 1:1-3

4:4 Ezra 3:3

*4:6ff Esth 1:1; Dan 9:1
*4:7 2 Kin 18:26; Dan 2:4

*4:10 v. 1

4:12 Ezra 5:3,9

4:13 v. 20; Ezra 7:24

---

[2]Or, *Xerxes* [3]I.e., Euphrates, and so throughout this context

---

4:2 *Esarhaddon*, see note to 2 Kin. 17:24.
4:5 *Darius* reigned 522–486 B.C.
4:6–23 Chronologically this unit, concerning the city walls (not the temple), belongs between chapters 6 and 7.
4:6 *Ahasuerus*, this is Xerxes (486–465 B.C.).
4:7 *Artaxerxes* reigned 465–423 B.C.
4:10 *Osnappar*, that is, Ashurbanipal. See note to 2 Kin. 17:24.

16 "We inform the king that, if that city is rebuilt and the walls finished, as a result you will have no possession in *the province* beyond the River."

17 *Then* the king sent an answer to Rehum the commander, to Shimshai the scribe, and to the rest of their colleagues who live in Samaria and in the rest of *the provinces* beyond the River: "Peace. And now

18 the document which you sent to us has been translated and read before me.

19 "And a decree has been issued by me, and a search has been made and it has been discovered that that city has risen up against the kings in past days, that rebellion and revolt have been perpetrated in it,

20 that mighty kings have ruled over Jerusalem, governing all *the provinces* beyond the River, and that tribute, custom, and toll were paid to them.

21 "So, now issue a decree to make these men stop *work,* that the city may not be rebuilt until a decree is issued by me.

22 "And beware of being negligent in carrying out this *matter;* why should damage increase to the detriment of the kings?"

23 Then as soon as the copy of King Artaxerxes' document was read before Rehum and Shimshai the scribe and their colleagues, they went in haste to Jerusalem to the Jews and stopped them by force of arms.

24 Then work on the house of God in Jerusalem ceased, and it was stopped until the second year of the reign of Darius king of Persia.

3. *Rebuilding the temple under Haggai and Zechariah*

a. *The work begun*

5 When the prophets, Haggai the prophet and Zechariah the son of Iddo, prophesied to the Jews who were in Judah and Jerusalem, in the name of the God of Israel, who was over them,

2 then Zerubbabel the son of Shealtiel and Jeshua the son of Jozadak arose and began to rebuild the house of God which is in Jerusalem; and the prophets of God were with them supporting them.

b. *An investigation instituted*

3 At that time Tattenai, the governor of *the province* beyond the River, and Shethar-bozenai and their colleagues came to them and spoke to them thus, "Who issued you a decree to rebuild this [4]temple and to finish this structure?"

4 Then we told them accordingly what the names of the men were who were reconstructing this building.

5 But the eye of their God was on the elders of the Jews, and they did not stop them until a report should come to Darius, and then a written reply be returned concerning it.

c. *Tattenai's letter to Darius*

6 *This is* the copy of the letter which Tattenai, the governor of *the province* beyond the River, and Shethar-bozenai and his colleagues the officials, who were beyond the River, sent to Darius the king.

7 They sent a report to him in which it was written thus: "To Darius the king, all peace.

8 "Let it be known to the king, that we have gone to the province of Judah, to the house of the great God, which is being built with huge stones, and beams are being laid in the walls; and this work is going on with great care and is succeeding in their hands.

9 "Then we asked those elders and said to them thus, 'Who issued you a decree to rebuild this temple and to finish this structure?'

10 "We also asked them their names so as to inform you, and that we might write down the names of the men who were at their head.

11 "And thus they answered us, saying, 'We are the servants of the God of heaven and earth and are rebuilding the temple that was built many years ago, which a great king of Israel built and finished.

5:12
2 Chr 36:16,
17;
2 Kin 24:2;
25:8,9,11
5:13
Ezra 1:1
12 'But because our fathers had provoked the God of heaven to wrath, He gave them into the hand of Nebuchadnezzar king of Babylon, the Chaldean, *who* destroyed this temple and deported the people to Babylon.

13 'However, in the first year of Cyrus king of Babylon, King Cyrus issued a decree to rebuild this house of God.

[4]Lit., *house,* and so throughout this context

14 'And also the gold and silver utensils of the house of God which Nebuchadnezzar had taken from the temple in Jerusalem, and brought them to the temple of Babylon, these King Cyrus took from the temple of Babylon, and they were given to one whose name was Sheshbazzar, whom he had appointed governor.

15 'And he said to him, "Take these utensils, go *and* deposit them in the temple in Jerusalem, and let the house of God be rebuilt in its place."

16 'Then that Sheshbazzar came *and* laid the foundations of the house of God in Jerusalem; and from then until now it has been under construction, and it is not *yet* completed.'

17 "And now, if it pleases the king let a search be conducted in the king's treasure house, which is there in Babylon, if it be that a decree was issued by King Cyrus to rebuild this house of God at Jerusalem; and let the king send to us his decision concerning this *matter*."

d. *Darius's search and reply*

6 Then King Darius issued a decree, and search was made in the [5]archives, where the treasures were stored in Babylon.

2 And in [6]Ecbatana in the fortress, which is in the province of Media, a scroll was found and there was written in it as follows: "Memorandum—

3 "In the first year of King Cyrus, Cyrus the king issued a decree: '*Concerning* the house of God at Jerusalem, let the temple, the place where sacrifices are offered, be rebuilt and let its foundations be retained, its height being 60 cubits and its width 60 cubits;

4 with three layers of huge stones, and one layer of timbers. And let the cost be paid from the royal treasury.

5 'And also let the gold and silver utensils of the temple of God, which Nebuchadnezzar took from the temple in Jerusalem and brought to Babylon, be returned and brought to their places in the temple in Jerusalem; and you shall put *them* in the house of God.'

6 "Now *therefore*, Tattenai, governor of *the province* beyond the River, Shetharbozenai, and your colleagues, the officials of *the provinces* beyond the River, keep away from there.

7 "Leave this work on the house of God alone; let the governor of the Jews and the elders of the Jews rebuild this house of God on its site.

8 "Moreover, I issue a decree concerning what you are to do for these elders of Judah in the rebuilding of this house of God: the full cost is to be paid to these people from the royal treasury out of the taxes of *the provinces* beyond the River, and that without delay.

9 "And whatever is needed, both young bulls, rams, and lambs for a burnt offering to the God of heaven, and wheat, salt, wine, and anointing oil, as the priests in Jerusalem request, *it* is to be given to them daily without fail,

10 that they may offer [7]acceptable sacrifices to the God of heaven and pray for the life of the king and his sons.

11 "And I issued a decree that any man who violates this edict, a timber shall be drawn from his house and he shall be impaled on it and his house shall be made a refuse heap on account of this.

12 "And may the God who has caused His name to dwell there overthrow any king or people who attempts to change *it*, so as to destroy this house of God in Jerusalem. I, Darius, have issued *this* decree, let *it* be carried out with all diligence!"

e. *The rebuilding of the temple completed*

13 Then Tattenai, the governor of *the province* beyond the River, Shetharbozenai, and their colleagues carried out *the decree* with all diligence, just as King Darius had sent.

14 And the elders of the Jews were successful in building through the prophesying of Haggai the prophet and Zechariah the son of Iddo. And they finished building according to the command of the God of Israel and the decree of Cyrus, Darius, and Artaxerxes king of Persia.

15 And this temple was completed on the third day of the month Adar; it was the sixth year of the reign of King Darius.

---

[5]Lit., *house of the books*   [6]Aram., *Achmetha*   [7]Lit., *pleasing* or *sweet-smelling sacrifices*

6:14 *Artaxerxes* is a later addition. He did not reign until fifty years after the temple was completed.   **6:15** *sixth year*, 515 B.C.

Cross references (margin):

5:14 Ezra 1:7; 6:5; Dan 5:2; v. 16; Ezra 1:8

5:16 Ezra 3:8,10; 6:15

5:17 Ezra 6:1,2

6:1 Ezra 5:17

6:3 Ezra 1:1

6:4 1 Kin 6:36

6:5 Ezra 1:7,8; 5:14

6:6 v. 13; Ezra 5:3

6:10 Ezra 7:23

6:11 Ezra 7:26; Dan 2:5; 3:29

6:12 Deut 12:5; 11

6:13 v. 6

*6:14 Ezra 5:1,2; 1:1; v. 12; Ezra 7:1

f. The temple dedicated: the Passover and Feast
of Unleavened Bread celebrated

6:16
1 Kin 8:63;
2 Chr 7:5
*6:17
Ezra 8:35

16   And the sons of Israel, the priests, the Levites, and the rest of the exiles, celebrated the dedication of this house of God with joy.

17   And they offered for the dedication of this temple of God 100 bulls, 200 rams, 400 lambs, and as a sin offering for all Israel 12 male goats, corresponding to the number of the tribes of Israel.

6:18
2 Chr 35:5;
1 Chr 23:6;
Num 3:6; 8:9
6:19
Ezra 1:11;
Ex 12:6
6:20
2 Chr 29:34;
30:15; 35:11
6:21
Neh 9:2;
10:28;
Ezra 9:11
*6:22
Ex 12:15;
Ezra 7:27;
1:1; 6:2

18   Then they appointed the priests to their divisions and the Levites in their orders for the service of God in Jerusalem, as it is written in the book of Moses.

19   And the exiles observed the Passover on the fourteenth of the first month.

20   For the priests and the Levites had purified themselves together; all of them were pure. Then they slaughtered the Passover *lamb* for all the exiles, both for their brothers the priests and for themselves.

21   And the sons of Israel who returned from exile and all those who had separated themselves from the impurity of the nations of the land to *join* them, to seek the LORD God of Israel, ate *the Passover.*

22   And they observed the Feast of Unleavened Bread seven days with joy, for the LORD had caused them to rejoice, and had turned the heart of the king of Assyria toward them to encourage them in the work of the house of God, the God of Israel.

III. *The return of Ezra and the reform that followed*

(7:1–10:44)

A. *Ezra's genealogy and career*

7:1
1 Chr 6:4-14;
vv. 12,21;
Neh 2:1

7   Now after these things, in the reign of Artaxerxes king of Persia, *there went up* Ezra son of Seraiah, son of Azariah, son of Hilkiah,

2   son of Shallum, son of Zadok, son of Ahitub,

3   son of Amariah, son of Azariah, son of Meraioth,

4   son of Zerahiah, son of Uzzi, son of Bukki,

5   son of Abishua, son of Phinehas, son of Eleazar, son of Aaron the chief priest.

7:6
vv. 9,11,12,
21,28

6   This Ezra went up from Babylon, and he was a scribe skilled in the law of Moses, which the LORD God of Israel had given; and the king granted him all he requested because the hand of the LORD his God *was* upon him.

*7:7
Ezra 8:1-20

7   And some of the sons of Israel and some of the priests, the Levites, the singers, the gatekeepers, and the temple servants went up to Jerusalem in the seventh year of King Artaxerxes.

8   And he came to Jerusalem in the fifth month, which was in the seventh year of the king.

7:9
v. 6

9   For on the first of the first month he began to go up from Babylon; and on the first of the fifth month he came to Jerusalem, because the good hand of his God *was* upon him.

7:10
Ps 119:45;
v. 25;
Neh 8:1-8

10   For Ezra had set his heart to study the law of the LORD, and to practice *it,* and to teach *His* statutes and ordinances in Israel.

B. *Ezra's commission from Artaxerxes*

11   Now this is the copy of the decree which King Artaxerxes gave to Ezra the priest, the scribe, learned in the words of the commandments of the LORD and His statutes to Israel:

7:12
Ezek 26:7;
Dan 2:37

12   "Artaxerxes, king of kings, to Ezra the priest, the scribe of the law of the God of heaven, perfect *peace.* And now

13   I have issued a decree that any of the people of Israel and their priests and the Levites in my kingdom who are willing to go to Jerusalem, may go with you.

7:14
Esth 1:14

14   "Forasmuch as you are sent by the king and his seven counselors to inquire

---

6:17 The return of the remnant was accompanied by the rebuilding of the temple, which never attained the glory of the Solomonic temple. Neither was there a restoration of the kingship or of the earlier theocracy. Nothing in Scripture indicates that the shekinah glory of God filled this temple as in the case of Solomon's house of worship. The temple itself was enlarged and embellished by Herod the Great and his immediate successors. It was finally destroyed in A.D. 70

when Jerusalem fell to the legions of Titus.
6:22 A Persian king is meant. The reason for the Assyrian designation is not clear.
7:7 *seventh year.* If Artaxerxes I, then it would be 458 B.C.; but if Artaxerxes II, then 397 B.C. Some suggest that the number "thirty" (which begins with the same letter as "seventh" and "year")) has accidentally dropped out. If so, then Ezra came in 428 B.C.

concerning Judah and Jerusalem according to the law of your God which is in your hand,

15   and to bring the silver and gold, which the king and his counselors have freely offered to the God of Israel, whose dwelling is in Jerusalem,

16   with all the silver and gold which you shall find in the whole province of Babylon, along with the freewill offering of the people and of the priests, who offered willingly for the house of their God which is in Jerusalem;

17   with this money, therefore, you shall diligently buy bulls, rams, and lambs, with their grain offerings and their libations and offer them on the altar of the house of your God which is in Jerusalem.

18   "And whatever seems good to you and to your brothers to do with the rest of the silver and gold, you may do according to the will of your God.

19   "Also the utensils which are given to you for the service of the house of your God, deliver in full before the God of Jerusalem.

20   "And the rest of the needs for the house of your God, for which you may have occasion to provide, provide *for it* from the royal treasury.

21   "And I, even I King Artaxerxes, issue a decree to all the treasurers who are *in the provinces* beyond the River, that whatever Ezra the priest, the scribe of the law of the God of heaven, may require of you, it shall be done diligently,

22   *even* up to 100 talents of silver, 100 kors of wheat, 100 baths of wine, 100 baths of oil, and salt as needed.

23   "Whatever is commanded by the God of heaven, let it be done with zeal for the house of the God of heaven, lest there be wrath against the kingdom of the king and his sons.

24   "We also inform you that it is not allowed to impose tax, tribute or toll *on* any of the priests, Levites, singers, doorkeepers, Nethinim, or servants of this house of God.

25   "And you, Ezra, according to the wisdom of your God which is in your hand, appoint magistrates and judges that they may judge all the people who are in *the province* beyond the River, *even* all those who know the laws of your God; and you may teach anyone who is ignorant *of them*.

26   "And whoever will not observe the law of your God and the law of the king, let judgment be executed upon him strictly, whether for death or for banishment or for confiscation of goods or for imprisonment."

C. *Ezra's song of praise*

27   Blessed be the LORD, the God of our fathers, who has put *such a thing* as this in the king's heart, to adorn the house of the LORD which is in Jerusalem,

28   and has extended lovingkindness to me before the king and his counselors and before all the king's mighty princes. Thus I was strengthened according to the hand of the LORD my God upon me, and I gathered leading men from Israel to go up with me.

D. *The list of the returning remnant*

8 Now these are the heads of their fathers' *households* and the genealogical enrollment of those who went up with me from Babylon in the reign of King Artaxerxes:

2   of the sons of Phinehas, Gershom; of the sons of Ithamar, Daniel; of the sons of David, Hattush;

3   of the sons of Shecaniah *who was* of the sons of Parosh, Zechariah and with him 150 males *who were in* the genealogical list;

4   of the sons of Pahath-moab, Eliehoenai the son of Zerahiah and 200 males with him;

5   of the sons of Shecaniah, the son of Jahaziel and 300 males with him;

6   and of the sons of Adin, Ebed the son of Jonathan and 50 males with him;

7   and of the sons of Elam, Jeshaiah the son of Athaliah and 70 males with him;

8   and of the sons of Shephatiah, Zebadiah the son of Michael and 80 males with him;

9   of the sons of Joab, Obadiah the son of Jehiel and 218 males with him;

10   and of the sons of Shelomith, the son of Josiphiah and 160 males with him;

11   and of the sons of Bebai, Zechariah the son of Bebai and 28 males with him;

7:15
2 Chr 6:2;
Ezra 6:12
7:16
Ezra 8:25;
1 Chr 29:6,9;
Ezra 1:4,6
7:17
Num 15:4-13;
Deut 12:5-11

7:20
Ezra 6:4

7:21
v. 6

7:23
Ezra 6:10

7:25
Ex 18:21;
Deut 16:18;
v. 10

7:27
1 Chr 29:10;
Ezra 6:22
7:28
Ezra 9:9;
vv. 6,9

8:2
1 Chr 3:22

8:3
Ezra 2:3

12   and of the sons of Azgad, Johanan the son of Hakkatan and 110 males with him;

13   and of the sons of Adonikam, the last ones, these being their names, Eliphelet, Jeuel, and Shemaiah and 60 males with them;

14   and of the sons of Bigvai, Uthai and Zabbud and 70 males with them.

E. *The selection of temple servants*

8:15
vv. 21,31;
Ezra 7:7

15   Now I assembled them at the river that runs to Ahava, where we camped for three days; and when I observed the people and the priests, I did not find any Levites there.

16   So I sent for Eliezer, Ariel, Shemaiah, Elnathan, Jarib, Elnathan, Nathan, Zechariah, and Meshullam, leading men, and for Joiarib and Elnathan, teachers.

8:17
Ezra 2:43

17   And I sent them to Iddo the leading man at the place Casiphia; and I told them what to say to Iddo *and* his brothers, the temple servants at the place Casiphia, *that is,* to bring ministers to us for the house of our God.

8:18
Ezra 7:6

18   And according to the good hand of our God upon us they brought us a man of insight of the sons of Mahli, the son of Levi, the son of Israel, namely Sherebiah, and his sons and brothers, 18 men;

19   and Hashabiah and Jeshaiah of the sons of Merari, with his brothers and their sons, 20 men;

8:20
Ezra 2:43

20   and 220 of the temple servants, whom David and the princes had given for the service of the Levites, all of them designated by name.

F. *The return to the land*

1. *A fast proclaimed*

8:21
2 Chr 20:3;
Is 58:3,5

21   Then I proclaimed a fast there at the river of Ahava, that we might humble ourselves before our God to seek from Him a safe journey for us, our little ones, and all our possessions.

8:22
Ezra 7:6,9,
28; Ps 33:18,
19; 34:16;
2 Chr 15:2

22   For I was ashamed to request from the king troops and horsemen to protect us from the enemy on the way, because we had said to the king, "The hand of our God is favorably disposed to all those who seek Him, but His power and His anger are against all those who forsake Him."

8:23
2 Chr 33:13

23   So we fasted and sought our God concerning this *matter*, and He listened to our entreaty.

2. *The treasure cared for*

24   Then I set apart twelve of the leading priests, Sherebiah, Hashabiah, and with them ten of their brothers;

8:25
Ezra 7:15,16

25   and I weighed out to them the silver, the gold, and the utensils, the offering for the house of our God which the king and his counselors and his princes, and all Israel present *there,* had offered.

8:26
Ezra 1:9-11

26   Thus I weighed into their hands 650 talents of silver, and silver utensils *worth* 100 talents, *and* 100 gold talents,

27   and 20 gold bowls, *worth* 1,000 darics; and two utensils of fine shiny bronze, precious as gold.

8:28
Lev 21:6-8;
22:2,3
8:29
vv. 33,34

28   Then I said to them, "You are holy to the Lord, and the utensils are holy; and the silver and the gold are a freewill offering to the Lord God of your fathers.

29   "Watch and keep *them* until you weigh *them* before the leading priests, the Levites, and the heads of the fathers' *households* of Israel at Jerusalem, *in* the chambers of the house of the Lord."

30   So the priests and the Levites accepted the weighed out silver and gold and the utensils, to bring *them* to Jerusalem to the house of our God.

3. *The departure from Ahava and arrival at Jerusalem*

8:31
Ezra 7:6,9,28

31   Then we journeyed from the river Ahava on the twelfth of the first month to go to Jerusalem; and the hand of our God was over us, and He delivered us from the hand of the enemy and the ambushes by the way.

8:32
Neh 2:11

32   Thus we came to Jerusalem and remained there three days.

8:33
vv. 26,30

33   And on the fourth day the silver and the gold and the utensils were weighed out in the house of our God into the hand of Meremoth the son of Uriah the priest, and with him *was* Eleazar the son of Phinehas; and with them *were* the Levites, Jozabad the son of Jeshua and Noadiah the son of Binnui.

34 Everything *was* numbered and weighed, and all the weight was recorded at that time.

35 The exiles who had come from the captivity offered burnt offerings to the God of Israel: 12 bulls for all Israel, 96 rams, 77 lambs, 12 male goats for a sin offering, all as a burnt offering to the LORD.

36 Then they delivered the king's edicts to the king's satraps, and to the governors *in the provinces* beyond the River, and they supported the people and the house of God.

G. *The reformation of the people*

1. *Ezra bemoans the mixed marriages*

9 Now when these things had been completed, the princes approached me, saying, "The people of Israel and the priests and the Levites have not separated themselves from the peoples of the lands, according to their abominations, *those* of the Canaanites, the Hittites, the Perizzites, the Jebusites, the Ammonites, the Moabites, the Egyptians, and the Amorites.

2 "For they have taken some of their daughters *as wives* for themselves and for their sons, so that the holy race has intermingled with the peoples of the lands; indeed, the hands of the princes and the rulers have been foremost in this unfaithfulness."

3 And when I heard about this matter, I tore my garment and my robe, and pulled some of the hair from my head and my beard, and sat down appalled.

4 Then everyone who trembled at the words of the God of Israel on account of the unfaithfulness of the exiles gathered to me, and I sat appalled until the evening offering.

2. *Ezra's prayer*

5 But at the evening offering I arose from my humiliation, even with my garment and my robe torn, and I fell on my knees and stretched out my hands to the LORD my God;

6 and I said, "O my God, I am ashamed and embarrassed to lift up my face to Thee, my God, for our iniquities have risen above our heads, and our guilt has grown even to the heavens.

7 "Since the days of our fathers to this day we *have been* in great guilt, and on account of our iniquities we, our kings *and* our priests have been given into the hand of the kings of the lands, to the sword, to captivity, and to plunder and to open shame, as *it is* this day.

8 "But now for a brief moment grace has been *shown* from the LORD our God, to leave us an escaped remnant and to give us a peg in His holy place, that our God may enlighten our eyes and grant us a little reviving in our bondage.

9 "For we are slaves; yet in our bondage, our God has not forsaken us, but has extended lovingkindness to us in the sight of the kings of Persia, to give us reviving to raise up the house of our God, to restore its ruins, and to give us a wall in Judah and Jerusalem.

10 "And now, our God, what shall we say after this? For we have forsaken Thy commandments,

11 which Thou hast commanded by Thy servants the prophets, saying, 'The land which you are entering to possess is an unclean land with the uncleanness of the peoples of the lands, with their abominations which have filled it from end to end *and* with their impurity.

12 'So now do not give your daughters to their sons nor take their daughters to your sons, and never seek their peace or their prosperity, that you may be strong and eat the good *things* of the land and leave *it* as an inheritance to your sons forever.'

13 "And after all that has come upon us for our evil deeds and our great guilt, since Thou our God hast requited *us* less than our iniquities *deserve*, and hast given us an escaped remnant as this,

14 shall we again break Thy commandments and intermarry with the peoples who commit these abominations? Wouldst Thou not be angry with us to the point of destruction, until there is no remnant nor any who escape?

15 "O LORD God of Israel, Thou art righteous, for we have been left an escaped remnant, as *it is* this day; behold, we are before Thee in our guilt, for no one can stand before Thee because of this."

8:35
Ezra 2:1;
6:17

8:36
Ezra 7:21

9:1
Ezra 6:21;
Neh 9:2;
Lev 18:24-30

9:2
Ezra 10:2,18;
Ex 22:31;
Neh 13:3

9:3
Job 1:20;
Neh 1:4
9:4
Ezra 10:3;
Ex 29:39

9:5
Ex 9:29,33

9:6
Dan 9:7,8;
2 Chr 28:9;
Rev 18:5
9:7
Dan 9:5,6;
Deut 28:36,
64; Dan 9:7,8

9:8
Is 22:23;
Ps 13:3; 34:5

9:9
Neh 9:36;
Ezra 7:28

9:11
Ezra 6:21

9:12
Deut 7:3;
23:6;
Prov 13:22
9:13
vv. 6-8

9:14
v. 2;
Neh 13:23,
27; Deut 9:8,
14
9:15
Neh 9:33;
Dan 9:14;
v. 6; Ps 130:3

3. Ezra's reform

10 Now while Ezra was praying and making confession, weeping and prostrating himself before the house of God, a very large assembly, men, women, and children, gathered to him from Israel; for the people wept bitterly.

2 And Shecaniah the son of Jehiel, one of the sons of Elam, answered and said to Ezra, "We have been unfaithful to our God, and have married foreign women from the peoples of the land; yet now there is hope for Israel in spite of this.

3 "So now let us make a covenant with our God to put away all the wives and their children, according to the counsel of [8]my lord and of those who tremble at the commandment of our God; and let it be done according to the law.

4 "Arise! For *this* matter is your responsibility, but we will be with you; be courageous and act."

5 Then Ezra rose and made the leading priests, the Levites, and all Israel, take oath that they would do according to this proposal; so they took the oath.

6 Then Ezra rose from before the house of God and went into the chamber of Jehohanan the son of Eliashib. Although he went there, he did not eat bread, nor drink water, for he was mourning over the unfaithfulness of the exiles.

7 And they made a proclamation throughout Judah and Jerusalem to all the exiles, that they should assemble at Jerusalem,

8 and that whoever would not come within three days, according to the counsel of the leaders and the elders, all his possessions should be forfeited and he himself excluded from the assembly of the exiles.

9 So all the men of Judah and Benjamin assembled at Jerusalem within the three days. It was the ninth month on the twentieth of the month, and all the people sat in the open square *before* the house of God, trembling because of this matter and the heavy rain.

10 Then Ezra the priest stood up and said to them, "You have been unfaithful and have married foreign wives adding to the guilt of Israel.

11 "Now, therefore, make confession to the LORD God of your fathers, and do His will; and separate yourselves from the peoples of the land and from the foreign wives."

12 Then all the assembly answered and said with a loud voice, "That's right! As you have said, so it is our duty to do.

13 "But there are many people, it is the rainy season, and we are not able to stand in the open. Nor *can* the task *be done* in one or two days, for we have transgressed greatly in this matter.

14 "Let our leaders represent the whole assembly and let all those in our cities who have married foreign wives come at appointed times, together with the elders and judges of each city, until the fierce anger of our God on account of this matter is turned away from us."

15 Only Jonathan the son of Asahel and Jahzeiah the son of Tikvah opposed this, with Meshullam and Shabbethai the Levite supporting them.

16 But the exiles did so. And Ezra the priest selected men *who were* heads of fathers' *households* for *each of* their father's households, all of them by name. So they convened on the first day of the tenth month to investigate the matter.

17 And they finished *investigating* all the men who had married foreign wives by the first of the first month.

4. The list of the offending priests

18 And among the sons of the priests who had married foreign wives were found of the sons of Jeshua the son of Jozadak, and his brothers: Maaseiah, Eliezer, Jarib, and Gedaliah.

19 And they pledged to put away their wives, and being guilty, *they offered* a ram of the flock for their offense.

20 And of the sons of Immer *there were* Hanani and Zebadiah;

21 and of the sons of Harim: Maaseiah, Elijah, Shemaiah, Jehiel, and Uzziah;

22 and of the sons of Pashhur: Elioenai, Maaseiah, Ishmael, Nethanel, Jozabad, and Elasah.

Margin references:

10:1 Dan 9:4,20; 2 Chr 20:9
*10:2 Ezra 9:2; Neh 13:27
10:3 2 Chr 34:31; v. 44; Ezra 9:4; Deut 7:2,3
10:4 1 Chr 28:10
10:5 Neh 5:12
*10:6 Deut 9:18
10:9 v. 3; Ezra 9:4
10:11 Lev 26:40; v. 3
10:14 2 Chr 29:10; 30:8
10:16 Ezra 4:1
10:19 2 Kin 10:15; 2 Chr 30:8; Lev 5:15; 6:6

---

[8]Or, *the Lord*

10:2 *Shecaniah,* convicted of his sin, evidences true repentance.

10:6 *Jehohanan.* Perhaps Johanan, the grandson of Eliashib (Neh. 12:22).

23 And of Levites *there were* Jozabad, Shimei, Kelaiah (that is, Kelita), Pethahiah, Judah, and Eliezer.

24 And of the singers *there was* Eliashib; and of the gatekeepers: Shallum, Telem, and Uri.

25 And of Israel, of the sons of Parosh *there were* Ramiah, Izziah, Malchijah, Mijamin, Eleazar, Malchijah, and Benaiah;

26 and of the sons of Elam: Mattaniah, Zechariah, Jehiel, Abdi, Jeremoth, and Elijah;

27 and of the sons of Zattu: Elioenai, Eliashib, Mattaniah, Jeremoth, Zabad, and Aziza;

28 and of the sons of Bebai: Jehohanan, Hananiah, Zabbai, *and* Athlai;

29 and of the sons of Bani: Meshullam, Malluch, and Adaiah, Jashub, Sheal, *and* Jeremoth;

30 and of the sons of Pahath-moab: Adna, Chelal, Benaiah, Maaseiah, Mattaniah, Bezalel, Binnui, and Manasseh;

31 and *of* the sons of Harim: Eliezer, Isshijah, Malchijah, Shemaiah, Shimeon,

32 Benjamin, Malluch, *and* Shemariah;

33 of the sons of Hashum: Mattenai, Mattattah, Zabad, Eliphelet, Jeremai, Manasseh, *and* Shimei.

34 of the sons of Bani: Maadai, Amram, Uel,

35 Benaiah, Bedeiah, Cheluhi,

36 Vaniah, Meremoth, Eliashib,

37 Mattaniah, Mattenai, Jaasu,

38 Bani, Binnui, Shimei,

39 Shelemiah, Nathan, Adaiah,

40 Machnadebai, Shashai, Sharai,

41 Azarel, Shelemiah, Shemariah,

42 Shallum, Amariah, *and* Joseph.

43 Of the sons of Nebo *there were* Jeiel, Mattithiah, Zabad, Zebina, Jaddai, Joel, *and* Benaiah.

44 All these had married foreign wives, and some of them had wives *by whom* they had children.

10:23
Ex 6:25

10:25
v. 1

10:44
v. 3

INTRODUCTION TO
THE BOOK OF
NEHEMIAH

Authorship and Background: The book of Nehemiah, named for its leading figure, is part of the book of Ezra in the Hebrew Bible. Internal evidence suggests two separate sources: the material that concludes the Chronicler's history (Ezra 1-10; Neh. 8-10) and the memoirs of Nehemiah (1-7,11-13). External evidence (for example, Elephantine letter #30 noted in the Introduction to Ezra) indicates that very little of the history or the memoirs may be dated after about 400 B.C. The two sources were put together by the author, but it is difficult to say just when this happened. Scholars have differed as to whether Nehemiah followed Ezra or vice versa. Nehemiah, like Ezra, is one of the five historical books that are part of the Hagiographa, which include the poetical books and the Megilloth (the Scrolls).

Nehemiah was a cupbearer for Artaxerxes. His name means "whom God hath comforted." The return of the first remnant occurred almost a hundred years before Nehemiah went back to Jerusalem. His call to service came as the result of a discouraging report brought to him at the Persian court by a kinsman named Hanani. He went to Jerusalem with the permission of Artaxerxes. A man of great energy and self-denial, he was able to cope successfully with plots laid against the Jews by neighboring peoples.

Characteristics: The first part of the book is autobiographical, containing the memoirs of Nehemiah. It is a personal report of his own activities that was incorporated into the book. These memoirs and the book of Ezra supply most of our knowledge of Jewish history from 538 to 430 B.C. Like Ezra, there are lists found in Nehemiah: one is geographical (11:25-35); another itemizes the gifts to the temple (7:70-72). The portion of the book that contains the memoirs of Nehemiah differs markedly from the remainder of the book. The style is somewhat disjointed and the account disconnected.

Contents:

I. The rebuilding of the walls and the reform movement of Nehemiah (1:1-7:73a): Nehemiah hears from Jerusalem, prays, and seeks permission to return. He arrives in Jerusalem, inspects the walls, and encourages the people to build. A conflict arises from neighboring officials. The rebuilding of the gates. Sanballat's opposition. Nehemiah defends the poor and stops usury. Sanballat, Shemaiah, and Tobiah fail to halt the work. The wall is finished and Jerusalem resettled. The genealogy of the exiles.

II. The reading of the Law and the renewing of the covenant (7:73b-10:39): The people are assembled and the Law read. They are enjoined to celebrate; the Feast of Booths is held. A penitential psalm is sung praising God as Creator and remembering former mercies in Egypt, in the exodus, the wanderings, and in the conquest of Canaan. A plea for mercy and salvation is made. A pledge for reform is drawn up and signed by officials, priests, Levites, and laymen. Its legislative acts include prohibition against mixed marriages, the observance of the Sabbath, the temple tax, wood offering, first fruits, tithes, and a pledge to support the temple.

III. The reconstituting of Jerusalem: Nehemiah's second reform movement (11:1-13:31): The listing of those who repeopled Jerusalem, and the names of the towns outside Jerusalem that were settled. A list of the priests and Levites. The walls of Jerusalem are dedicated: the Levites and musicians are assembled, rites of purification celebrated, the city circumambulated, and sacrifices offered. The ideal community is described. Nehemiah expels Tobiah, gathers support for the Levites, engages in Sabbath and mixed-marriage reforms.

THE BOOK OF
NEHEMIAH

I. *The rebuilding of the walls and the reform movement*
of Nehemiah (1:1–7:73a)

A. *Introduction*

1. *Nehemiah's sorrow*

1 The words of Nehemiah the son of Hacaliah.
Now it happened in the month Chislev, *in* the twentieth year, while I was in Susa the ¹capitol,
2   that Hanani, one of my brothers, and some men from Judah came; and I asked them concerning the Jews who had escaped *and* had survived the captivity, and about Jerusalem.
3   And they said to me, "The remnant there in the province who survived the captivity are in great distress and reproach, and the wall of Jerusalem is broken down and its gates are burned with fire."
4   Now it came about when I heard these words, I sat down and wept and mourned for days; and I was fasting and praying before the God of heaven.
5   And I said, "I beseech Thee, O LORD God of heaven, the great and awesome God, who preserves the covenant and lovingkindness for those who love Him and keep His commandments,
6   let Thine ear now be attentive and Thine eyes open to hear the prayer of Thy servant which I am praying before Thee now, day and night, on behalf of the sons of Israel Thy servants, confessing the sins of the sons of Israel which we have sinned against Thee; I and my father's house have sinned.
7   "We have acted very corruptly against Thee and have not kept the commandments, nor the statutes, nor the ordinances which Thou didst command Thy servant Moses.
8   "Remember the word which Thou didst command Thy servant Moses, saying, 'If you are unfaithful I will scatter you among the peoples;
9   but if you return to Me and keep My commandments and do them, though those of you who have been scattered were in the most remote part of the heavens, I will gather them from there and will bring them to the place where I have chosen to cause My name to dwell.'
10   "And they are Thy servants and Thy people whom Thou didst redeem by Thy great power and by Thy strong hand.
11   "O Lord, I beseech Thee, may Thine ear be attentive to the prayer of Thy servant and the prayer of Thy servants who delight to revere Thy name, and make Thy servant successful today, and grant him compassion before this man."
Now I was the cupbearer to the king.

2. *Nehemiah's request to go to Jerusalem*

2 And it came about in the month Nisan, in the twentieth year of King Artaxerxes, that wine *was* before him, and I took up the wine and gave it to the king. Now I had not been sad in his presence.
2   So the king said to me, "Why is your face sad though you are not sick? This is nothing but sadness of heart." Then I was very much afraid.

¹Or, *palace* or *citadel*

Marginal references:
*1:1 Neh 10:1; 2:1; Esth 1:2; Dan 8:2
1:3 Neh 7:6; 2:17; 2:3
1:4 Ezra 9:3; 10:1; Neh 2:4
1:5 Neh 4:14; 9:32; Ex 20:6
1:6 Dan 9:17; Ezra 10:1; Dan 9:20; 2 Chr 29:6
1:7 Dan 9:5; Deut 28:14, 15
1:8 Lev 26:33
1:9 Deut 30:2-4; 12:5
1:10 Deut 9:29; Dan 9:15
*1:11 v. 6
2:1 Neh 1:1; Ezra 7:1; Neh 1:11
2:2 Prov 15:13

1:1 *Chislev*, latter part of November and early December; *twentieth year* of Artaxerxes I, that is 445 B.C.
1:11 *cupbearer*. Since ancient monarchs were always in danger of poisoning, the cupbearer had to be the most faithful, trustworthy servant. In most cases he was a eunuch, and such may have been the case with Nehemiah; especially since he was also in contact with the queen (2:6). Deuteronomy 23:1 excludes emasculated persons from the Jewish community, but Nehemiah may have been excepted.

3   And I said to the king, "Let the king live forever. Why should my face not be sad when the city, the place of my fathers' tombs, lies desolate and its gates have been consumed by fire?"

2:3
Dan 2:4;
Neh 1:3

4   Then the king said to me, "What would you request?" So I prayed to the God of heaven.

2:4
Neh 1:4

5   And I said to the king, "If it please the king, and if your servant has found favor before you, send me to Judah, to the city of my fathers' tombs, that I may rebuild it."

6   Then the king said to me, the queen sitting beside him, "How long will your journey be, and when will you return?" So it pleased the king to send me, and I gave him a definite time.

2:6
Neh 5:14;
13:6

7   And I said to the king, "If it please the king, let letters be given me for the governors *of the provinces* beyond the River, that they may allow me to pass through until I come to Judah,

2:7
Ezra 7:21;
8:36

8   and a letter to Asaph the keeper of the king's forest, that he may give me timber to make beams for the gates of the fortress which is by the [2]temple, for the wall of the city, and for the house to which I will go." And the king granted *them* to me because the good hand of my God *was* on me.

2:8
Neh 7:2;
v. 18;
Ezra 7:6

3. *Nehemiah's journey to Jerusalem:*
his inspection of the walls

9   Then I came to the governors *of the provinces* beyond the River and gave them the king's letters. Now the king had sent with me officers of the army and horsemen.

2:9
v. 7;
Ezra 8:22

10   And when Sanballat the Horonite and Tobiah the Ammonite official heard *about it,* it was very displeasing to them that someone had come to seek the welfare of the sons of Israel.

2:10
v. 19;
Neh 4:1

11   So I came to Jerusalem and was there three days.

12   And I arose in the night, I and a few men with me. I did not tell anyone what my God was putting into my mind to do for Jerusalem and there was no animal with me except the animal on which I was riding.

13   So I went out at night by the Valley Gate in the direction of the Dragon's Well and *on* to the Refuse Gate, inspecting the walls of Jerusalem which were broken down and its gates which were consumed by fire.

2:13
Neh 3:13;
vv. 3,17;
Neh 1:3

14   Then I passed on to the Fountain Gate and the King's Pool, but there was no place for my mount to pass.

2:14
Neh 3:15;
2 Kin 20:20

15   So I went up at night by the ravine and inspected the wall. Then I entered the Valley Gate again and returned.

16   And the officials did not know where I had gone or what I had done; nor had I as yet told the Jews, the priests, the nobles, the officials, or the rest who did the work.

4. *Nehemiah's determination to rebuild;*
the opposition of Sanballat and Tobiah

17   Then I said to them, "You see the bad situation we are in, that Jerusalem is desolate and its gates burned by fire. Come, let us rebuild the wall of Jerusalem that we may no longer be a reproach."

2:17
Neh 1:3

18   And I told them how the hand of my God had been favorable to me, and also about the king's words which he had spoken to me. Then they said, "Let us arise and build." So they put their hands to the good *work.*

2:18
v. 8;
2 Sam 2:7

19   But when Sanballat the Horonite, and Tobiah the Ammonite official, and Geshem the Arab heard *it,* they mocked us and despised us and said, "What is this thing you are doing? Are you rebelling against the king?"

2:19
Ps 44:13;
Neh 6:6

20   So I answered them and said to them, "The God of heaven will give us success; therefore we His servants will arise and build, but you have no portion, right, or memorial in Jerusalem."

2:20
v. 4

[2]Lit., *house*

B. *The rebuilding of the walls*

1. *The workers and the places they worked*

3 Then Eliashib the high priest arose with his brothers the priests and built the Sheep Gate; they consecrated it and hung its doors. They consecrated the wall to the Tower of the Hundred *and* the Tower of Hananel.

2 And next to him the men of Jericho built, and next to them Zaccur the son of Imri built.

3 Now the sons of Hassenaah built the Fish Gate; they laid its beams and hung its doors with its bolts and bars.

4 And next to them Meremoth the son of Uriah the son of Hakkoz made repairs. And next to him Meshullam the son of Berechiah the son of Meshezabel made repairs. And next to him Zadok the son of Baana also made repairs.

5 Moreover, next to him the Tekoites made repairs, but their nobles did not support the work of their masters.

6 And Joiada the son of Paseah and Meshullam the son of Besodeiah repaired the Old Gate; they laid its beams and hung its doors, with its bolts and its bars.

7 Next to them Melatiah the Gibeonite and Jadon the Meronothite, the men of Gibeon and of Mizpah, also made repairs for the official seat of the governor *of the province* beyond the River.

8 Next to him Uzziel the son of Harhaiah of the goldsmiths made repairs. And next to him Hananiah, one of the perfumers, made repairs, and they restored Jerusalem as far as the Broad Wall.

9 And next to them Rephaiah the son of Hur, the official of half the district of Jerusalem, made repairs.

10 Next to him Jedaiah the son of Harumaph made repairs opposite his house. And next to him Hattush the son of Hashabneiah made repairs.

11 Malchijah the son of Harim and Hasshub the son of Pahath-moab repaired another section and the Tower of Furnaces.

12 And next to him Shallum the son of Hallohesh, the official of half the district of Jerusalem, made repairs, he and his daughters.

13 Hanun and the inhabitants of Zanoah repaired the Valley Gate. They built it and hung its doors with its bolts and its bars, and a thousand cubits of the wall to the Refuse Gate.

14 And Malchijah the son of Rechab, the official of the district of Beth-haccherem repaired the Refuse Gate. He built it and hung its doors with its bolts and its bars.

15 Shallum the son of Col-hozeh, the official of the district of Mizpah, repaired the Fountain Gate. He built it, covered it, and hung its doors with its bolts and its bars, and the wall of the Pool of Shelah at the king's garden as far as the steps that descend from the city of David.

16 After him Nehemiah the son of Azbuk, official of half the district of Beth-zur, made repairs as far as *a point* opposite the tombs of David, and as far as the artificial pool and the house of the mighty men.

17 After him the Levites carried out repairs *under* Rehum the son of Bani. Next to him Hashabiah, the official of half the district of Keilah, carried out repairs for his district.

18 After him their brothers carried out repairs *under* Bavvai the son of Henadad, official of *the other* half of the district of Keilah.

19 And next to him Ezer the son of Jeshua, the official of Mizpah, repaired another section, in front of the ascent of the armory at the Angle.

20 After him Baruch the son of Zabbai zealously repaired another section, from the Angle to the doorway of the house of Eliashib the high priest.

21 After him Meremoth the son of Uriah the son of Hakkoz repaired another section, from the doorway of Eliashib's house even as far as the end of his house.

22 And after him the priests, the men of the ³valley, carried out repairs.

23 After them Benjamin and Hasshub carried out repairs in front of their house. After them Azariah the son of Maaseiah, son of Ananiah carried out repairs beside his house.

---

³Lit., *circle*; i.e., lower Jordan valley

3:5 *Masters* may be a reference to Nehemiah.   **3:15** *Shelah*, that is, Siloam.

Cross references (left margin):

3:1 — vv. 20,32; Neh 6:1; 7:1; 12:39; Jer 31:38
3:2 — Neh 7:36
3:3 — Neh 12:39
3:6 — Neh 12:39
3:7 — Neh 2:7
3:8 — vv. 31,32; Neh 12:38
3:9 — vv. 12,17
3:11 — Neh 12:38
3:12 — v. 9
3:13 — Neh 2:13
*3:15 — Neh 2:14; 2 Kin 25:4; Neh 12:37
3:16 — vv. 9,12,17; 2 Kin 20:20
3:19 — v. 15; 2 Chr 26:9
3:20 — v. 1; Neh 13:7
3:22 — Neh 12:28

24 After him Binnui the son of Henadad repaired another section, from the house of Azariah as far as the Angle and as far as the corner.

25 Palal the son of Uzai *made repairs* in front of the Angle and the tower projecting from the upper house of the king, which is by the court of the guard. After him Pedaiah the son of Parosh *made repairs*.

26 And the temple servants living in Ophel *made repairs* as far as the front of the Water Gate toward the east and the projecting tower.

27 After him the Tekoites repaired another section in front of the great projecting tower and as far as the wall of Ophel.

28 Above the Horse Gate the priests carried out repairs, each in front of his house.

29 After them Zadok the son of Immer carried out repairs in front of his house. And after him Shemaiah the son of Shecaniah, the keeper of the East Gate, carried out repairs.

30 After him Hananiah the son of Shelemiah, and Hanun the sixth son of Zalaph, repaired another section. After him Meshullam the son of Berechiah carried out repairs in front of his own quarters.

31 After him Malchijah one of the goldsmiths, carried out repairs as far as the house of the temple servants and of the merchants, in front of the Inspection Gate and as far as the upper room of the corner.

32 And between the upper room of the corner and the Sheep Gate the goldsmiths and the merchants carried out repairs.

2. The opposition to the work

a. The stratagems of Sanballat and Tobiah

4 Now it came about that when Sanballat heard that we were rebuilding the wall, he became furious and very angry and mocked the Jews.

2 And he spoke in the presence of his brothers and the wealthy *men* of Samaria and said, "What are these feeble Jews doing? Are they going to restore *it* for themselves? Can they offer sacrifices? Can they finish in a day? Can they revive the stones from the dusty rubble even the burned ones?"

3 Now Tobiah the Ammonite *was* near him and he said, "Even what they are building—if a fox should jump on *it*, he would break their stone wall down!"

4 Hear, O our God, how we are despised! Return their reproach on their own heads and give them up for plunder in a land of captivity.

5 Do not forgive their iniquity and let not their sin be blotted out before Thee, for they have demoralized the builders.

6 So we built the wall and the whole wall was joined together to half its *height*, for the people had a mind to work.

7 Now it came about when Sanballat, Tobiah, the Arabs, the Ammonites, and the Ashdodites heard that the repair of the walls of Jerusalem went on, *and* that the breaches began to be closed, they were very angry.

8 And all of them conspired together to come *and* fight against Jerusalem and to cause a disturbance in it.

9 But we prayed to our God, and because of them we set up a guard against them day and night.

10 Thus in Judah it was said,

"The strength of the burden bearers is failing,
Yet there is much rubbish;
And we ourselves are unable
To rebuild the wall."

11 And our enemies said, "They will not know or see until we come among them, kill them, and put a stop to the work."

12 And it came about when the Jews who lived near them came and told us ten times, "They will come up against us from every place where you may turn,"

13 then I stationed *men* in the lowest parts of the space behind the wall, the exposed places, and I stationed the people in families with their swords, spears, and bows.

14 When I saw *their fear*, I rose and spoke to the nobles, the officials, and the rest of the people: "Do not be afraid of them; remember the Lord who is great and

---

3:24
v. 19

3:25
Jer 32:2

3:26
Neh 7:46;
11:21; 8:1

3:28
2 Kin 11:16;
2 Chr 23:15;
Jer 31:40

3:31
vv. 8,32

3:32
v. 1

4:1
Neh 2:10,19

4:2
v. 10

4:3
Neh 2:10,19

4:4
Ps 123:3,4;
79:12

4:5
Ps 69:27,28;
Jer 18:23

4:7
v. 1

*4:9
Ps 50:15

4:13
vv. 17,18

4:14
Num 14:9;
Deut 1:29;
2 Sam 10:12

4:9 Prayer and works are perfectly illustrated here. We are to pray as though we had never worked and work as though we had never prayed.

awesome, and fight for your brothers, your sons, your daughters, your wives, and your houses."

4:15
2 Sam 17:14;
Job 5:12

15   And it happened when our enemies heard that it was known to us, and that God had frustrated their plan, then all of us returned to the wall, each one to his work.

16   And it came about from that day on, that half of my servants carried on the work while half of them held the spears, the shields, the bows, and the breastplates; and the captains *were* behind the whole house of Judah.

17   Those who were rebuilding the wall and those who carried burdens took *their* load with one hand doing the work and the other holding a weapon.

18   As for the builders, each *wore* his sword girded at his side as he built, while the trumpeter *stood* near me.

19   And I said to the nobles, the officials, and the rest of the people, "The work is great and extensive, and we are separated on the wall far from one another.

4:20
Ex 14:14;
Deut 1:30;
Josh 23:10

20   "At whatever place you hear the sound of the trumpet, rally to us there. Our God will fight for us."

21   So we carried on the work with half of them holding spears from dawn until the stars appeared.

22   At that time I also said to the people, "Let each man with his servant spend the night within Jerusalem so that they may be a guard for us by night and a laborer by day."

23   So neither I, my brothers, my servants, nor the men of the guard who followed me, none of us removed our clothes, each *took* his weapon *even to* the water.

b. Disaffection among the Jews themselves

*5:1
Lev 25:35;
Deut 15:7

5 Now there was a great outcry of the people and of their wives against their Jewish brothers.

2   For there were those who said, "We, our sons and our daughters, are many; therefore let us get grain that we may eat and live."

3   And there were others who said, "We are mortgaging our fields, our vineyards, and our houses that we might get grain because of the famine."

5:4
Ezra 4:13;
7:24
5:5
Gen 37:27;
Lev 25:39

4   Also there were those who said, "We have borrowed money for the king's tax *on* our fields and our vineyards.

5   "And now our flesh is like the flesh of our brothers, our children like their children. Yet behold, we are forcing our sons and our daughters to be slaves, and some of our daughters are forced into bondage *already*, and we are helpless because our fields and vineyards belong to others."

6   Then I was very angry when I had heard their outcry and these words.

5:7
Ex 22:25;
Lev 25:36

7   And I consulted with myself, and contended with the nobles and the rulers and said to them, "You are exacting usury, each from his brother!" Therefore, I held a great assembly against them.

5:8
Lev 25:48

8   And I said to them, "We according to our ability have redeemed our Jewish brothers who were sold to the nations; now would you even sell your brothers that they may be sold to us?" Then they were silent and could not find a word *to* say.

5:9
2 Sam 12:14;
Neh 4:4;
Rom 2:24

9   Again I said, "The thing which you are doing is not good; should you not walk in the fear of our God because of the reproach of the nations, our enemies?

10   "And likewise I, my brothers and my servants, are lending them money and grain. Please, let us leave off this usury.

11   "Please, give back to them this very day their fields, their vineyards, their olive groves, and their houses, also the hundredth *part* of the money and of the grain, the new wine, and the oil that you are exacting from them."

5:12
Ezra 10:5

12   Then they said, "We will give *it* back and will require nothing from them; we will do exactly as you say." So I called the priests and took an oath from them that they would do according to this promise.

5:13
Acts 18:6;
Neh 8:6

13   I also shook out the front of my garment and said, "Thus may God shake out every man from his house and from his possessions who does not fulfill this promise; even thus may he be shaken out and emptied." And all the assembly said, "Amen!" And they praised the LORD. Then the people did according to this promise.

5:14
Neh 13:6;
Ezra 4:13,14

14   Moreover, from the day that I was appointed to be their governor in the land

---

5:1 A reason for the *great outcry* was the exaction of interest (v. 7) by the rich when they loaned money to the poor. This was forbidden, according to Deut. 23:20.

of Judah, from the twentieth year to the thirty-second year of King Artaxerxes, *for* twelve years, neither I nor my kinsmen have eaten the governor's food *allowance*.

15   But the former governors who were before me laid burdens on the people and took from them bread and wine besides forty shekels of silver; even their servants domineered the people. But I did not do so because of the fear of God.

16   And I also [4]applied myself to the work on this wall; we did not buy any land, and all my servants were gathered there for the work.

17   Moreover, *there were* at my table one hundred and fifty Jews and officials, besides those who came to us from the nations that were around us.

18   Now that which was prepared for each day was one ox *and* six choice sheep, also birds were prepared for me; and once in ten days all sorts of wine *were furnished* in abundance. Yet for all this I did not demand the governor's food *allowance*, because the servitude was heavy on this people.

19   Remember me, O my God, for good, *according to* all that I have done for this people.

c. The continued difficulties from Sanballat and Tobiah

6 Now it came about when it was reported to Sanballat, Tobiah, to Geshem the Arab, and to the rest of our enemies that I had rebuilt the wall, and *that* no breach remained in it, although at that time I had not set up the doors in the gates,

2   that Sanballat and Geshem sent *a message* to me, saying, "Come, let us meet together at [5]Chephirim in the plain of Ono." But they were planning to harm me.

3   So I sent messengers to them, saying, "I am doing a great work and I cannot come down. Why should the work stop while I leave it and come down to you?"

4   And they sent *messages* to me four times in this manner, and I answered them in the same way.

5   Then Sanballat sent his servant to me in the same manner a fifth time with an open letter in his hand.

6   In it was written, "It is reported among the nations, and Gashmu says, that you and the Jews are planning to rebel; therefore you are rebuilding the wall. And you are to be their king, according to these reports.

7   "And you have also appointed prophets to proclaim in Jerusalem concerning you, 'A king is in Judah!' And now it will be reported to the king according to these reports. So come now, let us take counsel together."

8   Then I sent *a message* to him saying, "Such things as you are saying have not been done, but you are inventing them in your own mind."

9   For all of them were *trying* to frighten us, thinking, "They will become discouraged with the work and it will not be done." But now, *O God*, strengthen my hands.

10   And when I entered the house of Shemaiah the son of Delaiah, son of Mehetabel, who was confined at home, he said, "Let us meet together in the house of God, within the temple, and let us close the doors of the temple, for they are coming to kill you, and they are coming to kill you at night."

11   But I said, "Should a man like me flee? And could one such as I go into the temple to save his life? I will not go in."

12   Then I perceived that surely God had not sent him, but he uttered *his* prophecy against me because Tobiah and Sanballat had hired him.

13   He was hired for this reason, that I might become frightened and act accordingly and sin, so that they might have an evil report in order that they could reproach me.

14   Remember, O my God, Tobiah and Sanballat according to these works of theirs, and also Noadiah the prophetess and the rest of the prophets who were *trying* to frighten me.

15   So the wall was completed on the twenty-fifth of *the month* Elul, in fifty-two days.

16   And it came about when all our enemies heard *of it*, and all the nations surrounding us saw *it*, they lost their confidence; for they recognized that this work had been accomplished with the help of our God.

[4]Or, *held fast*   [5]Another reading is, one of *the villages*

6:15 *fifty-two days.* This probably refers to the last phase of completion. According to Josephus, it took two years and four months to rebuild the walls.

5:15
v. 9

5:17
1 Kin 18:19

5:18
1 Kin 4:22, 23; 2 Thess 3:8

5:19
Neh 13:14, 22,31

6:1
Neh 2:10,19; 4:1,7; 3:1,3

6:2
1 Chr 8:12

6:6
Neh 2:19

6:10
Jer 36:5

6:12
Ezek 13:22

6:13
v. 6

6:14
Neh 13:29; Ezek 13:17

6:16
Neh 2:10; 4:1,7; Ex 14:25; Ps 126:2

17   Also in those days many letters went from the nobles of Judah to Tobiah, and Tobiah's *letters* came to them.

18   For many in Judah were bound by oath to him because he was the son-in-law of Shecaniah the son of Arah, and his son Jehohanan had married the daughter of Meshullam the son of Berechiah.

19   Moreover, they were speaking about his good deeds in my presence and reported my words to him. Then Tobiah sent letters to frighten me.

C. The new order at Jerusalem and list of returning exiles

1. The appointment of Hanani and Hananiah

7 Now it came about when the wall was rebuilt and I had set up the doors, and the gatekeepers and the singers and the Levites were appointed,

2   that I put Hanani my brother, and Hananiah the commander of the fortress, in charge of Jerusalem, for he was a faithful man and feared God more than many.

3   Then I said to them, "Do not let the gates of Jerusalem be opened until the sun is hot, and while they are standing *guard*, let them shut and bolt the doors. Also appoint guards from the inhabitants of Jerusalem, each at his post, and each in front of his own house."

4   Now the city was large and spacious, but the people in it were few and the houses were not built.

2. The genealogy of the returning remnant

5   Then my God put it into my heart to assemble the nobles, the officials, and the people to be enrolled by genealogies. Then I found the book of the genealogy of those who came up first in which I found the following record:

6   These are the people of the province who came up from the captivity of the exiles whom Nebuchadnezzar the king of Babylon had carried away, and who returned to Jerusalem and Judah, each to his city,

7   who came with Zerubbabel, Jeshua, Nehemiah, Azariah, Raamiah, Nahamani, Mordecai, Bilshan, Mispereth, Bigvai, Nehum, Baanah.
The number of men of the people of Israel:

8   the sons of Parosh, 2,172;
9   the sons of Shephatiah, 372;
10   the sons of Arah, 652;
11   the sons of Pahath-moab of the sons of Jeshua and Joab, 2,818;
12   the sons of Elam, 1,254;
13   the sons of Zattu, 845;
14   the sons of Zaccai, 760;
15   the sons of Binnui, 648;
16   the sons of Bebai, 628;
17   the sons of Azgad, 2,322;
18   the sons of Adonikam, 667;
19   the sons of Bigvai, 2,067;
20   the sons of Adin, 655;
21   the sons of Ater, of Hezekiah, 98;
22   the sons of Hashum, 328;
23   the sons of Bezai, 324;
24   the sons of Hariph, 112;
25   the sons of Gibeon, 95;
26   the men of Bethlehem and Netophah, 188;
27   the men of Anathoth, 128;
28   the men of Beth-azmaveth, 42;
29   the men of Kiriath-jearim, Chephirah, and Beeroth, 743;
30   the men of Ramah and Geba, 621;
31   the men of Michmas, 122;
32   the men of Bethel and Ai, 123;
33   the men of the other Nebo, 52;
34   the sons of the other Elam, 1,254;
35   the sons of Harim, 320;
36   the men of Jericho, 345;
37   the sons of Lod, Hadid, and Ono, 721;
38   the sons of Senaah, 3,930.

7:1 Neh 6:1,15
7:2 Neh 2:8
7:6 Ezra 2:1-70
7:7 Ezra 2:2
7:12 Ezra 2:7
7:17 see Ezra 2:12
7:23 Ezra 2:17
7:27 Ezra 2:23
7:34 Ezra 2:31

39 The priests: the sons of Jedaiah of the house of Jeshua, 973;	**7:39** Ezra 2:36
40 the sons of Immer, 1,052;	
41 the sons of Pashhur, 1,247;	
42 the sons of Harim, 1,017.	
43 The Levites: the sons of Jeshua, of Kadmiel, of the sons of Hodevah, 74.	**7:43** Ezra 2:40
44 The singers: the sons of Asaph, 148.	

45 The gatekeepers: the sons of Shallum, the sons of Ater, the sons of Talmon, the sons of Akkub, the sons of Hatita, the sons of Shobai, 138.

46 The temple servants: the sons of Ziha, the sons of Hasupha, the sons of Tabbaoth,

7:46 Ezra 2:43

47   the sons of Keros, the sons of Sia, the sons of Padon,
48   the sons of Lebana, the sons of Hagaba, the sons of Shalmai,
49   the sons of Hanan, the sons of Giddel, the sons of Gahar,
50   the sons of Reaiah, the sons of Rezin, the sons of Nekoda,
51   the sons of Gazzam, the sons of Uzza, the sons of Paseah,
52   the sons of Besai, the sons of Meunim, the sons of Nephushesim,
53   the sons of Bakbuk, the sons of Hakupha, the sons of Harhur,
54   the sons of Bazlith, the sons of Mehida, the sons of Harsha,
55   the sons of Barkos, the sons of Sisera, the sons of Temah,
56   the sons of Neziah, the sons of Hatipha.

57 The sons of Solomon's servants: the sons of Sotai, the sons of Sophereth, the sons of Perida,

7:57 Ezra 2:55

58   the sons of Jaala, the sons of Darkon, the sons of Giddel,

59   the sons of Shephatiah, the sons of Hattil, the sons of Pochereth-hazzebaim, the sons of Amon.

60   All the temple servants and the sons of Solomon's servants *were* 392.

7:60 v. 46

61 And these *were* they who came up from Tel-melah, Tel-harsha, Cherub, Addon, and Immer; but they could not show their fathers' houses or their descendants, whether they were of Israel:

62   the sons of Delaiah, the sons of Tobiah, the sons of Nekoda, 642.

63   And of the priests: the sons of Hobaiah, the sons of Hakkoz, the sons of Barzillai, who took a wife of the daughters of Barzillai, the Gileadite, and was named after them.

7:63 Ezra 2:61

64   These searched *among* their ancestral registration, but it could not be located; therefore they were considered unclean *and excluded* from the priesthood.

65   And the governor said to them that they should not eat from the most holy things until a priest arose with Urim and Thummim.

7:65 Neh 8:9; 10:1

66 The whole assembly together *was* 42,360,

67   besides their male and their female servants, of whom *there were* 7,337; and they had 245 male and female singers.

68   Their horses were 736; their mules, 245;

69   *their* camels, 435; *their* donkeys, 6,720.

70 And some from among the heads of fathers' *households* gave to the work. The governor gave to the treasury 1,000 gold drachmas, 50 basins, 530 priests' garments.

7:70 Neh 8:9

71   And some of the heads of fathers' *households* gave into the treasury of the work 20,000 gold drachmas, and 2,200 silver minas.

7:71 Ezra 2:69

72   And that which the rest of the people gave was 20,000 gold drachmas and 2,000 silver minas, and 67 priests' garments.

73 Now the priests, the Levites, the gatekeepers, the singers, some of the people, the temple servants, and all Israel, lived in their cities.

7:73 Ezra 3:1

And when the seventh month came, the sons of Israel *were* in their cities.

II. *The reading of the Law and the renewing of the covenant (7:73b–10:39)*

A. *The Law read and explained*

8 And all the people gathered as one man at the square which was in front of the Water Gate, and they asked Ezra the scribe to bring the book of the law of Moses which the LORD had given to Israel.

8:1 Ezra 3:1; Neh 3:26; Ezra 7:6

2   Then Ezra the priest brought the law before the assembly of men, women, and all who *could* listen with understanding, on the first day of the seventh month.

8:2 Deut 31:11, 12; Lev 23:24

3 And he read from it before the square which was in front of the Water Gate from early morning until midday, in the presence of men and women, those who could understand; and all the people were attentive to the book of the law.

4 And Ezra the scribe stood at a wooden podium which they had made for the purpose. And beside him stood Mattithiah, Shema, Anaiah, Uriah, Hilkiah, and Maaseiah on his right hand; and Pedaiah, Mishael, Malchijah, Hashum, Hashbaddanah, Zechariah, *and* Meshullam on his left hand.

5 And Ezra opened the book in the sight of all the people for he was standing above all the people; and when he opened it, all the people stood up.

6 Then Ezra blessed the LORD the great God. And all the people answered, "Amen, Amen!" while lifting up their hands; then they bowed low and worshiped the LORD with *their* faces to the ground.

7 Also Jeshua, Bani, Sherebiah, Jamin, Akkub, Shabbethai, Hodiah, Maaseiah, Kelita, Azariah, Jozabad, Hanan, Pelaiah, and the Levites, explained the law to the people while the people *remained* in their place.

8 And they read from the book, from the law of God, translating to give the sense so that they understood the reading.

9 Then Nehemiah, who was the governor, and Ezra the priest *and* scribe, and the Levites who taught the people said to all the people, "This day is holy to the LORD your God; do not mourn or weep." For all the people were weeping when they heard the words of the law.

10 Then he said to them, "Go, eat of the fat, drink of the sweet, and send portions to him who has nothing prepared; for this day is holy to our Lord. Do not be grieved, for the joy of the LORD is your strength."

11 So the Levites calmed all the people, saying, "Be still, for the day is holy; do not be grieved."

12 And all the people went away to eat, to drink, to send portions and to celebrate a great festival, because they understood the words which had been made known to them.

B. *The Feast of Tabernacles celebrated*

13 Then on the second day the heads of fathers' *households* of all the people, the priests, and the Levites were gathered to Ezra the scribe that they might gain insight into the words of the law.

14 And they found written in the law how the LORD had commanded through Moses that the sons of Israel should live in booths during the feast of the seventh month.

15 So they proclaimed and circulated a proclamation in all their cities and in Jerusalem, saying, "Go out to the hills, and bring olive branches, and wild olive branches, myrtle branches, palm branches, and branches of *other* leafy trees, to make booths, as it is written."

16 So the people went out and brought *them* and made booths for themselves, each on his roof, and in their courts, and in the courts of the house of God, and in the square at the Water Gate, and in the square at the Gate of Ephraim.

17 And the entire assembly of those who had returned from the captivity made booths and lived in them. The sons of Israel had indeed not done so from the days of Joshua the son of Nun to that day. And there was great rejoicing.

18 And he read from the book of the law of God daily, from the first day to the last day. And they celebrated the feast seven days, and on the eighth day *there was* a solemn assembly according to the ordinance.

C. *The covenant renewed*

1. *Separation from unbelievers*

9 Now on the twenty-fourth day of this month the sons of Israel assembled with fasting, in sackcloth, and with dirt upon them.

2 And the descendants of Israel separated themselves from all foreigners, and stood and confessed their sins and the iniquities of their fathers.

3 While they stood in their place, they read from the book of the law of the

---

Cross references (margin):

8:6 Neh 5:13; Gen 14:22; Ex 4:31

8:7 2 Chr 17:7-9

8:9 Neh 7:65,70; 12:26; Num 29:1; Deut 16:14, 15

8:10 Deut 26:11, 13

8:12 vv. 10,7,8

8:13 Lev 23:34,42

8:15 Lev 23:4; Deut 16:16; Lev 23:40

8:16 Jer 32:29; Neh 12:39; 2 Kin 14:13

8:17 2 Chr 30:21

8:18 Deut 31:11; Lev 23:36; Num 29:35

*9:1 Neh 8:2; Ezra 8:23; 1 Sam 4:12

9:2 Ezra 10:11; Neh 13:3,30

8:8 *give the sense.* Since Aramaic was rapidly replacing Hebrew as the language of the average Jew, some interpreters take vv. 7,8 to mean that Ezra's aides gave a Targum, Aramaic translation of the Hebrew text, so that all would clearly understand. **9:1** *fasting,* see note to Lev. 16:29.

LORD their God for a fourth of the day; and for *another* fourth they confessed and worshiped the LORD their God.

4   Now on the Levites' platform stood Jeshua, Bani, Kadmiel, Shebaniah, Bunni, Sherebiah, Bani, *and* Chenani, and they cried with a loud voice to the LORD their God.

5   Then the Levites, Jeshua, Kadmiel, Bani, Hashabneiah, Sherebiah, Hodiah, Shebaniah, *and* Pethahiah, said, "Arise, bless the LORD your God forever and ever!

O may Thy glorious name be blessed
And exalted above all blessing and praise!

2. *The penitential psalm*

6   "Thou alone art the LORD.
Thou hast made the heavens,
The heaven of heavens with all their host,
The earth and all that is on it,
The seas and all that is in them.
Thou dost give life to all of them
And the heavenly host bows down before Thee.

7   "Thou art the LORD God,
Who chose Abram
And brought him out from Ur of the Chaldees,
And gave him the name Abraham.

8   "And Thou didst find his heart faithful before Thee,
And didst make a covenant with him
To give *him* the land of the Canaanite,
Of the Hittite and the Amorite,
Of the Perizzite, the Jebusite, and the Girgashite—
To give *it* to his descendants.
And Thou hast fulfilled Thy promise,
For Thou art righteous.

9   "Thou didst see the affliction of our fathers in Egypt,
And didst hear their cry by the Red Sea.

10 "Then Thou didst perform signs and wonders against Pharaoh,
Against all his servants and all the people of his land;
For Thou didst know that they acted arrogantly toward them,
And didst make a name for Thyself as *it is* this day.

11 "And Thou didst divide the sea before them,
So they passed through the midst of the sea on dry ground;
And their pursuers Thou didst hurl into the depths,
Like a stone into raging waters.

12 "And with a pillar of cloud Thou didst lead them by day,
And with a pillar of fire by night
To light for them the way
In which they were to go.

13 "Then Thou didst come down on Mount Sinai,
And didst speak with them from heaven;
Thou didst give to them just ordinances and true laws,
Good statutes and commandments.

14 "So Thou didst make known to them Thy holy sabbath,
And didst lay down for them commandments, statutes, and law,
Through Thy servant Moses.

15 "Thou didst provide bread from heaven for them for their hunger,
Thou didst bring forth water from a rock for them for their thirst,
And Thou didst tell them to enter in order to possess
The land which Thou didst swear to give them.

16 "But they, our fathers, acted arrogantly;
They [6]became stubborn and
would not listen to Thy commandments.

[6]Lit., *stiffened their neck*

9:7 Chaldees, Babylon.

9:3 Neh 8:4
9:4 Neh 8:7
9:5 1 Chr 29:13
9:6 2 Kin 19:15; Gen 1:1; Ps 36:6; Col 1:17
*9:7 Gen 11:31; 12:1; 17:5
9:8 Gen 15:6, 18-21; Josh 21:43-45
9:9 Ex 3:7; 14:10-12
9:10 Ex 5:2; 9:16
9:11 Ex 14:21; 15:5,10
9:12 Ex 13:21,22
9:13 Ex 19:20; 20:1; Ps 19:7-9
9:14 Gen 2:3; Ex 20:8,11
9:15 Ex 16:14; 17:6; Num 20:7-13; Deut 1:8
9:16 Ps 106:6; Deut 31:27

9:17
Ps 78:11;
Num 14:4;
Ex 34:6,7

17 "And they refused to listen,
And did not remember Thy wondrous deeds which Thou hadst
performed among them;
So they [7]became stubborn and appointed a leader to return to their
slavery in Egypt.
But Thou art a God of forgiveness,
Gracious and compassionate,
Slow to anger, and abounding in lovingkindness;
And Thou didst not forsake them.

9:18
Ex 32:4

18 "Even when they made for themselves
A calf of molten metal
And said, 'This is your God
Who brought you up from Egypt,'
And committed great [8]blasphemies,

9:19
vv. 27,31,12

19 Thou, in Thy great compassion,
Didst not forsake them in the wilderness;
The pillar of cloud did not leave them by day,
To guide them on their way,
Nor the pillar of fire by night, to light for them the way in which
they were to go.

9:20
Num 11:17;
Is 63:11-14;
Ex 16:15;
17:6
9:21
Deut 2:7;
8:4; 29:5

20 "And Thou didst give Thy good Spirit to instruct them,
Thy manna Thou didst not withhold from their mouth,
And Thou didst give them water for their thirst.

21 "Indeed, forty years Thou didst provide for them in the wilderness
and they were not in want;
Their clothes did not wear out, nor did their feet swell.

9:22
Num 21:21-35

22 "Thou didst also give them kingdoms and peoples,
And Thou didst allot *them* to them as a boundary.
And they took possession of the land of Sihon the king of Heshbon,
And the land of Og the king of Bashan.

9:23
Gen 15:5

23 "And Thou didst make their sons numerous as the stars of heaven,
And Thou didst bring them into the land
Which Thou hadst told their fathers to enter and possess.

9:24
Josh 21:43;
18:1

24 "So their sons entered and possessed the land.
And Thou didst subdue before them the inhabitants of the land, the
Canaanites,
And Thou didst give them into their hand, with their kings, and the
peoples of the land,
To do with them as they desired.

9:25
Deut 3:9;
Num 13:27;
Deut 6:11;
32:15;
1 Kin 8:66

25 "And they captured fortified cities and a fertile land.
They took possession of houses full of every good thing,
Hewn cisterns, vineyards, olive groves,
Fruit trees in abundance.
So they ate, were filled, and grew fat,
And reveled in Thy great goodness.

9:26
Judg 2:11;
1 Kin 14:9;
2 Chr 36:16;
v. 30

26 "But they became disobedient and rebelled against Thee,
And cast Thy law behind their backs
And killed Thy prophets who had admonished them
So that they might return to Thee,
And they committed great [8]blasphemies.

9:27
Judg 2:14;
Deut 4:29;
Judg 2:16,18

27 "Therefore Thou didst deliver them into the hand of their oppressors
who oppressed them,
But when they cried to Thee in the time of their distress,
Thou didst hear from heaven, and according to Thy great
compassion
Thou didst give them deliverers who delivered them from the hand
of their oppressors.

9:28
Judg 3:11;
Ps 106:43

28 "But as soon as they had rest, they did evil again before Thee;
Therefore Thou didst abandon them to the hand of their enemies, so
that they ruled over them.
When they cried again to Thee, Thou didst hear from heaven,

---

[7]Lit., *stiffened their neck*   [8]Lit., *acts of contempt*

And many times Thou didst rescue them according to Thy
  compassion,

29   And admonished them in order to turn them back to Thy law.
  Yet they acted arrogantly and did not listen to Thy commandments
    but sinned against Thine ordinances,
  By which if a man observes them he shall live.
  And they turned a stubborn shoulder and stiffened their neck, and
    would not listen.

30   "However, Thou didst bear with them for many years,
  And admonished them by Thy Spirit through Thy prophets,
  Yet they would not give ear.
  Therefore Thou didst give them into the hand of the peoples of the
    lands.

31   "Nevertheless, in Thy great compassion Thou didst not make an end
    of them or forsake them,
  For Thou art a gracious and compassionate God.

32   "Now therefore, our God, the great, the mighty, and the awesome
    God, who dost keep covenant and lovingkindness,
  Do not let all the hardship seem insignificant before Thee,
  Which has come upon us, our kings, our princes, our priests, our
    prophets, our fathers, and on all Thy people,
  From the days of the kings of Assyria to this day.

33   "However, Thou art just in all that has come upon us;
  For Thou hast dealt faithfully, but we have acted wickedly.

34   "For our kings, our leaders, our priests, and our fathers have not kept
    Thy law
  Or paid attention to Thy commandments and Thine admonitions
    with which Thou hast admonished them.

35   "But they, in their own kingdom,
  With Thy great goodness which Thou didst give them,
  With the broad and rich land which Thou didst set before them,
  Did not serve Thee or turn from their evil deeds.

36   "Behold, we are slaves today,
  And as to the land which Thou didst give to our fathers to eat of its
    fruit and its bounty,
  Behold, we are slaves on it.

37   "And its abundant produce is for the kings
  Whom Thou hast set over us because of our sins;
  They also rule over our bodies
  And over our cattle as they please,
  So we are in great distress.

38   "Now because of all this
  We are making an agreement in writing;
  And on the sealed document *are the names of* our leaders, our Levites
    and our priests."

3. Those who signed the covenant

10 Now on the sealed document *were the names of:* Nehemiah the governor, the son of Hacaliah, and Zedekiah,

2   Seraiah, Azariah, Jeremiah,
3   Pashhur, Amariah, Malchijah,
4   Hattush, Shebaniah, Malluch,
5   Harim, Meremoth, Obadiah,
6   Daniel, Ginnethon, Baruch,
7   Meshullam, Abijah, Mijamin,
8   Maaziah, Bilgai, Shemaiah. These *were* the priests.
9   And the Levites: Jeshua the son of Azaniah, Binnui of the sons of Henadad, Kadmiel;
10   also their brothers Shebaniah, Hodiah, Kelita, Pelaiah, Hanan,
11   Mica, Rehob, Hashabiah,
12   Zaccur, Sherebiah, Shebaniah,
13   Hodiah, Bani, Beninu.

9:29
vv. 26,30,16;
Lev 18:5;
Zech 7:11

9:30
2 Kin 17:13;
Acts 7:51,52

9:31
Jer 4:27

9:32
Neh 1:5;
2 Kin 15:19;
17:3

9:33
Jer 12:1;
Dan 9:5,6,8

9:35
Deut 28:47

9:36
Deut 28:48

9:37
Deut 28:33

9:38
2 Chr 29:10;
34:31

10:1
Neh 9:38

14 The leaders of the people: Parosh, Pahath-moab, Elam, Zattu, Bani,
15 Bunni, Azgad, Bebai,
16 Adonijah, Bigvai, Adin,
17 Ater, Hezekiah, Azzur,
18 Hodiah, Hashum, Bezai,
19 Hariph, Anathoth, Nebai,
20 Magpiash, Meshullam, Hezir,
21 Meshezabel, Zadok, Jaddua,
22 Pelatiah, Hanan, Anaiah,
23 Hoshea, Hananiah, Hasshub,
24 Hallohesh, Pilha, Shobek,
25 Rehum, Hashabnah, Maaseiah,
26 Ahiah, Hanan, Anan,
27 Malluch, Harim, Baanah.

4. Resumé of the covenant

a. Mixed marriages

10:28
Ezra 2:36-58;
Neh 9:2

28 Now the rest of the people, the priests, the Levites, the gatekeepers, the singers, the temple servants, and all those who had separated themselves from the peoples of the lands to the law of God, their wives, their sons and their daughters, all those who had knowledge and understanding,

10:29
Neh 5:12;
2 Chr 34:31

29 are joining with their kinsmen, their nobles, and are taking on themselves a curse and an oath to walk in God's law, which was given through Moses, God's servant, and to keep and to observe all the commandments of GOD our Lord, and His ordinances and His statutes;

10:30
Ex 34:16;
Deut 7:3

30 and that we will not give our daughters to the peoples of the land or take their daughters for our sons.

b. Observance of the Sabbath

10:31
Neh 13:15-22;
Ex 23:10,11;
Deut 15:1,2

31 As for the peoples of the land who bring wares or any grain the sabbath day to sell, we will not buy from them on the sabbath or a holy day and we will forego *the crops* the seventh year and the exaction of every debt.

c. The promise to fulfill specific covenant obligations

*10:32
Ex 30:11-16

32 We also placed ourselves under obligation to contribute yearly one third of a shekel for the service of the house of our God:

33 for the showbread, for the continual grain offering, for the continual burnt offering, the sabbaths, the new moon, for the appointed times, for the holy things and for the sin offerings to make atonement for Israel, and all the work of the house of our God.

10:34
Neh 11:1;
13:31

34 Likewise we cast lots for the supply of wood *among* the priests, the Levites, and the people in order that they might bring it to the house of our God, according to our fathers' households, at fixed times annually, to burn on the altar of the LORD our God as it is written in the law;

10:35
Ex 23:19;
Deut 26:2
10:36
Ex 13:2;
Num 18:15,16

35 and in order that they might bring the first fruits of our ground and the first fruits of all the fruit of every tree to the house of the LORD annually,

36 and bring to the house of our God the first-born of our sons and of our cattle, and the first-born of our herds and our flocks as it is written in the law, for the priests who are ministering in the house of our God.

10:37
Lev 23:17;
Neh 13:5,9;
Lev 27:30

37 We will also bring the first of our dough, our contributions, the fruit of every tree, the new wine and the oil to the priests at the chambers of the house of our God, and the tithe of our ground to the Levites, for the Levites are they who receive the tithes in all the rural towns.

10:38
Num 18:26;
Neh 13:12,13

38 And the priest, the son of Aaron, shall be with the Levites when the Levites receive tithes, and the Levites shall bring up the tenth of the tithes to the house of our God, to the chambers of the storehouse.

10:39
Deut 12:6;
Neh 13:10,11

39 For *the sons of Israel and the sons of Levi* shall bring the contributions of the grain, the new wine and the oil, to the chambers; there are the utensils of the sanctuary, the priests who are ministering, the gatekeepers, and the singers. Thus we will not neglect the house of our God.

10:32 *third . . . shekel.* The *levy fixed by Moses* (2 Chr. 24:6)   (Matt. 17:24).
in Ex. 30:13 is *half a shekel*, the regulation in Jesus' day   **10:33** *showbread.* Read Ex. 25:30.

III. *The reconstituting of Jerusalem:*
Nehemiah's second reform movement (11:1–13:31)

A. *The repeopling of Jerusalem*

11 Now the leaders of the people lived in Jerusalem, but the rest of the people cast lots to bring one out of ten to live in Jerusalem, the holy city, while nine-tenths *remained* in the *other* cities.

2   And the people blessed all the men who volunteered to live in Jerusalem.

11:1
Neh 10:34;
v. 18; Is 48:2

B. *The key people in Jerusalem*

3   Now these are the heads of the provinces who lived in Jerusalem, but in the cities of Judah each lived on his own property in their cities—the Israelites, the priests, the Levites, the temple servants and the descendants of Solomon's servants.

4   And some of the sons of Judah and some of the sons of Benjamin lived in Jerusalem. From the sons of Judah: Athaiah the son of Uzziah, the son of Zechariah, the son of Amariah, the son of Shephatiah, the son of Mahalalel, of the sons of Perez;

5   and Maaseiah the son of Baruch, the son of Col-hozeh, the son of Hazaiah, the son of Adaiah, the son of Joiarib, the son of Zechariah, the son of the Shilonite.

6   All the sons of Perez who lived in Jerusalem were 468 able men.

7   Now these are the sons of Benjamin: Sallu the son of Meshullam, the son of Joed, the son of Pedaiah, the son of Kolaiah, the son of Maaseiah, the son of Ithiel, the son of Jeshaiah;

8   and after him Gabbai *and* Sallai, 928.

9   And Joel the son of Zichri was their overseer, and Judah the son of Hassenuah was second in command of the city.

10   From the priests: Jedaiah the son of Joiarib, Jachin,

11   Seraiah the son of Hilkiah, the son of Meshullam, the son of Zadok, the son of Meraioth, the son of Ahitub, the leader of the house of God,

12   and their [9]kinsmen who performed the work of the temple, 822; and Adaiah the son of Jeroham, the son of Pelaliah, the son of Amzi, the son of Zechariah, the son of Pashhur, the son of Malchijah,

13   and his kinsmen, heads of fathers' *households*, 242; and Amashsai the son of Azarel, the son of Ahzai, the son of Meshillemoth, the son of Immer,

14   and their brothers, valiant warriors, 128. And their overseer was Zabdiel, the son of Haggedolim.

15   Now from the Levites: Shemaiah the son of Hasshub, the son of Azrikam, the son of Hashabiah, the son of Bunni;

16   and Shabbethai and Jozabad, from the leaders of the Levites, who were in charge of the outside work of the house of God;

17   and Mattaniah the son of Mica, the son of Zabdi, the son of Asaph, who was the leader in beginning the thanksgiving at prayer, and Bakbukiah, the second among his brethren; and Abda the son of Shammua, the son of Galal, the son of Jeduthun.

18   All the Levites in the holy city *were* 284.

19   Also the gatekeepers, Akkub, Talmon, and their brethren, who kept watch at the gates, *were* 172.

20   And the rest of Israel, of the priests, *and* of the Levites, *were* in all the cities of Judah, each on his own inheritance.

21   But the temple servants were living in Ophel, and Ziha and Gishpa were in charge of the temple servants.

22   Now the overseer of the Levites in Jerusalem was Uzzi the son of Bani, the son of Hashabiah, the son of Mattaniah, the son of Mica, from the sons of Asaph, who were the singers for the service of the house of God.

23   For *there was* a commandment from the king concerning them and a firm regulation for the song leaders day by day.

24   And Pethahiah the son of Meshezabel, of the sons of Zerah the son of Judah, was the king's representative in all matters concerning the people.

11:3
1 Chr 9:2,3;
v. 20;
Ezra 2:43;
Neh 7:57
11:4
1 Chr 9:3ff

11:7
v. 4

11:10
1 Chr 9:10

11:16
1 Chr 26:29

11:18
v. 1

11:21
Neh 3:26

11:22
vv. 9,14

11:23
Ezra 6:8;
7:20;
Neh 12:47

[9]Lit., *brothers*, and so throughout this context

C. *The villages settled outside Jerusalem*

*11:25
Josh 14:15;
13:9,17

25 Now as for the villages with their fields, some of the sons of Judah lived in Kiriath-arba and its [10]towns, in Dibon and its towns, and in Jekabzeel and its villages,
26 and in Jeshua, in Moladah and Beth-pelet,
27 and in Hazar-shual, in Beersheba and its towns,
28 and in Ziklag, in Meconah and in its towns,
29 and in En-rimmon, in Zorah and in Jarmuth,
30 Zanoah, Adullam, and their villages, Lachish and its fields, Azekah and its towns. So they encamped from Beersheba as far as the valley of Hinnom.
31 The sons of Benjamin also *lived* from Geba *onward*, at Michmash and Aija, at Bethel and its towns,
32 at Anathoth, Nob, Ananiah,
33 Hazor, Ramah, Gittaim,
34 Hadid, Zeboim, Neballat,
35 Lod and Ono, the valley of craftsmen.
36 And from the Levites, *some* divisions in Judah belonged to Benjamin.

D. *The genealogies of the priests and Levites*

12:1
Ezra 2:1,2;
see
Neh 10:2-8

12 Now these are the priests and the Levites who came up with Zerubbabel the son of Shealtiel, and Jeshua: Seraiah, Jeremiah, Ezra,
2 Amariah, Malluch, Hattush,
3 Shecaniah, Rehum, Meremoth,
4 Iddo, Ginnethoi, Abijah,
5 Mijamin, Maadiah, Bilgah,
6 Shemaiah and Joiarib, Jedaiah,

12:7
Ezra 3:2

7 Sallu, Amok, Hilkiah, and Jedaiah. These were the heads of the priests and their kinsmen in the days of Jeshua.

12:8
Neh 11:17

8 And the Levites *were* Jeshua, Binnui, Kadmiel, Sherebiah, Judah, *and* Mattaniah *who was* in charge of the songs of thanksgiving, he and his brothers.
9 Also Bakbukiah and Unni, their brothers, stood opposite them in *their* service divisions.
10 And Jeshua became the father of Joiakim, and Joiakim became the father of Eliashib, and Eliashib became the father of Joiada,
11 and Joiada became the father of Jonathan, and Jonathan became the father of Jaddua.
12 Now in the days of Joiakim the priests, the heads of fathers' *households* were: of Seraiah, Meraiah; of Jeremiah, Hananiah;
13 of Ezra, Meshullam; of Amariah, Jehohanan;
14 of Malluchi, Jonathan; of Shebaniah, Joseph;
15 of Harim, Adna; of Meraioth, Helkai;
16 of Iddo, Zechariah; of Ginnethon, Meshullam;
17 of Abijah, Zichri; of Miniamin, of Moadiah, Piltai;
18 of Bilgah, Shammua; of Shemaiah, Jehonathan;
19 of Joiarib, Mattenai; of Jedaiah, Uzzi;
20 of Sallai, Kallai; of Amok, Eber;
21 of Hilkiah, Hashabiah; of Jedaiah, Nethanel.
22 As for the Levites, the heads of fathers' *households* were registered in the days of Eliashib, Joiada, and Johanan, and Jaddua; so *were* the priests in the reign of Darius the Persian.

*12:23
1 Chr 9:14ff

23 The sons of Levi, the heads of fathers' *households*, were registered in the Book of the Chronicles up to the days of Johanan the son of Eliashib.

12:24
Neh 11:17

24 And the heads of the Levites *were* Hashabiah, Sherebiah, and Jeshua the son of Kadmiel, with their brothers opposite them, to praise *and* give thanks, as prescribed by David the man of God, division corresponding to division.

12:25
1 Chr 26:15

25 Mattaniah, and Bakbukiah, Obadiah, Meshullam, Talmon, *and* Akkub were gatekeepers keeping watch at the storehouses of the gates.

12:26
Neh 8:9;
Ezra 7:6,11

26 These *served* in the days of Joiakim the son of Jeshua, the son of Jozadak,

---

[10]Lit., *daughters*, and so through this ch.

11:25 *villages with their fields.* This probably means the adjoining land.

12:11 *Jonathan* is a scribal error for *Johanan* (vv. 22,23).
12:23 *son*, that is, grandson.

and in the days of Nehemiah the governor and of Ezra the priest *and* scribe.

E. *Dedication of the city walls*

27   Now at the dedication of the wall of Jerusalem they sought out the Levites from all their places, to bring them to Jerusalem so that they might celebrate the dedication with gladness, with hymns of thanksgiving and with songs *to the accompaniment* of cymbals, harps, and lyres.   12:27
1 Chr 25:6

28   So the sons of the singers were assembled from the district around Jerusalem, and from the villages of the Netophathites,   12:28
1 Chr 9:16

29   from Beth-gilgal, and from *their* fields in Geba and Azmaveth, for the singers had built themselves villages around Jerusalem.

30   And the priests and the Levites purified themselves; they also purified the people, the gates, and the wall.   12:30
Neh 13:22,30

31   Then I had the leaders of Judah come up on top of the wall, and I appointed two great choirs, the first proceeding to the right on top of the wall toward the Refuse Gate.   12:31
v. 38;
Neh 2:13;
3:13

32   Hoshaiah and half of the leaders of Judah followed them,

33   with Azariah, Ezra, Meshullam,

34   Judah, Benjamin, Shemaiah, Jeremiah,

35   and some of the sons of the priests with trumpets; *and* Zechariah the son of Jonathan, the son of Shemaiah, the son of Mattaniah, the son of Micaiah, the son of Zaccur, the son of Asaph,   12:35
Num 10:2,8

36   and his kinsmen, Shemaiah, Azarel, Milalai, Gilalai, Maai, Nethanel, Judah *and* Hanani, with the musical instruments of David the man of God. And Ezra the scribe went before them.   *12:36
1 Chr 23:5

37   And at the Fountain Gate they went directly up the steps of the city of David by the stairway of the wall above the house of David to the Water Gate on the east.   12:37
Neh 2:14;
3:15; 3:26

38   The second choir proceeded to the left, while I followed them with half of the people on the wall, above the Tower of Furnaces, to the Broad Wall,   12:38
v. 31;
Neh 3:11; 3:8

39   and above the Gate of Ephraim, by the Old Gate, by the Fish Gate, the Tower of Hananel, and the Tower of the Hundred, as far as the Sheep Gate, and they stopped at the Gate of the Guard.   12:39
Neh 8:16;
3:6; 3:3; 3:1;
3:25

40   Then the two choirs took their stand in the house of God. So did I and half of the officials with me;

41   and the priests, Eliakim, Maaseiah, Miniamin, Micaiah, Elioenai, Zechariah, and Hananiah, with the trumpets;

42   and Maaseiah, Shemaiah, Eleazar, Uzzi, Jehohanan, Malchijah, Elam, and Ezer. And the singers sang, with Jezrahiah *their* leader,

43   and on that day they offered great sacrifices and rejoiced because God had given them great joy, even the women and children rejoiced, so that the joy of Jerusalem was heard from afar.

F. *The appointment of collectors, singers, and gatekeepers*

44   On that day men were also appointed over the chambers for the stores, the contributions, the first fruits, and the tithes, to gather into them from the fields of the cities the portions required by the law for the priests and Levites; for Judah rejoiced over the priests and Levites who served.   12:44
Neh 13:5,12,
13

45   For they performed the worship of their God and the service of purification, together with the singers and the gatekeepers in accordance with the command of David *and* of his son Solomon.   12:45
1 Chr 25:1;
26:1

46   For in the days of David and Asaph, in ancient times, *there were* leaders of the singers, songs of praise and hymns of thanksgiving to God.   12:46
2 Chr 29:30

47   And so all Israel in the days of Zerubbabel and Nehemiah gave the portions due the singers and the gatekeepers as each day required, and set apart the consecrated *portion* for the Levites, and the Levites set apart the consecrated *portion* for the sons of Aaron.   12:47
Neh 11:23;
Num 18:21

12:36 That Ezra and Nehemiah (v. 38) headed the two companies is in accord with 8:9, which indicates that the two were contemporaries during part of their activities: Nehemiah as governor, Ezra as priest.

G. Nehemiah's final reforms

1. The people separated

13 On that day they read aloud from the book of Moses in the hearing of the people; and there was found written in it that no Ammonite or Moabite should ever enter the assembly of God,

2 because they did not meet the sons of Israel with bread and water, but hired Balaam against them to curse them. However, our God turned the curse into a blessing.

3 So it came about, that when they heard the law, they excluded all foreigners from Israel.

2. Tobiah's furniture cast out of the temple

4 Now prior to this, Eliashib the priest, who was appointed over the chambers of the house of our God, being related to Tobiah,

5 had prepared a large room for him, where formerly they put the grain offerings, the frankincense, the utensils, and the tithes of grain, wine and oil prescribed for the Levites, the singers and the gatekeepers, and the contributions for the priests.

6 But during all this *time* I was not in Jerusalem, for in the thirty-second year of Artaxerxes king of Babylon I had gone to the king. After some time, however, I asked leave from the king,

7 and I came to Jerusalem and learned about the evil that Eliashib had done for Tobiah, by preparing a room for him in the courts of the house of God.

8 And it was very displeasing to me, so I threw all of Tobiah's household goods out of the room.

9 Then I gave an order and they cleansed the rooms; and I returned there the utensils of the house of God with the grain offerings and the frankincense.

3. The support of the priesthood begun

10 I also discovered that the portions of the Levites had not been given *them*, so that the Levites and the singers who performed the service had gone away, each to his own field.

11 So I reprimanded the officials and said, "Why is the house of God forsaken?" Then I gathered them together and restored them to their posts.

12 All Judah then brought the tithe of the grain, wine, and oil into the storehouses.

13 And in charge of the storehouses I appointed Shelemiah the priest, Zadok the scribe, and Pedaiah of the Levites, and in addition to them was Hanan the son of Zaccur, the son of Mattaniah; for they were considered reliable, and it was their task to distribute to their kinsmen.

14 Remember me for this, O my God, and do not blot out my loyal deeds which I have performed for the house of my God and its services.

4. Sabbath reforms instituted

15 In those days I saw in Judah some who were treading wine presses on the sabbath, and bringing in sacks of grain and loading *them* on donkeys, as well as wine, grapes, figs, and all kinds of loads; and they brought *them* into Jerusalem on the sabbath day. So I admonished *them* on the day they sold food.

16 Also men of Tyre were living there *who* imported fish and all kinds of merchandise, and sold *them* to the sons of Judah on the sabbath, even in Jerusalem.

17 Then I reprimanded the nobles of Judah and said to them, "What is this evil thing you are doing, by profaning the sabbath day?

18 "Did not your fathers do the same so that our God brought on us, and on this city, all this trouble? Yet you are adding to the wrath on Israel by profaning the sabbath."

19 And it came about that just as it grew dark at the gates of Jerusalem before

13:1 *written,* see Deut. 23:3–6. This was not carried out in the case of Ruth.
13:2 *Balaam . . . to curse them.* Read Num. 22:6 in this connection.
13:15 Three of the recurring sins of God's people were: (1) Sabbath-breaking (Num. 15:32–36; Neh. 13:17,18; Is.

58:13,14; Ezek. 20:13; 22:8); (2) intermarriage with the heathen (Deut. 7:3,4; 1 Kin. 11:1,2; Neh. 13:23,25); and (3) idolatry (1 Kin. 21:26; 2 Kin. 17:12; Ezek. 6:1–5; Zech. 13:2). These had to be faced and dealt with by appropriate disciplinary measures if the nation was to carry on its witness.

the sabbath, I commanded that the doors should be shut and that they should not open them until after the sabbath. Then I stationed some of my servants at the gates *that* no load should enter on the sabbath day.

20   Once or twice the traders and merchants of every kind of merchandise spent the night outside Jerusalem.

21   Then I warned them and said to them, "Why do you spend the night in front of the wall? If you do so again, I will use force against you." From that time on they did not come on the sabbath.

13:21
v. 15

22   And I commanded the Levites that they should purify themselves and come as gatekeepers to sanctify the sabbath day. *For* this also remember me, O my God, and have compassion on me according to the greatness of Thy lovingkindness.

13:22
Neh 12:30;
vv. 14,31

5. *Marriage reforms*

23   In those days I also saw that the Jews had married women from Ashdod, Ammon, *and* Moab.

13:23
Ezra 9:2

24   As for their children, half spoke in the language of Ashdod, and none of them was able to speak the language of Judah, but the language of his own people.

25   So I contended with them and cursed them and struck some of them and pulled out their hair, and made them swear by God, "You shall not give your daughters to their sons, nor take of their daughters for your sons or for yourselves.

13:25
vv. 11,17;
Deut 25:2;
Ezra 10:29,30

26   "Did not Solomon king of Israel sin regarding these things? Yet among the many nations there was no king like him, and he was loved by his God, and God made him king over all Israel; nevertheless the foreign women caused even him to sin.

13:26
1 Kin 11:1;
3:13;
2 Chr 1:12;
1 Kin 11:4ff

27   "Do we then hear about you that you have committed all this great evil by acting unfaithfully against our God by marrying foreign women?"

13:27
v. 23;
Ezra 10:2

28   Even one of the sons of Joiada, the son of Eliashib the high priest, was a son-in-law of Sanballat the Horonite, so I drove him away from me.

*13:28
Neh 12:10;
2:10,19

29   Remember them, O my God, because they have defiled the priesthood and the covenant of the priesthood and the Levites.

13:29
Neh 6:14;
Num 25:13

6. *Conclusion*

30   Thus I purified them from everything foreign and appointed duties for the priests and the Levites, each in his task,

13:30
Neh 10:30

31   and *I arranged* for the supply of wood at appointed times and for the first fruits. Remember me, O my God, for good.

13:31
Neh 10:34;
vv. 14,22

13:28 *drove him away from me.* Josephus tells how Sanballat arranged for a political marriage of his daughter to Manasseh, a priest. While Josephus dates the event about a century later, he may well have been describing this very expulsion. Evidently the grandson of Eliashib refused to put his wife away, so Nehemiah drove him out. The priest took with him a copy of the Pentateuch (this ancient copy is still in the possession of a small colony of Samaritans), and on Mt. Gerizim the Samaritan temple was erected.

INTRODUCTION TO

THE BOOK OF

ESTHER

Authorship and Background: The name Esther, a Persian word meaning "Star," derives from the principal character of the book. Her Hebrew name was Hadassah, meaning "Myrtle." The book appears in the last section of the Hebrew Bible among the Five Scrolls, *Megilloth,* which also include Ruth, Song of Solomon, Ecclesiastes, and Lamentations. Esther, the last of the five, is considered by Judaism as "the Scroll" par excellence. The events described took place at Shushan (Susa), the Persian capital, in the reign of Ahasuerus (486-465 B.C.), known usually as Xerxes, the Greek spelling of his name. The book is filled with Persian loan words and accurate information about the palace, customs, and history of the Persian empire. Some scholars believe the book was composed in the Maccabean period (about 168 B.C.), but the Persian atmosphere argues for a date not later than the conquest of the Persian empire by Alexander the Great (331 B.C.). Tradition has dated the book within the reign of Artaxerxes Longimanus (465-424 B.C.), as does Josephus. Because 9:20,23,29 note that Mordecai wrote certain instructions, some have thought him to be the author (e.g., Clement of Alexandria). Others have ascribed the authorship to Ezra (e.g., Augustine), but in all probability the author was an unknown Jew who lived in Persia and had access to oral and written sources.

Characteristics: Esther contains no reference to Palestine or to the return of the exiles from Babylon, although it is fervently patriotic. The author stresses God's providential watch and care, but the name of God is never mentioned, nor are we told that the Jews offered prayers or supplications to God during their trials. The book explains the origin of the Feast of Purim, and it became a Jewish tradition to read the book annually as a part of the Purim ritual. The literary style is one of skillful composition: the story moves smoothly, and the element of suspense is sustained in a developing plot with a final denouement. The author uses no adjectives to describe the characters, who are instead made known by their concrete actions; and through the use of literary techniques he achieves great vividness.

Contents:

I. Intrigues in the court at Susa (1:1-2:23): Drunken Ahasuerus asks Vashti to display herself. She refuses and is deposed. Mordecai's cousin Esther is chosen to replace Vashti. Mordecai discovers a plot against Ahasuerus's life that is foiled.

II. The struggle between the houses of Mordecai and Haman (3:1-9:19): Haman becomes vizier. Mordecai refuses to bow before him. Haman plots to kill all the Jews. Mordecai appeals to Esther for help. She points out that she may die if she seeks the king without prior permission. She yields to Mordecai, asking the Jews to fast and says, " . . . if I perish, I perish" (4:16). She approaches Ahasuerus, who holds out the golden scepter. She invites the king and Haman to her banquet. Haman prepares the gallows for Mordecai. The king wishes to honor Mordecai and asks Haman what he should do. Haman thinks the honor is to be for himself but is required to honor Mordecai. Esther pleads with the king for her life and her people's lives. She points the finger of accusation at Haman, who is hanged on his own gallows. Mordecai is set over the house of Haman. The Jews defend themselves and slay their enemies.

III. The Feast of Purim: observance and regulations (9:20-10:3): The two days' festival instituted. Mordecai is advanced further and the Jews prosper.

THE BOOK OF

ESTHER

I. Intrigues in the court at Susa (1:1–2:23)

A. The riches and splendor of Ahasuerus

1 Now it took place in the days of Ahasuerus, the Ahasuerus who reigned from India to Ethiopia over 127 provinces,
2 in those days as King Ahasuerus sat on his royal throne which *was* in Susa the capital,
3 in the third year of his reign, he gave a banquet for all his princes and attendants, the army *officers* of Persia and Media, the nobles, and the princes of his provinces being in his presence.
4 And he displayed the riches of his royal glory and the splendor of his great majesty for many days, 180 days.
5 And when these days were completed, the king gave a banquet lasting seven days for all the people who were present in Susa the capital, from the greatest to the least, in the court of the garden of the king's palace.
6 *There were hangings of* fine white and violet linen held by cords of fine purple linen on silver rings and marble columns, *and* couches of gold and silver on a mosaic pavement of porphyry, marble, mother-of-pearl, and precious stones.
7 Drinks were served in golden vessels of various kinds, and the royal wine was plentiful according to the king's bounty.
8 And the drinking was *done* according to the law, there was no compulsion, for so the king had given orders to each official of his household that he should do according to the desires of each person.
9 Queen Vashti also gave a banquet for the women in the palace which belonged to King Ahasuerus.

B. The removal of Queen Vashti

1. Vashti's refusal

10 On the seventh day, when the heart of the king was merry with wine, he commanded Mehuman, Biztha, Harbona, Bigtha, Abagtha, Zethar, and Carkas, the seven eunuchs who served in the presence of King Ahasuerus,
11 to bring Queen Vashti before the king with *her* royal crown in order to display her beauty to the people and the princes, for she was beautiful.
12 But Queen Vashti refused to come at the king's command delivered by the eunuchs. Then the king became very angry and his wrath burned within him.

2. Vashti's removal

13 Then the king said to the wise men who understood the times—for it was the custom of the king so *to speak* before all who knew law and justice,
14 and were close to him: Carshena, Shethar, Admatha, Tarshish, Meres, Marsena, and Memucan, the seven princes of Persia and Media who had access to the king's presence and sat in the first place in the kingdom—
15 "According to law, what is to be done with Queen Vashti, because she did not obey the command of King Ahasuerus *delivered* by the eunuchs?"
16 And in the presence of the king and the princes, Memucan said, "Queen Vashti has wronged not only the king but *also* all the princes, and all the peoples who are in all the provinces of King Ahasuerus.
17 "For the queen's conduct will become known to all the women causing them to look with contempt on their husbands by saying, 'King Ahasuerus commanded Queen Vashti to be brought in to his presence, but she did not come.'

*1:1
Ezra 4:6;
Dan 9:1;
Esth 8:9;
9:30
1:2
Neh 1:1
1:3
Esth 2:18
1:5
Esth 7:7,8
1:6
Ezek 23:41;
Amos 6:4
1:7
Esth 2:18
1:10
Judg 16:25;
Esth 7:9
1:13
Jer 10:7;
Dan 2:12;
1 Chr 12:32
1:14
2 Kin 25:19
1:17
Eph 5:33

1:1 *Ahasuerus.* He has been identified as Xerxes (486–465 B.C.).   1:12 Vashti's refusal eventually cost her the crown. (See 2:4.)

18 "And this day the ladies of Persia and Media who have heard of the queen's conduct will speak in *the same way* to all the king's princes, and there will be plenty of contempt and anger.

19 "If it pleases the king, let a royal edict be issued by him and let it be written in the laws of Persia and Media so that it cannot be repealed, that Vashti should come no more into the presence of King Ahasuerus, and let the king give her royal position to another who is more worthy than she.

20 "And when the king's edict which he shall make is heard throughout all his kingdom, great as it is, then all women will give honor to their husbands, great and small."

21 And *this* word pleased the king and the princes, and the king did as Memucan proposed.

22 So he sent letters to all the king's provinces, to each province according to its script and to every people according to their language, that every man should be the master in his own house and the one who speaks in the language of his own people.

C. Esther made queen

1. The search for a queen

2 After these things when the anger of King Ahasuerus had subsided, he remembered Vashti and what she had done and what had been decreed against her.

2 Then the king's attendants, who served him, said, "Let beautiful young virgins be sought for the king.

3 "And let the king appoint overseers in all the provinces of his kingdom that they may gather every beautiful young virgin to Susa the capital, to the harem, into the custody of Hegai, the king's eunuch, who was in charge of the women; and let their cosmetics be given *them*.

4 "Then let the young lady who pleases the king be queen in place of Vashti." And the matter pleased the king, and he did accordingly.

2. Esther's background

5 *Now* there was a Jew in Susa the capital whose name was Mordecai, the son of Jair, the son of Shimei, the son of Kish, a Benjamite,

6 who had been taken into exile from Jerusalem with the captives who had been exiled with Jeconiah king of Judah, whom Nebuchadnezzar the king of Babylon had exiled.

7 And he was bringing up Hadassah, that is Esther, his uncle's daughter, for she had neither father nor mother. Now the young lady was beautiful of form and face, and when her father and her mother died, Mordecai took her as his own daughter.

8 So it came about when the command and decree of the king were heard and many young ladies were gathered to Susa the capital into the custody of Hegai, that Esther was taken to the king's palace into the custody of Hegai, who was in charge of the women.

9 Now the young lady pleased him and found favor with him. So he quickly provided her with her cosmetics and food, gave her seven choice maids from the king's palace, and transferred her and her maids to the best place in the harem.

10 Esther did not make known her people or her kindred, for Mordecai had instructed her that she should not make *them* known.

11 And every day Mordecai walked back and forth in front of the court of the harem to learn how Esther was and how she fared.

3. Ahasuerus chooses Esther

12 Now when the turn of each young lady came to go in to King Ahasuerus, after the end of her twelve months under the regulations for the women—for the days of their beautification were completed as follows: six months with oil of myrrh and six months with spices and the cosmetics for women—

13 the young lady would go in to the king in this way: anything that she desired was given her to take with her from the harem to the king's palace.

*1:19 Esth 8:8; Dan 6:8
1:20 Eph 5:22; Col 3:18
1:22 Esth 8:9; Eph 5:22-24; 1 Tim 2:12
2:1 Esth 7:10; 1:19,20
2:3 vv. 8,15
2:5 Esth 3:2
2:6 2 Kin 24:14, 15; 24:6
*2:7 v. 15
2:8 vv. 3,15
2:9 vv. 3,12
2:10 v. 20

1:19 *Persia and Media*, Medes and Persians in Dan. 5:28, which is the correct chronological order; *cannot be repealed.* The idea of immutability is also stated in 8:8 and Dan. 6:8.

2:7 *Hadassah*, that is, Myrtle; *Esther*, either from the Persian word "star," or the Babylonian goddess "Ishtar"; *his uncle's daughter*, indicating that Mordecai adopted his cousin as his daughter.

14   In the evening she would go in and in the morning she would return to the second harem, to the custody of Shaashgaz, the king's eunuch who was in charge of the concubines. She would not again go in to the king unless the king delighted in her and she was summoned by name.

15   Now when the turn of Esther, the daughter of Abihail the uncle of Mordecai who had taken her as his daughter, came to go in to the king, she did not request anything except what Hegai, the king's eunuch who was in charge of the women, advised. And Esther found favor in the eyes of all who saw her.

16   So Esther was taken to King Ahasuerus to his royal palace in the tenth month which is the month Tebeth, in the seventh year of his reign.

17   And the king loved Esther more than all the women, and she found favor and kindness with him more than all the virgins, so that he set the royal crown on her head and made her queen instead of Vashti.

18   Then the king gave a great banquet, Esther's banquet, for all his princes and his servants; he also made a holiday for the provinces and gave gifts according to the king's bounty.

D. The plot to kill Ahasuerus and its failure

19   And when the virgins were gathered together the second time, then Mordecai was sitting at the king's gate.

20   Esther had not yet made known her kindred or her people, even as Mordecai had commanded her, for Esther did what Mordecai told her as she had done when under his care.

21   In those days, while Mordecai was sitting at the king's gate, Bigthan and Teresh, two of the king's officials from those who guarded the door, became angry and sought to lay hands on King Ahasuerus.

22   But the plot became known to Mordecai, and he told Queen Esther, and Esther informed the king in Mordecai's name.

23   Now when the plot was investigated and found *to be so*, they were both hanged on a ¹gallows; and it was written in the Book of the Chronicles in the king's presence.

II. *The struggle between the houses of Mordecai and Haman (3:1–9:19)*

A. *The elevation of Haman: the refusal of Mordecai to bow*

3 After these events King Ahasuerus promoted Haman, the son of Hammedatha the Agagite, and advanced him and established his authority over all the princes who *were* with him.

2   And all the king's servants who were at the king's gate bowed down and paid homage to Haman; for so the king had commanded concerning him. But Mordecai neither bowed down nor paid homage.

3   Then the king's servants who were at the king's gate said to Mordecai, "Why are you transgressing the king's command?"

4   Now it was when they had spoken daily to him and he would not listen to them, that they told Haman to see whether Mordecai's reason would stand; for he had told them that he was a Jew.

5   When Haman saw that Mordecai neither bowed down nor paid homage to him, Haman was filled with rage.

6   But he disdained to lay hands on Mordecai alone; for they had told him *who* the people of Mordecai *were;* therefore Haman sought to destroy all the Jews, the people of Mordecai, who *were* throughout the whole kingdom of Ahasuerus.

¹Lit., *tree*

2:15 v. 6; Esth 9:29 / 2:17 Esth 1:11 / 2:18 Esth 1:3; 1:7 / 2:20 v. 10 / 2:21 Esth 6:2 / 2:22 Esth 6:1,2 / *2:23 Esth 10:2 / *3:1 Esth 5:11; v. 10 / 3:2 Esth 2:19; v. 5 / 3:3 v. 2 / 3:5 v. 2; Esth 5:9 / 3:6 Ps 83:4

2:16 *seventh year.* Four years after the deposition of Vashti. **2:19** *sitting at the king's gate.* Mordecai's relationship to Esther had not yet been disclosed. **2:23** *Book of the Chronicles,* the court records of daily events, not the Biblical books. **3:1** Haman is here called a descendant of the line of Agag. An Amalekite king named Agag is mentioned in 1 Sam. 15 as the last survivor of a tribe that was destroyed by King Saul at God's command. If the old rabbinic tradition is correct in tracing Haman's ancestry from this Agag, we may see in this episode another chapter in the conflict between the line of Jacob and that of Esau (for Esau was an ancestor of Amalek). But a more likely explanation of the term "Agagite" is that it refers to a district in the Persian empire called Agag (spoken of in an Assyrian inscription of King Sargon). Haman's father, Hammedatha, had a Persian name and so did all of his sons (9:7–9). This would hardly have been the case in a family of Amalekite descent.

B. *Haman's plot against the Jews*

3:7
Esth 9:24;
Ezra 6:15

7 In the first month, which is the month Nisan, in the twelfth year of King Ahasuerus, Pur, that is the lot, was cast before Haman from day to day and from month *to month*, until the twelfth month, that is the month Adar.

3:8
Ezra 4:12-15;
Acts 16:20

8 Then Haman said to King Ahasuerus, "There is a certain people scattered and dispersed among the peoples in all the provinces of your kingdom; their laws are different from *those* of all *other* people, and they do not observe the king's laws, so it is not in the king's interest to let them remain.

9 "If it is pleasing to the king, let it be decreed that they be destroyed, and I will pay ten thousand talents of silver into the hands of those who carry on the *king's* business, to put into the king's treasuries."

3:10
Esth 8:2;
Gen 41:42;
Esth 7:6

10 Then the king took his signet ring from his hand and gave it to Haman, the son of Hammedatha the Agagite, the enemy of the Jews.

11 And the king said to Haman, "The silver is yours, and the people *also*, to do with them as you please."

3:12
Esth 8:8-10;
1 Kin 21:8

12 Then the king's scribes were summoned on the thirteenth day of the first month, and it was written just as Haman commanded to the king's satraps, to the governors who were over each province, and to the princes of each people, each province according to its script, each people according to its language, being written in the name of King Ahasuerus and sealed with the king's signet ring.

3:13
Esth 8:10-14

13 And letters were sent by couriers to all the king's provinces to destroy, to kill, and to annihilate all the Jews, both young and old, women and children, in one day, the thirteenth *day* of the twelfth month, which is the month Adar, and to seize their possessions as plunder.

3:14
Esth 8:13,14

14 A copy of the edict to be issued as law in every province was published to all the peoples so that they should be ready for this day.

3:15
Esth 8:15

15 The couriers went out impelled by the king's command while the decree was issued in Susa the capital; and while the king and Haman sat down to drink, the city of Susa was in confusion.

C. *Mordecai appeals to Esther for help*

*4:1ff
Esth 3:8-10;
Jon 3:5,6;
Ezek 27:30

4 When Mordecai learned all that had been done, he tore his clothes, put on sackcloth and ashes, and went out into the midst of the city and wailed loudly and bitterly.

2 And he went as far as the king's gate, for no one was to enter the king's gate clothed in sackcloth.

4:3
Is 58:5

3 And in each and every province where the command and decree of the king came, there was great mourning among the Jews, with fasting, weeping, and wailing; and many lay on sackcloth and ashes.

4 Then Esther's maidens and her eunuchs came and told her, and the queen writhed in great anguish. And she sent garments to clothe Mordecai that he might remove his sackcloth from him, but he did not accept *them*.

5 Then Esther summoned Hathach from the king's eunuchs, whom the king had appointed to attend her, and ordered him *to go* to Mordecai to learn what this *was* and why it *was*.

6 So Hathach went out to Mordecai to the city square in front of the king's gate.

4:7
Esth 3:9

7 And Mordecai told him all that had happened to him, and the exact amount of money that Haman had promised to pay to the king's treasuries for the destruction of the Jews.

4:8
Esth 3:14,15

8 He also gave him a copy of the text of the edict which had been issued in Susa for their destruction, that he might show Esther and inform her, and to order her to go in to the king to implore his favor and to plead with him for her people.

9 And Hathach came back and related Mordecai's words to Esther.

10 Then Esther spoke to Hathach and ordered him *to reply* to Mordecai:

4:11
Esth 5:1; 6:4;
Dan 2:9;
Esth 5:2; 8:4

11 "All the king's servants and the people of the king's provinces know that for any man or woman who comes to the king to the inner court who is not summoned, he has but one law, that he be put to death, unless the king holds out to him the

---

4:1 *sackcloth.* A dark-colored garment made of coarse material woven from camels' and goats' hair. It was worn when mourning (as here) in hopes of averting national catastrophe.

4:1–3 *tore his clothes.* These were outward signs of mourning. (Today, the tearing of clothes has been modified to the wearing of a black ribbon by some Jews.)

golden scepter so that he may live. And I have not been summoned to come to the king for these thirty days."

12   And they related Esther's words to Mordecai.

13   Then Mordecai told *them* to reply to Esther, "Do not imagine that you in the king's palace can escape any more than all the Jews.

14   "For if you remain silent at this time, relief and deliverance will arise for the Jews from another place and you and your father's house will perish. And who knows whether you have not attained royalty for such a time as this?"

15   Then Esther told *them* to reply to Mordecai,

16   "Go, assemble all the Jews who are found in Susa, and fast for me; do not eat or drink for three days, night or day. I and my maidens also will fast in the same way. And thus I will go in to the king, which is not according to the law; and if I perish, I perish."

17   So Mordecai went away and did just as Esther had commanded him.

D. *Esther's intervention*

1. *Her appeal to Ahasuerus*

5 Now it came about on the third day that Esther put on her royal robes and stood in the inner court of the king's palace in front of the king's rooms, and the king was sitting on his royal throne in the throne room, opposite the entrance to the palace.

2   And it happened when the king saw Esther the queen standing in the court, she obtained favor in his sight; and the king extended to Esther the golden scepter which was in his hand. So Esther came near and touched the top of the scepter.

3   Then the king said to her, "What is *troubling* you, Queen Esther? And what is your request? Even to half of the kingdom it will be given to you."

4   And Esther said, "If it please the king, may the king and Haman come this day to the banquet that I have prepared for him."

5   Then the king said, "Bring Haman quickly that we may do as Esther desires." So the king and Haman came to the banquet which Esther had prepared.

6   And, as they drank their wine at the banquet, the king said to Esther, "What is your petition, for it shall be granted to you. And what is your request? Even to half of the kingdom it shall be done."

7   So Esther answered and said, "My petition and my request is:

8   if I have found favor in the sight of the king, and if it please the king to grant my petition and do what I request, may the king and Haman come to the banquet which I shall prepare for them, and tomorrow I will do as the king says."

2. *Haman's plan against Mordecai*

9   Then Haman went out that day glad and pleased of heart; but when Haman saw Mordecai in the king's gate, and that he did not stand up or tremble before him, Haman was filled with anger against Mordecai.

10   Haman controlled himself, however, went to his house, and sent for his friends and his wife Zeresh.

11   Then Haman recounted to them the glory of his riches, and the number of his sons, and every *instance* where the king had magnified him, and how he had promoted him above the princes and servants of the king.

12   Haman also said, "Even Esther the queen let no one but me come with the king to the banquet which she had prepared; and tomorrow also I am invited by her with the king.

13   "Yet all of this does not satisfy me every time I see Mordecai the Jew sitting at the king's gate."

14   Then Zeresh his wife and all his friends said to him, "Have a gallows fifty cubits high made and in the morning ask the king to have Mordecai hanged on it, then go joyfully with the king to the banquet." And the advice pleased Haman, so he had the gallows made.

E. *The deliverance of the Jews*

1. *Haman's plot and its failure*

6 During that night the king could not sleep so he gave an order to bring the book of records, the chronicles, and they were read before the king.

4:15
Esth 5:1

5:1
Esth 4:16;
4:11; 6:4

5:2
Prov 21:1;
Esth 4:11;
8:4

5:3
Esth 7:2;
Mark 6:23

5:5
Esth 6:14

5:6
Esth 7:2; v. 3

5:8
Esth 7:3; 8:5;
6:14

5:9
Esth 2:19;
3:5

5:10
Esth 6:13

5:11
Esth 9:7-10;
3:1

5:12
v. 8

5:13
v. 9

5:14
Esth 6:4; 7:9,
10

6:1
Dan 6:18;
Esth 2:23;
10:2

6:2
Esth 2:21,22

2   And it was found written what Mordecai had reported concerning Bigthana and Teresh, two of the king's eunuchs who were doorkeepers, that they had sought to lay hands on King Ahasuerus.

3   And the king said, "What honor or dignity has been bestowed on Mordecai for this?" Then the king's servants who attended him said, "Nothing has been done for him."

6:4
Esth 4:11;
5:1; 5:14

4   So the king said, "Who is in the court?" Now Haman had just entered the outer court of the king's palace in order to speak to the king about hanging Mordecai on the gallows which he had prepared for him.

5   And the king's servants said to him, "Behold, Haman is standing in the court." And the king said, "Let him come in."

6:6
vv. 7,9,11

6   So Haman came in and the king said to him, "What is to be done for the man whom the king desires to honor?" And Haman said to himself, "Whom would the king desire to honor more than me?"

7   Then Haman said to the king, "For the man whom the king desires to honor,

6:8
1 Kin 1:33

8   let them bring a royal robe which the king has worn, and the horse on which the king has ridden, and on whose head a royal crown has been placed;

6:9
Gen 41:43

9   and let the robe and the horse be handed over to one of the king's most noble princes and let them array the man whom the king desires to honor and lead him on horseback through the city square, and proclaim before him, 'Thus it shall be done to the man whom the king desires to honor.' "

10   Then the king said to Haman, "Take quickly the robes and the horse as you have said, and do so for Mordecai the Jew, who is sitting at the king's gate; do not fall short in anything of all that you have said."

11   So Haman took the robe and the horse, and arrayed Mordecai, and led him *on horseback* through the city square, and proclaimed before him, "Thus it shall be done to the man whom the king desires to honor."

6:12
2 Sam 15:30

12   Then Mordecai returned to the king's gate. But Haman hurried home, mourning, with *his* head covered.

6:13
Esth 5:10

13   And Haman recounted to Zeresh his wife and all his friends everything that had happened to him. Then his wise men and Zeresh his wife said to him, "If Mordecai, before whom you have begun to fall, is of Jewish origin, you will not overcome him, but will surely fall before him."

6:14
Esth 5:8

14   While they were still talking with him, the king's eunuchs arrived and hastily brought Haman to the banquet which Esther had prepared.

2. *The downfall of Haman*

7 Now the king and Haman came to drink *wine* with Esther the queen.

7:2
Esth 5:6; 5:3

2   And the king said to Esther on the second day also as they drank their wine at the banquet, "What is your petition, Queen Esther? It shall be granted you. And what is your request? Even to half of the kingdom it shall be done."

7:3
Esth 5:8; 8:5

3   Then Queen Esther answered and said, "If I have found favor in your sight, O king, and if it please the king, let my life be given me as my petition, and my people as my request;

7:4
Esth 3:9,13

4   for we have been sold, I and my people, to be destroyed, to be killed and to be annihilated. Now if we had only been sold as slaves, men and women, I would have remained silent, for the trouble would not be commensurate with the annoyance to the king."

5   Then King Ahasuerus asked Queen Esther, "Who is he, and where is he, who would presume to do thus?"

7:6
Esth 3:10

6   And Esther said, "A foe and an enemy, is this wicked Haman!" Then Haman became terrified before the king and queen.

7   And the king arose in his anger from drinking wine *and went* into the palace garden; but Haman stayed to beg for his life from Queen Esther, for he saw that harm had been determined against him by the king.

7:8
Esth 1:6

8   Now when the king returned from the palace garden into the place where they were drinking wine, Haman was falling on the couch where Esther was. Then the king said, "Will he even assault the queen with me in the house?" As the word went out of the king's mouth, they covered Haman's face.

7:9
Esth 1:10;
5:14; Ps 7:16;
Prov 11:5,6

9   Then Harbonah, one of the eunuchs who *were* before the king said, "Behold indeed, the gallows standing at Haman's house fifty cubits high, which Haman

made for Mordecai who spoke good on behalf of the king!" And the king said, "Hang him on it."

10   So they hanged Haman on the gallows which he had prepared for Mordecai, and the king's anger subsided.

3. The promotion of Mordecai

8 On that day King Ahasuerus gave the house of Haman, the enemy of the Jews, to Queen Esther; and Mordecai came before the king, for Esther had disclosed what he was to her.

2   And the king took off his signet ring which he had taken away from Haman, and gave it to Mordecai. And Esther set Mordecai over the house of Haman.

4. Esther's request and Ahasuerus's decree

3   Then Esther spoke again to the king, fell at his feet, wept, and implored him to avert the evil *scheme* of Haman the Agagite and his plot which he had devised against the Jews.

4   And the king extended the golden scepter to Esther. So Esther arose and stood before the king.

5   Then she said, "If it pleases the king and if I have found favor before him and the matter *seems* proper to the king and I am pleasing in his sight, let it be written to revoke the letters devised by Haman, the son of Hammedatha the Agagite, which he wrote to destroy the Jews who are in all the king's provinces.

6   "For how can I endure to see the calamity which shall befall my people, and how can I endure to see the destruction of my kindred?"

7   So King Ahasuerus said to Queen Esther and to Mordecai the Jew, "Behold, I have given the house of Haman to Esther, and him they have hanged on the gallows because he had stretched out his hands against the Jews.

8   "Now you write to the Jews as you see fit, in the king's name, and seal *it* with the king's signet ring; for a decree which is written in the name of the king and sealed with the king's signet ring may not be revoked."

9   So the king's scribes were called at that time in the third month (that is, the month Sivan), on the twenty-third day; and it was written according to all that Mordecai commanded to the Jews, the satraps, the governors, and the princes of the provinces which *extended* from India to Ethiopia, 127 provinces, to every province according to its script, and to every people according to their language, as well as to the Jews according to their script and their language.

10   And he wrote in the name of King Ahasuerus, and sealed it with the king's signet ring, and sent letters by couriers on horses, riding on steeds sired by the royal stud.

11   In them the king granted the Jews who were in each and every city *the right* to assemble and to defend their lives, to destroy, to kill, and to annihilate the entire army of any people or province which might attack them, including children and women, and to plunder their spoil,

12   on one day in all the provinces of King Ahasuerus, the thirteenth *day* of the twelfth month (that is, the month Adar).

13   A copy of the edict to be issued as law in each and every province, was published to all the peoples, so that the Jews should be ready for this day to avenge themselves on their enemies.

14   The couriers, hastened and impelled by the king's command, went out, riding on the royal steeds; and the decree was given out in Susa the capital.

5. The victory of the Jews

15   Then Mordecai went out from the presence of the king in royal robes of blue and white, with a large crown of gold and a garment of fine linen and purple; and the city of Susa shouted and rejoiced.

16   For the Jews there was light and gladness and joy and honor.

17   And in each and every province, and in each and every city, wherever the king's commandment and his decree arrived, there was gladness and joy for the Jews, a feast and a holiday. And many among the peoples of the land became Jews, for the dread of the Jews had fallen on them.

8:1 *house of Haman*, that is, his property.
8:9 *their script and their language*, probably Hebrew in the old script, not the square script of the Aramaic language.

Marginal references:

*8:1 Esth 7:6; 2:7
8:2 Esth 3:10
8:4 Esth 4:11; 5:2
8:5 Esth 5:8; 7:3; 3:13
8:6 Esth 7:4; 9:1
8:7 v. 1
8:8 v. 10; Esth 3:12; 1:19
*8:9 Esth 3:12; 1:1; 1:22
8:10 1 Kin 21:8; Esth 3:12,13
8:11 Esth 9:2,10, 15,16; 3:13
8:13 Esth 3:14
8:15 Esth 3:15
8:17 Esth 9:2,19, 27

9:1
Esth 8:12;
v. 17;
Esth 3:13

9 Now in the twelfth month (that is, the month Adar), on the thirteenth day when the king's command and edict were about to be executed, on the day when the enemies of the Jews hoped to gain the mastery over them, it was turned to the contrary so that the Jews themselves gained the mastery over those who hated them.

9:2
vv. 15-18;
Esth 8:11;
Ps 71:13,24;
Esth 8:17
9:3
Ezra 8:36

2   The Jews assembled in their cities throughout all the provinces of King Ahasuerus to lay hands on those who sought their harm; and no one could stand before them, for the dread of them had fallen on all the peoples.

3   Even all the princes of the provinces, the satraps, the governors, and those who were doing the king's business assisted the Jews, because the dread of Mordecai had fallen on them.

4   Indeed, Mordecai was great in the king's house, and his fame spread throughout all the provinces; for the man Mordecai became greater and greater.

9:5
2 Sam 3:1;
Prov 4:18

5   Thus the Jews struck all their enemies with the sword, killing and destroying; and they did what they pleased to those who hated them.

6   And in Susa the capital the Jews killed and destroyed five hundred men,

7   and Parshandatha, Dalphon, Aspatha,

8   Poratha, Adalia, Aridatha,

9   Parmashta, Arisai, Aridai, and Vaizatha,

9:10
Esth 5:11;
8:11

10   the ten sons of Haman the son of Hammedatha, the Jews' enemy; but they did not lay their hands on the plunder.

6. The hanging of Haman's sons

11   On that day the number of those who were killed in Susa the capital was reported to the king.

9:12
Esth 7:2

12   And the king said to Queen Esther, "The Jews have killed and destroyed five hundred men and the ten sons of Haman in Susa the capital. What then have they done in the rest of the king's provinces! Now what is your petition? It shall even be granted you. And what is your further request? It shall also be done."

9:13
Esth 8:11

13   Then said Esther, "If it pleases the king, let tomorrow also be granted to the Jews who are in Susa to do according to the edict of today; and let Haman's ten sons be hanged on the gallows."

14   So the king commanded that it should be done so; and an edict was issued in Susa, and Haman's ten sons were hanged.

9:15
v. 10

15   And the Jews who were in Susa assembled also on the fourteenth day of the month Adar and killed three hundred men in Susa, but they did not lay their hands on the plunder.

7. The Feast of Purim begun

9:16
vv. 2,10,15

16   Now the rest of the Jews who *were* in the king's provinces assembled, to defend their lives and rid themselves of their enemies, and kill 75,000 of those who hated them; but they did not lay their hands on the plunder.

9:17
vv. 1,21

17   *This was done* on the thirteenth day of the month Adar, and on the fourteenth day they rested and made it a day of feasting and rejoicing.

9:18
vv. 2,21

18   But the Jews who were in Susa assembled on the thirteenth and the fourteenth of the same month, and they rested on the fifteenth day and made it a day of feasting and rejoicing.

9:19
Deut 16:11,
14; v. 22;
Neh 8:10

19   Therefore the Jews of the rural areas, who live in the rural towns, make the fourteenth day of the month Adar *a* holiday for rejoicing and feasting and sending portions *of food* to one another.

III. *The Feast of Purim:*
observance and regulations (9:20–10:3)

A. *The permanent establishment of Purim*

20   Then Mordecai recorded these events, and he sent letters to all the Jews who were in all the provinces of King Ahasuerus, both near and far,

21   obliging them to celebrate the fourteenth day of the month Adar, and the fifteenth day of the same month, annually,

9:22
v. 19

22   because on those days the Jews rid themselves of their enemies, and *it was a* month which was turned for them from sorrow into gladness and from mourning

into a holiday; that they should make them days of feasting and rejoicing and sending portions *of food* to one another and gifts to the poor.

23   Thus the Jews undertook what they had started to do, and what Mordecai had written to them.

24   For Haman the son of Hammedatha, the Agagite, the adversary of all the Jews, had schemed against the Jews to destroy them, and had cast Pur, that is the lot, to disturb them and destroy them.

9:24
Esth 3:6,7

25   But when it came to the king's attention, he commanded by letter that his wicked scheme which he had devised against the Jews, should return on his own head, and that he and his sons should be hanged on the gallows.

9:25
Esth 7:4-10;
3:6-15;
Ps 7:16

26   Therefore they called these days Purim after the name of Pur. And because of the instructions in this letter, both what they had seen in this regard and what had happened to them,

*9:26
v. 20

27   the Jews established and made a custom for themselves, and for their descendants, and for all those who allied themselves with them, so that they should not fail to celebrate these two days according to their regulation, and according to their appointed time annually.

9:27
Esth 8:17;
v. 20,21

28   So these days were to be remembered and celebrated throughout every generation, every family, every province, and every city; and these days of Purim were not to fail from among the Jews, or their memory fade from their descendants.

B. *The approval of Esther*

29   Then Queen Esther, daughter of Abihail, with Mordecai the Jew, wrote with full authority to confirm this second letter about Purim.

9:29
Esth 2:15;
vv. 20,21

30   And he sent letters to all the Jews, to the 127 provinces of the kingdom of Ahasuerus, namely, words of peace and truth,

9:30
Esth 1:1

31   to establish these days of Purim at their appointed times, just as Mordecai the Jew and Queen Esther had established for them, and just as they had established for themselves and for their descendants with instructions for their times of fasting and their lamentations.

*9:31
Esth 4:3

32   And the command of Esther established these customs for Purim, and it was written in the book.

*9:32
v. 26

C. *The power and might of Mordecai*

10 Now King Ahasuerus laid a tribute on the land and on the coastlands of the sea.

10:1
Is 24:15

2   And all the accomplishments of his authority and strength, and the full account of the greatness of Mordecai, to which the king advanced him, are they not written in the Book of the Chronicles of the Kings of Media and Persia?

10:2
Esth 8:15;
9:4; 2:23

3   For Mordecai the Jew was second *only* to King Ahasuerus and great among the Jews, and in favor with the multitude of his kinsmen, one who sought the good of his people and one who spoke for the welfare of his whole nation.

10:3
Gen 41:40;
Neh 2:10

9:26 *Purim*. The first mention of this feast outside of Scripture is in 2 Maccabees 15:36, where it is called "the day before Mordecai's [Mardocheus in the KJV] day."
9:31 *fasting*. The thirteenth day of Adar became Esther's Fast, a prelude to the joyous days of Purim.
9:32 The Feast of Purim was inaugurated by Mordecai

(9:20) to commemorate the deliverance of the Jews from wicked Haman (3:7-15; 9:24-26). It commenced on the fourteenth day of the twelfth month and lasted two days. It is thought that John 5:1 may refer to the celebration of this feast. The Jews bound themselves and their descendants to keep this feast forever (9:27,28).

INTRODUCTION TO
THE BOOK OF
JOB

Authorship and Background: The book derives its title from the central character, Job, whose name some have taken to mean "he who turns to God." Other meanings have been proposed, but the evidence is not clear. The author of the book is unknown, although Jewish tradition suggested writers from Moses to the time of Ahasuerus. It was probably written during the Solomonic age.

Sometimes regarded as parable, the book appears to be a historical poem describing actual events that took place during the patriarchal age, in the land of Uz, which probably lay in southeastern Edom. Job was a wealthy man, living a seminomadic life, free from worldly cares, when sudden catastrophe struck and he was faced with the problem of human suffering. The book was written for the purpose of seeking an answer to questions concerning the reason for human suffering and why a loving God allows it.

Characteristics: This epic poem has been acknowledged by many as one of the great literary works of all time. It has a magnificence and sublimity that defy analysis. In scope and treatment it moves majestically through the problem of suffering, seeking to resolve the dilemma in terms of human understanding. The friends of Job are skillfully depicted and their arguments cogently presented. Through their words, as well as through the words of Job himself, one is able to classify the characters, who, in some sense, are representative of men everywhere. The author does not find his solution in the dogmatic assertions of Job's friends, who shortsightedly suppose that Job has personally sinned; rather he comes, full circle, back to God and bows in acceptance of the will of God, which he may not always understand, for "we see in a mirror dimly."

Contents:

IV. The voice of God (38:1-42:6): God calls Job to account. He rehearses the marvels of the inanimate world, the animal world, and his own mighty power. Job responds to the divine Word in repentance and confession, renouncing human words and wisdom. He rejoices in his experience of God.

V. Epilogue (42:7-17): Poetry gives way to prose as Job's friends are condemned. Job's spiritual blessings are recounted. His material possessions are restored, a new family is given him, and he dies in fullness of age.

THE BOOK OF
JOB

I. *The prologue (1:1–2:13)*

A. *Job and his background*

*1:1
Jer 25:20;
Ezek 14:14;
James 5:11;
Gen 6:9;
17:1;
Ex 18:21
1:2
Job 42:13
1:3
Job 42:12
1:5
Ex 19:10;
Gen 8:20;
1 Kin 21:10,
13

1 There was a man in the land of Uz, whose name was Job, and that man was blameless, upright, fearing God, and turning away from evil.

2 And seven sons and three daughters were born to him.

3 His possessions also were 7,000 sheep, 3,000 camels, 500 yoke of oxen, 500 female donkeys, and very many servants; and that man was the greatest of all the men of the east.

4 And his sons used to go and hold a feast in the house of each one on his day, and they would send and invite their three sisters to eat and drink with them.

5 And it came about, when the days of feasting had completed their cycle, that Job would send and consecrate them, rising up early in the morning and offering burnt offerings *according to* the number of them all; for Job said, "Perhaps my sons have sinned and cursed God in their hearts." Thus Job did continually.

B. *The controversy of Satan with God*

1. *God grants Satan permission to test Job*

*1:6
Job 38:7;
1 Chr 21:1
1:7
1 Pet 5:8
1:8
Job 42:7,8;
v. 1
*1:9
1 Tim 6:5
1:10
Job 29:2-6;
Ps 128:1,2;
Job 31:25
1:11
Job 2:5;
19:21

6 Now there was a day when the sons of God came to present themselves before the LORD, and [1]Satan also came among them.

7 And the LORD said to Satan, "From where do you come?" Then Satan answered the LORD and said, "From roaming about on the earth and walking around on it."

8 And the LORD said to Satan, "Have you considered My servant Job? For there is no one like him on the earth, a blameless and upright man, fearing God and turning away from evil."

9 Then Satan answered the LORD, "Does Job fear God for nothing?

10 "Hast Thou not made a hedge about him and his house and all that he has, on every side? Thou hast blessed the work of his hands, and his possessions have increased in the land.

11 "But put forth Thy hand now and touch all that he has; he will surely curse Thee to Thy face."

12 Then the LORD said to Satan, "Behold, all that he has is in your power, only do not put forth your hand on him." So Satan departed from the presence of the LORD.

2. *Satan takes away Job's wealth and children*

1:15
Job 6:19
1:16
Gen 19:24;
Lev 10:2;

13 Now it happened on the day when his sons and his daughters were eating and drinking wine in their oldest brother's house,

14 that a messenger came to Job and said, "The oxen were plowing and the donkeys feeding beside them,

15 and the Sabeans attacked and took them. They also slew the servants with the edge of the sword, and I alone have escaped to tell you."

16 While he was still speaking, another also came and said, "The fire of God fell

[1]I.e., the adversary; so through chs. 1 and 2

1:1 *the land of Uz*, probably located in Edom (cf. Lam. 4:21), east of the territory occupied by Israel.

1:6 *the sons of God*, i.e., the angels. Among the angels we meet *Satan* (the adversary).

1:9 *Does Job fear God for nothing?* The question of Job's motivation was a subtle attack on God's providence. The accuser implies that love and loyalty can always be bought.

1:12 *in your power*. This suggests that God had delegated a limited jurisdiction to Satan. God explicitly forbade any harm to Job's person, however.

1:14 Job lost his wealth (vv. 14–17); he lost his children (vv. 18,19); and he lost his health (2:1–8). Since these are among life's most precious possessions, the loss of them was designed to lead to defection from God. Having lost all of these things, his own life seemed hardly worth preserving.

from heaven and burned up the sheep and the servants and consumed them, and I alone have escaped to tell you.''

17 While he was still speaking, another also came and said, "The Chaldeans formed three bands and made a raid on the camels and took them and slew the servants with the edge of the sword; and I alone have escaped to tell you.''

18 While he was still speaking, another also came and said, "Your sons and your daughters were eating and drinking wine in their oldest brother's house,

19 and behold, a great wind came from across the wilderness and struck the four corners of the house, and it fell on the young people and they died; and I alone have escaped to tell you.''

3. Job exhibits patience

20 Then Job arose and tore his robe and shaved his head, and he fell to the ground and worshiped.

21 And he said,
"Naked I came from my mother's womb,
And naked I shall return there.
The LORD gave and the LORD has taken away.
Blessed be the name of the LORD.''

22 Through all this Job did not sin nor did he blame God.

C. Satan's second request of God

1. Satan's request granted

2 Again there was a day when the sons of God came to present themselves before the LORD, and Satan also came among them to present himself before the LORD.

2 And the LORD said to Satan, "Where have you come from?" Then Satan answered the LORD and said, "From roaming about on the earth, and walking around on it.''

3 And the LORD said to Satan, "Have you considered My servant Job? For there is no one like him on the earth, a blameless and upright man fearing God and turning away from evil. And he still holds fast his integrity, although you incited Me against him, to ruin him without cause.''

4 And Satan answered the LORD and said, "Skin for skin! Yes, all that a man has he will give for his life.

5 "However, put forth Thy hand, now, and touch his bone and his flesh; he will curse Thee to Thy face.''

6 So the LORD said to Satan, "Behold, he is in your power, only spare his life.''

2. Satan afflicts Job physically

7 Then Satan went out from the presence of the LORD, and smote Job with sore boils from the sole of his foot to the crown of his head.

8 And he took a potsherd to scrape himself while he was sitting among the ashes.

3. Job's continued patience

9 Then his wife said to him, "Do you still hold fast your integrity? Curse God and die!''

10 But he said to her, "You speak as one of the foolish women speaks. Shall we indeed accept good from God and not accept adversity?" In all this Job did not sin with his lips.

D. The friends of Job

11 Now when Job's three friends heard of all this adversity that had come upon

Cross-references (right margin):
- Num 11:1-3; 2 Kin 1:10
- **1:17** Gen 11:28,31
- **1:18** vv. 4,13
- **1:19** Jer 4:11; 13:24
- **1:20** Gen 37:29; 1 Pet 5:6
- **1:21** Eccl 5:15; 1 Tim 6:7; Job 2:10; Eph 5:20; 1 Thess 5:18
- *1:22 Job 2:10
- **2:1** Job 1:6
- **2:2** Job 1:7
- **2:3** Job 1:1,8; 27:5,6; 9:17
- **2:5** Job 1:11
- **2:6** Job 1:12
- **2:7** Job 7:5
- **2:8** Job 42:6; Ezek 27:30; Matt 11:21
- **2:10** Job 1:21,22; Ps 39:1
- *2:11 1 Chr 1:45; Gen 25:2; Job 42:11

1:22 *blame God*, literally, "reproach God." Job did not understand the reason for the calamities he experienced, but he did not question God's sovereign rights over His creatures.

2:4 *Skin for skin* is probably a proverbial expression (used by tradesmen). The loss of possessions and loved ones may be regarded as secondary. Satan insists that Job will renounce his loyalty to God if He will bring affliction on his body.

2:9 *Curse God, and die!* Afflicted with a loathsome disease,

Job might well think life intolerable. His wife suggests that he curse God and accept the penalty, death (cf. Lev. 24:10–16).

2:11 *when Job's three friends heard.* There is no reason to question the good intent of Job's friends. They learned that Job was afflicted, and they came to be of help. Their homes appear to have been in northern Arabia. Teman is the name of an Edomite clan (Gen. 36:4,11), and the Shuhites appear to be a brother tribe to Midian (cf. Gen. 25:2; 1 Chr. 1:32). There are no references to the Naamathites other than those

him, they came each one from his own place, Eliphaz the Temanite, Bildad the Shuhite, and Zophar the Naamathite; and they made an appointment together to come to sympathize with him and comfort him.

2:12
Josh 7:6;
Lam 2:10;
Ezek 27:30

12   And when they lifted up their eyes at a distance, and did not recognize him, they raised their voices and wept. And each of them tore his robe, and they threw dust over their heads toward the sky.

2:13
Gen 50:10;
Ezek 3:15

13   Then they sat down on the ground with him for seven days and seven nights with no one speaking a word to him, for they saw that *his* pain was very great.

II. *Job's discussions with his friends (3:1–31:40)*

A. *Job's lament of misery and despair*

1. *He curses the day of his birth*

3 Afterward Job opened his mouth and cursed the day of his *birth*.
2   And Job said,

*3:3
Job 10:18;
Jer 20:14

3   "Let the day perish on which I was to be born,
  And the night *which* said, 'A boy is conceived.'

4   "May that day be darkness;
  Let not God above care for it,
  Nor light shine on it.

3:5
Job 10:21;
Ps 23:4;
Jer 2:6

5   "Let darkness and black gloom claim it;
  Let a cloud settle on it;
  Let the blackness of the day terrify it.

3:6
Job 23:17

6   "*As for* that night, let darkness seize it;
  Let it not rejoice among the days of the year;
  Let it not come into the number of the months.

7   "Behold, let that night be barren;
  Let no joyful shout enter it.

*3:8
Job 41:10

8   "Let those curse it who curse the day,
  Who are prepared to rouse Leviathan.

3:9
Job 41:18

9   "Let the stars of its twilight be darkened;
  Let it wait for light but have none,
  Neither let it see the breaking dawn;

10   Because it did not shut the opening of my *mother's* womb,
  Or hide trouble from my eyes.

2. *He asks why he did not die*

*3:11
Job 10:18

11   "Why did I not die at birth,
  Come forth from the womb and expire?

3:12
Gen 30:3;
Is 66:12

12   "Why did the knees receive me,
  And why the breasts, that I should suck?

13   "For now I would have lain down and been quiet;
  I would have slept then, I would have been at rest,

3:14
Job 12:17,18;
15:28

14   With kings and *with* counselors of the earth,
  Who rebuilt ruins for themselves;

15   Or with princes who had gold,
  Who were filling their houses *with* silver.

3:16
Eccl 6:3

16   "Or like a miscarriage which is discarded, I would not be,
  As infants that never saw light.

3:17
Job 17:16

17   "There the wicked cease from raging,
  And there the weary are at rest.

18   "The prisoners are at ease together;
  They do not hear the voice of the taskmaster.

19   "The small and the great are there,
  And the slave is free from his master.

---

in the book of Job.

3:3 Although he would not curse God, Job did curse the day of his birth. He wished that he had never been born (3:3–10) or that he might have been born dead (3:11–19).

3:8 *Leviathan,* the legendary sea monster, was thought to swallow up the sun in times of eclipse. Had Leviathan been aroused, the day of Job's birth might never have dawned!

3:11 *Why did I not die at birth . . . ?* Job wished that he had never been born or that he had died as soon as he was born. Jesus said, *"Blessed are the barren . . . and the breasts that never nursed."* (Luke 23:29), but in blessing the barren womb He never cursed the fruitful one. Job here curses life and welcomes death and the grave as a great blessing. He was sadly mistaken and unwilling to make the most of affliction.

3. He cries out in his agony

20   "Why is light given to him who suffers,
And life to the bitter of soul;

21   Who long for death, but there is none,
And dig for it more than for hidden treasures;

22   Who rejoice greatly,
They exult when they find the grave?

23   *Why is light given* to a man whose way is hidden,
And whom God has hedged in?

24   "For my groaning comes at the sight of my food,
And my cries pour out like water.

25   "For what I fear comes upon me,
And what I dread befalls me.

26   "I am not at ease, nor am I quiet,
And I am not at rest, but turmoil comes."

B. *The first cycle of speeches*

1. *The speech of Eliphaz*

a. *God does not punish the righteous*

4 Then Eliphaz the Temanite answered,
2   "If one ventures a word with you, will you become impatient?
But who can refrain from speaking?

3   "Behold you have admonished many,
And you have strengthened weak hands.

4   "Your words have helped the tottering to stand,
And you have strengthened feeble knees.

5   "But now it has come to you, and you are impatient;
It touches you, and you are dismayed.

6   "Is not your ²fear *of God* your confidence,
And the integrity of your ways your hope?

7   "Remember now, who *ever* perished being innocent?
Or where were the upright destroyed?

8   "According to what I have seen, those who plow iniquity
And those who sow trouble harvest it.

9   "By the breath of God they perish,
And by the blast of His anger they come to an end.

10   "The roaring of the lion and the voice of the *fierce* lion,
And the teeth of the young lions are broken.

11   "The lion perishes for lack of prey,
And the whelps of the lioness are scattered.

b. *Sinful man must perish*

12   "Now a word was brought to me stealthily,
And my ear received a whisper of it.

13   "Amid disquieting thoughts from the visions of the night,

²Or, *reverence*

---

*3:20
1 Sam 1:10;
Prov 31:6;
Is 38:15;
Ezek 27:31
3:21
Rev 9:6

3:23
Job 19:6,8,
12; Lam 3:7
3:24
Ps 42:3,4

*4:2
Job 32:18-20
*4:3
Is 35:3;
Heb 12:12
4:4
Is 35:3;
Heb 12:12
4:5
Job 6:14;
19:21
4:6
Job 1:1

*4:7
Ps 37:25

4:8
Prov 22:8;
Hos 10:13;
Gal 6:7,8
4:9
Job 15:30;
Is 30:33;
Ps 59:13
4:10
Ps 58:6
4:11
Ps 34:10

4:12
Job 26:14

3:20 *the bitter of soul.* This describes Job during the days following his affliction. Conscious that he has not committed some great sin, he cannot understand the reason for his suffering. He had refused to "curse God," but in his distress he does question the reason for his trials.

4:1 The speeches of Eliphaz, Bildad, Zophar, and Elihu are poetic in form. They constitute a true record of what was said, but this does not mean that what Job's friends said was necessarily true. God Himself passes adverse judgment on Eliphaz, Bildad, and Zophar (42:7–9). Nevertheless, some of the statements made by these men are true and are quoted as Scripture in the New Testament (e.g., the statements of Eliphaz in 5:11–13, echoed in Luke 1:52 and quoted in 1 Cor. 3:19).

4:2 In substance, the argument of Eliphaz is as follows: (1) If Job had been a righteous man, he would have had confidence in God rather than wishing to die; (2) Job's suffering could be explained by the maxim that as a man sows so shall

he reap (4:8,9); and (3) Job should submit to God's chastening with a humble repentance, which would enable him to regain his former prosperity. Eliphaz's maxims contain truth; but unfortunately they did not apply to Job's case, for he was not being punished for some secret sin he had committed, as the three comforters (Eliphaz, Bildad, and Zophar) implied.

4:3 *you have admonished many.* A tribute to the godly influence of Job in earlier times. Eliphaz implies that the godly Job, who has helped others so often, is now in need of help himself.

4:7 *who ever perished being innocent?* This expresses the philosophy of Job's friends. They assure him that only the wicked suffer. The logic of their position is that since Job is suffering, he must be wicked. Therefore they consider it their duty to urge Job to confess his sin and to trust in the mercy of God.

When deep sleep falls on men,

4:14
Jer 23:9

14 Dread came upon me, and trembling,
And made all my bones shake.

15 "Then a ³spirit passed by my face;
The hair of my flesh bristled up.

16 "It stood still, but I could not discern its appearance;
A form *was* before my eyes;
There was silence, then I heard a voice:

4:17
Job 9:2;
35:10

17 'Can mankind be just before God?
Can a man be pure before his Maker?

4:18
Job 15:15

18 'He puts no trust even in His servants;
And against His angels He charges error.

4:19
Job 10:9;
22:16

19 'How much more those who dwell in houses of clay,
Whose foundation is in the dust,
Who are crushed before the moth!

4:20
Ps 90:5,6;
Job 20:7

20 'Between morning and evening they are broken in pieces;
Unobserved, they perish forever.

4:21
Job 36:12

21 'Is not their tent-cord plucked up within them?
They die, yet without wisdom.'

c. Punishment the fruit of unrighteousness

5:1
Job 15:15

5 "Call now, is there anyone who will answer you?
And to which of the holy ones will you turn?

5:2
Prov 12:16

2 "For vexation slays the foolish man,
And anger kills the simple.

5:3
Ps 37:35

3 "I have seen the foolish taking root,
And I cursed his abode immediately.

5:4
Amos 5:12

4 "His sons are far from safety,
They are even ⁴oppressed in the gate,
Neither is there a deliverer.

5:5
Job 18:8-10

5 "His harvest the hungry devour,
And take it to a *place of* thorns;
And the schemer is eager for their wealth.

6 "For affliction does not come from the dust,
Neither does trouble sprout from the ground,

5:7
Job 14:1

7 For man is born for trouble,
As sparks fly upward.

d. Eliphaz implores Job to seek God

5:8
Ps 35:23

8 "But as for me, I would seek God,
And I would place my cause before God;

5:9
Ps 40:5;
72:18

9 Who does great and unsearchable things,
Wonders without number.

5:10
Ps 65:9

10 "He gives rain on the earth,
And sends water on the fields,

5:11
1 Sam 2:7;
Ps 113:7

11 So that He sets on high those who are lowly,
And those who mourn are lifted to safety.

5:12
Neh 4:15;
Ps 33:10;
Is 8:10

12 "He frustrates the plotting of the shrewd,
So that their hands cannot attain success.

13 "He captures the wise by their own shrewdness
And the advice of the cunning is quickly thwarted.

5:14
Job 12:25;
Deut 28:29

14 "By day they meet with darkness,
And grope at noon as in the night.

5:15
Ps 35:10

15 "But He saves from the sword of their mouth,
And the poor from the hand of the mighty.

5:16
Ps 107:42

16 "So the helpless has hope,
And unrighteousness must shut its mouth.

5:17
Ps 94:12;
James 1:12;
Heb 12:5-11

17 "Behold, how happy is the man whom God reproves,
So do not despise the discipline of the Almighty.

³Or, *breath passed over* ⁴Lit., *crushed*

4:15 *a spirit passed by my face.* Eliphaz made his appeal to Job on the basis of a night vision. His mystical experience is deemed sufficient to accuse Job of sin.

18   "For He inflicts pain, and gives relief;
       He wounds, and His hands *also* heal.

19   "From six troubles He will deliver you,
       Even in seven evil will not touch you.

20   "In famine He will redeem you from death,
       And in war from the power of the sword.

21   "You will be hidden from the scourge of the tongue,
       Neither will you be afraid of violence when it comes.

22   "You will laugh at violence and famine,
       Neither will you be afraid of wild beasts.

23   "For you will be in league with the stones of the field;
       And the beasts of the field will be at peace with you.

24   "And you will know that your tent is secure,
       For you will visit your abode and fear no loss.

25   "You will know also that your descendants will be many,
       And your offspring as the grass of the earth.

26   "You will come to the grave in full vigor,
       Like the stacking of grain in its season.

27   "Behold this, we have investigated it, thus it is;
       Hear it, and know for yourself."

2. Job's reply to Eliphaz

a. He complains that God will not let him die

6 Then Job answered,

2   "Oh that my vexation were actually weighed,
       And laid in the balances together with my iniquity!

3   "For then it would be heavier than the sand of the seas,
       Therefore my words have been rash.

4   "For the arrows of the Almighty are within me;
       Their poison my spirit drinks;
       The terrors of God are arrayed against me.

5   "Does the wild donkey bray over *his* grass,
       Or does the ox low over his fodder?

6   "Can something tasteless be eaten without salt,
       Or is there any taste in the white of an egg?

7   "My soul refuses to touch *them;*
       They are like loathsome food to me.

8   "Oh that my request might come to pass,
       And that God would grant my longing!

9   "Would that God were willing to crush me;
       That He would loose His hand and cut me off!

10   "But it is still my consolation,
       And I rejoice in unsparing pain,
       That I have not denied the words of the Holy One.

11   "What is my strength, that I should wait?
       And what is my end, that I should endure?

12   "Is my strength the strength of stones,
       Or is my flesh bronze?

13   "Is it that my help is not within me,
       And that deliverance is driven from me?

b. Job calls his friends unfaithful

14   "For the despairing man *there should be* kindness from his friend;
       Lest he forsake the fear of the Almighty.

15   "My brothers have acted deceitfully like a wadi,
       Like the torrents of wadis which vanish,

16   Which are turbid because of ice,
       And into which the snow melts.

17   "When they become waterless, they are silent,
       When it is hot, they vanish from their place.

18   "The paths of their course wind along,
       They go up into nothing and perish.

5:18 Is 30:26
5:19 Ps 34:19; 91:10
5:20 Ps 33:19; 144:10
5:21 Ps 31:20; 91:5,6
5:22 Ps 91:13; Ezek 34:25
5:23 Ps 91:12; Is 11:6-9
5:24 Job 8:6; 21:9
5:25 Ps 72:16; 112:2
5:26 Gen 15:15; Prov 9:11

6:2 Job 31:6
6:3 Prov 27:3
6:4 Ps 38:2; Job 21:20; Ps 88:15

6:8 Job 14:13
6:9 1 Kin 19:4
6:10 Job 23:11,12; Lev 19:2; Is 57:15; Hos 11:9
6:11 Job 21:4
6:13 Job 26:2,3

6:15 Ps 38:11; Jer 15:18
6:17 Job 24:19

6:19
Gen 25:15;
Is 21:14;
1 Kin 10:1
6:20
Jer 14:3

19 "The caravans of Tema looked,
   The travelers of Sheba hoped for them.

20 "They were disappointed for they had trusted,
   They came there and were confounded.

c. He asks for evidences of his sins

21 "Indeed, you have now become such,
   You see a terror and are afraid.

22 "Have I said, 'Give me *something*,'
   Or, 'Offer a bribe for me from your wealth,'

23 Or, 'Deliver me from the hand of the adversary,'
   Or, 'Redeem me from the hand of the tyrants'?

24 "Teach me, and I will be silent;
   And show me how I have erred.

6:25
Eccl 12:10,11

25 "How painful are honest words!
   But what does your argument prove?

6:26
Job 8:2

26 "Do you intend to reprove *my* words,
   When the words of one in despair belong to the wind?

6:27
Joel 3:3;
2 Pet 3:3
6:28
Job 27:4

27 "You would even cast *lots* for the orphans,
   And barter over your friend.

28 "And now please look at me,
   And *see* if I lie to your face.

29 "Desist now, let there be no injustice;
   Even desist, my righteousness is yet in it.

6:30
Job 27:4;
12:11

30 "Is there injustice on my tongue?
   Cannot my palate discern calamities?

d. He argues against hope

7:1
Job 10:17;
14:14;
Is 40:2;
Job 14:6
7:2
Lev 19:13
7:3
Lam 1:7;
Ps 6:6
7:4
Deut 28:67

7 "Is not man forced to labor on earth,
   And *are not* his days like the days of a hired man?

2 "As a slave who pants for the shade,
   And as a hired man who eagerly waits for his wages,

3 So am I allotted months of vanity,
   And nights of trouble are appointed me.

4 "When I lie down I say,
   'When shall I arise?'
   But the night continues,
   And I am continually tossing until dawn.

5 "My flesh is clothed with worms and a crust of dirt;
   My skin hardens and runs.

7:6
Job 9:25;
13:15; 17:15,
16

6 "My days are swifter than a weaver's shuttle,
   And come to an end without hope.

e. He prays to his God

7:7
Ps 78:39;
Job 9:25

7 "Remember that my life is *but* breath,
   My eye will not again see good.

7:8
Job 20:9;
v. 21

8 "The eye of him who sees me will behold me no more;
   Thine eyes *will be* on me, but I will not be.

7:9
Job 30:15;
11:8;
2 Sam 12:23
7:10
Job 10:21;
Ps 103:16

9 "When a cloud vanishes, it is gone,
   So he who goes down to Sheol does not come up.

10 "He will not return again to his house,
   Nor will his place know him anymore.

7:11
Ps 40:9;
1 Sam 1:10

11 "Therefore, I will not restrain my mouth;
   I will speak in the anguish of my spirit,
   I will complain in the bitterness of my soul.

7:12
Ezek 32:2,3

12 "Am I the sea, or the sea monster,
   That Thou dost set a guard over me?

7:13
Job 9:27

13 "If I say, 'My bed will comfort me,
   My couch will ease my complaint,'

7:14
Job 9:34

14 Then Thou dost frighten me with dreams
   And terrify me by visions;

7:15
1 Kin 19:4

15 So that my soul would choose suffocation,
   Death rather than my pains.

16 "I waste away; I will not live forever.
    Leave me alone, for my days are *but* a breath.

17 "What is man that Thou dost magnify him,
    And that Thou art concerned about him,

18 That Thou dost examine him every morning,
    And try him every moment?

19 "Wilt Thou never turn Thy gaze away from me,
    Nor let me alone until I swallow my spittle?

20 "Have I sinned? What have I done to Thee,
    O watcher of men?
    Why hast Thou set me as Thy target,
    So that I am a burden to myself?

21 "Why then dost Thou not pardon my transgression
    And take away my iniquity?
    For now I will lie down in the dust;
    And Thou wilt seek me, but I will not be."

3. The speech of Bildad: Bildad calls Job a hypocrite and urges repentance

8 Then Bildad the Shuhite answered,
2 "How long will you say these *things*,
    And the words of your mouth be a mighty wind?

3 "Does God pervert justice
    Or does the Almighty pervert what is right?

4 "If your sons sinned against Him,
    Then He delivered them into the power of their transgression.

5 "If you would seek God
    And implore the compassion of the Almighty,

6 If you are pure and upright,
    Surely now He would rouse Himself for you
    And restore your righteous estate.

7 "Though your beginning was insignificant,
    Yet your end will increase greatly.

8 "Please inquire of past generations,
    And consider the things searched out by their fathers.

9 "For we are *only* of yesterday and know nothing,
    Because our days on earth are as a shadow.

10 "Will they not teach you *and* tell you,
    And bring forth words from their minds?

11 "Can the papyrus grow up without marsh?
    Can the rushes grow without water?

12 "While it is still green *and* not cut down,
    Yet it withers before any *other* plant.

13 "So are the paths of all who forget God,
    And the hope of the godless will perish,

14 Whose confidence is fragile,
    And whose trust a spider's web.

15 "He trusts in his house, but it does not stand;
    He holds fast to it, but it does not endure.

16 "He thrives before the sun,
    And his shoots spread out over his garden.

17 "His roots wrap around a rock pile,
    He grasps a house of stones.

18 "If he is removed from his place,
    Then it will deny him, *saying,* 'I never saw you.'

19 "Behold, this is the joy of His way;

7:16
Job 10:1;
Eccl 7:15
7:17
Ps 8:4; 144:3;
Heb 2:6

7:20
Job 35:3,6;
v. 12;
Job 16:12

*7:21
Job 10:14;
Ps 104:29;
v. 8

8:3
Gen 18:25;
Deut 32:4;
2 Chr 19:7;
Dan 9:14;
Rom 3:5
8:4
Job 1:5,18,19
8:5
Job 5:8;
11:13; 9:15
8:6
Ps 7:6
8:7
Job 42:12

*8:8
Deut 4:32;
32:7;
Job 15:18
8:9
Gen 47:9;
1 Chr 29:15;
Job 7:5

8:12
Ps 129:6;
Jer 17:6
8:13
Ps 9:17;
Job 11:20;
Prov 10:28
8:14
Is 59:5,6
8:15
Job 27:18

8:16
Ps 37:35;
80:11

8:18
Job 7:10;
Ps 37:36
8:19
Job 20:5;
Eccl 1:4

7:21 *Why then dost Thou not pardon my transgression?* Job insists that no sin he has committed has harmed God. Let God forgive Job, for he does not merit the sore chastisement he has experienced. The words represent a "reasoning with God" and need not be deemed irreverent.
8:1 Bildad presents much the same argument as Eliphaz. He contends that if Job will stop rebelling against his suffer-ing and acknowledge the justice of God's dealings with him, he will soon regain his prosperity.
8:8 *consider the things searched out by their fathers.* Bildad appeals to history and tradition in seeking to convince Job of his error. Bildad's philosophy is similar to that of Eliphaz, but his appeal is on the basis of scholarship rather than mystical experience.

And out of the dust others will spring.

8:20
Job 4:7;
21:30
8:21
Ps 126:2;
132:16
8:22
Ps 35:26;
109:29; v. 15

20 "Lo, God will not reject *a man of* integrity,
Nor will He support the evildoers.

21 "He will yet fill your mouth with laughter,
And your lips with shouting.

22 "Those who hate you will be clothed with shame;
And the tent of the wicked will be no more."

4. *Job answers Bildad*

a. *The doctrine and proof of God's justice*

9 Then Job answered,

9:2
Ps 143:2;
Rom 3:20

2 "In truth I know that this is so,
But how can a man be in the right before God?

3 "If one wished to dispute with Him,
He could not answer Him once in a thousand *times.*

9:4
Job 36:5;
2 Chr 13:12
9:5
Mic 1:4

4 "Wise in heart and mighty in strength,
Who has defied Him without harm?

5 "*It is God* who removes the mountains, they know not *how,*
When He overturns them in His anger;

9:6
Is 2:19,21;
Hag 2:6;
Heb 12:26;
Job 26:11

6 Who shakes the earth out of its place,
And its pillars tremble;

7 Who commands the sun not to shine,
And sets a seal upon the stars;

9:8
Gen 1:6;
Ps 104:2,3
9:9
Gen 1:16;
Job 38:31;
Amos 5:8
9:10
Ps 71:15

8 Who alone stretches out the heavens,
And tramples down the waves of the sea;

9 Who makes the Bear, Orion, and the Pleiades,
And the chambers of the south;

10 Who does great things, unfathomable,
And wondrous works without number.

9:11
Job 23:8,9;
35:14
9:12
Is 45:9;
Rom 9:20;
Job 11:10

11 "Were He to pass by me, I would not see Him;
Were He to move past *me,* I would not perceive Him.

12 "Were He to snatch away, who could restrain Him?
Who could say to Him, 'What art Thou doing?'

b. *Job acknowledges himself a sinner*

*9:13
Job 26:12;
Is 30:7
9:14
vv. 3,32

13 "God will not turn back His anger;
Beneath Him crouch the helpers of Rahab.

14 "How then can I answer Him,
And choose my words before Him?

9:15
Job 10:15;
8:5

15 "For though I were right, I could not answer;
I would have to implore the mercy of my judge.

16 "If I called and He answered me,
I could not believe that He was listening to my voice.

9:17
Job 16:12,14;
2:3
9:18
Job 27:2

17 "For He bruises me with a tempest,
And multiplies my wounds without cause.

18 "He will not allow me to get my breath,
But saturates me with bitterness.

19 "If *it is a matter* of power, behold, *He is* the strong one!
And if *it is a matter* of justice, who can summon Him?

9:20
vv. 15,29

20 "Though I am righteous, my mouth will condemn me;
Though I am guiltless, He will declare me guilty.

9:21
Job 1:1; 7:16

21 "I am guiltless;
I do not take notice of myself;
I despise my life.

9:22
Eccl 9:2,3;
Ezek 21:3
9:23
Ps 64:4;
Heb 11:36;
1 Pet 1:7

22 "It is *all* one; therefore I say,
'He destroys the guiltless and the wicked.'

23 "If the scourge kills suddenly,
He mocks the despair of the innocent.

24 "The earth is given into the hand of the wicked;

9:13 *the helpers of Rahab.* Rahab is a mythological figure who symbolizes the power of evil over which Yahweh, Israel's God, gained a significant victory in primordial times (cf. Is. 51:9). Job depicts God as gaining a victory over Rahab's helpers. The Babylonian creation epic (*Enuma Elish,* iv, 105ff.) describes the victory of Marduk, god of Babylon, over Tiâmat, an evil deity who likewise had helpers "who marched at her side."

He covers the faces of its judges.
If *it is* not *He,* then who is it?"

c. *Job's complaint against God*

25 "Now my days are swifter than a runner;
They flee away, they see no good.
26 "They slip by like reed boats,
Like an eagle that swoops on its prey.
27 "Though I say, 'I will forget my complaint,
I will leave off my *sad* countenance and be cheerful,'
28 I am afraid of all my pains,
I know that Thou wilt not acquit me.
29 "I am accounted wicked,
Why then should I toil in vain?
30 "If I should wash myself with snow
And cleanse my hands with lye,
31 Yet Thou wouldst plunge me into the pit,
And my own clothes would abhor me.
32 "For *He is* not a man as I am that I may answer Him,
That we may go to court together.
33 "There is no umpire between us,
Who may lay his hand upon us both.
34 "Let Him remove His rod from me,
And let not dread of Him terrify me.
35 "*Then* I would speak and not fear Him;
But I am not like that in myself.

d. *Job's persistence in complaint*

10 "I loathe my own life;
I will give full vent to my complaint;
I will speak in the bitterness of my soul.
2 "I will say to God, 'Do not condemn me;
Let me know why Thou dost contend with me.
3 'Is it right for Thee indeed to oppress,
To reject the labor of Thy hands,
And to look favorably on the schemes of the wicked?
4 'Hast Thou eyes of flesh?
Or dost Thou see as a man sees?
5 'Are Thy days as the days of a mortal,
Or Thy years as man's years,
6 That Thou shouldst seek for my guilt,
And search after my sin?
7 'According to Thy knowledge I am indeed not guilty;
Yet there is no deliverance from Thy hand.

e. *Job acknowledges God as creator and preserver*

8 'Thy hands fashioned and made me altogether,
And wouldst Thou destroy me?
9 'Remember now, that Thou hast made me as clay;
And wouldst Thou turn me into dust again?
10 'Didst Thou not pour me out like milk,
And curdle me like cheese;
11 Clothe me with skin and flesh,
And knit me together with bones and sinews?
12 'Thou hast granted me life and lovingkindness;
And Thy care has preserved my spirit.
13 'Yet these things Thou hast concealed in Thy heart;
I know that this is within Thee:

f. *Job again complains against God*

14 If I sin, then Thou wouldst take note of me,
And wouldst not acquit me of my guilt.
15 'If I am wicked, woe to me!
And if I am righteous, I dare not lift up my head.

9:24
Job 10:3;
12:6; 12:17

9:25
Job 7:6,7

9:26
Hab 1:8

9:27
Job 7:13

9:28
Ps 119:120;
Job 7:21
9:29
v. 20

9:30
Jer 2:22

9:32
Eccl 6:10;
Rom 9:20;
v. 3; Ps 143:2
9:33
1 Sam 2:25
9:34
Job 13:21;
Ps 39:10
9:35
Job 13:22

10:1
1 Kin 19:4;
Job 7:16;
7:11

10:2
Job 9:29;
Hos 4:1
10:3
v. 8;
Job 21:16;
22:18

10:4
1 Sam 16:7

10:5
Ps 90:4;
2 Pet 3:8

10:7
Job 9:21;
9:12

10:8
Ps 119:73

10:9
Gen 2:7;
3:19; Is 64:8
10:10
Ps 139:14-16

10:12
Job 33:4

10:14
Job 13:27;
9:28
10:15
Is 3:11;
Job 9:12,15;
Ps 25:8

I am sated with disgrace and conscious of my misery.

16 'And should *my head* be lifted up, Thou wouldst hunt me like a lion;
And again Thou wouldst show Thy power against me.

17 'Thou dost renew Thy witnesses against me,
And increase Thine anger toward me,
Hardship after hardship is with me.

18 'Why then hast Thou brought me out of the womb?
Would that I had died and no eye had seen me!

19 'I should have been as though I had not been,
Carried from womb to tomb.'

20 "Would He not let my few days alone?
Withdraw from me that I may have a little cheer

21 Before I go—and I shall not return—
To the land of darkness and deep shadow;

22 The land of utter gloom as darkness *itself,*
Of deep shadow without order,
And which shines as the darkness."

5. *The speech of Zophar*

a. *He accuses Job of lying and hypocrisy*

11 Then Zophar the Naamathite answered,

2 "Shall a multitude of words go unanswered,
And a talkative man be acquitted?

3 "Shall your boasts silence men?
And shall you scoff and none rebuke?

4 "For you have said, 'My teaching is pure,
And I am innocent in your eyes.'

5 "But would that God might speak,
And open His lips against you,

6 And show you the secrets of wisdom!
For sound wisdom has two sides.
Know then that God forgets a part of your iniquity.

b. *He argues for God's sovereignty and infinity*

7 "Can you discover the depths of God?
Can you discover the limits of the Almighty?

8 "*They are* high as the heavens, what can you do?
Deeper than Sheol, what can you know?

9 "Its measure is longer than the earth,
And broader than the sea.

10 "If He passes by or shuts up,
Or calls an assembly, who can restrain Him?

11 "For He knows false men,
And He sees iniquity without investigating.

12 "And an idiot will become intelligent
When the foal of a wild donkey is born a man.

c. *He assures Job of restoration upon repentance and reformation*

13 "If you would direct your heart right,
And spread out your hand to Him;

14 If iniquity is in your hand, put it far away,
And do not let wickedness dwell in your tents.

15 "Then, indeed, you could lift up your face without *moral* defect,
And you would be steadfast and not fear.

16 "For you would forget *your* trouble,
As waters that have passed by, you would remember *it.*

17 "And your life would be brighter than noonday;
Darkness would be like the morning.

Cross-reference column (left margin):
10:16 Is 38:13; Lam 3:10; Job 5:9
10:17 Job 16:8; 7:1
10:18 Job 3:11
10:20 Job 14:1; 7:16,19; 9:27
10:21 Ps 88:12; 23:4
11:2 Job 8:2
11:3 James 3:5; Job 17:2; 21:3
11:4 Job 6:10; 10:7
*11:6 Job 28:21; Ezra 9:13
11:7 Eccl 3:11; Rom 11:33
11:8 Job 22:12; 17:16
11:10 Job 9:12; Rev 3:7
11:11 Job 34:21-25; Ps 10:14
11:13 Ps 78:8; 88:9
11:14 Job 22:23; Ps 101:3
11:15 1 John 3:21; Ps 27:3
11:16 Is 65:16; Job 22:11
11:17 Ps 37:6; 112:4; Is 58:8,10

11:1 Zophar repeats the same arguments of Bildad and Eliphaz. He thinks Job is a liar and a hypocrite and that his evil plight is the just consequence of his sins.
11:6 *God forgets a part of your iniquity.* Zophar dogmatically insists that Job is a hypocrite who deserves more, not less, suffering. His appeal is neither to mysticism (Eliphaz) nor scholarship (Bildad), but to his own conviction of right and wrong.

18	"Then you would trust, because there is hope; And you would look around and rest securely.	**11:18** Ps 3:5; Prov 3:24
19	"You would lie down and none would disturb *you*, And many would entreat your favor.	**11:19** v. 18
20	"But the eyes of the wicked will fail, And there will be no escape for them; And their hope is to breathe their last."	**11:20** Deut 28:65; Jer 15:9

6. *Job's reply to Zophar*

a. *Job denies the accusations*

12 Then Job responded,
2 "Truly then you are the people,
And with you wisdom will die!

3	"But I have intelligence as well as you; I am not inferior to you. And who does not know such things as these?	**12:3** Job 13:2
4	"I am a joke to my friends. The one who called on God, and He answered him; The just *and* blameless *man* is a joke.	**12:4** Job 6:10,20; 21:3; Ps 91:15; Job 6:29
5	"He who is at ease holds calamity in contempt, As prepared for those whose feet slip.	**12:5** Ps 123:4
6	"The tents of the destroyers prosper, And those who provoke God are secure, Whom God brings into ⁵their power.	**12:6** Job 9:24; 21:9; 22:18

b. *He argues that God is watching over all*

7	"But now ask the beasts, and let them teach you; And the birds of the heavens, and let them tell you.	
8	"Or speak to the earth, and let it teach you; And let the fish of the sea declare to you.	
9	"Who among all these does not know That the hand of the Lᴏʀᴅ has done this,	**12:9** Is 41:20
10	In whose hand is the life of every living thing, And the breath of all mankind?	**12:10** Acts 17:28; Job 27:3; 33:4
11	"Does not the ear test words, As the palate tastes its food?	**12:11** Job 34:3
12	"Wisdom is with aged men, *With* long life is understanding.	**12:12** Job 32:7

c. *He enlarges on God's providences*

13	"With Him are wisdom and might; To Him belong counsel and understanding.	**12:13** Job 9:4; 11:6
14	"Behold, He tears down, and it cannot be rebuilt; He imprisons a man, and there can be no release.	**12:14** Job 19:10; 37:7
15	"Behold, He restrains the waters, and they dry up; And He sends them out, and they inundate the earth.	**12:15** 1 Kin 8:35; Gen 7:11
16	"With Him are strength and sound wisdom, The misled and the misleader belong to Him.	**12:16** v. 13; Job 13:7,9
17	"He makes counselors walk barefoot, And makes fools of judges.	**12:17** Job 3:14; 19:9; 9:24
18	"He loosens the bond of kings, And binds their loins with a girdle.	**12:18** Ps 116:16
19	"He makes priests walk barefoot, And overthrows the secure ones.	
20	"He deprives the trusted ones of speech, And takes away the discernment of the elders.	**12:20** Job 32:9
21	"He pours contempt on nobles, And loosens the belt of the strong.	**12:21** Ps 107:40; v. 18

⁵Lit., *his*

12:2 *with you wisdom will die.* Job resorts to irony in conceding that his friends are the embodiment of wisdom. They "know it all"; and when they are gone, wisdom will be dead also!

12:7 *But now ask the beasts.* Although Job's friends profess wisdom, he insists that they can learn from beast and bird.

12:22
Dan 2:22;
1 Cor 4:5;
Job 3:5

12:23
Ps 107:38;
Is 9:3;
Jer 25:9;
Deut 12:20;
Ps 78:61

12:24
v. 20;
Ps 107:40

12:25
Job 5:14;
Ps 107:27

13:1
Job 12:9

13:2
Job 12:3

13:3
Job 23:3,4;
v. 15

13:4
Ps 119:69;
Jer 23:32

13:5
Prov 17:28

13:7
Job 36:4

13:9
Ps 44:21;
Gal 6:7

13:10
v. 8

13:11
Job 31:23

13:12
Job 15:3

13:13
v. 5

13:14
1 Sam 19:5

13:15
Ps 23:4;
Prov 14:32;
Job 27:5

13:16
Ps 5:5

13:17
Job 21:2

13:18
Job 23:4; 9:2

*13:19
Is 50:8;
Job 40:4

13:20
Job 9:34

13:21
Ps 39:10

13:22
Job 14:15

22 "He reveals mysteries from the darkness,
And brings the deep darkness into light.
23 "He makes the nations great, then destroys them;
He enlarges the nations, then leads them away.
24 "He deprives of intelligence the chiefs of the earth's people,
And makes them wander in a pathless waste.
25 "They grope in darkness with no light,
And He makes them stagger like a drunken man.

d. Job's resentment of his friends

13 "Behold, my eye has seen all *this*,
My ear has heard and understood it.
2 "What you know I also know.
I am not inferior to you.
3 "But I would speak to the Almighty,
And I desire to argue with God.
4 "But you smear with lies;
You are all worthless physicians.
5 "O that you would be completely silent,
And that it would become your wisdom!
6 "Please hear my argument,
And listen to the contentions of my lips.
7 "Will you speak what is unjust for God,
And speak what is deceitful for Him?
8 "Will you show partiality for Him?
Will you contend for God?
9 "Will it be well when He examines you?
Or will you deceive Him as one deceives a man?
10 "He will surely reprove you,
If you secretly show partiality.
11 "Will not His majesty terrify you,
And the dread of Him fall on you?
12 "Your memorable sayings are proverbs of ashes,
Your defenses are defenses of clay.

e. Job's defense of his own integrity

13 "Be silent before me so that I may speak;
Then let come on me what may.
14 "Why should I take my flesh in my teeth,
And put my life in my hands?
15 "Though He slay me,
I will hope in Him.
Nevertheless I will argue my ways before Him.
16 "This also will be my salvation,
For a godless man may not come before His presence.
17 "Listen carefully to my speech,
And let my declaration *fill* your ears.
18 "Behold now, I have prepared my case;
I know that I will be vindicated.
19 "Who will contend with me?
For then I would be silent and die.
20 "Only two things do not do to me,
Then I will not hide from Thy face:
21 Remove Thy hand from me,
And let not the dread of Thee terrify me.
22 "Then call, and I will answer;
Or let me speak, then reply to me.

13:19 Job here claims that he is righteous, guiltless of any such unconfessed sin as would warrant his present sufferings. Therefore he can only suppose that God is treating him capriciously and arbitrarily, and is at a loss to understand why.

f. Job asks for the number of his sins
and complains of God's severe dealings

23   "How many are my iniquities and sins?
       Make known to me my rebellion and my sin.

13:23
1 Sam 26:18

24   "Why dost Thou hide Thy face,
       And consider me Thine enemy?

13:24
Deut 32:20;
Ps 13:1;
Job 19:11

25   "Wilt Thou cause a driven leaf to tremble?
       Or wilt Thou pursue the dry chaff?

13:25
Is 42:3

26   "For Thou dost write bitter things against me,
       And dost make me to inherit the iniquities of my youth.

13:26
Ps 25:7

27   "Thou dost put my feet in the stocks,
       And dost watch all my paths;
       Thou dost set a limit for the soles of my feet,

13:27
Job 33:11

28   While I am decaying like a rotten thing,
       Like a garment that is moth-eaten.

13:28
Is 50:9;
James 5:2

g. Job speaks to God

14   "Man, who is born of woman,
       Is short-lived and full of turmoil.

14:1
Job 5:7;
Eccl 2:23

2   "Like a flower he comes forth and withers.
       He also flees like a shadow and does not remain.

14:2
Ps 90:5,6;
James 1:10;
1 Pet 1:24

3   "Thou also dost open Thine eyes on him,
       And bring him into judgment with Thyself.

14:3
Ps 144:3;
143:2

4   "Who can make the clean out of the unclean?
       No one!

14:4
Ps 51:2,10;
John 3:6;
Rom 5:12;
Eph 2:3

5   "Since his days are determined,
       The number of his months is with Thee,
       And his limits Thou hast set so that he cannot pass.

*14:5
Ps 139:16;
Job 21:21;
Acts 17:26

6   "Turn Thy gaze from him that he may rest,
       Until he fulfills his day like a hired man.

14:6
Job 7:19; 7:1

7   "For there is hope for a tree,
       When it is cut down, that it will sprout again,
       And its shoots will not fail.

8   "Though its roots grow old in the ground,
       And its stump dies in the dry soil,

9   At the scent of water it will flourish
       And put forth sprigs like a plant.

14:9
Is 55:10

10   "But man dies and lies prostrate.
       Man expires, and where is he?

14:10
Job 13:19

11   "*As* water evaporates from the sea,
       And a river becomes parched and dried up,

14:11
Is 19:5

12   So man lies down and does not rise.
       Until the heavens be no more,
       He will not awake nor be aroused out of his sleep.

14:12
Ps 102:26;
Acts 3:21;
Rev 20:11;
21:1

13   "Oh that Thou wouldst hide me in Sheol,
       That Thou wouldst conceal me until Thy wrath returns *to Thee*,
       That Thou wouldst set a limit for me and remember me!

14:13
Is 26:20

14   "If a man dies, will he live *again?*
       All the days of my struggle I will wait,
       Until my change comes.

14:14
Job 7:1

15   "Thou wilt call, and I will answer Thee;
       Thou wilt long for the work of Thy hands.

14:15
Job 13:22

16   "For now Thou dost number my steps,
       Thou dost not observe my sin.

14:16
Job 10:6;
31:4; 34:21;
Prov 5:21;
Jer 32:19

17   "My transgression is sealed up in a bag,
       And Thou dost wrap up my iniquity.

14:17
Deut 32:34;
Hos 13:12

18   "But the falling mountain crumbles away,
       And the rock moves from its place;

14:18
Job 18:4

19   Water wears away stones,

14:5 Man's days: (1) are numbered, not numberless; (2) are set by the will of God, who has determined how long he shall live and when he shall die; and (3) cannot be increased or diminished.

14:19
Job 7:6
Its torrents wash away the dust of the earth;
So Thou dost destroy man's hope.

*14:20
Job 34:20;
James 1:10
20 "Thou dost forever overpower him and he departs;
Thou dost change his appearance and send him away.

14:21
Eccl 9:5;
Is 63:16
21 "His sons achieve honor, but he does not know *it*;
Or they become insignificant, but he does not perceive it.

22 "But his body pains him,
And he mourns only for himself."

C. *The second cycle of speeches*

1. *Eliphaz's second speech*

a. *Job's own words condemn him*

15 Then Eliphaz the Temanite responded,
*15:2
Job 6:26
2 "Should a wise man answer with windy knowledge,
And fill himself with the east wind?

3 "Should he argue with useless talk,
Or with words which are not profitable?

4 "Indeed, you do away with reverence,
And hinder meditation before God.

15:5
Ps 36:3;
Prov 16:23;
Job 5:12,13
15:6
Job 9:20;
Luke 19:22
5 "For your guilt teaches your mouth,
And you choose the language of the crafty.

6 "Your own mouth condemns you, and not I;
And your own lips testify against you.

b. *Job is deluding himself*

15:7
Job 38:4,21;
Ps 90:2;
Prov 8:25
15:8
Rom 11:34;
Job 12:2
15:9
Job 13:2
15:10
Job 32:6,7
7 "Were you the first man to be born,
Or were you brought forth before the hills?

8 "Do you hear the secret counsel of God,
And limit wisdom to yourself?

9 "What do you know that we do not know?
What do you understand that we do not?

10 "Both the gray-haired and the aged are among us,
Older than your father.

15:11
Job 36:15,16;
2 Cor 1:3,4;
Zech 1:13
11 "Are the consolations of God too small for you,
Even the word *spoken* gently with you?

c. *Job is condemned before God*

12 "Why does your heart carry you away?
And why do your eyes flash,

15:13
Job 33:13
13 That you should turn your spirit against God,
And allow *such* words to go out of your mouth?

15:14
Job 14:4;
Prov 20:9;
Eccl 7:20;
Job 25:4;
Ps 51:5
15:15
Job 4:18;
25:5
15:16
Ps 14:1,3;
Job 34:7
14 "What is man, that he should be pure,
Or he who is born of a woman, that he should be righteous?

15 "Behold, He puts no trust in His holy ones,
And the heavens are not pure in His sight;

16 How much less one who is detestable and corrupt,
Man, who drinks iniquity like water!

d. *The end of an evil man*

17 "I will tell you, listen to me;
And what I have seen I will also declare;

15:18
Job 8:8
18 What wise men have told,
And have not concealed from their fathers,

19 To whom alone the land was given,

14:20 *Thou dost forever overpower him.* Man is an unequal match against God, and he cannot hope to defeat the divine purposes.

15:1 Eliphaz (ch. 15), Bildad (ch. 18), and Zophar (ch. 20) paint vivid pictures of the terrors that befall the wicked in this life. They cannot answer Job's rebuttals, for the stubborn fact remains that experience simply does not bear out their dogma that the wicked receive their just retribution in this life, and that no injustice ever befalls those who are righteous. In chapters 27 and 28 Job himself speaks of God's

ultimate justice outside this present visible world. In chapters 29–31 he complains that God deals capriciously with the world at present.

15:2 *Should a wise man answer with windy knowledge . . . ?* Eliphaz begins the second round of speeches on a more hostile note than his earlier address. Job's friends are angered that Job will not accept their counsel, and their words contain threats as well as rebukes for this terribly tormented man.

And no alien passed among them.

20 "The wicked man writhes in pain all *his* days,
And numbered are the years stored up for the ruthless.

21 "Sounds of terror are in his ears,
While at peace the destroyer comes upon him.

22 "He does not believe that he will return from darkness,
And he is destined for the sword.

23 "He wanders about for food, saying, 'Where is it?'
He knows that a day of darkness is at hand.

24 "Distress and anguish terrify him,
They overpower him like a king ready for the attack,

25 Because he has stretched out his hand against God,
And conducts himself arrogantly against the Almighty.

26 "He rushes headlong at Him
With his massive shield.

27 "For he has covered his face with his fat,
And made his thighs heavy with flesh.

28 "And he has lived in desolate cities,
In houses no one would inhabit,
Which are destined to become ruins.

29 "He will not become rich, nor will his wealth endure;
And his grain will not bend down to the ground.

30 "He will not escape from darkness;
The flame will wither his shoots,
And by the breath of His mouth he will go away.

31 "Let him not trust in emptiness, deceiving himself;
For emptiness will be his reward.

32 "It will be accomplished before his time,
And his palm branch will not be green.

33 "He will drop off his unripe grape like the vine,
And will cast off his flower like the olive tree.

34 "For the company of the godless is barren,
And fire consumes the tents of the corrupt.

35 "They conceive mischief and bring forth iniquity,
And their mind prepares deception.''

2. Job's second reply to Eliphaz

a. *He charges his friends with unkindness*

16 Then Job answered,

2 "I have heard many such things;
Sorry comforters are you all.

3 "Is there *no* limit to windy words?
Or what plagues you that you answer?

4 "I too could speak like you,
If I were in your place.
I could compose words against you,
And shake my head at you.

5 "I could strengthen you with my mouth,
And the solace of my lips could lessen *your pain*.

b. *He alleges that God is angry with him*

6 "If I speak, my pain is not lessened,
And if I hold back, what has left me?

7 "But now He has exhausted me;
Thou hast laid waste all my company.

8 "And Thou hast shriveled me up,
It has become a witness;
And my leanness rises up against me,
It testifies to my face.

9 "His anger has torn me and hunted me down,

Cross references (right margin)

*15:20
Job 27:13

15:21
Job 18:11;
20:25;
1 Thess 5:3
15:22
v. 30;
Job 27:14
15:23
Ps 59:15;
109:10;
Job 18:12

15:25
Job 36:9

15:27
Ps 17:10

15:29
Job 27:16,17

15:30
Job 5:14;
22:20; 4:9

15:31
Is 59:4

15:32
Job 22:16;
Ps 55:23;
Job 18:16
15:33
Hab 3:17
15:34
Job 16:7;
8:22
15:35
Ps 7:14;
Is 59:4;
Hos 10:13

*16:2
Job 13:4

16:3
Job 6:26

16:4
Ps 22:7;
109:25;
Lam 2:15;
Matt 27:39

16:7
Job 7:3; v. 20

16:8
Job 10:17;
19:20

16:9
Ps 35:16;
Job 13:24

15:20 *The wicked man.* Here Eliphaz refers to Job, supposing that he (Job) will see himself in this description.
16:2 *sorry comforters are you all.* This expresses Job's opinion of those who professed to be friends but acted like enemies.

He has gnashed at me with His teeth;
My adversary glares at me.

16:10
Ps 22:13;
Lam 3:30;
Mic 5:1;
Ps 35:15

10   "They have gaped at me with their mouth,
They have slapped me on the cheek with contempt;
They have massed themselves against me.

16:11
Job 1:15,17

11   "God hands me over to ruffians,
And tosses me into the hands of the wicked.

16:12
Job 9:17

12   "I was at ease, but He shattered me,
And He has grasped me by the neck and shaken me to pieces;
He has also set me up as His target.

16:13
Job 19:12;
27:22; 20:25

13   "His arrows surround me.
Without mercy He splits my kidneys open;
He pours out my gall on the ground.

16:14
Job 9:17;
Joel 2:7

14   "He breaks through me with breach after breach;
He runs at me like a warrior.

16:15
Gen 37:34;
Job 30:19

15   "I have sewed sackcloth over my skin,
And thrust my horn in the dust.

16:16
v. 20

16   "My face is flushed from weeping,
And deep darkness is on my eyelids,

16:17
Job 27:4

17   Although there is no violence in my hands,
And my prayer is pure.

c. His conscience is clear

16:18
Is 26:21;
Ps 66:18,19

18   "O earth, do not cover my blood,
And let there be no *resting* place for my cry.

16:19
Rom 1:9

19   "Even now, behold, my witness is in heaven,
And my advocate is on high.

16:20
v. 7;
Lam 2:19

20   "My friends are my scoffers;
My eye weeps to God.

16:21
1 Kin 8:45;
Ps 9:4

21   "O that a man might plead with God
As a man with his neighbor!

16:22
Eccl 12:5

22   "For when a few years are past,
I shall go the way of no return.

d. Job's appeal to God against the verdict of his friends

17:1
Ps 88:3,4

17   "My spirit is broken, my days are extinguished,
The grave is *ready* for me.

17:2
v. 6;
1 Sam 1:6,7

2   "Surely mockers are with me,
And my eye gazes on their provocation.

17:3
Ps 119:122;
Prov 6:1

3   "Lay down, now, a pledge for me with Thyself;
Who is there that will be my guarantor?

17:4
Job 12:20

4   "For Thou hast kept their heart from understanding;
Therefore Thou wilt not exalt *them*.

17:5
Lev 19:16;
Job 11:20

5   "He who informs against friends for a share *of the spoil*,
The eyes of his children also shall languish.

17:6
Job 30:9,10

6   "But He has made me a byword of the people,
And I am one at whom men spit.

17:7
Job 16:16;
16:8

7   "My eye has also grown dim because of grief,
And all my members are as a shadow.

17:8
Job 22:19

8   "The upright shall be appalled at this,
And the innocent shall stir up himself against the godless.

17:9
Prov 4:18;
Job 22:30

9   "Nevertheless the righteous shall hold to his way,
And he who has clean hands shall grow stronger and stronger.

17:10
Job 12:2

10   "But come again all of you now,
For I do not find a wise man among you.

17:11
Job 7:6

11   "My days are past, my plans are torn apart,
Even the wishes of my heart.

12   "They make night into day, *saying*,
'The light is near,' in the presence of darkness.

17:13
Job 3:13

13   "If I look for Sheol as my home,
I make my bed in the darkness;

17:14
Ps 16:10;
Job 21:26;
24:20

14   If I call to the pit, 'You are my father';

15 To the worm, 'my mother and my sister';
    Where now is my hope?
    And who regards my hope?
16 "Will it go down with me to Sheol?
    Shall we together go down into the dust?"

3. Bildad's second speech

a. He reproves Job as haughty and obstinate

18 Then Bildad the Shuhite responded,
2 "How long will you hunt for words?
    Show understanding and then we can talk.
3   "Why are we regarded as beasts,
    As stupid in your eyes?
4   "O you who tear yourself in your anger—
    For your sake is the earth to be abandoned,
    Or the rock to be moved from its place?

b. He describes the misery and ruin of the wicked

5   "Indeed, the light of the wicked goes out,
    And the flame of his fire gives no light.
6   "The light in his tent is darkened,
    And his lamp goes out above him.
7   "His vigorous stride is shortened,
    And his own scheme brings him down.
8   "For he is thrown into the net by his own feet,
    And he steps on the webbing.
9   "A snare seizes *him* by the heel,
    And a trap snaps shut on him.
10 "A noose for him is hidden in the ground,
    And a trap for him on the path.
11 "All around terrors frighten him,
    And harry him at every step.
12 "His strength is famished,
    And calamity is ready at his side.
13 "His skin is devoured by disease,
    The first-born of death devours his limbs.
14 "He is torn from the security of his tent,
    And they march him before the king of terrors.
15 "There dwells in his tent nothing of his;
    Brimstone is scattered on his habitation.
16 "His roots are dried below,
    And his branch is cut off above.
17 "Memory of him perishes from the earth,
    And he has no name abroad.
18 "He is driven from light into darkness,
    And chased from the inhabited world.
19 "He has no offspring or posterity among his people,
    Nor any survivor where he sojourned.
20 "Those in the west are appalled at his fate,
    And those in the east are seized with horror.
21 "Surely such are the dwellings of the wicked,
    And this is the place of him who does not know God."

4. Job's second reply to Bildad

a. Job reproves his friends

19 Then Job responded,
2 "How long will you torment me,
    And crush me with words?
3   "These ten times you have insulted me,
    You are not ashamed to wrong me.
4   "Even if I have truly erred,
    My error lodges with me.

17:15
Job 7:6
17:16
Jon 2:6;
Job 3:17-19

18:3
Ps 73:22;
Job 36:14
18:4
Job 13:14;
14:18

18:5
Prov 13:9;
20:20; 24:20

18:7
Prov 4:12;
Job 5:13
18:8
Job 22:10;
Ps 9:15; 35:8
18:9
Ps 140:5;
Job 5:5
18:10
Ps 69:22

18:11
Job 15:21;
Jer 6:25; 20:3
18:12
Is 8:21

18:14
Job 8:22;
15:21
18:15
Ps 11:6

18:16
Is 5:24;
Hos 9:1-16;
Amos 2:9;
Mal 4:1;
Job 15:30,32
18:17
Ps 34:16;
Prov 2:22;
10:7
18:18
Job 5:14;
27:21-23
18:19
Is 14:22;
Jer 22:30
18:21
Jer 9:3;
1 Thess 4:5

19:4
Job 6:24

19:5 Ps 35:26; 38:16	5	"If indeed you vaunt yourselves against me, And prove my disgrace to me,
19:6 Job 27:2; 18:8-10	6	Know then that God has wronged me, And has closed His net around me.
19:7 Job 30:20	7	"Behold, I cry, 'Violence!' but I get no answer; I shout for help, but there is no justice.

b. *God the author of his afflictions*

19:8 Job 3:23; 30:26	8	"He has walled up my way so that I cannot pass; And He has put darkness on my paths.
19:9 Ps 89:44; 89:39	9	"He has stripped my honor from me, And removed the crown from my head.
19:10 Job 12:14; 7:6; 24:20	10	"He breaks me down on every side, and I am gone; And He has uprooted my hope like a tree.
19:11 Job 16:9; 13:24	11	"He has also kindled His anger against me, And considered me as His enemy.
19:12 Job 30:12	12	"His troops come together, And build up their way against me, And camp around my tent.

c. *He is deserted of men*

	13	"He has removed my brothers far from me, And my acquaintances are completely estranged from me.
19:14 v. 19	14	"My relatives have failed, And my intimate friends have forgotten me.
19:15 Gen 14:14; Eccl 2:7	15	"Those who live in my house and my maids consider me a stranger. I am a foreigner in their sight.
	16	"I call to my servant, but he does not answer, I have to implore him with my mouth.
	17	"My breath is offensive to my wife, And I am loathsome to my own brothers.
19:18 2 Kin 2:23	18	"Even young children despise me; I rise up and they speak against me.
19:19 Ps 38:11; 55:13	19	"All my associates abhor me, And those I love have turned against me.

d. *His plea for pity*

19:20 Job 33:21; Ps 102:5	20	"My bone clings to my skin and my flesh, And I have escaped *only* by the skin of my teeth.
19:21 Job 6:14; Ps 38:2	21	"Pity me, pity me, O you my friends, For the hand of God has struck me.
19:22 Job 16:11	22	"Why do you persecute me as God *does*, And are not satisfied with my flesh?
19:23 Is 30:8	23	"Oh that my words were written! Oh that they were inscribed in a book!
19:24 Jer 17:1	24	"That with an iron stylus and lead They were engraved in the rock forever!

e. *His unshakable confidence in the living Redeemer*

*19:25 Ps 78:35; Is 43:14; Jer 50:34 *19:26 Matt 5:8; 1 Cor 13:12;	25	"And as for me, I know that my Redeemer lives, And at the last He will take His stand on the earth.
	26	"Even after my skin is destroyed,

19:25 *I know that my Redeemer lives.* As Job's friends had been unable to convince him of his guilt, so he was unable to convince them of his innocence. In the agony of the hour, however, Job gave expression to the great assurance that God was his vindicator (or Redeemer).

19:26 The doctrine of the resurrection is latent in the Old Testament and clearly revealed in the New Testament teaching. Old Testament references include Ps. 16:10; 49:15; Is. 26:19; Dan. 12:2; and Hos. 13:14. In apostolic times the Jews in general expected a resurrection of the body (John 11:24; Heb. 6:1,2). While it was denied by the Sadducees, it was basic in the thinking of the Pharisees (Acts 23:6-8). Jesus taught and accepted the bodily resur-

rection as an indisputable fact (Matt. 22:29-32; Luke 14:14; John 5:28,29). His apostles preached it constantly (Acts 4:2; 17:18; 24:15). Believers embrace the truth of a resurrection with hope and look forward to it with anticipation (Dan. 12:13; 2 Cor. 5:1; Phil. 3:11). The credibility of a resurrection is attested to by the resurrection of Christ Himself and of others (Matt. 9:25; Luke 7:14; John 11:44; Heb. 11:35). It should be noted that *from my flesh I shall see God* is a better translation of the Hebrew here than that given by some others who translate: *without my flesh.* It makes the doctrine of the resurrection of the body more explicit. But even if we construe it as *without my flesh* (which is not linguistically legitimate), the following verse, *my eyes*

Yet from my flesh I shall see God;

27   Whom I myself shall behold,
And whom my eyes shall see and not another.
My heart faints within me.

28   "If you say, 'How shall we persecute him?'
And 'What pretext for a case against him can we find?'

29   *Then* be afraid of the sword for yourselves,
For wrath *brings* the punishment of the sword,
So that you may know there is judgment."

5. *Zophar's second discourse: the misery and ruin that await the wicked*

20 Then Zophar the Naamathite answered,

2   "Therefore my disquieting thoughts make me respond,
Even because of my inward agitation.

3   "I listened to the reproof which insults me,
And the spirit of my understanding makes me answer.

4   "Do you know this from of old,
From the establishment of man on earth,

5   That the triumphing of the wicked is short,
And the joy of the godless momentary?

6   "Though his loftiness reaches the heavens,
And his head touches the clouds,

7   He perishes forever like his refuse;
Those who have seen him will say, 'Where is he?'

8   "He flies away like a dream, and they cannot find him;
Even like a vision of the night he is chased away.

9   "The eye which saw him sees him no more,
And his place no longer beholds him.

10   "His sons favor the poor,
And his hands give back his wealth.

11   "His bones are full of his youthful vigor,
But it lies down with him in the dust.

12   "Though evil is sweet in his mouth,
And he hides it under his tongue,

13   *Though* he desires it and will not let it go,
But holds it in his mouth,

14   *Yet* his food in his stomach is changed
To the venom of cobras within him.

15   "He swallows riches,
But will vomit them up;
God will expel them from his belly.

16   "He sucks the poison of cobras;
The viper's tongue slays him.

17   "He does not look at the streams,
The rivers flowing with honey and curds.

18   "He returns what he has attained
And cannot swallow *it;*
As to the riches of his trading,
He cannot even enjoy *them.*

19   "For he has oppressed *and* forsaken the poor;
He has seized a house which he has not built.

20   "Because he knew no quiet within him
He does not retain anything he desires.

21   "Nothing remains for him to devour,
Therefore his prosperity does not endure.

22   "In the fulness of his plenty he will be cramped;
The hand of everyone who suffers will come *against* him.

23   "When he fills his belly,
God will send His fierce anger on him

Marginal references:

1 John 3:2
19:27
Ps 73:26
19:28
Ps 69:26
19:29
Job 22:4

20:3
Job 19:3
20:4
Deut 4:32
20:5
Ps 37:35;
73:19
20:6
Is 14:13,14;
Obad 3,4
20:7
Job 4:20;
7:10; 8:18
20:8
Ps 73:20;
90:5;
Job 18:18;
27:21-23
20:9
Job 7:8,10
20:10
Job 5:4;
27:16,17
20:11
Job 13:26;
21:26
20:12
Prov 20:17;
Ps 10:7

20:16
Deut 32:24,
33
20:17
Job 29:6;
Deut 32:13,
14
20:18
vv. 10,15

20:19
Job 24:2-4;
35:9

20:20
Eccl 5:13,14

20:21
Job 15:29

20:23
Ps 78:30,31

---

shall see, makes mention of the possession and use of a body after death.

And will rain *it* on him while he is eating.

| 20:24
Is 24:18;
Jer 48:43;
Amos 5:19
20:25
Job 16:13;
18:11 | 24 | "He may flee from the iron weapon,
But the bronze bow will pierce him. |
| | 25 | "It is drawn forth and comes out of his back,
Even the glittering point from his gall.
Terrors come upon him, |
| 20:26
Job 18:18;
Ps 21:9 | 26 | Complete darkness is held in reserve for his treasures,
And unfanned fire will devour him;
It will consume the survivor in his tent. |
| 20:27
Deut 31:28 | 27 | "The heavens will reveal his iniquity,
And the earth will rise up against him. |
| 20:28
Deut 28:31;
Job 21:30 | 28 | "The increase of his house will depart;
His possessions will flow away in the day of His anger. |
| 20:29
Job 27:13 | 29 | "This is the wicked man's portion from God,
Even the heritage decreed to him by God." |

6. *Job's second reply to Zophar*

a. *He pleads to speak without interruption*

21 Then Job answered,
2 "Listen carefully to my speech,
And let this be your *way of* consolation.

| 21:3
Job 16:10 | 3 | "Bear with me that I may speak;
Then after I have spoken, you may mock. |
| 21:4
Job 6:11 | 4 | "As for me, is my complaint to man?
And why should I not be impatient? |
| 21:5
Judg 18:19;
Job 29:9;
40:4 | 5 | "Look at me, and be astonished,
And put *your* hand over *your* mouth. |
| | 6 | "Even when I remember, I am disturbed,
And horror takes hold of my flesh. |

b. *The wicked often prosper in this life*

| 21:7
Job 12:6;
Ps 73:3,12;
Jer 12:1
21:8
Ps 17:14
21:9
Ps 73:5 | 7 | "Why do the wicked *still* live,
Continue on, also become very powerful? |
| | 8 | "Their descendants are established with them in their sight,
And their offspring before their eyes, |
| | 9 | Their houses are safe from fear,
Neither is the rod of God on them. |
| 21:10
Ex 23:26 | 10 | "His ox mates without fail;
His cow calves and does not abort. |
| | 11 | "They send forth their little ones like the flock,
And their children skip about. |
| 21:12
Ps 81:2;
Job 30:31 | 12 | "They sing to the timbrel and harp
And rejoice at the sound of the flute. |
| 21:13
Job 36:11 | 13 | "They spend their days in prosperity,
And suddenly they go down to Sheol. |
| 21:14
Job 22:17;
Prov 1:29 | 14 | "And they say to God, 'Depart from us!
We do not even desire the knowledge of Thy ways. |
| 21:15
Ex 5:2;
Job 34:9;
Mal 3:14 | 15 | 'Who is the Almighty, that we should serve Him,
And what would we gain if we entreat Him?' |
| 21:16
Job 22:18 | 16 | "Behold, their prosperity is not in their hand;
The counsel of the wicked is far from me. |

c. *A sovereign God does as He pleases
with righteous and wicked alike*

| 21:17
Job 18:5,6,12 | 17 | "How often is the lamp of the wicked put out,
Or *does* their calamity fall on them?
Does God apportion destruction in His anger? |
| 21:18
Ps 1:4 | 18 | "Are they as straw before the wind,
And like chaff which the storm carries away? |
| 21:19
Ex 20:5
21:20
Ps 75:8;
Is 51:17;
Jer 25:15;
Rev 14:10 | 19 | "*You say,* 'God stores away a man's iniquity for his sons.'
Let God repay him so that he may know *it.* |
| | 20 | "Let his own eyes see his decay,
And let him drink of the wrath of the Almighty. |

I have kept His way and not turned aside.

12 "I have not departed from the command of His lips;
  I have treasured the words of His mouth more than my necessary
    food.

23:12
John 4:32,34

13 "But He is unique and who can turn Him?
  And *what* His soul desires, that He does.

23:13
Job 9:12;
12:14;
Ps 115:3

14 "For He performs what is appointed for me,
  And many such *decrees* are with Him.

23:14
1 Thess 3:3

15 "Therefore, I would be dismayed at His presence;
  When I consider, I am terrified of Him.

16 "*It is* God *who* has made my heart faint,
  And the Almighty *who* has dismayed me,

23:16
Ps 22:14;
Jer 51:46

17 But I am not silenced by the darkness,
  Nor deep gloom *which* covers *me*.

23:17
Job 10:18,19;
19:8

b. The punishment of the wicked is not always seen

24 "Why are times not stored up by the Almighty,
  And why do those who know Him not see His days?

24:1
Ps 31:15;
Jer 46:10

2 "Some remove the landmarks;
  They seize and devour flocks.

24:2
Deut 19:14;
27:17; 28:31

3 "They drive away the donkeys of the orphans;
  They take the widow's ox for a pledge.

24:3
Ex 22:26;
Deut 24:6,10,
12,17;
Job 22:6

4 "They push the needy aside from the road;
  The poor of the land are made to hide themselves altogether.

24:4
Deut 24:14;
Prov 28:28

5 "Behold, as wild donkeys in the wilderness
  They go forth seeking food in their activity,
  As bread for *their* children in the desert.

24:5
Job 39:5-8;
Ps 104:23

6 "They harvest their fodder in the field,
  And they glean the vineyard of the wicked.

7 "They spend the night naked, without clothing,
  And have no covering against the cold.

24:7
Ex 22:26;
Job 22:6

8 "They are wet with the mountain rains,
  And they hug the rock for want of a shelter.

24:8
Lam 4:5

9 "Others snatch the orphan from the breast,
  And against the poor they take a pledge.

24:9
Deut 24:17

10 "They cause *the poor* to go about naked without clothing,
  And they take away the sheaves from the hungry.

11 "Within the walls they produce oil;
  They tread wine presses but thirst.

12 "From the city men groan,
  And the souls of the wounded cry out;
  Yet God does not pay attention to folly.

24:12
Jer 51:52;
Ezek 26:15;
Job 9:23,24

13 "Others have been with those who rebel against the light;
  They do not want to know its ways,
  Nor abide in its paths.

24:13
Is 5:20;
John 3:19

14 "The murderer arises at dawn;
  He kills the poor and the needy,
  And at night he is as a thief.

24:14
Mic 2:1;
Ps 10:8

15 "And the eye of the adulterer waits for the twilight,
  Saying, 'No eye will see me.'
  And he disguises his face.

24:15
Prov 7:9;
Ps 10:11

16 "In the dark they dig into houses,
  They shut themselves up by day;
  They do not know the light.

24:16
Ex 22:2

17 "For the morning is the same to him as thick darkness,
  For he is familiar with the terrors of thick darkness.

24:17
Ps 91:5

18 "They are insignificant on the surface of the water;
  Their portion is cursed on the earth.
  They do not turn toward the vineyards.

24:18
Job 9:26;
Ps 90:5

19 "Drought and heat consume the snow waters,
  So does Sheol *those who* have sinned.

24:19
Job 6:16,17;
21:13

20 "A mother will forget him;

24:20
Ps 31:12;
Prov 10:7
24:21
Job 22:9
24:22
Deut 28:66
24:23
Job 12:6;
11:11
24:24
Ps 37:10;
Job 14:21;
Is 17:5
24:25
Job 6:28;
27:4

The worm feeds sweetly till he is remembered no more.
And wickedness will be broken like a tree.

21 "He wrongs the barren woman,
And does no good for the widow.

22 "But He drags off the valiant by His power;
He rises, but no one has assurance of life.

23 "He provides them with security, and they are supported;
And His eyes are on their ways.

24 "They are exalted a little while, then they are gone;
Moreover, they are brought low and like everything gathered up;
Even like the heads of grain they are cut off.

25 "Now if it is not so, who can prove me a liar,
And make my speech worthless?"

3. Bildad's third speech: no one is righteous before God

25:2
Job 9:4;
Rev 1:6;
Job 22:12
25:3
James 1:17
25:4
Job 4:17;
Ps 143:2;
Job 14:4
25:5
Job 31:26;
15:15
25:6
Job 7:17;
Ps 22:6

25 Then Bildad the Shuhite answered,
2 "Dominion and awe belong to Him
Who establishes peace in His heights.

3 "Is there any number to His troops?
And upon whom does His light not rise?

4 "How then can a man be just with God?
Or how can he be clean who is born of woman?

5 "If even the moon has no brightness
And the stars are not pure in His sight,

6 How much less man, *that* maggot,
And the son of man, *that* worm!"

4. Job's third reply to Bildad:
he knows the greatness and majesty of God

26:2
Ps 71:9

26 Then Job responded,
2 "What a help you are to the weak!
How you have saved the arm without strength!

3 "What counsel you have given to *one* without wisdom!
What helpful insight you have abundantly provided!

4 "To whom have you uttered words?
And whose spirit was expressed through you?

*26:6
Ps 139:8,11;
Heb 4:13
26:7
Job 9:8
26:8
Prov 30:4
26:9
Ps 97:2
26:10
Job 38:8-11;
Prov 8:29;
Job 38:19,20,
24
26:12
Ex 14:21;
Is 51:15;
Jer 31:35
26:13
Job 9:8;
Is 27:1
26:14
Job 36:29

5 "The departed spirits tremble
Under the waters and their inhabitants.

6 "Naked is Sheol before Him
And [7]Abaddon has no covering.

7 "He stretches out the north over empty space,
And hangs the earth on nothing.

8 "He wraps up the waters in His clouds;
And the cloud does not burst under them.

9 "He obscures the face of the full moon,
And spreads His cloud over it.

10 "He has inscribed a circle on the surface of the waters,
At the boundary of light and darkness.

11 "The pillars of heaven tremble,
And are amazed at His rebuke.

12 "He quieted the sea with His power,
And by His understanding He shattered Rahab.

13 "By His breath the heavens are cleared;
His hand has pierced the fleeing serpent.

14 "Behold, these are the fringes of His ways;
And how faint a word we hear of Him!
But His mighty thunder, who can understand?"

[7]I.e., place of destruction

26:6 *Abaddon* means "destruction." Here it is used as a parallel to Sheol (cf. Prov. 15:11). In Rev. 9:11 it is used as a name for Satan himself, the prince of the bottomless pit.

6	Let Him weigh me with accurate scales, And let God know my integrity.	**31:6** Job 6:2,3; 27:5,6
7	"If my step has turned from the way, Or my heart followed my eyes, Or if any spot has stuck to my hands,	*31:7 Job 23:11; 9:30
8	Let me sow and another eat, And let my crops be uprooted.	**31:8** Lev 26:16; Job 20:18
9	"If my heart has been enticed by a woman, Or I have lurked at my neighbor's doorway,	**31:9** Job 24:15
10	May my wife grind for another, And let others kneel down over her.	**31:10** Jer 8:10
11	"For that would be a lustful crime; Moreover, it would be an iniquity *punishable by* judges.	**31:11** Gen 38:24; Deut 22:22-24
12	"For it would be fire that consumes to Abaddon, And would uproot all my increase.	**31:12** Job 15:30; 26:6; 20:28
13	"If I have despised the claim of my male or female slaves When they filed a complaint against me,	**31:13** Deut 24:14, 15
14	What then could I do when God arises, And when He calls me to account, what will I answer Him?	
15	"Did not He who made me in the womb make him, And the same one fashion us in the womb?	**31:15** Mal 2:10
16	"If I have kept the poor from *their* desire, Or have caused the eyes of the widow to fail,	**31:16** Job 20:19; 22:7,9
17	Or have eaten my morsel alone, And the orphan has not shared it	**31:17** Job 22:7; 29:12
18	(But from my youth he grew up with me as with a father, And from infancy I guided her),	
19	If I have seen anyone perish for lack of clothing, Or that the needy had no covering,	**31:19** Job 22:6; 29:13
20	If his loins have not thanked me, And if he has not been warmed with the fleece of my sheep,	**31:20** Deut 31:20
21	If I have lifted up my hand against the orphan, Because I saw I had support in the gate,	**31:21** Job 22:9
22	Let my shoulder fall from the socket, And my arm be broken off at the elbow.	**31:22** Job 38:15
23	"For calamity from God is a terror to me, And because of His majesty I can do nothing.	**31:23** v. 3; Job 13:11
24	"If I have put my confidence *in* gold, And called fine gold my trust,	**31:24** Mark 10:24
25	If I have gloated because my wealth was great, And because my hand had secured *so* much;	**31:25** Ps 62:10
26	If I have looked at the sun when it shone, Or the moon going in splendor,	**31:26** Deut 4:19; Ezek 8:16
27	And my heart became secretly enticed, And my hand threw a kiss from my mouth,	
28	That too would have been an iniquity *calling for* judgment, For I would have denied God above.	**31:28** v. 11
29	"Have I rejoiced at the extinction of my enemy, Or exulted when evil befell him?	**31:29** Prov 17:5
30	"No, I have not allowed my mouth to sin By asking for his life in a curse.	**31:30** Matt 5:44
31	"Have the men of my tent not said, 'Who can find one who has not been satisfied with his meat'?	**31:31** Job 22:7
32	"The alien has not lodged outside, *For* I have opened my doors to the traveler.	**31:32** Gen 19:2,3; Rom 12:13
33	"Have I covered my transgressions like Adam, By hiding my iniquity in my bosom,	**31:33** Gen 3:8;
34	Because I feared the great multitude, And the contempt of families terrified me,	**31:34** Ex 23:2

31:7 *Any spot* is otherwise "any thing." Job has been honest in all his relationships.

And kept silent and did not go out of doors?

35   "Oh that I had one to hear me!
      Behold, here is my signature;
      Let the Almighty answer me!
      And the indictment which my adversary has written,

36   Surely I would carry it on my shoulder;
      I would bind it to myself like a crown.

37   "I would declare to Him the number of my steps;
      Like a prince I would approach Him.

38   "If my land cries out against me,
      And its furrows weep together;

39   If I have eaten its fruit without money,
      Or have caused its owners to lose their lives,

40   Let briars grow instead of wheat,
      And stinkweed instead of barley."

The words of Job are ended.

III. *The speeches of Elihu (32:1–37:24)*

A. *Elihu's anger at Job for his justification of self*

32 Then these three men ceased answering Job, because he was righteous in his own eyes.

2   But the anger of Elihu the son of Barachel the Buzite, of the family of Ram burned; against Job his anger burned, because he justified himself before God.

3   And his anger burned against his three friends because they had found no answer, and yet had condemned Job.

4   Now Elihu had waited to speak to Job because they were years older than he.

5   And when Elihu saw that there was no answer in the mouth of the three men his anger burned.

6   So Elihu the son of Barachel the Buzite spoke out and said,
      "I am young in years and you are old;
      Therefore I was shy and afraid to tell you what I think.

7   "I thought age should speak,
      And increased years should teach wisdom.

8   "But it is a spirit in man,
      And the breath of the Almighty gives them understanding.

9   "The abundant *in years* may not be wise,
      Nor may elders understand justice.

10   "So I say, 'Listen to me,
      I too will tell what I think.'

11   "Behold, I waited for your words,
      I listened to your reasonings,
      While you pondered what to say.

12   "I even paid close attention to you,
      Indeed, there was no one who refuted Job,
      Not one of you who answered his words.

13   "Do not say,
      'We have found wisdom;
      God will rout him, not man.'

14   "For he has not arranged *his* words against me;
      Nor will I reply to him with your arguments.

15   "They are dismayed, they answer no more;
      Words have failed them.

16   "And shall I wait, because they do not speak,
      Because they stop *and* answer no more?

32:2 Elihu enters into the discussion between Job and his friends because he is dissatisfied with Job's contention that God deals capriciously with men in this life. On the other hand, he realizes that Job's three friends have not won the argument with Job, because they have defended too narrow a viewpoint. The substance of Elihu's argument is that God permitted Job's sufferings in order to achieve beneficial results in Job's life and faith. 36:6–15 contains the clearest statement of the theory of Elihu on suffering.

17	"I too will answer my share,	
	I also will tell my opinion.	
18	"For I am full of words;	**32:18**
	The spirit within me constrains me.	Acts 18:5
19	"Behold, my belly is like unvented wine,	**32:19**
	Like new wineskins it is about to burst.	Acts 9:17
20	"Let me speak that I may get relief;	
	Let me open my lips and answer.	
21	"Let me now be partial to no one;	**32:21**
	Nor flatter *any* man.	Lev 19:15; Matt 22:16
22	"For I do not know how to flatter,	**32:22**
	Else my Maker would soon take me away.	1 Thess 2:5

B. *God uses pain to chasten men*

33 "However now, Job, please hear my speech,
And listen to all my words.

2 "Behold now, I open my mouth,
My tongue in my mouth speaks.

3 "My words are *from* the uprightness of my heart;
And my lips speak knowledge sincerely.   **33:3** Job 6:28; 27:4; 36:4

4 "The Spirit of God has made me,
And the breath of the Almighty gives me life.   ***33:4** Gen 2:7; Job 27:3

5 "Refute me if you can;
Array yourselves before me, take your stand.   **33:5** v. 32; Job 13:18

6 "Behold, I belong to God like you;
I too have been formed out of the clay.

7 "Behold, no fear of me should terrify you,
Nor should my pressure weigh heavily on you.   **33:7** Job 9:34; 13:21; 2 Cor 2:5

8 "Surely you have spoken in my hearing,
And I have heard the sound of *your* words:

9 'I am pure, without transgression;
I am innocent and there is no guilt in me.   **33:9** Job 10:7; 13:23; 16:17

10 'Behold, He invents pretexts against me;
He counts me as His enemy.   **33:10** Job 13:24

11 'He puts my feet in the stocks;
He watches all my paths.'   **33:11** Job 13:27; 14:16

12 "Behold, let me tell you, you are not right in this,
For God is greater than man.

13 "Why do you complain against Him,
That He does not give an account of all His doings?   **33:13** Job 15:25; Is 45:9

14 "Indeed God speaks once,
Or twice, *yet* no one notices it.   **33:14** Ps 62:11

15 "In a dream, a vision of the night,
When sound sleep falls on men,
While they slumber in their beds,   **33:15** Num 12:6; Job 4:13

16 Then He opens the ears of men,
And seals their instruction,   **33:16** Job 36:10,15

17 That He may turn man aside *from his* conduct,
And keep man from pride;

18 He keeps back his soul from the pit,
And his life from passing over into Sheol.   **33:18** vv. 24,28,30

19 "Man is also chastened with pain on his bed,
And with unceasing complaint in his bones;   **33:19** Job 30:17

20 So that his life loathes bread,
And his soul favorite food.   **33:20** Ps 107:18

21 "His flesh wastes away from sight,   **33:21** Job 16:8; 19:20

33:4 The Holy Spirit is referred to by more than thirty names or titles in Scripture. Job here speaks of Him as the *Spirit of God* and the *breath of the Almighty*. Many of the names given indicate attributes or characteristics of the Holy Spirit. He is called the *Spirit of life* (Rom. 8:2), *spirit of wisdom . . . understanding . . . counsel and strength . . . knowledge* (Is. 11:2), *Spirit of truth* (John 14:17), and *spirit of holiness* (Rom. 1:4), among others. An exhaustive study of these titles would reveal much about the person and work of the Holy Spirit, the third person of the Trinity.

And his bones which were not seen stick out.

33:22 Ps 88:3	22	"Then his soul draws near to the pit, And his life to those who bring death.
33:23 Mic 6:8	**23**	"If there is an angel *as* mediator for him, One out of a thousand, To remind a man what is right for him,
33:24 Is 38:17	24	Then let him be gracious to him, and say, 'Deliver him from going down to the pit, I have found a ransom';
33:25 2 Kin 5:14	25	Let his flesh become fresher than in youth, Let him return to the days of his youthful vigor;
33:26 Job 22:27; 34:28; 22:26; Ps 51:12	26	Then he will pray to God, and He will accept him, That he may see His face with joy, And He may restore His righteousness to man.
33:27 Luke 15:21; Rom 6:21	27	"He will sing to men and say, 'I have sinned and perverted what is right, And it is not proper for me.
33:28 Ps 103:14; Job 22:28	28	'He has redeemed my soul from going to the pit, And my life shall see the light.'
33:29 Eph 1:11; 1 Cor 12:6; Phil 2:13	**29** 30	"Behold, God does all these oftentimes with men, To bring back his soul from the pit, That he may be enlightened with the light of life.
33:30 Ps 56:13	31	"Pay attention, O Job, listen to me; Keep silent and let me speak.
	32	"*Then* if you have anything to say, answer me; Speak, for I desire to justify you.
33:33 Ps 34:11	33	"If not, listen to me; Keep silent, and I will teach you wisdom."

C. God is not unjust

	34	Then Elihu continued and said, 2 "Hear my words, you wise men, And listen to me, you who know.
34:3 Job 12:11	3	"For the ear tests words, As the palate tastes food.
34:4 1 Thess 5:21	4	"Let us choose for ourselves what is right; Let us know among ourselves what is good.
34:5 Job 33:9; 27:2	5	"For Job has said, 'I am righteous, But God has taken away my right;
34:6 Jer 15:18; 30:12	6	Should I lie concerning my right? My wound is incurable, *though I am* without transgression.'
34:7 Job 15:16	7	"What man is like Job, Who drinks up derision like water,
34:8 Ps 50:18	8	Who goes in company with the workers of iniquity, And walks with wicked men?
34:9 Job 21:15; 35:3	9	"For he has said, 'It profits a man nothing When he is pleased with God.'
34:10 Job 8:3	**10**	"Therefore, listen to me, you men of understanding. Far be it from God to do wickedness, And from the Almighty to do wrong.
34:11 Ps 62:12; Matt 16:27; Rom 2:6; 2 Cor 5:10; Rev 22:12	11	"For He pays a man according to his work, And makes him find it according to his way.
	12	"Surely, God will not act wickedly, And the Almighty will not pervert justice.
34:12 Job 8:3	13	"Who gave Him authority over the earth? And who has laid *on Him* the whole world?
34:13 Job 38:5,6	14	"If He should determine to do so, If He should gather to Himself His spirit and His breath,
34:14 Ps 104:29	15	All flesh would perish together, And man would return to dust.
34:15 Is 40:6,7; Gen 3:19	**16**	"But if *you have* understanding, hear this;

17 Listen to the sound of my words.
"Shall one who hates justice rule?
And will you condemn a righteous mighty one,

18 Who says to a king, 'Worthless one,'
To nobles, 'Wicked ones';

19 Who shows no partiality to princes,
Nor regards the rich above the poor,
For they all are the work of His hands?

20 "In a moment they die, and at midnight
People are shaken and pass away,
And the mighty are taken away without a hand.

21 "For His eyes are upon the ways of a man,
And He sees all his steps.

22 "There is no darkness or deep shadow
Where the workers of iniquity may hide themselves.

23 "For He does not *need to* consider a man further,
That he should go before God in judgment.

24 "He breaks in pieces mighty men without inquiry,
And sets others in their place.

25 "Therefore He knows their works,
And He overthrows *them* in the night,
And they are crushed.

26 "He strikes them like the wicked
In a public place,

27 Because they turned aside from following Him,
And had no regard for any of His ways;

28 So that they caused the cry of the poor to come to Him,
And that He might hear the cry of the afflicted—

29 When He keeps quiet, who then can condemn?
And when He hides His face, who then can behold Him,
That is, in regard to both nation and man?—

30 So that godless men should not rule,
Nor be snares of the people.

31 "For has anyone said to God,
'I have borne *chastisement;*
I will not offend *anymore;*

32 Teach Thou me what I do not see;
If I have done iniquity,
I will do it no more'?

33 "Shall He recompense on your terms, because you have rejected *it?*
For you must choose, and not I;
Therefore declare what you know.

34 "Men of understanding will say to me,
And a wise man who hears me,

35 'Job speaks without knowledge,
And his words are without wisdom.

36 'Job ought to be tried to the limit,
Because he answers like wicked men.

37 'For he adds rebellion to his sin;
He claps his hands among us,
And multiplies his words against God.' "

35 Then Elihu continued and said,
2 "Do you think this is according to justice?
Do you say, 'My righteousness is more than God's'?

3 "For you say, 'What advantage will it be to You?
What profit shall I have, more than if I had sinned?'

4 "I will answer you,
And your friends with you.

5 "Look at the heavens and see;
And behold the clouds—they are higher than you.

6 "If you have sinned, what do you accomplish against Him?

34:17
2 Sam 23:3

34:18
Ex 22:28

34:19
Deut 10:17;
Gal 2:6;
Job 31:15

34:20
Ex 12:29;
Job 12:19

34:21
Job 31:4

34:22
Ps 139:12;
Amos 9:2,3

34:24
Dan 2:21

34:25
vv. 11,20

34:26
Job 26:12

34:27
1 Sam 15:11;
Ps 28:5;
Is 5:12

34:28
Job 35:9;
James 5:4;
Ex 22:23

34:29
1 Chr 22:9

34:30
v. 17

34:32
Job 35:11;
Ps 25:4

34:35
Job 35:16

34:36
Job 23:10;
22:15

35:2
Job 32:2

35:3
Job 34:9;
9:30,31

35:5
Job 22:12

35:6
Prov 8:36;
Jer 7:19

And if your transgressions are many, what do you do to Him?

35:7
Job 22:2,3;
Prov 9:12;
Luke 17:10

7 "If you are righteous, what do you give to Him?
Or what does He receive from your hand?

8 "Your wickedness is for a man like yourself,
And your righteousness is for a son of man.

35:9
Ex 2:23;
Job 12:19

9 "Because of the multitude of oppressions they cry out;
They cry for help because of the arm of the mighty.

35:10
Job 27:10;
Ps 42:8;
149:5;
Acts 16:25

10 "But no one says, 'Where is God my Maker,
Who gives songs in the night,

11 Who teaches us more than the beasts of the earth,
And makes us wiser than the birds of the heavens?'

35:11
Ps 94:12;
Luke 12:24

12 "There they cry out, but He does not answer
Because of the pride of evil men.

35:12
Prov 1:28
35:13
Job 27:9;
Prov 15:29;
Is 1:15;
Jer 11:11

13 "Surely God will not listen to an empty *cry*,
Nor will the Almighty regard it.

14 "How much less when you say you do not behold Him,
The case is before Him, and you must wait for Him!

35:14
Ps 37:5,6
35:15
Eccl 8:11
35:16
Job 34:37,35

15 "And now, because He has not visited *in* His anger,
Nor has He acknowledged transgression well,

16 So Job opens his mouth emptily;
He multiplies words without knowledge."

D. *The justice of God whose ways are inscrutable*

36 Then Elihu continued and said,
2 "Wait for me a little, and I will show you
That there is yet more to be said in God's behalf.

36:3
Job 8:3;
37:23

3 "I will fetch my knowledge from afar,
And I will ascribe righteousness to my Maker.

36:4
Job 33:3;
37:16

4 "For truly my words are not false;
One who is perfect in knowledge is with you.

36:5
Ps 22:24;
Job 12:13

5 "Behold, God is mighty but does not despise *any*;
He is mighty in strength of understanding.

36:6
Job 8:22;
5:15

6 "He does not keep the wicked alive,
But gives justice to the afflicted.

36:7
Ps 33:18;
113:8

7 "He does not withdraw His eyes from the righteous;
But with kings on the throne
He has seated them forever, and they are exalted.

36:8
Ps 107:10;
vv. 15,21

8 "And if they are bound in fetters,
And are caught in the cords of affliction,

36:9
Job 15:25

9 Then he declares to them their work
And their transgressions, that they have magnified themselves.

36:10
Job 33:16;
2 Kin 17:13

10 "And He opens their ear to instruction,
And commands that they return from evil.

36:11
Is 1:19,20

11 "If they hear and serve *Him*,
They shall end their days in prosperity,
And their years in pleasures.

36:12
Job 15:22;
4:21

12 "But if they do not hear, they shall perish by the sword,
And they shall die without knowledge.

36:13
Rom 2:5

13 "But the godless in heart lay up anger;
They do not cry for help when He binds them.

36:14
Job 15:32;
22:16

14 "They die in youth,
And their life *perishes* among the cult prostitutes.

36:15
Ps 119:67;
v. 10

15 "He delivers the afflicted in their affliction,
And opens their ear in *time of* oppression.

36:16
Hos 2:14;
Ps 118:5;
23:5

16 "Then indeed, He enticed you from the mouth of distress,
Instead of it, a broad place with no constraint;
And that which was set on your table was full of fatness.

17 "But you were full of judgment on the wicked;
Judgment and justice take hold *of you*.

36:18
Job 34:33;
Jon 4:4,9;
Job 33:24

18 "*Beware* lest wrath entice you to scoffing;
And do not let the greatness of the ransom turn you aside.

19 "Will your riches keep *you* from distress,

20 Or all the forces of *your* strength?
    "Do not long for the night,
    When people vanish in their place.

21 "Be careful, do not turn to evil;
    For you have preferred this to affliction.

22 "Behold, God is exalted in His power;
    Who is a teacher like Him?

23 "Who has appointed Him His way,
    And who has said, 'Thou hast done wrong'?

24 "Remember that you should exalt His work,
    Of which men have sung.

25 "All men have seen it;
    Man beholds from afar.

26 "Behold, God is exalted, and we do not know *Him*;
    The number of His years is unsearchable.

27 "For He draws up the drops of water,
    They distill rain from the mist,

28 Which the clouds pour down,
    They drip upon man abundantly.

29 "Can anyone understand the spreading of the clouds,
    The thundering of His pavilion?

30 "Behold, He spreads His lightning about Him,
    And He covers the depths of the sea.

31 "For by these He judges peoples;
    He gives food in abundance.

32 "He covers *His* hands with the lightning,
    And commands it to strike the mark.

33 "Its noise declares His presence;
    The cattle also, concerning what is coming up.

37 "At this also my heart trembles,
    And leaps from its place.

2   "Listen closely to the thunder of His voice,
    And the rumbling that goes out from His mouth.

3   "Under the whole heaven He lets it loose,
    And His lightning to the ends of the earth.

4   "After it, a voice roars;
    He thunders with His majestic voice;
    And He does not restrain the lightnings when His voice is heard.

5   "God thunders with His voice wondrously,
    Doing great things which we cannot comprehend.

6   "For to the snow He says, 'Fall on the earth,'
    And to the downpour and the rain, 'Be strong.'

7   "He seals the hand of every man,
    That all men may know His work.

8   "Then the beast goes into its lair,
    And remains in its den.

9   "Out of the south comes the storm,
    And out of the north the cold.

10 "From the breath of God ice is made,
    And the expanse of the waters is frozen.

11 "Also with moisture He loads the thick cloud;
    He disperses the cloud of His lightning.

12 "And it changes direction, turning around by His guidance,
    That it may do whatever He commands it
    On the face of the inhabited earth.

36:20
Job 34:20,25

36:21
Ps 66:18;
Heb 11:25
36:22
Is 40:13;
1 Cor 2:16
36:23
Job 34:13;
Job 8:3

36:24
2 Sam 7:26;
Ps 35:27;
59:16

*36:26
Ps 102:24

36:27
Ps 147:8

36:29
Job 37:11,16;
26:14

36:31
Job 37:13;
Ps 136:25
36:32
Job 37:15

36:33
Job 37:2

*37:2
Job 36:33

37:3
v. 12

37:4
Ps 29:3

37:5
Job 5:9;
36:26
37:6
Job 38:22;
36:27
*37:7
Job 12:14

37:8
Ps 104:22
37:9
Job 9:9;
Ps 147:17
37:10
Job 38:29;
Ps 147:17
37:11
Job 36:27,29;
v. 15
37:12
Ps 148:8;
Is 14:21;
27:6;
Prov 8:31

36:26 *we do not know Him,* i.e., God is infinite and unsearchable. Man knows that God is, but he does not know who or what God is, except as God chooses to reveal Himself.
37:2 *thunder* (v. 2) and *lightning* (v. 3) go together. They bespeak the power and the glory of God. One witnesses to the ear and the other to the eye. They are designed by God to attract the attention of men. Elihu here speaks as though these natural phenomena happened while he was engaged in conversation with Job.
37:7 *He seals the hand of every man.* Through His control of the elements God is able to control the actions of men. Thus in winter the farmer cannot plow, and in blizzards salesmen stay at home.

37:13 Ex 9:18; 1 Sam 12:18; Job 38:26; 1 Kin 18:45	13 "Whether for correction, or for His world, Or for lovingkindness, He causes it to happen.
37:14 Ps 111:2	14 "Listen to this, O Job, Stand and consider the wonders of God.
	15 "Do you know how God establishes them, And makes the lightning of His cloud to shine?
37:16 vv. 5,14,23; Job 36:4	16 "Do you know about the layers of the thick clouds, The wonders of one perfect in knowledge,
	17 You whose garments are hot, When the land is still because of the south wind?
37:18 Job 9:8; Ps 104:2; Is 44:24	18 "Can you, with Him, spread out the skies, Strong as a molten mirror?
	19 "Teach us what we shall say to Him; We cannot arrange *our case* because of darkness.
	20 "Shall it be told Him that I would speak? Or should a man say that he would be swallowed up?
	21 "And now men do not see the light which is bright in the skies; But the wind has passed and cleared them.
	22 "Out of the north comes golden *splendor;* Around God is awesome majesty.
37:23 1 Tim 6:16; Job 9:4; 8:3; Is 63:9	23 "The Almighty—we cannot find Him; He is exalted in power; And He will not do violence to justice and abundant righteousness.
***37:24** Matt 10:28; 11:25; 1 Cor 1:26	24 "Therefore men fear Him; He does not regard any who are wise of heart."

IV. *The voice of God (38:1–42:6)*

A. *God challenges Job*

38:1 Job 40:6 ***38:2** Job 42:3; 35:16; 1 Tim 1:7 **38:3** Job 40:7	**38** Then the LORD answered Job out of the whirlwind and said, 2 "Who is this that darkens counsel By words without knowledge? 3 "Now gird up your loins like a man, And I will ask you, and you instruct Me!

B. *God's creation*

38:4 Ps 104:5; Prov 8:29	4 "Where were you when I laid the foundation of the earth? Tell *Me*, if you have understanding,
	5 Who set its measurements, since you know? Or who stretched the line on it?
38:6 Job 26:7	6 "On what were its bases sunk? Or who laid its cornerstone,
38:7 Job 1:6	7 When the morning stars sang together, And all the sons of God shouted for joy?
38:8 Gen 1:9	8 "Or *who* enclosed the sea with doors, When, bursting forth, it went out from the womb;
38:9 Prov 30:4	9 When I made a cloud its garment, And thick darkness its swaddling band,
38:10 Job 26:10	10 And I placed boundaries on it, And I set a bolt and doors,
38:11 Ps 89:9	11 And I said, 'Thus far you shall come, but no farther; And here shall your proud waves stop'?
38:12 Ps 74:16	12 "Have you ever in your life commanded the morning,

---

37:24 Elihu argued that God cannot be charged with injustice (v. 23). Job's suffering was first designed to uphold God's glory before the cynicism of Satan. Job's suffering was also to serve the purpose of perfecting his sanctification. God's glory was upheld, to be sure, but God then permitted the trial to continue that Job might be conformed more to His image.
38:2 *words without knowledge.* Job's three friends could not

get him to confess sin, and Elihu was only partially helpful in the solution of the problem. Although Job was correct in insisting that his suffering was not the result of sin, he erred in thinking too highly of his own ability to rationalize the Creator's actions. The climax of the book is reached when God appears in theophany to show Job the greatness of creation and underscore man's ignorance and finiteness. This is done by a series of questions in chapters 38–41.

13 *And* caused the dawn to know its place;
    That it might take hold of the ends of the earth,
    And the wicked be shaken out of it?

14 "It is changed like clay *under* the seal;
    And they stand forth like a garment.

15 "And from the wicked their light is withheld,
    And the uplifted arm is broken.

C. Man's inability to probe the mystery of God's creation

16 "Have you entered into the springs of the sea?
    Or have you walked in the recesses of the deep?

17 "Have the gates of death been revealed to you?
    Or have you seen the gates of deep darkness?

18 "Have you understood the expanse of the earth?
    Tell *Me,* if you know all this.

19 "Where is the way to the dwelling of light?
    And darkness, where is its place,

20 That you may take it to its territory,
    And that you may discern the paths to its home?

21 "You know, for you were born then,
    And the number of your days is great!

22 "Have you entered the storehouses of the snow,
    Or have you seen the storehouses of the hail,

23 Which I have reserved for the time of distress,
    For the day of war and battle?

24 "Where is the way that the light is divided,
    Or the east wind scattered on the earth?

25 "Who has cleft a channel for the flood,
    Or a way for the thunderbolt;

26 To bring rain on a land without people,
    On a desert without a man in it,

27 To satisfy the waste and desolate land,
    And to make the seeds of grass to sprout?

28 "Has the rain a father?
    Or who has begotten the drops of dew?

29 "From whose womb has come the ice?
    And the frost of heaven, who has given it birth?

30 "Water becomes hard like stone,
    And the surface of the deep is imprisoned.

31 "Can you bind the chains of the Pleiades,
    Or loose the cords of Orion?

32 "Can you lead forth a constellation in its season,
    And guide the Bear with her satellites?

33 "Do you know the ordinances of the heavens,
    Or fix their rule over the earth?

34 "Can you lift up your voice to the clouds,
    So that an abundance of water may cover you?

35 "Can you send forth lightnings that they may go
    And say to you, 'Here we are'?

36 "Who has put wisdom in the innermost being,
    Or has given understanding to the mind?

37 "Who can count the clouds by wisdom,
    Or tip the water jars of the heavens,

38 When the dust hardens into a mass,
    And the clods stick together?

D. Man's inability to probe the mysteries of animal and bird life

39 "Can you hunt the prey for the lion,
    Or satisfy the appetite of the young lions,

Cross-references:

38:13 Ps 104:35
38:15 Job 18:5; Ps 10:15
38:16 Ps 77:19
38:17 Ps 9:13
38:18 Job 28:24
38:20 Job 26:10; 24:13
38:21 Job 15:7
38:22 Job 37:6
38:23 Ex 9:18; Josh 10:11; Is 30:30; Ezek 13:11, 13; Rev 16:21
38:24 Job 26:10; 27:21
38:25 Job 28:26
38:26 Job 36:27; Ps 107:35
38:27 Ps 104:13,14
38:28 Ps 147:8; Jer 14:22
38:29 Ps 147:16,17
38:31 Job 9:9; Amos 5:8
38:33 Job 31:35
38:34 v. 37; Job 22:11; 36:27,28
38:35 Job 36:32; 37:3
38:36 Job 32:8; Ps 51:6; Eccl 2:26; Job 32:8
38:39 Ps 104:21

38:40
Job 38:8;
Ps 17:12
38:41
Ps 147:9;
Matt 6:26

40 When they crouch in *their* dens,
 And lie in wait in *their* lair?

41 "Who prepares for the raven its nourishment,
 When its young cry to God,
 And wander about without food?

39:1
Ps 29:9

39 "Do you know the time the mountain goats give birth?
 Do you observe the calving of the deer?

2 "Can you count the months they fulfill,
 Or do you know the time they give birth?

39:3
1 Sam 4:19

3 "They kneel down, they bring forth their young,
 They get rid of their labor pains.

4 "Their offspring become strong, they grow up in the open field;
 They leave and do not return to them.

39:5
Job 6:5;
11:12; 24:5
39:6
Job 24:5;
Jer 2:24;
Hos 8:9;
Ps 107:34

5 "Who sent out the wild donkey free?
 And who loosed the bonds of the swift donkey,

6 To whom I gave the wilderness for a home,
 And the salt land for his dwelling place?

7 "He scorns the tumult of the city,
 The shoutings of the driver he does not hear.

8 "He explores the mountains for his pasture,
 And he searches after every green thing.

39:9
Num 23:22;
Deut 33:17

9 "Will the wild ox consent to serve you?
 Or will he spend the night at your manger?

10 "Can you bind the wild ox in a furrow with ropes?
 Or will he harrow the valleys after you?

11 "Will you trust him because his strength is great
 And leave your labor to him?

12 "Will you have faith in him that he will return your grain,
 And gather *it from* your threshing floor?

13 "The ostriches' wings flap joyously
 With the pinion and plumage of [12]love,

14 For she abandons her eggs to the earth,
 And warms them in the dust,

15 And she forgets that a foot may crush them,
 Or that a wild beast may trample them.

39:16
Lam 4:3;
v. 22
39:17
Job 35:11

16 "She treats her young cruelly, as if *they* were not hers;
 Though her labor be in vain, *she* is unconcerned;

17 Because God has made her forget wisdom,
 And has not given her a share of understanding.

18 "When she lifts herself on high,
 She laughs at the horse and his rider.

39:19
Ps 147:10

19 "Do you give the horse *his* might?
 Do you clothe his neck with a mane?

39:20
Joel 2:5;
Jer 8:16
39:21
Jer 8:6

20 "Do you make him leap like the locust?
 His majestic snorting is terrible.

21 "He paws in the valley, and rejoices in *his* strength;
 He goes out to meet the weapons.

22 "He laughs at fear and is not dismayed;
 And he does not turn back from the sword.

23 "The quiver rattles against him,
 The flashing spear and javelin.

39:24
Jer 4:19;
Ezek 7:14;
Amos 3:6
39:25
Josh 6:5;
Amos 1:14;
2:2

24 "With shaking and rage he races over the ground;
 And he does not stand still at the voice of the trumpet.

25 "As often as the trumpet *sounds* he says, 'Aha!'
 And he scents the battle from afar,
 And thunder of the captains, and the war cry.

26 "Is it by your understanding that the hawk soars,
 Stretching his wings toward the south?

[12]Or, *a stork*

27	"Is it at your command that the eagle mounts up,
	And makes his nest on high?
28	"On the cliff he dwells and lodges,
	Upon the rocky crag, an inaccessible place.
29	"From there he spies out food;
	His eyes see *it* from afar.
30	"His young ones also suck up blood;
	And where the slain are, there is he."

E. *Job's penitent submission*

40 Then the LORD said to Job,
2 "Will the faultfinder contend with the Almighty?
Let him who reproves God answer it."

3 Then Job answered the LORD and said,
4 "Behold, I am insignificant; what can I reply to Thee?
I lay my hand on my mouth.
5 "Once I have spoken, and I will not answer;
Even twice, and I will add no more."

F. *God's second speech*

1. *God challenges Job*

6 Then the LORD answered Job out of the storm, and said,
7 "Now gird up your loins like a man;
I will ask you, and you instruct Me.
8 "Will you really annul My judgment?
Will you condemn Me that you may be justified?
9 "Or do you have an arm like God,
And can you thunder with a voice like His?

10 "Adorn yourself with eminence and dignity;
And clothe yourself with honor and majesty.
11 "Pour out the overflowings of your anger;
And look on everyone who is proud, and make him low.
12 "Look on everyone who is proud, *and* humble him;
And tread down the wicked where they stand.
13 "Hide them in the dust together;
Bind them in the hidden *place*.
14 "Then I will also confess to you,
That your own right hand can save you.

2. *The God who made Behemoth cannot be overcome by man*

15 "Behold now, [13]Behemoth, which I made as well as you;
He eats grass like an ox.
16 "Behold now, his strength in his loins,
And his power in the muscles of his belly.
17 "He bends his tail like a cedar;
The sinews of his thighs are knit together.
18 "His bones are tubes of bronze;
His limbs are like bars of iron.

19 "He is the first of the ways of God;
Let his maker bring near his sword.
20 "Surely the mountains bring him food,
And all the beasts of the field play there.
21 "Under the lotus plants he lies down,
In the covert of the reeds and the marsh.
22 "The lotus plants cover him with shade;
The willows of the brook surround him.
23 "If a river rages, he is not alarmed;
He is confident, though the Jordan rushes to his mouth.
24 "Can anyone capture him when he is on watch,

[13]Or, *the hippopotamus*

39:27
Jer 46:16;
Obad 4

39:30
Matt 24:28;
Luke 17:37

40:1
Job 33:13;
13:3; 23:4;
31:35

40:4
Job 42:6;
29:9
40:5
Job 9:3,15

40:6
Job 38:1
40:7
Job 38:3;
42:4
40:8
Is 14:27;
Rom 3:4
40:9
2 Chr 32:8;
Jer 17:5;
Job 37:5
40:10
Ps 93:1;
104:1
40:11
Is 42:25;
2:12;
Dan 4:37
40:12
1 Sam 2:7;
Is 13:11;
63:3;
Job 36:20
40:14
Ps 20:6; 60:5;
108:6

40:15
v. 19

40:19
Job 41:33;
v. 15
40:20
Ps 104:26

40:22
Is 44:4

40:24
Prov 1:17

With barbs can anyone pierce *his* nose?

3. *The God who made Leviathan is superior to man*

41
1 "Can you draw out [14]Leviathan with a fishhook?
Or press down his tongue with a cord?
2 "Can you put a rope in his nose?
Or pierce his jaw with a hook?
3 "Will he make many supplications to you?
Or will he speak to you soft words?
4 "Will he make a covenant with you?
Will you take him for a servant forever?
5 "Will you play with him as with a bird?
Or will you bind him for your maidens?
6 "Will the traders bargain over him?
Will they divide him among the merchants?
7 "Can you fill his skin with harpoons,
Or his head with fishing spears?
8 "Lay your hand on him;
Remember the battle; you will not do it again!
9 "Behold, your expectation is false;
Will you be laid low even at the sight of him?

10 "No one is so fierce that he dares to arouse him;
Who then is he that can stand before Me?

11 "Who has given to Me that I should repay *him*?
Whatever is under the whole heaven is Mine.
12 "I will not keep silence concerning his limbs,
Or his mighty strength, or his orderly frame.
13 "Who can strip off his outer armor?
Who can come within his double mail?
14 "Who can open the doors of his face?
Around his teeth there is terror.
15 "*His* strong scales are *his* pride,
Shut up *as with* a tight seal.
16 "One is so near to another,
That no air can come between them.
17 "They are joined one to another;
They clasp each other and cannot be separated.

18 "His sneezes flash forth light,
And his eyes are like the eyelids of the morning.
19 "Out of his mouth go burning torches;
Sparks of fire leap forth.
20 "Out of his nostrils smoke goes forth,
As *from* a boiling pot and *burning* rushes.
21 "His breath kindles coals,
And a flame goes forth from his mouth.
22 "In his neck lodges strength,
And dismay leaps before him.
23 "The folds of his flesh are joined together,
Firm on him and immovable.
24 "His heart is as hard as a stone;
Even as hard as a lower millstone.
25 "When he raises himself up, the mighty fear;
Because of the crashing they are bewildered.
26 "The sword that reaches him cannot avail;
Nor the spear, the dart, or the javelin.
27 "He regards iron as straw,
Bronze as rotten wood.
28 "The arrow cannot make him flee;
Slingstones are turned into stubble for him.

[14]Or, *the crocodile*

41:1 *Leviathan*, identified often with the crocodile, may here be the mythological sea monster mentioned in 3:8: *Let those curse it . . . rouse Leviathan.*
41:12ff. Tells of an indomitable monster.

29 "Clubs are regarded as stubble;
He laughs at the rattling of the javelin.
30 "His underparts are *like* sharp potsherds;
He spreads out *like* a threshing sledge on the mire.
31 "He makes the depths boil like a pot;
He makes the sea like a jar of ointment.
32 "Behind him he makes a wake to shine;
One would think the deep to be gray-haired.
33 "Nothing on earth is like him,
One made without fear.
34 "He looks on everything that is high;
He is king over all the sons of pride."

4. *Job repentant*

42 Then Job answered the LORD, and said,
2 "I know that Thou canst do all things,
And that no purpose of Thine can be thwarted.
3 'Who is this that hides counsel without knowledge?'
"Therefore I have declared that which I did not understand,
Things too wonderful for me, which I did not know."
4 'Hear, now, and I will speak;
I will ask Thee, and do Thou instruct me.'
5 "I have heard of Thee by the hearing of the ear;
But now my eye sees Thee;
6 Therefore I retract,
And I repent in dust and ashes."

V. *Epilogue (42:7–17)*

A. *Job's prayer for his friends*

7 And it came about after the LORD had spoken these words to Job, that the LORD said to Eliphaz the Temanite, "My wrath is kindled against you and against your two friends, because you have not spoken of Me what is right as My servant Job has.

8 "Now therefore, take for yourselves seven bulls and seven rams, and go to My servant Job, and offer up a burnt offering for yourselves, and My servant Job will pray for you. For I will accept him so that I may not do with you *according to your* folly, because you have not spoken of Me what is right, as My servant Job has."

9 So Eliphaz the Temanite and Bildad the Shuhite *and* Zophar the Naamathite went and did as the LORD told them; and the LORD accepted Job.

B. *The latter end of Job*

10 And the LORD restored the fortunes of Job when he prayed for his friends, and the LORD increased all that Job had twofold.

11 Then all his brothers, and all his sisters, and all who had known him before, came to him, and they ate bread with him in his house; and they consoled him and comforted him for all the evil that the LORD had brought on him. And each one gave him one piece of money, and each a ring of gold.

12 And the LORD blessed the latter *days* of Job more than his beginning, and he had 14,000 sheep, and 6,000 camels, and 1,000 yoke of oxen, and 1,000 female donkeys.

13 And he had seven sons and three daughters.

14 And he named the first Jemimah, and the second Keziah, and the third Keren-happuch.

41:33
Job 40:19

42:2
Gen 18:14;
Matt 19:26;
Mark 10:27;
Luke 18:27;
2 Chr 20:6;
Is 14:27
***42:3**
Job 38:2;
Ps 40:5;
131:1; 139:6
42:4
Job 38:3;
40:7
42:5
Job 26:14;
Judg 13:22;
Is 6:5
42:6
Ezra 9:6;
Job 40:4

***42:7**
Job 32:3;
vv. 1-6;
40:3-5

42:8
Num 23:1;
Job 1:5;
James 5:15,16

***42:10**
Ps 14:7;
126:1
42:11
Job 19:13

42:12
Job 1:10; 8:7;
1:3

42:13
Job 1:2

42:1 Job now understands God's purpose.
42:3 *I did not understand.* Job's vision of God did not provide a full answer to the problem of his suffering, but it did bring satisfaction to the sufferer. God's wisdom and power, contrasted with Job's ignorance and weakness, brought Job to humility and penitence.
42:7 *not spoken . . . as My servant Job has.* Job's repentance did not mean that the friends were right in their charges. God tells them that they were wrong. They are instructed to offer appropriate sacrifices and are assured that Job will pray for them. This would involve Job's forgiving them for their hard words. God heard Job's prayer in behalf of his friends (v. 9) and Job's own renewed prosperity followed (v. 10).
42:10 *the LORD restored the fortunes of Job.* The number of sheep, camels, oxen, and donkeys at the end of Job's career is double that which he had before his trials (1:3).

15   And in all the land no women were found so fair as Job's daughters; and their father gave them inheritance among their brothers.

16   And after this Job lived 140 years, and saw his sons, and his grandsons, four generations.

17   And Job died, an old man and full of days.

INTRODUCTION TO

THE PSALMS

Authorship and Background: The Hebrew name for this book was "The Book of Praises." The present name derives from the Latin Vulgate, which followed the Septuagint. The authorship is varied and includes David, Solomon, Asaph, Moses, and others, who are anonymous. The final editing probably took place in the time of Ezra. Thus the dates when the individual psalms were written range through many centuries. The psalter was closely associated with the Pentateuch. The repeated reading of the latter led to the choice of certain psalms that were used on specific occasions and festivals such as the Feast of Booths. This would indicate that the Psalms were used liturgically in ancient times, just as they have been in the life of the church.

Characteristics: The Psalms have a unique place in Scripture. They cover the gamut of human emotions, from imprecatory cries to heavenly praises. They are marked by spiritual intensity springing out of personal experience in the worship of God. God, nature, history, sin, animals, and heavenly constellations find their way naturally into these exalted acts of worship and devotion. The book itself is divided into five sections or "books," each of which ends with a doxology. The last psalm is entirely given over to doxology. Eight categories of psalms may be distinguished: (1) personal psalms; (2) penitential psalms; (3) psalms of praise; (4) prayer psalms; (5) Messianic psalms; (6) historical psalms; (7) liturgical psalms; and (8) psalms that attribute majesty and power to God. Many of the psalms have features of more than one of these categories, although some have been identified more nearly with one group than any other. Thus Psalms 120 and 135 are often thought of as liturgical; Psalms 2, 22, 45, and 110 as Messianic; Psalms 18, 100, and 103 as psalms of praise; Psalms 23, 27, 34, and 37 as personal; and Psalms 32, 51, and 130 as penitential.

Contents: The five books in the psalter divide the psalms thus:

I. Psalms 1-41

II. Psalms 42-72

III. Psalms 73-89

IV. Psalms 90-106

V. Psalms 107-150

Note: The word *Selah* (Heb *sālal*, "to lift up") occurs seventy-one times in the Psalms, as well as three times in Habakkuk. It is generally agreed that the word is a liturgical or musical sign, although its precise meaning remains uncertain. In all probability, Selah was a direction to the orchestra, who had been playing softly in accompaniment to the singers' voices to "lift up loud" their music. Some suggest that the word was not in the original text, but first appeared as a marginal gloss and gradually found its way into the main body of the book over the centuries.

THE PSALMS

The following expressions occur often in the Psalms:

Selah   May mean *Pause, Crescendo* or *Musical Interlude*
Maskil   Possibly, *Contemplative,* or *Didactic,* or *Skillful Psalm*
Mikhtam   Possibly, *Epigrammatic Poem,* or *Atonement Psalm*
Sheol   The nether world

BOOK 1

I. *The happiness of the godly (1:1–3)*

1

1:1
Prov 4:14;
Job 21:16;
Ps 17:4; 26:5;
Jer 15:17

1   How blessed is the man who does not walk in the counsel of the
      wicked,
   Nor stand in the path of sinners,
   Nor sit in the seat of scoffers!

1:2
Ps 119:35;
Josh 1:8;
Ps 119:1

2   But his delight is in the law of the LORD,
   And in his law he meditates day and night.

1:3
Jer 17:8;
Ezek 47:12;
Gen 39:3;
Ps 128:2

3   And he will be like a tree *firmly* planted by streams of water,
   Which yields its fruit in its season,
   And its leaf does not wither;
   And in whatever he does, he prospers.

II. *The misery of the wicked (1:4–6)*

1:4
Job 21:18;
Is 17:13

4   The wicked are not so,
   But they are like chaff which the wind drives away.

1:5
Ps 5:5; 9:7;
8:16; 111:1;
149:1

5   Therefore the wicked will not stand in the judgment,
   Nor sinners in the assembly of the righteous.

1:6
Ps 37:18;
2 Tim 2:19;
Ps 9:3-6

6   For the LORD knows the way of the righteous,
   But the way of the wicked will perish.

I. *The Messiah's psalm (2:1–11)*

A. *The Messiah rejected*

2

*2:1ff
Acts 4:25;
Ps 21:11

1   Why are the nations in an uproar,
   And the peoples devising a vain thing?

2:2
Ps 48:4-6;
74:18,23;
John 1:41

2   The kings of the earth take their stand,
   And the rulers take counsel together
   Against the LORD and against His [1]Anointed:

2:3
Jer 5:5

3   "Let us tear their fetters apart,
   And cast away their cords from us!"

[1]Or, *Messiah*

2:1–11 Many of the Psalms were written almost a thousand years before the advent of Jesus Christ. Yet some of them evidently refer to Him, as the apostles made clear at Pentecost, and thereafter in the sermons of Acts. They could not fully apply to David himself or to any other person who has ever lived. It is possible, of course, to read Messianic implications into some psalms where such implications are, to say the least, doubtful. On the other hand, it is not unusual for a psalm to refer to David as a type of the Messianic king. Among the psalms that are clearly Messianic are: 2, 8, 16, 22, 45, 69, 72, 89, 110, and 132.

Psalm 2 probably has as its historical background some rebellion of the nations against David or some ruler of the Davidic line. Such a revolt is described as futile, however, for God has willed that His Anointed (the Davidic king) should rule all nations. Jesus as the Messiah (i.e., the Anointed One, the Son of David) brings ultimate fulfillment to words that could apply only in a limited sense to others who claimed descent from David.

This is a Messianic psalm. The *Anointed* of v. 2 is, in its ultimate application, Christ. Verse 6 uses historical language (*My King upon Zion, My holy mountain*), which may be employed to depict Christ ascended to the right hand of the Father. This same Christ shall reign over a reconstituted Zion in the future. *Thou art My Son* (v. 7), while applicable to human kings who are chosen of God, looks forward to the incarnation for its ultimate fulfillment. These words were to be confirmed at Christ's baptism: *This is My beloved Son, in whom I am well-pleased* (Matt. 3:17). The note sounded in v. 12 sets blessing and happiness for the faithful against anger and judgment for the unbelieving.

C. *God blesses the righteous*

7 But as for me, by Thine abundant lovingkindness I will enter Thy
house,
At Thy holy temple I will bow in reverence for Thee.

8 O LORD, lead me in Thy righteousness because of my foes;
Make Thy way straight before me.
9 There is nothing reliable in what they say;
Their inward part is destruction *itself*;
Their throat is an open grave;
They flatter with their tongue.
10 Hold them guilty, O God;
By their own devices let them fall!
In the multitude of their transgressions thrust them out,
For they are rebellious against Thee.

11 But let all who take refuge in Thee be glad,
Let them ever sing for joy;
And mayest Thou shelter them,
That those who love Thy name may exult in Thee.
12 For it is Thou who dost bless the righteous man, O LORD,
Thou dost surround him with favor as with a shield.

For the choir director; with stringed instruments, upon an eight-stringed lyre.
A Psalm of David.

I. *Prayer for mercy in time of trouble (6:1–10)*

A. *Prayer for mercy*

6

O LORD, do not rebuke me in Thine anger,
Nor chasten me in Thy wrath.
2 Be gracious to me, O LORD, for I *am* pining away;
Heal me, O LORD, for my bones are dismayed.
3 And my soul is greatly dismayed;
But Thou, O LORD—how long?

4 Return, O LORD, rescue my [8]soul;
Save me because of Thy lovingkindness.
5 For there is no [9]mention of Thee in death;
In Sheol who will give Thee thanks?

6 I am weary with my sighing;
Every night I make my bed swim,
I dissolve my couch with my tears.
7 My eye has wasted away with grief;
It has become old because of all my adversaries.

B. *Assurance of a good answer*

8 Depart from me, all you who do iniquity,
For the LORD has heard the voice of my weeping.
9 The LORD has heard my supplication,
The LORD receives my prayer.
10 All my enemies shall be ashamed and greatly dismayed;
They shall turn back, they shall suddenly be ashamed.

[8]Or, *life* [9]Or, *remembrance*

5:7
Ps 69:13;
28:2

5:8
Ps 27:11;
31:1
5:9
Deut 32:20;
Luke 11:44;
Rom 3:13;
Ps 12:2

5:10
Ps 9:16;
Lam 1:5;
Ps 107:10,11

5:11
Ps 2:12;
Is 65:13;
Zech 9:15;
Ps 69:36

5:12
Ps 112:2;
32:7,10

6:1
Ps 38:1; 2:5

6:2
Ps 51:1;
102:4,11;
41:4; 22:14
6:3
John 12:27;
Ps 90:13

6:4
Ps 17:13

6:5
Ps 30:9;
Is 38:18

6:6
Ps 69:3; 22:1;
42:3

6:7
Ps 31:9

6:8
Ps 119:115;
Luke 13:27;
Ps 5:5; 28:6
6:9
Ps 116:1;
66:19,20
6:10
Ps 71:24;
40:14; 73:19

A [10]Shiggaion of David, which he sang to the Lord concerning Cush, a Benjamite.

I. *The prayer of a wronged man (7:1–17)*

A. *David turns to God*

7
O LORD my God, in Thee I have taken refuge;
Save me from all those who pursue me, and deliver me,
2 Lest he tear my soul like a lion,
Dragging me away, while there is none to deliver.

B. *He pleads his innocence*

3 O LORD my God, if I have done this,
If there is injustice in my hands,
4 If I have rewarded evil to my friend,
Or have plundered him who without cause was my adversary,
5 Let the enemy pursue my soul and overtake *it*;
And let him trample my life down to the ground,
And lay my glory in the dust.   Selah.

C. *He cries for justice*

6 Arise, O LORD, in Thine anger;
Lift up Thyself against the rage of my adversaries,
And arouse Thyself for me; Thou hast appointed judgment.
7 And let the assembly of the peoples encompass Thee;
And over them return Thou on high.
8 The LORD judges the peoples;
Vindicate me, O LORD, according to my righteousness and my
integrity that is in me.
9 O let the evil of the wicked come to an end, but establish the
righteous;
For the righteous God tries the hearts and [11]minds.

D. *The fate of the wicked*

10 My shield is with God,
Who saves the upright in heart.
11 God is a righteous judge,
And a God who has indignation every day.

12 If a man does not repent, He will sharpen His sword;
He has bent His bow and made it ready.
13 He has also prepared for Himself deadly weapons;
He makes His arrows fiery shafts.
14 Behold, he travails with wickedness,
And he conceives mischief, and brings forth falsehood.
15 He has dug a pit and hollowed it out,
And has fallen into the hole which he made.
16 His mischief will return upon his own head,
And his violence will descend upon [12]his own pate.

E. *Praise to a righteous God*

17 I will give thanks to the LORD according to His righteousness,
And will sing praise to the name of the LORD Most High.

7:1 Ps 11:1; 31:15
7:2 Ps 17:12; 50:22
7:3 2 Sam 16:7; 1 Sam 24:11
7:4 1 Sam 24:7
7:6 Ps 3:7; 94:2; 44:23
7:7 Ps 68:18
7:8 Ps 96:13; 18:20; 35:24
7:9 Ps 34:21; Is 54:14; 1 Chr 28:9; Jer 11:20; Rev 2:23
7:10 Ps 18:2; 125:4
7:11 Ps 50:6; Is 34:2
7:12 Ezek 3:19; 33:9; Deut 32:41; Ps 21:12
7:13 Ps 64:7
7:14 Is 59:4; James 1:15
7:15 Job 4:8; Ps 9:15; Eccl 10:8
7:16 Ps 140:9; Esth 9:25
7:17 Ps 71:15,16; 9:2

[10]I.e., Dithyrambic rhythm, or, wild, passionate song   [11]Lit., *kidneys*, figurative for inner man   [12]I.e., the crown of his own head

For the choir director; on the Gittith. A Psalm of David.

I. *God's glory and man's honor (8:1–9)*

A. *God the great creator*

8 O LORD, our Lord,
How majestic is Thy name in all the earth,
Who hast displayed Thy splendor above the heavens!
2 From the mouth of infants and nursing babes Thou hast established
strength,
Because of Thine adversaries,
To make the enemy and the revengeful cease.

3 When I consider Thy heavens, the work of Thy fingers,
The moon and the stars, which Thou hast ordained;
4 What is man, that Thou dost take thought of him?
And the son of man, that Thou dost care for him?

B. *Man the chief agent of God*

5 Yet Thou hast made him a little lower than God,
And dost crown him with glory and majesty!
6 Thou dost make him to rule over the works of Thy hands;
Thou hast put all things under his feet,
7 All sheep and oxen,
And also the beasts of the field,
8 The birds of the heavens, and the fish of the sea,
Whatever passes through the paths of the seas.

9 O LORD, our Lord,
How majestic is Thy name in all the earth!

For the choir director; on [13]Muth-labben. A Psalm of David.

I. *Praise to God for deliverance (9:1–20)*

A. *Hymn of thanksgiving*

9 I will give thanks to the LORD with all my heart;
I will tell of all Thy wonders.
2 I will be glad and exult in Thee;
I will sing praise to Thy name, O Most High.

3 When my enemies turn back,
They stumble and perish before Thee.
4 For Thou hast maintained my just cause;
Thou dost sit on the throne judging righteously.
5 Thou hast rebuked the nations; Thou hast destroyed the wicked;
Thou hast blotted out their name forever and ever.
6 The enemy has come to an end in perpetual ruins,
And Thou hast uprooted the cities;
The very memory of them has perished.

B. *Faith in God's righteousness*

7 But the LORD [14]abides forever;
He has established His throne for judgment,
8 And He will judge the world in righteousness;
He will execute judgment for the peoples with equity.
9 The LORD also will be a stronghold for the oppressed,
A stronghold in times of trouble,

[13]I.e., "Death to the Son" [14]Or, *sits as king*

Marginal references

8:1 Ps 66:2; 148:13; 57:5, 11; 113:4
8:2 Matt 21:16; Ps 44:16
8:3 Ps 89:11; 102:5; 136:9
8:4 Job 7:17; Ps 144:3; Heb 2:6
*8:5 Ps 103:4; 21:5; Heb 2:9
8:6 Gen 1:26; Heb 2:8
8:9 v. 1

9:1 Ps 86:12; 26:7
9:2 Ps 5:11; 83:18
9:3 Ps 56:9; 27:2
9:4 Ps 140:12; 47:8; 67:4; 1 Pet 2:23
9:5 Deut 9:14
9:6 Ps 40:15; 34:16
9:7 Ps 29:10; 89:14
9:8 Ps 96:13
9:9 Ps 18:2; 32:7; 37:39

8:5 Psalm 8 contains a paradox—man is very little in comparison with the vastness of creation (3,4), yet God has given him a position of glory and honor (5–8). Jesus, who as Son of God is sovereign over all creation, in humility became man, taking upon Himself the title "Son of man" as an expression of His identification with mankind.

9:10
Ps 91:14;
37:28

10 And those who know Thy name will put their trust in Thee;
For Thou, O LORD, hast not forsaken those who seek Thee.

9:11
Ps 76:2;
105:1
9:12
Gen 9:5; v. 18

11 Sing praises to the LORD, who dwells in Zion;
Declare among the peoples His deeds.
12 For He who 15requires blood remembers them;
He does not forget the cry of the afflicted.

C. A prayer for help

9:13
Ps 30:10;
25:18; 38:19;
30:3

13 Be gracious to me, O LORD;
Behold my affliction from those who hate me,
Thou who dost lift me up from the gates of death;

9:14
Ps 106:2;
87:2; 13:5

14 That I may tell of all Thy praises,
That in the gates of the daughter of Zion
I may rejoice in Thy salvation.

D. A testimony to God's past judgments

9:15
Ps 7:15; 35:8

15 The nations have sunk down in the pit which they have made;
In the net which they hid, their own foot has been caught.

9:16
Is 64:2; v. 4

16 The LORD has made Himself known;
He has executed judgment.
In the work of his own hands the wicked is snared.   Higgaion Selah.

E. Assurance of, and prayer for, justice

9:17
Ps 49:14;
50:22;
Job 8:13
9:18
v. 12;
Ps 74:19
9:19
Ps 3:7;
2 Chr 14:11;
Ps 110:6
9:20
Ps 83:15;
Is 31:3

17 The wicked will return to Sheol,
Even all the nations who forget God.
18 For the needy will not always be forgotten,
Nor the hope of the afflicted perish forever.
19 Arise, O LORD, do not let man prevail;
Let the nations be judged before Thee.
20 Put them in fear, O LORD;
Let the nations know that they are but men.   Selah.

I. When judgment is delayed (10:1–18)

A. The evil acts of the wicked

10:1
Ps 22:1; 13:1

10 Why dost Thou stand afar off, O LORD?
Why dost Thou hide *Thyself* in times of trouble?

10:2
Ps 109:16;
7:15; 9:16

2 In pride the wicked hotly pursue the afflicted;
Let them be caught in the plots which they have devised.

10:3
Ps 94:4;
Job 1:5,11;
v. 13
10:4
v. 13; Ps 14:1

3 For the wicked boasts of his heart's desire,
And 16the greedy man curses *and* spurns the LORD.
4 The wicked, in the haughtiness of his countenance, does not seek
Him.
All his thoughts are, "There is no God."

5 His ways prosper at all times;
Thy judgments are on high, out of his sight;
As for all his adversaries, he snorts at them.

10:6
Ps 30:6;
49:11
10:7
Rom 3:14;
Ps 59:12;
73:8; 140:3
10:8
Prov 1:11;
Ps 94:6

6 He says to himself, "I shall not be moved;
Throughout all generations I shall not be in adversity."
7 His mouth is full of curses and deceit and oppression;
Under his tongue is mischief and wickedness.
8 He sits in the lurking places of the villages;
In the hiding places he kills the innocent;
His eyes stealthily watch for the unfortunate.

10:9
Ps 17:12;
59:3; v. 2;
140:5

9 He lurks in a hiding place as a lion in his lair;
He lurks to catch the afflicted;
He catches the afflicted when he draws him into his net.
10 He crouches, he bows down,
And the unfortunate fall 17by his mighty ones.

15I.e., avenges bloodshed   16Or, *blesses the greedy man*   17Or, *into his claws*

11   He says to himself, "God has forgotten;
He has hidden His face; He will never see it."

B. A prayer for relief and confidence of an answer

12   Arise, O LORD; O God, lift up Thy hand.
Do not forget the afflicted.

13   Why has the wicked spurned God?
He has said to himself, "Thou wilt not require *it*."

14   Thou hast seen *it*, for Thou hast beheld mischief and vexation to
        take it into Thy hand.
The unfortunate commits *himself* to Thee;
Thou hast been the helper of the orphan.

15   Break the arm of the wicked and the evildoer,
Seek out his wickedness until Thou dost find none.

16   The LORD is King forever and ever;
Nations have perished from His land.

17   O LORD, Thou hast heard the desire of the [18]humble;
Thou wilt strengthen their heart, Thou wilt incline Thine ear

18   To [19]vindicate the orphan and the oppressed,
That man who is of the earth may cause terror no more.

For the choir director. *A Psalm* of David.

I. The LORD our refuge and defense (11:1–7)

A. Temptation to distrust in trial

11

In the LORD I take refuge;
How can you say to my soul, "Flee *as* a bird to your mountain;

2   For, behold, the wicked bend the bow,
They make ready their arrow upon the string,
To shoot in darkness at the upright in heart.

3   If the foundations are destroyed,
What can the righteous do?"

B. Affirmation of faith in the LORD

4   The LORD is in His holy temple; the LORD's throne is in heaven;
His eyes behold, His eyelids test the sons of men.

5   The LORD tests the righteous and the wicked,
And the one who loves violence His soul hates.

6   Upon the wicked He will rain [20]snares;
Fire and brimstone and burning wind will be the portion of their
        cup.

7   For the LORD is righteous; He loves righteousness;
The upright will behold His face.

For the choir director; upon an eight-stringed lyre. A Psalm of David.

I. Good thoughts for bad times (12:1–8)

A. Prayer for help amidst the ungodly

12

Help, LORD, for the godly man ceases to be,
For the faithful disappear from among the sons of men.

2   They speak falsehood to one another;
With flattering lips and with a double heart they speak.

3   May the LORD cut off all flattering lips,
The tongue that speaks great things;

4   Who have said, "With our tongue we will prevail;
Our lips are our own; who is lord over us?"

18Or, *afflicted*   19Lit., *judge*   20Or, *coals of fire*

10:11
v. 4;
Job 22:13;
Ps 73:11

10:12
Mic 5:9;
Ps 9:12
10:13
v. 3

10:14
Job 11:11;
Jer 51:56;
Ps 37:5; 68:5;
Hos 14:3

10:15
Ps 37:17;
9:12

10:16
Ps 29:10;
Deut 8:20
10:17
Ps 145:19;
1 Chr 29:18;
Ps 34:15
10:18
Ps 82:3; 9:9;
Is 29:20

11:1
Ps 56:11

11:2
Ps 7:12; 64:3,
4

11:3
Ps 82:5

11:4
Ps 18:6;
103:19;
33:13; 34:15,
16
11:5
Gen 22:1;
James 1:12;
Ps 5:5
11:6
Ezek 38:22;
Jer 4:11,12;
Ps 75:8
11:7
Ps 7:9,11;
33:5; 17:15

12:1
Is 57:1

12:2
Ps 41:6;
55:21;
1 Chr 12:33
12:3
Ps 73:8,9

B. *Assurance of the LORD's deliverance*

12:5
Ps 10:18; 3:7;
34:6

5 "Because of the devastation of the afflicted, because of the groaning of
    the needy,
Now I will arise," says the LORD; "I will set him in the safety for
    which he longs."

12:6
Ps 18:30;
Prov 30:5
12:7
Ps 37:28

6 The words of the LORD are pure words;
As silver tried in a furnace on the earth, refined seven times.
7 Thou, O LORD, wilt keep them;
Thou wilt preserve him from this generation forever.

12:8
Ps 55:10,11

8 The wicked strut about on every side,
When 21vileness is exalted among the sons of men.

For the choir director. A Psalm of David.

I. The deserted soul (13:1–6)

A. His desperate plight

13:1
Job 13:24;
Ps 44:24;
88:14
13:2
Ps 42:4,9;
94:3

13 How long, O LORD? Wilt Thou forget me forever?
How long wilt Thou hide Thy face from me?
  2 How long shall I take counsel in my soul,
Having sorrow in my heart all the day?
How long will my enemy be exalted over me?

B. His prayer for help

13:3
Ps 5:1;
Ezra 9:8;
Jer 51:39
13:4
Jer 20:10;
Ps 25:2

3 Consider *and* answer me, O LORD, my God;
Enlighten my eyes, lest I sleep the *sleep of* death,
4 Lest my enemy say, "I have overcome him,"
Lest my adversaries rejoice when I am shaken.

C. His assurance of deliverance

13:5
Ps 52:8; 9:14

5 But I have trusted in Thy lovingkindness;
My heart shall rejoice in Thy salvation.

13:6
Ps 59:16;
116:7

6 I will sing to the LORD,
Because He has dealt bountifully with me.

For the choir director. A Psalm of David.

I. The principles and practices of the wicked (14:1–7)

*14:1
Ps 10:4;
53:1-6; 73:8;
Rom 3:10-12

14 The fool has said in his heart, "There is no God."
They are corrupt, they have committed abominable deeds;
There is no one who does good.

14:2
Ps 33:13;
92:6;
Ezra 6:21

2 The LORD has looked down from heaven upon the sons of men,
To see if there are any who understand,
Who seek after God.

14:3
Ps 58:3;
2 Pet 2:7;
Rev 22:11;
Ps 143:2

3 They have all turned aside; together they have become corrupt;
There is no one who does good, not even one.

14:4
Ps 82:5; 27:2;
79:6; Is 64:7

4 Do all the workers of wickedness not know,
Who eat up my people *as* they eat bread,
And do not call upon the Lord?

14:5
Ps 73:15

5 There they are in great dread,
For God is with the righteous generation.

14:6
Ps 9:9; 40:17

6 You would put to shame the counsel of the afflicted,
But the LORD is his refuge.

<hr>

21Or, *worthlessness*

14:1 In Matt. 5:22 Christ says that to call a brother a fool provokes danger of hell fire. Yet He Himself reproaches the Pharisees as *fools* (using the same word as in 5:22) when He exposes their shallow legalism in Matt. 23:17,19. Here in 14:1 God calls the atheist a fool. The distinction between passages of this type and the injunction in Matt. 5:22 lies in the attitude and authority of the one speaking. As the surrounding verses in Matt. 5 show, what Christ forbade was passing judgment on another in a spirit of contempt or hatred.

7 Oh, that the salvation of Israel would come out of Zion!
When the LORD [22]restores His captive people,
Jacob will rejoice, Israel will be glad.

A Psalm of David.

I. *The happiness of the holy (15:1–5)*

15 O LORD, who may abide in Thy tent?
Who may dwell on Thy holy hill?
2 He who walks with integrity, and works righteousness,
And speaks truth in his heart.
3 He does not slander with his tongue,
Nor does evil to his neighbor,
Nor takes up a reproach against his friend;
4 In whose eyes a reprobate is despised,
But who honors those who fear the LORD;
He swears to his own hurt, and does not change;
5 He does not put out his money [23]at interest,
Nor does he take a bribe against the innocent.
He who does these things will never be shaken.

A [24]Mikhtam of David.

I. *A Messianic prophecy (16:1–11)*

A. *Faith evidenced*

16 Preserve me, O God, for I take refuge in Thee.
2 I said to the LORD, "Thou art my Lord;
I have no good besides Thee."
3 As for the saints who are in the earth,
They are the majestic ones in whom is all my delight.
4 The sorrows of those who have bartered for another *god* will be
multiplied;
I shall not pour out their libations of blood,
Nor shall I take their names upon my lips.

B. *Calvary predicted*

5 The LORD is the portion of my inheritance and my cup;
Thou dost support my lot.
6 The lines have fallen to me in pleasant places;
Indeed, my heritage is beautiful to me.
7 I will bless the LORD who has counseled me;
Indeed, my mind instructs me in the night.
8 I have set the LORD continually before me;
Because He is at my right hand, I will not be shaken.

C. *The resurrection assured*

9 Therefore my heart is glad, and my glory rejoices;
My flesh also will dwell securely.
10 For Thou wilt not abandon my soul to Sheol;
Neither wilt Thou allow Thy Holy One to [25]undergo decay.
11 Thou wilt make known to me the path of life;
In Thy presence is fulness of joy;
In Thy right hand there are pleasures forever.

[22]Or, *restores the fortunes of His people* [23]I.e., to a fellow Israelite [24]Possibly Epigrammatic Poem, or, Atonement Psalm
[25]Or, *see corruption* or *the pit*

15:1 *Thy tent.* The tabernacle (tent of meeting) and, later, the temple were structures in which God made manifest His presence in the midst of His people. The psalmist asks, "Who is qualified to dwell in fellowship with God?"
16:10 This is a Messianic psalm in which the resurrection of Christ is predicted. Words that were of comfort to David and the righteous of all ages are quoted in Acts 2:27,31 as being fulfilled in Christ at His resurrection. In Acts 2:27 it is translated: *Thou wilt not abandon my soul to Hades.* However, the Hebrew word *nephesh* does not mean "soul" as distinct from "body," but often refers to the whole person.

A Prayer of David.

I. *David's desire for deliverance (17:1–15)*

A. *He pleads his integrity*

17 Hear a just cause, O Lord, give heed to my cry;
Give ear to my prayer, which is not from deceitful lips.

2 Let my judgment come forth from Thy presence;
Let Thine eyes look with equity.

3 Thou hast tried my heart;
Thou hast visited *me* by night;
Thou hast tested me and dost find [26]nothing;
I have purposed that my mouth will not transgress.

4 As for the deeds of men, by the word of Thy lips
I have kept from the paths of the violent.

5 My steps have held fast to Thy paths.
My feet have not slipped.

B. *He prays to be preserved*

6 I have called upon Thee, for Thou wilt answer me, O God;
Incline Thine ear to me, hear my speech.

7 Wondrously show Thy lovingkindness,
O Savior of those who take refuge at Thy right hand
From those who rise up *against them*.

8 Keep me as [27]the apple of the eye;
Hide me in the shadow of Thy wings,

9 From the wicked who despoil me,
My deadly enemies, who surround me.

C. *He describes his enemies*

10 They have closed their unfeeling *heart*;
With their mouth they speak proudly.

11 They have now surrounded us in our steps;
They set their eyes to cast *us* down to the ground.

12 He is like a lion that is eager to tear,
And as a young lion lurking in hiding places.

D. *He expresses his confidence in the Lord*

13 Arise, O Lord, confront him, bring him low;
Deliver my soul from the wicked with Thy sword,

14 From men with Thy hand, O Lord,
From men of the world, whose portion is in *this* life;
And whose belly Thou dost fill with Thy treasure;
They are satisfied with children,
And leave their abundance to their babes.

15 As for me, I shall behold Thy face in righteousness;
I will be satisfied with Thy likeness when I awake.

For the choir director. *A Psalm* of David the servant of the Lord, who spoke to the Lord the words of this song in the day that the Lord delivered him from the hand of all his enemies and from the hand of Saul. And he said,

I. *Hymn of deliverance (18:1–50)*

A. *He glories in the Lord*

18 "I love Thee, O Lord, my strength."
2   The Lord is my rock and my fortress and my deliverer,

17:1
Ps 9:4; 61:1;
55:1; Is 29:13
17:2
1 Chr 29:17

17:3
Ps 26:2;
66:10;
Job 23:10;
Jer 50:20;
Ps 39:1
17:4
Prov 1:15

17:5
Ps 44:18;
18:36

17:6
Ps 86:7; 88:2

17:7
Ps 31:21;
20:6

17:8
Deut 32:10;
Ps 36:7
17:9
Ps 31:20;
38:12; 109:3

17:10
Ps 73:7;
1 Sam 2:3;
Ps 31:18
17:11
Ps 88:17;
37:14
17:12
Ps 7:2; 10:9

17:13
Ps 73:18;
22:20; 7:12
17:14
Luke 16:8;
Ps 73:3-7;
Is 2:7;
Job 21:11

17:15
1 John 3:2;
Ps 4:6,7;
16:11

18:1
Ps 27:1
18:2
Ps 19:14;

[26]Or, *no evil device in me*   [27]Lit., *the pupil, the daughter of the eye*

My God, my rock, in whom I take refuge;
My shield and the horn of my salvation, my
  stronghold.

3 I call upon the LORD, who is worthy to be praised,
And I am saved from my enemies.

B. *He testifies to His deliverances*

4 The cords of death encompassed me,
And the torrents of [28]ungodliness terrified me.
5 The cords of Sheol surrounded me;
The snares of death confronted me.
6 In my distress I called upon the LORD,
And cried to my God for help;
He heard my voice out of His temple,
And my cry for help before Him came into His ears.

7 Then the earth shook and quaked;
And the foundations of the mountains were trembling
And were shaken, because He was angry.
8 Smoke went up out of His nostrils,
And fire from His mouth devoured;
Coals were kindled by it.
9 He bowed the heavens also, and came down
With thick darkness under His feet.
10 And He rode upon a cherub and flew;
And He sped upon the wings of the wind.
11 He made darkness His hiding place, His canopy around Him,
Darkness of waters, thick clouds of the skies.
12 From the brightness before Him passed His thick clouds,
Hailstones and coals of fire.
13 The LORD also thundered in the heavens,
And the Most High uttered His voice,
Hailstones and coals of fire.
14 And He sent out His arrows, and scattered them,
And lightning flashes in abundance, and routed them.
15 Then the channels of water appeared,
And the foundations of the world were laid bare
At Thy rebuke, O LORD,
At the blast of the breath of Thy nostrils.

16 He sent from on high, He took me;
He drew me out of many waters.
17 He delivered me from my strong enemy,
And from those who hated me, for they were too mighty for me.
18 They confronted me in the day of my calamity,
But the LORD was my stay.
19 He brought me forth also into a broad place;
He rescued me, because He delighted in me.

C. *He justifies his integrity*

20 The LORD has rewarded me according to my righteousness;
According to the cleanness of my hands He has recompensed me.
21 For I have kept the ways of the LORD,
And have not wickedly departed from my God.
22 For all His ordinances were before me,
And I did not put away His statutes from me.
23 I was also [29]blameless with Him,
And I kept myself from my iniquity.
24 Therefore the LORD has recompensed me according to my
  righteousness,
According to the cleanness of my hands in His eyes.

[28]Or, *destruction* [29]Lit., *complete*; or, *having integrity*

Ps 91:2;
40:17; 11:1;
59:11; 75:10;
9:9
18:3
Ps 48:1;
Num 10:9

18:4
Ps 116:3;
124:3,4
18:5
Ps 116:3;
Prov 14:27
18:6
Ps 86:7; 11:4;
34:15

18:7
Ps 68:7,8;
114:4,6

18:8
Deut 29:20;
Hab 3:5

18:9
Ps 144:5;
Ex 20:21
18:10
Ps 80:1;
104:3
18:11
Ps 97:2

18:12
Ps 104:2;
Is 30:30;
Ps 140:10
18:13
Ps 29:3;
104:7

18:14
Ps 7:13;
144:6;
Ex 14:24;
Judg 4:15
18:15
Ps 106:9;
76:6; Ex 15:8

18:16
Ps 144:7

18:17
v. 48;
Ps 35:10
18:18
Ps 59:16;
Is 10:20
18:19
Ps 31:8;
118:5; 37:23

18:20
Ps 7:8;
1 Kin 8:32;
Ps 24:4
18:21
Ps 119:33;
2 Chr 34:33;
Ps 119:102
18:22
Ps 119:30,83

18:24
1 Sam 26:23

18:25 Ps 62:12; Matt 5:7	**25**	With the kind Thou dost show Thyself kind; With the blameless Thou dost show Thyself blameless;
18:26 Job 25:5; Prov 3:34	26	With the pure Thou dost show Thyself pure; And with the crooked Thou dost show Thyself ³⁰astute.
18:27 Ps 72:12; Prov 6:17	27	For Thou dost save an afflicted people; But haughty eyes Thou dost abase.
18:28 Job 18:6; Ps 27:1; Job 29:3	28	For Thou dost light my lamp; The LORD my God illumines my darkness.
18:29 2 Cor 12:9; Heb 11:34	29	For by Thee I can ³¹run upon a troop; And by my God I can leap over a wall.
18:30 Deut 32:4; Ps 12:6; 17:7	**30**	As for God, His way is blameless; The word of the LORD is tried; He is a shield to all who take refuge in Him.

D. *He acknowledges that God has delivered him*

*18:31 Deut 32:31, 39; Ps 86:8-10; Is 45:5	31	For who is God, but the LORD? And who is a rock, except our God,
18:32 Is 45:5; Heb 13:21; 1 Pet 5:10	32	The God who girds me with strength, And makes my way blameless?
*18:33 Hab 3:19; Deut 32:13	33	He makes my feet like hinds' *feet*, And sets me upon my high places.
18:34 Ps 144:1; Job 20:24	34	He trains my hands for battle, So that my arms can bend a bow of bronze.
18:35 Deut 33:29; Ps 119:117; 138:6	35	Thou hast also given me the shield of Thy salvation, And Thy right hand upholds me; And Thy gentleness makes me great.
18:36 Ps 31:8; 71:5	36	Thou dost enlarge my steps under me, And my feet have not slipped.
18:37 Ps 44:5; 37:20	**37**	I pursued my enemies and overtook them, And I did not turn back until they were consumed.
18:38 Ps 110:6; 36:12; 47:3	38	I shattered them, so that they were not able to rise; They fell under my feet.
18:39 vv. 32,47	39	For Thou hast girded me with strength for battle; Thou hast subdued under me those who rose up against me.
18:40 Ps 21:21; 94:23	40	Thou hast also made my enemies turn their backs to me, And I ³²destroyed those who hated me.
18:41 Ps 50:22; Prov 1:28	41	They cried for help, but there was none to save, *Even* to the LORD, but He did not answer them.
18:42 Ps 83:13	42	Then I beat them fine as the dust before the wind; I emptied them out as the mire of the streets.

E. *He expresses confidence in the future*

18:43 Ps 35:1; Is 52:15; 55:5	**43**	Thou hast delivered me from the contentions of the people; Thou hast placed me as head of the nations; A people whom I have not known serve me.
18:44 Ps 66:3	44	As soon as they hear, they obey me; Foreigners ³³submit to me.
	45	Foreigners fade away, And come trembling out of their fortresses.
18:46 Ps 42:2; 51:14	**46**	The LORD lives, and blessed be my rock; And exalted be the God of my salvation,
18:47 Ps 94:1; 47:3	47	The God who executes vengeance for me, And subdues peoples under me.
18:48 Ps 143:9; 27:6; 140:1,4	48	He delivers me from my enemies; Surely Thou dost lift me above those who rise up against me; Thou dost rescue me from the violent man.
18:49 Rom 15:9; Ps 108:1	49	Therefore I will give thanks to Thee among the nations, O LORD,

³⁰Lit., *twisted*   ³¹Or, *crush a troop*   ³²Or, *silenced*   ³³I.e., give feigned obedience

---

18:31 *rock.* In a symbolic sense, this word expresses the firm foundation of God.

18:33 *hinds' feet. Hind* is a female member of the deer family.

50   And I will sing praises to Thy name.
      He gives great ³⁴deliverance to His king,
      And shows lovingkindness to His anointed,
      To David and his descendants forever.

18:50
Ps 144:10;
28:8; 89:4,29

For the choir director. A Psalm of David.

I. *The works and Word of God (19:1–14)*

A. *The revelation of God in creation*

19   The heavens are telling of the glory of God;
         And their expanse is declaring the work of His hands.
2   Day to day pours forth speech,
         And night to night reveals knowledge.
3   There is no speech, nor are there words;
         Their voice is not heard.
4   Their ³⁵line has gone out through all the earth,
         And their utterances to the end of the world.
         In them He has placed a tent for the sun,
5   Which is as a bridegroom coming out of his chamber;
         It rejoices as a strong man to run his course.
6   Its rising is from one end of the heavens,
         And its circuit to the other end of them;
         And there is nothing hidden from its heat.

19:1
Gen 1:6;
Is 40:22;
Rom 1:19,20
19:2
Ps 74:16

19:4
Rom 10:18

19:5
Eccl 1:5

*19:6
Ps 113:3;
Deut 30:4

B. *The revelation of God in the Word of God*

7   The law of the LORD is ³⁶perfect, restoring the soul;
         The testimony of the LORD is sure, making wise the simple.
8   The precepts of the LORD are right, rejoicing the heart;
         The commandment of the LORD is pure, enlightening the eyes.
9   The fear of the LORD is clean, enduring forever;
         The judgments of the LORD are true; they are righteous altogether.
10   They are more desirable than gold, yes, than much fine gold;
         Sweeter also than honey and the drippings of the honeycomb.
11   Moreover, by them Thy servant is warned;
         In keeping them there is great reward.
12   Who can discern *his* errors? Acquit me of hidden *faults*.
13   Also keep back Thy servant from presumptuous *sins*;
         Let them not rule over me;
         Then I shall be ³⁷blameless,
         And I shall be acquitted of great transgression.
14   Let the words of my mouth and the meditation of my heart
         Be acceptable in Thy sight,
         O LORD, my rock and my Redeemer.

19:7
Ps 119:142;
23:3; 93:5;
111:7;
119:98-100
19:8
Ps 119:128;
12:6; 119:30
19:9
Ps 119:42
19:10
Prov 8:10;
16:24
19:11
Ps 17:4;
Prov 29:18
19:12
Ps 139:6;
51:1,2; 90:8
19:13
Ps 119:33;
32:2; 25:11
19:14
Ps 104:34;
18:2;
Is 41:14;
43:14

For the choir director. A Psalm of David.

I. *A liturgy for the king (20:1–9)*

A. *Prayer for victory*

20   May the LORD answer you in the day of trouble!
         May the name of the God of Jacob set you *securely* on high!
2   May He send you help from the sanctuary,
         And support you from Zion!
3   May He remember all your meal offerings,
         And find your burnt offering acceptable!   Selah.

4   May He grant you your heart's desire,

20:1
Ps 102:2;
91:14; 36:7,
11; 59:1
20:2
Ps 3:4;
119:28
20:3
Ps 51:19

20:4
Ps 21:2;
145:19

³⁴I.e., victories   ³⁵Another reading is *sound*   ³⁶I.e., blameless   ³⁷Lit., *complete*

19:6 *its circuit.* The sun appears to run a course from east to
west across the sky. Scripture does not teach that the sun
revolves around the earth.

And fulfill all your [38]counsel!

20:5
Ps 9:14;
1 Sam 1:17

5 We will sing for joy over your victory,
And in the name of our God we will set up our banners.
May the LORD fulfill all your petitions.

B. Assurance of divine help

20:6
Ps 41:11;
Is 58:9;
Ps 28:8

6 Now I know that the LORD saves His anointed;
He will answer him from His holy heaven,
With the saving strength of His right hand.

20:7
Is 36:9;
2 Chr 32:8

7 Some *boast* in chariots, and some in horses;
But we will boast in the name of the LORD, our God.

20:8
Ps 37:24

8 They have bowed down and fallen;
But we have risen and stood upright.

20:9
Ps 3:7

9 Save, O LORD;
May the King answer us in the day we call.

For the choir director. A Psalm of David.

I. Praise for deliverance (21:1–13)

A. Thanksgiving for past victories

21:1
Ps 59:16,17;
9:14

21

O LORD, in Thy strength the king will be glad,
And in Thy [39]salvation how greatly he will rejoice!

21:2
Ps 37:4

2 [Thou hast given him his heart's desire,
And Thou hast not withheld the request of his lips.]   Selah.

21:3
Ps 59:10

3 For Thou dost meet him with the blessings of good things;
Thou dost set a crown of fine gold on his head.

21:4
Ps 133:3;
91:16

4 He asked life of Thee,
Thou didst give it to him,
Length of days forever and ever.

21:5
Ps 18:50;
45:3,4

5 His glory is great through Thy [39]salvation,
Splendor and majesty Thou dost place upon him.

21:6
1 Chr 17:27;
Ps 16:11

6 For Thou dost make him most blessed forever;
Thou dost make him joyful with gladness in Thy presence.

21:7
2 Kin 18:5;
Ps 16:8

7 For the king trusts in the LORD,
And through the lovingkindness of the Most High he will not be
shaken.

B. Assurance of future victories

21:8
Is 10:10

8 Your hand will find out all your enemies;
Your right hand will find out those who hate you.

21:9
Mal 4:1;
Lam 2:2

9 You will make them as a fiery oven in the time of your anger;
The LORD will swallow them up in His wrath,
And fire will devour them.

21:10
Deut 28:18;
Ps 37:28

10 Their [40]offspring Thou wilt destroy from the earth,
And their [41]descendants from among the sons of men.

21:11
Ps 2:1-3; 10:2

11 Though they intended evil against Thee,
And devised a plot,
They will not succeed.

21:12
Ps 18:40;
7:12,13

12 For Thou wilt make them turn their back;
Thou wilt aim with Thy bowstrings at their faces.

21:13
Ps 57:5; 81:1

13 Be Thou exalted, O LORD, in Thy strength;
We will sing and praise Thy power.

---

[38]Or, *purpose*   [39]Or, *victory*   [40]Lit., *fruit*   [41]Lit., *seed*

For the choir director; upon [42]Aijeleth Hashshahar. A Psalm of David.

I. *The suffering and the glory of Messiah predicted*
(22:1–31)

A. *Forsaken of God*

22
My God, my God, why hast Thou forsaken me?
Far from my deliverance are the words of my groaning.

2 O my God, I cry by day, but Thou dost not answer;
And by night, but I have no rest.

3 Yet Thou art holy,
O Thou who art enthroned upon the praises of Israel.

4 In Thee our fathers trusted;
They trusted, and Thou didst deliver them.

5 To Thee they cried out, and were delivered;
In Thee they trusted, and were not disappointed.

B. *Scorned by men*

6 But I am a worm, and not a man,
A reproach of men, and despised by the people.

7 All who see me sneer at me;
They [43]separate with the lip, they wag the head, *saying,*

8 "[44]Commit *yourself* to the LORD; let Him deliver him;
Let Him rescue him, because He delights in him."

9 Yet Thou art He who didst bring me forth from the womb;
Thou didst make me trust *when* upon my mother's breasts.

10 Upon Thee I was cast from birth;
Thou hast been my God from my mother's womb.

11 Be not far from me, for trouble is near;
For there is none to help.

C. *Encompassed by animals*

12 Many bulls have surrounded me;
Strong *bulls* of Bashan have encircled me.

13 They open wide their mouth at me,
As a ravening and a roaring lion.

14 I am poured out like water,
And all my bones are out of joint;
My heart is like wax;
It is melted within me.

15 My strength is dried up like a potsherd,
And my tongue cleaves to my jaws;
And Thou dost lay me in the dust of death.

D. *They pierce his hands; they cast lots for his raiment*

16 For dogs have surrounded me;
A band of evildoers has encompassed me;
They pierced my hands and my feet.

17 I can count all my bones.
They look, they stare at me;

18 They divide my garments among them,
And for my clothing they cast lots.

---

[42]Lit., *the hind of the morning*   [43]I.e., make mouths at me   [44]Another reading is *He committed* himself

---

Margin references:

*22:1 Matt 27:46; Ps 10:1
22:2 Ps 42:3
22:3 Ps 99:9; 35:8
David remembers God's faithfulness in the past.
22:5 Ps 107:6; 25:2,3; Rom 9:33
*22:6 Job 25:6; Is 41:14; Ps 31:11; Is 49:7
People scorned David because of his trust in God.
22:7 Matt 27:39; Mark 15:29
22:8 Matt 27:43; Mark 1:11
22:9 Ps 71:6
22:10 Is 46:3
22:11 Ps 72:12
22:12 Ps 68:30; Deut 32:14
22:13 Ps 35:21; 17:12
22:14 Job 30:16; Ps 31:10; 107:26
22:15 Ps 38:10; 137:6; 104:29
22:16 Ps 59:6; Matt 27:35
22:18 Matt 27:35

22:1 In language that expresses the thoughts of God's suffering people of all ages, Psalm 22 prophetically sets forth Christ's agonizing emotions on the cross. Verses 14–17 are graphic representations of the suffering He endured through crucifixion. Moreover, two specific details are foretold in this psalm. In v. 1 the fourth saying of Christ on the cross is enunciated for the first time (Matt. 27:46). In v. 18 the prophecy of the soldiers casting lots over Christ's seamless robe is foretold (Matt. 27:35; Luke 23:34; John 19:23,24).

22:6 A *worm* is trodden underfoot and treated with contempt.

E. *His prayer for deliverance*

19 But Thou, O LORD, be not far off;
O Thou my help, hasten to my assistance.

20 Deliver my soul from the sword,
My only *life* from the power of the dog.

21 Save me from the lion's mouth;
And from the horns of the wild oxen Thou dost answer me.

F. *Praise to the LORD*

22 I will tell of Thy name to my brethren;
In the midst of the assembly I will praise Thee.

23 You who fear the LORD, praise Him;
All you descendants of Jacob, glorify Him,
And stand in awe of Him, all you descendants of Israel.

24 For He has not despised nor abhorred the affliction of the afflicted;
Neither has He hidden His face from him;
But when he cried to Him for help, He heard.

25 From Thee *comes* my praise in the great assembly;
I shall pay my vows before those who fear Him.

G. *Salvation offered to all*

26 The [45]afflicted shall eat and be satisfied;
Those who seek Him will praise the LORD.
Let your heart live forever!

27 All the ends of the earth will remember and turn to the LORD,
And all the families of the nations will worship before Thee.

28 For the kingdom is the LORD's,
And He rules over the nations.

29 All the prosperous of the earth will eat and worship,
All those who go down to the dust will bow before Him,
Even he who cannot keep his soul alive.

30 Posterity will serve Him;
It will be told of the Lord to the *coming* generation.

31 They will come and will declare His righteousness
To a people who will be born, that He has performed *it*.

A Psalm of David.

I. *The LORD my shepherd (23:1–6)*

A. *He feeds and guides His sheep*

23
The LORD is my shepherd,
I shall not want.

2 He makes me lie down in green pastures;
He leads me beside quiet waters.

3 He restores my soul;
He guides me in the paths of righteousness
For His name's sake.

4 Even though I walk through the [46]valley of the shadow of death,
I fear no [47]evil; for Thou art with me;
Thy rod and Thy staff, they comfort me.

B. *He is host to His people forever*

5 Thou dost prepare a table before me in the presence of my enemies;
Thou hast anointed my head with oil;
My cup overflows.

Marginal references (left column):

22:19 — v. 11; Ps 70:5
22:20 — Ps 35:17
22:21 — v. 13; Ps 34:4
22:22 — Heb 2:12
22:23 — Ps 135:19; 86:12; 33:8
22:24 — Ps 102:17; 69:17; Heb 5:7
22:25 — Ps 35:18; 66:13
22:26 — Ps 107:9; 40:16; 69:32
22:27 — Ps 2:8; 86:9
22:28 — Ps 47:7,8; Matt 6:13
22:29 — Ps 47:7; Is 27:13; Ps 95:6
22:30 — Ps 102:28; 71:18
22:31 — Ps 78:6
*23:1 — Is 40:11; Jer 23:4; John 10:11; 1 Pet 2:25; Phil 4:19
23:2 — Ezek 34:14; Rev 7:17
23:3 — Ps 19:7; 5:8; 85:13; 143:11
23:4 — Ps 138:7; Job 3:5; Ps 27:1; Is 43:2
23:5 — Ps 78:19; 31:19; 92:10; 16:5

---

[45]Or, *poor*   [46]Or, *valley of deep darkness*   [47]Or, *harm*

23:1 This, the most famous of all the Psalms, has been
identified as Messianic, picturing Jesus as the *good shepherd*
(John 10:11) and the *great Shepherd* (Heb. 13:20).

6   Surely goodness and lovingkindness will follow me all the days of my
      life,
      And I will [48]dwell in the house of the LORD forever.

23:6
Ps 25:7,10;
27:4-6

A Psalm of David.

I. *Psalm to the King of glory (24:1–10)*

A. *The LORD the creator*

24   The earth is the LORD's, and [49]all it contains,
          The world, and those who dwell in it.
2   For He has founded it upon the seas,
          And established it upon the rivers.

24:1
Ex 9:29;
Job 41:11;
1 Cor 10:26;
Ps 89:11

B. *The character of the LORD's people*

3   Who may ascend into the hill of the LORD?
          And who may stand in His holy place?
4   He who has clean hands and a pure heart,
          Who has not lifted up his soul to falsehood,
          And has not sworn deceitfully.
5   He shall receive a blessing from the LORD
          And righteousness from the God of his salvation.
6   This is the generation of those who seek Him,
          Who seek Thy face—*even* Jacob.   Selah.

24:3
Ps 15:1; 2:6;
65:4
24:4
Job 17:9;
Matt 5:8;
Ps 15:4
24:5
Deut 11:26,
27; Is 46:13;
Ps 25:5
24:6
Ps 27:8

C. *The entry of the King of glory*

7   Lift up your heads, O gates,
          And be lifted up, O [50]ancient doors,
          That the King of glory may come in!
8   Who is the King of glory?
          The LORD strong and mighty,
          The LORD mighty in battle.
9   Lift up your heads, O gates,
          And lift *them* up, O [50]ancient doors,
          That the King of glory may come in!
10   Who is this King of glory?
          The LORD of hosts,
          He is the King of glory.   Selah.

24:7
Is 26:2;
1 Cor 2:8
24:8
Ps 89:13;
76:3-6
24:9
Zech 9:9;
Matt 21:5

A Psalm of David.

I. *Prayer for guidance and protection (25:1–22)*

A. *God's way sought*

25   To Thee, O LORD, I lift up my soul.
2   O my God, in Thee I trust,
          Do not let me be ashamed;
          Do not let my enemies exult over me.
3   Indeed, none of those who wait for Thee will be ashamed;
          Those who deal treacherously without cause will be ashamed.

4   Make me know Thy ways, O LORD;
          Teach me Thy paths.
5   Lead me in Thy truth and teach me,
          For Thou art the God of my salvation;
          For Thee I wait all the day.

25:1
Ps 86:4
25:2
Ps 31:6;
41:11
25:3
Is 49:23; 33:1
*25:4
Ps 5:8; 86:11
25:5
John 16:13;
Ps 24:5; 40:1

[48]Another reading is *return to*   [49]Lit., *its fulness*   [50]Lit., *everlasting*

25:4 Scripture everywhere affirms that God has a perfect will for every believer. Here, and in v. 5, David, whose trust is in God, prays that God will reveal that will to him. Then he exclaims triumphantly that God will guide him in the way he should go (vv. 9,10). This truth is set forth in Is. 30:20,21 and Col. 1:9. Romans 12:2 implies that a total self-surrender will enable the believer to experience God's perfect will for his life.

6 Remember, O LORD, Thy compassion and Thy lovingkindnesses,
   For they have been [51]from of old.
7 Do not remember the sins of my youth or my transgressions;
   According to Thy lovingkindness remember Thou me,
   For Thy goodness' sake, O LORD.

B. God's way made plain

8 Good and upright is the LORD;
   Therefore He instructs sinners in the way.
9 He leads the humble in justice,
   And He teaches the humble His way.
10 All the paths of the LORD are lovingkindness and truth
   To those who keep His covenant and His testimonies.
11 For Thy name's sake, O LORD,
   Pardon my iniquity, for it is great.

12 Who is the man who fears the LORD?
   He will instruct him in the way he should choose.
13 His soul will abide in prosperity,
   And his [52]descendants will inherit the land.
14 The secret of the LORD is for those who fear Him,
   And He will make them know His covenant.
15 My eyes are continually toward the LORD,
   For He will pluck my feet out of the net.

C. Prayer for deliverance

16 Turn to me and be gracious to me,
   For I am lonely and afflicted.
17 The troubles of my heart are enlarged;
   Bring me out of my distresses.
18 Look upon my affliction and my [53]trouble,
   And forgive all my sins.
19 Look upon my enemies, for they are many;
   And they hate me with violent hatred.
20 Guard my soul and deliver me;
   Do not let me be ashamed, for I take refuge in Thee.
21 Let integrity and uprightness preserve me,
   For I wait for Thee.
22 Redeem Israel, O God,
   Out of all his troubles.

A Psalm of David.

I. A plea for vindication (26:1–12)

A. Prayer for divine help

26

1 [54]Vindicate me, O LORD, for I have walked in my integrity;
   And I have trusted in the LORD without wavering.
2 Examine me, O LORD, and try me;
   Test my [55]mind and my heart.
3 For Thy lovingkindness is before my eyes,
   And I have walked in Thy truth.

B. David's defense of himself

4 I do not sit with [56]deceitful men,
   Nor will I go with pretenders.

Marginal references:

25:6 Ps 103:17; Is 63:15
25:7 Job 13:26; Jer 3:25; Ps 51:1
25:8 Ps 106:1; 92:15; 32:8
25:9 Ps 23:3; 27:11
25:10 Ps 40:11; 103:18
25:11 Ps 31:1; Rom 5:20
25:13 Prov 19:23; Ps 37:11
25:14 Prov 3:32; John 7:17
25:15 Ps 141:8
25:16 Ps 69:16
25:17 Ps 88:3; 107:6
25:18 2 Sam 16:12
25:19 Ps 3:1; 27:12
25:20 Ps 86:2
25:21 Ps 41:12; v. 3
25:22 Ps 130:8
*26:1 Ps 7:8; Prov 20:7; Ps 25:2; Heb 10:23
26:2 Ps 7:9; 66:10
26:3 2 Kin 20:3
26:4 Ps 1:1

[51]Lit., *everlasting* [52]Lit., *seed* [53]Lit., *toil* [54]Lit., *Judge* [55]Lit., *kidneys,* figurative for inner man [56]Or, *worthless*

26:1 False accusations, slander, and defamation are the lot of those who seek to serve God. In Matt. 5:11 and John 15:20 Jesus warned His disciples to expect this kind of treatment. David here appeals to the judgment of God over against the judgment of men, and is willing to let God examine and prove him, confident that his prayer is heard and he is safe.

5	I hate the assembly of evildoers, And I will not sit with the wicked.
6	I shall wash my hands in innocence, And I will go about Thine altar, O Lord,
7	That I may proclaim with the voice of thanksgiving, And declare all Thy wonders.

26:5
 Ps 139:21;
 1:1
 26:6
 Ps 73:13
 26:7
 Ps 35:18; 9:1

C. *His final plea for help*

8	O Lord, I love the habitation of Thy house, And the place where Thy glory dwells.
9	Do not take my soul away *along* with sinners, Nor my life with men of bloodshed,
10	In whose hands is a wicked scheme, And whose right hand is full of bribes.
11	But as for me, I shall walk in my integrity; Redeem me, and be gracious to me.
12	My foot stands on a level place; In the congregations I shall bless the Lord.

26:8
 Ps 27:4
 26:9
 Ps 28:3
 26:10
 1 Sam 8:3
 26:11
 v. 1; Ps 69:18
 26:12
 Ps 40:2;
 27:11; 22:22

A Psalm of David.

I. *David's song of confidence (27:1–6)*

27	The Lord is my light and my salvation; Whom shall I fear? The Lord is the defense of my life; Whom shall I dread?
2	When evildoers came upon me to devour my flesh, My adversaries and my enemies, they stumbled and fell.
3	Though a host encamp against me, My heart will not fear; Though war arise against me, In *spite of* this I shall be confident.
4	One thing I have asked from the Lord, that I shall seek: That I may dwell in the house of the Lord all the days of my life, To behold the [57]beauty of the Lord, And to [58]meditate in His temple.
5	For in the day of trouble He will conceal me in His tabernacle; In the secret place of His tent He will hide me; He will lift me up on a rock.
6	And now my head will be lifted up above my enemies around me; And I will offer in His tent sacrifices with shouts of joy; I will sing, yes, I will sing praises to the Lord.

27:1
 Is 60:19;
 Ex 15:2;
 Ps 62:2
 27:2
 Ps 14:4
 27:3
 Ps 3:6
 27:4
 Ps 26:8;
 90:17
 27:5
 Ps 31:20;
 40:2
 27:6
 Ps 3:3

II. *David's prayer for help (27:7–14)*

7	Hear, O Lord, when I cry with my voice, And be gracious to me and answer me.
8	*When Thou didst say*, "Seek My face," my heart said to Thee, "Thy face, O Lord, I shall seek."
9	Do not hide Thy face from me, Do not turn Thy servant away in anger; Thou hast been my help; Do not abandon me nor forsake me, O God of my salvation!
10	For my father and my mother have forsaken me, But the Lord will take me up.
11	Teach me Thy way, O Lord, And lead me in a level path, Because of my foes.
12	Do not deliver me over to the desire of my adversaries;

27:7
 Ps 39:12;
 13:3
 27:8
 Ps 24:6
 27:9
 Ps 69:17
 27:10
 Is 49:15;
 40:11
 27:11
 Ps 25:4;
 86:11; 5:8
 27:12
 Ps 41:2;
 35:11;

[57]Lit., *delightfulness*   [58]Lit., *inquire*

Matt 26:60 Acts 9:1	For false witnesses have risen against me, And such as breathe out violence.
27:13 Ps 31:19; Jer 11:19	13 *I would have despaired* unless I had believed that I would see the goodness of the LORD In the land of the living.
27:14 Ps 40:1; Josh 1:6	14 Wait for the LORD; Be strong, and let your heart take courage; Yes, wait for the LORD.

A Psalm of David.

I. *The prayer for help (28:1–5)*

28:1 Ps 83:1; 88:4	**28** To Thee, O LORD, I call; My rock, do not be deaf to me, Lest, if Thou be silent to me, I become like those who go down to the pit.
28:2 Ps 140:6; 5:7; 138:2	2 Hear the voice of my supplications when I cry to Thee for help, When I lift up my hands toward [59]Thy holy sanctuary.
28:3 Ps 26:9; 12:2; Jer 9:8	3 Do not drag me away with the wicked And with those who work iniquity; Who speak peace with their neighbors, While evil is in their hearts.
28:4 Rev 18:6	4 Requite them according to their work and according to the evil of their practices; Requite them according to the deeds of their hands; Repay them their [60]recompense.
28:5 Is 5:12	5 Because they do not regard the works of the LORD Nor the deeds of His hands, He will tear them down and not build them up.

II. *The assurance of an answer (28:6–9)*

28:6 Ps 116:1	**6** Blessed be the LORD, Because He has heard the voice of my supplication.
28:7 Ps 18:2; 13:5	7 The LORD is my strength and my shield; My heart trusts in Him, and I am helped; Therefore my heart exults, And with my song I shall thank Him.
28:8 Ps 20:6	8 The LORD is their strength, And He is a saving defense to His anointed.
28:9 Deut 9:29; Ezra 1:4	9 Save Thy people, and bless Thine inheritance; Be their shepherd also, and carry them forever.

A Psalm of David.

I. *The LORD of the thunderstorm (29:1–11)*

A. *Summons to give glory to God*

29:1 1 Chr 16:28, 29; Ps 96:7-9	**29** Ascribe to the LORD, O sons of the mighty, Ascribe to the LORD glory and strength.
29:2 2 Chr 20:21	2 Ascribe to the LORD the glory due to His name; Worship the LORD in holy array.

B. *God's power in the storm*

29:3 Job 37:4,5	**3** The voice of the LORD is upon the waters; The God of glory thunders, The LORD is over many waters.
29:4 Ps 68:33	4 The voice of the LORD is powerful, The voice of the LORD is majestic.
29:5 Is 2:13	5 The voice of the LORD breaks the cedars;

[59]Lit., *the innermost place of Thy sanctuary*   [60]Or, *dealings*

Yes, the LORD breaks in pieces the cedars of Lebanon.

6   And He makes Lebanon skip like a calf,
        And Sirion like a young wild ox.

7   The voice of the LORD hews out flames of fire.

8   The voice of the LORD shakes the wilderness;
        The LORD shakes the wilderness of Kadesh.

9   The voice of the LORD makes the deer to calve,
        And strips the forests bare,
        And in His temple everything says, "Glory!"

C. Prayer for the blessing of the LORD of the storm

10   The LORD sat *as King* at the flood;
        Yes, the LORD sits as King forever.

11   The LORD will give strength to His people;
        The LORD will bless His people with peace.

A Psalm; a Song at the Dedication of the House. *A Psalm* of David.

I. Song of deliverance (30:1–12)

A. Praise for deliverance

30   I will extol Thee, O LORD, for Thou hast lifted me up,
         And hast not let my enemies rejoice over me.

2   O LORD my God,
         I cried to Thee for help, and Thou didst heal me.

3   O LORD, Thou hast brought up my soul from Sheol;
         Thou hast kept me alive, that I should not go down to the pit.

B. Exhortation for others to praise the LORD

4   Sing praise to the LORD, you His godly ones,
         And give thanks to His holy name.

5   For His anger is but for a moment,
         His favor is for a lifetime;
         Weeping may last for the night,
         But a shout of joy *comes* in the morning.

6   Now as for me, I said in my prosperity,
         "I will never be moved."

7   O LORD, by Thy favor Thou hast made my mountain to stand
             strong;
         Thou didst hide Thy face, I was dismayed.

8   To Thee, O LORD, I called,
         And to the LORD I made supplication:

9   "What profit is there in my blood, if I go down to the pit?
         Will the dust praise Thee? Will it declare Thy faithfulness?

10   "Hear, O LORD, and be gracious to me;
         O LORD, be Thou my helper."

11   Thou hast turned for me my mourning into dancing;
         Thou hast loosed my sackcloth and girded me with gladness;

12   That *my* soul may sing praise to Thee, and not be silent.
         O LORD my God, I will give thanks to Thee forever.

For the choir director. A Psalm of David.

I. "My times are in thy hands" (31:1–24)

A. Trust in God and prayer for deliverance

31   In Thee, O LORD, I have taken refuge;
         Let me never be ashamed;

30:4 *His godly ones*, i.e., his pious ones.

Marginal references:

29:6
Ps 114:4;
Deut 3:9

29:8
Num 13:26

29:9
Ps 26:8

29:10
Ps 10:16

29:11
Ps 28:8;
37:11

30:1
Ps 28:9; 25:2

30:2
Ps 88:13; 6:2

30:3
Ps 86:13;
28:1

*30:4
Ps 149:1;
50:5; 97:12
30:5
Ps 103:9;
63:3

30:7
Ps 104:29

30:9
Ps 6:5

30:11
Ps 6:8;
Jer 31:4,13;
Ps 4:7
30:12
Ps 16:9; 44:8

31:1
Ps 22:5;
Is 49:23

| | 2 | In Thy righteousness deliver me. |

*31:2
Ps 71:2

2 Incline Thine ear to me, rescue me quickly;
Be Thou to me a rock of strength,
A stronghold to save me.

31:3
Ps 18:2; 23:3

3 For Thou art my rock and my fortress;
For Thy name's sake Thou wilt lead me and guide me.

31:4
Ps 25:15;
28:8

4 Thou wilt pull me out of the net which they have secretly laid
for me;
For Thou art my strength.

31:5
Luke 23:46;
Acts 7:59

5 Into Thy hand I commit my spirit;
Thou hast ransomed me, O LORD, God of truth.

31:6
Jon 2:8

6 I hate those who regard vain idols;
But I trust in the LORD.

31:7
Ps 90:14;
10:14;
John 10:27

7 I will rejoice and be glad in Thy lovingkindness,
Because Thou hast seen my affliction;
Thou hast known the troubles of my soul,

31:8
Deut 32:30;
Ps 4:1

8 And Thou hast not given me over into the hand of the enemy;
Thou hast set my feet in a large place.

B. *Complaints that require deliverance*

31:9
Ps 6:7

9 Be gracious to me, O LORD, for I am in distress;
My eye is wasted away from grief, my soul and my body *also*.

31:10
Ps 13:2;
39:11; 38:3

10 For my life is spent with sorrow,
And my years with sighing;
My strength has failed because of my iniquity,
And my body has wasted away.

31:11
Is 53:4;
Ps 38:11;
64:8

11 Because of all my adversaries, I have become a reproach,
Especially to my neighbors,
And an object of dread to my acquaintances;
Those who see me in the street flee from me.

31:12
Ps 88:4,5

12 I am forgotten as a dead man, out of mind,
I am like a broken vessel.

31:13
Jer 20:10;
Lam 2:20;
Matt 27:1

13 For I have heard the slander of many,
Terror is on every side;
While they took counsel together against me,
They schemed to take away my life.

31:14
Ps 140:6

14 But as for me, I trust in Thee, O LORD,
I say, "Thou art my God."

31:15
Job 24:1;
Ps 143:9

15 My times are in Thy hand;
Deliver me from the hand of my enemies, and from those who
persecute me.

31:16
Num 6:25;
Ps 4:6

16 Make Thy face to shine upon Thy servant;
Save me in Thy lovingkindness.

31:17
Ps 25:2,3

17 Let me not be put to shame, O LORD, for I call upon Thee;
Let the wicked be put to shame, let them be silent in Sheol.

31:18
Ps 120:2;
94:4

18 Let the lying lips be dumb,
Which speak arrogantly against the righteous
With pride and contempt.

C. *Praise to a delivering LORD*

31:19
Is 64:4;
Rom 11:22;
Ps 5:11

19 How great is Thy goodness,
Which Thou hast stored up for those who fear Thee,
Which Thou hast wrought for those who take refuge in Thee,
Before the sons of men!

31:20
Ps 27:5;
Job 5:21

20 Thou dost hide them in the secret place of Thy presence from the
conspiracies of man;
Thou dost keep them secretly in a shelter from the strife of tongues.

31:21
Ps 17:7;
1 Sam 23:7

21 Blessed be the LORD,
For He has made marvelous His lovingkindness to me in a besieged
city.

31:2 *rock*, i.e., strength and impregnability.

22	As for me, I said in my alarm, "I am cut off from before Thine eyes"; Nevertheless Thou didst hear the voice of my supplications When I cried to Thee.	**31:22** Ps 116:11; Lam 3:54
23	O love the LORD, all you His godly ones! The LORD preserves the faithful, And fully recompenses the proud doer.	**31:23** Ps 34:9; 145:20; 94:2
24	Be strong, and let your heart take courage, All you who hope in the LORD.	**31:24** Ps 27:14

A Psalm of David. A[61]*Maskil.*

I. *The penitent's psalm (32:1–11)*

A. *The blessedness of the forgiven*

32 2	How blessed is he whose transgression is forgiven, Whose sin is covered! How blessed is the man to whom the LORD does not impute iniquity, And in whose spirit there is no deceit!	**32:1** Ps 85:2 **32:2** 2 Cor 5:19; John 1:47

B. *Sin confessed and forgiven*

3 4	When I kept silent *about my sin*, my body wasted away Through my groaning all day long. For day and night Thy hand was heavy upon me; My vitality was drained away *as* with the fever heat of summer. Selah.	**32:3** Ps 39:2,3; 31:10; 38:8 **32:4** Job 33:7
5	I acknowledged my sin to Thee, And my iniquity I did not hide; I said, "I will confess my transgressions to the LORD"; And Thou didst forgive the guilt of my sin. Selah.	**32:5** Lev 26:40; Job 31:33; Prov 28:13; Ps 103:12
6	Therefore, let everyone who is godly pray to Thee in a time when Thou mayest be found; Surely in a flood of great waters they shall not reach him.	**32:6** Ps 69:13; 144:7; Is 43:2
7	Thou art my hiding place; Thou dost preserve me from trouble; Thou dost surround me with songs of deliverance. Selah.	**32:7** Ps 31:20; 121:7; Ex 15:1

C. *Exhortation to sinners to repent*

8 9	I will instruct you and teach you in the way which you should go; I will counsel you with My eye upon you. Do not be as the horse or as the mule which have no understanding, Whose trappings include bit and bridle to hold them in check, *Otherwise* they will not come near to you.	**32:8** Ps 25:8; 33:18 **32:9** James 3:3
10	Many are the sorrows of the wicked; But he who trusts in the LORD, lovingkindness shall surround him.	**32:10** Rom 2:9; Prov 16:20
11	Be glad in the LORD and rejoice, you righteous ones, And shout for joy, all you who are upright in heart.	**32:11** Ps 64:10

I. *Praise to the LORD who provides and delivers (33:1–22)*

A. *Exhortation to praise the LORD*

33 2	Sing for joy in the LORD, O you righteous ones; Praise is becoming to the upright. Give thanks to the LORD with the lyre; Sing praises to Him with a harp of ten strings.	**33:1** Ps 32:11; 147:1 **33:2** Ps 92:3
3	Sing to Him a new song; Play skillfully with a shout of joy.	**33:3** Ps 96:1; 98:4

[61]Possibly, *Contemplative* or *Didactic*, or *Skillful Psalm*

B. *Reasons for praising the* LORD

1. He is the LORD *the creator*

33:4 Ps 19:8; 119:90	4	For the word of the LORD is upright; And all His work is *done* in faithfulness.
33:5 Ps 11:7; 119:64	5	He loves righteousness and justice; The earth is full of the lovingkindness of the LORD.
33:6 Gen 11:3; Job 23:13	**6**	By the word of the LORD the heavens were made, And by the breath of His mouth all their host.
33:7 Ps 78:13	7	He gathers the waters of the sea together as a heap; He lays up the deeps in storehouses.
33:8 Ps 67:7; 96:9	8	Let all the earth fear the LORD; Let all the inhabitants of the world stand in awe of Him.
33:9 Gen 1:3; Ps 148:5	9	For He spoke, and it was done; He commanded, and it stood fast.

2. He is the LORD *of providence*

33:10 Is 8:10; 19:3	10	The LORD nullifies the counsel of the nations; He frustrates the plans of the peoples.
33:11 Job 23:13; Prov 19:21; Ps 40:5	11	The counsel of the LORD stands forever, The plans of His heart from generation to generation.
33:12 Ps 144:15; Ex 19:5; Deut 7:6	12	Blessed is the nation whose God is the LORD, The people whom He has chosen for His own inheritance.
33:13 Job 28:24; Ps 11:4	**13**	The LORD looks from heaven; He sees all the sons of men;
	14	From His dwelling place He looks out On all the inhabitants of the earth,
33:15 Jer 32:19	15	He who fashions the hearts of them all, He who understands all their works.
33:16 Ps 44:6	16	The king is not saved by a mighty army; A warrior is not delivered by great strength.
33:17 Ps 20:7; Prov 21:31	17	A horse is a false hope for victory; Nor does it deliver anyone by its great strength.

3. He is the deliverer of His people

33:18 Job 36:7; Ps 34:15; 147:11	**18**	Behold, the eye of the LORD is on those who fear Him, On those who hope for His lovingkindness,
33:19 Ps 37:19	19	To deliver their soul from death, And to keep them alive in famine.
33:20 Ps 130:6; 115:9	20	Our soul waits for the LORD; He is our help and our shield.
33:21 Zech 10:7; John 16:22	21	For our heart rejoices in Him, Because we trust in His holy name.
	22	Let Thy lovingkindness, O LORD, be upon us, According as we have hoped in Thee.

A Psalm of David when he feigned madness before Abimelech, who drove him away
and he departed.

I. *A psalm of praise and trust (34:1-22)*

A. *Praise for God's goodness*

34:1 Eph 5:20; Ps 71:6	**34**	I will bless the LORD at all times; His praise shall continually be in my mouth.
34:2 Jer 9:24; Ps 119:74	2	My soul shall make its boast in the LORD; The humble shall hear it and rejoice.
34:3 Luke 1:46	3	O magnify the LORD with me, And let us exalt His name together.
34:4 Matt 7:7; vv. 6,17,19	**4**	I sought the LORD, and He answered me, And delivered me from all my fears.
34:5 Ps 36:9; 25:3	5	They looked to Him and were radiant,

6   And their faces shall never be ashamed.
    This poor man cried and the LORD heard him,
    And saved him out of all his troubles.

34:6
vv. 4,17,19

B. *Exhortation to trust and seek the* LORD

7   The angel of the LORD encamps around those who fear Him,
    And rescues them.

34:7
Dan 6:22;
2 Kin 6:17

8   O taste and see that the LORD is good;
    How blessed is the man who takes refuge in Him!

34:8
1 Pet 2:3;
Ps 2:12

9   O fear the LORD, you His saints;
    For to those who fear Him, there is no want.

34:9
Ps 23:1

10 The young lions do lack and suffer hunger;
    But they who seek the LORD shall not be in want of any good thing.

34:10
Ps 84:11

C. *Warning against sin*

11 Come, you children, listen to me;
    I will teach you the fear of the LORD.

34:11
Ps 111:10

12 Who is the man who desires life,
    And loves *length of* days that he may see good?

34:12
1 Pet 3:10

13 Keep your tongue from evil,
    And your lips from speaking deceit.

34:13
1 Pet 2:22

14 Depart from evil, and do good;
    Seek peace, and pursue it.

34:14
Ps 37:27;
Heb 12:14

D. *The righteous delivered: the wicked condemned*

15 The eyes of the LORD are toward the righteous,
    And His ears are *open* to their cry.

34:15
Job 36:7;
Ps 33:18

16 The face of the LORD is against evildoers,
    To cut off the memory of them from the earth.

34:16
Jer 44:11;
Prov 10:7

17 *The righteous* cry and the LORD hears,
    And delivers them out of all their troubles.

34:17
Ps 145:19;
v. 19

18 The LORD is near to the brokenhearted,
    And saves those who are [62]crushed in spirit.

34:18
Ps 145:18;
Is 57:15

19 Many are the afflictions of the righteous;
    But the LORD delivers him out of them all.

34:19
Prov 24:16;
vv. 4,6,17

20 He keeps all his bones;
    Not one of them is broken.

34:20
John 19:36

21 Evil shall slay the wicked;
    And those who hate the righteous will be condemned.

34:21
Ps 94:23

22 The LORD redeems the soul of His servants;
    And none of those who take refuge in Him will be condemned.

34:22
1 Kin 1:29;
Ps 71:23

A Psalm of David.

I. *A prayer for help (35:1–28)*

A. *From persecution*

35
1   Contend, O LORD, with those who contend with me;
    Fight against those who fight against me.

35:1
Ps 43:1

2   Take hold of [63]buckler and shield,
    And rise up for my help.

3   Draw also the spear and the battle-axe to meet those who pursue me;
    Say to my soul, "I am your salvation."

35:3
Ps 62:2

4   Let those be ashamed and dishonored who seek my life;
    Let those be turned back and humiliated who devise evil against me.

35:4
Ps 70:2,3

5   Let them be like chaff before the wind,
    With the angel of the LORD driving *them* on.

35:5
Job 21:18;
Ps 1:4;
Is 29:5

6   Let their way be dark and slippery,
    With the angel of the LORD pursuing them.

35:6
Ps 73:18;
Jer 23:12

[62]Or, *contrite* [63]I.e., small shield

35:7 Ps 9:15	7	For without cause they hid their net for me; Without cause they dug a pit for my soul.
35:8 1 Thess 5:3	8	Let destruction come upon him unawares; And let the net which he hid catch himself; Into that very destruction let him fall.
35:9 Is 61:10; Luke 1:47	**9**	And my soul shall rejoice in the LORD; It shall exult in His salvation.
35:10 Ex 15:11; Ps 18:17; 37:14	10	All my bones will say, "LORD, who is like Thee, Who delivers the afflicted from him who is too strong for him, And the afflicted and the needy from him who robs him?"

B. *From slanderers*

35:11 Ps 27:12	11	Malicious witnesses rise up; They ask me of things that I do not know.
35:12 John 10:32	12	They repay me evil for good, *To* the bereavement of my soul.
35:13 Job 30:25; Ps 69:10	13	But as for me, when they were sick, my clothing was sackcloth; I humbled my soul with fasting; And my prayer kept returning to my bosom.
	14	I went about as though it were my friend or brother; I bowed down mourning, as one who sorrows for a mother.
35:15 Job 30:1,8	15	But at my [64]stumbling they rejoiced, and gathered themselves together; The smiters whom I did not know gathered together against me, They slandered me without ceasing.
35:16 Lam 2:16	16	Like godless jesters at a feast, They gnashed at me with their teeth.
35:17 Hab 1:13; Ps 22:20	**17**	Lord, how long wilt Thou look on? Rescue my soul from their ravages, My only *life* from the lions.
35:18 Ps 22:22,25	18	I will give Thee thanks in the great congregation; I will praise Thee among a mighty throng.

C. *From haters*

35:19 Ps 13:4; 38:19; Prov 6:13; Ps 69:4; John 15:25	19	Do not let those who are wrongfully my enemies rejoice over me; Neither let those who hate me without cause wink maliciously.
	20	For they do not speak peace, But they devise deceitful words against those who are quiet in the land.
35:21 Ps 22:13; 40:15	21	And they opened their mouth wide against me; They said, "Aha, aha, our eyes have seen it!"
35:22 Ex 3:7; Ps 28:1; 10:1	**22**	Thou hast seen it, O LORD, do not keep silent; O Lord, do not be far from me.
35:23 Ps 44:23	23	Stir up Thyself, and awake to my right, And to my cause, my God and my Lord.
35:24 Ps 9:4; v. 19	24	Judge me, O LORD my God, according to Thy righteousness; And do not let them rejoice over me.
35:25 Lam 2:16	25	Do not let them say in their heart, "Aha, our desire!" Do not let them say, "We have swallowed him up!"
35:26 Ps 40:14; 38:16	26	Let those be ashamed and humiliated altogether who rejoice at my distress; Let those be clothed with shame and dishonor who magnify themselves over me.
35:27 Ps 32:11; 9:4; 40:16; 147:11	**27**	Let them shout for joy and rejoice, who favor my vindication; And let them say continually, "The LORD be magnified, Who delights in the prosperity of His servant."
35:28 Ps 51:14	28	And my tongue shall declare Thy righteousness *And* Thy praise all day long.

64Or, *limping*

For the choir director. *A Psalm* of David the servant of the LORD.

I. *The sinfulness of sin (36:1–4)*

36 Transgression speaks to the ungodly within his heart;
There is no fear of God before his eyes.   **36:1** Rom 3:18

2 For it flatters him in his *own* eyes,
Concerning the discovery of his iniquity *and* the hatred *of it.*

3 The words of his mouth are wickedness and deceit;
He has ceased to be wise *and* to do good.   **36:3** Jer 4:22

4 He plans wickedness upon his bed;
He sets himself on a path that is not good;
He does not despise evil.   **36:4** Prov 4:16; Mic 2:1; Is 65:2

II. *The goodness and graciousness of God (36:5–12)*

5 Thy lovingkindness, O LORD, extends to the heavens,
Thy faithfulness *reaches* to the skies.

6 Thy righteousness is like the mountains of God;
Thy judgments are *like* a great deep.
O LORD, Thou preservest man and beast.   **36:6** Job 11:8; Ps 77:19; Rom 11:33

7 How precious is Thy lovingkindness, O God!
And the children of men take refuge in the shadow of Thy wings.   **36:7** Ruth 2:12

8 They drink their fill of the abundance of Thy house;
And Thou dost give them to drink of the river of Thy delights.   **36:8** Ps 65:4; Job 20:17; Rev 22:1

9 For with Thee is the fountain of life;
In Thy light we see light.   **36:9** Jer 2:13; 1 Pet 2:9

10 O continue Thy lovingkindness to those who know Thee,
And Thy righteousness to the upright in heart.

11 Let not the foot of pride come upon me,
And let not the hand of the wicked drive me away.

12 There the doers of iniquity have fallen;
They have been thrust down and cannot rise.   **36:12** Ps 140:10

A Psalm of David.

I. *The wisdom of an aged man (37:1–40)*

A. *The righteous will prosper: the wicked cut off*

37 Do not fret because of evildoers,
Be not envious toward wrongdoers.   **37:1** Ps 73:3; Prov 23:17

2 For they will wither quickly like the grass,
And fade like the green herb.   **37:2** Ps 90:5,6

3 Trust in the LORD, and do good;
Dwell in the land and [65]cultivate faithfulness.   **37:3** Ps 62:8; Deut 30:20; Is 40:11

4 Delight yourself in the LORD;
And He will give you the desires of your heart.   **37:4** Is 58:14

5 Commit your way to the LORD,
Trust also in Him, and He will do it.   *37:5 Ps 55:22; Prov 16:3; 1 Pet 5:7

6 And He will bring forth your righteousness as the light,
And your judgment as the noonday.   **37:6** Job 11:17; Mic 7:9

7 [66]Rest in the LORD and wait [67]patiently for Him;
Do not fret because of him who prospers in his way,
Because of the man who carries out wicked schemes.   **37:7** Ps 62:5; 40:1; vv. 1,8

8 Cease from anger, and forsake wrath;
Do not fret, *it leads* only to evildoing.   **37:8** Ps 73:3; Eph 4:26

9 For evildoers will be cut off,   **37:9** Is 60:21

[65]Or, *feed securely,* or, *feed on His faithfulness*   [66]Or, *Be still*   [67]Or, *longingly*

37:5 Anxiety or care is a form of sin in the believer. We are earnestly warned against it (Luke 21:34). Anxiety about earthly things is forbidden (Matt. 6:25: Luke 12:22,29; John 6:27), and may be conquered by: (1) trusting in God (Jer. 17:7,8; Dan. 3:15–18); (2) casting care upon God (55:22; Prov. 16:3; 1 Pet. 5:7); (3) claiming the promises of God (Heb. 13:6); and (4) thanking Him in advance for His answer to prayer (Phil. 4:6).

37:10 Job 24:24; 7:10 **37:11** Matt 5:5	10 11	But those who wait for the LORD, they will inherit the land. Yet a little while and the wicked man will be no more; And you will look carefully for his place, and he will not be *there*. But the humble will inherit the land, And will delight themselves in abundant prosperity.

B. *The comparison between the wicked and the righteous*

37:12 Ps 35:16	**12**	The wicked plots against the righteous, And gnashes at him with his teeth.
37:13 Ps 2:4; 1 Sam 26:10 **37:14** Ps 11:2; 35:10	13 14	The Lord laughs at him; For He sees his day is coming. The wicked have drawn the sword and bent their bow, To cast down the afflicted and the needy, To slay those who are upright in conduct.
37:15 Ps 9:16	15	Their sword will enter their own heart, And their bows will be broken.
37:16 Prov 15:16	**16**	Better is the little of the righteous Than the abundance of many wicked.
37:17 Job 38:15; Ps 10:15 **37:18** Ps 1:6	17 18	For the arms of the wicked will be broken; But the LORD sustains the righteous. The LORD knows the days of the blameless; And their inheritance will be forever.
37:19 Job 5:20; Ps 33:19 **37:20** Ps 72:27; 102:3	19 20	They will not be ashamed in the time of evil; And in the days of famine they will have abundance. But the wicked will perish; And the enemies of the LORD will be like the [68]glory of the pastures, They vanish—like smoke they vanish away.
37:21 Ps 112:5,9	21	The wicked borrows and does not pay back, But the righteous is gracious and gives.
37:22 Prov 3:33; Job 5:3	22	For those blessed by Him will inherit the land; But those cursed by Him will be cut off.

C. *The sure deliverance and security of the righteous*

37:23 1 Sam 2:9; Ps 147:11 **37:24** Prov 24:16; Ps 147:6 *37:25 Heb 13:5; Job 15:23	**23** 24 25	The steps of a man are established by the LORD; And He delights in his way. When he falls, he shall not be hurled headlong; Because the LORD is the One who holds his hand. I have been young, and now I am old; Yet I have not seen the righteous forsaken, Or his descendants begging bread.
37:26 v. 21; Ps 147:13	26	All day long he is gracious and lends; And his descendants are a blessing.
37:27 Ps 34:14; v. 18 **37:28** Ps 11:7; 21:10; Is 14:20	**27** 28	Depart from evil, and do good, So you will abide forever. For the LORD loves justice, And does not forsake His godly ones; They are preserved forever; But the descendants of the wicked will be cut off.
37:29 vv. 9,18	29	The righteous will inherit the land, And dwell in it forever.
37:30 Matt 12:35	30	The mouth of the righteous utters wisdom, And his tongue speaks justice.
37:31 Ps 40:8; Is 51:7; v. 23 **37:32** Ps 10:8	31 32	The law of his God is in his heart; His steps do not slip. The wicked spies upon the righteous, And seeks to kill him.

[68] I.e., flowers

37:25 Scripture abounds with promises for the supply of the material needs of God's people (e.g., Eph. 3:20; Phil. 4:19). What we *think* we need may differ from what God *knows* we need. Depending on his gifts and circumstances, the quantity for each believer varies. But every believer may claim God's promises for that legitimate supply he may secure from God in his particular situation.

33	The LORD will not leave him in his hand, Or let him be condemned when he is judged.	37:33 2 Pet 2:9; Ps 109:31
34	Wait for the LORD, and keep His way, And He will exalt you to inherit the land; When the wicked are cut off, you will see it.	37:34 Ps 27:14; 52:5,6
35	I have seen a violent, wicked man Spreading himself like a luxuriant tree in its native soil.	37:35 Job 5:3
36	Then he passed away, and lo, he was no more; I sought for him, but he could not be found.	37:36 Job 20:5
37	Mark the blameless man, and behold the upright; For the man of peace will have a posterity.	37:37 Is 57:1,2
38	But transgressors will be altogether destroyed; The posterity of the wicked will be cut off.	37:38 Ps 1:4; vv. 9, 20,28
39	But the salvation of the righteous is from the LORD; He is their strength in time of trouble.	37:39 Ps 3:8; 9:9
40	And the LORD helps them, and delivers them; He delivers them from the wicked, and saves them, Because they take refuge in Him.	37:40 Is 31:5; 1 Chr 5:20

A Psalm of David, for a memorial.

I. *The penitent's plea for mercy (38:1–22)*

A. *The extremity of his condition*

38	O LORD, rebuke me not in Thy wrath; And chasten me not in Thy burning anger.	38:1 Ps 6:1
2	For Thine arrows have sunk deep into me, And Thy hand has pressed down on me.	38:2 Job 6:4; Ps 32:4
3	There is no soundness in my flesh because of Thine indignation; There is no health in my bones because of my sin.	38:3 Is 1:6; Ps 6:2
4	For my iniquities are gone over my head; As a heavy burden they weigh too much for me.	38:4 Ezra 9:6
5	My wounds grow foul *and* fester. Because of my folly,	38:5 Ps 69:5
6	I am bent over and greatly bowed down; I go mourning all day long.	38:6 Ps 35:14; 42:9
7	For my loins are filled with burning; And there is no soundness in my flesh.	38:7 Ps 102:3; v. 3
8	I am benumbed and badly crushed; I groan because of the agitation of my heart.	38:8 Job 3:24; Ps 22:1

B. *His desire for deliverance*

9	Lord, all my desire is before Thee; And my sighing is not hidden from Thee.	38:9 Ps 10:17; 6:6
10	My heart throbs, my strength fails me; And the light of my eyes, even that has gone from me.	38:10 Ps 31:10; 6:7
11	My loved ones and my friends stand aloof from my plague; And my kinsmen stand afar off.	38:11 Ps 31:11; Luke 23:49
12	Those who seek my life lay snares *for me*; And those who seek to injure me have threatened destruction, And they devise treachery all day long.	38:12 Ps 54:3; 140:5; 35:4, 20
13	But I, like a deaf man, do not hear; And I am like a dumb man who does not open his mouth.	38:13 Ps 39:2,9
14	Yes, I am like a man who does not hear, And in whose mouth are no arguments.	

C. *His confidence in God*

15	For I hope in Thee, O LORD; Thou wilt answer, O Lord my God.	38:15 Ps 39:7; 17:6
16	For I said, "May they not rejoice over me, *Who*, when my foot slips, would magnify themselves against me."	38:16 Ps 13:4; 35:26

	17	For I am ready to fall,
38:17 Ps 13:2		And my [69]sorrow is continually before me.
***38:18** Ps 32:5; 2 Cor 7:9	18	For I confess my iniquity; I am full of anxiety because of my sin.
38:19 Ps 18:17; 35:19	19	But my enemies are vigorous *and* [70]strong; And many are those who hate me wrongfully.
38:20 Ps 35:12; 1 John 3:12	20	And those who repay evil for good, They oppose me, because I follow what is good.
38:21 Ps 35:22	21	Do not forsake me, O LORD; O my God, do not be far from me!
38:22 Ps 40:13,17; 27:1	22	Make haste to help me, O Lord, my salvation!

For the choir director, for Jeduthun. A Psalm of David.

I. In time of trouble (39:1–13)

A. *Silence in trouble*

***39:1** 1 Kin 2:4; Job 2:10; James 3:2	**39**	I said, "I will guard my ways, That I may not sin with my tongue; I will guard my mouth as with a muzzle, While the wicked are in my presence."
39:2 Ps 38:13	2	I was dumb and silent, I [71]refrained *even* from good; And my [69]sorrow grew worse.
	3	My heart was hot within me; While I was musing the fire burned; *Then* I spoke with my tongue:

B. *Desire for enlightenment*

39:4 Ps 90:12; 103:14	4	"LORD, make me to know my end, And what is the extent of my days, Let me know how transient I am.
39:5 Ps 89:47; 144:4; 62:9	5	"Behold, Thou hast made my days *as* handbreadths, And my lifetime as nothing in Thy sight, Surely every man at his best is a mere breath. Selah.
39:6 1 Pet 1:24; Ps 127:2; Job 27:17; Luke 12:20	6	"Surely every man walks about as [72]a phantom; Surely they make an uproar for nothing; He amasses *riches*, and does not know who will gather them.

C. *Prayer for deliverance*

39:7 Ps 38:15	7	"And now, Lord, for what do I wait? My hope is in Thee.
39:8 Ps 51:9; 44:13	8	"Deliver me from all my transgressions; Make me not the reproach of the foolish.
39:9 v. 2; Job 2:10	9	"I have become dumb, I do not open my mouth, Because it is Thou who hast done *it*.
39:10 Job 9:34; Ps 32:4	10	"Remove Thy plague from me; Because of the opposition of Thy hand, I am perishing.
39:11 2 Pet 2:16; Job 13:28; v. 5	11	"With reproofs Thou dost chasten a man for iniquity; Thou dost consume as a moth what is precious to him; Surely every man is a mere breath. Selah.
39:12 Ps 102:1; 56:8; Heb 11:13; 1 Pet 2:11	**12**	"Hear my prayer, O LORD, and give ear to my cry; Do not be silent at my tears; For I am a stranger with Thee, A sojourner like all my fathers.
39:13 Job 10:20; 14:10	13	"Turn Thy gaze away from me, that I may [73]smile *again*, Before I depart and am no more."

[69]Lit., *pain*   [70]Or, *numerous*   [71]Lit., *kept silence*   [72]Lit., *an image*   [73]Or, *become cheerful*

38:18 The penitent are patient under affliction.   **39:1** God's providences sometimes occasion doubt.

For the choir director. A Psalm of David.

I. *Delight in the will of the* LORD *(40:1–17)*

A. *His acknowledgment of God's delivering goodness*

40 I waited [74]patiently for the LORD;
And He inclined to me, and heard my cry.

2 He brought me up out of the pit of destruction, out of the miry clay;
And He set my feet upon a rock making my footsteps firm.

3 And He put a new song in my mouth, a song of praise to our God;
Many will see and fear,
And will trust in the LORD.

4 How blessed is the man who has made the LORD his trust,
And has not turned to the proud, nor to those who lapse into
falsehood.

5 Many, O LORD my God, are the wonders which Thou hast done,
And Thy thoughts toward us;
There is none to compare with Thee;
If I would declare and speak of them,
They would be too numerous to count.

B. *His grateful obedience*

6 Sacrifice and meal offering Thou hast not desired;
My ears Thou hast [75]opened;
Burnt offering and sin offering Thou hast not required.

7 Then I said, "Behold, I come;
In the scroll of the book it is written of me;

8 I delight to do Thy will, O my God;
Thy Law is within my heart."

9 I have proclaimed glad tidings of righteousness in the great
congregation;
Behold, I will not restrain my lips,
O LORD, Thou knowest.

10 I have not hidden Thy righteousness within my heart;
I have spoken of Thy faithfulness and Thy salvation;
I have not concealed Thy lovingkindness and Thy truth from the
great congregation.

C. *His prayer for mercy and grace*

11 Thou, O LORD, wilt not withhold Thy compassion from me;
Thy lovingkindness and Thy truth will continually preserve me.

12 For evils beyond number have surrounded me;
My iniquities have overtaken me, so that I am not able to see;
They are more numerous than the hairs of my head;
And my heart has failed me.

13 Be pleased, O LORD, to deliver me;
Make haste, O LORD, to help me.

14 Let those be ashamed and humiliated together
Who seek my [76]life to destroy it;
Let those be turned back and dishonored
Who delight [77]in my hurt.

15 Let those be appalled because of their shame
Who say to me, "Aha, aha!"

16 Let all who seek Thee rejoice and be glad in Thee;
Let those who love Thy salvation say continually,
"The LORD be magnified!"

Marginal references:

40:1 Ps 27:14; 34:15
40:2 Ps 69:2; 27:5
40:3 Ps 33:3
40:4 Ps 84:12
40:5 Ps 136:4; Is 55:8; Ps 139:18
*40:6 1 Sam 15:22
40:8 John 4:34; Rom 7:22; Ps 37:31
40:9 Ps 22:22; 119:13
40:10 Acts 20:20; Ps 89:1
40:11 Ps 43:3
40:12 Ps 116:3; 38:4; 69:4; 73:26
40:13 Ps 70:1
40:14 Ps 35:4; 63:9
40:15 Ps 70:3
40:16 Ps 70:4; 35:27

---

[74]Or, *intently*   [75]Lit., *dug*, or possibly, *pierced*   [76]Or, *soul*   [77]Or, *to injure me*

40:6 *ears Thou hast opened.* The psalmist speaks of the ear as open and ready to hear and act on God's Word.   **40:7** *the scroll of the book,* the Law of God.

17 Since I am afflicted and needy,
Let the Lord be mindful of me;
Thou art my help and my deliverer;
Do not delay, O my God.

For the choir director. A Psalm of David.

I. The psalm of the compassionate (41:1–13)

A. The blessedness of the compassionate

41 How blessed is he who considers the helpless;
The LORD will deliver him in a day of trouble.
2 The LORD will protect him, and keep him alive,
And he shall be called blessed upon the earth;
And do not give him over to the desire of his enemies.
3 The LORD will sustain him upon his sickbed;
In his illness, Thou dost [78]restore him to health.

B. The malice of false friends

4 As for me, I said, "O LORD, be gracious to me;
Heal my soul, for I have sinned against Thee."
5 My enemies speak evil against me,
"When will he die, and his name perish?"
6 And when he comes to see *me*, he speaks falsehood;
His heart gathers wickedness to itself;
When he goes outside, he tells it.
7 All who hate me whisper together against me;
Against me they devise my hurt, *saying,*
8 "A wicked thing is poured out upon him,
That when he lies down, he will not rise up again."
9 Even my close friend, in whom I trusted,
Who ate my bread,
Has lifted up his heel against me.
10 But Thou, O LORD, be gracious to me, and raise me up,
That I may repay them.

C. Integrity vindicated

11 By this I know that Thou art pleased with me,
Because my enemy does not shout in triumph over me.
12 As for me, Thou dost uphold me in my integrity,
And Thou dost set me in Thy presence forever.
13 Blessed be the LORD, the God of Israel,
From everlasting to everlasting.
Amen, and Amen.

BOOK 2

For the choir director. A Maskil of the sons of Korah.

I. The sorrow and consolation of the godly (42:1–11)

A. The sorrow of separation

42 As the deer [79]pants for the water brooks,
So my soul pants for Thee, O God.
2 My soul thirsts for God, for the living God;

[78]Lit., *turn all his bed*   [79]Lit., *longs for*

41:9 The psalmist's note that he is betrayed by a friend suggests the betrayal of Christ by Judas. Christ quoted this verse as He prophesied of His own betrayal in John 13:18, 19: *He who eats My bread has lifted up his heel against Me.*

Margin refs: 40:17 Ps 70:5; 41:1 Ps 82:3,4; Prov 14:21; 41:2 Ps 37:22,28; 27:12; 41:3 Ps 6:6; 41:4 Ps 6:2; 51:4; 41:5 Ps 38:12; 41:6 Ps 12:2; 41:7 Ps 56:5; 41:8 Ps 71:10,11; *41:9 Job 19:19; Ps 55:12; John 13:18; 41:10 Ps 3:3; 41:11 Ps 147:11; 25:2; 41:12 Ps 37:17; Job 36:7; 41:13 Ps 106:48; 42:1 Ps 119:131; 42:2 Ps 63:1; Jer 10:10; Ps 43:4

When shall I come and appear before God?
3   My tears have been my food day and night,
While *they* say to me all day long, "Where is your God?"
4   These things I remember, and I pour out my soul within me.
For I used to go along with the throng *and* lead them in procession
    to the house of God,
With the voice of joy and thanksgiving, a multitude keeping festival.

5   Why are you in despair, O my soul?
And *why* have you become disturbed within me?
Hope in God, for I shall again praise Him
For the help of His presence.

B. *The consolation and hope of the godly*

6   O my God, my soul is in despair within me;
Therefore I remember Thee from the land of the Jordan,
And the peaks of Hermon, from Mount Mizar.
7   Deep calls to deep at the sound of Thy waterfalls;
All Thy breakers and Thy waves have rolled over me.
8   The LORD will command His lovingkindness in the daytime;
And His song will be with me in the night,
A prayer to the God of my life.

9   I will say to God my rock, "Why hast Thou forgotten me?
Why do I go mourning because of the oppression of the enemy?"
10 As a shattering of my bones, my adversaries revile me,
While they say to me all day long, "Where is your God?"
11 Why are you in despair, O my soul?
And why have you become disturbed within me?
Hope in God, for I shall yet praise Him,
The help of my countenance, and my God.

I. *A plea for vindication (43:1–5)*

43
    Vindicate me, O God, and plead my case against an ungodly nation;
    O deliver me from the deceitful and unjust man!
2   For Thou art the God of my strength; why hast Thou rejected me?
Why do I go mourning because of the oppression of the enemy?

3   O send out Thy light and Thy truth, let them lead me;
Let them bring me to Thy holy hill,
And to Thy dwelling places.
4   Then I will go to the altar of God,
To God my exceeding joy;
And upon the lyre I shall praise Thee, O God, my God.

5   Why are you in despair, O my soul?
And why are you disturbed within me?
Hope in God, for I shall again praise Him,
The help of my countenance, and my God.

For the choir director. A Maskil of the sons of Korah.

I. *A prayer for deliverance (44:1–26)*

A. *Acknowledgment of past mercies*

44
    O God, we have heard with our ears,
    Our fathers have told us,
    The work that Thou didst in their days,
    In the days of old.
2   Thou with Thine own hand didst drive out the nations;
Then Thou didst plant them;
Thou didst afflict the peoples,
Then Thou didst spread them abroad.

Marginal references:

42:3 Ps 80:5; 79:10
42:4 Ps 62:8; Is 30:29; Ps 100:4

42:5 Ps 38:6; 77:3; Lam 3:24; Ps 44:3

42:7 Ps 88:7; Jon 2:3
42:8 Ps 57:3; Job 35:10; Ps 63:6; 149:5

42:9 Ps 38:6

42:10 v. 3

42:11 v. 5

43:1 Ps 26:1; 1 Sam 24:15; Ps 5:6
43:2 Ps 18:1; 44:9; 42:9
43:3 Ps 36:9; 42:4; 84:1

43:4 Ps 26:6; 33:2

43:5 Ps 42:5,11

44:1 Ex 12:26; Ps 78:3,12

44:2 Ex 15:17; Ps 78:55; 80:8

44:3 Josh 24:12; Ps 77:15; Deut 4:37; 7:7,8	3	For by their own sword they did not possess the land; And their own arm did not save them; But Thy right hand, and Thine arm, and the light of Thy presence, For Thou didst favor them.
44:4 Ps 74:12; 79:9	4	Thou art my King, O God; Command victories for Jacob.
44:5 Dan 8:4; Ps 108:13	5	Through Thee we will push back our adversaries; Through Thy name we will trample down those who rise up against us.
44:6 Ps 33:16	6	For I will not trust in my bow, Nor will my sword save me.
44:7 Ps 136:24; 53:5	7	But Thou hast saved us from our adversaries, And Thou hast put to shame those who hate us.
44:8 Ps 34:2; 30:12	8	In God we have boasted all day long, And we will give thanks to Thy name forever. Selah.

B. *Statement of present complaints*

44:9 Ps 60:1,10; 74:1	9	Yet Thou hast rejected *us* and brought us to dishonor, And dost not go out with our armies.
44:10 Lev 26:17; Josh 7:8; Ps 89:41	10	Thou dost cause us to turn back from the adversary; And those who hate us have taken spoil for themselves.
44:11 v. 22; Deut 4:27; 28:64;	11	Thou dost give us as sheep to be eaten, And hast scattered us among the nations.
Ps 106:27 **44:12** Is 52:3,4; Jer 15:13	12	Thou dost sell Thy people cheaply, And hast not [80]profited by their sale.
44:13 Ps 79:4; 80:6	13	Thou dost make us a reproach to our neighbors, A scoffing and a derision to those around us.
44:14 Jer 24:9; Ps 109:25	14	Thou dost make us a byword among the nations, A laughingstock among the peoples.
	15	All day long my dishonor is before me, And my humiliation has overwhelmed me,
44:16 Ps 74:10; 8:2	16	Because of the voice of him who reproaches and reviles, Because of the presence of the enemy and the avenger.

C. *Appeal to God for deliverance*

44:17 Dan 9:13; Ps 78:7,57	17	All this has come upon us, but we have not forgotten Thee, And we have not dealt falsely with Thy covenant.
44:18 Ps 78:57; Job 23:11	18	Our heart has not turned back, And our steps have not deviated from Thy way,
44:19 Ps 51:8; Job 3:5	19	Yet Thou hast crushed us in a place of jackals, And covered us with the shadow of death.
44:20 Ps 78:11; 68:31; 81:9	20	If we had forgotten the name of our God, Or extended our hands to a strange god;
44:21 Ps 139:1,2; Jer 17:10	21	Would not God find this out? For He knows the secrets of the heart.
44:22 Rom 8:36; Is 53:7	22	But for Thy sake we are killed all day long; We are considered as sheep to be slaughtered.
44:23 Ps 7:6; 78:65; 77:7	23	Arouse Thyself, why dost Thou sleep, O Lord? Awake, do not reject us forever.
44:24 Job 13:24; Ps 42:9	24	Why dost Thou hide Thy face, And forget our affliction and our oppression?
44:25 Ps 119:25	25	For our soul has sunk down into the dust; Our body cleaves to the earth.
44:26 Ps 35:2; 25:22	26	Rise up, be our help, And redeem us for the sake of Thy lovingkindness.

---

[80]Or, *set a high price on them*

For the choir director; according to the [81]Shoshannim. A Maskil of the sons of
Korah. A Song of Love.

I. *The king's marriage (45:1–17)*

A. *The king and his rule*

45 My heart [82]overflows with a good theme;
I address my verses to the King;
My tongue is the pen of a ready writer.

*45:1
Ezra 7:6*

2 Thou art fairer than the sons of men;
Grace is poured upon Thy lips;
Therefore God has blessed Thee forever.

45:2
Luke 4:22

3 Gird Thy sword on *Thy* thigh, O Mighty One,
In Thy splendor and Thy majesty!

45:3
Is 9:6

4 And in Thy majesty ride on victoriously,
For the cause of truth and meekness *and* righteousness;
Let Thy right hand teach Thee awesome things.

45:4
Rev 6:2

5 Thine arrows are sharp;
The peoples fall under Thee;
Thine arrows are in the heart of the King's enemies.

6 Thy throne, O God, is forever and ever;
A scepter of uprightness is the scepter of Thy kingdom.

45:6
Ps 93:2;
Heb 1:8,9;
Ps 98:9

7 Thou hast loved righteousness, and hated wickedness;
Therefore God, Thy God, has anointed Thee
With the oil of joy above Thy fellows.

45:7
Ps 33:5;
Is 61:1;
Ps 79:4; 21:6

8 All Thy garments are *fragrant with* myrrh and aloes *and* cassia;
Out of ivory palaces stringed instruments have made Thee glad.

45:8
Song 1:3

9 Kings' daughters are among Thy noble ladies;
At Thy right hand stands the queen in gold from Ophir.

45:9
Song 6:8;
1 Kin 2:19

B. *The bride and the wedding*

10 Listen, O daughter, give attention and incline your ear;
Forget your people and your father's house;

45:10
Deut 21:13

11 Then the King will desire your beauty;
Because He is your Lord, bow down to Him.

45:11
Ps 95:6;
Is 54:5

12 And the daughter of Tyre *will come* with a gift;
The rich among the people will entreat your favor.

*45:12
Ps 22:29

13 The King's daughter is all glorious within;
Her clothing is interwoven with gold.

45:13
Is 61:10

14 She will be led to the King in embroidered work;
The virgins, her companions who follow her,
Will be brought to Thee.

45:14
Song 1:4; v. 9

15 They will be led forth with gladness and rejoicing;
They will enter into the King's palace.

C. *The conclusion*

16 In place of your fathers will be your sons;
You shall make them princes in all the earth.

45:16
1 Pet 2:9;
Rev 1:6; 20:6

17 I will cause Thy name to be remembered in all generations;
Therefore the peoples will give Thee thanks forever and ever.

45:17
Mal 1:11;
Ps 138:4

[81]Possibly, *Lilies* [82]Lit., *is astir*

45:1 This psalm, describing in glowing terms the marriage
of an ancient king, and elaborating on the beauties of the
bride and the bridegroom, is considered by many to describe the relationship of Christ to His church. The words in
v. 6 when applied to an ancient king of the line of David
imply that he rules in behalf of God over Israel. As applied

to Christ the words are: *Thy throne, O God, is forever and ever*
(Heb. 1:8).
45:12 *Tyre*, the wealthy maritime state, is pictured bringing her gift to the bride. Hiram of Tyre assisted both David
and Solomon in their building projects.

For the choir director. *A Psalm* of the sons of Korah,[83]set to Alamoth. A Song.

I. *God our refuge and strength (46:1–11)*

A. *God our refuge*

46
| 46:1
Ps 14:6;
Deut 4:7;
Ps 9:9 |

God is our refuge and strength,
[84]A very present help in trouble.

2
| 46:2
Ps 23:4; 82:5;
18:7 |
Therefore we will not fear, though the earth should change,
And though the mountains slip into the heart of the sea;

3
| 46:3
Ps 93:3,4 |
Though its waters roar *and* foam,
Though the mountains quake at its swelling pride.   Selah.

B. *God our strength*

4
| 46:4
Is 8:7;
Ps 48:1,8;
Is 60:14 |
There is a river whose streams make glad the city of God,
The holy dwelling places of the Most High.

5
| 46:5
Is 12:6;
Ps 37:40 |
God is in the midst of her, she will not be moved;
God will help her when morning dawns.

6
| 46:6
Ps 2:1; 68:33;
Mic 1:4 |
The nations made an uproar, the kingdoms tottered;
He raised His voice, the earth melted.

7
| 46:7
2 Chr 13:12;
Ps 9:9 |
The LORD of hosts is with us;
The God of Jacob is our stronghold.   Selah.

C. *God our victory*

8
| 46:8
Ps 66:5;
Is 61:4 |
Come, behold the works of the LORD,
Who has wrought desolations in the earth.

9
| 46:9
Is 2:4;
Ps 76:3;
Ezek 39:9 |
He makes wars to cease to the end of the earth;
He breaks the bow and cuts the spear in two;
He burns the chariots with fire.

10
| 46:10
Ps 100:3;
Is 2:11,17 |
"Cease *striving* and know that I am God;
I will be exalted among the nations, I will be exalted in the earth."

11
The LORD of hosts is with us;
The God of Jacob is our stronghold.   Selah.

For the choir director. A Psalm of the sons of Korah.

I. *God the king of the earth (47:1–9)*

A. *The nations subdued*

47
| 47:1
Ps 98:8;
Is 55:12;
Ps 106:47 |
O Clap your hands, all peoples;
Shout to God with the voice of joy.

2
| 47:2
Deut 7:21 |
For the LORD Most High is to be feared,
A great King over all the earth.

3
| 47:3
Ps 18:47 |
He subdues peoples under us,
And nations under our feet.

4
| 47:4
1 Pet 1:4 |
He chooses our inheritance for us,
The glory of Jacob whom He loves.   Selah.

B. *God reigns over all the earth*

5
| 47:5
Ps 68:33;
98:6 |
God has ascended with a shout,
The LORD, with the sound of a trumpet.

6
| 47:6
Ps 68:4;
89:18 |
Sing praises to God, sing praises;
Sing praises to our King, sing praises.

7
| 47:7
1 Cor 14:15 |
For God is the King of all the earth;
Sing praises with a skillful psalm.

8
| 47:8
1 Chr 16:31 |
God reigns over the nations,
God sits on His holy throne.

9
| 47:9
Ps 72:11;
Rom 4:11,12;
Ps 89:18;
97:9 |
The princes of the people have assembled themselves *as* the people
        of the God of Abraham;
For the shields of the earth belong to God;
He is highly exalted.

[83]Possibly, *for soprano voices*   [84]Or, *Abundantly available for help*

A Song; a Psalm of the sons of Korah.

I. *A song of Zion (48:1–14)*

A. *Zion, city of our God*

48 Great is the LORD, and greatly to be praised,
In the city of our God, His holy mountain.
2 Beautiful in elevation, the joy of the whole earth,
Is Mount Zion *in* the far north,
The city of the great King.
3 God, in her palaces,
Has made Himself known as a stronghold.

B. *Zion established*

4 For, lo, the kings assembled themselves,
They passed by together.
5 They saw *it*, then they were amazed;
They were terrified, they fled in alarm.
6 Panic seized them there,
Anguish, as of a woman in childbirth.
7 With the east wind
Thou dost break the ships of Tarshish.
8 As we have heard, so have we seen
In the city of the LORD of hosts, in the city of our God;
God will establish her for ever.   Selah.

C. *Zion praising God*

9 We have thought on Thy lovingkindness, O God,
In the midst of Thy temple.
10 As is Thy name, O God,
So is Thy praise to the ends of the earth;
Thy right hand is full of righteousness.
11 Let Mount Zion be glad,
Let the daughters of Judah rejoice,
Because of Thy judgments.
12 Walk about Zion, and go around her;
Count her towers;
13 Consider her ramparts;
Go through her palaces;
That you may tell *it* to the next generation.
14 For such is God,
Our God forever and ever;
He will guide us [85]until death.

For the choir director. A Psalm of the sons of Korah.

I. *A sermon on the foolishness of trusting in riches (49:1–20)*

A. *The summons to hear*

49 Hear this, all peoples;
Give ear, all inhabitants of the world,
2 Both low and high,
Rich and poor together.
3 My mouth will speak wisdom;
And the meditation of my heart *will be* understanding.

48:1
Ps 96:4;
Zech 8:3
48:2
Ps 50:2;
Lam 2:15;
Matt 5:35
48:3
Ps 46:7

48:4
2 Sam 10:6-19
48:5
Ex 15:15

*48:7
Jer 18:17
48:8
Ps 87:5

48:9
Ps 26:3
48:10
Josh 7:9;
Is 41:10
48:11
Ps 97:8

48:13
Ps 122:7;
78:5-7

48:14
Ps 23:4

*49:1
Ps 78:1; 33:8

49:3
Ps 37:30;
119:130

---

[85]Some mss. and the Gr. read *forever*

48:7 *ships of Tarshish*, see note to 1 Kin. 10:22.   **49:1** These thoughts have universal application.

49:4 Ps 78:2; Num 12:8	4	I will incline my ear to a proverb; I will express my riddle on the harp.

B. *The limitations of wealth*

49:5 Ps 23:4	5	Why should I fear in days of adversity, When the iniquity of my foes surrounds me,
*49:6 Job 31:24	6	Even those who trust in their wealth, And boast in the abundance of their riches?
49:7 Matt 25:8,9; Job 36:18	7	No man can by any means redeem *his* brother, Or give to God a ransom for him—
49:8 Matt 16:26	8	For the redemption of his soul is costly, And he should cease *trying* forever—
49:9 Ps 22:29; 89:48	9	That he should live on eternally; That he should not [86]undergo decay.
49:10 Eccl 2:16,18	10	For he sees *that even* wise men die; The stupid and the senseless alike perish, And leave their wealth to others.
49:11 Ps 64:6; 10:6; Deut 3:14	11	Their [87]inner thought is, *that* their houses are forever, *And* their dwelling places to all generations; They have called their lands after their own names.
49:12 v. 20	12	But man in *his* pomp will not endure; He is like the beasts that perish.

C. *The end of those who trust in wealth*

*49:13 Luke 12:20	13	This is the way of those who are foolish, And of those after them who approve their words.　　　　Selah.
49:14 Ps 9:17; Dan 7:18; Mal 4:3; 1 Cor 6:2; Rev 2:26; Job 24:19	14	As sheep they are appointed for Sheol; Death shall be their shepherd; And the upright shall rule over them in the morning; And their form shall be for Sheol to consume, So that they have no habitation.
49:15 Ps 56:13; 73:24	15	But God will redeem my soul from the power of Sheol; For He will receive me.　　　　Selah.

D. *The final exhortation*

49:16 Ps 37:7	16	Do not be afraid when a man becomes rich, When the [88]glory of his house is increased;
49:17 Ps 17:14	17	For when he dies he will carry nothing away; His [88]glory will not descend after him.
49:18 Luke 12:19	18	Though while he lives he congratulates himself— And though *men* praise you when you do well for yourself—
49:19 Gen 15:15; Job 33:30	19	He shall go to the generation of his fathers; They shall never see the light.
49:20 v. 12	20	Man in *his* pomp, yet without understanding, Is like the beasts that perish.

A Psalm of Asaph.

I. *True and false religion (50:1–23)*

A. *God is the true judge*

50:1 Josh 22:22; Ps 113:3	**50**	The Mighty One, God, the LORD, has spoken, And summoned the earth from the rising of the sun to its setting.
50:2 Ps 48:2; Deut 33:2	2	Out of Zion, the perfection of beauty, God has shone forth.

[86]Or, *see corruption* or *the pit*　　[87]Some versions read *graves are their houses*　　[88]Or, *wealth*

49:6 Wealthy worldlings are guilty of three sins: (1) they trust in their wealth; (2) they boast of their wealth; and (3) they think they can keep their wealth forever.
49:13 The power of wealth is limited. It cannot: (1) keep one's dearest friend from death; (2) keep oneself from death at the appointed hour; or (3) affect one's condition after death. The poor of this world, rich in faith, are better off than the wealthy without faith.

3   May our God come and not keep silence;
    Fire devours before Him,
    And it is very tempestuous around Him.
4   He summons the heavens above,
    And the earth, to judge His people:
5   "Gather My godly ones to Me,
    Those who have made a covenant with Me by sacrifice."
6   And the heavens declare His righteousness,
    For God Himself is judge.   Selah.

B. *God judges the intent, not the outward form*

7   "Hear, O My people, and I will speak;
    O Israel, I will testify against you;
    I am God, your God.
8   "I do not reprove you for your sacrifices,
    And your burnt offerings are continually before Me.
9   "I shall take no young bull out of your house,
    Nor male goats out of your folds.
10 "For every beast of the forest is Mine,
    The cattle on a thousand hills.
11 "I know every bird of the mountains,
    And everything that moves in the field is [89]Mine.
12 "If I were hungry, I would not tell you;
    For the world is Mine, and all it contains.
13 "Shall I eat the flesh of bulls,
    Or drink the blood of male goats?
14 "Offer to God a sacrifice of thanksgiving,
    And pay your vows to the Most High;
15 And call upon Me in the day of trouble;
    I shall rescue you, and you will honor Me."

C. *Hypocrisy rebuked*

16 But to the wicked God says,
    "What right have you to tell of My statutes,
    And to take My covenant in your mouth?
17 "For you hate discipline,
    And you cast My words behind you.
18 "When you see a thief, you are pleased with him,
    And you associate with adulterers.
19 "You let your mouth loose in evil,
    And your tongue frames deceit.
20 "You sit and speak against your brother;
    You slander your own mother's son.
21 "These things you have done, and I kept silence;
    You thought that I was just like you;
    I will reprove you, and state *the case* in order before your eyes.

D. *The conclusion stated*

22 "Now consider this, you who forget God,
    Lest I tear *you* in pieces, and there be none to deliver.
23 "He who offers a sacrifice of thanksgiving honors Me;
    And to him who orders *his* way *aright*
    I shall show the salvation of God."

[89]Or, *in My mind*

50:3
Ps 96:13;
97:3;
Dan 7:10
50:4
Deut 4:26;
Is 1:2
50:5
Ps 30:4;
Ex 24:7; v. 8
50:6
Ps 89:5; 75:7

50:7
Ps 81:8;
Ex 20:2

50:8
Ps 40:6;
Hos 6:6
50:9
Ps 69:31

50:10
Ps 104:24

50:12
Ex 19:5

50:14
Heb 13:15;
Deut 23:21
50:15
Ps 91:15;
81:7; 22:23

50:16
Is 29:13

50:17
Rom 2:21,22;
Neh 9:26
50:18
Rom 1:32;
1 Tim 5:22
50:19
Ps 10:7; 52:2

50:20
Matt 10:21

50:21
Eccl 8:11;
Is 42:14;
Ps 90:8

50:22
Job 8:13;
Ps 9:17; 7:2
50:23
v. 14;
Ps 85:13;
91:16

For the choir director. A Psalm of David, when Nathan the prophet came to him, after he had gone in to Bathsheba.

I. The penitent's psalm (51:1–19)

A. David's prayer for forgiveness and confession of sin

II Sam 12

*51:1
Ps 4:1;
106:45;
Is 43:25;
Acts 3:19
51:2
Heb 9:14;
1 John 1:7
51:3
Is 59:12

51 Be gracious to me, O God, according to Thy lovingkindness;
According to the greatness of Thy compassion blot out my transgressions.

2 Wash me thoroughly from my iniquity,
And cleanse me from my sin.

3 For I know my transgressions,
And my sin is ever before me.

51:4
Gen 20:6;
Luke 15:21;
Rom 3:4

4 Against Thee, Thee only, I have sinned,
And done what is evil in Thy sight,
So that Thou [90]art justified when Thou dost speak,
And blameless when Thou dost judge.

51:5
Ps 58:3;
Job 14:4
51:6
Ps 15:2;
Prov 2:6
*51:7
Lev 14:4;
Heb 9:19;
Is 1:18
51:8
Ps 35:10
51:9
Jer 16:17

5 Behold, I was brought forth in iniquity,
And in sin my mother conceived me.

6 Behold, Thou dost desire truth in the innermost being,
And in the hidden part Thou wilt make me know wisdom.

7 Purify me with hyssop, and I shall be clean;
Wash me, and I shall be whiter than snow.

8 Make me to hear joy and gladness,
Let the bones which Thou hast broken rejoice.

9 Hide Thy face from my sins,
And blot out all my iniquities.

B. David's prayer and vow

51:10
Acts 15:9;
Eph 2:10;
Ps 78:37
*51:11
2 Kin 13:23;
Eph 4:30
51:12
Ps 13:5;
2 Cor 3:17
51:13
Acts 9:21,22;
Ps 22:27
51:14
2 Sam 12:9;
Ps 25:5;
35:28

10 Create in me a clean heart, O God,
And renew a steadfast spirit within me.

11 Do not cast me away from Thy presence,
And do not take Thy Holy Spirit from me.

12 Restore to me the joy of Thy salvation,
And sustain me with a willing spirit.

13 *Then* I will teach transgressors Thy ways, II Sam 12:14
And sinners will [91]be converted to Thee.

14 Deliver me from bloodguiltiness, O God, Thou God of my salvation;
Then my tongue will joyfully sing of Thy righteousness.

C. God's acceptance of the broken and contrite heart

51:15
Ps 9:14
51:16
1 Sam 15:22;
Ps 40:6
51:17
Ps 34:18

15 O Lord, open my lips,
That my mouth may declare Thy praise.

16 For Thou dost not delight in sacrifice, otherwise I would give it;
Thou art not pleased with burnt offering.

17 The sacrifices of God are a broken spirit;
A broken and a contrite heart, O God, Thou wilt not despise.

D. David's prayer for Zion

51:18
Is 51:3;
Ps 102:16

18 By Thy favor do good to Zion;

[90]Or, *mayest be in the right* [91]Or, *turn back*

51:1 This psalm is one of the great Biblical passages on confession and cleansing from the defilement of sin. David's repentance includes: (1) a godly sorrow for his sin; (2) confession of that sin; (3) a turning from sin; (4) forgiveness; (5) restoration; (6) rejoicing; and (7) a readiness to witness to others of the grace of God.
51:7 The leaves and heads of the hyssop plant are used as a spice or condiment. David uses it in connection with cleansing from the defilement of sin. Here it cannot mean the inward use of the plant, but rather its use as specified in Ex. 12:22, where the hyssop was dipped in the blood of the slain animal and the blood sprinkled on the lintel and two doorposts. See also Lev. 14:4–8 and Num. 19:17,18.
51:11 The *Holy Spirit* dwelled in the heart of David. This verse, therefore, does not mean that David is apprehensive that the indwelling Spirit may actually be withdrawn from him. But he does fear that the Holy Spirit may be so quenched within him that he may lose all sense of the presence of God. Thus David earnestly begs that the sense of God's presence not be removed, but that he may remain responsive to His leading and will, and that his blessed fellowship with Him may not be forever lost.

Build the walls of Jerusalem.
19   Then Thou wilt delight in righteous sacrifices,
     In burnt offering and whole burnt offering;
     Then young bulls will be offered on Thine altar.

For the choir director. A Maskil of David, when Doeg the Edomite came and told
Saul, and said to him, "David has come to the house of Ahimelech."

I. *The fate of the wicked (52:1–9)*

A. *The portrait of the wicked*

52
Why do you boast in evil, O mighty man?
The lovingkindness of God *endures* all day long.
2   Your tongue devises destruction,
     Like a sharp razor, O worker of deceit.
3   You love evil more than good,
     Falsehood more than speaking what is right.   Selah.
4   You love all words that devour,
     O deceitful tongue.

52:1
1 Sam 22:9;
Ps 94:4
52:2
Ps 50:19;
57:4; 59:7
52:3
Jer 9:4,5

52:4
Ps 120:3

B. *The end of the wicked*

5   But God will break you down forever;
     He will snatch you up, and tear you away from *your* tent,
     And uproot you from the land of the living.   Selah.
6   And the righteous will see and fear,
     And will laugh at him, *saying,*
7   "Behold, the man who would not make God his refuge,
     But trusted in the abundance of his riches,
     And was strong in his *evil* desire."

52:5
Prov 2:22;
Ps 27:13

52:6
Job 22:19;
Ps 37:34;
40:3
52:7
Ps 49:6

C. *The praise of the righteous*

8   But as for me, I am like a green olive tree in the house of God;
     I trust in the lovingkindness of God forever and ever.
9   I will give Thee thanks forever, because Thou hast done *it,*
     And I will wait on Thy name, for *it is* good, in the presence of Thy
     godly ones.

52:8
Jer 11:16;
Ps 13:5
52:9
Ps 30:12;
54:6

For the choir director; according to [92]Mahalath. A Maskil of David.

I. *The folly and wickedness of men (53:1–6)*

A. *The depravity of men*

53
The fool has said in his heart, "There is no God,"
They are corrupt, and have committed abominable injustice;
There is no one who does good.
2   God has looked down from heaven upon the sons of men,
     To see if there is anyone who understands,
     Who seeks after God.
3   Every one of them has turned aside; together they have become
        corrupt;
     There is no one who does good, not even one.

*53:1
Ps 14:1-7;
Rom 3:10

53:2
Ps 33:13

53:3
Rom 3:12

B. *The punishment by God*

4   Have the workers of wickedness no knowledge,

53:4
Jer 4:22

[92]I.e., sickness, a sad tone

53:1 See note on 14:1 on *fool.* The Hebrew word is *nabal,*
which means senseless or foolish—having no perception of
ethical and religious values (with the collateral idea of igno-
ble or disgraceful).
  This psalm should be compared with Psalm 14, with
which it is closely related. It is thought by some scholars

that Book II of the Psalms (chs 42–47) may have been used
in the northern kingdom and that the differences reflect
local usage. Psalms were adapted to liturgical usage, and
thus minor alterations in form occurred during their long
history.

Who eat up My people *as though* they ate bread,
And have not called upon God?

53:5
Lev 26:17,36;
Ezek 6:5

5   There they were in great fear *where* no fear had been;
For God scattered the bones of him who encamped against you;
You put *them* to shame, because God had rejected them.

C. *The prayer for salvation*

53:6
Ps 14:7

6   Oh, that the salvation of Israel would come out of Zion!
When God restores His captive people,
Let Jacob rejoice, let Israel be glad.

For the choir director; on stringed instruments. A Maskil of David, when the Ziphites
came and said to Saul, "Is not David hiding himself among us?"

I. *A song for the distressed (54:1–7)*

A. *Complaint and prayer for help*

54:1
Ps 20:1;
2 Chr 20:6
54:2
Ps 55:1; 5:1

54   Save me, O God, by Thy name,
And [93]vindicate me by Thy power.
2   Hear my prayer, O God;
Give ear to the words of my mouth.

54:3
Ps 86:14;
40:14; 36:1

3   For strangers have risen against me,
And violent men have sought my life;
They have not set God before them.   Selah.

B. *Assurance of God's favor and deliverance*

54:4
Ps 118:7;
41:12
54:5
Ps 94:23;
143:12; 89:49

4   Behold, God is my helper;
The Lord is the sustainer of my soul.
5   [94]He will recompense the evil to my foes;
Destroy them in Thy faithfulness.

54:6
Ps 50:14;
52:9
54:7
Ps 34:6;
59:10

6   Willingly I will sacrifice to Thee;
I will give thanks to Thy name, O LORD, for it is good.
7   For He has delivered me from all trouble;
And my eye has looked *with satisfaction* upon my enemies.

For the choir director; on stringed instruments. A Maskil of David.

I. *A song for those who have been betrayed (55:1–23)*

A. *David describes his distress*

55:1
Ps 61:1; 27:9

55   Give ear to my prayer, O God;
And do not hide Thyself from my supplication.

55:2
Ps 66:19;
77:3; Is 38:14
55:3
Ps 17:9;
2 Sam 16:7,8;
Ps 71:11

2   Give heed to me, and answer me;
I am restless in my complaint and [95]am surely distracted,
3   Because of the voice of the enemy,
Because of the pressure of the wicked;
For they bring down trouble upon me,
And in anger they bear a grudge against me.

55:4
Ps 116:3

4   My heart is in anguish within me,
And the terrors of death have fallen upon me.

55:5
Ps 119:120;
Job 21:6
55:6
Job 3:13

5   Fear and trembling come upon me;
And horror has overwhelmed me.
6   And I said, "Oh, that I had wings like a dove!
I would fly away and [96]be at rest.
7   "Behold, I would wander far away,
I would lodge in the wilderness.   Selah.

55:8
Is 4:6

8   "I would hasten to my place of refuge
From the stormy wind *and* tempest."

[93]Lit., *judge*   [94]Lit., *The evil will return*   [95]Or, *I must moan*   [96]Lit., *settle down*

B. *The treachery of a friend*

9 Confuse, O Lord, divide their tongues,
For I have seen violence and strife in the city.

10 Day and night they go around her upon her walls;
And iniquity and mischief are in her midst.

11 Destruction is in her midst;
Oppression and deceit do not depart from her streets.

12 For it is not an enemy who reproaches me,
Then I could bear *it*;
Nor is it one who hates me who has exalted himself against me,
Then I could hide myself from him.

13 But it is you, a man my equal,
My companion and my familiar friend.

14 We who had sweet [97]fellowship together,
Walked in the house of God in the throng.

15 Let death come deceitfully upon them;
Let them go down alive to Sheol,
For evil is in their dwelling, in their midst.

C. *David's confidence in God*

16 As for me, I shall call upon God,
And the LORD will save me.

17 Evening and morning and at noon, I will complain and murmur,
And He will hear my voice.

18 He will redeem my soul in peace from the battle *which is* against me,
For they are many *who strive* with me.

19 God will hear and answer them—
Even the one who sits enthroned from of old—   Selah.
With whom there is no change,
And who do not fear God.

20 He has put forth his hands against those who were at peace with
him;
He has [98]violated his covenant.

21 His speech was smoother than butter,
But his heart was war;
His words were softer than oil,
Yet they were drawn swords.

22 Cast your burden upon the LORD, and He will sustain you;
He will never allow the righteous to be shaken.

23 But Thou, O God, wilt bring them down to the pit of destruction;
Men of bloodshed and deceit will not live out half their days.
But I will trust in Thee.

For the choir director; according to Jonath elem rehokim. A Mikhtam of David, when
the Philistines seized him in Gath.

I. *A prayer for deliverance (56:1–13)*

A. *His petition for help*

56 Be gracious, O God, for man has trampled upon me;
Fighting all day long he oppresses me.

2 My foes have trampled upon me all day long,
For they are many who fight proudly against me.

3 When I am afraid,
I will put my trust in Thee.

4 In God, whose word I praise,
In God I have put my trust;
I shall not be afraid.
What can *mere* man do to me?

[97]Lit., *counsel* [98]Lit., *profaned*

55:9 Jer 6:7
55:11 Ps 5:9; 10:7
55:12 Ps 41:9
55:13 2 Sam 15:12; Ps 41:9; Jer 9:4 **55:14** Ps 42:4 **55:15** Ps 64:7; Num 16:30, 33
55:16 Ps 57:2,3
55:17 Ps 141:2; Dan 6:10; Acts 3:1; Ps 5:3 **55:18** Ps 103:4; 2 Chr 32:7,8 **55:19** Ps 78:59; Deut 33:27
55:20 Ps 7:4; 89:34
55:21 Ps 28:3; 57:4; Prov 5:3; Ps 59:7
55:22 Ps 37:5; Matt 6:25; 1 Pet 5:7; Ps 37:24 **55:23** Ps 73:18; 5:6; Job 15:32; Prov 10:27; Ps 25:2
56:1 Ps 57:1,3
56:2 Ps 57:3; 35:1
56:3 Ps 55:4,5; 11:1 **56:4** Ps 118:6; Heb 13:6

B. *The malice of his enemies*

56:5
Ps 41:7

5 All day long they [99]distort my words;
All their thoughts are against me for evil.

56:6
Ps 59:3;
140:2; 19:10,
11

6 They [100]attack, they lurk,
They watch my steps,
As they have waited *to take* my life.

56:7
Ps 36:12;
55:23

7 Because of wickedness, cast them forth,
In anger put down the peoples, O God!

C. *His trust in God without a fear*

56:8
Ps 139:3;
39:12;
Mal 3:16

8 Thou hast taken account of my wanderings;
Put my tears in Thy bottle;
Are *they* not in Thy book?

56:9
Ps 9:3; 102:2;
Rom 8:31

9 Then my enemies will turn back in the day when I call;
This I know, [101]that God is for me.

10 In God, *whose* word I praise,
In the LORD, *whose* word I praise,

11 In God I have put my [102]trust, I shall not be afraid.
What can man do to me?

D. *His gratitude for deliverance*

56:12
Ps 50:14

12 Thy vows are *binding* upon me, O God;
I will render thank offerings to Thee.

56:13
Ps 116:8;
Job 33:30

13 For Thou hast delivered my soul from death,
Indeed my feet from stumbling,
So that I may walk before God
In the light of the living.

For the choir director; *set to* [103]Al-tashheth. A Mikhtam of David, when he fled from
Saul, in the cave.

I. *David's deliverance from Saul (57:1–11)*

A. *A prayer and a complaint*

57:1
Ps 2:12; 17:8;
Is 26:20

57 Be gracious to me, O God, be gracious to me,
For my soul takes refuge in Thee;
And in the shadow of Thy wings I will take refuge,
Until destruction passes by.

57:2
Ps 138:8

2 I will cry to God Most High,
To God who accomplishes *all things* for me.

57:3
Ps 18:16;
56:2; 40:11

3 He will send from heaven and save me;
He reproaches him who tramples upon me.   Selah.
God will send forth His lovingkindness and His truth.

57:4
Ps 35:17;
Prov 30:14;
Ps 55:21

4 My soul is among lions;
I must lie among those who breathe forth fire,
Even the sons of men, whose teeth are spears and arrows,
And their tongue a sharp sword.

57:5
Ps 108:5

5 Be exalted above the heavens, O God;
Let Thy glory *be* above all the earth.

57:6
Ps 35:7;
145:14; 7:15;
Prov 28:10

6 They have [104]prepared a net for my steps;
My soul is bowed down;
They dug a pit before me;
They *themselves* have fallen into the midst of it.   Selah.

B. *Praise and thanksgiving*

57:7
Ps 108:1

7 My heart is steadfast, O God, my heart is steadfast;
I will sing, yes, I will sing praises!

57:8
Ps 16:9;
30:12; 150:3

8 Awake, my glory;

[99]Or, *trouble my affairs* [100]Or, *stir up strife* [101]Or, *because* [102]Or, *trust without fear* [103]Lit., *Do Not Destroy*
[104]Or, *spread*

Awake, harp and lyre,
I will awaken the dawn!
9   I will give thanks to Thee, O Lord, among the peoples;
    I will sing praises to Thee among the nations.
10 For Thy lovingkindness is great to the heavens,
    And Thy truth to the clouds.
11 Be exalted above the heavens, O God;
    Let Thy glory *be* above all the earth.

57:9
Ps 108:3

57:10
Ps 36:5

57:11
v. 5

For the choir director; *set to* Al-tashheth. A Mikhtam of David.

I. *The punishment of the wicked (58:1–11)*

A. *Their sins*

58
Do you indeed speak righteousness, O [105]gods?
Do you judge [106]uprightly, O sons of men?
2   No, in heart you work unrighteousness;
    On earth you weigh out the violence of your hands.
3   The wicked are estranged from the womb;
    These who speak lies go astray from birth.
4   They have venom like the venom of a serpent;
    Like a deaf cobra that stops up its ear,
5   So that it does not hear the voice of charmers,
    Or a skillful caster of spells.

58:1
Ps 82:2

58:2
Mal 3:15;
Ps 94:20
58:3
Ps 51:5;
Is 48:8;
Ps 53:3
58:4
Ps 140:3;
Eccl 10:11
58:5
Ps 81:11

B. *Their judgment*

6   O God, shatter their teeth in their mouth;
    Break out the fangs of the young lions, O Lord.
7   Let them flow away like water that runs off;
    When he aims his arrows, let them be as headless shafts.
8   *Let them be* as a snail which melts away as it goes along,
    Like the miscarriages of a woman which never see the sun.
9   Before your pots can feel *the fire of* thorns,
    He will sweep them away with a whirlwind, the green and the
    burning alike.

58:6
Job 4:10;
Ps 3:7
58:7
Josh 7:5;
Ps 112:10;
64:3
58:8
Job 3:16
58:9
Ps 118:12;
Prov 10:25

10 The righteous will rejoice when he sees the vengeance;
    He will wash his feet in the blood of the wicked.
11 And men will say, "Surely there is a reward for the righteous;
    Surely there is a God who judges on earth!"

58:10
Ps 64:10;
91:8; 68:23
58:11
Ps 18:20; 9:8

For the choir director; *set to* Al-tashheth. A Mikhtam of David, when Saul sent *men*,
and they watched the house in order to kill him.

I. *David's deliverance from Saul (59:1–17)*

A. *David's prayer for deliverance*

59
Deliver me from my enemies, O my God;
Set me *securely* on high away from those who rise up against me.
2   Deliver me from those who do iniquity,
    And save me from men of bloodshed.
3   For behold, they have set an ambush for my life;
    Fierce men [107]launch an attack against me,
    Not for my transgression nor for my sin, O Lord.
4   For no guilt of *mine*, they run and set themselves against me.
    Arouse Thyself to help me, and see!
5   And Thou, O Lord God of hosts, the God of Israel,
    Awake to punish all the nations;
    Do not be gracious to any *who are* treacherous in iniquity.   Selah.

59:1
Ps 143:9

59:2
Ps 28:3;
139:19
59:3
Ps 56:6

59:4
Ps 35:19,23

59:5
Ps 9:5;
Jer 18:23

[105]Or, *judges*   [106]Or, *uprightly the sons of men?*   [107]Or, *stir up strife*

B. *David's trust in God*

59:6
v. 14

6   They return at evening, they howl like a dog,
And go around the city.

59:7
Ps 57:4;
10:11

7   Behold, they belch forth with their mouth;
Swords are in their lips,
For, *they say,* "Who hears?"

59:8
Ps 37:13; 2:4

8   But Thou, O LORD, dost laugh at them;
Thou dost scoff at all the nations.

59:9
Ps 9:9

9   *Because of* [108]his strength I will watch for Thee,
For God is my stronghold.

59:10
Ps 21:3; 54:7

10   My God in His lovingkindness will meet me;
God will let me look *triumphantly* upon my foes.

C. *Prayer for defeat of the enemy*

59:11
Deut 4:9;
Ps 106:27;
84:9

11   Do not slay them, lest my people forget;
Scatter them by Thy power, and bring them down,
O Lord, our shield.

59:12
Prov 12:13;
Zeph 3:11;
Ps 10:7

12   *On account of* the sin of their mouth *and* the words of their lips,
Let them even be caught in their pride,
And on account of curses and lies which they utter.

59:13
Ps 104:35;
83:18

13   [109]Destroy *them* in wrath, [109]destroy *them*, that they may be no more;
That *men* may know that God rules in Jacob,
To the ends of the earth.   Selah.

59:14
v. 6

14   And they return at evening, they howl like a dog,
And go around the city.

15   They wander about [110]for food,
And growl if they are not satisfied.

D. *David's song of praise*

59:16
Ps 21:13;
101:1; 88:13;
v. 9; Ps 46:1

16   But as for me, I shall sing of Thy strength;
Yes, I shall joyfully sing of Thy lovingkindness in the morning,
For Thou hast been my stronghold,
And a refuge in the day of my distress.

59:17
vv. 9,10

17   O my strength, I will sing praises to Thee;
For God is my stronghold, the God who shows me lovingkindness.

For the choir director; according to [111]Shushan Eduth. A Mikhtam of David, to teach;
when he struggled with Aram-naharaim and with Aram-zobah, and Joab returned, and
smote twelve thousand of Edom in the Valley of Salt.

I. *A prayer for national deliverance (60:1–12)*

A. *Israel's distress*

60:1
Ps 44:9;
2 Sam 5:20;
Ps 79:5; 80:3

60

O God, Thou hast rejected us. Thou hast broken us;
Thou hast been angry; O, restore us.

60:2
Ps 18:7;
2 Chr 7:14

2   Thou hast made the land quake, Thou hast split it open;
Heal its breaches, for it totters.

60:03
Ps 71:20;
Is 51:17,22

3   Thou hast made Thy people experience hardship;
Thou hast given us wine to drink that makes us stagger.

60:4
Ps 20:5

4   Thou hast given a banner to those who fear Thee,
That it may be displayed because of the truth.   Selah.

60:5
Ps 108:6;
127:2; 17:7

5   That Thy beloved may be delivered,
Save with Thy right hand, and answer us!

B. *Claiming God's promise*

60:6
Ps 89:35;
Josh 1:6;
Gen 12:6

6   God has spoken in His [112]holiness:
"I will exult, I will portion out Shechem and measure out the valley of
Succoth.

---

[108]Many mss. and some ancient versions read *My strength*   [109]Lit., *Bring to an end*   [110]Or, *to devour*   [111]Lit., *The lily of testimony*   [112]Or, *sanctuary*

7   "Gilead is Mine, and Manasseh is Mine;
     Ephraim also is the helmet of My head;
     Judah is My [113]scepter.
8   "Moab is My washbowl;
     Over Edom I shall throw My shoe;
     Shout loud, O Philistia, because of Me!"

C. Plea for aid

9   Who will bring me into the besieged city?
     Who will lead me to Edom?
10   Hast not Thou Thyself, O God, rejected us?
     And wilt Thou not go forth with our armies, O God?
11   O give us help against the adversary,
     For deliverance by man is in vain.
12   Through God we shall do valiantly,
     And it is He who will tread down our adversaries.

For the choir director; on a stringed instrument. *A Psalm* of David.

I. *The prayer of the troubled heart (61:1–8)*

A. *The prayer of faith*

61
Hear my cry, O God;
Give heed to my prayer.
2   From the end of the earth I call to Thee, when my heart is faint;
     Lead me to the rock that is higher than I.
3   For Thou hast been a refuge for me,
     A tower of strength against the enemy.
4   Let me dwell in Thy tent forever;
     Let me take refuge in the shelter of Thy wings.   Selah.

B. *The song of praise*

5   For Thou hast heard my vows, O God;
     Thou hast given *me* the inheritance of those who fear Thy name.
6   Thou wilt prolong the king's life;
     His years will be as many generations.
7   He will abide before God forever;
     Appoint lovingkindness and truth, that they may preserve him.
8   So I will sing praise to Thy name forever,
     That I may pay my vows day by day.

For the choir director; according to Jeduthun. A Psalm of David.

I. *The trial of faith (62:1–4)*

62
My soul *waits* in silence for God only;
From Him is my salvation.
2   He only is my rock and my salvation,
     My stronghold; I shall not be greatly shaken.

3   How long will you assail a man,
     That you may murder *him*, all of you,
     Like a leaning wall, like a tottering fence?
4   They have counseled only to thrust him down from his high
          position;
     They delight in falsehood;
     They bless with their mouth,
     But inwardly they curse.   Selah.

[113]Or, *lawgiver*

Cross references (right margin):

60:7 Josh 13:31; Deut 33:17; Gen 49:10
60:8 2 Sam 8:1
60:10 v. 1; Ps 44:9
60:11 Ps 146:3
60:12 Num 24:18; Ps 44:5
61:1 Ps 64:1; 86:6
61:2 Ps 77:3; 18:2
61:3 Ps 62:7; Prov 18:10
61:4 Ps 23:6; 91:4
61:5 Ps 56:12; 86:11
61:6 Ps 21:4
61:7 Ps 41:12; 40:11
61:8 Ps 71:22; 65:1
62:1 Ps 33:20
62:2 Ps 89:26; v. 6
62:3 Is 30:13
62:4 Ps 4:2; 28:3

II. *The confidence of faith (62:5–7)*

5 My soul, wait in silence for God only,
For my hope is from Him.

62:6
v. 2

6 He only is my rock and my salvation,
My stronghold; I shall not be shaken.

62:7
Ps 85:9; 46:1

7 On God my salvation and my glory *rest*;
The rock of my strength, my refuge is in God.

III. *The exhortation to faith (62:8–12)*

62:8
Ps 37:3;
1 Sam 1:15;
Ps 42:4;
Lam 2:19

8 Trust in Him at all times, O people;
Pour out your heart before Him;
God is a refuge for us.   Selah.

62:9
Ps 39:5,11;
Is 40:15,17;
Rom 3:4

9 Men of low degree are only vanity, and men of rank are a lie;
In the balances they go up;
They are together lighter than breath.

62:10
Is 30:12;
61:8;
Job 31:25;
Ps 52:7;
1 Tim 6:7

10 Do not trust in oppression,
And do not vainly hope in robbery;
If riches increase, do not set *your* heart *upon them.*

62:11
Job 33:14;
1 Chr 29:11

11 [114]Once God has spoken;
[115]Twice I have heard this:
That power belongs to God;

62:12
Job 34:11;
Matt 16:27;
Col 3:25

12 And lovingkindness is Thine, O Lord,
For Thou dost recompense a man according to his work.

A Psalm of David, when he was in the wilderness of Judah.

I. *The thirsty soul (63:1–11)*

A. *The soul that thirsts for God*

63:1
Ps 42:2; 84:2

63

O God, Thou art my God; I shall seek Thee [116]earnestly;
My soul thirsts for Thee, my flesh yearns for Thee,
In a dry and weary land where there is no water.

63:2
Ps 27:4

2 Thus I have beheld Thee in the sanctuary,
To see Thy power and Thy glory.

63:3
Ps 69:16

3 Because Thy lovingkindness is better than life,
My lips will praise Thee.

63:4
Ps 104:33;
28:2

4 So I will bless Thee as long as I live;
I will lift up my hands in Thy name.

B. *The soul whose thirst is quenched by God*

63:5
Ps 36:8;
71:23

5 My soul is satisfied as with [117]marrow and fatness,
And my mouth offers praises with joyful lips.

63:6
Ps 42:8

6 When I remember Thee on my bed,
I meditate on Thee in the night watches,

63:7
Ps 27:9

7 For Thou hast been my help,
And in the shadow of Thy wings I sing for joy.

63:8
Ps 18:35

8 My soul clings to Thee;
Thy right hand upholds me.

*63:9ff
Ps 40:14;
55:15

9 But those who seek my life, to destroy it,
Will go into the depths of the earth.

10 They will be delivered over to the power of the sword;
They will be a prey for foxes.

63:11
Ps 21:1;
Deut 6:13;
Is 45:23

11 But the king will rejoice in God;
Everyone who swears by Him will glory,
For the mouths of those who speak lies will be stopped.

[114]Or, *One thing* [115]Or, *These two things I have heard* [116]Lit., *early* [117]Lit., *fat*

63:9ff. What a man is, finds its expression in what he does.   What he does, determines his destiny.

For the choir director. A Psalm of David.

I. *A prayer for help against secret enemies (64:1–10)*

A. *The appeal for aid: the enemies described*

64 Hear my voice, O God, in my [118]complaint;
Preserve my life from dread of the enemy.

2 Hide me from the secret counsel of evildoers,
From the tumult of those who do iniquity,

3 Who have sharpened their tongue like a sword.
They aimed bitter speech *as* their arrow,

4 To shoot from concealment at the blameless;
Suddenly they shoot at him, and do not fear.

5 They hold fast to themselves an evil purpose;
They talk of laying snares secretly;
They say, "Who can see them?"

6 They [119]devise injustices, *saying*,
"We are ready with a well-conceived plot";
For the inward thought and the heart of a man are [120]deep.

B. *God's judgment of the wicked*

7 But God will shoot at them with an arrow;
Suddenly they will be wounded.

8 So they will make him stumble;
Their own tongue is against them;
All who see them will shake the head.

9 Then all men will fear,
And will declare the work of God,
And will consider what He has done.

10 The righteous man will be glad in the LORD, and will take refuge in
Him;
And all the upright in heart will glory.

For the choir director. A Psalm of David. A Song.

I. *The power and goodness of God (65:1–13)*

A. *God's praise required*

65 There will be silence before Thee, *and* praise in Zion, O God;
And to Thee the vow will be performed.

2 O Thou who dost hear prayer,
To Thee all men come.

3 Iniquities prevail against me;
As for our transgressions, Thou dost forgive them.

4 How blessed is the one whom Thou dost choose, and bring near *to*
Thee,
To dwell in Thy courts.
We will be satisfied with the goodness of Thy house,
Thy holy temple.

B. *God's power manifested*

5 By awesome *deeds* Thou dost answer us in righteousness, O God of
our salvation,

[118]Or, *concern*   [119]Or, *search out*   [120]Or, *unsearchable*

64:1	Ps 55:2; 140:1
64:2	Ps 56:6; 59:2
64:3	Ps 58:7
64:4	Ps 11:2; 55:19
64:5	Ps 10:11
64:6	Ps 49:11
64:8	Ps 9:3; Prov 18:7; Ps 22:7
64:9	Jer 50:28
64:10	Ps 32:11; 25:20
65:1	Ps 116:18
65:2	Is 66:23
65:3	Ps 38:4; Heb 9:14
*65:4	Ps 33:12; 4:3; 36:8
65:5	Ps 66:3; 85:4; 22:27; 107:23

64:7 What the righteous man at life's worst is infinitely
better than what the wicked man has at life's best. Therefore choose righteousness, however unprepossessing it may
appear at first glance.
65:4 Every believer has access to God. Scripture reveals
various truths about this: (1) it is possible through Christ
alone (John 10:7,9; Rom. 5:2; Heb. 10:19); (2) it is by the
Holy Spirit (Eph. 2:18); (3) it is secured by the believer
through personal faith (Rom. 5:2; Eph. 3:12; Heb. 11:6);
and (4) mercy and grace are fruits that flow to the believer as
a consequence of it (Heb. 4:16).

Thou who art the trust of all the ends of the earth and of the farthest
sea;

*65:6 Ps 93:1	6	Who dost establish the mountains by His strength, Being girded with might;
65:7 Matt 8:26; Is 17:12	7	Who dost still the roaring of the seas, The roaring of their waves, And the tumult of the peoples.
	8	And they who dwell in the ends *of the earth* stand in awe of Thy signs; Thou dost make the dawn and the sunset shout for joy.

C. *God's bounty displayed*

65:9 Ps 68:9,10; 46:4; 104:14	9	Thou dost visit the earth, and cause it to overflow; Thou dost greatly enrich it; The stream of God is full of water; Thou dost prepare their grain, for thus Thou dost prepare the earth.
	10	Thou dost water its furrows abundantly; Thou dost settle its ridges; Thou dost soften it with showers; Thou dost bless its growth.
	11	Thou hast crowned the year with Thy bounty, And Thy paths drip *with* fatness.
65:12 Job 38:26,27; Ps 98:8	12	The pastures of the wilderness drip, And the hills gird themselves with rejoicing.
65:13 Ps 144:13; 72:16; 98:8	13	The meadows are clothed with flocks, And the valleys are covered with grain; They shout for joy, yes, they sing.

For the choir director. A Song. A Psalm.

I. *A psalm of thanksgivng (66:1–20)*

A. *For national deliverances*

*66:1 Ps 100:1 66:2 Ps 81:1; 79:9	**66**	Shout joyfully to God, all the earth; 2 Sing the glory of His name; Make His praise glorious.
66:3 Ps 65:5; 18:44	3	Say to God, "How awesome are Thy works! Because of the greatness of Thy power Thine enemies will give feigned obedience to Thee.
66:4 Ps 22:27; 67:3,4	4	"All the earth will worship Thee, And will sing praises to Thee; They will sing praises to Thy name." Selah.
66:5 Ps 46:8; 106:22	5	Come and see the works of God, *Who is* awesome in *His* deeds toward the sons of men.
66:6 Ex 14:21; Josh 3:6; Ps 105:43	6	He turned the sea into dry land; They passed through the river on foot; There let us rejoice in Him!
66:7 Ps 145:13; 11:4; 140:8	7	He rules by His might forever; His eyes keep watch on the nations; Let not the rebellious exalt themselves. Selah.
66:8 Ps 98:4	8	Bless our God, O peoples, And sound His praise abroad;
66:9 Ps 121:3	9	Who keeps us in life, And does not allow our feet to slip.
66:10 Ps 17:3; Is 48:10; Zech 13:9; 1 Pet 1:6,7	10	For Thou hast tried us, O God; Thou hast refined us as silver is refined.
	11	Thou didst bring us into the net; Thou didst lay an oppressive burden upon our loins.
66:11 Lam 1:13	12	Thou didst make men ride over our heads;

65:6 *girded with might.* See Ps. 93:1.   **66:1** He calls on all peoples to praise God.

We went through fire and through water;
Yet Thou didst bring us out into *a place of* abundance.

B. *For personal help*

13 I shall come into Thy house with burnt offerings;
I shall pay Thee my vows,
14 Which my lips uttered
And my mouth spoke when I was in distress.
15 I shall offer to Thee burnt offerings of fat beasts,
With the smoke of rams;
I shall make *an offering of* bulls with male goats.   Selah.

16 Come *and* hear, all who [121]fear God,
And I will tell of what He has done for my soul.
17 I cried to Him with my mouth,
And He was extolled with my tongue.
18 If I [122]regard wickedness in my heart,
The Lord will not hear;
19 But certainly God has heard;
He has given heed to the voice of my prayer.
20 Blessed be God,
Who has not turned away my prayer,
Nor His lovingkindness from me.

For the choir director; with stringed instruments. A Psalm. A Song.

I. *A missionary psalm (67:1–7)*

67 God be gracious to us and bless us,
And cause His face to shine upon us—   Selah.
2 That Thy way may be known on the earth,
Thy salvation among all nations.
3 Let the peoples praise Thee, O God;
Let all the peoples praise Thee.
4 Let the nations be glad and sing for joy;
For Thou wilt judge the peoples with uprightness,
And guide the nations on the earth.   Selah.
5 Let the peoples praise Thee, O God;
Let all the peoples praise Thee.
6 The earth has yielded its produce;
God, our God, blesses us.
7 God blesses us,
[123]That all the ends of the earth may fear Him.

For the choir director. A Psalm of David. A Song.

1. *The God of the whole earth (68:1–35)*

A. *The God of the exodus*

68 Let God arise, let His enemies be scattered;
And let those who hate Him flee before Him.
2 As smoke is driven away, *so* drive *them* away;
As wax melts before the fire,
So let the wicked perish before God.
3 But let the righteous be glad; let them exult before God;
Yes, let them rejoice with gladness.
4 Sing to God, sing praises to His name;
Lift up *a song* for Him who rides through the deserts,

121Or, *revere*   122Or, *had regarded . . . would not have heard*   123Or, *And let all . . . earth fear Him*

66:12
Is 51:23; 43:2

*66:13
Eccl 5:4

66:14
Ps 18:6

66:15
Ps 51:19;
Num 6:14

66:16
Ps 34:11;
71:15,24

*66:18
Job 36:21;
Is 1:15;
James 4:3
66:19
Ps 116:1,2
66:20
Ps 68:35;
22:24

67:1
Num 6:25;
Ps 4:6
67:2
Acts 18:25;
Titus 2:11

67:4
Ps 96:10;
98:9

67:5
v. 3

67:6
Lev 26:4;
Ps 85:12;
Ezek 34:27
67:7
Ps 33:8

68:1
Num 10:35;
Is 33:3
68:2
Is 9:18;
Hos 13:3;
Ps 97:5;
Mic 1:4
68:3
Ps 32:11
68:4
Ps 66:2;
Is 57:14;
40:3;
Ps 83:18

66:13 A vow once made must be fulfilled.
66:18 Sin (cherishing iniquity in the heart) is one of the reasons that prayers of believers remain unanswered. The first question the believer should ask himself is, "Is there any known, unconfessed sin in my life?"

Whose name is the LORD, and exult before Him.

5 A father of the fatherless and a judge [124]for the widows,
Is God in His holy habitation.

6 God makes a home for the lonely;
He leads out the prisoners into prosperity,
Only the rebellious dwell in a parched land.

B. *The God of the wilderness*

7 O God, when Thou didst go forth before Thy people,
When Thou didst march through the wilderness,   Selah.

8 The earth quaked;
The heavens also dropped *rain* at the presence of God;
Sinai itself *quaked* at the presence of God, the God of Israel.

9 Thou didst shed abroad a plentiful rain, O God;
Thou didst confirm Thine inheritance, when it was parched.

10 Thy creatures settled in it;
Thou didst provide in Thy goodness for the poor, O God.

C. *The God of Canaan conquest*

11 The Lord gives the command;
The women who proclaim the *good* tidings are a great host:

12 "Kings of armies flee, they flee,
And she who remains at home will divide the spoil!"

13 [125]When you lie down among the [126]sheepfolds,
You are like the wings of a dove covered with silver,
And its pinions with glistening gold.

14 When the Almighty scattered the kings there,
It was snowing in Zalmon.

D. *The God of Zion*

15 A mountain of God is the mountain of Bashan;
A mountain *of many* peaks is the mountain of Bashan.

16 Why do you look with envy, O mountains with *many* peaks,
At the mountain which God has desired for His abode?
Surely, the LORD will dwell *there* forever.

17 The chariots of God are [127]myriads, thousands upon thousands;
The Lord is among them *as at* Sinai, in holiness.

18 Thou hast ascended on high, Thou hast led captive *Thy* captives;
Thou hast received gifts among men,
Even *among* the rebellious also, that the LORD God may dwell *there*.

E. *The God of salvation*

19 Blessed be the Lord, who daily bears our burden,
The God *who* is our salvation.   Selah.

20 God is to us a God of deliverances;
And to GOD the Lord belong escapes from death.

21 Surely God will shatter the head of His enemies,
The hairy crown of him who goes on in his guilty deeds.

22 The Lord said, "I will bring *them* back from Bashan.
I will bring *them* back from the depths of the sea;

23 That your foot may shatter *them* in blood,
The tongue of your dogs *may have* its portion from *your* enemies."

Cross-references (left margin):
- **68:5** Ps 146:9; Deut 10:18; 26:15
- **68:6** Ps 113:9; Acts 21:6; Ps 107:34
- **68:7** Ex 13:21; Judg 4:14
- **68:8** Ex 19:16,18; Judg 5:4
- **68:9** Deut 11:11
- **68:10** Deut 26:5; Ps 74:19
- *68:12** Ps 135:11; 1 Sam 30:24
- **68:13** Gen 49:14
- *68:14** Josh 10:10
- **68:16** Deut 12:5; Ps 87:1,2
- **68:17** Deut 33:2; Dan 7:10
- **68:18** Acts 1:9; Eph 4:8; Judg 5:12; 1 Tim 1:13
- **68:19** Ps 55:22; 65:5
- **68:20** Ps 49:15; 56:13
- **68:21** Ps 110:6; 55:23
- **68:22** Num 21:33; Ex 14:22
- **68:23** Ps 58:10; 1 Kin 21:19

[124]Lit., *of*   [125]Lit., *If*   [126]Or, *cooking stones, or, saddle bags*   [127]Lit., *twice ten thousand*

68:12 *divide the spoil.* The spoil of battle was brought home by the victorious army. The wives would share the booty.
68:14 *Zalmon* was a mountain near Shechem (Judg. 9:48).

It is possible God used a snowstorm there to rout Israel's foes.

F. *The God of the sanctuary*

1. *The temple procession*

24 They have seen Thy procession, O God,
The procession of my God, my King, into the sanctuary.
25 The singers went on, the musicians after *them*,
In the midst of the maidens beating tambourines.
26 Bless God in the congregations,
Even the LORD, *you who are* of the fountain of Israel.
27 There is Benjamin, the youngest, ruling them,
The princes of Judah *in* their throng,
The princes of Zebulun, the princes of Naphtali.

2. *The nations acknowledge Him*

28 Your God has commanded your strength;
Show Thyself strong, O God, who hast acted on our behalf.
29 Because of Thy temple at Jerusalem
Kings will bring gifts to Thee.
30 Rebuke the beasts in the reeds,
The herd of bulls with the calves of the peoples,
Trampling under foot the pieces of silver;
He has scattered the peoples who delight in war.
31 Envoys will come out of Egypt;
Ethiopia will quickly stretch out her hands to God.

3. *Praise to the God of the whole earth*

32 Sing to God, O kingdoms of the earth;
Sing praises to the Lord,   Selah.
33 To Him who rides upon the highest heavens, which are from ancient times;
Behold, He speaks forth with His voice, a mighty voice.
34 Ascribe strength to God;
His majesty is over Israel,
And His strength is in the skies.
35 O God, *Thou art* awesome from Thy sanctuary.
The God of Israel Himself gives strength and power to the people.
Blessed be God!

For the choir director; according to [128]Shoshannim. *A Psalm* of David.

I. *A plea for deliverance: A Messianic psalm (69:1–36)*

A. *The prayer and problem of the psalmist*

69
2 Save me, O God,
For the waters have threatened my life.
I have sunk in deep mire, and there is no foothold;
I have come into deep waters, and a flood overflows me.
3 I am weary with my crying; my throat is parched;
My eyes fail while I wait for my God.
4 Those who hate me without a cause are more than the hairs of my head;
Those who would destroy me are powerful, being wrongfully my enemies,
What I did not steal, I then have to restore.

[128]Or possibly, *Lilies*

68:30 *the beasts in the reeds.* The hippopotamuses, symbolic of Egypt.
68:32 Verses 32–35 speak of a sovereign, omnipotent, and majestic God.
69:1 This is a psalm with Messianic implications. In all probability it serves a dual purpose: it refers to some experience in the life of David, yet at the same time it has typical reference to Jesus Christ. Matthew 27:34,48 is a literal fulfillment of v. 21. The strongest argument against the view that it had direct reference to the Messiah is found in v. 5, where sin is confessed. Christ was the sinless One to whom this could hardly apply. Yet David, though imperfect, could in certain respects serve as a type of the Messiah. See also note to 1 Sam. 16:13.

Cross-references (right margin):

68:24 Ps 77:13; 63:2
68:25 1 Chr 13:8; Judg 11:34
68:26 Ps 26:12; Deut 33:28; Is 48:1
68:27 1 Sam 9:21
68:29 Ps 72:10
*68:30 Ps 22:12; 89:10
68:31 Is 19:19; 45:14
68:33 Ps 18:10; Deut 10:14; Ps 44:6; 29:4
68:34 Ps 29:1
68:35 Ps 47:2; 29:11; 66:20
*69:1 vv. 14,15
69:2 Ps 40:2; Jon 2:3
69:3 Ps 6:6; 119:82; Is 38:14
69:4 Ps 35:19; John 15:25; Ps 38:19; 35:11

69:5
Ps 38:5;
44:21
69:6
2 Sam 12:14

5 O God, it is Thou who dost know my folly,
And my wrongs are not hidden from Thee.

6 May those who wait for Thee not be ashamed through me, O Lord
GOD of hosts;
May those who seek Thee not be dishonored through me, O God of
Israel,

69:7
Jer 15:15;
Ps 44:15
69:8
Ps 31:11;
Is 53:3
69:9
John 2:17;
Ps 89:50
69:10
Ps 35:13

7 Because for Thy sake I have borne reproach;
Dishonor has covered my face.

8 I have become estranged from my brothers,
And an alien to my mother's sons.

9 For zeal for Thy house has consumed me,
And the reproaches of those who reproach Thee have fallen on me.

10 When I wept in my soul with fasting,
It became my reproach.

69:11
Ps 35:13;
Jer 24:9
69:12
Job 30:9

11 When I made sackcloth my clothing,
I became a byword to them.

12 Those who sit in the gate talk about me,
And I *am* the song of the drunkards.

B. *The prayer for deliverance renewed*

69:13
Is 49:8;
2 Cor 6:2;
Ps 51:1

13 But as for me, my prayer is to Thee, O LORD, at an acceptable time;
O God, in the greatness of Thy lovingkindness,
Answer me with Thy saving truth.

69:14
v. 2; Ps 144:7

14 Deliver me from the mire, and do not let me sink;
May I be delivered from my foes, and from the deep waters.

69:15
Ps 124:4,5;
Num 16:33

15 May the flood of water not overflow me,
And may the deep not swallow me up,
And may the pit not shut its mouth on me.

69:16
Ps 63:3; 51:1;
25:16
69:17
Ps 27:9;
66:14
69:18
Ps 49:15

16 Answer me, O LORD, for Thy lovingkindness is good;
According to the greatness of Thy compassion, turn to me,

17 And do not hide Thy face from Thy servant,
For I am in distress; answer me quickly.

18 Oh draw near to my soul *and* redeem it;
Ransom me because of my enemies!

69:19
Ps 22:6,7;
Is 53:3

19 Thou dost know my reproach and my shame and my dishonor;
All my adversaries are [129]before Thee.

69:20
Jer 23:9;
Is 63:5;
Job 16:2
69:21
Matt 27:34;
John 19:29

20 Reproach has broken my heart, and I am so sick.
And I looked for sympathy, but there was none,
And for comforters, but I found none.

21 They also gave me [130]gall for my food,
And for my thirst they gave me vinegar to drink.

C. *Imprecation on his enemies*

69:22
Rom 11:9,10

22 May their table before them become a snare;
And when they are in peace, *may it become* a trap.

69:23
Is 6:9,10;
Dan 5:6
69:24
Ps 79:6

23 May their eyes grow dim so that they cannot see,
And make their loins shake continually.

24 Pour out Thine indignation on them,
And may Thy burning anger overtake them.

69:25
Matt 23:38;
Acts 1:20
69:26
Is 53:4

25 May their camp be desolate;
May none dwell in their tents.

26 For they have persecuted him whom Thou Thyself hast smitten,
And they tell of the pain of those whom Thou hast wounded.

27 Do Thou add iniquity to their iniquity,
And may they not come into Thy righteousness.

69:28
Ex 32:32;
Phil 4:3;
Luke 10:20

28 May they be blotted out of the book of life,
And may they not be recorded with the righteous.

[129]Or, *known to Thee*   [130]Or, *poison*

D. *Concluding song of praise and assurance*

29 But I am afflicted and in pain;
    May Thy salvation, O God, set me *securely* on high.

30 I will praise the name of God with song,
    And shall magnify Him with thanksgiving.

31 And it will please the LORD better than an ox
    Or a young bull with horns and hoofs.

32 The humble have seen *it and* are glad;
    You who seek God, let your heart revive.

33 For the LORD hears the needy,
    And does not despise His *who are* prisoners.

34 Let heaven and earth praise Him,
    The seas and everything that moves in them.

35 For God will save Zion and build the cities of Judah,
    That they may dwell there and possess it.

36 And the descendants of His servants will inherit it,
    And those who love His name will dwell in it.

For the choir director. *A Psalm* of David; for a memorial.

I. *Appeal for deliverance from persecutors (70:1–5)*

70 O God, *hasten* to deliver me;
    O LORD, hasten to my help!

2 Let those be ashamed and humiliated
    Who seek my life;
    Let those be turned back and dishonored
    Who delight in my hurt.

3 Let those be turned back because of their shame
    Who say, "Aha, aha!"

4 Let all who seek Thee rejoice and be glad in Thee;
    And let those who love Thy salvation say continually,
    "Let God be magnified."

5 But I am afflicted and needy;
    Hasten to me, O God!
    Thou art my help and my deliverer;
    O LORD, do not delay.

I. *The prayer of an aged man for deliverance (71:1–24)*

A. *The plea for help*

71 In Thee, O LORD, I have taken refuge;
    Let me never be ashamed.

2 In Thy righteousness deliver me, and rescue me;
    Incline Thine ear to me, and save me.

3 Be Thou to me a rock of habitation, to which I may continually
        come;
    Thou hast given commandment to save me,
    For Thou art my rock and my fortress.

4 Rescue me, O my God, out of the hand of the wicked,
    Out of the grasp of the wrong doer and ruthless man,

5 For Thou art my hope;
    O Lord GOD, *Thou art* my confidence from my youth.

6 By Thee I have been sustained from *my* birth;
    Thou art He who took me from my mother's womb;
    My praise is continually of Thee.

7 I have become a marvel to many;
    For Thou art my strong refuge.

8 My mouth is filled with Thy praise,
    And with Thy glory all day long.

9 Do not cast me off in the time of old age;

69:29
Ps 70:5; 59:1

69:30
Ps 28:7; 34:3;
50:14
69:31
Ps 50:13,14

69:32
Ps 34:2;
22:26
69:33
Ps 12:9; 68:6

69:34
Ps 96:11;
148:1;
Is 44:23;
49:13
69:35
Ps 51:18;
Is 44:26
69:36
Ps 102:28;
37:29

70:1
Ps 40:13

70:2
Ps 35:4,26

70:3
Ps 40:15

70:5
Ps 40:17;
141:1

71:1
Ps 25:2,3

71:2
Ps 31:1; 17:6

71:3
Ps 31:2,3;
44:4

71:4
Ps 140:1,4

71:5
Jer 17:7

71:6
Ps 22:9,10;
Is 46:3;
Ps 34:1

71:7
1 Cor 4:9;
Ps 61:3
71:8
Ps 35:28
71:9
v. 18

Do not forsake me when my strength fails.

71:10
Ps 56:6;
Matt 27:1

10 For my enemies have spoken against me;
And those who watch for my life have consulted together,

71:11
Ps 3:2; 7:2

11 Saying, "God has forsaken him;
Pursue and seize him, for there is no one to deliver."

71:12
Ps 35:22;
70:1

12 O God, do not be far from me;
O my God, hasten to my help!

71:13
Ps 35:4;
109:29; v. 24

13 Let those who are adversaries of my soul be ashamed *and* consumed;
Let them be covered with reproach and dishonor, who seek to
injure me.

14 But as for me, I will hope continually,
And will praise Thee yet more and more.

71:15
Ps 35:28;
40:5

15 My mouth shall tell of Thy righteousness,
And of Thy salvation all day long;
For I do not know the sum *of them*.

71:16
Ps 106:2;
51:14

16 I will come with the mighty deeds of the Lord GOD;
I will make mention of Thy righteousness, Thine alone.

71:17
Deut 4:5;
6:7; Ps 26:7

17 O God, Thou hast taught me from my youth;
And I still declare Thy wondrous deeds.

71:18
v. 9

18 And even when *I am* old and gray, O God, do not forsake me,
Until I declare Thy strength to *this* generation,
Thy power to all who are to come.

B. *Song of assurance and praise for deliverance*

71:19
Ps 57:10;
35:10

19 For Thy righteousness, O God, *reaches* to the heavens,
Thou who hast done great things;
O God, who is like Thee?

71:20
Ps 60:3;
Hos 6:1,2

20 Thou, who hast shown [131]me many troubles and distresses,
Wilt revive [131]me again,
And wilt bring [131]me up again from the depths of the earth.

21 Mayest Thou increase my greatness,
And turn *to* comfort me.

71:22
Ps 33:2;
78:41

22 I will also praise Thee with a harp,
Even Thy truth, O my God;
To Thee I will sing praises with the lyre,
O Thou Holy One of Israel.

71:23
Ps 5:11;
103:4

23 My lips will shout for joy when I sing praises to Thee;
And my soul, which Thou hast redeemed.

71:24
Ps 35:28;
v. 13

24 My tongue also will utter Thy righteousness all day long;
For they are ashamed, for they are humiliated who seek my hurt.

A Psalm of Solomon.

I. *A prayer for the king (72:1–20)*

A. *For justice*

***72:1**
Ps 24:5

72

Give the king Thy judgments, O God,
And Thy righteousness to the king's son.

72:2
Is 9:7;
Ps 82:3

2 May he judge Thy people with righteousness,
And [132]Thine afflicted with justice.

72:3
Ps 85:10;
Is 32:17

3 Let the mountains bring peace to the people,
And the hills in righteousness.

72:4
Is 11:4

4 May he vindicate the afflicted of the people,

[131]Another reading is *us* [132]Or, *Thy humble*

72:1 This Solomonic psalm depicts the reign and kingdom of God's ideal King; hence it finds fulfillment in Christ, the true Messiah. It goes far beyond any human empire. Messiah's kingdom goes from sea to sea, and from the river to the ends of the earth (v. 8). All kings of the earth fall before Him; all nations do Him homage (v. 11). His kingdom shall endure forever (v. 17). The King is immortal, omnipotent, and omniscient. The Hebrew text makes possible the use of the subjunctive mood (identified by the word "may"), or the declarative ("he shall," in the KJV). Since Solomon speaks of one who goes beyond human proportions, it is perfectly proper to accept the Messianic implications of the psalm as portraying what has come and will surely come to fruition in Jesus Christ.

Save the children of the needy,
And crush the oppressor.

B. *For length of days*

5 Let them fear Thee while the sun endures,
And as long as the moon, throughout all generations.
6 May he come down like rain upon the mown grass,
Like showers that water the earth.
7 In his days may the righteous flourish,
And abundance of peace till the moon is no more.

C. *For dominion*

8 May he also rule from sea to sea,
And from the River to the ends of the earth.
9 Let the nomads of the desert bow before him;
And his enemies lick the dust.
10 Let the kings of Tarshish and of the islands bring presents;
The kings of Sheba and Seba offer gifts.
11 And let all kings bow down before him,
All nations serve him.

D. *For compassion*

12 For he will deliver the needy when he cries for help,
The afflicted also, and him who has no helper.
13 He will have compassion on the poor and needy,
And the lives of the needy he will save.
14 He will rescue their life from oppression and violence;
And their blood will be precious in his sight;

E. *For an enduring name*

15 So may he live; and may the gold of Sheba be given to him;
And let them pray for him continually;
Let them bless him all day long.
16 May there be abundance of grain in the earth on top of the
    mountains;
Its fruit will wave like *the cedars of* Lebanon;
And may those from the city flourish like vegetation of the earth.
17 May his name endure forever;
May his name increase as long as the sun *shines*;
And let *men* bless themselves by him;
Let all nations call him blessed.

F. *Benediction*

18 Blessed be the LORD God, the God of Israel,
Who alone works wonders.
19 And blessed be His glorious name forever;
And may the whole earth be filled with His glory.
Amen, and Amen.

20 The prayers of David the son of Jesse are ended.

BOOK 3

A Psalm of Asaph.

I. *The end of the prosperous wicked (73:1–28)*

A. *The temptation to envy the wicked*

73 Surely God is good to Israel,
To those who are pure in heart!

72:5
Ps 89:36

72:6
2 Sam 23:4;
Hos 6:3
72:7
Ps 92:12

72:8
Ex 23:31;
Zech 9:10
72:9
Ps 74:14;
Is 49:23;
Mic 7:17
72:10
2 Chr 9:21;
Ps 68:29
72:11
Ps 49:23

72:12
Job 29:12

72:14
Ps 116:15

72:15
Is 60:6

72:16
Ps 104:16;
Job 5:25

72:17
Ps 89:36;
Gen 12:3;
22:18;
Luke 1:48

72:18
Ps 41:13;
106:48; 77:14
72:19
Neh 9:5;
Zech 14:9

73:1
Ps 86:5;
51:10

73:2 Ps 94:18	2	But as for me, my feet came close to stumbling; My steps had almost slipped.
73:3 Ps 37:1; Jer 12:1	3	For I was envious of the arrogant, *As* I saw the prosperity of the wicked.

B. *The prosperity of the wicked*

	4	For there are no pains in their death; And their body is fat.
73:5 Job 21:9	5	They are not in trouble *as other* men; Nor are they plagued like mankind.
73:6 Ps 109:18	6	Therefore pride is their necklace; The garment of violence covers them.
73:7 Job 15:27; Ps 17:10	7	Their eye bulges from fatness; The imaginations of *their* heart run riot.
73:8 Ps 53:1; Jude 16	8	They mock, and wickedly speak of oppression; They speak from on high.
	9	They have set their mouth against the heavens, And their tongue parades through the earth.

C. *The lament of the righteous*

	10	Therefore his people return to this place; And waters of abundance are drunk by them.
73:11 Job 22:13	11	And they say, "How does God know? And is there knowledge with the Most High?"
73:12 Ps 49:6; Jer 49:31	12	Behold, these are the wicked; And always at ease, they have increased *in* wealth.
73:13 Job 21:15; 34:9; 36:3; Ps 26:6	13	Surely in vain I have kept my heart pure, And washed my hands in innocence;
73:14 Ps 38:6; 118:18	14	For I have been stricken all day long, And chastened every morning.

D. *The solution to the dilemma*

	15	If I had said, "I will speak thus," Behold, I should have betrayed the generation of Thy children.
73:16 Eccl 8:17	16	When I pondered to understand this, It was troublesome in my sight
73:17 Ps 77:13; 37:38	17	Until I came into the sanctuary of God; *Then* I perceived their end.
73:18 Ps 35:6,8	18	Surely Thou dost set them in slippery places; Thou dost cast them down to destruction.
73:19 Num 16:21; Job 18:11	19	How they are destroyed in a moment! They are utterly swept away by sudden terrors!
73:20 Job 20:8; Ps 78:65; 1 Sam 2:30	20	Like a dream when one awakes, O Lord, when aroused, Thou wilt despise their form.

E. *The assurance that God delivers the righteous*

	21	When my heart was embittered, And I was pierced within,
73:22 Ps 49:10; Job 18:3	22	Then I was senseless and ignorant; I was *like* a beast before Thee.
	23	Nevertheless I am continually with Thee; Thou hast taken hold of my right hand.
73:24 Ps 32:8; 48:14	24	With Thy counsel Thou wilt guide me, And afterward receive me to glory.
73:25 Phil 3:8	**25**	Whom have I in heaven *but Thee*? And besides Thee, I desire nothing on earth.
73:26 Ps 84:2; 16:5	26	My flesh and my heart may fail, But God is the strength of my heart and my portion forever.
73:27 Ps 37:20; 119:155	27	For, behold, those who are far from Thee will perish; Thou hast destroyed all those who are unfaithful to Thee.
73:28	28	But as for me, the nearness of God is my good;

I have made the Lord GOD my refuge,
That I may tell of all Thy works.

Heb 10:22;
Ps 71:7; 40:5

A Maskil of Asaph.

I. *Complaint over a devastated land (74:1–23)*

A. *Appeal for help against the enemy*

74   O God, why hast Thou rejected *us* forever?
      Why does Thine anger smoke against the sheep of Thy pasture?
2   Remember Thy congregation, which Thou hast purchased of old,
      Which Thou hast redeemed to be the tribe of Thine inheritance;
      And this Mount Zion, where Thou hast dwelt.
3   Turn Thy footsteps toward the perpetual ruins;
      The enemy has damaged everything within the sanctuary.
4   Thine adversaries have roared in the midst of Thy meeting place;
      They have set up their own standards for signs.
5   It seems as if one had lifted up
      His axe in a forest of trees.
6   And now all its carved work
      They smash with hatchet and hammers.
7   They have burned Thy sanctuary to the ground;
      They have defiled the dwelling place of Thy name.
8   They said in their heart, "Let us completely subdue them."
      They have burned all the meeting places of God in the land.
9   We do not see our signs;
      There is no longer any prophet,
      Nor is there any among us who knows how long.
10   How long, O God, will the adversary revile,
      And the enemy spurn Thy name forever?
11   Why dost Thou withdraw Thy hand, even Thy right hand?
      From within Thy bosom, destroy *them!*

74:1
Ps 44:9,23;
Deut 29:20;
Ps 95:7
74:2
Deut 34:6;
Ps 77:15;
68:16
74:3
Is 61:4;
Ps 79:1
74:4
Lam 2:7;
Num 2:2
74:5
Jer 46:22

74:7
2 Kin 25:9
74:8
Ps 83:4

74:9
Ps 78:43;
1 Sam 3:1;
Ps 79:5
74:10
Ps 44:16;
Lev 24:16
74:11
Lam 2:3;
Ps 59:13

B. *Assurance of a sovereign God's power*

12   Yet God is my king from of old,
      Who works deeds of deliverance in the midst of the earth.
13   [133]Thou didst divide the sea by Thy strength;
      Thou didst break the heads of the sea monsters in the waters.
14   Thou didst crush the heads of Leviathan;
      Thou didst give him as food for the creatures of the wilderness.
15   Thou didst break open springs and torrents;
      Thou didst dry up ever-flowing streams.
16   Thine is the day, Thine also is the night;
      Thou hast prepared the light and the sun.
17   Thou hast established all the boundaries of the earth;
      Thou hast made summer and winter.

74:12
Ps 44:4
74:13
Ex 14:21;
Is 51:9

74:15
Ex 17:5,6;
Num 20:11;
Josh 3:13
74:16
Ps 104:19
74:17
Gen 8:22

C. *Final appeal for help*

18   Remember this, O LORD, that the enemy has reviled;
      And a foolish people has spurned Thy name.
19   Do not deliver the soul of Thy turtledove to the wild beast;
      Do not forget the life of Thine afflicted forever.
20   Consider the covenant;
      For the dark places of the land are full of the habitations of violence.
21   Let not the oppressed return dishonored;
      Let the afflicted and needy praise Thy name.
22   Do arise, O God, *and* plead Thine own cause;

74:18
v. 10; Ps 39:8
74:19
Song 2:14;
Ps 9:18
74:20
Gen 17:7;
Ps 106:45;
88:6
74:21
Ps 103:6;
35:10
74:22
Ps 43:1; v. 18

[133]Or, *Thou Thyself,* and so through v. 17

74:14 *Leviathan* was a many-headed mythological sea monster who became a symbol of evil throughout the Bible.   (Leviathan is probably the *sea monsters* of v. 13.)

74:23
v. 10; Ps 65:7

23 Remember how the foolish man reproaches Thee all day long.
Do not forget the voice of Thine adversaries,
The uproar of those who rise against Thee which ascends
continually.

For the choir director; *set to* Al-tashheth. A Psalm of Asaph, a Song.

I. *The justice of God (75:1–10)*

A. *Invocation*

75:1
Ps 79:13;
145:18; 44:1

75 We give thanks to Thee, O God, we give thanks,
For Thy name is near;
Men declare Thy wondrous works.

B. *Assurance of judgment*

2 "When I select an appointed time,
It is I who judge with equity.

75:3
Ps 46:6;
1 Sam 2:8
75:4
Zech 1:21

3 "The earth and all who dwell in it [134]melt;
It is I who have firmly set its pillars. Selah.
4 "I said to the boastful, 'Do not boast,'
And to the wicked, 'Do not lift up the horn;

75:5
Ps 94:4

5 Do not lift up your horn on high,
Do not speak with insolent pride.' "

C. *God is the judge*

75:6
Ps 3:3

6 For not from the east, nor from the west,
Nor from the desert *comes* exaltation;

75:7
Ps 50:6;
1 Sam 2:7;
Dan 2:21
75:8
Job 21:20;
Ps 60:3;
Jer 26:15;
Prov 23:30;
Ps 73:10

7 But God is the Judge;
He puts down one, and exalts another.
8 For a cup is in the hand of the LORD, and the wine foams;
It is well mixed, and He pours out of this;
Surely all the wicked of the earth must drain *and* drink down
its dregs.

D. *Praise to Him*

75:9
Ps 40:10

9 But as for me, I will declare *it* forever;
I will sing praises to the God of Jacob.

75:10
Ps 89:17;
148:14

10 And all the horns of the wicked He will cut off,
But the horns of the righteous will be lifted up.

For the choir director; on stringed instruments. A Psalm of Asaph, a Song.

I. *The victorious power of God (76:1–12)*

76:1
Ps 48:3

76 God is known in Judah;
His name is great in Israel.

76:2
Ps 27:5; 9:11

2 And His tabernacle is in Salem;
His dwelling place also is in Zion.

76:3
Ps 46:9

3 There He broke the flaming arrows,
The shield, and the sword, and the weapons of war. Selah.

4 Thou art resplendent,
More majestic than the mountains of prey.

76:5
Is 46:12;
Ps 13:3

5 The stouthearted were plundered;
They sank into sleep;
And none of the warriors could use his hands.

76:6
Ex 15:1,21;
Ps 78:53
76:7
Ps 96:4;
Nah 1:6

6 At Thy rebuke, O God of Jacob,
Both rider and horse were cast into a dead sleep.
7 Thou, even Thou, art to be feared;
And who may stand in Thy presence when once Thou art angry?

[134]Or, *totter*

8 Thou didst cause judgment to be heard from heaven;
  The earth feared, and was still,
9 When God arose to judgment,
  To save all the humble of the earth. **Selah.**
10 For the wrath of man shall praise Thee;
  With a remnant of wrath Thou shalt gird Thyself.

11 Make vows to the LORD your God and fulfill *them*;
  Let all who are around Him bring gifts to Him who is to be feared.
12 He will cut off the spirit of princes;
  He is feared by the kings of the earth.

For the choir director; according to Jeduthun. A Psalm of Asaph.

I. Comfort in the memory of God's mighty deeds (77:1–20)

A. The call for help

77
   My voice *rises* to God, and I will cry aloud;
   My voice *rises* to God, and He will hear me.
2 In the day of my trouble I sought the Lord;
  In the night my hand was stretched out [135]without weariness;
  My soul refused to be comforted.
3 *When* I remember God, then I am disturbed;
  When I sigh, then my spirit grows faint. **Selah.**
4 Thou hast held my eyelids *open*;
  I am so troubled that I cannot speak.
5 I have considered the days of old,
  The years of long ago.
6 I will remember my song in the night;
  I will meditate with my heart;
  And my spirit ponders.

7 Will the Lord reject forever?
  And will He never be favorable again?
8 Has His lovingkindness ceased forever?
  Has *His* promise come to an end forever?
9 Has God forgotten to be gracious?
  Or has He in anger withdrawn His compassion? **Selah.**
10 Then I said, "It is my grief,
  That the right hand of the Most High has changed."

B. God's former wonders

11 I shall remember the deeds of the LORD;
  Surely I will remember Thy wonders of old.
12 I will meditate on all Thy work,
  And muse on Thy deeds.
13 Thy way, O God, is holy;
  What god is great like our God?
14 Thou art the God who workest wonders;
  Thou hast made known Thy strength among the peoples.
15 Thou hast by Thy power redeemed Thy people,
  The sons of Jacob and Joseph. **Selah.**
16 The waters saw Thee, O God;
  The waters saw Thee, they were in anguish;
  The deeps also trembled.
17 The clouds poured out water;
  The skies gave forth a sound;
  Thy arrows flashed here and there.
18 The sound of Thy thunder was in the whirlwind;
  The lightnings lit up the world;
  The earth trembled and shook.

[135]Lit., *and did not grow numb*

76:8
Ezek 38:20;
2 Chr 20:29, 30
76:9
Ps 9:7-9; 72:4
76:10
Ex 9:16;
Rom 9:17

76:11
Ps 50:14;
68:29
76:12
Ps 68:35

77:1
Ps 3:4

77:2
Ps 50:15;
Is 26:9,16

77:3
Ps 142:3;
143:4

77:5
Deut 32:7;
Ps 143:5;
Is 51:9
77:6
Ps 42:8; 4:4

77:7
Ps 74:1; 85:1

77:8
Ps 89:49;
2 Pet 3:9
77:9
Is 49:15;
Ps 25:6
77:10
Ps 31:22;
44:2,3

77:11
Ps 143:5

77:13
Ps 73:17;
Ex 15:11

77:15
Ex 6:6;
Deut 9:29

77:16
Ex 14:21

77:17
Judg 5:4;
Ps 68:33;
2 Sam 22:15
77:18
2 Sam 22:8

| 77:19
Hab 3:15;
Ex 14:28 | 19 | Thy way was in the sea,
And Thy paths in the mighty waters,
And Thy footprints may not be known. |
| 77:20
Ex 13:21;
Is 63:11-13;
Ex 6:26 | 20 | Thou didst lead Thy people like a flock,
By the hand of Moses and Aaron. |

A Maskil of Asaph.

I. God's guidance despite His people's unfaithfulness (78:1–72)

A. The call to hear and heed

78:1 Is 51:4	**78** **1**	Listen, O my people, to my instruction; Incline your ears to the words of my mouth.
78:2 Matt 13:35	2	I will open my mouth in a parable; I will utter dark sayings of old,
78:3 Ps 44:1	3	Which we have heard and known, And our fathers have told us.
78:4 Ex 12:26; Ps 22:30; 71:17	4	We will not conceal them from their children, But tell to the generation to come the praises of the LORD, And His strength and His wondrous works that He has done.
78:5 Ps 147:19; Deut 4:9	5	For He established a testimony in Jacob, And appointed a law in Israel, Which He commanded our fathers, That they should teach them to their children,
78:6 Ps 102:18	6	That the generation to come might know, *even* the children *yet* to be born, *That* they may arise and tell *them* to their children,
78:7 Deut 6:12; 27:1	7	That they should put their confidence in God, And not forget the works of God, But keep His commandments,
78:8 Ezek 20:18; Ex 32:9; v. 37	8	And not be like their fathers, A stubborn and rebellious generation, A generation that did not [136]prepare its heart, And whose spirit was not faithful to God.

B. The sins of Israel

1. The Ephraimites' disobedience

78:9 1 Chr 12:2; Judg 20:39	9	The sons of Ephraim were archers equipped with bows, *Yet* they turned back in the day of battle.
78:10 2 Kin 18:12; Ps 119:1	10	They did not keep the covenant of God, And refused to walk in His law;
78:11 Ps 106:13	11	And they forgot His deeds, And His miracles that He had shown them.
78:12 Ex 7-12; Num 13:22; Is 19:11,13; Ezek 30:14	12	He wrought wonders before their fathers, In the land of Egypt, in the field of Zoan.
78:13 Ex 14:21; 15:8	13	He divided the sea, and caused them to pass through; And He made the waters stand up like a heap.
78:14 Ex 13:21	14	Then He led them with the cloud by day, And all the night with a light of fire.
78:15 Num 20:11; 1 Cor 10:4	15	He split the rocks in the wilderness, And gave *them* abundant drink like the ocean depths.
	16	He brought forth streams also from the rock, And caused waters to run down like rivers.

2. Lusting for flesh in the wilderness

| 78:17
Deut 9:22;
Heb 3:16 | 17 | Yet they still continued to sin against Him,
To rebel against the Most High in the desert. |
| 78:18
Ex 16:2;
1 Cor 10:9 | 18 | And in their heart they put God to the test |

136Or, *put right*

By asking food according to their desire.
19 Then they spoke against God;
    They said, "Can God prepare a table in the wilderness?
20 "Behold, He struck the rock, so that waters gushed out,
    And streams were overflowing;
    Can He give bread also?
    Will He provide meat for His people?"

21 Therefore the LORD heard and was full of wrath,
    And a fire was kindled against Jacob,
    And anger also mounted against Israel;
22 Because they did not believe in God,
    And did not trust in His salvation.
23 Yet He commanded the clouds above,
    And opened the doors of heaven;
24 And He rained down manna upon them to eat,
    And gave them food from heaven.
25 Man did eat the bread of angels;
    He sent them food in abundance.
26 He caused the east wind to blow in the heavens;
    And by His power He directed the south wind.
27 When He rained meat upon them like the dust,
    Even winged fowl like the sand of the seas,
28 Then He let *them* fall in the midst of their camp,
    Round about their dwellings.
29 So they ate and were well filled;
    And their desire He gave to them.
30 Before they had satisfied their desire,
    While their food was in their mouths,
31 The anger of God rose against them,
    And killed some of their stoutest ones,
    And subdued the choice men of Israel.

3. Israel's sinful waywardness

32 In spite of all this they still sinned,
    And did not believe in His wonderful works.
33 So He brought their days to an end in futility,
    And their years in sudden terror.

34 When He killed them, then they sought Him,
    And returned and searched diligently for God;
35 And they remembered that God was their rock,
    And the Most High God their Redeemer.
36 But they deceived Him with their mouth,
    And lied to Him with their tongue.
37 For their heart was not steadfast toward Him,
    Nor were they faithful in His covenant.
38 But He, being compassionate, forgave *their* iniquity, and did not
        destroy *them*;
    And often He restrained His anger,
    And did not arouse all His wrath.
39 Thus He remembered that they were but flesh,
    A wind that passes and does not return.

4. Israel's forgetfulness of past mercies

40 How often they rebelled against Him in the wilderness,
    And grieved Him in the desert!
41 And again and again they [137]tempted God,
    And pained the Holy One of Israel.
42 They did not remember His power,
    The day when He redeemed them from the adversary,
43 When He performed His signs in Egypt,

137Or, *put to the test*

78:19	Num 11:4
78:20	Num 20:11
78:21	Num 11:1
78:22	Heb 3:18
78:23	Mal 3:10
78:24	John 6:31
78:26	Num 11:31
78:27	Ps 105:40
78:29	Num 11:20
78:31	Num 11:33
78:32	Num 14,16, 17; v. 22
78:33	Num 14:29, 35
78:34	Hos 5:15
78:35	Deut 32:4; Is 41:14
78:36	Ezek 33:31; Ex 32:7,8
78:38	Num 14:18; Is 48:9; 1 Kin 21:29
78:39	Ps 103:14; Gen 6:3; Job 7:7,16
78:40	Ps 95:8-10; Heb 3:16
78:41	Num 14:22; Ps 89:18

78:44 Ex 7:20	44	And His marvels in the field of Zoan, And turned their rivers to blood, And their streams, they could not drink.
78:45 Ex 8:24; Ps 105:31; Ex 8:6	45	He sent among them swarms of flies, which devoured them, And frogs which destroyed them.
	46	He gave also their crops to the grasshopper, And the product of their labor to the locust.
78:47 Ex 9:25	47	He destroyed their vines with hailstones, And their sycamore trees with frost.
78:48 Ex 9:23	48	He gave over their cattle also to the hailstones, And their herds to bolts of lightning.
78:49 Ex 15:7	49	He sent upon them His burning anger, Fury, and indignation, and trouble, A band of destroying angels.
	50	He leveled a path for His anger; He did not spare their soul from death, But gave over their life to the plague,
78:51 Ex 12:29; Ps 106:22	51	And smote all the first-born in Egypt, The first *issue* of their virility in the tents of Ham.
78:52 Ps 77:20	52	But He led forth His own people like sheep, And guided them in the wilderness like a flock;
78:53 Ex 14:19,27	53	And He led them safely, so that they did not fear; But the sea engulfed their enemies.
78:54 Ex 15:17; Ps 44:3	**54**	So He brought them to His holy land, To this hill country which His right hand had gained.
78:55 Ps 44:2; 105:11	55	He also drove out the nations before them, And He apportioned them for an inheritance by measurement, And made the tribes of Israel dwell in their tents.

5. *Israel's idolatry in Canaan*

78:56 vv. 18,40	56	Yet they [138]tempted and rebelled against the Most High God, And did not keep His testimonies.
78:57 Ezek 20:27, 28; Hos 7:16	57	But turned back and acted treacherously like their fathers; They turned aside like a treacherous bow.
78:58 Deut 32:16, 21; 12:2; 1 Kin 11:7	58	For they provoked Him with their high places, And aroused His jealousy with their graven images.
	59	When God heard, He was filled with wrath, And greatly abhorred Israel;
78:60 1 Sam 4:11	60	So that He abandoned the dwelling place at Shiloh, The tent which He had pitched among men,
78:61 Judg 18:30	61	And gave up His strength to captivity, And His glory into the hand of the adversary.
78:62 1 Sam 4:10	62	He also delivered His people to the sword, And was filled with wrath at His inheritance.
78:63 Jer 7:34	63	Fire devoured His young men; And His virgins had no wedding songs.
78:64 1 Sam 22:18; Job 27:15	64	His priests fell by the sword; And His widows could not weep.
78:65 Is 42:13	**65**	Then the Lord awoke as *if from* sleep, Like a warrior overcome by wine.
78:66 1 Sam 5:6	66	And He drove His adversaries backward; He put on them an everlasting reproach.

C. *Judah and David chosen*

	67	He also rejected the tent of Joseph, And did not choose the tribe of Ephraim,
78:68 Ps 87:2	68	But chose the tribe of Judah, Mount Zion which He loved.
78:69 1 Sam 6:1-38	69	And He built His sanctuary like the heights, Like the earth which He has founded forever.

[138]Or, *put to the test*

70	He also chose David His servant,	**78:70** 1 Sam 16:11, 12
	And took him from the sheepfolds;	
71	From the care of the ewes with suckling lambs He brought him,	**78:71** 2 Sam 7:8; Gen 33:13;
	To shepherd Jacob His people,	2 Sam 5:2;
	And Israel His inheritance.	1 Chr 11:2
72	So he shepherded them according to the integrity of his heart,	**78:72** 1 Kin 9:4
	And guided them with his skillful hands.	

A Psalm of Asaph.

I. *Lament over the destruction of Jerusalem (79:1–13)*

A. *The evil described*

79	O God, the nations have invaded Thine inheritance;	**79:1** Ex 15:17; Ps 74:2;
	They have defiled Thy holy temple;	2 Kin 25:9;
	They have laid Jerusalem in ruins.	Mic 3:12
2	They have given the dead bodies of Thy servants for food to the	**79:2** Jer 7:33
	birds of the heavens,	
	The flesh of Thy godly ones to the beasts of the earth.	
3	They have poured out their blood like water round about Jerusalem;	**79:3** Jer 14:16
	And there was no one to bury them.	
4	We have become a reproach to our neighbors,	**79:4** Ps 44:13
	A scoffing and derision to those around us.	

B. *The help of God besought*

5	How long, O LORD? Wilt Thou be angry forever?	**79:5** Ps 74:1,9; Zeph 3:8
	Will Thy jealousy burn like fire?	
6	Pour out Thy wrath upon the nations which do not know Thee,	**79:6** Jer 10:25; Rev 16:1;
	And upon the kingdoms which do not call upon Thy name.	Is 45:4,5;
7	For they have devoured Jacob,	2 Thess 1:8
	And laid waste his habitation.	
8	Do not remember the iniquities of *our* forefathers against us;	**79:8** Is 64:9
	Let Thy compassion come quickly to meet us;	
	For we are brought very low.	
9	Help us, O God of our salvation, for the glory of Thy name;	**79:9** 2 Chr 14:11; Jer 14:7
	And deliver us, and forgive our sins, for Thy name's sake.	
10	Why should the nations say, "Where is their God?"	**79:10** Ps 42:10; 94:1,2
	Let there be known among the nations in our sight,	
	Vengeance for the blood of Thy servants, which has been shed.	
11	Let the groaning of the prisoner come before Thee;	**79:11** Ps 102:20
	According to the greatness of Thy power preserve those who are	
	doomed to die.	
12	And return to our neighbors sevenfold into their bosom	**79:12** Is 65:6,7; Jer 32:18;
	The reproach with which they have reproached Thee, O Lord.	Luke 6:38;
13	So we Thy people and the sheep of Thy pasture	Ps 74:18,22
	Will give thanks to Thee forever;	**79:13** Ps 74:1; 95:7;
	To all generations we will tell of Thy praise.	Is 43:21

For the choir director; *set to* El Shoshannim; Eduth. A Psalm of Asaph.

I. *Israel's prayer for deliverance from calamities (80:1–19)*

A. *The call for help*

80	Oh, give ear, Shepherd of Israel,	**80:1** Ps 23:1; 77:20; 99:1
	Thou who dost lead Joseph like a flock;	
	Thou who art enthroned *above* the cherubim, shine forth!	
2	Before Ephraim and Benjamin and Manasseh, stir up Thy power,	**80:2** Ps 35:23
	And come to save us!	
3	O God, restore us,	**80:3** Lam 5:21;
	And cause Thy face to shine *upon us*, and we will be saved.	Num 6:25

B. *Israel's problem*

<table>
<tr><td>80:4
Ps 85:5</td><td>4</td><td>O LORD God *of* hosts,
How long wilt Thou be angry with the prayer of Thy people?</td></tr>
<tr><td>80:5
Ps 42:3;
102:9</td><td>5</td><td>Thou hast fed them with the bread of tears,
And Thou hast made them to drink tears in large measure.</td></tr>
<tr><td>80:6
Ps 44:13;
79:4</td><td>6</td><td>Thou dost make us [139]an object of contention to our neighbors;
And our enemies laugh among themselves.</td></tr>
<tr><td></td><td>7</td><td>O God *of* hosts, restore us,
And cause Thy face to shine *upon us*, [140]and we will be saved.</td></tr>
</table>

C. *Israel a wasted vine*

<table>
<tr><td>80:8
Is 5:1,7;
Jer 2:21;
Ezek 15:6;
Ps 44:2</td><td>8</td><td>Thou didst remove a vine from Egypt;
Thou didst drive out the nations, and didst plant it.</td></tr>
<tr><td>80:9
Hos 14:5</td><td>9</td><td>Thou didst clear *the ground* before it,
And it took deep root and filled the land.</td></tr>
<tr><td></td><td>10</td><td>The mountains were covered with its shadow;
And the cedars of God with its boughs.</td></tr>
<tr><td></td><td>11</td><td>It was sending out its branches to the sea,
And its shoots to the River.</td></tr>
<tr><td>80:12
Ps 89:40;
Nah 2:2</td><td>12</td><td>Why hast Thou broken down its hedges,
So that all who pass *that* way pick its *fruit*?</td></tr>
<tr><td>80:13
Jer 5:6</td><td>13</td><td>A boar from the forest eats it away,
And whatever moves in the field feeds on it.</td></tr>
</table>

D. *The call for help repeated*

<table>
<tr><td>80:14
Is 63:15</td><td>14</td><td>O God *of* hosts, turn again now, we beseech Thee;
Look down from heaven and see, and take care of this vine,</td></tr>
<tr><td></td><td>15</td><td>Even the shoot which Thy right hand has planted,
And on the son whom Thou hast strengthened for Thyself.</td></tr>
<tr><td>80:16
Ps 39:11;
76:6</td><td>16</td><td>It is burned with fire, it is cut down;
They perish at the rebuke of Thy countenance.</td></tr>
<tr><td>80:17
Ps 89:21</td><td>17</td><td>Let Thy hand be upon the man of Thy right hand,
Upon the son of man whom Thou didst make strong for Thyself.</td></tr>
<tr><td>80:18
Is 50:5;
Ps 71:20</td><td>18</td><td>Then we shall not turn back from Thee;
Revive us, and we will call upon Thy name.</td></tr>
<tr><td></td><td>19</td><td>O LORD God of hosts, restore us;
Cause Thy face to shine *upon us*, and we will be saved.</td></tr>
</table>

For the choir director; on the Gittith. *A Psalm* of Asaph.

I. *The goodness of God and the waywardness of Israel* (81:1–16)

A. *The call to praise*

<table>
<tr><td>81:1
Ps 59:16;
66:1</td><td>81</td><td>Sing for joy to God our strength;
Shout joyfully to the God of Jacob.</td></tr>
<tr><td></td><td>2</td><td>Raise a song, strike the timbrel,
The sweet sounding lyre with the harp.</td></tr>
<tr><td>81:3
Num 10:10;
Lev 23:24</td><td>3</td><td>Blow the trumpet at the new moon,
At the full moon, on our feast day.</td></tr>
<tr><td></td><td>4</td><td>For it is a statute for Israel,
An ordinance of the God of Jacob.</td></tr>
<tr><td>81:5
Ex 11:4</td><td>5</td><td>He established it for a testimony in Joseph,
When he went throughout the land of Egypt.
I heard a language that I did not know:</td></tr>
</table>

B. *The goodness of God to Israel*

<table>
<tr><td>81:6
Is 9:4; 10:27</td><td>6</td><td>"I relieved his shoulder of the burden,
His hands were freed from the basket.</td></tr>
</table>

[139]Lit., *a strife to*   [140]Or, *that we may*

7 "You called in trouble, and I rescued you;
   I answered you in the hiding place of thunder;
   I proved you at the waters of Meribah.   Selah.

8 "Hear, O My people, and I will admonish you;
   O Israel, if you would listen to Me!

9 "Let there be no strange god among you;
   Nor shall you worship any foreign god.

10 "I, the LORD, am your God,
   Who brought you up from the land of Egypt;
   Open your mouth wide and I will fill it.

C. *God's yearning for a backslidden people*

11 "But My people did not listen to My voice;
   And Israel did not obey Me.

12 "So I gave them over to the stubbornness of their heart,
   To walk in their own devices.

13 "Oh that My people would listen to Me,
   That Israel would walk in My ways!

14 "I would quickly subdue their enemies,
   And turn My hand against their adversaries.

15 "Those who hate the LORD would pretend obedience to Him;
   And their time *of punishment* would be forever.

16 "But I would feed you with the finest of the wheat;
   And with honey from the rock I would satisfy you."

A Psalm of Asaph.

I. *Unjust judgments rebuked (82:1–8)*

82 God takes His stand in His own congregation;
   He judges in the midst of the rulers.

2 How long will you judge unjustly,
   And show partiality to the wicked?   Selah.

3 Vindicate the weak and fatherless;
   Do justice to the afflicted and destitute.

4 Rescue the weak and needy;
   Deliver *them* out of the hand of the wicked.

5 They do not know nor do they understand;
   They walk about in darkness;
   All the foundations of the earth are shaken.

6 I said, "You are gods,
   And all of you are sons of the Most High.

7 "Nevertheless you will die like men,
   And fall like *any* one of the princes."

8 Arise, O God, judge the earth!
   For it is Thou who dost possess all the nations.

A Song, a Psalm of Asaph.

I. *A prayer for God to confound the enemies (83:1–18)*

A. *Prayer to judge Israel's enemies*

83 O God, do not remain quiet;
   Do not be silent and, O God, do not be still.

2 For, behold, Thine enemies make an uproar;
   And those who hate Thee have exalted themselves.

3 They make shrewd plans against Thy people,
   And conspire together against Thy treasured ones.

4 They have said, "Come, and let us wipe them out as a nation,
   That the name of Israel be remembered no more."

5 For they have conspired together with one mind;
   Against Thee do they make a covenant:

81:7
Ex 2:23;
Ps 50:15;
Ex 19:19;
17:6,7
81:8
Ps 50:7
81:9
Deut 32:12;
Is 43:12
81:10
Ex 20:2;
Ps 103:5

81:11
Ex 32:1
81:12
Acts 7:42;
Rom 1:24
81:13
Deut 5:29;
Is 48:18;
Ps 128:1
81:14
Ps 47:3;
Amos 1:8

81:16
Deut 32:13;
Ps 147:14

82:1
Is 3:13;
Ex 21:6
82:2
Ps 58:1;
Deut 1:17;
Prov 18:5
82:3
Deut 24:17
82:4
Job 29:12

82:5
Mic 3:1;
Ps 11:3

82:6
John 10:34;
Ps 89:26
82:7
Ps 49:12;
Ezek 31:14
82:8
Ps 12:5;
Mic 7:2,7;
Ps 2:8;
Rev 11:15

83:1
Ps 28:1;
109:1
83:2
Ps 2:1; 81:15

83:3
Ps 27:5

83:4
Esth 3:6

83:5
Ps 2:2

83:6 2 Chr 20:1, 10,11	6	The tents of Edom and the Ishmaelites; Moab, and the Hagrites;
	7	Gebal, and Ammon, and Amalek; Philistia with the inhabitants of Tyre;
	8	Assyria also has joined with them; They have become a help to the children of Lot. Selah.

B. *The prayer of imprecation*

83:9 Judg 4:22,23	9	Deal with them as with Midian, As with Sisera *and* Jabin, at the torrent of Kishon,
	10	Who were destroyed at En-dor, Who became as dung for the ground.
83:11 Judg 8:12,21	11	Make their nobles like Oreb and Zeeb, And all their princes like Zebah and Zalmunna,
83:12 2 Chr 20:11; Ps 132:13	12	Who said, "Let us possess for ourselves The pastures of God."
83:13 Is 17:13; Ps 35:5	13	O my God, make them like the [141]whirling dust; Like chaff before the wind.
83:14 Deut 32:22	14	Like fire that burns the forest, And like a flame that sets the mountains on fire,
83:15 Job 9:17	15	So pursue them with Thy tempest, And terrify them with Thy storm.
	16	Fill their faces with dishonor, That they may seek Thy name, O LORD.
83:17 Ps 70:2	17	Let them be ashamed and dismayed forever; And let them be humiliated and perish,
83:18 Ps 59:13; Ex 6:3; Ps 92:8	18	That they may know that Thou alone, whose name is the LORD, Art the Most High over all the earth.

For the choir director; on the Gittith. A Psalm of the sons of Korah.

I. *Longing to be in the sanctuary (84:1–12)*

A. *Longing for the courts of the LORD*

84:1 Ps 27:4	**84** 1	How lovely are Thy dwelling places, O LORD of hosts!
84:2 Ps 42:1,2	2	My soul longed and even yearned for the courts of the LORD; My heart and my flesh sing for joy to the living God.

B. *Blessedness in the LORD's house*

84:3 Ps 43:4; 5:2	3	The bird also has found a house, And the swallow a nest for herself, where she may lay her young, Even Thine altars, O LORD of hosts, My King and my God.
84:4 Ps 65:4	4	How blessed are those who dwell in Thy house! They are ever praising Thee. Selah.

C. *Blessedness of this pilgrim journey*

84:5 Ps 81:1	5	How blessed is the man whose strength is in Thee; In whose heart are the highways *to* Zion!
*84:6 2 Sam 4:23; Ps 107:35	6	Passing through the valley of [142]Baca, they make it a spring, The early rain also covers it with blessings.
84:7 Prov 4:18; 2 Cor 3:18; Deut 16:16; Ps 42:2	7	They go from strength to strength, *Every one of them* appears before God in Zion.

D. *Expression of petition and trust*

	8	O LORD God of hosts, hear my prayer;

141Or, *tumbleweed* 142Probably, *Weeping* or *Balsam trees*

84:6 *valley of Baca*, a normally dry valley in which the balsam tree flourishes.

9 Give ear, O God of Jacob!   Selah.
Behold our shield, O God,
And look upon the face of Thine anointed.
10 For a day in Thy courts is better than a thousand *outside*.
I would rather stand at the threshold of the house of my God,
Than dwell in the tents of wickedness.
11 For the LORD God is a sun and shield;
The LORD gives grace and glory;
No good thing does He withhold from those who walk uprightly.
12 O LORD of hosts,
How blessed is the man who trusts in Thee!

For the choir director. A Psalm of the sons of Korah.

I. Prayer for mercy to Israel (85:1–13)

A. The LORD's past mercies

85 O LORD, Thou didst show favor to Thy land;
Thou didst [143]restore the captivity of Jacob.
2 Thou didst forgive the iniquity of Thy people;
Thou didst cover all their sin.   Selah.
3 Thou didst withdraw all Thy fury;
Thou didst turn away from Thy burning anger.

B. The prayer for revival

4 Restore us, O God of our salvation,
And cause Thine indignation toward us to cease.
5 Wilt Thou be angry with us forever?
Wilt Thou prolong Thine anger to all generations?
6 Wilt Thou not Thyself revive us again,
That Thy people may rejoice in Thee?
7 Show us Thy lovingkindness, O LORD,
And grant us Thy salvation.

C. The steadfast love and faithfulness of the LORD

8 I will hear what God the LORD will say;
For He will speak peace to His people, to His godly ones;
But let them not turn back to folly.
9 Surely His salvation is near to those who [144]fear Him,
That glory may dwell in our land.
10 Lovingkindness and truth have met together;
Righteousness and peace have kissed each other.
11 Truth springs from the earth;
And righteousness looks down from heaven.
12 Indeed, the LORD will give what is good;
And our land will yield its produce.
13 Righteousness will go before Him,
And will make His footsteps into a way.

A Prayer of David.

I. A prayer for deliverance from trouble (86:1–17)

A. Appeal for help in trouble

86 Incline Thine ear, O LORD, *and* answer me;
For I am afflicted and needy.
2 Do preserve my soul, for I am a godly man;
O Thou my God, save Thy servant who trusts in Thee.

[143]Or, *restore the fortunes*   [144]Or, *reverence*

84:11 *sun,* a source of light, life, and fruitfulness.

86:3 Ps 57:1; 88:9	3	Be gracious to me, O Lord, For to Thee I cry all day long.
86:4 Ps 25:1; 143:8	4	Make glad the soul of Thy servant, For to Thee, O Lord, I lift up my soul.
86:5 Ps 130:7; 145:9; Joel 2:13	5	For Thou, Lord, art good, and ready to forgive, And abundant in lovingkindness to all who call upon Thee.
86:6 Ps 55:1	6	Give ear, O LORD, to my prayer; And give heed to the voice of my supplications!
86:7 Ps 50:15; 17:6	7	In the day of my trouble I shall call upon Thee, For Thou wilt answer me.

B. *Adoration of God*

86:8 Ex 15:11; Ps 89:6; Deut 3:24	8	There is no one like Thee among the gods, O Lord; Nor are there any works like Thine.
86:9 Ps 22:31; Is 43:7; Rev 15:4	9	All nations whom Thou hast made shall come and worship before Thee, O Lord; And they shall glorify Thy name.
86:10 Ex 15:11; Ps 72:18; Deut 6:4; Mark 12:29	10	For Thou art great and doest wondrous deeds; Thou alone art God.

C. *Petition and thanksgiving*

86:11 Ps 25:4	**11**	Teach me Thy way, O LORD; I will walk in Thy truth; Unite my heart to fear Thy name.
86:12 Ps 111:1	12	I will give thanks to Thee, O Lord my God, with all my heart, And will glorify Thy name forever.
86:13 Ps 30:3	13	For Thy lovingkindness toward me is great, And Thou hast delivered my soul from the depths of Sheol.

D. *Assurance of God's mercy and grace*

86:14 Ps 54:3	**14**	O God, arrogant men have risen up against me, And a band of violent men have sought my life, And they have not set Thee before them.
86:15 Ex 34:6; Neh 9:17; Ps 103:8; Joel 2:13	15	But Thou, O Lord, art a God merciful and gracious, Slow to anger and abundant in lovingkindness and truth.
86:16 Ps 25:16; 68:35; 116:16	16	Turn to me, and be gracious to me; Oh grant Thy strength to Thy servant, And save the son of Thy handmaid.
86:17 Ps 112:10; 118:13	17	Show me a sign for good, That those who hate me may see *it*, and be ashamed, Because Thou, O LORD, hast helped me and comforted me.

A Psalm of the sons of Korah. A Song.

I. *The privileges of citizenship in Zion (87:1–7)*

	87	His foundation is in the holy mountains.
87:2 Ps 78:67		2 The LORD loves the gates of Zion More than all the *other* dwelling places of Jacob.
87:3 Is 60:1	3	Glorious things are spoken of you, O city of God. Selah.
	4	"I shall mention [145]Rahab and Babylon among those who know Me; Behold, Philistia and Tyre with Ethiopia: 'This one was born there.' "
87:5 Ps 48:8	5	But of Zion it shall be said, "This one and that one were born in her"; And the Most High Himself will establish her.
87:6 Ezek 13:9	6	The LORD shall count when He registers the peoples,

[145]I.e., Egypt

87:4 *Rahab*, the name of a mythological monster used symbolically of Egypt. The word means "the haughty,"   "arrogant." See also Is. 30:7.

"This one was born there."   Selah.

7   Then those who sing as well as those who play the flutes *shall say*,
    "All my springs *of joy* are in you."

87:7
Ps 36:9

A Song. A Psalm of the sons of Korah. For the choir director; according to Mahalath
Leannoth. A Maskil of Heman the Ezrahite.

I. *A petition to be saved from death (88:1–18)*

A. *The psalmist's petition*

88   O LORD, the God of my salvation,
        I have cried out by day and in the night before Thee.
2   Let my prayer come before Thee;
    Incline Thine ear to my cry!

88:1
Ps 27:9;
51:14
88:2
Ps 18:6; 86:1

B. *The psalmist's troubles*

3   For my soul has had enough troubles,
    And my life has drawn near to Sheol.
4   I am reckoned among those who go down to the pit;
    I have become like a man without strength,
5   Forsaken among the dead,
    Like the slain who lie in the grave,
    Whom Thou dost remember no more,
    And they are cut off from Thy hand.
6   Thou hast put me in the lowest pit,
    In dark places, in the depths.
7   Thy wrath has rested upon me,
    And Thou hast afflicted me with all Thy waves.   Selah.
8   Thou hast removed my acquaintances far from me;
    Thou hast made me an [146]object of loathing to them;
    I am shut up and cannot go out.
9   My eye has wasted away because of affliction;
    I have called upon Thee every day, O LORD;
    I have spread out my hands to Thee.

88:3
Ps 107:18,26
88:4
Ps 28:1
88:5
Is 53:8

88:6
Ps 86:13;
143:3; 69:15
88:7
Ps 42:7
88:8
Job 19:13;
Ps 31:11;
142:4;
Lam 3:7
88:9
Ps 38:10;
86:3;
Job 11:13;
Ps 143:6

C. *The psalmist's questions*

10   Wilt Thou perform wonders for the dead?
     Will the departed spirits rise *and* praise Thee?   Selah.
11   Will Thy lovingkindness be declared in the grave,
     Thy faithfulness in Abaddon?
12   Will Thy wonders be made known in the darkness?
     And Thy righteousness in the land of forgetfulness?

88:10
Ps 6:5;
Is 38:18

88:12
Job 10:21

13   But I, O LORD, have cried out to Thee for help,
     And in the morning my prayer comes before Thee.
14   O LORD, why dost Thou reject my soul?
     Why dost Thou hide Thy face from me?

88:13
Ps 5:3;
119:147
88:14
Job 13:24;
Ps 13:1

D. *The psalmist's closing complaints*

15   I was afflicted and about to die from my youth on;
     I suffer Thy terrors; I am overcome.
16   Thy burning anger has passed over me;
     Thy terrors have destroyed me.
17   They have surrounded me like water all day long;
     They have encompassed me altogether.
18   Thou hast removed lover and friend far from me;
     My acquaintances are *in* darkness.

88:15
Job 6:4

88:17
Ps 22:16

88:18
Job 19:13;
Ps 31:11;
38:11

[146]Lit., *abomination to them*

A Maskil of Ethan the Ezrahite.

I. *God's covenant with David and Israel's afflictions (89:1–52)*

A. *The covenant with David*

89
I will sing of the lovingkindness of the LORD forever;
To all generations I will make known Thy faithfulness with my mouth.

2 For I have said, "Lovingkindness will be built up forever;
In the heavens Thou wilt establish Thy faithfulness."

3 "I have made a covenant with My chosen;
I have sworn to David My servant,

4 I will establish your seed forever,
And build up your throne to all generations."   Selah.

B. *Praise to a faithful and mighty God*

5 And the heavens will praise Thy wonders, O LORD;
Thy faithfulness also in the assembly of the holy ones.

6 For who in the skies is comparable to the LORD?
Who among the sons of the mighty is like the LORD,

7 A God greatly feared in the council of the holy ones,
And awesome above all those who are around Him?

8 O LORD God of hosts, who is like Thee, O mighty LORD?
Thy faithfulness also surrounds Thee.

9 Thou dost rule the swelling of the sea;
When its waves rise, Thou dost still them.

10 Thou Thyself didst crush Rahab like one who is slain;
Thou didst scatter Thine enemies with Thy mighty arm.

11 The heavens are Thine, the earth also is Thine;
The world and [147]all it contains, Thou hast founded them.

12 The north and the south, Thou hast created them;
Tabor and Hermon shout for joy at Thy name.

13 Thou hast a strong arm;
Thy hand is mighty, Thy right hand is exalted.

14 Righteousness and justice are the foundation of Thy throne;
Lovingkindness and truth go before Thee.

15 How blessed are the people who know the [148]joyful sound!
O LORD, they walk in the light of Thy countenance.

16 In Thy name they rejoice all the day,
And by Thy righteousness they are exalted.

17 For Thou art the glory of their strength,
And by Thy favor our horn is exalted.

18 For our shield belongs to the LORD,
[149]And our king to the Holy One of Israel.

C. *God's promises to David and his seed*

19 Once Thou didst speak in vision to Thy godly ones,

[147]Lit., *its fulness* [148]Or, *blast of the trumpet, shout of joy* [149]Or, *Even to the Holy One of Israel our King*

89:1 This psalm is related to the Davidic covenant (see note to 2 Sam. 7:4 on the subject). It reaffirms the divine promise of a line that will be established and will endure forever (v. 36). The psalm has Messianic implications, and this prophetic word looks to the rule of Jesus Christ. After the fall of Jerusalem in 587 B.C., which resulted in the loss of Jewish independence, there was no throne to be occupied by a descendant of David. This may be explained simply by observing that the purpose and plan of God was not changed by the changing fortunes of the royal house. An unbroken line of those who would have been eligible for the throne continued. The suspension of royal authority during these centuries was the consequence of chastening for sin. In a spiritual sense, the Lord Jesus Christ fulfilled the covenant promise by occupying the glorious heavenly counterpart of David's throne after His ascension.
89:19 Visions (like this one granted to Nathan, cf. 1 Chr. 17:15) were often the means by which God made His will known to men, both in the Old and New Testaments (Num. 12:6; Acts 16:9). These visions sometimes: (1) occurred at night (Gen. 46:2; Dan. 2:19); (2) occurred when the recipient was in a trance (Num. 24:16; Acts 11:5); (3) were not fully understood by the recipient (Dan. 7:15; Acts 10:17); and (4) were claimed by false prophets (Jer. 14:14; 23:16). Examples of those who experienced dreams include: (1) Abraham (Gen. 15:1); (2) Moses (Ex. 3:2,3); (3) Samuel (1 Sam. 3:2–15); (4) Paul (Acts 9:3,12; 16:9); (5) Peter (Acts 10:9–17); and (6) John (Rev. 1:12ff.).

	And didst say, "I have given help to one who is mighty;
	I have exalted one chosen from the people.
20	"I have found David My servant;
	With My holy oil I have anointed him,
21	With whom My hand will be established;
	My arm also will strengthen him.

20
Acts 13:22;
1 Sam 16:1,12

20 "I have found David My servant;
With My holy oil I have anointed him,

21 With whom My hand will be established;
My arm also will strengthen him.

22 "The enemy will not [150]deceive him,
Nor the son of wickedness afflict him.

89:22
2 Sam 7:10

23 "But I shall crush his adversaries before him,
And strike those who hate him.

89:23
2 Sam 7:9

24 "And My faithfulness and My lovingkindness will be with him,
And in My name his horn will be exalted.

89:24
2 Sam 7:15

25 "I shall also set his hand on the sea,
And his right hand on the rivers.

26 "He will cry to Me, 'Thou art my Father,
My God, and the rock of my salvation.'

89:26
2 Sam 7:14;
22:47

27 "I also shall make him *My* first-born,
The highest of the kings of the earth.

89:27
Col 1:15;
Num 24:7;
Rev 1:5

28 "My lovingkindness I will keep for him forever,
And My covenant shall be confirmed to him.

89:28
Is 55:3

29 "So I will establish his descendants forever,
And his throne as the days of heaven.

89:29
Is 9:7;
Jer 33:17;
Deut 11:21

30 "If his sons forsake My law,
And do not walk in My judgments,

89:30
2 Sam 7:14

31 If they [151]violate My statutes,
And do not keep My commandments,

32 Then I will visit their transgression with the rod,
And their iniquity with stripes.

89:32
2 Sam 7:14

33 "But I will not break off My lovingkindness from him,
Nor deal falsely in My faithfulness.

89:33
2 Sam 7:15

34 "My covenant I will not violate,
Nor will I alter the utterance of My lips.

89:34
Deut 7:9;
Num 23:19

35 "[152]Once I have sworn by My holiness;
I will not lie to David.

89:35
Amos 4:2

36 "His descendants shall endure forever,
And his throne as the sun before Me.

89:36
Ps 72:5

37 "It shall be established forever like the moon,
And the witness in the sky is faithful."   Selah.

D. *A plea for renewal of the covenant*

1. *The punishment of the* LORD

38 But Thou hast cast off and rejected,
Thou hast been full of wrath against Thine anointed.

89:38
1 Chr 28:9;
Deut 32:19

39 Thou hast spurned the covenant of Thy servant;
Thou hast profaned his crown in the dust.

89:39
Lam 5:16

40 Thou hast broken down all his walls;
Thou hast brought his strongholds to ruin.

89:40
Ps 80:12;
Lam 2:2,5

41 All who pass along the way plunder him;
He has become a reproach to his neighbors.

89:41
Ps 44:13

42 Thou hast exalted the right hand of his adversaries;
Thou hast made all his enemies rejoice.

89:42
Ps 13:2; 80:6

43 Thou dost also turn back the edge of his sword,
And hast not made him stand in battle.

89:43
Ps 44:10

44 Thou hast made his splendor to cease,
And cast his throne to the ground.

89:44
Ezek 28:7

45 Thou hast shortened the days of his youth;
Thou hast covered him with shame.   Selah.

89:45
Ps 102:23;
44:15

2. *The prayer for renewal*

46 How long, O LORD?

89:46
Ps 79:5

---

[150]Or, *exact usury from him*   [151]Lit., *profane*   [152]Or, *One thing*

Wilt Thou hide Thyself forever?
Will Thy wrath burn like fire?

89:47
Job 7:7; 10:9;
14:1; Ps 39:5
47 Remember what my span of life is;
For what vanity Thou hast created all the sons of men!

89:48
Ps 49:9;
Heb 11:5
48 What man can live and not see death?
Can he deliver his soul from the power of Sheol?   Selah.

*89:49
2 Sam 7:15;
Ps 54:5
49 Where are Thy former lovingkindnesses, O Lord,
Which Thou didst swear to David in Thy faithfulness?

89:50
Ps 69:9,19
50 Remember, O Lord, the reproach of Thy servants;
How I do bear in my bosom *the reproach of* all the many peoples,

89:51
Ps 74:10
51 With which Thine enemies have reproached, O Lord,
With which they have reproached the footsteps of Thine anointed.

89:52
Ps 41:13
52 Blessed be the Lord forever!
Amen and Amen.

BOOK 4

A Prayer of Moses the man of God.

I. *God's eternity and man's transitoriness (90:1–17)*

A. *Eternal God and transitory man*

90:1
Deut 33:27;
Ezek 11:16

90

Lord, Thou hast been our [153]dwelling place in all generations.
2   Before the mountains were born,

90:2
Prov 8:25;
Ps 102:25;
93:2
Or Thou didst give birth to the earth and the world,
Even from everlasting to everlasting, Thou art God.

90:3
Gen 3:19
3 Thou dost turn man back into dust,
And dost say, "Return, O children of men."

90:4
2 Pet 3:8;
Ps 39:5
4 For a thousand years in Thy sight
Are like yesterday when it passes by,
Or *as* a watch in the night.

90:5
Job 27:20;
Ps 73:20;
103:15;
Is 40:6
5 Thou hast swept them away like a flood, they fall asleep;
In the morning they are like grass which sprouts anew.

90:6
Job 14:2;
Ps 92:7
6 In the morning it flourishes, and sprouts anew;
Toward evening it fades, and withers away.

7 For we have been consumed by Thine anger,
And by Thy wrath we have been dismayed.

90:8
Ps 50:21;
Jer 16:17;
Ps 19:12
8 Thou hast placed our iniquities before Thee,
Our secret *sins* in the light of Thy presence.

90:9
Ps 78:33
9 For all our days have declined in Thy fury;
We have finished our years like a sigh.

90:10
Eccl 12:2-7
10 As for the days of our life, they contain seventy years,
Or if due to strength, eighty years,
Yet their pride is *but* labor and sorrow;
For soon it is gone and we fly away.

90:11
Ps 76:7
11 Who understands the power of Thine anger,
And Thy fury, according to the fear that is due Thee?

90:12
Ps 39:4
12 So teach us to number our days,
That we may present to Thee a heart of wisdom.

B. *A prayer for God's favor*

*90:13
Deut 32:26;
Ps 135:14
13 Do return, O Lord; how long *will it be*?

89:49 The word here translated *faithfulness* ('*emunah*) has to do with truth. God is a God of truth, that is, He keeps His own character. This is also said of Christ, who is the truth (John 7:18; 14:6). The Holy Spirit is correspondingly called the Spirit of truth (John 14:17). The Word of God is itself called the truth (John 17:17). Believers are called upon to serve and worship God and walk according to truth (Josh. 24:14; 1 Sam. 12:24; John 4:24). God's truth should be known, believed in, and obeyed from the heart (Rom. 2:8; 2 Thess. 2:12,13; 1 Tim. 4:3; 2 Tim. 2:25). Of particular significance is the injunction to handle aright the Word of truth (2 Tim. 2:15).

153Or, *hiding place;* some ancient mss. read *place of refuge*

And be sorry for Thy servants.

14 O satisfy us in the morning with Thy lovingkindness,
That we may sing for joy and be glad all our days.

15 Make us glad according to the days Thou hast afflicted us,
And the years we have seen [154]evil.

16 Let Thy work appear to Thy servants,
And Thy majesty to their children.

17 And let the favor of the Lord our God be upon us;
And do [155]confirm for us the work of our hands;
Yes, [155]confirm the work of our hands.

I. *The security of the godly (91:1–16)*

A. *The promise of security*

91
He who dwells in the shelter of the Most High
Will abide in the shadow of the Almighty.

2 I will say to the Lord, "My refuge and my fortress,
My God, in whom I trust!"

3 For it is He who delivers you from the snare of the trapper,
And from the deadly pestilence.

4 He will cover you with His pinions,
And under His wings you may seek refuge;
His faithfulness is a shield and bulwark.

5 You will not be afraid of the terror by night,
Or of the arrow that flies by day;

6 Of the pestilence that stalks in darkness,
Or of the destruction that lays waste at noon.

7 A thousand may fall at your side,
And ten thousand at your right hand;
But it shall not approach you.

8 You will only look on with your eyes,
And see the recompense of the wicked.

B. *The witness of the psalmist*

9 For you have made the Lord, my refuge,
Even the Most High, your dwelling place.

10 No evil will befall you,
Nor will any plague come near your tent.

11 For He will give His angels charge concerning you,
To guard you in all your ways.

12 They will bear you up in their hands,
Lest you strike your foot against a stone.

13 You will tread upon the lion and cobra,
The young lion and the serpent you will trample down.

C. *The witness of the Lord*

14 "Because he has loved Me, therefore I will deliver him;
I will set him *securely* on high, because he has known My name.

15 "He will call upon Me, and I will answer him;
I will be with him in trouble;
I will rescue him, and honor him.

16 "With a long life I will satisfy him,
And let him behold My salvation."

[154]Or, *trouble*   [155]Or, *give permanence to*

90:13 *return*, i.e., turn from your anger.   **91:1** Only those who abide in God are safe.

90:14
Ps 65:4; 85:6

90:16
Hab 3:2;
1 Kin 8:11
90:17
Ps 27:4;
Is 26:12

*91:1
Ps 27:5;
31:20; 17:8
91:2
Ps 142:5

91:3
Ps 124:7

91:4
Is 51:16;
Ps 57:1;
40:11; 35:2

91:5
Ps 23:4;
Song 3:8;
Ps 64:4
91:6
v. 10;
Job 5:22

91:8
Ps 37:34;
Mal 1:5

91:10
Prov 12:21

91:11
Ps 34:7;
Matt 4:6;
Luke 4:10;
Heb 1:14

91:13
Luke 10:19

91:14
Ps 145:20;
59:1; 9:10
91:15
Ps 50:15;
1 Sam 2:30;
John 12:26

91:16
Ps 21:4;
50:23

A Psalm, a Song for the Sabbath day.

I. *Praise for the Lord's goodness (92:1–15)*

A. *The command to give thanks*

92 It is good to give thanks to the LORD,
And to sing praises to Thy name, O Most High;
2 To declare Thy lovingkindness in the morning,
And Thy faithfulness by night,
3 With the ten-stringed lute, and with the harp;
With resounding music upon the lyre.
4 For Thou, O LORD, hast made me glad by what Thou hast done,
I will sing for joy at the works of Thy hands.

B. *The end of the wicked*

5 How great are Thy works, O LORD!
Thy thoughts are very deep.
6 A senseless man has no knowledge;
Nor does a stupid man understand this:
7 That when the wicked sprouted up like grass,
And all who did iniquity flourished,
It *was only* that they might be destroyed forevermore.
8 But Thou, O LORD, art on high forever.
9 For, behold, Thine enemies, O LORD,
For, behold, Thine enemies will perish;
All who do iniquity will be scattered.
10 But Thou hast exalted my horn like *that of* the wild ox;
I have been anointed with fresh oil.
11 And my eye has looked *exultantly* upon my foes,
My ears hear of the evildoers who rise up against me.

C. *The end of the righteous*

12 The righteous man will flourish like the palm tree,
He will grow like a cedar in Lebanon.
13 Planted in the house of the LORD,
They will flourish in the courts of our God.
14 They will still yield fruit in old age;
They shall be [156]full of sap and very green,
15 To declare that the LORD is upright;
He is my rock, and there is no unrighteousness in Him.

I. *The majesty of the Lord (93:1–5)*

93 The LORD reigns, He is clothed with majesty;
The LORD has clothed and girded Himself with strength;
Indeed, the world is firmly established, it will not be moved.
2 Thy throne is established from of old;
Thou art from everlasting.

3 The floods have lifted up, O LORD,
The floods have lifted up their voice;
The floods lift up their pounding waves.
4 More than the sounds of many waters,
Than the mighty breakers of the sea,
The LORD on high is mighty.
5 Thy testimonies are fully confirmed;
Holiness befits Thy house,
O LORD, forevermore.

[156]Lit., *fat and*

Marginal references

92:1 — Ps 157:1
92:2 — Ps 89:1
92:3 — 1 Chr 23:5; Ps 33:2
92:5 — Ps 40:5; Is 28:29; Rom 11:33
92:6 — Ps 73:22
92:7 — Ps 90:5; 94:4; 37:38; 93:4
92:8 — Ps 83:18
92:9 — Ps 68:1; 89:10
92:10 — Ps 89:17; 23:5
92:11 — Ps 54:7; 59:10
92:12 — Ps 52:8; Is 65:22; Hos 14:5,6; Ps 104:16
92:13 — Ps 80:15; 100:4
92:14 — Is 37:31
92:15 — Ps 25:8; Deut 32:4; Rom 9:14
93:1 — Ps 96:10; 97:1; 99:1; 104:1; 65:6
93:2 — Ps 45:6; 90:2
93:3 — Ps 98:7,8
93:4 — Ps 65:7; 89:9
93:5 — Ps 19:7; 1 Cor 3:17

741

I. *An appeal to avenge (94:1–23)*

A. *The cry for vengeance on the wicked*

O L<small>ORD</small>, God of vengeance;
O God of vengeance, shine forth!
Rise up, O Judge of the earth;
Render recompense to the proud.
How long shall the wicked, O L<small>ORD</small>,
How long shall the wicked exult?
They pour forth *words*, they speak arrogantly;
All who do wickedness vaunt themselves.
They crush Thy people, O L<small>ORD</small>,
And afflict Thy heritage.
They slay the widow and the stranger,
And murder the orphans.

7 And they have said, "The L<small>ORD</small> does not see,
Nor does the God of Jacob pay heed."

8 Pay heed, you senseless among the people;
And when will you understand, stupid ones?

9 He who planted the ear, does He not hear?
He who formed the eye, does He not see?

10 He who chastens the nations, will He not rebuke,
Even He who teaches man knowledge?

11 The L<small>ORD</small> knows the thoughts of man,
That they are a *mere* breath.

B. *The L<small>ORD</small> will not forsake His people*

12 Blessed is the man whom Thou dost chasten, O L<small>ORD</small>,
And dost teach out of Thy law;

13 That Thou mayest grant him relief from the days of adversity,
Until a pit is dug for the wicked.

14 For the L<small>ORD</small> will not abandon His people,
Nor will He forsake His inheritance.

15 For judgment will again be righteous;
And all the upright in heart will follow it.

C. *The psalmist seeks the L<small>ORD</small>*

16 Who will stand up for me against evildoers?
Who will take his stand for me against those who do wickedness?

17 If the L<small>ORD</small> had not been my help,
My soul would soon have dwelt in *the abode of* silence.

18 If I should say, "My foot has slipped,"
Thy lovingkindness, O L<small>ORD</small>, will hold me up.

19 When my anxious thoughts multiply within me,
Thy consolations delight my soul.

20 Can a throne of destruction be allied with Thee,
One which devises mischief by decree?

21 They band themselves together against the life of the righteous,
And condemn the innocent to death.

22 But the L<small>ORD</small> has been my stronghold,
And my God the rock of my refuge.

23 And He has brought back their wickedness upon them,
And will destroy them in their evil;
The L<small>ORD</small> our God will destroy them.

I. *A call to praise the L<small>ORD</small> (95:1–11)*

A. *The praise to be sung*

95 O come, let us sing for joy to the L<small>ORD</small>;
Let us shout joyfully to the rock of our salvation.

94:1
Deut 32:35;
Nah 1:2;
Ps 50:2
94:2
Ps 7:6;
Gen 18:25;
Ps 31:23
94:3
Job 20:5
94:4
Ps 31:18;
10:3

94:6
Is 10:2

94:7
Ps 10:11

94:8
Ps 92:6

94:9
Ex 4:11;
Prov 20:12
94:10
Ps 44:2;
Job 35:11;
Is 28:26
94:11
1 Cor 3:20

94:12
Job 5:17;
Heb 12:5
94:13
Ps 49:5; 9:15

94:14
1 Sam 12:22;
Rom 11:1,2

94:16
Is 28:21;
Ps 59:2

94:17
Ps 124:1

94:18
Ps 38:16

94:19
Is 66:13

94:20
Amos 6:3;
Is 10:1
94:21
Ps 56:6;
Matt 27:1;
Prov 17:15
94:22
Ps 59:9; 71:7
94:23
Ps 7:16

95:1
Ps 100:1;
Deut 32:15;
2 Sam 22:47

95:2 Mic 6:6; Ps 100:4; 81:2	2	Let us come before His presence with thanksgiving; Let us shout joyfully to Him with psalms.
95:3 Ps 96:4; 97:9; 135:5	3	For the LORD is a great God, And a great King above all gods,
	4	In whose hand are the depths of the earth; The peaks of the mountains are His also.
95:5 Gen 1:9,10	5	The sea is His, for it was He who made it; And His hands formed the dry land.
95:6 Ps 99:5,9; 2 Chr 6:13; Ps 100:3	6	Come, let us worship and bow down; Let us kneel before the LORD our Maker.
95:7 Ps 79:13; 100:3; Heb 3:7-11	7	For He is our God, And we are the people of His pasture, and the sheep of His hand. Today, if you would hear His voice,

B. *The warning to be followed*

95:8 Ex 17:2,7; Deut 6:16	8	Do not harden your hearts, as at [157]Meribah, As in the day of [158]Massah in the wilderness;
95:9 Ps 78:18; 1 Cor 10:9	9	"When your fathers tested Me, They tried Me, though they had seen My work.
95:10 Heb 3:10,17	10	"For forty years I loathed *that* generation, And said they are a people who err in their heart, And they do not know My ways.
95:11 Heb 4:3,5	11	"Therefore I swore in My anger, Truly they shall not enter into My rest."

I. *A call to worship the LORD (96:1–13).*

A. *The call to praise the LORD*

96:1 1 Chr 16:23-33	**96**	Sing to the LORD a new song; Sing to the LORD, all the earth.
96:2 Ps 71:15	2	Sing to the LORD, bless His name; Proclaim good tidings of His salvation from day to day.
96:3 Ps 145:12	3	Tell of His glory among the nations, His wonderful deeds among all the peoples.
96:4 Ps 145:3; 18:3; 95:3	4	For great is the LORD, and greatly to be praised; He is to be feared above all gods.
96:5 1 Chr 16:26; Ps 115:15	5	For all the gods of the peoples are idols, But the LORD made the heavens.
96:6 Ps 104:1	6	Splendor and majesty are before Him, Strength and beauty are in His sanctuary.

B. *All the earth to praise the LORD*

96:7 Ps 29:1,2	7	[159]Ascribe to the LORD, O families of the peoples, [159]Ascribe to the LORD glory and strength.
96:8 Ps 79:9	8	[159]Ascribe to the LORD the glory of His name; Bring an offering, and come into His courts.
96:9 Ps 29:2	9	Worship the LORD in [160]holy attire; Tremble before Him, all the earth.

C. *The LORD the righteous judge*

96:10 Ps 93:1; 67:4	10	Say among the nations, "The LORD reigns; Indeed, the world is firmly established, it will not be moved; He will judge the peoples with [161]equity."
96:11 Ps 97:1; 98:7	11	Let the heavens be glad, and let the earth rejoice; Let the sea roar, and all it contains;
	12	Let the field exult, and all that is in it. Then all the trees of the forest will sing for joy
96:13 Ps 67:4; Rev 19:11	13	Before the LORD, for He is coming; For He is coming to judge the earth.

[157]Or, *place of strife* [158]Or, *temptation* [159]Lit., *Give* [160]Or, *the splendor of holiness* [161]Or, *uprightness*

He will judge the world in righteousness,
And the peoples in His faithfulness.

I. The power and dominion of the Lord (97:1–12)

A. The reign of the Lord

97 The Lord reigns; let the earth rejoice;
Let the many [162]islands be glad.
2 Clouds and thick darkness surround Him;
Righteousness and justice are the foundation of His throne.
3 Fire goes before Him,
And burns up His adversaries round about.
4 His lightnings lit up the world;
The earth saw and trembled.
5 The mountains melted like wax at the presence of the Lord,
At the presence of the Lord of the whole earth.

B. The exaltation of the Lord

6 The heavens declare His righteousness,
And all the peoples have seen His glory.
7 Let all those be ashamed who serve graven images,
Who boast themselves of idols;
Worship Him, all you gods.
8 Zion heard *this* and was glad,
And the daughters of Judah have rejoiced
Because of Thy judgments, O Lord.
9 For Thou art the Lord Most High over all the earth;
Thou art exalted far above all gods.

C. The deliverance of the righteous by the Lord

10 Hate evil, you who love the Lord,
Who preserves the souls of His godly ones;
He delivers them from the hand of the wicked.
11 Light is sown *like seed* for the righteous,
And gladness for the upright in heart.
12 Be glad in the Lord, you righteous ones;
And give thanks to His holy name.

A Psalm.

I. A call to praise the righteous Lord (98:1–9)

A. The song of salvation

98 O sing to the Lord a new song,
For He has done wonderful things,
His right hand and His holy arm have [163]gained the victory for Him.
2 The Lord has made known His salvation;
He has revealed His righteousness in the sight of the nations.
3 He has remembered His lovingkindness and His faithfulness to the
house of Israel;
All the ends of the earth have seen the salvation of our God.

B. The summons of men to praise

4 Shout joyfully to the Lord, all the earth;
Break forth and sing for joy and sing praises.
5 Sing praises to the Lord with the lyre;
With the lyre and the sound of melody.
6 With trumpets and the sound of the horn
Shout joyfully before the King, the Lord.

162Or, *coastlands*   163Or, *accomplished salvation*

97:1
Ps 96:10,11

97:2
1 Kin 8:12;
Ps 18:11;
89:14
97:3
Ps 18:8;
Dan 7:10;
Hab 3:5;
Heb 12:29
97:4
Ps 77:18
97:5
Mic 1:4;
Josh 3:11

97:6
Ps 50:6

97:7
Ex 20:4;
Lev 26:1;
Heb 1:6
97:8
Ps 48:11

97:9
Ps 83:18;
Ex 18:11;
Ps 95:3

97:10
Ps 34:14;
Amos 5:15;
Prov 2:8;
Ps 37:39;
Dan 3:28
97:11
Job 22:28;
Ps 112:4
97:12
Ps 32:11;
30:4

98:1
Ps 33:3; 40:5;
Ex 15:6;
Is 52:10
98:2
Rom 3:25

98:3
Luke 1:54;
Is 49:6

98:4
Ps 100:1

98:6
Num 10:10

C. *The summons of nature to praise*

98:7
Ps 96:11;
24:1

7 Let the sea roar and all it contains,
The world and those who dwell in it.

98:8
Ps 93:3;
65:12

8 Let the rivers clap their hands;
Let the mountains sing together for joy

98:9
Ps 96:10,13

9 Before the LORD; for He is coming to judge the earth;
He will judge the world with righteousness,
And the peoples with equity.

I. *Praise to a holy God (99:1–9)*

A. *The summons to praise*

99:1
Ex 25:22

99 The LORD reigns, let the peoples tremble;
He is enthroned *above* the cherubim, let the earth shake!

99:2
Ps 97:9

2 The LORD is great in Zion,
And He is exalted above all the peoples.

3 Let them praise Thy great and awesome name;
Holy is He.

99:4
Ps 11:7; 17:2;
103:6

4 And the strength of the King loves [164]justice;
Thou hast established equity;
Thou hast executed [164]justice and righteousness in Jacob.

99:5
Ps 132:7;
Lev 19:2

5 Exalt the LORD our God,
And worship at His footstool;
Holy is He.

B. *Reasons for praise*

99:6
Jer 15:1;
Ex 14:15;
1 Sam 7:9

6 Moses and Aaron were among His priests,
And Samuel was among those who called on His name;
They called upon the LORD, and He answered them.

99:7
Ex 33:9

7 He spoke to them in the pillar of cloud;
They kept His testimonies,
And the statute that He gave them.

99:8
Ps 106:44;
Num 14:20;
Deut 9:20

8 O LORD our God, Thou didst answer them;
Thou wast a forgiving God to them,
And *yet* an avenger of their *evil* deeds.

99:9
Ps 34:3

9 Exalt the LORD our God,
And worship at His holy hill;
For holy is the LORD our God.

A Psalm for Thanksgiving.

I. *All men exhorted to praise God (100:1–5)*

100:1
Ps 98:4

100 Shout joyfully to the LORD, all the earth.
2   Serve the LORD with gladness;
Come before Him with joyful singing.

100:3
Ps 46:10;
95:6,7

3 Know that the LORD Himself is God;
It is He who has made us, and [165]not we ourselves;
We are His people and the sheep of His pasture.

100:4
Ps 95:2; 96:2

4 Enter His gates with thanksgiving,
And His courts with praise.
Give thanks to Him; bless His name.

100:5
Ps 25:8;
119:90

5 For the LORD is good;
His lovingkindness is everlasting,
And His faithfulness to all generations.

[164]Or, *judgment*   [165]Some mss. read *His we are*

98:7 As the whole creation has groaned under sin, so shall it exult when it is delivered.
99:5 *Holy is He.* Holiness sums up all of God's moral perfections. Therefore we should all worship Him.
99:6 These great saints worshiped the LORD God in: (1) their earnest prayers (v. 6); and (2) their holy lives (v. 7).

A Psalm of David.

I. *A profession of integrity (101:1–8)*

A. *David's desire for personal integrity*

101 I will sing of lovingkindness and justice,
To Thee, O LORD, I will sing praises.
2　I will give heed to the [166]blameless way.
When wilt Thou come to me?
I will walk within my house in the integrity of my heart.
3　I will set no worthless thing before my eyes;
I hate the work of those who fall away;
It shall not fasten its grip on me.
4　A perverse heart shall depart from me;
I will know no evil.

B. *David's desire for integrity in others*

5　Whoever secretly slanders his neighbor, him I will destroy;
No one who has a haughty look and an arrogant heart will I endure.

6　My eyes shall be upon the faithful of the land, that they may dwell
with me;
He who walks in a [166]blameless way is the one who will minister
to me.
7　He who practices deceit shall not dwell within my house;
He who speaks falsehood shall not maintain his position before me.
8　Every morning I will [167]destroy all the wicked of the land,
So as to cut off from the city of the LORD all those who do iniquity.

A Prayer of the Afflicted, when he is faint, and pours out his complaint before the
LORD.

I. *Appeal for mercy and for Zion (102:1–28)*

A. *The sufferings of the psalmist*

102 Hear my prayer, O LORD!
And let my cry for help come to Thee.
2　Do not hide Thy face from me in the day of my distress;
Incline Thine ear to me;
In the day when I call answer me quickly.
3　For my days have been consumed in smoke,
And my bones have been scorched like a hearth.
4　My heart has been smitten like grass and has withered away,
Indeed, I forget to eat my bread.
5　Because of the loudness of my groaning
My bones cling to my flesh.
6　I resemble a pelican of the wilderness;
I have become like an owl of the waste places.
7　I lie awake,
I have become like a lonely bird on a housetop.

8　My enemies have reproached me all day long;
Those who deride me have used my *name* as a curse.
9　For I have eaten ashes like bread,
And mingled my drink with weeping,
10　Because of Thine indignation and Thy wrath;
For Thou hast lifted me up and cast me away.
11　My days are like a lengthened shadow;
And I wither away like grass.

[166]Or, *way of integrity* [167]Or, *silence*

101:1
Ps 89:1

101:2
1 Sam 18:14;
1 Kin 9:4

101:3
Deut 15:9;
Ps 40:4

101:4
Prov 11:20

101:5
Ps 50:20;
Prov 6:17

101:6
Ps 119:1

101:8
Ps 75:10;
118:10-12

102:1
Ex 2:23;
1 Sam 9:16
102:2
Ps 69:17;
71:2

102:3
James 4:14;
Job 30:30;
Ps 31:10
102:4
Ps 37:2
102:5
Lam 4:8

102:6
Is 34:11

102:7
Ps 77:4;
38:11

102:8
Acts 26:11;
23:12
102:9
Ps 42:3

102:10
Ps 38:3;
Job 30:22
102:11
Job 14:2; v. 4

B. *The eternal God the refuge of Zion*

102:12
Ps 9:7;
Lam 5:19;
Ps 135:13

12 But Thou, O LORD, dost abide forever;
And Thy name to all generations.

102:13
Is 60:10;
Zech 1:12;
Ps 75:2

13 Thou wilt arise *and* have compassion on Zion;
For it is time to be gracious to her,
For the appointed time has come.

14 Surely Thy servants find pleasure in her stones,
And feel pity for her dust.

102:15
1 Kin 8:43;
Ps 138:4

15 So the nations will fear the name of the LORD,
And all the kings of the earth Thy glory.

102:16
Is 60:1,2

16 For the LORD has built up Zion;
He has appeared in His glory.

102:17
Neh 1:6

17 He has regarded the prayer of the destitute,
And has not despised their prayer.

102:18
Rom 15:4;
Ps 22:31

18 This will be written for the generation to come;
That a people yet to be created may praise the LORD.

102:19
Deut 26:15;
Ps 33:13

19 For He looked down from His holy height;
From heaven the LORD gazed upon the earth,

102:20
Ps 79:11

20 To hear the groaning of the prisoner;
To set free those who were doomed to death;

102:21
Ps 22:22

21 That *men* may tell of the name of the LORD in Zion,
And His praise in Jerusalem;

102:22
Ps 86:9

22 When the peoples are gathered together,
And the kingdoms, to serve the LORD.

C. *The assurance of deliverance*

102:23
Job 21:21

23 He has weakened my strength in the way;
He has shortened my days.

102:24
Is 38:10;
Ps 90:2;
Hab 1:12

24 I say, "O my God, do not take me away in the midst of my days,
Thy years are throughout all generations.

102:25
Gen 1:1;
Heb 1:10;
Ps 96:5

25 "Of old Thou didst found the earth;
And the heavens are the work of Thy hands.

102:26
Is 34:4;
Matt 24:35;
2 Pet 3:7,10;
Rev 20:11

26 "Even they will perish, but Thou dost endure;
And all of them will wear out like a garment;
Like clothing Thou wilt change them, and they will be changed.

102:27
Mal 3:6;
Heb 13:8;
James 1:17

27 "But Thou art the same,
And Thy years will not come to an end.

102:28
Ps 69:36;
89:4

28 "The children of Thy servants will continue,
And their descendants will be established before Thee."

A Psalm of David.

I. *An exhortation to bless the* LORD *(103:1–22)*

A. *The exhortation to self*

103:1
Ps 104:1;
33:21

103 Bless the LORD, O my soul;
And all that is within me, *bless* His holy name.

2 Bless the LORD, O my soul,
And forget none of His benefits;

103:3
Ps 130:8;
Is 43:25;
Ex 15:26

3 Who pardons all your iniquities;
Who heals all your diseases;

103:4
Ps 49:15;
5:12

4 Who redeems your life from the pit;
Who crowns you with lovingkindness and compassion;

103:5
Is 40:31

5 Who satisfies your [168]years with good things,
So that your youth is renewed like the eagle.

B. *God's mercies a reason to bless Him*

6 The LORD performs righteous deeds,
And judgments for all who are oppressed.

[168]Or, *desire*

7 He made known His ways to Moses,
His acts to the sons of Israel.

8 The LORD is compassionate and gracious,
Slow to anger and abounding in lovingkindness.

9 He will not always strive *with us*;
Nor will He keep *His anger* forever.

10 He has not dealt with us according to our sins,
Nor rewarded us according to our iniquities.

11 For as high as the heavens are above the earth,
So great is His lovingkindness toward those who [169]fear Him.

12 As far as the east is from the west,
So far has He removed our transgressions from us.

13 Just as a father has compassion on *his* children,
So the LORD has compassion on those who fear Him.

C. *God's everlasting love*

14 For He Himself knows [170]our frame;
He is mindful that we are *but* dust.

15 As for man, his days are like grass;
As a flower of the field, so he flourishes.

16 When the wind has passed over it, it is no more;
And its place acknowledges it no longer.

17 But the lovingkindness of the LORD is from everlasting to everlasting
on those who [169]fear Him,
And His righteousness to children's children,

18 To those who keep His covenant,
And who remember His precepts to do them.

D. *The universal call to bless God's name*

19 The LORD has established His throne in the heavens;
And His [171]sovereignty rules over all.

20 Bless the LORD, you His angels,
Mighty in strength, who perform His word,
Obeying the voice of His word!

21 Bless the LORD, all you His hosts,
You who serve Him, doing His will.

22 Bless the LORD, all you works of His,
In all places of His dominion;
Bless the LORD, O my soul!

I. *Praise to God the creator and sustainer (104:1–35)*

A. *The beginning of creation*

104 Bless the LORD, O my soul!
O LORD my God, Thou art very great;
Thou art clothed with splendor and majesty,

2 Covering Thyself with light as with a cloak,
Stretching out heaven like a *tent* curtain.

3 [172]He lays the beams of His upper chambers in the waters;
He makes the clouds His chariot;
He walks upon the wings of the wind;

4 He makes [173]the winds His messengers,
[174]Flaming fire His ministers.

B. *The foundations of the earth*

5 He established the earth upon its foundations,
So that it will not [175]totter forever and ever.

6 Thou didst cover it with the deep as with a garment;
The waters were standing above the mountains.

103:8
Ex 34:6;
Neh 9:17;
Ps 145:8
103:9
Ps 30:5;
Is 57:16;
Jer 3:5
103:10
Ezra 9:13
103:11
Ps 36:5
103:12
2 Sam 12:13;
Is 38:17;
Heb 9:26
103:13
Mal 3:17

103:14
Is 29:16;
Gen 3:19

103:15
1 Pet 1:24;
Job 14:1,2
103:16
Job 7:10

103:18
Deut 7:9

103:19
Ps 11:4; 47:2
103:20
Ps 148:2;
Matt 6:10;
Heb 1:14
103:21
Ps 148:2

104:1
Ps 103:1

104:2
Dan 7:9;
Is 40:22
104:3
Amos 9:6;
Is 19:1;
Ps 18:10
104:4
Heb 1:7

104:5
Job 26:7;
Ps 24:2
104:6
Gen 7:19

169Or, *revere* 170I.e., what we are made of 171Or, *kingdom* 172Lit., *Who*, so through v. 4, and vv. 13, 14 173Or, *His*
angels, spirits 174Or, *His ministers flames of fire* 175Or, *move out of place*

7   At Thy rebuke they fled;
    At the sound of Thy thunder they hurried away.

104:8
Ps 33:7

8   The mountains rose; the valleys sank down
    To the place which Thou didst establish for them.

104:9
Job 38:10,11;
Jer 5:22

9   Thou didst set a boundary that they may not pass over;
    That they may not return to cover the earth.

C. *The springs in the valleys*

104:10
Ps 107:35

10   He sends forth springs in the valleys;
    They flow between the mountains;

104:11
Job 39:5

11   They give drink to every beast of the field;
    The wild donkeys quench their thirst.

104:12
Matt 8:20

12   Beside them the birds of the heavens dwell;
    They lift up *their* voices among the branches.

104:13
Ps 65:9;
147:8

13   He waters the mountains from His upper chambers;
    The earth is satisfied with the fruit of His works.

D. *The fruitfulness of the earth*

104:14
Ps 147:8;
Job 38:27;
Gen 1:29;
Job 28:5

14   He causes the grass to grow for the cattle,
    And vegetation for the labor of man,
    So that he may bring forth food from the earth,

104:15
Judg 9:13;
Ps 23:5

15   And wine which makes man's heart glad,
    So that he may make *his* face glisten with oil,
    And food which sustains man's heart.

16   The trees of the LORD drink their fill,
    The cedars of Lebanon which He planted,

17   Where the birds build their nests,
    And the stork, whose home is the fir trees.

104:18
Prov 30:26

18   The high mountains are for the wild goats;
    The cliffs are a refuge for the rock badgers.

E. *The moon and the sun*

104:19
Gen 1:14

19   He made the moon for the seasons;
    The sun knows the place of its setting.

104:20
Is 45:7

20   Thou dost appoint darkness and it becomes night,
    In which all the beasts of the forest prowl about.

104:21
Job 38:39

21   The young lions roar after their prey,
    And seek their food from God.

22   *When* the sun rises they withdraw,
    And lie down in their dens.

104:23
Gen 3:19

23   Man goes forth to his work
    And to his labor until evening.

F. *The creatures of the sea*

104:24
Ps 40:5;
Prov 3:19;
Ps 65:9

24   O LORD, how many are Thy works!
    In wisdom Thou hast made them all;
    The earth is full of Thy [176]possessions.

25   There is the sea, great and broad,
    In which are swarms without number,
    Animals both small and great.

104:26
Ps 107:23;
Job 41:1

26   There the ships move along,
    And [177]Leviathan, which Thou hast formed to sport in it.

G. *God the sustainer of life*

104:27
Ps 136:25;
145:14

27   They all wait for Thee,
    To give them their food in [178]due season.

28   Thou dost give to them, they gather *it* up;
    Thou dost open Thy hand, they are satisfied with good.

104:29
Job 34:14;
Ps 146:4;
Eccl 12:7

29   Thou dost hide Thy face, they are dismayed;

[176]Or, *creatures*   [177]Or, *a sea monster*   [178]Lit., *its appointed time*

Thou dost take away their [179]spirit, they expire,
And return to their dust.
30 Thou dost send forth Thy [179]Spirit, they are created;
And Thou dost renew the face of the ground.

H. *Concluding praise to a mighty God*

31 Let the glory of the LORD endure forever;
Let the LORD be glad in His works;
32 He looks at the earth, and it trembles;
He touches the mountains, and they smoke.
33 I will sing to the LORD as long as I live;
I will sing praise to my God while I have my being.
34 Let my meditation be pleasing to Him;
As for me, I shall be glad in the LORD.
35 Let sinners be consumed from the earth,
And let the wicked be no more.
Bless the LORD, O my soul.
Praise the LORD!

I. *Praise to a covenant-keeping God (105:1–45)*

A. *The call to thanksgiving*

105 Oh give thanks to the LORD, call upon His name;
Make known His deeds among the peoples.
2 Sing to Him, sing praises to Him;
[180]Speak of all His wonders.
3 Glory in His holy name;
Let the heart of those who seek the LORD be glad.
4 Seek the LORD and His strength;
Seek His face continually.
5 Remember His wonders which He has done,
His marvels, and the judgments uttered by His mouth,
6 O seed of Abraham, His servant,
O sons of Jacob, His chosen ones!

B. *The Abrahamic covenant*

7 He is the LORD our God;
His judgments are in all the earth.

8 He has remembered His covenant forever,
The word which He commanded to a thousand generations,
9 *The covenant* which He made with Abraham,
And His oath to Isaac.
10 Then He confirmed it to Jacob for a statute,
To Israel as an everlasting covenant,
11 Saying, "To you I will give the land of Canaan
As the portion of your inheritance,"
12 When they were only a few men in number,
Very few, and strangers in it.
13 And they wandered about from nation to nation,
From *one* kingdom to another people.
14 He permitted no man to oppress them,
And He reproved kings for their sakes:
15 "Do not touch My anointed ones,
And do My prophets no harm."

C. *God sends Joseph to Egypt*

16 And He called for a famine upon the land;
He broke the whole staff of bread.
17 He sent a man before them,

179Or, *breath*   180Or, *Meditate on*

104:30
Is 32:15;
Ezek 37:9

104:31
Gen 1:31

104:32
Ps 97:4,5;
144:5
104:33
Ps 63:4;
146:2

104:35
Ps 59:13;
37:10; v. 1

105:1
1 Chr 16:8;
Ps 145:12
105:2
Ps 77:12

105:3
Ps 33:21

105:4
Ps 27:8

105:5
Ps 77:11

105:7
Is 26:9

105:8
Luke 1:72

105:9
Gen 17:2;
22:16; 26:3
105:10
Gen 28:13-15

105:11
Gen 13:15;
15:18
105:12
Gen 34:30;
Deut 7:7;
Heb 11:9

105:14
Gen 35:5;
12:17

105:16
Gen 41:54;
Lev 26:26;
Is 3:1;
105:17
Gen 45:5;
37:28,36

Joseph, *who* was sold as a slave.

105:18 Gen 39:20	18	They afflicted his feet with fetters, He himself was laid in irons;
105:19 Gen 40:20,21; Ps 66:10	19	Until the time that his word came to pass, The word of the LORD tested him.
105:20 Gen 41:14	20	The king sent and released him, The ruler of peoples, and set him free.
105:21 Gen 41:40	21	He made him lord of his house, And ruler over all his possessions,
	22	To imprison his princes at will, That he might teach his elders wisdom.

D. *Israel in Egypt*

105:23 Gen 46:6; Acts 13:17	23	Israel also came into Egypt; Thus Jacob sojourned in the land of Ham.
105:24 Ex 1:7	24	And He caused His people to be very fruitful, And made them stronger than their adversaries.
105:25 Ex 1:8,10	**25**	He turned their heart to hate His people, To deal craftily with His servants.

E. *Moses and the plagues*

*105:26 Ex 3:10; Num 16:5	26	He sent Moses His servant, *And* Aaron whom He had chosen.
105:27 Ex 7-12; Ps 78:43	27	They performed His wondrous acts among them, And miracles in the land of Ham.
105:28 Ex 10:22; Ps 99:7	28	He sent darkness and made *it* dark; And they did not rebel against His words.
105:29 Ex 7:20	29	He turned their waters into blood, And caused their fish to die.
105:30 Ex 8:6	30	Their land swarmed with frogs *Even* in the chambers of their kings.
105:31 Ex 8:16,21	31	He spoke, and there came a swarm of flies *And* gnats in all their territory.
105:32 Ex 9:23	32	He gave them hail for rain, *And* flaming fire in their land.
	33	He struck down their vines also and their fig trees, And shattered the trees of their territory.
105:34 Ex 10:4; Ps 73:46	34	He spoke, and locusts came, And young locusts, even without number,
	35	And ate up all vegetation in their land, And ate up the fruit of their ground.
105:36 Ex 12:29; Ps 78:51	36	He also struck down all the first-born in their land, The first fruits of all their vigor.

F. *The exodus and the wanderings*

*105:37 Ex 12:35	**37**	Then He brought them out with silver and gold; And among His tribes there was not one who stumbled.
105:38 Ex 12:33	38	Egypt was glad when they departed; For the dread of them had fallen upon them.
105:39 Ex 13:21; Neh 9:12	39	He spread a cloud for a [181]covering, And fire to illumine by night.
105:40 Ex 16:12ff; Ps 78:24ff	40	They asked, and He brought quail, And satisfied them with the bread of heaven.
105:41 Ex 17:6; Ps 78:15,16; 1 Cor 10:4	41	He opened the rock, and water flowed out; It ran in the dry places *like* a river.
105:42 v. 8	42	For He remembered His holy word *With* Abraham His servant;

[181]Or, *curtain*

105:26 God delivered Israel from Egypt: (1) by human instrumentalities (Moses and Aaron); (2) by overcoming Pharaoh's resistance; and (3) by circumstances that gave Israel wealth, health, respect, and joy.

105:37 *He brought them out.* God's guidance was provided: (1) by His Holy Word; (2) by His Spirit; and (3) by circumstances.

G. The settlement of Canaan

43 And He brought forth His people with joy,
    His chosen ones with a joyful shout.
44 He gave them also the lands of the nations,
    That they might take possession of *the fruit of* the peoples' labor,
45 So that they might keep His statutes,
    And observe His laws,
    Praise the LORD!

I. *Praise to God who has mercy on a sinful people* (106:1–48)

A. *The prayer for mercy*

106 Praise the LORD!
Oh give thanks to the LORD, for He is good;
For His lovingkindness is everlasting.
2 Who can speak of the mighty deeds of the LORD,
   Or can show forth all His praise?
3 How blessed are those who keep justice,
   Who practice righteousness at all times!

4 Remember me, O LORD, in *Thy* favor toward Thy people;
   Visit me with Thy salvation,
5 That I may see the prosperity of Thy chosen ones,
   That I may rejoice in the gladness of Thy nation,
   That I may glory with Thine [182]inheritance.

B. *Israel's sin at the Red Sea (cf. Exod. 14:10–12)*

6 We have sinned like our fathers,
   We have committed iniquity, we have behaved wickedly.
7 Our fathers in Egypt did not understand Thy wonders;
   They did not remember Thine abundant kindnesses,
   But rebelled by the sea, at the [183]Red Sea.
8 Nevertheless He saved them for the sake of His name,
   That He might make His power known.
9 Thus He rebuked the [183]Red Sea and it dried up;
   And He led them through the deeps, as through the wilderness.
10 So He saved them from the hand of the one who hated *them*,
   And redeemed them from the hand of the enemy.
11 And the waters covered their adversaries;
   Not one of them was left.
12 Then they believed His words;
   They sang His praise.

C. *Israel's sins in the wilderness (cf. Num. 11)*

13 They quickly forgot His works;
   They did not wait for His counsel,
14 But craved intensely in the wilderness,
   And tempted God in the desert.
15 So He gave them their request,
   But sent a wasting disease among them.

[Marginal references:]
105:44 Deut 6-10; Josh 13:7
105:45 Deut 6:21-25
*106:1 Ps 105:1; 100:5; 1 Chr 16:34
106:2 Ps 145:4,12
106:3 Ps 15:2
106:4 Ps 119:132
106:5 Ps 1:3; 118:15; 105:3
106:6 Dan 9:5
106:7 Ps 78:11,42; Ex 14:11
106:8 Ex 9:16
106:9 Ex 14:21; Ps 18:15; 78:11,42; Is 63:11-14
106:10 Ex 14:30; Ps 107:2
106:11 Ex 14:28; 15:5
106:12 Ex 14:31; 15:1-21
106:13 Ex 15:24
106:14 1 Cor 10:6,9
*106:15 Num 11:31; Is 10:16

[182]I.e., people [183]Lit., *Sea of Reeds*

106:1 This is the first of what has been called the "Hallelujah Psalms," for the word "Hallelujah" is, as it were, the inscription. The others are Ps. 106, 111–113, 117, 135, 146–50.

106:15 Here a spiritual principle is laid down that has value for all ages. In the instance cited, the children of Israel insisted on having meat when God provided manna. It was not His will for them to have meat; but since they insisted on obtaining what they wanted, God gave it to them. In return for meat they received spiritual poverty. Insistence on having our own preference (rather than God's) can lead only to unfortunate consequences at a cost higher than the anticipated benefits.

D. The sin of Dathan and Abiram (cf. Num. 16; Deut. 11:6)

106:16
Num 16:1-3

16 When they became envious of Moses in the camp,
And of Aaron, the holy one of the LORD,

106:17
Deut 11:6

17 The earth opened and swallowed up Dathan,
And engulfed the company of Abiram.

106:18
Num 16:35

18 And a fire blazed up in their company;
The flame consumed the wicked.

E. The golden calf at Horeb (cf. Exod. 32; Deut. 9:8–21)

106:19
Ex 32:14

19 They made a calf in Horeb,
And worshiped a molten image.

106:20
Jer 2:11;
Rom 1:23

20 Thus they exchanged their glory
For the image of an ox that eats grass.

106:21
Ps 78:11;
Deut 10:21

21 They forgot God their Savior,
Who had done great things in Egypt,

106:22
Ps 105:27

22 Wonders in the land of Ham,
And awesome things by the [184]Red Sea.

106:23
Ex 32:10;
32:11-14

23 Therefore He said that He would destroy them,
Had not Moses His chosen one stood in the breach before Him,
To turn away His wrath from destroying *them.*

F. The refusal to enter Canaan (cf. Num. 13–14)

106:24
Deut 8:7;
Heb 3:18,19

24 Then they despised the pleasant land;
They did not believe in His word,

106:25
Num 14:2

25 But grumbled in their tents;
They did not listen to the voice of the LORD.

106:26
Num 14:28-35;
Heb 11:3

26 Therefore He swore to them,
That He would cast them down in the wilderness,

106:27
Ps 44:11

27 And that He would cast their seed among the nations,
And scatter them in the lands.

G. Baal of Peor (cf. Num. 25)

*106:28
Num 25:2,3

28 They joined themselves also to Baal-peor,
And ate sacrifices offered to the dead.

29 Thus they provoked *Him* to anger with their deeds;
And the plague broke out among them.

106:30
Num 25:7

30 Then Phinehas stood up and interposed;
And so the plague was stayed.

106:31
Num 25:11-13

31 And it was reckoned to him for righteousness,
To all generations forever.

H. Israel's sin at Meribah (cf. Num. 20:2–13)

106:32
Num 20:3,13;
Ps 81:7

32 They also provoked *Him* to wrath at the waters of [185]Meribah,
So that it went hard with Moses on their account;

106:33
Num 20:10

33 Because they were rebellious against His Spirit,
He spoke rashly with his lips.

I. Israel's idolatry in Canaan

*106:34
Judg 1:21;
Deut 7:2,16

34 They did not destroy the peoples,
As the LORD commanded them,

106:35
Judg 3:5,6

35 But they mingled with the nations,
And learned their practices,

106:36
Judg 2:12

36 And served their idols,
Which became a snare to them.

---

[184]Lit., *Sea of Reeds*   [185]Lit., *strife*

106:28 *sacrifices offered to the dead.* Heathen sacrifices are offered to dead gods in contrast to the living God of Israel. This was one of Israel's recurring sins.
106:34 Israel sinned against God in that: (1) they disobeyed and did not destroy the nations as God commanded them; (2) they intermarried with the heathen and took over their evil practices; (3) they served their idols, which became a snare to them; and (4) they even went so far as to offer human sacrifices, which were explicitly forbidden.

37 They even sacrificed their sons and their daughters to the demons,
38 And shed innocent blood,
    The blood of their sons and their daughters,
    Whom they sacrificed to the idols of Canaan;
    And the land was polluted with the blood.
39 Thus they became unclean in their practices,
    And played the harlot in their deeds.

J. Israel's punishment

40 Therefore the anger of the Lord was kindled against His people,
    And He abhorred His inheritance.
41 Then He gave them into the hand of the nations;
    And those who hated them ruled over them.
42 Their enemies also oppressed them,
    And they were subdued under their power.
43 Many times He would deliver them;
    They, however, were rebellious in their counsel,
    And so sank down in their iniquity.

K. God's mercy

44 Nevertheless He looked upon their distress,
    When He heard their cry;
45 And He remembered His covenant for their sake,
    And relented according to the greatness of His lovingkindness.
46 He also made them objects of compassion
    In the presence of all their captors.

L. Final appeal and doxology

47 Save us, O Lord our God,
    And gather us from among the nations,
    To give thanks to Thy holy name,
    And glory in Thy praise.
48 Blessed be the Lord, the God of Israel,
    From everlasting even to everlasting.
    And let all the people say, "Amen."
    Praise the Lord!

BOOK 5

I. Thanksgiving to a delivering God (107:1–43)

A. The call to praise

107 Oh give thanks to the Lord, for He is good;
    For His lovingkindness is everlasting.
2   Let the redeemed of the Lord say so,
    Whom He has redeemed from the hand of the adversary,
3   And gathered from the lands,
    From the east and from the west,
    From the north and from the south.

B. Deliverance from the desert

4   They wandered in the wilderness in a desert region;
    They did not find a way to an inhabited city.
5   They were hungry and thirsty;
    Their soul fainted within them.

Cross-references:
106:37 2 Kin 17:7
106:38 Ps 94:21; Num 35:33
106:39 Ezek 20:18; Lev 17:7; Num 15:39
106:40 Ps 78:59
106:41 Judg 2:14; Neh 9:27
106:43 Judg 2:16-18
*106:44 Judg 3:9; 10:10
106:45 Ps 105:8; Judg 2:18
106:46 Ezra 9:9; Jer 42:12
106:47 1 Chr 16:35, 36; Ps 147:2
106:48 Ps 41:13
*107:1 Ps 106:1
107:2 Ps 106:10
107:3 Ps 106:47; Is 43:5,6
107:4 Num 14:33; 32:13

106:44 God visited them with His anger, but He did not forget them. This grace is ever displayed toward those whom God has redeemed, however far they stray from the fold.
107:1 The recurring sequence expressed in this psalm is as follows: (1) men ought to praise the Lord for His goodness and His delivering mercies; (2) men soon forget what they ought to remember; (3) men turn from God to sin; (4) God uses judgment to bring them to repentance; (5) men sense their need for deliverance and call on God; (6) God delivers them; and (7) they then praise God for His deliverance.

107:6 Ps 50:15	6	Then they cried out to the LORD in their trouble; He delivered them out of their distresses.
107:7 Ezra 8:21	7	He led them also by a straight way, To go to an inhabited city.
107:8 vv. 15,21,31	8	Let them give thanks to the LORD for His lovingkindness, And for His wonders to the sons of men!
107:9 Ps 22:26; Luke 1:53	9	For He has satisfied the thirsty soul, And the hungry soul He has filled with what is good.

C. Deliverance from the prison

107:10 Luke 1:79; Job 36:8	**10**	There were those who dwelt in darkness and in the shadow of death, Prisoners in misery and chains,
107:11 Ps 106:7; 2 Chr 36:16	11	Because they had rebelled against the words of God, And spurned the counsel of the Most High.
107:12 Ps 22:11	12	Therefore He humbled their heart with labor; They stumbled and there was none to help.
107:13 v. 6	13	Then they cried out to the LORD in their trouble; He saved them out of their distresses.
107:14 Ps 116:16; Luke 13:16; Acts 12:7	14	He brought them out of darkness and the shadow of death, And broke their bands apart.
107:15 vv. 8,21,31	15	Let them give thanks to the LORD for His lovingkindness, And for His wonders to the sons of men!
107:16 Is 45:2	16	For He has shattered gates of bronze, And cut bars of iron asunder.

D. Deliverance of the sick

107:17 Is 65:6,7	**17**	Fools, because of their rebellious way, And because of their iniquities, were afflicted.
107:18 Job 33:20,22; Ps 9:13; 88:3	18	Their soul abhorred all kinds of food; And they drew near to the gates of death.
	19	Then they cried out to the LORD in their trouble; He saved them out of their distresses.
107:20 Matt 8:8; Ps 30:2; 103:3	20	He sent His word and healed them, And delivered *them* from their [186]destructions.
	21	Let them give thanks to the LORD for His lovingkindness, And for His wonders to the sons of men!
107:22 Lev 7:12; Ps 50:14; 9:11; 73:28; 118:17	22	Let them also offer sacrifices of thanksgiving, And tell of His works with joyful singing.

E. Deliverance from the sea

	23	Those who go down to the sea in ships, Who do business on great waters;
	24	They have seen the works of the LORD, And His wonders in the deep.
107:25 Ps 105:31,34; Jon 1:4; Ps 93:3,4	25	For He spoke and raised up a stormy wind, Which lifted up the waves of the sea.
107:26 Ps 22:14; 119:28	26	They rose up to the heavens, they went down to the depths; Their soul melted away in *their* misery.
107:27 Job 12:25	27	They reeled and staggered like a drunken man, And [187]were at their wits' end.
107:28 vv. 6,13,19	28	Then they cried to the LORD in their trouble, And He brought them out of their distresses.
107:29 Ps 89:9; Matt 8:26	29	He caused the storm to be still, So that the waves of the sea were hushed.
	30	Then they were glad because they were quiet; So He guided them to their desired haven.
107:31 vv. 8,15,21	31	Let them give thanks to the LORD for His lovingkindness, And for His wonders to the sons of men!
107:32 Ps 22:22,25; 35:18	32	Let them extol Him also in the congregation of the people, And praise Him at the seat of the elders.

[186]Or, *pits*   [187]Lit., *all their wisdom was swallowed up*

F. The LORD who blesses the earth

33 He [188]changes rivers into a wilderness,
And springs of water into a thirsty ground;

34 A fruitful land into a salt waste,
Because of the wickedness of those who dwell in it.

35 He changes a wilderness into a pool of water,
And a dry land into springs of water;

36 And there He makes the hungry to dwell,
So that they may establish an inhabited city,

37 And sow fields, and plant vineyards,
And gather a fruitful harvest.

38 Also He blesses them and they multiply greatly;
And He does not let their cattle decrease.

G. The lovingkindnesses of the LORD

39 When they are diminished and bowed down
Through oppression, misery, and sorrow,

40 He pours contempt upon princes,
And makes them wander in a pathless waste.

41 But He sets the needy securely on high away from affliction,
And makes *his* families like a flock.

42 The upright see it, and are glad;
But all unrighteousness shuts its mouth.

43 Who is wise? Let him give heed to these things;
And consider the lovingkindnesses of the LORD.

A Song, a Psalm of David.

I. A song of confidence in God (108:1-13)
(cf. Pss. 57:7-11; 60:5-12)

A. Thanksgiving to the LORD

108 My heart is steadfast, O God;
I will sing, I will sing praises, even with my soul.

2 Awake, harp and lyre;
I will awaken the dawn!

3 I will give thanks to Thee, O LORD, among the peoples;
And I will sing praises to Thee among the nations.

4 For Thy lovingkindness is great above the heavens;
And Thy truth *reaches* to the skies.

5 Be exalted, O God, above the heavens,
And Thy glory above all the earth.

B. Pleading God's promises

6 That Thy beloved may be delivered,
Save with Thy right hand, and answer me!

7 God has spoken in His [189]holiness:
"I will exult, I will portion out Shechem,
And measure out the valley of Succoth.

8 "Gilead is Mine, Manasseh is Mine;
Ephraim also is the helmet of My head;
Judah is My [190]scepter.

9 "Moab is My washbowl;
Over Edom I shall throw My shoe;
Over Philistia I will shout aloud."

C. The cry for help

10 Who will bring me into the besieged city?
Who will lead me to Edom?

Reference column:

107:33
Ps 74:15

107:34
Gen 13:10;
14:3; 19:25
107:35
Ps 114:8;
Is 41:18

107:37
Is 65:21

107:38
Gen 12:2;
17:16,20;
Ex 1:7

107:39
Ezek 5:11;
Ps 57:6
107:40
Job 12:21,24

107:41
1 Sam 2:8;
Ps 113:7-9
107:42
Job 22:19;
Ps 52:6;
Job 5:16;
Ps 63:11;
Rom 3:19
107:43
Ps 64:9;
Jer 9:12;
Hos 14:9

108:1
Ps 57:7

108:2
Ps 57:8-11

108:4
Ps 113:4

108:6
Ps 60:5-12

108:8
Ps 60:7

---

[188]Or, *turns rivers into a desert*   [189]Or, *sanctuary*   [190]Or, *lawgiver*

108:11 Ps 44:9	11 Hast not Thou Thyself, O God, rejected us? And wilt Thou not go forth with our armies, O God?
	12 Oh give us help against the adversary, For deliverance by man is in vain.
	13 Through God we shall do valiantly; And it is He who will tread down our adversaries.

For the choir director. A Psalm of David.

I. *A psalm of anathema (109:1–31)*

A. *The cry for help*

109:1 Ps 83:1	**109** O God of my praise, Do not be silent!
109:2 Ps 52:4; 120:2	2 For they have opened the wicked and deceitful mouth against me; They have spoken against me with a lying tongue.
109:3 Ps 69:4	3 They have also surrounded me with words of hatred, And fought against me without cause.
109:4 Ps 38:20; 69:13	4 In return for my love they act as my accusers; But I am *in* prayer.
109:5 Ps 35:12; 38:20	5 Thus they have repaid me evil for good, And hatred for my love.

B. *The imprecation*

109:6 Zech 3:1	**6** Appoint a wicked man over him; And let an accuser stand at his right hand.
109:7 Prov 28:9	7 When he is judged, let him come forth guilty; And let his prayer become sin.
109:8 Acts 1:20	8 Let his days be few; Let another take his office.
109:9 Ex 22:24	9 Let his children be fatherless, And his wife a widow.
	10 Let his children wander about and beg; And let them seek *sustenance* far from their ruined homes.
109:11 Job 5:5; 18:9	11 Let the creditor seize all that he has; And let strangers plunder the product of his labor.
109:12 Is 9:17	12 Let there be none to extend lovingkindness to him, Nor any to be gracious to his fatherless children.
109:13 Ps 37:28; Prov 10:7	13 Let his posterity be cut off; In a following generation let their name be blotted out.
109:14 Ex 20:5; Neh 4:5; Jer 18:23	**14** Let the iniquity of his fathers be remembered before the LORD, And do not let the sin of his mother be blotted out.
109:15 Ps 34:16	15 Let them be before the LORD continually, That He may cut off their memory from the earth;
109:16 Ps 37:14,32	16 Because he did not remember to show lovingkindness, But persecuted the afflicted and needy man, And the despondent in heart, to put *them* to death.
109:17 Prov 14:14; Ezek 35:6	17 He also loved cursing, so it came to him; And he did not delight in blessing, so it was far from him.
109:18 Ps 73:6; Num 5:22	18 But he clothed himself with cursing as with his garment, And it entered into his body like water, And like oil into his bones.
	19 Let it be to him as a garment with which he covers himself, And for a belt with which he constantly girds himself.
109:20 Ps 94:23; 2 Tim 4:14; Ps 71:10	20 Let this be the reward of my accusers from the LORD, And of those who speak evil against my soul.

C. *The cry for help continued*

109:21 Ps 79:9; 69:16	**21** But Thou, O GOD, the Lord, deal *kindly* with me for Thy name's sake; Because Thy lovingkindness is good, deliver me;

F. The LORD who blesses the earth

33 He [188]changes rivers into a wilderness,
And springs of water into a thirsty ground;

34 A fruitful land into a salt waste,
Because of the wickedness of those who dwell in it.

35 He changes a wilderness into a pool of water,
And a dry land into springs of water;

36 And there He makes the hungry to dwell,
So that they may establish an inhabited city,

37 And sow fields, and plant vineyards,
And gather a fruitful harvest,

38 Also He blesses them and they multiply greatly;
And He does not let their cattle decrease.

G. The lovingkindnesses of the LORD

39 When they are diminished and bowed down
Through oppression, misery, and sorrow,

40 He pours contempt upon princes,
And makes them wander in a pathless waste.

41 But He sets the needy securely on high away from affliction,
And makes *his* families like a flock.

42 The upright see it, and are glad;
But all unrighteousness shuts its mouth.

43 Who is wise? Let him give heed to these things;
And consider the lovingkindnesses of the LORD.

A Song, a Psalm of David.

I. A song of confidence in God (108:1–13)
(cf. Pss. 57:7–11; 60:5–12)

A. Thanksgiving to the LORD

108
My heart is steadfast, O God;
I will sing, I will sing praises, even with my soul.

2 Awake, harp and lyre;
I will awaken the dawn!

3 I will give thanks to Thee, O LORD, among the peoples;
And I will sing praises to Thee among the nations.

4 For Thy lovingkindness is great above the heavens;
And Thy truth *reaches* to the skies.

5 Be exalted, O God, above the heavens,
And Thy glory above all the earth.

B. Pleading God's promises

6 That Thy beloved may be delivered,
Save with Thy right hand, and answer me!

7 God has spoken in His [189]holiness:
"I will exult, I will portion out Shechem,
And measure out the valley of Succoth.

8 "Gilead is Mine, Manasseh is Mine;
Ephraim also is the helmet of My head;
Judah is My [190]scepter.

9 "Moab is My washbowl;
Over Edom I shall throw My shoe;
Over Philistia I will shout aloud."

C. The cry for help

10 Who will bring me into the besieged city?
Who will lead me to Edom?

Marginal references:

107:33 Ps 74:15
107:34 Gen 13:10; 14:3; 19:25
107:35 Ps 114:8; Is 41:18
107:37 Is 65:21
107:38 Gen 12:2; 17:16,20; Ex 1:7
107:39 Ezek 5:11; Ps 57:6
107:40 Job 12:21,24
107:41 1 Sam 2:8; Ps 113:7-9
107:42 Job 22:19; Ps 52:6; Job 5:16; Ps 63:11; Rom 3:19
107:43 Ps 64:9; Jer 9:12; Hos 14:9
108:1 Ps 57:7
108:2 Ps 57:8-11
108:4 Ps 113:4
108:6 Ps 60:5-12
108:8 Ps 60:7

188Or, *turns rivers into a desert*   189Or, *sanctuary*   190Or, *lawgiver*

<table>
<tr><td>

108:11
Ps 44:9

</td><td>

11 Hast not Thou Thyself, O God, rejected us?
   And wilt Thou not go forth with our armies, O God?
12 Oh give us help against the adversary,
   For deliverance by man is in vain.
13 Through God we shall do valiantly;
   And it is He who will tread down our adversaries.

</td></tr>
</table>

For the choir director. A Psalm of David.

I. *A psalm of anathema (109:1–31)*

A. *The cry for help*

<table>
<tr><td>

109:1
Ps 83:1

</td><td>

109 O God of my praise,
      Do not be silent!

</td></tr>
<tr><td>

109:2
Ps 52:4;
120:2

</td><td>

2 For they have opened the wicked and deceitful mouth against me;
   They have spoken against me with a lying tongue.

</td></tr>
<tr><td>

109:3
Ps 69:4

</td><td>

3 They have also surrounded me with words of hatred,
   And fought against me without cause.

</td></tr>
<tr><td>

109:4
Ps 38:20;
69:13

</td><td>

4 In return for my love they act as my accusers;
   But I am *in* prayer.

</td></tr>
<tr><td>

109:5
Ps 35:12;
38:20

</td><td>

5 Thus they have repaid me evil for good,
   And hatred for my love.

</td></tr>
</table>

B. *The imprecation*

<table>
<tr><td>

109:6
Zech 3:1

</td><td>

6 Appoint a wicked man over him;
   And let an accuser stand at his right hand.

</td></tr>
<tr><td>

109:7
Prov 28:9

</td><td>

7 When he is judged, let him come forth guilty;
   And let his prayer become sin.

</td></tr>
<tr><td>

109:8
Acts 1:20

</td><td>

8 Let his days be few;
   Let another take his office.

</td></tr>
<tr><td>

109:9
Ex 22:24

</td><td>

9 Let his children be fatherless,
   And his wife a widow.
10 Let his children wander about and beg;
   And let them seek *sustenance* far from their ruined homes.

</td></tr>
<tr><td>

109:11
Job 5:5; 18:9

</td><td>

11 Let the creditor seize all that he has;
   And let strangers plunder the product of his labor.

</td></tr>
<tr><td>

109:12
Is 9:17

</td><td>

12 Let there be none to extend lovingkindness to him,
   Nor any to be gracious to his fatherless children.

</td></tr>
<tr><td>

109:13
Ps 37:28;
Prov 10:7

</td><td>

13 Let his posterity be cut off;
   In a following generation let their name be blotted out.

</td></tr>
<tr><td>

109:14
Ex 20:5;
Neh 4:5;
Jer 18:23

</td><td>

14 Let the iniquity of his fathers be remembered before the Lord,
   And do not let the sin of his mother be blotted out.

</td></tr>
<tr><td>

109:15
Ps 34:16

</td><td>

15 Let them be before the Lord continually,
   That He may cut off their memory from the earth;

</td></tr>
<tr><td>

109:16
Ps 37:14,32

</td><td>

16 Because he did not remember to show lovingkindness,
   But persecuted the afflicted and needy man,
   And the despondent in heart, to put *them* to death.

</td></tr>
<tr><td>

109:17
Prov 14:14;
Ezek 35:6

</td><td>

17 He also loved cursing, so it came to him;
   And he did not delight in blessing, so it was far from him.

</td></tr>
<tr><td>

109:18
Ps 73:6;
Num 5:22

</td><td>

18 But he clothed himself with cursing as with his garment,
   And it entered into his body like water,
   And like oil into his bones.
19 Let it be to him as a garment with which he covers himself,
   And for a belt with which he constantly girds himself.

</td></tr>
<tr><td>

109:20
Ps 94:23;
2 Tim 4:14;
Ps 71:10

</td><td>

20 Let this be the reward of my accusers from the Lord,
   And of those who speak evil against my soul.

</td></tr>
</table>

C. *The cry for help continued*

<table>
<tr><td>

109:21
Ps 79:9;
69:16

</td><td>

21 But Thou, O God, the Lord, deal *kindly* with me for Thy name's
     sake;
   Because Thy lovingkindness is good, deliver me;

</td></tr>
</table>

His glory is above the heavens.

5   Who is like the LORD our God,
    Who is enthroned on high,
6   Who humbles Himself to behold
    The things that are in heaven and in the earth?
7   He raises the poor from the dust,
    And lifts the needy from the ash heap,
8   To make *them* sit with princes,
    With the princes of His people.
9   He makes the barren woman abide in the house
    As a joyful mother of children.
    Praise the LORD!

I. *In remembrance of Israel's delivering God (114:1–8)*

114 When Israel went forth from Egypt,
    The house of Jacob from a people of strange language,
2   Judah became His sanctuary,
    Israel, His dominion.
3   The sea looked and fled;
    The Jordan turned back.
4   The mountains skipped like rams,
    The hills, like lambs.
5   What ails you, O sea, that you flee?
    O Jordan, that you turn back?
6   O mountains, that you skip like rams?
    O hills, like lambs?
7   Tremble, O earth, before the Lord,
    Before the God of Jacob,
8   Who turned the rock into a pool of water,
    The flint into a fountain of water.

I. *Give glory to God (115:1–18)*

A. *To God alone belongs glory*

115 Not to us, O LORD, not to us,
    But to Thy name give glory
    Because of Thy lovingkindness, because of Thy truth.
2   Why should the nations say,
    "Where, now, is their God?"

B. *The evil of idols*

3   But our God is in the heavens;
    He does whatever He pleases.
4   Their idols are silver and gold,
    The work of man's hands.
5   They have mouths, but they cannot speak;
    They have eyes, but they cannot see;
6   They have ears, but they cannot hear;
    They have noses, but they cannot smell;
7   They have hands, but they cannot feel;
    They have feet, but they cannot walk;
    They cannot make a sound with their throat.
8   Those who make them will become like them,
    Everyone who trusts in them.

C. *Israel enjoined to trust the LORD*

9   O Israel, trust in the LORD;

113:5
Ps 89:6;
103:19
113:6
Ps 11:4;
138:6;
Is 57:15
113:7
1 Sam 2:8;
Ps 107:41
113:8
Job 36:7
113:9
1 Sam 2:5;
Ps 68:6;
Is 54:1

114:1
Ex 13:3
114:2
Ex 19:6;
29:45,46
114:3
Ex 14:21;
Josh 3:13,16
114:4
Ps 29:6;
Hab 3:6
114:5
Hab 3:6

114:7
Ps 96:9

114:8
Ex 17:6;
Num 20:11;
Ps 107:35;
Deut 8:15

115:1
Is 48:11;
Ezek 36:32;
Ps 96:8
*115:2
Ps 42:3;
79:10

115:3
Ps 103:19;
135:6;
Dan 4:35
115:4
Deut 4:28;
Ps 135:15-17;
Jer 10:3ff
115:5
Jer 10:5

115:8
Ps 135:18

115:9
Ps 118:2-4;
33:20

115:2 *Where, now, is their God?* This is asked by those whose hearts are full of human folly, who do not believe in an invisible God beyond the reach of man's sense perceptions.

He is their help and their shield.

115:11
Ps 135:20
10 O house of Aaron, trust in the LORD;
He is their help and their shield.

11 You who [194]fear the LORD, trust in the LORD;
He is their help and their shield.

D. The LORD will bless Israel

12 The LORD has been mindful of us; He will bless *us*;
He will bless the house of Israel;
He will bless the house of Aaron.

115:13
Ps 128:1,4
13 He will bless those who [194]fear the LORD,
The small together with the great.

115:14
Deut 1:11
14 May the LORD give you increase,
You and your children.

115:15
Gen 14:19;
1:1; Ps 96:5
15 May you be blessed of the LORD,
Maker of heaven and earth.

115:16
Ps 89:11; 8:6
16 The heavens are the heavens of the LORD;
But the earth He has given to the sons of men.

115:17
Ps 6:5; 31:17
17 The dead do not praise the LORD,
Nor *do* any who go down into silence;

115:18
Ps 113:2
18 But as for us, we will bless the LORD
From this time forth and forever.
Praise the LORD!

I. Hymn of thanksgiving for deliverance (116:1–19)

A. Acknowledgment of God's deliverance

116:1
Ps 18:1;
66:19
116:2
Ps 40:1
116 I love the LORD, because He hears
My voice *and* my supplications.
2 Because He has inclined His ear to me,
Therefore I shall call *upon Him* as long as I live.

116:3
Ps 18:4-6
3 The cords of death encompassed me,
And the terrors of Sheol came upon me;
I found distress and sorrow.

116:4
Ps 118:5;
22:20
4 Then I called upon the name of the LORD:
"O LORD, I beseech Thee, save my life!"

116:5
Ps 103:8;
Ezra 9:15;
Neh 9:8;
Ps 145:17;
Ex 34:6
116:6
Ps 19:7; 79:8
116:7
Jer 6:16;
Matt 11:29;
Ps 13:6
116:8
Ps 56:13
116:9
Ps 27:13
5 Gracious is the LORD, and righteous;
Yes, our God is compassionate.
6 The LORD preserves the simple;
I was brought low, and He saved me.
7 Return to your rest, O my soul,
For the LORD has dealt bountifully with you.
8 For Thou hast rescued my soul from death,
My eyes from tears,
My feet from stumbling.
9 I shall walk before the LORD
In the land of the living.

116:10
2 Cor 4:13
10 I believed when I said,
"I am greatly afflicted."

116:11
Ps 31:22;
Rom 3:4
11 I said in my alarm,
"All men are liars."

B. Resolve to pay his vows

12 What shall I render to the LORD
For all His benefits toward me?

116:13
Ps 16:5;
80:18
116:14
Ps 22:25;
Jon 2:9
13 I shall lift up the cup of salvation,
And call upon the name of the LORD.
14 I shall pay my vows to the LORD,
Oh *may it be* in the presence of all His people.

[194]Or, *revere*

15   Precious in the sight of the LORD
         Is the death of His godly ones.
16   O LORD, surely I am Thy servant,
         I am Thy servant, the son of Thy handmaid,
         Thou hast loosed my bonds.
17   To Thee I shall offer a sacrifice of thanksgiving,
         And call upon the name of the LORD.
18   I shall pay my vows to the LORD,
         Oh *may it be* in the presence of all His people,
19   In the courts of the LORD's house,
         In the midst of you, O Jerusalem.
         Praise the LORD!

I. *Extol Him for His steadfast love (117:1,2)*

117 Praise the LORD, all nations;
         Laud Him, all peoples!
2   For His lovingkindness [195]is great toward us,
         And the truth of the LORD is everlasting.
         Praise the LORD!

I. *Thanks to the LORD (118:1–29)*

A. *The LORD's mercy*

118 Give thanks to the LORD, for He is good;
         For His lovingkindness is everlasting.
2   Oh let Israel say,
         "His lovingkindness is everlasting."
3   Oh let the house of Aaron say,
         "His lovingkindness is everlasting."
4   Oh let those who [196]fear the LORD say,
         "His lovingkindness is everlasting."

B. *The LORD's answer to prayer*

5   From *my* distress I called upon the LORD;
         The LORD answered me *and set me* in a large place.
6   The LORD is for me; I will not fear;
         What can man do to me?
7   The LORD is for me among those who help me;
         Therefore I shall look *with satisfaction* on those who hate me.
8   It is better to take refuge in the LORD
         Than to trust in man.
9   It is better to take refuge in the LORD
         Than to trust in princes.

C. *The LORD's deliverance*

10   All nations surrounded me;
         In the name of the LORD I will surely cut them off.
11   They surrounded me, yes, they surrounded me;
         In the name of the LORD I will surely cut them off.
12   They surrounded me like bees;
         They were extinguished as a fire of thorns;
         In the name of the LORD I will surely cut them off.
13   You pushed me violently so that I was falling,
         But the LORD helped me.
14   The LORD is my strength and song,
         And He has become my salvation.

Cross references (right margin):

116:15 — Ps 72:14
116:16 — Ps 119:125; 143:12; 86:16
116:17 — Ps 50:14; v. 13
116:18 — v. 14
116:19 — Ps 96:8; 135:2
117:1 — Rom 15:11
117:2 — Ps 100:5
118:1 — Ps 106:1; 136:1
118:2 — Ps 115:9
118:5 — Ps 120:1; 18:19
118:6 — Ps 27:1; Heb 13:6; Ps 56:4,11
118:7 — Ps 54:4; 59:10
118:8 — Ps 40:4; Jer 17:5
118:9 — Ps 146:3
118:10 — Ps 3:6; 18:40
118:12 — Deut 1:44; Ps 58:9
118:13 — Ps 140:4; 86:17
118:14 — Ex 15:2; Is 12:2

---

[195]Lit., *prevails over us*   [196]Or, *revere*

D. *The LORD's mighty right hand*

118:15
Ps 68:3;
89:13

118:16
Ex 15:6

118:17
Hab 1:12;
Ps 73:28
118:18
2 Cor 6:9

118:19
Is 26:2

118:20
Ps 24:7;
Is 35:8;
Rev 22:14
118:21
Ps 116:1;
v. 14

118:22
Matt 21:42;
Mark 12:10;
Luke 20:17;
Acts 4:11;
Eph 2:20;
1 Pet 2:4,7

118:26
Matt 21:9;
Mark 11:9;
Luke 13:35;
19:38;
John 12:13
118:27
1 Kin 18:39;
Esth 8:16;
1 Pet 2:9
118:28
Ex 15:2;
Is 25:1
118:29
v. 1

15 The sound of joyful shouting and salvation is in the tents of the
  righteous;
The right hand of the LORD does valiantly.

16 The right hand of the LORD is exalted;
The right hand of the LORD does valiantly.

17 I shall not die, but live,
And tell of the works of the LORD.

18 The LORD has disciplined me severely,
But He has not given me over to death.

19 Open to me the gates of righteousness;
I shall enter through them, I shall give thanks to the LORD.

20 This is the gate of the LORD;
The righteous will enter through it.

21 I shall give thanks to Thee, for Thou hast answered me;
And Thou hast become my salvation.

E. *The LORD's wisdom*

22 The stone which the builders rejected
Has become the chief corner *stone.*

23 This is [197]the LORD's doing;
It is marvelous in our eyes.

24 This is the day which the LORD has made;
Let us rejoice and be glad in it.

25 O LORD, do save, we beseech Thee;
O LORD, we beseech Thee, do send prosperity!

26 Blessed is the one who comes in the name of the LORD;
We have blessed you from the house of the LORD.

27 The LORD is God, and He has given us light;
Bind the festival sacrifice with cords to the horns of the altar.

F. *The doxology*

28 Thou art my God, and I give thanks to Thee;
Thou art my God, I extol Thee.

29 Give thanks to the LORD, for He is good;
For His lovingkindness is everlasting.

א Aleph.

I. *The law of the LORD (119:1–176)*

A. *The blessedness of those who keep His law*

*****119:1**
Ps 101:2,6;
128:1
119:2
vv. 22,10;
Deut 6:5
119:3
1 John 3:9;
5:18

119:6
v. 80

119:7
v. 62

119

How blessed are those whose way is [198]blameless,
Who walk in the law of the LORD.

2 How blessed are those who observe His testimonies,
Who seek Him with all *their* heart.

3 They also do no unrighteousness;
They walk in His ways.

4 Thou hast ordained Thy precepts,
That we should keep *them* diligently.

5 Oh that my ways may be established
To keep Thy statutes!

6 Then I shall not be ashamed
When I look upon all Thy commandments.

7 I shall give thanks to Thee with uprightness of heart,
When I learn Thy righteous judgments.

8 I shall keep Thy statutes;
Do not forsake me utterly!

[197]Lit., *from the LORD* [198]Lit., *complete,* or, *having integrity*

119:1 This psalm has twenty-two sections arranged according to the Hebrew alphabet.

ב Beth.

B. *Holiness the fruit of keeping God's law*

9 How can a young man keep his way pure?
By keeping *it* according to Thy word.

10 With all my heart I have sought Thee;
Do not let me wander from Thy commandments.

11 Thy word I have treasured in my heart,
That I may not sin against Thee.

12 Blessed art Thou, O LORD;
Teach me Thy statutes.

13 With my lips I have told of
All the ordinances of Thy mouth.

14 I have rejoiced in the way of Thy testimonies,
As much as in all riches.

15 I will meditate on Thy precepts,
And regard Thy ways.

16 I shall delight in Thy statutes;
I shall not forget Thy word.

ג Gimel.

C. *Eyes to behold the truth of God's law*

17 Deal bountifully with Thy servant,
That I may live and keep Thy word.

18 Open my eyes, that I may behold
Wonderful things from Thy law.

19 I am a stranger in the earth;
Do not hide Thy commandments from me.

20 My soul is crushed with longing
After Thine ordinances at all times.

21 Thou dost rebuke the arrogant, the cursed,
Who wander from Thy commandments.

22 Take away reproach and contempt from me,
For I observe Thy testimonies.

23 Even though princes sit and talk against me,
Thy servant meditates on Thy statutes.

24 Thy testimonies also are my delight;
They are my counselors.

ד Daleth.

D. *Prayer to understand God's precepts*

25 My soul cleaves to the dust;
Revive me according to Thy word.

26 I have told of my ways, and Thou hast answered me;
Teach me Thy statutes.

27 Make me understand the way of Thy precepts,
So I will meditate on Thy wonders.

28 My soul weeps because of grief;
Strengthen me according to Thy word.

29 Remove the false way from me,
And graciously grant me Thy law.

30 I have chosen the faithful way;

119:9
2 Chr 6:16

119:10
2 Chr 15:15;
vv. 21,118
*119:11
Ps 37:31;
Luke 2:19,51
119:12
vv. 26,64,68,
108,124,135,
171
119:13
Ps 40:9; v. 72

119:15
vv. 23,48,78;
Ps 1:2
119:16
Ps 1:2

119:17
Ps 13:6

119:19
Gen 47:9;
1 Chr 29:15;
Ps 39:12;
2 Cor 5:6;
Heb 11:13
119:20
Ps 42:1,2
119:21
vv. 10,118
119:22
Ps 39:8
119:23
v. 15

119:24
v. 16

119:25
Ps 44:25;
v. 37
119:26
v. 12

119:27
Ps 145:5

119:28
Ps 107:26;
20:2;
1 Pet 5:10

119:11 Why do believers say the Bible is the Word of God? (See also note to 2 Tim. 3:16.) The reasons are as follows: (1) the Old Testament writers affirmed that they were speaking the Word of God and not the word of man. "Thus says the LORD," or an equivalent, is found more than two thousand times in the Old Testament (2 Sam. 23:1–3; Is. 8:1,11; Jer. 1:9; 5:14; 7:27; 13:12; Ezek. 3:4; Mic. 5:10; Hab. 2:2, etc.); (2) the apostles regarded the whole of Scripture as the infallible Word of God (1 Cor. 14:37; Gal. 1:11, 12; 1 Thess. 2:13; 2 Tim. 3:16; 2 Pet. 1:21); (3) Jesus Christ unqualifiedly endorsed the Scriptures as the inspired Word of God (Matt. 5:18; John 10:35; etc.); (4) fulfilled prophecy unmistakably demonstrates the authoritativeness of Scripture (Deut. 28:37,63–65; Is. 13:19–22; Jer. 46:19,20; 51:37; Ezek. 29:15; 30:6; Nah. 3:1,4–6; Zeph. 2:13,14; Luke 21:24); (5) archaeology confirms the accuracy of Scripture; and (6) the pragmatic test, the fact that it performs what it promises (that it works in actual human experience in response to faith), also shows the Bible to be the Word of God (34:8; John 7:17).

I have placed Thine ordinances *before me.*

119:31
Deut 11:22

31 I cleave to Thy testimonies;
O LORD, do not put me to shame!

119:32
1 Kin 4:29;
Is 60:5;
2 Cor 6:11

32 I shall run the way of Thy commandments,
For Thou wilt enlarge my heart.

ה He.

E. *Perseverance based on God's promises*

119:33
vv. 5,12

33 Teach me, O LORD, the way of Thy statutes,
And I shall observe it to the end.

119:34
v. 73;
Prov 2:6;
James 1:5

34 Give me understanding, that I may observe Thy law,
And keep it with all *my* heart.

119:35
v. 16

35 Make me walk in the path of Thy commandments,
For I delight in it.

119:36
1 Kin 8:58;
Luke 12:15

36 Incline my heart to Thy testimonies,
And not to *dishonest* gain.

119:37
Is 33:15;
Ps 71:20

37 Turn away my eyes from looking at vanity,
And revive me in Thy ways.

119:38
2 Sam 7:25

38 Establish Thy word to Thy servant,
As that which produces reverence for Thee.

39 Turn away my reproach which I dread,
For Thine ordinances are good.

119:40
vv. 20,25

40 Behold, I long for Thy precepts;
Revive me through Thy righteousness.

ו Vav.

F. *Salvation through the law of the LORD*

119:41
vv. 77,116

41 May Thy lovingkindnesses also come to me, O LORD,
Thy salvation according to Thy word;

119:42
Prov 27:11

42 So I shall have an answer for him who reproaches me,
For I trust in Thy word.

43 And do not take the word of truth utterly out of my mouth,
For I wait for Thine ordinances.

44 So I will keep Thy law continually,
Forever and ever.

45 And I will walk at liberty,
For I seek Thy precepts.

119:46
Matt 10:18;
Acts 26:1,2

46 I will also speak of Thy testimonies before kings,
And shall not be ashamed.

119:47
v. 16

47 And I shall delight in Thy commandments,
Which I love.

119:48
v. 15

48 And I shall lift up my hands to Thy commandments,
Which I love;
And I will meditate on Thy statutes.

ז Zayin.

G. *The law of the LORD a source of hope and comfort*

49 Remember the word to Thy servant,
In which Thou hast made me hope.

119:50
Rom 15:4

50 This is my comfort in my affliction,
That Thy word has revived me.

119:51
Jer 20:7;
v. 157;
Job 23:11;
Ps 44:18

51 The arrogant utterly deride me,
Yet I do not turn aside from Thy law.

119:52
Ps 103:18

52 I have remembered Thine ordinances from [199]of old, O LORD,
And comfort myself.

119:53
Ezra 9:3;
Ps 89:30

53 Burning indignation has seized me because of the wicked,
Who forsake Thy law.

54 Thy statutes are my songs

[199]Or, *everlasting*

55 In the house of my pilgrimage.
    O LORD, I remember Thy name in the night,
    And keep Thy law.
56 This has become mine,
    That I observe Thy precepts.

119:55
Ps 63:6

ח Heth.

H. The LORD our portion

57 The LORD is my portion;
    I have promised to keep Thy words.
58 I entreated Thy favor with all *my* heart;
    Be gracious to me according to Thy word.
59 I considered my ways,
    And turned my feet to Thy testimonies.
60 I hastened and did not delay
    To keep Thy commandments.
61 The cords of the wicked have encircled me,
    But I have not forgotten Thy law.
62 At midnight I shall rise to give thanks to Thee
    Because of Thy righteous ordinances.
63 I am a companion of all those who fear Thee,
    And of those who keep Thy precepts.
64 The earth is full of Thy lovingkindness, O LORD;
    Teach me Thy statutes.

119:57
Ps 16:5;
Deut 33:9
119:58
1 Kin 13:6;
v. 41
119:59
Luke 15:17,
18

119:61
Ps 140:5;
v. 83
119:62
Acts 16:25

119:63
Ps 101:6

119:64
Ps 33:5; v. 12

ט Teth.

I. The law of the LORD taught by affliction

65 Thou hast dealt well with Thy servant,
    O LORD, according to Thy word.
66 Teach me good discernment and knowledge,
    For I believe in Thy commandments.
67 Before I was afflicted I went astray,
    But now I keep Thy word.
68 Thou art good and doest good;
    Teach me Thy statutes.
69 The arrogant [200]have forged a lie against me;
    With all *my* heart I will observe Thy precepts.
70 Their heart is covered with fat,
    But I delight in Thy law.
71 It is good for me that I was afflicted,
    That I may learn Thy statutes.
72 The law of Thy mouth is better to me
    Than thousands of gold and silver *pieces*.

119:67
v. 71;
Jer 31:18,19;
Heb 12:11
119:68
Ps 106:1;
Deut 8:16;
v. 12
119:69
Job 13:4;
v. 56
119:70
Ps 17:10;
Is 6:10; v. 16
119:72
v. 127;
Ps 19:10;
Prov 8:10,11,
19

י Yodh.

J. Fellowship based upon the law of the LORD

73 Thy hands made me and [201]fashioned me;
    Give me understanding, that I may learn Thy commandments.
74 May those who fear Thee see me and be glad,
    Because I wait for Thy word.
75 I know, O LORD, that Thy judgments are righteous,
    And that in faithfulness Thou hast afflicted me.
76 O may Thy lovingkindness comfort me,
    According to Thy word to Thy servant.
77 May Thy compassion come to me that I may live,
    For Thy law is my delight.
78 May the arrogant be ashamed, for they subvert me with a lie;
    But I shall meditate on Thy precepts.

119:73
Job 10:8;
Ps 138:8;
v. 34
119:74
Ps 34:2; v. 43
119:75
Heb 12:10

119:77
vv. 41,47

119:78
Jer 50:32;
vv. 86,15

---

[200]Lit., *besmear me with lies* [201]Lit., *established*

119:80
vv. 1,46

119:81
Ps 84:2

119:82
Ps 69:3

119:83
Job 30:30

119:84
Ps 39:4;
Rev 6:10
119:85
Ps 35:7

119:86
v. 78;
Ps 35:19;
109:26
119:87
Is 58:2

119:89
Matt 24:34,
35; 1 Pet 1:25
119:90
Ps 36:5;
148:6;
Eccl 1:4
119:91
Jer 33:25
119:92
vv. 16,50

119:93
vv. 16,25

119:94
vv. 146,45

119:97
Ps 1:2

119:98
v. 130;
Deut 4:6
119:99
v. 15

119:100
Job 32:7-9

119:101
Prov 1:15

119:103
Ps 19:10

79 May those who fear Thee turn to me,
Even those who know Thy testimonies.
80 May my heart be blameless in Thy statutes,
That I may not be ashamed.

 כ Kaph.

K. A longing for peace

81 My soul languishes for Thy salvation;
I wait for Thy word.
82 My eyes fail *with longing* for Thy word,
While I say, "When wilt Thou comfort me?"
83 Though I have become like a wineskin in the smoke,
I do not forget Thy statutes.
84 How many are the days of Thy servant?
When wilt Thou execute judgment on those who persecute me?
85 The arrogant have dug pits for me,
Men who are not in accord with Thy law.
86 All Thy commandments are faithful;
They have persecuted me with a lie; help me!
87 They almost destroyed me on earth,
But as for me, I did not forsake Thy precepts.
88 Revive me according to Thy lovingkindness,
So that I may keep the testimony of Thy mouth.

ל Lamedh.

L. The immutability of the law of the LORD

89 Forever, O LORD,
Thy word [202]is settled in heaven.
90 Thy faithfulness *continues* throughout all generations;
Thou didst establish the earth, and it stands.
91 They stand this day according to Thine ordinances,
For all things are Thy servants.
92 If Thy law had not been my delight,
Then I would have perished in my affliction.
93 I will never forget Thy precepts,
For by them Thou hast revived me.
94 I am Thine, save me;
For I have sought Thy precepts.
95 The wicked wait for me to destroy me;
I shall diligently consider Thy testimonies.
96 I have seen a limit to all perfection;
Thy commandment is exceedingly broad.

מ Mem.

M. The love of the law of the LORD

97 O how I love Thy law!
It is my meditation all the day.
98 Thy commandments make me wiser than my enemies,
For they are ever mine.
99 I have more insight than all my teachers,
For Thy testimonies are my meditation.
100 I understand more than the aged,
Because I have observed Thy precepts.
101 I have restrained my feet from every evil way,
That I may keep Thy word.
102 I have not turned aside from Thine ordinances,
For Thou Thyself hast taught me.
103 How sweet are Thy words to my taste!

[202]Lit., *stands firm*

104 *Yes, sweeter* than honey to my mouth!
From Thy precepts I get understanding;
Therefore I hate every false way.

נ Nun.

N. *The law of the LORD a lamp to the feet*

105 Thy word is a lamp to my feet,
And a light to my path.
106 I have sworn, and I will confirm it,
That I will keep Thy righteous ordinances.
107 I am exceedingly afflicted;
Revive me, O LORD, according to Thy word.
108 O accept the freewill offerings of my mouth, O LORD,
And teach me Thine ordinances.
109 My life is continually [203]in my hand,
Yet I do not forget Thy law.
110 The wicked have laid a snare for me,
Yet I have not gone astray from Thy precepts.
111 I have inherited Thy testimonies forever,
For they are the joy of my heart.
112 I have inclined my heart to perform Thy statutes
Forever, *even* to the end.

ס Samekh.

O. *The law of the LORD a hiding place*

113 I hate those who are double-minded,
But I love Thy law.
114 Thou art my hiding place and my shield;
I wait for Thy word.
115 Depart from me, evildoers,
That I may observe the commandments of my God.
116 Sustain me according to Thy word, that I may live;
And do not let me be ashamed of my hope.
117 Uphold me that I may be safe,
That I may have regard for Thy statutes continually.
118 Thou hast rejected all those who wander from Thy statutes,
For their deceitfulness is useless.
119 Thou hast removed all the wicked of the earth *like* dross;
Therefore I love Thy testimonies.
120 My flesh trembles for fear of Thee,
And I am afraid of Thy judgments.

ע Ayin.

P. *The psalmist has kept the law of the LORD*

121 I have done justice and righteousness;
Do not leave me to my oppressors.
122 Be surety for Thy servant for good;
Do not let the arrogant oppress me.
123 My eyes fail *with longing* for Thy salvation,
And for Thy righteous word.
124 Deal with Thy servant according to Thy lovingkindness,
And teach me Thy statutes.
125 I am Thy servant; give me understanding,
That I may know Thy testimonies.
126 It is time for the LORD to act,
For they have broken Thy law.
127 Therefore I love Thy commandments
Above gold, yes, above fine gold.

[203]I.e., in danger

119:104	vv. 128,130
119:105	Prov 6:23
119:106	Neh 10:29
119:107	v. 25
119:108	Hos 14:2; Heb 13:15; v. 12
119:109	Job 13:14; v. 16
119:110	Ps 140:5; 141:9; v. 10
119:111	Deut 33:4; vv. 14:162
119:112	v. 33
119:113	James 1:8; v. 47
119:114	Ps 32:7; 91:1; v. 74
119:115	Ps 6:8; 139:19; Matt 7:23
119:116	Ps 54:4; 25:2; Rom 5:5; 9:33
119:118	v. 21
119:119	Ezek 22:18
119:120	Hab 3:16
119:122	Job 17:3
119:123	vv. 81,82
119:124	v. 12
119:125	Ps 116:16
119:127	Ps 19:10

119:128 v. 104	128	Therefore I esteem right all *Thy* precepts concerning everything, I hate every false way.

פ Pe.

Q. *Prayer for grace to keep the law of the* Lord

119:129 vv. 18,22	**129**	Thy testimonies are wonderful; Therefore my soul observes them.
119:130 Prov 6:23; Ps 19:7	130	The unfolding of Thy words gives light; It gives understanding to the simple.
119:131 Ps 42:1; v. 20	131	I opened my mouth wide and panted, For I longed for Thy commandments.
119:132 Ps 25:16	132	Turn to me and be gracious to me, After Thy manner with those who love Thy name.
119:133 Ps 17:15; 19:13	133	Establish my footsteps in Thy word, And do not let any iniquity have dominion over me.
119:134 Ps 142:6	134	Redeem me from the oppression of man, That I may keep Thy precepts.
119:135 Ps 4:6; v. 12	135	Make Thy face shine upon Thy servant, And teach me Thy statutes.
119:136 Jer 9:1; Ezek 9:4	136	My eyes shed streams of water, Because they do not keep Thy law.

צ Tsadhe.

R. *The* Lord *and His law are righteous*

119:137 Ezra 9:15; Neh 9:13; Jer 12:1	**137**	Righteous art Thou, O Lord, And upright are Thy judgments.
119:138 Ps 19:7-9	138	Thou hast commanded Thy testimonies in righteousness And exceeding faithfulness.
119:139 Ps 69:9	139	My zeal has consumed me, Because my adversaries have forgotten Thy words.
119:140 Ps 12:6	140	Thy word is very pure, Therefore Thy servant loves it.
	141	I am small and despised, *Yet* I do not forget Thy precepts.
119:142 Ps 19:9; vv. 151,160	142	Thy righteousness is an everlasting righteousness, And Thy law is truth.
119:143 vv. 24,77	143	Trouble and anguish have come upon me; *Yet* Thy commandments are my delight.
119:144 Ps 19:9; vv. 34,73	144	Thy testimonies are righteous forever; Give me understanding that I may live.

ק Qoph.

S. *A cry for salvation*

119:145 vv. 10,22,55	**145**	I cried with all my heart; answer me, O Lord! I will observe Thy statutes.
	146	I cried to Thee; save me, And I shall keep Thy testimonies.
	147	I rise before dawn and cry for help; I wait for Thy words.
119:148 Ps 5:3	148	My eyes anticipate the night watches, That I may meditate on Thy word.
119:149 vv. 40,154	149	Hear my voice according to Thy lovingkindness; Revive me, O Lord, according to Thine ordinances.
	150	Those who follow after wickedness draw near; They are far from Thy law.
119:151 Ps 145:18; v. 142	151	Thou art near, O Lord, And all Thy commandments are truth.
119:152 Luke 21:33	152	Of old I have known from Thy testimonies, That Thou hast founded them forever.

ר Resh.

T. *Keeping the law of the* Lord *in adversity*

153 Look upon my affliction and rescue me,
For I do not forget Thy law.

154 Plead my cause and redeem me;
Revive me according to Thy word.

155 Salvation is far from the wicked,
For they do not seek Thy statutes.

156 Great are Thy mercies, O Lord;
Revive me according to Thine ordinances.

157 Many are my persecutors and my adversaries,
Yet I do not turn aside from Thy testimonies.

158 I behold the treacherous and loathe *them*,
Because they do not keep Thy word.

159 Consider how I love Thy precepts;
Revive me, O Lord, according to Thy lovingkindness.

160 The sum of Thy word is truth,
And every one of Thy righteous ordinances is everlasting.

ש Shin.

U. *Prayer for deliverance from persecution*

161 Princes persecute me without cause,
But my heart stands in awe of Thy words.

162 I rejoice at Thy word,
As one who finds great spoil.

163 I hate and despise falsehood,
But I love Thy law.

164 Seven times a day I praise Thee,
Because of Thy righteous ordinances.

165 Those who love Thy law have great peace,
And nothing causes them to stumble.

166 I hope for Thy salvation, O Lord,
And do Thy commandments.

167 My soul keeps Thy testimonies,
And I love them exceedingly.

168 I keep Thy precepts and Thy testimonies,
For all my ways are before Thee.

ת Tav.

V. *The closing general petition*

169 Let my cry come before Thee, O Lord;
Give me understanding according to Thy word.

170 Let my supplication come before Thee;
Deliver me according to Thy word.

171 Let my lips utter praise,
For Thou dost teach me Thy statutes.

172 Let my tongue sing of Thy word,
For all Thy commandments are righteousness.

173 Let Thy hand be ready to help me,
For I have chosen Thy precepts.

174 I long for Thy salvation, O Lord,
And Thy law is my delight.

175 Let my soul live that it may praise Thee,
And let Thine ordinances help me.

176 I have gone astray like a lost sheep; seek Thy servant,

119:153
v. 50;
Prov 3:1
119:154
1 Sam 24:15;
v. 134
119:155
Job 5:4
119:156
2 Sam 24:14

119:157
Ps 7:1; v. 51
119:158
Ps 139:21

119:159
vv. 47,88
119:160
Ps 139:17;
v. 142

119:161
1 Sam 24:11

119:162
1 Sam 30:16

*119:164
vv. 7,160
119:165
Prov 3:2;
Is 26:3; 32:17
119:166
v. 174;
Gen 49:18

119:168
v. 22;
Prov 5:21

119:169
Ps 18:6;
vv. 27,65
119:170
Ps 28:2; 31:2

119:171
Ps 51:15;
94:12

119:173
Ps 37:24
119:174
vv. 166,24
119:175
Is 55:3
*119:176
Is 53:6; v. 16

119:164 *Seven times a day*, i.e., again and again, according to some interpreters. Rabbi Solomon understood it literally: men should praise God twice in the morning before reading the Ten Commandments, and once after; twice in the evening before reading them, and twice after.

119:176 Men, like sheep, display folly and ingratitude as they go astray. God, the shepherd, through love, searches for and finds the lost sheep—a fitting climax to this, the longest of the psalms.

For I do not forget Thy commandments.

A Song of Ascents.

I. *A prayer for deliverance (120:1-7)*

A. *From lying lips*

120:1
Ps 102:2;
Jon 2:2
120:2
Prov 12:22;
Ps 52:4

120:4
Ps 45:5;
140:10

*120:5
Gen 10:2;
Ezek 27:13;
Gen 25:13;
Jer 49:28
120:7
Ps 55:21

120 In my trouble I cried to the LORD,
And He answered me.
2 Deliver my soul, O LORD, from lying lips,
From a deceitful tongue.
3 What shall be given to you, and what more shall be done to you,
You deceitful tongue?
4 Sharp arrows of the warrior,
With the *burning* coals of the broom tree.

B. *From haters of peace*

5 Woe is me, for I sojourn in Meshech,
For I dwell among the tents of Kedar!
6 Too long has my soul had its dwelling
With those who hate peace.
7 I am *for* peace, but when I speak,
They are for war.

A Song of Ascents.

I. *The LORD my keeper (121:1-8)*

121 I will lift up my eyes to the mountains;
From whence shall my help come?
2 My help *comes* from the LORD,
Who made heaven and earth.
3 He will not allow your foot to slip;
He who keeps you will not slumber.
4 Behold, He who keeps Israel
Will neither slumber nor sleep.

5 The LORD is your keeper;
The LORD is your shade on your right hand.
6 The sun will not smite you by day,
Nor the moon by night.
7 The LORD will [204]protect you from all evil;
He will keep your soul.
8 The LORD will [204]guard your going out and your coming in
From this time forth and forever.

121:2
Ps 124:8;
115:15
121:3
Ps 66:9;
127:1

121:5
Is 25:4;
Ps 16:8
121:6
Ps 91:5;
Is 49:10;
Rev 7:16
121:7
Ps 91:10-12
121:8
Deut 28:6

A Song of Ascents, of David.

I. *The peace of Jerusalem (122:1-9)*

A. *The house of the LORD*

122:1
Is 2:3;
Zech 8:21

122:3
Ps 48:13
122:4
Deut 16:16;
Ex 16:34

122 I was glad when they said to me,
"Let us go to the house of the LORD."
2 Our feet are standing
Within your gates, O Jerusalem,
3 Jerusalem, that is built
As a city that is compact together;
4 To which the tribes go up, even the tribes of the LORD—

204Or, *keep*

120:5 *Meshech . . . Kedar* (cf. Gen. 10:2; 25:13). The reference is to the Gentile peoples among whom the psalmist lived. *Kedar* refers both to the region and the people.

An ordinance for Israel—
To give thanks to the name of the LORD.

5 For there thrones were set for judgment,
The thrones of the house of David.

122:5
Deut 17:8;
2 Chr 19:8

B. *The prayer for its peace and prosperity*

6 Pray for the peace of Jerusalem:
"May they prosper who love you.

7 "May peace be within your walls,
And prosperity within your palaces."

8 For the sake of my brothers and my friends,
I will now say, "May peace be within you."

9 For the sake of the house of the LORD our God
I will seek your good.

122:6
Ps 51:18

122:9
Neh 2:10

A Song of Ascents.

I. *A song of confidence in God (123:1–4)*

A. *Looking to the LORD*

123 To Thee I lift up my eyes,
O Thou who art enthroned in the heavens!
2 Behold, as the eyes of servants *look* to the hand of their master,
As the eyes of a maid to the hand of her mistress;
So our eyes *look* to the LORD our God,
Until He shall be gracious to us.

123:1
Ps 121:1;
141:8; 2:4;
11:4
123:2
Prov 27:18;
Ps 25:15

B. *Prayer for mercy*

3 Be gracious to us, O LORD, be gracious to us;
For we are greatly filled with contempt.

4 Our soul is greatly filled
With the scoffing of those who are at ease,
And with the contempt of the proud.

123:3
Ps 4:1; 51:1

123:4
Ps 79:4

A Song of Ascents, of David.

I. *Thanksgiving for a supernatural deliverance (124:1–8)*

A. *God alone the deliverer*

124 "Had it not been the LORD who was on our side,"
Let Israel now say,
2 "Had it not been the LORD who was on our side,
When men rose up against us;

3 Then they would have swallowed us alive,
When their anger was kindled against us;

4 Then the waters would have engulfed us,
The stream would have swept over our soul;

5 Then the raging waters would have swept over our soul."

124:1
Ps 94:17;
129:1

124:3
Ps 56:1; 57:3;
Prov 1:12

124:5
Ps 69:2

B. *Praise to the deliverer*

6 Blessed be the LORD,
Who has not given us to be torn by their teeth.

7 Our soul has escaped as a bird out of the snare of the trapper;
The snare is broken and we have escaped.

8 Our help is in the name of the LORD,
Who made heaven and earth.

124:6
Ps 27:2
124:7
Prov 6:5;
Ps 91:3
124:8
Ps 121:2;
Gen 1:1

A Song of Ascents.

I. The LORD the protector of His people (125:1–5)

125:1
Ps 46:5

125:2
Zech 2:5;
Ps 121:8

125:3
Prov 22:8;
Is 14:5;
Ps 55:20

125:4
Ps 119:68;
7:10; 94:15
125:5
Prov 2:15;
Ps 128:6

125 Those who trust in the LORD
Are as Mount Zion, which cannot be moved, but abides forever.
2 As the mountains surround Jerusalem,
So the LORD surrounds His people
From this time forth and forever.
3 For the scepter of wickedness shall not rest upon the land of the
righteous;
That the righteous may not put forth their hands to do wrong.
4 Do good, O LORD, to those who are good,
And to those who are upright in their hearts.
5 But as for those who turn aside to their crooked ways,
The LORD will lead them away with the doers of iniquity.
Peace be upon Israel.

A Song of Ascents.

I. A song of thanks for God's deliverance (126:1–6)

*126:1
Ps 85:1;
Acts 12:9
126:2
Job 8:21;
Ps 51:14;
71:19

126:3
Is 25:9

126:4
Is 35:6; 43:19

126:5
Jer 31:16;
Is 35:10

126 When the LORD brought back the captive ones of Zion,
We were like those who dream.
2 Then our mouth was filled with laughter,
And our tongue with joyful shouting;
Then they said among the nations,
"The LORD has done great things for them."
3 The LORD has done great things for us;
We are glad.
4 Restore our captivity, O LORD,
As the streams in the South.
5 Those who sow in tears shall reap with joyful shouting.
6 He who goes to and fro weeping, carrying *his* bag of seed,
Shall indeed come again with a shout of joy, bringing his sheaves
with him.

A Song of Ascents, of Solomon.

I. The vanity of work without God (127:1–5)

*127:1
Ps 78:69;
121:4

127:2
Gen 3:17;
Job 11:18,19

*127:3
Gen 33:5;
Josh 24:3,4;
Deut 28:4

127:5
Job 5:4;
Prov 27:11

127 Unless the LORD builds the house,
They labor in vain who build it;
Unless the LORD guards the city,
The watchman keeps awake in vain.
2 It is vain for you to rise up early,
To retire late,
To eat the bread of painful labors;
For He gives to His beloved *even in his* sleep.
3 Behold, children are a gift of the LORD;
The fruit of the womb is a reward.
4 Like arrows in the hand of a warrior,
So are the children of one's youth.
5 How blessed is the man whose quiver is full of them;
They shall not be ashamed,
When they speak with their enemies in the gate.

126:1 Many commentators think this psalm refers to some great deliverance of Israel out of difficulty and bondage, in all probability their return to the land from Babylon in Ezra's time. Israel's liberation is directly attributed to God when the weeping (v. 6) of the captives turns to shouts of joy upon deliverance.

127:1 Men are ambitious to found a family and to continue the family name. But to found a family and to leave God out of the picture is to labor futilely.
127:3 Children are the gift of God and should be trained as such. They are a source of great joy to their parents and are their strength and defense.

A Song of Ascents.

I. *The family that fears the Lord is blessed (128:1–6)*

A. *The blessedness of the individual*

128 How blessed is everyone who fears the Lord,
Who walks in His ways.
2 When you shall eat of the [205]fruit of your hands,
You will be happy and it will be well with you.

B. *The blessedness of the home*

3 Your wife shall be like a fruitful vine,
Within your house,
Your children like olive plants
Around your table.

4 Behold, for thus shall the man be blessed
Who fears the Lord.

C. *The blessedness of the nation*

5 The Lord bless you from Zion,
And may you see the prosperity of Jerusalem all the days of your
life.

6 Indeed, may you see your children's children.
Peace be upon Israel!

A Song of Ascents.

I. *A prayer for the shame of Israel's enemies (129:1–8)*

129 "Many times they have persecuted me from my youth up,"
Let Israel now say,
2 "Many times they have persecuted me from my youth up;
Yet they have not prevailed against me.

3 "The plowers plowed upon my back;
They lengthened their furrows."

4 The Lord is righteous;
He has cut in two the cords of the wicked.

5 May all who hate Zion,
Be put to shame and turned backward,

6 Let them be like grass upon the housetops,
Which withers before it grows up;

7 With which the reaper does not fill his hand,
Or the binder of sheaves his bosom;

8 Nor do those who pass by say,
"The blessing of the Lord be upon you;
We bless you in the name of the Lord."

A Song of Ascents.

I. *The soul that waits on God (130:1–8)*

A. *The cry for help*

130 Out of the depths I have cried to Thee, O Lord.
2 Lord, hear my voice!
Let Thine ears be attentive

[205]Lit., *labor*

Cross references:
*128:1 Ps 112:1; 119:3
128:2 Is 3:10; Ezek 23:29; Eccl 8:12
128:3 Ezek 19:10; Ps 52:8; 144:12
128:5 Ps 134:3; 20:2; 122:9
128:6 Gen 50:23; Job 42:16; Ps 125:5
*129:1 Ps 88:15; Hos 2:15; Ps 124:1
129:2 Matt 16:18
129:4 Ps 119:137
129:5 Mic 4:11; Ps 71:13
129:6 Ps 37:2
129:8 Ruth 2:4; Ps 118:26
*130:1 Ps 42:7; 69:2
130:2 Ps 64:1; 2 Chr 6:40; Ps 28:2

128:1 This psalm is one that has been thought by many to have been sung at Israelite marriages. It teaches that family prosperity depends on the blessing of God.
129:1 This psalm was penned after the captivity began. The writer refers to the many tribulations endured by Israel, even as far back as the bondage in Egypt.
130:1 Man can expect no help apart from God; but no soul is beyond God's help. Each helpless soul should prayerfully seek the help of God for deliverance.

To the voice of my supplications.

130:3
Ps 76:7

3 If Thou, Lᴏʀᴅ, shouldst mark iniquities,
O Lord, who could stand?

130:4
Ex 34:7;
Is 55:7;
1 Kin 8:40;
Jer 33:8

4 But there is forgiveness with Thee,
That Thou mayest be feared.

B. The patient waiting

130:5
Ps 33:20;
Is 8:17;
Ps 119:81

5 I wait for the Lᴏʀᴅ, my soul does wait,
And in His word do I hope.

130:6
Ps 63:6;
119:147

6 My soul *waits* for the Lord
More than the watchmen for the morning;
Indeed, more than the watchmen for the morning.

C. Exhortation to hope

130:7
Ps 131:3;
Is 55:7

7 O Israel, hope in the Lᴏʀᴅ;
For with the Lᴏʀᴅ there is lovingkindness,
And with Him is abundant redemption.

130:8
Luke 1:68

8 And He will redeem Israel
From all his iniquities.

A Song of Ascents, of David.

I. The song of a humble and a quiet heart (131:1–3)

*131:1
Ps 101:5;
Is 5:15;
Rom 12:16

131 O Lᴏʀᴅ, my heart is not proud, nor my eyes haughty;
Nor do I involve myself in great matters,
Or in things too difficult for me.

131:2
Ps 62:1;
Matt 18:3;
1 Cor 14:20

2 Surely I have composed and quieted my soul;
Like a weaned child *rests* against his mother,
My soul is like a weaned child within me.

131:3
Ps 130:7

3 O Israel, hope in the Lᴏʀᴅ
From this time forth and forever.

A Song of Ascents.

I. David and the ark of the Lᴏʀᴅ (132:1–18)

A. David's vow

132 Remember, O Lᴏʀᴅ, on David's behalf,
All his affliction;

132:2
Gen 49:24

2 How he swore to the Lᴏʀᴅ,
And vowed to the Mighty One of Jacob,

3 "Surely I will not enter my house,
Nor lie on my bed;

132:4
Prov 6:4

4 I will not give sleep to my eyes,
Or slumber to my eyelids;

132:5
Acts 7:46

5 Until I find a place for the Lᴏʀᴅ,
A dwelling place for the Mighty One of Jacob."

B. The fulfillment of David's vow

*132:6
1 Sam 17:12;
7:1;
1 Chr 13:5

6 Behold, we heard of it in Ephrathah;
We found it in the field of Jaar.

132:7
Ps 4:7; 99:5

7 Let us go into His dwelling place;
Let us worship at His footstool.

132:8
Num 10:35;
2 Chr 6:41;
Ps 78:61

8 Arise, O Lᴏʀᴅ, to Thy resting place;
Thou and the ark of Thy strength.

9 Let Thy priests be clothed with righteousness;

131:1 The humility of David is expressed by the absence of a proud heart, of the "high look" (*my eyes haughty*), and of overweening ambition to strive after things beyond his knowledge and reach. Rather, he takes on the humility characteristic of a little child at its mother's breast. This is the opposite of the proud, who are always fretful and discontented, never satisfied or even at rest.
132:6 *Ephrathah* means "fruitful land." Although usually used of Bethlehem (Gen. 35:19), here it appears to refer to Kiriath-jearim (1 Sam. 7:1,2).

And let Thy godly ones sing for joy.

10   For the sake of David Thy servant,
Do not turn away the face of Thine anointed.

C. The promise of the LORD to David and to Zion

11   The LORD has sworn to David,
A truth from which He will not turn back;
"Of the fruit of your body I will set upon your throne.

12   "If your sons will keep My covenant,
And My testimony which I will teach them,
Their sons also shall sit upon your throne forever."

13   For the LORD has chosen Zion;
He has desired it for His habitation.

14   "This is My resting place forever;
Here I will dwell, for I have desired it.

15   "I will abundantly bless her provision;
I will satisfy her needy with bread.

16   "Her priests also I will clothe with salvation;
And her godly ones will sing aloud for joy.

17   "There I will cause the horn of David to spring forth;
I have prepared a lamp for Mine anointed.

18   "His enemies I will clothe with shame;
But upon himself his crown shall shine."

A Song of Ascents, of David.

I. Brotherly unity (133:1–3)

133 Behold, how good and how pleasant it is
For brothers to dwell together in unity!

2   It is like the precious oil upon the head,
Coming down upon the beard,
Even Aaron's beard,
Coming down upon the edge of his robes.

3   It is like the dew of Hermon,
Coming down upon the mountains of Zion;
For there the LORD commanded the blessing—life forever.

A Song of Ascents.

I. An exhortation for the night watch (134:1–3)

134 Behold, bless the LORD, all servants of the LORD,
Who serve by night in the house of the LORD!

2   Lift up your hands to the sanctuary,
And bless the LORD.

3   May the LORD bless you from Zion,
He who made heaven and earth.

I. Praise to the LORD (135:1–21)

A. The exhortation to praise

135 Praise the LORD!
Praise the name of the LORD;
Praise *Him*, O servants of the LORD,

2   You who stand in the house of the LORD,
In the courts of the house of our God!

3   Praise the LORD, for the LORD is good;
Sing praises to His name, for it is lovely.

Cross references:

132:9 v.16; Job 29:14; Is 61:10
132:11 Ps 89:3,4; 2 Sam 7:12; 2 Chr 6:16
132:12 Luke 1:32; Acts 2:30
132:13 Ps 48:1,2; 68:16
132:14 v. 8
132:15 Ps 147:14; 107:9
132:16 v. 9
132:17 Ezek 29:21; Luke 1:69; 1 Kin 11:36; 15:4; 2 Chr 21:7
132:18 Ps 35:26; 109:29
133:1 Gen 13:8; Heb 13:1
*133:2 Ex 30:25; 39:24
133:3 Deut 4:48; Lev 25:21; Deut 28:8; Ps 42:8
*134:1 Ps 103:21; 135:1,2; 1 Chr 9:33
134:2 Ps 28:2; 1 Tim 2:8
134:3 Ps 124:8; 128:5
135:1 Ps 113:1; 134:1
135:2 Luke 2:37; Ps 92:13
135:3 Ps 119:68; 147:1

133:2 *Precious oil* was used for anointing the priests.
134:1 The greeting is to the priests and Levites who had the night watch in the temple.

135:4
Deut 7:6,7;
10:15;
Ex 19:5;
1 Pet 2:9
4 For the LORD has chosen Jacob for Himself,
Israel for His own possession.

B. The greatness of the LORD

135:5
Ps 48:1; 97:9
5 For I know that the LORD is great,
And that our Lord is above all gods.

135:6
Ps 115:3
6 Whatever the LORD pleases, He does,
In heaven and in earth, in the seas and in all deeps.

135:7
Jer 10:13;
Job 28:25;
Zech 10:1;
Job 38:22
7 He causes the vapors to ascend from the ends of the earth;
Who makes lightnings for the rain;
Who brings forth the wind from His treasuries.

C. The deliverances of the LORD

135:8
Ex 12:12;
Ps 78:51
8 He smote the first-born of Egypt,
Both of man and beast.

135:9
Ps 78:43;
136:15
9 He sent signs and wonders into your midst, O Egypt,
Upon Pharaoh and all his servants.

135:10
Num 21:24;
Ps 136:17
10 He smote many nations,
And slew mighty kings,

135:11
Num 21:21-26,
33-35;
Josh 12:7
11 Sihon, king of the Amorites,
And Og, king of Bashan,
And all the kingdoms of Canaan;

135:12
Ps 78:55
12 And He gave their land as a heritage,
A heritage to Israel His people.

D. The vindication of the LORD

135:13
Ex 3:15;
Ps 102:12
13 Thy name, O LORD, is everlasting,
Thy remembrance, O LORD, throughout all generations.

135:14
Deut 32:36;
Ps 106:45
14 For the LORD will judge His people,
And will have compassion on His servants.

E. The idolatry of the nations

135:15
Ps 115:4-8
15 The idols of the nations are *but* silver and gold,
The work of man's hands.
16 They have mouths, but they do not speak;
They have eyes, but they do not see;
17 They have ears, but they do not hear;
Nor is there any breath at all in their mouths.
18 Those who make them will be like them,
Yes, everyone who trusts in them.

F. Concluding exhortation to praise

135:19
Ps 115:9
19 O house of Israel, bless the LORD;
O house of Aaron, bless the LORD;

135:20
Ps 118:4
20 O house of Levi, bless the LORD;
You who [206]revere the LORD, bless the LORD.

135:21
Ps 134:3;
132:14
21 Blessed be the LORD from Zion,
Who dwells in Jerusalem.
Praise the LORD!

I. Praise to the God of eternal mercy (136:1–26)

A. The exhortation to give thanks

136:1
Ps 106:1;
107:1; 118:1;
1 Chr 16:34;
2 Chr 20:21
136 Give thanks to the LORD, for He is good;
For His lovingkindness is everlasting.
2 Give thanks to the God of gods,
For His lovingkindness is everlasting.

136:2
Deut 10:17
3 Give thanks to the Lord of lords,
For His lovingkindness is everlasting.

206Or, *fear*

B. *Praise to God the creator*

4 To Him who alone does great wonders,
   For His lovingkindness is everlasting;
5 To Him who made the heavens with skill,
   For His lovingkindness is everlasting;
6 To Him who spread out the earth above the waters,
   For His lovingkindness is everlasting;
7 To Him who made *the* great lights,
   For His lovingkindness is everlasting:
8 The sun to rule by day,
   For His lovingkindness is everlasting,
9 The moon and stars to rule by night,
   For His lovingkindness is everlasting.

C. *Praise to God the deliverer of Israel*

10 To Him who smote the Egyptians in their first-born,
    For His lovingkindness is everlasting,
11 And brought Israel out from their midst,
    For His lovingkindness is everlasting,
12 With a strong hand and an outstretched arm,
    For His lovingkindness is everlasting;
13 To Him who divided the Red Sea asunder,
    For His lovingkindness is everlasting,
14 And made Israel pass through the midst of it,
    For His lovingkindness is everlasting,
15 But He overthrew Pharaoh and his army in the Red Sea,
    For His lovingkindness is everlasting.
16 To Him who led His people through the wilderness,
    For His lovingkindness is everlasting;
17 To Him who smote great kings,
    For His lovingkindness is everlasting,
18 And slew mighty kings,
    For His lovingkindness is everlasting:
19 Sihon, king of the Amorites,
    For His lovingkindness is everlasting,
20 And Og, king of Bashan,
    For His lovingkindness is everlasting,
21 And gave their land as a heritage,
    For His lovingkindness is everlasting,
22 Even a heritage to Israel His servant,
    For His lovingkindness is everlasting.

D. *Praise to the God of lovingkindnesses*

23 Who remembered us in our low estate,
    For His lovingkindness is everlasting,
24 And has rescued us from our adversaries,
    For His lovingkindness is everlasting;
25 Who gives food to all flesh,
    For His lovingkindness is everlasting.

E. *Closing thanksgiving*

26 Give thanks to the God of heaven,
    For His lovingkindness is everlasting.

I. *A hymn of the exiles in Babylon (137:1–9)*

A. *Their present plight*

137 By the rivers of Babylon,
     There we sat down and wept,
     When we remembered Zion.
2   Upon the willows in the midst of it

136:4
Ps 72:18

136:5
Gen 1:1;
Prov 3:19;
Jer 51:15
136:6
Gen 1:9;
Ps 24:2;
Jer 10:12
136:7
Gen 1:14,16
136:8
Gen 1:16

136:10
Ex 12:29;
Ps 135:8
136:11
Ex 12:51

136:12
Ex 6:6;
Ps 44:3;
Deut 4:34
136:13
Ex 14:21;
Ps 78:13
136:14
Ex 14:22
136:15
Ex 14:27;
Ps 135:9
136:16
Ex 13:18;
15:22;
Deut 8:15
136:17
Ps 135:10-12

136:21
Josh 12:1

136:23
Ps 113:7

136:24
Ps 107:2

136:25
Ps 104:27;
145:15

137:1
Ezek 1:1,3;
Neh 1:4

137:3
Ps 80:6

We hung our harps.

3 For there our captors demanded of us songs,
And our tormentors mirth, *saying,*
"Sing us one of the songs of Zion."

B. Their remembrance of Zion

4 How can we sing the LORD's song
In a foreign land?

5 If I forget you, O Jerusalem,
May my right hand forget *her skill.*

137:6
Ezek 3:26

6 May my tongue cleave to the roof of my mouth,
If I do not remember you,
If I do not exalt Jerusalem
Above my chief joy.

C. Their cry for vengeance

137:7
Jer 49:7;
Lam 4:22;
Ezek 25:12;
Obad 10-14

7 Remember, O LORD, against the sons of Edom
The day of Jerusalem,
Who said, "Raze it, raze it,
To its very foundation."

137:8
Is 13:1,6;
Jer 25:12;
50:15;
Rev 18:6
137:9
2 Kin 8:12;
Is 13:16

8 O daughter of Babylon, you devastated one,
How blessed will be the one who repays you
With the recompense with which you have repaid us.

9 How blessed will be the one who seizes and dashes your little ones
Against the rock.

A Psalm of David.

I. The LORD the faithful God (138:1–8)

A. David's acknowledgment of God's faithfulness

138:1
Ps 111:1;
95:3; 96:4
138:2
Ps 28:2;
1 Kin 8:29,
30; Is 42:21

138
I will give Thee thanks with all my heart;
I will sing praises to Thee before the gods.

2 I will bow down toward Thy holy temple,
And give thanks to Thy name for Thy lovingkindness and Thy
truth;
For Thou hast magnified Thy word according to all Thy name.

138:3
Ps 118:5;
28:7; 46:1

3 On the day I called Thou didst answer me;
Thou didst make me bold with strength in my soul.

B. All the kings shall praise the LORD

138:4
Ps 102:15

4 All the kings of the earth will give thanks to Thee, O LORD,
When they have heard the words of Thy mouth.

5 And they will sing of the ways of the LORD.
For great is the glory of the LORD.

138:6
Ps 113:5,6;
Is 57:15;
Prov 3:34;
James 4:6

6 For though the LORD is exalted,
Yet He regards the lowly;
But the haughty He knows from afar.

C. David's confidence in God's faithfulness

138:7
Ps 23:3,4;
71:20;
Jer 41:25;
Ps 20:6
138:8
Ps 57:2;
Phil 1:6;
Ps 136:1;
27:9;
Job 10:3,8;
14:15

7 Though I walk in the midst of trouble, Thou wilt revive me;
Thou wilt stretch forth Thy hand against the wrath of my enemies,
And Thy right hand will save me.

8 The LORD will accomplish what concerns me;
Thy lovingkindness, O LORD, is everlasting;
Do not forsake the works of Thy hands.

For the choir director. A Psalm of David.

I. *The prayer of a believing heart (139:1–24)*

A. *The omniscient God*

139 O LORD, Thou hast searched me and known *me*.
2   Thou dost know when I sit down and when I rise up;
Thou dost understand my thought from afar.
3 Thou dost scrutinize my path and my lying down,
And art intimately acquainted with all my ways.
4 Even before there is a word on my tongue,
Behold, O LORD, Thou dost know it all.
5 Thou hast enclosed me behind and before,
And laid Thy hand upon me.
6 *Such* knowledge is too wonderful for me;
It is *too* high, I cannot attain to it.

B. *The omnipresent God*

7 Where can I go from Thy Spirit?
Or where can I flee from Thy presence?
8 If I ascend to heaven, Thou art there;
If I make my bed in Sheol, behold, Thou art there.
9 If I take the wings of the dawn,
If I dwell in the remotest part of the sea,
10 Even there Thy hand will lead me,
And Thy right hand will lay hold of me.
11 If I say, "Surely the darkness will overwhelm me,
And the light around me will be night,"
12 Even the darkness is not dark to Thee,
And the night is as bright as the day.
Darkness and light are alike *to Thee*.

C. *The God of creation*

13 For Thou didst form my inward parts;
Thou didst weave me in my mother's womb.
14 I will give thanks to Thee, for [207]I am fearfully and wonderfully
made;
Wonderful are Thy works,
And my soul knows it very well.
15 My frame was not hidden from Thee,
When I was made in secret,
And skillfully wrought in the depths of the earth.
16 Thine eyes have seen my unformed substance;
And in Thy book they were all written,
The days that were ordained *for me*,
When as yet there was not one of them.

17 How precious also are Thy thoughts to me, O God!
How vast is the sum of them!
18 If I should count them, they would outnumber the sand.
When I awake, I am still with Thee.

[207]Some ancient versions read *Thou art fearfully wonderful*

139:1 In this psalm, the omniscience and omnipresence of God are emphasized. Verses 1,2,4,6 stress that God is all-knowing; 7–13 present God as being everywhere present and affirm that man cannot find a refuge too hidden or remote from His presence; 15,16 deal with God's foreknowledge of men before they are fashioned in human form.
139:8ff. Even though the psalmist speaks of God as being everywhere, yet he is not a pantheist. God is distinct from His creation. He fills His creation and sustains it, but He is independent of it and cannot be mingled with it.
139:13ff. This God who is the creator also made man according to His own desire, under His inquiring eye, and by His own power. The marvelous body of man, his rational faculties, and the composite nature of his being—body and soul—show the work of God.

Margin references:

*139:1 Ps 17:3; Jer 12:3
139:2 2 Kin 19:27; Matt 9:4; John 2:24
139:3 Job 31:4
139:4 Heb 4:13
139:5 Ps 34:7; Job 9:33
139:6 Rom 11:33; Job 42:3

139:7 Jer 23:24; Jon 1:3
*139:8ff Amos 9:2-4; Job 26:6; Prov 15:11
139:10 Ps 23:2,3
139:11 Job 22:13
139:12 Job 34:22; Dan 2:22; Heb 4:13

*139:13ff Ps 119:73; Job 10:11
139:14 Ps 40:5

139:17 Ps 40:5

D. *Concluding prayer for the wicked and for self*

139:19
Is 11:4;
Ps 119:115

19 O that Thou wouldst slay the wicked, O God;
Depart from me, therefore, men of bloodshed.

139:20
Jude 15

20 For they speak against Thee wickedly,
And Thine enemies take *Thy name* in vain.

139:21
Ps 119:158

21 Do I not hate those who hate Thee, O LORD?
And do I not loathe those who rise up against Thee?

22 I hate them with the utmost hatred;
They have become my enemies.

Does David come under conviction in v. 23??

139:23
Job 31:6;
Ps 26:2;
Jer 11:20

23 Search me, O God, and know my heart;
Try me and know my anxious thoughts;

139:24
Prov 15:9;
Ps 5:8;
143:10

24 And see if there be any hurtful way in me,
And lead me in the everlasting way.

For the choir director. A Psalm of David.

I. *Prayer for protection against enemies (140:1–13)*

A. *Petition for deliverance from the wicked*

140:1
Ps 17:13;
18:48

140

Rescue me, O LORD, from evil men;
Preserve me from violent men,

140:2
Ps 36:4; 56:6

2 Who devise evil things in *their* hearts;
They continually stir up wars.

140:3
Ps 57:4; 68:4;
James 3:8

3 They sharpen their tongues as a serpent;
Poison of a viper is under their lips.   Selah.

140:4
Ps 71:4

4 Keep me, O LORD, from the hands of the wicked;
Preserve me from violent men,
Who have purposed to [208]trip up my feet.

140:5
Ps 35:7; 31:4;
141:9

5 The proud have hidden a trap for me, and cords;
They have spread a net by the wayside;
They have set snares for me.   Selah.

B. *A cry for God to hear*

140:6
Ps 16:2;
143:1; 116:1

6 I said to the LORD, "Thou art my God;
Give ear, O LORD, to the voice of my supplications.

140:7
Ps 28:8;
144:10

7 "O GOD the Lord, the strength of my salvation,
Thou hast covered my head in the day of battle.

140:8
Ps 112:10;
10:2

8 "Do not grant, O LORD, the desires of the wicked;
Do not promote his *evil* device, *lest* they be exalted.   Selah.

C. *A prayer of imprecation*

140:9
Ps 7:16

9 "As for the head of those who surround me,
May the mischief of their lips cover them.

140:10
Ps 11:6; 21:9;
36:12

10 "May burning coals fall upon them;
May they be cast into the fire,
Into deep pits from which they cannot rise.

140:11
Ps 34:21

11 "May a slanderer not be established in the earth;
May evil hunt the violent man [209]speedily."

D. *Expression of confidence in the LORD*

140:12
Ps 9:4; 35:10

12 I know that the LORD will maintain the cause of the afflicted,
And justice for the poor.

140:13
Ps 97:12;
11:7

13 Surely the righteous will give thanks to Thy name;
The upright will dwell in Thy presence.

[208]Lit., *push violently*   [209]Lit., *thrust upon thrust*

A Psalm of David.

I. *The conduct of a good man in trouble (141:1–10)*

A. *The appeal to the LORD*

141
O LORD, I call upon Thee; hasten to me!
Give ear to my voice when I call to Thee!
2 May my prayer be counted as incense before Thee;
The lifting up of my hands as the evening offering.

B. *The prayer for an upright heart*

3 Set a guard, O LORD, over my mouth;
Keep watch over the door of my lips.
4 Do not incline my heart to any evil thing,
To practice deeds of wickedness
With men who do iniquity;
And do not let me eat of their delicacies.

C. *The end of the wicked*

5 Let the righteous smite me in kindness and reprove me;
It is oil upon the head;
Do not let my head refuse it,
For still my prayer is against their wicked deeds.
6 Their judges are thrown down by the sides of the rock,
And they hear my words, for they are pleasant.
7 As when one plows and breaks open the earth,
Our bones have been scattered at the mouth of Sheol.

D. *His eyes are upon God*

8 For my eyes are toward Thee, O GOD, the Lord;
In Thee I take refuge; do not leave me defenseless.
9 Keep me from the jaws of the trap which they have set for me,
And from the snares of those who do iniquity.
10 Let the wicked fall into their own nets,
While I pass by safely.

Maskil of David, when he was in the cave. A Prayer.

I. *The prisoner's prayer (142:1–7)*

A. *The appeal of the prisoner*

142
I Cry aloud with my voice to the LORD;
I make supplication with my voice to the LORD.
2 I pour out my complaint before Him;
I declare my trouble before Him.

B. *The plight of the prisoner*

3 When my spirit was overwhelmed within me,
Thou didst know my path.
In the way where I walk
They have hidden a trap for me.
4 Look to the right and see;
For there is no one who regards me;
There is no escape for me;
No one cares for my soul.

C. *The prayer for deliverance*

5 I cried out to Thee, O LORD;
I said, "Thou art my refuge,
My portion in the land of the living.

141:1
Ps 22:19;
70:5; 143:1
141:2
Rev 5:8; 8:3;
Ps 134:2;
Ex 29:39

141:4
Ps 119:36;
Prov 23:6

141:5
Prov 9:8;
Ps 23:5;
35:14

141:7
Ps 53:5

141:8
Ps 25:15;
2:12; 27:9
141:9
Ps 38:12;
140:5
141:10
Ps 35:8

142:1
Ps 77:1; 30:8

142:2
Is 26:16

142:3
Ps 143:4;
140:5

142:4
Ps 31:11;
Job 11:20;
Jer 30:17

142:5
Ps 46:1; 16:5;
27:13

142:6
Ps 17:1; 79:8;
116:6

6   "Give heed to my cry,
       For I am brought very low;
       Deliver me from my persecutors,
       For they are too strong for me.

142:7
Ps 146:7;
13:6

7   "Bring my soul out of prison,
       So that I may give thanks to Thy name;
       The righteous will surround me,
       For Thou wilt deal bountifully with me."

A Psalm of David.

I. *The prayer of a soul in distress (143:1–12)*

A. *The complaint of the psalmist*

143:1
Ps 140:6;
89:1,2; 71:2

143 Hear my prayer, O LORD,
       Give ear to my supplications!
       Answer me in Thy faithfulness, in Thy righteousness!

143:2
Job 14:3;
4:17;
Ps 130:3;
Eccl 7:20;
Rom 3:20

2   And do not enter into judgment with Thy servant,
       For in Thy sight no man living is righteous.

3   For the enemy has persecuted my soul;
       He has crushed my life to the ground;
       He has made me dwell in dark places, like those who have long been
         dead.

143:4
Ps 142:3;
Lam 3:11

4   Therefore my spirit is overwhelmed within me;
       My heart is [210]appalled within me.

143:5
Ps 77:5;
77:12; 105:2

5   I remember the days of old;
       I meditate on all Thy doings;
       I muse on the work of Thy hands.

143:6
Ps 88:9; 63:1

6   I stretch out my hands to Thee;
       My soul *longs* for Thee, as a parched land.   Selah.

B. *The prayer for deliverance*

143:7
Ps 69:17;
27:9; 28:1

7   Answer me quickly, O LORD, my spirit fails;
       Do not hide Thy face from me,
       Lest I become like those who go down to the pit.

143:8
Ps 90:14;
25:2; 27:11;
25:1

8   Let me hear Thy lovingkindness in the morning;
       For I trust in Thee;
       Teach me the way in which I should walk;
       For to Thee I lift up my soul.

143:9
Ps 31:15

9   Deliver me, O LORD, from my enemies;
       I take refuge in Thee.

143:10
Ps 25:4,5;
Neh 9:20;
Ps 23:3

10   Teach me to do Thy will,
       For Thou art my God;
       Let Thy good Spirit lead me on level ground.

143:11
Ps 119:25;
31:1

11   For the sake of Thy name, O LORD, revive me.
       In Thy righteousness bring my soul out of trouble.

143:12
Ps 54:5; 52:5;
116:16

12   And in Thy lovingkindness cut off my enemies,
       And destroy all those who afflict my soul;
       For I am Thy servant.

A *Psalm* of David.

I. *The warrior's psalm (144:1–15)*

A. *Praise to a great God*

144:1
Ps 18:2,34

144 Blessed be the LORD, my rock,
       Who trains my hands for war,
       And my fingers for battle;

144:2
Ps 91:2; 59:9;
84:9; 18:39

2   My lovingkindness and my fortress,

210Or, *desolate*

My stronghold and my deliverer;
My shield and He in whom I take refuge;
Who subdues my people under me.

3   O Lord, what is man, that Thou dost take knowledge of him?
Or the son of man, that Thou dost think of him?
4   Man is like a mere breath;
His days are like a passing shadow.

B. *Prayer for help and deliverance*

5   Bow Thy heavens, O Lord, and come down;
Touch the mountains, that they may smoke.
6   Flash forth lightning and scatter them;
Send out Thine arrows and confuse them.
7   Stretch forth Thy hand from on high;
Rescue me and deliver me out of great waters,
Out of the hand of aliens
8   Whose mouths speak deceit,
And whose right hand is a right hand of falsehood.

9   I will sing a new song to Thee, O God;
Upon a harp of ten strings I will sing praises to Thee,
10   Who dost give salvation to kings;
Who dost rescue David His servant from the evil sword.
11   Rescue me, and deliver me out of the hand of aliens,
Whose mouth speaks deceit,
And whose right hand is a right hand of falsehood.

C. *Prayer for prosperity for the people of God*

12   Let our sons in their youth be as grown-up plants,
And our daughters as corner pillars fashioned as for a palace;
13   *Let* our garners be full, furnishing every kind of produce,
And our flocks bring forth thousands and ten thousands in our
fields;
14   *Let* our cattle bear,
Without mishap and without loss,
Let there be no outcry in our streets!
15   How blessed are the people who are so situated;
How blessed are the people whose God is the Lord!

A Psalm of Praise, of David.

I. *The goodness of God (145:1–21)*

A. *The greatness of the Lord*

145 I will extol Thee, my God, O King;
And I will bless Thy name forever and ever.
2   Every day I will bless Thee,
And I will praise Thy name forever and ever.
3   Great is the Lord, and highly to be praised;
And His greatness is unsearchable.
4   One generation shall praise Thy works to another,
And shall declare Thy mighty acts.
5   On the glorious splendor of Thy majesty,
And on Thy wonderful works, I will meditate.
6   And men shall speak of the power of Thine awesome acts;
And I will tell of Thy greatness.
7   They shall eagerly utter the memory of Thine abundant goodness,
And shall shout joyfully of Thy righteousness.

B. *The graciousness of the Lord*

8   The Lord is gracious and merciful;
Slow to anger and great in lovingkindness.

144:3 Ps 8:4; Heb 2:6 **144:4** Ps 39:11; 102:11
144:5 Ps 18:9; Is 64:1; Ps 104:32 **144:6** Ps 18:13,14; 7:13 **144:7** Ps 69:1,14; 18:44 **144:8** Ps 12:2; Is 44:20
144:9 Ps 33:2,3
144:10 Ps 18:50; 140:7 **144:11** Ps 12:2; Is 44:20
144:12 Ps 128:3
144:15 Ps 33:12
145:1 Ps 30:1; 5:2; 34:1 **145:2** Ps 71:6 **145:3** Ps 96:4; Job 5:9; Rom 11:33 **145:4** Is 38:19 **145:5** v. 12; Ps 119:27 **145:6** Ps 66:3; Deut 32:3 **145:7** Is 63:7; Ps 51:14
145:8 Ex 34:6; Ps 86:5,15

145:9
Ps 100:5;
Na 1:7
145:10
Ps 19:1;
68:26

9 The LORD is good to all,
  And His mercies are over all His works.
10 All Thy works shall give thanks to Thee, O LORD,
  And Thy godly ones shall bless Thee.
11 They shall speak of the glory of Thy kingdom,
  And talk of Thy power;

145:12
Ps 105:1;
v. 54
145:13
Ps 146:10;
2 Pet 1:11

12 To make known to the sons of men Thy mighty acts,
  And the glory of the majesty of Thy kingdom.
13 Thy kingdom is an everlasting kingdom,
  And Thy dominion *endures* throughout all generations.

C. *The goodness of the* LORD

145:14
Ps 37:24;
146:8
145:15
Ps 104:27

14 The LORD sustains all who fall,
  And raises up all who are bowed down.
15 The eyes of all look to Thee,
  And Thou dost give them their food in due time.

145:16
Ps 124:28

16 Thou dost open Thy hand,
  And dost satisfy the desire of every living thing.

17 The LORD is righteous in all His ways,
  And kind in all His deeds.

145:18
Deut 4:7;
John 4:24
145:19
Ps 37:4;
Prov 15:29

18 The LORD is near to all who call upon Him,
  To all who call upon Him in truth.
19 He will fulfill the desire of those who fear Him;
  He will also hear their cry and will save them.

145:20
Ps 31:23;
97:10; 9:5
145:21
Ps 71:8; 65:2;
v. 1,2

20 The LORD keeps all who love Him;
  But all the wicked, He will destroy.
21 My mouth will speak the praise of the LORD;
  And all flesh will bless His holy name forever and ever.

I. *An exhortation to trust God (146:1–10)*

A. *The vanity of trusting men*

146:1
Ps 103:1

146 Praise the LORD!
  Praise the LORD, O my soul!

146:2
Ps 104:33

2 I will praise the LORD while I live;
  I will sing praises to my God while I have my being.

146:3
Ps 118:8;
Is 2:22
146:4
Ps 104:29;
Eccl 12:7;
Ps 33:10

3 Do not trust in princes,
  In mortal man, in whom there is no salvation.
4 His spirit departs, he returns to the earth;
  In that very day his thoughts perish.

B. *The wisdom of trusting God*

146:5
Ps 144:15;
71:5
146:6
Ps 115:15;
Acts 14:15;
Ps 117:2

5 How blessed is he whose help is the God of Jacob,
  Whose hope is in the LORD his God;
6 Who made heaven and earth,
  The sea and all that is in them;
  Who keeps faith forever;

146:7
Ps 103:6;
107:9; 68:6

7 Who executes justice for the oppressed;
  Who gives food to the hungry.
  The LORD sets the prisoners free.

146:8
Matt 9:30;
John 9:7;
Ps 145:14;
11:7

8 The LORD opens *the eyes of* the blind;
  The LORD raises up those who are bowed down;
  The LORD loves the righteous;

146:9
Ex 22:21;
Deut 10:18;
Ps 68:5;
147:6
146:10
Ex 15:18;
Ps 10:16;
Rev 11:15

9 The LORD protects the strangers;
  He supports the fatherless and the widow;
  But He thwarts the way of the wicked.
10 The LORD will reign forever,
  Thy God, O Zion, to all generations.
  Praise the LORD!

I. *The L*ORD *of might and grace (147:1–20)*

A. *The God of might in history*

147 Praise the LORD!
For it is good to sing praises to our God;
For [211]it is pleasant *and* praise is becoming.

2 The LORD builds up Jerusalem;
He gathers the outcasts of Israel.

3 He heals the brokenhearted,
And binds up their [212]wounds.

4 He counts the number of the stars;
He gives names to all of them.

5 Great is our Lord, and abundant in strength;
His understanding is infinite.

6 The LORD [213]supports the afflicted;
He brings down the wicked to the ground.

B. *The God who sustains life*

7 Sing to the LORD with thanksgiving;
Sing praises to our God on the lyre,

8 Who covers the heavens with clouds,
Who provides rain for the earth,
Who makes grass to grow on the mountains.

9 He gives to the beast its food,
And to the young ravens which cry.

10 He does not delight in the strength of the horse;
He does not take pleasure in the legs of a man.

11 The LORD favors those who fear Him,
Those who wait for His lovingkindness.

C. *Israel exhorted to praise God*

12 Praise the LORD, O Jerusalem!
Praise your God, O Zion!

13 For He has strengthened the bars of your gates;
He has blessed your sons within you.

14 He makes peace in your borders;
He satisfies you with the finest of the wheat.

15 He sends forth His command to the earth;
His word runs very swiftly.

16 He gives snow like wool;
He scatters the frost like ashes.

17 He casts forth His ice as fragments;
Who can stand before His cold?

18 He sends forth His word and melts them;
He causes His wind to blow and the waters to flow.

19 He declares His words to Jacob,
His statutes and His ordinances to Israel.

20 He has not dealt thus with any nation;
And as for His ordinances, they have not known them.
Praise the LORD!

I. *Nature's praise of the L*ORD *(148:1–14)*

A. *The heavens to praise the L*ORD

148 Praise the LORD!
Praise the LORD from the heavens;
Praise Him in the heights!

2 Praise Him, all His angels;

211Or, *He is gracious* 212Lit., *sorrows* 213Or, *relieves*

147:2 See Neh. 12:27 in this connection.   **147:4** God has infinite power and knowledge.

Cross-references (right margin):

147:1 Ps 135:3; 33:1
*147:2 Ps 102:16; Deut 30:3
147:3 Is 61:1; 30:26
*147:4 Is 40:26
147:5 Ps 48:1; Is 40:28
147:6 Ps 146:8,9
147:7 Ps 33:2
147:8 Job 38:26; Ps 104:13
147:9 Ps 104:27; Job 38:41
147:10 Ps 33:16,17; 1 Sam 16:7
147:11 Ps 102:15
147:13 Ps 37:26
147:14 Is 60:17; Ps 132:15
147:15 Job 37:12; Ps 104:4
147:16 Job 37:6; 38:29
147:18 Ps 33:9; 107:25
147:19 Deut 33:2; Mal 4:4
147:20 Deut 4:32
148:2 Ps 103:20,21

Praise Him, all His hosts!
3   Praise Him, sun and moon;
Praise Him, all stars of light!

148:4
1 Kin 8:27;
Gen 1:7
148:5
Gen 1:1;
Ps 33:6,9
148:6
Ps 89:37;
Jer 33:25;
Job 38:33

4   Praise Him, highest heavens,
And the waters that are above the heavens!
5   Let them praise the name of the LORD,
For He commanded and they were created.
6   He has also established them forever and ever;
He has made a decree which will not pass away.

B. The earth to praise the LORD

148:7
Ps 74:13

7   Praise the LORD from the earth,
Sea monsters and all deeps;

148:8
Ps 147:15-18

8   Fire and hail, snow and clouds;
Stormy wind, fulfilling His word;

148:9
Is 44:23;
49:13; 55:12

9   Mountains and all hills;
Fruit trees and all cedars;
10 Beasts and all cattle;
Creeping things and winged fowl;
11 Kings of the earth and all peoples;
Princes and all judges of the earth;
12 Both young men and virgins;
Old men and children.

148:13
Ps 8:1;
Is 12:4;
Ps 113:4

13 Let them praise the name of the LORD,
For His name alone is exalted;
His glory is above earth and heaven.

148:14
Ps 75:10;
Deut 10:21;
Eph 2:17

14 And He has lifted up a horn for His people,
Praise for all His godly ones;
Even for the sons of Israel, a people near to Him.
Praise the LORD!

I. The LORD's love of Israel (149:1–9)

A. Exhortation to sing a new song

149:1
Ps 33:3;
35:18

149 Praise the LORD!
Sing to the LORD a new song,
And His praise in the congregation of the godly ones.

149:2
Ps 95:6; 47:6

2   Let Israel be glad in his Maker;
Let the sons of Zion rejoice in their King.

149:3
Ps 150:4;
81:2
149:4
Ps 35:27;
132:16

3   Let them praise His name with dancing;
Let them sing praises to Him with timbrel and lyre.
4   For the LORD takes pleasure in His people;
He will beautify the afflicted ones with salvation.

B. Exhortation to execute vengeance on the nations

149:5
Ps 132:16;
Job 35:10
149:6
Ps 66:17;
Heb 4:12;
Rev 1:16

5   Let the godly ones exult in glory;
Let them sing for joy on their beds.
6   *Let* the high praises of God *be* in their mouth,
And a two-edged sword in their hand,
7   To execute vengeance on the nations,
And punishment on the peoples;
8   To bind their kings with chains,
And their nobles with fetters of iron;

149:9
Ezek 28:26;
Ps 148:14

9   To execute on them the judgment written;
This is an honor for all His godly ones.
Praise the LORD!

I. Let everything praise the LORD (150:1–6)

150:1
Ps 102:19;
19:1

150 Praise the LORD!
Praise God in His sanctuary;
Praise Him in His mighty expanse.

2　Praise Him for His mighty deeds;
　Praise Him according to His excellent greatness.

3　Praise Him with trumpet sound;
　Praise Him with harp and lyre.

4　Praise Him with timbrel and dancing;
　Praise Him with stringed instruments and pipe.

5　Praise Him with loud cymbals;
　Praise Him with resounding cymbals.

6　Let everything that has breath praise the LORD.
　Praise the LORD!

150:2
Ps 145:5,6;
Deut 3:24
150:3
Ps 149:3
150:4
Ex 15:20;
Is 38:20
150:5
1 Chr 13:8;
15:16
150:6
Ps 145:21

INTRODUCTION TO
THE PROVERBS

Authorship and Background: Solomon was the author of much of the book of Proverbs. The book itself, however, does not derive completely from Solomon's day. Some of the proverbs are said to be "the words of the wise" (22:17; 24:23); others were copied out by the scribes of Hezekiah's day, and the last two chapters of the book were composed by Agur and Lemuel. Thus the final arrangement of the book cannot be dated before 700 B.C. In 1 Kin. 4:30, Solomon's wisdom is compared with that of Egypt and the "sons of the east." Archaeology has brought to light a large body of wisdom literature from the ancient Near East. The Egyptian "Wisdom of Amenemope" has many parallels to the section of Proverbs (22:17-24:23) called "the words of the wise."

Characteristics: A proverb is a short, pithy saying centering in an antithesis or comparison. There is no necessary connection between the proverbs in the order in which they are given. They are aimed primarily at giving an outline of ethical regulations for daily life. The sayings are of practical import and cover a diversity of subjects such as knowledge, morality, chastity, control of the tongue, association with others, laziness, and justice. The contents do not yield to an orderly analysis. The book is cast in poetic form, usually in couplets. The sayings are a distillation of the wisdom of that age. There are stern warnings against sin, and ultimate punishment is promised. The source of wisdom is "the fear of the LORD."

Contents:

I. Wisdom (1:1-9:18): Introduction. Wisdom is to be sought. Listeners are exhorted to seek it. The benefits and blessings of wisdom are described. It is commended to students. Marriage is commended and warnings against licentiousness, and exhortation to faithfulness, follow. Warnings about suretyship, indolence, perversity, and the seven sins. Warnings against adultery. Men are exhorted to follow wisdom, which occupies an exalted position. Wisdom and folly are contrasted.

II. Proverbs of Solomon (10:1-22:16): The rewards of righteous and unrighteous living. Certain aspects of wickedness are dealt with. The conduct of good and bad men contrasted. Conduct and paternal discipline. The fear of God in the life of man. The secret of the happy. How God watches over life. The perils and blessings of life described. Thumbnail sketches in character. Sundry teachings: wine and strong drink; hearing ear and seeing eye; deceit; the spirit of man. Man finds no victory apart from God. The law of cause and effect stated.

III. Sundry sayings (22:17-24:34): Things men should avoid: exploiting the poor; temper; suretyship. Instruction on table manners, miserliness, the rights of the helpless. Folly and wisdom are compared. Sayings of the wise.

IV. Miscellaneous sayings of Solomon (25:1-29:27): Law courts and litigation. Fools and scoundrels described; sluggards. Human relationships. Conduct in the light of pure religion. God and society; rulers and justice.

V. The words of Agur (30:1-33): Agur records his personal reflections on life. His varied sayings: unfilial conduct; the four ways; the four intolerable things; the four tiny things; the four comely things; the closing admonition.

VI. The words of Lemuel: the folly of lust and strong drink (31:1-9): The duties of kingship; warnings against lust and intemperance. He urges righteous rule and justice for the needy.

VII. The virtuous woman (31:10-31): The perfect wife and mother is praised by her husband and children.

VI.   The words of Lemuel: the folly of lust and strong drink (31:1–9); The duties of kings: warnings against injustice and appeal for righteous rule and justice for the needy.

VII.   The virtuous woman (31:10–31): The perfect wife and mother is praised by her husband and children.

THE PROVERBS

I. *Wisdom (1:1–9:18)*

A. *Authorship*

*1:1
1 Kin 4:32;
Eccl 12:9

1 The proverbs of Solomon the son of David, king of Israel:

B. *The purpose*

2   To know wisdom and instruction,
    To discern the sayings of understanding,

1:3
Prov 19:20;
2:9
3   To receive instruction in wise behavior,
    Righteousness, justice and equity;

1:4
Prov 8:5,12;
2:10,11
4   To give prudence to the naive,
    To the youth knowledge and discretion,

1:5
Prov 9:9;
14:6
5   A wise man will hear and increase in learning,
    And a man of understanding will acquire wise counsel,

1:6
Ps 78:2
6   To understand a proverb and a figure,
    The words of the wise and their riddles.

C. *The major theme*

1:7
Job 28:28;
Ps 111:10;
Eccl 12:13
7   The fear of the LORD is the beginning of knowledge;
    Fools despise wisdom and instruction.

D. *Warnings against violence*

1:8
Prov 4:1;
6:20
8   Hear, my son, your father's instruction,
    And do not forsake your mother's teaching;

1:9
Prov 4:9;
Gen 41:42
9   Indeed, they are a graceful wreath to your head,
    And ornaments about your neck.

1:10
Deut 13:8;
Eph 5:11
10   My son, if sinners entice you,
     Do not consent.

1:11
Prov 12:6;
v. 18
11   If they say, "Come with us,
     Let us lie in wait for blood,
     Let us ambush the innocent without cause;

1:12
Ps 124:3;
28:1
12   Let us swallow them alive like Sheol,
     Even whole, as those who go down to the pit;

13   We shall find all *kinds* of precious wealth,
     We shall fill our houses with spoil;

14   Throw in your lot with us,
     We shall all have one purse,"

1:15
Ps 1:1;
119:101
15   My son, do not walk in the way with them.
     Keep your feet from their path,

1:16
Is 59:7
16   For their feet run to evil,
     And they hasten to shed blood.

17   Indeed, it is useless to spread the net
     In the eyes of any bird;

18   But they lie in wait for their own blood;
     They ambush their own lives.

1:19
Prov 15:27
19   So are the ways of everyone who gains by violence;
     It takes away the life of its possessors.

E. *Warning against the neglect of wisdom*

1:20
Prov 8:1
20   Wisdom shouts in the street,

1:1 *The proverbs of Solomon.* Although Solomon is credited with the book of Proverbs, not all of them originated with   him. (See Introduction for authorship and background.)

She lifts her voice in the square;

21 At the head of the noisy *streets* she cries out;
At the entrance of the gates in the city, she utters her sayings:

22 "How long, O naive ones, will you love simplicity?
And scoffers delight themselves in scoffing,
And fools hate knowledge?

23 "Turn to my reproof,
Behold, I will pour out my spirit on you;
I will make my words known to you.

24 Because I called, and you refused;
I stretched out my hand, and no one paid attention;

25 And you neglected all my counsel,
And did not want my reproof;

26 I will even laugh at your calamity;
I will mock when your dread comes,

27 When your dread comes like a storm,
And your calamity comes on like a whirlwind,
When distress *and* anguish come on you.

28 "Then they will call on me, but I will not answer;
They will seek me diligently, but they shall not find me,

29 Because they hated knowledge,
And did not choose the fear of the LORD.

30 "They would not accept my counsel,
They spurned all my reproof.

31 "So they shall eat of the fruit of their own way,
And be satiated with their own devices.

32 "For the waywardness of the naive shall kill them,
And the complacency of fools shall destroy them.

33 "But he who listens to me shall live securely,
And shall be at ease from the dread of evil."

F. *The reward of seeking wisdom*

2 My son, if you will receive my sayings,
And treasure my commandments within you,

2 Make your ear attentive to wisdom,
Incline your heart to understanding;

3 For if you cry for discernment,
Lift your voice for understanding;

4 If you seek her as silver,
And search for her as for hidden treasures;

5 Then you will discern the fear of the LORD,
And discover the knowledge of God.

6 For the LORD gives wisdom;
From His mouth *come* knowledge and understanding.

7 He stores up sound wisdom for the upright;
He is a shield to those who walk in integrity,

8 Guarding the paths of justice,
And He preserves the way of His godly ones.

9 Then you will discern righteousness and justice
And equity *and* every good course.

10 For wisdom will enter your heart,
And knowledge will be pleasant to your soul;

11 Discretion will guard you,
Understanding will watch over you,

12 To deliver you from the way of evil,
From the man who speaks perverse things;

13 From those who leave the paths of uprightness,
To walk in the ways of darkness;

14 Who delight in doing evil,
And rejoice in the perversity of evil;

15 Whose paths are crooked,
And who are devious in their ways;

16 To deliver you from the strange woman,

1:22
vv. 4,32;
Ps 1:1; v. 29

1:23
Joel 2:28

1:24
Is 65:12;
Zech 7:11;
Rom 10:21
1:25
Ps 107:11;
Luke 7:30;
Prov 15:10
1:26
Ps 2:4;
Prov 6:15;
10:24

1:28
Is 1:15;
Ezek 8:18;
Mic 3:4;
Zech 7:13

1:30
Ps 81:11

1:31
Job 4:8;
Prov 14:14;
Is 3:11;
Jer 6:19
1:32
Jer 2:19
1:33
Ps 25:12

2:1
Prov 4:10

2:2
Prov 3:1

2:4
Prov 3:14;
Matt 13:44
2:5
Prov 1:7

2:6
1 Kin 3:9,12;
James 1:5
2:7
Ps 84:11

2:8
1 Sam 2:9;
Ps 66:9
2:9
Prov 8:20;
4:18
2:10
Prov 14:33;
22:18
2:11
Prov 6:22

2:13
John 3:19
2:14
Prov 10:23;
Jer 11:15
2:15
Ps 125:5
2:16
Prov 6:24;
23:27

From the adulteress who flatters with her words;

2:17
Mal 2:14,15

17 That leaves the companion of her youth,
And forgets the covenant of her God;

2:18
Prov 7:27

18 For her house sinks down to death,
And her tracks *lead* to the dead;

19 None who go to her return again,
Nor do they reach the paths of life.

G. *Walking in the way of wisdom*

20 So you will walk in the way of good men,
And keep to the paths of the righteous.

2:21
Ps 37:29;
28:10

21 For the upright will live in the land,
And the blameless will remain in it;

2:22
Ps 37:38;
Deut 28:63

22 But the wicked will be cut off from the land,
And the treacherous will be uprooted from it.

H. *The blessing of wisdom*

3:1
Prov 4:5;
Ex 20:6;
Deut 30:16

3 My son, do not forget my teaching,
But let your heart keep my commandments;

3:2
Prov 4:10;
Ps 119:165

2 For length of days and years of life,
And peace they will add to you.

3:3
2 Sam 15:20;
Prov 1:9; 7:3

3 Do not let kindness and truth leave you;
Bind them around your neck,
Write them on the tablet of your heart.

3:4
Prov 8:5;
Ps 111:10

4 So you will find favor and good repute
In the sight of God and man.

3:5
Ps 37:3,5;
Jer 9:23

5 Trust in the LORD with all your heart,
And do not lean on your own understanding.

3:6
1 Chr 28:9;
Is 45:13

6 In all your ways acknowledge Him,
And He will make your paths straight.

3:7
Rom 12:16;
Prov 16:6

7 Do not be wise in your own eyes;
Fear the LORD and turn away from evil.

3:8
Job 21:24

8 It will be healing to your body,
And refreshment to your bones.

3:9
Is 43:23;
Ex 23:19

9 Honor the LORD from your wealth,
And from the first of all your produce;

3:10
Deut 28:8

10 So your barns will be filled with plenty,
And your vats will overflow with new wine.

3:11
Heb 12:5,6

11 My son, do not reject the discipline of the LORD,
Or loathe His reproof,

3:12
Deut 8:5

12 For whom the LORD loves He reproves,
Even as a father, the son in whom he delights.

I. *Wisdom more precious than wealth*

3:13
Prov 8:32,34

13 How blessed is the man who finds wisdom,
And the man who gains understanding.

3:14
Job 28:13;
Prov 8:10,19

14 For its profit is better than the profit of silver,
And its gain than fine gold.

3:15
Job 28:18;
Prov 8:11

15 She is more precious than jewels;
And nothing you desire compares with her.

3:16
Prov 8:18

16 Long life is in her right hand;
In her left hand are riches and honor.

3:17
Prov 16:7

17 Her ways are pleasant ways,
And all her paths are peace.

3:18
Prov 11:30;
Gen 2:9

18 She is a tree of life to those who take hold of her,
And happy are all who hold her fast.

3:19
Ps 104:24

19 The LORD by wisdom founded the earth;
By understanding He established the heavens.

3:20
Gen 7:11;
Job 36:28

20 By His knowledge the deeps were broken up,
And the skies drip with dew.

J. The wise inherit honor

21 My son, let them not depart from your sight;
    Keep sound wisdom and discretion,
22 So they will be life to your soul,
    And adornment to your neck.
23 Then you will walk in your way securely,
    And your foot will not stumble.
24 When you lie down, you will not be afraid;
    When you lie down, your sleep will be sweet.
25 Do not be afraid of sudden fear,
    Nor of the onslaught of the wicked when it comes;
26 For the LORD will be your confidence,
    And will keep your foot from being caught.

27 Do not withhold good from those to whom it is due,
    When it is in your power to do *it*.
28 Do not say to your neighbor, "Go, and come back,
    And tomorrow I will give *it*,"
    When you have it with you.
29 Do not devise harm against your neighbor,
    While he lives in security beside you.
30 Do not contend with a man without cause,
    If he has done you no harm.
31 Do not envy a man of violence,
    And do not choose any of his ways.
32 For the crooked *man* is an abomination to the LORD;
    But He is intimate with the upright.
33 The curse of the LORD is on the house of the wicked,
    But He blesses the dwelling of the righteous.
34 Though He scoffs at the scoffers,
    Yet He gives grace to the afflicted.
35 The wise will inherit honor,
    But fools display dishonor.

K. Admonitions of a father to his son

1. *The command to obtain wisdom*

4
    Hear, *O* sons, the instruction of a father,
    And give attention that you may gain understanding,
2   For I give you sound teaching;
    Do not abandon my instruction.
3   When I was a son to my father,
    Tender and the only son in the sight of my mother,
4   Then he taught me and said to me,
    "Let your heart hold fast my words;
    Keep my commandments and live;
5   Acquire wisdom! Acquire understanding!
    Do not forget, nor turn away from the words of my mouth.
6   "Do not forsake her, and she will guard you;
    Love her, and she will watch over you.
7   "The beginning of wisdom *is*: Acquire wisdom;
    And with all your acquiring, get understanding.
8   "Prize her, and she will exalt you;
    She will honor you if you embrace her.
9   "She will place on your head a garland of grace;
    She will present you with a crown of beauty."

2. *Contrast of the wise and the wicked*

10 Hear, my son, and accept my sayings,
    And the years of your life will be many.
11 I have directed you in the way of wisdom;
    I have led you in upright paths.
12 When you walk, your steps will not be impeded;

3:22
Prov 4:22;
1:9
3:23
Prov 4:12
3:24
Ps 3:5
3:25
Ps 91:5;
Job 5:21
3:27
Rom 13:7;
Gal 6:10
3:28
Lev 19:13
3:29
Prov 14:22
3:30
Rom 12:18
3:31
Ps 37:1;
Prov 24:1
3:32
Prov 11:20;
Ps 25:14
3:33
Deut 11:28;
Mal 2:2;
Job 8:6
3:34
James 4:6;
1 Pet 5:5
4:1
Prov 1:8; 2:2
4:3
1 Chr 22:5
4:4
1 Chr 28:9;
Prov 7:2
4:5
v. 7;
Prov 16:16
4:6
2 Thess 2:10
4:7
Prov 23:23
4:8
1 Sam 2:30
4:9
Prov 1:9
4:10
Prov 2:1; 3:2
4:11
1 Sam 12:23
4:12
Ps 18:36;

Prov 3:23
And if you run, you will not stumble.
13 Take hold of instruction; do not let go.
    Guard her, for she is your life.

4:14
Ps 1:1;
Prov 1:15
14 Do not enter the path of the wicked,
    And do not proceed in the way of evil men.
15 Avoid it, do not pass by it;
    Turn away from it and pass on.

4:16
Ps 36:4;
Mic 2:1
16 For they cannot sleep unless they do evil,
    And they are robbed of sleep unless they make *someone* stumble.
17 For they eat the bread of wickedness,
    And drink the wine of violence.

4:18
Is 26:7;
2 Sam 23:4;
Dan 12:3
18 But the path of the righteous is like the light of dawn,
    That shines brighter and brighter until the full day.

4:19
Job 18:5;
Is 59:9,10;
Jer 23:12;
John 12:35
19 The way of the wicked is like darkness;
    They do not know over what they stumble.

3. *Positive instructions to a son*

20 My son, give attention to my words;
    Incline your ear to my sayings.

4:21
Prov 3:21;
7:1,2
21 Do not let them depart from your sight;
    Keep them in the midst of your heart.

4:22
Prov 3:8;
12:18
22 For they are life to those who find them,
    And health to all their whole body.

4:23
Matt 12:34;
Mark 7:21;
Luke 6:45
23 Watch over your heart with all diligence,
    For from it *flow* the springs of life.

4:24
Prov 6:12;
19:1
24 Put away from you a deceitful mouth,
    And put devious lips far from you.
25 Let your eyes look directly ahead,
    And let your gaze be fixed straight in front of you.

4:26
Heb 12:13;
Ps 119:5
26 Watch the path of your feet,
    And all your ways will be established.

4:27
Deut 5:32;
28:14;
Prov 1:15
27 Do not turn to the right nor to the left;
    Turn your foot from evil.

L. *Instruction on marriage*

1. *Warning against unchastity*

5:1
Prov 4:20;
22:17
5 My son, give attention to my wisdom,
       Incline your ear to my understanding;

5:2
Mal 2:7
2   That you may observe discretion,
    And your lips may reserve knowledge.

5:3
Prov 2:16;
Ps 55:21
3   For the lips of an adulteress drip honey,
    And smoother than oil is her speech;

5:4
Eccl 7:26;
Ps 57:4
4   But in the end she is bitter as wormwood,
    Sharp as a two-edged sword.

5:5
Prov 7:27
5   Her feet go down to death,
    Her steps lay hold of Sheol.
6   She does not ponder the path of life;
    Her ways are unstable, she does not know *it*.

5:7
Prov 7:24;
Ps 119:102
7   Now then, *my* sons, listen to me,
    And do not depart from the words of my mouth.

5:8
Prov 7:25;
9:14
8   Keep your way far from her,
    And do not go near the door of her house,
9   Lest you give your vigor to others,
    And your years to the cruel one;
10 Lest strangers be filled with your strength,
    And your hard-earned goods *go* to the house of an alien;
11 And you groan at your latter end,
    When your flesh and your body are consumed;

5:12
Prov 1:29;
12:1
12 And you say, "How I have hated instruction!
    And my heart spurned reproof!
13 "And I have not listened to the voice of my teachers,

Nor inclined my ear to my instructors!

14 "I was almost in utter ruin
In the midst of the assembly and congregation."

2. Marital joys and responsibilities

15 Drink water from your own cistern,
And fresh water from your own well.

16 Should your springs be dispersed abroad,
Streams of water in the streets?

17 Let them be yours alone,
And not for strangers with you.

18 Let your fountain be blessed,
And rejoice in the wife of your youth.

19 *As* a loving hind and a graceful doe,
Let her breasts satisfy you at all times;
Be exhilarated always with her love.

20 For why should you, my son, be exhilarated with an adulteress,
And embrace the bosom of a foreigner?

21 For the ways of a man are before the eyes of the LORD,
And He watches all his paths.

22 His own iniquities will capture the wicked,
And he will be held with the cords of his sin.

23 He will die for lack of instruction,
And in the greatness of his folly he will go astray.

M. Warning against suretyship

6 My son, if you have become surety for your neighbor,
Have given a pledge for a stranger,

2 *If* you have been snared with the words of your mouth,
Have been caught with the words of your mouth,

3 Do this then, my son, and deliver yourself;
Since you have come into the hand of your neighbor,
Go, humble yourself, and importune your neighbor.

4 Do not give sleep to your eyes,
Nor slumber to your eyelids;

5 Deliver yourself like a gazelle from *the hunter's* hand,
And like a bird from the hand of the fowler.

N. Warning against idleness

6 Go to the ant, O sluggard,
Observe her ways and be wise,

7 Which, having no chief,
Officer or ruler,

8 Prepares her food in the summer,
And gathers her provision in the harvest.

9 How long will you lie down, O sluggard?
When will you arise from your sleep?

10 "A little sleep, a little slumber,
A little folding of the hands to rest"—

11 And your poverty will come in like a vagabond,
And your need like an armed man.

O. Warning against sowing discord

12 A worthless person, a wicked man,
Is the one who walks with a false mouth,

13 Who winks with his eyes, who signals with his feet,
Who points with his fingers;

14 Who *with* perversity in his heart devises evil continually,
Who spreads strife.

15 Therefore his calamity will come suddenly;
Instantly he will be broken, and there will be no healing.

5:16
Prov 9:17

5:18
Eccl 9:9;
Mal 2:14
5:19
Song 2:9; 4:5;
7:3

5:20
Prov 2:16;
7:5
5:21
Job 31:4;
34:21;
Prov 15:3;
Jer 16:17;
32:19;
Hos 7:2;
Heb 4:13
5:22
Ps 9:15
5:23
Job 4:21;
36:12
6:1
Prov 11:15;
17:18; 20:16;
22:26; 27:13

6:4
Ps 132:4
6:5
Ps 91:3

6:6
Prov 30:24,25

6:8
Prov 10:5
6:9
Prov 24:33

6:11
Prov 10:4;
13:4; 20:4

6:12
Prov 16:27;
10:32
6:13
Ps 35:19;
Prov 10:10
6:14
Mic 2:1; v. 19
6:15
Prov 24:22;
Jer 19:11;
2 Chr 36:16

P. *Warning against seven sins*

16   There are six things which the LORD hates,
         Yes, seven which are an abomination to Him:

6:17
Ps 18:27;
120:2; Is 1:15
6:18
Gen 6:5;
Prov 1:16
6:19
Ps 27:12; v. 4

17   Haughty eyes, a lying tongue,
      And hands that shed innocent blood,

18   A heart that devises wicked plans,
      Feet that run rapidly to evil,

19   A false witness *who* utters lies,
      And one who spreads strife among brothers.

Q. *Warning against adultery*

6:20
Prov 7:1; 1:8

20   My son, observe the commandment of your father,
         And do not forsake the teaching of your mother;

6:21
Prov 3:3

21   Bind them continually on your heart;
      Tie them around your neck.

6:22
Prov 3:23,24

22   When you walk about, they will guide you;
      When you sleep, they will watch over you;
      And when you awake, they will talk to you.

6:23
Ps 19:8

23   For the commandment is a lamp, and the teaching is light;
      And reproofs for discipline are the way of life,

6:24
Prov 2:16;
5:3

24   To keep you from the evil woman,
      From the smooth tongue of the adulteress.

6:25
Matt 5:28

25   Do not desire her beauty in your heart,
      Nor let her catch you with her eyelids.

6:26
Prov 29:3;
7:23;
Ezek 13:18

26   For on account of a harlot *one is reduced* to a loaf of bread,
      And an adulteress hunts for the precious life.

27   Can a man take fire in his bosom,
      And his clothes not be burned?

28   Or can a man walk on hot coals,
      And his feet not be scorched?

6:29
Ezek 18:6;
33:26

29   So is the one who goes in to his neighbor's wife;
      Whoever touches her will not go unpunished.

30   Men do not despise a thief if he steals
      To satisfy himself when he is hungry;

6:31
Ex 22:1-4

31   But when he is found, he must repay sevenfold;
      He must give all the substance of his house.

6:32
Prov 7:7

32   The one who commits adultery with a woman is lacking sense;
      He who would destroy himself does it.

33   Wounds and disgrace he will find,
      And his reproach will not be blotted out.

6:34
Prov 27:4;
11:4

34   For jealousy enrages a man,
      And he will not spare in the day of vengeance.

35   He will not accept any ransom,
      Nor will he be content though you give many gifts.

R. *The folly of yielding to a harlot*

7:1
Prov 2:1

7   My son, keep my words,
        And treasure my commandments within you.

7:2
Prov 4:4;
Deut 32:10

2   Keep my commandments and live,
     And my teaching as the apple of your eye.

7:3
Deut 6:8;
Prov 3:3

3   Bind them on your fingers;
     Write them on the tablet of your heart.

4   Say to wisdom, "You are my sister,"
     And call understanding *your* intimate friend;

7:5
Prov 2:16;
5:3; 6:24

5   That they may keep you from an adulteress,
     From the foreigner who flatters with her words.

6   For at the window of my house
     I looked out through my lattice,

7:6ff. Proverbs are frequently addressed to the young to warn them of the pitfalls into which they may be led by sin. The youth will assuredly hear the voice of the temptress (7:21), but he must spurn her entreaty and heed the call of wisdom (8:1).

797

I saw among the naive,
scerned among the youths,
oung man lacking sense,
sing through the street near her corner;
d he takes the way to her house,
the twilight, in the evening,
the middle of the night and *in* the darkness.
nd behold, a woman *comes* to meet him,
Dressed as a harlot and cunning of heart.
She is boisterous and rebellious;
Her feet do not remain at home;
She is now in the streets, now in the squares,
And lurks by every corner.
So she seizes him and kisses him,
And with a brazen face she says to him:
"I was due to offer peace offerings;
Today I have paid my vows.

15 "Therefore I have come out to meet you,
To seek your presence earnestly, and I have found you.
16 "I have spread my couch with coverings,
With colored linens of Egypt.
17 "I have sprinkled my bed
With myrrh, aloes and cinnamon.
18 "Come, let us drink our fill of love until morning;
Let us delight ourselves with caresses.
19 "For the man is not at home,
He has gone on a long journey;
20 He has taken a bag of money with him,
At full moon he will come home."
21 With her many persuasions she entices him;
With her flattering lips she seduces him.
22 Suddenly he follows her,
As an ox goes to the slaughter,
Or as *one in* fetters to the discipline of a fool,
23 Until an arrow pierces through his liver;
As a bird hastens to the snare,
So he does not know that it *will cost him* his life.

24 Now therefore, *my* sons, listen to me,
And pay attention to the words of my mouth.
25 Do not let your heart turn aside to her ways,
Do not stray into her paths.
26 For many are the victims she has cast down,
And numerous are all her slain.
27 Her house is the way to Sheol,
Descending to the chambers of death.

S. *Wisdom personified*

1. *The call of wisdom*

8
Does not wisdom call,
And understanding lift up her voice?
2 On top of the heights beside the way,
Where the paths meet, she takes her stand;
3 Beside the gates, at the opening to the city,
At the entrance of the doors, she cries out:
4 "To you, O men, I call,
And my voice is to the sons of men.
5 "O naive ones, discern prudence;
And, O fools, discern wisdom.

7:7
Prov 1:22;
6:32

7:8
vv. 12,27

7:9
Job 24:15

7:11
Prov 9:13;
1 Tim 5:13
7:12
Prov 23:28

*7:14
Prov 7:11,16

7:16
Prov 31:22;
Is 19:9

7:21
Prov 5:3

7:23
Eccl 9:12

7:24
Prov 5:7

7:25
Prov 5:8

7:26
Prov 9:18

7:27
Prov 2:18;
5:5; 9:18

8:1
Prov 1:20;
9:3

8:3
Job 29:7

8:5
Prov 1:4,22;
32

7:14 *I was due to offer peace offerings.* The flesh of sacrificial peace offerings had to be eaten the day on which they were offered, or the following day. The temptress told her in- tended victim that she had just offered her sacrifices, which would mean that a plentiful supply of meat was in her house. She would prepare a sumptuous feast with it.

8:6 Prov 22:20; 23:16	6 "Listen, for I shall speak noble things; And the opening of my lips *will produce* right things.
8:7 Ps 37:30	7 "For my mouth will utter truth; And wickedness is an abomination to my lips.
	8 "All the utterances of my mouth are in righteousness; There is nothing crooked or perverted in them.
8:9 Prov 14:6; 3:13	9 "They are all straightforward to him who understands, And right to those who find knowledge.
8:10 Prov 3:14,15	10 "Take my instruction, and not silver, And knowledge rather than choicest gold.
8:11 Job 28:18; Prov 3:15	11 "For wisdom is better than jewels; And all desirable things can not compare with her.
8:12 v. 5; Prov 1:4	**12** "I, wisdom, dwell with prudence, And I find knowledge *and* discretion.

8:13
Prov 16:6;
16:18; 15:9;
6:12
	13 "The fear of the LORD is to hate evil;
	     Pride and arrogance and the evil way,
	     And the perverted mouth, I hate.

8:14 Prov 1:25; 2:7; Eccl 7:19	14 "Counsel is mine and sound wisdom; I am understanding, power is mine.
8:15 Dan 2:21; Rom 13:1	15 "By me kings reign, And rulers decree justice.
	16 "By me princes rule, and nobles, All who judge rightly.
8:17 1 Sam 2:30; Ps 91:14; John 14:21; James 1:5	17 "I love those who love me; And those who diligently seek me will find me.
8:18 Prov 3:16; Matt 6:33	18 "Riches and honor are with me, Enduring wealth and righteousness.
8:19 Prov 3:14; 10:20	19 "My fruit is better than gold, even pure gold, And my yield than choicest silver.
	20 "I walk in the way of righteousness, In the midst of the paths of justice,
8:21 Prov 24:4	21 To endow those who love me with wealth, That I may fill their treasuries.

2. *The eternity of wisdom*

*8:22 Prov 3:19	**22** "The LORD possessed me at the beginning of His way, Before His works of old.
8:23 John 17:5	23 "From everlasting I was established, From the beginning, from the earliest times of the earth.
	24 "When there were no depths I was brought forth, When there were no springs abounding with water.
8:25 Ps 90:2	25 "Before the mountains were settled, Before the hills I was brought forth;
	26 While He had not yet made the earth and the fields, Nor the first dust of the world.
8:27 Prov 3:19; Job 26:10	27 "When He established the heavens, I was there, When He inscribed a circle on the face of the deep,
	28 When He made firm the skies above, When the springs of the deep became fixed,

8:29
Job 38:10;
Ps 104:9;
Job 38:6
	29 When He set for the sea its boundary,
	     So that the water should not transgress His command,
	     When He marked out the foundations of the earth;

8:30
John 1:1-3
	30 Then I was beside Him, *as* a master workman;
	     And I was daily *His* delight,
	     Rejoicing always before Him,

8:31 Ps 16:3	31 Rejoicing in the world, His earth, And *having* my delight in the sons of men.

8:22 Wisdom is personified in the passage from v. 22 to the end of the chapter. Wisdom is depicted as having been with God from the time of creation, thus having a claim on all men who would know life in its fullness (8:35,36). The New Testament writers looked on Christ as the Incarnate Wisdom (cf. John 8:51 with Prov. 8:35,36; Rom. 1:24–30).

3. *The invitation to wisdom*

32 "Now therefore, *O* sons, listen to me,
For blessed are they who keep my ways.

33 "Heed instruction and be wise,
And do not neglect *it.*

34 "Blessed is the man who listens to me,
Watching daily at my gates,
Waiting at my doorposts.

35 "For he who finds me finds life,
And obtains favor from the LORD.

36 "But he who sins against me injures himself;
All those who hate me love death."

T. *Wisdom and folly contrasted*

1. *The invitation of wisdom*

9 Wisdom has built her house,
She has hewn out her seven pillars;

2 She has prepared her food, she has mixed her wine;
She has also set her table;

3 She has sent out her maidens, she calls
From the tops of the heights of the city:

4 "Whoever is naive, let him turn in here!"
To him who lacks understanding she says,

5 "Come, eat of my food,
And drink of the wine I have mixed.

6 "Forsake *your* folly and live,
And proceed in the way of understanding."

2. *Interlude*

7 He who corrects a scoffer gets dishonor for himself,
And he who reproves a wicked man *gets* insults for himself.

8 Do not reprove a scoffer, lest he hate you,
Reprove a wise man, and he will love you.

9 Give *instruction* to a wise man, and he will be still wiser,
Teach a righteous man, and he will increase *his* learning.

10 The fear of the LORD is the beginning of wisdom,
And the knowledge of the Holy One is understanding.

11 For by me your days will be multiplied,
And years of life will be added to you.

12 If you are wise, you are wise for yourself,
And if you scoff, you alone will bear it.

3. *The invitation of the foolish woman*

13 The woman of folly is boisterous,
She is naive, and knows nothing.

14 And she sits at the doorway of her house,
On a seat by the high places of the city,

15 Calling to those who pass by,
Who are making their paths straight:

16 "Whoever is naive, let him turn in here,"
And to him who lacks understanding she says,

17 "Stolen water is sweet;
And bread *eaten* in secret is pleasant."

18 But he does not know that the dead are there,
That her guests are in the depths of Sheol.

8:32
Prov 5:7;
Ps 119:1,2;
Luke 11:28
8:33
Prov 4:1
8:34
Prov 3:13,18

8:35
Prov 4:22;
12:2
8:36
Prov 20:2

9:1
Matt 16:18;
Eph 2:20,22;
1 Pet 2:5
9:2
Matt 22:4;
Luke 14:16,
17
9:3
Ps 68:11;
Matt 22:3;
Prov 8:1,2
9:4
Prov 8:5;
6:32
9:5
Song 5:1;
Is 55:1;
John 6:27
9:6
Ezek 11:20;
37:24

9:7
Prov 23:9

9:8
Matt 7:6;
Ps 141:5
9:9
Prov 1:5
9:10
Job 28:28;
Prov 1:7
9:11
Prov 3:16;
10:27
9:12
Prov 19:29

*9:13
Prov 7:11;
5:6
9:14
v. 3

9:16
v. 4

9:17
Prov 20:17

9:18
Prov 7:27

9:13 Verses 13–18 describe the feast of folly, in which the guests wrong themselves, wrong God, and wrong their fellowmen by sitting down at the wicked table of the woman of folly.

II. *Proverbs of Solomon (10:1–22:16)*

A. *The upright and the wicked*

10 The proverbs of Solomon.

A wise son makes a father glad,
But a foolish son is a grief to his mother.

2 Ill-gotten gains do not profit,
But righteousness delivers from death.

3 The Lord will not allow the righteous to hunger,
But He will thrust *aside* the craving of the wicked.

4 Poor is he who works with a negligent hand,
But the hand of the diligent makes rich.

5 He who gathers in summer is a son who acts wisely,
But he who sleeps in harvest is a son who acts shamefully.

6 Blessings are on the head of the righteous,
But the mouth of the wicked conceals violence.

7 The memory of the righteous is blessed,
But the name of the wicked will rot.

8 The wise of heart will receive commands,
But a babbling fool will be thrown down.

9 He who walks in integrity walks securely,
But he who perverts his ways will be found out.

10 He who winks the eye causes trouble,
And a babbling fool will be thrown down.

11 The mouth of the righteous is a fountain of life,
But the mouth of the wicked conceals violence.

12 Hatred stirs up strife,
But love covers all transgressions.

13 On the lips of the discerning, wisdom is found,
But a rod is for the back of him who lacks understanding.

14 Wise men store up knowledge,
But with the mouth of the foolish, ruin is at hand.

15 The rich man's wealth is his fortress,
The ruin of the poor is their poverty.

16 The wages of the righteous is life,
The income of the wicked, punishment.

17 He is *on* the path of life who heeds instruction,
But he who forsakes reproof goes astray.

18 He who conceals hatred *has* lying lips,
And he who spreads slander is a fool.

19 When there are many words, transgression is unavoidable,
But he who restrains his lips is wise.

20 The tongue of the righteous is *as* choice silver,
The heart of the wicked is *worth* little.

21 The lips of the righteous feed many,
But fools die for lack of understanding.

22 It is the blessing of the Lord that makes rich,
And He adds no sorrow to it.

B. *Fear of the Lord prolongs life*

23 Doing wickedness is like sport to a fool;
And *so is* wisdom to a man of understanding.

24 What the wicked fears will come upon him,
And the desire of the righteous will be granted.

25 When the whirlwind passes, the wicked is no more,
But the righteous *has* an everlasting foundation.

26 Like vinegar to the teeth and smoke to the eyes,
So is the lazy one to those who send him.

27 The fear of the Lord prolongs life,
But the years of the wicked will be shortened.

28 The hope of the righteous is gladness,
But the expectation of the wicked perishes.

ay of the LORD is a stronghold to the upright,
   in to the workers of iniquity.
ighteous will never be shaken,
   he wicked will not dwell in the land.
mouth of the righteous flows with wisdom,
   he perverted tongue will be cut out.
lips of the righteous bring forth what is acceptable,
   the mouth of the wicked, what is perverted.

C. *The godless and the upright*

alse balance is an abomination to the LORD,
   a just weight is His delight.
nen pride comes, then comes dishonor,
But with the humble is wisdom.
The integrity of the upright will guide them,
But the falseness of the treacherous will destroy them.

4 Riches do not profit in the day of wrath,
   But righteousness delivers from death.
5 The righteousness of the blameless will smooth his way,
   But the wicked will fall by his own wickedness.
6 The righteousness of the upright will deliver them,
   But the treacherous will be caught by *their own* greed.
7 When a wicked man dies, *his* expectation will perish,
   And the hope of strong men perishes.
8 The righteous is delivered from trouble,
   But the wicked takes his place.
9 With *his* mouth the godless man destroys his neighbor,
   But through knowledge the righteous will be delivered.
10 When it goes well with the righteous, the city rejoices,
   And when the wicked perish, there is glad shouting.
11 By the blessing of the upright a city is exalted,
   But by the mouth of the wicked it is torn down.

D. *The trustworthy and the talebearer*

12 He who despises his neighbor lacks sense,
   But a man of understanding keeps silent.
13 He who goes about as a talebearer reveals secrets,
   But he who is trustworthy conceals a matter.
14 Where there is no guidance, the people fall,
   But in abundance of counselors there is victory.
15 He who is surety for a stranger will surely suffer for it,
   But he who hates going surety is safe.
16 A gracious woman attains honor,
   And violent men attain riches.
17 The merciful man does himself good,
   But the cruel man does himself harm.
18 The wicked earns deceptive wages,
   But he who sows righteousness *gets* a true reward.
19 He who is steadfast in righteousness *will attain* to life,
   And he who pursues evil *will bring about* his own death.
20 The perverse in heart are an abomination to the LORD,
   But the blameless in *their* walk are His delight.
21 Assuredly, the evil man will not go unpunished,
   But the descendants of the righteous will be delivered.
22 *As* a ring of gold in a swine's snout,
   So is a beautiful woman who lacks [1]discretion.
23 The desire of the righteous is only good,
   But the expectation of the wicked is wrath.

E. *The man who gives freely*

24 There is one who scatters, yet increases all the more,

[1]Lit., *taste*

10:29
Ps 28:8;
Prov 21:15
10:30
Ps 37:29
10:31
Ps 37:30;
Prov 17:20

11:1
Lev 19:35;
Deut 25:13-16
11:2
Prov 16:18
11:3
Prov 13:6

11:4
Ezek 7:19;
Zeph 1:18;
Gen 7:1

11:6
Eccl 10:8

11:7
Prov 10:28

11:8
Prov 21:18

11:10
Prov 28:12

11:11
Prov 29:8

11:12
Prov 14:21;
10:19
11:13
Lev 19:16;
Prov 20:19;
1 Tim 5:13;
Prov 19:11
11:14
Prov 15:22;
20:18; 24:6
11:16
Prov 31:30

11:17
Matt 5:7;
25:34-36
11:18
Hos 10:12;
Gal 6:8,9

11:20
Prov 12:22;
Ps 119:1
11:21
Prov 16:5;
Ps 112:2

11:23
Rom 2:8,9

11:24
Prov 13:7;
19:17

And there is one who withholds what is justly due, but *it rests* in want.

11:25
2 Cor 9:6-10;
Matt 5:7

25 The generous man will be prosperous,
And he who waters will himself be watered.

11:26
Amos 8:5,6;
Job 29:13

26 He who withholds grain, the people will curse him,
But blessing will be on the head of him who sells *it*.

11:27
Esth 7:10;
Ps 7:15; 10:2

27 He who diligently seeks good seeks favor,
But he who searches after evil, it will come to him.

11:28
Ps 52:7;
Mark 10:24;
1 Tim 6:17;
Ps 1:3;
Jer 17:8

28 He who trusts in his riches will fall,
But the righteous will flourish like the *green* leaf.

29 He who troubles his own house will inherit wind,
And the foolish will be servant to the wisehearted.

11:30
1 Cor 9:19;
James 5:20

30 The fruit of the righteous is a tree of life,
And he who is wise wins souls.

11:31
Prov 13:21;
2 Sam 22:21,
25

31 If the righteous will be rewarded in the earth,
How much more the wicked and the sinner!

F. *The discipline of knowledge*

12:1
Prov 9:8;
15:10

12 Whoever loves discipline loves knowledge,
But he who hates reproof is stupid.

12:2
Prov 8:35

2 A good man will obtain favor from the LORD,
But He will condemn a man who devises evil.

12:3
Prov 10:25

3 A man will not be established by wickedness,
But the root of the righteous will not be moved.

12:4
Prov 31:23;
1 Cor 11:7;
Prov 14:30

4 An excellent wife is the crown of her husband,
But she who shames *him* is as rottenness in his bones.

5 The thoughts of the righteous are just,
But the counsels of the wicked are deceitful.

12:6
Prov 1:11;
14:3

6 The words of the wicked lie in wait for blood,
But the mouth of the upright will deliver them.

12:7
Ps 37:36;
Matt 7:24

7 The wicked are overthrown and are no more,
But the house of the righteous will stand.

8 A man will be praised according to his insight,
But one of perverse mind will be despised.

G. *Care for life and land*

9 Better is he who is lightly esteemed and has a servant,
Than he who honors himself and lacks bread.

12:10
Deut 25:4

10 A righteous man has regard for the life of his beast,
But the compassion of the wicked is cruel.

12:11
Prov 28:19;
Judg 9:4

11 He who tills his land will have plenty of bread,
But he who pursues vain *things* lacks sense.

12 The wicked desires the booty of evil men,
But the root of the righteous yields *fruit*.

12:13
Prov 18:7;
2 Pet 2:9

13 An evil man is ensnared by the transgression of his lips,
But the righteous will escape from trouble.

12:14
Prov 13:2;
Job 34:11;
Is 3:10,11

14 A man will be satisfied with good by the fruit of his words,
And the deeds of a man's hands will return to him.

H. *The wise and the foolish*

12:15
Prov 14:12;
Luke 18:11

15 The way of a fool is right in his own eyes,
But a wise man is he who listens to counsel.

12:16
Prov 29:11

16 A fool's vexation is known at once,
But a prudent man conceals dishonor.

12:17
Prov 14:5

17 He who speaks truth tells what is right,
But a false witness, deceit.

12:18
Ps 57:4

18 There is one who speaks rashly like the thrusts of a sword,
But the tongue of the wise brings healing.

12:19
Ps 52:5

19 Truthful lips will be established forever,
But a lying tongue is only for a moment.

12:20
v. 5

20 Deceit is in the heart of those who devise evil,
But counselors of peace have joy.

21	No harm befalls the righteous,	**12:21**
	But the wicked are filled with trouble.	Ps 91:10; 1 Pet 3:13; Prov 14:14
22	Lying lips are an abomination to the LORD,	**12:22**
	But those who deal faithfully are His delight.	Prov 6:17; 11:20; Rev 22:15
23	A prudent man conceals knowledge,	**12:23**
	But the heart of fools proclaims folly.	Prov 13:16; 15:2
24	The hand of the diligent will rule,	
	But the slack *hand* will be put to forced labor.	
25	Anxiety in the heart of a man weighs it down,	**12:25**
	But a good word makes it glad.	Prov 15:13; Is 50:4
26	The righteous is a guide to his neighbor,	
	But the way of the wicked leads them astray.	
27	A slothful man does not roast his prey,	
	But the precious possession of a man *is* diligence.	
28	In the way of righteousness is life,	**12:28**
	And in *its* pathway there is no death.	Prov 11:19

I. *The source of great wealth*

13	A wise son *accepts his* father's discipline,	**13:1**
	But a scoffer does not listen to rebuke.	Prov 10:1; 15:12
2	From the fruit of a man's mouth he enjoys good,	**13:2**
	But the desire of the treacherous is violence.	Prov 12:14
3	The one who guards his mouth preserves his life;	**13:3**
	The one who opens wide his lips comes to ruin.	Ps 39:1; James 3:2
4	The soul of the sluggard craves and *gets* nothing,	**13:4**
	But the soul of the diligent is made fat.	Prov 10:4
5	A righteous man hates falsehood,	
	But a wicked man acts disgustingly and shamefully.	
6	Righteousness guards the one whose way is blameless,	**13:6**
	But wickedness subverts the sinner.	Prov 11:3,5
7	There is one who pretends to be rich, but has nothing;	**13:7**
	Another pretends to be poor, but has great wealth.	Prov 11:24; Luke 12:20, 21,33; 2 Cor 6:10
8	The ransom of a man's life is his riches,	
	But the poor hears no rebuke.	
9	The light of the righteous ²rejoices,	**13:9**
	But the lamp of the wicked goes out.	Job 18:5; Prov 24:20
10	Through presumption comes nothing but strife,	**13:10**
	But with those who receive counsel is wisdom.	Prov 11:14
11	Wealth *obtained* by fraud dwindles,	**13:11**
	But the one who gathers by labor increases *it*.	Prov 10:2; 14:23

J. *The source of hope*

12	Hope deferred makes the heart sick,	*****13:12**
	But desire fulfilled is a tree of life.	v. 19
13	The one who despises the word will be in debt to it,	**13:13**
	But the one who fears the commandment will be rewarded.	2 Chr 36:16
14	The teaching of the wise is a fountain of life,	**13:14**
	To turn aside from the snares of death.	Prov 10:11; Ps 18:5
15	Good understanding produces favor,	**13:15**
	But the way of the treacherous is hard.	Prov 3:4; 21:8
16	Every prudent man acts with knowledge,	**13:16**
	But a fool displays folly.	Prov 12:23; 15:2
17	A wicked messenger falls into adversity,	**13:17**
	But a faithful envoy *brings* healing.	Prov 25:13
18	Poverty and shame *will come* to him who neglects discipline,	**13:18**
	But he who regards reproof will be honored.	Prov 15:5,31, 32
19	Desire realized is sweet to the soul,	
	But it is an abomination to fools to depart from evil.	
20	He who walks with wise men will be wise,	**13:20**
		Prov 15:31; 28:19

²I.e., shines brightly

13:12 Hope includes a desire for the thing wanted and also an expectation that it will come. If the desire is present but not the expectation, it is not true hope.

But the companion of fools will suffer harm.

13:21
Ps 32:10

21 Adversity pursues sinners,
But the righteous will be rewarded with prosperity.

13:22
Job 27:16,17;
Prov 28:8;
Eccl 2:26

22 A good man leaves an inheritance to his children's children,
And the wealth of the sinner is stored up for the righteous.

13:23
Prov 12:11

23 Abundant food *is* in the fallow ground of the poor,
But it is swept away by injustice.

13:24
Prov 19:18;
22:15; 29:15,
17

24 He who spares his rod hates his son,
But he who loves him disciplines him diligently.

13:25
Ps 34:10;
37:3

25 The righteous has enough to satisfy his appetite,
But the stomach of the wicked is in want.

K. *The upright and the wicked*

14:1
Prov 24:3

14

The wise woman builds her house,
But the foolish tears it down with her own hands.

14:2
Prov 19:1;
Rom 2:4

2 He who walks in his uprightness fears the LORD,
But he who is crooked in his ways despises Him.

14:3
Prov 12:6

3 In the mouth of the foolish is a rod for *his* back,
But the lips of the wise will preserve them.

4 Where no oxen are, the manger is clean,
But much increase *comes* by the strength of the ox.

14:5
Ex 20:16;
Prov 6:19;
12:17

5 A faithful witness will not lie,
But a false witness speaks lies.

14:6
Prov 24:7;
8:9; 17:24

6 A scoffer seeks wisdom, and *finds* none,
But knowledge is easy to him who has understanding.

7 Leave the presence of a fool,
Or you will not discern words of knowledge.

14:8
Prov 15:21;
v. 24

8 The wisdom of the prudent is to understand his way,
But the folly of fools is deceit.

9 Fools mock at sin,
But among the upright there is good will.

10 The heart knows its own bitterness,
And a stranger does not share its joy.

14:11
Prov 3:33;
12:7; 15:25

11 The house of the wicked will be destroyed,
But the tent of the upright will flourish.

14:12
Prov 16:25;
Rom 6:21

12 There is a way *which seems* right to a man,
But its end is the way of death.

14:13
Prov 5:4;
Eccl 2:2

13 Even in laughter the heart may be in pain,
And the end of joy may be grief.

14:14
Prov 1:31;
12:14

14 The backslider in heart will have his fill of his own ways,
But a good man will *be satisfied* with his.

15 The naive believes everything,
But the prudent man considers his steps.

14:16
Prov 22:3

16 A wise man is cautious and turns away from evil,
But a fool is arrogant and careless.

14:17
v. 29

17 A quick-tempered man acts foolishly,
And a man of evil devices is hated.

14:18
Prov 18:15

18 The naive inherit folly,
But the prudent are crowned with knowledge.

14:19
Prov 11:29

19 The evil will bow down before the good,
And the wicked at the gates of the righteous.

L. *The rich and the poor*

14:20
Prov 19:7

20 The poor is hated even by his neighbor,
But those who love the rich are many.

14:21
Prov 11:12;
Ps 41:1

21 He who despises his neighbor sins,
But happy is he who is gracious to the poor.

22 Will they not go astray who devise evil?
But kindness and truth *will be to* those who devise good.

23 In all labor there is profit,
But mere talk *leads* only to poverty.

24 The crown of the wise is their riches,

But the folly of fools is foolishness.

25 A truthful witness saves lives,
But he who speaks lies is treacherous.

26 In the ³fear of the LORD there is strong confidence,
And his children will have refuge.

27 The ³fear of the LORD is a fountain of life,
That one may avoid the snares of death.

28 In a multitude of people is a king's glory,
But in the dearth of people is a prince's ruin.

29 He who is slow to anger has great understanding,
But he who is quick-tempered exalts folly.

30 A tranquil heart is life to the body,
But passion is rottenness to the bones.

31 He who oppresses the poor reproaches his Maker,
But he who is gracious to the needy honors Him.

32 The wicked is thrust down by his wrongdoing,
But the righteous has a refuge when he dies.

33 Wisdom rests in the heart of one who has understanding,
But in the bosom of fools it is made known.

34 Righteousness exalts a nation,
But sin is a disgrace to *any* people.

35 The king's favor is toward a servant who acts wisely,
But his anger is toward him who acts shamefully.

M. *The tongue of the wise*

15 A gentle answer turns away wrath,
But a harsh word stirs up anger.

2 The tongue of the wise makes knowledge acceptable,
But the mouth of fools spouts folly.

3 The eyes of the LORD are in every place,
Watching the evil and the good.

4 A soothing tongue is a tree of life,
But perversion in it crushes the spirit.

5 A fool rejects his father's discipline,
But he who regards reproof is prudent.

6 Much wealth is *in* the house of the righteous,
But trouble is in the income of the wicked.

7 The lips of the wise spread knowledge,
But the hearts of fools are not so.

8 The sacrifice of the wicked is an abomination to the LORD,
But the prayer of the upright is His delight.

9 The way of the wicked is an abomination to the LORD,
But He loves him who pursues righteousness.

10 Stern discipline is for him who forsakes the way;
He who hates reproof will die.

11 Sheol and Abaddon *lie open* before the LORD,
How much more the hearts of men!

12 A scoffer does not love one who reproves him,
He will not go to the wise.

N. *The reward of a cheerful heart*

13 A joyful heart makes a cheerful face,
But when the heart is sad, the spirit is broken.

14 The mind of the intelligent seeks knowledge,
But the mouth of fools feeds on folly.

15 All the days of the afflicted are bad,
But a cheerful heart *has* a continual feast.

³Or, *reverence*

14:25
v. 5
14:26
Prov 19:23;
Is 33:6
14:27
Prov 13:14

*14:29
Prov 16:32;
James 1:19;
Prov 29:20
14:30
Prov 12:4
14:31
Prov 17:5;
v. 21
14:32
Job 13:15;
Ps 23:4;
2 Cor 1:9;
2 Tim 4:18
14:33
Prov 2:10;
12:16
14:34
Prov 11:11
14:35
Matt 24:45

15:1
Judg 8:1-3;
1 Sam 25:10-13
15:2
Prov 12:23;
13:16
15:3
Job 34:21;
Heb 4:13

15:5
Prov 13:1,18

15:8
Is 1:11;
Jer 6:20;
Mic 6:7
15:9
Prov 21:21;
1 Tim 6:11
15:10
Prov 1:29-32;
5:12
15:11
Job 26:6;
Ps 139:8;
2 Chr 6:30
15:12
Prov 13:1;
Amos 5:10

15:13
Prov 17:22;
12:25

15:15
v. 13

14:29 Anger may be either sinful or righteous, depending on the reason for the anger. As an expression of mere human passion, it is a work of the flesh (Gal. 5:20) and is forbidden to the Christian. Illustrations of justifiable anger were fur- nished by: (1) Jesus (Mark 3:5); (2) Moses (Ex. 11:8); and (3) Nehemiah (Neh. 5:6). Sinful anger was illustrated by: (1) Cain (Gen. 4:5,6); (2) Jonah (Jon. 4:4); and (3) the priests who condemned Stephen (Acts 7:54).

15:16
Ps 37:16;
Prov 16:8;
1 Tim 6:6
15:17
Prov 17:1
15:18
Prov 26:21;
29:22; 14:29
15:19
Prov 22:5

16 Better is a little with the fear of the LORD,
    Than great treasure and turmoil with it.
17 Better is a dish of vegetables where love is,
    Than a fattened ox and hatred with it.
18 A hot-tempered man stirs up strife,
    But the slow to anger pacifies contention.
19 The way of the sluggard is as a hedge of thorns,
    But the path of the upright is a highway.

15:20
Prov 10:1;
30:17

20 A wise son makes a father glad,
    But a foolish man despises his mother.

O. *Instruction in wisdom*

15:21
Prov 10:23;
Eph 5:15
15:22
Prov 11:14;
20:18
15:23
Prov 25:11

21 Folly is joy to him who lacks sense,
    But a man of understanding walks straight.
22 Without consultation, plans are frustrated,
    But with many counselors they succeed.
23 A man has joy in an apt answer,
    And how delightful is a timely word!

15:24
Prov 4:18

24 The path of life *leads* upward for the wise,
    That he may keep away from Sheol below.

15:25
Prov 12:7;
Ps 68:5,6
15:26
Prov 6:16-19;
16:24
15:27
Prov 28:25;
1 Tim 6:10;
Is 33:15
15:28
1 Pet 3:15
15:29
Ps 34:16;
145:18

25 The LORD will tear down the house of the proud,
    But He will establish the boundary of the widow.
26 Evil plans are an abomination to the LORD,
    But pleasant words are pure.
27 He who profits illicitly troubles his own house,
    But he who hates bribes will live.
28 The heart of the righteous ponders how to answer,
    But the mouth of the wicked pours out evil things.
29 The LORD is far from the wicked,
    But He hears the prayer of the righteous.
30 Bright eyes gladden the heart;
    Good news puts fat on the bones.

15:31
v. 5

31 He whose ear listens to the life-giving reproof
    Will dwell among the wise.

15:32
Prov 1:7;
8:36; 15:5
15:33
Prov 1:7;
18:12

32 He who neglects discipline despises himself,
    But he who listens to reproof acquires understanding.
33 The fear of the LORD is the instruction for wisdom,
    And before honor *comes* humility.

P. *The LORD weighs the way of man*

16:1
Prov 19:21

16 The plans of the heart belong to man,
    But the answer of the tongue is from the LORD.

16:2
Prov 21:2

2   All the ways of a man are clean in his own sight,
    But the LORD weighs the motives.

16:3
Ps 37:5

3   Commit your works to the LORD,
    And your plans will be established.

16:4
Is 43:7;
Job 21:30
16:5
Prov 6:17;
11:21
16:6
Dan 4:27;
Prov 14:16
16:7
2 Chr 17:10

4   The LORD has made everything for its own purpose,
    Even the wicked for the day of evil.
5   Everyone who is proud in heart is an abomination to the LORD;
    Assuredly, he will not be unpunished.
6   By lovingkindness and truth iniquity is atoned for,
    And by the fear of the LORD one keeps away from evil.
7   When a man's ways are pleasing to the LORD,
    He makes even his enemies to be at peace with him.
8   Better is a little with righteousness
    Than great income with injustice.

16:9
Ps 37:23;
Prov 20:24;
Jer 10:23

9   The mind of man plans his way,
    But the LORD directs his steps.
10 A divine decision is in the lips of the king;
    His mouth should not err in judgment.

16:11
Prov 11:1

11 A just balance and scales belong to the LORD;
    All the weights of the bag are His concern.

Q. *Wisdom the fountain of life*

12 It is an abomination for kings to commit wickedness,
For a throne is established on righteousness.

13 Righteous lips are the delight of kings,
And he who speaks right is loved.

14 The wrath of a king is *as* messengers of death,
But a wise man will appease it.

15 In the light of a king's face is life,
And his favor is like a cloud with the spring rain.

16 How much better it is to get wisdom than gold!
And to get understanding is to be chosen above silver.

17 The highway of the upright is to depart from evil;
He who watches his way preserves his life.

18 Pride *goes* before destruction,
And a haughty spirit before stumbling.

19 It is better to be of a humble spirit with the lowly,
Than to divide the spoil with the proud.

20 He who gives attention to the word shall find good,
And blessed is he who trusts in the LORD.

21 The wise in heart will be called discerning,
And sweetness of speech increases persuasiveness.

22 Understanding is a fountain of life to him who has it,
But the discipline of fools is folly.

23 The heart of the wise teaches his mouth,
And adds persuasiveness to his lips.

24 Pleasant words are a honeycomb,
Sweet to the soul and healing to the bones.

R. *The wicked ways of man*

25 There is a way *which seems* right to a man,
But its end is the way of death.

26 A worker's appetite works for him,
For his hunger urges him *on*.

27 A worthless man digs up evil,
While his words are as a scorching fire.

28 A perverse man spreads strife,
And a slanderer separates intimate friends.

29 A man of violence entices his neighbor,
And leads him in a way that is not good.

30 He who winks his eyes *does so* to devise perverse things;
He who compresses his lips brings evil to pass.

31 A gray head is a crown of glory;
It is found in the way of righteousness.

32 He who is slow to anger is better than the mighty,
And he who rules his spirit, than he who captures a city.

33 The lot is cast into the lap,
But its every decision is from the LORD.

S. *Fine speech and false speech*

17 Better is a dry morsel and quietness with it
Than a house full of feasting with strife.

2 A servant who acts wisely will rule over a son who acts shamefully,
And will share in the inheritance among brothers.

Marginal references

16:12 Prov 25:5
16:13 Prov 14:35
16:14 Prov 19:12
16:15 Job 29:23
16:16 Prov 8:10,19
16:18 Prov 11:2
16:20 Ps 2:12; 34:8; Jer 17:7
16:22 Prov 13:14; 7:22
16:23 Prov 37:30
16:25 Prov 14:12
16:27 Prov 6:12,14, 18; James 3:6
16:28 Prov 15:18; 17:9
16:29 Prov 1:10
16:31 Prov 20:29
16:32 Prov 19:11
17:1 Prov 15:17
17:2 Prov 10:5

16:33 God's providence is that foresight and arrangement in advance of actual happenings by which God accomplishes the ends He has purposed beforehand. The preservation of God's creation continues through His providence. Thus it may be said that nature serves the purposes of God, and man is likewise subject to His providence. For example: (1) the days of our years are numbered by His providence (Gen. 6:3); (2) God saves or destroys life at His pleasure (Gen. 7:23; 8:1,21; 19:29; Ps. 18:17); (3) nothing can befall man without God's knowledge (Matt. 10:29,30); and (4) the flowers of the field and birds of the air are subject to His providence (Matt. 6:25–33). At the same time, man's freedom and responsibility are taught (Is. 1:16; Jer. 21:8). The existence of problems connected with this doctrine in no way destroys its truth; and the solutions are often given by God in Scripture. Thus the answer to the question, "Does not the suffering of the righteous contradict that moral order that requires the wicked to be punished and the righteous rewarded?" is given in Job by the conclusion that the suffering of the righteous is a needful discipline that purifies the life and demonstrates the true believer's love for God.

17:3
Prov 27:21;
Ps 26:2
3   The refining pot is for silver and the furnace for gold,
    But the LORD tests hearts.

4   An evildoer listens to wicked lips,
    A liar pays attention to a destructive tongue.

17:5
Prov 14:31;
Job 31:29
5   He who mocks the poor reproaches his Maker;
    He who rejoices at calamity will not go unpunished.

17:6
Prov 13:22
6   Grandchildren are the crown of old men,
    And the glory of sons is their fathers.

7   Excellent speech is not fitting for a fool;
    Much less are lying lips to a prince.

17:8
Prov 21:14;
Is 1:23;
Amos 5:12
8   A bribe is a charm in the sight of its owner;
    Wherever he turns, he prospers.

17:9
Prov 10:12;
James 5:20;
1 Pet 4:8;
Prov 16:28
9   He who covers a transgression seeks love,
    But he who repeats a matter separates intimate friends.

10 A rebuke goes deeper into one who has understanding
    Than a hundred blows into a fool.

11 A rebellious man seeks only evil,
    So a cruel messenger will be sent against him.

17:12
Hos 13:8
12 Let a man meet a bear robbed of her cubs,
    Rather than a fool in his folly.

T. The price of wisdom

17:13
Ps 109:4,5;
Jer 18:20
13 He who returns evil for good,
    Evil will not depart from his house.

17:14
Prov 20:3
14 The beginning of strife is *like* letting out water,
    So abandon the quarrel before it breaks out.

17:15
Ex 23:7;
Is 5:23
15 He who justifies the wicked, and he who condemns the righteous,
    Both of them alike are an abomination to the LORD.

16 Why is there a price in the hand of a fool to buy wisdom,
    When he has no sense?

17:17
Ruth 1:16;
Prov 18:24
17 A friend loves at all times,
    And a brother is born for adversity.

17:18
Prov 6:1
18 A man lacking in sense pledges,
    And becomes surety in the presence of his neighbor.

17:19
Prov 29:22;
16:18
19 He who loves transgression loves strife;
    He who raises his door seeks destruction.

17:20
James 3:8
20 He who has a crooked mind finds no good,
    And he who is perverted in his language falls into evil.

17:21
Prov 10:1;
19:13
21 He who begets a fool *does so* to his sorrow,
    And the father of a fool has no joy.

17:22
Prov 15:13;
Ps 22:15
22 A joyful heart is good medicine,
    But a broken spirit dries up the bones.

17:23
Ex 23:8
23 A wicked man receives a bribe from the bosom
    To pervert the ways of justice.

17:24
Eccl 2:14
24 Wisdom is in the presence of the one who has understanding,
    But the eyes of a fool are on the ends of the earth.

17:25
Prov 10:1
25 A foolish son is a grief to his father,
    And bitterness to her who bore him.

17:26
Prov 18:5
26 It is also not good to fine the righteous,
    Nor to strike the noble for *their* uprightness.

17:27
James 1:19
27 He who restrains his words has knowledge,
    And he who has a cool spirit is a man of understanding.

17:28
Job 13:5
28 Even a fool, when he keeps silent, is considered wise;
    When he closes his lips, he is *counted* prudent.

U. Words of the wise and the foolish

18

He who separates himself seeks *his own* desire,
He quarrels against all sound wisdom.

18:2
Prov 12:23
2   A fool does not delight in understanding,
    But only in revealing his own mind.

3   When a wicked man comes, contempt also comes,
    And with dishonor *comes* reproach.

4	The words of a man's mouth are deep waters; The fountain of wisdom is a bubbling brook.	**18:4** Prov 20:5; 10:11
5	To show partiality to the wicked is not good, *Nor* to thrust aside the righteous in judgment.	**18:5** Lev 19:15; Deut 1:17; Prov 24:23
6	A fool's lips bring strife, And his mouth calls for blows.	
7	A fool's mouth is his ruin, And his lips are the snare of his soul.	**18:7** Prov 10:14; Eccl 10:12
8	The words of a whisperer are like dainty morsels, And they go down into the innermost parts of the body.	**18:8** Prov 26:22
9	He also who is slack in his work Is brother to him who destroys.	**18:9** Prov 28:24
10	The name of the LORD is a strong tower; The righteous runs into it and is safe.	**18:10** 2 Sam 22:3; Ps 18:2
11	A rich man's wealth is his strong city, And like a high wall in his own imagination.	**18:11** Prov 10:15
12	Before destruction the heart of man is haughty, But humility *goes* before honor.	**18:12** Prov 11:2
13	He who gives an answer before he hears, It is folly and shame to him.	**18:13** John 7:51
14	The spirit of a man can endure his sickness, But a broken spirit who can bear?	
15	The mind of the prudent acquires knowledge, And the ear of the wise seeks knowledge.	
16	A man's gift makes room for him, And brings him before great men.	**18:16** Gen 32:20; 1 Sam 25:27
17	The first to plead his case *seems* just, *Until* another comes and examines him.	
18	The lot puts an end to contentions, And decides between the mighty.	**18:18** Prov 16:33
19	A brother offended *is harder to be won* than a strong city, And contentions are like the bars of a castle.	
20	With the fruit of a man's mouth his stomach will be satisfied; He will be satisfied *with* the product of his lips.	**18:20** Prov 12:14
21	Death and life are in the power of the tongue, And those who love it will eat its fruit.	**18:21** Matt 12:37
22	He who finds a wife finds a good thing, And obtains favor from the LORD.	**18:22** Prov 19:14; 8:35
23	The poor man utters supplications, But the rich man answers roughly.	*18:23** James 2:3
24	A man of *many* friends *comes* to ruin, But there is a friend who sticks closer than a brother.	**18:24** Prov 17:17

V. *Contrasts of wealth and poverty*

19	Better is a poor man who walks in his integrity Than he who is perverse in speech and is a fool.	**19:1** Prov 28:6
2	Also it is not good for a person to be without knowledge, And he who makes haste with his feet errs.	
3	The foolishness of man subverts his way, And his heart rages against the LORD.	**19:3** Prov 11:3; Ps 37:7
4	Wealth adds many friends, But a poor man is separated from his friend.	**19:4** Prov 14:20
5	A false witness will not go unpunished, And he who tells lies will not escape.	**19:5** Ex 23:1; Prov 6:19
6	Many will entreat the favor of a generous man, And every man is a friend to him who gives gifts.	**19:6** Prov 29:26; 17:8
7	All the brothers of a poor man hate him; How much more do his friends go far from him! He pursues *them with* words, *but* they are gone.	**19:7** v. 4; Ps 38:11
8	He who gets wisdom loves his own soul;	**19:8** Prov 16:20

18:19 *contentions are like the bars of a castle*. It is as difficult to settle the problems of brethren who quarrel, as to storm a castle.

18:23 This stresses man's fallen condition.

		He who keeps understanding will find good.
19:9 v. 5	9	A false witness will not go unpunished, And he who tells lies will perish.
19:10 Eccl 10:6,7	10	Luxury is not fitting for a fool; Much less for a slave to rule over princes.
19:11 James 1:19; Prov 16:32	11	A man's discretion makes him slow to anger, And it is his glory to overlook a transgression.
19:12 Prov 16:14; Hos 14:5	12	The king's wrath is like the roaring of a lion, But his favor is like dew on the grass.
19:13 Prov 10:1; 21:9	13	A foolish son is destruction to his father, And the contentions of a wife are a constant dripping.
19:14 2 Cor 12:14; Prov 18:22	14	House and wealth are an inheritance from fathers, But a prudent wife is from the LORD.
*__19:15__ Prov 6:9; 10:4	15	Laziness casts into a deep sleep, And an idle man will suffer hunger.
*__19:16__ Luke 10:28	16	He who keeps the commandment keeps his soul, *But* he who is careless of his ways will die.
19:17 Eccl 11:1; Matt 10:42; 2 Cor 9:6-8; Heb 6:10	17	He who is gracious to a poor man lends to the LORD, And He will repay him for his good deed.

W. *Advice and instruction*

19:18 Prov 13:24	18	Discipline your son while there is hope, And do not desire his death.
	19	*A man of* great anger shall bear the penalty, For if you rescue *him*, you will only have to do it again.
19:20 Prov 8:33	20	Listen to counsel and accept discipline, That you may be wise the rest of your days.
19:21 Prov 16:1,9; Ps 33:10,11	21	Many are the plans in a man's heart, But the counsel of the LORD, it will stand.
	22	What is desirable in a man is his ⁴kindness, And *it is* better to be a poor man than a liar.
19:23 1 Tim 4:8; Ps 25:13; Prov 12:21	23	The fear of the LORD *leads* to life, So that one may sleep satisfied, untouched by evil.
19:24 Prov 26:15	24	The sluggard buries his hand in the dish, *And* will not even bring it back to his mouth.
19:25 Prov 21:11; 9:8	25	Strike a scoffer and the naive may become shrewd, But reprove one who has understanding and he will gain knowledge.
19:26 Prov 28:24; 17:2	26	He who assaults *his* father *and* drives *his* mother away Is a shameful and disgraceful son.
	27	Cease listening, my son, to discipline, *And you will* stray from the words of knowledge.
19:28 Job 15:16	28	A rascally witness makes a mockery of justice, And the mouth of the wicked spreads iniquity.
19:29 Prov 10:13; 26:3	29	Judgments are prepared for scoffers, And blows for the back of fools.

X. *The integrity of the righteous*

20:1 Gen 9:21; Is 5:22	**20**	Wine is a mocker, strong drink a brawler, And whoever is intoxicated by it is not wise.
20:2 Prov 19:12; 8:36; 1 Kin 2:23	2	The terror of a king is like the growling of a lion; He who provokes him to anger forfeits his own life.
20:3 Prov 17:14	3	Keeping away from strife is an honor for a man, But any fool will quarrel.
20:4 Prov 10:4; 19:15,24	4	The sluggard does not plow after the autumn, So he begs during the harvest and has nothing.
20:5 Prov 18:4	5	A plan in the heart of a man is *like* deep water, But a man of understanding draws it out.
20:6 Prov 25:14; Matt 6:2; Luke 18:11; Ps 12:1; Luke 18:8	6	Many a man proclaims his own loyalty, But who can find a trustworthy man?

⁴Or, *loyalty*

19:15 This has the same meaning as v. 24.   **19:16** *his ways,* i.e., the divine commandments.

7   A righteous man who walks in his integrity—
    How blessed are his sons after him.

8   A king who sits on the throne of justice
    Disperses all evil with his eyes.

9   Who can say, "I have cleansed my heart,
    I am pure from my sin"?

10 Differing weights and differing measures,
    Both of them are abominable to the LORD.

11 It is by his deeds that a lad distinguishes himself
    If his conduct is pure and right.

12 The hearing ear and the seeing eye,
    The LORD has made both of them.

13 Do not love sleep, lest you become poor;
    Open your eyes, *and* you will be satisfied with food.

14 "Bad, bad," says the buyer;
    But when he goes his way, then he boasts.

Y. *The hastily-gotten inheritance*

15 There is gold, and an abundance of jewels;
    But the lips of knowledge are a more precious thing.

16 Take his garment when he becomes surety for a stranger;
    And for foreigners, hold him in pledge.

17 Bread obtained by falsehood is sweet to a man,
    But afterward his mouth will be filled with gravel.

18 Prepare plans by consultation,
    And make war by wise guidance.

19 He who goes about as a slanderer reveals secrets,
    Therefore do not associate with a gossip.

20 He who curses his father or his mother,
    His lamp will go out in time of darkness.

21 An inheritance gained hurriedly at the beginning,
    Will not be blessed in the end.

22 Do not say, "I will repay evil";
    Wait for the LORD, and He will save you.

23 Differing weights are an abomination to the LORD,
    And a false scale is not good.

24 Man's steps are *ordained* by the LORD,
    How then can man understand his way?

25 It is a snare for a man to say rashly, "It is holy!"
    And after the vows to make inquiry.

26 A wise king winnows the wicked,
    And drives the *threshing* wheel over them.

27 The spirit of man is the lamp of the LORD,
    Searching all the innermost parts of his being.

28 Loyalty and truth preserve the king,
    And he upholds his throne by righteousness.

29 The glory of young men is their strength,
    And the honor of old men is their gray hair.

30 Stripes that wound scour away evil,
    And strokes *reach* the innermost parts.

Z. *The treasures of the wicked*

21 The king's heart is *like* channels of water in the hand of the LORD;
    He turns it wherever He wishes.

2   Every man's way is right in his own eyes,
    But the LORD weighs the hearts.

3   To do righteousness and justice
    Is desired by the LORD rather than sacrifice.

4   Haughty eyes and a proud heart,

Marginal references:

20:7 2 Cor 1:12; Ps 37:26
20:8 v. 26
20:9 1 Kin 8:46; 1 John 1:8
20:10 Deut 25:13; v. 23
20:11 Matt 7:16
20:12 Ex 4:11
20:13 Prov 6:9,10; Rom 12:11
20:16 Prov 27:13
20:17 Prov 9:17
20:18 Prov 15:22; 24:6; Luke 14:31
20:19 Prov 11:13; Rom 16:18
20:20 Matt 15:4; Job 18:5
20:21 Prov 28:20
20:22 Rom 12:17; 1 Pet 3:9; Ps 27:14
20:24 Ps 37:23; Prov 16:9; Jer 10:23
20:25 Eccl 5:4,5
20:26 v. 8
*20:27 1 Cor 2:11
20:28 Prov 29:14
20:29 Prov 16:31
21:2 Prov 16:2; 24:12; Luke 16:15
21:3 1 Sam 15:22; Prov 15:8; Is 1:11-17; Hos 6:6; Mic 6:7,8
*21:4 Prov 6:17

20:27 *The spirit of man is the lamp of the LORD.* The spirit that God has placed in man illuminates his thoughts and motives, bringing to light all that is unworthy, and making it possible for man to attain to the purposes for which he was created.

21:4 The pride of man is a great sin that is condemned in

The lamp of the wicked, is sin.
5 The plans of the diligent *lead* surely to advantage,
But everyone who is hasty *comes* surely to poverty.
6 The getting of treasures by a lying tongue
Is a fleeting vapor, the pursuit of death.
7 The violence of the wicked will drag them away,
Because they refuse to act with justice.
8 The way of a guilty man is crooked,
But as for the pure, his conduct is upright.
9 It is better to live in a corner of a roof,
Than in a house shared with a contentious woman.
10 The soul of the wicked desires evil;
His neighbor finds no favor in his eyes.
11 When the scoffer is punished, the naive becomes wise;
But when the wise is instructed, he receives knowledge.
12 The righteous one considers the house of the wicked,
Turning the wicked to ruin.

21:5 Prov 10:4; 28:22 **21:6** 2 Pet 2:3 **21:7** Prov 10:25 **21:9** Prov 25:24 **21:10** Prov 2:14; 14:21 **21:11** Prov 19:25 **21:12** Prov 14:11

AA. *The treasures of the wise*

13 He who shuts his ear to the cry of the poor
Will also cry himself and not be answered.
14 A gift in secret subdues anger,
And a bribe in the bosom, strong wrath.
15 The execution of justice is joy for the righteous,
But is terror to the workers of iniquity.
16 A man who wanders from the way of understanding
Will rest in the assembly of the dead.
17 He who loves pleasure *will become* a poor man;
He who loves wine and oil will not become rich.
18 The wicked is a ransom for the righteous,
And the treacherous is in the place of the upright.
19 It is better to live in a desert land,
Than with a contentious and vexing woman.
20 There is precious treasure and oil in the dwelling of the wise,
But a foolish man swallows it up.
21 He who pursues righteousness and loyalty
Finds life, righteousness and honor.
22 A wise man scales the city of the mighty,
And brings down the stronghold in which they trust.
23 He who guards his mouth and his tongue,
Guards his soul from troubles.
24 "Proud," "Haughty," "Scoffer," are his names,
Who acts with insolent pride.
25 The desire of the sluggard puts him to death,
For his hands refuse to work;
26 All day long he is craving,
While the righteous gives and does not hold back.
27 The sacrifice of the wicked is an abomination,
How much more when he brings it with evil intent!
28 A false witness will perish,
But the man who listens *to the truth* will speak forever.
29 A wicked man shows a bold face,
But as for the upright, he makes his way sure.
30 There is no wisdom and no understanding
And no counsel against the LORD.
31 The horse is prepared for the day of battle,
But victory belongs to the LORD.

21:13 Matt 18:30-34; 1 John 3:17; James 2:13 **21:14** Prov 18:16; 19:6 **21:16** Ps 49:14 **21:18** Prov 11:8 **21:19** v. 9 **21:20** Prov 22:4; Job 20:15,18 **21:21** Matt 5:6 **21:22** Eccl 9:15,16 **21:23** Prov 12:13; James 3:2 **21:24** Ps 1:1; Prov 1:22; Jer 48:29 **21:25** Prov 13:4; 20:4 **21:26** Ps 37:26; Matt 5:42; **21:27** Is 66:3; Jer 6:20; Amos 5:22 **21:28** Prov 19:5,9 **21:29** Eccl 8:1 **21:30** Is 8:9,10; Jer 9:23; Acts 5:39 **21:31** Is 31:1; Ps 3:8; 1 Cor 15:28

Scripture (1 Sam. 2:3; Ps. 101:5; 131:1; Prov. 6:16,17; 16:5). It is characteristic of: (1) false teachers (1 Tim. 1:3, 4); (2) the wicked (Hab. 2:4,5; Rom. 1:30); (3) Satan (1 Tim. 3:6); and (4) those who love the world (1 John 2:16). Pride leads to anger, contentiousness toward others, and deception of oneself (Prov. 21:24; 28:25; Jer. 49:16); its fruits are shame, debasement, and punishment (Prov. 11:2; 29:23; Zeph. 2:10,11). Believers should avoid it because God resists the proud (James 4:6; 1 Pet. 5:5) and bestows no blessing on them except chastisement.

BB. *The value of a good name*

22 A *good* name is to be more desired than great riches,
Favor is better than silver and gold.

2 The rich and the poor have a common bond,
The LORD is the maker of them all.

3 The prudent sees the evil and hides himself,
But the naive go on, and are punished for it.

4 The reward of humility *and* the fear of the LORD
Are riches, honor and life.

5 Thorns *and* snares are in the way of the perverse;
He who guards himself will be far from them.

6 Train up a child in the way he should go,
Even when he is old he will not depart from it.

7 The rich rules over the poor,
And the borrower *becomes* the lender's slave.

8 He who sows iniquity will reap vanity,
And the rod of his fury will perish.

9 He who is generous will be blessed,
For he gives some of his food to the poor.

10 Drive out the scoffer, and contention will go out,
Even strife and dishonor will cease.

11 He who loves purity of heart
And whose speech is gracious, the king is his friend.

12 The eyes of the LORD preserve knowledge,
But He overthrows the words of the treacherous man.

13 The sluggard says, "There is a lion outside;
I shall be slain in the streets!"

14 The mouth of an adulteress is a deep pit;
He who is cursed of the LORD will fall into it.

15 Foolishness is bound up in the heart of a child;
The rod of discipline will remove it far from him.

16 He who oppresses the poor to make much for himself
Or who gives to the rich, *will* only *come to* poverty.

III. *Sundry sayings (22:17–24:34)*

A. *Hear the words of the wise*

17 Incline your ear and hear the words of the wise,
And apply your mind to my knowledge;

18 For it will be pleasant if you keep them within you,
That they may be ready on your lips.

19 So that your trust may be in the LORD,
I have taught you today, even you.

20 Have I not written to you excellent things
Of counsels and knowledge,

21 To make you know the certainty of the words of truth
That you may correctly answer to him who sent you?

22 Do not rob the poor because he is poor,
Or crush the afflicted at the gate;

23 For the LORD will plead their case,
And take the life of those who rob them.

24 Do not associate with a man *given* to anger;
Or go with a hot-tempered man,

25 Lest you learn his ways,
And find a snare for yourself.

26 Do not be among those who give pledges,
Among those who become sureties for debts.

27 If you have nothing with which to pay,

22:1	Eccl 7:1
22:3	Prov 14:16; 27:12
22:5	Prov 15:19
22:6	Eph 6:4
22:7	Prov 18:23; James 2:6
22:8	Prov 24:16; Ps 125:3
22:9	2 Cor 9:6
22:10	Prov 18:6; 26:20
22:11	Matt 5:8; Prov 16:13
22:12	Prov 21:12
22:13	Prov 26:13
22:14	Prov 2:16; 5:3; 23:27; Eccl 7:26
*22:15	Prov 13:24; 23:14
22:17	Prov 5:1; 23:12
22:18	Prov 2:10
22:19	Prov 3:5
22:20	Prov 8:6,10
22:21	Luke 1:3,4
22:22	Zech 7:10; Mal 3:5
22:23	1 Sam 25:39; Ps 12:5; 35:10; Prov 23:11
22:26	Prov 11:15

22:15 *Foolishness,* or delinquency, comes naturally to youth. Correction and discipline are a virtual necessity if the young are to live useful lives.

Why should he take your bed from under you?

28 Do not move the ancient boundary
Which your fathers have set.

29 Do you see a man skilled in his work?
He will stand before kings;
He will not stand before obscure men.

B. *The desire for delicacies*

23

When you sit down to dine with a ruler,
Consider carefully what is before you;

2 And put a knife to your throat,
If you are a man of *great* appetite.

3 Do not desire his delicacies,
For it is deceptive food.

4 Do not weary yourself to gain wealth,
Cease from your consideration *of it*.
5 When you set your eyes on it, it is gone.
For *wealth* certainly makes itself wings,
Like an eagle that flies *toward* the heavens.

6 Do not eat the bread of a selfish man,
Or desire his delicacies;

7 For as he thinks within himself, so he is.
He says to you, "Eat and drink!"
But his heart is not with you.
8 You will vomit up the morsel you have eaten,
And waste your compliments.

9 Do not speak in the hearing of a fool,
For he will despise the wisdom of your words.

10 Do not move the ancient boundary,
Or go into the fields of the fatherless;
11 For their Redeemer is strong;
He will plead their case against you.
12 Apply your heart to discipline,
And your ears to words of knowledge.

13 Do not hold back discipline from the child,
Although you beat him with the rod, he will not die.
14 You shall beat him with the rod,
And deliver his soul from Sheol.

C. *Wise words to a son*

15 My son, if your heart is wise,
My own heart also will be glad;

16 And my inmost being will rejoice,
When your lips speak what is right.

17 Do not let your heart envy sinners,
But *live* in the fear of the LORD always.
18 Surely there is a future,
And your hope will not be cut off.

19 Listen, my son, and be wise,
And direct your heart in the way.
20 Do not be with heavy drinkers of wine,
Or with gluttonous eaters of meat;
21 For the heavy drinker and the glutton will come to poverty,
And drowsiness will clothe *a man* with rags.
22 Listen to your father who begot you,

22:28 *Boundary* refers to the marker that designated the boundaries of property. To remove the boundary was to encroach on the property of a neighbor.

23:11 *Their Redeemer* was the next of kin, who had the responsibility for repurchasing the family estate that had become alienated (Lev. 25:25).

And do not despise your mother when she is old."

23 Buy truth, and do not sell *it,*
    Get wisdom and instruction and understanding.

24 The father of the righteous will greatly rejoice,
    And he who begets a wise son will be glad in him.

25 Let your father and your mother be glad,
    And let her rejoice who gave birth to you.

26 Give me your heart, my son,
    And let your eyes delight in my ways.

27 For a harlot is a deep pit,
    And an adulterous woman is a narrow well.

28 Surely she lurks as a robber,
    And increases the faithless among men.

29 Who has woe? Who has sorrow?
    Who has contentions? Who has complaining?
    Who has wounds without cause?
    Who has redness of eyes?

30 Those who linger long over wine,
    Those who go to taste mixed wine.

31 Do not look on the wine when it is red,
    When it sparkles in the cup,
    When it goes down smoothly;

32 At the last it bites like a serpent,
    And stings like a viper.

33 Your eyes will see strange things,
    And your mind will utter perverse things.

34 And you will be like one who lies down in the middle of the sea,
    Or like one who lies down on the top of a ⁵mast.

35 "They struck me, *but* I did not become ill;
    They beat me, *but* I did not know *it.*
    When shall I awake?
    I will seek another drink."

24 Do not be envious of evil men,
    Nor desire to be with them;

2 For their minds devise violence,
    And their lips talk of trouble.

D. *Wisdom weighed*

3 By wisdom a house is built,
    And by understanding it is established;

4 And by knowledge the rooms are filled
    With all precious and pleasant riches.

5 A wise man is strong,
    And a man of knowledge increases power.

6 For by wise guidance you will wage war,
    And in abundance of counselors there is victory.

7 Wisdom is too high for a fool,
    He does not open his mouth in the gate.

8 He who plans to do evil,
    Men will call him a schemer.

9 The devising of folly is sin,
    And the scoffer is an abomination to men.

10 If you are slack in the day of distress,
    Your strength is limited.

11 Deliver those who are being taken away to death,
    And those who are staggering to slaughter, O hold *them* back.

⁵Or, *lookout*

Eph 6:1
23:23
Prov 4:5,7;
Matt 13:44
23:24
Prov 10:1;
15:20
23:26
Prov 3:1; 4:4;
Ps 1:2
23:27
Prov 22:14
23:28
Prov 7:12;
Eccl 7:26
23:29
Is 5:11,22
23:30
Eph 5:18;
Ps 75:8
23:33
Prov 2:12
23:35
Jer 5:3
24:1
Ps 37:1; 73:3;
Prov 3:31
24:2
Jer 22:17;
Job 15:35
24:3
Prov 9:1
24:5
Prov 21:22
24:6
Luke 14:31
24:7
Ps 10:5
24:8
Prov 6:14;
Rom 1:30
24:10
Jer 51:46;
Heb 12:3
24:11
Ps 82:4;
Is 58:6,7

24:12 Prov 21:2; Eccl 5:8; Ps 121:3-5; 94:9-11; Prov 12:14	12	If you say, "See, we did not know this," Does He not consider *it* who weighs the hearts? And does He not know *it* who keeps your soul? And will He not render to man according to his work?

E. *Counsel to a son*

24:13 Song 5:1	**13**	My son, eat honey, for it is good, Yes, the honey from the comb is sweet to your taste;
24:14 Prov 2:10	14	Know *that* wisdom is thus for your soul; If you find *it*, then there will be a future, And your hope will not be cut off.
24:15 Ps 10:9,10	**15**	Do not lie in wait, O wicked man, against the dwelling of the 　righteous; Do not destroy his resting place;
24:16 Ps 34:19; Mic 7:8; v. 22	16	For a righteous man falls seven times, and rises again, But the wicked stumble in *time of* calamity.
24:17 Job 31:29; Obad 12	**17**	Do not rejoice when your enemy falls, And do not let your heart be glad when he stumbles;
	18	Lest the LORD see *it* and be displeased, And He turn away His anger from him.
24:19 Ps 37:1	**19**	Do not fret because of evildoers, Or be envious of the wicked;
24:20 Prov 13:9	20	For there will be no future for the evil man; The lamp of the wicked will be put out.
24:21 Rom 13:1-7; 1 Pet 2:17	**21**	My son, fear the LORD and the king; Do not associate with those who are given to change;
	22	For their calamity will rise suddenly, And who knows the ruin *that comes* from both of them?

F. *Sayings of the wise*

24:23 Prov 1:6; 18:5; Lev 19:15; Deut 1:17	**23**	These also are sayings of the wise. To show partiality in judgment is not good.
24:24 Prov 17:15	24	He who says to the wicked, "You are righteous," Peoples will curse him, nations will abhor him;
24:25 Prov 28:23	25	But to those who rebuke the *wicked* will be delight, And a good blessing will come upon them.
	26	He kisses the lips Who gives a right answer.
	27	Prepare your work outside, And make it ready for yourself in the field; Afterwards, then, build your house.
24:28 Prov 25:18; Eph 4:25	**28**	Do not be a witness against your neighbor without cause, And do not deceive with your lips.
24:29 Prov 20:22; Matt 5:39; Rom 12:17	29	Do not say, "Thus I shall do to him as he has done to me; I will render to the man according to his work."
24:30 Prov 6:6-11	**30**	I passed by the field of the sluggard, And by the vineyard of the man lacking sense;
	31	And behold, it was completely overgrown with thistles, Its surface was covered with nettles, And its stone wall was broken down.
	32	When I saw, I reflected upon it; I looked, *and* received instruction.
24:33 Prov 6:9; 20:13	33	"A little sleep, a little slumber, A little folding of the hands to rest,"
	34	Then your poverty will come *as* a robber, And your want like an armed man.

IV. *Miscellaneous sayings of Solomon (25:1–29:27)*

A. *Counsel for the king's presence*

25 These also are proverbs of Solomon which the men of Hezekiah, king of Judah, transcribed.

2 It is the glory of God to conceal a matter,
But the glory of kings is to search out a matter.

3 *As* the heavens for height and the earth for depth,
So the heart of kings is unsearchable.

4 Take away the dross from the silver,
And there comes out a vessel for the smith;

5 Take away the wicked *from* before the king,
And his throne will be established in righteousness.

6 Do not claim honor in the presence of the king,
And do not stand in the place of great men;

7 For it is better that it be said to you, "Come up here,"
Than that you should be put lower in the presence of the prince,
Whom your eyes have seen.

8 Do not go out hastily to argue *your case;*
Otherwise, what will you do in the end,
When your neighbor puts you to shame?

9 Argue your case with your neighbor,
And do not reveal the secret of another,

10 Lest he who hears *it* reproach you,
And the evil report about you not pass away.

11 *Like* apples of gold in settings of silver
Is a word spoken in right circumstances.

12 *Like* an earring of gold and an ornament of fine gold
Is a wise reprover to a listening ear.

13 Like the cold of snow in the time of harvest
Is a faithful messenger to those who send him,
For he refreshes the soul of his masters.

14 *Like* clouds and wind without rain
Is a man who boasts of his gifts falsely.

B. *The neighbor and the enemy*

15 By forbearance a ruler may be persuaded,
And a soft tongue breaks the bone.

16 Have you found honey? Eat *only* what you need,
Lest you have it in excess and vomit it.

17 Let your foot rarely be in your neighbor's house,
Lest he become weary of you and hate you.

18 *Like* a club and a sword and a sharp arrow
Is a man who bears false witness against his neighbor.

19 *Like* a bad tooth and an unsteady foot
Is confidence in a faithless man in time of trouble.

20 *Like* one who takes off a garment on a cold day, *or like* vinegar on soda,
Is he who sings songs to a troubled heart.

21 If your enemy is hungry, give him food to eat;
And if he is thirsty, give him water to drink;

22 For you will heap burning coals on his head,
And the LORD will reward you.

23 The north wind brings forth rain,
And a backbiting tongue, an angry countenance.

24 It is better to live in a corner of the roof
Than in a house shared with a contentious woman.

25 *Like* cold water to a weary soul,
So is good news from a distant land.

26 *Like* a trampled spring and a polluted well
Is a righteous man who gives way before the wicked.

25:1
Prov 1:1

25:2
Deut 29:29;
Ezra 6:1

25:4
2 Tim 2:21

25:5
Prov 20:8;
16:12

25:7
Luke 14:7-11

25:8
Matt 5:25

25:9
Matt 18:15;
Prov 11:13

25:11
Prov 15:23

25:12
Prov 15:31;
20:12
25:13
v. 25;
Prov 13:17

25:14
Prov 20:6;
Jude 12

25:15
Gen 32:4;
1 Sam 25:24;
Prov 15:1;
16:14
25:16
v. 27

25:18
Ps 57:4;
Prov 12:18

25:21
Ex 23:4,5;
Matt 5:44;
Rom 12:20
25:22
2 Sam 16:12
25:23
Ps 101:5

25:24
Prov 21:9

25:25
v. 13;
Prov 15:30
25:26
Ezek 32:2;
34:18,19

25:27 v. 16; Prov 27:2	27	It is not good to eat much honey, Nor is it glory to search out one's own glory.
25:28 Prov 16:32	28	*Like* a city that is broken into *and* without walls Is a man who has no control over his spirit.

C. *The fool and his folly*

26:1 1 Sam 12:17	**26**	Like snow in summer and like rain in harvest, So honor is not fitting for a fool.
26:2 Num 23:8; Deut 23:5	2	Like a sparrow in *its* flitting, like a swallow in *its* flying, So a curse without cause does not alight.
26:3 Ps 32:9	3	A whip is for the horse, a bridle for the donkey, And a rod for the back of fools.
26:4 Prov 23:9; 29:9	4	Do not answer a fool according to his folly, Lest you also be like him.
26:5 Matt 16:1-4; 21:24-27	5	Answer a fool as his folly *deserves*, Lest he be wise in his own eyes.
	6	He cuts off *his own* feet, *and* drinks violence Who sends a message by the hand of a fool.
26:7 v. 9	7	*Like* the legs *which* hang down from the lame, So is a proverb in the mouth of fools.
26:8 v. 1	8	Like one who binds a stone in a sling, So is he who gives honor to a fool.
26:9 v. 7	9	*Like* a thorn *which* falls into the hand of a drunkard, So is a proverb in the mouth of fools.
	10	*Like* an archer who wounds everyone, So is he who hires a fool or who hires those who pass by.
26:11 2 Pet 2:22; Ex 8:15	11	Like a dog that returns to its vomit Is a fool who repeats his folly.
26:12 v. 5; Prov 3:7; 29:20	12	Do you see a man wise in his own eyes? There is more hope for a fool than for him.

D. *The lazy man and the lying tongue*

26:13 Prov 22:13	13	The sluggard says, "There is a lion in the road! A lion is in the open square!"
	14	*As* the door turns on its hinges, So *does* the sluggard on his bed.
26:15 Prov 19:24	15	The sluggard buries his hand in the dish; He is weary of bringing it to his mouth again.
	16	The sluggard is wiser in his own eyes Than seven men who can give a discreet answer.
26:17 Prov 3:30	17	*Like* one who takes a dog by the ears Is he who passes by *and* meddles with strife not belonging to him.
26:18 Is 50:11	18	Like a madman who throws Firebrands, arrows and death,
26:19 Prov 24:28	19	So is the man who deceives his neighbor, And says, "Was I not joking?"
26:20 Prov 16:28; 22:10	20	For lack of wood the fire goes out, And where there is no whisperer, contention quiets down.
26:21 Prov 15:18	21	*Like* charcoal to hot embers and wood to fire, So is a contentious man to kindle strife.
26:22 Prov 18:8	22	The words of a whisperer are like dainty morsels, And they go down into the innermost parts of the body.
	23	*Like* an earthen vessel overlaid with silver dross Are burning lips and a wicked heart.
26:24 Prov 10:18; 12:20	24	He who hates disguises *it* with his lips, But he lays up deceit in his heart.
26:25 Ps 28:3; Jer 9:8	25	When he speaks graciously, do not believe him, For there are seven abominations in his heart.
26:26 Matt 23:28; Luke 8:17	26	*Though his* hatred covers itself with guile, His wickedness will be revealed before the assembly.
26:27 Ps 7:15; Prov 28:10; Eccl 10:8	27	He who digs a pit will fall into it, And he who rolls a stone, it will come back on him.

28	A lying tongue hates those it crushes,	**26:28** Prov 29:5
	And a flattering mouth works ruin.	

E. *Wisdom for today and tomorrow*

27	Do not boast about tomorrow,	**27:1** Luke 12:19, 20;
	For you do not know what a day may bring forth.	James 4:14
2	Let another praise you, and not your own mouth;	**27:2** Prov 25:27;
	A stranger, and not your own lips.	2 Cor 10:12, 18
3	A stone is heavy and the sand weighty,	**27:3** Prov 12:16
	But the provocation of a fool is heavier than both of them.	
4	Wrath is fierce and anger is a flood,	
	But who can stand before jealousy?	
5	Better is open rebuke	**27:5** Prov 28:23
	Than love that is concealed.	
6	Faithful are the wounds of a friend,	
	But deceitful are the kisses of an enemy.	
7	A sated man loathes honey,	**27:7** Prov 25:16
	But to a famished man any bitter thing is sweet.	
8	Like a bird that wanders from her nest,	
	So is a man who wanders from his home.	
9	Oil and perfume make the heart glad,	
	So a man's counsel is sweet to his friend.	
10	Do not forsake your own friend or your father's friend,	**27:10** 2 Chr 10:6-8;
	And do not go to your brother's house in the day of your calamity;	Prov 17:17; 18:24
	Better is a neighbor who is near than a brother far away.	
11	Be wise, my son, and make my heart glad,	**27:11** Prov 10:1;
	That I may reply to him who reproaches me.	23:15; Ps 119:42
12	A prudent man sees evil *and* hides himself,	**27:12** Prov 22:3
	The naive proceed *and* pay the penalty.	
13	Take his garment when he becomes surety for a stranger;	**27:13** Prov 20:16
	And for an adulterous woman hold him in pledge.	
14	He who blesses his friend with a loud voice early in the morning,	
	It will be reckoned a curse to him.	
15	A constant dripping on a day of steady rain	**27:15** Prov 19:13
	And a contentious woman are alike;	
16	He who would restrain her restrains the wind,	
	And grasps oil with his right hand.	

F. *Man never satisfied*

17	Iron sharpens iron,	
	So one man sharpens another.	
18	He who tends the fig tree will eat its fruit;	**27:18** 1 Cor 9:7;
	And he who cares for his master will be honored.	Luke 12:42-44; 19:17
19	As in water face *reflects* face,	
	So the heart of man *reflects* man.	
20	Sheol and Abaddon are never satisfied,	**27:20** Hab 2:5;
	Nor are the eyes of man ever satisfied.	Eccl 1:8
21	The crucible is for silver and the furnace for gold,	**27:21** Luke 6:26
	And a man *is tested* by the praise accorded him.	
22	Though you pound a fool in a mortar with a pestle along with	**27:22** Prov 23:35;
	crushed grain,	Jer 5:3
	Yet his folly will not depart from him.	
23	Know well the condition of your flocks,	
	And pay attention to your herds;	
24	For riches are not forever,	**27:24** Prov 23:5;
	Nor does a crown *endure* to all generations.	Job 19:9
25	*When* the grass disappears, the new growth is seen,	**27:25** Ps 104:14
	And the herbs of the mountains are gathered in,	
26	The lambs *will be* for your clothing,	
	And the goats *will bring* the price of a field,	
27	And *there will be* goats' milk enough for your food,	

For the food of your household,
And sustenance for your maidens.

G. *The wicked and the righteous*

28 The wicked flee when no one is pursuing,
But the righteous are bold as a lion.

2 By the transgression of a land many are its princes,
But by a man of understanding *and* knowledge, so it endures.

3 A poor man who oppresses the lowly
Is *like* a driving rain which leaves no food.

4 Those who forsake the law praise the wicked,
But those who keep the law strive with them.

5 Evil men do not understand justice,
But those who seek the LORD understand all things.

6 Better is the poor who walks in his integrity,
Than he who is crooked though he be rich.

7 He who keeps the law is a discerning son,
But he who is a companion of gluttons humiliates his father.

8 He who increases his wealth by interest and usury,
Gathers it for him who is gracious to the poor.

9 He who turns away his ear from listening to the law,
Even his prayer is an abomination.

10 He who leads the upright astray in an evil way
Will himself fall into his own pit,
But the blameless will inherit good.

11 The rich man is wise in his own eyes,
But the poor who has understanding sees through him.

12 When the righteous triumph, there is great glory,
But when the wicked rise, men hide themselves.

13 He who conceals his transgressions will not prosper,
But he who confesses and forsakes *them* will find compassion.

14 How blessed is the man who fears always,
But he who hardens his heart will fall into calamity.

15 *Like* a roaring lion and a rushing bear
Is a wicked ruler over a poor people.

16 A leader who is a great oppressor lacks understanding,
But he who hates unjust gain will prolong *his* days.

17 A man who is laden with the guilt of human blood
Will be a fugitive until death; let no one support him.

18 He who walks blamelessly will be delivered,
But he who is crooked will fall all at once.

19 He who tills his land will have plenty of food,
But he who follows empty *pursuits* will have poverty in plenty.

20 A faithful man will abound with blessings,
But he who makes haste to be rich will not go unpunished.

21 To show partiality is not good,
Because for a piece of bread a man will transgress.

22 A man with an evil eye hastens after wealth,
And does not know that want will come upon him.

23 He who rebukes a man will afterward find *more* favor
Than he who flatters with the tongue.

24 He who robs his father or his mother,
And says, "It is not a transgression,"
Is the companion of a man who destroys.

25 An arrogant man stirs up strife,
But he who trusts in the LORD will prosper.

26 He who trusts in his own heart is a fool,
But he who walks wisely will be delivered.

27 He who gives to the poor will never want,
But he who shuts his eyes will have many curses.

28 When the wicked rise, men hide themselves;
But when they perish, the righteous increase.

H. *The reign of the righteous*

29
A man who hardens *his* neck after much reproof
Will suddenly be broken beyond remedy.

2 When the righteous increase, the people rejoice,
But when a wicked man rules, people groan.

3 A man who loves wisdom makes his father glad,
But he who keeps company with harlots wastes *his* wealth.

4 The king gives stability to the land by justice,
But a man who takes bribes overthrows it.

5 A man who flatters his neighbor
Is spreading a net for his steps.

6 By transgression an evil man is ensnared,
But the righteous sings and rejoices.

7 The righteous is concerned for the rights of the poor,
The wicked does not understand *such* concern.

8 Scorners set a city aflame,
But wise men turn away anger.

9 When a wise man has a controversy with a foolish man,
The foolish man either rages or laughs, and there is no rest.

10 Men of bloodshed hate the blameless,
But the upright are concerned for his life.

11 A fool always loses his temper,
But a wise man holds it back.

12 If a ruler pays attention to falsehood,
All his ministers *become* wicked.

13 The poor man and the oppressor have this in common:
The LORD gives light to the eyes of both.

14 If a king judges the poor with truth,
His throne will be established forever.

15 The rod and reproof give wisdom,
But a child who gets his own way brings shame to his mother.

16 When the wicked increase, transgression increases;
But the righteous will see their fall.

17 Correct your son, and he will give you comfort;
He will also delight your soul.

18 Where there is no vision, the people are unrestrained,
But happy is he who keeps the law.

19 A slave will not be instructed by words *alone;*
For though he understands, there will be no response.

20 Do you see a man who is hasty in his words?
There is more hope for a fool than for him.

21 He who pampers his slave from childhood
Will in the end find him to be a son.

22 An angry man stirs up strife,
And a hot-tempered man abounds in transgression.

23 A man's pride will bring him low,
But a humble spirit will obtain honor.

24 He who is a partner with a thief hates his own life;
He hears the oath but tells nothing.

25 The fear of man brings a snare,
But he who trusts in the LORD will be exalted.

26 Many seek the ruler's favor,
But justice for man *comes* from the LORD.

27 An unjust man is abominable to the righteous,
And he who is upright in the way is abominable to the wicked.

V. *The words of Agur (30:1–33)*

A. *Personal observations*

30
The words of Agur the son of Jakeh, the oracle.
The man declares to Ithiel, to Ithiel and Ucal:

2 Surely I am more stupid than any man,

29:1
1 Sam 2:25;
2 Chr 36:16;
Prov 6:15
29:2
Esth 8:15;
Prov 28:15
29:3
Prov 10:1;
5:9,10;
Luke 15:13
29:5
Ps 5:9
29:6
Prov 22:5;
Ex 15:1
29:7
Job 29:16;
Ps 41:1
29:8
Prov 11:11;
16:14
29:10
1 John 3:12
29:11
Prov 12:16;
19:11
29:13
Ps 13:3
29:14
Ps 72:4;
Is 11:4;
Prov 16:12;
25:5
29:15
Prov 13:24;
10:1
29:16
Ps 37:36;
58:10; 91:8;
92:11
29:17
v. 15;
Prov 10:1
29:18
1 Sam 3:1;
Amos 8:11,
12;
John 13:17
29:20
James 1:19;
Prov 26:12
29:22
Prov 15:18;
17:19
29:23
Job 22:29;
Is 66:2;
Dan 4:30;
Matt 23:12
29:24
Lev 5:1
29:25
Gen 12:12;
Ps 91:1-16
29:26
Is 49:4
*30:1
Prov 31:1
30:2
Ps 73:22

And I do not have the understanding of a man.

30:3
Prov 9:10

3   Neither have I learned wisdom,
Nor do I have the knowledge of the Holy One.

30:4
John 3:13;
Ps 104:3;
Is 40:12;
Job 38:8,9;
Is 45:18

4   Who has ascended into heaven and descended?
Who has gathered the wind in His fists?
Who has wrapped the waters in His garment?
Who has established all the ends of the earth?
What is His name or His son's name?
Surely you know!

30:5
Ps 12:6;
18:30; 84:11

5   Every word of God is tested;
He is a shield to those who take refuge in Him.

30:6
Deut 4:2;
12:32;
Rev 22:18

6   Do not add to His words
Lest He reprove you, and you be proved a liar.

7   Two things I asked of Thee,
Do not refuse me before I die:

30:8
Matt 6:11

8   Keep deception and lies far from me,
Give me neither poverty nor riches;
Feed me with the food that is my portion,

30:9
Deut 8:12;
Neh 9:25;
Job 31:24;
Hos 13:6

9   Lest I be full and deny *Thee* and say, "Who is the LORD?"
Or lest I be in want and steal,
And profane the name of my God.

B. *Numerical proverbs*

30:10
Eccl 7:21

10   Do not slander a slave to his master,
Lest he curse you and you be found guilty.

30:11
Prov 20:20

11   There is a ⁶kind of *man* who curses his father,
And does not bless his mother.

30:12
Luke 18:11

12   There is a kind who is pure in his own eyes,
Yet is not washed from his filthiness.

30:13
Ps 131:1;
Prov 6:17

13   There is a kind—oh how lofty are his eyes!
And his eyelids are raised *in arrogance*.

30:14
Job 29:17;
Ps 52:2; 14:4;
Amos 8:4

14   There is a kind of *man* whose teeth are *like* swords,
And his jaw teeth *like* knives,
To devour the afflicted from the earth,
And the needy from among men.

15   The leech has two daughters,
"Give," "Give."
There are three things that will not be satisfied,
Four that will not say, "Enough":

30:16
Prov 27:20

16   Sheol, and the barren womb,
Earth that is never satisfied with water,
And fire that never says, "Enough."

30:17
Gen 9:22;
Prov 23:22;
Deut 28:26

17   The eye that mocks a father,
And scorns a mother,
The ravens of the valley will pick it out,
And the young eagles will eat it.

18   There are three things which are too wonderful for me,
Four which I do not understand:

19   The way of an eagle in the sky,
The way of a serpent on a rock,
The way of a ship in the middle of the sea,
And the way of a man with a maid.

30:20
Prov 5:6

20   This is the way of an adulterous woman:
She eats and wipes her mouth,
And says, "I have done no wrong."

21   Under three things the earth quakes,

⁶Or, *generation;* so through v. 14

30:1 *words of Agur*. Agur and Lemuel (31:1) left writings   about them otherwise.
incorporated into the book of Proverbs. We know nothing

	And under four, it cannot bear up:	
22	Under a slave when he becomes king,	**30:22** Prov 19:10
	And a fool when he is satisfied with food,	
23	Under an unloved woman when she gets a husband,	
	And a maidservant when she supplants her mistress.	

24	Four things are small on the earth,	
	But they are exceedingly wise:	
25	The ants are not a strong folk,	**30:25** Prov 6:6-8
	But they prepare their food in the summer;	
26	The badgers are not mighty folk,	**30:26** Ps 104:18
	Yet they make their houses in the rocks;	
27	The locusts have no king,	
	Yet all of them go out in ranks;	
28	The lizard you may grasp with the hands,	
	Yet it is in kings' palaces.	

29	There are three things which are stately in *their* march,	
	Even four which are stately when they walk:	
30	The lion *which* is mighty among beasts	**30:30** Judg 14:18; Mic 5:8
	And does not retreat before any,	
31	The strutting cock, the male goat also,	
	And a king *when his* army is with him.	

32	If you have been foolish in exalting yourself	**30:32** Job 21:5; 40:4; Mic 7:16
	Or if you have plotted *evil, put your* hand on your mouth.	
33	For the churning of milk produces butter,	**30:33** Prov 10:12; 29:22
	And pressing the nose brings forth blood;	
	So the churning of anger produces strife.	

VI. *The words of Lemuel: the folly of lust and strong drink (31:1–9)*

31	The words of King Lemuel, the oracle which his mother taught him.	**31:1** Prov 30:1
2	What, O my son?	**31:2** Is 49:15
	And what, O son of my womb?	
	And what, O son of my vows?	
3	Do not give your strength to women,	**31:3** Prov 5:9; Deut 17:17; 1 Kin 11:1; Neh 13:26
	Or your ways to that which destroys kings.	
4	It is not for kings, O Lemuel,	**31:4** Eccl 10:17; Prov 20:1
	It is not for kings to drink wine,	
	Or for rulers to desire strong drink,	**31:5** Hos 4:11
5	Lest they drink and forget what is decreed,	
	And pervert the rights of all the afflicted.	
6	Give strong drink to him who is perishing,	
	And wine to him whose life is bitter.	
7	Let him drink and forget his poverty,	
	And remember his trouble no more.	
8	Open your mouth for the dumb,	**31:8** Job 29:12-17
	For the rights of all the unfortunate.	
9	Open your mouth, judge righteously,	**31:9** Lev 19:15; Deut 1:16
	And defend the rights of the afflicted and needy.	

VII. *The virtuous woman (31:10–31)*

10	An excellent wife, who can find?	**31:10** Prov 12:4; 19:14
	For her worth is far above jewels.	
11	The heart of her husband trusts in her,	
	And he will have no lack of gain.	
12	She does him good and not evil	
	All the days of her life.	
13	She looks for wool and flax,	**31:13** vv. 21-24
	And works with her hands in delight.	
14	She is like merchant ships;	
	She brings her food from afar.	

31:15
Rom 12:11;
Luke 12:42

15 She rises also while it is still night,
And gives food to her household,
And portions to her maidens.

16 She considers a field and buys it;
From her earnings she plants a vineyard.

17 She girds herself with strength,
And makes her arms strong.

18 She senses that her gain is good;
Her lamp does not go out at night.

19 She stretches out her hands to the distaff,
And her hands grasp the spindle.

31:20
Eph 4:28;
Heb 13:16
31:21
1 Sam 1:24

20 She extends her hand to the poor;
And she stretches out her hands to the needy.

21 She is not afraid of the snow for her household,
For all her household are clothed with scarlet.

22 She makes coverings for herself;
Her clothing is fine linen and purple.

31:23
Ruth 4:1,11;
Prov 12:4

23 Her husband is known in the gates,
When he sits among the elders of the land.

24 She makes linen garments and sells *them,*
And supplies belts to the tradesmen.

31:25
v. 17

25 Strength and dignity are her clothing,
And she smiles at the future.

31:26
Prov 10:31

26 She opens her mouth in wisdom,
And the teaching of kindness is on her tongue.

31:27
Prov 19:15

27 She looks well to the ways of her household,
And does not eat the bread of idleness.

28 Her children rise up and bless her;
Her husband *also,* and he praises her, *saying:*

31:29
Prov 12:4

29 "Many daughters have done nobly,
But you excel them all."

31:30
Prov 6:25;
22:4

30 Charm is deceitful and beauty is vain,
But a woman who fears the LORD, she shall be praised.

31 Give her the product of her hands,
And let her works praise her in the gates.

INTRODUCTION TO

ECCLESIASTES

OR THE PREACHER

Authorship and Background: Traditionally, Ecclesiastes has been ascribed to Solomon, and it is thought to be the expression of the thinking of his later years. Actually, only the first section of the book gives any evidence of Solomonic authorship, and even there Solomon is not specifically named. Many scholars suggest a postexilic date for the book (ca. 430-400 B.C. or later). Since Luther's time, it has been thought that Ecclesiastes was composed by a later writer who put Solomon's thoughts in the form in which we now have them. The title "Ecclesiastes" is derived from the Septuagint title signifying "The Preacher." The Hebrew name is *Qoheleth*.

Characteristics: This is one of the most difficult Old Testament books. The vocabulary contains obscure, perplexing words, and the style is disjointed. References are made to customs, incidents, circumstances, and sayings easily understood by those to whom the work was addressed but lost to the modern mind. The material is not logically connected, which suggests that it is a collection of diverse fragments brought together in one book. Despite all of this, and the fact that the book cannot be outlined adequately, a message of tremendous significance is to be found in its critique of religion that has been secularized, and of men whose thoughts have been misguided. Stressing that the search for happiness and satisfaction in earthly pursuits apart from God always ends in "vanity of vanities" (1:2; 12:8), Ecclesiastes bears witness to the climactic statement that while man cannot reconcile all of his problems in this life, he can safely trust God who knows the end from the beginning and who will ultimately justify His ways.

Contents:

I. First discourse: the vanity of human wisdom (1:1-2:26): All is vanity. This is shown in experience, as men seek wisdom, pleasure, and wealth. Neither philosophy, pleasure, nor a middle pathway between them solves the problem. In life, man's days are pain; in death, he leaves it all behind him.

II. Second discourse: the disappointing experiences of life (3:1-5:20): There is a time and a season for all things, but ultimately all must go the same way. Society has its evils of oppression and its industry governed by envy. Idleness and contentment are no solution. Success produces enemies. The desire to possess and loneliness are common ills. Ambition is to strive after wind. Worship and service are vain. Government oppresses, avarice is evil, and wealth is a gift of God to be enjoyed by those fortunate enough to experience it.

III. Third discourse: the vanity of wealth and honor (6:1-8:17): It is vain to have wealth that cannot be enjoyed; life itself is vanity. There is wisdom in death. Asceticism and excess are harmful. Moral pride is sin. Man opposes himself because of sin. He knows not the hour of his death and cannot avert it; he has power to hurt others. The ends of the righteous and the wicked are often the same, yet man cannot know the answer.

IV. Fourth discourse: leaving with God the injustices of this life (9:1-12:8): Look for death, which is inevitable. Enjoy life while you can. Time and chance happen to all men. Be wise. Cultivate wisdom and avoid folly. Revere those in authority over you. Perform charitable works. Days of darkness will be many. Rejoice in God. Man is a creature of time; remember your Creator in the days of your youth.

V. Conclusion: considering life in the light of eternity (12:9-14): The preacher has taught men well. The sum of it all is this: "Fear God and keep His commandments, because this applies to every person."

ECCLESIASTES
OR THE PREACHER

I. First discourse: the vanity of human wisdom (1:1–2:26)

A. The theme advanced: the vanity of human effort and experience

1 1 The words of the Preacher, the son of David, king in Jerusalem.
2 "¹Vanity of vanities," says the Preacher,
"¹Vanity of vanities! All is vanity."

3 What advantage does man have in all his work
Which he does under the sun?

B. The theme demonstrated

1. The meaningless cycle of life

4 A generation goes and a generation comes,
But the earth remains forever.
5 Also, the sun rises and the sun sets;
And hastening to its place it rises there *again*.
6 Blowing toward the south,
Then turning toward the north,
The wind continues swirling along;
And on its circular courses the wind returns.
7 All the rivers flow into the sea,
Yet the sea is not full.
To the place where the rivers flow,
There they flow again.
8 All things are wearisome;
Man is not able to tell *it*.
The eye is not satisfied with seeing,
Nor is the ear filled with hearing.
9 That which has been is that which will be,
And that which has been done is that which will be done.
So, there is nothing new under the sun.
10 Is there anything of which one might say,
"See this, it is new"?
Already it has existed for ages
Which were before us.
11 There is no remembrance of earlier things;
And also of the later things which will occur,
There will be for them no remembrance
Among those who will come later *still*.

2. The vanity of human wisdom

12 I, the Preacher, have been king over Israel in Jerusalem.
13 And I set my mind to seek and explore by wisdom concerning all that has

¹Or, *Futility of futilities*

*1:1
v. 12;
Eccl 7:27;
12:8-10
*1:2
Ps 39:5,6;
62:9; 144:4;
Eccl 12:8
1:3
Eccl 2:22; 3:9

1:4
Ps 104:5;
119:90
1:5
Ps 19:5,6
1:6
Eccl 11:5;
John 3:8

1:8
Prov 27:20

1:9
Eccl 2:12;
3:15

1:11
Eccl 2:16; 9:5

1:12
v. 1
1:13
v. 17;
Eccl 3:10

1:1 The author of Ecclesiastes uses the name *Qoheleth*, traditionally rendered *The Preacher*. The word means "the gatherer" and can refer to the gatherer of people, or one who gathers wise sayings and proverbs. The fact that the name of Solomon is not used has led many to suggest that the writer, while drawing on Solomon's experiences in his opening discourse, did not wish to identify himself specifi-cally with the king. The words of Solomon may be incorporated into a work written some time after Solomon's reign. **1:2** *Vanity* as used here alludes to the uselessness and emptiness of life that is not lived in fellowship with God and in accord with the divine will. The solution to this problem of life's vanity is forcibly stated by the orator in 12:13,14.

been done under heaven. *It* is a grievous task *which* God has given to the sons of men to be afflicted with.

1:14
Eccl 2:11,17

14   I have seen all the works which have been done under the sun, and behold, all is vanity and striving after wind.

1:15
Eccl 7:13

15   What is crooked cannot be straightened, and what is lacking cannot be counted.

1:16
1 Kin 3:12,
13; 4:30;
10:23;
Eccl 2:9

16   I said to myself, "Behold, I have magnified and increased wisdom more than all who were over Jerusalem before me; and my mind has observed a wealth of wisdom and knowledge."

1:17
Eccl 2:3,12;
7:23,25

17   And I set my mind to know wisdom and to know madness and folly; I realized that this also is striving after wind.

1:18
Eccl 12:12

18   Because in much wisdom there is much grief, and increasing knowledge *results in* increasing pain.

3. *The vanity of pleasure and wealth*

2:1
Luke 12:19;
Eccl 1:2

2 I said to myself, "Come now, I will test you with pleasure. So enjoy yourself." And behold, it too was futility.

2:2
Prov 14:13;
Eccl 7:6

2   I said of laughter, "It is madness," and of pleasure, "What does it accomplish?"

3   I explored with my mind *how* to stimulate my body with wine while my mind was guiding *me* wisely, and how to take hold of folly, until I could see what good there is for the sons of men to do under heaven the few years of their lives.

2:4
1 Kin 7:1-12;
Song 8:10,11

4   I enlarged my works: I built houses for myself, I planted vineyards for myself;

2:5
Song 4:16;
5:1; Neh 2:8

5   I made gardens and parks for myself, and I planted in them all kinds of fruit trees;

6   I made ponds of water for myself from which to irrigate a forest of growing trees.

7   I bought male and female slaves, and I had homeborn slaves. Also I possessed flocks and herds larger than all who preceded me in Jerusalem.

2:8
1 Kin 9:28;
10:10,14,21;
4:21; 20:14;
2 Sam 19:35

8   Also, I collected for myself silver and gold, and the treasure of kings and provinces. I provided for myself male and female singers and the pleasures of men—many concubines.

2:9
Eccl 1:16

9   Then I became great and increased more than all who preceded me in Jerusalem. My wisdom also stood by me.

2:10
Eccl 3:22;
5:18; 9:9

10   And all that my eyes desired I did not refuse them. I did not withhold my heart from any pleasure, for my heart was pleased because of all my labor and this was my reward for all my labor.

2:11
Eccl 1:3,14

11   Thus I considered all my activities which my hands had done and the labor which I had exerted, and behold all was ²vanity and striving after wind and there was no profit under the sun.

4. *Both the fool and the wise must die*

2:12
Eccl 1:17;
7:25

12   So I turned to consider wisdom, madness and folly, for what *will* the man *do* who will come after the king *except* what has already been done?

2:13
Eccl 7:11,12

13   And I saw that wisdom excels folly as light excels darkness.

2:14
Prov 17:24;
Ps 49:10;
Eccl 9:2,3,11

14   The wise man's eyes are in his head, but the fool walks in darkness. And yet I know that one fate befalls them both.

2:15
Eccl 6:8,11

15   Then I said to myself, "As is the fate of the fool, it will also befall me. Why then have I been extremely wise?" So I said to myself, "This too is vanity."

2:16
Eccl 1:11;
9:5; v. 14

16   For there is no lasting remembrance of the wise man *as* with the fool, inasmuch as *in* the coming days all will be forgotten. And how the wise man and the fool alike die!

2:17
Eccl 4:2;
vv. 22,23

17   So I hated life, for the work which had been done under the sun was grievous to me; because everything is futility and striving after wind.

5. *The futility of leaving fruit of toil to undeserving heirs*

2:18
v. 11;
Ps 39:6;
49:10

18   Thus I hated all the fruit of my labor for which I had labored under the sun, for I must leave it to the man who will come after me.

19   And who knows whether he will be a wise man or a fool? Yet he will have

---

²Or, *futility*, and so throughout this context

control over all the fruit of my labor for which I have labored by acting wisely under the sun. This too is vanity.

20   Therefore I completely despaired of all the fruit of my labor for which I had labored under the sun.

2:20
v. 11

21   When there is a man who has labored with wisdom, knowledge and skill, then he gives his legacy to one who has not labored with them. This too is vanity and a great evil.

2:21
Eccl 4:4;
v. 18

22   For what does a man get in all his labor and in his striving with which he labors under the sun?

2:22
Eccl 1:3; 3:9

23   Because all his days his task is painful and grievous; even at night his mind does not rest. This too is vanity.

2:23
Job 5:7; 14:1;
Eccl 1:18;
Ps 127:2

6. *The godly must be content with what God gives them*

24   There is nothing better for a man *than* to eat and drink and tell himself that his labor is good. This also I have seen, that it is from the hand of God.

2:24
Eccl 3:12,13,
22; 5:18; 8:15

25   For who can eat and who can have enjoyment without Him?

26   For to a person who is good in His sight He has given wisdom and knowledge and joy, while to the sinner He has given the task of gathering and collecting so that he may give to one who is good in God's sight. This too is vanity and striving after wind.

2:26
Job 32:8;
27:16,17;
Eccl 1:14

II. *Second discourse: the disappointing experiences of life*
(3:1–5:20)

A. *The prudent attitude toward life*

1. *A time for everything*

3 There is an appointed time for everything. And there is a time for every event under heaven—

3:1
v. 17;
Eccl 8:6

2   A time to give birth, and a time to die;
A time to plant, and a time to uproot what is planted.

3:2
Heb 9:27

3   A time to kill, and a time to heal;
A time to tear down, and a time to build up.

4   A time to weep, and a time to laugh;
A time to mourn, and a time to dance.

3:4
Rom 12:15;
Ps 126:2;
Ex 15:20

5   A time to throw stones, and a time to gather stones;
A time to embrace, and a time to shun embracing.

3:5
1 Cor 7:5

6   A time to search, and a time to give up as lost;
A time to keep, and a time to throw away.

7   A time to tear apart, and a time to sew together;
A time to be silent, and a time to speak.

3:7
Amos 5:13

8   A time to love, and a time to hate;
A time for war, and a time for peace.

3:8
Luke 14:26

9   What profit is there to the worker from that in which he toils?

3:9
Eccl 1:3

2. *Uselessness of human striving*

10   I have seen the task which God has given the sons of men with which to occupy themselves.

3:10
Eccl 1:13

11   He has made everything ³appropriate in its time. He has also set eternity in their heart, yet so that man will not find out the work which God has done from the beginning even to the end.

3:11
Gen 1:31;
Eccl 8:17;
Rom 11:33

12   I know that there is nothing better for them than to rejoice and to do good in one's lifetime;

13   moreover, that every man who eats and drinks sees good in all his labor—it is the gift of God.

3:13
Eccl 2:24;
5:19

14   I know that everything God does will remain forever; there is nothing to add to it and there is nothing to take from it, for God has *so* worked that men should fear Him.

3:14
James 1:17;
Eccl 5:7; 1:3;
3:9

15   That which is has been already, and that which will be has already been, for God seeks what has passed by.

3:15
Eccl 1:9; 6:10

³Lit., *beautiful*

3. Man must make the best of this present life

16   Furthermore, I have seen under the sun *that* in the place of justice there is wickedness, and in the place of righteousness there is wickedness.

17   I said to myself, "God will judge both the righteous man and the wicked man," for a time for every matter and for every deed is there.

18   I said to myself concerning the sons of men, "God has surely tested them in order for them to see that they are but beasts."

19   For the fate of the sons of men and the fate of beasts is the same. As one dies so dies the other; indeed, they all have the same breath and there is no advantage for man over beast, for all is vanity.

20   All go to the same place. All came from the dust and all return to the dust.

21   Who knows that the breath of man ascends upward and the breath of the beast descends downward to the earth?

22   And I have seen that nothing is better than that man should be happy in his activities, for that is his lot. For who will bring him to see what will occur after him?

B. The disappointments of earthly life

1. Oppression makes life a dubious blessing

4   Then I looked again at all the acts of oppression which were being done under the sun. And behold *I saw* the tears of the oppressed and *that* they had no one to comfort *them;* and on the side of their oppressors was power, but they had no one to comfort *them.*

2   So I congratulated the dead who are already dead more than the living who are still living.

3   But better *off* than both of them is the one who has never existed, who has never seen the evil activity that is done under the sun.

2. Life's trials better faced by partners than alone

4   And I have seen that every labor and every skill which is done is *the result of* rivalry between a man and his neighbor. This too is vanity and striving after wind.

5   The fool folds his hands and consumes his own flesh.

6   One hand full of rest is better than two fists full of labor and striving after wind.

7   Then I looked again at vanity under the sun.

8   There was a certain man without a dependent, having neither a son nor a brother, yet there was no end to all his labor. Indeed, his eyes were not satisfied with riches *and he never asked,* "And for whom am I laboring and depriving myself of pleasure?" This too is vanity and it is a grievous task.

9   Two are better than one because they have a good return for their labor.

10   For if either of them falls, the one will lift up his companion. But woe to the one who falls when there is not another to lift him up.

11   Furthermore, if two lie down together they keep warm, but how can one be warm *alone?*

12   And if one can overpower him who is alone, two can resist him. A cord of three *strands* is not quickly torn apart.

3. Instability of political fame

13   A poor, yet wise lad is better than an old and foolish king who no longer knows *how* to receive instruction.

14   For he has come out of prison to become king, even though he was born poor in his kingdom.

15   I have seen all the living under the sun throng to the side of the second lad who replaces him.

16   There is no end to all the people, to all who were before them, and even the ones who will come later will not be happy with him, for this too is vanity and striving after wind.

Marginal references:

3:17
Matt 16:27;
Rom 2:6-8;
2 Cor 5:10;
2 Thess 1:6,
7; v. 1

3:19
Ps 73:22;
Eccl 9:12

3:20
Gen 3:19;
Eccl 12:7

3:21
Eccl 12:7

3:22
Eccl 2:24;
5:18; 6:12;
8:7; 10:14

4:1
Eccl 3:16;
5:8; Is 5:7;
Lam 1:9

4:2
Job 3:11-26;
Eccl 2:17

4:3
Eccl 6:3

4:4
Eccl 2:21;
1:14

4:5
Prov 6:10;
Is 9:20

4:6
Prov 15:16,
17; 16:8

4:8
Prov 27:20;
1 John 2:16

4:11
1 Kin 1:1

4:13
Eccl 9:15

4:14
Gen 41:14,
41-43

4:16
Eccl 1:14

C. *The futility of the self-seeking life*

1. *Warnings against certain sins*

5 ...ur seps as you go to the house of God, and draw near to listen rather ...ffer the sacrifice of fools; for they do not know they are doing evil. ...ot be hasty in word or impulsive in thought to bring up a matter in the ...God. For God is in heaven and you are on the earth; therefore let your ...w.

...'the dream comes through much effort, and the voice of a fool through ...ds.

...en you make a vow to God, do not be late in paying it, for *He takes* no ...fools. Pay what you vow! ...is better that you should not vow than that you should vow and not pay. ...o not let your speech cause you to sin and do not say in the presence of the ...er *of God* that it was a mistake. Why should God be angry on account of ...ice and destroy the work of your hands?

For in many dreams and in many words there is emptiness. Rather, fear ...d.

2. *The end of the oppressor and the covetous*

8 If you see oppression of the poor and denial of justice and righteousness in the province, do not be shocked at the sight, for one official watches over another official, and there are higher officials over them.

9 After all, a king who cultivates the field is an advantage to the land.

10 He who loves money will not be satisfied with money, nor he who loves abundance *with its* income. This too is vanity.

11 When good things increase, those who consume them increase. So what is the advantage to their owners except to look on?

12 The sleep of the working man is pleasant, whether he eats little or much. But the full stomach of the rich man does not allow him to sleep.

13 There is a grievous evil *which* I have seen under the sun: riches being hoarded by their owner to his hurt.

14 When those riches were lost through a bad investment and he had fathered a son, then there was nothing to support him.

15 As he had come naked from his mother's womb, so will he return as he came. He will take nothing from the fruit of his labor that he can carry in his hand.

16 And this also is a grievous evil—exactly as a man is born, thus will he die. So, what is the advantage to him who toils for the wind?

17 Throughout his life *he* also eats in darkness with great vexation, sickness and anger.

3. *Making the best of what God gives*

18 Here is what I have seen to be good and fitting: to eat, to drink and enjoy oneself in all one's labor in which he toils under the sun *during* the few years of his life which God has given him; for this is his reward.

19 Furthermore, as for every man to whom God has given riches and wealth, He has also empowered him to eat from them and to receive his reward and rejoice in his labor; this is the gift of God.

20 For he will not often consider the years of his life, because God keeps him occupied with the gladness of his heart.

III. *Third discourse: the vanity of wealth and honor*
(6:1–8:17)

A. *Ambition and desire frustrated*

6 There is an evil which I have seen under the sun and it is prevalent among men—

2 a man to whom God has given riches and wealth and honor so that his soul lacks nothing of all that he desires, but God has not empowered him to eat from them, for a foreigner enjoys them. This is vanity and a severe affliction.

Cross references:

5:1 Ex 3:5; Is 1:12; 1 Sam 15:22; Prov 15:8, 21-27; Hos 6:6
5:2 Prov 20:25; 10:19;
Matt 6:7
*5:4 Deut 23:21-23; Ps 50:14; 76:11; 66:13, 14
5:5 Prov 20:25; Acts 5:4
5:7 Eccl 3:14; 12:13
5:8 Eccl 4:1; Ps 12:5; 58:11; 82:1
*5:10 Eccl 2:10,11
5:11 Eccl 2:9
5:12 Prov 3:24
5:13 Eccl 6:1,2
5:15 Job 1:21; Ps 49:17; 1 Tim 6:7
5:16 Eccl 1:3; Prov 11:29
5:17 Eccl 2:23
5:18 Eccl 2:10,24; 3:22
5:19 2 Chr 1:12; Eccl 2:24; 3:13; 6:2
6:1 Eccl 5:13
6:2 1 Kin 3:13; Ps 17:14; 73:7

5:4 See note to Num. 6:2 on vows.   **5:10** See note to 1 Tim. 6:10 on money.

6:3
2 Kin 9:35;
Is 14:19,20;
Jer 22:19;
Eccl 4:3

3 If a man fathers a hundred *children* and lives many years, however be, but his soul is not satisfied with good things, and he does not even h₁ they burial, *then* I say, "Better the miscarriage than he,

4 for it comes in futility and goes into obscurity; and its name is *cover* obscurity.

5 "It never sees the sun and it never knows *anything;* it is better off t₁

6 "Even if the *other* man lives a thousand years twice and does not enjoy things—do not all go to one place?"

6:7
Prov 16:26
6:8
Eccl 2:15

7 All a man's labor is for his mouth and yet the appetite is not satis₁

8 For what advantage does the wise man have over the fool? What *advan.* does the poor man have, knowing *how* to walk before the living?

6:9
Eccl 11:9;
1:14
6:10
Eccl 1:9;
Job 9:32;
Is 45:9;
Jer 49:19

9 What the eyes see is better than what the soul desires. This too is futility an₁ a striving after wind.

10 Whatever exists has already been named, and it is known what man is; for he₁ cannot dispute with him who is stronger than he is.

11 For there are many words which increase futility. What *then* is the advantage to a man?

6:12
James 4:14;
Ps 39:6;
Eccl 8:7

12 For who knows what is good for a man during *his* lifetime, *during* the few years of his futile life? He will spend them like a shadow. For who can tell a man what will be after him under the sun?

B. *Counsels of prudence in a sin-corrupted world*

1. *Choosing the better*

7:1
Prov 15:30;
22:1; Eccl 4:2

7 A good name is better than a good ointment,
And the day of *one's* death is better than the day of one's birth.

7:2
Eccl 2:16;
Ps 90:12

2 It is better to go to a house of mourning
Than to go to a house of feasting,
Because that is the end of every man,
And the living takes *it* to heart.

7:3
2 Cor 7:10

3 Sorrow is better than laughter,
For when a face is sad a heart may be happy.

4 The mind of the wise is in the house of mourning,
While the mind of fools is in the house of pleasure.

7:5
Ps 141:5;
Prov 13:18;
15:31,32
7:6
Ps 118:12;
Eccl 2:2

5 It is better to listen to the rebuke of a wise man
Than for one to listen to the song of fools.

6 For as the crackling of thorn bushes under a pot,
So is the laughter of the fool,
And this too is futility.

7:7
Ex 23:8;
Deut 16:19
7:8
v. 1;
Prov 14:29;
Gal 5:22;
Eph 4:2

7 For oppression makes a wise man mad,
And a bribe corrupts the heart.

8 The end of a matter is better than its beginning;
Patience of spirit is better than haughtiness of spirit.

2. *The value of wisdom over wealth*

7:9
Prov 14:17;
James 1:19

9 Do not be eager in your heart to be angry,
For anger resides in the bosom of fools.

10 Do not say, "Why is it that the former days were better than these?"
For it is not from wisdom that you ask about this.

7:11
Prov 8:10,11

11 Wisdom along with an inheritance is good
And an advantage to those who see the sun.

7:12
Eccl 9:18;
Prov 3:18;
8:35

12 For wisdom is protection *just as* money is protection.
But the advantage of knowledge is that wisdom preserves the lives of
its possessors.

7:13
Eccl 3:11;
8:17; 1:15;
Is 14:27
7:14
Eccl 3:4;
Deut 8:5

13 Consider the work of God,
For who is able to straighten what He has bent?

14 In the day of prosperity be happy,
But in the day of adversity consider—
God has made the one as well as the other
So that man may not discover anything *that will be* after him.

3. *Asceticism and excess contrasted*

15 I have seen everything during my lifetime of futility; there is a righteous

man who perishes in his righteousness, and there is a wicked man who prolongs *his life* in his wickedness.

16   Do not be excessively righteous, and do not be overly wise. Why should you ruin yourself?

17   Do not be excessively wicked, and do not be a fool. Why should you die before your time?

18   It is good that you grasp one thing, and also not let go of the other; for the one who fears God comes forth with both of them.

4. *The value of wisdom and wickedness of folly*

19   Wisdom strengthens a wise man more than ten rulers who are in a city.

20   Indeed, there is not a righteous man on earth who *continually* does good and who never sins.

21   Also, do not take seriously all words which are spoken, lest you hear your servant cursing you.

22   For you also have realized that you likewise have many times cursed others.

23   I tested all this with wisdom, *and* I said, "I will be wise," but it was far from me.

24   What has been is remote and exceedingly mysterious. Who can discover it?

25   I directed my mind to know, to investigate, and to seek wisdom and an explanation, and to know the evil of folly and the foolishness of madness.

5. *Wicked womanhood discussed*

26   And I discovered more bitter than death the woman whose heart is snares and nets, whose hands are chains. One who is pleasing to God will escape from her, but the sinner will be captured by her.

27   "Behold, I have discovered this," says the Preacher, "*adding* one thing to another to find an explanation,

28   which I am still seeking but have not found. I have found one man among a thousand, but I have not found a woman among all these.

29   "Behold, I have found only this, that God made men upright, but they have sought out many devices."

C. *Expediency in an imperfect world*

1. *The acceptance of authority*

8 Who is like the wise man and who knows the interpretation of a matter? A man's wisdom illumines him and causes his stern face to beam.

2   I say, "Keep the command of the king because of the oath before God.

3   "Do not be in a hurry to leave him. Do not join in an evil matter, for he will do whatever he pleases."

4   Since the word of the king is authoritative, who will say to him, "What are you doing?"

5   He who keeps a *royal* command experiences no trouble, for a wise heart knows the proper time and procedure.

6   For there is a proper time and procedure for every delight, when a man's trouble is heavy upon him.

7   If no one knows what will happen, who can tell him when it will happen?

8   No man has authority to restrain the wind with the wind, or authority over the day of death; and there is no discharge in the time of war, and evil will not deliver those who practice it.

9   All this I have seen and applied my mind to every deed that has been done under the sun wherein a man has exercised authority over *another* man to his hurt.

2. *The judgment of the wicked*

10   So then, I have seen the wicked buried, those who used to go in and out from the holy place, and they are *soon* forgotten in the city where they did thus. This too is futility.

11   Because the sentence against an evil deed is not executed quickly, therefore the hearts of the sons of men among them are given fully to do evil.

8:1 Compare with the words in Deut. 28:50.   8:8 Man cannot prevent the inevitable.

8:12
Is 65:20;
Ps 37:11,18,
19;
Prov 1:32,33;
Is 3:10,11
8:13
v. 8; Is 3:11;
Eccl 6:12
8:14
Ps 73:14;
Eccl 7:15;
Job 21:7;
Mal 3:15
8:15
Eccl 2:24;
3:12,13; 5:18;
9:7
8:16
Eccl 1:13,14;
2:23
8:17
Job 5:9;
Eccl 3:11;
Rom 11:33;
Eccl 8:7;
Ps 73:16
9:1
Deut 33:3;
Job 12:10;
Ps 119:109;
v. 6;
Eccl 10:14
9:2
Job 9:22;
Eccl 6:6; 7:2
9:3
v. 2;
Eccl 8:11;
1:17
*9:5
Job 14:21;
Eccl 1:11;
2:16;
Ps 88:12;
Is 26:14
9:6
Eccl 3:22
9:7
Eccl 8:15
*9:8
Rev 3:4;
Ps 23:5
9:9
Eccl 6:12;
7:15
9:10
Rom 12:11;
Col 3:23;
Is 38:10

12 Although a sinner does evil a hundred *times* and may lengthen his *life*, still I know that it will be well for those who fear God, who fear Him openly.
13 But it will not be well for the evil man and he will not lengthen his days like a shadow, because he does not fear God.

3. *Injustices in this life*

14 There is futility which is done on the earth, that is, there are righteous men to whom it happens according to the deeds of the wicked. On the other hand, there are evil men to whom it happens according to the deeds of the righteous. I say that this too is futility.
15 So I commended pleasure, for there is nothing good for a man under the sun except to eat and to drink and to be merry, and this will stand by him in his toils *throughout* the days of his life which God has given him under the sun.

4. *The ways of God are inscrutable*

16 When I gave my heart to know wisdom and to see the task which has been done on the earth (even though one should never sleep day or night),
17 and I saw every work of God, *I concluded* that man cannot discover the work which has been done under the sun. Even though man should seek laboriously, he will not discover; and though the wise man should say, "I know," he cannot discover.

IV. *Fourth discourse: leaving with God the injustices of this life (9:1–12:8)*

A. *Make the best of this life*

1. *Death inevitable for both the good and the evil*

9 For I have taken all this to my heart and explain it that righteous men, wise men, and their deeds are in the hand of God. Man does not know whether *it will be* love or hatred; anything awaits him.
2 It is the same for all. There is one fate for the righteous and for the wicked; for the good, for the clean, and for the unclean; for the man who offers a sacrifice and for the one who does not sacrifice. As the good man is, so is the sinner; as the swearer is, so is the one who is afraid to swear.
3 This is an evil in all that is done under the sun, that there is one fate for all men. Furthermore, the hearts of the sons of men are full of evil, and insanity is in their hearts throughout their lives. Afterwards they *go* to the dead.
4 For whoever is joined with all the living, there is hope; surely a live dog is better than a dead lion.
5 For the living know they will die; but the dead do not know anything, nor have they any longer a reward, for their memory is forgotten.
6 Indeed their love, their hate, and their zeal have already perished, and they will no longer have a share in all that is done under the sun.

2. *Enjoy life while you can*

7 Go *then*, eat your bread in happiness, and drink your wine with a cheerful heart; for God has already approved your works.
8 Let your clothes be white all the time, and let not oil be lacking on your head.
9 Enjoy life with the woman whom you love all the days of your fleeting life which He has given to you under the sun; for this is your reward in life, and in your toil in which you have labored under the sun.
10 Whatever your hand finds to do, verily, do *it* with all your might; for there is no activity or planning or wisdom in Sheol where you are going.

9:5 From this verse some have adduced the dogma of *soul sleep* for the dead until the resurrection. The doctrine of soul sleep is not Biblical. The problem is solved when one understands that the Bible is a book of *progressive revelation*. The Old Testament does not have the full-orbed Biblical doctrine of the intermediate state after death. The person and nature of God are not fully disclosed in the Pentateuch. The mystery of the New Testament church is by no means fully revealed in the Old Testament. Since revelation is progres-sive, it is important that the principle of interpretation known as the analogy of Scripture be employed: that the Old Testament be interpreted by the New Testament; that the clear portions of Scripture take precedence over the obscure. In brief, no single portion of the Bible should be interpreted apart from its relation to the totality of the Word of God.
9:8 *White* garments would be worn on festive occasions; *oil* on the head produced a cooling and refreshing effect.

3. *Chance operates for all*

11   I again saw under the sun that the race is not to the swift, and the battle is not to the warriors, and neither is bread to the wise, nor wealth to the discerning, nor favor to men of ability; for time and chance overtake them all.

12   Moreover, man does not know his time: like fish caught in a treacherous net, and birds trapped in a snare, so the sons of men are ensnared at an evil time when it suddenly falls on them.

4. *Wisdom is superior*

13   Also this I came to see as wisdom under the sun, and it impressed me.

14   There was a small city with few men in it and a great king came to it, surrounded it, and constructed large siegeworks against it.

15   But there was found in it a poor wise man and he delivered the city by his wisdom. Yet no one remembered that poor man.

16   So I said, "Wisdom is better than strength." But the wisdom of the poor man is despised and his words are not heeded.

17   The words of the wise heard in quietness are *better* than the shouting of a ruler among fools.

18   Wisdom is better than weapons of war, but one sinner destroys much good.

B. *Life is uncertain and folly baneful*

1. *Folly hurtful; wisdom helpful*

10 Dead flies make a perfumer's oil stink, so a little foolishness is weightier than wisdom *and* honor.

2   A wise man's heart *directs him* toward the right, but the foolish man's heart *directs him* toward the left.

3   Even when the fool walks along the road his sense is lacking, and he demonstrates to everyone *that* he is a fool.

4   If the ruler's temper rises against you, do not abandon your position, because composure allays great offenses.

5   There is an evil I have seen under the sun, like an error which goes forth from the ruler—

6   folly is set in many exalted places while rich men sit in humble places.

7   I have seen slaves *riding* on horses and princes walking like slaves on the land.

8   He who digs a pit may fall into it, and a serpent may bite him who breaks through a wall.

9   He who quarries stones may be hurt by them, and he who splits logs may be endangered by them.

10   If the axe is dull and he does not sharpen *its* edge, then he must exert more strength. Wisdom has the advantage of giving success.

11   If the serpent bites before being charmed, there is no profit for the charmer.

2. *The folly of empty talk*

12   Words from the mouth of a wise man are gracious, while the lips of a fool consume him;

13   the beginning of his talking is folly, and the end of it is wicked madness.

14   Yet the fool multiplies words. No man knows what will happen, and who can tell him what will come after him?

15   The toil of a fool *so* wearies him that he does not *even* know how to go to a city.

3. *Concluding maxims*

16   Woe to you, O land, whose king is a lad and whose princes feast in the morning.

9:11
Amos 2:14, 15;
Deut 8:17,18;
1 Sam 6:9
9:12
Eccl 8:7;
Prov 29:6;
Is 24:18;
Luke 21:34, 35

9:15
Eccl 4:13;
2:16; 8:10
9:16
Prov 21:22;
Eccl 7:19
9:17
Eccl 7:5;
10:12
9:18
v. 16;
Josh 7:1,11, 12

10:3
Prov 13:16;
18:2
10:4
Eccl 8:3;
1 Sam 25:24-33;
Prov 25:15
10:5
Eccl 5:6
10:6
Esth 3:1
10:7
Prov 19:10;
Esth 6:8
10:8
Ps 7:15;
Prov 26:27

10:11
Ps 58:4,5;
Jer 8:17

10:12
Prov 10:32;
Luke 4:22;
Prov 10:14;
18:7
10:13
Eccl 7:25
*10:14**
Prov 15:2;
Eccl 3:22;
6:12; 8:7

*10:16**
Is 3:4,5,12;
5:11

10:14 *the fool multiplies words.* But the wide use of words does not necessarily make a man a fool. The value of speech is obvious, and right speech is a powerful instrument for good even as foolish words are a powerful instrument for evil or for folly. Even the wise man must be dextrous in the use of words, for they reveal what the heart really is like.

Everywhere Scripture warns men about the use of words. **10:16** Israel experienced this in a painful way in the lives of men like Absalom and Rehoboam, who were absurd and self-willed, destitute of those virtues that make for a good ruler.

10:17
Prov 31:4;
Is 5:11
*10:18
Prov 24:30-34
10:19
Ps 104:15;
Eccl 7:12
*10:20
Ex 22:28;
Acts 23:5;
2 Kin 6:12;
Luke 12:3

17   Blessed are you, O land, whose king is of nobility and whose princes eat at the appropriate time—for strength, and not for drunkenness.

18   Through indolence the rafters sag, and through slackness the house leaks.

19   *Men* prepare a meal for enjoyment, and wine makes life merry, and money is the answer to everything.

20   Furthermore, in your bedchamber do not curse a king, and in your sleeping rooms do not curse a rich man, for a bird of the heavens will carry the sound, and the winged creature will make the matter known.

C. How to invest a life

1. *Works of charity*

11:1
Is 32:20;
Deut 15:10;
Prov 19:17;
Matt 10:42;
2 Cor 9:8;
Gal 6:9,10;
Heb 6:10
*11:2
Ps 112:9;
Luke 6:30;
1 Tim 6:18,
19; Eccl 12:1
11:5
John 3:8;
Ps 139:14,15
11:6
Eccl 9:10
11:7
Eccl 7:11
11:8
Eccl 9:7; 12:1

11 Cast your bread on the surface of the waters, for you will find it after many days.

2   Divide your portion to seven, or even to eight, for you do not know what misfortune may occur on the earth.

3   If the clouds are full, they pour out rain upon the earth; and whether a tree falls toward the south or toward the north, wherever the tree falls, there it lies.

4   He who watches the wind will not sow and he who looks at the clouds will not reap.

5   Just as you do not know the path of the wind and how bones *are formed* in the womb of the pregnant woman, so you do not know the activity of God who makes all things.

6   Sow your seed in the morning, and do not be idle in the evening, for you do not know whether morning or evening sowing will succeed, or whether both of them alike will be good.

7   The light is pleasant, and *it is* good for the eyes to see the sun.

8   Indeed, if a man should live many years, let him rejoice in them all, and let him remember the days of darkness, for they shall be many. Everything that is to come *will be* futility.

2. *A misspent youth brings retribution*

11:9
Eccl 2:10;
Num 15:39;
Eccl 3:17;
12:14;
Rom 14:10
*11:10
2 Cor 7:1;
2 Tim 2:22

9   Rejoice, young man, during your childhood, and let your heart be pleasant during the days of young manhood. And follow the impulses of your heart and the desires of your eyes. Yet know that God will bring you to judgment for all these things.

10   So, remove vexation from your heart and put away pain from your body, because childhood and the prime of life are fleeting.

3. *Injunction to live for God*

*12:1ff
Ps 63:6;
119:55;
Eccl 11:8;
2 Sam 19:35

12 Remember also your Creator in the days of your youth, before the evil days come and the years draw near when you will say, "I have no delight in them";

2   before the sun, the light, the moon, and the stars are darkened, and clouds return after the rain;

3   in the day that the watchmen of the house tremble, and mighty men stoop, the grinding ones stand idle because they are few, and those who look through windows grow dim;

12:4
Jer 25:10;
2 Sam 19:35

4   and the doors on the street are shut as the sound of the grinding mill is low, and one will arise at the sound of the bird, and all the daughters of song will sing softly.

12:5
Job 17:13;
Jer 9:17

5   Furthermore, men are afraid of a high place and of terrors on the road; the almond tree blossoms, the grasshopper drags himself along, and the caperberry is ineffective. For man goes to his eternal home while mourners go about in the street.

10:18 *Slackness* results in deterioration of soul and home.
10:20 Men may become vocal because of indignation over evil, but prudence often dictates silence. Even the words one thinks are spoken in secret may come to light most unexpectedly, as, for example, *Elisha . . . tells the king of Israel the words that you speak in your bedroom* (2 Kin. 6:12).
11:2 *seven, or even to eight.* This is a Hebrew idiom to indicate an indefinite number. The climactic use of numbers adds emphasis and was a common poetic device in the Near East.

11:10 Life has both inward and outward troubles: pain that comes to the flesh and to the mind. All must experience some of both, but one can infer that obedience to the commandments of a loving God will save man from many of these afflictions and that he will be abundantly supplied with a full measure of grace to endure those things that cannot be avoided.
12:1ff This is a superb narrative (figuratively speaking) on the advent of old age, its effect on our mind, body, and soul, and on the gradual deterioration of all.

6 *Remember Him* before the silver cord is broken and the golden bowl is crushed, the pitcher by the well is shattered and the wheel at the cistern is crushed;

7 then the dust will return to the earth as it was, and the spirit will return to God who gave it.

8 "Vanity of vanities," says the Preacher, "all is vanity!"

V. Conclusion: considering life in the light of eternity (12:9–14)

A. The Preacher's purpose

9 In addition to being a wise man, the Preacher also taught the people knowledge; and he pondered, searched out and arranged many proverbs.

10 The Preacher sought to find delightful words and to write words of truth correctly.

B. The value of the Preacher's word

11 The words of wise men are like goads, and masters of *these* collections are like well-driven nails; they are given by one Shepherd.

12 But beyond this, my son, be warned: the writing of many books is endless, and excessive devotion *to books* is wearying to the body.

C. The concluding injunction

13 The conclusion, when all has been heard, *is:* fear God and keep His commandments, because this *applies to* every person.

14 For God will bring every act to judgment, everything which is hidden, whether it is good or evil.

12:7 Man's spirit returns to God neither to sleep nor to perish, but to be judged.

12:10 Truth is often harsh, but it can be stated so as to cause the least possible offense. Regard for truth should not keep men from clothing it in garments of beauty.

12:13 Ecclesiastes has depicted the spiritual pilgrimage of a man concerned with the meaning of life. He has entertained many and frequently contradictory thoughts in his quest for the highest good. He could not solve the riddle of life by anything he discovered or observed "under the sun."

The end of his quest did not provide a philosophical answer to the questions that plagued him, but it did provide a brief summary of that which makes life, with all its bewildering facets, meaningful. It does not take worldly wisdom to *fear God*—i.e., walk in reverence before the LORD, and to *keep his commandments*—i.e., bring the totality of life into subjection to His will. This is a summary of God's demands on His people, His law that served as a tutor until Christ came (Gal. 3:24). In any age, and at any time, man may safely trust God.

Margin references:

*12:7
Gen 3:19;
Job 34:15;
Ps 90:3;
Job 34:14;
Is 57:16;
Zech 12:1
12:8
Eccl 1:2

12:9
1 Kin 4:32

*12:10
Prov 10:32;
22:20,21

12:11
Eccl 7:5;
Acts 2:37;
Ezra 9:8;
Is 22:23

*12:13
Deut 4:2;
Eccl 8:5;
Mic 6:8
12:14
Matt 10:26;
12:36;
1 Cor 4:5

INTRODUCTION TO

THE SONG OF SOLOMON

Authorship and Background: The opening verse of the book ascribes the song to Solomon, who is known to have composed songs as well as proverbs (1 Kin. 4:32). Internal evidence suggests that the book was written before the division of the kingdom. Assuming the Solomonic authorship, the book must have been written in the tenth century B.C., although some of its phraseology was changed at a later date. This would account for the Greek and Persian words in it. Many English versions prefer the title "Song of Solomon"; the Greek and Latin versions follow the Hebrew title "The Song of Songs," which signifies "The Best of Songs."

Love songs were popular in all ancient lands. The Chester Beatty Papyrus No. 1 is an entire book of love songs in seven long cantos (called "houses") that are put alternately into the mouths of two sweethearts who address each other as "brother" and "sister" (cf. 5:1,2; 8:1). Lovesickness plays a great part in both.

Characteristics: The Song of Solomon is rich in oriental imagery and filled with beautiful descriptions of local scenery. Accepted in its best sense, it is an idyll of love and courtship. Various interpretations have been given to this remarkable book. It is regarded by some as a type of allegory, while others look upon it as a drama. According to the Shepherd Hypothesis, Solomon seeks to alienate the affections of the young lady from her lover, but she resists his temptations and the king finally allows her to return home. Perhaps the view that is most acceptable is that the book presents love and marriage in the proper Biblical framework, since marriage is ordained of God for man. It avoids both the error of lust and that of asceticism. The highest, purest, and most lofty elements of this honorable relationship are expressed. The marriage tie is used to illustrate the relationship of Yahweh to Israel in the Old Testament, and of Christ to the church in the New Testament. If this book is taken as an allegory, Solomon is a type of Christ and the bride is a type of the church.

Contents:

I. The bride and bridegroom (1:1-2:7): The bride speaks of her love for her beloved. She describes his beauty as she sees it. He praises her. She delights in his fellowship.

II. The praise of her beloved (2:8-3:5): The bridegroom takes the initiative. He invites her to come with him. She acknowledges her submission to his love. Her beloved disappears; she seeks and finds him.

III. In praise of the bride (3:6-5:1): Solomon draws near; betrothal and marriage are discussed. Solomon bursts into song twice. The Shulammite appeals to him and he responds.

IV. A troubled love (5:2-7:9): Her beloved comes and departs. She searches for him and depicts what he is like. She claims him for herself. When she finds him, he praises her. She recounts for him her recent experience. He praises her as the daughter of a prince. She asks him to join her in the open fields and countryside.

V. The unbroken communion (7:10-8:14): The Shulammite declares her love and devotion to her beloved. Before leaving he asks to hear her voice. She looks for his early return.

THE SONG OF SOLOMON

I. *The bride and bridegroom (1:1–2:7)*

A. *Inscription*

1 The [1]Song of Songs, which is Solomon's.

1:1
1 Kin 4:32

B. *The bride awaits her lover*

2 "[2]May he kiss me with the kisses of his mouth!
For your love is better than wine.
3 "Your oils have a pleasing fragrance,
Your name is *like* purified oil;
Therefore the maidens love you.
4 "Draw me after you *and* let us run *together!*
The king has brought me into his chambers."

"[3]We will rejoice in you and be glad;
We will extol your love more than wine.
Rightly do they love you."

5 "[2]I am black but lovely,
O daughters of Jerusalem,
Like the tents of Kedar,
Like the curtains of Solomon.
6 "Do not stare at me because I am swarthy,
For the sun has burned me.
My mother's sons were angry with me;
They made me caretaker of the vineyards,
But I have not taken care of my own vineyard.
7 "Tell me, O you whom my soul loves,
Where do you pasture *your flock,*
Where do you make *it* lie down at noon?
For why should I be like one who veils herself
Beside the flocks of your companions?"

8 "[4]If you yourself do not know,
Most beautiful among women,
Go forth on the trail of the flock,
And pasture your young goats
By the tents of the shepherds.

C. *Bride and bridegroom meet*

9 "To me, my darling, you are like
My mare among the chariots of Pharaoh.
10 "Your cheeks are lovely with ornaments,
Your neck with strings of beads."

11 "[3]We will make for you ornaments of gold
With beads of silver."

12 "[2]While the king was at his table,
My perfume gave forth its fragrance.
13 "My beloved is to me a pouch of myrrh
Which lies all night between my breasts.
14 "My beloved is to me a cluster of henna blossoms
In the vineyards of Engedi."

1:2
Song 4:10

1:3
Song 4:10;
Eccl 7:1

1:4
Ps 45:14,15

1:5
Song 2:14;
4:3; 2:7; 5:8

1:6
Ps 69:8;
Song 8:11

1:7
Song 3:1-4;
2:16; 8:13

1:8
Song 5:9; 6:1

1:9
Song 2:2,10,
13;
2 Chr 1:16
1:10
5:13

1:14
Song 4:13

[1]Or, *Best of the Songs* [2]BRIDE [3]CHORUS [4]BRIDEGROOM

<table>
<tr><td>

1:15
Song 4:1;
5:12

</td><td>**15**</td><td>

"[5]How beautiful you are, my darling,
How beautiful you are!
Your eyes are *like* doves."

</td></tr>
<tr><td></td><td>**16**</td><td>

"[6]How handsome you are, my beloved,
And so pleasant!
Indeed, our couch is luxuriant!

</td></tr>
<tr><td>

1:17
1 Kin 6:9,10;
2 Chr 3:5

</td><td>17</td><td>

"The beams of our houses are cedars,
Our rafters, cypresses.

</td></tr>
</table>

2

<table>
<tr><td>

2:1
Is 35:1,2;
Song 5:13;
7:2

</td><td></td><td>

"[6]I am the rose of Sharon,
The lily of the valleys."

</td></tr>
<tr><td></td><td>**2**</td><td>

"[5]Like a lily among the thorns,
So is my darling among the maidens."

</td></tr>
<tr><td>

2:3
Song 8:5;
4:13

</td><td>**3**</td><td>

"[6]Like an apple tree among the trees of the forest,
So is my beloved among the young men.
In his shade I took great delight and sat down,
And his fruit was sweet to my taste.

</td></tr>
<tr><td>

2:4
Ps 20:5

</td><td>4</td><td>

"He has brought me to *his* banquet hall,
And his banner over me is love.

</td></tr>
<tr><td>

2:5
Song 7:8; 5:8

</td><td>5</td><td>

"Sustain me with raisin cakes,
Refresh me with apples,
Because I am lovesick.

</td></tr>
<tr><td>

2:6
Song 8:3

</td><td>6</td><td>

"*Let* his left hand be under my head
And his right hand embrace me."

</td></tr>
<tr><td>

2:7
Song 3:5; 8:4

</td><td>**7**</td><td>

"[5]I adjure you, O daughters of Jerusalem,
By the gazelles or by the hinds of the field,
That you will not arouse or awaken *my* love,
Until she pleases."

</td></tr>
</table>

II. *The praise of her beloved (2:8–3:5)*

A. *Her praise by day*

<table>
<tr><td>

2:8
v. 17

</td><td>**8**</td><td>

"[6]Listen! My beloved!
Behold, he is coming,
Climbing on the mountains,
Leaping on the hills!

</td></tr>
<tr><td>

2:9
v. 17

</td><td>9</td><td>

"My beloved is like a gazelle or a young stag.
Behold, he is standing behind our wall,
He is looking through the windows,
He is peering through the lattice.

</td></tr>
<tr><td>

2:10
v. 13

</td><td>**10**</td><td>

"My beloved responded and said to me,
'Arise, my darling, my beautiful one,
And come along.

</td></tr>
<tr><td></td><td>11</td><td>

'For behold, the winter is past,
The rain is over *and* gone.

</td></tr>
<tr><td>

2:12
Ps 74:19

</td><td>12</td><td>

'The flowers have *already* appeared in the land;
The time has arrived for pruning *the vines*,
And the voice of the turtledove has been heard in our land.

</td></tr>
<tr><td>

2:13
Matt 24:32;
Song 7:12;
v. 10

</td><td>13</td><td>

'The fig tree has ripened its figs,
And the vines in blossom have given forth *their* fragrance.
Arise, my darling, my beautiful one,
And come along!' "

</td></tr>
<tr><td>

2:14
Song 5:2;
Jer 48:28;
Song 8:13;
1:5

</td><td>14</td><td>

"O my dove, in the clefts of the rock,
In the secret place of the steep pathway,
Let me see your form,
Let me hear your voice;
For your voice is sweet,
And your form is lovely."

</td></tr>
</table>

[5]BRIDEGROOM [6]BRIDE

15 "Catch the foxes for us,
    The little foxes that are ruining the vineyards,
    While our vineyards are in blossom."

16 "My beloved is mine, and I am his;
    He pastures *his flock* among the lilies.

17 "Until the cool of the day when the shadows flee away,
    Turn, my beloved, and be like a gazelle
    Or a young stag on the mountains of Bether."

B. *Her praise by night*

3 "[7]On my bed night after night I sought him
       Whom my soul loves;
       I sought him but did not find him.

2   'I must arise now and go about the city;
       In the streets and in the squares
       I must seek him whom my soul loves.'
       I sought him but did not find him.

3   "The watchmen who make the rounds in the city found me,
       And I said, 'Have you seen him whom my soul loves?'

4   "Scarcely had I left them
       When I found him whom my soul loves;
       I held on to him and would not let him go,
       Until I had brought him to my mother's house,
       And into the room of her who conceived me."

5   "[8]I adjure you, O daughters of Jerusalem,
       By the gazelles or by the hinds of the field,
       That you will not arouse or awaken *my* love,
       Until she pleases."

III. *In praise of the bride (3:6–5:1)*

A. *The bridegroom comes*

6   "[9]What is this coming up from the wilderness
       Like columns of smoke,
       Perfumed with myrrh and frankincense,
       With all scented powders of the merchant?

7   "Behold, it is the *traveling* couch of Solomon;
       Sixty mighty men around it,
       Of the mighty men of Israel.

8   "All of them are wielders of the sword,
       Expert in war;
       Each man has his sword at his side,
       Guarding against the terrors of the night.

9   "King Solomon has made for himself a sedan chair
       From the timber of Lebanon.

10   "He made its posts of silver,
       Its back of gold
       And its seat of purple fabric,
       With its interior lovingly fitted out
       By the daughters of Jerusalem.

11   "Go forth, O daughters of Zion,
       And gaze on King Solomon with the crown
       With which his mother has crowned him
       On the day of his wedding,
       And on the day of his gladness of heart."

[7]BRIDE [8]BRIDEGROOM [9]CHORUS

2:15
Ezek 13:4

2:16
Song 6:3;
7:10
2:17
Song 4:6;
vv. 8,9

*3:1
Is 26:9;
Song 1:7; 5:6

3:2
Jer 5:1

3:3
Song 5:7

3:4
Song 8:2

3:5
Song 2:7; 8:4

3:6
Song 8:5;
1:13; 4:6,14

3:8
Jer 50:9;
Ps 45:3; 91:5

3:10
Song 1:5

3:11
Song 3:16,17

3:1 Verses 1–5 are probably a song in which the Shulammite (the bride) relates a dream. Her sleeping as well as her
waking hours are always centered in her beloved.

B. *His proposal accepted*

<table>
<tr><td>4:1
Song 1:15;
5:12; 6:5,7</td><td>4</td><td></td><td>"[10]How beautiful you are, my darling,
How beautiful you are!
Your eyes are *like* doves behind your veil;
Your hair is like a flock of goats
That have descended from Mount Gilead.</td></tr>
<tr><td>4:2
Song 6:6</td><td></td><td>2</td><td>"Your teeth are like a flock of *newly* shorn ewes
Which have come up from *their* washing,
All of which bear twins,
And not one among them has lost her young.</td></tr>
<tr><td>4:3
Song 6:7</td><td></td><td>3</td><td>"Your lips are like a scarlet thread,
And your mouth is lovely.
Your temples are like a slice of a pomegranate
Behind your veil.</td></tr>
<tr><td>4:4
Song 7:4;
Neh 3:19</td><td></td><td>4</td><td>"Your neck is like the tower of David
Built with rows of stones,
On which are hung a thousand shields,
All the round shields of the mighty men.</td></tr>
<tr><td>4:5
Song 7:3;
2:16; 6:2,3</td><td></td><td>5</td><td>"Your two breasts are like two fawns,
Twins of a gazelle,
Which feed among the lilies.</td></tr>
<tr><td>4:6
Song 2:17;
v. 14</td><td></td><td>6</td><td>"Until the cool of the day
When the shadows flee away,
I will go my way to the mountain of myrrh
And to the hill of frankincense.</td></tr>
<tr><td>4:7
Song 1:15</td><td></td><td>7</td><td>"You are altogether beautiful, my darling,
And there is no blemish in you.</td></tr>
<tr><td>4:8
Song 5:1;
Deut 3:9</td><td></td><td>8</td><td>"*Come* with me from Lebanon, *my* bride,
May you come with me from Lebanon.
Journey down from the summit of Amana,
From the summit of Senir and Hermon,
From the dens of lions,
From the mountains of leopards.</td></tr>
<tr><td>4:9
vv. 10,12;
Prov 1:9;
Ezek 16:11</td><td></td><td>9</td><td>"You have made my heart beat faster, my sister, *my* bride;
You have made my heart beat faster with a single *glance* of your
    eyes,
With a single strand of your necklace.</td></tr>
<tr><td>4:10
Song 1:2-4</td><td></td><td>10</td><td>"How beautiful is your love, my sister, *my* bride!
How much better is your love than wine,
And the fragrance of your oils
Than all *kinds* of spices!</td></tr>
<tr><td>4:11
Prov 5:3;
24:13;
Gen 27:27;
Hos 14:6</td><td></td><td>11</td><td>"Your lips, *my* bride, drip honey;
Honey and milk are under your tongue,
And the fragrance of your garments is like the fragrance of Lebanon.</td></tr>
<tr><td>4:12
Prov 5:15-18;
Gen 29:3</td><td></td><td>12</td><td>"A garden locked is my sister, *my* bride,
A rock garden locked, a spring sealed up.</td></tr>
<tr><td>4:13
Eccl 2:5;
Song 6:11;
7:12; v. 16;
Song 1:14</td><td></td><td>13</td><td>"Your shoots are an orchard of pomegranates
With choice fruits, henna with nard plants,</td></tr>
<tr><td>4:14
Song 1:12;
Ex 30:23;
v. 6;
Song 3:6;
John 19:39</td><td></td><td>14</td><td>Nard and saffron, calamus and cinnamon,
With all the trees of frankincense,
Myrrh and aloes, along with all the finest spices.</td></tr>
<tr><td>4:15
John 4:10;
7:38</td><td></td><td>15</td><td>"*You are* a garden spring,
A well of fresh water,
And streams *flowing* from Lebanon."</td></tr>
<tr><td>4:16
Song 5:1; 6:2</td><td></td><td>16</td><td>"[11]Awake, O north *wind*,
And come, *wind of* the south;
Make my garden breathe out *fragrance*,
Let its spices be wafted abroad.
May my beloved come into his garden
And eat its choice fruits!"</td></tr>
</table>

[10]BRIDEGROOM   [11]BRIDE

5

"[12]I have come into my garden, my sister, *my* bride;
I have gathered my myrrh along with my balsam.
I have eaten my honeycomb and my honey;
I have drunk my wine and my milk.
Eat, friends;
Drink and imbibe deeply, O lovers.' "

5:1
Song 6:2; 4:9,
11,14;
Luke 15:7,
10; John 3:29

IV. *A troubled love (5:2–7:9)*

A. *Her disturbing dream*

2 "[13]I was asleep, but my heart was awake.
A voice! My beloved was knocking:
'Open to me, my sister, my darling,
My dove, my perfect one!
For my head is drenched with dew,
My locks with the damp of the night.'

5:2
Song 4:9; 6:9;
v. 11

3 "I have taken off my dress,
How can I put it on *again?*
I have washed my feet,
How can I dirty them *again?*

5:3
Luke 11:7;
Gen 19:2

4 "My beloved extended his hand through the opening,
And my feelings were aroused for him.

5 "I arose to open to my beloved;
And my hands dripped with myrrh,
And my fingers with liquid myrrh,
On the handles of the bolt.

5:5
v. 13

6 "I opened to my beloved,
But my beloved had turned away *and* had gone!
My heart went out *to him* as he spoke.
I searched for him, but I did not find him;
I called him, but he did not answer me.

5:6
Song 6:1; 3:1;
Prov 1:28

7 "The watchmen who make the rounds in the city found me,
They struck me *and* wounded me;
The guardsmen of the walls took away my shawl from me.

5:7
Song 3:3

8 "I adjure you, O daughters of Jerusalem,
If you find my beloved,
As to what you will tell him:
For I am lovesick."

5:8
Song 2:7; 3:5;
2:5

9 "[14]What kind of beloved is your beloved,
O most beautiful among women?
What kind of beloved is your beloved,
That thus you adjure us?"

5:9
Song 1:8; 6:1

10 "[13]My beloved is dazzling and ruddy,
Outstanding among ten thousand.

11 "His head is *like* gold, pure gold;
His locks are *like* clusters of dates,
And black as a raven.

12 "His eyes are like doves,
Beside streams of water,
Bathed in milk,
And reposed in *their* setting.

5:12
Song 1:15;
4:1

13 "His cheeks are like a bed of balsam,
Banks of sweet-scented herbs;
His lips are lilies,
Dripping with liquid myrrh.

5:13
Song 6:2; 2:1

14 "His hands are rods of gold
Set with beryl;
His abdomen is carved ivory
Inlaid with sapphires.

[12]BRIDEGROOM   [13]BRIDE   [14]CHORUS

15 "His legs are pillars of alabaster
    Set on pedestals of pure gold;
    His appearance is like Lebanon,
    Choice as the cedars.

5:16
Song 7:9;
2 Sam 1:23

16 "His mouth is *full of* sweetness.
    And he is wholly desirable.
    This is my beloved and this is my friend,
    O daughters of Jerusalem."

6:1
Song 5:6; 1:8

6

[15]"Where has your beloved gone,
    O most beautiful among women?
    Where has your beloved turned,
    That we may seek him with you?"

6:2
Song 4:16;
5:1,13; 1:7;
2:1

2 "[16]My beloved has gone down to his garden,
    To the beds of balsam,
    To pasture *his flock* in the gardens
    And gather lilies.

6:3
Song 2:16;
7:10

3 "I am my beloved's and my beloved is mine,
    He who pastures *his flock* among the lilies."

B. The bridegroom's inner thoughts of his beloved

*6:4
Song 1:15;
v. 10

4 "[17]You are as beautiful as Tirzah, my darling,
    As lovely as Jerusalem,
    As awesome as an army with banners.

6:5
Song 4:1

5 "Turn your eyes away from me,
    For they have confused me;
    Your hair is like a flock of goats
    That have descended from Gilead.

6:6
Song 4:2

6 "Your teeth are like a flock of ewes
    Which have come up from *their* washing,
    All of which bear twins,
    And not one among them has lost her young.

6:7
Song 4:3

7 "Your temples are like a slice of a pomegranate
    Behind your veil.

6:8
1 Kin 11:3;
Song 1:3

8 "There are sixty queens and eighty concubines,
    And maidens without number;

6:9
Song 2:14;
5:2;
Gen 30:13

9 *But* my dove, my perfect one, is unique:
    She is her mother's only *daughter;*
    She is the pure *child* of the one who bore her.
    The maidens saw her and called her blessed,
    The queens and the concubines *also*, and they praised her, *saying,*

6:10
v. 4

10 'Who is this that grows like the dawn,
    As beautiful as the full moon,
    As pure as the sun,
    As awesome as an army with banners?'

6:11
Song 7:12

11 "I went down to the orchard of nut trees
    To see the blossoms of the valley,
    To see whether the vine had budded
    Or the pomegranates had bloomed.

12 "Before I was aware, my soul set me
    Over the chariots of my noble people."

*6:13
Judg 21:21;
Gen 32:2

13 "[15]Come back, come back, O Shulammite;
    Come back, come back, that we may gaze at you!"

    "[17]**W**hy should you gaze at the Shulammite,
    As at the dance of the two companies?

---

[15]CHORUS [16]BRIDE [17]BRIDEGROOM

6:4 *Tirzah* was the capital of the northern kingdom until the time of Omri, who built Samaria (1 Kin. 16:15–24). Here the beauty of Tirzah is compared to that of Jerusalem.

6:13 The *Shulammite* came from Shulem (probably a variant of Shunem), a village in the plain of Esdraelon (check here 1 Sam. 28:4 and 2 Kin. 4:8).

7

"How beautiful are your feet in sandals,
O prince's daughter!
The curves of your hips are like jewels,
The work of the hands of an artist.

7:1
Ps 45:13

2 "Your navel is *like* a round goblet
Which never lacks mixed wine;
Your belly is like a heap of wheat
Fenced about with lilies.

3 "Your two breasts are like two fawns,
Twins of a gazelle.

7:3
Song 4:5

4 "Your neck is like a tower of ivory,
Your eyes *like* the pools in Heshbon
By the gate of Bath-rabbim;
Your nose is like the tower of Lebanon,
Which faces toward Damascus.

7:4
Song 4:4

5 "Your head crowns you like Carmel,
And the flowing locks of your head are like purple threads;
The king is captivated by *your* tresses.

7:5
Is 35:2

6 "How beautiful and how delightful you are,
My love, with *all* your charms!

7:6
Song 1:15,16

7 "Your stature is like a palm tree,
And your breasts are *like its* clusters.

8 "I said, 'I will climb the palm tree,
I will take hold of its fruit stalks.'
Oh, may your breasts be like clusters of the vine,
And the fragrance of your breath like apples,

7:8
Song 2:5

9 And your mouth like the best wine!"

"[18]It goes *down* smoothly for my beloved,
Flowing gently *through* the lips of those who fall asleep.

V. *The unbroken communion (7:10–8:14)*

A. *The bride gives her love*

10 "I am my beloved's,
And his desire is for me.

7:10
Song 2:16;
6:3; Ps 45:11

11 "Come, my beloved, let us go out into the country,
Let us spend the night in the villages.

12 "Let us rise early *and go* to the vineyards;
Let us see whether the vine has budded
And its blossoms have opened,
And whether the pomegranates have bloomed.
There I will give you my love.

7:12
Song 6:11

13 "The mandrakes have given forth fragrance;
And over our doors are all choice *fruits,*
Both new and old,
Which I have saved up for you, my beloved.

*7:13
Gen 30:14;
Song 2:3;
4:13,16

8

"Oh that you were like a brother to me
Who nursed at my mother's breasts.
If I found you outdoors, I would kiss you;
No one would despise me, either.

2 "I would lead you *and* bring you
Into the house of my mother, who used to instruct me;
I would give you spiced wine to drink from the juice of my
pomegranates.

8:2
Song 3:4

3 "Let his left hand be under my head,

8:3
Song 2:6

[18]BRIDE

7:13 *Mandrakes* were thought to produce feelings of love (cf. Gen. 30:14–16). Mandrakes were also associated with magic.

And his right hand embrace me."

8:4
Song 2:7; 3:5

4 "[19]I want you to swear, O daughters of Jerusalem,
Do not arouse or awaken *my* love,
Until she pleases."

B. *The beauty of love*

8:5
Song 3:6; 2:3

5 "[20]Who is this coming up from the wilderness,
Leaning on her beloved?"

"[19]Beneath the apple tree I awakened you;
There your mother was in labor with you,
There she was in labor *and* gave you birth.

8:6
Is 49:16;
Jer 22:24;
Hag 2:23;
Prov 6:34

6 "Put me like a [21]seal over your heart,
Like a seal on your arm.
For love is as strong as death,
Jealousy is as severe as Sheol;
Its flashes are flashes of fire,
The *very* flame of the LORD.

7 "Many waters cannot quench love,
Nor will rivers overflow it;
If a man were to give all the riches of his house for love,
It would be utterly despised."

8:8
Ezek 16:7

8 "[20]We have a little sister,
And she has no breasts;
What shall we do for our sister
On the day when she is spoken for?

9 "If she is a wall,
We shall build on her a battlement of silver;
But if she is a door,
We shall barricade her with planks of cedar."

10 "[22]I was a wall, and my breasts were like towers;
Then I became in his eyes as one who finds peace.

8:11
Eccl 2:4;
Matt 21:33;
Song 1:6; 2:3;
Is 7:23

11 "Solomon had a vineyard at Baal-hamon;
He entrusted the vineyard to caretakers;
Each one was to bring a thousand *shekels* of silver for its fruit.

12 "My very own vineyard is at my disposal;
The thousand *shekels* are for you, Solomon,
And two hundred are for those who take care of its fruit."

8:13
Song 1:7;
2:14

13 "[19]O you who sit in the gardens,
My companions are listening for your voice—
Let me hear it!"

8:14
Song 2:17;
4:6

14 "[22]Hurry, my beloved,
And be like a gazelle or a young stag
On the mountains of spices."

[19]BRIDEGROOM   [20]CHORUS   [21]Or, *signet*   [22]BRIDE

8:9 *A wall* is here symbolic of resistance to attack. The her innocence.
brothers think of their sister as resisting any who attack

INTRODUCTION TO
THE BOOK OF
ISAIAH

Authorship and Background: This book contains the prophecies of Isaiah (whose name means "Yahweh is salvation"), the son of Amoz, who lived in Jerusalem and prophesied mainly about Judah and Jerusalem. He took up his prophetic office in the year King Uzziah died and continued that ministry during the reigns of Jotham, Ahaz, and Hezekiah. Hosea and Micah were among his contemporaries. Isaiah's ministry lasted more than fifty years (ca. 740-687 B.C.), after which, according to tradition, he was sawn in pieces during the persecutions that raged after the accession of Manasseh (cf. Heb. 11:37).

The authorship of the latter half of Isaiah, beginning with chapter 40, has been the subject of much dispute. Unquestionably, there is a distinct break at the end of chapter 39. The difference may be explained in one of two ways. The traditional view holds that 40-66 were composed later in Isaiah's life and are predictive prophecy. Others assume that because of the Babylonian setting of this unit, it was composed by some great unknown prophet who wrote *after* the events occurred rather than before. A variant of this view suggests a school of Isaiah in which the prophet's disciples spoke in the name of their teacher after his death. Once prediction is regarded as a fundamental part of the prophet's message, there is no compelling reason for denying the unity of the book, although, as in other books, later editing probably took place.

Characteristics: By Isaiah's time, Solomon's kingdom had been divided into northern and southern kingdoms for many years. The southern kingdom (ca. 740 B.C.) faced attack by Israel (northern kingdom) and Syria. Assyria overcame Syria and threatened Israel. Samaria fell and Israel was taken captive (722 B.C.). Assyria now threatened Judah (southern kingdom), which looked toward Egypt for help. Isaiah wrote historically and prophetically. Chapters 36-39 are a record of his own life and activity during the days of Hezekiah. The remainder of the first half is devoted to prophecies concerning Judah and Jerusalem, and Judah with respect to Egypt and Assyria. The language of Isaiah is energetic and forceful. Beginning with chapter 40, the language becomes solemn, filled with pathos and marked by poetical outbursts of moving grandeur. The latter half of the book is replete with his messages of redemption and Messianic hope. Employing figures of rocks, forests, mountains, flocks of rams, trees of cedar and acacia, and moving torrents of flowing waters, Isaiah paints a graphic picture. In no other place in the Old Testament is there to be found a more realistic view of Calvary than in Isaiah 53.

Contents:

I. Volume of rebuke and promise (1:1-6:13): Isaiah arraigns the people of Judah, charging them with sin and rebellion. He exhorts them to repent and promises forgiveness, pronouncing ultimate judgment if they do not. He prophesies about a glorious future for Judah in the last days and sketches the present sins of the people. The parable of the vineyard follows, with a prophecy of invasion. Isaiah delineates his own call and commission.

II. Volume of Immanuel (7:1-12:6): Isaiah prophesies the coming of Immanuel to Ahaz. He speaks of the impending Assyrian invasion. Two other signs are given: one is the sign of Shear-jashub; the other the sign of Maher-shalal-hash-baz.

III. Volume of burdens on heathen nations (13:1-23:18): Isaiah prophesies: the fall of

Babylon; the defeat of Assyria; Palestine to have worse oppressors; Moab to be judged; Syria (Damascus) to become a heap; Israel to be doomed; Ethiopia to be trodden down; a confused and fearful Egypt to be taken captive; Sennacherib to invade Judah; the visions of Edom (Dumah) and Arabia; Jerusalem to be overcome and Shebna removed; and Tyre to be overthrown and restored.

IV. First volume of general rebuke and promise (24:1-27:13): The whole world to be judged. The song of praise for judgment. It is the righteous God who must judge and whose mercy brings salvation.

V. Volume of woes on the unbelievers of Israel (28:1-33:24): Isaiah prophesies that Judah's alliance with Egypt is death; it is a shame. Egypt itself will fall. Jerusalem also shall fall but will be restored. Her salvation is of God.

VI. Second volume of general rebuke and promise (34:1-35:10): The destruction of the hostile nations is prophesied, and the restoration of Zion promised. The desert shall blossom, the sick will be made well, the ground will bring forth fruit, and the captives will return with singing.

VII. The volume of Hezekiah (36:1-39:8): Sennacherib's invasion. Isaiah prophesies his defeat. The Babylonian captivity foretold. Hezekiah recovers from sickness and foolishly displays his wealth.

VIII. Volume of comfort and assurance (40:1-66:24): The deliverance of God's people announced. God has power to save them. The agent of deliverance is God's Servant. Israel is His servant-nation. Cyrus is God's servant-king who shall bring to pass God's will. Babylon falls and the people go back to Jerusalem. The coming Servant King is pictured followed by a description of His reign and kingdom. It shall be permanent; men are invited to enter into it; the rules and requirements of the kingdom are laid down; there shall be judgment on its foes. At last there shall be a sifting at the final day of judgment.

THE BOOK OF

ISAIAH

I. *Volume of rebuke and promise (1:1–6:13)*

A. *Rebellion confronted with judgment and grace*

1. *Superscription*

1 The vision of Isaiah the son of Amoz, concerning Judah and Jerusalem which he saw during the reigns of Uzziah, Jotham, Ahaz, *and* Hezekiah, kings of Judah.

2. *Judah's ingratitude*

2   Listen, O heavens, and hear, O earth;
    For the LORD speaks,
    "Sons I have reared and brought up,
    But they have revolted against Me.

3   "An ox knows its owner,
    And a donkey its master's manger,
    But Israel does not know,
    My people do not understand."

4   Alas, sinful nation,
    People weighed down with iniquity,
    Offspring of evildoers,
    Sons who act corruptly!
    They have abandoned the LORD,
    They have despised the Holy One of Israel,
    They have turned away from Him.

5   Where will you be stricken again,
    As you continue in *your* rebellion?
    The whole head is sick,
    And the whole heart is faint.

6   From the sole of the foot even to the head
    There is nothing sound in it,
    Only bruises, welts, and raw wounds,
    Not pressed out or bandaged,
    Nor softened with oil.

7   Your land is desolate,
    Your cities are burned with fire,
    Your fields—strangers are devouring them in your presence;
    It is desolation, as overthrown by strangers.

8   And the daughter of Zion is left like a shelter in a vineyard,
    Like a watchman's hut in a cucumber field, like a besieged city.

*1:1	Num 12:6; Is 2:1; 2 Kin 15:1, 13,32; 16:1; 18:1
1:2	Deut 23:1
1:3	Jer 8:7; 9:3,6
1:4	Is 14:20; v. 28; Is 5:24
*1:5	Is 31:6; 33:24
1:6	Job 2:7; Ps 38:3; Is 30:26; Luke 10:34
1:7	Is 6:11; Jer 44:6
1:8	Job 27:18

1:1 Isaiah was a prophet. "The Hebrew word for 'prophet' means literally 'one who is inspired by God.' The prophets . . . all felt themselves to be spiritual leaders commissioned by God to warn their contemporaries of the perils of wickedness, to point the way to true religion, and to give guidance on moral issues. . . . Though prophecy was primarily concerned with current situations, the prophets realized that tomorrow is inherent in today. They foresaw the outcome of Israel's national crises and her evil patterns of living. Time and again their predictions of impending doom were fulfilled. When Jerusalem fell in 587 B.C., as prophets had warned for generations, people saw prophecy fulfilled in history. This gave the post-Exilic prophets great prestige" (Madelaine S. and J. Lane Miller, *Harper's Bible Dictionary*, Harper and Row, p. 582).
Scripture reveals that all three persons of the Trinity cooperate in the bestowal of the prophetic gift (Jer. 1:5; Jon. 1:2; 3:2; 1 Cor. 12:10,11; Eph. 4:11; Rev. 11:3). The New Testament letters are striking examples of the exercise of the prophetic gift as it relates to instruction, reproof, and exhortation. Only occasionally (as in Rom. 9:23–26; 1 Thess. 4:13–17; 2 Thess. 2:3,4) do they contain predictive material. Whether the New Testament gift of prophecy in the postapostolic age includes the gift of prediction is not clear. At best, it would be rare and more often simulated than real.

1:5 *The whole head is sick.* In 701 B.C., Sennacherib of Assyria invaded Judah and despoiled the countryside. Jerusalem alone was spared (2 Kin. 18:13–16). Isaiah 1:5–9 describes the plight of Judah following Sennacherib's invasion.

1:9
Rom 9:29;
Is 10:20-22

9   Unless the LORD of hosts
Had left us a few survivors,
We would be like Sodom,
We would be like Gomorrah.

3. *God's requirement of a holy life*

1:10
Is 28:14; 3:9;
Ezek 16:46;
Rev 11:8

10   Hear the word of the LORD,
You rulers of Sodom;
Give ear to the instruction of our God,
You people of Gomorrah.

1:11
1 Sam 15:22;
Jer 6:20;
Mic 6:7

11   "What are your multiplied sacrifices to Me?"
Says the LORD.
"I have had enough of burnt offerings of rams,
And the fat of fed cattle.
And I take no pleasure in the blood of bulls, lambs, or goats.

1:12
Ex 23:17

12   "When you come to appear before Me,
Who requires of you this trampling of My courts?

*1:13
Is 66:3;
1 Chr 23:31;
Ex 12:16;
Jer 7:9,10

13   "Bring your worthless offerings no longer,
Incense is an abomination to Me.
New moon and sabbath, the calling of assemblies—
I cannot endure iniquity and the solemn assembly.

1:14
Num 28:11;
Lev 23:2;
Is 7:13; 43:24

14   "I hate your new moon *festivals* and your appointed feasts,
They have become a burden to Me.
I am weary of bearing *them*.

1:15
1 Kin 8:22;
Is 8:17; 59:2;
Mic 3:4;
Is 59:3

15   "So when you spread out your hands *in prayer*,
I will hide My eyes from you,
Yes, even though you multiply prayers,
I will not listen.
Your hands are covered with blood.

1:16
Jer 4:14;
Is 52:11;
55:7; Jer 25:5

16   "Wash yourselves, make yourselves clean;
Remove the evil of your deeds from My sight.
Cease to do evil;

1:17
Jer 22:3;
Is 58:6;
Ps 82:3

17   Learn to do good;
Seek justice,
Reprove the ruthless;
Defend the orphan,
Plead for the widow.

4. *The choice: repentance or destruction*

1:18
Is 43:26;
Ps 51:7;
Rev 7:14

18   "Come now, and let us reason together,"
Says the LORD,
"Though your sins are as scarlet,
They will be as white as snow;
Though they are red like crimson,
They will be like wool.

*1:19
Deut 30:15,
16
1:20
Is 3:25; 34:16

19   "If you consent and obey,
You will eat the best of the land;

20   "But if you refuse and rebel,
You will be devoured by the sword."
Truly, the mouth of the LORD has spoken.

5. *The promise to redeem Zion after judgment*

1:21
Jer 2:20;
Is 59:7

21   How the faithful city has become a harlot,
She *who* was full of justice!
Righteousness once lodged in her,
But now murderers.

1:22
Ezek 22:18

22   Your silver has become dross,

1:13 *Worthless offerings* were sacrifices devoid of any spiritual content. The forms of religion might be observed by those who had no real love of God or their fellowman. In v. 15 Isaiah complains that some who make religious profession are actually murderers.

1:19 *If you consent and obey.* This expresses the condition for renewed blessing. Isaiah makes it clear that a formal relationship of the people (i.e., Israel) to God is not enough to ensure God's favor.

Both supply and support, the whole supply of bread,
And the whole supply of water;

2 The mighty man and the warrior,
The judge and the prophet,
The diviner and the elder,

3 The captain of fifty and the honorable man,
The counselor and the expert artisan,
And the skillful enchanter.

4 And I will make mere lads their princes
And capricious children will rule over them,

5 And the people will be oppressed,
Each one by another, and each one by his neighbor;
The youth will storm against the elder,
And the inferior against the honorable.

6 When a man lays hold of his brother in his father's house, *saying,*
"You have a cloak, you shall be our ruler,
And these ruins will be under your charge,"

7 On that day will he protest, saying,
"I will not be *your* healer,
For in my house there is neither bread nor cloak;
You should not appoint me ruler of the people."

8 For Jerusalem has stumbled, and Judah has fallen,
Because their speech and their actions are against the Lord,
To rebel against His glorious presence.

9 The expression of their faces bears witness against them.
And they display their sin like Sodom;
They do not *even* conceal *it.*
Woe to them!
For they have brought evil on themselves.

10 Say to the righteous that *it will go* well *with them,*
For they will eat the fruit of their actions.

11 Woe to the wicked! *It will go* badly *with him,*
For what he deserves will be done to him.

12 O My people! Their oppressors are children,
And women rule over them.
O My people! Those who guide you lead *you* astray,
And confuse the direction of your paths.

13 The Lord arises to contend,
And stands to judge the people.

14 The Lord enters into judgment with the elders and princes of His
people,
"It is you who have devoured the vineyard;
The plunder of the poor is in your houses.

15 "What do you mean by crushing My people,
And grinding the face of the poor?"
Declares the Lord God of hosts.

16 Moreover, the Lord said, "Because the daughters of Zion are
proud,
And walk with heads held high and seductive eyes,
And go along with mincing steps,
And tinkle the bangles on their feet,

17 Therefore the Lord will afflict the scalp of the daughters of Zion
with scabs,
And the Lord will make their foreheads bare."

18 In that day the Lord will take away the beauty of *their* anklets, headbands,
crescent ornaments,

19 dangling earrings, bracelets, veils,

20 headdresses, ankle chains, sashes, perfume boxes, amulets,

Cross-references

3:2 — 2 Kin 24:14
*3:4 — Eccl 10:16
3:5 — Mic 7:3-6; Is 9:19
3:6 — Is 4:1
3:7 — Ezek 34:4
3:8 — Is 1:7; 6:11; 9:17; 65:3,5
3:9 — Is 1:10; Gen 13:13
3:10 — Deut 28:1-14
3:11 — Is 65:6,7
*3:12 — v. 4; Is 9:16
3:13 — Is 66:16; Mic 6:2
3:14 — Ezek 20:35, 36; Is 10:1,2; James 2:6
3:15 — Ps 94:5
3:16 — Is 4:4
3:17 — Is 47:3
3:18 — Judg 8:21
3:20 — Ex 39:28

3:4 *I will make mere lads their princes,* i.e., they shall have youthful, inexperienced rulers adding to their problems.
3:12 *women rule over them.* In 3:16,17 the prophet describes the haughty and wanton women of Jerusalem. Although the prophetess Deborah served as a judge in Israel (Judg. 4:4), the only woman ruler during the monarchy was the wicked Athaliah (2 Kin. 11:1-16).

3:21 Ezek 16:12	21 finger rings, nose rings, 22 festal robes, outer tunics, cloaks, money purses, 23 hand mirrors, undergarments, turbans, and veils.
3:24 Prov 31:24; Is 22:12; 15:3	24 Now it will come about that instead of sweet perfume there will be putrefaction; Instead of a belt, a rope; Instead of well-set hair, a plucked-out scalp; Instead of fine clothes, a donning of sackcloth; And branding instead of beauty.
3:25 Is 1:20; 65:12	25 Your men will fall by the sword, And your mighty ones in battle.
3:26 Jer 14:2; Lam 2:10	26 And her gates will lament and mourn; And deserted she will sit on the ground.

4 For seven women will take hold of one man in that day, saying, "We will eat our own bread and wear our own clothes, only let us be called by your name; take away our reproach!"

*4:1
Is 13:12;
2 Thess 3:12;
Is 54:4

d. Blessedness of revived Israel under Messiah

2 In that day the Branch of the LORD will be beautiful and glorious, and the fruit of the earth *will* be the pride and the adornment of the survivors of Israel. **3** And it will come about that he who is left in Zion and remains in Jerusalem will be called holy—everyone who is recorded for life in Jerusalem. **4** When the Lord has washed away the filth of the daughters of Zion, and purged the bloodshed of Jerusalem from her midst, by the spirit of judgment and the spirit of burning, **5** then the LORD will create over the whole area of Mount Zion and over her assemblies a cloud by day, even smoke, and the brightness of a flaming fire by night; for over all the glory will be a canopy. **6** And there will be a shelter to *give* shade from the heat by day, and refuge and protection from the storm and the rain.

*4:2
Is 11:1;
Zech 3:8;
6:12;
Ps 72:16;
Is 10:20
*4:3
Is 28:5;
60:21; 52:1;
Luke 10:20
4:4
Is 3:16,24;
1:15; 28:6;
Mal 3:2,3
4:5
Ex 13:21;
Is 60:1,2
4:6
Is 25:4

C. Judah to be exiled for unfaithfulness

1. The parable of the vineyard

*5:1 Ps 80:8; Matt 21:33; Mark 12:1; Luke 20:9 5:2 Jer 2:21; Matt 21:19; Mark 11:13; Luke 13:6	5 Let me sing now for my well-beloved A song of my beloved concerning His vineyard. My well-beloved had a vineyard on a fertile hill. 2 And He dug it all around, removed its stones, And planted it with the choicest vine. And He built a tower in the middle of it, And hewed out a wine vat in it; Then He expected *it* to produce *good* grapes, But it produced *only* worthless ones.
5:3 Matt 21:40	3 "And now, O inhabitants of Jerusalem and men of Judah, Judge between Me and My vineyard.
*5:4 Matt 23:37	4 "What more was there to do for My vineyard that I have not done in it? Why, when I expected *it* to produce *good* grapes did it produce worthless ones?
*5:5 Ps 89:40; Is 6:13;	5 "So now let Me tell you what I am going to do to My vineyard:

4:1 *seven women will take hold of one man,* i.e., they shall need a protector in a time of anarchy. The men will have been decimated in battle. Seven is a conventional number, meaning "many" in a context such as this. *take away our reproach,* i.e., shame or contempt here.
4:2 The *Branch* is an Old Testament name for Christ. It is a reference to the Messianic king as the descendant of the promised line of David. The word itself comes from the Hebrew *tsemach,* meaning a "sprout." In Jer. 23:5 and 33:15 it is referred to as the *righteous Branch,* and, finally, as the personal name of the Messiah in Zech. 3:8 and 6:12. In Isaiah, Christ is the *branch of the LORD.* In Jeremiah He is David's *righteous Branch.* In Zechariah He is *the man ... Branch.* (Cf. the closely related title in Is. 11:1 of the

shoot . . . from the stem of Jesse.)
4:3 *he who is left in Zion.* The prophet has depicted the judgment of God that would fall on the wicked. Here he depicts the righteous remnant protected by the presence of God in the cloud (by day) and fire (by night), reminiscent of the period of wilderness wandering.
5:1 *My well-beloved had a vineyard.* The prophet uses a parable to show God's care for Israel, and their ingratitude and disobedience. God cared for the vineyard (Israel), but received in return worthless grapes (5:4).
5:4 *What more was there to do . . . ?* Israel is given opportunity to answer the charge. There must be some reason for the worthless grapes. What had the beloved failed to do?
5:5 *I will remove its hedge.* The hedge was built to protect

I will remove its hedge and it will be consumed;
I will break down its wall and it will become trampled
    ground.

6   "And I will lay it waste;
It will not be pruned or hoed,
But briars and thorns will come up.
I will also charge the clouds to rain no rain on it."

7   For the vineyard of the LORD of hosts is the house of Israel,
And the men of Judah His delightful plant.
Thus He looked for justice, but behold, bloodshed;
For righteousness, but behold, a cry of distress.

2. Judah guilty of seven sins
a. Selfish greed

8   Woe to those who add house to house *and* join field to field,
Until there is no more room,
So that you have to live alone in the midst of the land!

9   In my ears the LORD of hosts *has sworn,* "Surely, many houses shall
    become desolate,
Even great and fine ones, without occupants.

10 "For ten acres of vineyard will yield *only* one ¹bath *of wine,*
And a homer of seed will yield *but* an ²ephah of grain."

b. Self-indulgence

11 Woe to those who rise early in the morning that they may pursue
    strong drink;
Who stay up late in the evening that wine may inflame them!

12 And their banquets are *accompanied* by lyre and harp, by tambourine
    and flute, and by wine;
But they do not pay attention to the deeds of the LORD,
Nor do they consider the work of His hands.

13 Therefore My people go into exile for their lack of knowledge;
And their honorable men are famished,
And their multitude is parched with thirst.

14 Therefore Sheol has enlarged its throat and opened its mouth
    without measure;
And Jerusalem's splendor, her multitude, her din *of revelry,*
    and the jubilant within her, descend *into it.*

15 So the *common* man will be humbled, and the man of *importance*
    abased,
The eyes of the proud also will be abased.

16 But the LORD of hosts will be exalted in judgment,
And the holy God will show Himself holy in righteousness.

17 Then the lambs will graze as in their pasture,
And strangers will eat in the waste places of the wealthy.

c. Cynical materialism

18 Woe to those who drag iniquity with the cords of falsehood,
And sin as if with cart ropes;

19 Who say, "Let Him make speed, let Him hasten His work, that we
    may see *it;*
And let the purpose of the Holy One of Israel draw near
And come to pass, that we may know *it!*"

d. Perversion of the standards of morality

20 Woe to those who call evil good, and good evil;
Who substitute darkness for light and light for darkness;

¹I.e., Approx. 10½ gal.   ²I.e., Approx. one bu.

Ps 80:12;
Is 10:6;
Luke 21:24;
Rev 11:2

5:6
Is 24:1,3;
Heb 6:8;
1 Kin 8:35

5:7
Ps 80:8-11;
Is 3:14,15

5:8
Mic 2:2

5:9
Is 22:14;
6:11,12

5:10
Is 7:23;
Ezek 45:11

5:11
Prov 23:29,
30;
Eccl 10:16

5:12
Amos 6:5,6;
Job 34:27;
Ps 28:5

5:13
Hos 4:6;
Is 1:3; 3:3;
9:14,15

*5:14
Prov 30:16;
Num 16:30-34;
Ps 141:7

5:15
Is 2:9,11

5:16
Is 2:11,17;
8:13; 29:23

5:18
Is 59:4-8

5:19
Ezek 12:22;
2 Pet 3:3,4

5:20
Prov 17:15;
Matt 6:22,23;
Luke 11:34,
35

---

the vineyard and ensure a good vintage. It had failed in its purpose. God, too, had placed a protecting hedge around Israel. When removed, Israel's powerful enemies could quickly devastate her.

5:14 *Sheol has enlarged its throat.* The nether world is personified and portrayed as a monster that opens its mouth and swallows the proud inhabitants of Jerusalem.

Who substitute bitter for sweet, and sweet for bitter!

e. *Intellectual pride and self-sufficiency*

5:21
Rom 12:16

21   Woe to those who are wise in their own eyes,
And clever in their own sight!

f. *Intemperance*

5:22
v. 11

22   Woe to those who are heroes in drinking wine,
And valiant men in mixing strong drink;

g. *Loss of integrity*

5:23
Is 10:1,2;
Ps 94:21

23   Who justify the wicked for a bribe,
And take away the rights of the ones who are in the right!

3. *God's judgment against Judah*

5:24
Is 9:18,19;
Job 18:16;
Hos 5:12;
Acts 13:41

24   Therefore, as a tongue of fire consumes stubble,
And dry grass collapses into the flame,
So their root will become like rot and their blossom
blow away as dust;
For they have rejected the law of the Lord of hosts,
And despised the word of the Holy One of Israel.

5:25
2 Kin 22:13;
Jer 4:24;
Is 14:19;
9:12,17,21;
23:11

25   On this account the anger of the Lord has burned against His
people,
And He has stretched out His hand against them and struck them
down,
And the mountains quaked; and their corpses lay like refuse in the
middle of the streets.
For all this His anger is not spent,
But His hand is still stretched out.

*5:26
Is 13:2,3;
7:18;
Deut 28:49;
Is 13:4,5
5:27
Joel 2:7,8;
Dan 5:6

26   He will also lift up a standard to the distant nation,
And will whistle for it from the ends of the earth;
And behold, it will come with speed swiftly.

27   No one in it is weary or stumbles,
None slumbers or sleeps;
Nor is the belt at its waist undone,
Nor its sandal strap broken.

5:28
Ps 7:12,13;
Jer 4:13

28   Its arrows are sharp, and all its bows are bent;
The hoofs of its horses seem like flint, and its *chariot* wheels like a
whirlwind.

5:29
Jer 51:38;
Is 10:6; 42:22

29   Its roaring is like a lioness, and it roars like young lions;
It growls as it seizes the prey,
And carries *it* off with no one to deliver *it*.

5:30
Is 17:12; 8:22

30   And it shall growl over it in that day like the roaring of the sea.
If one looks to the land, behold, there is darkness *and* distress;
Even the light is darkened by its clouds.

D. *Isaiah cleansed and commissioned*

1. *God's holiness revealed*

*6:1
Is 1:1;
2 Kin 15:7;
1 Kin 22:9
*6:2
Rev 4:8;
Ezek 1:11
6:3
Rev 4:8;
Ps 72:19

6 In the year of King Uzziah's death, I saw the Lord sitting on a throne, lofty and
exalted, with the train of His robe filling the temple.
2   Seraphim stood above Him, each having six wings; with two he covered his
face, and with two he covered his feet, and with two he flew.
3   And one called out to another and said,
"Holy, Holy, Holy, is the Lord of hosts,
The whole earth is full of His glory."

5:26 *He will also lift up a standard.* God will signal for a
distant nation of warriors (probably Assyria) to punish sinful Israel. This is but one of the many threats to be found in
Isaiah.
6:1 Here, and in vv. 5–8, the prophet recalls Uzziah's
horrible death from leprosy. Israel's king dies, but Israel's
God lives forever.
6:2 *Seraphim* in Hebrew signifies that which is burning and

dazzling. The word is used of angelic beings only in Isaiah,
and no explanation of the term is given in the Bible. The
Jews generally believed that the seraphim were a higher
order of celestial beings, a theory supported by the fact that
they worship and glorify God. This would certainly imply
that they are moral beings rather than mere symbolic figures
of some sort.

4　And the foundations of the thresholds trembled at the voice of him who called out, while the temple was filling with smoke.

2. Isaiah's repentance, confession, and cleansing

5　Then I said,
"Woe is me, for I am ruined!
Because I am a man of unclean lips,
And I live among a people of unclean lips;
For my eyes have seen the King, the LORD of hosts."

6　Then one of the seraphim flew to me, with a burning coal in his hand which he had taken from the altar with tongs.
7　And he touched my mouth *with it* and said, "Behold, this has touched your lips; and your iniquity is taken away, and your sin is forgiven."

3. *His commission to preach*

8　Then I heard the voice of the Lord, saying, "Whom shall I send, and who will go for Us?" Then I said, "Here am I. Send me!"
9　And He said, "Go, and tell this people:
'Keep on listening, but do not perceive;
Keep on looking, but do not understand.'
10　"Render the hearts of this people insensitive,
Their ears dull,
And their eyes dim,
Lest they see with their eyes,
Hear with their ears,
Understand with their hearts,
And return and be healed."
11　Then I said, "Lord, how long?" And He answered,
"Until cities are devastated *and* without inhabitant,
Houses are without people,
And the land is utterly desolate,
12　"The LORD has removed men far away,
And the forsaken places are many in the midst of the land.
13　"Yet there will be a tenth portion in it,
And it will again be *subject* to burning,
Like a terebinth or an oak
Whose stump remains when it is felled.
The holy seed is its stump."

II. *Volume of Immanuel (7:1–12:6)*

A. *Immanuel rejected by the wisdom of this world*

1. *The northern coalition*

7　Now it came about in the days of Ahaz, the son of Jotham, the son of Uzziah, king of Judah, that Rezin the king of Aram and Pekah the son of Remaliah, king of Israel, went up to Jerusalem to *wage* war against it, but could not conquer it.
2　When it was reported to the house of David, saying, "The Arameans have camped in Ephraim," his heart and the hearts of his people shook as the trees of the forest shake with the wind.

2. *God's answer on behalf of His people*

3　Then the LORD said to Isaiah, "Go out now to meet Ahaz, you and your son Shear-jashub, at the end of the conduit of the upper pool, on the highway to the fuller's field,
4　and say to him, 'Take care, and be calm, have no fear and do not be

6:5
Ex 33:20;
Jer 9:3-8;
51:57

6:7
Jer 1:9;
Is 40:2;
1 John 1:7

6:8
Ezek 10:5;
Acts 9:4;
26:19
6:9
Ezek 3:11;
Matt 13:14,
15;
Mark 4:12;
Luke 8:10;
John 12:40;
Rom 11:8
*6:10
Ps 119:70;
Jer 5:21

6:11
Mic 3:12

6:12
Jer 4:29

*6:13
Is 1:9;
Job 14:7;
Ezra 9:2

7:1
2 Kin 16:1;
15:37; 15:25

7:2
v. 13; Is 8:12

*7:3
Is 10:21;
2 Kin 18:17
7:4
Is 30:15;
10:24; 35:4

6:10 *Render the hearts of this people insensitive.* Isaiah was to declare the purposes of God, even though the people would reject his ministry. His faithful proclamation would result in rebellion—hardness of heart.
6:13 *The holy seed is its stump.* From the stump that is left after the tree is cut down, a new nation will arise. Attention is on the faithful remnant with whom God will work.

7:3 *the conduit of the upper pool.* Ahaz, threatened by an alliance of Israel and Syria, checked the water supplies of Jerusalem. In the event of a siege, water was necessary for survival. Ephraim was one of the tribes of Israel (the northern kingdom), and Ephraim and Israel are used synonymously (v. 2).

fainthearted because of these two stubs of smoldering firebrands, on account of the fierce anger of Rezin and Aram, and the son of Remaliah.

5 'Because Aram, *with* Ephraim and the son of Remaliah, has planned evil against you, saying,

6 "Let us go up against Judah and terrorize it, and make for ourselves a breach in its walls, and set up the son of Tabeel as king in the midst of it,"

7 thus says the Lord GOD, "It shall not stand nor shall it come to pass.

8 "For the head of Aram is Damascus and the head of Damascus is Rezin (now within another 65 years Ephraim will be shattered, *so that it is* no longer a people),

9 and the head of Ephraim is Samaria and the head of Samaria is the son of Remaliah. If you will not believe, you surely shall not last." ' "

3. *The sign of Immanuel and the child who will typify Him*

10 Then the LORD spoke again to Ahaz, saying,

11 "Ask a sign for yourself from the LORD your God; make *it* deep as Sheol or high as heaven."

12 But Ahaz said, "I will not ask, nor will I test the LORD!"

13 Then he said, "Listen now, O house of David! Is it too slight a thing for you to try the patience of men, that you will try the patience of my God as well?

14 "Therefore the Lord Himself will give you a sign: Behold, a virgin will be with child and bear a son, and she will call His name [3]Immanuel.

15 "He will eat curds and honey at the time He knows *enough* to refuse evil and choose good.

16 "For before the boy will know *enough* to refuse evil and choose good, the land whose two kings you dread will be forsaken.

17 "The LORD will bring on you, on your people, and on your father's house such days as have never come since the day that Ephraim separated from Judah, the king of Assyria."

18 And it will come about in that day, that the LORD will whistle for the fly that is in the remotest part of the rivers of Egypt, and for the bee that is in the land of Assyria.

19 And they will all come and settle on the steep ravines, on the ledges of the cliffs, on all the thorn bushes, and on all the watering places.

20 In that day the Lord will shave with a razor, hired from regions beyond the Euphrates (*that is*, with the king of Assyria), the head and the hair of the legs; and it will also remove the beard.

21 Now it will come about in that day that a man may keep alive a heifer and a pair of sheep;

22 and it will happen that because of the abundance of the milk produced he will eat curds, for everyone that is left within the land will eat curds and honey.

23 And it will come about in that day, that every place where there used to be a thousand vines, *valued* at a thousand *shekels* of silver, will become briars and thorns.

Cross-references (margin):
7:7 Is 8:10
7:8 Is 17:1-3
*7:9 2 Chr 20:20
7:11 Is 37:30; 38:7,8; 2 Kin 19:29
*7:14 Matt 1:23; Luke 1:31; Is 9:6; 8:8
7:15 v. 22
7:16 Is 8:4
7:17 2 Chr 28:19; 1 Kin 12:16
7:18 Is 5:26
7:19 Is 2:19; Jer 16:16
7:20 Is 24:1; Ezek 5:1-4; Is 10:5,15; 8:7
7:23 Is 5:6

---

[3]I.e., God is with us

7:6 Ahaz had refused to join Israel and Syria in opposing Assyria. The two states to the north determined to depose Ahaz and place their own puppet on the throne of Jerusalem.

7:9 *If you will not believe, you surely shall not last.* At this time of crisis, Ahaz was weak in faith. Isaiah urged him to trust the LORD, assuring him that this was the only basis for confidence. Although stated in the negative, the positive is implied, "If you believe, surely you shall last" and you need not fear your enemies.

7:14 *Behold, a virgin will be with child.* When Ahaz refused to ask for a sign to strengthen his faith, at the explicit command of the LORD through Isaiah (7:10–12), he was given a sign that would indicate that the enemy would soon be removed (7:16). The word rendered *virgin* denotes an adolescent of marriageable age. The *sign* is that such a young woman would give birth to a child to be named *Immanuel*, "with us, God." This, itself, would be an expression of faith, which was lacking in Ahaz. During the childhood of Immanuel there would be no agricultural crops because of the devastation wrought by invading armies, so his diet would be limited to *curds and honey* (7:15) until he reached the age of discernment between good and evil (7:16). About three years later Damascus fell (732 B.C.), followed a decade later by Samaria (722 B.C.). *Immanuel* was intended to serve as a sign to the people. It may be compared with *Shear-jashub* (7:3), meaning "a remnant shall return" and *Maher-shalal-hash-baz* (8:3), "Swift is the booty, speedy is the prey." In 8:18 Isaiah and his sons are depicted as *signs and wonders in Israel from the LORD of hosts.* Although it is clear that Immanuel lived in the days of Ahaz and his immediate successors, we cannot identify him with certainty. The young woman, his mother, may have been the wife of Isaiah, a woman of the royal family, or any woman of Judah. This deliverance promised to Ahaz is declared to be typical in Matt. 1:23. The antitype of the "young woman" is the Virgin Mary, who miraculously gives birth to *Immanuel*, a name or title for Jesus, God manifest in the flesh (see Luke 1:26–38). The deliverance to be achieved by Him transcends the national problems of ancient Judah and her neighbors; the salvation that He brings is salvation from sin, man's greatest enemy.

24   *People* will come there with bows and arrows because all the land will be briars and thorns.

25   And as for all the hills which used to be cultivated with the hoe, you will not go there for fear of briars and thorns; but they will become a place for pasturing oxen and for sheep to trample.

B. *The coming war and the future deliverer*

1. *Sign of Maher-shalal-hash-baz*

8 Then the LORD said to me, "Take for yourself a large tablet and write on it in ordinary letters: Swift is the booty, speedy is the prey.

2   "And I will take to Myself faithful witnesses for testimony, Uriah the priest and Zechariah the son of Jeberechiah."

3   So I approached the prophetess, and she conceived and gave birth to a son. Then the LORD said to me, "Name him [4]Maher-shalal-hash-baz;

4   for before the boy knows how to cry out 'My father' or 'My mother,' the wealth of Damascus and the spoil of Samaria will be carried away before the king of Assyria."

2. *The river overflowing its banks*

5   And again the LORD spoke to me further, saying,

6   "Inasmuch as these people have rejected the gently flowing waters of Shiloah,
      And rejoice in Rezin and the son of Remaliah;

7   "Now therefore, behold, the Lord is about to bring on them the
          strong and abundant waters of the Euphrates,
      Even the king of Assyria and all his glory;
      And it will rise up over all its channels and go over all its banks.

8   "Then it will sweep on into Judah, it will overflow and pass through,
      It will reach even to the neck;
      And the spread of its wings will fill the breadth of your land, O
          Immanuel.

3. *The stone of stumbling*

9   "Be broken, O peoples, and be shattered;
      And give ear, all remote places of the earth.
      Gird yourselves, yet be shattered;
      Gird yourselves, yet be shattered.

10   "Devise a plan but it will be thwarted;
      State a proposal, but it will not stand,
      For God is with us."

11   For thus the LORD spoke to me with mighty power and instructed me not to walk in the way of this people, saying,

12   "You are not to say, '*It is* a conspiracy!'
      In regard to all that this people call a conspiracy,
      And you are not to fear what they fear or be in dread
          of *it*.

13   "It is the LORD of hosts whom you should regard as holy.
      And He shall be your fear,
      And He shall be your dread.

14   "Then He shall become a sanctuary;
      But to both the houses of Israel, a stone to strike and a rock to
          stumble over,

---

[4]I.e., swift is the booty, speedy is the prey

Cross references (right margin):

7:25 — Is 5:17
8:1 — Is 30:8; Hab 2:2
8:2 — 2 Kin 16:10
8:4 — Is 7:16; 7:8,9
*8:6 — Neh 3:15; John 9:7; Is 7:1,2,6
8:7 — Is 17:12,13; 7:20; 10:5,6
8:8 — Is 10:6; 30:28; 7:14
8:10 — Job 5:12; Is 7:7; Rom 8:31
8:11 — Ezek 3:14; 2:8
8:12 — Is 7:2; 1 Pet 3:14,15
8:13 — Is 5:16; 29:23; Num 20:12
8:14 — Ezek 11:16; Luke 2:34; Rom 9:33; 1 Pet 2:8

8:3 The sign given to Ahaz has a double fulfillment. The first fulfillment is specified here. The birth of this son was not a virgin birth in the same sense that the birth of Christ was. The prophetess, who may have been a virgin at the time 7:14 was spoken, after entering into a normal marriage relationship with Isaiah, gave birth to Maher-shalal-hash-baz. Some hold that this little boy with the long name was therefore a type of the Messianic Immanuel. Others do not. The second fulfillment of this sign occurred in the birth of Christ, who was Himself the true Immanuel. (See also note

to 7:14.)
The prophetess is the wife of Isaiah. She bears her title because of her relationship to the prophet, not because of any prophetic gift of her own.
8:6 *the . . . waters of Shiloah*, the modern Ain Silwan, are located southwest of Mt. Moriah. The quiet waters of Shiloah are contrasted with the turbulent *waters of the Euphrates* of 8:7. Since Judah has rejected Shiloah, symbolic of God's rule, she would be overwhelmed by the king of Assyria, from beyond the Euphrates.

And a snare and a trap for the inhabitants of Jerusalem.

8:15
Is 28:13;
Matt 21:44;
Luke 20:18;
Rom 9:32

15   "And many will stumble over them,
Then they will fall and be broken;
They will even be snared and caught."

4. *Command to trust the* LORD

8:16
vv. 1,2;
Dan 12:4
8:17
Is 54:8;
Hab 2:3
8:18
Heb 2:13;
Ps 71:7;
Zech 3:8
8:19
1 Sam 28:8;
Is 19:3; 30:2;
45:11
8:20
Luke 16:29;
Mic 3:6
8:21
Is 9:20,21;
Rev 16:11

16   Bind up the testimony, seal the law among my disciples.

17   And I will wait for the LORD who is hiding His face from the house of Jacob; I will even look eagerly for Him.

18   Behold, I and the children whom the LORD has given me are for signs and wonders in Israel from the LORD of hosts, who dwells on Mount Zion.

19   And when they say to you, "Consult the mediums and the spiritists who whisper and mutter," should not a people consult their God? *Should they consult* the dead on behalf of the living?

20   To the law and to the testimony! If they do not speak according to this word, it is because they have no dawn.

21   And they will pass through the land hard-pressed and famished, and it will turn out that when they are hungry, they will be enraged and curse their king and their God as they face upward.

8:22
Is 5:30; 9:1

22   Then they will look to the earth, and behold, distress and darkness, the gloom of anguish; and *they will be* driven away into darkness.

5. *The birth of the Messianic king*

*9:1
2 Kin 15:29;
2 Chr 16:4

9 But there will be no *more* gloom for her who was in anguish; in earlier times He treated the land of Zebulun and the land of Naphtali with contempt, but later on He shall make *it* glorious, by the way of the sea, on the other side of Jordan, Galilee of the Gentiles.

9:2
Matt 4:15,16

2   The people who walk in darkness
Will see a great light;
Those who live in a dark land,
The light will shine on them.

9:3
Is 26:15;
35:10;
1 Sam 30:16

3   Thou shalt multiply the nation,
Thou shalt increase their gladness;
They will be glad in Thy presence
As with the gladness of harvest,
As men rejoice when they divide the spoil.

9:4
Is 10:27;
14:4; 10:26

4   For Thou shalt break the yoke of their burden and the staff on their shoulders,
The rod of their oppressor, as at the battle of Midian.

9:5
Is 2:4
*9:6

5   For every boot of the booted warrior in the *battle* tumult,
And cloak rolled in blood, will be for burning, fuel for the fire.

Is 7:14;
Luke 2:11;
John 3:16;
Matt 28:18;
1 Cor 15:25;
Is 28:29;
10:21; 63:16;
Eph 2:14
9:7

6   For a child will be born to us, a son will be given to us;
And the government will rest on His shoulders;
And His name will be called Wonderful Counselor, Mighty God,
Eternal Father, Prince of Peace.

Dan 2:44;
Luke 1:32,
33; Is 16:15;
11:4,5; 37:32

7   There will be no end to the increase of *His* government or of peace,
On the throne of David and over his kingdom,
To establish it and to uphold it with justice and righteousness
From now on and forevermore.
The zeal of the LORD of hosts will accomplish this.

9:1 *In earlier times,* 734 B.C., Tiglath-pileser III deprived Israel of Ephraim, Zebulun, and Naphtali (2 Kin. 15:29); *later on,* looks forward to a time of restoration. Matthew 4:13–17 sees a fulfillment of these words in Jesus' preaching in Galilee.

9:6 *For a child will be born to us.* Although some commentators see this as a prophecy of Hezekiah's birth, it is more probable that the words express hope for a future deliverance. This would take place in the *later on* of 9:1. This proclamation of the birth of the Messiah king undoubtedly refers to the Lord Jesus Christ as the God-Man. The title

Eternal Father is more literally "Father of Eternity" in the sense that He, as Creator, begot all things. Thus it does not involve any confusion between the Father and the Son in the Holy Trinity. The title *Prince of Peace* refers to the spiritual peace of the regenerate believer. The titles applied to Christ in this verse are only a few of the many ascribed to Him in Scripture. Among the others are: *God* (Is. 40:9; John 20:28), *the Almighty* (Rev. 1:8), *the bread of life* (John 6:35), *good shepherd* (John 10:14), *Lord of glory* (1 Cor. 2:8), *Son of David* (Matt. 9:27), *King of kings* (Rev. 17:14), and *Lamb* (Rev. 13:8).

C. The doom of boastful (Ephraim) Samaria

1. Samaria's pride

8   The Lord sends a message against Jacob,
And it falls on Israel.

9   And all the people know *it*,
That is, Ephraim and the inhabitants of Samaria,
Asserting in pride and in arrogance of heart:

10   "The bricks have fallen down,
But we will rebuild with smooth stones;
The sycamores have been cut down,
But we will replace *them* with cedars."

11   Therefore the LORD raises against them adversaries from Rezin,
And spurs their enemies on,

12   The Arameans on the east and the Philistines on the west;
And they devour Israel with gaping jaws.
In *spite of* all this His anger does not turn away,
And His hand is still stretched out.

2. Samaria's hypocrisy

13   Yet the people do not turn back to Him who struck them,
Nor do they seek the LORD of hosts.

14   So the LORD cuts off head and tail from Israel,
Both palm branch and bulrush in a single day.

15   The head is the elder and honorable man,
And the prophet who teaches falsehood is the tail.

16   For those who guide this people are leading *them* astray;
And those who are guided by them are brought to confusion.

17   Therefore the Lord does not take pleasure in their young men,
Nor does He have pity on their orphans or their widows;
For every one of them is godless and an evildoer,
And every mouth is speaking foolishness.
In *spite of* all this His anger does not turn away,
And His hand is still stretched out.

3. The self-destructiveness of sin

18   For wickedness burns like a fire;
It consumes briars and thorns;
It even sets the thickets of the forest aflame,
And they roll upward in a column of smoke.

19   By the fury of the LORD of hosts the land is burned up,
And the people are like fuel for the fire;
No man spares his brother.

20   And they slice off *what is* on the right hand but *still* are hungry,
And they eat *what is* on the left hand but they are not satisfied;
Each of them eats the flesh of his own arm.

21   Manasseh *devours* Ephraim, and Ephraim Manasseh,
And together they are against Judah.
In *spite of* all this His anger does not turn away,
And His hand is still stretched out.

4. The oppressors doomed to captivity

10   Woe to those who enact evil statutes,
And to those who constantly record unjust decisions,

2   So as to deprive the needy of justice,
And rob the poor of My people of *their* rights,
In order that widows may be their spoil,
And that they may plunder the orphans.

3   Now what will you do in the day of punishment,
And in the devastation which will come from afar?
To whom will you flee for help?
And where will you leave your wealth?

9:9
Is 7:8,9;
46:12

9:11
Is 7:1,8

9:12
2 Kin 16:6;
2 Chr 28:18;
Ps 79:7;
Is 5:25

9:13
Jer 5:3;
Hos 7:10;
Is 31:1
9:14
Is 19:15;
Rev 18:8
9:15
Is 3:2,3;
28:15
9:16
Is 3:12
9:17
Jer 18:21;
Is 27:11;
10:6;
Mic 7:2;
Is 5:25

9:18
Is 10:17;
Mal 4:1

9:19
Is 10:6;
Joel 2:3;
Is 1:31; 24:6;
Mic 7:2,6
9:20
Is 8:21,22;
49:26

9:21
Is 5:25

10:1
Ps 94:20

10:2
Is 5:23; 1:23

10:3
Job 31:14;
Hos 9:7;
Luke 19:44;
Is 5:26; 20:6

10:4 Is 24:22; 22:2; 5:25	4 Nothing *remains* but to crouch among the captives Or fall among the slain. In *spite of* all this His anger does not turn away, And His hand is still stretched out.

D. *The false empire vanquished: a glorious empire to come*

1. *God's instrument of judgment shall in turn be judged*

a. *Assyria, the rod, to be destroyed*

***10:5** Jer 51:20	5 Woe to Assyria, the rod of My anger And the staff in whose hands is My indignation,
10:6 Is 9:17,19; Jer 34:22; Is 5:25,29	6 I send it against a godless nation And commission it against the people of My fury To capture booty and to seize plunder, And to trample them down like mud in the streets.
10:7 Gen 50:20	7 Yet it does not so intend Nor does it plan so in its heart, But rather it is its purpose to destroy, And to cut off many nations.

10:8
2 Kin 18:24,
34; 19:10ff
10:9
Amos 6:2;
2 Chr 35:20;
2 Kin 16:9
10:10
2 Kin 19:17,
18
	8 For it says, "Are not my princes all kings?
	9 "Is not Calno like Carchemish,
	    Or Hamath like Arpad,
	    Or Samaria like Damascus?
	10 "As my hand has reached to the kingdoms of the idols,
	    Whose graven images *were* greater than those of Jerusalem and
	        Samaria,
	11 Shall I not do to Jerusalem and her images
	    Just as I have done to Samaria and her idols?"

10:12 2 Kin 19:31; Jer 50:18; Is 37:23	**12** So it will be that when the Lord has completed all His work on Mount Zion and on Jerusalem, *He will say*, "I will punish the fruit of the arrogant heart of the king of Assyria and the pomp of his haughtiness."

10:13
Is 37:24;
Ezek 28:4;
Dan 4:30
	13 For he has said,
	    "By the power of my hand and by my wisdom I did *this*,
	    For I have understanding;
	    And I removed the boundaries of the peoples,
	    And plundered their treasures,
	    And like a mighty man I brought down *their* inhabitants,

10:14
Job 31:25
	14 And my hand reached to the riches of the peoples like a nest,
	    And as one gathers abandoned eggs, I gathered all the earth;
	    And there was not one that flapped its wing or opened *its* beak or
	        chirped."

10:15
Jer 51:20;
Rom 9:20,21;
v. 5
	15 Is the axe to boast itself over the one who chops with it?
	    Is the saw to exalt itself over the one who wields it?
	    That would be like a club wielding those who lift it,
	    Or like a rod lifting *him who* is not wood.

10:16
Is 17:4;
Ps 106:15;
v. 18
	16 Therefore the Lord, the GOD of hosts, will send a wasting disease
	        among his stout warriors;
	    And under his glory a fire will be kindled like a burning flame.

10:17
Is 30:33;
37:23; 27:4
10:18
Jer 21:14
	17 And the light of Israel will become a fire and his Holy One a flame,
	    And it will burn and devour his thorns and his briars in a single day.
	18 And He will destroy the glory of his forest and of his fruitful garden,
	        both soul and body;
	    And it will be as when a sick man wastes away.

10:19 Is 21:17	19 And the rest of the trees of his forest will be so small in number That a child could write them down.

b. *A remnant of Israel to be saved*

10:20 2 Kin 16:7; 2 Chr 28:20; Is 17:7,8	**20** Now it will come about in that day that the remnant of Israel, and those of the house of Jacob who have escaped, will never again rely on the one who struck them, but will truly rely on the LORD, the Holy One of Israel.

10:5 *Assyria, the rod of My anger.* God used Assyria to humble sinful Israel and Judah. The proud Assyrian, how-   ever, would be humbled in due time (10:12).

21 A remnant will return, the remnant of Jacob, to the mighty God.
22 For though your people, O Israel, may be like the sand of the sea,
    Only a remnant within them will return;
    A destruction is determined, overflowing with righteousness.
23 For a complete destruction, one that is decreed, the Lord GOD of hosts will execute in the midst of the whole land.
24 Therefore thus says the Lord GOD of hosts, "O My people who dwell in Zion, do not fear the Assyrian who strikes you with the rod and lifts up his staff against you, the way Egypt *did*.
25 "For in a very little while My indignation *against you* will be spent, and My anger *will be directed* to their destruction."
26 And the LORD of hosts will arouse a scourge against him like the slaughter of Midian at the rock of Oreb; and His staff will be over the sea, and He will lift it up the way *He did* in Egypt.
27 So it will be in that day, that his burden will be removed from your shoulders and his yoke from your neck, and the yoke will be broken because of fatness.
28 He has come against Aiath,
    He has passed through Migron;
    At Michmash he deposited his baggage.
29 They have gone through the pass, *saying*,
    "Geba will be our lodging place."
    Ramah is terrified, and Gibeah of Saul has fled away.
30 Cry aloud with your voice, O daughter of Gallim!
    Pay attention, Laishah *and* wretched Anathoth!
31 Madmenah has fled.
    The inhabitants of Gebim have sought refuge.
32 Yet today he will halt at Nob;
    He shakes his fist at the mountain of the daughter of Zion, the hill of
      Jerusalem.
33 Behold, the Lord, the GOD of hosts, will lop off the boughs with a
      terrible crash;
    Those also who are tall in stature will be cut down,
    And those who are lofty will be abased.
34 And He will cut down the thickets of the forest with an iron *axe*,
    And Lebanon will fall by the Mighty One.

2. The age of Messiah

a. *The Branch out of Jesse*

11 Then a shoot will spring from the stem of Jesse,
    And a branch from his roots will bear fruit.
2 And the Spirit of the LORD will rest on Him,
    The spirit of wisdom and understanding,
    The spirit of counsel and strength,
    The spirit of knowledge and the fear of the LORD.
3 And He will delight in the fear of the LORD,
    And He will not judge by what His eyes see,
    Nor make a decision by what His ears hear;
4 But with righteousness He will judge the poor,
    And decide with fairness for the afflicted of the earth;
    And He will strike the earth with the rod of His mouth,
    And with the breath of His lips He will slay the wicked.
5 Also righteousness will be the belt about His loins,
    And faithfulness the belt about His waist.
6 And the wolf will dwell with the lamb,
    And the leopard will lie down with the kid,
    And the calf and the young lion [5]and the fatling together;

[5]Some versions read *will feed together*

Cross-reference column:

10:21 Is 6:13; 9:6
10:22 Rom 9:27,28; Is 28:22
10:23 Dan 9:27
10:24 Ps 87:5,6; Is 37:6; Ex 5:14-16
10:25 Is 17:14; v. 5
10:26 Is 37:36-38; Judg 7:25; Ex 14:16,27
10:27 Is 9:4; 30:23
10:28 1 Sam 14:2; 13:2,5; 17:22
10:29 Josh 21:17; 18:25; 1 Sam 10:26
10:30 1 Sam 25:44; Josh 21:18
10:31 Josh 15:31
10:32 1 Sam 21:1; Neh 11:32; Is 13:2; 37:22
10:33 Amos 2:9

*11:1 Zech 6:12; Rev 5:5; Acts 13:23; Is 4:2
11:2 Is 61:1; Matt 3:16; John 1:32
11:3 John 2:25; 7:24
11:4 Is 9:7; 3:14; 29:19; Mal 4:6; Job 4:9; 2 Thess 2:8
11:5 Eph 6:14; Is 25:1
11:6 Is 65:25

11:1 *a shoot . . . from the stem of Jesse*. Jesse, the father of David, is likened to a tree. Judgment on Israel may be likened to the felling of the tree. The judgment is not final, however, for the stump will produce a new shoot. Thus God's covenant with David is fulfilled. This description of the ideal king of David's line is interpreted in the New Testament as being fulfilled in Christ. (See especially Rev. 5:5.)

And a little boy will lead them.

11:7
Is 65:25

7 Also the cow and the bear will graze;
   Their young will lie down together;
   And the lion will eat straw like the ox.

8 And the nursing child will play by the hole of the cobra,
   And the weaned child will put his hand on the viper's den.

11:9
Job 5:23;
Hab 2:14

9 They will not hurt or destroy in all My holy mountain,
   For the earth will be full of the knowledge of the LORD
   As the waters cover the sea.

b. Messiah to restore Israel

11:10
Rom 15:12;
John 3:14,15;
Luke 2:32;
Is 14:3

10 Then it will come about in that day
    That the nations will resort to the root of Jesse,
    Who will stand as a signal for the peoples;
    And His resting place will be glorious.

11:11
Zech 10:10;
Mic 7:12;
Is 66:19

11 Then it will happen on that day that the Lord
    Will again recover the second time with His hand
    The remnant of His people, who will remain,
    From Assyria, Egypt, Pathros, Cush, Elam, Shinar, Hamath,
    And from the islands of the sea.

11:12
v. 10;
Zech 10:6;
Is 24:16

12 And He will lift up a standard for the nations,
    And will assemble the banished ones of Israel,
    And will gather the dispersed of Judah
    From the four corners of the earth.

11:13
Jer 3:18;
Ezek 37:16,
17,22;
Hos 1:11

13 Then the jealousy of Ephraim will depart,
    And those who harass Judah will be cut off;
    Ephraim will not be jealous of Judah,
    And Judah will not harass Ephraim.

11:14
Dan 11:41;
Joel 3:19;
Is 16:14;
25:10

14 And they will swoop down on the slopes of the Philistines on the
        west;
    Together they will plunder the sons of the east;
    They will possess Edom and Moab;
    And the sons of Ammon will be subject to them.

*11:15
Is 43:16;
19:16; 7:20;
8:7

15 And the LORD will utterly destroy
    The tongue of the Sea of Egypt;
    And He will wave His hand over the River
    With His scorching wind;
    And He will strike it into seven streams,
    And make *men* walk over dry-shod.

11:16
Is 19:23;
62:10;
Ex 14:26-29;
Is 51:10;
63:12,13

16 And there will be a highway from Assyria
    For the remnant of His people who will be left,
    Just as there was for Israel
    In the day that they came up out of the land of Egypt.

3. Thanksgiving for God's salvation

12:1
Is 26:1; 25:1;
40:1,2

12 Then you will say on that day,
    "I will give thanks to Thee, O LORD;
    For although Thou wast angry with me,
    Thine anger is turned away,
    And Thou dost comfort me.

12:2
Is 33:2; 26:3;
Ex 15:2;
Ps 118:14

2 "Behold, God is my salvation,
   I will trust and not be afraid;
   For the LORD GOD is my strength and song,
   And He has become my salvation."

12:3
John 4:10;
7:37,38;
Is 41:18

3 Therefore you will joyously draw water
   From the springs of salvation.

4 And in that day you will say,
   "Give thanks to the LORD, call on His name.
   Make known His deeds among the peoples;
   Make *them* remember that His name is exalted."

11:15 *the tongue of the Sea of Egypt.* The Gulf of Suez. God is depicted as providing a passageway for the safe return of His people, as He did at the exodus.

5 Praise the LORD in song, for He has done excellent things;
Let this be known throughout the earth.

6 Cry aloud and shout for joy, O inhabitant of Zion,
For great in your midst is the Holy One of Israel.

III. *Volume of burdens upon heathen nations (13:1–23:18)*

A. *First burden of Babylon*

1. *The doom of Babylon*

13 The oracle concerning Babylon which Isaiah the son of Amoz saw.
2 Lift up a standard on the [6]bare hill,
Raise your voice to them,
Wave the hand that they may enter the doors of the nobles.

3 I have commanded My consecrated ones,
I have even called My mighty warriors,
My proudly exulting ones,
To *execute* My anger.

4 A sound of tumult on the mountains,
Like that of many people!
A sound of the uproar of kingdoms,
Of nations gathered together!
The LORD of hosts is mustering the army for battle.

5 They are coming from a far country
From the farthest horizons,
The LORD and His instruments of indignation,
To destroy the whole land.

6 Wail, for the day of the LORD is near!
It will come as destruction from the Almighty.

7 Therefore all hands will fall limp,
And every man's heart will melt.

8 And they will be terrified,
Pains and anguish will take hold of *them*;
They will writhe like a woman in labor,
They will look at one another in astonishment,
Their faces aflame.

9 Behold, the day of the LORD is coming,
Cruel, with fury and burning anger,
To make the land a desolation;
And He will exterminate its sinners from it.

10 For the stars of heaven and their constellations
Will not flash forth their light;
The sun will be dark when it rises,
And the moon will not shed its light.

11 Thus I will punish the world for its evil,
And the wicked for their iniquity;
I will also put an end to the arrogance of the proud,
And abase the haughtiness of the ruthless.

12 I will make mortal man scarcer than pure gold,
And mankind than the gold of Ophir.

13 Therefore I shall make the heavens tremble,
And the earth will be shaken from its place
At the fury of the LORD of hosts
In the day of His burning anger.

14 And it will be that like a hunted gazelle,
Or like sheep with none to gather *them*,
They will each turn to his own people,
And each one flee to his own land.

15 Anyone who is found will be thrust through,
And anyone who is captured will fall by the sword.

16 Their little ones also will be dashed to pieces
Before their eyes;

[6]Or, *wind-swept mountain*

12:5
Is 24:14;
Ex 15:1;
Ps 98:1
12:6
Zeph 3:14;
Is 49:26

13:1
Jer chs. 50,51
13:2
Jer 50:2;
51:25;
Is 10:32
13:3
Joel 3:11;
Ps 149:2

13:4
Is 5:30

13:5
Is 5:26;
42:13; 10:5;
24:1

13:6
Zeph 1:7;
Is 10:25;
Joel 1:15
13:7
Ezek 7:17;
21:7
13:8
Is 21:3; 26:17

13:9
Is 66:15,16

13:10
Is 5:30;
Joel 2:10;
Matt 24:29;
Mark 13:24;
Luke 21:25
13:11
Is 26:21;
11:4; 2:11;
Jer 48:29

13:12
Is 4:1; 6:11,
12
13:13
Is 34:4; 51:6;
Jer 10:10;
Amos 8:8;
Hag 2:6

13:14
1 Kin 22:17;
Jer 50:16;
51:9

13:15
Is 14:19

13:16
Ps 137:9;
Nah 3:10;
Zech 14:2

Their houses will be plundered
And their wives ravished.

17 Behold, I am going to stir up the Medes against them,
Who will not value silver or take pleasure in gold,

18 And *their* bows will mow down the young men,
They will not even have compassion on the fruit of the womb,
Nor will their eye pity children.

19 And Babylon, the beauty of kingdoms, the glory of the Chaldeans'
pride,
Will be as when God overthrew Sodom and Gomorrah.

20 It will never be inhabited or lived in from generation to generation;
Nor will the Arab pitch *his* tent there,
Nor will shepherds make *their flocks* lie down there.

21 But desert creatures will lie down there,
And their houses will be full of owls,
Ostriches also will live there, and shaggy goats will frolic there.

22 And hyenas will howl in their fortified towers
And jackals in their luxurious palaces.
Her *fateful* time also will soon come
And her days will not be prolonged.

2. Taunt against the king of Babylon

14 When the LORD will have compassion on Jacob, and again choose Israel, and settle them in their own land, then strangers will join them and attach themselves to the house of Jacob.

2 And the peoples will take them along and bring them to their place, and the house of Israel will possess them as an inheritance in the land of the LORD as male servants and female servants; and they will take their captors captive, and will rule over their oppressors.

3 And it will be in the day when the LORD gives you rest from your pain and turmoil and harsh service in which you have been enslaved,

4 that you will take up this taunt against the king of Babylon, and say,
"How the oppressor has ceased,
And how fury has ceased!

5 "The LORD has broken the staff of the wicked,
The scepter of rulers

6 Which used to strike the peoples in fury with unceasing strokes,
Which subdued the nations in anger with unrestrained persecution.

7 "The whole earth is at rest *and* is quiet;
They break forth into shouts of joy.

8 "Even the cypress trees rejoice over you, *and* the cedars of Lebanon,
saying,
'Since you were laid low, no *tree* cutter comes up against us.'

9 "Sheol from beneath is excited over you to meet you when you come;
It arouses for you the spirits of the dead, all the leaders of the earth;
It raises all the kings of the nations from their thrones.

10 "They will all respond and say to you,
'Even you have been made weak as we,
You have become like us.

11 'Your pomp *and* the music of your harps
Have been brought down to Sheol;
Maggots are spread out *as your bed* beneath you,
And worms are your covering.'

12 "How you have fallen from heaven,

Side references (left column):

*13:17 / Is 21:2; Jer 51:11; Dan 5:28
13:18 / 2 Kin 8:12; Ezek 9:5,10
13:19 / Is 21:9; Dan 4:30; Gen 19:24; Deut 29:23; Jer 49:18
*13:20 / Jer 51:37-43
*13:21 / Is 34:11-15
13:22 / Jer 51:33
14:1 / Ps 102:13; Zech 1:17; 2:12; Is 60:4, 5,10; Eph 2:12-19
14:2 / Is 49:22; 60:9,10; 66:20; 60:14
14:3 / Is 40:2
14:4 / Is 13:19; Hab 2:6; Rev 18:6
14:6 / Is 10:14; 47:6
14:8 / Is 55:12
14:9 / Ezek 32:21
14:11 / Is 5:14; Ezek 28:13; Is 51:8
*14:12 / Is 34:4; Luke 10:18

13:17 *the Medes,* an ancient Aryan (Iranian) people located southwest of the Caspian Sea, joined forces with the Babylonians (Chaldeans) to bring about the destruction of Nineveh (612 B.C.). Subsequently, however, the Medes were incorporated into the Persian empire, which, under Cyrus, captured Babylon (539 B.C.).

13:20 Scripture foretold the utter ruin of Babylon and prophesied that it should never be rebuilt. It never has to this day. Consonant with the prophecy, then, it is proper to conclude that the Babylon of the Apocalypse (Rev. 17) is

not a literal one. Undoubtedly it is a political and ecclesiastical combination of which the Old Testament Babylon is a prophetic type and example.

13:21 *shaggy goats.* In myth, part goat, part man.

14:12 Scripture uses many names for Satan. Among them are (1) *liar* (John 8:44); (2) *prince of the power of the air* (Eph. 2:2); (3) *your adversary, the devil* (1 Pet. 5:8); and (4) *the dragon, the serpent of old, who is the devil and Satan* (Rev. 20:2). His origin is obscure, but 14:12-15; Ezek. 28:12-19; and Luke 10:18 throw light on it. Satan is (1) very

O star of the morning, son of the dawn!
You have been cut down to the earth,
You who have weakened the nations!

13 "But you said in your heart,
'I will ascend to heaven;
I will raise my throne above the stars of God,
And I will sit on the mount of assembly
In the recesses of the north.

14 'I will ascend above the heights of the clouds;
I will make myself like the Most High.'

15 "Nevertheless you will be thrust down to Sheol,
To the recesses of the pit.

16 "Those who see you will gaze at you,
They will ponder over you, *saying,*
'Is this the man who made the earth tremble,
Who shook kingdoms,

17 Who made the world like a wilderness
And overthrew its cities,
Who did not allow his prisoners to *go* home?'

18 "All the kings of the nations lie in glory,
Each in his own tomb.

19 "But you have been cast out of your tomb
Like a rejected branch,
Clothed with the slain who are pierced with a sword,
Who go down to the stones of the pit,
Like a trampled corpse.

20 "You will not be united with them in burial,
Because you have ruined your country,
You have slain your people.
May the offspring of evildoers not be mentioned forever.

21 "Prepare for his sons a place of slaughter
Because of the iniquity of their fathers.
They must not arise and take possession of the earth
And fill the face of the world with cities."

22 "And I will rise up against them," declares the LORD of hosts, "and will cut off from Babylon name and survivors, offspring and posterity," declares the LORD.

23 "I will also make it a possession for the hedgehog, and swamps of water, and I will sweep it with the broom of destruction," declares the LORD of hosts.

B. *The overthrow of Assyria*

24 The LORD of hosts has sworn saying, "Surely, just as I have intended so it has happened, and just as I have planned so it will stand,

25 to break Assyria in My land, and I will trample him on My mountains. Then his yoke will be removed from them, and his burden removed from their shoulder.

26 "This is the plan devised against the whole earth; and this is the hand that is stretched out against all the nations.

27 "For the LORD of hosts has planned, and who can frustrate *it*? And as for His stretched-out hand, who can turn it back?"

Marginal references:

14:13 Ezek 28:2; Dan 8:10
14:14 Is 47:8; 2 Thess 2:4
14:15 Matt 11:23
14:16 Jer 50:23
14:17 Joel 2:3; Is 45:13
14:19 Is 22:16-18; Jer 41:7,9; Is 5:25
14:20 Job 18:19; Ps 21:10; 37:28; Is 31:2
14:21 Ex 20:5; Is 13:16; Matt 23:35; Is 27:6
14:22 Is 26:14; Prov 10:7; Is 47:9
14:23 Is 34:11-15; Zeph 2:14; Is 13:6
14:24 Is 45:23; 55:8,9; Acts 4:28
14:25 Is 10:12,27
14:26 Is 23:9; Ex 15:12
14:27 2 Chr 20:6; Is 43:13; Dan 4:31,35

---

wicked (1 John 3:8); (2) very shrewd and cunning (2 Cor. 11:3,13–15; Rev. 12:9); and (3) the great enemy of God, who has many helpers (Luke 8:30; 11:15; Eph. 6:12). Actually Satan is already a defeated foe (John 12:31). His destiny and doom are sure. At last he will be cast into the lake of fire and there be tormented day and night forever (Rev. 20:10). Satan's works are numerous and various: (1) he tempts the servants of God (2 Cor. 2:11; 1 Thess. 3:5); (2) he blinds men's eyes (2 Cor. 4:3,4); (3) he seeks to destroy the Word of God (Mark 4:15); (4) he becomes regnant in individuals or takes up his abode in their hearts (John 13:27); (5) he accuses believers before God (Rev. 12:10); and (6) he seeks to harass and molest the servants of God (1 Thess. 2:18; 1 Pet. 5:8). Christians are commanded to resist the devil (James 4:7); to watch and pray (Matt. 26:41); and to employ the shield of faith (Eph. 6:16). Satan is responsible for sin, having led Adam and Eve to sin in the Garden.

In this particular passage (14:12) the title *star of the*

morning (or, Lucifer) is used. This taunt is addressed by the denizens of Sheol to the *king of Babylon* (v. 4), but the dimensions of the God-defying ambition expressed in vv. 13,14 surpass anything that could be put into the mouth of a mere human being (even hyperbolically). No human king is ever represented in any ancient Semitic literature, either Hebrew or pagan, as vaunting himself to set his throne above the heights of the clouds like the Most High God. Therefore the best interpretation of this passage is to see in the human king of Babylon a tool in the hand of the devil himself, who has empowered and directed him in his opposition to God's people and cause.

O star of the morning, son of the dawn! As the morning star quickly disappears when the sun rises, so the Babylonian king, brilliant in his hour, will soon be removed from his place. The Babylonian worship of Ishtar, later equated with Venus, an astral deity, may have occasioned the figure of speech used of the Babylonian ruler.

C. Burden of Philistia

14:28
2 Kin 16:20
14:29
Jer 47:1-7;
2 Chr 26:6

28 In the year that King Ahaz died this oracle came:
29 "Do not rejoice, O Philistia, all of you,
Because the rod that struck you is broken;
For from the serpent's root a viper will come out,
And its fruit will be a flying serpent.

14:30
Is 3:14,15;
7:21; 8:21;
Jer 25:16,20

30 "And those who are most helpless will eat,
And the needy will lie down in security;
I will destroy your root with famine,
And it will kill off your survivors.

14:31
Is 3:26; v. 29;
Jer 1:14;
Is 34:16

31 "Wail, O gate; cry, O city;
Melt away, O Philistia, all of you;
For smoke comes from the north,
And there is no straggler in his ranks.

14:32
Is 37:9;
Ps 87:1,5;
Zeph 3:12;
Zech 11:11

32 "How then will one answer the messengers of the nation?
That the LORD has founded Zion,
And the afflicted of His people will seek refuge in it."

D. Burden of Moab

1. Scenes of her coming devastation

15:1
Is 11:14;
Jer 48;
Ezek 25:8-11;
Jer 48:41
15:2
Lev 21:5

15 The oracle concerning Moab.
Surely in a night Ar of Moab is devastated *and* ruined;
Surely in a night Kir of Moab is devastated *and* ruined.
2 They have gone up to the temple and *to* Dibon, *even* to the high
places to weep.
Moab wails over Nebo and Medeba;
Everyone's head is bald *and* every beard is cut off.

15:3
Jon 3:6-8;
Jer 48:38;
Is 22:4

3 In their streets they have girded themselves with sackcloth;
On their housetops and in their squares
Everyone is wailing, dissolved in tears.
4 Heshbon and Elealeh also cry out,
Their voice is heard all the way to Jahaz;
Therefore the armed men of Moab cry aloud;
His soul trembles within him.

15:5
Jer 48:5,31,
34; Is 59:7

5 My heart cries out for Moab;
His fugitives are as far as Zoar *and* Eglath-shelishiyah,
For they go up the ascent of Luhith weeping;
Surely on the road to Horonaim they raise a cry of distress over *their*
ruin.

15:6
Is 19:5-7;
Joel 1:10-12

6 For the waters of Nimrim are desolate.
Surely the grass is withered, the tender grass died out,
There is no green thing.

15:7
Is 30:6

7 Therefore the abundance *which* they have acquired and stored up
They carry off over the brook of Arabim.
8 For the cry of distress has gone around the territory of Moab,
Its wail *goes* as far as Eglaim and its wailing even to Beer-elim.

15:9
2 Kin 17:25;
Jer 50:17

9 For the waters of Dimon are full of blood;
Surely I will bring added *woes* upon Dimon,
A lion upon the fugitives of Moab and upon the remnant of the land.

2. Moab's pride and fall

16:1
2 Kin 3:4;
14:7; Is 10:32

16 Send the *tribute* lamb to the ruler of the land,
From Sela by way of the wilderness to the mountain of the daughter
of Zion.

16:2
Num 21:13,
14

2 Then, like fleeing birds *or* scattered nestlings,
The daughters of Moab will be at the fords of the Arnon.

16:3
Is 25:4

3 "Give *us* advice, make a decision;
Cast your shadow like night at high noon;
Hide the outcasts, do not betray the fugitive.

16:4
Is 9:4; 54:14

4 "Let the outcasts of Moab stay with you;
Be a hiding place to them from the destroyer."
For the extortioner has come to an end, destruction has ceased,

869

...essors have completely *disappeared* from the land.
...rone will even be established in lovingkindness,
...d a judge will sit on it in faithfulness in the tent of David;
5 ...reover, he will seek justice
...d be prompt in righteousness.

...Ve have heard of the pride of Moab, an excessive pride;
Even of his arrogance, pride, and fury;
His idle boasts are false.
Therefore Moab shall wail; everyone of Moab shall wail.
You shall moan for the raisin cakes of Kir-hareseth
As those who are utterly stricken.
For the fields of Heshbon have withered, the vines of Sibmah *as
well*;
The lords of the nations have trampled down its choice clusters
Which reached as far as Jazer *and* wandered to the deserts;
Its tendrils spread themselves out *and* passed over the sea.

9   Therefore I will weep bitterly for Jazer, for the vine of Sibmah;
I will drench you with my tears, O Heshbon and Elealeh;
For the shouting over your summer fruits and your harvest has
fallen away.

10 And gladness and joy are taken away from the fruitful field;
In the vineyards also there will be no cries of joy or jubilant
shouting,
No treader treads out wine in the presses,
For I have made the shouting to cease.

11 Therefore my heart intones like a harp for Moab,
And my inward feelings for Kir-hareseth.

12 So it will come about when Moab presents himself,
When he wearies himself upon *his* high place,
And comes to his sanctuary to pray,
That he will not prevail.

13 This is the word which the LORD spoke earlier concerning Moab.
14 But now the LORD speaks, saying, "Within three years, as a hired man
would count them, the glory of Moab will be degraded along with all *his* great
population, and *his* remnant will be very small *and* impotent."

E. *Burden of Damascus and Samaria*

1. *The crushing of Damascus and Ephraim*

17 The oracle concerning Damascus.
"Behold, Damascus is about to be removed from being a city,
And it will become a fallen ruin.

2   "The cities of Aroer are forsaken;
They will be for flocks to lie down in,
And there will be no one to frighten *them*.

3   "The fortified city will disappear from Ephraim,
And sovereignty from Damascus
And the remnant of Aram;
They will be like the glory of the sons of Israel,"
Declares the LORD of hosts.

2. *Survival of an idol-hating remnant*

4   Now it will come about in that day that the glory of Jacob will fade,
And the fatness of his flesh will become lean.

5   It will be even like the reaper gathering the standing grain,
As his arm harvests the ears,
Or it will be like one gleaning ears of grain
In the valley of Rephaim.

6   Yet gleanings will be left in it like the shaking of an olive tree,
Two *or* three olives on the topmost bough,

16:5
Dan 7:14;
Mic 4:7;
Luke 1:33;
Is 9:7

16:6
Jer 48:29,30;
Zeph 2:8,10

16:7
1 Chr 16:3;
2 Kin 3:25;
Jer 48:31

16:8
Is 15:4;
Num 32:38;
Jer 48:32

16:9
Jer 48:32;
Is 15:4;
Jer 40:10,12

16:10
Is 24:7,8;
Jer 48:33;
Job 24:11

16:11
Is 15:5;
63:15;
Jer 48:36
16:12
Jer 48:35;
1 Kin 18:29;
Is 15:2;
2 Kin 19:12

*16:14
Is 21:16;
25:10

17:1
2 Kin 16:9;
Jer 49:23;
Amos 1:3;
Zech 9:1;
Is 8:4; 10:9
17:2
Jer 7:33

17:3
Is 7:16; 8:4

17:4
Is 10:3,16

17:5
Jer 51:33;
2 Sam 5:18,22

17:6
Is 24:13;
27:12

16:14 *three years, as a hired man.* A hired man labors only as
long as he must. The simile means "no more than three

years," as is indicated at the start of the verse.

Four *or* five on the branches of a fruitful tree,
Declares the LORD, the God of Israel.

17:7
Is 10:20;
Mic 7:7

7 In that day man will have regard for his Maker,
And his eyes will look to the Holy One of Israel.

17:8
Is 27:9;
30:22; 31:7;
Ex 34:13;
Deut 7:5

8 And he will not have regard for the altars, the work of his hands,
Nor will he look to that which his fingers have made,
Even the [7]Asherim and incense stands.

3. *The imminent horrors of invasion*

17:9
Is 7:25

9 In that day their strong cities will be like forsaken places in the
    forest,
Or like branches which they abandoned before the sons of Israel;
And the land will be a desolation.

17:10
Is 51:13;
Ps 68:19;
Is 26:4; 30:29

10 For you have forgotten the God of your salvation
And have not remembered the rock of your refuge.
Therefore you plant delightful plants
And set them with vine slips of a strange *god*.

17:11
Ps 90:6;
Job 4:8

11 In the day that you plant *it* you carefully fence *it* in,
And in the morning you bring your seed to blossom;
But the harvest will be a heap
In a day of sickliness and incurable pain.

17:12
Jer 6:23;
Ezek 43:2;
Ps 18:4

12 Alas, the uproar of many peoples
Who roar like the roaring of the seas,
And the rumbling of nations
Who rush on like the rumbling of mighty waters!

17:13
Is 33:3;
Ps 9:5;
Is 13:14;
29:5; 41:15,
16

13 The nations rumble on like the rumbling of many waters,
But He will rebuke them and they will flee far away,
And be chased like chaff in the mountains before the wind,
Or like whirling dust before a gale.

17:14
Is 41:12;
2 Kin 19:35

14 At evening time, behold, *there is* terror!
Before morning they are no more.
Such *will be* the portion of those who plunder us,
And the lot of those who pillage us.

F. *Burden of Ethiopia*

*18:1
Is 20:3-5;
Ezek 30:4,5,
9; Zeph 2:12;
3:10
18:2
Ex 2:3; v. 7;
2 Chr 12:2-4

18 Alas, oh land of whirring wings
Which lies beyond the rivers of [8]Cush,

2 Which sends envoys by the sea,
Even in papyrus vessels on the surface of the waters.
Go, swift messengers, to a nation tall and smooth,
To a people feared far and wide,
A powerful and oppressive nation
Whose land the rivers divide.

18:3
Ps 49:1;
Is 5:26; 26:11

3 All you inhabitants of the world and dwellers on earth,
As soon as a standard is raised on the mountains, you will see *it*,
And as soon as the trumpet is blown, you will hear *it*.

18:4
Is 26:21;
2 Sam 23:4;
Is 26:19

4 For thus the LORD has told me,
"I will look from My dwelling place quietly
Like dazzling heat in the sunshine,
Like a cloud of dew in the heat of harvest."

18:5
Ezek 17:6-10;
Is 27:11

5 For before the harvest, as soon as the bud blossoms
And the flower becomes a ripening grape,
Then He will cut off the sprigs with pruning knives
And remove *and* cut away the spreading branches.

18:6
Is 46:11;
56:9; Jer 7:33

6 They will be left together for mountain birds of prey,
And for the beasts of the earth;
And the birds of prey will spend the summer *feeding* on them,

[7]I.e., wooden symbols of a female deity   [8]Or, *Ethiopia*

18:1 *land of whirring wings*. This refers to the numerous insects of the Nile Valley. *Cush*. Or Ethiopia. An Ethiopian dynasty was ruling Egypt during Isaiah's lifetime.

And all the beasts of the earth will spend harvest time on them.

7 At that time a gift of homage will be brought to the LORD of hosts
From a people tall and smooth,
Even from a people feared far and wide,
A powerful and oppressive nation,
Whose land the rivers divide—
To the place of the name of the LORD of hosts, *even* Mount Zion.

G. *Burden of Egypt*

1. *The doom of Egypt*

19 The oracle concerning Egypt.
Behold, the LORD is riding on a swift cloud, and is about to come to
Egypt;
The idols of Egypt will tremble at His presence,
And the heart of the Egyptians will melt within them.

2 "So I will incite Egyptians against Egyptians;
And they will each fight against his brother, and each against his
neighbor,
City against city, *and* kingdom against kingdom.

3 "Then the spirit of the Egyptians will be demoralized within them;
And I will confound their strategy,
So that they will resort to idols and ghosts of the dead,
And to mediums and spiritists.

4 "Moreover, I will deliver the Egyptians into the hand of a cruel
master,
And a mighty king will rule over them," declares the Lord GOD of
hosts.

5 And the waters from the sea will dry up,
And the river will be parched and dry.

6 And the canals will emit a stench,
The streams of Egypt will thin out and dry up;
The reeds and rushes will rot away.

7 The bulrushes by the Nile, by the edge of the Nile
And all the sown fields by the Nile
Will become dry, be driven away, and be no more.

8 And the fishermen will lament,
And all those who cast a line into the Nile will mourn,
And those who spread nets on the waters will pine away.

9 Moreover, the manufacturers of linen made from combed flax
And the weavers of white cloth will be utterly dejected.

10 And the pillars *of Egypt* will be crushed;
All the hired laborers will be grieved in soul.

11 The princes of Zoan are mere fools;
The advice of Pharaoh's wisest advisers has become stupid.
How can you *men* say to Pharaoh,
"I am a son of the wise, a son of ancient kings"?

12 Well then, where are your wise men?
Please let them tell you,
And let them understand what the LORD of hosts
Has purposed against Egypt.

13 The princes of Zoan have acted foolishly,
The princes of Memphis are deluded;
Those who are the cornerstone of her tribes
Have led Egypt astray.

14 The LORD has mixed within her a spirit of distortion;
They have led Egypt astray in all that it does,
As a drunken man staggers in his vomit.

18:7
Ps 68:31;
Is 45:14;
Zeph 3:10;
Zech 14:16,
17

*19:1
Is 13:1;
Jer 46:13-26;
Ezek chs. 29,
30; Ps 18:10;
104:3;
Ex 12:12;
Jer 43:12
19:2
Judg 7:22;
1 Sam 14:16,
20;
2 Chr 20:23;
Matt 10:21,36
19:3
vv. 11-14;
Is 8:19

19:4
Is 20:4;
Jer 46:26;
Ezek 29:19

19:5
Jer 51:36;
Ezek 30:12
19:6
Ex 7:18;
Is 37:25; 15:6

19:7
Is 23:3,10

19:9
Prov 7:16;
Ezek 27:7
19:10
Ps 11:3

19:11
Num 13:22;
1 Kin 4:30;
Acts 7:22

19:12
1 Cor 1:20;
Is 14:24;
Rom 9:17

19:13
Jer 2:16;
Ezek 30:13;
Zech 10:4
19:14
Is 29:10;
Matt 17:17;
Is 3:12; 9:16;
28:7

19:1 *the LORD is riding on a swift cloud.* The Canaanite Baal was a god of fertility, who was described as the rider of the clouds. The figure of speech is used of the God of Israel (cf. Ps. 18:10; 104:3), who brings fertility to the land and hastens to bring blessing to His faithful people and to execute judgment on the wicked.

19:15
Is 9:14,15

15   And there will be no work for Egypt
      Which *its* head or tail, *its* palm branch or bulrush, may do.

2. God's people will triumph over Egypt

19:16
Jer 51:30;
Is 2:19;
11:15; 30:32

16   In that day the Egyptians will become like women, and they will tremble and be in dread because of the waving of the hand of the LORD of hosts, which He is going to wave over them.

19:17
Is 14:24

17   And the land of Judah will become a terror to Egypt; everyone to whom it is mentioned will be in dread of it, because of the purpose of the LORD of hosts which He is purposing against them.

*19:18
Is 45:23;
65:16

18   In that day five cities in the land of Egypt will be speaking the language of Canaan and swearing *allegiance* to the LORD of hosts; one will be called the City of [9]Destruction.

3. The final conversion and deliverance of Egypt

*19:19
Is 56:7;
Gen 28:18;
Ex 24:4;
Josh 22:10,
26,27
19:20
Is 43:3,11;
49:25
19:21
Is 11:9;
Mal 1:11;
Is 44:5
19:22
Is 30:26;
27:13; 45:14
19:23
Is 11:16;
27:13

19   In that day there will be an altar to the LORD in the midst of the land of Egypt, and a pillar to the LORD near its border.
20   And it will become a sign and a witness to the LORD of hosts in the land of Egypt; for they will cry to the LORD because of oppressors, and He will send them a Savior and a Champion, and He will deliver them.
21   Thus the LORD will make Himself known to Egypt, and the Egyptians will know the LORD in that day. They will even worship with sacrifice and offering, and will make a vow to the LORD and perform it.
22   And the LORD will strike Egypt, striking but healing; so they will return to the LORD, and He will respond to them and will heal them.
23   In that day there will be a highway from Egypt to Assyria, and the Assyrians will come into Egypt and the Egyptians into Assyria, and the Egyptians will worship with the Assyrians.
24   In that day Israel will be the third *party* with Egypt and Assyria, a blessing in the midst of the earth,

19:25
Is 45:14;
Hos 2:23;
Eph 2:10

25   whom the LORD of hosts has blessed, saying, "Blessed is Egypt My people, and Assyria the work of My hands, and Israel My inheritance."

4. Egypt to be conquered by Assyria

*20:1
2 Kin 18:17;
1 Sam 5:1
20:2
Zech 13:4;
Ezek 24:17,
23;
1 Sam 19:24;
Mic 1:8
20:3
Is 8:18; 37:9;
43:3
20:4
Is 19:4; 3:17;
Jer 13:22,26
20:5
2 Kin 18:21;
Is 30:3,5,7;
Ezek 29:6,7
20:6
Is 10:3; 30:7;
Matt 23:33;
Heb 2:3

20 In the year that the commander came to Ashdod, when Sargon the king of Assyria sent him and he fought against Ashdod and captured it,
2   at that time the LORD spoke through Isaiah the son of Amoz, saying, "Go and loosen the sackcloth from your hips, and take your shoes off your feet." And he did so, going naked and barefoot.
3   And the LORD said, "Even as My servant Isaiah has gone naked and barefoot three years as a sign and token against Egypt and Cush,
4   so the king of Assyria will lead away the captives of Egypt and the exiles of Cush, young and old, naked and barefoot with buttocks uncovered, to the shame of Egypt.
5   "Then they shall be dismayed and ashamed because of Cush their hope and Egypt their boast.
6   "So the inhabitants of this coastland will say in that day, 'Behold, such is our hope, where we fled for help to be delivered from the king of Assyria; and we, how shall we escape?'"

H. The defeat of Babylon by Medo-Persia

21:1
Is 31:1;
Jer 51:42;
Zech 9:14
21:2
Is 33:1;
13:17;
Jer 49:34

21 The oracle concerning the [10]wilderness of the sea.
      As windstorms in the Negev sweep on,
      It comes from the wilderness, from a terrifying land.
2   A harsh vision has been shown to me;

[9]Some ancient mss. and versions read *the Sun*   [10]Or, *sandy wastes, sea country*

19:18 *the language of Canaan.* This was the language (Hebrew) adopted by the Israelite patriarchs after their entrance into Canaan.
19:19 *an altar to the LORD in the midst of the land of Egypt.* The prophet depicts a future day when Egypt will call on the LORD and worship Him at an altar in Egypt. Josephus once stated that Onias IV, who built an altar at Leontopolis (154 B.C.), appealed to this text.
20:1 *Ashdod*, a Philistine city, was allied with Egypt against Assyria. Sargon's commander took the city in 711 B.C., and was later besieged by Sennacherib and other aggressors.

The treacherous one still deals treacherously, *and* the destroyer still
destroys.
Go up, Elam, lay siege, Media;
I have made an end of all the groaning she has caused.

3   For this reason my loins are full of anguish;
Pains have seized me like the pains of a woman in labor.
I am so bewildered I cannot hear, so terrified I cannot see.

4   My mind reels, horror overwhelms me;
The twilight I longed for has been turned for me into trembling.

5   They set the table, they [11]spread out the cloth, they eat, they drink;
"Rise up, captains, oil the shields,"

6   For thus the Lord says to me,
"Go, station the lookout, let him report what he sees.

7   "When he sees riders, horsemen in pairs,
A train of donkeys, a train of camels,
Let him pay close attention, very close attention."

8   Then the lookout called,
"O Lord, I stand continually by day on the watchtower,
And I am stationed every night at my guard post.

9   "Now behold, here comes a troop of riders, horsemen in pairs."
And one answered and said, "Fallen, fallen is Babylon;
And all the images of her gods are shattered on the
ground."

10   O my threshed *people*, and my afflicted of the threshing floor!
What I have heard from the LORD of hosts,
The God of Israel, I make known to you.

I. *Burden of (Edom) Dumah*

11   The oracle concerning Edom.
One keeps calling to me from Seir,
"Watchman, [12]how far gone is the night?
Watchman, [12]how far gone is the night?"

12   The watchman says,
"Morning comes but also night.
If you would inquire, inquire;
Come back again."

J. *Burden of Arabia*

13   The oracle about Arabia.
In the thickets of Arabia you must spend the night,
O caravans of Dedanites.

14   Bring water for the thirsty,
O inhabitants of the land of Tema,
Meet the fugitive with bread.

15   For they have fled from the swords,
From the drawn sword, and from the bent bow,
And from the press of battle.

16   For thus the Lord said to me, "In a year, as a hired man would count it, all
the splendor of Kedar will terminate;
17   and the remainder of the number of bowmen, the mighty men of the sons of
Kedar, will be few; for the LORD God of Israel has spoken."

K. *Burden of Jerusalem, the valley of vision*

1. *Heedless of warning, the city to fall*

22   The oracle concerning the valley of vision.
What is the matter with you now, that you have all gone up to the
housetops?

---

[11]Or, *spread out the rugs;* or possibly, *arranged the seating*   [12]Lit., *what is the time of the night?*

Cross-references (right margin):

21:3   Is 15:5; 16:11; 13:8
21:4   Deut 28:67
21:5   Jer 51:39,57; Dan 5:1-4
21:7   v. 9
21:8   Hab 2:1
21:9   Jer 51:8; Rev 14:8; 18:2; Is 46:1; Jer 50:2; 51:44
21:10   Jer 51:33
*21:11   Gen 25:14; 32:3
*21:13   Is 13:1; Jer 49:28; 1 Chr 1:9,32
21:14   Gen 25:15; Job 6:19
21:15   Is 13:14,15; 17:13
*21:16   Is 16:14; 17:4; Ps 120:5; Is 60:7
21:17   Is 10:19; Num 23:19; Zech 1:6
22:1   Is 13:1; Joel 3:12,14; Is 15:3

21:11 *Edom* means silence.
21:13 The Dedanites were apparently a commercial people
who carried on an extensive trade with Tyre and Damascus.
21:16 Isaiah's prophecy concerning Kedar was quickly
fulfilled.

22:2
Is 32:13;
Jer 14:18;
Lam 2:20
2 You who were full of noise,
You boisterous town, you exultant city;
Your slain were not slain with the sword,
Nor did they die in battle.

22:3
Is 21:15
3 All your rulers have fled together,
And have been captured without the bow;
All of you who were found were taken captive together,
Though they had fled far away.

22:4
Is 15:3;
Jer 4:19; 9:1
4 Therefore I say, "Turn your eyes away from me,
Let me weep bitterly,
Do not try to comfort me concerning the destruction of the daughter
of my people."

22:5
Is 37:3; 63:3;
Lam 1:5; 2:2;
v. 1
5 For the Lord GOD of hosts has a day of panic, subjugation, and
confusion
In the valley of vision,
A breaking down of walls
And a crying to the mountain.

22:6
Jer 49:35;
2 Kin 16:9
6 And Elam took up the quiver
With the chariots, infantry, *and* horsemen;
And Kir uncovered the shield.

22:7
2 Chr 32:1
7 Then your choicest valleys were full of chariots,
And the horsemen took up fixed positions at the gate.

22:8
2 Chr 32:3-5,
30; 1 Kin 7:2;
10:17
22:9
Neh 3:16
8 And He removed the defense of Judah.
In that day you depended on the weapons of the house of the forest,
9 And you saw that the breaches
In the *wall* of the city of David were many;
And you collected the waters of the lower pool.

10 Then you counted the houses of Jerusalem,
And you tore down houses to fortify the wall.

22:11
2 Kin 25:4;
20:20;
2 Chr 32:3,4;
Is 37:26
11 And you made a reservoir between the two walls
For the waters of the old pool.
But you did not depend on Him who made it,
Nor did you take into consideration Him who planned it long ago.

22:12
Joel 1:13;
Is 15:2;
Mic 1:16
12 Therefore in that day the Lord GOD of hosts, called *you* to weeping,
to wailing,
To shaving the head, and to wearing sackcloth.

22:13
Is 5:11,22;
56:12;
1 Cor 15:32
13 Instead, there is gaiety and gladness,
Killing of cattle and slaughtering of sheep,
Eating of meat and drinking of wine:
"Let us eat and drink, for tomorrow we may die."

22:14
Is 5:9; 65:7,
20
14 But the LORD of hosts revealed Himself to me,
"Surely this iniquity shall not be forgiven you
Until you die," says the Lord GOD of hosts.

2. Corrupt Shebna to be replaced by Eliakim

22:15
2 Kin 18:37;
Is 36:3
15 Thus says the Lord GOD of hosts,
"Come, go to this steward,
To Shebna, who is in charge of the *royal* household,

22:16
2 Sam 18:18;
2 Chr 16:14;
Matt 27:60
16 'What right do you have here,
And whom do you have here,
That you have hewn a tomb for yourself here,
You who hew a tomb on the height,
You who carve a resting place for yourself in the rock?

17 'Behold, the LORD is about to hurl you headlong, O man.
And He is about to grasp you firmly,

22:18
Is 17:13;
Job 18:18
18 *And* roll you tightly like a ball,
To be cast into a vast country;
There you will die,
And there your splendid chariots will be,
You shame of your master's house.'

22:19
Job 40:11,12;
Ezek 17:24
19 "And I will depose you from your office,
And I will pull you down from your station.

20   "Then it will come about in that day,
      That I will summon My servant Eliakim the son of Hilkiah
21   And I will clothe him with your tunic,
      And tie your sash securely about him,
      I will entrust him with your authority,
      And he will become a father to the inhabitants of Jerusalem and to
            the house of Judah.
22   "Then I will set the key of the house of David on his shoulder,
      When he opens no one will shut,
      When he shuts no one will open.
23   "And I will drive him *like* a peg in a firm place,
      And he will become a throne of glory to his father's house.
24 "So they will hang on him all the glory of his father's house, offspring and
issue, all the least of vessels, from bowls to all the jars.
25 "In that day," declares the LORD of hosts, "the peg driven in a firm place will
give way; it will even break off and fall, and the load hanging on it will be cut off,
for the LORD has spoken."

L. *The burden of Tyre*

1. *The fall of Tyre predicted*

23   The oracle concerning Tyre.
      Wail, O ships of Tarshish,
      For *Tyre* is destroyed, without house *or* harbor;
      It is reported to them from the land of Cyprus.
2   Be silent, you inhabitants of the coastland,
      You merchants of Sidon;
      Your messengers crossed the sea
3   And *were* on many waters.
      The grain of the Nile, the harvest of the River was her revenue;
      And she was the market of nations.
4   Be ashamed, O Sidon;
      For the sea speaks, the stronghold of the sea, saying,
      "I have neither travailed nor given birth,
      I have neither brought up young men *nor* reared virgins."
5   When the report *reaches* Egypt,
      They will be in anguish at the report of Tyre.
6   Pass over to Tarshish;
      Wail, O inhabitants of the coastland.
7   Is this your jubilant *city*,
      Whose origin is from antiquity,
      Whose feet used to carry her to colonize distant places?

8   Who has planned this against Tyre, the bestower of crowns,
      Whose merchants were princes, whose traders were the honored of
            the earth?
9   The LORD of hosts has planned it to defile the pride of all beauty,
      To despise all the honored of the earth.
10   Overflow your land like the Nile, O daughter of Tarshish,
      There is no more restraint.
11   He has stretched His hand out over the sea,
      He has made the kingdoms tremble;
      The LORD has given a command concerning Canaan to demolish its
            strongholds.
12   And He has said, "You shall exult no more, O crushed virgin
            daughter of Sidon.

Cross references (right margin):

*22:20
2 Kin 18:18;
Is 36:3

*22:22
Rev 3:7;
Is 7:2,13;
Job 12:14

22:23
Ezra 9:8;
Job 36:7

22:25
v. 23;
Is 46:11;
Mic 4:4

*23:1
Jer 25:22;
47:4;
Ezek chs. 26,
27,28; v. 12

23:2
Is 47:5

23:3
Jer 2:18;
Ezek 27:3-23

23:4
Ezek 28:21,
22

23:7
Is 22:2; 32:13

23:9
Is 2:11;
13:11;
Job 40:11,12;
Is 5:13; 9:15

23:11
Is 14:26;
50:2; 25:2

23:12
Rev 18:22;
Is 47:1; v. 1

22:20 Eliakim (whose name means "God will establish") is a type of Christ. As a leader and representative of the godly remnant of Isaiah's day who still believed and obeyed God, he stood in contrast to the worldy-minded Shebna (who doubtless advocated ignoring Isaiah's warnings against alliance with idolatrous Egypt). To Eliakim the key of the house of David was to be given. He was granted power to open and to shut; and no man would shut what he had opened or open what he had shut. The type is fulfilled in

Rev. 3:7. *My servant Eliakim* contrasts his person and work with Shebna, who sought his own ends.
22:22 *the key of the house of David.* The symbol of royal authority (cf. Rev. 3:7, where Christ holds the key of David).
23:1 *ships of Tarshish.* A term used of merchant ships in the Old Testament. Tarshish probably refers to Tartesus, a city on the Quadalquivir River in Spain (cf. 2:16), which had been colonized by Tyrians. See also note to 1 Kin. 10:22.

> Arise, pass over to Cyprus; even there you will find no rest."

23:13
Is 10:5,7

13 Behold, the land of the Chaldeans—this is the people *which* was not; Assyria appointed it for desert creatures—they erected their siege towers, they stripped its palaces, they made it a ruin.

23:14
v. 1

14 Wail, O ships of Tarshish,
For your stronghold is destroyed.

2. Tyre to be restored after seventy years

23:15
Jer 25:11,22

15 Now it will come about in that day that Tyre will be forgotten for seventy years like the days of one king. At the end of seventy years it will happen to Tyre as *in* the song of the harlot:
16 Take *your* harp, walk about the city,
O forgotten harlot;
Pluck the strings skillfully, sing many songs,
That you may be remembered.

23:17
Rev 17:2

17 And it will come about at the end of seventy years that the LORD will visit Tyre. Then she will go back to her harlot's wages, and will play the harlot with all the kingdoms on the face of the earth.

23:18
Is 60:5-9;
Zech 14:20

18 And her gain and her harlot's wages will be set apart to the LORD; it will not be stored up or hoarded, but her gain will become sufficient food and choice attire for those who dwell in the presence of the LORD.

IV. *First volume of general rebuke and promise*
(24:1–27:13)

A. *Sermon I: universal judgment for universal sin*

1. Devouring judgment meted out to all classes

*24:1
vv. 19,20;
Is 13:13,14

24 Behold, the LORD lays the earth waste, devastates it, distorts its surface, and scatters its inhabitants.

24:2
Hos 4:9;
Lev 25:36,37;
Deut 23:19,
20

2 And the people will be like the priest, the servant like his master, the maid like her mistress, the buyer like the seller, the lender like the borrower, the creditor like the debtor.

24:3
Is 6:11,12

3 The earth will be completely laid waste and completely despoiled, for the LORD has spoken this word.

24:4
Is 33:9; 2:12

4 The earth mourns *and* withers, the world fades *and* withers, the exalted of the people of the earth fade away.

*24:5
Gen 3:17;
Num 35:33;
Is 59:12

5 The earth is also polluted by its inhabitants, for they transgressed laws, violated statutes, broke the everlasting covenant.

24:6
Is 34:5;
Mal 4:6;
Is 5:24; 9:19

6 Therefore, a curse devours the earth, and those who live in it are held guilty. Therefore, the inhabitants of the earth are burned, and few men are left.

24:7
Is 16:8-10;
Joel 1:10-12

7 The new wine mourns,
The vine decays,
All the merry-hearted sigh.

24:8
Jer 7:34;
16:9; 25:10;
Ezek 26:13;
Hos 2:11;
Rev 18:22

8 The gaiety of tambourines ceases,
The noise of revelers stops,
The gaiety of the harp ceases.

24:9
Is 5:11,20,22

9 They do not drink wine with song;
Strong drink is bitter to those who drink it.

24:10
Is 23:1

10 The city of chaos is broken down;
Every house is shut up so that none may enter.

24:11
Jer 14:2;
46:12;
Is 16:10;
32:13

11 There is an outcry in the streets concerning the wine;
All joy turns to gloom.
The gaiety of the earth is banished.

24:12
Is 14:31; 45:2

12 Desolation is left in the city,
And the gate is battered to ruins.

24:13
Is 17:5,6

13 For thus it will be in the midst of the earth among the peoples,
As the shaking of an olive tree,
As the gleanings when the grape harvest is over.

24:1 *the LORD lays the earth waste.* In apocalyptic form the prophet envisions a guilty world in chaos.
24:5 Three sins are mentioned: (1) they *transgressed laws* of

creation; (2) they *violated statutes* of revealed religion; and (3) they broke the *covenant* of God's agreement with them.

2. *The grateful remnant praise God*

14   They raise their voices, they shout for joy.
     They cry out from the west concerning the majesty of the LORD.
15   Therefore glorify the LORD in the east,
     The name of the LORD, the God of Israel
     In the coastlands of the sea.

24:14
Is 12:6; 42:10

24:15
Is 25:3;
Mal 1:11;
Is 66:19

3 *Sure judgment and a new age*

16   From the ends of the earth we hear songs, "Glory to the Righteous
     One,"
     But I say, "Woe to me! Woe to me! Alas for me!
     The treacherous deal treacherously,
     And the treacherous deal very treacherously."
17   Terror and pit and snare
     Confront you, O inhabitant of the earth.
18   Then it will be that he who flees the report of disaster will fall into
     the pit,
     And he who climbs out of the pit will be caught in the snare;
     For the windows above are opened, and the foundations
     of the earth shake.
19   The earth is broken asunder,
     The earth is split through,
     The earth is shaken violently.
20   The earth reels to and fro like a drunkard,
     And it totters like a shack,
     For its transgression is heavy upon it,
     And it will fall, never to rise again.
21   So it will happen in that day,
     That the LORD will punish the host of heaven, on high,
     And the kings of the earth, on earth.
22   And they will be gathered together
     Like prisoners in the dungeon,
     And will be confined in prison;
     And after many days they will be punished.
23   Then the moon will be abashed and the sun ashamed,
     For the LORD of hosts will reign on Mount Zion and in Jerusalem,
     And *His* glory will be before His elders.

24:16
Is 11:12;
28:5; Jer 5:11

24:17
1 Kin 19:17

24:18
Jer 48:43,44;
Gen 7:11;
Ps 18:7

24:19
v. 1; Jer 4:23

24:20
Is 19:14;
66:24;
Dan 11:19;
Amos 8:14

24:21
Is 10:12; v. 4;
Ps 76:12

24:22
Is 10:4;
42:22;
Ezek 38:8;
Zech 9:11,12

24:23
Is 13:10;
60:19;
Zech 14:6,7;
Mic 4:7;
Heb 12:22

B. *Sermon II: praise to the LORD*

1. *For past judgments*

25   O LORD, Thou art my God;
     I will exalt Thee, I will give thanks to Thy name;
     For Thou hast worked wonders,
     Plans *formed* long ago, with perfect faithfulness.
2   For Thou hast made a city into a heap,
     A fortified city into a ruin;
     A palace of strangers is a city no more,
     It will never be rebuilt.
3   Therefore a strong people will glorify Thee;
     Cities of ruthless nations will revere Thee.
4   For Thou hast been a defense for the helpless,
     A defense for the needy in his distress,
     A refuge from the storm, a shade from the heat;
     For the breath of the ruthless
     Is like a *rain* storm *against* a wall.
5   Like heat in drought, Thou dost subdue the uproar of aliens;
     Like heat by the shadow of a cloud, the song of the ruthless is
     silenced.

25:1
Ps 118:28;
98:1;
Num 23:19

25:2
Is 17:1;
13:22; 32:14

25:4
Is 14:32;
11:4; 32:2;
49:25

25:5
Jer 51:54-56

2. For salvation yet to come

6 And the LORD of hosts will prepare a lavish banquet for all peoples
 on this mountain;
 A banquet of aged wine, choice pieces with marrow,
 And refined, aged wine.

7 And on this mountain He will swallow up the covering which is over
 all peoples,
 Even the veil which is stretched over all nations.

8 He will swallow up death for all time,
 And the Lord GOD will wipe tears away from all faces,
 And He will remove the reproach of His people from all the earth;
 For the LORD has spoken.

9 And it will be said in that day,
 "Behold, this is our God for whom we have waited that He might
 save us.
 This is the LORD for whom we have waited;
 Let us rejoice and be glad in His salvation."

10 For the hand of the LORD will rest on this mountain,
 And Moab will be trodden down in his place
 As straw is trodden down in the water of a manure pile.

11 And he will spread out his hands in the middle of it
 As a swimmer spreads out *his hands* to swim,
 But *the Lord* will lay low his pride together with the trickery of his
 hands.

12 And the unassailable fortifications of your walls He will bring down,
 Lay low, *and* cast to the ground, even to the dust.

C. Sermon III: song of rejoicing

1. Praise to the LORD as Israel's defender

26 In that day this song will be sung in the land of Judah:
 "We have a strong city;
 He sets up walls and ramparts for security.

2 "Open the gates, that the righteous nation may enter,
 The one that remains faithful.

3 "The steadfast of mind Thou wilt keep in perfect peace,
 Because he trusts in Thee.

4 "Trust in the LORD forever,
 For in GOD the LORD, *we have* an everlasting Rock.

5 "For He has brought low those who dwell on high, the unassailable
 city;
 He lays it low, He lays it low to the ground, He casts it to the dust.

6 "The foot will trample it,
 The feet of the afflicted, the steps of the helpless."

7 The way of the righteous is smooth;
 O Upright One, make the path of the righteous level.

8 Indeed, *while following* the way of Thy judgments, O LORD,
 We have waited for Thee eagerly;
 Thy name, even Thy memory, is the desire of *our* souls.

9 At night my soul longs for Thee,
 Indeed, my spirit within me seeks Thee diligently;
 For when the earth experiences Thy judgments
 The inhabitants of the world learn righteousness.

2. The doom of persistent wrongdoers

10 *Though* the wicked is shown favor,
 He does not learn righteousness;
 He deals unjustly in the land of uprightness,
 And does not perceive the majesty of the LORD.

Cross-references (left margin):

*25:6 — Is 2:2-4; Prov 9:2; Matt 22:4; Dan 7:14; Matt 8:11

*25:8 — Hos 13:14; 1 Cor 15:54; Rev 7:17; 21:4; Is 54:4

25:9 — Is 40:9; 30:18; 33:22; 66:10; Ps 20:5

25:10 — Is 16:14

26:1 — Is 4:2; 12:1; 14:31; 60:18

26:2 — Is 60:11,18; 61:3; 62:1,2

26:4 — Is 12:2; 17:10

26:5 — Is 25:12; Job 40:11-13

26:6 — Is 28:3; 3:14, 15

26:7 — Is 57:2; 42:16

26:8 — Is 51:4; 56:1; v. 13; Ex 3:15

26:9 — Ps 63:6; Is 55:6; Hos 5:15

26:10 — Rom 2:4; Is 22:12,13; Hos 11:7; John 5:37,38

25:6 *a lavish banquet.* The prophet envisions a great victory banquet on Mt. Zion. God has delivered His people (25:4, 5).

25:8 *swallow up death.* Death is forever abolished. God's presence with His people transcends time. Tears are washed away.

11 O Lord, Thy hand is lifted up *yet* they do not see it.
They see *Thy* zeal for the people and are put to shame;
Indeed, fire will devour Thine enemies.

12 Lord, Thou wilt establish peace for us,
Since Thou hast also performed for us all our works.

13 O Lord our God, other masters besides Thee have ruled us;
But through Thee alone we confess Thy name.

14 The dead will not live, the departed spirits will not rise;
Therefore Thou hast punished and destroyed them,
And Thou hast wiped out all remembrance of them.

3. *Israel's prayer for deliverance answered*

15 Thou hast increased the nation, O Lord,
Thou hast increased the nation, Thou art glorified;
Thou hast extended all the borders of the land.

16 O Lord, they sought Thee in distress;
They could only whisper a prayer,
Your chastening was upon them.

17 As the pregnant woman approaches *the time* to give birth,
She writhes *and* cries out in her labor pains,
Thus were we before Thee, O Lord.

18 We were pregnant, we writhed *in labor*,
We gave birth, as it were, *only* to wind.
We could not accomplish deliverance for the earth
Nor were inhabitants of the world born.

19 Your dead will live;
Their corpses will rise.
You who lie in the dust, awake and shout for joy,
For your dew is as the dew of the dawn,
And the earth will give birth to the departed spirits.

4. *Appeal to take refuge in God alone*

20 Come, my people, enter into your rooms,
And close your doors behind you;
Hide for a little while,
Until indignation runs *its* course.

21 For behold, the Lord is about to come out from His place
To punish the inhabitants of the earth for their iniquity;
And the earth will reveal her bloodshed,
And will no longer cover her slain.

27 In that day the Lord will punish Leviathan the fleeing serpent,
With His fierce and great and mighty sword,
Even Leviathan the twisted serpent;
And He will kill the dragon who *lives* in the sea.

D. *Sermon IV: punishment for oppressors; preservation of God's people*

1. *Future prosperity of Israel*

2 In that day,
"A vineyard of wine, sing of it!

26:12 The word *peace* is used in different ways in Scripture. The root idea of the word denotes prosperity and well-being such as was enjoyed during Solomon's reign (1 Kin. 4:20,25), an earthly state of blessedness, wholeness, and right relations that will be permanently enjoyed under Messiah's rule (Mic. 3,4). A second use of *peace* is the absence of war. This kind of peace can come only after the second advent of Christ. Until that time Christ revealed that there would be *wars and rumors of wars* (Matt. 24:6–14). Two other uses of *peace* in Scripture have spiritual connotations and refer to the relationship of saints to God. The first kind of spiritual *peace* concerns justification of believers.

Having been justified by faith, *we have peace with God* (Rom. 5:1). This is a matter of legal status, in which all charges against believers have been completely dropped and they have been acquitted for Christ's sake. The other kind of spiritual *peace* is the *peace of God, which surpasses all comprehension* (Phil. 4:7). This condition is one of inner tranquility amid vicissitude and trouble.
26:13 *other masters besides Thee,* i.e., other gods.
26:19 *Your dead,* i.e., God's faithful people, Israel.
26:20 See especially Ps. 30:5.
27:1 *Leviathan* was a mythological sea monster that became the symbol of evil, which must be destroyed.

Marginal references: 26:11 Is 5:12; 9:7; 10:17; 66:15, 24 · *26:12 v. 3; Is 64:8 · *26:13 Is 2:8; 10:11; 63:7 · 26:14 Is 8:19; Hab 2:19; Is 10:3 · 26:15 Is 9:3; 33:17 · 26:16 Hos 5:15 · 26:17 Is 13:8; John 16:21 · 26:18 Is 33:11; Ps 17:14 · *26:19 Ezek 37:1-14; Dan 12:2 · *26:20 Ex 12:22,23; Ps 30:5; Is 54:7,8; 2 Cor 4:17 · 26:21 Mic 1:3; Jude 14; Is 13:11; Job 16:18 · *27:1 Is 34:5,6; Job 3:8; Ps 74:14; Is 51:9 · 27:2 Ps 5:7; 80:8; Jer 2:21

27:3 Is 58:11; 31:5; 1 Sam 2:9	3	"I, the LORD, am its keeper; I water it every moment. Lest anyone damage it, I guard it night and day.
27:4 2 Sam 23:6; Is 33:12	4	"I have no wrath. Should someone give Me briars *and* thorns in battle, *Then* I would step on them, I would burn them completely.
27:5 Is 25:4; Job 22:21	5	"Or let him rely on My protection, Let him make peace with Me, Let him make peace with Me."
27:6 Is 37:31; Hos 14:5,6	6	In the days to come Jacob will take root, Israel will blossom and sprout; And they will fill the whole world with fruit.

2. *Exile a means of purging Israel*

27:7 Is 10:12,17	7	Like the striking of Him who has struck them, has He struck them? Or like the slaughter of His slain, have they been slain?
27:8 Job 23:6; Jer 10:23; Ps 78:38	8	Thou didst contend with them by banishing them, by driving them away. With His fierce wind He has expelled *them* on the day of the east wind.
27:9 Is 1:25; Rom 11:27; Is 17:8	9	Therefore through this Jacob's iniquity will be forgiven; And this will be the full price of the pardoning of his sin: When he makes all the altar stones like pulverized chalk stones; *When* Asherim and incense altars will not stand.
27:10 Is 32:13,14; Jer 26:6,18	10	For the fortified city is isolated, A homestead forlorn and forsaken like the desert; There the calf will graze, And there it will lie down and feed on its branches.
27:11 Deut 32:28; Is 1:3; Jer 8:7; Deut 32:18; Is 43:1,7; 44:2,21,24	11	When its limbs are dry, they are broken off; Women come *and* make a fire with them. For they are not a people of discernment, Therefore their Maker will not have compassion on them. And their Creator will not be gracious to them.

3. *The future regathering of Israel*

27:12 Is 11:11; Gen 15:18; Deut 30:3,4	12	And it will come about in that day, that the LORD will start *His* threshing from the flowing stream of the Euphrates to the brook of Egypt; and you will be gathered up one by one, O sons of Israel.
27:13 Lev 25:9; Matt 24:31; Rev 11:15; Is 19:23-25	13	It will come about also in that day that a great trumpet will be blown; and those who were perishing in the land of Assyria and who were scattered in the land of Egypt will come and worship the LORD in the holy mountain at Jerusalem.

V. *Volume of woes upon the unbelievers of Israel*
(28:1–33:24)

A. *Sermon I: God's dealing with drunkards and scoffers*

1. *Woe upon the drunkards of Samaria*

28:1 vv. 3,4,7	**28**	Woe to the proud crown of the drunkards of Ephraim, And to the fading flower of its glorious beauty, Which is at the head of the fertile valley Of those who are overcome with wine!
28:2 Is 40:10; 30:30; Ezek 13:11; Is 29:6; 30:28	2	Behold, the Lord has a strong and mighty *agent;* As a storm of hail, a tempest of destruction, Like a storm of mighty overflowing waters, He has cast *it* down to the earth with *His* hand.
28:3 vv. 1,18	3	The proud crown of the drunkards of Ephraim is trodden under foot.
28:4 Hos 9:10; Mic 7:1; Nah 3:12	4	And the fading flower of its glorious beauty, Which is at the head of the fertile valley, Will be like the first-ripe fig prior to summer;

Which one sees,
And as soon as it is in his hand,
He swallows it.

5   In that day the LORD of hosts will become a beautiful crown
    And a glorious diadem to the remnant of His people;
6   A spirit of justice for him who sits in judgment,
    A strength to those who repel the onslaught at the gate.
7   And these also reel with wine and stagger from strong drink:
    The priest and the prophet reel with strong drink,
    They are confused by wine, they stagger from strong drink;
    They reel while having visions,
    They totter *when rendering* judgment.
8   For all the tables are full of filthy vomit, without a *single clean* place.

2. Scoffers to be scourged by Assyria

9   "To whom would He teach knowledge?
    And to whom would He interpret the message?
    Those *just* weaned from milk?
    Those *just* taken from the breast?
10 "For *He says,*
    'Order on order, order on order,
    Line on line, line on line,
    A little here, a little there.' "
11 Indeed, He will speak to this people
    Through stammering lips and a foreign tongue,
12 He who said to them, "Here is rest, give rest to the weary,"
    And, "Here is repose," but they would not listen.
13 So the word of the LORD to them will be,
    "Order on order, order on order,
    Line on line, line on line,
    A little here, a little there,"
    That they may go and stumble backward, be broken, snared, and
        taken captive.
14 Therefore, hear the word of the LORD, O scoffers,
    Who rule this people who are in Jerusalem,
15 Because you have said, "We have made a covenant with death,
    And with Sheol we have made a pact.
    The overwhelming scourge will not reach us when it
        passes by,
    For we have made falsehood our refuge and we have
        concealed ourselves with deception."
16 Therefore thus says the Lord GOD,
    "Behold, I am laying in Zion a stone, a tested stone,
    A costly cornerstone *for* the foundation, firmly placed.
    He who believes *in it* will not be disturbed.
17 "And I will make justice the measuring line,
    And righteousness the level;
    Then hail shall sweep away the refuge of lies,
    And the waters shall overflow the secret place.
18 "And your covenant with death shall be canceled,
    And your pact with Sheol shall not stand;
    When the overwhelming scourge passes through,
    Then you become its trampling *place.*
19 "As often as it passes through, it will seize you.

Cross references (right column):

28:5 Is 41:16; 62:3; 4:2
28:6 Is 11:2; 32:15; 25:4
28:7 Prov 20:1; Hos 4:11; Is 56:10,12
28:8 Jer 48:26
28:9 v. 26; Ps 131:2; Heb 5:12,13
28:10 Neh 9:30
28:11 1 Cor 14:21
28:12 Jer 6:16; Matt 11:28,29
28:13 Matt 21:44
28:14 v. 22; Is 29:20
*28:15 vv. 18,2; Is 59:3,4; 29:15
*28:16 Ps 118:22; Matt 21:42; Acts 4:11; Rom 9:33; 10:11; Eph 2:20; 1 Pet 2:4-6
28:17 Is 5:16; v. 2
28:18 v. 15
28:19 Is 50:4; Ps 88:15; Jer 15:8

28:15 *a covenant with death, and with Sheol.* The proud in Israel insist that they have no fear of the future because they have entered into alliance with Egypt against Assyria. Allusion may be to the Egyptian gods of the nether world. **28:16** Scripture often makes reference to Christ as the stone of protection, deliverance, and judgment. We should exercise caution in the use of typology, but in this case analogies should be carefully studied: (1) Christ the Rock was smitten for our sins (Ex. 17:6; Num. 20:8, see also 1 Cor. 10:4); (2) Christ is the smiting stone that destroys the final world power (Dan. 2:34); (3) the stone of the Messianic kingdom becomes a great mountain and fills the whole earth (Dan. 2:35); (4) Christ is here (28:16) the chief cornerstone and also in Eph. 2:20 and 1 Pet. 2:6; and (5) Christ is a stone of stumbling and a rock of judgment over which men will fall (Rom. 9:32,33; 1 Cor. 1:23; 1 Pet. 2:8). *a tested stone.* God Himself provides the only sure foundation on which Israel may build. *be disturbed,* i.e., be anxious.

For morning after morning it will pass through, *anytime* during the
  day or night.
And it will be sheer terror to understand what it means."

20 The bed is too short on which to stretch out,
    And the blanket is too small to wrap oneself in.

*28:21
2 Sam 5:20;
1 Chr 14:11;
Josh 10:10,
12;
2 Sam 5:25;
1 Chr 14:16;
Lam 3:33
28:22
v. 14;
Is 10:22,23

21 For the LORD will rise up as *at* Mount Perazim,
    He will be stirred up as in the valley of Gibeon;
    To do His task, His unusual task,
    And to work His work, His extraordinary work.
22 And now do not carry on as scoffers,
    Lest your fetters be made stronger;
    For I have heard from the Lord GOD of hosts,
    Of decisive destruction on all the earth.

3. *Parable of the farmer*

23 Give ear and hear my voice,
    Listen and hear my words.
24 Does the farmer plow continually to plant seed?
    Does he *continually* turn and harrow the ground?
25 Does he not level its surface,
    And sow dill and scatter cummin,
    And plant wheat in rows,
    Barley in its place, and rye within its area?
26 For his God instructs and teaches him properly.

28:27
Amos 1:3

27 For dill is not threshed with a threshing sledge,
    Nor is the cartwheel driven over cummin;
    But dill is beaten out with a rod, and cummin with a club.
28 *Grain for* bread is crushed,
    Indeed, he does not continue to thresh it forever.
    Because the wheel of *his* cart and his horses *eventually* damage *it*,
    He does not thresh it longer.

28:29
Is 9:6; 31:2;
Rom 11:33

29 This also comes from the LORD of hosts,
    Who has made *His* counsel wonderful and *His* wisdom great.

B. *Sermon II: the doom of blind hypocrites*

1. *The careless Jews are to be humbled*

*29:1
2 Sam 5:9;
vv. 9,13
29:2
Is 3:26;
Lam 2:5

29

Woe, O Ariel, Ariel the city *where* David *once* camped!
Add year to year, observe *your* feasts on schedule.
2 And I will bring distress to Ariel,
   And she shall be *a city of* lamenting and mourning;
   And she shall be like an Ariel to me.

29:3
Luke 19:43,
44

3 And I will camp against you encircling *you*,
   And I will set siegeworks against you,
   And I will raise up battle towers against you.

29:4
Is 8:19;
Lev 20:6;
Deut 18:10,
11;
1 Sam 28:8,
15;
2 Chr 33:6

4 Then you shall be brought low;
   From the earth you shall speak,
   And from the dust *where* you are prostrate,
   Your words *shall come*.
   Your voice shall also be like that of a spirit from the ground,
   And your speech shall whisper from the dust.

2. *Sudden destruction of Israel's foes*

29:5
Is 17:13,14;
25:3-5; 30:13;
1 Thess 5:3
29:6
Is 28:2;
Matt 24:7;
Mark 13:8;
Luke 21:11;
Rev 11:13,19;
16:18

5 But the multitude of your enemies shall become like fine dust,
   And the multitude of the ruthless ones like the chaff which blows
     away;
   And it shall happen instantly, suddenly.
6 From the LORD of hosts you will be punished with thunder and
     earthquake and loud noise,

28:21 *Mount Perazim* was the site of a Philistine defeat
(2 Sam. 5:20). *the valley of Gibeon*, cf. 1 Chr. 14:16.

29:1 *Ariel*, a poetic name for Jerusalem. The Targum
defines Ariel here and in Ezek. 43:15,16 as *altar*.

With whirlwind and tempest and the flame of a consuming fire.

7 And the multitude of all the nations who wage war against Ariel,
Even all who wage war against her and her stronghold, and who distress her,
Shall be like a dream, a vision of the night.

8 And it will be as when a hungry man dreams—
And behold, he is eating;
But when he awakens, his hunger is not satisfied,
Or as when a thirsty man dreams—
And behold, he is drinking,
But when he awakens, behold, he is faint,
And his thirst is not quenched.
Thus the multitude of all the nations shall be,
Who wage war against Mount Zion.

3. *The folly of trying to deceive God with a sham faith*

9 Be delayed and wait.
Blind yourselves and be blind.
They become drunk, but not with wine;
They stagger, but not with strong drink.

10 For the LORD has poured over you a spirit of deep sleep,
He has shut your eyes, the prophets;
And He has covered your heads, the seers.

11 And the entire vision shall be to you like the words of a sealed book, which when they give it to the one who is literate, saying, "Please read this," he will say, "I cannot, for it is sealed."

12 Then the book will be given to the one who is illiterate, saying, "Please read this." And he will say, "I cannot read."

13 Then the Lord said,
"Because this people draw near with their words
And honor Me with their lip service,
But they remove their hearts far from Me,
And their reverence for Me consists of tradition learned *by rote,*

14 Therefore behold, I will once again deal marvelously with this people, wondrously marvelous;
And the wisdom of their wise men shall perish,
And the discernment of their discerning men shall be concealed.

15 Woe to those who deeply hide their plans from the LORD,
And whose deeds are *done* in a dark place,
And they say, "Who sees us?" or "Who knows us?"

16 You turn *things* around!
Shall the potter be considered as equal with the clay,
That what is made should say to its maker, "He did not make me";
Or what is formed say to him who formed it, "He has no understanding"?

4. *Future deliverance of God's people from blindness*

17 Is it not yet just a little while
Before Lebanon will be turned into a fertile field,
And the fertile field will be considered as a forest?

18 And on that day the deaf shall hear words of a book,
And out of *their* gloom and darkness the eyes of the blind shall see.

19 The afflicted also shall increase their gladness in the LORD,
And the needy of mankind shall rejoice in the Holy One of Israel.

20 For the ruthless will come to an end, and the scorner will be finished,
Indeed all who are intent on doing evil will be cut off;

21 Who cause a person to be indicted by a word,
And ensnare him who adjudicates at the gate,
And defraud the one in the right with meaningless arguments.

29:7
Mic 4:11,12;
Zech 12:9;
Job 20:8;
Ps 73:20

*29:8
Is 54:17

29:9
Is 51:17,21, 22

29:10
Rom 11:8;
Ps 69:23;
Is 6:9,10;
Mic 3:6

29:11
Is 27:7; 8:16;
Dan 12:4,9;
Matt 13:11

29:13
Ezek 33:31;
Matt 15:8,9;
Mark 7:6,7

29:14
Hab 1:5;
Jer 8:9; 49:7;
1 Cor 1:19

29:15
Is 30:1;
57:12;
Ps 94:7

29:16
Is 45:9;
Jer 18:1-6;
Rom 9:19-21

29:17
Is 32:15

29:18
Is 35:5; v. 11

29:19
Is 61:1;
Matt 11:5;
James 2:5

29:20
v. 5; Is 28:14,
22; 59:4

29:21
Amos 5:10,
12;
Prov 28:21

29:8 The Assyrians dreamed of conquering Jerusalem, but awakened from their dreams in great disap- pointment and failure.

5. *Jacob's reproach rolled away*

29:22
Is 41:8;
45:17; 54:4

22 Therefore thus says the LORD, who redeemed Abraham, concerning the house of Jacob,
"Jacob shall not now be ashamed, nor shall his face now turn pale;

29:23
Is 49:20-26;
45:11; 5:16;
8:13

23 But when he sees his children, the work of My hands, in his midst,
They will sanctify My name;
Indeed, they will sanctify the Holy One of Jacob,
And will stand in awe of the God of Israel.

29:24
Is 28:7

24 "And those who err in mind will know the truth,
And those who criticize will accept instruction.

C. *Sermon III: trust in man versus trust in God*

1. *Sinful reliance upon Egypt*

30:1
v. 9; Is 29:15;
8:11,12

30 "Woe to the rebellious children," declares the LORD,
"Who execute a plan, but not Mine,
And make an alliance, but not of My Spirit,
In order to add sin to sin;

*30:2
Is 31:1;
Num 27:21;
Josh 9:14;
1 Kin 22:7;
Jer 21:2

2 Who proceed down to Egypt,
Without consulting Me,
To take refuge in the safety of Pharaoh,
And to seek shelter in the shadow of Egypt!

30:3
Is 20:5;
Jer 37:3,5

3 "Therefore the safety of Pharaoh will be your shame,
And the shelter in the shadow of Egypt, your humiliation.

30:4
Is 19:11

4 "For their princes are at Zoan,
And their ambassadors arrive at Hanes.

30:5
Jer 2:36; v. 7

5 "Everyone will be ashamed because of a people who cannot profit them,
Who are not for help or profit, but for shame and also for reproach."

2. *The embassy to Egypt of no avail*

*30:6
Is 46:1,2;
8:22; 14:29;
15:7

6 The oracle concerning the beasts of the Negev.
Through a land of distress and anguish,
From where *come* lioness and lion, viper and flying serpent,
They carry their riches on the backs of young donkeys
And their treasures on camels' humps,
To a people who cannot profit *them*;

*30:7
Jer 37:7;
v. 15

7 Even Egypt, whose help is vain and empty.
Therefore, I have called her
"Rahab who has been exterminated."

3. *Rebellious Judah to be crushed*

30:8
Is 8:1;
Hab 2:2

8 Now go, write it on a tablet before them
And inscribe it on a scroll,
That it may serve in the time to come
As a witness forever.

30:9
v. 1; Is 28:15;
24:5

9 For this is a rebellious people, false sons,
Sons who refuse to listen
To the instruction of the LORD;

30:10
Is 29:10;
5:20;
1 Kin 22:8,13

10 Who say to the seers, "You must not see *visions*";
And to the prophets, "You must not prophesy to us what is right,
Speak to us pleasant words,
Prophesy illusions.

30:2 *proceed down to Egypt*, i.e., seek to make an alliance with the Egyptians. In a time of national crisis Judah preferred to lean on the arm of flesh rather than to put trust in God. The sin was that of making an alliance with idol-worshiping Egypt without seeking God. Had they sought God and been told to make an alliance it would have been a different matter entirely. The grossness of their sin lay in the fact that they seemed to have greater confidence in Egypt than they had in God. They are told: (1) their strength lies in resting and waiting expectantly for God to intervene for them (v. 15); (2) Egypt's help is sure to prove

worthless and empty (v. 7); and (3) God is willing and eager to be gracious to His sinning people when they turn to Him with repentant faith (v. 18).
30:6 *beasts of the Negev.* The wilderness must be traversed en route to Egypt.
30:7 *Rahab who has been exterminated.* An allusion to a primordial sea monster familiar from Semitic mythology. There is irony in the prophet's charge. Egypt is arrogant, like Rahab, but sits still and fails to help her allies. Judah should not trust her. Cf. 51:9.

11   "Get out of the way, turn aside from the path,
        Let us hear no more about the Holy One of Israel."
12   Therefore thus says the Holy One of Israel,
        "Since you have rejected this word,
        And have put your trust in oppression and guile, and have relied on
          them,
13   Therefore this iniquity will be to you
        Like a breach about to fall,
        A bulge in a high wall,
        Whose collapse comes suddenly in an instant.
14   "And whose collapse is like the smashing of a potter's jar;
        So ruthlessly shattered
        That a sherd will not be found among its pieces
        To take fire from a hearth,
        Or to scoop water from a cistern."
15   For thus the Lord GOD, the Holy One of Israel, has said,
        "In repentance and rest you shall be saved,
        In quietness and trust is your strength."
        But you were not willing,
16   And you said, "No, for we will flee on horses,"
        Therefore you shall flee!
      "And we will ride on swift *horses*,"
        Therefore those who pursue you shall be swift.
17   One thousand *shall flee* at the threat of one *man*,
        You shall flee at the threat of five;
        Until you are left as a flag on a mountain top,
        And as a signal on a hill.

4. *God's promise to a repentant people*

18   Therefore the LORD longs to be gracious to you,
        And therefore He waits on high to have compassion on you.
        For the LORD is a God of justice;
        How blessed are all those who long for Him.
19   O people in Zion, inhabitant in Jerusalem, you will weep no longer. He will
surely be gracious to you at the sound of your cry; when He hears it, He will answer
you.
20   Although the Lord has given you bread of privation and water of oppression, *He*, your Teacher will no longer hide Himself, but your eyes will behold your
Teacher.
21   And your ears will hear a word behind you, "This is the way, walk in it,"
whenever you turn to the right or to the left.
22   And you will defile your graven images, overlaid with silver, and your
molten images plated with gold. You will scatter them as an impure thing; *and* say
to them, "Be gone!"
23   Then He will give *you* rain for the seed which you will sow in the ground,
and bread *from* the yield of the ground, and it will be rich and plenteous; on that day
your livestock will graze in a roomy pasture.
24   Also the oxen and the donkeys which work the ground will eat salted fodder,
which has been winnowed with shovel and fork.
25   And on every lofty mountain and on every high hill there will be streams
running with water on the day of the great slaughter, when the towers fall.
26   And the light of the moon will be as the light of the sun, and the light of the
sun will be seven times *brighter*, like the light of seven days, on the day the LORD
binds up the fracture of His people and heals the bruise He has inflicted.

5. *Israel's enemies to be smitten*

27   Behold, the name of the LORD comes from a remote place;
        Burning is His anger, and dense is *His* smoke;
        His lips are filled with indignation,
        And His tongue is like a consuming fire;
28   And His breath is like an overflowing torrent,
        Which reaches to the neck,
        To shake the nations back and forth in a sieve,

Cross references (right margin):

30:11 Job 21:14

30:12 Is 5:24; 59:13

30:13 Is 26:21; Ps 62:3; Is 29:5

30:14 Ps 2:9; Jer 19:10,11

30:15 Is 7:4; 28:12; 32:17

30:16 Is 31:1,3

30:17 Lev 26:8; Deut 28:25; 32:30; Josh 23:10

30:18 Is 42:14; 33:5; 5:16; 25:9

30:19 Is 65:9; 60:20; 61:1-3; Matt 7:7-11

30:20 1 Kin 22:27; Ps 80:5; 74:9; Amos 8:11

30:21 Is 35:8,9; Prov 3:6; Is 29:24

30:22 Is 2:20; 31:7; 46:6; Matt 4:10

30:23 Ps 65:9-13; Is 65:21,22; 32:20

30:26 Is 60:19,20; Rev 21:23; 22:5; Is 61:1; 1:6; Jer 33:6

30:27 Is 59:19; 10:5,13,17; 66:15

30:28 Is 11:4; 2 Thess 2:8; Is 8:8; 37:29

And to *put* in the jaws of the peoples the bridle which leads to ruin.

29 You will have songs as in the night when you keep the festival;
And gladness of heart as when one marches to *the sound of* the flute,
To go to the mountain of the LORD, to the Rock of Israel.

30 And the LORD will cause His voice of authority to be heard.
And the descending of His arm to be seen in fierce anger,
And *in* the flame of a consuming fire,
In cloudburst, downpour, and hailstones.

31 For at the voice of the LORD Assyria will be terrified,
When He strikes with the rod.

32 And every blow of the rod of punishment,
Which the LORD will lay on him,
Will be with *the music of* tambourines and lyres;
And in battles, brandishing weapons, He will fight them.

33 For [13]Topheth has long been ready,
Indeed, it has been prepared for the king.
He has made it deep and large,
A pyre of fire with plenty of wood;
The breath of the LORD, like a torrent of brimstone, sets it afire.

D. *Sermon IV: Israel's deliverance by divine intervention*

1. *Folly of reliance on Egypt*

31 Woe to those who go down to Egypt for help,
And rely on horses,
And trust in chariots because they are many,
And in horsemen because they are very strong,
But they do not look to the Holy One of Israel, nor seek
the LORD!

2 Yet He also is wise and will bring disaster,
And does not retract His words,
But will arise against the house of evildoers,
And against the help of the workers of iniquity.

3 Now the Egyptians are men, and not God,
And their horses are flesh and not spirit;
So the LORD will stretch out His hand,
And he who helps will stumble
And he who is helped will fall,
And all of them will come to an end together.

2. *The call to trust in the LORD*

4 For thus says the LORD to me,
"As the lion or the young lion growls over his prey,
Against which a band of shepherds is called out,
Will not be terrified at their voice, nor disturbed at their noise,
So will the LORD of hosts come down to wage war on Mount Zion
and on its hill."

5 Like flying birds so the LORD of hosts will protect Jerusalem.
He will protect and deliver *it;*
He will pass over and rescue *it.*

6 Return to Him from whom you have deeply defected, O sons of Israel.

7 For in that day every man will cast away his silver idols and his gold idols,
which your hands have made as a sin.

8 And the Assyrian will fall by a sword not of man,
And a sword not of man will devour him.
So he will not escape the sword,
And his young men will become forced laborers.

9 "And his rock will pass away because of panic,
And his princes will be terrified at the standard,"
Declares the LORD, whose fire is in Zion and whose furnace is
in Jerusalem.

---

13 I.e., the place of human sacrifice to Molech

Cross references (margin)

30:29 Ps 42:4; Is 2:3; 17:10
30:30 Is 28:2; 32:19
30:31 Is 31:8
30:32 Is 10:24; Jer 31:4; Ezek 32:10
30:33 Jer 7:3; 19:6; vv. 27,28; Is 34:9
31:1 Is 30:2; Ezek 17:15; Is 2:7; Ps 20:7; Dan 9:13; Is 10:17
31:2 Is 28:29; Rom 16:27; Is 45:7; Num 23:19; Is 14:20; 22:14
31:3 Ezek 28:9; Is 36:9; 9:17; 30:5,7
31:4 Hos 11:10; Amos 3:8; Is 42:13
31:5 Ps 91:4; Is 17:13
31:6 Is 44:22; 1:2,5
31:7 Is 2:20
31:8 Is 10:12; 66:16; 21:15; 14:2
31:9 Deut 32:31, 37; Is 5:26; 10:16

3. Israel's ultimate deliverance

32 Behold, a king will reign righteously,
And princes will rule justly.

2 And each will be like a refuge from the wind,
And a shelter from the storm,
Like streams of water in a dry country,
Like the shade of a huge rock in a parched land.

3 Then the eyes of those who see will not be blinded,
And the ears of those who hear will listen.

4 And the mind of the hasty will discern the truth,
And the tongue of the stammerers will hasten to speak clearly.

5 No longer will the fool be called noble,
Or the rogue be spoken of as generous.

6 For a fool speaks nonsense,
And his heart inclines toward wickedness,
To practice ungodliness and to speak error against the LORD,
To keep the hungry person unsatisfied
And to withhold drink from the thirsty.

7 As for a rogue, his weapons are evil;
He devises wicked schemes
To destroy the afflicted with slander,
Even though the needy one speaks what is right.

8 But the noble man devises noble plans;
And by noble plans he stands.

4. After calamity, restoration

9 Rise up you women who are at ease,
And hear my voice;
Give ear to my word,
You complacent daughters.

10 Within a year and a few days,
You will be troubled, O complacent daughters;
For the vintage is ended,
And the fruit gathering will not come.

11 Tremble, you women who are at ease;
Be troubled, you complacent daughters;
Strip, undress, and put sackcloth on your waist,

12 Beat your breasts for the pleasant fields, for the fruitful vine,

13 For the land of my people in which thorns and briars shall come up;
Yea, for all the joyful houses, and for the jubilant city.

14 Because the palace has been abandoned, the populated city forsaken.
Hill and watch-tower have become caves forever,
A delight for wild donkeys, a pasture for flocks;

15 Until the Spirit is poured out upon us from on high,
And the wilderness becomes a fertile field
And the fertile field is considered as a forest.

16 Then justice will dwell in the wilderness,
And righteousness will abide in the fertile field.

17 And the work of righteousness will be peace,
And the service of righteousness, quietness and confidence forever.

18 Then my people will live in a peaceful habitation,
And in secure dwellings and in undisturbed resting places;

19 And it will hail when the forest comes down,
And the city will be utterly laid low.

Cross-references (right margin):

*32:1
Is 9:6,7;
Jer 23:5;
Zech 9:9
32:2
Is 4:6; 35:6;
41:18; 43:19,
20
32:3
Is 29:18
32:4
Is 29:24
32:5
1 Sam 25:25
32:6
Is 59:7,13;
10:6; 9:15,16;
3:15
32:7
Jer 5:26-28;
Is 11:4; 5:23
32:8
2 Cor 9:6-11
32:9
Is 47:8; 28:23
32:10
Is 5:5,6
32:11
Is 22:12; 47:2
32:12
Nah 2:7
32:13
Is 34:13; 22:2
32:14
Is 13:22;
6:11; 13:21
32:15
Is 11:2;
Ezek 39:29;
Joel 2:28;
Is 29:17; 35:2
32:16
Is 33:5
*32:17
Rom 14:17;
James 3:18;
Is 30:15
32:19
Is 30:30;
Zech 11:2

32:1 *a king will reign righteously.* This expresses the hope of the Old Testament saints. Surrounded by oppression, and often ruled by weak, unworthy kings, the godly in Israel looked to the day when a righteous king would reign.
32:17 Assurance is the Christian's firm conviction that he has been saved, and will be kept by faith through the power of the Holy Spirit. The basis of all assurance derives from the promises of God. It is the product of faith (Eph. 3:12; 2 Tim. 1:12; Heb. 10:22). Believers can be assured of: (1) salvation (12:2; John 3:17; Acts 16:30,31); (2) eternal life (1 John 5:13); (3) peace (Rom. 5:1); (4) a glorious resurrection (Phil. 3:21); (5) a kingdom (Heb. 12:28); and (6) a crown (2 Tim. 4:7,8; James 1:12).

<table>
<tr><td>32:20
Is 30:24</td><td>20</td><td>How blessed will you be, you who sow beside all waters,
Who let out freely the ox and the donkey.</td></tr>
</table>

E. *Sermon V: the punishment of the treacherous and the triumph of the L*ORD

1. *Treacherous Gentiles will be spoiled*

<table>
<tr><td>33:1
Is 21:2;
Hab 2:8;
Is 24:16;
Jer 25:12-14;
Matt 7:2</td><td>33</td><td>Woe to you, O destroyer,
While you were not destroyed;
And he who is treacherous, while *others* did not deal treacherously
    with him.
As soon as you shall finish destroying, you shall be destroyed;
As soon as you shall cease to deal treacherously, *others* shall deal
    treacherously with you.</td></tr>
<tr><td>33:2
Is 25:9</td><td>2</td><td>O LORD, be gracious to us; we have waited for Thee.
Be Thou their strength every morning,
Our salvation also in the time of distress.</td></tr>
<tr><td>33:3
Is 17:13;
Jer 25:30,31</td><td>3</td><td>At the sound of the tumult peoples flee;
At the lifting up of Thyself nations disperse.</td></tr>
<tr><td></td><td>4</td><td>And your spoil is gathered *as* the caterpillar gathers;
As locusts rushing about, men rush about on it.</td></tr>
<tr><td>33:5
Ps 97:9</td><td>5</td><td>The LORD is exalted, for He dwells on high;
He has filled Zion with justice and righteousness.</td></tr>
<tr><td>33:6
v. 20;
Is 45:17;
11:9;
Matt 6:33</td><td>6</td><td>And He shall be the stability of your times,
A wealth of salvation, wisdom, and knowledge;
The fear of the LORD is his treasure.</td></tr>
</table>

2. *Judah's distress described*

<table>
<tr><td>33:7
2 Kin 18:18,
37</td><td>7</td><td>Behold, their brave men cry in the streets,
The ambassadors of peace weep bitterly.</td></tr>
<tr><td>33:8
Is 35:8; 24:5</td><td>8</td><td>The highways are desolate, the traveler has ceased,
He has broken the covenant, he has despised the cities,
He has no regard for man.</td></tr>
<tr><td>33:9
Is 24:4; 2:13;
35:2</td><td>9</td><td>The land mourns and pines away,
Lebanon is shamed and withers;
Sharon is like a desert plain,
And Bashan and Carmel lose *their foliage.*</td></tr>
</table>

3. *Prediction of God's vengeance*

<table>
<tr><td>33:10
Ps 12:5</td><td>10</td><td>"Now I will arise," says the LORD,
"Now I will be exalted, now I will be lifted up.</td></tr>
<tr><td>33:11
Ps 7:14;
Is 59:4</td><td>11</td><td>"You have conceived chaff, you will give birth to stubble;
My breath will consume you like a fire.</td></tr>
<tr><td>33:12
Is 9:18; 10:17</td><td>12</td><td>"And the peoples will be burned to lime,
Like cut thorns which are burned in the fire.</td></tr>
<tr><td>33:13
Is 49:1</td><td>13</td><td>"You who are far away, hear what I have done;
And you who are near, acknowledge My might."</td></tr>
<tr><td>33:14
Is 32:11;
30:27,30;
9:18,19</td><td>14</td><td>Sinners in Zion are terrified;
Trembling has seized the godless.
"Who among us can live with the consuming fire?
Who among us can live with continual burning?"</td></tr>
<tr><td>33:15
Ps 15:2; 24:4;
119:37</td><td>15</td><td>He who walks righteously, and speaks with sincerity,
He who rejects unjust gain,
And shakes his hands so that they hold no bribe;
He who stops his ears from hearing about bloodshed,
And shuts his eyes from looking upon evil;</td></tr>
<tr><td>33:16
Is 25:4; 26:1;
49:10</td><td>16</td><td>He will dwell on the heights;
His refuge will be the impregnable rock;
His bread will be given *him;*
His water will be sure.</td></tr>
</table>

4. *Promise of safety and joy under Messiah*

17 Your eyes will see the King in His beauty;
They will behold a far-distant land.

18 Your heart will meditate on terror:
"Where is he who counts?
Where is he who weighs?
Where is he who counts the towers?"

19 You will no longer see a fierce people,
A people of unintelligible speech which no one comprehends,
Of a stammering tongue which no one understands.

20 Look upon Zion, the city of our appointed feasts;
Your eyes shall see Jerusalem an undisturbed habitation,
A tent which shall not be folded,
Its stakes shall never be pulled up
Nor any of its cords be torn apart.

21 But there the majestic *One*, the Lord, shall be for us
A place of rivers *and* wide canals,
On which no boat with oars shall go,
And on which no mighty ship shall pass—

22 For the Lord is our judge,
The Lord is our lawgiver,
The Lord is our king;
He will save us—

23 Your tackle hangs slack;
It cannot hold the base of its mast firmly,
Nor spread out the sail.
Then the prey of an abundant spoil will be divided;
The lame will take the plunder.

24 And no resident will say, "I am sick";
The people who dwell there will be forgiven *their* iniquity.

VI. *Second volume of general rebuke and promise*
(34:1–35:10)

A. *Sermon I: destruction of the nations who are enemies of God*

1. *The judgment on the nations*

34 Draw near, O nations, to hear; and listen, O peoples!
Let the earth and all it contains hear, and the world and all that
springs from it.

2 For the Lord's indignation is against all the nations,
And *His* wrath against all their armies;
He has utterly destroyed them,
He has given them over to slaughter.

3 So their slain will be thrown out,
And their corpses will give off their stench,
And the mountains will be drenched with their blood.

4 And all the host of heaven will wear away,
And the sky will be rolled up like a scroll;
All their hosts will also wither away
As a leaf withers from the vine,
Or as *one* withers from the fig tree.

2. *The example of Edom*

5 For My sword is satiated in heaven,
Behold it shall descend for judgment upon Edom,
And upon the people whom I have devoted to destruction.

6 The sword of the Lord is filled with blood,
It is sated with fat, with the blood of lambs and goats,
With the fat of the kidneys of rams.
For the Lord has a sacrifice in Bozrah,
And a great slaughter in the land of Edom.

33:17	vv. 21,22; Is 26:15
33:18	Is 17:14; 1 Cor 1:20
33:19	2 Kin 19:32; Deut 28:49, 50; Jer 5:15
33:20	Ps 48:12; 46:5; 125:1,2; Is 37:33; 54:2
33:21	Is 41:18
33:22	Is 2:4; James 4:12; v. 17; Zech 9:9; Is 35:4
33:23	2 Kin 7:8,16
33:24	Jer 30:17; 50:20
34:1	Ps 49:1; Deut 32:1
34:2	Is 26:20,21; 13:5; 30:25
34:3	Joel 2:20; Ezek 14:19
34:4	Ezek 32:7,8; Joel 2:31; Matt 24:29; 2 Pet 3:10; Rev 6:13,14
34:5	Jer 46:10; 49:7; Mal 1:4
34:6	Jer 49:13; Is 63:1

34:7 Ps 22:21; 68:30; Is 29:9; 49:26	7	Wild oxen shall also fall with them, And young bulls with strong ones; Thus their land shall be soaked with blood, And their dust become greasy with fat.
34:8 Is 63:4	8	For the LORD has a day of vengeance, A year of recompense for the cause of Zion.
34:9 Deut 29:23	9	And its streams shall be turned into pitch, And its loose earth into brimstone, And its land shall become burning pitch.
34:10 Is 66:24; Rev 14:11; 19:3; Mal 1:4; Ezek 29:11	10	It shall not be quenched night or day; Its smoke shall go up forever; From generation to generation it shall be desolate; None shall pass through it forever and ever.
34:11 Is 14:23; Zeph 2:14; Rev 18:2; 2 Kin 21:13; Lam 2:8	11	But pelican and hedgehog shall possess it, And owl and raven shall dwell in it; And He shall stretch over it the line of desolation And the plumb line of emptiness.
	12	Its nobles—there is no one there *Whom* they may proclaim king— And all its princes shall be nothing.
34:13 Is 13:22; 32:13; Jer 9:11; 10:22	13	And thorns shall come up in its fortified towers, Nettles and thistles in its fortified cities; It shall also be a haunt of jackals *And* an abode of ostriches.
34:14 Is 13:21	14	And the desert creatures shall meet with the wolves, The hairy goat also shall cry to its kind; Yes, the night monster shall settle there And shall find herself a resting place.
34:15 Deut 14:13	15	The tree snake shall make its nest and lay *eggs* there, And it will hatch and gather *them* under its protection. Yes, the hawks shall be gathered there, Every one with its kind.
*34:16 Is 30:8; 40:5	**16**	Seek from the book of the LORD, and read: Not one of these will be missing; None will lack its mate. For His mouth has commanded, And His Spirit has gathered them.
34:17 Jer 13:25; vv. 10,11	17	And He has cast the lot for them, And His hand has divided it to them by line. They shall possess it forever; From generation to generation they shall dwell in it.

B. *Sermon II: the return to Zion promised*

*35:1f Is 55:12; 51:3	**35**	The wilderness and the desert will be glad, And the Arabah will rejoice and blossom; Like the crocus
35:2 Is 32:15; v. 10; Is 60:13; 25:9	2	It will blossom profusely And rejoice with rejoicing and shout of joy. The glory of Lebanon will be given to it, The majesty of Carmel and Sharon. They will see the glory of the LORD, The majesty of our God.
35:3 Job 4:3,4; Heb 12:12	3	Encourage the exhausted, and strengthen the feeble.
35:4 Is 1:24; 34:8; Ps 145:19	4	Say to those with anxious heart, "Take courage, fear not. Behold, your God will come *with* vengeance; The recompense of God will come, But He will save you."

34:16 *the book of the LORD.* The fulfillment may be compared with its prophecy in Scripture, where it will be seen that the thing prophesied has come to pass.
35:1,2 The contrast in these opening verses is conspicuous. From wilderness and dry land there shall come: (1) gladness and rejoicing; (2) fertility, for the desert shall blossom; (3) beauty, after dryness and sterility; (4) glory and majesty; and (5) *the glory of the LORD.*

5	Then the eyes of the blind will be opened, And the ears of the deaf will be unstopped.
6	Then the lame will leap like a deer, And the tongue of the dumb will shout for joy. For waters will break forth in the wilderness And streams in the Arabah.
7	And the scorched land will become a pool, And the thirsty ground springs of water; In the haunt of jackals, its resting place, Grass *becomes* reeds and rushes.
8	And a highway will be there, a roadway, And it will be called the Highway of Holiness. The unclean will not travel on it, But it *will* be for him who walks *that* way, And fools will not wander *on it*.
9	No lion will be there, Nor will any vicious beast go up on it; These will not be found there. But the redeemed will walk *there*,
10	And the ransomed of the LORD will return, And come with joyful shouting to Zion, With everlasting joy upon their heads. They will find gladness and joy, And sorrow and sighing will flee away.

Margin references:
35:5 Is 29:18; Matt 11:5; John 9:6,7
35:6 Matt 15:30; John 5:8,9; Acts 3:8; Matt 9:32; Is 41:18; 43:19; John 7:38
35:7 Is 49:10; 34:13
35:8 Is 62:10; Matt 7:13,14; Jer 14:8
35:9 Is 30:6; 34:14; 62:12
35:10 Is 51:11; 25:8; 65:19; Rev 7:17; 21:4

VII. *Volume of Hezekiah (36:1–39:8)*

A. *Sennacherib's challenge to the people of God*

1. *His demand for Judah to submit*

36 Now it came about in the fourteenth year of King Hezekiah, Sennacherib king of Assyria came up against all the fortified cities of Judah and seized them.

2 And the king of Assyria sent Rabshakeh from Lachish to Jerusalem to King Hezekiah with a large army. And he stood by the conduit of the upper pool on the highway of the fuller's field.

3 Then Eliakim the son of Hilkiah, who was over the household, and Shebna the scribe, and Joah the son of Asaph, the recorder, came out to him.

4 Then Rabshakeh said to them, "Say now to Hezekiah, 'Thus says the great king, the king of Assyria, "What is this confidence that you have?

5 "I say, 'Your counsel and strength for the war are only empty words.' Now on whom do you rely, that you have rebelled against me?

6 "Behold, you rely on the staff of this crushed reed, *even* on Egypt; on which if a man leans, it will go into his hand and pierce it. So is Pharaoh king of Egypt to all who rely on him.

7 "But if you say to me, 'We trust in the LORD our God,' is it not He whose high places and whose altars Hezekiah has taken away, and has said to Judah and to Jerusalem, 'You shall worship before this altar'?

8 "Now therefore, come make a bargain with my master the king of Assyria, and I will give you two thousand horses, if you are able on your part to set riders on them.

9 "How then can you repulse one official of the least of my master's servants, and rely on Egypt for chariots and for horsemen?

10 "And have I now come up without the LORD's approval against this land to destroy it? The LORD said to me, 'Go up against this land, and destroy it.'"'"

2. *Direct summons to the people to surrender*

11 Then Eliakim and Shebna and Joah said to Rabshakeh, "Speak now to your

Margin references:
36:1 2 Kin 18:13; Is 1:1
*36:2 2 Kin 18:17-20; Is 7:3
36:3 Is 22:15,20
36:4 2 Kin 18:19
36:5 2 Kin 18:7
36:6 Ezek 29:6,7; Is 30:3,5,7
*36:7 2 Kin 18:4,5
36:9 Is 37:29; 20:5
*36:11 Ezra 4:7; v. 13

servants in Aramaic, for we understand *it*; and do not speak with us in Judean, in the hearing of the people who are on the wall.''

12   But Rabshakeh said, "Has my master sent me only to your master and to you to speak these words, *and* not to the men who sit on the wall, *doomed* to eat their own dung and drink their own urine with you?''

36:13
2 Chr 32:18

13   Then Rabshakeh stood and cried with a loud voice in Judean, and said, "Hear the words of the great king, the king of Assyria.

36:14
Is 37:10

14   "Thus says the king, 'Do not let Hezekiah deceive you, for he will not be able to deliver you;

36:15
v. 18

15   nor let Hezekiah make you trust in the LORD, saying, "The LORD will surely deliver us, this city shall not be given into the hand of the king of Assyria.''

36:16
Zech 3:10;
Prov 5:15

16   'Do not listen to Hezekiah,' for thus says the king of Assyria, 'Make your peace with me and come out to me, and eat each of his vine and each of his fig tree and drink each of the waters of his own cistern,

17   until I come and take you away to a land like your own land, a land of grain and new wine, a land of bread and vineyards.

36:18
v. 15

18   *'Beware* lest Hezekiah misleads you, saying, "The LORD will deliver us.'' Has any one of the gods of the nations delivered his land from the hand of the king of Assyria?

36:19
Is 37:11-13;
2 Kin 17:6
36:20
1 Kin 20:23,
28; v. 15

19   'Where are the gods of Hamath and Arpad? Where are the gods of Sepharvaim? And when have they delivered Samaria from my hand?

20   'Who among all the gods of these lands have delivered their land from my hand, that the LORD should deliver Jerusalem from my hand?' ''

21   But they were silent and answered him not a word; for the king's commandment was, "Do not answer him.''

36:22
v. 3; Is 22:15,
20

22   Then Eliakim the son of Hilkiah, who was over the household, and Shebna the scribe and Joah the son of Asaph, the recorder, came to Hezekiah with their clothes torn and told him the words of Rabshakeh.

B. *God's answer to Sennacherib*

1. *Hezekiah's appeal to God*

37:1
2 Kin 19:1-37

37 And when King Hezekiah heard *it*, he tore his clothes, covered himself with sackcloth and entered the house of the LORD.

37:2
Is 22:15,20

2   Then he sent Eliakim who was over the household with Shebna the scribe and the elders of the priests, covered with sackcloth, to Isaiah the prophet, the son of Amoz.

37:3
Is 26:16-18

3   And they said to him, "Thus says Hezekiah, 'This day is a day of distress, rebuke, and rejection; for children have come to birth, and there is no strength to deliver.

37:4
Is 36:15,18,
20

4   'Perhaps the LORD your God will hear the words of Rabshakeh, whom his master the king of Assyria has sent to reproach the living God, and will rebuke the words which the LORD your God has heard. Therefore, offer a prayer for the remnant that is left.' ''

2. *God's first assurance of deliverance*

5   So the servants of King Hezekiah came to Isaiah.

37:6
Is 7:4; 35:4

6   And Isaiah said to them, "Thus you shall say to your master, 'Thus says the LORD, "Do not be afraid because of the words that you have heard, with which the servants of the king of Assyria have blasphemed Me.

37:7
vv. 9,37,38

7   "Behold, I will put a spirit in him so that he shall hear a rumor and return to his own land. And I will make him fall by the sword in his own land." ' ''

3. *Blasphemous challenge from Assyria*

8   Then Rabshakeh returned and found the king of Assyria fighting against Libnah, for he had heard that the king had left Lachish.

*37:9
v. 7; Is 18:1;
20:5

9   When he heard *them* say concerning Tirhakah king of Cush, "He has come out to fight against you," and when he heard *it* he sent messengers to Hezekiah, saying,

37:10
Is 36:15

10   "Thus you shall say to Hezekiah king of Judah, 'Do not let your God in whom

---

37:9 *Tirhakah* is known in history as "Taharkah," the next-to-the-last king of the Twenty-fifth (or Ethiopian)   Dynasty in Egypt.

you trust deceive you, saying, "Jerusalem shall not be given into the hand of the king of Assyria."

11   'Behold, you have heard what the kings of Assyria have done to all the lands, destroying them completely. So will you be spared?

12   'Did the gods of those nations which my fathers have destroyed deliver them, *even* Gozan and Haran and Rezeph and the sons of Eden who *were* in Telassar?

13   'Where is the king of Hamath, the king of Arpad, the king of the city of Sepharvaim, *and of* Hena and Ivvah?'"

4. Hezekiah's prayer to the LORD

14   Then Hezekiah took the letter from the hand of the messengers and read it, and he went up to the house of the LORD and spread it out before the LORD.

15   And Hezekiah prayed to the LORD saying,

16   "O LORD of hosts, the God of Israel, who art enthroned *above* the cherubim, Thou art the God, Thou alone, of all the kingdoms of the earth. Thou hast made heaven and earth.

17   "Incline Thine ear, O LORD, and hear; open Thine eyes, O LORD, and see; and listen to all the words of Sennacherib, who sent *them* to reproach the living God.

18   "Truly, O LORD, the kings of Assyria have devastated all the countries and their lands,

19   and have cast their gods into the fire, for they were not gods but the work of men's hands, wood and stone. So they have destroyed them.

20   "And now, O LORD our God, deliver us from his hand that all the kingdoms of the earth may know that Thou alone, LORD, art God."

5. God's second answer: Sennacherib shall be crushed

21   Then Isaiah the son of Amoz sent *word* to Hezekiah, saying, "Thus says the LORD, the God of Israel, 'Because you have prayed to Me about Sennacherib king of Assyria,

22   this is the word that the LORD has spoken against him:
  "She has despised you and mocked you,
  The virgin daughter of Zion;
  She has shaken *her* head behind you,
  The daughter of Jerusalem!

23   "Whom have you reproached and blasphemed?
  And against whom have you raised *your* voice,
  And haughtily lifted up your eyes?
  Against the Holy One of Israel!

24   "Through your servants you have reproached the Lord,
  And you have said, 'With my many chariots I came up to the heights
    of the mountains,
  To the remotest parts of Lebanon;
  And I cut down its tall cedars *and* its choice cypresses.
  And I will go to its highest peak, its thickest forest.

25   'I dug *wells* and drank waters,
  And with the sole of my feet I dried up
  All the rivers of Egypt.'

26   "Have you not heard?
  Long ago I did it,
  From ancient times I planned it.
  Now I have brought it to pass,
  That you should turn fortified cities into ruinous heaps.

27   "Therefore their inhabitants were short of strength,
  They were dismayed and put to shame;
  They were *as* the vegetation of the field and *as* the green herb,
  As grass on the housetops is scorched before it is grown up.

28   "But I know your sitting down,
  And your going out and your coming in,
  And your raging against Me.

29   "Because of your raging against Me,
  And because your arrogance has come up to My ears,
  Therefore I will put My hook in your nose,
  And My bridle in your lips,

37:11
Is 10:9-11;
36:18-20
37:12
2 Kin 17:6;
18:11;
Gen 11:31;
12:1-4;
Acts 7:2

37:16
Ex 25:22;
Deut 10:17;
Is 42:5; 45:12
37:17
Dan 9:18;
Ps 74:22; v. 4
37:18
2 Kin 15:29;
1 Chr 5:26;
Nah 2:11,12
37:19
Is 2:8; 26:14
37:20
Is 25:9;
Ps 46:10;
Ezek 36:23

37:21
v. 2

37:22
Jer 14:17;
Lam 2:13;
Zech 2:10;
Job 16:4

37:23
v. 4; Is 2:11;
5:15,21;
Ezek 39:7;
Hab 1:12

37:24
Is 8:7,8;
10:18,33,34;
14:8

37:26
Is 40:21,28;
Acts 2:23;
4:27,28;
Is 46:11;
10:6; 17:1

37:27
Is 40:7;
Ps 129:6

37:28
Ps 139:1

37:29
Is 10:12;
30:28;
Ezek 38:4;
v. 34

And I will turn you back by the way which you came.

30 "Then this shall be the sign for you: you shall eat this year what grows of itself, in the second year what springs from the same, and in the third year sow, reap, plant vineyards, and eat their fruit.

31 "And the surviving remnant of the house of Judah shall again take root downward and bear fruit upward.

32 "For out of Jerusalem shall go forth a remnant, and out of Mount Zion survivors. The zeal of the LORD of hosts shall perform this." '

33 "Therefore, thus says the LORD concerning the king of Assyria, 'He shall not come to this city, or shoot an arrow there; neither shall he come before it with a shield, nor throw up a mound against it.

34 'By the way that he came, by the same he shall return, and he shall not come to this city,' declares the LORD.

35 'For I will defend this city to save it for My own sake and for My servant David's sake.' "

6. *The fulfillment of God's promise*

36 Then the angel of the LORD went out, and struck 185,000 in the camp of the Assyrians; and when men arose early in the morning, behold, all of these were dead.

37 So Sennacherib, king of Assyria, departed and returned *home*, and lived at Nineveh.

38 And it came about as he was worshiping in the house of Nisroch his god, that Adrammelech and Sharezer his sons killed him with the sword; and they escaped into the land of Ararat. And Esarhaddon his son became king in his place.

C. *Hezekiah's sickness and recovery*

1. *His prayer: God's answer*

38 In those days Hezekiah became mortally ill. And Isaiah the prophet the son of Amoz came to him and said to him, "Thus says the LORD, 'Set your house in order, for you shall die and not live.' "

2 Then Hezekiah turned his face to the wall, and prayed to the LORD,

3 and said, "Remember now, O LORD, I beseech Thee, how I have walked before Thee in truth and with a whole heart, and have done what is good in Thy sight." And Hezekiah wept bitterly.

4 Then the word of the LORD came to Isaiah, saying,

5 "Go and say to Hezekiah, 'Thus says the LORD, the God of your father David, "I have heard your prayer, I have seen your tears; behold, I will add fifteen years to your life.

6 "And I will deliver you and this city from the hand of the king of Assyria; and I will defend this city." '

7 "And this shall be the sign to you from the LORD, that the LORD will do this thing that He has spoken:

8 "Behold, I will cause the shadow on the stairway, which has gone down with the sun on the stairway of Ahaz, to go back ten steps." So the sun's *shadow* went back ten steps on the stairway on which it had gone down.

2. *His psalm of praise*

9 A writing of Hezekiah king of Judah, after his illness and recovery:

10   I said, "In the middle of my life
        I am to enter the gates of Sheol;
        I am to be deprived of the rest of my years."

11   I said, "I shall not see the LORD,
        The LORD in the land of the living;
        I shall look on man no more among the inhabitants of the world.

12   "Like a shepherd's tent my dwelling is pulled up and removed
            from me;
        As a weaver I rolled up my life.
        He cuts me off from the loom;
        From day until night Thou dost make an end of me.

13   "I composed *my soul* until morning.
        Like a lion—so He breaks all my bones,
        From day until night Thou dost make an end of me.

37:30
Lev 25:5,11

37:31
v. 4; Is 4:2;
10:20; 27:6

37:32
v. 4;
2 Kin 19:31;
Is 9:7;
Zech 1:14

37:33
Jer 6:6; 32:24

37:35
2 Kin 20:6;
Is 38:6; 48:9,
11

37:36
2 Kin 19:35;
Is 10:12,33,
34

37:38
Jer 51:27;
Ezra 4:2

38:1
2 Kin 20:1-6,
9-11;
2 Chr 32:24;
2 Sam 17:23

38:3
Neh 13:14;
2 Kin 18:5,6;
1 Chr 28:9;
29:19;
Deut 6:18

38:5
2 Kin 18:2,13

38:6
Is 37:35

38:7
Is 7:11

38:8
2 Kin 20:9-11;
Josh 10:12-14

38:10
Ps 102:24;
107:18;
Job 17:11,15;
2 Cor 1:9

38:11
Ps 27:13;
116:9

38:12
2 Cor 5:1,4;
Heb 1:12;
Job 7:6; 6:9;
Ps 73:14

38:13
Job 10:16;
16:12;
Ps 51:8; 32:4

And *who* taught Him in the path of justice and taught Him
  knowledge,
And informed Him of the way of understanding?
15 Behold, the nations are like a drop from a bucket,
And are regarded as a speck of dust on the scales;
Behold, He lifts up the islands like fine dust.
16 Even Lebanon is not enough to burn,
Nor its beasts enough for a burnt offering.
17 All the nations are as nothing before Him,
They are regarded by Him as less than nothing and meaningless.

c. Contrast between idols and the living God

18 To whom then will you liken God?
Or what likeness will you compare with Him?
19 *As for* the idol, a craftsman casts it,
A goldsmith plates it with gold,
And a silversmith *fashions* chains of silver.
20 He who is too impoverished for *such* an offering
Selects a tree that does not rot;
He seeks out for himself a skillful craftsman
To prepare an idol that will not totter.

21 Do you not know? Have you not heard?
Has it not been declared to you from the beginning?
Have you not understood from the foundations of the earth?
22 It is He who [14]sits above the [15]vault of the earth,
And its inhabitants are like grasshoppers,
Who stretches out the heavens like a curtain
And spreads them out like a tent to dwell in.
23 He *it is* who reduces rulers to nothing,
Who makes the judges of the earth meaningless.
24 [16]Scarcely have they been planted,
[16]Scarcely have they been sown,
[16]Scarcely has their stock taken root in the earth,
But He merely blows on them, and they wither,
And the storm carries them away like stubble.
25 "To whom then will you liken Me
That I should be *his* equal?" says the Holy One.
26 Lift up your eyes on high
And see who has created these *stars*,
The One who leads forth their host by number,
He calls them all by name;
Because of the greatness of His might and the strength of *His* power
Not one *of them* is missing.

d. God's faithfulness and empowering grace

27 Why do you say, O Jacob, and assert, O Israel,
"My way is hidden from the LORD,
And the justice due me escapes the notice of my God"?
28 Do you not know? Have you not heard?
The Everlasting God, the LORD, the Creator of the ends of the earth
Does not become weary or tired.
His understanding is inscrutable.
29 He gives strength to the weary,
And to *him who* lacks might He increases power.
30 Though youths grow weary and tired,
And vigorous young men stumble badly,
31 Yet those who wait for the LORD
Will gain new strength;
They will mount up *with* wings like eagles,
They will run and not get tired,
They will walk and not become weary.

[14]Or, *is enthroned* [15]Or, *circle* [16]Or, *Not even*

40:14
Job 38:4;
21:22

40:15
Jer 10:10;
Is 17:13; 29:5

40:17
Is 29:7; 30:28

40:18
v. 25; Is 46:5;
Mic 7:18;
Acts 17:29
40:19
Is 41:6,7;
44:12;
Jer 10:3
40:20
Is 41:7;
Jer 10:3-5

40:21
Ps 19:1;
Acts 14:17;
Rom 1:19
40:22
Job 22:14;
Num 13:33;
Is 42:5;
44:24;
Ps 104:2
40:23
Job 12:21;
Ps 107:40;
Is 5:21
40:24
Is 17:10,11;
v. 7; Is 17:13;
41:16

40:25
v. 18

40:26
Is 51:6; 42:5;
Ps 147:4;
89:11-13;
Is 34:16

40:27
Is 49:4,14;
54:8;
Luke 18:7,8;
Is 25:1
40:28
Ps 90:2;
147:5;
Rom 11:33

40:29
Is 50:4;
Jer 31:25;
Is 41:10
40:30
Jer 6:11;
Is 9:17
40:31
Ps 103:5;
2 Cor 4:8-10,
16;
Deut 32:11;
2 Cor 4:1;
Heb 12:3

2. *The God of providence challenges unbelievers*

a. *God's providence based on omnipotence*

41:1
Zech 2:13;
Is 40:31;
34:1; 43:26

41 "Coastlands, listen to Me in silence,
And let the peoples gain new strength;
Let them come forward, then let them speak;
Let us come together for judgment.

41:2
Is 45:1-3;
46:11; 42:6;
2 Chr 36:23;
Is 29:5; 40:24

2 "Who has aroused one from the east
Whom He calls in righteousness to His feet?
He delivers up nations before him,
And subdues kings.
He makes them like dust with his sword,
As the wind-driven chaff with his bow.

3 "He pursues them, passing on in safety,
By a way he had not been traversing with his feet.

41:4
Is 44:7;
46:10; 43:10;
44:6;
Rev 1:17;
22:13

4 "Who has performed and accomplished *it*,
Calling forth the generations from the beginning?
'I, the Lord, am the first, and with the last. I am He.' "

41:5
Ps 67:7

5 The coastlands have seen and are afraid;
The ends of the earth tremble;
They have drawn near and have come.

41:6
Is 40:19

6 Each one helps his neighbor,
And says to his brother, "Be strong!"

41:7
Is 40:19,20

7 So the craftsman encourages the smelter,
And he who smooths *metal* with the hammer *encourages* him who
beats the anvil,
Saying of the soldering, "It is good";
And he fastens it with nails,
That it should not totter.

b. *God's servant, Israel, an instrument of His providence*

41:8
Is 44:1;
2 Chr 20:7;
James 2:23

8 "But you, Israel, My servant,
Jacob whom I have chosen,
Descendant of Abraham My friend,

41:9
Is 11:11;
43:5-7; 42:1;
Ps 135:4

9 "You whom I have taken from the ends of the earth,
And called from its remotest parts,
And said to you, 'You are My servant,
I have chosen you and not rejected you.

41:10
Is 43:5;
Rom 8:31;
Is 44:2

10 'Do not fear, for I am with you;
Do not anxiously look about you, for I am your God.
I will strengthen you, surely I will help you,
Surely I will uphold you with My righteous right hand.'

c. *His chosen people will overcome their foes*

*41:11
Is 45:24;
17:13

11 "Behold, all those who are angered at you will be shamed and
dishonored;
Those who contend with you will be as nothing, and will perish.

41:12
Is 17:14;
29:20

12 "You will seek those who quarrel with you, but will not find them,
Those who war with you will be as nothing, and non-existent.

41:13
Is 42:6; v. 10

13 "For I am the Lord your God, who upholds your right hand,
Who says to you, 'Do not fear, I will help you.'

*41:14
Job 25:6;
Is 43:14

14 "Do not fear, you worm Jacob, you men of Israel;
I will help you," declares the Lord, "and your
Redeemer is the Holy One of Israel.

41:11 The Christian life is a warfare. There is no release from it until death. There are Biblical principles that throw light on this problem. The warfare is directed against known enemies such as: (1) Satan (2 Cor. 2:11; Eph. 6:11, 12); (2) the flesh (Rom. 7:23; Gal. 5:17; 1 Pet. 2:11); (3) the world (John 16:33; 1 John 5:4,5); and (4) death (1 Cor. 15:26; Heb. 2:14,15). Saints are exhorted: (1) to be spiritually armed (Eph. 6:14–18); (2) to be watchful (1 Pet. 5:8);

(3) to be sober (1 Thess. 5:6); and (4) to exercise faith (1 Tim. 1:18,19). There are assurances of victory (Rom. 8:37; 16:20; Gal. 5:24; 1 John 5:4,5); also the certainty of rewards (Rev. 2:17; 3:5; 21:7).
41:14 *you worm Jacob.* This is actually a term of compassion and love. A worm on the ground is at the mercy of any who might trample on it. God will help His helpless worm, Jacob-Israel.

15	"Behold, I have made you a new, sharp threshing sledge with double edges; You will thresh the mountains, and pulverize *them,* And will make the hills like chaff.	**41:15** Mic 4:13
16	"You will winnow them, and the wind will carry them away, And the storm will scatter them; But you will rejoice in the LORD, You will glory in the Holy One of Israel.	**41:16** Jer 51:2; Is 45:25

d. *God will deliver and prosper His people*

17	"The afflicted and needy are seeking water, but there is none, And their tongue is parched with thirst; I, the LORD, will answer them Myself, *As* the God of Israel I will not forsake them.	**41:17** Is 43:20; 30:19; 42:16
18	"I will open rivers on the bare heights, And springs in the midst of the valleys; I will make the wilderness a pool of water, And the dry land fountains of water.	**41:18** Is 35:6,7; 43:19
19	"I will put the cedar in the wilderness, The acacia, and the myrtle, and the olive tree; I will place the juniper in the desert, Together with the box tree and the cypress,	
20	That they may see and recognize, And consider and gain insight as well, That the hand of the LORD has done this, And the Holy One of Israel has created it.	**41:20** Is 40:5; Job 12:9

e. *God's omnipotence shown by foretelling the future*

21	"Present your case," the LORD says. "Bring forward your strong *arguments,*" The King of Jacob says.	**41:21** v. 1; Is 43:15
22	Let them bring forth and declare to us what is going to take place; As for the former *events,* declare what they *were,* That we may consider them, and know their outcome; Or announce to us what is coming.	**41:22** Is 45:21; 43:9
23	Declare the things that are going to come afterward, That we may know that you are gods; Indeed, do good or evil, that we may anxiously look about us and fear together.	**41:23** Is 42:9; 44:7, 8; 45:3; John 13:19; Jer 10:5
24	Behold, you are of no account, And your work amounts to nothing; He who chooses you is an abomination.	**41:24** Ps 115:8; Is 44:9; 1 Cor 8:4; v. 29
25	"I have aroused one from the north, and he has come; From the rising of the sun he will call on My name; And he will come upon rulers as *upon* mortar, Even as the potter treads clay."	**41:25** v. 2; Is 10:6
26	Who has declared *this* from the beginning, that we might know? Or from former times, that we may say, "*He is* right!"? Surely there was no one who declared, Surely there was no one who proclaimed, Surely there was no one who heard your words.	**41:26** Is 44:7; 45:21; Hab 2:18,19
27	"Formerly *I said* to Zion, 'Behold, here they are.' And to Jerusalem, 'I will give a messenger of good news.'	**41:27** v. 4; Is 40:9
28	"But when I look, there is no one, And there is no counselor among them Who, if I ask, can give an answer.	**41:28** Is 63:5; 40:13,14; 46:7
29	"Behold, all of them are [17]false; Their works are worthless, Their molten images are wind and emptiness.	**41:29** v. 24; Is 44:9; Jer 5:13

[17]Another reading is *nothing*

3. *God's servant: individual and national*

a. *The mission of the servant*

42

42:1
Is 43:10;
53:11;
Matt 12:18-20;
3:16,17; 17:5;
Is 2:4

"Behold, My Servant, whom I uphold;
My chosen one *in whom* My soul delights.
I have put My Spirit upon Him;
He will bring forth justice to the nations.

2 "He will not cry out or raise *His voice,*
Nor make His voice heard in the street.

42:3
Is 57:15;
Ps 72:2

3 "A bruised reed He will not break,
And a dimly burning wick He will not extinguish;
He will faithfully bring forth justice.

42:4
Is 40:28;
vv. 10,12

4 "He will not be disheartened or crushed,
Until He has established justice in the earth;
And the coastlands will wait expectantly for His law."

b. *The servant a light to the nations*

42:5
Is 44:24;
Zech 12:1;
Acts 17:25

5 Thus says God the LORD,
Who created the heavens and stretched them out,
Who spread out the earth and its offspring,
Who gives breath to the people on it,
And spirit to those who walk in it,

42:6
Is 43:1; 49:6,
8; Luke 2:32;
Acts 13:47

6 "I am the LORD, I have called you in righteousness,
I will also hold you by the hand and watch over you,
And I will appoint you as a covenant to the people,
As a light to the nations,

42:7
Is 35:5; 61:1;
Luke 4:18;
2 Tim 2:26;
Heb 2:14
42:8
Is 48:11

7 To open blind eyes,
To bring out prisoners from the dungeon,
And those who dwell in darkness from the prison.

8 "I am the LORD, that is My name;
I will not give My glory to another,
Nor My praise to graven images.

42:9
Is 48:3,6

9 "Behold, the former things have come to pass,
Now I declare new things;
Before they spring forth I proclaim *them* to you."

c. *Song of praise to the LORD*

42:10
Is 33:3; 40:3;
98:1; 107:23

10 Sing to the LORD a new song,
Sing His praise from the end of the earth!
You who go down to the sea, and all that is in it.
You islands and those who dwell on them.

11 Let the wilderness and its cities lift up *their voices,*
The settlements where Kedar inhabits.
Let the inhabitants of Sela sing aloud,
Let them shout for joy from the tops of the mountains.

42:12
Is 24:15; v. 4

12 Let them give glory to the LORD,
And declare His praise in the coastlands.

42:13
Is 9:7;
Ex 15:3;
Hos 11:10;
Is 66:14-16

13 The LORD will go forth like a warrior,
He will arouse *His* zeal like a man of war.
He will utter a shout, yes, He will raise a war cry.
He will prevail against His enemies.

d. *Idolators to be punished; backsliders restored*

42:14
Is 57:11

14 "I have kept silent for a long time,
I have kept still and restrained Myself.
Now like a woman in labor I will groan,
I will both gasp and pant.

42:15
Is 2:12-16;
44:27

15 "I will lay waste the mountains and hills,
And wither all their vegetation;
I will make the rivers into coastlands,
And dry up the ponds.

42:11 *the settlements where Kedar inhabits.* They were occupied by nomads of the Syrian desert. They would see the
glory of Israel's God as He brought His People back from
exile.

16   "And I will lead the blind by a way they do not know,
     In paths they do not know I will guide them.
     I will make darkness into light before them
     And rugged places into plains.
     These are the things I will do,
     And I will not leave them undone."

17   They shall be turned back and be utterly put to shame,
     Who trust in idols,
     Who say to molten images,
     "You are our gods."

e. Blindness of the servant-nation and its punishment

18 Hear, you deaf!
     And look, you blind, that you may see.

19   Who is blind but My servant,
     Or so deaf as My messenger whom I send?
     Who is so blind as he that is at peace *with Me,*
     Or so blind as the servant of the LORD?

20   You have seen many things, but you do not observe *them;*
     Your ears are open, but none hears.

21   The LORD was pleased for His righteousness' sake
     To make the law great and glorious.

22   But this is a people plundered and despoiled;
     All of them are trapped in caves,
     Or are hidden away in prisons;
     They have become a prey with none to deliver *them,*
     And a spoil, with none to say, "Give *them* back!"

23 Who among you will give ear to this?
     Who will give heed and listen hereafter?

24   Who gave Jacob up for spoil, and Israel to plunderers?
     Was it not the LORD, against whom we have sinned,
     And in whose ways they were not willing to walk,
     And whose law they did not obey?

25   So He poured out on him the heat of His anger
     And the fierceness of battle;
     And it set him aflame all around,
     Yet he did not recognize *it;*
     And it burned him, but he paid no attention.

4. Redemption by grace

a. God's love will support, redeem, and restore His people

43 But now, thus says the LORD, your Creator, O Jacob,
     And He who formed you, O Israel,
     "Do not fear, for I have redeemed you;
     I have called you by name; you are Mine!

2   "When you pass through the waters, I will be with you;
     And through the rivers, they will not overflow you.
     When you walk through the fire, you will not be scorched,
     Nor will the flame burn you.

3   "For I am the LORD your God,
     The Holy One of Israel, your Savior;
     I have given Egypt as your ransom,
     Cush and Seba in your place.

4   "Since you are precious in My sight,
     Since you are honored and I love you,
     I will give *other* men in your place and *other* peoples in exchange for
         your life.

5   "Do not fear, for I am with you;
     I will bring your offspring from the east,
     And gather you from the west.

42:16
Is 29:18;
Luke 1:78,
79; 3:5;
Is 41:17

42:17
Ps 97:7;
Is 1:29;
44:11; 45:16

42:19
Is 43:8;
Ezek 12:2

42:20
Jer 6:10

42:21
Is 58:13

42:22
Is 24:18,22;
10:6

42:24
Is 30:15;
48:18

42:25
Is 5:25;
2 Kin 25:9;
Hos 7:9

43:1
vv. 7,15,21;
Is 44:2,6,21

43:2
Ps 66:12;
Deut 31:6,8;
Dan 3:25,27

*43:3
Ex 20:2;
v. 11;
Prov 11:8;
21:18

43:4
Is 63:9

43:5
Is 41:10,14;
44:2;
Jer 30:10,11;
46:27,28

43:3 *Egypt as your ransom.* Persia is compensated for the   Seba (conquered by Cambyses, son of Cyrus).
loss of the Israelites by being assigned Egypt, Ethiopia, and

43:6
Ps 107:3;
Is 14:2

6 "I will say to the north, 'Give *them* up!'
And to the south, 'Do not hold *them* back.'
Bring My sons from afar,
And My daughters from the ends of the earth,

43:7
Ps 100:3;
Is 29:23;
Eph 2:10;
v. 1

7 Everyone who is called by My name,
And whom I have created for My glory,
Whom I have formed, even whom I have made."

b. The servant-nation a witness to the world

43:8
Is 6:9; 42:19;
Ezek 12:2

8 Bring out the people who are blind, even though they have eyes,
And the deaf, even though they have ears.

43:9
Is 41:21,22,
26

9 All the nations have gathered together
In order that the peoples may be assembled.
Who among them can declare this
And proclaim to us the former things?
Let them present their witnesses that they may be justified,
Or let them hear and say, "It is true."

43:10
Is 44:8; 42:1;
41:4; 44:6

10 "You are My witnesses," declares the LORD,
"And My servant whom I have chosen,
In order that you may know and believe Me,
And understand that I am He.
Before Me there was no God formed,
And there will be none after Me.

43:11
Is 45:21

11 "I, even I, am the LORD;
And there is no savior besides Me.

43:12
Deut 32:16;
Ps 81:9;
v. 10; Is 44:8

12 "It is I who have declared and saved and proclaimed,
And there was no strange *god* among you;
So you are My witnesses," declares the LORD,
"And I am God.

43:13
Ps 90:2;
Job 9:12;
Is 14:27

13 "Even from eternity I am He;
And there is none who can deliver out of My hand;
I act and who can reverse it?"

c. The Redeemer will restore His people from Babylon

43:14
Is 41:14;
13:14,15

14 Thus says the LORD your Redeemer, the Holy One of Israel,
"For your sake I have sent to Babylon,
And will bring them all down as fugitives,
[18]Even the Chaldeans, into the ships in which they rejoice.

15 "I am the LORD, your Holy One,
The Creator of Israel, your King."

43:16
Ex 14:16;
Ps 77:19;
Is 51:10;
Josh 3:13
43:17
Ex 14:4-9,25

16 Thus says the LORD,
Who makes a way through the sea
And a path through the mighty waters,

17 Who brings forth the chariot and the horse,
The army and the mighty man
(They will lie down together *and* not rise again;
They have been quenched *and* extinguished like a wick):

43:18
Jer 16:14

18 "Do not call to mind the former things,
Or ponder things of the past.

43:19
2 Cor 5:17;
Rev 21:5;
Ex 17:6;
Num 20:11;
Is 35:6

19 "Behold, I will do something new,
Now it will spring forth;
Will you not be aware of it?
I will even make a roadway in the wilderness,
Rivers in the desert.

43:20
Is 48:21

20 "The beasts of the field will glorify Me;
The jackals and the ostriches;
Because I have given waters in the wilderness
And rivers in the desert,
To give drink to My chosen people.

43:21
v. 1;
Ps 102:18;
Luke 1:74,75

21 "The people whom I formed for Myself,
Will declare My praise.

[18]Another reading is *As for the Chaldeans, their rejoicing is* turned *into lamentations*

And he will perform all My desire.'
And he declares of Jerusalem, 'She will be built,'
And of the temple, 'Your foundation will be laid.' ''

b. Promise of victory to Cyrus

45 Thus says the LORD to Cyrus His anointed,
Whom I have taken by the right hand,
To subdue nations before him,
And to loose the loins of kings;
To open doors before him so that gates will not be shut:

2 "I will go before you and make the rough places smooth;
I will shatter the doors of bronze, and cut through their iron bars.

3 "And I will give you the treasures of darkness,
And hidden wealth of secret places,
In order that you may know that it is I,
The LORD, the God of Israel, who calls you by your name.

4 "For the sake of Jacob My servant,
And Israel My chosen *one*,
I have also called you by your name;
I have given you a title of honor
Though you have not known Me.

5 "I am the LORD, and there is no other;
Besides Me there is no God.
I will gird you, though you have not known Me;

6 That men may know from the rising to the setting of the sun
That there is no one besides Me.
I am the LORD, and there is no other,

c. The folly of striving with God

7 The One forming light and creating darkness,
Causing well-being and creating calamity;
I am the LORD who does all these.

8 "Drip down, O heavens, from above,
And let the clouds pour down righteousness;
Let the earth open up and salvation bear fruit,
And righteousness spring up with it.
I, the LORD, have created it.

9 "Woe to *the one* who quarrels with his Maker—
An earthenware vessel among the vessels of earth!
Will the clay say to the potter, 'What are you doing?'
Or the thing you are making *say*, 'He has no hands'?

10 "Woe to him who says to a father, 'What are you begetting?'
Or to a woman, 'To what are you giving birth?' ''

11 Thus says the LORD, the Holy One of Israel, and his Maker:
"Ask Me about the things to come concerning My sons,
And you shall commit to Me the work of My hands.

12 "It is I who made the earth, and created man upon it.
I stretched out the heavens with My hands,
And I ordained all their host.

13 "I have aroused him in righteousness,
And I will make all his ways smooth;

Cross references (right margin):

45:1 Is 44:28; 41:13; Jer 50:3,35; v. 5
45:2 Is 40:4; Ps 107:16; Jer 51:30
45:3 Jer 41:8; Is 43:1
45:4 Is 41:8; 43:1; Acts 17:23
45:5 v. 6; Is 44:6, 8; Ps 18:39
45:6 Mal 1:11; Is 43:5; v. 5
*45:7 Is 42:16; Ps 104:20; Amos 3:6
45:8 Ps 72:6; 85:11; Is 12:3; 60:21
45:9 Is 29:16; Rom 9:20,21
45:11 Is 43:15; 54:5; 8:19; Jer 31:9; 60:21
45:12 v. 18; Is 42:5; Neh 9:6
45:13 Is 41:2; v. 2; Is 44:28; 52:3

44:28 This prediction of the rebuilding of the temple at Jerusalem was made 150 years before Cyrus's decree to rebuild it was promulgated. His decree was given in the first year of his reign over Babylon, about 538 B.C. (Ezra 1:1,2; 6:3). The new temple was known as the second temple, and it remained as the center of Jewish worship until the fall of Jerusalem in A.D. 70. It was desecrated by Antiochus Epiphanes in 168 B.C., an event that was predicted by Daniel (Dan. 9:27; 11:31). In New Testament days the temple was repaired and improved by Herod the Great and his successors over a period of forty-six years (John 2:20). Jesus often taught in this temple (Mark 14:49), and He predicted its utter destruction (Matt. 24:2; Mark 13:2; Luke 21:6). It was the curtain (veil) of this temple that was torn in two at Christ's death (Matt. 27:51). No Gentile was ever permitted to enter its inner courts (Acts 21:27–30).

45:7 The KJV translation, "I make peace, and create evil," has led to the idea that God is the author of sin. The NAS translation is more accurate, since this word for "evil" (ra') is often used of physical evil or calamity, rather than moral evil. God is not the author of sin. Man has the power of free will and contrary choice. Since all sin is basically rebellion against God, it is impossible for Him to have created it.

He will build My city, and will let My exiles go free,
Without any payment or reward," says the LORD of hosts.

d. *The future conversion of the Gentiles*

14 Thus says the LORD,
"The products of Egypt and the merchandise of Cush
And the Sabeans, men of stature,
Will come over to you and will be yours;
They will walk behind you, they will come over in chains
And will bow down to you;
They will make supplication to you:
'Surely, God is with you, and there is none else,
No other God.'"

15 Truly, Thou art a God who hides Himself,
O God of Israel, Savior!

16 They will be put to shame and even humiliated, all of them;
The manufacturers of idols will go away together in humiliation.

17 Israel has been saved by the LORD
With an everlasting salvation;
You will not be put to shame or humiliated
To all eternity.

18 For thus says the LORD, who created the heavens
(He is the God who formed the earth and made it,
He established it and did not create it a waste place,
But formed it to be inhabited),
"I am the LORD, and there is none else.

19 "I have not spoken in secret,
In some dark land;
I did not say to the offspring of Jacob,
'Seek Me in a waste place';
I, the LORD, speak righteousness
Declaring things that are upright.

e. *The heathen invited to be saved by faith in the LORD*

20 "Gather yourselves and come;
Draw near together, you fugitives of the nations;
They have no knowledge,
Who carry about their wooden idol,
And pray to a god who cannot save.

21 "Declare and set forth *your case;*
Indeed, let them consult together.
Who has announced this from of old?
Who has long since declared it?
Is it not I, the LORD?
And there is no other God besides Me,
A righteous God and a Savior;
There is none except Me.

22 "Turn to Me, and be saved, all the ends of the earth;
For I am God, and there is no other.

23 "I have sworn by Myself,
The word has gone forth from My mouth in righteousness
And will not turn back,
That to Me every knee will bow, every tongue will swear *allegiance.*

24 "They will say of Me, 'Only in the LORD are righteousness and
strength.'
Men will come to Him,
And all who were angry at Him shall be put to shame.

25 "In the LORD all the offspring of Israel
Will be justified, and will glory."

Cross references (left margin):
- **45:14** Is 14:1,2; Ps 149:8; Is 49:23; Jer 16:19; 1 Cor 14:25; v. 5
- **45:15** Is 8:17; 43:3
- **45:16** Is 44:9,11
- **45:17** Is 26:4; Rom 11:26; Is 49:23
- **45:18** Is 42:5; v. 12; Gen 1:2,26; v. 5
- **45:19** Is 48:16; 41:8; Jer 29:13,14; Is 63:1; 44:8
- **45:20** Is 43:9; 44:18,19; Jer 10:5; Is 46:6,7
- **45:21** Is 41:23,26; v. 5; Is 43:3, 11
- ***45:22** Num 21:8,9; Is 30:15; 49:6,12
- **45:23** Is 62:8; Rom 14:11; Is 55:11; 65:16
- **45:24** Is 54:17; 41:11
- **45:25** Is 53:11; 60:19

45:22 Verse 20 speaks of great idolatry. But a loving God extends a universal call to all people. It is clear that all need to be saved and that all who come can be saved.

7. Lessons from Babylon's fall and Israel's preservation

a. Babylon's helpless idols and the omnipotent God

46
Bel has bowed down, Nebo stoops over;
　　Their images are *consigned* to the beasts and the cattle.
　　The things that you carry are burdensome,
　　A load for the weary *beast*.

2
They stooped over, they have bowed down together;
　　They could not rescue the burden,
　　But have themselves gone into captivity.

3
"Listen to Me, O house of Jacob,
　　And all the remnant of the house of Israel,
　　You who have been borne by Me from birth,
　　And have been carried from the womb;

4
Even to your old age, I shall be the same,
　　And even to your graying years I shall bear *you!*
　　I have done *it*, and I shall carry *you;*
　　And I shall bear *you*, and I shall deliver *you*.

5
"To whom would you liken Me,
　　And make Me equal and compare Me,
　　That we should be alike?

6
"Those who lavish gold from the purse
　　And weigh silver on the scale
　　Hire a goldsmith, and he makes it *into* a god;
　　They bow down, indeed they worship it.

7
"They lift it upon the shoulder and carry it;
　　They set it in its place and it stands *there*.
　　It does not move from its place.
　　Though one may cry to it, it cannot answer;
　　It cannot deliver him from his distress.

8
"Remember this, and be assured;
　　Recall it to mind, you transgressors.

9
"Remember the former things long past,
　　For I am God, and there is no other;
　　I am God, and there is no one like Me,

10
Declaring the end from the beginning
　　And from ancient times things which have not been done,
　　Saying, 'My purpose will be established,
　　And I will accomplish all My good pleasure';

11
Calling a bird of prey from the east,
　　The man of My purpose from a far country.
　　Truly I have spoken; truly I will bring it to pass.
　　I have planned *it, surely* I will do it.

12
"Listen to Me, you stubborn-minded,
　　Who are far from righteousness.

13
"I bring near My righteousness, it is not far off;
　　And My salvation will not delay.
　　And I will grant salvation in Zion,
　　And My glory for Israel.

b. Judgment against merciless Babylon

47
"Come down and sit in the dust,
　　O virgin daughter of Babylon;
　　Sit on the ground without a throne,
　　O daughter of the Chaldeans.
　　For you shall no longer be called tender and delicate.

2
"Take the millstones and grind meal.
　　Remove your veil, strip off the skirt,

Cross references (right margin):

*46:1
Jer 50:2-4;
Is 45:20

46:2
Jer 43:12,13

46:3
v. 12;
Is 45:19;
10:21,22;
63:9

46:4
Is 43:13;
Ps 71:18

46:5
Is 40:18,25

46:6
Is 40:19;
44:15,17

46:7
v. 1; Is 40:20;
44:17; 41:26,
28; 45:20

46:8
Is 44:19,21;
48:8
46:9
Is 45:5,21;
41:26,27

46:10
Is 45:21;
14:24;
Acts 5:39

46:11
Is 18:6; 41:2,
25; 37:26

46:12
v. 3; Is 48:4;
Jer 2:5
46:13
Is 61:11;
43:7; 44:23

47:1
Jer 48:18;
46:11; 51:33

46:1 *Bel has bowed down, Nebo stoops over.* Bel-Marduk was the principal god of Babylon; Nebo was the Babylonian god of writing and patron of Borsippa.

Uncover the leg, cross the rivers.

47:3
Ezek 16:37;
Is 34:8; 63:4

3 "Your nakedness will be uncovered,
Your shame also will be exposed;
I will take vengeance and will not spare a man."

47:4
Is 41:14

4 Our Redeemer, the LORD of hosts is His name,
The Holy One of Israel.

47:5
Is 23:2;
13:10;
Is 13:19;
Dan 2:37

5 "Sit silently, and go into darkness,
O daughter of the Chaldeans;
For you will no more be called
The queen of kingdoms.

47:6
Zech 1:15;
Is 43:28;
10:14;
Deut 28:50

6 "I was angry with My people,
I profaned My heritage,
And gave them into your hand.
You did not show mercy to them,
On the aged you made your yoke very heavy.

47:7
v. 5; Is 42:25;
45:21

7 "Yet you said, 'I shall be a queen forever.'
These things you did not consider,
Nor remember the outcome of them.

c. Babylon's false security amid wickedness

47:8
Is 32:9,11;
Zeph 2:15;
Rev 18:7

8 "Now, then, hear this, you sensual one,
Who dwells securely,
Who says in your heart,
'I am, and there is no one besides me.
I shall not sit as a widow,
Nor shall I know loss of children.'

47:9
Is 13:16,18;
1 Thess 5:3;
Nah 3:4

9 "But these two things shall come on you suddenly in one day:
Loss of children and widowhood.
They shall come on you in full measure
In spite of your many sorceries,
In spite of the great power of your spells.

47:10
Ps 52:7;
Is 29:15;
44:20; v. 8

10 "And you felt secure in your wickedness and said,
'No one sees me,'
Your wisdom and your knowledge, they have deluded you;
For you have said in your heart,
'I am, and there is no one besides me.'

47:11
Is 57:1;
1 Thess 5:3;
v. 9

11 "But evil will come on you
Which you will not know how to charm away;
And disaster will fall on you
For which you cannot atone,
And destruction about which you do not know
Will come on you suddenly.

d. Helplessness of Babylon to avert her fall

47:12
v. 9

12 "Stand *fast* now in your spells
And in your many sorceries
With which you have labored from your youth;
Perhaps you will be able to profit,
Perhaps you may cause trembling.

47:13
Is 57:10;
Dan 2:2

13 "You are wearied with your many counsels;
Let now the astrologers,
Those who prophesy by the stars,
Those who predict by the new moons,
Stand up and save you from what will come upon you.

47:14
Nah 1:10;
Mal 4:1

14 "Behold, they have become like stubble,
Fire burns them;
They cannot deliver themselves from the power of the flame;
There will be no coal to warm by,
Nor a fire to sit before!

47:15
Rev 18:11;
Is 43:13; 46:7

15 "So have those become to you with whom you have labored,
Who have trafficked with you from your youth;
Each has wandered in his own way.
There is none to save you.

8. *Israel punished and returned to her land*
a. *The prophecy of captivity fulfilled*

48 "Hear this, O house of Jacob, who are named Israel
And who came forth from the loins of Judah,
Who swear by the name of the LORD
And invoke the God of Israel,
But not in truth nor in righteousness.

2 "For they call themselves after the holy city,
And lean on the God of Israel;
The LORD of hosts is His name.

3 "I declared the former things long ago
And they went forth from My mouth, and I proclaimed them.
Suddenly I acted, and they came to pass.

4 "Because I know that you are obstinate,
And your neck is an iron sinew,
And your forehead bronze,

5 Therefore I declared *them* to you long ago,
Before they took place I proclaimed *them* to you,
Lest you should say, 'My idol has done them,
And my graven image and my molten image have commanded
    them.'

6 "You have heard; look at all this.
And you, will you not declare it?
I proclaim to you new things from this time,
Even hidden things which you have not known.

7 "They are created now and not long ago;
And before today you have not heard them,
Lest you should say, 'Behold, I knew them.'

8 "You have not heard, you have not known.
Even from long ago your ear has not been open,
Because I knew that you would deal very treacherously;
And you have been called a rebel from birth.

b. *God's glory upheld by Israel's affliction*

9 "For the sake of My name I delay My wrath,
And *for* My praise I restrain *it* for you,
In order not to cut you off.

10 "Behold, I have refined you, but not as silver;
I have tested you in the furnace of affliction.

11 "For My own sake, for My own sake, I will act;
For how can *My name* be profaned?
And My glory I will not give to another.

c. *God to send Cyrus against Babylon*

12 "Listen to Me, O Jacob, even Israel whom I called;
I am He, I am the first, I am also the last.

13 "Surely My hand founded the earth,
And My right hand spread out the heavens;
When I call to them, they stand together.

14 "Assemble, all of you, and listen!
Who among them has declared these things?
The LORD loves him; he shall carry out His good pleasure on
    Babylon,
And His arm *shall be against* the Chaldeans.

15 "I, even I, have spoken; indeed I have called him,
I have brought him, and He will make his ways successful.

16 "Come near to Me, listen to this:
From the first I have not spoken in secret,
From the time it took place, I was there.
And now the Lord GOD has sent Me, and His Spirit."

d. *A chastened Israel to flee from Babylon and return home*

17 Thus says the LORD, your Redeemer, the Holy One of Israel;

48:1
Is 46:12;
Num 24:7;
Ps 68:26;
Is 45:23

48:2
Is 52:1;
Mic 3:11;
Rom 2:17

48:3
Is 41:22;
42:9; 43:9;
44:7,8; 45:21;
Josh 21:45
48:4
Ezek 2:4;
Ex 32:9;
Deut 31:27;
Ezek 3:7-9
48:5
Ezek 2:4; 3:7

48:6
Is 42:9; 43:19

48:8
Is 42:25;
46:8; Ps 58:3

48:9
v. 11;
Ps 78:38;
Is 30:18
48:10
Jer 9:7;
Ezek 22:18-22;
Jer 11:4
48:11
v. 9;
Deut 32:26;
Ezek 20:9;
Is 42:8

48:12
Deut 32:39;
Is 41:4;
Rev 1:17;
22:13
48:13
Ps 102:25;
Is 40:26
48:14
Is 43:9;
45:21; 46:10,
11;
Jer 50:21-29

48:15
Is 41:2; 45:1,
2
48:16
Is 41:1;
45:19; 43:13;
Zech 2:9,11

48:17
Is 43:14;
Ps 32:8

"I am the LORD your God, who teaches you to profit,
Who leads you in the way you should go.

48:18
Deut 32:29;
Ps 119:165;
Is 61:10,11

18 "If only you had paid attention to My commandments!
Then your well-being would have been like a river,
And your righteousness like the waves of the sea.

48:19
Gen 22:17;
Jer 33:22;
Is 56:5; 66:22

19 "Your descendants would have been like the sand,
And your offspring like its grains;
Their name would never be cut off or destroyed from My presence."

48:20
Jer 50:8;
Is 42:10;
62:11; 43:1

20 Go forth from Babylon! Flee from the Chaldeans!
Declare with the sound of joyful shouting, proclaim this,
Send it out to the end of the earth;
Say, "The LORD has redeemed His servant Jacob."

48:21
Is 41:17;
Ex 17:6;
Ps 105:41

21 And they did not thirst when He led them through the deserts.
He made the water flow out of the rock for them;
He split the rock, and the water gushed forth.

48:22
Is 57:21

22 "There is no peace for the wicked," says the LORD.

B. Part II: God's servant-king Redeemer

1. God's servant-king to restore Israel and bring light to the Gentiles

a. Messiah's call and commission; message to Israel and the heathen

49:1
Is 42:4;
66:19; 44:2,
24; Is 7:14;
9:6;
Matt 1:20;
Gal 1:15

49 Listen to Me, O islands,
And pay attention, you peoples from afar.
The LORD called Me from the womb;
From the body of My mother He named Me.

49:2
Is 11:4;
Heb 4:12;
Is 51:16;
Hab 3:11

2 And He has made My mouth like a sharp sword;
In the shadow of His hand He has concealed Me,
And He has also made Me a select arrow;
He has hidden Me in His quiver.

49:3
Is 42:1; 44:23

3 And He said to Me, "You are My Servant, Israel,
In Whom I will show My glory."

49:4
Is 65:23

4 But I said, "I have toiled in vain,
I have spent My strength for nothing and vanity;
Yet surely the justice due to Me is with the LORD,
And My reward with My God."

49:5
Is 44:2,23;
27:12; 43:4;
12:2

5 And now says the LORD, who formed Me from the womb to be His
      Servant,
To bring Jacob back to Him, in order that Israel might be gathered
      to Him
(For I am honored in the sight of the LORD,
And My God is My strength),

49:6
Is 42:6;
Luke 2:32;
Acts 13:47;
26:23

6 He says, "It is too small a thing that You should be My Servant
To raise up the tribes of Jacob, and to restore the preserved ones of
      Israel;
I will also make You a light of the nations
So that My salvation may reach to the end of the earth."

49:7
Is 48:17;
53:3;
Ps 22:6-8;
Is 52:15;
66:23

7 Thus says the LORD, the Redeemer of Israel, and its Holy One,
To the despised One,
To the One abhorred by the nation,
To the Servant of rulers,
"Kings shall see and arise,
Princes shall also bow down;
Because of the LORD who is faithful, the Holy One of Israel who has
      chosen You."

b. God's deliverance and care of His redeemed

49:8
Ps 69:13;
2 Cor 6:2;
Is 42:6; 44:26

8 Thus says the LORD, "In a favorable time I have answered You,
And in a day of salvation I have helped You;
And I will keep You and give You for a covenant of the people,
To restore the land, to make them inherit the desolate heritages;

49:9
Is 42:7;

9 Saying to those who are bound, 'Go forth,'

To those who are in darkness, 'Show yourselves.'
Along the roads they will feed,
And their pasture will be on all bare heights.

10   "They will not hunger or thirst,
Neither will the scorching heat or sun strike them down;
For He who has compassion on them will lead them,
And will guide them to springs of water.

11   "And I will make all My mountains a road,
And My highways will be raised up.

12   "Behold, these shall come from afar;
And lo, these *will come* from the north and from the west,
And these from the land of Sinim."

13   Shout for joy, O heavens! And rejoice, O earth!
Break forth into joyful shouting, O mountains!
For the LORD has comforted His people,
And will have compassion on His afflicted.

c. *Zion assured of God's continuing love*

14   But Zion said, "The LORD has forsaken me,
And the Lord has forgotten me."

15   "Can a woman forget her nursing child,
And have no compassion on the son of her womb?
Even these may forget, but I will not forget you.

16   "Behold, I have inscribed you on the palms *of My hands;*
Your walls are continually before Me.

17   "Your builders hurry;
Your destroyers and devastators
Will depart from you.

18   "Lift up your eyes and look around;
All of them gather together, they come to you.
As I live," declares the LORD,
"You shall surely put on all of them as jewels, and bind them on as a
bride.

19   "For your waste and desolate places, and your destroyed land—
Surely now you will be too cramped for the inhabitants,
And those who swallowed you will be far away.

20   "The children of whom you were bereaved will yet say in your ears,
'The place is too cramped for me;
Make room for me that I may live *here.*'

21   "Then you will say in your heart,
'Who has begotten these for me,
Since I have been bereaved of my children,
And am barren, an exile and a wanderer?
And who has reared these?
Behold, I was left alone;
From where did these come?'"

d. *Glorious restoration of Israel along with converted Gentiles*

22   Thus says the Lord GOD,
"Behold, I will lift up My hand to the nations,
And set up My standard to the peoples;
And they will bring your sons in *their* bosom,
And your daughters will be carried on *their* shoulders.

23   "And kings will be your guardians,
And their princesses your nurses.
They will bow down to you with their faces to the earth,
And lick the dust of your feet;
And *you* will know that I am the LORD;
Those who hopefully wait for Me will not be put to shame.

	Luke 4:18; Is 41:18
49:10	Rev 7:16; Ps 121:6; Is 14:1; 40:11; 41:17
49:11	Is 40:4; 62:10
49:12	Is 43:5,6
49:13	Is 44:23; 40:1; 54:7,8, 10; Rev 12:12; 18:20
49:14	Is 40:27
49:15	Is 44:21
49:16	Song 8:6; Is 62:6,7
49:17	v. 19
49:18	Is 60:4; 43:5; 45:23; 52:1
49:19	Is 51:3; 54:1, 2; Zech 10:10; Ps 56:1,2
49:20	Is 54:1-3
49:21	Is 54:6,7; 27:10; 5:13; 1:8
49:22	Is 62:10; 60:4; 66:20
***49:23**	Is 60:16; 45:14; Ps 72:9; Mic 7:17; Is 43:10; 25:9; Ps 25:3

49:23 *those who hopefully wait for Me.* People are always impatient and in haste. God is never in a hurry. Thus a long time elapsed between the promise of the Redeemer and His advent. A long time has passed between the first advent of Jesus and His second return. There is the sure promise of God, however, that those who wait for Him *will not be put to shame,* i.e., God will justify their confidence for having waited.

24 "Can the prey be taken from the mighty man,
  Or the captives of a tyrant be rescued?"

49:25
Is 14:1,2;
25:9

25 Surely, thus says the LORD,
  "Even the captives of the mighty man will be taken away,
  And the prey of the tyrant will be rescued;
  For I will contend with the one who contends with you,
  And I will save your sons.

49:26
Is 9:4,20;
45:6; 43:3;
v. 7

26 "And I will feed your oppressors with their own flesh,
  And they will become drunk with their own blood as with sweet
     wine;
  And all flesh will know that I, the LORD, am your Savior,
  And your Redeemer, the Mighty One of Jacob."

2. Sinfulness of Israel contrasted with obedience of the servant

a. The LORD separated from His wife, Israel, by sin

*50:1
Deut 24:1,3;
Jer 3:8;
Is 54:6,7;
Deut 32:30;
Is 52:3; 48:8

50 Thus says the LORD,
  "Where is the certificate of divorce,
  By which I have sent your mother away?
  Or to whom of My creditors did I sell you?
  Behold, you were sold for your iniquities,
  And for your transgressions your mother was sent away.

*50:2
Is 65:12;
66:4;
Num 11:23;
Is 59:1;
Ex 14:21;
Josh 3:16

2 "Why was there no man when I came?
  When I called, *why* was there none to answer?
  Is My hand so short that it cannot ransom?
  Or have I no power to deliver?
  Behold, I dry up the sea with My rebuke,
  I make the rivers a wilderness;
  Their fish stink for lack of water,
  And die of thirst.

50:3
Is 13:10;
Rev 6:12

3 "I clothe the heavens with blackness,
  And I make sackcloth their covering."

b. Obedient response of the servant, the true Israel

50:4
Is 54:13;
Jer 31:25;
Ps 143:8

4 The Lord GOD has given Me the tongue of disciples,
  That I may know how to sustain the weary one with a word.
  He awakens *Me* morning by morning,
  He awakens My ear to listen as a disciple.

50:5
Ps 40:6;
Matt 26:39;
John 8:29;
14:31;
Phil 2:8

5 The Lord GOD has opened My ear;
  And I was not disobedient,
  Nor did I turn back.

50:6
Is 53:5;
Matt 26:67;
Luke 22:63

6 I gave My back to those who strike *Me*,
  And My cheeks to those who pluck out the beard;
  I did not cover My face from humiliation and spitting.

50:7
Is 49:8; 54:4;
Ezek 3:8,9

7 For the Lord GOD helps Me,
  Therefore, I am not disgraced;
  Therefore, I have set My face like flint,
  And I know that I shall not be ashamed.

50:8
Rom 8:32-34

8 He who vindicates Me is near;
  Who will contend with Me?
  Let us stand up to each other;
  Who has a case against Me?
  Let him draw near to Me.

50:9
Is 41:10;
54:17; 5:18

9 Behold, the Lord GOD helps Me;
  Who is he who condemns Me?
  Behold, they will all wear out like a garment;
  The moth will eat them.

c. Exhortation to trust the LORD

50:10
Is 49:2,3; 9:2;
Eph 5:8;
Is 12:2

10 Who is among you that fears the LORD,

50:1 *Where . . . ?* The question is rhetorical. The implied answer is that there is no bill of divorcement. Israel was never divorced, never sold to creditors, still the beloved of God although estranged from Him by sin.

50:2 *Is My hand so short . . . ?* Israel had been taken captive, not because God was unable to deliver her, but because of her sins. Yet a sovereign God still could easily fulfill His promise of deliverance.

That obeys the voice of His servant,
That walks in darkness and has no light?
Let him trust in the name of the LORD and rely on his God.

11 Behold, all you who kindle a fire,
Who encircle yourselves with firebrands,
Walk in the light of your fire
And among the brands you have set ablaze.
This you will have from My hand;
And you will lie down in torment.

3. Encouragement to trust in God, not fearing man

a. God's mercy to Abraham bestowed on his descendants

51 "Listen to me, you who pursue righteousness,
Who seek the LORD:
Look to the rock from which you were hewn,
And to the quarry from which you were dug.

2 "Look to Abraham your father,
And to Sarah who gave birth to you in pain;
When *he was* one I called him,
Then I blessed him and multiplied him."

3 Indeed, the LORD will comfort Zion;
He will comfort all her waste places.
And her wilderness He will make like Eden,
And her desert like the garden of the LORD;
Joy and gladness will be found in her,
Thanksgiving and sound of a melody.

b. Trust in the eternal Creator, not fearing man

4 "Pay attention to Me, O My people;
And give ear to Me, O My nation;
For a law will go forth from Me,
And I will set My justice for a light of the peoples.

5 "My righteousness is near, My salvation has gone forth,
And My arms will judge the peoples;
The coastlands will wait for Me,
And for My arm they will wait expectantly.

6 "Lift up your eyes to the sky,
Then look to the earth beneath;
For the sky will vanish like smoke,
And the earth will wear out like a garment,
And its inhabitants will die in like manner,
But My salvation shall be forever,
And My righteousness shall not wane.

7 "Listen to Me, you who know righteousness,
A people in whose heart is My law;
Do not fear the reproach of man,
Neither be dismayed at their revilings.

8 "For the moth will eat them like a garment,
And the grub will eat them like wool.
But My righteousness shall be forever,
And My salvation to all generations."

c. Prayer that God will again deliver Israel

9 Awake, awake, put on strength, O arm of the LORD;
Awake as in the days of old, the generations of long ago.
Was it not Thou who cut Rahab in pieces,
Who pierced the dragon?

10 Was it not Thou who dried up the sea,
The waters of the great deep;
Who made the depths of the sea a pathway
For the redeemed to cross over?

11 So the ransomed of the LORD will return,
And come with joyful shouting to Zion;

50:11
Ps 35:8;
Is 65:13-15

51:1
v. 7; Ps 94:15

51:2
Rom 4:16;
Heb 11:11,
12; Gen 12:1;
24:35

51:3
Is 40:1; 52:9;
Joel 2:3;
Gen 13:10;
Is 66:10

51:4
Ps 50:7;
Is 2:3; 42:4,6

51:5
Is 46:13;
40:10; 42:4;
63:5

51:6
Is 40:26;
Ps 102:26;
Matt 24:35;
2 Pet 3:10;
Is 45:17

51:7
v. 1;
Ps 37:31;
Matt 5:11;
Acts 5:41

51:8
Is 50:9; v. 6

51:9
Is 52:1;
Deut 4:34;
Ps 89:10;
74:13;
Ezek 29:3

51:10
Ex 14:21;
Is 43:16;
63:9,16

51:11
Is 35:10;
60:19;

And everlasting joy *will be* on their heads.
They will obtain gladness and joy,
And sorrow and sighing will flee away.

d. The Lord the Maker will faithfully deliver His people

12 "I, even I, am He who comforts you.
Who are you that you are afraid of man who dies,
And of the son of man who is made like grass;

13 That you have forgotten the Lord your Maker,
Who stretched out the heavens,
And laid the foundations of the earth;
That you fear continually all day long because of the fury of the
    oppressor,
As he makes ready to destroy?
But where is the fury of the oppressor?

14 "The exile will soon be set free, and will not die in the dungeon, nor will his
bread be lacking.

15 "For I am the Lord your God, who stirs up the sea and its waves roar (the
Lord of hosts is His name).

16 "And I have put My words in your mouth, and have covered you with the
shadow of My hand, to establish the heavens, to found the earth, and to say to Zion,
'You are My people.' "

4. Israel summoned to awaken and return

a. Her cup of wrath has been drunk

17 Rouse yourself! Rouse yourself! Arise, O Jerusalem,
You who have drunk from the Lord's hand the cup of His anger;
The chalice of reeling you have drained to the dregs.

18 There is none to guide her among all the sons she has borne;
Nor is there one to take her by the hand among all the sons she has
    reared.

19 These two things have befallen you;
Who will mourn for you?
The devastation and destruction, famine and sword,
How shall I comfort you?

20 Your sons have fainted,
They lie *helpless* at the head of every street,
Like an antelope in a net,
Full of the wrath of the Lord,
The rebuke of your God.

21 Therefore, please hear this, you afflicted,
Who are drunk, but not with wine:

22 Thus says your Lord, the Lord, even your God
Who contends for His people,
"Behold, I have taken out of your hand the cup of reeling;
The chalice of My anger,
You will never drink it again.

23 "And I will put it into the hand of your tormentors,
Who have said to you, 'Lie down that we may walk over you.'
You have even made your back like the ground,
And like the street for those who walk over *it*."

b. God will restore Jerusalem for His own glory

52

Awake, awake,
Clothe yourself in your strength, O Zion;
Clothe yourself in your beautiful garments,
O Jerusalem, the holy city.
For the uncircumcised and the unclean
Will no more come into you.

2 Shake yourself from the dust, rise up,
O captive Jerusalem;
Loose yourself from the chains around your neck,
O captive daughter of Zion.

6. Israel's blessing through the servant
a. Captive Israel multiplied and enlarged

54 "Shout for joy, O barren one, you who have borne no *child;*
Break forth into joyful shouting and cry aloud, you who have not travailed;
For the sons of the desolate one *will be* more numerous
Than the sons of the married woman," says the LORD.

54:1
Gal 4:27;
1 Sam 2:5;
Is 62:4

2 "Enlarge the place of your tent;
Stretch out the curtains of your dwellings, spare not;
Lengthen your cords,
And strengthen your pegs.

54:2
Is 49:19,20

3 "For you will spread abroad to the right and to the left.
And your descendants will possess nations,
And they will resettle the desolate cities.

54:3
Is 43:5,6;
49:19,23

b. The LORD's exiled wife restored

4 "Fear not, for you will not be put to shame;
Neither feel humiliated, for you will not be disgraced;
But you will forget the shame of your youth,
And the reproach of your widowhood you will remember no more.

54:4
Is 45:17;
Jer 31:19;
Is 4:1; 25:8

5 "For your husband is your Maker,
Whose name is the LORD of hosts;
And your Redeemer is the Holy One of Israel,
Who is called the God of all the earth.

54:5
Jer 3:14;
Is 43:14;
48:17; 6:3

6 "For the LORD has called you,
Like a wife forsaken and grieved in spirit,
Even like a wife of *one's* youth when she is rejected,"
Says your God.

54:6
Is 62:4

7 "For a brief moment I forsook you,
But with great compassion I will gather you.

54:7
Is 26:20; 43:5

8 "In an outburst of anger
I hid My face from you for a moment;
But with everlasting lovingkindness I will have compassion on you,"
Says the LORD your Redeemer.

54:8
Is 60:10;
v. 10;
Is 49:10,13;
v. 5

c. Promise of God's unchanging favor

9 "For this is like the days of Noah to Me;
When I swore that the waters of Noah
Should not flood the earth again,
So I have sworn that I will not be angry with you,
Nor will I rebuke you.

54:9
Gen 9:11;
Is 12:1

10 "For the mountains may be removed and the hills may shake,
But My lovingkindness will not be removed from you,
And My covenant of peace will not be shaken,"
Says the LORD who has compassion on you.

54:10
Is 51:6;
Ps 89:33,34;
v. 8

d. Future radiance of the new Jerusalem

11 "O afflicted one, storm-tossed, and not comforted,
Behold, I will set your stones in antimony,
And your foundations I will lay in sapphires.

54:11
1 Chr 29:2;
Rev 21:18

12 "Moreover, I will make your battlements of rubies,
And your gates of crystal,
And your entire wall of precious stones.

13 "And all your sons will be taught of the LORD;
And the well-being of your sons will be great.

54:13
Jer 31:34;
John 6:45;
Ps 119:165

14 "In righteousness you will be established;
You will be far from oppression, for you will not fear;
And from terror, for it will not come near you.

54:14
Is 62:1; 9:4;
14:3; v. 4

15 "If anyone fiercely assails *you* it will not be from Me.
Whoever assails you will fall because of you.

54:15
Is 41:11-16

16 "Behold, I Myself have created the smith who blows the fire of coals,
And brings out a weapon for its work;
And I have created the destroyer to ruin.

<table>
<tr><td>

54:17
Is 29:8; 50:8,
9; 45:24

</td><td>

17   "No weapon that is formed against you shall prosper;
       And every tongue that accuses you in judgment you will condemn.
       This is the heritage of the servants of the LORD,
       And their vindication is from Me," declares the LORD.

</td></tr>
</table>

7. Grace for trusting sinners

a. The repentant to be blessed

55:1
Is 41:17;
John 4:14;
7:37;
Matt 13:44;
Rev 3:18
55:2
Hos 8:7;
Is 62:8,9;
25:6

55

1   "Ho! Every one who thirsts, come to the waters;
       And you who have no money come, buy and eat.
       Come, buy wine and milk
       Without money and without cost.

2   "Why do you spend money for what is not bread,
       And your wages for what does not satisfy?
       Listen carefully to Me, and eat what is good,
       And delight yourself in abundance.

55:3
Is 51:4;
Rom 10:5;
Is 61:8;
Acts 13:34

3   "Incline your ear and come to Me.
       Listen, that you may live;
       And I will make an everlasting covenant with you,
       According to the faithful mercies shown to David.

55:4
Jer 30:9;
Ezek 34:23,
24; Dan 9:25
55:5
Is 49:6,12,23;
Zech 8:22;
Is 60:9

4   "Behold, I have made him a witness to the peoples,
       A leader and commander for the peoples.

5   "Behold, you will call a nation you do not know,
       And a nation which knows you not will run to you,
       Because of the LORD your God, even the Holy One of Israel;
       For He has glorified you."

b. Repentant sinners commanded to seek the LORD

55:6
Ps 32:6;
Is 49:8;
2 Cor 6:1,2
*55:7
Is 1:16; 59:7;
31:6; 54:8,10;
44:22

6   Seek the LORD while He may be found;
       Call upon Him while He is near.

7   Let the wicked forsake his way,
       And the unrighteous man his thoughts;
       And let him return to the LORD,
       And He will have compassion on him;
       And to our God,
       For He will abundantly pardon.

8   "For My thoughts are not your thoughts,
       Neither are your ways My ways," declares the LORD.

55:9
Ps 103:11

9   "For *as* the heavens are higher than the earth,
       So are My ways higher than your ways,
       And My thoughts than your thoughts.

c. The efficacy of God's word

55:10
Is 30:23;
2 Cor 9:10

10   "For as the rain and the snow come down from heaven,
       And do not return there without watering the earth,
       And making it bear and sprout,
       And furnishing seed to the sower and bread to the eater;

55:11
Is 45:23;
59:21; 46:10

11   So shall My word be which goes forth from My mouth;
       It shall not return to Me empty,
       Without accomplishing what I desire,
       And without succeeding *in the matter* for which I sent it.

d. The joyous return of the redeemed

55:12
Is 51:11;
54:10,13;
44:23;
1 Chr 16:33

12   "For you will go out with joy,
       And be led forth with peace;
       The mountains and the hills will break forth into shouts of joy
         before you,
       And all the trees of the field will clap *their* hands.

13   "Instead of the thorn bush the cypress will come up;

55:7 A pardon is an official warrant of remission of penalty. God alone can grant a pardon, although the assurance of such pardon may be communicated to men by God's agents. Several conditions inhere when a pardon is granted: (1) the person to whom the pardon is granted is acknowledgedly guilty of transgression (Ps. 51:3,4; Luke 15:18; 18:13); (2) the guilty transgressor must forsake his wickedness, i.e., repent (Acts 3:19; 17:30); (3) the guilty transgressor must turn to God, who alone can grant pardon (v. 6; Acts 26:20; 1 Thess. 1:9); and (4) God's mercy is available in a pardon when the guilty transgressor repents and turns to God (v. 7; Jer. 33:3,8; Luke 24:47.

And instead of the nettle the myrtle will come up;
And it will be a memorial to the LORD,
For an everlasting sign which will not be cut off."

55:13
Is 41:19;
32:13; 63:12,
14; 19:20

8. Gentiles included in Israel's blessing

a. Admonition to maintain a godly witness

56 Thus says the LORD,
"Preserve justice, and do righteousness,
For My salvation is about to come
And My righteousness to be revealed.

56:1
Is 61:8; 46:13

2 "How blessed is the man who does this,
And the son of man who takes hold of it;
Who keeps from profaning the sabbath,
And keeps his hand from doing any evil."

56:2
Is 58:13

b. Promised blessing to childless believers

3 Let not the foreigner who has joined himself to the LORD say,
"The LORD will surely separate me from His people."
Neither let the eunuch say, "Behold, I am a dry tree."

56:3
v. 6;
Acts 8:27

4 For thus says the LORD,
"To the eunuchs who keep My sabbaths,
And choose what pleases Me,
And hold fast My covenant,

56:4
vv. 2,6

5 To them I will give in My house and within My walls a memorial,
And a name better than that of sons and daughters;
I will give them an everlasting name which will not
be cut off.

56:5
v. 7; Is 66:20;
26:1; 62:2;
48:19

c. Believing Gentiles included in God's covenant people

6 "Also the foreigners who join themselves to the LORD,
To minister to Him, and to love the name of the LORD,
To be His servants, every one who keeps from profaning the
sabbath,
And holds fast My covenant;

56:6
Is 60:10;
61:5; vv. 2,4

7 Even those I will bring to My holy mountain,
And make them joyful in My house of prayer.
Their burnt offerings and their sacrifices will be acceptable on My
altar;
For My house will be called a house of prayer for all the peoples."

8 The Lord GOD, who gathers the dispersed of Israel, declares,
"Yet *others* I will gather to them, to those *already* gathered."

*56:7
Is 11:9;
65:25;
Rom 12:1;
Heb 13:15;
Matt 21:13;
Mark 11:17;
Luke 19:46
56:8
Is 11:12;
60:3-11;
John 10:16

9. Condemnation of the wicked rulers of Israel

a. Israel's wicked prophets

9 All you beasts of the field,
All you beasts in the forest,
Come to eat.

56:9
Jer 12:9

10 His watchmen are blind,
All of them know nothing.
All of them are dumb dogs unable to bark,
Dreamers lying down, who love to slumber;

56:10
Is 29:9-14;
Nah 3:18

11 And the dogs are greedy, they are not satisfied.
And they are shepherds who have no understanding;
They have all turned to their own way,
Each one to his unjust gain, to the last one.

12 "Come," *they* say, "let us get wine, and let us drink heavily of strong
drink;
And tomorrow will be like today, only more so."

56:7 Private and family prayers do not exhaust our responsibility to God. Public prayer is also required of believers. We are exhorted so to pray (Heb. 10:25), and God promises to hear and to answer this kind of prayer (2 Chr. 7:14,16; Matt. 18:19). Scripture abounds in examples of godly people who engaged in public prayer.

b. Heavenly reward of persecuted believers

57:1
Ps 12:1;
Is 42:25;
47:7,11

57 The righteous man perishes, and no man takes it to heart;
And devout men are taken away, while no one understands.
For the righteous man is taken away from evil,

57:2
Is 26:7

2 He enters into peace;
They rest in their beds,
Each one who walked in his upright way.

c. The wicked Jews sacrifice their children to idols

57:3
Matt 16:4;
Is 1:21

3 "But come here, you sons of a sorceress,
Offspring of an adulterer and a prostitute.

57:4
Is 48:8

4 "Against whom do you jest?
Against whom do you open wide your mouth
And stick out your tongue?
Are you not children of rebellion,
Offspring of deceit,

57:5
2 Kin 16:4;
Lev 18:21;
2 Kin 16:3;
Jer 7:31

5 *Who* inflame yourselves among the oaks,
Under every luxuriant tree,
Who slaughter the children in the ravines,
Under the clefts of the crags?

57:6
Jer 3:9; 7:18;
5:9,29

6 "Among the smooth *stones* of the ravine
Is your portion, they are your lot;
Even to them you have poured out a libation,
You have made a grain offering.
Shall I relent concerning these things?

d. Idolatrous worship on the "high places"

57:7
Ezek 16:16;
23:41

7 "Upon a high and lofty mountain
You have made your bed.
You also went up there to offer sacrifice.

57:8
Ezek 23:7,18;
16:26,28

8 "And behind the door and the doorpost
You have set up your sign;
Indeed, far removed from Me, you have uncovered yourself;
And have gone up and made your bed wide.
And you have made an agreement for yourselves with them,
You have loved their bed,
You have looked on *their* manhood.

57:9
Ezek 23:16,
40

9 "And you have journeyed to the king with oil
And increased your perfumes;
You have sent your envoys a great distance,
And made *them* go down to Sheol.

57:10
Is 47:13;
Jer 2:25

10 "You were tired out by the length of your road,
Yet you did not say, 'It is hopeless.'
You found renewed strength,
Therefore you did not faint.

e. Idols are helpless to deliver

57:11
Is 51:12;
Jer 2:32; v. 1;
Ps 50:21

11 "Of whom were you worried and fearful,
When you lied, and did not remember Me,
Nor give *Me* a thought?
Was I not silent even for a long time
So you do not fear Me?

12 "I will declare your righteousness and your deeds,
But they will not profit you.

57:13
Jer 22:20;
Is 25:4;
60:21; 65:9

13 "When you cry out, let your collection *of idols* deliver you.
But the wind will carry all of them up,
And a breath will take *them away.*
But he who takes refuge in Me shall inherit the land,
And shall possess My holy mountain."

f. Compassion for the repentant, but no peace for the wicked

57:14
Is 62:10;
Jer 18:15

14 And it shall be said,
"Build up, build up, prepare the way,
Remove *every* obstacle out of the way of My people."

15 For thus says the high and exalted One
Who lives forever, whose name is Holy,
"I dwell *on* a high and holy place,
And *also* with the contrite and lowly of spirit
In order to revive the spirit of the lowly
And to revive the heart of the contrite.

57:15
Is 52:13;
40:28; 66:1;
Ps 34:18;
51:17; 14:2,3;
Is 61:1

16 "For I will not contend forever,
Neither will I always be angry;
For the spirit would grow faint before Me,
And the breath *of those whom* I have made.

57:16
Gen 6:3;
Ps 85:5;
103:9;
Mic 7:18;
Job 34:14;
Is 42:5

17 "Because of the iniquity of his unjust gain I was angry and struck
him;
I hid *My face* and was angry,
And he went on turning away, in the way of his heart.

57:17
Jer 6:13;
Is 1:4

18 "I have seen his ways, but I will heal him;
I will lead him and restore comfort to him and to his mourners,

57:18
Is 53:5;
52:12; 61:1-3

19 Creating the praise of the lips.
Peace, peace to him who is far and to him who is near,"
Says the LORD, "and I will heal him."

57:19
Heb 13:15;
Acts 2:39;
Eph 2:17

20 But the wicked are like the tossing sea,
For it cannot be quiet,
And its waters toss up refuse and mud.

57:20
Job 18:5-14

21 "There is no peace," says my God, "for the wicked."

57:21
Is 48:22

C. Part III: the program of peace

1. Contrast between true and false worship

a. Right and wrong fasting

58 "Cry loudly, do not hold back;
Raise your voice like a trumpet,
And declare to My people their transgression,
And to the house of Jacob their sins.

58:1
Is 48:8; 50:1;
59:12

2 "Yet they seek Me day by day, and delight to know My ways,
As a nation that has done righteousness,
And has not forsaken the ordinance of their God.
They ask Me *for* just decisions,
They delight in the nearness of God.

58:2
Is 1:11; 48:1;
59:13; 29:13

3 'Why have we fasted and Thou dost not see?
Why have we humbled ourselves and Thou dost not notice?'
Behold, on the day of your fast you find *your* desire,
And drive hard all your workers.

58:3
Mal 3:14;
Is 22:12,13

4 "Behold, you fast for contention and strife and to strike with a wicked
fist.
You do not fast like *you do* today to make your voice heard on high.

58:4
1 Kin 21:9,
12,13; Is 59:2

5 "Is it a fast like this which I choose, a day for a man to humble
himself?
Is it for bowing one's head like a reed,
And for spreading out sackcloth and ashes as a bed?
Will you call this a fast, even an acceptable day to the LORD?

58:5
Zech 7:5;
Esth 4:3;
Job 2:8

6 "Is this not the fast which I choose,
To loosen the bonds of wickedness,
To undo the bands of the yoke,
And to let the oppressed go free,
And break every yoke?

58:6
Neh 5:10-12;
Jer 34:9

7 "Is it not to divide your bread with the hungry,
And bring the homeless poor into the house;
When you see the naked, to cover him;
And not to hide yourself from your own flesh?

58:7
Ezek 18:7,16;
Matt 25:35;
Job 31:19;
Gen 29:14;
Neh 5:5

b. Protection and blessing for the righteous

8 "Then your light will break out like the dawn,
And your recovery will speedily spring forth;
And your righteousness will go before you;

58:8
v. 10;
Is 30:26;
62:1;
Ex 14:19;
Is 52:12

The glory of the LORD will be your rear guard.

58:9
Is 55:6; v. 6;
Ps 12:2

9 "Then you will call, and the LORD will answer;
You will cry, and He will say, 'Here I am.'
If you remove the yoke from your midst,
The pointing of the finger, and speaking wickedness,

58:10
v. 7; Ps 37:6

10 And if you give yourself to the hungry,
And satisfy the desire of the afflicted,
Then your light will rise in darkness,
And your gloom *will become* like midday.

58:11
Is 49:10;
41:17; 66:14;
John 4:14;
7:38

11 "And the LORD will continually guide you,
And satisfy your desire in scorched places,
And give strength to your bones;
And you will be like a watered garden,
And like a spring of water whose waters do not fail.

58:12
Is 49:8;
44:28; 30:13;
Amos 9:11

12 "And those from among you will rebuild the ancient ruins;
You will raise up the age-old foundations;
And you will be called the repairer of the breach,
The restorer of the streets in which to dwell.

c. The reward for keeping the Sabbath

*58:13
Is 56:2;
Ps 84:2,10;
Is 55:8; 59:13

13 "If because of the sabbath, you turn your foot
From doing your *own* pleasure on My holy day,
And call the sabbath a delight, the holy *day* of the LORD honorable,
And shall honor it, desisting from your *own* ways,
From seeking your *own* pleasure,
And speaking *your own* word,

58:14
Is 61:10;
Deut 32:13;
Is 1:19,20

14 Then you will take delight in the LORD,
And I will make you ride on the heights of the earth;
And I will feed you *with* the heritage of Jacob your father,
For the mouth of the LORD has spoken."

2. Confessing national wickedness, Israel is rescued by God's grace

a. Iniquity keeps Israel from God's deliverance

59:1
Num 11:23;
Is 50:2; 58:9

59 Behold, the LORD's hand is not so short
That it cannot save;
Neither is His ear so dull
That it cannot hear.

59:2
Is 1:15; 58:4

2 But your iniquities have made a separation between you and your God,
And your sins have hidden *His* face from you, so that He does not hear.

59:3
Is 1:15;
Jer 2:30;
v. 13;
Is 28:15

3 For your hands are defiled with blood,
And your fingers with iniquity;
Your lips have spoken falsehood,
Your tongue mutters wickedness.

59:4
vv. 14,15;
Is 30:12;
Job 15:35;
Ps 7:14

4 No one sues righteously and no one pleads honestly.
They trust in confusion, and speak lies.
They conceive mischief, and bring forth iniquity.

59:5
Is 14:29;
Job 8:14

5 They hatch adders' eggs and weave the spider's web;
He who eats of their eggs dies,
And *from* that which is crushed a snake breaks forth.

59:6
Is 28:20;
57:12; 58:4

6 Their webs will not become clothing,
Nor will they cover themselves with their works;
Their works are works of iniquity,
And an act of violence is in their hands.

59:7
Rom 3:15-17;
Is 65:2

7 Their feet run to evil,
And they hasten to shed innocent blood;
Their thoughts are thoughts of iniquity;

58:13 Matthew 28:1 talks about the Christian Sabbath. The principle of the Sabbath is to set a day apart in a special way for God's service and fellowship, rather than to use it for personal recreation and pleasure. There is no reason to suppose that the same blessings promised for faithful adherence to the Old Testament Sabbath will not be accorded to those who faithfully and regularly gather to worship Him in divine services and in private devotions. Historically, profanation of the Lord's Day leads to spiritual decline and withdrawal of God's blessing. (See Neh. 13:17,18.)

Devastation and destruction are in their highways.
8   They do not know the way of peace,
    And there is no justice in their tracks;
    They have made their paths crooked;
    Whoever treads on them does not know peace.

b. Israel's confession of sins

9   Therefore, justice is far from us,
    And righteousness does not overtake us;
    We hope for light, but behold, darkness;
    For brightness, but we walk in gloom.
10 We grope along the wall like blind men,
    We grope like those who have no eyes;
    We stumble at midday as in the twilight,
    Among those who are vigorous we are like dead men.
11 All of us growl like bears,
    And moan sadly like doves;
    We hope for justice, but there is none,
    For salvation, *but* it is far from us.
12 For our transgressions are multiplied before Thee,
    And our sins testify against us;
    For our transgressions are with us,
    And we know our iniquities:
13 Transgressing and denying the LORD,
    And turning away from our God,
    Speaking oppression and revolt,
    Conceiving *in* and uttering from the heart lying words.
14 And justice is turned back,
    And righteousness stands far away;
    For truth has stumbled in the street,
    And uprightness cannot enter.
15 Yes, truth is lacking;
    And he who turns aside from evil makes himself a prey.

Now the LORD saw,
And it was displeasing in His sight that there was no justice.

c. God intervenes to redeem Zion

16 And He saw that there was no man,
    And was astonished that there was no one to intercede;
    Then His own arm brought salvation to Him;
    And His righteousness upheld Him.
17 And He put on righteousness like a breastplate,
    And a helmet of salvation on His head;
    And He put on garments of vengeance for clothing,
    And wrapped Himself with zeal as a mantle.
18 According to *their* deeds, so He will repay,
    Wrath to His adversaries, recompense to His enemies;
    To the coastlands He will make recompense.
19 So they will fear the name of the LORD from the west
    And His glory from the rising of the sun,
    For He will come like a rushing stream,
    Which the wind of the LORD drives.
20 "And a Redeemer will come to Zion,
    And to those who turn from transgression in Jacob," declares the
        LORD.
21 "And as for Me, this is My covenant with them," says the LORD: "My Spirit
which is upon you, and My words which I have put in your mouth, shall not depart
from your mouth, nor from the mouth of your offspring, nor from the mouth of
your offspring's offspring," says the LORD, "from now and forever."

59:8
vv. 9,11;
Ps 125:5;
v. 14

59:9
v. 14; Is 5:30;
8:21,22

59:10
Deut 28:29;
Job 5:14;
Amos 8:9;
Is 8:14,15

59:11
Is 38:14;
Ezek 7:16;
vv. 9,14

59:12
Is 58:1;
Jer 14:7

59:13
Josh 24:27;
Titus 1:16;
Is 30:12;
vv. 3,4

59:14
Is 1:21;
46:12; 48:1

59:15
Is 5:23;
1:21-23

59:16
Is 63:5;
Ezek 22:30;
Ps 98:1

59:17
Eph 6:14;
1 Thess 5:8;
Is 63:2,3

59:18
Is 65:6,7;
66:6

59:19
Ps 113:3;
Is 66:12

59:20
Rom 11:26,
27;
Ezek 18:30,
31; Acts 2:38,
39

59:21
Jer 31:31-34;
Is 44:3,26;
54:10;
Jer 32:40

3. *The future glory of Zion*

a. *The dawn of Zion's glory*

60

"Arise, shine; for your light has come,
And the glory of the LORD has risen upon you.

2 "For behold, darkness will cover the earth,
And deep darkness the peoples;
But the LORD will rise upon you,
And His glory will appear upon you.

3 "And nations will come to your light,
And kings to the brightness of your rising.

b. *Converted Gentiles to adore Israel's God*

4 "Lift up your eyes round about, and see;
They all gather together, they come to you.
Your sons will come from afar,
And your daughters will be carried in the arms.

5 "Then you will see and be radiant,
And your heart will thrill and rejoice;
Because the abundance of the sea will be turned to you,
The wealth of the nations will come to you.

6 "A multitude of camels will cover you,
The young camels of Midian and Ephah;
All those from Sheba will come;
They will bring gold and frankincense,
And will bear good news of the praises of the LORD.

7 "All the flocks of Kedar will be gathered together to you,
The rams of Nebaioth will minister to you;
They will go up with acceptance on My altar,
And I shall glorify My glorious house.

8 "Who are these who fly like a cloud,
And like the doves to their lattices?

9 "Surely the coastlands will wait for Me;
And the ships of Tarshish *will come* first,
To bring your sons from afar,
Their silver and their gold with them,
For the name of the LORD your God,
And for the Holy One of Israel because He has glorified you.

c. *Millennial peace and supremacy of God's people*

10 "And foreigners will build up your walls,
And their kings will minister to you;
For in My wrath I struck you,
And in My favor I have had compassion on you.

11 "And your gates will be open continually;
They will not be closed day or night,
So that *men* may bring to you the wealth of the nations,
With their kings led in procession.

12 "For the nation and the kingdom which will not serve you will perish,
And the nations will be utterly ruined.

13 "The glory of Lebanon will come to you,
The juniper, the box tree, and the cypress together,
To beautify the place of My sanctuary;
And I shall make the place of My feet glorious.

14 "And the sons of those who afflicted you will come bowing to you,
And all those who despised you will bow themselves at the soles of
your feet;
And they will call you the city of the LORD,
The Zion of the Holy One of Israel.

d. *Prosperity and peace of the Messianic kingdom*

15 "Whereas you have been forsaken and hated

With no one passing through,
I will make you an everlasting pride,
A joy from generation to generation.

16 "You will also suck the milk of nations,
And will suck the breast of kings;
Then you will know that I, the LORD, am your Savior,
And your Redeemer, the Mighty One of Jacob.

60:16
Is 49:23;
66:11; 63:8,
16

17 "Instead of bronze I will bring gold,
And instead of iron I will bring silver,
And instead of wood, bronze,
And instead of stones, iron.
And I will make peace your administrators,
And righteousness your overseers.

18 "Violence will not be heard again in your land,
Nor devastation or destruction within your borders;
But you will call your walls salvation, and your gates
praise.

60:18
Is 54:14;
51:19; 26:1;
v. 11

19 "No longer will you have the sun for light by day,
Nor for brightness will the moon give you light;
But you will have the LORD for an everlasting light,
And your God for your glory.

60:19
Rev 21:23;
22:5; Is 9:2;
Zech 2:5

20 "Your sun will set no more,
Neither will your moon wane;
For you will have the LORD for an everlasting light,
And the days of your mourning will be finished.

60:20
Is 30:26;
65:19

21 "Then all your people *will be* righteous;
They will possess the land forever,
The branch of My planting,
The work of My hands,
That I may be glorified.

60:21
Is 52:1;
Ps 37:11,22;
Is 29:23;
45:11

22 "The smallest one will become a clan,
And the least one a mighty nation.
I, the LORD, will hasten it in its time."

60:22
Is 51:2

4. *Good tidings of salvation*

a. *The commission to preach the good tidings*

61 The Spirit of the Lord GOD is upon me,
Because the LORD has anointed me
To bring good news to the afflicted,
He has sent me to bind up the brokenhearted,
To proclaim liberty to captives,
And freedom to prisoners;

*61:1f
Is 11:2;
Luke 4:18;
Ps 45:7;
Is 57:15; 42:7

2 To proclaim the favorable year of the LORD,
And the day of vengeance of our God;
To comfort all who mourn,

61:2
Is 49:8; 34:8;
57:18;
Matt 5:4

3 To grant those who mourn *in* Zion,
Giving them a garland instead of ashes,
The oil of gladness instead of mourning,
The mantle of praise instead of a spirit of fainting.
So they will be called oaks of righteousness,
The planting of the LORD, that He may be glorified.

61:3
Is 60:20;
Ps 45:7;
Is 60:21

b. *Exaltation of Zion in the final age*

4 Then they will rebuild the ancient ruins,
They will raise up the former devastations,
And they will repair the ruined cities,

61:4
Is 49:8;
Ezek 36:33

60:7 *Kedar . . . Nebaioth*, tribes of nomadic Ishmaelites.

60:15 The persecution and hatred of the Jews, still God's people, at last shall cease.

61:1,2 This Scripture is quoted by Jesus Christ and applied to Himself (Luke 4:18,19). It must have been for a definite reason that He stopped in the middle of v. 2. He

ended with: *to proclaim the . . . year of the LORD* as designating the age of grace that would continue until His coming again. With His second advent, *the day of vengeance of our God* (v. 2) is to take place. Christ stated that the very day He quoted this Scripture was the day it was fulfilled in their hearing. The remainder of it will be fully and inexorably fulfilled when He returns to earth the second time.

The desolations of many generations.

61:5
Is 60:10

5　And strangers will stand and pasture your flocks,
　　And foreigners will be your farmers and your vinedressers.

61:6
Is 66:21;
60:5,11

6　But you will be called the priests of the LORD;
　　You will be spoken of *as* ministers of our God.
　　You will eat the wealth of nations,
　　And in their riches you will boast.

61:7
Is 54:4; 40:2;
Zech 9:12;
Is 60:15;
Ps 16:11

7　Instead of your shame *you will have a* double *portion,*
　　And *instead of* humiliation they will shout for joy over their portion.
　　Therefore they will possess a double *portion* in their land,
　　Everlasting joy will be theirs.

61:8
Is 30:18; 55:3

8　For I, the LORD, love justice,
　　I hate robbery in the burnt offering;
　　And I will faithfully give them their recompense,
　　And I will make an everlasting covenant with them.

61:9
Is 54:3; 44:3

9　Then their offspring will be known among the nations,
　　And their descendants in the midst of the peoples.
　　All who see them will recognize them
　　Because they are the offspring *whom* the LORD has blessed.

c. Song of praise for God's redemptive love

61:10
Is 12:1,2;
49:4,18;
Rev 21:2

10　I will rejoice greatly in the LORD,
　　My soul will exult in my God;
　　For He has clothed me with garments of salvation,
　　He has wrapped me with a robe of righteousness,
　　As a bridegroom decks himself with a garland,
　　And as a bride adorns herself with her jewels.

61:11
Is 55:10;
45:23,24;
Ps 72:3;
85:11;
Is 60:18

11　For as the earth brings forth its sprouts,
　　And as a garden causes the things sown in it to spring up,
　　So the Lord GOD will cause righteousness and praise
　　To spring up before all the nations.

5. Zion restored and glorified

a. God's promise to honor Israel as a wife

62:1
Is 61:11;
52:10

62　For Zion's sake I will not keep silent,
　　And for Jerusalem's sake I will not keep quiet,
　　Until her righteousness goes forth like brightness,
　　And her salvation like a torch that is burning.

62:2
Is 60:3; vv. 4,
12; Is 65:15

2　And the nations will see your righteousness,
　　And all kings your glory;
　　And you will be called by a new name,
　　Which the mouth of the LORD will designate.

62:3
Zech 9:16

3　You will also be a crown of beauty in the hand of the LORD,
　　And a royal diadem in the hand of your God.

62:4
Hos 1:10;
Is 54:6,7;
Jer 32:41;
3:14

4　It will no longer be said to you, "Forsaken,"
　　Nor to your land will it any longer be said, "Desolate";
　　But you will be called, "My delight is in her,"
　　And your land, "Married";
　　For the LORD delights in you,
　　And *to Him* your land will be married.

62:5
Is 65:19

5　For *as* a young man marries a virgin,
　　So your sons will marry you;
　　And *as* the bridegroom rejoices over the bride,
　　So your God will rejoice over you.

b. Zion to have rest without fear

62:6
Is 52:8;
Jer 6:17;
Ezek 3:17;
Ps 74:2

6　On your walls, O Jerusalem, I have appointed watchmen;
　　All day and all night they will never keep silent.
　　You who remind the LORD, take no rest for yourselves;

62:7
Matt 15:21-28;
Luke 18:1-8;
Jer 33:9

7　And give Him no rest until He establishes
　　And makes Jerusalem a praise in the earth.

62:8
Is 45:23;
Deut 28:31,
33; Jer 5:17

8　The LORD has sworn by His right hand and by His strong arm,
　　"I will never again give your grain *as* food for your enemies;

Nor will foreigners drink your new wine, for which you have
    labored.''

9   But those who garner it will eat it, and praise the LORD;
    And those who gather it will drink it in the courts of My sanctuary.

62:9
Is 65:13,
21-23

c. God's favor on His holy people

10   Go through, go through the gates;
    Clear the way for the people;
    Build up, build up the highway;
    Remove the stones, lift up a standard over the peoples.

62:10
Is 57:14;
49:11; 11:10,
12

11   Behold, the LORD has proclaimed to the end of the earth,
    Say to the daughter of Zion, "Lo, your salvation comes;
    Behold His reward is with Him, and His recompense before Him.''

12   And they will call them, "The holy people,
    The redeemed of the LORD'';
    And you will be called, "Sought out, a city not forsaken.''

62:11
Is 49:6;
Zech 9:9;
Matt 21:5;
Is 51:1; 40:10
62:12
Is 4:3; 51:10;
v. 4

d. God's wrath on Zion's foes

63   Who is this who comes from Edom,
    With garments of glowing colors from Bozrah,
    This One who is majestic in His apparel,
    Marching in the greatness of His strength?
"It is I who speak in righteousness, mighty to save.''

*63:1
Is 34:5,6;
Amos 1:12;
Zeph 3:17

2   Why is Your apparel red,
    And Your garments like the one who treads in the wine press?

63:2
Rev 19:13,15

3   "I have trodden the wine trough alone,
    And from the peoples there was no man with Me.
    I also trod them in My anger,
    And trampled them in My wrath;
    And their lifeblood is sprinkled on My garments,
    And I stained all My raiment.

63:3
Is 22:5; 28:3;
Mic 7:10;
Rev 19:15

4   "For the day of vengeance was in My heart,
    And My year of redemption has come.

63:4
Is 34:8; 61:2

5   "And I looked, and there was no one to help,
    And I was astonished and there was no one to uphold;
    So My own arm brought salvation to Me,
    And My wrath upheld Me.

63:5
Is 59:16;
Ps 98:1;
Is 52:10

6   "And I trod down the peoples in My anger,
    And made them drunk in My wrath,
    And I poured out their lifeblood on the earth.''

63:6
Is 65:12;
51:17,21,22;
34:3

6. Remembering past mercies, repentant Israel pleads to God for deliverance

a. Israel the elect of God

7   I shall make mention of the lovingkindnesses of the LORD, the
    praises of the LORD,
    According to all that the LORD has granted us,
    And the great goodness toward the house of Israel,
    Which He has granted them according to His compassion,
    And according to the multitude of His lovingkindnesses.

*63:7
Is 54:8,10;
1 Kin 8:66;
Ps 51:1

8   For He said, "Surely, they are My people,
    Sons who will not deal falsely.''
    So He became their Savior.

9   In all their affliction He was afflicted,
    And the angel of His presence saved them;
    In His love and in His mercy He redeemed them;
    And He lifted them and carried them all the days of old.

63:9
Judg 10:16;
Ex 23:20-23;
Deut 7:7,8;
Ex 19:4;
Deut 1:31

b. God's deliverance in Moses' day

10   But they rebelled

63:10
Ps 78:40;

63:1 *Edom* had acted treacherously against Israel at the time of the fall of Jerusalem. Isaiah pictures the judgment on his people's foe.

63:7 *lovingkindnesses.* God's vindication of His people and judgment on their enemies is evidence of His love, a love that continues even in their disobedience.

Acts 7:51; Eph 4:30; Ps 106:40		And grieved His Holy Spirit; Therefore, He turned Himself to become their enemy, He fought against them.
63:11 Ps 106:44,45; Ex 14:30; Is 51:9,10; Num 11:17	11	Then His people remembered the days of old, of Moses. Where is He who brought them up out of the sea with the shepherds of His flock? Where is He who put His Holy Spirit in the midst of them,
63:12 Ex 15:6; 14:21; Is 50:10,11	12	Who caused His glorious arm to go at the right hand of Moses, Who divided the waters before them to make for Himself an everlasting name,
63:13 Ps 106:9	13	Who led them through the depths? Like the horse in the wilderness, they did not stumble;
63:14 Deut 32:12	14	As the cattle which go down into the valley, The Spirit of the LORD gave them rest. So didst Thou lead Thy people, To make for Thyself a glorious name.

c. Chastened Judah appeals to her Father and Redeemer

63:15
Deut 26:15;
Ps 80:14;
Jer 31:20;
Hos 11:8
	15	Look down from heaven, and see from Thy holy and glorious
		  habitation;
		Where are Thy zeal and Thy mighty deeds?
		The stirrings of Thy heart and Thy compassion are restrained
		  toward me.

63:16 Is 64:8; 51:2; 44:6; 60:16	16	For Thou art our Father, though Abraham does not know us, And Israel does not recognize us. Thou, O LORD, art our Father, Our Redeemer from of old is Thy name.
63:17 Ezek 14:7-9; Is 29:13,14; Num 10:36	17	Why, O LORD, dost Thou cause us to stray from Thy ways, And harden our heart from fearing Thee? Return for the sake of Thy servants, the tribes of Thy heritage.
63:18 Deut 7:6; Ps 74:3-7	18	Thy holy people possessed Thy sanctuary for a little while, Our adversaries have trodden it down.
63:19 Lam 3:43-45	19	We have become like those over whom Thou hast never ruled, Like those who were not called by Thy name.

d. God is besought for help against the heathen

64:1 Ps 144:5; Judg 5:5	**64**	Oh, that Thou wouldst rend the heavens and come down, That the mountains might quake at Thy presence—
64:2 Jer 5:22	2	As fire kindles the brushwood, as fire causes water to boil— To make Thy name known to Thine adversaries, That the nations may tremble at Thy presence!
64:3 Ps 65:5; 66:3, 5; 106:22	3	When Thou didst awesome things which we did not expect, Thou didst come down, the mountains quaked at Thy presence.
64:4 1 Cor 2:9; Is 40:31	4	For from of old they have not heard nor perceived by ear, Neither has the eye seen a God besides Thee, Who acts in behalf of the one who waits for Him.

e. Confession of iniquity

64:5 Ex 20:24; Is 56:1; 63:7, 10	5	Thou dost meet him who rejoices in doing righteousness, Who remembers Thee in Thy ways. Behold, Thou wast angry, for we sinned, We continued in them a long time; And shall we be saved?
64:6 Is 6:5; 46:12; Ps 90:5,6; Is 50:1	6	For all of us have become like one who is unclean, And all our righteous deeds are like a filthy garment; And all of us wither like a leaf, And our iniquities, like the wind, take us away.
64:7 Is 59:4; 27:5; 54:8; 9:18	7	And there is no one who calls on Thy name, Who arouses himself to take hold of Thee; For Thou hast hidden Thy face from us, And hast delivered us into the power of our iniquities.

f. Appeal for pardon and restoration

64:8 Is 63:16; 29:16; 60:21	8	But now, O LORD, Thou art our Father,

We are the clay, and Thou our potter;
And all of us are the work of Thy hand.

9 Do not be angry beyond measure, O LORD,
Neither remember iniquity forever;
Behold, look now, all of us are Thy people.

10 Thy holy cities have become a wilderness,
Zion has become a wilderness,
Jerusalem a desolation.

11 Our holy and beautiful house,
Where our fathers praised Thee,
Has been burned *by* fire;
And all our precious things have become a ruin.

12 Wilt Thou restrain Thyself at these things, O LORD?
Wilt Thou keep silent and afflict us beyond measure?

64:9
Is 60:10;
43:25; 63:8

64:10
Is 6:11

64:11
Is 63:18;
Ps 74:5-7;
Is 7:23

64:12
Is 42:14;
Ps 83:1

7. The judgment and redemption of God's people

a. Retribution for idolatrous, hypocritical Israel

65 "I permitted Myself to be sought by those who did not ask *for Me*;
I permitted Myself to be found by those who did not seek Me.
I said, 'Here am I, here am I,'
To a nation which did not call on My name.

2 "I have spread out My hands all day long to a rebellious people,
Who walk *in* the way which is not good, following their own thoughts,

3 A people who continually provoke Me to My face,
Offering sacrifices in gardens and burning incense on bricks;

4 Who sit among graves, and spend the night in secret places;
Who eat swine's flesh,
And the broth of unclean meat is *in* their pots.

5 "Who say, 'Keep to yourself, do not come near me,
For I am holier than you!'
These are smoke in My nostrils,
A fire that burns all the day.

6 "Behold, it is written before Me,
I will not keep silent, but I will repay;
I will even repay into their bosom,

7 Both their own iniquities and the iniquities of their fathers together," says the LORD.
"Because they have burned incense on the mountains,
And scorned Me on the hills,
Therefore I will measure their former work into their bosom."

65:1
Rom 10:20;
Hos 1:10

65:2
Rom 10:21;
Is 30:1,9;
59:7

65:3
Is 3:8; 66:3,
17

65:4
Lev 11:7;
Is 66:3,17

65:5
Matt 9:11;
Luke 18:9-12

65:6
Ps 50:3;
79:12;
Jer 16:18

65:7
Is 30:13,14;
57:7;
Ezek 20:27,
28; Jer 5:29

b. The righteous to have an inheritance but apostates to be destroyed

8 Thus says the LORD,
"As the new wine is found in the cluster,
And one says, 'Do not destroy it, for there is benefit in it,'
So I will act on behalf of My servants
In order not to destroy all of them.

9 "And I will bring forth offspring from Jacob,
And an heir of My mountains from Judah;
Even My chosen ones shall inherit it,
And My servants shall dwell there.

10 "And Sharon shall be a pasture land for flocks,
And the valley of Achor a resting place for herds,
For My people who seek Me.

11 "But you who forsake the LORD,
Who forget My holy mountain,
Who set a table for Fortune,
And who fill *cups* with mixed wine for Destiny,

12 I will destine you for the sword,

*65:9f
Is 45:19,25;
49:8; 57:13;
32:18

65:10
Is 33:9;
Josh 7:24;
Hos 2:15

65:11
Deut 29:24,
25; Is 56:7

65:9,10 God's chosen people shall dwell in Palestine.

65:12 Is 34:5,6; 63:6; 2 Chr 36:15, 16; Prov 1:24; Jer 7:13	And all of you shall bow down to the slaughter. Because I called, but you did not answer; I spoke, but you did not hear. And you did evil in My sight, And chose that in which I did not delight."

c. The obedient blessed; the disobedient punished

65:13 Is 1:19; 8:21; 41:17,18; 5:13; 66:5,14	13	Therefore, thus says the Lord GOD, "Behold, My servants shall eat, but you shall be hungry. Behold, My servants shall drink, but you shall be thirsty. Behold, My servants shall rejoice, but you shall be put to shame.
65:14 Matt 8:12; Luke 13:28	14	"Behold, My servants shall shout joyfully with a glad heart, But you shall cry out with a heavy heart, And you shall wail with a broken spirit.
65:15 Zech 8:13; Is 62:2	15	"And you will leave your name for a curse to My chosen ones, And the Lord GOD will slay you. But My servants will be called by another name.
65:16 Ps 72:17; 31:5; Is 45:23; Jer 31:12	16	"Because he who is blessed in the earth Shall be blessed by the God of truth; And he who swears in the earth Shall swear by the God of truth; Because the former troubles are forgotten, And because they are hidden from My sight!

d. Messianic bliss in the new age

*65:17 2 Pet 3:13; Is 43:18	17	"For behold, I create new heavens and a new earth; And the former things shall not be remembered or come to mind.
65:18 Is 61:10	18	"But be glad and rejoice forever in what I create; For behold, I create Jerusalem for rejoicing, And her people for gladness.
65:19 Is 62:5; 35:10; Rev 7:17	19	"I will also rejoice in Jerusalem, and be glad in My people; And there will no longer be heard in her The voice of weeping and the sound of crying.
65:20 Deut 4:40; Eccl 8:12,13	20	"No longer will there be in it an infant who lives but a few days, Or an old man who does not live out his days; For the youth will die at the age of one hundred And the one who does not reach the age of one hundred Shall be thought accursed.
65:21 Amos 9:14; Is 37:30	21	"And they shall build houses and inhabit them; They shall also plant vineyards and eat their fruit.
65:22 Is 62:8,9; Ps 92:12-14; Deut 32:46, 47	22	"They shall not build, and another inhabit, They shall not plant, and another eat; For as the lifetime of a tree, so shall be the days of My people, And My chosen ones shall wear out the work of their hands.
65:23 Is 55:2; 61:9	23	"They shall not labor in vain, Or bear children for calamity; For they are the offspring of those blessed by the LORD, And their descendants with them.
65:24 Dan 9:27	24	"It will also come to pass that before they call, I will answer; and while they are still speaking, I will hear.
65:25 Is 11:6,7,9; Gen 3:14	25	"The wolf and the lamb shall graze together, and the lion shall eat straw like the ox; and dust shall be the serpent's food. They shall do no evil or harm in all My holy mountain," says the LORD.

8. The final judgments of the LORD

a. God's doom on the unrepentant

66:1 1 Kin 8:27; 2 Chr 6:18; Matt 5:34,35; Jer 7:4; Acts 7:49,50	**66**	Thus says the LORD, "Heaven is My throne, and the earth is My footstool. Where then is a house you could build for Me? And where is a place that I may rest?
	2	"For My hand made all these things,

65:17 Isaiah here seems to be speaking of the era described by John in Rev. 21:1.

Thus all these things came into being," declares the LORD.
"But to this one I will look,
    To him who is humble and contrite of spirit, and who trembles at
        My word.

3   *"But* he who kills an ox is *like* one who slays a man;
    He who sacrifices a lamb is *like* the one who breaks a dog's neck;
    He who offers a grain offering *is like one who offers* swine's blood;
    He who burns incense is *like* the one who blesses an idol.
    As they have chosen their *own* ways,
    And their soul delights in their abominations,
4   So I will choose their punishments,
    And I will bring on them what they dread.
    Because I called, but no one answered;
    I spoke, but they did not listen.
    And they did evil in My sight,
    And chose that in which I did not delight."

b. *The deliverance of the believing remnant*

5   Hear the word of the LORD, you who tremble at His word:
    "Your brothers who hate you, who exclude you for My name's sake,
    Have said, 'Let the LORD be glorified, that we may see your joy.'
    But they will be put to shame.
6   "A voice of uproar from the city, a voice from the temple,
    The voice of the LORD who is rendering recompense to His enemies.

7   "Before she travailed, she brought forth;
    Before her pain came, she gave birth to a boy.
8   "Who has heard such a thing? Who has seen such things?
    Can a land be born in one day?
    Can a nation be brought forth all at once?
    As soon as Zion travailed, she also brought forth her sons.
9   "Shall I bring to the point of birth, and not give delivery?" says the
        LORD.
    "Or shall I who gives delivery shut *the womb?* " says your God.

c. *Comfort and prosperity in the Messianic age*

10   "Be joyful with Jerusalem and rejoice for her, all you who love her;
    Be exceedingly glad with her, all you who mourn over her,
11   That you may nurse and be satisfied with her comforting breasts,
    That you may suck and be delighted with her bountiful bosom."
12   For thus says the LORD, "Behold, I extend peace to her like a river,
    And the glory of the nations like an overflowing stream;
    And you shall be nursed, you shall be carried on the hip and
        fondled on the knees.
13   "As one whom his mother comforts, so I will comfort you;
    And you shall be comforted in Jerusalem."
14   Then you shall see *this*, and your heart shall be glad,
    And your bones shall flourish like the new grass;
    And the hand of the LORD shall be made known to His servants,
    But He shall be indignant toward His enemies.

d. *The wicked consigned to judgment*

15   For behold, the LORD will come in fire
    And His chariots like the whirlwind,
    To render His anger with fury,
    And His rebuke with flames of fire.
16   For the LORD will execute judgment by fire
    And by His sword on all flesh,
    And those slain by the LORD will be many.
17   "Those who sanctify and purify themselves *to go* to the gardens,
    Following one in the center,
    Who eat swine's flesh, detestable things, and mice,
    Shall come to an end altogether," declares the LORD.

66:2
Is 40:26;
57:15;
Matt 5:3,4;
v. 5

66:3
Is 1:11,13;
65:2,4

66:4
Prov 1:24;
Is 65:12;
Jer 7:13

66:5
v. 2; Is 60:15;
Matt 5:10-12;
Luke 13:17

66:6
Is 6:1,8; 65:6

66:7
Is 37:3

66:8
Is 64:4

66:10
Is 65:18;
Ps 26:8;
137:6
66:11
Is 60:16
66:12
Is 48:18;
60:4,5

66:13
2 Cor 1:3,4

66:14
Is 33:20;
Zech 10:7;
Is 58:11;
Ezra 7:9;
Is 34:2

66:15
Is 31:9;
2 Thess 1:8;
Ps 78:16

66:16
Is 30:30;
65:12; 34:3

66:17
Is 65:3,4;
Ps 37:20

e. God glorified in Israel and Gentile converts

66:18
Is 59:7;
45:22-25
66:19
Is 62:10;
42:12

18 "For I know their works and their thoughts; the time is coming to gather all nations and tongues. And they shall come and see My glory.

19 "And I will set a sign among them and will send survivors from them to the nations: Tarshish, Put, Lud, Meshech, Rosh, Tubal, and Javan, to the distant coastlands that have neither heard My fame nor seen My glory. And they will declare My glory among the nations.

66:20
Is 60:4;
65:11,25;
52:11

20 "Then they shall bring all your brethren from all the nations as a grain offering to the LORD, on horses, in chariots, in litters, on mules, and on camels, to My holy mountain Jerusalem," says the LORD, "just as the sons of Israel bring their grain offering in a clean vessel to the house of the LORD.

66:21
Is 61:6;
1 Pet 2:5,9

21 "I will also take some of them for priests and for Levites," says the LORD.

f. Heaven for the righteous; eternal fire for the wicked

66:22
Is 65:17;
2 Pet 3:13;
Rev 21:1;
Is 65:22,23;
56:5
66:23
Is 1:13,14;
49:7
66:24
Is 5:25;
24:20;
Mark 9:48;
Is 1:31;
Dan 12:2

22   "For just as the new heavens and the new earth
          Which I make will endure before Me," declares the LORD,
          "So your offspring and your name will endure.

23   "And it shall be from new moon to new moon
          And from sabbath to sabbath,
          All mankind will come to bow down before Me," says the LORD.

24   "Then they shall go forth and look
          On the corpses of the men
          Who have transgressed against Me.
          For their worm shall not die,
          And their fire shall not be quenched;
          And they shall be an abhorrence to all mankind."

INTRODUCTION TO
THE BOOK OF
JEREMIAH

Authorship and Background: This book is named after Jeremiah the prophet, who was the son of Hilkiah. He was born in the priest-city of Anathoth and was called to be a prophet around 627 B.C., when he was but twenty years of age. He began his ministry in the reign of Josiah and continued in his office for about fifty years. The northern kingdom had already fallen. Judah, the southern kingdom, had suffered many reverses and was declining. Jeremiah prophesied during the closing days of that kingdom and lived through the invasion of Nebuchadnezzar, who destroyed Jerusalem. The international situation of that time involved a threefold battle for world supremacy among Assyria, Babylon, and Egypt. Assyria was broken under the heel of Babylon; and Babylon, in the battle of Carchemish in 605 B.C., crushed Egypt too. Judah was caught between the upper and nether millstones in the struggle, only to fall under the hand of the Babylonian oppressor.

The prophecies in the book of Jeremiah are not arranged in chronological order. The book itself was written by Baruch, who was Jeremiah's faithful amanuensis. Jeremiah dictated much of the work to him. In Jer. 36:32 it is stated that "many similar words were added to them," i.e., to the dictated words of Jeremiah. This has led some to conclude that the book contains more than the words of Jeremiah. Chapter 52 is almost identical with 2 Kin. 24, 25. The problem has been further complicated by the fact that the Septuagint version of Jeremiah differs markedly from the Hebrew text in arrangement and length (it is more than 2500 words shorter). The Septuagint translators seem to have edited the Hebrew text in the process of translation.

Characteristics: Jeremiah predicts the fall of Judah and the seventy-year captivity. He regards himself as the true spokesman of Yahweh against false prophets like Hananiah. He claims that they are not sent by Yahweh, even though they think themselves to be sincere. They hate him fiercely and bring pressure to bear on the king. Jeremiah records his personal history in all of these political and religious intrigues of the day. He loses politically, but wins spiritually. He feels his sense of aloneness, agonizing over the sins of the people and the sure judgment to come. While he shrinks from his task, he is unable to remain silent. He speaks in parables, warns of apostasy, and employs burning words of rebuke, contempt, and doom. Beneath them lies the aching heart of the patriot who senses that Israel's security cannot be divorced from faith in God and a right covenantal relationship and obedience.

Contents:

I. Prophecies under Josiah and Jehoiakim (1:1-20:18): Jeremiah's call. His prophecy that Jerusalem will fall because the people are immoral and wicked. Judgment lies before them. Their sinful impenitence in their religious worship threatens them with judgment. They are idolatrous and obdurate, and this too calls for judgment. God must judge them because He punishes those who refuse to repent; nor will He hear Jeremiah's prayer of intercession. He strengthens His prophet for the task He has given him. The parable of the potter and the clay illustrating the breaking of Jerusalem by the breaking of the pottery. Jeremiah is placed in stocks and offers his complaint to God.

II. Prophecies under Jehoiakim and Zedekiah (21:1-39:18): Zedekiah asks about Nebuchadnezzar; Jeremiah suggests surrender. He calls for the people to amend their ways, and urges them not to lament over Shallum. He rebukes Jehoiakim (Eliakim) and pronounces judgment on Coniah (Jehoiachin). He warns against the false prophets. He uses the vision of the two baskets of figs as a symbol: the good figs represent the people in captivity; the bad figs Zedekiah and the judgment to come. He prophesies the seventy-year captivity, the fall of Babylon, and the destruction of the temple. Jeremiah's trial, his warning against false prophets. He promises a return from captivity and speaks of the new covenant. As a token he buys land in Anathoth. Jerusalem shall be restored, and they shall have a new king—the Branch. He describes the siege of Jerusalem. Jehoiakim destroys Jeremiah's roll. Zedekiah asks for prayer. Jeremiah is imprisoned. He and Zedekiah consult secretly. Jerusalem is captured.

III. Prophecies after the fall of Jerusalem (40:1-45:5): Jeremiah returns to Gedaliah at Mizpah. Ishmael conspires against Gedaliah, who is murdered. Jeremiah warns against flight to Egypt. He is abducted and prophesies in Egypt against Egypt and Judah. He encourages Baruch.

IV. Prophecies against heathen nations (46:1-51:64): Jeremiah pronounces doom on Egypt by the Chaldeans. He also prophesies the doom of Philistia, Moab, Ammon, Edom, Damascus (Syria), Kedar (Arabia), Hazor, Elam, and Babylon.

V. Historical appendix (52:1-34): The fall of Jerusalem described again: the rebellion, capture, destruction, the booty, the slain, the captives, and the disposition of Jehoiachin.

THE BOOK OF

JEREMIAH

I. *Prophecies under Josiah and Jehoiakim (1:1–20:18)*

A. *The prophet's call and commission*

1. *Superscription*

1 The words of Jeremiah, the son of Hilkiah, of the priests who were in Anathoth in the land of Benjamin,
2 to whom the word of the LORD came in the days of Josiah, the son of Amon, king of Judah, in the thirteenth year of his reign.
3 It came also in the days of Jehoiakim, the son of Josiah, king of Judah, until the end of the eleventh year of Zedekiah, the son of Josiah, king of Judah, until the exile of Jerusalem in the fifth month.

2. *His personal call from God*

4   Now the word of the LORD came to me saying,
5   "Before I formed you in the womb I knew you,
      And before you were born I consecrated you;
      I have appointed you a prophet to the nations."
6   Then I said, "Alas, Lord GOD!
      Behold, I do not know how to speak,
      Because I am a youth."
7   But the LORD said to me,
      "Do not say, 'I am a youth,'
      Because everywhere I send you, you shall go,
      And all that I command you, you shall speak.
8   "Do not be afraid of them,
      For I am with you to deliver you," declares the LORD.
9   Then the LORD stretched out His hand and touched my mouth, and the LORD said to me,
      "Behold, I have put My words in your mouth.
10   "See, I have appointed you this day over the nations and over the
            kingdoms,
      To pluck up and to break down,
      To destroy and to overthrow,
      To build and to plant."

3. *Vision of the almond rod and the boiling pot*

11   And the word of the LORD came to me saying, "What do you see, Jeremiah?" And I said, "I see a rod of an almond tree."
12   Then the LORD said to me, "You have seen well, for I am watching over My word to perform it."
13   And the word of the LORD came to me a second time saying, "What do you see?" And I said, "I see a boiling pot, facing away from the north."
14   Then the LORD said to me, "Out of the north the evil will break forth on all the inhabitants of the land.
15   "For, behold, I am calling all the families of the kingdoms of the north," declares the LORD; "and they will come, and they will set each one his throne at the

1:1	2 Chr 35:25; 1 Chr 6:60; Is 32:7-9
1:2	1 Kin 13:2; 2 Kin 21:18, 24
1:3	Jer 25:1; 39:2; 52:12
*1:5	Ps 139:15,16; Is 49:1,5
1:6	Ex 4:10; Is 6:5
1:8	Ezek 2:6; Jer 15:20
1:9	Is 6:7; Ex 4:11-16
1:10	Jer 18:7; 2 Cor 10:4,5
*1:11	Jer 24:3
1:13	Zech 4:2; Ezek 11:3,7; 24:3
1:14	Jer 4:6; 6:1
1:15	Is 22:7; Jer 9:11

1:5 From this Scripture we may learn much about the operation of God's will: (1) God had a master plan for the life of Jeremiah before he was even born; (2) God's call in connection with this will was effectual—Jeremiah voluntarily became what God wanted; (3) God provided the means by which it was possible for Jeremiah to do the will of God; (4) Jeremiah's excuses for avoiding the divine call were puerile and unworthy; and (5) Jeremiah was not able to stay silent even when he wanted to do so (20:9).
1:11 *almond.* Jeremiah uses a word play based on the fact that the Hebrew word for almond (*shaqed*) is formed on the root of the verb "to be wakeful," "to watch." The almond is so named because it awakens early, i.e., blossoms in January-February.

entrance of the gates of Jerusalem, and against all its walls round about, and against all the cities of Judah.

1:16
Deut 28:20;
Jer 17:13;
7:9; 10:3-5

16 "And I will pronounce My judgments on them concerning all their wickedness, whereby they have forsaken Me and have offered sacrifices to other gods, and worshiped the works of their own hands.

1:17
1 Kin 18:46;
Ex 3:12;
Ezek 2:6

17 "Now, gird up your loins, and arise, and speak to them all which I command you. Do not be dismayed before them, lest I dismay you before them.

1:18
Is 50:7;
Jer 6:27;
15:20

18 "Now behold, I have made you today as a fortified city, and as a pillar of iron and as walls of bronze against the whole land, to the kings of Judah, to its princes, to its priests and to the people of the land.

1:19
Jer 11:19;
15:10,11; v. 8

19 "And they will fight against you, but they will not overcome you, for I am with you to deliver you," declares the LORD.

B. *First movement: God's summons to Judah for judgment*

1. *Sermon I: unfaithful Israel*

a. *Israel's early fidelity*

2:1
Jer 1:2,11
2:2
Jer 7:2; 11:6;
Ezek 16:8;
Deut 2:7

2 Now the word of the LORD came to me saying,
2 "Go and proclaim in the ears of Jerusalem, saying, 'Thus says the LORD,
"I remember concerning you the devotion of your youth,
The love of your betrothals,
Your following after Me in the wilderness,
Through a land not sown.

*2:3
Ex 19:5,6;
Jer 30:16;
50:7

3 "Israel was holy to the LORD,
The first of His harvest;
All who ate of it became guilty;
Evil came upon them," declares the LORD.'"

b. *Israel forsakes the LORD*

4 Hear the word of the LORD, O house of Jacob, and all the families of the house of Israel.

2:5
Is 5:4;
Mic 6:3;
Jer 8:19;
2 Kin 17:15

5 Thus says the LORD,
"What injustice did your fathers find in Me,
That they went far from Me
And walked after emptiness and became empty?

2:6
Ex 20:2;
Is 63:11;
Hos 13:4;
Deut 8:15;
32:10

6 "And they did not say, 'Where is the LORD
Who brought us up out of the land of Egypt,
Who led us through the wilderness,
Through a land of deserts and of pits,
Through a land of drought and of deep darkness,
Through a land that no one crossed
And where no man dwelt?'

2:7
Num 13:27;
Lev 18:25;
Ps 78:58

7 "And I brought you into the fruitful land,
To eat its fruit and its good things.
But you came and defiled My land,
And My inheritance you made an abomination.

2:8
Jer 10:21;
Mal 2:6,7;
Rom 2:20;
Jer 23:13;
16:19

8 "The priests did not say, 'Where is the LORD?'
And those who handle the law did not know Me;
The rulers also transgressed against Me,
And the prophets prophesied by Baal
And walked after things that did not profit.

2:9
Ezek 20:35,
36; Mic 6:2
2:10
Is 23:12;
Jer 49:28

9 "Therefore I will yet contend with you," declares the LORD,
"And with your sons' sons I will contend.
10 "For cross to the coastlands of Kittim and see,
And send to Kedar and observe closely,
And see if there has been such *a thing* as this!

*2:11
Mic 4:5;
Ps 106:20;
Rom 1:23

11 "Has a nation changed gods,
When they were not gods?
But My people have changed their glory

2:3 *the first of His harvest.* As the first fruits, Israel was consecrated to God. The metaphor, however, suggests that there would be a later harvest extending beyond Israel.

2:11 *A nation* here means "a heathen nation." The heathen remain true to their idols, but Israel has rejected the true God.

For that which does not profit.
12   "Be appalled, O heavens, at this,
And shudder, be very desolate," declares the LORD.
13   "For My people have committed two evils:
They have forsaken Me,
The fountain of living waters,
To hew for themselves cisterns,
Broken cisterns,
That can hold no water.

c. Consequences of Israel's apostasy

14   "Is Israel a slave? Or is he a homeborn servant?
Why has he become a prey?
15   "The young lions have roared at him,
They have roared loudly.
And they have made his land a waste;
His cities have been destroyed, without inhabitant.
16   "Also the men of Memphis and Tahpanhes
Have shaved the crown of your head.
17   "Have you not done this to yourself,
By your forsaking the LORD your God,
When He led you in the way?
18   "But now what are you doing on the road to Egypt,
To drink the waters of the Nile?
Or what are you doing on the road to Assyria,
To drink the waters of the Euphrates?
19   "Your own wickedness will correct you,
And your apostasies will reprove you;
Know therefore and see that it is evil and bitter
For you to forsake the LORD your God,
And the dread of Me is not in you," declares the Lord GOD of hosts.

d. Israel to be punished for her idolatry

20   "For long ago I broke your yoke
And tore off your bonds;
But you said, 'I will not serve!'
For on every high hill
And under every green tree
You have lain down as a harlot.
21   "Yet I planted you a choice vine,
A completely faithful seed.
How then have you turned yourself before Me
Into the degenerate shoots of a foreign vine?
22   "Although you wash yourself with lye
And use much soap,
The stain of your iniquity is before Me," declares the Lord GOD.
23   "How can you say, 'I am not defiled,
I have not gone after the Baals'?
Look at your way in the valley!
Know what you have done!
You are a swift young camel entangling her ways,
24   A wild donkey accustomed to the wilderness,
That sniffs the wind in her passion.
In *the time of* her heat who can turn her away?
All who seek her will not become weary;
In her month they will find her.
25   "Keep your feet from being unshod
And your throat from thirst;
But you said, 'It is hopeless!

Cross references (right margin):

2:13
Ps 36:9;
Jer 17:13;
John 4:14;
Jer 14:3

2:14
Ex 4:22;
Jer 5:19
2:15
Jer 50:17; 4:7

2:16
Jer 44:1;
43:7-9; 48:45
2:17
Jer 4:18;
Deut 32:10

2:18
Is 30:1,2;
Josh 13:3;
Jer 50:17

2:19
Is 3:9;
Hos 5:5;
11:7;
Jer 5:24;
Ps 36:1

*2:20
Lev 26:13;
v. 25;
Deut 12:2;
Is 57:5,7

2:21
Ex 15:17;
Is 5:4

2:22
Jer 4:14

*2:23
Prov 30:12;
Jer 9:14; 7:31

2:24
Jer 14:6

2:25
Jer 18:12;
14:10;
Deut 32:16

2:20 *every high hill.* Idolatrous Baal worship took place at "high places." Israel adopted this heathen custom for the worship of Baal, and also adopted the idolatries of Baal worship in her worship of Yahweh.

2:23 *the valley,* i.e., the "Valley of Hinnom," where infants were sacrificed in the Molech cult. This valley is located southwest of Jerusalem . . . located south and west of Jerusalem, and included within present day Jerusalem.

No! For I have loved strangers,
And after them I will walk.'

2:26
Jer 48:27

26 "As the thief is shamed when he is discovered,
So the house of Israel is shamed;
They, their kings, their princes,
And their priests, and their prophets,

2:27
Jer 3:9;
18:17; 22:23;
Is 26:16

27 Who say to a tree, 'You are my father,'
And to a stone, 'You gave me birth.'
For they have turned *their* back to Me,
And not *their* face;
But in the time of their trouble they will say,
'Arise and save us.'

2:28
Deut 32:37;
Is 45:20;
Jer 11:13

28 "But where are your gods
Which you made for yourself?
Let them arise, if they can save you
In the time of your trouble;
For *according to* the number of your cities
Are your gods, O Judah.

e. *The punishment is at hand*

2:29
Jer 5:1; 6:13

29 "Why do you contend with Me?
You have all transgressed against Me," declares the LORD.

2:30
Is 1:5;
Jer 26:20-24

30 "In vain I have struck your sons;
They accepted no chastening.
Your sword has devoured your prophets
Like a destroying lion.

2:31
Is 45:19;
Deut 32:15

31 "O generation, heed the word of the LORD.
Have I been a wilderness to Israel,
Or a land of thick darkness?
Why do My people say, 'We *are free to* roam;
We will come no more to Thee'?

2:32
Is 17:10;
Hos 8:14

32 "Can a virgin forget her ornaments,
Or a bride her attire?
Yet My people have forgotten Me
Days without number.

33 "How well you prepare your way
To seek love!
Therefore even the wicked women
You have taught your ways.

2:34
Jer 19:4;
Ex 22:2

34 "Also on your skirts is found
The lifeblood of the innocent poor;
You did not find them breaking in.
But in spite of all these things,

2:35
v. 23;
Jer 25:31;
1 John 1:8,10

35 Yet you said, 'I am innocent;
Surely His anger is turned away from me.'
Behold, I will enter into judgment with you
Because you say, 'I have not sinned.'

2:36
v. 23;
Hos 12:1;
Is 30:3;
2 Chr 28:16,
20,21

36 "Why do you go around so much
Changing your way?
Also, you shall be put to shame by Egypt
As you were put to shame by Assyria.

2:37
2 Sam 13:19;
Jer 37:7-10

37 "From this *place* also you shall go out
With your hands on your head;
For the LORD has rejected those in whom you trust,
And you shall not prosper with them."

f. *Let Judah repent and turn to the LORD*

*3:1
Deut 24:4;

3 *God* says, "If a husband divorces his wife,
And she goes from him,

3:1 God knew that the captivity was about to occur. He knew what Judah would do. Yet vv. 1-5 bespeak the mercy of God. He urges repentance and a return to Himself in the light of imminent judgment. Had Judah obeyed God, the judgment would have been delayed or averted. Once again the inevitability of ultimate judgment for disobedience is made plain.

And belongs to another man,
Will he still return to her?
Will not that land be completely polluted?
But you are a harlot *with* many lovers;
Yet you turn to Me," declares the LORD.

2 "Lift up your eyes to the bare heights and see;
Where have you not been violated?
By the roads you have sat for them
Like an Arab in the desert,
And you have polluted a land
With your harlotry and with your wickedness.

3 "Therefore the showers have been withheld,
And there has been no spring rain.
Yet you had a harlot's forehead;
You refused to be ashamed.

4 "Have you not just now called to Me,
'My Father, Thou art the friend of my youth?

5 'Will He be angry forever?
Will He be indignant to the end?'
Behold, you have spoken
And have done evil things,
And you have had your way."

2. Sermon II: the warning example of exiled Samaria
a. The ten tribes dispersed but urged to repent

6 Then the LORD said to me in the days of Josiah the king, "Have you seen what faithless Israel did? She went up on every high hill and under every green tree, and she was a harlot there.

7 "And I thought, 'After she has done all these things, she will return to Me'; but she did not return, and her treacherous sister Judah saw it.

8 "And I saw that for all the adulteries of faithless Israel, I had sent her away and given her a writ of divorce, yet her treacherous sister Judah did not fear; but she went and was a harlot also.

9 "And it came about because of the lightness of her harlotry, that she polluted the land and committed adultery with stones and trees.

10 "And yet in spite of all this her treacherous sister Judah did not return to Me with all her heart, but rather in deception," declares the LORD.

11 And the LORD said to me, "Faithless Israel has proved herself more righteous than treacherous Judah.

12 "Go, and proclaim these words toward the north and say,
'Return, faithless Israel,' declares the LORD;
'I will not look upon you in anger.
For I am gracious,' declares the LORD;
'I will not be angry forever.

13 'Only acknowledge your iniquity,
That you have transgressed against the LORD your God
And have scattered your favors to the strangers under every green tree,
And you have not obeyed My voice,' declares the LORD.

14 'Return, O faithless sons,' declares the LORD;
'For I am a master to you,
And I will take you one from a city and two from a family,
And I will bring you to Zion.'

15 "Then I will give you shepherds after My own heart, who will feed you on knowledge and understanding.

16 "And it shall be in those days when you are multiplied and increased in the land," declares the LORD, "they shall say no more, 'The ark of the covenant of the

Jer 2:20; Ezek 16:26, 28,29; Zech 1:3
*3:2 Deut 12:2; Jer 2:20; Prov 23:28; Jer 2:7
3:3 Lev 26:19; Jer 6:15; Ezek 3:7
3:4 v. 19; Ps 71:17
3:5 v. 12; Is 57:16
*3:6 Jer 7:24; 17:2
3:7 Ezek 16:46, 47
3:8 2 Kin 17:6; Is 50:1; Ezek 23:11
3:9 Jer 2:7,27
3:10 Hos 7:14
3:11 Ezek 16:51; v. 7
3:12 2 Kin 17:6; Ps 86:15
3:13 Deut 30:1-3; Jer 2:20,25; Deut 12:2
3:14 Hos 2:19; Jer 50:4,5
3:15 Jer 23:4; Acts 20:28
3:16 Is 65:17

3:2 *like an Arab in the desert*. The Arab was free to approach or attack any who passed through his wilderness abode. Israel was equally ready to embrace her *lovers*, the gods of the land.

3:6 Scripture repeatedly warns men of impending judg-ment. Here Jeremiah uses Samaria (already dispersed) as a warning to Judah that a similar judgment will fall on her. But men seem all too prone to disregard such warnings, as the apostle Peter pointed out, using the illustrations of Noah, Sodom and Gomorrah, and Balaam (2 Pet. 2:1–16).

LORD.' And it shall not come to mind, nor shall they remember it, nor shall they miss *it*, nor shall it be made again.

3:17
Jer 17:12;
v. 19; Is 60:9;
Jer 11:8

17 "At that time they shall call Jerusalem 'The Throne of the LORD,' and all the nations will be gathered to it, to Jerusalem, for the name of the LORD; nor shall they walk anymore after the stubbornness of their evil heart.

3:18
Is 11:13;
Hos 1:11;
Jer 31:8;
Amos 9:15

18 "In those days the house of Judah will walk with the house of Israel, and they will come together from the land of the north to the land that I gave your fathers as an inheritance.

3:19
Dan 8:9;
Ps 16:6;
Is 63:16

19 "Then I said,
'How I would set you among My sons,
    And give you a pleasant land,
    The most beautiful inheritance of the nations!'
And I said, 'You shall call Me, My Father,
    And not turn away from following Me.'

3:20
vv. 6,7;
Is 48:8

20 "Surely, as a woman treacherously departs from her lover,
    So you have dealt treacherously with Me,
    O house of Israel," declares the LORD.

3:21
Is 15:2;
Jer 2:32

21 A voice is heard on the bare heights,
    The weeping *and* the supplications of the sons of Israel;
    Because they have perverted their way,
    They have forgotten the LORD their God.

3:22
v. 14;
Hos 6:1;
14:4; Jer 31:6

22 "Return, O faithless sons,
    I will heal your faithlessness."
"Behold, we come to Thee;
    For Thou art the LORD our God.

*3:23
Ps 121:1,2;
3:8

23 "Surely, the hills are a deception,
    A tumult *on* the mountains.
    Surely, in the LORD our God
    Is the salvation of Israel.

3:24
Jer 8:16

24 "But the shameful thing has consumed the labor of our fathers since our youth, their flocks and their herds, their sons and their daughters.

3:25
Ezra 9:7;
Jer 22:21

25 "Let us lie down in our shame, and let our humiliation cover us; for we have sinned against the LORD our God, we and our fathers, since our youth even to this day. And we have not obeyed the voice of the LORD our God."

4:1
Jer 3:1,22;
Joel 2:12;
Jer 7:3,7

4 "If you will return, O Israel," declares the LORD,
    "*Then* you should return to Me.
    And if you will put away your detested things from My presence,
    And will not waver,

4:2
Deut 10:20;
Gen 22:18;
Gal 3:8;
Is 45:25;
1 Cor 1:31

2 And you will swear, 'As the LORD lives,'
    In truth, in justice, and in righteousness;
    Then the nations will bless themselves in Him,
    And in Him they will glory."

b. *Judah promised a similar judgment*

(1) JUDGMENT TO COME FROM THE NORTH

4:3
Hos 10:12;
Matt 13:7,22

3 For thus says the LORD to the men of Judah and to Jerusalem,
    "Break up your fallow ground,
    And do not sow among thorns.

4:4
Deut 10:16;
30:6;
Jer 9:26;
Rom 2:28,29;
Jer 21:12;
Mark 9:43,48

4 "Circumcise yourselves to the LORD
    And remove the foreskins of your heart,
    Men of Judah and inhabitants of Jerusalem,
    Lest My wrath go forth like fire
    And burn with none to quench it,
    Because of the evil of your deeds."

4:5
Jer 6:1; 8:14

5 Declare in Judah and proclaim in Jerusalem, and say,
    "Blow the trumpet in the land;
    Cry aloud and say,
    'Assemble yourselves, and let us go

3:23 *the hills are a deception*, i.e., no help will come from the idolatrous worship associated with the high places, whereas Israel can find real help in *the* LORD *our God*.

6   "Lift up a standard toward Zion!
     Seek refuge, do not stand *still*,
     For I am bringing evil from the north,
     And great destruction.

7   "A lion has gone up from his thicket,
     And a destroyer of nations has set out;
     He has gone out from his place
     To make your land a waste.
     Your cities will be ruins
     Without inhabitant.

8   "For this, put on sackcloth,
     Lament and wail;
     For the fierce anger of the LORD
     Has not turned back from us."

9   "And it shall come about in that day," declares the LORD, "that the heart of the king and the heart of the princes will fail; and the priests will be appalled, and the prophets will be astounded."

10   Then I said, "Ah, Lord GOD! Surely Thou hast utterly deceived this people and Jerusalem, saying, 'You will have peace'; whereas a sword touches the throat."

11   In that time it will be said to this people and to Jerusalem, "A scorching wind from the bare heights in the wilderness in the direction of the daughter of My people—not to winnow, and not to cleanse,

12   a wind too strong for this—will come at My command; now I will also pronounce judgments against them.

13   "Behold, he goes up like clouds,
     And his chariots like the whirlwind;
     His horses are swifter than eagles.
     Woe to us, for we are ruined!"

14   Wash your heart from evil, O Jerusalem,
     That you may be saved.
     How long will your wicked thoughts
     Lodge within you?

15   For a voice declares from Dan,
     And proclaims wickedness from Mount Ephraim.

16   "Report *it* to the nations, now!
     Proclaim over Jerusalem,
     'Besiegers come from a far country,
     And lift their voices against the cities of Judah.

17   'Like watchmen of a field they are against her round about,
     Because she has rebelled against Me,' declares the LORD.

18   "Your ways and your deeds
     Have brought these things to you.
     This is your evil. How bitter!
     How it has touched your heart!"

19   My soul, my soul! I am in anguish! Oh, my heart!
     My heart is pounding in me;
     I cannot be silent,
     Because you have heard, O my soul,
     The sound of the trumpet,
     The alarm of war.

20   Disaster on disaster is proclaimed,
     For the whole land is devastated;
     Suddenly my tents are devastated,
     My curtains in an instant.

21   How long must I see the standard,
     And hear the sound of the trumpet?

22   "For My people are foolish,
     They know Me not;

4:6
Jer 1:13-15;
6:1,22

***4:7**
2 Kin 24:1;
Jer 5:6;
Dan 7:4;
Jer 25:9;
Is 1:7;
Jer 2:15

4:8
Is 22:12;
Jer 6:26;
30:24

4:9
Is 22:3-5;
29:9,10

4:10
Ezek 14:9;
2 Thess 2:11;
Jer 5:12;
14:13

4:11
Jer 51:1;
Ezek 17:10;
Hos 13:15

4:12
Jer 1:16

4:13
Is 19:1; 5:28;
Deut 28:49;
Lam 4:19;
Is 3:8

4:14
Is 1:16;
James 4:8;
Jer 6:19;
13:27

***4:15**
Jer 8:16

4:16
Jer 5:6,15;
Is 39:3;
Ezek 21:22

4:17
2 Kin 25:1,4;
Jer 5:23

4:18
Ps 107:17;
Is 50:1;
Jer 2:17,19

4:19
Is 15:5;
16:11; 21:3;
22:4; Jer 9:1,
10

4:20
Ps 42:7;
Ezek 7:26;
Jer 10:20

4:22
Jer 10:8; 2:8;
Rom 16:19

4:7 A *lion* is a metaphor for Nebuchadnezzar, the king who destroyed Jerusalem.
4:15 *Dan* was in the far north of Palestine. The enemy would first be seen at Dan as he moved from the east through the Fertile Crescent.

They are stupid children,
And they have no understanding.
They are shrewd to do evil,
But to do good they do not know."

23 I looked on the earth, and behold, *it was* formless and void;
And to the heavens, and they had no light.

24 I looked on the mountains, and behold, they were quaking,
And all the hills moved to and fro.

25 I looked, and behold, there was no man,
And all the birds of the heavens had fled.

26 I looked, and behold, the fruitful land was a wilderness,
And all its cities were pulled down
Before the LORD, before His fierce anger.

27 For thus says the LORD,
"The whole land shall be a desolation,
Yet I will not execute a complete destruction.

28 "For this the earth shall mourn,
And the heavens above be dark,
Because I have spoken, I have purposed,
And I will not change My mind, nor will I turn from it."

29 At the sound of the horseman and bowman every city flees;
They go into the thickets and climb among the rocks;
Every city is forsaken,
And no man dwells in them.

30 And you, O desolate one, what will you do?
Although you dress in scarlet,
Although you decorate *yourself with* ornaments of gold,
Although you enlarge your eyes with paint,
In vain you make yourself beautiful;
Your lovers despise you;
They seek your life.

31 For I heard a cry as of a woman in labor,
The anguish as of one giving birth to her first child,
The cry of the daughter of Zion gasping for breath,
Stretching out her hands, *saying,*
"Ah, woe is me, for I faint before murderers."

(2) FUTILE SEARCH FOR AN UPRIGHT MAN

5 "Roam to and fro through the streets of Jerusalem,
And look now, and take note.
And seek in her open squares,
If you can find a man,
If there is one who does justice, who seeks truth,
Then I will pardon her.

2 "And although they say, 'As the LORD lives,'
Surely they swear falsely."

3 O LORD, do not Thine eyes look for truth?
Thou hast smitten them,
But they did not weaken;
Thou hast consumed them,
But they refused to take correction.
They have made their faces harder than rock;
They have refused to repent.

4 Then I said, "They are only the poor,
They are foolish;
For they do not know the way of the LORD
Or the ordinance of their God.

5 "I will go to the great
And will speak to them,
For they know the way of the LORD,
And the ordinance of their God."
But they too, with one accord, have broken the yoke

4:23
Gen 1:2;
Is 24:19
4:24
Is 5:25;
Ezek 38:20
4:25
Zeph 1:3

4:26
Jer 9:10

4:27
Jer 12:11,12;
5:10,18;
30:11; 46:28
4:28
Hos 4:3;
Is 5:30; 50:3;
Num 23:19;
Jer 7:16
4:29
Jer 6:23;
16:16

4:30
Jer 13:21;
2 Kin 9:30;
Ezek 23:40;
Jer 22:20,22

4:31
Jer 13:21;
Is 42:14;
1:15;
Lam 1:17

5:1
2 Chr 16:9;
Ezek 22:30;
Gen 18:23,26,
32

5:2
Titus 1:16;
Jer 4:2; 7:9
5:3
Is 1:5; 9:13;
Jer 2:30;
Zeph 3:2;
Jer 7:26;
19:15

5:4
Jer 4:22; 8:7

5:5
Mic 3:1;
Ps 2:3

(6) THE BESIEGERS ENCOURAGED AGAINST JERUSALEM

6   For thus says the LORD of hosts,
      "Cut down her trees,
      And cast up a siege against Jerusalem.
      This is the city to be punished,
      In whose midst there is only oppression.

6:6 Deut 20:19, 20; Jer 32:24; 22:17

7   "As a well keeps its waters fresh,
      So she keeps fresh her wickedness.
      Violence and destruction are heard in her;
      Sickness and wounds are ever before Me.

6:7 Is 57:20; Ps 55:9-11; Jer 20:8; Ezek 7:11,23

8   "Be warned, O Jerusalem,
      Lest I be alienated from you;
      Lest I make you a desolation,
      A land not inhabited."

6:8 Jer 7:28; Ezek 23:18; Hos 9:12

9   Thus says the LORD of hosts,
      "They will thoroughly glean as the vine the remnant of Israel;
      Pass your hand again like a grape gatherer
      Over the branches."

6:9 Jer 49:9; 8:3

10   To whom shall I speak and give warning,
      That they may hear?
      Behold, their ears are closed,
      And they cannot listen.
      Behold, the word of the LORD has become a reproach to them;
      They have no delight in it.

6:10 Jer 7:26; Acts 7:51; Jer 20:8

11   But I am full of the wrath of the LORD;
      I am weary with holding *it* in.
      "Pour *it* out on the children in the street,
      And on the gathering of young men together;
      For both husband and wife shall be taken,
      The aged and the very old.

6:11 Job 32:18,19; Jer 20:9; 9:21

12   "And their houses shall be turned over to others,
      Their fields and their wives together;
      For I will stretch out My hand
      Against the inhabitants of the land," declares the LORD.

6:12 Deut 28:30; Jer 8:10; 15:6

13   "For from the least of them even to the greatest of them,
      Everyone is greedy for gain,
      And from the prophet even to the priest
      Everyone deals falsely.

6:13 Is 56:11; Jer 8:10; 22:17; Mic 3:5,11

14   "And they have healed the brokenness of My people superficially,
      Saying, 'Peace, peace,'
      But there is no peace.

6:14 Jer 8:11; Ezek 13:10; Jer 4:10; 23:17

15   "Were they ashamed because of the abomination they have done?
      They were not even ashamed at all;
      They did not even know how to blush.
      Therefore they shall fall among those who fall;
      At the time that I punish them,
      They shall be cast down," says the LORD.

6:15 Jer 3:3; 8:12

(7) REFUSAL TO REPENT DESPITE IMPENDING RUIN

16   Thus says the LORD,
      "Stand by the ways and see and ask for the ancient paths,
      Where the good way is, and walk in it;
      And you shall find rest for your souls.
      But they said, 'We will not walk *in it.*'

6:16 Is 8:20; Jer 18:15; Mal 4:4; Luke 16:29; Matt 11:29

17   "And I set watchmen over you, *saying,*
      'Listen to the sound of the trumpet!'
      But they said, 'We will not listen.'

6:17 Is 21:11; 58:1; Jer 25:4; Ezek 3:17; Hab 2:1

18   "Therefore hear, O nations,
      And know, O congregation, what is among them.

19   "Hear, O earth: behold, I am bringing disaster on this people,
      The fruit of their plans,
      Because they have not listened to My words,
      And as for My law, they have rejected it also.

6:19 Is 1:2; Jer 19:3,15; Prov 1:31; Jer 8:9

6:20
Is 1:11;
Amos 5:21;
Mic 6:6;
Is 60:6;
Jer 7:21
20 "For what purpose does frankincense come to Me from Sheba,
And the sweet cane from a distant land?
Your burnt offerings are not acceptable,
And your sacrifices are not pleasing to Me."

6:21
Is 8:14;
Jer 13:16;
9:21,22
21 Therefore, thus says the LORD,
"Behold, I am laying stumbling blocks before this people.
And they will stumble against them,
Fathers and sons together;
Neighbor and friend will perish."

(8) THE INVADER WILL SUDDENLY DESTROY

6:22
Jer 1:15;
5:15; 10:22;
50:41-43;
Neh 1:9
22 Thus says the LORD,
"Behold, a people is coming from the north land,
And a great nation will be aroused from the remote parts of the earth.

6:23
Jer 4:29;
50:42; Is 5:30
23 "They seize bow and spear;
They are cruel and have no mercy;
Their voice roars like the sea,
And they ride on horses,
Arrayed as a man for the battle
Against you, O daughter of Zion!"

6:24
Jer 4:31;
13:21; 49:24;
50:43
24 We have heard the report of it;
Our hands are limp.
Anguish has seized us,
Pain as of a woman in childbirth.

6:25
Jer 14:18;
12:12; 20:10
25 Do not go out into the field,
And do not walk on the road,
For the enemy has a sword,
Terror is on every side.

6:26
Jer 4:8;
25:34;
Mic 1:10;
Zech 12:10
26 O daughter of my people, put on sackcloth
And roll in ashes;
Mourn as for an only son,
A lamentation most bitter.
For suddenly the destroyer
Will come upon us.

6:27
Jer 1:18;
15:20; 9:7
27 "I have made you an assayer *and* a tester among My people,
That you may know and assay their way."

6:28
Jer 5:23; 9:4;
Ezek 22:18
28 All of them are stubbornly rebellious,
Going about as a talebearer.
They are bronze and iron;
They, all of them, are corrupt.

6:29
Jer 15:19
29 The bellows blow fiercely,
The lead is consumed by the fire;
In vain the refining goes on,
But the wicked are not separated.

6:30
Jer 7:29
30 They call them rejected silver,
Because the LORD has rejected them.

C. Second movement: Sermon III: the great temple-sermon

1. First indictment: idolatry and immorality

*7:1f
Jer 26:1,2
7:2
Jer 17:19; 2:4
7 The word that came to Jeremiah from the LORD, saying,
2 "Stand in the gate of the LORD's house and proclaim there this word, and say, 'Hear the word of the LORD, all you of Judah, who enter by these gates to worship the LORD!'"

7:3
Jer 18:11;
26:13
*7:4
Mic 3:11
3 Thus says the LORD of hosts, the God of Israel, "Amend your ways and your deeds, and I will let you dwell in this place.
4 "Do not trust in deceptive words, saying, 'This is the temple of the LORD, the temple of the LORD, the temple of the LORD.'

7:1,2 Here, as elsewhere in Scripture, the writer professes that the words he speaks are not his own words but originate with God. This is characteristic of the Old Testament prophets, who often preface their message with, "Thus says the LORD" or some similar phrase. *Hear the word of the LORD* is Jeremiah's way of introducing a message that had been directly given to him by God. This is the essence of revelation.

5 "For if you truly amend your ways and your deeds, if you truly practice justice between a man and his neighbor,

6 *if* you do not oppress the alien, the orphan, or the widow, and do not shed innocent blood in this place, nor walk after other gods to your own ruin,

7 then I will let you dwell in this place, in the land that I gave to your fathers forever and ever.

8 "Behold, you are trusting in deceptive words to no avail.

9 "Will you steal, murder, and commit adultery, and swear falsely, and offer sacrifices to Baal, and walk after other gods that you have not known,

10 then come and stand before Me in this house, which is called by My name, and say, 'We are delivered!'—that you may do all these abominations?

11 "Has this house, which is called by My name, become a den of robbers in your sight? Behold, I, even I, have seen *it*," declares the LORD.

12 "But go now to My place which was in Shiloh, where I made My name dwell at the first, and see what I did to it because of the wickedness of My people Israel.

13 "And now, because you have done all these things," declares the LORD, "and I spoke to you, rising up early and speaking, but you did not hear, and I called you but you did not answer,

14 therefore, I will do to the house which is called by My name, in which you trust, and to the place which I gave you and your fathers, as I did to Shiloh.

15 "And I will cast you out of My sight, as I have cast out all your brothers, all the offspring of Ephraim.

16 "As for you, do not pray for this people, and do not lift up cry or prayer for them, and do not intercede with Me; for I do not hear you.

17 "Do you not see what they are doing in the cities of Judah and in the streets of Jerusalem?

18 "The children gather wood, and the fathers kindle the fire, and the women knead dough to make cakes for the queen of heaven; and *they* pour out libations to other gods in order to spite Me.

19 "Do they spite Me?" declares the LORD. "Is it not themselves *they spite*, to their own shame?"

20 Therefore thus says the Lord GOD, "Behold, My anger and My wrath will be poured out on this place, on man and on beast and on the trees of the field and on the fruit of the ground; and it will burn and not be quenched."

21 Thus says the LORD of hosts, the God of Israel, "Add your burnt offerings to your sacrifices and eat flesh.

22 "For I did not speak to your fathers, or command them in the day that I brought them out of the land of Egypt, concerning burnt offerings and sacrifices.

23 "But this is what I commanded them, saying, 'Obey My voice, and I will be your God, and you will be My people; and you will walk in all the way which I command you, that it may be well with you.'

24 "Yet they did not obey or incline their ear, but walked in *their own* counsels *and* in the stubbornness of their evil heart, and went backward and not forward.

25 "Since the day that your fathers came out of the land of Egypt until this day, I have sent you all My servants the prophets, daily rising early and sending *them*.

26 "Yet they did not listen to Me or incline their ear, but stiffened their neck; they did evil more than their fathers.

27 "And you shall speak all these words to them, but they will not listen to you; and you shall call to them, but they will not answer you.

28 "And you shall say to them, 'This is the nation that did not obey the voice of the LORD their God or accept correction; truth has perished and has been cut off from their mouth.

29 'Cut off your hair and cast *it* away,
And take up a lamentation on the bare heights;
For the LORD has rejected and forsaken
The generation of His wrath.'

30 "For the sons of Judah have done that which is evil in My sight," declares the LORD, "they have set their detestable things in the house which is called by My name, to defile it.

Marginal references:

7:5 Jer 4:1,2; 22:3
7:6 Deut 6:14,15; 8:19; Jer 13:10
7:8 Jer 13:25
7:9 Ex 20:3; Jer 11:13,17; 19:4
7:10 Ezek 23:39; Jer 32:34; 2:23,35
7:11 Matt 21:13; Mark 11:17; Luke 19:46
*7:12 Jer 26:6; 1 Sam 4:10,11
7:13 2 Chr 36:15; Jer 35:17; Is 65:12
7:14 1 Kin 9:7; vv. 4,12
7:15 Jer 15:1; 2 Kin 17:23; Ps 78:67
7:16 Ex 32:10; Jer 11:14; 15:1
*7:18 Jer 44:17; 19:13; 11:17
7:19 Deut 32:16, 21
7:20 Jer 6:11,12; 8:13; 11:16
7:21 Is 1:11; Amos 5:21; Hos 8:13
7:22 1 Sam 15:22; Ps 51:16; Hos 6:6
7:23 Ex 15:26; Lev 26:12; Is 3:10
7:24 Ps 81:11,12; Jer 15:6
7:25 Jer 25:4; Luke 11:49
7:26 Jer 19:15; 16:12
7:27 Ezek 2:7; 3:7; Is 50:2
7:28 Jer 6:17; 5:3; 9:5
7:29 Is 15:2; Jer 16:6; Jer 3:21; 14:19
7:30 2 Kin 21:4; 2 Chr 33:4,5, 7; Jer 23:11; Dan 9:27

7:4 *the temple of the LORD.* The false prophets insisted that God would never allow the heathen Babylonians to defile His temple.
7:12 *Shiloh* had been the site of a sanctuary to Israel's God, but it was destroyed by the Philistines (cf. 1 Sam. 4:10). Jerusalem could not expect its iniquities to be overlooked.
7:18 *the queen of heaven.* Ishtar, the Babylonian fertility goddess, later identified with Venus.

*7:31
2 Kin 23:10;
Jer 19:5;
Ps 106:38;
Deut 17:3
7:32
Jer 19:5,7,11;
2 Kin 23:10

31 "And they have built the high places of Topheth, which is in the valley of the son of Hinnom, to burn their sons and their daughters in the fire, which I did not command, and it did not come into My mind.

32 "Therefore, behold, days are coming," declares the LORD, "when it will no more be called Topheth, or the valley of the son of Hinnom, but the valley of the Slaughter; for they will bury in Topheth because there is no *other* place.

7:34
Is 24:7,8;
Ezek 26:13;
Hos 2:11;
Rev 18:23;
Is 1:7

33 "And the dead bodies of this people will be food for the birds of the sky, and for the beasts of the earth; and no one will frighten *them away.*

34 "Then I will make to cease from the cities of Judah and from the streets of Jerusalem the voice of joy and the voice of gladness, the voice of the bridegroom and the voice of the bride; for the land will become a ruin.

8:1
Ezek 6:5

8 "At that time," declares the LORD, "they will bring out the bones of the kings of Judah, and the bones of its princes, and the bones of the priests, and the bones of the prophets, and the bones of the inhabitants of Jerusalem from their graves.

8:2
Acts 7:42;
Jer 22:19

2 "And they will spread them out to the sun, the moon, and to all the host of heaven, which they have loved, and which they have served, and which they have gone after, and which they have sought, and which they have worshiped. They will not be gathered or buried; they will be as dung on the face of the ground.

8:3
Job 3:21;
7:15,16;
Rev 9:6;
Jer 23:3,8

3 "And death will be chosen rather than life by all the remnant that remains of this evil family, that remains in all the places to which I have driven them," declares the LORD of hosts.

2. Second indictment: stubbornly unrepentant, they must be exiled

8:4
Prov 24:16

4 "And you shall say to them, 'Thus says the LORD,
   "Do *men* fall and not get up again?
   Does one turn away and not repent?

8:5
Jer 5:6; 7:24;
5:27; 9:6

5 "Why then has this people, Jerusalem,
   Turned away in continual apostasy?
   They hold fast to deceit,
   They refuse to return.

8:6
Ps 14:2;
Ezek 22:30;
Rev 9:20;
Job 39:21-25

6 "I have listened and heard,
   They have spoken what is not right;
   No man repented of his wickedness,
   Saying, 'What have I done?'
   Everyone turned to his course,
   Like a horse charging into the battle.

8:7
Is 1:3;
Song 2:12;
Jer 5:4,5

7 "Even the stork in the sky
   Knows her seasons;
   And the turtledove and the swift and the thrush
   Observe the time of their migration;
   But My people do not know
   The ordinance of the LORD.

8:8
Jer 4:22;
Rom 2:17

8 "How can you say, 'We are wise,
   And the law of the LORD is with us'?
   But behold, the lying pen of the scribes
   Has made *it* into a lie.

8:9
Jer 6:15,19

9 "The wise men are put to shame,
   They are dismayed and caught;
   Behold, they have rejected the word of the LORD,
   And what kind of wisdom do they have?

8:10
Deut 28:30;
Is 56:11

10 "Therefore I will give their wives to others,
   Their fields to new owners;
   Because from the least even to the greatest
   Everyone is greedy for gain;
   From the prophet even to the priest
   Everyone practices deceit.

7:31 *I did not command.* Human sacrifice such as that practiced at Hinnom was explicitly contrary to God's command. Indeed, note: *and it did not come into My mind.*

11   "And they heal the brokenness of the daughter of My people
      superficially,
  Saying, 'Peace, peace,'
  But there is no peace.

12   "Were they ashamed because of the abomination they had done?
  They certainly were not ashamed,
  And they did not know how to blush;
  Therefore they shall fall among those who fall;
  At the time of their punishment they shall be brought down,"
  Declares the LORD.

13   "I will surely snatch them away," declares the LORD;
  "There will be no grapes on the vine,
  And no figs on the fig tree,
  And the leaf shall wither;
  And what I have given them shall pass away." ' "

14   Why are we sitting still?
  Assemble yourselves, and let us go into the fortified cities,
  And let us perish there,
  Because the LORD our God has doomed us
  And given us poisoned water to drink,
  For we have sinned against the LORD.

15   *We* waited for peace, but no good *came;*
  For a time of healing, but behold, terror!

16   From Dan is heard the snorting of his horses;
  At the sound of the neighing of his stallions
  The whole land quakes;
  For they come and devour the land and its fulness,
  The city and its inhabitants.

17   "For behold, I am sending serpents against you,
  Adders, for which there is no charm,
  And they will bite you," declares the LORD.

18   My sorrow is beyond healing,
  My heart is faint *within me!*

19   Behold, listen! The cry of the daughter of my people from a distant
      land:
  "Is the LORD not in Zion? Is her King not within her?"
  "Why have they provoked Me with their graven images, with
      foreign idols?"

20   "Harvest is past, summer is ended,
  And we are not saved."

21   For the brokenness of the daughter of my people I am broken;
  I mourn, dismay has taken hold of me.

22   Is there no balm in Gilead?
  Is there no physician there?
  Why then has not the health of the daughter of my people been
      restored?

3. *Third indictment: faithless and truthless,*
they must be scattered and slain

9   Oh, that my head were waters,
  And my eyes a fountain of tears,
  That I might weep day and night
  For the slain of the daughter of my people!

2   O that I had in the desert
  A wayfarers' lodging place;
  That I might leave my people,

8:11 *superficially.* False prophets sought to encourage the people with assurances of peace, when actually the sins of the Israelites were to lead them to the judgment of the exile. (Also see note to 5:31 on false prophets.)

8:16 *Dan,* see note to 4:15.
8:22 *balm.* Gilead produced a medicinal balm. Israel's sickness could not be healed by such balm, however.

*(margin references: *8:11 Jer 6:14; Ezek 13:10; 8:12 Jer 3:3; 6:21; 10:15; 8:13 Jer 14:12; Ezek 22:20,21; Is 5:2; Joel 1:7; Matt 21:19; 8:14 Jer 4:5; 35:11; 9:15; Matt 27:34; Jer 3:25; 14:20; 8:15 Jer 14:19; *8:16 Jer 4:15; Judg 5:22; Jer 3:24; 10:25; 8:17 Num 21:6; Ps 58:4,5; 8:19 Jer 4:16; Is 39:3; Jer 14:9; Deut 32:21; Ps 31:6; 8:21 Jer 14:17; Joel 2:6; Nah 2:10; *8:22 Gen 37:25; Jer 14:19; 30:13; 9:1 Is 22:4; Lam 2:11; Jer 6:26; 8:21,22; 9:2 Is 55:6,7; Jer 5,7,8,11; 12:1,6)*

And go from them!
For all of them are adulterers,
An assembly of treacherous men.

9:3
Ps 64:3;
Is 59:4;
Jer 4:22;
1 Sam 2:12;
Hos 4:1
3   "And they bend their tongue *like* their bow;
Lies and not truth prevail in the land;
For they proceed from evil to evil,
And they do not know Me," declares the LORD.

9:4
v. 8; Jer 12:6;
Gen 27:35;
Jer 6:28
4   "Let everyone be on guard against his neighbor,
And do not trust any brother;
Because every brother deals craftily,
And every neighbor goes about as a slanderer.

9:5
Mic 6:12;
Jer 12:13;
51:58,64
5   "And everyone deceives his neighbor,
And does not speak the truth,
They have taught their tongue to speak lies;
They weary themselves committing iniquity.

9:6
Jer 5:27;
11:10;
John 3:19,20
6   "Your dwelling is in the midst of deceit;
Through deceit they refuse to know Me," declares the LORD.

9:7
Is 1:25;
Mal 3:3;
Hos 11:8
7   Therefore thus says the LORD of hosts,
"Behold, I will refine them and assay them;
For what *else* can I do, because of the daughter of My people?

9:8
Ps 12:2; 28:3;
Jer 5:26
8   "Their tongue is a deadly arrow;
It speaks deceit;
With his mouth one speaks peace to his neighbor,
But inwardly he sets an ambush for him.

9:9
Jer 5:9,29
9   "Shall I not punish them for these things?" declares the LORD.
"On a nation such as this
Shall I not avenge Myself?

9:10
Jer 4:24-26;
Hos 4:3;
Ezek 14:15
10 "For the mountains I will take up a weeping and wailing,
And for the pastures of the wilderness a dirge,
Because they are laid waste, so that no one passes through,
And the lowing of the cattle is not heard;
Both the birds of the sky and the beasts have fled; they are gone.

9:11
Is 25:2;
13:22; 34:13;
Jer 4:27; 26:9
11 "And I will make Jerusalem a heap of ruins,
A haunt of jackals;
And I will make the cities of Judah a desolation, without
    inhabitant."

9:12
Ps 107:43;
Hos 14:9;
Jer 23:10,16
12 Who is the wise man that may understand this? And *who is* he to whom the mouth of the LORD has spoken, that he may declare it? Why is the land ruined, laid waste like a desert, so that no one passes through?

9:13
Jer 5:19;
Ps 89:30
13 And the LORD said, "Because they have forsaken My law which I set before them, and have not obeyed My voice nor walked according to it,

9:14
Rom 1:21-24;
Gal 1:14;
1 Pet 1:18
14 but have walked after the stubbornness of their heart and after the Baals, as their fathers taught them,"

9:15
Jer 8:14;
23:15
15 therefore thus says the LORD of hosts, the God of Israel, "behold, I will feed them, this people, with wormwood and give them poisoned water to drink.

9:16
Lev 26:33;
Deut 28:64;
Jer 44:27;
Ezek 5:2
16 "And I will scatter them among the nations, whom neither they nor their fathers have known; and I will send the sword after them until I have annihilated them."

9:17
2 Chr 35:25;
Eccl 12:5;
Amos 5:16
17 Thus says the LORD of hosts,
"Consider and call for the mourning women, that they may come;
And send for the wailing women, that they may come!

9:18
Jer 14:17
18 "And let them make haste, and take up a wailing for us,
That our eyes may shed tears,
And our eyelids flow with water.

9:19
Jer 4:13;
7:15; 15:1
19 "For a voice of wailing is heard from Zion,
'How are we ruined!
We are put to great shame,
For we have left the land,
Because they have cast down our dwellings.'"

9:20
Is 32:9
20 Now hear the word of the LORD, O you women,
And let your ear receive the word of His mouth;

      Teach your daughters wailing,
      And everyone her neighbor a dirge.

21   For death has come up through our windows;
      It has entered our palaces
      To cut off the children from the streets,
      The young men from the town squares.

4. *Conclusion: true wisdom is knowing the LORD; idolatry brings destruction*

22   Speak, "Thus declares the LORD,
      'The corpses of men will fall like dung on the open field,
      And like the sheaf after the reaper,
      But no one will gather *them*.' "

23   Thus says the LORD, "Let not a wise man boast of his wisdom, and let not the mighty man boast of his might, let not a rich man boast of his riches;

24   but let him who boasts boast of this, that he understands and knows Me, that I am the LORD who exercises lovingkindness, justice, and righteousness on earth; for I delight in these things," declares the LORD.

25   "Behold, the days are coming," declares the LORD, "that I will punish all who are circumcised and yet uncircumcised—

26   Egypt, and Judah, and Edom, and the sons of Ammon, and Moab, and all those inhabiting the desert who clip the hair on their temples; for all the nations are uncircumcised, and all the house of Israel are uncircumcised of heart."

10 Hear the word which the LORD speaks to you, O house of Israel.
2   Thus says the LORD,
      "Do not learn the way of the nations,
      And do not be terrified by the signs of the heavens
      Although the nations are terrified by them;

3   For the customs of the peoples are delusion;
      Because it is wood cut from the forest,
      The work of the hands of a craftsman with a cutting tool.

4   "They decorate *it* with silver and with gold;
      They fasten it with nails and with hammers
      So that it will not totter.

5   "Like a scarecrow in a cucumber field are they,
      And they cannot speak;
      They must be carried,
      Because they cannot walk!
      Do not fear them,
      For they can do no harm,
      Nor can they do any good."

6   There is none like Thee, O LORD;
      Thou art great, and great is Thy name in might.
7   Who would not fear Thee, O King of the nations?
      Indeed it is Thy due!
      For among all the wise men of the nations,
      And in all their kingdoms,
      There is none like Thee.

8   But they are altogether stupid and foolish
      In their discipline of delusion—their idol is wood!
9   Beaten silver is brought from Tarshish,
      And gold from Uphaz,
      The work of a craftsman and of the hands of a goldsmith;
      Violet and purple are their clothing;
      They are all the work of skilled men.

9:21 Jer 15:7; 18:21; 6:11

9:22 Jer 8:2; 16:4

9:23 Eccl 9:11; Is 10:8-12; Ps 49:6-9
9:24 1 Cor 1:31; 2 Cor 10:17; Gal 6:14; Ps 36:5,7; Mic 7:18
*9:25 Rom 2:8,9
9:26 Jer 25:23; Lev 26:41; Ezek 44:7; Rom 2:28

10:2 Lev 18:3; Is 47:12-14

10:3 Is 40:19; 45:20

10:4 v. 14; Is 41:7

10:5 Ps 115:5; 1 Cor 12:2; Is 46:1,7; 41:23

10:6 Deut 33:26; Is 12:6; Jer 32:18
10:7 Ps 22:28; Dan 2:27,28; 1 Cor 1:19,20

10:8 v. 14; Jer 4:22; 2:27
*10:9 Is 40:19; Ps 72:10; Dan 10:5; Ps 115:4

9:25 *circumcised and yet uncircumcised.* Yahweh makes a distinction between the external rite of circumcision and the Israelite motivated by spiritual considerations. The external mark was not enough. The words stipulate that spiritual devotion is necessary.

10:9 *Uphaz* may be a variant of Ophir, the more modern rendering. This would place it in southwest Arabia. Daniel 10:5 also refers to Uphaz in connection with gold.

10:10 Is 65:16; Jer 4:2; 50:46; Ps 76:7	10	But the LORD is the true God; He is the living God and the everlasting King. At His wrath the earth quakes, And the nations cannot endure His indignation.
10:11 Ps 96:5; Is 2:18; Zeph 2:11	**11**	Thus you shall say to them, "The gods that did not make the heavens and the earth shall perish from the earth and from under the heavens."
10:12 Jer 51:15-19; Ps 78:69; Job 9:8; Is 40:22	**12**	*It is* He who made the earth by His power, Who established the world by His wisdom; And by His understanding He has stretched out the heavens.
10:13 Ps 29:3-9; Job 36:27-29; Ps 135:7	13	When He utters His voice, *there is* a tumult of waters in the heavens, And He causes the clouds to ascend from the end of the earth; He makes lightning for the rain, And brings out the wind from His storehouses.
10:14 Jer 51:17; Is 42:17; Hab 2:18	14	Every man is stupid, devoid of knowledge; Every goldsmith is put to shame by his idols; For his molten images are deceitful, And there is no breath in them.
10:15 Jer 8:19; 51:18	15	They are worthless, a work of mockery; In the time of their punishment they will perish.
10:16 Ps 73:26; Jer 51:19; Is 45:7; Deut 32:9; Jer 31:35	16	The portion of Jacob is not like these; For the Maker of all is He, And Israel is the tribe of His inheritance; The LORD of hosts is His name.
10:17 Ezek 12:3-12	**17**	Pick up your bundle from the ground, You who dwell under siege!
10:18 1 Sam 25:29; Ezek 6:10	18	For thus says the LORD, "Behold, I am slinging out the inhabitants of the land At this time, And will cause them distress, That they may be found."
10:19 Jer 4:19,31; 14:17; Mic 7:9	**19**	Woe is me, because of my injury! My wound is incurable. But I said, "Truly this is a sickness, And I must bear it."
10:20 Jer 4:20; 31:15; Is 51:18	20	My tent is destroyed, And all my ropes are broken; My sons have gone from me and are no more. There is no one to stretch out my tent again Or to set up my curtains.
10:21 Jer 2:8; 23:2	21	For the shepherds have become stupid And have not sought the LORD; Therefore they have not prospered, And all their flock is scattered.
*10:22 Jer 4:15; 1:14; 9:11	22	The sound of a report! Behold, it comes— A great commotion out of the land of the north— To make the cities of Judah A desolation, a haunt of jackals.
10:23 Prov 20:24; Is 26:7	**23**	I know, O LORD, that a man's way is not in himself; Nor is it in a man who walks to direct his steps.
10:24 Ps 6:1	24	Correct me, O LORD, but with justice; Not with Thine anger, lest Thou bring me to nothing.
10:25 Ps 79:6,7; Job 18:21; Jer 8:16; 50:7,17	25	Pour out Thy wrath on the nations that do not know Thee, And on the families that do not call Thy name; For they have devoured Jacob; They have devoured him and consumed him, And have laid waste his habitation.

10:22 *the land of the north.* It first hears the report of the advance of Nebuchadnezzar's armies.

D. *Third movement: signs of judgments and deliverances to come*

1. *Sermon IV: the broken covenant and the marred waistcloth*

a. *Judah has broken the covenant*

11 The word which came to Jeremiah from the LORD, saying, 2 "Hear the words of this covenant, and speak to the men of Judah and to the inhabitants of Jerusalem;

3 and say to them, 'Thus says the LORD, the God of Israel, "Cursed is the man who does not heed the words of this covenant

4 which I commanded your forefathers in the day that I brought them out of the land of Egypt, from the iron furnace, saying, 'Listen to My voice, and do according to all which I command you; so you shall be My people, and I will be your God,'

5 in order to confirm the oath which I swore to your forefathers, to give them a land flowing with milk and honey, as *it is* this day.' " ' " Then I answered and said, "Amen, O LORD."

6 And the LORD said to me, "Proclaim all these words in the cities of Judah and in the streets of Jerusalem, saying, 'Hear the words of this covenant and do them.

7 'For I solemnly warned your fathers in the day that I brought them up from the land of Egypt, even to this day, warning persistently, saying, "Listen to My voice."

8 'Yet they did not obey or incline their ear, but walked, each one, in the stubbornness of his evil heart; therefore I brought on them all the words of this covenant, which I commanded *them* to do, but they did not.' "

9 Then the LORD said to me, "A conspiracy has been found among the men of Judah and among the inhabitants of Jerusalem.

10 "They have turned back to the iniquities of their ancestors who refused to hear My words, and they have gone after other gods to serve them; the house of Israel and the house of Judah have broken My covenant which I made with their fathers."

11 Therefore thus says the LORD, "Behold I am bringing disaster on them which they will not be able to escape; though they will cry to Me, yet I will not listen to them.

12 "Then the cities of Judah and the inhabitants of Jerusalem will go and cry to the gods to whom they burn incense, but they surely will not save them in the time of their disaster.

13 "For your gods are as many as your cities, O Judah; and as many as the streets of Jerusalem are the altars you have set up to the shameful thing, altars to burn incense to Baal.

14 "Therefore do not pray for this people, nor lift up a cry or prayer for them; for I will not listen when they call to Me because of their disaster.

15   "What right has My beloved in My house
        When she has done many vile deeds?
        Can the sacrificial flesh take away from you your disaster,
        So *that* you can rejoice?"

16   The LORD called your name,
        "A green olive tree, beautiful in fruit and form";
        With the noise of a great tumult
        He has kindled fire on it,
        And its branches are worthless.

17   And the LORD of hosts, who planted you, has pronounced evil against you because of the evil of the house of Israel and of the house of Judah, which they have done to provoke Me by offering up sacrifices to Baal.

b. *Her corruption makes doom inevitable*

18   Moreover, the LORD made it known to me and I knew it;
        Then Thou didst show me their deeds.
19   But I was like a gentle lamb led to the slaughter;

---

*11:3
Deut 27:26;
Gal 3:10
11:4
Ex 24:3-8;
Deut 4:20;
1 Kin 8:51;
Jer 7:23; 24:7
11:5
Ex 13:5;
Deut 7:12;
Jer 32:22;
28:6
11:6
Jer 3:12; v. 2;
Rom 2:13
11:7
1 Sam 8:9;
Jer 7:13,25
11:8
Jer 7:26;
Mic 7:9;
Lev 26:14-43
11:9
Ezek 22:25;
Hos 6:9
11:10
1 Sam 15:11;
Jer 13:10;
Judg 2:11-13;
Jer 3:6-11
11:11
v. 17;
Jer 25:35;
v. 14;
Jer 14:12
11:12
Deut 32:37;
Jer 44:17
11:13
Jer 2:28;
3:24; 7:9
11:14
Ex 32:10;
v. 11;
Ps 66:18
11:15
Jer 12:7;
13:27; 4:22
11:16
Ps 52:8; 83:2;
Jer 21:14
11:17
Jer 12:2;
16:10,11;
32:27
11:18
1 Sam 23:11,
12
11:19
Is 53:7;

11:3 Jeremiah here is speaking of the broken covenant (see note to Deut. 29:1). The failure of Israel to keep the terms and conditions of this covenant could lead only to judgment and dispersion, according to the promises of God in that covenant.

And I did not know that they had devised plots against me, *saying,*
"Let us destroy the tree with its fruit,
And let us cut him off from the land of the living,
That his name be remembered no more."

20 But, O Lᴏʀᴅ of hosts, who judges righteously,
Who tries the feelings and the heart,
Let me see Thy vengeance on them,
For to Thee have I committed my cause.

21 Therefore thus says the Lᴏʀᴅ concerning the men of Anathoth, who seek your life, saying, "Do not prophesy in the name of the Lᴏʀᴅ, that you might not die at our hand";

22 therefore, thus says the Lᴏʀᴅ of hosts, "Behold, I am about to punish them! The young men will die by the sword, their sons and daughters will die by famine;

23 and a remnant will not be left to them, for I will bring disaster on the men of Anathoth—the year of their punishment."

12 Righteous art Thou, O Lᴏʀᴅ, that I would plead *my* case with Thee;
Indeed I would discuss matters of justice with Thee:
Why has the way of the wicked prospered?
Why are all those who deal in treachery at ease?

2 Thou hast planted them, they have also taken root;
They grow, they have even produced fruit.
Thou art near to their lips
But far from their mind.

3 But Thou knowest me, O Lᴏʀᴅ;
Thou seest me;
And Thou dost examine my heart's *attitude* toward Thee.
Drag them off like sheep for the slaughter
And set them apart for a day of carnage!

4 How long is the land to mourn
And the vegetation of the countryside to wither?
For the wickedness of those who dwell in it,
Animals and birds have been snatched away,
Because *men* have said, "He will not see our latter ending."

5 "If you have run with footmen and they have tired you out,
Then how can you compete with horses?
If you fall down in a land of peace,
How will you do in the thicket of the Jordan?

6 "For even your brothers and the household of your father,
Even they have dealt treacherously with you,
Even they have cried aloud after you.
Do not believe them, although they may say nice things to you."

7 "I have forsaken My house,
I have abandoned My inheritance;
I have given the beloved of My soul
Into the hand of her enemies.

8 "My inheritance has become to Me
Like a lion in the forest;
She has roared against Me;
Therefore I have come to hate her.

9 "Is My inheritance like a speckled bird of prey to Me?
Are the birds of prey against her on every side?
Go, gather all the beasts of the field,
Bring them to devour!

10 "Many shepherds have ruined My vineyard,
They have trampled down My field;
They have made My pleasant field

12:1 *that I would plead my case with Thee.* The prophet was disturbed at the prosperity of the wicked and brought his complaint to God.
12:5 *horses.* Jeremiah is told that his trials will become greater rather than less. Instead of competing with *footmen* he will have to race horses! *The thicket* was the place where lions and other wild beasts lurked.

A desolate wilderness.

11 "It has been made a desolation,
Desolate, it mourns before Me;
The whole land has been made desolate,
Because no man lays it to heart.

12 "On all the bare heights in the wilderness
Destroyers have come,
For a sword of the LORD is devouring
From one end of the land even to the other;
There is no peace for anyone.

13 "They have sown wheat and have reaped thorns,
They have strained themselves to no profit.
But be ashamed of your harvest
Because of the fierce anger of the LORD."

14 Thus says the LORD concerning all My wicked neighbors who strike at the inheritance with which I have endowed My people Israel, "Behold I am about to uproot them from their land and will uproot the house of Judah from among them.

15 "And it will come about that after I have uprooted them, I will again have compassion on them; and I will bring them back, each one to his inheritance and each one to his land.

16 "Then it will come about that if they will really learn the ways of My people, to swear by My name, 'As the LORD lives,' even as they taught My people to swear by Baal, then they will be built up in the midst of My people.

17 "But if they will not listen, then I will uproot that nation, uproot and destroy it," declares the LORD.

c. Five warnings to Judah: the marred waistcloth in the mud

13 Thus the LORD said to me, "Go and buy yourself a linen waistband, and put it around your waist, but do not put it in water."

2 So I bought the waistband in accordance with the word of the LORD and put it around my waist.

3 Then the word of the LORD came to me a second time, saying,

4 "Take the waistband that you have bought, which is around your waist, and arise, go to the Euphrates and hide it there in a crevice of the rock."

5 So I went and hid it by the Euphrates, as the LORD had commanded me.

6 And it came about after many days that the LORD said to me, "Arise, go to the Euphrates and take from there the waistband which I commanded you to hide there."

7 Then I went to the Euphrates and dug, and I took the waistband from the place where I had hidden it; and lo, the waistband was ruined, it was totally worthless.

8 Then the word of the LORD came to me, saying,

9 "Thus says the LORD, 'Just so will I destroy the pride of Judah and the great pride of Jerusalem.

10 'This wicked people, who refuse to listen to My words, who walk in the stubbornness of their hearts and have gone after other gods to serve them and to bow down to them, let them be just like this waistband, which is totally worthless.

11 'For as the waistband clings to the waist of a man, so I made the whole household of Israel and the whole household of Judah cling to Me,' declares the LORD, 'that they might be for Me a people, for renown, for praise, and for glory; but they did not listen.'

12 "Therefore you are to speak this word to them, 'Thus says the LORD, the God of Israel, "Every jug is to be filled with wine." ' And when they say to you, 'Do we not very well know that every jug is to be filled with wine?'

13 then say to them, 'Thus says the LORD, "Behold I am about to fill all the inhabitants of this land—the kings that sit for David on his throne, the priests, the prophets and all the inhabitants of Jerusalem—with drunkenness!

14 "And I will dash them against each other, both the fathers and the sons together," declares the LORD. "I will not show pity nor be sorry nor have compassion that I should not destroy them." ' "

15 Listen and give head, do not be haughty,
For the LORD has spoken.

13:12 Every jug is to be filled with wine, i.e., everything gets what it is fitted for.

13:16 Ps 96:8; Is 59:9; Jer 23:12; 2:6	16	Give glory to the LORD your God, Before He brings darkness And before your feet stumble On the dusky mountains, And while you are hoping for light He makes it into deep darkness, *And* turns *it* into gloom.
13:17 Mal 2:2; Jer 9:1; 14:17; 23:1,2	17	But if you will not listen to it, My soul will sob in secret for *such* pride; And my eyes will bitterly weep And flow down with tears, Because the flock of the LORD has been taken captive.
*13:18 2 Chr 33:12, 19; Is 3:20; Ezek 24:17, 23	18	Say to the king and the queen mother, "Take a lowly seat, For your beautiful crown Has come down from your head."
13:19 Jer 32:44; 20:4; 52:27-30	19	The cities of the Negev have been locked up, And there is no one to open *them*; All Judah has been carried into exile, Wholly carried into exile.
13:20 Jer 6:22; v. 17	**20**	"Lift up your eyes and see Those coming from the north. Where is the flock that was given you, Your beautiful sheep?
13:21 Jer 5:31; 2:25; 4:31	21	"What will you say when He appoints over you— And you yourself had taught them— Former companions to be head over you? Will not pangs take hold of you, Like a woman in childbirth?
13:22 Deut 7:17; Jer 5:19; 16:10	22	"And if you say in your heart, 'Why have these things happened to me?' Because of the magnitude of your iniquity Your skirts have been removed, And your heels have been exposed.
13:23 Prov 27:22; Jer 4:22	23	"Can the Ethiopian change his skin Or the leopard his spots? *Then* you also can do good Who are accustomed to do evil.
13:24 Jer 9:16; 4:11; 18:17	24	"Therefore I will scatter them like drifting straw To the desert wind.
13:25 Ps 11:6; Jer 2:32; 3:21	25	"This is your lot, the portion measured to you From Me," declares the LORD, "Because you have forgotten Me And trusted in falsehood.
13:26 Ezek 16:37; Hos 2:10	26	"So I Myself have also stripped your skirts off over your face, That your shame may be seen.
13:27 Jer 5:7,8; 11:15; 2:20; 4:14; Hos 8:5	27	"As for your adulteries and your *lustful* neighings, The lewdness of your prostitution On the hills in the field, I have seen your abominations. Woe to you, O Jerusalem! How long will you remain unclean?"

2. Sermon V: the exile inevitable, yet Judah will some day be restored

a. Judah beyond deliverance: drought, sword, famine must come

14:1 Jer 17:8 **14:2** Is 3:26; Jer 8:21; 11:11; 46:12	**14**	That which came as the word of the LORD to Jeremiah in regard to the drought:
	2	"Judah mourns, And her gates languish

13:18 *the king,* Jehoiachin. *the queen mother,* Nehushta (2 Kin. 24:8).

They sit on the ground in mourning,
And the cry of Jerusalem has ascended.

3   "And their nobles have sent their servants for water;
They have come to the cisterns and found no water.
They have returned with their vessels empty;
They have been put to shame and humiliated,
And they cover their heads.

14:3
1 Kin 18:5;
2 Kin 18:31;
2 Sam 15:30

4   "Because the ground is cracked,
For there has been no rain on the land;
The farmers have been put to shame,
They have covered their heads.

14:4
Joel 1:19,20;
Jer 3:3;
Joel 1:11

5   "For even the doe in the field has given birth only to abandon *her
young*,
Because there is no grass.

14:5
Is 15:6

6   "And the wild donkeys stand on the bare heights;
They pant for air like jackals,
Their eyes fail
For there is no vegetation.

14:6
Jer 2:24;
Joel 1:18

7   "Although our iniquities testify against us,
O LORD, act for Thy name's sake!
Truly our apostasies have been many,
We have sinned against Thee.

14:7
Is 59:12;
Jer 5:6; 8:5

8   "Thou Hope of Israel,
Its Savior in time of distress,
Why art Thou like a stranger in the land
Or like a traveler who has pitched his *tent* for the night?

14:8
Jer 17:13;
Is 43:3; 63:8;
Ps 50:15

9   "Why art Thou like a man dismayed,
Like a mighty man who cannot save?
Yet Thou art in our midst, O LORD,
And we are called by Thy name;
Do not forsake us!"

14:9
Is 50:2;
Jer 8:19;
15:16;
Is 63:19

10   Thus says the LORD to this people, "Even so they have loved to wander; they have not kept their feet in check. Therefore the LORD does not accept them; now He will remember their iniquity and call their sins to account."

14:10
Jer 2:25;
6:20;
Hos 8:13

11   So the LORD said to me, "Do not pray for the welfare of this people.

14:11
Ex 32:10;
Jer 7:16

12   "When they fast, I am not going to listen to their cry; and when they offer burnt offering and grain offering, I am not going to accept them. Rather I am going to make an end of them by the sword, famine and pestilence."

14:12
Is 1:15;
Jer 11:11;
6:20; 7:21;
9:16; 21:9

13   But, "Ah, Lord GOD!" I said, "Look, the prophets are telling them, 'You will not see the sword nor will you have famine, but I will give you lasting peace in this place.' "

14:13
Jer 5:12;
23:17; 6:14

14   Then the LORD said to me, "The prophets are prophesying falsehood in My name. I have neither sent them nor commanded them nor spoken to them; they are prophesying to you a false vision, divination, futility and the deception of their own minds.

14:14
Jer 5:31;
27:15; 23:16,
26;
Ezek 12:24

15   "Therefore thus says the LORD concerning the prophets who are prophesying in My name, although it was not I who sent them—yet they keep saying, 'There shall be no sword or famine in this land'—by sword and famine those prophets shall meet their end!

14:15
Jer 5:12,13;
Ezek 14:10

16   "The people also to whom they are prophesying will be thrown out into the streets of Jerusalem because of the famine and the sword; and there will be no one to bury them—*neither* them, *nor* their wives, nor their sons, nor their daughters—for I shall pour out their *own* wickedness on them.

14:16
Is 9:16;
Jer 7:33; 8:1,
2; 13:22-25

17   "And you will say this word to them,
'Let my eyes flow down with tears night and day,
And let them not cease;
For the virgin daughter of my people has been crushed with a
mighty blow,
With a sorely infected wound.

14:17
Jer 9:1;
Lam 1:15,16;
Jer 10:19;
30:14,15

18   'If I go out to the country,
Behold, those slain with the sword!
Or if I enter the city,
Behold, diseases of famine!

14:18
Jer 6:25;
Ezek 7:15;
Jer 6:13; 2:8;
5:5

For both prophet and priest
Have gone roving about in the land that they do not know.' "

14:19
Jer 6:30;
30:13; 8:15;
1 Thess 5:3

19   Hast Thou completely rejected Judah?
     Or hast Thou loathed Zion?
     Why hast Thou stricken us so that we are beyond healing?
     We waited for peace, but nothing good *came;*
     And for a time of healing, but behold, terror!

14:20
Jer 3:25; 8:14

20   We know our wickedness, O LORD,
     The iniquity of our fathers, for we have sinned against Thee.

14:21
v. 7; Jer 3:17;
17:12

21   Do not despise *us*, for Thine own name's sake;
     Do not disgrace the throne of Thy glory;
     Remember *and* do not annul Thy covenant with us.

14:22
Is 41:29;
Jer 10:3;
5:24; Is 41:4;
43:10;
Lam 3:26

22   Are there any among the idols of the nations who give rain?
     Or can the heavens grant showers?
     Is it not Thou, O LORD our God?
     Therefore we hope in Thee,
     For Thou art the one who hast done all these things.

         b. *Not even the intercession of Moses or Samuel*
                    could avert judgment

15:1
Ezek 14:14,
20; Ex 32:11,
12;
1 Sam 7:9;
12:23;
2 Kin 17:20;
Jer 7:15;
10:20

15 Then the LORD said to me, "Even though Moses and Samuel were to stand before Me, My heart would not be with this people; send them away from My presence and let them go!

2 "And it shall be that when they say to you, 'Where should we go?' then you are to tell them, 'Thus says the LORD:

15:2
Jer 43:11;
Ezek 5:2,12;
Zech 11:9

     "Those *destined* for death, to death;
       And those *destined* for the sword, to the sword;
       And those *destined* for famine, to famine;
       And those *destined* for captivity, to captivity." '

15:3
Lev 26:16;
1 Kin 21:23,
24;
Deut 28:26;
Jer 7:33

3 "And I shall appoint over them four kinds *of doom*," declares the LORD: "the sword to slay, the dogs to drag off, and the birds of the sky and the beasts of the earth to devour and destroy.

15:4
Deut 28:25;
2 Kin 21:11ff;
23:26

4 "And I shall make them an object of horror among all the kingdoms of the earth because of Manasseh, the son of Hezekiah, the king of Judah, for what he did in Jerusalem.

15:5
Ps 69:20;
Is 51:19;
Jer 16:5

5   "Indeed, who will have pity on you, O Jerusalem,
     Or who will mourn for you,
     Or who will turn aside to ask about your welfare?

15:6
Jer 6:19;
7:24; 6:11,12;
7:16

6   "You who have forsaken Me," declares the LORD,
     "You keep going backward.
     So I will stretch out My hand against you and destroy you;
     I am tired of relenting!

15:7
Jer 51:2;
18:21; 5:3

7   "And I will winnow them with a winnowing fork
     At the gates of the land;
     I will bereave *them* of children, I will destroy My people;
     They did not repent of their ways.

15:8
Is 3:25,26;
Jer 22:7; 6:4

8   "Their widows will be more numerous before Me
     Than the sand of the seas;
     I will bring against them, against the mother of a young man,
     A destroyer at noonday;
     I will suddenly bring down on her
     Anguish and dismay.

15:9
1 Sam 2:5;
Is 47:9;
Jer 6:4;
Amos 8:9;
Jer 50:12;
21:7

9   "She who bore seven *sons* pines away;
     Her breathing is labored.
     Her sun has set while it was yet day;
     She has been shamed and humiliated.
     So I shall give over their survivors to the sword
     Before their enemies," declares the LORD.

15:10
Job 3:1;
Jer 20:14;
Deut 23:19

10   Woe to me, my mother, that you have borne me
     As a man of strife and a man of contention to all the land!
     I have neither lent, nor have men lent money to me,
     Yet everyone curses me.

11   The LORD said, "Surely I will set you free for *purposes of* good;
      Surely I will cause the enemy to make supplication to you
      In a time of disaster and a time of distress.

15:11
Is 41:10;
Jer 39:11,12;
40:4,5

12   "Can anyone smash iron,
      Iron from the north, or bronze?

15:12
Jer 28:14

13   "Your wealth and your treasures
      I will give for booty without cost,
      Even for all your sins
      And within all your borders.

15:13
Ps 44:12;
Jer 17:3;
Is 52:3,5

14   "Then I will cause your enemies to bring *it*
      Into a land you do not know;
      For a fire has been kindled in My anger,
      It will burn upon you."

15:14
Jer 16:13;
17:4;
Deut 32:22

c. *Jeremiah encouraged to persevere*

15   Thou who knowest, O LORD,
      Remember me, take notice of me,
      And take vengeance for me on my persecutors.
      Do *not*, in view of Thy patience, take me away;
      Know that for Thy sake I endure reproach.

15:15
Jer 12:3;
20:11;
Ps 69:7-9

16   Thy words were found and I ate them,
      And Thy words became for me a joy and the delight of my heart;
      For I have been called by Thy name,
      O LORD God of hosts.

15:16
Ezek 3:1-3;
Ps 119:72;
Jer 14:9

17   I did not sit in the circle of merrymakers,
      Nor did I exult.
      Because of Thy hand *upon me* I sat alone,
      For Thou didst fill me with indignation.

15:17
Jer 16:8;
Ezek 3:24,25

18   Why has my pain been perpetual
      And my wound incurable, refusing to be healed?
      Wilt Thou indeed be to me like a deceptive *stream*
      With water that is unreliable?

15:18
Jer 30:15;
Mic 1:9;
Jer 14:3

19   Therefore, thus says the LORD,
      "If you return, then I will restore you—
      Before Me you will stand;
      And if you extract the precious from the worthless,
      You will become My spokesman.
      They for their part may turn to you,
      But as for you, you must not turn to them.

15:19
Jer 4:1;
Ezek 22:26

20   "Then I will make you to this people
      A fortified wall of bronze;
      And though they fight against you,
      They will not prevail over you;
      For I am with you to save you
      And deliver you," declares the LORD.

15:20
Jer 1:18,19;
20:11;
Is 41:10

21   "So I will deliver you from the hand of the wicked,
      And I will redeem you from the grasp of the violent."

15:21
Jer 20:13;
31:11

3. *Sermon VI: the sign of Jeremiah's unmarried state*

a. *Command to remain unmarried lest his children should perish*

16 The word of the LORD also came to me saying,

2   "You shall not take a wife for yourself nor have sons or daughters in this place."

16:1
Jer 1:2,4
16:2
1 Cor 7:26

3   For thus says the LORD concerning the sons and daughters born in this place, and concerning their mothers who bear them, and their fathers who beget them in this land:

16:3
Jer 6:11;
15:8; 6:21

4   "They will die of deadly diseases, they will not be lamented or buried; they will be as dung on the surface of the ground and come to an end by sword and famine, and their carcasses will become food for the birds of the sky and for the beasts of the earth."

16:4
Ps 83:10;
Jer 9:22;
15:3; 34:20

5   For thus says the LORD, "Do not enter a house of mourning, or go to lament

16:5
Ezek 24:16-23;

Jer 12:12;
13:14

16:6
Ezek 9:6;
Jer 41:5; 47:5
16:7
Ezek 24:17;
Hos 9:4
16:8
Jer 15:17

16:9
Jer 7:34;
25:10;
Hos 2:11;
Rev 18:23
16:10
Deut 29:24;
1 Kin 9:8,9;
Jer 5:19

16:11
Jer 22:9;
Ezek 11:21;
1 Pet 4:3

16:12
Jer 7:26;
13:10;
Eccl 9:3

16:13
Deut 4:26-28;
28:36;
Jer 15:4; 5:19

16:14
Is 43:18;
Jer 23:7,8;
Ex 20:2

16:15
Ps 106:47;
Is 11:11-16;
Jer 24:6

16:16
Amos 4:2;
Hab 1:14,15;
Mic 7:2;
Is 2:21
16:17
Ps 90:8;
1 Cor 4:5;
Heb 4:13;
Jer 2:22
16:18
Rev 18:6;
Ezek 11:18,
21
16:19
Jer 15:11;
Ps 14:6;
Hab 2:18,19

16:20
Is 37:19;
Jer 2:11;
Gal 4:8
16:21
Ps 9:16;
Jer 33:2;
Amos 5:8

*17:1
Jer 2:22;
Job 19:24;
Prov 3:3;
2 Cor 3:3
17:2
Jer 7:18;
Ex 34:13;
Jer 3:6
17:3
Jer 26:18;
15:13

or to console them; for I have withdrawn My peace from this people," declares the LORD, "*My* lovingkindness and compassion.

6 "Both great men and small will die in this land; they will not be buried, they will not be lamented, nor will anyone gash himself or shave his head for them.

7 "Neither will men break *bread* in mourning for them, to comfort anyone for the dead, nor give them a cup of consolation to drink for anyone's father or mother.

8 "Moreover you shall not go into a house of feasting to sit with them to eat and drink."

9 For thus says the LORD of hosts, the God of Israel: "Behold, I am going to eliminate from this place, before your eyes and in your time, the voice of rejoicing and the voice of gladness, the voice of the groom and the voice of the bride.

10 "Now it will come about when you tell this people all these words that they will say to you, 'For what reason has the LORD declared all this great calamity against us? And what is our iniquity, or what is our sin which we have committed against the LORD our God?'

11 "Then you are to say to them, '*It is* because your forefathers have forsaken Me,' declares the LORD, 'and have followed other gods and served them and bowed down to them; but Me they have forsaken and have not kept My law.

12 'You too have done evil, *even* more than your forefathers; for behold, you are each one walking according to the stubbornness of his own evil heart, without listening to Me.

13 'So I will hurl you out of this land into the land which you have not known, neither you nor your fathers; and there you will serve other gods day and night, for I shall grant you no favor.'

14 "Therefore behold, days are coming," declares the LORD, "when it will no longer be said, 'As the LORD lives, who brought up the sons of Israel out of the land of Egypt,'

15 but, 'As the LORD lives, who brought up the sons of Israel from the land of the north and from all the countries where He had banished them.' For I will restore them to their own land which I gave to their fathers.

16 "Behold, I am going to send for many fishermen," declares the LORD, "and they will fish for them; and afterwards I shall send for many hunters, and they will hunt them from every mountain and every hill, and from the clefts of the rocks.

17 "For My eyes are on all their ways; they are not hidden from My face, nor is their iniquity concealed from My eyes.

18 "And I will first doubly repay their iniquity and their sin, because they have polluted My land; they have filled My inheritance with the carcasses of their detestable idols and with their abominations."

19 O LORD, my strength and my stronghold,
And my refuge in the day of distress,
To Thee the nations will come
From the ends of the earth and say,
"Our fathers have inherited nothing but falsehood,
Futility and things of no profit."

20 Can man make gods for himself?
Yet they are not gods!

21 "Therefore behold, I am going to make them know—
This time I will make them know
My power and My might;
And they shall know that My name is the LORD."

b. *Idolatry Judah's sin: her only hope, the* LORD

17 The sin of Judah is written down with an iron stylus;
With a diamond point it is engraved upon the tablet of their heart,
And on the horns of their altars,

2 As they remember their children,
So they *remember* their altars and their Asherim
By green trees on the high hills.

3 O mountain of Mine in the countryside,
I will give over your wealth and all your treasures for booty,

---

17:1 *iron stylus*, for use on rock. Jeremiah suggests that no ordinary pen would do. Israel's sin cannot be effaced, and punishment must be imposed on her.

Your high places for sin throughout your borders.

4   And you will, even of yourself, let go of your inheritance
That I gave you;
And I will make you serve your enemies
In the land which you do not know;
For you have kindled a fire in My anger
Which will burn forever.

17:4
Jer 12:7;
15:14; 7:20

5   Thus says the LORD,
"Cursed is the man who trusts in mankind
And makes flesh his strength,
And whose heart turns away from the LORD.

17:5
Is 30:1-3;
2 Chr 32:8

6   "For he will be like a bush in the desert
And will not see when prosperity comes,
But will live in stony wastes in the wilderness,
A land of salt without inhabitant.

17:6
Jer 48:6;
Deut 29:23

7   "Blessed is the man who trusts in the LORD
And whose trust is the LORD.

17:7
Ps 34:8;
84:12; 40:4;
Prov 16:20

8   "For he will be like a tree planted by the water,
That extends its roots by a stream
And will not fear when the heat comes;
But its leaves will be green,
And it will not be anxious in a year of drought
Nor cease to yield fruit.

17:8
Ps 1:3;
Jer 14:1-6

9   "The heart is more deceitful than all else
And is desperately sick;
Who can understand it?

17:9
Mark 7:21,
22;
Rom 7:11;
Eph 4:22

10   "I, the LORD, search the heart,
I test the mind,
Even to give to each man according to his ways,
According to the results of his deeds.

17:10
1 Sam 16:7;
Jer 11:20;
20:12;
Rom 8:27;

11   "As a partridge that hatches eggs which it has not laid,
So is he who makes a fortune, but unjustly;
In the midst of his days it will forsake him,
And in the end he will be a fool."

Jer 32:19;
Rom 2:6
17:11
Jer 6:13;
8:10; 22:13,
17

12   A glorious throne on high from the beginning
Is the place of our sanctuary.

17:12
Jer 3:17;
14:21

13   O LORD, the hope of Israel,
All who forsake Thee will be put to shame.
Those who turn away on earth will be written down,
Because they have forsaken the fountain of living water, even the
LORD.

17:13
Jer 14:8;
Ps 73:27;
Is 1:28;
Jer 2:13,17

14   Heal me, O LORD, and I will be healed;
Save me and I will be saved,
For Thou art my praise.

17:14
Jer 30:17;
Ps 54:1;
Deut 10:21;
Ps 109:1

15   Look, they keep saying to me,
"Where is the word of the LORD?
Let it come now!"

17:15
Is 5:19;
Amos 5:18

16   But as for me, I have not hurried away from *being* a shepherd after
Thee,
Nor have I longed for the woeful day;
Thou Thyself knowest the utterance of my lips
Was in Thy presence.

17:16
Jer 1:6; 12:3

17   Do not be a terror to me;
Thou art my refuge in the day of disaster.

17:17
Ps 88:15;
Jer 16:19

18   Let those who persecute me be put to shame, but as for me, let me
not be put to shame;
Let them be dismayed, but let me not be dismayed.
Bring on them a day of disaster,
And crush them with twofold destruction!

17:18
Ps 35:4,26;
35:8;
Jer 16:18

4. *Sabbath observance stressed*

19 Thus the LORD said to me, "Go and stand in the public gate, through which the kings of Judah come in and go out, as well as in all the gates of Jerusalem;

20 and say to them, 'Listen to the word of the LORD, kings of Judah, and all Judah, and all inhabitants of Jerusalem, who come in through these gates:

21 'Thus says the LORD, "Take heed for yourselves, and do not carry any load on the sabbath day or bring anything in through the gates of Jerusalem.

22 "And you shall not bring a load out of your houses on the sabbath day nor do any work, but keep the sabbath day holy, as I commanded your forefathers.

23 "Yet they did not listen or incline their ears, but stiffened their necks in order not to listen or take correction.

24 "But it will come about, if you listen attentively to Me," declares the LORD, "to bring no load in through the gates of this city on the sabbath day, but to keep the sabbath day holy by doing no work on it,

25 then there will come in through the gates of this city kings and princes sitting on the throne of David, riding in chariots and on horses, they and their princes, the men of Judah, and the inhabitants of Jerusalem; and this city will be inhabited forever.

26 "They will come in from the cities of Judah and from the environs of Jerusalem, from the land of Benjamin, from the lowland, from the hill country, and from the Negev, bringing burnt offerings, sacrifices, grain offerings and incense, and bringing sacrifices of thanksgiving to the house of the LORD.

27 "But if you do not listen to Me to keep the sabbath day holy by not carrying a load and coming in through the gates of Jerusalem on the sabbath day, then I shall kindle a fire in its gates, and it will devour the palaces of Jerusalem and not be quenched." ' "

5. *Sermon VII: the sign of the potter's house and the broken vessel*

a. *First symbol: the potter and the clay*

18 The word which came to Jeremiah from the LORD saying,
2 "Arise and go down to the potter's house, and there I shall announce My words to you."

3 Then I went down to the potter's house, and there he was, making something on the wheel.

4 But the vessel that he was making of clay was spoiled in the hand of the potter; so he remade it into another vessel, as it pleased the potter to make.

5 Then the word of the LORD came to me saying,

6 "Can I not, O house of Israel, deal with you as this potter *does*?" declares the LORD. "Behold, like the clay in the potter's hand, so are you in My hand, O house of Israel.

7 "At one moment I might speak concerning a nation or concerning a kingdom to uproot, to pull down, or to destroy *it;*

8 if that nation against which I have spoken turns from its evil, I will [4]relent concerning the calamity I planned to bring on it.

9 "Or at another moment I might speak concerning a nation or concerning a kingdom to build up or to plant *it;*

10 if it does evil in My sight by not obeying My voice, then I will [4]think better of the good with which I had promised to bless it.

11 "So now then, speak to the men of Judah and against the inhabitants of Jerusalem saying, 'Thus says the LORD, "Behold, I am fashioning calamity against you and devising a plan against you. Oh turn back, each of you from his evil way, and reform your ways and your deeds." '

12 "But they will say, 'It's hopeless! For we are going to follow our own plans, and each of us will act according to the stubbornness of his evil heart.'

13 "Therefore thus says the LORD,
'Ask now among the nations,
Who ever heard the like of this?
The virgin of Israel

[4]Lit., *repent (of)*

17:21 The Sabbath was made for man, not man for the Sabbath. Israel, by breaking the Sabbath, was helping to break herself. Moreover, judgment must follow.

Has done a most appalling thing.

14 'Does the snow of Lebanon forsake the rock of the open country?
Or is the cold flowing water *from* a foreign *land* ever snatched away?

15 'For My people have forgotten Me,
They burn incense to worthless gods
And they have stumbled from their ways,
From the ancient paths,
To walk in bypaths,
Not on a highway,

16 To make their land a desolation,
An object of perpetual hissing;
Everyone who passes by it will be astonished
And shake his head.

17 'Like an east wind I will scatter them
Before the enemy;
I will show them My back and not *My* face
In the day of their calamity.' "

18 Then they said, "Come and let us devise plans against Jeremiah. Surely the law is not going to be lost to the priest, nor counsel to the sage, nor the *divine* word to the prophet! Come on and let us strike at him with *our* tongue, and let us give no heed to any of his words."

19 Do give heed to me, O LORD,
And listen to what my opponents are saying!

20 Should good be repaid with evil?
For they have dug a pit for me.
Remember how I stood before Thee
To speak good on their behalf,
So as to turn away Thy wrath from them.

21 Therefore, give their children over to famine,
And deliver them up to the power of the sword;
And let their wives become childless and widowed.
Let their men also be smitten to death,
Their young men struck down by the sword in battle.

22 May an outcry be heard from their houses,
When Thou suddenly bringest raiders upon them;
For they have dug a pit to capture me
And hidden snares for my feet.

23 Yet Thou, O LORD, knowest
All their deadly designs against me;
Do not forgive their iniquity
Or blot out their sin from Thy sight.
But may they be overthrown before Thee;
Deal with them in the time of Thine anger!

b. Second symbol: the broken flask

19 Thus says the LORD, "Go and buy a potter's earthenware jar, and *take* some of the elders of the people and some of the senior priests.

2 "Then go out to the valley of Ben-hinnom, which is by the entrance of the potsherd gate; and proclaim there the words that I shall tell you,

3 and say, 'Hear the word of the LORD, O kings of Judah and inhabitants of Jerusalem: thus says the LORD of hosts, the God of Israel, "Behold I am about to bring a calamity upon this place, at which the ears of everyone that hears of it will tingle.

4 "Because they have forsaken Me and have made this an alien place and have burned sacrifices in it to other gods that neither they nor their forefathers nor the kings of Judah had *ever* known, and *because* they have filled this place with the blood of the innocent

5 and have built the high places of Baal to burn their sons in the fire as burnt offerings to Baal, a thing which I never commanded or spoke of, nor did it *ever* enter My mind;

6 therefore, behold, days are coming," declares the LORD, "when this place will no longer be called Topheth or the valley of Ben-hinnom, but rather the valley of Slaughter.

18:15 Is 65:7; Jer 7:9; 6:16; Is 57:14; 62:10
18:16 Jer 25:9; 50:13; 48:27
18:17 Job 27:21; Jer 13:24; 2:27; 46:21
18:18 Jer 11:19; Mal 2:7; Jer 8:8; 5:13; 20:10; 43:2
18:20 Ps 35:7; 57:6; 106:23
18:21 Ps 109:9,10; Is 13:18; Jer 15:8; Ezek 22:25; Jer 9:21; 11:22
18:22 Jer 6:26; Ps 140:5
18:23 Ps 109:14; Is 2:9; Jer 6:15,21; 7:20
19:1 Jer 18:2; v. 10; Num 11:16; 2 Kin 19:2
19:2 Josh 15:8; Jer 7:31
19:3 Jer 17:20; 1 Sam 3:11; 4:18
19:4 Deut 28:20; Is 65:11; 2 Kin 21:16; Jer 2:34
19:5 Jer 32:35; 2 Kin 17:17; Lev 18:21
19:6 Jer 7:32; Josh 15:8

19:7
Jer 15:2,9;
Ps 79:2;
Jer 16:4

7 "And I shall make void the counsel of Judah and Jerusalem in this place, and I shall cause them to fall by the sword before their enemies and by the hand of those who seek their life; and I shall give over their carcasses as food for the birds of the sky and the beasts of the earth.

19:8
Jer 18:16;
49:13;
1 Kin 9:8;
2 Chr 7:21

8 "I shall also make this city a desolation and an *object of* hissing; everyone who passes by it will be astonished and hiss because of all its disasters.

19:9
Deut 28:53,
55; Is 9:20;
Lam 4:10

9 "And I shall make them eat the flesh of their sons and the flesh of their daughters, and they will eat one another's flesh in the siege and in the distress with which their enemies and those who seek their life will distress them.'' '

19:10
v. 1

10 "Then you are to break the jar in the sight of the men who accompany you

19:11
Ps 2:9;
Is 30:14;
Rev 2:27;
Jer 7:32

11 and say to them, 'Thus says the LORD of hosts, "Just so shall I break this people and this city, even as one breaks a potter's vessel, which cannot again be repaired; and they will bury in Topheth because there is no *other* place for burial.

12 "This is how I shall treat this place and its inhabitants," declares the LORD, "so as to make this city like Topheth.

19:13
Jer 52:13;
7:18;
Ezek 20:28;
Acts 7:42

13 "And the houses of Jerusalem and the houses of the kings of Judah will be defiled like the place Topheth, because of all the houses on whose rooftops they burned sacrifices to all the heavenly host and poured out libations to other gods."' "

19:14
Jer 26:2

14 Then Jeremiah came from Topheth, where the LORD had sent him to prophesy; and he stood in the court of the LORD's house and said to all the people:

19:15
Jer 7:26;
17:23;
Ps 58:4

15 "Thus says the LORD of hosts, the God of Israel, 'Behold, I am about to bring on this city and all its towns the entire calamity that I have declared against it, because they have stiffened their necks so as not to heed My words.' "

c. Jeremiah must preach despite persecution

20:1
1 Chr 24:14;
2 Kin 25:18
*20:2
Jer 1:19;
Job 13:27;
Jer 37:13;
38:7

20 When Pashhur the priest, the son of Immer, who was chief officer in the house of the LORD, heard Jeremiah prophesying these things,

2 Pashhur had Jeremiah the prophet beaten, and put him in the stocks that were at the upper Benjamin Gate, which was by the house of the LORD.

20:3
v. 1

3 Then it came about on the next day, when Pashhur released Jeremiah from the stocks, that Jeremiah said to him, "Pashhur is not the name the LORD has called you, but rather [5]Magor-missabib.

20:4
Job 18:11-21;
Jer 29:21;
21:4-10;
52:27

4 "For thus says the LORD, 'Behold, I am going to make you a terror to yourself and to all your friends; and while your eyes look on, they will fall by the sword of their enemies. So I shall give over all Judah to the hand of the king of Babylon, and he will carry them away as exiles to Babylon and will slay them with the sword.

20:5
Jer 15:13;
17:3;
2 Kin 20:17;
2 Chr 36:10;
Jer 3:24

5 'I shall also give over all the wealth of this city, all its produce, and all its costly things; even all the treasures of the kings of Judah I shall give over to the hand of their enemies, and they will plunder them, take them away, and bring them to Babylon.

20:6
v. 1;
Jer 28:15-17;
14:13-15;
29:21

6 'And you, Pashhur, and all who live in your house will go into captivity; and you will enter Babylon, and there you will die, and there you will be buried, you and all your friends to whom you have falsely prophesied.' "

20:7
Jer 1:6-8;
Mic 3:8;
Jer 38:19

7 O LORD, Thou hast deceived me and I was deceived;
Thou hast overcome me and prevailed.
I have become a laughingstock all day long;
Everyone mocks me.

20:8
Jer 6:7,10;
2 Chr 36:16

8 For each time I speak, I cry aloud;
I proclaim violence and destruction,
Because for me the word of the LORD has resulted
In reproach and derision all day long.

*20:9
1 Kin 19:3,4;
Ps 39:3;
Job 32:18-20;
Acts 4:20

9 But if I say, "I will not remember Him
Or speak anymore in His name,"
Then in my heart it becomes like a burning fire
Shut up in my bones;

[5]I.e., terror on every side

20:2 Jeremiah is often called the "weeping prophet." His ministry had to be carried on in the midst of apostasy without repentance. He suffered persecution because of his faithful preaching. His life is a shining example of a stalwart prophet who faithfully proclaimed a message that his people did not wish to hear and which they rejected. Here Jeremiah is flogged for his faithfulness to God and then placed in stocks.

20:9 Jeremiah was crushed and in great distress of spirit before God, but he stood before the people heroically warning the princes, the priests, and the people of the consequences of their sins. He would have preferred to be silent and not to *speak anymore in His name*, but there was the feeling of the *burning fire*. He had to speak out for God.

And I am weary of holding *it* in,
And I cannot endure *it.*

10   For I have heard the whispering of many,
"Terror on every side!
Denounce *him;* yes, let us denounce him!"
All my trusted friends,
Watching for my fall, say:
"Perhaps he will be deceived, so that we may prevail against him
And take our revenge on him."

20:10
Ps 31:13;
41:9;
Luke 11:53,
54

11   But the LORD is with me like a dread champion;
Therefore my persecutors will stumble and not prevail.
They will be utterly ashamed, because they have failed,
With an everlasting disgrace that will not be forgotten.

20:11
Jer 1:8,19;
15:20; 17:18;
23:40

12   Yet, O LORD of hosts, Thou who dost test the righteous,
Who seest the mind and the heart;
Let me see Thy vengeance on them;
For to Thee I have set forth my cause.

20:12
Jer 11:20;
17:10;
Ps 54:7;
59:10

13   Sing to the LORD, praise the LORD!
For He has delivered the soul of the needy one
From the hand of evildoers.

20:13
Jer 31:7;
Ps 35:9,10;
Jer 15:21

14   Cursed be the day when I was born;
Let the day not be blessed when my mother bore me!

20:14
Job 3:3;
Jer 15:10

15   Cursed be the man who brought the news
To my father, saying,
"A baby boy has been born to you!"
And made him very happy.

20:15
Gen 21:6,7

16   But let that man be like the cities
Which the LORD overthrew without [6]relenting,
And let him hear an outcry in the morning
And a shout of alarm at noon;

*20:16
Gen 19:25;
Jer 18:22

17   Because he did not kill me before birth,
So that my mother would have been my grave,
And her womb ever pregnant.

20:17
Job 3:10,11;
10:18,19

18   Why did I ever come forth from the womb
To look on trouble and sorrow,
So that my days have been spent in shame?

20:18
Job 3:20;
Ps 90:9;
Jer 3:25

II. Prophecies under Jehoiakim and Zedekiah (21:1–39:18)

A. Nebuchadnezzar is God's instrument to punish Jerusalem

1. Sermon I: God's judgment on the wicked kings and prophets of Judah

a. Zedekiah's prayer for deliverance and God's negative answer

21 The word which came to Jeremiah from the LORD when King Zedekiah sent to him Pashhur the son of Malchijah, and Zephaniah the priest, the son of Maaseiah, saying,

21:1
2 Kin 24:17,
18; Jer 38:1;
2 Kin 25:18;

2   "Please inquire of the LORD on our behalf, for Nebuchadnezzar king of Babylon is warring against us; perhaps the LORD will deal with us according to all His wonderful acts, that *the enemy* may withdraw from us."

Jer 29:25;
37:3
21:2
Jer 37:3,7

3   Then Jeremiah said to them, "You shall say to Zedekiah as follows:

4   'Thus says the LORD God of Israel, "Behold, I am about to turn back the weapons of war which are in your hands, with which you are warring against the king of Babylon and the Chaldeans who are besieging you outside the wall; and I shall gather them into the center of this city.

21:4
Zech 14:2

5   "And I Myself shall war against you with an outstretched hand and a mighty arm, even in anger and wrath and great indignation.

21:5
Is 63:10;
Jer 32:37

6   "I shall also strike down the inhabitants of this city, both man and beast; they will die of a great pestilence.

21:6
Jer 7:20;
14:12

---

[6]Lit., *being sorry*

20:16 *The cities,* in this verse, refer to Sodom and Gomorrah.

7 "Then afterwards," declares the LORD, "I shall give over Zedekiah king of Judah and his servants and the people, even those who survive in this city from the pestilence, the sword, and the famine, into the hand of Nebuchadnezzar king of Babylon, and into the hand of their foes, and into the hand of those who seek their lives; and he will strike them down with the edge of the sword. He will not spare them nor have pity nor compassion." '

8 "You shall also say to this people, 'Thus says the LORD, "Behold, I set before you the way of life and the way of death.

9 "He who dwells in this city will die by the sword and by famine and by pestilence; but he who goes out and falls away to the Chaldeans who are besieging you will live, and he will have his own life as booty.

10 "For I have set My face against this city for harm and not for good," declares the LORD. "It will be given into the hand of the king of Babylon, and he will burn it with fire." '

11 "Then say to the household of the king of Judah, 'Hear the word of the LORD,
12 O house of David, thus says the LORD:
"Administer justice every morning;
And deliver the person who has been robbed from the power of his oppressor,
That My wrath may not go forth like fire
And burn with none to extinguish it,
Because of the evil of their deeds.

13 "Behold, I am against you, O valley dweller,
O rocky plain," declares the LORD,
"You men who say, 'Who will come down against us?
Or who will enter into our habitations?'

14 "But I shall punish you according to the results of your deeds," declares the LORD,
"And I shall kindle a fire in its forest
That it may devour all its environs." ' "

b. Woe pronounced on the four evil kings
and their dishonest prophets

(1) THE WICKED KINGS, AND MESSIAH THE TRUE KING

22 Thus says the LORD, "Go down to the house of the king of Judah, and there speak this word,
2 and say, 'Hear the word of the LORD, O king of Judah, who sits on David's throne, you and your servants and your people who enter these gates.
3 'Thus says the LORD, "Do justice and righteousness, and deliver the one who has been robbed from the power of his oppressor. Also do not mistreat or do violence to the stranger, the orphan, or the widow; and do not shed innocent blood in this place.
4 "For if you men will indeed perform this thing, then kings will enter the gates of this house, sitting in David's place on his throne, riding in chariots and on horses, even the king himself and his servants and his people.
5 "But if you will not obey these words, I swear by Myself," declares the LORD, "that this house will become a desolation." ' "
6 For thus says the LORD concerning the house of the king of Judah:
"You are like Gilead to Me,
Like the summit of Lebanon;
Yet most assuredly I shall make you like a wilderness,
Like cities which are not inhabited.
7 "For I shall set apart destroyers against you,
Each with his weapons;
And they will cut down your choicest cedars
And throw them on the fire.
8 "And many nations will pass by this city; and they will say to one another, 'Why has the LORD done thus to this great city?'

9 "Then they will answer, 'Because they forsook the covenant of the LORD their God and bowed down to other gods and served them.'"

10 Do not weep for the dead or mourn for him,
But weep continually for the one who goes away;
For he will never return
Or see his native land.

11 For thus says the LORD in regard to Shallum the son of Josiah, king of Judah, who became king in the place of Josiah his father, who went forth from this place, "He will never return there;

12 but in the place where they led him captive, there he will die and not see this land again.

13 "Woe to him who builds his house without righteousness
And his upper rooms without justice,
Who uses his neighbor's services without pay
And does not give him his wages,

14 Who says, 'I will build myself a roomy house
With spacious upper rooms,
And cut out its windows,
Paneling it with cedar and painting it bright red.'

15 "Do you become a king because you are competing in cedar?
Did not your father eat and drink,
And do justice and righteousness?
Then it was well with him.

16 "He pled the cause of the afflicted and needy;
Then it was well.
Is not that what it means to know Me?"
Declares the LORD.

17 "But your eyes and your heart
Are intent only upon your own dishonest gain,
And on shedding innocent blood
And on practicing oppression and extortion."

18 Therefore thus says the LORD in regard to Jehoiakim the son of Josiah, king of Judah,
"They will not lament for him:
'Alas, my brother!' or, 'Alas, sister!'
They will not lament for him:
'Alas for the master!' or, 'Alas for his splendor!'

19 "He will be buried with a donkey's burial,
Dragged off and thrown out beyond the gates of Jerusalem.

20 "Go up to Lebanon and cry out,
And lift up your voice in Bashan;
Cry out also from Abarim,
For all your lovers have been crushed.

21 "I spoke to you in your prosperity;
But you said, 'I will not listen!'
This has been your practice from your youth,
That you have not obeyed My voice.

22 "The wind will sweep away all your shepherds,
And your lovers will go into captivity;
Then you will surely be ashamed and humiliated
Because of all your wickedness.

23 "You who dwell in Lebanon,
Nested in the cedars,
How you will groan when pangs come upon you,
Pain like a woman in childbirth!

24 "As I live," declares the LORD, "even though [7]Coniah the son of Jehoiakim king of Judah were a signet ring on My right hand, yet I would pull you off;

25 and I shall give you over into the hand of those who are seeking your life,

[7]I.e., Jehoiachin

22:10 the dead, viz., Josiah, who was killed at Megiddo. (Read 2 Kin. 23:29.) | 22:11 Shallum, also known as Jehoahaz.

Cross references (right margin):

22:9 2 Kin 22:17; 2 Chr 34:25
*22:10 2 Kin 22:20; v. 18; Jer 16:7; 44:14
*22:11 2 Kin 23:30, 34
22:13 Mic 3:10; Hab 2:9; James 5:4
22:14 Is 5:8,9; 2Sa 7:2
22:15 2 Kin 23:25; Jer 7:5; 42:6
22:16 Ps 72:1-4,12, 13; 1 Chr 28:9; Jer 9:24
22:17 Jer 6:13; 8:10; 6:6
22:18 1 Kin 13:30; Jer 34:5
22:19 Jer 36:30
22:20 Deut 32:49; Jer 2:25; 3:1
22:21 Jer 13:10; 19:15; 3:24, 25; 32:30
22:22 Jer 5:13; 30:14; Is 65:13; Jer 20:11
22:23 Jer 4:31; 6:24
22:24 Jer 37:1; Song 8:6; Hag 2:23
22:25 2 Kin 24:15, 16; Jer 34:20

yes, into the hand of those whom you dread, even into the hand of Nebuchadnezzar king of Babylon, and into the hand of the Chaldeans.

22:26
2 Kin 24:15;
2 Chr 36:10;
2 Kin 24:8

26 "I shall hurl you and your mother who bore you into another country where you were not born, and there you will die.

27 "But as for the land to which they desire to return, they will not return to it.

*22:28
Ps 31:12;
Jer 48:38;
Hos 8:8;
Jer 15:1; 17:4

28   "Is this man Coniah a despised, shattered jar?
         Or is he an undesirable vessel?
         Why have he and his descendants been hurled out
         And cast into a land that they had not known?

22:29
Deut 32:1;
Jer 6:19;
Mic 1:2

29   "O land, land, land,
         Hear the word of the LORD!

22:30
1 Chr 3:16,
17; Matt 1:12

30   "Thus says the LORD,
         'Write this man down childless,
         A man who will not prosper in his days;
         For no man of his descendants will prosper
         Sitting on the throne of David
         Or ruling again in Judah.' "

23:1
Ezek 13:3;
Jer 10:21;
50:6;
Ezek 34:31

23 "Woe to the shepherds who are destroying and scattering the sheep of My pasture!" declares the LORD.

2   Therefore thus says the LORD God of Israel concerning the shepherds who are tending My people: "You have scattered My flock and driven them away, and have not attended to them; behold, I am about to attend to you for the evil of your deeds," declares the LORD.

23:3
Is 11:11-16;
Jer 32:37;
Ezek 34:13-16

3   "Then I Myself shall gather the remnant of My flock out of all the countries where I have driven them and shall bring them back to their pasture; and they will be fruitful and multiply.

23:4
Jer 3:15;
Ezek 34:23;
Jer 30:10;
John 6:39;
10:28

4   "I shall also raise up shepherds over them and they will tend them; and they will not be afraid any longer, nor be terrified, nor will any be missing," declares the LORD.

*23:5
Is 4:2; 11:1;
53:2;
Jer 33:14-16;
Zech 3:8;
6:12; Is 9:7;
Luke 1:32,33

5   "Behold, *the* days are coming," declares the LORD,
       "When I shall raise up for David a righteous Branch;
         And He will reign as king and act wisely
         And do justice and righteousness in the land.

23:6
Deut 33:28;
Zech 14:11;
Is 7:14; 9:6;
Matt 1:21-23;
Jer 33:16;
Rom 3:22;
1 Cor 1:30

6   "In His days Judah will be saved,
         And Israel will dwell securely;
         And this is His name by which He will be called,
         'The LORD our righteousness.'

7   "Therefore behold, *the* days are coming," declares the LORD, "when they will no longer say, 'As the LORD lives, who brought up the sons of Israel from the land of Egypt,'

23:7
Is 43:18,19;
Jer 16:14,15

8   but, 'As the LORD lives, who brought up and led back the descendants of the household of Israel from *the* north land and from all the countries where I had driven them.' Then they will live on their own soil."

(2) FALSE PROPHETS SHALL DIE IN MISERY AND SHAME

23:9
Hab 3:16;
Jer 20:8,9

9   As for the prophets:
         My heart is broken within me,
         All my bones tremble;
         I have become like a drunken man,
         Even like a man overcome with wine,
         Because of the LORD
         And because of His holy words.

23:10
Jer 5:7,8;
Hos 4:2,3;
Jer 9:10; 12:4

10   For the land is full of adulterers;
         For the land mourns because of the curse.
         The pastures of the wilderness have dried up.
         Their course also is evil,
         And their might is not right.

23:11
Jer 6:13;
8:10; 7:9,10;
32:34

11   "For both prophet and priest are polluted;

22:28 *Coniah,* another name for Jehoiachin.
23:5 *a righteous Branch,* or a true shoot from the old stock of David. Kings of the Davidic line had become guilty of

injustice and oppression. The godly in Israel looked, however, to the prophetic promise that a righteous king would one day arise as the LORD's anointed (or Messiah).

Even in My house I have found their wickedness," declares the LORD.

12 "Therefore their way will be like slippery paths to them,
    They will be driven away into the gloom and fall down in it;
    For I shall bring calamity upon them,
    The year of their punishment," declares the LORD.

23:12
Ps 35:6;
John 12:35;
Jer 11:23

13 "Moreover, among the prophets of Samaria I saw an offensive thing:
    They prophesied by Baal and led My people Israel astray.
14 "Also among the prophets of Jerusalem I have seen a horrible thing:
    The committing of adultery and walking in falsehood;
    And they strengthen the hands of evildoers,
    So that no one has turned back from his wickedness.
    All of them have become to Me like Sodom,
    And her inhabitants like Gomorrah.

23:13
Hos 9:7,8;
Jer 2:8
23:14
Jer 5:30;
29:23;
Ezek 13:22;
Is 1:9,10;
Jer 20:16

15 "Therefore thus says the LORD of hosts concerning the prophets,
    'Behold, I am going to feed them wormwood
    And make them drink poisonous water,
    For from the prophets of Jerusalem
    Pollution has gone forth into all the land.' "

23:15
Jer 8:14; 9:15

16 Thus says the LORD of hosts,
    "Do not listen to the words of the prophets who are prophesying to
        you.
    They are leading you into futility;
    They speak a vision of their own imagination,
    Not from the mouth of the LORD.

23:16
Jer 27:9,10;
14:14; 9:12,
20

17 "They keep saying to those who despise Me,
    'The LORD has said, "You will have peace" ';
    And as for everyone who walks in the stubbornness of his own heart,
    They say, 'Calamity will not come upon you.'

23:17
Jer 8:11;
13:10; 18:12;
5:12;
Mic 3:11

18 "But who has stood in the council of the LORD,
    That he should see and hear His word?
    Who has given heed to His word and listened?

23:18
Job 15:8;
33:31

19 "Behold, the storm of the LORD has gone forth in wrath,
    Even a whirling tempest;
    It will swirl down on the head of the wicked.

23:19
Jer 25:32;
30:23

20 "The anger of the LORD will not turn back
    Until He has performed and carried out the purposes of His heart;
    In the last days you will clearly understand it.

23:20
Jer 30:24;
Gen 49:1

21 "I did not send *these* prophets,
    But they ran.
    I did not speak to them,
    But they prophesied.

23:21
Jer 14:14;
27:15; 29:9

22 "But if they had stood in My council,
    Then they would have announced My words to My people,
    And would have turned them back from their evil way
    And from the evil of their deeds.

23:22
Jer 9:12;
35:15;
1 Thess 1:9,
10

23 "Am I a God who is near," declares the LORD,
    "And not a God far off?

23:23
Ps 139:1-10;
Jer 50:51

24 "Can a man hide himself in hiding places,
    So I do not see him?" declares the LORD.
    "Do I not fill the heavens and the earth?" declares the LORD.

23:24
Ps 139:7-12;
Is 29:15;
Amos 9:2;
1 Kin 8:27

25 "I have heard what the prophets have said who prophesy falsely in My name,
saying, 'I had a dream, I had a dream!'

23:25
Jer 8:6;
14:14; 29:8

26 "How long? Is there *anything* in the hearts of the prophets who prophesy
falsehood, even *these* prophets of the deception of their own heart,

27 who intend to make My people forget My name by their dreams which they
relate to one another, just as their fathers forgot My name because of Baal?

23:27
Judg 3:7;
8:33,34
*23:28
Jer 9:12,20

28 "The prophet who has a dream may relate *his* dream, but let him who has My

---

23:28 *The prophet who has a dream may relate his dream.* The
dreams, however, were not to be confused with true proph-   ecy, i.e., the *word* handed down by the LORD.

word speak My word in truth. What does straw have *in common* with grain?" declares the LORD.

29 "Is not My word like fire?" declares the LORD, "and like a hammer which shatters a rock?

30 "Therefore behold, I am against the prophets," declares the LORD, "who steal My words from each other.

31 "Behold, I am against the prophets," declares the LORD, "who use their tongues and declare, '*The Lord* declares.'

32 "Behold, I am against those who have prophesied false dreams," declares the LORD, "and related them, and led My people astray by their falsehoods and reckless boasting; yet I did not send them or command them, nor do they furnish this people the slightest benefit," declares the LORD.

33 "Now when this people or the prophet or a priest asks you saying, 'What is the [8]oracle of the LORD?' then you shall say to them, 'What oracle?' The LORD declares, 'I shall abandon you.'

34 "Then as for the prophet or the priest or the people who say, 'The oracle of the LORD,' I shall bring punishment upon that man and his household.

35 "Thus shall each of you say to his neighbor and to his brother, 'What has the LORD answered?' or, 'What has the LORD spoken?'

36 "For you will no longer remember the oracle of the LORD, because every man's own word will become the oracle, and you have perverted the words of the living God, the LORD of hosts, our God.

37 "Thus you will say to *that* prophet, 'What has the LORD answered you?' and, 'What has the LORD spoken?'

38 "For if you say, 'The oracle of the LORD!' surely thus says the LORD, 'Because you said this word, "The oracle of the LORD!" I have also sent to you, saying, "You shall not say, 'The oracle of the LORD!' " ' '

39 "Therefore behold, I shall surely forget you and cast you away from My presence, along with the city which I gave you and your fathers.

40 "And I will put an everlasting reproach on you and an everlasting humiliation which will not be forgotten.' "

c. The sign of the good and the bad figs

24 After Nebuchadnezzar king of Babylon had carried away captive Jeconiah the son of Jehoiakim, king of Judah, and the officials of Judah with the craftsmen and smiths from Jerusalem and had brought them to Babylon, the LORD showed me: behold, two baskets of figs set before the temple of the LORD!

2 One basket had very good figs, like first-ripe figs; and the other basket had very bad figs, which could not be eaten due to rottenness.

3 Then the LORD said to me, "What do you see, Jeremiah?" And I said, "Figs, the good figs, very good; and the bad *figs,* very bad, which cannot be eaten due to rottenness."

4 Then the word of the LORD came to me, saying,

5 "Thus says the LORD God of Israel, 'Like these good figs, so I will regard as good the captives of Judah, whom I have sent out of this place *into* the land of the Chaldeans.

6 'For I will set My eyes on them for good, and I will bring them again to this land; and I will build them up and not overthrow them, and I will plant them and not pluck *them* up.

7 'And I will give them a heart to know Me, for I am the LORD; and they will be My people, and I will be their God, for they will return to Me with their whole heart.

8 'But like the bad figs which cannot be eaten due to rottenness—indeed, thus says the LORD—so I will abandon Zedekiah king of Judah and his officials, and the remnant of Jerusalem who remain in this land, and the ones who dwell in the land of Egypt.

9 'And I will make them a terror *and an* evil for all the kingdoms of the earth, as a reproach and a proverb, a taunt and a curse in all places where I shall scatter them.

10 'And I will send the sword, the famine, and the pestilence upon them until they are destroyed from the land which I gave to them and their forefathers.' "

---

[8]Or, *burden,* and so throughout the ch.

23:29
Jer 5:14;
20:9;
2 Cor 10:4,5
23:30
Ezek 13:8
23:31
v. 17
23:32
vv. 25,28
23:33
Is 13:1;
Hab 1:1;
Mal 1:1; v. 39
23:34
Lam 2:14;
Zech 13:3
23:35
Jer 33:3; 42:4
23:36
Jer 10:10
23:38
v. 36
23:39
Jer 7:14,15;
Ezek 8:18
23:40
Jer 20:11
24:1
Amos 8:1;
2 Kin 24:10-16;
2 Chr 36:10;
Jer 22:24;
29:2
24:2
Nah 3:12;
Jer 27:19
24:3
Jer 1:11,13
24:5
Nah 1:7;
Zech 13:9
24:6
Jer 29:10;
Ezek 11:17;
Jer 33:7;
42:10
24:7
Jer 31:33;
32:40;
Zech 8:8;
Heb 8:10;
Jer 29:13
*24:8
Jer 29:17;
39:5,9;
44:26-30
24:9
Jer 15:4;
29:18; 34:17;
1 Kin 9:7;
Ps 44:13,14;
Is 65:15
24:10
Is 51:19;
Jer 21:9; 27:8

2. Sermon II: the vision of the end coming
upon Judah and the heathen

a. The captivity of Judah and the end of Babylon

25 The word that came to Jeremiah concerning all the people of Judah, in the fourth year of Jehoiakim the son of Josiah, king of Judah (that was the first year of Nebuchadnezzar king of Babylon),

2 which Jeremiah the prophet spoke to all the people of Judah and to all the inhabitants of Jerusalem, saying,

3 "From the thirteenth year of Josiah the son of Amon, king of Judah, even to this day, these twenty-three years the word of the LORD has come to me, and I have spoken to you again and again, but you have not listened.

4 "And the LORD has sent to you all His servants the prophets again and again, but you have not listened nor inclined your ear to hear,

5 saying, 'Turn now everyone from his evil way and from the evil of your deeds, and dwell on the land which the LORD has given to you and your forefathers forever and ever;

6 and do not go after other gods to serve them and to worship them, and do not provoke Me to anger with the work of your hands, and I will do you no harm.'

7 "Yet you have not listened to Me," declares the LORD, "in order that you might provoke Me to anger with the work of your hands to your own harm.

8 "Therefore thus says the LORD of hosts, 'Because you have not obeyed My words,

9 behold, I will send and take all the families of the north,' declares the LORD, 'and *I will send* to Nebuchadnezzar king of Babylon, My servant, and will bring them against this land, and against its inhabitants, and against all these nations round about; and I will utterly destroy them, and make them a horror, and a hissing, and an everlasting desolation.

10 'Moreover, I will take from them the voice of joy and the voice of gladness, the voice of the bridegroom and the voice of the bride, the sound of the millstones and the light of the lamp.

11 'And this whole land shall be a desolation and a horror, and these nations shall serve the king of Babylon seventy years.

12 'Then it will be when seventy years are completed I will punish the king of Babylon and that nation,' declares the LORD, 'for their iniquity, and the land of the Chaldeans; and I will make it an everlasting desolation.

13 'And I will bring upon that land all My words which I have pronounced against it, all that is written in this book, which Jeremiah has prophesied against all the nations.

14 '(For many nations and great kings shall make slaves of them, even them; and I will recompense them according to their deeds, and according to the work of their hands.)' "

b. The cup of wrath visited on the nations

15 For thus the LORD, the God of Israel, says to me, "Take this cup of the wine of wrath from My hand, and cause all the nations, to whom I send you, to drink it.

16 "And they shall drink and stagger and go mad because of the sword that I will send among them."

17 Then I took the cup from the LORD's hand, and made all the nations drink, to whom the LORD sent me:

18 Jerusalem and the cities of Judah, and its kings *and* its princes, to make them a ruin, a horror, a hissing, and a curse, as it is this day;

19 Pharaoh king of Egypt, his servants, his princes, and all his people;

20 and all the foreign people, all the kings of the land of Uz, all the kings of the land of the Philistines (even Ashkelon, Gaza, Ekron, and the remnant of Ashdod);

21 Edom, Moab, and the sons of Ammon;

25:1 Jer 36:1; 2 Kin 24:1,2
25:2 Jer 18:11
25:3 Jer 1:2; 2 Chr 34:1-3, 8; Jer 36:2; 7:13; 22:21
25:4 Jer 7:13,25; 26:5
25:5 Is 55:6,7; Jer 4:1; 7:7
25:6 Deut 6:14; 8:19;
25:7 Jer 35:15 Deut 32:21; 2 Kin 17:17; 21:15; Jer 7:19
*25:9 Jer 1:15; 27:6; 18:16
25:10 Is 24:7; Ezek 26:13; Eccl 12:4; Is 47:2
*25:11 Jer 4:27; 12:11,12; Dan 9:2
25:12 Ezra 1:1; Jer 29:10; Is 13:14; 13:19; 14:23
25:14 Jer 50:9; 51:27,28; 50:41; 51:6, 24
25:15 Ps 75:8; Is 51:17
25:16 Jer 51:7; Nah 3:11
25:17 v. 28; Ezek 43:3
25:18 Is 51:17; Jer 24:9; 44:22
25:19 Jer 46:2-28
25:20 Job 1:1; Jer 47:1-7; Is 20:1
25:21 Jer 49:1-22; 48:1-47

24:8 Even flight to Egypt provided no safety.
25:9 *My servant*, i.e., under God's control.
25:11 Jeremiah states the length of the captivity (seventy years). Some compute it from 605 B.C., when the first deportation took place (2 Kin. 24:10–15); others start with 586 B.C., when the final deportation occurred and the temple was destroyed (2 Chr. 36:17–20). In the former case the captivity terminated in 538 B.C., with the decree of Cyrus for the return of the remnant to the land (Ezra 1:1–3); in the latter case, the terminating date would be 516 B.C., when the second temple was completed. Seventy may, on the other hand, be a conventional round number (ten times seven). In this instance it would not be necessary to press for the exact length of time the Jews were in servitude to Babylon.

22   and all the kings of Tyre, all the kings of Sidon, and the kings of the coastlands which are beyond the sea;

23   and Dedan, Tema, Buz, and all who cut the corners *of their hair;*

24   and all the kings of Arabia and all the kings of the foreign people who dwell in the desert;

25   and all the kings of Zimri, all the kings of Elam, and all the kings of Media;

26   and all the kings of the north, near and far, one with another; and all the kingdoms of the earth which are upon the face of the ground, and the king of Sheshach shall drink after them.

27   "And you shall say to them, 'Thus says the Lord of hosts, the God of Israel, "Drink, be drunk, vomit, fall, and rise no more because of the sword which I will send among you." '

28   "And it will be, if they refuse to take the cup from your hand to drink, then you will say to them, 'Thus says the Lord of hosts: "You shall surely drink!

29   "For behold, I am beginning to work calamity in *this* city which is called by My name, and shall you be completely free from punishment? You will not be free from punishment; for I am summoning a sword against all the inhabitants of the earth," declares the Lord of hosts.'

c. The vengeance of the LORD

30   "Therefore you shall prophesy against them all these words, and you shall say to them,

> 'The Lord will roar from on high,
> And utter His voice from His holy habitation;
> He will roar mightily against His fold.
> He will shout like those who tread *the grapes,*
> Against all the inhabitants of the earth.

31   'A clamor has come to the end of the earth,
> Because the Lord has a controversy with the nations.
> He is entering into judgment with all flesh;
> As for the wicked, He has given them to the sword,' declares the
>   Lord."

32   Thus says the Lord of hosts,

> "Behold, evil is going forth
> From nation to nation,
> And a great storm is being stirred up
> From the remotest parts of the earth.

33   "And those slain by the Lord on that day shall be from one end of the earth to the other. They shall not be lamented, gathered, or buried; they shall be like dung on the face of the ground.

34   "Wail, you shepherds, and cry;
> And wallow *in ashes,* you masters of the flock;
> For the days of your slaughter and your dispersions have come,
> And you shall fall like a choice vessel.

35   "Flight shall perish from the shepherds,
> And escape from the masters of the flock.

36   *"Hear* the sound of the cry of the shepherds,
> And the wailing of the masters of the flock!
> For the Lord is destroying their pasture.

37   "And the peaceful folds are made silent
> Because of the fierce anger of the Lord.

38   "He has left His hiding place like the lion;
> For their land has become a horror
> Because of the fierceness of the oppressing *sword,*
> And because of His fierce anger."

3. Four contests between Jeremiah and the false prophets

a. Jeremiah arrested and released: Uriah murdered

26   In the beginning of the reign of Jehoiakim the son of Josiah, king of Judah, this word came from the Lord, saying,

2   "Thus says the Lord, 'Stand in the court of the Lord's house, and speak to

all the cities of Judah, who have come to worship *in* the LORD's house, all the words that I have commanded you to speak to them. Do not omit a word!

3 'Perhaps they will listen and everyone will turn from his evil way, that I may repent of the calamity which I am planning to do to them because of the evil of their deeds.'

4 "And you will say to them, 'Thus says the LORD, "If you will not listen to Me, to walk in My law, which I have set before you,

5 to listen to the words of My servants the prophets, whom I have been sending to you again and again, but you have not listened;

6 then I will make this house like Shiloh, and this city I will make a curse to all the nations of the earth."' "

7 And the priests and the prophets and all the people heard Jeremiah speaking these words in the house of the LORD.

8 And when Jeremiah finished speaking all that the LORD had commanded *him* to speak to all the people, the priests and the prophets and all the people seized him, saying, "You must die!

9 "Why have you prophesied in the name of the LORD saying, 'This house will be like Shiloh, and this city will be desolate, without inhabitant'?" And all the people gathered about Jeremiah in the house of the LORD.

10 And when the princes of Judah heard these things, they came up from the king's house to the house of the LORD and sat in the entrance of the New Gate of the LORD's *house.*

11 Then the priests and the prophets spoke to the officials and to all the people, saying, "A death sentence for this man! For he has prophesied against this city as you have heard in your hearing."

12 Then Jeremiah spoke to all the officials and to all the people, saying, "The LORD sent me to prophesy against this house and against this city all the words that you have heard.

13 "Now therefore amend your ways and your deeds, and obey the voice of the LORD your God; and the LORD will change His mind about the misfortune which He has pronounced against you.

14 "But as for me, behold, I am in your hands; do with me as is good and right in your sight.

15 "Only know for certain that if you put me to death, you will bring innocent blood on yourselves, and on this city, and on its inhabitants; for truly the LORD has sent me to you to speak all these words in your hearing."

16 Then the officials and all the people said to the priests and to the prophets, "No death sentence for this man! For he has spoken to us in the name of the LORD our God."

17 Then some of the elders of the land rose up and spoke to all the assembly of the people, saying,

18 "Micah of Moresheth prophesied in the days of Hezekiah king of Judah; and he spoke to all the people of Judah, saying, 'Thus the LORD of hosts has said,
> "Zion will be plowed *as* a field,
> And Jerusalem will become ruins,
> And the mountain of the house as the high places of a forest."' "

19 "Did Hezekiah king of Judah and all Judah put him to death? Did he not fear the LORD and entreat the favor of the LORD, and the LORD changed His mind about the misfortune which He had pronounced against them? But we are committing a great evil against ourselves."

20 Indeed, there was also a man who prophesied in the name of the LORD, Uriah the son of Shemaiah from Kiriath-jearim; and he prophesied against this city and against this land words similar to all those of Jeremiah.

21 When King Jehoiakim and all his mighty men and all the officials heard his words, then the king sought to put him to death; but Uriah heard *it,* and he was afraid and fled, and went to Egypt.

22 Then King Jehoiakim sent men to Egypt: Elnathan the son of Achbor and *certain* men with him *went* into Egypt.

23 And they brought Uriah from Egypt and led him to King Jehoiakim, who

---

26:3 Jer 36:3-7; 18:8
26:4 Lev 26:14; Deut 28:15; Jer 17:27; 32:23; 44:10, 23
26:5 2 Kin 9:7; Jer 25:3,4
26:6 1 Sam 4:10, 11; Is 65:15; Jer 24:9
26:8 Jer 20:1,2; 11:19; 18:23
*26:9 Jer 9:11; 33:10
*26:10 Jer 36:10
26:11 Jer 18:23; Deut 18:20; Matt 26:66; Jer 38:4; Acts 6:11-14
26:12 Jer 1:17,18; 5:6; 46:16
26:13 Jer 7:3,5; 18:11; Joel 2:14; Jon 3:9; 4:2
26:14 Jer 38:5
26:15 Prov 6:16,17; Jer 7:6
26:16 v. 11; Acts 5:34-39; 23:9,29; 25:25; 26:31
26:18 Mic 1:1; Ps 79:1; Mic 3:12; Zech 8:3
26:19 2 Chr 29:6-11; 32:26; 2 Sam 24:16; Acts 5:39
26:20 Josh 9:17; 1Sa 6:21; 7:2
26:21 1 Kin 19:2-4; Matt 10:23,28
26:22 Jer 36:12
26:23 Jer 2:30

26:9 *Shiloh,* cf. 7:12. Jeremiah cited Shiloh as an example of the fact that even a sanctuary of the LORD could be destroyed when God brings judgment on His people. The false prophets insisted that the temple was inviolable. **26:10** *the princes.* These were officials of the palace, not to be mistaken for royalty.

slew him with a sword, and cast his dead body into the burial place of the common people.

24 But the hand of Ahikam the son of Shaphan was with Jeremiah, so that he was not given into the hands of the people to put him to death.

b. Jeremiah testifies again that Nebuchadnezzar will conquer

27 In the beginning of the reign of Zedekiah the son of Josiah, king of Judah, this word came to Jeremiah from the LORD, saying—

2   thus says the LORD to me—"Make for yourself bonds and yokes and put them on your neck,

3   and send word to the king of Edom, to the king of Moab, to the king of the sons of Ammon, to the king of Tyre, and to the king of Sidon by the messengers who come to Jerusalem to Zedekiah king of Judah.

4   "And command them *to go* to their masters, saying, 'Thus says the LORD of hosts, the God of Israel, thus you shall say to your masters,

5   "I have made the earth, the men and the beasts which are on the face of the earth by My great power and by My outstretched arm, and I will give it to the one who is pleasing in My sight.

6   "And now I have given all these lands into the hand of Nebuchadnezzar king of Babylon, My servant, and I have given him also the wild animals of the field to serve him.

7   "And all the nations shall serve him, and his son, and his grandson, until the time of his own land comes; then many nations and great kings will make him their servant.

8   "And it will be, *that* the nation or the kingdom which will not serve him, Nebuchadnezzar king of Babylon, and which will not put its neck under the yoke of the king of Babylon, I will punish that nation with the sword, with famine, and with pestilence," declares the LORD, "until I have destroyed it by his hand.

9   "But as for you, do not listen to your prophets, your diviners, your dreamers, your soothsayers, or your sorcerers, who speak to you, saying, 'You shall not serve the king of Babylon.'

10   "For they prophesy a lie to you, in order to remove you far from your land; and I will drive you out, and you will perish.

11   "But the nation which will bring its neck under the yoke of the king of Babylon and serve him, I will let remain on its land," declares the LORD, "and they will till it and dwell in it." ' "

12   And I spoke words like all these to Zedekiah king of Judah, saying, "Bring your necks under the yoke of the king of Babylon, and serve him and his people, and live!

13   "Why will you die, you and your people, by the sword, famine, and pestilence, as the LORD has spoken to that nation which will not serve the king of Babylon?

14   "So do not listen to the words of the prophets who speak to you, saying, 'You shall not serve the king of Babylon,' for they prophesy a lie to you;

15   for I have not sent them," declares the LORD, "but they prophesy falsely in My name, in order that I may drive you out, and that you may perish, you and the prophets who prophesy to you."

16   *Then* I spoke to the priests and to all this people, saying, "Thus says the LORD: Do not listen to the words of your prophets who prophesy to you, saying, 'Behold, the vessels of the LORD's house will now shortly be brought again from Babylon'; for they are prophesying a lie to you.

17   "Do not listen to them; serve the king of Babylon, and live! Why should this city become a ruin?

18   "But if they are prophets, and if the word of the LORD is with them, let them now entreat the LORD of hosts, that the vessels which are left in the house of the LORD, in the house of the king of Judah, and in Jerusalem, may not go to Babylon.

19   "For thus says the LORD of hosts concerning the pillars, concerning the sea, concerning the stands, and concerning the rest of the vessels that are left in this city,

20   which Nebuchadnezzar king of Babylon did not take when he carried into exile Jeconiah the son of Jehoiakim, king of Judah, from Jerusalem to Babylon, and all the nobles of Judah and Jerusalem.

21   "Yes, thus says the LORD of hosts, the God of Israel, concerning the vessels

26:24
2 Kin 22:12-14;
Jer 39:14

27:1
Jer 26:1

27:2
Jer 28:10,13

27:3
Jer 25:21,22

27:5
Jer 10:12;
51:15;
Ps 115:15,16;
Acts 17:26
27:6
Ezek 29:18-20;
Jer 25:9;
28:14
27:7
Jer 44:30;
46:13; 25:12;
Is 14:4-6
27:8
Jer 38:17-19;
Ezek 17:19-21;
Jer 29:17,18;
Ezek 14:21
27:9
Ex 22:18;
Deut 18:10;
Is 8:19;
Mal 3:5
27:10
Jer 23:25;
8:19; 32:31
27:11
Jer 21:9

27:12
Jer 28:1

27:13
Ezek 18:31

27:14
Jer 14:14;
Ezek 13:22
27:15
Jer 23:21,25;
6:13-15;
14:15,16
27:16
2 Chr 36:7,
10; Jer 28:3;
Dan 1:2;
v. 10

27:17
v. 13

27:18
1 Sam 7:8;
12:19,23

27:19
2 Kin 25:13,
17;
Jer 52:17-23
27:20
2 Kin 24:14-16;
Jer 24:1

that are left in the house of the LORD, and in the house of the king of Judah, and in Jerusalem,

22 'They shall be carried to Babylon, and they shall be there until the day I visit them,' declares the LORD. 'Then I will bring them back and restore them to this place.' "

c. Jeremiah exposes Hananiah and foretells his death

28 Now it came about in the same year, in the beginning of the reign of Zedekiah king of Judah, in the fourth year, in the fifth month, that Hananiah the son of Azzur, the prophet, who was from Gibeon, spoke to me in the house of the LORD in the presence of the priests and all the people, saying,

2 "Thus says the LORD of hosts, the God of Israel, 'I have broken the yoke of the king of Babylon.

3 'Within two years I am going to bring back to this place all the vessels of the LORD's house, which Nebuchadnezzar king of Babylon took away from this place and carried to Babylon.

4 'I am also going to bring back to this place Jeconiah the son of Jehoiakim, king of Judah, and all the exiles of Judah who went to Babylon,' declares the LORD, 'for I will break the yoke of the king of Babylon.' "

5 Then the prophet Jeremiah spoke to the prophet Hananiah in the presence of the priests and in the presence of all the people who were standing in the house of the LORD,

6 and the prophet Jeremiah said, "Amen! May the LORD do so; may the LORD confirm your words which you have prophesied to bring back the vessels of the LORD's house and all the exiles, from Babylon to this place.

7 "Yet hear now this word which I am about to speak in your hearing and in the hearing of all the people!

8 "The prophets who were before me and before you from ancient times prophesied against many lands and against great kingdoms, of war and of calamity and of pestilence.

9 "The prophet who prophesies of peace, when the word of the prophet shall come to pass, then that prophet will be known as one whom the LORD has truly sent."

10 Then Hananiah the prophet took the yoke from the neck of Jeremiah the prophet and broke it.

11 And Hananiah spoke in the presence of all the people, saying, "Thus says the LORD, 'Even so will I break within two full years, the yoke of Nebuchadnezzar king of Babylon from the neck of all the nations.' " Then the prophet Jeremiah went his way.

12 And the word of the LORD came to Jeremiah, after Hananiah the prophet had broken the yoke from off the neck of the prophet Jeremiah, saying,

13 "Go and speak to Hananiah, saying, 'Thus says the LORD, "You have broken the yokes of wood, but you have made instead of them yokes of iron."

14 'For thus says the LORD of hosts, the God of Israel, "I have put a yoke of iron on the neck of all these nations, that they may serve Nebuchadnezzar king of Babylon; and they shall serve him. And I have also given him the beasts of the field." ' "

15 Then Jeremiah the prophet said to Hananiah the prophet, "Listen now, Hananiah, the LORD has not sent you, and you have made this people trust in a lie.

16 "Therefore thus says the LORD, 'Behold, I am about to remove you from the face of the earth. This year you are going to die, because you have counseled rebellion against the LORD.' "

17 So Hananiah the prophet died in the same year in the seventh month.

Cross references (margin)

27:22 2 Kin 25:13; 2 Chr 36:18; Jer 29:10; 32:5; Ezra 1:7; 7:19

*28:1 Jer 27:1,3,12; Josh 9:3; 10:12

*28:3 2 Kin 24:13; 2 Chr 36:10; Jer 27:12

28:4 Jer 22:24,26, 27; 27:8

28:5 v. 1

28:6 1 Kin 1:36; Jer 11:5

28:7 1 Kin 22:28

28:8 1 Kin 14:15; Is 5:5-7; Joel 1:20; Amos 1:2; Nah 1:2

28:9 Deut 18:22

28:10 Jer 27:2

28:11 Jer 14:14; 27:10

28:12 Jer 1:2

28:13 Ps 107:16; Is 45:2

28:14 Deut 28:48; Jer 27:6-8; 25:11

28:15 Jer 29:31; Ezek 13:22

28:16 Deut 6:15; 13:5; Jer 29:32

28:1 Every age of history has both its true and its false prophets. Wherever there is the real there is sure to be the counterfeit. Jeremiah found in Hananiah the antithesis of all he stood for. The people were probably in doubt as to whose prophecies they should accept, although they might have inclined toward those of Hananiah as being far more to their liking. But God did not long leave them without a sign to confirm the truth of Jeremiah's message. Jeremiah prophesied the death of Hananiah himself, and in the very year of the prophecy it came to pass. This sign should have convinced the people, but it did not. (See 28:1–17.)

should be noted that while God is consistent with Himself, His dealings with His people vary from generation to generation. The false prophets of Jeremiah's day prophesied that God would spare Jerusalem and protect His temple. This had been God's word through Isaiah at the time of Sennacherib's invasion (Is. 37:6,7), but God's word through Jeremiah was one of victory for Nebuchadnezzar and the enemies of Judah. (Read 32:26–35.)
28:3 Hananiah insisted that temple treasures and captives from Jerusalem would be returned from Babylon within two years.

d. *Jeremiah assures the captives they are safer in Babylon,*
for Jerusalem will be destroyed

29 Now these are the words of the letter which Jeremiah the prophet sent from Jerusalem to the rest of the elders of the exile, the priests, the prophets, and all the people whom Nebuchadnezzar had taken into exile from Jerusalem to Babylon.

2 (This was after King Jeconiah and the queen mother, the court officials, the princes of Judah and Jerusalem, the craftsmen and the smiths had departed from Jerusalem.)

3 *The letter was sent* by the hand of Elasah the son of Shaphan, and Gemariah the son of Hilkiah, whom Zedekiah king of Judah sent to Babylon to Nebuchadnezzar king of Babylon, saying,

4 "Thus says the LORD of hosts, the God of Israel, to all the exiles whom I have sent into exile from Jerusalem to Babylon,

5 'Build houses and live *in them;* and plant gardens, and eat their produce.

6 'Take wives and become the fathers of sons and daughters, and take wives for your sons and give your daughters to husbands, that they may bear sons and daughters; and multiply there and do not decrease.

7 'And seek the welfare of the city where I have sent you into exile, and pray to the LORD on its behalf; for in its welfare you will have welfare.'

8 "For thus says the LORD of hosts, the God of Israel, 'Do not let your prophets who are in your midst and your diviners deceive you, and do not listen to the dreams which they dream.

9 'For they prophesy falsely to you in My name; I have not sent them,' declares the LORD.

10 "For thus says the LORD, 'When seventy years have been completed for Babylon, I will visit you and fulfill My good word to you, to bring you back to this place.

11 'For I know the plans that I have for you,' declares the LORD, 'plans for welfare and not for calamity to give you a future and a hope.

12 'Then you will call upon Me and come and pray to Me, and I will listen to you.

13 'And you will seek Me and find *Me,* when you search for Me with all your heart.

14 'And I will be found by you,' declares the LORD, 'and I will restore your fortunes and will gather you from all the nations and from all the places where I have driven you,' declares the LORD, 'and I will bring you back to the place from where I sent you into exile.'

15 "Because you have said, 'The LORD has raised up prophets for us in Babylon'—

16 for thus says the LORD concerning the king who sits on the throne of David, and concerning all the people who dwell in this city, your brothers who did not go with you into exile—

17 thus says the LORD of hosts, 'Behold, I am sending upon them the sword, famine, and pestilence, and I will make them like split-open figs that cannot be eaten due to rottenness.

18 'And I will pursue them with the sword, with famine and with pestilence; and I will make them a terror to all the kingdoms of the earth, to be a curse, and a horror, and a hissing, and a reproach among all the nations where I have driven them,

19 because they have not listened to My words,' declares the LORD, 'which I sent to them again and again by My servants the prophets; but you did not listen,' declares the LORD.

20 "You, therefore, hear the word of the LORD, all you exiles, whom I have sent away from Jerusalem to Babylon.

21 "Thus says the LORD of hosts, the God of Israel, concerning Ahab the son of Kolaiah and concerning Zedekiah the son of Maaseiah, who are prophesying to you

---

Marginal references (left column):

29:1
vv. 25,29

29:2
2 Kin 24:12-16;
Jer 22:24-28;
24:1; 28:4

*29:4ff
Is 10:5,6;
Jer 24:5

29:6
Jer 16:2-4

29:7
Ezra 6:10;
Dan 4:19;
1 Tim 2:2
29:8
Jer 27:9;
14:14; 23:21,
25,27
29:9
Jer 27:15;
v. 31
29:10
2 Chr 36:21,
22; Jer 25:12;
27:22;
Dan 9:2
29:11
Is 40:9-11;
Jer 30:18-22;
31:17
29:12
Ps 50:15;
Jer 33:3;
Ps 145:19
29:13
1 Chr 22:19;
2 Chr 22:9;
Jer 24:7
29:14
Deut 30:1-10;
Jer 30:3;
Is 43:5,6;
Jer 3:14

29:16
Jer 38:2,3,
17-23

29:17
Jer 27:8;
32:24; 24:3,
8-10

29:18
Is 65:15;
Jer 42:18;
25:9

29:19
Jer 6:19;
25:4; 26:5

29:20
Jer 24:5

29:21
vv. 8,9

29:4-23 In his letter to the captives in Babylon, Jeremiah sought to counteract two errors: (1) false prophets had assured them of a speedy return. Jeremiah stated that they would be in Babylon a long time. They should build houses, marry, raise families, and pray for the well-being of the land in which they were exiles. (2) Discouragement might lead them to think their exile would be endless. It would indeed be long—*seventy years* (29:10); but when God's people sought Him wholeheartedly (29:13), they would find Him. The exile was brought about because of sin, but when sin was forsaken by the people, God's purposes in mercy would then be realized.

falsely in My name, 'Behold, I will deliver them into the hand of Nebuchadnezzar king of Babylon, and he shall slay them before your eyes.

22 'And because of them a curse shall be used by all the exiles from Judah who are in Babylon, saying, "May the LORD make you like Zedekiah and like Ahab, whom the king of Babylon roasted in the fire,   `29:22` Is 65:15; Dan 3:6

23 because they have acted foolishly in Israel, and have committed adultery with their neighbors' wives, and have spoken words in My name falsely, which I did not command them; and I am He who knows, and am a witness," declares the LORD.' "   `29:23` 2Sa 13:12; Prov 5:21; Jer 16:17

24 And to Shemaiah the Nehelamite you shall speak, saying,   `29:24` vv. 31,32

25 "Thus says the LORD of hosts, the God of Israel, 'Because you have sent letters in your own name to all the people who are in Jerusalem, and to Zephaniah the son of Maaseiah, the priest, and to all the priests, saying,   `29:25` vv. 1,29; 2 Kin 25:18; Jer 21:1

26 "The LORD has made you priest instead of Jehoiada the priest, to be the overseer in the house of the LORD over every madman who prophesies, to put him in the stocks and in the iron collar,   `29:26` Jer 20:1; 2 Kin 9:11; Acts 26:24; Jer 20:2

27 now then, why have you not rebuked Jeremiah of Anathoth who prophesies to you?

28 "For he has sent to us in Babylon, saying, 'The exile will be long; build houses and live in them and plant gardens and eat their produce.' " ' "   `29:28` vv. 1,5,10

29 And Zephaniah the priest read this letter to Jeremiah the prophet.   `29:29` v. 25

30 Then came the word of the LORD to Jeremiah, saying,

31 "Send to all the exiles, saying, 'Thus says the LORD concerning Shemaiah the Nehelamite, "Because Shemaiah has prophesied to you, although I did not send him, and he has made you trust in a lie,"   `29:31` vv. 20,24; Jer 14:14,15; 28:15

32 therefore thus says the LORD, "Behold, I am about to punish Shemaiah the Nehelamite and his descendants; he shall not have anyone living among this people, and he shall not see the good that I am about to do to My people," declares the LORD, "because he has preached rebellion against the LORD." ' "   `29:32` Jer 36:31; 22:30; 17:6; 28:16

B. The glorious future of latter-day Israel and their new covenant

1. Sermon III: ultimate deliverance and blessing of the reunited kingdom

a. Israel restored; the heathen judged

30 The word which came to Jeremiah from the LORD, saying,

2 "Thus says the LORD, the God of Israel, 'Write all the words which I have spoken to you in a book.   `30:2` Jer 25:13; Hab 2:2

3 'For, behold, days are coming,' declares the LORD, 'when I will restore the fortunes of My people Israel and Judah.' The LORD says, 'I will also bring them back to the land that I gave to their forefathers, and they shall possess it.' "   `30:3` Jer 29:10; Ps 53:6; Zeph 3:20; Jer 16:15; Ezek 20:42

4 Now these are the words which the LORD spoke concerning Israel and concerning Judah,

5 "For thus says the LORD,
'I have heard a sound of terror,
Of dread, and there is no peace.   `30:5` Is 5:30; Amos 5:16-18

6 'Ask now, and see,
If a male can give birth.
Why do I see every man
With his hands on his loins, as a woman in childbirth?
And why have all faces turned pale?   `30:6` Jer 4:31; 6:24

7 'Alas! for that day is great,
There is none like it;
And it is the time of Jacob's distress,
But he will be saved from it.   `*30:7` Is 2:12; Joel 2:11; Lam 1:12; Jer 2:27,28; v. 10

8 'And it shall come about on that day,' declares the LORD of hosts, 'that I will break his yoke from off their neck, and will tear off their bonds; and strangers shall no longer make them their slaves.   `30:8` Is 9:4; Jer 27:2; Ezek 34:27

30:7 *he will be saved from it.* The exile, while long, will not be permanent. God will deliver His people from their affliction.

*30:9
Is 55:3,4;
Ezek 34:23;
37:24;
Hos 3:5;
Luke 1:69;
Acts 2:30;
13:23
30:10
Is 43:5; 44:2;
Jer 46:27,28;
Is 60:4;
Jer 33:16;
Mic 4:4
30:11
Jer 46:28;
4:27; 10:24

9 'But they shall serve the LORD their God, and David their king, whom I will raise up for them.

10 'And fear not, O Jacob My servant,' declares the LORD,
'And do not be dismayed, O Israel;
For behold, I will save you from afar,
And your offspring from the land of their captivity.
And Jacob shall return, and shall be quiet and at ease,
And no one shall make him afraid.

11 'For I am with you,' declares the LORD, 'to save you;
For I will destroy completely all the nations where I have scattered you,
Only I will not destroy you completely.
But I will chasten you justly,
And will by no means leave you unpunished.'

30:12
v. 15;
Jer 15:18

12 "For thus says the LORD,
'Your wound is incurable,
And your injury is serious.

30:13
Jer 14:19;
46:11

13 'There is no one to plead your cause;
No healing for your sore,
No recovery for you.

30:14
Lam 1:2; 2:4,
5; Jer 5:6;
32:30-35

14 'All your lovers have forgotten you,
They do not seek you;
For I have wounded you with the wound of an enemy,
With the punishment of a cruel one,
Because your iniquity is great
And your sins are numerous.

15 'Why do you cry out over your injury?
Your pain is incurable.
Because your iniquity is great
And your sins are numerous,
I have done these things to you.

30:16
Is 33:1;
41:11;
Jer 10:25;
50:10

16 'Therefore all who devour you shall be devoured;
And all your adversaries, every one of them, shall go into captivity;
And those who plunder you shall be for plunder,
And all who prey upon you I will give for prey.

30:17
Jer 8:22;
22:33; 33:24

17 'For I will restore you to health
And I will heal you of your wounds,' declares the LORD,
'Because they have called you an outcast, saying:
"It is Zion; no one cares for her." '

*30:18
Jer 31:23;
Ps 102:13;
Jer 31:4,
38-40

18 "Thus says the LORD,
'Behold, I will restore the fortunes of the tents of Jacob
And have compassion on his dwelling places;
And the city shall be rebuilt on its ruin,
And the palace shall stand on its rightful place.

30:19
Is 35:10;
Jer 31:4,12,
13; 33:10,11,
22

19 'And from them shall proceed thanksgiving
And the voice of those who make merry;
And I will multiply them, and they shall not be diminished;
I will also honor them, and they shall not be insignificant.

30:20
Is 54:13;
Jer 31:17;
Is 54:14

20 'Their children also shall be as formerly,
And their congregation shall be established before Me;
And I will punish all their oppressors.

30:21
Num 16:5;
Jer 50:44

21 'And their leader shall be one of them,
And their ruler shall come forth from their midst;
And I will bring him near, and he shall approach Me;
For who would dare to risk his life to approach Me?' declares the LORD.

30:22
Jer 32:38;
Ezek 11:20;
36:28;
Zech 13:9

22 'And you shall be My people,
And I will be your God.' "

30:9 With the restoration, Jeremiah promised a Davidic king, a future ideal ruler who would inherit the promises made to David.

30:18 rebuilt on its ruin. Assurance that Jerusalem would be rebuilt.

23   Behold, the tempest of the LORD!
       Wrath has gone forth,
       A sweeping tempest;
       It will burst on the head of the wicked.

24   The fierce anger of the LORD will not turn back,
       Until He has performed, and until He has accomplished
       The intent of His heart;
       In the latter days you will understand this.

b. *Restoration and blessing of both Ephraim and Judah*

31 "At that time," declares the LORD, "I will be the God of all the families of
Israel, and they shall be My people."

2   Thus says the LORD,
       "The people who survived the sword
       Found grace in the wilderness—
       Israel, when it went to find its rest."

3   The LORD appeared to him from afar, *saying*,
       "I have loved you with an everlasting love;
       Therefore I have drawn you with lovingkindness.

4   "Again I will build you, and you shall be rebuilt,
       O virgin of Israel!
       Again you shall take up your tambourines,
       And go forth to the dances of the merrymakers.

5   "Again you shall plant vineyards
       On the hills of Samaria;
       The planters shall plant
       And shall enjoy *them*.

6   "For there shall be a day when watchmen
       On the hills of Ephraim shall call out,
       'Arise, and let us go up *to* Zion,
       To the LORD our God.' "

7   For thus says the LORD,
       "Sing aloud with gladness for Jacob,
       And shout among the chiefs of the nations;
       Proclaim, give praise, and say,
       'O LORD, save Thy people,
       The remnant of Israel.'

8   "Behold, I am bringing them from the north country,
       And I will gather them from the remote parts of the earth,
       Among them the blind and the lame,
       The woman with child and she who is in labor with child, together;
       A great company, they shall return here.

9   "With weeping they shall come,
       And by supplication I will lead them;
       I will make them walk by streams of waters,
       On a straight path in which they shall not stumble;
       For I am a father to Israel,
       And Ephraim is My first-born."

10   Hear the word of the LORD, O nations,
       And declare in the coastlands afar off,
       And say, "He who scattered Israel will gather him,
       And keep him as a shepherd keeps his flock."

11   For the LORD has ransomed Jacob,
       And redeemed him from the hand of him who was stronger than he.

12   "And they shall come and shout for joy on the height of Zion,
       And they shall be radiant over the bounty of the LORD—
       Over the grain, and the new wine, and the oil,
       And over the young of the flock and the herd;
       And their life shall be like a watered garden,

Marginal references:

*30:23f — Jer 23:19,20; 25:32

30:24 — Jer 4:8; 23:20

31:1 — Jer 30:22,24; Is 41:10; Rom 11:26-28
*31:2 — Num 14:20; Josh 1:13; Is 63:14

31:3 — Deut 7:8; Ps 25:6; Hos 11:4

31:4 — Jer 30:19

31:5 — Is 65:21; Jer 50:19

31:6 — Is 2:3; Mic 4:2

31:7 — Ps 14:7; Deut 28:13; Is 61:9; Ps 28:9; Is 37:31

31:8 — Jer 3:18; 23:8; Is 43:6; Ezek 20:34, 41; Is 42:16; 40:11

31:9 — Is 43:19; 49:10,11; 64:8; Jer 3:4, 19

31:10 — Is 66:19; Jer 50:19; Is 40:11

31:11 — Is 44:23; 48:20; Jer 50:34; Is 49:24,25
31:12 — Ezek 17:23; Hos 3:5; Is 58:11; 35:10; 65:19; Rev 21:4

30:23,24 Except for a few words, these verses repeat 23:19,20 verbatim.
31:2 *grace in the wilderness*, cf. Hos. 2:14,15. Away from the land of "milk and honey," the remnant of Israel would find grace, for God loves them with an everlasting love (v. 3).

And they shall never languish again.

31:13
Ps 30:11;
Zech 8:4,5;
Is 61:3; 51:11

13   "Then the virgin shall rejoice in the dance,
     And the young men and the old, together,
     For I will turn their mourning into joy,
     And will comfort them, and give them joy for their sorrow.

31:14
v. 25;
Jer 50:19

14   "And I will fill the soul of the priests with abundance,
     And My people shall be satisfied with My goodness," declares the
     LORD.

*31:15
Matt 2:17,18;
Gen 37:35;
Ps 77:2;
Jer 10:20

15   Thus says the LORD,
     "A voice is heard in Ramah,
     Lamentation *and* bitter weeping.
     Rachel is weeping for her children;
     She refuses to be comforted for her children,
     Because they are no more."

31:16
Is 25:8;
30:19;
Heb 6:10;
vv. 4,5;
Jer 30:3;
Ezek 11:17

16   Thus says the LORD,
     "Restrain your voice from weeping,
     And your eyes from tears;
     For your work shall be rewarded," declares the LORD,
     "And they shall return from the land of the enemy.

31:17
Jer 29:11

17   "And there is hope for your future," declares the LORD,
     "And *your* children shall return to their own territory.

31:18
Job 5:17;
Ps 94:12;
Hos 4:16;
Ps 80:3,7,19;
Jer 17:14;
Acts 3:26

18   "I have surely heard Ephraim grieving,
     'Thou hast chastised me, and I was chastised,
     Like an untrained calf;
     Bring me back that I may be restored,
     For Thou art the LORD my God.

31:19
Ezek 36:31;
Zech 12:10;
Ezek 21:12;
Jer 3:25;
Ps 25:7;
Jer 22:21

19   'For after I turned back, I repented;
     And after I was instructed, I smote on *my* thigh;
     I was ashamed, and also humiliated,
     Because I bore the reproach of my youth.'

31:20
Hos 11:8;
Gen 43:30;
Is 63:15;
55:7;
Hos 14:4

20   "Is Ephraim My dear son?
     Is he a delightful child?
     Indeed, as often as I have spoken against him,
     I certainly *still* remember him;
     Therefore My heart yearns for him;
     I will surely have mercy on him," declares the LORD.

31:21
Jer 6:16;
50:5;
Is 48:20; v. 4

21   "Set up for yourself roadmarks,
     Place for yourself guideposts;
     Direct your mind to the highway,
     The way by which you went.
     Return, O virgin of Israel,
     Return to these your cities.

31:22
Jer 2:18,23,
36; 49:4

22   "How long will you go here and there,
     O faithless daughter?
     For the LORD has created a new thing in the earth—
     A woman will encompass a man."

31:23
Jer 30:18;
32:44;
Is 1:26;
Jer 50:7;
Zech 8:3

23   Thus says the LORD of hosts, the God of Israel, "Once again they will speak
     this word in the land of Judah and in its cities, when I restore their fortunes,
     'The LORD bless you, O abode of righteousness,
        O holy hill!'

31:24
Jer 33:12,13

24   "And Judah and all its cities will dwell together in it, the farmer and they who
     go about with flocks.

31:25
Matt 5:6

25   "For I satisfy the weary ones and refresh everyone who languishes."

31:27
Ezek 36:9-11;
Hos 2:23

26   At this I awoke and looked, and my sleep was pleasant to me.

27   "Behold, days are coming," declares the LORD, "when I will sow the house of
     Israel and the house of Judah with the seed of man and with the seed of beast.

31:28
Jer 44:27;
1:10

28   "And it will come about that as I have watched over them to pluck up, to

---

31:15 The mother of Joseph (and thus of the tribes of
Ephraim and Manasseh) and Benjamin is depicted weeping
because her children are taken into exile. Verses 16 and 17
are filled with a promise of their return, however. The
northern kingdom, which fell to Assyria in 722 B.C., was in
large measure descended from Rachel. The words are also
applied to the horrors of Herod's massacre of male children
near Bethlehem (Matt. 2:17,18).

break down, to overthrow, to destroy, and to bring disaster, so I will watch over them to build and to plant," declares the LORD.

29   "In those days they will not say again,
       'The fathers have eaten sour grapes,
       And the children's teeth are set on edge.'

30 "But everyone will die for his own iniquity; each man who eats the sour grapes, his teeth will be set on edge.

31 "Behold, days are coming," declares the LORD, "when I will make a new covenant with the house of Israel and with the house of Judah,

32   not like the covenant which I made with their fathers in the day I took them by the hand to bring them out of the land of Egypt, My covenant which they broke, although I was a husband to them," declares the LORD.

33 "But this is the covenant which I will make with the house of Israel after those days," declares the LORD, "I will put My law within them, and on their heart I will write it; and I will be their God, and they shall be My people.

34 "And they shall not teach again, each man his neighbor and each man his brother, saying, 'Know the LORD,' for they shall all know Me, from the least of them to the greatest of them," declares the LORD, "for I will forgive their iniquity, and their sin I will remember no more."

35   Thus says the LORD,
       Who gives the sun for light by day,
       And the fixed order of the moon and the stars for light by night,
       Who stirs up the sea so that its waves roar;
       The LORD of hosts is His name:

36   "If this fixed order departs
       From before Me," declares the LORD,
       "Then the offspring of Israel also shall cease
       From being a nation before Me forever."

37   Thus says the LORD,
       "If the heavens above can be measured,
       And the foundations of the earth searched out below,
       Then I will also cast off all the offspring of Israel
       For all that they have done," declares the LORD.

38 "Behold, days are coming," declares the LORD, "when the city shall be rebuilt for the LORD from the Tower of Hananel to the Corner Gate.

39 "And the measuring line shall go out farther straight ahead to the hill Gareb; then it will turn to Goah.

40 "And the whole valley of the dead bodies and of the ashes, and all the fields as far as the brook Kidron, to the corner of the Horse Gate toward the east, shall be holy to the LORD; it shall not be plucked up, or overthrown anymore forever."

2. Sermon IV: the glorious restoration of Israel after the captivity

a. Jeremiah's land purchase a sign of restoration to the land

32 The word that came to Jeremiah from the LORD in the tenth year of Zedekiah king of Judah, which was the eighteenth year of Nebuchadnezzar.

2   Now at that time the army of the king of Babylon was besieging Jerusalem, and Jeremiah the prophet was shut up in the court of the guard, which was in the house of the king of Judah,

3   because Zedekiah king of Judah had shut him up, saying, "Why do you prophesy, saying, 'Thus says the LORD, "Behold, I am about to give this city into the hand of the king of Babylon, and he will take it;

4   and Zedekiah king of Judah shall not escape out of the hand of the Chaldeans, but he shall surely be given into the hand of the king of Babylon, and he shall speak with him face to face, and see him eye to eye;

5   and he shall take Zedekiah to Babylon, and he shall be there until I visit him," declares the LORD. "If you fight against the Chaldeans, you shall not succeed" ' ? "

6   And Jeremiah said, "The word of the LORD came to me, saying,

---

Cross-references (margin):

31:29 Ezek 18:2

31:30 Deut 24:16; Ezek 18:4,20; Gal 6:5,7

*31:31 Jer 32:40; Ezek 37:26; Heb 8:8-12

31:32 Ex 19:5; 24:6-8; Deut 1:31; Jer 11:7,8; 3:14

31:33 Jer 32:40; 24:7; 32:38

31:34 1 Thess 4:9; Is 54:13; John 6:45; Mic 7:18; Rom 11:27

31:35 Gen 1:16; Ps 19:1-6; Jer 10:16

31:36 Is 54:9,10; Jer 33:20; Amos 9:8,9

31:37 Jer 33:22-26

31:38 Neh 3:1; Zech 14:10; 2 Kin 14:13

31:40 Jer 7:32; 2 Sam 15:23; 2 Kin 23:6; Joel 3:17

32:1 2 Kin 25:1,2; Jer 39:1; 25:1

32:2 Neh 3:25; Jer 37:21; 39:14

32:3 2 Kin 6:31, 32; Jer 26:8, 9; 34:2,3

32:4 Jer 38:18,23; 39:5

32:5 Jer 39:7; 27:22; 34:4,5; 21:4

31:31 Jeremiah here speaks of a *new covenant*. Reference is made to this in Rom. 11:26–36 and Heb. 8:8–12. The contrast here is between the tables of the law written on stones and the law of God written in the hearts of men. It is "new," not in the sense that it has no continuity with the past, but rather in that the graciousness of God would then be fully revealed, bestowing on man what he could not earn by his own effort or good works.

32:7
Jer 1:1;
Lev 25:25;
Ruth 4:4

7 'Behold, Hanamel the son of Shallum your uncle is coming to you, saying, "Buy for yourself my field which is at Anathoth, for you have the right of redemption to buy it." '

32:8
vv. 2,7,25

8 "Then Hanamel my uncle's son came to me in the court of the guard according to the word of the LORD, and said to me, 'Buy my field, please, that is at Anathoth, which is in the land of Benjamin; for you have the right of possession and the redemption is yours; buy it for yourself.' Then I knew that this was the word of the LORD.

*32:9
Gen 23:16;
24:22;
Ex 21:32

9 "And I bought the field which was at Anathoth from Hanamel my uncle's son, and I weighed out the silver for him, seventeen shekels of silver.

32:10
Ruth 4:1,9

10 "And I signed and sealed the deed, and called in witnesses, and weighed out the silver on the scales.

32:11
Luke 2:27

11 "Then I took the deeds of purchase, both the sealed *copy containing* the terms and conditions, and the open *copy;*

32:12
Jer 36:4;
51:59

12 and I gave the deed of purchase to Baruch the son of Neriah, the son of Mahseiah, in the sight of Hanamel my uncle's *son*, and in the sight of the witnesses who signed the deed of purchase, before all the Jews who were sitting in the court of the guard.

13 "And I commanded Baruch in their presence, saying,

*32:14
vv. 10-12

14 'Thus says the LORD of hosts, the God of Israel, "Take these deeds, this sealed deed of purchase, and this open deed, and put them in an earthenware jar, that they may last a long time."

32:15
Jer 33:12,13;
Zech 3:10

15 'For thus says the LORD of hosts, the God of Israel, "Houses and fields and vineyards shall again be bought in this land." '

16 "After I had given the deed of purchase to Baruch the son of Neriah, then I prayed to the LORD, saying,

32:17
Jer 1:6; 4:10;
2 Kin 19:15;
Is 40:26-28

17 'Ah Lord GOD! Behold, Thou hast made the heavens and the earth by Thy great power and by Thine outstretched arm! Nothing is too difficult for Thee,

32:18
Ex 34:7;
Jer 20:11;
10:16

18 who showest lovingkindness to thousands, but repayest the iniquity of fathers into the bosom of their children after them, O great and mighty God. The LORD of hosts is His name;

*32:19
Is 28:29;
Jer 16:17;
17:10

19 great in counsel and mighty in deed, whose eyes are open to all the ways of the sons of men, giving to everyone according to his ways and according to the fruit of his deeds;

32:20
Ex 9:16;
Dan 9:15

20 who hast set signs and wonders in the land of Egypt, *and* even to this day both in Israel and among mankind; and Thou hast made a name for Thyself, as at this day.

32:21
Ex 6:6;
1 Chr 17:21

21 'And Thou didst bring Thy people Israel out of the land of Egypt with signs and with wonders, and with a strong hand and with an outstretched arm, and with great terror;

32:22
Ex 3:8,17;
Jer 11:5

22 and gavest them this land, which Thou didst swear to their forefathers to give them, a land flowing with milk and honey.

32:23
Jer 2:7; 26:4;
44:10;
Neh 9:26;
Jer 11:8;
Dan 9:10-14

23 'And they came in and took possession of it, but they did not obey Thy voice or walk in Thy law; they have done nothing of all that Thou commandedst them to do; therefore Thou hast made all this calamity come upon them.

32:24
Jer 33:4;
Ezek 14:21;
Deut 4:26;
Zech 1:6

24 'Behold, the siege mounds have reached the city to take it; and the city is given into the hand of the Chaldeans who fight against it, because of the sword, the famine, and the pestilence; and what Thou hast spoken has come to pass; and, behold, Thou seest it.

32:25
vv. 8,24

25 'And Thou hast said to me, O Lord GOD, "Buy for yourself the field with money, and call in witnesses"—although the city is given into the hand of the Chaldeans.' "

26 Then the word of the LORD came to Jeremiah, saying,

32:6,9 Somehow the Holy Spirit conveyed to Jeremiah the will of God. *For all who are being led by the Spirit of God, these are the sons of God* (Rom. 8:14), then as now. But it is important to observe that the spoken word of 32:7 was confirmed by circumstances in 32:8: *Then I knew that this was the word of the LORD.* The purchase of the field by Jeremiah was simply a token from God that there would be a restoration of that land after the captivity.
32:14 *an earthenware jar.* This served as a safe deposit box. The Dead Sea Scrolls from Qumran were preserved in large jars for two thousand years.

32:19 God is sovereign over His universe. His purposes do not change and His counsels are true. Of His purposes and counsels Scripture says: (1) they are wise and wonderful (Is. 28:29); (2) they are great (32:19); (3) they are immutable or unchangeable (Heb. 6:17); (4) they are eternal (Eph. 3:11); and (5) they cannot be disannulled (Is. 14:27). Furthermore, the counsels and purposes of God: (1) are not understood by evil men (Mic. 4:12); and (2) are rejected by unregenerate men, even those of a religious profession (Luke 7:30).

27 "Behold, I am the LORD, the God of all flesh; is anything too difficult for Me?"

28 Therefore thus says the LORD, "Behold, I am about to give this city into the hand of the Chaldeans and into the hand of Nebuchadnezzar king of Babylon, and he shall take it.

29 "And the Chaldeans who are fighting against this city shall enter and set this city on fire and burn it, with the houses where *people* have offered incense to Baal on their roofs and poured out libations to other gods to provoke Me to anger.

30 "Indeed the sons of Israel and the sons of Judah have been doing only evil in My sight from their youth; for the sons of Israel have been only provoking Me to anger by the work of their hands," declares the LORD.

31 "Indeed this city has been to Me *a provocation of* My anger and My wrath from the day that they built it, even to this day, that it should be removed from before My face,

32 because of all the evil of the sons of Israel and the sons of Judah, which they have done to provoke Me to anger—they, their kings, their leaders, their priests, their prophets, the men of Judah, and the inhabitants of Jerusalem.

33 "And they have turned *their* back to Me, and not *their* face; though *I* taught them, teaching again and again, they would not listen and receive instruction.

34 "But they put their detestable things in the house which is called by My name, to defile it.

35 "And they built the high places of Baal that are in the valley of Ben-hinnom to cause their sons and their daughters to pass through *the fire* to Molech, which I had not commanded them nor had it entered My mind that they should do this abomination, to cause Judah to sin.

36 "Now therefore thus says the LORD God of Israel concerning this city of which you say, 'It is given into the hand of the king of Babylon by sword, by famine, and by pestilence.'

37 "Behold, I will gather them out of all the lands to which I have driven them in My anger, in My wrath, and in great indignation; and I will bring them back to this place and make them dwell in safety.

38 "And they shall be My people, and I will be their God;

39 and I will give them one heart and one way, that they may fear Me always, for their own good, and for *the good of* their children after them.

40 "And I will make an everlasting covenant with them that I will not turn away from them, to do them good; and I will put the fear of Me in their hearts so that they will not turn away from Me.

41 "And I will rejoice over them to do them good, and I will faithfully plant them in this land with all My heart and with all My soul.

42 "For thus says the LORD, 'Just as I brought all this great disaster on this people, so I am going to bring on them all the good that I am promising them.

43 'And fields shall be bought in this land of which you say, "It is a desolation, without man or beast; it is given into the hand of the Chaldeans."

44 'Men shall buy fields for money, sign and seal deeds, and call in witnesses in the land of Benjamin, in the environs of Jerusalem, in the cities of Judah, in the cities of the hill country, in the cities of the lowland, and in the cities of the [9]Negev; for I will restore their fortunes,' declares the LORD."

b. *Beyond the exile: restoration of Jerusalem under the righteous Branch*

33 Then the word of the LORD came to Jeremiah the second time, while he was still confined in the court of the guard, saying,

2 "Thus says the LORD who made *the earth*, the LORD who formed it to establish it, the LORD is His name,

3 'Call to Me, and I will answer you, and I will tell you great and mighty things, which you do not know.'

4 "For thus says the LORD God of Israel concerning the houses of this city, and concerning the houses of the kings of Judah, which are broken down *to make a defense* against the siege mounds and against the sword,

5 'While *they* are coming to fight with the Chaldeans, and to fill them with the corpses of men whom I have slain in My anger and in My wrath, and I have hidden My face from this city because of all their wickedness:

[9]I.e., South country

32:27
Num 16:22

32:28
Jer 34:2,3

32:29
Jer 21:10;
37:8,10;
52:13; 19:13

32:30
Jer 2:7;
22:21; 25:7

32:31
2 Kin 23:27;
24:3

32:32
Is 1:4-6;
Dan 9:8

32:33
Jer 2:27;
Ezek 8:16;
Jer 35:15

32:34
Jer 7:30,31;
Ezek 8:5,6

32:35
Jer 7:31;
19:5;
Lev 18:21;
1 Kin 11:33

32:37
Deut 30:3;
Jer 23:3,6;
Zech 14:11

32:38
Jer 30:22;
31:33

32:39
Jer 24:7;
Ezek 11:19,
20; 37:25

32:40
Is 55:3;
31:31,33;
Ezek 39:29

32:41
Deut 30:9;
Zeph 3:17;
Amos 9:15

32:42
Jer 31:28;
Zech 8:14,15;
Jer 33:14

32:43
vv. 15,25

32:44
Jer 17:26;
33:7,11,26

33:1
Jer 32:2,3

33:2
Jer 10:16;
51:19;
Ex 15:3

33:3
Ps 50:15;
Jer 29:12;
32:17,27;
Is 48:6

33:4
Jer 32:13,14,
24

33:5
Is 8:17;
Jer 21:10

33:6
Is 66:12;
Gal 5:22,23
33:7
Jer 32:44;
Amos 9:14,15
33:8
Mic 7:18;
Zech 13:1;
Heb 9:13,14

33:9
Is 62:7;
Jer 13:11;
Is 60:5

33:10
Jer 32:43;
26:9; 34:22

33:11
Is 35:10;
51:3,11;
1 Chr 16:8,
34;
2 Chr 5:13;
Lev 7:12

33:12
Is 65:10;
Ezek 34:12-14

33:13
Jer 17:26;
Lev 27:32;
Luke 15:4

33:14
Jer 23:5;
Ezek 34:23-25
33:15
Is 4:2; 11:1;
Zech 3:8;
Ps 72:1-5
33:16
Jer 23:6;
Is 45:24,25;
Phil 3:9
33:17
2 Sam 7:16;
1 Kin 2:4;
Luke 1:32,33
33:18
Deut 18:1;
24:8;
Heb 13:15
33:20
Ps 89:37;
Is 54:9;
Jer 31:36
33:21
Ps 89:34
33:22
Gen 15:5;
22:17;
Jer 30:19
33:24
Neh 4:2-4;
Ezek 36:2

33:25
Ps 74:16,17;
Jer 31:35,36
33:26
Jer 31:37;
Is 14:1;
Hos 1:7; 2:23

6 'Behold, I will bring to it health and healing, and I will heal them; and I will reveal to them an abundance of peace and truth.

7 'And I will restore the fortunes of Judah and the fortunes of Israel, and I will rebuild them as they were at first.

8 'And I will cleanse them from all their iniquity by which they have sinned against Me, and I will pardon all their iniquities by which they have sinned against Me, and by which they have transgressed against Me.

9 'And [10]it shall be to Me a name of joy, praise, and glory before all the nations of the earth, which shall hear of all the good that I do for them, and they shall fear and tremble because of all the good and all the peace that I make for it.'

10 "Thus says the LORD, 'Yet again there shall be heard in this place, of which you say, "It is a waste, without man and without beast," *that is,* in the cities of Judah and in the streets of Jerusalem that are desolate, without man and without inhabitant and without beast,

11 the voice of joy and the voice of gladness, the voice of the bridegroom and the voice of the bride, the voice of those who say,

"Give thanks to the LORD of hosts,
For the LORD is good,
For His lovingkindness is everlasting";

and of those who bring a thank offering into the house of the LORD. For I will restore the fortunes of the land as they were at first,' says the LORD.

12 "Thus says the LORD of hosts, 'There shall again be in this place which is waste, without man or beast, and in all its cities, a habitation of shepherds who rest their flocks.

13 'In the cities of the hill country, in the cities of the lowland, in the cities of the Negev, in the land of Benjamin, in the environs of Jerusalem, and in the cities of Judah, the flocks shall again pass under the hands of the one who numbers them,' says the LORD.

14 'Behold, days are coming,' declares the LORD, 'when I will fulfill the good word which I have spoken concerning the house of Israel and the house of Judah.

15 'In those days and at that time I will cause a righteous Branch of David to spring forth; and He shall execute justice and righteousness on the earth.

16 'In those days Judah shall be saved, and Jerusalem shall dwell in safety; and this is *the name* by which she shall be called: the LORD is our righteousness.'

17 "For thus says the LORD, 'David shall never lack a man to sit on the throne of the house of Israel;

18 and the Levitical priests shall never lack a man before Me to offer burnt offerings, to burn grain offerings, and to prepare sacrifices continually.' "

19 And the word of the LORD came to Jeremiah, saying,

20 "Thus says the LORD, 'If you can break My covenant for the day, and My covenant for the night, so that day and night will not be at their appointed time,

21 then My covenant may also be broken with David My servant that he shall not have a son to reign on his throne, and with the Levitical priests, My ministers.

22 'As the host of heaven cannot be counted, and the sand of the sea cannot be measured, so I will multiply the descendants of David My servant and the Levites who minister to Me.' "

23 And the word of the LORD came to Jeremiah, saying,

24 "Have you not observed what this people have spoken, saying, 'The two families which the LORD chose, He has rejected them'? Thus they despise My people, no longer are they as a nation in their sight.

25 "Thus says the LORD, 'If My covenant *for* day and night *stand* not, *and* the fixed patterns of heaven and earth I have not established,

26 then I would reject the descendants of Jacob and David My servant, not taking from his descendants rulers over the descendants of Abraham, Isaac, and Jacob. But I will restore their fortunes and will have mercy on them.' "

---

[10]I.e., this city

33:17 *David shall never lack a man,* i.e., the Davidic dynasty shall be permanent. (See footnote on the Davidic covenant, 2 Sam. 7:4.) It does not necessarily imply that there would always be an occupant on the throne of David, but only that the Davidic line would never die out, and that the descendants of David would never be permanently cut off from royal authority in the Holy Land. So understood, the Davidic covenant allowed for a temporary discontinuance of effective royal authority on the part of his dynasty, but at the same time it did guarantee that his posterity would ultimately exercise permanent and enduring sovereignty. At the annunciation to the Virgin Mary, the angel made it clear that Jesus Christ was the fulfillment of this covenant promise (Luke 1:32).

C. *Encounters between Jeremiah and the kings of Judah*

1. *Zedekiah condemned for breaking his promise to slaves*

34 The word which came to Jeremiah from the LORD, when Nebuchadnezzar king of Babylon and all his army, with all the kingdoms of the earth that were under his dominion and all the peoples, were fighting against Jerusalem and against all its cities, saying,

2 "Thus says the LORD God of Israel, 'Go and speak to Zedekiah king of Judah and say to him: "Thus says the LORD, 'Behold, I am giving this city into the hand of the king of Babylon, and he will burn it with fire.

3 'And you will not escape from his hand, for you will surely be captured and delivered into his hand; and you will see the king of Babylon eye to eye, and he will speak with you face to face, and you will go to Babylon.' " '

4 "Yet hear the word of the LORD, O Zedekiah king of Judah! Thus says the LORD concerning you, 'You will not die by the sword.

5 'You will die in peace; and as spices were burned for your fathers, the former kings who were before you, so they will burn spices for you; and they will lament for you, "Alas, lord!" ' For I have spoken the word," declares the LORD.

6 Then Jeremiah the prophet spoke all these words to Zedekiah king of Judah in Jerusalem

7 when the army of the king of Babylon was fighting against Jerusalem and against all the remaining cities of Judah, *that is*, Lachish and Azekah, for they *alone* remained as fortified cities among the cities of Judah.

8 The word which came to Jeremiah from the LORD, after King Zedekiah had made a covenant with all the people who were in Jerusalem to proclaim release to them:

9 that each man should set free his male servant and each man his female servant, a Hebrew man or a Hebrew woman; so that no one should keep them, a Jew his brother, in bondage.

10 And all the officials and all the people obeyed, who had entered into the covenant that each man should set free his male servant and each man his female servant, so that no one should keep them any longer in bondage; they obeyed, and set *them free*.

11 But afterward they turned around and took back the male servants and the female servants, whom they had set free, and brought them into subjection for male servants and for female servants.

12 Then the word of the LORD came to Jeremiah from the LORD, saying,

13 "Thus says the LORD God of Israel, 'I made a covenant with your forefathers in the day that I brought them out of the land of Egypt, from the house of bondage, saying,

14 "At the end of seven years each of you shall set free his Hebrew brother, who has been sold to you and has served you six years, you shall send him out free from you; but your forefathers did not obey Me, or incline their ear to Me.

15 "Although recently you *had* turned and done what is right in My sight, each man proclaiming release to his neighbor, and you had made a covenant before Me in the house which is called by My name.

16 "Yet you turned and profaned My name, and each man took back his male servant and each man his female servant, whom you had set free according to their desire, and you brought them into subjection to be your male servants and female servants." '

17 "Therefore thus says the LORD, 'You have not obeyed Me in proclaiming release each man to his brother, and each man to his neighbor. Behold, I am proclaiming a release to you,' declares the LORD, 'to the sword, to the pestilence, and to the famine; and I will make you a terror to all the kingdoms of the earth.

18 'And I will give the men who have transgressed My covenant, who have not fulfilled the words of the covenant which they made before Me, *when* they cut the calf in two and passed between its parts—

19 the officials of Judah, and the officials of Jerusalem, the court officers, and the priests, and all the people of the land, who passed between the parts of the calf—

20 and I will give them into the hand of their enemies and into the hand of those who seek their life. And their dead bodies shall be food for the birds of the sky and the beasts of the earth.

21 'And Zedekiah king of Judah and his officials I will give into the hand of their

34:1
2 Kin 25:1ff;
Jer 39:1;
1:15;
Dan 2:37,38

34:2
Jer 22:1,2;
37:1-4;
Jer 32:29

34:3
Jer 32:4;
2 Kin 25:6,7;
Jer 39:6,7

34:5
2 Chr 16:14;
21:19;
Jer 22:18

34:7
2 Chr 11:9;
2 Kin 18:13;
19:8

34:8
Ex 21:2;
Lev 25:10

34:9
Neh 5:11;
Lev 25:39-46

34:11
v. 21;
Jer 37:5;
Hos 6:4

34:13
Ex 24:3,7,8;
Deut 15:22

34:14
Ex 21:2;
23:10;
Deut 15:12;
1 Sam 8:7,8;
2 Kin 17:13,
14
34:15
2 Kin 23:3;
Neh 10:29;
Jer 7:10,11;
32:34
34:16
Ex 20:7;
Lev 19:12
34:17
Matt 7:2;
Gal 6:7;
Deut 28:25,
64

34:18
Deut 17:2;
Hos 6:7;
Gen 15:10,17

34:19
v. 10

34:20
Jer 11:21;
7:33; 19:7

34:21
Jer 37:5,11

enemies, and into the hand of those who seek their life, and into the hand of the army of the king of Babylon which has gone away from you.

22   'Behold, I am going to command,' declares the LORD, 'and I will bring them back to this city; and they shall fight against it and take it and burn it with fire; and I will make the cities of Judah a desolation without inhabitant.' "

2. The faithfulness of the Rechabites
emphasizes the guilt of Judah

35 The word which came to Jeremiah from the LORD in the days of Jehoiakim the son of Josiah, king of Judah, saying,

2   "Go to the house of the Rechabites, and speak to them, and bring them into the house of the LORD, into one of the chambers, and give them wine to drink."

3   Then I took Jaazaniah the son of Jeremiah, son of Habazziniah, and his brothers, and all his sons, and the whole house of the Rechabites,

4   and I brought them into the house of the LORD, into the chamber of the sons of Hanan the son of Igdaliah, the man of God, which was near the chamber of the officials, which was above the chamber of Maaseiah the son of Shallum, the doorkeeper.

5   Then I set before the men of the house of the Rechabites pitchers full of wine, and cups; and I said to them, "Drink wine!"

6   But they said, "We will not drink wine, for Jonadab the son of Rechab, our father, commanded us, saying, 'You shall not drink wine, you or your sons, forever.

7   'And you shall not build a house, and you shall not sow seed, and you shall not plant a vineyard or own one; but in tents you shall dwell all your days, that you may live many days in the land where you sojourn.'

8   "And we have obeyed the voice of Jonadab the son of Rechab, our father, in all that he commanded us, not to drink wine all our days, we, our wives, our sons, or our daughters,

9   nor to build ourselves houses to dwell in; and we do not have vineyard or field or seed.

10   "We have only dwelt in tents, and have obeyed, and have done according to all that Jonadab our father commanded us.

11   "But it came about, when Nebuchadnezzar king of Babylon came up against the land, that we said, 'Come and let us go to Jerusalem before the army of the Chaldeans and before the army of the Arameans.' So we have dwelt in Jerusalem."

12   Then the word of the LORD came to Jeremiah, saying,

13   "Thus says the LORD of hosts, the God of Israel, 'Go and say to the men of Judah and the inhabitants of Jerusalem, "Will you not receive instruction by listening to My words?" declares the LORD.

14   "The words of Jonadab the son of Rechab, which he commanded his sons not to drink wine, are observed. So they do not drink *wine* to this day, for they have obeyed their father's command. But I have spoken to you again and again; yet you have not listened to Me.

15   "Also I have sent to you all My servants the prophets, sending *them* again and again, saying: 'Turn now every man from his evil way, and amend your deeds, and do not go after other gods to worship them, then you shall dwell in the land which I have given to you and to your forefathers; but you have not inclined your ear or listened to Me.

16   'Indeed, the sons of Jonadab the son of Rechab have observed the command of their father which he commanded them, but this people has not listened to Me.' " '

17   "Therefore thus says the LORD, the God of hosts, the God of Israel, 'Behold, I am bringing on Judah and on all the inhabitants of Jerusalem all the disaster that I have pronounced against them; because I spoke to them but they did not listen, and I have called them but they did not answer.' "

18   Then Jeremiah said to the house of the Rechabites, "Thus says the LORD of hosts, the God of Israel, 'Because you have obeyed the command of Jonadab your father, kept all his commands, and done according to all that he commanded you;

19   therefore thus says the LORD of hosts, the God of Israel, "Jonadab the son of Rechab shall not lack a man to stand before Me always." ' "

Cross references (margin):

34:22
Jer 37:8,10;
4:7; 33:10;
44:22

35:1
2 Kin 24:1;
Jer 1:3; 27:20
*35:2
2 Kin 10:15;
1 Chr 2:55;
1 Kin 6:5

35:4
Deut 33:1;
1 Kin 12:22;
2 Kin 12:9;
25:18;
1 Chr 9:18,19
35:5
Amos 2:12

35:6
2 Kin 10:15;
1 Chr 2:55;
Lev 10:9;
Luke 1:15
35:7
Gen 25:27;
Heb 11:9;
Ex 20:12;
Eph 6:2,3
35:8
Prov 1:8,9;
Eph 6:1;
Col 3:20
35:9
v. 7
35:10
vv. 6,7

35:11
2 Kin 24:1,2;
Jer 4:5-7;
8:14

35:13
Is 28:9-12;
Jer 32:33

35:14
2 Chr 36:15;
Jer 7:13;
25:3; Is 30:9;
50:2

35:15
Jer 26:5;
32:33;
Is 1:16,17;
Jer 4:1;
18:11; 7:6;
13:10; 22:4;
34:14
35:16
v. 14

35:17
Jer 19:3,15;
Mic 3:12;
Prov 1:24;
Is 65:12;
66:4; Jer 7:13

35:19
Jer 33:17;
15:19

35:2 *Rechabites.* A nomadic tribe of Kenite descent that refused to take part in urban culture and vowed not to drink   intoxicating beverages.

3. Jehoiakim's arrogance in burning the scroll; the scroll rewritten

36 And it came about in the fourth year of Jehoiakim the son of Josiah, king of Judah, that this word came to Jeremiah from the LORD, saying,

2 "Take a scroll and write on it all the words which I have spoken to you concerning Israel, and concerning Judah, and concerning all the nations, from the day I *first* spoke to you, from the days of Josiah, even to this day.

3 "Perhaps the house of Judah will hear all the calamity which I plan to bring on them, in order that every man will turn from his evil way; then I will forgive their iniquity and their sin."

4 Then Jeremiah called Baruch the son of Neriah, and Baruch wrote at the dictation of Jeremiah all the words of the LORD, which He had spoken to him, on a scroll.

5 And Jeremiah commanded Baruch, saying, "I am restricted; I cannot go into the house of the LORD.

6 "So you go and read from the scroll which you have written at my dictation the words of the LORD to the people in the LORD's house on a fast day. And also you shall read them to all *the people of* Judah who come from their cities.

7 "Perhaps their supplication will come before the LORD, and everyone will turn from his evil way, for great is the anger and the wrath that the LORD has pronounced against this people."

8 And Baruch the son of Neriah did according to all that Jeremiah the prophet commanded him, reading from the book the words of the LORD in the LORD's house.

9 Now it came about in the fifth year of Jehoiakim the son of Josiah, king of Judah, in the ninth month, that all the people in Jerusalem and all the people who came from the cities of Judah to Jerusalem proclaimed a fast before the LORD.

10 Then Baruch read from the book the words of Jeremiah in the house of the LORD in the chamber of Gemariah the son of Shaphan the scribe, in the upper court, at the entry of the New Gate of the LORD's house, to all the people.

11 Now when Micaiah the son of Gemariah, the son of Shaphan, had heard all the words of the LORD from the book,

12 he went down to the king's house, into the scribe's chamber. And, behold, all the officials were sitting there—Elishama the scribe, and Delaiah the son of Shemaiah, and Elnathan the son of Achbor, and Gemariah the son of Shaphan, and Zedekiah the son of Hananiah, and all the *other* officials.

13 And Micaiah declared to them all the words that he had heard, when Baruch read from the book to the people.

14 Then all the officials sent Jehudi the son of Nethaniah, the son of Shelemiah, the son of Cushi, to Baruch, saying, "Take in your hand the scroll from which you have read to the people and come." So Baruch the son of Neriah took the scroll in his hand and went to them.

15 And they said to him, "Sit down please, and read it to us." So Baruch read it to them.

16 Now it came about when they had heard all the words, they turned in fear one to another and said to Baruch, "We will surely report all these words to the king."

17 And they asked Baruch, saying, "Tell us please, how did you write all these words? *Was it* at his dictation?"

18 Then Baruch said to them, "He dictated all these words to me, and I wrote them with ink on the book."

19 Then the officials said to Baruch, "Go, hide yourself, you and Jeremiah, and do not let anyone know where you are."

20 So they went to the king in the court, but they had deposited the scroll in the chamber of Elishama the scribe, and they reported all the words to the king.

21 Then the king sent Jehudi to get the scroll, and he took it out of the chamber of Elishama the scribe. And Jehudi read it to the king as well as to all the officials who stood beside the king.

22 Now the king was sitting in the winter house in the ninth month, with *a fire* burning in the brazier before him.

23 And it came about, when Jehudi had read three or four columns, *the king* cut it with a scribe's knife and threw *it* into the fire that was in the brazier, until all the scroll was consumed in the fire that was in the brazier.

36:1
2 Kin 24:1;
Jer 25:1,3
36:2
vv. 6,23,28;
Zech 5:1;
Jer 1:9,10;
25:9-29; 25:3
36:3
v. 7; Jer 26:3;
Is 55:7;
Jer 18:8;
Jon 3:8;
Mark 4:12;
Acts 3:19
36:4
v. 18;
Jer 32:12;
v. 14;
Ezek 2:9
36:5
Jer 32:2; 33:1

36:7
2 Kin 22:13;
Jer 4:4; 21:5

36:8
v. 6

36:9
v. 6;
Esth 4:16;
Jon 3:5
36:10
Jer 26:10

36:11
v. 13

36:12
vv. 20,25;
Jer 26:22

36:13
2 Kin 22:10;
36:14; v. 21

36:15
v. 21

36:16
v. 24;
Acts 24:25;
Jer 13:18;
Amos 7:10,11

36:18
v. 4

36:19
v. 26;
Jer 26:20-24
36:20
v. 12

36:21
v. 14;
2 Chr 34:18

36:22
Amos 3:15

36:23
v. 29

24   Yet the king and all his servants who heard all these words were not afraid, nor did they rend their garments.

25   Even though Elnathan and Delaiah and Gemariah entreated the king not to burn the scroll, he would not listen to them.

26   And the king commanded Jerahmeel the king's son, Seraiah the son of Azriel, and Shelemiah the son of Abdeel to seize Baruch the scribe and Jeremiah the prophet, but the LORD hid them.

27   Then the word of the LORD came to Jeremiah after the king had burned the scroll and the words which Baruch had written at the dictation of Jeremiah, saying,

28   "Take again another scroll and write on it all the former words that were on the first scroll which Jehoiakim the king of Judah burned.

29   "And concerning Jehoiakim king of Judah you shall say, 'Thus says the LORD, "You have burned this scroll, saying, 'Why have you written on it that the king of Babylon shall certainly come and destroy this land, and shall make man and beast to cease from it?' "

30   'Therefore thus says the LORD concerning Jehoiakim king of Judah, "He shall have no one to sit on the throne of David, and his dead body shall be cast out to the heat of the day and the frost of the night.

31   "I shall also punish him and his descendants and his servants for their iniquity, and I shall bring on them and the inhabitants of Jerusalem and the men of Judah all the calamity that I have declared to them—but they did not listen." ' "

32   Then Jeremiah took another scroll and gave it to Baruch the son of Neriah, the scribe, and he wrote on it at the dictation of Jeremiah all the words of the book which Jehoiakim king of Judah had burned in the fire; and many similar words were added to them.

4. Jeremiah's arrest and imprisonment

37 Now Zedekiah the son of Josiah whom Nebuchadnezzar king of Babylon had made king in the land of Judah, reigned as king in place of Coniah the son of Jehoiakim.

2   But neither he nor his servants nor the people of the land listened to the words of the LORD which He spoke through Jeremiah the prophet.

3   Yet King Zedekiah sent Jehucal the son of Shelemiah, and Zephaniah the son of Maaseiah, the priest, to Jeremiah the prophet, saying, "Please pray to the LORD our God on our behalf."

4   Now Jeremiah was *still* coming in and going out among the people, for they had not *yet* put him in the prison.

5   Meanwhile, Pharaoh's army had set out from Egypt; and when the Chaldeans who had been besieging Jerusalem heard the report about them, they lifted the *siege* from Jerusalem.

6   Then the word of the LORD came to Jeremiah the prophet, saying,

7   "Thus says the LORD God of Israel, 'Thus you are to say to the king of Judah, who sent you to Me to inquire of Me: "Behold, Pharaoh's army which has come out for your assistance is going to return to its own land of Egypt.

8   "The Chaldeans will also return and fight against this city, and they will capture it and burn it with fire." '

9   "Thus says the LORD, 'Do not deceive yourselves, saying, "The Chaldeans will surely go away from us," for they will not go.

10   'For even if you had defeated the entire army of Chaldeans who were fighting against you, and there were *only* wounded men left among them, each man in his tent, they would rise up and burn this city with fire.' "

11   Now it happened, when the army of the Chaldeans had lifted *the siege* from Jerusalem because of Pharaoh's army,

12   that Jeremiah went out from Jerusalem to go to the land of Benjamin in order to take possession of *some* property there among the people.

13   While he was at the Gate of Benjamin, a captain of the guard whose name was Irijah, the son of Shelemiah the son of Hananiah was there; and he arrested Jeremiah the prophet, saying, "You are going over to the Chaldeans!"

14   But Jeremiah said, "A lie! I am not going over to the Chaldeans"; yet he would not listen to him. So Irijah arrested Jeremiah and brought him to the officials.

15   Then the officials were angry at Jeremiah and beat him, and they put him in jail in the house of Jonathan the scribe, which they had made into the prison.

16   For Jeremiah had come into the dungeon, that is, the vaulted cell; and Jeremiah stayed there many days.

17   Now King Zedekiah sent and took him *out;* and in his palace the king secretly asked him and said, "Is there a word from the LORD?" And Jeremiah said, "There is!" Then he said, "You will be given into the hand of the king of Babylon!"

18   Moreover Jeremiah said to King Zedekiah, "*In* what *way* have I sinned against you, or against your servants, or against this people, that you have put me in prison?

19   "Where then are your prophets who prophesied to you, saying, 'The king of Babylon will not come against you or against this land'?

20   "But now, please listen, O my lord the king; please let my petition come before you, and do not make me return to the house of Jonathan the scribe, that I may not die there."

21   Then King Zedekiah gave commandment, and they committed Jeremiah to the court of the guardhouse and gave him a loaf of bread daily from the bakers' street, until all the bread in the city was gone. So Jeremiah remained in the court of the guardhouse.

5. Jeremiah cast into the miry pit; rescued by Ebed-melech

38 Now Shephatiah the son of Mattan, and Gedaliah the son of Pashhur, and Jucal the son of Shelemiah, and Pashhur the son of Malchijah heard the words that Jeremiah was speaking to all the people, saying,

2   "Thus says the LORD, 'He who stays in this city will die by the sword and by famine and by pestilence, but he who goes out to the Chaldeans will live and have his *own* life as booty and stay alive.'

3   "Thus says the LORD, 'This city will certainly be given into the hand of the army of the king of Babylon, and he will capture it.' "

4   Then the officials said to the king, "Now let this man be put to death, inasmuch as he is discouraging the men of war who are left in this city and all the people, by speaking such words to them; for this man is not seeking the well-being of this people, but rather their harm."

5   So King Zedekiah said, "Behold, he is in your hands; for the king can *do* nothing against you."

6   Then they took Jeremiah and cast him into the cistern *of* Malchijah the king's son, which was in the court of the guardhouse; and they let Jeremiah down with ropes. Now in the cistern there was no water but only mud, and Jeremiah sank into the mud.

7   But Ebed-melech the Ethiopian, a eunuch, while he was in the king's palace, heard that they had put Jeremiah into the cistern. Now the king was sitting in the Gate of Benjamin;

8   and Ebed-melech went out from the king's palace and spoke to the king, saying,

9   "My lord the king, these men have acted wickedly in all that they have done to Jeremiah the prophet whom they have cast into the cistern; and he will die right where he is because of the famine, for there is no more bread in the city."

10   Then the king commanded Ebed-melech the Ethiopian, saying, "Take thirty men from here under your authority, and bring up Jeremiah the prophet from the cistern before he dies."

11   So Ebed-melech took the men under his authority and went into the king's palace to *a place* beneath the storeroom and took from there worn-out clothes and worn-out rags and let them down by ropes into the cistern to Jeremiah.

12   Then Ebed-melech the Ethiopian said to Jeremiah, "Now put these worn-out clothes and rags under your armpits under the ropes"; and Jeremiah did so.

13   So they pulled Jeremiah up with the ropes and lifted him out of the cistern, and Jeremiah stayed in the court of the guardhouse.

14   Then King Zedekiah sent and had Jeremiah the prophet brought to him at

---

37:16
Jer 38:6

37:17
Jer 38:5,
14-16,24-27

37:18
Dan 6:22;
John 10:32;
Acts 25:8,11,
25

37:19
Jer 2:28;
6:14; 29:31

37:20
Jer 36:7;
38:26; 18:23

37:21
Jer 32:3;
38:13,28;
Is 33:16;
Jer 38:9;
52:6; 39:14,
15

38:1
Jer 37:3;
21:1,8

38:2
Jer 21:9;
42:17; 45:5

38:3
Jer 21:10;
32:3

*38:4
Jer 18:23;
26:11;
1 Kin 18:17,
18; 21:20;
Amos 7:10;
Acts 16:20;
Jer 29:7

38:5
2 Sam 3:39

38:6
Jer 37:21;
Acts 16:24;
Zech 9:11

*38:7
Jer 39:16;
37:13;
Amos 5:10

38:9
Jer 37:21;
52:6

38:11
v. 6

38:13
Jer 37:21;
39:14,15

38:14
Jer 21:1,2;
37:17; 15:11;
42:2-5,20

38:4 Jeremiah appeared to his nationalistic compatriots to be guilty of treason and betrayal of the nation to Nebuchadnezzar, and for that reason his enemies sought to have him killed. Jeremiah himself knew that he was only fulfilling his God-given mission, and yet it resulted in his being cast into a vile dungeon where he sank into the mud (vv. 6,11–13). Scripture nowhere affirms that God's servants will be exempted from persecution and tribulation as a reward for their faithfulness. On the contrary, it implies that affliction and hardship may be their portion (Heb. 11:32–37). But God does promise grace and strength sufficient to triumph in adversity (2 Cor. 1:3–7; 9:8; Eph. 3:20; Phil. 4:6,7,l9).

38:7 *a eunuch.* The word may be rendered simply "an officer." Eunuchs were frequently employed in oriental courts, where some attained considerable power.

the third entrance that is in the house of the LORD; and the king said to Jeremiah, "I am going to ask you something; do not hide anything from me."

15 Then Jeremiah said to Zedekiah, "If I tell you, will you not certainly put me to death? Besides, if I give you advice, you will not listen to me."

16 But King Zedekiah swore to Jeremiah in secret saying, "As the LORD lives, who made this life for us, surely I will not put you to death nor will I give you over to the hand of these men who are seeking your life."

17 Then Jeremiah said to Zedekiah, "Thus says the LORD God of hosts, the God of Israel, 'If you will indeed go out to the officers of the king of Babylon, then you will live, this city will not be burned with fire, and you and your household will survive.

18 'But if you will not go out to the officers of the king of Babylon, then this city will be given over to the hand of the Chaldeans; and they will burn it with fire, and you yourself will not escape from their hand.' "

19 Then King Zedekiah said to Jeremiah, "I dread the Jews who have gone over to the Chaldeans, lest they give me over into their hand and they abuse me."

20 But Jeremiah said, "They will not give you over. Please obey the LORD in what I am saying to you, that it may go well with you and you may live.

21 "But if you keep refusing to go out, this is the word which the LORD has shown me:

22 'Then behold, all of the women who have been left in the palace of the king of Judah are going to be brought out to the officers of the king of Babylon; and those women will say,

"Your close friends
Have misled and overpowered you;
While your feet were sunk in the mire,
They turned back."

23 'They will also bring out all your wives and your sons to the Chaldeans, and you yourself will not escape from their hand, but will be seized by the hand of the king of Babylon, and this city will be burned with fire.' "

24 Then Zedekiah said to Jeremiah, "Let no man know about these words and you will not die.

25 "But if the officials hear that I have talked with you and come to you and say to you, 'Tell us now what you said to the king, and what the king said to you; do not hide it from us, and we will not put you to death,'

26 then you are to say to them, 'I was presenting my petition before the king, not to make me return to the house of Jonathan to die there.' "

27 Then all the officials came to Jeremiah and questioned him. So he reported to them in accordance with all these words which the king had commanded; and they ceased speaking with him, since the conversation had not been overheard.

28 So Jeremiah stayed in the court of the guardhouse until the day that Jerusalem was captured.

6. The fall of Jerusalem and the capture of Zedekiah; special blessing for Ebed-melech

39 Now it came about when Jerusalem was captured in the ninth year of Zedekiah king of Judah, in the tenth month, Nebuchadnezzar king of Babylon and all his army came to Jerusalem and laid siege to it;

2 in the eleventh year of Zedekiah, in the fourth month, in the ninth day of the month, the city wall was breached.

3 Then all the officials of the king of Babylon came in and sat down at the Middle Gate: Nergal-sar-ezer, Samgar-nebu, Sar-sekim the Rab-saris, Nergal-sar-ezer the Rab-mag, and all the rest of the officials of the king of Babylon.

4 And it came about, when Zedekiah the king of Judah and all the men of war saw them, that they fled and went out of the city at night by way of the king's garden through the gate between the two walls; and he went out toward the [1] Arabah.

5 But the army of the Chaldeans pursued them and overtook Zedekiah in the plains of Jericho; and they seized him and brought him up to Nebuchadnezzar king of Babylon at Riblah in the land of Hamath, and he passed sentence on him.

6 Then the king of Babylon slew the sons of Zedekiah before his eyes at Riblah; the king of Babylon also slew all the nobles of Judah.

[1] I.e., Jordan valley

38:15
Luke 22:67, 68
38:16
Jer 37:17; Is 57:16; Zech 12:1; vv. 4-6
38:17
Ps 80:7,14; 1 Chr 17:24; Ezek 8:4; 2 Kin 24:12; 26:27-30
38:18
Jer 27:8; 32:4; 34:3
38:19
Is 51:12,13; John 12:42; 19:12,13; Jer 39:9; 2 Chr 30:10; Neh 4:1
38:20
Jer 11:4,8; 7:23; Is 55:3
38:22
Jer 6:12; 8:10; 43:6
38:23
Jer 39:6; 41:10
38:25
vv. 4-6,27
38:26
Jer 37:15,20
38:27
1 Sam 10:15, 16; 16:2-5
38:28
Jer 37:21; 39:14
39:1
2 Kin 25:1-4; Jer 52:4-7; Ezek 24:1,2
39:2
2 Kin 25:4; Jer 52:7
39:3
Jer 38:17
39:4
2 Kin 25:4; Jer 52:7; Amos 2:14; 2 Chr 32:5
39:5
Jer 32:4; 38:18,23; Josh 4:13; 2 Kin 23:33
39:6
2 Kin 25:7; Jer 34:19-21

7 He then blinded Zedekiah's eyes and bound him in fetters of bronze to bring him to Babylon.

8 The Chaldeans also burned with fire the king's palace and the houses of the people, and they broke down the walls of Jerusalem.

9 And as for the rest of the people who were left in the city, the deserters who had gone over to him and the rest of the people who remained, Nebuzaradan the captain of the bodyguard carried *them* into exile in Babylon.

10 But some of the poorest people who had nothing, Nebuzaradan the captain of the bodyguard left behind in the land of Judah, and gave them vineyards and fields at that time.

11 Now Nebuchadnezzar king of Babylon gave orders about Jeremiah through Nebuzaradan the captain of the bodyguard, saying,

12 "Take him and look after him, and do nothing harmful to him; but rather deal with him just as he tells you."

13 So Nebuzaradan the captain of the bodyguard sent *word*, along with Nebu-shazban the Rab-saris, and Nergal-sar-ezer the Rab-mag, and all the leading officers of the king of Babylon;

14 they even sent and took Jeremiah out of the court of the guardhouse and entrusted him to Gedaliah, the son of Ahikam, the son of Shaphan, to take him home. So he stayed among the people.

15 Now the word of the LORD had come to Jeremiah while he was confined in the court of the guardhouse, saying,

16 "Go and speak to Ebed-melech the Ethiopian, saying, 'Thus says the LORD of hosts, the God of Israel, "Behold, I am about to bring My words on this city for disaster and not for prosperity; and they will take place before you on that day.

17 "But I will deliver you on that day," declares the LORD, "and you shall not be given into the hand of the men whom you dread.

18 "For I will certainly rescue you, and you will not fall by the sword; but you will have your *own* life as booty, because you have trusted in Me," declares the LORD.'"

III. Prophecies after the fall of Jerusalem (40:1–45:5)

A. Jeremiah's ministry among the remnant in Judah

1. Released by Nebuzaradan, Jeremiah lives in Mizpah with Governor Gedaliah

40 The word which came to Jeremiah from the LORD after Nebuzaradan captain of the bodyguard had released him from Ramah, when he had taken him bound in chains, among all the exiles of Jerusalem and Judah, who were being exiled to Babylon.

2 Now the captain of the bodyguard had taken Jeremiah and said to him, "The LORD your God promised this calamity against this place;

3 and the LORD has brought *it* on and done just as He promised. Because you *people* sinned against the LORD and did not listen to His voice, therefore this thing has happened to you.

4 "But now, behold, I am freeing you today from the chains which are on your hands. If you would prefer to come with me to Babylon, come *along,* and I will look after you; but if you would prefer not to come with me to Babylon, never mind. Look, the whole land is before you; go wherever it seems good and right for you to go."

5 As Jeremiah was still not going back, *he said,* "Go on back then to Gedaliah the son of Ahikam, the son of Shaphan, whom the king of Babylon has appointed over the cities of Judah, and stay with him among the people; or else go anywhere it seems right for you to go." So the captain of the bodyguard gave him a ration and a gift and let him go.

6 Then Jeremiah went to Mizpah to Gedaliah the son of Ahikam and stayed with him among the people who were left in the land.

7 Now all the commanders of the forces that were in the field, they and their men, heard that the king of Babylon had appointed Gedaliah the son of Ahikam over the land and that he had put him in charge of the men, women and children, those of the poorest of the land who had not been exiled to Babylon.

8 So they came to Gedaliah at Mizpah, along with Ishmael the son of

39:7
2 Kin 25:7;
Jer 52:11;
Ezek 12:13;
Jer 32:5
39:8
2 Kin 25:9,
10; Jer 38:18;
52:13
39:9
2 Kin 25:11,
20;
Jer 52:12-16;
24:8; 38:19
39:10
2 Kin 25:12;
Jer 52:16
39:11
Jer 1:8;
15:20,21;
Acts 24:23

39:14
Jer 38:28;
40:1-6;
2 Kin 22:12,
14;
2 Chr 34:20

39:16
Jer 38:7,12;
21:10;
Dan 9:12;
Zech 1:6
39:17
Ps 41:1,2;
50:15
39:18
Jer 21:9;
45:5;
Ps 34:22;
Jer 17:7,8

40:1
Jer 39:9,11,
14; 31:15;
Eph 6:20

40:2
Jer 22:8,9;
50:7
40:3
Deut 29:24,
25; Dan 9:11

40:4
Jer 39:11,12;
Gen 20:15

40:5
Jer 39:14;
2 Kin 25:23;
v. 4;
Jer 52:34

40:6
Jer 39:14;
Judg 20:1
40:7
2 Kin 25:23,
24; Jer 39:10;
52:16

40:8
Jer 41:1

Nethaniah, and Johanan and Jonathan the sons of Kareah, and Seraiah the son of Tanhumeth, and the sons of Ephai the Netophathite, and Jezaniah the son of the Maacathite, *both* they and their men.

40:9
2 Kin 25:24;
Jer 27:11;
38:17-20

9   Then Gedaliah the son of Ahikam, the son of Shaphan, swore to them and to their men, saying, "Do not be afraid of serving the Chaldeans; stay in the land and serve the king of Babylon, that it may go well with you.

40:10
v. 6;
Jer 35:19;
39:10; v. 12;
Jer 48:32

10   "Now as for me, behold, I am going to stay at Mizpah to stand *for you* before the Chaldeans who come to us; but as for you, gather in wine and summer fruit and oil, and put *them* in your *storage* vessels, and live in your cities that you have taken over."

40:11
Is 16:4;
1 Sam 11:1;
12:12;
Is 11:14

11   Likewise also all the Jews who were in Moab and among the sons of Ammon and in Edom, and who were in all the *other* countries, heard that the king of Babylon had left a remnant for Judah and that he had appointed over them Gedaliah the son of Ahikam, the son of Shaphan.

40:12
Jer 43:5;
v. 10

12   Then all the Jews returned from all the places to which they had been driven away and came to the land of Judah, to Gedaliah at Mizpah, and gathered in wine and summer fruit in great abundance.

40:13
v. 8

13   Now Johanan the son of Kareah and all the commanders of the forces that were in the field came to Gedaliah at Mizpah,

40:14
Jer 41:10

14   and said to him, "Are you well aware that Baalis the king of the sons of Ammon has sent Ishmael the son of Nethaniah to take your life?" But Gedaliah the son of Ahikam did not believe them.

40:15
1 Sam 26:8;
2 Sam 21:17;
Jer 42:2

15   Then Johanan the son of Kareah spoke secretly to Gedaliah in Mizpah, saying, "Let me go and kill Ishmael the son of Nethaniah, and not a man will know! Why should he take your life, so that all the Jews who are gathered to you should be scattered and the remnant of Judah perish?"

40:16
Matt 10:16

16   But Gedaliah the son of Ahikam said to Johanan the son of Kareah, "Do not do this thing, for you are telling a lie about Ishmael."

2. After murdering Gedaliah, Ishmael is routed by Johanan

41:1
2 Kin 25:25;
Jer 40:6,8,14

41 Now it came about in the seventh month that Ishmael the son of Nethaniah, the son of Elishama, of the royal family and *one* of the chief officers of the king, along with ten men, came to Mizpah to Gedaliah the son of Ahikam. While they were eating bread together there in Mizpah,

41:2
2 Kin 25:25;
Jer 40:5

2   Ishmael the son of Nethaniah and the ten men who were with him arose and struck down Gedaliah the son of Ahikam, the son of Shaphan, with the sword and put to death the one whom the king of Babylon had appointed over the land.

3   Ishmael also struck down all the Jews who were with him, *that is* with Gedaliah at Mizpah, and the Chaldeans who were found there, the men of war.

4   Now it happened on the next day after the killing of Gedaliah, when no one knew about *it*,

41:5
Gen 33:18;
Josh 18:1;
1 Kin 16:24,
29; Jer 16:6;
2 Kin 25:9
41:6
Jer 50:4

5   that eighty men came from Shechem, from Shiloh, and from Samaria with their beards shaved off and their clothes torn and their bodies gashed, having grain offerings and incense in their hands to bring to the house of the LORD.

6   Then Ishmael the son of Nethaniah went out from Mizpah to meet them, weeping as he went; and it came about as he met them that he said to them, "Come to Gedaliah the son of Ahikam!"

41:7
Is 59:7;
Ezek 22:27

7   Yet it turned out that as soon as they came inside the city, Ishmael the son of Nethaniah and the men that were with him slaughtered them, *and cast them* into the cistern.

8   But ten men who were found among them said to Ishmael, "Do not put us to death; for we have stores of wheat, barley, oil and honey hidden in the field." So he refrained and did not put them to death along with their companions.

41:9
1 Kin 15:22;
2 Chr 16:6

9   Now as for the cistern where Ishmael had cast all the corpses of the men whom he had struck down because of Gedaliah, it was the one that King Asa had made on account of Baasha, king of Israel; Ishmael the son of Nethaniah filled it with the slain.

41:10
Jer 40:11,12;
43:6; 40:7,14

10   Then Ishmael took captive all the remnant of the people who were in Mizpah, the king's daughters and all the people who were left in Mizpah, whom Nebuzaradan the captain of the bodyguard had put under the charge of Gedaliah the son of Ahikam; thus Ishmael the son of Nethaniah took them captive and proceeded to cross over to the sons of Ammon.

41:11
Jer 40:7,8,
13-16

11   But Johanan the son of Kareah and all the commanders of the forces that

were with him heard of all the evil that Ishmael the son of Nethaniah had done.

12   So they took all the men and went to fight with Ishmael the son of Nethaniah and they found him by the great pool that is in Gibeon.

13   Now it came about, as soon as all the people who were with Ishmael saw Johanan the son of Kareah and the commanders of the forces that were with him, they were glad.

14   So all the people whom Ishmael had taken captive from Mizpah turned around and came back, and went to Johanan the son of Kareah.

15   But Ishmael the son of Nethaniah escaped from Johanan with eight men and went to the sons of Ammon.

16   Then Johanan the son of Kareah and all the commanders of the forces that were with him took from Mizpah all the remnant of the people whom he had recovered from Ishmael the son of Nethaniah, after he had struck down Gedaliah the son of Ahikam, *that is,* the men who were soldiers, *the* women, *the* children, and *the* eunuchs, whom he had brought back from Gibeon.

17   And they went and stayed in Geruth Chimham, which is beside Bethlehem, in order to proceed into Egypt

18   because of the Chaldeans; for they were afraid of them, since Ishmael the son of Nethaniah had struck down Gedaliah the son of Ahikam, whom the king of Babylon had appointed over the land.

3. Jeremiah warns the remnant not to flee to Egypt

42 Then all the commanders of the forces, Johanan the son of Kareah, Jezaniah the son of Hoshaiah, and all the people both small and great approached

2   and said to Jeremiah the prophet, "Please let our petition come before you, and pray for us to the LORD your God, *that is* for all this remnant; because we are left *but* a few out of many, as your own eyes *now* see us,

3   that the LORD your God may tell us the way in which we should walk and the thing that we should do."

4   Then Jeremiah the prophet said to them, "I have heard *you.* Behold, I am going to pray to the LORD your God in accordance with your words; and it will come about that the whole message which the LORD will answer you I will tell you. I will not keep back a word from you."

5   Then they said to Jeremiah, "May the LORD be a true and faithful witness against us, if we do not act in accordance with the whole message with which the LORD your God will send you to us.

6   "Whether *it* is pleasant or unpleasant, we will listen to the voice of the LORD our God to whom we are sending you, in order that it may go well with us when we listen to the voice of the LORD our God."

7   Now it came about at the end of ten days that the word of the LORD came to Jeremiah.

8   Then he called for Johanan the son of Kareah, and all the commanders of the forces that were with him, and for all the people both small and great,

9   and said to them, "Thus says the LORD the God of Israel, to whom you sent me to present your petition before Him:

10   'If you will indeed stay in this land, then I will build you up and not tear you down, and I will plant you and not uproot you; for I shall relent concerning the calamity that I have inflicted on you.

11   'Do not be afraid of the king of Babylon, whom you are *now* fearing; do not be afraid of him,' declares the LORD, 'for I am with you to save you and deliver you from his hand.

12   'I will also show you compassion, so that he will have compassion on you and restore you to your own soil.

13   'But if you are going to say, "We will not stay in this land," so as not to listen to the voice of the LORD your God,

14   saying, "No, but we will go to the land of Egypt, where we shall not see war or hear the sound of a trumpet or hunger for bread, and we will stay there";

15   then in that case listen to the word of the LORD, O remnant of Judah. Thus says the LORD of hosts, the God of Israel, "If you really set your mind to enter Egypt, and go in to reside there,

16   then it will come about that the sword, which you are afraid of will overtake you there in the land of Egypt; and the famine, about which you are anxious, will follow closely after you there *in* Egypt; and you will die there.

42:17
Jer 44:13,14,
28

42:18
Jer 7:20;
33:5;
Is 65:15;
Jer 29:18;
22:10,27
42:19
Deut 17:16;
Is 30:1-7;
Neh 9:26,29,
30
42:20
v. 2

42:21
Jer 43:1;
Ezek 2:7;
Jer 43:4
42:22
Jer 43:11;
Hos 9:6

17 "So all the men who set their mind to go to Egypt to reside there will die by the sword, by famine, and by pestilence; and they will have no survivors or refugees from the calamity that I am going to bring on them."'"

18 For thus says the LORD of hosts, the God of Israel, "As My anger and wrath have been poured out on the inhabitants of Jerusalem, so My wrath will be poured out on you when you enter Egypt. And you will become a curse, an object of horror, an imprecation, and a reproach; and you will see this place no more."

19 The LORD has spoken to you, O remnant of Judah, "Do not go into Egypt!" You should clearly understand that today I have testified against you.

20 For you have *only* deceived yourselves; for it is you who sent me to the LORD your God, saying, "Pray for us to the LORD our God; and whatever the LORD our God says, tell us so, and we will do it."

21 So, I have told you today, but you have not obeyed the LORD your God, even in whatever He has sent me to *tell* you.

22 Therefore you should now clearly understand that you will die by the sword, by famine, and by pestilence, in the place where you wish to go to reside.

B. *Jeremiah's ministry among the refugees in Egypt*

1. *God's warning rejected, the Jews migrate to Tahpanhes*

43:1
Jer 26:8;
51:63;
42:10-18
43:2
Jer 42:1;
2 Chr 36:13;
Jer 42:5
43:3
Jer 38:4

43:4
Jer 42:5,6,
10-12
43:5
Jer 40:11,12

43:6
Jer 41:10;
39:10; 40:7

43:7
Jer 44:1

43 But it came about, as soon as Jeremiah whom the LORD their God had sent, had finished telling all the people all the words of the LORD their God—that is, all these words—

2 that Azariah the son of Hoshaiah, and Johanan the son of Kareah, and all the arrogant men said to Jeremiah, "You are telling a lie! The LORD our God has not sent you to say, 'You are not to enter Egypt to reside there';

3 but Baruch the son of Neriah is inciting you against us to give us over into the hand of the Chaldeans, so they may put us to death or exile us to Babylon."

4 So Johanan the son of Kareah and all the commanders of the forces, and all the people, did not obey the voice of the LORD, so as to stay in the land of Judah.

5 But Johanan the son of Kareah and all the commanders of the forces took the entire remnant of Judah who had returned from all the nations to which they had been driven away, in order to reside in the land of Judah—

6 the men, the women, the children, the king's daughters and every person that Nebuzaradan the captain of the bodyguard had left with Gedaliah the son of Ahikam and grandson of Shaphan, together with Jeremiah the prophet and Baruch the son of Neriah—

7 and they entered the land of Egypt (for they did not obey the voice of the LORD) and went in as far as Tahpanhes.

2. *Prophecy of the invasion of Egypt by Chaldea*

43:8
Jer 2:16;
44:1; 46:14

43:10
Jer 25:9,11;
27:5,6; 31:20

43:11
Is 19:1-25;
Jer 44:13;
46:13;
Ezek 29:19,
20; Jer 15:2
43:12
Is 19:1;
Jer 46:25;
Ezek 30:13

8 Then the word of the LORD came to Jeremiah in Tahpanhes, saying,

9 "Take *some* large stones in your hands and hide them in the mortar in the brick *terrace* which is at the entrance of Pharaoh's palace in Tahpanhes, in the sight of some *of the* Jews;

10 and say to them, 'Thus says the LORD of hosts, the God of Israel, "Behold, I am going to send and get Nebuchadnezzar the king of Babylon, My servant, and I am going to set his throne *right* over these stones that I have hidden; and he will spread his canopy over them.

11 "He will also come and strike the land of Egypt; those who are *meant* for death *will be given over* to death, and those for captivity to captivity, and those for the sword to the sword.

12 "And I shall set fire to the temples of the gods of Egypt, and he will burn them and take them captive. So he will wrap himself with the land of Egypt as a shepherd wraps himself with his garment, and he will depart from there safely.

13 "He will also shatter the obelisks of Heliopolis, which is in the land of Egypt; and the temples of the gods of Egypt he will burn with fire."'"

3. *The refugees to perish in Egypt*

44:1
Jer 46:14;
43:7; Is 19:13
44:2
Jer 9:11;
34:22;
Mic 3:12

44 The word that came to Jeremiah for all the Jews living in the land of Egypt, those who were living in Migdol, Tahpanhes, Memphis, and the land of Pathros, saying,

2 "Thus says the LORD of hosts, the God of Israel, 'You yourselves have seen all

the calamity that I have brought on Jerusalem and all the cities of Judah; and behold, this day they are in ruins and no one lives in them,

3   because of their wickedness which they committed so as to provoke Me to anger by continuing to burn sacrifices *and* to serve other gods whom they had not known, *neither* they, you, nor your fathers.

4   'Yet I sent you all My servants the prophets, again and again, saying, "Oh, do not do this abominable thing which I hate."

5   'But they did not listen or incline their ears to turn from their wickedness, so as not to burn sacrifices to other gods.

6   'Therefore My wrath and My anger were poured out and burned in the cities of Judah and in the streets of Jerusalem, so they have become a ruin and a desolation as it is this day.

7   'Now then thus says the LORD God of hosts, the God of Israel, "Why are you doing great harm to yourselves, so as to cut off from you man and woman, child and infant, from among Judah, leaving yourselves without remnant,

8   provoking Me to anger with the works of your hands, burning sacrifices to other gods in the land of Egypt, where you are entering to reside, so that you might be cut off and become a curse and a reproach among all the nations of the earth?

9   "Have you forgotten the wickedness of your fathers, the wickedness of the kings of Judah, and the wickedness of their wives, your own wickedness, and the wickedness of your wives, which they committed in the land of Judah and in the streets of Jerusalem?

10   "But they have not become contrite even to this day, nor have they feared nor walked in My law or My statutes, which I have set before you and before your fathers." '

11   "Therefore thus says the LORD of hosts, the God of Israel, 'Behold, I am going to set My face against you for woe, even to cut off all Judah.

12   'And I will take away the remnant of Judah who have set their mind on entering the land of Egypt to reside there, and they will all meet their end in the land of Egypt; they will fall by the sword *and* meet their end by famine. Both small and great will die by the sword and famine; and they will become a curse, an object of horror, an imprecation and a reproach.

13   'And I will punish those who live in the land of Egypt, as I have punished Jerusalem, with the sword, with famine, and with pestilence.

14   'So there will be no refugees or survivors for the remnant of Judah who have entered the land of Egypt to reside there and then to return to the land of Judah, to which they are longing to return and live; for none will return except *a few* refugees.' "

15   Then all the men who were aware that their wives were burning sacrifices to other gods, along with all the women who were standing by, *as* a large assembly, including all the people who were living in Pathros in the land of Egypt, responded to Jeremiah, saying,

16   "As for the message that you have spoken to us in the name of the LORD, we are not going to listen to you!

17   "But rather we will certainly carry out every word that has proceeded from our mouths, by burning sacrifices to the queen of heaven and pouring out libations to her, just as we ourselves, our forefathers, our kings and our princes did in the cities of Judah and in the streets of Jerusalem; for *then* we had plenty of food, and were well off, and saw no misfortune.

18   "But since we stopped burning sacrifices to the queen of heaven and pouring out libations to her, we have lacked everything and have met our end by the sword and by famine."

19   "And," *said the women,* "when we were burning sacrifices to the queen of heaven, and were pouring out libations to her, was it without our husbands that we made for her *sacrificial* cakes in her image and poured out libations to her?"

20   Then Jeremiah said to all the people, to the men and women—even to all the people who were giving him *such* an answer—saying,

21   "As for the smoking sacrifices that you burned in the cities of Judah and in the streets of Jerusalem, you and your forefathers, your kings and your princes, and the people of the land, did not the LORD remember them, and did not *all this* come into His mind?

44:3
Ezek 8:17,18;
Dan 9:5;
Is 3:8;
Jer 19:4;
Deut 13:6;
32:17
44:4
2 Chr 36:15;
Jer 7:25;
25:4; 26:5;
Ezek 8:10
44:5
Jer 11:8,10;
13:10
44:6
Jer 42:18
44:7
Jer 26:19;
Ezek 33:11;
Jer 9:21;
51:22
44:8
2 Kin 17:15-17;
Jer 25:6,7;
42:18
44:9
Jer 7:9,10,17,
18
44:10
Jer 6:15;
8:12; 26:4;
32:23
44:11
Lev 26:17;
Jer 21:10;
Amos 9:4
44:12
Jer 42:15-18,
22
44:13
Jer 11:22;
21:9; 24:10;
42:17,22
44:14
Jer 22:26,27;
Is 4:2; 10:20;
v. 28;
Rom 9:27
***44:15**
Jer 5:1-5
44:16
Jer 8:6,12;
13:10
***44:17**
2 Kin 17:16;
Jer 7:18;
Hos 2:5-9;
Phil 3:19
44:18
Jer 40:12
44:19
Jer 7:18;
Num 30:6,7
44:21
Ezek 8:10,11;
16:24;
Is 64:9;
Jer 14:10;
Hos 7:2

44:15 *Pathros,* a section of Upper Egypt.   **44:17** *the queen of heaven,* cf. 7:18.

22 "So the LORD was no longer able to endure *it*, because of the evil of your deeds, because of the abominations which you have committed; thus your land has become a ruin, an object of horror and a curse, without an inhabitant, as *it is* this day.

23 "Because you have burned sacrifices and have sinned against the LORD and not obeyed the voice of the LORD or walked in His law, His statutes or His testimonies, therefore this calamity has befallen you, as *it has* this day.' "

24 Then Jeremiah said to all the people, including all the women, "Hear the word of the LORD, all Judah who are in the land of Egypt,

25 thus says the LORD of hosts, the God of Israel, as follows: 'As for you and your wives, you have spoken with your mouths and fulfilled *it* with your hands, saying, "We will certainly perform our vows that we have vowed, to burn sacrifices to the queen of heaven and pour out libations to her." Go ahead and confirm your vows, and certainly perform your vows!'

26 "Nevertheless hear the word of the LORD, all Judah who are living in the land of Egypt, 'Behold, I have sworn by My great name,' says the LORD, 'never shall My name be invoked again by the mouth of any man of Judah in all the land of Egypt, saying, "As the Lord GOD lives."

27 'Behold, I am watching over them for harm and not for good, and all the men of Judah who are in the land of Egypt will meet their end by the sword and by famine until they are completely gone.

28 'And those who escape the sword will return out of the land of Egypt to the land of Judah few in number. Then all the remnant of Judah who have gone to the land of Egypt to reside there will know whose word will stand, Mine or theirs.

29 'And this will be the sign to you,' declares the LORD, 'that I am going to punish you in this place, so that you may know that My words will surely stand against you for harm.'

30 "Thus says the LORD, 'Behold, I am going to give over Pharaoh Hophra king of Egypt to the hand of his enemies, to the hand of those who seek his life, just as I gave over Zedekiah king of Judah to the hand of Nebuchadnezzar king of Babylon, *who was* his enemy and was seeking his life.' "

C. *Encouragement to Baruch, Jeremiah's secretary*

45 This is the message which Jeremiah the prophet spoke to Baruch the son of Neriah, when he had written down these words in a book at Jeremiah's dictation, in the fourth year of Jehoiakim the son of Josiah, king of Judah, saying:

2 "Thus says the LORD the God of Israel to you, O Baruch:

3 'You said, "Ah, woe is me! For the LORD has added sorrow to my pain; I am weary with my groaning and have found no rest." '

4 "Thus you are to say to him, 'Thus says the LORD, "Behold, what I have built I am about to tear down, and what I have planted I am about to uproot, that is, the whole land."

5 'But you, are you seeking great things for yourself? Do not seek *them;* for behold, I am going to bring disaster on all flesh,' declares the LORD, 'but I will give your life to you as booty in all the places where you may go.' ' "

IV. *Prophecies against heathen nations (46:1–51:64)*

A. *Prophecies against Egypt*

1. *Nebuchadnezzar will crush Neco at Carchemish*

46 That which came as the word of the LORD to Jeremiah the prophet concerning the nations.

2 To Egypt, concerning the army of Pharaoh Neco king of Egypt, which was by the Euphrates River at Carchemish, which Nebuchadnezzar king of Babylon defeated in the fourth year of Jehoiakim the son of Josiah, king of Judah:

3   "Line up the shield and buckler,
      And draw near for the battle!
4   "Harness the horses,
      And mount the steeds,
      And take your stand with helmets *on!*
      Polish the spears,
      Put on the scale-armor!

5　　"Why have I seen *it*?
　　　　They are terrified,
　　　　They are drawing back,
　　　　And their mighty men are defeated
　　　　And have taken refuge in flight,
　　　　Without facing back;
　　　　Terror is on every side!"
　　　　Declares the LORD.

　　　　　　　　　　　　　　　　　46:5
　　　　　　　　　　　　　　　　　Is 42:17;
　　　　　　　　　　　　　　　　　Ezek 39:18;
　　　　　　　　　　　　　　　　　Jer 6:25;
　　　　　　　　　　　　　　　　　49:29

6　　Let not the swift man flee,
　　　　Nor the mighty man escape;
　　　　In the north beside the river Euphrates
　　　　They have stumbled and fallen.

　　　　　　　　　　　　　　　　　46:6
　　　　　　　　　　　　　　　　　Is 30:16;
　　　　　　　　　　　　　　　　　Dan 11:19

7　　Who is this that rises like the Nile,
　　　　Like the rivers whose waters surge about?

　　　　　　　　　　　　　　　　　46:7
　　　　　　　　　　　　　　　　　Jer 47:2

8　　Egypt rises like the Nile,
　　　　Even like the rivers whose waters surge about;
　　　　And He has said, "I will rise and cover *that* land;
　　　　I will surely destroy the city and its inhabitants."

　　　　　　　　　　　　　　　　　46:8
　　　　　　　　　　　　　　　　　Is 37:24;
　　　　　　　　　　　　　　　　　10:13

9　　Go up, you horses, and drive madly, you chariots,
　　　　That the mighty men may march forward:
　　　　Ethiopia and Put, that handle the shield,
　　　　And the Lydians, that handle *and* bend the bow.

　　　　　　　　　　　　　　　　　46:9
　　　　　　　　　　　　　　　　　Jer 47:3;
　　　　　　　　　　　　　　　　　Nah 2:4; 3:9;
　　　　　　　　　　　　　　　　　Is 66:19

10　　For that day belongs to the Lord GOD of hosts,
　　　　A day of vengeance, so as to avenge Himself on His foes;
　　　　And the sword will devour and be satiated
　　　　And drink its fill of their blood;
　　　　For there will be a slaughter for the Lord GOD of hosts,
　　　　In the land of the north by the river Euphrates.

　　　　　　　　　　　　　　　　　46:10
　　　　　　　　　　　　　　　　　Is 13:6;
　　　　　　　　　　　　　　　　　Joel 1:15;
　　　　　　　　　　　　　　　　　2:1;
　　　　　　　　　　　　　　　　　Jer 50:15,28;
　　　　　　　　　　　　　　　　　Is 34:6;
　　　　　　　　　　　　　　　　　Zeph 1:7

11　　Go up to Gilead and obtain balm,
　　　　O virgin daughter of Egypt!
　　　　In vain have you multiplied remedies;
　　　　There is no healing for you.

　　　　　　　　　　　　　　　　　46:11
　　　　　　　　　　　　　　　　　Jer 8:22;
　　　　　　　　　　　　　　　　　51:8; Is 47:1;
　　　　　　　　　　　　　　　　　Jer 31:4,21;
　　　　　　　　　　　　　　　　　30:13;
　　　　　　　　　　　　　　　　　Ezek 30:21

12　　The nations have heard of your shame,
　　　　And the earth is full of your cry *of distress;*
　　　　For one warrior has stumbled over another,
　　　　And both of them have fallen down together.

　　　　　　　　　　　　　　　　　46:12
　　　　　　　　　　　　　　　　　Jer 2:36;
　　　　　　　　　　　　　　　　　Nah 3:8-10;
　　　　　　　　　　　　　　　　　Jer 14:2

2. Nebuchadnezzar will ravage Memphis and Thebes

13　*This is* the message which the LORD spoke to Jeremiah the prophet about the coming of Nebuchadnezzar king of Babylon to smite the land of Egypt:

　　　　　　　　　　　　　　　　　46:13
　　　　　　　　　　　　　　　　　Is 19:1;
　　　　　　　　　　　　　　　　　Jer 43:10,11

14　　"Declare in Egypt and proclaim in Migdol,
　　　　Proclaim also in Memphis and Tahpanhes;
　　　　Say, 'Take your stand and get yourself ready,
　　　　For the sword has devoured those around you.'

　　　　　　　　　　　　　　　　　*46:14
　　　　　　　　　　　　　　　　　Jer 44:1;
　　　　　　　　　　　　　　　　　43:8;
　　　　　　　　　　　　　　　　　Nah 2:13

15　　"Why have your mighty ones become prostrate?
　　　　They do not stand because the LORD has thrust them down.

16　　"They have repeatedly stumbled;
　　　　Indeed, they have fallen one against another.
　　　　Then they said, 'Get up! And let us go back
　　　　To our own people and our native land
　　　　Away from the sword of the oppressor.'

　　　　　　　　　　　　　　　　　46:16
　　　　　　　　　　　　　　　　　Lev 26:36,37;
　　　　　　　　　　　　　　　　　Jer 51:9;
　　　　　　　　　　　　　　　　　50:16

17　　"They cried there, 'Pharaoh king of Egypt *is but* a big noise;
　　　　He has let the appointed time pass by!'

　　　　　　　　　　　　　　　　　46:17
　　　　　　　　　　　　　　　　　Is 19:11-16

18　　"As I live," declares the King
　　　　Whose name is the LORD of hosts,
　　　　"Surely one shall come *who looms up* like Tabor among the
　　　　　　mountains,
　　　　Or like Carmel by the sea.

　　　　　　　　　　　　　　　　　46:18
　　　　　　　　　　　　　　　　　Jer 48:15;
　　　　　　　　　　　　　　　　　Ps 89:12;
　　　　　　　　　　　　　　　　　1 Kin 18:42

19　　"Make your baggage ready for exile,
　　　　O daughter dwelling in Egypt,
　　　　For Memphis will become a desolation;

　　　　　　　　　　　　　　　　　46:19
　　　　　　　　　　　　　　　　　Jer 48:18;
　　　　　　　　　　　　　　　　　Is 20:4; v. 4;
　　　　　　　　　　　　　　　　　Ezek 30:13

46:14 *Migdol . . . Memphis and Tahpanhes,* all cities of Egypt.

It will even be burned down *and* bereft of inhabitants.

46:20
Jer 50:11;
v. 24

20   "Egypt is a pretty heifer,
      But a horsefly is coming from the north—it is coming!

46:21
v. 5;
Ps 37:13;
Jer 50:27

21   "Also her mercenaries in her midst
      Are like fattened calves,
      For even they too have turned back *and* have fled away together;
      They did not stand *their ground*.
      For the day of their calamity has come upon them,
      The time of their punishment.

46:22
Is 29:4

22   "Its sound moves along like a serpent;
      For they move on like an army
      And come to her as woodcutters with axes.

46:23
Is 10:34;
Jer 21:14;
Judg 6:5;
Joel 2:25

23   "They have cut down her forest," declares the LORD;
      "Surely it will no *more* be found,
      Even though they are *now* more numerous than locusts
      And are without number.

46:24
v. 19;
Jer 1:15

24   "The daughter of Egypt has been put to shame,
      Given over to the power of the people of the north."

46:25
Jer 43:12;
Ezek 30:14-16;
Jer 44:30;
Ezek 30:13;
Is 20:5

25   The LORD of hosts, the God of Israel, says, "Behold, I am going to punish Amon of Thebes, and Pharaoh, and Egypt along with her gods and her kings, even Pharaoh and those who trust in him.

46:26
Jer 44:30;
Ezek 32:11;
29:11-14

26   "And I shall give them over to the power of those who are seeking their lives, even into the hand of Nebuchadnezzar king of Babylon and into the hand of his officers. Afterwards, however, it will be inhabited as in the days of old," declares the LORD.

3. *Israel will be restored, and the enemy powers will be destroyed*

46:27
Is 41:13;
43:5;
Jer 30:10,11;
23:3,4,6;
50:19

27   "But as for you, O Jacob My servant, do not fear,
      Nor be dismayed, O Israel!
      For, see, I am going to save you from afar,
      And your descendants from the land of their captivity;
      And Jacob shall return and be undisturbed
      And secure, with no one making *him* tremble.

46:28
Is 8:9,10;
Jer 1:19;
4:27;
Amos 9:8,9;
Jer 10:24;
30:11

28   "O Jacob My servant, do not fear," declares the LORD,
      "For I am with you.
      For I shall make a full end of all the nations
      Where I have driven you,
      Yet I shall not make a full end of you;
      But I shall correct you properly
      And by no means leave you unpunished."

B. *Prophecy against Philistia*

47:1
Jer 25:17,20;
Amos 1:6;
Zeph 2:4

47   That which came as the word of the LORD to Jeremiah the prophet concerning the Philistines, before Pharaoh conquered Gaza.

47:2
Is 14:31;
Jer 46:20,24;
Is 8:7; 15:2-5;
Jer 46:12

2   Thus says the LORD:
      "Behold, waters are going to rise from the north
      And become an overflowing torrent,
      And overflow the land and all its fulness,
      The city and those who live in it;
      And the men will cry out,
      And every inhabitant of the land will wail.

47:3
Jer 8:16;
Nah 3:2

3   "Because of the noise of the galloping hoofs of his stallions,
      The tumult of his chariots, *and* the rumbling of his wheels,
      The fathers have not turned back for *their* children,
      Because of the limpness of *their* hands,

47:4
Is 14:31;
23:5,6,11;
Joel 3:4;
Zech 9:2-4;
Gen 10:14

4   On account of the day that is coming
      To destroy all the Philistines,
      To cut off from Tyre and Sidon
      Every ally that is left;
      For the LORD is going to destroy the Philistines,
      The remnant of the coastland of Caphtor.

47:5
Mic 1:16;

5   "Baldness has come upon Gaza;

Ashkelon has been ruined.
O remnant of their valley,
How long will you gash yourself?

6 "Ah, sword of the LORD,
How long will you not be quiet?
Withdraw into your sheath;
Be at rest and stay still.

7 "How can it be quiet,
When the LORD has given it an order?
Against Ashkelon and against the seacoast—
There He has assigned it."

C. Prophecy against Moab

48 Concerning Moab.
Thus says the LORD of hosts, the God of Israel,
"Woe to Nebo, for it has been destroyed;
Kiriathaim has been put to shame, it has been captured;
The lofty stronghold has been put to shame and shattered.

2 "There is praise for Moab no longer;
In Heshbon they have devised calamity against her:
'Come and let us cut her off from *being* a nation!'
You too, [12]Madmen, will be silenced;
The sword will follow after you.

3 "The sound of an outcry from Horonaim,
'Devastation and great destruction!'

4 "Moab is broken,
Her little ones have sounded out a cry *of distress*.

5 "For by the ascent of Luhith
They will ascend with continual weeping;
For at the descent of Horonaim
They have heard the anguished cry of destruction.

6 "Flee, save your lives,
That you may be like a juniper in the wilderness.

7 "For because of your trust in your own achievements and treasures,
Even you yourself will be captured;
And Chemosh will go off into exile
Together with his priests and his princes.

8 "And a destroyer will come to every city,
So that no city will escape;
The valley also will be ruined,
And the plateau will be destroyed,
As the LORD has said.

9 "Give wings to Moab,
For she will flee away;
And her cities will become a desolation,
Without inhabitants in them.

10 "Cursed be the one who does the LORD's work negligently,
And cursed be the one who restrains his sword from blood.

11 "Moab has been at ease since his youth;
He has also been undisturbed on his lees,
Neither has he been emptied from vessel to vessel,
Nor has he gone into exile.
Therefore he retains his flavor,
And his aroma has not changed.

12 "Therefore behold, the days are coming," declares the LORD, "when I shall send to him those who tip *vessels*, and they will tip him over, and they will empty his vessels and shatter his jars.

13 "And Moab will be ashamed of Chemosh, as the house of Israel was ashamed of Bethel, their confidence.

[12]I.e., a city of Moab

48:5 Similar to the lament in Is. 15:5.   **48:7** *Chemosh* was the god of Moab.

48:14 Is 10:13-16	14 "How can you say, 'We are mighty warriors, And men valiant for battle'?
48:15 Jer 50:27; 46:18	15 "Moab has been destroyed, and men have gone up to his cities; His choicest young men have also gone down to the slaughter," Declares the King, whose name is the LORD of hosts.
48:16 Is 13:22	16 "The disaster of Moab will soon come, And his calamity has swiftly hastened.
48:17 Jer 9:17-20; Is 14:5	17 "Mourn for him, all you who *live* around him, Even all of you who know his name; Say, 'How has the mighty scepter been broken, A staff of splendor!'
48:18 Is 47:1; Jer 46:19; v. 8	18 "Come down from your glory And sit on the parched ground, O daughter dwelling in Dibon, For the destroyer of Moab has come up against you, He has ruined your strongholds.
48:19 Deut 2:36; 1 Sam 4:13,16	19 "Stand by the road and keep watch, O inhabitant of Aroer; Ask him who flees and her who escapes *And* say, 'What has happened?'
48:20 Is 16:7; Num 21:13	20 "Moab has been put to shame, for it has been shattered. Wail and cry out; Declare by the Arnon That Moab has been destroyed.
48:21 vv. 8,34; Josh 13:18	21 "Judgment has also come upon the plain, upon Holon, Jahzah, and against Mephaath, 22 against Dibon, Nebo, and Beth-diblathaim, 23 against Kiriathaim, Beth-gamul, and Beth-meon,
48:24 Amos 2:2 **48:25** Ps 75:10; Ezek 30:21 **48:26** Jer 25:15,27	24 against Kerioth, Bozrah, and all the cities of the land of Moab, far and near. 25 "The horn of Moab has been cut off, and his arm broken," declares the LORD. 26 "Make him drunk, for he has become arrogant toward the LORD; so Moab will wallow in his vomit, and he also will become a laughingstock.
48:27 Zeph 2:8; Jer 2:26; 18:16 **48:28** Jer 49:16; Ps 55:6,7; Song 2:14	27 "Now was not Israel a laughingstock to you? Or was he caught among thieves? For each time you speak about him you shake *your head in scorn.* 28 "Leave the cities and dwell among the crags, O inhabitants of Moab, And be like a dove that nests Beyond the mouth of the chasm.
48:29 Is 16:6; Zeph 2:8; Ps 138:6 **48:30** Is 37:28; 16:6	29 "We have heard of the pride of Moab—he *is* very proud— Of his haughtiness, his pride, his arrogance and his self-exaltation. 30 "I know his fury," declares the LORD, "But it is futile; His idle boasts have accomplished nothing.
48:31 Is 15:5; 16:7, 11	31 "Therefore I shall wail for Moab, Even for all Moab shall I cry out; I will moan for the men of Kir-heres.
48:32 Is 16:8,9; Num 21:32	32 "More than the weeping for Jazer I shall weep for you, O vine of Sibmah! Your tendrils stretched across the sea, They reached to the sea of Jazer; Upon your summer fruits and your grape harvest The destroyer has fallen.
48:33 Is 16:10; Joel 1:12; Is 5:10; Hag 2:16	33 "So gladness and joy are taken away From the fruitful field, even from the land of Moab. And I have made the wine to cease from the wine presses; No one will tread *them* with shouting, The shouting will not be shouts *of joy.*
48:34 Is 15:4-6	34 "From the outcry at Heshbon even to Elealeh, even to Jahaz they have raised their voice, from Zoar even to Horonaim *and to* Eglath-shelishiyah; for even the waters of Nimrim will become desolate.
48:35 Is 15:2; 16:12; Jer 7:9; 11:13	35 "And I shall make an end of Moab," declares the LORD, "the one who offers *sacrifice* on the high place and the one who burns incense to his gods.

36 "Therefore My heart wails for Moab like flutes; My heart also wails like flutes for the men of Kir-heres. Therefore they have lost the abundance it produced.

37 "For every head is bald and every beard cut short; there are gashes on all the hands and sackcloth on the loins.

38 "On all the housetops of Moab and in its streets there is lamentation everywhere; for I have broken Moab like an undesirable vessel," declares the LORD.

39 "How shattered it is! *How* they have wailed! How Moab has turned his back—he is ashamed! So Moab will become a laughingstock and an object of terror to all around him."

40   For thus says the LORD,
         "Behold, one will fly swiftly like an eagle,
         And spread out his wings against Moab.

41   "Kerioth has been captured
         And the strongholds have been seized,
         So the hearts of the mighty men of Moab in that day
         Will be like the heart of a woman in labor.

42   "And Moab will be destroyed from *being* a people
         Because he has become arrogant toward the LORD.

43   "Terror, pit, and snare are *coming* upon you,
         O inhabitant of Moab," declares the LORD.

44   "The one who flees from the terror
         Will fall into the pit,
         And the one who climbs up out of the pit
         Will be caught in the snare;
         For I shall bring upon her, *even* upon Moab,
         The year of their punishment," declares the LORD.

45   "In the shadow of Heshbon
         The fugitives stand without strength;
         For a fire has gone forth from Heshbon,
         And a flame from the midst of Sihon,
         And it has devoured the forehead of Moab
         And the scalps of the riotous revelers.

46   "Woe to you, Moab!
         The people of Chemosh have perished;
         For your sons have been taken away captive,
         And your daughters into captivity.

47   "Yet I will restore the fortunes of Moab
         In the latter days," declares the LORD.
         Thus far the judgment on Moab.

D. *Prophecies against Ammon, Edom, Kedar, and Elam*

1. *The Ammonites to go into captivity*

49   Concerning the sons of Ammon.
         Thus says the LORD:
         "Does Israel have no sons?
         Or has he no heirs?
         Why then has Malcam taken possession of Gad
         And his people settled in its cities?

2   "Therefore behold, the days are coming," declares the LORD,
         "That I shall cause a trumpet blast of war to be heard
         Against Rabbah of the sons of Ammon;
         And it will become a desolate heap,
         And her towns will be set on fire.
         Then Israel will take possession of his possessors,"
         Says the LORD.

3   "Wail, O Heshbon, for Ai has been destroyed!
         Cry out, O daughters of Rabbah,
         Gird yourselves with sackcloth and lament,
         And rush back and forth inside the walls;
         For Malcam will go into exile

48:36
Is 16:11; 15:7
48:37
Is 15:2,3;
Jer 47:5
48:38
Jer 22:28;
25:34
48:39
Ezek 26:16

48:40
Jer 49:22;
Dan 7:4;
Hos 8:1;
Is 8:8
48:41
Is 21:3;
Jer 30:6;
49:22,24;
Mic 4:9

48:42
v. 2; Ps 83:4;
v. 26;
Is 37:23
48:43
Is 24:17,18;
Lam 3:47
48:44
1 Kin 19:17;
Jer 11:23;
46:21

48:45
v. 2;
Num 21:21,
26,28,29;
24:17

48:46
Num 21:29;
v. 7

48:47
Jer 49:6,39

*49:1
Ezek 21:28;
25:2;
Amos 1:13;
Zeph 2:8,9

*49:2
Jer 4:19;
Ezek 21:20;
Is 14:2

49:3
Jer 48:2;
Josh 7:2-5;
8:1-29;
Is 32:11;
Jer 4:8; 48:7

49:1 *Malcam* was the god of Ammon.   **49:2** *Rabbah*, the capital of the Ammonites.

Together with his priests and his princes.

4   "How boastful you are about the valleys!
     Your valley is flowing *away*,
     O backsliding daughter
     Who trusts in her treasures, *saying*,
     'Who will come against me?'

5   "Behold, I am going to bring terror upon you,"
     Declares the Lord GOD of hosts,
     "From all *directions* around you;
     And each of you will be driven out headlong,
     With no one to gather the fugitives together.

6   "But afterward I will restore
     The fortunes of the sons of Ammon,"
     Declares the LORD.

2. Edom to be devastated and dispossessed

7   Concerning Edom.
     Thus says the LORD of hosts,
     "Is there no longer any wisdom in Teman?
     Has good counsel been lost to the prudent?
     Has their wisdom decayed?

8   "Flee away, turn back, dwell in the depths,
     O inhabitants of Dedan,
     For I will bring the disaster of Esau upon him
     At the time I punish him.

9   "If grape gatherers came to you,
     Would they not leave gleanings?
     If thieves *came* by night,
     They would destroy *only* until they had enough.

10   "But I have stripped Esau bare,
     I have uncovered his hiding places
     So that he will not be able to conceal himself;
     His offspring has been destroyed along with his relatives
     And his neighbors, and he is no more.

11   "Leave your orphans behind, I will keep *them* alive;
     And let your widows trust in Me."

12   For thus says the LORD, "Behold, those who were not sentenced to drink the cup will certainly drink *it*, and are you the one who will be completely acquitted? You will not be acquitted, but you will certainly drink *it*.

13   "For I have sworn by Myself," declares the LORD, "that Bozrah will become an object of horror, a reproach, a ruin and a curse; and all its cities will become perpetual ruins."

14   I have heard a message from the LORD,
     And an envoy is sent among the nations, *saying*,
     "Gather yourselves together and come against her,
     And rise up for battle!"

15   "For behold, I have made you small among the nations,
     Despised among men.

16   "As for the terror of you,
     The arrogance of your heart has deceived you,
     O you who live in the clefts of the rock,
     Who occupy the height of the hill.
     Though you make your nest as high as an eagle's,
     I will bring you down from there," declares the LORD.

17   "And Edom will become an object of horror; everyone who passes by it will be horrified and will hiss at all its wounds.

18   "Like the overthrow of Sodom and Gomorrah with its neighbors," says the LORD, "no one will live there, nor will a son of man reside in it.

19   "Behold, one will come up like a lion from the thickets of the Jordan against a perennially watered pasture; for in an instant I shall make him run away from it, and whoever is chosen I shall appoint over it. For who is like Me, and who will summon Me *into court?* And who then is the shepherd who can stand against Me?"

20   Therefore hear the plan of the LORD which He has planned against Edom,

and His purposes which He has purposed against the inhabitants of Teman: surely they will drag them off, *even* the little ones of the flock; surely He will make their pasture desolate because of them.

21 The earth has quaked at the noise of their downfall. There is an outcry! The noise of it has been heard at the Red Sea.

22 Behold, He will mount up and swoop like an eagle, and spread out His wings against Bozrah; and the hearts of the mighty men of Edom in that day will be like the heart of a woman in labor.

23 Concerning Damascus.

"Hamath and Arpad are put to shame,
For they have heard bad news;
They are disheartened.
There is anxiety by the sea,
It cannot be calmed.

24 "Damascus has become helpless;
She has turned away to flee,
And panic has gripped her;
Distress and pangs have taken hold of her
Like a woman in childbirth.

25 "How the city of praise has not been deserted,
The town of My joy!

26 "Therefore, her young men will fall in her streets,
And all the men of war will be silenced in that day," declares the LORD of hosts.

27 "And I shall set fire to the wall of Damascus,
And it will devour the fortified towers of Ben-hadad."

3. *Kedar and Hazor to be ravaged by Nebuchadnezzar*

28 Concerning Kedar and the kingdoms of Hazor, which Nebuchadnezzar king of Babylon defeated. Thus says the LORD,

"Arise, go up to Kedar
And devastate the men of the east.

29 "They will take away their tents and their flocks;
They will carry off for themselves
Their tent curtains, all their goods, and their camels,
And they will call out to one another, 'Terror on every side!'

30 "Run away, flee! Dwell in the depths,
O inhabitants of Hazor," declares the LORD;
"For Nebuchadnezzar king of Babylon has formed a plan against you
And devised a scheme against you.

31 "Arise, go up against a nation which is at ease,
Which lives securely," declares the LORD.
"It has no gates or bars;
They dwell alone.

32 "And their camels will become plunder,
And the multitude of their cattle for booty,
And I shall scatter to all the winds those who cut the
corners *of their hair;*
And I shall bring their disaster from every side," declares the LORD.

33 "And Hazor will become a haunt of jackals,
A desolation forever;
No one will live there,
Nor will a son of man reside in it."

4. *The Elamites to be dispersed and their rulers slain; a remnant to return*

34 That which came as the word of the LORD to Jeremiah the prophet concerning Elam, at the beginning of the reign of Zedekiah king of Judah, saying,

35 "Thus says the LORD of hosts,
'Behold, I am going to break the bow of Elam,
The finest of their might.

36 'And I shall bring upon Elam the four winds

49:20 Jer 50:45; Mal 1:3,4
49:21 Jer 50:46; Ezek 26:15,18
49:22 Jer 4:13; 48:40,41
49:23 2 Chr 16:2; Jer 39:5; Is 10:9; 57:20
49:24 v. 22; Jer 6:24; 30:6; 48:41
49:25 Jer 33:9; 51:41
49:26 Jer 50:30; 51:4; Amos 4:10
49:27 Jer 43:12; Amos 1:3-5; 1 Kin 15:18-20
49:28 Is 21:16,17; Jer 2:10; Ezek 27:21; Is 11:14
49:29 Jer 6:25; 20:3,10; 46:5
49:30 Jer 25:9
49:31 Is 47:8; Ezek 38:11; Deut 33:28
49:32 Ezek 12:14,15; Jer 9:26; 25:23
49:33 Jer 10:22; Zeph 2:9,13-15
49:34 Ezek 32:24; 2 Kin 24:17,18; Jer 28:1
49:35 Is 22:6; Jer 51:56

49:36 Rev 7:1; Ezek 5:10; Amos 9:9	From the four ends of heaven, And shall scatter them to all these winds; And there will be no nation To which the outcasts of Elam will not go.
49:37 Jer 8:9; 17:18; 6:19; 30:24; 9:16	37 'So I shall shatter Elam before their enemies And before those who seek their lives; And I shall bring calamity upon them, Even My fierce anger,' declares the LORD, 'And I shall send out the sword after them Until I have consumed them.
	38 'Then I shall set My throne in Elam, And I shall destroy out of it king and princes,' Declares the LORD.
49:39 Jer 48:47	39 'But it will come about in the last days That I shall restore the fortunes of Elam,' " Declares the LORD.

E. Prophecies against Babylon

1. Babylon to become an uninhabited waste; the Jews to return home

50:1 Is 13:1; Rev 14:8	**50** The word which the LORD spoke concerning Babylon, the land of the Chaldeans, through Jeremiah the prophet:
*50:2 Jer 51:27,31; Is 46:1; Jer 51:44,47	2 "Declare and proclaim among the nations. Proclaim it and lift up a standard. Do not conceal it but say, 'Babylon has been captured, Bel has been put to shame, Marduk has been shattered; Her images have been put to shame, her idols have been shattered.'
*50:3 Jer 51:48; 9:10; Zeph 1:3	3 "For a nation has come up against her out of the north; it will make her land an object of horror, and there will be no inhabitant in it. Both man and beast have wandered off, they have gone away!
50:4 Hos 1:11; Ezra 3:12,13; Jer 31:9; Zech 12:10; Hos 3:5	4 "In those days and at that time," declares the LORD, "the sons of Israel will come, both they and the sons of Judah as well; they will go along weeping as they go, and it will be the LORD their God they will seek.
	5 "They will ask for the way to Zion, turning their faces in its direction; they will come that they may join themselves to the LORD in an everlasting covenant that will not be forgotten.
50:6 Is 53:6; Ezek 34:15, 16; Jer 23:11-14; 2:20; 3:6,23; 33:12	6 "My people have become lost sheep; Their shepherds have led them astray. They have made them turn aside on the mountains; They have gone along from mountain to hill And have forgotten their resting place.
50:7 Jer 40:2,3; 31:23; 14:8; 17:13	7 "All who came upon them have devoured them; And their adversaries have said, 'We are not guilty, Inasmuch as they have sinned against the LORD who is the habitation of righteousness, Even the LORD, the hope of their fathers.'
50:8 Jer 51:6,45; Rev 18:4	8 "Wander away from the midst of Babylon, And go forth from the land of the Chaldeans; Be also like male goats at the head of the flock.
50:9 Jer 51:1,2	9 "For behold, I am going to arouse and bring up against Babylon A horde of great nations from the land of the north, And they will draw up their battle lines against her; From there she will be taken captive. Their arrows will be like an expert warrior Who does not return empty-handed.
*50:10 Jer 51:24,35; Rev 17:16	10 "And Chaldea will become plunder; All who plunder her will have enough," declares the LORD.

50:2 *Bel . . . Marduk*, names of the god of Babylon.
50:3 *out of the north.* Here the reference is to Media, north of Babylon.

50:10 Destroyed Babylon will never be rebuilt. (Read 50:39.)

11 "Because you are glad, because you are jubilant,
    O you who pillage My heritage,
    Because you skip about like a threshing heifer
    And neigh like stallions,

50:11
Jer 12:14;
46:20

12 Your mother will be greatly ashamed,
    She who gave you birth will be humiliated.
    Behold, *she will be* the least of the nations,
    A wilderness, a parched land, and a desert.

50:12
Jer 22:6;
51:43

13 "Because of the indignation of the LORD she will not be inhabited,
    But she will be completely desolate;
    Everyone who passes by Babylon will be horrified
    And will hiss because of all her wounds.

50:13
Jer 25:12;
49:17

14 "Draw up your battle lines against Babylon on every side,
    All you who bend the bow,
    Shoot at her, do not be sparing with *your* arrows,
    For she has sinned against the LORD.

50:14
Jer 49:35;
Hab 2:8,17

15 "Raise your battle cry against her on every side!
    She has given herself up, her pillars have fallen,
    Her walls have been torn down.
    For this is the vengeance of the LORD:
    Take vengeance on her;
    As she has done *to others, so* do to her.

50:15
Jer 51:14;
1 Chr 29:24;
Ezek 17:18;
Jer 51:44,58;
46:10

16 "Cut off the sower from Babylon,
    And the one who wields the sickle at the time of harvest;
    From before the sword of the oppressor
    They will each turn back to his own people,
    And they will each flee to his own land.

50:16
Joel 1:11;
Jer 51:9

17 "Israel is a scattered flock, the lions have driven *them* away. The first one *who* devoured him was the king of Assyria, and this last one *who* has broken his bones is Nebuchadnezzar king of Babylon.

50:17
Jer 2:15;
2 Kin 17:6;
24:10,14

18 "Therefore thus says the LORD of hosts, the God of Israel: 'Behold, I am going to punish the king of Babylon and his land, just as I punished the king of Assyria.

50:18
Is 10:12;
Ezek 31:3,11,
12

19 'And I shall bring Israel back to his pasture, and he will graze on Carmel and Bashan, and his desire will be satisfied in the hill country of Ephraim and Gilead.

*50:19
Jer 31:10;
33:12; 31:5

20 'In those days and at that time,' declares the LORD, 'search will be made for the iniquity of Israel, but there will be none; and for the sins of Judah, but they will not be found; for I shall pardon those whom I leave as a remnant.'

50:20
Jer 31:34;
Mic 7:19;
Is 1:9;
Jer 33:8

21 "Against the land of ¹³Merathaim, go up against it,
    And against the inhabitants of ¹⁴Pekod.
    Slay and utterly destroy them," declares the LORD,
    "And do according to all that I have commanded you.

*50:21
Ezek 23:23;
Is 10:6;
44:28; 48:14;
Jer 34:22

22 "The noise of battle is in the land,
    And great destruction.

50:22
Jer 51:54-56

23 "How the hammer of the whole earth
    Has been cut off and broken!
    How Babylon has become
    An object of horror among the nations!

50:23
Is 14:6;
Jer 51:20-24

24 "I set a snare for you, and you were also caught, O Babylon,
    While you yourself were not aware;
    You have been found and also seized
    Because you have engaged in conflict with the LORD."

50:24
Jer 48:43,44;
51:8,31,39,
57; Dan 5:30,
31

25 The LORD has opened His armory
    And has brought forth the weapons of His indignation,
    For it is a work of the Lord GOD of hosts
    In the land of the Chaldeans.

50:25
Is 13:5;
Jer 51:12,25,
55

26 Come to her from the farthest border;
    Open up her barns,
    Pile her up like heaps

50:26
v. 41;
Is 14:23

---

¹³Or, *Double Rebellion*   ¹⁴Or, *Punishment*

50:19 This is a promise of Israel's ultimate return.
50:21 *Merathaim*, "double rebellion," a reference to southern Babylonia. *Pekod*, "punishment," a reference to a
people in eastern Babylonia.

And utterly destroy her,
Let nothing be left to her.

27 Put all her young bulls to the sword;
Let them go down to the slaughter!
Woe be upon them, for their day has come,
The time of their punishment.

28 There is a sound of fugitives and refugees from the land of Babylon,
To declare in Zion the vengeance of the LORD our God,
Vengeance for His temple.

29 "Summon [15]many against Babylon,
All those who bend the bow:
Encamp against her on every side,
Let there be no escape.
Repay her according to her work;
According to all that she has done, *so* do to her;
For she has become arrogant against the LORD,
Against the Holy One of Israel.

30 "Therefore her young men will fall in her streets,
And all her men of war will be silenced in that day," declares the LORD.

31 "Behold, I am against you, O arrogant one,"
Declares the Lord GOD of hosts,
"For your day has come,
The time when I shall punish you.

32 "And the arrogant one will stumble and fall
With no one to raise him up;
And I shall set fire to his cities,
And it will devour all his environs."

33 Thus says the LORD of hosts,
"The sons of Israel are oppressed,
And the sons of Judah as well;
And all who took them captive have held them fast,
They have refused to let them go.

34 "Their Redeemer is strong, the LORD of hosts is His name;
He will vigorously plead their case,
So that He may bring rest to the earth,
But turmoil to the inhabitants of Babylon.

35 "A sword against the Chaldeans," declares the LORD,
"And against the inhabitants of Babylon,
And against her officials and her wise men!

36 "A sword against the oracle priests, and they will become fools!
A sword against her mighty men, and they will be shattered!

37 "A sword against their horses and against their chariots,
And against all the foreigners who are in the midst of her,
And they will become women!
A sword against her treasures, and they will be plundered!

38 "A drought on her waters, and they will be dried up!
For it is a land of idols,
And they are mad over fearsome idols.

39 "Therefore the desert creatures will live *there* along with the jackals;
The ostriches also will live in it,
And it will never again be inhabited
Or dwelt in from generation to generation.

40 "As when God overthrew Sodom
And Gomorrah with its neighbors," declares the LORD,
"No man will live there,
Nor will *any* son of man reside in it.

41 "Behold, a people is coming from the north,

[15]Another reading is *archers*

50:29 Babylon has defied the true God. Therefore she shall be requited.

Cross references (left margin):

50:27 Is 34:7; Ezek 7:7; Jer 48:44

50:28 Is 48:20; Jer 51:6; 51:10,11

*50:29 Jer 51:56; Rev 18:6; Is 47:10

50:30 Is 13:17,18; Jer 49:26; 51:56,57

50:31 Jer 21:13; Nah 2:13

50:32 Is 10:12-15; Jer 21:14; 49:27

50:33 Is 14:17; 58:6

50:34 Is 43:14; Jer 15:21; 31:11; 32:18; 51:19,36; Is 14:3-7

50:35 Dan 5:1,2,7, 8,30

50:36 Is 44:25; Jer 49:22

50:37 Jer 51:21,22; 25:30; Ezek 30:5; Jer 51:30; Nah 3:13

50:38 Jer 51:32,36, 42,47,52

50:39 Is 13:21,22; Jer 51:37; Is 13:20

50:40 Gen 19:25; Jer 49:18; Luke 17:28-30

50:41 cf. v. 3; Jer 6:22; Rev 17:16

And a great nation and many kings
Will be aroused from the remote parts of the earth.

42　"They seize *their* bow and javelin;
They are cruel and have no mercy.
Their voice roars like the sea,
And they ride on horses,
Marshalled like a man for the battle
Against you, O daughter of Babylon.

50:42
Jer 6:23;
Is 13:18; 5:30

43　"The king of Babylon has heard the report about them,
And his hands hang limp;
Distress has gripped him,
Agony like a woman in childbirth.

50:43
Jer 51:31;
49:24

44　"Behold, one will come up like a lion from the thicket of the Jordan to a perennially watered pasture; for in an instant I shall make them run away from it, and whoever is chosen I shall appoint over it. For who is like Me, and who will summon Me *into court?* And who then is the shepherd who can stand before Me?"

50:44
Jer 49:19-21;
Is 46:9;
Job 41:10;
Jer 49:19

45　Therefore hear the plan of the LORD which He has planned against Babylon, and His purposes which He has purposed against the land of the Chaldeans: surely they will drag them off, *even* the little ones of the flock; surely He will make their pasture desolate because of them.

50:45
Is 14:24;
Jer 51:11;
49:20

46　At the shout, "Babylon has been seized!" the earth is shaken, and an outcry is heard among the nations.

50:46
Rev 18:9;
Ezek 27:28

2. Babylon to be destroyed by the Medes

51　Thus says the LORD:
"Behold, I am going to arouse against Babylon
And against the inhabitants of [16]Leb-kamai
The spirit of a destroyer.

51:1
Jer 4:11;
Hos 13:15

2　"And I shall dispatch foreigners to Babylon that they may winnow her
And may devastate her land;
For on every side they will be opposed to her
In the day of *her* calamity.

51:2
Is 41:16;
Jer 15:7;
Matt 3:12

3　"Let not him who bends his bow bend *it,*
Nor let him rise up in his scale-armor;
So do not spare her young men;
Devote all her army to destruction.

51:3
Jer 50:14;
46:4; 50:21

4　"And they will fall down slain in the land of the Chaldeans,
And pierced through in their streets."

51:4
Jer 49:26;
50:30,37

5　For neither Israel nor Judah has been forsaken
By his God, the LORD of hosts,
Although their land is full of guilt
Before the Holy One of Israel.

51:5
Is 54:7,8;
Jer 33:24-26

6　Flee from the midst of Babylon,
And each of you save his life!
Do not be destroyed in her punishment;
For this is the LORD's time of vengeance;
He is going to render recompense to her.

51:6
Jer 50:8;
Rev 18:4;
Num 16:26;
Jer 50:15;
25:14

7　Babylon has been a golden cup in the hand of the LORD,
Intoxicating all the earth.
The nations have drunk of her wine;
Therefore the nations are going mad.

51:7
Rev 17:4;
Jer 25:15;
Rev 14:8;
18:3;
Jer 25:16

8　Suddenly Babylon has fallen and been broken;
Wail over her!
Bring balm for her pain;
Perhaps she may be healed.

51:8
Is 21:9;
Rev 14:8;
18:2;
Jer 48:20;
Rev 18:9,11,
19

9　We applied healing to Babylon, but she was not healed;
Forsake her and let us each go to his own country,
For her judgment has reached to heaven
And towers up to the very skies.

51:9
Is 13:14;
Jer 50:16;
Rev 18:5

10　The LORD has brought about our vindication;
Come and let us recount in Zion

51:10
Ps 37:6;
Jer 51:11;
Is 40:2;
Jer 50:28

[16]Cryptic name for Chaldea

The work of the LORD our God!

51:11
Jer 46:4;
Joel 3:9,10;
Jer 50:3,9,28

11 Sharpen the arrows, fill the quivers!
The LORD has aroused the spirit of the kings of the Medes,
Because His purpose is against Babylon to destroy it;
For it is the vengeance of the LORD, vengeance for His temple.

51:12
Is 13:2;
Jer 50:2

12 Lift up a signal against the walls of Babylon;
Post a strong guard,
Station sentries,
Place men in ambush!
For the LORD has both purposed and performed
What He spoke concerning the inhabitants of Babylon.

51:13
Rev 17:1,15

13 O you who dwell by many waters,
Abundant in treasures,
Your end has come,
The measure of your end.

51:14
Jer 49:13;
Amos 6:8;
Nah 3:15;
Jer 50:15

14 The LORD of hosts has sworn by Himself:
"Surely I will fill you with a population like locusts,
And they will cry out with shouts of victory over you."

*51:15ff
Gen 1:1,6;
Jer 10:12-16;
Acts 14:15;
Rom 1:20;
Job 9:8;
Ps 104:2;
Is 40:22

15 *It is* He who made the earth by His power,
Who established the world by His wisdom,
And by His understanding He stretched out the heavens.

51:16
Ps 18:13;
Jer 10:13;
Ps 135:7

16 When He utters His voice, *there is* a tumult of waters in the heavens,
And He causes the clouds to ascend from the end of the earth;
He makes lightning for the rain,
And brings forth the wind from His storehouses.

51:17
Jer 10:14;
50:2;
Hab 2:18,19

17 All mankind is stupid, devoid of knowledge;
Every goldsmith is put to shame by his idols,
For his molten images are deceitful,
And there is no breath in them.

51:18
Jer 10:15

18 They are worthless, a work of mockery;
In the time of their punishment they will perish.

51:19
Jer 10:16;
50:34

19 The portion of Jacob is not like these;
For the Maker of all is He,
And of the tribe of His inheritance;
The LORD of hosts is His name.

51:20
Is 10:5,15;
Jer 50:23;
Is 41:15,16;
Mic 4:12,13

20 *He says,* "You are My war-club, *My* weapon of war;
And with you I shatter nations,
And with you I destroy kingdoms.

51:22
2 Chr 36:17

21 "And with you I shatter the horse and his rider,
22 And with you I shatter the chariot and its rider,
And with you I shatter man and woman,
And with you I shatter old man and youth,
And with you I shatter young man and virgin,

51:23
v. 57

23 And with you I shatter the shepherd and his flock,
And with you I shatter the farmer and his team,
And with you I shatter governors and prefects.

51:24
Jer 50:10,15,
29

24 "But I will repay Babylon and all the inhabitants of Chaldea for all their evil
that they have done in Zion before your eyes," declares the LORD.

*51:25
Jer 50:31;
Zech 4:7;
Rev 8:8

25 "Behold, I am against you, O destroying mountain,
Who destroy the whole earth," declares the LORD,
"And I will stretch out My hand against you,
And roll you down from the crags
And I will make you a burnt out mountain.

51:26
v. 29;
Jer 50:13

26 "And they will not take from you *even* a stone for a corner
Nor a stone for foundations,
But you will be desolate forever," declares the LORD.

*51:27
Is 13:2;

27 Lift up a signal in the land,
Blow a trumpet among the nations!

51:15–19 These verses are borrowed from 10:12–16. (Moffatt eliminates them altogether here in chapter 51.)
51:25 *O destroying mountain,* a symbol of power. *a burnt out mountain,* an extinct volcano.

51:27 *Ararat, Minni and Ashkenaz.* Areas north of Babylon: Assyrian Urartu (part of modern Armenia); Mannai (southwest of Lake Van); Ashguzu (south of Lake Urmiah).

Consecrate the nations against her,
Summon against her the kingdoms of Ararat, Minni and Ashkenaz;
Appoint a marshal against her,
Bring up the horses like bristly locusts.

28   Consecrate the nations against her,
The kings of the Medes,
Their governors and all their prefects,
And every land of their dominion.

29   So the land quakes and writhes,
For the purposes of the LORD against Babylon stand,
To make the land of Babylon
A desolation without inhabitants.

30   The mighty men of Babylon have ceased fighting,
They stay in the strongholds;
Their strength is exhausted,
They are becoming *like* women;
Their dwelling places are set on fire,
The bars of her *gates* are broken.

31   One courier runs to meet another,
And one messenger to meet another,
To tell the king of Babylon
That his city has been captured from end *to end;*

32   The fords also have been seized,
And they have burned the marshes with fire,
And the men of war are terrified.

33   For thus says the LORD of hosts, the God of Israel:
"The daughter of Babylon is like a threshing floor
At the time it is stamped firm;
Yet in a little while the time of harvest will come for her."

34   "Nebuchadnezzar king of Babylon has devoured me *and* crushed me,
He has set me down *like* an empty vessel;
He has swallowed me like a monster,
He has filled his stomach with my delicacies;
He has washed me away.

35   "May the violence *done* to me and to my flesh be upon Babylon,"
The inhabitant of Zion will say;
And, "May my blood be upon the inhabitants of Chaldea,"
Jerusalem will say.

36   Therefore thus says the LORD,
"Behold, I am going to plead your case
And exact full vengeance for you;
And I shall dry up her sea
And make her fountain dry.

37   "And Babylon will become a heap *of ruins*, a haunt of jackals,
An object of horror and hissing, without inhabitants.

38   "They will roar together like young lions,
They will growl like lions' cubs.

39   "When they become heated up, I shall serve *them* their banquet
And make them drunk, that they may become jubilant
And may sleep a perpetual sleep
And not wake up," declares the LORD.

40   "I shall bring them down like lambs to the slaughter,
Like rams together with male goats.

41   "How [17]Sheshak has been captured,
And the praise of the whole earth been seized!
How Babylon has become an object of horror among the nations!

42   "The sea has come up over Babylon;
She has been engulfed with its tumultuous waves.

43   "Her cities have become an object of horror,
A parched land and a desert,

Jer 50:2; 25:14; 50:41, 42
51:28 v. 11
51:29 Jer 8:16; 10:10; 50:46; Amos 8:8; Is 13:19,20; 47:11
51:30 Ps 76:5; Jer 50:36,37; Is 13:7,8; Lam 2:9; Amos 1:5; Nah 3:13
51:31 2 Chr 30:6; 2 Sam 18:19-31; Jer 50:24
51:32 Jer 50:37,38
51:33 Is 21:10; 41:15; Hab 3:12; Is 17:5-7; Hos 6:11; Joel 3:13
51:34 Jer 50:17; Is 24:1-3; Amos 8:4
51:35 Ps 137:8; v. 24
51:36 Ps 140:12; Jer 50:34; Rom 12:19; Jer 50:38
51:37 Is 13:22; Jer 50:39; Rev 18:2
Jer 49:33; 50:13
51:39 Jer 25:27
51:40 Jer 50:27
51:41 Jer 25:26; Is 13:19; Jer 49:25
51:42 Is 8:7,8; Dan 9:26
51:43 Jer 50:12; Is 13:20

---

[17]Cryptic name for Babylon

A land in which no man lives,
And through which no son of man passes.

51:44
Is 46:1;
Jer 50:2;
vv. 34,58

44   "And I shall punish Bel in Babylon,
And I shall make what he has swallowed come out of his mouth;
And the nations will no longer stream to him.
Even the wall of Babylon has fallen down!

51:45
v. 6; Jer 50:8;
Rev 18:4;
Acts 2:40

45   "Come forth from her midst, My people,
And each of you save yourselves
From the fierce anger of the LORD.

51:46
Jer 46:27,28;
2 Kin 19:7;
Is 13:3-5;
19:2

46   "Now lest your heart grow faint,
And you be afraid at the report that *will be* heard in the land—
For the report will come one year,
And after that another report in another year,
And violence *will be* in the land
With ruler against ruler—

51:47
Is 46:1,2;
v. 52;
Jer 50:2;
50:12,35-37

47   Therefore behold, days are coming
When I shall punish the idols of Babylon;
And her whole land will be put to shame,
And all her slain will fall in her midst.

51:48
Is 44:23;
49:13;
Rev 12:12;
18:20; vv. 11,
27

48   "Then heaven and earth and all that is in them
Will shout for joy over Babylon,
For the destroyers will come to her from the north,"
Declares the LORD.

51:49
Jer 50:29

49   Indeed Babylon is to fall *for* the slain of Israel,
As also for Babylon the slain of all the earth have fallen.

51:50
v. 45;
Ps 137:6

50   You who have escaped the sword,
Depart! Do not stay!
Remember the LORD from afar,
And let Jerusalem come to your mind.

51:51
Ps 79:4

51   We are ashamed because we have heard reproach;
Disgrace has covered our faces,
For aliens have entered
The holy places of the LORD's house.

51:52
v. 47;
Jer 50:38

52   "Therefore behold, the days are coming," declares the LORD,
"When I shall punish her idols,
And the mortally wounded will groan throughout her land.

51:53
Is 14:12,13;
Jer 49:16;
Is 13:3

53   "Though Babylon should ascend to the heavens,
And though she should fortify her lofty stronghold,
From Me destroyers will come to her," declares the LORD.

51:54
Jer 50:46

54   The sound of an outcry from Babylon,
And of great destruction from the land of the Chaldeans!

51:55
v. 42

55   For the LORD is going to destroy Babylon,
And He will make *her* loud noise vanish from her.
And their waves will roar like many waters;
The tumult of their voices sounds forth.

51:56
v. 48;
Hab 2:8;
Ps 94:1,2;
vv. 6,24

56   For the destroyer is coming against her, against Babylon,
And her mighty men will be captured,
Their bows are shattered;
For the LORD is a God of recompense,
He will fully repay.

51:57
v. 39;
Ps 76:5,6;
Jer 46:18;
48:15

57   "And I shall make her princes and her wise men drunk,
Her governors, her prefects, and her mighty men,
That they may sleep a perpetual sleep and not wake up,"
Declares the King, whose name is the LORD of hosts.

51:58
v. 44;
Jer 50:15;
Hab 2:13;
v. 64

58   Thus says the LORD of hosts,
"The broad wall of Babylon will be completely razed,
And her high gates will be set on fire;
So the peoples will toil for nothing,
And the nations become exhausted *only* for fire."

51:44 *Bel*, or Bel-Marduk, the god of Babylon.   likewise be punished.
51:47 Idolatrous Babylon, who has punished Israel, shall

59 The message which Jeremiah the prophet commanded Seraiah the son of Neriah, the grandson of Mahseiah, when he went with Zedekiah the king of Judah to Babylon in the fourth year of his reign. (Now Seraiah was quartermaster.)

60 So Jeremiah wrote in a single scroll all the calamity which would come upon Babylon, *that is*, all these words which have been written concerning Babylon.

61 Then Jeremiah said to Seraiah, "As soon as you come to Babylon, then see that you read all these words aloud,

62 and say, 'Thou, O Lord, hast promised concerning this place to cut it off, so that there will be nothing dwelling in it, whether man or beast, but it will be a perpetual desolation.'

63 "And it will come about as soon as you finish reading this scroll, you will tie a stone to it and throw it into the middle of the Euphrates,

64 and say, 'Just so shall Babylon sink down and not rise again, because of the calamity that I am going to bring upon her; and they will become exhausted.'" Thus far are the words of Jeremiah.

V. Historical appendix (52:1–34)

A. Zedekiah's reign

52 Zedekiah was twenty-one years old when he became king, and he reigned eleven years in Jerusalem; and his mother's name was Hamutal the daughter of Jeremiah of Libnah.

2 And he did evil in the sight of the Lord like all that Jehoiakim had done.

3 For through the anger of the Lord *this* came about in Jerusalem and Judah until He cast them out from His presence. And Zedekiah rebelled against the king of Babylon.

B. Siege and fall of Jerusalem

4 Now it came about in the ninth year of his reign, on the tenth day of the tenth month, that Nebuchadnezzar king of Babylon came, he and all his army, against Jerusalem, camped against it, and built a siege wall all around it.

5 So the city was under siege until the eleventh year of King Zedekiah.

6 On the ninth day of the fourth month the famine was so severe in the city that there was no food for the people of the land.

7 Then the city was broken into, and all the men of war fled and went forth from the city at night by way of the gate between the two walls which *was* by the king's garden, though the Chaldeans were all around the city. And they went by way of the Arabah.

8 But the army of the Chaldeans pursued the king and overtook Zedekiah in the plains of Jericho, and all his army was scattered from him.

9 Then they captured the king and brought him up to the king of Babylon at Riblah in the land of Hamath; and he passed sentence on him.

10 And the king of Babylon slaughtered the sons of Zedekiah before his eyes, and he also slaughtered all the princes of Judah in Riblah.

11 Then he blinded the eyes of Zedekiah; and the king of Babylon bound him with bronze fetters and brought him to Babylon, and put him in prison until the day of his death.

12 Now on the tenth day of the fifth month, which was the nineteenth year of King Nebuchadnezzar, king of Babylon, Nebuzaradan the captain of the bodyguard, who was in the service of the king of Babylon, came to Jerusalem.

13 And he burned the house of the Lord, the king's house, and all the houses of Jerusalem; even every large house he burned with fire.

14 So all the army of the Chaldeans who *were* with the captain of the guard broke down all the walls around Jerusalem.

15 Then Nebuzaradan the captain of the guard carried away into exile some of the poorest of the people, the rest of the people who were left in the city, the deserters who had deserted to the king of Babylon, and the rest of the artisans.

16 But Nebuzaradan the captain of the guard left some of the poorest of the land to be vinedressers and plowmen.

17 Now the bronze pillars which belonged to the house of the Lord and the stands and the bronze sea, which were in the house of the Lord, the Chaldeans broke in pieces and carried all their bronze to Babylon.

51:59
Jer 32:12;
28:1

51:60
Jer 30:2,3;
36:2,4,32

51:62
Jer 25:12;
50:3,39;
v. 43;
Ezek 35:9
51:63
Rev 18:21

51:64
Nah 1:8,9;
v. 58

52:1
2 Kin 24:18;
2 Chr 36:11-13

52:2
Jer 36:30,31
52:3
Is 3:1,4,5;
2 Chr 36:13

52:4
2 Kin 25:1-7;
Jer 39:1;
Ezek 24:1,2;
Jer 32:24

52:6
Jer 38:9

52:7
Jer 39:2;
39:4-7

52:8
Jer 21:7;
32:4; 34:21;
37:17; 38:23
52:9
Jer 32:4;
2 Kin 25:6;
Jer 39:5
52:10
Jer 39:6
52:11
Jer 39:7;
Ezek 12:13

52:12
2 Kin 25:8-21;
Jer 39:9

52:13
2 Chr 36:19;
Lam 2:7;
Mic 3:12;
Jer 39:8
52:14
2 Kin 25:10
52:15
2 Kin 25:11;
Jer 39:9

52:16
2 Kin 25:12;
Jer 39:10;
40:2-6
52:17
1 Kin 7:15-36;
Jer 27:19-22

52:18
1 Kin 7:40,45

52:19
1 Kin 7:49,50

52:20
1 Kin 7:47

52:21
1 Kin 7:15

52:22
1 Kin 7:16,
20,42

52:24
2 Kin 25:18;
Jer 21:1;
29:25; 37:3;
35:4

52:26
vv. 12,15,16;
2 Kin 25:20,
21; v. 9
52:27
Is 6:11,12;
Jer 13:19;
Ezek 33:28;
Mic 4:10

52:28
2 Kin 24:2,3,
12-16;
Neh 7:6;
Dan 1:1-3
52:30
2 Kin 25:11;
Jer 39:9

52:31
2 Kin 25:27-30;
Gen 40:13

52:33
Gen 41:14,42;
2 Sam 9:13;
1 Kin 2:7
52:34
2 Sam 9:10

18   And they also took away the pots, the shovels, the snuffers, the basins, the pans, and all the bronze vessels which were used in *temple* service.

19   The captain of the guard also took away the bowls, the firepans, the basins, the pots, the lampstands, the pans and the libation bowls, what was fine gold and what was fine silver.

20   The two pillars, the one sea, and the twelve bronze bulls that were under the sea, *and* the stands, which King Solomon had made for the house of the LORD—the bronze of all these vessels was beyond weight.

21   As for the pillars, the height of each pillar was eighteen cubits, and it was twelve cubits in circumference and four fingers in thickness, *and* hollow.

22   Now a capital of bronze was on it; and the height of each capital was five cubits, with network and pomegranates upon the capital all around, all of bronze. And the second pillar was like these, including pomegranates.

23   And there were ninety-six exposed pomegranates; all the pomegranates *numbered* a hundred on the network all around.

24   Then the captain of the guard took Seraiah the chief priest and Zephaniah the second priest, with the three officers of the temple.

25   He also took from the city one official who was overseer of the men of war, and seven of the king's advisers who were found in the city, and the scribe of the commander of the army who mustered the people of the land, and sixty men of the people of the land who were found in the midst of the city.

26   And Nebuzaradan the captain of the guard took them and brought them to the king of Babylon at Riblah.

27   Then the king of Babylon struck them down and put them to death at Riblah in the land of Hamath. So Judah was led away into exile from its land.

C. *The deportations*

28   These are the people whom Nebuchadnezzar carried away into exile: in the seventh year 3,023 Jews;

29   in the eighteenth year of Nebuchadnezzar 832 persons from Jerusalem;

30   in the twenty-third year of Nebuchadnezzar, Nebuzaradan the captain of the guard carried into exile 745 Jewish people; there were 4,600 persons in all.

D. *The honor accorded Jehoiachin*

31   Now it came about in the thirty-seventh year of the exile of Jehoiachin king of Judah, in the twelfth month, on the twenty-fifth of the month, that Evil-merodach king of Babylon, in the *first* year of his reign, showed favor to Jehoiachin king of Judah and brought him out of prison.

32   Then he spoke kindly to him and set his throne above the thrones of the kings who *were* with him in Babylon.

33   So Jehoiachin changed his prison clothes, and had his meals in the king's presence regularly all the days of his life.

34   And for his allowance, a regular allowance was given him by the king of Babylon, a daily portion all the days of his life until the day of his death.

INTRODUCTION TO

THE LAMENTATIONS

OF JEREMIAH

Authorship and Background: Tradition has assigned the authorship of this book to the prophet Jeremiah. The title of the book appears as "The Lamentations of Jeremiah" in the Septuagint and Greek uncial manuscripts. However, the rabbinical and Talmud writers referred to it simply as Lamentations. In the Hebrew Bible the book appears in the Writings (Hagiographa) and is the third of the five Megilloth (Scrolls), which include the Song of Solomon, Ruth, Ecclesiastes, and Esther. The style of Lamentations differs from that of Jeremiah. Many believe that the author was a younger contemporary of Jeremiah, an eyewitness, in which event the book was composed around 540 B.C.

Characteristics: The writer pens this elegy in sorrow and lament over the fall of Jerusalem and the destruction of the temple. His work takes the form of an acrostic in the first four chapters. Each chapter has twenty-two verses, except chapter 3, which has sixty-six. The verses are arranged alphabetically (from *aleph* to *tau*). Chapter 3 employs the same design, but for each letter of the alphabet the author allots three verses instead of one. For some reason the last chapter, which has twenty-two verses, is not in acrostic form.

The author expresses deep grief over the evil that has befallen Jerusalem and the people of God. Throughout there is a sense of horror over what has taken place. The judgment of God for sin is prominently featured in the book, and yet hope is expressed that the people will profit from their experience. The book serves to memorialize for the Jews the destruction of Jerusalem in 587 B.C. To this day they read Lamentations in their synagogues on the ninth of Ab, when they mourn the destruction of Jerusalem.

Contents:

I. Jerusalem desolate and forsaken (1:1-22): The desolation of Jerusalem occasioned by her sin. A cry for compassion.

II. God's judgment explained, and repentance urged (2:1-22): God has judged His people; He is their enemy. The horrors of famine. Jerusalem's false prophets. A call to supplication.

III. The prophet's lament and hope (3:1-66): The cry of affliction; the prophet has shared in the suffering. He hopes for the mercies of God, and calls for conversion. Sin has its sorrows. A prayer for Jerusalem.

IV. The condition of Zion, past and present, contrasted (4:1-22): What Jerusalem was and now is. Consequences of her sin. Edom to be punished.

V. The prayer for mercy amid affliction (5:1-22): An appeal for mercy and confession of sin. A final plea to God.

THE LAMENTATIONS
OF JEREMIAH

I. *Jerusalem desolate and forsaken (1:1–22)*

A. *Description of her desolation*

1:1
Is 3:26; 54:4;
Ezra 4:20;
Jer 40:9

1 How lonely sits the city
That was full of people!
She has become like a widow
Who was *once* great among the nations!
She who was a princess among the provinces
Has become a forced laborer!

1:2
Ps 6:6;
Jer 2:25; 4:30

2 She weeps bitterly in the night,
And her tears are on her cheeks;
She has none to comfort her
Among all her lovers.
All her friends have dealt treacherously with her;
They have become her enemies.

1:3
Jer 13:19;
Deut 28:64,
65;
2 Kin 25:4,5

3 Judah has gone into exile under affliction,
And under harsh servitude;
She dwells among the nations,
But she has found no rest;
All her pursuers have overtaken her
In the midst of distress.

1:4
Jer 9:11;
10:22;
Joel 1:8-13

4 The roads of Zion are in mourning
Because no one comes to the appointed feasts.
All her gates are desolate;
Her priests are groaning,
Her virgins are afflicted,
And she herself is bitter.

1:5
Deut 28:43,
44; Jer 30:14,
15; 39:9;
52:28

5 Her adversaries have become her masters,
Her enemies prosper;
For the LORD has caused her grief
Because of the multitude of her transgressions;
Her little ones have gone away
As captives before the adversary.

1:6
Jer 13:18;
2 Kin 25:4,5

6 And all her majesty
Has departed from the daughter of Zion;
Her princes have become like bucks
That have found no pasture;
And they have fled without strength
Before the pursuer.

1:7
Ps 42:4;
Is 5:1-4;
Jer 37:7;
Lam 4:17;
Jer 48:27

7 In the days of her affliction and homelessness
Jerusalem remembers all her precious things
That were from the days of old
When her people fell into the hand of the adversary,
And no one helped her.
The adversaries saw her,
They mocked at her ruin.

*1:8
1 Kin 8:46;
vv. 5,20,17;
Jer 13:22,26;
vv. 4,11,21,
22

8 Jerusalem sinned greatly,
Therefore she has become an unclean thing.
All who honored her despise her
Because they have seen her nakedness;
Even she herself groans and turns away.

9 Her uncleanness was in her skirts;

She did not consider her future;
Therefore she has fallen astonishingly;
She has no comforter.
"See, O LORD, my affliction,
For the enemy has magnified himself!"

*1:9
Ezek 24:13;
Deut 32:29;
Is 47:7;
Jer 13:17,18;
16:7

10 The adversary has stretched out his hand
Over all her precious things,
For she has seen the nations enter her sanctuary,
The ones whom Thou didst command
That they should not enter into Thy congregation.

1:10
Is 64:10,11;
Jer 51:51;
Deut 23:3

11 All her people groan seeking bread;
They have given their precious things for food
To restore their lives themselves.
"See, O LORD, and look,
For I am despised."

1:11
Jer 38:9;
52:6;
1 Sam 30:12

B. Acknowledgment of her sin

12 "Is it nothing to all you who pass this way?
Look and see if there is any pain like my pain
Which was severely dealt out to me,
Which the LORD inflicted on the day of His fierce anger.

1:12
Jer 18:16;
48:27; v. 18;
Jer 30:23,24;
4:8

13 "From on high He sent fire into my bones,
And it prevailed *over them;*
He has spread a net for my feet;
He has turned me back;
He has made me desolate,
Faint all day long.

1:13
Job 30:30;
Hab 3:16;
Job 19:6;
Jer 44:6

14 "The yoke of my transgressions is bound;
By His hand they are knit together;
They have come upon my neck;
He has made my strength fail;
The Lord has given me into the hands
Of *those against whom* I am not able to stand.

1:14
Deut 28:48;
Is 47:6;
Jer 28:13,14;
32:3,5;
Ezek 25:4,7

15 "The Lord has rejected all my strong men
In my midst;
He has called an appointed time against me
To crush my young men;
The Lord has trodden *as in* a wine press
The virgin daughter of Judah.

1:15
Is 41:2;
Jer 13:24;
18:21;
Is 28:18;
Mic 7:10;
Rev 14:19

16 "For these things I weep;
My eyes run down with water;
Because far from me is a comforter,
One who restores my soul;
My children are desolate
Because the enemy has prevailed."

1:16
Jer 13:17;
14:17;
Lam 2:18;
vv. 2,9

17 Zion stretches out her hands;
There is no one to comfort her;
The LORD has commanded concerning Jacob
That the ones round about him should be his adversaries;
Jerusalem has become an unclean thing among them.

1:17
Jer 4:31;
2 Kin 24:2-4;
v. 8

18 "The LORD is righteous;
For I have rebelled against His command;
Hear now, all peoples,
And behold my pain;
My virgins and my young men
Have gone into captivity.

1:18
Jer 12:1;
1 Sam 12:14;
v. 12;
Deut 28:32,
41

19 "I called to my lovers, *but* they deceived me;
My priests and my elders perished in the city,
While they sought food to restore their strength themselves.

1:19
Jer 30:14;
14:15;
Lam 2:20

1:8 *her nakedness.* Sin leaves one without adequate cover- ing.

1:9 *in her skirts,* i.e., for all to see. Her sins are now public knowledge.

1:20
Is 16:11;
Jer 4:19;
Lam 2:11;
Deut 32:29;
Ezek 7:15

20 "See, O LORD, for I am in distress;
My spirit is greatly troubled;
My heart is overturned within me,
For I have been very rebellious.
In the street the sword slays;
In the house it is like death.

1:21
Lam 2:15;
Is 14:5,6;
Jer 30:16

21 "They have heard that I groan;
There is no one to comfort me;
All my enemies have heard of my calamity;
They are glad that Thou hast done it.
Oh, that Thou wouldst bring the day which Thou hast proclaimed,
That they may become like me.

1:22
Neh 4:4,5;
Ps 137:7,8

22 "Let all their wickedness come before Thee;
And deal with them as Thou hast dealt with me
For all my transgressions;
For my groans are many, and my heart is faint."

II. *God's judgment explained; repentance urged*
(2:1–22)

A. *The judgment of the LORD*

*2:1
Lam 3:43,44;
Ezek 28:14-16;
Is 64:11;
Ps 99:5;
132:7

2 How the Lord has covered the daughter of Zion
With a cloud in His anger!
He has cast from heaven to earth
The glory of Israel,
And has not remembered His footstool
In the day of His anger.

*2:2
Ps 21:9;
Lam 3:43;
Mic 5:11,14;
Is 25:12;
Ps 89:39

2 The Lord has swallowed up; He has not spared
All the habitations of Jacob.
In His wrath He has thrown down
The strongholds of the daughter of Judah;
He has brought them down to the ground;
He has profaned the kingdom and its princes.

2:3
Ps 75:5,10;
74:11;
Jer 21:4,5;
21:14

3 In fierce anger He has cut off
All the strength of Israel;
He has drawn back His right hand
From before the enemy.
And He has burned in Jacob like a flaming fire
Consuming round about.

2:4
Lam 3:12,13;
Ezek 24:25;
Is 42:25;
Jer 7:20

4 He has bent His bow like an enemy,
He has set His right hand like an adversary
And slain all that were pleasant to the eye;
In the tent of the daughter of Zion
He has poured out His wrath like fire.

2:5
Jer 30:14;
6:26; 9:17-20

5 The Lord has become like an enemy.
He has swallowed up Israel;
He has swallowed up all its palaces;
He has destroyed its strongholds
And multiplied in the daughter of Judah
Mourning and moaning.

2:6
Jer 7:14;
52:13;
Lam 1:4;
Zeph 3:18;
Lam 4:16,20;
5:12

6 And He has violently treated His tabernacle like a garden *booth;*
He has destroyed His appointed meeting place;
For I have caused to be forgotten
The appointed feast and sabbath in Zion,
And He has despised king and priest
In the indignation of His anger.

2:7
Is 64:11;
Ezek 7:20-22;
Jer 33:4,5;
Ps 74:4

7 The Lord has rejected His altar,
He has abandoned His sanctuary;
He has delivered into the hand of the enemy
The walls of her palaces.
They have made a noise in the house of the LORD

2:1 *Zion* here means Jerusalem.   **2:2** *Jacob* here is another name for Israel.

8   The LORD determined to destroy
    The wall of the daughter of Zion.
    He has stretched out a line,
    He has not restrained His hand from destroying;
    And He has caused rampart and wall to lament;
    They have languished together.

    Jer 5:10;
    2 Kin 21:13;
    Is 34:11;
    3:26; Jer 14:2

9   Her gates have sunk into the ground,
    He has destroyed and broken her bars.
    Her king and her princes are among the nations;
    The law is no more;
    Also, her prophets find
    No vision from the LORD.

    2:9
    Neh 1:3;
    Jer 51:30;
    Deut 28:36;
    2 Kin 24:15;
    2 Chr 15:3;
    Jer 14:14;
    23:16;
    Ezek 7:26

10 The elders of the daughter of Zion
    Sit on the ground, they are silent.
    They have thrown dust on their heads;
    They have girded themselves with sackcloth.
    The virgins of Jerusalem
    Have bowed their heads to the ground.

    2:10
    Job 2:13;
    Is 3:26;
    Amos 8:3;
    Job 2:12;
    Ezek 27:30,
    31; Is 15:3;
    Lam 1:4

11 My eyes fail because of tears,
    My spirit is greatly troubled;
    My heart is poured out on the earth,
    Because of the destruction of the daughter of my people,
    When little ones and infants faint
    In the streets of the city.

    2:11
    Ps 6:7;
    Lam 3:48;
    1:20;
    Job 16:13;
    Ps 22:14;
    Lam 4:4

12 They say to their mothers,
    "Where is grain and wine?"
    As they faint like a wounded man
    In the streets of the city,
    As their life is poured out
    On their mothers' bosom.

    2:12
    Jer 5:17;
    Lam 4:4;
    Job 30:16

13 How shall I admonish you?
    To what shall I compare you,
    O daughter of Jerusalem?
    To what shall I liken you as I comfort you,
    O virgin daughter of Zion?
    For your ruin is as vast as the sea;
    Who can heal you?

    2:13
    Lam 1:12;
    Is 37:22;
    Jer 14:17;
    8:22;
    30:12-15

B. The false prophets of Zion

14 Your prophets have seen for you
    False and foolish *visions;*
    And they have not exposed your iniquity
    So as to restore you from captivity,
    But they have seen for you false and misleading oracles.

    2:14
    Jer 2:8; 29:8,
    9; Is 58:1;
    Jer 23:36;
    Ezek 22:25,
    28

15 All who pass along the way
    Clap their hands *in derision* at you;
    They hiss and shake their heads
    At the daughter of Jerusalem,
    "Is this the city of which they said,
    'The perfection of beauty,
    A joy to all the earth'?"

    *2:15
    Jer 19:8;
    Zeph 2:15;
    Is 37:22;
    Ps 48:2; 50:2

16 All your enemies
    Have opened their mouths wide against you;
    They hiss and gnash *their* teeth.
    They say, "We have swallowed *her* up!
    Surely this is the day for which we waited;
    We have reached *it,* we have seen *it.*"

    2:16
    Ps 22:13;
    Lam 3:46;
    Ps 37:12;
    56:2;
    Obad 12-15

17 The LORD has done what He purposed;
    He has accomplished His word
    Which He commanded from days of old.

    2:17
    Deut 28:15;
    Jer 18:11;
    vv. 1,2;

2:15 Jerusalem, *The perfection of beauty,* is desolate and deserted.

Ps 35:24,26; Lam 1:5		He has thrown down without sparing, And He has caused the enemy to rejoice over you; He has exalted the might of your adversaries.
2:18 Hos 7:14; Jer 9:1; Lam 1:2,16	18	Their heart cried out to the Lord, "O wall of the daughter of Zion, Let *your* tears run down like a river day and night; Give yourself no relief; Let your eyes have no rest.
2:19 Ps 42:3; Is 26:9; Ps 62:8; Is 51:20	19	"Arise, cry aloud in the night At the beginning of the night watches; Pour out your heart like water Before the presence of the Lord; Lift up your hands to Him For the life of your little ones Who are faint because of hunger At the head of every street."
*2:20 Jer 19:9; 14:15; Lam 4:13,16	20	See, O LORD, and look! With whom hast Thou dealt thus? Should women eat their offspring, The little ones who were born healthy? Should priest and prophet be slain In the sanctuary of the Lord?
2:21 2 Chr 36:17; Jer 6:11; Ps 78:62,63; Jer 13:14; Zech 11:6	21	On the ground in the streets Lie young and old, My virgins and my young men Have fallen by the sword. Thou hast slain *them* in the day of Thine anger, Thou hast slaughtered, not sparing.
2:22 Ps 31:13; Jer 6:25; Hos 9:12,13	22	Thou didst call as in the day of an appointed feast My terrors on every side; And there was no one who escaped or survived In the day of the LORD's anger. Those whom I bore and reared, My enemy annihilated them.

III. *The prophet's lament and hope (3:1–66)*

A. *Lament over Zion's tragic condition*

3:1 Job 19:21; Jer 15:17,18	**3**	I am the man who has seen affliction Because of the rod of His wrath.
3:2 Is 59:9; Jer 4:23	2	He has driven me and made me walk In darkness and not in light.
3:3 Is 5:25	3	Surely against me He has turned His hand Repeatedly all the day.
3:4 Job 16:8; Ps 51:8; Is 38:13; Jer 50:17	4	He has caused my flesh and my skin to waste away, He has broken my bones.
3:5 Job 19:8; Jer 23:15	5	He has besieged and encompassed me with bitterness and hardship.
3:6 Ps 88:5,6	6	In dark places He has made me dwell, Like those who have long been dead.
3:7 Job 3:23; Jer 40:4	7	He has walled *me* in so that I cannot go out; He has made my chain heavy.
3:8 Job 30:20; Ps 22:2	8	Even when I cry out and call for help, He shuts out my prayer.
3:9 Hos 2:6; Is 63:17	9	He has blocked my ways with hewn stone; He has made my paths crooked.
3:10 Job 10:16; Is 38:13	10	He is to me like a bear lying in wait, *Like* a lion in secret places.
3:11 Hos 6:1	11	He has turned aside my ways and torn me to pieces; He has made me desolate.
3:12 Ps 7:12,13; Job 7:20	12	He bent His bow And set me as a target for the arrow.

2:20 *eat their offspring.* Famine produced inhuman conditions (cf. 2 Kin. 6:26–29).

13	He made the arrows of His quiver To enter into my inward parts.	**3:13** Job 6:4
14	I have become a laughingstock to all my people, Their *mocking* song all the day.	**3:14** Jer 20:7; Job 30:9
15	He has filled me with bitterness, He has made me drunk with wormwood.	**3:15** Jer 9:15
16	And He has broken my teeth with gravel; He has made me cower in the dust.	**3:16** Prov 20:17; Jer 6:26
17	And my soul has been rejected from peace; I have forgotten happiness.	**3:17** Jer 12:12
18	So I say, "My strength has perished, And *so has* my hope from the LORD."	**3:18** Ps 31:22
19	Remember my affliction and my wandering, the wormwood and bitterness.	**3:19** Jer 9:15
20	Surely my soul remembers And is bowed down within me.	**3:20** Ps 42:5,6,11

B. *The mercies of God recalled and trust expressed*

21	This I recall to my mind, Therefore I have hope.	**3:21** Ps 130:7
22	The LORD's lovingkindnesses indeed never cease, For His compassions never fail.	**3:22** Mal 3:6
23	*They* are new every morning; Great is Thy faithfulness.	**3:23** Zeph 3:5
24	"The LORD is my portion," says my soul, "Therefore I have hope in Him."	**3:24** Ps 16:5; 33:18
25	The LORD is good to those who wait for Him, To the person who seeks Him.	**3:25** Is 25:9; 30:18; 26:9
26	*It is* good that he waits silently For the salvation of the LORD.	**3:26** Ps 37:7; 40:1; Is 30:15
27	*It is* good for a man that he should bear The yoke in his youth.	**3:27** Ps 94:12
28	Let him sit alone and be silent Since He has laid *it* on him.	**3:28** Jer 15:17
29	Let him put his mouth in the dust, Perhaps there is hope.	**3:29** Job 16:15; Jer 31:17
30	Let him give his cheek to the smiter; Let him be filled with reproach.	**3:30** Is 50:6; Matt 5:39
31	For the Lord will not reject forever,	**3:31** Ps 94:14
32	For if He causes grief, Then He will have compassion According to His abundant lovingkindness.	**3:32** Ps 78:38; Hos 11:8
33	For He does not afflict willingly, Or grieve the sons of men.	**3:33** Ezek 33:11; Heb 12:10
34	To crush under His feet All the prisoners of the land,	
35	To deprive a man of justice In the presence of the Most High,	**3:35** Ps 140:12
36	To defraud a man in his lawsuit— Of these things the Lord does not approve.	**3:36** Hab 1:13
37	Who is there who speaks and it comes to pass, Unless the Lord has commanded *it*?	**3:37** Ps 33:9
38	*Is it* not from the mouth of the Most High That both good and ill go forth?	**3:38** Job 2:10; Is 45:7; Jer 32:42
39	Why should *any* living mortal, or *any* man, Offer complaint in view of his sins?	**3:39** Mic 7:9; Heb 12:5,6

C. *Israel exhorted to turn to God*

40	Let us examine and probe our ways, And let us return to the LORD.	**3:40** Ps 119:59; 2 Cor 13:5
41	We lift up our heart and hands	**3:41** Ps 25:1; 28:2

3:42
Dan 9:5;
Jer 5:7,9
42   Toward God in heaven;
We have transgressed and rebelled,
Thou hast not pardoned.

3:43
Lam 2:21;
Ps 83:15
43   Thou hast covered *Thyself* with anger
And pursued us;
Thou hast slain *and* hast not spared.

3:44
Ps 97:2; v. 8
44   Thou hast covered Thyself with a cloud
So that no prayer can pass through.

3:45
1 Cor 4:13
45   *Mere* offscouring and refuse Thou hast made us
In the midst of the peoples.

3:46
Lam 2:16
3:47
Is 24:17;
Jer 48:43;
Is 51:19
46   All our enemies have opened their mouths against us.
47   Panic and pitfall have befallen us,
Devastation and destruction;

3:48
Lam 1:16;
2:11,18
48   My eyes run down with streams of water
Because of the destruction of the daughter of my people.

3:49
Ps 77:2
3:50
Is 63:15
49   My eyes pour down unceasingly,
Without stopping,
50   Until the LORD looks down
And sees from heaven.

51   My eyes bring pain to my soul
Because of all the daughters of my city.

3:52
Ps 35:7
52   My enemies without cause
Hunted me down like a bird;

3:53
Jer 37:16
53   They have silenced me in the pit
And have placed a stone on me.

3:54
Ps 69:2;
Is 38:10
54   Waters flowed over my head;
I said, "I am cut off!"

D. *The cry for vengeance against Israel's enemies*

3:55
Jon 2:2
55   I called on Thy name, O LORD,
Out of the lowest pit.

3:56
Ps 116:1,2
56   Thou hast heard my voice,
"Do not hide Thine ear from my *prayer for* relief,
From my cry for help."

3:57
Ps 145:18;
Is 41:10,14
57   Thou didst draw near when I called on Thee;
Thou didst say, "Do not fear!"

3:58
Jer 51:36;
Ps 71:23
58   O Lord, Thou didst plead my soul's cause;
Thou hast redeemed my life.

3:59
Jer 18:19,20;
Ps 35:23
59   O LORD, Thou hast seen my oppression;
Judge my case.

3:60
Jer 11:19,20;
18:18
60   Thou hast seen all their vengeance,
All their schemes against me.

3:61
Lam 5:1
61   Thou hast heard their reproach, O LORD,
All their schemes against me.

3:62
Ezek 36:3
62   The lips of my assailants and their whispering
Are against me all day long.

3:63
Ps 139:2
63   Look on their sitting and their rising;
I am their mocking song.

3:64
Ps 28:4
64   Thou wilt recompense them, O LORD,
According to the work of their hands.

3:65
Is 6:10
65   Thou wilt give them hardness of heart,
Thy curse will be on them.

3:66
Ps 8:3
66   Thou wilt pursue them in anger and destroy them
From under the heavens of the LORD!

IV. *The condition of Zion, past and present, contrasted*
(4:1-22)

A. *The effects of the siege*

4:1
Ezek 7:19-22;
Jer 52:13,14
4   How dark the gold has become,
How the pure gold has changed!
The sacred stones are poured out

       At the corner of every street.

2   The precious sons of Zion,
       Weighed against fine gold,
       How they are regarded as earthen jars,
       The work of a potter's hands!

4:2
Is 51:18;
30:14;
Jer 19:11

3   Even jackals offer the breast,
       They nurse their young;
       But the daughter of my people has become cruel
       Like ostriches in the wilderness.

4:3
Is 34:13;
49:15;
Job 39:14,16

4   The tongue of the infant cleaves
       To the roof of its mouth because of thirst;
       The little ones ask for bread,
       But no one breaks *it* for them.

4:4
Jer 14:3;
Lam 2:12

5   Those who ate delicacies
       Are desolate in the streets;
       Those reared in purple
       Embrace ash pits.

4:5
Jer 6:2;
Amos 6:3-7;
Ps 113:7

6   For the iniquity of the daughter of my people
       Is greater than the sin of Sodom,
       Which was overthrown as in a moment,
       And no hands were turned toward her.

4:6
Ezek 16:48;
Gen 19:23;
Jer 20:16

7   Her consecrated ones were purer than snow,
       They were whiter than milk;
       They were more ruddy *in* body than corals,
       Their polishing *was* like lapis lazuli.

4:7
Ps 51:7

8   Their appearance is blacker than soot,
       They are not recognized in the streets;
       Their skin is shriveled on their bones,
       It is withered, it has become like wood.

4:8
Job 30:30;
Lam 5:10;
Ps 102:5

9   Better are those slain with the sword
       Than those slain with hunger;
       For they pine away, being stricken
       For lack of the fruits of the field.

4:9
Jer 15:2;
Ezek 24:23

10   The hands of compassionate women
       Boiled their own children;
       They became food for them
       Because of the destruction of the daughter of my people.

4:10
Lam 2:20;
2 Kin 6:29;
Deut 28:57

11   The LORD has accomplished His wrath,
       He has poured out His fierce anger;
       And He has kindled a fire in Zion
       Which has consumed its foundations.

4:11
Jer 7:20;
v. 22;
Deut 32:22;
Jer 21:14

12   The kings of the earth did not believe,
       Nor *did* any of the inhabitants of the world,
       That the adversary and the enemy
       Could enter the gates of Jerusalem.

4:12
1 Kin 9:8,9;
Jer 21:13

B. *The uselessness of the false prophets*

13   Because of the sins of her prophets
       And the iniquities of her priests,
       Who have shed in her midst
       The blood of the righteous,

4:13
Jer 5:31;
6:13;
Ezek 22:26;
Mic 3:11,12;
Matt 23:31

14   They wandered, blind, in the streets;
       They were defiled with blood
       So that no one could touch their garments.

4:14
Is 56:10;
59:9,10;
Jer 19:4; 2:34

15   "Depart! Unclean!" they cried of themselves.
       "Depart, depart, do not touch!"
       So they fled and wandered;
       Men among the nations said,
       "They shall not continue to dwell *with us.*"

4:15
Lev 13:45;
Jer 49:5

16   The presence of the LORD has scattered them;
       He will not continue to regard them.
       They did not honor the priests,
       They did not favor the elders.

4:16
Lam 5:12

C. *The absence of external help*

4:17
2 Kin 24:7;
Is 20:5;
Jer 37:7;
Ezek 29:16

17 Yet our eyes failed;
Looking for help was useless.
In our watching we have watched
For a nation that could not save.

4:18
2 Kin 25:4;
Ezek 7:2,3;
Amos 8:2

18 They hunted our steps
So that we could not walk in our streets;
Our end drew near,
Our days were finished
For our end had come.

4:19
Deut 28:49;
Jer 4:13;
Hab 1:8

19 Our pursuers were swifter
Than the eagles of the sky.
They chased us on the mountains;
They waited in ambush for us in the wilderness.

4:20
2 Sam 1:14;
19:21;
Ezek 12:13;
19:4,8

20 The breath of our nostrils, the LORD's anointed,
Was captured in their pits,
Of whom we had said, "Under his shadow
We shall live among the nations."

D. *Closing refrain*

*4:21
Is 34:7;
Amos 1:11,
12; Obad 1,
16

21 Rejoice and be glad, O daughter of Edom,
Who dwells in the land of Uz;
But the cup will come around to you as well,
You will become drunk and make yourself naked.

4:22
Is 40:2;
Mal 1:3,4

22 *The punishment* of your iniquity has been completed, O daughter of
Zion;
He will exile you no longer.
But He will punish your iniquity, O daughter of Edom,
He will expose your sins!

V. *The prayer for mercy amid affliction (5:1–22)*

A. *Acknowledgment of their sin and evil condition*

5:1
Ps 89:50;
44:13-16

5 Remember, O LORD, what has befallen us;
Look, and see our reproach!

5:2
Ps 79:1;
Zeph 1:13

2 Our inheritance has been turned over to strangers,
Our houses to aliens.

5:3
Jer 15:8;
18:21

3 We have become orphans without a father,
Our mothers are like widows.

5:4
Is 3:1

4 We have to pay for our drinking water,
Our wood comes *to us* at a price.

5:5
Jer 28:14;
Neh 9:36,37

5 Our pursuers are at our necks;
We are worn out, there is no rest for us.

5:6
Jer 2:36;
Hos 5:13;
7:11; 9:3

6 We have submitted to Egypt *and* Assyria to get enough bread.

7 Our fathers sinned, *and* are no more;
It is we who have borne their iniquities.

5:7
Jer 14:20;
16:12

8 Slaves rule over us;
There is no one to deliver us from their hand.

5:8
Neh 5:15;
Zech 11:6

9 We get our bread at the risk of our lives
Because of the sword in the wilderness.

5:10
Lam 4:8

10 Our skin has become as hot as an oven,
Because of the burning heat of famine.

5:11
Is 13:16;
Zech 14:2

11 They ravished the women in Zion,
The virgins in the cities of Judah.

5:12
Lam 4:16

12 Princes were hung by their hands;
Elders were not respected.

5:13
Jer 7:18

13 Young men worked at the grinding mill;
And youths stumbled under *loads* of wood.

5:14
Lam 4:8;
Jer 7:34

14 Elders are gone from the gate,

4:21 *O daughter of Edom.* The Edomites side with the Babylonians against Judah in the months before the fall of Jerusalem (587 B.C.). Edom, as a result, profited from Is- rael's tragedy but was herself punished in the end (cf. Ezek. 25:12–14; 35:5; Obad. 11–14).

	Young men from their music.	
15	The joy of our hearts has ceased;	**5:15** Jer 25:10
	Our dancing has been turned into mourning.	
16	The crown has fallen from our head;	**5:16** Ps 89:39; Is 3:9-11
	Woe to us, for we have sinned!	
17	Because of this our heart is faint;	**5:17** Is 1:5; Ps 6:7
	Because of these things our eyes are dim;	
18	Because of Mount Zion which lies desolate,	**5:18** Ps 74:2,3; Neh 4:3
	Foxes prowl in it.	

B. *Their prayer for mercy*

19	Thou, O Lord, dost rule forever;	**5:19** Ps 9:7; 102:12,25-27; 45:6
	Thy throne is from generation to generation.	
20	Why dost Thou forget us forever;	**5:20** Ps 13:1
	Why dost Thou forsake us so long?	
21	Restore us to Thee, O Lord, that we may be restored;	**5:21** Jer 31:18
	Renew our days as of old,	
22	Unless Thou hast utterly rejected us,	**5:22** Jer 7:29; Is 64:9
	And art exceedingly angry with us.	

INTRODUCTION TO
THE BOOK OF
EZEKIEL

Authorship and Background: This book is the work of Ezekiel, whose name means "God strengtheneth," or "God is strong." Ezekiel belonged to a priestly family and was the son of Buzi. As a young man he was carried away captive to Babylon, along with Jehoiachin, a decade before the destruction of Jerusalem. In captivity he lived in Telabib on the river Chebar. He was married and had his own home. Ezekiel's call to the prophetic office came in the fourth month of the fifth year of the captivity. He prophesied for more than two decades and undoubtedly knew both Daniel and Jeremiah. On the day that the siege of Jerusalem began, his wife died suddenly. Ezekiel wrote in Babylon but often addressed the Jews in Jerusalem, describing situations and events in that city. This has caused some to question whether the book was composed in Babylon at the indicated time, despite the internal evidences favoring authorship by Ezekiel in Babylon.

Characteristics: Ezekiel writes as one whose main burden is judgment. In a sense, he closely parallels the writer of the Revelation in the New Testament. No one exposes the sins of the people of God more openly or pronounces judgment more explicitly. Through the use of parables, oratory, and logic he arraigns Judah and does it in language that causes men to draw back in horror. He discloses the wrath of God against sin in the strongest language. Ezekiel uses his vivid imagination and often engages in symbolic actions. Occasionally a ray of hope shines through his utterances in the first half of the book. In the second half he prophesies the doom of Judah's conquerors and neighbors. Following the news of the fall of Jerusalem, people flock to hear the one whose prophecy has been fulfilled. Then it is that he speaks of the restoration of the people of God with hope and assurance. He is the forerunner of the apocalyptic writers of a later day.

Contents:

I. The divine judgment on Judah and Jerusalem (1:1-24:27): The call of Ezekiel in the vision of the glory of God enthroned on the four cherubim. He is commissioned to be a watchman, to speak and to be silent as God moves him. He prophesies the fall of Jerusalem by symbolic act and by word of mouth. It will occur because of the unbelief and hypocrisy of the people as illustrated by false prophets, and in spite of the idea that God will not punish His own people. He argues that Jerusalem has become a harlot. Judah has trusted her armies and fails to understand the righteousness of God as shown by the proverb of the sour grapes and the pictures of the lioness and the vine. God will judge Jerusalem because He wants a holy people. By parables of forest fire and the two harlots, as well as the boiling pot, he shows that God must punish the sins of His people.

II. The prophecies against the surrounding nations (25:1-32:32): Ezekiel pronounces doom on Ammon, Moab, and Philistia. Tyre is condemned for her pride and her insults to Jerusalem. The fall of Tyre is described. Sidon is condemned for not knowing the LORD and shall be destroyed by sword and pestilence. Egypt is guilty of treachery and pride, and Nebuchadnezzar will be the instrument of punishment. Pharaoh will fall.

III. Israel restored (33:1-39:29): The prophet watchman who will warn of danger is described. There is the promise of a good Shepherd, along with a restored land, a new heart among the people, and new life as illustrated in the vision of the valley of dry bones that come

21   Whenever those went, these went; and whenever those stood still, these stood still. And whenever those rose from the earth, the wheels rose close beside them; for the spirit of the living beings *was* in the wheels.

22   Now over the heads of the living beings *there was* something like an expanse, like the awesome gleam of crystal, extended over their heads.

23   And under the expanse their wings *were stretched out* straight, one toward the other; each one also had two wings covering their bodies on the one side and on the other.

24   I also heard the sound of their wings like the sound of abundant waters as they went, like the voice of the Almighty, a sound of tumult like the sound of an army camp; whenever they stood still, they dropped their wings.

25   And there came a voice from above the expanse that was over their heads; whenever they stood still, they dropped their wings.

26   Now above the expanse that was over their heads there was something resembling a throne, like lapis lazuli in appearance; and on that which resembled a throne, high up, *was* a figure with the appearance of a man.

27   Then I noticed from the appearance of His loins and upward something like glowing metal that looked like fire all around within it, and from the appearance of His loins and downward I saw something like fire; and *there was* a radiance around Him.

28   As the appearance of the rainbow in the clouds on a rainy day, so *was* the appearance of the surrounding radiance. Such *was* the appearance of the likeness of the glory of the LORD. And when I saw *it*, I fell on my face and heard a voice speaking.

3. *The commissions of Ezekiel*
a. *To go to the house of Israel*

2 Then He said to me, "Son of man, stand on your feet that I may speak with you!"

2   And as He spoke to me the Spirit entered me and set me on my feet; and I heard *Him* speaking to me.

3   Then He said to me, "Son of man, I am sending you to the sons of Israel, to a rebellious people who have rebelled against Me; they and their fathers have transgressed against Me to this very day.

4   "And I am sending you to them who are stubborn and obstinate children; and you shall say to them, 'Thus says the Lord GOD.'

5   "As for them, whether they listen or not—for they are a rebellious house—they will know that a prophet has been among them.

6   "And you, son of man, neither fear them nor fear their words, though thistles and thorns are with you and you sit on scorpions; neither fear their words nor be dismayed at their presence, for they are a rebellious house.

7   "But you shall speak My words to them whether they listen or not, for they are rebellious.

b. *To eat the scroll*

8   "Now you, son of man, listen to what I am speaking to you; do not be rebellious like that rebellious house. Open your mouth and eat what I am giving you."

9   Then I looked, behold, a hand was extended to me; and lo, a scroll *was* in it.

10   When He spread it out before me, it was written on the front and back; and written on it were lamentations, mourning and woe.

3 Then He said to me, "Son of man, eat what you find; eat this scroll, and go, speak to the house of Israel."

2   So I opened my mouth, and He fed me this scroll.

3   And He said to me, "Son of man, feed your stomach, and fill your body with

---

1:21
Ezek 10:17

1:22
Ezek 10:1

1:23
vv. 6,4

1:24
Ezek 10:5;
43:2;
Rev 1:15;
19:6;
2 Kin 7:6
1:25
v. 22
1:26
Ezek 10:1;
Ex 24:10;
Ezek 43:6,7;
Rev 1:13
1:27
v. 4; Ezek 8:2

*1:28
Rev 4:3;
10:1;
Ezek 3:23;
8:4;
Dan 8:17;
Rev 1:17

*2:1
Dan 10:11

*2:2
Dan 8:18;
Ezek 3:24
2:3
Jer 3:25;
Ezek 20:18,
30
2:4
Jer 5:3;
Ezek 3:7
2:5
Ezek 3:11,26,
27; 33:33
2:6
Jer 1:8,17;
Is 9:18;
Mic 7:4;
Ezek 3:9
2:7
Jer 1:7,17

2:8
Is 50:5;
Rev 10:9

2:9
Ezek 8:3; 3:1
2:10
Rev 8:13

3:1
Ezek 2:8,9

1:28 *the likeness of the glory of the* LORD. Ezekiel saw a vision of Israel's God. Although invisible, He revealed Himself to Ezekiel in the manner described in chapter 1 (cf. Isaiah's vision, Is. 6). **2:1** Ezekiel is addressed as *Son of man*, et passim, a term stressing the prophet's humanity. Although given celestial visions, Ezekiel was but a "son of man," i.e., a human being. The term later came to be used in a Messianic sense to describe the representative man, the Son of man who would establish God's rule over the earth and usher in the Messianic age (cf. Dan. 7:9–13). This usage does not occur in Ezekiel, however. **2:2** *the Spirit.* This is the Spirit of God.

3:3
Rev 10:9,10;
Jer 15:16;
Ps 19:10;
119:103

this scroll which I am giving you." Then I ate it, and it was sweet as honey in my mouth.

c. To speak God's message to Israel

3:4
v. 11

4 Then He said to me, "Son of man, go to the house of Israel and speak with My words to them.

*3:5
Jon 1:2;
Is 28:11;
33:19

5 "For you are not being sent to a people of unintelligible speech or difficult language, *but* to the house of Israel,

3:6
Matt 11:21,
23;
Acts 13:46-48

6 nor to many peoples of unintelligible speech or difficult language, whose words you cannot understand. But I have sent you to them who should listen to you;

3:7
John 15:20;
Ezek 2:4

7 yet the house of Israel will not be willing to listen to you, since they are not willing to listen to Me. Surely the whole house of Israel is stubborn and obstinate.

3:8
Jer 1:18;
15:20

8 "Behold, I have made your face as hard as their faces, and your forehead as hard as their foreheads.

3:9
Is 50:7;
Mic 3:8;
Ezek 2:6

9 "Like emery harder than flint I have made your forehead. Do not be afraid of them or be dismayed before them, though they are a rebellious house."

3:10
vv. 1-3

10 Moreover, He said to me, "Son of man, take into your heart all My words which I shall speak to you, and listen closely.

3:11
Ezek 2:5,7

11 "And go to the exiles, to the sons of your people, and speak to them and tell them, whether they listen or not, 'Thus says the Lord GOD.' "

d. The visit to Babylon

3:12
Ezek 8:3;
Acts 8:39; 2:2

12 Then the Spirit lifted me up, and I heard a great rumbling sound behind me, "Blessed be the glory of the LORD in His place."

3:13
Ezek 1:24;
10:5,16,17

13 And I *heard* the sound of the wings of the living beings touching one another, and the sound of the wheels beside them, even a great rumbling sound.

*3:14
Jer 6:11;
Ezek 1:3; 8:1

14 So the Spirit lifted me up and took me away; and I went embittered in the rage of my spirit, and the hand of the LORD was strong on me.

3:15
Ezek 1:1;
Job 2:13

15 Then I came to the exiles who lived beside the river Chebar at Tel-abib, and I sat there seven days where they were living, causing consternation among them.

e. The message of the watchman given

*3.16ff

16 Now it came about at the end of seven days that the word of the LORD came to me, saying,

3:17
Ezek 33:7-9;
Is 52:8;
56:10;
Jer 6:17

17 "Son of man, I have appointed you a watchman to the house of Israel; whenever you hear a word from My mouth, warn them from Me.

3:18
Gen 2:17;
Ezek 33:6;
John 8:21,24

18 "When I say to the wicked, 'You shall surely die'; and you do not warn him or speak out to warn the wicked from his wicked way that he may live, that wicked man shall die in his iniquity, but his blood I will require at your hand.

3:19
Ezek 33:3,9;
Acts 18:6;
20:26

19 "Yet if you have warned the wicked, and he does not turn from his wickedness or from his wicked way, he shall die in his iniquity; but you have delivered yourself.

3:20
Ezek 18:24;
33:12,13;
Jer 6:21

20 "Again, when a righteous man turns away from his righteousness and commits iniquity, and I place an obstacle before him, he shall die; since you have not warned him, he shall die in his sin, and his righteous deeds which he has done shall not be remembered; but his blood I will require at your hand.

3:21
Acts 20:31;
v. 19

21 "However, if you have warned the righteous man that the righteous should not sin, and he does not sin, he shall surely live because he took warning; and you have delivered yourself."

f. The commission to confinement

3:22
v. 14;
Ezek 8:4;
Acts 9:6

22 And the hand of the LORD was on me there, and He said to me, "Get up, go out to the plain, and there I will speak to you."

3:23
Ezek 1:28;
1:1

23 So I got up and went out to the plain; and behold, the glory of the LORD was standing there, like the glory which I saw by the river Chebar, and I fell on my face.

3:24
Ezek 2:2

24 The Spirit then entered me and made me stand on my feet, and He spoke with me and said to me, "Go, shut yourself up in your house.

3:5 *unintelligible speech or difficult language,* i.e., deep of lip and heavy of tongue.
3:14 *embittered in the rage of my spirit,* i.e., the prophet was both depressed and excited. Insufficient, he was mastered by God's mighty hand.
3:16–21 As a watchman, Ezekiel was responsible to sound

the alarm of impending catastrophe. Faithlessness on his part would mean the destruction of his people. Faithfulness could not ensure safety, for his message might go unheeded. Nevertheless, the prophet must be faithful to his God-appointed task.

25 "As for you, son of man, they will put ropes on you and bind you with them, so that you cannot go out among them.

26 "Moreover, I will make your tongue stick to the roof of your mouth so that you will be dumb, and cannot be a man who rebukes them, for they are a rebellious house.

27 "But when I speak to you, I will open your mouth, and you will say to them, 'Thus says the Lord GOD.' He who hears, let him hear; and he who refuses, let him refuse; for they are a rebellious house.

B. The coming destruction of Jerusalem

1. The symbol of the siege

4 "Now you son of man, get yourself a brick, place it before you, and inscribe a city on it, Jerusalem.

2 "Then lay siege against it, build a siege wall, raise up a ramp, pitch camps, and place battering rams against it all around.

3 "Then get yourself an iron plate and set it up as an iron wall between you and the city, and set your face toward it so that it is under siege, and besiege it. This is a sign to the house of Israel.

2. The symbol of the punishment

4 "As for you, lie down on your left side, and lay the iniquity of the house of Israel on it; you shall bear their iniquity for the number of days that you lie on it.

5 "For I have assigned you a number of days corresponding to the years of their iniquity, three hundred and ninety days; thus you shall bear the iniquity of the house of Israel.

6 "When you have completed these, you shall lie down a second time, *but* on your right side, and bear the iniquity of the house of Judah; I have assigned it to you for forty days, a day for each year.

7 "Then you shall set your face toward the siege of Jerusalem with your arm bared, and prophesy against it.

8 "Now behold, I will put ropes on you so that you cannot turn from one side to the other, until you have completed the days of your siege.

3. The symbol of the consequences of the siege

9 "But as for you, take wheat, barley, beans, lentils, millet and spelt, put them in one vessel and make them into bread for yourself; you shall eat it according to the number of the days that you lie on your side, three hundred and ninety days.

10 "And your food which you eat *shall be* twenty shekels a day by weight; you shall eat it from time to time.

11 "And the water you drink will be the sixth part of a hin by measure; you shall drink it from time to time.

12 "And you shall eat it as a barley cake, having baked *it* in their sight over human dung."

13 Then the LORD said, "Thus shall the sons of Israel eat their bread unclean among the nations where I shall banish them."

14 But I said, "Ah, Lord GOD! Behold, I have never been defiled; for from my youth until now I have never eaten what died of itself or was torn by beasts, nor has any unclean meat ever entered my mouth."

15 Then He said to me, "See, I shall give you cow's dung in place of human dung over which you will prepare your bread."

16 Moreover, He said to me, "Son of man, behold, I am going to break the staff of bread in Jerusalem, and they will eat bread by weight and with anxiety, and drink water by measure and in horror,

17 because bread and water will be scarce; and they will be appalled with one another and waste away in their iniquity.

3:25	Ezek 4:8
3:26	Ezek 24:27; Luke 1:20, 22;
	Ezek 2:5-7
3:27	Ezek 24:27; 33:22; vv. 11, 9,26
***4:1**	Is 20:2; Ezek 5:1
4:2	Ezek 21:22
4:3	Ezek 5:2; 12:6,11; 24:24,27
4:4	Lev 10:17; Num 18:1
4:5	Num 14:34
4:7	v. 3; Ezek 21:2
4:8	Ezek 3:25
4:9	v. 5
4:10	v. 16
4:12	Is 36:12
4:13	Hos 9:3
4:14	Ezek 9:8; Acts 10:14; Ex 22:31; Lev 17:15; Deut 14:3; Is 65:4
4:16	Lev 26:26; Is 3:1; Ezek 5:16; 14:13
4:17	Lev 26:39; Ezek 24:23

4:1 *get yourself a brick.* Ezekiel was ordered to draw a plan of Jerusalem on a clay tablet such as the Babylonians used as writing material. He then would enact a mock battle to depict the coming siege.

4. The symbol of Jerusalem's fate

a. What will happen to the people

5 "As for you, son of man, take a sharp sword; take and use it *as* a barber's razor on your head and beard. Then take scales for weighing and divide the hair.

2 "One third you shall burn in the fire at the center of the city, when the days of the siege are completed. Then you shall take one third and strike *it* with the sword all around the city, and one third you shall scatter to the wind; and I will unsheathe a sword behind them.

3 "Take also a few in number from them and bind them in the edges of your robes.

4 "And take again some of them and throw them into the fire, and burn them in the fire; from it a fire will spread to all the house of Israel.

b. Jerusalem's fate the result of sin (idolatry)

5 "Thus says the Lord GOD, 'This is Jerusalem; I have set her at the center of the nations, with lands around her.

6 'But she has rebelled against My ordinances more wickedly than the nations and against My statutes more than the lands which surround her; for they have rejected My ordinances and have not walked in My statutes.'

7 "Therefore, thus says the Lord GOD, 'Because you have more turmoil than the nations which surround you, and have not walked in My statutes, nor observed My ordinances, nor observed the ordinances of the nations which surround you,'

8 therefore, thus says the Lord GOD, 'Behold, I, even I, am against you, and I will execute judgments among you in the sight of the nations.

9 'And because of all your abominations, I will do among you what I have not done, and the like of which I will never do again.

10 'Therefore, fathers will eat *their* sons among you, and sons will eat their fathers; for I will execute judgments on you, and scatter all your remnant to every wind.

11 'So as I live,' declares the Lord GOD, 'surely, because you have defiled My sanctuary with all your detestable idols and with all your abominations, therefore I will also withdraw, and My eye shall have no pity and I will not spare.

12 'One third of you will die by plague or be consumed by famine among you, one third will fall by the sword around you, and one third I will scatter to every wind, and I will unsheathe a sword behind them.

13 'Thus My anger will be spent, and I will satisfy My wrath on them, and I shall be appeased; then they will know that I, the LORD, have spoken in My zeal when I have spent My wrath upon them.

14 'Moreover, I will make you a desolation and a reproach among the nations which surround you, in the sight of all who pass by.

15 'So it will be a reproach, a reviling, a warning and an object of horror to the nations who surround you, when I execute judgments against you in anger, wrath, and raging rebukes. I, the LORD, have spoken.

16 'When I send against them the deadly arrows of famine which were for the destruction of those whom I shall send to destroy you, then I shall also intensify the famine upon you, and break the staff of bread.

17 'Moreover, I will send on you famine and wild beasts, and they will bereave you of children; plague and bloodshed also will pass through you, and I will bring the sword on you. I, the LORD, have spoken.'"

C. The oracle of the mountains

1. The high places to be destroyed

6 And the word of the LORD came to me saying,
2 "Son of man, set your face toward the mountains of Israel, and prophesy against them,

3 and say, 'Mountains of Israel, listen to the word of the Lord GOD! Thus says the Lord GOD to the mountains, the hills, the ravines and the valleys: "Behold, I Myself am going to bring a sword on you, and I will destroy your high places.

4 "So your altars will become desolate, and your incense altars will be smashed; and I shall make your slain fall in front of your idols.

5 "I shall also lay the dead bodies of the sons of Israel in front of their idols; and I shall scatter your bones around your altars.

6 "In all your dwellings, cities will become waste and the high places will be desolate, that your altars may become waste and desolate, your idols may be broken and brought to an end, your incense altars may be cut down, and your works may be blotted out.

7 "And the slain will fall among you, and you will know that I am the LORD.

2. A remnant to be preserved

8 "However, I shall leave a remnant, for you will have those who escaped the sword among the nations when you are scattered among the countries.

9 "Then those of you who escape will remember Me among the nations to which they will be carried captive, how I have been hurt by their adulterous hearts which turned away from Me, and by their eyes, which played the harlot after their idols; and they will loathe themselves in their own sight for the evils which they have committed, for all their abominations.

10 "Then they will know that I am the LORD; I have not said in vain that I would inflict this disaster on them.' "

3. Israel to know the LORD by His judgments

11 "Thus says the Lord GOD, 'Clap your hand, stamp your foot, and say, "Alas, because of all the evil abominations of the house of Israel, which will fall by sword, famine, and plague!

12 "He who is far off will die by the plague, and he who is near will fall by the sword, and he who remains and is besieged will die by the famine. Thus shall I spend My wrath on them.

13 "Then you will know that I am the LORD, when their slain are among their idols around their altars, on every high hill, on all the tops of the mountains, under every green tree, and under every leafy oak—the places where they offered soothing aroma to all their idols.

14 "So throughout all their habitations I shall stretch out My hand against them and make the land more desolate and waste than the wilderness toward Diblah; thus they will know that I am the LORD." ' "

D. The oracle of the coming end

1. The disaster in the land

7 Moreover, the word of the LORD came to me saying,
2 "And you, son of man, thus says the Lord GOD to the land of Israel, 'An end! The end is coming on the four corners of the land.

3 'Now the end is upon you, and I shall send My anger against you; I shall judge you according to your ways, and I shall bring all your abominations upon you.

4 'For My eye will have no pity on you, nor shall I spare you, but I shall bring your ways upon you, and your abominations will be among you; then you will know that I am the LORD!'

5 "Thus says the Lord GOD, 'A disaster, unique disaster, behold it is coming!

6 'An end is coming; the end has come! It has awakened against you; behold, it has come!

7 'Your doom has come to you, O inhabitant of the land. The time has come, the day is near—tumult rather than joyful shouting on the mountains.

8 'Now I will shortly pour out My wrath on you, and spend My anger against you, judge you according to your ways, and bring on you all your abominations.

9 'And My eye will show no pity, nor will I spare. I will repay you according to your ways, while your abominations are in your midst; then you will know that I, the LORD, do the smiting.

10 'Behold, the day! Behold, it is coming! Your doom has gone forth; the rod has budded, arrogance has blossomed.

11 'Violence has grown into a rod of wickedness. None of them shall remain, none of their multitude, none of their wealth, nor anything eminent among them.

12 'The time has come, the day has arrived. Let not the buyer rejoice nor the seller mourn; for wrath is against all their multitude.

13 'Indeed, the seller will not regain what he sold as long as they both live; for the vision regarding all their multitude will not be averted, nor will any of them maintain his life by his iniquity.

Cross references (margin)

6:6 Lev 26:31; Zech 13:2

6:7 Ezek 11:10, 12

6:8 Jer 44:28; Ezek 5:2,12; 12:16; 14:22

6:9 Jer 51:50; Ps 78:40; Is 7:13; Ezek 43:24; 20:7,24; 20:43 — *God has hurt feelings See Gen 6:6*

6:10 v. 7

6:11 Ezek 21:14; 25:6; 5:12; 7:15

6:12 Dan 9:7; Ezek 5:13

6:13 v. 7; Jer 2:20; Hos 4:13; Is 57:5

6:14 Is 5:25; Ezek 14:13; Num 33:46

7:2 Amos 8:2; Ezek 11:13; Rev 7:1; 20:8

7:3 vv. 8,9,27

7:4 Ezek 5:11; 8:18; 11:21; 6:7

7:5 2 Kin 21:12, 13

7:6 vv. 2,10

7:7 v. 12; Is 22:5

7:8 Ezek 20:8,21; 6:12; v. 3

7:10 v. 7; Is 10:5

7:11 Jer 6:7; 16:5, 6; Ezek 24:16, 22

7:12 vv. 5-7,10; 1 Cor 7:30; v. 14

2. The desolation of the inhabitants within and without

14 'They have blown the trumpet and made everything ready, but no one is going to the battle; for My wrath is against all their multitude.

15 'The sword is outside, and the plague and the famine are within. He who is in the field will die by the sword; famine and the plague will also consume those in the city.

16 'Even when their survivors escape, they will be on the mountains like doves of the valleys, all of them mourning, each over his own iniquity.

17 'All hands will hang limp, and all knees will become like water.

18 'And they will gird themselves with sackcloth, and shuddering will overwhelm them; and shame *will be* on all faces, and baldness on all their heads.

19 'They shall fling their silver into the streets, and their gold shall become an abhorrent thing; their silver and their gold shall not be able to deliver them in the day of the wrath of the LORD. They cannot satisfy their appetite, nor can they fill their stomachs, for their iniquity has become an occasion of stumbling.

20 'And they transformed the beauty of His ornaments into pride, and they made the images of their abominations *and* their detestable things with it; therefore I will make it an abhorrent thing to them.

21 'And I shall give it into the hands of the foreigners as plunder and to the wicked of the earth as spoil, and they will profane it.

22 'I shall also turn My face from them, and they will profane My secret place; then robbers will enter and profane it.

23 'Make the chain, for the land is full of bloody crimes, and the city is full of violence.

3. The profanation of the holy places

24 'Therefore, I shall bring the worst of the nations, and they will possess their houses. I shall also make the pride of the strong ones cease, and their holy places will be profaned.

25 'When anguish comes, they will seek peace, but there will be none.

26 'Disaster will come upon disaster, and rumor will be *added* to rumor; then they will seek a vision from a prophet, but the law will be lost from the priest and counsel from the elders.

27 'The king will mourn, the prince will be clothed with horror, and the hands of the people of the land will tremble. According to their conduct I shall deal with them, and by their judgments I shall judge them. And they will know that I am the LORD.'"

E. *The vision of abominations in Jerusalem*

1. *Idolatry in the temple*

a. *The background of the vision*

8 And it came about in the sixth year, on the fifth *day* of the sixth month, as I was sitting in my house with the elders of Judah sitting before me, that the hand of the Lord GOD fell on me there.

2 Then I looked, and behold, a likeness as the appearance of a man; from His loins and downward *there was* the appearance of fire, and from His loins and upward the appearance of brightness, like the appearance of glowing metal.

3 And He stretched out the form of a hand and caught me by a lock of my head; and the Spirit lifted me up between earth and heaven and brought me in the visions of God to Jerusalem, to the entrance of the north gate of the inner *court*, where the seat of the idol of jealousy, which provokes to jealousy, was *located*.

4 And behold, the glory of the God of Israel *was* there, like the appearance which I saw in the plain.

b. *The image of jealousy*

5 Then He said to me, "Son of man, raise your eyes, now, toward the north." So I raised my eyes toward the north, and behold, to the north of the altar gate *was* this idol of jealousy at the entrance.

6 And He said to me, "Son of man, do you see what they are doing, the great

---

8:5 *idol of jealousy,* i.e., an image that provokes the LORD to jealousy (cf. Ex. 20:5).

abominations which the house of Israel are committing here, that I should be far from My sanctuary? But yet you will see still greater abominations."

c. *The worship of idols and pictures*

7   Then He brought me to the entrance of the court, and when I looked, behold, a hole in the wall.

8   And He said to me, "Son of man, now dig through the wall." So I dug through the wall, and behold, an entrance.

9   And He said to me, "Go in and see the wicked abominations that they are committing here."

10   So I entered and looked, and behold, every form of creeping things and beasts *and* detestable things, with all the idols of the house of Israel, were carved on the wall all around.

11   And standing in front of them were seventy elders of the house of Israel, with Jaazaniah the son of Shaphan standing among them, each man with his censer in his hand, and the fragrance of the cloud of incense rising.

12   Then He said to me, "Son of man, do you see what the elders of the house of Israel are committing in the dark, each man in the room of his carved images? For they say, 'The LORD does not see us; the LORD has forsaken the land.'"

13   And He said to me, "Yet you will see still greater abominations which they are committing."

d. *The worship of Tammuz*

14   Then He brought me to the entrance of the gate of the LORD's house which *was* toward the north; and behold, women were sitting there weeping for Tammuz.

15   And He said to me, "Do you see *this*, son of man? Yet you will see still greater abominations than these."

e. *The worship of the sun*

16   Then He brought me into the inner court of the LORD's house. And behold, at the entrance to the temple of the LORD, between the porch and the altar, *were* about twenty-five men with their backs to the temple of the LORD and their faces toward the east; and they were prostrating themselves eastward toward the sun.

f. *The call to judgment*

17   And He said to me, "Do you see *this*, son of man? Is it too light a thing for the house of Judah to commit the abominations which they have committed here, that they have filled the land with violence and provoked Me repeatedly? For behold, they are putting the twig to their nose.

18   "Therefore, I indeed shall deal in wrath. My eye will have no pity nor shall I spare; and though they cry in My ears with a loud voice, yet I shall not listen to them."

2. *The slaughter of the idolaters*

a. *The marking of the innocent*

9 Then He cried out in my hearing with a loud voice saying, "Draw near, O executioners of the city, each with his destroying weapon in his hand."

2   And behold, six men came from the direction of the upper gate which faces north, each with his shattering weapon in his hand; and among them was a certain man clothed in linen with a writing case at his loins. And they went in and stood beside the bronze altar.

3   Then the glory of the God of Israel went up from the cherub on which it had been, to the threshold of the temple. And He called to the man clothed in linen at whose loins was the writing case.

4   And the LORD said to him, "Go through the midst of the city, *even* through

---

Cross-references (margin)

8:6 vv. 9,17; Ezek 5:11; 7:22,24; vv. 11,14,16

8:10 Ex 20:4; Ezek 14:3

8:11 Jer 19:1; Num 16:17, 35; Ezek 16:18; 23:41

8:12 Ezek 9:9

8:13 Ezek 9:3

*8:14 Ezek 44:4; 46:9

8:16 Ezek 11:1; Jer 2:27; Deut 4:19; Job 31:26; Jer 44:17

8:17 Ezek 9:9; Mic 2:2; Jer 7:18,19; Ezek 16:26

8:18 Ezek 5:13; 7:4; 9:5,10; Is 1:15; Jer 11:11; Mic 3:4; Zech 7:13

*9:2 Ezek 10:2; Rev 15:6

*9:3 Ezek 8:4; 10:4,18; 11:22,23

*9:4 Ex 12:7; 1 Pet 4:17; Rev 7:3; 9:4;

8:14 *Tammuz* was a Babylonian vegetation deity who was believed to vanish into the nether world during the dry season when plants and streams dried up. Public dirges marked the departure of Tammuz. The women of Jerusalem, taking part in this idolatrous worship, gave evidence of the hold of idolatry in the Holy City.

9:2 *writing case at his loins.* It was customary in the East for men to wear the writing case or inkhorn (KJV) in the girdle.

9:3 *the glory of the God of Israel.* The visible manifestation

and evidence of God's presence with His people. In a vision, Ezekiel saw the glory leave the Holy of Holies and linger at the threshold (9:3). Then it hovered over the city and paused on the Mount of Olives (11:23). Slowly, reluctantly, God was leaving His people. After the departure of the glory of God, the city was defenseless before its enemies.

9:4 *the men who sigh and groan,* i.e., those who disapprove of the city's idolatry. They are marked for safety. All others are to be destroyed.

Ps 119:53,
136; Jer 13:17
the midst of Jerusalem, and put a mark on the foreheads of the men who sigh and groan over all the abominations which are being committed in its midst.''

b. *The slaughter of the guilty*

*9:5
Ezek 5:11;
7:4,9
9:6
2 Chr 36:17;
Rev 9:4;
Jer 25:29;
Amos 3:2;
Ezek 8:11,12,
16
9:7
2 Chr 36:17;
Ezek 7:20-22;
6:4
9:8
1 Chr 21:16;
Josh 7:6;
Ezek 11:13
9:9
Ezek 7:23;
22:29; 8:12
9:10
Is 65:6;
Ezek 8:18;
7:4; 11:21
5   But to the others He said in my hearing, ''Go through the city after him and strike; do not let your eye have pity, and do not spare.

6   ''Utterly slay old men, young men, maidens, little children, and women, but do not touch any man on whom is the mark; and you shall start from My sanctuary.'' So they started with the elders who *were* before the temple.

7   And He said to them, ''Defile the temple and fill the courts with the slain. Go out!'' Thus they went out and struck down *the people* in the city.

8   Then it came about as they were striking and I *alone* was left, that I fell on my face and cried out saying, ''Alas, Lord GOD! Art Thou destroying the whole remnant of Israel by pouring out Thy wrath on Jerusalem?''

9   Then He said to me, ''The iniquity of the house of Israel and Judah is very, very great, and the land is filled with blood, and the city is full of perversion; for they say, 'The LORD has forsaken the land, and the LORD does not see!'

10   ''But as for Me, My eye will have no pity nor shall I spare, but I shall bring their conduct upon their heads.''

11   Then behold, the man clothed in linen at whose loins was the writing case reported, saying, ''I have done just as Thou hast commanded me.''

3. *The departure of the LORD from the sanctuary*

*10:1
Ezek 1:22,26;
Rev 4:2

10:2
Ezek 9:2,3;
v. 13; Is 6:6;
Rev 8:5
10:3
Ezek 8:3,16

10:4
Ezek 1:28;
9:3;
Ex 40:34,35;
1 Kin 8:10,11
10:5
Ezek 1:24

10:6
v. 2

10:7
Ezek 1:13

10:8
Ezek 1:8

10:9
Ezek 1:15,16

10:11
Ezek 1:17;
v. 22
10:12
Rev 4:6,8;
Ezek 1:18
10:13
v. 2
10 Then I looked, and behold, in the expanse that was over the heads of the cherubim something like a sapphire stone, in appearance resembling a throne, appeared above them.

2   And He spoke to the man clothed in linen and said, ''Enter between the whirling wheels under the cherubim, and fill your hands with coals of fire from between the cherubim, and scatter *them* over the city.'' And he entered in my sight.

3   Now the cherubim were standing on the right side of the temple when the man entered, and the cloud filled the inner court.

4   Then the glory of the LORD went up from the cherub to the threshold of the temple, and the temple was filled with the cloud, and the court was filled with the brightness of the glory of the LORD.

5   Moreover, the sound of the wings of the cherubim was heard as far as the outer court, like the voice of God Almighty when He speaks.

6   And it came about when He commanded the man clothed in linen, saying, ''Take fire from between the whirling wheels, from between the cherubim,'' he entered and stood beside a wheel.

7   Then the cherub stretched out his hand from between the cherubim to the fire which *was* between the cherubim, took some and put it into the hands of the one clothed in linen, who took *it* and went out.

8   And the cherubim appeared to have the form of a man's hand under their wings.

9   Then I looked, and behold, four wheels beside the cherubim, one wheel beside each cherub; and the appearance of the wheels *was* like the gleam of a Tarshish stone.

10   And as for their appearance, all four of them had the same likeness, as if one wheel were within another wheel.

11   When they moved, they went in *any of* their four directions without turning as they went; but they followed in the direction which they faced, without turning as they went.

12   And their whole body, their backs, their hands, their wings, and the wheels were full of eyes all around, the wheels belonging to all four of them.

13   The wheels were called in my hearing, the whirling wheels.

9:5 *Go through . . . and strike*, i.e., spare neither female nor aged; save only those *on whom is the mark* (v. 6).
10:1 The Scripture describes the cherubim as winged creatures of great splendor and power in the service of the LORD. In Genesis we are told God placed the cherubim at the east of the Garden of Eden to keep Adam and Eve from the sacred tree (Gen. 3:24). Golden figures of two cherubim were on either end of the lid or mercy seat of the ark of the covenant, bowing before the presence of the LORD and touching each other with the tips of their outstretched wings (Ex. 25:18–21). Figures of cherubim were also embroidered into the veil or curtain that separated the Holy of Holies from the holy place (Ex. 26:31). In the book of Revelation the cherubim are spoken of as living creatures, four in number, who stand in the midst of and around the throne of God (Rev. 4:6,7). Some hold that the reference in 28:14 to the cherub goes beyond the king of Tyre and speaks of Satan, whose fall may have been described in Is. 14:12–14. (Read also 1:26.)

14　And each one had four faces. The first face *was* the face of a cherub, the second face *was* the face of a man, the third the face of a lion, and the fourth the face of an eagle.

15　Then the cherubim rose up. They are the living beings that I saw by the river Chebar.

16　Now when the cherubim moved, the wheels would go beside them; also when the cherubim lifted up their wings to rise from the ground, the wheels would not turn from beside them.

17　When the cherubim stood still, the wheels would stand still; and when they rose up, the wheels would rise with them; for the spirit of the living beings *was* in them.

18　Then the glory of the LORD departed from the threshold of the temple and stood over the cherubim.

19　When the cherubim departed, they lifted their wings and rose up from the earth in my sight with the wheels beside them; and they stood still at the entrance of the east gate of the LORD's house. And the glory of the God of Israel hovered over them.

20　These are the living beings that I saw beneath the God of Israel by the river Chebar; so I knew that they *were* cherubim.

21　Each one had four faces and each one four wings, and beneath their wings *was* the form of human hands.

22　As for the likeness of their faces, they were the same faces whose appearance I had seen by the river Chebar. Each one went straight ahead.

4. *The ungodly rulers of the nation to be punished*

11　Moreover, the Spirit lifted me up and brought me to the east gate of the LORD's house which faced eastward. And behold, *there were* twenty-five men at the entrance of the gate, and among them I saw Jaazaniah son of Azzur and Pelatiah son of Benaiah, leaders of the people.

2　And He said to me, "Son of man, these are the men who devise iniquity and give evil advice in this city,

3　who say, 'Is not *the time* near to build houses? This *city* is the pot and we are the flesh.'

4　"Therefore, prophesy against them, son of man, prophesy!"

5　Then the Spirit of the LORD fell upon me, and He said to me, "Say, 'Thus says the LORD, "So you think, house of Israel, for I know your thoughts.

6　"You have multiplied your slain in this city, filling its streets with them."

7　'Therefore, thus says the Lord GOD, "Your slain whom you have laid in the midst of the city are the flesh, and this *city* is the pot; but I shall bring you out of it.

8　"You have feared a sword; so I will bring a sword upon you," the Lord GOD declares.

9　"And I shall bring you out of the midst of the city, and I shall deliver you into the hands of strangers and execute judgments against you.

10　"You will fall by the sword. I shall judge you to the border of Israel; so you shall know that I am the LORD.

11　"This *city* will not be a pot for you, nor will you be flesh in the midst of it, *but* I shall judge you to the border of Israel.

12　"Thus you will know that I am the LORD; for you have not walked in My statutes nor have you executed My ordinances, but have acted according to the ordinances of the nations around you." ' "

13　Now it came about as I prophesied, that Pelatiah son of Benaiah died. Then I fell on my face and cried out with a loud voice and said, "Alas, Lord GOD! Wilt Thou bring the remnant of Israel to a complete end?"

14　Then the word of the LORD came to me, saying,

15　"Son of man, your brothers, your relatives, your fellow exiles, and the whole house of Israel, all of them, *are those* to whom the inhabitants of Jerusalem have said, 'Go far from the LORD; this land has been given us as a possession.'

16　"Therefore say, 'Thus says the Lord GOD, "Though I had removed them far away among the nations, and though I had scattered them among the countries, yet I was a sanctuary for them a little while in the countries where they had gone." '

17　"Therefore say, 'Thus says the Lord GOD, "I shall gather you from the peoples and assemble you out of the countries among which you have been scattered, and I shall give you the land of Israel." '

10:14
Ezek 1:6,10;
Rev 4:7

10:15
Ezek 1:3,5

10:16
Ezek 1:19

10:17
Ezek 1:12,20,
21

10:18
v. 4

10:19
11:1,22

10:20
v. 15;
Ezek 1:22;
1:1
10:21
Ezek 1:6,8
10:22
Ezek 1:10,12

11:1
Ezek 3:12,14;
8:3; 10:19;
8:16

11:2
Is 30:1;
Mic 2:1
11:3
Ezek 12:22,
27; 2 Pet 3:4;
Jer 1:13;
Ezek 24:3,6
11:4
Ezek 3:4,17
11:5
Ezek 2:2;
3:24;
Jer 11:20;
Ezek 38:10
11:6
Ezek 7:23;
22:3,4
11:7
Ezek 24:3,6,
10,11;
Mic 3:3; v. 9
11:9
Ps 106:41;
Ezek 5:8
11:10
2 Kin 25:19-21;
Jer 52:10;
2 Kin 14:25;
Ezek 6:7
11:11
v. 3
11:12
v. 10;
Ezek 18:8,9;
8:10,14,16
11:13
v. 1; Ezek 9:8
11:15
Ezek 33:24

11:16
Is 8:14

11:17
Jer 24:5;
Ezek 28:25;
34:13

18 "When they come there, they will remove all its detestable things and all its abominations from it.

19 "And I shall give them one heart, and shall put a new spirit within them. And I shall take the heart of stone out of their flesh and give them a heart of flesh,

20 that they may walk in My statutes and keep My ordinances, and do them. Then they will be My people, and I shall be their God.

21 "But as for those whose hearts go after their detestable things and abominations, I shall bring their conduct down on their heads," declares the Lord GOD.

5. The glory of the LORD departs from Jerusalem

22 Then the cherubim lifted up their wings with the wheels beside them, and the glory of the God of Israel hovered over them.

23 And the glory of the LORD went up from the midst of the city, and stood over the mountain which is east of the city.

24 And the Spirit lifted me up and brought me in a vision by the Spirit of God to the exiles in Chaldea. So the vision that I had seen left me.

25 Then I told the exiles all the things that the LORD had shown me.

F. The reasons for the fall of Jerusalem

1. Unbelief of the people

a. The sign of the exile's baggage

12 Then the word of the LORD came to me saying,

2 "Son of man, you live in the midst of the rebellious house, who have eyes to see but do not see, ears to hear but do not hear; for they are a rebellious house.

3 "Therefore, son of man, prepare for yourself baggage for exile and go into exile by day in their sight; even go into exile from your place to another place in their sight. Perhaps they will understand though they are a rebellious house.

4 "And bring your baggage out by day in their sight, as baggage for exile. Then you will go out at evening in their sight, as those going into exile.

5 "Dig a hole through the wall in their sight and go out through it.

6 "Load the baggage on your shoulder in their sight, and carry it out in the dark. You shall cover your face so that you can not see the land, for I have set you as a sign to the house of Israel."

7 And I did so, as I had been commanded. By day I brought out my baggage like the baggage of an exile. Then in the evening I dug through the wall with my hands; I went out in the dark and carried the baggage on my shoulder in their sight.

8 And in the morning the word of the LORD came to me, saying,

9 "Son of man, has not the house of Israel, the rebellious house, said to you, 'What are you doing?'

10 "Say to them, 'Thus says the Lord GOD, "This burden concerns the prince in Jerusalem, as well as all the house of Israel who are in it."'

11 "Say, 'I am a sign to you. As I have done, so it will be done to them; they will go into exile, into captivity.'

12 "And the prince who is among them will load his baggage on his shoulder in the dark and go out. They will dig a hole through the wall to bring it out. He will cover his face so that he can not see the land with his eyes.

13 "I shall also spread My net over him, and he will be caught in My snare. And I shall bring him to Babylon in the land of the Chaldeans; yet he will not see it, though he will die there.

14 "And I shall scatter to every wind all who are around him, his helpers and all his troops; and I shall draw out a sword after them.

15 "So they will know that I am the LORD when I scatter them among the nations, and spread them among the countries.

16 "But I shall spare a few of them from the sword, the famine, and the pestilence that they may tell all their abominations among the nations where they go, and may know that I am the LORD."

b. The sign of eating and drinking with quaking

17 Moreover, the word of the LORD came to me saying,

12:10 *the prince in Jerusalem*, i.e., Zedekiah, who was to be blinded before being taken as a prisoner to Babylon. (See   Jer. 52:11: *Then he blinded the eyes of Zedekiah*.)

18 "Son of man, eat your bread with trembling, and drink your water with quivering and anxiety.

19 "Then say to the people of the land, 'Thus says the Lord GOD concerning the inhabitants of Jerusalem in the land of Israel, "They will eat their bread with anxiety and drink their water with horror, because their land will be stripped of its fulness on account of the violence of all who live in it.

20 "And the inhabited cities will be laid waste, and the land will be a desolation. So you will know that I am the LORD." ' "

c. The word of the LORD to the house of Israel

21 Then the word of the LORD came to me saying,

22 "Son of man, what is this proverb you *people* have concerning the land of Israel, saying, 'The days are long and every vision fails'?

23 "Therefore say to them, 'Thus says the Lord GOD, "I will make this proverb cease so that they will no longer use it as a proverb in Israel." But tell them, "The days draw near as well as the fulfillment of every vision.

24 "For there will no longer be any false vision or flattering divination within the house of Israel.

25 "For I the LORD shall speak, and whatever word I speak will be performed. It will no longer be delayed, for in your days, O rebellious house, I shall speak the word and perform it," declares the Lord GOD.' "

26 Furthermore, the word of the LORD came to me saying,

27 "Son of man, behold, the house of Israel is saying, 'The vision that he sees is for many years *from now*, and he prophesies of times far off.'

28 "Therefore say to them, 'Thus says the Lord GOD, "None of My words will be delayed any longer. Whatever word I speak will be performed," ' " declares the Lord GOD.

2. Heeding false prophets and prophetesses

a. The prophecy against the false prophets

13 Then the word of the LORD came to me saying,
2 "Son of man, prophesy against the prophets of Israel who prophesy, and say to those who prophesy from their own inspiration, 'Listen to the word of the LORD!

3 'Thus says the Lord GOD, "Woe to the foolish prophets who are following their own spirit and have seen nothing.

4 "O Israel, your prophets have been like foxes among ruins.

5 "You have not gone up into the breaches, nor did you build the wall around the house of Israel to stand in the battle on the day of the LORD.

6 "They see falsehood and lying divination who are saying, 'The LORD declares,' when the LORD has not sent them; yet they hope for the fulfillment of *their* word.

7 "Did you not see a false vision and speak a lying divination when you said, 'The LORD declares,' but it is not I who have spoken?" ' "

8 Therefore, thus says the Lord GOD, "Because you have spoken falsehood and seen a lie, therefore behold, I am against you," declares the Lord GOD.

9 "So My hand will be against the prophets who see false visions and utter lying divinations. They will have no place in the council of My people, nor will they be written down in the register of the house of Israel, nor will they enter the land of Israel, that you may know that I am the Lord GOD.

10 "It is definitely because they have misled My people by saying, 'Peace!' when there is no peace. And when anyone builds a wall, behold, they plaster it over with whitewash;

11 *so* tell those who plaster it over with whitewash, that it will fall. A flooding rain will come, and you, O hailstones, will fall; and a violent wind will break out.

12 "Behold, when the wall has fallen, will you not be asked, 'Where is the plaster with which you plastered *it*?' "

13 Therefore, thus says the Lord GOD, "I will make a violent wind break out in My wrath. There will also be in My anger a flooding rain and hailstones to consume *it* in wrath.

14 "So I shall tear down the wall which you plastered over with whitewash and bring it down to the ground, so that its foundation is laid bare; and when it falls, you will be consumed in its midst. And you will know that I am the LORD.

12:18 Ezek 4:16
12:19 Ezek 4:16; 23:33; Zech 7:14
12:20 Ezek 5:14; 36:3
12:22 Ezek 16:44; 11:3; v. 27; Amos 6:3; 2 Pet 3:4
12:23 Joel 2:1; Zeph 1:14
12:24 Ezek 13:23; Zech 13:2-4
12:25 v. 28; Is 55:11; Dan 9:12; Hab 1:5; v. 2
12:27 v. 22; Dan 10:14; 2 Pet 3:4
12:28 v. 25; Matt 24:48-50
13:2 Jer 37:19; v. 17; Jer 14:14; 23:16,26; Amos 7:16
13:3 Lam 2:14; Jer 23:28-32
13:5 Ps 106:23,30; Ezek 22:30; Is 58:12; Ezek 7:19
13:6 v. 22; Ezek 22:28; Jer 28:15
13:7 Ezek 22:28
13:8 Ezek 21:29; 5:8
13:9 Ezra 2:59,62; Neh 7:5; Ps 69:28; Ezek 11:10, 12
13:10 Jer 50:6; 8:11; v. 16; Ezek 22:28
13:11 Ezek 38:22
13:13 v. 11; Is 30:30; Rev 11:19; 16:21
13:14 Mic 1:6; v. 9; Ezek 14:8

15 "Thus I shall spend My wrath on the wall and on those who have plastered it over with whitewash; and I shall say to you, 'The wall is gone and its plasterers are gone,

13:16
Ezek 6:14;
Is 57:21

16 *along with* the prophets of Israel who prophesy to Jerusalem, and who see visions of peace for her when there is no peace,' declares the Lord GOD.

b. *The prophecy against the false prophetesses*

13:17
Ezek 20:46;
21:2; v. 2

17 "Now you, son of man, set your face against the daughters of your people who are prophesying from their own inspiration. Prophesy against them,

13:18
Ezek 22:25;
2 Pet 2:14

18 and say, 'Thus says the Lord GOD, "Woe to the women who sew *magic* bands on all wrists, and make veils for the heads of *persons* of every stature to hunt down lives! Will you hunt down the lives of My people, but preserve the lives *of others* for yourselves?

13:19
Ezek 20:39;
Prov 28:21;
Mic 3:5;
Jer 23:14,17

19 "And for handfuls of barley and fragments of bread, you have profaned Me to My people to put to death some who should not die and to keep others alive who should not live, by your lying to My people who listen to lies." ' "

13:20
v. 17

20 Therefore, thus says the Lord GOD, "Behold, I am against your *magic* bands by which you hunt lives there as birds, and I will tear them off your arms; and I will let them go, even those lives whom you hunt as birds.

13:21
Ps 124:7; v. 9

21 "I will also tear off your veils and deliver My people from your hands, and they will no longer be in your hands to be hunted; and you will know that I am the LORD.

13:22
Amos 5:12;
Jer 23:14;
Ezek 33:14-16

22 "Because you disheartened the righteous with falsehood when I did not cause him grief, but have encouraged the wicked not to turn from his wicked way *and* preserve his life,

13:23
v. 6;
Ezek 12:24;
Mic 3:6; v. 9;
Ezek 14:8

23 therefore, you women will no longer see false visions or practice divination, and I will deliver My people out of your hand. Thus you will know that I am the LORD."

3. *The idolatry of the elders*

a. *Hypocrisy rebuked*

14:1
Ezek 8:1;
20:1; 33:31

14 Then some elders of Israel came to me and sat down before me.
2 And the word of the LORD came to me saying,

14:3
Ezek 20:16;
7:19;
Jer 11:11;
Ezek 20:3,31

3 "Son of man, these men have set up their idols in their hearts, and have put right before their faces the stumbling block of their iniquity. Should I be consulted by them at all?

14:4
v. 7

4 "Therefore speak to them and tell them, 'Thus says the Lord GOD, "Any man of the house of Israel who sets up his idols in his heart, puts right before his face the stumbling block of his iniquity, and *then* comes to the prophet, I the LORD will be brought to give him an answer in the matter in view of the multitude of his idols,

14:5
Is 1:4;
Jer 2:11;
Zech 11:8

5 in order to lay hold of the hearts of the house of Israel who are estranged from Me through all their idols." '

b. *Repentance urged*

14:6
Is 2:20;
30:22;
Ezek 18:30;
8:6

6 "Therefore say to the house of Israel, 'Thus says the Lord GOD, "Repent and turn away from your idols, and turn your faces away from all your abominations.

14:7
Ex 12:48;
20:10; v. 4

7 "For anyone of the house of Israel or of the immigrants who stay in Israel who separates himself from Me, sets up his idols in his heart, puts right before his face the stumbling block of his iniquity, and *then* comes to the prophet to inquire of Me for himself, I the LORD will be brought to answer him in My own person.

14:8
Jer 44:11;
Ezek 15:7;
Is 65:15;
Ezek 5:15;
6:7

8 "And I shall set My face against that man and make him a sign and a proverb, and I shall cut him off from among My people. So you will know that I am the LORD.

14:9
1 Kin 22:23;
Job 12:16;
Jer 4:10;
2 Thess 2:11;
Jer 14:15

9 "But if the prophet is prevailed upon to speak a word, it is I, the LORD, who have prevailed upon that prophet, and I will stretch out My hand against him and destroy him from among My people Israel.

10 "And they will bear *the punishment of* their iniquity; as the iniquity of the inquirer is, so the iniquity of the prophet will be,

14:11
Ezek 44:10,
15; 11:20;
37:27

11 in order that the house of Israel may no longer stray from Me and no longer defile themselves with all their transgressions. Thus they will be My people, and I shall be their God," ' declares the Lord GOD."

c. The presence of some righteous cannot effect the deliverance of the wicked

12 Then the word of the LORD came to me saying,

13 "Son of man, if a country sins against Me by committing unfaithfulness, and I stretch out My hand against it, destroy its supply of bread, send famine against it, and cut off from it both man and beast,

14 even *though* these three men, Noah, Daniel, and Job were in its midst, by their *own* righteousness they could *only* deliver themselves," declares the Lord GOD.

15 "If I were to cause wild beasts to pass through the land, and they depopulated it, and it became desolate so that no one would pass through it because of the beasts,

16 *though* these three men were in its midst, as I live," declares the Lord GOD, "they could not deliver either *their* sons or *their* daughters. They alone would be delivered, but the country would be desolate.

17 "Or *if* I should bring a sword on that country and say, 'Let the sword pass through the country and cut off man and beast from it,'

18 even *though* these three men were in its midst, as I live," declares the Lord GOD, "they could not deliver either *their* sons or *their* daughters, but they alone would be delivered.

19 "Or *if* I should send a plague against that country and pour out My wrath in blood on it, to cut off man and beast from it,

20 even *though* Noah, Daniel, and Job were in its midst, as I live," declares the Lord GOD, "they could not deliver either *their* son or *their* daughter. They would deliver only themselves by their righteousness."

21 For thus says the Lord GOD, "How much more when I send My four severe judgments against Jerusalem: sword, famine, wild beasts, and plague to cut off man and beast from it!

22 "Yet, behold, survivors will be left in it who will be brought out, *both* sons and daughters. Behold, they are going to come forth to you and you will see their conduct and actions; then you will be comforted for the calamity which I have brought against Jerusalem for everything which I have brought upon it.

23 "Then they will comfort you when you see their conduct and actions, for you will know that I have not done in vain whatever I did to it," declares the Lord GOD.

G. The punishment both certain and necessary

1. The example of the vine

15 Then the word of the LORD came to me saying,
2 "Son of man, how is the wood of the vine *better* than any wood of a branch which is among the trees of the forest?

3 "Can wood be taken from it to make anything, or can *men* take a peg from it on which to hang any vessel?

4 "If it has been put into the fire for fuel, *and* the fire has consumed both of its ends, and its middle part has been charred, is it *then* useful for anything?

5 "Behold, while it is intact, it is not made into anything. How much less, when the fire has consumed it and it is charred, can it still be made into anything!

6 "Therefore, thus says the Lord GOD, 'As the wood of the vine among the trees of the forest, which I have given to the fire for fuel, so have I given up the inhabitants of Jerusalem;

7 and I set My face against them. *Though* they have come out of the fire, yet the fire will consume them. Then you will know that I am the LORD, when I set My face against them.

8 'Thus I will make the land desolate, because they have acted unfaithfully,' " declares the Lord GOD.

2. The example of the unfaithful wife

a. The foundling child, Israel

16 Then the word of the LORD came to me saying,
2 "Son of man, make known to Jerusalem her abominations,

Marginal references:

14:13 Ezek 15:8; 6:14; 5:16; vv. 17,19,21

*14:14 Jer 15:1; Gen 6:8; Dan 1:6; Job 1:1,5; vv. 16,18,20
14:15 Ezek 5:17
14:16 vv. 14,18,20; Ezek 18:20

14:17 Ezek 5:12; 21:3,4; 25:13; Zeph 1:3
14:18 v. 14

14:19 v. 21; Ezek 38:22; 7:8
14:20 v. 14

14:21 Ezek 5:17; Jer 15:2,3; Rev 6:8

14:22 Ezek 12:16; 7:16; 20:43; 16:54

14:23 Jer 22:8,9

15:2 Is 5:1-7; Jer 2:21; Hos 10:1

15:4 v. 6; Ezek 19:14; John 15:6

15:6 v. 2; Ezek 17:3-10

15:7 Lev 17:10; Ezek 14:8; Is 24:18; Ezek 6:7; 7:4; 14:8
15:8 Ezek 14:13

16:2 Ezek 20:4; 22:2; 8:9-17

14:14 So certain was the fall of Jerusalem as predicted here that not even intercession on the part of Israel's holiest saints would forestall it. The best that Noah, Daniel, and Job could do with their godly petitions would be to save themselves but no one else among their countrymen, so awful was the apostasy of Ezekiel's generation.

*16:3
Ezek 21:30;
v. 45

16:4
Hos 2:3

16:5
Deut 32:10

16:6
v. 22; Ex 19:4

16:7
Ex 1:7; v. 22

16:8
Ruth 3:9;
Gen 22:16-18;
Ex 24:7,8;
19:5; Jer 2:2

16:10
v. 13

16:11
Ezek 23:40;
Gen 24:22,47;
Prov 1:9

16:13
Deut 32:13,
14;
1 Sam 10:1

16:14
Ps 50:2;
Lam 2:15

16:15
Is 57:8;
Jer 2:20;
Ezek 23:3,8,
11,12
16:16
v. 10;
Ezek 6:3,6;
Hos 2:8
16:17
Ezek 7:20
16:18
v. 10

16:19
Hos 2:8

16:20
2 Kin 16:3;
Is 57:5

16:21
2 Kin 17:17;
Jer 19:5
16:22
Hos 11:1;
vv. 4-6

16:24
Is 57:5,7;
Jer 2:20; 3:2
16:25
Prov 9:14;
v. 15

3   and say, 'Thus says the Lord GOD to Jerusalem, "Your origin and your birth are from the land of the Canaanite, your father was an Amorite and your mother a Hittite.

4   "As for your birth, on the day you were born your navel cord was not cut, nor were you washed with water for cleansing; you were not rubbed with salt or even wrapped in cloths.

5   "No eye looked with pity on you to do any of these things for you, to have compassion on you. Rather you were thrown out into the open field, for you were abhorred on the day you were born.

6   "When I passed by you and saw you squirming in your blood, I said to you *while you were* in your blood, 'Live!' I said to you while you were in your blood, 'Live!'

7   "I made you numerous like plants of the field. Then you grew up, became tall, and reached the age for fine ornaments; *your* breasts were formed and your hair had grown. Yet you were naked and bare.

b. Its rescue by God

8   "Then I passed by you and saw you, and behold, you were at the time for love; so I spread My skirt over you and covered your nakedness. I also swore to you and entered into a covenant with you so that you became Mine," declares the Lord GOD.

9   "Then I bathed you with water, washed off your blood from you, and anointed you with oil.

10   "I also clothed you with embroidered cloth, and put sandals of porpoise skin on your feet; and I wrapped you with fine linen and covered you with silk.

11   "And I adorned you with ornaments, put bracelets on your hands, and a necklace around your neck.

12   "I also put a ring in your nostril, earrings in your ears, and a beautiful crown on your head.

13   "Thus you were adorned with gold and silver, and your dress was of fine linen, silk, and embroidered cloth. You ate fine flour, honey, and oil; so you were exceedingly beautiful and advanced to royalty.

14   "Then your fame went forth among the nations on account of your beauty, for it was perfect because of My splendor which I bestowed on you," declares the Lord GOD.

c. The harlotry of the rescued foundling

15   "But you trusted in your beauty and played the harlot because of your fame, and you poured out your harlotries on every passer-by who might be *willing*.

16   "And you took some of your clothes, made for yourself high places of various colors, and played the harlot on them, which should never come about nor happen.

17   "You also took your beautiful jewels *made* of My gold and of My silver, which I had given you, and made for yourself male images that you might play the harlot with them.

18   "Then you took your embroidered cloth and covered them, and offered My oil and My incense before them.

19   "Also My bread which I gave you, fine flour, oil, and honey with which I fed you, you would offer before them for a soothing aroma; so it happened," declares the Lord GOD.

20   "Moreover, you took your sons and daughters whom you had borne to Me, and you sacrificed them to idols to be devoured. Were your harlotries so small a matter?

21   "You slaughtered My children, and offered them up to idols by causing them to pass through *the fire*.

22   "And besides all your abominations and harlotries you did not remember the days of your youth, when you were naked and bare and squirming in your blood.

23   "Then it came about after all your wickedness ('Woe, woe to you!' declares the Lord GOD),

24   that you built yourself a shrine and made yourself a high place in every square.

25   "You built yourself a high place at the top of every street, and made your

---

16:3 *from the land of the Canaanite.* Ezekiel stresses the non-Israelite origin of Jerusalem. Amorites, Hittites, and   Canaanites left their mark on later Israelite history.

beauty abominable; and you spread your legs to every passer-by to multiply your harlotry.

26 "You also played the harlot with the Egyptians, your lustful neighbors, and multiplied your harlotry to make Me angry.

27 "Behold now, I have stretched out My hand against you and diminished your rations. And I delivered you up to the desire of those who hate you, the daughters of the Philistines, who are ashamed of your lewd conduct.

28 "Moreover, you played the harlot with the Assyrians because you were not satisfied; you even played the harlot with them and still were not satisfied.

29 "You also multiplied your harlotry with the land of merchants, Chaldea, yet even with this you were not satisfied." '"

30 "How languishing is your heart," declares the Lord GOD, "while you do all these things, the actions of a bold-faced harlot.

31 "When you built your shrine at the beginning of every street and made your high place in every square, in disdaining money, you were not like a harlot.

32 "You adulteress wife, who takes strangers instead of her husband!

33 "Men give gifts to all harlots, but you give your gifts to all your lovers to bribe them to come to you from every direction for your harlotries.

34 "Thus you are different from those women in your harlotries, in that no one plays the harlot as you do, because you give money and no money is given you; thus you are different."

d. The promised punishment for harlotry

35   Therefore, O harlot, hear the word of the LORD.

36   Thus says the Lord GOD, "Because your lewdness was poured out and your nakedness uncovered through your harlotries with your lovers and with all your detestable idols, and because of the blood of your sons which you gave to idols,

37   therefore, behold, I shall gather all your lovers with whom you took pleasure, even all those whom you loved and all those whom you hated. So I shall gather them against you from every direction and expose your nakedness to them that they may see all your nakedness.

38 "Thus I shall judge you, like women who commit adultery or shed blood are judged; and I shall bring on you the blood of wrath and jealousy.

39 "I shall also give you into the hands of your lovers, and they will tear down your shrines, demolish your high places, strip you of your clothing, take away your jewels, and will leave you naked and bare.

40 "They will incite a crowd against you, and they will stone you and cut you to pieces with their swords.

41 "And they will burn your houses with fire and execute judgments on you in the sight of many women. Then I shall stop you from playing the harlot, and you will also no longer pay your lovers.

42 "So I shall calm My fury against you, and My jealousy will depart from you, and I shall be pacified and angry no more.

43 "Because you have not remembered the days of your youth but have enraged Me by all these things, behold, I in turn will bring your conduct down on your own head," declares the Lord GOD, "so that you will not commit this lewdness on top of all your other abominations.

e. The sin worse than that of Sodom and Samaria

44   "Behold, everyone who quotes proverbs will quote this proverb concerning you, saying, 'Like mother, like daughter.'

45 "You are the daughter of your mother, who loathed her husband and children. You are also the sister of your sisters, who loathed their husbands and children. Your mother was a Hittite and your father an Amorite.

46 "Now your older sister is Samaria, who lives north of you with her daughters; and your younger sister, who lives south of you, is Sodom with her daughters.

47 "Yet you have not merely walked in their ways or done according to their abominations; but, as if that were too little, you acted more corruptly in all your conduct than they.

48 "As I live," declares the Lord GOD, "Sodom, your sister, and her daughters, have not done as you and your daughters have done.

16:48 Sodom, your sister, and her daughters, have not done. If God destroyed Sodom because of its awful sins, there is no

reason why Israel, whose sins are greater, should be spared.

16:26
Ezek 8:17;
20:7,8;
23:19-21
16:27
Ezek 14:13;
20:33,34;
2 Chr 28:18,
19
16:28
2 Kin 16:7,
10;
2 Chr 28:23
16:29
Ezek 23:14-17
16:30
Jer 3:3
16:31
v. 24; Is 52:3

16:33
Is 30:6;
Hos 8:9,10

16:36
v. 15;
Ezek 23:10,
18,29;
Jer 19:5
16:37
Jer 13:22,26;
Hos 2:10;
Nah 3:5;
Is 47:3
16:38
Lev 20:10;
Ezek 23:45;
Jer 18:21
16:39
Ezek 21:31;
vv. 24,31;
Ezek 23:26
16:40
Ezek 23:46,
47; John 8:5,
7
16:41
Deut 13:16;
2 Kin 25:9;
Jer 52:13;
Ezek 23:10,
27
16:42
Ezek 5:13;
Is 54:9,10;
Ezek 39:29
16:43
Ps 78:42;
v. 22;
Ezek 6:9;
11:21; 22:31
16:44
Ezek 12:22,
23

16:46
Gen 13:11-13;
Is 1:10
16:47
2 Kin 21:9;
Ezek 5:6,7

*16:48
Matt 10:15;
11:24

16:49
Is 3:9;
Gen 13:10;
Luke 12:16-20;
Ezek 18:7,12,
16
16:50
Ezek 7:10
16:51
Ezek 5:6;
Jer 3:11;
Matt 12:41,42
16:52
vv. 54,61,47,
48,51

49 "Behold, this was the guilt of your sister Sodom: she and her daughters had arrogance, abundant food, and careless ease, but she did not help the poor and needy.

50 "Thus they were haughty and committed abominations before Me. Therefore I removed them when I saw *it*.

51 "Furthermore, Samaria did not commit half of your sins, for you have multiplied your abominations more than they. Thus you have made your sisters appear righteous by all your abominations which you have committed.

52 "Also bear your disgrace in that you have made judgment favorable for your sisters. Because of your sins in which you acted more abominably than they, they are more in the right than you. Yes, be also ashamed and bear your disgrace, in that you made your sisters appear righteous.

f. The promise of restoration

16:53
vv. 60,61;
Is 19:24,25
16:54
Ezek 14:22,
23
16:55
v. 53;
Ezek 36:11;
Mal 3:4

53 "Nevertheless, I will restore their captivity, the captivity of Sodom and her daughters, the captivity of Samaria and her daughters, and along with them your own captivity,

54 in order that you may bear your humiliation, and feel ashamed for all that you have done when you become a consolation to them.

55 "And your sisters, Sodom with her daughters and Samaria with her daughters, will return to their former state, and you with your daughters will *also* return to your former state.

56 "As *the name of* your sister Sodom was not heard from your lips in your day of pride,

16:57
2 Kin 16:5;
2 Chr 28:18;
Ezek 5:14
16:58
Ezek 23:49
16:59
Ezek 17:13;
Deut 29:12
*16:60
Jer 2:2;
Hos 2:15;
Jer 32:40;
Ezek 37:26
16:61
Ezek 20:43;
Is 54:1; 60:4;
Jer 31:31
16:62
Ezek 20:37;
Hos 2:19,20;
Ezek 20:43,
44
16:63
v. 61;
Rom 3:19

57 before your wickedness was uncovered, so now you have become the reproach of the daughters of Edom, and of all who are around her, of the daughters of the Philistines—those surrounding *you* who despise you.

58 "You have borne *the penalty of* your lewdness and abominations," the LORD declares.

59 For thus says the Lord GOD, "I will also do with you as you have done, you who have despised the oath by breaking the covenant.

60 "Nevertheless, I will remember My covenant with you in the days of your youth, and I will establish an everlasting covenant with you.

61 "Then you will remember your ways and be ashamed when you receive your sisters, *both* your older and your younger; and I will give them to you as daughters, but not because of your covenant.

62 "Thus I will establish My covenant with you, and you shall know that I am the LORD,

63 in order that you may remember and be ashamed, and never open your mouth anymore because of your humiliation, when I have forgiven you for all that you have done," the Lord GOD declares.

3. The two eagles and the cedar

a. The allegory presented

17:2
Ezek 20:49;
24:3
17:3
Jer 22:23

17 Now the word of the LORD came to me saying,

2 "Son of man, propound a riddle, and speak a parable to the house of Israel,

3 saying, 'Thus says the Lord GOD, "A great eagle with great wings, long pinions and a full plumage of many colors, came to Lebanon and took away the top of the cedar.

4 "He plucked off the topmost of its young twigs and brought it to a land of merchants; he set it in a city of traders.

17:5
Deut 8:7-9;
Is 44:4
17:6
v. 14

5 "He also took some of the seed of the land and planted it in fertile soil. He placed *it* beside abundant waters; he set it *like* a willow.

6 "Then it sprouted and became a low, spreading vine with its branches turned toward him, but its roots remained under it. So it became a vine, and yielded shoots and sent out branches.

16:60 Here we see unfolded the amazing grace of a faithful and patient God. He chose Israel and made her great, only to have her rebel against Him. Justice demanded severest punishment, but God's grace and loving-kindness, nevertheless, promised for Israel a future restoration with all the blessings of an enduring covenant. The Scripture seems to teach that His dispersed people will someday be regathered to their ancestral land.

b. The allegory interpreted

7 "But there was another great eagle with great wings and much plumage; and behold, this vine bent its roots toward him and sent out its branches toward him from the beds where it was planted, that he might water it.

8 "It was planted in good soil beside abundant waters, that it might yield branches and bear fruit, *and* become a splendid vine."'

9 "Say, 'Thus says the Lord GOD, "Will it thrive? Will he not pull up its roots and cut off its fruit, so that it withers—so that all its sprouting leaves wither? And neither by great strength nor by many people can it be raised from its roots *again*.

10 "Behold, though it is planted, will it thrive? Will it not completely wither as soon as the east wind strikes it—wither on the beds where it grew?"'"

11 Moreover, the word of the LORD came to me saying,

12 "Say now to the rebellious house, 'Do you not know what these things *mean?*' Say, 'Behold, the king of Babylon came to Jerusalem, took its king and princes, and brought them to him in Babylon.

13 'And he took one of the royal family and made a covenant with him, putting him under oath. He also took away the mighty of the land,

14 that the kingdom might be in subjection, not exalting itself, *but* keeping his covenant, that it might continue.

15 'But he rebelled against him by sending his envoys to Egypt that they might give him horses and many troops. Will he succeed? Will he who does such things escape? Can he indeed break the covenant and escape?

16 'As I live,' declares the Lord GOD, 'Surely in the country of the king who put him on the throne, whose oath he despised, and whose covenant he broke, in Babylon he shall die.

17 'And Pharaoh with *his* mighty army and great company will not help him in the war, when they cast up mounds and build siege walls to cut off many lives.

18 'Now he despised the oath by breaking the covenant, and behold, he pledged his allegiance, yet did all these things; he shall not escape.'"

19 Therefore, thus says the Lord GOD, "As I live, surely My oath which he despised and My covenant which he broke, I will inflict on his head.

20 "And I will spread My net over him, and he will be caught in My snare. Then I will bring him to Babylon and enter into judgment with him there *regarding* the unfaithful act which he has committed against Me.

21 "And all the choice men in all his troops will fall by the sword, and the survivors will be scattered to every wind; and you will know that I, the LORD, have spoken."

c. The goodly cedar a type of Messiah

22 Thus says the Lord GOD, "I shall also take *a sprig* from the lofty top of the cedar and set *it* out; I shall pluck from the topmost of its young twigs a tender one, and I shall plant *it* on a high and lofty mountain.

23 "On the high mountain of Israel I shall plant it, that it may bring forth boughs and bear fruit, and become a stately cedar. And birds of every kind will nest under it; they will nest in the shade of its branches.

24 "And all the trees of the field will know that I am the LORD; I bring down the high tree, exalt the low tree, dry up the green tree, and make the dry tree flourish. I am the LORD; I have spoken, and I will perform *it.*"

H. The justice of a righteous God

1. The soul that sins shall die

18 Then the word of the LORD came to me saying,

2 "What do you mean by using this proverb concerning the land of Israel saying,

'The fathers eat the sour grapes,
But the children's teeth are set on edge'?

3 "As I live," declares the Lord GOD, "you are surely not going to use this proverb in Israel anymore.

4 "Behold, all souls are Mine; the soul of the father as well as the soul of the son is Mine. The soul who sins will die.

17:7 / v. 15
17:8 / v. 5
17:9 / vv. 10,15-21
17:10 / v. 15; Ezek 19:14; Hos 13:15
17:12 / Ezek 2:5; 12:9; v. 3; 2 Kin 24:11-16
17:13 / 2 Kin 24:15-17; 2 Chr 36:13
17:14 / v. 6; Ezek 29:14
17:15 / 2 Kin 24:20; 2 Chr 36:13
17:16 / vv. 13,18,19; Jer 52:11; Ezek 12:13
17:17 / Jer 37:7; Ezek 29:6,7; 4:2
17:18 / Lam 5:6
17:19 / Ezek 16:59
17:20 / Ezek 12:13; 32:3; 20:36
17:21 / 2 Kin 25:5, 11; Ezek 12:14; 6:7,10
17:22 / Is 11:1; Jer 23:5; Zech 3:8; Ezek 36:36; 20:40
17:23 / Is 2:2,3; Ezek 20:40; Hos 14:5-7; Matt 13:31,32
17:24 / Ps 96:12; Ezek 21:26; 19:12; 22:14; 24:14
18:2 / Jer 31:29; Lam 5:7
18:3 / vv. 11,20,30
18:4 / Is 42:5; v. 20; Rom 6:23

2. *The righteous man shall live*

5 "But if a man is righteous, and practices justice and righteousness,
6 and does not eat at the mountain *shrines* or lift up his eyes to the idols of the house of Israel, or defile his neighbor's wife, or approach a woman during her menstrual period—
7 if a man does not oppress anyone, but restores to the debtor his pledge, does not commit robbery, *but* gives his bread to the hungry, and covers the naked with clothing,
8 if he does not lend *money* on interest or take increase, *if* he keeps his hand from iniquity, *and* executes true justice between man and man,
9 *if* he walks in My statutes and My ordinances so as to deal faithfully—he is righteous *and* will surely live," declares the Lord GOD.

3. *The wicked son of a righteous man shall die*

10 "Then he may have a violent son who sheds blood, and who does any of these things to a brother
11 (though he himself did not do any of these things), that is, he even eats at the mountain *shrines*, and defiles his neighbor's wife,
12 oppresses the poor and needy, commits robbery, does not restore a pledge, but lifts up his eyes to the idols, *and* commits abomination,
13 he lends *money* on interest and takes increase; will he live? He will not live! He has committed all these abominations, he will surely be put to death; his blood will be on his own head.

4. *The righteous son of a wicked man shall live*

14 "Now behold, he has a son who has observed all his father's sins which he committed, and observing does not do likewise.
15 "He does not eat at the mountain *shrines* or lift up his eyes to the idols of the house of Israel, or defile his neighbor's wife,
16 or oppress anyone, or retain a pledge, or commit robbery, *but* he gives his bread to the hungry, and covers the naked with clothing,
17 he keeps his hand from the poor, does not take interest or increase, *but* executes My ordinances, and walks in My statutes; he will not die for his father's iniquity, he will surely live.
18 "As for his father, because he practiced extortion, robbed *his* brother, and did what was not good among his people, behold, he will die for his iniquity.
19 "Yet you say, 'Why should the son not bear the punishment for the father's iniquity?' When the son has practiced justice and righteousness, and has observed all My statutes and done them, he shall surely live.
20 "The person who sins will die. The son will not bear the punishment for the father's iniquity, nor will the father bear the punishment for the son's iniquity; the righteousness of the righteous will be upon himself, and the wickedness of the wicked will be upon himself.

5. *The wicked man who repents shall live*

21 "But if the wicked man turns from all his sins which he has committed and observes all My statutes and practices justice and righteousness, he shall surely live; he shall not die.
22 "All his transgressions which he has committed will not be remembered against him; because of his righteousness which he has practiced, he will live.
23 "Do I have any pleasure in the death of the wicked," declares the Lord GOD, "rather than that he should turn from his ways and live?
24 "But when a righteous man turns away from his righteousness, commits iniquity, and does according to all the abominations that a wicked man does, will he live? All his righteous deeds which he has done will not be remembered for his treachery which he has committed and his sin which he has committed; for them he will die.

6. *The way of the LORD is just*

25 "Yet you say, 'The way of the Lord is not right.' Hear now, O house of Israel! Is My way not right? Is it not your ways that are not right?
26 "When a righteous man turns away from his righteousness, commits iniqui-

ty, and dies because of it, for his iniquity which he has committed he will die.

27 "Again, when a wicked man turns away from his wickedness which he has committed and practices justice and righteousness, he will save his life.

18:27
v. 21

28 "Because he considered and turned away from all his transgressions which he had committed, he shall surely live; he shall not die.

18:28
vv. 22,30,31

29 "But the house of Israel says, 'The way of the Lord is not right.' Are My ways not right, O house of Israel? Is it not your ways that are not right?

18:29
v. 25

7. The command to repent

30 "Therefore I will judge you, O house of Israel, each according to his conduct," declares the Lord GOD. "Repent and turn away from all your transgressions, so that iniquity may not become a stumbling block to you.

18:30
Ezek 7:3;
33:20;
Matt 3:2;
Rev 2:5

31 "Cast away from you all your transgressions which you have committed, and make yourselves a new heart and a new spirit! For why will you die, O house of Israel?

18:31
Is 1:16,17;
55:7;
Ezek 11:19;
36:26

32 "For I have no pleasure in the death of anyone who dies," declares the Lord GOD. "Therefore, repent and live."

18:32
Ezek 33:11;
2 Pet 3:9

I. Lamentation over the princes of Israel

1. The case of Jehoahaz

19 "As for you, take up a lamentation for the princes of Israel,
2   and say,

'What was your mother?
A lioness among lions!
She lay down among young lions,
She reared her cubs.

19:1
Ezek 26:17;
27:2
19:2
Nah 2:11,12;
Is 5:29;
Zech 11:3

3 'When she brought up one of her cubs,
He became a lion,
And he learned to tear *his* prey;
He devoured men.

19:3
2 Kin 23:31,
32; v. 6

4 'Then nations heard about him;
He was captured in their pit,
And they brought him with hooks
To the land of Egypt.

19:4
2 Kin 23:33;
2 Chr 36:4

2. The case of Jehoiachin

5 'When she saw, as she waited,
That her hope was lost,
She took another of her cubs
And made him a young lion.

19:5
2 Kin 23:34

6 'And he walked about among the lions;
He became a young lion,
He learned to tear *his* prey;
He devoured men.

19:6
2 Kin 24:9;
v. 3

7 'And he destroyed their fortified towers
And laid waste their cities;
And the land and its fulness were appalled
Because of the sound of his roaring.

19:7
Ezek 12:19;
30:12

8 'Then nations set against him
On every side from *their* provinces,
And they spread their net over him;
He was captured in their pit.

19:8
2 Kin 24:2;
v. 4

9 'And they put him in a cage with hooks
And brought him to the king of Babylon;
They brought him in hunting nets
So that his voice should be heard no more
On the mountains of Israel.

19:9
2 Chr 36:6;
Jer 22:18;
Ezek 6:2

18:25 Sinful men habitually charge God with injustice. This is the normal response of guilty but unrepentant sinners. Scripture does reveal that God's ways are not our ways (Is. 55:8,9), but it also states that whatever God does is right (Rom. 9:20–24). In the final judgment, every mouth will be stopped and all will have to confess that God's judgments are wholly righteous and according to truth (Rev. 19:2).

3. *The case of Zedekiah*

19:10
Ps 80:8-11

10   'Your mother was like a vine in your vineyard,
        Planted by the waters;
        It was fruitful and full of branches
        Because of abundant waters.

19:11
Ezek 31:3;
Dan 4:11

11   'And it had strong branches *fit* for scepters of rulers,
        And its height was raised above the clouds
        So that it was seen in its height with the mass of its branches.

19:12
Jer 31:28;
Ezek 28:17;
17:10;
Hos 13:15

12   'But it was plucked up in fury;
        It was cast down to the ground;
        And the east wind dried up its fruit.
        Its strong branch was torn off
        So that it withered;
        The fire consumed it.

19:13
Hos 2:3

13   'And now it is planted in the wilderness,
        In a dry and thirsty land.

19:14
Ezek 15:4;
Lam 4:20

14   'And fire has gone out from *its* branch;
        It has consumed its shoots *and* fruit,
        So that there is not in it a strong branch,
        A scepter to rule.' ''

This is a lamentation, and has become a lamentation.

J. *The abominations of Israel*

1. *Ezekiel commanded to answer the elders*

20:1
Ezek 8:1,11;
12; 9:6

20 Now it came about in the seventh year, in the fifth *month*, on the tenth of the month, that certain of the elders of Israel came to inquire of the LORD, and sat before me.

2   And the word of the LORD came to me saying,

20:3
v. 31;
Ezek 14:3;
Mic 3:7

3   "Son of man, speak to the elders of Israel, and say to them, 'Thus says the Lord GOD, "Do you come to inquire of Me? As I live," declares the Lord GOD, "I will not be inquired of by you."'

20:4
Ezek 16:2;
22:2

4   "Will you judge them, will you judge them, son of man? Make them know the abominations of their fathers;

2. *Israel's idolatry in Egypt*

20:5
Ex 6:7;
Deut 7:6;
Ex 6:2,3;
20:2

5   and say to them, 'Thus says the Lord GOD, "On the day when I chose Israel and swore to the descendants of the house of Jacob and made Myself known to them in the land of Egypt, when I swore to them, saying, I am the LORD your God,

20:6
Ex 3:8,17;
Deut 8:7-9;
Jer 32:22;
Ps 48:2;
Dan 8:9

6   on that day I swore to them, to bring them out from the land of Egypt into a land that I had selected for them, flowing with milk and honey, which is the glory of all lands.

20:7
Ezek 18:31;
Deut 29:16,
18; Ex 20:2

7   "And I said to them, 'Cast away, each of you, the detestable things of his eyes, and do not defile yourselves with the idols of Egypt; I am the LORD your God.'

8   "But they rebelled against Me and were not willing to listen to Me; they did not cast away the detestable things of their eyes, nor did they forsake the idols of Egypt.

20:8
Is 63:10;
Ezek 7:8

Then I resolved to pour out My wrath on them, to accomplish My anger against them in the midst of the land of Egypt.

20:9
Ex 32:12;
Num 14:13ff;
Ezek 36:21;
39:7

9   "But I acted for the sake of My name, that it should not be profaned in the sight of the nations among whom they *lived*, in whose sight I made Myself known to them by bringing them out of the land of Egypt.

3. *Israel's rebellion in the wilderness*

20:10
Ex 13:18

10   "So I took them out of the land of Egypt and brought them into the wilderness.

20:11
Deut 4:8;
Lev 18:5;
Rom 10:5;
Gal 3:12

11   "And I gave them My statutes and informed them of My ordinances, by which, if a man observes them, he will live.

20:12
Ex 31:13,17;
v. 20

12   "And also I gave them My sabbaths to be a sign between Me and them, that they might know that I am the LORD who sanctifies them.

20:13
Num 14:22;
Ps 78:40;
95:8-10;

13   "But the house of Israel rebelled against Me in the wilderness. They did not walk in My statutes, and they rejected My ordinances, by which, if a man observes

them, he will live; and My sabbaths they greatly profaned. Then I resolved to pour out My wrath on them in the wilderness, to annihilate them.

14 "But I acted for the sake of My name, that it should not be profaned in the sight of the nations, before whose sight I had brought them out.

15 "And also I swore to them in the wilderness that I would not bring them into the land which I had given them, flowing with milk and honey, which is the glory of all lands,

16 because they rejected My ordinances, and as for My statutes, they did not walk in them; they even profaned My sabbaths, for their heart continually went after their idols.

17 "Yet My eye spared them rather than destroying them, and I did not cause their annihilation in the wilderness.

18 "And I said to their children in the wilderness, 'Do not walk in the statutes of your fathers, or keep their ordinances, or defile yourselves with their idols.

19 'I am the LORD your God; walk in My statutes, and keep My ordinances, and observe them.

20 'And sanctify My sabbaths; and they shall be a sign between Me and you, that you may know that I am the LORD your God.'

21 "But the children rebelled against Me; they did not walk in My statutes, nor were they careful to observe My ordinances, by which, *if* a man observes them, he will live; they profaned My sabbaths. So I resolved to pour out My wrath on them, to accomplish My anger against them in the wilderness.

22 "But I withdrew My hand and acted for the sake of My name, that it should not be profaned in the sight of the nations in whose sight I had brought them out.

23 "Also I swore to them in the wilderness that I would scatter them among the nations and disperse them among the lands,

24 because they had not observed My ordinances, but had rejected My statutes, and had profaned My sabbaths, and their eyes were on the idols of their fathers.

25 "And I also gave them statutes that were not good and ordinances by which they could not live;

26 and I pronounced them unclean because of their gifts, in that they caused all their first-born to pass through *the fire* so that I might make them desolate, in order that they might know that I am the LORD." '

4. *Israel's idolatry in Canaan*

27 "Therefore, son of man, speak to the house of Israel, and say to them, 'Thus says the Lord GOD, "Yet in this your fathers have blasphemed Me by acting treacherously against Me.

28 "When I had brought them into the land which I swore to give to them, then they saw every high hill and every leafy tree, and they offered there their sacrifices, and there they presented the provocation of their offering. There also they made their soothing aroma, and there they poured out their libations.

29 "Then I said to them, 'What is the high place to which you go?' So its name is called ¹Bamah to this day." '

5. *God refuses to be inquired of*

30 "Therefore, say to the house of Israel, 'Thus says the Lord GOD, "Will you defile yourselves after the manner of your fathers and play the harlot after their detestable things?

31 "And when you offer your gifts, when you cause your sons to pass through the fire, you are defiling yourselves with all your idols to this day. And shall I be inquired of by you, O house of Israel? As I live," declares the Lord GOD, "I will not be inquired of by you.

6. *God to purge Israel*

32 "And what comes into your mind will not come about, when you say: 'We will be like the nations, like the tribes of the lands, serving wood and stone.'

33 "As I live," declares the Lord GOD, "surely with a mighty hand and with an outstretched arm and with wrath poured out, I shall be king over you.

34 "And I shall bring you out from the peoples and gather you from the lands

¹Or, *High Place*

Prov 1:25;
Num 14:29;
Ps 106:23
20:14
vv. 9,22;
Ezek 36:22,
23
20:15
Num 14:28;
Ps 95:11; v. 6
20:16
Num 15:39;
Ps 78:37;
Amos 5:25

20:18
Deut 4:3-6;
Zech 1:4; v. 7
20:19
Ex 6:7; 20:2;
Deut 5:32
20:20
v. 12

20:21
Num 25:1;
vv. 8,13,16

20:22
v. 17;
Ps 78:38;
vv. 9,14
20:23
Lev 26:33;
Deut 28:64;
Ps 106:27;
Jer 15:4
20:24
vv. 13,16;
Ezek 6:9
20:25
Ps 81:12;
Rom 1:24;
2 Thess 2:11
20:26
v. 30;
2 Kin 17:17;
2 Chr 28:3;
Ezek 16:20,
21; 6:7
20:27
Ezek 2:7;
Rom 2:24;
Ezek 18:24;
39:23,26
20:28
Is 57:5-7;
Ezek 6:13;
16:19

20:30
v. 43;
Jer 7:26;
16:12

20:31
Ps 106:37-39;
Jer 7:31;
Ezek 16:20

20:32
Ezek 11:5;
16:16;
Jer 2:25;
44:17
20:33
Jer 21:5
20:34
v. 38;

Jer 42:18;
44:6;
Lam 2:4
20:35
Ezek 17:20
where you are scattered, with a mighty hand and with an outstretched arm and with wrath poured out;

35   and I shall bring you into the wilderness of the peoples, and there I shall enter into judgment with you face to face.

20:36
vv. 13,21;
1 Cor 10:5-10;
Deut 32:10
20:37
Lam 27:32;
Jer 33:13;
Ezek 16:60,
62
36   "As I entered into judgment with your fathers in the wilderness of the land of Egypt, so I will enter into judgment with you," declares the Lord GOD.

37   "And I shall make you pass under the rod, and I shall bring you into the bond of the covenant;

20:38
Ezek 34:17,
20; Amos 9:9,
10; Jer 44:14;
Ezek 6:7
20:39
Jer 44:25,26;
Amos 4:4;
Is 1:13;
Ezek 23:38,
39
38   and I shall purge from you the rebels and those who transgress against Me; I shall bring them out of the land where they sojourn, but they will not enter the land of Israel. Thus you will know that I am the LORD.

39   "As for you, O house of Israel," thus says the Lord GOD, "Go, serve everyone his idols; but later, you will surely listen to Me, and My holy name you will profane no longer with your gifts and with your idols.

7. God to show mercy on the obedient

20:40
Ezek 17:23;
Mic 4:1;
Ezek 37:22,
24; Is 56:7;
60:7; Mal 3:4
20:41
Eph 5:2;
Phil 4:18
40   "For on My holy mountain, on the high mountain of Israel," declares the Lord GOD, "there the whole house of Israel, all of them, will serve Me in the land; there I shall accept them, and there I shall seek your contributions and the choicest of your gifts, with all your holy things.

41   "As a soothing aroma I shall accept you, when I bring you out from the peoples and gather you from the lands where you are scattered; and I shall prove Myself holy among you in the sight of the nations.

20:42
Ezek 34:13;
36:24
42   "And you will know that I am the LORD, when I bring you into the land of Israel, into the land which I swore to give to your forefathers.

20:43
Ezek 16:61;
Hos 5:15;
Ezek 36:31;
Zech 12:10
20:44
Ezek 24:44;
36:22
43   "And there you will remember your ways and all your deeds, with which you have defiled yourselves; and you will loathe yourselves in your own sight for all the evil things that you have done.

44   "Then you will know that I am the LORD when I have dealt with you for My name's sake, not according to your evil ways or according to your corrupt deeds, O house of Israel," declares the Lord GOD.' "

8. The prophecy against the south

20:46
Ezek 6:2;
21:2
20:47
Jer 21:14;
17:24; 21:4
45   Now the word of the LORD came to me saying,

46   "Son of man, set your face toward Teman, and speak out against the south, and prophesy against the forest land of the Negev,

47   and say to the forest of the Negev, 'Hear the word of the LORD: thus says the Lord GOD, "Behold, I am about to kindle a fire in you, and it shall consume every green tree in you, as well as every dry tree; the blazing flame will not be quenched, and the whole surface from south to north will be burned by it.

20:48
Jer 7:20;
17:27
20:49
Ezek 17:2;
Matt 13:13,14
48   "And all flesh will see that I, the LORD, have kindled it; it shall not be quenched." ' "

49   Then I said, "Ah Lord GOD! They are saying of me, 'Is he not *just* speaking parables?' "

K. The prophecies of the sharpened sword

1. The sword drawn from the sheath

21:2
Ezek 20:46;
Amos 7:16
21:3
Jer 21:13;
Ezek 5:8;
vv. 9-11,19;
Job 9:22
21:4
Ezek 20:47
21 And the word of the LORD came to me saying,

2   "Son of man, set your face toward Jerusalem, and speak against the sanctuaries, and prophesy against the land of Israel;

3   and say to the land of Israel, 'Thus says the LORD, "Behold, I am against you; and I shall draw My sword out of its sheath and cut off from you the righteous and the wicked.

4   "Because I shall cut off from you the righteous and the wicked, therefore My sword shall go forth from its sheath against all flesh from south *to* north.

21:5
Ezek 20:48;
Jer 23:20;
Nah 1:9
21:6
Is 22:4
21:7
Ezek 7:26;
5   "Thus all flesh will know that I, the LORD, have drawn My sword out of its sheath. It will not return *to its sheath* again." '

6   "As for you, son of man, groan with breaking heart and bitter grief, groan in their sight.

7   "And it will come about when they say to you, 'Why do you groan?' that you will say, 'Because of the news that is coming; and every heart will melt, all hands

will be feeble, every spirit will faint, and all knees will be weak as water. Behold, it comes and it will happen,' declares the Lord GOD."

2. The sword sharpened

8   Again the word of the LORD came to me saying,
9   "Son of man, prophesy and say, 'Thus says the LORD.' Say,
    'A sword, a sword sharpened
    And also polished!
10 'Sharpened to make a slaughter,
    Polished to flash like lightning!'
Or shall we rejoice, the rod of My son despising every tree?
11 "And it is given to be polished, that it may be handled; the sword is sharpened and polished, to give it into the hand of the slayer.
12 "Cry out and wail, son of man; for it is against My people, it is against all the officials of Israel. They are delivered over to the sword with My people, therefore strike *your* thigh.
13 "For *there is* a testing; and what if even the rod which despises will be no more?" declares the Lord GOD.
14 "You therefore, son of man, prophesy, and clap *your* hands together; and let the sword be doubled the third time, the sword for the slain. It is the sword for the great one slain, which surrounds them,
15 that *their* hearts may melt, and many fall at all their gates. I have given the glittering sword. Ah! It is made *for striking* like lightning, it is wrapped up *in readiness* for slaughter.
16 "Show yourself sharp, go to the right; set yourself; go to the left, wherever your edge is appointed.
17 "I shall also clap My hands together, and I shall appease My wrath; I, the LORD, have spoken."

3. The sword wielded by Babylon

18 And the word of the LORD came to me saying,
19 "As for you, son of man, make two ways for the sword of the king of Babylon to come; both of them will go out of one land. And make a signpost; make it at the head of the way to the city.
20 "You shall mark a way for the sword to come to Rabbah of the sons of Ammon, and to Judah into fortified Jerusalem.
21 "For the king of Babylon stands at the parting of the way, at the head of the two ways, to use divination; he shakes the arrows, he consults the household idols, he looks at the liver.
22 "Into his right hand came the divination, 'Jerusalem,' to set battering rams, to open the mouth for slaughter, to lift up the voice with a battle cry, to set battering rams against the gates, to cast up mounds, to build a siege wall.
23 "And it will be to them like a false divination in their eyes; they have *sworn* solemn oaths. But he brings iniquity to remembrance, that they may be seized.
24 "Therefore, thus says the Lord GOD, 'Because you have made your iniquity to be remembered, in that your transgressions are uncovered, so that in all your deeds your sins appear—because you have come to remembrance, you will be seized with the hand.

4. The punishment of the prince of Israel

25 'And you, O slain, wicked one, the prince of Israel, whose day has come, in the time of the punishment of the end,'
26 thus says the Lord GOD, 'Remove the turban, and take off the crown; this will *be* no more the same. Exalt that which is low, and abase that which is high.
27 'A ruin, a ruin, a ruin, I shall make it. This also will be no more, until He comes whose right it is; and I shall give it *to Him*.'

5. The sentence against the Ammonites

28 "And you, son of man, prophesy and say, 'Thus says the Lord GOD concerning the sons of Ammon and concerning their reproach,' and say: 'A sword, a sword

---

Is 13:7;
Ezek 7:17;
22:14

21:9
Deut 32:41

21:10
Is 34:5,6;
v. 15

21:11
vv. 15,19

21:12
Jer 31:19

21:14
Num 24:10;
Ezek 6:11;
Lev 26:21,24;
Ezek 30:24
21:15
vv. 7,10

21:17
v. 14;
Ezek 22:13;
5:13

21:19
Ezek 4:1-3;
v. 15

21:20
Jer 49:2;
Ezek 25:5;
Amos 1:14
*21:21
Num 23:23;
Prov 16:33;
Judg 17:5
21:22
Jer 51:14;
Ezek 4:2

21:23
Ezek 17:13,
15,16,18;
29:16

21:25
Ezek 7:2,3,7;
35:5
21:26
Jer 13:18;
Ezek 16:12;
17:24;
Luke 1:52
21:27
Hag 2:21,22;
Ps 2:6;
Jer 23:5,6;
Ezek 34:24;
37:24
21:28
Jer 49:1;
Ezek 25:2,3;
Zeph 2:8;

Is 31:8;
Jer 12:12

21:29
Ezek 13:6-9;
22:28; v. 25;
Ezek 35:5
21:30
Jer 47:6,7;
Ezek 16:3
21:31
Ezek 7:8;
14:19; 22:20,
21; Jer 6:22,
23; 51:20,21
21:32
Mal 4:1;
Ezek 25:10

22:2
Ezek 20:4;
24:6-9;
Nah 3:1;
Ezek 16:2;
20:4
22:3
vv. 6,27;
Ezek 23:37,
45
22:4
2 Kin 21:16;
Ezek 24:7,8;
21:25; 5:14,
15; 16:57
22:5
Is 22:5
22:6
Is 1:23
22:7
Deut 27:16;
Ex 22:21,22
22:8
v. 26;
Lev 19:30;
Ezek 23:38,
39
22:9
Ezek 18:6,11,
15
22:10
Lev 18:8,19;
Ezek 18:6
22:11
Ezek 18:11;
Lev 18:15;
18:9
22:12
Mic 7:2,3;
Lev 25:36;
19:13;
Jer 3:21
22:13
Ezek 21:17;
Is 33:15; v. 3
22:14
Ezek 21:7;
24:14
22:15
Deut 4:27;
Zech 4:17;
Ezek 23:27

22:18
Is 1:22;
Jer 6:28

22:20
v. 21; Mal 3:2

is drawn, polished for the slaughter, to cause it to consume, that it may be like lightning—

29 while they see for you false visions, while they divine lies for you—to place you on the necks of the wicked who are slain, whose day has come, in the time of the punishment of the end.

30 'Return it to its sheath. In the place where you were created, in the land of your origin, I shall judge you.

31 'And I shall pour out My indignation on you; I shall blow on you with the fire of My wrath, and I shall give you into the hand of brutal men, skilled in destruction.

32 'You will be fuel for the fire; your blood will be in the midst of the land. You will not be remembered, for I, the LORD, have spoken.'"

L. The sins of Jerusalem

1. The indictment

22 Then the word of the LORD came to me saying,

2 "And you, son of man, will you judge, will you judge the bloody city? Then cause her to know all her abominations.

3 "And you shall say, 'Thus says the Lord GOD, "A city shedding blood in her midst, so that her time will come, and that makes idols, contrary to her interest, for defilement!

4 "You have become guilty by the blood which you have shed, and defiled by your idols which you have made. Thus you have brought your day near and have come to your years; therefore I have made you a reproach to the nations, and a mocking to all the lands.

5 "Those who are near and those who are far from you will mock you, you of ill repute, full of turmoil.

6 "Behold, the rulers of Israel, each according to his power, have been in you for the purpose of shedding blood.

7 "They have treated father and mother lightly within you. The alien they have oppressed in your midst; the fatherless and the widow they have wronged in you.

8 "You have despised My holy things and profaned My sabbaths.

9 "Slanderous men have been in you for the purpose of shedding blood, and in you they have eaten at the mountain shrines. In your midst they have committed acts of lewdness.

10 "In you they have uncovered their fathers' nakedness; in you they have humbled her who was unclean in her menstrual impurity.

11 "And one has committed abomination with his neighbor's wife, and another has lewdly defiled his daughter-in-law. And another in you has humbled his sister, his father's daughter.

12 "In you they have taken bribes to shed blood; you have taken interest and profits, and you have injured your neighbors for gain by oppression, and you have forgotten Me," declares the Lord GOD.

13 "Behold, then, I smite My hand at your dishonest gain which you have acquired and at the bloodshed which is among you.

14 "Can your heart endure, or can your hands be strong, in the days that I shall deal with you? I, the LORD, have spoken and shall act.

15 "And I shall scatter you among the nations, and I shall disperse you through the lands, and I shall consume your uncleanness from you.

16 "And you will profane yourself in the sight of the nations, and you will know that I am the LORD."'"

2. The promise of God's wrath

17 And the word of the LORD came to me saying,

18 "Son of man, the house of Israel has become dross to Me; all of them are bronze and tin and iron and lead in the furnace; they are the dross of silver.

19 "Therefore, thus says the Lord GOD, 'Because all of you have become dross, therefore, behold, I am going to gather you into the midst of Jerusalem.

20 'As they gather silver and bronze and iron and lead and tin into the furnace to blow fire on it in order to melt it, so I shall gather you in My anger and in My wrath, and I shall lay you there and melt you.

21 'And I shall gather you and blow on you with the fire of My wrath, and you will be melted in the midst of it.

22 'As silver is melted in the furnace, so you will be melted in the midst of it; and you will know that I, the LORD, have poured out My wrath on you.' "

3. The indictment extended to all classes

23 And the word of the LORD came to me saying,

24 "Son of man, say to her, 'You are a land that is not cleansed or rained on in the day of indignation.'

25 "There is a conspiracy of her prophets in her midst, like a roaring lion tearing the prey. They have devoured lives; they have taken treasure and precious things; they have made many widows in the midst of her.

26 "Her priests have done violence to My law and have profaned My holy things; they have made no distinction between the holy and the profane, and they have not taught the difference between the unclean and the clean; and they hide their eyes from My sabbaths, and I am profaned among them.

27 "Her princes within her are like wolves tearing the prey, by shedding blood and destroying lives in order to get dishonest gain.

28 "And her prophets have smeared whitewash for them, seeing false visions and divining lies for them, saying, 'Thus says the Lord GOD,' when the LORD has not spoken.

29 "The people of the land have practiced oppression and committed robbery, and they have wronged the poor and needy and have oppressed the sojourner without justice.

30 "And I searched for a man among them who should build up the wall and stand in the gap before Me for the land, that I should not destroy it; but I found no one.

31 "Thus I have poured out My indignation on them; I have consumed them with the fire of My wrath; their way I have brought upon their heads," declares the Lord GOD.

M. The harlotry of Oholah (Samaria) and Oholibah (Jerusalem)

1. Introduction

23 The word of the LORD came to me again saying,
2 "Son of man, there were two women, the daughters of one mother;
3 and they played the harlot in Egypt. They played the harlot in their youth; there their breasts were pressed, and there their virgin bosom was handled.

4 "And their names were Oholah the elder and Oholibah her sister. And they became Mine, and they bore sons and daughters. And as for their names, Samaria is Oholah, and Jerusalem is Oholibah.

2. The sin of Oholah

5 "And Oholah played the harlot while she was Mine; and she lusted after her lovers, after the Assyrians, her neighbors,
6 who were clothed in purple, governors and officials, all of them desirable young men, horsemen riding on horses.

7 "And she bestowed her harlotries on them, all of whom were the choicest men of Assyria; and with all whom she lusted after, with all their idols she defiled herself.

8 "And she did not forsake her harlotries from the time in Egypt; for in her youth men had lain with her, and they handled her virgin bosom and poured out their lust on her.

9 "Therefore, I gave her into the hand of her lovers, into the hand of the Assyrians, after whom she lusted.

10 "They uncovered her nakedness; they took her sons and her daughters, but they slew her with the sword. Thus she became a byword among women, and they executed judgments on her.

3. The sin of Oholibah

11 "Now her sister Oholibah saw this, yet she was more corrupt in her lust than she, and her harlotries were more than the harlotries of her sister.

12 "She lusted after the Assyrians, governors and officials, the ones near, magnificently dressed, horsemen riding on horses, all of them desirable young men.

13 "And I saw that she had defiled herself; they both took the same way.

23:14
Ezek 8:10;
16:29;
Jer 22:14
23:15
Is 22:21
23:16
v. 20
23:17
vv. 28,30
23:18
v. 10; Jer 6:8
23:19
vv. 14,3
23:20
Ezek 16:26
23:21
v. 3
23:22
v. 28;
Ezek 16:37
23:23
Ezek 21:19;
2 Kin 24:2;
Jer 50:21;
vv. 6,12
23:24
Ezek 21:15,
19; Jer 47:3;
Ezek 16:40;
Jer 39:5,6
23:25
Ezek 8:17,18;
Zeph 1:18;
v. 47;
Ezek 20:47,
48; 22:20,21
23:26
Ezek 16:39
23:27
Ezek 16:41;
22:15; vv. 3,
19
23:28
Ezek 16:37
23:29
v. 26;
Ezek 16:39
23:30
vv. 7,17;
Jer 2:18-20;
Ezek 6:9
23:32
Is 51:17;
Jer 25:15;
Ezek 22:4,5
23:33
Jer 25:15,16,
27; Ezek 4:16
23:34
Ps 75:8;
Is 51:17
23:35
Jer 3:21;
Hos 8:14;
1 Kin 14:9;
Neh 9:26

14 "So she increased her harlotries. And she saw men portrayed on the wall, images of the Chaldeans portrayed with vermilion,

15 girded with belts on their loins, with flowing turbans on their heads, all of them looking like officers, like the Babylonians in Chaldea, the land of their birth.

16 "And when she saw them she lusted after them and sent messengers to them in Chaldea.

17 "And the Babylonians came to her to the bed of love, and they defiled her with their harlotry. And when she had been defiled by them, she became disgusted with them.

18 "And she uncovered her harlotries and uncovered her nakedness; then I became disgusted with her, as I had become disgusted with her sister.

19 "Yet she multiplied her harlotries, remembering the days of her youth, when she played the harlot in the land of Egypt.

20 "And she lusted after their paramours, whose flesh is like the flesh of donkeys and whose issue is like the issue of horses.

21 "Thus you longed for the lewdness of your youth, when the Egyptians handled your bosom because of the breasts of your youth.

4. The punishment of Oholibah

22 "Therefore, O Oholibah, thus says the Lord GOD, 'Behold I will arouse your lovers against you, from whom you were alienated, and I will bring them against you from every side:

23 the Babylonians and all the Chaldeans, Pekod and Shoa and Koa, and all the Assyrians with them; desirable young men, governors and officials all of them, officers and men of renown, all of them riding on horses.

24 'And they will come against you with weapons, chariots, and wagons, and with a company of peoples. They will set themselves against you on every side with buckler and shield and helmet; and I shall commit the judgment to them, and they will judge you according to their customs.

25 'And I will set My jealousy against you, that they may deal with you in wrath. They will remove your nose and your ears; and your survivors will fall by the sword. They will take your sons and your daughters; and your survivors will be consumed by the fire.

26 'They will also strip you of your clothes and take away your beautiful jewels.

27 'Thus I shall make your lewdness and your harlotry brought from the land of Egypt to cease from you, so that you will not lift up your eyes to them or remember Egypt anymore.'

28 "For thus says the Lord GOD, 'Behold, I will give you into the hand of those whom you hate, into the hand of those from whom you were alienated.

29 'And they will deal with you in hatred, take all your property, and leave you naked and bare. And the nakedness of your harlotries shall be uncovered, both your lewdness and your harlotries.

30 'These things will be done to you because you have played the harlot with the nations, because you have defiled yourself with their idols.

31 'You have walked in the way of your sister; therefore I will give her cup into your hand.'

32 "Thus says the Lord GOD,
'You will drink your sister's cup,
Which is deep and wide.
You will be laughed at and held in derision;
It contains much.

33 'You will be filled with drunkenness and sorrow,
The cup of horror and desolation,
The cup of your sister Samaria.

34 'And you will drink it and drain it.
Then you will gnaw its fragments
And tear your breasts;
for I have spoken,' declares the Lord GOD.

35 "Therefore, thus says the Lord GOD, 'Because you have forgotten Me and cast Me behind your back, bear now the punishment of your lewdness and your harlotries.'"

5. *The judgment of the* Lord *on Oholah and Oholibah*

36 Moreover, the Lord said to me, "Son of man, will you judge Oholah and Oholibah? Then declare to them their abominations.

37 "For they have committed adultery, and blood is on their hands. Thus they have committed adultery with their idols and even caused their sons, whom they bore to Me, to pass through *the fire* to them as food.

38 "Again, they have done this to Me: they have defiled My sanctuary on the same day and have profaned My sabbaths.

39 "For when they had slaughtered their children for their idols, they entered My sanctuary on the same day to profane it; and lo, thus they did within My house.

40 "Furthermore, they have even sent for men who come from afar, to whom a messenger was sent; and lo, they came—for whom you bathed, painted your eyes, and decorated yourselves with ornaments;

41 and you sat on a splendid couch with a table arranged before it, on which you had set My incense and My oil.

42 "And the sound of a carefree multitude was with her; and drunkards were brought from the wilderness with men of the common sort. And they put bracelets on the hands of the women and beautiful crowns on their heads.

43 "Then I said concerning her who was worn out by adulteries, 'Will they now commit adultery with her when she is *thus*?'

44 "But they went in to her as they would go in to a harlot. Thus they went in to Oholah and to Oholibah, the lewd women.

45 "But they, righteous men, will judge them with the judgment of adulteresses, and with the judgment of women who shed blood, because they are adulteresses and blood is on their hands.

46 "For thus says the Lord God, 'Bring up a company against them, and give them over to terror and plunder.

47 'And the company will stone them with stones and cut them down with their swords; they will slay their sons and their daughters and burn their houses with fire.

48 'Thus I shall make lewdness cease from the land, that all women may be admonished and not commit lewdness as you have done.

49 'And your lewdness will be requited upon you, and you will bear the penalty of *worshiping* your idols; thus you will know that I am the Lord God.' "

N. *The allegory of the boiling pot*

24 And the word of the Lord came to me in the ninth year, in the tenth month, on the tenth of the month, saying,

2 "Son of man, write the name of the day, this very day. The king of Babylon has laid siege to Jerusalem this very day.

3 "And speak a parable to the rebellious house, and say to them, 'Thus says the Lord God,

"Put on the pot, put *it* on, and also pour water in it;

4   Put in it the pieces,
Every good piece, the thigh, and the shoulder;
Fill *it* with choice bones.

5   "Take the choicest of the flock,
And also pile wood under the pot.
Make it boil vigorously.
Also seethe its bones in it."

6 'Therefore, thus says the Lord God,
"Woe to the bloody city,
To the pot in which there is rust
And whose rust has not gone out of it!
Take out of it piece after piece,
Without making a choice.

7 "For her blood is in her midst;
She placed it on the bare rock;
She did not pour it on the ground
To cover it with dust.

8 "That it may cause wrath to come up to take vengeance,
I have put her blood on the bare rock,
That it may not be covered."

23:36
Ezek 20:4;
22:2; Is 58:1
23:37
vv. 3,45;
Ezek 16:20,
21,36,45
23:38
Ezek 5:11;
7:20; 22:8
23:39
2 Kin 21:4

23:40
Is 57:9;
2 Ki 9:30;
Jer 4:30;
Ezek 16:13-16
23:41
Esth 1:6;
Amos 6:4;
Prov 7:17;
Hos 2:8
23:42
Ezek 16:49;
Jer 51:7;
Ezek 16:11,
12

23:45
Ezek 16:38;
Hos 6:5;
Lev 20:10

23:46
v. 24;
Ezek 16:40;
Jer 15:4;
24:9; 29:18
23:47
Ezek 16:40;
2 Chr 36:17,
19;
Ezek 24:21;
Jer 39:8
23:48
v. 27;
Ezek 22:15;
2 Pet 2:6
23:49
v. 35;
Ezek 6:7;
20:38,42,44
24:1
Ezek 1:2;
8:1; 20:1;
26:1
24:2
Is 8:1;
2 Kin 25:1;
Jer 39:1; 52:4
24:3
Ezek 17:2;
Jer 1:13;
Ezek 11:3
24:4
Ezek 22:19-22;
Mic 3:2,3
24:5
v. 10

24:6
v. 9;
Ezek 22:3;
Mic 7:2;
Joel 3:3;
Nah 3:10

24:7
Ezek 23:37,
45;
Lev 17:13;
Deut 12:16

24:8
Matt 7:2

24:9
v. 6; Nah 3:1;
Hab 2:12

9   'Therefore, thus says the Lord God,
    "Woe to the bloody city!
    I also shall make the pile great.

24:10
v. 5

10   "Heap on the wood, kindle the fire,
    Boil the flesh well,
    And mix in the spices,
    And let the bones be burned.

24:11
Ezek 21:10;
22:15

11   "Then set it empty on its coals,
    So that it may be hot,
    And its bronze may glow,
    And its filthiness may be melted in it,
    Its rust consumed.

12   "She has wearied *Me* with toil,
    Yet her great rust has not gone from her;
    Let her rust *be* in the fire!

24:13
Jer 6:28-30;
Ezek 22:24;
5:13; 8:18;
16:42

13   "In your filthiness is lewdness.
    Because I *would* have cleansed you,
    Yet you are not clean,
    You will not be cleansed from your filthiness again,
    Until I have spent My wrath on you.

24:14
1 Sam 15:29;
Is 55:11;
Ezek 9:10;
18:30; 36:19

14 "I, the Lord, have spoken; it is coming and I shall act. I shall not relent, and I shall not pity, and I shall not be sorry; according to your ways and according to your deeds I shall judge you," declares the Lord God.' "

O. The death of Ezekiel's wife

15   And the word of the Lord came to me saying,

*24:16
Job 23:2;
Jer 16:5;
22:10; 13:17

16 "Son of man, behold, I am about to take from you the desire of your eyes with a blow; but you shall not mourn, and you shall not weep, and your tears shall not come.

24:17
Jer 16:5-7;
2 Sam 15:30;
Mic 3:7

17 "Groan silently; make no mourning for the dead. Bind on your turban, and put your shoes on your feet, and do not cover *your* mustache, and do not eat the bread of men."

18 So I spoke to the people in the morning, and in the evening my wife died. And in the morning I did as I was commanded.

24:19
Ezek 12:9;
37:18

19 And the people said to me, "Will you not tell us what these things that you are doing mean for us?"

20 Then I said to them, "The word of the Lord came to me saying,

24:21
Jer 7:14;
Ps 27:4;
Jer 6:11;
Ezek 23:47

21 'Speak to the house of Israel, "Thus says the Lord God, 'Behold, I am about to profane My sanctuary, the pride of your power, the desire of your eyes, and the delight of your soul; and your sons and your daughters whom you have left behind will fall by the sword.

24:22
Jer 16:6,7;
v. 17

22 'And you will do as I have done; you will not cover *your* mustache, and you will not eat the bread of men.

24:23
Job 27:15;
Ps 78:64;
Ezek 33:10

23 'And your turbans will be on your heads and your shoes on your feet. You will not mourn, and you will not weep; but you will rot away in your iniquities, and you will groan to one another.

24:24
Ezek 4:3;
12:6,11;
Jer 17:15;
Ezek 6:7;
25:5

24 'Thus Ezekiel will be a sign to you; according to all that he has done you will do; when it comes, then you will know that I am the Lord God.' "

24:25
Jer 11:22

25 'As for you, son of man, will *it* not be on the day when I take from them their stronghold, the joy of their pride, the desire of their eyes, and their heart's delight, their sons and their daughters,

24:26
Ezek 33:21f

26 that on that day he who escapes will come to you with information for *your* ears?

24:27
Ezek 3:26,27;
33:22; v. 24

27 'On that day your mouth will be opened to him who escaped, and you will speak and be dumb no longer. Thus you will be a sign to them, and they will know that I am the Lord.' "

24:16 *the desire of your eyes,* Ezekiel's wife. *with a blow.* The death of Ezekiel's wife occurred in a sudden and striking manner, making it obvious that it was a providential visitation of God and there was to be no grief.
24:18 Ezekiel here represents the case of the obedient servant who is faithful to God despite personal disappointment and sorrow. This lesson needs to be learned by every servant of God, each one of whom is called upon to live above life's tragic moments and to find his highest happiness in his Father in heaven.

II. *The prophecies against the surrounding nations*
(25:1–32:32)

A. *Ammon*

25 And the word of the LORD came to me saying,
2 "Son of man, set your face toward the sons of Ammon, and prophesy against them,   *25:2
3   and say to the sons of Ammon, 'Hear the word of the Lord GOD! Thus says the Lord GOD, "Because you said, 'Aha!' against My sanctuary when it was profaned, and against the land of Israel when it was made desolate, and against the house of Judah when they went into exile,
4   therefore, behold, I am going to give you to the sons of the east for a possession, and they will set their encampments among you and make their dwellings among you; they will eat your fruit and drink your milk.
5   "And I shall make Rabbah a pasture for camels and the sons of Ammon a resting place for flocks. Thus you will know that I am the LORD."
6   'For thus says the Lord GOD, "Because you have clapped your hands and stamped your feet and rejoiced with all the scorn of your soul against the land of Israel,
7   therefore, behold, I have stretched out My hand against you, and I shall give you for spoil to the nations. And I shall cut you off from the peoples and make you perish from the lands; I shall destroy you. Thus you will know that I am the LORD."

B. *Moab*

8   'Thus says the Lord GOD, "Because Moab and Seir say, 'Behold, the house of Judah is like all the nations,'
9   therefore, behold, I am going to deprive the flank of Moab of *its* cities, of its cities which are on its frontiers, the glory of the land, Beth-jeshimoth, Baal-meon, and Kiriathaim,
10   and I will give it for a possession, along with the sons of Ammon, to the sons of the east, that the sons of Ammon may not be remembered among the nations.
11   "Thus I will execute judgments on Moab, and they will know that I am the LORD."

C. *Edom*

12   'Thus says the Lord GOD, "Because Edom has acted against the house of Judah by taking vengeance, and has incurred grievous guilt, and avenged themselves upon them,"
13   therefore, thus says the Lord GOD, "I will also stretch out My hand against Edom and cut off man and beast from it. And I will lay it waste; from Teman even to Dedan they will fall by the sword.
14   "And I will lay My vengeance on Edom by the hand of My people Israel. Therefore, they will act in Edom according to My anger and according to My wrath; thus they will know My vengeance," declares the Lord GOD.

D. *Philistia*

15   'Thus says the Lord GOD, "Because the Philistines have acted in revenge and have taken vengeance with scorn of soul to destroy with everlasting enmity,"
16   therefore, thus says the Lord GOD, "Behold, I will stretch out My hand against the Philistines, even cut off the Cherethites and destroy the remnant of the seacoast.
17   "And I will execute great vengeance on them with wrathful rebukes; and they will know that I am the LORD when I lay My vengeance on them." ' "

Marginal references:
*25:2 Jer 27:3; Ezek 21:28; Amos 1:13; Zeph 2:8,9
25:3 Prov 17:5; Ezek 26:2
25:4 Ezek 21:31
25:5 Ezek 21:20; Is 17:2; Zeph 2:14
25:6 Job 27:23; Lam 2:15; Zeph 2:8,10
25:7 Ezek 26:5; Amos 1:14, 15; Ezek 6:14
25:8 Is chs. 15,16; Jer 48:1;
Amos 2:1; Ezek 35:2,5
*25:9 Num 33:49; 32:3,38; 32:37
25:10 v. 4; Ezek 21:32
25:11 Ezek 5:15; 11:9
*25:12 Lam 4:21,22; Ezek 35:2; Amos 1:11; Obad 10-16
25:13 Amos 1:12; Jer 25:23
25:14 Is 11:14; Jer 49:2
25:15 Jer 25:20; Is 14:29-31; Joel 3:4; 2 Chr 28:18
25:16 Zeph 2:4,5; 1 Sam 30:14; Jer 47:1-7
25:17 Ezek 5:15; Ps 9:16

25:2 The Ammonites were descendants of the younger daughter of Lot, who bore her father a son, Ben-ammi, by incest. Ben-ammi was the father of the Ammonites, who turned out to be inveterate enemies of the true people of God. (See Gen. 19:33–38.)
25:9 The Moabites were descendants of Moab, the son of Lot's elder daughter. She bore Moab by her father in an incestuous relationship. The Moabites and the Ammonites were prohibited by the Mosaic Law from entering the congregation of Israel until the tenth generation. (See Gen. 19:33–38; Deut. 23:3.)
25:12 See note to Gen. 36:9 for information on the Edomites.

E. *Tyre*

1. *Prediction of its doom*

26 Now it came about in the eleventh year, on the first of the month, that the word of the LORD came to me saying,

2 "Son of man, because Tyre has said concerning Jerusalem, 'Aha, the gateway of the peoples is broken; it has opened to me. I shall be filled, *now that* she is laid waste,'

3 therefore, thus says the Lord GOD, 'Behold, I am against you, O Tyre, and I will bring up many nations against you, as the sea brings up its waves.

4 'And they will destroy the walls of Tyre and break down her towers; and I will scrape her debris from her and make her a bare rock.

5 'She will be a place for the spreading of nets in the midst of the sea, for I have spoken,' declares the Lord GOD, 'and she will become spoil for the nations.

6 'Also her daughters who are on the mainland will be slain by the sword, and they will know that I am the LORD.'"

2. *Nebuchadnezzar the agent of destruction*

7 For thus says the Lord GOD, "Behold, I will bring upon Tyre from the north Nebuchadnezzar king of Babylon, king of kings, with horses, chariots, cavalry, and a great army.

8 "He will slay your daughters on the mainland with the sword; and he will make siege walls against you, cast up a mound against you, and raise up a large shield against you.

9 "And the blow of his battering rams he will direct against your walls, and with his axes he will break down your towers.

10 "Because of the multitude of his horses, the dust *raised by* them will cover you; your walls will shake at the noise of cavalry and wagons and chariots, when he enters your gates as men enter a city that is breached.

11 "With the hoofs of his horses he will trample all your streets. He will slay your people with the sword; and your strong pillars will come down to the ground.

12 "Also they will make a spoil of your riches and a prey of your merchandise, break down your walls and destroy your pleasant houses, and throw your stones and your timbers and your debris into the water.

13 "So I will silence the sound of your songs, and the sound of your harps will be heard no more.

14 "And I will make you a bare rock; you will be a place for the spreading of nets. You will be built no more, for I the LORD have spoken," declares the Lord GOD.

3. *Lamentation of the princes of the sea*

15 Thus says the Lord GOD to Tyre, "Shall not the coastlands shake at the sound of your fall when the wounded groan, when the slaughter occurs in your midst?

16 "Then all the princes of the sea will go down from their thrones, remove their robes, and strip off their embroidered garments. They will clothe themselves with trembling; they will sit on the ground, tremble every moment, and be appalled at you.

17 "And they will take up a lamentation over you and say to you,
'How you have perished, O inhabited one,
From the seas, O renowned city,
Which was mighty on the sea,
She and her inhabitants,
Who imposed her terror
On all her inhabitants!

18 'Now the coastlands will tremble

Marginal references (left column):

*26:2
Is ch. 23;
Jer 25:22;
Ezek 25:3;
36:2
26:3
Mic 4:11;
Is 5:30;
Jer 50:42
26:4
Amos 1:10
26:5
Ezek 27:32;
29:19
26:6
Ezek 25:5

26:7
Jer 27:3-6;
Ezra 7:12;
Dan 2:37;
Ezek 23:24
26:8
v. 6;
Ezek 21:22;
Jer 6:6; 32:24
26:9
Ezek 21:22

26:10
Jer 4:13;
39:3;
Ezek 27:28
26:11
Hab 1:8;
Is 26:5;
Jer 43:13
26:12
v. 5

26:13
Is 14:11;
25:10;
Is 23:16;
Rev 18:22
26:14
vv. 4,5;
Mal 1:4;
Is 14:27

26:15
v. 18;
Ezek 31:16

26:16
Ezek 27:35;
Jon 3:6;
Job 2:13

26:17
Ezek 27:32;
Rev 18:9;
Is 23:4;
Ezek 28:2

26:18
v. 15*

26:2 The overthrow of Tyre was predicted by Isaiah long before the time of Ezekiel (see Is. 23). The reference here is to Nebuchadnezzar's coming siege and the permanent desolation of this splendid and wealthy maritime city. Old Tyre was located on the shore of the mainland, whereas New Tyre was built on an island one-half mile offshore. Nebuchadnezzar seems to have reduced Old Tyre after a thirteen years' siege, although it is not certain that he was able to storm the island. At any rate, it came under Persian suzerainty under Cyrus the Great and fell for the last time under the attack of Alexander the Great in 332 B.C. Unable to capture it by ships, he built a stone causeway all the way out to the island itself. From that day to this its glory has never been recovered, and it stands as a monument to fulfilled prophecy that declared that it should become a bare uninhabited rock fit only for the spreading of fish nets (26:4,5, 14,21; 27:36; 28:2–9).

> On the day of your fall;
> Yes, the coastlands which are by the sea
> Will be terrified at your passing.'"

4. *Tyre to go down to the pit*

19 For thus says the Lord GOD, "When I shall make you a desolate city, like the cities which are not inhabited, when I shall bring up the deep over you, and the great waters will cover you,

20 then I shall bring you down with those who go down to the pit, to the people of old, and I shall make you dwell in the lower parts of the earth, like the ancient waste places, with those who go down to the pit, so that you will not be inhabited; but I shall set glory in the land of the living.

21 "I shall bring terrors on you, and you will be no more; though you will be sought, you will never be found again," declares the Lord GOD.

5. *The lamentation over Tyre*

a. *The beauty and wealth of Tyre*

27 Moreover, the word of the LORD came to me saying,

2 "And you, son of man, take up a lamentation over Tyre;

3 and say to Tyre, who dwells at the entrance to the sea, merchant of the peoples to many coastlands, 'Thus says the Lord GOD,
"O Tyre, you have said, 'I am perfect in beauty.'

4 "Your borders are in the heart of the seas;
Your builders have perfected your beauty.

5 "They have made all *your* planks of fir trees from Senir;
They have taken a cedar from Lebanon to make a mast for you.

6 "Of oaks from Bashan they have made your oars;
With ivory they have inlaid your deck of boxwood from the
coastlands of Cyprus.

7 "Your sail was of fine embroidered linen from Egypt
So that it became your distinguishing mark;
Your awning was blue and purple from the coastlands
of Elishah.

8 "The inhabitants of Sidon and Arvad were your rowers;
Your wise men, O Tyre, were aboard; they were your pilots.

9 "The elders of Gebal and her wise men were with you repairing your
seams;
All the ships of the sea and their sailors were with you in order to
deal in your merchandise.

b. *The armies of Tyre*

10 "Persia and Lud and Put were in your army, your men of war. They hung shield and helmet in you; they set forth your splendor.

11 "The sons of Arvad and your army were on your walls, *all* around, and the Gammadim were in your towers. They hung their shields on your walls, *all* around; they perfected your beauty.

c. *The commerce of Tyre*

12 "Tarshish was your customer because of the abundance of all *kinds* of wealth; with silver, iron, tin, and lead, they paid for your wares.

13 "Javan, Tubal, and Meshech, they were your traders; with the lives of men and vessels of bronze they paid for your merchandise.

14 "Those from Beth-togarmah gave horses and war horses and mules for your wares.

15 "The sons of Dedan were your traders. Many coastlands were your market; ivory tusks and ebony they brought as your payment.

16 "Aram was your customer because of the abundance of your goods; they paid for your wares with emeralds, purple, embroidered work, fine linen, coral, and rubies.

17 "Judah and the land of Israel, they were your traders; with the wheat of Minnith, cakes, honey, oil, and balm they paid for your merchandise.

18 "Damascus was your customer because of the abundance of your goods, because of the abundance of all *kinds* of wealth, because of the wine of Helbon and white wool.

26:20
Ezek 32:18,
24; Amos 9:2;
Jer 33:9

26:21
Ezek 27:36;
28:19; v. 14

27:2
Ezek 28:12
27:3
Ezek 28:2;
v. 33;
Ezek 28:12
27:4
vv. 25-27

27:5
Deut 3:9

27:6
Zech 11:2;
Is 2:13;
Jer 2:10

27:8
1 Kin 9:27

27:9
1 Kin 5:18;
v. 27

27:10
Ezek 30:5;
38:5; v. 11
27:11
vv. 3,8,10

27:12
2 Chr 20:36;
Is 23:6,10;
vv. 18,33
27:13
Gen 10:2;
Is 66:19;
Rev 18:13
27:14
Gen 10:3;
Ezek 38:6
27:15
Gen 10:7;
Rev 18:12
27:16
Ezek 28:13;
16:13,18
27:17
Judg 11:33;
Jer 8:22
27:18
Jer 49:23;
Ezek 47:16-18;
vv. 12,33

19 "Vedan and Javan paid for your wares from Uzal; wrought iron, cassia, and sweet cane were among your merchandise.

20 "Dedan traded with you in saddlecloths for riding.

21 "Arabia and all the princes of Kedar, they were your customers for lambs, rams, and goats; for these they were your customers.

22 "The traders of Sheba and Raamah, they traded with you; they paid for your wares with the best of all *kinds* of spices, and with all *kinds* of precious stones, and gold.

23 "Haran, Canneh, Eden, the traders of Sheba, Asshur, *and* Chilmad traded with you.

24 "They traded with you in choice garments, in clothes of blue and embroidered work, and in carpets of many colors, *and* tightly wound cords, *which were* among your merchandise.

d. *The ruin of Tyre*

25 "The ships of Tarshish were the carriers for your merchandise.
And you were filled and were very glorious
In the heart of the seas.

26 "Your rowers have brought you
Into great waters;
The east wind has broken you
In the heart of the seas.

27 "Your wealth, your wares, your merchandise,
Your sailors, and your pilots,
Your repairers of seams, your dealers in merchandise,
And all your men of war who are in you,
With all your company that is in your midst,
Will fall into the heart of the seas
On the day of your overthrow.

28 "At the sound of the cry of your pilots
The pasture lands will shake.

29 "And all who handle the oar,
The sailors, *and* all the pilots of the sea
Will come down from their ships;
They will stand on the land,

30 And they will make their voice heard over you
And will cry bitterly.
They will cast dust on their heads,
They will wallow in ashes.

31 "Also they will make themselves bald for you
And gird themselves with sackcloth;
And they will weep for you in bitterness of soul
With bitter mourning.

32 "Moreover, in their wailing they will take up a lamentation for you
And lament over you:
'Who is like Tyre,
Like her who is silent in the midst of the sea?'

33 'When your wares went out from the seas,
You satisfied many peoples;
With the abundance of your wealth and your merchandise
You enriched the kings of earth.

34 'Now that you are broken by the seas
In the depths of the waters,
Your merchandise and all your company
Have fallen in the midst of you.

35 'All the inhabitants of the coastlands
Are appalled at you,
And their kings are horribly afraid;
They are troubled in countenance.

36 'The merchants among the peoples hiss at you;
You have become terrified,
And you will be no more.' " " "

Marginal references:

27:20 v. 15
27:21 Jer 25:24; 49:28; Is 60:7
27:22 Gen 10:7; 1 Kin 10:1,2; Is 60:6
27:23 Gen 11:31; 2 Kin 19:12; Amos 1:5

27:25 Is 2:16; 23:14; v. 4

27:26 Ezek 26:19; Ps 48:7; vv. 4,25,27

27:27 Prov 11:4; Rev 18:9-19

27:28 Ezek 26:15

27:29 Rev 18:17-19

27:30 Job 2:12; Rev 18:19; Esth 4:1,3; Jer 6:26

27:31 Jer 16:6; Ezek 29:18; Is 22:12; 16:9

27:32 v. 2; Ezek 26:17; Rev 18:18

27:33 Rev 18:19

27:34 vv. 26,27; Ezek 26:19; Zech 9:3,4

27:35 Ezek 26:15, 16; 32:10

27:36 Jer 18:16; Zeph 2:15; Ezek 26:21; Ps 37:10,36

F. Prophecies against Tyre and Sidon

1. The pride of Tyre the reason for its ruin

28 The word of the LORD came again to me saying,
2 "Son of man, say to the leader of Tyre, 'Thus says the Lord GOD,
"Because your heart is lifted up
And you have said, 'I am a god,
I sit in the seat of gods,
In the heart of the seas';
Yet you are a man and not God,
Although you make your heart like the heart of God—

3   Behold, you are wiser than Daniel;
There is no secret that is a match for you.

4   "By your wisdom and understanding
You have acquired riches for yourself,
And have acquired gold and silver for your treasuries.

5   "By your great wisdom, by your trade
You have increased your riches,
And your heart is lifted up because of your riches—

6   Therefore, thus says the Lord GOD,
'Because you have made your heart
Like the heart of God,

7   Therefore, behold, I will bring strangers upon you,
The most ruthless of the nations.
And they will draw their swords
Against the beauty of your wisdom
And defile your splendor.

8   'They will bring you down to the pit,
And you will die the death of those who are slain
In the heart of the seas.

9   'Will you still say, "I am a god,"
In the presence of your slayer,
Although you are a man and not God,
In the hands of those who wound you?

10   'You will die the death of the uncircumcised
By the hand of strangers,
For I have spoken!' declares the Lord GOD!" ' "

2. The lamentation over Tyre

11   Again the word of the LORD came to me saying,
12 "Son of man, take up a lamentation over the king of Tyre, and say to him,
'Thus says the Lord GOD,
"You had the seal of perfection,
Full of wisdom and perfect in beauty.

13   "You were in Eden, the garden of God;
Every precious stone was your covering:
The ruby, the topaz, and the diamond;
The beryl, the onyx, and the jasper;
The lapis lazuli, the turquoise, and the emerald;
And the gold, the workmanship of your settings and sockets,
Was in you.
On the day that you were created
They were prepared.

14   "You were the anointed cherub who covers,
And I placed you there.
You were on the holy mountain of God;
You walked in the midst of the stones of fire.

15   "You were blameless in your ways

Marginal references:

28:2 Ezek 27:25-27; Is 31:3; v. 6

28:3 Dan 1:20

28:4 Ezek 27:33

28:5 Ps 62:10; Zech 9:3; Hos 13:6

28:6 v. 2

28:7 Ezek 26:7; 30:11; 31:12; 32:12; v. 17

28:8 Ezek 32:30; 27:26,27,34

28:9 v. 2

28:10 Ezek 31:18; 32:19,21,25, 27

28:12 Ezek 27:2; v. 3; Ezek 27:3

28:13 Ezek 31:8,9; 36:35

28:14 Ex 25:20; v. 16; Ezek 20:40; Rev 18:16
28:15 Ezek 27:3,4; Is 14:12; vv. 17,18

28:2 *In the heart of the seas.* Tyre occupied an island one-half mile from the Phoenician coast. From the island stronghold, Tyre was able to withstand Nebuchadnezzar's siege for thirteen years. As an island fortress it was almost impregnable for that day.

From the day you were created,
Until unrighteousness was found in you.

28:16
Ezek 27:12ff;
8:17;
Gen 3:24;
v. 14

16 "By the abundance of your trade
You were internally filled with violence,
And you sinned;
Therefore I have cast you as profane
From the mountain of God.
And I have destroyed you, O covering cherub,
From the midst of the stones of fire.

28:17
vv. 2,5;
Ezek 31:10;
27:3,4; 26:16

17 "Your heart was lifted up because of your beauty;
You corrupted your wisdom by reason of your splendor.
I cast you to the ground;
I put you before kings,
That they may see you.

28:18
v. 16;
Amos 1:9,10;
Mal 4:3

18 "By the multitude of your iniquities,
In the unrighteousness of your trade,
You profaned your sanctuaries.
Therefore I have brought fire from the midst of you;
It has consumed you,
And I have turned you to ashes on the earth
In the eyes of all who see you.

28:19
Ezek 26:21;
27:36;
Jer 51:64

19 "All who know you among the peoples
Are appalled at you;
You have become terrified,
And you will be no more."'"

3. Sidon to perish by pestilence and the sword

20 And the word of the LORD came to me saying,
21 "Son of man, set your face toward Sidon, prophesy against her,
22 and say, 'Thus says the Lord GOD,
"Behold, I am against you, O Sidon,
And I shall be glorified in your midst.
Then they will know that I am the LORD, when I execute judgments
in her,
And I shall manifest My holiness in her.

28:21
Ezek 6:2;
25:2; Is 23:4,
12;
Ezek 32:30
28:22
Ezek 26:3;
39:13;
Ps 9:16;
v. 26;
Ezek 38:16
28:23
Ezek 38:22;
Jer 51:52;
vv. 24,26

23 "For I shall send pestilence to her
And blood to her streets,
And the wounded will fall in her midst
By the sword upon her on every side;
Then they will know that I am the LORD.

4. The recovery of the house of Israel

28:24
Num 33:55;
Josh 23:13;
Is 55:13;
Ezek 25:6;
36:5
28:25
Is 11:12;
Jer 32:37;
Ezek 20:41;
Jer 23:8;
27:11;
Ezek 37:25
28:26
Jer 23:6;
Is 65:21;
Amos 9:13,14

24 "And there will be no more for the house of Israel a prickling brier or a painful thorn from any round about them who scorned them; then they will know that I am the Lord GOD."

25 'Thus says the Lord GOD, "When I gather the house of Israel from the peoples among whom they are scattered, and shall manifest My holiness in them in the sight of the nations, then they will live in their land which I gave to My servant Jacob.

26 "And they will live in it securely; and they will build houses, plant vineyards, and live securely, when I execute judgments upon all who scorn them round about them. Then they will know that I am the LORD their God."'"

G. The prophecies against Egypt

1. The word against Pharaoh

a. Pharaoh's sin of pride

*29:2
Ezek 28:21;
Jer 44:30;
Is 19:1;
Jer 25:19;
46:2,25
29:3
Jer 44:30;
Ezek 28:22;
Is 27:1; 51:9;
Ezek 32:2

29 In the tenth year, in the tenth *month*, on the twelfth of the month, the word of the LORD came to me saying,

2 "Son of man, set your face against Pharaoh, king of Egypt, and prophesy against him and against all Egypt.

3 "Speak and say, 'Thus says the Lord GOD,
"Behold, I am against you, Pharaoh, king of Egypt,

The great monster that lies in the midst of his rivers,
That has said, 'My Nile is mine, and I myself have made it.'

4 "And I shall put hooks in your jaws,
And I shall make the fish of your rivers cling to your scales.
And I shall bring you up out of the midst of your rivers,
And all the fish of your rivers will cling to your scales.

5 "And I shall abandon you to the wilderness, you and all the fish of
your rivers;
You will fall on the open field; you will not be brought together or
gathered.
I have given you for food to the beasts of the earth and to the birds
of the sky.

b. Egypt's judgment

6 "Then all the inhabitants of Egypt will know that I am the LORD,
Because they have been *only* a staff *made* of reed to the house of
Israel.

7 "When they took hold of you with the hand,
You broke and tore all their hands;
And when they leaned on you,
You broke and made all their loins quake."

8 'Therefore, thus says the Lord GOD, "Behold, I shall bring upon you a
sword, and I shall cut off from you man and beast.

9 "And the land of Egypt will become a desolation and waste. Then they will
know that I am the LORD.

Because you said, 'The Nile is mine, and I have made *it*,'

c. The desolation and restoration of Egypt

10 therefore, behold, I am against you and against your rivers, and I will make
the land of Egypt an utter waste and desolation, from Migdol *to* Syene and even to
the border of Ethiopia.

11 "A man's foot will not pass through it, and the foot of a beast will not pass
through it, and it will not be inhabited for forty years.

12 "So I shall make the land of Egypt a desolation in the midst of desolated
lands. And her cities, in the midst of cities that are laid waste, will be desolate forty
years; and I shall scatter the Egyptians among the nations and disperse them among
the lands."

13 'For thus says the Lord GOD, "At the end of forty years I shall gather the
Egyptians from the peoples among whom they were scattered.

14 "And I shall turn the fortunes of Egypt and shall make them return to the
land of Pathros, to the land of their origin; and there they will be a lowly kingdom.

15 "It will be the lowest of the kingdoms; and it will never again lift itself up
above the nations. And I shall make them so small that they will not rule over the
nations.

16 "And it will never again be the confidence of the house of Israel, bringing to
mind the iniquity of their having turned to Egypt. Then they will know that I am
the Lord GOD."'"

2. Nebuchadnezzar to receive Egypt as his wages

17 Now in the twenty-seventh year, in the first *month*, on the first of the month,
the word of the LORD came to me saying,

18 "Son of man, Nebuchadnezzar king of Babylon made his army labor hard
against Tyre; every head was made bald, and every shoulder was rubbed bare. But
he and his army had no wages from Tyre for the labor that he had performed
against it."

19 Therefore, thus says the Lord GOD, "Behold, I shall give the land of Egypt
to Nebuchadnezzar king of Babylon. And he will carry off her wealth, and capture
her spoil and seize her plunder; and it will be wages for his army.

29:2 God plainly foretold the overthrow of Egypt (Is. 19:1–15; Jer. 43:8–13; Ezek. 29–31). This prophecy was later fulfilled by Nebuchadnezzar in his invasions of 572 and 568 B.C., when Egypt was reduced to the status of *the lowest of the kingdoms* (29:15). From the Persian conquest by Cambyses (ca. 524 B.C.) until the present generation, the land of the Nile has for the most part been subject either to foreign powers (Alexander the Great, Rome, Arabia, Turkey) or to a foreign dynasty.
29:18 *labor hard against Tyre*. Nebuchadnezzar besieged Tyre for thirteen years before it fell in 572 B.C. (See note to 28:2 for location of Tyre.)

29:20
Is 45:1-3;
Jer 25:9
29:21
Ps 132:17;
Ezek 24:27;
33:22;
Luke 21:15;
Ezek 6:7; v. 6

20 "I have given him the land of Egypt *for* his labor which he performed, because they acted for Me," declares the Lord GOD.

21 "On that day I shall make a horn sprout for the house of Israel, and I shall open your mouth in their midst. Then they will know that I am the LORD."

3. The nearness of Egypt's doom

a. The LORD's vengeance on Egypt

30:2
Is 13:6;
Ezek 21:12;
Joel 1:5,11,13
30:3
Ezek 7:7,12;
Joel 2:1;
Obad 15;
Zeph 1:7;
v. 18
30:4
vv. 11,5,9;
Ezek 29:19

30 The word of the LORD came again to me saying,
2 "Son of man, prophesy and say, 'Thus says the Lord GOD,
   "Wail, 'Alas for the day!'
3   "For the day is near,
      Even the day of the LORD is near;
      It will be a day of clouds,
      A time *of doom* for the nations.
4   "And a sword will come upon Egypt,
      And anguish will be in Ethiopia,
      When the slain fall in Egypt,
      They take away her wealth,
      And her foundations are torn down.

30:5
Jer 25:20,24

5 "Ethiopia, Put, Lud, all Arabia, Libya, and the people of the land that is in league will fall with them by the sword."

b. The fall of Egypt's supporters

30:6
Is 20:3-6;
Ezek 29:10

6 'Thus says the LORD,
   "Indeed, those who support Egypt will fall,
   And the pride of her power will come down;
   From Migdol *to* Syene
   They will fall within her by the sword,"
   Declares the Lord GOD.

30:7
Ezek 29:12

7   "And they will be desolate
      In the midst of the desolated lands;
      And her cities will be
      In the midst of the devastated cities.

30:8
Ezek 29:6;
9:16; vv. 14,
16,5,6

8   "And they will know that I am the LORD,
      When I set a fire in Egypt
      And all her helpers are broken.

30:9
Is 18:1,2;
Ezek 38:11;
32:9,10

9 "On that day messengers will go forth from Me in ships to frighten secure Ethiopia; and anguish will be on them as on the day of Egypt; for, behold, it comes!"

c. The advent of Nebuchadnezzar

30:10
Ezek 29:19

10 'Thus says the Lord GOD,
   "I will also make the multitude of Egypt cease
   By the hand of Nebuchadnezzar king of Babylon.

30:11
Ezek 28:7;
v. 4

11 "He and his people with him,
   The most ruthless of the nations,
   Will be brought in to destroy the land;
   And they will draw their swords against Egypt
   And fill the land with the slain.

30:12
Is 19:5,6;
Ezek 29:3,9

12   "Moreover, I will make the Nile canals dry
      And sell the land into the hands of evil men.
      And I will make the land desolate,
      And all that is in it,
      By the hand of strangers; I, the LORD, have spoken.

d. The vengeance of the LORD on Egypt

30:13
Is 19:1;
Zech 13:2;
v. 16;
Zech 10:11;
Is 19:16
30:14
Ezek 29:14;
Ps 78:12,43;
vv. 15,16

13 'Thus says the Lord GOD,
   "I will also destroy the idols
   And make the images cease from Memphis.
   And there will no longer be a prince in the land of Egypt;
   And I will put fear in the land of Egypt.
14   "And I will make Pathros desolate,
      Set a fire in Zoan,

And execute judgments on [2]Thebes.

15 "And I will pour out My wrath on [3]Sin,
The stronghold of Egypt;
I will also cut off the multitude of Thebes.

30:15
Jer 46:25;
v. 16

16 "And I will set a fire in Egypt;
Sin will writhe in anguish,
Thebes will be breached,
And [4]Memphis *will have* distresses daily.

30:16
vv. 8,13-15

17 "The young men of [5]On and of Pi-beseth
Will fall by the sword,
And the women will go into captivity.

18 "And in Tehaphnehes the day will be dark
When I break there the yoke bars of Egypt.
Then the pride of her power will cease in her;
A cloud will cover her,
And her daughters will go into captivity.

30:18
Jer 43:8-13;
Ezek 34:27;
v. 3

19 "Thus I will execute judgments on Egypt,
And they will know that I am the LORD."' "

30:19
vv. 14,25,26

e. *The arms of Pharaoh to be broken*

20 And it came about in the eleventh year, in the first *month*, on the seventh of the month, that the word of the LORD came to me saying,

21 "Son of man, I have broken the arm of Pharaoh king of Egypt; and, behold, it has not been bound up for healing or wrapped with a bandage, that it may be strong to hold the sword.

30:21
Ps 10:15;
Jer 46:11

22 "Therefore, thus says the Lord GOD, 'Behold, I am against Pharaoh king of Egypt and will break his arms, both the strong and the broken; and I will make the sword fall from his hand.

30:22
Ezek 29:3;
Ps 37:17

23 'And I will scatter the Egyptians among the nations and disperse them among the lands.

30:23
Ezek 29:12;
v. 26

24 'For I will strengthen the arms of the king of Babylon and put My sword in his hand; and I will break the arms of Pharaoh, so that he will groan before him with the groanings of a wounded man.

30:24
vv. 10,25;
Zech 10:12;
Zeph 2:12;
Ezek 26:15;
21:14,25

25 'Thus I will strengthen the arms of the king of Babylon, but the arms of Pharaoh will fall. Then they will know that I am the LORD, when I put My sword into the hand of the king of Babylon and he stretches it out against the land of Egypt.

30:25
vv. 24,22,11;
Is 5:25

26 'When I scatter the Egyptians among the nations and disperse them among the lands, then they will know that I am the LORD.' "

30:26
Ezek 29:12

4. *The allegory of the great cedar*

a. *Egypt likened to a great cedar*

31 And it came about in the eleventh year, in the third *month*, on the first of the month, that the word of the LORD came to me saying,

2 "Son of man, say to Pharaoh king of Egypt, and to his multitude,
'Whom are you like in your greatness?

31:2
Ezek 29:19;
30:10; v. 18

3 'Behold, Assyria *was* a cedar in Lebanon
With beautiful branches and forest shade,
And very high;
And its top was among the clouds.

31:3
Nah 3:1ff;
Ezek 17:23;
vv. 5,10

4 'The waters made it grow, the deep made it high.
With its rivers it continually extended all around its planting place,
And it sent out its channels to all the trees of the field.

31:4
Ezek 17:5,8;
Rev 17:1,15

5 'Therefore its height was loftier than all the trees of the field
And its boughs became many and its branches long
Because of many waters as it spread them out.

31:5
Ps 37:35;
Ezek 17:5

6 'All the birds of the heavens nested in its boughs,
And under its branches all the beasts of the field gave birth,
And all great nations lived under its shade.

31:6
Ezek 17:23;
Dan 4:12;
Matt 13:32;
Mark 4:32;
Luke 13:19

7 'So it was beautiful in its greatness, in the length of its branches;
For its roots extended to many waters.

31:7
vv. 2,9

[2]Or, *No* [3]Or, *Pelusium* [4]Or, *Noph* [5]Or, *Aven*

8   'The cedars in God's garden could not match it;
     The cypresses could not compare with its boughs,
     And the plane trees could not match its branches.
     No tree in God's garden could compare with it in its beauty.

9   'I made it beautiful with the multitude of its branches,
     And all the trees of Eden, which were in the garden of God, were
     jealous of it.

b. The fall of the cedar (Egypt) into the pit

10   'Therefore, thus says the Lord GOD, "Because it is high in stature, and it has
set its top among the clouds, and its heart is haughty in its loftiness,
11   therefore, I will give it into the hand of a despot of the nations; he will
thoroughly deal with it. According to its wickedness I have driven it away.
12   "And alien tyrants of the nations have cut it down and left it; on the mountains and in all the valleys its branches have fallen, and its boughs have been broken
in all the ravines of the land. And all the peoples of the earth have gone down from
its shade and left it.
13   "On its ruin all the birds of the heavens will dwell. And all the beasts of the
field will be on its *fallen* branches
14   in order that all the trees by the waters may not be exalted in their stature,
nor set their top among the clouds, nor their well-watered mighty ones stand *erect* in
their height. For they have all been given over to death, to the earth beneath, among
the sons of men, with those who go down to the pit."

15   'Thus says the Lord GOD, "On the day when it went down to Sheol I caused
lamentations; I closed the deep over it and held back its rivers. And *its* many waters
were stopped up, and I made Lebanon mourn for it, and all the trees of the field
wilted away on account of it.

16   "I made the nations quake at the sound of its fall when I made it go down to
Sheol with those who go down to the pit; and all the well-watered trees of Eden, the
choicest and best of Lebanon, were comforted in the earth beneath.
17   "They also went down with it to Sheol to those who were slain by the sword;
and those who were its strength lived under its shade among the nations.
18   "To which among the trees of Eden are you thus equal in glory and greatness?
Yet you will be brought down with the trees of Eden to the earth beneath; you will
lie in the midst of the uncircumcised, with those who were slain by the sword. So is
Pharaoh and all his multitude!" ' declares the Lord GOD."

5. The lamentation over Pharaoh

a. The evils that shall befall him

32 And it came about in the twelfth year, in the twelfth *month*, on the first of the
month, that the word of the LORD came to me saying,
2   "Son of man, take up a lamentation over Pharaoh king of Egypt, and say to
him,

     'You compared yourself to a young lion of the nations,
     Yet you are like the monster in the seas;
     And you burst forth in your rivers,
     And muddied the waters with your feet,
     And fouled their rivers.' "

3   Thus says the Lord GOD,
     "Now I will spread My net over you
     With a company of many peoples,
     And they shall lift you up in My net.

4   "And I will leave you on the land;
     I will cast you on the open field.
     And I will cause all the birds of the heavens to dwell on you,
     And I will satisfy the beasts of the whole earth with you.

5   "And I will lay your flesh on the mountains,
     And fill the valleys with your refuse.

6   "I will also make the land drink the discharge of your blood,
     As far as the mountains,
     And the ravines shall be full of you.

7   "And when *I* extinguish you,
     I will cover the heavens, and darken their stars;

I will cover the sun with a cloud,
And the moon shall not give its light.

8   "All the shining lights in the heavens
I will darken over you
And will set darkness on your land,"
Declares the Lord GOD.

b. The dispersal of the peoples

9   "I will also trouble the hearts of many peoples, when I bring your destruction among the nations, into lands which you have not known.

10   "And I will make many peoples appalled at you, and their kings shall be horribly afraid of you when I brandish My sword before them; and they shall tremble every moment, every man for his own life, on the day of your fall."

11   For thus says the Lord GOD, "The sword of the king of Babylon shall come upon you.

12   "By the swords of the mighty ones I will cause your multitude to fall; all of them are tyrants of the nations,
And they shall devastate the pride of Egypt,
And all its multitude shall be destroyed.

13   "I will also destroy all its cattle from beside many waters;
And the foot of man shall not muddy them anymore,
And the hoofs of beasts shall not muddy them.

14   "Then I will make their waters settle,
And will cause their rivers to run like oil,"
Declares the Lord GOD.

15   "When I make the land of Egypt a desolation,
And the land is destitute of that which filled it,
When I smite all those who live in it,
Then they shall know that I am the LORD.

16   "This is a lamentation and they shall chant it. The daughters of the nations shall chant it. Over Egypt and over all her multitude they shall chant it," declares the Lord GOD.

6. The lamentation over Egypt:
the nations Egypt will join in the pit

17   And it came about in the twelfth year, on the fifteenth of the month, that the word of the LORD came to me saying,

18   "Son of man, wail for the multitude of Egypt, and bring it down, her and the daughters of the powerful nations, to the nether world, with those who go down to the pit;

19   'Whom do you surpass in beauty?
Go down and make your bed with the uncircumcised.'

20   "They shall fall in the midst of those who are slain by the sword. She is given over to the sword; they have drawn her and all her multitudes away.

21   "The strong among the mighty ones shall speak of him and his helpers from the midst of Sheol, 'They have gone down, they lie still, the uncircumcised, slain by the sword.'

22   "Assyria is there and all her company; her graves are round about her. All of them are slain, fallen by the sword,

23   whose graves are set in the remotest parts of the pit, and her company is round about her grave. All of them are slain, fallen by the sword, who spread terror in the land of the living.

24   "Elam is there and all her multitude around her grave; all of them slain, fallen by the sword, who went down uncircumcised to the lower parts of the earth, who instilled their terror in the land of the living, and bore their disgrace with those who went down to the pit.

25   "They have made a bed for her among the slain with all her multitude. Her graves are around it, they are all uncircumcised, slain by the sword (although their terror was instilled in the land of the living), and they bore their disgrace with those who go down to the pit; they were put in the midst of the slain.

26   "Meshech, Tubal and all their multitude are there; their graves surround them. All of them were slain by the sword uncircumcised, though they instilled their terror in the land of the living.

Is 34:4;
13:10;
Joel 2:31;
3:15;
Amos 8:9;
Matt 24:29;
Rev 6:12,13

32:9
Ezek 28:19;
Rev 18:10-15;
Ex 15:14-16
32:10
Ezek 27:35;
26:16;
Jer 46:10
32:11
Jer 46:26;
Ezek 30:4
32:12
Ezek 28:7;
31:12; 30:18

32:13
Ezek 29:8,11

32:15
Ezek 29:12,
19,20;
Ps 9:16;
Ezek 6:7

32:16
2 Sam 1:17;
2 Chr 35:25;
Ezek 26:17

32:18
vv. 2,16;
Mic 1:8;
Ezek 26:20;
31:14; v. 24
32:19
Ezek 31:2,18;
28:10; vv. 21,
24,29

32:21
Is 1:31; 14:9,
10; vv. 27,31,
32

32:22
Ezek 31:3,16

32:23
Is 14:15;
vv. 24-27,32

32:24
Jer 49:34-39;
Ps 27:13;
Is 38:11;
Jer 11:19;
vv. 25,30
32:25
Ps 139:8;
vv. 19,23,24

32:26
Gen 10:2;
Ezek 27:13;
38:2; vv. 19,
32

32:27
Is 14:18,19,
21,23

27 "Nor do they lie beside the fallen heroes of the uncircumcised, who went down to Sheol with their weapons of war, and whose swords were laid under their heads; but the punishment for their iniquity rested on their bones, though the terror of *these* heroes *was* once in the land of the living.

32:28
v. 19

28 "But in the midst of the uncircumcised you will be broken and lie with those slain by the sword.

32:29
Is 34:5-15;
Jer 49:7-22;
Ezek 25:13

29 "There also is Edom, its kings, and all its princes, who for *all* their might are laid with those slain by the sword; they will lie with the uncircumcised, and with those who go down to the pit.

32:30
Ezek 38:6,15;
39:2; 28:21

30 "There also are the chiefs of the north, all of them, and all the Sidonians, who in spite of the terror resulting from their might, in shame went down with the slain. So they lay down uncircumcised with those slain by the sword, and bore their disgrace with those who go down to the pit.

32:31
vv. 18,21;
Ezek 31:16

31 "These Pharaoh will see, and he will be comforted for all his multitude slain by the sword, *even* Pharaoh and all his army," declares the Lord GOD.

32:32
vv. 19-24

32 "Though I instilled a terror of him in the land of the living, yet he will be made to lie down among *the* uncircumcised *along* with those slain by the sword, *even* Pharaoh and all his multitude," declares the Lord GOD.

III. *Israel restored (33:1–39:29)*

A. *The prophet watchman*

1. *Ezekiel as Israel's watchman*

33 And the word of the LORD came to me saying,

33:2
Ezek 3:11;
Jer 12:12;
Zech 13:7;
2 Sam 18:24,
25;
2 Kin 9:17

2 "Son of man, speak to the sons of your people, and say to them, 'If I bring a sword upon a land, and the people of the land take one man from among them and make him their watchman;

33:3
Hos 8:1;
Joel 2:1

3 and he sees the sword coming upon the land, and he blows on the trumpet and warns the people,

33:4
Jer 6:17;
Zech 1:4;
Ezek 18:13;
Acts 18:6

4 then he who hears the sound of the trumpet and does not take warning, and a sword comes and takes him away, his blood will be on his *own* head.

33:5
Heb 11:7

5 'He heard the sound of the trumpet, but did not take warning; his blood will be on himself. But had he taken warning, he would have delivered his life.

33:6
Is 56:10,11;
v. 8;
Ezek 3:18,20

6 'But if the watchman sees the sword coming and does not blow the trumpet, and the people are not warned, and a sword comes and takes a person from them, he is taken away in his iniquity; but his blood I will require from the watchman's hand.'

33:7
Ezek 3:17-21;
Jer 26:2;
Acts 5:20

7 "Now as for you, son of man, I have appointed you a watchman for the house of Israel; so you will hear a message from My mouth, and give them warning from Me.

33:8
vv. 14,6

8 "When I say to the wicked, 'O wicked man, you shall surely die,' and you do not speak to warn the wicked from his way, that wicked man shall die in his iniquity, but his blood I will require from your hand.

33:9
Acts 13:40,
41,46;
Ezek 3:19,21

9 "But if you on your part warn a wicked man to turn from his way, and he does not turn from his way, he will die in his iniquity; but you have delivered your life.

2. *The watchman's message of righteousness*

33:10
Ezek 18:2;
24:23; 37:11

10 "Now as for you, son of man, say to the house of Israel, 'Thus you have spoken, saying, "Surely our transgressions and our sins are upon us, and we are rotting away in them; how then can we survive?" '

33:11
2 Sam 14:14;
Ezek 18:23,
32; 2 Pet 3:9;
Ezek 18:30,
31

11 "Say to them, 'As I live!' declares the Lord GOD, 'I take no pleasure in the death of the wicked, but rather that the wicked turn from his way and live. Turn back, turn back from your evil ways! Why then will you die, O house of Israel?'

33:12
Ezek 3:20;
2 Chr 7:14

12 "And you, son of man, say to your fellow citizens, 'The righteousness of a righteous man will not deliver him in the day of his transgression, and as for the wickedness of the wicked, he will not stumble because of it in the day when he turns from his wickedness; whereas a righteous man will not be able to live by his righteousness on the day when he commits sin.'

33:13
Ezek 3:20;
18:24;
2 Pet 2:20,21

13 "When I say to the righteous he will surely live, and he *so* trusts in his righteousness that he commits iniquity, none of his righteous deeds will be remembered; but in that same iniquity of his which he has committed he will die.

14 "But when I say to the wicked, 'You will surely die,' and he turns from his sin and practices justice and righteousness,

15 *if a* wicked man restores a pledge, pays back what he has taken by robbery, walks by the statutes which ensure life without committing iniquity, he will surely live; he shall not die.

16 "None of his sins that he has committed will be remembered against him. He has practiced justice and righteousness; he will surely live.

17 "Yet your fellow citizens say, 'The way of the Lord is not right,' when it is their own way that is not right.

18 "When the righteous turns from his righteousness and commits iniquity, then he shall die in it.

19 "But when the wicked turns from his wickedness and practices justice and righteousness, he will live by them.

20 "Yet you say, 'The way of the Lord is not right.' O house of Israel, I will judge each of you according to his ways."

3. *The tidings of Jerusalem's fall*

21 Now it came about in the twelfth year of our exile, on the fifth of the tenth month, that the refugees from Jerusalem came to me, saying, "The city has been taken."

22 Now the hand of the LORD had been upon me in the evening, before the refugees came. And He opened my mouth at the time *they* came to me in the morning; so my mouth was opened, and I was no longer speechless.

4. *The desolation to come upon the remnant*

23 Then the word of the LORD came to me saying,

24 "Son of man, they who live in these waste places in the land of Israel are saying, 'Abraham was *only* one, yet he possessed the land; so to us who are many the land has been given as a possession.'

25 "Therefore, say to them, 'Thus says the Lord GOD, "You eat *meat* with the blood *in it,* lift up your eyes to your idols as you shed blood. Should you then possess the land?

26 "You rely on your sword, you commit abominations, and each of you defiles his neighbor's wife. Should you then possess the land?" '

27 "Thus you shall say to them, 'Thus says the Lord GOD, "As I live, surely those who are in the waste places will fall by the sword, and whoever is in the open field I will give to the beasts to be devoured, and those who are in the strongholds and in the caves will die of pestilence.

28 "And I shall make the land a desolation and a waste, and the pride of her power will cease; and the mountains of Israel will be desolate, so that no one will pass through.

29 "Then they will know that I am the LORD, when I make the land a desolation and a waste because of all their abominations which they have committed." '

5. *The people will hear but not heed Ezekiel*

30 "But as for you, son of man, your fellow citizens who talk about you by the walls and in the doorways of the houses, speak to one another, each to his brother, saying, 'Come now, and hear what the message is which comes forth from the LORD.'

31 "And they come to you as people come, and sit before you *as* My people, and hear your words, but they do not do them, for they do the lustful desires *expressed* by their mouth, *and* their heart goes after their gain.

32 "And behold, you are to them like a sensual song by one who has a beautiful voice and plays well on an instrument; for they hear your words, but they do not practice them.

33 "So when it comes to pass—as surely it will—then they will know that a prophet has been in their midst."

B. *The prophecy concerning the shepherds of Israel*

1. *Indictment of the shepherds who failed to care for their sheep*

34 Then the word of the LORD came to me saying,
2 "Son of man, prophesy against the shepherds of Israel. Prophesy and say

---

33:14 Ezek 3:18,19; 18:27
33:15 Lev 6:2,4,5; Num 5:6,7; Luke 19:8; Ezek 20:11
33:16 Ezek 18:22
33:17 Ezek 18:25, 29; v. 20
33:18 Ezek 18:26
33:19 vv. 12,14
33:20 Ezek 18:25; v. 17

33:21 Ezek 1:2; 24:26; 2 Kin 25:4
33:22 Ezek 1:3; 24:27; Luke 1:64

33:24 Ezek 36:4; Is 51:2; Acts 7:5
33:25 Deut 12:16; Ezek 20:24; 22:6,9
33:26 Ezek 18:6; 22:11
33:27 Ezek 39:4; 1 Sam 13:6; Is 2:19
33:28 Jer 44:2,6,22; Ezek 7:24; 36:34,35
33:29 Ezek 23:33, 35

33:30 vv. 2,17; Is 29:13; 58:2

33:31 Ezek 14:1; 20:1; 8:1; Ps 78:36,37; Is 29:13; Matt 13:22

33:33 1 Sam 3:20; Ezek 2:5

34:2 Jer 10:21; vv. 8-10,14, 15; John 10:11; 21:15-17

to those shepherds, 'Thus says the Lord GOD, "Woe, shepherds of Israel who have been feeding themselves! Should not the shepherds feed the flock?

3 "You eat the fat and clothe yourselves with the wool, you slaughter the fat *sheep* without feeding the flock.

4 "Those who are sickly you have not strengthened, the diseased you have not healed, the broken you have not bound up, the scattered you have not brought back, nor have you sought for the lost; but with force and with severity you have dominated them.

5 "And they were scattered for lack of a shepherd, and they became food for every beast of the field and were scattered.

6 "My flock wandered through all the mountains and on every high hill, and My flock was scattered over all the surface of the earth; and there was no one to search or seek *for them.*" ' "

7 Therefore, you shepherds, hear the word of the LORD:

8 "As I live," declares the Lord GOD, "surely because My flock has become a prey, My flock has even become food for all the beasts of the field for lack of a shepherd, and My shepherds did not search for My flock, but *rather* the shepherds fed themselves and did not feed My flock;

9 therefore, you shepherds, hear the word of the LORD:

10 'Thus says the Lord GOD, "Behold, I am against the shepherds, and I shall demand My sheep from them and make them cease from feeding sheep. So the shepherds will not feed themselves anymore, but I shall deliver My flock from their mouth, that they may not be food for them." ' "

2. *The* LORD *the shepherd of the sheep*

11 For thus says the Lord GOD, "Behold, I Myself will search for My sheep and seek them out.

12 "As a shepherd cares for his herd in the day when he is among his scattered sheep, so I will care for My sheep and will deliver them from all the places to which they were scattered on a cloudy and gloomy day.

13 "And I will bring them out from the peoples and gather them from the countries and bring them to their own land; and I will feed them on the mountains of Israel, by the streams, and in all the inhabited places of the land.

14 "I will feed them in a good pasture, and their grazing ground will be on the mountain heights of Israel. There they will lie down in good grazing ground, and they will feed in rich pasture on the mountains of Israel.

15 "I will feed My flock and I will lead them to rest," declares the Lord GOD.

16 "I will seek the lost, bring back the scattered, bind up the broken, and strengthen the sick; but the fat and the strong I will destroy. I will feed them with judgment.

3. *The* LORD'*s judgment between sheep and sheep*

17 "And as for you, My flock, thus says the Lord GOD, 'Behold, I will judge between one sheep and another, between the rams and the male goats.

18 'Is it too slight a thing for you that you should feed in the good pasture, that you must tread down with your feet the rest of your pastures? Or that you should drink of the clear waters, that you must foul the rest with your feet?

19 'And as for My flock, they must eat what you tread down with your feet, and they must drink what you foul with your feet!' "

20 Therefore, thus says the Lord GOD to them, "Behold, I, even I, will judge between the fat sheep and the lean sheep.

21 "Because you push with side and with shoulder, and thrust at all the weak with your horns, until you have scattered them abroad,

22 therefore, I will deliver My flock, and they will no longer be a prey; and I will judge between one sheep and another.

4. *The Messiah as the new shepherd*

23 "Then I will set over them one shepherd, My servant David, and he will feed them; he will feed them himself and be their shepherd.

34:23 *one shepherd.* The Davidic king will rule the united kingdom (Israel and Judah, cf. 37:15–18). Israel and Judah are also the *two nations* mentioned in 35:10.

34:3
Is 56:11;
Zech 11:16;
Ezek 22:25,
27
34:4
Zech 11:16;
Matt 9:36;
Luke 15:4;
1 Pet 5:3
34:5
Jer 10:21;
50:6,7;
Jer 23:2;
Matt 9:36

34:8
Acts 20:29;
vv. 5,6,2

34:10
Ezek 3:18;
Heb 13:17;
vv. 2,8

34:11
Ezek 11:17;
20:41
34:12
John 10:16;
Ezek 30:3;
Joel 2:2

34:13
Is 65:9,10;
Jer 23:3;
Ezek 37:22;
Is 30:25
34:14
Ps 23:1,2;
Ezek 20:40;
28:25,26

34:16
Matt 18:11;
Luke 5:32;
Is 49:26

34:17
Ezek 20:37,
38;
Zech 10:3;
Matt 25:32,33
34:18
2 Sam 7:19

34:20
v. 17

34:21
Deut 33:17;
Dan 8:4
34:22
vv. 5,8,10,17

*34:23
Is 40:11;
Jer 23:4,5;
30:9; Hos 3:5

24 "And I, the LORD, will be their God, and My servant David will be prince among them; I, the LORD, have spoken.

5. The LORD's covenant of peace

25 "And I will make a covenant of peace with them and eliminate harmful beasts from the land, so that they may live securely in the wilderness and sleep in the woods.

26 "And I will make them and the places around My hill a blessing. And I will cause showers to come down in their season; they will be showers of blessing.

27 "Also the tree of the field will yield its fruit, and the earth will yield its increase, and they will be secure on their land. Then they will know that I am the LORD, when I have broken the bars of their yoke and have delivered them from the hand of those who enslaved them.

28 "And they will no longer be a prey to the nations, and the beasts of the earth will not devour them; but they will live securely, and no one will make *them* afraid.

29 "And I will establish for them a renowned planting place, and they will not again be victims of famine in the land, and they will not endure the insults of the nations anymore.

30 "Then they will know that I, the LORD their God, am with them, and that they, the house of Israel, are My people," declares the Lord GOD.

31 "As for you, My sheep, the sheep of My pasture, you are men, and I am your God," declares the Lord GOD.

C. The prophecy against Mount Seir

35 Moreover, the word of the LORD came to me saying,
2 "Son of man, set your face against Mount Seir, and prophesy against it,
3 and say to it, 'Thus says the Lord GOD,
"Behold, I am against you, Mount Seir,
And I will stretch out My hand against you,
And I will make you a desolation and a waste.
4 "I will lay waste your cities,
And you will become a desolation.
Then you will know that I am the LORD.

5 "Because you have had everlasting enmity and have delivered the sons of Israel to the power of the sword at the time of their calamity, at the time of the punishment of the end,

6 therefore, as I live," declares the Lord GOD, "I will give you over to bloodshed, and bloodshed will pursue you; since you have not hated bloodshed, therefore bloodshed will pursue you.

7 "And I will make Mount Seir a waste and a desolation, and I will cut off from it the one who passes through and returns.

8 "And I will fill its mountains with its slain; on your hills and in your valleys and in all your ravines those slain by the sword will fall.

9 "I will make you an everlasting desolation, and your cities will not be inhabited. Then you will know that I am the LORD.

10 "Because you have said, 'These two nations and these two lands will be mine, and we will possess them,' although the LORD was there,

11 therefore, as I live," declares the Lord GOD, "I will deal *with you* according to your anger and according to your envy which you showed because of your hatred against them; so I will make Myself known among them when I judge you.

12 "Then you will know that I, the LORD, have heard all your revilings which you have spoken against the mountains of Israel saying, 'They are laid desolate; they are given to us for food.'

13 "And you have spoken arrogantly against Me and have multiplied your words against Me; I have heard."

14 'Thus says the Lord GOD, "As all the earth rejoices, I will make you a desolation.

15 "As you rejoiced over the inheritance of the house of Israel because it was desolate, so I will do to you. You will be a desolation, O Mount Seir, and all Edom, all of it. Then they will know that I am the LORD."'

35:10 *two nations,* i.e., Judah and Israel.

D. *The restoration of Israel*

1. *Judgment on Israel's oppressors*

36 "And you, son of man, prophesy to the mountains of Israel and say, 'O mountains of Israel, hear the word of the LORD.

2 'Thus says the Lord GOD, "Because the enemy has spoken against you, 'Aha!' and, 'The everlasting heights have become our possession,'

3 therefore, prophesy and say, 'Thus says the Lord GOD, "For good cause they have made you desolate and crushed you from every side, that you should become a possession of the rest of the nations, and you have been taken up in the talk and the whispering of the people."'"

4 'Therefore, O mountains of Israel, hear the word of the Lord GOD. Thus says the Lord GOD to the mountains and to the hills, to the ravines and to the valleys, to the desolate wastes and to the forsaken cities, which have become a prey and a derision to the rest of the nations which are round about,

5 therefore, thus says the Lord GOD, "Surely in the fire of My jealousy I have spoken against the rest of the nations, and against all Edom, who appropriated My land for themselves as a possession with wholehearted joy *and* with scorn of soul, to drive it out for a prey."

6 'Therefore, prophesy concerning the land of Israel, and say to the mountains and to the hills, to the ravines and to the valleys, "Thus says the Lord GOD, 'Behold, I have spoken in My jealousy and in My wrath because you have endured the insults of the nations.'

7 "Therefore, thus says the Lord GOD, 'I have sworn that surely the nations which are around you will themselves endure their insults.

2. *Israel to be returned*

8 'But you, O mountains of Israel, you will put forth your branches and bear your fruit for My people Israel; for they will soon come.

9 'For, behold, I am for you, and I will turn to you, and you shall be cultivated and sown.

10 'And I will multiply men on you, all the house of Israel, all of it; and the cities will be inhabited, and the waste places will be rebuilt.

11 'And I will multiply on you man and beast; and they will increase and be fruitful; and I will cause you to be inhabited as you were formerly and will treat you better than at the first. Thus you will know that I am the LORD.

12 'Yes, I will cause men—My people Israel—to walk on you and possess you, so that you will become their inheritance and never again bereave them of children.'

13 "Thus says the Lord GOD, 'Because they say to you, "You are a devourer of men and have bereaved your nation of children,"

14 therefore, you will no longer devour men, and no longer bereave your nation of children,' declares the Lord GOD.

15 "And I will not let you hear insults from the nations anymore, nor will you bear disgrace from the peoples any longer, nor will you cause your nation to stumble any longer," declares the Lord GOD.'"

3. *Israel's punishment due to idolatry*

16 Then the word of the LORD came to me saying,

17 "Son of man, when the house of Israel was living in their own land, they defiled it by their ways and their deeds; their way before Me was like the uncleanness of a woman in her impurity.

18 "Therefore, I poured out My wrath on them for the blood which they had shed on the land, because they had defiled it with their idols.

19 "Also I scattered them among the nations, and they were dispersed throughout the lands. According to their ways and their deeds I judged them.

20 "When they came to the nations where they went, they profaned My holy name, because it was said of them, 'These are the people of the LORD; yet they have come out of His land.'

21 "But I had concern for My holy name, which the house of Israel had profaned among the nations where they went.

36:7 Israel's shame was only temporary.

4. The LORD Himself to regather Israel

22 "Therefore, say to the house of Israel, 'Thus says the Lord GOD, "It is not for your sake, O house of Israel, that I am about to act, but for My holy name, which you have profaned among the nations where you went.

23 "And I will vindicate the holiness of My great name which has been profaned among the nations, which you have profaned in their midst. Then the nations will know that I am the LORD," declares the Lord GOD, "when I prove Myself holy among you in their sight.

24 "For I will take you from the nations, gather you from all the lands, and bring you into your own land.

25 "Then I will sprinkle clean water on you, and you will be clean; I will cleanse you from all your filthiness and from all your idols.

26 "Moreover, I will give you a new heart and put a new spirit within you; and I will remove the heart of stone from your flesh and give you a heart of flesh.

27 "And I will put My Spirit within you and cause you to walk in My statutes, and you will be careful to observe My ordinances.

28 "And you will live in the land that I gave to your forefathers; so you will be My people, and I will be your God.

29 "Moreover, I will save you from all your uncleanness; and I will call for the grain and multiply it, and I will not bring a famine on you.

30 "And I will multiply the fruit of the tree and the produce of the field, that you may not receive again the disgrace of famine among the nations.

31 "Then you will remember your evil ways and your deeds that were not good, and you will loathe yourselves in your own sight for your iniquities and your abominations.

32 "I am not doing *this* for your sake," declares the Lord GOD, "let it be known to you. Be ashamed and confounded for your ways, O house of Israel!"

5. The cities to be inhabited; the waste places rebuilt

33 'Thus says the Lord GOD, "On the day that I cleanse you from all your iniquities, I will cause the cities to be inhabited, and the waste places will be rebuilt.

34 "And the desolate land will be cultivated instead of being a desolation in the sight of everyone who passed by.

35 "And they will say, 'This desolate land has become like the garden of Eden; and the waste, desolate, and ruined cities are fortified *and* inhabited.'

36 "Then the nations that are left round about you will know that I, the LORD, have rebuilt the ruined places *and* planted that which was desolate; I, the LORD, have spoken and will do it."

6. The people to increase in number

37 'Thus says the Lord GOD, "This also I will let the house of Israel ask Me to do for them: I will increase their men like a flock.

38 "Like the flock for sacrifices, like the flock at Jerusalem during her appointed feasts, so will the waste cities be filled with flocks of men. Then they will know that I am the LORD."'"

E. The vision of the dry bones in the valley: Israel to be regathered

37 The hand of the LORD was upon me, and He brought me out by the Spirit of the LORD and set me down in the middle of the valley; and it was full of bones.

2 And He caused me to pass among them round about, and behold, *there were* very many on the surface of the valley; and lo, *they were* very dry.

3 And He said to me, "Son of man, can these bones live?" And I answered, "O Lord GOD, Thou knowest."

4 Again He said to me, "Prophesy over these bones, and say to them, 'O dry bones, hear the word of the LORD.'

5 "Thus says the Lord GOD to these bones, 'Behold, I will cause [6]breath to enter you that you may come to life.

6 'And I will put sinews on you, make flesh grow back on you, cover you with

---

[6]Or, *spirit*, and so throughout this context

Marginal references:

36:22 Ps 106:8
36:23 Ezek 20:41; Ps 126:2; Ezek 28:25; 39:27
36:24 Ezek 34:13; 37:21
36:25 Is 52:15; Heb 10:22; Zech 13:1
36:26 Ps 51:10; Ezek 11:19
36:27 Ezek 11:19; 37:14
36:28 Jer 30:22; Ezek 11:20; 37:27
36:29 Zech 13:1
36:30 Ezek 34:27, 29; Hos 2:21-23
36:31 Ezek 16:61-63; 20:43; 6:9
36:32 Ezek 20:44; v. 22
36:33 v. 25; Zech 8:7,8; Is 58:12; v. 10
36:34 v. 9
36:35 Is 51:3; Ezek 31:9; Joel 2:3
36:36 Ezek 39:27, 28; 22:14; 37:14
36:38 1 Kin 8:63; vv. 33-35; Zech 11:17
37:1 Ezek 1:3; 8:3; 11:24; Luke 4:1; Acts 8:39
37:2 v. 11
37:3 Is 26:19; Deut 32:39; 1 Sam 2:6
37:4 vv. 9,12; Is 42:18; Ezek 36:1
37:5 Ps 104:29,30; vv. 9,10

*37:6
Ezek 6:7;
Joel 2:27
37:7
Jer 13:5-7;
Ezek 38:19

37:9
Ps 104:30;
v. 5;
Hos 13:14
37:10
vv. 5,6;
Rev 11:11
*37:11
Ezek 36:10;
39:25;
Ps 141:7;
Is 49:14
37:12
Is 26:19;
Hos 13:14;
v. 25;
Ezek 36:24;
Amos 9:14,15
37:13
Ezek 6:7;
vv. 6,12
37:14
Ezek 36:27;
39:29; 36:36

37:16
Num 17:2;
2 Chr 11:11-17;
15:9
37:17
vv. 22-24
37:18
Ezek 12:9;
24:19
37:19
Zech 10:6;
vv. 16,17

37:21
Ezek 36:24;
39:27

37:22
Is 11:13;
Jer 3:18;
Hos 1:11;
Ezek 34:23
37:23
Ezek 11:18;
43:7; 36:25;
36:28

37:24
Jer 30:9;
Is 40:11;
Hos 3:5;
Ezek 36:27
37:25
Ezek 28:25;
36:28;
Zech 6:12
37:26
Is 55:3;
Ezek 36:10;
20:40; 43:7

skin, and put breath in you that you may come alive; and you will know that I am the LORD.' "

7 So I prophesied as I was commanded; and as I prophesied, there was a noise, and behold, a rattling; and the bones came together, bone to its bone.

8 And I looked, and behold, sinews were on them, and flesh grew, and skin covered them; but there was no breath in them.

9 Then He said to me, "Prophesy to the breath, prophesy, son of man, and say to the breath, 'Thus says the Lord GOD, "Come from the four winds, O breath, and breathe on these slain, that they come to life." ' "

10 So I prophesied as He commanded me, and the breath came into them, and they came to life, and stood on their feet, an exceedingly great army.

11 Then He said to me, "Son of man, these bones are the whole house of Israel; behold, they say, 'Our bones are dried up, and our hope has perished. We are completely cut off.'

12 "Therefore prophesy, and say to them, 'Thus says the Lord GOD, "Behold, I will open your graves and cause you to come up out of your graves, My people; and I will bring you into the land of Israel.

13 "Then you will know that I am the LORD, when I have opened your graves and caused you to come up out of your graves, My people.

14 "And I will put My [7]Spirit within you, and you will come to life, and I will place you on your own land. Then you will know that I, the LORD, have spoken and done it," declares the LORD.' "

F. The union of the two sticks (Israel and Judah)

15 The word of the LORD came again to me saying,

16 "And you, son of man, take for yourself one stick and write on it, 'For Judah and for the sons of Israel, his companions'; then take another stick and write on it, 'For Joseph, the stick of Ephraim and all the house of Israel, his companions.'

17 "Then join them for yourself one to another into one stick, that they may become one in your hand.

18 "And when the sons of your people speak to you saying, 'Will you not declare to us what you mean by these?'

19 say to them, 'Thus says the Lord GOD, "Behold, I will take the stick of Joseph, which is in the hand of Ephraim, and the tribes of Israel, his companions; and I will put them with it, with the stick of Judah, and make them one stick, and they will be one in My hand." '

20 "And the sticks on which you write will be in your hand before their eyes.

21 "And say to them, 'Thus says the Lord GOD, "Behold, I will take the sons of Israel from among the nations where they have gone, and I will gather them from every side and bring them into their own land;

22 and I will make them one nation in the land, on the mountains of Israel; and one king will be king for all of them; and they will no longer be two nations, and they will no longer be divided into two kingdoms.

23 "And they will no longer defile themselves with their idols, or with their detestable things, or with any of their transgressions; but I will deliver them from all their [8]dwelling places in which they have sinned, and will cleanse them. And they will be My people, and I will be their God.

24 "And My servant David will be king over them, and they will all have one shepherd; and they will walk in My ordinances, and keep My statutes, and observe them.

25 "And they shall live on the land that I gave to Jacob My servant, in which your fathers lived; and they will live on it, they, and their sons, and their sons' sons, forever; and David My servant shall be their prince forever.

26 "And I will make a covenant of peace with them; it will be an everlasting covenant with them. And I will place them and multiply them, and will set My sanctuary in their midst forever.

[7]Or, breath   [8]Another reading is *backslidings*

37:6 *you will know that I am the LORD*, i.e., God will prove both His deity and His sovereignty by reviving Israel, which is pictured as dead (dry) bones in need of resurrection. **37:11** Verses 11–14 contain the explanation of the vision of the dry bones. The regathering of Israel is in view here, an event that is still future. The fulfillment of this prophetic promise is guaranteed by the Word of the LORD: *I . . . have spoken and done it.*

27 "My dwelling place also will be with them; and I will be their God, and they will be My people.

28 "And the nations will know that I am the LORD who sanctifies Israel, when My sanctuary is in their midst forever." ' "

G. The prophecy of Gog and Magog

1. The hordes of Gog to be assembled

38 And the word of the LORD came to me saying,

2 "Son of man, set your face toward Gog of the land of Magog, the prince of Rosh, Meshech, and Tubal, and prophesy against him,

3 and say, 'Thus says the Lord GOD, "Behold, I am against you, O Gog, prince of Rosh, Meshech, and Tubal.

4 "And I will turn you about, and put hooks into your jaws, and I will bring you out, and all your army, horses and horsemen, all of them splendidly attired, a great company *with* buckler and shield, all of them wielding swords;

5 Persia, Ethiopia, and Put with them, all of them *with* shield and helmet;

6 Gomer with all its troops; Beth-togarmah *from* the remote parts of the north with all its troops—many peoples with you.

7 "Be prepared, and prepare yourself, you and all your companies that are assembled about you, and be a guard for them.

8 "After many days you will be summoned; in the latter years you will come into the land that is restored from the sword, *whose inhabitants* have been gathered from many nations to the mountains of Israel which had been a continual waste; but its people were brought out from the nations, and they are living securely, all of them.

9 "And you will go up, you will come like a storm; you will be like a cloud covering the land, you and all your troops, and many peoples with you."

2. The evil scheme of Gog

10 'Thus says the Lord GOD, "It will come about on that day, that thoughts will come into your mind, and you will devise an evil plan,

11 and you will say, 'I will go up against the land of [9]unwalled villages. I will go against those who are at rest, that live securely, all of them living without walls, and having no bars or gates,

12 to capture spoil and to seize plunder, to turn your hand against the waste places which are *now* inhabited, and against the people who are gathered from the nations, who have acquired cattle and goods, who live at the center of the world.'

13 "Sheba, and Dedan, and the merchants of Tarshish, with all its villages, will say to you, 'Have you come to capture spoil? Have you assembled your company to seize plunder, to carry away silver and gold, to take away cattle and goods, to capture great spoil?' " '

3. Gog descends on Israel

14 "Therefore, prophesy, son of man, and say to Gog, 'Thus says the Lord GOD, "On that day when My people Israel are living securely, will you not know *it*?

15 "And you will come from your place out of the remote parts of the north, you and many peoples with you, all of them riding on horses, a great assembly and a mighty army;

16 and you will come up against My people Israel like a cloud to cover the land. It will come about in the last days that I shall bring you against My land, in order that the nations may know Me when I shall be sanctified through you before their eyes, O Gog."

4. The defeat of Gog

17 'Thus says the Lord GOD, "Are you the one of whom I spoke in former days

[9]Or, *open country*

Cross references (margin):

37:27 Lev 26:11; John 1:14
37:28 Ezek 36:23; 20:12
*38:2 Ezek 39:1; Rev 20:8
38:3 Ezek 39:1
38:4 2 Kin 19:28; Ezek 39:2
38:5 Ezek 27:10; 30:4,5
38:6 Gen 10:2; Ezek 27:14
38:7 Jer 46:3; 51:12
38:8 Is 24:22; Ezek 36:24
38:9 Is 28:2; Joel 2:2
38:10 Mic 2:1
38:11 Zech 2:4; Jer 49:31; v. 8
38:12 Is 10:6; Ezek 29:19; v. 8
38:13 Ezek 27:22; 27:15; Nah 2:11-13
38:14 Jer 23:6; Zech 2:5,8
38:15 v. 6; Ezek 39:2
38:16 Ezek 36:23; 39:21
38:17 Is 34:1-6

38:2 Gog is the ruler of the land called Magog. Magog, Meshech, and Tubal are mentioned in Gen. 10:2 as sons of Japheth. They have been identified with the Goths, the Cretans, the Scythians, and the Russians. Although positive identification is not possible, these peoples appear in Rev. 20:8 as furnishing leadership for the final rebellion against God. The fearsome dimensions of this cataclysm may be seen by two statistics: (1) the weapons of the defeated enemy will provide fuel enough for seven years (39:9); and (2) it will require seven months to bury the innumerable corpses left on the battlefield (39:14).

through My servants the prophets of Israel, who prophesied in those days for *many* years that I would bring you against them?

18 "And it will come about on that day, when Gog comes against the land of Israel," declares the Lord GOD, "that My fury will mount up in My anger.

19 "And in My zeal and in My blazing wrath I declare *that* on that day there will surely be a great earthquake in the land of Israel.

20 "And the fish of the sea, the birds of the heavens, the beasts of the field, all the creeping things that creep on the earth, and all the men who are on the face of the earth will shake at My presence; the mountains also will be thrown down, the steep pathways will collapse, and every wall will fall to the ground.

21 "And I shall call for a sword against him on all My mountains," declares the Lord GOD. "Every man's sword will be against his brother.

22 "And with pestilence and with blood I shall enter into judgment with him; and I shall rain on him, and on his troops, and on the many peoples who are with him, a torrential rain, with hailstones, fire, and brimstone.

23 "And I shall magnify Myself, sanctify Myself, and make Myself known in the sight of many nations; and they will know that I am the LORD."'

5. *The slaughtered hordes of Gog to be buried*

39 "And you, son of man, prophesy against Gog, and say, 'Thus says the Lord GOD, "Behold, I am against you, O Gog, prince of Rosh, Meshech, and Tubal;

2 and I shall turn you around, drive you on, take you up from the remotest parts of the north, and bring you against the mountains of Israel.

3 "And I shall strike your bow from your left hand, and dash down your arrows from your right hand.

4 "You shall fall on the mountains of Israel, you and all your troops, and the peoples who are with you; I shall give you as food to every kind of predatory bird and beast of the field.

5 "You will fall on the open field; for it is I who have spoken," declares the Lord GOD.

6 "And I shall send fire upon Magog and those who inhabit the coastlands in safety; and they will know that I am the LORD.

7 "And My holy name I shall make known in the midst of My people Israel; and I shall not let My holy name be profaned anymore. And the nations will know that I am the LORD, the Holy One in Israel.

8 "Behold, it is coming and it shall be done," declares the Lord GOD. "That is the day of which I have spoken.

9 "Then those who inhabit the cities of Israel will go out, and make fires with the weapons and burn *them*, both shields and bucklers, bows and arrows, war clubs and spears and for seven years they will make fires of them.

10 "And they will not take wood from the field or gather firewood from the forests, for they will make fires with the weapons; and they will take the spoil of those who despoiled them, and seize the plunder of those who plundered them," declares the Lord GOD.

11 "And it will come about on that day that I shall give Gog a burial ground there in Israel, the valley of those who pass by east of the sea, and it will block off the passers-by. So they will bury Gog there with all his multitude, and they will call *it* the valley of Hamon-gog.

12 "For seven months the house of Israel will be burying them in order to cleanse the land.

13 "Even all the people of the land will bury *them;* and it will be to their renown *on* the day that I glorify Myself," declares the Lord GOD.

14 "And they will set apart men who will constantly pass through the land, burying those who were passing through, even those left on the surface of the ground, in order to cleanse it. At the end of seven months they will make a search.

15 "And as those who pass through the land pass through and anyone sees a man's bone, then he will set up a marker by it until the buriers have buried it in the valley of Hamon-gog.

16 "And even *the* name of *the* city will be Hamonah. So they will cleanse the land."'

6. *The sacrificial feast of the* LORD

17 "And as for you, son of man, thus says the Lord GOD, 'Speak to every kind of bird and to every beast of the field, "Assemble and come, gather from every side to My sacrifice which I am going to sacrifice for you, as a great sacrifice on the mountains of Israel, that you may eat flesh and drink blood.

18 "You shall eat the flesh of mighty men, and drink the blood of the princes of the earth, as *though they were* rams, lambs, goats, and bulls, all of them fatlings of Bashan.

19 "So you will eat fat until you are glutted, and drink blood until you are drunk, from My sacrifice which I have sacrificed for you.

20 "And you will be glutted at My table with horses and charioteers, with mighty men and all the men of war," declares the Lord GOD.

21 "And I shall set My glory among the nations; and all the nations will see My judgment which I have executed, and My hand which I have laid on them.

22 "And the house of Israel will know that I am the LORD their God from that day onward.

23 "And the nations will know that the house of Israel went into exile for their iniquity because they acted treacherously against Me, and I hid My face from them; so I gave them into the hand of their adversaries, and all of them fell by the sword.

24 "According to their uncleanness and according to their transgressions I dealt with them, and I hid My face from them." ' "

7. *The regathering of God's people:* *Israel shall know the* LORD

25 Therefore thus says the Lord GOD, "Now I shall restore the fortunes of Jacob, and have mercy on the whole house of Israel; and I shall be jealous for My holy name.

26 "And they shall [10]forget their disgrace and all their treachery which they [11]perpetrated against Me, when they live securely on their *own* land with no one to make them afraid.

27 "When I bring them back from the peoples and gather them from the lands of their enemies, then I shall be sanctified through them in the sight of the many nations.

28 "Then they will know that I am the LORD their God because I made them go into exile among the nations, and then gathered them *again* to their own land; and I will leave none of them there any longer.

29 "And I will not hide My face from them any longer, for I shall have poured out My Spirit on the house of Israel," declares the Lord GOD.

IV. *Israel in the land in the kingdom age (40:1–48:35)*

A. *The new temple arrangements*

1. *Introduction*

40 In the twenty-fifth year of our exile, at the beginning of the year, on the tenth of the month, in the fourteenth year after the city was taken, on that same day the hand of the LORD was upon me and He brought me there.

2 In the visions of God He brought me into the land of Israel, and set me on a very high mountain; and on it to the south *there was* a structure like a city.

3 So He brought me there; and behold, there was a man whose appearance was like the appearance of bronze, with a line of flax and a measuring rod in his hand; and he was standing in the gateway.

4 And the man said to me, "Son of man, see with your eyes, hear with your ears, and give attention to all that I am going to show you; for you have been brought here in order to show *it* to you. Declare to the house of Israel all that you see."

5 And behold, there was a wall on the outside of the temple all around, and in the man's hand was a measuring rod of six cubits, *each of which was* a cubit and a

[10]Another reading is *bear*   [11]Lit., *did treacherously*

39:25 *Jacob*, the one whose name was changed to *Israel*.
39:26 *they shall forget their disgrace.* "They have borne their   shame" in the KJV.

Reference column:

39:17
v. 4;
Rev 19:17;
Is 34:6,7;
Jer 46:10;
Zeph 1:7
39:18
Rev 19:18;
Deut 32:14;
Ps 22:12;
Amos 4:1

39:20
Ps 76:6;
Ezek 38:4;
Rev 19:18
39:21
Ezek 38:16,
23; v. 13
39:22
vv. 7,28
39:23
Ezek 36:18-20,
23; 20:27;
v. 26; Is 59:2;
v. 29
39:24
Ezek 36:19;
v. 23

*39:25
Jer 30:3,18;
Ezek 34:13;
36:24; 20:40;
Hos 1:11
*39:26
Ezek 34:25-28;
Is 17:2;
Mic 4:4
39:27
Ezek 28:25,
26; 36:23,24;
38:16
39:28
Ezek 34:30;
v. 22

39:29
Is 32:15;
Ezek 36:27;
37:14;
Joel 2:28;
Acts 2:17

40:1
Ezek 33:21;
1:2,3

40:2
Ezek 8:3;
Dan 7:1,7;
Ezek 17:23;
Rev 21:10
40:3
Ezek 1:7;
Dan 10:6;
Ezek 47:3;
Rev 11:1;
21:15
40:4
Ezek 44:5;
43:10;
Jer 26:2;
Acts 20:27
40:5
Ezek 42:20

handbreadth. So he measured the thickness of the wall, one rod; and the height, one rod.

2. The outer court: the east gate

40:6
vv. 20,26

6   Then he went to the gate which faced east, went up its steps, and measured the threshold of the gate, one rod in width; and the other threshold *was* one rod in width.

40:7
vv. 10-16,21,
29,33,36

7   And the guardroom *was* one rod long and one rod wide; and *there were* five cubits between the guardrooms. And the threshold of the gate by the porch of the gate facing inward *was* one rod.

8   Then he measured the porch of the gate facing inward, one rod.

9   And he measured the porch of the gate, eight cubits; and its side pillars, two cubits. And the porch of the gate was faced inward.

40:10
v. 7

10   And the guardrooms of the gate toward the east *numbered* three on each side; the three of them had the same measurement. The side pillars also had the same measurement on each side.

11   And he measured the width of the gateway, ten cubits, and the length of the gate, thirteen cubits.

12   And *there was* a barrier *wall* one cubit *wide* in front of the guardrooms on each side; and the guardrooms *were* six cubits *square* on each side.

13   And he measured the gate from the roof of the one guardroom to the roof of the other, a width of twenty-five cubits from *one* door to *the* door opposite.

40:14
vv. 9,16;
1 Chr 28:6;
Is 62:9;
Ezek 42:1

14   And he made the side pillars sixty cubits *high;* the gate *extended* round about to the side pillar of the courtyard.

15   And *from* the front of the entrance gate to the front of the inner porch of the gate *was* fifty cubits.

40:16
1 Kin 6:4;
vv. 21,22,26,
31,34,37

16   And *there were* shuttered windows *looking* toward the guardrooms, and toward their side pillars within the gate all around, and likewise for the porches. And *there were* windows all around inside; and on *each* side pillar *were* palm tree ornaments.

3. The thirty chambers about the court

40:17
Rev 11:2;
1 Chr 9:26;
2 Chr 31:11;
Ezek 41:6;
45:5

17   Then he brought me into the outer court, and behold, *there were* chambers and a pavement, made for the court all around; thirty chambers faced the pavement.

18   And the pavement (*that is,* the lower pavement) *was* by the side of the gates, corresponding to the length of the gates.

40:19
vv. 23,27

19   Then he measured the width from the front of the lower gate to the front of the exterior of the inner court, a hundred cubits on the east and on the north.

4. The north gate of the outer court

40:20
v. 6

20   And *as for* the gate of the outer court which faced the north, he measured its length and its width.

40:21
vv. 7,16,30,
15,13

21   And it had three guardrooms on each side; and its side pillars and its porches had the same measurement as the first gate. Its length *was* fifty cubits, and the width twenty-five cubits.

40:22
vv. 16,6,26,
31,34,37,49

22   And its windows, and its porches, and its palm tree ornaments *had* the same measurements as the gate which faced toward the east; and it was reached by seven steps, and its porch *was* in front of them.

40:23
vv. 19,27

23   And the inner court had a gate opposite the gate on the north as well as *the gate* on the east; and he measured a hundred cubits from gate to gate.

5. The south gate of the outer court

40:24
v. 21

24   Then he led me toward the south, and behold, there was a gate toward the south; and he measured its side pillars and its porches according to those same measurements.

40:25
vv. 16,22,21,
33

25   And the gate and its porches had windows all around like those other windows; the length *was* fifty cubits and the width twenty-five cubits.

40:26
vv. 6,22,16

26   And *there were* seven steps going up to it, and its porches *were* in front of them; and it had palm tree ornaments on its side pillars, one on each side.

40:27
vv. 23,32,19

27   And the inner court had a gate toward the south; and he measured from gate to gate toward the south, a hundred cubits.

6. *The gates of the inner court*

28 Then he brought me to the inner court by the south gate; and he measured the south gate according to those same measurements.

29 Its guardrooms also, its side pillars, and its porches *were* according to those same measurements. And the gate and its porches had windows all around; it *was* fifty cubits long and twenty-five cubits wide.

30 And *there were* porches all around, twenty-five cubits long and five cubits wide.

31 And its porches *were* toward the outer court; and palm tree ornaments *were* on its side pillars, and its stairway had eight steps.

32 And he brought me into the inner court toward the east. And he measured the gate according to those same measurements.

33 Its guardrooms also, its side pillars, and its porches *were* according to those same measurements. And the gate and its porches had windows all around; it *was* fifty cubits long and twenty-five cubits wide.

34 And its porches *were* toward the outer court; and palm tree ornaments *were* on its side pillars, on each side, and its stairway had eight steps.

35 Then he brought me to the north gate; and he measured *it* according to those same measurements,

36 *with* its guardrooms, its side pillars, and its porches. And the gate had windows all around; the length *was* fifty cubits and the width twenty-five cubits.

37 And its side pillars *were* toward the outer court; and palm tree ornaments *were* on its side pillars on each side, and its stairway had eight steps.

7. *The tables of sacrifice*

38 And a chamber with its doorway was by the side pillars at the gates; there they rinse the burnt offering.

39 And in the porch of the gate *were* two tables on each side, on which to slaughter the burnt offering, the sin offering, and the guilt offering.

40 And on the outer side, as one went up to the gateway toward the north, were two tables; and on the other side of the porch of the gate *were* two tables.

41 Four tables *were* on each side next to the gate; *or,* eight tables on which they slaughter *sacrifices.*

42 And for the burnt offering *there were* four tables of hewn stone, a cubit and a half long, a cubit and a half wide, and one cubit high, on which they lay the instruments with which they slaughter the burnt offering and the sacrifice.

43 And the double hooks, one handbreadth in length, were installed in the house all around; and on the tables *was* the flesh of the offering.

8. *The chambers for the priests*

44 And from the outside to the inner gate were chambers for the singers in the inner court, *one of* which was at the side of the north gate, with its front toward the south, and one at the side of the east gate facing toward the north.

45 And he said to me, "This is the chamber which faces toward the south, *intended* for the priests who keep charge of the temple;

46 but the chamber which faces toward the north is for the priests who keep charge of the altar. These are the sons of Zadok, who from the sons of Levi come near to the LORD to minister to Him."

47 And he measured the court, a *perfect* square, a hundred cubits long and a hundred cubits wide; and the altar was in front of the temple.

9. *The vestibule of the temple*

48 Then he brought me to the porch of the temple and measured *each* side pillar of the porch, five cubits on each side; and the width of the gate was three cubits on each side.

49 The length of the porch was twenty cubits, and the width eleven cubits; and at the stairway by which it was ascended *were* columns belonging to the side pillars, one on each side.

40:28
vv. 32,35

40:29
vv. 7,10,21,
16,22,25

40:30
vv. 16,21,25

40:31
vv. 16,22,26,
34,37
40:32
vv. 28-31,35

40:33
vv. 29,16,21

40:34
vv. 16,22,37

40:35
Ezek 44:4;
47:2

40:36
vv. 7,29,16,
21
40:37
vv. 16,35

40:38
Ezek 41:10;
42:13;
2 Chr 4:6
40:39
Lev 4:2,3;
5:6; 6:6; 7:1

40:41
vv. 39,40

40:42
v. 39;
Ex 20:25

40:44
vv. 23,27,17,
38;
1 Chr 6:31;
25:1-7
40:45
vv. 17,38;
Lev 8:35;
1 Chr 9:23;
2 Chr 13:11
40:46
vv. 17,38;
Num 18:5;
Ezek 44:15;
43:19;
1 Kin 2:35
40:47
vv. 19,23,27

40:49
1 Kin 6:3;
2 Kin 7:21;
Jer 52:17-23;
Rev 3:12

B. *The new temple*

1. *The nave and the holy place*

41 Then he brought me to the nave and measured the side pillars; six cubits wide on each side *was* the width of the side pillar.
2   And the width of the entrance *was* ten cubits, and the sides of the entrance were five cubits on each side. And he measured the length of the nave, forty cubits, and the width, twenty cubits.
3   Then he went inside and measured each side pillar of the doorway, two cubits, and the doorway, six cubits *high;* and the width of the doorway, seven cubits.
4   And he measured its length, twenty cubits, and the width, twenty cubits, before the nave; and he said to me, "This is the most holy *place.*"

2. *The side chambers*

5   Then he measured the wall of the temple, six cubits; and the width of the side chambers, four cubits, all around about the house on every side.
6   And the side chambers were in three stories, one above another, and thirty in each story; and the side chambers extended to the wall which *stood* on their inward side all around, that they might be fastened, and not be fastened into the wall of the temple *itself*.
7   And the side chambers surrounding the temple were wider at each successive story. Because the structure surrounding the temple went upward by stages on all sides of the temple, therefore the width of the temple *increased* as it went higher; and thus one went up from the lowest *story* to the highest by way of the second *story.*
8   I saw also that the house had a raised platform all around; the foundations of the side chambers were a full rod of six long cubits *in height.*
9   The thickness of the outer wall of the side chambers was five cubits. But the free space between the side chambers belonging to the temple
10   and the *outer* chambers *was* twenty cubits in width all around the temple on every side.
11   And the doorways of the side chambers toward the free space *consisted of* one doorway toward the north and another doorway toward the south; and the width of the free space was five cubits all around.

3. *The building facing the temple on the west*

12   And the building that *was* in front of the separate area at the side toward the west *was* seventy cubits wide; and the wall of the building was five cubits thick all around, and its length *was* ninety cubits.

4. *The measurements of the temple and the yard*

13   Then he measured the temple, a hundred cubits long; the separate area with the building and its walls *were* also a hundred cubits long.
14   Also the width of the front of the temple and *that of* the separate areas along the east *side totaled* a hundred cubits.
15   And he measured the length of the building along the front of the separate area behind it, with a gallery on each side, a hundred cubits; *he* also *measured* the inner nave and the porches of the court.

5. *The interior decorations*

16   The thresholds, the latticed windows, and the galleries round about their three stories, opposite the threshold, were paneled with wood all around, and *from* the ground to the windows (but the windows were covered),
17   over the entrance, and to the inner house, and on the outside, and on all the wall all around inside and outside, by measurement.
18   And it was carved with cherubim and palm trees; and a palm tree was between cherub and cherub, and every cherub had two faces,
19   a man's face toward the palm tree on one side, and a young lion's face toward the palm tree on the other side; they were carved on all the house all around.
20   From the ground to above the entrance cherubim and palm trees were carved, as well as *on* the wall of the nave.
21   The doorposts of the nave were square; as for the front of the sanctuary, the appearance of one doorpost was like that of the other.

41:1
Ezek 40:2,3,
17; vv. 21,23;
Ezek 40:9
41:2
1 Kin 6:2,17;
2 Chr 3:3
41:3
Ezek 40:16;
v. 1
41:4
1 Kin 6:20;
2 Chr 3:8
41:5
vv. 6-11
41:6
1 Kin 6:5,6
41:7
1 Kin 6:8
41:8
Ezek 40:5
41:9
v. 11
41:10
Ezek 40:17
41:11
v. 9
41:12
vv. 13-15;
Ezek 42:1
41:13
Ezek 40:47;
vv. 13-15
41:14
Ezek 40:47
41:15
Ezek 42:1,10,
13; 40:6;
v. 25
41:16
vv. 25,26;
Ezek 40:16;
v. 15;
Ezek 42:3;
1 Kin 6:15
41:18
1 Kin 6:29;
7:36;
Ezek 40:16;
2 Chr 3:5
41:19
Ezek 1:10;
10:14
41:20
v. 18
41:21
1 Kin 6:33;
Ezek 40:9,14

22   The altar *was* of wood, three cubits high, and its length two cubits; its corners, its base, and its sides *were* of wood. And he said to me, "This is the table that is before the LORD."

23   And the nave and the sanctuary each had a double door.

24   And each of the doors had two leaves, two swinging leaves; two *leaves* for one door and two leaves for the other.

25   Also there were carved on them, on the doors of the nave, cherubim and palm trees like those carved on the walls; and *there was* a threshold of wood on the front of the porch outside.

26   And *there were* latticed windows and palm trees on one side and on the other, on the sides of the porch; thus *were* the side chambers of the house and the thresholds.

C. *The priests' chambers: north and south*

42 Then he brought me out into the outer court, the way toward the north; and he brought me to the chamber which *was* opposite the separate area and opposite the building toward the north.

2   Along the length, *which was* a hundred cubits, *was* the north door; the width *was* fifty cubits.

3   Opposite the twenty *cubits* which belonged to the inner court, and opposite the pavement which belonged to the outer court, *was* gallery corresponding to gallery in three stories.

4   And before the chambers *was* an inner walk ten cubits wide, a way of one *hundred* cubits; and their openings *were* on the north.

5   Now the upper chambers *were* smaller because the galleries took more *space* away from them than from the lower and middle ones in the building.

6   For they *were* in three stories and had no pillars like the pillars of the courts; therefore *the upper chambers* were set back from the ground upward, more than the lower and middle ones.

7   As for the outer wall by the side of the chambers, toward the outer court facing the chambers, its length *was* fifty cubits.

8   For the length of the chambers which *were* in the outer court *was* fifty cubits; and behold, *the length of those* facing the temple *was* a hundred cubits.

9   And below these chambers *was* the entrance on the east side, as one enters them from the outer court.

10   In the thickness of the wall of the court toward the east, facing the separate area and facing the building, *there were* chambers.

11   And the way in front of them *was* like the appearance of the chambers which *were* on the north, according to their length so was their width; and all their exits *were* both according to their arrangements and openings.

12   And corresponding to the openings of the chambers which were toward the south was an opening at the head of the way, the way in front of the wall toward the east, as one enters them.

13   Then he said to me, "The north chambers *and* the south chambers, which are opposite the separate area, they are the holy chambers where the priests who are near to the LORD shall eat the most holy things. There they shall lay the most holy things, the grain offering, the sin offering, and the guilt offering; for the place is holy.

14   "When the priests enter, then they shall not go out into the outer court from the sanctuary without laying there their garments in which they minister, for they are holy. They shall put on other garments; then they shall approach that which is for the people."

D. *The measurements of the temple area*

15   Now when he had finished measuring the inner house, he brought me out by the way of the gate which faced toward the east, and measured it all around.

16   He measured on the east side with the measuring reed five hundred reeds, by the measuring reed.

17   He measured on the north side five hundred reeds by the measuring reed.

18   On the south side he measured five hundred reeds with the measuring reed.

19   He turned to the west side, *and* measured five hundred reeds with the measuring reed.

42:20
Ezek 40:5;
Zech 2:5;
Ezek 45:2

20   He measured it on the four sides; it had a wall all around, the length five hundred and the width five hundred, to divide between the holy and the profane.

E. The return of the LORD to the temple

1. His glory enters the temple

43:1
Ezek 10:19;
44:1; 46:1
*43:2
Ezek 11:23;
1:24;
Rev 1:15;
18:1;
Ezek 10:4

43 Then he led me to the gate, the gate facing toward the east; 2   and behold, the glory of the God of Israel was coming from the way of the east. And His voice was like the sound of many waters; and the earth shone with His glory.

43:3
Ezek 1:4,28;
Jer 1:10;
Ezek 1:3;
3:23

3   And *it was* like the appearance of the vision which I saw, like the vision which I saw when He came to destroy the city. And the visions *were* like the vision which I saw by the river Chebar; and I fell on my face.

43:4
Ezek 10:19;
44:2

4   And the glory of the LORD came into the house by the way of the gate facing toward the east.

43:5
Ezek 3:14;
8:3;
1 Kin 8:10,
11; Ezek 44:4

5   And the Spirit lifted me up and brought me into the inner court; and behold, the glory of the LORD filled the house.

2. The message of the LORD

43:6
Ezek 1:26;
40:3

6   Then I heard one speaking to me from the house, while a man was standing beside me.

43:7
Ps 47:8;
Ezek 1:26;
37:26,28;
Jer 16:18;
Ezek 6:5,13

7   And He said to me, "Son of man, *this is* the place of My throne and the place of the soles of My feet, where I will dwell among the sons of Israel forever. And the house of Israel will not again defile My holy name, neither they nor their kings, by their harlotry and by the [12]corpses of their kings [13]when they die,

43:8
Ezek 8:3;
23:39; 44:7

8   by setting their threshold by My threshold, and their door post beside My door post, with *only* the wall between Me and them. And they have defiled My holy name by their abominations which they have committed. So I have consumed them in My anger.

43:9
Ezek 18:30,
31

9   "Now let them put away their harlotry and the [12]corpses of their kings far from Me; and I will dwell among them forever.

43:10
Ezek 40:4;
v. 11

10   "As for you, son of man, describe the temple to the house of Israel, that they may be ashamed of their iniquities; and let them measure the plan.

43:11
Ezek 44:5;
12:3; 11:20;
36:27

11   "And if they are ashamed of all that they have done, make known to them the design of the house, its structure, its exits, its entrances, all its designs, all its statutes, and all its laws. And write *it* in their sight, so that they may observe its whole design and all its statutes, and do them.

43:12
Ezek 40:2

12   "This is the law of the house: its entire area on the top of the mountain all around *shall be* most holy. Behold, this is the law of the house.

3. The measurements of the altar of burnt offering

43:13
Ezek 40:5;
41:8

13   "And these are the measurements of the altar by cubits (the cubit being a cubit and a handbreadth): the base *shall be* a cubit, and the width a cubit, and its border on its edge round about one span; and this *shall be* the *height of the* base of the altar.

43:14
vv. 17,20;
Ezek 45:19

14   "And from the base on the ground to the lower ledge *shall be* two cubits, and the width one cubit; and from the smaller ledge to the larger ledge *shall be* four cubits, and the width one cubit.

43:15
Ex 27:2;
Lev 9:9;
1 Kin 1:50

15   "And the altar hearth *shall be* four cubits; and from the altar hearth shall extend upwards four horns.

43:16
Ex 27:1

16   "Now the altar hearth *shall be* twelve *cubits* long by twelve wide, square in its four sides.

43:17
Ex 20:26;
Ezek 40:6

17   "And the ledge *shall be* fourteen *cubits* long by fourteen wide in its four sides, the border around it *shall be* half a cubit, and its base *shall be* a cubit round about; and its steps shall face the east."

4. Instructions for the consecration of the altar

43:18
Ezek 2:1;
Ex 40:29;
Lev 1:5

18   And He said to me, "Son of man, thus says the Lord GOD, 'These are the

---

[12]Or, *monuments*   [13]Or, *in their high places*

43:2 *the glory of the God of Israel was coming from the way of the east* (cf. 9:3). It had gone eastward as a token of the fact that God was delivering Jerusalem to its enemies. Its return was a token that God was about to take up His abode in the midst of His people again.

statutes for the altar on the day it is built, to offer burnt offerings on it and to sprinkle blood on it.

19 'And you shall give to the Levitical priests who are from the offspring of Zadok, who draw near to Me to minister to Me,' declares the Lord GOD, 'a young bull for a sin offering.

20 'And you shall take some of its blood, and put it on its four horns, and on the four corners of the ledge, and on the border round about; thus you shall cleanse it and make atonement for it.

21 'You shall also take the bull for the sin offering; and it *shall be* burned in the appointed place of the house, outside the sanctuary.

22 'And on the second day you shall offer a male goat without blemish for a sin offering; and they shall cleanse the altar, as they cleansed *it* with the bull.

23 'When you have finished cleansing *it*, you shall present a young bull without blemish and a ram without blemish from the flock.

24 'And you shall present them before the LORD, and the priests shall throw salt on them, and they shall offer them up as a burnt offering to the LORD.

25 'For seven days you shall prepare daily a goat for a sin offering; also a young bull and a ram from the flock, without blemish, shall be prepared.

26 'For seven days they shall make atonement for the altar and purify it; so shall they consecrate it.

27 'And when they have completed the days, it shall be that on the eighth day and onward, the priests shall offer your burnt offerings on the altar, and your peace offerings; and I will accept you,' declares the Lord GOD."

F. The rules of the sanctuary

1. The east gate and the prince

44 Then He brought me back by the way of the outer gate of the sanctuary, which faces the east; and it was shut.

2 And the LORD said to me, "This gate shall be shut; it shall not be opened, and no one shall enter by it, for the LORD God of Israel has entered by it; therefore it shall be shut.

3 "As for the prince, he shall sit in it as prince to eat bread before the LORD; he shall enter by way of the porch of the gate, and shall go out by the same way."

2. The exclusion of the uncircumcised

4 Then He brought me by way of the north gate to the front of the house; and I looked, and behold, the glory of the LORD filled the house of the LORD, and I fell on my face.

5 And the LORD said to me, "Son of man, mark well, see with your eyes, and hear with your ears all that I say to you concerning all the statutes of the house of the LORD and concerning all its laws; and mark well the entrance of the house, with all exits of the sanctuary.

6 "And you shall say to the rebellious ones, to the house of Israel, 'Thus says the Lord GOD, "Enough of all your abominations, O house of Israel,

7 when you brought in foreigners, uncircumcised in heart and uncircumcised in flesh, to be in My sanctuary to profane it, *even* My house, when you offered My food, the fat and the blood; for they made My covenant void—*this* in addition to all your abominations.

8 "And you have not kept charge of My holy things yourselves, but you have set *foreigners* to keep charge of My sanctuary."

3. The exclusion of the idolatrous Levites

9 'Thus says the Lord GOD, "No foreigner, uncircumcised in heart and

---

Marginal references (right column):

*43:19
1 Kin 2:35;
Ezek 44:15;
Num 16:5,40;
v. 23;
Ezek 45:18,
19

43:21
Ex 29:14;
Heb 13:11
43:22
vv. 25,20,26

43:23
Ex 29:1

43:24
Lev 2:13;
Mark 9:49,
50; Col 4:6
43:25
Ex 29:35,36;
Lev 8:33

43:27
Lev 9:1; 3:1;
17:5;
Ezek 20:40

44:1
Ezek 42:14;
43:1
44:2
Ezek 43:4

44:3
Ezek 37:25;
Gen 31:54;
1 Cor 10:18;
Ezek 46:2,8

44:4
Ezek 40:20,
40; 3:23;
43:5; 1:28;
Rev 15:8
44:5
Ezek 40:4;
43:10,11

44:6
Ezek 2:5;
3:9; 45:9;
1 Pet 4:3
44:7
Ex 12:43-49;
Lev 26:41;
Deut 10:16;
Jer 4:4; 9:26;
Lev 22:25;
Gen 17:14
44:8
Num 18:7
44:9
v. 7;
Zech 14:21

---

uncircumcised in flesh, of all the foreigners who are among the sons of Israel, shall enter My sanctuary.

10 "But the Levites who went far from Me, when Israel went astray, who went astray from Me after their idols, shall bear the punishment for their iniquity.

11 "Yet they shall be ministers in My sanctuary, having oversight at the gates of the house and ministering in the house; they shall slaughter the burnt offering and the sacrifice for the people, and they shall stand before them to minister to them.

12 "Because they ministered to them before their idols and became a stumbling block of iniquity to the house of Israel, therefore I have sworn against them," declares the Lord GOD, "that they shall bear the punishment for their iniquity.

13 "And they shall not come near to Me to serve as a priest to Me, nor come near to any of My holy things, to the things that are most holy; but they shall bear their shame and their abominations which they have committed.

14 "Yet I will appoint them to keep charge of the house, of all its service, and of all that shall be done in it.

4. The service of the Levitical sons of Zadok: their duties

15 "But the Levitical priests, the sons of Zadok, who kept charge of My sanctuary when the sons of Israel went astray from Me, shall come near to Me to minister to Me; and they shall stand before Me to offer Me the fat and the blood," declares the Lord GOD.

16 "They shall enter My sanctuary; they shall come near to My table to minister to Me and keep My charge.

17 "And it shall be that when they enter at the gates of the inner court, they shall be clothed with linen garments; and wool shall not be on them while they are ministering in the gates of the inner court and in the house.

18 "Linen turbans shall be on their heads, and linen undergarments shall be on their loins; they shall not gird themselves with *anything which makes them* sweat.

19 "And when they go out into the outer court, into the outer court to the people, they shall put off their garments in which they have been ministering and lay them in the holy chambers; then they shall put on other garments that they may not transmit holiness to the people with their garments.

20 "Also they shall not shave their heads, yet they shall not let their locks grow long; they shall only trim *the hair of* their heads.

21 "Nor shall any of the priests drink wine when they enter the inner court.

22 "And they shall not marry a widow or a divorced woman but shall take virgins from the offspring of the house of Israel, or a widow who is the widow of a priest.

23 "Moreover, they shall teach My people *the difference* between the holy and the profane, and cause them to discern between the unclean and the clean.

24 "And in a dispute they shall take their stand to judge; they shall judge it according to My ordinances. They shall also keep My laws and My statutes in all My appointed feasts, and sanctify My sabbaths.

25 "And they shall not go to a dead person to defile *themselves;* however, for father, for mother, for son, for daughter, for brother, or for a sister who has not had a husband, they may defile themselves.

26 "And after he is cleansed, seven days shall [14]elapse for him.

27 "And on the day that he goes into the sanctuary, into the inner court to minister in the sanctuary, he shall offer his sin offering," declares the Lord GOD.

28 "And it shall be with regard to an inheritance for them, *that* I am their inheritance; and you shall give them no possession in Israel—I am their possession.

29 "They shall eat the grain offering, the sin offering, and the guilt offering; and every devoted thing in Israel shall be theirs.

30 "And the first of all the first fruits of every kind and every contribution of every kind, from all your contributions, shall be for the priests; you shall also give to the priest the first of your dough to cause a blessing to rest on your house.

31 "The priests shall not eat any bird or beast that has died a natural death or has been torn to pieces.

G. The land for priests and prince

45 "And when you shall divide by lot the land for inheritance, you shall offer an allotment to the LORD, a holy portion of the land; the length shall be the

[14]Lit., *be counted*

length of 25,000 *cubits*, and the width shall be 10,000. It shall be holy within all its boundary round about.

2 "Out of this there shall be for the holy place a square round about five hundred by five hundred *cubits*, and fifty cubits for its open space round about.

3 "And from this area you shall measure a length of 25,000 *cubits*, and a width of 10,000 *cubits;* and in it shall be the sanctuary, the most holy place.

4 "It shall be the holy portion of the land; it shall be for the priests, the ministers of the sanctuary, who come near to minister to the LORD, and it shall be a place for their houses and a holy place for the sanctuary.

5 "And *an area* 25,000 *cubits* in length and 10,000 in width shall be for the Levites, the ministers of the house, *and* for their possession cities to dwell in.

6 "And you shall give the city possession of *an area* 5,000 *cubits* wide and 25,000 *cubits* long, alongside the [15]allotment of the holy portion; it shall be for the whole house of Israel.

7 "And the prince shall have *land* on either side of the holy [15]allotment and the property of the city, adjacent to the holy [15]allotment and the property of the city, on the west side toward the west and on the east side toward the east, and in length comparable to one of the portions, from the west border to the east border.

8 "This shall be his land for a possession in Israel; so My princes shall no longer oppress My people, but they shall give *the rest of* the land to the house of Israel according to their tribes."

9 'Thus says the Lord GOD, "Enough, you princes of Israel; put away violence and destruction, and practice justice and righteousness. Stop your expropriations from My people," declares the Lord GOD.

H. *Additional instructions*

1. *Just balances*

10 "You shall have just balances, a just ephah, and a just bath.

11 "The ephah and the bath shall be the same quantity, so that the bath may contain a tenth of a homer, and the ephah a tenth of a homer; their standard shall be according to the homer.

12 "And the shekel shall be twenty gerahs; twenty shekels, twenty-five shekels, *and* fifteen shekels shall be your maneh.

2. *The cereal offerings*

13 "This is the offering that you shall offer: a sixth of an ephah from a homer of wheat; a sixth of an ephah from a homer of barley;

14 and the prescribed portion of oil (*namely,* the bath of oil), a tenth of a bath from *each* kor (*which is* ten baths *or* a homer, for ten baths are a homer);

15 and one sheep from *each* flock of two hundred from the watering places of Israel—for a grain offering, for a burnt offering, and for peace offerings, to make atonement for them," declares the Lord GOD.

16 "All the people of the land shall give to this offering for the prince in Israel.

17 "And it shall be the prince's part *to provide* the burnt offerings, the grain offerings, and the libations, at the feasts, on the new moons, and on the sabbaths, at all the appointed feasts of the house of Israel; he shall provide the sin offering, the grain offering, the burnt offering, and the peace offerings, to make atonement for the house of Israel."

3. *The offerings at sacred seasons*

18 'Thus says the Lord GOD, "In the first *month,* on the first of the month, you shall take a young bull without blemish and cleanse the sanctuary.

19 "And the priest shall take some of the blood from the sin offering and put *it* on the door posts of the house, on the four corners of the ledge of the altar, and on the posts of the gate of the inner court.

20 "And thus you shall do on the seventh *day* of the month for everyone who goes astray or is naive; so you shall make atonement for the house.

21 "In the first *month,* on the fourteenth day of the month, you shall have the Passover, a feast of seven days; unleavened bread shall be eaten.

[15]Or, *contribution*

45:2
Ezek 42:20

45:3
Ezek 48:10

45:4
v. 1;
Ezek 48:10,
11

45:5
Ezek 48:13

45:6
Ezek 48:15

45:7
Ezek 46:16-18;
48:21

45:8
Is 11:3-5;
Jer 23:5;
Ezek 22:27;
46:18;
Josh 11:23
45:9
Ezek 44:6;
Jer 6:7; 22:3;
Neh 5:1-5

45:10
Lev 19:35,36;
Prov 11:1
45:11
Is 5:10

45:12
Ex 30:13;
Lev 27:25;
Num 3:47

45:15
v. 17;
Lev 1:4; 6:30

45:17
Ezek 46:4-12;
1 Kin 8:64;
2 Chr 31:3;
Lev 23:1-44;
Ezek 43:27

45:18
Ezek 46:1,3,
6; Lev 16:16
45:19
Ezek 43:20

45:20
Lev 4:27;
16:20; vv. 15,
18
45:21
Ex 12:18;
Lev 23:5,6;
Num 9:2,3;
28:16,17

45:22
Lev 4:14
22 "And on that day the prince shall provide for himself and all the people of the land a bull for a sin offering.

45:23
Lev 23:8;
Num 28:16-25;
Job 42:8
23 "And *during* the seven days of the feast he shall provide as a burnt offering to the LORD seven bulls and seven rams without blemish on every day of the seven days, and a male goat daily for a sin offering.

24 "And he shall provide as a grain offering an ephah with a bull, an ephah with a ram, and a hin of oil with an ephah.

45:25
Lev 23:34;
Num 29:12;
Deut 16:13
25 "In the seventh *month*, on the fifteenth day of the month, at the feast, he shall provide like this, seven days for the sin offering, the burnt offering, the grain offering, and the oil."

4. *The new moon and Sabbath offerings of the prince*

46:1
Ezek 45:17-19
46 'Thus says the Lord GOD, "The gate of the inner court facing east shall be shut the six working days; but it shall be opened on the sabbath day, and opened on the day of the new moon.

46:2
v. 8;
Ezek 44:3;
45:9; v. 12
2 "And the prince shall enter by way of the porch of the gate from outside and stand by the post of the gate. Then the priests shall provide his burnt offering and his peace offerings, and he shall worship at the threshold of the gate and then go out; but the gate shall not be shut until the evening.

46:3
Luke 1:10;
v. 1
3 "The people of the land shall also worship at the doorway of that gate before the LORD on the sabbaths and on the new moons.

46:4
Ezek 45:17
4 "And the burnt offering which the prince shall offer to the LORD on the sabbath day shall be six lambs without blemish and a ram without blemish;

46:5
Ezek 45:24;
vv. 7,11
5 and the grain offering shall be an ephah with the ram, and the grain offering with the lambs as much as he is able to give, and a hin of oil with an ephah.

46:6
v. 1
6 "And on the day of the new moon *he shall offer* a young bull without blemish, also six lambs and a ram, *which* shall be without blemish.

46:7
v. 5
7 "And he shall provide a grain offering, an ephah with the bull, and an ephah with the ram, and with the lambs as much as he is able, and a hin of oil with an ephah.

46:8
Ezek 44:3;
v. 2
8 "And when the prince enters, he shall go in by way of the porch of the gate and go out by the same way.

5. *Entering and leaving the temple*

46:9
Ex 23:14-17;
Deut 16:16
9 "But when the people of the land come before the LORD at the appointed feasts, he who enters by way of the north gate to worship shall go out by way of the south gate. And he who enters by way of the south gate shall go out by way of the north gate. No one shall return by way of the gate by which he entered but shall go straight out.

10 "And when they go in, the prince shall go in among them; and when they go out, he shall go out.

6. *Rules for sacrifice*

46:11
Ezek 45:17;
vv. 5,7
11 "And at the festivals and the appointed feasts the grain offering shall be an ephah with a bull and an ephah with a ram, and with the lambs as much as one is able to give, and a hin of oil with an ephah.

46:12
2 Chr 29:31;
Ezek 44:3;
v. 2;
Ezek 45:17
12 "And when the prince provides a freewill offering, a burnt offering, or peace offerings *as* a freewill offering to the LORD, the gate facing east shall be opened for him. And he shall provide his burnt offering and his peace offerings as he does on the sabbath day. Then he shall go out, and the gate shall be shut after he goes out.

46:13
Ex 29:38;
Num 28:3;
Is 50:4
46:14
Num 28:5
13 "And you shall provide a lamb a year old without blemish for a burnt offering to the LORD daily; morning by morning you shall provide it.

14 "Also you shall provide a grain offering with it morning by morning, a sixth of an ephah, and a third of a hin of oil to moisten the fine flour, a grain offering to the LORD continually by a perpetual ordinance.

46:15
Ex 29:42;
Num 28:6
15 "Thus they shall provide the lamb, the grain offering, and the oil, morning by morning, for a continual burnt offering."

7. *The prince and the laws of inheritance*

46:16
2 Chr 21:3;
46:17
Lev 27:10
16 'Thus says the Lord GOD, "If the prince gives a gift *out of* his inheritance to any of his sons, it shall belong to his sons; it is their possession by inheritance.

17 "But if he gives a gift from his inheritance to one of his servants, it shall be his

until the year of liberty; then it shall return to the prince. His inheritance *shall be* only his sons'; it shall belong to them.

18 "And the prince shall not take from the people's inheritance, thrusting them out of their possession; he shall give his sons inheritance from his own possession so that My people shall not be scattered, anyone from his possession." ' "

8. *The kitchens for the temple*

19 Then he brought me through the entrance, which *was* at the side of the gate, into the holy chambers for the priests, which faced north; and behold, there *was* a place at the extreme rear toward the west.

20 And he said to me, "This is the place where the priests shall boil the guilt offering and the sin offering, *and* where they shall bake the grain offering, in order that they may not bring *them* out into the outer court to transmit holiness to the people."

21 Then he brought me out into the outer court and led me across to the four corners of the court; and behold, in every corner of the court *there was* a *small* court.

22 In the four corners of the court *there were* enclosed courts, forty *cubits* long and thirty wide; these four in the corners *were* the same size.

23 And *there was* a row *of masonry* round about in them, around the four of them, and boiling places were made under the rows round about.

24 Then he said to me, "These are the boiling places where the ministers of the house shall boil the sacrifices of the people."

I. *The river flowing from the temple*

47 Then he brought me back to the door of the house; and behold, water was flowing from under the threshold of the house toward the east, for the house faced east. And the water was flowing down from under, from the right side of the house, from south of the altar.

2 And he brought me out by way of the north gate and led me around on the outside to the outer gate by way of *the gate* that faces east. And behold, water was trickling from the south side.

3 When the man went out toward the east with a line in his hand, he measured a thousand cubits, and he led me through the water, water *reaching* the ankles.

4 Again he measured a thousand and led me through the water, water *reaching* the knees. Again he measured a thousand and led me through *the water*, water *reaching* the loins.

5 Again he measured a thousand; *and it was* a river that I could not ford, for the water had risen, *enough* water to swim in, a river that could not be forded.

6 And he said to me, "Son of man, have you seen *this*?" Then he brought me back to the bank of the river.

7 Now when I had returned, behold, on the bank of the river there *were* very many trees on the one side and on the other.

8 Then he said to me, "These waters go out toward the eastern region and go down into the Arabah; then they go toward the sea, being made to flow into the sea, and the waters *of the sea* become fresh.

9 "And it will come about that every living creature which swarms in every place where the river goes, will live. And there will be very many fish, for these waters go there, and *the others* become fresh; so everything will live where the river goes.

10 "And it will come about that fishermen will stand beside it; from Engedi to Eneglaim there will be a place for the spreading of nets. Their fish will be according to their kinds, like the fish of the Great Sea, very many.

11 "But its swamps and marshes will not become fresh; they will be left for salt.

12 "And by the river on its bank, on one side and on the other, will grow all *kinds of* trees for food. Their leaves will not wither, and their fruit will not fail. They will bear every month because their water flows from the sanctuary, and their fruit will be for food and their leaves for healing."

47:7 The river that Ezekiel saw bringing refreshment to the parched Judean wilderness corresponds to that described in Rev. 22:1–2 as *coming from the throne of God and of the Lamb.* Jesus spoke of *rivers of living water flowing from* the heart of the believer (John 7:37–39). In each instance the symbolic language describes blessing that finds its source in God and that brings refreshment to all it touches.

J. The boundaries of the land

47:13
Num 34:2-12;
Gen 48:5;
1 Chr 5:1;
Ezek 48:4
47:14
Gen 12:7;
Deut 1:8;
Ezek 20:5,6
47:15
Num 34:8;
Ezek 48:1
47:16
vv. 17,20;
Ezek 48:1;
v. 18
47:17
Num 34:9;
Ezek 48:1;
v. 16
47:18
v. 16;
Jer 50:19;
Gen 13:10,11
47:19
Ezek 48:28;
Deut 32:51;
Is 27:12
47:20
Num 34:6;
vv. 10,15;
Ezek 48:1;
Amos 6:14

47:22
Num 26:55,
56; Is 56:6,7;
Rom 10:12;
Eph 2:12-14;
3:6; Col 3:11

13 Thus says the Lord GOD, "This *shall be* the boundary by which you shall divide the land for an inheritance among the twelve tribes of Israel; Joseph *shall have two* portions.

14 "And you shall divide it for an inheritance, each one equally with the other; for I swore to give it to your forefathers, and this land shall fall to you as an inheritance.

15 "And this *shall be* the boundary of the land: on the north side, from the Great Sea *by* the way of Hethlon, to the entrance of Zedad;

16 Hamath, Berothah, Sibraim, which is between the border of Damascus and the border of Hamath; Hazer-hatticon, which is by the border of Hauran.

17 "And the boundary shall extend from the sea *to* Hazar-enan *at* the border of Damascus, and on the north toward the north is the border of Hamath. This is the north side.

18 "And the east side, from between Hauran, Damascus, Gilead, and the land of Israel, *shall be* the Jordan; from the *north* border to the eastern sea you shall measure. This is the east side.

19 "And the south side toward the south *shall extend* from Tamar as far as the waters of Meribath-kadesh, to the brook *of Egypt, and* to the Great Sea. This is the south side toward the south.

20 "And the west side *shall be* the Great Sea, from the *south* border to a point opposite Lebo-hamath. This is the west side.

21 "So you shall divide this land among yourselves according to the tribes of Israel.

22 "And it will come about that you shall divide it by lot for an inheritance among yourselves and among the aliens who stay in your midst, who bring forth sons in your midst. And they shall be to you as the native-born among the sons of Israel; they shall be allotted an inheritance with you among the tribes of Israel.

23 "And it will come about that in the tribe with which the alien stays, there you shall give *him* his inheritance," declares the Lord GOD.

K. The division of the land

1. The land allotted to the north

48:1
Ezek 47:15-17,
20;
Josh 19:40-48

48:2
Josh 19:24-31

48:3
Josh 19:32-39

48:4
Josh 13:29-31;
17:1-11
48:5
Josh 16:5-9;
17:8-10,14-18
48:6
Josh 13:15-21

48:7
Josh 15:1-63

48 "Now these are the names of the tribes: from the northern extremity, beside the way of Hethlon to Lebo-hamath, *as far as* Hazar-enan *at* the border of Damascus, toward the north beside Hamath, running from east to west, Dan, one *portion*.

2 "And beside the border of Dan, from the east side to the west side, Asher, one *portion*.

3 "And beside the border of Asher, from the east side to the west side, Naphtali, one *portion*.

4 "And beside the border of Naphtali, from the east side to the west side, Manasseh, one *portion*.

5 "And beside the border of Manasseh, from the east side to the west side, Ephraim, one *portion*.

6 "And beside the border of Ephraim, from the east side to the west side, Reuben, one *portion*.

7 "And beside the border of Reuben, from the east side to the west side, Judah, one *portion*.

2. The allotment for the priests and Levites

48:8
Ezek 45:1-6

48:10
Ezek 44:28;
45:4; v. 8

8 "And beside the border of Judah, from the east side to the west side, shall be the [16]allotment which you shall set apart, 25,000 *cubits* in width, and in length like one of the portions, from the east side to the west side; and the sanctuary shall be in the middle of it.

9 "The allotment that you shall set apart to the LORD *shall be* 25,000 *cubits* in length, and 10,000 in width.

10 "And the holy allotment shall be for these, *namely* for the priests, toward the north 25,000 *cubits in length,* toward the west 10,000 in width, toward the east

[16]Or, *contribution*, and so throughout this context

10,000 in width, and toward the south 25,000 in length; and the sanctuary of the LORD shall be in its midst.

11 *"It shall be* for the priests who are sanctified of the sons of Zadok, who have kept My charge, who did not go astray when the sons of Israel went astray, as the Levites went astray.

12 "And it shall be an allotment to them from the allotment of the land, a most holy place, by the border of the Levites.

13 "And alongside the border of the priests the Levites *shall have* 25,000 *cubits* in length and 10,000 in width. The whole length *shall be* 25,000 *cubits* and the width 10,000.

14 "Moreover, they shall not sell or exchange any of it, or alienate this choice *portion* of land; for it is holy to the LORD.

3. The allotment for the city

15 "And the remainder, 5,000 *cubits* in width and 25,000 in length, shall be for common use for the city, for dwellings and for open spaces; and the city shall be in its midst.

16 "And these *shall be* its measurements: the north side 4,500 *cubits*, the south side 4,500 *cubits*, the east side 4,500 *cubits*, and the west side 4,500 *cubits*.

17 "And the city shall have open spaces: on the north 250 *cubits*, on the south 250 *cubits*, on the east 250 *cubits*, and on the west 250 *cubits*.

18 "And the remainder of the length alongside the holy allotment shall be 10,000 *cubits* toward the east, and 10,000 toward the west; and it shall be alongside the holy allotment. And its produce shall be food for the workers of the city.

19 "And the workers of the city, out of all the tribes of Israel, shall cultivate it.

20 "The whole allotment *shall be* 25,000 by 25,000 *cubits;* you shall set apart the holy allotment, a square, with the property of the city.

4. The allotment for the prince

21 "And the remainder *shall be* for the prince, on the one side and on the other of the holy allotment and of the property of the city; in front of the 25,000 *cubits* of the allotment toward the east border and westward in front of the 25,000 toward the west border, alongside the portions, *it shall be* for the prince. And the holy allotment and the sanctuary of the house shall be in the middle of it.

22 "And exclusive of the property of the Levites and the property of the city, *which* are in the middle of that which belongs to the prince, *everything* between the border of Judah and the border of Benjamin shall be for the prince.

5. The land allotted to the south of the sacred portion

23 "As for the rest of the tribes: from the east side to the west side, Benjamin, one *portion.*

24 "And beside the border of Benjamin, from the east side to the west side, Simeon, one *portion.*

25 "And beside the border of Simeon, from the east side to the west side, Issachar, one *portion.*

26 "And beside the border of Issachar, from the east side to the west side, Zebulun, one *portion.*

27 "And beside the border of Zebulun, from the east side to the west side, Gad, one *portion.*

28 "And beside the border of Gad, at the south side toward the south, the border shall be from Tamar to the waters of Meribath-kadesh, to the brook *of Egypt,* to the Great Sea.

29 "This is the land which you shall divide by lot to the tribes of Israel for an inheritance, and these are their *several* portions," declares the Lord GOD.

6. The city named "The LORD is there"

30 "And these are the exits of the city: on the north side, 4,500 *cubits* by measurement;

31 shall be the gates of the city, named for the tribes of Israel, three gates toward the north: the gate of Reuben, one; the gate of Judah, one; the gate of Levi, one.

32 "And on the east side, 4,500 *cubits,* shall be three gates: the gate of Joseph, one; the gate of Benjamin, one; the gate of Dan, one.

48:11
Ezek 44:15,
10,12

48:12
Ezek 45:4

48:13
Ezek 45:3

48:14
Lev 25:32-34

48:15
Ezek 42:20;
45:6

48:16
Rev 21:16

48:17
Ezek 45:2

48:18
v. 8

48:19
Ezek 45:6
48:20
v. 16

48:21
Ezek 34:24;
45:7; vv. 22,
8,10

48:23
vv. 1-7;
Josh 18:21-28
48:24
Josh 19:1-9

48:25
Josh 19:17-23

48:26
Josh 19:10-16

48:27
Josh 13:24-28

48:28
Ezek 47:19,
20

48:29
Ezek 47:13-20

48:30
vv. 31-34

48:31
Rev 21:12,13

48:35
Jer 23:6;
33:16; 3:17;
Joel 3:21;
Zech 2:10;
Rev 21:3;
22:3

33 "And on the south side, 4,500 *cubits* by measurement, shall be three gates: the gate of Simeon, one; the gate of Issachar, one; the gate of Zebulun, one.

34 "On the west side, 4,500 *cubits, shall be* three gates: the gate of Gad, one; the gate of Asher, one; the gate of Naphtali, one.

35 *"The city shall be* 18,000 *cubits* round about; and the name of the city from *that* day *shall be,* 'The LORD is there.'"

INTRODUCTION TO
THE BOOK OF
DANIEL

Authorship and Background: Conservative scholarship has always acknowledged that Daniel wrote this book, as the internal evidences indicate. Daniel was carried away to Babylon as a captive while he was still a boy. According to the traditional view he lived and prophesied when Babylon was the most powerful empire of its day, and himself watched the activities of a number of famous monarchs (of whom Nebuchadnezzar is best known to Bible students) for almost three quarters of a century.

The Jews and early Christians universally accepted the book as genuine, and it was not until Porphyry's day (ca. A.D. 260) that doubt was cast on the traditional view. Many critical scholars object to a sixth-century date, claiming that the book must have been written *after* the events described took place, not before, since the predictions were so specifically fulfilled by the time of the Maccabean struggle for independence (165 B.C.). A mediating viewpoint acknowledges the historical Daniel and the Babylonian setting in the first portion of the book, and attributes the latter part of the book to the Maccabean period, thus assuming a dual authorship. Even if one were to assume that the book was written in the Maccabean period, there are still important prophecies relating to future events such as the time of the end (Dan. 11:35,40,45) that had not been fulfilled by 165 B.C.

Perhaps more than any other book, Daniel has been used to develop contradictory schemes of prophetic interpretation. Yet no comprehensive Christian world view can be developed without its use. Daniel's panoramic vision includes the period of Gentile ascendancy after Calvary and sweeps on to the end of the age.

Characteristics: Daniel is written in Aramaic and Hebrew: the Aramaic portions pertain to the Gentile nations in general, the Hebrew portions to the Jewish nation in particular. It is an apocalyptic work, rich in symbol and imagery. The author upholds a philosophy of history in which the sovereign God rules and overrules among men and nations. Direct divine intervention in the affairs of men may be seen in the account of the fiery furnace (3:14ff.), the degradation of Nebuchadnezzar (4:33ff.), Belshazzar's downfall (5:25ff.), and Daniel in the lions' den (6:16ff.). Daniel's visions of the beasts, the seventy weeks, and the end time require careful study and interpretation. The style of writing is somewhat similar to the Revelation of John in the New Testament.

Contents:

I. Daniel and his friends (1:1-6:28): The personal history of Daniel is related and his rise to power noted. Nebuchadnezzar has a dream that cannot be interpreted. Daniel alone is able to tell the king the meaning of the vision. He reveals the secret of four world empires, and God's eternal and universal kingdom. Nebuchadnezzar sets up an image of gold. The three Jews refuse to bow before the image and are cast into the fiery furnace, from which they are delivered by God. Nebuchadnezzar has another vision that Daniel interprets, and the king is degraded and restored. The story of Belshazzar follows, in which pride overtakes him. His vision is interpreted by Daniel, who prophesies the end of his kingdom, which is taken over by Darius. Darius's decree against prayer to God leads to Daniel's being placed in the lions' den, from which God delivers him.

II. The final dream and visions (7:1-12:13): Daniel portrays the beast vision of a lion, a bear, a leopard, and a fourth beast with ten horns. The interpretation is given. Then follows the vision of the ram and the goat with its interpretation. This is succeeded by the vision of the seventy weeks and his vision of the glory of God. He foresees the movement of history from Darius to Antiochus Epiphanes on to the end of the age. The book closes with a prophecy of a "time of distress" and a command to seal the book, "until the time of the end."

THE BOOK OF
DANIEL

I. *Daniel and his friends (1:1–6:28)*

A. *The training and testing of the remnant*

1. *The hostages captured*

1 In the third year of the reign of Jehoiakim king of Judah, Nebuchadnezzar king of Babylon came to Jerusalem and besieged it.

2 And the Lord gave Jehoiakim king of Judah into his hand, along with some of the vessels of the house of God; and he brought them to the land of Shinar, to the house of his ¹god, and he brought the vessels into the treasury of his ¹god.

2. *Daniel and his three friends chosen as students*

3 Then the king ordered Ashpenaz, the chief of his ²officials, to bring in some of the sons of Israel, including some of the royal family and of the nobles,

4 youths in whom was no defect, who were good-looking, showing intelligence in every *branch of* wisdom, endowed with understanding, and discerning knowledge, and who had ability for serving in the king's court; and *he ordered him* to teach them the ³literature and language of the Chaldeans.

5 And the king appointed for them a daily ration from the king's choice food and from the wine which he drank, and *appointed* that they should be educated three years, at the end of which they were to enter the king's personal service.

6 Now among them from the sons of Judah were Daniel, Hananiah, Mishael and Azariah.

7 Then the commander of the officials assigned *new* names to them; and to Daniel he assigned *the name* Belteshazzar, to Hananiah Shadrach, to Mishael Meshach, and to Azariah Abed-nego.

3. *The trial of their faith*

8 But Daniel made up his mind that he would not defile himself with the king's choice food or with the wine which he drank; so he sought *permission* from the commander of the officials that he might not defile himself.

9 Now God granted Daniel favor and compassion in the sight of the commander of the officials,

10 and the commander of the officials said to Daniel, "I am afraid of my lord the king, who has appointed your food and your drink; for why should he see your faces looking more haggard than the youths who are your own age? Then you would make me forfeit my head to the king."

11 But Daniel said to the overseer whom the commander of the officials had appointed over Daniel, Hananiah, Mishael and Azariah,

12 "Please test your servants for ten days, and let us be given some vegetables to eat and water to drink.

13 "Then let our appearance be observed in your presence, and the appearance of the youths who are eating the king's choice food; and deal with your servants according to what you see."

---

¹Or, *gods* ²Or, *eunuchs*, and so throughout the ch. ³Or, *writing*

1:1
2 Kin 24:1;
2 Chr 36:6
*1:2
Jer 27:19,20;
Is 11:11;
Zech 5:11

1:3
2 Kin 20:17,
18; Is 39:7
*1:4
2 Sam 14:25;
Dan 2:4

*1:5ff
vv. 8,18;
1 Kin 10:8;
v. 19
1:6
Ezek 14:14,
20; 28:3
1:7
Dan 4:8;
5:12; 2:49;
3:12

1:8
Deut 32:38;
Ezek 4:13;
Hos 9:3
1:9
Job 5:15,16;
Ps 106:46;
Prov 16:7
1:10
v. 7

1:12
v. 16

1:2 Judah was defeated and taken captive by Babylon. Punished by God because of idolatry, the Jews were delivered into the hands of the Babylonian king. In Babylon they were preserved and, having learned the evil of idolatry, were prepared by God to return that they might be the people through whom the Savior of men might come.

Shinar, or Babylonia, a name for the land of the Chaldeans.

1:4 *literature . . . Chaldeans.* The cuneiform writing system and the Semitic Akkadian (Assyro-Babylonian) language.

1:5–7 The Babylonians sought to win the Jewish captives to loyalty to Nebuchadnezzar and his court. To this end a three-fold program was adopted: (1) the Jewish youths were given new names, suggesting their change in loyalty; (2) they were subjected to a three-year training program; and (3) they were provided with the best food Babylon could offer. Although cooperative where possible, Daniel determined to be faithful to the Law of God, and God caused him to prosper.

14 So he listened to them in this matter and tested them for ten days.

15 And at the end of ten days their appearance seemed better and they were fatter than all the youths who had been eating the king's choice food.

16 So the overseer continued to withhold their choice food and the wine they were to drink, and kept giving them vegetables.

4. The reward of their faith

17 And as for these four youths, God gave them knowledge and intelligence in every *branch of* literature and wisdom; Daniel even understood all *kinds of* visions and dreams.

18 Then at the end of the days which the king had specified for presenting them, the commander of the officials presented them before Nebuchadnezzar.

19 And the king talked with them, and out of them all not one was found like Daniel, Hananiah, Mishael and Azariah; so they entered the king's personal service.

20 And as for every matter of wisdom and understanding about which the king consulted them, he found them ten times better than all the magicians *and* conjurers who *were* in all his realm.

21 And Daniel continued until the first year of Cyrus the king.

B. Nebuchadnezzar's dream of the image and the stone

1. Nebuchadnezzar's forgotten dream

2 Now in the second year of the reign of Nebuchadnezzar, Nebuchadnezzar had dreams; and his spirit was troubled and his sleep left him.

2 Then the king gave orders to call in the ⁴magicians, the conjurers, the sorcerers and the ⁵Chaldeans, to tell the king his dreams. So they came in and stood before the king.

3 And the king said to them, "I had a dream, and my spirit is anxious to understand the dream."

4 Then the Chaldeans spoke to the king in Aramaic: "O king, live forever! Tell the dream to your servants, and we will declare the interpretation."

5 The king answered and said to the Chaldeans, "The command from me is firm: if you do not make known to me the dream and its interpretation, you will be torn limb from limb, and your houses will be made a rubbish heap.

6 "But if you declare the dream and its interpretation, you will receive from me gifts and a reward and great honor; therefore declare to me the dream and its interpretation."

7 They answered a second time and said, "Let the king tell the dream to his servants, and we will declare the interpretation."

8 The king answered and said, "I know for certain that you are bargaining for time, inasmuch as you have seen that the command from me is firm,

9 that if you do not make the dream known to me, there is only one decree for you. For you have agreed together to speak lying and corrupt words before me until the situation is changed; therefore tell me the dream, that I may know that you can declare to me its interpretation."

10 The Chaldeans answered the king and said, "There is not a man on earth who could declare the matter for the king, inasmuch as no great king or ruler has *ever* asked anything like this of any magician, conjurer or Chaldean.

11 "Moreover, the thing which the king demands is difficult, and there is no one else who could declare it to the king except gods, whose dwelling place is not with *mortal* flesh."

12 Because of this the king became indignant and very furious, and gave orders to destroy all the wise men of Babylon.

13 So the decree went forth that the wise men should be slain; and they looked for Daniel and his friends to kill *them.*

---

⁴Or, *soothsayer priests*   ⁵Or, *master astrologers*, and so throughout this context

---

2:2 *Chaldeans.* The term may be used for the Neo-Babylonians, who, under Nabopolassar, established an empire in Mesopotamia; or for astrologers, because Chaldeans were noted for astral studies. In this verse, however, Chal-deans refers to "wise men."

2:4 *O king.* These words begin the Aramaic section of Daniel that extends to 7:28.

Cross references (margin):

1:15 — Ex 23:25; Prov 10:22
1:16 — v. 12
1:17 — 1 Kin 3:12; James 1:5,17; Dan 2:19; 7:1; 8:1
1:18 — vv. 5,3,7
1:19 — Gen 41:46; 1 Kin 10:8; Jer 15:1
1:20 — Dan 2:27,28; 46,48; 2:2
1:21 — Dan 6:28; 10:1
2:1 — Gen 41:8; Dan 4:5; Esth 6:1; Dan 6:18
*2:2 — Gen 41:8; Ex 7:11; vv. 10,27; Dan 5:7
2:3 — Gen 40:8; 41:15; Dan 4:5
*2:4 — Is 36:11; 1 Kin 1:31; Dan 3:9; 5:10; 6:6,21
2:5 — Ezra 6:11; v. 12; Dan 3:29
2:6 — Dan 5:7,16,29
2:7 — v. 4
2:9 — Esth 4:11; Is 41:23
2:10 — v. 27
2:11 — Dan 5:11; Is 57:15
2:12 — v. 5
2:13 — Dan 1:19,20

2. Daniel interpreting Nebuchadnezzar's dream

a. His request for God to reveal the dream

14 Then Daniel replied with discretion and discernment to Arioch, the captain of the king's bodyguard, who had gone forth to slay the wise men of Babylon; **15** he answered and said to Arioch, the king's commander, "For what reason is the decree from the king *so* urgent?" Then Arioch informed Daniel about the matter.
16 So Daniel went in and requested of the king that he would give him time, in order that he might declare the interpretation to the king.
17 Then Daniel went to his house and informed his friends, Hananiah, Mishael and Azariah, about the matter,
18 in order that they might request compassion from the God of heaven concerning this mystery, so that Daniel and his friends might not be destroyed with the rest of the wise men of Babylon.
19 Then the mystery was revealed to Daniel in a night vision. Then Daniel blessed the God of heaven;

b. His hymn of thanksgiving

20 Daniel answered and said,
"Let the name of God be blessed forever and ever,
For wisdom and power belong to Him.
21 "And it is He who changes the times and the epochs;
He removes kings and establishes kings;
He gives wisdom to wise men,
And knowledge to men of understanding.
22 "It is He who reveals the profound and hidden things;
He knows what is in the darkness,
And the light dwells with Him.
23 "To Thee, O God of my fathers, I give thanks and praise,
For Thou hast given me wisdom and power;
Even now Thou hast made known to me what we requested of Thee,
For Thou hast made known to us the king's matter."

c. Before the king, Daniel glorifies God

24 Therefore, Daniel went in to Arioch, whom the king had appointed to destroy the wise men of Babylon; he went and spoke to him as follows: "Do not destroy the wise men of Babylon! Take me into the king's presence, and I will declare the interpretation to the king."
25 Then Arioch hurriedly brought Daniel into the king's presence and spoke to him as follows: "I have found a man among the exiles from Judah who can make the interpretation known to the king!"
26 The king answered and said to Daniel, whose name was Belteshazzar, "Are you able to make known to me the dream which I have seen and its interpretation?"
27 Daniel answered before the king and said, "As for the mystery about which the king has inquired, neither wise men, conjurers, magicians, *nor* diviners are able to declare *it* to the king.
28 "However, there is a God in heaven who reveals mysteries, and He has made known to King Nebuchadnezzar what will take place in the latter days. This was your dream and the visions in your mind *while* on your bed.
29 "As for you, O king, *while* on your bed your thoughts turned to what would take place in the future; and He who reveals mysteries has made known to you what will take place.
30 "But as for me, this mystery has not been revealed to me for any wisdom residing in me more than *in any other* living man, but for the purpose of making the interpretation known to the king, and that you may understand the thoughts of your mind.

d. Nebuchadnezzar's dream unfolded

31 "You, O king, were looking and behold, there was a single great statue; that

2:14
v. 24;
Jer 52:12,14
2:15
Dan 3:22;
vv. 1-12

2:16
Dan 1:19

2:18
Is 37:4;
Jer 33:3;
Dan 9:9
2:19
vv. 22,27-29;
Num 12:6;
Job 33:15,16

2:20
Ps 113:2;
Jer 32:19;
vv. 21-23
2:21
Esth 1:13;
Dan 7:25;
Job 12:18;
Ps 75:6,7;
James 1:5
2:22
Job 12:22;
Ps 25:14;
139:11,12;
Is 45:7;
Jer 23:24;
Dan 5:11,14;
James 1:17
2:23
Gen 31:42;
v. 21;
Dan 1:17;
vv. 18,29,30
2:24
vv. 12-14

2:25
Gen 41:14;
Dan 1:6;
5:13; 6:13

2:26
Dan 1:7;
vv. 3-7
2:27
vv. 2,10

2:28
Gen 40:8;
41:16; 49:1;
Is 2:2;
Mic 4:1;
Dan 4:5
2:29
vv. 22,28

2:30
Gen 41:16;
Is 45:3;
Ps 139:2

*__*2:31__
Dan 7:7;
Hab 1:7

2:31 Nebuchadnezzar's dream of the image is capable of very certain interpretation, except for those parts of it that have not yet been fulfilled. The four metals comprising the image stand for four empires: the Babylonian empire of
Nebuchadnezzar (2:37,38); the Medo-Persian empire (breast and arms of silver as per 2:32,39 and the leopard of 7:6); the Grecian empire under Alexander the Great and his successors (2:39); and the Roman empire, the mightiest of

statue, which was large and of extraordinary splendor, was standing in front of you, and its appearance was awesome.

2:32
vv. 38,39

32 "The head of that statue *was made* of fine gold, its breast and its arms of silver, its belly and its thighs of bronze,

2:33
vv. 40-43
2:34
Dan 8:25;
Zech 4:6;
Is 2:9; 60:12
2:35
Ps 1:4;
Hos 13:3;
Ps 37:10,36;
Is 2:2,3

33 its legs of iron, its feet partly of iron and partly of clay.

34 "You continued looking until a stone was cut out without hands, and it struck the statue on its feet of iron and clay, and crushed them.

35 "Then the iron, the clay, the bronze, the silver and the gold were crushed all at the same time, and became like chaff from the summer threshing floors; and the wind carried them away so that not a trace of them was found. But the stone that struck the statue became a great mountain and filled the whole earth.

e. The four earthly kingdoms

2:36
v. 24
2:37
Is 47:5;
Jer 27:6,7;
Ezek 26:7;
Ezra 1:2;
Ps 62:11
2:38
Jer 27:6;
Dan 4:21,22;
v. 32
2:39
v. 32
2:40
Dan 7:7,23
2:41
v. 33

36 "This *was* the dream; now we shall tell its interpretation before the king.

37 "You, O king, are the king of kings, to whom the God of heaven has given the kingdom, the power, the strength, and the glory;

38 and wherever the sons of men dwell, *or* the beasts of the field, or the birds of the sky, He has given *them* into your hand and has caused you to rule over them all. You are the head of gold.

39 "And after you there will arise another kingdom inferior to you, then another third kingdom of bronze, which will rule over all the earth.

40 "Then there will be a fourth kingdom as strong as iron; inasmuch as iron crushes and shatters all things, so, like iron that breaks in pieces, it will crush and break all these in pieces.

41 "And in that you saw the feet and toes, partly of potter's clay and partly of iron, it will be a divided kingdom; but it will have in it the toughness of iron, inasmuch as you saw the iron mixed with common clay.

42 "And *as* the toes of the feet *were* partly of iron and partly of pottery, *so* some of the kingdom will be strong and part of it will be brittle.

43 "And in that you saw the iron mixed with common clay, they will combine with one another in the seed of men; but they will not adhere to one another, even as iron does not combine with pottery.

f. God's eternal kingdom

*2:44
Ps 2:9;
Is 60:12;
1 Cor 15:24

44 "And in the days of those kings the God of heaven will set up a kingdom which will never be destroyed, and *that* kingdom will not be left for another people; it will crush and put an end to all these kingdoms, but it will itself endure forever.

*2:45
Is 28:16;
v. 35;
Dan 8:25;
v. 29;
Mal 1:11;
Gen 41:28,32

45 "Inasmuch as you saw that a stone was cut out of the mountain without hands and that it crushed the iron, the bronze, the clay, the silver, and the gold, the great God has made known to the king what will take place in the future; so the dream is true, and its interpretation is trustworthy."

3. Nebuchadnezzar glorifies God and promotes Daniel

2:46
Dan 8:17;
Acts 10:25;
14:13; 28:6;
Rev 19:10
2:47
Dan 11:36;
vv. 22,28
2:48
v. 6; Dan 4:9;
5:11

46 Then King Nebuchadnezzar fell on his face and did homage to Daniel, and gave orders to present to him an offering and fragrant incense.

47 The king answered Daniel and said, "Surely your God is a God of gods and a Lord of kings and a revealer of mysteries, since you have been able to reveal this mystery."

48 Then the king promoted Daniel and gave him many great gifts, and he made him ruler over the whole province of Babylon and chief prefect over all the wise men of Babylon.

49 And Daniel made request of the king, and he appointed Shadrach, Meshach

---

them all (2:40). The Roman empire was to be divided into two segments, Eastern and Western empires (the two legs); then ten toes are mentioned. It is concerning these that interpreters disagree. Some hold that the Roman empire represented by the ten toes will reappear at the close of the age in the form of a ten-nation confederacy under the leadership of the "Beast," or final world-dictator. This same school usually holds that the *stone* of 2:35 will strike a final blow at the end of the age. To still others it appears that a blow was struck by the death and resurrection of Christ and that in a sense His kingdom is filling the whole earth. But the final and consummate fulfillment of this prophetic Scripture came in Christ, for the fifth kingdom is said to eradicate the previous empires altogether, and to take their

place. In a spiritual form, Christ's kingdom is already present, and He reigns in the hearts of believers and in His church. The consummation of His kingdom awaits His second coming.
2:44 See note to 2:31. Some hold that this verse lends itself well to the millennial interpretation. Nothing in history has yet approximated the ten toes of the image. Therefore, this aspect of the prophecy appears to be definitely future. At that time the kingdom that now exists only in a spiritual sense and not in a literal one will become dominant in the world scene, attaining political supremacy over all the earth. The stone of v. 45 refers to Christ and His second advent.
2:45 *the great God.* The God of Israel.

and Abed-nego over the administration of the province of Babylon, while Daniel *was* at the king's court.

C. The golden image and the fiery furnace

1. *The abomination: the compulsory state religion*

3 Nebuchadnezzar the king made an image of gold, the height of which *was* sixty cubits *and* its width six cubits; he set it up on the plain of Dura in the province of Babylon.

2   Then Nebuchadnezzar the king sent *word* to assemble the satraps, the prefects and the governors, the counselors, the treasurers, the judges, the magistrates and all the rulers of the provinces to come to the dedication of the image that Nebuchadnezzar the king had set up.

3   Then the satraps, the prefects and the governors, the counselors, the treasurers, the judges, the magistrates and all the rulers of the provinces were assembled for the dedication of the image that Nebuchadnezzar the king had set up; and they stood before the image that Nebuchadnezzar had set up.

4   Then the herald loudly proclaimed: "To you the command is given, O peoples, nations and *men of every* language,

5   that at the moment you hear the sound of the horn, flute, lyre, trigon, psaltery, bagpipe, and all kinds of music, you are to fall down and worship the golden image that Nebuchadnezzar the king has set up.

6   "But whoever does not fall down and worship shall immediately be cast into the midst of a furnace of blazing fire."

7   Therefore at that time, when all the peoples heard the sound of the horn, flute, lyre, trigon, psaltery, bagpipe, and all kinds of music, all the peoples, nations and *men of every* language fell down *and* worshiped the golden image that Nebuchadnezzar the king had set up.

2. *The accusation and trial of Shadrach, Meshach, and Abednego*

8   For this reason at that time certain Chaldeans came forward and brought charges against the Jews.

9   They responded and said to Nebuchadnezzar the king: "O king, live forever!

10   "You yourself, O king, have made a decree that every man who hears the sound of the horn, flute, lyre, trigon, psaltery, and bagpipe, and all kinds of music, is to fall down and worship the golden image.

11   "But whoever does not fall down and worship shall be cast into the midst of a furnace of blazing fire.

12   "There are certain Jews whom you have appointed over the administration of the province of Babylon, *namely* Shadrach, Meshach and Abed-nego. These men, O king, have disregarded you; they do not serve your gods or worship the golden image which you have set up."

13   Then Nebuchadnezzar in rage and anger gave orders to bring Shadrach, Meshach and Abed-nego; then these men were brought before the king.

14   Nebuchadnezzar responded and said to them, "Is it true, Shadrach, Meshach and Abed-nego, that you do not serve my gods or worship the golden image that I have set up?

15   "Now if you are ready, at the moment you hear the sound of the horn, flute, lyre, trigon, psaltery, and bagpipe, and all kinds of music, to fall down and worship the image that I have made, *very well*. But if you will not worship, you will immediately be cast into the midst of a furnace of blazing fire; and what god is there who can deliver you out of my hands?"

16   Shadrach, Meshach and Abed-nego answered and said to the king, "O Nebuchadnezzar, we do not need to give you an answer concerning this matter.

17   "If it be *so*, our God whom we serve is able to deliver us from the furnace of blazing fire; and He will deliver us out of your hand, O king.

18   "But *even if He does* not, let it be known to you, O king, that we are not going to serve your gods or worship the golden image that you have set up."

3. *The sentence and its execution*

19   Then Nebuchadnezzar was filled with wrath, and his facial expression was

2:49	Dan 3:12; Esth 2:19,21; Dan 3:2
3:1	Is 46:6; Hab 2:19; v. 30; Dan 2:48
3:2	vv. 3,27
3:4	Is 40:9; 58:1; Rev 18:2; Dan 4:1; 6:25
3:5	vv. 7,10,15
3:6	vv. 11,15,21; Jer 29:22; Rev 14:11
3:7	vv. 4,5
3:8	Dan 4:7; 6:12
3:9	Dan 2:4; 5:10
3:10	vv. 4-6; Dan 6:2; vv. 5,7,15
3:12	Dan 2:49; 1:7; 6:13
3:13	Dan 2:12; v. 19
3:14	Is 46:1; Jer 50:2; v. 1
3:15	vv. 5,6; Ex 5:2; Is 36:18-20; Dan 2:47
3:16	v. 12
3:17	Ps 27:1,2; Is 26:3,4; Jer 15:20,21
3:18	v. 28
3:19	v. 13; Dan 5:6; v. 12

altered toward Shadrach, Meshach and Abed-nego. He answered by giving orders to heat the furnace seven times more than it was usually heated.

3:20
vv. 23-25

20   And he commanded certain valiant warriors who *were* in his army to tie up Shadrach, Meshach and Abed-nego, in order to cast *them* into the furnace of blazing fire.

3:21
v. 27

21   Then these men were tied up in their trousers, their coats, their caps and their *other* clothes, and were cast into the midst of the furnace of blazing fire.

3:22
Ex 12:33;
Dan 2:15

22   For this reason, because the king's command *was* urgent and the furnace had been made extremely hot, the flame of the fire slew those men who carried up Shadrach, Meshach and Abed-nego.

3:23
v. 21

23   But these three men, Shadrach, Meshach and Abed-nego, fell into the midst of the furnace of blazing fire *still* tied up.

4. *The miraculous deliverance and the fourth man*

24   Then Nebuchadnezzar the king was astounded and stood up in haste; he responded and said to his high officials, "Was it not three men we cast bound into the midst of the fire?" They answered and said to the king, "Certainly, O king."

*3:25
Is 43:2; v. 28

25   He answered and said, "Look! I see four men loosed *and* walking *about* in the midst of the fire without harm, and the appearance of the fourth is like a son of *the* gods!"

3:26
v. 17;
Dan 4:2

26   Then Nebuchadnezzar came near to the door of the furnace of blazing fire; he responded and said, "Shadrach, Meshach and Abed-nego, come out, you servants of the Most High God, and come here!" Then Shadrach, Meshach and Abed-nego came out of the midst of the fire.

3:27
v. 2; Is 43:2;
Heb 11:34;
v. 21

27   And the satraps, the prefects, the governors and the king's high officials gathered around *and* saw in regard to these men that the fire had no effect on the bodies of these men nor was the hair of their head singed, nor were their trousers damaged, nor had the smell of fire *even* come upon them.

5. *Nebuchadnezzar glorifies God*

3:28
vv. 15,25;
Acts 5:19;
12:7; Ps 34:7,
8; Jer 17:7;
v. 18

28   Nebuchadnezzar responded and said, "Blessed be the God of Shadrach, Meshach and Abed-nego, who has sent His angel and delivered His servants who put their trust in Him, violating the king's command, and yielded up their bodies so as not to serve or worship any god except their own God.

3:29
Dan 6:26;
v. 12;
Dan 2:5;
2:47; 6:27

29   "Therefore, I make a decree that any people, nation or tongue that speaks anything offensive against the God of Shadrach, Meshach and Abed-nego shall be torn limb from limb and their houses reduced to a rubbish heap, inasmuch as there is no other god who is able to deliver in this way."

3:30
Dan 2:49

30   Then the king caused Shadrach, Meshach and Abed-nego to prosper in the province of Babylon.

D. *Nebuchadnezzar's insanity*

1. *The frightening dream that could not be interpreted*

4:1
Dan 6:25

4 Nebuchadnezzar the king to all the peoples, nations, and *men of every* language that live in all the earth: "May your peace abound!

4:2
Dan 3:26

2   "It has seemed good to me to declare the signs and wonders which the Most High God has done for me.

4:3
Dan 6:27;
v. 34;
Dan 2:44;
6:26

3   "How great are His signs,
        And how mighty are His wonders!
        His kingdom is an everlasting kingdom,
        And His dominion is from generation to generation.

4:4
Is 47:7,8

4   "I, Nebuchadnezzar, was at ease in my house and flourishing in my palace.

4:5
Dan 2:28,29;
2:1

5   "I saw a dream and it made me fearful; and *these* fantasies *as I* lay on my bed and the visions in my mind kept alarming me.

4:6
Dan 2:2

6   "So I gave orders to bring into my presence all the wise men of Babylon, that they might make known to me the interpretation of the dream.

4:7
Dan 2:2

7   "Then the magicians, the conjurers, the Chaldeans, and the diviners came in,

---

3:25 This may well be a theophany: an appearance of Christ in the Old Testament. The fourth person in the fire appeared to Nebuchadnezzar to be *like a son of the gods*. Spiritually here is a lesson for all believers. Christ promises to go with His people and to succor and help them in the midst of temporal affliction suffered for His sake (Heb. 2:18). He has promised never to forsake His own (Matt. 28:20; Heb. 13:5).

and I related the dream to them; but they could not make its interpretation known to me.

2. The king narrates the dream to Daniel

8 "But finally Daniel came in before me, whose name is Belteshazzar according to the name of my god, and in whom is [6]a spirit of the holy gods; and I related the dream to him, *saying,*

9 'O Belteshazzar, chief of the magicians, since I know that a spirit of the holy gods is in you and no mystery baffles you, tell *me* the visions of my dream which I have seen, along with its interpretation.

10 'Now *these were* the visions in my mind *as I lay* on my bed: I was looking, and behold, *there was* a tree in the midst of the earth, and its height *was* great.

11 'The tree grew large and became strong,
And its height reached to the sky,
And it *was* visible to the end of the whole earth.

12 'Its foliage *was* beautiful and its fruit abundant,
And in it *was* food for all.
The beasts of the field found shade under it,
And the birds of the sky dwelt in its branches,
And all living creatures fed themselves from it.

13 'I was looking in the visions in my mind *as I lay* on my bed, and behold, an *angelic* watcher, a holy one, descended from heaven.

14 'He shouted out and spoke as follows:
"Chop down the tree and cut off its branches,
Strip off its foliage and scatter its fruit;
Let the beasts flee from under it,
And the birds from its branches.

15 "Yet leave the stump with its roots in the ground,
But with a band of iron and bronze *around it*
In the new grass of the field;
And let him be drenched with the dew of heaven,
And let him share with the beasts in the grass of the earth.

16 "Let his mind be changed from *that of* a man,
And let a beast's mind be given to him,
And let seven periods of time pass over him.

17 "This sentence is by the decree of the *angelic* watchers,
And the decision is a command of the holy ones,
In order that the living may know
That the Most High is ruler over the realm of mankind,
And bestows it on whom He wishes,
And sets over it the lowliest of men."

18 'This is the dream *which* I, King Nebuchadnezzar, have seen. Now you, Belteshazzar, tell *me* its interpretation, inasmuch as none of the wise men of my kingdom is able to make known to me the interpretation; but you are able, for a spirit of the holy gods is in you.'

3. Daniel's interpretation and warning

19 "Then Daniel, whose name is Belteshazzar, was appalled for a while as his thoughts alarmed him. The king responded and said, 'Belteshazzar, do not let the dream or its interpretation alarm you.' Belteshazzar answered and said, 'My lord, *if only* the dream applied to those who hate you, and its interpretation to your adversaries!

20 'The tree that you saw, which became large and grew strong, whose height reached to the sky and was visible to all the earth,

21 and whose foliage *was* beautiful and its fruit abundant, and in which *was* food for all, under which the beasts of the field dwelt and in whose branches the birds of the sky lodged—

22 it is you, O king; for you have become great and grown strong, and your

---

[6]Or possibly, *the Spirit of the holy God,* and so throughout this context

---

4:9 *a spirit of the holy gods.* Nebuchadnezzar was a polytheist. Thus he could recognize Daniel as a man whose God or gods had showed themselves strong.

Marginal references

4:8 — Dan 1:7; 2:26; Dan 5:11,14

*4:9 — Dan 2:48; 5:11; 2:47; 2:4,5

4:10 — vv. 5,20; Ezek 31:3-6

4:11 — vv. 20,22

4:12 — Ezek 31:6,7; Lam 4:20; Matt 13:32; Luke 13:19

4:13 — Dan 7:1; vv. 17,23; Dan 8:13; Zech 14:5

4:14 — Ezek 31:10-14; Matt 3:10; Ezek 31:12, 13

4:15 — Job 14:7-9; v. 32

4:16 — Dan 7:25; 11:13; 12:7

4:17 — Ps 9:16; vv. 2,25; Dan 5:18,19; Dan 11:21

4:18 — Gen 41:8,15; Dan 5:8,15; vv. 7-9

4:19 — Dan 7:15,28; 2 Sam 18:32; Jer 29:7

4:20 — vv. 10-12

4:21 — see v. 12

4:22 — 2 Sam 12:7; Dan 2:37,38; 5:18,19; Jer 27:6-8

majesty has become great and reached to the sky and your dominion to the end of the earth.

23 'And in that the king saw an *angelic* watcher, a holy one, descending from heaven and saying, "Chop down the tree and destroy it; yet leave the stump with its roots in the ground, but with a band of iron and bronze *around it* in the new grass of the field, and let him be drenched with the dew of heaven, and let him share with the beasts of the field until seven periods of time pass over him''';

24 this is the interpretation, O king, and this is the decree of the Most High, which has come upon my lord the king:

25 that you be driven away from mankind, and your dwelling place be with the beasts of the field, and you be given grass to eat like cattle and be drenched with the dew of heaven; and seven periods of time will pass over you, until you recognize that the Most High is ruler over the realm of mankind, and bestows it on whomever He wishes.

26 'And in that it was commanded to leave the stump with the roots of the tree, your kingdom will be assured to you after you recognize that *it is* Heaven *that* rules.

27 'Therefore, O king, may my advice be pleasing to you: break away now from your sins by *doing* righteousness, and from your iniquities by showing mercy to *the* poor, in case there may be a prolonging of your prosperity.'

4. The king's punishment for pride

28 "All *this* happened to Nebuchadnezzar the king.

29 "Twelve months later he was walking on the *roof of* the royal palace of Babylon.

30 "The king reflected and said, 'Is this not Babylon the great, which I myself have built as a royal residence by the might of my power and for the glory of my majesty?'

31 "While the word *was* in the king's mouth, a voice came from heaven, *saying,* 'King Nebuchadnezzar, to you it is declared: sovereignty has been removed from you,

32 and you will be driven away from mankind, and your dwelling place *will be* with the beasts of the field. You will be given grass to eat like cattle, and seven periods of time will pass over you, until you recognize that the Most High is ruler over the realm of mankind, and bestows it on whomever He wishes.'

33 "Immediately the word concerning Nebuchadnezzar was fulfilled; and he was driven away from mankind and began eating grass like cattle, and his body was drenched with the dew of heaven, until his hair had grown like eagles' *feathers* and his nails like birds' *claws*.

5. The king's repentance and recovery

34 "But at the end of that period I, Nebuchadnezzar, raised my eyes toward heaven, and my reason returned to me, and I blessed the Most High and praised and honored Him who lives forever;

For His dominion is an everlasting dominion,
And His kingdom *endures* from generation to generation.

35 "And all the inhabitants of the earth are accounted as nothing,
But He does according to His will in the host of heaven
And *among* the inhabitants of earth;
And no one can ward off His hand
Or say to Him, 'What hast Thou done?'

36 "At that time my reason returned to me. And my majesty and splendor were restored to me for the glory of my kingdom, and my counselors and my nobles began seeking me out; so I was reestablished in my sovereignty, and surpassing greatness was added to me.

37 "Now I Nebuchadnezzar praise, exalt, and honor the King of heaven, for all His works are true and His ways just, and He is able to humble those who walk in pride."

Marginal references:

4:23 vv. 13-17; Dan 5:21
4:24 vv. 17,2; Job 40:11,12; Ps 107:40
4:25 Dan 5:21; Ps 83:18; Jer 27:5
4:26 Matt 21:25; Luke 15:18
4:27 Is 55:6,7; Ezek 18:21, 22; Ps 41:1-3; 1 Kin 21:29
*4:28ff Zech 1:6
4:30 Hab 2:4; v. 25; Dan 5:20,21; Is 37:24,25
4:31 Dan 5:5; vv. 13,14,23
4:32 v. 25
4:33 Dan 5:21
*4:34 vv. 16,25,32, 36,2; Dan 5:18,21; 12:7; Rev 4:10; Luke 1:33
4:35 Is 40:15,17; Ps 135:6; Is 43:13; 45:9; Rom 9:20
4:36 vv. 34,30; Dan 2:31; v. 26
4:37 Ps 33:4,5; Ex 18:11; Dan 5:20

4:28ff. God was patient, waiting twelve months before executing His sentence on Nebuchadnezzar. Pride was punished as the king became a brute in the shape of a man.

4:34 *I blessed the Most High.* Nebuchadnezzar could worship Daniel's God, although still remaining loyal to his own gods—the gods of Babylon.

E. Belshazzar's feast and punishment for defying God

1. The profanation of the temple vessels

5 Belshazzar the king held a great feast for a thousand of his nobles, and he was drinking wine in the presence of the thousand.

2   When Belshazzar tasted the wine, he gave orders to bring the gold and silver vessels which Nebuchadnezzar his father had taken out of the temple which *was* in Jerusalem, in order that the king and his nobles, his wives, and his concubines might drink from them.

3   Then they brought the gold vessels that had been taken out of the temple, the house of God which *was* in Jerusalem; and the king and his nobles, his wives, and his concubines drank from them.

4   They drank the wine and praised the gods of gold and silver, of bronze, iron, wood, and stone.

2. The handwriting on the wall

5   Suddenly the fingers of a man's hand emerged and began writing opposite the lampstand on the plaster of the wall of the king's palace, and the king saw the back of the hand that did the writing.

6   Then the king's face grew pale, and his thoughts alarmed him; and his hip joints went slack, and his knees began knocking together.

7   The king called aloud to bring in the conjurers, the Chaldeans and the diviners. The king spoke and said to the wise men of Babylon, "Any man who can read this inscription and explain its interpretation to me will be clothed with purple, and *have* a necklace of gold around his neck, and have authority as third *ruler* in the kingdom."

8   Then all the king's wise men came in, but they could not read the inscription or make known its interpretation to the king.

9   Then King Belshazzar was greatly alarmed, his face grew *even* paler, and his nobles were perplexed.

3. The queen mother turns Belshazzar to Daniel

10   The queen entered the banquet hall because of the words of the king and his nobles; the queen spoke and said, "O king, live forever! Do not let your thoughts alarm you or your face be pale.

11   "There is a man in your kingdom in whom is a spirit of the holy gods; and in the days of your father, illumination, insight, and wisdom like the wisdom of the gods were found in him. And King Nebuchadnezzar, your father, your father the king, appointed him chief of the magicians, conjurers, Chaldeans, *and* diviners.

12   "*This was* because an extraordinary spirit, knowledge and insight, interpretation of dreams, explanation of enigmas, and solving of difficult problems were found in this Daniel, whom the king named Belteshazzar. Let Daniel now be summoned, and he will declare the interpretation."

13   Then Daniel was brought in before the king. The king spoke and said to Daniel, "Are you that Daniel who is one of the exiles from Judah, whom my father the king brought from Judah?

14   "Now I have heard about you that a spirit of the gods is in you, and that illumination, insight, and extraordinary wisdom have been found in you.

15   "Just now the wise men *and* the conjurers were brought in before me that they might read this inscription and make its interpretation known to me, but they could not declare the interpretation of the message.

Marginal references:
*5:1 Esth 1:3
5:2 Dan 1:2; Jer 52:19; v.23
5:4 v. 23; Rev 9:20
5:5 Dan 4:31; v. 24
5:6 Dan 4:5,19; Nah 2:10; Ezek 7:17; 21:7
5:7 Is 47:13; Dan 2:6; Ezek 16:11; Dan 6:2,3
5:8 Dan 2:10,27; 4:7
5:9 Is 21:2-4; Jer 6:24; v. 6
*5:10 Dan 2:4; 3:9
*5:11 Dan 2:47,48; 4:8,9,18; 1:17
5:12 Dan 6:3; 1:7
5:13 Dan 2:25; 6:13; 1:1,2
5:14 vv. 11,12

5:1 A few decades ago the historicity of Belshazzar was in doubt. Secular history seemed to give no confirmation of his actual existence. But in the light of cuneiform records more recently discovered, it has been admitted by all that he was a real person, who was a viceroy to his father Nabonidus. The historical reliability of Daniel relative to Belshazzar can no longer be seriously questioned. This still leaves unconfirmed the identity of Darius the Mede (who is stated by Daniel to have assumed the rule over Babylonia immediately after the overthrow of the Chaldeans), for whom there were no historical and archaeological evidences. But more recently strong arguments have been advanced that favor his identification with the Gubaru, whom Cyrus appointed as governor of Babylonia after the death of Ugbaru (who survived his brilliant capture of Babylon by only three weeks). Gubaru the Mede continued in office until 521 B.C., although Cyrus himself seems to have assumed the title of king of Babylon within two years after Gubaru's appointment.

5:10 *The queen.* Probably the queen mother, Nebuchadnezzar's widow, is meant.

5:11 *your father.* Actually Belshazzar was the son of Nabonidus, a usurper. It is possible that Nebuchadnezzar was Belshazzar's grandfather on his mother's side. The terms "father" and "son" do not bear the same exact connotation in Hebrew that they do in Western languages. Jesus was termed the "son of David," although many generations intervened between Him and David.

5:16
Gen 40:8;
vv.7,29

5:17
2 Kin 5:16

5:18
v. 21;
Dan 2:37,38;
4:17;
Jer 27:5-7
5:19
Dan 3:4;
2:12,13

5:20
Dan 4:30,37;
2 Kin 17:14;
2 Chr 36:13;
Jer 13:18
5:21
Dan 4:32-34;
4:16;
Ezek 17:24;
Dan 4:34,35

5:22
2 Chr 33:23;
36:12
5:23
Jer 50:29;
vv. 3,4;
Ps 115:5,6;
Hab 2:18,19;
Job 12:10;
31:4;
Jer 10:23

5:24
v. 5
*5:25

*5:26
Is 13:6,17;
Jer 27:7;
50:41-43
5:27
Job 31:6;
Ps 62:9

5:29
vv. 7,16

*5:30
Is 21:4-9;
Jer 51:31,39,
57
*5:31
Dan 6:1; 9:1

6:1
Esth 1:1;
Dan 5:31

16 "But I personally have heard about you, that you are able to give interpretations and solve difficult problems. Now if you are able to read the inscription and make its interpretation known to me, you will be clothed with purple and *wear a* necklace of gold around your neck, and you will have authority as the third *ruler* in the kingdom."

4. Daniel announces God's judgment

17 Then Daniel answered and said before the king, "Keep your gifts for yourself, or give your rewards to someone else; however, I will read the inscription to the king and make the interpretation known to him.

18 "O king, the Most High God granted sovereignty, grandeur, glory, and majesty to Nebuchadnezzar your father.

19 "And because of the grandeur which He bestowed on him, all the peoples, nations, and *men of every* language feared and trembled before him; whomever he wished he killed, and whomever he wished he spared alive; and whomever he wished he elevated, and whomever he wished he humbled.

20 "But when his heart was lifted up and his spirit became so proud that he behaved arrogantly, he was deposed from his royal throne, and *his* glory was taken away from him.

21 "He was also driven away from mankind, and his heart was made like *that of* beasts, and his dwelling place *was* with the wild donkeys. He was given grass to eat like cattle, and his body was drenched with the dew of heaven, until he recognized that the Most High God is ruler over the realm of mankind, and *that* He sets over it whomever He wishes.

22 "Yet you, his son, Belshazzar, have not humbled your heart, even though you knew all this,

23 but you have exalted yourself against the Lord of heaven; and they have brought the vessels of His house before you, and you and your nobles, your wives and your concubines have been drinking wine from them; and you have praised the gods of silver and gold, of bronze, iron, wood and stone, which do not see, hear or understand. But the God in whose hand are your life-breath and your ways, you have not glorified.

24 "Then the hand was sent from Him, and this inscription was written out.

25 "Now this is the inscription that was written out: 'MENĒ, MENĒ, TEKĒL, UPHARSIN.'

26 "This is the interpretation of the message: 'MENĒ'—God has numbered your kingdom and put an end to it.

27 " 'TEKĒL'—you you have been weighed on the scales and found deficient.

28 " 'PERĒS'—your kingdom has been divided and given over to the Medes and Persians."

5. Daniel rewarded and Belshazzar slain

29 Then Belshazzar gave orders, and they clothed Daniel with purple and *put a* necklace of gold around his neck, and issued a proclamation concerning him that he *now* had authority as the third *ruler* in the kingdom.

30 That same night Belshazzar the Chaldean king was slain.

31 So Darius the Mede received the kingdom at about the age of sixty-two.

F. Daniel preserved in the lions' den

1. The conspiracy against Daniel

6 It seemed good to Darius to appoint 120 satraps over the kingdom, that they should be in charge of the whole kingdom,

5:25 *MENE.* The Aramaic of the weight known as a *maneh.* The verb from which it is derived means "to number." *TEKEL.* The Aramaic of the weight known as a "shekel." The related verb means "to weigh." *upharsin.* The Aramaic plural of the half-maneh weight. The related verb means "to divide."
5:26 Daniel interpreted the names of the weights in terms of their related forms: "numbered, numbered, weighed, and divided." *PERES*, the singular of *upharsin,* also suggests the name Persians (Aramaic, *paras*).
5:30 At least two ancient historians (Xenophon and Herodotus) have recorded the fall of Babylon. The Euphra-

tes River ran through the city. Under the cover of night it was diverted from its normal channel by the Medo-Persian invaders. While the inhabitants of Babylon, imagining themselves secure behind their mighty walls, amused themselves in drunken carousal, two Babylonian deserters led the conquering hosts into the city by the dry bed of the river. The defending garrison found itself attacked from within the city itself and was helpless to withstand the invaders. Belshazzar himself was slain that same night as the Persian troops raged through the city.
5:31 *Darius the Mede,* probably the one who took the city in the name of Cyrus.

2   and over them three commissioners (of whom Daniel was one), that these satraps might be accountable to them, and that the king might not suffer loss.

3   Then this Daniel began distinguishing himself among the commissioners and satraps because he possessed an extraordinary spirit, and the king planned to appoint him over the entire kingdom.

4   Then the commissioners and satraps began trying to find a ground of accusation against Daniel in regard to government affairs; but they could find no ground of accusation or *evidence of* corruption, inasmuch as he was faithful, and no negligence or corruption was *to be* found in him.

5   Then these men said, "We shall not find any ground of accusation against this Daniel unless we find *it* against him with regard to the law of his God."

6   Then these commissioners and satraps came by agreement to the king and spoke to him as follows: "King Darius, live forever!

7   "All the commissioners of the kingdom, the prefects and the satraps, the high officials and the governors have consulted together that the king should establish a statute and enforce an injunction that anyone who makes a petition to any god or man besides you, O king, for thirty days, shall be cast into the lions' den.

8   "Now, O king, establish the injunction and sign the document so that it may not be changed, according to the law of the Medes and Persians, which may not be revoked."

9   Therefore King Darius signed the document, that is, the injunction.

2. Daniel detected, tried, and sentenced

10   Now when Daniel knew that the document was signed, he entered his house (now in his roof chamber he had windows open toward Jerusalem); and he continued kneeling on his knees three times a day, praying and giving thanks before his God, as he had been doing previously.

11   Then these men came by agreement and found Daniel making petition and supplication before his God.

12   Then they approached and spoke before the king about the king's injunction, "Did you not sign an injunction that any man who makes a petition to any god or man besides you, O king, for thirty days, is to be cast into the lions' den?" The king answered and said, "The statement is true, according to the law of the Medes and Persians, which may not be revoked."

13   Then they answered and spoke before the king, "Daniel, who is one of the exiles from Judah, pays no attention to you, O king, or to the injunction which you signed, but keeps making his petition three times a day."

14   Then, as soon as the king heard this statement, he was deeply distressed and set *his* mind on delivering Daniel; and even until sunset he kept exerting himself to rescue him.

15   Then these men came by agreement to the king and said to the king, "Recognize, O king, that it is a law of the Medes and Persians that no injunction or statute which the king establishes may be changed."

16   Then the king gave orders, and Daniel was brought in and cast into the lions' den. The king spoke and said to Daniel, "Your God whom you constantly serve will Himself deliver you."

17   And a stone was brought and laid over the mouth of the den; and the king sealed it with his own signet ring and with the signet rings of his nobles, so that nothing might be changed in regard to Daniel.

18   Then the king went off to his palace and spent the night fasting, and no entertainment was brought before him; and his sleep fled from him.

3. Daniel delivered and his foes punished

19   Then the king arose with the dawn, at the break of day, and went in haste to the lions' den.

6:2
Dan 2:48,49;
Ezra 4:22
6:3
Dan 1:20;
5:12,14;
Esth 10:3
6:4
Gen 43:18;
v.22

6:6
v. 21;
Neh 2:3;
Dan 2:4
6:7
Dan 3:2,27;
Ps 59:3;
Dan 3:6;
v. 16
6:8
vv. 12,15;
Esth 1:19;
8:8
6:9
Ps 118:9;
146:3

6:10
1 Kin 8:48,
49; Ps 95:6;
55:17;
1 Thess 5:17,
18
6:11
v.6

6:12
Dan 3:8;
Acts 16:19-21

6:13
Dan 1:6;
5:13;
Esth 3:8;
Dan 3:12;
Acts 5:29
6:14
Mark 6:26

6:15
Esth 8:8; v.8

6:16
Jer 38:5;
vv. 7,20;
Ps 37:39,40
6:17
Lam 3:55;
Matt 27:66

6:18
2 Sam 12:16,
17; Esth 6:1;
Dan 2:1

6:9 Some have objected that this episode is of legendary character for the reason that no king would ever have consented to such a decree as this, exalting himself to a position of exclusive worship even in preference to the gods themselves. But the historical situation prevailing at the beginning of the Persian rule over Babylon made it seem a clever stroke of statesmanship. Imposing such a regulation on the diverse nations of the empire, clinging with superstitious loyalty to their local gods, would have enforced the lesson

that Persia was the new sovereign over them all, and no appeal to the gods would avail to challenge the authority of the new conquerors. So even though the new measure was a foolish and iniquitous one, it might have commended itself to worldly wisdom on purely political grounds.
6:16 This event occurred when Daniel was an old man (probably over eighty). It reveals his unbroken devotion to God and his refusal to compromise conscience for temporal advantage.

6:20
vv. 26,27;
Jer 32:17;
Dan 3:17
6:21
Dan 2:4; v. 6
6:22
Acts 12:11;
2 Tim 4:17;
Heb 11:33;
1 Sam 24:10
6:23
vv. 14,18;
Dan 3:25,27;
Is 26:3;
Heb 11:33
6:24
2 Kin 14:6;
Ps 54:5;
Is 38:13

20   And when he had come near the den to Daniel, he cried out with a troubled voice. The king spoke and said to Daniel, "Daniel, servant of the living God, has your God, whom you constantly serve, been able to deliver you from the lions?"

21   Then Daniel spoke to the king, "O king, live forever!

22   "My God sent His angel and shut the lions' mouths, and they have not harmed me, inasmuch as I was found innocent before Him; and also toward you, O king, I have committed no crime."

23   Then the king was very pleased and gave orders for Daniel to be taken up out of the den. So Daniel was taken up out of the den, and no injury whatever was found on him, because he had trusted in his God.

24   The king then gave orders, and they brought those men who had maliciously accused Daniel, and they cast them, their children, and their wives into the lions' den; and they had not reached the bottom of the den before the lions overpowered them and crushed all their bones.

4. Darius acknowledges Daniel's God

6:25
Ezra 1:1,2;
Esth 3:12;
8:9; Dan 4:1;
1 Pet 1:2
6:26
Dan 3:29;
Ps 99:1;
Dan 4:34;
Ps 93:1,2;
Dan 4:3;
7:14,27
6:27
v. 22;
Dan 4:3
6:28
Ezra 1:1,2;
Dan 1:21;
10:1

25   Then Darius the king wrote to all the peoples, nations, and *men of every* language who were living in all the land: "May your peace abound!

26   "I make a decree that in all the dominion of my kingdom men are to fear and tremble before the God of Daniel;

For He is the living God and enduring forever,
And His kingdom is one which will not be destroyed,
And His dominion *will be* forever.

27   "He delivers and rescues and performs signs and wonders
In heaven and on earth,
Who has *also* delivered Daniel from the power of the lions."

28   So this Daniel enjoyed success in the reign of Darius and in the reign of Cyrus the Persian.

II. The final dream and visions (7:1–12:13)

A. The vision of the four beasts

1. The four beasts of Babylon, Persia, Greece, and Rome

7:1
Dan 5:1,22,
30; 1:17;
vv. 7,13,15;
Jer 36:4,32

7 In the first year of Belshazzar king of Babylon Daniel saw a dream and visions in his mind *as he lay* on his bed; then he wrote the dream down *and* related the *following* summary of it.

2   Daniel said, "I was looking in my vision by night, and behold, the four winds of heaven were stirring up the great sea.

7:3
v. 17;
Rev 13:1

3   "And four great beasts were coming up from the sea, different from one another.

*7:4
Jer 48:40;
Ezek 17:3;
Hab 1:8

4   "The first *was* like a lion and had *the* wings of an eagle. I kept looking until its wings were plucked, and it was lifted up from the ground and made to stand on two feet like a man; a human mind also was given to it.

*7:5
Dan 2:39

5   "And behold, another beast, a second one, resembling a bear. And it was raised up on one side, and three ribs *were* in its mouth between its teeth; and thus they said to it, 'Arise, devour much meat!'

7:6
v. 12

6   "After this I kept looking, and behold, another one, like a leopard, which had on its back four wings of a bird; the beast also had four heads, and dominion was given to it.

7:7
Rev 12:3;
13:1; 17:3

7   "After this I kept looking in the night visions, and behold, a fourth beast, dreadful and terrifying and extremely strong; and it had large iron teeth. It devoured and crushed, and trampled down the remainder with its feet; and it was different from all the beasts that were before it, and it had ten horns.

*7:8
vv. 20,21;
Rev 9:7;
vv. 11,25

8   "While I was contemplating the horns, behold, another horn, a little one, came up among them, and three of the first horns were pulled out by the roots

---

7:4 *lion . . . wings of an eagle.* Winged lions have been excavated at Nimrud and Babylon. Here they symbolize the Babylonian empire.
7:5 *another beast.* The vision comprised four beasts in all. In addition to the winged lion, Daniel describes a bear, a leopard, and an unnamed *dreadful and terrifying* beast (v. 7). These have been interpreted as meaning: Babylon, Media, Persia, and Greece; or Babylon, Medo-Persia, Greece, and

Rome.
7:8 *another horn, a little one.* Horns are symbolic of power. In Daniel ten are used of kings. Those who interpret the fourth kingdom as Greece identify the "little horn" with Antiochus Epiphanes, the Seleucid ruler who sought to suppress Jewish worship. Those who identify the fourth kingdom with Rome, interpret the "little horn" as a reference to a future antichrist.

before it; and behold, this horn possessed eyes like the eyes of a man, and a mouth uttering great *boasts*.

2. *The everlasting kingdom of the Son of man*

9   "I kept looking
      Until thrones were set up,
      And the Ancient of Days took *His* seat;
      His vesture *was* like white snow,
      And the hair of His head like pure wool.
      His throne *was* ablaze with flames,
      Its wheels *were* a burning fire.

10   "A river of fire was flowing
      And coming out from before Him;
      Thousands upon thousands were attending Him,
      And myriads upon myriads were standing before Him;
      The court sat,
      And the books were opened.

11   "Then I kept looking because of the sound of the boastful words which the horn was speaking; I kept looking until the beast was slain, and its body was destroyed and given to the burning fire.

12   "As for the rest of the beasts, their dominion was taken away, but an extension of life was granted to them for an appointed period of time.

13   "I kept looking in the night visions,
      And behold, with the clouds of heaven
      One like a Son of Man was coming,
      And He came up to the Ancient of Days
      And was presented before Him.

14   "And to Him was given dominion,
      Glory and a kingdom,
      That all the peoples, nations, and *men of every* language
      Might serve Him.
      His dominion is an everlasting dominion
      Which will not pass away;
      And His kingdom is one
      Which will not be destroyed.

3. *The dream explained*

15   "As for me, Daniel, my spirit was distressed within me, and the visions in my mind kept alarming me.

16   "I approached one of those who were standing by and began asking him the exact meaning of all this. So he told me and made known to me the interpretation of these things:

17   'These great beasts, which are four *in number*, are four kings *who* will arise from the earth.

18   'But the saints of the Highest One will receive the kingdom and possess the kingdom forever, for all ages to come.'

19   "Then I desired to know the exact meaning of the fourth beast, which was different from all the others, exceedingly dreadful, with its teeth of iron and its claws of bronze, *and which* devoured, crushed, and trampled down the remainder with its feet,

20   and *the meaning* of the ten horns that *were* on its head, and the other *horn* which came up, and before which three *of them* fell, namely, that horn which had eyes and a mouth uttering great *boasts*, and which was larger in appearance than its associates.

21   "I kept looking, and that horn was waging war with the saints and overpowering them

Cross-references (margin)

*7:9
Mark 9:3;
Rev 1:14;
Ezek 1:13,26;
10:2,6

7:10
Ps 50:3; 97:3;
Is 30:33;
Rev 5:11;
20:12

7:11
vv. 7,8;
Rev 19:20

7:12
vv. 3-6

*7:13
Ezek 1:26;
Matt 24:30;
26:64;
Mark 13:26;
Luke 21:27;
Rev 1:7,13

7:14
Ps 2:6-8;
1 Cor 15:27;
Eph 1:22;
Phil 2:9-11;
Ps 72:11;
102:22;
Dan 2:44;
Mic 4:7;
Heb 12:28

7:15
vv. 1,28

7:16
Rev 5:5;
7:13,14;
Dan 8:16,17

7:17
v. 3

7:18
Is 60:12-14;
Rev 2:26;
20:4
7:19
vv. 7,8

7:21
Rev 13:7

7:9 Verses 9–14 describe future events. The *Son of Man* is none other than the Lord Jesus Christ, whose kingdom is to be eternal and before whom the nations of the earth shall bow. One should not, however, expect precise details in this general statement about the final outcome of world history.
7:13 *a Son of Man*. This is the Hebrew idiom for a human being. The one who appeared in Daniel's vision was human, in contrast to the beasts that represented the nations. The term "Son of Man" was later used more generally as a title of the Messiah, and is so used in the New Testament. The coming of Christ has been repeatedly foretold in the Scriptures of the Old Testament prophets. Jesus Christ Himself spoke of His second coming (Matt. 25:31; John 14:3). So did the apostles (Acts 2:30; 1 Tim. 6:14), and the angels who relayed God's message to the disciples (Acts 1:10,11).

7:22
vv. 9,13;
1 Cor 6:2,3;
v. 18

7:23
vv. 7,19

*7:24
vv. 7,8;
Rev 17:12

7:25
Is 37:23;
Dan 8:24,25;
Rev 13:5;
17:6; 18:24;
Dan 2:21;
12:7;
Rev 12:14
7:26
vv. 10,22
7:27
vv. 14,18,22;
Luke 1:33;
John 12:34;
Rev 11:15;
Ps 2:6-12;
Is 60:12
7:28
v. 15;
Dan 8:27;
Luke 2:19

8:1
Dan 7:1,15,
28
8:2
Dan 7:2,15;
Esth 1:2;
Ezek 32:24;
v. 16
*8:3
Dan 10:5;
v. 20
8:4
v. 7

*8:5
v. 21

8:6
v. 3

8:7
Dan 11:11;
7:7

8:8
2 Chr 26:16;
Dan 5:20;
v. 22;
Dan 7:2;
Rev 7:1

*8:9
v. 23;
Dan 11:16,41

22 until the Ancient of Days came, and judgment was passed in favor of the saints of the Highest One, and the time arrived when the saints took possession of the kingdom.

23 "Thus he said: 'The fourth beast will be a fourth kingdom on the earth, which will be different from all the *other* kingdoms, and it will devour the whole earth and tread it down and crush it.

24 'As for the ten horns, out of this kingdom ten kings will arise; and another will arise after them, and he will be different from the previous ones and will subdue three kings.

25 'And he will speak out against the Most High and wear down the saints of the Highest One, and he will intend to make alterations in times and in law; and they will be given into his hand for a time, times, and half a time.

26 'But the court will sit *for judgment,* and his dominion will be taken away, annihilated and destroyed forever.

27 'Then the sovereignty, the dominion, and the greatness of *all* the kingdoms under the whole heaven will be given to the people of the saints of the Highest One; His kingdom *will be* an everlasting kingdom, and all the dominions will serve and obey Him.'

28 "At this point the revelation ended. As for me, Daniel, my thoughts were greatly alarming me and my face grew pale, but I kept the matter to myself."

B. The vision of the ram and the male goat

1. The ram of Medo-Persia and the male goat of Greece

8 In the third year of the reign of Belshazzar the king a vision appeared to me, Daniel, subsequent to the one which appeared to me previously.

2 And I looked in the vision, and it came about while I was looking, that I was in the citadel of Susa, which is in the province of Elam; and I looked in the vision, and I myself was beside the Ulai Canal.

3 Then I lifted my gaze and looked, and behold, a ram which had two horns was standing in front of the canal. Now the two horns *were* long, but one *was* longer than the other, with the longer one coming up last.

4 I saw the ram butting westward, northward, and southward, and no *other* beasts could stand before him, nor was there anyone to rescue from his power; but he did as he pleased and magnified *himself.*

5 While I was observing, behold, a male goat was coming from the west over the surface of the whole earth without touching the ground; and the goat *had* a conspicuous horn between his eyes.

6 And he came up to the ram that had the two horns, which I had seen standing in front of the canal, and rushed at him in his mighty wrath.

7 And I saw him come beside the ram, and he was enraged at him; and he struck the ram and shattered his two horns, and the ram had no strength to withstand him. So he hurled him to the ground and trampled on him, and there was none to rescue the ram from his power.

8 Then the male goat magnified *himself* exceedingly. But as soon as he was mighty, the large horn was broken; and in its place there came up four conspicuous *horns* toward the four winds of heaven.

2. The little horn

9 And out of one of them came forth a rather small horn which grew exceedingly great toward the south, toward the east, and toward the [7]Beautiful *Land.*

[7]I.e., Palestine

7:24 The ten horns (representing ten kings or kingdoms) parallel the earlier vision of the ten toes (ch. 2). Verse 27 indicates that the king who shall emerge as ruler over all will ultimately be defeated by Christ's kingdom. The little horn here, who defeats three of the ten kings, is not to be confused with the little horn of 8:9, for he is said to emerge from the fourth kingdom (the latter-day Roman empire), whereas the little horn of chapter 8 comes from the third kingdom (the Greek empire established by Alexander the Great).

8:3 *two horns,* representing Media and Persia (cf. 8:20).

8:5 *male goat,* i.e., Greece (cf. 8:21). *a conspicuous horn,* Alexander the Great (cf. 8:21).

8:9 In chapter 8 Daniel returns to the ram and the male-goat visions that represent the second and the third of the four great kingdoms. They have been spoken of as the bronze and silver kingdoms of chapter 2 and the bear and leopard kingdoms of 7:5,6. The two kingdoms here in view are those of Medo-Persia and Greece. The little horn here is identified by some with Antiochus Epiphanes (175–164 B.C.), who in 168 B.C. profaned the Jewish temple and sought to stamp out the Jewish religion altogether. They also hold that Antiochus was a type of the final world-dictator (the "beast" of Revelation) who is yet to come. For this reason both Antiochus (the type) and the "beast" (the antitype) are called by the same name: the little horn.

10   And it grew up to the host of heaven and caused some of the host and some of the stars to fall to the earth, and it trampled them down.

11   It even magnified *itself* to be equal with the Commander of the host; and it removed the regular sacrifice from Him, and the place of His sanctuary was thrown down.

12   And on account of transgression the host will be given over *to the horn* along with the regular sacrifice; and it will fling truth to the ground and perform *its will* and prosper.

13   Then I heard a holy one speaking, and another holy one said to that particular one who was speaking, "How long will the vision *about* the regular sacrifice apply, while the transgression causes horror, so as to allow both the holy place and the host to be trampled?"

14   And he said to me, "For 2,300 evenings *and* mornings; then the holy place will be properly restored."

3. Gabriel's explanation of the vision

15   And it came about when I, Daniel, had seen the vision, that I sought to understand it; and behold, standing before me was one who looked like a man.

16   And I heard the voice of a man between *the banks of* Ulai, and he called out and said, "Gabriel, give this *man* an understanding of the vision."

17   So he came near to where I was standing, and when he came I was frightened and fell on my face; but he said to me, "Son of man, understand that the vision pertains to the time of the end."

18   Now while he was talking with me, I sank into a deep sleep with my face to the ground; but he touched me and made me stand upright.

19   And he said, "Behold, I am going to let you know what will occur at the final period of the indignation, for *it* pertains to the appointed time of the end.

20   "The ram which you saw with the two horns represents the kings of Media and Persia.

21   "And the shaggy goat *represents* the kingdom of Greece, and the large horn that is between his eyes is the first king.

22   "And the broken *horn* and the four *horns that* arose in its place *represent* four kingdoms *which* will arise from *his* nation, although not with his power.

23   "And in the latter period of their rule,
        When the transgressors have run *their course,*
        A king will arise
        Insolent and skilled in intrigue.

24   "And his power will be mighty, but not by his *own* power,
        And he will destroy to an extraordinary degree
        And prosper and perform *his will;*
        He will destroy mighty men and the holy people.

25   "And through his shrewdness
        He will cause deceit to succeed by his influence;
        And he will magnify *himself* in his heart,
        And he will destroy many while *they are* at ease.
        He will even oppose the Prince of princes,
        But he will be broken without human agency.

26   "And the vision of the evenings and mornings
        Which has been told is true;
        But keep the vision secret,
        For *it* pertains to many days *in the future.*"

27   Then I, Daniel, was exhausted and sick for days. Then I got up *again* and carried on the king's business; but I was astounded at the vision, and there was none to explain *it.*

C. The vision of the seventy weeks

1. Daniel's persistent, promise-claiming prayer

9 In the first year of Darius the son of Ahasuerus, of Median descent, who was made king over the kingdom of the Chaldeans—

2   in the first year of his reign I, Daniel, observed in the books the number of

---

8:10
Rev 12:4

*8:11
Dan 11:36, 37; Josh 5:14; Dan 11:31; 12:11; Ezek 46:13, 14

8:13
Dan 4:13,23; 12:6,8; Rev 11:2

8:15
v. 1;
Dan 7:13
8:16
Dan 9:21;
Luke 1:19,26
8:17
Ezek 1:28;
Rev 1:17

8:18
Dan 10:9,16, 18; Ezek 2:2
8:19
Hab 2:3

8:21
v. 5;
Dan 10:20
8:22
v. 8

8:24
Dan 11:36

8:25
Dan 11:21;
v. 11;
Dan 2:34,45

8:26
Dan 10:1;
12:4,9; 10:14

8:27
Dan 7:28;
Hab 3:16

9:1
Dan 5:31;
11:1
*9:2
2 Chr 36:21;

8:11 *the Commander,* God Himself.
8:14 *evenings and mornings,* i.e., successive evenings and

mornings, 1,150 days.
9:2 *the number of the years* (cf. Jer 25:11). Daniel realized

Jer 29:10;
Zech 7:5

9:3
Neh 1:4;
Jer 29:12;
James 4:8
9:4
Deut 7:21;
Neh 9:32;
Deut 7:9
9:5
Ps 106:6;
Lam 1:18,20;
v. 11
9:6
2 Chr 36:15,
16; v. 8
9:7
Jer 23:6;
33:16;
Amos 9:9

9:8
vv. 6,5

9:9
Neh 9:17;
Ps 130:4
9:10
2 Kin 17:13-15;
18:12
9:11
Is 1:4-6;
Jer 8:5,10;
Deut 27:15

9:12
Is 44:26;
Zech 1:6;
Ezek 5:9

9:13
Is 9:13;
Jer 2:30

9:14
Jer 31:28;
44:27; vv. 7,
10

9:15
Ex 6:1,6;
Jer 32:21;
Neh 9:10;
Jer 32:20
9:16
1 Sam 12:7;
Ps 31:1;
Zech 8:3

9:17
Num 6:25;
Lam 5:18
9:18
Is 37:17;
Jer 25:29;
36:7

9:19
Ps 44:23;
74:10,11

9:20
v. 3; Is 58:9;
6:5
*9:21
Dan 8:16;
Is 6:2;
Dan 8:18;
10:10,16,18
9:23
Dan 10:12;
Luke 1:28;
Matt 24:15

the years which was *revealed as* the word of the LORD to Jeremiah the prophet for the completion of the desolations of Jerusalem, *namely*, seventy years.

3   So I gave my attention to the Lord God to seek *Him by* prayer and supplications, with fasting, sackcloth, and ashes.

4   And I prayed to the LORD my God and confessed and said, "Alas, O Lord, the great and awesome God, who keeps His covenant and lovingkindness for those who love Him and keep His commandments,

5   we have sinned, committed iniquity, acted wickedly, and rebelled, even turning aside from Thy commandments and ordinances.

6   "Moreover, we have not listened to Thy servants the prophets, who spoke in Thy name to our kings, our princes, our fathers, and all the people of the land.

7   "Righteousness belongs to Thee, O Lord, but to us open shame, as it is this day—to the men of Judah, the inhabitants of Jerusalem, and all Israel, those who are nearby and those who are far away in all the countries to which Thou hast driven them, because of their unfaithful deeds which they have committed against Thee.

8   "Open shame belongs to us, O Lord, to our kings, our princes, and our fathers, because we have sinned against Thee.

9   "To the Lord our God belong compassion and forgiveness, for we have rebelled against Him;

10   nor have we obeyed the voice of the LORD our God, to walk in His teachings which He set before us through His servants the prophets.

11   "Indeed all Israel has transgressed Thy law and turned aside, not obeying Thy voice; so the curse has been poured out on us, along with the oath which is written in the law of Moses the servant of God, for we have sinned against Him.

12   "Thus He has confirmed His words which He had spoken against us and against our rulers who ruled us, to bring on us great calamity; for under the whole heaven there has not been done *anything* like what was done to Jerusalem.

13   "As it is written in the law of Moses, all this calamity has come on us; yet we have not sought the favor of the LORD our God by turning from our iniquity and giving attention to Thy truth.

14   "Therefore, the LORD has kept the calamity in store and brought it on us; for the LORD our God is righteous with respect to all His deeds which He has done, but we have not obeyed His voice.

15   "And now, O Lord our God, who hast brought Thy people out of the land of Egypt with a mighty hand and hast made a name for Thyself, as it is this day—we have sinned, we have been wicked.

16   "O Lord, in accordance with all Thy righteous acts, let now Thine anger and Thy wrath turn away from Thy city Jerusalem, Thy holy mountain; for because of our sins and the iniquities of our fathers, Jerusalem and Thy people *have become* a reproach to all those around us.

17   "So now, our God, listen to the prayer of Thy servant and to his supplications, and for Thy sake, O Lord, let Thy face shine on Thy desolate sanctuary.

18   "O my God, incline Thine ear and hear! Open Thine eyes and see our desolations and the city which is called by Thy name; for we are not presenting our supplications before Thee on account of any merits of our own, but on account of Thy great compassion.

19   "O Lord, hear! O Lord, forgive! O Lord, listen and take action! For Thine own sake, O my God, do not delay, because Thy city and Thy people are called by Thy name."

2. Gabriel's appearance and the interpretation

20   Now while I was speaking and praying, and confessing my sin and the sin of my people Israel, and presenting my supplication before the LORD my God in behalf of the holy mountain of my God,

21   while I was still speaking in prayer, then the man Gabriel, whom I had seen in the vision previously, came to me in *my* extreme weariness about the time of the evening offering.

22   And he gave *me* instruction and talked with me, and said, "O Daniel, I have now come forth to give you insight with understanding.

23   "At the beginning of your supplications the command was issued, and I have

---

(perceived in the books) that the seventy years of exile and   **9:21** *the man Gabriel.* Gabriel appeared in human form.
devastation must be nearing an end.

come to tell *you*, for you are highly esteemed; so give heed to the message and gain understanding of the vision.

24 "Seventy weeks have been decreed for your people and your holy city, to finish the transgression, to make an end of sin, to make atonement for iniquity, to bring in everlasting righteousness, to seal up vision and prophecy, and to anoint the most holy *place*.

25 "So you are to know and discern *that* from the issuing of a decree to restore and rebuild Jerusalem until Messiah the Prince *there will be* seven weeks and sixty-two weeks; it will be built again, with plaza and moat, even in times of distress.

26 "Then after the sixty-two weeks the Messiah will be cut off and have nothing, and the people of the prince who is to come will destroy the city and the sanctuary. And its end *will come* with a flood; even to the end there will be war; desolations are determined.

27 "And he will make a firm covenant with the many for one week, but in the middle of the week he will put a stop to sacrifice and grain offering; and on the wing of abominations *will come* one who makes desolate, even until a complete destruction, one that is decreed, is poured out on the one who makes desolate."

*9:24
Is 55:10;
Rom 5:10;
Acts 3:14

*9:25
Ezra 4:24;
Neh 2:1-8;
3:1;
John 1:41;
4:25; Is 9:6

*9:26
Is 53:8;
Mark 9:12;
Luke 19:43,
44; Nah 1:8

*9:27
Dan 11:31;
Matt 24:15;
Luke 21:20;
Is 10:23

D. *The vision of the last days*

1. *Daniel's vision of an angel*

10 In the third year of Cyrus king of Persia a message was revealed to Daniel, who was named Belteshazzar; and the message was true and *one of* great conflict, but he understood the message and had an understanding of the vision.

10:1
Dan 6:28;
1:7; 8:26;
2:21

2 In those days I, Daniel, had been mourning for three entire weeks.

10:2
Ezra 9:4,5;
Neh 1:4

3 I did not eat any tasty food, nor did meat or wine enter my mouth, nor did I use any ointment at all, until the entire three weeks were completed.

4 And on the twenty-fourth day of the first month, while I was by the bank of the great river, that is, the Tigris,

10:4
Dan 8:2;
Gen 2:14

9:24 The prophecy of the seventy weeks has been variously interpreted. One conclusion seems self-evident. Each *week* or "heptad" must be a period of seven years or a total of 490 years. Daniel divides this period into three parts: the first has seven weeks or forty-nine years, the second has sixty-two weeks or 434 years, and the third has one week or seven years. Some interpreters hold that the entire seventy weeks were to follow one upon another without interruption. This interpretation, however, encounters the difficulty that, according to the received Hebrew text of v. 25, there are to elapse only sixty-nine weeks, after which time (according to v. 26) the Anointed One is to be cut off. (Moreover, a full 490 years can hardly be made out between any of the eligible decrees—538, 457, and 445 B.C.—and the cutting off of the Messiah.) Others hold that only sixty-nine weeks were fulfilled by the time the Anointed One was cut off at Calvary, and that the last week belongs to the period of the great tribulation. The early church fathers held this view. Some of those who hold to the latter view interpret the New Testament church age as an unrevealed mystery during Old Testament times, constituting a "parenthesis" until the beginning of the seventieth week. (Others who hold to the deferment of the seventieth week acknowledge that the New Testament church was quite frequently alluded to in the Old Testament.) The *terminus a quo* for the commencement of these sixty-nine weeks of years is stated to be *from the issuing of a decree to restore and rebuild Jerusalem* (v. 25). This may refer to the divine decree, or one of three historical edicts: (1) the decree of King Cyrus in 538 B.C. (Ezra 1:1-4); (2) the order of Artaxerxes to Ezra in 457 B.C. (which apparently involved authority to erect the walls of Jerusalem, cf. Ezra 7:6,7; 9:9); and (3) the order to Nehemiah in 445 B.C. to carry through the rebuilding of the walls (which Ezra had not been able to accomplish). Of these choices, (1) must be ruled out as coming nowhere near to the time of Christ's ministry; and (3) comes out too late, unless lunar years are used for the computation. Only (2) comes out right according to regular solar years, for it yields the result as A.D. 27, or the commencement of Christ's ministry. Ezra and Nehemiah render an account of the rebuilding of Jerusalem in forty-nine years and troublous times. Then follow the sixty-two weeks, after which Mes-

siah was cut off for sin. One's view of the remaining week is colored by his whole scheme of prophetic interpretation. Still others hold that the numbers are used symbolically, as in 12:11,12, and that the passage "covers the whole period of time from Daniel to the consummation of all things," Herbert C. Leupold, *Exposition of Daniel* (Augsburg Publishing House), p. 405.
9:25 *and sixty-two weeks*. The time of rebuilding the city and land subsequent to the return from exile.
9:26 *the Messiah will be cut off*. Some scholars identify the "Messiah" with Onias III, the high priest who was deposed by Antiochus Epiphanes in 175 B.C. The KJV as well as the NAS identify the "Messiah" with Jesus, the Christ (anointed). Historically, the Christian church has tended to interpret the passage Messianically. *destroy the city*. If the reference is to Onias III, the destruction is that described in 1 Maccabees 1:31,32,38; 3:45. If interpreted Messianically, the reference is to the destruction of Jerusalem, A.D. 70.
9:27 *will put a stop to sacrifice and grain offering*. Antiochus outlawed the rites of the Jewish faith. Similarly, in A.D. 70, the temple was destroyed and sacrifices ended. *one that is decreed*. The prophet knows that God holds the ultimate key to history, and even the *one who makes desolate* must stand before God. The phrase "abomination of desolation" is used variantly three times in Daniel (9:27; 11:31; 12:11) and once in Matthew (24:15). This significant expression probably has three prophetic references: (1) in 11:31 it refers to Antiochus Epiphanes, whose troops desecrated the temple in 168 B.C. and suspended the daily burnt offering and other services. He erected an idol-altar in place of the altar of burnt offering (apparently a statue of Zeus Olympus) and entered into the Holy of Holies. (2) In 9:27 and 12:11, and Mark 13:14 it seems to refer to a desecration that shall take place in the end, during the period of the great tribulation. And (3) in Matt. 24:15 (cf. Luke 21:19–24) it probably refers also to the destruction of Jerusalem in A.D. 70 by Titus, whose legions triumphantly brought their eagle-topped army standards into holy precincts. Others hold that the ninth chapter gives us "a rather comprehensive description of the New Testament Antichrist" (Leupold, *Exposition of Daniel*, p. 437).
10:3 Check Dan. 1:8 in this connection.

5   I lifted my eyes and looked, and behold, there was a certain man dressed in linen, whose waist was girded with *a belt of* pure gold of Uphaz.

6   His body also was like beryl, his face had the appearance of lightning, his eyes were like flaming torches, his arms and feet like the gleam of polished bronze, and the sound of his words like the sound of a tumult.

7   Now I, Daniel, alone saw the vision, while the men who were with me did not see the vision; nevertheless, a great dread fell on them, and they ran away to hide themselves.

8   So I was left alone and saw this great vision; yet no strength was left in me, for my natural color turned to a deathly pallor, and I retained no strength.

9   But I heard the sound of his words; and as soon as I heard the sound of his words, I fell into a deep sleep on my face, with my face to the ground.

2. Daniel strengthened, encouraged, and promised further revelations

10   Then behold, a hand touched me and set me trembling on my hands and knees.

11   And he said to me, "O Daniel, man of high esteem, understand the words that I am about to tell you and stand upright, for I have now been sent to you." And when he had spoken this word to me, I stood up trembling.

12   Then he said to me, "Do not be afraid, Daniel, for from the first day that you set your heart on understanding *this* and on humbling yourself before your God, your words were heard, and I have come in response to your words.

13   "But the prince of the kingdom of Persia was withstanding me for twenty-one days; then behold, Michael, one of the chief princes, came to help me, for I had been left there with the kings of Persia.

14   "Now I have come to give you an understanding of what will happen to your people in the latter days, for the vision pertains to the days yet *future*."

15   And when he had spoken to me according to these words, I turned my face toward the ground and became speechless.

16   And behold, one who resembled a human being was touching my lips; then I opened my mouth and spoke, and said to him who was standing before me, "O my lord, as a result of the vision anguish has come upon me, and I have retained no strength.

17   "For how can such a servant of my lord talk with such as my lord? As for me, there remains just now no strength in me, nor has any breath been left in me."

18   Then *this* one with human appearance touched me again and strengthened me.

19   And he said, "O man of high esteem, do not be afraid. Peace be with you; take courage and be courageous!" Now as soon as he spoke to me, I received strength and said, "May my lord speak, for you have strengthened me."

20   Then he said, "Do you understand why I came to you? But I shall now return to fight against the prince of Persia; so I am going forth, and behold, the prince of Greece is about to come.

21   "However, I will tell you what is inscribed in the writing of truth. Yet there is no one who stands firmly with me against these *forces* except Michael your prince.

3. The interpretation of Daniel's vision

a. From the Persian Empire to the death of Alexander (323 B.C.)

11 "And in the first year of Darius the Mede, I arose to be an encouragement and a protection for him.

10:13 *the prince of the kingdom of Persia.* Each nation is thought to have a guardian angel. *Michael,* regarded as the guardian of Israel, came to Daniel's aid.

10:20 *the prince of Greece.* After his difficulties with Persia (*I shall now return to fight against the prince of Persia*), Israel faced even greater problems with the Greeks as well as with their successors.

11:1ff. This chapter points forward to specific rulers of the Near East during the last few centuries before Christ. The following outline will help to understand the historical fulfillment of this prophecy: (1) the four kings of v. 2 (although this cannot be stated dogmatically) were the Persian rulers Cyrus, Cambyses, Darius Hystaspes, and Xerxes (Ahasuerus, who attempted the conquest of Greece in 480

B.C.); (2) the mighty king of v. 4 was Alexander the Great, who conquered the Persian empire, ca. 330 B.C.; (3) the division of his kingdom after his death into four parts included Greece, the Asiatic Near East, Egypt, and Asia Minor; (4) the king of the south in v. 5 was Ptolemy I of Egypt (323–285 B.C.) and *one of his princes,* his son Ptolemy II (who reigned during the development of the Septuagint, and who added various islands and seaport cities to the Egyptian realm); (5) in v. 6 the daughter of Ptolemy II (Berenice) was married to Antiochus II of the Asiatic or "Syrian" empire; but she and her husband were both murdered by his divorced wife; (6) Berenice's brother, Ptolemy III, avenged her death by invading and pillaging the whole realm of Syria (vv. 7–9); (7) the two sons of v. 10 were

2 "And now I will tell you the truth. Behold, three more kings are going to arise in Persia. Then a fourth will gain far more riches than all *of them;* as soon as he becomes strong through his riches, he will arouse the whole *empire* against the realm of Greece.

3 "And a mighty king will arise, and he will rule with great authority and do as he pleases.

4 "But as soon as he has arisen, his kingdom will be broken up and parceled out toward the four points of the compass, though not to his *own* descendants, nor according to his authority which he wielded; for his sovereignty will be uprooted and *given* to others besides them.

b. Wars between the Ptolemaic and Seleucid Empires

5 "Then the king of the South will grow strong, along with *one* of his princes who will gain ascendancy over him and obtain dominion; his domain *will be* a great dominion *indeed*.

6 "And after some years they will form an alliance, and the daughter of the king of the South will come to the king of the North to carry out a peaceful arrangement. But she will not retain her position of power, nor will he remain with his power, but she will be given up, along with those who brought her in, and the one who sired her, as well as he who supported her in *those* times.

7 "But one of the descendants of her line will arise in his place, and he will come against *their* army and enter the fortress of the king of the North, and he will deal with them and display *great* strength.

8 "And also their gods with their metal images *and* their precious vessels of silver and gold he will take into captivity to Egypt, and he on his part will refrain from *attacking* the king of the North for *some* years.

9 "Then the latter will enter the realm of the king of the South, but will return to his *own* land.

10 "And his sons will mobilize and assemble a multitude of great forces; and one of them will keep on coming and overflow and pass through, that he may again wage war up to his *very* fortress.

11 "And the king of the South will be enraged and go forth and fight with the king of the North. Then the latter will raise a great multitude, but *that* multitude will be given into the hand of the *former*.

12 "When the multitude is carried away, his heart will be lifted up, and he will cause tens of thousands to fall; yet he will not prevail.

13 "For the king of the North will again raise a greater multitude than the former, and after an interval of some years he will press on with a great army and much equipment.

14 "Now in those times many will rise up against the king of the South; the violent ones among your people will also lift themselves up in order to fulfill the vision, but they will fall down.

15 "Then the king of the North will come, cast up a siege mound, and capture a well-fortified city; and the forces of the South will not stand *their ground*, not even their choicest troops, for there will be no strength to make a stand.

16 "But he who comes against him will do as he pleases, and no one will *be able*

*11:2 Dan 8:26; 8:21
*11:3 Dan 8:4,5,21
11:4 Dan 8:8,22; Ezek 37:9; Zech 2:6; Rev 7:1
*11:5 vv. 9,11,14, 25,40
*11:6 vv. 13,15,40
*11:7 vv. 19,38,39
11:8 Is 37:19; 46:1,2; Jer 43:12,13
*11:10 Is 8:8; Jer 46:7,8; Dan 9:26; v. 7
*11:11 v. 5; Dan 8:7; vv. 13,10
*11:13 Dan 4:16; 12:7
*11:15 Jer 6:6; Ezek 4:2; 17:17

Seleucus III and Antiochus III (grandsons of Antiochus II), who vigorously pushed down to the borders of Egypt (v. 10); (8) Ptolemy IV enjoyed a temporary success over Antiochus III at the Battle of Raphia (217 B.C.) and recaptured Palestine from him (vv. 11,12); (9) fifteen years later Antiochus III launched a new and successful counterattack and annexed Palestine (*the Beautiful Land*) permanently to the Seleucid empire (vv. 13–16); (10) Cleopatra (v. 17) was given in marriage to Ptolemy V by her father Antiochus III; (11) in vv. 18,19 Antiochus invaded Asia Minor and Greece but was defeated by the Romans at Magnesia in 190 B.C.; (12) in vv. 21–35 the history of Antiochus Epiphanes (175–164 B.C.) is traced; and (13) in vv. 36–45 the primary reference is to Antiochus Epiphanes, who was a type of the antichrist yet to come, but many features of this prediction were not fulfilled in the career of the historical Epiphanes and can only find fulfillment in the end time.
11:2 *three more kings.* The identification of the three kings and the fourth is uncertain. The fourth is probably Xerxes, who campaigned against the Greeks.
11:3 *a mighty king,* Alexander the Great.

11:5 *the king of the South,* Ptolemy I, Lagi (son of Lagos), of Egypt. *one of his princes,* Seleucus I, Nicator, founder of the Seleucid kingdom in Syria.
11:6 *the daughter of the king of the South.* This woman, Berenice, was murdered, with her child, after being supplanted by her husband's first wife. The attempted alliance thus ended in failure.
11:7 *one of the descendants of her line.* The brother of Berenice became Ptolemy III of Egypt. He marched against Syria and brought home much booty.
11:9 *the latter.* Seleucus II attempted a counterblow against Egypt.
11:10 *his sons.* Seleucus III and Antiochus III (the Great).
11:11 *the king of the South.* Ptolemy IV, Philopater.
11:12 *the multitude.* The army of Antiochus.
11:13 *after an interval of some years.* Fourteen years after his defeat at Raphia (217 B.C.), Antiochus again campaigned against Egypt.
11:15 *a well-fortified city.* Antiochus routed the army of Ptolemy at Panion (198 B.C.). From this time Seleucid control of Palestine was undisputed.

*11:16
Dan 8:4,7;
Josh 1:5
*11:17
2 Kin 12:17;
Ezek 4:3,7

to withstand him; he will also stay *for a time* in the Beautiful Land, with destruction in his hand.

17 "And he will set his face to come with the power of his whole kingdom, bringing with him a proposal of peace which he will put into effect; he will also give him the daughter of women to ruin it. But she will not take a stand *for him* or be on his side.

*11:18
Is 66:19;
Jer 31:10;
Hos 12:14

18 "Then he will turn his face to the coastlands and capture many. But a commander will put a stop to his scorn against him; moreover, he will repay him for his scorn.

11:19
Ps 27:2;
Job 20:8;
Ezek 26:21
*11:20
Is 60:17

19 "So he will turn his face toward the fortresses of his own land, but he will stumble and fall and be found no more.

20 "Then in his place one will arise who will send an oppressor through the ⁸Jewel of *his* kingdom; yet within a few days he will be shattered, though neither in anger nor in battle.

c. Antiochus Epiphanes's persecution of the Jews

*11:21
vv. 24,32,34

21 "And in his place a despicable person will arise, on whom the honor of kingship has not been conferred, but he will come in a time of tranquility and seize the kingdom by intrigue.

*11:22
v. 10;
Dan 8:10,11
11:23
Dan 8:25

22 "And the overflowing forces will be flooded away before him and shattered, and also the prince of the covenant.

23 "And after an alliance is made with him he will practice deception, and he will go up and gain power with a small *force of* people.

11:24
v. 21;
Ezek 34,14

24 "In a time of tranquility he will enter the richest *parts* of the realm, and he will accomplish what his fathers never did, nor his ancestors; he will distribute plunder, booty, and possessions among them, and he will devise his schemes against strongholds, but *only* for a time.

25 "And he will stir up his strength and courage against the king of the South with a large army; so the king of the South will mobilize an extremely large and mighty army for war; but he will not stand, for schemes will be devised against him.

11:26
vv. 10,40

26 "And those who eat his choice food will destroy him, and his army will overflow, but many will fall down slain.

11:27
Ps 52:1; 64:6;
Jer 9:3-5;
vv. 35,40;
Hab 2:3

27 "As for both kings, their hearts will be *intent* on evil, and they will speak lies *to each other* at the same table; but it will not succeed, for the end is still *to come* at the appointed time.

28 "Then he will return to his land with much plunder; but his heart will be *set* against the holy covenant, and he will take action and *then* return to his *own* land.

29 "At the appointed time he will return and come into the South, but this last time it will not turn out the way it did before.

*11:30
Gen 10:4;
Num 24:24;
Jer 2:10

30 "For ships of Kittim will come against him; therefore he will be disheartened, and will return and become enraged at the holy covenant and take action; so he will come back and show regard for those who forsake the holy covenant.

*11:31
Dan 8:11;
9:27;
Matt 24:15;
Mark 13:14
11:32
vv. 21,34;
Mic 5:7-9

31 "And forces from him will arise, desecrate the sanctuary fortress, and do away with the regular sacrifice. And they will set up the abomination of desolation.

32 "And by smooth *words* he will turn to godlessness those who act wickedly toward the covenant, but the people who know their God will display strength and take action.

11:33
Matt 24:9;
John 16:2;
Heb 11:36-38
*11:34
Matt 7:15;
Rom 16:18

33 "And those who have insight among the people will give understanding to the many; yet they will fall by sword and by flame, by captivity and by plunder, for *many* days.

34 "Now when they fall they will be granted a little help, and many will join with them in hypocrisy.

⁸Lit., *adornment;* i.e., probably Jerusalem and its temple

11:16 *the Beautiful Land,* the Land of Israel.
11:17 *the daughter of women.* Cleopatra, daughter of Antiochus, was given in marriage to the Egyptian king. Antiochus actually desired to gain control of Egypt for himself, thus *to ruin it. she will not take a stand.* Egypt did not come under the control of Antiochus.
11:18 *a commander.* The Roman consul, Scipio, defeated Antiochus at Magnesia near Smyrna (190 B.C.).
11:20 *in his place.* Antiochus the Great was succeeded by his son Seleucus IV. The *oppressor* whom he sent was Heliodorus, who ultimately murdered the king.

11:21 *a despicable person.* Antiochus Epiphanes, son of Antiochus the Great.
11:22 *the prince of the covenant.* The Jewish high priest, Onias III.
11:25 *the king of the South.* Ptolemy VI, Philometor.
11:28 *the holy covenant.* The Jewish faith.
11:30 *ships of Kittim.* Roman intervention is described in terms of ships from Kittim.
11:31 *the abomination of desolation.* A statue of Zeus.
11:34 *a little help.* The Maccabees, who rebelled against Antiochus.

35 "And some of those who have insight will fall, in order to refine, purge, and make them pure, until the end time; because *it is* still *to come* at the appointed time.

36 "Then the king will do as he pleases, and he will exalt and magnify himself above every god, and will speak monstrous things against the God of gods; and he will prosper until the indignation is finished, for that which is decreed will be done.

37 "And he will show no regard for the gods of his fathers or for the desire of women, nor will he show regard for any *other* god; for he will magnify himself above *them* all.

38 "But instead he will honor a god of fortresses, a god whom his fathers did not know; he will honor *him* with gold, silver, costly stones, and treasures.

39 "And he will take action against the strongest of fortresses with *the help of* a foreign god; he will give great honor to those who acknowledge *him*, and he will cause them to rule over the many, and will parcel out land for a price.

d. The similar career of the antitype of Antiochus at the time of the end

40 "And at the end time the king of the South will collide with him, and the king of the North will storm against him with chariots, with horsemen, and with many ships; and he will enter countries, overflow *them*, and pass through.

41 "He will also enter the Beautiful Land, and many *countries* will fall; but these will be rescued out of his hand: Edom, Moab and the foremost of the sons of Ammon.

42 "Then he will stretch out his hand against *other* countries, and the land of Egypt will not escape.

43 "But he will gain control over the hidden treasures of gold and silver, and over all the precious things of Egypt; and Libyans and Ethiopians *will follow* at his heels.

44 "But rumors from the East and from the North will disturb him, and he will go forth with great wrath to destroy and annihilate many.

45 "And he will pitch the tents of his royal pavilion between the seas and the beautiful Holy Mountain; yet he will come to his end, and no one will help him.

e. The end of the tribulation and the resurrection of the dead

12 "Now at that time Michael, the great prince who stands *guard* over the sons of your people, will arise. And there will be a time of distress such as never occurred since there was a nation until that time; and at that time your people, everyone who is found written in the book, will be rescued.

2 "And many of those who sleep in the dust of the ground will awake, these to everlasting life, but the others to disgrace *and* everlasting contempt.

3 "And those who have insight will shine brightly like the brightness of the expanse of heaven, and those who lead the many to righteousness, like the stars forever and ever.

4 "But as for you, Daniel, conceal these words and seal up the book until the end of time; many will go back and forth, and knowledge will increase."

f. The sealing of the prophecy until the time of the end

5 Then I, Daniel, looked and behold, two others were standing, one on this bank of the river, and the other on that bank of the river.

6 And one said to the man dressed in linen, who was above the waters of the river, "How long *will it be* until the end of *these* wonders?"

7 And I heard the man dressed in linen, who was above the waters of the river, as he raised his right hand and his left toward heaven, and swore by Him who lives forever that it would be for a time, times, and half *a time;* and as soon as they finish shattering the power of the holy people, all these *events* will be completed.

8 As for me, I heard but could not understand; so I said, "My lord, what *will be* the outcome of these *events?*"

11:35 *will fall,* i.e., suffer martyrdom.
11:37 *the desire of women.* Probably Tammuz-Adonis, whose worship was popular with women (cf. Eze. 8:14).
11:38 *a god of fortresses.* Probably Jupiter Capitolinus (Zeus), for whom he built a temple at Antioch.
11:39 *a foreign god.* Possibly a reference to the Gentile garrisons in Jerusalem.
11:40 *at the end time.* When the destined time for Antio-

chus's end has arrived. *the king of the South.* Ptolemy Philometor.
11:41 *the Beautiful Land,* i.e., the Land of Israel.
12:1 *at that time.* Following the destruction of Antiochus, Daniel envisions the final consummation and ushering in of God's kingdom.
12:5 *two others,* i.e., angels.

12:9
vv. 13,4
12:10
Dan 11:35;
Is 32:6,7
*12:11f
Dan 8:11-14;
Matt 24:15
12:12
Is 30:18;
Rev 11:2
12:13
vv. 9,4;
Rev 14:13

9   And he said, "Go *your way*, Daniel, for *these* words are concealed and sealed up until the end time.

10 "Many will be purged, purified and refined; but the wicked will act wickedly, and none of the wicked will understand, but those who have insight will understand.

11 "And from the time that the regular sacrifice is abolished, and the abomination of desolation is set up, *there will be* 1,290 days.

12 "How blessed is he who keeps waiting and attains to the 1,335 days!

13 "But as for you, go *your way* to the end; then you will enter into rest and rise *again* for your allotted portion at the end of the age."

12:11,12 In these two verses the figures 1,290 and 1,335 are given. It is impossible to be dogmatic about their precise significance as to the future fulfillment. In all probability, however, they point to the last days and speak of that persecution that the antichrist will direct against the saints of God when he removes the worship of the true God and oppresses believers. The 1,290 days reflect the truth that the period of the tribulation and of the rule of antichrist is limited, and the 1,335 days indicate that those who maintain their true faith through the period of persecution will emerge into a time of great blessing.

INTRODUCTION TO

THE BOOK OF

HOSEA

Authorship and Background: The name of the author, Hosea, the son of Beeri, means "salvation" and is related to the root word for Joshua. He lived in the eighth century B.C. and was a prophet in the northern kingdom during the reign of Jeroboam. His ministry overlapped that of Amos, Isaiah, and Micah during an age that was marked by religious apostasy. Instead of putting their trust in God, the leaders of the northern kingdom courted the favor, or by bribery tried to buy the favor, of Assyria and Egypt. In their religious practices they kept the name of God but took over the ritual and practices of Baal worship. There was gross immorality, and the priests reaped a rich harvest by increasing their own incomes from the sin offerings.

Characteristics: Hosea writes out of the acute agony of personal grief. He is commanded to marry a woman who then proves faithless ("a wife of harlotry"). He reclaims her after she sins and writes in the white heat of severe judgment, but also with tenderness. These extremes are intermingled in beautiful fashion as Hosea uses his personal tragedy to illustrate the relationship of Israel to God. His wife Gomer's three children are given symbolic names that proclaim Israel's unfaithfulness. The first is Jezreel, so named to signify the avenging of the blood of Jezreel on the dynasty of Jehu (2 Kin. 10:1-14); Lo-ruhamah signifies "no [more] mercy" to be extended to the northern kingdom; and Lo-ammi signifies "not my people," a symbol of God's rejection of the apostate Israelite kingdom.

Contents:

I. Hosea's marital experiences and their fruits (1:1-3:5): Gomer is a symbol of Israel's unfaithfulness. God's judgment is expressed in the names of their three children: Jezreel, Lo-ruhamah, and Lo-ammi. He describes Gomer's adultery. His pronouncement of judgment, His tenderness toward her, and her restoration.

II. Israel's unfaithfulness to the God of covenant love (4:1-13:16): Hosea accuses Israel of adultery. He is severe in judgment and tender in mercy, looking to restoration. He repeats accusations of her adultery and renders severe judgment that her prayers will not be heard, her cities will be destroyed, and her people taken captive. He repeats in two sequences the cycle of adultery, judgment, tenderness, and restoration.

III. Forgiveness and blessing in response to repentance (14:1-9): He encourages repentance and promises blessing in response to repentance.

THE BOOK OF

HOSEA

I. Hosea's marital experiences and their fruits (1:1–3:5)

A. Superscription

1:1
Rom 9:25;
2 Kin 5:1-7;
2 Chr 27:1-9;
2 Kin 16:1-20;
2 Chr 28:1-27;
2 Kin 18:1-20;
2 Chr 29:1-32;
2 Kin 13:13;
14:23-29

1 The word of the LORD which came to Hosea the son of Beeri, during the days of Uzziah, Jotham, Ahaz, *and* Hezekiah, kings of Judah, and during the days of Jeroboam the son of Joash, king of Israel.

B. Hosea's marriage to Gomer

*1:2
Hos 3:1;
Jer 3:1,12,14;
Hos 2:5; 3:5

2 When the LORD first spoke through Hosea, the LORD said to Hosea, "Go, take to yourself a wife of harlotry, and *have* children of harlotry; for the land commits flagrant harlotry, forsaking the LORD."

3 So he went and took Gomer the daughter of Diblaim, and she conceived and bore him a son.

*1:4
2 Kin 10:1-14;
15:10

4 And the LORD said to him, "Name him Jezreel; for yet a little while, and I will punish the house of Jehu for the bloodshed of Jezreel, and I will put an end to the kingdom of the house of Israel.

1:5
2 Kin 15:29

5 "And it will come about on that day, that I will break the bow of Israel in the valley of Jezreel."

*1:6
vv. 3,9;
Hos 2:4

6 Then she conceived again and gave birth to a daughter. And the LORD said to him, "Name her [1]Lo-ruhamah, for I will no longer have compassion on the house of Israel, that I should ever forgive them.

1:7
Is 30:18;
Jer 25:5,6;
Zech 9:9,10

7 "But I will have compassion on the house of Judah and deliver them by the LORD their God, and will not deliver them by bow, sword, battle, horses, or horsemen."

8 When she had weaned Lo-ruhamah, she conceived and gave birth to a son.

*1:9
v. 6

9 And the LORD said, "Name him [2]Lo-ammi, for you are not My people and I am not your God."

C. The prophecy of restoration

*1:10
Gen 32:12;
Jer 33:22;
Rom 9:25-27;
v. 9; Is 63:16;
64:8

10 Yet the number of the sons of Israel
Will be like the sand of the sea,
Which cannot be measured or numbered;
And it will come about that, in the place
Where it is said to them,
"You are not My people,"
It will be said to them,
"*You are* the sons of the living God."

1:11
Is 11:12;
Jer 23:5,6;
Ezek 37:21-24;
Hos 3:5

11 And the sons of Judah and the sons of Israel will be gathered together,
And they will appoint for themselves one leader,
And they will go up from the land,
For great will be the day of Jezreel.

---

[1]I.e., she has not obtained compassion   [2]I.e., not my people

---

1:2 *the land commits flagrant harlotry.* Hosea's own domestic unhappiness served as the background for the prophet's message. Just as Gomer had been unfaithful to Hosea, so Israel had been unfaithful to God.
1:4 *the house of Jehu.* It was responsible for the death of Joram of Israel, Ahaziah of Judah, and Jezebel (2 Kin. 9). Jehu's zeal for the extermination of the Baal cult does not justify his murderous acts.

1:6 Lo-ruhamah is called *Not pitied* in the RSV.
1:9 Lo-ammi is called *Not my people* in the RSV.
1:10 Hosea prophesied the judgment of God on faithless Israel but, with the eye of faith, he looked forward to the day when Israel would be restored to a place of honor and blessing. The new name, *sons of the living God*, indicates that this indeed will come about.

D. *Gomer a symbol of Israel*

1. *Her adultery*

2 Say to your brothers, "³Ammi," and to your sisters, "⁴Ruhamah." | 2:1 v. 23

2   "Contend with your mother, contend,
      For she is not my wife, and I am not her husband;
      And let her put away her harlotry from her face,
      And her adultery from between her breasts, | 2:2 v. 5; Hos 4:5; Is 50:1; Hos 1:2

3   Lest I strip her naked
      And expose her as on the day when she was born.
      I will also make her like a wilderness,
      Make her like desert land,
      And slay her with thirst. | 2:3 Ezek 16:7,22, 39; Is 32:13, 14; Amos 8:11

4   "Also, I will have no compassion on her children,
      Because they are children of harlotry. | 2:4 Jer 13:14; Ezek 8:18

5   "For their mother has played the harlot;
      She who conceived them has acted shamefully.
      For she said, 'I will go after my lovers,
      Who give *me* my bread and my water,
      My wool and my flax, my oil and my drink.' | 2:5 Is 1:21; Jer 3:1,2,6; 44:17,18

2. *Gomer's judgment*

6   "Therefore, behold, I will hedge up her way with thorns,
      And I will build a wall against her so that she cannot find her paths. | 2:6 Job 3:23; 19:8; Hos 9:6; 10:8

7   "And she will pursue her lovers, but she will not overtake them;
      And she will seek them, but will not find *them*.
      Then she will say, 'I will go back to my first husband,
      For it was better for me then than now!' | 2:7 Jer 2:2; 3:1; Ezek 16:8; Hos 13:6

8   "For she does not know that it was I who gave her the grain, the new wine, and the oil,
      And lavished on her silver and gold,
      Which they used for Baal. | 2:8 Is 1:3; Ezek 16:19; Hos 8:4

9   "Therefore, I will take back My grain at harvest time
      And My new wine in its season.
      I will also take away My wool and My flax
      Given to cover her nakedness. | 2:9 Hos 8:7; 9:2

10   "And then I will uncover her lewdness
      In the sight of her lovers,
      And no one will rescue her out of My hand. | 2:10 Ezek 16:37

11   "I will also put an end to all her gaiety,
      Her feasts, her new moons, her sabbaths,
      And all her festal assemblies. | 2:11 Jer 7:34; 16:9; Amos 8:10; Is 1:13,14

12   "And I will destroy her vines and fig trees,
      Of which she said, 'These are my wages
      Which my lovers have given me.'
      And I will make them a forest,
      And the beasts of the field will devour them. | 2:12 v. 5; Is 5:5; Hos 13:8

13   "And I will punish her for the days of the Baals
      When she used to offer sacrifices to them
      And adorn herself with her earrings and jewelry,
      And follow her lovers, so that she forgot Me," declares the LORD. | 2:13 Ezek 16:12, 17; Hos 4:6; 8:14; 13:6

3. *Her restoration promised*

14   "Therefore, behold, I will allure her,
      Bring her into the wilderness,
      And speak kindly to her. | *2:14 Ezek 20:33-38

15   "Then I will give her her vineyards from there, | *2:15 Ezek 28:25, 26; Josh 7:26;

³I.e., my people   ⁴I.e., she has obtained compassion

2:14 *I will allure her.* God's love for faithless Israel has not changed. In the land of Canaan she is tempted by the Baalim, but God states His purpose to take His people into the wilderness, where He will be able to *speak kindly* (literally, speak to her heart).
2:15 *a door of hope.* There was no hope for faithless Israel in Canaan. Achor (trouble) in exile was the only way she could be restored to her place of favor with God.

And the valley of Achor as a door of hope.
And she will sing there as in the days of her youth,
As in the day when she came up from the land of Egypt.

16   "And it will come about in that day," declares the LORD,
"That you will call Me [5]Ishi
And will no longer call Me [6]Baali.

17   "For I will remove the names of the Baals from her mouth,
So that they will be mentioned by their names no more.

18   "In that day I will also make a covenant for them
With the beasts of the field,
The birds of the sky,
And the creeping things of the ground.
And I will abolish the bow, the sword, and war from the land,
And will make them lie down in safety.

19   "And I will betroth you to Me forever;
Yes, I will betroth you to Me in righteousness and in justice,
In lovingkindness and in compassion,

20   And I will betroth you to Me in faithfulness.
Then you will know the LORD.

21   "And it will come about in that day that I will respond," declares the
LORD.
"I will respond to the heavens, and they will respond to the earth,

22   And the earth will respond to the grain, to the new wine, and to the
oil,
And they will respond to [7]Jezreel.

23   "And I will sow her for Myself in the land.
I will also have compassion on her who had not obtained
compassion,
And I will say to those who were not My people,
'You are My people!'
And they will say, '*Thou art* my God!' "

4. *Her restoration accomplished*

3 Then the LORD said to me, "Go again, love a woman *who* is loved by *her* husband, yet an adulteress, even as the LORD loves the sons of Israel, though they turn to other gods and love raisin cakes."

2   So I bought her for myself for fifteen *shekels* of silver and a homer and a half of barley.

3   Then I said to her, "You shall stay with me for many days. You shall not play the harlot, nor shall you have a man; so I will also be toward you."

4   For the sons of Israel will remain for many days without king or prince, without sacrifice or *sacred* pillar, and without ephod or household idols.

5   Afterward the sons of Israel will return and seek the LORD their God and David their king; and they will come trembling to the LORD and to His goodness in the last days.

II. *Israel's unfaithfulness to the God of covenant love*
(4:1–13:16)

A. *Israel's adultery*

4 Listen to the word of the LORD, O sons of Israel,
For the LORD has a case against the inhabitants of the land,
Because there is no faithfulness or kindness
Or knowledge of God in the land.

2   *There is* swearing, deception, murder, stealing, and adultery.
They employ violence, so that bloodshed follows bloodshed.

3   Therefore the land mourns,
And everyone who lives in it languishes
Along with the beasts of the field and the birds of the sky;
And also the fish of the sea disappear.

[5]I.e., my Husband   [6]I.e., my Master, or, my Baal   [7]I.e., God sows

4 Yet let no one find fault, and let none offer reproof;
For your people are like those who contend with the priest.

5 So you will stumble by day,
And the prophet also will stumble with you by night;
And I will destroy your mother.

6 My people are destroyed for lack of knowledge.
Because you have rejected knowledge,
I also will reject you from being My priest.
Since you have forgotten the law of your God,
I also will forget your children.

7 The more they multiplied, the more they sinned against Me;
I will change their glory into shame.

8 They feed on the sin of My people,
And direct their desire toward their iniquity.

9 And it will be, like people, like priest;
So I will punish them for their ways,
And repay them for their deeds.

10 And they will eat, but not have enough;
They will play the harlot, but not increase,
Because they have stopped giving heed to the LORD.

11 Harlotry, wine, and new wine take away the understanding.

12 My people consult their wooden idol, and their *diviner's* wand
informs them;
For a spirit of harlotry has led *them* astray,
And they have played the harlot, *departing* from their God.

13 They offer sacrifices on the tops of the mountains
And burn incense on the hills,
Under oak, poplar, and terebinth,
Because their shade is pleasant.
Therefore your daughters play the harlot,
And your brides commit adultery.

14 I will not punish your daughters when they play the harlot
Or your brides when they commit adultery,
For *the men* themselves go apart with harlots
And offer sacrifices with temple prostitutes;
So the people without understanding are ruined.

15 Though you, Israel, play the harlot,
Do not let Judah become guilty;
Also do not go to Gilgal,
Or go up to Beth-aven,
And take the oath:
"As the LORD lives!"

16 Since Israel is stubborn
Like a stubborn heifer,
Can the LORD now pasture them
Like a lamb in a large field?

17 Ephraim is joined to idols;
Let him alone.

18 Their liquor gone,
They play the harlot continually;
Their rulers dearly love shame.

19 The wind wraps them in its wings,
And they will be ashamed because of their sacrifices.

B. *God's severity toward Israel*

5 Hear this, O priests!
Give heed, O house of Israel!
Listen, O house of the king!
For the judgment applies to you,
For you have been a snare at Mizpah,
And a net spread out on Tabor.

Cross references

4:4 Ezek 3:26; Deut 17:12
4:5 Hos 5:5; Ezek 14:3,7; Hos 2:2,5
4:6 v. 1; Mal 2:7, 8; Hos 2:13; 8:1,12
4:7 Hos 10:1; 13:6; Hab 2:16; Mal 2:9
4:8 Hos 10:13; Is 56:11
4:9 Is 24:2; Jer 5:31; Hos 9:9
4:10 Lev 26:26; Mic 6:14; Hos 7:14; 9:17
4:11 Hos 5:4; Is 28:7
4:12 Jer 2:27; Hab 2:19; Hos 5:4; 9:1
4:13 Jer 3:6; Ezek 6:13; Hos 2:13; 11:2; Amos 7:17; Rom 1:28
4:14 v. 18; Deut 23:17; vv. 6,11
4:15 Amos 4:4; 1 Kin 12:28, 29
4:16 Ps 78:8; Is 5:17; 7:25
4:17 Ps 81:12; v. 4
4:18 vv. 14,7
4:19 Hos 12:1; 13:15; Is 1:29
5:1 Hos 4:1; 6:9

	2 And the revolters have gone deep in depravity, But I will chastise all of them.
5:3 Amos 3:2; Hos 6:10	3 I know Ephraim, and Israel is not hidden from Me; For now, O Ephraim, you have played the harlot, Israel has defiled itself.
5:4 Hos 4:11,12	4 Their deeds will not allow them To return to their God. For a spirit of harlotry is within them, And they do not know the LORD.
5:5 Hos 7:10; 4:5; Ezek 23:31-35	5 Moreover, the pride of Israel testifies against him, And Israel and Ephraim stumble in their iniquity; Judah also has stumbled with them.
5:6 Mic 6:6,7; Is 1:15; Ezek 8:6	6 They will go with their flocks and herds To seek the LORD, but they will not find *Him*; He has withdrawn from them.
5:7 Is 48:8; Hos 6:7; 2:4, 11,12	7 They have dealt treacherously against the LORD, For they have borne illegitimate children. Now the new moon will devour them with their land.
5:8 Hos 9:9; 10:9; Is 10:29,30; Hos 4:15	**8** Blow the horn in Gibeah, The trumpet in Ramah. Sound an alarm at Beth-aven: "Behind you, Benjamin!"
5:9 Is 37:3; 46:10; Zech 1:6	9 Ephraim will become a desolation in the day of rebuke; Among the tribes of Israel I declare what is sure.
5:10 Deut 19:14; Ezek 7:8; Ps 93:3,4	10 The princes of Judah have become like those who move a boundary; On them I will pour out My wrath like water.
5:11 Hos 9:16	11 Ephraim is oppressed, crushed in judgment, Because he was determined to follow *man's* command.
5:12 Ps 39:11; Prov 12:4	12 Therefore I am like a moth to Ephraim, And like rottenness to the house of Judah.
5:13 Jer 30:12; Hos 7:11; 8:9; 10:6; 14:3	13 When Ephraim saw his sickness, And Judah his wound, Then Ephraim went to Assyria And sent to King Jareb. But he is unable to heal you, Or to cure you of your wound.
5:14 Hos 13:7,8; Ps 50:22; Mic 5:8	14 For I *will be* like a lion to Ephraim, And like a young lion to the house of Judah. I, even I, will tear to pieces and go away, I will carry away, and there will be none to deliver.
5:15 Is 64:7-9; Jer 2:27; Hos 3:5	15 I will go away *and* return to My place Until they acknowledge their guilt and seek My face; In their affliction they will earnestly seek Me.

C. Repentance and restoration

6:1 Jer 50:4,5; Hos 5:14; 14:4; Is 30:26	**6** "Come, let us return to the LORD. For He has torn *us*, but He will heal us; He has wounded *us*, but He will bandage us.
***6:2** Ps 30:5	2 "He will revive us after two days; He will raise us up on the third day That we may live before Him.
6:3 Is 2:3; Mic 4:2; Ps 19:6; Mic 5:2; Joel 2:23	3 "So let us know, let us press on to know the LORD. His going forth is as certain as the dawn; And He will come to us like the rain, Like the spring rain watering the earth."

D. Israel's unfaithfulness restated

	4 What shall I do with you, O Ephraim?

6:2 Israel shall be as dead people during the period of God's wrath. Yet Hosea affirms that within a short time *(after two days)* God will cause His people to live in His sight.

What shall I do with you, O Judah?
For your loyalty is like a morning cloud,
And like the dew which goes away early.

5 Therefore I have hewn *them* in pieces by the prophets;
I have slain them by the words of My mouth;
And the judgments on you are *like* the light that goes forth.

6 For I delight in loyalty rather than sacrifice,
And in the knowledge of God rather than burnt offerings.

7 But like Adam they have transgressed the covenant;
There they have dealt treacherously against Me.

8 Gilead is a city of wrongdoers,
Tracked with bloody *footprints*.

9 And as raiders wait for a man,
So a band of priests murder on the way to Shechem;
Surely they have committed crime.

10 In the house of Israel I have seen a horrible thing;
Ephraim's harlotry is there, Israel has defiled itself.

11 Also, O Judah, there is a harvest appointed for you,
When I restore the fortunes of My people.

7

When I would heal Israel,
The iniquity of Ephraim is uncovered,
And the evil deeds of Samaria,
For they deal falsely;
The thief enters in,
Bandits raid outside,

2 And they do not consider in their hearts
That I remember all their wickedness.
Now their deeds are all around them;
They are before My face.

3 With their wickedness they make the king glad,
And the princes with their lies.

4 They are all adulterers
Like an oven heated by the baker,
Who ceases to stir up *the fire*
From the kneading of the dough until it is leavened.

5 On the day of our king, the princes became sick with the heat of wine;
He stretched out his hand with scoffers,

6 For their hearts are like an oven
As they approach their plotting;
Their anger smolders all night,
In the morning it burns like a flaming fire.

7 All of them are hot like an oven,
And they consume their rulers;
All their kings have fallen.
None of them calls on Me.

8 Ephraim mixes himself with the nations;
Ephraim has become a cake not turned.

9 Strangers devour his strength,
Yet he does not know *it*;
Gray hairs also are sprinkled on him,
Yet he does not know *it*.

10 Though the pride of Israel testifies against him,
Yet they have neither returned to the LORD their God,
Nor have they sought Him, for all this.

11 So Ephraim has become like a silly dove, without sense;
They call to Egypt, they go to Assyria.

12 When they go, I will spread My net over them;

6:4 Hos 7:1; 11:8; 13:3
6:5 Jer 1:10,18; Heb 4:12; v. 3
6:6 Matt 9:13; Ps 50:8,9; Hos 2:20
6:7 Hos 8:1; 5:7
6:8 Hos 4:2
6:9 Hos 7:1; Jer 7:9,10; Ezek 22:9; 23:27
6:10 Jer 5:30,31; Hos 5:3
6:11 Joel 3:13; Zeph 2:7
7:1 v. 13; Hos 6:4; 11:8; 4:2; 6:9
7:2 Hos 8:13; 9:9; Amos 8:7; Jer 2:19; Hos 4:9
7:3 v. 5; Mic 7:3; Hos 4:2; 11:12; Rom 1:32
7:4 Jer 9:2; 23:10
7:5 Is 28:1,7,8
7:7 Ps 21:9; v. 16; Is 64:7
7:8 Ps 106:35; v. 11; Hos 5:13
7:9 Is 1:7; Hos 4:6
7:10 Hos 5:5; vv. 7,14; Hos 5:4
***7:11** Hos 11:11; 4:6,11,14; v. 16; Hos 5:13; 8:9; 12:1

7:11 *call to Egypt . . . go to Assyria.* These two world powers sought to control Palestine. The Israelite kings and their nobles were torn between the pro-Egyptian and pro-Assyrian factions at court. Hosea sees this vacillation as evidence of distrust in God.

7:12 Ezek 12:13	I will bring them down like the birds of the sky. I will chastise them in accordance with the proclamation to their assembly.
7:13 Hos 9:12,17; Jer 14:10; Ezek 34:6; v. 1; Matt 23:37	13 Woe to them, for they have strayed from Me! Destruction is theirs, for they have rebelled against Me! I would redeem them, but they speak lies against Me.
7:14 Jer 3:10; Amos 2:8; Mic 2:11; Hos 13:16	14 And they do not cry to Me from their heart When they wail on their beds; For the sake of grain and new wine they assemble themselves, They turn away from Me.
7:15 Hos 11:13; Nah 1:9	15 Although I trained *and* strengthened their arms, Yet they devise evil against Me.
7:16 Ps 78:57; v. 7; Ezek 23:32	16 They turn, *but* not upward, They are like a deceitful bow; Their princes will fall by the sword Because of the insolence of their tongue. This *will be* their derision in the land of Egypt.

E. *The fruit of Israel's sin*

1. *God's sentence upon them*

8:1 Hos 5:8; Hab 1:8; Hos 6:7; 4:6	**8** *Put* the trumpet to your lips! Like an eagle *the enemy comes* against the house of the LORD, Because they have transgressed My covenant, And rebelled against My law.
8:2 Hos 7:14	2 They cry out to Me, "My God, we of Israel know Thee!"
	3 Israel has rejected the good; The enemy will pursue him.
8:4 Hos 13:10,11; 2:8	4 They have set up kings, but not by Me; They have appointed princes, but I did not know *it.* With their silver and gold they have made idols for themselves, That they might be cut off.
8:5 v. 6; Hos 10:5; 13:2; Jer 13:27	5 He has rejected your calf, O Samaria, saying, "My anger burns against them!" How long will they be incapable of innocence?
8:6 Hos 13:2	6 For from Israel is even this! A craftsman made it, so it is not God; Surely the calf of Samaria will be broken to pieces.
8:7 Hos 10:12,13; Is 66:15; Nah 1:3	7 For they sow the wind, And they reap the whirlwind. The standing grain has no heads; It yields no grain. Should it yield, strangers would swallow it up.
8:8 Jer 51:34; Hos 13:15	8 Israel is swallowed up; They are now among the nations Like a vessel in which no one delights.
8:9 Hos 7:11; Jer 2:24; Ezek 16:3	9 For they have gone up to Assyria, *Like* a wild donkey all alone; Ephraim has hired lovers.
8:10 Ezek 16:37; 22:40; Jer 42:2	10 Even though they hire *allies* among the nations, Now I will gather them up; And they will begin to diminish Because of the burden of the king of princes.
8:11 Hos 10:1; 12:11	11 Since Ephraim has multiplied altars for sin, They have become altars of sinning for him.
8:12 v. 1; Hos 4:6	12 Though I wrote for him ten thousand *precepts* of My law, They are regarded as a strange thing.
8:13 Jer 7:21; Hos 7:2; 1 Cor 4:5; Hos 4:9; 9:7; 9:3,6	13 As for My sacrificial gifts, They sacrifice the flesh and eat *it,* *But* the LORD has taken no delight in them. Now He will remember their iniquity,

And punish *them* for their sins;
They will return to Egypt.

14 For Israel has forgotten his Maker and built palaces;
    And Judah has multiplied fortified cities,
    But I will send a fire on its cities that it may consume its palatial
        dwellings.

2. Israel's riches to be taken away

9   Do not rejoice, O Israel, with exultation like the nations!
        For you have played the harlot, forsaking your God.
        You have loved *harlots'* earnings on every threshing floor.

2   Threshing floor and wine press will not feed them,
    And the new wine will fail them.

3   They will not remain in the LORD's land,
    But Ephraim will return to Egypt,
    And in Assyria they will eat unclean *food.*

4   They will not pour out libations of wine to the LORD,
    Their sacrifices will not please Him.
    Their bread will be like mourners' bread;
    All who eat of it will be defiled,
    For their bread will be for themselves *alone*;
    It will not enter the house of the LORD.

5   What will you do on the day of the appointed festival
    And on the day of the feast of the LORD?

6   For behold, they will go because of destruction;
    Egypt will gather them up, Memphis will bury them.
    Weeds will take over their treasures of silver;
    Thorns *will be* in their tents.

7   The days of punishment have come,
    The days of retribution have come;
    Let Israel know *this*!
    The prophet is a fool,
    The inspired man is demented,
    Because of the grossness of your iniquity,
    And *because* your hostility is *so* great.

8   Ephraim *was* a watchman with my God, a prophet;
    Yet the snare of a bird catcher is in all his ways,
    And there is *only* hostility in the house of his God.

9   They have gone deep in depravity
    As in the days of Gibeah;
    He will remember their iniquity,
    He will punish their sins.

3. Israel's population to decline

10 I found Israel like grapes in the wilderness;
    I saw your forefathers as the earliest fruit on the fig tree in its first
        season.
    But they came to Baal-peor and devoted themselves to [8]shame,
    And they became as detestable as that which they loved.

11 As for Ephraim, their glory will fly away like a bird—
    No birth, no pregnancy, and no conception!

12 Though they bring up their children,
    Yet I will bereave them until not a man is left.
    Yes, woe to them indeed when I depart from them!

13 Ephraim, as I have seen,
    Is planted in a pleasant meadow like Tyre;
    But Ephraim will bring out his children for slaughter.

8I.e., Baal

9:6 *Memphis will bury them.* The place of refuge to which they will flee will prove to be a place of death. They flee from God, expecting life, but they will discover instead that they will inherit death.

9:10 *they came to Baal-peor.* The Moabites invited the Israelites to their licentious fertility cult at Baal-peor (Num. 25:1–4). Baal worship became prevalent in Israel during the time of the judges (Judg. 2:11–13).

8:14
Hos 2:13;
13:6;
Jer 17:27

9:1
Is 22:12,13;
Hos 10:5;
4:12;
Jer 44:17
9:2
Hos 2:9

9:3
Jer 2:7;
Hos 8:13;
Ezek 4:13;
Hos 7:11
9:4
Jer 6:20;
Hos 5:6;
8:13;
Hag 2:14

9:5
Is 10:3;
Jer 5:31;
Joel 1:13
*9:6
v. 3; Jer 2:16;
Ezek 30:13,
16; Is 5:6;
Hos 10:8

9:7
Jer 10:15;
Mic 7:4;
Is 34:8;
Jer 16:18;
Ezek 14:9,10

9:8
Hos 5:1

9:9
Is 31:6;
Judg 19:12;
Hos 5:8;
10:9; 7:2;
8:13

*9:10
Mic 7:1;
Jer 24:2;
Num 25:3;
Hos 4:14;
Jer 11:13

9:11
Hos 4:7;
10:5; v. 14
9:12
v. 16;
Hos 7:13

9:13
Ezek 27:3,4

9:14 v. 11; Luke 23:29	14 Give them, O LORD—what wilt Thou give? Give them a miscarrying womb and dry breasts.
9:15 Hos 4:9; 7:2; 12:2; Is 1:23	**15** All their evil is at Gilgal; Indeed, I came to hate them there! Because of the wickedness of their deeds I will drive them out of My house! I will love them no more; All their princes are rebels.
9:16 Hos 5:11; 8:7; v. 12	16 Ephraim is stricken, their root is dried up, They will bear no fruit. Even though they bear children, I will slay the precious ones of their womb.
9:17 Hos 4:10; Deut 28:65	17 My God will cast them away Because they have not listened to Him; And they will be wanderers among the nations.

4. *Israel's idols to be destroyed*

10:1 Ezek 15:1-5; Hos 8:11; 3:4	**10** Israel is a luxuriant vine; He produces fruit for himself. The more his fruit, The more altars he made; The richer his land, The better he made the *sacred* pillars.
10:2 1 Kin 18:21; Matt 6:24; Hos 13:16; v. 8	2 Their heart is faithless; Now they must bear their guilt. The LORD will break down their altars *And* destroy their *sacred* pillars.
10:3 Ps 12:4	**3** Surely now they will say, "We have no king, For we do not revere the LORD. As for the king, what can he do for us?"
10:4 Ezek 17:13-19; Hos 4:2; Deut 31:16, 17	4 They speak *mere* words, With worthless oaths they make covenants; And judgment sprouts like poisonous weeds in the furrows of the field.
10:5 Hos 8:5,6; 9:11	5 The inhabitants of Samaria will fear For the calf of Beth-aven. Indeed, its people will mourn for it, And its idolatrous priests will cry out over it, Over its glory, since it has departed from it.
10:6 Hos 11:5; 5:13; 4:7; Is 30:3; Jer 7:24	6 The thing itself will be carried to Assyria As tribute to King Jareb; Ephraim will be seized with shame, And Israel will be ashamed of its own counsel.
10:7 Hos 13:11	7 Samaria will be cut off *with* her king, Like a stick on the surface of the water.
10:8 v. 5; 1 Kin 12:30; v. 2; Hos 9:6; Luke 23:30; Rev 6:16	8 Also the high places of Aven, the sin of Israel, will be destroyed; Thorn and thistle will grow on their altars, Then they will say to the mountains, "Cover us!" And to the hills, "Fall on us!"

5. *Israel's fortresses to be destroyed*

10:9 Hos 5:8; 9:9	9 From the days of Gibeah you have sinned, O Israel; There they stand! Will not the battle against the sons of iniquity overtake them in Gibeah?
10:10 Ezek 5:13; Hos 4:9	10 When it is My desire, I will chastise them; And the peoples will be gathered against them When they are bound for their double guilt.
10:11 Jer 50:11; Hos 4:16; Jer 28:14; Ps 66:12	**11** And Ephraim is a trained heifer that loves to thresh, But I will come over her fair neck *with a yoke*; I will harness Ephraim,

Judah will plow, Jacob will harrow for himself.

12 Sow with a view to righteousness,
Reap in accordance with kindness;
Break up your fallow ground,
For it is time to seek the LORD
Until He comes to rain righteousness on you.

13 You have plowed wickedness, you have reaped injustice,
You have eaten the fruit of lies.
Because you have trusted in your way, in your numerous warriors,

14 Therefore, a tumult will arise among your people,
And all your fortresses will be destroyed,
As Shalman destroyed Beth-arbel on the day of battle,
When mothers were dashed in pieces with *their* children.

15 Thus it will be done to you at Bethel because of your great
wickedness.
At dawn the king of Israel will be completely cut off.

6. Israel to be a captive of Assyria

11 When Israel *was* a youth I loved him,
And out of Egypt I called My son.

2 The more they called them,
The more they went from them;
They kept sacrificing to the Baals
And burning incense to idols.

3 Yet it is I who taught Ephraim to walk,
I took them in My arms;
But they did not know that I healed them.

4 I led them with cords of a man, with bonds of love,
And I became to them as one who lifts the yoke from their jaws;
And I bent down *and* fed them.

5 They will not return to the land of Egypt;
But Assyria—he will be their king,
Because they refused to return *to Me*.

6 And the sword will whirl against their cities,
And will demolish their gate bars
And consume *them* because of their counsels.

7 So My people are bent on turning from Me.
Though they call them to *the One* on high,
None at all exalts *Him*.

F. God's tenderness toward Israel

8 How can I give you up, O Ephraim?
How can I surrender you, O Israel?
How can I make you like Admah?
How can I treat you like Zeboiim?
My heart is turned over within Me,
All my compassions are kindled.

9 I will not execute My fierce anger;
I will not destroy Ephraim again.
For I am God and not man, the Holy One in your midst,
And I will not come in wrath.

G. Israel to be restored

10 They will walk after the LORD,

11:3 God had tenderly cared for Ephraim-Israel in the day of her immaturity. When Israel "grew up," the Baals took the place of God in worship and affection.
11:5 The northern kingdom lasted for two hundred years. Hosea prophesies its downfall, which was accomplished by Shalmaneser V and Sargon II in 722 B.C.. Israel was never to be restored as a nation after her expulsion from the promised land, as Judah was after the Babylonian captivity.

There is a sense in which the northern kingdom and the southern kingdom shall be united in a single realm in the last days (14:4–8; Isa. 11:13). Comparison of 2:1,23 with Rom. 9:24,25 indicates that this prophecy of the restoration of the ten tribes was to be fulfilled, at least in part, by the filling in of their vacant ranks by Gentile Christians. Hence, in that sense, the Gentile believers shall become His people.

He will roar like a lion;
Indeed He will roar,
And *His* sons will come trembling from the west.

11:11
Is 11:11;
60:8;
Ezek 28:25,
26

11 They will come trembling like birds from Egypt,
And like doves from the land of Assyria;
And I will settle them in their houses, declares the LORD.

H. *Ephraim's unfaithfulness restated; her doom predicted*

1. *The sin of Ephraim*

11:12
Hos 4:2; 7:3

12 Ephraim surrounds Me with lies,
And the house of Israel with deceit;
Judah is also unruly against God,
Even against the Holy One who is faithful.

12:1
2 Kin 17:4;
Is 30:6

12
Ephraim feeds on wind,
And pursues the east wind continually;
He multiplies lies and violence.
Moreover, he makes a covenant with Assyria,
And oil is carried to Egypt.

2. *The judgment on Jacob*

12:2
Mic 6:2;
Hos 4:9

2 The LORD also has a dispute with Judah,
And will punish Jacob according to his ways;
He will repay him according to his deeds.

12:3
Gen 25:26;
32:24,28
12:4
Gen 32:26;
28:12-15

3 In the womb he took his brother by the heel,
And in his maturity he contended with God.

4 Yes, he wrestled with the angel and prevailed;
He wept and sought His favor.
He found Him at Bethel,
And there He spoke with us,

12:5
Ex 3:15

5 Even the LORD, the God of hosts;
The LORD is His name.

12:6
Mic 6:8;
Hos 6:6;
Mic 7:7

6 Therefore, return to your God,
Observe kindness and justice,
And wait for your God continually.

3. *Ephraim's sins enlarged on*

12:7
Amos 8:5;
Mic 6:11

7 A merchant, in whose hands are false balances,
He loves to oppress.

12:8
Hos 13:6;
Rev 3:17;
Hos 4:8; 14:1

8 And Ephraim said, "Surely I have become rich,
I have found wealth for myself;
In all my labors they will find in me
No iniquity, which *would be* sin."

12:9
Hos 11:1;
13:4;
Lev 23:42;
Neh 8:17
12:10
2 Kin 17:13;
Jer 7:25;
Ezek 17:2;
20:49
12:11
Hos 6:8;
4:15; 9:15;
10:1,2

9 But I *have been* the LORD your God since the land of Egypt;
I will make you live in tents again,
As in the days of the appointed festival.

10 I have also spoken to the prophets,
And I gave numerous visions;
And through the prophets I gave parables.

11 Is there iniquity *in* Gilead?
Surely they are worthless.
In Gilgal they sacrifice bulls,
Yes, their altars are like the stone heaps
Beside the furrows of the field.

12:12
Gen 28:5;
29:20

12 Now Jacob fled to the land of Aram,
And Israel worked for a wife,
And for a wife he kept *sheep.*

12:13
Ex 13:3

13 But by a prophet the LORD brought Israel from Egypt,
And by a prophet he was kept.

12:14
Ezek 18:10-13;
Dan 11:18;
Mic 6:16

14 Ephraim has provoked to bitter anger;
So his Lord will leave his bloodguilt on him,
And bring back his reproach to him.

4. *Ephraim's doom predicted*

13 When Ephraim spoke, *there was* trembling.
He exalted himself in Israel,
But through Baal he did wrong and died.

2 And now they sin more and more,
And make for themselves molten images,
Idols skillfully made from their silver,
All of them the work of craftsmen.
They say of them, "Let the men who sacrifice kiss
the calves!"

3 Therefore, they will be like the morning cloud,
And like dew which soon disappears,
Like chaff which is blown away from the threshing floor,
And like smoke from a chimney.

4 Yet I *have been* the LORD your God
Since the land of Egypt;
And you were not to know any god except Me,
For there is no savior besides Me.

5 I cared for you in the wilderness,
In the land of drought.

6 As *they had* their pasture, they became satisfied,
And being satisfied, their heart became proud;
Therefore, they forgot Me.

7 So I will be like a lion to them;
Like a leopard I will lie in wait by the wayside.

8 I will encounter them like a bear robbed of her cubs,
And I will tear open their chests;
There I will also devour them like a lioness,
As a wild beast would tear them.

9 *It is* your destruction, O Israel,
That *you are* against Me, against your help.

10 Where now is your king
That he may save you in all your cities,
And your judges of whom you requested,
"Give me a king and princes"?

11 I gave you a king in My anger,
And took him away in My wrath.

12 The iniquity of Ephraim is bound up;
His sin is stored up.

13 The pains of childbirth come upon him;
He is not a wise son,
For it is not the time that he should delay at the opening
of the womb.

14 Shall I ransom them from the power of Sheol?
Shall I redeem them from death?
O Death, where are your thorns?
O Sheol, where is your sting?
Compassion will be hidden from My sight.

15 Though he flourishes among the reeds,
An east wind will come,
The wind of the LORD coming up from the wilderness;
And his fountain will become dry,
And his spring will be dried up;
It will plunder *his* treasury of every precious article.

16 Samaria will be held guilty,
For she has rebelled against her God.
They will fall by the sword,
Their little ones will be dashed in pieces,
And their pregnant women will be ripped open.

Cross-references:
13:1 Judg 8:1; 12:1; Hos 2:8-17
13:2 Is 46:6; Hos 8:6
13:3 Hos 6:4; Dan 2:35; Ps 68:2
13:4 Hos 12:9; Is 43:11
13:5 Deut 2:7; 8:15; 32:10
13:6 Deut 8:12,14; 32:15; Hos 2:13; 4:6; 8:14
13:7 Lam 3:10; Jer 5:6
13:8 2 Sam 17:8; Ps 50:22
13:10 2 Kin 17:4; Hos 8:4
13:11 1 Sam 8:7; 1 Kin 14:7-10
13:12 Deut 32:34; Rom 2:5
13:13 Mic 4:9,10; Is 37:3; 66:9
13:14 Ezek 37:12,13; 1 Cor 15:54,55; Rom 11:29
13:15 Hos 10:1; Ezek 17:10; 19:12; Jer 51:36; 20:5
13:16 Hos 10:2; 7:14; Is 13:16; Hos 10:14; 2 Kin 15:16

III. *Forgiveness and blessing in response to repentance*
(14:1–9)

A. *The call to repent*

<table>
<tr><td>

14:1
Hos 10:12;
14:6;
Joel 2:13
14:2
Mic 7:18,19;
Heb 13:15

</td><td>

14

2

</td><td>

Return, O Israel, to the LORD your God,
For you have stumbled because of your iniquity.
Take words with you and return to the LORD.
Say to Him, "Take away all iniquity,
And receive *us* graciously,
That we may present the fruit of our lips.

</td></tr>
<tr><td>

*14:3
Hos 5:13;
Is 31:1;
Hos 8:6;
13:2;
Ps 10:14

</td><td>3</td><td>

"Assyria will not save us,
We will not ride on horses;
Nor will we say again, 'Our god,'
To the work of our hands;
For in Thee the orphan finds mercy."

</td></tr>
</table>

B. *The promise of blessing*

<table>
<tr><td>

14:4
Zeph 3:17;
Is 12:1

</td><td>4</td><td>

I will heal their apostasy,
I will love them freely,
For My anger has turned away from them.

</td></tr>
<tr><td>

14:5
Job 29:19;
Matt 6:28;
Is 35:2

</td><td>5</td><td>

I will be like the dew to Israel;
He will blossom like the lily,
And he will take root like *the cedars of* Lebanon.

</td></tr>
<tr><td>

14:6
Ps 52:8;
Song 4:11

</td><td>6</td><td>

His shoots will sprout,
And his beauty will be like the olive tree,
And his fragrance like *the cedars of* Lebanon.

</td></tr>
<tr><td>

14:7
Ps 91:4;
Ezek 17:23;
Hos 2:21,22

</td><td>7</td><td>

Those who live in his shadow
Will again raise grain,
And they will blossom like the vine.
His renown *will be* like the wine of Lebanon.

</td></tr>
<tr><td>

*14:8
v. 3; Is 41:19;
Ezek 17:23

</td><td>8</td><td>

O Ephraim, what more have I to do with idols?
It is I who answer and look after you.
I am like a luxuriant cypress;
From Me comes your fruit.

</td></tr>
</table>

C. *The postscript*

<table>
<tr><td>

14:9
Ps 107:43;
Acts 13:10;
Is 26:7; 1:28

</td><td>9</td><td>

Whoever is wise, let him understand these things;
Whoever is discerning, let him know them.
For the ways of the LORD are right,
And the righteous will walk in them,
But transgressors will stumble in them.

</td></tr>
</table>

14:3 *Assyria will not save us, we will not ride on horses.* The hope of Israel is neither in Assyria nor Egypt. In reality, Israel is a helpless orphan, dependent on God for mercy and protection. If there is to be any deliverance, it must come from Israel's God.

14:8 *From Me comes your fruit.* Israel will enjoy the blessing of fruitfulness when she turns to the Lord in confession and renunciation of sin (14:1,2).

INTRODUCTION TO

THE BOOK OF

JOEL

Authorship and Background: Joel, the son of Pethuel, is the author of this book. His is a common name occurring often in the Old Testament, meaning "Yahweh is God." The evidences for the dating of the book are inconclusive. Many conservatives hold that the internal evidence supports the preexilic view that it was written before 800 B.C. Other scholars prefer a sixth-century date. If the former view is correct, it was probably written during the reign of Joash, in the ninth century B.C. In the Jewish canon the book was placed between Hosea and Amos. There are similarities between the prophecies of Amos and Joel (cf. Joel 3:16 and Amos 1:2; Joel 3:18 and Amos 9:13). Joel was intimately acquainted with Judah and Jerusalem. His prophecy deals largely with a locust invasion of the area, which God will send as a judgment and as a warning sign of future disaster.

Characteristics: Joel's book has been described as a literary gem that highlights his writing ability and his purity of style. He carefully polishes and beautifies his work as perhaps no other Old Testament writer does. The language is forceful, and the description of the locust invasion minutely accurate. He employs a historical incident to foretell the coming judgment of God against Judah, and from there he goes on to the judgments of the "day of the LORD," which are still future. His prophecy of the outpouring of the Spirit (2:28-32) is quoted by Peter in Acts 2:16ff. as being fulfilled at Pentecost. In all, his work is characterized by strength, tenderness, and sublimity.

Contents:

  I. The plague of locusts (1:1-2:27): Joel describes the plague of locusts and calls the people to repentance. They are urged to see, mourn, and fast. He further exhorts them to tremble, repent, fast, and pray.

 II. The judgment of God and His blessing in the last days (2:28-3:21): God's mercy drives away the locusts and sends an abundant harvest. God pours out His Spirit on all flesh. He blesses His people and punishes their enemies.

THE BOOK OF

JOEL

I. *The plague of locusts (1:1–2:27)*

A. *Superscription*

1:1
Jer 1:2;
Ezek 1:3;
Hos 1:1;
Acts 2:16
1:2
Hos 4:1; 5:1;
v. 14; Joel 2:2
1:3
Ps 78:4

1 The word of the Lord that came to Joel, the son of Pethuel.
2 Hear this, O elders,
And listen, all inhabitants of the land.
Has *anything like* this happened in your days
Or in your fathers' days?
3 Tell your sons about it,
And *let* your sons *tell* their sons,
And their sons the next generation.

B. *The plague and drought described*

1:4
Deut 28:38;
Joel 2:25;
Nah 3:15,16;
Is 33:4

4 What the gnawing locust has left, the swarming locust has eaten;
And what the swarming locust has left, the creeping locust has
eaten;
And what the creeping locust has left, the stripping locust has eaten.

1:5
Joel 3:3;
Is 32:10

5 Awake, drunkards, and weep;
And wail, all you wine drinkers,
On account of the sweet wine
That is cut off from your mouth.

1:6
Joel 2:2,11;
Rev 9:8

6 For a nation has invaded my land,
Mighty and without number;
Its teeth are the teeth of a lion,
And it has the fangs of a lioness.

1:7
Is 5:6;
Amos 4:9

7 It has made my vine a waste,
And my fig tree splinters.
It has stripped them bare and cast *them* away;
Their branches have become white.

1:8
v. 13;
Amos 8:10
1:9
Joel 2:14,17

8 Wail like a virgin girded with sackcloth
For the bridegroom of her youth.
9 The grain offering and the libation are cut off
From the house of the Lord.
The priests mourn,
The ministers of the Lord.

1:10
Is 24:4,7;
Hos 9:2

10 The field is ruined,
The land mourns,
For the grain is ruined,
The new wine dries up,
Fresh oil fails.

1:11
Jer 14:3,4;
Is 17:11;
Jer 9:12

11 Be ashamed, O farmers,
Wail, O vinedressers,
For the wheat and the barley;
Because the harvest of the field is destroyed.

*1:12
Hab 3:17,18;
Is 16:10;
24:11;
Jer 48:33

12 The vine dries up,
And the fig tree fails;
The pomegranate, the palm also, and the apple tree,
All the trees of the field dry up.
Indeed, rejoicing dries up
From the sons of men.

1:12 *The vine dries up.* Despite all of the labors of the keepers of the field, the earth gives forth no harvest. The husbandmen labor in hope but are disappointed. Then fol-lows the call to the priests to prepare their hearts in private for their public duty of fasting and praying to God for help.

13	Gird yourselves *with sackcloth*, And lament, O priests; Wail, O ministers of the altar! Come, spend the night in sackcloth, O ministers of my God, For the grain offering and the libation Are withheld from the house of your God.	**1:13** v. 8; Jer 4:8; v. 9; Joel 2:17; 1 Kin 21:27
14	Consecrate a fast, Proclaim a solemn assembly; Gather the elders *And* all the inhabitants of the land To the house of the LORD your God, And cry out to the LORD.	**1:14** 2 Chr 20:3,4; Joel 2:15,16; v. 2; Jon 3:8
15	Alas for the day! For the day of the LORD is near, And it will come as destruction from the Almighty.	***1:15** Jer 30:7; Is 13:6,9; Joel 2:1,11,31
16	Has not food been cut off before our eyes, Gladness and joy from the house of our God?	**1:16** Is 3:7; Deut 12:6,7; Ps 43:4
17	The seeds shrivel under their clods; The storehouses are desolate, The barns are torn down, For the grain is dried up.	**1:17** Is 17:10,11
18	How the beasts groan! The herds of cattle wander aimlessly Because there is no pasture for them; Even the flocks of sheep suffer.	**1:18** 1 Kin 18:5; Jer 14:5,6; Hos 4:3
19	To Thee, O LORD, I cry; For fire has devoured the pastures of the wilderness, And the flame has burned up all the trees of the field.	**1:19** Ps 50:15; Jer 9:10; Joel 2:3
20	Even the beasts of the field pant for Thee; For the water brooks are dried up, And fire has devoured the pastures of the wilderness.	**1:20** Job 38:41; Ps 104:21; 1 Kin 17:7; 18:5

C. *The coming day of the LORD*

2	Blow a trumpet in Zion, And sound an alarm on My holy mountain! Let all the inhabitants of the land tremble, For the day of the LORD is coming; Surely it is near,	***2:1** Jer 4:5; Num 10:9; Zeph 1:14-16; vv. 11,31; Joel 1:15
2	A day of darkness and gloom, A day of clouds and thick darkness. As the dawn is spread over the mountains, *So* there is a great and mighty people; There has never been *anything* like it, Nor will there be again after it To the years of many generations.	**2:2** Amos 5:18; Joel 1:6; Lam 1:12; Joel 1:2
3	A fire consumes before them, And behind them a flame burns. The land is like the garden of Eden before them, But a desolate wilderness behind them, And nothing at all escapes them.	**2:3** Joel 1:19,20; Gen 2:8; Is 51:3; Ps 105:34,35
4	Their appearance is like the appearance of horses; And like war horses, so they run.	**2:4** Rev 9:7
5	With a noise as of chariots They leap on the tops of the mountains, Like the crackling of a flame of fire consuming the stubble, Like a mighty people arranged for battle.	**2:5** Rev 9:9; Is 5:24; 30:30
6	Before them the people are in anguish; All faces turn pale.	**2:6** Is 13:8; Nah 2:10; Jer 30:6

1:15 *Alas for the day!* This is a day of terror because of the evils that come with it, and due to the sins of the people.
2:1 *The day of the LORD.* This is still in the future. It will come at the end of the age. It must be remembered that the prophets looked in a horizontal direction from one mountaintop to another, rather than from a vertical vantage point. This is the way the nearness of which Joel spoke is to be understood in this context.

2:7 Is 5:26,27; v. 9	7	They run like mighty men; They climb the wall like soldiers; And they each march in line, Nor do they deviate from their paths.
	8	They do not crowd each other; They march everyone in his path. When they burst through the defenses, They do not break ranks.
2:9 v. 7; Jer 9:21; John 10:1	9	They rush on the city, They run on the wall; They climb into the houses, They enter through the windows like a thief.
2:10 Ps 18:7; Is 13:10; Joel 3:15; Matt 24:29	10	Before them the earth quakes, The heavens tremble, The sun and the moon grow dark, And the stars lose their brightness.
2:11 Joel 3:16; Amos 1:2; vv. 2,25; Jer 50:34; Rev 18:8; Joel 3:14; Ezek 22:14	11	And the LORD utters His voice before His army; Surely His camp is very great, For strong is he who carries out His word. The day of the LORD is indeed great and very awesome, And who can endure it?

D. *The call to repentance*

2:12 Jer 4:1; Hos 12:6	12	"Yet even now," declares the LORD, "Return to Me with all your heart, And with fasting, weeping, and mourning;
2:13 Ps 34:18; Is 57:15; 2 Sam 1:11; Jon 4:2; Jer 18:8; 42:10	13	And rend your heart and not your garments." Now return to the LORD your God, For He is gracious and compassionate, Slow to anger, abounding in lovingkindness, And relenting of evil.
*2:14 Jer 26:3; Hag 2:19; Joel 1:9,13	14	Who knows whether He will *not* turn and relent, And leave a blessing behind Him, *Even* a grain offering and a libation For the LORD your God?
*2:15 Num 10:3; v. 1; Jer 36:9; Joel 1:14	15	Blow a trumpet in Zion, Consecrate a fast, proclaim a solemn assembly,
2:16 Ex 19:10,22; Ps 19:5	16	Gather the people, sanctify the congregation, Assemble the elders, Gather the children and the nursing infants. Let the bridegroom come out of his room And the bride out of her *bridal* chamber.
2:17 Ezek 8:16; Matt 23:35; Joel 1:9; Deut 9:26-29; Is 37:20; Ps 44:13; 42:10	17	Let the priests, the LORD's ministers, Weep between the porch and the altar, And let them say, "Spare Thy people, O LORD, And do not make Thine inheritance a reproach, A byword among the nations. Why should they among the peoples say, 'Where is their God?'"

E. *The promised deliverance following repentance*

2:18 Zech 1:14; Is 60:10	18	Then the LORD will be zealous for His land, And will have pity on His people.
2:19 Hos 2:21,22; Ezek 34:29; 36:15	19	And the LORD will answer and say to His people, "Behold, I am going to send you grain, new wine, and oil, And you will be satisfied *in full* with them; And I will never again make you a reproach among the nations.
*2:20 Jer 1:14,15; Zech 14:8;	20	"But I will remove the northern *army* far from you,

---

2:14 *Who knows whether He will not turn and relent?* Joel describes a desolated land in which there is neither food for man nor pasture for beasts (1:17,18). He calls on the people to turn to God, with the thought and hope that God might then turn to them in blessing.

2:15 *Blow a trumpet.* A call to humiliation and public fasting, not an uncommon practice for God's people (see 2 Chr. 20).

2:20 *the northern army.* Israel's enemies habitually came from the north (cf. Jer. 1:14).

And I will drive it into a parched and desolate land,
And its vanguard into the eastern sea,
And its rear guard into the western sea.
And its stench will arise and its foul smell will come up,
For it has done great things."

Deut 11:24;
Is 34:3;
Amos 4:10

21 Do not fear, O land, rejoice and be glad,
For the LORD has done great things.

2:21
Jer 30:10;
v. 26

22 Do not fear, beasts of the field,
For the pastures of the wilderness have turned green,
For the tree has borne its fruit,
The fig tree and the vine have yielded in full.

2:22
Ps 65:12,13

23 So rejoice, O sons of Zion,
And be glad in the LORD your God;
For He has given you the ¹early rain for *your* vindication.
And He has poured down for you the rain,
The ¹early and ²latter rain as before.

2:23
Ps 149:2;
Is 41:16;
Deut 11:14;
Jer 5:24;
Hos 6:3

24 And the threshing floors will be full of grain,
And the vats will overflow with the new wine and oil.

2:24
Amos 9:13;
Mal 3:10
*2:25
Joel 1:4

25 "Then I will make up to you for the years
That the swarming locust has eaten,
The creeping locust, the stripping locust, and the gnawing locust,
My great army which I sent among you.

26 "And you shall have plenty to eat and be satisfied,
And praise the name of the LORD your God,
Who has dealt wondrously with you;
Then My people will never be put to shame.

2:26
Is 62:9;
Ps 67:5-7;
Is 25:1; 45:17

27 "Thus you will know that I am in the midst of Israel,
And that I am the LORD your God
And there is no other;
And My people will never be put to shame.

2:27
Joel 3:17,21;
Is 45:1,21;
49:23

II. The judgment of God and His blessing in the last days
(2:28–3:21)

A. The promised outpouring of the Spirit

28 "And it will come about after this
That I will pour out My Spirit on all mankind;
And your sons and daughters will prophesy,
Your old men will dream dreams,
Your young men will see visions.

*2:28
Acts 2:17-21;
Ezek 39:29;
Is 40:5

29 "And even on the male and female servants
I will pour out My Spirit in those days.

2:29
1 Cor 12:13;
Gal 3:28

30 "And I will display wonders in the sky and on the earth,
Blood, fire, and columns of smoke.

2:30
Matt 24:29;

31 "The sun will be turned into darkness,
And the moon into blood,
Before the great and awesome day of the LORD comes.

Luke 21:11,
25; Acts 2:19
2:31
Is 13:9,10;
Matt 24:29;

32 "And it will come about that whoever calls on the name of the LORD
Will be delivered;
For on Mount Zion and in Jerusalem
There will be those who escape,
As the LORD has said,
Even among the survivors whom the LORD calls.

Mal 4:1,5;
Rev 6:12
2:32
Is 46:13;
Mic 4:7;
Rom 9:27

¹I.e., autumn   ²I.e., spring

2:25 *I will make up to you . . . years.* After the years of judgment and devastation, God will give a comparable period of blessing and plenty.
2:28 *on all mankind.* God's Spirit had come upon prophets, priests, and kings during Old Testament times. Joel looked to a future day when the gifts of the Spirit would come to old and young, men and women, without regard to external

office or function. In the New Testament, Peter stated that this prophecy was fulfilled on the day of Pentecost when the Holy Spirit baptized the church (Acts 2:17–21). There may be, however, some elements in this prediction that are to find still further fulfillment in the end time, or the ultimate phase of the "last days," e.g., the supernatural signs and meteoric phenomena of v. 30.

B. *The restoration of Judah and the judgment of her enemies*

3:1
Jer 30:3;
Ezek 38:14
*3:2
Is 66:16;
Ezek 34:6;
35:10; 36:1-5

3 "For behold, in those days and at that time,
When I restore the fortunes of Judah and Jerusalem,
2   I will gather all the nations,
And bring them down to the valley of Jehoshaphat.
Then I will enter into judgment with them there
On behalf of My people and My inheritance, Israel,
Whom they have scattered among the nations;
And they have divided up My land.

3:3
Obad 11;
Nah 3:10

3   "They have also cast lots for My people,
Traded a boy for a harlot,
And sold a girl for wine that they may drink.

3:4
Amos 1:9,10;
Ezek 25:12,
17

4   "Moreover, what are you to Me, O Tyre, Sidon, and all the regions of
Philistia? Are you rendering Me a recompense? But if you do recompense Me,
swiftly and speedily I will return your recompense on your head.

3:5
2 Kin 12:18;
2 Chr 21:16,
17

5   "Since you have taken My silver and My gold, brought My precious treasures
to your temples,
6   and sold the sons of Judah and Jerusalem to the Greeks in order to remove
them far from their territory,

3:7
Is 43:5,6;
Jer 23:8
3:8
Is 14:2;
60:14;
Ezek 23:42;
Jer 6:20

7   behold, I am going to arouse them from the place where you have sold them,
and return your recompense on your head.
8   "Also I will sell your sons and your daughters into the hand of the sons of
Judah, and they will sell them to the Sabeans, to a distant nation," for the LORD has
spoken.

3:9
Is 8:9,10;
Jer 51:27,28;
6:4; 46:3,4;
Zech 14:2,3
3:10
Is 2:4;
Mic 4:3;
Zech 12:8
3:11
Ezek 38:15,
16; Is 13:3

9   Proclaim this among the nations:
Prepare a war; rouse the mighty men!
Let all the soldiers draw near, let them come up!
10   Beat your plowshares into swords,
And your pruning hooks into spears;
Let the weak say, "I am a mighty man."
11   Hasten and come, all you surrounding nations,
And gather yourselves there.
Bring down, O LORD, Thy mighty ones.

3:12
Is 2:4; 3:13

12   Let the nations be aroused
And come up to the valley of Jehoshaphat,
For there I will sit to judge
All the surrounding nations.

3:13
Matt 13:39;
Rev 14:15;
Is 63:3;
Rev 14:19
3:14
Is 34:2-8;
Joel 1:15; 2:1
3:15
Joel 2:10,31

13   Put in the sickle, for the harvest is ripe.
Come, tread, for the wine press is full;
The vats overflow, for their wickedness is great.
14   Multitudes, multitudes in the valley of decision!
For the day of the LORD is near in the valley of decision.
15   The sun and moon grow dark,
And the stars lose their brightness.

3:16
Amos 1:2;
Joel 2:11;
Hag 2:6;
Jer 17:17

16   And the LORD roars from Zion
And utters His voice from Jerusalem,
And the heavens and the earth tremble.
But the LORD is a refuge for His people
And a stronghold to the sons of Israel.

C. *Everlasting blessing for God's people*

3:17
v. 21;
Ezek 20:40;
Obad 17;
Is 52:1;
Nah 1:15

17   Then you will know that I am the LORD your God,
Dwelling in Zion My holy mountain.
So Jerusalem will be holy,
And strangers will pass through it no more.

3:18
Amos 9:13;
Is 30:25;
35:6;

18   And it will come about in that day
That the mountains will drip with sweet wine,
And the hills will flow with milk,

3:2 *Jehoshaphat* means "Yahweh has judged." The name
expresses the reality of judgment that would be meted out to
the godless there.

And all the brooks of Judah will flow with water;
And a spring will go out from the house of the LORD,
To water the valley of Shittim.

19 Egypt will become a waste,
And Edom will become a desolate wilderness,
Because of the violence done to the sons of Judah,
In whose land they have shed innocent blood.

20 But Judah will be inhabited forever,
And Jerusalem for all generations.

21 And I will avenge their blood which I have not avenged,
For the LORD dwells in Zion.

Margin references:
Ezek 47:1-12;
Rev 22:1

*3:19
Obad 10

3:20
Ezek 37:25;
Amos 9:15

3:21
Ezek 36:25;
v. 17

3:19 *Egypt will become a waste.* The enemies of Israel will be confounded when a spiritually revived Israel enjoys God's blessing in the land He has given her (3:18–21).

INTRODUCTION TO
THE BOOK OF
AMOS

Authorship and Background: The author, Amos, a minor prophet whose name means "burden" or "burden-bearer," is not to be confused with Isaiah's father, Amoz. Amos came from Tekoa, a town about six miles southeast of Bethlehem. He was a herdsman and also a cultivator of sycamore trees, the fruit of which was eaten by the poorer people. Some two hundred years before Amos prophesied, the Davidic kingdom had been broken into two parts, the northern and southern kingdoms. Although Amos lived in Judah, he spoke for God to the northern kingdom from their religious center at Bethel. He prophesied during the reign of Jeroboam II, which dates his writing about the middle of the eighth century B.C.

Characteristics: Amos writes as one accustomed to the perils and hardships of a shepherd's life. He knows the caravan customs and the marketplaces of his day. He is familiar with the gross inequalities between rich and poor. He sees the rich getting richer and the poor getting poorer. Filled with a sense of his divine call, he champions the oppressed. He is a rugged and a stern man, fearless and dynamic. Judgment and punishment are his familiar themes. He speaks against moral rottenness, selfishness, greed, immorality, and oppression of the poor. He notes the absence of justice for the oppressed. He condemns the idolatry of God's people and arraigns the Gentile nations that will also experience the judgment of God. His style is simple, yet it is pure and energetic; it is rich in metaphor and vivid in symbol. Nature is the source of his figures, and they speak through him with a loud voice.

Contents:

I. The prediction of judgment on the surrounding nations (1:1-2:16): Amos prophesies that the nations that sin shall experience divine punishment: this includes Damascus (Syria), Gaza (Philistia), Tyre (Phoenicia), Teman and Bozrah (Edom), Rabbah (Ammon), and Kerioth (Moab). Jerusalem will also suffer, and Israel is doomed because of her sins and the abuse of her privileges.

II. The judgment against Israel (3:1-6:14): Amos elaborates on the judgment against Israel. God has spoken against Israel; Amos must proclaim that message. The judgment must be published among the heathen. It is a just judgment, because the rich lived in luxury while oppressing the poor; idolatry is rampant and she is incorrigible. He laments the judgment and exhorts the people to repent. He prophesies exile beyond Damascus and speaks of their coming desolation and want.

III. The five visions of the coming judgment and blessings to follow (7:1-9:15): The locust plague averted by Amos's prayer. The judgment of fire also is averted. The plumb line, a symbol of God's determined judgment. Amaziah tells Amos to keep out of Israel. Amos cannot heed him because God has called him to prophesy. The vision of the basket of summer fruit, a sign that judgment is at hand. The LORD beside the altar, a sign that awful judgment, sure and just, is upon them. Amos foresees the restoration of the booth of David and the blessings of the kingdom in the age to come.

THE BOOK OF

AMOS

I. *The prediction of judgment on the surrounding nations*
(1:1–2:16)

A. *Superscription and theme*

1 The words of Amos, who was among the sheepherders from Tekoa, which he envisioned in visions concerning Israel in the days of Uzziah king of Judah, and in the days of Jeroboam son of Joash, king of Israel, two years before the earthquake.

2 And he said,
"The LORD roars from Zion,
And from Jerusalem He utters His voice;
And the shepherds' pasture grounds mourn,
And the summit of Carmel dries up."

1:1
2 Sam 14:2;
2 Kin 14:23-29;
Zech 14:5

1:2
Jer 25:30;
Joel 3:16;
1:18,19;
Amos 9:3

B. *Prophecy against Damascus*

3 Thus says the LORD,
"For three transgressions of Damascus and for four
I will not revoke its *punishment*,
Because they threshed Gilead with *implements* of sharp iron.
4 "So I will send fire upon the house of Hazael,
And it will consume the citadels of Ben-hadad.
5 "I will also break the *gate* bar of Damascus,
And cut off the inhabitant from the valley of Aven,
And him who holds the scepter, from Beth-eden;
So the people of Aram will go exiled to Kir,"
Says the LORD.

*1:3
Is 7:8; 8:4;
v. 13

1:4
Jer 49:27;
1 Kin 20:1;
2 Kin 6:24
1:5
Jer 51:30;
2 Kin 16:9;
Amos 9:7

C. *Prophecy against Gaza (Philistia)*

6 Thus says the LORD,
"For three transgressions of Gaza and for four
I will not revoke its *punishment*,
Because they deported an entire population
To deliver *it* up to Edom.
7 "So I will send fire upon the wall of Gaza,
And it will consume her citadels.
8 "I will also cut off the inhabitant from Ashdod,
And him who holds the scepter, from Ashkelon;
I will even unleash My power upon Ekron,
And the remnant of the Philistines will perish,"
Says the Lord GOD.

1:6
1 Sam 6:17;
Jer 47:1,5;
v. 9; Obad 11

1:7
Jer 47:1; v. 6

1:8
Zeph 2:4;
Zech 9:6;
Ps 81:14;
Ezek 25:16

D. *Prophecy against Tyre (Phoenicia)*

9 Thus says the LORD,
"For three transgressions of Tyre and for four
I will not revoke its *punishment*,
Because they delivered up an entire population to Edom
And did not remember *the* covenant of brotherhood.
10 "So I will send fire upon the wall of Tyre,
And it will consume her citadels."

1:9
Is 23:1-18;
Ezek 26:2-4;
1 Kin 5:1;
9:11-14

1:10
Zech 9:4

1:3 *For three transgressions of Damascus and for four.* The numbers "three" and "four" are used in a way in which emphasis and climax are presented. Amos was addressing Israel, the northern kingdom. He first pronounced judgment on Israel's enemies, then her sister kingdom Judah (2:4,5), and, finally, upon Israel (2:6–16 and the remainder of the book), although in some passages the whole nation is involved.

E. *Prophecy against Edom*

1:11
Is 34:5,6;
63:1-6;
Jer 49:7-22;
Obad 10-12;
Is 57:16;
Mic 7:18

11 Thus says the LORD,
   "For three transgressions of Edom and for four
   I will not revoke its *punishment*,
   Because he pursued his brother with the sword,
   While he stifled his compassion;
   His anger also tore continually,
   And he maintained his fury forever.

1:12
Jer 49:7,20;
Obad 9,10

12 "So I will send fire upon Teman,
   And it will consume the citadels of Bozrah."

F. *Prophecy against Ammon*

1:13
Jer 49:1-6;
Ezek 25:2-7;
2 Kin 15:16

13 Thus says the LORD,
   "For three transgressions of the sons of Ammon and for four
   I will not revoke its *punishment*,
   Because they ripped open the pregnant women of Gilead
   In order to enlarge their borders.

1:14
Jer 49:2;
Amos 2:2;
Ezek 21:22;
Is 29:6; 30:30

14 "So I will kindle a fire on the wall of Rabbah,
   And it will consume her citadels
   Amid war cries on the day of battle
   And a storm on the day of tempest.

1:15
Jer 49:3

15 "Their king will go into exile,
   He and his princes together," says the LORD.

G. *Prophecy against Moab*

*2:1
Is chs. 15,16;
Jer ch. 48;
Zeph 2:8,9

2 Thus says the LORD,
   "For three transgressions of Moab and for four
   I will not revoke its *punishment*,
   Because he burned the bones of the king of Edom to lime.

2:2
Jer 48:41,45

2 "So I will send fire upon Moab,
   And it will consume the citadels of Kerioth;
   And Moab will die amid tumult,
   With war cries and the sound of a trumpet.

2:3
Amos 5:7,12;
6:12; Ps 2:10;
Is 40:23;
Jer 48:7

3 "I will also cut off the judge from her midst,
   And slay all her princes with him," says the LORD.

H. *Prophecies against the chosen people*

1. *Judah*

2:4
2 Kin 17:19;
Joel 3:2;
Jer 6:19; 8:9;
Dan 9:11;
Is 28:15;
Jer 16:19;
Ezek 20:13,
16,18

4 Thus says the LORD,
   "For three transgressions of Judah and for four
   I will not revoke its *punishment*,
   Because they rejected the law of the LORD
   And have not kept His statutes;
   Their lies also have led them astray,
   Those after which their fathers walked.

2:5
Jer 17:27;
Hos 8:14

5 "So I will send fire upon Judah,
   And it will consume the citadels of Jerusalem."

2. *Israel*

2:6
2 Kin 18:12;
Joel 3:3;
Amos 5:11;
12; 8:6

6 Thus says the LORD,
   "For three transgressions of Israel and for four
   I will not revoke its *punishment*,
   Because they sell the righteous for money
   And the needy for a pair of sandals.

2:7
Amos 8:4;
5:12;

7 "These who pant after the *very* dust of the earth on the head of the
   helpless

2:1 Amos insists that the moral law is applicable to all peoples. Here he describes the atrocity of one Gentile nation (Moab) against a second (Edom).

Also turn aside the way of the humble;
And a man and his father resort to the same girl
In order to profane My holy name.

8 "And on garments taken as pledges they stretch out beside every altar,
And in the house of their God they drink the wine of those who have been fined.

9 "Yet it was I who destroyed the Amorite before them,
Though his height *was* like the height of cedars
And he *was* strong as the oaks;
I even destroyed his fruit above and his root below.

10 "And it was I who brought you up from the land of Egypt,
And I led you in the wilderness forty years
That you might take possession of the land of the Amorite.

11 "Then I raised up some of your sons to be prophets
And some of your young men to be Nazirites.
Is this not so, O sons of Israel?" declares the LORD.

12 "But you made the Nazirites drink wine,
And you commanded the prophets saying, 'You shall not prophesy!'

13 "Behold, I am weighted down beneath you
As a wagon is weighted down when filled with sheaves.

14 "Flight will perish from the swift,
And the stalwart will not strengthen his power,
Nor the mighty man save his life.

15 "He who grasps the bow will not stand *his ground*,
The swift of foot will not escape,
Nor will he who rides the horse save his life.

16 "Even the bravest among the warriors will flee naked in that day,"
declares the LORD.

II. *The judgment against Israel (3:1–6:14)*

A. *The relation of Israel to God*

3 Hear this word which the LORD has spoken against you, sons of Israel, against the entire family which He brought up from the land of Egypt,

2 "You only have I chosen among all the families of the earth;
Therefore, I will punish you for all your iniquities."

3 Do two men walk together unless they have made an appointment?

4 Does a lion roar in the forest when he has no prey?
Does a young lion growl from his den unless he has captured *something*?

5 Does a bird fall into a trap on the ground when there is no bait in it?
Does a trap spring up from the earth when it captures nothing at all?

6 If a trumpet is blown in a city will not the people tremble?
If a calamity occurs in a city has not the LORD done it?

7 Surely the Lord GOD does nothing
Unless He reveals His secret counsel
To His servants the prophets.

8 A lion has roared! Who will not fear?
The Lord GOD has spoken! Who can but prophesy?

B. *The sins of Samaria*

9 Proclaim on the citadels in Ashdod and on the citadels in the land of Egypt and say, "Assemble yourselves on the mountains of Samaria and see *the* great tumults within her and *the* oppressions in her midst.

10 "But they do not know how to do what is right," declares the LORD, "these who hoard up violence and devastation in their citadels."

11 Therefore, thus says the Lord GOD,

Cross references (right column):

Lev 20:3;
Hos 4:14

2:8
1 Cor 8:10;
Ex 22:26;
Amos 4:1; 6:6

*2:9
Deut 2:31;
Num 13:33;
Is 5:24;
Mal 4:1

2:10
Ex 12:51;
Deut 2:7;
Ex 3:8

2:11
Jer 7:25;
Num 6:2,3

2:12
Is 30:10;
Jer 11:21;
Amos 7:12,
13; Mic 2:6
2:13
Joel 3:13
2:14
Is 30:16,17;
Jer 9:23;
Ps 33:16
2:15
Jer 51:56;
Ezek 39:3;
Is 31:3
2:16
Jer 48:41

3:1
Jer 8:3;
13:11;
Amos 2:10;
9:7
*3:2
Deut 7:6;
Jer 14:20;
Ezek 20:36;
Luke 12:47;
Rom 2:9
3:3
Lev 26:23,24
3:4
Hos 11:10
3:6
Jer 6:1;
Hos 5:8;
Is 14:24-27;
45:7
3:7
Gen 18:17;
John 15:15;
Rev 10:7
3:8
Amos 1:2;
Jon 1:1; 3:1;
Jer 20:9;
Acts 4:20
3:9
Amos 1:8;
4:1; 6:1; 8:6
3:10
Jer 4:22;
Amos 5:7;
6:12;
Zech 5:3,4

2:9 *I who destroyed the Amorite.* Because of their sins, the Amorites were expelled from Canaan, and the land was given to Israel as an inheritance. Now, Amos asserts, Israel is guilty of sins comparable to those of the Amorites.

3:2 *You only have I chosen.* God's sovereign choice of Israel placed Israel under solemn obligation to serve Him faithfully. Privilege involves responsibility.

3:11
Amos 6:14;
2:14; 2:5

"An enemy, even one surrounding the land,
Will pull down your strength from you
And your citadels will be looted."

*3:12
1 Sam 17:34-37;
Amos 6:4;
Ps 132:3

12 Thus says the LORD,
"Just as the shepherd snatches from the lion's mouth a
couple of legs or a piece of an ear,
So will the sons of Israel dwelling in Samaria be snatched away—
With *the* corner of a bed and *the* cover of a couch!

3:13
Ezek 2:7

13 "Hear and testify against the house of Jacob,"
Declares the Lord GOD, the God of hosts.

3:14
v.2;
Amos 4:4;
5:5,6

14 "For on the day that I punish Israel's transgressions,
I will also punish the altars of Bethel;
The horns of the altar will be cut off,
And they will fall to the ground.

3:15
Jer 36:22;
Judg 3:20;
1 Kin 22:39

15 "I will also smite the winter house together with the summer house;
The houses of ivory will also perish
And the great houses will come to an end,"
Declares the LORD.

*4:1
Ps 22:12;
Ezek 39:18;
Amos 3:9;
6:1; 5:11;
8:6; 2:8; 6:6

4 Hear this word, you cows of Bashan who are on the mountain of
Samaria,
Who oppress the poor, who crush the needy,
Who say to your husbands, "Bring now, that we may drink!"

*4:2
Ps 89:25;
Amos 6:8;
8:7; Is 37:29;
Ezek 38:4;
29:4

2 The Lord GOD has sworn by His holiness,
"Behold, the days are coming upon you
When they will take you away with meat hooks,
And the last of you with fish hooks.

4:3
Jer 52:7;
Ezek 12:5

3 "You will go out *through* breaches *in the walls,*
Each one straight before her,
And you will be cast to Harmon," declares the LORD.

C. Israel's failure to return to God

4:4
Amos 3:14;
5:5;
Hos 4:15;
Num 28:3,4;
Deut 14:28

4 "Enter Bethel and transgress;
In Gilgal multiply transgression!
Bring your sacrifices every morning,
Your tithes every three days.

4:5
Lev 7:13;
22:18,21;
Hos 9:1,10

5 "Offer a thank offering also from that which is leavened,
And proclaim freewill offerings, make them known.
For so you love *to do,* you sons of Israel,"
Declares the Lord GOD.

4:6
Is 3:1;
Jer 14:18;
5:3; Hag 2:17

6 "But I gave you also cleanness of teeth in all your cities
And lack of bread in all your places,
Yet you have not returned to Me," declares the LORD.

4:7
Deut 11:17;
2 Chr 7:13;
Ex 9:4,26;
10:22,23

7 "And furthermore, I withheld the rain from you
While *there were* still three months until harvest.
Then I would send rain on one city
And on another city I would not send rain;
One part would be rained on,
While the part not rained on would dry up.

4:8
Jer 14:4;
Ezek 4:16;
Jer 3:7

8 "So two or three cities would stagger to another city to drink water,
But would not be satisfied;
Yet you have not returned to Me," declares the LORD.

4:9
Deut 28:22;
Hag 2:17;
Joel 1:4;
2:25; Jer 3:10

9 "I smote you with scorching *wind* and mildew;
And the caterpillar was devouring
Your many gardens and vineyards, fig trees and olive trees;
Yet you have not returned to Me," declares the LORD.

4:10
Ex 9:3,6;

10 "I sent a plague among you after the manner of Egypt;

3:12 *a couple of legs or a piece of an ear.* Only a very small
remnant of Israel shall be spared the coming judgment.
4:1 *you cows of Bashan.* Amos spoke scornfully of the
Israelite women, who are likened to the fat cows of Bashan.

(Bashan was rich, grain-producing land.)
4:2 *they will take you away with meat hooks.* Assyrian reliefs
depict prisoners actually led along the road with hooks in
their lips.

I slew your young men by the sword along with your captured
   horses,
And I made the stench of your camp rise up in your nostrils;
Yet you have not returned to Me," declares the LORD.

11 "I overthrew you as God overthrew Sodom and Gomorrah,
And you were like a firebrand snatched from a blaze;
Yet you have not returned to Me," declares the LORD.

12 "Therefore, thus I will do to you, O Israel;
Because I shall do this to you,
Prepare to meet your God, O Israel."

13 For behold, He who forms mountains and creates the wind
And declares to man what are His thoughts,
He who makes dawn into darkness
And treads on the high places of the earth,
The LORD God of hosts is His name.

D. *The LORD's lamentation over Israel*

5 2 Hear this word which I take up for you as a dirge, O house of Israel.
She has fallen, she will not rise again—
The virgin Israel.
She *lies* neglected on her land;
There is none to raise her up.

3 For thus says the Lord GOD,
"The city which goes forth a thousand *strong*
Will have a hundred left,
And the one which goes forth a hundred *strong*
Will have ten left to the house of Israel."

E. *The call to repentance*

4 For thus says the LORD to the house of Israel,
"Seek Me that you may live.

5 "But do not resort to Bethel,
And do not come to Gilgal,
Nor cross over to Beersheba;
For Gilgal will certainly go into captivity,
And Bethel will come to trouble.

6 "Seek the LORD that you may live,
Lest He break forth like a fire, O house of Joseph,
And it consume with none to quench *it* for Bethel,

7 *For* those who turn justice into wormwood
And cast righteousness down to the earth."

8 He who made the Pleiades and Orion
And changes deep darkness into morning,
Who also darkens day *into* night,
Who calls for the waters of the sea
And pours them out on the surface of the earth,
The LORD is His name.

9 It is He who flashes forth *with* destruction upon the strong,
So that destruction comes upon the fortress.

10 They hate him who reproves in the gate,
And they abhor him who speaks *with* integrity.

11 Therefore, because you impose heavy rent on the poor
And exact a tribute of grain from them,
Though you have built houses of well-hewn stone,
Yet you will not live in them;
You have planted pleasant vineyards, yet you will not drink
   their wine.

12 For I know your transgressions are many and your sins are great,
You who distress the righteous *and* accept bribes,
And turn aside the poor in the gate.

Cross references (right margin):

Deut 28:27,
60; Jer 11:22;
18:21; 48:15;
Joel 2:20;
Is 9:13

4:11
Is 13:19;
Zech 3:2;
Jer 23:14

4:12
v. 2;
Ezek 13:5

4:13
Jer 10:13;
Ps 139:2;
Dan 2:28;
Jer 13:16;
Mic 1:3;
Amos 5:8,27;
9:6

5:1
Ezek 19:1
5:2
Jer 14:17;
Amos 8:14;
Is 51:18;
Jer 50:32

5:3
Is 6:13;
Amos 6:9

5:4
Jer 29:3;
Is 55:3
*5:5
Amos 4:4;
1 Sam 7:16;
11:14;
Amos 8:14

5:6
Is 55:3,6,7;
v. 14;
Deut 4:24;
Amos 3:14
5:7
Amos 6:12

*5:8
Job 9:9;
12:22;
Is 42:16;
Amos 8:9;
Ps 104:6-9;
Amos 9:6;
4:13

5:9
Is 29:5;
Mic 5:11

5:10
Is 29:21;
1 Kin 22:8;
Is 59:15
5:11
Amos 3:9;
8:6; 3:15;
6:11;
Mic 6:15

5:12
Amos 2:6,7;
Is 29:21

5:5 *Beersheba*, a sanctuary used by Israel.   5:8 *Pleiades and Orion*, constellations.

<table>
<tr><td>5:13
Eccl 3:7</td><td>13</td><td>Therefore, at such a time the prudent person keeps silent, for it is an evil time.</td></tr>
<tr><td>5:14
v. 6; Mic 3:11</td><td>14</td><td>Seek good and not evil, that you may live;
And thus may the LORD God of hosts be with you,
Just as you have said!</td></tr>
<tr><td>5:15
Ps 97:10;
Rom 12:9;
Joel 2:14;
Mic 5:3,7,8</td><td>15</td><td>Hate evil, love good,
And establish justice in the gate!
Perhaps the LORD God of hosts
May be gracious to the remnant of Joseph.</td></tr>
<tr><td>5:16
Jer 9:17;
Joel 1:11;
2 Chr 35:25</td><td>16</td><td>Therefore, thus says the LORD God of hosts, the Lord,
"There is wailing in all the plazas,
And in all the streets they say, 'Alas! Alas!'
They also call the farmer to mourning
And professional mourners to lamentation.</td></tr>
<tr><td>5:17
Is 16:10;
Jer 48:33;
Nah 1:2</td><td>17</td><td>"And in all the vineyards *there is* wailing,
Because I shall pass through the midst of you," says the LORD.</td></tr>
</table>

F. The double woe for Israel

1. Exile beyond Damascus

<table>
<tr><td>*5:18
Is 5:19;
Joel 1:15;
2:1,11,31;
2 Pet 3:4;
Jer 30:7
5:19
Jer 48:44</td><td>18</td><td>Alas, you who are longing for the day of the LORD,
For what purpose *will* the day of the LORD *be* to you?
It *will be* darkness and not light;</td></tr>
<tr><td></td><td>19</td><td>As when a man flees from a lion,
And a bear meets him,
Or goes home, leans his hand against the wall,
And a snake bites him.</td></tr>
<tr><td>5:20
Is 13:10;
Zeph 1:15</td><td>20</td><td>*Will* not the day of the LORD *be* darkness instead of light,
Even gloom with no brightness in it?</td></tr>
<tr><td>5:21
Is 1:11-16;
Lev 26:31
5:22
Is 66:3;
Mic 6:6,7;
Amos 4:5</td><td>21</td><td>"I hate, I reject your festivals,
Nor do I delight in your solemn assemblies.</td></tr>
<tr><td></td><td>22</td><td>"Even though you offer up to Me burnt offerings and your grain offerings,
I will not accept *them*;
And I will not *even* look at the peace offerings of your fatlings.</td></tr>
<tr><td>5:23
Amos 6:4,5;
8:10
5:24
Jer 22:3;
Ezek 45:9;
Mic 6:8</td><td>23</td><td>"Take away from Me the noise of your songs;
I will not even listen to the sound of your harps.</td></tr>
<tr><td></td><td>24</td><td>"But let justice roll down like waters
And righteousness like an ever-flowing stream.</td></tr>
<tr><td>5:25
Deut 32:17;
Ezek 20:8,16,
24; Acts 7:42</td><td>25</td><td>"Did you present Me with sacrifices and grain offerings in the wilderness for forty years, O house of Israel?</td></tr>
<tr><td></td><td>26</td><td>"You also carried along Sikkuth your king and Kiyyun, your images, the star of your gods which you made for yourselves.</td></tr>
<tr><td>5:27
2 Kin 17:6;
Amos 4:13</td><td>27</td><td>"Therefore, I will make you go into exile beyond Damascus," says the LORD, whose name is the God of hosts.</td></tr>
</table>

2. Oppression, desolation, and want predicted

<table>
<tr><td>*6:1
Is 32:9-11;
Luke 6:24;
Ex 19:5;
Amos 3:2</td><td>6</td><td>Woe to those who are at ease in Zion,
And to those who *feel* secure in the mountain of Samaria,
The distinguished men of the foremost of nations,
To whom the house of Israel comes.</td></tr>
<tr><td>6:2
Jer 2:10;
Is 10:9;
2 Kin 18:34;
2 Chr 26:6;
Nah 3:8</td><td>2</td><td>Go over to Calneh and look,
And go from there to Hamath the great,
Then go down to Gath of the Philistines.
Are they better than these kingdoms,
Or is their territory greater than yours?</td></tr>
<tr><td>6:3
Is 56:12;
Amos 9:10</td><td>3</td><td>Do you put off the day of calamity,</td></tr>
</table>

5:18 *the day of the LORD.* In popular thought, this was the day when Israel's enemies would be confounded, and the Israelites vindicated before all the world as the LORD's chosen people. Amos, like other prophets, states that Israel herself must face judgment.
6:1 *at ease.* Conscious of God's great acts of deliverance in Israel's past history, many took it for granted that no harm could ever befall the chosen nation.

And would you bring near the seat of violence?

4   Those who recline on beds of ivory
And sprawl on their couches,
And eat lambs from the flock
And calves from the midst of the stall,

5   Who improvise to the sound of the harp,
And like David have composed songs for themselves,

6   Who drink wine from sacrificial bowls
While they anoint themselves with the finest of oils,
Yet they have not grieved over the ruin of Joseph.

7   Therefore, they will now go into exile at the head of the exiles,
And the sprawlers' banqueting will pass away.

8   The Lord GOD has sworn by Himself, the LORD God of hosts has
declared:
"I loathe the arrogance of Jacob,
And I detest his citadels;
Therefore, I will deliver up *the* city and all it contains."

9   And it will be, if ten men are left in one house, they will die.
10   Then one's uncle, or his undertaker, will lift him up to carry out *his* bones
from the house, and he will say to the one who is in the innermost part of the house,
"Is anyone else with you?" And that one will say, "No one." Then he will answer,
"Keep quiet. For the name of the LORD is not to be mentioned."
11   For behold, the LORD is going to command that the great house be smashed
to pieces and the small house to fragments.
12   Do horses run on rocks?
Or does one plow them with oxen?
Yet you have turned justice into poison,
And the fruit of righteousness into [1]wormwood,

13   You who rejoice in [2]Lo-debar,
And say, "Have we not by our *own* strength taken [3]Karnaim for
ourselves?"

14   "For behold, I am going to raise up a nation against you,
O house of Israel," declares the LORD God of hosts,
"And they will afflict you from the entrance of Hamath
To the brook of the Arabah.

III. The five visions of the coming judgment and blessings
to follow (7:1–9:15)

A. The plague of locusts

7 Thus the Lord GOD showed me, and behold, He was forming a locust-swarm
when the spring crop began to sprout. And behold, the spring crop *was* after the
king's mowing.
2   And it came about, when it had finished eating the vegetation of the land,
that I said,
"Lord GOD, please pardon!
How can Jacob stand,
For he is small?"
3   The LORD changed His mind about this.
"It shall not be," said the LORD.

B. The fire devouring the deep

4   Thus the Lord GOD showed me, and behold, the Lord GOD was calling to
contend *with them* by fire, and it consumed the great deep and began to consume the
farm land.
5   Then I said,
"Lord GOD, please stop!
How can Jacob stand, for he is small?"
6   The LORD changed His mind about this.
"This too shall not be," said the Lord GOD.

[1]I.e., bitterness [2]Lit., *a thing of nothing* [3]Lit., *a pair of horns*

6:4
Amos 3:15;
3:12;
Ezek 34:2,3
6:5
Is 5:12;
Amos 5:23;
1 Chr 23:5
6:6
Amos 2:8;
4:1;
Gen 37:25;
Ezek 9:4
6:7
Amos 7:11,
17;
Dan 5:4-6,30;
v. 4
6:8
Jer 51:14;
Heb 6:13;
Deut 32:19;
Ps 106:40;
Amos 3:10,
11; Hos 11:6
6:9
Amos 5:3
6:10
Amos 5:13;
8:3
6:11
Is 55:11;
Amos 3:15
6:12
Is 59:13,14;
Hos 10:4;
Amos 5:7
6:13
Ps 75:4,5
6:14
Jer 5:15;
Amos 3:11;
Num 34:8;
1 Kin 8:65
7:1
vv. 4,7;
Amos 8:1;
Joel 1:4;
Amos 4:9;
Nah 3:15
7:2
Ex 10:14,15;
Ezek 9:8;
11:13;
Is 37:4;
Jer 42:2
7:3
Deut 32:36;
Jer 26:19;
Jon 3:10
7:4
Is 66:15,16;
Amos 2:5
7:5
v. 2
7:6
v. 3

C. The vision of the plumb line:
Amos told to leave the land

7 Thus He showed me, and behold, the Lord was standing by a vertical wall, with a plumb line in His hand.

8 And the LORD said to me, "What do you see, Amos?" And I said, "A plumb line." Then the Lord said,

"Behold I am about to put a plumb line
In the midst of My people Israel.
I will spare them no longer.

9 "The high places of Isaac will be desolated
And the sanctuaries of Israel laid waste.
Then shall I rise up against the house of Jeroboam with the sword."

10 Then Amaziah, the priest of Bethel, sent *word* to Jeroboam, king of Israel, saying, "Amos has conspired against you in the midst of the house of Israel; the land is unable to endure all his words.

11 "For thus Amos says, 'Jeroboam will die by the sword and Israel will certainly go from its land into exile.' "

12 Then Amaziah said to Amos, "Go, you seer, flee away to the land of Judah, and there eat bread and there do your prophesying!

13 "But no longer prophesy at Bethel, for it is a sanctuary of the king and a royal residence."

14 Then Amos answered and said to Amaziah, "I am not a prophet, nor am I the son of a prophet; for I am a herdsman and a grower of sycamore figs.

15 "But the LORD took me from following the flock and the LORD said to me, 'Go prophesy to My people Israel.'

16 "And now hear the word of the LORD: you are saying, 'You shall not prophesy against Israel nor shall you speak against the house of Isaac.'

17 "Therefore, thus says the LORD, 'Your wife will become a harlot in the city, your sons and your daughters will fall by the sword, your land will be parceled up by a *measuring* line, and you yourself will die upon unclean soil. Moreover, Israel will certainly go from its land into exile.' "

D. The basket of summer fruit

1. The vision of Israel's ruin

8 Thus the Lord GOD showed me, and behold, *there was* a basket of summer fruit.
2 And He said, "What do you see, Amos?" And I said, "A basket of summer fruit." Then the LORD said to me, "The end has come for My people Israel. I will spare them no longer.

3 "The songs of the palace will turn to wailing in that day," declares the Lord GOD. "Many *will be* the corpses; in every place they will cast them forth in silence."

2. The lust for money

4 Hear this, you who trample the needy, to do away with the humble of the land,

5 saying,
"When will the new moon be over,
So that we may sell grain,
And the sabbath, that we may open the wheat *market*,
To make the bushel smaller and the shekel bigger,
And to cheat with dishonest scales,

6 So as to buy the helpless for money
And the needy for a pair of sandals,
And *that* we may sell the refuse of the wheat?"

7 The LORD has sworn by the pride of Jacob,
"Indeed, I will never forget any of their deeds,

8 "Because of this will not the land quake

Cross-references (margin)

7:8
Amos 8:2;
Is 28:17;
34:11;
Lam 2:8;
Mic 7:18

7:9
Hos 10:8;
Mic 1:5;
Is 63:18;
2 Kin 15:10
*7:10
1 Kin 12:32;
2 Kin 14:23;
Jer 26:8-11
7:11
vv. 9,17

*7:13
Amos 2:12;
1 Kin 12:32;
13:1
*7:14
1 Kin 20:35;
2 Kin 2:5;
4:38;
2 Chr 19:2;
Amos 1:1
7:15
2 Sam 7:8;
Amos 3:8;
Jer 7:1;
Ezek 2:3,4
7:16
Amos 2:12;
Ezek 21:2;
Mic 2:6
7:17
Jer 29:21;
Hos 4:13,14;
Jer 14:16;
Ezek 4:13;
Hos 9:3

8:2
Amos 7:8;
Jer 24:3;
Ezek 7:2

8:3
Amos 5:23;
6:9,10

8:4
Ps 14:4;
Amos 5:11,12
8:5
2 Kin 4:23;
Neh 13:15,
16; Mic 6:10,
11

8:6
Amos 2:6

8:7
Amos 6:8;
Deut 33:26,
29; Hos 8:13;
9:9

7:10 *Amos has conspired against you.* Amos, a native of Tekoa in the southern kingdom (Judah), was looked upon as a foreigner who was stirring up trouble in the north. He was told that he was not welcome at Bethel, a shrine of the northern kingdom.

7:13 *Bethel,* see note to Gen. 28:19.
7:14 *I am not a prophet.* Amos insisted that he was not a professional prophet but a layman to whom God had entrusted a message.

And everyone who dwells in it mourn?
Indeed, all of it will rise up like the Nile,
And it will be tossed about,
And subside like the Nile of Egypt.

9 "And it will come about in that day," declares the Lord GOD,
"That I shall make the sun go down at noon
And make the earth dark in broad daylight.

10 "Then I shall turn your festivals into mourning
And all your songs into lamentation;
And I will bring sackcloth on everyone's loins
And baldness on every head.
And I will make it like *a time of* mourning for an only son,
And the end of it will be like a bitter day.

3. *The famine of the Word of God*

11 "Behold, days are coming," declares the Lord GOD,
"When I will send a famine on the land,
Not a famine for bread or a thirst for water,
But rather for hearing the words of the LORD.

12 "And people will stagger from sea to sea,
And from the north even to the east;
They will go to and fro to seek the word of the LORD,
But they will not find *it*.

13 "In that day the beautiful virgins
And the young men will faint from thirst.

14 "*As for* those who swear by the guilt of Samaria,
Who say, 'As your god lives, O Dan,'
And, 'As the way of Beersheba lives,'
They will fall and not rise again."

E. *The destruction of the sanctuary*

9 I saw the Lord standing beside the altar, and He said,
"Smite the capitals so that the thresholds will shake,
And break them on the heads of them all!
Then I will slay the rest of them with the sword;
They will not have a fugitive who will flee,
Or a refugee who will escape.

2 "Though they dig into Sheol,
From there shall My hand take them;
And though they ascend to heaven,
From there will I bring them down.

3 "And though they hide on the summit of Carmel,
I will search them out and take them from there;
And though they conceal themselves from My sight on the floor of
the sea,
From there I will command the serpent and it will bite them.

4 "And though they go into captivity before their enemies,
From there I will command the sword that it slay them,
And I will set My eyes against them for evil and not for good."

5 And the Lord GOD of hosts,
The One who touches the land so that it melts,
And all those who dwell in it mourn,
And all of it rises up like the Nile
And subsides like the Nile of Egypt;

6 The One who builds His upper chambers in the heavens,
And has founded His vaulted dome over the earth,
He who calls for the waters of the sea
And pours them out on the face of the earth,
The LORD is His name.

7 "Are you not as the sons of Ethiopia to Me,
O sons of Israel?" declares the LORD.

8:8
Is 5:25;
Hos 4:3;
Amos 9:5

8:9
Is 13:10;
Jer 15:9;
Mic 3:6;
Amos 4:13;
5:8

8:10
Amos 5:21;
6:4,5;
Jer 48:37;
Ezek 7:18;
Jer 6:26;
Zech 12:10

8:11
1 Sam 3:1;
2 Chr 15:3;
Ezek 7:26;
Mic 3:6

8:12
Ezek 20:3,31

8:13
Lam 1:18;
Is 41:17;
Hos 2:3
8:14
Hos 4:15;
1 Kin 12:28,
29; Amos 5:5

9:1
Amos 3:14;
Zeph 2:14;
Hab 3:13;
v. 4;
Amos 2:14

9:2
Ps 139:8;
Jer 51:53;
Obad 4

9:3
Amos 1:2;
Jer 16:16,17;
Is 27:1

9:4
Lev 26:33;
Ezek 5:12;
Jer 44:11

9:5
Mic 1:4;
Amos 8:8

9:6
Ps 104:3;
Amos 5:8;
4:13

*9:7
Is 43:3;
Amos 2:10;
3:1;

Deut 2:23; Jer 47:4; Amos 1:5		"Have I not brought up Israel from the land of Egypt, And the Philistines from Caphtor and the Arameans from Kir?
9:8 Jer 44:27; vv. 4,10; Jer 30:11; Joel 2:32	8	"Behold, the eyes of the Lord GOD are on the sinful kingdom, And I will destroy it from the face of the earth; Nevertheless, I will not totally destroy the house of Jacob," Declares the LORD.
9:9 Is 30:28	9	"For behold, I am commanding, And I will shake the house of Israel among all nations As *grain* is shaken in a sieve, But not a kernel will fall to the ground.
9:10 Amos 8:14; 6:3	10	"All the sinners of My people will die by the sword, Those who say, 'The calamity will not overtake or confront us.'

F. *The promise of Messianic blessing*

1. *Restoration of the Davidic kingdom*

*9:11 Acts 15:16, 17; Ps 80:12; Is 63:11; Jer 46:26	11	"In that day I will raise up the fallen booth of David, And wall up its breaches; I will also raise up its ruins, And rebuild it as in the days of old;
9:12 Obad 19; Is 11:14; 43:7	12	That they may possess the remnant of Edom And all the nations who are called by My name," Declares the LORD who does this.

2. *The productivity of the earth*

9:13 Lev 26:5; Joel 3:18	13	"Behold, days are coming," declares the LORD, "When the plowman will overtake the reaper And the treader of grapes him who sows seed; When the mountains will drip sweet wine, And all the hills will be dissolved.

3. *Kingdom blessings*

9:14 Is 60:4; Jer 30:18; Is 61:4; Ezek 36:35; 28:26	14	"Also I will restore the captivity of My people Israel, And they will rebuild the ruined cities and live *in them,* They will also plant vineyards and drink their wine, And make gardens and eat their fruit.
9:15 Jer 24:6; 31:28; Is 60:21; Jer 32:41; Ezek 34:28	15	"I will also plant them on their land, And they will not again be rooted out from their land Which I have given them," Says the LORD your God.

9:7 *the Philistines from Caphtor.* Israel gloried in the fact that God had brought her ancestors from Egypt and had given them an inheritance in Canaan. Amos reminded them that Philistines and Syrians were also under the providential care of God.
9:11 *In that day.* Amos had prophesied the destruction of Israel, but he held forth the hope of a glorious future, when the people would be planted again in their own land with God's blessing. In the New Testament, James, in Acts 15:16,17, quotes this passage as evidence that the call of the Gentiles into the church was in accord with Old Testament prophecy. Some think that Amos also here prophesied the re-establishment of the house of David following the second advent of Christ, when the Savior will sit upon the throne of David according to promise (Luke 1:32).

INTRODUCTION TO

THE BOOK OF

OBADIAH

Authorship and Background: We know little or nothing about the author of this book, which is the shortest in the Old Testament. The name Obadiah means "servant of Yahweh," and is found frequently in the Old Testament. The date of the book is open to question. The traditional view is that it was written before the book of Jeremiah. Many scholars construe the reference to the captivity of Jerusalem (11-14) as pointing to a date of composition subsequent to 586 B.C. The people of Edom participated in four plunderings of Jerusalem in a three-hundred-year period, beginning in the ninth century B.C. It was in connection with these depredations that Obadiah wrote.

The burden of Obadiah's prophecy concerned Edom. The Edomites were descendants of Esau and had always been enemies of the sons of Jacob. The Herods of Jesus' day came from Edomite stock. Following the destruction of Jerusalem in A.D. 70, the Edomites are heard of no more.

Characteristics: Obadiah prophesies the destruction and extinction of Edom. This is a suitable divine judgment on the nation for its unbrotherly conduct toward the people of God, to whom they have been cruel, and whose goods they have plundered. The latter part of Obadiah's prophecy deals with the day of the LORD, when judgment will come on Edom and other nations, but deliverance will be in Zion. Israel will overcome its conquerors and extend itself to the four points of the compass. The earlier part of the book is unrelieved in its spirit of judgment. There is no hope for Edom and no mention of repentance and salvation. The message is of only doom and destruction. Nations shall reap as they have sown. But the latter part of the prophecy is encouraging to Israel and ends with the promise that "the kingdom will be the LORD's."

Contents:

 I. The judgment against Edom (1-14): Edom will be destroyed. It is guilty of the sin of pride and has wronged its brother, Judah.

 II. The day of the LORD (15-21): As nations sow, so shall they reap. Judgment will come. Judah will be free, holy, and rich. The enemy will be destroyed. Judah's boundaries will be enlarged, and the nation will return from dispersion. The kingdom shall be the LORD's.

THE BOOK OF

OBADIAH

I. *The judgment against Edom (1–14)*

A. *The fall of Edom predicted*

*1 Is 34:5; Ezek 25:12; Joel 3:19; Jer 49:14; Is 30:4; Jer 6:4,5	**1** The vision of Obadiah. Thus says the Lord GOD concerning Edom— We have heard a report from the LORD, And an envoy has been sent among the nations saying, "Arise and let us go against her for battle"—
	2 "Behold, I will make you small among the nations; You are greatly despised.
*3 Is 16:6; Jer 49:16; 2 Kin 14:7; Is 14:13-15; Rev 18:7	**3** "The arrogance of your heart has deceived you, You who live in the clefts of the rock, In the loftiness of your dwelling place, Who say in your heart, 'Who will bring me down to earth?'
4 Job 20:6; Hab 2:9; Is 14:13-15	**4** "Though you build high like the eagle, Though you set your nest among the stars, From there I will bring you down," declares the LORD.

B. *Edom's destruction to be complete*

5 Jer 49:9; vv. 9,10; Is 17:6	**5** "If thieves came to you, If robbers by night— O how you will be ruined!— Would they not steal *only* until they had enough? If grape gatherers came to you, Would they not leave *some* gleanings?
*6 Jer 49:10	**6** "O how Esau will be ransacked, And his hidden treasures searched out!
7 Jer 30:14; 38:22; Ps 41:9; Jer 49:7	**7** "All the men allied with you Will send you forth to the border, And the men at peace with you Will deceive you and overpower you. *They who eat* your bread Will set an ambush for you. (There is no understanding in him.)
8 Job 5:12; Is 29:14	**8** "Will I not on that day," declares the LORD, "Destroy wise men from Edom And understanding from the mountain of Esau?
9 Jer 49:22; Amos 1:12; Hab 3:3; v. 5	**9** "Then your mighty men will be dismayed, O Teman, In order that everyone may be cut off from the mountain of Esau by slaughter.

C. *Edom's sins laid bare*

10 Ps 137:7; Joel 3:19; Amos 1:11	**10** "Because of violence to your brother Jacob, You will be covered *with* shame, And you will be cut off forever.
*11 Ps 137:7; Joel 3:3; Nah 3:10	**11** "On the day that you stood aloof, On the day that strangers carried off his wealth, And foreigners entered his gate

---

1 See note to Gen. 36:9 on Edomites.
3 Arrogance of heart is deceptive, fostered in this instance by the fact that Edom was located on a rock that seemed impregnable. Moreover, arrogance led to presumption, Edom assuming that it was perfectly safe. But God would bring it to nothing anyway.
6 *how Esau will be ransacked.* Jacob (Israel) and Esau

(Edom) were brothers, and the rivalry between the brothers developed into hostility among their descendants (cf. Gen. 27:40).
11 *On the day that you stood aloof.* When the territory of Israel was attacked, brother Edom should have come to her aid. Instead, Edom rejoiced over the destruction of the Israelite territory.

And cast lots for Jerusalem—
You too were as one of them.

12 "Do not gloat over your brother's day,
The day of his misfortune.
And do not rejoice over the sons of Judah
In the day of their destruction;
Yes, do not boast
In the day of *their* distress.

12
Mic 4:11;
Ezek 35:15;
36:5;
Ps 31:18

13 "Do not enter the gate of My people
In the day of their disaster.
Yes, you, do not gloat over their calamity
In the day of their disaster.
And do not loot their wealth
In the day of their disaster.

13
Ezek 35:5,10;
36:2,3

14 "And do not stand at the fork of the road
To cut down their fugitives;
And do not imprison their survivors
In the day of their distress.

II. The day of the LORD (15–21)

A. The judgment of all nations

15 "For the day of the LORD draws near on all the nations.
As you have done, it will be done to you.
Your dealings will return on your own head.

15
Ezek 30:3;
Joel 1:15;
Jer 50:29;
Hab 2:8;
Ezek 35:11

16 "Because just as you drank on My holy mountain,
All the nations will drink continually.
They will drink and swallow,
And become as if they had never existed.

16
Jer 49:12,13;
25:15,16

B. Deliverance in Zion: the kingdom of the LORD

17 "But on Mount Zion there will be those who escape,
And it will be holy.
And the house of Jacob will possess their possessions.

17
Is 4:2,3;
Amos 9:11-15

18 "Then the house of Jacob will be a fire
And the house of Joseph a flame;
But the house of Esau *will be* as stubble.
And they will set them on fire and consume them,
So that there will be no survivor of the house of Esau,"
For the LORD has spoken.

*18
Is 10:17;
Jer 11:23;
Amos 1:8

19 Then *those of* the ¹Negev will possess the mountain of Esau,
And *those of* the ²Shephelah the Philistine *plain*;
Also, they will possess the territory of Ephraim and the territory of
    Samaria,
And Benjamin *will possess* Gilead.

*19
Amos 9:12;
Is 11:14;
Zeph 2:7;
Jer 31:5;
32:44

20 And the exiles of this host of the sons of Israel,
Who are *among* the Canaanites as far as Zarephath,
And the exiles of Jerusalem who are in Sepharad
Will possess the cities of the Negev.

*20
1 Kin 17:9;
Jer 32:44;
33:13

21 The deliverers will ascend Mount Zion
To judge the mountain of Esau,
And the kingdom will be the LORD's.

21
Neh 9:27;
Ps 22:28;
67:4;
Dan 2:44;
Zech 14:9

¹I.e., South country   ²I.e., the foothills

---

14 *To cut down their fugitives.* Edom refused to allow fugitives from Israel to enter Edomite territory.
18 Edom sprang from Esau; Israel from Jacob. Edom shall be consumed, Israel saved.
19 *Negev,* see note to Gen. 12:9. Located south of Judah, Negev was relatively waterless. It included a series of rolling hills and was the favored home of the early Israelites. *Shephelah:* a geographical term for the region between the coastal plain of Philistia and the high central ranges of The Land of Israel.

20 *this host.* This is a reference to Halah, mentioned in 2 Kin. 17:6; 18:11; and 1 Chr. 5:26 as one of the places to which the Assyrians deported the prisoners from Samaria. This implies that it must have been somewhere in the neighborhood of the city of Nineveh. *Sepharad,* a place to which the Jews were sent as captives, the location of which has never been determined to the satisfaction of all. Locations in Spain, Assyria, etc., have been proposed, but there is nothing to substantiate these claims.

INTRODUCTION TO
THE BOOK OF
JONAH

Authorship and Background: Who wrote this book is nowhere plainly stated. The chief character is Jonah, the son of Amittai. *Jonah* means "dove." According to 2 Kin. 14:25, he lived in Gath-hepher, just north of Nazareth, during the reign of Jeroboam II. The time period was the eighth century B.C., when Hosea and Amos were also prophesying. The length of Jonah's ministry cannot be determined. Conservatives generally accept the book as history since the names and locations are historical. They infer that Jesus' references to Jonah in the New Testament (Matt. 12:39,40; Luke 11:29,30) imply the historicity of the book. Some scholars suggest that an unknown author attempted to depict the great theological truth of God's universal concern and wove a parabolic story around the historical character of Jonah. Nineveh, the city that is central in Jonah, was the capital of the world empire of Assyria, an empire that stood for three hundred years. It was a brutally militaristic nation, hated by other peoples of western Asia. Proud Assyria represented heathen defiance against God.

Characteristics: The greater part of Jonah is a biographical narrative. No effort is made to disregard Jonah's disobedience. The account is chronologically progressive and straightforward. One event follows on another. Behind the story lies the truth of God's saving concern for all nations. Its implications for Israel cannot be overlooked. Here is a Gentile nation that, when faced with judgment, was willing to repent. Israel must do no less if she is to escape punishment for her unfaithfulness in the face of much greater blessings of God. Jonah also has prophetic significance relative to the death, burial, and resurrection of Jesus Christ, typically pointing to the One who is "greater than Jonah" and whose own experience fulfilled the prophetic word (Matt 12:40,41).

Contents:

I. The disobedient and suffering prophet (1:1-17): God calls Jonah to go to Nineveh. He flees toward Tarshish. A storm rises on the sea. Jonah is cast overboard and is swallowed by a great fish.

II. The repentant and delivered prophet (2:1-10): Jonah repents; he prays from the fish's belly and is delivered.

III. The reluctantly obedient prophet (3:1-10): God calls Jonah the second time to go to Nineveh. He obeys God. He preaches repentance and deferment of judgment. Nineveh repents and judgment is averted.

IV. The God of unlimited mercy (4:1-11): Jonah is angry because Nineveh is saved. He is sheltered by a plant that withers. He is distressed. God applies this as a parable to Nineveh, the object of His unlimited mercy.

THE BOOK OF
JONAH

I. *The disobedient and suffering prophet (1:1–17)*

1 The word of the LORD came to Jonah the son of Amittai saying,
2 "Arise, go to Nineveh the great city, and cry against it, for their wickedness has come up before Me."
3 But Jonah rose up to flee to Tarshish from the presence of the LORD. So he went down to Joppa, found a ship which was going to Tarshish, paid the fare, and went down into it to go with them to Tarshish from the presence of the LORD.
4 And the LORD hurled a great wind on the sea and there was a great storm on the sea so that the ship was about to break up.
5 Then the sailors became afraid, and every man cried to his god, and they threw the cargo which was in the ship into the sea to lighten *it* for them. But Jonah had gone below into the hold of the ship, lain down, and fallen sound asleep.
6 So the captain approached him and said, "How is it that you are sleeping? Get up, call on your god. Perhaps *your* god will be concerned about us so that we will not perish."
7 And each man said to his mate, "Come, let us cast lots so we may learn on whose account this calamity *has struck* us." So they cast lots and the lot fell on Jonah.
8 Then they said to him, "Tell us, now! On whose account *has* this calamity *struck* us? What is your occupation? And where do you come from? What is your country? From what people are you?"
9 And he said to them, "I am a Hebrew, and I fear the LORD God of heaven who made the sea and the dry land."
10 Then the men became extremely frightened and they said to him, "How could you do this?" For the men knew that he was fleeing from the presence of the LORD, because he had told them.
11 So they said to him, "What should we do to you that the sea may become calm for us?"—for the sea was becoming increasingly stormy.
12 And he said to them, "Pick me up and throw me into the sea. Then the sea will become calm for you, for I know that on account of me this great storm *has come* upon you."
13 However, the men rowed *desperately* to return to land but they could not, for the sea was becoming *even* stormier against them.
14 Then they called on the LORD and said, "We earnestly pray, O LORD, do not let us perish on account of this man's life and do not put innocent blood on us; for Thou, O LORD, hast done as Thou hast pleased."
15 So they picked up Jonah, threw him into the sea, and the sea stopped its raging.
16 Then the men feared the LORD greatly, and they offered a sacrifice to the LORD and made vows.
17 And the LORD appointed a great fish to swallow Jonah, and Jonah was in the stomach of the fish three days and three nights.

*1:1
2 Kin 14:25;
Matt 12:39
1:2
Jon 3:2,3;
4:1; Ezra 9:6
*1:3
Ps 139:7,9,
10; Acts 9:36
1:4
Ps 107:25
1:5
Acts 27:18;
1 Sam 24:3
1:6
Ps 107:28;
Jon 3:9
1:7
Josh 7:14;
1 Sam 10:20;
14:41,42;
Acts 1:26
1:8
Josh 7:14;
1 Sam 14:43
*1:9
Ps 146:6;
Acts 17:24
1:10
Job 27:22
1:12
2 Sam 24:17;
John 11:50;
1 Chr 21:17
1:13
Prov 21:30
*1:14
v. 16;
Deut 21:8;
Ps 115:3
1:15
Ps 89:9;
107:29;
Luke 8:24
1:16
1 Sam 6:2-5;
Mark 4:41
*1:17
Jon 4:6;
Matt 12:40;
16:4;
Luke 11:30

1:1 *Jonah the son of Amittai.* A prophet in Israel during the reign of Jeroboam II (2 Kin. 14:25).
1:3 *to Tarshish,* probably Tartessus in southwestern Spain. See also note to 1 Kin. 10:22.
1:9 *a Hebrew.* The term is frequently used by Israelites in situations in which they must identify themselves to foreigners (cf. Gen. 40:15; Ex. 2:6). *fear the LORD.* This means to have a reverential trust in Him. It also encompasses the idea of a hatred of sin. The common sense of "fear" as apprehension or dread does not exhaust the meaning of the word.
1:14 *do not let us perish,* i.e., do not let the innocent suffer with the guilty.
1:17 Jonah and Christ are compared with each other.

Christ Himself points out in a simile in Matt. 12:40 that as Jonah was in the belly of the fish (the Greek term is *Ketos,* or sea monster) for three days and nights, so would Christ be raised from the dead on the third day. Some have theorized that Jonah actually died and was resuscitated on his ejection from the fish's stomach. But since he was as good as dead while in the creature's digestive tract, the typical meaning is in no sense violated by his having been entombed alive in the fish. Many have been distracted by supposed scientific difficulties in the account of Jonah's preservation in the belly of the fish and have thus lost sight of the true lesson to be learned from Jonah's life and experience. Whether God created a special whale or other huge fish unlike those known to zoology is of no consequence. The God who

II. *The repentant and delivered prophet (2:1–10)*

2:1
Ps 130:1
2:2
Ps 18:4-6

2 Then Jonah prayed to the LORD his God from the stomach of the fish,
2 and he said,
"I called out of my distress to the LORD,
And He answered me.
I cried for help from the depth of Sheol;
Thou didst hear my voice.

2:3
Ps 88:6; 42:7

3 "For Thou hadst cast me into the deep,
Into the heart of the seas,
And the current engulfed me.
All Thy breakers and billows passed over me.

2:4
Ps 31:22;
1 Kin 8:38
2:5
Ps 69:1;
Lam 3:54

4 "So I said, 'I have been expelled from Thy sight.
Nevertheless I will look again toward Thy holy temple.'
5 "Water encompassed me to the point of death.
The great deep engulfed me,
Weeds were wrapped around my head.

2:6
Ps 16:10

6 "I descended to the roots of the mountains.
The earth with its bars *was* around me forever,
But Thou hast brought up my life from the pit, O LORD my God.

2:7
Ps 142:3;
77:10,11;
18:6

7 "While I was fainting away,
I remembered the LORD;
And my prayer came to Thee,
Into Thy holy temple.

2:8
2 Kin 17:15;
Ps 31;6;
Jer 10:8;
16:19
*2:9
Ps 50:14;
Hos 14:2;
Heb 13:15;
Job 22:27;
Ps 3:8
2:10
Jon 1:17

8 "Those who regard vain idols
Forsake their faithfulness,
9 But I will sacrifice to Thee
With the voice of thanksgiving.
That which I have vowed I will pay.
Salvation is from the LORD."
10 Then the LORD commanded the fish, and it vomited Jonah up onto the dry land.

III. *The reluctantly obedient prophet (3:1–10)*

*3:1
Jon 1:1,2

3 Now the word of the LORD came to Jonah the second time, saying,
2 "Arise, go to Nineveh the great city and proclaim to it the proclamation which I am going to tell you."
3 So Jonah arose and went to Nineveh according to the word of the LORD. Now Nineveh was [1]an exceedingly great city, a three days' walk.
4 Then Jonah began to go through the city one day's walk; and he cried out and said, "Yet forty days and Nineveh will be overthrown."

3:5
Dan 9:3;
Joel 1:14;
Jer 31:34
3:6
Job 2:8;
Jer 6:25;
Dan 9:3
3:7
v. 5;
2 Chr 20:3
3:8
Ps 130:1;
Jon 1:6,14;
Is 55:6,7;
Jer 18:11
3:9
2 Sam 12:22;
Joel 2:14
3:10
Jer 31:18;

5 Then the people of Nineveh believed in God; and they called a fast and put on sackcloth from the greatest to the least of them.
6 When the word reached the king of Nineveh, he arose from his throne, laid aside his robe from him, covered *himself* with sackcloth, and sat on the ashes.
7 And he issued a proclamation and it said, "In Nineveh by the decree of the king and his nobles: Do not let man, beast, herd, or flock taste a thing. Do not let them eat or drink water.
8 "But both man and beast must be covered with sackcloth; and let men call on God earnestly that each may turn from his wicked way and from the violence which is in his hands.
9 "Who knows, God may turn and relent, and withdraw His burning anger so that we shall not perish?"
10 When God saw their deeds, that they turned from their wicked way, then

[1]Lit., *a great city to God*

---

created all things must retain the power to create a unique specimen for a special purpose if it suits His purpose. Tradition has interpreted Christ's reference to Jonah (Matt. 12:39,40) as implying the historicity of the event.
2:9 *That which I have vowed I will pay.* As a prophet, Jonah had vowed obedience. His flight from God's revealed will was a breaking of a solemn vow.
3:1 The story of Jonah falls naturally into five sections: (1)

Jonah commissioned (1:2); (2) Jonah disobedient (1:3); (3) Jonah repentant (2:1–7); (4) Jonah delivered (2:10); and (5) Jonah recommissioned (3:1–3).
3:4 *"Yet forty days and Nineveh will be overthrown."* This statement has an implied condition—"unless she repents." As a matter of fact, Nineveh repented and was not overthrown in forty days, much to the displeasure of Jonah.

God relented concerning the calamity which He had declared He would bring upon them. And He did not do *it*.

Ex 32:14;
Jer 18:8;
Amos 7:3,6

IV. *The God of unlimited mercy (4:1–11)*

4 But it greatly displeased Jonah, and he became angry.
2   And he prayed to the LORD and said, "Please LORD, was not this what I said while I was still in my *own* country? Therefore, in order to forestall this I fled to Tarshish, for I knew that Thou art a gracious and compassionate God, slow to anger and abundant in lovingkindness, and one who relents concerning calamity.
3   "Therefore now, O LORD, please take my life from me, for death is better to me than life."
4   And the LORD said, "Do you have good reason to be angry?"
5   Then Jonah went out from the city and sat east of it. There he made a shelter for himself and sat under it in the shade until he could see what would happen in the city.
6   So the LORD God appointed a plant and it grew up over Jonah to be a shade over his head to deliver him from his discomfort. And Jonah was extremely happy about the plant.
7   But God appointed a worm when dawn came the next day, and it attacked the plant and it withered.
8   And it came about when the sun came up that God appointed a scorching east wind, and the sun beat down on Jonah's head so that he became faint and begged with *all* his soul to die, saying, "Death is better to me than life."
9   Then God said to Jonah, "Do you have good reason to be angry about the plant?" And he said, "I have good reason to be angry, even to death."
10   Then the LORD said, "You had compassion on the plant for which you did not work, and *which* you did not cause to grow, which came up overnight and perished overnight.
11   "And should I not have compassion on Nineveh, the great city in which there are more than 120,000 persons who do not know *the difference* between their right and left hand, as well as many animals?" ✱

4:1
vv. 4,9;
Matt 20:15;
Luke 15:28
*4:2
Jon 1:3;
Ex 34:6;
Ps 86:5;
Joel 2:13
4:3
1 Kin 19:4;
v. 8;
Job 7:15,16
4:4
v. 9;
Matt 20:11,15
4:5
1 Kin 19:9,13

4:7
Joel 1:12

*4:9
v. 4

*4:11
Jon 1:2; 3:2,
3; Deut 1:39;
Ps 36:6

4:2 *I knew that Thou art a gracious and compassionate God.* Jonah, as a loyal Israelite, wanted the hated Assyrian capital to be destroyed. He did not resist God's first command to go to Nineveh because of fear for his own safety, but because of fear that his message might bring the Ninevites to repentance, and thus ensure their deliverance from divine judgment. The book of Jonah stresses the fact that God's love transcends all national distinctions and embraces the most unlovely.
4:9 *Do you have good reason . . . ?* God reasons with Jonah in order to reprove him, to show him the error of his ways, and to produce in him a humble and a contrite spirit. Jonah

might well have resisted this outburst, since his earlier disobedience had resulted in his imprisonment in the belly of the fish. Evidently he had not learned all that he might have from his previous experience.
4:11 *And should I not have compassion on Nineveh?* Jonah was concerned about a plant that grew quickly, and just as quickly disappeared. This in itself was not wrong, but Jonah was reminded that his concern should include the people of Nineveh, who were of greater value in God's sight than a plant. Even cattle were spared the suffering that would have fallen on unrepentant Nineveh.

✱ God has compassion on the animals, too.

INTRODUCTION TO

THE BOOK OF

MICAH

Authorship and Background: The author's name, Micah, is an abbreviation of the Hebrew words that mean "Who is like Yahweh?" Micah came from Moresheth, which was located near Gath, some thirty miles from Jerusalem. He ministered during the reigns of Jotham, Ahaz, and Hezekiah (1:1) and was a contemporary of Hosea and Isaiah in the latter half of the eighth century B.C. As a prophet, Micah spoke to both Judah and Israel, usually referring to them by the names of their capital cities. A rural resident, he appears to have been less familiar with the politics of Jerusalem than his contemporary Isaiah, who lived and prophesied in that city. However, Micah lived near the coastal road over which traders, pilgrims, and soldiers had passed for hundreds of years. He must have observed the traffic between Egypt and Jerusalem and noted the corrupting influence of this entangling foreign alliance. His ministry extended over a long period of time.

Characteristics: The contents of this book form blocks of material indicating that the messages were delivered at different times. The style itself is varied. The language of Micah is direct, rugged, indignant, and convincing. Some of it rises to lofty heights and is beautiful. He exhibits great tenderness as he pleads with the people of God. His messages are moral and religious, with little regard for the political situation. He prophesied briefly against Israel, and these prophecies were fulfilled within a short period of time. He prophesied similar doom for Judah because of her sins. Amid his gloomy predictions are signs of hope and blessing if the people will repent. Seeing far beyond the moment of his writing, he alludes to God's promise of ultimate salvation through the appearance of the divine Savior and the establishment of God's glorious kingdom. Peculiar to Micah is the statement in 5:2 that Matt. 2:5 quotes, and explains as being fulfilled in the birth of Christ in Bethlehem of Judea.

Contents:

   I. The pronouncement of judgment on Israel and Judah (1:1-2:13): Micah records his vision concerning Samaria and Jerusalem. Both are guilty of sinning against God. The fall of each is predicted. He mourns their end, which is occasioned by their iniquity and listening to false prophets. A remnant will be saved.

   II. The judgment followed by restoration and the reign of Messiah (3:1-5:15): Micah arraigns the cruel princes. He assails the false prophets. He derides them for their false sense of security. There will be a restored Zion with law and peace. There will be victory. A Ruler will come forth from Bethlehem bringing peace to the "ends of the earth" (5:4). They should trust in their king and not in the idols of men.

   III. Divine punishment followed by divine mercy (6:1-7:20): The LORD invites His people to reason with Him. He speaks of what He has done for them in the past and appeals to them "to do justice, to love kindness, and to walk humbly with your God" (6:8). The sin of commercial dishonesty is denounced. Moral barrenness and vicious exploitation and idolatry are lamented. God's judgment is just, but in mercy God will bring them back to Himself. Micah closes with a psalm of praise to the mercy of God, who "does not retain His anger forever, because He delights in unchanging love."

THE BOOK OF

MICAH

I. *The pronouncement of judgment on Israel and Judah*
(1:1–2:13)

A. *Introductory heading*

1 The word of the LORD which came *to* Micah of Moresheth in the days of Jotham, Ahaz, *and* Hezekiah, kings of Judah, which he saw concerning Samaria and Jerusalem.

1:1
Jer 26:18;
2 Kin 15:5,7,
32-38;
16:1-20;
18:1-21

B. *God's anger against Samaria and Judah*

2   Hear, O peoples, all of you;
        Listen, O earth and all it contains,
        And let the Lord GOD be a witness against you,
        The Lord from His holy temple.

1:2
Jer 6:19;
22:29;
Ps 50:7; 11:4

3   For behold, the LORD is coming forth from His place.
        He will come down and tread on the high places of the
          earth.

1:3
Is 26:21;
Amos 4:13

4   The mountains will melt under Him,
        And the valleys will be split,
        Like wax before the fire,
        Like water poured down a steep place.

1:4
Is 64:1,2;
Nah 1:5

5   All this is for the rebellion of Jacob
        And for the sins of the house of Israel.
        What is the rebellion of Jacob?
        Is it not Samaria?
        What is the high place of Judah?
        Is it not Jerusalem?

1:5
Is 28:1;
Amos 8:14;
2 Chr 34:3,4

6   For I will make Samaria a heap of ruins in the open country,
        Planting places for a vineyard.
        I will pour her stones down into the valley,
        And will lay bare her foundations.

*1:6
Jer 31:5;
Amos 5:11;
Ezek 13:14

7   All of her idols will be smashed,
        All of her earnings will be burned with fire,
        And all of her images I will make desolate,
        For she collected *them* from a harlot's earnings,
        And to the earnings of a harlot they will return.

1:7
Deut 9:21;
2 Chr 34:7;
Is 23:17

8   Because of this I must lament and wail,
        I must go barefoot and naked;
        I must make a lament like the jackals
        And a mourning like the ostriches.

1:8
Is 22:4;
32:11; 13:21,
22

9   For her wound is incurable,
        For it has come to Judah;
        It has reached the gate of my people,
        Even to Jerusalem.

1:9
Jer 30:12,15;
2 Kin 18:13;
v. 12

10   Tell it not in Gath,
        Weep not at all.
        At [1]Beth-le-aphrah roll yourself in the dust.

1:10
2 Sam 1:20

11   Go on your way, inhabitant of [2]Shaphir, in shameful nakedness.
        The inhabitant of [3]Zaanan does not escape.
        The lamentation of [4]Beth-ezel: "He will take from you its support."

1:11
Ezek 23:29

[1]I.e., house of dust   [2]I.e., pleasantness   [3]I.e., going out   [4]I.e., house of removal

---

1:6 See 2 Kin. 17:1–18 for the literal fulfillment of this prophecy that the northern kingdom of Israel would be taken into captivity by Assyria.

1:12 Is 59:9-11; Jer 14:19	12	For the inhabitant of [5]Maroth Becomes weak waiting for good, Because a calamity has come down from the LORD To the gate of Jerusalem.
1:13 2 Kin 14:19; Is 36:2	13	Harness the chariot to the team of horses, O inhabitant of Lachish— She was the beginning of sin To the daughter of Zion— Because in you were found The rebellious acts of Israel.
1:14 2 Kin 16:8; Josh 15:44; Jer 15:18	14	Therefore, you will give parting gifts On behalf of Moresheth-gath The houses of Achzib *will* become a deception To the kings of Israel.
1:15 Josh 15:44; Mic 5:2; Josh 12:15; 2 Sam 23:13	15	Moreover, I will bring on you The one who takes possession, O inhabitant of [6]Mareshah. The glory of Israel will enter Adullam.
1:16 Is 15:2; 22:12; Lam 4:5; Amos 7:11,17	16	Make yourself bald and cut off your hair, Because of the children of your delight; Extend your baldness like the eagle, For they will go from you into exile.

C. *The cause of God's anger*

1. *Their sins described*

2:1 Is 32:7; Nah 1:11; Hos 7:6,7; Prov 3:27	2	Woe to those who scheme iniquity, Who work out evil on their beds! When morning comes, they do it, For it is in the power of their hands.
2:2 Amos 8:4; Is 5:8; 1 Kin 21:1-15	2	They covet fields and then seize *them*, And houses, and take *them* away. They rob a man and his house, A man and his inheritance.

2. *God's purpose to punish*

2:3 Amos 3:1,2; Deut 28:48; Jer 18:11; Is 2:11,12; Amos 5:13	3	Therefore, thus says the LORD, "Behold, I am planning against this family a calamity From which you cannot remove your necks; And you will not walk haughtily, For it will be an evil time.
2:4 Hab 2:6; Mic 1:8; Is 24:3; Jer 4:13; 6:12; 8:10	4	"On that day they will take up against you a taunt And utter a bitter lamentation *and* say, 'We are completely destroyed! He exchanges the portion of my people; How He removes it from me! To the apostate He apportions our fields.'
2:5 Josh 18:4,10	5	"Therefore, you will have no one stretching a measuring line For you by lot in the assembly of the LORD.
2:6 Is 30:10; Amos 2:12; 7:16; Mic 3:6; 6:16	6	'Do not speak out,' *so* they speak out. *But if* they do not speak out concerning these things, Reproaches will not be turned back.
2:7 Is 50:2; 59:1; Jer 15:16; Ps 15:2; 84:11	7	"Is it being said, O house of Jacob: 'Is the Spirit of the LORD impatient? Are these His doings?' Do not My words do good To the one walking uprightly?
2:8 Jer 12:8; Mic 3:2,3; 7:2,3; Ps 120:6,7	8	"Recently My people have arisen as an enemy— You strip the robe off the garment, From unsuspecting passers-by,

[5]I.e., bitterness   [6]I.e., possession

From those returned from war.

9　"The women of My people you evict,
　　Each *one* from her pleasant house.
　　From her children you take My splendor forever.

10　"Arise and go,
　　For this is no place of rest
　　Because of the uncleanness that brings on destruction,
　　A painful destruction.

11　"If a man walking after wind and falsehood
　　Had told lies *and said,*
　　'I will speak out to you concerning wine and liquor,'
　　He would be spokesman to this people.

3. God's purpose of future deliverance

12　"I will surely assemble all of you, Jacob,
　　I will surely gather the remnant of Israel.
　　I will put them together like sheep in the fold;
　　Like a flock in the midst of its pasture
　　They will be noisy with men.

13　"The breaker goes up before them;
　　They break out, pass through the gate, and go out by it.
　　So their king goes on before them,
　　And the LORD at their head."

II. *The judgment followed by restoration and the reign of Messiah (3:1–5:15)*

A. *Sins denounced and the destruction of Jerusalem foretold*

3 And I said,
　　"Hear now, heads of Jacob
　　And rulers of the house of Israel.
　　Is it not for you to know justice?

2　"You who hate good and love evil,
　　Who tear off their skin from them
　　And their flesh from their bones,

3　And who eat the flesh of my people,
　　Strip off their skin from them,
　　Break their bones,
　　And chop *them* up as for the pot
　　And as meat in a kettle."

4　Then they will cry out to the LORD,
　　But He will not answer them.
　　Instead, He will hide His face from them at that time,
　　Because they have practiced evil deeds.

5　Thus says the LORD concerning the prophets
　　Who lead my people astray;
　　When they have *something* to bite with their teeth,
　　They cry, "Peace,"
　　But against him who puts nothing in their mouths,
　　They declare holy war.

6　Therefore *it will be* night for you—without vision,
　　And darkness for you—without divination.
　　The sun will go down on the prophets,
　　And the day will become dark over them.

7　The seers will be ashamed
　　And the diviners will be embarrassed.
　　Indeed, they will all cover *their* mouths
　　Because there is no answer from God.

8　On the other hand I am filled with power—
　　With the Spirit of the LORD—
　　And with justice and courage
　　To make known to Jacob his rebellious act,

2:9	Jer 10:20
2:10	Lev 18:25,28, 29; Deut 12:9; Ps 106:38
2:11	Jer 5:13,31; Is 28:7; 30:10,11
2:12	Mic 4:6,7; 5:7,8; 7:18; Jer 33:22
2:13	Hos 3:5; Is 52:12
3:1	Jer 5:4,5
3:2	Mic 2:8; 7:2, 3; Ezek 22:27
3:3	Ps 14:4; Zeph 3:3; Ezek 34:2,3; 11:3
3:4	Ps 18:41; Prov 1:28; Is 1:15; Zech 7:13; Is 59:2; Mic 7:13
3:5	Is 56:10; Ezek 13:10; Jer 14:14,15; Mic 2:11; Jer 6:14; Ezek 13:18, 19
3:6	Is 8:20,22; Ezek 13:23; Amos 8:9
3:7	Zech 13:4; Is 44:25; Mic 7:16; 1 Sam 28:6; v. 4
3:8	Is 61:1,2; 58:1

Even to Israel his sin.

3:9
v. 1; Is 1:23

9   Now hear this, heads of the house of Jacob
And rulers of the house of Israel,
Who abhor justice
And twist everything that is straight,

3:10
Jer 22:13;
Ezek 22:27;
Hab 2:12
*3:11
Is 1:23;
Hos 4:18;
Jer 6:13;
Is 48:2;
Jer 7:4

10   Who build Zion with bloodshed
And Jerusalem with violent injustice.

11   Her leaders pronounce judgment for a bribe,
Her priests instruct for a price,
And her prophets divine for money.
Yet they lean on the LORD saying,
"Is not the LORD in our midst?
Calamity will not come upon us."

*3:12
Jer 26:18;
Mic 4:1,2

12   Therefore, on account of you,
Zion will be plowed as a field,
Jerusalem will become a heap of ruins,
And the mountain of the temple *will become* high places of a forest.

B. Promise of the coming of God's kingdom

1. *Law and peace*

4:1
Is 2:2-4;
Ezek 17:22;
43:12;
Jer 3:17

4   And it will come about in the last days
That the mountain of the house of the LORD
Will be established as the chief of the mountains.
It will be raised above the hills,
And the peoples will stream to it.

*4:2
Zech 2:11;
14:16;
Jer 31:6;
Is 54:13;
42:1-4;
Zech 14:8,9

2   And many nations will come and say,
"Come and let us go up to the mountain of the LORD
And to the house of the God of Jacob,
That He may teach us about His ways
And that we may walk in His paths."
For from Zion will go forth the law,
Even the word of the LORD from Jerusalem.

4:3
Is 2:4;
Joel 3:10;
Ps 72:7

3   And He will judge between many peoples
And render decisions for mighty, distant nations.
Then they will hammer their swords into plowshares
And their spears into pruning hooks;
Nation will not lift up sword against nation,
And never again will they train for war.

4:4
1 Kin 4:25;
Zech 3:10;
Is 1:20; 40:5

4   And each of them will sit under his vine
And under his fig tree,
With no one to make *them* afraid,
For the mouth of the LORD of hosts has spoken.

*4:5
2 Kin 17:29;
Is 26:8,13;
Zech 10:12

5   Though all the peoples walk
Each in the name of his god,
As for us, we will walk
In the name of the LORD our God forever and ever.

2. *God's victorious reign*

*4:6
Ezek 34:16;
Zeph 3:19;
Ps 147:2;
Ezek 34:13

6   "In that day," declares the LORD,
"I will assemble the lame,
And gather the outcasts,
Even those whom I have afflicted.

4:7
Mic 2:12;
5:7,8; 7:18;
Is 9:6;
Dan 7:14;
Luke 1:33;
Rev 11:15

7   "I will make the lame a remnant,
And the outcasts a strong nation,
And the LORD will reign over them in Mount Zion
From now on and forever.

3:11 *Calamity will not come upon us.* Past blessings and deliverances gave the people of Israel a false sense of security.
3:12 *Zion will be plowed as a field*, i.e., all buildings will be destroyed and it will lose its identity as a city.
4:2 *For from Zion will go forth the law.* Micah depicts a restored Zion that will be a means of blessing to all peoples.
4:5 *Each in the name of his god.* All men are religious and will worship some god; if not the true God it will be a false one, an idol.
4:6 God's flock is helpless, afflicted, and scattered, but God will gather them again.

8   "And as for you, tower of the flock,
Hill of the daughter of Zion,
To you it will come—
Even the former dominion will come,
The kingdom of the daughter of Jerusalem.

9   "Now, why do you cry out loudly?
Is there no king among you,
Or has your counselor perished,
That agony has gripped you like a woman in childbirth?

10 "Writhe and labor to give birth,
Daughter of Zion,
Like a woman in childbirth,
For now you will go out of the city,
Dwell in the field,
And go to Babylon.
There you will be rescued;
There the LORD will redeem you
From the hand of your enemies.

11 "And now many nations have been assembled against you
Who say, 'Let her be polluted,
And let our eyes gloat over Zion.'

12 "But they do not know the thoughts of the LORD,
And they do not understand His purpose;
For He has gathered them like sheaves to the threshing floor.

13 "Arise and thresh, daughter of Zion,
For your horn I will make iron
And your hoofs I will make bronze,
That you may pulverize many peoples,
That you may devote to the LORD their unjust gain
And their wealth to the Lord of all the earth.

5   "Now muster yourselves in troops, daughter of troops;
They have laid siege against us;
With a rod they will smite the judge of Israel on the cheek.

3. The coming Messiah and His reign

2 "But as for you, Bethlehem Ephrathah,
Too little to be among the clans of Judah,
From you One will go forth for Me to be ruler in Israel.
His goings forth are from long ago,
From the days of eternity."

3 Therefore, He will give them *up* until the time
When she who is in labor has borne a child.
Then the remainder of His brethren
Will return to the sons of Israel.

4 And He will arise and shepherd *His flock*
In the strength of the LORD,
In the majesty of the name of the LORD His God.
And they will remain,
Because at that time He will be great
To the ends of the earth.

5 And this One will be *our* peace.

References: 4:8 Mic 2:12; Is 1:26; Zech 9:10 — 4:9 Jer 8:19; Is 13:8; Jer 30:6 — *4:10 Hos 2:14; Is 45:13; Mic 7:8-12; Is 48:20; 52:9-12 — 4:11 Lam 2:16; Obad 12; Mic 7:10 — 4:12 Is 55:8; Rom 11:33; Is 21:10 — 4:13 Is 41:15; Dan 2:44; Zech 4:14 — 5:1 Jer 5:7; 1 Kin 22:24; Lam 3:30 — *5:2 Matt 2:6; 1 Sam 17:12; 23:23; Luke 2:4; Is 9:6 — 5:3 Mic 4:10; Hos 11:8; Is 10:20-22 — 5:4 Is 40:11; Ezek 34:23; Is 52:13; Luke 1:32 — 5:5 Is 9:6; Rev 11:15; Is 8:7,8

4:10 It is significant that Micah, like his great contemporary Isaiah, was granted a revelation of the Babylonian captivity of 586–537 B.C., and even in an age when Babylon was only a vassal of Assyria. Thus these two eighth-century prophets foresaw events that transpired in the sixth century B.C.
5:2 This verse was not written merely to impress the reader with the fact of predictive prophecy, but it serves to link the Messiah with the Davidic line. As a "Son of David" the Messiah would come from the city of David's birth, Bethlehem. In Matt. 2:5 it is apparent that the Jews accepted this prophecy as genuine. A second truth emerges from Micah's prophecy: the Son existed long before His birth in Bethlehem, and was active in the history of redemption. The Hebrew word here translated *His goings forth* refers to His origin and therefore points to the occasions when the LORD "went forth" to reveal His truth to His people or to redeem them from bondage or peril. (The translation *from the days of eternity* refers to events in ancient patriarchal or Davidic history in the three instances where it occurs elsewhere in the Old Testament.)

When the Assyrian invades our land,
When he tramples on our citadels,
Then we will raise against him
Seven shepherds and eight leaders of men.

5:6
Nah 2:11-13;
Zeph 2:13;
Gen 10:8;
Is 37:36,37

6   And they will shepherd the land of Assyria with the sword,
The land of Nimrod at its entrances;
And He will deliver *us* from the Assyrian
When he attacks our land
And when he tramples our territory.

5:7
Mic 2:12;
Deut 32:2;
Hos 14:5

7   Then the remnant of Jacob
Will be among many peoples
Like dew from the LORD,
Like showers on vegetation
Which do not wait for man
Or delay for the sons of men.

5:8
Mic 4:13;
Zech 10:5;
Hos 5:14;
Ps 50:22

8   And the remnant of Jacob
Will be among the nations,
Among many peoples
Like a lion among the beasts of the forest,
Like a young lion among flocks of sheep,
Which, if he passes through,
Tramples down and tears,
And there is none to rescue.

5:9
Ps 10:12;
21:8; Is 26:11

9   Your hand will be lifted up against your adversaries,
And all your enemies will be cut off.

5:10
Is 2:7;
Hos 14:3;
Zech 9:10

10   "And it will be in that day," declares the LORD,
"That I will cut off your horses from among you
And destroy your chariots.

5:11
Is 1:7;
Hos 10:14;
Amos 5:9

11   "I will also cut off the cities of your land
And tear down all your fortifications.

5:12
Deut 18:10-12;
Is 2:6

12   "I will cut off sorceries from your hand,
And you will have fortunetellers no more.

5:13
Zech 13:2;
Is 2:8

13   "I will cut off your carved images
And your *sacred* pillars from among you,
So that you will no longer bow down
To the work of your hands.

5:14
Ex 34:13;
Is 17:8; 27:9

14   "I will root out your Asherim from among you
And destroy your cities.

5:15
Ps 149:7;
Is 65:12

15   "And I will execute vengeance in anger and wrath
On the nations which have not obeyed."

III. *Divine punishment followed by divine mercy (6:1–7:20)*

A. *God's complaint against a rebellious people*

6:1
Ps 50:1;
Ezek 6:2,3

6   Hear now what the LORD is saying,
"Arise, plead your case before the mountains,
And let the hills hear your voice.

6:2
Deut 32:1;
Hos 12:2;
Is 1:8;
Hos 4:1

2   "Listen, you mountains, to the indictment of the LORD,
And you enduring foundations of the earth,
Because the LORD has a case against His people;
Even with Israel He will dispute.

6:3
Ps 50:7;
Jer 2:5;
Is 43:22,23

3   "My people, what have I done to you,
And how have I wearied you? Answer Me.

6:4
Ex 12:51;
Deut 4:20;
7:8; Ps 77:20;
Ex 15:20

4   "Indeed, I brought you up from the land of Egypt
And ransomed you from the house of slavery,
And I sent before you Moses, Aaron, and Miriam.

6:5
Num 22:5,6;
Rev 2:14;
Num 25:1;
Josh 4:19

5   "My people, remember now
What Balak king of Moab counseled
And what Balaam son of Beor answered him,
And from Shittim to Gilgal,
In order that you might know the righteous acts of the LORD."

... high?
... nt offerings,

_0911_ _0916_

... delight in thousands of rams,
... rivers of oil?
... sent my first-born *for* my rebellious acts,
... uit of my body for the sin of my soul?
... he has told you, O man, what is good;
And what does the LORD require of you
But to do justice, to love kindness,
And to walk humbly with your God?

*6:8
Deut 10:12;
1 Sam 15:22;
Hos 6:6;
12:6; Is 56:1;
57:15; 66:2

9   The voice of the LORD will call to the city—
     And it is sound wisdom to fear Thy name:
     "Hear, O tribe. Who has appointed its time?

10   "Is there yet a man in the wicked house,
     Along with treasures of wickedness,
     And a short measure *that is* cursed?

11   "Can I justify wicked scales
     And a bag of deceptive weights?

12   "For the rich men of *the* city are full of violence,
     Her residents speak lies,
     And their tongue is deceitful in their mouth.

13   "So also I will make *you* sick, striking you down,
     Desolating *you* because of your sins.

14   "You will eat, but you will not be satisfied,
     And your [7]vileness will be in your midst.
     You will *try to* remove *for safekeeping,*
     But you will not preserve *anything,*
     And what you do preserve I will give to the sword.

15   "You will sow but you will not reap.
     You will tread the olive but will not anoint yourself with oil;
     And the grapes, but you will not drink wine.

16   "The statutes of Omri
     And all the works of the house of Ahab are observed;
     And in their devices you walk.
     Therefore, I will give you up for destruction
     And your inhabitants for derision,
     And you will bear the reproach of My people."

6:12
Amos 6:3,4;
Mic 2:1,2;
Jer 9:3,5;
Hos 7:13;
Amos 2:4;
Is 3:8

B. *The confession of sin and the hope of mercy*

7   Woe is me! For I am
     Like the fruit pickers and the grape gatherers.
     There is not a cluster of grapes to eat,
     Or a first-ripe fig *which* I crave.

2   The godly person has perished from the land,
     And there is no upright *person* among men.
     All of them lie in wait for bloodshed;
     Each of them hunts the other with a net.

3   Concerning evil, both hands do it well.
     The prince asks, also the judge, for a bribe,

[7]Or possibly, *garbage* or *excreta*

6:7 *Shall I present my first-born . . . ?* Human sacrifice was practiced by apostate Israelites who took part in Molech worship, although it was distinctly forbidden in Israel. Cf. 2 Kin. 16:3; 21:2,6; Jer. 7:31; 19:4–6.
6:8 Some have supposed that this passage teaches that God's only requirement for salvation is a virtuous life, religious dogma being comparatively nonessential. But such an interpretation completely overlooks the setting in which this pronouncement is given. It is addressed not to the heathen or the human race in general, but only to that special section of mankind that stands in a covenant rela-

tionship to Him. In Micah's generation the dominant issue was the insufficiency of a dead faith that did not eventuate in a holy life. God lays emphasis here on the fruits of a sincere belief and trust in Him, as opposed to an empty and hypocritical profession of faith. The same emphasis is found in the New Testament letter of James.
6:16 *The statutes of Omri.* They enforced the worship of Baal. See 1 Kin. 16:25–32 and 18:19–40 for a description of the life of Omri and of Elijah's triumphs over Omri's son Ahab.

And a great man speaks the desire of his soul;
So they weave it together.

7:4
Ezek 2:6;
28:24;
Nah 1:10;
Is 10:3;
Hos 9:7;
Is 22:5

4 The best of them is like a briar,
The most upright like a thorn hedge.
The day when you post a watchman,
Your punishment will come.
Then their confusion will occur.

7:5
Jer 9:4

5 Do not trust in a neighbor;
Do not have confidence in a friend.
From her who lies in your bosom
Guard your lips.

7:6
Ezek 22:7;
Matt 10:21,
35:36;
Luke 12:53

6 For son treats father contemptuously,
Daughter rises up against her mother,
Daughter-in-law against her mother-in-law;
A man's enemies are the men of his own household.

7:7
Hab 2:1;
Ps 130:5; 4:3

7 But as for me, I will watch expectantly for the LORD;
I will wait for the God of my salvation.
My God will hear me.

7:8
Prov 24:17;
Lam 4:21;
Ps 37:24;
Is 9:2

8 Do not rejoice over me, O my enemy.
Though I fall I will rise;
Though I dwell in darkness, the LORD is a light for me.

7:9
Lam 3:29,40;
Is 42:7,16;
56:1

9 I will bear the indignation of the LORD
Because I have sinned against Him,
Until He pleads my case and executes justice for me.
He will bring me out to the light,
And I will see His righteousness.

7:10
Ps 35:26;
Is 51:23;
Zech 10:5

10 Then my enemy will see,
And shame will cover her who said to me,
"Where is the LORD your God?"
My eyes will look on her;
At that time she will be trampled down,
Like mire of the streets.

7:11
Is 54:11;
Zeph 2:2
7:12
Is 11:16;
19:23-25

11 It will be a day for building your walls.
On that day will your boundary be extended.

12 It will be a day when they will come to you
From Assyria and the cities of Egypt,
From Egypt even to the Euphrates,
Even from sea to sea and mountain to mountain.

7:13
Jer 25:11;
Mic 6:13;
Is 3:10,11;
Mic 3:4
7:14
Mic 5:4;
Ps 23:4;
Jer 50:19;
Amos 9:11

13 And the earth will become desolate because of her inhabitants,
On account of the fruit of their deeds.

14 Shepherd Thy people with Thy scepter,
The flock of Thy possession
Which dwells by itself in the woodland,
In the midst of a fruitful field.
Let them feed in Bashan and Gilead
As in the days of old.

7:15
Ex 3:20;
20:34;
Ps 78:12
7:16
Job 21:5;
Mic 3:7

15 "As in the days when you came out from the land of Egypt,
I will show you miracles."

16 Nations will see and be ashamed
Of all their might.
They will put their hand on their mouth,
Their ears will be deaf.

7:17
Ps 72:9;
Is 49:23;
Deut 32:24;
Ps 18:45;
Is 59:19

17 They will lick the dust like a serpent,
Like reptiles of the earth.
They will come trembling out of their fortresses;
To the LORD our God they will come in dread,
And they will be afraid before Thee.

7:18
Ex 34:7,9;
Is 43:25;
Jer 32:41

18 Who is a God like Thee, who pardons iniquity
And passes over the rebellious act of the remnant of His possession?
He does not retain His anger forever,
Because He delights in unchanging love.

7:19
Jer 50:20;

19 He will again have compassion on us;

He will tread our iniquities under foot.
Yes, Thou wilt cast all their sins
Into the depths of the sea.
20 Thou wilt give truth to Jacob
And unchanging love to Abraham,
Which Thou didst swear to our forefathers
From the days of old.

Is 38:17;
43:25;
Jer 31:34

7:20
Luke 1:55,
72; Deut 7:8,
12

INTRODUCTION TO
THE BOOK OF
NAHUM

Authorship and Background: The writer of this book, Nahum the Elkoshite, apparently was from Judah, but the location of the town of Elkosh is unknown. Nahum means "consolation," "comfort," or "relief." He was a contemporary of Zephaniah, Habakkuk, and Jeremiah. He prophesied during the second half of the seventh century B.C., prior to the destruction of Nineveh in 612 B.C. The exact date of the book is unknown, but it was probably composed around 620 B.C. Since the sack of No (i.e., No-amon or Thebes) is an accomplished fact (ca. 663 B.C., by Ashurbanipal of Assyria), and the sack of Nineveh is impending (612 B.C.), the book can be dated between these two events.

The earlier prophecy of Jonah forecasted the divine judgment that would fall on Nineveh unless its people repented. When Nahum wrote, however, the day of opportunity for Nineveh had passed; there is no mention of repentance. The messages of these two prophecies, separated by a century and a half, illustrate the patience of God in dealing with sinning nations.

Characteristics: Nahum writes in white heat of the downfall of Nineveh. He breathes out a spirit of divine judgment. His prediction in poetic form is vivid and forceful and may be compared favorably with the Song of Deborah in Judg. 5. Burning with moral indignation, he speaks with great plainness concerning two major themes. First he points to Nineveh's ruthless military power, stating that "all those who take up the sword shall perish by the sword" (Matt. 26:52). God is against such tyrants (2:11-13), and is responsible for their overthrow and destruction. He also denounces dishonest merchantmen who acquire wealth at the expense of morality and honesty. God is also against such (3:5). Nahum's only word to the Judeans is for them to observe their religious feasts and to fulfill their religious obligations (1:15). The language of Nahum in describing the siege and final fall of Nineveh is graphic and amazingly accurate in its details.

Contents:

I. The psalm of the LORD's majesty (1:1-15): Nahum describes the majesty and power of an angry God who will punish His enemies. God's verdict is against Nineveh, and there shall be relief for Judah.

II. The siege and fall of Nineveh (2:1-13): Nahum describes the coming of the destroyer, the siege, and the sacking of the city; its final overthrow.

III. The reasons for Nineveh's destruction (3:1-19): Nahum describes Nineveh's lies, thievery, harlotry, and witchcraft. God's verdict is righteous. He reminds Nineveh of the fate of Thebes (No-amon). Let Nineveh prepare for war; it will do her no good. She shall be destroyed.

THE BOOK OF

NAHUM

I. The psalm of the LORD's majesty (1:1–15)

1 The ¹oracle of Nineveh. The book of the vision of Nahum the Elkoshite.
2 A jealous and avenging God is the LORD;
The LORD is avenging and wrathful.
The LORD takes vengeance on His adversaries,
And He reserves wrath for His enemies.

3 The LORD is slow to anger and great in power,
And the LORD will by no means leave *the guilty* unpunished.
In whirlwind and storm is His way,
And clouds are the dust beneath His feet.

4 He rebukes the sea and makes it dry;
He dries up all the rivers.
Bashan and Carmel wither;
The blossoms of Lebanon wither.

5 Mountains quake because of Him,
And the hills dissolve;
Indeed the earth is upheaved by His presence,
The world and all the inhabitants in it.

6 Who can stand before His indignation?
Who can endure the burning of His anger?
His wrath is poured out like fire,
And the rocks are broken up by Him.

7 The LORD is good,
A stronghold in the day of trouble,
And He knows those who take refuge in Him.

8 But with an overflowing flood
He will make a complete end of its site,
And will pursue His enemies into darkness.

9 Whatever you devise against the LORD,
He will make a complete end of it.
Distress will not rise up twice.

10 Like tangled thorns,
And like those who are drunken with their drink,
They are consumed
As stubble completely withered.

11 From you has gone forth
One who plotted evil against the LORD,
A wicked counselor.

12 Thus says the LORD,
"Though they are at full *strength* and likewise many,
Even so, they will be cut off and pass away.
Though I have afflicted you,
I will afflict you no longer.

13 "So now, I will break his yoke bar from upon you,

¹Or, *burden*

*1:1
Is 13:1;
Hab 1:1;
Nah 2:8; 3:7;
Zeph 2:13
1:2
Ex 20:5;
Deut 4:24;
32:35,41;
Ps 94:1
1:3
Ex 34:6,7;
Ps 103:8;
Is 29:6;
Ps 104:3
1:4
Ps 106:9;
Is 33:9

1:5
Ex 19:18;
Mic 1:4;
Is 24:1,20
1:6
Jer 10:10;
Mal 3:2;
Is 66:15;
1 Kin 19:11
1:7
1 Chr 16:34;
Ps 28:8

1:8
Is 28:2,18;
13:9,10

1:9
Ps 2:1;
Is 28:22
1:10
2 Sam 23:6;
Mal 4:1

1:11
v. 9;
Ezek 11:2

1:12
Is 10:16-19,
33,34; 54:7,8

1:13
Is 9:4;
Jer 2:20

1:1 The city of Nineveh was situated on the Tigris River. It was the ancient capital of Assyria. The might of the Assyrian empire seemed absolutely invincible, yet its downfall was here plainly predicted—a prediction later fulfilled in detail. During the age of Jonah (c. 770 B.C.), judgment had been averted from Nineveh because the city had repented. But now in the seventh century Nahum was prophesying its utter destruction, as did his contemporary, Zephaniah (Zeph. 2:13–15). In 612 B.C. the Chaldeans and the Medes finally closed in on Nineveh and laid it under siege for two years before it fell. So complete was its devastation that two hundred years later Xenophon could pass by the ruins without being able to discover its name from the local inhabitants. Alexander the Great later fought the battle of Arbela in 331 B.C., not far from the site where Nineveh had stood. It was not until 1845 that the site was identified and the ruins uncovered. Archaeological investigations there have confirmed the Biblical account of its destruction.

And I will tear off your shackles."

1:14
Is 46:1,2;
Mic 5:13,14;
Ezek 32:22,
23

14 The LORD has issued a command concerning you:
"Your name will no longer be perpetuated.
I will cut off idol and image
From the house of your gods.
I will prepare your grave,
For you are contemptible."

1:15
Is 40:9;
Ps 52:7;
Rom 10:15;
Lev 23:2,4;
Is 52:1;
Joel 3:17;
Is 29:7,8

15 Behold, on the mountains the feet of him who brings good news,
Who announces peace!
Celebrate your feasts, O Judah;
Pay your vows.
For never again will the wicked one pass through you;
He is cut off completely.

II. *The siege and fall of Nineveh (2:1–13)*

2:1
Jer 51:20-23;
Nah 3:12,14

2 The one who scatters has come up against you.
Man the fortress, watch the road;
Strengthen your back, summon all *your* strength.

2:2
Is 60:15;
Ezek 37:21-23

2 For the LORD will restore the splendor of Jacob
Like the splendor of Israel,
Even though devastators have devastated them
And destroyed their vine branches.

2:3
Ezek 23:14,
15; Job 39:23

3 The shields of his mighty men are *colored* red,
The warriors are dressed in scarlet,
The chariots are *enveloped* in flashing steel
When he is prepared *to march,*
And the cypress *spears* are brandished.

2:4
Ezek 26:10;
Jer 4:13

4 The chariots race madly in the streets,
They rush wildly in the squares,
Their appearance is like torches,
They dash to and fro like lightning flashes.

2:5
Nah 3:18;
Jer 46:12

5 He remembers his nobles;
They stumble in their march,
They hurry to her wall,
And the mantelet is set up.

2:6
Nah 3:18

6 The gates of the rivers are opened,
And the palace is dissolved.

2:7
Is 59:11;
32:12

7 And it is fixed:
She is stripped, she is carried away,
And her handmaids are moaning like the sound of doves,
Beating on their breasts.

2:8
Nah 3:7;
Jer 46:5; 47:3

8 Though Nineveh *was* like a pool of water throughout her days,
Now they are fleeing;
"Stop, stop,"
But no one turns back.

9 Plunder the silver!
Plunder the gold!
For there is no limit to the treasure—
Wealth from every kind of desirable object.

2:10
Ps 22:14;
Is 13:7,8;
Joel 2:6

10 She is emptied! Yes, she is desolate and waste!
Hearts are melting and knees knocking!
Also anguish is in the whole body,
And all their faces are grown pale!

2:11
Is 5:29;
Jer 4:7;
Nah 3:1

11 Where is the den of the lions
And the feeding place of the young lions,
Where the lion, lioness, and lion's cub prowled,
With nothing to disturb *them?*

2:12
Is 10:6-14;
Jer 51:34

12 The lion tore enough for his cubs,
Killed *enough* for his lionesses,
And filled his lairs with prey
And his dens with torn flesh.

13 "Behold, I am against you," declares the LORD of hosts. "I will burn up her chariots in smoke, a sword will devour your young lions, I will cut off your prey from the land, and no longer will the voice of your messengers be heard."

III. The reasons for Nineveh's destruction (3:1–19)

A. The sin of Nineveh

3
Woe to the bloody city, completely full of lies *and* pillage;
Her prey never departs.

2 The noise of the whip,
The noise of the rattling of the wheel,
Galloping horses,
And bounding chariots!

3 Horsemen charging,
Swords flashing, spears gleaming,
Many slain, a mass of corpses,
And countless dead bodies—
They stumble over the dead bodies!

4 *All* because of the many harlotries of the harlot,
The charming one, the mistress of sorceries,
Who sells nations by her harlotries
And families by her sorceries.

5 "Behold, I am against you," declares the LORD of hosts;
"And I will lift up your skirts over your face,
And show to the nations your nakedness
And to the kingdoms your disgrace.

6 "I will throw filth on you
And make you vile,
And set you up as a spectacle.

7 "And it will come about that all who see you
Will shrink from you and say,
'Nineveh is devastated!
Who will grieve for her?'
Where will I seek comforters for you?"

B. The justness of the judgment

8 Are you better than [2]No-amon,
Which was situated by the waters of the Nile,
With water surrounding her,
Whose rampart *was* the sea,
Whose wall *consisted* of the sea?

9 Ethiopia was *her* might,
And Egypt too, without limits.
Put and Lubim were among her helpers.

10 Yet she became an exile,
She went into captivity;
Also her small children were dashed to pieces
At the head of every street;
They cast lots for her honorable men,
And all her great men were bound with fetters.

11 You too will become drunk,
You will be hidden.
You too will search for a refuge from the enemy.

12 All your fortifications are fig trees with ripe fruit—
When shaken, they fall into the eater's mouth.

[2]I.e., the city of Amon: Thebes

Cross references:
2:13 Nah 3:5; Ps 46:9; Is 49:24,25
*3:1 Ezek 24:6,9
3:2 Nah 2:3,4; Jer 47:3
3:3 Hab 3:11; Is 34:3; 66:16; 2 Kin 19:35
3:4 Is 23:17; Rev 17:1,2; Is 47:9; Rev 18:3
3:5 Nah 2:13; Is 47:2,3; Jer 13:22; Ezek 16:37
3:6 Job 9:31; Mal 2:9; Is 14:16; Jer 51:37
3:7 Jer 51:9; Nah 2:8; Zeph 2:13; Is 51:19; Jer 15:5
*3:8 Jer 46:25; Ezek 30:14-16; Is 19:6-8
3:9 Is 20:5; Ezek 27:10; 30:5; 38:5; 2 Chr 12:3; 16:8
3:10 Is 20:4; 13:16; Hos 13:16; Lam 2:19; Joel 3:3; Obad 11
3:11 Jer 25:27; Is 2:10,19
3:12 Is 28:4; Rev 6:13

3:1 Nahum states what is constantly taught in Scripture—that as we sow, thus we must reap. The spiritual laws of cause and effect must prevail and vindicate the timeless principles of justice and equity. Sin and wickedness yield a harvest of destruction.
3:8 *Are you better than No-amon?* No-amon, or Thebes, located 400 miles south of modern Cairo, was one of the great cities of the ancient world. Nahum probably refers to the destruction of Thebes by Ashurbanipal (663 B.C.). So if Thebes, the Egyptian capital of a brilliant dynasty, could be destroyed, why not Nineveh?

3:13 Jer 50:37; 51:30; Ps 147:13	13	Behold, your people are women in your midst! The gates of your land are opened wide to your enemies; Fire consumes your gate bars.
3:14 2 Chr 32:3,4, 11; Nah 2:1	14	Draw for yourself water for the siege! Strengthen your fortifications! Go into the clay and tread the mortar! Take hold of the brick mold!
3:15 v. 13; Joel 1:4	15	There fire will consume you, The sword will cut you down; It will consume you as the locust *does*. Multiply yourself like the creeping locust, Multiply yourself like the swarming locust.
3:16 Is 23:8	16	You have increased your traders more than the stars of heaven— The creeping locust strips and flies away.
3:17 Jer 51:27; Rev 9:7	17	Your guardsmen are like the swarming locust. Your marshals are like hordes of grasshoppers Settling in the stone walls on a cold day. The sun rises and they flee, And the place where they are is not known.
3:18 Ps 76:5,6; Is 56:10; Jer 51:57; Nah 2:5; 1 Kin 22:17 ***3:19** Mic 1:9; Lam 2:15; Zeph 2:15	18	Your shepherds are sleeping, O king of Assyria; Your nobles are lying down. Your people are scattered on the mountains, And there is no one to regather *them*.
	19	There is no relief for your breakdown, Your wound is incurable. All who hear about you Will clap *their* hands over you, For on whom has not your evil passed continually?

3:19 *All who hear about you.* The Assyrians sought to rule all of western Asia, and they were universally hated. Nineveh was destroyed, never to rise again.

INTRODUCTION TO

THE BOOK OF

HABAKKUK

Authorship and Background: Little is known about the author of this book except his name. The title of the book in the Septuagint is *Ambakoum*. Jerome thought the name Habakkuk came from a Hebrew root meaning "to clasp." There is some reason to think the name may derive from an Assyrian word signifying a vegetable or a plant. Habakkuk probably prophesied just before the invasion of Judah by the Chaldeans, which would place the date of the book close to the end of the seventh century B.C. He was a contemporary of Jeremiah, whose ministry was much longer than his. The national catastrophe, which was imminent and which had been predicted before the prophet's day, had now come, and Habakkuk spoke and lived to see the fulfillment of his words.

Characteristics: Habakkuk engages in a soliloquy between himself and God. He arraigns God rather than Judah, implying that He allows injustice and wickedness to go unchecked. He asks age-old questions: "Why are the wicked ruling classes allowed to oppress the weak in Jewish society?" God answers, "I will punish them by the Chaldean invasion" (cf. Hab. 1:1-11). Next he asks how God can allow wicked Judah to be punished by a nation that itself is more wicked than Judah. His sense of justice is violated by such a thought. God replies that this result is in accord with the divine purpose. Habakkuk seeks further light as he acknowledges that the judgment of God against Judah is just. Then it is that God reveals that the Chaldeans in their turn shall be destroyed, and at last the people of God will possess the earth. Habakkuk writes passionately and inquiringly. Some of his phrases: "the righteous will live by his faith" (2:4); "the earth will be filled with the knowledge of the glory of the LORD, as the waters cover the sea" (2:14); "in wrath remember mercy" (3:2) stand out as precious jewels in splendid array.

Contents:

I. Habakkuk's first question (1:1-4): Why does wrong seem to triumph?

II. God's first answer (1:5-11): Judean wrongdoers will be punished.

III. Habakkuk's second question (1:12-2:1): Why does God allow the more wicked to punish the less wicked?

IV. God's second answer (2:2-20): Chaldea, in turn, will be punished. The righteous shall live by his faith.

V. The prayer of Habakkuk (3:1-19): He asks God in wrath to remember mercy. God replies that He is mighty to punish the wicked and to save those who repent. Habakkuk closes with praise, "the Lord GOD is my strength" (3:19).

THE BOOK OF

HABAKKUK

I. Habakkuk's first question: why does evil go unpunished?
(1:1–4)

1:1
Is 13:1;
Nah 1:1

1 The ¹oracle which Habakkuk the prophet saw.

1:2
Ps 13:1,2;
22:1,2

2 How long, O LORD, will I call for help,
And Thou wilt not hear?
I cry out to Thee, "Violence!"
Yet Thou dost not save.

1:3
v. 13;
Jer 20:8

3 Why dost Thou make me see iniquity,
And cause *me* to look on wickedness?
Yes, destruction and violence are before me;
Strife exists and contention arises.

*1:4
Ps 119:126;
22:12; Is 5:20

4 Therefore, the law is ignored
And justice is never upheld.
For the wicked surround the righteous;
Therefore, justice comes out perverted.

II. God's first answer: He will use the Chaldeans
to punish (1:5–11)

1:5
Acts 13:41;
Is 29:9,14

5 "Look among the nations! Observe!
Be astonished! Wonder!
Because *I* am doing something in your days—
You would not believe if you were told.

*1:6
2 Kin 24:2;
Jer 4:11-13;
5:15; 8:10

6 "For behold, I am raising up the Chaldeans,
That fierce and impetuous people
Who march throughout the earth
To seize dwelling places which are not theirs.

1:7
Is 18:2,7;
Jer 39:5-9

7 "They are dreaded and feared.
Their justice and authority originate with themselves.

1:8
Jer 4:13; 5:6;
Ezek 17:3;
Hos 8:1

8 "Their horses are swifter than leopards
And keener than wolves in the evening.
Their horsemen come galloping,
Their horsemen come from afar;
They fly like an eagle swooping *down* to devour.

1:9
Hab 2:5

9 "All of them come for violence.
Their horde of faces *moves* forward.
They collect captives like sand.

*1:10
2 Chr 36:6,
10; Is 10:9;
14:16;
Jer 32:24;
Ezek 26:8

10 "They mock at kings,
And rulers are a laughing matter to them.
They laugh at every fortress,
And heap up rubble to capture it.

1:11
Jer 4:11,12;
2:3; Dan 4:30

11 "Then they will sweep through *like* the wind and pass on.
But they will be held guilty,
They whose strength is their god."

---

¹Or, *burden*

1:4 *the law is ignored*, i.e., the law had lost its authority. It was both disregarded and perverted.
1:6 *The Chaldeans* were a tribe in southern Babylon that, under Nabopolassar, became independent of Assyria and,

under Nebuchadnezzar, dominated all of western Asia including Judea, which fell in 586 B.C.
1:10 *They laugh at every fortress*, i.e., every fortress will fall before their attack.

III. *Habakkuk's second question: why will God use the more wicked to punish the less wicked? (1:21–2:1)*

12 Art Thou not from everlasting,
O LORD, my God, my Holy One?
We will not die.
Thou, O LORD, hast appointed them to judge;
And Thou, O Rock, hast established them to correct.

1:12
Deut 33:27;
Ps 90:2;
Is 10:5-7;
Deut 32:4

13 *Thine* eyes are too pure to approve evil,
And Thou canst not look on wickedness *with favor*.
Why dost Thou look with favor
On those who deal treacherously?
Why art Thou silent when the wicked swallow up
Those more righteous than they?

1:13
Jer 12:1,2;
Is 24:16;
Ps 50:21;
56:1,2

14 *Why* hast Thou made men like the fish of the sea,
Like creeping things without a ruler over them?

1:14
Eccl 9:12

15 *The Chaldeans* bring all of them up with a hook,
Drag them away with their net,
And gather them together in their fishing net.
Therefore, they rejoice and are glad.

1:15
Jer 16:16;
Amos 4:2;
Ps 10:9

16 Therefore, they offer a sacrifice to their net.
And burn incense to their fishing net;
Because through these things their catch is large,
And their food is plentiful.

17 Will they therefore empty their net
And continually slay nations without sparing?

1:17
Is 19:8; 14:5,
6

2 I will stand on my guard post
And station myself on the rampart;
And I will keep watch to see what He will speak to me,
And how I may reply when I am reproved.

2:1
Is 21:8,11;
Ps 5:3; 85:8

IV. *God's second answer: the Chaldeans shall be punished also (2:2–20)*

A. *Chaldea is greedy*

2 Then the LORD answered me and said,
"Record the vision
And inscribe *it* on tablets,
That the one who reads it may run.

2:2
Deut 27:8;
Is 8:1;
Rev 1:19

3 "For the vision is yet for the appointed time;
It hastens toward the goal, and it will not fail.
Though it tarries, wait for it;
For it will certainly come, it will not delay.

2:3
Dan 8:17,19;
10:14;
Ezek 12:25;
Heb 10:37,38

4 "Behold, as for the proud one,
His soul is not right within him;
But the righteous will live by his faith.

*2:4
Rom 1:17;
Gal 3:11;
Heb 10:38,39

5 "Furthermore, wine betrays the haughty man,
So that he does not stay at home.
He enlarges his appetite like Sheol,
And he is like death, never satisfied.
He also gathers to himself all nations
And collects to himself all peoples.

*2:5
Prov 20:1;
21:24;
2 Kin 14:10;
Jer 25:9

6 "Will not all of these take up a taunt-song against him,
Even mockery *and* insinuations against him,

*2:6ff
Jer 50:13;
v. 12;
Ezek 18:12;
Amos 2:8

2:4 This verse is quoted three times with variation in the New Testament (Rom. 1:17; Gal. 3:11; Heb. 10:38,39) as proof of the proposition that salvation is granted by grace through faith. 2:4 might be rendered, "Behold his soul is puffed up; it is not upright in him; but a righteous man by his faith [or, faithfulness] shall live." The Jewish Talmud states that Habakkuk reduced the 613 commandments of Moses to one: "the righteous will live by his faith." In effect, this is true.
2:5 See note to Deut. 32:22 on Sheol, the underworld abode.
2:6ff. These verses tell of the dooms that will befall evildoers.

And say, 'Woe to him who increases what is not his—
For how long—
And makes himself rich with loans?'

2:7
Prov 29:1

7 "Will not your creditors rise up suddenly,
And those who collect from you awaken?
Indeed, you will become plunder for them.

2:8
Is 33:1;
Zech 2:8;
v. 17

8 "Because you have looted many nations,
All the remainder of the peoples will loot you—
Because of human bloodshed and violence done to the land,
To the town and all its inhabitants.

B. *Chaldea is covetous*

2:9
Jer 22:13;
Ezek 22:27;
Jer 49:16

9 "Woe to him who gets evil gain for his house
To put his nest on high
To be delivered from the hand of calamity!

2:10
2 Kin 9:26;
v. 16;
Prov 1:18;
Jer 26:29

10 "You have devised a shameful thing for your house
By cutting off many peoples;
So you are sinning against yourself.

2:11
Josh 24:27;
Luke 19:40

11 "Surely the stone will cry out from the wall,
And the rafter will answer it from the framework.

C. *Chaldea is cruel*

2:12
Mic 3:10;
Nah 3:1

12 "Woe to him who builds a city with bloodshed
And founds a town with violence!

2:13
Is 50:11;
Jer 51:58

13 "Is it not indeed from the LORD of hosts
That peoples toil for fire,
And nations grow weary for nothing?

** 2:14
Is 11:9;
Zech 14:8,9

14 ⌐ "For the earth will be filled
   With the knowledge of the glory of the LORD,
 ⌐ As the waters cover the sea.

2:15
Is 28:7,8;
Hos 7:5

15 "Woe to you who make your neighbors drink,
Who mix in your venom even to make *them* drunk
So as to look on their nakedness!

2:16
v. 10;
Lam 4:21;
Jer 25:15,27;
Nah 3:6

16 "You will be filled with disgrace rather than honor.
Now you yourself drink and expose your *own* nakedness.
The cup in the LORD's right hand will come around to you,
And utter disgrace *will come* upon your glory.

2:17
Zech 11:1;
v. 8;
Jer 51:35

17 "For the violence done to Lebanon will overwhelm you,
And the devastation of *its* beasts by which you terrified them,
Because of human bloodshed and violence done to the land,
To the town and all its inhabitants.

D. *Chaldea is idolatrous*

2:18
Is 42:17;
Jer 2:27,28;
10:8,14;
Zech 10:2;
Ps 115:4,8

18 "What profit is the idol when its maker has carved it,
Or an image, a teacher of falsehood?
For *its* maker trusts in his *own* handiwork
When he fashions speechless idols.

2:19
Jer 2:27,28;
1 Kin 18:26-29;
Jer 10:9,14;
Ps 135:17

19 "Woe to him who says to a *piece of* wood, 'Awake!'
To a dumb stone, 'Arise!'
And that is *your* teacher?
Behold, it is overlaid with gold and silver,
And there is no breath at all inside it.

2:20
Mic 1:2;
Zeph 1:7;
Zech 2:13

20 "But the LORD is in His holy temple.
Let all the earth be silent before Him."

V. *The prayer of Habakkuk (3:1–19)*

A. *"In wrath remember mercy"*

3:2
Job 42:5,6;
Ps 119:120;
Jer 10:7;
Ps 85:6;
Is 54:8

3 A prayer of Habakkuk the prophet, according to ²Shigionoth.
2 LORD, I have heard the report about Thee *and* I fear.

²I.e., A highly emotional poetic form

O LORD, revive Thy work in the midst of the years,
In the midst of the years make it known;
In wrath remember mercy.

B. *God dooms the wicked and saves the repentant*

3 God comes from Teman,
And the Holy One from Mount Paran.   Selah.

His splendor covers the heavens,
And the earth is full of His praise.

4 *His* radiance is like the sunlight;
He has rays *flashing* from His hand,
And there is the hiding of His power.

5 Before Him goes pestilence,
And plague comes after Him.

6 He stood and surveyed the earth;
He looked and startled the nations.
Yes, the perpetual mountains were shattered,
The ancient hills collapsed.
His ways are everlasting.

7 I saw the tents of Cushan under distress,
The tent curtains of the land of Midian were trembling.

8 Did the LORD rage against the rivers,
Or *was* Thine anger against the rivers,
Or *was* Thy wrath against the sea,
That Thou didst ride on Thy horses,
On Thy chariots of salvation?

9 Thy bow was made bare,
The rods of chastisement were sworn.   Selah.
Thou didst cleave the earth with rivers.

10 The mountains saw Thee *and* quaked;
The downpour of waters swept by.
The deep uttered forth its voice,
It lifted high its hands.

11 Sun *and* moon stood in their places;
They went away at the light of Thine arrows,
At the radiance of Thy gleaming spear.

12 In indignation Thou didst march through the earth;
In anger Thou didst trample the nations.

13 Thou didst go forth for the salvation of Thy people,
For the salvation of Thine anointed.
Thou didst strike the head of the house of the evil
To lay him open from thigh to neck.   Selah.

14 Thou didst pierce with his own spears
The head of his throngs.
They stormed in to scatter us;
Their exultation *was* like those
Who devour the oppressed in secret.

15 Thou didst tread on the sea with Thy horses,
On the surge of many waters.

C. *Habakkuk's unwavering faith*

16 I heard and my inward parts trembled,
At the sound my lips quivered.
Decay enters my bones,
And in my place I tremble.
Because I must wait quietly for the day of distress,
For the people to arise *who* will invade us.

17 Though the fig tree should not blossom,

Reference column:

*3:3
Amos 1:12;
Deut 33:2;
Ps 113:4;
48:10

3:4
Ps 18:12;
Job 26:14

3:5
Ex 12:29,30;
Num 16:46-49

3:6
Ps 35:5;
114:1-6;
Mic 5:2

*3:7
Ex 15:14-16;
Judg 7:24,25

3:8
Ex 7:19,20;
14:16,21;
Deut 33:26;
Ps 68:17

3:9
Gen 26:3;
Deut 7:8;
Ps 78:16;
105:41

3:10
Ps 114:1-6;
98:7,8;
Ex 14:22

3:11
Josh 10:12-14;
Ps 18:9,11,14

3:12
Ps 68:7;
Is 41:15;
Jer 51:33

3:13
Ex 15:2;
Ps 68:19,20;
110:6;
Ezek 13:14

3:14
Judg 7:22;
Dan 11:40;
Zech 9:14;
Ps 10:8;
64:2-5

3:15
Ps 77:19;
Ex 15:8

3:16
Jer 23:9; 5:15

*3:17ff
Joel 1:18;
Jer 5:17

3:3 *God comes from Teman.* Teman was a district of Edom.
The prophet describes the coming of God to deliver His
people in language reminiscent of the exodus from Egypt
(cf. Deut. 33:3).

3:7 *Cushan* was a Bedouin tribe, settled near Edom, as was
Midian. Nothing more is known about it.
3:17–19 These verses are universally quoted.

And there be no fruit on the vines,
Though the yield of the olive should fail,
And the fields produce no food,
Though the flock should be cut off from the fold,
And there be no cattle in the stalls,

18 Yet I will exult in the LORD,
    I will rejoice in the God of my salvation.

19 The Lord GOD is my strength,
    And He has made my feet like hinds' *feet*,
    And makes me walk on my high places.

For the choir director, on my stringed instruments.

*3:18
Is 61:10;
Ps 46:1-5;
Is 12:2
3:19
2 Sam 22:34;
Ps 18:33;
Deut 33:29

3:18 Habakkuk rejoices in the God he knows.

INTRODUCTION TO
THE BOOK OF
ZEPHANIAH

Authorship and Background: This book was written by Zephaniah, whose name means "he whom Yahweh has hidden, or protected." He was the son of Cushi, the son of Gedaliah, the son of Amariah, the son of Hizkiah (which is the same in Hebrew as Hezekiah). If this was King Hezekiah, Zephaniah was of royal blood. In this event, he would have been a prince as well as a prophet. He lived in Jerusalem and wrote during the reign of Josiah, probably around 625 B.C. Nahum was a contemporary. It is possible the reforms made by Josiah were urged on him by Zephaniah.

A knowledge of general world history is helpful to an understanding of the book. For fifty years before Zephaniah's day, Assyria had reigned supreme. That kingdom was apparently at its zenith (although its end came less than twenty years later). Manasseh (ca. 687-642 B.C.) had ruled in Jerusalem for the benefit of Assyria and was very wicked. He was followed by his wicked son Amon, who reigned briefly. Then came the godly grandson, Josiah, under whom reforms were instituted. He recovered the Book of the Law given by Moses and enforced its injunctions on the people. During his reign, the power of Assyria declined. The death of Ashurbanipal in 626 B.C. marked the beginning of the end of Assyria. It was replaced shortly thereafter by Babylonia, under the Chaldean dynasty.

Characteristics: Zephaniah is the last of the minor prophets before the captivity. He writes to announce the approaching judgment, the impending day of wrath for Judah. He speaks out of youth, with vigor and zeal. His pronouncements of judgment are forthright and unsparing. He exhibits his strong convictions, along with a moral earnestness and spiritual sensitivity. The book itself bears evidence of his rhetorical powers, and these are further strengthened by his use of figures of speech. The immediate reference to approaching judgment is to the invasion by Nebuchadnezzar, but the eschatological reference to the day of wrath is as vivid as it is terrible. The author of the medieval hymn, "Dies Irae," got his inspiration from this description by Zephaniah. Zephaniah envisions judgment for the surrounding nations, but he holds forth hope for the people of God to foresee their ultimate deliverance and the restoration of Israel. God will be in their midst and rejoice over them.

Contents:

    I. The day of the LORD (1:1-2:3): God will judge Judah. She is guilty of idolatry and of trusting in riches. The goods of the people of Judah will be plundered and their houses be laid waste. The day of the LORD is near. They are called on to repent and to seek the LORD that they may be delivered.

  II. The judgment of the nations (2:4-15): Gaza and the Philistines will be destroyed; the seacoasts will be desolate and uninhabited. God will return the land to Judah and be mindful of her. Moab will become like Sodom; Ammon will become like Gomorrah; the LORD will be terrible against them. The Ethiopians will be slain. Nineveh will become a desolation, and the nation of Assyria will be utterly destroyed.

III. The sin of Jerusalem and the future salvation (3:1-20): Jerusalem is rebellious; she does not heed, nor accept correction, trust the LORD, or draw near to her God. She will be destroyed because of her sins of rebellion, oppression, disobedience, distrust, and the faithlessness of her political leaders and her priests. Deliverance is to come, and the LORD calls for the people to wait for Him. Blessing is promised to the remnant of Judah and to the whole Israel of God. They may rejoice because the LORD will be in their midst; He will gather them together and promises to "restore your fortunes before your eyes."

THE BOOK OF
ZEPHANIAH

I. *The day of the* LORD *(1:1–2:3)*

A. *Introduction*

1 The word of the LORD which came to Zephaniah son of Cushi, son of Gedaliah, son of Amariah, son of Hezekiah, in the days of Josiah son of Amon, king of Judah,

1:1
2 Kin 22:1-23,
34; 21:18-26

B. *The judgment on Judah*

2 "I will completely remove all *things*
From the face of the earth," declares the LORD.

1:2
Ezek 33:27

3 "I will remove man and beast;
I will remove the birds of the sky
And the fish of the sea,
And the ruins along with the wicked;
And I will cut off man from the face of the earth," declares the LORD.

1:3
Is 6:11,12;
Jer 9:10;
Ezek 7:19

4 "So I will stretch out My hand against Judah
And against all the inhabitants of Jerusalem.
And I will cut off the remnant of Baal from this place,
And the names of the idolatrous priests along with the priests.

1:4
Ezek 6:14;
Mic 5:13;
Hos 10:5

5 "And those who bow down on the housetops to the host of heaven,
And those who bow down *and* swear to the LORD and *yet* swear by Milcom,

*1:5
Jer 19:13;
5:2,7; 49:1

6 And those who have turned back from following the LORD,
And those who have not sought the LORD or inquired of Him."

1:6
Is 1:4;
Jer 2:13;

7 Be silent before the Lord GOD!
For the day of the LORD is near,
For the LORD has prepared a sacrifice,
He has consecrated His guests.

Is 9:13;
Hos 7:7
*1:7
Hab 2:20;
Zech 2:13;
Is 13:6; v. 14;
Is 34:6;

8 "Then it will come about on the day of the LORD's sacrifice,
That I will punish the princes, the king's sons,
And all who clothe themselves with foreign garments.

Jer 46:10
*1:8
Is 24:21;
Jer 39:6;

9 "And I will punish on that day all who leap on the *temple* threshold,
Who fill the house of their lord with violence and deceit.

Is 2:6
*1:9
Jer 5:27;

10 "And on that day," declares the LORD,
"There will be the sound of a cry from the Fish Gate,
A wail from the ¹Second Quarter,
And a loud crash from the hills.

Amos 3:10
1:10
Amos 8:3;
2 Chr 33:14;
34:22;
Ezek 6:13

11 "Wail, O inhabitants of the ¹Mortar,
For all the people of Canaan will be silenced;
All who weigh out silver will be cut off.

1:11
James 5:1;
Zeph 2:5;
Hos 9:6

12 "And it will come about at that time
That I will search Jerusalem with lamps,
And I will punish the men

*1:12
Jer 16:16,17;
Jer 48:11;
Amos 6:1;
Ezek 8:12;
9:9

¹I.e., a district of Jerusalem

1:5 *Milcom* was a god of the Ammonites. He was also called "Molech," or "Moloch," which were simply variants of the name lacking the *-om* ending. He seems to have been identical with the god Baal in his aspect as the "king-god."
1:7 *the* LORD *has prepared a sacrifice*, i.e., a slaughter of people who rebelled against Him.
  In this verse and v. 14 the prophet has in mind a double fulfillment. The earlier preliminary judgment was inflicted when Nebuchadnezzar invaded Judah. But the final and climactic *day of the* LORD is yet future and remains to be fulfilled at the end of the present age.
1:8 *Foreign garments* identifies the wearer as a follower of the foreign idols.
1:9 *all who leap on the temple threshold.* This is a foreign custom associated with pagan superstitions.
1:12 *The* LORD *will not do good or evil*, i.e., the LORD will do nothing. Those who have such sentiments live in practical disregard of God and His claims on their lives.

Who are stagnant in spirit,
Who say in their hearts,
'The LORD will not do good or evil!'

1:13
Deut 28:30,
39;
Amos 5:11;
Mic 6:15

13 "Moreover, their wealth will become plunder,
And their houses desolate;
Yes, they will build houses but not inhabit *them,*
And plant vineyards but not drink their wine."

C. *The day of wrath*

1:14
Joel 2:1,11

14 Near is the great day of the LORD,
Near and coming very quickly;
Listen, the day of the LORD!
In it the warrior cries out bitterly.

1:15
Is 22:5;
Jer 30:7;
Amos 5:18-20

15 A day of wrath is that day,
A day of trouble and distress,
A day of destruction and desolation,
A day of darkness and gloom,
A day of clouds and thick darkness,

1:16
Jer 4:19;
Is 2:12-15

16 A day of trumpet and battle cry,
Against the fortified cities
And the high corner towers.

1:17
Jer 10:18;
Is 59:10;
Ps 79:3;
Jer 9:22

17 And I will bring distress on men,
So that they will walk like the blind,
Because they have sinned against the LORD;
And their blood will be poured out like dust,
And their flesh like dung.

1:18
Prov 11:4;
Zeph 3:8;
vv. 2,3

18 Neither their silver nor their gold
Will be able to deliver them
On the day of the LORD's wrath;
And all the earth will be devoured
In the fire of His jealousy,
For He will make a complete end,
Indeed a terrifying one,
Of all the inhabitants of the earth.

D. *The call to repentance*

2:1
Joel 1:14;
Jer 3:3; 6:15
2:2
Is 17:13;
Hos 13:3;
Nah 1:6;
Zeph 1:18

2 Gather yourselves together, yes, gather,
O nation without shame,
Before the decree takes effect—
The day passes like the chaff—
Before the burning anger of the LORD comes upon you,
Before the day of the LORD's anger comes upon you.

2:3
Amos 5:6;
Ps 76:9;
Amos 5:14,
15; Ps 57:1

3 Seek the LORD,
All you humble of the earth
Who have carried out His ordinances;
Seek righteousness, seek humility.
Perhaps you will be hidden
In the day of the LORD's anger.

II. *The judgment of the nations (2:4–15)*

A. *Gaza and the Philistines*

2:4
Amos 1:7,8;
Zech 9:5-7

4 For Gaza will be abandoned,
And Ashkelon a desolation;
Ashdod will be driven out at noon,
And Ekron will be uprooted.

*2:5
Ezek 25:16;
Amos 3:1;
Is 14:29-31;
Zeph 3:6

5 Woe to the inhabitants of the seacoast,
The nation of the ²Cherethites!
The word of the LORD is against you,

²I.e., a segment of the Philistines with roots in Crete

2:5 *Cherethites,* i.e., Cretans.

O Canaan, land of the Philistines;
And I will destroy you,
So that there will be no inhabitant.

6 So the seacoast will be pastures,
With caves for shepherds and folds for flocks.

7 And the coast will be
For the remnant of the house of Judah,
They will pasture on it.
In the houses of Ashkelon they will lie down at evening;
For the LORD their God will care for them
And restore their fortune.

B. *Moab and Ammon*

8 "I have heard the taunting of Moab
And the revilings of the sons of Ammon,
With which they have taunted My people
And become arrogant against their territory.

9 "Therefore, as I live," declares the LORD of hosts,
The God of Israel,
"Surely Moab will be like Sodom,
And the sons of Ammon like Gomorrah—
A place possessed by nettles and salt pits,
And a perpetual desolation.
The remnant of My people will plunder them,
And the remainder of My nation will inherit them."

10 This they will have in return for their pride, because they have taunted and become arrogant against the people of the LORD of hosts.

11 The LORD will be terrifying to them, for He will starve all the gods of the earth; and all the coastlands of the nations will bow down to Him, everyone from his *own* place.

C. *Ethiopia and Assyria*

12 "You also, O Ethiopians, will be slain by My sword."
13 And He will stretch out His hand against the north
And destroy Assyria,
And He will make Nineveh a desolation,
Parched like the wilderness.

14 And flocks will lie down in her midst,
All beasts which range in herds;
Both the pelican and the hedgehog
Will lodge in the tops of her pillars;
Birds will sing in the window,
Desolation *will be* on the threshold;
For He has laid bare the cedar work.

15 This is the exultant city
Which dwells securely,
Who says in her heart,
"I am, and there is no one besides me."
How she has become a desolation,
A resting place for beasts!
Everyone who passes by her will hiss
And wave his hand *in contempt.*

III. *The sin of Jerusalem and the future salvation (3:1–20)*

A. *The woe on Jerusalem*

3
Woe to her who is rebellious and defiled,
The tyrannical city!
2 She heeded no voice;
She accepted no instruction.

Cross references (margin):
2:6 Is 17:2
2:7 Mic 4:7; Is 32:14; Ps 80:14; Luke 1:68; Ps 126:1,4
*2:8 Ezek 25:3,6, 8; Jer 49:1
2:9 Is 15:1-16,14; Amos 1:13; Deut 29:23; Is 11:14
2:10 Is 16:6; Jer 48:29; v. 8
2:11 Joel 2:11; Zeph 1:4; 3:9; Mal 1:11; Is 24:15
2:12 Is 18:1
2:13 Is 14:26; 10:12; Nah 3:7
2:14 v. 6; Is 13:21; 34:11,14; Jer 22:14
2:15 Is 22:2; 47:8; 32:14; Jer 18:16; 19:8
3:1 Jer 5:23; Ezek 23:30; Jer 6:6
3:2 Jer 22:21; 5:3; Ps 78:22; 73:28

2:8 See notes to Ezek. 25:2; 25:9.

She did not trust in the LORD;
She did not draw near to her God.

3:3
Ezek 22:27;
Hab 1:8

3   Her princes within her are roaring lions;
Her judges are wolves at evening;
They leave nothing for the morning.

3:4
Hos 9:7;
Ezek 22:26

4   Her prophets are reckless, treacherous men;
Her priests have profaned the sanctuary.
They have done violence to the law.

3:5
vv. 15,17;
Deut 32:4;
Jer 3:3

5   The LORD is righteous within her;
He will do no injustice.
Every morning He brings His justice to light;
He does not fail.
But the unjust knows no shame.

3:6
Zeph 1:16;
Is 6:11;
Zeph 2:5

6   "I have cut off nations;
Their corner towers are in ruins.
I have made their streets desolate,
With no one passing by;
Their cities are laid waste,
Without a man, without an inhabitant.

3:7
v. 2; Jer 7:7;
Hos 9:9

7   "I said, 'Surely you will revere Me,
Accept instruction.'
So her dwelling will not be cut off
According to all that I have appointed concerning her.
But they were eager to corrupt all their deeds.

B. The deliverance that is to come

1. The call to wait

3:8
Ps 27:14;
Zeph 2:2;
Joel 3:2;
Zeph 1:18

8   "Therefore, wait for Me," declares the LORD,
"For the day when I rise up to the prey.
Indeed, My decision is to gather nations,
To assemble kingdoms,
To pour out on them My indignation,
All My burning anger;
For all the earth will be devoured
By the fire of My zeal.

*3:9
Is 19:18;
Ps 22:27;
Zeph 2:11

9   "For then I will give to the peoples purified lips,
That all of them may call on the name of the LORD,
To serve Him shoulder to shoulder.

3:10
Ps 68:31;
Is 18:1,7;
60:6,7

10   "From beyond the rivers of Ethiopia
My worshipers, My dispersed ones,
Will bring My offerings.

3:11
Is 45:17;
Joel 2:26,27;
Is 2:12; 5:15;
Ezek 20:40

11   "In that day you will feel no shame
Because of all your deeds
By which you have rebelled against Me;
For then I will remove from your midst
Your proud, exulting ones,
And you will never again be haughty
On My holy mountain.

3:12
Is 14:32;
Nah 1:7

12   "But I will leave among you
A humble and lowly people,
And they will take refuge in the name of the LORD.

3:13
Mic 4:7;
Is 60:21;
Zech 8:3,16;
Rev 14:5;
Ezek 34:28;
Mic 4:4

13   "The remnant of Israel will do no wrong
And tell no lies,
Nor will a deceitful tongue
Be found in their mouths;
For they shall feed and lie down
With no one to make them tremble."

3:9 *Purified lips* refers to the honoring of God's name.   worship of the LORD.
Idolatrous worship is put aside in favor of the purity of the

2. The call to rejoice

14 Shout for joy, O daughter of Zion!
Shout *in triumph*, O Israel!
Rejoice and exult with all *your* heart,
O daughter of Jerusalem!

15 The LORD has taken away *His* judgments against you,
He has cleared away your enemies.
The King of Israel, the LORD, is in your midst;
You will fear disaster no more.

16 In that day it will be said to Jerusalem:
"Do not be afraid, O Zion;
Do not let your hands fall limp.

17 "The LORD your God is in your midst,
A victorious warrior.
He will exult over you with joy,
He will be quiet in His love,
He will rejoice over you with shouts of joy.

18 "I will gather those who grieve about the appointed feasts—
They came from you, O *Zion*;
The reproach *of exile* is a burden on them.

19 "Behold, I am going to deal at that time
With all your oppressors,
I will save the lame
And gather the outcast,
And I will turn their shame into praise and renown
In all the earth.

20 "At that time I will bring you in,
Even at the time when I gather you together;
Indeed, I will give you renown and praise
Among all the peoples of the earth,
When I restore your fortunes before your eyes,"
Says the LORD.

3:14
Is 12:6;
Zech 2:10

3:15
Ezek 37:26-28;
v. 5; Is 54:14

3:16
Is 35:3,4;
Heb 12:12

*3:17
vv. 5,15;
Is 63:1; 62:5

3:19
Is 60:14;
Ezek 34:16;
Mic 4:6,7

3:20
Ezek 37:12,
21; Is 56:5;
66:22;
Zeph 2:7

3:17 God is love (1 John 4:8). This pure and holy love is described in Scripture as being: (1) sovereign (Deut. 7:8; 10:15); (2) everlasting (Jer. 31:3); (3) indissoluble (Rom. 8:39); and (4) never failing (Is. 49:15,16). The measure of God's love may be seen in the advent of Jesus and His death on the cross of Calvary for the sins of the world. God's love, in turn, has been poured into our hearts by the Holy Spirit (Rom. 5:5).

INTRODUCTION TO
THE BOOK OF
HAGGAI

Authorship and Background: This book is the work of Haggai, about whom almost nothing is known except his name. The period covered by his life cannot be fixed with accuracy. He may possibly have been a boy at the time of the exile and have seen the temple of Solomon. Some think he was born during the time of the captivity, and even in the land of the captivity. He returned with the remnant after the exile and, with his contemporary Zechariah, labored toward the common goal of securing the rebuilding of the temple. He wrote the four discourses that make up this prophecy, during a four-month period in the year 520 B.C. The rebuilding of the temple was his general theme.

From 605 B.C., Judah was under the dominion of Babylon. Her rebellion finally led to the destruction of the temple and the burning of the city of Jerusalem. Seventy years of captivity ensued. Then, under an edict of King Cyrus of Persia, a remnant numbering some forty thousand returned to the land. Led by Zerubbabel the governor and Joshua the high priest, they began the rebuilding of the city. The foundation of the temple was laid right away, but the work was thereafter delayed for fifteen years due to the machinations of hostile neighbors. King Darius ascended the Persian throne in 521 B.C. and was favorable to the Jews. The preaching and encouragement of Haggai and Zechariah resulted in the work on the temple being resumed in 520 B.C. It was finished in 516 or 515 B.C.

Characteristics: Haggai acts as a goad for God. He urges on the people the task of rebuilding the temple. He rebukes the people for their indolence and spurs them on to finish the work. There are no lofty flights of oratory. His style appears somewhat dull and prosaic. He speaks plainly and directly, briefly and tersely. His words give no clue to his person. He shrouds himself in his work as a prophet of God, as an intermediary bearing a letter. He is one of the few prophets who has the privilege of seeing his dream fulfilled. In his day the temple is finished.

Contents:

I. The call to rebuild the temple: the first prophecy (1:1-15): Haggai accuses the Jews of building their own homes and neglecting the temple. God has not blessed them. The path of obedience is to rebuild the temple. God will help and they will be blessed.

II. Comfort and hope: the second message (2:1-9): Haggai assures Zerubbabel and Joshua that God is present; His Spirit is among them. He will shake the nations and fill His house with His glory. The latter splendor will be greater than the former.

III. Holiness versus uncleanness and God's blessing: third message (2:10-19): The Word of the LORD comes to Haggai. Holy flesh in the skirt of the garment will not make other things holy when touched; but an unclean person by touching the same things can make them unholy. God's people are unclean, so their works are unclean. God has withheld His blessing because of disobedience, and the earth does not yield its fruit. If the people will be obedient, then immediate blessing will follow.

IV. Zerubbabel, the servant of Yahweh: fourth message (2:20-23): The Word of the LORD comes the second time. God tells Zerubbabel that He will shake the heavens and earth; He will overthrow the foreign masters; horses and riders will go down. God will make Zerubbabel like a signet ring, for Zerubbabel is God's servant.

THE BOOK OF
HAGGAI

I. *The call to rebuild the temple: the first prophecy (1:1–15)*

A. *Objections and response*

1 In the second year of Darius the king, on the first day of the sixth month, the word of the LORD came by the prophet Haggai to Zerubbabel the son of Shealtiel, governor of Judah, and to Joshua the son of Jehozadak, the high priest saying,

2 "Thus says the LORD of hosts, 'This people says, "The time has not come, *even* the time for the house of the LORD to be rebuilt." ' "

3 Then the word of the LORD came by Haggai the prophet saying,

4 "Is it time for you yourselves to dwell in your paneled houses while this house *lies* desolate?"

5 Now therefore, thus says the LORD of hosts, "Consider your ways!

6 "You have sown much, but harvest little; *you* eat, but *there is* not *enough* to be satisfied; *you* drink, but *there is* not *enough* to become drunk; *you* put on clothing, but no one is warm *enough*; and he who earns, earns wages *to put* into a purse with holes."

7 Thus says the LORD of hosts, "Consider your ways!

8 "Go up to the mountains, bring wood and rebuild the temple, that I may be pleased with it and be glorified," says the LORD.

9 "*You* look for much, but behold, *it comes* to little; when you bring *it* home, I blow it *away*. Why?" declares the LORD of hosts, "Because of My house which *lies* desolate, while each of you runs to his own house.

10 "Therefore, because of you the sky has withheld its dew, and the earth has withheld its produce.

11 "And I called for a drought on the land, on the mountains, on the grain, on the new wine, on the oil, on what the ground produces, on men, on cattle, and on all the labor of your hands."

B. *The call to rebuild obeyed*

12 Then Zerubbabel the son of Shealtiel, and Joshua the son of Jehozadak, the high priest, with all the remnant of the people, obeyed the voice of the LORD their God and the words of Haggai the prophet, as the LORD their God had sent him. And the people showed reverence for the LORD.

13 Then Haggai, the messenger of the LORD, spoke by the commission of the LORD to the people saying, " 'I am with you,' declares the LORD."

14 So the LORD stirred up the spirit of Zerubbabel the son of Shealtiel, governor of Judah, and the spirit of Joshua the son of Jehozadak, the high priest, and the spirit of all the remnant of the people; and they came and worked on the house of the LORD of hosts, their God,

15 on the twenty-fourth day of the sixth month in the second year of Darius the king.

II. *Comfort and hope: the second message (2:1–9)*

2 On the twenty-first of the seventh month, the word of the LORD came by Haggai the prophet saying,

2 "Speak now to Zerubbabel the son of Shealtiel, governor of Judah, and to Joshua the son of Jehozadak, the high priest, and to the remnant of the people saying,

3 'Who is left among you who saw this temple in its former glory? And how do you see it now? Does it not seem to you like nothing in comparison?

4 'But now take courage, Zerubbabel,' declares the LORD, 'take courage also, Joshua son of Jehozadak, the high priest, and all you people of the land take

---

1:1
Zech 1:1;
1 Chr 3:17;
Ezra 3:2;
Zech 6:11

1:2
v. 15

1:4
2 Sam 7:2;
v. 9
1:5
Lam 3:40
1:6
Deut 28:38;
Mic 6:14;
Zech 8:10

1:7
v. 1
1:8
Ezra 3:7;
Ps 132:13,14;
Hag 2:7,9
1:9
v. 6; Is 40:7

1:10
Lev 26:19;
Deut 28:23;
1 Kin 8:35
1:11
Mal 3:9-11;
Deut 28:22;
Hag 2:17

1:12
Hag 2:2;
Is 1:19; 50:10

1:13
Mal 2:7; 3:1;
Matt 28:30;
Rom 8:31
1:14
2 Chr 36:22;
Ezra 1:1; 5:2,
8

2:3
Ezra 3:12;
Zech 4:10
2:4
Zech 8:9;
Acts 7:9

courage,' declares the LORD, 'and work; for I am with you,' says the LORD of hosts.

5 'As for the promise which I made you when you came out of Egypt, My Spirit is abiding in your midst; do not fear!'

6 "For thus says the LORD of hosts, 'Once more in a little while, I am going to shake the heavens and the earth, the sea also and the dry land.

7 'And I will shake all the nations; and they will come with the wealth of all nations; and I will fill this house with glory,' says the LORD of hosts.

8 'The silver is Mine, and the gold is Mine,' declares the LORD of hosts.

9 'The latter glory of this house will be greater than the former,' says the LORD of hosts, 'and in this place I shall give peace,' declares the LORD of hosts."

III. Holiness versus uncleanness and God's blessing:
third message (2:10–19)

10 On the twenty-fourth of the ninth *month*, in the second year of Darius, the word of the LORD came to Haggai the prophet saying,

11 "Thus says the LORD of hosts, 'Ask now the priests *for* a ruling:

12 'If a man carries holy meat in the fold of his garment, and touches bread with this fold, or cooked food, wine, oil, or any *other* food, will it become holy?'" And the priests answered and said, "No."

13 Then Haggai said, "If one who is unclean from a corpse touches any of these, will *the latter* become unclean?" And the priests answered and said, "It will become unclean."

14 Then Haggai answered and said, " 'So is this people. And so is this nation before Me,' declares the LORD, 'and so is every work of their hands; and what they offer there is unclean.

15 'But now, do consider from this day onward: before one stone was placed on another in the temple of the LORD,

16 from that time *when* one came to a *grain* heap of twenty *measures*, there would be only ten; and *when* one came to the wine vat to draw fifty measures, there would be *only* twenty.

17 'I smote you *and* every work of your hands with blasting wind, mildew, and hail; yet you *did* not *come back* to Me,' declares the LORD.

18 'Do consider from this day onward, from the twenty-fourth day of the ninth *month*; from the day when the temple of the LORD was founded, consider:

19 'Is the seed still in the barn? Even including the vine, the fig tree, the pomegranate, and the olive tree, it has not borne *fruit*. Yet from this day on I will bless *you.*' "

IV. Zerubbabel, the servant of Yahweh:
fourth message (2:20–23)

20 Then the word of the LORD came a second time to Haggai on the twenty-fourth *day* of the month saying,

21 "Speak to Zerubbabel governor of Judah saying, 'I am going to shake the heavens and the earth.

22 'And I will overthrow the thrones of kingdoms and destroy the power of the kingdoms of the nations; and I will overthrow the chariots and their riders, and the horses and their riders will go down, everyone by the sword of another.'

23 'On that day,' declares the LORD of hosts, 'I will take you, Zerubbabel, son of Shealtiel, my servant,' declares the LORD, 'and I will make you like a signet *ring*, for I have chosen you,' " declares the LORD of hosts.

Marginal references

2:5 Ex 29:45,46; Neh 9:20; Is 63:11,14
*2:6 Heb 12:26; Is 10:25; 29:17; v. 21
2:7 Dan 2:44; Is 60:4-9
*2:9 Is 66:12; Zech 2:5
2:10 vv. 1,20
*2:11 Lev 10:10; Deut 33:10; Mal 2:7
2:12 Ezek 44:19; Matt 23:19
2:13 Num 19:11, 22
2:14 Prov 15:8; Is 1:11-15
2:15 Hag 1:5; Ezra 3:10; 4:24
2:16 Hag 1:6,9; Zech 8:10
2:17 1 Kin 8:37; Amos 4:9; Is 9:13
2:18 Zech 8:9
2:19 Zech 8:12
2:20ff v. 10
2:21 Hag 1:14; Zech 4:6-10; Heb 12:26
2:22 Dan 2:44; Mic 5:10; Zech 4:6; 2 Chr 20:23
2:23 Song 8:6; Jer 22:24; Is 42:1; 43:10

2:6 *I am going to shake the heavens.* Political upheavals and earthquakes would be used by God to accomplish His purposes. The earthly confusion would be but evidence that God was preparing to act.
2:9 *greater than the former.* This should not be taken as referring to external splendor, for in that respect the temple of Solomon greatly surpassed this new edifice under construction by Zerubbabel. It refers rather to the spiritual glory that would be granted it when Jesus of Nazareth Himself entered its courts and preached the gospel to Israel in its precincts.
2:11 *Ask now the priests for a ruling,* i.e., to illustrate from the law. If they do this the people will learn that: (1) it is impossible for sacred things to communicate holiness to the things they touch; and (2) any person who is unclean will contaminate everything he touches.

INTRODUCTION TO

THE BOOK OF

ZECHARIAH

Authorship and Background: The author, Zechariah, whose name means "whom Yahweh hath remembered," was the son of Berechiah. His grandfather, Iddo, returned from the exile with Zerubbabel and Joshua (Neh. 12:1,4,7). In all probability Zechariah was attached to the priesthood. He was a contemporary of Haggai, beginning his prophetic ministry in 520 B.C. The historical background of the book is identical to that of Haggai. The main divisions of Zechariah (1-8,9-14) are markedly dissimilar in style and subject matter. Some have therefore supposed that the book is the work of different authors. Those who accept the unity of the authorship account for the differences by concluding that the latter section of the prophecy was composed some decades after the first part. The first part is historical and the second apocalyptic, resulting in distinct styles in the two sections of the book.

Characteristics: Zechariah concerns himself with the rebuilding of the temple in the first part of his prophecy. He aims to encourage the people to continue the work, which has been interrupted for some years. Then he looks into the future, to distant events not yet fulfilled. Whereas his contemporary, Haggai, uses plain and simple language, Zechariah employs symbolic language such as was common to the Babylonians, and to Daniel and Ezekiel. Often it is difficult to determine the precise meaning of what Zechariah says, although the main lines of the book are plain enough. Zechariah contributes more to angelology than any other Old Testament writer, not excluding Daniel.

In the first section he urges the people to repent and warns them not to act as their forefathers did, upon whom the judgment of God fell in the captivity. He notes that the consequences of God's judgment are still in force. The question is, how long will this continue? In a series of visions, Zechariah discloses God's plan to pour out His anger on the nations, but to allow the rebuilding of Jerusalem and the temple. He teaches the people the meaning of worship.

Beginning with chapter 9, Zechariah looks into the future. This section is filled with Messianic references and passages that deal with the end of the age. He foresees the day of the LORD, when the kingdom will be set up, Israel restored, the nations judged, and God and His kingdom triumphant.

Contents:

I. Messages during the building of the temple (1:1-8:23): Zechariah calls on his people to repent and return to God. He recounts his visions: the red horse speaks of God watching over Judah; the four horns and four smiths show the defeat of Judah's enemies; the measuring line is the vision of what Jerusalem is yet to be; Joshua reclothed in clean raiment indicates that the promise of God includes removal of sin, and moral and spiritual reformation of the people; the golden lampstand fed by the two olive trees is a message to Zerubbabel that success in rebuilding comes from the Spirit, for the day of small things is not to be despised; the flying scroll vision pronounces a curse on those who steal and perjure themselves; the vision of the woman sitting in the ephah deals with iniquity "in all the land" (5:6), teaching that even in restored Israel the spirit of lawlessness will exist; and the four chariots symbolize God's spirits released for the fulfillment of God's plans for His people. Joshua, who represents the Branch, is crowned. The deputation from Bethel asks whether the fasts are to be kept. Obey God's law; disobedience the cause of the captivity. God promises to restore His people. Finish rebuilding the temple. Love truth and peace; fast days will become feast days. The nation will gather at Jerusalem to seek the LORD and pray before Him.

II. Messages after the building of the temple (9:1-14:21): Sidon, Tyre, and Philistia fall. Jerusalem is spared for the coming of its king. Judah is restored. Temporal prosperity is promised. Wickedness will not go unpunished; Jerusalem is destroyed. The shepherd-king is rejected; false shepherds replace the true shepherd. God delivers Jerusalem, which becomes penitent and is restored. The land is cleansed. The shepherd is stricken, and Jerusalem falls. The shepherd comes victoriously; he is enthroned; his enemies are defeated; and ultimately the glory of Jerusalem is established and all nations come to worship the king.

THE BOOK OF
ZECHARIAH

I. *Messages during the building of the temple (1:1–8:23)*

A. *First message: call for national repentance*

1 In the eighth month of the second year of Darius, the word of the LORD came to Zechariah the prophet, the son of Berechiah, the son of Iddo saying,

2 "The LORD was very angry with your fathers.

3 "Therefore say to them, 'Thus says the LORD of hosts, "Return to Me,"' declares the LORD of hosts, "that I may return to you," says the LORD of hosts.

4 "Do not be like your fathers, to whom the former prophets proclaimed, saying, 'Thus says the LORD of hosts, "Return now from your evil ways and from your evil deeds."' But they did not listen or give heed to Me," declares the LORD.

5 "Your fathers, where are they? And the prophets, do they live forever?

6 "But did not My words and My statutes, which I commanded My servants the prophets, overtake your fathers? Then they repented and said, 'As the LORD of hosts purposed to do to us in accordance with our ways and our deeds, so He has dealt with us.'"'"

B. *Second message: the eight visions of God's care for Israel*

1. *The horsemen among the myrtles*

7 On the twenty-fourth day of the eleventh month, which is the month Shebat, in the second year of Darius, the word of the LORD came to Zechariah the prophet, the son of Berechiah, the son of Iddo, as follows:

8 I saw at night, and behold, a man was riding on a red horse, and he was standing among the myrtle trees which were in the ravine, with red, sorrel, and white horses behind him.

9 Then I said, "My lord, what are these?" And the angel who was speaking with me said to me, "I will show you what these are."

10 And the man who was standing among the myrtle trees answered and said, "These are those whom the LORD has sent to patrol the earth."

11 So they answered the angel of the LORD who was standing among the myrtle trees, and said, "We have patrolled the earth, and behold, all the earth is peaceful and quiet."

12 Then the angel of the LORD answered and said, "O LORD of hosts, how long wilt Thou have no compassion for Jerusalem and the cities of Judah, with which Thou hast been indignant these seventy years?"

13 And the LORD answered the angel who was speaking with me with gracious words, comforting words.

14 So the angel who was speaking with me said to me, "Proclaim, saying, 'Thus says the LORD of hosts, "I am exceedingly jealous for Jerusalem and Zion.

15 "But I am very angry with the nations who are at ease; for while I was only a little angry, they furthered the disaster."

16 'Therefore, thus says the LORD, "I will return to Jerusalem with compassion; My house will be built in it," declares the LORD of hosts, "and a measuring line will be stretched over Jerusalem."'

17 "Again, proclaim, saying, 'Thus says the LORD of hosts, "My cities will again overflow with prosperity, and the LORD will again comfort Zion and again choose Jerusalem."'"

1:1
Ezra 4:24;
Hag 1:1;
Neh 12:4,16

1:3
Is 31:6;
Mal 3:7;
James 4:8
1:4
2 Chr 36:15;
Hos 14:1;
Jer 6:17;
11:7,8
1:6
Jer 12:16,17;
Lam 2:17

1:8
Josh 5:13;
Rev 6:4;
Zech 6:2-7
1:9
Zech 2:3; 4:5

1:10
Heb 1:14

*1:11
Is 14:7

1:12
Hab 1:2;
Dan 9:2

1:13
Zech 4:1;
Is 40:1,2
1:14
Zech 8:2

1:15
Ps 123:4;
Amos 1:11
*1:16
Is 54:8;
Zech 2:1,2,10

1:17
Is 44:26;
51:3;
Zech 2:12;
3:2

1:11 *all the earth is peaceful and quiet.* The earth was at peace, but Jerusalem was still oppressed by external foes and troubled by dissident groups within.

1:16 *a measuring line.* It would be used as a preparation for building.

2. The four horns and the four smiths

18 Then I lifted up my eyes and looked, and behold, *there were* four horns.
19 So I said to the angel who was speaking with me, "What are these?" And he answered me, "These are the horns which have scattered Judah, Israel, and Jerusalem."

20 Then the LORD showed me four craftsmen.
21 And I said, "What are these coming to do?" And he said, "These are the horns which have scattered Judah, so that no man lifts up his head; but these *craftsmen* have come to terrify them, to throw down the horns of the nations who have lifted up *their* horns against the land of Judah in order to scatter it."

3. The measuring line of Jerusalem

2 Then I lifted up my eyes and looked, and behold, *there was* a man with a measuring line in his hand.
2 So I said, "Where are you going?" And he said to me, "To measure Jerusalem, to see how wide it is and how long it is."
3 And behold, the angel who was speaking with me was going out, and another angel was coming out to meet him,
4 and said to him, "Run, speak to that young man, saying, 'Jerusalem will be inhabited without walls, because of the multitude of men and cattle within it.
5 'For I,' declares the LORD, 'will be a wall of fire around her, and I will be the glory in her midst.' "
6 "Ho there! Flee from the land of the north," declares the LORD, "for I have dispersed you as the four winds of the heavens," declares the LORD.
7 "Ho, Zion! Escape, you who are living with the daughter of Babylon."
8 For thus says the LORD of hosts, "After glory He has sent me against the nations which plunder you, for he who touches you, touches the apple of His eye.
9 "For behold, I will wave My hand over them, so that they will be plunder for their slaves. Then you will know that the LORD of hosts has sent Me.
10 "Sing for joy and be glad, O daughter of Zion; for behold I am coming and I will dwell in your midst," declares the LORD.
11 "And many nations will join themselves to the LORD in that day and will become My people. Then I will dwell in your midst, and you will know that the LORD of hosts has sent Me to you.
12 "And the LORD will possess Judah as His portion in the holy land, and will again choose Jerusalem.
13 "Be silent, all flesh, before the LORD; for He is aroused from His holy habitation."

4. Joshua as the symbol of the priestly nation

3 Then he showed me Joshua the high priest standing before the angel of the LORD, and Satan standing at his right hand to accuse him.
2 And the LORD said to Satan, "The LORD rebuke you, Satan! Indeed, the LORD who has chosen Jerusalem rebuke you! Is this not a brand plucked from the fire?"
3 Now Joshua was clothed with filthy garments and standing before the angel.
4 And he spoke and said to those who were standing before him saying, "Remove the filthy garments from him." Again he said to him, "See, I have taken your iniquity away from you and will clothe you with festal robes."
5 Then I said, "Let them put a clean turban on his head." So they put a clean turban on his head and clothed him with garments, while the angel of the LORD was standing by.
6 And the angel of the LORD admonished Joshua saying,
7 "Thus says the LORD of hosts, 'If you will walk in My ways, and if you will perform My service, then you will also govern My house and also have charge of My courts, and I will grant you free access among these who are standing *here*.
8 'Now listen, Joshua the high priest, you and your friends who are sitting in

Marginal cross-references

1:20 Is 44:12; 54:16
1:21 Ps 75:10
2:1 Zech 1:18; Ezek 40:3
2:2 Ezek 40:3; Rev 21:15-17
*2:4 Ezek 38:11; Jer 30:19
2:5 Is 26:1; Zech 9:8; Rev 21:23
2:6 Is 48:20; Jer 1:14; Ezek 17:21
2:8 Is 60:7-9; Deut 32:10
2:9 Is 11:15; Zech 4:9
2:10 Is 12:6; Zeph 3:14; Lev 26:12; Ezek 37:27
2:12 Deut 32:9; Zech 1:17
2:13 Hab 2:20; Ps 78:65; Is 51:9
3:1 Hag 1:1; Ps 109:6
3:2 Jude 9,23; Am 4:11
3:4 Is 43:25; Rev 19:8
3:5 Ex 29:6
3:7 1 Kin 3:14; Ezek 44:16; Deut 17:9; Zech 4:14
*3:8 Is 20:3; Ezek 12:11;

2:4 This prophecy about Jerusalem points to a future age when it becomes a large and populous city, too large to be contained within walls, and one that will be indwelt by the glory of God. Note particularly that v. 11 refers to the Gentiles, who have been grafted into the stock of Israel by faith (Rom. 11:13–25).

3:8 *the Branch*, i.e., the Messiah appears here as a Messianic title, referring to Christ as the descendant of David. At His first advent the Jews were blinded and unable to discern His presence. At the end of the age He will be received by Israel in faith and submission. But from the time of His Easter victory He will be constantly building up His spiri-

front of you—indeed they are men who are a symbol, for behold, I am going to bring in My servant the Branch.

9 'For behold, the stone that I have set before Joshua; on one stone are seven eyes. Behold, I will engrave an inscription on it,' declares the LORD of hosts, 'and I will remove the iniquity of that land in one day.

10 'In that day,' declares the LORD of hosts, 'every one of you will invite his neighbor to *sit* under *his* vine and under *his* fig tree.' "

5. The lampstand and the two olive trees

4 Then the angel who was speaking with me returned, and roused me as a man who is awakened from his sleep.

2 And he said to me, "What do you see?" And I said, "I see, and behold, a lampstand all of gold with its bowl on the top of it, and its seven lamps on it with seven spouts belonging to each of the lamps which are on the top of it;

3 also two olive trees by it, one on the right side of the bowl and the other on its left side."

4 Then I answered and said to the angel who was speaking with me saying, "What are these, my lord?"

5 So the angel who was speaking with me answered and said to me, "Do you not know what these are?" And I said, "No, my lord."

6 Then he answered and said to me, "This is the word of the LORD to Zerubbabel saying, 'Not by might nor by power, but by My Spirit,' says the LORD of hosts.

7 'What are you, O great mountain? Before Zerubbabel *you will become* a plain; and he will bring forth the top stone with shouts of "Grace, grace to it!" ' "

8 Also the word of the LORD came to me saying,

9 "The hands of Zerubbabel have laid the foundation of this house, and his hands will finish *it*. Then you will know that the LORD of hosts has sent me to you.

10 "For who has despised the day of small things? But these seven will be glad when they see the plumb line in the hand of Zerubbabel—*these are* the eyes of the LORD which range to and fro throughout the earth."

11 Then I answered and said to him, "What are these two olive trees on the right of the lampstand and on its left?"

12 And I answered the second time and said to him, "What are the two olive branches which are beside the two golden pipes, which empty the golden *oil* from themselves?"

13 So he answered me saying, "Do you not know what these are?" And I said, "No, my lord."

14 Then he said, "These are the two anointed ones, who are standing by the Lord of the whole earth."

6. The flying scroll

5 Then I lifted up my eyes again and looked, and behold, *there was* a flying scroll.

2 And he said to me, "What do you see?" And I answered, "I see a flying scroll; its length is twenty cubits and its width ten cubits."

3 Then he said to me, "This is the curse that is going forth over the face of the whole land; surely everyone who steals will be purged away according to the writing on one side, and everyone who swears will be purged away according to the writing on the other side.

4 "I will make it go forth," declares the LORD of hosts, "and it will enter the house of the thief and the house of the one who swears falsely by My name; and it will spend the night within that house and consume it with its timber and stones."

7. The ephah of iniquity carried back to Babylon

5 Then the angel who was speaking with me went out, and said to me, "Lift up now your eyes, and see what this is, going forth."

6 And I said, "What is it?" And he said, "This is the ephah going forth." Again he said, "This is their appearance in all the land

7 (and behold, a lead cover was lifted up); and this is a woman sitting inside the ephah."

Marginal references:

4:2
Is 4:2; 53:2;
Jer 33:15

3:9
Is 28:16;
Zech 4:10;
Jer 31:34;
Mic 7:18
3:10
1 Kin 4:25;
Is 36:16

4:1
Zech 1:9; 2:3;
Dan 8:18
4:2
Ex 25:31;
Rev 1:12;
Ex 25:37;
Rev 4:5
4:3
Rev 11:4

4:5
Zech 1:9

4:6
Hag 2:4,5;
Hos 1:7;
Eph 6:17
4:7
Jer 51:25;
Ps 118:22;
Ezra 3:10,11

4:9
Ezra 3:10;
6:15;
Zech 2:9,11;
6:15;
Is 48:16;
Zech 2:8
4:10
Hag 2:3;
Zech 3:9;
Rev 8:2;
Zech 1:10
4:11
v. 3

4:14
Rev 11:4;
Zech 3:1-7;
Mic 4:13

5:1
Ezek 2:9

5:3
Jer 26:6;
Ex 20:15;
Mal 3:8,9;
v. 4

5:4
Mal 3:5;
Hos 4:2,3;
Lev 14:45;
Hab 2:9-11

5:5
Zech 1:9,18

5:6
Lev 19:36;
Amos 8:5

---

tual temple, the church (cf. 1 Pet. 2:5), as is indicated by 6:12–15.

8   Then he said, "This is Wickedness!" And he threw her down into the middle of the ephah and cast the lead weight on its opening.

9   Then I lifted up my eyes and looked, and there two women were coming out with the wind in their wings; and they had wings like the wings of a stork, and they lifted up the ephah between the earth and the heavens.

10   And I said to the angel who was speaking with me, "Where are they taking the ephah?"

11   Then he said to me, "To build a temple for her in the land of Shinar; and when it is prepared, she will be set there on her own pedestal."

8. The four chariots of divine judgment

6 Now I lifted up my eyes again and looked, and behold, four chariots were coming forth from between the two mountains; and the mountains *were* bronze mountains.

2   With the first chariot *were* red horses, with the second chariot black horses,

3   with the third chariot white horses, and with the fourth chariot strong dappled horses.

4   Then I spoke and said to the angel who was speaking with me, "What are these, my lord?"

5   And the angel answered and said to me, "These are the four spirits of heaven, going forth after standing before the Lord of all the earth,

6   with one of which the black horses are going forth to the north country; and the white ones go forth after them, while the dappled ones go forth to the south country.

7   "When the strong ones went out, they were eager to go to patrol the earth." And He said, "Go, patrol the earth." So they patrolled the earth.

8   Then He cried out to me and spoke to me saying, "See, those who are going to the land of the north have appeased My wrath in the land of the north."

9. Sequel: Joshua crowned as a type of the Branch

9   The word of the LORD also came to me saying,

10   "Take *an offering* from the exiles, from Heldai, Tobijah, and Jedaiah; and you go the same day and enter the house of Josiah the son of Zephaniah, where they have arrived from Babylon.

11   "And take silver and gold, make an *ornate* crown, and set *it* on the head of Joshua the son of Jehozadak, the high priest.

12   "Then say to him, 'Thus says the LORD of hosts, "Behold, a man whose name is Branch, for He will branch out from where He is; and He will build the temple of the LORD.

13   "Yes, it is He who will build the temple of the LORD, and He who will bear the honor and sit and rule on His throne. Thus, He will be a priest on His throne, and the counsel of peace will be between the two offices." '

14   "Now the crown will become a reminder in the temple of the LORD to Helem, Tobijah, Jedaiah, and Hen the son of Zephaniah.

15   "And those who are far off will come and build the temple of the LORD." Then you will know that the LORD of hosts has sent me to you. And it will take place, if you completely obey the LORD your God.

C. Third message: the meaning of true piety

1. The inquiry about extra fasts

7 Then it came about in the fourth year of King Darius, that the word of the LORD came to Zechariah on the fourth *day* of the ninth month, *which is* Chislev.

2   Now *the town of* Bethel had sent Sharezer and Regemmelech and their men to seek the favor of the LORD,

3   speaking to the priests who belong to the house of the LORD of hosts, and to the prophets saying, "Shall I weep in the fifth month and abstain, as I have done these many years?"

Cross references (left margin):

5:8 Hos 12:7; Amos 8:5; Mic 6:11
5:9 v. 5; Jer 8:7
*5:11 Jer 29:5,28; Gen 10:10
*6:1 Zech 1:18; 5:9; v. 5
6:2 Rev 6:4,5
6:3 Rev 6:2
6:4 Zech 5:10
6:5 Jer 49:36; Ezek 37:9; Matt 24:31; Rev 7:1
6:6 Jer 1:14; Ezek 1:4; Dan 11:5
6:7 Zech 1:10
6:8 Ezek 5:13
6:9 Zech 1:1; 7:1; 8:1
6:10 Jer 28:6
6:11 Ezra 3:2; Hag 1:1
6:12 Is 11:1; Zech 3:8; Is 53:2
6:13 Is 9:6; 22:24; 9:7; Ps 110:1,4
6:14 v. 11
6:15 Is 57:19; 60:10; Zech 4:9; 3:7
7:1 Zech 1:1,7; Neh 1:1
7:2 Jer 26:19; Zech 8:21
*7:3 Jer 52:12; Zech 8:19; 12:12-14

5:11 *in the land of Shinar* (Babylon). Iniquity was symbolically taken from Judah to Babylon and left there.
6:1 *four chariots,* i.e., *the four spirits* (v. 5).

7:3 *in the fifth month . . . abstain.* Commemorating the destruction of Jerusalem (587 B.C.).

2. The fourfold answer

a. The hypocrisy of their fasts

4 Then the word of the LORD of hosts came to me saying,

5 "Say to all the people of the land and to the priests, 'When you fasted and mourned in the fifth and seventh months these seventy years, was it actually for Me that you fasted?

6 'And when you eat and drink, do you not eat for yourselves and do you not drink for yourselves?

7 'Are not *these* the words which the LORD proclaimed by the former prophets, when Jerusalem was inhabited and prosperous with its cities around it, and the Negev and the foothills were inhabited?'"

b. The exile a result of their oppressions

8 Then the word of the LORD came to Zechariah saying,

9 "Thus has the LORD of hosts said, 'Dispense true justice, and practice kindness and compassion each to his brother;

10 and do not oppress the widow or the orphan, the stranger or the poor; and do not devise evil in your hearts against one another.'

11 "But they refused to pay attention, and turned a stubborn shoulder and stopped their ears from hearing.

12 "And they made their hearts *like* flint so that they could not hear the law and the words which the LORD of hosts had sent by His Spirit through the former prophets; therefore great wrath came from the LORD of hosts.

13 "And it came about that just as He called and they would not listen, so they called and I would not listen," says the LORD of hosts;

14 "but I scattered them with a storm wind among all the nations whom they have not known. Thus the land is desolated behind them, so that no one went back and forth, for they made the pleasant land desolate."

c. God's intention to restore Jerusalem

8 Then the word of the LORD of hosts came saying,

2 "Thus says the LORD of hosts, 'I am exceedingly jealous for Zion, yes, with great wrath I am jealous for her.'

3 "Thus says the LORD, 'I will return to Zion and will dwell in the midst of Jerusalem. Then Jerusalem will be called the City of Truth, and the mountain of the LORD of hosts *will be called* the Holy Mountain.'

4 "Thus says the LORD of hosts, 'Old men and old women will again sit in the ¹streets of Jerusalem, each man with his staff in his hand because of age.

5 'And the ¹streets of the city will be filled with boys and girls playing in its ¹streets.'

6 "Thus says the LORD of hosts, 'If it is too difficult in the sight of the remnant of this people in those days, will it also be too difficult in My sight?' declares the LORD of hosts.

7 "Thus says the LORD of hosts, 'Behold, I am going to save My people from the land of the east and from the land of the west;

8 and I will bring them *back*, and they will live in the midst of Jerusalem, and they will be My people and I will be their God in truth and righteousness.'

9 "Thus says the LORD of hosts, 'Let your hands be strong, you who are listening in these days to these words from the mouth of the prophets, *those* who *spoke* in the day that the foundation of the house of the LORD of hosts was laid, to the end that the temple might be built.

10 'For before those days there was no wage for man or any wage for animal; and for him who went out or came in there was no peace because of his enemies, and I set all men one against another.

11 'But now I will not treat the remnant of this people as in the former days,' declares the LORD of hosts.

12 'For *there will be* peace for the seed: the vine will yield its fruit, the land will yield its produce, and the heavens will give their dew; and I will cause the remnant of this people to inherit all these *things*.

¹Or, *squares*

7:5 God's people performed the rites and ceremonies, but not for God's glory.

Cross references
*7:5
Is 58:5;
Zech 8:19;
Jer 41:1;
Rom 14:6

7:7
Zech 1:4;
Jer 22:21;
17:26

7:9
Ezek 18:8;
Zech 8:16;
Mic 6:8
7:10
Deut 24:17;
Jer 7:6;
Mic 2:1
7:11
Jer 11:10;
17:23; 5:21;
Acts 7:57
7:12
Ezek 11:19;
36:26;
Neh 9:29,30;
Dan 9:11
7:13
Prov 1:24;
Is 1:15;
Mic 3:4
7:14
Deut 4:27;
Jer 23:19;
44:6; Is 60:15

8:2
Zech 1:14

8:3
Zech 1:16;
2:10,11;
Jer 31:23

8:4
Is 65:20

8:5
Jer 30:19,20

8:6
Ps 118:23;
Jer 32:17,27

8:7
Is 11:11;
43:5,6;
Amos 9:14
8:8
Zech 10:10;
Ezek 37:25;
Zech 2:11
8:9
Hag 2:4;
Ezra 5:1

8:10
Hag 1:6

8:11
Ps 103:9;
Is 12:1
8:12
Joel 2:22;
Hag 1:10;
Is 61:7

8:13
Jer 42:18;
Gen 12:2;
Ruth 4:11
13 'And it will come about that just as you were a curse among the nations, O house of Judah and house of Israel, so I will save you that you may become a blessing. Do not fear; let your hands be strong.'

8:14
Jer 31:28;
Ezek 24:14
14 "For thus says the LORD of hosts, 'Just as I purposed to do harm to you when your fathers provoked Me to wrath,' says the LORD of hosts, 'and I have not relented,

8:15
Jer 29:11;
v. 13
15 so I have again purposed in these days to do good to Jerusalem and to the house of Judah. Do not fear!

8:16
Zech 7:9;
Eph 4:25
16 'These are the things which you should do: speak the truth to one another; judge with truth and judgment for peace in your 2gates.

8:17
Prov 3:29;
Zech 7:10;
5:4; Hab 1:13
17 'Also let none of you devise evil in your heart against another, and do not love perjury; for all these are what I hate,' declares the LORD.'"

d. The nations to seek the LORD in Jerusalem

18 Then the word of the LORD of hosts came to me saying,

8:19
Zech 7:3,5;
Jer 39:2;
52:4; Is 12:1;
v. 16
19 "Thus says the LORD of hosts, 'The fast of the fourth, the fast of the fifth, the fast of the seventh, and the fast of the tenth *months* will become joy, gladness, and cheerful feasts for the house of Judah; so love truth and peace.'

20 "Thus says the LORD of hosts, '*It will* yet *be* that peoples will come, even the inhabitants of many cities.

8:21
Mic 4:1,2
21 'And the inhabitants of one will go to another saying, "Let us go at once to entreat the favor of the LORD, and to seek the LORD of hosts; I will also go."

8:22
Is 60:3;
66:23; v. 21
22 'So many peoples and mighty nations will come to seek the LORD of hosts in Jerusalem and to entreat the favor of the LORD.'

*8:23
Is 45:14,24;
60:14;
1 Cor 14:25;
2 Chr 15:5;
Is 19:2
23 "Thus says the LORD of hosts, 'In those days ten men from all the nations will grasp the garment of a Jew saying, "Let us go with you, for we have heard that God is with you."'"

II. *Messages after the building of the temple (9:1—14:21)*

A. *Messiah king rejected, triumphant*

1. *The coming of the king announced*

9 The burden of the word of the LORD is against the land of Hadrach, with Damascus as its resting place (for the eyes of men, especially of all the tribes of Israel, are toward the LORD),

9:2
Jer 49:23;
Ezek 28:3-5,
12,21
2 And Hamath also, which borders on it;
Tyre and Sidon, though they are very wise.

9:3
2 Sam 24:7;
Ezek 27:33;
1 Kin 10:21,
27
3 For Tyre built herself a fortress
And piled up silver like dust,
And gold like the mire of the streets.

9:4
Is 23:1;
Ezek 28:18
4 Behold, the Lord will dispossess her
And cast her wealth into the sea;
And she will be consumed with fire.

9:5
Amos 1:6-8
5 Ashkelon will see *it* and be afraid.
Gaza too will writhe in great pain;
Also Ekron, for her expectation has been confounded.
Moreover, the king will perish from Gaza,
And Ashkelon will not be inhabited.

9:6
Amos 1:6-8
6 And a mongrel race will dwell in Ashdod,
And I will cut off the pride of the Philistines.

9:7
Ezek 25:15-17
7 And I will remove their blood from their mouth,
And their detestable things from between their teeth.
Then they also will be a remnant for our God,
And be like a clan in Judah,
And Ekron like a Jebusite.

9:8
Zech 2:5;
Is 52:1;
54:14; 60:18
8 But I will camp around My house because of an army,
Because of him who passes by and returns;
And no oppressor will pass over them anymore,
For now I have seen with My eyes.

2I.e., the place where court was held

8:23 This prophecy has not been fulfilled as yet. Undoubt-edly it awaits the time when Jerusalem shall become the center of the worship of God, and Jewish Christians will be foremost leaders in world evangelism.

9 Rejoice greatly, O daughter of Zion!
Shout *in triumph*, O daughter of Jerusalem!
Behold, your king is coming to you;
He is just and endowed with salvation,
Humble, and mounted on a donkey,
Even on a colt, the foal of a donkey.

10 And I will cut off the chariot from Ephraim,
And the horse from Jerusalem;
And the bow of war will be cut off.
And He will speak peace to the nations;
And His dominion will be from sea to sea,
And from the ³River to the ends of the earth.

2. The program of the king

a. Israel delivered from captivity

11 As for you also, because of the blood of *My* covenant with you,
I have set your prisoners free from the waterless pit.
12 Return to the stronghold, O prisoners who have the hope;
This very day I am declaring that I will restore double to you.

b. Triumph over the Greek oppressor

13 For I will bend Judah as My bow,
I will fill the bow with Ephraim.
And I will stir up your sons, O Zion, against your sons, O Greece;
And I will make you like a warrior's sword.
14 Then the LORD will appear over them,
And His arrow will go forth like lightning;
And the Lord GOD will blow the trumpet,
And will march in the storm winds of the south.
15 The LORD of hosts will defend them.
And they will devour, and trample on the sling stones;
And they will drink, *and* be boisterous as with wine;
And they will be filled like a *sacrificial* basin,
Drenched like the corners of the altar.
16 And the LORD their God will save them in that day
As the flock of His people;
For *they are as* the stones of a crown,
Sparkling in His land.
17 For what comeliness and beauty *will be* theirs!
Grain will make the young men flourish, and new wine the virgins.

c. The complete redemption of God's people

10 Ask rain from the LORD at the time of the spring rain—
The LORD who makes the storm clouds;
And He will give them showers of rain, vegetation in the field
    to *each* man.
2 For the teraphim speak iniquity,
And the diviners see lying visions,
And tell false dreams;
They comfort in vain.
Therefore *the people* wander like sheep,
They are afflicted, because there is no shepherd.
3 "My anger is kindled against the shepherds,
And I will punish the male goats;
For the LORD of hosts has visited His flock, the house of Judah,
And will make them like His majestic horse in battle.
4 "From them will come the cornerstone,
From them the tent peg,

³I.e., Euphrates

9:9 This passage predicts the triumphal entry of Christ into Jerusalem on the Sunday of Passion Week. Coming as king, Christ was to be acclaimed by the people with shouts of "Hosanna to the Son of David! . . . " (Matt. 21:9), even though their adulation proved to be short-lived by Good Friday.

From them the bow of battle,
From them every ruler, *all* of them together.

10:5
2 Sam 22:43;
Hag 2:22

5   "And they will be as mighty men,
Treading down *the enemy* in the mire of the streets in battle;
And they will fight, for the Lord *will be* with them;
And the riders on horses will be put to shame.

10:6
v. 12;
Zech 9:16;
8:8; 1:1,6;
13:9

6   "And I shall strengthen the house of Judah,
And I shall save the house of Joseph,
And I shall bring them back,
Because I have had compassion on them;
And they will be as though I had not rejected them,
For I am the Lord their God, and I will answer them.

10:7
Zech 9:13,15;
Is 54:13

7   "And Ephraim will be like a mighty man,
And their heart will be glad as if *from* wine;
Indeed, their children will see *it* and be glad,
Their heart will rejoice in the Lord.

10:8
Is 5:26;
Jer 33:22;
Ezek 36:11

8   "I will whistle for them to gather them together,
For I have redeemed them;
And they will be as numerous as they were before.

10:9
Ezek 6:9

9   "When I scatter them among the peoples,
They will remember Me in far countries,
And they with their children will live and come back.

10:10
Is 11:11;
Jer 50:19;
Is 49:19,20

10 "I will bring them back from the land of Egypt,
And gather them from Assyria;
And I will bring them into the land of Gilead and Lebanon,
Until no *room* can be found for them.

10:11
Is 51:9,10;
19:5-7;
Zeph 2:13;
Ezek 30:13

11 "And He will pass through the sea *of* distress,
And strike the waves in the sea,
So that all the depths of the Nile will dry up;
And the pride of Assyria will be brought down,
And the scepter of Egypt will depart.

10:12
Mic 4:5

12 "And I shall strengthen them in the Lord,
And in His name they will walk," declares the Lord.

3. *The rejection of the king*

a. *The proud in Israel humbled*

11:1
Jer 22:6,7;
Ezek 31:3
11:2
Is 32:19

11

Open your doors, O Lebanon,
That a fire may feed on your cedars.

2   Wail, O cypress, for the cedar has fallen,
Because the glorious *trees* have been destroyed;
Wail, O oaks of Bashan,
For the impenetrable forest has come down.

11:3
Jer 25:34-36;
50:44

3   There is a sound of the shepherds' wail,
For their glory is ruined;
There is a sound of the young lions' roar,
For the pride of the Jordan is ruined.

b. *The good shepherd rejected by His people*

11:4
v. 7
11:5
Jer 50:7;
Hos 12:8

4   Thus says the Lord my God, "Pasture the flock *doomed* to slaughter.

5   "Those who buy them slay them and go unpunished, and *each of* those who sell them says, 'Blessed be the Lord, for I have become rich!' And their own shepherds have no pity on them.

11:6
Jer 13:14;
Zech 14:13;
Mic 5:8

6   "For I shall no longer have pity on the inhabitants of the land," declares the Lord; "but behold, I shall cause the men to fall, each into another's power and into the power of his king; and they will strike the land, and I shall not deliver *them* from their power."

11:7
Zeph 3:12;
Ezek 37:16;
vv. 10,14

7   So I pastured the flock *doomed* to slaughter, hence the afflicted of the flock. And I took for myself two staffs: the one I called Favor, and the other I called Union; so I pastured the flock.

11:8
Hos 5:7

8   Then I annihilated the three shepherds in one month, for my soul was impatient with them, and their soul also was weary of me.

9   Then I said, "I will not pasture you. What is to die, let it die, and what is to

be annihilated, let it be annihilated; and let those who are left eat one another's flesh."

10   And I took my staff, Favor, and cut it in pieces, to break my covenant which I had made with all the peoples.

11   So it was broken on that day, and ⁴thus the afflicted of the flock who were watching me realized that it was the word of the LORD.

12   And I said to them, "If it is good in your sight, give *me* my wages; but if not, never mind!" So they weighed out thirty *shekels* of silver as my wages.

13   Then the LORD said to me, "Throw it to the potter, *that* magnificent price at which I was valued by them." So I took the thirty *shekels* of silver and threw them to the potter in the house of the LORD.

14   Then I cut my second staff, Union, in pieces, to break the brotherhood between Judah and Israel.

c. *The false shepherd described*

15   And the LORD said to me, "Take again for yourself the equipment of a foolish shepherd.

16   "For behold, I am going to raise up a shepherd in the land who will not care for the perishing, seek the scattered, heal the broken, or sustain the one standing, but will devour the flesh of the fat *sheep* and tear off their hoofs.

17   "Woe to the worthless shepherd
Who leaves the flock!
A sword will be on his arm
And on his right eye!
His arm will be totally withered,
And his right eye will be blind."

B. *The rejected king enthroned*

1. *Repentant Israel triumphant*

a. *Downfall of heathen attackers of Jerusalem*

12 The ⁵burden of the word of the LORD concerning Israel. *Thus* declares the LORD who stretches out the heavens, lays the foundation of the earth, and forms the spirit of man within him,

2   "Behold, I am going to make Jerusalem a cup that causes reeling to all the peoples around; and when the siege is against Jerusalem, it will also be against Judah.

3   "And it will come about in that day that I will make Jerusalem a heavy stone for all the peoples; all who lift it will be severely injured. And all the nations of the earth will be gathered against it.

4   "In that day," declares the LORD, "I will strike every horse with bewilderment, and his rider with madness. But I will watch over the house of Judah, while I strike every horse of the peoples with blindness.

5   "Then the clans of Judah will say in their hearts, 'A strong support for us are the inhabitants of Jerusalem through the LORD of hosts, their God.'

b. *Israel's power to vanquish all foes*

6   "In that day I will make the clans of Judah like a firepot among pieces of wood and a flaming torch among sheaves, so they will consume on the right hand and on the left all the surrounding peoples, while the inhabitants of Jerusalem again dwell on their own sites in Jerusalem.

7   "The LORD also will save the tents of Judah first in order that the glory of the house of David and the glory of the inhabitants of Jerusalem may not be magnified above Judah.

8   "In that day the LORD will defend the inhabitants of Jerusalem, and the one who is feeble among them in that day will be like David, and the house of David *will be* like God, like the angel of the LORD before them.

9   "And it will come about in that day that I will set about to destroy all the nations that come against Jerusalem.

c. *Repentance of Israel for piercing their king*

10   "And I will pour out on the house of David and on the inhabitants of

⁴Another reading is *the sheep dealers who*   ⁵Or, *oracle*

11:9
Jer 15:2;
43:11
11:10
v. 7;
Jer 14:21
11:11
Zeph 3:12

11:12
1 Kin 5:6;
Gen 37:28;
Ex 21:32;
Matt 26:15;
27:9,10
11:13
Matt 27:9

11:15
Ezek 34:2-4

11:16
Jer 23:2;
Ezek 34:2-6

11:17
Jer 23:1;
John 10:12;
Ezek 30:21,
22; Mic 3:6,7

12:1
Is 42:5;
57:16;
Heb 12:9
12:2
Is 51:22,23;
Zech 14:14

12:3
Dan 2:34,35,
44,45;
Matt 21:44;
Zech 14:2
12:4
Ps 76:6;
Ezek 38:4;
Zech 9:10
12:5
Zech 10:6,12

12:6
Is 10:17,18;
Obad 18;
Zech 2:4;
8:3-5

12:7
Jer 30:18;
Amos 9:11

12:8
Zech 9:14,15;
Mic 7:8;
Ps 8:5; 82:6

12:9
v. 3;
Zech 14:2,3

12:10
Is 44:3;
Ezek 39:29;
Joel 2:28;

John 19:34;
Rev 1:7;
Jer 6:26;
Amos 8:10

12:11
2 Kin 23:29

12:12
Matt 24:30;
Rev 1:7

13:1
Jer 2:13;
Heb 9:14;
Ps 51:2,7;
Ezek 36:25
13:2
Ex 23:13;
Hos 2:17;
Jer 23:14,15;
Ezek 36:25,
29
13:3
Jer 23:34;
Deut 18:20;
13:6-11
13:4
Mic 3:6,7;
2 Kin 1:8;
Matt 3:4
13:5
Amos 7:14

13:6
2 Kin 9:24

13:7
Jer 47:6;
Mic 5:2,4;
Jer 23:5,6;
Is 53:4,5,10;
Matt 26:31;
Is 1:25
13:8
Is 6:13

13:9
Is 48:10;
1 Pet 1:6;
Zech 10:6;
Jer 30:22;
Hos 2:23

*14:1
Is 13:9;
Joel 2:1;
Mal 4:1; v. 14
14:2
Zech 12:2,3;
Is 13:6;
Zech 13:8
14:3
Zech 9:14,15

14:4
Ezek 11:23;

Jerusalem, the Spirit of grace and of supplication, so that they will look on Me whom they have pierced; and they will mourn for Him, as one mourns for an only son, and they will weep bitterly over Him, like the bitter weeping over a first-born.

11 "In that day there will be great mourning in Jerusalem, like the mourning of Hadadrimmon in the plain of Megiddo.

12 "And the land will mourn, every family by itself; the family of the house of David by itself, and their wives by themselves; the family of the house of Nathan by itself, and their wives by themselves;

13 the family of the house of Levi by itself, and their wives by themselves; the family of the Shimeites by itself, and their wives by themselves;

14 all the families that remain, every family by itself, and their wives by themselves.

d. Israel cleansed and evil cut off

13 "In that day a fountain will be opened for the house of David and for the inhabitants of Jerusalem, for sin and for impurity.

2 "And it will come about in that day," declares the LORD of hosts, "that I will cut off the names of the idols from the land, and they will no longer be remembered; and I will also remove the prophets and the unclean spirit from the land.

3 "And it will come about that if anyone still prophesies, then his father and mother who gave birth to him will say to him, 'You shall not live, for you have spoken falsely in the name of the LORD'; and his father and mother who gave birth to him will pierce him through when he prophesies.

4 "Also it will come about in that day that the prophets will each be ashamed of his vision when he prophesies, and they will not put on a hairy robe in order to deceive;

5 but he will say, 'I am not a prophet; I am a tiller of the ground, for a man sold me as a slave in my youth.'

6 "And one will say to him, 'What are these wounds between your arms?' Then he will say, 'Those with which I was wounded in the house of my friends.'

2. Israel purged, delivered, and triumphant

a. Israel chastened after rejecting the king

7   "Awake, O sword, against My Shepherd,
     And against the man, My Associate,"
     Declares the LORD of hosts.
     "Strike the Shepherd that the sheep may be scattered;
     And I will turn My hand against the little ones.

8   "And it will come about in all the land,"
     Declares the LORD,
     "That two parts in it will be cut off and perish;
     But the third will be left in it.

9   "And I will bring the third part through the fire,
     Refine them as silver is refined,
     And test them as gold is tested.
     They will call on My name,
     And I will answer them;
     I will say, 'They are My people,'
     And they will say, 'The LORD is my God.' "

b. Jerusalem delivered by the LORD

14 Behold, a day is coming for the LORD when the spoil taken from you will be divided among you.

2   For I will gather all the nations against Jerusalem to battle, and the city will be captured, the houses plundered, the women ravished, and half of the city exiled, but the rest of the people will not be cut off from the city.

3   Then the LORD will go forth and fight against those nations, as when He fights on a day of battle.

4   And in that day His feet will stand on the Mount of Olives, which is in front of Jerusalem on the east; and the Mount of Olives will be split in its middle from east

---

14:1 The coming of Christ here predicted when Jerusalem will be rescued from complete destruction by a miraculous   divine interposition.

to west by a very large valley, so that half of the mountain will move toward the north and the other half toward the south.

5   And you will flee by the valley of My mountains, for the valley of the mountains will reach to Azel; yes, you will flee just as you fled before the earthquake in the days of Uzziah king of Judah. Then the LORD, my God, will come, *and* all the holy ones with Him!

6   And it will come about in that day that there will be no light; the luminaries will dwindle.

7   For it will be a unique day which is known to the LORD, neither day nor night, but it will come about that at evening time there will be light.

8   And it will come about in that day that living waters will flow out of Jerusalem, half of them toward the eastern sea and the other half toward the western sea; it will be in summer as well as in winter.

9 And the LORD will be king over all the earth; in that day the LORD will be *the only* one, and His name *the only* one.

c. Judah's king supreme over the earth

10   All the land will be changed into a plain from Geba to Rimmon south of Jerusalem; but Jerusalem will rise and remain on its site from Benjamin's Gate as far as the place of the First Gate to the Corner Gate, and from the Tower of Hananel to the king's wine presses.

11   And people will live in it, and there will be no more curse, for Jerusalem will dwell in security.

12   Now this will be the plague with which the LORD will strike all the peoples who have gone to war against Jerusalem; their flesh will rot while they stand on their feet, and their eyes will rot in their sockets, and their tongue will rot in their mouth.

13   And it will come about in that day that a great panic from the LORD will fall on them; and they will seize one another's hand, and the hand of one will be lifted against the hand of another.

14   And Judah also will fight at Jerusalem; and the wealth of all the surrounding nations will be gathered, gold and silver and garments in great abundance.

15   So also like this plague, will be the plague on the horse, the mule, the camel, the donkey, and all the cattle that will be in those camps.

d. The nations subjugated and Israel holy

16   Then it will come about that any who are left of all the nations that went against Jerusalem will go up from year to year to worship the King, the LORD of hosts, and to celebrate the Feast of Booths.

17   And it will be that whichever of the families of the earth does not go up to Jerusalem to worship the King, the LORD of hosts, there will be no rain on them.

18   And if the family of Egypt does not go up or enter, then no *rain will fall* on them; it will be the plague with which the LORD smites the nations who do not go up to celebrate the Feast of Booths.

19   This will be the punishment of Egypt, and the punishment of all the nations who do not go up to celebrate the Feast of Booths.

20   In that day there will *be inscribed* on the bells of the horses, "HOLY TO THE LORD." And the cooking pots in the LORD's house will be like the bowls before the altar.

21   And every cooking pot in Jerusalem and in Judah will be holy to the LORD of hosts; and all who sacrifice will come and take of them and boil in them. And there will no longer be a Canaanite in the house of the LORD of hosts in that day.

Mic 1:3,4;
Hab 3:6

14:5
Amos 1:1;
Is 66:15,16;
Matt 25:31;
Jude 14

14:7
Is 30:26;
Rev 21:23
14:8
Ezek 47:1;
Joel 3:18;
Rev 22:1
***14:9**
Rev 11:15;
Is 45:21-24;
Eph 4:5,6

14:10
Amos 9:11;
Zech 12:6;
Jer 37:13;
38:7; 31:38

14:11
Zech 2:4;
Rev 22:3;
Jer 23:5,6
14:12
Deut 28:21,
22
14:13
1 Sam 14:15,
20;
Zech 11:6;
Ezek 38:21
14:14
Zech 12:2,5;
Is 23:18
14:15
v. 12

14:16
Is 60:6,7,9;
66:23; v. 9

14:17
vv. 9,16;
Amos 4:7
14:18
v. 12

14:19
v. 12

14:20
Ex 28:36-38;
Zech 9:15

14:21
Neh 8:10;
1 Cor 10:31;
Ezek 44:9;
Zech 9:8

14:9 This verse assures every believer of an ultimate answer to the prayer, "Thy kingdom come." In its consummation, Christ's kingdom will embrace all the earth, and the prayer for the spiritual unity of all believers will be more perfectly fulfilled (John 17:21).

INTRODUCTION TO

THE BOOK OF

MALACHI

Authorship and Background: Almost nothing is known about Malachi, whose name means "My messenger" (3:1). According to synagogue tradition he followed after Zechariah and Haggai and thus came before or during Nehemiah's day. This prophecy, the last book in the canon of the Old Testament Scripture, was written probably in the fifth century, either before or during the time of Nehemiah. It was followed by the four hundred "silent years." At the time of the writing, the temple in Jerusalem had been rebuilt, but the glorious kingdom for which the people looked had not yet come. Times were hard because of drought, famine, and blighted crops. These hardships had been met by sloth, indifference, and spiritual lethargy. The people had been in the land after the captivity for almost a hundred years and the walls of Jerusalem had been rebuilt, but present circumstances made them apathetic. They doubted the love of God and wondered whether there was any divine justice. Since the wicked prospered, they questioned whether there was profit in walking penitently before God and obeying His commandments. Against such a background this book was written. Malachi is divided into three chapters in the Hebrew Bible and into four chapters in the English Bible.

Characteristics: Malachi writes as a man of great spiritual force who speaks with the authority of God's Word. His love for the people of God is intense; he has a high conception of the duties of the priesthood and is devoted to the religious ceremonies in the temple. He speaks his message in the street and the marketplace. His writing is in the form of a dialogue, of question and answer; this is both a literary device and also the result of his actual experiences among men. He tries to respond to questions rationally and logically because men demand that their objections be met and his own assertions be justified. Basically, he seeks to answer the question relating to the justice of God. If God is good, why do the wicked prosper and the righteous suffer hardship? His first reply is that the people of God have neglected Him and have been disloyal to Him. Secondly, he argues that cruelty and faithlessness do not go unpunished, as the fate of the Edomites indicates.

Malachi reassures the people that the Messiah will surely come, but He will bring judgment on them because of their sins. The catalogue of their sins is similar to those recorded in the memoirs of Nehemiah, his contemporary. The people offer blemished animals for sacrifice. They neglect to pay their tithes. The priesthood is corrupt, mercenary, and debased. The people have loose marriage morals; divorce is common and intermarriage with the heathen too frequent. Malachi challenges the people to pay their tithes, obey God, and see how He will bless them. He foresees a day when God will destroy the wicked and vindicate the righteous. The coming of the prophet Elijah will precede that day.

Contents:

I. The apostasy and sin of Israel (1:1-2:17): Malachi shows that God is a loving Father, as demonstrated by Jacob's election. Israel is a son who has dishonored his Father by neglecting His law and offering profane sacrifices. God's holiness has been despised by their mixed marriages and divorces. God is wearied by their words.

II. The judgment for sinners and blessings for the penitent (3:1-4:6): God will send His messenger before Him. God is like a refiner's fire and fuller's soap; He does not change. His people have robbed Him by failing to pay their tithes, and thus they will be cursed. Those who are faithful will be God's special possession. The day of the LORD is coming when the wicked will be consumed and the righteous rewarded. The people are urged to keep the Law and look for the forerunner, Elijah, "before the coming of the great and terrible day of the LORD" (4:5).

THE BOOK OF
MALACHI

I. *The apostasy and sin of Israel (1:1–2:17)*

A. *God's love for Israel shown by the fall of Edom*

1:1
Nah 1:1;
Hab 1:1
1:2
Is 41:8,9;
Jer 31:3;
Rom 9:13
1:3
Jer 49:18;
Ezek 35:3-9

1 The oracle of the word of the LORD to Israel through Malachi. **2** "I have loved you," says the LORD. But you say, "How has Thou loved us?" "*Was* not Esau Jacob's brother?" declares the LORD. "Yet I have loved Jacob; **3** but I have hated Esau, and I have made his mountains a desolation, and *appointed* his inheritance for the jackals of the wilderness."

4 Though Edom says, "We have been beaten down, but we will return and build up the ruins"; thus says the LORD of hosts, "They may build, but I will tear down; and *men* will call them the wicked territory, and the people toward whom the LORD is indignant forever."

1:5
Ps 35:27;
Job 42:8

5 And your eyes will see this and you will say, "The LORD be magnified beyond the border of Israel!"

B. *The sins of the priesthood*

1:6
Ex 20:12;
Mal 2:10;
Luke 6:46;
Mal 3:5;
2:1-9
1:7
Lev 21:6,8;
v. 12
1:8
Lev 22:22

6 " 'A son honors *his* father, and a servant his master. Then if I am a father, where is My honor? And if I am a master, where is My respect?' says the LORD of hosts to you, O priests who despise My name. But you say, 'How have we despised Thy name?'

7 "*You* are presenting defiled food upon My altar. But you say, 'How have we defiled Thee?' In that you say, 'The table of the LORD is to be despised.'

8 "But when you present the blind for sacrifice, is it not evil? And when you present the lame and sick, is it not evil? Why not offer it to your governor? Would he be pleased with you? Or would he receive you kindly?" says the LORD of hosts.

1:9
Amos 5:22;
Lev 23:34-44

9 "But now will you not entreat God's favor, that He may be gracious to us? With such an offering on your part, will He receive any of you kindly?" says the LORD of hosts.

1:10
Is 1:13;
Jer 14:10-12;
Hos 5:6

10 "Oh that there were one among you who would shut the gates, that you might not uselessly kindle *fire on* My altar! I am not pleased with you," says the LORD of hosts, "nor will I accept an offering from you.

1:11
Is 45:6; 60:3,
5,6; Rev 8:3;
Jer 10:6,7

11 "For from the rising of the sun, even to its setting, My name *will be* great among the nations, and in every place incense is going to be offered to My name, and a grain offering *that is* pure; for My name *will be* great among the nations," says the LORD of hosts.

1:12
Deut 28:15;
v. 7

12 "But you are profaning it, in that you say, 'The table of the Lord is defiled, and as for its fruit, its food is to be despised.'

1:13
Is 43:22;
61:8;
Lev 22:20

13 "You also say, 'My, how tiresome it is!' And you disdainfully sniff at it," says the LORD of hosts, "and you bring what was taken by robbery, and *what is* lame or sick; so you bring the offering! Should I receive that from your hand?" says the LORD.

1:14
Lev 22:18-20;
Zech 14:9;
Zeph 2:11

14 "But cursed be the swindler who has a male in his flock, and vows it, but sacrifices a blemished animal to the Lord, for I am a great King," says the LORD of hosts, "and My name is feared among the nations."

C. *The warning to the priesthood*

2:1
vv. 7,8
2:2
Lev 26:14;
Deut 28:15-20

2 "And now, this commandment is for you, O priests. **2** "If you do not listen, and if you do not take it to heart to give honor to My name," says the LORD of hosts, "then I will send the curse upon you, and I will curse your blessings; and indeed, I have cursed them *already*, because you are not taking *it* to heart.

2:3
Nah 3:6;
Ex 29:14

3 "Behold, I am going to rebuke your offspring, and I will spread refuse on your faces, the refuse of your feasts; and you will be taken away with it.

4 "Then you will know that I have sent this commandment to you, that My covenant may continue with Levi," says the LORD of hosts.

5 "My covenant with him was *one of* life and peace, and I gave them to him *as an object of* reverence; so he revered Me, and stood in awe of My name.

6 "True instruction was in his mouth, and unrighteousness was not found on his lips; he walked with Me in peace and uprightness, and he turned many back from iniquity.

7 "For the lips of a priest should preserve knowledge, and men should seek instruction from his mouth; for he is the messenger of the LORD of hosts.

8 "But as for you, you have turned aside from the way; you have caused many to stumble by the instruction; you have corrupted the covenant of Levi," says the LORD of hosts.

9 "So I also have made you despised and abased before all the people, just as you are not keeping My ways, but are showing partiality in the instruction.

10 "Do we not all have one father? Has not one God created us? Why do we deal treacherously each against his brother so as to profane the covenant of our fathers?

11 "Judah has dealt treacherously, and an abomination has been committed in Israel and in Jerusalem; for Judah has profaned the sanctuary of the LORD which He loves, and has married the daughter of a foreign god.

12 "*As* for the man who does this, may the LORD cut off from the tents of Jacob *everyone* who awakes and answers, or who presents an offering to the LORD of hosts.

13 "And this is another thing you do: you cover the altar of the LORD with tears, with weeping and with groaning, because He no longer regards the offering or accepts *it with* favor from your hand.

14 "Yet you say, 'For what reason?' Because the LORD has been a witness between you and the wife of your youth, against whom you have dealt treacherously, though she is your companion and your wife by covenant.

15 "But not one has done *so* who has a remnant of the Spirit. And what did *that* one *do* while he was seeking a godly offspring? Take heed then, to your spirit, and let no one deal treacherously against the wife of your youth.

16 "For I hate divorce," says the LORD, the God of Israel, "and him who covers his garment with wrong," says the LORD of hosts. "So take heed to your spirit, that you do not deal treacherously."

17 You have wearied the LORD with your words. Yet you say, "How have we wearied *Him*?" In that you say, "Everyone who does evil is good in the sight of the LORD, and He delights in them," or, "Where is the God of justice?"

II. The judgment for sinners and the blessings for the penitent (3:1–4:6)

A. The sending of the Messiah

3 "Behold, I am going to send My messenger, and he will clear the way before Me. And the Lord, whom you seek, will suddenly come to His temple; and the messenger of the covenant, in whom you delight, behold, He is coming," says the LORD of hosts.

2 "But who can endure the day of His coming? And who can stand when He appears? For He is like a refiner's fire and like fullers' soap.

3 "And He will sit as a smelter and purifier of silver, and He will purify the sons of Levi and refine them like gold and silver, so that they may present to the LORD offerings in righteousness.

4 "Then the offering of Judah and Jerusalem will be pleasing to the LORD, as in the days of old and as in former years.

5 "Then I will draw near to you for judgment; and I will be a swift witness against the sorcerers and against the adulterers and against those who swear falsely, and against those who oppress the wage earner in his wages, the widow and the orphan, and those who turn aside the alien, and do not fear Me," says the LORD of hosts.

2:4
Num 3:45;
18:21
2:5
Num 25:12;
Ezek 34:25;
Deut 33:9
2:6
Deut 33:8-10;
Jer 23:22;
James 5:20
2:7
Lev 10:11;
Jer 18:18;
Num 27:21
2:8
Mal 3:7;
Jer 18:15;
Ezek 44:10
2:9
1 Sam 2:30;
Deut 1:17;
Mic 3:11
2:10
Is 63:16;
1 Cor 8:6;
Jer 9:4,5;
Ex 19:4-6
*2:11
Jer 3:7-9;
Ezra 9:1;
Neh 13:23
2:12
Hos 9:12;
Mal 1:10,13
2:13
Jer 11:14;
14:12
2:14
Prov 5:18;
2:17

2:15
Gen 2:24;
Matt 19:4;
Ex 20:14;
Lev 20:10
2:16
Deut 24:1;
Matt 5:31,32;
Ps 73:6;
Is 59:6
2:17
Is 43:24;
5:19,20

*3:1
Matt 11:10;
Mark 1:2;
Luke 1:76;
7:27

3:2
Ezek 22:14;
Zech 13:9;
Matt 3:10-12;
1 Cor 3:13-15
3:3
Is 1:25;
Zech 13:9
3:4
Mal 1:11
3:5
Deut 18:10;
Ezek 22:9-11;
Zech 5:4;
Lev 19:13

2:11 Intermarriage was a serious problem.　　　　3:1 *My messenger* heralds the Messianic age.

B. *The sins of the people*

3:6
Num 23:19;
James 1:17

6 "For I, the LORD, do not change; therefore you, O sons of Jacob, are not consumed.

3:7
Acts 7:51;
Zech 1:3

7 "From the days of your fathers you have turned aside from My statutes, and have not kept *them*. Return to Me, and I will return to you," says the LORD of hosts. "But you say, 'How shall we return?'

*3:8
Neh 13:10-12

8 "Will a man ¹rob God? Yet you are robbing Me! But you say, 'How have we robbed Thee?' In tithes and offerings.

3:9
Mal 2:2

9 "You are cursed with a curse, for you are ¹robbing Me, the whole nation *of you!*

3:10
Prov 3:9,10;
Ps 78:23-29;
2 Chr 31:10

10 "Bring the whole tithe into the storehouse, so that there may be food in My house, and test Me now in this," says the LORD of hosts, "if I will not open for you the windows of heaven, and pour out for you a blessing until ²it overflows.

3:11
Joel 1:4; 2:25

11 "Then I will rebuke the devourer for you, so that it may not destroy the fruits of the ground; nor will your vine in the field cast *its grapes*," says the LORD of hosts.

3:12
Is 61:9; 62:4

12 "And all the nations will call you blessed, for you shall be a delightful land," says the LORD of hosts.

C. *The distinction between the good and the evil*

3:13
Mal 2:17

13 "Your words have been arrogant against Me," says the LORD. "Yet you say, 'What have we spoken against Thee?'

3:14
Ps 73:13;
Jer 2:25;
18:12; Is 58:3

14 "You have said, 'It is in vain to serve God; and what profit is it that we have kept His charge, and that we have walked in mourning before the LORD of hosts?

3:15
Mal 4:1;
Jer 7:10

15 'So now we call the arrogant blessed; not only are the doers of wickedness built up, but they also test God and escape.' "

3:16
Ps 34:15;
56:8;
Rev 20:12

16 Then those who ³feared the LORD spoke to one another, and the LORD gave attention and heard *it*, and a book of remembrance was written before Him for those who ³fear the LORD and who esteem His name.

3:17
1 Pet 2:9;
Is 26:20

17 "And they will be Mine," says the LORD of hosts, "on the day that I prepare *My* own possession, and I will spare them as a man spares his own son who serves him."

3:18
Gen 18:25;
Amos 5:15

18 So you will again distinguish between the righteous and the wicked, between one who serves God and one who does not serve Him.

4:1
Joel 2:31;
Obad 18;
Amos 2:9

4 "For behold, the day is coming, burning like a furnace; and all the arrogant and every evildoer will be chaff; and the day that is coming will set them ablaze," says the LORD of hosts, "so that it will leave them neither root nor branch."

4:2
Mal 3:16;
Luke 1:78;
Eph 5:14

2 "But for you who ³fear My name the sun of righteousness will rise with healing in its wings; and you will go forth and skip about like calves from the stall.

4:3
Mic 7:10;
Zech 10:5

3 "And you will tread down the wicked, for they shall be ashes under the soles of your feet on the day which I am preparing," says the LORD of hosts.

D. *Conclusion*

1. *The command to obedience*

4:4
Ex 20:3

4 "Remember the law of Moses My servant, *even the* statutes and ordinances which I commanded him in Horeb for all Israel.

2. *The coming of Elijah before the day of the LORD*

*4:5
Matt 11:14;
Mark 9:11;
Luke 1:17

5 "Behold, I am going to send you Elijah the prophet before the coming of the great and terrible day of the LORD.

6 "And he will restore the hearts of the fathers to *their* children, and the hearts of the children to their fathers, lest I come and smite the land with a curse."

¹Or, *defraud(ing)*   ²Or, *there is not room enough*   ³Or, *revere(d)*

3:8 The law of the tithe is set forth in the Mosaic system. But the tithe was already recognized as obligatory before Moses, since even Abraham paid a tenth to Melchizedek (Gen. 14:18–20; Heb. 7:1–4). The New Testament does not prescribe the tithe as a legal requirement, but the Christian can do no less for God under grace than the Jew did under law. The tithe is therefore an outward evidence of an inward committment and springs from one's love of God. (See also note to 1 Cor. 16:2.)
4:5 *Elijah* is depicted as the forerunner, heralding the

coming of the day of the LORD. This prophecy of the coming of Elijah envisions two fulfillments, one at the first advent of Christ and the other in connection with the day of the LORD. Christ identified John the Baptist's coming as a preliminary fulfillment of this prophecy (Matt. 11:14; see also Luke 1:17; 9:8,19; John 1:21). The final fulfillment is probably that portrayed in Rev. 11:3–6. Elijah also appeared at the transfiguration of Christ (Matt. 17:1–5; Mark 9:2–13; Luke 9:28–36).

New Testament

NEW AMERICAN STANDARD BIBLE

INTRODUCTION TO
THE GOSPEL ACCORDING TO
MATTHEW

Authorship and Background: The titles by which the four Gospels are known, "According to Matthew," "According to Mark," "According to Luke," and "According to John," were not composed by the authors, but were added later and represent the thinking of the early church. Any consideration of their authorship must include the fact that in none of them does the author identify himself by name. The first book in the New Testament was accepted and canonized as having for its author the apostle Matthew, also called Levi, a former tax-gatherer (Matt. 9:9; Mark 2:14,15; Luke 5:27-29). There is no further specific information about him, although later traditions concerning his ministry and death are recorded by different writers.

There is no way of fixing the precise date when the Gospel was written. Some prefer a date between A.D. 60 and 70; others take it to have been written between A.D. 80 and 90.

Characteristics: The importance of this Gospel is shown by the fact that it is placed first, and that the early Christian writers quoted from it more often than they did from any other Gospel. Note that:

(1) The strongly Hebraic character of the book identifies its author as a Jewish Christian writing for Jewish readers. Properly, then, this book should come first in the New Testament, since it connects Jesus Christ with God's promises to, and covenants with, David and Abraham (1:1). Christ's mission to Israel is emphasized, and the Old Testament Scriptures are abundantly cited as having been fulfilled in the person and ministry of Jesus. He is "the son of David," "the King of the Jews," the Messiah whom God had promised to Israel. "The kingdom of heaven" (and its equivalent, "the kingdom of God") is the key phrase and the subject of much of the teaching, especially the parables.

(2) The orderly arrangement of the teachings of Jesus into discourses shows the author to have been a teacher, concerned with the urgent need of preserving and transmitting the lessons of the Great Teacher. There are five great discourses: the Sermon on the Mount (chs. 5-7), the missionary instructions to the Twelve (ch. 10), the parables of the kingdom (ch. 13), greatness and forgiveness in the Christian community (ch. 18), and the discourse on last things (chs. 24-25). Much of the material is arranged in groups of threes, fives, and sevens for greater ease in teaching and learning.

(3) Interest in the organized life of the Christian church is shown, for only in this Gospel does the word "church" (*ekklēsia*) appear (16:18; 18:17). Along with this, other teachings emphasize principles and conduct in the Christian fellowship (especially in ch. 18).

(4) Prominence is given to Christ's teachings on the end of the age and the second coming, particularly in the parables in chapter 13 and the Olivet discourse in chapters 24-25.

Contents:

I. Genealogy and birth of the Messiah (1:1-2:23)

II. John the Baptist; baptism and temptation of Christ (3:1-4:11)

III. Public ministry in Galilee (4:12-18:35): Teaching, calling of the disciples, miracles, healings, conflicts with Jewish leaders. Appointment of the Twelve and their missionary work; death of John the Baptist and period of retirement, with special training of the Twelve. The great confession at Caesarea Philippi and the transfiguration.

IV. From Galilee to Jerusalem (19:1-20:34)

V. The last week in Jerusalem (21:1-28:15): Triumphal entry, cleansing of the temple, cursing of the fig tree. Disputes with Pharisees and Sadducees; the apocalyptic discourse. The Supper, Gethsemane, arrest, trial, crucifixion, death, and resurrection.

VI. The appearance in Galilee and the Great Commission (28:16-20)

THE GOSPEL ACCORDING TO
MATTHEW

I. Genealogy and birth of the Messiah (1:1–2:23)

A. The genealogy of Jesus (1:1–17; cf. Luke 3:23–38)

1 The book of the genealogy of Jesus Christ, the son of David, the son of Abraham.

2 To Abraham was born Isaac; and to Isaac, Jacob; and to Jacob, ¹Judah and his brothers;

3 and to Judah were born Perez and Zerah by Tamar; and to Perez was born Hezron; and to Hezron, Ram;

4 and to Ram was born Amminadab; and to Amminadab, Nahshon; and to Nahshon, Salmon;

5 and to Salmon was born Boaz by Rahab; and to Boaz was born Obed by Ruth; and to Obed, Jesse;

6 and to Jesse was born David the king.
And to David was born Solomon by her *who had been the wife* of Uriah;

7 and to Solomon was born Rehoboam; and to Rehoboam, Abijah; and to Abijah, Asa;

8 and to Asa was born Jehoshaphat; and to Jehoshaphat, Joram; and to Joram, Uzziah;

9 and to Uzziah was born Jotham; and to Jotham, Ahaz; and to Ahaz, Hezekiah;

10 and to Hezekiah was born Manasseh; and to Manasseh, Amon; and to Amon, Josiah;

11 and to Josiah were born Jeconiah and his brothers, at the time of the deportation to Babylon.

12 And after the deportation to Babylon, to Jeconiah was born Shealtiel; and to Shealtiel, Zerubbabel;

13 and to Zerubbabel was born Abiud; and to Abiud, Eliakim; and to Eliakim, Azor;

14 and to Azor was born Zadok; and to Zadok, Achim; and to Achim, Eliud;

15 and to Eliud was born Eleazar; and to Eleazar, Matthan; and to Matthan, Jacob;

16 and to Jacob was born Joseph the husband of Mary, by whom was born Jesus, who is called Christ.

17 Therefore all the generations from Abraham to David are fourteen generations; and from David to the deportation to Babylon fourteen generations; and from the deportation to Babylon to *the time of* Christ fourteen generations.

B. The birth of Jesus (1:18–25; Luke 1:26–35; 2:1–7)

18 Now the birth of Jesus Christ was as follows. When His mother Mary had

---

¹Gr., *Judas*. Names of Old Testament characters will be given in their Old Testament form.

1:5 The Davidic line, and thus the line of Christ, was racially mixed in that it included Gentiles as well as Hebrew ancestors. Ruth, the wife of Boaz and great-grandmother of David, was a Moabitess (Ruth 1:4). Thus there was Gentile blood in the Messianic line. Most interpreters assume that the Rahab of this verse refers to the Gentile harlot of Josh. 2:1 (see also Heb. 11:31).
1:16 The difference between the accounts of the genealogy of Jesus in Matthew and Luke is usually explained by the fact that Matthew records the genealogy of Joseph as the legal (rather than the natural) father of Jesus. Luke, on the other hand, appears to trace the genealogy of Jesus through Mary, His mother, which accounts for an almost completely different set of ancestors listed from Eli to David (Luke

3:23–31). It is assumed that Eli was Joseph's father-in-law. Mary's name is not mentioned before Eli's because it was not customary among the Jews to trace genealogy through a female.
1:17 The gospel writer divides the forty-two generations from Abraham to Christ into three groups of fourteen generations each: Abraham to David, David to the Babylonian captivity, and from the Babylonian captivity to Christ. In order to maintain the total of forty-two generations, Matthew omitted some names and used others twice, e.g., Jeconiah is the last name in the second group (v. 11) and the first name in the third group (v. 12).
Several generations are omitted, for example, Joash, Amaziah, and Azariah, between Uzziah and Jotham (v. 9).

1:1
Ps 132:11;
Is 11:1;
Luke 1:32;
John 7:42;
Acts 2:30;
13:23;
Rom 1:3;
Gen 12:3;
22:18;
Gal 3:16
1:2
Gen 21:2,3;
25:26; 29:35
1:3
Gen 38:27ff;
Ruth 4:18ff;
1 Chr 2:5,9ff
1:6
1 Sam 16:1;
17:1;
2 Sam 12:24
1:7
1 Chr 3:10
1:10
2 Kin 20:21;
1 Chr 3:13
1:11
2 Kin 24:14-16;
Jer 27:20;
39:9; Dan 1:3
1:12
1 Chr 3:17,19
*1:16
Luke 1:27
*1:17
vv. 11,12

been betrothed to Joseph, before they came together she was found to be with child by the Holy Spirit.

*1:19
Deut 24:1

19   And Joseph her husband, being a righteous man, and not wanting to disgrace her, desired [2]to put her away secretly.

20   But when he had considered this, behold, an angel of the Lord appeared to him in a dream, saying, "Joseph, son of David, do not be afraid to take Mary as your wife; for that which has been [3]conceived in her is of the Holy Spirit.

1:21
Luke 2:21;
2:11;
John 1:29;
Acts 4:12;
13:3,38

21   "And she will bear a Son; and you shall call His name Jesus, for it is He who will save His people from their sins."

22   Now all this took place that what was spoken by the Lord through the prophet might be fulfilled, saying,

*1:23
Is 7:14

23   "BEHOLD, THE VIRGIN SHALL BE WITH CHILD, AND SHALL BEAR A SON, AND THEY SHALL CALL HIS NAME IMMANUEL," which translated means, "GOD WITH US."

24   And Joseph arose from his sleep, and did as the angel of the Lord commanded him, and took *her* as his wife,

1:25
Ex 13:2;
Luke 2:21

25   and [4]kept her a virgin until she gave birth to a Son; and he called His name Jesus.

C. The visit of the wise men (2:1–12)

*2:1
Luke 2:4-7;
1:5
2:2
Jer 23:5;
Zech 9:9;
Mark 15:2;
John 1:49

2 Now after Jesus was born in Bethlehem of Judea in the days of Herod the king, behold, [5]magi from the east arrived in Jerusalem, saying,

2   "Where is He who has been born King of the Jews? For we saw His star in the east, and have come to worship Him."

3   And when Herod the king heard it, he was troubled, and all Jerusalem with him.

4   And gathering together all the chief priests and scribes of the people, he *began* to inquire of them where the Christ was to be born.

2:5
John 7:42

5   And they said to him, "In Bethlehem of Judea, for so it has been written by the prophet,

2:6
Mic 5:2;
John 21:16

6   'AND YOU, BETHLEHEM, LAND OF JUDAH,
ARE BY NO MEANS LEAST AMONG THE LEADERS OF JUDAH;
FOR OUT OF YOU SHALL COME FORTH A RULER,
WHO WILL SHEPHERD MY PEOPLE ISRAEL.' "

7   Then Herod secretly called the magi, and ascertained from them the time the star appeared.

8   And he sent them to Bethlehem, and said, "Go and make careful search for the Child; and when you have found *Him*, report to me, that I too may come and worship Him."

9   And having heard the king, they went their way; and lo, the star, which they had seen in the east, went on before them, until it came and stood over where the Child was.

*2:11
Matt 1:18;
12:46;
Ps 72:10;
Is 60:2

10   And when they saw the star, they rejoiced exceedingly with great joy.

11   And they came into the house and saw the Child with Mary His mother; and

[2]Or, *to divorce her* [3]Lit., *begotten* [4]Lit., *was not knowing her* [5]Pronounced may-ji, a caste of wise men specializing in astrology, medicine and natural science

---

1:19 Jewish betrothal could be dissolved only by a formal act in which the man gave the woman a certificate of divorce. Joseph planned to do this quietly, in order to avoid a public scandal.

1:23 This statement stresses the fact that the birth of Christ was a literal fulfillment of Isaiah's prophecy (Is. 7:14). The specific Greek word for *virgin* (*parthenos*) is quoted here from the standard Greek translation of the Old Testament. The fact that Christ had no human father, but was miraculously conceived in the womb of Mary by the divine act of the Holy Spirit, shows Him to be in a unique sense the Son of God.

2:1a Herod the Great, the son of an Idumean chieftain named Antipater, was a cunning and crafty schemer who ingratiated himself with Julius Caesar. The Romans appointed him procurator of Judea in 47 B.C., and in 37 B.C. elevated him to the rank of king, after which the last reigning descendant of the Maccabean dynasty, Antigonus, was executed. By fawning and flattery he managed to remain in the good graces of Rome through every change of imperial government. In his domestic life he was so ruthless and cruel that even Augustus could say, "I would rather be

Herod's dog than his son." Herod renovated the temple of the LORD in Jerusalem and was still on the throne when Christ was born in 5 or 4 B.C.. He died shortly after the massacre of the infants of Bethlehem.

2:1b The term for *magi* is the Greek form of the Old Persian *magav*. These *magoi* constituted a priestly caste that originated in Media. They specialized in dreams and omens and, according to Herodotus (Book i. 107, 120; Book vii. 19, 37, 113), claimed the gift of prophecy. The term *magos* came to be applied later to others, not of Median stock, like the Jew Bar-Jesus (Acts 13:6) and the Samaritan Simon (Acts 8:9), who used incantations and magical methods like theirs. But these *magoi* who visited Bethlehem were Eastern in origin and doubtlessly came from Persia or Media. Having somehow heard of the promise of a Messianic king in Judea, and having observed a new and brilliant star portending His birth, they were ready to be guided by it to His birthplace. Their adoration of the Christ-child was a token of the later submission of the Gentile world to the Jewish Messiah.

2:11 There is no way of determining how long after the birth of Christ the wise men arrived in Bethlehem. That

they fell down and worshiped Him; and opening their treasures they presented to
Him gifts of gold and frankincense and myrrh.

12   And having been warned *by God* in a dream not to return to Herod, they
departed for their own country by another way.

2:12
Matt 2:22;
Acts 10:22;
Heb 11:7

D. The flight into Egypt (2:13–18)

13   Now when they had departed, behold, an angel of the Lord *appeared to
Joseph in a dream, saying, "Arise and take the Child and His mother, and flee to
Egypt, and remain there until I tell you; for Herod is going to search for the Child
to destroy Him."

2:13
v. 19

14   And he arose and took the Child and His mother by night, and departed for
Egypt;

2:14
Hos 11:1;
Ex 4:22

15   and was there until the death of Herod, that what was spoken by the Lord
through the prophet might be fulfilled, saying, "OUT OF EGYPT DID I CALL MY
SON."

16   Then when Herod saw that he had been tricked by the magi, he became very
enraged, and sent and slew all the male children who were in Bethlehem and in all
its environs, from two years old and under, according to the time which he had
ascertained from the magi.

17   Then that which was spoken through Jeremiah the prophet was fulfilled,
saying,

18   "A VOICE WAS HEARD IN RAMAH,
            WEEPING AND GREAT MOURNING,
            RACHEL WEEPING FOR HER CHILDREN;
            AND SHE REFUSED TO BE COMFORTED,
            BECAUSE THEY WERE NO MORE."

2:18
Jer 31:15

E. From Egypt to Nazareth (2:19–23; cf. Mark 1:9; Luke 1:26)

19   But when Herod was dead, behold, an angel of the Lord *appeared in a
dream to Joseph in Egypt, saying,

2:19
Matt 1:20;
v. 13

20   "Arise and take the Child and His mother, and go into the land of Israel; for
those who sought the Child's life are dead."

21   And he arose and took the Child and His mother, and came into the land of
Israel.

22   But when he heard that Archelaus was reigning over Judea in place of his
father Herod, he was afraid to go there. And being warned *by God* in a dream, he
departed for the regions of Galilee,

*2:22
v. 12;
Matt 3:13;
Luke 2:39

23   and came and resided in a city called Nazareth, that what was spoken
through the prophets might be fulfilled, "He shall be called a Nazarene."

2:23
Luke 1:26;
Is 11:1;
Mark 1:24

II. John the Baptist; baptism and temptation of Christ (3:1–4:11)

A. The ministry of John the Baptist (3:1–12; Mark 1:1–8; Luke 3:2–17; John 1:6–8,19–28)

3 Now in those days John the Baptist *came, preaching in the wilderness of
Judea, saying,

2   "Repent, for the kingdom of heaven is at hand."

3:2
Dan 2:44;
Matt 4:7;
10:7

---

they did not see the babe on the night of His birth is clear
from the fact that the family was in a house (2:11), and that
King Herod ordered all male children up to two years of age
to be slain (2:16), in accordance with the information given
him by the wise men concerning the time of the star's
appearance (2:7), presumably the night Christ was born.
2:16 Evidently the wise men had indicated to Herod the
exact time when they had seen the natal star in the East, and
thus afforded him an idea as to how old the infant king
might be when they finally arrived in Palestine and visited
Bethlehem. Yet the fact that Herod ordered the execution of
all male babies two years of age and under does not necessarily mean that Jesus was as old as two. He may have been
not more than twelve months, and Herod may simply have
ordered all within that age-span to be killed to make certain
that the Messiah Himself should be slain. It is estimated

that the number of children slain would not have exceeded
forty or fifty.

2:22 Archelaus is mentioned only here in the Bible. He was
the older of two sons of Herod the Great by Malthace, a
Samaritan woman. The Roman emperor, Caesar Augustus,
made him ethnarch (not king) of Judea, Samaria, and Idumea. Archelaus was the worst of all of Herod's sons. During
his rule of nine years the people under him suffered greatly,
and they at last appealed to Augustus to depose him. Augustus banished him to Vienna in A.D. 6. Joseph feared Archelaus and for this reason left for Galilee, which was under
the control of Antipas. After the deportation of Archelaus,
Judea was placed under the rule of Roman procurators until
A.D. 41.

3:1 See note to Luke 1:57 on John the Baptist.

3:3
Is 40:3;
Mark 1:3;
Luke 3:4;
John 1:23;
Luke 1:76

3 For this is the one referred to by Isaiah the prophet, saying,

"THE VOICE OF ONE CRYING IN THE WILDERNESS,
'MAKE READY THE WAY OF THE LORD,
MAKE HIS PATHS STRAIGHT!'"

3:4
2 Kin 1:8;
Zech 13:4;
Lev 11:22

4 Now John himself had a garment of camel's hair, and a leather belt about his waist; and his food was locusts and wild honey.

5 Then Jerusalem was going out to him, and all Judea, and all the district around the Jordan;

3:6
Acts 19:4,18

6 and they were being baptized by him in the Jordan River, as they confessed their sins.

*3:7
Matt 12:34;
23:33;
Rom 5:9;
1 Thess 1:10

7 But when he saw many of the Pharisees and Sadducees coming for baptism, he said to them, "You brood of vipers, who warned you to flee from the wrath to come?

3:8
Acts 26:20

8 "Therefore bring forth fruit in keeping with repentance;

3:9
John 8:33,39;
Acts 13:26;
Rom 4:1,11,
16

9 and do not suppose that you can say to yourselves, 'We have Abraham for our father'; for I say to you, that God is able from these stones to raise up children to Abraham.

3:10
Matt 7:19

10 "And the axe is already laid at the root of the trees; every tree therefore that does not bear good fruit is cut down and thrown into the fire.

3:11
Acts 1:5;
11:16; 19:4;
Is 4:4;
Acts 2:3,4

11 "As for me, I baptize you [6]with water for repentance, but He who is coming after me is mightier than I, and I am not fit to remove His sandals; He will baptize you with the Holy Spirit and fire.

3:12
Mal 3:3;
Matt 13:30

12 "And His winnowing fork is in His hand, and He will thoroughly clear His threshing floor; and He will gather His wheat into the barn, but He will burn up the chaff with unquenchable fire."

B. The baptism of Jesus (3:13–17; Mark 1:9–11; Luke 3:21,22)

3:13
John 1:31-34

13 Then Jesus *arrived from Galilee at the Jordan coming to John, to be baptized by him.

14 But John tried to prevent Him, saying, "I have need to be baptized by You, and do You come to me?"

15 But Jesus answering said to him, "Permit it at this time; for in this way it is fitting for us to fulfill all righteousness." Then he *permitted Him.

3:16
Is 11:2; 42:1;
John 1:32

16 And after being baptized, Jesus went up immediately from the water; and behold, the heavens were opened, and he saw the Spirit of God descending as a dove, and coming upon Him,

*3:17
Ps 2:7;
Matt 12:18;
17:5;
Mark 9:7;
Luke 9:35

17 and behold, a voice out of the heavens, saying, "This is [7]My beloved Son, in whom I am well-pleased."

[6]The Gr. here can be translated in, with or by   [7]Lit., My Son, the Beloved

---

3:7a The Pharisees were probably the most influential of the Jewish sects among the people. Their main tenet was separation from everything non-Jewish. They held generally to the following practices and ideas: (1) careful observance of the Law, to which they added many detailed requirements and special interpretations; (2) belief in the immortality of the soul, resurrection of the body, and retribution in the future life; (3) belief in the existence of angels and spirits; (4) belief that God would deliver Israel and restore her to a position of power and prestige; and (5) belief in a doctrine of divine providence along with the freedom of the will. But their most characteristic teaching was that the faithful Jew earned merit with God by scrupulously observing the niceties of the Law. They perverted the Law into a system of merit-earning that virtually excluded the principle of justification by grace through faith. The Pharisees were openly hostile to Christ because He consistently practiced what they rejected and condemned (e.g., Matt. 98:3, 11,14; Luke 5:21). Christ therefore exposed them as legalists and severely condemned their hypocrisy (e.g., 6:2,5,16; 12:34; 23:33; Mark 7:6, etc.).
3:7b The Sadducees were one of several Jewish sects. Their name is usually thought to be derived from Zadok,

who was a high priest in the reign of David. Their membership came largely from the priestly nobility, whereas the Pharisees enjoyed a wider following among all Jewish social classes. The Sadducees often clashed with the Pharisees both in theological and political matters. They were particularly opposed to the oral law meticulously observed by the Pharisees (known as "the tradition of the elders"), accepting only the written Law of Moses as binding. In their interpretation of Scripture they disagreed with the Pharisees in denying the following doctrines: (1) the bodily resurrection of the dead; (2) the future punishments and rewards of the dead on the day of judgment; (3) the existence of angels and spirits; and (4) an overruling divine providence or "fate," as opposed to an unconditional free will. While they are not mentioned in the New Testament as often as the Pharisees, this group opposed Christ just as vigorously as they did. Christ refuted and denounced Sadducees on several occasions (16:1–4,6–12; 22:23–33), although Scripture records His condemnation of them less frequently than His condemnation of the Pharisees (16:6,11).
3:17 This is My beloved Son. Jesus here begins His public ministry.

C. The temptation in the wilderness
(4:1–11; Mark 1:12,13; Luke 4:1–13)

4 Then Jesus was led up by the Spirit into the wilderness to be tempted by the devil.

2 And after He had fasted forty days and forty nights, He [8]then became hungry.

3 And the tempter came and said to Him, "If You are the Son of God, command that these stones become bread."

4 But He answered and said, "It is written, 'MAN SHALL NOT LIVE ON BREAD ALONE, BUT ON EVERY WORD THAT PROCEEDS OUT OF THE MOUTH OF GOD.'"

5 Then the devil *took Him into the holy city; and he had Him stand on the pinnacle of the temple,

6 and *said to Him, "If You are the Son of God throw Yourself down; for it is written,

'HE WILL GIVE HIS ANGELS CHARGE CONCERNING YOU';

and

'ON *their* HANDS THEY WILL BEAR YOU UP,
LEST YOU STRIKE YOUR FOOT AGAINST A STONE.'"

7 Jesus said to him, "On the other hand, it is written, 'YOU SHALL NOT [9]PUT THE LORD YOUR GOD TO THE TEST.'"

8 Again, the devil *took Him to a very high mountain, and *showed Him all the kingdoms of the world, and their glory;

9 and he said to Him, "All these things will I give You, if You fall down and worship me."

10 Then Jesus *said to him, "Begone, Satan! For it is written, 'YOU SHALL WORSHIP THE LORD YOUR GOD, AND SERVE HIM ONLY.'"

11 Then the devil *left Him; and behold, angels came and *began* to minister to Him.

III. Public ministry in Galilee (4:12–18:35)

A. The beginning of Jesus' Galilean ministry
(4:12–17; Mark 1:14,15; Luke 4:14,15; John 4:43–45)

12 Now when He heard that John had been taken into custody, He withdrew into Galilee;

13 and leaving Nazareth, He came and settled in Capernaum, which is by the sea, in the region of Zebulun and Naphtali.

14 *This was* to fulfill what was spoken through Isaiah the prophet, saying,

15 "THE LAND OF ZEBULUN AND THE LAND OF NAPHTALI,
BY THE WAY OF THE SEA, BEYOND THE JORDAN, GALILEE OF THE
[10]GENTILES—

16 "THE PEOPLE WHO WERE SITTING IN DARKNESS SAW A GREAT LIGHT,
AND TO THOSE WHO WERE SITTING IN THE LAND AND SHADOW OF
DEATH,
UPON THEM A LIGHT DAWNED."

17 From that time Jesus began to preach and say, "Repent, for the kingdom of heaven is at hand."

B. The call of James and John
(4:18–25; cf. Mark 1:16–20; Luke 5:1–11)

18 And walking by the Sea of Galilee, He saw two brothers, Simon who was called Peter, and Andrew his brother, casting a net into the sea; for they were fishermen.

4:2
Ex 34:28;
1 Kin 19:8
4:3
1 Thess 3:5
4:4
Deut 8:3
4:5
Neh 11:1;
Dan 9:24;
Matt 27:53;
Rev 21:10
4:6
Ps 91:11,12

This was a 2 temptation to doubt God

4:7
Deut 6:16

4:10
1 Chr 21:1;
Deut 6:13
4:11
Matt 26:53;
Luke 22:43;
Heb 1:14

4:15
Is 9:1,2

4:16
Is 42:7;
Luke 2:32

***4:17**
Matt 3:2;
10:7

4:18
John 1:35-42

---

[8]Lit., *later, afterward* [9]Or, *tempt . . . God* [10]Or, *nations*

4:1 See note to Luke 4:2 on the temptation of Jesus. (This was at the start of His ministry.)
4:13 From now on Capernaum was Jesus' home in Galilee (cf. Mark 2:1; 3:20). Capernaum, the hometown of Simon and Andrew (Mark 1:29), was an important town at the north end of the Sea of Galilee, on the border of the province of Galilee. The international highway ran through there, hence the tax office (9:9; Mark 2:13,14).
4:17 The phrase *kingdom of heaven* is synonymous with the

phrase *kingdom of God*, used in Mark and Luke (although Matthew sometimes uses *the kingdom of God*, cf. 12:28; 19:24; 21:31,43). Thus, in this particular instance, Matthew quotes Jesus as using the Hebrew or Aramaic phrase, *kingdom of God* (where "heaven" is a respectful equivalent to the name of God), whereas Mark 1:15 quotes the identical saying in the form more familiar to Gentile readers, *kingdom of God*. As in many other instances, the writers express the same truth in a variety of words and phrases.

19 And He *said to them, "Follow Me, and I will make you fishers of men."

20 And they immediately left the nets, and followed Him.

21 And going on from there He saw two other brothers, James the *son of Zebedee, and John his brother, in the boat with Zebedee their father, mending their nets; and He called them.

22 And they immediately left the boat and their father, and followed Him.

23 And *Jesus* was going about in all Galilee, teaching in their synagogues, and proclaiming the gospel of the kingdom, and healing every kind of disease and every kind of sickness among the people.

24 And the news about Him went out into all Syria; and they brought to Him all who were ill, taken with various diseases and pains, demoniacs, epileptics, paralytics; and He healed them.

25 And great multitudes followed Him from Galilee and Decapolis and Jerusalem and Judea and *from* beyond the Jordan.

C. The Sermon on the Mount (5:1–7:29; Luke 6:20–49)

1. The Beatitudes (5:1–12; Luke 6:20–23)

5 And when He saw the multitudes, He went up on the mountain; and after He sat down, His disciples came to Him.

2 And opening His mouth He *began* to teach them, saying,

3 "Blessed are the poor in spirit, for theirs is the kingdom of heaven.

4 "Blessed are those who mourn, for they shall be comforted.

5 "Blessed are the [11]gentle, for they shall inherit the earth.

6 "Blessed are those who hunger and thirst for righteousness, for they shall be satisfied.

7 "Blessed are the merciful, for they shall receive mercy.

8 "Blessed are the pure in heart, for they shall see God.

9 "Blessed are the peacemakers, for they shall be called sons of God.

10 "Blessed are those who have been persecuted for the sake of righteousness, for theirs is the kingdom of heaven.

11 "Blessed are you when *men* cast insults at you, and persecute you, and say all kinds of evil against you falsely, on account of Me.

12 "Rejoice, and be glad, for your reward in heaven is great, for so they persecuted the prophets who were before you.

2. What the believer is like (5:13–16)

13 "You are the salt of the earth; but if the salt has become tasteless, how will it be made salty *again*? It is good for nothing anymore, except to be thrown out and trampled under foot by men.

14 "You are the light of the world. A city set on a hill cannot be hidden.

15 "Nor do *men* light a lamp, and put it under the peck-measure, but on the lampstand; and it gives light to all who are in the house.

16 "Let your light shine before men in such a way that they may see your good works, and glorify your Father who is in heaven.

3. The righteousness required (5:17–20)

17 "Do not think that I came to abolish the Law or the Prophets; I did not come to abolish, but to fulfill.

11Or, *humble, meek*

4:24 Demon possession is presented in Scripture as a dreadful reality. The supposition that the demoniacs of the Gospels were only mentally ill is fallacious, for Mark 1:32 and Luke 6:17,18 distinguish clearly between demon possession and bodily disease. Christ spoke to the demons themselves as well as to the victims possessed by them, and commanded them to depart (8:32; 17:18; Mark 1:23,34; 9:25). In Luke 8:32 the demons are stated to have left those whom they had possessed and to have entered into a herd of swine. In 8:31 and Mark 9:26 the personalities and characteristics of the demons are clearly distinguished from those possessed by them. In Jewish and Biblical thought demons are believed to be part of the whole spiritual hierarchy of evil headed by Satan.
5:1 The impression is usually given that the Sermon on the

Mount (5–7) was spoken on a single occasion during the early ministry of our Lord. Many hold that these three chapters contain teachings of Jesus that were given on numerous occasions. Undoubtedly, much that Jesus said has not been recorded, and many of His utterances were probably repeated in different places and on various occasions.
5:17 Christ was neither lawless nor a lawbreaker. In all things He obeyed God's laws (John 8:46; 1 Pet. 2:21–23), and in His teaching freed the law from its human accretions and false interpretations. His followers today are not under the yoke of the Mosaic Law with its ceremonial regulations (Acts 15:10; Gal. 5:1). They have been adopted as sons in the household of God; this does not mean, however, that they are free to break whatever God has made binding. The ceremonial law has been rendered obsolete by the cross, and

18 "For truly I say to you, until heaven and earth pass away, not the smallest letter or stroke shall pass away from the Law, until all is accomplished.

19 "Whoever then annuls one of the least of these commandments, and so teaches others, shall be called least in the kingdom of heaven; but whoever keeps and teaches *them*, he shall be called great in the kingdom of heaven.

20 "For I say to you, that unless your righteousness surpasses *that* of the scribes and Pharisees, you shall not enter the kingdom of heaven.

4. *The sixth commandment (5:21–26)*

21 "You have heard that the ancients were told, 'YOU SHALL NOT COMMIT MURDER' and 'Whoever commits murder shall be [12]liable to the court.'

22 "But I say to you that everyone who is angry with his brother [13]shall be guilty before the court; and whoever shall say to his brother, '[14]Raca,' shall be guilty before [15]the supreme court; and whoever shall say, 'You fool,' shall be guilty *enough to go* into the [16]fiery hell.

23 "If therefore you are presenting your offering at the altar, and there remember that your brother has something against you,

24 leave your offering there before the altar, and go your way; first be reconciled to your brother, and then come and present your offering.

25 "Make friends quickly with your opponent at law while you are with him on the way, in order that your opponent may not deliver you to the judge, and the judge to the officer, and you be thrown into prison.

26 "Truly I say to you, you shall not come out of there, until you have paid up the last [17]cent.

5. *The seventh commandment*
(5:27–32; cf. 19:9; Mark 10:11; Luke 16:18)

27 "You have heard that it was said, 'YOU SHALL NOT COMMIT ADULTERY';

28 but I say to you, that everyone who looks on a woman to lust for her has committed adultery with her already in his heart.

29 "And if your right eye makes you stumble, tear it out, and throw it from you; for it is better for you that one of the parts of your body perish, than for your whole body to be thrown into hell.

30 "And if your right hand makes you stumble, cut it off, and throw it from you; for it is better for you that one of the parts of your body perish, than for your whole body to go into hell.

31 "And it was said, 'WHOEVER SENDS HIS WIFE AWAY, LET HIM GIVE HER A CERTIFICATE OF DIVORCE';

32 but I say to you that everyone who divorces his wife, except for *the* cause of unchastity, makes her commit adultery; and whoever marries a divorced woman commits adultery.

6. *The law of oaths (5:33–37)*

33 "Again, you have heard that the ancients were told, 'YOU SHALL NOT MAKE FALSE VOWS, BUT SHALL FULFILL YOUR VOWS TO THE LORD.'

34 "But I say to you, make no oath at all, either by heaven, for it is the throne of God,

---

Marginal references:

5:18 Luke 16:17

5:19 James 2:10

*5:21f Ex 20:13; Deut 5:17
5:22 1 John 3:15; James 2:20

5:23 Matt 8:4; 23:19

5:25 Prov 25:8; Luke 12:57-59

*5:27 Ex 20:14; Deut 5:18
5:28 Job 31:1; Prov 6:25
*5:29 Matt 18:9; Mark 9:43-47

*5:31 Deut 24:1-4; Mark 10:11, 12; Luke 16:18

5:33 Lev 19:12; Num 30:2; Deut 23:21; Matt 23:16
5:34 James 5:12; Is 66:1

---

[12]Or, *guilty before*　[13]Some mss. insert here: *without cause*　[14]Aramaic for *empty-head* or, *good for nothing*　[15]Lit., *the Sanhedrin*　[16]Lit., *Gehenna of fire*　[17]Lit., *quadrans* (equaling two lepta or mites), i.e., 1/64 of a denarius

---

yet the basic moral law continues in force even for Christians. The children of God must obey its demands, not as a condition of salvation, but as the fruit of a transformed life.
5:21,22 Christ did not abolish the Old Testament law concerning murder. Rather, He taught that the righteousness of God's children must exceed that of the scribes and Pharisees (v. 20). These Jewish teachers defined sin as consisting principally in the overt act; Jesus showed that it consists principally in the intention of the heart. Thus murder begins when hatred or hostility rises up in the human heart; such hostility renders a man guilty before God even though the hater or despiser is restrained from murder only by the fear of retribution. The evil desire within the soul is the root of the sin to which it logically leads, and God condemns it as such.
5:27 As with murder, so with adultery. Christ defines the

sin as consisting in the evil thought. In Jesus' day the teaching was prevalent that adultery consisted only in the overt act. Thus a man had not broken the law unless and until the act itself was performed. His heart could be filled with adulterous thoughts, but this was not regarded as sinful. Jesus provided the correct interpretation and understanding of what had always been the heart of the moral law relative to adultery even in the Old Testament.
5:29 This utterance of Jesus is not to be taken literally, for He did not mean for men to pluck out their eyes or cut off their hands. Sin is so dangerous, however, that "it is better to lose the eye and the hand that thus offend than to give way to the sin, and perish eternally in it," (Matthew Henry, *Commentary on the Whole Bible*, Fleming H. Revell Co., vol. 5, p. 61).
5:31 See note to 19:3 on divorce.

35 or by the earth, for it is the footstool of His feet, or by Jerusalem, for it is THE CITY OF THE GREAT KING.

36 "Nor shall you make an oath by your head, for you cannot make one hair white or black.

37 "But let your statement be, 'Yes, yes' or 'No, no'; and anything beyond these is of evil.

7. The law of retaliation (5:38–42)

38 "You have heard that it was said, 'AN EYE FOR AN EYE, AND A TOOTH FOR A TOOTH.'

39 "But I say to you, do not resist him who is evil; but whoever slaps you on your right cheek, turn to him the other also.

40 "And if anyone wants to sue you, and take your [18]shirt, let him have your [19]coat also.

41 "And whoever shall force you to go one mile, go with him two.

42 "Give to him who asks of you, and do not turn away from him who wants to borrow from you.

8. The law of love (5:43–48)

43 "You have heard that it was said, 'YOU SHALL LOVE YOUR NEIGHBOR, and hate your enemy.'

44 "But I say to you, love your enemies, and pray for those who persecute you

45 in order that you may be sons of your Father who is in heaven; for He causes His sun to rise on the evil and the good, and sends rain on the righteous and the unrighteous.

46 "For if you love those who love you, what reward have you? Do not even the tax-gatherers do the same?

47 "And if you greet your brothers only, what do you do more than others? Do not even the Gentiles do the same?

48 "Therefore you are to be perfect, as your heavenly Father is perfect.

D. The Sermon on the Mount continued: religious observances (6:1–34)

1. Giving of alms (6:1–4)

6 "Beware of practicing your righteousness before men to be noticed by them; otherwise you have no reward with your Father who is in heaven.

2 "When therefore you give alms, do not sound a trumpet before you, as the hypocrites do in the synagogues and in the streets, that they may be honored by men. Truly I say to you, they have their reward in full.

3 "But when you give alms, do not let your left hand know what your right hand is doing

4 that your alms may be in secret; and your Father who sees in secret will repay you.

2. Praying (6:5–15; cf. Luke 11:1–4)

5 "And when you pray, you are not to be as the hypocrites; for they love to stand and pray in the synagogues and on the street corners, in order to be seen by men. Truly I say to you, they have their reward in full.

6 "But you, when you pray, go into your inner room, and when you have shut your door, pray to your Father who is in secret, and your Father who sees in secret will repay you.

7 "And when you are praying, do not use meaningless repetition, as the Gentiles do, for they suppose that they will be heard for their many words.

Cross-references (left margin):

5:38 Ex 21:24; Lev 24:20; Deut 19:21
5:39 Prov 24:29; Luke 6:29; Rom 12:17, 19; 1 Cor 6:7; 1 Pet 3:9
5:42 Deut 15:8; Luke 6:30
5:43 Lev 19:18; Deut 23:6; Ps 41:10
5:44 Rom 12:14; Acts 7:60; 1 Cor 4:12; 1 Pet 2:23
5:45 Job 25:3
*5:48 Lev 19:2; Col 1:28; James 1:4
6:1 Matt 23:5
6:2 Rom 12:8
6:4 Col 3:23,24
6:5 Mark 11:25; Luke 18:10-14
6:6 2 Kin 4:33
6:7 Eccl 5:2; 1 Kin 18:26, 29

---

[18]Or, tunic; i.e., garment worn next to the body   [19]Or, cloak; i.e., outer garment

---

5:48 The word *perfect* (Greek *teleios*) is derived from *telos*, meaning "end," "goal," "limit." It therefore signifies "attaining to the end, complete, mature." But here the comparison is made between God and His children, and so the word must mean more than "mature." From the context we can deduce that the God-like quality that must characterize a true believer is the quality of self-disinterested love and kindness for others, even for those who deserve no kindness. This kind of "perfectness" consists in the basic intention or attitude of the believer, rather than in absolute sinlessness. This is perfectly possible for believers who, by faith, draw from Him the grace to maintain that attitude of kindly benevolence and sincere desire for the good of others.

8   "Therefore do not be like them; for your Father knows what you need, before you ask Him.

9   "Pray, then, in this way:
    'Our Father who art in heaven,
    Hallowed be Thy name.

10   Thy kingdom come.
    Thy will be done,
    On earth as it is in heaven.

11   'Give us this day our daily bread.

12   'And forgive us our debts, as we also have forgiven our debtors.

13   'And do not lead us into temptation, but deliver us from evil. [For
    Thine is the kingdom, and the power, and the glory, forever.
    Amen.]'

14   "For if you forgive men for their transgressions, your heavenly Father will also forgive you.

15   "But if you do not forgive men, then your Father will not forgive your transgressions.

3. Fasting (6:16–18)

16   "And whenever you fast, do not put on a gloomy face as the hypocrites *do*, for they neglect their appearance in order to be seen fasting by men. Truly I say to you, they have their reward in full.

17   "But you, when you fast, anoint your head, and wash your face

18   so that you may not be seen fasting by men, but by your Father who is in secret; and your Father who sees in secret will repay you.

4. The Christian and the world (6:19–34)

a. True riches (6:19–21)

19   "Do not lay up for yourselves treasures upon earth, where moth and rust destroy, and where thieves break in and steal.

20   "But lay up for yourselves treasures in heaven, where neither moth nor rust destroys, and where thieves do not break in or steal;

21   for where your treasure is, there will your heart be also.

b. Light or darkness (6:22,23)

see Mt 20:15 "Is Your eye envious..."
eye = your will

22   "The lamp of the body is the eye; if therefore your eye is clear, your whole body will be full of light.

23   "But if your eye is bad, your whole body will be full of darkness. If therefore the light that is in you is darkness, how great is the darkness!

c. God or mammon (6:24)

Lk 16:11   If you have not been faithful in who will entrust true riches to you?

24   "No one can serve two masters; for either he will hate the one and love the other, or he will hold to one and despise the other. You cannot serve God and [20]mammon.

d. Trust or anxiety (6:25–34; cf. Luke 12:22–31)

25   "For this reason I say to you, do not be anxious for your life, *as to* what you shall eat, or what you shall drink; nor for your body, *as to* what you shall put on. Is not life more than food, and the body than clothing?

26   "Look at the birds of the air, that they do not sow, neither do they reap, nor gather into barns, and *yet* your heavenly Father feeds them. Are you not worth much more than they?

27   "And which of you by being anxious can add a *single* cubit to his life's span?

[20]Or, *riches*

6:10
Matt 26:39,42

6:11
Prov 30:8
6:12
Matt 18:21
6:13
John 17:15;
2 Thess 3:3;
James 1:13
6:14
Mark 11:25,
26; Eph 4:32;
Col 3:13
6:15
Matt 18:35

6:16
Is 58:5

6:18
vv. 4,6

6:19
Prov 23:4;
1 Tim 6:17
Heb 13:5;
James 5:1
6:20
Luke 12:33,
34; 18:22;
1 Tim 6:19;
1 Pet 1:4

6:22
Matt 20:15;
Mark 7:22;
Luke 11:34-36

*6:24
Luke 16:13

6:25
Ps 55:22;
Phil 4:6;
1 Pet 5:7
6:26
Job 38:41;
Ps 147:9;
Luke 12:24
6:27
Ps 39:5

6:9 This is the model for all true prayer. It begins with adoration and the interests of God's kingdom; then follows the plea for forgiveness and the petition for individual needs. Ever since Christ taught it, this has been the most widely used prayer of the Bible, and it is repeated by millions of Christians every day of the year. Some have imagined that there is an Old Testament legalism in asking for forgiveness as we forgive others (6:12,14,15). This is a grave misunderstanding. Our forgiveness is not granted to us on condition that we furnish God with merit of any kind, not even the merit of forgiving others. It is only that our refusal to forgive others unavoidably involves our denial of the whole principle of forgiveness as such, and therefore our rejection of God's forgiveness toward us. He who does not forgive his fellowman has not repented of his own sin, and hence cannot find forgiveness for himself.

6:24 See note to Luke 16:9 on mammon.

28 "And why are you anxious about clothing? Observe how the lilies of the field grow; they do not toil nor do they spin,

6:29
1 Kin 10:4-7

29 yet I say to you that even Solomon in all his glory did not clothe himself like one of these.

6:30
Matt 8:26;
14:31; 16:8

30 "But if God so arrays the grass of the field, which is *alive* today and tomorrow is thrown into the furnace, *will He* not much more *do so for* you, O men of little faith?

31 "Do not be anxious then, saying, 'What shall we eat?' or 'What shall we drink?' or 'With what shall we clothe ourselves?'

6:32
v. 8

32 "For all these things the Gentiles eagerly seek; for your heavenly Father knows that you need all these things.

6:33
Matt 19:28;
Mark 10:29,
30;
Luke 18:29,
30

33 "But seek first His kingdom and His righteousness; and all these things shall be added to you.

34 "Therefore do not be anxious for tomorrow; for tomorrow will care for itself. *Each* day has enough trouble of its own.

E. *Sermon on the Mount concluded (7:1–29)*

1. *Censure and reproof (7:1–6; Luke 6:37–42)*

*7:1
Mark 4:24;
Rom 2:1;
14:10;
1 Cor 4:3

7 "Do not judge lest you be judged.
2 "For in the way you judge, you will be judged; and by your standard of measure, it will be measured to you.

3 "And why do you look at the speck that is in your brother's eye, but do not notice the log that is in your own eye?

4 "Or how can you say to your brother, 'Let me take the speck out of your eye,' and behold, the log is in your own eye?

5 "You hypocrite, first take the log out of your own eye, and then you will see clearly to take the speck out of your brother's eye.

7:6
Prov 9:7,8;
Acts 13:45

6 "Do not give what is holy to dogs, and do not throw your pearls before swine, lest they trample them under their feet, and turn and tear you to pieces.

2. *Prayer and the Golden Rule (7:7–12; cf. Luke 11:9–13)*

*7:7
Mark 11:24;
John 15:7;
16:23,24;
James 4:3;
1 John 3:22;
5:14,15
7:8
Jer 29:12,13

7 "Ask, and it shall be given to you; seek, and you shall find; knock, and it shall be opened to you.

8 "For everyone who asks receives, and he who seeks finds, and to him who knocks it shall be opened.

9 "Or what man is there among you, when his son shall ask him for a loaf, will give him a stone?

10 "Or if he shall ask for a fish, he will not give him a snake, will he?

11 "If you then, being evil, know how to give good gifts to your children, how much more shall your Father who is in heaven give what is good to those who ask Him!

7:12
Luke 6:31;
Rom 13:8-10;
Gal 5:14

12 "Therefore, however you want people to treat you, so treat them, for this is the Law and the Prophets.

3. *The narrow and the wide gates (7:13,14)*

7:13
Luke 13:24

13 "Enter by the narrow gate; for the gate is wide, and the way is broad that leads to destruction, and many are those who enter by it.

14 "For the gate is small, and the way is narrow that leads to life, and few are those who find it.

4. *The test of false prophets (7:15–20)*

7:15
Jer 23:16;
Matt 24:11,
24;
Mark 13:22;
2 Pet 2:1;
1 John 4:1;
Rev 16:13;
19:20; 20:10;
Acts 20:29
7:16
Matt 12:33;
Mark 3:10;
James 3:12

15 "Beware of the false prophets, who come to you in sheep's clothing, but inwardly are ravenous wolves.

16 "You will know them by their fruits. Grapes are not gathered from thorn *bushes*, nor figs from thistles, are they?

17 "Even so, every good tree bears good fruit; but the bad tree bears bad fruit.

18 "A good tree cannot produce bad fruit, nor can a bad tree produce good fruit.

7:1 This verse cannot be construed as teaching that believers are never to exercise judgment relative to the doctrine or the actions of others. It does teach that those who do judge, will themselves be judged by the same standards they use in their judgments of others. Therefore one should be careful to employ standards of judgment by which he himself would be happy to be judged in his own conduct and convictions.
7:7 See note to Luke 11:1 on principles of prayer.

19 "Every tree that does not bear good fruit is cut down and thrown into the fire.
20 "So then, you will know them by their fruits.

5. *Profession versus possession (7:21–29)*

21 "Not everyone who says to Me, 'Lord, Lord,' will enter the kingdom of heaven; but he who does the will of My Father who is in heaven.

22 "Many will say to Me on that day, 'Lord, Lord, did we not prophesy in Your name, and in Your name cast out demons, and in Your name perform many miracles?'

23 "And then I will declare to them, 'I never knew you; DEPART FROM ME, YOU WHO PRACTICE LAWLESSNESS.'

24 "Therefore everyone who hears these words of Mine, and acts upon them, may be compared to a wise man, who built his house upon the rock.

25 "And the rain descended, and the floods came, and the winds blew, and burst against that house; and *yet* it did not fall, for it had been founded upon the rock.

26 "And everyone who hears these words of Mine, and does not act upon them, will be like a foolish man, who built his house upon the sand.

27 "And the rain descended, and the floods came, and the winds blew, and burst against that house; and it fell, and great was its fall."

28 The result was that when Jesus had finished these words, the multitudes were amazed at His teaching;

29 for He was teaching them as *one* having authority, and not as their scribes.

F. *Miracles of Jesus (1) (8:1–17)*

1. *The leper cleansed (8:1–4; Mark 1:40–45; Luke 5:12–16)*

8 And when He had come down from the mountain, great multitudes followed Him.

2 And behold, a leper came to Him, and bowed down to Him, saying, "Lord, if You are willing, You can make me clean."

3 And He stretched out His hand and touched him, saying, "I am willing; be cleansed." And immediately his leprosy was cleansed.

4 And Jesus *said to him, "See that you tell no one; but go, show yourself to the priest, and present the offering that Moses commanded, for a testimony to them."

2. *The centurion's servant healed (8:5–13; Luke 7:1–10)*

5 And when He had entered Capernaum, a centurion came to Him, entreating Him,

6 and saying, "Lord, my servant is lying paralyzed at home, suffering great pain."

7 And He *said to him, "I will come and heal him."

8 But the centurion answered and said, "Lord, I am not worthy for You to come under my roof, but just say the word, and my servant will be healed.

9 "For I, too, am a man under authority, with soldiers under me; and I say to this one, 'Go!' and he goes, and to another, 'Come!' and he comes, and to my slave, 'Do this!' and he does *it.*"

10 Now when Jesus heard *this,* He marveled, and said to those who were following, "Truly I say to you, I have not found such great faith with anyone in Israel.

11 "And I say to you, that many shall come from east and west, and [21]recline *at the table* with Abraham, and Isaac, and Jacob, in the kingdom of heaven;

[21]Or, *dine*

Cross-references (right margin):

7:19 Matt 3:10; Luke 3:9; John 15:2,6

*7:21 Hos 8:2 Matt 25:11, 12; Acts 19:13; Rom 2:13; James 1:22
7:22 Matt 25:12; Luke 13:25-27
7:23 Ps 6:8; Matt 25:12; Luke 13:25, 27
7:24 Luke 6:47-49; James 1:22-25

7:28 Matt 11:1; 13:53; 19:1; 26:1; 13:54; Mark 1:22; 6:2; Luke 4:32; John 7:46

8:2 Matt 9:18; 15:25; 18:26; 20:20; John 9:38

8:4 Lev 14:3,4, 10; Mark 3:12; 5:43; 7:36; 8:30; 9:9

8:8 Ps 107:20

8:11 Is 49:12; 59:19; Mal 1:11; Luke 13:29; Acts 10:45

7:21 The title *Lord* (Greek *kyrios*) is used of Jesus Christ almost seven hundred times. In combination with Jesus and Christ, the title has a threefold significance: Jesus is savior; Christ is the anointed of God; and, as Lord, He is master of life. The title *kyrios* was also used as an equivalent of Yahweh in the old Greek translation of the Old Testament, and it is so used in the New Testament as well, both in quotations from the Old Testament and in other contexts where God in heaven is referred to as *an angel of the Lord* (2:19), or *the kingdom of our Lord* (Rev. 11:15). Therefore an identifi-cation of Jesus Christ with Yahweh Himself is involved in this title of *kyrios*, or "Lord."

8:1 Matthew presents Christ as the Savior who manifested His power over nature (8:23–27), death (9:18–26), demons (8:28–34), and disease (8:1–17; 9:27–34). His miracles were only one aspect of His ministry and did not represent the principal goal of His mission. They were evidences that would enable men to know that this was the Son of God and that His authority to forgive and cleanse was of divine origin (cf. 9:1–8).

8:12
Matt 13:42,
50; 22:13;
25:30;
Luke 13:28
12   but the sons of the kingdom shall be cast out into the outer darkness; in that place there shall be weeping and gnashing of teeth."
13   And Jesus said to the centurion, "Go your way; let it be done to you as you have believed." And the servant was healed that *very* hour.

3. Peter's mother-in-law healed (8:14–17; Mark 1:29–34; Luke 4:28–41)

8:14
1 Cor 9:5
14   And when Jesus had come to Peter's home, He saw his mother-in-law lying sick in bed with a fever.
15   And He touched her hand, and the fever left her; and she arose, and waited on Him.
16   And when evening had come, they brought to Him many who were demon-possessed; and He cast out the spirits with a word, and healed all who were ill
8:17
Is 53:4
17   in order that what was spoken through Isaiah the prophet might be fulfilled, saying, "HE HIMSELF TOOK OUR INFIRMITIES, AND CARRIED AWAY OUR DISEASES."

G. Impulsive and reluctant followers (8:18–22; Luke 9:57–62)

8:18
Mark 4:35;
Luke 8:22
18   Now when Jesus saw a crowd around Him, He gave orders to depart to the other side.
19   And a certain scribe came and said to Him, "Teacher, I will follow You wherever You go."
20   And Jesus *said to him, "The foxes have holes, and the birds of the air *have* nests; but the Son of Man has nowhere to lay His head."
21   And another of the disciples said to Him, "Lord, permit me first to go and bury my father."
*8:22
Matt 9:9;
John 1:43;
21:19
22   But Jesus *said to him, "Follow Me; and allow the dead to bury their own dead."

H. Miracles of Jesus (2) (8:23–9:8)

1. The storm stilled (8:23–27; Mark 4:36–41; Luke 8:22–25)

23   And when He got into the boat, His disciples followed Him.
24   And behold, there arose a great storm in the sea, so that the boat was covered with the waves; but He Himself was asleep.
25   And they came to *Him,* and awoke Him, saying, "Save *us,* Lord; we are perishing!"
*8:26
Mt. 6:30;
14:31; 16:8;
Ps 65:7; 89:9;
107:29
26   And He *said to them, "Why are you timid, you men of little faith?" Then He arose, and rebuked the winds and the sea; and it became perfectly calm.
27   And the men marveled, saying, "What kind of a man is this, that even the winds and the sea obey Him?"

2. Demons cast out (8:28–34; Mark 5:1–20; Luke 8:26–39)

8:29
Judg 11:12;
2 Sam 16:10;
Mark 1:24;
John 2:4
28   And when He had come to the other side into the country of the Gadarenes, two men who were demon-possessed met Him as they were coming out of the tombs; *they were* so exceedingly violent that no one could pass by that road.
29   And behold, they cried out, saying, "What do we have to do with You, Son of God? Have You come here to torment us before the time?"
30   Now there was at a distance from them a herd of many swine feeding.
31   And the demons *began* to entreat Him, saying, "If You are *going to* cast us out, send us into the herd of swine."
32   And He said to them, "Begone!" And they came out, and went into the swine, and behold, the whole herd rushed down the steep bank into the sea and perished in the waters.
33   And the herdsmen ran away, and went to the city, and reported everything, including the *incident* of the demoniacs.

8:20 Jesus called Himself the *Son of Man* about eighty times in the New Testament. That name is used over thirty times in Matthew alone. Jesus used it to describe His office as Messiah, but He tended to avoid the term Messiah itself because of the improper connotations attached to it by the people of His day. (They conceived of the coming Messiah as an irresistible military conqueror who would restore the political empire of David.) *Son of Man* is first used with a Messianic connotation in Dan. 7:13, and there it is applied to a heavenly figure to whom everlasting dominion over all

the earth is granted by the Ancient of Days. By His own person and work, Jesus invested this title with its full Messianic and redemptive significance.
8:22 *Follow Me.* Jesus makes it clear that His command takes precedence over all other duties.
8:26 From 8:1–9:34 Christ sets forth His credentials in the form of miracles, to demonstrate His power to save man from sin and death. Thus He cleansed the leper, healed the sick, cast out demons, raised the dead, and stilled the storm at sea.

34　And behold, the whole city came out to meet Jesus; and when they saw Him, they entreated *Him* to depart from their region.

3. *A paralytic healed and forgiven (9:1–8; Mark 2:1–12; Luke 5:17–26)*

9 And getting into a boat, He crossed over, and came to His own city.
2　And behold, they were bringing to Him a paralytic, lying on a bed; and Jesus seeing their faith said to the paralytic, "Take courage, My son, your sins are forgiven."
3　And behold, some of the scribes said to themselves, "This *fellow* blasphemes."
4　And Jesus knowing their thoughts said, "Why are you thinking evil in your hearts?
5　"For which is easier, to say, 'Your sins are forgiven,' or to say, 'Rise, and walk'?
6　"But in order that you may know that the Son of Man has authority on earth to forgive sins"—then He *said to the paralytic—"Rise, take up your bed, and go home."
7　And he rose, and went home.
8　But when the multitudes saw *this*, they were filled with awe, and glorified God, who had given such authority to men.

I. *Matthew called (9:9–13; Mark 2:13–17; Luke 5:27–32)*

9　And as Jesus passed on from there, He saw a man, called Matthew, sitting in the tax office; and He *said to him, "Follow Me!" And he rose, and followed Him.
10　And it happened that as He was reclining *at the table* in the house, behold many tax-gatherers and sinners came and were dining with Jesus and His disciples.
11　And when the Pharisees saw *this*, they said to His disciples, "Why is your Teacher eating with the tax-gatherers and sinners?"
12　But when He heard this, He said, "*It is* not those who are healthy who need a physician, but those who are sick.
13　"But go and learn what *this* means, 'I DESIRE COMPASSION, [22]AND NOT SACRIFICE,' for I did not come to call the righteous, but sinners."

J. *The question about fasting*
(9:14–17; Mark 2:18–22; Luke 5:33–39)

14　Then the disciples of John *came to Him, saying, "Why do we and the Pharisees fast, but Your disciples do not fast?"
15　And Jesus said to them, "The attendants of the bridegroom cannot mourn as long as the bridegroom is with them, can they? But the days will come when the bridegroom is taken away from them, and then they will fast.
16　"But no one puts a patch of unshrunk cloth on an old garment; for the patch pulls away from the garment, and a worse tear results.
17　"Nor do *men* put new wine into old wineskins; otherwise the wineskins burst, and the wine pours out, and the wineskins are ruined; but they put new wine into fresh wineskins, and both are preserved."

K. *Miracles of Jesus (3) (9:18–34)*

1. *The issue of blood stopped and the dead raised*
(9:18–26; Mark 5:21–43; Luke 8:40–56)

18　While He was saying these things to them, behold, there came a *synagogue* official, and bowed down before Him, saying, "My daughter has just died; but come and lay Your hand on her, and she will live."

[22]I.e., more than

9:6 *authority . . . to forgive sins.* This is quite different from the authority to declare that sins have been forgiven. God alone can forgive sins, but anyone may declare that a man's sins have been forgiven by God so long as God's requirements have been met.
9:10 *tax-gatherers and sinners.* These *sinners* were not notorious scoundrels or criminals; rather they were ordinary people who did not observe all the minute prescriptions of ceremonial laws prized by the Pharisees, especially laws

having to do with food and social relations with non-Jews. Jesus was accused of being a friend of tax collectors and sinners because He associated with them. The Pharisees' attitude may be seen in their contemptuous words (Luke 7:34), which reveal the bitterness of their criticism of Jesus for befriending such people. Against such self-righteousness Jesus told the parable of the Pharisee and the tax collector, both of whom went to the temple to pray (Luke 18:9–14).

Marginal references:

8:34 see 1 Kin 17:18; Luke 5:8; Acts 16:39

9:1 Matt 4:13
9:2 Matt 9:22; Mark 6:50; 10:49; Acts 23:11

9:4 Matt 12:25; Luke 6:8; 9:47; 11:17

9:8 Matt 5:16; 15:31; Luke 7:16; 13:13; 17:15; 23:47; John 15:8; Acts 4:21; 11:18; 21:20

9:11 Matt 11:19; Gal 2:15

9:13 Hos 6:6; Mic 6:6-8; Matt 12:7; 1 Tim 1:15

9:14 Luke 18:12

9:15 John 3:29; Acts 13:2,3; 14:23

9:16 Luke 5:36

9:18 Matt 8:2; John 9:38

9:20
Matt 14:36;
Mark 3:10
9:21
see Luke 6:19
9:22
Mark 10:52;
Luke 7:50;
17:19; 18:42;
Matt 9:9;
15:28
9:23
see
2 Chr 35:25;
Jer 9:17;
16:6;
Ezek 24:17
9:24
see
John 11:13;
Acts 20:10

19   And Jesus rose and *began* to follow him, and *so did* His disciples.

20   And behold, a woman who had been suffering from a hemorrhage for twelve years, came up behind Him and touched the fringe of His cloak;

21   for she was saying to herself, "If I only touch His garment, I shall get well."

22   But Jesus turning and seeing her said, "Daughter, take courage; your faith has made you well." And at once the woman was made well.

23   And when Jesus came into the official's house, and saw the flute-players, and the crowd in noisy disorder,

24   He *began* to say, "Depart; for the girl has not died, but is asleep." And they *began* laughing at Him.

25   But when the crowd had been put out, He entered and took her by the hand; and the girl arose.

26   And this news went out into all that land.

2. Sight to the blind and speech to the dumb (9:27–34)

9:27
Matt 15:22;
Mark 10:47,
48;
Luke 18:38,
39

27   And as Jesus passed on from there, two blind men followed Him, crying out, and saying, "Have mercy on us, Son of David!"

28   And after He had come into the house, the blind men came up to Him, and Jesus *said to them, "Do you believe that I am able to do this?" They *said to Him, "Yes, Lord."

9:29
see v. 22;
Matt 8:13
9:30
Matt 8:4;
17:9
9:31
Mark 7:36
9:32
Matt 12:22-24;
Luke 11:14

29   Then He touched their eyes, saying, "Be it done to you according to your faith."

30   And their eyes were opened. And Jesus sternly warned them, saying, "See here, let no one know *about this!*"

31   But they went out, and spread the news about Him in all that land.

32   And as they were going out, behold, a dumb man, demon-possessed, was brought to Him.

33   And after the demon was cast out, the dumb man spoke; and the multitudes marveled, saying, "Nothing like this was ever seen in Israel."

9:34
Matt 12:24;
Mark 3:22;
Luke 11:15

34   But the Pharisees were saying, "He casts out the demons by the ruler of the demons."

L. The need for workers (9:35–38)

9:35
Mark 6:6;
Luke 13:22
9:36
Mark 6:34;
Ezek 34:5;
Zech 10:2
9:37
Luke 10:2;
John 4:35

35   And Jesus was going about all the cities and the villages, teaching in their synagogues, and proclaiming the gospel of the kingdom, and healing every kind of disease and every kind of sickness.

36   And seeing the multitudes, He felt compassion for them, because they were distressed and downcast like sheep without a shepherd.

37   Then He *said to His disciples, "The harvest is plentiful, but the workers are few.

38   "Therefore beseech the Lord of the harvest to send out workers into His harvest."

M. The names and mission of the Twelve
(10:1–15; Mark 6:7–13; Luke 9:1–16)

10:1
Mark 3:13-15;
Luke 6:14-16;
Acts 1:13

10 And having summoned His twelve disciples, He gave them authority over unclean spirits, to cast them out, and to heal every kind of disease and every kind of sickness.

*10:4
Luke 6:15;
Acts 1:13;
John 13:26
10:5
Luke 9:52;
Acts 8:5,25
10:6
Matt 15:24;
Ezek 34:5
10:7
Matt 3:2;
Luke 10:9

2   Now the names of the twelve apostles are these: The first, Simon, who is called Peter, and Andrew his brother; and James the *son* of Zebedee, and John his brother;

3   Philip and Bartholomew; Thomas and Matthew the tax-gatherer; James the *son* of Alphaeus, and Thaddaeus;

4   Simon the Zealot, and Judas Iscariot, the one who betrayed Him.

5   These twelve Jesus sent out after instructing them, saying, "Do not go in *the* way of *the* Gentiles, and do not enter *any* city of the Samaritans;

6   but rather go to the lost sheep of the house of Israel.

7   "And as you go, preach, saying, 'The kingdom of heaven is at hand.'

10:2 For *apostle* and its definition see note to Luke 6:13.
10:4 The Greek name *Kananaios* represents the Aramaic *kan'an*, meaning "zealous" or "zealot." Perhaps Simon the Zealot had formerly belonged to the extremist party of Zealots who advocated the overthrow of the Roman power by revolution and force.

8 "Heal *the* sick, raise *the* dead, cleanse *the* lepers, cast out demons; freely you received, freely give.

9 "Do not acquire gold, or silver, or copper for your money belts,

10 or a bag for *your* journey, or even two tunics, or sandals, or a staff; for the worker is worthy of his support.

11 "And into whatever city or village you enter, inquire who is worthy in it; and abide there until you go away.

12 "And as you enter the house, give it your greeting.

13 "And if the house is worthy, let your *greeting of* peace come upon it; but if it is not worthy, let your *greeting of* peace return to you.

14 "And whoever does not receive you, nor heed your words, as you go out of that house or that city, shake off the dust of your feet.

15 "Truly I say to you, it will be more tolerable for *the* land of Sodom and Gomorrah in the day of judgment, than for that city.

N. *The servant and suffering* *(10:16–23; cf. Mark 13:9–13; Luke 21:12–19)*

16 "Behold, I send you out as sheep in the midst of wolves; therefore be shrewd as serpents, and innocent as doves.

17 "But beware of men; for they will deliver you up to *the* courts, and scourge you in their synagogues;

18 and you shall even be brought before governors and kings for My sake, as a testimony to them and to the Gentiles.

19 "But when they deliver you up, do not become anxious about how or what you will speak; for it shall be given you in that hour what you are to speak.

20 "For it is not you who speak, but *it is* the Spirit of your Father who speaks in you.

21 "And brother will deliver up brother to death, and a father *his* child; and children will rise up against parents, and cause them to be put to death.

22 "And you will be hated by all on account of My name, but it is the one who has endured to the end who will be saved.

23 "But whenever they persecute you in this city, flee to the next; for truly I say to you, you shall not finish *going through* the cities of Israel, until the Son of Man comes.

O. *The servant's encouragement (10:24–33; cf. Luke 12:2–9)*

24 "A disciple is not above his teacher, nor a slave above his master.

25 "It is enough for the disciple that he become as his teacher, and the slave as his master. If they have called the head of the house Beelzebul, how much more the members of his household!

26 "Therefore do not fear them, for there is nothing covered that will not be revealed, and hidden that will not be known.

27 "What I tell you in the darkness, speak in the light; and what you hear *whispered* in *your* ear, proclaim upon the housetops.

28 "And do not fear those who kill the body, but are unable to kill the soul; but rather fear Him who is able to destroy both soul and body in hell.

29 "Are not two sparrows sold for a [23]cent? And *yet* not one of them will fall to the ground apart from your Father.

30 "But the very hairs of your head are all numbered.

31 "Therefore do not fear; you are of more value than many sparrows.

32 "Everyone therefore who shall confess Me before men, I will also confess him before My Father who is in heaven.

33 "But whoever shall deny Me before men, I will also deny him before My Father who is in heaven.

Marginal references:

10:10
1 Cor 9:7;
1 Tim 5:18

10:14
Luke 10:10,
11;
Acts 13:51;
18:6
10:15
Matt 11:22

10:16
Luke 10:3;
Rom 16:19

10:18
Acts 25:24-26

10:20
2 Sam 23:2;
John 16:7-11;
Acts 4:8

10:22
Luke 21:17;
Dan 12:12;
Matt 24:13;
Mark 13:13

10:24
Luke 6:40;
John 13:16;
15:20
*10:25
Matt 12:24;
Mark 3:22;
Luke 11:15
10:26
Mark 4:22;
Luke 8:17;
12:2,3
10:28
Is 8:12,13;
Heb 10:31

10:30
Luke 21:18;
Acts 27:34
10:32
Rom 10:9;
2 Tim 2:12;
Rev 3:5

---

[23]Gr., *assarion*, the smallest copper coin

10:25 The Philistine deity *Beelzebul* was called by the Old Testament writers *Baalzebub*, meaning "lord of the flies." (See note to 2 Kin. 1:2.) In the New Testament, Beelzebul is the name derived from an Aramaic form that meant, "lord of the high house," or "lord of the temple." The people of Jesus' day believed that Beelzebul was the prince of de-mons. Therefore it is appropriate to assume, as most commentators do, that this is another name for Satan. The Pharisees accused Jesus of being in league with Beelzebul in exorcising demons (12:24,27; Mark 3:22; Luke 11:15,18, 19).

P. *The servant and the cross (10:34–39)*

10:34
Luke 12:51-53;
Mark 13:12
34 "Do not think that I came to bring peace on the earth; I did not come to bring peace, but a sword.

10:35
Mic 7:6
35 "For I came to SET A MAN AGAINST HIS FATHER, AND A DAUGHTER AGAINST HER MOTHER, AND A DAUGHTER-IN-LAW AGAINST HER MOTHER-IN-LAW;

10:36
Mic 7:6
36 and A MAN'S ENEMIES WILL BE THE MEMBERS OF HIS HOUSEHOLD.

10:37
Luke 14:26
37 "He who loves father or mother more than Me is not worthy of Me; and he who loves son or daughter more than Me is not worthy of Me.

10:38
Matt 16:24
38 "And he who does not take his cross and follow after Me is not worthy of Me.

10:39
Matt 16:25;
Luke 17:33;
John 12:25
39 "He who has found his life shall lose it, and he who has lost his life for My sake shall find it.

Q. *The servant and the reward (10:40–11:1)*

10:40
Luke 9:48;
John 12:44;
Gal 4:14
40 "He who receives you receives Me, and he who receives Me receives Him who sent Me.

41 "He who receives a prophet in *the* name of a prophet shall receive a prophet's reward; and he who receives a righteous man in the name of a righteous man shall receive a righteous man's reward.

10:42
Matt 25:40;
Heb 6:10
42 "And whoever in the name of a disciple gives to one of these little ones even a cup of cold water to drink, truly I say to you he shall not lose his reward."

11 And it came about that when Jesus had finished giving instructions to His twelve disciples, He departed from there to teach and preach in their cities.

R. *John the Baptist's last message (11:2–19; Luke 7:18–35)*

11:2
Matt 14:3;
Mark 6:17;
Luke 9:7ff
2 Now when John in prison heard of the works of Christ, he sent *word* by his disciples,

11:3
John 11:27
3 and said to Him, "Are You the Expected One, or shall we look for someone else?"

4 And Jesus answered and said to them, "Go and report to John what you hear and see:

11:5
Is 35:4-6;
61:1;
Luke 4:18,19
5 *the* BLIND RECEIVE SIGHT and *the* lame walk, *the* lepers are cleansed and *the* deaf hear, and *the* dead are raised up, and *the* POOR HAVE THE GOSPEL PREACHED TO THEM.

11:6
Is 8:14,15;
Rom 9:32;
1 Pet 2:8
6 "And blessed is he who keeps from stumbling over Me."

11:7
Matt 3:1
7 And as these were going *away,* Jesus began to speak to the multitudes about John, "What did you go out into the wilderness to look at? A reed shaken by the wind?

8 "But what did you go out to see? A man dressed in soft *clothing*? Behold, those who wear soft *clothing* are in kings' palaces.

11:9
Luke 1:76
9 "But why did you go out? To see a prophet? Yes, I say to you, and one who is more than a prophet.

11:10
Mal 3:1;
Mark 1:2
10 "This is the one about whom it is written,
'BEHOLD, I SEND MY MESSENGER BEFORE YOUR FACE,
WHO WILL PREPARE YOUR WAY BEFORE YOU.'

11 "Truly, I say to you, among those born of women there has not arisen *anyone* greater than John the Baptist; yet he who is least in the kingdom of heaven is greater than he.

12 "And from the days of John the Baptist until now the kingdom of heaven suffers violence, and violent men take it by force.

11:14
Mal 4:5;
Matt 17:12;
Luke 1:17
13 "For all the prophets and the Law prophesied until John.

14 "And if you care to accept *it,* he himself is Elijah, who was to come.

11:15
Matt 13:9,43;
Mark 4:23;
Rev 3:9
15 "He who has ears to hear, let him hear.

16 "But to what shall I compare this generation? It is like children sitting in the market places, who call out to the other *children,*

11:11 The statement *he who is least in the kingdom of heaven is greater than he* (John) is enigmatic. Jesus probably meant that while John was the greatest prophet of the age preceding Calvary and the resurrection, he died before the bestowal of the baptism of the Holy Spirit on the church at Pentecost. Those who have received this blessed Comforter as their permanent possession—"Christ in you, the hope of glory"—enjoy a more privileged status and a more intimate access to God than even the greatest of the Old Testament saints. According to another interpretation, Jesus was in this phrase referring to Himself, "he who is least in the kingdom of heaven is greater than he [John]."

17 and say, 'We played the flute for you, and you did not dance; we sang a dirge, and you did not mourn.'
18 "For John came neither eating nor drinking, and they say, 'He has a demon!'
19 "The Son of Man came eating and drinking, and they say, 'Behold, a gluttonous man and a drunkard, a friend of tax-gatherers and sinners!' Yet wisdom is vindicated by her deeds."

11:19
Matt 9:11;
Luke 15:2

S. The judgment of the unrepentant (11:20–24; cf. Luke 10:12–15)

20 Then He began to reproach the cities in which most of His miracles were done, because they did not repent.
21 "Woe to you, Chorazin! Woe to you, Bethsaida! For if the miracles had occurred in Tyre and Sidon which occurred in you, they would have repented long ago in sackcloth and ashes.
22 "Nevertheless I say to you, it shall be more tolerable for Tyre and Sidon in *the* day of judgment, than for you.
23 "And you, Capernaum, will not be exalted to heaven, will you? You shall descend to Hades; for if the miracles had occurred in Sodom which occurred in you, it would have remained to this day.
24 "Nevertheless I say to you that it shall be more tolerable for the land of Sodom in *the* day of judgment, than for you."

11:21
Jon 3:7,8

11:22
v. 24;
Matt 10:15
11:23
Is 14:13;
Lam 2:1

11:24
Matt 10:15

T. Jesus who reveals the Father (11:25–30; cf. Luke 10:21,22)

25 At that time Jesus answered and said, "I praise Thee, O Father, Lord of heaven and earth, that Thou didst hide these things from *the* wise and intelligent and didst reveal them to babes.
26 "Yes, Father, for thus it was well-pleasing in Thy sight.
27 "All things have been handed over to Me by My Father; and no one knows the Son, except the Father; nor does anyone know the Father, except the Son, and anyone to whom the Son wills to reveal *Him*.
28 "Come to Me, all who are weary and heavy-laden, and I will give you rest.
29 "Take My yoke upon you, and learn from Me, for I am gentle and humble in heart; and YOU SHALL FIND REST FOR YOUR SOULS.
30 "For My yoke is easy, and My load is light."

11:25
1 Cor 1:26-29

11:27
Matt 28:18;
John 3:35;
13:3; 17:2
11:28
see Jer 31:25;
John 7:37
11:29
John 13:15;
Phil 2:5;
1 Pet 2:21;
1 John 2:6;
Jer 6:16

U. Jesus the Lord of the Sabbath (12:1–8; Mark 2:23–28; Luke 6:1–5)

12 At that time Jesus went on the Sabbath through the grainfields, and His disciples became hungry and began to pick the heads *of grain* and eat.
2 But when the Pharisees saw it, they said to Him, "Behold, Your disciples do what is not lawful to do on a Sabbath."
3 But He said to them, "Have you not read what David did, when he became hungry, he and his companions;
4 how he entered the house of God, and they ate the consecrated bread, which was not lawful for him to eat, nor for those with him, but for the priests alone?
5 "Or have you not read in the Law, that on the Sabbath the priests in the temple break the Sabbath, and are innocent?
6 "But I say to you, that something greater than the temple is here.
7 "But if you had known what this means, 'I DESIRE COMPASSION, AND NOT A SACRIFICE,' you would not have condemned the innocent.
8 "For the Son of Man is Lord of the Sabbath."

12:1
Deut 23:25

12:2
v. 10;
Luke 13:14;
14:3;
John 5:10;
7:23; 9:16
*12:3
1 Sam 21:6
*12:4
Ex 25:30;
Lev 24:5,9
12:5
Num 28:9,10
*12:6
vv. 41,42
12:7
Hos 6:6;
Matt 9:13

V. The healing of the withered hand on the Sabbath (12:9–14; Mark 3:1–6; Luke 6:6–11)

9 And departing from there, He went into their synagogue.
10 And behold, *there was* a man with a withered hand. And they questioned

12:10
Luke 13:14;
14:3;
John 9:16

12:3 Jesus often answered the criticisms of His opponents by citing Old Testament precedents to explain and justify His own conduct. He cited two incidents: (1) David and his companions, fleeing from Saul, ate the bread of the presence, which was eaten only by priests (1 Sam. 21:1–6): the lesson is that human need takes precedence over ceremonial regulations; and (2) priests in the temple worked on the Sabbath by offering prescribed sacrifices (cf. Num. 28:9, 10). If in the service of the temple they broke the Sabbath law, so could Christ's disciples. For His disciples served the greater temple, namely, the kingdom of God.
12:4 See note to Mark 2:25 for information on the consecrated bread.
12:6 *greater than the temple.* This is supported by vv. 41,42.

Him, saying, "Is it lawful to heal on the Sabbath?"—in order that they might accuse Him.

12:11
Luke 14:5

11   And He said to them, "What man shall there be among you, who shall have one sheep, and if it falls into a pit on the Sabbath, will he not take hold of it, and lift it out?

12:12
Matt 10:31

12   "Of how much more value then is a man than a sheep! So then, it is lawful to do good on the Sabbath."

13   Then He *said to the man, "Stretch out your hand!" And he stretched it out, and it was restored to normal, like the other.

12:14
Matt 27:1;
Mark 3:6;
Luke 6:11;
John 5:18;
11:53

14   But the Pharisees went out, and counseled together against Him, *as to* how they might destroy Him.

W. Jesus heals many (12:15–21; Mark 3:7–12; cf. Luke 6:17–19)

12:15
Matt 10:23;
19:2
12:16
Matt 9:30

15   But Jesus, aware of *this*, withdrew from there. And many followed Him, and He healed them all,

16   and warned them not to make Him known,

17   in order that what was spoken through Isaiah the prophet, might be fulfilled, saying,

12:18
Is 42:1-4

18   "Behold, My Servant whom I have chosen;
       My Beloved in whom My soul is well-pleased;
       I will put My Spirit upon Him,
       And He shall proclaim justice to the Gentiles.

19   "He will not quarrel, nor cry out;
       Nor will anyone hear His voice in the streets.

20   "A battered reed He will not break off,
       And a smoldering wick He will not put out,
       Until He leads justice to victory.

21   "And in His name the Gentiles will hope."

X. Jesus answers the Pharisees' slander (12:22–37; Mark 3:20–30; Luke 11:14–23)

12:22
Matt 9:32,33

22   Then there was brought to Him a demon-possessed man *who was* blind and dumb, and He healed him, so that the dumb man spoke and saw.

12:23
Matt 9:27

23   And all the multitudes were amazed, and *began* to say, "This *man* cannot be the Son of David, can he?"

12:24
Matt 9:34;
10:25;
John 7:20;
8:52; 10:20
12:25
Matt 9:4

24   But when the Pharisees heard it, they said, "This man casts out demons only by Beelzebul the ruler of the demons."

25   And knowing their thoughts He said to them, "Any kingdom divided against itself is laid waste; and any city or house divided against itself shall not stand.

26   "And if Satan casts out Satan, he is divided against himself; how then shall his kingdom stand?

12:27
Matt 9:34;
10:25;
Acts 19:13
12:28
Dan 2:44;
7:14;
Luke 1:33;
17:20,21
12:30
Mark 9:40;
Luke 9:50
*12:31
Luke 12:10

27   "And if I by Beelzebul cast out demons, by whom do your sons cast them out? Consequently they shall be your judges.

28   "But if I cast out demons by the Spirit of God, then the kingdom of God has come upon you.

29   "Or how can anyone enter the strong man's house and carry off his property, unless he first binds the strong *man*? And then he will plunder his house.

30   "He who is not with Me is against Me; and he who does not gather with Me scatters.

31   "Therefore I say to you, any sin and blasphemy shall be forgiven men, but blasphemy against the Spirit shall not be forgiven.

12:32
Matt 11:19;
13:55;
John 7:12,52

32   "And whoever shall speak a word against the Son of Man, it shall be forgiven him; but whoever shall speak against the Holy Spirit, it shall not be forgiven him, either in this age, or in the *age* to come.

12:33
Matt 7:17;
Luke 6:43,44
12:34
Matt 3:7;
23:33;
Luke 6:45

33   "Either make the tree good, and its fruit good; or make the tree bad, and its fruit bad; for the tree is known by its fruit.

34   "You brood of vipers, how can you, being evil, speak what is good? For the mouth speaks out of that which fills the heart.

35   "The good man out of *his* good treasure brings forth what is good; and the evil man out of *his* evil treasure brings forth what is evil.

12:31 See note to Mark 3:29.

36 "And I say to you, that every careless word that men shall speak, they shall render account for it in the day of judgment.

37 "For by your words you shall be justified, and by your words you shall be condemned."

Y. Warning against seeking signs (12:38–45; Luke 11:29–32)

38 Then some of the scribes and Pharisees answered Him, saying, "Teacher, we want to see a sign from You." | **12:38** Matt 16:1; Mark 8:11, 12; John 2:18; 6:30; 1 Cor 1:22

39 But He answered and said to them, "An evil and adulterous generation craves for a sign; and *yet* no sign shall be given to it but the sign of Jonah the prophet; | *****12:39** Matt 16:4

40 for just as JONAH WAS THREE DAYS AND THREE NIGHTS IN THE BELLY OF THE SEA MONSTER, so shall the Son of Man be three days and three nights in the heart of the earth. | **12:40** Jon 1:17

41 "The men of Nineveh shall stand up with this generation at the judgment, and shall condemn it because they repented at the preaching of Jonah; and behold, something greater than Jonah is here. | **12:41** Jon 1:2; 3:5

42 "*The* Queen of *the* South shall rise up with this generation at the judgment and shall condemn it, because she came from the ends of the earth to hear the wisdom of Solomon; and behold, something greater than Solomon is here. | **12:42** 1 Kin 10:2; 2 Chr 9:1

43 "Now when the unclean spirit goes out of a man, it passes through waterless places, seeking rest, and does not find *it*.

44 "Then it says, 'I will return to my house from which I came'; and when it comes, it finds it unoccupied, swept, and put in order.

45 "Then it goes, and takes along with it seven other spirits more wicked than itself, and they go in and live there; and the last state of that man becomes worse than the first. That is the way it will also be with this evil generation." | **12:45** 2 Pet 2:20

Z. Christ's true kindred (12:46–50; Mark 3:31–35; Luke 8:19–21)

46 While He was still speaking to the multitudes, behold, His mother and brothers were standing outside, seeking to speak to Him. | **12:46** Matt 13:55; Mark 6:3; John 2:12; 7:3,5; Acts 1:4; 1 Cor 9:5; Gal 1:9

47 And someone said to Him, "Behold, Your mother and Your brothers are standing outside seeking to speak to You."

48 But He answered the one who was telling Him and said, "Who is My mother and who are My brothers?"

49 And stretching out His hand toward His disciples, He said, "Behold, My mother and My brothers!

50 "For whoever does the will of My Father who is in heaven, he is My brother and sister and mother." | **12:50** John 15:14

AA. Jesus teaches in parables (13:1–52)

1. The sower (13:1–23)

a. The story of the sower (13:1–9; Mark 4:1–9; Luke 8:4–8)

13 On that day Jesus went out of the house, and was sitting by the sea. 2 And great multitudes gathered to Him, so that He got into a boat and sat down, and the whole multitude was standing on the beach. | **13:2** Luke 5:3

3 And He spoke many things to them in parables, saying, "Behold, the sower went out to sow;

4 and as he sowed, some *seeds* fell beside the road, and the birds came and ate them up.

5 "And others fell upon the rocky places, where they did not have much soil; and immediately they sprang up, because they had no depth of soil.

6 "But when the sun had risen, they were scorched; and because they had no root, they withered away.

12:36 Words are an index to the heart. Careless words inevitably will reap their just reward in the judgment. Words, of course, are neither good nor bad in themselves. The kind of words, the intended meaning, and the heart intention make them either good or bad. See here the note to 2 Cor. 5:10 on the judgment seat of Christ.
12:39 *adulterous.* The sense of the word here is not debasement, but a turning away from God.

13:3a A *parable* is an earthly story with a heavenly meaning. Spiritual truth is unfolded in everyday language and figures. The details of a parable should not be pressed beyond the principal object of the comparison. Each parable has a main point and was spoken to make that point easily apparent.
13:3b See note to Mark 4:3 on the sower.

7 "And others fell among the thorns, and the thorns came up and choked them out.

8 "And others fell on the good soil, and *yielded a crop, some a hundredfold, some sixty, and some thirty.

9 "He who has ears, let him hear."

b. The reason for parables (13:10–17; Mark 4:10–12; Luke 8:9–10)

10 And the disciples came and said to Him, "Why do You speak to them in parables?"

11 And He answered and said to them, "To you it has been granted to know the mysteries of the kingdom of heaven, but to them it has not been granted.

12 "For whoever has, to him shall *more* be given, and he shall have an abundance; but whoever does not have, even what he has shall be taken away from him.

13 "Therefore I speak to them in parables; because while seeing they do not see, and while hearing they do not hear, nor do they understand.

14 "And in their case the prophecy of Isaiah is being fulfilled, which says,

'YOU WILL KEEP ON HEARING, BUT WILL NOT UNDERSTAND;
AND YOU WILL KEEP ON SEEING, BUT WILL NOT PERCEIVE;
15   FOR THE HEART OF THIS PEOPLE HAS BECOME DULL,
AND WITH THEIR EARS THEY SCARCELY HEAR,
AND THEY HAVE CLOSED THEIR EYES
LEST THEY SHOULD SEE WITH THEIR EYES,
AND HEAR WITH THEIR EARS,
AND UNDERSTAND WITH THEIR HEART AND RETURN,
AND I SHOULD HEAL THEM.'

16 "But blessed are your eyes, because they see; and your ears, because they hear.

17 "For truly I say to you, that many prophets and righteous men desired to see what you see, and did not see *it*; and to hear what you hear, and did not hear *it*.

c. The parable of the sower explained (13:18–23; Mark 4:13–20; Luke 8:11–15)

18 "Hear then the parable of the sower.

19 "When anyone hears the word of the kingdom, and does not understand it, the evil *one* comes and snatches away what has been sown in his heart. This is the one on whom seed was sown beside the road.

20 "And the one on whom seed was sown on the rocky places, this is the man who hears the word, and immediately receives it with joy;

21   yet he has no *firm* root in himself, but is *only* temporary, and when affliction or persecution arises because of the word, immediately he falls away.

22 "And the one on whom seed was sown among the thorns, this is the man who hears the word, and the worry of the world, and the deceitfulness of riches choke the word, and it becomes unfruitful.

23 "And the one on whom seed was sown on the good soil, this is the man who hears the word and understands it; who indeed bears fruit, and brings forth, some a hundredfold, some sixty, and some thirty."

2. The wheat and the tares (13:24–30; cf. Mark 4:26–29)

24 He presented another parable to them, saying, "The kingdom of heaven may be compared to a man who sowed good seed in his field.

25 "But while men were sleeping, his enemy came and sowed [24]tares also among the wheat, and went away.

26 "But when the wheat sprang up and bore grain, then the tares became evident also.

27 "And the slaves of the landowner came and said to him, 'Sir, did you not sow good seed in your field? How then does it have tares?'

28 "And he said to them, 'An enemy has done this!' And the slaves *said to him, 'Do you want us, then, to go and gather them up?'

[24]Or, *darnel,* a weed resembling wheat

13:18 The parable of the sower was readily understood by the listeners, who were quite familiar with the rocky soil from which they wrested their living. The parable is more difficult to comprehend for those whose experiences are limited to fertile, non-rocky soil, such as is found in many areas of the world.

Cross-references (margin):
13:8 Gen 26:12
13:9 Matt 11:15
13:11 Matt 11:25; 19:11; John 6:65; 1 Cor 2:10; 1 John 2:27
13:12 Matt 25:29; Luke 19:26
13:13 Jer 5:21; Ezek 12:2
13:14 Is 6:9,10; Ezek 12:2; John 12:40; Acts 28:26, 27; Rom 11:8
13:15 Heb 5:11
13:16 Matt 16:17; Luke 10:23, 24; John 20:29
13:17 Heb 11:13; 1 Pet 1:10,11
13:19 Matt 4:23
13:21 Matt 11:6
13:22 Rom 12:2; 1 Cor 1:20; 2 Cor 4:4; Gal 1:4; Eph 2:2; Matt 19:23; 1 Tim 6:9,10, 17
13:23 v. 8
13:24 Luke 13:18, 20

29 "But he *said, 'No; lest while you are gathering up the tares, you may root up the wheat with them.

30 'Allow both to grow together until the harvest; and in the time of the harvest I will say to the reapers, "First gather up the tares and bind them in bundles to burn them up; but gather the wheat into my barn." ' "   **13:30** Matt 3:12

3. The grain of mustard seed
(13:31,32; Mark 4:30–32; Luke 13:18,19)

31 He presented another parable to them, saying, "The kingdom of heaven is like a mustard seed, which a man took and sowed in his field;   *13:31 see Is 2:2,3; Mic 4:1

32 and this is smaller than all *other* seeds; but when it is full grown, it is larger than the garden plants, and becomes a tree, so that THE BIRDS OF THE AIR come and NEST IN ITS BRANCHES."   13:32 Ps 104:12; Ezek 17:23; 31:6; Dan 4:12

4. The leaven (13:33–35; Luke 13:20,21)

33 He spoke another parable to them, "The kingdom of heaven is like leaven, which a woman took, and hid in three pecks of meal, until it was all leavened."   *13:33 Gen 18:6; Gal 5:9

34 All these things Jesus spoke to the multitudes in parables, and He did not speak to them without a parable,   13:34 Mark 4:33,34

35 so that what was spoken through the prophet might be fulfilled, saying,
"I WILL OPEN MY MOUTH IN PARABLES;
I WILL UTTER THINGS HIDDEN SINCE THE FOUNDATION OF THE
WORLD."   *13:35 Ps 78:2; Rom 16:25, 26; 1 Cor 2:7; Eph 3:9; Col 1:26

5. The wheat and the tares explained (13:36–43)

36 Then He left the multitudes, and went into the house. And His disciples came to Him, saying, "Explain to us the parable of the tares of the field."

37 And He answered and said, "The one who sows the good seed is the Son of Man,   13:38 Matt 24:14; 28:19; Luke 24:47; John 8:44; 1 John 3:10

38 and the field is the world; and *as for* the good seed, these are the sons of the kingdom; and the tares are the sons of the evil *one;*

39 and the enemy who sowed them is the devil, and the harvest is the end of the age; and the reapers are angels.   13:39 Joel 3:13; Matt 24:3; 28:20; Rev 14:15

40 "Therefore just as the tares are gathered up and burned with fire, so shall it be at the end of the age.   13:40 1 Cor 10:11; Heb 9:26

41 "The Son of Man will send forth His angels, and they will gather out of His kingdom all stumbling blocks, and those who commit lawlessness,   13:41 Matt 24:31

42 and will cast them into the furnace of fire; in that place there shall be weeping and gnashing of teeth.   13:42 Matt 8:12; v. 50; Matt 24:51; 25:30; Luke 13:28

43 "Then THE RIGHTEOUS WILL SHINE FORTH AS THE SUN in the kingdom of their Father. He who has ears, let him hear.   13:43 Dan 12:3; Matt 11:15

6. The hidden treasure (13:44)

44 "The kingdom of heaven is like a treasure hidden in the field, which a man

---

13:29 This parable teaches us that there are always true and false believers within the fellowship of those who profess to belong to God. It is not always possible to distinguish the false from the true. While great harm may come from the presence of unbelievers, yet great harm may also come from human efforts to separate the false from the true. Scripture does warrant the exclusion of those who are not true believers if and when they can be positively identified (Titus 3:10). As the interpretation of the parable makes clear (vv. 36–43), the final separation is made by the Judge of all, the Son of Man.

Indeed, there may be a further lesson that one cannot judge the success or failure of a movement by the smallness of its beginnings. *For who has despised the day of small things* shall rejoice (Zech. 4:10). The Lord Jesus left behind a small company of despised followers from whom little could be expected. Yet from them came the seeds of history's greatest movement.
13:31 This parable has for its central teaching the growth and spread of the gospel throughout the world. Commencing as a tiny seed, it becomes a giant tree. The present-day existence of a worldwide church in some measure represents a fulfillment of this prophetic word.

13:33 In the New Testament, *leaven* is used metaphorically in an evil sense: (1) of the doctrines of the Pharisees and Sadducees (16:6,12; see also Mark 8:15; Luke 12:1); (2) of ungodly professors of the true faith (1 Cor. 5:6,7); (3) of false teachers of Christianity (Gal. 5:8,9); and (4) of malice and evil (1 Cor. 5:8). On the other hand, it seems to be used to illustrate the influence of the gospel here (and in the parallel passage, Luke 13:21). *Leaven* suggests permeation and its silent working. Only a small amount of leaven was needed for a large quantity of dough, a small amount affecting something like thirty-six quarts of dough. So the kingdom message, apparently insignificant, permeates the whole world.

In the Old Testament: (1) it was forbidden to use leaven during the Passover (Ex. 12:15–20); (2) leaven was not to be offered with the blood of sacrifice (Ex. 34:25); and (3) it was not to be offered with cereal offerings that were burned on the altar (Lev. 2:11; 10:12). It was permitted, however, with thank offerings (Lev. 7:13) and with the presentation of the first fruits of wheat (Lev. 23:17).
13:35 The parables of Jesus were not understood either by the multitudes or by the disciples of the Lord: He explained *everything privately to His own disciples* (Mark 4:34).

*13:44
see Phil 3:7,
8; Is 55:1
found and hid; and from joy over it he goes and sells all that he has, and buys that field.

7. *The pearl (13:45)*

45 "Again, the kingdom of heaven is like a merchant seeking fine pearls,

46 and upon finding one pearl of great value, he went and sold all that he had, and bought it.

8. *The dragnet (13:47–52)*

*13:47
Matt 22:10
47 "Again, the kingdom of heaven is like a dragnet cast into the sea, and gathering *fish* of every kind;

48 and when it was filled, they drew it up on the beach; and they sat down, and gathered the good *fish* into containers, but the bad they threw away.

13:49
Matt 25:32
49 "So it will be at the end of the age; the angels shall come forth, and take out the wicked from among the righteous,

13:50
v. 42
50 and will cast them into the furnace of fire; there shall be weeping and gnashing of teeth.

51 "Have you understood all these things?" They *said to Him, "Yes."

52 And He said to them, "Therefore every scribe who has become a disciple of the kingdom of heaven is like a head of a household, who brings forth out of his treasure things new and old."

BB. *Second rejection of Jesus at Nazareth (13:53–58; Mark 6:1–6; Luke 4:16–30)*

13:53
Matt 7:28;
11:1; 19:1;
26:1
13:54
Matt 4:23;
7:28
53 And it came about that when Jesus had finished these parables, He departed from there.

54 And coming to His home town He *began* teaching them in their synagogue, so that they became astonished, and said, "Where *did* this man *get* this wisdom, and *these* miraculous powers?

*13:55
Luke 3:23;
John 6:42
55 "Is not this the carpenter's son? Is not His mother called Mary, and His brothers, James and Joseph and Simon and Judas?

56 "And His sisters, are they not all with us? Where then *did* this man *get* all these things?"

13:57
John 4:44
57 And they took offense at Him. But Jesus said to them, "A prophet is not without honor except in his home town, and in his *own* household."

58 And He did not do many miracles there because of their unbelief.

CC. *Death of John the Baptist (14:1–12; Mark 6:14–29; Luke 9:7–9)*

14:1
Mark 8:15;
Luke 3:1,19;
8:3; 13:31;
23:7,8;
Acts 4:27;
12:1
*14:3
Luke 3:19,20
14:4
Lev 18:16;
20:21
14:5
Matt 21:26;
Luke 20:6

14 At that time Herod the tetrarch heard the news about Jesus,

2 and said to his servants, "This is John the Baptist; he has risen from the dead; and that is why miraculous powers are at work in him."

3 For when Herod had John arrested, he bound him, and put him in prison on account of Herodias, the wife of his brother Philip.

4 For John had been saying to him, "It is not lawful for you to have her."

5 And although he wanted to put him to death, he feared the multitude, because they regarded him as a prophet.

6 But when Herod's birthday came, the daughter of Herodias danced before *them* and pleased Herod.

7 Thereupon he promised with an oath to give her whatever she asked.

8 And having been prompted by her mother, she *said, "Give me here on a platter the head of John the Baptist."

13:44 This parable has for its central teaching the incomparable value of the gospel, which will cause a man to forsake everything that he may possess the greatest of all. All else when compared to this is of no value whatever (16:26). Another possible interpretation would be the equation of this discoverer with Christ Himself, who sacrificed all that He had in order to purchase the treasure of His church.
13:45 The pearl and the hidden treasure are similar in general meaning. In the case of the pearl, Christ suggests that the one who seeks it will find salvation. And when he discovers this one pearl he will gladly sell all else for it. Here again, however, the purchaser may represent the Lord Jesus Himself.
13:47 The dragnet represents the kingdom of God. The net is cast into the sea and when drawn to land has in it a mixed company. The good represent the converted, and the bad the unconverted. At the end of the age the righteous will be separated from the unrighteous by the angels of God. Needless to say, this parable precludes the idea of a wholly converted world at the end of the age.
13:55 See note to Mark 6:3 on the family of Jesus.
14:3 See note to Luke 1:57 on John the Baptist. See also note to Mark 6:17 on Philip the brother of Herod Antipas.

9   And although he was grieved, the king commanded *it* to be given because of his oaths, and because of his dinner guests.

10   And he sent and had John beheaded in the prison.

11   And his head was brought on a platter and given to the girl; and she brought *it* to her mother.

12   And his disciples came and took away the body and buried it; and they went and reported to Jesus.

DD. *The five thousand fed*
(14:13–21; Mark 6:30–44; Luke 9:10–17; John 6:1–13; cf. Matt. 15:32–38)

13   Now when Jesus heard *it*, He withdrew from there in a boat, to a lonely place by Himself; and when the multitudes heard *of this*, they followed Him on foot from the cities.

14   And when He went ashore, He saw a great multitude, and felt compassion for them, and healed their sick.

15   And when it was evening, the disciples came to Him, saying, "The place is desolate, and the time is already past; so send the multitudes away, that they may go into the villages and buy food for themselves."

16   But Jesus said to them, "They do not need to go away; you give them *something* to eat!"

17   And they *said to Him, "We have here only five loaves and two fish."

18   And He said, "Bring them here to Me."

19   And ordering the multitudes to recline on the grass, He took the five loaves and the two fish, and looking up toward heaven, He blessed *the food*, and breaking the loaves He gave them to the disciples, and the disciples *gave* to the multitudes,

20   and they all ate, and were satisfied. And they picked up what was left over of the broken pieces, twelve full baskets.

21   And there were about five thousand men who ate, aside from women and children.

EE. *Jesus walks on the sea (14:22–36; Mark 6:45–52; John 6:15–21)*

22   And immediately He made the disciples get into the boat, and go ahead of Him to the other side, while He sent the multitudes away.

23   And after He had sent the multitudes away, He went up to the mountain by Himself to pray; and when it was evening, He was there alone.

24   But the boat was already many [25]stadia away from the land, battered by the waves; for the wind was contrary.

25   And in the [26]fourth watch of the night He came to them, walking on the sea.

26   And when the disciples saw Him walking on the sea, they were frightened, saying, "It is a ghost!" And they cried out for fear.

27   But immediately Jesus spoke to them, saying, "Take courage, it is I; do not be afraid."

28   And Peter answered Him and said, "Lord, if it is You, command me to come to You on the water."

29   And He said, "Come!" And Peter got out of the boat, and walked on the water and came toward Jesus.

30   But seeing the wind, he became afraid, and beginning to sink, he cried out, saying, "Lord, save me!"

31   And immediately Jesus stretched out His hand and took hold of him, and *said to him, "O you of little faith, why did you doubt?"

32   And when they got into the boat, the wind stopped.

33   And those who were in the boat worshiped Him, saying, "You are certainly God's Son!"

34   And when they had crossed over, they came to land at Gennesaret.

35   And when the men of that place recognized Him, they sent into all that surrounding district and brought to Him all who were sick;

36   and they *began* to entreat Him that they might just touch the fringe of His cloak; and as many as touched *it* were cured.

[25]A *stadion* was about 600 feet   [26]I.e., 3–6 a.m.

14:14
Matt 9:36

14:17
Matt 16:9

14:19
1 Sam 9:13;
Matt 15:36;
Mark 14:22;
Luke 24:30

14:23
Luke 6:12;
9:28

14:26
see
Luke 24:37
14:27
Matt 9:2;
17:7; 28:10;
Rev 1:17

14:31
Matt 6:30;
8:26; 16:8

14:33
Ps 2:7;
Matt 16:16;
26:63;
Luke 4:41;
John 11:27;
Acts 8:37;
Rom 1:4
14:36
Matt 9:20;
Mark 3:10

14:25 See note to Mark 6:48 on *fourth watch*.
14:29 Peter stepped out of the boat on to the water in faith. Doubt overtook him and he began to sink. True faith must persevere and does not end when the initial step has been taken. Peter had only beginning faith.

FF. Ceremonial and real defilement (15:1-20; Mark 7:1-23)

15 Then some Pharisees and scribes *came to Jesus from Jerusalem, saying,
2   "Why do Your disciples transgress the tradition of the elders? For they do not wash their hands when they eat bread."

3   And He answered and said to them, "And why do you yourselves transgress the commandment of God for the sake of your tradition?

4   "For God said, 'HONOR YOUR FATHER AND MOTHER,' and, 'HE WHO SPEAKS EVIL OF FATHER OR MOTHER, LET HIM BE PUT TO DEATH.'

5   "But you say, 'Whoever shall say to *his* father or mother, "Anything of mine you might have been helped by has been given *to God*,"

6   he is not to honor his father [27]or his mother[28].' And *thus* you invalidated the word of God for the sake of your tradition.

7   "You hypocrites, rightly did Isaiah prophesy of you, saying,

8   'THIS PEOPLE HONORS ME WITH THEIR LIPS,
     BUT THEIR HEART IS FAR AWAY FROM ME.

9   'BUT IN VAIN DO THEY WORSHIP ME,
     TEACHING AS DOCTRINES THE PRECEPTS OF MEN.' "

10   And after He called the multitude to Him, He said to them, "Hear, and understand.

11   "Not what enters into the mouth defiles the man, but what proceeds out of the mouth, this defiles the man."

12   Then the disciples *came and *said to Him, "Do You know that the Pharisees were offended when they heard this statement?"

13   But He answered and said, "Every plant which My heavenly Father did not plant shall be rooted up.

14   "Let them alone; they are blind guides [29]of the blind. And if a blind man guides a blind man, both will fall into a pit."

15   And Peter answered and said to Him, "Explain the parable to us."

16   And He said, "Are you still lacking in understanding also?

17   "Do you not understand that everything that goes into the mouth passes into the stomach, and is eliminated?

18   "But the things that proceed out of the mouth come from the heart, and those defile the man.

19   "For out of the heart come evil thoughts, murders, adulteries, fornications, thefts, false witness, slanders.

20   "These are the things which defile the man; but to eat with unwashed hands does not defile the man."

GG. Journey toward Tyre and Sidon (15:21-28; Mark 7:24-30)

21   And Jesus went away from there, and withdrew into the district of Tyre and Sidon.

22   And behold, a Canaanite woman came out from that region, and *began* to cry out, saying, "Have mercy on me, O Lord, Son of David; my daughter is cruelly demon-possessed."

23   But He did not answer her a word. And His disciples came to *Him* and kept asking Him, saying, "Send her away, for she is shouting out after us."

24   But He answered and said, "I was sent only to the lost sheep of the house of Israel."

25   But she came and *began* to bow down before Him, saying, "Lord, help me!"

26   And He answered and said, "It is not good to take the children's bread and throw it to the dogs."

27   But she said, "Yes, Lord; but even the dogs feed on the crumbs which fall from their masters' table."

28   Then Jesus answered and said to her, "O woman, your faith is great; be it done for you as you wish." And her daughter was healed at once.

HH. Multitudes healed (15:29-31; Mark 7:31-37)

29   And departing from there, Jesus went along by the Sea of Galilee, and having gone up to the mountain, He was sitting there.

30   And great multitudes came to Him, bringing with them *those who were* lame,

[marginal references]
15:2
Luke 11:38

15:4
Ex 20:12;
Deut 5:16;
Eph 6:2
15:5
Ex 21:17;
Lev 20:9;
Deut 27:16

15:9
Col 2:18-22

15:11
Acts 10:14,
15; 1 Tim 4:3

15:13
Is 60:21;
John 15:2;
1 Cor 3:9ff
15:14
Matt 23:16;
Luke 6:39;
Rom 2:19
15:15
Matt 13:36
15:16
Matt 16:9
15:18
Matt 12:34;
James 3:6
15:19
Gal 5:19-21;
1 Cor 6:9,10;
Rom 14:14

15:22
Matt 9:27;
4:24

15:24
Matt 10:6,23

15:25
Matt 8:2;
18:26; 20:20;
John 9:38

15:28
Matt 9:22,28;
Mark 10:52;
Luke 7:50;
17:19

15:30
Luke 7:22

[27]Many mss. do not contain *or his mother*   [28]I.e., by supporting them with it   [29]Some mss. do not contain *of the blind*

crippled, blind, dumb, and many others, and they laid them down at His feet; and He healed them,

31   so that the multitude marveled as they saw the dumb speaking, the crippled restored, and the lame walking, and the blind seeing; and they glorified the God of Israel.

II. The four thousand fed (15:32–39; Mark 8:1–9)

32   And Jesus called His disciples to Him, and said, "I feel compassion for the multitude, because they have remained with Me now three days and have nothing to eat; and I do not wish to send them away hungry, lest they faint on the way."

33   And the disciples *said to Him, "Where would we get so many loaves in a desolate place to satisfy such a great multitude?"

34   And Jesus *said to them, "How many loaves do you have?" And they said, "Seven, and a few small fish."

35   And He directed the multitude to sit down on the ground;

36   and He took the seven loaves and the fish; and giving thanks, He broke them and started giving them to the disciples, and the disciples *in turn*, to the multitudes.

37   And they all ate, and were satisfied, and they picked up what was left over of the broken pieces, seven large baskets full.

38   And those who ate were four thousand men, besides women and children.

39   And sending away the multitudes, He got into the boat, and came to the region of Magadan.

JJ. The Pharisees and Sadducees demand a sign from heaven (16:1–12; Mark 8:11–21)

16 And the Pharisees and Sadducees came up, and testing Him asked Him to show them a sign from heaven.

2   But He answered and said to them, "When it is evening, you say, '*It will be* fair weather, for the sky is red.'

3   "And in the morning, '*There will be* a storm today, for the sky is red and threatening.' Do you know how to discern the appearance of the sky, but cannot *discern* the signs of the times?

4   "An evil and adulterous generation seeks after a sign; and a sign will not be given it, except the sign of Jonah." And He left them, and went away.

5   And the disciples came to the other side and had forgotten to take bread.

6   And Jesus said to them, "Watch out and beware of the leaven of the Pharisees and Sadducees."

7   And they began to discuss among themselves, saying, "*It is* because we took no bread."

8   But Jesus, aware of this, said, "You men of little faith, why do you discuss among yourselves that you have no bread?

9   "Do you not yet understand or remember the five loaves of the five thousand, and how many baskets you took up?

10   "Or the seven loaves of the four thousand, and how many large baskets you took up?

11   "How is it that you do not understand that I did not speak to you concerning bread? But beware of the leaven of the Pharisees and Sadducees."

12   Then they understood that He did not say to beware of the leaven of bread, but of the teaching of the Pharisees and Sadducees.

KK. Peter's confession (16:13–20; Mark 8:27–30; Luke 9:18–21)

13   Now when Jesus came into the district of Caesarea Philippi, He *began* asking His disciples, saying, "Who do people say that the Son of Man is?"

14   And they said, "Some *say* John the Baptist; and others, Elijah; but still others, Jeremiah, or one of the prophets."

15   He *said to them, "But who do you say that I am?"

15:31 Matt 9:8

15:32 Matt 9:36

15:36 Matt 14:19; 1 Sam 9:13

16:1 Matt 12:38; Luke 11:16, 29; 12:54-56

*16:4 Jon 3:4,5; Matt 12:39

16:6 Luke 12:1

16:8 Matt 6:30; 8:26; 14:31
16:9 Matt 14:17-21

16:10 Matt 15:34-38

16:14 Matt 14:2; John 1:21

16:4 In answer to the request for a sign from heaven, that is, some extraordinary or miraculous act that would prove Jesus' divine authority, Jesus replied that no sign would be given that evil and faithless generation except the sign of Jonah. As Luke 11:29,30,32 show, this referred to Jonah's message of imminent destruction unless the people of Nineveh repented: in the same way the Son of Man was a sign to His generation.

In 12:39,40 the sign of Jonah is explained as referring to his three days and nights in the fish's belly, as a type of Christ's burial and resurrection. In Mark 8:11-13 Jesus refused to give any sign: *no sign shall be given to this generation.*

16:16
Matt 14:33;
John 6:69;
11:27
16:17
1 Cor 15:50;
Gal 1:6;
Eph 6:12
*16:18
John 1:42
*16:19
Matt 18:18;
John 20:23
16:20
Mark 3:12;
5:43; 7:36;
9:9

16   And Simon Peter answered and said, "Thou art the Christ, the Son of the living God."

17   And Jesus answered and said to him, "Blessed are you, Simon Barjona, because flesh and blood did not reveal *this* to you, but My Father who is in heaven.

18   "And I also say to you that you are Peter, and upon this rock I will build My church; and the gates of Hades shall not overpower it.

19   "I will give you the keys of the kingdom of heaven; and whatever you shall bind on earth shall be bound in heaven, and whatever you shall loose on earth shall be loosed in heaven."

20   Then He warned the disciples that they should tell no one that He was the Christ.

LL. *Christ foretells His death, resurrection, and second coming* (16:21–28; Mark 8:31–9:1; Luke 9:22–27)

16:21
Matt 17:22,
23; 20:17-19;
Luke 17:25

21   From that time Jesus Christ began to show His disciples that He must go to Jerusalem, and suffer many things from the elders and chief priests and scribes, and be killed, and be raised up on the third day.

22   And Peter took Him aside and began to rebuke Him, saying, "God forbid *it*, Lord! This shall never happen to You."

23   But He turned and said to Peter, "Get behind Me, Satan! You are a stumbling block to Me; for you are not setting your mind on God's interests, but man's."

*16:24
Matt 10:38,
39;
Luke 14:27;
17:33;
John 12:25

24   Then Jesus said to His disciples, "If anyone wishes to come after Me, let him deny himself, and take up his cross, and follow Me.

25   "For whoever wishes to save his life shall lose it; but whoever loses his life for My sake shall find it.

26   "For what will a man be profited, if he gains the whole world, and forfeits his soul? Or what will a man give in exchange for his soul?

16:27
Matt 10:33;
Luke 12:9;
1 John 2:18;
Rom 2:6;
Rev 22:12
16:28
Matt 10:23;
1 Cor 16:22;
1 Thess
4:15-18;
Rev 1:7;
James 5:7
17:1
Matt 26:37;
Mark 5:37;
13:2

27   "For the Son of Man is going to come in the glory of His Father with His angels; and WILL THEN RECOMPENSE EVERY MAN ACCORDING TO HIS DEEDS.

28   "Truly I say to you, there are some of those who are standing here who shall not taste death until they see the Son of Man coming in His kingdom."

MM. *The transfiguration* (17:1–13; Mark 9:2–13; Luke 9:28–36)

17   And six days later Jesus *took with Him Peter and James and John his brother, and *brought them up to a high mountain by themselves.

2   And He was transfigured before them; and His face shone like the sun, and His garments became as white as light.

3   And behold, Moses and Elijah appeared to them, talking with Him.

4   And Peter answered and said to Jesus, "Lord, it is good for us to be here; if

---

16:18 Some have interpreted this verse to mean that Christ founded His church on Peter himself. But such an interpretation overlooks some very important elements in this conversation. It is plain that Christ was making a play on words, for *Peter* and *rock* are *Petros* and *petra* in the Greek. The church is not built on Peter or any other individual as its foundation stone, for Peter makes it clear in 1 Pet. 2:4–8 that Christ Himself is the only cornerstone of the church (cf. also Eph. 2:20–22). The church, then, is built on the person of the Lord Jesus, and its membership includes only those who have confessed Him as Peter did. The "gates of Hades" cannot prevail against this church, for Christ has risen again from the dead and will keep His body safe from the onslaughts of death.
16:19 The keys of the kingdom were not given to Peter alone. They were for all of the apostles and for the church in all ages (cf. 18:18). Nor is it to be supposed that the power of the keys includes the power of any individual to forgive sins. The Greek tense of the verbs *shall be bound* and *shall be loosed* means "shall have been." Thus men of God have the power to declare that God has forgiven the sins of those who have repented and received Christ by faith. No one may pronounce absolution, but anyone may announce that sins have been forgiven when gospel terms have been met. In 18:18 Jesus uses the same words in speaking to all the apostles. In John 20:23 Jesus, in identical language, be-

stows this "power of the keys" on all of the apostles and not simply on Peter alone. Yet Peter made the first significant use of the "keys" in Acts 2 when he preached the gospel to all the pilgrims at Pentecost and proclaimed the message of salvation to them.
16:23 In 16:17 Jesus said to Peter, *"Blessed are you."* In this verse He rebukes Peter sharply. Peter knew that Jesus was the Christ, but he apparently misunderstood the nature of His approaching sacrifice and went so far as to try to deter Jesus from fulfilling His divine mission. Jesus regarded any interference that would take Him out of the will of His Father as satanic. Hence, the rebuke now, after His blessing earlier.
16:24 It is important to notice that Christ does not speak here of self-denial in the sense of denying things to oneself, but rather in the sense of denying self as a life principle. The self-life belongs to the old, unconverted state of existence. But the new believer renounces the demands of the old ego altogether, for the old ego has been crucified with Christ (cf. Gal. 2:20). The true Christian is dead to the world, to the old life, and to the old self; he is alive to God, and Christ is his new life principle (cf. Rom. 6:6–13; Col. 3:1–4). The "cross" that he is to take up as he follows Christ is nothing less than the instrument of death, for that is what the cross was to Christ Himself.
17:2 See note to Mark 9:2 on transfiguration.

You wish, I will make three tabernacles here, one for You, and one for Moses, and one for Elijah."

5   While he was still speaking, behold, a bright cloud overshadowed them; and behold, a voice out of the cloud, saying, "This is My beloved Son, with whom I am well-pleased; listen to Him!"

6   And when the disciples heard *this*, they fell on their faces and were much afraid.

7   And Jesus came to *them* and touched them and said, "Arise, and do not be afraid."

8   And lifting up their eyes, they saw no one, except Jesus Himself alone.

9   And as they were coming down from the mountain, Jesus commanded them, saying, "Tell the vision to no one until the Son of Man has risen from the dead."

10   And His disciples asked Him, saying, "Why then do the scribes say that Elijah must come first?"

11   And He answered and said, "Elijah is coming and will restore all things;

12   but I say to you, that Elijah already came, and they did not recognize him, but did to him whatever they wished. So also the Son of Man is going to suffer at their hands."

13   Then the disciples understood that He had spoken to them about John the Baptist.

NN. The epileptic boy cured (17:14–21; Mark 9:14–29; Luke 9:37–43)

14   And when they came to the multitude, a man came up to Him, falling on his knees before Him, and saying,

15   "Lord, have mercy on my son, for he is a lunatic, and is very ill; for he often falls into the fire, and often into the water.

16   "And I brought him to Your disciples, and they could not cure him."

17   And Jesus answered and said, "O unbelieving and perverted generation, how long shall I be with you? How long shall I put up with you? Bring him here to Me."

18   And Jesus rebuked him, and the demon came out of him, and the boy was cured at once.

19   Then the disciples came to Jesus privately and said, "Why could we not cast it out?"

20   And He *said to them, "Because of the littleness of your faith; for truly I say to you, if you have faith as a mustard seed, you shall say to this mountain, 'Move from here to there,' and it shall move; and nothing shall be impossible to you.

21   [" 30But this kind does not go out except by prayer and fasting."]

OO. Jesus again foretells His death and resurrection (17:22,23; Mark 9:30–32; Luke 9:43–45)

22   And while they were gathering together in Galilee, Jesus said to them, "The Son of Man is going to be delivered into the hands of men;

23   and they will kill Him, and He will be raised on the third day." And they were deeply grieved.

PP. The drachma in the fish's mouth (17:24–27)

24   And when they had come to Capernaum, those who collected the 31 two-drachma *tax* came to Peter, and said, "Does your teacher not pay the 31 two-drach-ma *tax*?"

25   He *said, "Yes." And when he came into the house, Jesus spoke to him first, saying, "What do you think, Simon? From whom do the kings of the earth collect customs or poll-tax, from their sons or from strangers?"

17:5
2 Pet 1:17;
Matt 3:17;
Is 42:1;
Acts 3:22,23

17:7
Matt 14:27

17:9
Matt 8:4;
16:20;
Mark 3:12;
5:43; 7:36
17:10
Mal 4:5;
Matt 11:14
*17:11
Mal 4:6;
Luke 1:16,17
17:12
Matt 11:14;
14:3,10;
16:21

17:15
Matt 4:24

*17:20
Matt 21:21;
Mark 11:23;
Luke 17:6;
1 Cor 12:9

17:22
Matt 16:21;
20:17;
Luke 18:31;
24:6,7

*17:24
Ex 30:13;
38:26

17:25
Rom 13:7;
Matt 22:17,19

30Many mss. do not contain this verse   31Equivalent to two denarii or two days' wages paid as a temple tax

---

17:11 See note to Mal. 4:5 on Elijah.
17:20 *nothing shall be impossible.* This cannot be interpreted without reservation. True faith is rooted in the conviction that the particular thing anticipated is the will of God. But many things are not the will of God and are excluded from this promise.

17:24 The annual temple tax of *two-drachma* was paid by all free Jewish males over twenty years of age (cf. Ex. 30:11–16). The Greek coin equivalent to the Hebrew half-shekel was the double drachma (didrachma); the *stater* in v. 27 is worth two didrachmas.

26   And upon his saying, "From strangers," Jesus said to him, "Consequently the sons are exempt.

27   "But, lest we give them offense, go to the sea, and throw in a hook, and take the first fish that comes up; and when you open its mouth, you will find a [32]stater. Take that and give it to them for you and Me."

17:27
Matt 5:29,30;
18:6,8;
Luke 17:2;
John 6:61;
1 Cor 8:13

QQ. Discourse on humility (18:1–9; Mark 9:33–37; Luke 9:46–48)

18 At that time the disciples came to Jesus, saying, "Who then is greatest in the kingdom of heaven?"

2   And He called a child to Himself and set him before them,

3   and said, "Truly I say to you, unless you are converted and become like children, you shall not enter the kingdom of heaven.

18:3
Matt 19:14;
Mark 10:15;
Luke 18:17;
1 Pet 2:2

4   "Whoever then humbles himself as this child, he is the greatest in the kingdom of heaven.

18:4
Matt 20:27;
23:11

5   "And whoever receives one such child in My name receives Me;

18:5
Matt 10:40;
Luke 18:17

6   but whoever causes one of these little ones who believe in Me to stumble, it is better for him that a heavy millstone be hung around his neck, and that he be drowned in the depth of the sea.

18:6
Luke 17:1,2

7   "Woe to the world because of *its* stumbling blocks! For it is inevitable that stumbling blocks come; but woe to that man through whom the stumbling block comes!

18:7
Luke 17:1;
1 Cor 11:19

8   "And if your hand or your foot causes you to stumble, cut it off and throw it from you; it is better for you to enter life crippled or lame, than having two hands or two feet, to be cast into the eternal fire.

*18:8
Matt 5:29,30;
Mark 9:43,45

9   "And if your eye causes you to stumble, pluck it out, and throw it from you. It is better for you to enter life with one eye, than having two eyes, to be cast into the fiery hell.

*18:9
Matt 5:29;
Mark 9:47;
Matt 17:27

RR. The lost sheep (18:10–14; Luke 15:4–7)

10   "See that you do not despise one of these little ones, for I say to you, that their angels in heaven continually behold the face of My Father who is in heaven.

18:10
Ps 34:7;
Acts 12:11;
Heb 1:14

11   [" [33]For the Son of Man has come to save that which was lost.]

12   "What do you think? If any man has a hundred sheep, and one of them has gone astray, does he not leave the ninety-nine on the mountains and go and search for the one that is straying?

13   "And if it turns out that he finds it, truly I say to you, he rejoices over it more than over the ninety-nine which have not gone astray.

14   "Thus it is not *the* will of your Father who is in heaven that one of these little ones perish.

SS. The treatment of offenders (18:15–35)

1. Church discipline (18:15–20)

15   "And if your brother sins[34], go and reprove him in private; if he listens to you, you have won your brother.

18:15
Lev 19:17;
Luke 17:3;
Gal 6:1;
James 5:19,20

16   "But if he does not listen *to you*, take one or two more with you, so that BY THE MOUTH OF TWO OR THREE WITNESSES EVERY FACT MAY BE CONFIRMED.

18:16
Deut 19:15;
John 8:17;
2 Cor 13:1;
Heb 10:28

17   "And if he refuses to listen to them, tell it to the church; and if he refuses to

*18:17
1 Cor 6:1-6;
2 Thess 3:6,
14

---

[32]Or, *shekel*, worth four drachmas   [33]Most ancient mss. do not contain this verse   [34]Many mss. add here: *against you*

18:8 See note to 5:29 explaining this verse.
18:9 *Fiery hell* or *Gehenna of fire* (spelled Geenna in the Greek) is the Aramaic form of the Hebrew *Gehinnom*, which means the *Valley of Hinnom.* This term is used for the place of the eternal punishment of the wicked dead. Body and soul are cast into *Gehenna*, and unquenchable fire is used as the symbol of this unending torment. In the Old Testament, the Valley of Hinnom (Topheth) was the place where, in the idolatrous reigns of Ahaz and Manasseh, helpless infants were immolated by fire and where the gruesome idol of Molech was worshiped. Josiah later defiled Topheth and converted it into the city dump, where a smoldering fire was continually burning. Thus it became a very fit symbol for hell itself. Indeed, the KJV usually translates the word for Gehenna as "hell." And yet this is confusing, since it translates the Greek *Hades* (Hebrew *Sheol*) as "hell" also. The

NAS translates it here in 18:9, and also in 5:22, as *fiery hell* but renders it simply as *hell* in 5:29,30; 10:28; 23:15,33; Mark 9:43,45,47; Luke 12:5; and James 3:6, but always with a footnote indicating that it is the Greek word *Gehenna.*
18:17 God, who ordained the church, has likewise ordained its government and its order. Order in the church is to be maintained by church discipline, and the effective sanction to enforce discipline is excommunication. Scripture enjoins the churches to maintain sound doctrine (1 Tim. 1:3; Titus 1:13) and to see that order prevails (1 Cor. 11:34; Titus 1:5). Offenders are to be dealt with and rebuked (1 Tim. 5:20; 2 Tim. 4:2). Sincere believers are to submit to discipline (Heb. 13:17), which has for its end decency and order (1 Cor. 14:40) as well as the correction of the offender (2 Cor. 10:8; 13:10). Unrepentant offenders who refuse to accept discipline should be excommunicated

listen even to the church, let him be to you as a Gentile and a tax-gatherer.

18 "Truly I say to you, whatever you shall bind on earth shall be bound in heaven; and whatever you loose on earth shall be loosed in heaven.

19 "Again I say to you, that if two of you agree on earth about anything that they may ask, it shall be done for them by My Father who is in heaven.

20 "For where two or three have gathered together in My name, there I am in their midst."

2. The law of forgiveness (18:21–35)

21 Then Peter came and said to Him, "Lord, how often shall my brother sin against me and I forgive him? Up to seven times?"

22 Jesus *said to him, "I do not say to you, up to seven times, but up to seventy times seven.

23 "For this reason the kingdom of heaven may be compared to a certain king who wished to settle accounts with his slaves.

24 "And when he had begun to settle *them,* there was brought to him one who owed him [35]ten thousand talents.

25 "But since he did not have *the means* to repay, his lord commanded him to be sold, along with his wife and children and all that he had, and repayment to be made.

26 "The slave therefore falling down, prostrated himself before him, saying, 'Have patience with me, and I will repay you everything.'

27 "And the lord of that slave felt compassion and released him and forgave him the debt.

28 "But that slave went out and found one of his fellow slaves who owed him a hundred [36]denarii; and he seized him and *began* to choke *him,* saying, 'Pay back what you owe.'

29 "So his fellow slave fell down and *began* to entreat him, saying, 'Have patience with me and I will repay you.'

30 "He was unwilling however, but went and threw him in prison until he should pay back what was owed.

31 "So when his fellow slaves saw what had happened, they were deeply grieved and came and reported to their lord all that had happened.

32 "Then summoning him, his lord *said to him, 'You wicked slave, I forgave you all that debt because you entreated me.

33 'Should you not also have had mercy on your fellow slave, even as I had mercy on you?'

34 "And his lord, moved with anger, handed him over to the torturers until he should repay all that was owed him.

35 "So shall My heavenly Father also do to you, if each of you does not forgive his brother from your heart."

IV. From Galilee to Jerusalem (19:1–20:34)

A. Jesus goes to Judea (19:1,2)

19 And it came about that when Jesus had finished these words, He departed from Galilee, and came into the region of Judea beyond the Jordan;

2 and great multitudes followed Him, and He healed them there.

B. Jesus' teaching on marriage (19:3–12; Mark 10:2–12)

3 And *some* Pharisees came to Him, testing Him, and saying, "Is it lawful *for a man* to divorce his wife for any cause at all?"

---

[35]About $10,000,000 in silver content but worth much more in buying power   [36]The denarius was equivalent to one day's wage

---

18:18 Matt 16:19; John 20:23
18:19 Matt 5:24; 1 John 5:14

18:21 Gen 4:24; Luke 17:4
18:22 Matt 6:14; Mark 11:25; Col 3:13
***18:23** Matt 25:19

18:25 Luke 7:42; 2 Kin 4:1; Neh 5:5,8

18:26 Matt 8:2

18:35 Matt 6:14; Mark 11:26; James 2:13

19:1 Mark 10:1; John 10:40
19:2 Matt 4:23

***19:3** Matt 5:31

---

from the fellowship (1 Cor. 5:3–5,13), not simply as a penalty, but to bring them to repentance.
18:23 This parable teaches us the absolute necessity of forgiveness. The unmerciful servant, having been forgiven a debt of unheard-of proportions (for 10,000 talents exceeded the wealth of Croesus himself), refused to forgive a fellow servant for an obligation only one twenty-thousandth of one percent as great as his own. Since we have been forgiven the heaviest of all debts, it is incumbent on us to forgive others whose debt to us is nothing compared to that for which we have been forgiven.
19:3 Jesus' teachings on divorce are found in 5:31,32; 19:3–9; Mark 10:2–12; Luke 16:18. In 1 Cor. 7:10,11 Paul attributes his teaching on divorce to the Lord, by which he means he is reporting the teaching of Jesus. In all these passages divorce is forbidden; in 5:32 and 19:9 a single exception is made, and a man is allowed to divorce his wife in the case of infidelity. (See note to Deut. 24:1 on divorce.)

19:4
Gen 1:27; 5:2

19:5
Gen 2:24;
1 Cor 6:16;
Eph 5:31

19:7
Deut 24:1-4;
Matt 5:31

19:9
Mark 5:32;
Luke 16:18;
1 Cor 7:10-13

19:11
1 Cor 7:7-9

4   And He answered and said, "Have you not read, that He who created *them* from the beginning MADE THEM MALE AND FEMALE,

5   and said, 'FOR THIS CAUSE A MAN SHALL LEAVE HIS FATHER AND MOTHER, AND SHALL CLEAVE TO HIS WIFE; AND THE TWO SHALL BECOME ONE FLESH'?

6   "Consequently they are no longer two, but one flesh. What therefore God has joined together, let no man separate."

7   They *said to Him, "Why then did Moses command to GIVE HER A CERTIFICATE OF DIVORCE AND SEND *her* AWAY?"

8   He *said to them, "Because of your hardness of heart, Moses permitted you to divorce your wives; but from the beginning it has not been this way.

9   "And I say to you, whoever divorces his wife, except for immorality, and marries another woman commits adultery."

10   The disciples *said to Him, "If the relationship of the man with his wife is like this, it is better not to marry."

11   But He said to them, "Not all men *can* accept this statement, but *only* those to whom it has been given.

12   "For there are eunuchs who were born that way from their mother's womb; and there are eunuchs who were made eunuchs by men; and there are *also* eunuchs who made themselves eunuchs for the sake of the kingdom of heaven. He who is able to accept *this*, let him accept *it*."

C. *Jesus blesses little children*
(19:13–15; Mark 10:13–16; Luke 18:15–17)

13   Then *some* children were brought to Him so that He might lay His hands on them and pray; and the disciples rebuked them.

19:14
Matt 18:3;
1 Cor 14:20;
1 Pet 2:2

14   But Jesus said, "Let the children alone, and do not hinder them from coming to Me; for the kingdom of heaven belongs to such as these."

15   And after laying His hands on them, He departed from there.

D. *The rich young ruler*
(19:16–30; Mark 10:17–31; Luke 18:18–30)

19:16
Lev 18:5;
Luke 10:25

16   And behold, one came to Him and said, "Teacher, what good thing shall I do that I may obtain eternal life?"

17   And He said to him, "Why are you asking Me about what is good? There is *only* One who is good; but if you wish to enter into life, keep the commandments."

19:18
Ex 20:13;
Deut 5:17;
Rom 13:9;
James 2:11
19:19
Lev 19:18;
Matt 22:39;
Rom 13:9;
Gal 5:14

18   He *said to Him, "Which ones?" And Jesus said, "YOU SHALL NOT COMMIT MURDER; YOU SHALL NOT COMMIT ADULTERY; YOU SHALL NOT STEAL; YOU SHALL NOT BEAR FALSE WITNESS;

19   HONOR YOUR FATHER AND MOTHER; and YOU SHALL LOVE YOUR NEIGHBOR AS YOURSELF."

20   The young man *said to Him, "All these things I have kept; what am I still lacking?"

19:21
Matt 6:20;
Luke 12:33;
16:9;
Acts 2:45;
4:34,35

21   Jesus said to him, "If you wish to be complete, go *and* sell your possessions and give to *the* poor, and you shall have treasure in heaven; and come, follow Me."

22   But when the young man heard this statement, he went away grieved; for he was one who owned much property.

19:23
Matt 13:22;
1 Cor 1:26;
1 Tim 6:9,10

23   And Jesus said to His disciples, "Truly I say to you, it is hard for a rich man to enter the kingdom of heaven.

24   "And again I say to you, it is easier for a camel to go through the eye of a needle, than for a rich man to enter the kingdom of God."

25   And when the disciples heard *this*, they were very astonished and said, "Then who can be saved?"

19:26
Gen 18:14;
Job 42:2;
Jer 32:17;
Zech 8:6
19:27
Matt 4:20;
Luke 5:11

26   And looking upon *them* Jesus said to them, "With men this is impossible, but with God all things are possible."

27   Then Peter answered and said to Him, "Behold, we have left everything and followed You; what then will there be for us?"

19:28
Matt 20:21;
Luke 22:28-30;
Rev 3:21

28   And Jesus said to them, "Truly I say to you, that you who have followed Me, in the regeneration when the Son of Man will sit on His glorious throne, you also shall sit upon twelve thrones, judging the twelve tribes of Israel.

29   "And everyone who has left houses or brothers or sisters or father or

mother[37] or children or farms for My name's sake, shall receive many times as much, and shall inherit eternal life.

30 "But many *who are* first will be last; and *the* last, first.

E. *Parable of the householder (20:1–16)*

20 "For the kingdom of heaven is like a landowner who went out early in the morning to hire laborers for his vineyard.

2 "And when he had agreed with the laborers for a [38]denarius for the day, he sent them into his vineyard. 9am

3 "And he went out about the [39]third hour and saw others standing idle in the market place;

4 and to those he said, 'You too go into the vineyard, and whatever is right I will give you.' And *so* they went. noon

5 "Again he went out about the [40]sixth and the ninth hour, and did the same thing. 5pm

6 "And about the [41]eleventh *hour* he went out, and found others standing; and he *said to them, 'Why have you been standing here idle all day long?'

7 "They *said to him, 'Because no one hired us.' He *said to them, 'You too go into the vineyard.'

8 "And when evening had come, the owner of the vineyard *said to his fore-man, 'Call the laborers and pay them their wages, beginning with the last *group* to the first.'

9 "And when those *hired* about the eleventh hour came, each one received a [38]denarius.

10 "And when those *hired* first came, they thought that they would receive more; and they also received each one a [38]denarius.

11 "And when they received it, they grumbled at the landowner,

12 saying, 'These last men have worked *only* one hour, and you have made them equal to us who have borne the burden and the scorching heat of the day.'

13 "But he answered and said to one of them, 'Friend, I am doing you no wrong; did you not agree with me for a [38]denarius?

14 'Take what is yours and go your way, but I wish to give to this last man the same as to you.

15 'Is it not lawful for me to do what I wish with what is my own? Or is your eye envious because I am generous?' See Eph 2:8 re grace + faith

16 "Thus the last shall be first, and the first last."

F. *Christ foretells His crucifixion and resurrection (20:17–19; Mark 10:32–34; Luke 18:31–34)*

17 And as Jesus was about to go up to Jerusalem, He took the twelve *disciples* aside by themselves, and on the way He said to them,

18 "Behold, we are going up to Jerusalem; and the Son of Man will be delivered to the chief priests and scribes, and they will condemn Him to death,

19 and will deliver Him to the Gentiles to mock and scourge and crucify *Him*, and on the third day He will be raised up."

G. *Ambition of James and John (20:20–28; Mark 10:35–45)*

20 Then the mother of the sons of Zebedee came to Him with her sons, bowing down, and making a request of Him.

21 And He said to her, "What do you wish?" She *said to Him, "Command that in Your kingdom these two sons of mine may sit, one on Your right and one on Your left."

22 But Jesus answered and said, "You do not know what you are asking for.

[Reference column:]

19:30
Matt 20:16;
Luke 13:30

*20:1
Matt 13:24;
21:28,33

20:8
Lev 19:3;
Deut 24:15

20:12
Jon 4:8;
Luke 12:55;
James 1:11
20:13
Matt 22:12;
26:50

20:15
Deut 15:9;
Matt 6:23;
Mark 7:22
20:16
Matt 19:30

20:18
Matt 16:21

20:19
Matt 16:21;
27:2;
Acts 2:23;
3:13

20:20
Matt 4:21;
8:2; 9:18;
John 9:38
20:21
Matt 19:28

20:22
Matt 26:39,
42;
Luke 22:42;
John 18:11

---

[37]Many mss. add here, *or wife* [38]The denarius was equivalent to one day's wage [39]I.e., 9 a.m. [40]I.e., Noon and 3 p.m. [41]I.e., 5 p.m.

20:1 The major teaching of this parable is that God bestows His grace of salvation (represented by the denarius) upon all those who respond to His call regardless of human merit. Length of years in the service of the Lord does not insure to the convert any more blessed a heaven than to the sinner who turns to God in faith at the eleventh hour. The principle in operation here is grace only, and merit has nothing to do with it.
20:3 The working day began at 6:00 A.M., at which time the householder went to the marketplace to hire workers for the day (v. 1); he returned at 9:00 A.M. (v. 3), 12:00 noon, 3:00 P.M. (v. 5), and at 5:00 P.M. (v. 6) when only one hour of the day was left.

Are you able to drink the cup that I am about to drink?" They *said to Him, "We are able."

23   He *said to them, "My cup you shall drink; but to sit on My right and on *My* left, this is not Mine to give, but it is for those for whom it has been prepared by My Father."

20:24
Luke 22:24,
25
*20:25
Luke 22:25-27
20:26
Matt 23:11;
Mark 9:35;
Luke 9:48
20:28
John 13:4;
Phil 2:7;
John 13:14;
Is 53:10;
1 Tim 2:6;
Titus 2:14;
1 Pet 1:19;
Matt 26:28;
Heb 9:28
20:30
Matt 9:27

24   And hearing *this*, the ten became indignant with the two brothers.

25   But Jesus called them to Himself, and said, "You know that the rulers of the Gentiles lord it over them, and *their* great men exercise authority over them.

26   "It is not so among you, but whoever wishes to become great among you shall be your servant,

27   and whoever wishes to be first among you shall be your slave;

28   just as the Son of Man did not come to be served, but to serve, and to give His life a ransom for many."

H. *Healing two blind men near Jericho* (20:29–34; Mark 10:46–52; Luke 18:35–43)

29   And as they were going out from Jericho, a great multitude followed Him.

30   And behold, two blind men sitting by the road, hearing that Jesus was passing by, cried out, saying, "Lord, have mercy on us, Son of David!"

31   And the multitude sternly told them to be quiet; but they cried out all the more, saying, "Lord, have mercy on us, Son of David!"

32   And Jesus stopped and called them, and said, "What do you want Me to do for you?"

33   They *said to Him, "Lord, *we want* our eyes to be opened."

34   And moved with compassion, Jesus touched their eyes; and immediately they regained their sight and followed Him.

V. *The last week in Jerusalem* (21:1–28:15)

A. *The triumphal entry* (21:1–11; Mark 11:1–11; Luke 19:29–44; John 12:12–19)

21   And when they had approached Jerusalem and had come to Bethphage, to the Mount of Olives, then Jesus sent two disciples,

2   saying to them, "Go into the village opposite you, and immediately you will find a donkey tied *there* and a colt with her; untie *them*, and bring *them* to Me.

3   "And if anyone says something to you, you shall say, 'The Lord has need of them,' and immediately he will send them."

4   Now this took place that what was spoken through the prophet might be fulfilled, saying,

5   "SAY TO THE DAUGHTER OF ZION,
    'BEHOLD YOUR KING IS COMING TO YOU,
    GENTLE, AND MOUNTED ON A DONKEY,
    EVEN ON A COLT, THE FOAL OF A BEAST OF BURDEN.' "

6   And the disciples went and did just as Jesus had directed them,

7   and brought the donkey and the colt, and laid on them their garments, on which He sat.

8   And most of the multitude spread their garments in the road, and others were cutting branches from the trees, and spreading them in the road.

9   And the multitudes going before Him, and those who followed after were crying out, saying,
    "Hosanna to the Son of David;
    BLESSED IS HE WHO COMES IN THE NAME OF THE LORD;
    Hosanna in the highest!"

10   And when He had entered Jerusalem, all the city was stirred, saying, "Who is this?"

20:25 Christ draws a contrast here between the ambition of the natural, once-born man, who covets power and glory for himself, and the ambition of the redeemed, twice-born man, who lives not for self *but for Him who died and rose again on their behalf* (2 Cor. 5:15). The Christ-centered believer is ambitious only for the performance of God's holy will and the display of His self-sacrificing love. Just as his Savior came to serve rather than to be served (v. 28), so the

true Christian lives to bless and serve others rather than himself. Spiritual stature (*whoever wishes to become great among you*, v. 26) will be measured by God according to how close a resemblance the believer bears to the Christ of the cross.

21:9 *Hosanna*, meaning "save we pray thee," occurs six times in the gospels.

11   And the multitudes were saying, "This is the prophet Jesus, from Nazareth in Galilee."

B. Second cleansing of the temple
(21:12–17; Mark 11:15–19; Luke 19:45–48; cf. John 2:13–22)

12   And Jesus entered the temple and cast out all those who were buying and selling in the temple, and overturned the tables of the moneychangers and the seats of those who were selling doves.

13   And He *said to them, "It is written, 'MY HOUSE SHALL BE CALLED A HOUSE OF PRAYER'; but you are making it a ROBBERS' DEN.'"

14   And the blind and the lame came to Him in the temple, and He healed them.

15   But when the chief priests and the scribes saw the wonderful things that He had done, and the children who were crying out in the temple and saying, "Hosanna to the Son of David," they became indignant,

16   and said to Him, "Do You hear what these are saying?" And Jesus *said to them, "Yes; have you never read, 'OUT OF THE MOUTH OF INFANTS AND NURSING BABES THOU HAST PREPARED PRAISE FOR THYSELF'?"

17   And He left them and went out of the city to Bethany, and lodged there.

C. The barren fig tree (21:18–22; Mark 11:12–14,20–25)

18   Now in the morning, when He returned to the city, He became hungry.

19   And seeing a lone fig tree by the road, He came to it, and found nothing on it except leaves only; and He *said to it, "No longer shall there ever be any fruit from you." And at once the fig tree withered.

20   And seeing this, the disciples marveled, saying, "How did the fig tree wither at once?"

21   And Jesus answered and said to them, "Truly I say to you, if you have faith, and do not doubt, you shall not only do what was done to the fig tree, but even if you say to this mountain, 'Be taken up and cast into the sea,' it shall happen.

22   "And all things you ask in prayer, believing, you shall receive."

D. Christ's authority challenged
(21:23–27; Mark 11:27–33; Luke 20:1–8)

23   And when He had come into the temple, the chief priests and the elders of the people came to Him as He was teaching, and said, "By what authority are You doing these things, and who gave You this authority?"

24   And Jesus answered and said to them, "I will ask you one thing too, which if you tell Me, I will also tell you by what authority I do these things.

25   "The baptism of John was from what source, from heaven or from men?" And they began reasoning among themselves, saying, "If we say, 'From heaven,' He will say to us, 'Then why did you not believe him?'

26   "But if we say, 'From men,' we fear the multitude; for they all hold John to be a prophet."

27   And answering Jesus, they said, "We do not know." He also said to them, "Neither will I tell you by what authority I do these things.

E. Parable of the two sons (21:28–32)

28   "But what do you think? A man had two sons, and he came to the first and said, 'Son, go work today in the vineyard.'

29   "And he answered and said, 'I will, sir'; and he did not go.

30   "And he came to the second and said the same thing. But he answered and said, 'I will not'; yet he afterward regretted it and went.

31   "Which of the two did the will of his father?" They *said, "The latter." Jesus *said to them, "Truly I say to you that the tax-gatherers and harlots will get into the kingdom of God before you.

32   "For John came to you in the way of righteousness and you did not believe him; but the tax-gatherers and harlots did believe him; and you, seeing this, did not even feel remorse afterward so as to believe him.

21:22 See note to Luke 11:1 on the principles of prayer and faith.

F. Parable of the wicked tenants
(21:33–46; Mark 12:1–12; Luke 20:9–19)

33 "Listen to another parable. There was a landowner who PLANTED A VINEYARD AND PUT A WALL AROUND IT AND DUG A WINE PRESS IN IT, AND BUILT A TOWER, and rented it out to vine-growers, and went on a journey.

34 "And when the harvest time approached, he sent his slaves to the vine-growers to receive his produce.

35 "And the vine-growers took his slaves and beat one, and killed another, and stoned a third.

36 "Again he sent another group of slaves larger than the first; and they did the same thing to them.

37 "But afterward he sent his son to them, saying, 'They will respect my son.'

38 "But when the vine-growers saw the son, they said among themselves, 'This is the heir; come, let us kill him, and seize his inheritance.'

39 "And they took him, and threw him out of the vineyard, and killed him.

40 "Therefore when the owner of the vineyard comes, what will he do to those vine-growers?"

41 They *said to Him, "He will bring those wretches to a wretched end, and will rent out the vineyard to other vine-growers, who will pay him the proceeds at the *proper* seasons."

42 Jesus *said to them, "Did you never read in the Scriptures,

'THE STONE WHICH THE BUILDERS REJECTED,
THIS BECAME THE CHIEF CORNER *stone;*
THIS CAME ABOUT FROM THE LORD,
AND IT IS MARVELOUS IN OUR EYES'?

43 "Therefore I say to you, the kingdom of God will be taken away from you, and be given to a nation producing the fruit of it.

44 "And he who falls on this stone will be broken to pieces; but on whomever it falls, it will scatter him like dust."

45 And when the chief priests and the Pharisees heard His parables, they understood that He was speaking about them.

46 And when they sought to seize Him, they feared the multitudes, because they held Him to be a prophet.

G. Parable of the marriage feast (22:1–14; Luke 14:15–24)

22 And Jesus answered and spoke to them again in parables, saying,
2 "The kingdom of heaven may be compared to a king, who gave a wedding feast for his son.

3 "And he sent out his slaves to call those who had been invited to the wedding feast, and they were unwilling to come.

4 "Again he sent out other slaves saying, 'Tell those who have been invited, "Behold, I have prepared my dinner; my oxen and my fattened livestock are *all* butchered and everything is ready; come to the wedding feast."'

5 "But they paid no attention and went their way, one to his own farm, another to his business,

6 and the rest seized his slaves and mistreated them and killed them.

7 "But the king was enraged and sent his armies, and destroyed those murderers, and set their city on fire.

8 "Then he *said to his slaves, 'The wedding is ready, but those who were invited were not worthy.

9 'Go therefore to the main highways, and as many as you find *there*, invite to the wedding feast.'

10 "And those slaves went out into the streets, and gathered together all they found, both evil and good; and the wedding hall was filled with dinner guests.

11 "But when the king came in to look over the dinner guests, he saw there a man not dressed in wedding clothes,

12 and he *said to him, 'Friend, how did you come in here without wedding clothes?' And he was speechless.

13 "Then the king said to the servants, 'Bind him hand and foot, and cast him

---

into the outer darkness; in that place there shall be weeping and gnashing of teeth.'

14 "For many are called, but few *are* chosen."

H. *Three questions by the Jewish rulers (22:15–40)*

1. *Taxes to Caesar (22:15–22; Mark 12:13–17; Luke 20:19–26)*

15 Then the Pharisees went and counseled together how they might trap Him in what He said.

16 And they *sent their disciples to Him, along with the Herodians, saying, "Teacher, we know that You are truthful and teach the way of God in truth, and defer to no one; for You are not partial to any.

17 "Tell us therefore, what do You think? Is it lawful to give a poll-tax to Caesar, or not?"

18 But Jesus perceived their malice, and said, "Why are you testing Me, you hypocrites?

19 "Show Me the coin *used* for the poll-tax." And they brought Him a denarius.

20 And He *said to them, "Whose likeness and inscription is this?"

21 They *said to Him, "Caesar's." Then He *said to them, "Then render to Caesar the things that are Caesar's; and to God the things that are God's."

22 And hearing *this*, they marveled, and leaving Him, they went away.

2. *The Sadducees and the resurrection*
 (22:23–33; Mark 12:18–27; Luke 20:27–38)

23 On that day *some* Sadducees (who say there is no resurrection) came to Him and questioned Him,

24 saying, "Teacher, Moses said, 'IF A MAN DIES, HAVING NO CHILDREN, HIS BROTHER AS NEXT OF KIN SHALL MARRY HIS WIFE, AND RAISE UP AN OFFSPRING TO HIS BROTHER.'

25 "Now there were seven brothers with us; and the first married and died, and having no offspring left his wife to his brother;

26 so also the second, and the third, down to the seventh.

27 "And last of all, the woman died.

28 "In the resurrection therefore whose wife of the seven shall she be? For they all had her."

29 But Jesus answered and said to them, "You are mistaken, not understanding the Scriptures, or the power of God.

30 "For in the resurrection they neither marry, nor are given in marriage, but are like angels in heaven.

31 "But regarding the resurrection of the dead, have you not read that which was spoken to you by God, saying,

32 'I AM THE GOD OF ABRAHAM, AND THE GOD OF ISAAC, AND THE GOD OF JACOB'? He is not the God of the dead but of the living."

33 And when the multitudes heard *this*, they were astonished at His teaching.

3. *The great commandment*
 (22:34–40; Mark 12:28–34)

34 But when the Pharisees heard that He had put the Sadducees to silence, they gathered themselves together.

35 And one of them, [42]a lawyer, asked Him *a question*, testing Him,

36 "Teacher, which is the great commandment in the Law?"

37 And He said to him, " 'YOU SHALL LOVE THE LORD YOUR GOD WITH ALL YOUR HEART, AND WITH ALL YOUR SOUL, AND WITH ALL YOUR MIND.'

38 "This is the great and foremost commandment.

39 "The second is like it, 'YOU SHALL LOVE YOUR NEIGHBOR AS YOURSELF.'

40 "On these two commandments depend the whole Law and the Prophets."

[42]I.e., an expert in the Mosaic law

Marginal references:

22:13 Matt 8:12; Luke 13:28

*22:16 Mark 3:6; 8:15

22:17 Matt 17:25

22:21 Rom 13:7

22:23 Acts 23:8

22:24 Deut 25:5

22:29 John 20:9

22:32 Ex 3:6,16; Acts 7:32; Heb 11:16

22:33 Matt 7:28

22:35 Luke 7:30; 10:25; 11:45; 14:3

22:37 Deut 6:5

22:39 Lev 19:18; Matt 19:19; Rom 13:9; Gal 5:14; James 2:8

22:40 Matt 7:12

22:16 The Herodians are mentioned three times in the New Testament (here and in Mark 3:6; 12:13). Apparently they constituted a political party and were followers of the dynasty of Herod. Archelaus, the son of Herod, became ethnarch of Judea but was deposed (ca. A.D. 6 or 7) and replaced by Roman procurators. The Herodians seem to have favored the return of the old dynasty over Judea. They allied themselves with the Pharisees against Jesus because both of these parties recognized in Christ their greatest opponent. Their differences were subordinated to a temporary alliance until they had disposed of Christ.

22:25 See note to Deut. 25:5–10.

I. Christ's unanswerable question
(22:41–46; Mark 12:35–37; Luke 20:41–44)

41 Now while the Pharisees were gathered together, Jesus asked them a question,

22:42
Matt 9:27

42 saying, "What do you think about the Christ, whose son is He?" They *said to Him, *"The son of David."*

43 He *said to them, "Then how does David in the Spirit call Him 'Lord,' saying,

*22:44
Ps 110:1;
Acts 2:34;
Heb 1:13;
10:13

44 'THE LORD SAID TO MY LORD,
  "SIT AT MY RIGHT HAND,
  UNTIL I PUT THINE ENEMIES BENEATH THY FEET" '?

45 "If David then calls Him 'Lord,' how is He his son?"

22:46
Mark 12:34;
Luke 20:40

46 And no one was able to answer Him a word, nor did anyone dare from that day on to ask Him another question.

J. The warning against Pharisaism
(23:1–12; Mark 12:38–40; Luke 20:45–47)

23 Then Jesus spoke to the multitudes and to His disciples,

*23:2
Ezra 7:6,25;
Neh 8:4

2 saying, "The scribes and the Pharisees have seated themselves in the chair of Moses;

3 therefore all that they tell you, do and observe; but do not do according to their deeds; for they say *things,* and do not do *them.*

23:4
Luke 11:46;
Acts 15:10;
Gal 6:13
*23:5
Matt 6:1,2,5,
16; Deut 6:8
23:6
Luke 11:43;
14:7; 20:46

4 "And they tie up heavy loads, and lay them on men's shoulders; but they themselves are unwilling to move them with *so much as* a finger.

5 "But they do all their deeds to be noticed by men; for they broaden their [43]phylacteries, and lengthen the tassels *of their garments.*

6 "And they love the place of honor at banquets, and the chief seats in the synagogues,

7 and respectful greetings in the market places, and being called by men, Rabbi.

23:8
James 3:1

8 "But do not be called Rabbi; for One is your Teacher, and you are all brothers.

23:9
Mal 1:6

9 "And do not call *anyone* on earth your father; for One is your Father, He who is in heaven.

10 "And do not be called leaders; for One is your Leader, *that is,* Christ.

23:11
Matt 20:26
23:12
Luke 14:11;
18:14;
James 4:6;
1 Pet 5:5

11 "But the greatest among you shall be your servant.

12 "And whoever exalts himself shall be humbled; and whoever humbles himself shall be exalted.

K. The woes upon the Pharisees (23:13–36)

23:13
Luke 11:52

13 "But woe to you, scribes and Pharisees, hypocrites, because you shut off the kingdom of heaven from men; for you do not enter in yourselves, nor do you allow those who are entering to go in.

14 ["[44]Woe to you, scribes and Pharisees, hypocrites, because you devour widows' houses, even while for a pretense you make long prayers; therefore you shall receive greater condemnation.]

15 "Woe to you, scribes and Pharisees, hypocrites, because you travel about on sea and land to make one proselyte; and when he becomes one, you make him twice as much a son of hell as yourselves.

*23:16
v. 24;
Matt 15:14;
5:33-35

16 "Woe to you, blind guides, who say, 'Whoever swears by the temple, that is nothing; but whoever swears by the gold of the temple, he is obligated.'

[43]I.e., small boxes containing Scripture texts worn for religious purposes   [44]This verse not found in the earliest mss.

22:44 The first use of *Lord* in this verse means God; the second *Lord* means Messiah.
23:2 See note to 3:7a on Pharisees.
23:5 *Phylacteries* (sometimes called frontlets) were small leather cases containing strips of vellum on which were written the words from Ex. 13:1–10,11–16; Deut. 6:4–9; 11:13–21. Two such cases (called *tephillim,* "prayers") were worn, one on the forehead and one on the arm, in literal obedience to the injunctions of Ex. 13:16; Deut. 6:8; 11:18.
The *tassels* were four in number, one at each corner of the cloak, worn by men as a sign of religious devotion in

accordance with Num. 15:38–41. To *broaden their phylacteries, and lengthen the tassels of their garments* was to parade their piety before people.
23:16 Jesus condemns the scribes and Pharisees because they have made unbiblical distinctions by which they have permitted men to violate their oaths. He who takes an oath by the temple is exempt from keeping his oath, but if the oath is taken by the gold of the temple, he is bound to keep it. Jesus teaches that the temple (or altar) sanctifies the gold, and a vow made there, i.e., swearing *by Him who dwells within it* (v. 21) is equally binding, despite the casuistry. So

17 "You fools and blind men; which is more important, the gold, or the temple that sanctified the gold?

18 "And, 'Whoever swears by the altar, *that* is nothing, but whoever swears by the offering upon it, he is obligated.'

19 "You blind men, which is more important, the offering or the altar that sanctifies the offering?

20 "Therefore he who swears, swears *both* by the altar and by everything on it.

21 "And he who swears by the temple, swears *both* by the temple and by Him who dwells within it.

22 "And he who swears by heaven, swears *both* by the throne of God and by Him who sits upon it.

23 "Woe to you, scribes and Pharisees, hypocrites! For you tithe mint and dill and cummin, and have neglected the weightier provisions of the law: justice and mercy and faithfulness; but these are the things you should have done without neglecting the others.

24 "You blind guides, who strain out a gnat and swallow a camel!

25 "Woe to you, scribes and Pharisees, hypocrites! For you clean the outside of the cup and of the dish, but inside they are full of robbery and self-indulgence.

26 "You blind Pharisee, first clean the inside of the cup and of the dish, so that the outside of it may become clean also.

27 "Woe to you, scribes and Pharisees, hypocrites! For you are like whitewashed tombs which on the outside appear beautiful, but inside they are full of dead men's bones and all uncleanness.

28 "Even so you too outwardly appear righteous to men, but inwardly you are full of hypocrisy and lawlessness.

29 "Woe to you, scribes and Pharisees, hypocrites! For you build the tombs of the prophets and adorn the monuments of the righteous,

30 and say, 'If we had been *living* in the days of our fathers, we would not have been partners with them in *shedding* the blood of the prophets.'

31 "Consequently you bear witness against yourselves, that you are sons of those who murdered the prophets.

32 "Fill up then the measure *of the guilt* of your fathers.

33 "You serpents, you brood of vipers, how shall you escape the sentence of hell?

34 "Therefore, behold, I am sending you prophets and wise men and scribes; some of them you will kill and crucify, and some of them you will scourge in your synagogues, and persecute from city to city,

35 that upon you may fall *the guilt of* all the righteous blood shed on earth, from the blood of righteous Abel to the blood of Zechariah, the son of Berechiah, whom you murdered between the temple and the altar.

36 "Truly I say to you, all these things shall come upon this generation.

L. *The lament over Jerusalem (23:37–39; Luke 13:34–35)*

37 "O Jerusalem, Jerusalem, who kills the prophets and stones those who are sent to her! How often I wanted to gather your children together, the way a hen gathers her chicks under her wings, and you were unwilling.

38 "Behold, your house is being left to you desolate!

39 "For I say to you, from now on you shall not see Me until you say, 'BLESSED IS HE WHO COMES IN THE NAME OF THE LORD!' "

M. *The Olivet Discourse (24:1–25:46; Mark 13; Luke 21)*

1. *The course of this age (24:1–14; Mark 13:3–13; Luke 21:5–19)*

24 And Jesus came out from the temple and was going away when His disciples came up to point out the temple buildings to Him.

2 And He answered and said to them, "Do you not see all these things? Truly

---

Cross references (right margin):

23:17 Ex 30:29
23:19 Ex 29:37
23:22 Ps 11:4; Matt 5:34
23:23 Matt 11:42; Lev 27:30; Mic 6:8
23:24 v. 16
23:25 Mark 7:4; Luke 11:39
23:27 Luke 11:44; Acts 23:3
23:29 Luke 11:47, 48
23:31 Acts 7:51,52
23:32 1 Thess 2:16
23:33 Matt 3:7; 5:22
23:34 Luke 11:49; 2 Chr 36:15, 16
*23:35 Gen 4:8; Heb 11:4; Zech 1:1; 2 Chr 24:21
23:36 Matt 10:23; 24:34
23:37 2 Chr 24:21
23:39 Ps 118:26; Matt 21:9
24:1 Mark 13:1
*24:2 Matt 26:61; 27:39,40; Luke 19:44; John 2:19

---

also in Mark 7:11 Jesus says that no man has a right to break a commandment on the ground that to keep it is to violate an oath, for wicked men would then use rash oaths to nullify the commandments of the Lord.
23:35 *Zechariah* is the Old Testament prophet whose book bears his name. 2 Chronicles 24:20ff. relates the murder of a Zechariah (son of Jehoiada the priest). It may be that this Zechariah is meant. Since 2 Chronicles is last in the Hebrew Bible (Luke does not link Zechariah to anyone), the saying *from the blood of Abel to the blood of Zechariah* in Luke 11:51 could mean "from the first to the last murder in the Bible."
24:2 The principle of predictive prophecy is exemplified throughout the Scriptures. In the New Testament many prophecies are given concerning the future, some of which have already been fulfilled in subsequent history, and others that await future fulfillment. The Olivet Discourse (chs.

I say to you, not one stone here shall be left upon another, which will not be torn down."

3   And as He was sitting on the Mount of Olives, the disciples came to Him privately, saying, "Tell us, when will these things be, and what *will be* the sign of Your coming, and of the end of the age?"

4   And Jesus answered and said to them, "See to it that no one misleads you.

5   "For many will come in My name, saying, 'I am the Christ,' and will mislead many.

6   "And you will be hearing of wars and rumors of wars; see that you are not frightened, for *those things* must take place, but *that* is not yet the end.

7   "For nation will rise against nation, and kingdom against kingdom, and in various places there will be famines and earthquakes.

8   "But all these things are *merely* the beginning of birth pangs.

9   "Then they will deliver you to tribulation, and will kill you, and you will be hated by all nations on account of My name.

10   "And at that time many will fall away and will deliver up one another and hate one another.

11   "And many false prophets will arise, and will mislead many.

12   "And because lawlessness is increased, most people's love will grow cold.

13   "But the one who endures to the end, he shall be saved.

14   "And this gospel of the kingdom shall be preached in the whole world for a witness to all the nations, and then the end shall come.

2. The great tribulation (24:15–28; Mark 13:14–23; Luke 21:20–24)

15   "Therefore when you see the ABOMINATION OF DESOLATION which was spoken of through Daniel the prophet, standing in the holy place (**let the reader understand**),

16   then let those who are in Judea flee to the mountains;

17   let him who is on the housetop not go down to get the things out that are in his house;

18   and let him who is in the field not turn back to get his cloak.

19   "But woe to those who are with child and to those who nurse babes in those days!

20   "But pray that your flight may not be in the winter, or on a Sabbath;

21   for then there will be a great tribulation, such as has not occurred since the beginning of the world until now, nor ever shall.

22   "And unless those days had been cut short, no life would have been saved; but for the sake of the elect those days shall be cut short.

23   "Then if anyone says to you, 'Behold, here is the Christ,' or 'There *He is*,' do not believe *him*.

24   "For false Christs and false prophets will arise and will show great signs and wonders, so as to mislead, if possible, even the elect.

25   "Behold, I have told you in advance.

26   "If therefore they say to you, 'Behold, He is in the wilderness,' do not go forth, *or*, 'Behold, He is in the inner rooms,' do not believe *them*.

27   "For just as the lightning comes from the east, and flashes even to the west, so shall the coming of the Son of Man be.

28   "Wherever the corpse is, there the vultures will gather.

3. The coming of the Son of Man
(24:29–31; Mark 13:24–27; Luke 21:25–28)

29   "But immediately after the tribulation of those days THE SUN WILL BE DARKENED, AND THE MOON WILL NOT GIVE ITS LIGHT, AND THE STARS WILL FALL from the sky, and the powers of the heavens will be shaken,

30   and then the sign of the Son of Man will appear in the sky, and then all the tribes of the earth will mourn, and they will see the SON OF MAN COMING ON THE CLOUDS OF THE SKY with power and great glory.

Cross references (left margin):

24:4 Jer 29:8; 2 Thess 2:3
24:5 vv. 11,23,24; 1 John 2:18
24:7 Is 19:2; Hag 2:22; Zech 14:13
24:9 Matt 10:17, 22; John 15:18; 16:2
24:10 Matt 11:6
24:11 Matt 7:15; Acts 20:29; 1 Tim 4:1
24:13 Matt 10:22; Rev 2:7
*24:14 Rom 10:18; Col 1:6,23
24:15 Dan 9:27; 11:31; 12:11; Acts 21:28; 1 Cor 15:52; 1 Thess 4:16
24:21 Dan 12:1; Joel 2:2
24:22 Is 65:8,9
24:23 Luke 17:23; 21:8
24:24 2 Thess 2:9-11; Rev 13:13
24:27 Luke 17:24
24:29 Is 13:10; Ezek 32:7; Joel 2:10; Rev 8:12
24:30 Dan 7:13; Matt 16:27; Rev 1:7

23–25) and Revelation contain much prophecy that is yet to come to pass.
24:3 In the Olivet Discourse the disciples of Jesus asked two major questions: (1) *When will these things be?* i.e., the destruction of the buildings of the temple; and (2) *What will be the sign of Your coming* parousia, *and of the* full *end of the*

age? All that Jesus had to say to these questions is not recorded in the Gospel of Matthew alone.
24:14 Prior to the end of the age, the gospel must be preached to all nations for a witness. Since the end has not come, we know that this obligation has not yet been completely fulfilled.

31 "And He will send forth His angels with A GREAT TRUMPET and THEY WILL GATHER TOGETHER His elect from the four winds, from one end of the sky to the other.

4. The parable of the fig tree
(24:32–35; Mark 13:28–31; Luke 21:29–33)

32 "Now learn the parable from the fig tree: when its branch has already become tender, and puts forth its leaves, you know that summer is near;

33 even so you too, when you see all these things, recognize that He is near, *right* at the door.

34 "Truly I say to you, this generation will not pass away until all these things take place.

35 "Heaven and earth will pass away, but My words shall not pass away.

5. Watchfulness (24:36–44; Mark 13:32–37; Luke 21:34–36)

36 "But of that day and hour no one knows, not even the angels of heaven, nor the Son, but the Father alone.

37 "For the coming of the Son of Man will be just like the days of Noah.

38 "For as in those days which were before the flood they were eating and drinking, they were marrying and giving in marriage, until the day that Noah entered the ark,

39 and they did not understand until the flood came and took them all away; so shall the coming of the Son of Man be.

40 "Then there shall be two men in the field; one will be taken, and one will be left.

41 "Two women *will be* grinding at the mill; one will be taken, and one will be left.

42 "Therefore be on the alert, for you do not know which day your Lord is coming.

43 "But be sure of this, that if the head of the house had known at what time of the night the thief was coming, he would have been on the alert and would not have allowed his house to be broken into.

44 "For this reason you be ready too; for the Son of Man is coming at an hour when you do not think *He will.*

6. Faithful and unfaithful servants (24:45–51; Luke 12:42–46)

45 "Who then is the faithful and sensible slave whom his master put in charge of his household to give them their food at the proper time?

46 "Blessed is that slave whom his master finds so doing when he comes.

47 "Truly I say to you, that he will put him in charge of all his possessions.

48 "But if that evil slave says in his heart, 'My master is not coming for a long time,'

49 and shall begin to beat his fellow slaves and eat and drink with drunkards;

50 the master of that slave will come on a day when he does not expect *him* and at an hour which he does not know,

51 and shall cut him in pieces and assign him a place with the hypocrites; weeping shall be there and the gnashing of teeth.

7. The parable of the ten virgins (25:1–13)

25 "Then the kingdom of heaven will be comparable to ten virgins, who took their lamps, and went out to meet the bridegroom.

2 "And five of them were foolish, and five were prudent.

3 "For when the foolish took their lamps, they took no oil with them,

4 but the prudent took oil in flasks along with their lamps.

Cross-references (right margin):

24:31 Is 27:13; Zech 9:14

24:33 James 5:9

*24:34 Matt 16:28; 23:36

24:35 Matt 5:18

24:37 Gen 6:5; 7:6–23; Luke 17:26, 27

24:40 Luke 17:34, 35

24:42 Matt 25:13; Luke 12:40

24:43 1 Thess 5:2; 2 Pet 3:10; Rev 3:3; 16:15

24:44 1 Thess 5:6

24:45 Matt 25:21,23

24:46 Rev 16:15

24:49 Luke 21:34

24:51 Matt 8:12; 13:42,50; 25:30

*25:1 Matt 13:24; Luke 12:35–38; Rev 19:7; 21:2,9

25:2 Matt 7:24; 10:16; 24:45

24:34 A *generation* in the Old Testament was usually thought of as forty years. The problem here is whether Jesus was referring to the generation of men who were alive at that time or to the generation of men who would be alive at the time of the second advent. In the former case it would mean that He prophesied His second advent as taking place within no more than forty years after His death and resurrection. Only in the sense that the destruction of Jerusalem took place in A.D. 70 was it true that any of Christ's contemporaries lived to see the fulfillment of *these things*. In the latter case, the *generation* would refer to those living at the time of the earliest of the signs concerning the end; they will live to see the fulfillment of them all.

25:1 The teaching of this parable is the contrast between watchful preparation and careless security. The whole idea of the parable is that Christians should watch, be ready, be prepared for the coming of the Lord.

5 "Now while the bridegroom was delaying, they all got drowsy and *began* to sleep.

6 "But at midnight there was a shout, 'Behold, the bridegroom! Come out to meet *him*.'

7 "Then all those virgins rose, and trimmed their lamps.

8 "And the foolish said to the prudent, 'Give us some of your oil, for our lamps are going out.'

9 "But the prudent answered, saying, 'No, there will not be enough for us and you *too*; go instead to the dealers and buy *some* for yourselves.'

V8 - The fool recognizes his short coming, but has excuses or covers it up.

10 "And while they were going away to make the purchase, the bridegroom came, and those who were ready went in with him to the wedding feast; and the door was shut.

11 "And later the other virgins also came, saying, 'Lord, lord, open up for us.'

12 "But he answered and said, 'Truly I say to you, I do not know you.'

13 "Be on the alert then, for you do not know the day nor the hour.

8. *The parable of the talents (25:14-30)*

14 "For *it is* just like a man *about* to go on a journey, who called his own slaves, and entrusted his possessions to them.

15 "And to one he gave five talents, to another, two, and to another, one, each according to his own ability; and he went on his journey.

16 "Immediately the one who had received the five talents went and traded with them, and gained five more talents.

17 "In the same manner the one who *had received* the two *talents* gained two more.

18 "But he who received the one *talent* went away and dug in the ground, and hid his master's money.

19 "Now after a long time the master of those slaves *came and *settled accounts with them.

20 "And the one who had received the five talents came up and brought five more talents, saying, 'Master, you entrusted five talents to me; see, I have gained five more talents.'

21 "His master said to him, 'Well done, good and faithful slave; you were faithful with a few things, I will put you in charge of many things, enter into the joy of your master.'

22 "The one also who *had received* the two talents came up and said, 'Master, you entrusted to me two talents; see, I have gained two more talents.'

23 "His master said to him, 'Well done, good and faithful slave; you were faithful with a few things, I will put you in charge of many things; enter into the joy of your master.'

24 "And the one also who had received the one talent came up and said, 'Master, I knew you to be a hard man, reaping where you did not sow, and gathering where you scattered no *seed*.

25 'And I was afraid, and went away and hid your talent in the ground; see, you have what is yours.'

*Lev 25:37
usury prohibited
w/ poor debtors*

26 "But his master answered and said to him, 'You wicked, lazy slave, you knew that I reap where I did not sow, and gather where I scattered no *seed*.

27 'Then you ought to have put my money in the bank, and on my arrival I would have received my *money* back with interest.

28 'Therefore take away the talent from him, and give it to the one who has the ten talents.'

29 "For to everyone who has shall *more* be given, and he shall have an abundance; but from the one who does not have, even what he does have shall be taken away.

30 "And cast out the worthless slave into the outer darkness; in that place there shall be weeping and gnashing of teeth.

25:14 Christ here teaches that the use men make of the gifts God has given is vitally important. Responsibility is bestowed in proportion to each person's native endowments, and these may be misused, abused, or properly used. The servant with the one talent was guilty not only of failing to use properly what he had been given, but also of slandering his lord as a greedy and cruel master. (This attitude characterizes those who refuse to accept God's grace as a loving Father, but who project onto Him the smallness and pettiness of their own unconverted nature, and therefore regard Him only as a tyrant who makes impossible demands.) The lord's response to this false and fruitless servant is that by his own estimate of his master he stands condemned. He should have made an effort to measure up to the expectations of his allegedly rapacious master.

9. The judgment (25:31–46)

31 "But when the Son of Man comes in His glory, and all the angels with Him, then He will sit on His glorious throne.

32 "And all the nations will be gathered before Him; and He will separate them from one another, as the shepherd separates the sheep from the goats;

33 and He will put the sheep on His right, and the goats on the left.

34 "Then the King will say to those on His right, 'Come, you who are blessed of My Father, inherit the kingdom prepared for you from the foundation of the world.

35 'For I was hungry, and you gave Me *something* to eat; I was thirsty, and you gave Me drink; I was a stranger, and you invited Me in;

36 naked, and you clothed Me; I was sick, and you visited Me; I was in prison, and you came to Me.'

37 "Then the righteous will answer Him, saying, 'Lord, when did we see You hungry, and feed You, or thirsty, and give You drink?

38 'And when did we see You a stranger, and invite You in, or naked, and clothe You?

39 'And when did we see You sick, or in prison, and come to You?'

40 "And the King will answer and say to them, 'Truly I say to you, to the extent that you did it to one of these brothers of Mine, *even* the least *of them*, you did it to Me.'

41 "Then He will also say to those on His left, 'Depart from Me, accursed ones, into the eternal fire which has been prepared for the devil and his angels;

42 for I was hungry, and you gave Me *nothing* to eat; I was thirsty, and you gave Me nothing to drink;

43 I was a stranger, and you did not invite Me in; naked, and you did not clothe Me; sick, and in prison, and you did not visit Me.'

44 "Then they themselves also will answer, saying, 'Lord, when did we see You hungry, or thirsty, or a stranger, or naked, or sick, or in prison, and did not take care of You?'

45 "Then He will answer them, saying, 'Truly I say to you, to the extent that you did not do it to one of the least of these, you did not do it to Me.'

46 "And these will go away into eternal punishment, but the righteous into eternal life."

N. The trial and condemnation of Jesus (26:1–27:26)

1. The plot to kill Jesus
(26:1–5,14–16; Mark 14:1–2,10–11; Luke 22:1–6)

26 And it came about that when Jesus had finished all these words, He said to His disciples,

2 "You know that after two days the Passover is coming, and the Son of Man is *to be* delivered up for crucifixion."

3 Then the chief priests and the elders of the people were gathered together in the court of the high priest, named Caiaphas;

4 and they plotted together to seize Jesus by stealth, and kill *Him*.

5 But they were saying, "Not during the festival, lest a riot occur among the people."

2. Anointing of Jesus by Mary of Bethany
(26:6–13; Mark 14:3–9; John 12:1–8)

6 Now when Jesus was in Bethany, at the home of Simon the leper,

7 a woman came to Him with an alabaster vial of very costly perfume, and she poured it upon His head as He reclined *at the table*.

8 But the disciples were indignant when they saw *this*, and said, "Why this waste?

Cross-references (margin):

25:31 Matt 16:27; 19:28
25:32 Ezek 34:17, 20
25:34 Luke 12:32; 1 Cor 6:9; 15:50; Gal 5:21; Rev 13:8; 17:8
25:35 Is 58:7; Ezek 18:7; James 1:27; Heb 13:2
25:36 James 2:15, 16; 2 Tim 1:16
25:40 Prov 14:31; 19:17; Matt 10:42; Heb 6:10
25:41 Matt 7:23; Mark 9:48; Luke 16:24; Jude 7; 2 Pet 2:4

Their eyes did not see. need & their hearts did not respond with compassion.

25:45 Prov 14:31; 17:5
*25:46 Dan 12:2; John 5:29; Rom 2:7; Gal 6:8

26:1 Matt 7:28; 11:1; 13:53; 19:1
26:2 John 13:1
26:3 Ps 2:2; John 11:47-53
26:4 Matt 12:14
26:5 Matt 27:24

26:6 Matt 21:17

25:46 Eternal death, or everlasting punishment, is the unavoidable consequence of unforgiven sin (Rom. 6:16,21, 23; 8:13). It differs from the mere physical death that all people, saints and sinners alike, must endure. It assumes its final and most terrible form at the Last Judgment (see note to Rev. 20:11,12). It is variously described in Scripture as *disgrace and everlasting contempt* (Dan. 12:2), *destruction* (Rom. 9:22), *second death* (Rev. 2:11), and *wrath to come* (1 Thess. 1:10). It is characterized by unending torment (Rev. 20:10; 21:8). Christ Himself says of hell that it is a place *where their worm does not die, and the fire is not quenched* (Mark 9:48). God alone can inflict this eternal death (10:28; James 4:12), and Christ alone is the way of escape (John 3:16; 8:51; Acts 4:12).

26:7 *a woman*, see note to Luke 7:36ff. for her identity.

9 "For this *perfume* might have been sold for a high price and *the money* given to the poor."

10 But Jesus, aware of this, said to them, "Why do you bother the woman? For she has done a good deed to Me.

26:11
Deut 15:11
26:12
John 19:40

11 "For the poor you have with you always; but you do not always have Me.

12 "For when she poured this perfume upon My body, she did it to prepare Me for burial.

13 "Truly I say to you, wherever this gospel is preached in the whole world, what this woman has done shall also be spoken of in memory of her."

3. *The bargain of Judas Iscariot (26:14–16, vv. 1–5)*

14 Then one of the twelve, named Judas Iscariot, went to the chief priests,

26:15
Ex 21:32
Zech 11:12

15 and said, "What are you willing to give me to deliver Him up to you?" And they weighed out to him thirty pieces of silver.

16 And from then on he *began* looking for a good opportunity to betray Him.

4. *The Last Supper (26:17–35)*

a. *The Passover prepared (26:17–19; Mark 14:12–16; Luke 22:7–13)*

17 Now on the first *day* of Unleavened Bread the disciples came to Jesus, saying, "Where do You want us to prepare for You to eat the Passover?"

26:18
John 7:6,8;
12:23; 13:1;
17:1

18 And He said, "Go into the city to a certain man, and say to him, 'The Teacher says, "My time is at hand; I *am to* keep the Passover at your house with My disciples."'"

26:19
Deut 16:5-8

19 And the disciples did as Jesus had directed them; and they prepared the Passover.

b. *The Passover eaten*
(26:20–25; Mark 14:17–21; Luke 22:14–18; see John 13:1–30)

20 Now when evening had come, He was reclining *at the table* with the twelve disciples.

21 And as they were eating, He said, "Truly I say to you that one of you will betray Me."

22 And being deeply grieved, they each one began to say to Him, "Surely not I, Lord?"

26:23
Ps 41:9;
Luke 22:21;
John 13:18;
Is 53;
Dan 9:26;
Luke 24:25;
Acts 17:2,3;
1 Cor 15:3

23 And He answered and said, "He who dipped his hand with Me in the bowl is the one who will betray Me.

24 "The Son of Man *is to* go, just as it is written of Him; but woe to that man by whom the Son of Man is betrayed! It would have been good for that man if he had not been born."

25 And Judas, who was betraying Him, answered and said, "Surely it is not I, Rabbi?" He *said to him, "You have said *it* yourself."

*26:26
1 Cor 10:16;
11:23-25

c. *The Lord's Supper instituted*
(26:26–29; Mark 14:22–25; Luke 22:19–24)

26 And while they were eating, Jesus took *some* bread, and after a blessing, He broke *it* and gave *it* to the disciples, and said, "Take, eat; this is My body."

*26:28
Ex 24:6-8;
Matt 20:28;
Mark 1:4;
Heb 9:20

27 And when He had taken a cup and given thanks, He gave *it* to them, saying, "Drink from it, all of you;

28 for this is My blood of the covenant, which is poured out for many for forgiveness of sins.

26:14 *Judas Iscariot* secured his ignominious reputation as the betrayer of Jesus Christ. Certain facts connected with his life are of interest. His name *Judas* is the Greek form of the Hebrew name *Judah*. *Iscariot* is taken by some to mean *man of Kerioth*, a town in Judea. Except for Judas Iscariot, all of the other disciples came from Galilee. Generally, the Judeans looked down on the Galileans, and this may have been a possible cause for alienation between Judas and the other disciples. Judas was called along with the Eleven to be an apostle. He is always listed, however, as the last of the Twelve. He was a dishonest coveter who sold Christ for a few pieces of silver. Scripture informs us that Christ knew that Judas would betray Him even before he was chosen as a disciple (see John 6:64,70,71). It is difficult to reconcile the freedom of choice that Judas exercised in betraying Christ and the divine foreordination that assured he would

do so (Acts 1:15–17,20). Yet both appear in the Scriptures. Christ announced that it *would have been good for that man if he had not been born* (26:24). Judas's sin differed from the denial of Peter in that it was deliberate, calculated, and premeditated, whereas the sin of Peter was one of weakness and sudden capitulation in the face of enormous stress. Many have raised the question as to whether Judas Iscariot partook of the bread and the wine at the institution of the Lord's Supper. Most modern interpreters think he did not. The accounts of his death were written by Matthew (27:3–10) and Luke (Acts 1:16–20). A reconciliation of the accounts has been difficult. However, he reaped the just deserts of his wicked actions, and his life stands as a constant warning against betrayal of Christ (e.g., see Heb. 6:6).
26:26 See note to Mark 14:22 on the Lord's Supper.
26:28 The mercy of God makes possible the forgiveness of

29 "But I say to you, I will not drink of this fruit of the vine from now on until that day when I drink it new with you in My Father's kingdom."

d. Peter's denial foretold
(26:30–35; Mark 14:27–31; Luke 22:31–34; see John 14–17)

30 And after singing a hymn, they went out to the Mount of Olives.

31 Then Jesus *said to them, "You will all fall away because of Me this night, for it is written, 'I WILL STRIKE DOWN THE SHEPHERD, AND THE SHEEP OF THE FLOCK SHALL BE SCATTERED.'

32 "But after I have been raised, I will go before you to Galilee."

33 But Peter answered and said to Him, "*Even* though all may fall away because of You, I will never fall away."

34 Jesus said to him, "Truly I say to you that this *very* night, before a cock crows, you shall deny Me three times."

35 Peter *said to Him, "Even if I have to die with You, I will not deny You." All the disciples said the same thing too.

5. Jesus in Gethsemane (26:36–56)

a. Jesus' agony
(26:36–46; Mark 14:32–42; Luke 22:39–46; cf. John 18:1)

36 Then Jesus *came with them to a place called Gethsemane, and *said to His disciples, "Sit here while I go over there and pray."

37 And He took with Him Peter and the two sons of Zebedee, and began to be grieved and distressed.

38 Then He *said to them, "My soul is deeply grieved, to the point of death; remain here and keep watch with Me."

39 And He went a little beyond *them*, and fell on His face and prayed, saying, "My Father, if it is possible, let this cup pass from Me; yet not as I will, but as Thou wilt."

40 And He *came to the disciples and *found them sleeping, and *said to Peter, "So, you *men* could not keep watch with Me for one hour?

41 "Keep watching and praying, that you may not enter into temptation; the spirit is willing, but the flesh is weak."

42 He went away again a second time and prayed, saying, "My Father, if this cannot pass away unless I drink it, Thy will be done."

43 And again He came and found them sleeping, for their eyes were heavy.

44 And He left them again, and went away and prayed a third time, saying the same thing once more.

45 Then He *came to the disciples, and *said to them, "Are you still sleeping and taking your rest? Behold, the hour is at hand and the Son of Man is being betrayed into the hands of sinners.

46 "Arise, let us be going; behold, the one who betrays Me is at hand!"

b. Jesus' betrayal and arrest
(26:47–56; Mark 14:43–50; Luke 22:47–53; John 18:1–11)

47 And while He was still speaking, behold, Judas, one of the twelve, came up, accompanied by a great multitude with swords and clubs, from the chief priests and elders of the people.

48 Now he who was betraying Him gave them a sign, saying, "Whomever I shall kiss, He is the one; seize Him."

49 And immediately he went to Jesus and said, "Hail, Rabbi!" and kissed Him.

26:30
Mark 14:26
26:31
John 16:32;
Matt 11:6;
Zech 13:7
26:32
Matt 28:7,10,
16
26:34
John 13:38
26:35
John 13:37

26:37
Matt 4:21
26:38
John 12:27
*26:39
John 12:27;
Matt 20:22;
John 6:38;
Phil 2:8
26:40
v. 38
26:41
Matt 6:13;
Luke 11:4
26:42
John 4:34;
5:30; 6:38

26:45
v. 18;
John 12:23,
27; 13:1; 17:1

26:49
v. 25

sins (Dan. 9:9). The sacrifice of Christ is the ground of forgiveness (Acts 13:38; Eph. 1:7; Heb. 9:22; 1 John 1:7). Forgiveness implies: (1) limitlessness (18:22); (2) infiniteness (Ps. 103:12); (3) completeness (Col. 2:13); and (4) God remembers sins no more (Is. 44:22; Jer. 31:34). The only sin that can never be forgiven is the sin of turning away from the Holy Spirit (12:31; Mark 3:29; 1 John 5:16), who alone can bring about repentance and faith.

26:39 The *cup* of which Jesus speaks has been the subject of much discussion. Two views prevail generally. The first one suggests that the God-man in His humanity prayed for some other way than Calvary to redeem man. But since Calvary was the Father's only way, Jesus accepted it in His humanity, for He prayed: *not as I will, but as Thou wilt.* Those who hold the second view contend that Christ always prayed according to the will of His Father and that in the garden He feared that Satan would kill Him before He made atonement at Calvary. Thus He prayed for deliverance in the garden so that He might go to Calvary; but He was willing to die in the garden if God so willed. In this view His prayer was answered, and He was spared to go to the cross. Perhaps more plausible than either view is a third explanation, that He shrank with a holy abhorrence from the approaching experience of complete identification with the defiling sin of the human race on the cross, and the complete forsakenness that this would temporarily entail (*My God, My God, why hast Thou forsaken Me?* (27:46). This was the horrid cup from which He shrank; nevertheless, He was willing finally to exalt the Father's will above His own and drink it to the dregs.

26:50
Matt 20:13;
22:12

26:52
Gen 9:6;
Rev 13:10

26:53
2 Kin 6:17;
Dan 7:10

26:54
v. 24;
Luke 24:25,
44,46

26:56
v. 54

26:58
John 18:15

26:60
Ps 27:12;
35:11;
Acts 6:13;
Deut 19:15

26:61
Matt 27:40

26:63
Is 53:7;
Matt 27:12,
14; Lev 5:1;
John 18:33

26:64
Ps 110:1;
Dan 7:13;
Matt 16:27,28

26:65
Num 14:6;
Acts 14:14;
Lev 24:16

26:66
John 19:7

50   And Jesus said to him, "Friend, *do* what you have come for." Then they came and laid hands on Jesus and seized Him.

51   And behold, one of those who were with Jesus reached and drew out his sword, and struck the slave of the high priest, and cut off his ear.

52   Then Jesus *said to him, "Put your sword back into its place; for all those who take up the sword shall perish by the sword.

53   "Or do you think that I cannot appeal to My Father, and He will at once put at My disposal more than twelve [45]legions of angels?

54   "How then shall the Scriptures be fulfilled, that it must happen this way?"

55   At that time Jesus said to the multitudes, "Have you come out with swords and clubs to arrest Me as against a robber? Every day I used to sit in the temple teaching and you did not seize Me.

56   "But all this has taken place that the Scriptures of the prophets may be fulfilled." Then all the disciples left Him and fled.

6. Jesus before Caiaphas
(26:57–68; Mark 14:53–65; cf. Luke 22:54; John 18:12–14,19–25)

57   And those who had seized Jesus led Him away to Caiaphas, the high priest, where the scribes and the elders were gathered together.

58   But Peter also was following Him at a distance as far as the courtyard of the high priest, and entered in, and sat down with the officers to see the outcome.

59   Now the chief priests and the whole Council kept trying to obtain false testimony against Jesus, in order that they might put Him to death;

60   and they did not find *any*, even though many false witnesses came forward. But later on two came forward,

61   and said, "This man stated, 'I am able to destroy the temple of God and to rebuild it in three days.'"

62   And the high priest stood up and said to Him, "Do You make no answer? What is it that these men are testifying against You?"

63   But Jesus kept silent. And the high priest said to Him, "I adjure You by the living God, that You tell us whether You are the Christ, the Son of God."

64   Jesus *said to him, "You have said it *yourself*; nevertheless I tell you, hereafter you shall see THE SON OF MAN SITTING AT THE RIGHT HAND OF POWER, and COMING ON THE CLOUDS OF HEAVEN."

65   Then the high priest tore his robes, saying, "He has blasphemed! What further need do we have of witnesses? Behold, you have now heard the blasphemy;

66   what do you think?" They answered and said, "He is deserving of death!"

[45]A legion equaled 6,000 troops

26:57 Caiaphas, the high priest, was the son-in-law of Annas, who had previously been high priest himself. Caiaphas was appointed to his position by the procurator who preceded Pontius Pilate, Valerius Gratus. He remained as high priest until A.D. 37, when he was removed by Vitellius. As a person, Caiaphas was guilty of hypocrisy and cloaked his hatred of Christ under the guise of religious pretensions and patriotic loyalty. It was he who recommended the action that would bring Christ to Calvary (John 11:49–53). He and his cohorts used Judas Iscariot to further their nefarious scheme (26:3ff.). When Christ appeared before Caiaphas, He remained silent until pressed to answer the question, "*I adjure You by the living God, that You tell us whether You are the Christ, the Son of God*" (26:63). To this Christ responded that He was (26:64). Having failed to convict Christ on the testimony of perjurers, Caiaphas now condemned Him on the charge of blasphemy, disregarding both religious scruples and common justice. So it was that Christ was sentenced to be crucified.
26:59 The *Council*, or *Sanhedrin* (Jewish Supreme Court) of this verse was a familiar institution. The origins of the Sanhedrin are somewhat obscure, but it was a firmly developed body during the life of Jesus. The name was applied primarily to the highest court of justice and the supreme council at Jerusalem, but it was also used to designate the lower courts of justice. The Sanhedrin at Jerusalem was called the *Great Sanhedrin*. There were seventy-one members of this body, although at times the membership was spoken of as seventy. Apparently the difference in the figures depended on whether the president of the body was to

be included in the total number. Normally the members of the Sanhedrin were called *elders*, and they generally were selected for membership in the body from among the chief priests and the scribes. How the members were elected and how vacancies were filled is not known. In order to be eligible for membership, tradition has it that a man had to be learned, humble, and popular with his people. At the trial of Jesus, the high priest Caiaphas appears to have been the president of the Sanhedrin, but there is no evidence that the presidency belonged to the high priest as such. The *Little Sanhedrin* with its twenty-three members passed judgment on cases other than those that were reserved exclusively for the *Great Sanhedrin*. When the lower courts were unable to reach a decision, the case was taken to the last court of appeal, which was the supreme court of justice. Cases involving life and death came before the Little Sanhedrin, although important ones were referred to the Great Sanhedrin for judgment. The decisions of the Great Sanhedrin were binding on all. The court met in the Hall of Hewn Stone in Jerusalem. The members were seated in a semi-circle so that each could see the others. In cases involving life and death, the vote was taken beginning with the younger members so that they could not be influenced by the votes of the older ones. No fewer than twenty-three members could be in attendance in such cases. In the event a verdict of guilty was reached by a majority of one, the number of members in attendance had to be increased. Only when the full court was assembled could a man be declared guilty of a crime worthy of capital punishment by a majority of one.

67　Then they spat in His face and beat Him with their fists; and others slapped Him,

68　and said, "Prophesy to us, You Christ; who is the one who hit You?"

26:67
Is 53:3;
Matt 27:30;
John 19:3

7. Peter's denial of Jesus
(26:69–75; Mark 14:66–72; Luke 22:55–63; John 18:15–18,25–27)

69　Now Peter was sitting outside in the courtyard, and a certain servant-girl came to him and said, "You too were with Jesus the Galilean."

70　But he denied *it* before them all, saying, "I do not know what you are talking about."

71　And when he had gone out to the gateway, another *servant-girl* saw him and *said to those who were there, "This man was with Jesus of Nazareth."

72　And again he denied *it* with an oath, "I do not know the man."

73　And a little later the bystanders came up and said to Peter, "Surely you too are *one* of them; for the way you talk gives you away."

74　Then he began to curse and swear, "I do not know the man!" And immediately a cock crowed.

75　And Peter remembered the word which Jesus had said, "Before a cock crows, you will deny Me three times." And he went out and wept bitterly.

26:75
v. 34;
John 13:38

8. Jesus delivered to Pilate by the Sanhedrin
(27:1–2; Mark 15:1; Luke 23:1; John 18:28)

27 Now when morning had come, all the chief priests and the elders of the people took counsel against Jesus to put Him to death;

2　and they bound Him, and led Him away, and delivered Him up to Pilate the governor.

27:2
Matt 20:19;
Acts 3:13

9. The death of Judas Iscariot (27:3–10; cf. Acts 1:16–20)

3　Then when Judas, who had betrayed Him, saw that He had been condemned, he felt remorse and returned the thirty pieces of silver to the chief priests and elders,

27:3
Matt 26:14,15

4　saying, "I have sinned by betraying innocent blood." But they said, "What is that to us? See *to that* yourself!"

27:4
v. 24

5　And he threw the pieces of silver into the sanctuary and departed; and he went away and hanged himself.

27:5
Acts 1:18

6　And the chief priests took the pieces of silver and said, "It is not lawful to put them into the temple treasury, since it is the price of blood."

7　And they counseled together and with the money bought the Potter's Field as a burial place for strangers.

8　For this reason that field has been called the Field of Blood to this day.

9　Then that which was spoken through Jeremiah the prophet was fulfilled, saying, "AND THEY TOOK THE THIRTY PIECES OF SILVER, THE PRICE OF THE ONE WHOSE PRICE HAD BEEN SET by the sons of Israel;

27:8
Acts 1:19
*27:9f
Zech 11:12,
13

10　AND THEY GAVE THEM FOR THE POTTER'S FIELD, AS THE LORD DIRECTED ME."

10. Jesus before Pontius Pilate
(27:11–26; Mark 15:2–15; Luke 23:3–25; John 18:29–40)

a. Jesus questioned (27:11–14)

11　Now Jesus stood before the governor, and the governor questioned Him, saying, "Are You the King of the Jews?" And Jesus said to him, "*It is as* you say."

12　And while He was being accused by the chief priests and elders, He made no answer.

27:12
Matt 26:63;
John 19:9

13　Then Pilate *said to Him, "Do You not hear how many things they testify against You?"

27:13
Matt 26:62;
John 19:10

14　And He did not answer him with regard to even a *single* charge, so that the governor was quite amazed.

27:14
1 Tim 6:13

26:69　See note to Mark 14:71 for Peter's denial of Christ.
27:9,10　This quotation has been taken from Zech. 11:12–13, and so its attribution to Jeremiah has been regarded as inaccurate. Actually, however, there is no reference to a *field* in the Zechariah passage; and yet the whole point of the quotation is the field purchased with Judas's money. But Jer. 32:6–9 refers to a field that Jeremiah purchased for a certain number of shekels, and this field is mentioned as a place for burial. Thus Matthew combines here a reference both to Zechariah and to Jeremiah and assigns the combined quotation to Jeremiah only, both because he was the more prominent prophet of the two, and because the potter's field figures so importantly in his prophecy.

15   Now at *the* feast the governor was accustomed to release for the multitude *any* one prisoner whom they wanted.

16   And they were holding at that time a notorious prisoner, called Barabbas.

17   When therefore they were gathered together, Pilate said to them, "Whom do you want me to release for you? Barabbas, or Jesus who is called Christ?"

18   For he knew that because of envy they had delivered Him up.

27:19
Acts 12:21;
v. 24

19   And while he was sitting on the judgment seat, his wife sent to him, saying, "Have nothing to do with that righteous Man; for last night I suffered greatly in a dream because of Him."

27:20
Acts 3:14

20   But the chief priests and the elders persuaded the multitudes to ask for Barabbas, and to put Jesus to death.

21   But the governor answered and said to them, "Which of the two do you want me to release for you?" And they said, "Barabbas."

22   Pilate *said to them, "Then what shall I do with Jesus who is called Christ?" They all *said, "Let Him be crucified!"

23   And he said, "Why, what evil has He done?" But they kept shouting all the more, saying, "Let Him be crucified!"

b. *Barabbas released and Jesus delivered (27:24–26)*

27:24
Matt 26:5;
Deut 21:6-8;
Ps 26:6; v. 19

24   And when Pilate saw that he was accomplishing nothing, but rather that a riot was starting, he took water and washed his hands in front of the multitude, saying, "I am innocent of this Man's blood; see *to that* yourselves."

27:25
Josh 2:19;
Acts 5:28

25   And all the people answered and said, "His blood *be* on us and on our children!"

27:26
Is 53:5

26   Then he released Barabbas for them; but after having Jesus scourged, he delivered Him to be crucified.

O. *The crucifixion and burial of Jesus (27:27–66)*

1. *Jesus crowned with thorns (27:27–31; Mark 15:16–20; cf. John 19:2,3)*

27:27
John 18:28,
33; Acts 10:1

27   Then the soldiers of the governor took Jesus into the Praetorium and gathered the whole *Roman* cohort around Him.

28   And they stripped Him, and put a scarlet robe on Him.

27:29
Ps 69:19;
Is 53:3

29   And after weaving a crown of thorns, they put it on His head, and a reed in His right hand; and they kneeled down before Him and mocked Him, saying, "Hail, King of the Jews!"

27:30
Matt 26:67;
Mark 10:34;
14:65
27:31
Is 53:7

30   And they spat on Him, and took the reed and *began* to beat Him on the head.

31   And after they had mocked Him, they took His robe off and put His garments on Him, and led Him away to crucify *Him*.

2. *Jesus crucified* (27:32–44; Mark 15:21–32; Luke 23:32–43; John 19:17–24)

27:32
Heb 13:12

32   And as they were coming out, they found a man of Cyrene named Simon, whom they pressed into service to bear His cross.

33   And when they had come to a place called Golgotha, which means Place of a Skull,

27:34
Ps 69:21

34   they gave Him wine to drink mingled with gall; and after tasting *it*, He was unwilling to drink.

27:35
Ps 22:18

35   And when they had crucified Him, they divided up His garments among themselves, casting lots;

27:36
v. 54

36   and sitting down, they *began* to keep watch over Him there.

37   And they put up above His head the charge against Him which read, "THIS IS JESUS THE KING OF THE JEWS."

27:37 All four gospels contain a report of the inscription that specified Jesus' offense: that of presuming to kingly status in opposition to the authority of Rome. The charge on which the accused had been convicted was inscribed on a placard that was normally carried in front of him as he made his way to the place of execution, and then was either affixed to his gallows or hung around his neck. When Christ was crucified, it was apparently placed above His head. Each gospel writer specifies certain elements of the charge on which Christ was crucified. The full inscription seems to have been: *This is Jesus of Nazareth the King of the Jews*. It was written in Greek, Hebrew, and Latin, repesenting the universal language of the day, the language of the Jews, and the legal language of the governing power of Rome. One satisfactory reconciliation of the slight variations in the wording of this superscription is as follows. Matthew records the inscription in its Aramaic (Hebrew) form: "This is Jesus the King of the Jews." Mark and Luke record it in its Latin form: "The King of the Jews" (Mark), or "This is the King of the Jews" (Luke). John recalls the Greek version: "Jesus the Nazarene, the King of the Jews." In other words, the versions in the three languages were not absolutely identical, and they contained variations that were faithfully recorded in the four gospel accounts.

38   At that time two robbers *were crucified with Him, one on the right and one on the left.

39   And those passing by were hurling abuse at Him, wagging their heads,

40   and saying, "You who *are going to* destroy the temple and rebuild it in three days, save Yourself! If You are the Son of God, come down from the cross."

41   In the same way the chief priests also, along with the scribes and elders, were mocking *Him,* and saying,

42   "He saved others; He cannot save Himself. He is the King of Israel; let Him now come down from the cross, and we shall believe in Him.

43   "HE TRUSTS IN GOD; LET HIM DELIVER *Him* now, IF HE TAKES PLEASURE IN HIM; for He said, 'I am the Son of God.' "

44   And the robbers also who had been crucified with Him were casting the same insult at Him.

3. *The death of Christ*
(27:45–50; Mark 15:33–41; Luke 23:41–49; John 19:28–37)

45   Now from the [46]sixth hour darkness fell upon all the land until the [47] ninth hour.

46   And about the ninth hour Jesus cried out with a loud voice, saying, "ELI, ELI, LAMA SABACHTHANI?" that is, "MY GOD, MY GOD, WHY HAST THOU FORSAKEN ME?"

47   And some of those who were standing there, when they heard it, *began* saying, "This man is calling for Elijah."

48   And immediately one of them ran, and taking a sponge, he filled it with sour wine, and put it on a reed, and gave Him a drink.

49   But the rest *of them* said, "Let us see whether Elijah will come to save Him."[48]

50   And Jesus cried out again with a loud voice, and yielded up *His* spirit.

4. *Redemption completed (27:51–56; Heb. 9:8–14; 10:19–20)*

51   And behold, the veil of the temple was torn in two from top to bottom, and the earth shook; and the rocks were split,

52   and the tombs were opened; and many bodies of the saints who had fallen asleep were raised;

53   and coming out of the tombs after His resurrection they entered the holy city and appeared to many.

54   Now the centurion, and those who were with him keeping guard over Jesus, when they saw the earthquake and the things that were happening, became very frightened and said, "Truly this was the Son of God!"

55   And many women were there looking on from a distance, who had followed Jesus from Galilee, ministering to Him,

56   among whom was Mary Magdalene, *along with* Mary the mother of James and Joseph, and the mother of the sons of Zebedee.

5. *Jesus laid in the tomb*
(27:57–61; Mark 15:42–47; Luke 23:50–56; John 19:38–42)

57   And when it was evening, there came a rich man from Arimathea, named Joseph, who himself had also become a disciple of Jesus.

58   This man went to Pilate and asked for the body of Jesus. Then Pilate ordered *it* to be given over *to him.*

---

[46]I.e., noon   [47]I.e., 3 p.m.   [48]Some early mss. add: *And another took a spear and pierced His side, and there came out water and blood.* (cf. John 19:34)

27:38 Is 53:12
27:39 Ps 22:7; 109:25
27:40 Matt 26:61; Acts 6:14; John 2:19
27:42 John 1:49; 12:13
27:43 Ps 22:8
27:45 Amos 8:9
***27:46** Ps 22:1
27:48 Ps 69:21
***27:51** Ex 26:31; Heb 9:3; v. 54
27:54 Matt 3:17; 17:5
27:55 Luke 8:2,3
27:56 Mark 15:40, 47; Luke 24:10
27:57 Acts 13:29

27:46 See note to Luke 23:34 on the seven last words.
27:50 Christ was not killed by Satan, nor was He overcome by the natural processes of dissolution. He Himself declared that no man could take His life from Him. He stated that He had the power to lay it down and the power to take it up again (John 10:14–18). Thus His death was a voluntary one; His act one of free choice in obedience to the Father's will.
27:51 The tearing of the veil signified: (1) that full atonement had been made (Heb. 10:19,20); (2) that Christ had gone through the veil into the most holy place, into the presence of God Himself (Heb. 9:12,24); (3) that Christ as mediating high priest made unnecessary any human priesthood standing between man and God (Heb. 7:23–28); and

(4) that all believers have immediate access, without the benefit of any priesthood except that of Christ, to the presence and favor of God (Rom. 5:2; Eph. 2:18; 3:12).
27:52 This miracle is mentioned only by Matthew. There are no simple answers to the many questions that it raises. We do not know which saints rose (the account says *many*), nor do we know whether they continued in resurrection as bodies and eventually died and were again buried. Verse 53 makes it appear that they came out of their graves *after* the resurrection of Christ and entered into the city of Jerusalem, where they appeared to many people. Matthew Henry suggests that these resurrected saints ascended with Christ to glory, although this is simply an inference.

59   And Joseph took the body and wrapped it in a clean linen cloth,

27:60
Matt 28:2;
Mark 16:4

60   and laid it in his own new tomb, which he had hewn out in the rock; and he rolled a large stone against the entrance of the tomb and went away.

61   And Mary Magdalene was there, and the other Mary, sitting opposite the grave.

6. *The tomb sealed and guarded (27:62–66)*

62   Now on the next day, which is *the one* after the preparation, the chief priests and the Pharisees gathered together with Pilate,

27:63
Matt 16:21;
17:23; 20:19;
Mark 8:31;
10:34;
Luke 9:22;
18:33; 24:6,7;
John 2:19

63   and said, "Sir, we remember that when He was still alive that deceiver said, 'After three days I *am to* rise again.'

64   "Therefore, give orders for the grave to be made secure until the third day, lest the disciples come and steal Him away and say to the people, 'He has risen from the dead,' and the last deception will be worse than the first."

65   Pilate said to them, "You have a guard; go, make it *as* secure as you know how."

27:66
v. 60;
Matt 28:11-15

66   And they went and made the grave secure, and along with the guard they set a seal on the stone.

P. *The resurrection of Jesus Christ (28:1–10; Mark 16:1–8; Luke 24:1–11; John 20:1–18)*

28:1
Luke 8:2;
Matt 27:56

28   Now after the Sabbath, as it began to dawn toward the first *day* of the week, Mary Magdalene and the other Mary came to look at the grave.

28:2
Matt 27:51,60

2   And behold, a severe earthquake had occurred, for an angel of the Lord descended from heaven and came and rolled away the stone and sat upon it.

28:3
Dan 7:9;
10:6;
Mark 9:3;
John 20:12;
Acts 1:10

3   And his appearance was like lightning, and his garment as white as snow;

4   and the guards shook for fear of him, and became like dead men.

5   And the angel answered and said to the women, "Do not be afraid; for I know that you are looking for Jesus who has been crucified.

28:5
v. 10;
Matt 14:27
*28:6
Matt 12:40;
16:21; 17:23;
20:19

6   "He is not here, for He has risen, just as He said. Come, see the place where He was lying.

7   "And go quickly and tell His disciples that He has risen from the dead; and behold, He is going before you into Galilee, there you will see Him; behold, I have told you."

28:7
Matt 26:32;
v. 16

8   And they departed quickly from the tomb with fear and great joy and ran to report it to His disciples.

28:9
John 20:14-18

9   And behold, Jesus met them and greeted them. And they came up and took hold of His feet and worshiped Him.

28:10
Rom 8:29;
Heb 2:11

10   Then Jesus *said to them, "Do not be afraid; go and take word to My brethren to leave for Galilee, and there they shall see Me."

Q. *The bribing of the soldiers (28:11–15)*

28:11
Matt 27:65,66

11   Now while they were on their way, behold, some of the guard came into the city and reported to the chief priests all that had happened.

12   And when they had assembled with the elders and counseled together, they gave a large sum of money to the soldiers,

13   and said, "You are to say, 'His disciples came by night and stole Him away while we were asleep.'

28:14
Matt 27:2

14   "And if this should come to the governor's ears, we will win him over and keep you out of trouble."

15   And they took the money and did as they had been instructed; and this story was widely spread among the Jews, *and is* to this day.

28:6 Christ's resurrection is spoken of by Peter in Acts 2:25–31 as a fulfillment of David's utterance in Ps. 16:10. Christ Himself plainly foretold that He would rise from the dead in 20:19 and John 10:18. Other witnesses to the historicity of the resurrection include: (1) the eleven apostles (Acts 1:3); (2) Paul (Acts 9:3–8; 1 Cor. 15:8; (3) five hundred brethren who met the risen Jesus at one time (1 Cor. 15:6); and (4) the hard-headed and skeptical Thomas, who would accept no testimony but that of his own fingers and eyes (John 20:24–29). Paul demonstrated conclusively (1 Cor. 15) that the Christian faith stands or falls on the resurrection. Without any question he was speaking of a physical resurrection in the same body (although glorified) as that in which Christ was crucified. He appeared in a body that could be seen and felt, and that still bore the prints of the nails. The resurrection guarantees: (1) that Christ is truly the Son of God (Rom. 1:4); (2) that the Father accepted His atoning work and approved it as effective for redemption (Rom. 4:25); (3) that the believer has an advocate before the Father (Rom. 8:34); (4) that he may enjoy the assurance of eternal life (John 14:19; 1 Pet. 1:3–5); and (5) that believers will also be raised and that they shall be like their risen Lord (1 Cor. 15:49; Phil. 3:21; 1 John 3:2).

VI. *The appearance in Galilee; the Great Commission*
(28:16–20; Mark 16:15–18)

16 But the eleven disciples proceeded to Galilee, to the mountain which Jesus had designated.

17 And when they saw Him, they worshiped *Him*; but some were doubtful.

18 And Jesus came up and spoke to them, saying, "All authority has been given to Me in heaven and on earth.

19 "Go therefore and make disciples of all the nations, baptizing them in the name of the Father and the Son and the Holy Spirit,

20 teaching them to observe all that I commanded you; and lo, I am with you always, even to the end of the age."

28:16
v. 7;
Matt 26:32
28:18
Dan 7:13,14;
Luke 10:22;
Phil 2:9,10;
1 Pet 3:22
***28:19**
Luke 24:47;
Acts 1:8
28:20
Acts 2:42;
Mt 18:20;
Acts 18:10

28:19a This Scripture is the warrant for water baptism. Indeed baptism is not optional with a believer; it is, rather, the express command of Christ. To dismiss it as a merely psychological transaction is to do violence to the Word of God. Christians generally have been united in the conviction that baptism is commanded, but they have been divided on almost every other aspect of the subject. Some insist that immersion is the only mode of baptism. Others believe that the Scripture teaches baptism by pouring (affusion) or by sprinkling (aspersion). Some baptize infants on the analogy of Old Testament circumcision (cf. Gen. 17; Col. 2:11–13); others insist that only those who are old enough to make a personal decision for Christ ought to be baptized. Some call baptism a sacrament and others regard it as an ordinance. The rite is administered in the name of the Father, Son, and Holy Spirit in accordance with Christ's command in this verse.

28:19b The Christian church has always been trinitarian.

This means that God is one in essence, eternally subsisting in three persons: Father, Son, and Holy Spirit. Here the word *name* is in the singular, intimating that the three persons of the Trinity are one in substance and equality, yet three in person. Biblical evidences for the Trinity include Matt. 3:16,17; Rom. 8:9; 1 Cor. 12:3–6; 2 Cor. 13:14; Eph. 4:4–6; 1 Pet. 1:2; Jude 20,21; Rev. 1:4,5. There is no other way of reconciling consistently all that the Bible says about God except by understanding Him as a Trinity (rather than as a mere Unity or as three separate Gods). All of the members of the Trinity are accorded the attributes of deity, and each member has an office that He uniquely fulfills. God the Father sent God the Son. It was the Son who died on Calvary. It was the Father and the Son who sent the Holy Spirit, who seals and indwells each believer. Salvation is the work of the Trinity (Father, Son, and Holy Spirit), as stated in 2 Thess. 2:13,14 and Titus 3:4–6.

INTRODUCTION TO
THE GOSPEL ACCORDING TO
MARK

Authorship and Background: From earliest times the second Gospel was ascribed to John Mark, whose name does not appear in the Gospels. Some think he was the young man present at the arrest of Jesus (14:51,52). From Acts and the epistles it appears that John Mark was the son of Mary, whose home in Jerusalem was used as a meeting place by the Jerusalem church (Acts 12:12). His cousin Barnabas (Col. 4:10) and Paul took him with them when they returned from Jerusalem to Antioch (Acts 12:25). He went with them on their first missionary journey as far as Perga, from which he returned to Jerusalem (Acts 13:5,13). Paul and Barnabas parted company over whether Mark should go with them on their second journey, Barnabas taking Mark with him to Cyprus (Acts 15:37-39). Years later Mark was with Paul when he wrote to the Colossians and to Philemon (Col. 4:10; Philem. 24), and later Paul asked for him (2 Tim. 4:11). Moreover, he was with Peter in "Babylon" (probably Rome), according to 1 Pet. 5:13.

Mark himself was not one of the Twelve, but his Gospel (claimed by many to have been the first one to be written as over against the tradition of Matthew's priority) has all the earmarks of a firsthand witness, who was, from all early accounts, none other than Simon Peter, from whom Mark obtained his information.

It is generally agreed that the Gospel was written before A.D. 70; some date it as early as A.D. 50, while others place it around A.D. 65.

Characteristics: This Gospel is the shortest of the four, and most of its contents are also to be found in Matthew or Luke. It presents a vivid, vigorous, straightforward account of the public ministry of Jesus, culminating in His passion, death, and resurrection. The events of the last week in Jerusalem occupy over one-third of the book, with the climactic end of the ministry dominating the entire account. From the ministry of John the Baptist to the resurrection of Jesus, the emphasis is on the mighty acts of the Son of God, vividly described with an abundance of detail. Comparatively less attention is devoted to the teachings of Jesus, although there are blocks of teachings, such as the parables in chapter 4 and the apocalyptic discourse in chapter 13. In this book Jesus is (1) the Son of God (1:1; 15:39); and (2) the Son of Man, who is destined to be betrayed, to suffer and die (8:31; 9:31; 10:33-34; 14:21), and who will come in the power and glory of the Father (8:38; 13:26; 14:62).

In the key verse of the Gospel, Jesus discloses that the Son of Man is the suffering servant of God, who will "give His life a ransom for many" (10:45).

Contents:

I. The beginning of the gospel message (1:1-13): John the Baptist; Jesus' baptism and wilderness temptation.

II. Public ministry in Galilee (1:14-9:50): Calling of disciples, cures, miracles, and teachings. Disputes with the religious leaders; appointment of the Twelve; parables of the kingdom; and feedings of the multitudes. The disclosure at Caesarea Philippi and the transfiguration.

III. From Galilee to Jerusalem (10:1-52)

IV. The last week in Jerusalem (11:1-16:8): Triumphal entry, cursing of the fig tree, cleansing of the temple. Disputes with Pharisees and Sadducees; the apocalyptic discourse. The Supper, Gethsemane, arrest, trial, crucifixion, death, and resurrection.

V. Appearances of the risen Christ (16:9-20)

THE GOSPEL ACCORDING TO
MARK

I. The beginning of the gospel message (1:1–13)

A. The ministry of John the Baptist
(1:1–8; Matt. 3:1–12; Luke 3:2–17; John 1:6–8,19–28)

1:1
Matt 4:3
1:2
Mal 3:1;
Matt 11:10;
Luke 7:27
1:3
Is 40:3

This prophecy
was approx
700 BC

1 The beginning of the gospel of Jesus Christ, [1]the Son of God.
2 As it is written in Isaiah the prophet,

"BEHOLD, I SEND MY MESSENGER BEFORE YOUR FACE,
WHO WILL PREPARE YOUR WAY;
3 THE VOICE OF ONE CRYING IN THE WILDERNESS,
'MAKE READY THE WAY OF THE LORD,
MAKE HIS PATHS STRAIGHT.' "

*1:4
Acts 13:24;
Luke 1:77

4 John the Baptist appeared in the wilderness [2]preaching a baptism of repentance for the forgiveness of sins.
5 And all the country of Judea was going out to him, and all the people of Jerusalem; and they were being baptized by him in the Jordan River, confessing their sins.

1:6
Lev 11:22

6 And John was clothed with camel's hair and *wore* a leather belt around his waist, and his diet was locusts and wild honey.

1:7
Acts 13:25

7 And he was preaching, and saying, "After me One is coming who is mightier than I, and I am not fit to stoop down and untie the thong of His sandals.

1:8
Acts 1:5;
Is 44:3;
Joel 2:28

8 "I baptized you [3]with water; but He will baptize you [3]with the Holy Spirit."

B. The baptism of Jesus (1:9–11; Matt. 3:13–17; Luke 3:21,22)

This book starts
w/ Jesus' adult
ministry

1:9
Matt 2:23

9 And it came about in those days that Jesus came from Nazareth in Galilee, and was baptized by John in the Jordan.

1:10
John 1:32

10 And immediately coming up out of the water, He saw the heavens opening, and the Spirit like a dove descending upon Him;

1:11
Ps 2:7;
Is 42:1

11 and a voice came out of the heavens: "Thou art My beloved Son, in Thee I am well-pleased."

C. The temptation of Jesus (1:12,13; Matt. 4:1–11; Luke 4:1–13)

12 And immediately the Spirit *impelled Him *to go* out into the wilderness.
13 And He was in the wilderness forty days being tempted by Satan; and He was with the wild beasts, and the angels were ministering to Him.

---

[1]Many mss. do not contain *the Son of God*   [2]Or, *proclaiming*   [3]The Gr. here can be translated *in, with* or *by*

1:4 John belonged to the Old Testament dispensation, and his baptism of repentance, though its purpose was the forgiveness of sins, fell short of Christian baptism. The Christian church did not yet exist, and the disciples of John and those who were to be the followers of Jesus were not joined together. John did not administer baptism in the name of the Trinity, nor did he baptize with the Holy Spirit (who had not yet been given to the church, John 7:39). Paul felt it necessary to baptize again those who had known only John's baptism (Acts 18:24–19:7).
1:12 See note to Luke 4:2 on the temptation of Jesus.
1:13 Angels are heavenly messengers of God whose purpose is to execute His will or communicate it to mankind. The term *angel* (both the Hebrew *mal'akh* and the Greek *angellos*) means "messenger," and ordinarily is used to refer to a higher order of spirits who dwell in the very presence of God. But it also refers to the devil's angels (Matt. 25:41), and seems to be applied to the pastors who serve as God's messengers to the congregations of the seven churches of Asia (Rev. 1–3). In Gen. 16:7–14; 22:11–19; Ex. 3:2–4;

Judg. 2:1; 6:11–14; and 13:3 the presence of deity in angelic form is obvious. The Greek word for *angel* (sometimes translated *messenger*) is also used for men in passages like Luke 7:24; James 2:25. Angels are stated in Scripture to be: (1) created beings (Col. 1:16); (2) innumerable (Dan. 7:10; Heb. 12:22; Rev. 5:11); (3) of different orders and ranks (Dan. 10:13; Jude 9); (4) powerful (2 Kin. 19:35; Ps. 103:20; 2 Thess. 1:7); (5) spirits without material bodies (Heb. 1:14); (6) not bound by physical limitations (Acts 12:5–10); (7) possessed of great wisdom (2 Sam. 14:20); and (8) capable of assuming human form (1 Chr. 21:16,20; John 20:12). In their work angels: (1) guide the destinies of nations (Dan. 10:13,20); (2) minister to the people of God (1 Kin. 19:5–7; Ps. 91:10–12; Acts 12:7; Heb. 1:14); (3) execute God's judgments (2 Kin. 19:35; Acts 12:23; Rev. 16:1); (4) will accompany Christ at His second coming (Matt. 25:31; 2 Thess. 1:7,8); and (5) transmitted the law to Moses and the Israelites (Ps. 68:17; Acts 7:53; Heb. 2:2). Aside from Satan only two are named, one the archangel Michael and the other Gabriel, to whom were entrusted

II. *Public ministry in Galilee (1:14–9:50)*

A. *The beginning of Jesus' Galilean ministry*
(1:14,15; Matt. 4:12–17; Luke 4:14,15; John 4:43–45)

14 And after John had been taken into custody, Jesus came into Galilee, preaching the gospel of God,

15 and saying, "The time is fulfilled, and the kingdom of God is at hand; repent and believe in the gospel."

B. *The call of the first four disciples*
(1:16–20; Matt. 4:18–22; Luke 5:1–11; cf. John 1:40–42)

16 And as He was going along by the Sea of Galilee, He saw Simon and Andrew, the brother of Simon, casting a net in the sea; for they were fishermen.

17 And Jesus said to them, "Follow Me, and I will make you become fishers of men."

18 And they immediately left the nets and followed Him.

19 And going on a little farther, He saw James the *son* of Zebedee, and John his brother, who were also in the boat mending the nets.

20 And immediately He called them; and they left their father Zebedee in the boat with the hired servants, and went away to follow Him.

C. *The unclean spirit cast out (1:21–28; Luke 4:31–37)*

21 And they *went into Capernaum; and immediately on the Sabbath He entered the synagogue and *began* to teach.

22 And they were amazed at His teaching; for He was teaching them as *one* having authority, and not as the scribes.

23 And just then there was in their synagogue a man with an unclean spirit; and he cried out,

24 saying, "What do we have to do with You, Jesus [4]of Nazareth? Have You come to destroy us? I know who You are—the Holy One of God!"

25 And Jesus rebuked him, saying, "Be quiet, and come out of him!"

26 And throwing him into convulsions, the unclean spirit cried out with a loud voice, and came out of him.

27 And they were all amazed, so that they debated among themselves, saying, "What is this? A new teaching with authority! He commands even the unclean spirits, and they obey Him."

28 And immediately the news about Him went out everywhere into all the surrounding district of Galilee.

D. *Peter's mother-in-law healed*
(1:29–31; Matt. 8:14–17; Luke 4:38–41)

29 And immediately after they had come out of the synagogue, they came into the house of Simon and Andrew, with James and John.

30 Now Simon's mother-in-law was lying sick with a fever; and immediately they *spoke to Him about her.

31 And He came to her and raised her up, taking her by the hand, and the fever left her, and she [5]waited on them.

E. *The sick healed; demons cast out*
(1:32–34; Matt. 8:16–17; Luke 4:40–41)

32 And when evening had come, after the sun had set, they *began* bringing to Him all who were ill and those who were demon-possessed.

33 And the whole city had gathered at the door.

34 And He healed many who were ill with various diseases, and cast out many demons; and He was not permitting the demons to speak, because they [6]knew who He was.

---

[4]Lit., *the Nazarene* [5]Or, *served* [6]Some mss. read: *knew Him to be Christ*

special assignments (Dan. 8:16; 9:21; 10:13,21; 12:1,2; Luke 1:19,26; 1 Thess. 4:16; Jude 9). Man is said to be a little lower than the angels, and Christ shared in this low estate in His humiliation (Heb. 2:6–9).

Margin references:

1:14 Matt 4:23

1:15 Gal 4:4; Eph 1:10; Acts 20:21

[handwritten note] Andrew had heard John the Baptist (Jn 1: 40) earlier.

1:18 Matt 19:27

1:21 Matt 4:23

1:22 Matt 7:28

1:24 Matt 8:29; Mark 10:47; 14:67; John 6:69; Acts 3:14

1:25 v. 34

1:27 Mark 10:24, 32

1:29 vv. 21,23

1:32 Mark 4:24

1:34 Matt 4:23; Mark 3:12; Acts 16:17,18

F. *First preaching tour in Galilee*
(1:35–39; cf. Luke 4:42–44)

1:35
Matt 14:23;
Luke 5:16

The prayer in v.35
formed the basis
for Jesus' clear
focus in v.38!

35   And in the early morning, while it was still dark, He arose and went out and departed to a lonely place, and was praying there.

36   And Simon and his companions hunted for Him;

37   and they found Him, and *said to Him, "Everyone is looking for You."

1:38
Is 61:1

38   And He *said to them, "Let us go somewhere else to the towns nearby, in order that I may preach there also; for that is what I came out for."

1:39
Matt 4:23-25

39   And He went into their synagogues throughout all Galilee, preaching and casting out the demons.

G. *The leper cleansed (1:40–45; Matt. 8:1–4; Luke 5:12–16)*

1:40
Mark 10:17

unusual to touch
a leper

40   And a leper *came to Him, beseeching Him and falling on his knees before Him, and saying to Him, "If You are willing, You can make me clean."

41   And moved with compassion, He stretched out His hand, and touched him, and *said to him, "I am willing; be cleansed."

42   And immediately the leprosy left him and he was cleansed.

43   And He sternly warned him and immediately sent him away,

1:44
Lev 13:49;
14:2-32

44   and He *said to him, "See that you say nothing to anyone; but go, show yourself to the priest and offer for your cleansing what Moses commanded, for a testimony to them."

1:45
Luke 5:15;
Matt 28:15;
Mark 2:13;
Luke 5:17;
John 6:2

45   But he went out and began to proclaim it freely and to spread the news about, to such an extent that Jesus could no longer publicly enter a city, but [7]stayed out in unpopulated areas; and they were coming to Him from everywhere.

H. *A paralytic healed and forgiven*
(2:1–12; Matt. 9:1–8; Luke 5:17–26)

2   And when He had come back to Capernaum several days afterward, it was heard that He was at home.

2:2
v. 13

It may
have been
a 1-sided
relationship
by a
paralytic, but

2   And many were gathered together, so that there was no longer room, even near the door; and He was speaking the word to them.

2:3
Matt 4:24

3   And they *came, bringing to Him a paralytic, carried by four men.

It was the
friends' faith
that resulted in
the healing!

4   And being unable to get to Him because of the crowd, they removed the roof above Him; and when they had dug an opening, they let down the pallet on which the paralytic was lying.

5   And Jesus seeing their faith *said to the paralytic, "My [8]son, your sins are forgiven."

*2:7
Is 43:25

6   But there were some of the scribes sitting there and reasoning in their hearts,

7   "Why does this man speak that way? He is blaspheming; who can forgive sins but God alone?"

8   And immediately Jesus, aware in His spirit that they were reasoning that way within themselves, *said to them, "Why are you reasoning about these things in your hearts?

9   "Which is easier, to say to the paralytic, 'Your sins are forgiven'; or to say, 'Arise, and take up your pallet and walk'?

10   "But in order that you may know that the Son of Man has authority on earth to forgive sins"—He *said to the paralytic—

11   "I say to you, rise, take up your pallet and go home."

2:12
Matt 9:33

12   And he rose and immediately took up the pallet and went out in the sight of all; so that they were all amazed and were glorifying God, saying, "We have never seen anything like this."

I. *Matthew called (2:13–17; Matt. 9:9–13; Luke 5:27–32)*

2:13
Mark 1:45

13   And He went out again by the seashore; and all the multitude were coming to Him, and He was teaching them.

2:14
Matt 8:22

14   And as He passed by, He saw Levi the *son* of Alphaeus sitting in the tax office, and He *said to him, "Follow Me!" And he rose and followed Him.

[7]Lit., *was*   [8]Lit., *child*

2:7   The scribes asked the right question but came to the wrong conclusion, so far as Christ's authority was concerned. It is true that only God can forgive sins. But as the Son of Man, Jesus exercised this divine prerogative on earth, of which He gave conclusive proof by healing the paralytic (vv. 10–12).

15 And it came about that He was reclining *at the table* in his house, and many tax-gatherers and sinners were dining with Jesus and His disciples; for there were many of them, and they were following Him.

16 And when the scribes of the Pharisees saw that He was eating with the sinners and tax-gatherers, they *began* saying to His disciples, "Why is He eating and drinking with tax-gatherers and sinners?"

17 And hearing this, Jesus *said to them, *"It is* not those who are healthy who need a physician, but those who are sick; I did not come to call the righteous, but sinners."

J. The question about fasting
(2:18–22; Matt. 9:14–17; Luke 5:33–39)

18 And John's disciples and the Pharisees were fasting; and they *came and *said to Him, "Why do John's disciples and the disciples of the Pharisees fast, but Your disciples do not fast?"

19 And Jesus said to them, "While the bridegroom is with them, the attendants of the bridegroom do not fast, do they? So long as they have the bridegroom with them, they cannot fast.

20 "But the days will come when the bridegroom is taken away from them, and then they will fast in that day.

21 "No one sews a patch of unshrunk cloth on an old garment; otherwise the patch pulls away from it, the new from the old, and a worse tear results.

22 "And no one puts new wine into old wineskins; otherwise the wine will burst the skins, and the wine is lost, and the skins *as well;* but *one puts* new wine into fresh wineskins."

K. Jesus the Lord of the Sabbath
(2:23–28; Matt. 12:1–8; Luke 6:1–5)

23 And it came about that He was passing through the grainfields on the Sabbath, and His disciples began to make their way along while picking the heads *of grain.*

24 And the Pharisees were saying to Him, "See here, why are they doing what is not lawful on the Sabbath?"

25 And He *said to them, "Have you never read what David did when he was in need and became hungry, he and his companions;

26 how he entered the house of God in the time of Abiathar *the* high priest, and ate the consecrated bread, which is not lawful for *anyone* to eat except the priests, and he gave *it* also to those who were with him?"

27 And He was saying to them, "The Sabbath was made for man, and not man for the Sabbath.

28 "Consequently, the Son of Man is Lord even of the Sabbath."

L. Jesus heals on the Sabbath (3:1–6; Matt. 12:9–14; Luke 6:6–11)

3 And He entered again into a synagogue; and a man was there with a withered hand.

Marginal references:
- 2:16 Acts 23:9
- 2:17 Luke 19:10; 1 Tim 1:15
- 2:20 Luke 17:22
- 2:23 Deut 23:25
- 2:26 1 Sam 21:1-6; 2 Sam 8:17; Ex 29:32,33; Lev 24:9
- *2:27 Ex 23:12; Deut 5:14
- 3:1 Mark 1:21,39

2:18 From the teachings of Jesus and the New Testament record of the practice of the apostolic church, it does not appear that early Christians fasted regularly as a religious duty. The answer Jesus gave to the question as to why His disciples did not fast shows He regarded fasting as an expression of sorrow, and thus incompatible with the joy His disciples shared in company with Him, like the joy of a wedding feast (a common figure of the Messianic age). In Matt. 6:16–18 Jesus teaches that fasting as a religious observance is of value only if practiced without ostentation, for the sole purpose of pleasing God.

In the apostolic church there are references to fasting on occasions of crisis and decision, particularly in the choosing of leaders for church work (cf. Acts 13:2,3; 14:23).

2:21 See note to Luke 5:36 on cloth and wine.

2:25 Every week the priests prepared twelve loaves of bread in accordance with instructions in Lev. 24:5–9, and laid them on the table before God on the Sabbath (cf. Ex. 25:30; 35:13; 39:36). When the twelve fresh loaves were placed on the table, the priests could eat the old loaves if they so desired.

2:27 In Gen. 2:2 the statement is made that God rested on the seventh day. That is the first mention of the Biblical doctrine of the Sabbath. Among the children of Israel the seventh day, or Saturday, was the Sabbath. Indeed, this was a part of the Mosaic Law (Ex. 20:9–11). Eventually it became hedged about by all kinds of artificial and hairsplitting regulations so that in Jesus' day one could not even walk beyond a certain distance without breaking the Law. The phrase *a Sabbath day's journey* (defined as about a thousand yards) illustrates this legal restriction (Acts 1:12). Christ enunciated two major principles concerning the Sabbath: (1) it was made for man, not vice versa (see also Matt. 12:1–8; Luke 6:1–5); and (2) certain types of work were permissible even on the Sabbath—works of mercy and works of necessity. To pluck grain for food was a work of necessity; and to pull an ox out of a hole was a work of mercy, so also to care for the healing of the sick.

After the incident in Ch.2, this represents the positive side of the Sabbath

3:2
Luke 14:1;
20:20;
Matt 12:10

Dual meaning; the pharisees were also plotting to kill Jesus.

v.6.- The Pharisees and Herodians were enemies.

3:6
Matt 12:14;
22:16;
Mark 12:13

v5- He was angry, they showed no compassion

3:7
Matt 4:25

3:8
Matt 11:21

3:10
Matt 4:23;
Mark 5:29,
34; 6:56; 8:22

*3:11
Mark 1:23,
24;
Luke 4:41;
Matt 14:33

3:12
Mark 1:25,34

3:13
Matt 5:1;
Luke 9:1

v15- See Lk 6:12 Jesus prayed all night first

3:16

3 points to the job description
John 1:42

v22- They resorted to a logically inconsistent argument

3:20
Mark 6:31

Jesus was pulled
3:21
John 10:20;
Acts 26:24

1 way- by family
3:22
Matt 9:34;
10:25;
by crowd
John 7:20;
by pharisees 8:48,52

3:23
Mark 4:2ff

Jesus gave a gracious response to the Pharisees spiteful charge.

3:27
Is 49:24,25

2 And they were watching Him *to see* if He would heal him on the Sabbath, in order that they might accuse Him.

3 And He *said to the man with the withered hand, "Rise and *come* forward!"

4 And He *said to them, "Is it lawful on the Sabbath to do good or to do harm, to save a life or to kill?" But they kept silent.

5 And after looking around at them with anger, grieved at their hardness of heart, He *said to the man, "Stretch out your hand." And he stretched it out, and his hand was restored.

6 And the Pharisees went out and immediately *began* taking counsel with the Herodians against Him, *as to* how they might destroy Him.

M. *Jesus heals many (3:7–12; Matt. 12:15–21; cf. Luke 6:17–19)*

7 And Jesus withdrew to the sea with His disciples; and a great multitude from Galilee followed; and *also* from Judea,

8 and from Jerusalem, and from Idumea, and beyond the Jordan, and the vicinity of Tyre and Sidon, a great multitude heard of all that He was doing and came to Him.

9 And He told His disciples that a boat should stand ready for Him because of the multitude, in order that they might not crowd Him;

10 for He had healed many, with the result that all those who had afflictions pressed about Him in order to touch Him.

11 And whenever the unclean spirits beheld Him, they would fall down before Him and cry out, saying, "You are the Son of God!"

12 And He earnestly warned them not to make Him known.

N. *The appointing of the Twelve*
(3:13–19; Matt. 10:1–4; Luke 6:12–16)

13 And He *went up to the mountain and *summoned those whom He Himself wanted, and they came to Him.

14 And He appointed twelve[9], ① that they might be with Him, and ② that He might send them out to preach,

15 ③ and to have authority to cast out the demons.

16 And He appointed the twelve: Simon (to whom He gave the name Peter),

17 and James, the *son* of Zebedee, and John the brother of James (to them He gave the name Boanerges, which means, "Sons of Thunder");

18 and Andrew, and Philip, and Bartholomew, and Matthew, and Thomas, and James the *son* of Alphaeus, and Thaddaeus, and Simon the Zealot;

19 and Judas Iscariot, who also betrayed Him.

O. *Jesus answers the slander of the Pharisees*
(3:20–27; Matt. 12:22–45; Luke 11:14–23)

20 And He *came [10]home, and the multitude *gathered again, to such an extent that they could not even eat a meal.

21 And when His own [11]people heard *of this*, they went out to take custody of Him; for they were saying, "He has lost His senses."

22 And the scribes who came down from Jerusalem were saying, "He is possessed by Beelzebul," and "He casts out the demons by the ruler of the demons."

23 And He called them to Himself and began speaking to them in parables, "How can Satan cast out Satan?

24 "And if a kingdom is divided against itself, that kingdom cannot stand.

25 "And if a house is divided against itself, that house will not be able to stand.

26 "And if Satan has risen up against himself and is divided, he cannot stand, but he is finished!

27 "But no one can enter the strong man's house and plunder his property unless he first binds the strong man, and then he will plunder his house.

---

[9]Some early mss. add: *whom He named apostles*   [10]Lit., *into a house*   [11]Or, *kinsmen*

3:11 The unclean spirits had knowledge that Jesus was the Son of God; yet this knowledge did not issue in salvation. So people may profess belief in all the major doctrines of the Christian faith and still be unregenerate.

Perhaps the "blasphemy" in v 28 is for a person to equate themselves w/ God & the Holy Spirit. See Mark 14:62-63 where Christ equated himself to God and was accused of blasphemy.

v28- See Jn 3:19

P. The unforgivable sin (3:28–30)

28 "Truly I say to you, all sins shall be forgiven the sons of men, and whatever blasphemies they utter;

29 but whoever blasphemes against the Holy Spirit never has forgiveness, but is guilty of an eternal sin"—

30 because they were saying, "He has an unclean spirit."

3:28
Luke 12:10

Q. Christ's true kindred (3:31–35; Matt. 12:46–50; Luke 8:19–21)

31 And His mother and His brothers *arrived, and standing outside they sent *word* to Him, and called Him.

32 And a multitude was sitting around Him, and they *said to Him, "Behold, Your mother and Your brothers [12] are outside looking for You."

33 And answering them, He *said, "Who are My mother and My brothers?"

34 And looking about on those who were sitting around Him, He *said, "Behold, My mother and My brothers!

35 "For whoever does the will of God, he is My brother and sister and mother."

3:31
Matt 12:46;
Luke 8:19

R. Jesus teaches in parables (4:1–34)

1. Parable of the sower (4:1–9; Matt. 13:1–9; Luke 8:4–8)

4 And He began to teach again by the sea. And such a very great multitude gathered to Him that He got into a boat in the sea and sat down; and the whole multitude was by the sea on the land.

2 And He was teaching them many things in parables, and was saying to them in His teaching,

3 "Listen *to this*! Behold, the sower went out to sow;

4 and it came about that as he was sowing, some *seed* fell beside the road, and the birds came and ate it up.

5 "And other *seed* fell on the rocky *ground* where it did not have much soil; and immediately it sprang up because it had no depth of soil.

6 "And after the sun had risen, it was scorched; and because it had no root, it withered away.

7 "And other *seed* fell among the thorns, and the thorns came up and choked it, and it yielded no crop.

8 "And other *seeds* fell into the good soil and as they grew up and increased, they yielded a crop and produced thirty, sixty, and a hundredfold."

9 And He was saying, "He who has ears to hear, let him hear."

4:1
Mark 2:13;
3:7

4:2
Mark 3:23

Is the problem He is addressing the cost of discipleship. i.e. rejection of god's message

v4 - this represents wasted seed

4:8
John 15:5;
Col 1:6
4:9
Matt 11:15

Don't deliberately hide your fruit [illegible]

2. The reason for parables (4:10–12; Matt. 13:10–17; Luke 8:9–10)

10 And as soon as He was alone, His followers, along with the twelve, *began* asking Him *about* the parables.

11 And He was saying to them, "To you has been given the mystery of the kingdom of God; but those who are outside get everything in parables,

12 in order that WHILE SEEING, THEY MAY SEE AND NOT PERCEIVE; AND WHILE HEARING, THEY MAY HEAR AND NOT UNDERSTAND LEST THEY RETURN AND BE FORGIVEN."

See Is. 6:9-10
Jn 12:37-40
4:11
1 Cor 5:12; fulfillment
Col 4:5; of prophecy
1 Thess 4:12;
1 Tim 3:7
*4:12
Is 6:9;
John 12:40;
Acts 28:26;
Rom 11:8

3. The parable of the sower explained (4:13–20; Matt. 13:18–23; Luke 8:11–15)

13 And He *said to them, "Do you not understand this parable? And how will you understand all the parables?

[12]Later mss. add: *and Your sisters*

3:29 Blaspheming the Holy Spirit is the unpardonable sin (Matt. 12:31,32; Luke 12:10). To commit this sin one must consciously, persistently, deliberately, and maliciously reject the testimony of the Spirit to the deity and saving power of the Lord Jesus. Since only the Holy Spirit can convince and convert the unsaved, a continuous and final rejection of His wooing and His witness shuts off the only possible avenue whereby the saving work of Christ is applied to the sinner in his need.

4:3 Three elements are significant in this parable: the seed, the sower, and the soil. Note that two of the elements are identical in each instance. It is the same seed and the same sower. The one factor that accounts for the variety of results is the soil. Accepting the principle that the soil means the hearer, then it follows that there are four kinds of people who hear the gospel, and of them only one brings forth enduring or acceptable fruit.

4:12 *they may see and not perceive.* This would appear to mean that Jesus used parables in order to hide the truth, not to reveal it. The words of 4:12 are a summary of Is. 6:9,10, which speak of the prophet's message in terms of its rejection by the people of Israel. The blindness of the people and their unwillingness to repent and receive God's forgiveness came as the result of their willful rejection of God's message through His prophet. This same pattern of rejection and blindness was repeated in Christ's ministry of teaching, as the lengthier parallel in Matt. 13:13–15 makes abundantly clear.

Perhaps we are
the sowers of
the word?

14 "The sower sows the word.
15 "And these are the ones who are beside the road where the word is sown; and when they hear, immediately Satan comes and takes away the word which has been sown in them.

4:15
Mark 2:23,26

Is the soil
actually our
will?

16 "And in a similar way these are the ones on whom seed was sown on the rocky places, who, when they hear the word, immediately receive it with joy;
17 and they have no *firm* root in themselves, but are *only* temporary; then, when affliction or persecution arises because of the word, immediately they fall away.
18 "And others are the ones on whom seed was sown among the thorns; these are the ones who have heard the word,
19 and the worries of the [13]world, and the deceitfulness of riches, and the desires for other things enter in and choke the word, and it becomes unfruitful.
20 "And those are the ones on whom seed was sown on the good soil; and they hear the word and accept it, and bear fruit, thirty, sixty, and a hundredfold."

4. The parable of the candle (4:21–25; cf. Matt. 5:15; Luke 8:16; 11:33)

Don't deliberately
hide your fruit-
fulness.

21 And He was saying to them, "A lamp is not brought to be put under a peck-measure, is it, or under a bed? Is it not *brought* to be put on the lampstand?
22 "For nothing is hidden, except to be revealed; nor has *anything* been secret, but that it should come to light.

4:22
Matt 10:26;
Luke 8:17;
12:2
4:23
Matt 11:15
4:24
Matt 7:2;
Luke 6:38
4:25
Matt 13:12;
25:29;
Luke 8:18;
19:26
*4:26
Matt 13:24

23 "If any man has ears to hear, let him hear."
24 And He was saying to them, "Take care what you listen to. By your standard of measure it shall be measured to you; and more shall be given you besides.

Is this
fair?

25 "For whoever has, to him shall *more* be given; and whoever does not have, even what he has shall be taken away from him."

5. The parable of growing grain (4:26–29)

26 And He was saying, "The kingdom of God is like a man who casts seed upon the soil;

See a variation
of this parable
in Matt 13:24-30

27 and goes to bed at night and gets up by day, and the seed sprouts up and grows—how, he himself does not know.
28 "The soil produces crops by itself; first the blade, then the head, then the mature grain in the head.

4:29
Rev 14:15

29 "But when the crop permits, he immediately puts in the sickle, because the harvest has come."

6. The parable of the mustard seed
(4:30–34; Matt. 13:31,32; Luke 13:18,19)

4:30
Matt 13:24

30 And He said, "How shall we [14]picture the kingdom of God, or by what parable shall we present it?

Even the small
powerless
creatures such as
birds have a
"home" in the
kingdom — this
shows Jesus'
compassion

31 "*It is* like a mustard seed, which, when sown upon the soil, though it is smaller than all the seeds that are upon the soil,
32 yet when it is sown, grows up and becomes larger than all the garden plants and forms large branches; so that THE BIRDS OF THE [15]AIR can NEST UNDER ITS SHADE."

4:33
John 16:12
4:34
Matt 13:34;
John 16:25

33 And with many such parables He was speaking the word to them as they were able to hear it;
34 and He did not speak to them without a parable; but He was explaining everything privately to His own disciples.

S. The storm stilled (4:35–41; Matt. 8:23–27; Luke 8:22–25)

35 And on that day, when evening had come, He *said to them, "Let us go over to the other side."

4:36
Mark 5:2,21

36 And leaving the multitude, they *took Him along with them, just as He was, in the boat; and other boats were with Him.
37 And there *arose a fierce gale of wind, and the waves were breaking over the boat so much that the boat was already filling up.

---

[13]Or, *age* [14]Lit., *compare* [15]Or, *sky*

4:26 The law of growth is the central teaching of this parable. The kingdom of God has steadily enlarged itself during the centuries since Christ died and rose again. This growth has not always been perceptible, but in His own way, God knows how to bring forth abundant fruit from the gospel seed that has been planted.

38   And He Himself was in the stern, asleep on the cushion; and they *awoke Him and *said to Him, "Teacher, do You not care that we are perishing?"

39   And being aroused, He rebuked the wind and said to the sea, "Hush, be still." And the wind died down and it became perfectly calm.

40   And He said to them, "Why are you so timid? How is it that you have no faith?"

41   And they became very much afraid and said to one another, "Who then is this, that even the wind and the sea obey Him?" ← *Didn't the disciples yet realize that Christ was the Son of God?*

T. Demons cast out (5:1–20; Matt. 8:28–34; Luke 8:26–39)

5   And they came to the other side of the sea, into the country of the Gerasenes.

2   And when He had come out of the boat, immediately a man from the tombs with an unclean spirit met Him,

3   and he had his dwelling among the tombs. And no one was able to bind him anymore, even with a chain;

4   because he had often been bound with shackles and chains, and the chains had been torn apart by him, and the shackles broken in pieces, and no one was strong enough to subdue him.

5   And constantly night and day, among the tombs and in the mountains, he was crying out and gashing himself with stones.

6   And seeing Jesus from a distance, he ran up and bowed down before Him;

7   and crying out with a loud voice, he *said, "What do I have to do with You, Jesus, Son of the Most High God? I implore You by God, do not torment me!"

8   For He had been saying to him, "Come out of the man, you unclean spirit!"

9   And He was asking him, "What is your name?" And he *said to Him, "My name is Legion; for we are many."

10   And he *began* to entreat Him earnestly not to send them out of the country.

11   Now there was a big herd of swine feeding there on the mountain.

12   And *the demons* entreated Him, saying, "Send us into the swine so that we may enter them."

13   And He gave them permission. And coming out, the unclean spirits entered the swine; and the herd rushed down the steep bank into the sea, about two thousand *of them;* and they were drowned in the sea.

14   And their herdsmen ran away and reported it in the city and *out* in the country. And *the people* came to see what it was that had happened.

15   And they *came to Jesus and *observed the man who had been demon-possessed sitting down, clothed and in his right mind, the very man who had had the "legion"; and they became frightened.

16   And those who had seen it described to them how it had happened to the demon-possessed man, and *all* about the swine.

17   And they began to entreat Him to depart from their region.

18   And as He was getting into the boat, the man who had been demon-possessed was entreating Him that he might accompany Him.

19   And He did not let him, but He *said to him, "Go home to your people and report to them [16]what great things the Lord has done for you, and *how* He had mercy on you."

20   And he went away and began to proclaim in Decapolis what great things Jesus had done for him; and everyone marveled.

U. The woman with the issue of blood healed and Jairus's daughter raised (5:21–43; Matt. 9:18–26; Luke 8:40–56)

21   And when Jesus had crossed over again in the boat to the other side, a great multitude gathered about Him; and He stayed by the seashore.

22   And one of the synagogue officials named Jairus *came up, and upon seeing Him, *fell at His feet,   *sign of respect*

23   and *entreated Him earnestly, saying, "My little daughter is at the point of death; *please* come and lay Your hands on her, that she may get well and live."

[16]Or, *everything that*

Margin references
4:40 Matt 14:31, 32; Mark 16:14

5:2 Matt 4:1; 1:23

5:6 Matt 4:9; 18:26
*5:7 Matt 8:29; 4:3; Luke 8:28; Acts 16:17; Heb 7:1

5:15 vv. 16,18; Matt 4:24; v. 9

5:18 Acts 16:39

5:20 Mark 7:31; Matt 4:25

5:21 Matt 9:1
5:22 Luke 8:49; 13:14; Acts 13:15; 18:8,17
5:23 Mark 6:5; 7:32; 8:23; Acts 9:17; 28:8

5:7   The question *"What do I have to do with You . . . ?"* is found also in the parallels, Matt. 8:29; Luke 8:28 (see also Matt. 27:19; Mark 1:24; Luke 4:34; John 2:4). The question is patterned after a Semitic idiom by which the speaker rejects any kind of interference on the part of the person he addresses (in the Old Testament see 2 Sam. 16:10; 19:22; also Judg. 11:12; 1 Kin. 17:18). The question is thus a protest, "What do You want with me?"

24 And He went off with him; and a great multitude was following Him and pressing in on Him.

5:25 Lev 15:25

25 And a woman who had had a hemorrhage for twelve years,
26 and had endured much at the hands of many physicians, and had spent all that she had and was not helped at all, but rather had grown worse,
27 after hearing about Jesus, came up in the crowd behind *Him,* and touched His cloak.
28 For she thought, "If I just touch His garments, I shall get well."

5:29 v. 34

29 And immediately the flow of her blood was dried up; and she felt in her body that she was healed of her affliction.

5:30 Luke 5:17

30 And immediately Jesus, perceiving in Himself that the power *proceeding* from Him had gone forth, turned around in the crowd and said, "Who touched My garments?"
31 And His disciples said to Him, "You see the multitude pressing in on You, and You say, 'Who touched Me?' "
32 And He looked around to see the woman who had done this.
33 But the woman fearing and trembling, aware of what had happened to her, came and fell down before Him, and told Him the whole truth.

5:34 Luke 7:50; 8:48; Acts 16:36; James 2:16

34 And He said to her, "Daughter, your faith has made you well; go in peace, and be healed of your affliction."

5:35 v. 22

35 While He was still speaking, they *came from the *house of* the synagogue official, saying, "Your daughter has died; why trouble the Teacher anymore?"

5:36 Luke 8:50

36 But Jesus, overhearing what was being spoken, *said to the synagogue official, "Do not be afraid *any longer,* only believe."

5:37 Matt 17:1; 26:37

37 And He allowed no one to follow with Him, except Peter and James and John the brother of James.

5:38 v. 22

38 And they *came to the house of the synagogue official; and He *beheld a commotion, and *people* loudly weeping and wailing.

5:39 John 11:11

39 And entering in, He *said to them, "Why make a commotion and weep? The child has not died, but is asleep."
40 And they *began* laughing at Him. But putting them all out, He *took along the child's father and mother and His own companions, and *entered *the room* where the child was.

5:41 Luke 7:14; Acts 9:40

41 And taking the child by the hand, He *said to her, "Talitha kum!" (which translated means, "Little girl, I say to you, arise!").
42 And immediately the girl rose and *began* to walk; for she was twelve years old. And immediately they were completely astounded.

5:43 Matt 8:4

43 And He gave them strict orders that no one should know about this; and He said that *something* should be given her to eat.

She was an outcast—just like the demoniac

The woman must have been ostracized because she was unclean. This would have made Jesus unclean too.

Why does Jesus inspire such fear? 5:17, 5:33, 5:36

She was at the end of her rope, broke, and in trouble. Jesus made her acknowledge her neediness ???

V. *Second rejection of Jesus at Nazareth*
(6:1–6; Matt. 13:53–58; Luke 4:16–30)

6 And He went out from there, and He *came into His home town; and His disciples *followed Him.

6:2 Matt 4:23; 7:28; Mark 1:21

2 And when the Sabbath had come, He began to teach in the synagogue; and the many listeners were astonished, saying, "Where did this man *get* these things, and what is *this* wisdom given to Him, and such miracles as these performed by His hands?

*6:3 Matt 12:46; 11:6

3 "Is not this the carpenter, the son of Mary, and brother of James, and Joses, and Judas, and Simon? Are not His sisters here with us?" And they took offense at Him.

6:4 John 4:44

4 And Jesus said to them, "A prophet is not without honor except in his home town and among his *own* relatives and in his *own* household."

6:3 Jesus is here called *the carpenter;* in Matt. 13:55, *the carpenter's son;* and Luke 4:22 has *Joseph's son.* It is probable that by calling him *the son of Mary* here in 6:3 a slur was intended, since ordinarily a man was called the son of his father, not of his mother.

Jesus' sisters are mentioned here, but no names are given; his brothers are named here and in Matt. 13:55: James, Joseph (or, Joses), Simon, and Judas. The brothers are also referred to in John 7:3–10 and Acts 1:14. In Gal. 1:19 Paul speaks of James, the Lord's brother, the same James of Acts 12:17; 15:13–21; 1 Cor. 15:7. From these references it is surmised that none of Jesus' brothers believed in Him prior to the resurrection.

The way in which the New Testament speaks of the brothers and sisters of Jesus implies that they were the children of Joseph and Mary; there is no New Testament warrant for later theories that they were Joseph's children by a previous marriage, or that they were cousins of Jesus, not brothers and sisters.

55   and ran about that whole country and began to carry about on their pallets those who were sick, to the place they heard He was.

56   And wherever He entered villages, or cities, or countryside, they were laying the sick in the market places, and entreating Him that they might just touch the fringe of His cloak; and as many as touched it were being cured.

BB. *Ceremonial and real defilement: the Pharisees rebuked*
(7:1-23; Matt. 15:1-20)

7 And the Pharisees and some of the scribes gathered together around Him when they had come from Jerusalem,

2   and had seen that some of His disciples were eating their bread with impure hands, that is, unwashed.

3   (For the Pharisees and all the Jews do not eat unless they carefully wash their hands, *thus* observing the traditions of the elders;

4   and *when they come* from the market place, they do not eat unless they cleanse themselves; and there are many other things which they have received in order to observe, such as the washing of cups and pitchers and copper pots.)

5   And the Pharisees and the scribes *asked Him, "Why do Your disciples not walk according to the tradition of the elders, but eat their bread with impure hands?"

6   And He said to them, "Rightly did Isaiah prophesy of you hypocrites, as it is written,

'THIS PEOPLE HONORS ME WITH THEIR LIPS,
BUT THEIR HEART IS FAR AWAY FROM ME.

7   'BUT IN VAIN DO THEY WORSHIP ME,
TEACHING AS DOCTRINES THE PRECEPTS OF MEN.'

8   "Neglecting the commandment of God, you hold to the tradition of men."

9   He was also saying to them, "You nicely set aside the commandment of God in order to keep your tradition.

10   "For Moses said, 'HONOR YOUR FATHER AND YOUR MOTHER'; and, 'HE WHO SPEAKS EVIL OF FATHER OR MOTHER, LET HIM BE PUT TO DEATH';

11   but you say, 'If a man says to *his* father or *his* mother, anything of mine you might have been helped by is Corban (that is to say, [19]given *to God*),'

12   you no longer permit him to do anything for *his* father or *his* mother;

13   *thus* invalidating the word of God by your tradition which you have handed down; and you do many things such as that."

14   And after He called the multitude to Him again, He *began* saying to them, "Listen to Me, all of you, and understand.

15   there is nothing outside the man which going into him can defile him; but the things which proceed out of the man are what defile the man.

16   ["[20]If any man has ears to hear, let him hear."]

17   And when leaving the multitude, He had entered the house, His disciples questioned Him about the parable.

18   And He *said to them, "Are you so lacking in understanding also? Do you not understand that whatever goes into the man from outside cannot defile him;

19   because it does not go into his heart, but into his stomach, and is eliminated?" (*Thus He* declared all foods clean.)

20   And He was saying, "That which proceeds out of the man, that is what defiles the man.

21   "For from within, out of the heart of men, proceed the evil thoughts, fornications, thefts, murders, adulteries,

22   deeds of coveting *and* wickedness, *as well as* deceit, sensuality, envy, slander, pride *and* foolishness.

23   "All these evil things proceed from within and defile the man."

Cross references (right margin):

6:56
Mark 3:10;
Matt 9:20

*7:3
v. 5
Acts 10:14,
28; 11:8
7:4
Matt 23:25;
Luke 11:39

7:5
vv. 3,8,9,13;
Gal 1:14

7:6
Is 29:13

7:8
vv. 5,9,13
7:9
vv. 5,8,13

7:10
Ex 20:12;
Deut 5:6;
Ex 21:17;
Lev 20:9
7:11
Matt 23:18

7:13
vv. 5,8,9

7:17
Mark 9:28

7:19
Rom 14:1-12;
Col 2:16;
Luke 11:41;
Acts 10:15;
11:9

7:22
Matt 6:23;
20:15

---

[19]Or, *a gift, an offering*   [20]Many mss. do not contain this verse

---

7:1   See note to Matt. 3:7a on the Pharisees.
7:3   One Greek word in this verse has not been translated. The word is *pugme,* "fist," and the statement is literally, "they wash their hands with (or, to) the fist." Some translate "with the fist"; others, "as far as the wrist (or, elbow)"; others, in a more general sense, "carefully." There is no general agreement as to the precise meaning of the word here.

CC. Journey toward Tyre and Sidon: the Syrophoenician woman's daughter healed (7:24–30; Matt. 15:21–28)

7:24
Matt 11:21

24   And from there He arose and went away to the region of Tyre[21]. And when He had entered a house, He wanted no one to know *of it;* yet He could not escape notice.

25   But after hearing of Him, a woman whose little daughter had an unclean spirit, immediately came and fell at His feet.

26   Now the woman was a [22]Gentile, of the Syrophoenician race. And she kept asking Him to cast the demon out of her daughter.

27   And He was saying to her, "Let the children be satisfied first, for it is not good to take the children's bread and throw it to the dogs."

28   But she answered and *said to Him, "Yes, Lord, *but* even the dogs under the table feed on the children's crumbs."

The woman acknowledges that she is a "dog."

29   And He said to her, "Because of this answer go your way; the demon has gone out of your daughter."

30   And going back to her home, she found the child lying on the bed, the demon having departed.

DD. A deaf mute healed (7:31–37; Matt. 15:29–31)

Decapolis was where the former demoniac lived Ch. 5:20

31   And again He went out from the region of Tyre, and came through Sidon to the Sea of Galilee, within the region of Decapolis.

7:32
Mark 5:23;
Matt 9:32;
Luke 11:14

32   And they *brought to Him one who was deaf and spoke with difficulty, and they *entreated Him to lay His hand upon him.

7:33
Mark 8:23

33   And He took him aside from the multitude by himself, and put His fingers into his ears, and after spitting, He touched his tongue *with the saliva;*

7:34
Mark 6:41;
8:12

34   and looking up to heaven with a deep sigh, He *said to him, "Ephphatha!" that is, "Be opened!"

7:35
Is 35:5,6

35   And his ears were opened, and the impediment of his tongue was removed, and he *began* speaking plainly.

7:36
Mark 1:44;
5:43

36   And He gave them orders not to tell anyone; but the more He ordered them, the more widely they continued to proclaim it.

37   And they were utterly astonished, saying, "He has done all things well; He makes even the deaf to hear, and the dumb to speak."

EE. The four thousand fed (8:1–10; Matt. 15:32–39)

8 In those days again, when there was a great multitude and they had nothing to eat, He called His disciples and *said to them,

8:2
Matt 9:36

2   "I feel compassion for the multitude because they have remained with Me now three days, and have nothing to eat;

3 days – Jesus lets people recognize their own needs.

3   and if I send them away hungry to their home, they will faint on the way; and some of them have come from a distance."

4   And His disciples answered Him, "Where will anyone be able to *find enough to* satisfy these men with bread here in a desolate place?"

8:5
Mark 6:38

5   And He was asking them, "How many loaves do you have?" And they said, "Seven."

6   And He *directed the multitude to sit down on the ground; and taking the seven loaves, He gave thanks and broke them, and started giving them to His disciples to serve to them, and they served them to the multitude.

8:7
Matt 14:19;
Mark 6:41

7   They also had a few small fish; and after He had blessed them, He ordered these to be served as well.

our god is a god of extravagance

8   And they ate and were satisfied; and they picked up seven large baskets full of what was left over of the broken pieces.

9   And about four thousand were *there;* and He sent them away.

10   And immediately He entered the boat with His disciples, and came to the district of Dalmanutha.

---

[21]Some early mss. add: *and Sidon*   [22]Lit., *Greek*

8:10 This place has not been identified. Some manuscripts of Mark have "Magdala," a town on the west side of the Sea of Galilee; other manuscripts (like the parallel passage in Matt. 15:39) have *Magadan,* which is possibly the town of Megiddo, more than twenty miles distant from the Sea of Galilee. It is suggested that the same locality may have been known by two or three different names.

FF. *The Pharisees seek a sign from heaven* (8:11–21; Matt. 16:1–10)

11 And the Pharisees came out and began to argue with Him, seeking from Him a sign from heaven, to test Him.

12 And sighing deeply in His spirit, He *said, "Why does this generation seek for a sign? Truly I say to you, no sign shall be given to this generation."

13 And leaving them, He again embarked and went away to the other side.

14 And they had forgotten to take bread; and did not have more than one loaf in the boat with them.

15 And He was giving orders to them, saying, "Watch out! Beware of the leaven of the Pharisees and the leaven of Herod."

16 And they *began* to discuss with one another *the fact* that they had no bread.

17 And Jesus, aware of this, *said to them, "Why do you discuss *the fact* that you have no bread? Do you not yet see or understand? Do you have a hardened heart?

18 "HAVING EYES, DO YOU NOT SEE? AND HAVING EARS, DO YOU NOT HEAR? And do you not remember,

19 when I broke the five loaves for the five thousand, how many baskets full of broken pieces you picked up?" They *said to Him, "Twelve."

20 "And when *I broke* the seven for the four thousand, how many large baskets full of broken pieces did you pick up?" And they *said to Him, "Seven."

21 And He was saying to them, "Do you not yet understand?"

GG. *The blind man healed near Bethsaida* (8:22–26)

22 And they *came to Bethsaida. And they *brought a blind man to Him, and *entreated Him to touch him.

23 And taking the blind man by the hand, He brought him out of the village; and after spitting on his eyes, and laying His hands upon him, He asked him, "Do you see anything?"

24 And he looked up and said, "I see men, for I am seeing *them* like trees, walking about."

25 Then again He laid His hands upon his eyes; and he looked intently and was restored, and *began* to see everything clearly.

26 And He sent him to his home, saying, "Do not even enter the village."

HH. *Peter's confession* (8:27–30; Matt. 16:13–20; Luke 9:18–21)

27 And Jesus went out, along with His disciples, to the villages of Caesarea Philippi; and on the way He questioned His disciples, saying to them, "Who do people say that I am?"

28 And they told Him, saying, "John the Baptist; and others *say* Elijah; but others, one of the prophets."

29 And He *continued* by questioning them, "But who do you say that I am?" Peter *answered and *said to Him, "Thou art the Christ."

30 And He warned them to tell no one about Him.

II. *Jesus foretells His death, resurrection, and second coming* (8:31–9:1; Matt. 16:21–28; Luke 9:22–27)

31 And He began to teach them that the Son of Man must suffer many things and be rejected by the elders and the chief priests and the scribes, and be killed, and after three days rise again.

32 And He was stating the matter plainly. And Peter took Him aside and began to rebuke Him.

33 But turning around and seeing His disciples, He rebuked Peter, and *said, "Get behind Me, Satan; for you are not setting your mind on [23]God's interests, but man's."

34 And He summoned the multitude with His disciples, and said to them, "If anyone wishes to come after Me, let him deny himself, and take up his cross, and follow Me.

[23]Lit., *the things of God*

Marginal references:

8:11 Matt 12:38, 39; Luke 11:29; John 6:30
8:12 Mark 7:34
8:15 Luke 12:1; Mark 16:4; 12:13
8:17 Mark 6:52; Is 6:9,10
8:19 Matt 14:20; Mark 6:43; Luke 9:17; John 6:13
8:20 vv. 6-9; Matt 15:37
8:21 Mark 6:52
8:22 Matt 11:21; Mark 6:45; Luke 9:10
8:23 Mark 7:33; 5:23
8:26 Matt 8:4
8:27 John 6:66-69
8:28 Mark 6:14
*8:29 John 6:69; 11:27
8:30 Mark 9:9
8:32 John 18:20
8:33 Matt 4:10
8:34 Matt 10:38; Luke 14:27

8:35
Matt 10:39;
Luke 17:33;
John 12:25

35 "For whoever wishes to save his life shall lose it; but whoever loses his life for My sake and the gospel's shall save it.

36 "For what does it profit a man to gain the whole world, and forfeit his soul?

37 "For what shall a man give in exchange for his soul?

8:38
Matt 10:33;
Luke 12:9;
Matt 8:20;
Mark 13:26

38 "For whoever is ashamed of Me and My words in this adulterous and sinful generation, the Son of Man will also be ashamed of him when He comes in the glory of His Father with the holy angels."

9:1
Matt 24:30;
25:31;
Mark 13:30;
Luke 22:18

9 And He was saying to them, "Truly I say to you, there are some of those who are standing here who shall not taste death until they see the kingdom of God after it has come with power."

JJ. The transfiguration (9:2–13; Matt. 17:1–8; Luke 9:28–36)

*9:2
Mark 5:37;
13:3

2 And six days later, Jesus *took with Him Peter and James and John, and *brought them up to a high mountain by themselves. And He was transfigured before them;

9:3
Matt 28:3

3 and His garments became radiant and exceedingly white, as no launderer on earth can whiten them.

4 And Elijah appeared to them along with Moses; and they were talking with Jesus.

9:5
Matt 23:7

5 And Peter answered and *said to Jesus, "Rabbi, it is good for us to be here; and let us make three tabernacles, one for You, and one for Moses, and one for Elijah."

6 For he did not know what to answer; for they became terrified.

9:7
2 Pet 1:17,18;
Mark 1:11

7 Then a cloud formed, overshadowing them, and a voice came out of the cloud, "This is My beloved Son, listen to Him!"

8 And all at once they looked around and saw no one with them anymore, except Jesus alone.

9:9
Mark 5:43;
7:36; 8:30

9 And as they were coming down from the mountain, He gave them orders not to relate to anyone what they had seen, until the Son of Man should rise from the dead.

10 And they seized upon that statement, discussing with one another what rising from the dead might mean.

*9:11
Matt 11:14

11 And they asked Him, saying, *"Why is it* that the scribes say that Elijah must come first?"

9:12
Ps 22:6;
Luke 23:11;
Phil 2:7

12 And He said to them, "Elijah does first come and restore all things. And *yet* how is it written of the Son of Man that He should suffer many things and be treated with contempt?

9:13
Matt 11:14;
Luke 1:17

13 "But I say to you, that Elijah has indeed come, and they did to him whatever they wished, just as it is written of him."

KK. The demoniac boy cured (9:14–29; Matt. 17:14–21; Luke 9:37–43)

14 And when they came *back* to the disciples, they saw a large crowd around them, and *some* scribes arguing with them.

9:15
Mark 14:33;
16:5,6

15 And immediately, when the entire crowd saw Him, they were amazed, and *began* running up to greet Him.

16 And He asked them, "What are you discussing with them?"

17 And one of the crowd answered Him, "Teacher, I brought You my son, possessed with a spirit which makes him mute;

18 and whenever it seizes him, it dashes him *to the ground* and he foams *at the mouth*, and grinds his teeth, and stiffens out. And I told Your disciples to cast it out, and they could not *do it.*"

19 And He *answered them and *said, "O unbelieving generation, how long

9:2 The transfiguration of Christ is recorded by Matthew, Mark, and Luke. The accounts supplement each other somewhat, for no single one supplies all the details. Most scholars today believe that the event occurred on Mt. Hermon. Christ called it a vision (Greek *horama*, Matt. 17:9), but this does not imply that it was unreal. The clear indication is that Moses and Elijah were actually there in person, since it is said that the three disciples saw the two (Luke 9:32). This solemn interview and donning of the garments of heavenly radiance were intended as a foretaste of Christ's glory. The disciples were greatly strengthened in their faith, as they heard the voice from the cloud declare, *"This is My beloved Son; listen to Him"* (v. 7). When Moses and Elijah were suddenly removed from the scene to leave *Jesus alone*, the disciples were shown that in Him the Old Testament law and prophecy were fulfilled. Peter always remembered this episode as an event of deep significance and was careful to remind his readers that he was an actual eyewitness of *His majesty* (2 Pet. 1:16–18).
9:11 See note to Mal. 4:5 on Elijah.

shall I be with you? How long shall I put up with you? Bring him to Me!"

20   And they brought the boy to Him. And when he saw Him, immediately the spirit threw him into a convulsion, and falling to the ground, he *began* rolling about and foaming *at the mouth*.

21   And He asked his father, "How long has this been happening to him?" And he said, "From childhood.

22   "And it has often thrown him both into the fire and into the water to destroy him. But if You can do anything, take pity on us and help us!"

23   And Jesus said to him, " 'If You can!' All things are possible to him who believes."

24   Immediately the boy's father cried out and *began* saying, "I do believe; help my unbelief."

25   And when Jesus saw that a crowd was rapidly gathering, He rebuked the unclean spirit, saying to it, "You deaf and dumb spirit, I command you, come out of him and do not enter him again."

26   And after crying out and throwing him into terrible convulsions, it came out; and *the boy* became so much like a corpse that most *of them* said, "He is dead!"

27   But Jesus took him by the hand and raised him; and he got up.

28   And when He had come into *the* house, His disciples *began* questioning Him privately, "Why could we not cast it out?"

29   And He said to them, "This kind cannot come out by anything but prayer[24]."

LL. *Jesus again foretells His death and resurrection* (9:30–32; Matt. 17:22–23; Luke 9:43–45)

30   And from there they went out and *began* to go through Galilee, and He was unwilling for anyone to know *about it*.

31   For He was teaching His disciples and telling them, "The Son of Man is to be [25]delivered into the hands of men, and they will kill Him; and when He has been killed, He will rise three days later."

32   But they did not understand *this* statement, and they were afraid to ask Him.

MM. *Discourse on humility* (9:33–50; Matt. 18:1–5; Luke 9:46–48)

33   And they came to Capernaum; and when He was in the house, He *began* to question them, "What were you discussing on the way?"

34   But they kept silent, for on the way they had discussed with one another which *of them was* the greatest.

35   And sitting down, He called the twelve and *said to them, "If anyone wants to be first, he shall be last of all, and servant of all."

36   And taking a child, He set him before them, and taking him in His arms, He said to them,

37   "Whoever receives one child like this in My name receives Me; and whoever receives Me does not receive Me, but Him who sent Me."

38   John said to Him, "Teacher, we saw someone casting out demons in Your name, and we tried to hinder him because he was not following us."

39   But Jesus said, "Do not hinder him, for there is no one who shall perform a miracle in My name, and be able soon afterward to speak evil of Me.

40   "For he who is not against us is [26]for us.

41   "For whoever gives you a cup of water to drink because of your name as *followers* of Christ, truly I say to you, he shall not lose his reward.

42   "And whoever causes one of these little ones who believe to stumble, it would

---

[24]Many mss. add: *and fasting*   [25]Or, *betrayed*   [26]Or, *on our side*

Side references:

9:20
Mark 1:26

*9:23
Mark 11:23;
Luke 17:6;
John 11:40

9:25
v. 15

9:28
Mark 7:17

9:31
Matt 16:21;
Mark 8:31

9:32
John 12:16

9:34
Luke 22:24

9:35
Matt 20:26,
27;
Mark 10:43;
Luke 22:26
9:36
Mark 10:16
9:37
Matt 10:40;
John 12:44;
13:20
*9:38
Num 11:27-29

9:40
Matt 12:30
9:41
Matt 10:42

9:42
Luke 17:1,2;
1 Cor 8:12

See Mk 10:15

9:23 This statement of Jesus has been misconstrued by well-meaning believers who accept it as an unqualified promise. Believing faith must be based on evidences of the will of God. That which is asked for personal desires or passions (James 4:3) is asked amiss and therefore cannot be asked in faith (i.e., in faith that such self-seeking requests are truly the will of God). For a believer to ask God to change the color of his skin, for example, or his sex, or to restore his youth when he is old hardly falls within the purview of this promise. Nor does it imply that deliverance from death is always God's will either, since other Scripture indicates that it is *appointed for men to die once* (Heb. 9:27).

Unbroken or continued physical existence is not the will of God. But faith that is impelled by a sincere desire for God's glory and is based on a known promise of Scripture or on an inward assurance generated by the Holy Spirit will surely be rewarded with a divine answer.

9:38 The disciples here fell into the sin of sectarianism. They forbade the man to perform miracles in Christ's name simply because he was not a member of their particular group. Jesus rebuked them for this attitude—an attitude that has been prevalent in the church since then, and which calls for rebuke.

be better for him if, with a heavy millstone hung around his neck, he had been cast into the sea.

*9:43
Matt 5:29,30;
5:22; 25:41
43 "And if your hand causes you to stumble, cut it off; it is better for you to enter life crippled, than having your two hands, to go into hell, into the unquenchable fire,

44 [27where THEIR WORM DOES NOT DIE, AND THE FIRE IS NOT QUENCHED.]

9:45
Matt 5:22
45 "And if your foot causes you to stumble, cut it off; it is better for you to enter life lame, than having your two feet, to be cast into hell,

46 [27where THEIR WORM DOES NOT DIE, AND THE FIRE IS NOT QUENCHED.]

9:47
Matt 5:29
47 "And if your eye causes you to stumble, cast it out; it is better for you to enter the kingdom of God with one eye, than having two eyes, to be cast into hell,

9:48
Is 66:24
*9:49
Lev 2:13
9:50
Matt 5:13;
Luke 14:34,
35; Col 4:6;
Rom 12:18;
2 Cor 13:11;
1 Thess 5:13
48 where THEIR WORM DOES NOT DIE, AND THE FIRE IS NOT QUENCHED.

49 "For everyone will be salted with fire.

50 "Salt is good; but if the salt becomes unsalty, with what will you make it salty again? Have salt in yourselves, and be at peace with one another."

III. From Galilee to Jerusalem (10:1–52)

A. Jesus goes to Judea (10:1)

10:1
Matt 19:1;
John 10:40;
11:7
10 And rising up, He *went from there to the region of Judea, and beyond the Jordan; and crowds *gathered around Him again, and, according to His custom, He once more *began* to teach them.

B. Jesus teaches about marriage (10:2–12; Matt. 19:3–12)

2 And *some* Pharisees came up to Him, testing Him, and *began* to question Him whether it was lawful for a man to divorce a wife.

3 And He answered and said to them, "What did Moses command you?"

10:4
Deut 24:1-4;
Matt 5:31;
19:7
4 And they said, "Moses permitted *a man* TO WRITE A CERTIFICATE OF DIVORCE AND SEND *her* AWAY."

5 But Jesus said to them, "Because of your hardness of heart he wrote you this commandment.

10:6
Gen 1:27; 5:2
10:7
Gen 2:24;
1 Cor 6:16
6 "But from the beginning of creation, *God* MADE THEM MALE AND FEMALE.

7 "FOR THIS CAUSE A MAN SHALL LEAVE HIS FATHER AND MOTHER, 28

8 AND THE TWO SHALL BECOME ONE FLESH; consequently they are no longer two, but one flesh.

9 "What therefore God has joined together, let no man separate."

10 And in the house the disciples *began* questioning Him about this again.

*10:11
Matt 5:32;
Luke 16:18;
Rom 7:3;
1 Cor 7:10,11
11 And He *said to them, "Whoever divorces his wife and marries another woman commits adultery against her;

12 and if she herself divorces her husband and marries another man, she is committing adultery."

C. Jesus blesses little children
(10:13–16; Matt. 19:13–15; Luke 18:15–17)

13 And they were bringing children to Him so that He might touch them; and the disciples rebuked them.

14 But when Jesus saw this, He was indignant and said to them, "Permit the children to come to Me; do not hinder them; for the kingdom of God belongs to such as these.

10:15
Matt 18:3;
1 Cor 14:20;
1 Pet 2:2
10:16
Mark 9:36
15 "Truly I say to you, whoever does not receive the kingdom of God like a child shall not enter it *at all*."

16 And He took them in His arms and *began* blessing them, laying His hands upon them.

27Vv. 44 and 46, which are identical with v. 48, are not found in the best ancient mss.   28Some mss. add: *and shall cleave to his wife*

9:43 See here the note to Matt. 5:29.
9:49 At least fifteen different explanations of the meaning of this verse have been proposed. Most commentators see an allusion to Lev. 2:13, which contains instructions on seasoning the cereal offerings with the salt of the covenant. Salt generally represents preservation, or dedication, while fire

is often used as a figure for purification. Moffatt translates this verse, "Everyone has to be consecrated by the fire of the discipline."
10:5 See note to Matt. 19:3 on divorce.
10:11 See note to Matt. 5:27 on adultery.

D. The rich young ruler: the peril of riches
(10:17–31; Matt. 19:16–30; Luke 18:18–30)

17 And as He was setting out on a journey, a man ran up to Him and knelt before Him, and *began* asking Him, "Good Teacher, what shall I do to inherit eternal life?"

18 And Jesus said to him, "Why do you call Me good? No one is good except God alone.

19 "You know the commandments, 'DO NOT MURDER, DO NOT COMMIT ADULTERY, DO NOT STEAL, DO NOT BEAR FALSE WITNESS, Do not defraud, HONOR YOUR FATHER AND MOTHER.'"

20 And he said to Him, "Teacher, I have kept all these things from my youth up."

21 And looking at him, Jesus felt a love for him, and said to him, "One thing you lack: go and sell all you possess, and give to the poor, and you shall have treasure in heaven; and come, follow Me."

22 But at these words his face fell, and he went away grieved, for he was one who owned much property.

23 And Jesus, looking around, *said to His disciples, "How hard it will be for those who are wealthy to enter the kingdom of God!"

24 And the disciples were amazed at His words. But Jesus *answered again and *said to them, "Children, how hard it is [29]to enter the kingdom of God!

25 "It is easier for a camel to go through the eye of a needle than for a rich man to enter the kingdom of God."

26 And they were even more astonished and said to Him, "Then who can be saved?"

27 Looking upon them, Jesus *said, "With men it is impossible, but not with God; for all things are possible with God."

28 Peter began to say to Him, "Behold, we have left everything and followed You."

29 Jesus said, "Truly I say to you, there is no one who has left house or brothers or sisters or mother or father or children or farms, for My sake and for the gospel's sake,

30 but that he shall receive a hundred times as much now in the present age, houses and brothers and sisters and mothers and children and farms, along with persecutions; and in the age to come, eternal life.

31 "But many *who are* first, will be last; and the last, first."

E. Christ foretells His crucifixion and resurrection
(10:32–34; Matt. 20:17–19; Luke 18:31–34)

32 And they were on the road, going up to Jerusalem, and Jesus was walking on ahead of them; and they were amazed, and those who followed were fearful. And again He took the twelve aside and began to tell them what was going to happen to Him,

33 *saying,* "Behold, we are going up to Jerusalem, and the Son of Man will be [30]delivered to the chief priests and the scribes; and they will condemn Him to death, and will deliver Him to the Gentiles.

34 "And they will mock Him and spit upon Him, and scourge Him, and kill Him, and three days later He will rise again."

F. Ambition of James and John (10:35–45; Matt. 20:20–28)

35 And James and John, the two sons of Zebedee, *came up to Him, saying to Him, "Teacher, we want You to do for us whatever we ask of You."

36 And He said to them, "What do you want Me to do for you?"

37 And they said to Him, "Grant that we may sit in Your glory, one on Your right, and one on *Your* left."

38 But Jesus said to them, "You do not know what you are asking for. Are you able to drink the cup that I drink, or to be baptized with the baptism with which I am baptized?"

---

[29]Later mss. insert: *for those who trust in wealth*   [30]Or, *betrayed*

10:25 *eye of a needle,* probably a narrow gate through which it was difficult for a camel to pass. Riches often are a hindrance that keep men from the kingdom of God.

Cross references:

10:17 Mark 1:40; Luke 10:25; Eph 1:18

10:19 Ex 20:12-16; Deut 5:16-20

10:21 Matt 6:20; Luke 12:33; Acts 2:35; 4:34,35

10:23 Matt 19:23; Luke 18:24

10:24 Ps 52:7; 62:10; 1 Tim 6:17

10:27 Jer 32:17

10:28 Matt 4:20-22

10:29 Matt 6:33

10:31 Matt 20:16; Luke 13:30

10:32 Mark 8:31; 9:31; Luke 9:22

10:34 Matt 26:67; 27:30; Mark 14:65

10:37 Matt 19:28; Luke 22:30

10:38 Luke 12:50; John 18:11

10:39
Acts 12:2;
Rev 1:9;
10:41;
Luke 22:25-27

39   And they said to Him, "We are able." And Jesus said to them, "The cup that I drink you shall drink; and you shall be baptized with the baptism with which I am baptized.

40   "But to sit on My right or on *My* left, this is not Mine to give; but it is for those for whom it has been prepared."

41   And hearing this, the ten began to feel indignant with James and John.

42   And calling them to Himself, Jesus *said to them, "You know that those who are recognized as rulers of the Gentiles lord it over them; and their great men exercise authority over them.

10:43
Matt 9:35

43   "But it is not so among you, but whoever wishes to become great among you shall be your servant;

44   and whoever wishes to be first among you shall be slave of all.

10:45
John 13:14;
1 Tim 2:5,6

45   "For even the Son of Man did not come to be served, but to serve, and to give His life a ransom for many."

AN EXAMPLE OF GRACE

G. Bartimaeus receives his sight
(10:46–52; Matt. 20:29–34; Luke 18:35–43)

Bartimaeus = Son of Timaeus.
Timaeus = God, or honor
Admission of Need

46   And they *came to Jericho. And as He was going out from Jericho with His disciples and a great multitude, a blind beggar *named* Bartimaeus, the son of Timaeus, was sitting by the road.

10:47
Matt 9:27

Shaming voices

47   And when he heard that it was Jesus the Nazarene, he began to cry out and say, "Jesus, Son of David, have mercy on me!"

48   And many were sternly telling him to be quiet, but he kept crying out all the more, "Son of David, have mercy on me!"

49   And Jesus stopped and said, "Call him *here*." And they *called the blind man, saying to him, "Take courage, arise! He is calling for you."

50   And casting aside his cloak, he jumped up, and came to Jesus.

10:51
John 20:16;
Matt 23:7
10:52
Matt 9:22;
Mark 5:34;
Luke 7:50;
8:48; 17:19

51   And answering him, Jesus said, "What do you want Me to do for you?" And the blind man said to Him, "[31]Rabboni, *I want* to regain my sight!"

52   And Jesus said to him, "Go your way; your faith has made you well." And immediately he regained his sight and *began* following Him on the road.

IV. *The last week in Jerusalem (11:1–16:8)*

A. *The triumphal entry*
(11:1–11; Matt. 21:1–11; Luke 19:29–44; John 12:12–19)

*11:1
Matt 21:17

11   And as they *approached Jerusalem, at Bethphage and Bethany, near the Mount of Olives, He *sent two of His disciples,

2   and *said to them, "Go into the village opposite you, and immediately as you enter it, you will find a colt tied *there*, on which no one yet has ever sat; untie it and bring it *here*.

3   "And if anyone says to you, 'Why are you doing this?' you say, 'The Lord has need of it'; and immediately he will send it back here."

11:4
Mark 14:16

4   And they went away and found a colt tied at the door outside in the street; and they *untied it.

5   And some of the bystanders were saying to them, "What are you doing, untying the colt?"

6   And they spoke to them just as Jesus had told *them,* and they gave them permission.

7   And they *brought the colt to Jesus and put their garments on it; and He sat upon it.

8   And many spread their garments in the road, and others *spread* leafy branches which they had cut from the fields.

11:9
Ps 118:26;
Matt 23:39

9   And those who went before, and those who followed after, were crying out,
   "Hosanna!
        BLESSED IS HE WHO COMES IN THE NAME OF THE LORD;

10   Blessed *is* the coming kingdom of our father David;
        Hosanna in the highest!"

[31]I.e., My Master

11:1 Bethany was a village some two miles southeast of Jerusalem (John 11:18), the home of Lazarus and his sisters Martha and Mary (John 11:1). Bethphage was closer to Jerusalem, probably less than a mile away, somewhat like a suburb of the city.

11   And He entered Jerusalem *and came* into the temple; and after looking all around, He departed for Bethany with the twelve, since it was already late.

11:11
Matt 21:10,
11,17

B. *The barren fig tree*
(11:12–14,20–25; Matt. 21:18–22)

12   And on the next day, when they had departed from Bethany, He became hungry.

11:12
Luke 13:6-9

13   And seeing at a distance a fig tree in leaf, He went *to see* if perhaps He would find anything on it; and when He came to it, He found nothing but leaves, for it was not the season for figs.

14   And He answered and said to it, "May no one ever eat fruit from you again!" And His disciples were listening.

C. *Second cleansing of the temple*
(11:15–19; Matt. 21:12–17; Luke 19:45–48; cf. John 2:13–22)

15   And they *came to Jerusalem. And He entered the temple and began to cast out those who were buying and selling in the temple, and overturned the tables of the moneychangers and the seats of those who were selling doves;

16   and He would not permit anyone to carry goods through the temple.

17   And He *began* to teach and say to them, "Is it not written, 'MY HOUSE SHALL BE CALLED A HOUSE OF PRAYER FOR ALL THE NATIONS'? But you have made it a ROBBERS' DEN."

*11:17
Is 56:7;
Jer 7:11

18   And the chief priests and the scribes heard *this*, and *began* seeking how to destroy Him; for they were afraid of Him, for all the multitude was astonished at His teaching.

11:18
Matt 21:46;
7:28;
Mark 1:22;
Luke 4:32

19   And whenever evening came, they would go out of the city.

D. *The power of faith (11:20–25)*

20   And as they were passing by in the morning, they saw the fig tree withered from the roots *up*.

11:20
Matt 21:19

21   And being reminded, Peter *said to Him, "Rabbi, behold, the fig tree which You cursed has withered."

11:21
Matt 23:7

22   And Jesus *answered saying to them, "Have faith in God.

11:22
Matt 17:20

23   "Truly I say to you, whoever says to this mountain, 'Be taken up and cast into the sea,' and does not doubt in his heart, but believes that what he says is going to happen, it shall be *granted* him.

11:23
Matt 21:21;
Luke 17:6

24   "Therefore I say to you, all things for which you pray and ask, believe that you have received them, and they shall be *granted* you.

*11:24
Matt 7:7;
John 14:13,
14; 15:7;
16:23,24;
James 1:5,6

25   "And whenever you stand praying, forgive, if you have anything against anyone; so that your Father also who is in heaven may forgive you your transgressions.

11:25
Matt 6:14,15;
Col 3:13

26   ["³²But if you do not forgive, neither will your Father who is in heaven forgive your transgressions."]

E. *Christ's authority challenged*
(11:27–33; Matt. 21:23–27; Luke 20:1–8)

27   And they *came again to Jerusalem. And as He was walking in the temple, the chief priests, and scribes, and elders *came to Him,

28   and *began* saying to Him, "By what authority are You doing these things, or who gave You this authority to do these things?"

29   And Jesus said to them, "I will ask you one question, and you answer Me, and *then* I will tell you by what authority I do these things.

30   "Was the baptism of John from heaven, or from men? Answer Me."

³²Many mss. do not contain this verse

11:17 For the convenience of those who came to the temple during the great national feasts, the animal vendors provided sacrificial animals that would meet the proper requirements of ritual cleanliness and soundness, while the moneychangers exchanged the foreign currency of the Jews of the dispersion into the proper half-shekel coin required for payment of the annual temple tax. All this traffic took place in the court of the Gentiles, where non-Jews were allowed to come in order to participate in the temple worship of the Jews. The traders were converting God's house into a bazaar, making it impossible for devout Gentiles to worship in the temple, thus voiding the words of Is. 56:7, quoted by Jesus, that God's house was *a house of prayer for all the peoples.*

11:24 See note to Luke 11:1 on principles of prayer.

31 And they *began* reasoning among themselves, saying, "If we say, 'From heaven,' He will say, 'Then why did you not believe him?'

11:32
Matt 14:5

32 "But shall we say, 'From men'?"—they were afraid of the multitude, for all considered John to have been a prophet indeed.

33 And answering Jesus, they *said, "We do not know." And Jesus *said to them, "Neither will I tell you by what authority I do these things."

F. *Parable of the wicked tenants*
(12:1–12; Matt. 21:33–46; Luke 20:9–19)

*12:1
Is 5:1-7

12 And He began to speak to them in parables: "A man PLANTED A VINEYARD, AND PUT A WALL AROUND IT, AND DUG A VAT UNDER THE WINE PRESS, AND BUILT A TOWER, and rented it out to 33vine-growers and went on a journey.

2 "And at the *harvest* time he sent a slave to the vine-growers, in order to receive *some* of the produce of the vineyard from the vine-growers.

3 "And they took him, and beat him, and sent him away empty-handed.

4 "And again he sent them another slave, and they wounded him in the head, and treated him shamefully.

5 "And he sent another, and that one they killed; and *so with* many others, beating some, and killing others.

12:6
cf. Heb 1:1-3

6 "He had one more *to send*, a beloved son; he sent him last *of all* to them, saying, 'They will respect my son.'

7 "But those vine-growers said to one another, 'This is the heir; come, let us kill him, and the inheritance will be ours!'

8 "And they took him, and killed him, and threw him out of the vineyard.

9 "What will the owner of the vineyard do? He will come and destroy the vine-growers, and will give the vineyard to others.

12:10
Ps 118:22,23;
Acts 4:11;
1 Pet 2:7

10 "Have you not even read this Scripture:
'THE STONE WHICH THE BUILDERS REJECTED,
THIS BECAME THE CHIEF CORNER *stone*;

11 THIS CAME ABOUT FROM THE LORD,
AND IT IS MARVELOUS IN OUR EYES'?"

12:12
Matt 21:45,
46;
Mark 11:18;
Matt 22:22

12 And they were seeking to seize Him; and *yet* they feared the multitude; for they understood that He spoke the parable against them. And *so* they left Him, and went away.

G. *Three questions by the Jewish rulers (12:13–34)*

1. *Paying taxes to Caesar*
(12:13–17; Matt. 22:15–22; Luke 20:20–26)

*12:13
Mark 3:6;
Luke 11:54

13 And they *sent some of the Pharisees and Herodians to Him, in order to trap Him in a statement.

14 And they *came and *said to Him, "Teacher, we know that You are truthful, and defer to no one; for You are not partial to any, but teach the way of God in truth. Is it lawful to pay a poll-tax to Caesar, or not?

15 "Shall we pay, or shall we not pay?" But He, knowing their hypocrisy, said to them, "Why are you testing Me? Bring Me a 34denarius to look at."

16 And they brought *one*. And He *said to them, "Whose likeness and inscription is this?" And they said to Him, "Caesar's."

12:17
Rom 13:7

17 And Jesus said to them, "Render to Caesar the things that are Caesar's, and to God the things that are God's." And they were amazed at Him.

2. *The Sadducees and the resurrection*
(12:18–27; Matt. 22:23–33; Luke 20:27–38)

18 And *some* Sadducees (who say that there is no resurrection) *came to Him, and *began* questioning Him, saying,

12:19
Deut 25:5

19 "Teacher, Moses wrote for us that IF A MAN'S BROTHER DIES, and leaves behind a wife, AND LEAVES NO CHILD, HIS BROTHER SHOULD TAKE THE WIFE, AND RAISE UP OFFSPRING TO HIS BROTHER.

33Or, *tenant farmers*, also vv. 2, 7, 9   34The denarius was equivalent to one day's wage

---

12:1 See note to Luke 20:9 on the parable of the wicked tenants.

12:13 See note to Matt. 22:16 for information on the Herodians.

20 "There were seven brothers; and the first took a wife, and died, leaving no offspring.

21 "And the second one took her, and died, leaving behind no offspring; and the third likewise;

22 and *so* all seven left no offspring. Last of all the woman died also.

23 "In the resurrection, [35]when they rise again, which one's wife will she be? For all seven had her as wife."

24 Jesus said to them, "Is this not the reason you are mistaken, that you do not understand the Scriptures, or the power of God?

25 "For when they rise from the dead, they neither marry, nor are given in marriage, but are like angels in heaven.

26 "But regarding the fact that the dead rise again, have you not read in the book of Moses, in the *passage about the burning* bush, how God spoke to him, saying, 'I AM THE GOD OF ABRAHAM, AND THE GOD OF ISAAC, AND THE GOD OF JACOB'?

27 "He is not the God of the dead, but of the living; you are greatly mistaken."

3. *The great commandment (12:28–34; Matt. 22:34–40)*

28 And one of the scribes came and heard them arguing, and recognizing that He had answered them well, asked Him, "What commandment is the foremost of all?"

29 Jesus answered, "The foremost is, 'HEAR, O ISRAEL! THE LORD OUR GOD IS ONE LORD;

30 AND YOU SHALL LOVE THE LORD YOUR GOD WITH ALL YOUR HEART, AND WITH ALL YOUR SOUL, AND WITH ALL YOUR MIND, AND WITH ALL YOUR STRENGTH.'

31 "The second is this, 'YOU SHALL LOVE YOUR NEIGHBOR AS YOURSELF.' There is no other commandment greater than these."

32 And the scribe said to Him, "Right, Teacher, You have truly stated that HE IS ONE; AND THERE IS NO ONE ELSE BESIDES HIM;

33 AND TO LOVE HIM WITH ALL THE HEART AND WITH ALL THE UNDERSTANDING AND WITH ALL THE STRENGTH, AND TO LOVE ONE'S NEIGHBOR AS HIMSELF, is much more than all burnt offerings and sacrifices."

34 And when Jesus saw that he had answered intelligently, He said to him, "You are not far from the kingdom of God." And after that, no one would venture to ask Him any more questions.

H. *Christ's unanswerable question (12:35–37; Matt. 22:41–46; Luke 20:41–44)*

35 And Jesus answering *began* to say, as He taught in the temple, "How *is it that* the scribes say that the Christ is the son of David?

36 "David himself said in the Holy Spirit,
'THE LORD SAID TO MY LORD,
"SIT AT MY RIGHT HAND,
UNTIL I PUT THINE ENEMIES BENEATH THY FEET."'

37 "David himself calls Him 'Lord'; and *so* in what sense is He his son?" And the great crowd enjoyed listening to Him.

I. *Jesus' warning against the scribes (12:38–40; Matt. 23:1–12; Luke 20:45–47)*

38 And in His teaching He was saying: "Beware of the scribes who like to walk around in long robes, and *like* respectful greetings in the market places,

39 and chief seats in the synagogues, and places of honor at banquets,

40 who devour widows' houses, and for appearance's sake offer long prayers; these will receive greater condemnation."

---

[35]Most ancient mss. do not contain *when they rise again*

12:28 For a discussion of scribes in the Old Testament see note on 2 Sam. 8:17. In Jesus' day the scribes were characterized both by their activities and their attitudes. Of them Scripture says: (1) they were often Pharisees (Acts 23:9); (2) they were doctors of the Old Testament law (check Matt. 22:35 with Mark 12:28); (3) they were looked upon as experts in the Old Testament Scriptures (Matt. 2:4; 17:10; Mark 12:35); (4) they suffered from the sin of pride (12:38, 39); (5) they sat on Moses' seat (Matt. 23:2); (6) they were condemned by Christ (Matt. 23:15); (7) they helped to secure Christ's crucifixion (Luke 23:10); and (8) they actively persecuted the believers (Acts 4:5,18,21; 6:12).

Marginal references:

12:25 1 Cor 15:42, 49,52
12:26 Ex 3:6

*12:28 Luke 10:25-28; 20:39

12:29 Deut 6:4

12:31 Lev 19:18; Rom 13:9; Gal 5:14; James 2:8
12:32 Deut 4:39; Is 45:6,14; 46:9
12:33 1 Sam 15:22; Hos 6:6; Mic 6:6-8
12:34 Matt 22:46

12:35 Matt 26:55; 9:27
12:36 Ps 110:1; Acts 2:34,35; Heb 1:13

12:37 John 12:9

12:38 Luke 11:43

J. *The widow's penny* (12:41–44)

12:41
John 8:20;
2 Kin 12:9

41 And He sat down opposite the treasury, and *began* observing how the multitude were putting money into the treasury; and many rich people were putting in large sums.

42 And a poor widow came and put in two small copper coins, which amount to a cent.

12:43
2 Cor 8:12

43 And calling His disciples to Him, He said to them, "Truly I say to you, this poor widow put in more than all the contributors to the treasury;

44 for they all put in out of their surplus, but she, out of her poverty, put in all she owned, all she had to live on."

K. *The Olivet Discourse* (13:1–37; Matt. 24; Luke 21)

1. *Course of the present age* (13:1–13; Matt. 24:1–14; Luke 21:5–19)

13 And as He was going out of the temple, one of His disciples *said to Him, "Teacher, behold ³⁶what wonderful stones and what wonderful buildings!"

13:2
Luke 19:44;
Mark 14:58;
15:29;
Acts 6:14
13:3
Mark 5:37;
9:2

2 And Jesus said to him, "Do you see these great buildings? Not one stone shall be left upon another which will not be torn down."

3 And as He was sitting on the Mount of Olives opposite the temple, Peter and James and John and Andrew were questioning Him privately,

4 "Tell us, when will these things be, and what *will be* the sign when all these things are going to be fulfilled?"

13:5
Eph 5:6;
1 Thess 2:3
13:6
John 8:24

5 And Jesus began to say to them, "See to it that no one misleads you.

6 "Many will come in My name, saying, 'I am *He!*' and will mislead many.

7 "And when you hear of wars and rumors of wars, do not be frightened; *those things* must take place; but *that is* not yet the end.

8 "For nation will arise against nation, and kingdom against kingdom; there will be earthquakes in various places; there will *also* be famines. These things are *merely* the beginning of birth pangs.

13:9
Matt 10:17

9 "But be on your guard; for they will deliver you to *the* courts, and you will be flogged in *the* synagogues, and you will stand before governors and kings for My sake, as a testimony to them.

10 "And the gospel must first be preached to all the nations.

13:11
Matt 10:19;
Luke 12:11

11 "And when they arrest you and deliver you up, do not be anxious beforehand about what you are to say, but say whatever is given you in that hour; for it is not you who speak, but *it is* the Holy Spirit.

13:12
Mic 7:6;
Matt 10:21
13:13
John 15:21;
Matt 10:22;
Rev 2:10

12 "And brother will deliver brother to death, and a father *his* child; and children will rise up against parents and have them put to death.

13 "And you will be hated by all on account of My name, but the one who endures to the end, he shall be saved.

2. *The great tribulation* (13:14–23; Matt. 24:15–28; Luke 21:20–24)

*13:14
Dan 9:27;
11:31; 12:11

14 "But when you see the ABOMINATION OF DESOLATION standing where it should not be (let the reader understand), then let those who are in Judea flee to the mountains.

15 "And let him who is on the housetop not go down, or enter in, to get anything out of his house;

16 and let him who is in the field not turn back to get his cloak.

13:17
Luke 23:29

17 "But woe to those who are with child and to those who nurse babes in those days!

18 "But pray that it may not happen in the winter.

13:19
Dan 9:26;
12:1; Joel 2:2

19 "For those days will be a *time of* tribulation such as has not occurred since the beginning of the creation which God created, until now, and never shall.

20 "And unless the Lord had shortened *those* days, no life would have been saved; but for the sake of the elect whom He chose, He shortened the days.

13:21
Luke 17:23;
21:8

21 "And then if anyone says to you, 'Behold, here is the Christ'; or, 'Behold, *He* is there'; do not believe *him;*

³⁶Lit., *how great*

12:42 Scripture always treats widows sympathetically.
13:4 See note to Matt. 24:3 for information on the Olivet Discourse.

13:14 See note to Dan. 9:27 on the abomination of desolation.

22   for false Christs and false prophets will arise, and will show signs and wonders, in order, if possible, to lead the elect astray.

23   "But take heed; behold, I have told you everything in advance.

3. The second advent of Christ
(13:24–27; Matt. 24:29–31; Luke 21:25–28)

24   "But in those days, after that tribulation, THE SUN WILL BE DARKENED, AND THE MOON WILL NOT GIVE ITS LIGHT,

25   AND THE STARS WILL BE FALLING from heaven, and the powers that are in the heavens will be shaken.

26   "And then they will see THE SON OF MAN COMING IN CLOUDS with great power and glory.

27   "And then He will send forth the angels, and will gather together His elect from the four winds, from the farthest end of the earth, to the farthest end of heaven.

4. The parable of the fig tree
(13:28–31; Matt. 24:32–35; Luke 21:29–33)

28   "Now learn the parable from the fig tree: when its branch has already become tender, and puts forth its leaves, you know that summer is near.

29   "Even so, you too, when you see these things happening, recognize that He is near, *right* at the door.

30   "Truly I say to you, this [37]generation will not pass away until all these things take place.

31   "Heaven and earth will pass away, but My words will not pass away.

5. Watchfulness (13:32–37; Matt. 24:32–35; Luke 21:29–33)

32   "But of that day or hour no one knows, not even the angels in heaven, nor the Son, but the Father *alone*.

33   "Take heed, keep on the alert; for you do not know when the *appointed* time is.

34   "*It is* like a man, away on a journey, *who* upon leaving his house and putting his slaves in charge, *assigning* to each one his task, also commanded the doorkeeper to stay on the alert.

35   "Therefore, be on the alert—for you do not know when the master of the house is coming, whether in the evening, at midnight, at cockcrowing, or in the morning—

36   lest he come suddenly and find you asleep.

37   "And what I say to you I say to all, 'Be on the alert!' "

L. The plot to kill Jesus
(14:1,2,10,11; Matt. 26:1–5,14–16; Luke 22:1–6)

14 Now the Passover and Unleavened Bread was two days off; and the chief priests and the scribes were seeking how to seize Him by stealth, and kill *Him*;

[37]Or, race

Cross references (right margin):

13:22 Matt 7:15; John 4:48
13:23 2 Pet 3:17
13:24 Zeph 1:15
13:26 Dan 7:13; Matt 16:27; Mark 14:62; 1 Thess 4:16; 2 Thess 1:7, 10
13:30 Mark 9:1
13:31 Matt 5:18; Luke 16:17
13:32 Acts 1:7
13:33 Eph 6:18; Col 4:2; 1 Thess 5:6
13:34 Matt 25:14
13:35 Luke 12:35-40
*14:1 John 11:55; 13:1; Matt 12:14

13:27 *from the four winds.* This means "from every direction," "from the four points of the compass." *from the farthest end of the earth, to the farthest end of heaven.* This probably means "from one end of the world to the other," i.e., from the whole earth. This saying seems to combine two Old Testament phrases: "from one end of the earth to the other end" (cf. Deut. 13:7), and "from one end of the heavens to the other" (cf. Deut. 4:32).

13:37 Watchfulness is required of all God's servants (Matt. 25:13; Luke 21:36; 1 Thess. 5:6; 1 Pet. 4:7). (The term used in all these passages is *grēgoreō:* be awake, keep awake, be alert and on guard, watch out.) They must watch with courage (1 Cor. 16:13), with prayer (Luke 21:36; Eph. 6:18), and with thanksgiving (Col. 4:2). There is blessedness in watching (Luke 12:37; Rev. 16:15). Believers are to watch eagerly for Christ's second advent, since they do not know at what time He may return to earth (Matt. 24:42; 25:13; Mark 13:35,36).

14:1 This feast also celebrated the deliverance from Egypt (cf. Ex. 12:15; Deut. 16:3). It began on the fifteenth day of Nisan, immediately after Passover, and lasted until the twenty-first. During this time no leavened bread was to be eaten, in commemoration of the flight from Egypt when the people ate unleavened bread only, "the bread of affliction." The feasts of Passover and Unleavened Bread were celebrated as one feast (cf. Luke 22:1).

Passover (Hebrew *pesah*, from the verb *pasah*, "pass over") commemorated the ancient Hebrews' deliverance from the Egyptian bondage, in particular the night when the Lord "passed over" the homes of the Hebrews in the slaughter of the first-born of Egypt (cf. Ex. 12:13,23,27). It was celebrated on the fourteenth day of the month of Nisan (March-April), and was one of the three great religious celebrations of the Jews, at which time all Jewish males over twelve years of age were supposed to go to Jerusalem. (See note to Ex. 12:11.)

2   for they were saying, "Not during the festival, lest there be a riot of the people."

M. *Jesus anointed by Mary of Bethany*
(14:3–9; Matt. 26:6–13; John 12:1–8)

*14:3
Luke 7:37-39;
Matt 21:17

3   And while He was in Bethany at the home of Simon the leper, and reclining *at the table*, there came a woman with an alabaster vial of very costly perfume of pure nard; *and* she broke the vial and poured it over His head.

4   But some were indignantly *remarking* to one another, "Why has this perfume been wasted?

5   "For this perfume might have been sold for over three hundred [38] denarii, and *the money* given to the poor." And they were scolding her.

6   But Jesus said, "Let her alone; why do you bother her? She has done a good deed to Me.

14:7
Deut 15:11

7   "For the poor you always have with you, and whenever you wish, you can do them good; but you do not always have Me.

14:8
John 19:20

8   "She has done what she could; she has anointed My body beforehand for the burial.

9   "And truly I say to you, wherever the gospel is preached in the whole world, that also which this woman has done shall be spoken of in memory of her."

N. *The bargain of Judas Iscariot (14:10,11)*

*14:10
Luke 22:3,4;
John 6:71

10   And Judas Iscariot, who was one of the twelve, went off to the chief priests, in order to betray Him to them.

11   And they were glad when they heard *this*, and promised to give him money. And he *began* seeking how to betray Him at an opportune time.

O. *The Last Supper (14:12–25)*

1. *The Passover prepared (14:12–16; Matt. 26:17–19; Luke 22:7–13)*

14:12
Ex 12:11

12   And on the first day of Unleavened Bread, when the Passover *lamb* was being sacrificed, His disciples *said to Him, "Where do You want us to go and prepare for You to eat the Passover?"

13   And He *sent two of His disciples, and *said to them, "Go into the city, and a man will meet you carrying a pitcher of water; follow him;

14   and wherever he enters, say to the owner of the house, 'The Teacher says, "Where is My guest room in which I may eat the Passover with My disciples?" '

15   "And he himself will show you a large upper room furnished *and* ready; and prepare for us there."

16   And the disciples went out, and came to the city, and found *it* just as He had told them; and they prepared the Passover.

2. *The Passover eaten*
(14:17–21; Matt. 26:20–25; Luke 22:14–18; see John 13:1–30)

17   And when it was evening He *came with the twelve.

14:18
vv. 44,45

18   And as they were reclining *at the table* and eating, Jesus said, "Truly I say to you that one of you will betray Me—one who is eating with Me."

19   They began to be grieved and to say to Him one by one, "Surely not I?"

20   And He said to them, "*It is* one of the twelve, one who dips with Me in the bowl.

21   "For the Son of Man *is to* go, just as it is written of Him; but woe to that man by whom the Son of Man is betrayed! *It would have been* good for that man if he had not been born."

3. *The Lord's Supper instituted*
(14:22–25; Matt. 26:26–29; Luke 22:19–24)

*14:22
Mark 6:41;
8:6;
Luke 24:30;
1 Cor 11:23-25

22   And while they were eating, He took *some* bread, and after a blessing He broke *it*; and gave *it* to them, and said, "Take *it*; this is My body."

[38]The denarius was equivalent to one day's wage

14:3 See note to Luke 7:36ff. on the various Marys.
14:10 See note to Matt. 26:14 on Judas Iscariot.
14:22 "The Lord's Supper," also known as the *Eucharist*

(or Thanksgiving), was instituted by Christ at His last meal before the crucifixion, and it is recorded in Matthew and Luke as well as here in Mark. Paul specifically refers to its

23   And when He had taken a cup, *and* given thanks, He gave *it* to them; and they all drank from it.

24   And He said to them, "This is My blood of the covenant, which is poured out for many.

25   "Truly I say to you, I shall never again drink of the fruit of the vine until that day when I drink it new in the kingdom of God."

P. Peter's denial foretold
(14:26–31; Matt. 26:30–35; Luke 22:31–34; see John 14–17)

26   And after singing a hymn, they went out to the Mount of Olives.

27   And Jesus *said to them, "You will all fall away, because it is written, 'I WILL STRIKE DOWN THE SHEPHERD, AND THE SHEEP SHALL BE SCATTERED.'

28   "But after I have been raised, I will go before you to Galilee."

29   But Peter said to Him, "*Even* though all may fall away, yet I will not."

30   And Jesus *said to him, "Truly I say to you, that you yourself this very night, before a cock crows twice, shall three times deny Me."

31   But *Peter* kept saying insistently, "*Even* if I have to die with You, I will not deny You!" And they all were saying the same thing, too.

Q. Jesus in Gethsemane (14:32–52)

1. His agony (14:32–42; Matt. 26:36–46; Luke 22:39–46; cf. John 18:1)

32   And they *came to a place named Gethsemane; and He *said to His disciples, "Sit here until I have prayed."

33   And He *took with Him Peter and James and John, and began to be very distressed and troubled.

34   And He *said to them, "My soul is deeply grieved to the point of death; remain here and keep watch."

35   And He went a little beyond *them,* and fell to the ground, and *began* to pray that if it were possible, the hour might pass Him by.

36   And He was saying, "Abba! Father! All things are possible for Thee; remove this cup from Me; yet not what I will, but what Thou wilt."

37   And He *came and *found them sleeping, and *said to Peter, "Simon, are you asleep? Could you not keep watch for one hour?

38   "Keep watching and praying, that you may not come into temptation; the spirit is willing, but the flesh is weak."

39   And again He went away and prayed, saying the same words.

40   And again He came and found them sleeping, for their eyes were very heavy; and they did not know what to answer Him.

41   And He *came the third time, and *said to them, "Are you still sleeping and taking your rest? It is enough; the hour has come; behold, the Son of Man is being betrayed into the hands of sinners.

42   "Arise, let us be going; behold, the one who betrays Me is at hand!"

2. Jesus' betrayal and arrest
(14:43–52; Matt. 26:47–56; Luke 22:47–53; John 18:1–11)

43   And immediately while He was still speaking, Judas, one of the twelve, *came up, accompanied by a multitude with swords and clubs, from the chief priests and the scribes and the elders.

44   Now he who was betraying Him had given them a signal, saying, "Whomever I shall kiss, He is the one; seize Him, and lead Him away under guard."

45   And after coming, he immediately went to Him, saying, "Rabbi!" and kissed Him.

46   And they laid hands on Him, and seized Him.

47   But a certain one of those who stood by drew his sword, and struck the slave of the high priest, and cut off his ear.

Marginal references: 14:23 1 Cor 10:16 · 14:24 Ex 24:8; Heb 9:20 · 14:26 Matt 21:1 · 14:27 Zech 13:7 · 14:28 Mark 16:7 · 14:29 John 13:37,38 · 14:30 vv. 66-72; John 13:38 · 14:34 John 12:27 · 14:35 v. 41 · 14:36 Rom 8:15; Gal 4:6; John 5:30; 6:38 · 14:38 Matt 6:13; Luke 11:4; Rom 7:23; Gal 5:17 · 14:41 v. 35; John 13:1 · 14:45 Matt 23:7

institution by Christ in 1 Cor. 11:23ff. It was prefigured in the Old Testament by the Passover meal (Ex. 12:21–28; 1 Cor. 5:7,8). It is to be observed until the second advent of Christ and includes the requirement of an earnest self-examination as one partakes of the bread and the wine representing the body and blood of our Lord. The early church practiced this ordinance or sacrament at very frequent intervals (Acts 2:42 and 20:7). Only believers are permitted by Scripture to partake of the Lord's Supper; unworthy partakers are those who do not truly repent and do not discern Christ's body. These are said to be guilty of His shed blood and broken body and will be judged for their sin (1 Cor. 11:27–30).

48   And Jesus answered and said to them, "Have you come out with swords and clubs to arrest Me, as against a robber?

14:49
Mark 12:35;
Is 53:7ff;
Luke 19:47;
John 18:19-21
14:50
Ps 88:8; v. 27

49   "Every day I was with you in the temple teaching, and you did not seize Me; but *this has happened* that the Scriptures might be fulfilled."

50   And they all left Him and fled.

51   And a certain young man was following Him, wearing *nothing but* a linen sheet over *his* naked *body;* and they *seized him.

52   But he left the linen sheet behind, and escaped naked.

R. *Jesus before Caiaphas*
(14:53–65; Matt. 26:57–68; cf. Luke 22:54; John 18:12–14,19–25)

53   And they led Jesus away to the high priest; and all the chief priests and the elders and the scribes *gathered together.

14:54
v. 68;
Matt 26:3;
John 18:18

54   And Peter had followed Him at a distance, right into the courtyard of the high priest; and he was sitting with the officers, and warming himself at the fire.

55   Now the chief priests and the whole [39]Council kept trying to obtain testimony against Jesus to put Him to death; and they were not finding any.

56   For many were giving false testimony against Him, and *yet* their testimony was not consistent.

57   And some stood up and *began* to give false testimony against Him, saying,

14:58
Mark 15:29;
John 2:19;
Acts 6:14

58   "We heard Him say, 'I will destroy this temple made with hands, and in three days I will build another made without hands.' "

59   And not even in this respect was their testimony consistent.

60   And the high priest stood up *and came* forward and questioned Jesus, saying, "Do You make no answer? What is it that these men are testifying against You?"

*14:61
Is 53:7

61   But He kept silent, and made no answer. Again the high priest was questioning Him, and saying to Him, "Are You the Christ, the Son of the Blessed *One?*"

14:62
Dan 7:13;
Matt 24:30;
Mark 13:26
14:63
Num 14:6;
Acts 14:14
14:64
Lev 24:16
14:65
Mark 10:34;
Esth 7:8;
Luke 22:64

62   And Jesus said, "I am; and you shall see THE SON OF MAN SITTING AT THE RIGHT HAND OF POWER, and COMING WITH THE CLOUDS OF HEAVEN."

63   And tearing his clothes, the high priest *said, "What further need do we have of witnesses?

64   "You have heard the blasphemy; how does it seem to you?" And they all condemned Him to be deserving of death.

65   And some began to spit at Him, and to blindfold Him, and to beat Him with their fists, and to say to Him, "Prophesy!" And the officers received Him with slaps *in the face.*

S. *Peter's denial of Jesus*
(14:66–72; Matt. 26:69–75; Luke 22:55–62; John 18:15–18,25–27)

14:66
vv. 30,54

66   And as Peter was below in the courtyard, one of the servant-girls of the high priest *came,

14:67
v. 54;
Mark 1:24
14:68
v. 54

67   and seeing Peter warming himself, she looked at him, and *said, "You, too, were with Jesus the Nazarene."

68   But he denied *it,* saying, "I neither know nor understand what you are talking about." And he went out onto the porch. [40]

69   And the maid saw him, and began once more to say to the bystanders, "This is *one* of them!"

14:70
v. 68;
Acts 2:7

70   But again he was denying it. And after a little while the bystanders were again saying to Peter, "Surely you are *one* of them, for you are a Galilean too."

71   But he began to curse and swear, "I do not know this man you are talking about!"

14:72
v. 30

72   And immediately a cock crowed a second time. And Peter remembered how Jesus had made the remark to him, "Before a cock crows twice, you will deny Me three times." And he began to weep.

[39]Or, *Sanhedrin*   [40]Later mss. add: *and a cock crowed*

14:61 This Scripture may be considered to be a fulfillment of the prophecy of Is. 53:7: *He was oppressed and He was afflicted, yet He did not open his mouth; like a lamb that is led to slaughter, and like a sheep that is silent before its shearers, so He did not open His mouth.* (Cf. 1 Pet. 2:23.)
14:71 The gravity of Peter's words accentuates the gravity of his sin. He took an oath in the name of Almighty God and called down on himself all of the imprecations that attend such an oath. Then he testified to a falsehood when he swore he did not know Jesus Christ. The glory of grace is well illustrated in Peter's later life, for when he repented and was restored he became a flaming evangel for the One he had denied.

T. *Jesus before Pontius Pilate*
(15:1–15; Matt. 27:11–26; Luke 23:3–25; John 18:29–40)

1. *Pilate questions Jesus (15:1–5)*

15 And early in the morning the chief priests with the elders and scribes, and the whole [41]Council, immediately held a consultation; and binding Jesus, they led Him away, and delivered Him up to Pilate.

2 And Pilate questioned Him, "Are You the King of the Jews?" And answering He *said to him, "*It is as* you say."

3 And the chief priests *began* to accuse Him harshly.

4 And Pilate was questioning Him again, saying, "Do You make no answer? See how many charges they bring against You!"

5 But Jesus made no further answer; so that Pilate was amazed.

2. *Pilate releases Barabbas and delivers Jesus (15:6–15)*

6 Now at *the* feast he used to release for them *any* one prisoner whom they requested.

7 And the man named Barabbas had been imprisoned with the insurrectionists who had committed murder in the insurrection.

8 And the multitude went up and began asking him *to do* as he had been accustomed to do for them.

9 And Pilate answered them, saying, "Do you want me to release for you the King of the Jews?"

10 For he was aware that the chief priests had delivered Him up because of envy.

11 But the chief priests stirred up the multitude *to ask* him to release Barabbas for them instead.

12 And answering again, Pilate was saying to them, "Then what shall I do with Him whom you call the King of the Jews?"

13 And they shouted back, "Crucify Him!"

14 But Pilate was saying to them, "Why, what evil has He done?" But they shouted all the more, "Crucify Him!"

15 And wishing to satisfy the multitude, Pilate released Barabbas for them, and after having Jesus scourged, he delivered *Him* to be crucified.

U. *The crucifixion and burial of Jesus (15:16–47)*

1. *Jesus crowned with thorns*
(15:16–20; Matt. 27:27–31; cf. John 19:2,3)

16 And the soldiers took Him away into the palace (that is, the Praetorium), and they *called together the whole *Roman* [42]cohort.

17 And they *dressed Him up in purple, and after weaving a crown of thorns, they put it on Him;

18 and they began to acclaim Him, "Hail, King of the Jews!"

19 And they kept beating His head with a [43]reed, and spitting at Him, and kneeling and bowing before Him.

---

[41]Or, *Sanhedrin*   [42]Or, *battalion*   [43]Or, *staff* (made of a reed)

15:1 Pontius Pilate was the Roman procurator (called "governor" in the gospels) of the territory formerly ruled over by Archelaus, the son of Herod. It included generally Judea, Idumea, and Samaria. Nothing is known of Pilate's origins, although the idea that he was the descendant of a manumitted slave is undoubtedly spurious. Procurators usually came from the Roman equestrian class. Pilate came to Judea about the time John the Baptist began his ministry. He was responsible for the financial administration and collection of taxes for the Roman empire. Normally the subjugated peoples were allowed much freedom to rule themselves. The Sanhedrin was the supreme court of the Jews, but it did not have the power to impose a death sentence without the approval of the governor, who also carried out such executions. Pilate was constantly in some kind of struggle with the Jews, who were themselves turbulent and disaffected. He was capricious, willful, weak, rude, and overbearing. When Christ appeared before him he intended to release Him, but he was outmaneuvered by the Jews and finally capitulated to their demands that Jesus be crucified. Personal and political considerations outweighed his sense of justice and moral obligation. He was finally removed from his procuratorship after ten years' service. Fantastic legends grew up around his later life, none of which seem to have historical certification.

15:7 Barabbas was a well-known insurrectionist (cf. Matt. 27:16: *a notorious prisoner*), probably a leader in the insurrection referred to (cf. Luke 23:18,19,25). In John 18:40 he is called a robber (Greek *lestes*), a word used by Josephus, the Jewish historian, to describe rebels against the Roman power. This is the same word used of the two robbers crucified with Jesus (Matt. 27:38; Mark 15:27). Aside from these few verses, nothing else is known about Barabbas. Some manuscripts in Matt. 27:16,17 give his name as "Jesus Barabbas," and Origen of Alexandria, a church father, writer, and teacher of the third century, said this name occurred in some old copies of the Gospel of Matthew.

---

*15:1
Matt 5:22;
Luke 22:66;
23:1;
John 18:28

15:5
Is 53:7

15:6
Matt 27:15;
Luke 23:17;
John 18:39

15:11
Acts 3:14

15:15
John 19:1,16

15:16
Acts 10:1*

20   And after they had mocked Him, they took the purple off Him, and put His garments on Him. And they *led Him out to crucify Him.

2. Jesus crucified
(15:21–32; Matt. 27:32–44; Luke 23:32–43; John 19:17–24)

15:21
Luke 23:26;
Rom 16:13

21   And they *pressed into service a passer-by coming from the country, Simon of Cyrene (the father of Alexander and Rufus), to bear His cross.
22   And they *brought Him to the place Golgotha, which is translated, Place of a Skull.
23   And they tried to give Him wine mixed with myrrh; but He did not take it.

15:24
Ps 22:18

24   And they *crucified Him, and *divided up His garments among themselves, casting lots for them, to decide what each should take.
25   And it was the 44third hour when they crucified Him.
26   And the inscription of the charge against Him read, "THE KING OF THE JEWS."
27   And they *crucified two robbers with Him, one on His right and one on His left.
28   [45And the Scripture was fulfilled which says, "And He was numbered with transgressors."]

15:29
Ps 22:7;
Mark 13:2;
14:58;
John 2:19
15:31
Ps 22:8

29   And those passing by were hurling abuse at Him, wagging their heads, and saying, "Ha! You who are going to destroy the temple and rebuild it in three days,
30   save Yourself, and come down from the cross!"
31   In the same way the chief priests also, along with the scribes, were mocking Him among themselves and saying, "He saved others; He cannot save Himself.

15:32
vv. 26,27

32   "Let this Christ, the King of Israel, now come down from the cross, so that we may see and believe!" And those who were crucified with Him were casting the same insult at Him.

3. The death of Jesus
(15:33–41; Matt. 27:45–50; Luke 23:44–49; John 19:28–37)

33   And when the 46sixth hour had come, darkness fell over the whole land until the 47ninth hour.

15:34
Ps 22:1

34   And at the ninth hour Jesus cried out with a loud voice, "ELOI, ELOI, LAMA SABACHTHANI?" which is translated, "MY GOD, MY GOD, WHY HAST THOU FORSAKEN ME?"
35   And when some of the bystanders heard it, they began saying, "Behold, He is calling for Elijah."

15:36
Ps 69:21

36   And someone ran and filled a sponge with sour wine, put it on a reed, and gave Him a drink, saying, "Let us see whether Elijah will come to take Him down."
37   And Jesus uttered a loud cry, and breathed His last.

15:38
Heb 10:19,20
15:39
Mark 1:11;
9:7
15:40
Ps 38:11;
John 19:25;
Mark 16:1
15:41
Luke 8:1-3

38   And the veil of the temple was torn in two from top to bottom.
39   And when the centurion, who was standing right in front of Him, saw the way He breathed His last, he said, "Truly this man was the Son of God!"
40   And there were also some women looking on from a distance, among whom were Mary Magdalene, and Mary the mother of James the Less and Joses, and Salome.
41   And when He was in Galilee, they used to follow Him and minister to Him; and there were many other women who had come up with Him to Jerusalem.

4. Jesus laid in the tomb
(15:42–47; Matt. 27:57–61; Luke 23:50–56; John 19:38–42)

15:42
Deut 21:22,
23;
Matt 27:62
15:43
Acts 13:50;
17:12;
Luke 2:25,38

42   And when evening had already come, because it was the preparation day, that is, the day before the Sabbath,
43   Joseph of Arimathea came, a prominent member of the Council, who himself was waiting for the kingdom of God; and he gathered up courage and went in before Pilate, and asked for the body of Jesus.
44   And Pilate wondered if He was dead by this time, and summoning the centurion, he questioned him as to whether He was already dead.

15:45
v. 39

45   And ascertaining this from the centurion, he granted the body to Joseph.

44I.e., 9 a.m.   45Many mss. do not contain this verse   46I.e., noon   47I.e., 3 p.m.

15:23 This was probably intended to ease the pain, but Jesus refused such escape.

15:26 See note to Matt. 27:37 for the variations of the superscription on the cross.

46   And *Joseph* bought a linen cloth, took Him down, wrapped Him in the linen cloth, and laid Him in a tomb which had been hewn out in the rock; and he rolled a stone against the entrance of the tomb.

47   And Mary Magdalene and Mary the *mother* of Joses were looking on *to see* where He was laid.

V. The resurrection of Jesus Christ
(16:1–8; Matt. 28:1–10; Luke 24:1–11; John 20:1–18)

16 And when the Sabbath was over, Mary Magdalene, and Mary the *mother* of James, and Salome, bought spices, that they might come and anoint Him.   **16:1** Luke 23:56; John 19:39

2   And very early on the first day of the week, they *came to the tomb when the sun had risen.

3   And they were saying to one another, "Who will roll away the stone for us from the entrance of the tomb?"   **16:3** Mark 15:46

4   And looking up, they *saw that the stone had been rolled away, although it was extremely large.

5   And entering the tomb, they saw a young man sitting at the right, wearing a white robe; and they were amazed.   **16:5** Mark 9:15

6   And he *said to them, "Do not be amazed; you are looking for Jesus the Nazarene, who has been crucified. He has risen; He is not here; behold, *here is the* place where they laid Him.   **16:6** v. 5; Mark 1:24

7   "But go, tell His disciples and Peter, 'He is going before you into Galilee; there you will see Him, just as He said to you.' "   **16:7** Mark 14:28; John 21:1-23

8   And they went out and fled from the tomb, for trembling and astonishment had gripped them; and they said nothing to anyone, for they were afraid.

V. *Appearances of the risen Christ (16:9–20)*

9   [[48]Now after He had risen early on the first day of the week, He first appeared to Mary Magdalene, from whom He had cast out seven demons.   **16:9** John 20:11-18

10   She went and reported to those who had been with Him, while they were mourning and weeping.

11   And when they heard that He was alive, and had been seen by her, they refused to believe it.

12   And after that, He appeared in a different form to two of them, while they were walking along on their way to the country.   **16:12** Luke 24:13-35

13   And they went away and reported it to the others, but they did not believe them either.

14   And afterward He appeared to the eleven themselves as they were reclining *at the table;* and He reproached them for their unbelief and hardness of heart, because they had not believed those who had seen Him after He had risen.   **16:14** Luke 24:36-38; John 20:26

15   And He said to them, "Go into all the world and preach the gospel to all creation.   **16:15** Matt 28:18-20; Luke 24:47, 48

16   "He who has believed and has been baptized shall be saved; but he who has disbelieved shall be condemned.

17   "And these signs will accompany those who have believed: in My name they will cast out demons, they will speak with new tongues;

18   they will pick up serpents, and if they drink any deadly *poison,* it shall not hurt them; they will lay hands on the sick, and they will recover."

19   So then, when the Lord Jesus had spoken to them, He was received up into heaven, and sat down at the right hand of God.   **16:19** Luke 24:50, 51; Acts 1:9-11

20   And they went out and preached everywhere, while the Lord worked with them, and confirmed the word by the signs that followed.]

[49][*And they promptly reported all these instructions to Peter and his companions. And after that, Jesus Himself sent out through them from east to west the sacred and imperishable proclamation of eternal salvation.*]

[48]Some of the oldest mss. do not contain vv. 9-20   [49]A few later mss. and versions contain this paragraph, usually after verse 8; a few have it at the end of chapter.

INTRODUCTION TO
THE GOSPEL ACCORDING TO
LUKE

Authorship and Background: The third Gospel bears the name of Luke, "beloved physician" (Col. 4:14), friend and companion of Paul. The earliest references to the third Gospel name Luke as its author, the only known Gentile author in the New Testament. It is clear that the same author wrote the third Gospel and Acts, and according to the accounts in Acts and the epistles, he joined Paul and his party at Troas during the second missionary journey, going with them to Philippi (Acts 16:10-40). He apparently remained in Philippi until Paul's return there on the third missionary journey, and went on with him to Jerusalem (Acts 20:5-21:18) and Rome (Acts 27:1-28:16). He was with Paul when he wrote to the Colossians, to Philemon, and to Timothy (Col. 4:14; 2 Tim. 4:11; Philem. 24).

Opinions vary on the exact date of the book: some scholars place it before the destruction of Jerusalem in A.D. 70, while others prefer the period A.D. 80-90.

Characteristics: The nature and purpose of the book is explicitly stated (1:1-4; cf. also Acts 1:1-2). The identity of Theophilus, to whom the work is dedicated, is a matter of surmise. In writing "in consecutive order" (1:3) of the beginning, growth, and spread of the Christian movement, the author writes consciously as a historian, and his work is more nearly akin to history than any of the other Gospels (notice the precise dating of the beginning of John the Baptist's ministry in 3:1-2).

Called by one scholar "the most beautiful book ever written," the Gospel of Luke records the birth of Christ (2:7), and tells with consummate artistry and grace such parables as that of the good Samaritan (10:29-37), the rich man and Lazarus (16:19-31), and the prodigal son (15:11-32). The loveliest story of all is the narrative of the Emmaus appearance of the risen Lord (24:13-35).

Beautiful hymns adorn the book: the *Magnificat* of Mary (1:46-55), the *Benedictus* of Zechariah (1:67-79), the *Gloria in Excelsis* of the angels (2:14), and the *Nunc Dimittis* of Simeon (2:29-32).

A strong note of joy runs through the whole narrative, from the angels' song in 2:14 to the end of the story, as the disciples return to Jerusalem "with great joy, and were continually in the temple, praising God" (24:52,53; cf. also 15:7,10,24,32). Prominence is given to prayer (see 3:21; 5:16; 6:12; 11:1; 22:32; 23:34,46), and to the work of the Holy Spirit (see 4:1,14; 10:21; 24:49).

This Gospel sounds the note of universal relevance, with its message of "a light of revelation to the Gentiles" (2:32) and God's salvation proffered to all mankind (3:6). Women are accorded a prominent place: Mary, Elizabeth, Anna, Joanna, and Susanna; the women who helped Jesus (8:2,3); the widow of Nain (7:11,12); the sinful woman (7:36-50); Mary and Martha (10:38-42); the woman with the spirit of infirmity (13:10-17); and the women who mourned for Jesus on the way to Golgotha (23:27). Jesus' parables include those of the woman who lost her coin (15:8-10) and the widow who insisted on her rights (18:1-8). His gracious call to salvation also embraces society's outcasts: the "sinners," tax-gatherers, and Samaritans (see 10:29-37; 17:11-19; 18:9-14; 19:1-10).

The narrative reaches its climax in Christ's passion: before the book is even half finished, Jesus begins His journey to Jerusalem, where at Mount Olivet He will be received into heaven (9:51), in fulfillment of His destiny (9:31). The Passion Week is the climax and culmination of the whole Gospel, casting its spell over the entire narrative.

Contents:

THE GOSPEL ACCORDING TO

LUKE

I. Introduction (1:1–4)

1 Inasmuch as many have undertaken to compile an account of the things accomplished among us,

2 just as those who from the beginning were eyewitnesses and servants of the ¹word have handed them down to us,

3 it seemed fitting for me as well, having investigated everything carefully from the beginning, to write *it* out for you in consecutive order, most excellent Theophilus;

4 so that you might know the exact truth about the things you have been taught.

II. Birth and childhood of John the Baptist and of Jesus (1:5–2:52)

A. Birth of John the Baptist foretold (1:5–25)

5 In the days of Herod, king of Judea, there was a certain priest named Zacharias, of the division of ²Abijah; and he had a wife ³from the daughters of Aaron, and her name was Elizabeth.

6 And they were both righteous in the sight of God, walking blamelessly in all the commandments and requirements of the Lord.

7 And they had no child, because Elizabeth was barren, and they were both advanced in years.

8 Now it came about, while he was performing his priestly service before God in the *appointed* order of his division,

9 according to the custom of the priestly office, he was chosen by lot to enter the temple of the Lord and burn incense.

10 And the whole multitude of the people were in prayer outside at the hour of the incense offering.

11 And an angel of the Lord appeared to him, standing to the right of the altar of incense.

12 And Zacharias was troubled when he saw *him*, and fear gripped him.

13 But the angel said to him, "Do not be afraid, Zacharias, for your petition has been heard, and your wife Elizabeth will bear you a son, and you will give him the name John.

14 "And you will have joy and gladness, and many will rejoice at his birth.

15 "For he will be great in the sight of the Lord, and he will drink no wine or liquor; and he will be filled with the Holy Spirit, while yet in his mother's womb.

16 "And he will turn back many of the sons of Israel to the Lord their God.

17 "And it is he who will go *as a forerunner* before Him in the spirit and power of Elijah, TO TURN THE HEARTS OF THE FATHERS BACK TO THE CHILDREN, and the disobedient to the attitude of the righteous; so as to make ready a people prepared for the Lord."

18 And Zacharias said to the angel, "How shall I know this *for certain*? For I am an old man, and my wife is advanced in years."

19 And the angel answered and said to him, "I am Gabriel, who stands in the presence of God; and I have been sent to speak to you, and to bring you this good news.

20 "And behold, you shall be silent and unable to speak until the day when these

---

¹I.e., gospel ²Gr., *Abia* ³I.e., of priestly descent

1:5 Elizabeth is called *from the daughters of Aaron*, meaning she was of a priestly family.   **1:17** See note to Mal. 4:5 on the coming of Elijah.

Marginal references

1:2 — Heb 2:3; 1 Pet 5:1; 2 Pet 1:16; 1 John 1:1; Mark 1:1; John 15:27
1:3 — Acts 11:4; 18:23; 1:1
1:4 — John 20:31
*1:5 — Matt 2:1; 1 Chr 24:10
1:6 — Gen 7:1; 1 Kin 9:4; 2 Kin 20:3
1:8 — 1 Chr 24:19; 2 Chr 8:14
1:9 — Ex 30:7,8; 1 Chr 23:13; 2 Chr 29:11
1:10 — Lev 16:17
1:13 — vv. 30,60,63
1:14 — v. 58
1:15 — Num 6:3; Judg 13:4; Luke 7:33; Jer 1:5; Gal 1:15
1:16 — Mal 4:5,6
*1:17 — Matt 11:14; 17:13
1:18 — Gen 17:17; v. 34
1:19 — Dan 8:16; 9:21-23; Matt 18:10
1:20 — Ezek 3:26; 24:27

things take place, because you did not believe my words, which shall be fulfilled in their proper time."

21   And the people were waiting for Zacharias, and were wondering at his delay in the temple.

22   But when he came out, he was unable to speak to them; and they realized that he had seen a vision in the temple; and he kept making signs to them, and remained mute.   1:22
v. 62

23   And it came about, when the days of his priestly service were ended, that he went back home.

24   And after these days Elizabeth his wife became pregnant; and she kept herself in seclusion for five months, saying,

25   "This is the way the Lord has dealt with me in the days when He looked *with favor* upon *me,* to take away my disgrace among men."   1:25
Gen 30:23;
Is 4:1

B. *The birth of Jesus foretold: the annunciation*
(1:26–38; Matt. 1:18–25)

26   Now in the sixth month the angel Gabriel was sent from God to a city in Galilee, called Nazareth,   1:26
Matt 2:23

27   to a virgin engaged to a man whose name was Joseph, of the descendants of David; and the virgin's name was Mary.   1:27
Matt 1:16;
v. 19

28   And coming in, he said to her, "Hail, favored one! The Lord *is* with you."[4]   1:28
Dan 9:23;
10:19

29   But she was greatly troubled at *this* statement, and kept pondering what kind of salutation this might be.

30   And the angel said to her, "Do not be afraid, Mary; for you have found favor with God.

31   "And behold, you will conceive in your womb, and bear a son, and you shall name Him Jesus.   1:31
Is 7:14;
Luke 2:21

32   "He will be great, and will be called the Son of the Most High; and the Lord God will give Him the throne of His father David;   1:32
Mark 5:7;
Is 9:6,7;
Jer 23:5;
Rev 3:7

33   and He will reign over the house of Jacob forever; and His kingdom will have no end."   1:33
Dan 2:44;
7:14,27;
Matt 28:18;
Heb 1:8

34   And Mary said to the angel, "How can this be, since I am a virgin?"

35   And the angel answered and said to her, "The Holy Spirit will come upon you, and the power of the Most High will overshadow you; and for that reason the holy offspring shall be called the Son of God.   1:35
v. 32;
Mark 1:24;
Matt 4:3

36   "And behold, even your relative Elizabeth has also conceived a son in her old age; and she who was called barren is now in her sixth month.

37   "For nothing will be impossible with God."   1:37
Gen 18:14;
Jer 32:17;
Matt 19:26;
Mark 10:27;
Luke 18:27;
Rom 4:21

38   And Mary said, "Behold, the [5]bondslave of the Lord; be it done to me according to your word." And the angel departed from her.

C. *Mary visits Elizabeth*
(1:39–45)

39   Now at this time Mary arose and went with haste to the hill country, to a city of Judah,   1:39
v. 65

40   and entered the house of Zacharias and greeted Elizabeth.

41   And it came about that when Elizabeth heard Mary's greeting, the baby leaped in her womb; and Elizabeth was filled with the Holy Spirit.   1:41
v. 67

42   And she cried out with a loud voice, and said, "Blessed among women *are* you, and blessed *is* the fruit of your womb!   1:42
Judg 5:24;
Luke 11:27,
28

43   "And how has it *happened* to me, that the mother of my Lord should come to me?   1:43
Luke 2:11

44   "For behold, when the sound of your greeting reached my ears, the baby leaped in my womb for joy.

45   "And blessed *is* she who believed that there would be a fulfillment of what had been spoken to her by the Lord."

D. *The song of Mary (1:46–56)*

46   And Mary said:
"My soul exalts the Lord,   1:46
1 Sam 2:1-10;
Ps 34:2,3

47   "And my spirit has rejoiced in God my Savior.   1:47
Ps 35:9;
1 Tim 1:1;
2:3;
Titus 2:10;
Jude 25

[4]Later mss. add: *you are blessed among women*   [5]I.e., female slave

1:48
Ps 138:6;
Luke 11:27
1:49
Ps 71:19;
111:9
1:50
Ps 103:17
1:51
Ps 98:1;
Is 40:10;
Ps 33:10;
1 Pet 5:5
1:52
Job 5:11
1:53
Ps 34:10
1:54
Ps 98:3
1:55
Gen 17:19;
Ps 132:11;
Gal 3:16

48   "For He has had regard for the humble state of His bondslave;
      For behold, from this time on all generations will count me blessed.
49   "For the Mighty One has done great things for me;
      And holy is His name.
50   "AND HIS MERCY IS UPON GENERATION AFTER GENERATION
      TOWARD THOSE WHO FEAR HIM.
51   "He has done mighty deeds with His arm;
      He has scattered *those who were* proud in the thoughts of their heart.
52   "He has brought down rulers from *their* thrones,
      And has exalted those who were humble.
53   "HE HAS FILLED THE HUNGRY WITH GOOD THINGS;
      And sent away the rich empty-handed.
54   "He has given help to Israel His servant,
      In remembrance of His mercy,
55   As He spoke to our fathers,
      To Abraham and his offspring forever."

56   And Mary stayed with her about three months, and *then* returned to her home.

E. *Birth of John the Baptist (1:57–66)*

57   Now the time had come for Elizabeth to give birth, and she brought forth a son.

1:58
Gen 19:19
58   And her neighbors and her relatives heard that the Lord had displayed His great mercy toward her; and they were rejoicing with her.

1:59
Gen 17:12;
Lev 12:3
59   And it came about that on the eighth day they came to circumcise the child, and they were going to call him Zacharias, after his father.

60   And his mother answered and said, "No indeed; but he shall be called John."

61   And they said to her, "There is no one among your relatives who is called by that name."

1:62
v. 22
1:63
v. 13
62   And they made signs to his father, as to what he wanted him called.

63   And he asked for a tablet, and wrote as follows, "His name is John." And they were all astonished.

1:64
v. 20
64   And at once his mouth was opened and his tongue *loosed*, and he *began* to speak in praise of God.

1:66
Luke 2:19,
51; Gen 39:2;
Acts 11:21
1:67
v. 41;
Joel 2:28
65   And fear came on all those living around them; and all these matters were being talked about in all the hill country of Judea.

66   And all who heard them kept them in mind, saying, "What then will this child *turn out to* be?" For the hand of the Lord was certainly with him.

F. *The song of Zacharias: the "Benedictus"(1:67–80)*

1:68
Ps 72:18;
111:9;
Luke 7:16
*1:69
Ps 18:2;
89:17;
132:17;
Ezek 29:21
1:70
Jer 23:5;
Dan 9:24;
Acts 3:21;
Rom 1:2;
Mic 7:20;
Ps 105:8,9;
106:45;
Ezek 16:60

67   And his father Zacharias was filled with the Holy Spirit, and prophesied, saying:
68   "Blessed *be* the Lord God of Israel,
      For He has visited us and accomplished redemption for His people,
69   And has raised up a horn of salvation for us
      In the house of David His servant—
70   As He spoke by the mouth of His holy prophets from of old—
71   Salvation FROM OUR ENEMIES,
      And FROM THE HAND OF ALL WHO HATE US;
72   To show mercy toward our fathers,
      And to remember His holy covenant,

1:57 Information about John the Baptist, other than the New Testament accounts, is limited to what Josephus, the Jewish historian, wrote about him. John was the son of Zechariah and Elizabeth, both of whom were descendants of Aaron. He was about six months older than Jesus. The town of his birth is unknown, although Luke mentions a city in the hill country of Judah (1:39). John's early life may be summarized in several sentences: *the hand of the Lord was certainly with him* (1:66); *he continued to grow, and to become strong in spirit . . . lived in the deserts until the day of his public appearance* (1:80); *he will be great in the sight of the Lord, and . . . filled with the Holy Spirit* (1:15). He was imprisoned by

Herod prior to his execution, ca. A.D. 28. John, of course, was the forerunner of Jesus, and his ministry was prophetic. His chief preaching burden was the announcement of the coming kingdom, emphasizing the necessity for repentance and confession of sins (Matt. 3:1–12; Mark 1:4–8; Luke 3:3–18; John 1:19–28). Jesus said that no one born of woman was greater than John (Matt. 11:11).
1:69 *Horn* is often used as a metaphor in the Old Testament, meaning "power," "might" (cf. 1 Sam. 2:1,10; 2 Sam. 22:3; Ps. 18:2). The phrase *a horn of salvation* means therefore "a mighty savior" (Goodspeed), "a deliverer of victorious power" (New English Bible).

73   The oath which He swore to Abraham our father,

74   To grant us that we, being delivered from the hand of our enemies,
       Might serve Him without fear,

75   In holiness and righteousness before Him all our days.

76   "And you, child, will be called the prophet of the Most High;
       For you will go on BEFORE THE LORD TO PREPARE HIS WAYS;

77   To give to His people *the* knowledge of salvation
       By the forgiveness of their sins,

78   Because of the tender mercy of our God,
       With which the Sunrise from on high shall visit us,

79   TO SHINE UPON THOSE WHO SIT IN DARKNESS AND THE SHADOW OF
       DEATH,
       To guide our feet into the way of peace.''

80   And the child continued to grow, and to become strong in spirit, and he lived in the deserts until the day of his public appearance to Israel.

G. The birth of Jesus the Christ (2:1–7; Matt. 1:18–25)

2 Now it came about in those days that a decree went out from Caesar Augustus, that a census be taken of all [6]the inhabited earth.

2   This was the first census taken while [7]Quirinius was governor of Syria.

3   And all were proceeding to register for the census, everyone to his own city.

4   And Joseph also went up from Galilee, from the city of Nazareth, to Judea, to the city of David, which is called Bethlehem, because he was of the house and family of David,

5   in order to register, along with Mary, who was engaged to him, and was with child.

6   And it came about that while they were there, the days were completed for her to give birth.

7   And she gave birth to her first-born son; and she wrapped Him in cloths, and laid Him in a manger, because there was no room for them in the inn.

H. The angels and the shepherds (2:8–20)

8   And in the same region there were *some* shepherds staying out in the fields, and keeping watch over their flock by night.

9   And an angel of the Lord suddenly stood before them, and the glory of the Lord shone around them; and they were terribly frightened.

10   And the angel said to them, "Do not be afraid; for behold, I bring you good news of a great joy which shall be for all the people;

11   for today in the city of David there has been born for you a Savior, who is [8]Christ the Lord.

12   "And this *will be* a sign for you: you will find a baby wrapped in cloths, and lying in a manger."

13   And suddenly there appeared with the angel a multitude of the heavenly host praising God, and saying,

14   "Glory to God in the highest,
       And on earth peace among men [9]with whom He is pleased."

15   And it came about when the angels had gone away from them into heaven, that the shepherds *began* saying to one another, "Let us go straight to Bethlehem then, and see this thing that has happened which the Lord has made known to us."

16   And they came in haste and found their way to Mary and Joseph, and the baby as He lay in the manger.

Marginal references:

1:74 Rom 6:18; Heb 9:14
1:75 Eph 4:24; Titus 2:12
1:76 Mal 3:1; 4:5; Matt 11:9,10
1:77 Mark 1:4
1:79 Matt 9:2; Mark 4:16; Acts 26:18
1:80 Luke 2:40,52
2:1 Luke 3:1
2:4 Luke 1:27
2:9 Luke 1:11; Acts 5:19
*2:10 Matt 14:27
*2:11 John 4:42; Matt 1:16; 16:16; Luke 1:43; Acts 2:36
2:12 1 Sam 2:34; 2 Kin 19:29; Is 7:14
2:13 Dan 7:10; Rev 5:11
2:14 Is 57:19; Luke 1:79; Rom 5:1; Eph 1:9; Phil 2:13

---

[6]I.e., the Roman empire   [7]Gr., *Kyrenios*   [8]I.e., Messiah   [9]Lit., *of good pleasure;* or possibly, *of good will*

2:2 While many believe that Quirinius had nothing to do with this enrollment, conservative scholars generally accept Sir W. M. Ramsey's view that he controlled Syria's foreign relations and supervised the census. Luke's accuracy has been vindicated on other points.

2:10 The missionary aspect of the gospel and its primacy are stated again and again in Scripture. The message at Jesus' birth was a message for all people (2:30–32). Even Christ's model prayer had a missionary thrust to it: *Thy kingdom come. Thy will be done, On earth as it is in heaven* (Matt. 6:10). The first convert, Andrew, became a mission-

ary: *He found first his own brother Simon, and said to him, "We have found the Messiah"* . . . *He brought him to Jesus.* (John 1:41,42). The first apostolic sermon, addressed to representatives of all the language groups of that age, had a strong missionary motif: *For the promise is . . . for all who are far off* . . . (Acts 2:39). The Great Commission of the risen Lord (recorded for us at least three times) gives expression to His all-embracing concern for all men everywhere (Matt. 28:18–20; Luke 24:45–49; John 20:21).

2:11 *the city of David,* Bethlehem.

17   And when they had seen this, they made known the statement which had been told them about this Child.

18   And all who heard it wondered at the things which were told them by the shepherds.

2:19
v. 51
2:20
Matt 9:8

19   But Mary treasured up all these things, pondering them in her heart.

20   And the shepherds went back, glorifying and praising God for all that they had heard and seen, just as had been told them.

I. *The circumcision (2:21)*

2:21
Luke 1:59;
1:31

21   And when eight days were completed before His circumcision, His name was *then* called Jesus, the name given by the angel before He was conceived in the womb.

J. *The presentation in the temple (2:22–28)*

2:22
Lev 12:2-6

22   And when the days for their purification according to the law of Moses were completed, they brought Him up to Jerusalem to present Him to the Lord

2:23
Ex 13:2,12;
Num 3:13

23   (as it is written in the Law of the Lord, "EVERY *first-born* MALE THAT OPENS THE WOMB SHALL BE CALLED HOLY TO THE LORD"),

24   and to offer a sacrifice according to what was said in the Law of the Lord, "A PAIR OF TURTLEDOVES, OR TWO YOUNG PIGEONS."

2:25
v. 38;
Luke 23:51

25   And behold, there was a man in Jerusalem whose name was Simeon; and this man was righteous and devout, looking for the consolation of Israel; and the Holy Spirit was upon him.

2:26
Ps 89:48;
Heb 11:5

26   And it had been revealed to him by the Holy Spirit that he would not see death before he had seen the Lord's Christ.

2:27
v. 22

27   And he came in the Spirit into the temple; and when the parents brought in the child Jesus, to carry out for Him the custom of the Law,

28   then he took Him into his arms, and blessed God, and said,

K. *The song of Simeon (2:29–35)*

2:29
v. 26

29   "Now Lord, Thou dost let Thy bond-servant depart
        In peace, according to Thy word;

2:30
Is 52:10;
Luke 3:6

30   For my eyes have seen Thy salvation,

31   Which Thou hast prepared in the presence of all peoples,

2:32
Is 42:6; 49:6;
Acts 13:47;
26:23

32   A LIGHT OF REVELATION TO THE GENTILES,
        And the glory of Thy people Israel."

33   And His father and mother were amazed at the things which were being said about Him.

2:34
Matt 21:44;
1 Cor 1:23,
24;
2 Cor 2:16;
1 Pet 2:7,8

34   And Simeon blessed them, and said to Mary His mother, "Behold, this *Child* is appointed for the fall and rise of many in Israel, and for a sign to be opposed—

35   and a sword will pierce even your own soul—to the end that thoughts from many hearts may be revealed."

L. *The adoration of Anna (2:36–40)*

2:36
Acts 21:9;
Josh 19:24;
1 Tim 5:9

36   And there was a prophetess, Anna the daughter of Phanuel, of the tribe of Asher. She was advanced in years, having lived with a husband seven years after her marriage,

2:37
Acts 13:3;
1 Tim 5:5

37   and then as a widow to the age of eighty-four. And she never left the temple, serving night and day with fastings and prayers.

2:38
v. 25;
Luke 24:21

38   And at that very moment she came up and *began* giving thanks to God, and continued to speak of Him to all those who were looking for the redemption of Jerusalem.

2:39
v. 51

39   And when they had performed everything according to the Law of the Lord, they returned to Galilee, to their own city of Nazareth.

2:40
v. 52;
Luke 1:80

40   And the Child continued to grow and become strong, increasing in wisdom; and the grace of God was upon Him.

M. *The boy Jesus in the temple (2:41–52)*

2:41
Ex 23:15;
Deut 16:1-6

41   And His parents used to go to Jerusalem every year at the Feast of the Passover.

42 And when He became twelve, they went up *there* according to the custom of the Feast;

43 and as they were returning, after spending the full number of days, the boy Jesus stayed behind in Jerusalem. And His parents were unaware of it,

44 but supposed Him to be in the caravan, and went a day's journey; and they *began* looking for Him among their relatives and acquaintances.

45 And when they did not find Him, they returned to Jerusalem, looking for Him.

46 And it came about that after three days they found Him in the temple, sitting in the midst of the teachers, both listening to them, and asking them questions.

47 And all who heard Him were amazed at His understanding and His answers.

48 And when they saw Him, they were astonished; and His mother said to Him, "Son, why have You treated us this way? Behold, Your father and I have been anxiously looking for You."

49 And He said to them, "Why is it that you were looking for Me? Did you not know that I had to be in My Father's *house?*"

50 And they did not understand the statement which He had made to them.

51 And He went down with them, and came to Nazareth; and He continued in subjection to them; and His mother treasured all *these* things in her heart.

52 And Jesus kept increasing in wisdom and stature, and in favor with God and men.

III. *The ministry of John the Baptist*
(3:1–20; Matt. 3:1–12; Mark 1:1–8; John 1:6–8,19–28)

3 Now in the fifteenth year of the reign of Tiberius Caesar, when Pontius Pilate was governor of Judea, and Herod was tetrarch of Galilee, and his brother Philip was tetrarch of the region of Ituraea and Trachonitis, and Lysanias was tetrarch of Abilene,

2 in the high priesthood of Annas and Caiaphas, the word of God came to John, the son of Zacharias, in the wilderness.

3 And he came into all the district around the Jordan, preaching a baptism of repentance for the forgiveness of sins;

4 as it is written in the book of the words of Isaiah the prophet,
> "THE VOICE OF ONE CRYING IN THE WILDERNESS,
> 'MAKE READY THE WAY OF THE LORD,
> MAKE HIS PATHS STRAIGHT.

5 'EVERY RAVINE SHALL BE FILLED UP,
> AND EVERY MOUNTAIN AND HILL SHALL BE BROUGHT LOW;
> AND THE CROOKED SHALL BECOME STRAIGHT,
> AND THE ROUGH ROADS SMOOTH;

6 AND ALL FLESH SHALL SEE THE SALVATION OF GOD.' "

7 He therefore *began* saying to the multitudes who were going out to be baptized by him, "You brood of vipers, who warned you to flee from the wrath to come?

8 "Therefore bring forth fruits in keeping with repentance, and do not begin to say to yourselves, 'We have Abraham for our father,' for I say to you that God is able from these stones to raise up children to Abraham.

9 "And also the axe is already laid at the root of the trees; every tree therefore that does not bear good fruit is cut down and thrown into the fire."

10 And the multitudes were questioning him, saying, "Then what shall we do?"

11 And he would answer and say to them, "Let the man who has two tunics share with him who has none; and let him who has food do likewise."

12 And *some* [10]tax-gatherers also came to be baptized, and they said to him, "Teacher, what shall we do?"

13 And he said to them, "Collect no more than what you have been ordered to."

14 And *some* [11]soldiers were questioning him, saying, "And *what about* us,

---

2:47 Matt 7:28; Mark 1:22; Luke 4:22, 32; John 7:15,46
2:48 Mark 3:31-35
2:49 John 2:16
2:50 Mark 9:32; Luke 9:45
2:51 vv. 19,39
*2:52 v. 40; 1 Sam 2:26

3:1 Matt 27:2; 14:1
3:2 John 11:49; 18:13; Acts 4:6; Matt 26:3
3:4 Is 40:3-5

3:6 Ps 98:2; Is 52:10; Luke 2:30
3:7 Matt 12:34; 23:33
3:8 John 8:33,39
3:9 Matt 7:19; Heb 6:7,8
3:10 Acts 2:37
3:11 James 2:15,16
3:12 Luke 7:29
3:13 Luke 19:8
3:14 Ex 23:1; Lev 19:11

---

[10]I.e., Collectors of Roman taxes for profit   [11]I.e., men in active military service

2:46 *teachers,* authorities on Jewish religion.   **2:52** Read v. 40; 1 Sam. 2:26.

what shall we do?" And he said to them, "Do not take money from anyone by force, or accuse *anyone* falsely, and be content with your wages."

3:15
Acts 13:25

15 Now while the people were in a state of expectation and all were wondering in their hearts about John, as to whether he might be the Christ,

3:16
Acts 1:5;
11:16; 19:4

16 John answered and said to them all, "As for me, I baptize you with water; but One is coming who is mightier than I, and I am not fit to untie the thong of His sandals; He will baptize you with the Holy Spirit and fire.

3:17
Is 30:24;
Mic 4:12;
Matt 13:30

17 "And His winnowing fork is in His hand to thoroughly clear His threshing floor, and to gather the wheat into His barn; but He will burn up the chaff with unquenchable fire."

18 So with many other exhortations also he preached the gospel to the people.

3:19
Matt 14:3,4;
Mark 6:17,18

19 But when Herod the tetrarch was reproved by him on account of Herodias, his brother's wife, and on account of all the wicked things which Herod had done,

20 he added this also to them all, that he locked John up in prison.

IV. *The baptism and temptation of Jesus (3:21–4:13)*

A. *The baptism of Jesus (3:21,22; Matt. 3:13–17; Mark 1:9–11)*

3:21
Luke 5:16;
6:12; 9:18,28;
11:1
3:22
Ps 2:7;
Is 42:1;
Luke 9:35;
Acts 10:38;
2 Pet 1:17

21 Now it came about when all the people were baptized, that Jesus also was baptized, and while He was praying, heaven was opened,

22 and the Holy Spirit descended upon Him in bodily form like a dove, and a voice came out of heaven, "Thou art My beloved Son, in Thee I am well-pleased."

B. *The genealogy of Jesus (3:23–38; cf. Matt. 1:1–17)*

***3:23**
Matt 4:17;
Acts 1:1;
John 8:57;
Luke 1:27

23 And when He began His ministry, Jesus Himself was about thirty years of age, being supposedly *the* son of Joseph, the *son* of Eli,

24 the *son* of Matthat, the *son* of Levi, the *son* of Melchi, the *son* of Jannai, the *son* of Joseph,

25 the *son* of Mattathias, the *son* of Amos, the *son* of Nahum, the *son* of Hesli, the *son* of Naggai,

26 the *son* of Maath, the *son* of Mattathias, the *son* of Semein, the *son* of Josech, the *son* of Joda,

3:27
Matt 1:12

27 the *son* of Joanan, the *son* of Rhesa, the *son* of Zerubbabel, the *son* of Shealtiel, the *son* of Neri,

28 the *son* of Melchi, the *son* of Addi, the *son* of Cosam, the *son* of Elmadam, the *son* of Er,

29 the *son* of Joshua, the *son* of Eliezer, the *son* of Jorim, the *son* of Matthat, the *son* of Levi,

30 the *son* of Simeon, the *son* of Judah, the *son* of Joseph, the *son* of Jonam, the *son* of Eliakim,

3:31
2 Sam 5:14;
1 Chr 3:5
3:32
Ruth 4:18ff;
1 Chr 2:10ff

31 the *son* of Melea, the *son* of Menna, the *son* of Mattatha, the *son* of Nathan, the *son* of David,

32 the *son* of Jesse, the *son* of Obed, the *son* of Boaz, the *son* of Salmon, the *son* of Nahshon,

33 the *son* of Amminadab, the *son* of Admin, the *son* of Ram, the *son* of Hezron, the *son* of Perez, the *son* of Judah,

3:34
Gen 11:24,26

34 the *son* of Jacob, the *son* of Isaac, the *son* of Abraham, the *son* of Terah, the *son* of Nahor,

35 the *son* of Serug, the *son* of Reu, the *son* of Peleg, the *son* of Heber, the *son* of Shelah,

3:36
Gen 11:12;
5:6ff

36 the *son* of Cainan, the *son* of Arphaxad, the *son* of Shem, the *son* of Noah, the *son* of Lamech,

37 the *son* of Methuselah, the *son* of Enoch, the *son* of Jared, the *son* of Mahalaleel, the *son* of Cainan,

3:38
Gen 5:1,2

38 the *son* of Enosh, the *son* of Seth, the *son* of Adam, the *son* of God.

3:23 Matthew seems to trace the genealogy of Joseph, whereas Luke seems to record the genealogy of Mary. Joseph is called the *son of Eli* in Luke, apparently in order to conform with Jewish legal custom; this can only mean that he was the son of Eli in the sense that he was the husband of Eli's daughter. Luke carefully specifies that Jesus was not *really* Joseph's son. For Luke, a Greek, to trace Mary's genealogy is not inappropriate, for Luke always shows a special interest in the women who followed Jesus. While Matthew traces the genealogy of Jesus to Abraham, Luke traces it all the way back to Adam.

C. The wilderness temptation of Jesus
(4:1–13; Matt. 4:1–11; Mark 1:12,13)

4 And Jesus, full of the Holy Spirit, returned from the Jordan and was led about by the Spirit in the wilderness

2 for forty days, being tempted by the devil. And He ate nothing during those days; and when they had ended, He became hungry.

3 And the devil said to Him, "If You are the Son of God, tell this stone to become bread."

4 And Jesus answered him, "It is written, 'MAN SHALL NOT LIVE ON BREAD ALONE.'"

5 And he led Him up and showed Him all the kingdoms of the world in a moment of time.

6 And the devil said to Him, "I will give You all this domain and its glory; for it has been handed over to me, and I give it to whomever I wish.

7 "Therefore if You worship before me, it shall all be Yours."

8 And Jesus answered and said to him, "It is written, 'YOU SHALL WORSHIP THE LORD YOUR GOD AND SERVE HIM ONLY.'"

9 And he led Him to Jerusalem and had Him stand on the pinnacle of the temple, and said to Him, "If You are the Son of God, throw Yourself down from here;

10 for it is written,
'HE WILL GIVE HIS ANGELS CHARGE CONCERNING YOU TO GUARD YOU,'

11 and,
'ON *their* HANDS THEY WILL BEAR YOU UP,
LEST YOU STRIKE YOUR FOOT AGAINST A STONE.'"

12 And Jesus answered and said to him, "It is said, 'YOU SHALL NOT [12]PUT THE LORD YOUR GOD TO THE TEST.'"

13 And when the devil had finished every temptation, he departed from Him until an opportune time.

V. Public ministry in Galilee (4:14–9:50)

A. Jesus returns to Galilee
(4:14,15; Matt. 4:12–17; Mark 1:14,15; John 4:43–45)

14 And Jesus returned to Galilee in the power of the Spirit; and news about Him spread through all the surrounding district.

15 And He *began* teaching in their synagogues and was praised by all.

B. Jesus' first rejection at Nazareth (4:16–30)

16 And He came to Nazareth, where He had been brought up; and as was His custom, He entered the synagogue on the Sabbath, and stood up to read.

17 And the book of the prophet Isaiah was handed to Him. And He opened the book, and found the place where it was written,

18 "THE SPIRIT OF THE LORD IS UPON ME,
BECAUSE HE ANOINTED ME TO PREACH THE GOSPEL TO THE POOR.
HE HAS SENT ME TO PROCLAIM RELEASE TO THE CAPTIVES,
AND RECOVERY OF SIGHT TO THE BLIND,
TO SET FREE THOSE WHO ARE DOWNTRODDEN,

19 TO PROCLAIM THE FAVORABLE YEAR OF THE LORD."

20 And He closed the book, and gave it back to the attendant, and sat down; and the eyes of all in the synagogue were fixed upon Him.

21 And He began to say to them, "Today this Scripture has been fulfilled in your hearing."

[12]Or, *tempt . . . God*

Marginal references: 4:1 v. 14; Luke 2:27; *4:2 Ex 34:28; 1 Kin 19:8; 4:4 Deut 8:3; 4:6 John 12:31; 14:30; 1 John 5:19; 4:8 Deut 6:13; 4:10 Ps 91:11,12; 4:12 Deut 6:16; 4:13 John 14:30; Heb 4:15; 4:14 Matt 9:26; 4:15 Matt 9:35; 11:1; 4:16 Matt 13:54; Mark 6:1; Acts 13:14-16; 4:18 Is 61:1,2; Matt 12:18; *4:19 Lev 25:10; 4:20 v. 17

4:2 The Bible teaches two great truths about Jesus and sin: (1) He was tempted (Matt. 4:1; Mark 1:12,13; Luke 4:1–13); and (2) He was sinless (2 Cor. 5:21; Heb. 4:15; 1 John 3:5; cf. John 8:46). This means that it was possible for Christ to be tempted without sinning, and that He was sinless although tempted. In His humanity the possibility of sinning existed, yet He resisted temptation and perfectly fulfilled the law and will of God.

4:19 Jesus ended His quotation from Is. 61:1,2 just before the phrase, *to proclaim . . . the day of vengeance of our God,* although including the phrase *the favorable year of the Lord.* Undoubtedly He made this omission purposely, since the "day of vengeance" still awaits His second advent. The "favorable year of the Lord" was related to His first advent.

4:22
Ps 45:2;
Matt 13:54,
55; Mark 6:2,
3; John 6:42;
7:15
4:23
Mark 1:21ff;
2:1ff; v. 16
4:24
Matt 13:57;
Mark 6:4;
John 4:44
4:25
1 Kin 17:1,
8-16; 18:1;
James 5:17,18
4:27
2 Kin 5:1-14

22   And all were speaking well of Him, and wondering at the gracious words which were falling from His lips; and they were saying, "Is this not Joseph's son?"

23   And He said to them, "No doubt you will quote this proverb to Me, 'Physician, heal yourself! Whatever we heard was done at Capernaum, do here in your home town as well.' "

24   And He said, "Truly I say to you, no prophet is welcome in his home town.

25   "But I say to you in truth, there were many widows in Israel in the days of Elijah, when the sky was shut up for three years and six months, when a great famine came over all the land;

26   and yet Elijah was sent to none of them, but only to Zarephath, *in the land* of Sidon, to a woman who was a widow.

27   "And there were many lepers in Israel in the time of Elisha the prophet; and none of them was cleansed, but only Naaman the Syrian."

4:29
Num 15:35;
Acts 7:58;
Heb 13:12
4:30
John 8:49;
10:39

28   And all in the synagogue were filled with rage as they heard these things;

29   and they rose up and cast Him out of the city, and led Him to the brow of the hill on which their city had been built, in order to throw Him down the cliff.

30   But passing through their midst, He went His way.

C. Jesus performing miracles at Capernaum (4:31–44)

1. The casting out of the unclean spirit (4:31–37; Mark 1:21–28)

4:31
Matt 4:13

31   And He came down to Capernaum, a city of Galilee. And He was teaching them on the Sabbath;

4:32
Matt 7:28;
Mark 11:18;
John 7:46

32   and they were amazed at His teaching, for His message was with authority.

33   And there was a man in the synagogue possessed by the spirit of an unclean demon, and he cried out with a loud voice,

4:34
v. 41;
Ps 16:10;
Dan 9:24
4:35
vv. 39,41;
Matt 8:26;
Mark 4:39;
Luke 8:24
4:36
v. 32

34   "Ha! What do we have to do with You, Jesus of Nazareth? Have You come to destroy us? I know who You are—the Holy One of God!"

35   And Jesus rebuked him, saying, "Be quiet and come out of him!" And when the demon had thrown him down in *their* midst, he came out of him without doing him any harm.

36   And amazement came upon them all, and they *began* discussing with one another saying, "What is this message? For with authority and power He commands the unclean spirits, and they come out."

4:37
v. 14

37   And the report about Him was getting out into every locality in the surrounding district.

2. Peter's mother-in-law healed
(4:38,39; Matt. 8:14–17; Mark 1:29–34)

38   And He arose and *left* the synagogue, and entered Simon's home. Now Simon's mother-in-law was suffering from a high fever; and they made request of Him on her behalf.

4:39
vv. 35,41

39   And standing over her, He rebuked the fever, and it left her; and she immediately arose and waited on them.

3. Healing the sick; casting out demons
(4:40–44; Matt. 8:16–17; Mark 1:32–34)

4:40
Mark 5:23;
Matt 4:23

40   And while the sun was setting, all who had any sick with various diseases brought them to Him; and laying His hands on every one of them, He was healing them.

4:41
Matt 4:3; 8:4

41   And demons also were coming out of many, crying out and saying, "You are the Son of God!" And rebuking them, He would not allow them to speak, because they knew Him to be the Christ.

4:42
Mark 1:35-38

42   And when day came, He departed and went to a lonely place; and the multitudes were searching for Him, and came to Him, and tried to keep Him from going away from them.

43   But He said to them, "I must preach the kingdom of God to the other cities also, for I was sent for this purpose."

4:44
Matt 4:18-22;
Mark 1:16-20;
John 1:40-42

44   And He kept on preaching in the synagogues of [13]Judea.

[13]I.e., the country of the Jews (including Galilee); some mss. read *Galilee*

D. *The call of the first disciples*
(5:1–11; Matt. 4:18–22; Mark 1:16–20)

5 Now it came about that while the multitude were pressing around Him and listening to the word of God, He was standing by the lake of Gennesaret;

2   and He saw two boats lying at the edge of the lake; but the fishermen had gotten out of them, and were washing their nets.

3   And He got into one of the boats, which was Simon's, and asked him to put out a little way from the land. And He sat down and *began* teaching the multitudes from the boat.

4   And when He had finished speaking, He said to Simon, "Put out into the deep water and let down your nets for a catch."

5   And Simon answered and said, "Master, we worked hard all night and caught nothing, but at Your bidding I will let down the nets."

6   And when they had done this, they enclosed a great quantity of fish; and their nets *began* to break;

7   and they signaled to their partners in the other boat, for them to come and help them. And they came, and filled both of the boats, so that they began to sink.

8   But when Simon Peter saw *that*, he fell down at Jesus' feet, saying, "Depart from me, for I am a sinful man, O Lord!"

9   For amazement had seized him and all his companions because of the catch of fish which they had taken;

10   and so also James and John, sons of Zebedee, who were partners with Simon. And Jesus said to Simon, "Do not fear, from now on you will be catching men."

11   And when they had brought their boats to land, they left everything and followed Him.

E. *The leper cleansed (5:12–16; Matt. 8:1–4; Mark 1:40–45)*

12   And it came about that while He was in one of the cities, behold, *there was* a man full of leprosy; and when he saw Jesus, he fell on his face and implored Him, saying, "Lord, if You are willing, You can make me clean."

13   And He stretched out His hand, and touched him, saying, "I am willing; be cleansed." And immediately the leprosy left him.

14   And He ordered him to tell no one, "But go and show yourself to the priest, and make an offering for your cleansing, just as Moses commanded, for a testimony to them."

15   But the news about Him was spreading even farther, and great multitudes were gathering to hear *Him* and to be healed of their sicknesses.

16   But He Himself would *often* slip away to the wilderness and pray.

F. *A paralytic healed and forgiven*
(5:17–26; Matt. 9:1–8; Mark 2:1–12)

17   And it came about one day that He was teaching; and there were *some* Pharisees and teachers of the law sitting *there*, who had come from every village of Galilee and Judea and *from* Jerusalem; and the power of the Lord was *present* for Him to perform healing.

18   And behold, *some* men *were* carrying on a bed a man who was paralyzed; and they were trying to bring him in, and to set him down in front of Him.

19   And not finding any *way* to bring him in because of the crowd, they went up on the roof and let him down through the tiles with his stretcher, right in the center, in front of Jesus.

20   And seeing their faith, He said, "Friend, your sins are forgiven you."

21   And the scribes and the Pharisees began to reason, saying, "Who is this *man* who speaks blasphemies? Who can forgive sins, but God alone?"

22   But Jesus, aware of their reasonings, answered and said to them, "Why are you reasoning in your hearts?

5:3 Matt 13:1,2; Mark 4:1
5:4 John 21:6
5:5 Luke 8:24, 45; 9:33,49; 17:13
5:10 Matt 14:27
5:11 v. 28; Matt 19:29
***5:12** Luke 17:11-19
5:15 Matt 9:26; Luke 4:14,37
5:16 Matt 14:23; Mark 6:46; Luke 3:21; 6:12; 9:18,28; 11:1
5:17 Matt 15:1; Mark 5:30; Luke 6:19
5:19 Matt 24:17
5:20 Luke 7:48,49
5:21 Is 43:25

5:12 Leprosy was a common disease among the Hebrews. It was then almost incurable and was easily transmitted from one person to another. Lepers were: (1) ceremonially unclean (Lev. 13:8,11,22,44); (2) cut off from the house of God (2 Chr. 26:21); (3) excluded from the office of the priesthood (Lev. 22:2–4); (4) forbidden to associate with others (Num. 5:2; 12:14,15); and (5) under obligation in public to cry aloud that they were unclean (Lev. 13:45). Minute prescriptions were set up to detect and diagnose leprosy as well as rules to govern the cleansing of lepers. Biblically the disease of leprosy is used as a type of the spiritual disease of sin that cuts man off from communion with God until it is cleansed away. Jesus is the only cure for the leprosy of sin.

23 "Which is easier, to say, 'Your sins have been forgiven you,' or to say, 'Rise and walk'?

24 "But in order that you may know that the Son of Man has authority on earth to forgive sins,"—He said to the paralytic—"I say to you, rise, and take up your stretcher and go home."

25 And at once he rose up before them, and took up what he had been lying on, and went home, glorifying God.

5:26
Luke 7:16 26 And they were all seized with astonishment and *began* glorifying God; and they were filled with fear, saying, "We have seen remarkable things today."

G. The call of (Matthew) Levi
(5:27–32; Matt. 9:9–13; Mark 2:13–17)

27 And after that He went out, and noticed a [14]tax-gatherer named Levi, sitting in the tax office, and He said to him, "Follow Me."

5:28
v. 11 28 And he left everything behind, and rose and *began* to follow Him.

5:29
Luke 15:1 29 And Levi gave a big reception for Him in his house; and there was a great crowd of tax-gatherers and other *people* who were reclining *at the table* with them.

5:30
Acts 23:9 30 And the Pharisees and their scribes *began* grumbling at His disciples, saying, "Why do you eat and drink with the tax-gatherers and sinners?"

31 And Jesus answered and said to them, "*It is* not those who are well who need a physician, but those who are sick.

5:32
1 Tim 1:15 32 "I have not come to call the righteous but sinners to repentance."

H. The question about fasting
(5:33–39; Matt. 9:14–17; Mark 2:18–22)

5:33
Luke 7:18;
John 3:25,26 33 And they said to Him, "The disciples of John often fast and offer prayers; the *disciples* of the Pharisees also do the same; but Yours eat and drink."

34 And Jesus said to them, "You cannot make the attendants of the bridegroom fast while the bridegroom is with them, can you?

5:35
Luke 9:22;
17:22 35 "But *the* days will come; and when the bridegroom is taken away from them, then they will fast in those days."

36 And He was also telling them a parable: "No one tears a piece from a new garment and puts it on an old garment; otherwise he will both tear the new, and the piece from the new will not match the old.

37 "And no one puts new wine into old wineskins; otherwise the new wine will burst the skins, and it will be spilled out, and the skins will be ruined.

38 "But new wine must be put into fresh wineskins.

39 "And no one, after drinking old *wine* wishes for new; for he says, 'The old is good *enough*.' "

I. Jesus the Lord of the Sabbath
(6:1–5; Matt. 12:1–8; Mark 2:23–28)

*6:1
Deut 23:25 6 Now it came about that on a *certain* Sabbath He was passing through *some* grainfields; and His disciples were picking and eating the heads *of grain,* rubbing them in their hands.

6:2
Ex 20:10;
23:12;
Deut 5:14 2 But some of the Pharisees said, "Why do you do what is not lawful on the Sabbath?"

*6:3
1 Sam 21:6 3 And Jesus answering them said, "Have you not even read what David did when he was hungry, he and those who were with him,

6:4
Lev 24:9 4 how he entered the house of God, and took and ate the [15]consecrated bread which is not lawful for any to eat except the priests alone, and gave it to his companions?"

---

[14]I.e., Collector of Roman taxes for profit [15]Or, *showbread,* lit., *loaves of presentation*

5:27 The tax-gatherers (KJV, "publicans") were intensely hated by the Jews and were regarded as extortioners (3:13; 18:11; 19:8). Some of them became quite wealthy (19:2). Christ was condemned for associating with them (Matt. 9:11; 11:19). A number of them had already been influenced by John the Baptist (Matt. 21:32), and had received his baptism (3:12; 7:29). Many of them now listened to the preaching of Christ and embraced the gospel (Matt. 21:31; Mark 2:15; Luke 15:1). The apostle Matthew was a tax collector (Matt. 10:3).

5:36 The parables of the new cloth and the new wine are designed to teach the same general lesson: that it is unwise to bring together the old and the new. To mix the new and living kingdom of God with the obsolete legalistic system of the old Jewish dispensation is self-defeating. This was shown to be true after Pentecost, when it became necessary to separate the Christian church from the Judaistic community that still put its trust in works of religion and merit.
6:1 See note to Mark 2:27 for information on the Sabbath.
6:3 See note to Matt. 12:3 for further elaboration.

5   And He was saying to them, "The Son of Man is Lord of the Sabbath."

J. Jesus heals on the Sabbath
(6:6–11; Matt. 12:9–14; Mark 3:1–6)

6   And it came about on another Sabbath, that He entered the synagogue and was teaching; and there was a man there whose right hand was withered.

7   And the scribes and the Pharisees were watching Him closely, *to see* if He healed on the Sabbath, in order that they might find *reason* to accuse Him.

8   But He knew what they were thinking, and He said to the man with the withered hand, "Rise and come forward!" And he rose and came forward.

9   And Jesus said to them, "I ask you, is it lawful on the Sabbath to do good, or to do harm, to save a life, or to destroy it?"

10   And after looking around at them all, He said to him, "Stretch out your hand!" And he did *so*; and his hand was restored.

11   But they themselves were filled with rage, and discussed together what they might do to Jesus.

K. *The choosing of the Twelve*
(6:12–16; Matt. 10:1–4; Mark 3:13–19)

12   And it was at this time that He went off to the mountain to pray, and He spent the whole night in prayer to God.

13   And when day came, He called His disciples to Him; and chose twelve of them, whom He also named as apostles:

14   Simon, whom He also named Peter, and Andrew his brother; and James and John; and Philip and Bartholomew;

15   and Matthew and Thomas; James *the son* of Alphaeus, and Simon who was called the Zealot;

16   Judas *the son* of James, and Judas Iscariot, who became a traitor.

L. *Sermon on the Mount: Beatitudes and other teachings*
(6:17–26; cf. Matt. 5–7)

17   And He descended with them, and stood on a level place; and *there was* a great multitude of His disciples, and a great throng of people from all Judea and Jerusalem and the coastal region of Tyre and Sidon,

18   who had come to hear Him, and to be healed of their diseases; and those who were troubled with unclean spirits were being cured.

19   And all the multitude were trying to touch Him, for power was coming from Him and healing *them* all.

20   And turning His gaze on His disciples, He *began* to say, "Blessed *are* you who are poor, for yours is the kingdom of God.

21   "Blessed *are* you who hunger now, for you shall be satisfied. Blessed *are* you who weep now, for you shall laugh.

22   "Blessed are you when men hate you, and ostracize you, and cast insults at you, and spurn your name as evil, for the sake of the Son of Man.

23   "Be glad in that day, and leap *for joy*, for behold, your reward is great in heaven; for in the same way their fathers used to treat the prophets.

24   "But woe to you who are rich, for you are receiving your comfort in full.

25   "Woe to you who are well-fed now, for you shall be hungry. Woe *to you* who laugh now, for you shall mourn and weep.

26   "Woe *to you* when all men speak well of you, for in the same way their fathers used to treat the false prophets.

Cross-references: 6:6 Luke 13:14; 14:3; John 9:16 · 6:8 Matt 9:4 · *6:12 Matt 14:23; Luke 9:28 · *6:13 Mark 6:30 · 6:16 Jude 1 · 6:17 Matt 4:25; Mark 3:7,8 · 6:19 Matt 9:21; 14:36; Mark 3:10; Luke 5:17 · 6:21 Is 61:3 · 6:22 1 Pet 4:14; John 9:22; 16:2 · 6:23 Acts 5:41; Col 1:24; Mal 4:2; Acts 7:51 · 6:24 James 5:1; Luke 16:25 · 6:25 Is 65:13; Prov 14:13 · 6:26 John 15:19

6:12 The prayer life of Jesus shows that important acts were performed only after serious prayer had preceded them. Perhaps the most notable instance is His prayer in Gethsemane.
6:13 An *apostle* (from the Greek *apostolos*) is "one sent forth." He is an ambassador who not only bears a message but also represents the one who sends him. The New Testament office of apostle does not continue today because one of its indispensable qualifications was that an apostle must have actually seen the Lord and thus have become an eyewitness to His resurrection (24:48; Acts 1:8,22; 1 Cor. 9:1). A second qualification was the special call of the Holy Spirit, for no human authority could invest a man with this office (1 Cor. 12:28; Eph. 4:11). The apostles often enjoyed the ability to perform signs of an apostolic character, that is, wonders and "powers" (or miracles of healing). Incidentally, the number of the apostles was not limited to the twelve disciples. Scripture speaks of Paul, Barnabas, James, and perhaps Andronicus and Junius as apostles (Acts 14:14; Rom. 16:7; 1 Cor. 15:7; Gal. 1:19).

M. *The law of love (6:27–36; Matt. 5:43–48)*

27 "But I say to you who hear, love your enemies, do good to those who hate you,

28 bless those who curse you, pray for those who mistreat you.

29 "Whoever hits you on the cheek, offer him the other also; and whoever takes away your coat, do not withhold your shirt from him either.

30 "Give to everyone who asks of you, and whoever takes away what is yours, do not demand it back.

31 "And just as you want people to treat you, treat them in the same way.

32 "And if you love those who love you, what credit is *that* to you? For even sinners love those who love them.

33 "And if you do good to those who do good to you, what credit is *that* to you? For even sinners do the same.

34 "And if you lend to those from whom you expect to receive, what credit is *that* to you? Even sinners lend to sinners, in order to receive back the same *amount*.

35 "But love your enemies, and do good, and lend, expecting nothing in return; and your reward will be great, and you will be sons of the Most High; for He Himself is kind to ungrateful and evil *men*.

36 "Be merciful, just as your Father is merciful.

N. *Censure and reproof (6:37–45; Matt. 7:1–5)*

37 "And do not judge and you will not be judged; and do not condemn, and you will not be condemned; pardon, and you will be pardoned.

38 "Give, and it will be given to you; good measure, pressed down, shaken together, running over, they will pour into your lap. For by your standard of measure it will be measured to you in return."

39 And He also spoke a parable to them: "A blind man cannot guide a blind man, can he? Will they not both fall into a pit?

40 "A pupil is not above his teacher; but everyone, after he has been fully trained, will be like his teacher.

41 "And why do you look at the speck that is in your brother's eye, but do not notice the log that is in your own eye?

42 "Or how can you say to your brother, 'Brother, let me take out the speck that is in your eye,' when you yourself do not see the log that is in your own? You hypocrite, first take the log out of your own eye, and then you will see clearly to take out the speck that is in your brother's eye.

43 "For there is no good tree which produces bad fruit; nor, on the other hand, a bad tree which produces good fruit.

44 "For each tree is known by its own fruit. For men do not gather figs from thorns, nor do they pick grapes from a briar bush.

45 "The good man out of the good treasure of his heart brings forth what is good; and the evil *man* out of the evil *treasure* brings forth what is evil; for his mouth speaks from that which fills his heart.

O. *The parable of the two houses (6:46–49; Matt. 7:24–27)*

46 "And why do you call Me, 'Lord, Lord,' and do not do what I say?

47 "Everyone who comes to Me, and hears My words, and acts upon them, I will show you whom he is like:

48 he is like a man building a house, who dug deep and laid a foundation upon the rock; and when a flood rose, the torrent burst against that house and could not shake it, because it had been well built.

49 "But the one who has heard, and has not acted *accordingly*, is like a man who built a house upon the ground without any foundation; and the torrent burst against it and immediately it collapsed, and the ruin of that house was great."

P. *The centurion's servant healed (7:1–10; Matt. 8:5–13)*

7 When He had completed all His discourse in the hearing of the people, He went to Capernaum.

6:27
v. 35;
Rom 12:20
6:28
Luke 23:34;
Acts 7:60

6:30
Deut 15:7,8,
10;
Prov 21:26
6:31
Matt 7:12

6:35
vv. 27,30

6:37
Rom 2:1

6:38
Mark 4:24;
James 2:13

6:39
Matt 15:4

6:40
Matt 10:24;
John 13:16;
15:20

6:43
Matt 7:16,18,
20
6:44
Matt 12:33

6:45
Matt 12:34,
35;
Mark 7:20

6:46
Matt 7:21
6:47
James 1:22-25

7:1
Matt 7:28

6:48 The obvious meaning of this parable is the difference between a true and a false profession. The *rock* as a symbol of a true profession is quite appropriate and is analogous to Paul's reference to a solid foundation as a figure for those who live truly in Christ (1 Cor. 3:11). Peter's use of the metaphor of the stone is somewhat similar (1 Pet. 2:7,8).

2   And a certain centurion's slave, who was highly regarded by him, was sick and about to die.

3   And when he heard about Jesus, he sent some Jewish elders asking Him to come and save the life of his slave.

4   And when they had come to Jesus, they earnestly entreated Him, saying, "He is worthy for You to grant this to him;

5   for he loves our nation, and it was he who built us our synagogue."

6   Now Jesus *started* on His way with them; and when He was already not far from the house, the centurion sent friends, saying to Him, "Lord, do not trouble Yourself further, for I am not worthy for You to come under my roof;

7   for this reason I did not even consider myself worthy to come to You, but *just* say the word, and my servant will be healed.

8   "For I, too, am a man under authority, with soldiers under me; and I say to this one, 'Go!' and he goes; and to another, 'Come!' and he comes; and to my slave, 'Do this!' and he does it."

9   Now when Jesus heard this, He marveled at him, and turned and said to the multitude that was following Him, "I say to you, not even in Israel have I found such great faith."

10   And when those who had been sent returned to the house, they found the slave in good health.

Q. The raising of the widow's son (7:11–17)

11   And it came about soon afterwards, that He went to a city called Nain; and His disciples were going along with Him, accompanied by a large multitude.

12   Now as He approached the gate of the city, behold, a dead man was being carried out, the only son of his mother, and she was a widow; and a sizeable crowd from the city was with her.

13   And when the Lord saw her, He felt compassion for her, and said to her, "Do not weep."

14   And He came up and touched the coffin; and the bearers came to a halt. And He said, "Young man, I say to you, arise!"

15   And the dead man sat up, and began to speak. And *Jesus* gave him back to his mother.

16   And fear gripped them all, and they *began* glorifying God, saying, "A great prophet has arisen among us!" and, "God has visited His people!"

17   And this report concerning Him went out all over Judea, and in all the surrounding district.

R. John the Baptist's last message (7:18–35; Matt. 11:2–19)

18   And the disciples of John reported to him about all these things.

19   And summoning two of his disciples, John sent them to the Lord, saying, "Are You the Expected One, or do we look for someone else?"

20   And when the men had come to Him, they said, "John the Baptist has sent us to You, saying, 'Are You the Expected One, or do we look for someone else?'"

21   At that very time He cured many *people* of diseases and afflictions and evil spirits; and He granted sight to many *who were* blind.

22   And He answered and said to them, "Go and report to John what you have seen and heard: the BLIND RECEIVE SIGHT, *the* lame walk, *the* lepers are cleansed, and *the* deaf hear, *the* dead are raised up, *the* POOR HAVE THE GOSPEL PREACHED TO THEM.

23   "And blessed is he who keeps from stumbling over Me."

24   And when the messengers of John had left, He began to speak to the multitudes about John, "What did you go out into the wilderness to look at? A reed shaken by the wind?

25   "But what did you go out to see? A man dressed in soft clothing? Behold, those who are splendidly clothed and live in luxury are *found* in royal palaces.

26   "But what did you go out to see? A prophet? Yes, I say to you, and one who is more than a prophet.

27   "This is the one about whom it is written,

'BEHOLD, I SEND MY MESSENGER BEFORE YOUR FACE,
WHO WILL PREPARE YOUR WAY BEFORE YOU.'

28   "I say to you, among those born of women, there is no one greater than John; yet he who is least in the kingdom of God is greater than he."

7:9
v. 50

7:11
1 Kin 17:17-24;
2 Kin 4:32-37;
Mark 5:21-24,
35-43;
John 11:1-44

7:13
v. 19;
Luke 10:1;
11:1,39;
12:42; 13:15;
17:5,6; 18:6;
19:8; 22:61;
24:34
7:14
Luke 8:54;
John 11:43;
Acts 9:40
7:16
Luke 1:65;
John 6:14;
Luke 1:68

7:21
Matt 4:23;
Mark 3:10
7:22
Is 29:18,19;
35:5,6;
Luke 4:18

7:27
Mal 3:1;
Mark 1:2

7:29
Matt 21:32;
Luke 3:12
29   And when all the people and the [16]tax-gatherers heard *this*, they acknowledged God's justice, having been baptized with the baptism of John.

7:30
Matt 22:35;
Acts 20:27
30   But the Pharisees and the [17]lawyers rejected God's purpose for themselves, not having been baptized by John.

31   "To what then shall I compare the men of this generation, and what are they like?

32   "They are like children who sit in the market place and call to one another; and they say, 'We played the flute for you, and you did not dance; we sang a dirge, and you did not weep.'

7:33
Luke 1:15
33   "For John the Baptist has come eating no bread and drinking no wine; and you say, 'He has a demon!'

7:34
Luke 5:29;
15:1,2
34   "The Son of Man has come eating and drinking; and you say, 'Behold, a gluttonous man, and a drunkard, a friend of tax-gatherers and sinners!'

35   "Yet wisdom is vindicated by all her children."

S. *Jesus anointed: the sinful woman forgiven (7:36–50)*

*7:36ff
Matt 26:6-13;
Mark 14:3-9;
John 12:1-8
36   Now one of the Pharisees was requesting Him to dine with him. And He entered the Pharisee's house, and reclined *at the table*.

The pharisees measured every one else by their own yard stick. Simon wanted to observe Christ, but not to honor him.

37   And behold, there was a woman in the city who was a sinner; and when she learned that He was reclining *at the table* in the Pharisee's house, she brought an alabaster vial of perfume,

38   and standing behind *Him* at His feet, weeping, she began to wet His feet with her tears, and kept wiping them with the hair of her head, and kissing His feet, and anointing them with the perfume.

7:39
v. 16;
Luke 24:19;
John 6:14
39   Now when the Pharisee who had invited Him saw this, he said to himself, "If this man were a prophet He would know who and what sort of person this woman is who is touching Him, that she is a sinner."

V.39 Yet, as a prophet, Christ knew his thoughts.

40   And Jesus answered and said to him, "Simon, I have something to say to you." And he replied, "Say it, Teacher."

*7:41
Matt 18:28
41   "A certain moneylender had two debtors: one owed five hundred [18]denarii, and the other fifty.

42   "When they were unable to repay, he graciously forgave them both. Which of them therefore will love him more?"

43   Simon answered and said, "I suppose the one whom he forgave more." And He said to him, "You have judged correctly."

7:44
Gen 18:4;
19:2; 43:24;
Judg 19:21;
1 Tim 5:10
44   And turning toward the woman, He said to Simon, "Do you see this woman? I entered your house; you gave Me no water for My feet, but she has wet My feet with her tears, and wiped them with her hair.

45   "You gave Me no kiss; but she, since the time I came in, has not ceased to kiss My feet.

7:46
Ps 23:5
46   "You did not anoint My head with oil, but she anointed My feet with perfume.

47   "For this reason I say to you, her sins, which are many, have been forgiven, for she loved much; but he who is forgiven little, loves little."

7:48
Matt 9:2;
Mark 2:5;
Luke 5:20
48   And He said to her, "Your sins have been forgiven."

49   And those who were reclining *at the table* with Him began to say to themselves, "Who is this *man* who even forgives sins?"

7:50
Matt 9:22;
Mark 5:34;
Luke 8:48
50   And He said to the woman, "Your faith has saved you; go in peace."

[16]I.e., Collectors of Roman taxes for profit   [17]I.e., experts in the Mosaic law   [18]The denarius was equivalent to one day's wage

7:36ff.   There should not be any confusion between this incident, during the Galilean ministry of Christ, and a similar incident in Bethany of Judea, during the last week of our Lord's life (Matt. 26:6–13; Mark 14:3–9; John 12:1–8). In the one case the woman is unnamed; in the other she is identified as Mary, the sister of Martha and Lazarus (John 11:1,2); the host in Galilee was Simon the Pharisee (7:36, 40); in Bethany he was Simon the leper (Matt. 26:6; Mark 14:3); the concluding remarks of Jesus are quite dissimilar in the two incidents. Furthermore, there is no New Testament evidence for identifying the anonymous *sinner* of 7:37 with Mary Magdalene (cf. note to 8:2).

7:41   Christ here emphasizes the obligation of gratitude as incumbent on those who have been pardoned. The greater the wickedness from which one has been delivered, the greater the love he should normally show toward the person who delivered him. Incidental to this parable is the lesson taught through the life of the grateful woman. Christ accepted her outward works as an evidence of a genuine inner faith. She was saved by faith. Faith was instrumental in her salvation but not the ground of it. However, her salvation was manifested in outward conduct. (See also Titus 2:14; 3:4–8; James 2:14–26.)

T. Christ's companions on His second preaching tour (8:1–3)

8 And it came about soon afterwards, that He *began* going about from one city and village to another, proclaiming and preaching the kingdom of God; and the twelve were with Him,

2 and *also* some women who had been healed of evil spirits and sicknesses: Mary who was called Magdalene, from whom seven demons had gone out,

3 and Joanna the wife of Chuza, Herod's steward, and Susanna, and many others who were contributing to their support out of their private means.

U. Parable of the sower (8:4–8; Matt. 13:1–8; Mark 4:1–9)

4 And when a great multitude were coming together, and those from the various cities were journeying to Him, He spoke by way of a parable:

5 "The sower went out to sow his seed; and as he sowed, some fell beside the road; and it was trampled under foot, and the birds of the air ate it up.

6 "And other *seed* fell on rocky *soil*, and as soon as it grew up, it withered away, because it had no moisture.

7 "And other *seed* fell among the thorns; and the thorns grew up with it, and choked it out.

8 "And other *seed* fell into the good soil, and grew up, and produced a crop a hundred times as great." As He said these things, He would call out, "He who has ears to hear, let him hear."

V. The reason for parables (8:9,10; Matt. 13:1–17; Mark 4:10–12)

9 And His disciples *began* questioning Him as to what this parable might be.

10 And He said, "To you it has been granted to know the mysteries of the kingdom of God, but to the rest *it is* in parables, in order that SEEING THEY MAY NOT SEE, AND HEARING THEY MAY NOT UNDERSTAND.

W. The parable of the sower explained (8:11–18; Matt. 13:18–23; Mark 4:13–20)

11 "Now the parable is this: the seed is the word of God.

12 "And those beside the road are those who have heard; then the devil comes and takes away the word from their heart, so that they may not believe and be saved.

13 "And those on the rocky *soil are* those who, when they hear, receive the word with joy; and these have no *firm* root; they believe for a while, and in time of temptation fall away.

14 "And the *seed* which fell among the thorns, these are the ones who have heard, and as they go on their way they are choked with worries and riches and pleasures of *this* life, and bring no fruit to maturity.

15 "And the *seed* in the good soil, these are the ones who have heard the word in an honest and good heart, and hold it fast, and bear fruit with perseverance.

16 "Now no one after lighting a lamp covers it over with a container, or puts it under a bed; but he puts it on a lampstand, in order that those who come in may see the light.

17 "For nothing is hidden that shall not become evident, nor *anything* secret that shall not be known and come to light.

18 "Therefore take care how you listen; for whoever has, to him shall *more* be given; and whoever does not have, even what he thinks he has shall be taken away from him."

X. Christ's true kindred (8:19–21; Matt. 12:46–50; Mark 3:31–35)

19 And His mother and brothers came to Him, and they were unable to get to Him because of the crowd.

20 And it was reported to Him, "Your mother and Your brothers are standing outside, wishing to see You."

Margin references: 8:1 Matt 4:23; *8:2 Matt 27:55,56; 8:8 Matt 11:15; 8:10 Is 6:9,10; Jer 5:21; Ezek 12:2; 8:11 1 Thess 2:13; 1 Pet 1:23; *8:16 Matt 5:15; Mark 4:21; Luke 11:33; 8:17 Matt 10:26; Mark 4:22; Luke 12:2; 8:18 Matt 13:12; 25:29; Luke 19:26

8:2 The name *Magdalene* means "of (the town of) Magdala," a fishing village, also called Tarichaea, on the west side of the Sea of Galilee. This verse in Luke contains the only specific item of information about Mary's previous life: she had been freed from seven demons, presumably by Jesus. Nowhere in the New Testament is demon possession equated with immorality, or said to be the cause of immorality, and there is nothing in the gospels to support the frequent assertion that Mary had been a prostitute.
8:5 See note to Mark 4:3 for an explanation of the parable of the sower.
8:16 *a container*. Matt. 5:15 and Mark 4:21 have *a peck-measure*.

8:21
Luke 11:28;
John 15:14

8:22
Mark 6:47-52;
John 6:16-21

8:24
Luke 5:5;
4:39

8:28
Mark 1:24

8:31
Rom 10:7;
Rev 20:1,3

8:33
vv. 22,23

8:35
Luke 10:39

8:36
Matt 4:24

8:37
Acts 16:39

21 But He answered and said to them, "My mother and My brothers are these who hear the word of God and do it."

Y. The storm stilled (8:22–25; Matt. 8:23–27; Mark 4:36–41)

22 Now it came about on one of *those* days, that He and His disciples got into a boat, and He said to them, "Let us go over to the other side of the lake." And they launched out.
23 But as they were sailing along He fell asleep; and a fierce gale of wind descended upon the lake, and they *began* to be swamped and to be in danger.
24 And they came to Him and woke Him up, saying, "Master, Master, we are perishing!" And being aroused, He rebuked the wind and the surging waves, and they stopped, and it became calm.
25 And He said to them, "Where is your faith?" And they were fearful and amazed, saying to one another, "Who then is this, that He commands even the winds and the water, and they obey Him?"

Z. Demons cast out (8:26–39; Matt. 8:28–34; Mark 5:1–20)

26 And they sailed to the country of the Gerasenes, which is opposite Galilee.
27 And when He had come out onto the land, He was met by a certain man from the city who was possessed with demons; and who had not put on any clothing for a long time, and was not living in a house, but in the tombs.
28 And seeing Jesus, he cried out and fell before Him, and said in a loud voice, "What do I have to do with You, Jesus, Son of the Most High God? I beg You, do not torment me."
29 For He had been commanding the unclean spirit to come out of the man. For it had seized him many times; and he was bound with chains and shackles and kept under guard; and *yet* he would burst his fetters and be driven by the demon into the desert.
30 And Jesus asked him, "What is your name?" And he said, "Legion"; for many demons had entered him.
31 And they were entreating Him not to command them to depart into the abyss.
32 Now there was a herd of many swine feeding there on the mountain; and *the demons* entreated Him to permit them to enter the swine. And He gave them permission.
33 And the demons came out from the man and entered the swine; and the herd rushed down the steep bank into the lake, and were drowned.
34 And when the herdsmen saw what had happened, they ran away and reported it in the city and *out* in the country.
35 And *the people* went out to see what had happened; and they came to Jesus, and found the man from whom the demons had gone out, sitting down at the feet of Jesus, clothed and in his right mind; and they became frightened.
36 And those who had seen it reported to them how the man who was demon-possessed had been made well.
37 And all the people of the country of the Gerasenes and the surrounding district asked Him to depart from them; for they were gripped with great fear; and He got into a boat, and returned.
38 But the man from whom the demons had gone out was begging Him that he might accompany Him; but He sent him away, saying,
39 "Return to your house and describe what great things God has done for you." And he went away, proclaiming throughout the whole city what great things Jesus had done for him.

AA. The woman with the issue of blood healed and Jairus's daughter raised (8:40–56; Matt. 9:18–26; Mark 5:21–43)

40 And as Jesus returned, the multitude welcomed Him, for they had all been waiting for Him.
41 And behold, there came a man named Jairus, and he was an official of the synagogue; and he fell at Jesus' feet, and *began* to entreat Him to come to his house;
42 for he had an only daughter, about twelve years old, and she was dying. But as He went, the multitudes were pressing against Him.

43 And a woman who had a hemorrhage for twelve years, [19]and could not be healed by anyone,

44 came up behind Him, and touched the fringe of His cloak; and immediately her hemorrhage stopped.

45 And Jesus said, "Who is the one who touched Me?" And while they were all denying it, Peter said, "Master, the multitudes are crowding and pressing upon You."

46 But Jesus said, "Someone did touch Me, for I was aware that power had gone out of Me."

47 And when the woman saw that she had not escaped notice, she came trembling and fell down before Him, and declared in the presence of all the people the reason why she had touched Him, and how she had been immediately healed.

48 And He said to her, "Daughter, your faith has made you well; go in peace."

49 While He was still speaking, someone *came from *the house of* the synagogue official, saying, "Your daughter has died; do not trouble the Teacher anymore."

50 But when Jesus heard *this,* He answered him, "Do not be afraid *any longer;* only believe, and she shall be made well."

51 And when He had come to the house, He did not allow anyone to enter with Him, except Peter and John and James, and the girl's father and mother.

52 Now they were all weeping and lamenting for her; but He said, "Stop weeping, for she has not died, but is asleep."

53 And they *began* laughing at Him, knowing that she had died.

54 He, however, took her by the hand and called, saying, "Child, arise!"

55 And her spirit returned, and she rose immediately; and He gave orders for *something* to be given her to eat.

56 And her parents were amazed; but He instructed them to tell no one what had happened.

BB. *The mission of the Twelve (9:1–6; Matt. 10:1–15; Mark 6:7–13)*

9 And He called the twelve together, and gave them power and authority over all the demons, and to heal diseases.

2 And He sent them out to proclaim the kingdom of God, and to perform healing.

3 And He said to them, "Take nothing for *your* journey, neither a staff, nor a bag, nor bread, nor money; and do not *even* have two tunics apiece.

4 "And whatever house you enter, stay there, and take your leave from there.

5 "And as for those who do not receive you, as you go out from that city, shake off the dust from your feet as a testimony against them."

6 And departing, they *began* going about among the villages, preaching the gospel, and healing everywhere.

CC. *Death of John the Baptist (9:7–9; Matt. 14:1–12; Mark 6:14–39)*

7 Now Herod the tetrarch heard of all that was happening; and he was greatly perplexed, because it was said by some that John had risen from the dead,

8 and by some that Elijah had appeared, and by others, that one of the prophets of old had risen again.

9 And Herod said, "I myself had John beheaded; but who is this man about whom I hear such things?" And he kept trying to see Him.

DD. *The five thousand fed (9:10–17; Matt. 14:13–21; Mark 6:30–44; John 6:1–13; cf. Matt. 15:32–38)*

10 And when the apostles returned, they gave an account to Him of all that they had done. And taking them with Him, He withdrew by Himself to a city called Bethsaida.

11 But the multitudes were aware of this and followed Him; and welcoming

[19]Some mss. add *who had spent all her living upon physicians*

8:46 Here, and in the parallel Mark 5:30, reference is made to the *power* (Greek *dunamis*) that went forth from Jesus and healed the woman with the flow of blood. From the account, this took place without any conscious volition on the part of Jesus. In 5:17 it is reported that *the power of the Lord* was with Jesus for Him to perform healings, and 6:19 speaks of the power that came from Jesus and healed all. These passages point up the truth elsewhere expressed that Jesus healed and expelled demons by the power of God, or the Spirit of God (cf. 4:18; 11:20; Matt. 12:28).

Margin references: 8:45 Luke 5:5; *8:46 Luke 5:17; 6:19; 8:48 Luke 7:50; 17:19; 18:42; 8:49 v. 41; 8:52 Luke 23:27; John 11:11,13; 8:54 Luke 7:14; John 11:43; 8:56 Matt 8:4; Mark 3:12; 7:36; Luke 9:21; 9:1 Mark 3:13,14; 9:2 Luke 10:1,9; 9:3 Luke 10:4; 22:35; 9:5 Acts 13:51; 9:7 v. 19; 9:8 Matt 16:14; 9:9 Luke 23:8; 9:10 v. 17

them, He *began* speaking to them about the kingdom of God and curing those who had need of healing.

12 And the day began to decline, and the twelve came and said to Him, "Send the multitude away, that they may go into the surrounding villages and countryside and find lodging and get something to eat; for here we are in a desolate place."

9:13
2 Kin 4:42-44

13 But He said to them, "You give them *something* to eat!" And they said, "We have no more than five loaves and two fish, unless perhaps we go and buy food for all these people."

14 (For there were about five thousand men.) And He said to His disciples, "Have them recline *to eat* in groups of about fifty each."

15 And they did so, and had them all recline.

9:16
Luke 22:19;
24:30,31;
Acts 2:42;
20:11; 27:35

16 And He took the five loaves and the two fish, and looking up to heaven, He blessed them, and broke *them*, and kept giving *them* to the disciples to set before the multitude.

17 And they all ate and were satisfied; and the broken pieces which they had left over were picked up, twelve baskets *full*.

EE. *Peter's confession and Christ's death and resurrection foretold (9:18–27; Matt. 16:13–28; Mark 8:27–9:1)*

9:18
John 1:49;
6:66-69;
11:27
9:19
vv. 7,8;
Mark 9:11-13
*9:20
John 6:69

18 And it came about that while He was praying alone, the disciples were with Him, and He questioned them, saying, "Who do the multitudes say that I am?"

19 And they answered and said, "John the Baptist, and others *say* Elijah; but others, that one of the prophets of old has risen again."

20 And He said to them, "But who do you say that I am?" And Peter answered and said, "The Christ of God."

9:21
Matt 16:20
9:22
vv. 43-45;
Luke 18:31-34

21 But He warned them, and instructed *them* not to tell this to anyone,

22 saying, "The Son of Man must suffer many things, and be rejected by the elders and chief priests and scribes, and be killed, and be raised up on the third day."

9:23
Matt 10:38;
Luke 14:27

23 And He was saying to *them* all, "If anyone wishes to come after Me, let him deny himself, and take up his cross daily, and follow Me.

9:24
Matt 10:39

24 "For whoever wishes to save his life shall lose it, but whoever loses his life for My sake, he is the one who will save it.

9:25
John 12:25

25 "For what is a man profited if he gains the whole world, and loses or forfeits himself?

9:26
Matt 10:33;
Luke 12:9;
2 Tim 2:12;
1 John 2:28
9:27
Luke 22:18;
John 21:22

26 "For whoever is ashamed of Me and My words, of him will the Son of Man be ashamed when He comes in His glory, and *the glory* of the Father and of the holy angels.

27 "But I say to you truthfully, there are some of those standing here who shall not taste death until they see the kingdom of God."

FF. *The transfiguration (9:28–36; Matt. 17:1–8; Mark 9:2–13)*

9:28
Luke 3:21;
5:16; 6:12

28 And some eight days after these sayings, it came about that He took along Peter and John and James, and went up to the mountain to pray.

29 And while He was praying, the appearance of His face became different, and His clothing *became* white *and* gleaming.

30 And behold, two men were talking with Him; and they were Moses and Elijah,

9:31
2 Pet 1:15

31 who, appearing in glory, were speaking of His departure which He was about to accomplish at Jerusalem.

9:32
Matt 26:43;
Mark 14:40
9:33
Luke 5:8;
8:24,45;
17:13

32 Now Peter and his companions had been overcome with sleep; but when they were fully awake, they saw His glory and the two men standing with Him.

33 And it came about, as these were parting from Him, Peter said to Jesus, "Master, it is good for us to be here; and let us make three tabernacles: one for You, and one for Moses, and one for Elijah"—not realizing what he was saying.

34 And while he was saying this, a cloud formed and *began* to overshadow them; and they were afraid as they entered the cloud.

9:35
2 Pet 1:17,18;
Matt 3:17
9:36
Matt 17:9

35 And a voice came out of the cloud, saying, "This is My Son, *My* Chosen One; listen to Him!"

36 And when the voice had spoken, Jesus was found alone. And they kept silent, and reported to no one in those days any of the things which they had seen.

9:20 See note to Matt. 16:18 on Peter and the church.   **9:29** See note to Mark 9:2 on the transfiguration.

22 "All things have been handed over to Me by My Father, and no one knows who the Son is except the Father, and who the Father is except the Son, and anyone to whom the Son wills to reveal *Him*."

23 And turning to the disciples, He said privately, "Blessed *are* the eyes which see the things you see,

24 for I say to you, that many prophets and kings wished to see the things which you see, and did not see *them*, and to hear the things which you hear, and did not hear *them*."

D. *The good Samaritan (10:25–37)*

25 And behold, a certain lawyer stood up and put Him to the test, saying, "Teacher, what shall I do to inherit eternal life?"

26 And He said to him, "What is written in the Law? How does it read to you?"

27 And he answered and said, "YOU SHALL LOVE THE LORD YOUR GOD WITH ALL YOUR HEART, AND WITH ALL YOUR SOUL, AND WITH ALL YOUR STRENGTH, AND WITH ALL YOUR MIND; AND YOUR NEIGHBOR AS YOURSELF."

28 And He said to him, "You have answered correctly; DO THIS, AND YOU WILL LIVE."

29 But wishing to justify himself, he said to Jesus, "And who is my neighbor?"

30 Jesus replied and said, "A certain man was going down from Jerusalem to Jericho; and he fell among robbers, and they stripped him and beat him, and went off leaving him half dead.

31 "And by chance a certain priest was going down on that road, and when he saw him, he passed by on the other side.

32 "And likewise a Levite also, when he came to the place and saw him, passed by on the other side.

33 "But a certain Samaritan, who was on a journey, came upon him; and when he saw him, he felt compassion,

34 and came to him, and bandaged up his wounds, pouring oil and wine on *them*; and he put him on his own beast, and brought him to an inn, and took care of him.

35 "And on the next day he took out two [21]denarii and gave them to the innkeeper and said, 'Take care of him; and whatever more you spend, when I return, I will repay you.'

36 "Which of these three do you think proved to be a neighbor to the man who fell into the robbers' *hands?*"

37 And he said, "The one who showed mercy toward him." And Jesus said to him, "Go and do the same."

E. *Jesus visits Mary and Martha (10:38–42)*

38 Now as they were traveling along, He entered a certain village; and a woman named Martha welcomed Him into her home.

39 And she had a sister called Mary, who moreover was listening to the Lord's word, seated at His feet.

40 But Martha was distracted with all her preparations; and she came up *to Him*, and said, "Lord, do You not care that my sister has left me to do all the serving alone? Then tell her to help me."

41 But the Lord answered and said to her, "Martha, Martha, you are worried and bothered about so many things;

21The denarius was equivalent to one day's wage

10:30 The parable of the Good Samaritan cannot be understood apart from its context. A lawyer had asked Jesus what he must do to inherit eternal life. Jesus replied by reciting the first table of the Law: *love the Lord your God* (v. 27). Then Jesus gave the parable of the Good Samaritan, which had reference to the second table of the Law: Love your neighbor as yourself (v. 27). The Jew in Jesus' day acknowledged none as his neighbor except those who were Jews. In the parable the priest and the Levite failed to help one of their own, a fellow Jew. The Samaritan, who was hated by the Jews and who was not regarded as a neighbor, assisted the Jew. Jesus gained an admission from the lawyer that the true neighbor was the Samaritan—although the lawyer could not bring himself to use the word "Samaritan" but rather *the one who showed mercy toward him* (v. 37). But, this being true, he had to admit that the Jew must also show mercy to those who were not usually regarded as neighbors. The answer to the question of the lawyer, ". . . *what shall I do to inherit eternal life?*" (v. 25) was twofold: . . . *love the Lord your God with all your heart . . . and your neighbor as yourself* (v. 27). This, of course, must be understood as indicating a true and living faith, rather than a way of earning salvation, for Jesus elsewhere made it very clear that salvation was of faith alone, not of good works (John 6:28, 29; cf. Matt. 7:22,23).

What was the disciples' notion of prayer before chap 11? Were they expecting the long, windy prayers of the Pharisees?

10:42
Ps 27:4

42 but *only* a few things are necessary, really *only* one, for Mary has chosen the good part, which shall not be taken away from her."

F. Jesus' discourse on prayer (11:1–13; cf. Matt. 6:5–15)

V1- Even the disciples craved structure

*11:1
Mark 1:35;
Luke 3:21

V2 - when God's will is being done, God's Kingdom is present.

11 And it came about that while He was praying in a certain place, after He had finished, one of His disciples said to Him, "Lord, teach us to pray just as John also taught his disciples."

2 And He said to them, "When you pray, say:
'[22]Father, hallowed be Thy name.
Thy kingdom come.

3 'Give us each day our daily bread.

11:4
Matt 18:35;
Mark 11:25

4 'And forgive us our sins,
For we ourselves also forgive everyone who is indebted to us.
And lead us not into temptation.'"

V4 - Heb 4:15
Testing is our norm
James 1:13-14

W - worship
A - ask
F - forgive
T - Thank

5 And He said to them, "Suppose one of you shall have a friend, and shall go to him at midnight, and say to him, 'Friend, lend me three loaves;

6 for a friend of mine has come to me from a journey, and I have nothing to set before him';

7 and from inside he shall answer and say, 'Do not bother me; the door has already been shut and my children and I are in bed; I cannot get up and give you *anything*.'

*11:8
Luke 18:1-6
seeking is diff. from looking.

8 "I tell you, even though he will not get up and give him *anything* because he is his friend, yet because of his persistence he will get up and give him as much as he needs.

11:9
Matt 7:7-11;
18:19; 21:22;
Mark 11:24;
James 1:5-8;
1 John 5:14,
15

9 "And I say to you, ask, and it shall be given to you; seek, and you shall find; knock, and it shall be opened to you.

10 "For everyone who asks, receives; and he who seeks, finds; and to him who knocks, it shall be opened.

11 "Now suppose one of you fathers is asked by his son for a fish; he will not give him a snake instead of a fish, will he?

12 "Or *if* he is asked for an egg, he will not give him a scorpion, will he?

13 "If you then, being evil, know how to give good gifts to your children, how much more shall *your* heavenly Father give the Holy Spirit to those who ask Him?"

G. Jesus answers the slander of the Pharisees (11:14–28; Matt. 12:22–45; Mark 3:20–30)

11:14
Matt 9:32-34

14 And He was casting out a demon, and it was dumb; and it came about that when the demon had gone out, the dumb man spoke; and the multitudes marveled.

15 But some of them said, "He casts out demons by Beelzebul, the ruler of the demons."

11:16
Matt 16:1;
Mark 8:11
11:17
John 2:25

16 And others, to test *Him*, were demanding of Him a sign from heaven.

17 But He knew their thoughts, and said to them, "Any kingdom divided against itself is laid waste; and a house *divided* against itself falls.

18 "And if Satan also is divided against himself, how shall his kingdom stand? For you say that I cast out demons by Beelzebul.

19 "And if I by Beelzebul cast out demons, by whom do your sons cast them out? Consequently they shall be your judges.

11:20
Ex 8:19

20 "But if I cast out demons by the finger of God, then the kingdom of God has come upon you.

21 "When a strong *man*, fully armed, guards his own homestead, his possessions are undisturbed;

22 but when someone stronger than he attacks him and overpowers him, he

---

[22]Some mss. insert phrases from Matt. 6:9-13 to make the two passages closely similar

11:1 The conditions for effectual prayer include: (1) a right relationship of repentance and faith, for God never promises to answer the prayers of unbelievers, although He may occasionally choose to do so (2 Chr. 7:14; John 14:13,14); (2) an earnest and spiritual desire (1 Sam. 1:10,11; 2 Kin. 19:14-19; Luke 11:5-10); (3) a confidence in God that leads the petitioner to ask in simple trust (Matt. 7:7-11; James 4:2); (4) a faith that believes God is both able and willing to answer (Matt. 21:22; Heb. 11:1; 1 John 5:14,15); and (5) a

reception of the anticipated answer by faith, as we appropriate or lay hold of that which we have not yet received (Mark 11:24). While there are many hindrances to prayer, all of them may be comprehended under two general classifications: sin (Ps. 66:18) and unbelief (Matt. 21:22; James 1:6-8).
11:8 Here and in Luke 18:1-6 Jesus stresses the necessity for importunity in prayer if one is to prevail before God.

takes away from him all his armor on which he had relied, and distributes his plunder.

23 "He who is not with Me is against Me; and he who does not gather with Me, scatters.

24 "When the unclean spirit goes out of a man, it passes through waterless places seeking rest, and not finding any, it says, 'I will return to my house from which I came.'

25 "And when it comes, it finds it swept and put in order.

26 "Then it goes and takes *along* seven other spirits more evil than itself, and they go in and live there; and the last state of that man becomes worse than the first."

27 And it came about while He said these things, one of the women in the crowd raised her voice, and said to Him, "Blessed is the womb that bore You, and the breasts at which You nursed."

28 But He said, "On the contrary, blessed are those who hear the word of God, and observe it."

H. *Warning against seeking signs* (11:29–32; Matt. 12:38–42)

29 And as the crowds were increasing, He began to say, "This generation is a wicked generation; it seeks for a sign, and *yet* no sign shall be given to it but the sign of Jonah.

30 "For just as Jonah became a sign to the Ninevites, so shall the Son of Man be to this generation.

31 "The Queen of the South shall rise up with the men of this generation at the judgment and condemn them, because she came from the ends of the earth to hear the wisdom of Solomon; and behold, something greater than Solomon is here.

32 "The men of Nineveh shall stand up with this generation at the judgment and condemn it, because they repented at the preaching of Jonah; and behold, something greater than Jonah is here.

I. *The parable of the lighted lamp* (11:33–36)

33 "No one, after lighting a lamp, puts it away in a cellar, nor under a peck-measure, but on the lampstand, in order that those who enter may see the light.

34 "The lamp of your body is your eye; when your eye is clear, your whole body also is full of light; but when it is bad, your body also is full of darkness.

35 "Then watch out that the light in you may not be darkness.

36 "If therefore your whole body is full of light, with no dark part in it, it shall be wholly illumined, as when the lamp illumines you with its rays."

J. *Pharisaism exposed and denounced* (11:37–54)

37 Now when He had spoken, a Pharisee *asked Him to have lunch with him; and He went in, and reclined *at the table*.

38 And when the Pharisee saw it, he was surprised that He had not first ceremonially washed before the meal.

39 But the Lord said to him, "Now you Pharisees clean the outside of the cup and of the platter; but inside of you, you are full of robbery and wickedness.

40 "You foolish ones, did not He who made the outside make the inside also?

41 "But give that which is within as charity, and then all things are clean for you.

42 "But woe to you Pharisees! For you pay tithe of mint and rue and every *kind of* garden herb, and *yet* disregard justice and the love of God; but these are the things you should have done without neglecting the others.

43 "Woe to you Pharisees! For you love the front seats in the synagogues, and the respectful greetings in the market places.

44 "Woe to you! For you are like concealed tombs, and the people who walk over *them* are unaware *of it*."

45 And one of the [23]lawyers *said to Him in reply, "Teacher, when You say this, You insult us too."

46 But He said, "Woe to you lawyers as well! For you weigh men down with burdens hard to bear, while you yourselves will not even touch the burdens with one of your fingers.

11:23
Luke 9:50

11:26
Heb 10:26;
2 Pet 2:20

11:27
Luke 23:29

11:28
Luke 8:21;
John 15:14

11:29
Matt 16:4;
Mark 8:12;
v. 16

11:31
1 Kin 10:1;
2 Chr 9:1

11:32
Jon 3:5

11:33
Matt 5:15;
Mark 4:21;
Luke 8:16
11:34
Matt 6:22,23

11:37
Luke 7:36;
14:1
11:38
Mark 7:3,4
11:39
Matt 23:25,26

11:41
Luke 12:33;
Mark 7:19;
Titus 1:15
11:42
Matt 23:23;
Luke 18:12
11:43
Matt 23:6,7;
Mark 12:38,
39;
Luke 20:46
11:44
Matt 23:27

11:46
Matt 23:4

11:47
Matt 23:29-32;
Acts 7:51-53
47 "Woe to you! For you build the tombs of the prophets, and *it was* your fathers *who* killed them.

48 "Consequently, you are witnesses and approve the deeds of your fathers; because it was they who killed them, and you build *their tombs.*

11:49
Matt 23:34-36;
1 Cor 1:24;
Col 2:3
49 "For this reason also the wisdom of God said, 'I will send to them prophets and apostles, and *some* of them they will kill and *some* they will persecute,

50 in order that the blood of all the prophets, shed since the foundation of the world, may be charged against this generation,

11:51
Gen 4:8;
2 Chr 24:20,
21
51 from the blood of Abel to the blood of Zechariah, who perished between the altar and the house *of God;* yes, I tell you, it shall be charged against this generation.'

11:52
Matt 23:13
52 "Woe to you lawyers! For you have taken away the key of knowledge; you did not enter in yourselves, and those who were entering in you hindered."

53 And when He left there, the scribes and the Pharisees began to be very hostile and to question Him closely on many subjects,

11:54
Mark 12:13
54 plotting against Him, to catch *Him* in something He might say.

K. *Warning against the leaven of the Pharisees (12:1–12)*

12:1
Matt 16:6;
Mark 8:15;
Matt 16:12
12 Under these circumstances, after so many thousands of the multitude had gathered together that they were stepping on one another, He began saying to His disciples first *of all,* "Beware of the leaven of the Pharisees, which is hypocrisy.

12:2
Matt 10:26,
27;
Mark 4:22;
Luke 8:17;
Eph 5:13
2 "But there is nothing covered up that will not be revealed, and hidden that will not be known.

3 "Accordingly, whatever you have said in the dark shall be heard in the light, and what you have whispered in the inner rooms shall be proclaimed upon the housetops.

12:4
Matt 10:28-33;
John 15:14,15
4 "And I say to you, My friends, do not be afraid of those who kill the body, and after that have no more that they can do.

12:5
Heb 10:31
5 "But I will warn you whom to fear: fear the One who after He has killed has authority to cast into hell; yes, I tell you, fear Him!

cf. Matt 10:29
6 "Are not five sparrows sold for two cents? And *yet* not one of them is forgotten before God.

12:7
Matt 12:12;
Luke 21:18;
Acts 27:34
7 "Indeed, the very hairs of your head are all numbered. Do not fear; you are of more value than many sparrows.

12:8
Mark 8:38;
2 Tim 2:12;
1 John 2:23
8 "And I say to you, everyone who confesses Me before men, the Son of Man shall confess him also before the angels of God;

9 but he who denies Me before men shall be denied before the angels of God.

12:10
Matt 12:31,
32;
Mark 3:28,29
10 "And everyone who will speak a word against the Son of Man, it shall be forgiven him; but he who blasphemes against the Holy Spirit, it shall not be forgiven him.

12:11
Matt 10:19;
Mark 13:11;
Luke 21:14
11 "And when they bring you before the synagogues and the rulers and the authorities, do not become anxious about how or what you should speak in your defense, or what you should say;

12 for the Holy Spirit will teach you in that very hour what you ought to say."

L. *Parable of the rich fool: covetousness (12:13–21)*

13 And someone in the crowd said to Him, "Teacher, tell my brother to divide the *family* inheritance with me."

12:14
Mic 6:8;
Rom 2:1,3
14 But He said to him, "Man, who appointed Me a judge or arbiter over you?"

15 And He said to them, "Beware, and be on your guard against every form of greed; for not *even* when one has an abundance does his life consist of his possessions."

16 And He told them a parable, saying, "The land of a certain rich man was very productive.

12:16 Worldly-mindedness, or concern only for this life, is the dominant trait warned against in this parable. Christ here reiterates what He taught in the Sermon on the Mount (Matt. 6:20,32–34). Nowhere did He suggest that being wealthy is wrong or that we should disregard the practical requirements of this life. But when wealth becomes an end in itself and is not used with a sense of holy stewardship to God, then it becomes a snare and a delusion. Material riches present more temptations than usual to people of wealth, and therefore require special precautions. Sometimes wealth must be disposed of altogether if the soul is to be freed for whole-hearted fellowship with Christ (Matt. 19:16–24).

If this man's soul wasn't being used to love other people, what function did it serve?

17 "And he began reasoning to himself, saying, 'What shall I do, since I have no place to store my crops?'

18 "And he said, 'This is what I will do: I will tear down my barns and build larger ones, and there I will store all my grain and my goods.

19 'And I will say to my soul, "Soul, you have many goods laid up for many years *to come;* take your ease, eat, drink *and* be merry." '

20 "But God said to him, 'You fool! This *very* night your soul is required of you; and *now* who will own what you have prepared?'

21 "So is the man who lays up treasure for himself, and is not rich toward God."

M. *Trust or anxiety (12:22–34; cf. Matt. 6:25–34)*

22 And He said to His disciples, "For this reason I say to you, do not be anxious for *your* life, *as to* what you shall eat; nor for your body, *as to* what you shall put on.

23 "For life is more than food, and the body than clothing.

24 "Consider the ravens, for they neither sow nor reap; and they have no storeroom nor barn; and *yet* God feeds them; how much more valuable you are than the birds!

25 "And which of you by being anxious can add a *single* [24]cubit to his [25] life's span?

26 "If then you cannot do even a very little thing, why are you anxious about other matters?

27 "Consider the lilies, how they grow; they neither toil nor spin; but I tell you, even Solomon in all his glory did not clothe himself like one of these.

28 "But if God so arrays the grass in the field, which is *alive* today and tomorrow is thrown into the furnace, how much more *will He clothe* you, O men of little faith!

29 "And do not seek what you shall eat, and what you shall drink, and do not keep worrying.

30 "For all these things the nations of the world eagerly seek; but your Father knows that you need these things.

31 "But seek for His kingdom, and these things shall be added to you.

32 "Do not be afraid, little flock, for your Father has chosen gladly to give you the kingdom.

33 "Sell your possessions and give to charity; make yourselves purses which do not wear out, an unfailing treasure in heaven, where no thief comes near, nor moth destroys.

34 "For where your treasure is, there will your heart be also.

N. *Exhortation to vigilance (12:35–40)*

35 "Be dressed in readiness, and *keep* your lamps alight.

36 "And be like men who are waiting for their master when he returns from the wedding feast, so that they may immediately open *the door* to him when he comes and knocks.

37 "Blessed are those slaves whom the master shall find on the alert when he comes; truly I say to you, that he will gird himself *to serve,* and have them recline *at the table,* and will come up and wait on them.

38 "Whether he comes in the [26]second watch, or even in the [27]third, and finds *them* so, blessed are those *slaves.*

39 "And be sure of this, that if the head of the house had known at what hour the thief was coming, he would not have allowed his house to be broken into.

40 "You too, be ready; for the Son of Man is coming at an hour that you do not expect."

O. *Faithful and unfaithful servants (12:41–48; Matt. 24:45–51)*

41 And Peter said, "Lord, are You addressing this parable to us, or to everyone *else* as well?"

42 And the Lord said, "Who then is the faithful and sensible steward, whom

[24]I.e., One cubit equals approx. 18 in.   [25]Or, *height*   [26]I.e., 9 p.m. to midnight   [27]I.e., midnight to 3 a.m.

12:42 This parable emphasizes the need of conscientiousness in discharging one's obligations. The thought of possible delay in the return of Christ to earth should dispose no Christian to slothful ease or failure to do God's will. Jesus further indicates here that there is a time of judgment coming for the master's servants when rewards for faithfulness will be handed out, and unfaithfulness will be fittingly punished.

his master will put in charge of his servants, to give them their rations at the proper time?

43 "Blessed is that slave whom his master finds so doing when he comes.

44 "Truly I say to you, that he will put him in charge of all his possessions.

45 "But if that slave says in his heart, 'My master will be a long time in coming,' and begins to beat the slaves, *both* men and women, and to eat and drink and get drunk;

46 the master of that slave will come on a day when he does not expect *him,* and at an hour he does not know, and will cut him in pieces, and assign him a place with the unbelievers.

47 "And that slave who knew his master's will and did not get ready or act in accord with his will, shall receive many lashes,

48 but the one who did not know *it,* and committed deeds worthy of a flogging, will receive but few. And from everyone who has been given much shall much be required; and to whom they entrusted much, of him they will ask all the more.

P. Christ the great divider (12:49–59)

49 "I have come to cast fire upon the earth; and how I wish it were already kindled!

50 "But I have a baptism to undergo, and how distressed I am until it is accomplished!

51 "Do you suppose that I came to grant peace on earth? I tell you, no, but rather division;

52 for from now on five *members* in one household will be divided, three against two, and two against three.

53 "They will be divided, father against son, and son against father; mother against daughter, and daughter against mother; mother-in-law against daughter-in-law, and daughter-in-law against mother-in-law."

54 And He was also saying to the multitudes, "When you see a cloud rising in the west, immediately you say, 'A shower is coming,' and so it turns out.

55 "And when *you see* a south wind blowing, you say, 'It will be a hot day,' and it turns out *that way.*

56 "You hypocrites! You know how to analyze the appearance of the earth and the sky, but why do you not analyze this present time?

57 "And why do you not even on your own initiative judge what is right?

58 "For while you are going with your opponent to appear before the magistrate, on *your* way *there* make an effort to settle with him, in order that he may not drag you before the judge, and the judge turn you over to the constable, and the constable throw you into prison.

59 "I say to you, you shall not get out of there until you have paid the very last cent."

Q. Jesus' call to repentance (13:1–9)

13 Now on the same occasion there were some present who reported to Him about the Galileans, whose blood Pilate had mingled with their sacrifices.

2 And He answered and said to them, "Do you suppose that these Galileans were *greater* sinners than all *other* Galileans, because they suffered this *fate?*

3 "I tell you, no, but, unless you repent, you will all likewise perish.

4 "Or do you suppose that those eighteen on whom the tower in Siloam fell and killed them, were *worse* culprits than all the men who live in Jerusalem?

5 "I tell you, no, but unless you repent, you will all likewise perish."

6 And He *began* telling this parable: "A certain man had a fig tree which had been planted in his vineyard; and he came looking for fruit on it, and did not find any.

7 "And he said to the vineyard-keeper, 'Behold, for three years I have come

---

Marginal references:

12:47 Num 15:30; Deut 25:2
12:48 Lev 5:17
12:50 Mark 10:38; John 12:27
12:51 Matt 10:34-36; v. 49
12:53 Mic 7:6; Matt 10:21
12:54 Matt 16:2
12:55 Matt 20:12
12:56 Matt 16:3
12:58 Matt 5:25,26
12:59 Mark 12:42
*13:1 Matt 27:2
13:2 John 9:2,3
13:4 Luke 11:4
*13:6 Matt 21:19
13:7 Matt 3:10; 7:19; Luke 3:9

13:1 There is no further information on this incident. It may be inferred that some Galileans, while in the act of offering sacrifices in the temple in Jerusalem, were attacked and killed by Pilate's soldiers, so that their blood was mingled with that of their sacrifices. Pilate may have thought that these Galileans were planning an insurrection. An incident like this may explain the enmity that existed between Pilate and Herod Antipas, tetrarch of Galilee (23:12).

13:6 The parable of the barren fig tree had primary reference to the nation of Israel. For centuries God had been expecting Israel to bring forth fruit to repentance, but there had been none. Now Christ had come, but even He had been rejected; however, as this parable teaches, God, who is long-suffering, will grant more time for Israel to repent and turn at last to Him. But if the chosen people persist in their refusal to turn to God, they will finally be cut off.

looking for fruit on this fig tree without finding any. Cut it down! Why does it even use up the ground?'

8   "And he answered and said to him, 'Let it alone, sir, for this year too, until I dig around it and put in fertilizer;

9   and if it bears fruit next year, *fine;* but if not, cut it down.' "

R. A woman healed on the Sabbath (13:10–17)

10   And He was teaching in one of the synagogues on the Sabbath.

11   And behold, there was a woman who for eighteen years had had a sickness caused by a spirit; and she was bent double, and could not straighten up at all.

12   And when Jesus saw her, He called her over and said to her, "Woman, you are freed from your sickness."

13   And He laid His hands upon her; and immediately she was made erect again, and *began* glorifying God.

14   And the synagogue official, indignant because Jesus had healed on the Sabbath, *began* saying to the multitude in response, "There are six days in which work should be done; therefore come during them and get healed, and not on the Sabbath day."

15   But the Lord answered him and said, "You hypocrites, does not each of you on the Sabbath untie his ox or his donkey from the stall, and lead him away to water *him?*

16   "And this woman, a daughter of Abraham as she is, whom Satan has bound for eighteen long years, should she not have been released from this bond on the Sabbath day?"

17   And as He said this, all His opponents were being humiliated; and the entire multitude was rejoicing over all the glorious things being done by Him.

S. Parable of the mustard seed
(13:18,19; Matt. 13:31,32; Mark 4:30–32)

18   Therefore He was saying, "What is the kingdom of God like, and to what shall I compare it?

19   "It is like a mustard seed, which a man took and threw into his own garden; and it grew and became a tree; and THE BIRDS OF THE AIR NESTED IN ITS BRANCHES."

T. Parable of the leaven (13:20,21; Matt. 13:31,32)

20   And again He said, "To what shall I compare the kingdom of God?

21   "It is like leaven, which a woman took and hid in three pecks of meal, until it was all leavened."

U. The narrow door (13:22–30)

22   And He was passing through from one city and village to another, teaching, and proceeding on His way to Jerusalem.

23   And someone said to Him, "Lord, are there *just* a few who are being saved?" And He said to them,

24   "Strive to enter by the narrow door; for many, I tell you, will seek to enter and will not be able.

25   "Once the head of the house gets up and shuts the door, and you begin to stand outside and knock on the door, saying, 'Lord, open up to us!' then He will answer and say to you, 'I do not know where you are from.'

26   "Then you will begin to say, 'We ate and drank in Your presence, and You taught in our streets';

27   and He will say, 'I tell you, I do not know where you are from; DEPART FROM ME, ALL YOU EVILDOERS.'

28   "There will be weeping and gnashing of teeth there when you see Abraham and Isaac and Jacob and all the prophets in the kingdom of God, but yourselves being cast out.

29   "And they will come from east and west, and from north and south, and will recline *at the table* in the kingdom of God.

13:11
v. 16

13:13
Mark 5:23

13:14
Ex 20:9;
Luke 6:7;
14:3

13:15
Luke 7:13;
14:5

13:16
Luke 19:9

13:22
Luke 9:51

13:24
Matt 7:13

13:25
Matt 25:10-12;
7:23

13:27
Matt 7:23;
25:41
13:28
Matt 8:11,12

13:19   See note to Matt. 13:31 on the parable of the mustard seed.

13:21   See note to Matt. 13:33 on the parable of the leaven.

13:30 Matt 19:30; Mark 10:31

30 "And behold, *some* are last who will be first and *some* are first who will be last."

V. *Jesus sends a message to Herod and weeps over Jerusalem (13:31–35)*

31 Just at that time some Pharisees came up, saying to Him, "Go away and depart from here, for Herod wants to kill You."

13:32 Heb 2:10; 7:28

32 And He said to them, "Go and tell that fox, 'Behold, I cast out demons and perform cures today and tomorrow, and the third *day* I reach My goal.'

33 "Nevertheless I must journey on today and tomorrow and the next *day;* for it cannot be that a prophet should perish outside of Jerusalem.

13:34 Matt 23:37-39; Luke 19:41

34 "O Jerusalem, Jerusalem, *the city* that kills the prophets and stones those sent to her! How often I wanted to gather your children together, just as a hen *gathers* her brood under her wings, and you would not *have it!*

13:35 Ps 118:26; Matt 21:9; Luke 19:38

35 "Behold, your house is left to you *desolate;* and I say to you, you shall not see Me until *the time* comes when you say, 'BLESSED IS HE WHO COMES IN THE NAME OF THE LORD!'"

W. *Jesus heals on the Sabbath (14:1–6)*

Pharisees were watching Jesus

*14:1 Mark 3:2

14 And it came about when He went into the house of one of the leaders of the Pharisees on *the* Sabbath to eat bread, that they were watching Him closely.

2 And there, in front of Him was a certain man suffering from dropsy.

14:3 Matt 12:10; Mark 3:4; Luke 6:9

3 And Jesus answered and spoke to the lawyers and Pharisees, saying, "Is it lawful to heal on the Sabbath, or not?"

4 But they kept silent. And He took hold of him, and healed him, and sent him away.

14:5 Ex 23:5; Luke 13:15

5 And He said to them, "Which one of you shall have a son or an ox fall into a well, and will not immediately pull him out on a Sabbath day?"

6 And they could make no reply to this.

X. *Parable of the marriage feast (14:7–14)*

Jesus was watching the Pharisees too. Saw that they loved to show off.

14:7 Matt 23:6

7 And He *began* speaking a parable to the invited guests when He noticed how they had been picking out the places of honor *at the table;* saying to them,

*14:8 Prov 25:6,7

8 "When you are invited by someone to a wedding feast, do not take the place of honor, lest someone more distinguished than you may have been invited by him,

9 and he who invited you both shall come and say to you, 'Give place to this man,' and then in disgrace you proceed to occupy the last place.

14:10 Prov 25:6,7

10 "But when you are invited, go and recline at the last place, so that when the one who has invited you comes, he may say to you, 'Friend, move up higher'; then you will have honor in the sight of all who are at the table with you.

14:11 Matt 23:12; Luke 18:14; James 4:6; 1 Pet 5:5,6

11 "For everyone who exalts himself shall be humbled, and he who humbles himself shall be exalted."

12 And He also went on to say to the one who had invited Him, "When you give a luncheon or a dinner, do not invite your friends or your brothers or your relatives or rich neighbors, lest they also invite you in return, and repayment come to you.

Lev 21:18

14:13 v. 21

13 "But when you give a reception, invite *the* poor, *the* crippled, *the* lame, *the* blind,

14 and you will be blessed, since they do not have *the means* to repay you; for you will be repaid at the resurrection of the righteous."

Y. *Parable of the great banquet (14:15–24; Matt. 22:1–14)*

Who can be invited to partake of a banquet? — God's kingdom! See Rev 3:20 Is. 25:6

14:15 Rev 19:9

15 And when one of those who were reclining *at the table* with Him heard this, he said to Him, "Blessed is everyone who shall eat bread in the kingdom of God!"

16 But He said to him, "A certain man was giving a big dinner, and he invited many;

14:17 Prov 9:2,5

17 and at the dinner hour he sent his slave to say to those who had been invited, 'Come; for everything is ready now.'

14:1 See note to Mark 2:27 on the Sabbath.
14:8 Here Jesus gives a lesson on humility.
14:16 See Matt. 22:1–14 for a parable that sets forth the same truth. The Jews are the invited guests who decline to come; those gathered from the streets and lanes are the Gentiles who repent and believe. But the call to repentance and salvation is universal to both Jew and Gentile.

18 "But they all alike began to make excuses. The first one said to him, 'I have bought a piece of land and I need to go out and look at it; please consider me excused.'

19 "And another one said, 'I have bought five yoke of oxen, and I am going to try them out; please consider me excused.'

20 "And another one said, 'I have married a wife, and for that reason I cannot come.'

21 "And the slave came *back* and reported this to his master. Then the head of the household became angry and said to his slave, 'Go out at once into the streets and lanes of the city and bring in here the poor and crippled and blind and lame.'

22 "And the slave said, 'Master, what you commanded has been done, and still there is room.'

23 "And the master said to the slave, 'Go out into the highways and along the hedges, and compel *them* to come in, that my house may be filled.

24 'For I tell you, none of those men who were invited shall taste of my dinner.'"

Z. Counting the cost: (14:25–15:2)

1. *Parable of the tower and of the king going to war (14:25–33)*

25 Now great multitudes were going along with Him; and He turned and said to them,

26 "If anyone comes to Me, and does not [28]hate his own father and mother and wife and children and brothers and sisters, yes, and even his own life, he cannot be My disciple.

27 "Whoever does not carry his own cross and come after Me cannot be My disciple.

28 "For which one of you, when he wants to build a tower, does not first sit down and calculate the cost, to see if he has enough to complete it?

29 "Otherwise, when he has laid a foundation, and is not able to finish, all who observe it begin to ridicule him,

30 saying, 'This man began to build and was not able to finish.'

31 "Or what king, when he sets out to meet another king in battle, will not first sit down and take counsel whether he is strong enough with ten thousand *men* to encounter the one coming against him with twenty thousand?

32 "Or else, while the other is still far away, he sends a delegation and asks terms of peace.

33 "So therefore, no one of you can be My disciple who does not give up all his own possessions.

2. *Parable of the salt (14:34–15:2)*

34 "Therefore, salt is good; but if even salt has become tasteless, with what will it be seasoned?

35 "It is useless either for the soil or for the manure pile; it is thrown out. He who has ears to hear, let him hear."

15 Now all the tax-gatherers and the sinners were coming near Him to listen to Him.

2 And both the Pharisees and the scribes *began* to grumble, saying, "This man receives sinners and eats with them."

AA. Three parables of grace: (15:3–32)

1. *The lost sheep (15:3–7; Matt. 18:10–14)*

3 And He told them this parable, saying,

4 "What man among you, if he has a hundred sheep and has lost one of them,

[28]I.e., by comparison of his love for Me

Marginal references:
14:20 Deut 24:5; 1 Cor 7:33
14:21 v. 13
14:24 Matt 21:43; Acts 13:46
14:25 Matt 10:37,38
14:27 Matt 16:24; Mark 8:34; Luke 9:23
14:33 Luke 18:29, 30; Phil 3:7; Heb 11:26
14:34 Matt 5:13; Mark 9:50
14:35 Matt 11:15
15:1 Luke 5:29
15:2 Matt 9:11

14:26 This verse must be understood in the light of Matt. 10:37,38. The meaning is perfectly clear: no person nor any thing can be permitted to take precedence over the Lord Jesus.

15:3 Jesus spoke this parable to the Pharisees and scribes, who objected to His association with tax collectors and sinners. Jesus argues that since they considered themselves in the fold, they should be glad that He was seeking those who were outside the fold and who obviously, according to their ideas, needed to be brought back. Instead of criticizing Him they should have rejoiced.

does not leave the ninety-nine in the open pasture, and go after the one which is lost, until he finds it?

5 "And when he has found it, he lays it on his shoulders, rejoicing.

6 "And when he comes home, he calls together his friends and his neighbors, saying to them, 'Rejoice with me, for I have found my sheep which was lost!'

7 "I tell you that in the same way, there will be *more* joy in heaven over one sinner who repents, than over ninety-nine righteous persons who need no repentance.

2. The lost coin (15:8–10)

8 "Or what woman, if she has ten silver coins and loses one coin, does not light a lamp and sweep the house and search carefully until she finds it?

9 "And when she has found it, she calls together her friends and neighbors, saying, 'Rejoice with me, for I have found the coin which I had lost!'

10 "In the same way, I tell you, there is joy in the presence of the angels of God over one sinner who repents.'"

3. The lost son (15:11–32)

11 And He said, "A certain man had two sons;

12 and the younger of them said to his father, 'Father, give me the share of the estate that falls to me.' And he divided his wealth between them.

13 "And not many days later, the younger son gathered everything together and went on a journey into a distant country, and there he squandered his estate with loose living.

14 "Now when he had spent everything, a severe famine occurred in that country, and he began to be in need.

15 "And he went and attached himself to one of the citizens of that country, and he sent him into his fields to feed swine.

16 "And he was longing to fill his stomach with the pods that the swine were eating, and no one was giving *anything* to him.

17 "But when he came to his senses, he said, 'How many of my father's hired men have more than enough bread, but I am dying here with hunger!

18 'I will get up and go to my father, and will say to him, "Father, I have sinned against heaven, and in your sight;

19 I am no longer worthy to be called your son; make me as one of your hired men."'

20 "And he got up and came to his father. But while he was still a long way off, his father saw him, and felt compassion *for him*, and ran and embraced him, and kissed him.

21 "And the son said to him, 'Father, I have sinned against heaven and in your sight; I am no longer worthy to be called your son.'

22 "But the father said to his slaves, 'Quickly bring out the best robe and put it on him, and put a ring on his hand and sandals on his feet;

23 and bring the fattened calf, kill it, and let us eat and be merry;

24 for this son of mine was dead, and has come to life again; he was lost, and has been found.' And they began to be merry.

25 "Now his older son was in the field, and when he came and approached the house, he heard music and dancing.

26 "And he summoned one of the servants and *began* inquiring what these things might be.

15:8 The parable of the lost coin should not be separated from the parable of the lost sheep, for they are intimately connected. Duplicate parables portraying the same truths were not uncommonly used by Christ (5:36–39; 13:19–21). In this parable Jesus tells of the joy of the angels at the conversion of a single lost person. The application is plain. If the angels themselves rejoice, so ought all true believers to rejoice with them when a single soul is converted. By implication these words condemned the Pharisees and scribes for their criticism of Jesus' ministry to despised tax collectors and sinners.

15:11 The parable of the prodigal son must be understood in the light of the two parables that precede it: the lost sheep and the lost coin. The sheep and the coin are now replaced by a human being. The shepherd and the woman now become our Father in heaven. The son leaves his father's house with disastrous results. When he comes to himself, he returns to his father in repentance and is joyfully received. Here Jesus adds a sidelight that is not found in the two preceding parables. He introduces an elder brother who properly represents the self-righteous Pharisees and scribes, and who is not at all happy that his brother has returned. Instead of rejoicing he is envious and finds fault. Jesus points up the fact that these objectors are like the elder brother, for they are critical of His eating and drinking with tax collectors and sinners so that He might bring them back to the Father's house.

27 "And he said to him, 'Your brother has come, and your father has killed the fattened calf, because he has received him back safe and sound.'

28 "But he became angry, and was not willing to go in; and his father came out and *began* entreating him.

29 "But he answered and said to his father, 'Look! For so many years I have been serving you, and I have never neglected a command of yours; and *yet* you have never given me a kid, that I might be merry with my friends;

30 but when this son of yours came, who has devoured your wealth with harlots, you killed the fattened calf for him.'

31 "And he said to him, '*My* child, you have always been with me, and all that is mine is yours.

32 'But we had to be merry and rejoice, for this brother of yours was dead and *has begun* to live, and *was* lost and has been found.'"

BB. *Parable of the unrighteous steward (16:1–13)*

16 Now He was also saying to the disciples, "There was a certain rich man who had a steward, and this *steward* was reported to him as squandering his possessions.

2 "And he called him and said to him, 'What is this I hear about you? Give an account of your stewardship, for you can no longer be steward.'

3 "And the steward said to himself, 'What shall I do, since my master is taking the stewardship away from me? I am not strong enough to dig; I am ashamed to beg.

4 'I know what I shall do, so that when I am removed from the stewardship, they will receive me into their homes.'

5 "And he summoned each one of his master's debtors, and he *began* saying to the first, 'How much do you owe my master?'

6 "And he said, 'A hundred measures of oil.' And he said to him, 'Take your bill, and sit down quickly and write fifty.'

7 "Then he said to another, 'And how much do you owe?' And he said, 'A hundred measures of wheat.' He *said to him, 'Take your bill, and write eighty.'

8 "And his master praised the unrighteous steward because he had acted shrewdly; for the sons of this age are more shrewd in relation to their own kind than the sons of light.

9 "And I say to you, make friends for yourselves by means of the [29]mammon of unrighteousness; that when it fails, they may receive you into the eternal dwellings.

10 "He who is faithful in a very little thing is faithful also in much; and he who is unrighteous in a very little thing is unrighteous also in much.

11 "If therefore you have not been faithful in the *use of* unrighteous mammon, who will entrust the true *riches* to you?

12 "And if you have not been faithful in *the use of* that which is another's, who will give you that which is your own?

13 "No servant can serve two masters; for either he will hate the one, and love the other, or else he will hold to one, and despise the other. You cannot serve God and mammon."

CC. *Jesus answers the Pharisees (16:14–18)*

14 Now the Pharisees, who were lovers of money, were listening to all these things, and they were scoffing at Him.

15 And He said to them, "You are those who justify yourselves in the sight of men, but God knows your hearts; for that which is highly esteemed among men is detestable in the sight of God.

16 "The Law and the Prophets *were proclaimed* until John; since then the gospel of the kingdom of God is preached, and everyone is forcing his way into it.

[29]Or, *riches*

16:1 The parable of the dishonest steward was spoken to the followers of Jesus, but it was related in the hearing of the Pharisees. The parable taught Jesus' followers the importance of the proper use of this world's goods in the light of eternal values. Jesus did not suggest nor intend to imply that dishonesty is ultimately profitable. Rather He showed that if dishonest people use all of their ingenuity to promote their material welfare, so ought the people of God to use their energies to further their spiritual welfare.

16:9 *Mammon* means "wealth" or "property." Money or wealth, as such, is neither good nor bad, but it has use in this world, and thus shares in the general nature of unrighteousness. (See also Matt. 6:24; Luke 16:11–13.)

Margin references:

15:30 v. 12

LK 13:34 "Like a mother hen"...

15:32 v. 24

*16:1 Luke 15:13

Mt 18- Parable of the debtors

16:8 John 12:36; Eph 5:8; 1 Thess 5:5

*16:9 Matt 6:19,24; 19:21; Luke 11:41; 12:33

16:10 Matt 25:21; Luke 19:17

16:11 v. 9

16:13 Matt 6:24

Pharisees felt that wealth was a sign of God's approval.

16:14 2 Tim 3:2; Luke 23:35

16:15 Luke 10:29; 1 Sam 16:7; Prov 21:2; Acts 1:24

16:16 Matt 11:12, 13; 4:23

Hope is deferred reality,

16:17
Is 40:8;
Matt 5:17,18;
Luke 21:33
*16:18
Matt 5:31,32;
19:19;
Mark 10:11;
1 Cor 7:10,11

17 "But it is easier for heaven and earth to pass away than for one stroke of a letter of the Law to fail.

18 "Everyone who divorces his wife and marries another commits adultery; and he who marries one who is divorced from a husband commits adultery.

DD. *The rich man and Lazarus (16:19–31)*

This is the only parable where a protagonist is named.

16:20
Acts 3:2

Lazarus = He whom God helps.

Royal clothes were not an everyday wear,

16:22
John 13:23

16:23
Matt 11:23

Drew attn to himself, but v. 30; cf. day Matt 25:41

sabbath to be free from these things.

16:25
Luke 6:24

the greatest element in this parable is God's grace.

19 "Now there was a certain rich man, and he habitually dressed in purple and fine linen, gaily living in splendor <u>every day</u>.

20 "And a certain poor man named Lazarus was laid at his gate, covered with sores, *(ie dressed in sores)*

21 and longing to be fed with the *crumbs* which were falling from the rich man's table; besides, even the dogs were coming and licking his sores.

22 "Now it came about that the poor man died and he was carried away by the angels to Abraham's bosom; and the rich man also died and was buried.

23 "And in Hades he lifted up his eyes, being in torment, and *saw Abraham far away, and Lazarus in his bosom. *See Luke 3:8*

24 "And he cried out and said, 'Father Abraham, have mercy on me, and send Lazarus, that he may dip the tip of his finger in water and cool off my tongue; for I am in agony in this flame.'

25 "But Abraham said, 'Child, remember that during your life you received your good things, and likewise Lazarus bad things; but now he is being comforted here, and you are in agony.

26 'And besides all this, between us and you there is a great chasm fixed, in order that those who wish to come over from here to you may not be able, and *that* none may cross over from there to us.'

27 "And he said, 'Then I beg you, Father, that you send him to my father's house—

28 for I have five brothers—that he may warn them, lest they also come to this place of torment.'

16:29
Luke 4:17;
John 5:45-47;
Acts 15:21
16:30
Luke 3:8;
19:9

29 "But Abraham *said, 'They have Moses and the Prophets; let them hear them.'

30 "But he said, 'No, Father Abraham, but if someone goes to them from the dead, they will repent!'

31 "But he said to him, 'If they do not listen to Moses and the Prophets, neither will they be persuaded if someone rises from the dead.' "

EE. *Jesus' teaching on forgiveness and faith (17:1–10)*

17:1
Matt 18:6,7;
Mark 9:42;
1 Cor 11:19
17:2
1 Cor 8:12

17 And He said to His disciples, "It is inevitable that stumbling blocks should come, but woe to him through whom they come!

2 "It would be better for him if a millstone were hung around his neck and he were thrown into the sea, than that he should cause one of these little ones to stumble.

17:3
Matt 18:15

Foot...

3 "Be on your guard! If your brother sins, rebuke him; and if he repents, forgive him.

17:4
Matt 18:21,22

4 "And if he sins against you seven times a day, and returns to you seven times, saying, 'I repent,' forgive him."

17:5
Mark 6:30
17:6
Matt 17:20;
21:21;
Mark 9:23;
Luke 7:13

The disciples may have asked

5 And the apostles said to the Lord, "Increase our faith!"

6 And the Lord said, "If you had faith like a mustard seed, you would say to this mulberry tree, 'Be uprooted and be planted in the sea'; and it would obey you.

17:8
Luke 12:37

for a good thing, but for the wrong reasons ie personal 'aggrandizement'. The purpose of faith is to become a better servant.

7 "But which of you, having a slave plowing or tending sheep, will say to him when he has come in from the field, 'Come immediately and sit down to eat'?

8 "But will he not say to him, 'Prepare something for me to eat, and *properly* clothe yourself and serve me until I have eaten and drunk; and afterward you will eat and drink'?

9 "He does not thank the slave because he did the things which were commanded, does he?

10 "So you too, when you do all the things which are commanded you, say, 'We are unworthy slaves; we have done *only* that which we ought to have done.' "

16:18 See note to Matt. 19:3 on divorce.
16:19 This parable intends to teach two lessons: (1) worldly wealth is no guarantee of eternal bliss; and (2) warnings concerning destiny are to be found in Moses and the prophets.

FF. *The healing of the ten lepers (17:11–19)*

11 And it came about while He was on the way to Jerusalem, that He was passing between Samaria and Galilee.

12 And as He entered a certain village, ten leprous men who stood at a distance met Him;

13 and they raised their voices, saying, "Jesus, Master, have mercy on us!"

14 And when He saw them, He said to them, "Go and show yourselves to the priests." And it came about that as they were going, they were cleansed.

15 Now one of them, when he saw that he had been healed, turned back, glorifying God with a loud voice,

16 and he fell on his face at His feet, giving thanks to Him. And he was a Samaritan.

17 And Jesus answered and said, "Were there not ten cleansed? But the nine—where are they?

18 "Was no one found who turned back to give glory to God, except this foreigner?"

19 And He said to him, "Rise, and go your way; your faith [30]has made you well."

GG. *The coming of the kingdom (17:20,21)*

20 Now having been questioned by the Pharisees as to when the kingdom of God was coming, He answered them and said, "The kingdom of God is not coming with signs to be observed;

21 nor will they say, 'Look, here *it is!*' or, 'There *it is!*' For behold, the kingdom of God is in your midst."

HH. *Christ's second advent (17:22–37)*

22 And He said to the disciples, "The days shall come when you will long to see one of the days of the Son of Man, and you will not see it.

23 "And they will say to you, 'Look there! Look here!' Do not go away, and do not run after *them*.

24 "For just as the lightning, when it flashes out of one part of the sky, shines to the other part of the sky, so will the Son of Man be in His day.

25 "But first He must suffer many things and be rejected by this generation.

26 "And just as it happened in the days of Noah, so it shall be also in the days of the Son of Man:

27 they were eating, they were drinking, they were marrying, they were being given in marriage, until the day that Noah entered the ark, and the flood came and destroyed them all.

28 "It was the same as happened in the days of Lot: they were eating, they were drinking, they were buying, they were selling, they were planting, they were building;

29 but on the day that Lot went out from Sodom it rained fire and brimstone from heaven and destroyed them all.

30 "It will be just the same on the day that the Son of Man is revealed.

31 "On that day, let not the one who is on the housetop and whose goods are in the house go down to take them away; and likewise let not the one who is in the field turn back.

32 "Remember Lot's wife.

33 "Whoever seeks to keep his life shall lose it, and whoever loses *his life* shall preserve it.

34 "I tell you, on that night there will be two men in one bed; one will be taken, and the other will be left.

35 "There will be two women grinding at the same place; one will be taken, and the other will be left.

36 [" [31]Two men will be in the field; one will be taken and the other will be left."]

30Or, *has saved you*   31Many mss. do not contain this verse

17:21 The statement that *the kingdom of God is in your midst,* or "within you," means that it is already a spiritual reality that exists in the hearts of men. Any external evidence of this kingdom flows from the actions of men who have received Christ within themselves. If they have not done this, any external evidence is spurious. In outward form the kingdom will come fully with the second advent of Christ.

Marginal references:

17:11 Luke 9:51, 52; John 4:3, 4
17:12 Lev 13:46
17:14 Lev 13:2; 14:2; Matt 8:4
17:15 Matt 9:8
17:16 Matt 10:5
17:19 Matt 9:22; Mark 5:34; Luke 7:50; 8:48; 18:42
17:20 Luke 19:11; Acts 1:6
*17:21 v. 23
17:22 Matt 9:15; Mark 2:20; Luke 5:35
17:23 Matt 24:23; Mark 13:21; Luke 21:8
17:24 Matt 24:27
17:25 Matt 16:21; Luke 9:22
17:26 Matt 24:37-39; Gen ch. 7
17:28 Gen 18:20-33; 19:24,25
17:30 2 Thess 1:7
17:31 Matt 24:17, 18; Mark 13:15, 16
17:32 Gen 19:26
17:33 Matt 10:39; 16:25; Mark 8:35; Luke 9:24
17:34 Matt 24:40,41

| 17:37
Matt 24:28 | 37 And answering they *said to Him, "Where, Lord?" And He said to them, "Where the body *is*, there also will the vultures be gathered." |

II. Parable of the widow and the judge (18:1–8)

| 18:1
Luke 11:5-8;
Rom 12:12;
Eph 6:18;
Col 4:2;
1 Thess 5:17 | **18** Now He was telling them a parable to show that at all times they ought to pray and not to lose heart, |

The woman recognized her neediness — ie, not self-sufficient

2 saying, "There was in a certain city a judge who did not fear God, and did not respect man.

3 "And there was a widow in that city, and she kept coming to him, saying, 'Give me legal protection from my opponent.'

4 "And for a while he was unwilling; but afterward he said to himself, 'Even though I do not fear God nor respect man,

| 18:5
Luke 11:8 | 5 yet because this widow bothers me, I will give her legal protection, lest by continually coming she wear me out.' " |

| 18:6
Luke 7:13
18:7
Rev 6:10;
Rom 8:33;
Col 3:12;
2 Tim 2:10 | 6 And the Lord said, "Hear what the unrighteous judge *said;
7 now shall not God bring about justice for His elect, who cry to Him day and night, and will He delay long over them?
8 "I tell you that He will bring about justice for them speedily. However, when the Son of Man comes, will He find faith on the earth?" |

JJ. Parable of the Pharisee and the publican (18:9–14)

v 9-30 are all about discarding the baggage we bring to god.

| *18:9
Luke 16:15 | 9 And He also told this parable to certain ones who trusted in themselves that they were righteous, and viewed others with contempt: |

10 "Two men went up into the temple to pray, one a Pharisee, and the other a tax-gatherer.

Pharisee focuses on what he can do

| 18:11
Matt 6:5;
Mark 11:25 | 11 "The Pharisee stood and was praying thus to himself, 'God, I thank Thee that I am not like other people: swindlers, unjust, adulterers, or even like this tax-gatherer. |

12 'I fast twice a week; I pay tithes of all that I get.'

The sinner focuses on what God can do.

| *18:12
Matt 9:14;
Luke 11:42
18:13
Luke 23:48 | 13 "But the tax-gatherer, standing some distance away, was even unwilling to lift up his eyes to heaven, but was beating his breast, saying, 'God, be merciful to me, the sinner!' |

| 18:14
Matt 23:12;
Luke 14:11;
1 Pet 5:6 | 14 "I tell you, this man went down to his house justified rather than the other; for everyone who exalts himself shall be humbled, but he who humbles himself shall be exalted." |

when does this ultimate "exaltation" occur?

KK. Jesus and the little children
(18:15–17; Matt. 19:13–15; Mark 10:13–16)

15 And they were bringing even their babies to Him so that He might touch them, but when the disciples saw it, they *began* rebuking them.

16 But Jesus called for them, saying, "Permit the children to come to Me, and do not hinder them, for the kingdom of God belongs to such as these.

| 18:17
Matt 18:3 | 17 "Truly I say to you, whoever does not receive the kingdom of God like a child shall not enter it *at all*." |

LL. The rich young ruler
(18:18–30; Matt. 19:16–30; Mark 10:17–31)

| 18:18
Luke 10:25 | 18 And a certain ruler questioned Him, saying, "Good Teacher, what shall I do to inherit eternal life?" |

19 And Jesus said to him, "Why do you call Me good? No one is good except God alone.

| 18:20
Ex 20:12-16;
Deut 5:16-20;
Rom 13:9 | 20 "You know the commandments, 'DO NOT COMMIT ADULTERY, DO NOT MURDER, DO NOT STEAL, DO NOT BEAR FALSE WITNESS, HONOR YOUR FATHER AND MOTHER.' " |

21 And he said, "All these things I have kept from *my* youth."

18:9 This parable illustrates the difference between those who are trusting in their own works of self-righteousness for salvation, and those who are destitute of any self-righteousness and who seek God's mercy. The Greek word for *be merciful* in v. 13 is *hilaskomai* (to be propitiated), and its use indicates the desire of the publican that God be merciful. **18:12** The Mosaic Law prescribed only one day of fasting, the Day of Atonement referred to in Acts 27:9 (cf.

Lev. 16:29). Although fasting was not required by oral traditions, this Pharisee, and probably others like him, fasted two days a week, on Mondays and Thursdays. He went beyond the requirements of the Law and was quite proud of it. Other references to the frequent fasting of the Pharisees and the disciples of John the Baptist are to be found in Matt. 9:14; Mark 2:18; Luke 5:33. (See note on Mark 2:18 for Christian fasting.)

[handwritten margin note: The young ruler thought he was self-sufficient. There are other forms of s/s besides money.]

22   And when Jesus heard *this,* He said to him, "One thing you still lack; sell all that you possess, and distribute it to the poor, and you shall have treasure in heaven; and come, follow Me."

23   But when he had heard these things, he became very sad; for he was extremely rich.

24   And Jesus looked at him and said, "How hard it is for those who are wealthy to enter the kingdom of God!

25   "For it is easier for a camel to go through the eye of a needle, than for a rich man to enter the kingdom of God."

26   And they who heard it said, "Then who can be saved?"

27   But He said, "The things impossible with men are possible with God."

28   And Peter said, "Behold, we have left our own *homes,* and followed You."

29   And He said to them, "Truly I say to you, there is no one who has left house or wife or brothers or parents or children, for the sake of the kingdom of God,

30   who shall not receive many times as much at this time and in the age to come, eternal life."

[handwritten margin note: See Lk 14:33 No longer seek security in things]

MM. *Christ foretells His crucifixion and resurrection*
(18:31–34; Matt. 20:17–19; Mark 10:32–34)

31   And He took the twelve aside and said to them, "Behold, we are going up to Jerusalem, and all things which are written through the prophets about the Son of Man will be accomplished.

32   "For He will be delivered to the Gentiles, and will be mocked and mistreated and spit upon,

33   and after they have scourged Him, they will kill Him; and the third day He will rise again."

34   And they understood none of these things, and this saying was hidden from them, and they did not comprehend the things that were said.

NN. *Healing the blind man near Jericho*
(18:35–43; Matt. 20:29–34; Mark 10:46–52)

35   And it came about that as He was approaching Jericho, a certain blind man was sitting by the road, begging.

36   Now hearing a multitude going by, he *began* to inquire what this might be.

37   And they told him that Jesus of Nazareth was passing by.

38   And he called out, saying, "Jesus, Son of David, have mercy on me!"

39   And those who led the way were sternly telling him to be quiet; but he kept crying out all the more, "Son of David, have mercy on me!"

40   And Jesus stopped and commanded that he be brought to Him; and when he had come near, He questioned him,

41   "What do you want Me to do for you?" And he said, "Lord, *I want* to regain my sight!"

42   And Jesus said to him, "Receive your sight; your faith has made you well."

43   And immediately he regained his sight, and *began* following Him, glorifying God; and when all the people saw it, they gave praise to God.

OO. *The conversion of Zaccheus (19:1–10)*

19   And He entered and was passing through Jericho.

2   And behold, there was a man called by the name of Zaccheus; and he was a chief tax-gatherer, and he was rich.

3   And he was trying to see who Jesus was, and he was unable because of the crowd, for he was small in stature.

4   And he ran on ahead and climbed up into a sycamore tree in order to see Him, for He was about to pass through that way.

5   And when Jesus came to the place, He looked up and said to him, "Zaccheus, hurry and come down, for today I must stay at your house."

6   And he hurried and came down, and received Him gladly.

7   And when they saw it, they all *began* to grumble, saying, "He has gone to be the guest of a man who is a sinner."

8   And Zaccheus stopped and said to the Lord, "Behold, Lord, half of my possessions I will give to the poor, and if I have defrauded anyone of anything, I will give back four times as much."

Margin references:

18:22 Luke 12:33; Matt 19:21

18:24 Prov 11:28

18:27 Gen 18:14; Job 42:2; Jer 32:17; Luke 1:37 *[handwritten: Peter did have a wife]*
18:28 Luke 5:11
18:30 Matt 12:32

18:31 Luke 9:51; Ps 22

18:32 Matt 16:21; 27:2; Luke 23:1

18:34 Mark 9:32; Luke 9:45

18:38 Matt 9:27
18:39 v. 38

18:42 Matt 9:22; Mark 5:34; Luke 17:19
18:43 Matt 9:8; Luke 13:17

19:1 Luke 18:35

19:4 1 Kin 10:27; 1 Chr 27:28; Is 9:10

19:7 Matt 9:11; Luke 5:30
19:8 Luke 7:13; 3:14; Ex 22:1; Lev 6:5; Num 5:7; 2 Sam 12:6

19:9
Luke 3:8;
13:16;
Rom 4:16;
Gal 3:7
19:10
Matt 18:11

*19:11
Acts 1:6

19:12
Matt 25:14-30;
Mark 13:34

19:17
Luke 16:10

19:21
Matt 25:24

19:22
2 Sam 1:16;
Job 15:6;
Matt 25:26

19:26
Matt 13:12;
Luke 8:18

19:28
Mark 10:32;
Matt 21:17;
Luke 21:37

19:32
Luke 22:13

9   And Jesus said to him, "Today salvation has come to this house, because he, too, is a son of Abraham.

10   "For the Son of Man has come to seek and to save that which was lost."

PP. *The parable of the pounds (19:11-27)*

11   And while they were listening to these things, He went on to tell a parable, because He was near Jerusalem, and they supposed that the kingdom of God was going to appear immediately.

12   He said therefore, "A certain nobleman went to a distant country to receive a kingdom for himself, and *then* return.

13   "And he called ten of his slaves, and gave them ten ³²minas, and said to them, 'Do business *with this* until I come *back*.'

14   "But his citizens hated him, and sent a delegation after him, saying, 'We do not want this man to reign over us.'

15   "And it came about that when he returned, after receiving the kingdom, he ordered that these slaves, to whom he had given the money, be called to him in order that he might know what business they had done.

16   "And the first appeared, saying, 'Master, your mina has made ten minas more.'

17   "And he said to him, 'Well done, good slave, because you have been faithful in a very little thing, be in authority over ten cities.'

18   "And the second came, saying, 'Your mina, master, has made five minas.'

19   "And he said to him also, 'And you are to be over five cities.'

20   "And another came, saying, 'Master, behold your mina, which I kept put away in a handkerchief;

21   for I was afraid of you, because you are an exacting man; you take up what you did not lay down, and reap what you did not sow.'

22   "He *said to him, 'By your own words I will judge you, you worthless slave. Did you know that I am an exacting man, taking up what I did not lay down, and reaping what I did not sow?

23   'Then why did you not put the money in the bank, and having come, I would have collected it with interest?'

24   "And he said to the bystanders, 'Take the mina away from him, and give it to the one who has the ten minas.'

25   "And they said to him, 'Master, he has ten minas *already*.'

26   "I tell you, that to everyone who has shall *more* be given, but from the one who does not have, even what he does have shall be taken away.

27   "But these enemies of mine, who did not want me to reign over them, bring them here and slay them in my presence."

VII. *The last week in Jerusalem (19:28-24:53)*

A. *The triumphal entry (19:28-40; Matt. 21:1-11; Mark 11:1-11; John 12:12-19)*

28   And after He had said these things, He was going on ahead, ascending to Jerusalem.

29   And it came about that when He approached Bethphage and Bethany, near the mount that is called Olivet, He sent two of the disciples,

30   saying, "Go into the village opposite *you*, in which as you enter you will find a colt tied, on which no one yet has ever sat; untie it, and bring it *here*.

31   "And if anyone asks you, 'Why are you untying it?' thus shall you speak, 'The Lord has need of it.' "

32   And those who were sent went away and found it just as He had told them.

33   And as they were untying the colt, its owners said to them, "Why are you untying the colt?"

34   And they said, "The Lord has need of it."

³²A mina is equal to about 100 days' wages or nearly $20

19:11   The teaching of this parable is similar to that of the talents in Matt. 25:14ff. Christ indicated that diligence receives a fit reward, whereas slothfulness is punished. Undoubtedly He spoke of Himself as the nobleman and the servants as those who belong to Him and to His kingdom. In His kingdom there are faithful and unfaithful servants to whom appropriate rewards will be given. In this parable those who are not His servants and who refuse to have Him reign over them are slain.

35   And they brought it to Jesus, and they threw their garments on the colt, and put Jesus *on it*.

36   And as He was going, they were spreading their garments in the road.   **19:36** 2 Kin 9:13

37   And as He was now approaching, near the descent of the Mount of Olives, the whole multitude of the disciples began to praise God joyfully with a loud voice for all the miracles which they had seen,

38   saying,   **19:38** Ps 118:26; Luke 13:35; 2:14

"Blessed is the King who comes in the name of the Lord;
Peace in heaven and glory in the highest!"

39   And some of the Pharisees in the multitude said to Him, "Teacher, rebuke Your disciples."   **19:39** Matt 21:15,16

40   And He answered and said, "I tell you, if these become silent, the stones will cry out!"   **19:40** Hab 2:11

B. *Jesus weeps over Jerusalem (19:41–44)*

41   And when He approached, He saw the city and wept over it,

42   saying, "If you had known in this day, even you, the things which make for peace! But now they have been hidden from your eyes.   **19:41** Luke 13:34, 35

43   "For the days shall come upon you when your enemies will throw up a bank before you, and surround you, and hem you in on every side,   **19:43** Is 29:3; Jer 6:6; Ezek 4:2; Luke 21:20

44   and will level you to the ground and your children within you, and they will not leave in you one stone upon another, because you did not recognize the time of your visitation."   **19:44** Matt 24:2; Mark 13:2; Luke 21:6; 1 Pet 2:12

C. *Second cleansing of the temple*
(19:45–48; Matt. 21:12–17; Mark 11:15–19; cf. John 2:13–22)

45   And He entered the temple and began to cast out those who were selling,

46   saying to them, "It is written, 'And My house shall be a house of prayer,' but you have made it a robbers' den."   **19:46** Is 56:7

47   And He was teaching daily in the temple; but the chief priests and the scribes and the leading men among the people were trying to destroy Him,   **19:47** Matt 26:55; Mark 11:18; John 7:19

48   and they could not find anything that they might do, for all the people were hanging upon His words.

D. *Christ's authority challenged*
(20:1–8; Matt. 21:23–27; Mark 11:27–33)

20 And it came about on one of the days while He was teaching the people in the temple and preaching the gospel, that the chief priests and the scribes with the elders confronted *Him*,   **20:1** Matt 26:55; Luke 8:1

2   and they spoke, saying to Him, "Tell us by what authority You are doing these things, or who is the one who gave You this authority?"   **20:2** John 2:18; Acts 4:7; 7:27

3   And He answered and said to them, "I shall also ask you a question, and you tell Me:

4   "Was the baptism of John from heaven or from men?"

5   And they reasoned among themselves, saying, "If we say, 'From heaven,' He will say, 'Why did you not believe him?'

6   "But if we say, 'From men,' all the people will stone us to death, for they are convinced that John was a prophet."   **20:6** Matt 14:5; Luke 7:29

7   And they answered that they did not know where *it* came from.

8   And Jesus said to them, "Neither will I tell you by what authority I do these things."

E. *Parable of the wicked tenants*
(20:9–18; Matt. 21:33–46; Mark 12:1–12)

9   And He began to tell the people this parable: "A man planted a vineyard and rented it out to vine-growers, and went on a journey for a long time.   ***20:9** Is 5:1-7; Matt 25:14

10   "And at the *harvest* time he sent a slave to the vine-growers, in order that they might give him *some* of the produce of the vineyard; but the vine-growers beat him and sent him away empty-handed.

20:9 This parable apparently was directed against the Jews as a nation because of their rejection of Christ as their Messiah. He warned them of the dire consequences of their decision, as it related both to judgment upon their nation and to the inclusion of the Gentiles, who would be offered the kingdom they had rejected.

11 "And he proceeded to send another slave; and they beat him also and treated him shamefully, and sent him away empty-handed.

12 "And he proceeded to send a third; and this one also they wounded and cast out.

13 "And the owner of the vineyard said, 'What shall I do? I will send my beloved son; perhaps they will respect him.'

14 "But when the vine-growers saw him, they reasoned with one another, saying, 'This is the heir; let us kill him that the inheritance may be ours.'

15 "And they threw him out of the vineyard and killed him. What, therefore, will the owner of the vineyard do to them?

16 "He will come and destroy these vine-growers and will give the vineyard to others." And when they heard it, they said, "May it never be!"

17 But He looked at them and said, "What then is this that is written,

'THE STONE WHICH THE BUILDERS REJECTED,
THIS BECAME THE CHIEF CORNER *stone*'?

18 "Everyone who falls on that stone will be broken to pieces; but on whomever it falls, it will scatter him like dust."

F. Paying taxes to Caesar
(20:19–26; Matt. 22:15–22; Mark 12:13–17)

19 And the scribes and the chief priests tried to lay hands on Him that very hour, and they feared the people; for they understood that He spoke this parable against them.

20 And they watched Him, and sent spies who pretended to be righteous, in order that they might catch Him in some statement, so as to deliver Him up to the rule and the authority of the governor.

21 And they questioned Him, saying, "Teacher, we know that You speak and teach correctly, and You are not partial to any, but teach the way of God in truth.

22 "Is it lawful for us to pay taxes to Caesar, or not?"

23 But He detected their trickery and said to them,

24 "Show Me a [33]denarius. Whose likeness and inscription does it have?" And they said, "Caesar's."

25 And He said to them, "Then render to Caesar the things that are Caesar's, and to God the things that are God's."

26 And they were unable to catch Him in a saying in the presence of the people; and marveling at His answer, they became silent.

G. The Sadducees and the resurrection
(20:27–40; Matt. 22:23–33; Mark 12:18–27)

27 Now there came to Him some of the Sadducees (who say that there is no resurrection),

28 and they questioned Him, saying, "Teacher, Moses wrote for us that IF A MAN'S BROTHER DIES, having a wife, AND HE IS CHILDLESS, HIS BROTHER SHOULD TAKE THE WIFE AND RAISE UP OFFSPRING TO HIS BROTHER.

29 "Now there were seven brothers; and the first took a wife, and died childless;

30 and the second

31 and the third took her; and in the same way all seven died, leaving no children.

32 "Finally the woman died also.

33 "In the resurrection therefore, which one's wife will she be? For all seven had her as wife."

34 And Jesus said to them, "The sons of this age marry and are given in marriage,

35 but those who are considered worthy to attain to that age and the resurrection from the dead, neither marry, nor are given in marriage;

36 for neither can they die anymore, for they are like angels, and are sons of God, being sons of the resurrection.

37 "But that the dead are raised, even Moses showed, in the *passage about the*

Margin references:
20:16 Luke 19:27; Rom 3:4,6,31
20:17 Ps 118:22,23; 1 Pet 2:6
*20:18 Is 8:14,15
20:19 Luke 19:47
20:21 John 3:2
*20:25 Rom 13:7; Luke 23:2
20:27 Acts 23:6,8
20:28 Deut 25:5
20:36 Rom 8:16,17; 1 John 3:1,2
20:37 Ex 3:6

[33]The denarius was equivalent to one day's wage

20:18 A variation of Is. 8:14,15; Dan. 2:34.
20:25 God's due takes precedence over Caesar's due when one is forced to choose between them.

burning bush, where he calls the Lord THE GOD OF ABRAHAM, AND THE GOD OF ISAAC, AND THE GOD OF JACOB.

38　"Now He is not the God of the dead, but of the living; for all live to Him."

39　And some of the scribes answered and said, "Teacher, You have spoken well."

40　For they did not have courage to question Him any longer about anything.

H. *Christ's unanswerable question*
(20:41–44; Matt. 22:41–46; Mark 12:35–37)

41　And He said to them, "How *is it that* they say [34]the Christ is David's son?

42　"For David himself says in the book of Psalms,

'THE LORD SAID TO MY LORD,

"SIT AT MY RIGHT HAND,

43　UNTIL I MAKE THINE ENEMIES A FOOTSTOOL FOR THY FEET."'

44　"David therefore calls Him 'Lord,' and how is He his son?"

I. *Warning against the scribes*
(20:45–47; Matt. 23:1–12; Mark 12:38–40)

45　And while all the people were listening, He said to the disciples,

46　"Beware of the scribes, who like to walk around in long robes, and love respectful greetings in the market places, and chief seats in the synagogues, and places of honor at banquets,

47　who devour widows' houses, and for appearance's sake offer long prayers; these will receive greater condemnation."

J. *The widow's offering (21:1–4)*

21　And He looked up and saw the rich putting their gifts into the treasury.

2　And He saw a certain poor widow putting in two small copper coins.

3　And He said, "Truly I say to you, this poor widow put in more than all *of them;*

4　for they all out of their surplus put into the offering; but she out of her poverty put in all that she had to live on."

K. *The Olivet Discourse (21:5–38; Matt. 24; Mark 13)*

1. *The course of this age (21:5–19; Matt. 24:1–14; Mark 13:3–13)*

5　And while some were talking about the temple, that it was adorned with beautiful stones and votive gifts, He said,

6　"*As for* these things which you are looking at, the days will come in which there will not be left one stone upon another which will not be torn down."

7　And they questioned Him, saying, "Teacher, when therefore will these things be? And what *will be* the sign when these things are about to take place?"

8　And He said, "See to it that you be not misled; for many will come in My name, saying, 'I am *He*,' and, 'The time is at hand'; do not go after them.

9　"And when you hear of wars and disturbances, do not be terrified; for these things must take place first, but the end *does* not *follow* immediately."

10　Then He continued by saying to them, "Nation will rise against nation, and kingdom against kingdom,

11　and there will be great earthquakes, and in various places plagues and famines; and there will be terrors and great signs from heaven.

12　"But before all these things, they will lay their hands on you and will persecute you, delivering you to the synagogues and prisons, bringing you before kings and governors for My name's sake.

13　"It will lead to an opportunity for your testimony.

14　"So make up your minds not to prepare beforehand to defend yourselves;

15　for I will give you utterance and wisdom which none of your opponents will be able to resist or refute.

[34]I.e., the Messiah

20:38 Rom 6:10,11
20:40 Matt 22:46; Mark 12:34
20:42 Ps 110:1; Acts 2:34
20:46 Luke 11:43
21:1 Mark 12:41-44
21:2 Mark 12:42
*21:5 Mark 13:1
21:6 Luke 19:44
21:8 Mark 13:21; Luke 17:23
21:10 2 Chr 15:6; Is 19:2
21:12 John 16:2
21:13 Phil 1:12
21:14 Luke 12:11, 12
21:15 Luke 12:12

21:5 *some.* See note to Luke 21:7.
21:7 *they.* Probably the Peter, James, John, and Andrew in

Mark 13:3. Also see note to Matt. 24:3 on the Olivet Discourse.

21:16
Luke 12:52,
53
21:17
Matt 10:22
21:18
Matt 10:30;
Luke 12:7
21:19
Rev 2:7

16 "But you will be delivered up even by parents and brothers and relatives and friends, and they will put *some* of you to death,

17   and you will be hated by all on account of My name.

18 "Yet not a hair of your head will perish.

19 "By your endurance you will gain your lives.

2. The destruction of Jerusalem
(21:20–24; Matt. 24:15–28; Mark 13:14–23)

*21:20
Luke 19:43

20 "But when you see Jerusalem surrounded by armies, then recognize that her desolation is at hand.

21:21
Luke 17:31

21 "Then let those who are in Judea flee to the mountains, and let those who are in the midst of the city depart, and let not those who are in the country enter the city;

21:22
Is 63:4;
Dan 9:24-27;
Zech 11:1

22   because these are days of vengeance, in order that all things which are written may be fulfilled.

23 "Woe to those who are with child and to those who nurse babes in those days; for there will be great distress upon the land, and wrath to this people,

*21:24
Is 63:18;
Dan 8:13;
9:27; 12:7;
Rom 11:25;
Rev 11:2

24   and they will fall by the edge of the sword, and will be led captive into all the nations; and Jerusalem will be trampled under foot by the Gentiles until the times of the Gentiles be fulfilled.

3. The second advent of Christ
(21:25–28; Matt. 24:29–31; Mark 13:24–27)

21:25
2 Pet 3:10,12

25 "And there will be signs in sun and moon and stars, and upon the earth dismay among nations, in perplexity at the roaring of the sea and the waves,

26   men fainting from fear and the expectation of the things which are coming upon the world; for the powers of the heavens will be shaken.

21:27
Rev 1:7;
14:14
21:28
Luke 18:7

27 "And then they will see THE SON OF MAN COMING IN A CLOUD with power and great glory.

28 "But when these things begin to take place, straighten up and lift up your heads, because your redemption is drawing near."

4. The parable of the fig tree
(21:29–33; Matt. 24:32–35; Mark 13:28–31)

29   And He told them a parable: "Behold the fig tree and all the trees;

30   as soon as they put forth *leaves,* you see it and know for yourselves that summer is now near.

21:31
Matt 3:2

31 "Even so you, too, when you see these things happening, recognize that the kingdom of God is near.

32 "Truly I say to you, this generation will not pass away until all things take place.

21:33
Luke 16:17

33 "Heaven and earth will pass away, but My words will not pass away.

5. Watchfulness (21:34–38; Matt. 24:36–51; Mark 13:32–37)

21:34
Mark 4:19;
Luke 12:45;
1 Thess 5:6,7

34 "Be on guard, that your hearts may not be weighted down with dissipation and drunkenness and the worries of life, and that day come on you suddenly like a trap;

35   for it will come upon all those who dwell on the face of all the earth.

21:36
Luke 18:1

36 "But keep on the alert at all times, praying in order that you may have strength to escape all these things that are about to take place, and to stand before the Son of Man."

21:37
Luke 19:47;
Mark 11:19

37   Now during the day He was teaching in the temple, but at evening He would go out and spend the night on the mount that is called Olivet.

38   And all the people would get up early in the morning *to come* to Him in the temple to listen to Him.

21:20 This prophecy about Jerusalem was literally fulfilled in A.D. 70 when the city was destroyed by Roman legions under Titus. Josephus, the Jewish historian, in his *Wars of the Jews,* Books V and VI, describes the siege and taking of Jerusalem in some detail. From that day to this the city of Jerusalem has been *trampled under foot by the Gentiles* (v. 24).
21:24 Jesus speaks of the *times of the Gentiles.* His prophecy

includes the statement that Jerusalem will be trampled under during the length of this period. This implies that the times of the Gentiles will have an end and that then Jerusalem will be restored to the Jews. Romans 11:25 indicates that a hardening has come upon Israel until the *fulness of the Gentiles has come in.* When this occurs *all Israel will be saved* (Rom. 11:26).

L. The plot to kill Jesus
(22:1–6; Matt. 26:1–5,14–16; Mark 14:1–2,10–11)

22 Now the Feast of Unleavened Bread, which is called the Passover, was approaching.

2 And the chief priests and the scribes were seeking how they might put Him to death; for they were afraid of the people.

3 And Satan entered into Judas who was called Iscariot, belonging to the number of the twelve.

4 And he went away and discussed with the chief priests and officers how he might betray Him to them.

5 And they were glad, and agreed to give him money.

6 And he consented, and *began* seeking a good opportunity to betray Him to them apart from the multitude.

M. The Last Supper (22:7–30)

1. The Passover prepared (22:7–13; Matt. 26:17–19; Mark 14:12–16)

7 Then came the *first* day of Unleavened Bread on which the Passover *lamb* had to be sacrificed.

8 And He sent Peter and John, saying, "Go and prepare the Passover for us, that we may eat it."

9 And they said to Him, "Where do You want us to prepare it?"

10 And He said to them, "Behold, when you have entered the city, a man will meet you carrying a pitcher of water; follow him into the house that he enters.

11 "And you shall say to the owner of the house, 'The Teacher says to you, "Where is the guest room in which I may eat the Passover with My disciples?"'

12 "And he will show you a large, furnished, upper room; prepare it there."

13 And they departed and found *everything* just as He had told them; and they prepared the Passover.

2. The Passover eaten
(22:14–18; Matt. 26:20–25; Mark 14:17–21; see John 13:1–30)

14 And when the hour had come He reclined *at the table*, and the apostles with Him.

15 And He said to them, "I have earnestly desired to eat this Passover with you before I suffer;

16 for I say to you, I shall never again eat it until it is fulfilled in the kingdom of God."

17 And when He had taken a cup *and* given thanks, He said, "Take this and share it among yourselves;

18 for I say to you, I will not drink of the fruit of the vine from now on until the kingdom of God comes."

3. The Lord's Supper instituted
(22:19–30; Matt. 26:26–29; Mark 14:22–25)

19 And when He had taken *some* bread *and* given thanks, He broke *it*, and gave *it* to them, saying, "This is My body [35]which is given for you; do this in remembrance of Me."

20 And in the same way *He took* the cup after they had eaten, saying, "This cup which is poured out for you is the new covenant in My blood.

21 "But behold, the hand of the one betraying Me is with Me on the table.

22 "For indeed, the Son of Man is going as it has been determined; but woe to that man by whom He is betrayed!"

23 And they began to discuss among themselves which one of them it might be who was going to do this thing.

24 And there arose also a dispute among them *as to* which one of them was regarded to be greatest.

25 And He said to them, "The kings of the Gentiles lord it over them; and those who have authority over them are called 'Benefactors.'

---

[35]Some ancient mss. do not contain the remainder of v. 19 nor any of v. 20

22:3 See note to Matt. 26:14 on Judas Iscariot (cf. also note to John 13:27).

22:19 See note to Mark 14:22 on the Lord's Supper.

Marginal references:

22:1 John 11:47-53

22:2 Matt 12:14

*22:3 John 13:2

22:5 Zech 11:12

22:7 Ex 12:18-20; Deut 16:5-8
22:8 Luke 19:29; Acts 3:1

22:16 Luke 14:15; Rev 19:9

22:21 Matt 26:21-24; Mark 14:18-21; John 13:21-30
22:22 Acts 2:23; 4:28

22:24 Mark 9:34; Luke 9:46
22:25 Matt 20:25-28; Mark 10:42-45

22:26
Luke 9:48;
1 Pet 5:5
22:27
Luke 12:37

*22:28
Heb 2:18;
4:15
22:29
Luke 12:32;
2 Tim 2:12
22:30
Luke 14:15;
Rev 19:9;
Matt 19:28;
Rev 3:21
22:31
Job 1:6-12;
Amos 9:9
*22:32
John 17:9,15;
21:15-17

26 "But not so with you, but let him who is the greatest among you become as the youngest, and the leader as the servant.

27 "For who is greater, the one who reclines *at the table,* or the one who serves? Is it not the one who reclines *at the table*? But I am among you as the one who serves.

28 "And you are those who have stood by Me in My trials;

29 and just as My Father has granted Me a kingdom, I grant you

30 that you may eat and drink at My table in My kingdom, and you will sit on thrones judging the twelve tribes of Israel.

N. *Peter's denial foretold*
(22:31–38; Matt. 26:30–35; Mark 14:27–31; see John 14–17)

31 "Simon, Simon, behold, Satan has demanded *permission* to sift you like wheat;

32 but I have prayed for you, that your faith may not fail; and you, when once you have turned again, strengthen your brothers."

33 And he said to Him, "Lord, with You I am ready to go both to prison and to death!"

34 And He said, "I say to you, Peter, the cock will not crow today until you have denied three times that you know Me."

22:35
Matt 10:9;
Luke 9:3;
10:4

35 And He said to them, "When I sent you out without purse and bag and sandals, you did not lack anything, did you?" And they said, "*No,* nothing."

36 And He said to them, "But now, let him who has a purse take it along, likewise also a bag, and let him who has no sword sell his robe and buy one.

22:37
Is 53:12;
Mark 15:28

37 "For I tell you, that this which is written must be fulfilled in Me, 'AND HE WAS NUMBERED WITH TRANSGRESSORS'; for that which refers to Me has *its* fulfillment."

38 And they said, "Lord, look, here are two swords." And He said to them, "It is enough."

O. *Jesus in Gethsemane (22:39–53)*

1. *His agony (22:39–46; Matt. 26:36–46; Mark 14:32–43; cf. John 18:1)*

22:39
Luke 21:37

39 And He came out and proceeded as was His custom to the Mount of Olives; and the disciples also followed Him.

22:40
Matt 6:13

40 And when He arrived at the place, He said to them, "Pray that you may not enter into temptation."

41 And He withdrew from them about a stone's throw, and He knelt down and *began* to pray,

*22:42
Mark 10:38;
John 5:30;
18:11

42 saying, "Father, if Thou art willing, remove this cup from Me; yet not My will, but Thine be done."

43 Now an angel from heaven appeared to Him, strengthening Him.

44 And being in agony He was praying very fervently; and His sweat became like drops of blood, falling down upon the ground.

45 And when He rose from prayer, He came to the disciples and found them sleeping from sorrow,

22:46
v. 40

46 and said to them, "Why are you sleeping? Rise and pray that you may not enter into temptation."

2. *Jesus' betrayal and arrest*
(22:47–53; Matt. 26:47–56; Mark 14:43–50; John 18:1–11)

47 While He was still speaking, behold, a multitude *came,* and the one called Judas, one of the twelve, was preceding them; and he approached Jesus to kiss Him.

48 But Jesus said to him, "Judas, are you betraying the Son of Man with a kiss?"

22:49
v. 38

49 And when those who were around Him saw what was going to happen, they said, "Lord, shall we strike with the sword?"

22:28 *trials,* translated *temptation* in Matt. 6:13.
22:32 Intercessory prayer is that form of prayer in which believers entreat God in behalf of other people. Like other forms of prayer, it must meet the conditions that govern effective praying. We are commanded to engage in this form of prayer habitually (1 Tim. 2:1; James 5:14,16), interced-

ing for: (1) all classes of men, including kings and those in authority (1 Tim. 2:1,2); (2) ministers of the gospel (2 Cor. 1:11; Phil. 1:19); (3) persecutors (Matt. 5:44); and (4) friends (Job 42:8).
22:42 *this cup,* see note to Matt. 26:39.

50   And a certain one of them struck the slave of the high priest and cut off his right ear.

51   But Jesus answered and said, "Stop! No more of this." And He touched his ear and healed him.

52   And Jesus said to the chief priests and officers of the temple and elders who had come against Him, "Have you come out with swords and clubs as against a robber?

22:52
vv. 4,37

53   "While I was with you daily in the temple, you did not lay hands on Me; but this hour and the power of darkness are yours."

22:53
John 12:27

P. *Peter's denial of Jesus*
(22:54–71; Matt. 26:69–75; Mark 14:66–72; John 18:15–18,25–27)

54   And having arrested Him, they led Him *away*, and brought Him to the house of the high priest; but Peter was following at a distance.

22:54
Matt 26:58;
Mark 14:54

55   And after they had kindled a fire in the middle of the courtyard and had sat down together, Peter was sitting among them.

56   And a certain servant-girl, seeing him as he sat in the firelight, and looking intently at him, said, "This man was with Him too."

57   But he denied *it*, saying, "Woman, I do not know Him."

58   And a little later, another saw him and said, "You are *one* of them too!" But Peter said, "Man, I am not!"

59   And after about an hour had passed, another man *began* to insist, saying, "Certainly this man also was with Him, for he is a Galilean too."

60   But Peter said, "Man, I do not know what you are talking about." And immediately, while he was still speaking, a cock crowed.

61   And the Lord turned and looked at Peter. And Peter remembered the word of the Lord, how He had told him, "Before a cock crows today, you will deny Me three times."

22:61
v. 34

62   And he went out and wept bitterly.

63   And the men who were holding Jesus in custody were mocking Him, and beating Him,

22:63
Matt 26:67,
68;
Mark 14:65;
John 18:22,23

64   and they blindfolded Him and were asking Him, saying, "Prophesy, who is the one who hit You?"

65   And they were saying many other things against Him, blaspheming.

66   And when it was day, the [36]Council of elders of the people assembled, both chief priests and scribes, and they led Him away to their council *chamber*, saying,

22:66
Matt 27:1;
Mark 15:1
22:67
Matt 26:63-66;
Mark 14:61-63;
John 18:19-21

67   "If You are the Christ, tell us." But He said to them, "If I tell you, you will not believe;

68   and if I ask a question, you will not answer.

69   "But from now on THE SON OF MAN WILL BE SEATED AT THE RIGHT HAND of the power OF GOD."

70   And they all said, "Are You the Son of God, then?" And He said to them, "Yes, I am."

22:70
Matt 27:11;
Luke 23:3

71   And they said, "What further need do we have of testimony? For we have heard it ourselves from His own mouth."

Q. *Jesus before Pontius Pilate*
(23:1–25; Matt. 27:11–26; Mark 15:2–15; John 18:29–40)

1. *Pilate questions Jesus (23:1–5)*

23   Then the whole body of them arose and brought Him before Pilate.

23:1
Matt 27:2;
Mark 15:1;
John 18:28

2   And they began to accuse Him, saying, "We found this man misleading our nation and forbidding to pay taxes to Caesar, and saying that He Himself is Christ, a King."

23:2
Luke 20:22;
John 19:12

3   And Pilate asked Him, saying, "Are You the King of the Jews?" And He answered him and said, "*It is as* you say."

23:3
Luke 22:70;
1 Tim 6:13

4   And Pilate said to the chief priests and the multitudes, "I find no guilt in this man."

23:4
1 Pet 2:22

5   But they kept on insisting, saying, "He stirs up the people, teaching all over Judea, starting from Galilee, even as far as this place."

[36]Or, *Sanhedrin*

22:66 See note to Matt. 26:59 on Sanhedrin.   **23:1** See note to Mark 15:1 on Pilate.

2. Pilate sends Jesus to Herod (23:6–12)

6   But when Pilate heard it, he asked whether the man was a Galilean.

23:7
Luke 3:1

7   And when he learned that He belonged to Herod's jurisdiction, he sent Him to Herod, who himself also was in Jerusalem at that time.

23:8
Luke 9:9;
Matt 14:1;
Mark 6:14

8   Now Herod was very glad when he saw Jesus; for he had wanted to see Him for a long time, because he had been hearing about Him and was hoping to see some sign performed by Him.

9   And he questioned Him at some length; but He answered him nothing.

10   And the chief priests and the scribes were standing there, accusing Him vehemently.

23:11
Mark 15:17-19;
John 19:2,3
23:12
Acts 4:27

11   And Herod with his soldiers, after treating Him with contempt and mocking Him, dressed Him in a gorgeous robe and sent Him back to Pilate.

12   Now Herod and Pilate became friends with one another that very day; for before they had been at enmity with each other.

3. Pilate would free Jesus (23:13–17)

13   And Pilate summoned the chief priests and the rulers and the people,

23:14
vv. 2,4

14   and said to them, "You brought this man to me as one who incites the people to rebellion, and behold, having examined Him before you, I have found no guilt in this man regarding the charges which you make against Him.

15   "No, nor has Herod, for he sent Him back to us; and behold, nothing deserving death has been done by Him.

23:16
Matt 27:26;
Mark 15:15;
John 19:1

16   "I will therefore punish Him and release Him."

17   [[37]Now he was obliged to release to them at the feast one prisoner.]

4. Pilate releases Barabbas and delivers Jesus (23:18–25)

23:18
Matt 27:20-23;
Mark 15:11-14;
John 18:38-40;
19:14,15;
Acts 3:13,14

18   But they cried out all together, saying, "Away with this man, and release for us Barabbas!"

19   (He was one who had been thrown into prison for a certain insurrection made in the city, and for murder.)

20   And Pilate, wanting to release Jesus, addressed them again,

21   but they kept on calling out, saying, "Crucify, crucify Him!"

23:22
v. 16

22   And he said to them the third time, "Why, what evil has this man done? I have found in Him no guilt *demanding* death; I will therefore punish Him and release Him."

23   But they were insistent, with loud voices asking that He be crucified. And their voices *began* to prevail.

24   And Pilate pronounced sentence that their demand should be granted.

25   And he released the man they were asking for who had been thrown into prison for insurrection and murder, but he delivered Jesus to their will.

R. The crucifixion and burial of Jesus (23:26–56)

1. Jesus on the way to Calvary
(23:26–31; see Matt. 27:32; Mark 15:21)

23:26
John 19:17

26   And when they led Him away, they laid hold of one Simon of Cyrene, coming in from the country, and placed on him the cross to carry behind Jesus.

23:27
Luke 8:52

27   And there were following Him a great multitude of the people, and of women who were mourning and lamenting Him.

23:28
Luke 19:41-44;
21:23,24

28   But Jesus turning to them said, "Daughters of Jerusalem, stop weeping for Me, but weep for yourselves and for your children.

29   "For behold, the days are coming when they will say, 'Blessed are the barren, and the wombs that never bore, and the breasts that never nursed.'

23:30
Is 2:19;
Hos 10:8;
Rev 6:16
23:31
Ezek 20:47

30   "Then they will begin TO SAY TO THE MOUNTAINS, 'FALL ON US,' AND TO THE HILLS, 'COVER US.'

31   "For if they do these things in the green tree, what will happen in the dry?"

2. Jesus crucified
(23:32–38; Matt. 27:32–44; Mark 15:21–32; John 19:17–24)

23:32
Is 53:12

32   And two others also, who were criminals, were being led away to be put to death with Him.

---

[37]Many mss. do not contain this verse

33   And when they came to the place called The Skull, there they crucified Him and the criminals, one on the right and the other on the left.

34   But Jesus was saying, "Father, forgive them; for they do not know what they are doing." And they cast lots, dividing up His garments among themselves.

35   And the people stood by, looking on. And even the rulers were sneering at Him, saying, "He saved others; let Him save Himself if this is the Christ of God, His Chosen One."

36   And the soldiers also mocked Him, coming up to Him, offering Him sour wine,

37   and saying, "If You are the King of the Jews, save Yourself!"

38   Now there was also an inscription above Him, "THIS IS THE KING OF THE JEWS."

3. The penitent thief (23:39–43)

39   And one of the criminals who were hanged *there* was hurling abuse at Him, saying, "Are You not the Christ? Save Yourself and us!"

40   But the other answered, and rebuking him said, "Do you not even fear God, since you are under the same sentence of condemnation?

41   "And we indeed justly, for we are receiving what we deserve for our deeds; but this man has done nothing wrong."

42   And he was saying, "Jesus, remember me when You come in Your kingdom!"

43   And He said to him, "Truly I say to you, today you shall be with Me in Paradise."

4. The death of Jesus
(23:44–49; Matt. 27:45–50; Mark 15:33–41; John 19:28–37)

44   And it was now about [38]the sixth hour, and darkness fell over the whole land until [39]the ninth hour,

45   the sun being obscured; and the veil of the temple was torn in two.

46   And Jesus, crying out with a loud voice, said, "Father, INTO THY HANDS I COMMIT MY SPIRIT." And having said this, He breathed His last.

47   Now when the centurion saw what had happened, he *began* praising God, saying, "Certainly this man was innocent."

48   And all the multitudes who came together for this spectacle, when they observed what had happened, *began* to return, beating their breasts.

49   And all His acquaintances and the women who accompanied Him from Galilee, were standing at a distance, seeing these things.

5. Jesus laid in the tomb
(23:50–56; Matt. 27:57–61; Mark 15:42–47; John 19:38–42)

50   And behold, a man named Joseph, who was a member of the Council, a good and righteous man

51   (he had not consented to their plan and action), *a man* from Arimathea, a city of the Jews, who was waiting for the kingdom of God;

52   this man went to Pilate and asked for the body of Jesus.

53   And he took it down and wrapped it in a linen cloth, and laid Him in a tomb cut into the rock, where no one had ever lain.

54   And it was the preparation day, and the Sabbath was about to begin.

---

[38]I.e., 12 noon   [39]I.e., 3 p.m.

Marginal references:

*23:34 Ps 22:18; Acts 7:60
23:35 Ps 22:17
23:36 Ps 69:21; Matt 27:48
23:39 vv. 35,37
23:41 vv. 4,14,22
*23:43 2 Cor 12:3,4; Rev 2:7
23:45 Ex 26:31-35; Heb 9:8; 10:19
23:46 Ps 31:5; 1 Pet 2:23
23:47 Matt 27:54
23:49 Ps 38:11; Luke 8:2
23:51 Luke 2:25
*23:54 Matt 27:62

23:34 Chronologically, the seven last sayings of Christ on Calvary were spoken in the following order: (1) the word of forgiveness: *Father, forgive them* (23:34); (2) the word of salvation: *today you shall be with Me in Paradise* (23:43); (3) the word of affection: *Woman, behold, your son!* and *Behold, your mother!* (John 19:26,27); (4) the word of despair: *My God, My God, why hast Thou forsaken Me?* (Matt. 27:46; Mark 15:34); (5) the word of physical torment: *I am thirsty* (John 19:28); (6) the word of triumph: *It is finished!* (John 19:30); and (7) the word of committal: *Father, into Thy hands I commit My spirit!* (23:46). Note that Matthew and Mark record only one saying, and Luke and John three each.
23:38 See note to Matt. 27:37.

23:43 The Greek word for *Paradise (paradeisos)* comes from the Persian language as a loan word, and occurs two other times in the New Testament (2 Cor. 12:4; Rev. 2:7). The original meaning was *enclosed park* or a *pleasure ground,* but it came to be used in the Septuagint translation as a term for the Garden of Eden, and in the intertestamental period for a superterrestrial place of blessedness. As it is used here it can mean only heaven or the presence of God.
23:54 *Preparation day* was Friday (cf. Mark 15:42; John 19:31,42), the day on which the Jews made the necessary preparations to observe the Sabbath, when no work could be done. Sabbath began at sundown on Friday, being thus the day after preparation (cf. Matt. 27:62). The burial of Jesus, therefore, was completed before sundown on Friday.

23:55
v. 49

55   Now the women who had come with Him out of Galilee followed after, and saw the tomb and how His body was laid.

23:56
Mark 16:1;
Ex 12:16;
20:10

56   And they returned and prepared spices and perfumes.
And on the Sabbath they rested according to the commandment.

S. *The resurrection of Jesus Christ*
(24:1–11; Matt. 28:1–10; Mark 16:1–8; John 20:1–18)

24:1
Luke 23:56

24 But on the first day of the week, at early dawn, they came to the tomb, bringing the spices which they had prepared.

2   And they found the stone rolled away from the tomb,

3   but when they entered, they did not find the body of the Lord Jesus.

24:4
Acts 1:10;
12:7

4   And it happened that while they were perplexed about this, behold, two men suddenly stood near them in dazzling apparel;

5   and as *the women* were terrified and bowed their faces to the ground, *the men* said to them, "Why do you seek the living One among the dead?

24:6
Matt 17:22,
23;
Mark 9:30,
31; Luke 9:22

6   "He is not here, but He has risen. Remember how He spoke to you while He was still in Galilee,

7   saying that the Son of Man must be delivered into the hands of sinful men, and be crucified, and the third day rise again."

24:8
John 2:22
24:9
v. 46

8   And they remembered His words,

9   and returned from the tomb and reported all these things to the eleven and to all the rest.

24:10
Luke 8:1-3

10   Now they were Mary Magdalene and Joanna and Mary the *mother* of James; also the other women with them were telling these things to the apostles.

24:11
v. 35

11   And these words appeared to them as nonsense, and they would not believe them.

12   [⁴⁰But Peter arose and ran to the tomb; stooping and looking in, he *saw the linen wrappings only; and he went away to his home, marveling at that which had happened.]

T. *The walk to Emmaus (24:13–35)*

13   And behold, two of them were going that very day to a village named Emmaus, which was ⁴¹about seven miles from Jerusalem.

14   And they were conversing with each other about all these things which had taken place.

24:15
v. 36

15   And it came about that while they were conversing and discussing, Jesus Himself approached, and *began* traveling with them.

24:16
John 21:4

16   But their eyes were prevented from recognizing Him.

17   And He said to them, "What are these words that you are exchanging with one another as you are walking?" And they stood still, looking sad.

*24:18
John 19:25

18   And one of them, named Cleopas, answered and said to Him, "Are You the only one visiting Jerusalem and unaware of the things which have happened here in these days?"

24:19
Matt 21:11;
Luke 7:16;
13:33;
Acts 3:22
24:20
Luke 23:13

19   And He said to them, "What things?" And they said to Him, "The things about Jesus the Nazarene, who was a prophet mighty in deed and word in the sight of God and all the people,

20   and how the chief priests and our rulers delivered Him up to the sentence of death, and crucified Him.

*24:21
Luke 1:68

21   "But we were hoping that it was He who was going to redeem Israel. Indeed, besides all this, it is the third day since these things happened.

24:22
vv. 9,10

22   "But also some women among us amazed us. When they were at the tomb early in the morning,

23   and did not find His body, they came, saying that they had also seen a vision of angels, who said that He was alive.

24:24
v. 12

24   "And some of those who were with us went to the tomb and found it just exactly as the women also had said; but Him they did not see."

---

⁴⁰Some ancient mss. do not contain v. 12   ⁴¹I.e., 60 stadia, one stadion was about 600 feet

24:18 *Cleopas* is not the Clopas of John 19:25.   **24:21** Here the reference is to the Messiah.

25   And He said to them, "O foolish men and slow of heart to believe in all that the prophets have spoken!

26   "Was it not necessary for the Christ to suffer these things and to enter into His glory?"

27   And beginning with Moses and with all the prophets, He explained to them the things concerning Himself in all the Scriptures.

28   And they approached the village where they were going, and He acted as though He would go farther.

29   And they urged Him, saying, "Stay with us, for it is *getting* toward evening, and the day is now nearly over." And He went in to stay with them.

30   And it came about that when He had reclined *at the table* with them, He took the bread and blessed *it*, and breaking *it*, He *began* giving *it* to them.

31   And their eyes were opened and they recognized Him; and He vanished from their sight.

32   And they said to one another, "Were not our hearts burning within us while He was speaking to us on the road, while He was explaining the Scriptures to us?"

33   And they arose that very hour and returned to Jerusalem, and found gathered together the eleven and those who were with them,

34   saying, "The Lord has really risen, and has appeared to Simon."

35   And they *began* to relate their experiences on the road and how He was recognized by them in the breaking of the bread.

U. *Christ appears to the ten in Jerusalem* (24:36–43; John 20:19–25)

36   And while they were telling these things, He Himself stood in their midst. [42]

37   But they were startled and frightened and thought that they were seeing a spirit.

38   And He said to them, "Why are you troubled, and why do doubts arise in your hearts?

39   "See My hands and My feet, that it is I Myself; touch Me and see, for a spirit does not have flesh and bones as you see that I have."

40   [[43]And when He had said this, He showed them His hands and His feet.]

41   And while they still could not believe *it* for joy and were marveling, He said to them, "Have you anything here to eat?"

42   And they gave Him a piece of a broiled fish;

43   and He took it and ate *it* before them.

V. *The Great Commission* (24:44–49; cf. Matt. 28:18–20; John 20:21; Acts 1:8)

44   Now He said to them, "These are My words which I spoke to you while I was still with you, that all things which are written about Me in the Law of Moses and the Prophets and the Psalms must be fulfilled."

45   Then He opened their minds to understand the Scriptures,

46   and He said to them, "Thus it is written, that the Christ should suffer and rise again from the dead the third day;

47   and that repentance for forgiveness of sins should be proclaimed in His name to all the nations, beginning from Jerusalem.

48   "You are witnesses of these things.

49   "And behold, I am sending forth the promise of My Father upon you; but you are to stay in the city until you are clothed with power from on high."

Cross references (right margin):

24:26 Heb 2:10; 1 Pet 1:11
24:27 Gen 3:15; Num 21:9; Deut 18:15; Is 7:14; 9:6; 40:10,11; ch. 53; Ezek 34:23; Dan 9:24; Mic 7:20; Mal 3:1
24:28 Mark 6:48
24:30 Matt 14:19
24:33 Acts 1:14
24:34 1 Cor 15:5
24:37 Mark 6:49
24:39 John 20:27
24:41 John 21:5
24:43 Acts 10:41
24:44 Matt 16:21; Mark 8:31; Luke 9:22; 18:31
*24:46 Is 50:6; Hos 6:2; 1 Cor 15:3,4
24:47 Acts 5:31; 13:38; Matt 28:19
24:48 Acts 1:8
24:49 John 14:16; Acts 1:4

---

[42]Some ancient mss. insert *And He says to them, "Peace be to you."*   [43]Many mss. do not contain this verse

---

24:46 The bodily resurrection of Jesus Christ is clearly set forth as a historical event in the New Testament. The resurrection was necessary: (1) to make possible the forgiveness of sins (1 Cor. 15:17); (2) to fulfill the Scriptures (24:45,46); (3) to afford justification for believers (Rom. 4:25; 8:34); and (4) to furnish a solid basis for Christian hope (1 Cor. 15:19). The resurrection was brought to pass: (1) by the power of God (Acts 2:24; Rom. 8:11; Eph. 1:19,20); and (2) by the Lord Jesus Himself (John 2:19; 10:18).

W. Christ's ascension
(24:50–53; Mark 16:19–20; cf. Acts 1:9–11)

24:50
Acts 1:12

50 And He led them out as far as Bethany, and He lifted up His hands and blessed them.

24:51
2 Kin 2:11

51 And it came about that while He was blessing them, He parted from them. [44]

52 And they [45] returned to Jerusalem with great joy,

24:53
Acts 2:46

53 and were continually in the temple, praising God.

[44] Some mss. add *and was carried up into heaven* [45] Some mss. insert *worshiped Him, and*

INTRODUCTION TO

THE GOSPEL ACCORDING TO

JOHN

Authorship and Background: Unlike the other Gospels, the fourth Gospel refers to its author, as "the disciple whom Jesus loved . . . who . . . wrote these things" (21:20,24). This disciple, referred to in 13:23; 19:26; 20:2; and 21:7,20, is not identified by name. In every instance, except at the cross in 19:26, he is with Simon Peter, and he may be the "another disciple" who was with Peter when they went into the high priest's house at the trial of Jesus (18:15,16). The early writers who speak of the authorship of this Gospel identify "the beloved disciple" with the apostle John, the son of Zebedee.

The Gospels reveal that the apostle John, his father Zebedee, and his brother James were fishermen on Lake Galilee (Mark 1:19-20), and partners of Simon Peter (Luke 5:10). The two brothers were called "Boanerges," i.e., "Sons of Thunder" by Jesus (Mark 3:17). Their mother was probably Salome (cf. Mark 15:40 with Matt. 27:56). John and Peter were the two disciples sent in advance into Jerusalem to prepare for the Passover meal (Luke 22:8). John, James, and Peter were the only disciples to accompany Jesus at the raising of the daughter of Jairus (Mark 5:37-40), to the Mount of Transfiguration (Mark 9:2), and into the Garden of Gethsemane (Mark 14:33). The three were joined by Andrew when Jesus delivered His discourse on last things on Mount Olivet (Mark 13:3). John and his brother asked for the places of honor in Christ's glory (Mark 10:35-45), and suggested that fire descend from heaven on the inhospitable Samaritans (Luke 9:54).

After Pentecost, John was associated with Peter in Jerusalem (Acts 3:1-4:22) and on the Samaritan mission (Acts 8:14-25); Paul identified John as one of the three "pillar" apostles whom he saw on his postconversion visit to Jerusalem (Gal. 2:9-10).

The date most often suggested for the fourth Gospel is the last decade of the first century, A.D. 90-100; some date it earlier, near A.D. 70.

Characteristics: The book's purpose is formally stated in 20:30,31: it is a narrative of some of the signs Jesus performed, written in order that the readers might believe that Jesus is the Christ, the Son of God, and in this faith have life in His name.

The supreme question for faith is, "Who is Jesus?" This Gospel answers: (1) he is the "Word of God" (1:14); (2) the "Lamb of God" (1:29,36); (3) the "Messiah" (1:41); (4) the "Son of God" (1:49); (5) the "King of Israel" (1:49); and (6) the "Savior of the world" (4:42). The climax comes with Thomas's ringing confession, "My Lord and my God!" (20:28). In this Gospel seven "signs" of Jesus are recorded, which reveal the person and mission of Jesus: (1) the turning of water into wine (2:1-11); (2) the cure of the nobleman's son (4:46-54); (3) the cure of the paralytic (5:1-18); (4) the feeding of the multitude (6:6-13); (5) walking on the water (6:16-21); (6) giving sight to the blind (9:1-7); and (7) the raising of Lazarus (11:1-45). The purpose and effect of these "signs" are disclosed in 12:37-43: they will not believe because their eyes have been blinded.

There are also seven great "I am" sayings: (1) the bread of life (6:35); (2) the light of the world (8:12); (3) the door of the sheep (10:7); (4) the good shepherd (10:11); (5) the resurrection and the life (11:25); (6) the way, and the truth, and the life (14:6); and (7) the true vine (15:1).

The ministry of Jesus is controlled by "the hour," the decisive moment when God's purpose will be accomplished (2:4; 4:21,23; 5:25,28; 7:30; 8:20; 12:23,27; 13:1); the decisive climax is reached with the declaration of 17:1, "Father, the hour has come."

Contents:

THE GOSPEL ACCORDING TO

JOHN

I. Prologue (1:1–18)

A. The eternal Word (1:1–5)

1 In the beginning was the Word, and the Word was with God, and the Word was God.

2 He was in the beginning with God.

3 All things came into being by Him, and apart from Him nothing came into being that has come into being.

4 In Him was life, and the life was the light of men.

5 And the light shines in the darkness, and the darkness did not [1]comprehend it.

B. The ministry of John the Baptist
(1:6–8; see vv. 19–28; Matt. 3:1–12; Mark 1:1–8; Luke 3:2–17)

6 There [2]came a man, sent from God, whose name was John.

7 He came for a witness, that he might bear witness of the light, that all might believe through him.

8 He was not the light, but *came* that he might bear witness of the light.

C. The first advent of Jesus Christ and His rejection (1:9–13)

9 There was the true light [3]which, coming into the world, enlightens every man.

10 He was in the world, and the world was made through Him, and the world did not know Him.

11 He came to His [4]own, and those who were His own did not receive Him.

12 But as many as received Him, to them He gave the right to become children of God, *even* to those who believe in His name,

13 who were born not of blood, nor of the will of the flesh, nor of the will of man, but of God.

D. The witness of John the Baptist to the incarnate Word
(1:14–18)

14 And the Word became flesh, and dwelt among us, and we beheld His glory, glory as of the only begotten from the Father, full of grace and truth.

---

[1]Or, *overpower* [2]Or, *came into being* [3]Or, *which enlightens every man coming into the world* [4]Or, *own things, possessions, domain*

Cross references (right margin):

*1:1 Col 1:17; 1 John 1:1; Phil 2:6
1:3 Col 1:16; Heb 1:2
1:4 John 5:26; 11:25; 14:6
1:5 John 3:19; 9:5; 12:46
1:7 Acts 19:4
1:8 v. 20
1:9 Is 49:6; 1 John 2:8
1:10 Col 1:16; Heb 1:2
1:12 Gal 3:26; John 3:18; 1 John 5:13
1:13 John 3:5,6; James 1:18; 1 Pet 1:23
1:14 Rom 1:3; Gal 4:4; 1 Tim 3:16; Heb 2:14

1:1 The *Word* (from the Greek *logos*, meaning *reason* or *word*) is a designation for Christ Himself. Scripture makes a distinction between the *Word* of God *written*, the Scriptures, and the *Word* of God *incarnate*, or Jesus Christ in the flesh. John, in his prologue, speaks of Christ as the eternal, preexistent One who became flesh. We may say: (1) the *Word* existed before the world began; (2) *the Word was with God*, or distinct from, and yet in communion with, God the Father; (3) *the Word was God*, or identical in essence with God the Father; (4) through the Word, God brought into being the entire created universe, both the visible and the invisible (Col. 1:16; Heb. 1:2; 11:3); (5) the Word is the source of the physical, intellectual, moral, and spiritual life of man (1:4); and (6) God the Word became flesh, or incarnate as a true human being (1:14). In essence this is the same teaching as that of Paul, who said that in Christ *all the fulness of Deity dwells in bodily form* (Col. 2:9).
1:14 The incarnation is the fundamental part of the gospel. It is that act whereby the Son of God, being Himself God and of the same substance with the Father, nevertheless

condescended to assume human nature for the purpose of man's redemption and restoration. Of the incarnation it may be said: (1) Jesus of Nazareth was and is true God, having a divine nature and all the attributes of deity (Phil. 2:6; Col. 1:19; Heb. 1:8–10); (2) Jesus Christ became true man, having a natural human body and exhibiting those attributes that are common to humanity (Acts 3:22; Gal. 4:4; 1 Tim. 2:5; Heb. 2:14,17,18; 4:15); (3) Jesus Christ was both human and divine (Phil. 2:6–11); He was addressed by both divine and human titles, and divine as well as human attributes were ascribed to Him; and (4) Jesus Christ shall subsist forever as the God-man in His resurrected body (cf. Acts 1:11). The truth of the incarnation is so intimately intertwined with every other doctrine of the gospel, that if either His true humanity or His true deity is destroyed, Christianity cannot be sustained as genuine. (See 1 John 4:2,3, which emphasizes the necessity of this doctrine.)

Christ, the God-man, was both human and divine. Biblical evidences for the true humanity of Jesus are: (1) He was

*1:15 v. 30	15 John *bore witness of Him, and cried out, saying, "This was He of whom I said, 'He who comes after me has a higher rank than I, for He existed before me.'"
1:16 Eph 1:23; Col 1:19	16 For of His fulness we have all received, and grace upon grace.
*1:17 Rom 3:24	17 For the Law was given through Moses; grace and truth were realized through Jesus Christ.
*1:18 Ex 33:20; John 6:46; 1 John 4:9	18 No man has seen God at any time; the only begotten ⁵God, who is in the bosom of the Father, He has explained *Him*.

II. Revelation to old Israel:
the public ministry (1:19–12:50)

A. John's witness to himself (1:19–28)

19   And this is the witness of John, when the Jews sent to him priests and Levites from Jerusalem to ask him, "Who are you?"

1:20 John 3:28; Luke 3:15,16	20 And he confessed, and did not deny, and he confessed, "I am not the Christ."
*1:21 Matt 11:14; 16:14; Deut 18:15	21 And they asked him, "What then? Are you Elijah?" And he *said, "I am not." "Are you the Prophet?" And he answered, "No."
	22 They said then to him, "Who are you, so that we may give an answer to those who sent us? What do you say about yourself?"
1:23 Matt 3:1; Mark 1:3; Luke 3:4; Is 40:3	23 He said, "I am A VOICE OF ONE CRYING IN THE WILDERNESS, 'MAKE STRAIGHT THE WAY OF THE LORD,' as Isaiah the prophet said."
	24 Now they had been sent from the Pharisees.
	25 And they asked him, and said to him, "Why then are you baptizing, if you are not the Christ, nor Elijah, nor the Prophet?"
1:26 Acts 1:5	26 John answered them saying, "I baptize ⁶in water, *but* among you stands One whom you do not know.
1:27 vv. 15,30	27 "*It is* He who comes after me, the thong of whose sandal I am not worthy to untie."
1:28 John 3:26; 10:40	28 These things took place in Bethany beyond the Jordan, where John was baptizing.

B. John's witness to Jesus (1:29–34)

1:29 Is 53:7; 1 Pet 1:19	29 The next day he *saw Jesus coming to him, and *said, "Behold, the Lamb of God who takes away the sin of the world!
1:30 vv. 15,27	30 "This is He on behalf of whom I said, 'After me comes a Man who has a higher rank than I, for He existed before me.'
	31 "And I did not recognize Him, but in order that He might be manifested to Israel, I came baptizing ⁶in water."
1:32 Matt 3:16; Mark 1:10; Luke 3:22	32 And John bore witness saying, "I have beheld the Spirit descending as a dove out of heaven, and He remained upon Him.
1:33 Matt 3:11; Acts 1:5	33 "And I did not recognize Him, but He who sent me to baptize ⁶in water said

---

⁵Some later mss. read *Son*   ⁶The Gr. here can be translated *in, with* or *by*

born of our flesh (Matt. 1:16,25; 2:2; Luke 2:7,11); (2) He had a human soul (Matt. 26:38; Luke 23:46); (3) He was hungry, weary, and required sleep (Matt. 4:2; 8:24; 21:18; Mark 4:38; John 4:6); (4) He was scourged, nailed to the cross, and His side was pierced (Luke 23:33; John 19:1,34); and (5) He is stated to have been like man in all essentials except that He did not sin (John 8:46; Acts 3:22; Phil. 2:7,8; Heb. 2:14,17,18; 4:15; 1 Pet. 2:22).
1:15   See note to Luke 1:57 on the life of John the Baptist.
1:17   *Grace* may be defined as the "unmerited favor of God" toward a sinner; it is "everything for nothing to those who deserve the exact opposite." Grace is an attribute of God (Ex. 22:27; 33:19; Neh. 9:17; 1 Pet. 5:10). The supreme revelation of the grace of God is found in the incarnation, ministry, and atoning sacrifice of the Lord Jesus. Scripture teaches that: (1) justification is by grace (Rom. 3:24; Titus 3:7); (2) salvation is by grace at every point (Eph. 1:7,8); (3) election is by grace (Rom. 11:5,6); (4) faith is the gift of grace (Acts 18:27; Eph. 2:8,9); (5) spiritual gifts are of grace (Rom. 12:6); and (6) comfort, hope, and strength spring from grace (2 Cor. 12:9; 2 Thess. 2:16).
1:18   Scripture teaches that God is Spirit, hence He is not

material and not visible. At the same time there are Scriptures that appear to teach that men have beheld the presence of God (e.g., Gen. 32:30; Ex. 24:9,10; Judg. 13:22; Is. 6:1; Dan. 7:9). Several explanations have been suggested: (1) God may have assumed visible human forms on occasion for the purpose of communicating to men intelligibly (such appearances are called *theophanies*); (2) God may have been represented by proxy, either by a created angelic being who acted for God, or by "the angel of the LORD" (taken by many to be the preincarnate Christ); and (3) Scripture may have used symbolic language or figures of speech that are not intended literally (e.g., in Is. 6:1 it was evidently a vision; in Num. 12:8 God is simply indicating that Moses enjoyed a closer relationship to Him than did the children of Israel). The glory of Judaism lies in its revelation of the unity and spirituality of God; the glory of Christianity, in its revelation of the once-for-all incarnation of God in Jesus Christ.
1:21   The prophet referred to here (also in 1:25; 6:14; 7:40; Acts 3:22,23; 7:37) is the one spoken of by Moses in Deut. 18:15,18. He is identified in the New Testament, not with John the Baptist, but with Jesus who is also Priest and King.

[handwritten top margin: V8- You can visibly see the effect of the H.S., but not the H.S. himself]

8 "The wind blows where it wishes and you hear the sound of it, but do not know where it comes from and where it is going; so is everyone who is born of the Spirit."

9 Nicodemus answered and said to Him, "How can these things be?"

10 Jesus answered and said to him, "Are you the teacher of Israel, and do not understand these things?

11 "Truly, truly, I say to you, we speak that which we know, and bear witness of that which we have seen; and you do not receive our witness.

12 "If I told you earthly things and you do not believe, how shall you believe if I tell you heavenly things?

13 "And no one has ascended into heaven, but He who descended from heaven, *even* the Son of Man.

14 "And as Moses lifted up the serpent in the wilderness, even so must the Son of Man be lifted up; *[handwritten: Num 21:4-9]*

15 that whoever [9]believes may in Him have eternal life.

16 "For God so loved the world, that He gave His only begotten Son, that whoever believes in Him should not perish, but have eternal life.

17 "For God did not send the Son into the world to judge the world, but that the world should be saved through Him.

18 "He who believes in Him is not judged; he who does not believe has been judged already, because he has not believed in the name of the only begotten Son of God. *[handwritten: Perhaps we judge ourselves by our actions; God doesn't need to judge!]*

19 "And this is the judgment, that the light is come into the world, and men loved the darkness rather than the light; for their deeds were evil.

20 "For everyone who does evil hates the light, and does not come to the light, lest his deeds should be exposed.

21 "But he who practices the truth comes to the light, that his deeds may be manifested as having been wrought in God." *[handwritten: See Jn 19:39 The "end" of true story]*

H. *Jesus baptizes in Judea (3:22–24)*

22 After these things Jesus and His disciples came into the land of Judea, and there He was spending time with them and baptizing.

23 And John also was baptizing in Aenon near Salim, because there was much water there; and they were coming and were being baptized.

24 For John had not yet been thrown into prison.

I. *John's testimony to Jesus (3:25–36)*

25 There arose therefore a discussion on the part of John's disciples with a Jew about purification.

26 And they came to John and said to him, "Rabbi, He who was with you beyond the Jordan, to whom you have borne witness, behold, He is baptizing, and all are coming to Him."

27 John answered and said, "A man can receive nothing, unless it has been given him from heaven.

28 "You yourselves bear me witness, that I said, 'I am not the Christ,' but, 'I have been sent before Him.'

29 "He who has the bride is the bridegroom; but the friend of the bridegroom, who stands and hears him, rejoices greatly because of the bridegroom's voice. And so this joy of mine has been made full.

30 "He must increase, but I must decrease.

31 "He who comes from above is above all, he who is of the earth is from the earth and speaks of the earth. He who comes from heaven is above all.

32 "What He has seen and heard, of that He bears witness; and no man receives His witness.

33 "He who has received His witness has set his seal to *this*, that God is true.

34 "For He whom God has sent speaks the words of God; for He gives the Spirit without measure.

35 "The Father loves the Son, and has given all things into His hand.

36 "He who believes in the Son has eternal life; but he who does not obey the Son shall not see life, but the wrath of God abides on him."

[9]Some mss. read *believes in Him may have eternal life*

Cross-reference column:

3:8
1 Cor 2:11

3:9
John 6:52,60
3:10
Luke 2:46

3:11
John 7:16,17 *[handwritten: The "we" includes God the Father.]*

3:13
Prov 30:4; *[handwritten: v 14-]*
Acts 2:34; *[handwritten: Jesus was]*
Rom 10:6; *[handwritten: "lifted up"]*
Eph 4:9 *[handwritten: on the]*
3:14 *[handwritten: cross.]*
Num 21:9;
John 8:28;
12:34
3:15
v. 36;
John 20:21;
1 John
5:11-13
3:16
Rom 5:8;
1 John 4:9
3:17
John 5:36,38;
8:15; 12:47;
1 John 4:14
3:18
John 5:24;
1 John 4:9
3:19
John 1:4;
8:12
3:20
Eph 5:11,13
3:21
1 John 1:6
3:22
John 4:2

3:24
Matt 4:12;
14:3

3:25
John 2:6
3:26
John 1:7,28
3:27
1 Cor 4:7;
Heb 5:4
3:28
John 1:20,23
3:29
Mark 2:19,
20;
Matt 25:1;
John 15:11;
16:24
3:31
John 8:23;
1 John 4:5
3:32
v. 11;
John 8:26;
15:15
3:33
Rom 4:11;
15:28;
Eph 1:13;
4:30
3:34
Matt 12:18;
Luke 4:18
3:35
Matt 28:18;
John 5:20,22;
17:2
3:36
John 5:24;
6:47

J. *Jesus in Samaria (4:1–6)*

4:1
John 3:22,26

4 When therefore the Lord knew that the Pharisees had heard that Jesus was making and baptizing more disciples than John

2 (although Jesus Himself was not baptizing, but His disciples were),

4:3
John 3:22
*4:4
Luke 9:52
*4:5
Gen 33:19;
48:22;
Josh 24:32

3 He left Judea, and departed again into Galilee.

4 And He had to pass through Samaria.

5 So He *came to a city of Samaria, called Sychar, near the parcel of ground that Jacob gave to his son Joseph;

6 and Jacob's well was there. Jesus therefore, being wearied from His journey, was sitting thus by the well. It was about [10]the sixth hour.

K. *Jesus' discourse with the woman of Samaria (4:7–38)*

7 There *came a woman of Samaria to draw water. Jesus *said to her, "Give Me a drink."

4:8
vv. 5, 39
4:9
Matt 10:5;
Luke 9:52,
53; John 8:48

8 For His disciples had gone away into the city to buy food.

9 The Samaritan woman therefore *said to Him, "How is it that You, being a Jew, ask me for a drink since I am a Samaritan woman?" (For Jews have no dealings with Samaritans.)

4:10
Is 44:3;
John 7:37;
Rev 21:6;
22:17

10 Jesus answered and said to her, "If you knew the gift of God, and who it is who says to you, 'Give Me a drink,' you would have asked Him, and He would have given you living water."

11 She *said to Him, "Sir, You have nothing to draw with and the well is deep; where then do You get that living water?

4:12
v. 6

12 "You are not greater than our father Jacob, are You, who gave us the well, and drank of it himself, and his sons, and his cattle?"

13 Jesus answered and said to her, "Everyone who drinks of this water shall thirst again;

4:14
John 6:35;
7:38

14 but whoever drinks of the water that I shall give him shall never thirst; but the water that I shall give him shall become in him a well of water springing up to eternal life."

4:15
John 6:34

15 The woman *said to Him, "Sir, give me this water, so I will not be thirsty, nor come all the way here to draw."

Jesus tested her to see if she was sincere (she could have lied about her husband)

16 He *said to her, "Go, call your husband, and come here."

17 The woman answered and said, "I have no husband." Jesus *said to her, "You have well said, 'I have no husband';

18 for you have had five husbands, and the one whom you now have is not your husband; this you have said truly."

4:19
Luke 7:39

she in turn tested him to see what kind of prophet he was.

19 The woman *said to Him, "Sir, I perceive that You are a prophet.

4:20
Deut 11:29;
Josh 8:33;
Luke 9:53

20 "Our fathers worshiped in this mountain, and you *people* say that in Jerusalem is the place where men ought to worship."

4:21
Mal 1:11;
1 Tim 2:8

21 Jesus *said to her, "Woman, believe Me, an hour is coming when neither in this mountain, nor in Jerusalem, shall you worship the Father.

4:22
2 Kin 17:28-41;
Is 2:3;
Rom 3:1,2;
9:4,5

22 "You worship that which you do not know; we worship that which we know, for salvation is from the Jews.

4:23
John 5:25;
Phil 3:3

23 "But an hour is coming, and now is, when the true worshipers shall worship the Father in spirit and truth; for such people the Father seeks to be His worshipers.

4:24
Phil 3:3

24 "God is spirit, and those who worship Him must worship in spirit and truth."

4:25
John 1:41;
Matt 1:16

25 The woman *said to Him, "I know that Messiah is coming (He who is called Christ); when that One comes, He will declare all things to us."

[10]Perhaps 6 p.m. (Roman time)

4:4 The Samaritan village of Sychar (modern *Askar*) is on the east slope of Mt. Ebal, not too far removed from Mt. Gerizim. Some of the Syriac texts of the New Testament raise the question whether *Sychar* should not be *Shechem*. Recent excavations at Balatah, between Ebal and Gerizim, have shown it to be ancient Shechem, which is nearer to Jacob's well than the site of Askar. The Samaritans had their temple on Mt. Gerizim (although it was destroyed by John Hyrcanus in 128 B.C. and never rebuilt). The Passover was held annually on Mt. Gerizim, not far from the ruins of the temple, but the regular place of worship was probably at the base of Gerizim, not far from Shechem.
4:5 The Samaritans in Jesus' day formed a substantial element in the population. The Jews hated them and had

nothing to do with them. The Samaritans were a mixed people of Assyrian and Jewish blood. When the northern kingdom of Samaria had been conquered by the Assyrians and the Jews had been carried away, their territory was repopulated by Gentiles from the Assyrian empire. Over the centuries the Assyrians intermarried with Jews to form the hybrid group known as the Samaritans. The Jews did not accept them as their neighbors, and it was with this in view that Jesus spoke to the Jews the parable of the Good Samaritan. See also note to Luke 10:30 on the parable of the Good Samaritan.

The fact that Jesus ministered to Samaritans made Him suspect to the scribes and Pharisees. But Jesus came not to respect position; He came to call all sinners to repentance.

26   Jesus *said to her, "I who speak to you am *He.*"

27   And at this point His disciples came, and they marveled that He had been speaking with a woman; yet no one said, "What do You seek?" or, "Why do You speak with her?"

28   So the woman left her waterpot, and went into the city, and *said to the men,

29   "Come, see a man who told me all the things that I *have* done; this is not the Christ, is it?"

30   They went out of the city, and were coming to Him.

31   In the meanwhile the disciples were requesting Him, saying, "Rabbi, eat."

32   But He said to them, "I have food to eat that you do not know about."

33   The disciples therefore were saying to one another, "No one brought Him *anything* to eat, did he?"

34   Jesus *said to them, "My food is to do the will of Him who sent Me, and to accomplish His work.

35   "Do you not say, 'There are yet four months, and *then* comes the harvest'? Behold, I say to you, lift up your eyes, and look on the fields, that they are white for harvest.

36   "Already he who reaps is receiving wages, and is gathering fruit for life eternal; that he who sows and he who reaps may rejoice together.

37   "For in this *case* the saying is true, 'One sows, and another reaps.'

38   "I sent you to reap that for which you have not labored; others have labored, and you have entered into their labor."

L. *The conversion of Samaritans (4:39–42)*

39   And from that city many of the Samaritans believed in Him because of the word of the woman who testified, "He told me all the things that I *have* done."

40   So when the Samaritans came to Him, they were asking Him to stay with them; and He stayed there two days.

41   And many more believed because of His word;

42   and they were saying to the woman, "It is no longer because of what you said that we believe, for we have heard for ourselves and know that this One is indeed the Savior of the world."

M. *Jesus returns to Galilee*
(4:43–45; Matt. 4:12–17; Mark 1:14,15; Luke 4:14,15)

43   And after the two days He went forth from there into Galilee.

44   For Jesus Himself testified that a prophet has no honor in his own country.

45   So when He came to Galilee, the Galileans received Him, having seen all the things that He did in Jerusalem at the feast; for they themselves also went to the feast.

N. *The healing of the official's son (4:46–54)*

46   He came therefore again to Cana of Galilee where He had made the water wine. And there was a certain royal official, whose son was sick at Capernaum.

47   When he heard that Jesus had come out of Judea into Galilee, he went to Him, and was requesting *Him* to come down and heal his son; for he was at the point of death.

48   Jesus therefore said to him, "Unless you *people* see signs and wonders, you *simply* will not believe."

49   The royal official *said to Him, "Sir, come down before my child dies."

50   Jesus *said to him, "Go your way; your son lives." The man believed the word that Jesus spoke to him, and he started off.

51   And as he was now going down, *his* slaves met him, saying that his son was living.

52   So he inquired of them the hour when he began to get better. They said therefore to him, "Yesterday at the [11]seventh hour the fever left him."

53   So the father knew that *it was* at that hour in which Jesus said to him, "Your son lives"; and he himself believed, and his whole household.

54   This is again a second sign that Jesus performed, when He had come out of Judea into Galilee.

[11]Perhaps 7 p.m. (Roman time)

O. Jesus heals at Bethesda on the Sabbath (5:1–16)

5 After these things there was [12]a feast of the Jews, and Jesus went up to Jerusalem.

2 Now there is in Jerusalem by the sheep *gate* a pool, which is called in Hebrew Bethesda, having five porticoes.

3 In these lay a multitude of those who were sick, blind, lame, and withered, [[13]waiting for the moving of the waters;

4 for an angel of the Lord went down at certain seasons into the pool, and stirred up the water; whoever then first, after the stirring up of the water, stepped in was made well from whatever disease with which he was afflicted.]

5 And a certain man was there, who had been thirty-eight years in his sickness.

6 When Jesus saw him lying there, and knew that he had already been a long time *in that condition*, He *said to him, "Do you wish to get well?"

7 The sick man answered Him, "Sir, I have no man to put me into the pool when the water is stirred up, but while I am coming, another steps down before me."

8 Jesus *said to him, "Arise, take up your pallet, and walk."

9 And immediately the man became well, and took up his pallet and *began* to walk.

Now it was the Sabbath on that day.

10 Therefore the Jews were saying to him who was cured, "It is the Sabbath, and it is not permissible for you to carry your pallet."

11 But he answered them, "He who made me well was the one who said to me, 'Take up your pallet and walk.' "

12 They asked him, "Who is the man who said to you, 'Take up *your pallet*, and walk'?"

13 But he who was healed did not know who it was; for Jesus had slipped away while there was a crowd in *that* place.

14 Afterward Jesus *found him in the temple, and said to him, "Behold, you have become well; do not sin anymore, so that nothing worse may befall you."

15 The man went away, and told the Jews that it was Jesus who had made him well.

16 And for this reason the Jews were persecuting Jesus, because He was doing these things on the Sabbath.

P. Jesus claims to be God (5:17–24)

17 But He answered them, "My Father is working until now, and I Myself am working."

18 For this cause therefore the Jews were seeking all the more to kill Him, because He not only was breaking the Sabbath, but also was calling God His own Father, making Himself equal with God.

19 Jesus therefore answered and was saying to them, "Truly, truly, I say to you, the Son can do nothing of Himself, unless *it is* something He sees the Father doing; for whatever *the Father* does, these things the Son also does in like manner.

20 "For the Father loves the Son, and shows Him all things that He Himself is doing; and greater works than these will He show Him, that you may marvel.

21 "For just as the Father raises the dead and gives them life, even so the Son also gives life to whom He wishes.

22 "For not even the Father judges anyone, but He has given all judgment to the Son,

23 in order that all may honor the Son, even as they honor the Father. He who does not honor the Son does not honor the Father who sent Him.

24 "Truly, truly, I say to you, he who hears My word, and believes Him who sent Me, has eternal life, and does not come into judgment, but has passed out of death into life.

[12]Many mss. read *the feast*, i.e., the Passover   [13]Many mss. do not contain the remainder of v. 3 nor v. 4

5:18 Scripture asserts that on a number of occasions Jesus claimed to be divine. In this instance the Jews were perfectly aware that by the nature of Jesus' claim He made Himself *equal with God*. Either this was blasphemy or His claim was true. In the former case He deserved to die; in the latter case He was worthy of worship. One's attitude toward the deity of Christ is ever a dividing line between faith and unbelief.

Margin references: 5:2 Neh 3:1; 12:39 · 5:8 Matt 9:6; Mark 2:11; Luke 5:24 · 5:9 John 9:14 · 5:10 vv. 15,16; Neh 13:19; Jer 17:21; Matt 12:2; Mark 2:24; John 7:23; 9:16 · 5:14 Mark 2:5; John 8:11 · 5:17 John 9:4; 14:10 · *5:18 John 7:1,19; 10:30,33 · 5:19 John 8:28; 12:49; 14:10 · 5:20 John 3:35; 14:12 · 5:21 Rom 4:17; 8:11; John 11:25 · 5:22 John 9:39; Acts 17:31 · 5:23 Luke 10:16; 1 John 2:23 · 5:24 John 3:18; 12:44; 20:31; 1 John 5:13; 3:14

Handwritten notes: V. 6 After 38 years, was the man afraid to be healed for fear the prison of his disease? · V 14 — Grace came first, his obedience was in response to grace — not to earn it.

Q. *The two resurrections (5:25–29)*

25 "Truly, truly, I say to you, an hour is coming and now is, when the dead shall hear the voice of the Son of God; and those who hear shall live.

26 "For just as the Father has life in Himself, even so He gave to the Son also to have life in Himself;

27 and He gave Him authority to execute judgment, because He is *the* Son of Man.

28 "Do not marvel at this; for an hour is coming, in which all who are in the tombs shall hear His voice,

29 and shall come forth; those who did the good *deeds* to a resurrection of life, those who committed the evil *deeds* to a resurrection of judgment.

R. *The Father's witness to the Son (5:30–47)*

30 "I can do nothing on My own initiative. As I hear, I judge; and My judgment is just, because I do not seek My own will, but the will of Him who sent Me.

31 "If I *alone* bear witness of Myself, My testimony is not true.

32 "There is another who bears witness of Me, and I know that the testimony which He bears of Me is true.

33 "You have sent to John, and he has borne witness to the truth.

34 "But the witness which I receive is not from man, but I say these things that you may be saved.

35 "He was the lamp that was burning and was shining and you were willing to rejoice for a while in his light.

36 "But the witness which I have is greater than *that of* John; for the works which the Father has given Me to accomplish, the very works that I do, bear witness of Me, that the Father has sent Me.

37 "And the Father who sent Me, He has borne witness of Me. You have neither heard His voice at any time, nor seen His form.

38 "And you do not have His word abiding in you, for you do not believe Him whom He sent.

39 "[14]You search the Scriptures, because you think that in them you have eternal life; and it is these that bear witness of Me;

40 and you are unwilling to come to Me, that you may have life.

41 "I do not receive glory from men;

42 but I know you, that you do not have the love of God in yourselves.

43 "I have come in My Father's name, and you do not receive Me; if another shall come in his own name, you will receive him.

44 "How can you believe, when you receive glory from one another, and you do not seek the glory that is from the *one and* only God?

45 "Do not think that I will accuse you before the Father; the one who accuses you is Moses, in whom you have set your hope.

46 "For if you believed Moses, you would believe Me; for he wrote of Me.

47 "But if you do not believe his writings, how will you believe My words?"

S. *The five thousand fed (6:1–14; Matt. 14:13–21; Mark 6:30–44; Luke 9:10–17; cf. Matt. 15:32–38)*

6 After these things Jesus went away to the other side of the Sea of Galilee (or Tiberias).

2 And a great multitude was following Him, because they were seeing the signs which He was performing on those who were sick.

3 And Jesus went up on the mountain, and there He sat with His disciples.

4 Now the Passover, the feast of the Jews, was at hand.

5 Jesus therefore lifting up His eyes, and seeing that a great multitude was coming to Him, *said to Philip, "Where are we to buy bread, that these may eat?"

Marginal references:

5:25 John 4:21; 6:60; 8:43,47
5:26 John 6:57
5:27 Acts 10:42; 17:31
5:29 Dan 12:2; Acts 24:15; Matt 25:46
5:30 John 8:16; 4:34; 6:38
*5:31 John 8:14
5:32 John 8:18
5:33 John 1:7,15, 19,27,32
5:34 1 John 5:9
5:35 2 Pet 1:19; Matt 21:26
5:36 1 John 5:9; John 10:25; 14:11; 15:24
5:37 John 8:18; Deut 4:12; 1 Tim 1:17
5:38 John 3:17
5:39 Luke 24:25, 27; Acts 13:27
5:41 v. 44
5:43 Matt 24:5
5:44 Rom 2:29
5:45 John 9:28; Rom 2:17
5:46 Gen 3:15; Luke 24:27; Acts 26:22
5:47 Luke 16:29, 31
6:2 John 2:11
6:3 v. 15
6:4 John 2:13
6:5 John 1:43

---

[14]Or, (a command) *Search the Scriptures!*

5:31 In 8:14 Christ affirmed that His witness was in and of itself true and trustworthy and needed no corroborative testimony. In this encounter, however, the context makes it plain that Christ, for purposes of persuasion, yielded to the demands of the rabbis for a verification of His claims. This verse may well be paraphrased: "If I bear witness of myself alone, without other witnesses, my testimony is not true," i.e., not measuring up to the requirements of legal evidence. But Christ offered decisive witnesses: (1) the Father Himself (5:32,37); (2) John the Baptist (5:33); (3) His own miraculous works (5:36); (4) the Word of God (5:39); and (5) the prophecy of Moses (5:46; cf. Deut. 18:19).

6:6
2 Cor 13:5

6 And this He was saying to test him; for He Himself knew what He was intending to do.

7 Philip answered Him, "Two hundred [15]denarii worth of bread is not sufficient for them, for everyone to receive a little."

6:8
John 1:40
6:9
2 Kin 4:43

8 One of His disciples, Andrew, Simon Peter's brother, *said to Him,

9 "There is a lad here who has five barley loaves and two fish, but what are these for so many people?"

10 Jesus said, "Have the people sit down." Now there was much grass in the place. So the men sat down, in number about five thousand.

6:11
v. 23;
Matt 15:36

11 Jesus therefore took the loaves; and having given thanks, He distributed to those who were seated; likewise also of the fish as much as they wanted.

12 And when they were filled, He *said to His disciples, "Gather up the leftover fragments that nothing may be lost."

13 And so they gathered them up, and filled twelve baskets with fragments from the five barley loaves, which were left over by those who had eaten.

6:14
Gen 49:10;
Deut 18:15,
18;
Matt 11:3;
21:11

14 When therefore the people saw the sign which He had performed, they said, "This is of a truth the Prophet who is to come into the world."

T. Jesus walks on the sea
(6:15–21; Matt. 14:22–32; Mark 6:45–52)

*6:15
John 18:36

15 Jesus therefore perceiving that they were intending to come and take Him by force, to make Him king, withdrew again to the mountain by Himself alone.

16 Now when evening came, His disciples went down to the sea,

17 and after getting into a boat, they *started to* cross the sea to Capernaum. And it had already become dark, and Jesus had not yet come to them.

18 And the sea *began* to be stirred up because a strong wind was blowing.

19 When therefore they had rowed about three or four miles, they *beheld Jesus walking on the sea and drawing near to the boat; and they were frightened.

20 But He *said to them, "It is I; do not be afraid."

21 They were willing therefore to receive Him into the boat; and immediately the boat was at the land to which they were going.

U. Jesus' discourse on the bread of life (6:22–40)

6:22
vv. 2,16ff

22 The next day the multitude that stood on the other side of the sea saw that there was no other small boat there, except one, and that Jesus had not entered with His disciples into the boat, but *that* His disciples had gone away alone.

6:23
vv. 1,11

23 There came other small boats from Tiberias near to the place where they ate the bread after the Lord had given thanks.

6:24
Matt 14:34;
Mark 6:53

24 When the multitude therefore saw that Jesus was not there, nor His disciples, they themselves got into the small boats, and came to Capernaum, seeking Jesus.

25 And when they found Him on the other side of the sea, they said to Him, "Rabbi, when did You get here?"

6:26
vv. 24,30

26 Jesus answered them and said, "Truly, truly, I say to you, you seek Me, not because you saw signs, but because you ate of the loaves, and were filled.

6:27
Is 55:2; v. 54;
John 4:14;
3:35

27 "Do not work for the food which perishes, but for the food which endures to eternal life, which the Son of Man shall give to you, for on Him the Father, *even* God, has set His seal."

28 They said therefore to Him, "What shall we do, that we may work the works of God?"

6:29
1 John 3:23;
John 3:17

29 Jesus answered and said to them, "This is the work of God, that you believe in Him whom He has sent."

6:30
Matt 12:38;
Mark 8:11

30 They said therefore to Him, "What then do You do for a sign, that we may see, and believe You? What work do You perform?

6:31
Ex 16:15;
Num 11:8;
Neh 9:15;
Ps 78:24

31 "Our fathers ate the manna in the wilderness; as it is written, 'HE GAVE THEM BREAD OUT OF HEAVEN TO EAT.' "

---

[15]The denarius was equivalent to one day's wage

6:15 The multitude, astonished by the miracle of Christ's feeding them, was swept by a wave of enthusiasm and would have forced Jesus to lead them in their revolt against the Roman power. This information explains why Jesus had to compel His disciples to embark and leave the place, so that He might dismiss the crowds (Matt. 14:22; Mark 6:45). Obviously the disciples had been affected by the crowd's delirium and readily went along with them in their attempt to make Jesus their revolutionary leader.

32   Jesus therefore said to them, "Truly, truly, I say to you, it is not Moses who has given you the bread out of heaven, but it is My Father who gives you the true bread out of heaven.

33   "For the bread of God is [16]that which comes down out of heaven, and gives life to the world."

34   They said therefore to Him, "Lord, evermore give us this bread."

35   Jesus said to them, "I am the bread of life; he who comes to Me shall not hunger, and he who believes in Me shall never thirst.

36   "But I said to you, that you have seen Me, and yet do not believe.

37   "All that the Father gives Me shall come to Me, and the one who comes to Me I will certainly not cast out.

38   "For I have come down from heaven, not to do My own will, but the will of Him who sent Me.

39   "And this is the will of Him who sent Me, that of all that He has given Me I lose nothing, but raise it up on the last day.

40   "For this is the will of My Father, that everyone who beholds the Son and believes in Him, may have eternal life; and I Myself will raise him up on the last day."

V. The Jews dispute Jesus' claim (6:41–59)

41   The Jews therefore were grumbling about Him, because He said, "I am the bread that came down out of heaven."

42   And they were saying, "Is not this Jesus, the son of Joseph, whose father and mother we know? How does He now say, 'I have come down out of heaven'?"

43   Jesus answered and said to them, "Do not grumble among yourselves.

44   "No one can come to Me, unless the Father who sent Me draws him; and I will raise him up on the last day.

45   "It is written in the prophets, 'AND THEY SHALL ALL BE TAUGHT OF GOD.' Everyone who has heard and learned from the Father, comes to Me.

46   "Not that any man has seen the Father, except the One who is from God; He has seen the Father.

47   "Truly, truly, I say to you, he who believes has eternal life.

48   "I am the bread of life.

49   "Your fathers ate the manna in the wilderness, and they died.

50   "This is the bread which comes down out of heaven, so that one may eat of it and not die.

51   "I am the living bread that came down out of heaven; if anyone eats of this bread, he shall live forever; and the bread also which I shall give for the life of the world is My flesh."

52   The Jews therefore *began* to argue with one another, saying, "How can this man give us *His* flesh to eat?"

53   Jesus therefore said to them, "Truly, truly, I say to you, unless you eat the flesh of the Son of Man and drink His blood, you have no life in yourselves.

54   "He who eats My flesh and drinks My blood has eternal life, and I will raise him up on the last day.

55   "For My flesh is true food, and My blood is true drink.

56   "He who eats My flesh and drinks My blood abides in Me, and I in him.

57   "As the living Father sent Me, and I live because of the Father, so he who eats Me, he also shall live because of Me.

58   "This is the bread which came down out of heaven; not as the fathers ate, and died, he who eats this bread shall live forever."

59   These things He said in the synagogue, as He taught in Capernaum.

[16]Or, *He who comes*

Cross-references (right margin):

6:33 — v. 50
6:34 — John 4:15
*6:35 — vv. 48,51; John 4:14
6:36 — v. 26
6:37 — v. 39; John 17:2
6:38 — John 4:34; 5:30
6:39 — John 10:28; 17:12; 18:9
6:40 — vv. 27,47,54; John 3:15,16
6:42 — Luke 4:22; John 7:27,28; vv. 38,62
6:44 — Jer 31:3; Hos 11:4; John 12:32
6:45 — Is 54:13; Jer 31:34; Heb 8:10; 10:16
6:46 — John 1:18; 5:37; 7:29; 8:19
6:47 — John 3:16,18, 36; 5:24; 11:26
6:48 — vv. 35,51
6:49 — v. 31
6:50 — v. 33
6:51 — Heb 10:10
6:52 — John 9:16; 10:19
6:53 — Matt 26:26,28
6:54 — John 4:14
6:56 — John 15:4; 1 John 3:24; 4:15,16
6:57 — John 3:17
6:58 — vv. 49-51

6:35 While bread is not exactly a type of Christ, yet it is used metaphorically to illustrate the truth that He is life to the believer. The words *I am the bread of life* are no more to be taken literally than such similar affirmations as *I am the door* and *I am the vine.* Christ only means that as bread and water are necessary to sustain physical life, so He is necessary to sustain the spiritual life of the believer. But the figure goes even beyond this, for He states that those who eat of His bread and drink of the water from His fountain shall never hunger or thirst again. He fully and forever satisfies the heart's needs.

v54- The thought of eating blood would have been offensive to his hearers.

W. *The questioning disciples (6:60–65)*

6:60
v. 66
60 Many therefore of His disciples, when they heard *this* said, "This is a difficult statement; who can listen to it?"

6:61
Matt 11:6
61 But Jesus, conscious that His disciples grumbled at this, said to them, "Does this cause you to stumble?

6:62
John 3:13;
17:5
62 "*What* then if you should behold the Son of Man ascending where He was before?

6:63
2 Cor 3:6
63 "It is the Spirit who gives life; the flesh profits nothing; the words that I have spoken to you are spirit and are life.

6:64
John 2:25
64 "But there are some of you who do not believe." For Jesus knew from the beginning who they were who did not believe, and who it was that would betray Him.

6:65
vv. 37,44;
John 3:27
65 And He was saying, "For this reason I have said to you, that no one can come to Me, unless it has been granted him from the Father."

X. *Peter's great affirmation (6:66–71)*

6:66
v. 60
66 As a result of this many of His disciples withdrew, and were not walking with Him anymore.

6:67
Matt 10:2
67 Jesus said therefore to the twelve, "You do not want to go away also, do you?"

6:68
Matt 16:16;
Acts 5:20
68 Simon Peter answered Him, "Lord, to whom shall we go? You have words of eternal life.

6:69
Mark 8:29;
Luke 9:20
69 "And we have believed and have come to know that You are the Holy One of God."

6:70
John 15:16,
19; 13:27
70 Jesus answered them, "Did I Myself not choose you, the twelve, and *yet* one of you is a devil?"

6:71
John 13:26;
Mark 14:10
71 Now He meant Judas *the son* of Simon Iscariot, for he, one of the twelve, was going to betray Him.

Y. *Jesus and the Feast of Tabernacles (7:1–13)*

7:1
John 5:18
7 And after these things Jesus was walking in Galilee; for He was unwilling to walk in Judea, because the Jews were seeking to kill Him.

*7:2
Lev 23:34;
Deut 16:16
2 Now the feast of the Jews, the Feast of Booths, was at hand.

7:3
Matt 12:46;
Mark 3:31
3 His brothers therefore said to Him, "Depart from here, and go into Judea, that Your disciples also may behold Your works which You are doing.

4 "For no one does anything in secret, when he himself seeks to be *known* publicly. If You do these things, show Yourself to the world."

7:5
Mark 3:21
5 For not even His brothers were believing in Him.

7:6
Matt 26:18;
vv. 8,30
6 Jesus therefore *said to them, "My time is not yet at hand, but your time is always opportune.

7:7
John 15:18,
19; 3:19,20
7 "The world cannot hate you; but it hates Me because I testify of it, that its deeds are evil.

7:8
v. 6
8 "Go up to the feast yourselves; I do not go up to this feast because My time has not yet fully come."

9 And having said these things to them, He stayed in Galilee.

10 But when His brothers had gone up to the feast, then He Himself also went up, not publicly, but as it were, in secret.

7:11
John 11:56
11 The Jews therefore were seeking Him at the feast, and were saying, "Where is He?"

7:12
vv. 40-43
12 And there was much grumbling among the multitudes concerning Him; some were saying, "He is a good man"; others were saying, "No, on the contrary, He leads the multitude astray."

7:13
John 9:22;
12:42; 19:38
13 Yet no one was speaking openly of Him for fear of the Jews.

Z. *Jesus teaches in the temple (7:14–36)*

7:14
v. 28
14 But when it was now the midst of the feast Jesus went up into the temple, and *began to* teach.

7:2 The Feast of Booths (Tabernacles), starting on the fifteenth day of the seventh month, Tishri (September-October), and lasting eight days, commemorated the wilderness life of the Hebrews in their flight from Egypt. Every day in this period the priests brought water from the pool of Siloam and poured it out in libation on the altar of the temple (see the words of Jesus, vv. 37–39). (See also note to Ex. 23:16.)

15   The Jews therefore were marveling, saying, "How has this man become learned, having never been educated?"

16   Jesus therefore answered them, and said, "My teaching is not Mine, but His who sent Me.

17   "If any man is willing to do His will, he shall know of the teaching, whether it is of God, or *whether* I speak from Myself.

18   "He who speaks from himself seeks his own glory; but He who is seeking the glory of the one who sent Him, He is true, and there is no unrighteousness in Him.

19   "Did not Moses give you the Law, and *yet* none of you carries out the Law? Why do you seek to kill Me?"

20   The multitude answered, "You have a demon! Who seeks to kill You?"

21   Jesus answered and said to them, "I did one deed, and you all marvel.

22   "On this account Moses has given you circumcision (not because it is from Moses, but from the fathers), and on *the* Sabbath you circumcise a man.

23   "If a man receives circumcision on *the* Sabbath that the Law of Moses may not be broken, are you angry with Me because I made an entire man well on *the* Sabbath?

24   "Do not judge according to appearance, but judge with righteous judgment."

25   Therefore some of the people of Jerusalem were saying, "Is this not the man whom they are seeking to kill?

26   "And look, He is speaking publicly, and they are saying nothing to Him. The rulers do not really know that this is the Christ, do they?

27   "However, we know where this man is from; but whenever the Christ may come, no one knows where He is from."

28   Jesus therefore cried out in the temple, teaching and saying, "You both know Me and know where I am from; and I have not come of Myself, but He who sent Me is true, whom you do not know.

29   "I know Him; because I am from Him, and He sent Me."

30   They were seeking therefore to seize Him; and no man laid his hand on Him, because His hour had not yet come.

31   But many of the multitude believed in Him; and they were saying, "When the Christ shall come, He will not perform more signs than those which this man has, will He?"

32   The Pharisees heard the multitude muttering these things about Him; and the chief priests and the Pharisees sent officers to seize Him.

33   Jesus therefore said, "For a little while longer I am with you, then I go to Him who sent Me.

34   "You shall seek Me, and shall not find Me; and where I am, you cannot come."

35   The Jews therefore said to one another, "Where does this man intend to go that we shall not find Him? He is not intending to go to the Dispersion among the Greeks, and teach the Greeks, is He?

36   "What is this statement that He said, 'You will seek Me, and will not find Me; and where I am, you cannot come'?"

AA. *The last day of the feast (7:37–52)*

37   Now on the last day, the great *day* of the feast, Jesus stood and cried out, saying, "If any man is thirsty, let him come to Me and drink.

38   "He who believes in Me, as the Scripture said, 'From his innermost being shall flow rivers of living water.'"

39   But this He spoke of the Spirit, whom those who believed in Him were to receive; for the Spirit was not yet *given*, because Jesus was not yet glorified.

40   *Some* of the multitude therefore, when they heard these words, were saying, "This certainly is the Prophet."

41   Others were saying, "This is the Christ." Still others were saying, "Surely the Christ is not going to come from Galilee, is He?

42   "Has not the Scripture said that the Christ comes from the offspring of David, and from Bethlehem, the village where David was?"

Cross references (right margin):

7:15 Matt 13:54; Mark 6:2; Luke 4:22
7:16 John 3:11; 8:28; 12:49
7:17 John 8:43
7:18 John 5:41; 8:50
7:19 Ex 24:3; John 1:17; 11:53
7:20 John 8:48; 10:20
7:22 Lev 12:3; Gen 17:10
*7:23 Mark 3:5
7:24 Lev 19:15; John 8:15
7:26 v. 48
7:27 Matt 13:55; Mark 6:3; Luke 4:22
7:28 John 8:14; 8:26; 1:18
7:29 Matt 11:27; John 10:15
7:30 Matt 21:46; John 8:20
7:31 John 8:30; Matt 12:23
7:33 John 13:33; 16:16-19
7:34 John 8:21; 13:33
7:35 James 1:1; 1 Pet 1:1
7:37 Lev 23:36; Is 55:1; Rev 22:17
*7:38 Is 12:3; John 4:10,14
7:39 Joel 2:28; Acts 2:17,33; John 20:22; 12:23
7:40 Matt 21:11; John 1:21
7:41 John 1:46
7:42 Jer 23:5; Mic 5:2; Matt 2:5; Luke 2:4

7:23 Every male infant was circumcised on the eighth day. If the child had been born on the Sabbath, then the circumcision was performed on the Sabbath, in disregard of the Sabbath laws against work. If the Jews were willing to violate the Sabbath in order to keep the law of circumcision, how could they quarrel with Jesus for having healed the sick man on the Sabbath (5:8–10)?

7:38 No precise source for this quotation is found in the Old Testament. Commentators see parallels in Is. 12:3; 44:3; 58:11; Zech. 14:8.

7:43
John 9:16;
10:19
7:44
v. 30

7:46
Matt 7:28,29
7:47
v. 12

7:48
John 12:42

7:51
Deut 17:6;
19:15

8:5
Lev 20:10;
Deut 22:22

8:7
Deut 17:7;
Rom 2:1

8:9
Rom 2:22

8:11
John 3:18;
5:14

8:12
John 1:4; 9:5;
12:35
8:13
John 5:31
8:14
John 18:37;
13:3; 16:28;
7:28; 9:29
8:15
John 7:24;
3:17
8:16
John 5:30
8:17
Deut 17:6;
Matt 18:16
8:18
John 5:37
8:19
John 14:7;
16:3
8:20
Mark 12:41;
John 7:30

43 So there arose a division in the multitude because of Him.

44 And some of them wanted to seize Him, but no one laid hands on Him.

45 The officers therefore came to the chief priests and Pharisees, and they said to them, "Why did you not bring Him?"

46 The officers answered, "Never did a man speak the way this man speaks."

47 The Pharisees therefore answered them, "You have not also been led astray, have you?

48 "No one of the rulers or Pharisees has believed in Him, has he?

49 "But this multitude which does not know the Law is accursed."

50 Nicodemus *said to them (he who came to Him before, being one of them),

51 "Our Law does not judge a man, unless it first hears from him and knows what he is doing, does it?"

52 They answered and said to him, "You are not also from Galilee, are you? Search, and see that no prophet arises out of Galilee."

53 [17And everyone went to his home.

8 But Jesus went to the Mount of Olives.

BB. *The woman caught in adultery (8:2–11)*

2 And early in the morning He came again into the temple, and all the people were coming to Him; and He sat down and *began* to teach them.

3 And the scribes and the Pharisees *brought a woman caught in adultery, and having set her in the midst,

4 they *said to Him, "Teacher, this woman has been caught in adultery, in the very act.

5 "Now in the Law Moses commanded us to stone such women; what then do You say?"

6 And they were saying this, testing Him, in order that they might have grounds for accusing Him. But Jesus stooped down, and with His finger wrote on the ground.

7 But when they persisted in asking Him, He straightened up, and said to them, "He who is without sin among you, let him *be the* first to throw a stone at her."

8 And again He stooped down, and wrote on the ground.

9 And when they heard it, they *began* to go out one by one, beginning with the older ones, and He was left alone, and the woman, where she was, in the midst.

10 And straightening up, Jesus said to her, "Woman, where are they? Did no one condemn you?"

11 And she said, "No one, Lord." And Jesus said, "Neither do I condemn you; go your way. From now on sin no more."]

CC. *Jesus the light of the world: the claim and the testimony (8:12–20)*

12 Again therefore Jesus spoke to them, saying, "I am the light of the world; he who follows Me shall not walk in the darkness, but shall have the light of life."

13 The Pharisees therefore said to Him, "You are bearing witness of Yourself; Your witness is not true."

14 Jesus answered and said to them, "Even if I bear witness of Myself, My witness is true; for I know where I came from, and where I am going; but you do not know where I come from, or where I am going.

15 "You people judge according to the flesh; I am not judging anyone.

16 "But even if I do judge, My judgment is true; for I am not alone *in it*, but I and 18He who sent Me.

17 "Even in your law it has been written, that the testimony of two men is true.

18 "I am He who bears witness of Myself, and the Father who sent Me bears witness of Me."

19 And so they were saying to Him, "Where is Your Father?" Jesus answered, "You know neither Me, nor My Father; if you knew Me, you would know My Father also."

20 These words He spoke in the treasury, as He taught in the temple; and no one seized Him, because His hour had not yet come.

17John 7:53-8:11 is not found in most of the old mss.   18Many ancient mss. read *the Father who sent Me*

DD. *Jesus warns against unbelief (8:21–30)*

21   He said therefore again to them, "I go away, and you shall seek Me, and shall die in your sin; where I am going, you cannot come."   **8:21** John 7:34

22   Therefore the Jews were saying, "Surely He will not kill Himself, will He, since He says, 'Where I am going, you cannot come' ?"

23   And He was saying to them, "You are from below, I am from above; you are of this world, I am not of this world.   **8:23** John 3:31; 17:14

24   "I said therefore to you, that you shall die in your sins; for unless you believe that I am *He,* you shall die in your sins."   **8:24** Mark 13:6; John 4:26; 13:19

25   And so they were saying to Him, "Who are You?" Jesus said to them, "What have I been saying to you *from* the beginning?

26   "I have many things to speak and to judge concerning you, but He who sent Me is true; and the things which I heard from Him, these I speak to the world."   **8:26** John 7:28; 3:32; 15:15

27   They did not realize that He had been speaking to them about the Father.

28   Jesus therefore said, "When you lift up the Son of Man, then you will know that I am *He,* and I do nothing on My own initiative, but I speak these things as the Father taught Me.   **8:28** John 3:14; 12:32; 5:19; 3:11

29   "And He who sent Me is with Me; He has not left Me alone, for I always do the things that are pleasing to Him."   **8:29** John 4:34; 5:30; 6:38

30   As He spoke these things, many came to believe in Him.   **8:30** John 7:31; 10:42; 11:45

EE. *The true children of Abraham (8:31–59)*

31   Jesus therefore was saying to those Jews who had believed Him, "If you abide in My word, *then* you are truly disciples of Mine;   **8:31** John 15:7; 2 John 9

32   and you shall know the truth, and the truth shall make you free."   **8:32** Rom 8:2; James 2:12

33   They answered Him, "We are Abraham's offspring, and have never yet been enslaved to anyone; how is it that You say, 'You shall become free' ?"   **8:33** Matt 3:9

34   Jesus answered them, "Truly, truly, I say to you, everyone who commits sin is the slave of sin.   **8:34** Rom 6:16; 2 Pet 2:19

35   "And the slave does not remain in the house forever; the son does remain forever.   **8:35** Gal 4:30

36   "If therefore the Son shall make you free, you shall be free indeed.

37   "I know that you are Abraham's offspring; yet you seek to kill Me, because My word has no place in you.   **8:37** vv. 39,40

38   "I speak the things which I have seen with *My* Father; therefore you also do the things which you heard from *your* father."   **8:38** John 5:19,30; 14:10,24

39   They answered and said to Him, "Abraham is our father." Jesus *said to them, "If you are Abraham's children, do the deeds of Abraham.   **8:39** Rom 9:7; Gal 3:7

40   "But as it is, you are seeking to kill Me, a man who has told you the truth, which I heard from God; this Abraham did not do.   **8:40** v. 26

41   "You are doing the deeds of your father." They said to Him, "We were not born of fornication; we have one Father, *even* God."   **8:41** Is 63:16; 64:8

42   Jesus said to them, "If God were your Father, you would love Me; for I proceeded forth and have come from God, for I have not even come on My own initiative, but He sent Me.   **8:42** 1 John 5:1; John 16:27, 28; 17:8; 7:28

43   "Why do you not understand what I am saying? *It is* because you cannot hear My word.

44   "You are of *your* father the devil, and you want to do the desires of your father. He was a murderer from the beginning, and does not stand in the truth, because there is no truth in him. Whenever he speaks a lie, he speaks from his own *nature;* for he is a liar, and the father of lies.   **8:44** 1 John 3:8; vv. 38,41; 1 John 2:4; Matt 12:34

45   "But because I speak the truth, you do not believe Me.

46   "Which one of you convicts Me of sin? If I speak truth, why do you not believe Me?

47   "He who is of God hears the words of God; for this reason you do not hear *them,* because you are not of God."   **8:47** 1 John 4:6

48   The Jews answered and said to Him, "Do we not say rightly that You are a Samaritan and have a demon?"   **8:48** v. 52; John 7:20; 10:20

49   Jesus answered, "I do not have a demon; but I honor My Father, and you dishonor Me.

50   "But I do not seek My glory; there is One who seeks and judges.   **8:50** John 5:41

8:51
John 14:23;
15:20; 17:6;
Matt 16:28;
Heb 11:5
8:52
John 7:20;
14:23; 15:20;
17:6
8:53
John 4:12
8:54
v. 50;
John 16:14
8:55
John 7:28,29;
15:10
8:56
Matt 13:17;
Heb 11:13

*8:58
John 1:1;
17:5,24;
Rev 1:8
8:59
John 10:31;
11:8; 12:36

51 "Truly, truly, I say to you, if anyone keeps My word he shall never see death."

52 The Jews said to Him, "Now we know that You have a demon. Abraham died, and the prophets *also;* and You say, 'If anyone keeps My word, he shall never taste of death.'

53 "Surely You are not greater than our father Abraham, who died? The prophets died too; whom do You make Yourself out *to be?"*

54 Jesus answered, "If I glorify Myself, My glory is nothing; it is My Father who glorifies Me, of whom you say, 'He is our God';

55 and you have not come to know Him, but I know Him; and if I say that I do not know Him, I shall be a liar like you, but I do know Him, and keep His word.

56 "Your father Abraham rejoiced to see My day, and he saw *it* and was glad."

57 The Jews therefore said to Him, "You are not yet fifty years old, and have You seen Abraham?"

58 Jesus said to them, "Truly, truly, I say to you, before Abraham was born, I am."

59 Therefore they picked up stones to throw at Him; but Jesus hid Himself, and went out of the temple.

FF. *Jesus heals the man born blind (9:1–12)*

*9:2
v. 34;
Luke 13:2;
Ex 20:5;
Ezek 18:20
*9:3
John 11:4
9:4
John 11:9;
12:35
9:5
John 1:4;
8:12; 12:46
9:6
Mark 7:33;
8:23
9:7
v. 11;
Luke 13:4;
John 11:37

9:11
v. 7

9:14
John 5:9

9:15
v. 10
9:16
Matt 12:2;
John 7:43;
10:19
9:17
v. 15;
Matt 21:11
9:18
v. 22

9 And as He passed by, He saw a man blind from birth.
2 And His disciples asked Him, saying "Rabbi, who sinned, this man or his parents, that he should be born blind?"

3 Jesus answered, "*It was* neither *that* this man sinned, nor his parents; but *it was* in order that the works of God might be displayed in him.

4 "We must work the works of Him who sent Me, as long as it is day; night is coming, when no man can work.

5 "While I am in the world, I am the light of the world."

6 When He had said this, He spat on the ground, and made clay of the spittle, and applied the clay to his eyes,

7 and said to him, "Go, wash in the pool of Siloam" (which is translated, Sent). And so he went away and washed, and came *back* seeing.

8 The neighbors therefore, and those who previously saw him as a beggar, were saying, "Is not this the one who used to sit and beg?"

9 Others were saying, "This is he," *still* others were saying, "No, but he is like him." He kept saying, "I am the one."

10 Therefore they were saying to him, "How then were your eyes opened?"

11 He answered, "The man who is called Jesus made clay, and anointed my eyes, and said to me, 'Go to Siloam, and wash'; so I went away and washed, and I received sight."

12 And they said to him, "Where is He?" He *said, "I do not know."

GG. *The Pharisees question the healed man (9:13–23)*

13 They *brought to the Pharisees him who was formerly blind.

14 Now it was a Sabbath on the day when Jesus made the clay, and opened his eyes.

15 Again, therefore, the Pharisees also were asking him how he received his sight. And he said to them, "He applied clay to my eyes, and I washed, and I see."

16 Therefore some of the Pharisees were saying, "This man is not from God, because He does not keep the Sabbath." But others were saying, "How can a man who is a sinner perform such signs?" And there was a division among them.

17 They *said therefore to the blind man again, "What do you say about Him, since He opened your eyes?" And he said, "He is a prophet."

18 The Jews therefore did not believe *it* of him, that he had been blind, and had

---

8:58 The claim of Jesus that *before Abraham was born, I am* is one of the evidences of His pre-existence. The instant negative reaction of the Jews to His statement makes it apparent that to accept it was to acknowledge the uniqueness of His person. This they were not prepared to do, for then they would have had to worship Him as God.
9:2 The disciples evidently shared the common Jewish belief that sickness was invariably a penalty for sin. But the

fact that this man was blind from birth indicated that personal sin was not the cause of his affliction, and pointed to his parents as the ones responsible. Jesus reiterated what the book of Job had already taught: that sickness is not always the result of sin either by the individual or, as in this case, by his parents. Note that this is the only recorded case in which Jesus healed a person blind from birth.

received sight, until they called the parents of the very one who had received his sight,

19   and questioned them, saying, "Is this your son, who you say was born blind? Then how does he now see?"

20   His parents answered them and said, "We know that this is our son, and that he was born blind;

21   but how he now sees, we do not know; or who opened his eyes, we do not know. Ask him; he is of age, he shall speak for himself."

22   His parents said this because they were afraid of the Jews; for the Jews had already agreed, that if anyone should confess Him to be Christ, he should be put out of the synagogue.

23   For this reason his parents said, "He is of age; ask him."

HH. *The Pharisees question the healed man a second time (9:24–34)*

24   So a second time they called the man who had been blind, and said to him, "Give glory to God; we know that this man is a sinner."

25   He therefore answered, "Whether He is a sinner, I do not know; one thing I do know, that, whereas I was blind, now I see."

26   They said therefore to him, "What did He do to you? How did He open your eyes?"

27   He answered them, "I told you already, and you did not listen; why do you want to hear *it* again? You do not want to become His disciples too, do you?"

28   And they reviled him, and said, "You are His disciple, but we are disciples of Moses.

29   "We know that God has spoken to Moses; but as for this man, we do not know where He is from."

30   The man answered and said to them, "Well, here is an amazing thing, that you do not know where He is from, and *yet* He opened my eyes.

31   "We know that God does not hear sinners; but if anyone is God-fearing, and does His will, He hears him.

32   "Since the beginning of time it has never been heard that anyone opened the eyes of a person born blind.

33   "If this man were not from God, He could do nothing."

34   They answered and said to him, "You were born entirely in sins, and are you teaching us?" And they put him out.

II. *Jesus seeks the outcast (9:35–41)*

35   Jesus heard that they had put him out; and finding him, He said, "Do you believe in the Son of Man?"

36   He answered and said, "And who is He, Lord, that I may believe in Him?"

37   Jesus said to him, "You have both seen Him, and He is the one who is talking with you."

38   And he said, "Lord, I believe." And he worshiped Him.

39   And Jesus said, "For judgment I came into this world, that those who do not see may see; and that those who see may become blind."

40   Those of the Pharisees who were with Him heard these things, and said to Him, "We are not blind too, are we?"

41   Jesus said to them, "If you were blind, you would have no sin; but since you say, 'We see,' your sin remains.

JJ. *Jesus' discourse on the good (true) shepherd (10:1–18)*

10 "Truly, truly, I say to you, he who does not enter by the door into the fold of the sheep, but climbs up some other way, he is a thief and a robber.

2   "But he who enters by the door is a shepherd of the sheep.

Cross references (right margin):

9:22 John 7:13; 12:42; v. 34; Luke 6:22
9:23 v. 21
9:24 Josh 7:19; 1 Sam 6:5; v. 16
9:27 v. 15; John 5:25
9:28 John 5:45
9:29 John 8:14
9:31 Job 27:8,9; Ps 34:15; 66:18; Prov 15:29; 28:9; Is 1:15; Jer 11:11; Zech 7:13
9:33 v. 16
9:34 v. 2
9:35 Matt 14:33; 16:16; Mark 1:1; John 10:36
9:36 Rom 10:14
9:37 John 4:26
9:38 Matt 28:9
9:39 John 5:22,27; 3:19; Matt 13:13; 15:14
9:40 Rom 2:19
9:41 John 15:22,24
10:2 Mark 6:34; vv. 11,12

10:1 The story of the good shepherd is an *allegory*, not a *parable*. An allegory differs from a parable in one essential point, and that is that all the details in an allegory are relevant, whereas the details in a parable, for the most part, are incidental to the main idea. For example, in the parable of the mustard seed (Matt. 13:31,32), the connection between the seed, the tree, and the birds is casual. The main idea is the growth of the kingdom. But in the allegory of the good shepherd each detail is important. Thus Jesus is both the shepherd of the sheep and the door. Only through Him can the sheep enter the kingdom. Jesus, the shepherd, died for the sheep. Those who are not true sheep cannot enter the door. (See also the note to Matt. 13:3 on the definition of a parable.)

John the Baptist announced Christ's coming as the lamb of God.

3 "To him the doorkeeper opens, and the sheep hear his voice, and he calls his own sheep by name, and leads them out.

4 "When he puts forth all his own, he goes before them, and the sheep follow him because they know his voice.

5 "And a stranger they simply will not follow, but will flee from him, because they do not know the voice of strangers."

6 This figure of speech Jesus spoke to them, but they did not understand what those things were which He had been saying to them.

7 Jesus therefore said to them again, "Truly, truly, I say to you, I am the door of the sheep.

8 "All who came before Me are thieves and robbers, but the sheep did not hear them.

9 "I am the door; if anyone enters through Me, he shall be saved, and shall go in and out, and find pasture.

10 "The thief comes only to steal, and kill, and destroy; I came that they might have life, and might have *it* abundantly.

*10:11
Is 40:11;
Ezek 34:11-16,
23;
Heb 13:20;
1 Pet 5:4;
Rev 7:17;
1 John 3:16;
John 15:13

11 "I am the good shepherd; the good shepherd lays down His life for the sheep.

12 "He who is a hireling, and not a shepherd, who is not the owner of the sheep, beholds the wolf coming, and leaves the sheep, and flees, and the wolf snatches them, and scatters *them*.

13 "*He flees* because he is a hireling, and is not concerned about the sheep.

14 "I am the good shepherd; and I know My own, and My own know Me,

15 even as the Father knows Me and I know the Father; and I lay down My life for the sheep.

16 "And I have other sheep, which are not of this fold; I must bring them also, and they shall hear My voice; and they shall become one flock *with* one shepherd.

10:16
Is 56:8;
John 11:52;
Eph 2:14;
1 Pet 2:25
10:17
Is 53:7,8,12
10:18
John 2:19;
15:10;
Heb 5:8

17 "For this reason the Father loves Me, because I lay down My life that I may take it again.

18 "No one [19]has taken it away from Me, but I lay it down on My own initiative. I have authority to lay it down, and I have authority to take it up again. This commandment I received from My Father."

KK. The Jews divided (10:19–21)

The strong reaction was because Christ ate away the basis for their beliefs.

10:19
John 7:43;
9:16
*10:20
John 7:20;
8:48;
Mark 3:21
10:21
John 9:32,33;
Ex 4:11

19 There arose a division again among the Jews because of these words.

20 And many of them were saying, "He has a demon and is insane. Why do you listen to Him?"

21 Others were saying, "These are not the sayings of one demon-possessed. A demon cannot open the eyes of the blind, can he?"

LL. *Jesus the Christ the Son of God (10:22–42)*

22 At that time the Feast of the Dedication took place at Jerusalem;

23 it was winter, and Jesus was walking in the temple in the portico of Solomon.

24 The Jews therefore gathered around Him, and were saying to Him, "How long will You keep us in suspense? If You are the Christ, tell us plainly."

25 Jesus answered them, "I told you, and you do not believe; the works that I do in My Father's name, these bear witness of Me.

26 "But you do not believe, because you are not of My sheep.

27 "My sheep hear My voice, and I know them, and they follow Me;

[19]Many Gr. mss. read *takes*

10:11 Christ is called the *good shepherd* here, the *great Shepherd* (Heb. 13:20), and the *Chief Shepherd* (1 Pet. 5:4). We need not suppose that these words connote different aspects of the shepherd. They present Jesus as the One whose death on Calvary saves the sheep. The *good* shepherd gave His life; the *great* shepherd did the same through the blood of the eternal covenant; the *Chief* shepherd will come again for His sheep.

10:20 The Gospel of John records no instance of Christ's expelling demons. Several times in this Gospel, however, Jesus Himself is accused of having a demon, as one who imagines things (7:20), or as one who speaks wildly and makes extravagant claims (8:48–52), and appears to be insane (10:20,21).

10:22 The Feast of the Dedication was instituted long after the time of Moses. After the desecration of the temple by Antiochus Epiphanes in 168 B.C., Judas Maccabeus recaptured the city and had the sanctuary cleansed of the symbols of idolatry. This feast commemorated the rededication of the temple to God's worship once the defilement had been removed. It was celebrated for eight days in the winter month of *Chislev* (corresponding to December), according to the apocryphal books of the Maccabees. Daniel 11:31 refers to this profanation by Antiochus. Today it is known as Hannukah.

28   and I give eternal life to them, and they shall never perish; and no one shall snatch them out of My hand.

29   "[20]My Father, who has given *them* to Me, is greater than all; and no one is able to snatch *them* out of the Father's hand.

30   "I and the Father are one."

31   The Jews took up stones again to stone Him.

32   Jesus answered them, "I showed you many good works from the Father; for which of them are you stoning Me?"

33   The Jews answered Him, "For a good work we do not stone You, but for blasphemy; and because You, being a man, make Yourself out *to be* God."

34   Jesus answered them, "Has it not been written in your Law, 'I SAID, YOU ARE GODS'?

35   "If he called them gods, to whom the word of God came (and the Scripture cannot be broken),

36   do you say of Him, whom the Father sanctified and sent into the world, 'You are blaspheming,' because I said, 'I am the Son of God'?

37   "If I do not do the works of My Father, do not believe Me;

38   but if I do them, though you do not believe Me, believe the works, that you may know and understand that the Father is in Me, and I in the Father."

39   Therefore they were seeking again to seize Him, and He eluded their grasp.

40   And He went away again beyond the Jordan to the place where John was first baptizing, and He was staying there.

41   And many came to Him and were saying, "While John performed no sign, yet everything John said about this man was true."

42   And many believed in Him there.

MM. *The raising of Lazarus (11:1–57)*

1. *Jesus hears of Lazarus' death (11:1–4)*

11   Now a certain man was sick, Lazarus of Bethany, the village of Mary and her sister Martha.

2   And it was the Mary who anointed the Lord with ointment, and wiped His feet with her hair, whose brother Lazarus was sick.

3   The sisters therefore sent to Him, saying, "Lord, behold, he whom You love is sick."

4   But when Jesus heard it, He said, "This sickness is not unto death, but for the glory of God, that the Son of God may be glorified by it."

2. *Jesus goes to Lazarus' home (11:5–16)*

5   Now Jesus loved Martha, and her sister, and Lazarus.

6   When therefore He heard that he was sick, He stayed then two days *longer* in the place where He was.

7   Then after this He *said to the disciples, "Let us go to Judea again."

8   The disciples *said to Him, "Rabbi, the Jews were just now seeking to stone You, and are You going there again?"

[20]Some early mss. read *What My Father has given Me is greater than all*

Marginal references:
*10:28 John 17:2,3; 1 John 2:25; John 6:37,39
10:29 John 14:28; 17:2,6ff
10:30 John 17:21ff
10:31 John 8:59
10:33 John 5:18
10:34 Ps 82:6
10:36 John 6:69; 3:17; John 5:17,18
10:37 John 15:24
10:38 John 14:10, 11; 17:21
10:39 John 7:30; 8:59
10:40 John 1:28
10:41 John 2:11; 3:30
10:42 John 7:31; 11:45
11:1 Mark 11:1; Luke 10:38
11:2 Mark 14:3; Luke 7:38; John 12:3
11:3 Luke 7:13
11:4 v. 40; John 9:3
11:7 John 10:40
11:8 John 10:31

10:28 God promises eternal life to those who receive Christ (1:12) as Savior by faith (Eph. 2:8,9). True believers may know that they possess eternal life (1 John 5:13). The Greek word *aionios* means "age lasting." Thus eternal life has a beginning but no end. Believers shall never perish. They are kept by God's power through faith (1 Pet. 1:5). This does not mean that believers will never die physically; rather it means that believers will never suffer spiritual death, although their bodies die. The possession of eternal life guarantees to believers a resurrection hope when they will rise in their glorious resurrection bodies, for mortality and corruption must give way to immortality and to incorruption (1 Cor. 15).

10:35 The written Word of God originated in the mind of God, but it was written and compiled by men, humanly speaking. How then did the canon of Scripture come into being? The word *canon* means "rod" or "rule"—a standard of authoritative books containing God's revealed truth. This group of authoritative writings, called the Old Testament,

was recognized as God-given. In Jesus' day, the same books we now have in the Old Testament were accepted as sacred Scripture. Jesus Himself placed His stamp of approval on the Old Testament and embraced it as the Word of God. The New Testament canon developed gradually as the apostles wrote inspired letters to various churches in Asia Minor, Greece, and Rome. Copies of these wonderful letters were made and distributed to other churches. At the same time, of course, the first three Gospels were being written largely to inform new believers of the content of the gospel message that they might be prepared for baptism and for Christian service. Gradually the church of Jesus Christ recognized and accepted as sacred Scripture those books that now appear in the New Testament. Lists of these canonical letters and Gospels were gradually drawn up, perhaps as a safeguard against the spurious apocryphal "gospels" and letters produced by Gnostics and other heretics.

11:9
Luke 13:33;
John 9:4;
12:35

V10 - cf.
John 12:35

11:11
v. 3;
Matt 27:52;
Mark 5:39;
Acts 7:60

11:13
Matt 9:24;
Luke 8:52

V16 - This is the
same impulsive
Thomas
who
denied Christ.
11:16
Matt 10:3;
John 20:24-28

11:17
v. 39

11:18
v. 1
11:19
Job 2:11

11:21
vv. 2,32

V24,27
Martha moved
from belief in
a dogma
to a
belief in
a person
11:22
John 9:31
11:24
Dan 12:2;
John 5:28,29;
Acts 24:15
11:25
John 1:4;
5:26; 14:6;
3:36

John 5:19
The Son
can do nothing
of himself
11:26
John 6:47;
8:51
11:27
Matt 16:16;
John 6:14

11:28
Matt 26:18;
Luke 22:11

11:30
v. 20

11:31
v. 19

11:32
v. 21

"deeply moved" -
Lit. "snort
like a
horse", denoting
anger.
11:33
v. 38;
John 12:27;

11:35
Luke 19:41

11:37
John 9:6,7;
11:38
v. 33;
Matt 27:60;
Mark 15:46;
Luke 24:2;
John 20:1
11:39
v. 17

9 Jesus answered, "Are there not twelve hours in the day? If anyone walks in the day, he does not stumble, because he sees the light of this world."

10 "But if anyone walks in the night, he stumbles, because the light is not in him."

11 This He said, and after that He *said to them, "Our friend Lazarus has fallen asleep; but I go, that I may awaken him out of sleep."

12 The disciples therefore said to Him, "Lord, if he has fallen asleep, he will recover."

13 Now Jesus had spoken of his death, but they thought that He was speaking of literal sleep.

14 Then Jesus therefore said to them plainly, "Lazarus is dead,

15 and I am glad for your sakes that I was not there, so that you may believe; but let us go to him."

16 Thomas therefore, who is called Didymus, said to *his* fellow disciples, "Let us also go, that we may die with Him."

3. Jesus talks with Martha: "the resurrection and the life" (11:17–27)

17 So when Jesus came, He found that he had already been in the tomb four days.

18 Now Bethany was near Jerusalem, about two miles off;

19 and many of the Jews had come to Martha and Mary, to console them concerning *their* brother.

20 Martha therefore, when she heard that Jesus was coming, went to meet Him; but Mary still sat in the house.

21 Martha therefore said to Jesus, "Lord, if You had been here, my brother would not have died.

22 "Even now I know that whatever You ask of God, God will give You."

23 Jesus *said to her, "Your brother shall rise again."

24 Martha *said to Him, "I know that he will rise again in the resurrection on the last day."

25 Jesus said to her, "I am the resurrection and the life; he who believes in Me shall live even if he dies,

26 and everyone who lives and believes in Me shall never die. Do you believe this?"

27 She *said to Him, "Yes, Lord; I have believed that You are the Christ, the Son of God, *even* He who comes into the world."

4. Jesus talks with Mary (11:28–37)

28 And when she had said this, she went away, and called Mary her sister, saying secretly, "The Teacher is here, and is calling for you."

29 And when she heard it, she *arose quickly, and was coming to Him.

30 Now Jesus had not yet come into the village, but was still in the place where Martha met Him.

31 The Jews then who were with her in the house, and consoling her, when they saw that Mary rose up quickly and went out, followed her, supposing that she was going to the tomb to weep there.

32 Therefore, when Mary came where Jesus was, she saw Him, and fell at His feet, saying to Him, "Lord, if You had been here, my brother would not have died."

33 When Jesus therefore saw her weeping, and the Jews who came with her, *also* weeping, He was deeply moved in spirit, and was troubled,

34 and said, "Where have you laid him?" They *said to Him, "Lord, come and see."

35 Jesus wept.

36 And so the Jews were saying, "Behold how He loved him!"

37 But some of them said, "Could not this man, who opened the eyes of him who was blind, have kept this man also from dying?"

5. Jesus raises Lazarus from the dead (11:38–44)

38 Jesus therefore again being deeply moved within, *came to the tomb. Now it was a cave, and a stone was lying against it.

39 Jesus *said, "Remove the stone." Martha, the sister of the deceased, *said

to Him, "Lord, by this time there will be a stench, for he has been *dead* four days."

40 Jesus *said to her, "Did I not say to you, if you believe, you will see the glory of God?"

41 And so they removed the stone. And Jesus raised His eyes, and said, "Father, I thank Thee that Thou heardest Me.

42 "And I knew that Thou hearest Me always; but because of the people standing around I said it, that they may believe that Thou didst send Me."

43 And when He had said these things, He cried out with a loud voice, "Lazarus, come forth."

44 He who had died came forth, bound hand and foot with wrappings; and his face was wrapped around with a cloth. Jesus *said to them, "Unbind him, and let him go."

6. The Pharisees plot to kill Jesus (11:45–57)

45 Many therefore of the Jews, who had come to Mary and beheld what He had done, believed in Him.

46 But some of them went away to the Pharisees, and told them the things which Jesus had done.

47 Therefore the chief priests and the Pharisees convened a council, and were saying, "What are we doing? For this man is performing many signs.

48 "If we let Him *go on* like this, all men will believe in Him, and the Romans will come and take away both our place and our nation."

49 But a certain one of them, Caiaphas, who was high priest that year, said to them, "You know nothing at all,

50 nor do you take into account that it is expedient for you that one man should die for the people, and that the whole nation should not perish."

51 Now this he did not say on his own initiative; but being high priest that year, he prophesied that Jesus was going to die for the nation,

52 and not for the nation only, but that He might also gather together into one the children of God who are scattered abroad.

53 So from that day on they planned together to kill Him.

54 Jesus therefore no longer continued to walk publicly among the Jews, but went away from there to the country near the wilderness, into a city called Ephraim; and there He stayed with the disciples.

55 Now the Passover of the Jews was at hand, and many went up to Jerusalem out of the country before the Passover, to purify themselves.

56 Therefore they were seeking for Jesus, and were saying to one another, as they stood in the temple, "What do you think; that He will not come to the feast at all?"

57 Now the chief priests and the Pharisees had given orders that if anyone knew where He was, he should report it, that they might seize Him.

NN. Jesus anointed by Mary of Bethany
(12:1–11; Matt. 26:6–13; Mark 14:3–9)

12 Jesus, therefore, six days before the Passover, came to Bethany where Lazarus was, whom Jesus had raised from the dead.

2 So they made Him a supper there, and Martha was serving; but Lazarus was one of those reclining *at the table* with Him.

3 Mary therefore took a pound of very costly perfume of pure nard, and anointed the feet of Jesus, and wiped His feet with her hair; and the house was filled with the fragrance of the perfume.

4 But Judas Iscariot, one of His disciples, who was intending to betray Him, *said,

5 "Why was this perfume not sold for [21]three hundred denarii, and given to poor *people*?"

6 Now he said this, not because he was concerned about the poor, but because he was a thief, and as he had the money box, he used to pilfer what was put into it.

7 Jesus therefore said, "Let her alone, in order that she may keep [22]it for the day of My burial.

Marginal references:

- 11:40 vv. 4,23
- 11:41 John 17:1; Matt 11:25
- 11:42 John 12:30; 3:17
- 11:44 John 19:40; 20:7
- 11:45 v. 19; John 2:23
- 11:47 v. 57; Matt 26:3
- 11:49 Matt 26:3; John 18:13,14
- 11:50 John 18:14
- 11:52 Is 49:6; John 10:16
- 11:53 Matt 26:4
- *11:54 John 7:1; 2 Chr 13:19
- 11:55 Matt 26:1,2; Mark 14:1; Luke 22:1; John 12:1; Num 9:10; 2 Chr 30:17, 18
- 11:56 John 7:11
- 12:1 Luke 7:37-39; John 11:55
- 12:2 Luke 10:38
- *12:3 John 11:2; Mark 14:3
- 12:4 John 6:71
- 12:6 John 13:29; Luke 8:3
- 12:7 John 19:40

[21]Equivalent to 11 months' wages   [22]I.e., The custom of anointing for burial

---

11:54 *Ephraim*, a city located north of Jerusalem and possibly east of the Jordan.

12:3 *Mary*, the sister of Martha and Lazarus. (See note to Luke 7:36.)

12:8
Matt 26:11;
Mark 14:7
12:9
Mark 12:37;
Matt 11:43,44

12:11
v. 18;
John 11:45

8   "For the poor you always have with you, but you do not always have Me."

9   The great multitude therefore of the Jews learned that He was there; and they came, not for Jesus' sake only, but that they might also see Lazarus, whom He raised from the dead.

10   But the chief priests took counsel that they might put Lazarus to death also;

11   because on account of him many of the Jews were going away, and were believing in Jesus.

OO. The triumphal entry
(12:12–19; Matt. 21:1–11; Mark 11:1–11; Luke 19:29–44)

12:13
Ps 118:25,26;
John 1:49

12:15
Zech 9:9

12:16
Mark 9:32;
John 2:22;
14:26; 7:39

12   On the next day the great multitude who had come to the feast, when they heard that Jesus was coming to Jerusalem,

13   took the branches of the palm trees, and went out to meet Him, and *began* to cry out, "Hosanna! BLESSED IS HE WHO COMES IN THE NAME OF THE LORD, even the King of Israel."

14   And Jesus, finding a young donkey, sat on it; as it is written,

15   "FEAR NOT, DAUGHTER OF ZION; BEHOLD, YOUR KING IS COMING, SEATED ON A DONKEY'S COLT."

16   These things His disciples did not understand at the first; but when Jesus was glorified, then they remembered that these things were written of Him, and that they had done these things to Him.

17   And so the multitude who were with Him when He called Lazarus out of the tomb, and raised him from the dead, were bearing Him witness.

12:18
v. 11

12:19
John 11:47,48

18   For this cause also the multitude went and met Him, because they heard that He had performed this sign.

19   The Pharisees therefore said to one another, "You see that you are not doing any good; look, the world has gone after Him."

12:20
John 7:35;
Acts 11:20
12:21
John 1:44
12:23
John 13:1,32;
17:1;
Mark 14:35,
41
12:24
1 Cor 15:36
12:25
Matt 10:39;
Mark 8:35;
Luke 9:24;
14:26
12:26
John 14:3;
17:24;
1 Thess 4:17
12:27
Matt 26:38,
39;
Mark 14:34;
John 11:33
12:28
Matt 3:17;
17:5;
Mark 1:11;
9:7;
Luke 3:22;
9:35
12:30
John 11:42
***12:31**
John 16:11;
14:30;
2 Cor 4:4;
Eph 2:2
12:32
John 3:14;
8:28; 6:44
12:33
John 18:32
12:34
Ps 110:4;
Is 9:7;
Ezek 37:25

PP. Christ sought by the Gentiles: His last public discourse
(12:20–36)

20   Now there were certain Greeks among those who were going up to worship at the feast;

21   these therefore came to Philip, who was from Bethsaida of Galilee, and *began to* ask him, saying, "Sir, we wish to see Jesus."

22   Philip *came and *told Andrew; Andrew and Philip *came, and they *told Jesus.

23   And Jesus *answered them, saying, "The hour has come for the Son of Man to be glorified.

24   "Truly, truly, I say to you, unless a grain of wheat falls into the earth and dies, it remains by itself alone; but if it dies, it bears much fruit.

25   "He who loves his life loses it; and he who hates his life in this world shall keep it to life eternal.

26   "If anyone serves Me, let him follow Me; and where I am, there shall My servant also be; if anyone serves Me, the Father will honor him.

27   "Now My soul has become troubled; and what shall I say, 'Father, save Me from this hour'? But for this purpose I came to this hour.

28   "Father, glorify Thy name." There came therefore a voice out of heaven: "I have both glorified it, and will glorify it again."

29   The multitude therefore, who stood by and heard it, were saying that it had thundered; others were saying, "An angel has spoken to Him."

30   Jesus answered and said, "This voice has not come for My sake, but for your sakes.

31   "Now judgment is upon this world; now the ruler of this world shall be cast out.

32   "And I, if I be lifted up from the earth, will draw all men to Myself."

33   But He was saying this to indicate the kind of death by which He was to die.

34   The multitude therefore answered Him, "We have heard out of the Law that the Christ is to remain forever; and how can You say, 'The Son of Man must be lifted up'? Who is this Son of Man?"

12:31 Jesus never disputes the fact that Satan has power over this present evil world. (Compare, for example, Matt. 4:8–10; Luke 4:5–8; John 14:30; 16:11.) Here Jesus proclaims His victory over Satan and the sure end of his earthly reign. Jesus' death (v. 32) not only defeated Satan, but made possible the redemption of man.

35   Jesus therefore said to them, "For a little while longer the light is among you. Walk while you have the light, that darkness may not overtake you; he who walks in the darkness does not know where he goes.

36   "While you have the light, believe in the light, in order that you may become sons of light."

These things Jesus spoke, and He departed and hid Himself from them.

QQ. *The cause of unbelief*
(12:37–43)

37   But though He had performed so many signs before them, *yet* they were not believing in Him;

38   that the word of Isaiah the prophet might be fulfilled, which he spoke, "LORD, WHO HAS BELIEVED OUR REPORT? AND TO WHOM HAS THE ARM OF THE LORD BEEN REVEALED?"

39   For this cause they could not believe, for Isaiah said again,

40   "HE HAS BLINDED THEIR EYES, AND HE HARDENED THEIR HEART; LEST THEY SEE WITH THEIR EYES, AND PERCEIVE WITH THEIR HEART, AND BE CONVERTED, AND I HEAL THEM."

41   These things Isaiah said, because he saw His glory, and he spoke of Him.

42   Nevertheless many even of the rulers believed in Him, but because of the Pharisees they were not confessing *Him*, lest they should be put out of the synagogue;

43   for they loved the approval of men rather than the approval of God.

RR. *A summary of Jesus' claims (12:44–50)*

44   And Jesus cried out and said, "He who believes in Me does not believe in Me, but in Him who sent Me.

45   "And he who beholds Me beholds the One who sent Me.

46   "I have come *as* light into the world, that everyone who believes in Me may not remain in darkness.

47   "And if anyone hears My sayings, and does not keep them, I do not judge him; for I did not come to judge the world, but to save the world.

48   "He who rejects Me, and does not receive My sayings, has one who judges him; the word I spoke is what will judge him at the last day.

49   "For I did not speak on My own initiative, but the Father Himself who sent Me has given Me commandment, what to say, and what to speak.

50   "And I know that His commandment is eternal life; therefore the things I speak, I speak just as the Father has told Me."

III. *Revelation to new Israel: disclosures*
to the disciples (13:1–20:29)

A. *Washing the disciples' feet (13:1–20)*

13 Now before the Feast of the Passover, Jesus knowing that His hour had come that He should depart out of this world to the Father, having loved His own who were in the world, He loved them to the end.

2   And during supper, the devil having already put into the heart of Judas Iscariot, *the son* of Simon, to betray Him,

3   *Jesus*, knowing that the Father had given all things into His hands, and that He had come forth from God, and was going back to God,

4   *rose from supper, and *laid aside His garments; and taking a towel, He girded Himself about.

5   Then He *poured water into the basin, and began to wash the disciples' feet, and to wipe them with the towel with which He was girded.

6   And so He *came to Simon Peter. He *said to Him, "Lord, do You wash my feet?"

7   Jesus answered and said to him, "What I do you do not realize now, but you shall understand hereafter."

8   Peter *said to Him, "Never shall You wash my feet!" Jesus answered him, "If I do not wash you, you have no part with Me."

9   Simon Peter *said to Him, "Lord, not my feet only, but also my hands and my head."

Marginal references

12:35
Eph 5:8

12:36
Luke 16:8;
John 8:59

12:37
John 2:11

12:38
Is 53:1;
Rom 10:16

12:40
Is 6:9,10;
Matt 13:14

12:41
Is 6:1
12:42
John 7:48,13;
9:22

12:43
John 5:44

12:44
Matt 10:40;
John 5:24
12:45
John 14:9
12:46
John 1:4;
3:19; 8:12;
9:5
12:47
John 3:17
12:48
Luke 10:16;
Matt 10:15
12:49
John 14:31
12:50
John 8:28

13:1
John 11:55;
12:23; 16:28

13:2
John 6:70,71;
Mark 14:10
13:3
Matt 28:18;
Heb 2:8;
John 8:42;
16:28
13:4
Luke 22:27
13:5
Luke 7:44

13:8
John 3:5; 9:7

13:10
John 15:3

10 Jesus *said to him, "He who has bathed needs only to wash his feet, but is completely clean; and you are clean, but not all *of you.*"

13:11
John 6:64

11 For He knew the one who was betraying Him; for this reason He said, "Not all of you are clean."

12 And so when He had washed their feet, and taken His garments, and reclined *at the table* again, He said to them, "Do you know what I have done to you?

13:13
Luke 6:46;
Phil 2:11

13 "You call Me Teacher and Lord; and you are right, for *so* I am.

13:14
1 Pet 5:5

14 "If I then, the Lord and the Teacher, washed your feet, you also ought to wash one another's feet.

13:15
1 Pet 2:21

15 "For I gave you an example that you also should do as I did to you.

13:16
Matt 10:24;
Luke 6:40;
John 15:20

16 "Truly, truly, I say to you, a slave is not greater than his master; neither *is* one who is sent greater than the one who sent him.

13:17
Luke 11:28;
James 1:25

17 "If you know these things, you are blessed if you do them.

13:18
Ps 41:9;
Matt 26:23

18 "I do not speak of all of you. I know the ones I have chosen; but *it is* that the Scripture may be fulfilled, 'HE WHO EATS MY BREAD HAS LIFTED UP HIS HEEL AGAINST ME.'

13:19
John 14:29;
16:4; 8:24

19 "From now on I am telling you before *it* comes to pass, so that when it does occur, you may believe that I am *He.*

13:20
Matt 10:40;
Luke 10:16

20 "Truly, truly, I say to you, he who receives whomever I send receives Me; and he who receives Me receives Him who sent Me."

B. *Jesus dismisses Judas Iscariot, His betrayer* (13:21–30; Matt. 26:21–25; Mark 14:18–21; Luke 22:21–23)

13:21
John 12:27

21 When Jesus had said this, He became troubled in spirit, and testified, and said, "Truly, truly, I say to you, that one of you will betray Me."

22 The disciples *began* looking at one another, at a loss *to know* of which one He was speaking.

13:23
John 19:26;
20:2; 21:7,20

23 There was reclining on Jesus' breast one of His disciples, whom Jesus loved.

24 Simon Peter therefore *gestured to him, and *said to him, "Tell *us* who it is of whom He is speaking."

13:25
John 21:20

25 He, leaning back thus on Jesus' breast, *said to Him, "Lord, who is it?"

13:26
John 6:71

26 Jesus therefore *answered, "That is the one for whom I shall dip the morsel and give it to him." So when He had dipped the morsel, He *took and *gave it to Judas, *the son* of Simon Iscariot.

*13:27
Luke 22:3

27 And after the morsel, Satan then entered into him. Jesus therefore *said to him, "What you do, do quickly."

28 Now no one of those reclining *at the table* knew for what purpose He had said this to him.

13:29
John 12:5,6

29 For some were supposing, because Judas had the money box, that Jesus was saying to him, "Buy the things we have need of for the feast"; or else, that he should give something to the poor.

30 And so after receiving the morsel he went out immediately; and it was night.

C. *Jesus announces His departure (13:31–35)*

13:31
John 7:39;
14:13;
1 Pet 4:11

31 When therefore he had gone out, Jesus *said, "Now is the Son of Man glorified, and God is glorified in Him;

13:32
John 17:1

32 if God is glorified in Him, God will also glorify Him in Himself, and will glorify Him immediately.

13:33
John 7:33,34

33 "Little children, I am with you a little while longer. You shall seek Me; and as I said to the Jews, I now say to you also, 'Where I am going, you cannot come.'

13:34
Lev 19:18;
John 15:12;
1 Pet 1:22;
1 John 2:7;
3:11; 4:10

34 "A new commandment I give to you, that you love one another, even as I have loved you, that you also love one another.

13:35
1 John 3:14;
4:20

35 "By this all men will know that you are My disciples, if you have love for one another."

13:27 The devil apparently cannot be in more than one place at one time. The Scriptures do not attribute omnipresence to him, yet the number of fallen angels who do his bidding make him practically ubiquitous. Here, however, the devil himself took possession of the person of Judas Iscariot, making his abode in him, since he had allowed himself to be possessed by the devil. (This is parallel to the experience of true conversion, whereby a repentant believer allows himself to be possessed by the Holy Spirit of Christ.)

D. Peter's denial foretold (13:36–38)

36 Simon Peter *said to Him, "Lord, where are You going?" Jesus answered, "Where I go, you cannot follow Me now; but you shall follow later."

37 Peter *said to Him, "Lord, why can I not follow You right now? I will lay down my life for You."

38 Jesus *answered, "Will you lay down your life for Me? Truly, truly, I say to you, a cock shall not crow, until you deny Me three times.

E. Christ comforts His disciples (14:1–31)

1. The way, and the truth, and the life (14:1–11)

14 "Let not your heart be troubled; [23]believe in God, believe also in Me.
2 "In My Father's house are many dwelling places; if it were not so, I would have told you; for I go to prepare a place for you.

3 "And if I go and prepare a place for you, I will come again, and receive you to Myself; that where I am, *there* you may be also.

4 "[24]And you know the way where I am going."

5 Thomas *said to Him, "Lord, we do not know where You are going, how do we know the way?"

6 Jesus *said to him, "I am the way, and the truth, and the life; no one comes to the Father, but through Me.

7 "If you had known Me, you would have known My Father also; from now on you know Him, and have seen Him."

8 Philip *said to Him, "Lord, show us the Father, and it is enough for us."

9 Jesus *said to him, "Have I been so long with you, and *yet* you have not come to know Me, Philip? He who has seen Me has seen the Father; how do you say, 'Show us the Father'?

10 "Do you not believe that I am in the Father, and the Father is in Me? The words that I say to you I do not speak on My own initiative, but the Father abiding in Me does His works.

11 "Believe Me that I am in the Father, and the Father in Me; otherwise believe on account of the works themselves.

2. The promise of greater works (14:12–14)

12 "Truly, truly, I say to you, he who believes in Me, the works that I do shall he do also; and greater *works* than these shall he do; because I go to the Father.

13 "And whatever you ask in My name, that will I do, that the Father may be glorified in the Son.

14 "If you ask Me anything in My name, I will do *it*.

3. The promise of the Holy Spirit (14:15–24)

15 "If you love Me, you will keep My commandments.

16 "And I will ask the Father, and He will give you another Helper, that He may be with you forever;

17 *that is* the Spirit of truth, whom the world cannot receive, because it does not behold Him or know Him, *but* you know Him because He abides with you, and will be in you.

18 "I will not leave you as orphans; I will come to you.

Marginal references:

13:36 John 21:18; 2 Pet 1:14
13:37 Matt 26:33-35; Mark 14:29-31; Luke 22:33, 34
13:38 John 18:27
14:1 John 16:23,24
14:2 John 13:33
14:3 John 12:26
14:5 John 11:16
14:6 John 10:9; 8:32; 1:4; 11:25
14:7 John 8:19
14:9 John 12:45
14:10 John 10:38; 5:19; 12:49
14:11 John 5:36; 10:38
14:12 Matt 21:21; Luke 10:17
14:13 John 15:7,16; 16:23; James 1:5
14:15 John 15:10; 1 John 5:3
*14:16 John 15:26; 16:7; 1 John 2:1
14:17 John 16:13; 1 John 4:6; 1 Cor 2:14
14:18 vv. 3,28

---

[23]Or, *you believe in God*   [24]Many ancient authorities read *And where I go you know, and the way you know*

14:16 There are five passages in chapters 14–16 that speak of the ministry of the Holy Spirit: 14:15–17; 14:25,26; 15:26,27; 16:7–11; and 16:12–15. In these passages, the Holy Spirit is called *parakletos* four times (14:16,26; 15:26; 16:7), which the NAS translates *Helper* (KJV, "Comforter"). The verb *parakaleo*, from which this noun is formed, means "to encourage," "exhort," "comfort," and the noun *parakletos* itself refers to one who is called upon to intercede in behalf of, or to help, someone. In the only other New Testament passage where *parakletos* occurs (1 John 2:1) it is used of Christ and translated *Advocate*.

In the five passages in the Gospel of John, the Holy Spirit is defined and described both as to origin and as to mission. He is *the Holy Spirit* (14:26); *the Spirit of truth* (14:17; 15:26; 16:13); *another Helper* (14:16); the One who will take the place of Jesus with the disciples (16:7); the One whom the world cannot receive, but the disciples only (14:17). He proceeds from the Father (15:26), and is sent by the Father at Jesus' request (14:16), and in Jesus' name (14:26); alternately, Jesus Himself sends Him from the Father (15:26; 16:7). His ministry as teacher will be: (1) to remain with and in the disciples forever (14:16,17); (2) to teach them all things (14:26) and lead them into all the truth (16:13); (3) to speak, not on His own authority, but as directed by Jesus (16:13–15): He will thus bear witness to Jesus (15:26) and glorify Him (16:14), and remind the disciples of what Jesus taught (14:26); and (4) to announce future things to the disciples (16:13).

His ministry to the world will be that of convincing it of sin, of righteousness, and of judgment (16:8–11).

14:19
John 7:33;
16:16; 6:57

19 "After a little while the world will behold Me no more; but you *will* behold Me; because I live, you shall live also.

14:20
John 10:38

20 "In that day you shall know that I am in My Father, and you in Me, and I in you.

14:21
1 John 2:5;
5:3

21 "He who has My commandments and keeps them, he it is who loves Me; and he who loves Me shall be loved by My Father, and I will love him, and will disclose Myself to him."

14:22
Acts 1:13;
10:14,41

22 Judas (not Iscariot) *said to Him, "Lord, what then has happened that You are going to disclose Yourself to us, and not to the world?"

14:23
1 John 2:24;
Rev 3:20

23 Jesus answered and said to him, "If anyone loves Me, he will keep My word; and My Father will love him, and We will come to him, and make Our abode with him.

14:24
John 7:16;
8:28; 12:49

24 "He who does not love Me does not keep My words; and the word which you hear is not Mine, but the Father's who sent Me.

4. The promise of peace (14:25–31)

25 "These things I have spoken to you, while abiding with you.

14:26
John 15:26;
16:7,13;
1 John 2:20,
27

26 "But the Helper, the Holy Spirit, whom the Father will send in My name, He will teach you all things, and bring to your remembrance all that I said to you.

14:27
John 16:33;
Phil 4:7;
Col 3:15

27 "Peace I leave with you; My peace I give to you; not as the world gives, do I give to you. Let not your heart be troubled, nor let it be fearful.

14:28
vv. 3,18;
John 5:18;
10:29,30;
Phil 2:6

28 "You heard that I said to you, 'I go away, and I will come to you.' If you loved Me, you would have rejoiced, because I go to the Father; for the Father is greater than I.

29 "And now I have told you before it comes to pass, that when it comes to pass, you may believe.

14:29
John 13:19

14:30
John 12:31

30 "I will not speak much more with you, for the ruler of the world is coming, and he has nothing in Me;

14:31
John 10:18;
12:49; 18:1

31 but that the world may know that I love the Father, and as the Father gave Me commandment, even so I do. Arise, let us go from here.

F. Christel the true vine (15:1–17)

15:1
Is 5:1-7;
Ezek 19:10

15 "I am the true vine, and My Father is the vinedresser.
2 "Every branch in Me that does not bear fruit, He takes away; and every *branch* that bears fruit, He 25 prunes it, that it may bear more fruit.

15:3
John 13:10;
17:17;
Eph 5:26

3 "You are already clean because of the word which I have spoken to you.

15:4
1 John 2:6

4 "Abide in Me, and I in you. As the branch cannot bear fruit of itself, unless it abides in the vine, so neither *can* you, unless you abide in Me.

15:5
v. 16

5 "I am the vine, you are the branches; he who abides in Me, and I in him, he bears much fruit; for apart from Me you can do nothing.

15:6
v. 2

6 "If anyone does not abide in Me, he is thrown away as a branch, and dries up; and they gather them, and cast them into the fire, and they are burned.

15:7
John 14:13;
16:23

7 "If you abide in Me, and My words abide in you, ask whatever you wish, and it shall be done for you.

15:8
Matt 5:16;
John 8:31

8 "By this is My Father glorified, that you bear much fruit, and *so* prove to be My disciples.

9 "Just as the Father has loved Me, I have also loved you; abide in My love.

15:10
John 14:15,23

10 "If you keep My commandments, you will abide in My love; just as I have kept My Father's commandments, and abide in His love.

15:11
John 17:13

11 "These things I have spoken to you, that My joy may be in you, and *that* your joy may be made full.

15:12
John 13:34

12 "This is My commandment, that you love one another, just as I have loved you.

25 Lit., *cleanses*

15:2 Fruit-bearing is the normal product of regeneration. To be fruitless is abnormal and suggests the possiblity of a spurious conversion experience. Christ's statement that fruitless branches shall be removed is in line with James's statement that faith without works is a dead faith (James 2:26). At the same time Christ also makes it clear that *fruit* is not the final purpose of the believer's life, but rather a joyous and loving fellowship with God Himself. Nevertheless God purges the fruit-bearing Christian (painful though it may be) so that he becomes more fruitful.

15:9 Four relationships of love are expressed here: (1) the Father loves the Son; (2) the Son uses His Father's love for Him as a pattern of His love for the disciples (*as the Father has loved Me, I have also loved you*); the measure of His love is expressed by His death for those He loves (15:13); (3) His disciples are to love Him and to abide in His love (15:10); and (4) the disciples are likewise to love one another (15:17). Elsewhere, Scripture speaks of Christ's love for His church (Eph. 5:25) and affirms that nothing shall separate believers from His love (Rom. 8:38–39).

13 "Greater love has no one than this, that one lay down his life for his friends.

14 "You are My friends, if you do what I command you.

15 "No longer do I call you slaves, for the slave does not know what his master is doing; but I have called you friends, for all things that I have heard from My Father I have made known to you.

16 "You did not choose Me, but I chose you, and appointed you, that you should go and bear fruit, and *that* your fruit should remain, that whatever you ask of the Father in My name, He may give to you.

17 "This I command you, that you love one another.

G. The hatred of the world (15:18–16:4)

18 "If the world hates you, you know that it has hated Me before *it hated* you.

19 "If you were of the world, the world would love its own; but because you are not of the world, but I chose you out of the world, therefore the world hates you.

20 "Remember the word that I said to you, 'A slave is not greater than his master.' If they persecuted Me, they will also persecute you; if they kept My word, they will keep yours also.

21 "But all these things they will do to you for My name's sake, because they do not know the One who sent Me.

22 "If I had not come and spoken to them, they would not have sin, but now they have no excuse for their sin.

23 "He who hates Me hates My Father also.

24 "If I had not done among them the works which no one else did, they would not have sin; but now they have both seen and hated Me and My Father as well.

25 "But *they have done this* in order that the word may be fulfilled that is written in their Law, 'THEY HATED ME WITHOUT A CAUSE.'

26 "When the Helper comes, whom I will send to you from the Father, *that is* the Spirit of truth, who proceeds from the Father, He will bear witness of Me,

27 and you *will* bear witness also, because you have been with Me from the beginning.

16 "These things I have spoken to you, that you may be kept from stumbling.

2 "They will make you outcasts from the synagogue, but an hour is coming for everyone who kills you to think that he is offering service to God.

3 "And these things they will do, because they have not known the Father, or Me.

4 "But these things I have spoken to you, that when their hour comes, you may remember that I told you of them. And these things I did not say to you at the beginning, because I was with you.

H. The departure of Jesus and the coming of the Holy Spirit (16:5–11)

5 "But now I am going to Him who sent Me; and none of you asks Me, 'Where are You going?'

6 "But because I have said these things to you, sorrow has filled your heart.

7 "But I tell you the truth, it is to your advantage that I go away; for if I do not go away, the Helper shall not come to you; but if I go, I will send Him to you.

8 "And He, when He comes, will convict the world concerning sin, and righteousness, and judgment;

9 concerning sin, because they do not believe in Me;

10 and concerning righteousness, because I go to the Father, and you no longer behold Me;

11 and concerning judgment, because the ruler of this world has been judged.

I. The illuminating power of the Holy Spirit (16:12–15)

12 "I have many more things to say to you, but you cannot bear *them* now.

15:13 Rom 5:7,8; John 10:11
15:14 Matt 12:50
15:15 John 8:26
15:16 John 6:70; 14:13
15:17 v. 12
15:18 1 John 3:13
15:19 John 17:14
15:20 Matt 10:24; Luke 6:40; John 13:16
15:21 Matt 12:24; Luke 6:40; John 13:16
15:22 John 9:41; Rom 1:20
15:23 1 John 2:23
15:24 John 5:36
15:25 Ps 35:19; 69:4
15:26 John 14:16, 17,26; 1 John 2:1; 5:7
15:27 Luke 24:48; Acts 2:32; 3:15; 5:32; 10:39; 13:31; 1 John 4:14
16:1 John 15:18-27;
16:2 John 9:22; Acts 26:9,10; Is 66:5; Rev 6:9
16:3 John 15:21; 17:25; 1 John 3:1
16:4 John 13:19; 15:27
16:5 John 7:33; 13:36; 14:5
16:7 John 7:39; 14:16,26; 15:26
16:9 John 15:22
16:10 Acts 3:14; 7:52; 17:31; 1 Pet 3:18
16:11 John 12:31
***16:12** Mark 4:33

16:8 The Holy Spirit's ministry to the world is defined as that of convincing the world of sin, of righteousness, and of judgment: (1) of sin, which is defined basically as the refusal to accept Jesus and His message; (2) of righteousness, inasmuch as the death of Jesus was not the shameful defeat on the cross, but the return of the resurrected Jesus to the Father by which His mission and message were vindicated and shown to be true; and (3) of judgment, for the ministry, death, and resurrection of Jesus were the means whereby God condemned the evil ruler of this present age. **16:12** God's revelation is progressive. Christ revealed to the disciples only what they were then ready to receive and

16:13 John 14:17,26	13 "But when He, the Spirit of truth, comes, He will guide you into all the truth; for He will not speak on His own initiative, but whatever He hears, He will speak; and He will disclose to you what is to come.
16:14 John 7:39 **16:15** John 17:10	14 "He shall glorify Me; for He shall take of Mine, and shall disclose *it* to you. 15 "All things that the Father has are Mine; therefore I said, that He takes of Mine, and will disclose *it* to you.

J. *Jesus' farewell to His disciples (16:16–33)*

16:16 John 7:33; 14:18-24; 13:3 **16:17** vv. 16,5	16 "A little while, and you will no longer behold Me; and again a little while, and you will see Me." 17 *Some* of His disciples therefore said to one another, "What is this thing He is telling us, 'A little while, and you will not behold Me; and again a little while, and you will see Me'; and, 'because I go to the Father'?"
	18 And so they were saying, "What is this that He says, 'A little while'? We do not know what He is talking about."
16:19 Mark 9:32	19 Jesus knew that they wished to question Him, and He said to them, "Are you deliberating together about this, that I said, 'A little while, and you will not behold Me, and again a little while, and you will see Me'?
16:20 Luke 23:27; John 20:20	20 "Truly, truly, I say to you, that you will weep and lament, but the world will rejoice; you will be sorrowful, but your sorrow will be turned to joy.
16:21 1 Thess 5:3	21 "Whenever a woman is in travail she has sorrow, because her hour has come; but when she gives birth to the child, she remembers the anguish no more, for joy that a child has been born into the world.
16:22 vv. 6,16	22 "Therefore you too now have sorrow; but I will see you again, and your heart will rejoice, and no one takes your joy away from you.
16:23 Matt 7:7; John 14:13; 15:16 **16:24** John 15:11	23 "And in that day you will ask Me no question. Truly, truly, I say to you, if you shall ask the Father for anything, He will give it to you in My name. 24 "Until now you have asked for nothing in My name; ask, and you will receive, that your joy may be made full.
16:25 John 10:6; Matt 13:34	25 "These things I have spoken to you in figurative language; an hour is coming when I will speak no more to you in figurative language, but will tell you plainly of the Father.
	26 "In that day you will ask in My name, and I do not say to you that I will request the Father on your behalf;
16:27 John 14:21,23	27 for the Father Himself loves you, because you have loved Me, and have believed that I came forth from the Father.
16:28 John 13:3	28 "I came forth from the Father, and have come into the world; I am leaving the world again, and going to the Father."
16:29 v. 25	29 His disciples *said, "Lo, now You are speaking plainly, and are not using a figure of speech.
16:30 John 8:42	30 "Now we know that You know all things, and have no need for anyone to question You; by this we believe that You came from God."
	31 Jesus answered them, "Do you now believe?
16:32 Matt 26:31; Mark 14:27 ***16:33** John 14:27; Col 1:20; Rom 8:37; Rev 3:21	32 "Behold, an hour is coming, and has *already* come, for you to be scattered, each to his own *home*, and to leave Me alone; and *yet* I am not alone, because the Father is with Me. 33 "These things I have spoken to you, that in Me you may have peace. In the world you have tribulation, but take courage; I have overcome the world."

---

understand. But He told them to expect further revelation after His ascension at the coming of the Holy Spirit, and to accept this revelation as the Word of God. We may reasonably infer that this promise applies to the additional revealed truths contained in the New Testament.

16:33 The problem of suffering in the Old Testament is dealt with most fully in the book of Job. In the New Testament, Christ promised His people tribulation (from the Greek word, *thlipsis*, meaning "pressure" or "affliction"). Believers must be careful to distinguish the different forms of pressure and realize the sources from which they come. In general, there are three orders of affliction: (1) that which comes simply because we are alive and share in the fallen nature of the human race (experiences like natural catastrophe, sickness, bereavement, and death); (2) afflictions that (by God's permission) come to us from the malice of Satan because we have been delivered from his power and he strives to bring us back under bondage (1 Pet. 5:8); and (3) afflictions that come more directly from the hand of God Himself and are designed to purify or refine us (Job 23:10). These often overlap. Thus God can and does use the afflictions in the first two categories to accomplish His work in us. Yet Christians should be careful to avoid attributing to God, or even to Satan, that which they bring on themselves. Afflictions resulting from our own folly we must face up to as our personal responsibility.

K. *Christ's intercessory (high priestly) prayer (17:1–26)*

1. *The prayer to be glorified (17:1–5)*

17 These things Jesus spoke; and lifting up His eyes to heaven, He said, "Father, the hour has come; glorify Thy Son, that the Son may glorify Thee,

2 even as Thou gavest Him authority over all mankind, that to all whom Thou hast given Him, He may give eternal life.

3 "And this is eternal life, that they may know Thee, the only true God, and Jesus Christ whom Thou hast sent.

4 "I glorified Thee on the earth, having accomplished the work which Thou hast given Me to do.

5 "And now, glorify Thou Me together with Thyself, Father, with the glory which I had with Thee before the world was.

2. *The prayer for the disciples (17:6–19)*

6 "I manifested Thy name to the men whom Thou gavest Me out of the world; Thine they were, and Thou gavest them to Me, and they have kept Thy word.

7 "Now they have come to know that everything Thou hast given Me is from Thee;

8 for the words which Thou gavest Me I have given to them; and they received *them*, and truly understood that I came forth from Thee, and they believed that Thou didst send Me.

9 "I ask on their behalf; I do not ask on behalf of the world, but of those whom Thou hast given Me; for they are Thine;

10 and all things that are Mine are Thine, and Thine are Mine; and I have been glorified in them.

11 "And I am no more in the world; and *yet* they themselves are in the world, and I come to Thee. Holy Father, keep them in Thy name, *the name* which Thou hast given Me, that they may be one, even as We *are*.

12 "While I was with them, I was keeping them in Thy name which Thou hast given Me; and I guarded them, and not one of them perished but the son of perdition, that the Scripture might be fulfilled.

13 "But now I come to Thee; and these things I speak in the world, that they may have My joy made full in themselves.

14 "I have given them Thy word; and the world has hated them, because they are not of the world, even as I am not of the world.

15 "I do not ask Thee to take them out of the world, but to keep them from the evil *one*.

16 "They are not of the world, even as I am not of the world.

17 "Sanctify them in the truth; Thy word is truth.

18 "As Thou didst send Me into the world, I also have sent them into the world.

19 "And for their sakes I sanctify Myself, that they themselves also may be sanctified in truth.

3. *The prayer for the church (17:20–26)*

20 "I do not ask in behalf of these alone, but for those also who believe in Me through their word;

21 that they may all be one; even as Thou, Father, *art* in Me, and I in Thee, that they also may be in Us; that the world may believe that Thou didst send Me.

22 "And the glory which Thou hast given Me I have given to them; that they may be one, just as We are one;

Marginal references:

17:1 John 12:23; 13:32 — v. 3
17:2 Dan 7:14; Heb 2:8; John 6:37 — Def of eternal life
17:3 John 5:44; 3:34; 6:29,57
17:4 John 13:31; 4:34; 14:31 — v.5 glory, Rom 1:20–23
17:5 John 1:1; Phil 2:6
17:6 John 6:37,39
17:8 John 8:28; 16:27 — v.8 Christ came from God.
17:9 Luke 22:32; John 14:16
17:10 John 16:15
17:11 John 13:1; 7:33; Rev 19:12; John 10:30 — v11 Christ & the Father are one
17:12 Heb 2:13; John 6:39; 18:9; 6:70
17:14 John 15:19; 8:23
17:15 Matt 6:13
17:16 v. 14
17:17 John 15:3
17:18 John 20:21
17:19 John 15:13
*17:21 John 10:38
17:22 John 14:20

17:21 The communion of saints is a central theme in this high-priestly prayer of Christ. It is His will that His people be organically united with one another in life and experience as they are united in Him in spirit. The communion of saints consists in: (1) fellowship with the Father and the Son through the Spirit (1 John 1:3); (2) fellow-citizenship with the saints already in glory (Heb. 12:22–24); and (3) fellowship with other believers here on earth (Gal. 2:9; 1 John 1:3). This organic unity, whereby all regenerate believers belong to the mystical body of Christ, is here envisioned as a glorious spiritual reality to be brought to pass immediately by the cross, the resurrection, and the bestowal of the Spirit. Because of their spiritual solidarity in Christ, the saints partake of both privileges and obligations. On the one hand they enjoy a bond of fellowship far closer than blood. As Christ said (Mark 10:29–30), " . . . *there is no one who has left house or brothers or sisters or mother or father or children or farms, for My sake and for the gospel's sake, but that he shall receive a hundred times as much now in the present age, houses and brothers and sisters and mothers and children and farms, along with persecutions; and in the age to come, eternal life.*" On the other hand, the saints are under obligation to (1) pray for one another (2 Cor. 1:11; Eph. 6:18); (2) exhort one another (Col. 3:16; Heb. 10:25); and (3) comfort and edify one another (1 Thess. 4:18; 5:11). The unity of the saints is expressed in public worship and in the ordinances (or sacraments) of baptism and the Lord's Supper.

23   I in them, and Thou in Me, that they may be perfected in unity, that the world may know that Thou didst send Me, and didst love them, even as Thou didst love Me.

17:24
John 12:26;
Matt 25:34;
v. 5

24   "Father, I desire that they also, whom Thou hast given Me, be with Me where I am, in order that they may behold My glory, which Thou hast given Me; for Thou didst love Me before the foundation of the world.

17:25
John 15:21;
16:3; 7:29;
John 16:27

25   "O righteous Father, although the world has not known Thee, yet I have known Thee; and these have known that Thou didst send Me;

17:26
v. 6;
John 15:9

26   and I have made Thy name known to them, and will make it known; that the love wherewith Thou didst love Me may be in them, and I in them."

L. *Jesus' betrayal and arrest*
(18:1–11; Matt. 26:47–56; Mark 14:43–50; Luke 22:27–53)

18:1
2 Sam 15:23

18 When Jesus had spoken these words, He went forth with His disciples over the ravine of the Kidron, where there was a garden, into which He Himself entered, and His disciples.

18:2
Luke 21:37;
22:39

2   Now Judas also, who was betraying Him, knew the place; for Jesus had often met there with His disciples.

18:3
Acts 1:16

3   Judas then, having received the *Roman* cohort, and officers from the chief priests and the Pharisees, *came there with lanterns and torches and weapons.

18:4
John 6:64;
13:1,11; v. 7

4   Jesus therefore, knowing all the things that were coming upon Him, went forth, and *said to them, "Whom do you seek?"

5   They answered Him, "Jesus the Nazarene." He *said to them, "I am *He*." And Judas also who was betraying Him, was standing with them.

6   When therefore He said to them, "I am *He*," they drew back, and fell to the ground.

18:7
v. 4

7   Again therefore He asked them, "Whom do you seek?" And they said, "Jesus the Nazarene."

8   Jesus answered, "I told you that I am *He*; if therefore you seek Me, let these go their way,"

18:9
John 17:12

9   that the word might be fulfilled which He spoke, "Of those whom Thou hast given Me I lost not one."

10   Simon Peter therefore having a sword, drew it, and struck the high priest's slave, and cut off his right ear; and the slave's name was Malchus.

18:11
Matt 20:22

11   Jesus therefore said to Peter, "Put the sword into the sheath; the cup which the Father has given Me, shall I not drink it?"

M. *Jesus before the Jewish authorities*
(18:12–14; see vv. 19–24)

12   So the *Roman* cohort and the commander, and the officers of the Jews, arrested Jesus and bound Him,

18:13
Matt 26:57;
Mark 14:53;
Luke 22:54

13   and led Him to Annas first; for he was father-in-law of Caiaphas, who was high priest that year.

18:14
John 11:49-51

14   Now Caiaphas was the one who had advised the Jews that it was expedient for one man to die on behalf of the people.

N. *Peter's denial of Jesus* (18:15–18; vv. 25–27; Matt. 26:69–75;
Mark 14:66–72; Luke 22:55–62)

*18:15
Matt 26:58;
Mark 14:54;
Luke 22:54

15   And Simon Peter was following Jesus, and *so was* another disciple. Now that disciple was known to the high priest, and entered with Jesus into the court of the high priest,

16   but Peter was standing at the door outside. So the other disciple, who was known to the high priest, went out and spoke to the doorkeeper, and brought in Peter.

18:17
v. 25

17   The slave-girl therefore who kept the door *said to Peter, "You are not also *one* of this man's disciples, are you?" He *said, "I am not."

18:18
Mark 14:54,
67; John 21:9

18   Now the slaves and the officers were standing *there*, having made a charcoal fire, for it was cold and they were warming themselves; and Peter also was with them, standing and warming himself.

18:10 Only in John's Gospel is it recorded that it was Peter who cut off the ear of the high priest's servant. Matthew 26:51 and Mark 14:47 simply indicate that it was "one of them." Luke 22:50 does say *one of them*.

18:15 See note to Mark 14:71 on Peter's denial of Christ.

O. Jesus before the Jewish authorities
(18:19–27; see vv. 12–14)

19   The high priest therefore questioned Jesus about His disciples, and about His teaching.

20   Jesus answered him, "I have spoken openly to the world; I always taught in synagogues, and in the temple, where all the Jews come together; and I spoke nothing in secret.

21   "Why do you question Me? Question those who have heard what I spoke to them; behold, these know what I said."

22   And when He had said this, one of the officers standing by gave Jesus a blow, saying, "Is that the way You answer the high priest?"

23   Jesus answered him, "If I have spoken wrongly, bear witness of the wrong; but if rightly, why do you strike Me?"

24   Annas therefore sent Him bound to Caiaphas the high priest.

25   Now Simon Peter was standing and warming himself. They said therefore to him, "You are not also *one* of His disciples, are you?" He denied *it*, and said, "I am not."

26   One of the slaves of the high priest, being a relative of the one whose ear Peter cut off, *said, "Did I not see you in the garden with Him?"

27   Peter therefore denied *it* again; and immediately a cock crowed.

P. Jesus before Pontius Pilate
(18:28–19:16; Matt. 27:11–16; Mark 15:2–15; Luke 23:3–25)

1. Pilate demands the indictment (18:28–32)

28   They *led Jesus therefore from Caiaphas into the [26]Praetorium, and it was early; and they themselves did not enter into the Praetorium in order that they might not be defiled, but might eat the Passover.

29   Pilate therefore went out to them, and *said, "What accusation do you bring against this Man?"

30   They answered and said to him, "If this Man were not an evildoer, we would not have delivered Him up to you."

31   Pilate therefore said to them, "Take Him yourselves, and judge Him according to your law." The Jews said to him, "We are not permitted to put anyone to death,"

32   that the word of Jesus might be fulfilled, which He spoke, signifying by what kind of death He was about to die.

2. Pilate's first questioning of Jesus (18:33–38)

33   Pilate therefore entered again into the [26]Praetorium, and summoned Jesus, and said to Him, "Are You the King of the Jews?"

34   Jesus answered, "Are you saying this on your own initiative, or did others tell you about Me?"

35   Pilate answered, "I am not a Jew, am I? Your own nation and the chief priests delivered You up to me; what have You done?"

36   Jesus answered, "My kingdom is not of this world. If My kingdom were of

---

Cross references (right margin):

18:19 Matt 26:59-68; Mark 14:55-65; Luke 22:63-71
18:20 Matt 26:55; John 7:26
18:22 v. 3; John 19:3
18:23 Matt 5:39; Acts 23:2-5
*18:24 v. 13
18:25 v. 18
18:26 v. 10
18:27 John 13:38
18:28 Matt 27:1,2; Mark 15:1; Luke 23:1; John 11:55; Acts 11:3
*18:32 Matt 20:19; John 12:32,33
*18:33 vv. 28,29; John 19:9; Luke 23:3
*18:36 Matt 26:53; Luke 17:21; John 6:15

---

[26] I.e., governor's official residence

18:24 See note to Matt. 26:57 on Caiaphas, the high priest.
18:29 See note to Mark 15:1 on Pontius Pilate.
18:32 The Jewish method of execution was by stoning (cf. 8:5; Acts 7:58,59). But Jesus had said that He would be *lifted up* (3:14; 8:28; 12:32,34), which the evangelist here interprets as a prediction of His crucifixion, whereby He was lifted up from the earth.
18:33 *Praetorium*, official quarters of Pontius Pilate, praetorian guards, and high court officers. Jesus was crowned with thorns in the Praetorium (Mark 15:16,17).
18:36 Christ is King, but His kingdom is not of this present world system. His is a spiritual and eternal kingdom. According to the interpretation of many, the one-thousand-year reign spoken of in Rev. 20:4 refers to a future complete domination of Christ over the world. Although Christ did not come into the world in order to condemn mankind (3:17), His ultimate purpose is to impose God's judgment on the unrepentant and rebellious world system

and to wrest the control of world affairs from the grasp of Satan, who constantly aspires to become (for the present) the ruler of this world (12:31). Implicit in the kingship of Christ are three necessary elements: (1) He must have absolute sovereignty; (2) He must have a people to rule over; and (3) He must have a definite territory under His domain. In a spiritual sense, Christ has all of these now. He is seated at the right hand of the Father (Acts 2:34; Heb. 1:3; Rev. 3:21); in His church He certainly has a people to rule over; and the Father has committed to Him all authority in heaven and on earth (Matt. 28:18). In the plan of God it was never intended that Christ should set up an earthly kingdom during His first advent; apart from the cross He could not have been the *Lamb who has been slain* (Rev. 13:8), nor could He have taken away the *sin of the world* (1:29). He came the first time in humiliation to die on Calvary. He will come the second time in visible glory and irresistible power as *KING OF KINGS* (Rev. 19:16), Lord of the whole

this world, then My servants would be fighting, that I might not be delivered up to the Jews; but as it is, My kingdom is not [27]of this realm."

18:37
John 8:47;
1 John 3:19;
4:6

37 Pilate therefore said to Him, "So You are a king?" Jesus answered, "You say *correctly* that I am a king. For this I have been born, and for this I have come into the world, to bear witness to the truth. Everyone who is of the truth hears My voice."

18:38
John 19:4,6

38 Pilate *said to Him, "What is truth?"

And when he had said this, he went out again to the Jews, and *said to them, "I find no guilt in Him.

3. *The people demand Barabbas (18:39–40)*

18:39
Matt 27:15-18,
20-23;
Mark 15:6-15;
Luke 23:18-25
18:40
Acts 3:14

39 "But you have a custom, that I should release someone for you at the Passover; do you wish then that I release for you the King of the Jews?"
40 Therefore they cried out again, saying, "Not this Man, but Barabbas." Now Barabbas was a robber.

4. *Pilate scourges Jesus, and questions Him again (19:1–11)*

19:1
Matt 27:26
19:2
Matt 27:27-30;
Mark 15:16-19
19:3
John 18:22

19 Then Pilate therefore took Jesus, and scourged Him.
2 And the soldiers wove a crown of thorns and put it on His head, and arrayed Him in a purple robe;
3 and they *began* to come up to Him, and say, "Hail, King of the Jews!" and to give Him blows *in the face*.

19:4
v. 6;
John 18:38
19:5
v. 2

4 And Pilate came out again, and *said to them, "Behold, I am bringing Him out to you, that you may know that I find no guilt in Him."
5 Jesus therefore came out, wearing the crown of thorns and the purple robe. And *Pilate* *said to them, "Behold, the Man!"

19:6
Acts 3:13

6 When therefore the chief priests and the officers saw Him, they cried out, saying, "Crucify, crucify!" Pilate *said to them, "Take Him yourselves, and crucify Him, for I find no guilt in Him."

19:7
Lev 24:16;
Matt 26:63-66;
John 5:18;
10:33
19:9
Is 53:7;
Matt 27:12,14

7 The Jews answered him, "We have a law, and by that law He ought to die because He made Himself out *to be* the Son of God."
8 When Pilate therefore heard this statement, he was the more afraid;
9 and he entered into the [28]Praetorium again, and *said to Jesus, "Where are You from?" But Jesus gave him no answer.
10 Pilate therefore *said to Him, "You do not speak to me? Do You not know that I have authority to release You, and I have authority to crucify You?"

***19:11**
Rom 13:11;
John 18:28ff

11 Jesus answered, "You would have no authority over Me, unless it had been given you from above; for this reason he who delivered Me up to you has *the* greater sin."

5. *Pilate delivers Jesus (19:12–16)*

19:12
Luke 23:2

12 As a result of this Pilate made efforts to release Him, but the Jews cried out, saying, "If you release this Man, you are no friend of Caesar; everyone who makes himself out *to be* a king opposes Caesar."

19:13
Matt 27:19

13 When Pilate therefore heard these words, he brought Jesus out, and sat down on the judgment seat at a place called The Pavement, but in Hebrew, Gabbatha.

19:14
Matt 27:62;
Mark 15:25;
vv. 19,21

14 Now it was the day of preparation for the Passover; it was about the [29] sixth hour. And he *said to the Jews, "Behold, your King!"
15 They therefore cried out, "Away with *Him*, away with *Him*, crucify Him!" Pilate *said to them, "Shall I crucify your King?" The chief priests answered, "We have no king but Caesar."

19:16
Matt 27:26;
Mark 15:15;
Luke 23:25

16 So he then delivered Him to them to be crucified.

---

[27]Lit., *from here*   [28]I.e., governor's official residence   [29]Perhaps 6 a.m. (Roman time)

universe (Phil. 2:10,11).
19:11 *he who delivered Me up to you.* This is taken by some to allude to Caiaphas, the high priest under whose leadership the Jews *delivered (paradidomi, handed . . . over,* 18:30,

35) Jesus to Pilate. Caiaphas was thus ultimately responsible for Jesus' arrest and condemnation (18:14,28). Others refer the saying to Judas, who *delivered (paradidomi, betrayed,* 6:64,71; 12:4; 13:2,11,21; 18:2,5) Jesus.

Q. The crucifixion and burial of Jesus (19:17–42)

1. Jesus crucified
(19:17–27; Matt. 27:32–44; Mark 15:21–32; Luke 23:32–43)

17 They took Jesus therefore, and He went out, bearing His own cross, to the place called the Place of a Skull, which is called in Hebrew, Golgotha.

18 There they crucified Him, and with Him two other men, one on either side, and Jesus in between.

19 And Pilate wrote an inscription also, and put it on the cross. And it was written, "JESUS THE NAZARENE, THE KING OF THE JEWS."

20 Therefore this inscription many of the Jews read, for the place where Jesus was crucified was near the city; and it was written in Hebrew, Latin, *and* in Greek.

21 And so the chief priests of the Jews were saying to Pilate, "Do not write, 'The King of the Jews'; but that He said, 'I am King of the Jews.'"

22 Pilate answered, "What I have written I have written."

23 The soldiers therefore, when they had crucified Jesus, took His outer garments and made four parts, a part to every soldier and *also* the [30]tunic; now the tunic was seamless, woven in one piece.

24 They said therefore to one another, "Let us not tear it, but cast lots for it, *to decide* whose it shall be"; that the Scripture might be fulfilled, "THEY DIVIDED MY OUTER GARMENTS AMONG THEM, AND FOR MY CLOTHING THEY CAST LOTS."

25 Therefore the soldiers did these things. But there were standing by the cross of Jesus His mother, and His mother's sister, Mary the *wife* of Clopas, and Mary Magdalene.

26 When Jesus therefore saw His mother, and the disciple whom He loved standing nearby, He *said to His mother, "Woman, behold, your son!"

27 Then He *said to the disciple, "Behold, your mother!" And from that hour the disciple took her into his own *household.*

2. The death of Jesus
(19:28–37; Matt. 27:45–50; Mark 15:33–41; Luke 23:44–49)

28 After this, Jesus, knowing that all things had already been accomplished, in order that the Scripture might be fulfilled, *said, "I am thirsty."

29 A jar full of sour wine was standing there; so they put a sponge full of the sour wine upon *a branch of* hyssop, and brought it up to His mouth.

30 When Jesus therefore had received the sour wine, He said, "It is finished!" And He bowed His head, and gave up His spirit.

31 The Jews therefore, because it was the day of preparation, so that the bodies should not remain on the cross on the Sabbath (for that Sabbath was a high *day*), asked Pilate that their legs might be broken, and *that* they might be taken away.

32 The soldiers therefore came, and broke the legs of the first man, and of the other man who was crucified with Him;

33 but coming to Jesus, when they saw that He was already dead, they did not break His legs;

34 but one of the soldiers pierced His side with a spear, and immediately there came out blood and water.

35 And he who has seen has borne witness, and his witness is true; and he knows that he is telling the truth, so that you also may believe.

36 For these things came to pass, that the Scripture might be fulfilled, "NOT A BONE OF HIM SHALL BE BROKEN."

37 And again another Scripture says, "THEY SHALL LOOK ON HIM WHOM THEY PIERCED."

3. Jesus laid in the tomb
(19:38–42; Matt. 27:57–61; Mark 15:42–47; Luke 23:50–56)

38 And after these things Joseph of Arimathea, being a disciple of Jesus, but a

---

[30]Gr., *khiton*, the garment worn next to the skin

19:19 *cross,* see the note to Matt. 27:37.
19:25 Four women were standing at the foot of the cross: (1) Mary, the mother of Jesus (not mentioned as being at the cross in the other Gospels); (2) Mary's sister, who is probably to be equated with Salome (Mark 15:40), the wife of Zebedee and mother of James and John (Matt. 27:56); (3)

Mary, the wife of Clopas, mother of James the younger and Joses (Matt. 27:56; Mark 15:40); and (4) Mary Magdalene (Matt. 27:56; Mark 15:40).
19:28 See note to Luke 23:34 on the seven last words of Christ.

Marginal references:

19:17 Luke 23:26
19:21 v. 14
19:24 Ex 28:32; Ps 22:18
*19:25 Matt 27:55, 56; Mark 15:40, 41; Luke 23:49; 24:18; John 20:1,18
19:26 John 13:23; 20:2; 21:20; 2:4
*19:28 John 13:1; 17:4; Ps 69:21
19:30 John 17:4
19:31 Deut 21:23; Ex 12:16
19:32 v. 18
19:34 1 John 5:6,8
19:35 John 15:27; 21:24
19:36 Ex 12:46; Num 9:12; Ps 34:20
19:37 Zech 12:10

secret *one*, for fear of the Jews, asked Pilate that he might take away the body of Jesus; and Pilate granted permission. He came therefore, and took away His body.

19:39
John 3:1;
7:50

39   And Nicodemus came also, who had first come to Him by night; bringing a mixture of myrrh and aloes, about a hundred pounds *weight*.

19:40
John 11:44;
Matt 26:12;
John 20:5,7;
Luke 24:12

40   And so they took the body of Jesus, and bound it in linen wrappings with the spices, as is the burial custom of the Jews.

41   Now in the place where He was crucified there was a garden; and in the garden a new tomb, in which no one had yet been laid.

19:42
vv. 14,31,20,
41

42   Therefore on account of the Jewish day of preparation, because the tomb was nearby, they laid Jesus there.

R. *The resurrection of Jesus Christ*
(20:1–10; Matt. 28:1–10; Mark 16:1–8; Luke 24:1–11)

20:1
Matt 27:60,66

20 Now on the first *day* of the week Mary Magdalene *came early to the tomb, while it *was still dark, and *saw the stone *already* taken away from the tomb.

20:2
John 13:23;
19:26; 21:7,
20,24

2   And so she *ran and *came to Simon Peter, and to the other disciple whom Jesus loved, and *said to them, "They have taken away the Lord out of the tomb, and we do not know where they have laid Him."

20:3
Luke 24:12

3   Peter therefore went forth, and the other disciple, and they were going to the tomb.

4   And the two were running together; and the other disciple ran ahead faster than Peter, and came to the tomb first;

20:5
John 19:40

5   and stooping and looking in, he *saw the linen wrappings lying *there;* but he did not go in.

6   Simon Peter therefore also *came, following him, and entered the tomb; and he *beheld the linen wrappings lying *there,*

7   and the face-cloth, which had been on His head, not lying with the linen wrappings, but rolled up in a place by itself.

20:8
v. 4

8   So the other disciple who had first come to the tomb entered then also, and he saw and believed.

20:9
Matt 22:29;
Luke 24:26,
46

9   For as yet they did not understand the Scripture, that He must rise again from the dead.

10   So the disciples went away again to their own homes.

S. *Jesus appears to Mary Magdalene (20:11–18)*

*20:11
Mark 16:5;
v. 5

11   But Mary was standing outside the tomb weeping; and so, as she wept, she stooped and looked into the tomb;

20:12
Matt 28:2,3;
Mark 16:5;
Luke 24:4

12   and she *beheld two angels in white sitting, one at the head, and one at the feet, where the body of Jesus had been lying.

20:13
v. 2

13   And they *said to her, "Woman, why are you weeping?" She *said to them, "Because they have taken away my Lord, and I do not know where they have laid Him."

20:14
Matt 28:9;
John 21:4

14   When she had said this, she turned around, and *beheld Jesus standing *there,* and did not know that it was Jesus.

20:15
v. 13

15   Jesus *said to her, "Woman, why are you weeping? Whom are you seeking?" Supposing Him to be the gardener, she *said to Him, "Sir, if you have carried Him away, tell me where you have laid Him, and I will take Him away."

16   Jesus *said to her, "Mary!" She *turned and *said to Him in Hebrew, "Rabboni!" (which means, Teacher).

20:17
Matt 28:10;
v. 27;
John 7:33

17   Jesus *said to her, "Stop clinging to Me, for I have not yet ascended to the Father; but go to My brethren, and say to them, 'I ascend to My Father and your Father, and My God and your God.'"

20:18
Luke 24:10,
13

18   Mary Magdalene *came, announcing to the disciples, "I have seen the Lord," and *that* He had said these things to her.

20:11 The order of Christ's appearances after the resurrection seems to be as follows: (1) to Mary Magdalene and the other women (Matt. 28:9; Mark 16:9,10; John 20:11–18); (2) to the disciples on the Emmaus road (Mark 16:12; Luke 24:13–15); (3) to Peter (Luke 24:34; 1 Cor. 15:5); (4) to the ten in the upper room (20:19); (5) to the Eleven in the upper room with Thomas present (20:26; Mark 16:14; Luke 24:36); (6) to the disciples at the Sea of Tiberias (21:1–24); (7) to the Eleven on a mountain in Galilee (Matt. 28:16–20); (8) to the five hundred brethren (1 Cor. 15:6); (9) to James (1 Cor. 15:7); (10) to all the apostles (1 Cor. 15:7); and (11) to those who witnessed His ascension (Mark 16:19; Luke 24:50,51; Acts 1:3–12).

T. *Jesus appears to the ten in Jerusalem*
(20:19–25; Luke 24:36–43)

19 When therefore it was evening, on that day, the first *day* of the week, and when the doors were shut where the disciples were, for fear of the Jews, Jesus came and stood in their midst, and *said to them, "Peace *be* with you."

20 And when He had said this, He showed them both His hands and His side. The disciples therefore rejoiced when they saw the Lord.

21 Jesus therefore said to them again, "Peace *be* with you; as the Father has sent Me, I also send you."

22 And when He had said this, He breathed on them, and *said to them, "Receive the Holy Spirit.

23 "If you forgive the sins of any, *their sins* have been forgiven them; if you retain the *sins* of any, they have been retained."

24 But Thomas, one of the twelve, called Didymus, was not with them when Jesus came.

25 The other disciples therefore were saying to him, "We have seen the Lord!" But he said to them, "Unless I shall see in His hands the imprint of the nails, and put my finger into the place of the nails, and put my hand into His side, I will not believe."

U. *Jesus appears to Thomas and the ten (20:26–29)*

26 And after eight days again His disciples were inside, and Thomas with them. Jesus *came, the doors having been shut, and stood in their midst, and said, "Peace *be* with you."

27 Then He *said to Thomas, "Reach here your finger, and see My hands; and reach here your hand, and put it into My side; and be not unbelieving, but believing."

28 Thomas answered and said to Him, "My Lord and my God!"

29 Jesus *said to him, "Because you have seen Me, have you believed? Blessed *are* they who did not see, and *yet* believed."

IV. Conclusion (20:30,31)

30 Many other signs therefore Jesus also performed in the presence of the disciples, which are not written in this book;

31 but these have been written that you may believe that Jesus is the Christ, the Son of God; and that believing you may have life in His name.

V. Epilogue: (21:1–25)

A. *Jesus appears to the disciples at the Sea of Tiberias (21:1–14)*

21 After these things Jesus manifested Himself again to the disciples at the Sea of Tiberias, and He manifested *Himself* in this way.

2 There were together Simon Peter, and Thomas called Didymus, and Nathanael of Cana in Galilee, and the *sons* of Zebedee, and two others of His disciples.

3 Simon Peter *said to them, "I am going fishing." They *said to him, "We will also come with you." They went out, and got into the boat; and that night they caught nothing.

4 But when the day was now breaking, Jesus stood on the beach; yet the disciples did not know that it was Jesus.

5 Jesus therefore *said to them, "Children, you do not have any fish, do you?" They answered Him, "No."

6 And He said to them, "Cast the net on the right-hand side of the boat, and

---

20:23 See note on Matt. 16:19 on the keys of the kingdom.
20:28 "Deity of Christ." The watershed of Christian theology is how one answers the question, "What do you think of Christ? Whose son is He?" The Biblical evidences show conclusively that Christ is God. He is spoken of as eternally preexistent (Is. 9:6; John 1:1,2; Heb. 13:8; Rev. 22:13). He bore testimony to Himself that He was the only Son of God (Matt. 11:27; Mark 14:61,62; John 10:30; 14:9). In the New Testament letters He is sometimes referred to as God (Titus 2:13; 1 John 5:20). Attributes of deity are assigned to Him: (1) holiness (John 8:46; 2 Cor. 5:21; Heb. 7:26); (2)

omnipresence (Matt. 18:20; 28:20); (3) omnipotence (Matt. 28:18; Heb. 1:3; Rev. 1:8); (4) immutability (Heb. 1:11,12; 13:8); (5) creative activity (John 1:3; 1 Cor. 8:6; Col. 1:16,-17; Heb. 1:8,10); (6) His right to be worshiped (Matt. 2:11; 14:33; 28:9; Phil. 2:10; Heb. 1:6); and (7) His right to forgive sins (Mark 2:5,7,9,10; Luke 24:47; John 1:29; Acts 10:43; 1 John 1:7). The deity of Christ is the foundation of the Christian faith. The denial of it invalidates the entire structure of Christian theology.
21:1 The Sea (or Lake) of Tiberias was also called lake of Gennesaret (Luke 5:1) and the Sea of Galilee (John 6:1).

you will find *a catch."* They cast therefore, and then they were not able to haul it in because of the great number of fish.

7   That disciple therefore whom Jesus loved *said to Peter, "It is the Lord." And so when Simon Peter heard that it was the Lord, he put his outer garment on (for he was stripped *for work*), and threw himself into the sea.

8   But the other disciples came in the little boat, for they were not far from the land, but about one hundred yards away, dragging the net *full* of fish.

9   And so when they got out upon the land, they *saw a charcoal fire *already* laid, and fish placed on it, and bread.

10   Jesus *said to them, "Bring some of the fish which you have now caught."

11   Simon Peter went up, and drew the net to land, full of large fish, a hundred and fifty-three; and although there were so many, the net was not torn.

12   Jesus *said to them, "Come *and* have breakfast." None of the disciples ventured to question Him, "Who are You?" knowing that it was the Lord.

13   Jesus *came and *took the bread, and *gave them, and the fish likewise.

14   This is now the third time that Jesus was manifested to the disciples, after He was raised from the dead.

B. *Jesus questions Peter (21:15–23)*

15   So when they had finished breakfast, Jesus *said to Simon Peter, "Simon, *son* of John, do you love Me more than these?" He *said to Him, "Yes, Lord; You know that I love You." He *said to him, "Tend My lambs."

16   He *said to him again a second time, "Simon, *son* of John, do you love Me?" He *said to Him, "Yes, Lord; You know that I love You." He *said to him, "Shepherd My sheep."

17   He *said to him the third time, "Simon, *son* of John, do you love Me?" Peter was grieved because He said to him the third time, "Do you love Me?" And he said to Him, "Lord, You know all things; You know that I love You." Jesus *said to him, "Tend My sheep.

18   "Truly, truly, I say to you, when you were younger, you used to gird yourself, and walk wherever you wished; but when you grow old, you will stretch out your hands, and someone else will gird you, and bring you where you do not wish to *go."*

19   Now this He said, signifying by what kind of death he would glorify God. And when He had spoken this, He *said to him, "Follow Me!"

20   Peter, turning around, *saw the disciple whom Jesus loved following *them;* the one who also had leaned back on His breast at the supper, and said, "Lord, who is the one who betrays You?"

21   Peter therefore seeing him *said to Jesus, "Lord, and what about this man?"

22   Jesus *said to him, "If I want him to remain until I come, what *is that* to you? You follow Me!"

23   This saying therefore went out among the brethren that that disciple would not die; yet Jesus did not say to him that he would not die, but *only,* "If I want him to remain until I come, what *is that* to you?"

C. *The authentication (21:24,25)*

24   This is the disciple who bears witness of these things, and wrote these things; and we know that his witness is true.

25   And there are also many other things which Jesus did, which if they *were written in detail, I suppose that even the world itself *would not contain the books which *were written.

21:7 John 13:23; 20:2; v. 20
21:9 vv. 10,13
21:13 v. 9
21:14 John 20:19,26
*21:15 John 13:37; Matt 26:33; Mark 14:29
21:16 Matt 2:6; Acts 20:28; 1 Pet 5:2; Rev 7:17
21:17 John 16:30; v. 16
21:19 2 Pet 1:14
21:20 v. 7; John 13:25
21:22 Matt 16:27, 28; 25:31; 1 Cor 4:5; 11:26; Rev 2:25; 3:11; 22:7,20
21:23 Acts 1:15
21:24 John 15:27; 19:35
21:25 John 20:30

21:15 The question, *"Do you love Me more than these?"* is variously understood. Some believe that Jesus was asking, "Do you love Me more than you love these other disciples?" Others take it to mean, "Do you love Me more than these other disciples love Me?" Still others, "Do you love Me more than your boat, nets, and fishes?" It should also be noted that in vv. 15–17, Jesus' first two uses of the word *love* is from the Greek *agapaō,* meaning "high, devoted love." His third use of *love* is translated from *phileō,* the humbler word for love (as love for a friend). Peter makes no claim to superior love.

INTRODUCTION TO

THE

ACTS OF THE APOSTLES

Authorship and Background: As a companion volume to the Gospel of Luke (cf. 1:1-2 with Luke 1:1-4), Acts continues the story of the Christian movement, from the ascension of Christ to Paul's arrival in Rome some thirty years later. The author (for which see the Introduction to Luke) is a participant in some of the events recorded, as seen by the use of "we" and "us" in some passages (16:10-17; 20:5-21:18; 27:1-28:16).

It is generally assumed that Acts was written soon after Luke, so that its date of composition is placed A.D. 60-70 by some, A.D. 80-90 by others.

Characteristics: The book traces the development and spread of the Christian church, from the coming of the Holy Spirit at Pentecost to Paul's preaching the gospel in Rome "with all openness, unhindered" (28:31) for two whole years.

The title "Acts of the Apostles" is in some ways inadequate, for the book tells of the acts of only two of the twelve apostles: Peter, who dominates the early part of the book (1:15-12:17), and John (3:1-4:22; 8:14-25). The only other apostle of whom anything specific is said is James, brother of John, who was put to death by Herod Agrippa I (12:2). The other great names in the book are not of the Twelve: Stephen (6:8-7:60) and Philip (8:4-13,26-40; 21:8), two of the seven helpers chosen by the Jerusalem church; in addition there are Barnabas (4:36,37; 9:27; 11:22-30; 12:25-15:39), and James, brother of the Lord and leader in the Jerusalem church (cf. 1:14; 15:13-21; 21:18). The dominant figure is Paul, born Saul of Tarsus, first seen at the martyrdom of Stephen (7:58; 8:1). His conversion is narrated in 9:1-30 (with two other recitals of the event in 22:3-16; 26:4-18), and early activities in 11:25-30 and 12:25. From chapter 13 the book becomes in fact "The Acts of Paul," as the author traces the activity of the great apostle to the Gentiles in preaching throughout the Roman empire.

Many would call the book "The Acts of the Holy Spirit," since it is the Holy Spirit who empowers, directs, and confirms the work of the apostles and missionaries. Acts presents the thrilling account of the life of the early church, the opposition faced and overcome, the problems met and solved; and above all, it is the story of divine grace in its redemptive power in the lives of early believers.

The development of the Christian movement is told in terms of people and places; the author was necessarily selective and did not trace all developments or describe how the gospel was first preached in all regions. For example, how or by whom the work was started in Damascus and Rome is not stated. With broad strokes of his pen the author shows how the Christian message was originally proclaimed in Jerusalem, and then in all Judea and Samaria, and so throughout the empire to the capital city of Rome, in fulfillment of the Lord's command and promise (1:8). From this story the reader learns of early Christian worship and fellowship, of the bold witness of plain and simple laymen, and of the opposition of the Jews and of the authorities. The author is careful to point out that the Christians were not enemies of the empire: every time the missionaries were brought before Roman authorities they were absolved of all charges of sedition or insurrection.

Through all problems and opposition, by the power of the Holy Spirit in the lives of these early witnesses, "the word of the Lord continued to grow and to be multiplied" (12:24).

Contents:

Matthias chosen to take the place of Judas. Pentecost. Signs and wonders performed by the apostles; the choice of the seven helpers. Stephen, witness and martyr.

II. Judea, Samaria, and on to Antioch of Syria (8:4-12:25): Philip in Samaria and with the Ethiopian official. Conversion of Saul on the road to Damascus. Peter in the coast cities of Lydda, Joppa, and Caesarea. The planting of the gospel in Antioch of Syria.

III. Throughout the Roman empire with Paul (13:1-28:31):
   (1) First missionary journey (13:1-14:28)
   (2) The Jerusalem conference (15:1-35)
   (3) Second missionary journey (15:36-18:22)
   (4) Third missionary journey (18:23-21:16)
   (5) Paul a prisoner in Jerusalem, Caesarea, and Rome (21:17-28:31)

THE
ACTS OF THE APOSTLES

I. Jerusalem (1:1–8:3)

A. Introduction

1. Preface

1 The first account I composed, Theophilus, about all that Jesus began to do and teach, — **1:1** Luke 1:1-4

2 until the day when He was taken up, after He had by the Holy Spirit given orders to the apostles whom He had chosen. — **1:2** Matt 28:19

3 To these He also presented Himself alive, after His suffering, by many convincing proofs, appearing to them over *a period of* forty days, and speaking of the things concerning the kingdom of God. — **1:3** Matt 28:17; Luke 24:34, 36; 1 Cor 15:5-7

4 And gathering them together, He commanded them not to leave Jerusalem, but to wait for what the Father had promised, "Which," *He said,* "you heard of from Me; — **1:4** Luke 24:49; John 14:16

5 for John baptized with water, but you shall be baptized with the Holy Spirit not many days from now." — **1:5** Acts 11:16

2. The ascension

6 And so when they had come together, they were asking Him, saying, "Lord, is it at this time You are restoring the kingdom to Israel?" — **1:6** Matt 24:3

7 He said to them, "It is not for you to know times or epochs which the Father has fixed by His own authority; — **1:7** Matt 24:36; Mark 13:32

8 but you shall receive power when the Holy Spirit has come upon you; and you shall be My witnesses both in Jerusalem, and in all Judea and Samaria, and even to the remotest part of the earth." — **1:8** Acts 2:1-4; Luke 24:48; John 15:27

9 And after He had said these things, He was lifted up while they were looking on, and a cloud received Him out of their sight. — ***1:9** Luke 24:51; v. 2

10 And as they were gazing intently into the sky while He was departing, behold, two men in white clothing stood beside them; — **1:10** Luke 24:4; John 20:12

11 and they also said, "Men of Galilee, why do you stand looking into the sky? This Jesus, who has been taken up from you into heaven, will come in just the same way as you have watched Him go into heaven." — ***1:11** Matt 24:30; Mark 13:26; John 14:3

B. The origin of the church

1. The disciples in prayer

12 Then they returned to Jerusalem from the mount called Olivet, which is near Jerusalem, a Sabbath day's journey away. — **1:13** Acts 9:37,39; 20:8;

13 And when they had entered, they went up to the upper room, where they were staying; that is, Peter and John and James and Andrew, Philip and Thomas, Bartholomew and Matthew, James *the son* of Alphaeus, and Simon the Zealot, and Judas *the son* of James. — Matt 10:2-4; Mark 3:16-19; Luke 6:14-16 **1:14** Acts 2:1,46;

14 These all with one mind were continually devoting themselves to prayer, along with *the* women, and Mary the mother of Jesus, and with His brothers. — Luke 23:49, 55; Matt 12:46

1:9 Jesus left the earth forty days after the resurrection to ascend to the right hand of the Father. He was in the presence of the eleven disciples and two angels (or possibly two glorified men, such as Moses and Elijah, who had appeared on the Mount of Transfiguration). This episode took place on the Mount of Olives near Bethany (Luke 24:50). The disciples were assured that He would come back personally and physically. (See also Ps. 68:18; Eph. 4:8.)

1:11 Here we are told that Christ will return to earth in the same manner as He ascended into heaven. Elsewhere we learn that He will come: (1) in flaming fire (2 Thess. 1:7,8); (2) in His own heavenly glory (Matt. 25:31); (3) with His saints (1 Thess. 3:13); (4) as a thief in the night (1 Thess. 5:2; 2 Pet. 3:10; Rev. 16:15); (5) with a cry of command and the archangel's call (1 Thess. 4:16); (6) in company with the angels (2 Thess. 1:7); and (7) suddenly (Mark 13:36).

2. *The replacement of Judas Iscariot*

1:15
John 21:23;
Acts 6:3; 9:30
15 And at this time Peter stood up in the midst of the brethren (a gathering of about one hundred and twenty persons was there together), and said,

1:16
John 13:18
16 "Brethren, the Scripture had to be fulfilled, which the Holy Spirit foretold by the mouth of David concerning Judas, who became a guide to those who arrested Jesus.

1:17
John 6:70,71;
v. 25;
Acts 20:24;
21:19
17 "For he was counted among us, and received his portion in this ministry."

18 (Now this man acquired a field with the price of his wickedness; and falling headlong, he burst open in the middle and all his bowels gushed out.

1:18
Matt 27:3-10;
26:14,15
19 And it became known to all who were living in Jerusalem; so that in their own language that field was called Hakeldama, that is, Field of Blood.)

1:20
Ps 69:25;
109:8
20 "For it is written in the book of Psalms,

'LET HIS HOMESTEAD BE MADE DESOLATE,
AND LET NO MAN DWELL IN IT';

and,

'HIS OFFICE LET ANOTHER MAN TAKE.'

1:21
Luke 24:3
21 "It is therefore necessary that of the men who have accompanied us all the time that the Lord Jesus went in and out among us—

1:22
Mark 1:1;
v. 8;
Acts 2:32
22 beginning with the baptism of John, until the day that He was taken up from us—one of these should become a witness with us of His resurrection."

23 And they put forward two men, Joseph called Barsabbas (who was also called Justus), and Matthias.

1:24
1 Sam 16:7;
Jer 17:10;
Acts 15:8;
Rom 8:27
24 And they prayed, and said, "Thou, Lord, who knowest the hearts of all men, show which one of these two Thou hast chosen

25 to occupy this ministry and apostleship from which Judas turned aside to go to his own place."

*1:26
Lev 16:8
26 And they drew lots for them, and the lot fell to Matthias; and he was numbered with the eleven apostles.

C. *The advent of the Holy Spirit*

1. *The gift of the Spirit*

*2:1
Lev 23:15;
Deut 16:9;
Acts 1:14
2 And when the day of Pentecost had come, they were all together in one place.
2 And suddenly there came from heaven a noise like a violent, rushing wind, and it filled the whole house where they were sitting.

2:2
Acts 4:31
3 And there appeared to them tongues as of fire distributing themselves, and they rested on each one of them.

2:4
Acts 4:8,31;
9:17; 13:9,52;
1 Cor 12:10,
11; 14:21
4 And they were all filled with the Holy Spirit and began to speak with other tongues, as the Spirit was giving them utterance.

5 Now there were Jews living in Jerusalem, devout men, from every nation under heaven.

2:5
Acts 8:2
6 And when this sound occurred, the multitude came together, and were bewildered, because they were each one hearing them speak in his own language.

2:7
v. 12;
Acts 1:11
7 And they were amazed and marveled, saying, "Why, are not all these who are speaking Galileans?

2:9
1 Pet 1:1;
Acts 6:9;
16:6;
Rom 16:5;
1 Cor 16:19;
2 Cor 1:8
8 "And how is it that we each hear *them* in our own language to which we were born?

9 "Parthians and Medes and Elamites, and residents of Mesopotamia, Judea and Cappadocia, Pontus and Asia,

---

1:26 Matthias is chosen as an apostle to be, with the other apostles, *a witness . . . of His resurrection* (v.22). The primary function of the apostolic office is stressed throughout the narrative of the apostles' ministry in the early chapters of Acts. The central element of the apostolic message was the resurrection of Christ (cf. 2:32; 3:14,15; 4:1,2,10,33; 5:30–32; 10:39–41; 13:30,31). As these passages show, the apostles preached Christ's resurrection not simply as the resuscitation of one who had been dead, but as the proof and evidence of the fact that God had exalted Jesus to Messiah and Lord: His resurrection was at the same time His exaltation and enthronement as Leader and Savior (see especially 2:36; 5:31).

2:1 The *day of Pentecost* marks the birthday of the Christian church, of which the risen and exalted Christ is head. Note: (1) it was an altogether supernatural event, as evidenced by the suddenness of its occurrence; (2) the sound

like that of a rushing mighty wind revealed the presence of the Holy Spirit; (3) the tongues as of fire proclaiming Christ's message in the many different languages were a token of the ultimate preaching of the gospel to the ends of the earth; and (4) the symbol of fire itself typified the holy zeal and divinely empowered utterance of those who would speak forth the divine message.

Pentecost, from the Greek *pentekostē*, "fiftieth day," was celebrated on the sixth or seventh day of Sivan (May-June), fifty days after Passover. One of the three great annual feasts, it was called in Hebrew *the Feast of Weeks* (cf. Deut. 16:10), and was referred to also as *the day of the first fruits* (Num. 28:26), or *Feast of the Harvest* (Ex. 23:16). This was the Jewish feast of the wheat harvest. For details of its celebration see Lev. 23:15–21. It is further referred to in 20:16 and 1 Cor. 16:8.

10 Phrygia and Pamphylia, Egypt and the districts of Libya around Cyrene, and visitors from Rome, both Jews and [1]proselytes,

11 Cretans and Arabs—we hear them in our *own* tongues speaking of the mighty deeds of God."

12 And they all continued in amazement and great perplexity, saying to one another, "What does this mean?"

13 But others were mocking and saying, "They are full of sweet wine."

2. Peter's Pentecostal sermon

14 But Peter, taking his stand with the eleven, raised his voice and declared to them: "Men of Judea, and all you who live in Jerusalem, let this be known to you, and give heed to my words.

15 "For these men are not drunk, as you suppose, for it is *only* the [2]third hour of the day;

16 but this is what was spoken of through the prophet Joel:

17 'AND IT SHALL BE IN THE LAST DAYS,' God says,
      'THAT I WILL POUR FORTH OF MY SPIRIT UPON ALL MANKIND;
      AND YOUR SONS AND YOUR DAUGHTERS SHALL PROPHESY,
      AND YOUR YOUNG MEN SHALL SEE VISIONS,
      AND YOUR OLD MEN SHALL DREAM DREAMS;

18 EVEN UPON MY BONDSLAVES, BOTH MEN AND WOMEN,
      I WILL IN THOSE DAYS POUR FORTH OF MY SPIRIT
      And they shall prophesy.

19 'AND I WILL GRANT WONDERS IN THE SKY ABOVE,
      AND SIGNS ON THE EARTH BENEATH,
      BLOOD, AND FIRE, AND VAPOR OF SMOKE.

20 'THE SUN SHALL BE TURNED INTO DARKNESS,
      AND THE MOON INTO BLOOD,
      BEFORE THE GREAT AND GLORIOUS DAY OF THE LORD SHALL COME.

21 'AND IT SHALL BE, THAT EVERYONE WHO CALLS ON THE NAME OF THE
      LORD SHALL BE SAVED.'

22 "Men of Israel, listen to these words: Jesus the Nazarene, a man attested to you by God with miracles and wonders and signs which God performed through Him in your midst, just as you yourselves know—

23 this *Man*, delivered up by the predetermined plan and foreknowledge of God, you nailed to a cross by the hands of godless men and put *Him* to death.

24 "And God raised Him up again, putting an end to the agony of death, since it was impossible for Him to be held in its power.

25 "For David says of Him,
      'I WAS ALWAYS BEHOLDING THE LORD IN MY PRESENCE;
      FOR HE IS AT MY RIGHT HAND, THAT I MAY NOT BE SHAKEN.

26 'THEREFORE MY HEART WAS GLAD AND MY TONGUE EXULTED;
      MOREOVER MY FLESH ALSO WILL ABIDE IN HOPE;

27 BECAUSE THOU WILT NOT ABANDON MY SOUL TO HADES,
      NOR ALLOW THY HOLY ONE TO UNDERGO DECAY.

28 'THOU HAST MADE KNOWN TO ME THE WAYS OF LIFE;
      THOU WILT MAKE ME FULL OF GLADNESS WITH THY PRESENCE.'

29 "Brethren, I may confidently say to you regarding the patriarch David that he both died and was buried, and his tomb is with us to this day.

30 "And so, because he was a prophet, and knew that GOD HAD SWORN TO HIM WITH AN OATH TO SEAT *one* OF HIS DESCENDANTS UPON HIS THRONE,

31 he looked ahead and spoke of the resurrection of [3]the Christ, that HE WAS NEITHER ABANDONED TO HADES, NOR DID HIS flesh SUFFER DECAY.

32 "This Jesus God raised up again, to which we are all witnesses.

33 "Therefore having been exalted to the right hand of God, and having received from the Father the promise of the Holy Spirit, He has poured forth this which you both see and hear.

34 "For it was not David who ascended into heaven, but he himself says:
      'THE LORD SAID TO MY LORD,
      "SIT AT MY RIGHT HAND,

35   UNTIL I MAKE THINE ENEMIES A FOOTSTOOL FOR THY FEET."'

[1]I.e., Gentile converts to Judaism   [2]I.e., 9 a.m.   [3]I.e., the Messiah

---

2:12
v. 7

2:13
1 Cor 14:23

2:15
1 Thess 5:7

2:17
Joel 2:28-32;
Zech 12:10;
John 7:38;
Acts 10:45;
21:9

2:18
Acts 21:4,9,
10

2:20
Matt 24:29;
Mark 13:24;
Luke 21:25

2:21
Rom 10:13

2:22
John 3:2;
Acts 10:38;
John 4:48

2:23
Matt 26:24;
Luke 22:22;
Acts 3:18;
4:28; 3:13

2:24
Acts 3:15;
Rom 4:24;
2 Cor 4:14;
Eph 1:20;
Col 2:12;
Heb 13:20;
1 Pet 1:21

2:25
Ps 16:8-11

2:27
Matt 11:23;
Acts 13:35

2:29
Acts 7:8,9;
13:36;
1 Kin 2:10;
Neh 3:16

2:30
2 Sam 7:12,
13;
Ps 132:11;
Rom 1:3

2:31
Ps 16:10

2:32
v. 24;
Acts 1:8

2:33
Acts 5:31;
1:4;
John 7:39;
14:26; 15:26;
Acts 10:45

2:34
Ps 110:1;
Matt 22:44

36 "Therefore let all the house of Israel know for certain that God has made Him both Lord and Christ—this Jesus whom you crucified."

3. *The first ingathering of souls*

37 Now when they heard *this*, they were pierced to the heart, and said to Peter and the rest of the apostles, "Brethren, what shall we do?"

38 And Peter *said* to them, "Repent, and let each of you be baptized in the name of Jesus Christ for the forgiveness of your sins; and you shall receive the gift of the Holy Spirit.

39 "For the promise is for you and your children, and for all who are far off, as many as the Lord our God shall call to Himself."

40 And with many other words he solemnly testified and kept on exhorting them, saying, "Be saved from this perverse generation!"

41 So then, those who had received his word were baptized; and there were added that day about three thousand [4]souls.

42 And they were continually devoting themselves to the apostles' teaching and to fellowship, to the breaking of bread and to prayer.

4. *The brotherhood of believers*

43 And everyone kept feeling a sense of awe; and many wonders and signs were taking place through the apostles [5].

44 And all those who had believed [6]were together, and had all things in common;

45 and they *began* selling their property and possessions, and were sharing them with all, as anyone might have need.

46 And day by day continuing with one mind in the temple, and breaking bread from house to house, they were taking their meals together with gladness and sincerity of heart,

47 praising God, and having favor with all the people. And the Lord was adding to their number day by day those who were being saved.

D. *The church at work in Jerusalem*

1. *Peter's second sermon: healing of the lame man*

3 Now Peter and John were going up to the temple at the [7]ninth *hour*, the hour of prayer.

2 And a certain man who had been lame from his mother's womb was being carried along, whom they used to set down every day at the gate of the temple which is called Beautiful, in order to beg [8]alms of those who were entering the temple.

3 And when he saw Peter and John about to go into the temple, he *began* asking to receive alms.

4 And Peter, along with John, fixed his gaze upon him and said, "Look at us!"

5 And he *began* to give them his attention, expecting to receive something from them.

6 But Peter said, "I do not possess silver and gold, but what I do have I give to you: In the name of Jesus Christ the Nazarene—walk!"

7 And seizing him by the right hand, he raised him up; and immediately his feet and his ankles were strengthened.

8 And with a leap, he stood upright and *began* to walk; and he entered the temple with them, walking and leaping and praising God.

9 And all the people saw him walking and praising God;

10 and they were taking note of him as being the one who used to sit at the

[4]I.e., persons   [5]Some ancient mss. add *in Jerusalem; and great fear was upon all*   [6]Some ancient mss. do not contain *were*
[7]I.e., 3 p.m.   [8]Or, *a gift of charity*

2:47 The church (Greek *ekklesia*, the "called-out-assembly," or "congregation") is composed of those who have been regenerated by the Spirit of God. The invisible church includes those who have already died in the faith, those believers who are yet alive (some also include among these their infant children), and those who are yet to become members of the body of Christ. A professing church may include both those who are members of the true church and those who are not. The New Testament uses the word *church* both for local assemblies of believers and for the

church universal (e.g., 1 Cor. 1:2; 2 Cor. 1:1; Gal. 1:2; Eph. 1:22). Whether Israel in the Old Testament is to be equated with the church in the New Testament is a debatable question, although 7:38 speaks of the *congregation* [church] *in the wilderness*. Israel was a *true church*, but Eph. 3:5 states that the Jewish-Gentile New Testament church was a mystery not clearly revealed in the Old Testament. In a sense, therefore, the church had its beginnings at Pentecost. Israel looked forward to Calvary, the church looks back at it, but both are redeemed by it.

Beautiful Gate of the temple to *beg* alms, and they were filled with wonder and amazement at what had happened to him.

11   And while he was clinging to Peter and John, all the people ran together to them at the so-called portico of Solomon, full of amazement.

12   But when Peter saw *this*, he replied to the people, "Men of Israel, why do you marvel at this, or why do you gaze at us, as if by our own power or piety we had made him walk?

13   "The God of Abraham, Isaac, and Jacob, the God of our fathers, has glorified His servant Jesus, *the one* whom you delivered up, and disowned in the presence of Pilate, when he had decided to release Him.

14   "But you disowned the Holy and Righteous One, and asked for a murderer to be granted to you,

15   but put to death the Prince of life, *the one* whom God raised from the dead, *a fact* to which we are witnesses.

16   "And on the basis of faith in His name, *it is* the name of Jesus which has strengthened this man whom you see and know; and the faith which *comes* through Him has given him this perfect health in the presence of you all.

17   "And now, brethren, I know that you acted in ignorance, just as your rulers did also.

18   "But the things which God announced beforehand by the mouth of all the prophets, that His Christ should suffer, He has thus fulfilled.

19   "Repent therefore and return, that your sins may be wiped away, in order that times of refreshing may come from the presence of the Lord;

20   and that He may send Jesus, the Christ appointed for you,

21   whom heaven must receive until *the* period of restoration of all things about which God spoke by the mouth of His holy prophets from ancient time.

22   "Moses said, 'THE LORD GOD SHALL RAISE UP FOR YOU A PROPHET LIKE ME FROM YOUR BRETHREN; TO HIM YOU SHALL GIVE HEED in everything He says to you.

23   'And it shall be that every soul that does not heed that prophet shall be utterly destroyed from among the people.'

24   "And likewise, all the prophets who have spoken, from Samuel and *his* successors onward, also announced these days.

25   "It is you who are the sons of the prophets, and of the covenant which God made with your fathers, saying to Abraham, 'AND IN YOUR SEED ALL THE FAMILIES OF THE EARTH SHALL BE BLESSED.'

26   "For you first, God raised up His Servant, and sent Him to bless you by turning every one *of you* from your wicked ways."

2. *The beginning of opposition*

a. *Peter and John arrested*

4   And as they were speaking to the people, the priests and the captain of the temple *guard*, and the Sadducees, came upon them,

2   being greatly disturbed because they were teaching the people and proclaiming in Jesus the resurrection from the dead.

3   And they laid hands on them, and put them in jail until the next day, for it was already evening.

4   But many of those who had heard the message believed; and the number of the men came to be about five thousand.

b. *Peter's defense before the Sanhedrin*

5   And it came about on the next day, that their rulers and elders and scribes were gathered together in Jerusalem;

6   and Annas the high priest *was there*, and Caiaphas and John and Alexander, and all who were of high-priestly descent.

7   And when they had placed them in the center, they *began to* inquire, "By what power, or in what name, have you done this?"

8   Then Peter, filled with the Holy Spirit, said to them, "Rulers and elders of the people,

9   if we are on trial today for a benefit done to a sick man, as to how this man has been made well,

10   let it be known to all of you, and to all the people of Israel, that by the name of Jesus Christ the Nazarene, whom you crucified, whom God raised from the dead—by this *name* this man stands here before you in good health.

4:11
Ps 118:22;
Is 28:16;
Matt 21:42
4:12
Matt 1:21;
Acts 10:43;
1 Tim 2:5,6

11 "He is the STONE WHICH WAS REJECTED by you, THE BUILDERS, *but* WHICH BECAME THE VERY CORNER *stone*.

12 "And there is salvation in no one else; for there is no other name under heaven that has been given among men, by which we must be saved."

c. Peter and John set free

*4:13
v. 31;
Matt 11:25;
1 Cor 1:27

13 Now as they observed the confidence of Peter and John, and understood that they were uneducated and untrained men, they were marveling, and *began* to recognize them as having been with Jesus.

14 And seeing the man who had been healed standing with them, they had nothing to say in reply.

4:15
Matt 5:22

15 But when they had ordered them to go aside out of the Council, they *began* to confer with one another,

4:16
John 11:47;
Acts 3:7-10

16 saying, "What shall we do with these men? For the fact that a noteworthy miracle has taken place through them is apparent to all who live in Jerusalem, and we cannot deny it.

17 "But in order that it may not spread any further among the people, let us warn them to speak no more to any man in this name."

4:18
Acts 5:40

18 And when they had summoned them, they commanded them not to speak or teach at all in the name of Jesus.

4:19
Acts 5:28,29

19 But Peter and John answered and said to them, "Whether it is right in the sight of God to give heed to you rather than to God, you be the judge;

4:20
Acts 1:8; 2:32

20 for we cannot stop speaking what we have seen and heard."

21 And when they had threatened them further, they let them go (finding no basis on which they might punish them) on account of the people, because they were all glorifying God for what had happened;

22 for the man was more than forty years old on whom this miracle of healing had been performed.

d. The report to the church

23 And when they had been released, they went to their own *companions*, and reported all that the chief priests and the elders had said to them.

4:24
2 Kin 19:15

24 And when they heard *this*, they lifted their voices to God with one accord and said, "O Lord, it is Thou who DIDST MAKE THE HEAVEN AND THE EARTH AND THE SEA, AND ALL THAT IS IN THEM,

4:25
Ps 2:1;
Acts 1:16

25 who by the Holy Spirit, *through* the mouth of our father David Thy servant, didst say,

'WHY DID THE [9]GENTILES RAGE,
AND THE PEOPLES DEVISE FUTILE THINGS?

4:26
Heb 1:9

26 'THE KINGS OF THE EARTH TOOK THEIR STAND,
AND THE RULERS WERE GATHERED TOGETHER
AGAINST THE LORD, AND AGAINST HIS CHRIST.'

4:27
v. 30;
Luke 4:18;
John 10:36;
Matt 14:1;
Luke 23:12
4:28
Acts 2:23

27 "For truly in this city there were gathered together against Thy holy servant Jesus, whom Thou didst anoint, both Herod and Pontius Pilate, along with the Gentiles and the peoples of Israel,

28 to do whatever Thy hand and Thy purpose predestined to occur.

4:29
vv. 13,31;
Acts 9:27;
13:46; 28:31
4:30
Acts 2:43;
5:12; 3:6,16;
v. 27
4:31
Acts 2:2,4;
v. 29
*4:32
Acts 5:12;
2:44

29 "And now, Lord, take note of their threats, and grant that Thy bond-servants may speak Thy word with all confidence,

30 while Thou dost extend Thy hand to heal, and signs and wonders take place through the name of Thy holy servant Jesus."

31 And when they had prayed, the place where they had gathered together was shaken, and they were all filled with the Holy Spirit, and *began* to speak the word of God with boldness.

32 And the congregation of those who believed were of one heart and soul; and

[9]Or, *nations*

4:13 The description of the apostles Peter and John as *uneducated and untrained men* reflects the point of view of the members of the Sanhedrin, the chief priests, elders, and scribes. The apostles were Galileans, and were not professional scholars (*agrammatoi*, "unlearned") or ordained teachers of religion (*idiotai*, "laymen"), as were the members of the Sanhedrin. Their persuasive eloquence was, therefore, all the more astonishing.
4:32 A careful reading of 2:44,45; 4:32–37; and 6:1 shows

the nature, extent, and purpose of the communal sharing in the early church in Jerusalem. It was a purely voluntary act, and no one was coerced into surrendering his property to the church. As Peter told Ananias, the property belonged to him, and once he had sold it the money was his to do with as he pleased (5:4). The proceeds were distributed only to those in need, not to all members alike, and the distribution of the money was according to the needs of those being helped (2:45; 4:35). This was a genuine expression of Chris-

not one *of them* claimed that anything belonging to him was his own; but all things were common property to them.

33   And with great power the apostles were giving witness to the resurrection of the Lord Jesus, and abundant grace was upon them all.

34   For there was not a needy person among them, for all who were owners of land or houses would sell them and bring the proceeds of the sales,

35   and lay them at the apostles' feet; and they would be distributed to each, as any had need.

36   And Joseph, a Levite of Cyprian birth, who was also called Barnabas by the apostles (which translated means, Son of Encouragement),

37   and who owned a tract of land, sold it and brought the money and laid it at the apostles' feet.

3. Discipline in the church

a. Ananias

5 But a certain man named Ananias, with his wife Sapphira, sold a piece of property,

2   and kept back *some* of the price for himself, with his wife's full knowledge, and bringing a portion of it, he laid it at the apostles' feet.

3   But Peter said, "Ananias, why has Satan filled your heart to lie to the Holy Spirit, and to keep back *some* of the price of the land?

4   "While it remained *unsold*, did it not remain your own? And after it was sold, was it not under your control? Why is it that you have conceived this deed in your heart? You have not lied to men, but to God."

5   And as he heard these words, Ananias fell down and breathed his last; and great fear came upon all who heard of it.

6   And the young men arose and covered him up, and after carrying him out, they buried him.

b. Sapphira

7   Now there elapsed an interval of about three hours, and his wife came in, not knowing what had happened.

8   And Peter responded to her, "Tell me whether you sold the land for such and such a price?" And she said, "Yes, that was the price."

9   Then Peter *said* to her, "Why is it that you have agreed together to put the Spirit of the Lord to the test? Behold, the feet of those who have buried your husband are at the door, and they shall carry you out *as well*."

10   And she fell immediately at his feet, and breathed her last; and the young men came in and found her dead, and they carried her out and buried her beside her husband.

11   And great fear came upon the whole church, and upon all who heard of these things.

4. The first persecution

a. Converts multiplied

12   And at the hands of the apostles many signs and wonders were taking place among the people; and they were all with one accord in Solomon's portico.

13   But none of the rest dared to associate with them; however, the people held them in high esteem.

14   And all the more believers in the Lord, multitudes of men and women, were constantly added to *their number*;

15   to such an extent that they even carried the sick out into the streets, and laid them on cots and pallets, so that when Peter came by, at least his shadow might fall on any one of them.

16   And also the people from the cities in the vicinity of Jerusalem were coming

Marginal references:
- 4:33 Acts 1:8; 1:22
- 4:34 Acts 2:45
- 4:35 v. 37; Acts 5:2; 2:45; 6:1
- 4:37 v. 35; Acts 5:2
- 5:2 Acts 4:37
- *5:3 Deut 23:21; Luke 22:3; John 13:2,7; v. 9
- 5:5 vv. 10,11
- 5:6 John 19:40
- 5:8 v. 2
- 5:9 v. 3
- 5:10 v. 5
- 5:11 v. 5; Acts 19:17
- 5:12 Acts 2:43; 3:11; 4:32
- 5:13 Acts 2:47; 4:21
- 5:14 Acts 2:47; 11:24
- 5:15 Matt 9:21; 14:36; Acts 19:12

---

tian love and concern.
5:3 Scripture teaches that the Holy Spirit, the third person of the Trinity, is God and possesses the attributes of deity. In 5:3,4 He is equated with God. In Matt. 28:19 and 2 Cor. 13:14 He is linked with the Father and the Son in such a way as to imply He is equal, and one, with them. These attrib-

utes of deity are ascribed to Him: (1) eternity (Heb. 9:14); (2) omnipresence (Ps. 139:7-13); (3) omnipotence (Luke 1:35; Rom. 15:19); and (4) omniscience (1 Cor. 2:10). The Holy Spirit had a part in creation (Job 33:4). He was the divine author of Scripture (2 Pet. 1:21). He had a part in man's redemption (Heb. 9:14).

together, bringing people who were sick [10]or afflicted with unclean spirits; and they were all being healed.

b. The apostles imprisoned

5:17
Acts 15:5; 4:1

17 But the high priest rose up, along with all his associates (that is the sect of the Sadducees), and they were filled with jealousy;

5:18
Acts 4:3
5:19
Acts 12:7;
16:26
5:20
John 6:63,68

18 and they laid hands on the apostles, and put them in a public jail.

19 But an angel of the Lord during the night opened the gates of the prison, and taking them out he said,

20 "Go your way, stand and speak to the people in the temple the whole message of this Life."

5:21
Acts 4:5,6;
vv. 27,34,41

21 And upon hearing *this*, they entered into the temple about daybreak, and *began* to teach. Now when the high priest and his associates had come, they called the Council together, even all the Senate of the sons of Israel, and sent *orders* to the prison house for them to be brought.

22 But the officers who came did not find them in the prison; and they returned, and reported back,

23 saying, "We found the prison house locked quite securely and the guards standing at the doors; but when we had opened up, we found no one inside."

5:24
Acts 4:1

24 Now when the captain of the temple *guard* and the chief priests heard these words, they were greatly perplexed about them as to what would come of this.

25 But someone came and reported to them, "Behold, the men whom you put in prison are standing in the temple and teaching the people!"

5:26
Acts 4:21

26 Then the captain went along with the officers and *proceeded* to bring them *back* without violence (for they were afraid of the people, lest they should be stoned).

27 And when they had brought them, they stood them before the Council. And the high priest questioned them,

5:28
Acts 4:18;
2:33,36; 3:15;
7:52;
Matt 23:35;
27:25
5:29
Acts 4:19
5:30
Acts 3:13,15;
22:14; 10:39;
13:29;
Gal 3:13;
1 Pet 2:24
5:31
Acts 2:33;
Heb 2:10;
Acts 3:15
5:32
Luke 24:48;
John 15:26;
Rom 8:16
5:33
Acts 2:37;
7:54

28 saying, "We gave you strict orders not to continue teaching in this name, and behold, you have filled Jerusalem with your teaching, and intend to bring this man's blood upon us."

29 But Peter and the apostles answered and said, "We must obey God rather than men.

30 "The God of our fathers raised up Jesus, whom you had put to death by hanging Him on a cross.

31 "He is the one whom God exalted to His right hand as a Prince and a Savior, to grant repentance to Israel, and forgiveness of sins.

32 "And we are witnesses[11] of these things; and *so is* the Holy Spirit, whom God has given to those who obey Him."

c. The counsel of Gamaliel

33 But when they heard this, they were cut to the quick and were intending to slay them.

34 But a certain Pharisee named Gamaliel, a teacher of the Law, respected by all the people, stood up in the Council and gave orders to put the men outside for a short time.

35 And he said to them, "Men of Israel, take care what you propose to do with these men.

36 "For some time ago Theudas rose up, claiming to be somebody; and a group of about four hundred men joined up with him. And he was slain; and all who followed him were dispersed and came to nothing.

37 "After this man Judas of Galilee rose up in the days of the census, and drew away *some* people after him; he too perished, and all those who followed him were scattered.

5:38
Matt 15:13

38 "And so in the present case, I say to you, stay away from these men and let

[10]Lit., *and* [11]Some mss. add *in Him*, or, *of Him*

5:34 This Gamaliel, an elder, was a respected rabbi among whose pupils was Saul of Tarsus (22:3). He belonged to the liberal group of Jewish teachers who followed the interpretations of Hillel, a venerated Jewish rabbi who lived shortly before the time of Jesus.
5:36 There is no other extant reference to a revolutionary leader called Theudas who led a revolt against the Roman authorities. Josephus, the Jewish historian, mentions a

Theudas who led an ill-fated revolt in A.D. 44. The name was common, however, and there may have been two such revolutionaries with the same name.
5:37 According to Josephus, this Judas led a revolt against the census carried out by Quirinius in A.D. 6. Though he was defeated, his movement lived on in the Zealots, a revolutionary party dedicated to the overthrow of the Roman power by force.

them alone, for if this plan or action should be of men, it will be overthrown;
39   but if it is of God, you will not be able to overthrow them; or else you may even be found fighting against God.''
40   And they took his advice; and after calling the apostles in, they flogged them and ordered them to speak no more in the name of Jesus, and *then* released them.
41   So they went on their way from the presence of the Council, rejoicing that they had been considered worthy to suffer shame for *His* name.
42   And every day, in the temple and from house to house, they kept right on teaching and preaching Jesus *as* the Christ.

5. *The first deacons*

6 Now at this time while the disciples were increasing *in number,* a complaint arose on the part of the [12]Hellenistic *Jews* against the *native* Hebrews, because their widows were being overlooked in the daily serving *of food.*
2   And the twelve summoned the congregation of the disciples and said, "It is not desirable for us to neglect the word of God in order to serve tables.
3   "But select from among you, brethren, seven men of good reputation, full of the Spirit and of wisdom, whom we may put in charge of this task.
4   "But we will devote ourselves to prayer, and to the ministry of the word.''
5   And the statement found approval with the whole congregation; and they chose Stephen, a man full of faith and of the Holy Spirit, and Philip, Prochorus, Nicanor, Timon, Parmenas and Nicolas, a [13]proselyte from Antioch.
6   And these they brought before the apostles; and after praying, they laid their hands on them.
7   And the word of God kept on spreading; and the number of the disciples continued to increase greatly in Jerusalem, and a great many of the priests were becoming obedient to the faith.

6. *The first martyrdom*

a. *The arrest of Stephen*

8   And Stephen, full of grace and power, was performing great wonders and signs among the people.
9   But some men from what was called the Synagogue of the Freedmen, *including* both Cyrenians and Alexandrians, and some from Cilicia and Asia, rose up and argued with Stephen.
10   And *yet* they were unable to cope with the wisdom and the Spirit with which he was speaking.
11   Then they secretly induced men to say, "We have heard him speak blasphemous words against Moses and *against* God.''
12   And they stirred up the people, the elders and the scribes, and they came upon him and dragged him away, and brought him before the Council.
13   And they put forward false witnesses who said, "This man incessantly speaks against this holy place, and the Law;
14   for we have heard him say that this Nazarene, Jesus, will destroy this place and alter the customs which Moses handed down to us.''
15   And fixing their gaze on him, all who were sitting in the Council saw his face like the face of an angel.

b. *The defense of Stephen*

7 And the high priest said, "Are these things so?''
2   And he said, "Hear me, brethren and fathers! The God of glory appeared to our father Abraham when he was in Mesopotamia, before he lived in Haran,
3   and said to him, 'DEPART FROM YOUR COUNTRY AND YOUR RELATIVES, AND COME INTO THE LAND THAT I WILL SHOW YOU.'
4   "Then he departed from the land of the Chaldeans, and settled in Haran. And

Marginal references:

5:39 Acts 7:51; 9:5; 11:17
5:40 Matt 10:17; Mark 13:9
5:41 1 Pet 4:13,16; John 15:21
5:42 Acts 2:46; 8:35; 11:20; 17:18; Gal 1:16
*6:1 Acts 2:41,47; 9:29; 11:20; 4:35
*6:3 John 21:23; Acts 1:15
*6:5 Acts 11:19, 24; 8:5,26; 21:8
6:6 Acts 1:24; 8:17; 9:17; 13:3; 1 Tim 4:14; 5:22; 2 Tim 1:6
6:7 Acts 12:24; 19:20; Acts 13:8; 14:22; Gal 1:23; 6:10
6:10 Luke 21:15; Acts 5:39
6:11 Matt 26:59,60
6:13 Acts 7:58; 21:28
6:14 Matt 26:61; 15:1; 21:21; 26:3; 28:17
7:2 Acts 22:1; Ps 29:3; Gen 11:31; 15:7
7:3 Gen 12:1
7:4 Gen 12:5

---

[12]I.e., non-Palestinian Jews who normally spoke Greek   [13]I.e., a Gentile convert to Judaism

6:1 It is commonly understood that *Hellenistic Jews* spoke Greek and/or adopted some Greek customs, while *Hebrews* were more conservative Jews, perhaps largely natives of Jerusalem, who spoke Hebrew (or Aramaic) and abstained from Greek customs. Even in the early church a certain tension between the two groups was inevitable.

6:3 See note to 1 Tim. 3:8 on the office of deacon.
6:5 Nicolas, one of the seven who were chosen to serve in the Jerusalem church, was a proselyte. He is the first Gentile Christian to be identified by name. Notice that on the day of Pentecost there were proselytes from Rome in Jerusalem who heard Peter's message (2:10).

from there, after his father died, *God* removed him into this country in which you are now living.

5 "And He gave him no inheritance in it, not even a foot of ground; and *yet,* even when he had no child, He promised that HE WOULD GIVE IT TO HIM AS A POSSESSION, AND TO HIS OFFSPRING AFTER HIM.

6 "But God spoke to this effect, that his OFFSPRING WOULD BE ALIENS IN A FOREIGN LAND, AND THAT THEY WOULD BE ENSLAVED AND MISTREATED FOR FOUR HUNDRED YEARS.

7 " 'AND WHATEVER NATION TO WHICH THEY SHALL BE IN BONDAGE I MYSELF WILL JUDGE,' said God, 'AND AFTER THAT THEY WILL COME OUT AND [14]SERVE ME IN THIS PLACE.'

8 "And He gave him the covenant of circumcision; and so *Abraham* became the father of Isaac, and circumcised him on the eighth day; and Isaac *became the father of* Jacob, and Jacob *of* the twelve patriarchs.

9 "And the patriarchs became jealous of Joseph and sold him into Egypt. And *yet* God was with him,

10 and rescued him from all his afflictions, and granted him favor and wisdom in the sight of Pharaoh, king of Egypt; and he made him governor over Egypt and all his household.

11 "Now a famine came over all Egypt and Canaan, and great affliction *with it;* and our fathers could find no food.

12 "But when Jacob heard that there was grain in Egypt, he sent our fathers *there* the first time.

13 "And on the second *visit* Joseph made himself known to his brothers, and Joseph's family was disclosed to Pharaoh.

14 "And Joseph sent *word* and invited Jacob his father and all his relatives to come to him, seventy-five persons *in all.*

15 "And Jacob went down to Egypt and *there* passed away, he and our fathers.

16 "And *from there* they were removed to Shechem, and laid in the tomb which Abraham had purchased for a sum of money from the sons of Hamor in Shechem.

17 "But as the time of the promise was approaching which God had assured to Abraham, the people increased and multiplied in Egypt,

18 until THERE AROSE ANOTHER KING OVER EGYPT WHO KNEW NOTHING ABOUT JOSEPH.

19 "It was he who took shrewd advantage of our race, and mistreated our fathers so that they would expose their infants and they would not survive.

20 "And it was at this time that Moses was born; and he was lovely in the sight of God; and he was nurtured three months in his father's home.

21 "And after he had been exposed, Pharaoh's daughter took him away, and nurtured him as her own son.

22 "And Moses was educated in all the learning of the Egyptians, and he was a man of power in words and deeds.

23 "But when he was approaching the age of forty, it entered his mind to visit his brethren, the sons of Israel.

24 "And when he saw one *of them* being treated unjustly, he defended him and took vengeance for the oppressed by striking down the Egyptian.

25 "And he supposed that his brethren understood that God was granting them deliverance through him; but they did not understand.

26 "And on the following day he appeared to them as they were fighting together, and he tried to reconcile them in peace, saying, 'Men, you are brethren, why do you injure one another?'

27 "But the one who was injuring his neighbor pushed him away, saying, 'WHO MADE YOU A RULER AND JUDGE OVER US?

28 'YOU DO NOT MEAN TO KILL ME AS YOU KILLED THE EGYPTIAN YESTERDAY, DO YOU?'

29 "And at this remark MOSES FLED, AND BECAME AN ALIEN IN THE LAND OF MIDIAN, where he became the father of two sons.

30 "And after forty years had passed, AN ANGEL APPEARED TO HIM IN THE WILDERNESS OF MOUNT Sinai, IN THE FLAME OF A BURNING THORN BUSH.

Cross references (left margin):

7:5 Gen 12:7; 17:8; 26:3
7:6 Gen 15:13,14; Ex 12:40
7:7 Ex 3:12
7:8 Gen 17:9-11; 21:2-4; 25:26; 29:31ff
7:9 Gen 37:4,11, 28; 39:2,21, 23
7:10 Gen 41:37; 42:6
7:11 Gen 41:54
7:12 Gen 42:1,2
7:13 Gen 45:1-4
*7:14 Gen 45:9,10; 46:26,27; Deut 10:22
7:15 Gen 46:5; 49:33; Ex 1:6
*7:16 Gen 23:16; 33:19; Josh 24:32
7:17 Ex 1:7-9; Ps 105:24,25
7:19 Ex 1:10,11, 15-22
7:22 1 Kin 4:30; Is 19:11
7:23 Ex 2:11,12
7:30 Ex 3:1,2

[14]Or, *worship*

7:14 See note on Gen. 46:27.   **7:16** *a sum,* 400 shekels in Gen. 23:16.

31 "And when Moses saw it, he *began* to marvel at the sight; and as he approached to look *more* closely, there came the voice of the Lord:

32 'I AM THE GOD OF YOUR FATHERS, THE GOD OF ABRAHAM AND ISAAC AND JACOB.' And Moses shook with fear and would not venture to look. | 7:32 Ex 3:6

33 "BUT THE LORD SAID TO HIM, 'TAKE OFF THE SANDALS FROM YOUR FEET, FOR THE PLACE ON WHICH YOU ARE STANDING IS HOLY GROUND. | 7:33 Ex 3:5; Josh 5:15

34 'I HAVE CERTAINLY SEEN THE OPPRESSION OF MY PEOPLE IN EGYPT, AND HAVE HEARD THEIR GROANS, AND I HAVE COME DOWN TO DELIVER THEM; COME NOW, AND I WILL SEND YOU TO EGYPT.' | 7:34 Ex 3:7

35 "This Moses whom they disowned, saying, 'WHO MADE YOU A RULER AND A JUDGE?' is the one whom God sent *to be* both a ruler and a deliverer with the help of the angel who appeared to him in the thorn bush. | 7:35 Ex 14:19

36 "This man led them out, performing wonders and signs in the land of Egypt and in the Red Sea and in the wilderness for forty years. | 7:36 Ex 12:41; 14:21

37 "This is the Moses who said to the sons of Israel, 'GOD SHALL RAISE UP FOR YOU A PROPHET LIKE ME FROM YOUR BRETHREN.' | 7:37 Deut 18:15, 18; Acts 3:22

38 "This is the one who was in the congregation in the wilderness together with the angel who was speaking to him on Mount Sinai, and *who was* with our fathers; and he received living oracles to pass on to you. | 7:38 Ex 19:17; Is 63:9; Rom 3:2; Heb 5:12; 1 Pet 4:11

39 "And our fathers were unwilling to be obedient to him, but repudiated him and in their hearts turned back to Egypt,

40 SAYING TO AARON, 'MAKE FOR US GODS WHO WILL GO BEFORE US; FOR THIS MOSES WHO LED US OUT OF THE LAND OF EGYPT—WE DO NOT KNOW WHAT HAPPENED TO HIM.' | 7:40 Ex 32:1,23

41 "And at that time they made a calf and brought a sacrifice to the idol, and were rejoicing in the works of their hands. | 7:41 Ex 32:4,6; Ps 106:19

42 "But God turned away and delivered them up to serve the host of heaven; as it is written in the book of the prophets, 'IT WAS NOT TO ME THAT YOU OFFERED VICTIMS AND SACRIFICES FORTY YEARS IN THE WILDERNESS, WAS IT, O HOUSE OF ISRAEL? | 7:42 Ezek 20:25, 39; Amos 5:25,26

43 'YOU ALSO TOOK ALONG THE TABERNACLE OF MOLOCH AND THE STAR OF THE GOD ROMPHA, THE IMAGES WHICH YOU MADE TO WORSHIP THEM. I ALSO WILL REMOVE YOU BEYOND BABYLON.'

44 "Our fathers had the tabernacle of testimony in the wilderness, just as He who spoke to Moses directed *him* to make it according to the pattern which he had seen. | 7:44 Ex 25:9,40

45 "And having received it in their turn, our fathers brought it in with Joshua upon dispossessing the nations whom God drove out before our fathers, until the time of David. | 7:45 Josh 3:14-17; Ps 44:2

46 "And *David* found favor in God's sight, and asked that he might find a dwelling place for the [15]God of Jacob. | 7:46 2 Sam 7:8-16; Ps 132:1-5

47 "But it was Solomon who built a house for Him.

48 "However, the Most High does not dwell in *houses* made by *human* hands; as the prophet says: | 7:48 1 Kin 8:27; 2 Chr 2:6

49   'HEAVEN IS MY THRONE, | 7:49 Is 66:1,2; Matt 5:34,35
        AND EARTH IS THE FOOTSTOOL OF MY FEET;
        WHAT KIND OF HOUSE WILL YOU BUILD FOR ME?' says the Lord;
        'OR WHAT PLACE IS THERE FOR MY REPOSE?

50   'WAS IT NOT MY HAND WHICH MADE ALL THESE THINGS?'

51 "You men who are stiff-necked and uncircumcised in heart and ears are always resisting the Holy Spirit; you are doing just as your fathers did. | 7:51 Lev 26:41; Jer 6:10; 9:26

52 "Which one of the prophets did your fathers not persecute? And they killed those who had previously announced the coming of the Righteous One, whose betrayers and murderers you have now become; | 7:52 2 Chr 36:16; Matt 23:31, 37; Acts 3:14

53 you who received the law as ordained by angels, and *yet* did not keep it." | 7:53 Ex 20:1; Heb 2:2

[15]The earliest mss. read *house* instead of *God;* the Septuagint reads *God*

7:43 This quotation from Amos 5:25–27 employs the Greek form of the names of the two pagan deities, *Moloch* and *Rompha*, which in the Hebrew are called *Sikkuth* and *Kiyyun*. Moloch (or Molech) was the Canaanite deity to whom human sacrifices were offered.

Rompha is the Greek name for the Hebrew Kiyyun (or Chiun), which is taken to refer to Repa, the Egyptian god of the planet Saturn.

c. The stoning of Stephen

54 Now when they heard this, they were cut to the quick, and they *began* gnashing their teeth at him.

55 But being full of the Holy Spirit, he gazed intently into heaven and saw the glory of God, and Jesus standing at the right hand of God;

56 and he said, "Behold, I see the heavens opened up and the Son of Man standing at the right hand of God."

57 But they cried out with a loud voice, and covered their ears, and they rushed upon him with one impulse.

58 And when they had driven him out of the city, they *began* stoning *him*, and the witnesses laid aside their robes at the feet of a young man named Saul.

59 And they went on stoning Stephen as he called upon *the Lord* and said, "Lord Jesus, receive my spirit!"

60 And falling on his knees, he cried out with a loud voice, "Lord, do not hold this sin against them!" And having said this, he fell asleep.

8 And Saul was in hearty agreement with putting him to death.
And on that day a great persecution arose against the church in Jerusalem; and they were all scattered throughout the regions of Judea and Samaria, except the apostles.

d. The scattering of the church

2 And *some* devout men buried Stephen, and made loud lamentation over him.

3 But Saul *began* ravaging the church, entering house after house; and dragging off men and women, he would put them in prison.

II. Judea, Samaria, and on to Antioch of Syria (8:4–12:25)

A. The ministry of Philip

1. Philip at Samaria

4 Therefore, those who had been scattered went about preaching the word.

5 And Philip went down to the city of Samaria and *began* proclaiming Christ to them.

6 And the multitudes with one accord were giving attention to what was said by Philip, as they heard and saw the signs which he was performing.

7 For *in the case of* many who had unclean spirits, they were coming out *of them* shouting with a loud voice; and many who had been paralyzed and lame were healed.

8 And there was much rejoicing in that city.

2. Conversion of Simon the sorcerer

9 Now there was a certain man named Simon, who formerly was practicing magic in the city, and astonishing the people of Samaria, claiming to be someone great;

10 and they all, from smallest to greatest, were giving attention to him, saying, "This man is what is called the Great Power of God."

11 And they were giving him attention because he had for a long time astonished them with his magic arts.

12 But when they believed Philip preaching the good news about the kingdom of God and the name of Jesus Christ, they were being baptized, men and women alike.

13 And even Simon himself believed; and after being baptized, he continued on

---

8:1 *Saul* was the Hebrew name of Paul.

8:13 A miracle is commonly defined in the dictionaries as an effect in nature not attributable to any of the recognized operations of nature nor to the act of man, but indicative of superhuman power and serving as a sign or witness thereof; a wonderful work manifesting a power superior to the ordinary forces of nature. Whereas miracles were once regarded as an aid to faith, they now are stumbling blocks for a science-minded generation that has been taught to regard them as impossible. The Bible does not argue the case for miracles; it just assumes them. Efforts to explain away miracles of Scripture or to discount them are most unsuccessful. They are part of the very warp and woof of the Bible and cannot be excised from the holy record without rendering much of the narrative implausible and unmotivated. The supreme miracle is the incarnation of Jesus Christ, who is the Word of God and by whom the miracle of salvation is wrought.

with Philip; and as he observed signs and great miracles taking place, he was constantly amazed.

14 Now when the apostles in Jerusalem heard that Samaria had received the word of God, they sent them Peter and John,

15 who came down and prayed for them, that they might receive the Holy Spirit.

16 For He had not yet fallen upon any of them; they had simply been baptized in the name of the Lord Jesus.

17 Then they *began* laying their hands on them, and they were receiving the Holy Spirit.

18 Now when Simon saw that the Spirit was bestowed through the laying on of the apostles' hands, he offered them money,

19 saying, "Give this authority to me as well, so that everyone on whom I lay my hands may receive the Holy Spirit."

20 But Peter said to him, "May your silver perish with you, because you thought you could obtain the gift of God with money!

21 "You have no part or portion in this matter, for your heart is not right before God.

22 "Therefore repent of this wickedness of yours, and pray the Lord that if possible, the intention of your heart may be forgiven you.

23 "For I see that you are in the gall of bitterness and in the bondage of iniquity."

24 But Simon answered and said, "Pray to the Lord for me yourselves, so that nothing of what you have said may come upon me."

25 And so, when they had solemnly testified and spoken the word of the Lord, they started back to Jerusalem, and were preaching the gospel to many villages of the Samaritans.

3. Conversion of the Ethiopian eunuch

26 But an angel of the Lord spoke to Philip saying, "Arise and go south to the road that descends from Jerusalem to Gaza." (This is a desert *road*.)

27 And he arose and went; and behold, there was an Ethiopian eunuch, a court official of Candace, queen of the Ethiopians, who was in charge of all her treasure; and he had come to Jerusalem to worship.

28 And he was returning and sitting in his chariot, and was reading the prophet Isaiah.

29 And the Spirit said to Philip, "Go up and join this chariot."

30 And when Philip had run up, he heard him reading Isaiah the prophet, and said, "Do you understand what you are reading?"

31 And he said, "Well, how could I, unless someone guides me?" And he invited Philip to come up and sit with him.

32 Now the passage of Scripture which he was reading was this:
"HE WAS LED AS A SHEEP TO SLAUGHTER;
AND AS A LAMB BEFORE ITS SHEARER IS SILENT,
SO HE DOES NOT OPEN HIS MOUTH.

33 "IN HUMILIATION HIS JUDGMENT WAS TAKEN AWAY;
WHO SHALL RELATE HIS GENERATION?
FOR HIS LIFE IS REMOVED FROM THE EARTH."

34 And the eunuch answered Philip and said, "Please *tell me*, of whom does the prophet say this? Of himself, or of someone else?"

35 And Philip opened his mouth, and beginning from this Scripture he preached Jesus to him.

36 And as they went along the road they came to some water; and the eunuch *said, "Look! Water! What prevents me from being baptized?"

Marginal references:

8:14
v. 1

8:15
Acts 2:38

8:16
Acts 19:2;
Matt 28:19;
Acts 10:48;
19:5

8:17
Acts 6:6; 2:4

*arrogance &
selfish ambition
cf James 3:14*

8:20
Acts 2:38;
Matt 10:8;
2 Kin 5:16

8:21
Ps 78:37

8:23
Is 58:6;
Heb 12:15

8:25
Luke 16:28;
v. 40

8:26
Acts 5:19;
v. 5

*8:27
Ps 68:31;
Zeph 3:10;
John 12:20

*8:29
Acts 10:19;
11:12; 13:2;
20:23; 21:11

8:32
Is 53:7,8

8:35
Matt 5:2;
Luke 24:27;
Acts 17:2;
18:28; 5:42

8:36
Acts 10:47

8:27 As a Gentile convert to the Jewish faith, i.e., a prose-lyte, the Ethiopian eunuch had gone to Jerusalem to wor-ship in the temple, probably during one of the great feasts of the Jews. He is the second Gentile referred to specifically as a convert to the Christian faith (cf. note to 6:5 on Nicolas).
8:29 (For the person of the Holy Spirit see notes to John 14:16 and Acts 5:3.) The Holy Spirit fulfills many offices, among which are: (1) directing God's servants concerning where, when, and what to do or to preach (8:29; 10:19,20;

16:6,7; 1 Cor. 2:13); (2) choosing and commissioning work-ers for Christ's service (13:2; 20:28); (3) teaching the church the truth of Christ (John 14:26; 1 Cor. 12:3); (4) testifying to the Son and magnifying His glory (John 15:26; 16:14); (5) reproving sinners and convicting them of their guilt (John 16:8); and (6) communicating the truths of Scripture to men (1:16; 1 Pet. 1:11,12; 2 Pet. 1:21). The Holy Spirit may be resisted (7:51); He may be quenched (1 Thess. 5:19); and He may be grieved (Eph. 4:30).

37   [[16]And Philip said, "If you believe with all your heart, you may." And he answered and said, "I believe that Jesus Christ is the Son of God."]

38   And he ordered the chariot to stop; and they both went down into the water, Philip as well as the eunuch; and he baptized him.

8:39
1 Kin 18:12;
2 Kin 2:16;
Ezek 3:12,14

39   And when they came up out of the water, the Spirit of the Lord snatched Philip away; and the eunuch saw him no more, but went on his way rejoicing.

40   But Philip found himself at Azotus; and as he passed through he kept preaching the gospel to all the cities, until he came to Caesarea.

B. *The conversion of Saul (Paul)*

1. *His call on the Damascus road*

9:1
Acts 8:3;
22:4-16;
26:9-18

9 Now Saul, still breathing threats and murder against the disciples of the Lord, went to the high priest,

2   and asked for letters from him to the synagogues at Damascus, so that if he found any belonging to the Way, both men and women, he might bring them bound to Jerusalem.

9:3
Acts 22:6;
26:12;
1 Cor 15:8
9:4
Acts 22:7;
26:14

3   And it came about that as he journeyed, he was approaching Damascus, and suddenly a light from heaven flashed around him;

4   and he fell to the ground, and heard a voice saying to him, "Saul, Saul, why are you persecuting Me?"

5   And he said, "Who art Thou, Lord?" And He *said*, "I am Jesus whom you are persecuting,

6   but rise, and enter the city, and it shall be told you what you must do."

9:7
Acts 22:9;
26:13,14
9:8
Acts 22:11;
Gal 1:17

See Acts 26 for Paul's re-telling of his conversion

7   And the men who traveled with him stood speechless, hearing the voice, but seeing no one.

8   And Saul got up from the ground, and though his eyes were open, he could see nothing; and leading him by the hand, they brought him into Damascus.

9   And he was three days without sight, and neither ate nor drank.

2. *His baptism by Ananias*

9:10
Acts 22:12

10   Now there was a certain disciple at Damascus, named Ananias; and the Lord said to him in a vision, "Ananias." And he said, "Behold, *here am* I, Lord."

9:11
Acts 21:39;
22:3

11   And the Lord *said* to him, "Arise and go to the street called Straight, and inquire at the house of Judas for a man from Tarsus named Saul, for behold, he is praying,

12   and he has seen [17]in a vision a man named Ananias come in and lay his hands on him, so that he might regain his sight."

9:14
v. 21;
Acts 7:59;
1 Cor 1:2;
2 Tim 2:22
9:15
Acts 13:2;
Eph 3:7,8;
Gal 2:7,8;
Acts 25:22,
23; 26:1
***9:16**
Acts 20:23;
21:11;
2 Cor 11:23
9:17
Acts 22:12,
13; 8:17; 2:4;
4:31
9:19
Acts 26:20

13   But Ananias answered, "Lord, I have heard from many about this man, how much harm he did to Thy saints at Jerusalem;

14   and here he has authority from the chief priests to bind all who call upon Thy name."

15   But the Lord said to him, "Go, for he is a chosen [18]instrument of Mine, to bear My name before the Gentiles and kings and the sons of Israel;

16   for I will show him how much he must suffer for My name's sake."

17   And Ananias departed and entered the house, and after laying his hands on him said, "Brother Saul, the Lord Jesus, who appeared to you on the road by which you were coming, has sent me so that you may regain your sight, and be filled with the Holy Spirit."

18   And immediately there fell from his eyes something like scales, and he regained his sight, and he arose and was baptized;

19   and he took food and was strengthened.

Now for several days he was with the disciples who were at Damascus,

20   and immediately he *began* to proclaim Jesus in the synagogues, saying, "He is the Son of God."

---

[16]Many mss. do not contain this verse   [17]Some mss. do not contain *in a vision*   [18]Or, *vessel*

9:2 *Way* is a name used in the book of Acts for the Christian faith (see also 19:9,23; 24:14,22). It is *the way of God* (18:26), *the way of salvation* (16:17). All these passages aptly describe the faith that rests on Him who said, *I am the way*

(John 14:6).
9:16 This prophecy was accurately fulfilled in the life of Paul, who suffered greatly for the sake of Jesus. Those who follow Him do not necessarily live without suffering.

3. His preaching at Damascus

21   And all those hearing him continued to be amazed, and were saying, "Is this not he who in Jerusalem destroyed those who called on this name, and *who* had come here for the purpose of bringing them bound before the chief priests?"

22   But Saul kept increasing in strength and confounding the Jews who lived at Damascus by proving that this *Jesus* is the Christ.

4. His escape from the Jews

23   And when many days had elapsed, the Jews plotted together to do away with him,

24   but their plot became known to Saul. And they were also watching the gates day and night so that they might put him to death;

25   but his disciples took him by night, and let him down through *an opening in* the wall, lowering him in a large basket.

5. His reception in Jerusalem

26   And when he had come to Jerusalem, he was trying to associate with the disciples; and they were all afraid of him, not believing that he was a disciple.

27   But Barnabas took hold of him and brought him to the apostles and described to them how he had seen the Lord on the road, and that He had talked to him, and how at Damascus he had spoken out boldly in the name of Jesus.

28   And he was with them moving about freely in Jerusalem, speaking out boldly in the name of the Lord.

29   And he was talking and arguing with the Hellenistic *Jews;* but they were attempting to put him to death.

30   But when the brethren learned *of it,* they brought him down to Caesarea and sent him away to Tarsus.

31   So the church throughout all Judea and Galilee and Samaria enjoyed peace, being built up; and, going on in the fear of the Lord and in the comfort of the Holy Spirit, it continued to increase.

C. The ministry of Peter

1. Aeneas healed

32   Now it came about that as Peter was traveling through all *those parts,* he came down also to the saints who lived at Lydda.

33   And there he found a certain man named Aeneas, who had been bedridden eight years, for he was paralyzed.

34   And Peter said to him, "Aeneas, Jesus Christ heals you; arise, and make your bed." And immediately he arose.

35   And all who lived at Lydda and Sharon saw him, and they turned to the Lord.

2. Tabitha raised from the dead

36   Now in Joppa there was a certain disciple named Tabitha (which translated *in Greek* is called Dorcas); this woman was abounding with deeds of kindness and charity, which she continually did.

37   And it came about at that time that she fell sick and died; and when they had washed her body, they laid it in an upper room.

38   And since Lydda was near Joppa, the disciples, having heard that Peter was there, sent two men to him, entreating him, "Do not delay to come to us."

39   And Peter arose and went with them. And when he had come, they brought him into the upper room; and all the widows stood beside him weeping, and showing all the [19]tunics and garments that Dorcas used to make while she was with them.

40   But Peter sent them all out and knelt down and prayed, and turning to the

---

[19]Or, *inner garments*

Marginal references:

9:21 Acts 8:3; Gal 1:13,23

9:22 Acts 18:28

9:23 Acts 23:12; 25:3

9:24 2 Cor 11:32, 33

*9:26 Acts 22:17; Gal 1:17,18

9:27 Acts 4:36; vv. 20,22

9:29 Acts 6:1; 11:20; 2 Cor 11:26

9:31 Acts 8:1

9:32 v. 13

*9:34 Acts 3:6,16; 4:10

9:35 1 Chr 5:16; Acts 11:21

9:36 John 1:3; 1 Tim 2:10; Titus 3:8

9:37 Acts 1:13

9:38 Acts 11:26

9:39 Acts 6:1

9:40 Matt 9:25; Acts 7:60; Mark 5:41,42

9:26 The Christians might well suspect that Paul's conversion was a trap to ensnare them.
9:34 This was another manifestation of the many signs and wonders that were part of the apostolic period. They subsequently decreased and were seldom repeated. The greater part of the miracles recorded in Scripture occurred within a relatively short space of time, and they were connected with only a few names: Moses, Elijah, Elisha, Jesus, and the apostles.

body, he said, "Tabitha, arise." And she opened her eyes, and when she saw Peter, she sat up.

41   And he gave her his hand and raised her up; and calling the saints and widows, he presented her alive.

42   And it became known all over Joppa, and many believed in the Lord.

43   And it came about that he stayed many days in Joppa with a certain tanner, Simon.

3. The conversion of Cornelius

a. Cornelius' vision

10 Now *there was* a certain man at Caesarea named Cornelius, a centurion of what was called the Italian [20]cohort,

2   a devout man, and one who feared God with all his household, and gave many [21]alms to the *Jewish* people, and prayed to God continually.

3   About the [22]ninth hour of the day he clearly saw in a vision an angel of God who had *just* come in to him, and said to him, "Cornelius!"

4   And fixing his gaze upon him and being much alarmed, he said, "What is it, Lord?" And he said to him, "Your prayers and [23]alms have ascended as a memorial before God.

5   "And now dispatch *some* men to Joppa, and send for a man *named* Simon, who is also called Peter;

6   he is staying with a certain tanner *named* Simon, whose house is by the sea."

7   And when the angel who was speaking to him had departed, he summoned two of his servants and a devout soldier of those who were in constant attendance upon him,

8   and after he had explained everything to them, he sent them to Joppa.

b. Peter's vision

9   And on the next day, as they were on their way, and approaching the city, Peter went up on the housetop about the [24]sixth hour to pray.

10   And he became hungry, and was desiring to eat; but while they were making preparations, he fell into a trance;

11   and he *beheld the sky opened up, and a certain [25]object like a great sheet coming down, lowered by four corners to the ground,

12   and there were in it all *kinds of* four-footed animals and [26]crawling creatures of the earth and birds of the air.

13   And a voice came to him, "Arise, Peter, kill and eat!"

14   But Peter said, "By no means, Lord, for I have never eaten anything unholy and unclean."

15   And again a voice *came* to him a second time, "What God has cleansed, no *longer* consider unholy."

16   And this happened three times; and immediately the object was taken up into the sky.

c. The sending for Peter

17   Now while Peter was greatly perplexed in mind as to what the vision which he had seen might be, behold, the men who had been sent by Cornelius, having asked directions for Simon's house, appeared at the gate;

18   and calling out, they were asking whether Simon, who was also called Peter, was staying there.

19   And while Peter was reflecting on the vision, the Spirit said to him, "Behold, three men are looking for you.

20   "But arise, go downstairs, and accompany them without misgivings; for I have sent them Myself."

21   And Peter went down to the men and said, "Behold, I am the one you are looking for; what is the reason for which you have come?"

22   And they said, "Cornelius, a centurion, a righteous and God-fearing man

[20]Or, *battalion* [21]Or, *gifts of charity* [22]I.e., 3 p.m. [23]Or, *deeds of charity* [24]I.e., noon [25]Or, *vessel* [26]Or possibly, *reptiles*

10:1 Cornelius, the Roman centurion, is the third Gentile convert to be identified in the book of Acts (cf. notes on Nicolas the proselyte, 6:5; the Ethiopian eunuch, 8:27). The descent of the Holy Spirit on these Gentiles, Cornelius, his household and friends (10:24,44,45), marks a new phase in the spread of the gospel (11:15–18). So Peter refers to it later (15:7–9). Note that he needed a vision before he would preach to a Gentile.

well spoken of by the entire nation of the Jews, was *divinely* directed by a holy angel to send for you *to come* to his house and hear a message from you.''

23   And so he invited them in and gave them lodging.

And on the next day he arose and went away with them, and some of the brethren from Joppa accompanied him.

10:23
v. 45;
Acts 11:12

d. *Peter's visit to Cornelius*

24   And on the following day he entered Caesarea. Now Cornelius was waiting for them, and had called together his relatives and close friends.

25   And when it came about that Peter entered, Cornelius met him, and fell at his feet and worshiped *him*.

26   But Peter raised him up, saying, "Stand up; I too am *just* a man."

27   And as he talked with him, he entered, and found many people assembled.

28   And he said to them, "You yourselves know how unlawful it is for a man who is a Jew to associate with a foreigner or to visit him; and *yet* God has shown me that I should not call any man unholy or unclean.

29   "That is why I came without even raising any objection when I was sent for. And so I ask for what reason you have sent for me."

30   And Cornelius said, "Four days ago to this hour, I was praying in my house during the [27]ninth hour; and behold, a man stood before me in shining garments,

31   and he *said, 'Cornelius, your prayer has been heard and your alms have been remembered before God.

32   'Send therefore to Joppa and invite Simon, who is also called Peter, to come to you; he is staying at the house of Simon *the* tanner by the sea.'

33   "And so I sent to you immediately, and you have been kind enough to come. Now then, we are all here present before God to hear all that you have been commanded by the Lord."

10:26
Acts 24:14,
15; Rev 19:10
10:28
John 4:9;
18:28;
Acts 11:3;
15:8,9

10:30
Acts 1:10;
Matt 28:3;
Mark 16:5;
Luke 24:4

e. *Peter's sermon to Cornelius*

34   And opening his mouth, Peter said:

"**I** most certainly understand *now* that God is not one to show partiality,

35   but in every nation the man who fears Him and does what is right, is welcome to Him.

36   "The word which He sent to the sons of Israel, preaching peace through Jesus Christ (He is Lord of all)—

37   you yourselves know the thing which took place throughout all Judea, starting from Galilee, after the baptism which John proclaimed.

38   "*You know of* Jesus of Nazareth, how God anointed Him with the Holy Spirit and with power, and *how* He went about doing good, and healing all who were oppressed by the devil; for God was with Him.

39   "And we are witnesses of all the things He did both in the land of the Jews and in Jerusalem. And they also put Him to death by hanging Him on a cross.

40   "God raised Him up on the third day, and granted that He should become visible,

41   not to all the people, but to witnesses who were chosen beforehand by God, *that is*, to us, who ate and drank with Him after He arose from the dead.

42   "And He ordered us to preach to the people, and solemnly to testify that this is the One who has been appointed by God as Judge of the living and the dead.

43   "Of Him all the prophets bear witness that through His name everyone who believes in Him receives forgiveness of sins."

10:34
Deut 10:17;
Rom 2:11;
Eph 6:9;
Col 3:25;
1 Pet 1:17
10:35
Acts 15:9
10:36
Is 57:19;
Matt 28:18;
Rom 10:12;
Eph 1:20,22
10:38
Acts 2:22;
John 3:2

10:39
Luke 24:48;
Acts 5:30
10:40
Acts 2:24

10:41
John 14:17,
22; 21:13
10:42
Matt 28:19,
20;
Rom 14:9;
2 Cor 5:10;
1 Pet 4:5
10:43
Is 53:11;
Acts 26:22;
15:9;
Rom 10:11;
Gal 3:22

f. *The baptism of Cornelius*

44   While Peter was still speaking these words, the Holy Spirit fell upon all those who were listening to the message.

45   And all the circumcised believers who had come with Peter were amazed, because the gift of the Holy Spirit had been poured out upon the Gentiles also.

46   For they were hearing them speaking with tongues and exalting God. Then Peter answered,

47   "Surely no one can refuse the water for these to be baptized who have received the Holy Spirit just as we *did*, can he?"

48   And he ordered them to be baptized in the name of Jesus Christ. Then they asked him to stay on for a few days.

10:44
Acts 4:31;
8:15,16;
11:15; 15:8
10:45
v. 23;
Acts 11:18
10:47
Acts 8:36;
11:17
10:48
1 Cor 1:17;
Acts 2:38;
8:16; 19:5

[27]I.e., 3 to 4 p.m.

g. *Peter's defense of Gentile evangelization*

11 Now the apostles and the brethren who were throughout Judea heard that the Gentiles also had received the word of God.

2 And when Peter came up to Jerusalem, those who were circumcised took issue with him,

3 saying, "You went to uncircumcised men and ate with them."

4 But Peter began *speaking* and *proceeded* to explain to them in orderly sequence, saying,

5 "I was in the city of Joppa praying; and in a trance I saw a vision, a certain object coming down like a great sheet lowered by four corners from the sky; and it came right down to me,

6 and when I had fixed my gaze upon it and was observing it I saw the four-footed animals of the earth and the wild beasts and the [28]crawling creatures and the birds of the air.

7 "And I also heard a voice saying to me, 'Arise, Peter; kill and eat.'

8 "But I said, 'By no means, Lord, for nothing unholy or unclean has ever entered my mouth.'

9 "But a voice from heaven answered a second time, 'What God has cleansed, no longer consider unholy.'

10 "And this happened three times, and everything was drawn back up into the sky.

11 "And behold, at that moment three men appeared before the house in which we were *staying*, having been sent to me from Caesarea.

12 "And the Spirit told me to go with them without misgivings. And these six brethren also went with me, and we entered the man's house.

13 "And he reported to us how he had seen the angel standing in his house, and saying, 'Send to Joppa, and have Simon, who is also called Peter, brought here;

14 and he shall speak words to you by which you will be saved, you and all your household.'

15 "And as I began to speak, the Holy Spirit fell upon them, just as *He did* upon us at the beginning.

16 "And I remembered the word of the Lord, how He used to say, 'John baptized with water, but you shall be baptized with the Holy Spirit.'

17 "If God therefore gave to them the same gift as *He gave* to us also after believing in the Lord Jesus Christ, who was I that I could stand in God's way?"

18 And when they heard this, they quieted down, and glorified God, saying, "Well then, God has granted to the Gentiles also the repentance *that leads* to life."

D. *Barnabas at Antioch*

19 So then those who were scattered because of the persecution that arose in connection with Stephen made their way to Phoenicia and Cyprus and Antioch, speaking the word to no one except to Jews alone.

20 But there were some of them, men of Cyprus and Cyrene, who came to Antioch and *began* speaking to the [29]Greeks also, preaching the Lord Jesus.

21 And the hand of the Lord was with them, and a large number who believed turned to the Lord.

22 And the news about them reached the ears of the church at Jerusalem, and they sent Barnabas off to Antioch.

23 Then when he had come and witnessed the grace of God, he rejoiced and *began* to encourage them all with resolute heart to remain *true* to the Lord;

24 for he was a good man, and full of the Holy Spirit and of faith. And considerable numbers were brought to the Lord.

25 And he left for Tarsus to look for Saul;

26 and when he had found him, he brought him to Antioch. And it came about

---

Cross-references (left margin):

*11:2 Acts 10:45
11:3 Acts 10:28; Gal 2:12
11:4 Luke 1:3
11:5 Acts 10:9-32
11:9 Acts 10:15
11:12 Acts 8:29; 15:9; 10:23
11:13 Acts 10:30
11:15 Acts 10:44; 2:4
11:16 Matt 3:11; John 1:26,33; Acts 1:5; Joel 2:28; 3:18
11:17 Acts 10:45,47
11:18 Rom 10:12, 13; 2 Cor 7:10
11:19 Acts 8:1,4
*11:20 Acts 4:36; 6:5; 13:1; 5:42
11:21 Luke 1:66; Acts 2:47; 9:35
11:23 Acts 13:43; 14:22
11:24 Acts 6:5; v. 21; Acts 5:14
11:25 Acts 9:1,30
*11:26 Acts 26:28

---

[28]Or possibly, *reptiles*   [29]Some mss. read *Greek-speaking Jews*

11:2 The early church was constantly vexed by the problem of legalism, particularly as it related to circumcision. Paul addressed himself to this question definitively in his letter to the Galatians.

11:20 " . . . *speaking to the Greeks* . . . " The preaching of the gospel to the Greeks in Antioch by the Cypriot and Cyrenian evangelists marks the first systematic attempt to evangelize the Gentiles as a whole. This initial campaign was followed by the farspread missionary work of Paul in preaching throughout the whole Mediterranean world (cf. 14:27; 15:3).

11:26 It was in Antioch that the followers of Jesus were first called *Christians*, perhaps as a term of opprobrium. The word appears only two more times: 26:28 and 1 Pet. 4:16.

that for an entire year they met with the church, and taught considerable numbers; and the disciples were first called Christians in Antioch.

27 Now at this time some prophets came down from Jerusalem to Antioch.

28 And one of them named Agabus stood up and *began* to indicate by the Spirit that there would certainly be a great famine all over the world. And this took place in the *reign* of Claudius.

29 And in the proportion that any of the disciples had means, each of them determined to send *a contribution* for the relief of the brethren living in Judea.

30 And this they did, sending it in charge of Barnabas and Saul to the elders.

E. *Herod's persecution*

1. *Martyrdom of James; imprisonment of Peter*

12 Now about that time Herod the king laid hands on some who belonged to the church, in order to mistreat them.

2 And he had James the brother of John put to death with a sword.

3 And when he saw that it pleased the Jews, he proceeded to arrest Peter also. Now it was during the days of Unleavened Bread.

4 And when he had seized him, he put him in prison, delivering him to four squads of soldiers to guard him, intending after the Passover to bring him out before the people.

5 So Peter was kept in the prison, but prayer for him was being made fervently by the church to God.

2. *Deliverance of Peter*

6 And on the very night when Herod was about to bring him forward, Peter was sleeping between two soldiers, bound with two chains; and guards in front of the door were watching over the prison.

7 And behold, an angel of the Lord suddenly appeared, and a light shone in the cell; and he struck Peter's side and roused him, saying, "Get up quickly." And his chains fell off his hands.

8 And the angel said to him, "Gird yourself and put on your sandals." And he did so. And he *said to him, "Wrap your cloak around you and follow me."

9 And he went out and continued to follow, and he did not know that what was being done by the angel was real, but thought he was seeing a vision.

10 And when they had passed the first and second guard, they came to the iron gate that leads into the city, which opened for them by itself; and they went out and went along one street; and immediately the angel departed from him.

11 And when Peter came to himself, he said, "Now I know for sure that the Lord has sent forth His angel and rescued me from the hand of Herod and from all that the Jewish people were expecting."

3. *The testimony of Peter*

12 And when he realized *this*, he went to the house of Mary, the mother of John who was also called Mark, where many were gathered together and were praying.

13 And when he knocked at the door of the gate, a servant-girl named Rhoda came to answer.

14 And when she recognized Peter's voice, because of her joy she did not open the gate, but ran in and announced that Peter was standing in front of the gate.

11:27 Christian prophets are here mentioned for the first time. Both John the Baptist and Jesus are called prophets. Besides Agabus (see also 21:10), mention is made of the prophets in the church at Antioch (13:1), Judas and Silas are called prophets (15:32), and the four unmarried daughters of Philip the evangelist also prophesied (21:9). Elsewhere in the New Testament the prophets are referred to in 1 Cor. 12:28,29; 14:29,37; Eph. 4:11. It is not certain whether the prophets spoken of in Eph. 2:20 and 3:5 are Christian or Old Testament prophets.

11:28 *Claudius*, emperor from A.D. 41–54, nephew of the emperor Tiberius and grandson of Livia, the wife of Augustus. Agrippina, his last wife, was a niece. He adopted her son Nero.

11:30 This is the first mention in the New Testament of

Christian church officers called *elders* (or presbyters). In Acts, the elders in the Jerusalem church are referred to further in 15:2–23; 16:4; 21:18. Other references in Acts to elders are found in 14:23 and 20:17. Outside of Acts they are mentioned in 1 Tim. 4:14; 5:17,19; Titus 1:5; James 5:14; 1 Pet. 5:1,5; 2 John 1; 3 John 1. Nothing is said about the origin of church officers, but it is probable that the Christian elders were patterned in name and function after the Jewish elders of the synagogue. (See note to Titus 1:5.)

12:1 This is Herod Agrippa I, grandson of Herod the Great, born in 11 B.C. Reared in Rome, he was given the tetrarchies of Iturea, Trachonitis, and Gaulinitis (cf. Luke 3:1) in A.D. 37 by the Roman emperor Gaius, who also conferred on him the title of king. Later he was also given rule over Galilee and Perea, and still later, under Claudius, his rule was extended to include Judea and Samaria.

15 Gen 48:16; Matt 18:10 15 And they said to her, "You are out of your mind!" But she kept insisting that it was so. And they kept saying, "It is his angel."

16 But Peter continued knocking; and when they had opened *the door*, they saw him and were amazed.

12:17
Acts 13:16; 19:33; 21:40
17 But motioning to them with his hand to be silent, he described to them how the Lord had led him out of the prison. And he said, "Report these things to James and the brethren." And he departed and went to another place.

4. Herod's punishment of the guards

18 Now when day came, there was no small disturbance among the soldiers *as to* what could have become of Peter.

12:19
Acts 16:27; 27:42
19 And when Herod had searched for him and had not found him, he examined the guards and ordered that they be led away *to execution*. And he went down from Judea to Caesarea and was spending time there.

5. Herod's death

12:20
Matt 11:21; 1 Kin 5:9,11; Ezek 27:17
20 Now he was very angry with the people of Tyre and Sidon; and with one accord they came to him, and having won over Blastus the king's chamberlain, they were asking for peace, because their country was fed by the king's country.

21 And on an appointed day Herod, having put on his royal apparel, took his seat on the rostrum and *began* delivering an address to them.

22 And the people kept crying out, "The voice of a god and not of a man!"

12:23
1 Sam 25:38; 2 Sam 24:17
23 And immediately an angel of the Lord struck him because he did not give God the glory, and he was eaten by worms and died.

12:24
Acts 6:7; 19:20
24 But the word of the Lord continued to grow and to be multiplied.

12:25
Acts 13:5,13; 15:37
25 And Barnabas and Saul returned from Jerusalem when they had fulfilled their mission, taking along with *them* John, who was also called Mark.

III. Throughout the Roman Empire with Paul (13:1—28:31)

A. First missionary journey

1. The call of Paul and Barnabas

*13:1
Acts 11:22-26
13 Now there were at Antioch, in the church that was *there*, prophets and teachers: Barnabas, and Simeon who was called Niger, and Lucius of Cyrene, and Manaen who had been brought up with Herod the tetrarch, and Saul.

13:2
Acts 9:15; 22:21; 14:26
2 And while they were ministering to the Lord and fasting, the Holy Spirit said, "Set apart for Me Barnabas and Saul for the work to which I have called them."

13:3
Acts 6:65; 14:26
3 Then, when they had fasted and prayed and laid their hands on them, they sent them away.

2. Their ministry on Cyprus

13:4
vv. 2,3;
Acts 4:36
4 So, being sent out by the Holy Spirit, they went down to Seleucia and from there they sailed to Cyprus.

*13:5
Acts 9:20
5 And when they reached Salamis, they *began* to proclaim the word of God in the synagogues of the Jews; and they also had John as their helper.

13:6
Acts 8:9
6 And when they had gone through the whole island as far as Paphos, they found a certain magician, a Jewish false prophet whose name was Bar-Jesus,

13:7
vv. 8,12
7 who was with the proconsul, Sergius Paulus, a man of intelligence. This man summoned Barnabas and Saul and sought to hear the word of God.

13:8
Acts 8:9;
vv. 7,12;
Acts 6:7
8 But Elymas the magician (for thus his name is translated) was opposing them, seeking to turn the proconsul away from the faith.

13:1 *Teachers*, as a distinct group, are referred to here and in 1 Cor. 12:28,29; Eph. 4:11; Heb. 5:12; James 3:1. Paul's teaching ministry is often referred to (cf. 11:26; 15:35; 18:11; 20:20; 28:31), and he calls himself a teacher in 1 Tim. 2:7 and 2 Tim. 1:11.
13:5 The word *synagogue* comes from the Greek *synagōgē*—a place where people are brought together. The Old Testament does not make frequent reference to these places of worship. That they existed seems clear from Ps. 74:8. Although there are no precise historical references as to the date and place of origin of the synagogues, it would appear that they originated among the Jews of the Disper-

sion, especially during the last century of the Persian rule (440–330 B.C.). The services in the synagogues consisted of prayer, reading the Old Testament Scriptures, expounding the Scriptures, and praise and thanksgiving to God (Neh. 9:5; Matt. 6:5; Luke 4:16–21; Acts 13:15; 15:21). Christ Himself attended, taught, and preached in synagogues, and performed miracles before their congregations (Matt. 4:23; 12:9,10; Luke 4:16; 13:10–13). The apostles followed the practice of Christ in this respect (9:20; 13:5; 17:1,17), though rejection of the gospel message often compelled them to preach their message elsewhere than in synagogues (18:8).

9   But Saul, who was also *known as* Paul, filled with the Holy Spirit, fixed his gaze upon him,

10   and said, "You who are full of all deceit and fraud, you son of the devil, you enemy of all righteousness, will you not cease to make crooked the straight ways of the Lord?

11   "And now, behold, the hand of the Lord is upon you, and you will be blind and not see the sun for a time." And immediately a mist and a darkness fell upon him, and he went about seeking those who would lead him by the hand.

12   Then the proconsul believed when he saw what had happened, being amazed at the teaching of the Lord.

3. *Their ministry to Perga and Antioch*

13   Now Paul and his companions put out to sea from Paphos and came to Perga in Pamphylia; and John left them and returned to Jerusalem.

14   But going on from Perga, they arrived at Pisidian Antioch, and on the Sabbath day they went into the synagogue and sat down.

15   And after the reading of the Law and the Prophets the synagogue officials sent to them, saying, "Brethren, if you have any word of exhortation for the people, say it."

16   And Paul stood up, and motioning with his hand, he said,

"Men of Israel, and you who fear God, listen:

17   "The God of this people Israel chose our fathers, and made the people great during their stay in the land of Egypt, and with an uplifted arm He led them out from it.

18   "And for a period of about forty years He put up with them in the wilderness.

19   "And when He had destroyed seven nations in the land of Canaan, He distributed their land as an inheritance—*all of which took* about four hundred and fifty years.

20   "And after these things He gave *them* judges until Samuel the prophet.

21   "And then they asked for a king, and God gave them Saul the son of Kish, a man of the tribe of Benjamin, for forty years.

22   "And after He had removed him, He raised up David to be their king, concerning whom He also testified and said, 'I HAVE FOUND DAVID the son of Jesse, A MAN AFTER MY HEART, who will do all My will.'

23   "From the offspring of this man, according to promise, God has brought to Israel a Savior, Jesus,

24   after John had proclaimed before His coming a baptism of repentance to all the people of Israel.

25   "And while John was completing his course, he kept saying, 'What do you suppose that I am? I am not *He*. But behold, one is coming after me the sandals of whose feet I am not worthy to untie.'

26   "Brethren, sons of Abraham's family, and those among you who fear God, to us the word of this salvation is sent out.

27   "For those who live in Jerusalem, and their rulers, recognizing neither Him nor the utterances of the prophets which are read every Sabbath, fulfilled *these* by condemning *Him*.

28   "And though they found no ground for *putting Him to* death, they asked Pilate that He be executed.

29   "And when they had carried out all that was written concerning Him, they took Him down from the cross and laid Him in a tomb.

30   "But God raised Him from the dead;

31   and for many days He appeared to those who came up with Him from Galilee to Jerusalem, the very ones who are now His witnesses to the people.

32   "And we preach to you the good news of the promise made to the fathers,

33   that God has fulfilled this *promise* to our children in that He raised up Jesus, as it is also written in the second Psalm, 'THOU ART MY SON; TODAY I HAVE BEGOTTEN THEE.'

34   "*And as for the fact* that He raised Him up from the dead, no more to return to decay, He has spoken in this way: 'I WILL GIVE YOU THE HOLY *and* SURE *blessings* OF DAVID.'

35   "Therefore He also says in another *Psalm*, 'THOU WILT NOT ALLOW THY HOLY ONE TO UNDERGO DECAY.'

13:9	Acts 4:8
13:10	Matt 13:38; John 8:44; Hos 14:9
13:11	Ex 9:3
13:12	vv. 7,8; Acts 8:25
13:13	Acts 15:38
13:14	Acts 14:19, 21; 16:13
13:17	Deut 7:6-8
13:18	Ex 16:35; Deut 1:31
13:19	Deut 7:1; Josh 19:51
13:20	Judg 2:16; 1 Sam 3:20
13:21	1 Sam 8:5; 10:1
13:22	1 Sam 13:14; 15:23,26
13:23	Is 11:1; Matt 1:21; Rom 11:26
13:24	Matt 3:1; Luke 3:3
13:25	Matt 3:11; Luke 3:16
13:27	Luke 23:13; Acts 3:17; Luke 24:27
13:28	Matt 27:22
13:29	Luke 18:31; Matt 27:59
13:30	Matt 28:6
13:31	Matt 28:16; Luke 24:48
13:32	Gen 3:15; Rom 4:13
13:33	Ps 2:7
13:34	Is 55:3
13:35	Ps 16:10; Acts 2:27

36 "For David, after he had served the purpose of God in his own generation, fell asleep, and was laid among his fathers, and underwent decay;

37 but He whom God raised did not undergo decay.

38 "Therefore let it be known to you, brethren, that through Him forgiveness of sins is proclaimed to you,

39 and through Him everyone who believes is freed from all things, from which you could not be freed through the Law of Moses.

40 "Take heed therefore, so that the thing spoken of in the Prophets may not come upon *you*:

41   'BEHOLD, YOU SCOFFERS, AND MARVEL, AND PERISH;
    FOR I AM ACCOMPLISHING A WORK IN YOUR DAYS,
    A WORK WHICH YOU WILL NEVER BELIEVE, THOUGH SOMEONE SHOULD
        DESCRIBE IT TO YOU.' "

42 And as Paul and Barnabas were going out, the people kept begging that these things might be spoken to them the next Sabbath.

43 Now when *the meeting of* the synagogue had broken up, many of the Jews and of the God-fearing proselytes followed Paul and Barnabas, who, speaking to them, were urging them to continue in the grace of God.

44 And the next Sabbath nearly the whole city assembled to hear the word of God.

45 But when the Jews saw the crowds, they were filled with jealousy, and *began* contradicting the things spoken by Paul, and were blaspheming.

46 And Paul and Barnabas spoke out boldly and said, "It was necessary that the word of God should be spoken to you first; since you repudiate it, and judge yourselves unworthy of eternal life, behold, we are turning to the Gentiles.

47 "For thus the Lord has commanded us,
    'I HAVE PLACED YOU AS A LIGHT FOR THE GENTILES,
    THAT YOU SHOULD BRING SALVATION TO THE END OF THE EARTH.' "

48 And when the Gentiles heard this, they *began* rejoicing and glorifying the word of the Lord; and as many as had been appointed to eternal life believed.

49 And the word of the Lord was being spread through the whole region.

50 But the Jews aroused the devout women of prominence and the leading men of the city, and instigated a persecution against Paul and Barnabas, and drove them out of their district.

51 But they shook off the dust of their feet *in protest* against them and went to Iconium.

52 And the disciples were continually filled with joy and with the Holy Spirit.

4. *Their ministry at Iconium*

14 And it came about that in Iconium they entered the synagogue of the Jews together, and spoke in such a manner that a great multitude believed, both of Jews and of Greeks.

2 But the Jews who disbelieved stirred up the minds of the Gentiles, and embittered them against the brethren.

3 Therefore they spent a long time *there* speaking boldly *with reliance* upon the Lord, who was bearing witness to the word of His grace, granting that signs and wonders be done by their hands.

4 But the multitude of the city was divided; and some sided with the Jews, and some with the apostles.

5 And when an attempt was made by both the Gentiles and the Jews with their rulers, to mistreat and to stone them,

6 they became aware of it and fled to the cities of Lycaonia, Lystra and Derbe, and the surrounding region;

7 and there they continued to preach the gospel.

5. *Their ministry at Lystra*

8 And at Lystra there was sitting a certain man, without strength in his feet, lame from his mother's womb, who had never walked.

9 This man was listening to Paul as he spoke, who, when he had fixed his gaze upon him, and had seen that he had faith to be made well,

---

Marginal references (left column):

13:36 Acts 2:29; 1 Kin 2:10
13:38 Luke 24:47
*13:39 Rom 3:28; Acts 10:43
13:40 John 6:45
13:41 Hab 1:5
13:42 v. 14
13:43 Acts 11:23; 14:22
13:45 Acts 18:6; 1 Pet 4:4; Jude 10
13:46 v. 26; Acts 3:26; 18:6; 28:28
*13:47 Is 49:6; Luke 2:32
13:48 Acts 2:47; Rom 3:28ff
13:51 Matt 10:14; Mark 6:11; Luke 9:5; Acts 18:6
13:52 Acts 2:4
14:1 Acts 13:51; 13:5; 2:47; 18:4
14:3 Heb 2:4; John 4:48
14:4 Acts 17:4,5; v. 14
14:5 2 Tim 3:11
14:6 Matt 10:23
14:8 Acts 3:2
14:9 Acts 3:4; 10:4; Matt 9:28,29

13:39 See note to Hab. 2:4 on justification.   **13:47** Reflects God's concern for all men.

10   said with a loud voice, "Stand upright on your feet." And he leaped up and *began* to walk.

11   And when the multitudes saw what Paul had done, they raised their voice, saying in the Lycaonian language, "The gods have become like men and have come down to us."

12   And they *began* calling Barnabas, Zeus, and Paul, Hermes, because he was the chief speaker.

13   And the priest of Zeus, whose *temple* was just outside the city, brought oxen and garlands to the gates, and wanted to offer sacrifice with the crowds.

14   But when the apostles, Barnabas and Paul, heard of it, they tore their robes and rushed out into the crowd, crying out

15   and saying, "Men, why are you doing these things? We are also men of the same nature as you, and preach the gospel to you in order that you should turn from these ³⁰vain things to a living God, WHO MADE THE HEAVEN AND THE EARTH AND THE SEA, AND ALL THAT IS IN THEM.

16   "And in the generations gone by He permitted all the nations to go their own ways;

17   and yet He did not leave Himself without witness, in that He did good and gave you rains from heaven and fruitful seasons, satisfying your hearts with food and gladness."

18   And *even* saying these things, they with difficulty restrained the crowds from offering sacrifice to them.

6. Their return to Antioch

19   But Jews came from Antioch and Iconium, and having won over the multitudes, they stoned Paul and dragged him out of the city, supposing him to be dead.

20   But while the disciples stood around him, he arose and entered the city. And the next day he went away with Barnabas to Derbe.

21   And after they had preached the gospel to that city and had made many disciples, they returned to Lystra and to Iconium and to Antioch,

22   strengthening the souls of the disciples, encouraging them to continue in the faith, and *saying*, "Through many tribulations we must enter the kingdom of God."

23   And when they had appointed elders for them in every church, having prayed with fasting, they commended them to the Lord in whom they had believed.

24   And they passed through Pisidia and came into Pamphylia.

25   And when they had spoken the word in Perga, they went down to Attalia;

26   and from there they sailed to Antioch, from which they had been commended to the grace of God for the work that they had accomplished.

27   And when they had arrived and gathered the church together, they *began* to report all things that God had done with them and how He had opened a door of faith to the Gentiles.

28   And they spent a long time with the disciples.

B. The Jerusalem conference

1. The problem stated

15 And some men came down from Judea and *began* teaching the brethren, "Unless you are circumcised according to the custom of Moses, you cannot be saved."

2   And when Paul and Barnabas had great dissension and debate with them, *the brethren* determined that Paul and Barnabas and certain others of them should go up to Jerusalem to the apostles and elders concerning this issue.

3   Therefore, being sent on their way by the church, they were passing through both Phoenicia and Samaria, describing in detail the conversion of the Gentiles, and were bringing great joy to all the brethren.

4   And when they arrived at Jerusalem, they were received by the church and the apostles and the elders, and they reported all that God had done with them.

5   But certain ones of the sect of the Pharisees who had believed, stood up,

---

³⁰I.e., idols

Cross-references (right margin):

14:11 Acts 8:10; 28:6

14:15 Acts 10:26; James 5:17; 1 Sam 12:21; Jer 14:22; 1 Cor 8:4; Gen 1:1; Ps 146:6; Rev 14:7
14:16 Ps 81:12; Acts 17:30; 1 Pet 4:3
14:17 Acts 17:27; Rom 1:20; Deut 11:14; Job 5:10; Ps 65:10

14:19 Acts 13:45; 2 Cor 11:25; 2 Tim 3:11
14:20 vv. 22,28

14:22 Acts 11:23; 13:43; John 16:33; 1 Thess 3:3; 2 Tim 3:12
14:23 Titus 1:5; Acts 11:30; 13:3; 20:32
14:26 Acts 11:19; 13:1,3; 15:40
14:27 Acts 15:4,12; 21:19; 1 Cor 16:9; 2 Cor 2:12; Col 4:3

15:1 v. 24; Gal 2:12; v. 5; Gal 5:2; Acts 6:14
15:2 v. 7; Gal 2:2; Acts 11:30
*15:3 Acts 20:38; Rom 15:24; 1 Cor 16:6, 11; Acts 14:27
15:4 v. 12; Acts 14:27

15:3 Conversion connotes a change *from* one condition or state *to* another condition or state. Turning *from* something involves repentance. Turning *to* something involves faith. Both elements are at work in the experience of conversion.

saying, "It is necessary to circumcise them, and to direct them to observe the Law of Moses."

2. The council deciding

6 And the apostles and the elders came together to look into this matter.

7 And after there had been much debate, Peter stood up and said to them, "Brethren, you know that in the early days God made a choice among you, that by my mouth the Gentiles should hear the word of the gospel and believe.

8 "And God, who knows the heart, bore witness to them, giving them the Holy Spirit, just as He also did to us;

9 and He made no distinction between us and them, cleansing their hearts by faith.

10 "Now therefore why do you put God to the test by placing upon the neck of the disciples a yoke which neither our fathers nor we have been able to bear?

11 "But we believe that we are saved through the grace of the Lord Jesus, in the same way as they also are."

12 And all the multitude kept silent, and they were listening to Barnabas and Paul as they were relating what signs and wonders God had done through them among the Gentiles.

13 And after they had stopped speaking, James answered, saying, "Brethren, listen to me.

14 "Simeon has related how God first concerned Himself about taking from among the Gentiles a people for His name.

15 "And with this the words of the Prophets agree, just as it is written,

16 'AFTER THESE THINGS I will return,
AND I WILL REBUILD THE TABERNACLE OF DAVID WHICH HAS FALLEN,
AND I WILL REBUILD ITS RUINS,
AND I WILL RESTORE IT,

17 IN ORDER THAT THE REST OF MANKIND MAY SEEK THE LORD,
AND ALL THE GENTILES WHO ARE CALLED BY MY NAME,'

18 SAYS THE LORD, WHO MAKES THESE THINGS KNOWN FROM OF OLD.

19 "Therefore it is my judgment that we do not trouble those who are turning to God from among the Gentiles,

20 but that we write to them that they abstain from things contaminated by idols and from fornication and from what is strangled and from blood.

21 "For Moses from ancient generations has in every city those who preach him, since he is read in the synagogues every Sabbath."

3. The decision communicated

22 Then it seemed good to the apostles and the elders, with the whole church, to choose men from among them to send to Antioch with Paul and Barnabas—Judas called Barsabbas, and Silas, leading men among the brethren,

23 and they sent this letter by them,

"The apostles and the brethren who are elders, to the brethren in Antioch and Syria and Cilicia who are from the Gentiles, greetings.

24 "Since we have heard that some of our number to whom we gave no instruction have disturbed you with *their* words, unsettling your souls,

25 it seemed good to us, having become of one mind, to select men to send to you with our beloved Barnabas and Paul,

26 men who have risked their lives for the name of our Lord Jesus Christ.

27 "Therefore we have sent Judas and Silas, who themselves will also report the same things by word *of mouth*.

28 "For it seemed good to the Holy Spirit and to us to lay upon you no greater burden than these essentials:

Cross-references (margin)

15:7
Acts 10:19, 20; 20:24
15:8
Acts 1:24; 10:44,47
15:9
Acts 10:28, 34,43; 11:12
15:10
Matt 23:4; Gal 5:1
15:11
Rom 3:24; Eph 2:5-8; Titus 2:11; 3:4,5
*15:12
John 4:48; Acts 14:27
15:13
Acts 12:17
15:15
Acts 13:40
15:16
Amos 9:11, 12; Jer 12:15
15:20
v. 29;
1 Cor 8:7-13; 10:7,8,14-28; Rev 2:14,20; Gen 9:4; Lev 3:17; Deut 12:16, 23
15:21
Acts 13:15; 2 Cor 3:14,15
15:22
Acts 11:20; vv. 27,32,40
15:23
vv. 1,41; Acts 23:26; James 1:1
15:24
v. 1; Gal 1:7; 5:10
15:26
Acts 14:19; 1 Cor 15:30

15:12 This is a very significant passage of Scripture (vv. 12–18). From v. 12 it appears that the Jews felt there was no place for Gentiles in the gospel economy. James proved from the Old Testament Scriptures that the Gentiles were spoken of by the prophets, and furthermore, Paul later argued cogently that the Gentile believers constitute the new Israel (see Rom. 9–11 and Gal. 3). Despite this, God still has a concern for Israel, and Paul states that eventually *all Israel will be saved* (Rom. 11:26).

15:28 At the first church council the apostles and elders rendered a decision based on the guidance of the Holy Spirit. They were absolutely confident that He had revealed His will to them in arriving at this decision. But decisions made apart from the will and guidance of God are likely to prove wrong, and Scripture nowhere suggests that believers may safely rely on self-determined decisions, no matter how

29 that you abstain from things sacrificed to idols and from blood and from things strangled and from fornication; if you keep yourselves free from such things, you will do well. Farewell."

30 So, when they were sent away, they went down to Antioch; and having gathered the congregation together, they delivered the letter.

31 And when they had read it, they rejoiced because of its encouragement.

32 And Judas and Silas, also being prophets themselves, encouraged and strengthened the brethren with a lengthy message.

33 And after they had spent time *there*, they were sent away from the brethren in peace to those who had sent them out.

34 [³¹But it seemed good to Silas to remain there.]

35 But Paul and Barnabas stayed in Antioch, teaching and preaching, with many others also, the word of the Lord.

C. Second missionary journey

1. Asia Minor

a. Separation of Paul and Barnabas

36 And after some days Paul said to Barnabas, "Let us return and visit the brethren in every city in which we proclaimed the word of the Lord, *and see how they are.*"

37 And Barnabas was desirous of taking John, called Mark, along with them also.

38 But Paul kept insisting that they should not take him along who had deserted them in Pamphylia and had not gone with them to the work.

39 And there arose such a sharp disagreement that they separated from one another, and Barnabas took Mark with him and sailed away to Cyprus.

40 But Paul chose Silas and departed, being committed by the brethren to the grace of the Lord.

41 And he was traveling through Syria and Cilicia, strengthening the churches.

b. Selection of Timothy

16 And he came also to Derbe and to Lystra. And behold, a certain disciple was there, named Timothy, the son of a Jewish woman who was a believer, but his father was a Greek,

2 and he was well spoken of by the brethren who were in Lystra and Iconium.

3 Paul wanted this man to go with him; and he took him and circumcised him because of the Jews who were in those parts, for they all knew that his father was a Greek.

4 Now while they were passing through the cities, they were delivering the decrees, which had been decided upon by the apostles and elders who were in Jerusalem, for them to observe.

5 So the churches were being strengthened in the faith, and were increasing in number daily.

³¹Many mss. do not contain this verse

---

sensible they may seem.
15:36ff. Dissension existed between Paul and Barnabas over John Mark (see 15:39). The solution to their dissension lay in their decision to go their separate ways. It is not always possible, in this present life, for believers to work with everyone without dissension. While those who are in disagreement should go their own ways, it should be done without acrimony, recrimination, or hostility and bad feelings.
16:3 Paul circumcised Timothy despite his sturdy insistence that the rite was no longer necessary for salvation (Gal. 2:3–5). Doctrinal principle did not require it, but strategic considerations made it desirable under the peculiar circumstances at that time. Scripture lays down the maxim that if an act is inherently wrong it is never to be performed no matter how expedient it may seem. (E.g., it appeared expedient to David to have Uriah the Hittite slain lest his adultery with Bathsheba be discovered. God reproved him both for the adultery *and* the sin of murder, which were forbidden (2 Sam. 12:9). David did not slay Uriah himself, but was an accessory before the fact and was thus charged with the crime by God.) But many acts are not inherently wrong and may be performed or not performed, depending on what will best promote the gospel. Paul argued that eating meat offered to idols was not sinful in itself, but he would eat no meat if by doing so his brother would be offended. This is expediency (1 Cor. 8:1–13). Paul's quotation, *All things are lawful* (1 Cor. 6:12; 10:23), must be understood in the light of its context, for everywhere in Scripture it is recognized that there are acts that are always unlawful (e.g., the prohibitions expressed in the Ten Commandments that ever remain valid in principle). In the passage under consideration here, Paul had Timothy circumcised because it would enlarge the usefulness of his junior assistant for Christian evangelism to the Jews.

c. *The Macedonian call*

16:6
Acts 18:23;
2:9
16:7
v. 8;
Luke 24:49;
Rom 8:9;
Gal 4:6
16:8
v. 11;
2 Cor 2:12;
2 Tim 4:13
16:9
Acts 9:10;
18:5; 20:1,3;
27:2
*16:10
2 Cor 2:13

6 And they passed through the Phrygian and Galatian region, having been forbidden by the Holy Spirit to speak the word in Asia;

7 and when they had come to Mysia, they were trying to go into Bithynia, and the Spirit of Jesus did not permit them;

8 and passing by Mysia, they came down to Troas.

9 And a vision appeared to Paul in the night: a certain man of Macedonia was standing and appealing to him, and saying, "Come over to Macedonia and help us."

10 And when he had seen the vision, immediately we sought to go into Macedonia, concluding that God had called us to preach the gospel to them.

2. *The Macedonian ministry*

a. *At Philippi*

16:11
v. 8;
2 Tim 4:13
16:12
Phil 1:1;
Acts 18:5;
19:21,22,29;
20:1,3; 27:2
16:13
Acts 13:14
16:14
Luke 24:45
16:15
Acts 11:14;
Luke 24:29
16:16
Deut 18:11;
1 Sam 28:3,7
16:17
Mark 5:7

11 Therefore putting out to sea from Troas, we ran a straight course to Samothrace, and on the day following to Neapolis;

12 and from there to Philippi, which is a leading city of the district of Macedonia, a *Roman* colony; and we were staying in this city for some days.

13 And on the Sabbath day we went outside the gate to a riverside, where we were supposing that there would be a place of prayer; and we sat down and began speaking to the women who had assembled.

14 And a certain woman named Lydia, from the city of Thyatira, a seller of purple fabrics, a worshiper of God, was listening; and the Lord opened her heart to respond to the things spoken by Paul.

15 And when she and her household had been baptized, she urged us, saying, "If you have judged me to be faithful to the Lord, come into my house and stay." And she prevailed upon us.

16 And it happened that as we were going to the place of prayer, a certain slave-girl having a spirit of divination met us, who was bringing her masters much profit by fortunetelling.

17 Following after Paul and us, she kept crying out, saying, "These men are bond-servants of the Most High God, who are proclaiming to you the way of salvation."

18 And she continued doing this for many days. But Paul was greatly annoyed, and turned and said to the spirit, "I command you in the name of Jesus Christ to come out of her!" And it came out at that very moment.

16:19
Acts 19:25,
26; 15:40;
17:6,7;
James 2:6
16:20
Acts 17:6

19 But when her masters saw that their hope of profit was gone, they seized Paul and Silas and dragged them into the market place before the authorities,

20 and when they had brought them to the chief magistrates, they said, "These men are throwing our city into confusion, being Jews,

21 and are proclaiming customs which it is not lawful for us to accept or to observe, being Romans."

16:22
2 Cor 11:23,
25; 1 Thess
2:2
16:23
vv. 27,36
16:24
Jer 20:2,3

22 And the crowd rose up together against them, and the chief magistrates tore their robes off them, and proceeded to order *them* to be beaten with rods.

23 And when they had inflicted many blows upon them, they threw them into prison, commanding the jailer to guard them securely;

24 and he, having received such a command, threw them into the inner prison, and fastened their feet in the stocks.

16:25
Eph 5:19
16:26
Acts 4:31;
5:19; 12:7,10
16:27
Acts 12:19

25 But about midnight Paul and Silas were praying and singing hymns of praise to God, and the prisoners were listening to them;

26 and suddenly there came a great earthquake, so that the foundations of the prison house were shaken; and immediately all the doors were opened, and everyone's chains were unfastened.

27 And when the jailer had been roused out of sleep and had seen the prison doors opened, he drew his sword and was about to kill himself, supposing that the prisoners had escaped.

28 But Paul cried out with a loud voice, saying, "Do yourself no harm, for we are all here!"

16:10 For the first time the author of Acts associates himself with the narrative: *we sought to go into Macedonia, concluding that God had called us to preach the gospel to them.* This first so-called "we" section begins here, and it appears that Luke joined Paul and his group in Troas, went on with them to Philippi, but did not accompany them when they left Philippi (v. 40). The other "we" section begins in Philippi, some six or seven years later (20:5), and continues to the end of the book.

29 And he called for lights and rushed in and, trembling with fear, he fell down before Paul and Silas,

30 and after he brought them out, he said, "Sirs, what must I do to be saved?"

31 And they said, "Believe in the Lord Jesus, and you shall be saved, you and your household."

32 And they spoke the word of the Lord to him together with all who were in his house.

33 And he took them that *very* hour of the night and washed their wounds, and immediately he was baptized, he and all his *household*.

34 And he brought them into his house and set food before them, and rejoiced greatly, having believed in God with his whole household.

35 Now when day came, the chief magistrates sent their policemen, saying, "Release those men."

36 And the jailer reported these words to Paul, *saying*, "The chief magistrates have sent to release you. Now therefore, come out and go in peace."

37 But Paul said to them, "They have beaten us in public without trial, men who are Romans, and have thrown us into prison; and now are they sending us away secretly? No indeed! But let them come themselves and bring us out."

38 And the policemen reported these words to the chief magistrates. And they were afraid when they heard that they were Romans,

39 and they came and appealed to them, and when they had brought them out, they kept begging them to leave the city.

40 And they went out of the prison and entered *the house of* Lydia, and when they saw the brethren, they encouraged them and departed.

b. At Thessalonica

17 Now when they had traveled through Amphipolis and Apollonia, they came to Thessalonica, where there was a synagogue of the Jews.

2 And according to Paul's custom, he went to them, and for three Sabbaths reasoned with them from the Scriptures,

3 explaining and giving evidence that the Christ had to suffer and rise again from the dead, and *saying*, "This Jesus whom I am proclaiming to you is the Christ."

4 And some of them were persuaded and joined Paul and Silas, along with a great multitude of the God-fearing Greeks and a number of the leading women.

5 But the Jews, becoming jealous and taking along some wicked men from the market place, formed a mob and set the city in an uproar; and coming upon the house of Jason, they were seeking to bring them out to the people.

6 And when they did not find them, they *began* dragging Jason and some brethren before the city authorities, shouting, "These men who have upset [32] the world have come here also;

7 and Jason has welcomed them, and they all act contrary to the decrees of Caesar, saying that there is another king, Jesus."

8 And they stirred up the crowd and the city authorities who heard these things.

9 And when they had received a pledge from Jason and the others, they released them.

c. At Berea

10 And the brethren immediately sent Paul and Silas away by night to Berea; and when they arrived, they went into the synagogue of the Jews.

11 Now these were more noble-minded than those in Thessalonica, for they received the word with great eagerness, examining the Scriptures daily, *to see* whether these things were so.

12 Many of them therefore believed, along with a number of prominent Greek women and men.

13 But when the Jews of Thessalonica found out that the word of God had been proclaimed by Paul in Berea also, they came there likewise, agitating and stirring up the crowds.

14 And then immediately the brethren sent Paul out to go as far as the sea; and Silas and Timothy remained there.

15 Now those who conducted Paul brought him as far as Athens; and receiving

32Lit., *the inhabited earth*

16:30
Acts 2:37;
9:6; 22:10
16:31
John 3:16,36;
6:47; 1 John
5:10
16:33
v. 25
16:34
Acts 11:14
16:36
vv. 23,27
16:37
Acts 22:25-27
16:38
Acts 22:29
16:39
Matt 8:34
16:40
v. 14
17:1
Acts 27:2;
1 Thess 1:1;
2 Thess 1:1
17:2
Acts 9:20;
13:14; 16:13;
19:8
17:3
Luke 24:26,
46;
Acts 18:28;
Gal 3:1
17:4
Acts 15:22,
27,32,40
17:5
v. 13;
Rom 16:21
17:6
Acts 16:19,20
17:7
Luke 23:2;
John 19:12
17:9
v. 5
17:10
v. 14;
Acts 20:4;
v. 2
17:11
Is 34:16;
Luke 16:29;
John 5:39
17:14
vv. 6,10;
Acts 16:1
17:15
Acts 15:3;
vv. 16,21,22;
Acts 18:5

a command for Silas and Timothy to come to him as soon as possible, they departed.

3. The ministry in Greece

a. At Athens

17:16
2 Pet 2:8

16 Now while Paul was waiting for them at Athens, his spirit was being provoked within him as he was beholding the city full of idols.

17 So he was reasoning in the synagogue with the Jews and the God-fearing *Gentiles*, and in the market place every day with those who happened to be present.

*17:18
1 Cor 4:10;
Acts 4:2

18 And also some of the Epicurean and Stoic philosophers were conversing with him. And some were saying, "What would this idle babbler wish to say?" Others, "He seems to be a proclaimer of strange deities,"—because he was preaching Jesus and the resurrection.

17:19
Acts 23:19;
v. 22

19 And they took him and brought him to the Areopagus, saying, "May we know what this new teaching is which you are proclaiming?

20 "For you are bringing some strange things to our ears; we want to know therefore what these things mean."

21 (Now all the Athenians and the strangers visiting there used to spend their time in nothing other than telling or hearing something new.)

22 And Paul stood in the midst of the Areopagus and said, "Men of Athens, I observe that you are very religious in all respects.

23 "For while I was passing through and examining the objects of your worship, I also found an altar with this inscription, 'TO AN UNKNOWN GOD.' What therefore you worship in ignorance, this I proclaim to you.

17:24
Is 42:5;
Acts 14:15;
Matt 11:25;
Acts 7:48
17:25
Ps 50:10-12;
Is 42:5;
57:16;
Zech 12:1
17:26
Mal 2:10;
Deut 32:8
17:27
Rom 1:20;
Acts 14:17
17:28
Col 1:17;
Heb 1:3;
Epimenides;
Aratus,
Phaenomena,5
17:29
Is 40:18ff
*17:30
v. 23;
Acts 14:16;
Rom 3:25;
Luke 24:47;
Titus 2:11,
12; 1 Pet 1:14
17:31
Matt 10:15;
Acts 10:42;
Luke 22:22;
Acts 22:4
*17:34
vv. 19,22

24 "The God who made the world and all things in it, since He is Lord of heaven and earth, does not dwell in temples made with hands;

25 neither is He served by human hands, as though He needed anything, since He Himself gives to all life and breath and all things;

26 and He made from [33]one, every nation of mankind to live on all the face of the earth, having determined *their* appointed times, and the boundaries of their habitation,

27 that they should seek God, if perhaps they might grope for Him and find Him, though He is not far from each one of us;

28 for in Him we live and move and exist, as even some of your own poets have said, 'For we also are His offspring.'

29 "Being then the offspring of God, we ought not to think that the Divine Nature is like gold or silver or stone, an image formed by the art and thought of man.

30 "Therefore having overlooked the times of ignorance, God is now declaring to men that all everywhere should repent,

31 because He has fixed a day in which He will judge the world in righteousness through a Man whom He has appointed, having furnished proof to all men by raising Him from the dead."

32 Now when they heard of the resurrection of the dead, some *began* to sneer, but others said, "We shall hear you again concerning this."

33 So Paul went out of their midst.

34 But some men joined him and believed, among whom also were Dionysius the Areopagite and a woman named Damaris and others with them.

[33]Some later mss. read *one blood*

17:18 The Epicureans derived their philosophic teachings from their founder Epicurus, who was born 342 B.C. He lived in Athens during the later years of his life. He taught that the supreme good in life is pleasure or that which will bring man the greatest satisfaction. He argued that each man must consider the consequences of his actions and their effects on those who are related to him. The charge of the Stoics that his teaching led to sloth and sensuality was probably not justified. The Stoics also claimed that Epicurus was an atheist. The school of the Stoics was founded by Zeno (c. 278 B.C.). The key concept of Stoicism was to possess the courage never to submit or yield. It was a philosophy of indifference to either pleasure or pain. To both the Epicureans and the Stoics, the teaching of Paul was a novelty because it cut across the lines of their own teachings.

17:30 The doctrine of repentance is taught throughout the New Testament. No one can be regenerated without repentance. Repentance cannot confer salvation or merit it in any way, but it does bring a person to a place where the forgiving grace of God can meet him. There are five steps to genuine repentance: (1) a change of mind (Matt. 21:28,29; Luke 15:17,18; Acts 2:38); (2) godly sorrow for sin (Ps. 38:18; Luke 10:13; 18:9–14); (3) confession of sin (Luke 15:18; 18:13); (4) forsaking of sins (Prov. 28:13; Is. 55:7; see also John 8:11); and (5) turning to God as Savior and Lord (26:18; 1 Thess. 1:9).

17:34 Paul's ministry in Athens was evidently not too successful. It was one of the few places where no church was founded in connection with his preaching. He was discouraged, but when he came to Corinth God promised him fruit.

b. At Corinth

18 After these things he left Athens and went to Corinth.

2 And he found a certain Jew named Aquila, a native of Pontus, having recently come from Italy with his wife Priscilla, because Claudius had commanded all the Jews to leave Rome. He came to them,

3 and because he was of the same trade, he stayed with them and they were working; for by trade they were tent-makers.

4 And he was reasoning in the synagogue every Sabbath and trying to persuade Jews and Greeks.

5 But when Silas and Timothy came down from Macedonia, Paul *began* devoting himself completely to the word, solemnly testifying to the Jews that Jesus was the Christ.

6 And when they resisted and blasphemed, he shook out his garments and said to them, "Your blood *be* upon your own heads! I am clean. From now on I shall go to the Gentiles."

7 And he departed from there and went to the house of a certain man named Titius Justus, a worshiper of God, whose house was next to the synagogue.

8 And Crispus, the leader of the synagogue, believed in the Lord with all his household, and many of the Corinthians when they heard were believing and being baptized.

9 And the Lord said to Paul in the night by a vision, "Do not be afraid *any longer*, but go on speaking and do not be silent;

10 for I am with you, and no man will attack you in order to harm you, for I have many people in this city."

11 And he settled *there* a year and six months, teaching the word of God among them.

12 But while Gallio was proconsul of Achaia, the Jews with one accord rose up against Paul and brought him before the judgment seat,

13 saying, "This man persuades men to worship God contrary to the law."

14 But when Paul was about to open his mouth, Gallio said to the Jews, "If it were a matter of wrong or of vicious crime, O Jews, it would be reasonable for me to put up with you;

15 but if there are questions about words and names and your own law, look after it yourselves; I am unwilling to be a judge of these matters."

16 And he drove them away from the judgment seat.

17 And they all took hold of Sosthenes, the leader of the synagogue, and *began* beating him in front of the judgment seat. And Gallio was not concerned about any of these things.

c. The return to Antioch

18 And Paul, having remained many days longer, took leave of the brethren and put out to sea for Syria, and with him were Priscilla and Aquila. In Cenchrea he had his hair cut, for he was keeping a vow.

19 And they came to Ephesus, and he left them there. Now he himself entered the synagogue and reasoned with the Jews.

20 And when they asked him to stay for a longer time, he did not consent,

21 but taking leave of them and saying, "I will return to you again if God wills," he set sail from Ephesus.

D. Third missionary journey

1. At Galatia and Phrygia

22 And when he had landed at Caesarea, he went up and greeted the church, and went down to Antioch.

18:12 Achaia was the Roman province of which Corinth was the capital. The proconsul Gallio, brother of the philosopher Seneca and uncle of the poet Lucan, was appointed to his position by the emperor Claudius in July of A.D. 51.
18:18 For information on vows, see note to Num. 6:2.
18:19 Paul, for the first time, entered this city, which was to become an important center in the early Christian work. At the beginning of his second missionary tour he had been prevented by the Holy Spirit from preaching in the Roman province of Asia, of which Ephesus was the capital city (16:6). Now, at the end of this tour, he stayed only a few days, but returned to the city on his next tour and stayed there for three years (19:1–20:1; 20:31). On his return to Jerusalem he avoided the city, since he was in a hurry to reach Jerusalem by Pentecost (20:16), but at Miletus he summoned the elders of the church at Ephesus, addressed them in eloquent terms, and bade them farewell with the sad prediction that they would not see him again (20:17–38).

23   And having spent some time *there*, he departed and passed successively through the Galatian region and Phrygia, strengthening all the disciples.

2. At Ephesus

a. The preaching of Apollos

24   Now a certain Jew named Apollos, an Alexandrian by birth, an eloquent man, came to Ephesus; and he was mighty in the Scriptures.
25   This man had been instructed in the way of the Lord; and being fervent in spirit, he was speaking and teaching accurately the things concerning Jesus, being acquainted only with the baptism of John;
26   and he began to speak out boldly in the synagogue. But when Priscilla and Aquila heard him, they took him aside and explained to him the way of God more accurately.

27   And when he wanted to go across to Achaia, the brethren encouraged him and wrote to the disciples to welcome him; and when he had arrived, he helped greatly those who had believed through grace;

28   for he powerfully refuted the Jews in public, demonstrating by the Scriptures that Jesus was the Christ.

b. Paul's and John's disciples

19 And it came about that while Apollos was at Corinth, Paul having passed through the upper country came to Ephesus, and found some disciples,
2   and he said to them, "Did you receive the Holy Spirit when you believed?" And they *said* to him, "No, we have not even heard whether there is a Holy Spirit."

3   And he said, "Into what then were you baptized?" And they said, "Into John's baptism."

4   And Paul said, "John baptized with the baptism of repentance, telling the people to believe in Him who was coming after him, that is, in Jesus."
5   And when they heard this, they were baptized in the name of the Lord Jesus.

6   And when Paul had laid his hands upon them, the Holy Spirit came on them, and they *began* speaking with tongues and prophesying.
7   And there were in all about twelve men.

c. Paul in the synagogue and the hall of Tyrannus

8   And he entered the synagogue and continued speaking out boldly for three months, reasoning and persuading *them* about the kingdom of God.
9   But when some were becoming hardened and disobedient, speaking evil of the Way before the multitude, he withdrew from them and took away the disciples, reasoning daily in the school of Tyrannus.
10   And this took place for two years, so that all who lived in Asia heard the word of the Lord, both Jews and Greeks.

d. Miracles by Paul

11   And God was performing extraordinary miracles by the hands of Paul,
12   so that handkerchiefs or aprons were even carried from his body to the sick, and the diseases left them and the evil spirits went out.

13   But also some of the Jewish exorcists, who went from place to place, attempted to name over those who had the evil spirits the name of the Lord Jesus, saying, "I adjure you by Jesus whom Paul preaches."
14   And seven sons of one Sceva, a Jewish chief priest, were doing this.
15   And the evil spirit answered and said to them, "I recognize Jesus, and I know about Paul, but who are you?"
16   And the man, in whom was the evil spirit, leaped on them and subdued all of them and overpowered them, so that they fled out of that house naked and wounded.

17   And this became known to all, both Jews and Greeks, who lived in Ephesus; and fear fell upon them all and the name of the Lord Jesus was being magnified.
18   Many also of those who had believed kept coming, confessing and disclosing their practices.
19   And many of those who practiced magic brought their books together and *began* burning them in the sight of all; and they counted up the price of them and found it fifty thousand pieces of silver.

20   So the word of the Lord was growing mightily and prevailing.

e. Paul's future plans

21   Now after these things were finished, Paul purposed in the spirit to go to Jerusalem after he had passed through Macedonia and Achaia, saying, "After I have been there, I must also see Rome."

22   And having sent into Macedonia two of those who ministered to him, Timothy and Erastus, he himself stayed in Asia for a while.

f. Demetrius and the riot at Ephesus

23   And about that time there arose no small disturbance concerning the Way.

24   For a certain man named Demetrius, a silversmith, who made silver shrines of Artemis, was bringing no little business to the craftsmen;

25   these he gathered together with the workmen of similar *trades*, and said, "Men, you know that our prosperity depends upon this business.

26   "And you see and hear that not only in Ephesus, but in almost all of Asia, this Paul has persuaded and turned away a considerable number of people, saying that gods made with hands are no gods *at all*.

27   "And not only is there danger that this trade of ours fall into disrepute, but also that the temple of the great goddess Artemis be regarded as worthless and that she whom all of Asia and the world worship should even be dethroned from her magnificence."

28   And when they heard *this* and were filled with rage, they *began* crying out, saying, "Great is Artemis of the Ephesians!"

29   And the city was filled with the confusion, and they rushed with one accord into the theater, dragging along Gaius and Aristarchus, Paul's traveling companions from Macedonia.

30   And when Paul wanted to go into the assembly, the disciples would not let him.

31   And also some of the [34]Asiarchs who were friends of his sent to him and repeatedly urged him not to venture into the theater.

32   So then, some were shouting one thing and some another, for the assembly was in confusion, and the majority did not know for what cause they had come together.

33   And some of the crowd concluded *it was* Alexander, since the Jews had put him forward; and having motioned with his hand, Alexander was intending to make a defense to the assembly.

34   But when they recognized that he was a Jew, a *single* outcry arose from them all as they shouted for about two hours, "Great is Artemis of the Ephesians!"

35   And after quieting the multitude, the town clerk *said, "Men of Ephesus, what man is there after all who does not know that the city of the Ephesians is guardian of the temple of the great Artemis, and of the *image* which fell down from heaven?

36   "Since then these are undeniable facts, you ought to keep calm and to do nothing rash.

37   "For you have brought these men *here* who are neither robbers of temples nor blasphemers of our goddess.

38   "So then, if Demetrius and the craftsmen who are with him have a complaint against any man, the courts are in session and proconsuls are *available*; let them bring charges against one another.

39   "But if you want anything beyond this, it shall be settled in the lawful assembly.

40   "For indeed we are in danger of being accused of a riot in connection with today's affair, since there is no *real* cause *for it*; and in this connection we shall be unable to account for this disorderly gathering."

41   And after saying this he dismissed the assembly.

---

[34]I.e., political or religious officials of the province of Asia

---

19:24   The Ephesian goddess Artemis is not to be identified with the Greek virgin goddess Artemis (Diana in Latin), but was the great goddess of fertility of Asia Minor, who was known by several names and whose worship extended back to earliest times. The temple of Artemis at Ephesus was one of the seven great wonders of the ancient world.

19:31   *Asiarchs* were provincial officials who had charge of the festival of emperor worship. Only one man bore the title at a time, and the plural "Asiarchs" was probably used of the actual Asiarch and his predecessors in office. They were civic benefactors.

Marginal references:

19:20 Acts 6:7; 12:24

19:21 Rom 15:24-28

19:22 Acts 13:5; Rom 16:23; 2 Tim 4:20; v. 10

19:23 v. 9
*19:24 Acts 16:16,19

19:26 Ps 115:4; Is 44:10-20; Jer 10:3; Acts 17:29

19:28 Acts 18:19

19:29 Rom 16:23; 1 Cor 1:4; Acts 20:4; 27:2; Col 4:10; Philem 24

19:32 Acts 21:34

19:33 1 Tim 1:20; 2 Tim 4:14; Acts 12:17

19:35 Acts 18:19

19:37 Rom 2:22

19:38 Acts 13:7

3. Paul's last visit to Macedonia and Achaia

20:1
Acts 11:26;
1 Cor 16:5;
1 Tim 1:3

20 And after the uproar had ceased, Paul sent for the disciples and when he had exhorted them and taken his leave of them, he departed to go to Macedonia.

2 And when he had gone through those districts and had given them much exhortation, he came to Greece.

20:3
v. 19;
Acts 23:12;
25:3;
2 Cor 11:26

3 And *there* he spent three months, and when a plot was formed against him by the Jews as he was about to set sail for Syria, he determined to return through Macedonia.

20:4
Acts 19:29;
27:2; 16:1;
Eph 6:21;
Col 4:7;
2 Tim 4:12;
Titus 3:12;
Acts 21:29;
2 Tim 4:20

4 And he was accompanied by Sopater of Berea, *the son* of Pyrrhus; and by Aristarchus and Secundus of the Thessalonians; and Gaius of Derbe, and Timothy; and Tychicus and Trophimus of Asia.

4. From Philippi to Miletus

20:6
Acts 16:8;
2 Cor 2:12;
2 Tim 4:13

5 But these had gone on ahead and were waiting for us at Troas.

6 And we sailed from Philippi after the days of Unleavened Bread, and came to them at Troas within five days; and there we stayed seven days.

20:7
1 Cor 16:2;
Rev 1:10

7 And on the first day of the week, when we were gathered together to break bread, Paul *began* talking to them, intending to depart the next day, and he prolonged his message until midnight.

20:8
Acts 1:13

8 And there were many lamps in the upper room where we were gathered together.

9 And there was a certain young man named Eutychus sitting on the window sill, sinking into a deep sleep; and as Paul kept on talking, he was overcome by sleep and fell down from the third floor, and was picked up dead.

20:10
1 Kin 17:21;
Matt 9:23,24

10 But Paul went down and fell upon him and after embracing him, he said, "Do not be troubled, for his life is in him."

11 And when he had gone *back* up, and had broken the bread and eaten, he talked with them a long while, until daybreak, and so departed.

12 And they took away the boy alive, and were greatly comforted.

13 But we, going ahead to the ship, set sail for Assos, intending from there to take Paul on board; for thus he had arranged it, intending himself to go by land.

14 And when he met us at Assos, we took him on board and came to Mitylene.

20:15
v. 17;
2 Tim 4:20
20:16
Acts 18:19;
21:4,12;
19:21; 2:1;
1 Cor 16:8

15 And sailing from there, we arrived the following day opposite Chios; and the next day we crossed over to Samos; and the day following we came to Miletus.

16 For Paul had decided to sail past Ephesus in order that he might not have to spend time in Asia; for he was hurrying to be in Jerusalem, if possible, on the day of Pentecost.

5. Paul's defense before the Ephesian elders

20:17
Acts 11:30

17 And from Miletus he sent to Ephesus and called to him the elders of the church.

20:18
Acts 18:19;
19:1,10

18 And when they had come to him, he said to them,

"You yourselves know, from the first day that I set foot in Asia, how I was with you the whole time,

19 serving the Lord with all humility and with tears and with trials which came upon me through the plots of the Jews;

20:20
v. 27
20:21
Acts 18:5;
2:38; 24:24;
26:18
20:22
v. 16
20:23
Acts 21:4,11
20:24
Acts 21:13;
2 Cor 4:16;
Acts 1:17;
2 Cor 4:1;
Gal 1:1;
Titus 1:3
20:25
v. 38
20:26
Acts 18:6;
2 Cor 7:2
20:27
v. 20;
Acts 13:36

20 how I did not shrink from declaring to you anything that was profitable, and teaching you publicly and from house to house,

21 solemnly testifying to both Jews and Greeks of repentance toward God and faith in our Lord Jesus Christ.

22 "And now, behold, bound in spirit, I am on my way to Jerusalem, not knowing what will happen to me there,

23 except that the Holy Spirit solemnly testifies to me in every city, saying that bonds and afflictions await me.

24 "But I do not consider my life of any account as dear to myself, in order that I may finish my course, and the ministry which I received from the Lord Jesus, to testify solemnly of the gospel of the grace of God.

25 "And now, behold, I know that all of you, among whom I went about preaching the kingdom, will see my face no more.

26 "Therefore I testify to you this day, that I am innocent of the blood of all men.

27 "For I did not shrink from declaring to you the whole purpose of God.

28 "Be on guard for yourselves and for all the flock, among which the Holy

Spirit has made you overseers, to shepherd the church of God which He purchased with His own blood.

29 "I know that after my departure savage wolves will come in among you, not sparing the flock;

30 and from among your own selves men will arise, speaking perverse things, to draw away the disciples after them.

31 "Therefore be on the alert, remembering that night and day for a period of three years I did not cease to admonish each one with tears.

32 "And now I commend you to God and to the word of His grace, which is able to build *you* up and to give *you* the inheritance among all those who are sanctified.

33 "I have coveted no one's silver or gold or clothes.

34 "You yourselves know that these hands ministered to my *own* needs and to the men who were with me.

35 "In everything I showed you that by working hard in this manner you must help the weak and remember the words of the Lord Jesus, that He Himself said, 'It is more blessed to give than to receive.'"

36 And when he had said these things, he knelt down and prayed with them all.

37 And they *began* to weep aloud and embraced Paul, and repeatedly kissed him,

38 grieving especially over the word which he had spoken, that they should see his face no more. And they were accompanying him to the ship.

6. *Paul travels to Caesarea*

21 And when it came about that we had parted from them and had set sail, we ran a straight course to Cos and the next day to Rhodes and from there to Patara;

2 and having found a ship crossing over to Phoenicia, we went aboard and set sail.

3 And when we had come in sight of Cyprus, leaving it on the left, we kept sailing to Syria and landed at Tyre; for there the ship was to unload its cargo.

4 And after looking up the disciples, we stayed there seven days; and they kept telling Paul through the Spirit not to set foot in Jerusalem.

5 And when it came about that our days there were ended, we departed and started on our journey, while they all, with wives and children, escorted us until *we were* out of the city. And after kneeling down on the beach and praying, we said farewell to one another.

6 Then we went on board the ship, and they returned home again.

7 And when we had finished the voyage from Tyre, we arrived at Ptolemais; and after greeting the brethren, we stayed with them for a day.

8 And on the next day we departed and came to Caesarea; and entering the house of Philip the evangelist, who was one of the seven, we stayed with him.

9 Now this man had four virgin daughters who were prophetesses.

10 And as we were staying there for some days, a certain prophet named Agabus came down from Judea.

11 And coming to us, he took Paul's belt and bound his own feet and hands, and said, "This is what the Holy Spirit says: 'In this way the Jews at Jerusalem will bind the man who owns this belt and deliver him into the hands of the Gentiles.'"

12 And when we had heard this, we as well as the local residents *began* begging him not to go up to Jerusalem.

13 Then Paul answered, "What are you doing, weeping and breaking my heart? For I am ready not only to be bound, but even to die at Jerusalem for the name of the Lord Jesus."

14 And since he would not be persuaded, we fell silent, remarking, "The will of the Lord be done!"

15 And after these days we got ready and started on our way up to Jerusalem.

16 And *some* of the disciples from Caesarea also came with us, taking us to Mnason of Cyprus, a disciple of long standing with whom we were to lodge.

Cross references (margin):

*20:28
1 Tim 4:16;
1 Pet 5:2;
1 Cor 12:28;
1 Pet 1:19;
20:29;
Matt 7:15

20:31
Acts 19:10

20:32
Acts 14:23;
9:31; 26:18;
Eph 1:18;
Col 1:12;
3:24;
1 Pet 1:4
20:33
1 Cor 9:12;
2 Cor 7:2;
11:9; 12:17
20:34
Acts 18:3
20:35
Rom 15:1
20:36
Acts 9:40;
21:5
20:37
Gen 45:14
20:38
v. 25;
Acts 15:3

21:2
Acts 11:19

21:4
v. 11;
Acts 20:23
21:5
Acts 20:36

21:7
Acts 12:20;
1:15
21:8
Eph 4:11;
2 Tim 4:5;
Acts 6:5;
8:26,40
21:9
Acts 2:17;
Luke 2:36
21:10
Acts 11:28
21:11
v. 33;
Acts 20:23

21:13
Acts 20:24

21:14
Matt 26:42;
Luke 22:42

21:16
vv. 3,4

20:28 Many different names are applied by the New Testament to the church of Jesus Christ. These names are often descriptive and reveal much concerning the nature of the church. Among these designations are: (1) *His* [Christ's] body (Eph. 1:22,23; Col. 1:24); (2) *the flock of God* (1 Pet. 5:2); (3) *God's field, God's building* (1 Cor. 3:9); (4) the *temple of the living God* (2 Cor. 6:16); and (5) *the marriage of the Lamb* (Rev. 19:7).

E. *Paul a prisoner in Jerusalem, Caesarea, and Rome*

1. *Paul in Jerusalem*

17 And when we had come to Jerusalem, the brethren received us gladly.

18 And now the following day Paul went in with us to James, and all the elders were present.

19 And after he had greeted them, he *began* to relate one by one the things which God had done among the Gentiles through his ministry.

20 And when they heard it they *began* glorifying God; and they said to him, "You see, brother, how many thousands there are among the Jews of those who have believed, and they are all zealous for the Law;

21 and they have been told about you, that you are teaching all the Jews who are among the Gentiles to forsake Moses, telling them not to circumcise their children nor to walk according to the customs.

22 "What, then, is *to be done*? They will certainly hear that you have come.

23 "Therefore do this that we tell you. We have four men who are under a vow;

24 take them and purify yourself along with them, and pay their expenses in order that they may shave their heads; and all will know that there is nothing to the things which they have been told about you, but that you yourself also walk orderly, keeping the Law.

25 "But concerning the Gentiles who have believed, we wrote, having decided that they should abstain from meat sacrificed to idols and from blood and from what is strangled and from fornication."

26 Then Paul took the men, and the next day, purifying himself along with them, went into the temple, giving notice of the completion of the days of purification, until the sacrifice was offered for each one of them.

2. *Paul's imprisonment*

a. *His arrest*

27 And when the seven days were almost over, the Jews from Asia, upon seeing him in the temple, *began* to stir up all the multitude and laid hands on him,

28 crying out, "Men of Israel, come to our aid! This is the man who preaches to all men everywhere against our people, and the Law, and this place; and besides he has even brought Greeks into the temple and has defiled this holy place."

29 For they had previously seen Trophimus the Ephesian in the city with him, and they supposed that Paul had brought him into the temple.

30 And all the city was aroused, and the people rushed together; and taking hold of Paul, they dragged him out of the temple; and immediately the doors were shut.

31 And while they were seeking to kill him, a report came up to the [35] commander of the *Roman* cohort that all Jerusalem was in confusion.

32 And at once he took along *some* soldiers and centurions, and ran down to them; and when they saw the commander and the soldiers, they stopped beating Paul.

33 Then the commander came up and took hold of him, and ordered him to be bound with two chains; and he *began* asking who he was and what he had done.

34 But among the crowd some were shouting one thing *and* some another, and when he could not find out the facts on account of the uproar, he ordered him to be brought into the barracks.

35 And when he got to the stairs, it so happened that he was carried by the soldiers because of the violence of the mob;

36 for the multitude of the people kept following behind, crying out, "Away with him!"

b. *His defense*

37 And as Paul was about to be brought into the barracks, he said to the

[35]I.e., chiliarch, in command of one thousand troops

Cross-references (margin)

21:17 Acts 15:4
21:18 Acts 12:17; 15:13
21:19 Acts 14:27; 1:17; 20:24
21:20 Acts 22:3; Rom 10:2; Gal 1:14
21:21 v. 28; 1 Cor 7:18,19
*21:23 Acts 18:18
21:24 v. 26; Acts 24:18
21:25 Acts 15:20,29
21:26 Num 6:13; Acts 24:18
21:27 Acts 24:18; 26:21
21:28 Acts 24:5,6
*21:29 Acts 20:4; 18:19
21:30 Acts 26:21; 16:19
21:32 Acts 23:27
21:33 Acts 20:23; v. 11
21:34 Acts 19:32; v. 37
21:36 Luke 23:18; John 19:15; Acts 22:22
21:37 v. 34

21:23 See note to Num. 6:2 on vows.
21:29 Trophimus was a Gentile Christian from Ephesus (20:4) who accompanied Paul to Jerusalem. Gentiles were allowed in the temple area known as the Court of the Gentiles, but were forbidden, under pain of death, to go beyond the barrier that separated it from the inner courts of the temple. Notices in Greek and Latin were posted warning Gentiles to stay out. It was the report that Paul had taken a Gentile into the inner courts, where sacrifices were offered, that aroused the populace and caused the temple gates to be closed (v. 30), since the temple had presumably been defiled by the presence of a Gentile (v. 28).

commander, "May I say something to you?" And he *said, "Do you know Greek?

38   "Then you are not the Egyptian who some time ago stirred up a revolt and led the four thousand men of the Assassins out into the wilderness?"

39   But Paul said, "I am a Jew of Tarsus in Cilicia, a citizen of no insignificant city; and I beg you, allow me to speak to the people."

40   And when he had given him permission, Paul, standing on the stairs, motioned to the people with his hand; and when there was a great hush, he spoke to them in the Hebrew dialect, saying,

22 "Brethren and fathers, hear my defense which I now *offer* to you."
2   And when they heard that he was addressing them in the Hebrew dialect, they became even more quiet; and he *said,

3   "I am a Jew, born in Tarsus of Cilicia, but brought up in this city, educated under Gamaliel, strictly according to the law of our fathers, being zealous for God, just as you all are today.

4   "And I persecuted this Way to the death, binding and putting both men and women into prisons,

5   as also the high priest and all the Council of the elders can testify. From them I also received letters to the brethren, and started off for Damascus in order to bring even those who were there to Jerusalem as prisoners to be punished.

6   "And it came about that as I was on my way, approaching Damascus about noontime, a very bright light suddenly flashed from heaven all around me,

7   and I fell to the ground and heard a voice saying to me, 'Saul, Saul, why are you persecuting Me?'

8   "And I answered, 'Who art Thou, Lord?' And He said to me, 'I am Jesus the Nazarene, whom you are persecuting.'

9   "And those who were with me beheld the light, to be sure, but did not understand the voice of the One who was speaking to me.

10   "And I said, 'What shall I do, Lord?' And the Lord said to me, 'Arise and go on into Damascus; and there you will be told of all that has been appointed for you to do.'

11   "But since I could not see because of the brightness of that light, I was led by the hand by those who were with me, and came into Damascus.

12   "And a certain Ananias, a man who was devout by the standard of the Law, *and* well spoken of by all the Jews who lived there,

13   came to me, and standing near said to me, 'Brother Saul, receive your sight!' And at that very time I looked up at him.

14   "And he said, 'The God of our fathers has appointed you to know His will, and to see the Righteous One, and to hear an utterance from His mouth.

15   'For you will be a witness for Him to all men of what you have seen and heard.

16   'And now why do you delay? Arise, and be baptized, and wash away your sins, calling on His name.'

17   "And it came about when I returned to Jerusalem and was praying in the temple, that I fell into a trance,

18   and I saw Him saying to me, 'Make haste, and get out of Jerusalem quickly, because they will not accept your testimony about Me.'

19   "And I said, 'Lord, they themselves understand that in one synagogue after another I used to imprison and beat those who believed in Thee.

20   'And when the blood of Thy witness Stephen was being shed, I also was standing by approving, and watching out for the cloaks of those who were slaying him.'

21   "And He said to me, 'Go! For I will send you far away to the Gentiles.' "

22   And they listened to him up to this statement, and *then* they raised their

*21:38 Acts 5:36; Matt 24:26 21:39 Acts 9:11; 22:3 21:40 Acts 12:17; 22:2; 26:14 22:1 Acts 7:2 22:2 Acts 21:40 22:3 Acts 21:39; 20:4; Luke 10:39; Acts 26:5; 21:20 22:4 Acts 8:3; 26:9-11; Phil 3:6; 1 Tim 1:13 22:5 Luke 22:66; Acts 4:5; 9:2; 26:10,12 22:6 Acts 9:3; 26:12,13 22:9 Acts 9:7; 26:13 22:10 Acts 16:30 22:11 Acts 9:8 22:12 Acts 9:17; 10:22 *22:14 Acts 3:13; 5:30; 9:15; 26:16; 1 Cor 9:1; 15:8; Acts 7:52 22:15 Acts 23:11; 26:16 22:16 Acts 2:38; Heb 10:22; Acts 9:14; Rom 10:13 22:17 Acts 9:26; 10:10 22:19 v. 4; Acts 8:3; 26:11; Matt 10:17 22:20 Luke 11:48; Acts 8:1; Rom 1:32 22:21 Acts 9:15 *22:22 Acts 21:36; 25:24

21:38 The Egyptian who led this ill-fated revolt is referred to by the Jewish historian Josephus, who reported that he had gathered his followers on the Mount of Olives about the year A.D. 54 to see the walls of Jerusalem fall. He was attacked and his forces routed by Felix, but he himself escaped unharmed.
22:14 The title *the Righteous One* (Greek *dikaios*) is used of Christ here, as well as in 3:14 and 7:52; *the righteous* in 1 John 2:1. Righteousness is one of the attributes of the

Messiah (cf. Is. 32:1; 53:11), and it was natural that Christ should be called *the Righteous*.
22:22 The Jerusalem Jews listened carefully until Paul referred to the Gentiles, and then a riot broke out. In a similar way the Greeks in Athens listened attentively to Paul until he spoke of the resurrection of Christ; then the meeting broke up, for to the Greeks the idea of resurrection was nonsense (17:31,32).

voices and said, "Away with such a fellow from the earth, for he should not be allowed to live!"

23 And as they were crying out and throwing off their cloaks and tossing dust into the air,

24 the [36]commander ordered him to be brought into the barracks, stating that he should be examined by scourging so that he might find out the reason why they were shouting against him that way.

25 And when they stretched him out with thongs, Paul said to the centurion who was standing by, "Is it lawful for you to scourge a man who is a Roman and uncondemned?"

26 And when the centurion heard *this*, he went to the commander and told him, saying, "What are you about to do? For this man is a Roman."

27 And the commander came and said to him, "Tell me, are you a Roman?" And he said, "Yes."

28 And the commander answered, "I acquired this citizenship with a large sum of money." And Paul said, "But I was actually born *a citizen*."

29 Therefore those who were about to examine him immediately let go of him; and the commander also was afraid when he found out that he was a Roman, and because he had put him in chains.

c. His trial before the Sanhedrin

30 But on the next day, wishing to know for certain why he had been accused by the Jews, he released him and ordered the chief priests and all the Council to assemble, and brought Paul down and set him before them.

23 And Paul, looking intently at the Council, said, "Brethren, I have lived my life with a perfectly good conscience before God up to this day."

2 And the high priest Ananias commanded those standing beside him to strike him on the mouth.

3 Then Paul said to him, "God is going to strike you, you whitewashed wall! And do you sit to try me according to the Law, and in violation of the Law order me to be struck?"

4 But the bystanders said, "Do you revile God's high priest?"

5 And Paul said, "I was not aware, brethren, that he was high priest; for it is written, 'YOU SHALL NOT SPEAK EVIL OF A RULER OF YOUR PEOPLE.'"

6 But perceiving that one part were Sadducees and the other Pharisees, Paul *began* crying out in the Council, "Brethren, I am a Pharisee, a son of Pharisees; I am on trial for the hope and resurrection of the dead!"

7 And as he said this, there arose a dissension between the Pharisees and Sadducees; and the assembly was divided.

8 For the Sadducees say that there is no resurrection, nor an angel, nor a spirit; but the Pharisees acknowledge them all.

9 And there arose a great uproar; and some of the scribes of the Pharisaic party stood up and *began* to argue heatedly, saying, "We find nothing wrong with this man; suppose a spirit or an angel has spoken to him?"

10 And as a great dissension was developing, the [36]commander was afraid Paul would be torn to pieces by them and ordered the troops to go down and take him away from them by force, and bring him into the barracks.

11 But on the night *immediately* following, the Lord stood at his side and said, "Take courage; for as you have solemnly witnessed to My cause at Jerusalem, so you must witness at Rome also."

[36] I.e., chiliarch, in command of one thousand troops

22:25 Paul here claimed Roman citizenship. In his day, one was automatically a Roman citizen if both parents were Roman citizens. However, if the woman in a marriage was not a Roman citizen, children born of such a marriage were not entitled to Roman citizenship either. Roman citizenship was also secured by manumission and by grant to individuals or districts as a reward for various kinds of services rendered. The chief benefits accruing to those who held Roman citizenship were that they could not be scourged or put to death without the right to appeal to the emperor. Once an appeal was granted, the case was stopped until the emperor acted, but not all appeals to the emperor were granted. The accused, while waiting for his trial, might be kept in the common jail, housed in the home of a friend who vouched for his appearance, or placed either in the custody of a soldier to whom the accused was fastened with a chain or permitted to live in his own lodgings. Anyone falsely claiming Roman citizenship was guilty of a capital crime. In 25:11 Paul's appeal to Caesar was granted.
23:6 See note to Matt. 3:7.
23:11 The Lord appeared to Paul on the road to Damascus at his conversion (9:5; 22:8; 26:15); on his first visit to Jerusalem (22:17,18); in Corinth (18:9,10); and now on his last visit to Jerusalem.

d. His removal to Caesarea

12 And when it was day, the Jews formed a conspiracy and bound themselves under an oath, saying that they would neither eat nor drink until they had killed Paul.

13 And there were more than forty who formed this plot.

14 And they came to the chief priests and the elders, and said, "We have bound ourselves under a solemn oath to taste nothing until we have killed Paul.

15 "Now, therefore, you and the Council notify the commander to bring him down to you, as though you were going to determine his case by a more thorough investigation; and we for our part are ready to slay him before he comes near *the place.*"

16 But the son of Paul's sister heard of their ambush, and he came and entered the barracks and told Paul.

17 And Paul called one of the centurions to him and said, "Lead this young man to the commander, for he has something to report to him."

18 So he took him and led him to the commander and *said, "Paul the prisoner called me to him and asked me to lead this young man to you since he has something to tell you."

19 And the commander took him by the hand and stepping aside, *began* to inquire of him privately, "What is it that you have to report to me?"

20 And he said, "The Jews have agreed to ask you to bring Paul down tomorrow to the Council, as though they were going to inquire somewhat more thoroughly about him.

21 "So do not listen to them, for more than forty of them are lying in wait for him who have bound themselves under a curse not to eat or drink until they slay him; and now they are ready and waiting for the promise from you."

22 Therefore the commander let the young man go, instructing him, "Tell no one that you have notified me of these things."

23 And he called to him two of the centurions, and said, "Get two hundred soldiers ready by [37]the third hour of the night to proceed to Caesarea, with seventy horsemen and two hundred spearmen."

24 *They were* also to provide mounts to put Paul on and bring him safely to Felix the governor.

25 And he wrote a letter having this form:

26 "Claudius Lysias, to the most excellent governor Felix, greetings.

27 "When this man was arrested by the Jews and was about to be slain by them, I came upon them with the troops and rescued him, having learned that he was a Roman.

28 "And wanting to ascertain the charge for which they were accusing him, I brought him down to their Council;

29 and I found him to be accused over questions about their Law, but under no accusation deserving death or imprisonment.

30 "And when I was informed that there would be a plot against the man, I sent him to you at once, also instructing his accusers to bring charges against him before you."

31 So the soldiers, in accordance with their orders, took Paul and brought him by night to Antipatris.

32 But the next day, leaving the horsemen to go on with him, they returned to the barracks.

33 And when these had come to Caesarea and delivered the letter to the governor, they also presented Paul to him.

34 And when he had read it, he asked from what province he was; and when he learned that he was from Cilicia,

Cross references (right margin):

23:12 vv. 21,30; Acts 25:3
23:14 v. 21
23:15 Acts 22:30
23:16 Acts 21:34; v. 10
23:18 Eph 3:1
23:20 vv. 14,15
23:21 vv.12,14
23:23 v. 33
*23:24 Acts 24:1,3, 10; 25:14
23:26 Acts 24:3; 15:23
23:27 Acts 21:32, 33; 22:25-29
23:28 Acts 22:30
23:29 Acts 18:15; 25:19; 26:31
23:30 vv. 20,21; Acts 24:19; 25:16
23:32 v. 23
23:33 vv. 23,24,26
23:34 Acts 21:39

---

[37]I.e., 9 p.m.

23:24 Felix was the procurator of Judea, with both military and civil jurisdiction over his territory. His headquarters were in Caesarea, a seaport on the Mediterranean Sea. Felix was married to Drusilla, the youngest daughter of Herod Agrippa I, who deserted her husband Azizus, king of Emesa, for this Gentile (24:24). Felix's reputation was odious. He was of common origin, and his appointment apparently was due to the friendship of Pallas, who was a favorite of Claudius Caesar. Nero, who followed Claudius, confirmed Felix's appointment. During Paul's stay, there were serious riots that were quelled, but charges were leveled against Felix by the Jews and he was recalled to Rome. Pallas's influence protected him. Before departing for Rome, Felix sought the favor of the Jews by leaving Paul in prison (24:27).

*23:35
Acts 24:19;
25:16; 24:27
35   he said, "I will give you a hearing after your accusers arrive also," giving orders for him to be kept in Herod's [38]Praetorium.

e. Paul's defense at Caesarea

(1) PAUL BEFORE FELIX

24:1
Acts 23:2,30,
35
24 And after five days the high priest Ananias came down with some elders, with a certain attorney *named* Tertullus; and they brought charges to the governor against Paul.

2   And after *Paul* had been summoned, Tertullus began to accuse him, saying *to the governor,*

"Since we have through you attained much peace, and since by your providence reforms are being carried out for this nation,

24:3
Acts 23:26;
26:25
3   we acknowledge *this* in every way and everywhere, most excellent Felix, with all thankfulness.

4   "But, that I may not weary you any further, I beg you to grant us, by your kindness, a brief hearing.

24:5
Acts 16:20;
17:6; 21:28
5   "For we have found this man a real pest and a fellow who stirs up dissension among all the Jews throughout [39]the world, and a ringleader of the sect of the Nazarenes.

24:6
Acts 21:28
6   "And he even tried to desecrate the temple; and then we arrested him. [[40]And we wanted to judge him according to our own Law.

7   "But Lysias the commander came along, and with much violence took him out of our hands,

8   ordering his accusers to come before you.] And by examining him yourself concerning all these matters, you will be able to ascertain the things of which we accuse him."

24:9
1 Thess 2:16
24:10
Acts 23:24
9   And the Jews also joined in the attack, asserting that these things were so.

10   And when the governor had nodded for him to speak, Paul responded:

"Knowing that for many years you have been a judge to this nation, I cheerfully make my defense,

24:11
Acts 21:26
11   since you can take note of the fact that no more than twelve days ago I went up to Jerusalem to worship.

24:12
Acts 25:8;
28:17
12   "And neither in the temple, nor in the synagogues, nor in the city *itself* did they find me carrying on a discussion with anyone or causing a riot.

24:13
Acts 25:7
24:14
Acts 9:2; v. 5;
Acts 3:13;
26:22; 28:23
13   "Nor can they prove to you *the charges* of which they now accuse me.

14   "But this I admit to you, that according to the Way which they call a sect I do serve the God of our fathers, believing everything that is in accordance with the Law, and that is written in the Prophets;

24:15
Acts 23:6;
28:20;
Dan 12:2;
John 5:28,29
24:16
Acts 23:1
24:17
Acts 11:29,
30;
Rom 15:25-28;
2 Cor 8:1-4;
Gal 2:10
24:18
Acts 21:26,27
24:19
Acts 23:30
15   having a hope in God, which these men cherish themselves, that there shall certainly be a resurrection of both the righteous and the wicked.

16   "In view of this, I also do my best to maintain always a blameless conscience *both* before God and before men.

17   "Now after several years I came to bring [41]alms to my nation and to present offerings;

18   in which they found me *occupied* in the temple, having been purified, without *any* crowd or uproar. But *there were* certain Jews from Asia—

19   who ought to have been present before you, and to make accusation, if they should have anything against me.

20   "Or else let these men themselves tell what misdeed they found when I stood before the Council,

24:21
Acts 23:6
21   other than for this one statement which I shouted out while standing among them, 'For the resurrection of the dead I am on trial before you today.' "

22   But Felix, having a more exact knowledge about the Way, put them off, saying, "When Lysias the [42]commander comes down, I will decide your case."

24:23
Acts 23:35;
28:16; 23:16;
27:3
23   And he gave orders to the centurion for him to be kept in custody and *yet* have *some* freedom, and not to prevent any of his friends from ministering to him.

24   But some days later, Felix arrived with Drusilla, his wife who was a Jewess, and sent for Paul, and heard him *speak* about faith in Christ Jesus.

[38]I.e., governor's official residence   [39]Lit., *the inhabited earth*   [40]Many mss. do not contain the remainder of v. 6, v. 7, nor the first part of v. 8   [41]Or, *gifts to charity*   [42]I.e., chiliarch, in command of one thousand troops

23:35   Herod's Praetorium was the palace built by Herod the Great in Caesarea and used as a place of residence by the Roman procurators.

25   And as he was discussing righteousness, self-control and the judgment to come, Felix became frightened and said, "Go away for the present, and when I find time, I will summon you."

26   At the same time too, he was hoping that money would be given him by Paul; therefore he also used to send for him quite often and converse with him.

27   But after two years had passed, Felix was succeeded by Porcius Festus; and wishing to do the Jews a favor, Felix left Paul imprisoned.

24:25
Gal 5:23;
Acts 10:42

24:27
Acts 25:1,4,9,
14; 12:3;
23:35

(2) PAUL BEFORE FESTUS

25   Festus therefore, having arrived in the province, three days later went up to Jerusalem from Caesarea.

2   And the chief priests and the leading men of the Jews brought charges against Paul; and they were urging him,

3   requesting a concession against Paul, that he might have him brought to Jerusalem (*at the same time*, setting an ambush to kill him on the way).

4   Festus then answered that Paul was being kept in custody at Caesarea and that he himself was about to leave shortly.

5   "Therefore," he *said, "let the influential men among you go there with me, and if there is anything wrong about the man, let them prosecute him."

6   And after he had spent not more than eight or ten days among them, he went down to Caesarea; and on the next day he took his seat on the tribunal and ordered Paul to be brought.

7   And after he had arrived, the Jews who had come down from Jerusalem stood around him, bringing many and serious charges against him which they could not prove;

8   while Paul said in his own defense, "I have committed no offense either against the Law of the Jews or against the temple or against Caesar."

9   But Festus, wishing to do the Jews a favor, answered Paul and said, "Are you willing to go up to Jerusalem and stand trial before me on these *charges*?"

10   But Paul said, "I am standing before Caesar's tribunal, where I ought to be tried. I have done no wrong to *the* Jews, as you also very well know.

11   "If then I am a wrongdoer, and have committed anything worthy of death, I do not refuse to die; but if none of those things is *true* of which these men accuse me, no one can hand me over to them. I appeal to Caesar."

12   Then when Festus had conferred with his council, he answered, "You have appealed to Caesar, to Caesar you shall go."

25:2
Acts 24:1;
v. 15
25:3
Acts 23:12,15

25:4
Acts 24:23

25:7
Mark 15:3;
Luke 23:2,
10; Acts 24:5,
13
25:8
Acts 6:13;
24:12; 28:17
25:9
Acts 24:27;
v. 20

25:11
v. 25;
Acts 26:32;
28:19

(3) FESTUS AND AGRIPPA

13   Now when several days had elapsed, King Agrippa and Bernice arrived at Caesarea, and paid their respects to Festus.

14   And while they were spending many days there, Festus laid Paul's case before the king, saying, "There is a certain man left a prisoner by Felix;

15   and when I was at Jerusalem, the chief priests and the elders of the Jews brought charges against him, asking for a sentence of condemnation upon him.

16   "And I answered them that it is not the custom of the Romans to hand over any man before the accused meets his accusers face to face, and has an opportunity to make his defense against the charges.

17   "And so after they had assembled here, I made no delay, but on the next day took my seat on the tribunal, and ordered the man to be brought.

18   "And when the accusers stood up, they *began* bringing charges against him not of such crimes as I was expecting;

19   but they *simply* had some points of disagreement with him about their own religion and about a certain dead man, Jesus, whom Paul asserted to be alive.

20   "And being at a loss how to investigate such matters, I asked whether he was willing to go to Jerusalem and there stand trial on these matters.

25:14
Acts 24:27

25:15
Acts 24:1;
v. 2
25:16
vv. 4,5

25:17
vv. 6,10

25:19
Acts 18:15;
23:29
25:20
v. 9

25:1 Porcius Festus succeeded Felix in A.D. 60 as the procurator of Judea. Little is known of his family background. His suggestion to Paul that he stand trial in Jerusalem at the request of the Jews provoked Paul's appeal to Caesar. The appeal was allowed by Festus, since it was the inherent right of a Roman citizen to appeal to Caesar.
25:13 This Agrippa was Herod Agrippa II, the son of Herod Agrippa I. Paul appeared before him and his sister Bernice, of whom history has little good to report. Only

seventeen at the time of his father's death, young Agrippa succeeded in building up a kingdom by degrees. He tried to reconcile Judaism and Hellenism without great success. His enigmatic statement of 26:28 translated, *In a short time you will persuade me to become a Christian.* is open to various other interpretations: (KJV, "Almost thou persuadest me to be a Christian"; Berkeley, "You are with a little effort convincing enough to make me a Christian").

21 "But when Paul appealed to be held in custody for [43]the Emperor's decision, I ordered him to be kept in custody until I send him to Caesar."

22 And Agrippa *said* to Festus, "I also would like to hear the man myself." "Tomorrow," he *said, "you shall hear him."

23 And so, on the next day when Agrippa had come together with Bernice, amid great pomp, and had entered the auditorium [44]accompanied by the commanders and the prominent men of the city, at the command of Festus, Paul was brought in.

24 And Festus *said, "King Agrippa, and all you gentlemen here present with us, you behold this man about whom all the people of the Jews appealed to me, both at Jerusalem and here, loudly declaring that he ought not to live any longer.

25 "But I found that he had committed nothing worthy of death; and since he himself appealed to the Emperor, I decided to send him.

26 "Yet I have nothing definite about him to write to my lord. Therefore I have brought him before you *all* and especially before you, King Agrippa, so that after the investigation has taken place, I may have something to write.

27 "For it seems absurd to me in sending a prisoner, not to indicate also the charges against him."

(4) PAUL BEFORE AGRIPPA

26 And Agrippa said to Paul, "You are permitted to speak for yourself." Then Paul stretched out his hand and *proceeded* to make his defense:

2 "In regard to all the things of which I am accused by the Jews, I consider myself fortunate, King Agrippa, that I am about to make my defense before you today;

3 especially because you are an expert in all customs and questions among *the* Jews; therefore I beg you to listen to me patiently.

4 "So then, all Jews know my manner of life from my youth up, which from the beginning was spent among my *own* nation and at Jerusalem;

5 since they have known about me for a long time previously, if they are willing to testify, that I lived *as* a Pharisee according to the strictest sect of our religion.

6 "And now I am standing trial for the hope of the promise made by God to our fathers;

7 *the promise* to which our twelve tribes hope to attain, as they earnestly serve *God* night and day. And for this hope, O King, I am being accused by Jews.

8 "Why is it considered incredible among you *people* if God does raise the dead?

9 "So then, I thought to myself that I had to do many things hostile to the name of Jesus of Nazareth.

10 "And this is just what I did in Jerusalem; not only did I lock up many of the saints in prisons, having received authority from the chief priests, but also when they were being put to death I cast my vote against them.

11 "And as I punished them often in all the synagogues, I tried to force them to blaspheme; and being furiously enraged at them, I kept pursuing them even to foreign cities.

12 "While thus engaged as I was journeying to Damascus with the authority and commission of the chief priests,

13 at midday, O King, I saw on the way a light from heaven, brighter than the sun, shining all around me and those who were journeying with me.

14 "And when we had all fallen to the ground, I heard a voice saying to me in the Hebrew dialect, 'Saul, Saul, why are you persecuting Me? It is hard for you to kick against the goads.'

15 "And I said, 'Who art Thou, Lord?' And the Lord said, 'I am Jesus whom you are persecuting.

16 'But arise, and stand on your feet; for this purpose I have appeared to you, to appoint you a minister and a witness not only to the things which you have seen, but also to the things in which I will appear to you;

17 delivering you from the *Jewish* people and from the Gentiles, to whom I am sending you,

18 to open their eyes so that they may turn from darkness to light and from the dominion of Satan to God, in order that they may receive forgiveness of sins and an inheritance among those who have been sanctified by faith in Me.'

[43]Lit., *the Augustus* (in this case Nero) [44]Lit., *and with*

19 "Consequently, King Agrippa, I did not prove disobedient to the heavenly vision,

20   but *kept* declaring both to those of Damascus first, and *also* at Jerusalem and *then* throughout all the region of Judea, and *even* to the Gentiles, that they should repent and turn to God, performing deeds appropriate to repentance.

21   "For this reason *some* Jews seized me in the temple and tried to put me to death.

22   "And so, having obtained help from God, I stand to this day testifying both to small and great, stating nothing but what the Prophets and Moses said was going to take place;

23   that the Christ was to suffer, *and* that by reason of *His* resurrection from the dead He should be the first to proclaim light both to the *Jewish* people and to the Gentiles."

24   And while *Paul* was saying this in his defense, Festus *said in a loud voice, "Paul, you are out of your mind! *Your* great learning is driving you mad."

25   But Paul *said, "I am not out of my mind, most excellent Festus, but I utter words of sober truth.

26   "For the king knows about these matters, and I speak to him also with confidence, since I am persuaded that none of these things escape his notice; for this has not been done in a corner.

27   "King Agrippa, do you believe the Prophets? I know that you do."

28   And Agrippa *replied* to Paul, "In a short time you will persuade me to become a Christian."

29   And Paul *said*, "I would to God, that whether in a short or long time, not only you, but also all who hear me this day, might become such as I am, except for these chains."

30   And the king arose and the governor and Bernice, and those who were sitting with them,

31   and when they had drawn aside, they *began* talking to one another, saying, "This man is not doing anything worthy of death or imprisonment."

32   And Agrippa said to Festus, "This man might have been set free if he had not appealed to Caesar."

3. *Paul sent to Rome*

a. *The embarkation and voyage*

27 And when it was decided that we should sail for Italy, they proceeded to deliver Paul and some other prisoners to a centurion of the Augustan [45]cohort named Julius.

2   And embarking in an Adramyttian ship, which was about to sail to the regions along the coast of Asia, we put out to sea, accompanied by Aristarchus, a Macedonian of Thessalonica.

3   And the next day we put in at Sidon; and Julius treated Paul with consideration and allowed him to go to his friends and receive care.

4   And from there we put out to sea and sailed under the shelter of Cyprus because the winds were contrary.

5   And when we had sailed through the sea along the coast of Cilicia and Pamphylia, we landed at Myra in Lycia.

6   And there the centurion found an Alexandrian ship sailing for Italy, and he put us aboard it.

7   And when we had sailed slowly for a good many days, and with difficulty had arrived off Cnidus, since the wind did not permit us *to go* farther, we sailed under the shelter of Crete, off Salmone;

8   and with difficulty sailing past it we came to a certain place called Fair Havens, near which was the city of Lasea.

9   And when considerable time had passed and the voyage was now dangerous, since even the [46]fast was already over, Paul *began* to admonish them,

10   and said to them, "Men, I perceive that the voyage will certainly be *attended* with damage and great loss, not only of the cargo and the ship, but also of our lives."

[45]Or, *battalion* [46]I.e., Day of Atonement in September or October

Marginal references:

26:20 Acts 9:19-29; 22:17-20; 13:46; 9:15; 3:19; Matt 3:8; Luke 3:8
26:21 Acts 21:30,31
26:22 Luke 24:27, 44; Acts 24:14
26:23 Matt 26:24; 1 Cor 15:20; Col 1:18; Rev 1:5; Luke 2:32
26:24 2 Kin 9:11; John 10:20; 1Cor 1:23
26:25 Acts 23:26; 24:3
26:30 Acts 25:33
26:31 Acts 23:29
26:32 Acts 28:18; 25:11
27:1 Acts 25:12, 25; 10:1
27:2 Acts 19:29; 16:9; 17:1
27:3 Acts 24:23; 28:16
27:4 v. 7
27:5 Acts 6:9; 13:13
27:6 Acts 28:11; v. 1
27:7 vv. 4,12,13
*27:9 Lev 23:27-29
27:10 v. 21

27:9 This is the one Jewish fast prescribed by Mosaic Law, the Day of Atonement (cf. Lev. 16:29–34), on the tenth day of Tishri (September-October). Assuming this incident took place in the year A.D. 59, the Day of Atonement was about October 5.

11   But the centurion was more persuaded by the pilot and the captain of the ship, than by what was being said by Paul.

12   And because the harbor was not suitable for wintering, the majority reached a decision to put out to sea from there, if somehow they could reach Phoenix, a harbor of Crete, facing southwest and northwest, and spend the winter *there*.

27:13
vv. 7,12

13   And when a moderate south wind came up, supposing that they had gained their purpose, they weighed anchor and *began* sailing along Crete, close *inshore*.

27:14
Mark 4:37

14   But before very long there rushed down from the land a violent wind, called [47]Euraquilo;

15   and when the ship was caught *in it*, and could not face the wind, we gave way *to it*, and let ourselves be driven along.

16   And running under the shelter of a small island called Clauda, we were scarcely able to get the *ship's* boat under control.

27:17
vv. 26,29

17   And after they had hoisted it up, they used supporting cables in undergirding the ship; and fearing that they might run aground on *the shallows* of Syrtis, they let down the sea anchor, and so let themselves be driven along.

27:18
Jon 1:5; v. 38

18   The next day as we were being violently storm-tossed, they began to jettison the cargo;

19   and on the third day they threw the ship's tackle overboard with their own hands.

20   And since neither sun nor stars appeared for many days, and no small storm was assailing *us*, from then on all hope of our being saved was gradually abandoned.

27:21
vv. 10,7,12,
13

21   And when they had gone a long time without food, then Paul stood up in their midst and said, "Men, you ought to have followed my advice and not to have set sail from Crete, and incurred this damage and loss.

27:22
vv. 25,36

22   "And *yet* now I urge you to keep up your courage, for there shall be no loss of life among you, but *only* of the ship.

27:23
Acts 23:11;
5:19;
Rom 1:9

23   "For this very night an angel of the God to whom I belong and whom I serve stood before me,

27:24
Acts 23:11;
v. 44

24   saying, 'Do not be afraid, Paul; you must stand before Caesar; and behold, God has granted you all those who are sailing with you.'

27:25
vv. 22,36;
Rom 4:20,21

25   "Therefore, keep up your courage, men, for I believe God, that it will turn out exactly as I have been told.

27:26
Acts 28:1

26   "But we must run aground on a certain island."

b. The shipwreck

27   But when the fourteenth night had come, as we were being driven about in the Adriatic Sea, about midnight the sailors *began* to surmise that they were approaching some land.

28   And they took soundings, and found *it to be* twenty fathoms; and a little farther on they took another sounding and found *it to be* fifteen fathoms.

29   And fearing that we might run aground somewhere on the rocks, they cast four anchors from the stern and wished for daybreak.

27:30
v. 16

30   And as the sailors were trying to escape from the ship, and had let down the *ship's* boat into the sea, on the pretense of intending to lay out anchors from the bow,

31   Paul said to the centurion and to the soldiers, "Unless these men remain in the ship, you yourselves cannot be saved."

32   Then the soldiers cut away the ropes of the *ship's* boat, and let it fall away.

33   And until the day was about to dawn, Paul was encouraging them all to take some food, saying, "Today is the fourteenth day that you have been constantly watching and going without eating, having taken nothing.

27:34
1 Kin 1:52;
Matt 10:30;
Luke 12:7;
21:18

34   "Therefore I encourage you to take some food, for this is for your preservation; for not a hair from the head of any of you shall perish."

27:35
1 Sam 9:13;
Matt 15:36;
Mark 8:6;
John 6:11;
1 Tim 4:3,4

35   And having said this, he took bread and gave thanks to God in the presence of all; and he broke it and began to eat.

36   And all of them were encouraged, and they themselves also took food.

37   And all of us in the ship were two hundred and seventy-six persons.

27:36
vv. 22,25

38   And when they had eaten enough, they *began* to lighten the ship by throwing out the wheat into the sea.

27:38
v. 18

39   And when day came, they could not recognize the land; but they did observe

[47]I.e., a northeaster

a certain bay with a beach, and they resolved to [48]drive the ship onto it if they could.

40   And casting off the anchors, they left them in the sea while at the same time they were loosening the ropes of the rudders, and hoisting the foresail to the wind, they were heading for the beach.

41   But striking a reef where two seas met, they ran the vessel aground; and the prow stuck fast and remained immovable, but the stern *began* to be broken up by the force *of the waves.*

42   And the soldiers' plan was to kill the prisoners, that none *of them* should swim away and escape;

43   but the centurion, wanting to bring Paul safely through, kept them from their intention, and commanded that those who could swim should jump overboard first and get to land,

44   and the rest *should follow*, some on planks, and others on various things from the ship. And thus it happened that they all were brought safely to land.

c. The stopover at Malta

28 And when they had been brought safely through, then we found out that the island was called Malta.

2   And the natives showed us extraordinary kindness; for because of the rain that had set in and because of the cold, they kindled a fire and received us all.

3   But when Paul had gathered a bundle of sticks and laid them on the fire, a viper came out because of the heat, and fastened on his hand.

4   And when the natives saw the creature hanging from his hand, they *began* saying to one another, "Undoubtedly this man is a murderer, and though he has been saved from the sea, justice has not allowed him to live."

5   However he shook the creature off into the fire and suffered no harm.

6   But they were expecting that he was about to swell up or suddenly fall down dead. But after they had waited a long time and had seen nothing unusual happen to him, they changed their minds and *began* to say that he was a god.

7   Now in the neighborhood of that place were lands belonging to the leading man of the island, named Publius, who welcomed us and entertained us courteously three days.

8   And it came about that the father of Publius was lying *in bed* afflicted with *recurrent* fever and dysentery; and Paul went in *to see* him and after he had prayed, he laid his hands on him and healed him.

9   And after this had happened, the rest of the people on the island who had diseases were coming to him and getting cured.

10   And they also honored us with many marks of respect; and when we were setting sail, they supplied *us* with all we needed.

11   And at the end of three months we set sail on an Alexandrian ship which had wintered at the island, and which had the Twin Brothers for its figurehead.

12   And after we put in at Syracuse, we stayed there for three days.

13   And from there we sailed around and arrived at Rhegium, and a day later a south wind sprang up, and on the second day we came to Puteoli.

14   There we found *some* brethren, and were invited to stay with them for seven days; and thus we came to Rome.

15   And the brethren, when they heard about us, came from there as far as the Market of Appius and Three Inns to meet us; and when Paul saw them, he thanked God and took courage.

16   And when we entered Rome, Paul was allowed to stay by himself, with the soldier who was guarding him.

d. The arrival at Rome

17   And it happened that after three days he called together those who were the leading men of the Jews, and when they had come together, he *began* saying to them, "Brethren, though I had done nothing against our people, or the customs of our fathers, yet I was delivered prisoner from Jerusalem into the hands of the Romans.

18   "And when they had examined me, they were willing to release me because there was no ground for putting me to death.

[48]Some ancient mss. read *bring the ship safely ashore*

Marginal references:

27:39 / Acts 28:1

27:40 / v. 29

27:41 / 2 Cor 11:25

27:42 / Acts 12:19

27:43 / v. 3

27:44 / vv. 22,31

28:1 / Acts 27:26,39

28:2 / Rom 1:14; 1 Cor 14:11; Col 3:11

28:4 / Luke 13:2,4

28:5 / Luke 10:19
28:6 / Acts 14:11

28:8 / James 5:14, 15; Mark 5:23

28:11 / Acts 27:6

28:14 / Acts 1:15

28:16 / Acts 24:23; 27:3

28:17 / Acts 13:50; 25:8; 6:14

28:18 / Acts 22:24; 26:31,32; 23:29

19 "But when the Jews objected, I was forced to appeal to Caesar; not that I had any accusation against my nation.

20 "For this reason therefore, I requested to see you and to speak with you, for I am wearing this chain for the sake of the hope of Israel."

21 And they said to him, "We have neither received letters from Judea concerning you, nor have any of the brethren come here and reported or spoken anything bad about you.

22 "But we desire to hear from you what your views are; for concerning this sect, it is known to us that it is spoken against everywhere."

23 And when they had set a day for him, they came to him at his lodging in large numbers; and he was explaining to them by solemnly testifying about the kingdom of God, and trying to persuade them concerning Jesus, from both the Law of Moses and from the Prophets, from morning until evening.

24 And some were being persuaded by the things spoken, but others would not believe.

25 And when they did not agree with one another, they *began* leaving after Paul had spoken one *parting* word, "The Holy Spirit rightly spoke through Isaiah the prophet to your fathers,

26 saying,

'GO TO THIS PEOPLE AND SAY,

"YOU WILL KEEP ON HEARING, BUT WILL NOT UNDERSTAND;

AND YOU WILL KEEP ON SEEING, BUT WILL NOT PERCEIVE;

27 FOR THE HEART OF THIS PEOPLE HAS BECOME DULL,

AND WITH THEIR EARS THEY SCARCELY HEAR,

AND THEY HAVE CLOSED THEIR EYES;

LEST THEY SHOULD SEE WITH THEIR EYES,

AND HEAR WITH THEIR EARS,

AND UNDERSTAND WITH THEIR HEART AND RETURN,

AND I SHOULD HEAL THEM." '

28 "Let it be known to you therefore, that this salvation of God has been sent to the Gentiles; they will also listen."

29 [[49]And when he had spoken these words, the Jews departed, having a great dispute among themselves.]

30 And he stayed two full years in his own rented quarters, and was welcoming all who came to him,

31 preaching the kingdom of God, and teaching concerning the Lord Jesus Christ with all openness, unhindered.

[49]Many mss. do not contain this verse

INTRODUCTION TO
THE LETTER OF PAUL TO THE
ROMANS

Authorship and Background: Paul wrote to the Romans about A.D. 56. He was probably in Corinth during his three-month visit there (Acts 20:2,3; cf. 1 Cor. 16:5-7), at the end of his third missionary journey. Since he had never been in Rome, Paul expressed disappointment over his failure to visit the Christians there and spoke of his eagerness to see them (1:10-13; 15:22,23; cf. Acts 19:21). First, however, he had to go to Jerusalem with the relief offering raised by the churches in Macedonia and Achaia (15:25-27). Then after visiting Rome he planned to go to Spain, for which trip he hoped to enlist the approval and support of the Roman believers (15:24,28).

The Roman church was already widely known (1:8), and Paul was eager to minister to the Christians there, for mutual strength and blessing (1:11-13). Since it was his policy not to carry on intensive work where the gospel had been planted by others, Paul stated that he would see them in passing, so as not to trespass on another's field of work (15:20,22,28). His divine commission as an apostle to the Gentiles, however, made him anxious to preach the gospel in Rome also (1:13-15). He wrote, therefore, to acquaint the Romans with his message, thus preparing the way for his visit (15:14-17).

Characteristics: Paul sets forth in an orderly way his understanding of some of the fundamental principles of the gospel. The letter is more formal and less personal in tone than his other letters (except for ch. 16, for which see note).

It is not known who planted the gospel in Rome. On the day of Pentecost visitors from Rome were present in Jerusalem (Acts 2:10), and doubtlessly some of them carried the Christian message back to the imperial capital. Paul addressed himself both to Jews (2:17-4:25) and to Gentiles (1:13-15; 11:13). The proportion between the two in the Roman church nearly twenty-five years after Pentecost is unknown, but it would appear that the Gentiles outnumbered the Jews.

The theme is stated quite formally in 1:16,17. This is followed by the development and exposition of the truth that "the gospel . . . is the power of God for salvation to everyone who believes." Indeed, for Paul the true doctrine of justification is the truth of all truths, demanding attention because of the crisis in Galatia, Jewish unbelief, and pressing questions of ceremonialism. Justification is through faith alone: what this involves and what its consequences are in the lives of believers constitute the greater part of the letter. The apostle magnifies the grace of God in salvation, with the corresponding responsibility of the believer who lives under grace, not law. He rises to heights of inspired eloquence in chapter 8, which could be called "The Gospel of the Holy Spirit." Time and again the Spirit of God has used this letter to call God's people back to the foundational truths of the Christian faith.

Contents:

I. Introduction (1:1-17)

II. The world's need of God (1:18-3:20): Gentiles (1:18-2:16) and Jews (2:17-3:20) stand in need of salvation: all have sinned and fall short of the glory of God (3:23).

III. Justification by faith alone (3:21-8:39): Salvation is God's gracious gift: man is justified on the basis of faith alone, not of works. This is true both of Jews and Gentiles, and it means that the believer is to live a life of purity and holiness, since he lives under grace, not law. The Spirit enables the believer to live a triumphant life, and no power can separate him from God's love in Christ Jesus the Lord.

IV. **Jew and Gentile in the plan of God (9:1-11:36):** God has not forsaken His people; but His people have always been a minority, not the total number of the Israelites. They too are saved by grace through faith, as are the Gentiles, and both are within God's redemptive purposes: though we cannot fully understand it, we can rely on God's all-embracing mercy.

V. **Ethical teaching (12:1-15:13):** How God's grace works in the lives of believers; how they are to relate themselves to the state and its rights; how "strong" and "weak" Christians are to treat each other, living in harmony and accepting one another as God in Christ has accepted them all.

VI. **Conclusion and postscript (15:14-16:27)**

Note: Chapter 16 reads like a postscript and raises some questions, since in it Paul calls by name twenty-six people in a church he has never visited. Prisca and Aquila (vv. 3-5) shortly before this were in Ephesus (Acts 18:18,19; 1 Cor. 16:19) and later (2 Tim. 4:19) they are not in Rome, but probably Ephesus. Epaenetus (v. 5) is the first convert of the province of Asia, whose capital was Ephesus. Paul spent over three years in Ephesus, and chapter 16 is more easily understood if it was addressed to Ephesus, not Rome.

In addition, the oldest manuscript has the benediction of 16:25-27 at the end of chapter 15. In other copies it occurs at the end of chapters 14 and 16.

These facts have led some scholars to conclude that a copy of the epistle with chapter 16 added was sent to Ephesus and it is this copy that has survived. This is simply a conjecture, of course, and in no way affects the content or destination of chapters 1-15. The fact that there is no single clear omission of chapter 16 in the manuscripts is strong evidence of its integrity.

THE LETTER OF PAUL TO THE

ROMANS

I. Introduction (1:1–17)

A. Salutation

1 Paul, a bond-servant of Christ Jesus, called *as* an apostle, set apart for the gospel of God,

2 which He promised beforehand through His prophets in the holy Scriptures,

3 concerning His Son, who was born of a descendant of David according to the flesh,

4 who was declared the Son of God with power [1]by the resurrection from the dead, according to the spirit of holiness, Jesus Christ our Lord,

5 through whom we have received grace and apostleship to bring about *the* obedience of faith among all the Gentiles, for His name's sake,

6 among whom you also are the called of Jesus Christ;

7 to all who are beloved of God in Rome, called *as* saints: Grace to you and peace from God our Father and the Lord Jesus Christ.

B. Prayer of thanksgiving

8 First, I thank my God through Jesus Christ for you all, because your faith is being proclaimed throughout the whole world.

9 For God, whom I serve in my spirit in the *preaching of the* gospel of His Son, is my witness *as to* how unceasingly I make mention of you,

10 always in my prayers making request, if perhaps now at last by the will of God I may succeed in coming to you.

11 For I long to see you in order that I may impart some spiritual gift to you, that you may be established;

12 that is, that I may be encouraged together with you *while* among you, each of us by the other's faith, both yours and mine.

13 And I do not want you to be unaware, brethren, that often I have planned to come to you (and have been prevented thus far) in order that I might obtain some fruit among you also, even as among the rest of the Gentiles.

14 I am [2]under obligation both to Greeks and to barbarians, both to the wise and to the foolish.

15 Thus, for my part, I am eager to preach the gospel to you also who are in Rome.

*1:1
1 Cor 1:1;
Acts 9:15;
2 Cor 11:7
1:2
Acts 26:6;
Gal 3:8
1:3
John 1:14
1:4
Acts 13:33;
Heb 9:14
1:5
Gal 1:16;
Acts 6:7; 9:15
*1:7
1 Cor 1:2,3;
Gal 1:3;
Eph 1:2
1:8
Phil 1:3;
Acts 16:19
1:9
Phil 1:8;
Acts 24:14;
Eph 1:16
1:10
Rom 15:32
1:11
Rom 15:23
1:13
Rom 15:22
1:14
1 Cor 9:16;
Acts 28:2
1:15
Rom 12:18;
15:20

[1]Or, *as a result of* [2]Lit., *debtor*

1:1 Believers are called *slaves* (Greek *douloi*) of Jesus Christ. The distinction between *bond-servants* and *slaves* should be kept in mind. A bond-servant (*misthios* or *diakonos*) had certain rights and privileges. He was not mere chattel as a slave was. *Bond*-servants were engaged and paid for their labors, and when their terms of service expired. they were free to go. The slave was not free but was the property of his master his entire life. He had no rights or privileges. He was never free to go. Paul declares that true believers, for the sake of Christ, are also slaves to their fellow believers (2 Cor. 4:5).
1:7 *Saints* is the Greek *hagioi*, from *hagios*, meaning "set apart," "separated unto God," "holy." This title is applied in the New Testament to those who have been regenerated by faith in Christ. It points to the position of the believer as holy, and in sanctified possession of the Lord, indwelt by

the Holy Spirit. Experientially, the sanctified believer becomes more and more filled with Jesus Christ and conformed to His character, even though he will not become perfectly like Him until he is with Him and sees Him as He is (1 John 3:2).

The Fatherhood of God may be understood in two senses: (1) God is the Father of all men in the sense that He is their creator (all have been made by Him), just as a male parent is the father of all of his offspring. (2) God is especially the Father of those who believe. In this latter and special sense, God is not the Father of unbelievers at all (except as their creator). But He is the covenantal Father of all believers, for by the new birth they have become His children (1 John 3:2) and have been adopted into His family (Gal. 4:5).

C. *Theme*

16 For I am not ashamed of the gospel, for it is the power of God for salvation to everyone who believes, to the Jew first and also to the Greek.

17 For in it *the* righteousness of God is revealed from faith to faith; as it is written, "BUT THE RIGHTEOUS *man* SHALL LIVE BY FAITH."

II. *The world's need of God (1:18–3:20)*

A. *The Gentiles: guilty before God*

18 For the wrath of God is revealed from heaven against all ungodliness and unrighteousness of men, who suppress the truth in unrighteousness,

19 because that which is known about God is evident within them; for God made it evident to them.

20 For since the creation of the world His invisible attributes, His eternal power and divine nature, have been clearly seen, being understood through what has been made, so that they are without excuse.

21 For even though they knew God, they did not [3]honor Him as God, or give thanks; but they became futile in their speculations, and their foolish heart was darkened.

22 Professing to be wise, they became fools,

23 and exchanged the glory of the incorruptible God for an image in the form of corruptible man and of birds and four-footed animals and [4]crawling creatures.

24 Therefore God gave them over in the lusts of their hearts to impurity, that their bodies might be dishonored among them.

25 For they exchanged the truth of God for a lie, and worshiped and served the creature rather than the Creator, who is blessed forever. Amen.

26 For this reason God gave them over to degrading passions; for their women exchanged the natural function for that which is unnatural,

27 and in the same way also the men abandoned the natural function of the woman and burned in their desire toward one another, men with men committing indecent acts and receiving in their own persons the due penalty of their error.

28 And just as they did not see fit to acknowledge God any longer, God gave them over to a depraved mind, to do those things which are not proper,

29 being filled with all unrighteousness, wickedness, greed, evil; full of envy, murder, strife, deceit, malice; *they are* gossips,

30 slanderers, haters of God, insolent, arrogant, boastful, inventors of evil, disobedient to parents,

31 without understanding, untrustworthy, unloving, unmerciful;

32 and, although they know the ordinance of God, that those who practice such things are worthy of death, they not only do the same, but also give hearty approval to those who practice them.

B. *God's principles of judgment*

2 Therefore you are without excuse, every man *of you* who passes judgment, for in that you judge another, you condemn yourself; for you who judge practice the same things.

2 And we know that the judgment of God rightly falls upon those who practice such things.

3 And do you suppose this, O man, when you pass judgment upon those who practice such things and do the same *yourself*, that you will escape the judgment of God?

4 Or do you think lightly of the riches of His kindness and forbearance and patience, not knowing that the kindness of God leads you to repentance?

---

[3]Lit., *glorify*   [4]Or possibly, *reptiles*

Cross references (left margin):

*1:16
2 Tim 1:8;
1 Cor 1:18;
Acts 3:26;
Rom 2:9
1:17
Rom 3:21;
Gal 3:11;
Heb 10:38

*1:18ff
Eph 5:6;
Col 3:6
1:19
Acts 14:17

1:20
Ps 19:1-6

1:21
Jer 2:5;
Eph 4:17,18

1:22
Jer 10:14;
1:23
Ps 106:20;
Jer 2:11;
Acts 17:29
1:24
Eph 4:18,19;
1 Pet 4:3
1:25
Is 44:20;
Jer 10:14;
Rom 9:5
1:26
Lev 18:22;
Eph 4:19;
1 Thess 4:5
1:27
Lev 18:22;
20:13
1:28
Eph 4:19

1:30
Ps 5:5;
2 Tim 3:2
1:31
2 Tim 3:3
1:32
Rom 6:21;
Acts 8:1;
22:20

2:1
Rom 1:20;
2 Sam 12:5-7;
Matt 7:1,2

2:4
Eph 1:7; 2:7;
Rom 11:22;
3:25;
Ex 34:6;
2 Pet 3:9

1:16 The word *salvation* is derived from the Greek word *sōtēria*, meaning "safety" or "soundness." Comprehended under this term are such elements as "justification," "regeneration," "sanctification," "glorification," "redemption," "propitiation," "grace," and "forgiveness." Scripture states that salvation is: (1) of God (Ps. 37:39); (2) by and through Christ (Acts 4:12; Gal. 1:4; Heb. 2:10; 5:9); and (3) not of the works of men (11:6; Eph. 2:9; 2 Tim. 1:9; Titus 3:5). It has three aspects: past, present, and future.

That is, the believer has already been redeemed from the guilt and penalty of sin; he is now being delivered from its power; and he will at last be delivered from its presence and be perfectly conformed to Christ's image.
1:18ff. Instead of progression or evolution in religion, this account (vv. 18–32) indicates that there is retrogression. Men turn from God to idols and from purity to gross sinfulness, which they love and approve of.

5   But because of your stubbornness and unrepentant heart you are storing up wrath for yourself in the day of wrath and revelation of the righteous judgment of God,

6   who WILL RENDER TO EVERY MAN ACCORDING TO HIS DEEDS:

7   to those who by perseverance in doing good seek for glory and honor and immortality, eternal life;

8   but to those who are selfishly ambitious and do not obey the truth, but obey unrighteousness, wrath and indignation.

9   *There will be* tribulation and distress for every soul of man who does evil, of the Jew first and also of the Greek,

10   but glory and honor and peace to every man who does good, to the Jew first and also to the Greek.

11   For there is no partiality with God.

12   For all who have sinned without the Law will also perish without the Law; and all who have sinned under the Law will be judged by the Law;

13   for not the hearers of the Law are just before God, but the doers of the Law will be justified.

14   For when Gentiles who do not have the Law do instinctively the things of the Law, these, not having the Law, are a law to themselves,

15   in that they show the work of the Law written in their hearts, their conscience bearing witness, and their thoughts alternately accusing or else defending them,

16   on the day when, according to my gospel, God will judge the secrets of men through Christ Jesus.

C. The Jews: guilty before God

17   But if you bear the name "Jew," and rely upon the Law, and boast in God,

18   and know *His* will, and approve the things that are essential, being instructed out of the Law,

19   and are confident that you yourself are a guide to the blind, a light to those who are in darkness,

20   a corrector of the foolish, a teacher of the immature, having in the Law the embodiment of knowledge and of the truth,

21   you, therefore, who teach another, do you not teach yourself? You who preach that one should not steal, do you steal?

22   You who say that one should not commit adultery, do you commit adultery? You who abhor idols, do you rob temples?

23   You who boast in the Law, through your breaking the Law, do you dishonor God?

24   For "THE NAME OF GOD IS BLASPHEMED AMONG THE GENTILES BECAUSE OF YOU," just as it is written.

25   For indeed circumcision is of value, if you practice the Law; but if you are a transgressor of the Law, your circumcision has become uncircumcision.

26   If therefore the uncircumcised man keeps the requirements of the Law, will not his uncircumcision be regarded as circumcision?

Marginal references

2:5 Deut 32:34; Jude 6
2:6 Matt 16:27; 1 Cor 3:8; 2 Cor 5:10
2:8 Gal 5:20; 2 Thess 2:12
2:9 1 Pet 4:17
2:10 1 Pet 1:7; v. 9
2:11 Deut 10:17; Gal 2:6; Eph 6:9
*2:12 Rom 3:19; 1 Cor 9:21
2:13 James 1:22, 23,25
*2:14ff v. 15
*2:15 vv. 14,27
2:16 Eccl 12:14; 1 Cor 4:5; Acts 10:42; 1 Tim 1:11
2:17 v. 23; Mic 3:11; Rom 9:4
2:18 Phil 1:10
2:20 Rom 6:17; 2 Tim 1:13
2:21 Matt 23:3,4
2:22 Acts 19:37
2:23 v. 17
2:24 Is 52:5
2:25 Gal 5:3
2:26 1 Cor 7:19; Eph 2:11; Rom 8:4

2:12 The condition of those who die without hearing of Christ presents a very serious problem. However, although nothing specific is said about those who die without hearing the gospel, it appears that Scripture assigns those who die without receiving Christ to everlasting punishment. Men are not judged for refusing to accept Christ if they have never heard of Him. They are then judged in the light of their own consciences, but as Romans here teaches us, no man really lives up to the light of his conscience. There is no Scripture that supports the idea of a second chance for the unevangelized heathen. The belief that men without Christ are lost has always been a motive for missionary outreach. 2:14–16 The law of God may be defined as the revealed will of God. It is found imperfectly in human conscience and perfectly in the Scriptures. The *moral law* of God is summarized in the Ten Commandments (Ex. 20:2–27; Deut. 5:6–21). The judicial and ceremonial laws of the Old Testament were transitory and adapted to the needs of a particular people for a particular time. The moral law is of permanent significance for all peoples and has the greatest relevance for Christians as a guide to pleasing their heavenly Father. Even faith does not revoke this law.

2:15 Beginning with Adam and Eve, God gave man a conscience. In the Garden of Eden that conscience was uncorrupted. Subsequent to the fall, it was corrupted and depraved, but it was not totally erased. Conscience serves man as a witness to truth (2:15; Prov. 20:27), but moral choice determines whether a man will obey what his conscience dictates (Josh. 24:15). The conscience accuses men of sin (Gen. 42:21; 2 Sam. 24:10; Matt. 27:3,4), and its indictment will be confirmed in the last judgment when the books are opened. Every mouth will be stopped, and His judgment will be seen to be according to righteousness (Rev. 20:12–15). The spiritual Christian (1 Cor. 3:1) has a conscience cleansed of guilt by faith in the atoning merits of Jesus Christ; he maintains a clear conscience by a sincere purpose of self-surrender to God (6:13; 12:1,2) and immediate repentance and confession of any known sin (1 Cor. 11:31). In this sense it is possible to have a conscience blameless and void of offense (Acts 24:16; Rom. 9:1; 14:22). But conscience can be perfected and delivered from its bondage only through a genuine faith and trust in the atoning work of Christ (Heb. 9:14; 10:2ff.).

2:27
Matt 12:41
27   And will not he who is physically uncircumcised, if he keeps the Law, will he not judge you who though having the letter *of the Law* and circumcision are a transgressor of the Law?

2:28
Matt 3:9;
John 8:39;
Rom 9:6;
Gal 6:15
2:29
Col 2:11;
2 Cor 10:18;
1 Pet 3:4
28   For he is not a Jew who is one outwardly; neither is circumcision that which is outward in the flesh.

29   But he is a Jew who is one inwardly; and circumcision is that which is of the heart, by the Spirit, not by the letter; and his praise is not from men, but from God.

3:2
Deut 4:8;
Ps 147:19
3 Then what advantage has the Jew? Or what is the benefit of circumcision?
2   Great in every respect. First of all, that they were entrusted with the oracles of God.

3:3
Heb 4:2;
2 Tim 2:13
3   What then? If some did not believe, their unbelief will not nullify the faithfulness of God, will it?

3:4
John 3:33;
Ps 116:11;
51:4
4   May it never be! Rather, let God be found true, though every man *be found* a liar, as it is written,

"THAT THOU MIGHTEST BE JUSTIFIED IN THY WORDS,
AND MIGHTEST PREVAIL WHEN THOU ART JUDGED."

3:5
Rom 6:19;
Gal 3:15
5   But if our unrighteousness demonstrates the righteousness of God, what shall we say? The God who inflicts wrath is not unrighteous, is He? (I am speaking in human terms.)

3:6
Gen 18:25
3:7
v. 4
6   May it never be! For otherwise how will God judge the world?

7   But if through my lie the truth of God abounded to His glory, why am I also still being judged as a sinner?

3:8
Rom 6:1
8   And why not *say* (as we are slanderously reported and as some affirm that we say), "Let us do evil that good may come"? Their condemnation is just.

D. The world: guilty before God

3:9
Gal 3:22
9   What then? Are we better than they? Not at all; for we have already charged that both Jews and Greeks are all under sin;

3:10
Ps 14:1-3
10   as it is written,
"THERE IS NONE RIGHTEOUS, NOT EVEN ONE;
11   THERE IS NONE WHO UNDERSTANDS,
THERE IS NONE WHO SEEKS FOR GOD;
12   ALL HAVE TURNED ASIDE, TOGETHER THEY HAVE BECOME USELESS;
THERE IS NONE WHO DOES GOOD,
THERE IS NOT EVEN ONE."

3:13
Ps 5:9
13   "THEIR THROAT IS AN OPEN GRAVE,
WITH THEIR TONGUES THEY KEEP DECEIVING,"
"THE POISON OF ASPS IS UNDER THEIR LIPS";

3:14
Ps 10:7;
140:3
3:15
Is 59:7,8
14   "WHOSE MOUTH IS FULL OF CURSING AND BITTERNESS";
15   "THEIR FEET ARE SWIFT TO SHED BLOOD,
16   DESTRUCTION AND MISERY ARE IN THEIR PATHS,
17   AND THE PATH OF PEACE HAVE THEY NOT KNOWN."

3:18
Ps 36:1
3:19
John 10:34;
Rom 2:12
18   "THERE IS NO FEAR OF GOD BEFORE THEIR EYES."

19   Now we know that whatever the Law says, it speaks to those who are under the Law, that every mouth may be closed, and all the world may become accountable to God;

*3:20
Ps 143:2;
Acts 13:39;
Gal 2:16;
Rom 7:7
20   because by the works of the Law no flesh will be justified in His sight; for through the Law *comes* the knowledge of sin.

III. Justification by faith alone (3:21–8:39)

A. The means of salvation: faith

*3:21
Rom 1:17;
9:30; 1:2;
Acts 10:43
21   But now apart from the Law *the* righteousness of God has been manifested, being witnessed by the Law and the Prophets,

---

3:20 The *moral law* serves four definite purposes: (1) it exhibits the moral perfection of God; (2) it reveals the inexcusable guilt of man and convicts him as a hopeless sinner; (3) it provides a standard by which human society is, at least imperfectly, governed; and (4) it serves as a guide to believers as to how they may best please their redeeming God and do His will, which is to them the most important motive in life.

3:21 The word for *righteousness* (Greek *dikaiosynē*) is used in various ways in Scripture. At times it appears as an attribute of God, implying that He is faithful to what He is and to what He has promised. Or else it refers to His holy standard of moral purity in contrast to the sinfulness of man. God's reaction against sin is expressed in wrath or a holy displeasure toward all iniquity (1:18; Eph. 5:6). When used of man, *righteousness* refers to a perfect conformity to

22   even *the* righteousness of God through faith in Jesus Christ for all those who believe; for there is no distinction;

23   for all have sinned and fall short of the glory of God,

24   being justified as a gift by His grace through the redemption which is in Christ Jesus;

25   whom God displayed publicly as a propitiation in His blood through faith. *This was* to demonstrate His righteousness, because in the forbearance of God He passed over the sins previously committed;

26   for the demonstration, *I say,* of His righteousness at the present time, that He might be just and the justifier of the one who has faith in Jesus.

27   Where then is boasting? It is excluded. By what kind of law? Of works? No, but by a law of faith.

28   For we maintain that a man is justified by faith apart from works of the Law.

29   Or is God *the God* of Jews only? Is He not *the God* of Gentiles also? Yes, of Gentiles also,

30   since indeed God who will justify the circumcised by faith and the uncircumcised through faith is one.

31   Do we then nullify the Law through faith? May it never be! On the contrary, we establish the Law.

B. *The Old Testament proof: Abraham saved by faith*

4   What then shall we say that Abraham, our forefather according to the flesh, has found?

2   For if Abraham was justified by works, he has something to boast about; but not before God.

3   For what does the Scripture say? "AND ABRAHAM BELIEVED GOD, AND IT WAS RECKONED TO HIM AS RIGHTEOUSNESS."

4   Now to the one who works, his wage is not reckoned as a favor, but as what is due.

5   But to the one who does not work, but believes in Him who justifies the ungodly, his faith is reckoned as righteousness,

6   just as David also speaks of the blessing upon the man to whom God reckons righteousness apart from works:

7   "BLESSED ARE THOSE WHOSE LAWLESS DEEDS HAVE BEEN FORGIVEN,
       AND WHOSE SINS HAVE BEEN COVERED.

8   "BLESSED IS THE MAN WHOSE SIN THE LORD WILL NOT TAKE INTO
       ACCOUNT."

9   Is this blessing then upon the circumcised, or upon the uncircumcised also? For we say, "FAITH WAS RECKONED TO ABRAHAM AS RIGHTEOUSNESS."

10   How then was it reckoned? While he was circumcised, or uncircumcised? Not while circumcised, but while uncircumcised;

11   and he received the sign of circumcision, a seal of the righteousness of the

3:22
Rom 10:12;
Gal 3:28;
Col 3:11
*3:23
Gal 3:22
3:24
Rom 4:16;
Eph 1:7; 2:8;
Col 1:14;
Heb 9:12,15
*3:25
1 John 2:2;
Heb 9:14,28;
1 Pet 1:19
3:27
Rom 2:17,23;
4:2;
1 Cor 1:29-31;
Eph 2:9
3:28
Acts 13:39;
Eph 2:9
3:29
Rom 9:24;
Acts 10:34,35
3:30
Gal 3:8

4:2
1 Cor 1:31
4:3
Gen 15:6;
Gal 3:6;
James 2:23
4:4
Rom 11:6

4:7
Ps 32:1,2
4:8
2 Cor 5:19
4:9
Rom 3:30;
v. 3
4:11
Gen 17:10;
Luke 19:9

God's will and moral standards. The Scripture teaches that no man has ever been truly righteous in this sense since all have sinned against God (3:10,23). Yet the perfect righteousness of Jesus Christ is reckoned by grace to the justified believer, and the indwelling Holy Spirit imparts a power for godly living as an adopted child in God's holy family (3:21, 22; Phil. 3:9). Thus the believer's imputed righteousness springs from God's righteousness, made possible on God's terms by faith in Christ. *Faith* is the *means* by which God's righteousness becomes man's righteousness; *justification* is the *act* of God that makes man righteous when he evidences faith in Christ; *righteousness* is the *result* of justification and is apprehended through faith.

3:23 Sin is basically a violation of the moral law of God that is revealed in the Word of God and through conscience. The failure to conform to the law of God is attended by the gravest penalties (Ezek. 18:4,20). The evil motive is essential, however, to constitute an action as sinful. For example, culpability is not implied when one is accidentally responsible for the death of another. But if one deliberately intends to commit murder, that establishes the act as a grievous sin. Men cannot always read the hearts of others and so determine their true motives, but God always can (1 Chr. 28:9; Heb. 4:13). Sin already is present with a mere purpose or desire of evil, even before any overt offense is committed (Matt. 5:28).

3:25 Theologians have argued whether there is a difference between *expiation* and *propitiation*. In this passage Paul uses the Greek word *hilastērion*. It is also used in Heb. 9:5, where it is translated *mercy seat.* Some interpreters see a distinction between expiation and propitiation in that the former refers to ritual satisfaction for sins committed, and the latter has to do with the person offended. Charles Hodge speaks of the two words as correlative terms, "The sinner, or his guilt, is expiated; God, or justice, is propitiated," *Systematic Theology* (Wm. B. Eerdmans), vol. 2, p. 478. John Knox says, "A price must be paid; a penalty must be suffered; a sacrifice must be offered . . . Paul . . . undoubtedly finds in the life and death of Christ the indispensable atoning sacrifice," *The Interpreter's Bible* (Abingdon Press), vol. 9, pp. 433–34. In any event, man was reconciled to God by the death of Christ.

4:6 God declares sinners righteous, not because they are intrinsically righteous or have anything righteous in themselves, but simply because of their faith, through which the righteousness of Jesus Christ is reckoned to their account. The guilt and punishment of the believer were borne by Christ (Isa. 53:5,11; 2 Cor. 5:21; Gal. 3:13), and the righteousness of Christ, is reckoned to the believer's credit (1 Cor. 1:30; 2 Cor. 5:21; Phil. 3:9). The believer's guilt is laid on Christ, and Christ's merit is laid on the believer.

faith which he had while uncircumcised, that he might be the father of all who believe without being circumcised, that righteousness might be reckoned to them,

12   and the father of circumcision to those who not only are of the circumcision, but who also follow in the steps of the faith of our father Abraham which he had while uncircumcised.

4:13
Gen 17:4-6;
Gal 3:29

13   For the promise to Abraham or to his descendants that he would be heir of the world was not through the Law, but through the righteousness of faith.

4:14
Gal 3:18

14   For if those who are of the Law are heirs, faith is made void and the promise is nullified;

4:15
Rom 3:20;
7:8,10,11;
Gal 3:10

15   for the Law brings about wrath, but where there is no law, neither is there violation.

4:16
Rom 3:24;
9:8; 15:8

16   For this reason *it is* by faith, that *it might be* in accordance with grace, in order that the promise may be certain to all the descendants, not only to those who are of the Law, but also to those who are of the faith of Abraham, who is the father of us all,

4:17
Gen 17:5;
1 Cor 1:28

17   (as it is written, "A FATHER OF MANY NATIONS HAVE I MADE YOU") in the sight of Him whom he believed, *even* God, who gives life to the dead and calls into being that which does not exist.

4:18
Gen 15:5

18   In hope against hope he believed, in order that he might become a father of many nations, according to that which had been spoken, "SO SHALL YOUR DESCENDANTS BE."

4:19
Gen 17:17;
Heb 11:11

19   And without becoming weak in faith he contemplated his own body, now as good as dead since he was about a hundred years old, and the deadness of Sarah's womb;

20   yet, with respect to the promise of God, he did not waver in unbelief, but grew strong in faith, giving glory to God,

4:21
Gen 18:14;
Heb 11:19

21   and being fully assured that what He had promised, He was able also to perform.

22   Therefore also IT WAS RECKONED TO HIM AS RIGHTEOUSNESS.

4:23
Rom 15:4;
1 Cor 9:10;
10:11

23   Now not for his sake only was it written, that it was reckoned to him,

4:24
Rom 10:9;
Acts 2:24

24   but for our sake also, to whom it will be reckoned, as those who believe in Him who raised Jesus our Lord from the dead,

*4:25
Is 53:5,6;
2 Cor 5:21;
1 Cor 15:17

25   *He* who was delivered up because of our transgressions, and was raised because of our justification.

C. *The results of justification by faith*

5:1
Rom 3:28

5   Therefore having been justified by faith, we have peace with God through our Lord Jesus Christ,

5:2
Eph 2:18;
1 Cor 15:1;
Heb 3:6

2   through whom also we have obtained our introduction by faith into this grace in which we stand; and we exult in hope of the glory of God.

5:3
2 Cor 12:10;
James 1:2,3

3   And not only this, but we also exult in our tribulations, knowing that tribulation brings about perseverance;

5:5
Phil 1:20;
Eph 1:13

4   and perseverance, proven character; and proven character, hope;

5   and hope does not disappoint, because the love of God has been poured out within our hearts through the Holy Spirit who was given to us.

5:6
Gal 4:4;
Rom 4:25

6   For while we were still helpless, at the right time Christ died for the ungodly.

5:8
John 15:13;
1 Pet 3:18;
1 John 3:16

7   For one will hardly die for a righteous man; though perhaps for the good man someone would dare even to die.

8   But God demonstrates His own love toward us, in that while we were yet sinners, Christ died for us.

5:9
Rom 3:5,25;
Heb 9:14;
1 Thess 1:10

9   Much more then, having now been justified by His blood, we shall be saved from the wrath *of God* through Him.

5:10
Rom 11:28;
Col 1:21,22;
2 Cor 5:18;
Rom 8:34

10   For if while we were enemies, we were reconciled to God through the death of His Son, much more, having been reconciled, we shall be saved by His life.

4:25 *Dikaiosis*, the Greek word for *justification*, occurs only twice in the New Testament, although the verb *dikaioō*, "justify," is frequently used. It refers to the believer's relationship to God by reason of the righteousness of Christ that is imputed to him (cf. note to 4:6). Through justification the penalty of sin is cancelled and the rewards promised to the believer. No man can be justified by good works; no one is good enough to get to heaven (11:6; Gal. 2:16,21; 3:10,21; 5:3,4; Eph. 2:8,9; Phil. 3:9). Justification is more than a pardon. The demands of the law are not simply waived; they are fully satisfied. Thus the ground of justification is the atoning work of Christ on Calvary (3:24; 5:9,19; 8:1; 10:4; 1 Cor. 1:30; 2 Cor. 5:21; Phil. 3:9). Justification is made available to man by faith alone (Rom. 5:1; Eph. 2:8).

11   And not only this, but we also exult in God through our Lord Jesus Christ, through whom we have now received the reconciliation.

D. Christ the ground of our salvation

12   Therefore, just as through one man sin entered into the world, and death through sin, and so death spread to all men, because all sinned—

13   for until the Law sin was in the world; but sin is not imputed when there is no law.

14   Nevertheless death reigned from Adam until Moses, even over those who had not sinned in the likeness of the offense of Adam, who is a ⁵type of Him who was to come.

15   But the free gift is not like the transgression. For if by the transgression of the one the many died, much more did the grace of God and the gift by the grace of the one Man, Jesus Christ, abound to the many.

16   And the gift is not like *that which came* through the one who sinned; for on the one hand the judgment *arose* from one *transgression* resulting in condemnation, but on the other hand the free gift *arose* from many transgressions resulting in justification.

17   For if by the transgression of the one, death reigned through the one, much more those who receive the abundance of grace and of the gift of righteousness will reign in life through the One, Jesus Christ.

18   So then as through one transgression there resulted condemnation to all men, even so through one act of righteousness there resulted justification of life to all men.

19   For as through the one man's disobedience the many were made sinners, even so through the obedience of the One the many will be made righteous.

20   And the Law came in that the transgression might increase; but where sin increased, grace abounded all the more,

21   that, as sin reigned in death, even so grace might reign through righteousness to eternal life through Jesus Christ our Lord.

E. The believer's life in Christ

1. United in His death

6 What shall we say then? Are we to continue in sin that grace might increase?
2   May it never be! How shall we who died to sin still live in it?
3   Or do you not know that all of us who have been baptized into Christ Jesus have been baptized into His death?
4   Therefore we have been buried with Him through baptism into death, in order that as Christ was raised from the dead through the glory of the Father, so we too might walk in newness of life.
5   For if we have become united with *Him* in the likeness of His death, certainly we shall be also *in the likeness* of His resurrection,
6   knowing this, that our old self was crucified with *Him,* that our body of sin might be done away with, that we should no longer be slaves to sin;
7   for he who has died is freed from sin.
8   Now if we have died with Christ, we believe that we shall also live with Him,
9   knowing that Christ, having been raised from the dead, is never to die again; death no longer is master over Him.

⁵Or, *foreshadowing*

Cross-references (right column):

*5:12
Gen 2:17;
3:6,19;
1 Cor 15:21;
Rom 6:23
5:13
Rom 4:15
5:14
1 Cor 15:22,
45
5:15
vv. 12,18,19;
Is 53:11;
Acts 15:11
5:17
2 Tim 2:12;
Rev 22:5
5:18
v. 12;
Rom 4:25
5:19
v. 12;
Rom 11:32;
Phil 2:8
5:20
Rom 7:7,8;
Gal 3:19;
1 Tim 1:14
5:21
vv. 12,14;
John 1:17;
Rom 6:23

*6:1
Rom 3:5,8;
v. 15
6:2
Rom 7:4,6;
Gal 2:19;
Col 3:3;
1 Pet 2:24
6:3
Acts 2:38;
8:16; 19:5
6:4
Col 2:12;
Gal 6:15;
Eph 4:22-24;
Col 3:10
6:6
Eph 4:22;
Col 3:9;
Gal 2:20;
Rom 7:24
6:9
Rev 1:18

5:12 In this paragraph (5:12–21) Paul draws an analogy between Adam's sin and Christ's righteousness. Through Adam's disobedience, sin and death entered the world, and death spread to all men, because all sinned. Man is helpless to save himself from his lost condition, and death, as punishment for sin, is the lot of all. But in the righteousness (v. 18) or obedience (v. 19) of Jesus Christ, the situation is reversed, and instead of condemnation, man may have justification; instead of death, life (vv. 16–18). The sinner may now be declared righteous (v. 19), i.e., he may now be justified by God's free gift of righteousness. The analogy, as Paul makes clear (vv. 15,16,20), is not precise: God's grace is much more than man's trespass and sin.

Verse 18 might appear to mean that all men will be saved. But read in close connection with 19, it is clear that Paul is stating that Christ's redemptive work is available and efficacious for all men: there is not one who cannot be justified by God's free grace in Jesus.

6:1 Some have supposed that the dispensation of the gospel releases man from any obligation to keep the law of God. This error is known as *antinomianism* (opposition to moral law), and in its extreme form has led to the notion that the more man sins the more the grace of God abounds. Here, and in 3:8; 6:15–23, Paul conclusively refutes this view and shows that salvation means deliverance from the power of sin and death, not a continued thralldom to it.

6:10
Heb 7:27

6:11
v. 2; Gal 2:19

6:12
v. 14

6:13
Rom 7:5;
Col 3:5;
Rom 12:1

*6:14
Rom 8:2;
Gal 5:18

6:16
Rom 11:2;
Matt 6:24;
John 8:34;
2 Pet 2:19
6:17
Rom 1:8;
2 Tim 1:13
6:18
John 8:32;
Rom 8:2
6:19
Rom 3:5;
6:13; 12:1

6:20
Matt 6:24;
John 8:34
*6:21
Rom 7:5; 8:6,
13,21
6:22
John 8:32;
1 Cor 7:22;
1 Pet 2:16
6:23
Rom 5:12;
5:21; Gal 6:7,
8

7:2
1 Cor 7:39

7:3
Matt 5:32

7:4
Rom 6:2,11;
Gal 2:19;
Col 1:22

7:5
Rom 6:13,21;
Gal 5:19;
James 1:15
7:6
Rom 2:29;
2 Cor 3:6

*7:7
Ex 20:17;
Deut 5:21;
Rom 3:20;
5:20

10 For the death that He died, He died to sin, once for all; but the life that He lives, He lives to God.

11 Even so consider yourselves to be dead to sin, but alive to God in Christ Jesus.

12 Therefore do not let sin reign in your mortal body that you should obey its lusts,

13 and do not go on presenting the members of your body to sin *as* instruments of unrighteousness; but present yourselves to God as those alive from the dead, and your members *as* instruments of righteousness to God.

14 For sin shall not be master over you, for you are not under law, but under grace.

2. Slaves to righteousness

15 What then? Shall we sin because we are not under law but under grace? May it never be!

16 Do you not know that when you present yourselves to someone *as* slaves for obedience, you are slaves of the one whom you obey, either of sin resulting in death, or of obedience resulting in righteousness?

17 But thanks be to God that though you were slaves of sin, you became obedient from the heart to that form of teaching to which you were committed,

18 and having been freed from sin, you became slaves of righteousness.

19 I am speaking in human terms because of the weakness of your flesh. For just as you presented your members *as* slaves to impurity and to lawlessness, resulting in *further* lawlessness, so now present your members *as* slaves to righteousness, resulting in sanctification.

20 For when you were slaves of sin, you were free in regard to righteousness.

21 Therefore what benefit were you then deriving from the things of which you are now ashamed? For the outcome of those things is death.

22 But now having been freed from sin and enslaved to God, you derive your benefit, resulting in sanctification, and the outcome, eternal life.

23 For the wages of sin is death, but the free gift of God is eternal life in Christ Jesus our Lord.

3. Married to Christ

7 Or do you not know, brethren (for I am speaking to those who know the law), that the law has jurisdiction over a person as long as he lives?

2 For the married woman is bound by law to her husband while he is living; but if her husband dies, she is released from the law concerning the husband.

3 So then if, while her husband is living, she is joined to another man, she shall be called an adulteress; but if her husband dies, she is free from the law, so that she is not an adulteress, though she is joined to another man.

4 Therefore, my brethren, you also were made to die to the Law through the body of Christ, that you might be joined to another, to Him who was raised from the dead, that we might bear fruit for God.

5 For while we were in the flesh, the sinful passions, which were *aroused* by the Law, were at work in the members of our body to bear fruit for death.

6 But now we have been released from the Law, having died to that by which we were bound, so that we serve in newness of the ⁶Spirit and not in oldness of the letter.

4. The Christian struggle

7 What shall we say then? Is the Law sin? May it never be! On the contrary,

⁶Or, *spirit*

6:14 Paul's statements that *sin shall not be master over you* (v. 14), *having been freed from sin* (v. 18), and *having been freed from sin* (v. 22), show how dynamic a view he had of the salvation in Christ. Through God's grace, Christ truly delivers man from the slavery to sin, and makes him free under righteousness; instead of being an impotent and defeated subject under the dominion of sin, man is now set free and is able to obey God, to yield his life to God's demands, in a life of complete dedication (*sanctification*, vv. 19,22) to Him and look forward to eternal life. It is this boundless assurance of the reality of God's grace operating

in a man's life that enables Paul to describe in such glowing terms the new life in Christ.
6:21 *benefit* (Greek *karpos*), i.e., fruit.
7:7 This whole passage (7:7–25) dealing with Paul's experience with the law is one that is the subject of widely different interpretations. The principal question is whether Paul is speaking of his life before or after conversion. Perhaps the answer is not a sharp either/or but a both/and. Paul shows what God's law, itself holy, just, and good (v. 12), did for him. Before Paul was conscious of the law's demands he was unaware of his own sin and so, relatively speaking,

I would not have come to know sin except through the Law; for I would not have known about coveting if the Law had not said, "YOU SHALL NOT COVET."

8 But sin, taking opportunity through the commandment, produced in me coveting of every kind; for apart from the Law sin *is* dead.

9 And I was once alive apart from the Law; but when the commandment came, sin became alive, and I died;

10 and this commandment, which was to result in life, proved to result in death for me;

11 for sin, taking opportunity through the commandment, deceived me, and through it killed me.

12 So then, the Law is holy, and the commandment is holy and righteous and good.

13 Therefore did that which is good become *a cause of* death for me? May it never be! Rather it was sin, in order that it might be shown to be sin by effecting my death through that which is good, that through the commandment sin might become utterly sinful.

14 For we know that the Law is spiritual; but I am of flesh, sold into bondage to sin.

15 For that which I am doing, I do not understand; for I am not practicing what I *would* like to *do,* but I am doing the very thing I hate.

16 But if I do the very thing I do not wish *to do,* I agree with the Law, *confessing* that it is good.

17 So now, no longer am I the one doing it, but sin which indwells me.

18 For I know that nothing good dwells in me, that is, in my flesh; for the wishing is present in me, but the doing of the good *is* not.

19 For the good that I wish, I do not do; but I practice the very evil that I do not wish.

20 But if I am doing the very thing I do not wish, I am no longer the one doing it, but sin which dwells in me.

21 I find then the principle that evil is present in me, the one who wishes to do good.

22 For I joyfully concur with the law of God in the inner man,

23 but I see a different law in the members of my body, waging war against the law of my mind, and making me a prisoner of the law of sin which is in my members.

24 Wretched man that I am! Who will set me free from the body of this death?

25 Thanks be to God through Jesus Christ our Lord! So then, on the one hand I myself with my mind am serving the law of God, but on the other, with my flesh the law of sin.

5. *Life in the Spirit*

a. *Holiness a possibility*

8 There is therefore now no condemnation for those who are in Christ Jesus.
2 For the law of the Spirit of life in Christ Jesus has set [7]you free from the law of sin and of death.

3 For what the Law could not do, weak as it was through the flesh, God *did:* sending His own Son in the likeness of sinful flesh and *as an offering* for sin, He condemned sin in the flesh,

4 in order that the requirement of the Law might be fulfilled in us, who do not walk according to the flesh, but according to the Spirit.

5 For those who are according to the flesh set their minds on the things of the flesh, but those who are according to the Spirit, the things of the Spirit.

[7]Some ancient mss. read *me*

Marginal references:

7:8 v. 11; 1 Cor 15:56
7:10 Lev 18:5; Rom 10:5; Gal 3:12
7:12 1 Tim 1:8
7:15 Gal 5:17
7:16 v. 12
7:17 v. 20
7:18 v. 25
7:19 v. 15
7:20 v. 17
7:21 vv. 23,25
7:22 Ps 1:2; 2 Cor 4:16; Eph 3:16
7:23 Gal 5:17
7:24 Rom 6:6; 8:2
7:25 1 Cor 15:57
8:1 Rom 5:16
8:2 1 Cor 15:45; Rom 6:14,18; John 8:32,36
8:3 Acts 13:39; Heb 7:18; Phil 2:7; Heb 2:14
8:4 Gal 5:16,25
8:5 Gal 5:19-25

he was then *alive* (vv. 7,9); but with the knowledge of the law came the awareness of his own sin and guilt. Thus sin sprang to life and "killed" Paul. Sin is powerless apart from the law; the law itself is good, but sin works through it to convict a man of his own sinfulness (v. 13).

Paul's description of the civil war raging within him (vv. 15–24) is so intimate and vivid as to make it quite probable that he was talking of the paradox of the Christian life, stressing here the element of struggle, the recognition of one's own helplessness in attempting to live up to God's requirements. It is precisely the man who has experienced God's free grace and forgiveness who is the most acutely aware of his own sin and plight. The cry of despair, *Who will set me free from the body of this death?* (v. 24) is answered at once in the grateful assertion, *Thanks be to God through Jesus Christ our Lord!* (v. 25). God's grace is immeasurably greater than man's sin.

8:6
Rom 6:21;
Gal 6:8

6 For the mind set on the flesh is death, but the mind set on the Spirit is life and peace,

8:7
James 4:4

7 because the mind set on the flesh is hostile toward God; for it does not subject itself to the law of God, for it is not even able *to do so*;

8:8
Rom 7:5

8 and those who are in the flesh cannot please God.

8:9
1 Cor 3:16;
Gal 4:6;
Phil 1:19;
1 John 4:13

9 However, you are not in the flesh but in the Spirit, if indeed the Spirit of God dwells in you. But if anyone does not have the Spirit of Christ, he does not belong to Him.

8:10
Gal 2:20;
Eph 3:17

10 And if Christ is in you, though the body is dead because of sin, yet the spirit is alive because of righteousness.

8:11
Acts 2:24;
John 5:21;
1 Cor 6:14

11 But if the Spirit of Him who raised Jesus from the dead dwells in you, He who raised Christ Jesus from the dead will also give life to your mortal bodies [8]through His Spirit who indwells you.

b. Holiness a duty

12 So then, brethren, we are under obligation, not to the flesh, to live according to the flesh—

8:13
Gal 6:8;
Col 3:5

13 for if you are living according to the flesh, you must die; but if by the Spirit you are putting to death the deeds of the body, you will live.

8:14
Gal 5:18

14 For all who are being led by the Spirit of God, these are sons of God.

8:15
2 Tim 1:7;
Heb 2:15;
Gal 4:5,6

15 For you have not received a spirit of slavery leading to fear again, but you have received a spirit of adoption as sons by which we cry out, "Abba! Father!"

*8:16
2 Cor 1:22;
Eph 1:13

16 The Spirit Himself bears witness with our spirit that we are children of God,

8:17
Gal 4:7;
2 Tim 2:12;
1 Pet 4:13

17 and if children, heirs also, heirs of God and fellow heirs with Christ, if indeed we suffer with *Him* in order that we may also be glorified with *Him*.

6. The future glory

a. A sure hope

8:18
2 Cor 4:17;
Col 3:4;
1 Pet 5:1

18 For I consider that the sufferings of this present time are not worthy to be compared with the glory that is to be revealed to us.

8:19
Col 3:4;
1 Pet 1:7,13;
1 John 3:2

19 For the anxious longing of the creation waits eagerly for the revealing of the sons of God.

8:20
Gen 3:17-19;
Eccl 1:2

20 For the creation was subjected to futility, not of its own will, but because of Him who subjected it, [9]in hope

8:21
Acts 3:21;
Rom 6:21;
2 Pet 3:13;
Rev 21:1

21 that the creation itself also will be set free from its slavery to corruption into the freedom of the glory of the children of God.

22 For we know that the whole creation groans and suffers the pains of childbirth together until now.

8:23
2 Cor 1:22;
5:2,4; Gal 5:5

23 And not only this, but also we ourselves, having the first fruits of the Spirit, even we ourselves groan within ourselves, waiting eagerly for *our* adoption as sons, the redemption of our body.

24 For in hope we have been saved, but hope that is seen is not hope; for [10] why does one also hope for what he sees?

25 But if we hope for what we do not see, with perseverance we wait eagerly for it.

b. A sure help

8:26
Matt 20:22;
Eph 6:18

26 And in the same way the Spirit also helps our weakness; for we do not know how to pray as we should, but the Spirit Himself intercedes for *us* with groanings too deep for words;

8:27
Ps 139:1,2;
Luke 16:15;
Rev 2:23

27 and He who searches the hearts knows what the mind of the Spirit is, because He intercedes for the saints according to *the will* of God.

*8:28
v. 32

28 And we know that [11]God causes all things to work together for good to those who love God, to those who are called according to *His* purpose.

*8:29
Rom 11:2;
1 Pet 1:2,20;
Eph 1:5,11;
Phil 3:21;
Heb 1:6

29 For whom He foreknew, He also predestined *to become* conformed to the image of His Son, that He might be the first-born among many brethren;

[8]Some ancient mss. read *because of* [9]Some ancient mss. read *in hope; because the creation* [10]Some ancient mss. read *who hopes for what he sees?* [11]Some ancient mss. read *all things work together for good*

8:16 The Scripture defines the children of God as those who have received Christ as their Savior and are regenerated: *He gave the right to become children of God* (John 1:12). There is no Biblical basis for the common supposition that all men are by nature the children of God. By means of the new birth sinners not only become saints, they are also adopted into the family of God as His sons and daughters (John 1:13; 1 John 3:2) **8:28** *We know* is the Christian's certainty. **8:29** Predestination or foreordination may be defined as

30   and whom He predestined, these He also called; and whom He called, these He also justified; and whom He justified, these He also glorified.

c. *A certain salvation*

31   What then shall we say to these things? If God *is* for us, who *is* against us?

32   He who did not spare His own Son, but delivered Him up for us all, how will He not also with Him freely give us all things?

33   Who will bring a charge against God's elect? God is the one who justifies;

34   who is the one who condemns? Christ Jesus is He who died, yes, rather who was [12]raised, who is at the right hand of God, who also intercedes for us.

35   Who shall separate us from the love of [13]Christ? Shall tribulation, or distress, or persecution, or famine, or nakedness, or peril, or sword?

36   Just as it is written,

"FOR THY SAKE WE ARE BEING PUT TO DEATH ALL DAY LONG;
WE WERE CONSIDERED AS SHEEP TO BE SLAUGHTERED."

37   But in all these things we overwhelmingly conquer through Him who loved us.

38   For I am convinced that neither death, nor life, nor angels, nor principalities, nor things present, nor things to come, nor powers,

39   nor height, nor depth, nor any other created thing, shall be able to separate us from the love of God, which is in Christ Jesus our Lord.

IV. *Jew and Gentile in the plan of God (9:1–11:36)*

A. *Paul's sorrow for Israel*

9 I am telling the truth in Christ, I am not lying, my conscience bearing me witness in the Holy Spirit,

2   that I have great sorrow and unceasing grief in my heart.

3   For I could wish that I myself were accursed, *separated* from Christ for the sake of my brethren, my kinsmen according to the flesh,

4   who are Israelites, to whom belongs the adoption as sons and the glory and the covenants and the giving of the Law and the *temple* service and the promises,

5   whose are the fathers, and from whom is the Christ according to the flesh, who is over all, God blessed forever. Amen.

B. *The unbelief of the Jew not God's fault*

6   But *it is* not as though the word of God has failed. For they are not all Israel who are *descended* from Israel;

7   neither are they all children because they are Abraham's descendants, but: "THROUGH ISAAC YOUR DESCENDANTS WILL BE NAMED."

8   That is, it is not the children of the flesh who are children of God, but the children of the promise are regarded as descendants.

9   For this is a word of promise: "AT THIS TIME I WILL COME, AND SARAH SHALL HAVE A SON."

10   And not only this, but there was Rebekah also, when she had conceived *twins* by one man, our father Isaac;

11   for though *the twins* were not yet born, and had not done anything good or bad, in order that God's purpose according to *His* choice might stand, not because of works, but because of Him who calls,

12   it was said to her, "THE OLDER WILL SERVE THE YOUNGER."

---

[12]Some ancient mss. read *raised from the dead*   [13]Some ancient mss. read *God*

Cross references (right column):

8:30 Eph 1:5,11; Rom 9:24; 1 Cor 6:11
8:31 Rom 4:1; Ps 118:6
8:32 John 3:16; Rom 5:8;
4:25
8:33 Luke 18:7; Is 50:8,9
8:34 Col 3:1; Heb 1:3; 7:25; 9:24; 1 John 2:1
8:36 Ps 44:22; 2 Cor 4:11
8:37 1 Cor 15:57; Rev 1:5
8:38 Eph 1:21; 1 Pet 3:22
9:1 2 Cor 1:23; 11:10; 1 Tim 2:7
9:3 Ex 32:32
9:4 Acts 3:25; Ps 147:19; Heb 9:1
9:5 Col 1:16-19; John 1:1; Rom 1:25
*9:6 Num 23:19; Rom 2:28,29; Gal 6:16
9:7 Gal 4:23; Heb 11:18
9:8 Rom 8:14; Gal 3:29; 4:28
9:9 Gen 18:10
9:10 Gen 25:21
9:11 Rom 4:17; 8:28
9:12 Gen 25:23

---

that act of God by which the salvation of man is effected in accordance with the will of God. Some explain predestination as conditioned on a foreknowledge by which God simply foresees what men are going to do, and then ordains that it shall come to pass as He foresaw it. This involves an interpretation of God's foreknowledge that is hard to reconcile with His absolute sovereignty. Perhaps it is better to conclude that here we are confronted with a divine mystery in which God works out His sovereign will in such a way as to preserve inviolate that prerogative of free will that is implicit in the divine image (Gen. 1:27) in which man was created. Thus man may act freely, i.e., he can accept or reject God's free offer of the gift of eternal life through

Christ, though only the Holy Spirit can move him to accept it. At the same time his response to God's grace and truth are fully certain, foreknown and foreordained in the mind and will of God.

9:6 Paul distinguishes here between the physical and the spiritual descendants of Abraham: not all the former belong to the latter. The spiritual descendants are those who are children of promise, as was Isaac, who was born as a result of God's promise when it was impossible, humanly speaking (cf. 4:19), for him to have been conceived. So those who share Abraham's faith in God's promise, Jew or Gentile, are Abraham's real spiritual descendants.

13 Just as it is written, "JACOB I LOVED, BUT ESAU I HATED."

14 What shall we say then? There is no injustice with God, is there? May it never be!

15 For He says to Moses, "I WILL HAVE MERCY ON WHOM I HAVE MERCY, AND I WILL HAVE COMPASSION ON WHOM I HAVE COMPASSION."

16 So then it *does* not *depend* on the man who wills or the man who runs, but on God who has mercy.

17 For the Scripture says to Pharaoh, "FOR THIS VERY PURPOSE I RAISED YOU UP, TO DEMONSTRATE MY POWER IN YOU, AND THAT MY NAME MIGHT BE PRO-CLAIMED THROUGHOUT THE WHOLE EARTH."

18 So then He has mercy on whom He desires, and He hardens whom He desires.

19 You will say to me then, "Why does He still find fault? For who resists His will?"

20 On the contrary, who are you, O man, who answers back to God? The thing molded will not say to the molder, "Why did you make me like this," will it?

21 Or does not the potter have a right over the clay, to make from the same lump one vessel for honorable use, and another for common use?

22 What if God, although willing to demonstrate His wrath and to make His power known, endured with much patience vessels of wrath prepared for destruction?

23 And *He did so* in order that He might make known the riches of His glory upon vessels of mercy, which He prepared beforehand for glory,

24 *even* us, whom He also called, not from among Jews only, but also from among Gentiles.

25 As He says also in Hosea,
"I WILL CALL THOSE WHO WERE NOT MY PEOPLE, 'MY PEOPLE,'
AND HER WHO WAS NOT BELOVED, 'BELOVED.' "

26 "AND IT SHALL BE THAT IN THE PLACE WHERE IT WAS SAID TO THEM,
'YOU ARE NOT MY PEOPLE,'
THERE THEY SHALL BE CALLED SONS OF THE LIVING GOD."

27 And Isaiah cries out concerning Israel, "THOUGH THE NUMBER OF THE SONS OF ISRAEL BE AS THE SAND OF THE SEA, IT IS THE REMNANT THAT WILL BE SAVED;

28 FOR THE LORD WILL EXECUTE HIS WORD UPON THE EARTH, THOROUGHLY AND QUICKLY."

29 And just as Isaiah foretold,
"EXCEPT THE LORD OF SABAOTH HAD LEFT TO US A POSTERITY,
WE WOULD HAVE BECOME AS SODOM, AND WOULD HAVE RESEMBLED
GOMORRAH."

30 What shall we say then? That Gentiles, who did not pursue righteousness, attained righteousness, even the righteousness which is by faith;

31 but Israel, pursuing a law of righteousness, did not arrive at *that* law.

32 Why? Because *they did* not *pursue it* by faith, but as though *it were* by works. They stumbled over the stumbling stone,

33 just as it is written,
"BEHOLD, I LAY IN ZION A STONE OF STUMBLING AND A ROCK OF
OFFENSE,
AND HE WHO BELIEVES IN HIM WILL NOT BE DISAPPOINTED."

C. God's rejection the fault of the Jews

10 Brethren, my heart's desire and my prayer to God for them is for *their* salvation.

2 For I bear them witness that they have a zeal for God, but not in accordance with knowledge.

3 For not knowing about God's righteousness, and seeking to establish their own, they did not subject themselves to the righteousness of God.

Cross-references (left margin):

9:13 Mal 1:2,3
9:14 2 Chr 19:7
9:15 Ex 33:19
9:16 Eph 2:8
9:17 Ex 9:16
9:19 2 Chr 20:6; Job 23:13; Dan 4:35
9:20 Is 29:16; 64:8
*9:21 2 Tim 2:20
9:22 Rom 2:4
9:23 Eph 3:16; Rom 8:29,30
9:24 Rom 3:29
9:25 Hos 2:23; 1 Pet 2:10
9:26 Hos 1:10
9:27 Is 10:22,23; Gen 22:17; Hos 1:10
9:29 Is 1:4; 13:19; Jer 50:40
9:30 Rom 10:6; Gal 2:16; Heb 11:7
9:31 Rom 10:2,3; Gal 5:4
9:32 1 Pet 2:6,8
9:33 Is 28:16; Matt 21:42; Rom 10:11
10:2 Acts 21:20
*10:3 Rom 1:17; Phil 3:9

9:21 Read in isolation from other passages, this verse, and Paul's whole discussion of the subject here (vv. 14–24), might appear to teach that man is merely an important vessel in God's hands, and therefore completely without responsibility for his own actions and ultimate destiny. But seen in the context of other teachings, it is clear that Paul here is emphasizing God's freedom in His mercy: man's redemption, finally, is not due to his own will but solely to God's mercy (v. 16).

10:3 Self-righteousness shuts out God's righteousness, which is bestowed through faith in Christ, and replaces it with a spurious righteousness of man that has no standing before God (Is. 64:4; Mark 10:18). It is based on the false supposition that man in himself is right with God or can make himself right by his own efforts. Rejecting God's righteousness and substituting for it man's pretended right-

4   For Christ is the end of the law for righteousness to everyone who believes.
5   For Moses writes that the man who practices the righteousness which is based on law shall live by that righteousness.
6   But the righteousness based on faith speaks thus, "DO NOT SAY IN YOUR HEART, 'WHO WILL ASCEND INTO HEAVEN?' (that is, to bring Christ down),
7   or 'WHO WILL DESCEND INTO THE ABYSS?' (that is, to bring Christ up from the dead)."
8   But what does it say? "THE WORD IS NEAR YOU, IN YOUR MOUTH AND IN YOUR HEART"—that is, the word of faith which we are preaching,
9   that if you confess with your mouth Jesus *as* Lord, and believe in your heart that God raised Him from the dead, you shall be saved;
10 for with the heart man believes, resulting in righteousness, and with the mouth he confesses, resulting in salvation.
11 For the Scripture says, "WHOEVER BELIEVES IN HIM WILL NOT BE DISAPPOINTED."
12 For there is no distinction between Jew and Greek; for the same *Lord* is Lord of all, abounding in riches for all who call upon Him;
13 for "WHOEVER WILL CALL UPON THE NAME OF THE LORD WILL BE SAVED."
14 How then shall they call upon Him in whom they have not believed? And how shall they believe in Him whom they have not heard? And how shall they hear without a preacher?
15 And how shall they preach unless they are sent? Just as it is written, "HOW BEAUTIFUL ARE THE FEET OF THOSE WHO BRING GLAD TIDINGS OF GOOD THINGS!"
16 However, they did not all heed the glad tidings; for Isaiah says, "LORD, WHO HAS BELIEVED OUR REPORT?"
17 So faith *comes* from hearing, and hearing by the word of Christ.
18 But I say, surely they have never heard, have they? Indeed they have;
    "THEIR VOICE HAS GONE OUT INTO ALL THE EARTH,
    AND THEIR WORDS TO THE ENDS OF THE WORLD."
19 But I say, surely Israel did not know, did they? At the first Moses says,
    "I WILL MAKE YOU JEALOUS BY THAT WHICH IS NOT A NATION,
    BY A NATION WITHOUT UNDERSTANDING WILL I ANGER YOU."
20 And Isaiah is very bold and says,
    "I WAS FOUND BY THOSE WHO SOUGHT ME NOT,
    I BECAME MANIFEST TO THOSE WHO DID NOT ASK FOR ME."
21 But as for Israel He says, "ALL THE DAY LONG I HAVE STRETCHED OUT MY HANDS TO A DISOBEDIENT AND OBSTINATE PEOPLE."

D. Israel's rejection not final

1. The remnant

11 I say then, God has not rejected His people, has He? May it never be! For I too am an Israelite, a descendant of Abraham, of the tribe of Benjamin.
2   God has not rejected His people whom He foreknew. Or do you not know what the Scripture says in *the passage about* Elijah, how he pleads with God against Israel?
3   "Lord, THEY HAVE KILLED THY PROPHETS, THEY HAVE TORN DOWN THINE ALTARS, AND I ALONE AM LEFT, AND THEY ARE SEEKING MY LIFE."
4   But what is the divine response to him? "I HAVE KEPT for Myself SEVEN THOUSAND MEN WHO HAVE NOT BOWED THE KNEE TO BAAL."
5   In the same way then, there has also come to be at the present time a remnant according to *God's* gracious choice.
6   But if it is by grace, it is no longer on the basis of works, otherwise grace is no longer grace.
7   What then? That which Israel is seeking for, it has not obtained, but those who were chosen obtained it, and the rest were hardened;
8   just as it is written,
    "GOD GAVE THEM A SPIRIT OF STUPOR,

10:4 Gal 3:24; Rom 7:1-4
10:5 Neh 9:29; Ezek 20:11, 13,21; Rom 7:10
10:7 Heb 13:20
10:8 Deut 30:14
10:9 Matt 10:32; Luke 12:8; Acts 16:31
10:11 Is 28:16; Rom 9:33
10:12 Rom 3:22,29; Gal 3:28; Acts 10:36
10:13 Joel 2:32; Acts 2:21
10:15 Is 52:7
10:16 Heb 4:2; Is 53:1; John 12:38
*10:17 Gal 3:2,5; Col 3:16
10:18 Ps 19:4; Col 1:6,23; 1 Thess 1:8
10:19 Deut 32:21; Rom 11:11
10:20 Is 65:1; Rom 9:30
10:21 Is 65:2
11:1 1 Sam 12:22; Jer 31:37; 2 Cor 11:22; Phil 3:5
11:2 Ps 94:19; 1 Kin 19:10; Rom 8:29
11:4 1 Kin 19:18
11:5 2 Kin 19:4; Rom 9:27
11:6 Rom 4:4
11:7 Rom 9:18,31
11:8 Is 29:10; Deut 29:4; Matt 13:13,14

eousness is sinful folly.
10:17 A basic truth is taught here that bears on the missionary task of the church. Salvation is possible only when certain indispensable conditions are met. One must have faith (10:11), but faith is not possible unless the gospel is communicated, and the gospel can be communicated only by the preaching of the Word of God. Therefore the ultimate source from which salvation springs is necessarily the Word of God. This may be given to men a variety of ways, such as by word of mouth or the printed page; but however it is conveyed the Word of God is indispensable to salvation.

EYES TO SEE NOT AND EARS TO HEAR NOT,
DOWN TO THIS VERY DAY."

11:9
Ps 69:22,23

9   And David says,
"LET THEIR TABLE BECOME A SNARE AND A TRAP,
AND A STUMBLING BLOCK AND A RETRIBUTION TO THEM.

10   "LET THEIR EYES BE DARKENED TO SEE NOT,
AND BEND THEIR BACKS FOREVER."

2. Israel's future salvation

11:11
Acts 13:46;
Rom 10:19

11   I say then, they did not stumble so as to fall, did they? May it never be! But by their transgression salvation *has come* to the Gentiles, to make them jealous.

11:12
v. 25

12   Now if their transgression be riches for the world and their failure be riches for the Gentiles, how much more will their fulfillment be!

11:13
Acts 9:15;
Rom 15:16

13   But I am speaking to you who are Gentiles. Inasmuch then as I am an apostle of Gentiles, I magnify my ministry,

11:14
Rom 10:19;
1 Cor 7:16;
9:22

14   if somehow I might move to jealousy my fellow countrymen and save some of them.

11:15
Luke 15:24,
32

15   For if their rejection be the reconciliation of the world, what will *their* acceptance be but life from the dead?

11:16
Lev 23:10;
Num 15:18

16   And if the first piece *of dough* be holy, the lump is also; and if the root be holy, the branches are too.

*11:17
Jer 11:17;
Acts 2:39;
Eph 2:11,12

17   But if some of the branches were broken off, and you, being a wild olive, were grafted in among them and became partaker with them of the rich root of the olive tree,

18   do not be arrogant toward the branches; but if you are arrogant, *remember that* it is not you who supports the root, but the root *supports* you.

19   You will say then, "Branches were broken off so that I might be grafted in."

11:20
Rom 12:16;
2 Cor 1:24

20   Quite right, they were broken off for their unbelief, but you stand by your faith. Do not be conceited, but fear;

21   for if God did not spare the natural branches, neither will He spare you.

11:22
1 Cor 15:2;
Heb 3:6;
John 15:2

22   Behold then the kindness and severity of God; to those who fell, severity, but to you, God's kindness, if you continue in His kindness; otherwise you also will be cut off.

11:23
2 Cor 3:16

23   And they also, if they do not continue in their unbelief, will be grafted in; for God is able to graft them in again.

24   For if you were cut off from what is by nature a wild olive tree, and were grafted contrary to nature into a cultivated olive tree, how much more shall these who are the natural *branches* be grafted into their own olive tree?

*11:25
1 Cor 2:7-10;
Eph 3:3-5,9;
Rom 9:18

25   For I do not want you, brethren, to be uninformed of this mystery, lest you be wise in your own estimation, that a partial hardening has happened to Israel until the fulness of the Gentiles has come in;

11:26
Is 59:20,21

26   and thus all Israel will be saved; just as it is written,
"THE DELIVERER WILL COME FROM ZION,
HE WILL REMOVE UNGODLINESS FROM JACOB."

11:27
Is 27:9

27   "AND THIS IS MY COVENANT WITH THEM,
WHEN I TAKE AWAY THEIR SINS."

11:28
Deut 7:8;
10:15;
Rom 5:10;
9:5

28   From the standpoint of the gospel they are enemies for your sake, but from the standpoint of *God's* choice they are beloved for the sake of the fathers;

11:29
Num 23:19

29   for the gifts and the calling of God are irrevocable.

11:17 In his use of the figure of the olive tree, with some branches broken off and others grafted in, Paul constantly stresses the elements of unbelief and faith. It was through unbelief that the natural branches (Jews) were broken off (v. 20), and through faith that the branches of the wild olive tree (Gentiles) have been grafted in (v. 20). They will remain grafted in if they, the Gentiles, continue in God's kindness (v. 22), while the branches that have been broken off may be replaced in the tree if they abandon their unbelief (v. 23). All figures and analogies, whether that of a potter and his vessels (9:14–24), or of a gardener and his tree, are finally inadequate, of course, to carry the full meaning of the paradox of God's sovereignty and man's freedom; and the believer's proper response is that of thanksgiving and praise to God for His inscrutable ways (vv. 33–36).

11:25f One of the fundamental tenets of the gospel is that

a man is brought as an individual to God by His grace, irrespective of race: that God does not deal with national or racial blocs, as chosen or favored people; that no race has a privileged status with God; that there is only one way in which God deals with all individuals; that the new Israel is of all races and tongues. Yet at the same time Paul appears to be saying that God has not forgotten His people Israel: *a partial hardening has happened to Israel until the fulness of the Gentiles has come in . . . all Israel will be saved.* Certainly this is not to be understood to mean that every Israelite will be saved. But it cannot mean less than that substantial numbers of Israelites will turn to God in Christ before the end of the present age. The converts will be saved in exactly the same way and by the same means as anyone is being saved today.

30   For just as you once were disobedient to God, but now have been shown mercy because of their disobedience,

31   so these also now have been disobedient, in order that because of the mercy shown to you they also may now be shown mercy.

32   For God has shut up all in disobedience that He might show mercy to all.

3. Paul's concluding doxology

33   Oh, the depth of the riches both of the wisdom and knowledge of God! How unsearchable are His judgments and unfathomable His ways!

34   For WHO HAS KNOWN THE MIND OF THE LORD, OR WHO BECAME HIS COUNSELOR?

35   Or WHO HAS FIRST GIVEN TO HIM THAT IT MIGHT BE PAID BACK TO HIM AGAIN?

36   For from Him and through Him and to Him are all things. To Him *be* the glory forever. Amen.

V. Ethical teaching (12:1–15:13)

A. The call to full surrender

12   I urge you therefore, brethren, by the mercies of God, to present your bodies a living and holy sacrifice, acceptable to God, *which is* your spiritual service of worship.

2   And do not be conformed to this world, but be transformed by the renewing of your mind, that you may prove what the will of God is, that which is good and acceptable and perfect.

B. The use of God's gifts

3   For through the grace given to me I say to every man among you not to think more highly of himself than he ought to think; but to think so as to have sound judgment, as God has allotted to each a measure of faith.

4   For just as we have many members in one body and all the members do not have the same function,

5   so we, who are many, are one body in Christ, and individually members one of another.

6   And since we have gifts that differ according to the grace given to us, *let each exercise them accordingly:* if prophecy, according to the proportion of his faith;

7   if service, in his serving; or he who teaches, in his teaching;

8   or he who exhorts, in his exhortation; he who gives, with [14]liberality; he who leads, with diligence; he who shows mercy, with cheerfulness.

C. Christian conduct in personal relationships

9   Let love be without hypocrisy. Abhor what is evil; cling to what is good.

10   Be devoted to one another in brotherly love; give preference to one another in honor;

11   not lagging behind in diligence, fervent in spirit, serving the Lord;

12   rejoicing in hope, persevering in tribulation, devoted to prayer,

13   contributing to the needs of the saints, practicing hospitality.

14   Bless those who persecute [15]you; bless and curse not.

15   Rejoice with those who rejoice, and weep with those who weep.

16   Be of the same mind toward one another; do not be haughty in mind, but associate with the lowly. Do not be wise in your own estimation.

17   Never pay back evil for evil to anyone. Respect what is right in the sight of all men.

18   If possible, so far as it depends on you, be at peace with all men.

19   Never take your own revenge, beloved, but leave room for the wrath *of God,* for it is written, "VENGEANCE IS MINE, I WILL REPAY," says the Lord.

20   "BUT IF YOUR ENEMY IS HUNGRY, FEED HIM, AND IF HE IS THIRSTY, GIVE HIM A DRINK; FOR IN SO DOING YOU WILL HEAP BURNING COALS UPON HIS HEAD."

21   Do not be overcome by evil, but overcome evil with good.

[14]Or, *simplicity*   [15]Some ancient mss. do not contain *you*

Cross-references (right margin):

11:30 — Eph 2:2
11:32 — Rom 3:9; Gal 3:22,23
11:33 — Eph 3:8; Ps 92:5
11:34 — Is 40:13,14; 1 Cor 2:16; Job 36:22
11:36 — 1 Cor 8:6; Heb 2:10; Rom 16:27; Heb 13:21
12:1 — 2 Cor 10:1,2; Rom 6:13,16, 19; 1 Pet 2:5
12:2 — 1 Pet 1:14; 1 John 2:15; Eph 4:23; 5:10
12:3 — Rom 15:15; 2 Cor 10:13; Eph 4:7
12:4 — 1 Cor 12:12-14; Eph 4:4,16
12:6 — 1 Cor 7:7; 12:4,10; 1 Pet 4:10,11
12:7 — 1 Cor 12:28; 14:26
12:8 — Acts 15:32; Matt 6:1-3; 1 Tim 5:17; 2 Cor 9:7
12:12 — Heb 10:32, 36; Acts 1:14
12:13 — Rom 15:25; Heb 13:2
12:14 — Matt 5:44; Luke 6:28
12:16 — Rom 15:5; 11:25
12:17 — Prov 20:22; 2 Cor 8:21
12:18 — Mark 9:50; Rom 14:19
12:19 — Lev 19:18; Heb 10:30
12:20 — Prov 25:21, 22;
Matt 5:44; Luke 6:27

D. Christian conduct in relation to the state

13 Let every person be in subjection to the governing authorities. For there is no authority except from God, and those which exist are established by God.

2   Therefore he who resists authority has opposed the ordinance of God; and they who have opposed will receive condemnation upon themselves.

3   For rulers are not a cause of fear for good behavior, but for evil. Do you want to have no fear of authority? Do what is good, and you will have praise from the same;

4   for it is a minister of God to you for good. But if you do what is evil, be afraid; for it does not bear the sword for nothing; for it is a minister of God, an avenger who brings wrath upon the one who practices evil.

5   Wherefore it is necessary to be in subjection, not only because of wrath, but also for conscience' sake.

6   For because of this you also pay taxes, for *rulers* are servants of God, devoting themselves to this very thing.

7   Render to all what is due them: tax to whom tax *is due;* custom to whom custom; fear to whom fear; honor to whom honor.

E. *The call to love*

8   Owe nothing to anyone except to love one another; for he who loves his neighbor has fulfilled *the* law.

9   For this, "YOU SHALL NOT COMMIT ADULTERY, YOU SHALL NOT MURDER, YOU SHALL NOT STEAL, YOU SHALL NOT COVET," and if there is any other commandment, it is summed up in this saying, "YOU SHALL LOVE YOUR NEIGHBOR AS YOURSELF."

10   Love does no wrong to a neighbor; love therefore is the fulfillment of *the* law.

F. *Hope, the Christian motivation*

11   And this *do,* knowing the time, that it is already the hour for you to awaken from sleep; for now [16]salvation is nearer to us than when we believed.

12   The night is almost gone, and the day is at hand. Let us therefore lay aside the deeds of darkness and put on the armor of light.

13   Let us behave properly as in the day, not in carousing and drunkenness, not in sexual promiscuity and sensuality, not in strife and jealousy.

14   But put on the Lord Jesus Christ, and make no provision for the flesh in regard to *its* lusts.

G. *The Christian and matters of conscience*

1. *Not to judge*

14 Now accept the one who is weak in faith, *but* not for *the purpose of* passing judgment on his opinions.

2   One man has faith that he may eat all things, but he who is weak eats vegetables *only.*

3   Let not him who eats regard with contempt him who does not eat, and let not him who does not eat judge him who eats, for God has accepted him.

4   Who are you to judge the servant of another? To his own master he stands or falls; and stand he will, for the Lord is able to make him stand.

5   One man regards one day above another, another regards every day *alike.* Let each man be fully convinced in his own mind.

6   He who observes the day, observes it for the Lord, and he who eats, does so

[16]Or, *our salvation is nearer than when*

13:1   Rulers or authorities are said to be: (1) established by God (13:1); (2) a cause of fear for evildoers (13:3); (3) bearers of the sword to execute vengeance (13:4); (4) entitled to be respected and obeyed (13:2); and (5) entitled to gather taxes (13:6,7). See also 1 Pet. 2:13–17.
13:9   At least three statements of the believer's relationship to love as the governing principle of life may be found in the New Testament: (1) *You shall love your neighbor as yourself* (v. 9); (2) *Love does no wrong to a neighbor* (v. 10); and (3) the Golden Rule of Matt. 7:12. The proper use of these prin-

ciples in the relationships of men personally, nationally, and internationally would resolve most of our tensions and disputes. See also note to 1 Cor. 10:23.
13:11ff.   Paul argues that the Christian should be motivated in his conduct by the prospect of the return of the Lord. In fact, some have argued that this passage indicates Paul believed in an imminent return of Christ and taught it as revealed truth. However, chapter 11 shows that he expected an extended future or a long interval between the first and second coming.

for the Lord, for he gives thanks to God; and he who eats not, for the Lord he does not eat, and gives thanks to God.

7   For not one of us lives for himself, and not one dies for himself;

8   for if we live, we live for the Lord, or if we die, we die for the Lord; therefore whether we live or die, we are the Lord's.

9   For to this end Christ died and lived *again*, that He might be Lord both of the dead and of the living.

10   But you, why do you judge your brother? Or you again, why do you regard your brother with contempt? For we shall all stand before the judgment seat of God.

11   For it is written,

"AS I LIVE, SAYS THE LORD, EVERY KNEE SHALL BOW TO ME,
   AND EVERY TONGUE SHALL GIVE PRAISE TO GOD."

12   So then each one of us shall give account of himself to God.

2. Not to be a stumbling block

13   Therefore let us not judge one another anymore, but rather determine this—not to put an obstacle or a stumbling block in a brother's way.

14   I know and am convinced in the Lord Jesus that nothing is unclean in itself; but to him who thinks anything to be unclean, to him it is unclean.

15   For if because of food your brother is hurt, you are no longer walking according to love. Do not destroy with your food him for whom Christ died.

16   Therefore do not let what is for you a good thing be spoken of as evil;

17   for the kingdom of God is not eating and drinking, but righteousness and peace and joy in the Holy Spirit.

18   For he who in this *way* serves Christ is acceptable to God and approved by men.

19   So then [17]let us pursue the things which make for peace and the building up of one another.

20   Do not tear down the work of God for the sake of food. All things indeed are clean, but they are evil for the man who eats and gives offense.

21   It is good not to eat meat or to drink wine, or *to do anything* by which your brother stumbles.

22   The faith which you have, have as your own conviction before God. Happy is he who does not condemn himself in what he approves.

23   But he who doubts is condemned if he eats, because *his eating is* not from faith; and whatever is not from faith is sin.

3. To follow Christ's example

15 Now we who are strong ought to bear the weaknesses of those without strength and not *just* please ourselves.

2   Let each of us please his neighbor for his good, to his edification.

3   For even Christ did not please Himself; but as it is written, "THE REPROACHES OF THOSE WHO REPROACHED THEE FELL UPON ME."

4   For whatever was written in earlier times was written for our instruction, that through perseverance and the encouragement of the Scriptures we might have hope.

5   Now may the God who gives perseverance and encouragement grant you to be of the same mind with one another according to Christ Jesus;

[17]Many ancient mss. read *we pursue*

Marginal references:

14:7 2 Cor 5:15; Gal 2:20; Phil 1:20,21
*14:8 Phil 1:20
14:9 2 Cor 5:15; Acts 10:36
14:10 2 Cor 5:10
14:11 Is 45:23; Phil 2:10,11
14:12 Matt 12:36; 1 Pet 4:5
14:13 Matt 7:1; 1 Cor 8:13
*14:14 Acts 10:15; 1 Cor 8:7
14:15 Eph 5:2; 1 Cor 8:11
14:16 1 Cor 10:30
14:17 1 Cor 8:8; Rom 15:13
14:18 2 Cor 8:21
14:19 Ps 34:14; Heb 12:14; Rom 15:2
14:20 v. 15; 1 Cor 8:9-12
14:21 1 Cor 8:13
14:22 1 John 3:21
15:1 Rom 14:1; Gal 6:1,2
15:2 1 Cor 10:33; Rom 14:19
15:3 Ps 69:9; 2 Cor 8:9
15:4 Rom 4:23,24; 2 Tim 3:16,17
15:5 Rom 12:16; 1 Cor 1:10

14:8 The rules for Christian conduct may be determined in one of two ways: either by general principles laid down in Scripture, or else by specific Biblical injunctions. Thus, by way of principle, the Christian is told to walk: (1) so as to command the respect of others (1 Thess. 4:11,12); (2) fully pleasing to God (Col. 1:10); (3) in the Spirit (Gal. 5:25); (4) in newness of life (6:4); and (5) worthy of his calling (Eph. 4:1). By way of specific injunction the believer is commanded: (1) to control his body (1 Cor. 9:27); (2) to forgive those who wrong him (12:20); (3) to subdue anger (Eph. 4:26; James 1:19); (4) to have no fellowship with sinners (Ps. 1:1; 2 Thess. 3:6); and (5) to live peaceably with all men (12:18; Heb. 12:14).

14:14 *nothing is unclean in itself.* This must not be taken as a general statement that includes all acts of conduct. Rather it is specifically related to the matter of foods, as the next

verse demonstrates. Some Christians in Rome thought they should, for religious reasons, abstain from certain kinds of food, particularly meat (v. 2). Paul calls them *weak* (perhaps "immature" is a better word), and warns them not to pass judgment on those who did not abide by their scruples (vv. 3,4,10a), since those who ate did so with thanksgiving to God (v. 6). Those who were not bound by false scruples Paul called *strong* (15:1), and admonished them not to despise their weak brother (14:3,10b). Furthermore, they had the added responsibility of not hurting their weak brother by their example, for if a man ate what he thought was impure he thus transgressed his own conscience and was thereby injured. All foods are clean (v. 20): none is in itself unclean (v. 14), a statement reminiscent of Jesus' teaching and the evangelist's comment: *Thus He declared all foods clean* (Mark 7:18,19).

15:6
Rev 1:6

15:7
Rom 14:1

15:8
Matt 15:24;
Acts 3:25,26;
Rom 3:3;
2 Cor 1:20
15:9
Ps 18:49;
2 Sam 22:50
15:10
Deut 32:43
15:11
Ps 117:1

15:12
Is 11:10;
Matt 12:21;
Rev 5:5;
22:16

15:13
Rom 14:17;
1 Thess 1:5

6 that with one accord you may with one voice glorify the God and Father of our Lord Jesus Christ.

7 Wherefore, accept one another, just as Christ also accepted us to the glory of God.

8 For I say that Christ has become a servant to the circumcision on behalf of the truth of God to confirm the promises *given* to the fathers,

9 and for the Gentiles to glorify God for His mercy; as it is written,
"THEREFORE I WILL GIVE PRAISE TO THEE AMONG THE GENTILES,
   AND I WILL SING TO THY NAME."

10 And again he says,
"REJOICE, O GENTILES, WITH HIS PEOPLE."

11 And again,
"PRAISE THE LORD ALL YOU GENTILES,
   AND LET ALL THE PEOPLES PRAISE HIM."

12 And again Isaiah says,
"THERE SHALL COME THE ROOT OF JESSE,
   AND HE WHO ARISES TO RULE OVER THE GENTILES,
   IN HIM SHALL THE GENTILES HOPE."

13 Now may the God of hope fill you with all joy and peace in believing, that you may abound in hope by the power of the Holy Spirit.

VI. *Conclusion and postscript (15:14–16:27)*

A. *Paul's reasons for writing*

15:14
2 Pet 1:12;
1 Cor 8:1,7,
10

15:15
Rom 12:3;
Eph 3:7,8
15:16
Acts 9:15;
Rom 11:13;
Phil 2:17

15:17
Phil 3:3;
Heb 2:17; 5:1
15:18
Acts 15:12;
21:19;
Rom 1:5;
16:26
15:19
Acts 19:11;
2 Cor 12:12
15:20
2 Cor 10:15,
16
15:21
Is 52:15

14 And concerning you, my brethren, I myself also am convinced that you yourselves are full of goodness, filled with all knowledge, and able also to admonish one another.

15 But I have written very boldly to you on some points, so as to remind you again, because of the grace that was given me from God,

16 to be a minister of Christ Jesus to the Gentiles, ministering as a priest the gospel of God, that *my* offering of the Gentiles might become acceptable, sanctified by the Holy Spirit.

17 Therefore in Christ Jesus I have found reason for boasting in things pertaining to God.

18 For I will not presume to speak of anything except what Christ has accomplished through me, resulting in the obedience of the Gentiles by word and deed,

19 in the power of signs and wonders, in the power of the Spirit; so that from Jerusalem and round about as far as Illyricum I have fully preached the gospel of Christ.

20 And thus I aspired to preach the gospel, not where Christ was *already* named, that I might not build upon another man's foundation;

21 but as it is written,
"THEY WHO HAD NO NEWS OF HIM SHALL SEE,
   AND THEY WHO HAVE NOT HEARD SHALL UNDERSTAND."

B. *Paul's future plans*

15:22
Rom 1:13
15:23
Acts 19:21;
Rom 1:11
15:24
v. 28;
Acts 15:3
15:25
Acts 19:21;
24:27
15:26
2 Cor 8:1;
9:2; 1 Thess
1:7,8
15:27
1 Cor 9:11

22 For this reason I have often been hindered from coming to you;

23 but now, with no further place for me in these regions, and since I have had for many years a longing to come to you

24 whenever I go to Spain—for I hope to see you in passing, and to be helped on my way there by you, when I have first enjoyed your company for a while—

25 but now, I am going to Jerusalem serving the saints.

26 For Macedonia and Achaia have been pleased to make a contribution for the poor among the saints in Jerusalem.

27 Yes, they were pleased *to do so*, and they are indebted to them. For if the Gentiles have shared in their spiritual things, they are indebted to minister to them also in material things.

28 Therefore, when I have finished this, and have put my seal on this fruit of theirs, I will go on by way of you to Spain.

29 And I know that when I come to you, I will come in the fulness of the blessing of Christ.

30 Now I urge you, brethren, by our Lord Jesus Christ and by the love of the Spirit, to strive together with me in your prayers to God for me,

31 that I may be delivered from those who are disobedient in Judea, and *that* my service for Jerusalem may prove acceptable to the saints;

32 so that I may come to you in joy by the will of God and find *refreshing* rest in your company.

33 Now the God of peace be with you all. Amen.

C. *Commendations and greetings*

16 I commend to you our sister Phoebe, who is a servant of the church which is at Cenchrea;

2 that you receive her in the Lord in a manner worthy of the saints, and that you help her in whatever matter she may have need of you; for she herself has also been a helper of many, and of myself as well.

3 Greet Prisca and Aquila, my fellow workers in Christ Jesus,

4 who for my life risked their own necks, to whom not only do I give thanks, but also all the churches of the Gentiles;

5 also *greet* the church that is in their house. Greet Epaenetus, my beloved, who is the first convert to Christ from Asia.

6 Greet Mary, who has worked hard for you.

7 Greet Andronicus and Junias, my kinsmen, and my fellow prisoners, who are outstanding among the apostles, who also were in Christ before me.

8 Greet Ampliatus, my beloved in the Lord.

9 Greet Urbanus, our fellow worker in Christ, and Stachys my beloved.

10 Greet Apelles, the approved in Christ. Greet those who are of the *household* of Aristobulus.

11 Greet Herodion, my kinsman. Greet those of the *household* of Narcissus, who are in the Lord.

12 Greet Tryphaena and Tryphosa, workers in the Lord. Greet Persis the beloved, who has worked hard in the Lord.

13 Greet Rufus, a choice man in the Lord, also his mother and mine.

14 Greet Asyncritus, Phlegon, Hermes, Patrobas, Hermas and the brethren with them.

15 Greet Philologus and Julia, Nereus and his sister, and Olympas, and all the saints who are with them.

16 Greet one another with a holy kiss. All the churches of Christ greet you.

17 Now I urge you, brethren, keep your eye on those who cause dissensions and hindrances contrary to the teaching which you learned, and turn away from them.

18 For such men are slaves, not of our Lord Christ but of their own appetites; and by their smooth and flattering speech they deceive the hearts of the unsuspecting.

19 For the report of your obedience has reached to all; therefore I am rejoicing over you, but I want you to be wise in what is good, and innocent in what is evil.

20 And the God of peace will soon crush Satan under your feet.

The grace of our Lord Jesus be with you.

21 Timothy my fellow worker greets you, and *so do* Lucius and Jason and Sosipater, my kinsmen.

22 I, Tertius, who write this letter, greet you in the Lord.

23 Gaius, host to me and to the whole church, greets you. Erastus, the city treasurer greets you, and Quartus, the brother.

24 [[18]The grace of our Lord Jesus Christ be with you all. Amen.]

D. *Doxology*

25 Now to Him who is able to establish you according to my gospel and the preaching of Jesus Christ, according to the revelation of the mystery which has been kept secret for long ages past,

26 but now is manifested, and by the Scriptures of the prophets, according to the commandment of the eternal God, has been made known to all the nations, *leading* to obedience of faith;

27 to the only wise God, through Jesus Christ, be the glory forever. Amen.

[18]Many mss. do not contain this verse

Cross references (right margin):

15:30
Gal 5:22;
2 Cor 1:11;
Col 4:12

15:32
Rom 1:10;
Acts 18:21;
1 Cor 16:18
15:33
Rom 16:20;
2 Cor 13:11;
Phil 4:9;
Heb 13:20
16:1
Acts 18:18
16:2
Phil 2:29;
Rom 15:15,31

16:3
Acts 18:2;
2 Tim 4:19

16:5
1 Cor 16:15,
19; Col 4:15

16:9
2 Cor 5:17
16:10
2 Cor 5:17
16:11
vv. 7,21;
1 Cor 1:11

16:15
vv. 2,14

16:16
1 Cor 16:20;
2 Cor 13:12;
1 Thess 5:26
16:17
1 Tim 1:3;
6:3; Gal 1:8,
9; 2 Thess
3:6,14;
2 John 10
16:18
Phil 3:19;
Col 2:4
16:19
Rom 1:8;
Matt 10:16;
1 Cor 14:20
16:20
Rom 15:33;
Gen 3:15;
1 Cor 16:23;
1 Thess 5:28
16:21
Acts 16:1;
13:1; 17:5;
20:4; vv. 7,11

INTRODUCTION TO
THE FIRST LETTER OF PAUL TO THE
CORINTHIANS

Authorship and Background: Before writing this letter Paul had already written to the Corinthians (5:9). This earlier letter has not survived, unless its contents have been preserved in 2 Cor. 6:14-7:1, as some scholars believe. The Corinthian church then wrote to Paul about several matters (7:1) and sent the letter by a group that included Stephanas, Fortunatus, and Achaicus (16:17). It was in reply to this communication that Paul penned his second letter, known to us as 1 Corinthians. It appears to have been written in Ephesus, in A.D. 55, shortly before Pentecost and at the end of Paul's three-year stay there (16:8,19). It was probably delivered to Corinth by Timothy (cf. 16:10-11).

Paul first came to Corinth from Athens on his second missionary journey (Acts 18:1). He arrived with some misgivings (2:3), but went to work in typical fashion, with the help of Aquila and Priscilla (Acts 18:2-4). He was joined eventually by Silas and Timothy, and spent eighteen months in intensive work (Acts 18:11). When Gallio was appointed proconsul of Achaia, in A.D. 51, Paul's enemies sought to have him jailed, but with no success (Acts 18:12-17). After spending some more time in Corinth, Paul went to the port city of Cenchreae, and on to Antioch (Acts 18:18-22). In all, he must have spent close to two years in Corinth (probably A.D. 49-51), establishing the work in the city and throughout the province of Achaia (cf. Rom. 16:1 for Cenchrea, and "throughout Achaia" in 2 Cor. 1:1).

Characteristics: Corinth was a bustling metropolis, one of the largest centers of commerce and travel in the Roman empire. Its reputation for immorality was so notorious that the verb "to corinthianize," meaning to live an immoral life, was coined. It is small wonder that even in the church there were problems of immorality (ch. 5). Reports had also been brought by Chloe's family (or slaves) of factions in the church (1:11,12), and the letter from the church itself raised several questions that Paul dealt with (7:1; see further "now concerning" in 7:1; 7:25; 8:1; 12:1; 16:1, which seem to refer to specific questions in the letter). In no other letter is there so vivid and realistic a portrait of the problems and difficulties confronting a church in a pagan and corrupt society. Here one may see the early Christians, "warts and all," their weakness serving to magnify the greatness of God's grace and power. In this letter are the earliest reports of the Lord's Supper (11:20-34), the great hymn of love (ch. 13), and the gospel of the resurrection (ch. 15).

Contents:

I. Introduction (1:1-9)

II. Factions (1:10-4:21): The different parties of Paul, Apollos, Cephas, and Christ had broken the unity of the church and made a mockery of the lordship of Christ. Such factions are intolerable: the apostles are fellow servants, and it is God alone who supplies the life of the church (3:1-9), in which all are fellow members in the unity of Christ (3:21-23).

III. Sexual morality (5:1-7:40): Flagrant and unrepented immorality within the church has only one solution: the expulsion of the guilty from the Christian fellowship (5:1-13). All immorality is grievous sin against Christ: believers are His members and their bodies the temples of the Spirit (6:9-20). Christians should never appear in pagan courts in lawsuits against one another (6:1-8). Questions of marriage, celibacy, divorce, and remarriage are dealt with (7:1-40): sometimes Paul has a teaching from the Lord, at other times he gives his own judgment.

IV. Christian liberty (8:1-11:1): Christian life in a pagan society raised acute problems, especially that of table fellowship with pagans, which involved eating meat offered in pagan temples; where no spiritual offense is involved (8:8) Christian love imposes voluntary restrictions on personal conduct (8:8-13; 9:19-23; 10:24,31-33).

V. Public worship (11:2-14:40): Paul deals with women's dress (11:2-16); the Lord's Supper (11:17-34); spiritual gifts, their value and use (12:1-14:40). Love is the greatest of all gifts (13:1-13).

VI. The resurrection (15:1-58): The foundation of the Christian faith and message is the resurrection of Christ, the guarantee of the believer's own resurrection.

VII. Personal matters (16:1-24): The offering for the Christians in Judea; future plans for Paul and his companions; final exhortations and benediction.

THE FIRST LETTER OF PAUL TO THE
CORINTHIANS

I. Introduction (1:1–9)

A. Salutation

1 Paul, called *as* an apostle of Jesus Christ by the will of God, and Sosthenes our brother,

2 to the church of God which is at Corinth, to those who have been sanctified in Christ Jesus, saints by calling, with all who in every place call upon the name of our Lord Jesus Christ, their *Lord* and ours:

3 Grace to you and peace from God our Father and the Lord Jesus Christ.

B. *Thanksgiving*

4 I thank ¹my God always concerning you, for the grace of God which was given you in Christ Jesus,

5 that in everything you were enriched in Him, in all speech and all knowledge,

6 even as the testimony concerning Christ was confirmed in you,

7 so that you are not lacking in any gift, awaiting eagerly the revelation of our Lord Jesus Christ,

8 who shall also confirm you to the end, blameless in the day of our Lord Jesus Christ.

9 God is faithful, through whom you were called into fellowship with His Son, Jesus Christ our Lord.

II. *Factions (1:10–4:21)*

A. *Exhortation to unity*

10 Now I exhort you, brethren, by the name of our Lord Jesus Christ, that you all agree, and there be no divisions among you, but you be made complete in the same mind and in the same judgment.

11 For I have been informed concerning you, my brethren, by Chloe's *people*, that there are quarrels among you.

12 Now I mean this, that each one of you is saying, "I am of Paul," and "I of Apollos," and "I of Cephas," and "I of Christ."

13 Has Christ been divided? Paul was not crucified for you, was he? Or were you baptized in the name of Paul?

14 ²I thank God that I baptized none of you except Crispus and Gaius,

15 that no man should say you were baptized in my name.

16 Now I did baptize also the household of Stephanas; beyond that, I do not know whether I baptized any other.

17 For Christ did not send me to baptize, but to preach the gospel, not in cleverness of speech, that the cross of Christ should not be made void.

B. *The wisdom of men and the "foolishness of God"*

18 For the word of the cross is to those who are perishing foolishness, but to us who are being saved it is the power of God.

19 For it is written,

¹Some ancient mss. do not contain *my*   ²Some ancient mss. read *I give thanks that*

Reference column (left margin):

1:1 — Rom 1:1; 2 Cor 1:1; Eph 1:1; Col 1:1; Acts 18:17
1:2 — Acts 18:1; Rom 1:7; Acts 7:59
1:3 — Rom 1:7
1:4 — Rom 1:8
1:5 — 2 Cor 9:11; 8:7
1:6 — 2 Tim 1:8; Rev 1:2
1:7 — Phil 3:20; Titus 2:13; 2 Pet 3:12
1:9 — Is 49:7; 1 John 1:3
*1:10 — 2 Cor 13:11; Rom 12:16
1:13 — 2 Cor 11:4; Matt 28:19; Acts 2:38
1:14 — Acts 18:8; Rom 16:23
1:16 — 1 Cor 16:15
1:17 — John 4:2; Acts 10:48; 1 Cor 2:1,4, 13
1:18 — Acts 17:18; 1 Cor 15:2; Rom 1:16
1:19 — Is 29:14

1:10 Schism is the tearing of the body into warring parts. The Scripture here does not speak of separation caused by apostasy, but of divisions that arise about matters that are marginal to the gospel. Schism is condemned by God because it is destructive of the unity of His church and contrary to the will of Christ (1:13; 12:13; John 17:21–23). The existence of schism reveals carnality of spirit among the brethren (3:3). The great evil of schism is alluded to by Christ in Matt. 12:25, where He describes the downfall of a house divided against itself. Believers are commanded to avoid fellowship with those who create dissension within the body of the church (Rom. 16:17).

"I WILL DESTROY THE WISDOM OF THE WISE,
AND THE CLEVERNESS OF THE CLEVER I WILL SET ASIDE."

20   Where is the wise man? Where is the scribe? Where is the debater of this age? Has not God made foolish the wisdom of the world?

21   For since in the wisdom of God the world through its wisdom did not *come to know* God, God was well-pleased through the foolishness of the message preached to save those who believe.

22   For indeed Jews ask for signs, and Greeks search for wisdom;

23   but we preach [3]Christ crucified, to Jews a stumbling block, and to Gentiles foolishness,

24   but to those who are the called, both Jews and Greeks, Christ the power of God and the wisdom of God.

25   Because the foolishness of God is wiser than men, and the weakness of God is stronger than men.

26   For consider your calling, brethren, that there were not many wise according to the flesh, not many mighty, not many noble;

27   but God has chosen the foolish things of the world to shame the wise, and God has chosen the weak things of the world to shame the things which are strong,

28   and the base things of the world and the despised, God has chosen, the things that are not, that He might nullify the things that are,

29   that no man should boast before God.

30   But by His doing you are in Christ Jesus, who became to us wisdom from God, and righteousness and sanctification, and redemption,

31   that, just as it is written, "LET HIM WHO BOASTS, BOAST IN THE LORD."

See 1.Cor 15 about the centrality of the resurrection

2   And when I came to you, brethren, I did not come with superiority of speech or of wisdom, proclaiming to you the [4]testimony of God.

2   For I determined to know nothing among you except Jesus Christ, and Him crucified.

3   And I was with you in weakness and in fear and in much trembling.

4   And my message and my preaching were not in persuasive words of wisdom, but in demonstration of the Spirit and of power,

5   that your faith should not rest on the wisdom of men, but on the power of God.

C. True wisdom the gift of God

6   Yet we do speak wisdom among those who are mature; a wisdom, however, not of this age, nor of the rulers of this age, who are passing away;

7   but we speak God's wisdom in a mystery, the hidden *wisdom*, which God predestined before the ages to our glory;

8   *the wisdom* which none of the rulers of this age has understood; for if they had understood it, they would not have crucified the Lord of glory;

9   but just as it is written,
"THINGS WHICH EYE HAS NOT SEEN AND EAR HAS NOT HEARD,
AND *which* HAVE NOT ENTERED THE HEART OF MAN,
ALL THAT GOD HAS PREPARED FOR THOSE WHO LOVE HIM."

10   [5]For to us God revealed *them* through the Spirit; for the Spirit searches all things, even the depths of God.

11   For who among men knows the *thoughts* of a man except the spirit of the man, which is in him? Even so the *thoughts* of God no one knows except the Spirit of God.

12   Now we have received, not the spirit of the world, but the Spirit who is from God, that we might know the things freely given to us by God,

13   which things we also speak, not in words taught by human wisdom, but in those taught by the Spirit, combining spiritual *thoughts* with spiritual *words*. (James 3:15)

14   But a natural man does not accept the things of the Spirit of God; for they are

---

Cross references:

1:20 Is 33:18; Rom 1:22
1:21 Gal 1:15; 1 Tim 4:16; Heb 7:25
1:22 Matt 12:38
1:23 Gal 5:11; 1 Cor 2:14
1:24 Rom 1:4; Col 2:3
1:26 Rom 11:29
1:27 James 2:5
1:29 Eph 2:9
1:30 1 Cor 6:11; 1 Thess 5:23; Eph 1:7,14; Rom 3:24
1:31 Jer 9:23,24; 2 Cor 10:17
2:1 1 Cor 1:17
2:2 Gal 6:14; 1 Cor 1:23
2:4 Rom 15:19; 1 Cor 4:20
2:5 2 Cor 4:7; 6:7
2:6 Eph 4:13; Phil 3:15; 1 Cor 1:20; 1:28
2:8 Acts 7:2; James 2:1
2:9 Is 64:4; 65:17
2:10 Matt 16:17; Eph 3:3,5; John 14:26
2:11 Prov 20:27; Jer 17:9
2:12 Rom 8:15; 1 Cor 1:27
2:13 1 Cor 1:17
*2:14 1 Cor 1:18; James 3:15

---

[3]I.e., Messiah   [4]Some ancient mss. read *mystery*   [5]Some ancient mss. use *But*

2:14 The term here is *psychikos*, and designates the man who is dominated by his *psyche* or natural "soul" (that individuality or life-principle that man shares with animals, although his soul is possessed of a higher order of intelligence). The *psychikos* is the once-born man, the natural, fallen man, dead in trespasses and sins, without hope and without God (Eph. 2:1,12). The *natural* man is to be carefully distinguished from what the Bible calls the *carnal* man. The carnal (*sarkikos*) man is a Christian who is not fully surrendered to Christ and who lives largely under the domi-

foolishness to him, and he cannot understand them, because they are spiritually appraised.

15 But he who is spiritual appraises all things, yet he himself is appraised by no man.

16 For WHO HAS KNOWN THE MIND OF THE LORD, THAT HE SHOULD INSTRUCT HIM? But we have the mind of Christ.

3 And I, brethren, could not speak to you as to spiritual men, but as to men of flesh, as to babes in Christ.

2 I gave you milk to drink, not solid food; for you were not yet able *to receive it.* Indeed, even now you are not yet able,

3 for you are still fleshly. For since there is jealousy and strife among you, are you not fleshly, and are you not walking like mere men?

4 For when one says, "I am of Paul," and another, "I am of Apollos," are you not *mere* men?

D. *The apostles: co-workers together*

5 What then is Apollos? And what is Paul? Servants through whom you believed, even as the Lord gave *opportunity* to each one.

6 I planted, Apollos watered, but God was causing the growth.

7 So then neither the one who plants nor the one who waters is anything, but God who causes the growth.

8 Now he who plants and he who waters are one; but each will receive his own reward according to his own labor.

9 For we are God's fellow workers; you are God's field, God's building.

10 According to the grace of God which was given to me, as a wise master builder I laid a foundation, and another is building upon it. But let each man be careful how he builds upon it.

11 For no man can lay a foundation other than the one which is laid, which is Jesus Christ.

12 Now if any man builds upon the foundation with gold, silver, precious stones, wood, hay, straw,

13 each man's work will become evident; for the day will show it, because it is *to be* revealed with fire; and the fire itself will test the quality of each man's work.

14 If any man's work which he has built upon it remains, he shall receive a reward.

15 If any man's work is burned up, he shall suffer loss; but he himself shall be saved, yet so as through fire.

16 Do you not know that you are a temple of God, and *that* the Spirit of God dwells in you?

17 If any man destroys the temple of God, God will destroy him, for the temple of God is holy, and that is what you are.

18 Let no man deceive himself. If any man among you thinks that he is wise in this age, let him become foolish that he may become wise.

2:16
Is 40:13;
John 15:15

*3:1
1 Cor 2:15;
Rom 7:14;
1 Cor 2:14;
Heb 5:13
3:2
Heb 5:12,13;
1 Pet 2:2
3:3
1 Cor 1:11;
Gal 5:20;
James 3:16
3:4
1 Cor 1:12

3:8
Ps 62:12;
Gal 6:4,5
3:9
2 Cor 6:1;
Is 61:3;
Eph 2:20-22;
1 Pet 2:5
3:10
Rom 12:3;
15:20;
1 Cor 15:10
3:11
Is 28:6;
Eph 2:20
3:13
1 Cor 4:5;
2 Thess
1:7-10
*3:14
1 Cor 4:5;
9:17
3:15
Job 23:10;
Jude 23
*3:16
1 Cor 6:19;
2 Cor 6:16

3:18
Is 5:21;
1 Cor 8:2

nation of his fleshly nature (see, e.g., 3:3). But the *natural* man is without spiritual discernment, blinded by the prince of this world (John 12:40; 2 Cor. 4:4; 1 John 2:11). **3:1** Scripture distinguishes between two kinds of Christian walks. One walk is termed *carnal* and the other *spiritual*. The *carnal* believer is a converted believer whose life is fleshly (*sarkinos*) because he is under the domination of the *sarx* or self-relying, self-pleasing nature. Therefore he is not walking in full fellowship with the Lord Jesus nor is he wholly surrendered to the Spirit of God. He is not Spirit-filled, although he should be (Eph. 5:18); nor does his life reflect the fruit of the Spirit (Gal. 5:22,23). The *spiritual* (*pneumatikos*) Christian is one whose life is yielded to God and whose will is in subjection to the will of God. He is filled with the Spirit and men can see the evidences of spiritual vitality, for he produces the fruit of the Spirit in his life. An unbeliever is not spoken of as either *carnal* or *spiritual*. He is called a *natural* (*psychikos*) man. (See 2:14, where he is called the *natural* man.) **3:14** See also note to 2 Cor. 5:10 on the judgment seat of Christ. Salvation is by grace through faith. Rewards are determined according to works performed subsequent to

salvation. Scripture reveals that some will suffer *loss*, entering heaven by the skin of their teeth and with the smell of smoke on their garments (3:15). While works constitute the basis of the reward, yet the reward is of grace and not merit, since all of the believer's works are defective. God, however, judges the intent of the heart (1 Kin. 8:17–19). It should be clearly understood that a self-seeking desire for heavenly rewards has no proper place in the Christian's motivation, since he lives no longer for himself, but for Him who died for him (2 Cor. 5:15). But the rewards have value only as a demonstration of the grace and righteousness of God. The Christian desires them only as a display of the glory of God. **3:16** Paul uses the temple as a figure of the believer's body. Just as the Shekinah glory of God inhabited the Holy Place in the tabernacle and the temple, so the Holy Spirit indwells the believer, whose body becomes the temple of the Holy Spirit. Since the Holy Spirit indwells the believer, his body becomes holy, and care must be exercised not to defile it in any manner. Certainly the most compelling reason to live a life of holiness to the Lord is the fact that the Holy Spirit dwells in the believer.

19   For the wisdom of this world is foolishness before God. For it is written, "*He is* THE ONE WHO CATCHES THE WISE IN THEIR CRAFTINESS";

20   and again, "THE LORD KNOWS THE REASONINGS of the wise, THAT THEY ARE USELESS."

21   So then let no one boast in men. For all things belong to you,

22   whether Paul or Apollos or Cephas or the world or life or death or things present or things to come; all things belong to you,

23   and you belong to Christ; and Christ belongs to God.

E. *The ministry judged by God*

4 Let a man regard us in this manner, as servants of Christ, and stewards of the mysteries of God.

2   In this case, moreover, it is required of stewards that one be found trustworthy.

3   But to me it is a very small thing that I should be examined by you, or by *any* human court; in fact, I do not even examine myself.

4   For I am conscious of nothing against myself, yet I am not by this acquitted; but the one who examines me is the Lord.

5   Therefore do not go on passing judgment before 6the time, *but wait* until the Lord comes who will both bring to light the things hidden in the darkness and disclose the motives of *men's* hearts; and then each man's praise will come to him from God.

F. *The humility of the apostles*

6   Now these things, brethren, I have figuratively applied to myself and Apollos for your sakes, that in us you might learn not to exceed what is written, in order that no one of you might become arrogant in behalf of one against the other.

7   For who regards you as superior? And what do you have that you did not receive? But if you did receive it, why do you boast as if you had not received it?

8   You are already filled, you have already become rich, you have become kings without us; and *I* would indeed that you had become kings so that we also might reign with you.

9   For, I think, God has exhibited us apostles last of all, as men condemned to death; because we have become a spectacle to the world, both to angels and to men.

10   We are fools for Christ's sake, but you are prudent in Christ; we are weak, but you are strong; you are distinguished, but we are without honor.

11   To this present hour we are both hungry and thirsty, and are poorly clothed, and are roughly treated, and are homeless;

12   and we toil, working with our own hands; when we are reviled, we bless; when we are persecuted, we endure;

13   when we are slandered, we try to conciliate; we have become as the scum of the world, the dregs of all things, *even* until now.

G. *The appeal of Paul*

14   I do not write these things to shame you, but to admonish you as my beloved children.

15   For if you were to have countless tutors in Christ, yet *you would* not *have* many fathers; for in Christ Jesus I became your father through the gospel.

16   I exhort you therefore, be imitators of me.

17   For this reason I have sent to you Timothy, who is my beloved and faithful child in the Lord, and he will remind you of my ways which are in Christ, just as I teach everywhere in every church.

18   Now some have become arrogant, as though I were not coming to you.

19   But I will come to you soon, if the Lord wills, and I shall find out, not the words of those who are arrogant, but their power.

20   For the kingdom of God does not consist in words, but in power.

21   What do you desire? Shall I come to you with a rod or with love and a spirit of gentleness?

6I.e., the appointed time of judgment

3:19
Job 5:13;
1 Cor 1:20
3:20
Ps 94:11

3:21
1 Cor 4:6;
Rom 8:32

3:23
1 Cor 15:23;
2 Cor 10:7;
Gal 3:29

4:1
2 Cor 6:4;
1 Cor 9:17;
Rom 11:25;
16:25

4:4
2 Cor 1:12;
Rom 2:13
4:5
Rom 2:1;
2 Cor 10:18;
Rom 2:29

4:6
1 Cor 1:19,
31; 3:19,20;
1:12; 3:4
4:7
Rom 12:3,6

4:8
Rev 3:17,18

4:9
1 Cor 15:31;
2 Cor 11:23;
Rom 8:36;
Heb 10:33
4:10
1 Cor 1:18;
Acts 17:18;
1 Cor 3:18
4:11
Rom 8:35;
2 Cor 11:23-27
4:12
Acts 18:3;
1 Pet 3:9;
John 15:20;
Rom 8:35

4:14
1 Thess 2:11

4:15
1 Cor 1:30;
Philem 10
4:16
Phil 3:17;
1 Thess 1:6;
2 Thess 3:9

4:19
Acts 19:21;
2 Cor 1:15;
Rom 15:32
4:20
1 Thess 1:5
4:21
2 Cor 1:23;
13:10

III. Sexual morality (5:1–7:40)

A. Incest at Corinth

5 It is actually reported that there is immorality among you, and immorality of such a kind as does not exist even among the Gentiles, that someone has his father's wife.

2 And you have become arrogant, and have not mourned instead, in order that the one who had done this deed might be removed from your midst.

3 For I, on my part, though absent in body but present in spirit, have already judged him who has so committed this, as though I were present.

4 In the name of our Lord Jesus, when you are assembled, and I with you in spirit, with the power of our Lord Jesus,

5 *I have decided* to deliver such a one to Satan for the destruction of his flesh, that his spirit may be saved in the day of the Lord [7]Jesus.

B. *The duty to perform*

6 Your boasting is not good. Do you not know that a little leaven leavens the whole lump *of dough*?

7 Clean out the old leaven, that you may be a new lump, just as you are *in fact* unleavened. For Christ our Passover also has been sacrificed.

8 Let us therefore celebrate the feast, not with old leaven, nor with the leaven of malice and wickedness, but with the unleavened bread of sincerity and truth.

C. *The command to follow*

9 I wrote you in my letter not to associate with immoral people;

10 *I did* not at all *mean* with the immoral people of this world, or with the covetous and swindlers, or with idolaters; for then you would have to go out of the world.

11 But actually, I wrote to you not to associate with any so-called brother if he should be an immoral person, or covetous, or an idolater, or a reviler, or a drunkard, or a swindler—not even to eat with such a one.

12 For what have I to do with judging outsiders? Do you not judge those who are within *the church*?

13 But those who are outside, God judges. REMOVE THE WICKED MAN FROM AMONG YOURSELVES.

D. *Lawsuits and the Christian*

6 Does any one of you, when he has a case against his neighbor, dare to go to law before the unrighteous, and not before the saints?

2 Or do you not know that the saints will judge the world? And if the world is judged by you, are you not competent *to constitute* the smallest law courts?

3 Do you not know that we shall judge angels? How much more, matters of this life?

4 If then you have law courts dealing with matters of this life, do you appoint them as judges who are of no account in the church?

5 I say *this* to your shame. *Is it* so, *that* there is not among you one wise man who will be able to decide between his brethren,

6 but brother goes to law with brother, and that before unbelievers?

7 Actually, then, it is already a defeat for you, that you have lawsuits with one another. Why not rather be wronged? Why not rather be defrauded?

8 On the contrary, you yourselves wrong and defraud, and that *your* brethren.

E. *Kingdom standards*

9 Or do you not know that the unrighteous shall not inherit the kingdom of

[7]Some ancient mss. do not contain *Jesus*

Cross references (left margin):

5:1 Lev 18:8; Deut 22:30; 2 Cor 7:12
5:2 1 Cor 4:18; 2 Cor 7:7
5:3 Col 2:5
5:4 2 Thess 3:6; 2 Cor 2:10
5:5 1 Tim 1:20
5:6 James 4:16; Gal 5:9
*5:7 1 Pet 1:19
5:8 Deut 16:3; Mark 8:15
5:9 2 Cor 6:14; Eph 5:11; 2 Thess 3:14
5:10 1 Cor 10:27
*5:11 2 Thess 3:6; 1 Cor 10:7, 14,20,21
5:12 Mark 4:11; 1 Cor 6:1-4
5:13 Deut 13:5; 21:21
6:1 Matt 18:17
6:2 Dan 7:22; Matt 19:28; Luke 22:30
6:4 1 Cor 5:12
6:5 1 Cor 15:34; Acts 1:15
6:6 2 Cor 6:14,15
6:7 Matt 5:39,40; Rom 12:17
6:8 1 Thess 4:6
6:9 Gal 5:21; 1 Tim 1:10; Rev 22:15

5:7 Christ is called the Passover or Paschal lamb. This speaks of the fulfillment of the Old Testament type of the sacrificial lamb that foreshadowed Christ and His atoning sacrifice. (Here read the note to Ex. 12:11 on Passover.) **5:11** Scripture admonishes true believers to have no fellowship with the wicked works of darkness. Thus Paul lists here those sins that should cause believers to have no fellow-ship with so-called Christians who practice them. So strong is his warning against fellowship with them that he commands that they be driven from their midst (v. 13). Just as people having communicable diseases are isolated to keep them from infecting others, so Paul would protect believers by isolating these wicked persons from them.

God? Do not be deceived; neither fornicators, nor idolaters, nor adulterers, nor [8]effeminate, nor homosexuals,

10   nor thieves, nor *the* covetous, nor drunkards, nor revilers, nor swindlers, shall inherit the kingdom of God.

11   And such were some of you; but you were washed, but you were sanctified, but you were justified in the name of the Lord Jesus Christ, and in the Spirit of our God.

F. Chastity

12   All things are lawful for me, but not all things are profitable. All things are lawful for me, but I will not be mastered by anything.

13   Food is for the stomach, and the stomach is for food; but God will do away with both of them. Yet the body is not for immorality, but for the Lord; and the Lord is for the body.

14   Now God has not only raised the Lord, but will also raise us up through His power.

15   Do you not know that your bodies are members of Christ? Shall I then take away the members of Christ and make them members of a harlot? May it never be!

16   Or do you not know that the one who joins himself to a harlot is one body *with her?* For He says, "THE TWO WILL BECOME ONE FLESH."

17   But the one who joins himself to the Lord is one spirit *with Him.*

18   Flee immorality. Every *other* sin that a man commits is outside the body, but the immoral man sins against his own body.

19   Or do you not know that your body is a temple of the Holy Spirit who is in you, whom you have from God, and that you are not your own?

20   For you have been bought with a price: therefore glorify God in your body.

G. Marriage and celibacy

1. *Principles of marriage*

7 Now concerning the things about which you wrote, it is good for a man not to touch a woman.

2   But because of immoralities, let each man have his own wife, and let each woman have her own husband.

3   Let the husband fulfill his duty to his wife, and likewise also the wife to her husband.

4   The wife does not have authority over her own body, but the husband *does*; and likewise also the husband does not have authority over his own body, but the wife *does.*

5   Stop depriving one another, except by agreement for a time that you may devote yourselves to prayer, and come together again lest Satan tempt you because of your lack of self-control.

6   But this I say by way of concession, not of command.

7   [9]Yet I wish that all men were even as I myself am. However, each man has his own gift from God, one in this manner, and another in that.

8   But I say to the unmarried and to widows that it is good for them if they remain even as I.

[8]I.e., effeminate by perversion   [9]Some ancient mss. read *For*

Cross-references (right margin):

*6:11
Eph 2:2;
Col 3:7;
Titus 3:3

6:12
1 Cor 10:23

6:13
Matt 15:17;
Eph 5:23

6:14
Rom 6:5,8;
8:11;
2 Cor 4:14;
Eph 1:19
6:15
Rom 12:5;
1 Cor 12:27
6:16
Gen 2:4;
Matt 19:5;
Eph 5:31
6:17
John 17:21-23;
Gal 2:20
6:18
Rom 6:12;
Heb 13:4;
1 Thess 4:4
6:19
John 2:21;
Rom 14:7,8
6:20
1 Cor 7:23;
1 Pet 1:18,19;
Rev 5:9
7:1
vv. 8,26

7:3
1 Pet 3:7

7:5
Ex 19:15;
1 Sam 21:4,5;
1 Thess 3:5
7:6
2 Cor 8:8
7:7
v. 8;
1 Cor 9:5;
12:11;
Matt 19:12
7:8
vv. 1,26

6:11 There are two aspects to the Biblical use of the term "sanctification" (*hagiasmos,* from *hagios,* or "holy"). The first aspect refers to that act of grace whereby a believer is at conversion *set apart* from the world (and from self-seeking) to God as His sacred possession. In this sense we have already been perfectly sanctified in the sight of God (Heb. 10:10). The second aspect refers to that process of spiritual growth by which the believer dies more and more to self and sin and lives more and more to Christ and righteousness. Justification and regeneration are "once for all" acts. Sanctification is progressive and continues to the end of one's earthly life. In justification God did something *for* us. In sanctification God does something *in* us. Justification has to do with our *standing* before God; sanctification concerns our *character* and *conduct.* Sanctification proceeds from Father, Son, and Holy Spirit (6:ll; Rom. 15:16; 1 Thess. 5:23; Heb. 2:ll; 13:12). Negatively it implies the putting off of the old;

positively it connotes the putting on of the new (Rom. 6:11,12; Col. 3:5,8,12–17). The ultimate goal is to bring us into conformity to Jesus Christ (Rom. 8:28,29; 1 Thess. 4:3) and to His sinless perfection. Either upon death or at the coming of Christ we shall be made perfect in holiness, for we shall see Him as He is (1 John 3:2).

7:2 Scripture states that a man should have one wife (7:2–4; Gen. 2:24; Mark 10:6–8). As head of the house, man is to have authority over his wife (11:3; Gen. 3:16; Eph. 5:23). A husband has certain duties toward his wife other than the usual ones of support, protection, and care. They are: (1) to love her (Eph. 5:25; Col. 3:19); (2) to live considerately with her (1 Pet. 3:7); (3) to be faithful to her (Prov. 5:19; Mal. 2:14,15); and (4) to live with her for life (Matt. 19:3–9). A husband's duty to his wife precedes his obligations to parents and children; it is second only to his duty to God (Matt. 19:29; Luke 14:26).

7:9
1 Tim 5:14

9   But if they do not have self-control, let them marry; for it is better to marry than to burn.

2. *The Christian and divorce*

7:10
Mal 2:14;
Matt 5:32;
19:3-9;
Mark 10:11;
Luke 16:18

10   But to the married I give instructions, not I, but the Lord, that the wife should not leave her husband

11   (but if she does leave, let her remain unmarried, or else be reconciled to her husband), and that the husband should not send his wife away.

7:12
v. 6;
2 Cor 11:17

12   But to the rest I say, not the Lord, that if any brother has a wife who is an unbeliever, and she consents to live with him, let him not send her away.

13   And a woman who has an unbelieving husband, and he consents to live with her, let her not send her husband away.

7:14
Mal 2:15

14   For the unbelieving husband is sanctified through his wife, and the unbelieving wife is sanctified through her believing husband; for otherwise your children are unclean, but now they are holy.

*7:15
Rom 14:19;
1 Cor 14:33

15   Yet if the unbelieving one leaves, let him leave; the brother or the sister is not under bondage in such *cases*, but God has called [10]us to peace.

7:16
1 Pet 3:1

16   For how do you know, O wife, whether you will save your husband? Or how do you know, O husband, whether you will save your wife?

3. *The status quo*

7:17
Rom 12:3;
1 Cor 4:17;
14:33;
2 Cor 8:18;
11:28

17   Only, as the Lord has assigned to each one, as God has called each, in this manner let him walk. And thus I direct in all the churches.

18   Was any man called *already* circumcised? Let him not become uncircumcised. Has anyone been called in uncircumcision? Let him not be circumcised.

7:18
Acts 15:1,2
7:19
Gal 5:6; 6:15;
Rom 2:25

19   Circumcision is nothing, and uncircumcision is nothing, but *what matters is* the keeping of the commandments of God.

7:20
v. 24

20   Let each man remain in that condition in which he was called.

21   Were you called while a slave? Do not worry about it; but if you are able also to become free, rather do that.

7:22
John 8:32,36;
Philem 16;
Eph 6:6

22   For he who was called in the Lord while a slave, is the Lord's freedman; likewise he who was called while free, is Christ's slave.

7:23
1 Cor 6:20

23   You were bought with a price; do not become slaves of men.

24   Brethren, let each man remain with God in that *condition* in which he was called.

4. *Counsel to the unmarried*

*7:25
2 Cor 8:8,10;
1 Tim 1:13,16

25   Now concerning virgins I have no command of the Lord, but I give an opinion as one who by the mercy of the Lord is trustworthy.

7:26
vv. 1,8

26   I think then that this is good in view of the present distress, that it is good for a man to remain as he is.

27   Are you bound to a wife? Do not seek to be released. Are you released from a wife? Do not seek a wife.

28   But if you should marry, you have not sinned; and if a virgin should marry, she has not sinned. Yet such will have trouble in this life, and I am trying to spare you.

7:29
Rom 13:11,
12; v. 31

29   But this I say, brethren, the time has been shortened, so that from now on those who have wives should be as though they had none;

30   and those who weep, as though they did not weep; and those who rejoice, as though they did not rejoice; and those who buy, as though they did not possess;

7:31
1 Cor 9:18;
1 John 2:17

31   and those who use the world, as though they did not make full use of it; for the form of this world is passing away.

---

[10]Some ancient mss. read *you*

7:15 See note to Deut. 24:1 on divorce.
7:25 Paul did not belittle marriage. Indeed he entertained the very highest views of the marital estate (Eph. 5:22–33). Nor did he suggest that to remain single was, in his judgment, best for all men at all times. By way of advice (not command) he urged remaining single at that time because of the *present distress*. It was wise for those who had the gift of continence and a sincere purpose of devoting themselves to Christian service to refrain from marriage and its involvements. Presumably the *present distress* (v. 26) referred to the terrible persecutions that were to come, when Christians might be put under undue pressures to forswear Christ in order to save their wives and children from brutal torture and death. Or it may have been a reference to the imminent end of the age (vv. 28,31b). In any case, this recommendation was not meant to be binding on all Christians for all time.

32   But I want you to be free from concern. One who is unmarried is concerned about the things of the Lord, how he may please the Lord;

7:32
1 Tim 5:5

33   but one who is married is concerned about the things of the world, how he may please his [11]wife,

34   and *his interests* are divided. And the woman who is unmarried, and the virgin, is concerned about the things of the Lord, that she may be holy both in body and spirit; but one who is married is concerned about the things of the world, how she may please her husband.

7:34
Luke 10:40

35   And this I say for your own benefit; not to put a restraint upon you, but to promote what is seemly, and *to secure* undistracted devotion to the Lord.

5. *Asceticism and marriage*

36   But if any man thinks that he is acting unbecomingly toward his virgin *daughter*, if she should be of full age, and if it must be so, let him do what he wishes, he does not sin; let her marry.

37   But he who stands firm in his heart, being under no constraint, but has authority over his own will, and has decided this in his own heart, to keep his own virgin *daughter*, he will do well.

38   So then both he who gives his own virgin *daughter* in marriage does well, and he who does not give her in marriage will do better.

7:38
Heb 13:4

6. *Counsel to widows*

39   A wife is bound as long as her husband lives; but if her husband is dead, she is free to be married to whom she wishes, only in the Lord.

7:39
Rom 7:2;
2 Cor 6:14

40   But in my opinion she is happier if she remains as she is; and I think that I also have the Spirit of God.

7:40
v. 25

IV. *Christian liberty (8:1–11:1)*

A. *Food offered to idols*

8 Now concerning things sacrificed to idols, we know that we all have knowledge. Knowledge makes arrogant, but love edifies.

*8:1
Acts 15:20;
Rom 15:14;
14:3,10

2   If anyone supposes that he knows anything, he has not yet known as he ought to know;

8:2
1 Cor 3:18;
13:8,9,12;
1 Tim 6:4

3   but if anyone loves God, he is known by Him.

8:3
Gal 4:9;
Rom 8:29

4   Therefore concerning the eating of things sacrificed to idols, we know that [12]there is no such thing as an idol in the world, and that there is no God but one.

8:4
1 Cor 10:19;
Deut 6:4;
Eph 4:6

5   For even if there are so-called gods whether in heaven or on earth, as indeed there are many gods and many lords,

6   yet for us there is *but* one God, the Father, from whom are all things, and we *exist* for Him; and one Lord, Jesus Christ, by whom are all things, and we *exist* through Him.

8:6
Mal 2:10;
Rom 11:36;
Phil 2:11

7   However not all men have this knowledge; but some, being accustomed to the idol until now, eat *food* as if it were sacrificed to an idol; and their conscience being weak is defiled.

8:7
1 Cor 10:28;
Rom 14:14

8   But food will not commend us to God; we are neither the worse if we do not eat, nor the better if we do eat.

8:8
Rom 14:17

9   But take care lest this liberty of yours somehow become a stumbling block to the weak.

*8:9
Gal 5:13;
Rom 14:1,13,
20

10   For if someone sees you, who have knowledge, dining in an idol's temple, will not his conscience, if he is weak, be strengthened to eat things sacrificed to idols?

8:10
1 Cor 10:28,
32

11   For through your knowledge he who is weak is ruined, the brother for whose sake Christ died.

8:11
Rom 14:15,20

---

[11]Some mss. read *wife. And there is a difference also between the wife and the virgin. One who is unmarried is concerned* . . .
[12]I.e., has no real existence

8:1   In the sacrifice of animals in heathen temples only a token part of the animal was burned in sacrifice, while the remainder was disposed of in meat markets for sale to the public (10:25). Some Corinthian Christians believed that the eating of such meat involved idolatry, since the animal had been offered in idol worship (v. 7). Paul again stresses the fact that food has no moral or spiritual value in itself. Those who were immature in the faith, however, had scruples about this, and it was the strong Christian's responsibility to abstain from what in itself was innocent in order not to hurt his weak brother.
8:9   See note to Acts 16:3.

12 And thus, by sinning against the brethren and wounding their conscience when it is weak, you sin against Christ.

13 Therefore, if food causes my brother to stumble, I will never eat meat again, that I might not cause my brother to stumble.

B. *The law of expediency*

1. *Christian rights acknowledged*

9 Am I not free? Am I not an apostle? Have I not seen Jesus our Lord? Are you not my work in the Lord?

2 If to others I am not an apostle, at least I am to you; for you are the seal of my apostleship in the Lord.

3 My defense to those who examine me is this:

4 Do we not have a right to eat and drink?

5 Do we not have a right to take along a believing wife, even as the rest of the apostles, and the brothers of the Lord, and Cephas?

6 Or do only Barnabas and I not have a right to refrain from working?

7 Who at any time serves as a soldier at his own expense? Who plants a vineyard, and does not eat the fruit of it? Or who tends a flock and does not use the milk of the flock?

8 I am not speaking these things according to human judgment, am I? Or does not the Law also say these things?

9 For it is written in the Law of Moses, "YOU SHALL NOT MUZZLE THE OX WHILE HE IS THRESHING." God is not concerned about oxen, is He?

10 Or is He speaking altogether for our sake? Yes, for our sake it was written, because the plowman ought to plow in hope, and the thresher *to thresh* in hope of sharing *the crops*.

11 If we sowed spiritual things in you, is it too much if we should reap material things from you?

12 If others share the right over you, do we not more? Nevertheless, we did not use this right, but we endure all things, that we may cause no hindrance to the gospel of Christ.

13 Do you not know that those who perform sacred services eat the *food* of the temple, *and* those who attend regularly to the altar have their share with the altar?

14 So also the Lord directed those who proclaim the gospel to get their living from the gospel.

2. *Christian rights surrendered*

15 But I have used none of these things. And I am not writing these things that it may be done so in my case; for it would be better for me to die than have any man make my boast an empty one.

16 For if I preach the gospel, I have nothing to boast of, for I am under compulsion; for woe is me if I do not preach the gospel.

17 For if I do this voluntarily, I have a reward; but if against my will, I have a stewardship entrusted to me.

18 What then is my reward? That, when I preach the gospel, I may offer the gospel without charge, so as not to make full use of my right in the gospel.

19 For though I am free from all *men*, I have made myself a slave to all, that I might win the more.

20 And to the Jews I became as a Jew, that I might win Jews; to those who are under the Law, as under the Law, though not being myself under the Law, that I might win those who are under the Law;

21 to those who are without law, as without law, though not being without the law of God but under the law of Christ, that I might win those who are without law.

22 To the weak I became weak, that I might win the weak; I have become all things to all men, that I may by all means save some.

23 And I do all things for the sake of the gospel, that I may become a fellow partaker of it.

Cross references (margin)

8:13 Rom 14:21; 2 Cor 11:29

9:1 2 Cor 12:12; Acts 9:3,17; 18:9; 22:14; 18; 23:11; 1 Cor 3:6; 4:15

9:2 2 Cor 3:2,3

9:4 1 Thess 2:6; 2 Thess 3:8,9

9:5 1 Cor 7:7,8; Matt 12:46; 8:14

9:6 Acts 4:36

9:7 2 Cor 10:4; 1 Tim 1:18; Deut 20:6; Prov 27:18

9:9 Deut 25:4; 1 Tim 5:18

9:11 Rom 15:27

9:12 2 Cor 6:3; 11:12

9:13 Lev 6:16; Deut 18:1

*9:14 Matt 10:10; Luke 10:7

9:15 Acts 18:3; 2 Cor 11:10

9:16 Rom 1:14; Acts 9:15

9:17 1 Cor 3:8,14; Gal 2:7; Phil 1:16,17; Col 1:25

9:18 2 Cor 11:7; 12:13; 1 Cor 7:31

9:19 Gal 5:13; Matt 18:15; 1 Pet 3:1

9:20 Acts 16:3; 21:23; Rom 11:14; Gal 2:19

9:21 Rom 2:12,14; Gal 3:13; 1 Cor 7:22

9:14 Paul was not paid for his ministerial labors. In order to avoid all possible accusation of mercenary motives in propagating this revolutionary new religion, Paul supported himself by plying his trade as a tentmaker. At the same time he insisted that as a matter of principle, both he and all other ministers of the gospel are entitled to wages for their labors. Some have mistakenly concluded that Paul's own example should be binding on all Christian clergymen, but Paul's teaching itself refutes this position as unjustifiable. Galatians 6:6 reiterates what is taught here.

14 Does not even nature itself teach you that if a man has long hair, it is a dishonor to him,

15 but if a woman has long hair, it is a glory to her? For her hair is given to her for a covering.

16 But if one is inclined to be contentious, we have no other practice, nor have the churches of God.

B. *The Lord's Supper*

17 But in giving this instruction, I do not praise you, because you come together not for the better but for the worse.

18 For, in the first place, when you come together as a church, I hear that divisions exist among you; and in part, I believe it.

19 For there must also be factions among you, in order that those who are approved may have become evident among you.

20 Therefore when you meet together, it is not to eat the Lord's Supper,

21 for in your eating each one takes his own supper first; and one is hungry and another is drunk.

22 What! Do you not have houses in which to eat and drink? Or do you despise the church of God, and shame those who have nothing? What shall I say to you? Shall I praise you? In this I will not praise you.

23 For I received from the Lord that which I also delivered to you, that the Lord Jesus in the night in which He was betrayed took bread;

24 and when He had given thanks, He broke it, and said, "This is My body, which [14]is for you; do this in remembrance of Me."

25 In the same way *He took* the cup also, after supper, saying, "This cup is the new covenant in My blood; do this, as often as you drink *it*, in remembrance of Me."

26 For as often as you eat this bread and drink the cup, you proclaim the Lord's death until He comes.

27 Therefore whoever eats the bread or drinks the cup of the Lord in an unworthy manner, shall be guilty of the body and the blood of the Lord.

28 But let a man examine himself, and so let him eat of the bread and drink of the cup.

29 For he who eats and drinks, eats and drinks judgment to himself, if he does not judge the body rightly.

30 For this reason many among you are weak and sick, and a number sleep.

31 But if we judged ourselves rightly, we should not be judged.

32 But when we are judged, we are disciplined by the Lord in order that we may not be condemned along with the world.

33 So then, my brethren, when you come together to eat, wait for one another.

34 If anyone is hungry, let him eat at home, so that you may not come together for judgment. And the remaining matters I shall arrange when I come.

C. *The use of spiritual gifts*

1. *The gifts of the Spirit*

a. *The source of spiritual gifts*

12 Now concerning spiritual *gifts*, brethren, I do not want you to be unaware.

2 You know that when you were pagans, *you were* led astray to the dumb idols, however you were led.

3 Therefore I make known to you, that no one speaking by the Spirit of God says, "Jesus is accursed"; and no one can say, "Jesus is Lord," except by the Holy Spirit.

b. *Varieties of gifts*

4 Now there are varieties of gifts, but the same Spirit.

5 And there are varieties of ministries, and the same Lord.

6 And there are varieties of effects, but the same God who works all things in all *persons*.

7 But to each one is given the manifestation of the Spirit for the common good.

[14]Some ancient mss. read *is broken*

11:16
1 Cor 7:17

11:17
vv. 2,22

11:18
1 Cor 1:10-12

11:19
Matt 18:7;
Luke 17:1;
1 Tim 4:1;
Deut 13:3;
1 John 2:19
11:21
2 Pet 2:13;
Jude 12
11:22
1 Cor 10:32;
James 2:6
11:23
1 Cor 15:3;
Matt 26:26-28;
Mark 14:22-24;
Luke 22:17-20

11:25
2 Cor 3:6;
Luke 22:20

11:26
1 Cor 4:5;
John 14:3;
Acts 1:11;
Rev 1:7
11:27
Heb 10:29
11:28
2 Cor 13:5

11:31
Ps 32:5;
1 John 1:9
11:32
Ps 94:12;
Heb 12:7-10;
1 Cor 1:20
11:34
vv. 21,22;
1 Cor 4:19

12:1
1 Cor 14:1,
37; Rom 1:13
12:2
Eph 2:11,12;
1 Pet 4:3;
1 Thess 1:9;
Ps 115:5
12:3
1 John 4:2,3;
Rom 9:3;
10:9
12:4
Rom 12:4-7;
Heb 2:4
12:5
Eph 4:11

12:7
Eph 4:7

12:8
1 Cor 2:6,7;
Rom 15:4;
2 Cor 8:7
12:9
Matt 17:19,
20;
2 Cor 4:13;
vv. 28,30
*12:10
Gal 3:5;
Rom 12:6;
1 John 4:1;
Acts 2:4;
1 Cor 13:1
12:11
2 Cor 10:13;
Heb 2:4
*12:12
Rom 12:4;
Gal 3:16
12:13
Eph 2:18;
Gal 3:28;
Col 3:11;
John 7:37-39
12:18
vv. 28,11
12:20
v. 14
12:27
Eph 1:23;
4:12;
Col 1:18,24;
Eph 5:30;
Rom 12:5
*12:28
Eph 4:11;
2:30; 3:5;
Rom 12:6,8;
vv. 9,10
*12:30
v. 10
12:31
1 Cor 14:1,39

8 For to one is given the word of wisdom through the Spirit, and to another the word of knowledge according to the same Spirit;

9 to another faith by the same Spirit, and to another gifts of healing by the one Spirit,

10 and to another the effecting of miracles, and to another prophecy, and to another the distinguishing of spirits, to another *various* kinds of tongues, and to another the interpretation of tongues.

11 But one and the same Spirit works all these things, distributing to each one individually just as He wills.

c. *Unity in diversity*

12 For even as the body is one and *yet* has many members, and all the members of the body, though they are many, are one body, so also is Christ.

13 For by one Spirit we were all baptized into one body, whether Jews or Greeks, whether slaves or free, and we were all made to drink of one Spirit.

14 For the body is not one member, but many.

15 If the foot should say, "Because I am not a hand, I am not *a part* of the body," it is not for this reason any the less *a part* of the body.

16 And if the ear should say, "Because I am not an eye, I am not *a part* of the body," it is not for this reason any the less *a part* of the body.

17 If the whole body were an eye, where would the hearing be? If the whole were hearing, where would the sense of smell be?

18 But now God has placed the members, each one of them, in the body, just as He desired.

19 And if they were all one member, where would the body be?

20 But now there are many members, but one body.

21 And the eye cannot say to the hand, "I have no need of you"; or again the head to the feet, "I have no need of you."

22 On the contrary, it is much truer that the members of the body which seem to be weaker are necessary;

23 and those *members* of the body, which we deem less honorable, on these we bestow more abundant honor, and our unseemly *members come to* have more abundant seemliness,

24 whereas our seemly *members* have no need *of it.* But God has *so* composed the body, giving more abundant honor to that *member* which lacked,

25 that there should be no division in the body, but *that* the members should have the same care for one another.

26 And if one member suffers, all the members suffer with it; if *one* member is honored, all the members rejoice with it.

d. *Specific gifts*

27 Now you are Christ's body, and individually members of it.

28 And God has appointed in the church, first apostles, second prophets, third teachers, then miracles, then gifts of healings, helps, administrations, *various* kinds of tongues.

29 All are not apostles, are they? All are not prophets, are they? All are not teachers, are they? All are not *workers of* miracles, are they?

30 All do not have gifts of healings, do they? All do not speak with tongues, do they? All do not interpret, do they?

31 But earnestly desire the greater gifts.

12:10 For a definition of prophecy see note to Is. 1:1.
12:12 See note to John 17:21 on the communion of saints.
12:28 God calls men to specific offices in His church. This call includes the divine endowments that are given to men for their effectiveness in the work to which they have been called. The Trinity is involved in the bestowal of these enablements. In Eph. 4:11 the offices of the church (apostles, prophets, evangelists, pastors, teachers) are spoken of as gifts of Christ. Here in 12:28 they are called the gifts of God. In 12:8ff. Paul designates the Spirit as the One who gives the gifts of healing, tongues, etc. Hence it follows that these gifts are from the Father and the Son through the agency of the Holy Spirit. A genuine call to the office must carry with it divine enablement to discharge its functions.
12:30 The gift of tongues is referred to several times in the New Testament. At Pentecost the disciples proclaimed the gospel message with other tongues. The gift came from the Holy Spirit *as the Spirit was giving them utterance* (Acts 2:4). Here the gift was in known languages, or at least they were understood by the people who spoke these other languages. In 1 Corinthians the *tongues* are described as ecstatic utterances not corresponding to any known languages but giving direct expression to ineffable emotions and insights of the soul. Such tongues are not to be uttered in the church unless a Spirit-empowered interpreter is at hand to translate these utterances into intelligible discourse (14:28). Paul lists this gift as one of those bestowed by the Holy Spirit, but he classifies it as a lesser gift (12:7-11). Speaking in an unknown tongue cannot, as a matter of principle, be ruled out for the church age, but not all that goes by that name is genuine. Nor is speaking in tongues essential as an evidence of regeneration or sanctification.

And I show you a still more excellent way.

2. *The way of love*

a. *Love superior*

13 If I speak with the tongues of men and of angels, but do not have love, I have become a noisy gong or a clanging cymbal.

2   And if I have *the gift of* prophecy, and know all mysteries and all knowledge; and if I have all faith, so as to remove mountains, but do not have love, I am nothing.

3   And if I give all my possessions to feed *the poor*, and if I deliver my body [15]to be burned, but do not have love, it profits me nothing.

b. *Love defined*

4   Love is patient, love is kind, *and* is not jealous; love does not brag *and* is not arrogant,

5   does not act unbecomingly; it does not seek its own, is not provoked, does not take into account a wrong *suffered*,

6   does not rejoice in unrighteousness, but rejoices with the truth;

7   bears all things, believes all things, hopes all things, endures all things.

c. *Love imperishable*

8   Love never fails; but if *there are gifts of* prophecy, they will be done away; if *there are* tongues, they will cease; if *there is* knowledge, it will be done away.

9   For we know in part, and we prophesy in part;

10   but when the perfect comes, the partial will be done away.

11   When I was a child, I used to speak as a child, think as a child, reason as a child; when I became a man, I did away with childish things.

12   For now we see in a mirror dimly, but then face to face; now I know in part, but then I shall know fully just as I also have been fully known.

13   But now abide faith, hope, love, these three; but the greatest of these is love.

3. *The worth and use of spiritual gifts*

a. *Prophecy versus tongues*

14 Pursue love, yet desire earnestly spiritual *gifts*, but especially that you may prophesy.

2   For one who speaks in a tongue does not speak to men, but to God; for no one understands, but in *his* spirit he speaks mysteries.

3   But one who prophesies speaks to men for edification and exhortation and consolation.

4   One who speaks in a tongue edifies himself; but one who prophesies edifies the church.

5   Now I wish that you all spoke in tongues, but *even* more that you would prophesy; and greater is one who prophesies than one who speaks in tongues, unless he interprets, so that the church may receive edifying.

6   But now, brethren, if I come to you speaking in tongues, what shall I profit you, unless I speak to you either by way of revelation or of knowledge or of prophecy or of teaching?

7   Yet *even* lifeless things, either flute or harp, in producing a sound, if they do not produce a distinction in the tones, how will it be known what is played on the flute or on the harp?

8   For if the bugle produces an indistinct sound, who will prepare himself for battle?

9   So also you, unless you utter by the tongue speech that is clear, how will it be known what is spoken? For you will be speaking into the air.

10   There are, perhaps, a great many kinds of languages in the world, and no *kind* is without meaning.

11   If then I do not know the meaning of the language, I shall be to the one who speaks a barbarian, and the one who speaks will be a barbarian to me.

12   So also you, since you are zealous of spiritual *gifts*, seek to abound for the edification of the church.

13   Therefore let one who speaks in a tongue pray that he may interpret.

[15]Some ancient mss. read *that I may boast*

13:2
Acts 13:1;
1 Cor 14:1;
Matt 7:22;
1 Cor 12:9;
Matt 17:20;
21:21
13:3
Matt 6:2

13:4
Prov 10:12;
1 Pet 4:8
13:5
1 Cor 10:24;
2 Cor 5:19
13:6
2 John 4
13:7
Rom 15:1;
1 Cor 9:12

13:8
vv. 1,2

13:9
1 Cor 8:2

13:12
2 Cor 5:7;
Phil 3:12;
1 John 3:2;
1 Cor 8:3
13:13
1 Cor 16:14

14:1
1 Cor 16:14;
12:31; 12:1;
13:2
14:2
Acts 10:46;
1 Cor 12:10,
28,30; 13:1
14:3
vv. 5,12,17,
26; Acts 4:36

14:5
Num 11:29

14:6
v. 26;
1 Cor 12:8;
Rom 6:17

14:8
Num 10:9
14:9
1 Cor 9:26

14:11
Acts 28:2
14:12
vv. 4,5,17,26

14:15
Eph 5:19;
Col 3:16
14:16
1 Chr 16:36;
Ps 106:48;
Matt 15:36;
1 Cor 11:24
14:17
Rom 14:19

14   For if I pray in a tongue, my spirit prays, but my mind is unfruitful.
15   What is *the outcome* then? I shall pray with the spirit and I shall pray with the mind also; I shall sing with the spirit and I shall sing with the mind also.
16   Otherwise if you bless in the spirit *only*, how will the one who fills the place of the ungifted say the "Amen" at your giving of thanks, since he does not know what you are saying?
17   For you are giving thanks well enough, but the other man is not edified.
18   I thank God, I speak in tongues more than you all;
19   however, in the church I desire to speak five words with my mind, that I may instruct others also, rather than ten thousand words in a tongue.

14:20
Eph 4:14;
Heb 5:12,13;
Ps 131:2;
Rom 16:19;
1 Pet 2:2
14:21
John 10:34;
Is 28:11,12
14:22
v. 1
14:23
Acts 2:13

20   Brethren, do not be children in your thinking; yet in evil be babes, but in your thinking be mature.
21   In the Law it is written, "BY MEN OF STRANGE TONGUES AND BY THE LIPS OF STRANGERS I WILL SPEAK TO THIS PEOPLE, AND EVEN SO THEY WILL NOT LISTEN TO ME," says the Lord.
22   So then tongues are for a sign, not to those who believe, but to unbelievers; but prophecy *is for a sign*, not to unbelievers, but to those who believe.
23   If therefore the whole church should assemble together and all speak in tongues, and ungifted men or unbelievers enter, will they not say that you are mad?
24   But if all prophesy, and an unbeliever or an ungifted man enters, he is convicted by all, he is called to account by all;

14:25
John 4:19;
Luke 17:16;
Is 45:14;
Zech 8:23

25   the secrets of his heart are disclosed; and so he will fall on his face and worship God, declaring that God is certainly among you.

b. *Rules regarding the use of spiritual gifts*

14:26
1 Cor 12:7-10;
2 Cor 12:19;
Eph 4:12

26   What is *the outcome* then, brethren? When you assemble, each one has a psalm, has a teaching, has a revelation, has a tongue, has an interpretation. Let all things be done for edification.
27   If anyone speaks in a tongue, *it should be* by two or at the most three, and *each* in turn, and let one interpret;
28   but if there is no interpreter, let him keep silent in the church; and let him speak to himself and to God.

14:29
1 Cor 12:10

29   And let two or three prophets speak, and let the others pass judgment.
30   But if a revelation is made to another who is seated, let the first keep silent.
31   For you can all prophesy one by one, so that all may learn and all may be exhorted;

14:32
1 John 4:1
14:33
v. 40;
1 Cor 4:17;
11:16
14:34
1 Tim 2:11,
12; 1 Pet 3:1;
Gen 3:16

32   and the spirits of prophets are subject to prophets;
33   for God is not *a God* of confusion but of peace, as in all the churches of the saints.
34   Let the women keep silent in the churches; for they are not permitted to speak, but let them subject themselves, just as the Law also says.
35   And if they desire to learn anything, let them ask their own husbands at home; for it is improper for a woman to speak in church.
36   Was it from you that the word of God *first* went forth? Or has it come to you only?

14:37
2 Cor 10:7;
1 John 4:6

37   If anyone thinks he is a prophet or spiritual, let him recognize that the things which I write to you are the Lord's commandment.
38   But if anyone [16]does not recognize *this*, he is not recognized.

14:39
1 Cor 12:31

39   Therefore, my brethren, desire earnestly to prophesy, and do not forbid to speak in tongues.

14:40
v. 33

40   But let all things be done properly and in an orderly manner.

VI. *The resurrection (15:1–58)*

A. *The fact of the resurrection*

15:1
Gal 1:11;
Rom 2:16;
5:2
15:2
Rom 1:16;
11:22; Gal 3:4
15:3
1 Cor 11:23;
1 Pet 2:24;
Is 53:5-12;
Luke 24:25-27;
Acts 26:22,23

15 Now I make known to you, brethren, the gospel which I preached to you, which also you received, in which also you stand,
2   by which also you are saved, if you hold fast the word which I preached to you, unless you believed in vain.
3   For I delivered to you as of first importance what I also received, that Christ died for our sins according to the Scriptures,

16Some ancient mss. read *is ignorant, let him be ignorant*

4 and that He was buried, and that He was raised on the third day according to the Scriptures,

5 and that He appeared to Cephas, then to the twelve.

6 After that He appeared to more than five hundred brethren at one time, most of whom remain until now, but some have fallen asleep;

7 then He appeared to James, then to all the apostles;

8 and last of all, as it were to one untimely born, He appeared to me also.

9 For I am the least of the apostles, who am not fit to be called an apostle, because I persecuted the church of God.

10 But by the grace of God I am what I am, and His grace toward me did not prove vain; but I labored even more than all of them, yet not I, but the grace of God with me.

11 Whether then *it was* I or they, so we preach and so you believed.

B. *The necessity of the resurrection*

12 Now if Christ is preached, that He has been raised from the dead, how do some among you say that there is no resurrection of the dead?

13 But if there is no resurrection of the dead, not even Christ has been raised;

14 and if Christ has not been raised, then our preaching is vain, your faith also is vain.

15 Moreover we are even found *to be* false witnesses of God, because we witnessed against God that He raised [17]Christ, whom He did not raise, if in fact the dead are not raised.

16 For if the dead are not raised, not even Christ has been raised;

17 and if Christ has not been raised, your faith is worthless; you are still in your sins.

18 Then those also who have fallen asleep in Christ have perished.

19 If we have hoped in Christ in this life only, we are of all men most to be pitied.

C. *The assurance of the resurrection*

20 But now Christ has been raised from the dead, the first fruits of those who are asleep.

21 For since by a man *came* death, by a man also *came* the resurrection of the dead.

22 For as in Adam all die, so also in Christ all shall be made alive.

23 But each in his own order: Christ the first fruits, after that those who are Christ's at His coming,

24 then *comes* the end, when He delivers up the kingdom to the God and Father, when He has abolished all rule and all authority and power.

25 For He must reign until He has put all His enemies under His feet.

26 The last enemy that will be abolished is death.

27 For HE HAS PUT ALL THINGS IN SUBJECTION UNDER HIS FEET. But when He says, "All things are put in subjection," it is evident that He is excepted who put all things in subjection to Him.

28 And when all things are subjected to Him, then the Son Himself also will be subjected to the One who subjected all things to Him, that God may be all in all.

D. *The logic of the resurrection*

29 Otherwise, what will those do who are baptized for the dead? If the dead are not raised at all, why then are they baptized for them?

30 Why are we also in danger every hour?

31 I protest, brethren, by the boasting in you, which I have in Christ Jesus our Lord, I die daily.

32 If from human motives I fought with wild beasts at Ephesus, what does it

[17]I.e., the Messiah

Cross-references (right column)

15:4
Matt 16:21;
Ps 16:8-10;
Acts 2:24,25
15:5
Luke 24:34;
1 Cor 1:12;
Matt 28:17
15:7
Luke 24:33,
36,37;
Acts 1:3,4
15:8
Acts 9:3-8;
1 Cor 9:1;
Gal 1:16
15:9
Eph 3:8;
1 Tim 1:15;
Acts 8:3
15:10
Eph 3:7,8;
2 Cor 11:23;
3:5; Gal 2:8;
Phil 2:13
15:12
Acts 17:32;
23:8;
2 Tim 2:18
15:14
1 Thess 4:14
15:15
Acts 2:24

15:17
Rom 4:25

*15:18
1 Thess 4:16
15:19
2 Tim 3:12

15:20
1 Pet 1:3;
v. 23;
Acts 26:23;
Rev 1:5
15:21
Rom 5:12

15:24
Dan 7:14,27

15:25
Ps 110:1
15:26
2 Tim 1:10;
Rev 20:14
15:27
Ps 8:6;
Matt 28:18;
Heb 2:8
15:28
Phil 3:21;
1 Cor 3:23

15:30
2 Cor 11:26
15:31
Rom 8:36;
2 Cor 4:10;
11:23
15:32
2 Cor 1:8;
Luke 12:19

15:18 Death for the Christian is spoken of as sleep so far as the bodily nature is concerned (see also 1 Thess. 4:14). It is not something to be feared by believers but rather to be welcomed as a promotion to a higher estate. Paul speaks of it as a *gain* (Phil. 1:21). John calls it *blessed* (Rev. 14:13). Believers are at death ushered into Christ's presence (2 Cor. 5:8; Phil. 1:23) and exist in a state of blissful consciousness (Luke 16:19ff.). In joyous fellowship with Him they await the resurrection, when they will live in their glorious resurrection bodies for all eternity (1 Thess. 4:13ff.; Rev. 20:4–6).

profit me? If the dead are not raised, LET US EAT AND DRINK, FOR TOMORROW WE DIE.

33 Do not be deceived: "Bad company corrupts good morals."

34 Become sober-minded as you ought, and stop sinning; for some have no knowledge of God. I speak *this* to your shame.

E. *The nature of the resurrection body*

35 But someone will say, "How are the dead raised? And with what kind of body do they come?"

36 You fool! That which you sow does not come to life unless it dies;

37 and that which you sow, you do not sow the body which is to be, but a bare grain, perhaps of wheat or of something else.

38 But God gives it a body just as He wished, and to each of the seeds a body of its own.

39 All flesh is not the same flesh, but there is one *flesh* of men, and another flesh of beasts, and another flesh of birds, and another of fish.

40 There are also heavenly bodies and earthly bodies, but the glory of the heavenly is one, and the *glory* of the earthly is another.

41 There is one glory of the sun, and another glory of the moon, and another glory of the stars; for star differs from star in glory.

42 So also is the resurrection of the dead. It is sown a perishable *body*, it is raised an imperishable *body*;

43 it is sown in dishonor, it is raised in glory; it is sown in weakness, it is raised in power;

44 it is sown a natural body, it is raised a spiritual body. If there is a natural body, there is also a spiritual *body*.

45 So also it is written, "The first MAN, Adam, BECAME A LIVING SOUL." The last Adam *became* a life-giving spirit.

46 However, the spiritual is not first, but the natural; then the spiritual.

47 The first man is from the earth, earthy; the second man is from heaven.

48 As is the earthy, so also are those who are earthy; and as is the heavenly, so also are those who are heavenly.

49 And just as we have borne the image of the earthy, [18]we shall also bear the image of the heavenly.

50 Now I say this, brethren, that flesh and blood cannot inherit the kingdom of God; nor does the perishable inherit the imperishable.

F. *The Christian's confidence*

51 Behold, I tell you a mystery; we shall not all sleep, but we shall all be changed,

52 in a moment, in the twinkling of an eye, at the last trumpet; for the trumpet will sound, and the dead will be raised imperishable, and we shall be changed.

53 For this perishable must put on the imperishable, and this mortal must put on immortality.

54 But when this perishable will have put on the imperishable, and this mortal will have put on immortality, then will come about the saying that is written, "DEATH IS SWALLOWED UP in victory.

55 "O DEATH, WHERE IS YOUR VICTORY? O DEATH, WHERE IS YOUR STING?"

56 The sting of death is sin, and the power of sin is the law;

57 but thanks be to God, who gives us the victory through our Lord Jesus Christ.

58 Therefore, my beloved brethren, be steadfast, immovable, always abounding in the work of the Lord, knowing that your toil is not *in* vain in the Lord.

[18]Some ancient mss. read *let us also*

15:42 The resurrection body has been the subject of much discussion. Scripture teaches that it is a body analogous in some respects to the earthly body, but with this major difference: the corruption and mortality attached to the mortal body as a consequence of sin will be removed. It will become an immortal, incorruptible, perfected body without any of the limitations imposed by the fall, and as far superior to the mortal body as the grown wheat plant is superior to the seed from which it has sprung.
15:45 The Edenic covenant between God and Adam was conditioned on Adam's perfect obedience. It was thus a covenant of works. Adam, as representative and ancestor of the whole human race, fell from a state of obedience and so broke the indispensable condition of the covenant. What the first Adam did not do, the second Adam did. Christ, as representative and spiritual forefather of the redeemed, obeyed God perfectly and kept the whole law of God. He came to fulfill the divine law (Is. 42:21; Rom. 3:31), and His perfect obedience is contrasted with the disobedience of Adam (Rom. 5:19).

VII. *Personal matters (16:1–24)*

A. *The contribution for the poor*

16 Now concerning the collection for the saints, as I directed the churches of Galatia, so do you also.

2   On the first day of every week let each one of you put aside and save, as he may prosper, that no collections be made when I come.

3   And when I arrive, whomever you may approve, I shall send them with letters to carry your gift to Jerusalem;

4   and if it is fitting for me to go also, they will go with me.

B. *Paul's itinerary*

5   But I shall come to you after I go through Macedonia, for I am going through Macedonia;

6   and perhaps I shall stay with you, or even spend the winter, that you may send me on my way wherever I may go.

7   For I do not wish to see you now *just* in passing; for I hope to remain with you for some time, if the Lord permits.

8   But I shall remain in Ephesus until Pentecost;

9   for a wide door for effective *service* has opened to me, and there are many adversaries.

10   Now if Timothy comes, see that he is with you without cause to be afraid; for he is doing the Lord's work, as I also am.

11   Let no one therefore despise him. But send him on his way in peace, so that he may come to me; for I expect him with the brethren.

12   But concerning Apollos our brother, I encouraged him greatly to come to you with the brethren; and it was not at all *his* desire to come now, but he will come when he has opportunity.

C. *Concluding exhortations, greetings, and benediction*

13   Be on the alert, stand firm in the faith, act like men, be strong.

14   Let all that you do be done in love.

15   Now I urge you, brethren (you know the household of Stephanas, that they were the first fruits of Achaia, and that they have devoted themselves for ministry to the saints),

16   that you also be in subjection to such men and to everyone who helps in the work and labors.

17   And I rejoice over the coming of Stephanas and Fortunatus and Achaicus; because they have supplied what was lacking on your part.

18   For they have refreshed my spirit and yours. Therefore acknowledge such men.

19   The churches of Asia greet you. Aquila and Prisca greet you heartily in the Lord, with the church that is in their house.

20   All the brethren greet you. Greet one another with a holy kiss.

21   The greeting is in my own hand—Paul.

22   If anyone does not love the Lord, let him be accursed. Maranatha.

23   The grace of the Lord Jesus be with you.

24   My love be with you all in Christ Jesus. Amen.

16:1
Acts 24:17;
9:13; 16:6
*16:2
Acts 20:7;
2 Cor 9:4,5
16:3
2 Cor 8:18,19

16:5
Acts 19:21

16:6
Acts 15:3

16:7
Acts 18:21

16:10
Acts 16:1;
19:22;
1 Cor 15:58
16:11
1 Tim 4:12;
Acts 15:33
16:12
Acts 18:24;
1 Cor 1:12;
3:5,6

16:13
Phil 1:27;
2 Thess 2:15;
Eph 6:10
16:14
1 Cor 14:1
16:15
Rom 16:5;
2 Cor 8:4;
Heb 6:10
16:16
Heb 13:1
16:17
2 Cor 7:6,7;
11:9
16:18
2 Cor 7:13;
Phil 2:29
16:19
Acts 16:6;
Rom 16:5
*16:22
Eph 6:24;
Rom 9:3
16:23
Rom 16:20

16:2 Paul lays down the principles of Christian giving: (1) regular or periodic: on the first day of every week; (2) personal: each of you; (3) proportionate: as God prospers the giver; and (4) preventive: so that collections need not be taken hurriedly.

16:22 *Maranatha.* The English translation of this word is "Our Lord, come!" The word itself is a Greek translitera-

tion of the Aramaic *Marana tha.* This short prayer preserves the original language of worship and prayer of the early church, the language spoken by Jesus Himself. The word is found again in an ancient church book of teaching, *The Didache* (10:6), which was written perhaps in the first century of our era.

INTRODUCTION TO

THE SECOND LETTER OF PAUL TO THE

CORINTHIANS

Authorship and Background: Paul's letter to the Corinthians (known to us as 1 Corinthians) did not resolve the problems or reunite the factions. Although the story of the following events is not clearly spelled out, it can in part be reconstructed from 2 Corinthians. Instead of peace and harmony, the badly split church was plunged into greater controversy, and a full-fledged revolt was raised against Paul. Apparently some Jewish Christian leaders arrived, claiming to represent the Jerusalem apostles, and they detracted from Paul's apostolic commission and authority (11:4,5,12,13,20-23). There was one member of the church in Corinth who headed the revolt against Paul (2:5-8), and he evidently led the church, or a large part of it, to repudiate the apostle's leadership and authority.

Paul made a quick trip to Corinth, hoping to settle the controversy; he met with defeat, however, and returned to Ephesus. This seems clear from the references to a recent unhappy visit (2:1; 12:14; 13:1,2). As a result of this painful and humiliating experience, Paul wrote to the church again—his third letter—in stern and severe terms. He referred to this letter in 2:3,4,9; 7:8,12, and it is clear from what he said about it that he was not talking about 1 Corinthians. Has this "stern" letter survived? Some scholars feel that its contents have been preserved in 2 Cor. 10-13, although this opinion is not unanimous.

Paul sent this stern letter to the church, probably by Titus (7:6-8), with instructions for him to return with news from Corinth. After Titus's departure Paul himself went on to Troas, hoping to meet him there; anxious and distressed at not finding him in Troas he went on to Macedonia (2:12,13), where Titus met him (perhaps in Philippi) with good news: the crisis was past and the church was reconciled to Paul. With great joy and deep feeling Paul wrote the church the letter now known as 2 Corinthians, probably from Macedonia in A.D. 56.

A little later, maybe in the same year, Paul journeyed to Corinth, spending three months there (Acts 20:1-3), during which time he wrote to the Romans (cf. Introduction to Romans).

Characteristics: In no letter does Paul bare his feelings as he does in 2 Corinthians: he runs the whole gamut of emotion from hopeless despair to ecstatic joy, as he gives expression to his deep love and concern for his Corinthian brothers. The passionate defense of his apostolic commission and authority in chapters 10-13 is filled with sarcasm, denunciation, threats, and condemnation, and contrasts sharply with the joy and tenderness that overflow in chapters 1-9, a fact that lends some substance to the contention that chapters 10-13 are part of the "stern" letter. In any case, 2 Corinthians reflects a pastor's heart of love, as Paul attempts to guide his people into the paths of love and unity.

Contents:

I. Introduction (1:1-11)

II. The defense of the ministry (1:12-7:16): Paul briefly reviews his past relation with the church and launches into a lengthy and passionate defense of his apostolic commission and ministry (2:14-6:10). Paul is Christ's ambassador, messenger of God's reconciliation of the world to Himself (5:18-20).

III. The collection for the saints (8:1-9:15): Christian giving is the result of Christ's self-giving in our behalf (8:9), and should not be of necessity or compulsion, but out of gratitude and thanksgiving (9:6,7).

IV. Paul's personal defense and appeal (10:1-13:10): Paul defends himself from his opponents' denunciations, condemns their motives, and rebukes the church for being led astray by these false apostles, deceitful workmen, and servants of the devil (11:13-15). He pleads with the Corinthians to repent lest he return with authority and punishment (13:1-10).

V. Conclusion (13:11-14)

THE SECOND LETTER OF PAUL TO THE

CORINTHIANS

I. *Introduction (1:1–11)*

A. *Salutation*

1:1
Col 1:1;
1 Tim 1:1;
1 Cor 1:1

1 Paul, an apostle of Christ Jesus by the will of God, and Timothy *our* brother, to the church of God which is at Corinth with all the saints who are throughout Achaia:

1:2
Rom 1:7;
1 Cor 1:3;
Gal 1:3

2 Grace to you and peace from God our Father and the Lord Jesus Christ.

B. *Thanksgiving*

1:3
Eph 1:3;
1 Pet 1:3;
Rom 15:5

3 Blessed *be* the God and Father of our Lord Jesus Christ, the Father of mercies and God of all comfort;

1:4
2 Cor 7:6,7,
13

4 who comforts us in all our affliction so that we may be able to comfort those who are in any affliction with the comfort with which we ourselves are comforted by God.

1:5
2 Cor 4:10;
Col 1:24

5 For just as the sufferings of Christ are ours in abundance, so also our comfort is abundant through Christ.

1:6
2 Cor 4:15

6 But if we are afflicted, it is for your comfort and salvation; or if we are comforted, it is for your comfort, which is effective in the patient enduring of the same sufferings which we also suffer;

1:7
Rom 8:17;
2 Tim 2:12

7 and our hope for you is firmly grounded, knowing that as you are sharers of our sufferings, so also you are *sharers* of our comfort.

1:8
Acts 19:23;
1 Cor 15:32

8 For we do not want you to be unaware, brethren, of our affliction which came *to us* in Asia, that we were burdened excessively, beyond our strength, so that we despaired even of life;

1:9
Jer 17:5,7

9 indeed, we had the sentence of death within ourselves in order that we should not trust in ourselves, but in God who raises the dead;

1:10
2 Pet 2:9

10 who delivered us from so great a *peril of* death, and will deliver *us*, He on whom we have set our hope. And He will yet deliver us,

1:11
Rom 15:30;
Phil 1:19;
2 Cor 4:15

11 you also joining in helping us through your prayers, that thanks may be given by many persons on our behalf for the favor bestowed upon us through *the prayers of* many.

II. *The defense of the ministry (1:12–7:16)*

A. *Paul's change of plans*

1:12
2 Cor 2:17;
1 Cor 2:4,13

12 For our proud confidence is this, the testimony of our conscience, that in holiness and godly sincerity, not in fleshly wisdom but in the grace of God, we have conducted ourselves in the world, and especially toward you.

13 For we write nothing else to you than what you read and understand, and I hope you will understand until the end;

1:14
1 Cor 1:8

14 just as you also partially did understand us, that we are your reason to be proud as you also are ours, in the day of our Lord Jesus.

1:15
1 Cor 4:19;
Rom 1:11;
15:29

15 And in this confidence I intended at first to come to you, that you might twice receive a blessing;

1:16
1 Cor 16:5-7

16 that is, to pass your way into Macedonia, and again from Macedonia to come to you, and by you to be helped on my journey to Judea.

1:17
2 Cor 10:2,3

17 Therefore, I was not vacillating when I intended to do this, was I? Or that which I purpose, do I purpose according to the flesh, that with me there should be yes, yes and no, no *at the same time?*

1:18
1 Cor 1:9;
2 Cor 2:17

18 But as God is faithful, our word to you is not yes and no.

1:19
Matt 16:16;
1 Thess 1:1;
Heb 13:8

19 For the Son of God, Christ Jesus, who was preached among you by us—by me and Silvanus and Timothy—was not yes and no, but is yes in Him.

20   For as many as may be the promises of God, in Him they are yes; wherefore also by Him is our Amen to the glory of God through us.

21   Now He who establishes us with you in Christ and anointed us is God,

22   who also sealed us and gave *us* the Spirit in our hearts as a pledge.

B. *The reason for the change of plans*

23   But I call God as witness to my soul, that to spare you I came no more to Corinth.

24   Not that we lord it over your faith, but are workers with you for your joy; for in your faith you are standing firm.

2 But I determined this for my own sake, that I would not come to you in sorrow again.

2   For if I cause you sorrow, who then makes me glad but the one whom I made sorrowful?

3   And this is the very thing I wrote you, lest, when I came, I should have sorrow from those who ought to make me rejoice; having confidence in you all, that my joy would be *the joy* of you all.

4   For out of much affliction and anguish of heart I wrote to you with many tears; not that you should be made sorrowful, but that you might know the love which I have especially for you.

C. *Forgiveness of the penitent offender*

5   But if any has caused sorrow, he has caused sorrow not to me, but in some degree—in order not to say too much—to all of you.

6   Sufficient for such a one is this punishment which was *inflicted by* the majority,

7   so that on the contrary you should rather forgive and comfort *him*, lest somehow such a one be overwhelmed by excessive sorrow.

8   Wherefore I urge you to reaffirm *your* love for him.

9   For to this end also I wrote that I might put you to the test, whether you are obedient in all things.

10   But whom you forgive anything, I *forgive* also; for indeed what I have forgiven, if I have forgiven anything, *I did it* for your sakes in the presence of Christ,

11   in order that no advantage be taken of us by Satan; for we are not ignorant of his schemes.

D. *Paul's vindication of his ministry*

1. *A triumphant ministry*

12   Now when I came to Troas for the gospel of Christ and when a door was opened for me in the Lord,

13   I had no rest for my spirit, not finding Titus my brother; but taking my leave of them, I went on to Macedonia.

14   But thanks be to God, who always leads us in His triumph in Christ, and manifests through us the sweet aroma of the knowledge of Him in every place.

15   For we are a fragrance of Christ to God among those who are being saved and among those who are perishing;

16   to the one an aroma from death to death, to the other an aroma from life to life. And who is adequate for these things?

17   For we are not like many, [1]peddling the word of God, but as from sincerity, but as from God, we speak in Christ in the sight of God.

2. *A commended ministry*

3 Are we beginning to commend ourselves again? Or do we need, as some, letters of commendation to you or from you?

2   You are our letter, written in our hearts, known and read by all men;

3   being manifested that you are a letter of Christ, cared for by us, written not with ink, but with the Spirit of the living God, not on tablets of stone, but on tablets of human hearts.

[1]Or, *corrupting*

1:20
Rom 15:8,9;
1 Cor 14:16
1:21
1 Cor 1:8;
1 John 2:20,
27
1:22
Eph 1:13
1:23
Gal 1:20;
1 Cor 4:21;
2 Cor 2:3
1:24
1 Pet 5:3;
Rom 11:20;
1 Cor 15:1
2:1
2 Cor 1:23
2:2
2 Cor 7:8
2:3
2 Cor 12:21;
7:16; 8:22
2:4
2 Cor 7:8,9,
12
2:5
1 Cor 5:1,2
2:6
1 Cor 5:4,5
2:7
Gal 6:1;
Eph 4:32
2:9
Phil 2:22;
2 Cor 7:15;
10:6
2:11
Matt 4:10;
Luke 22:31;
2 Cor 4:4;
1 Pet 5:8
2:12
Acts 16:8;
1 Cor 16:9
2:13
2 Cor 7:5,6;
Mark 6:46;
Rom 15:26
2:14
Rom 6:17;
Eph 5:2;
Phil 4:18;
1 Cor 12:8
2:15
Eph 5:2;
Phil 4:18;
2 Cor 4:3
2:16
John 9:39;
1 Pet 2:7
2:17
2 Cor 4:2;
1:12; 12:19
3:1
2 Cor 5:12;
12:11;
Acts 18:27
3:2
1 Cor 9:2
3:3
Jer 31:33;
Ezek 11:19

3. A ministry of splendor

4   And such confidence we have through Christ toward God.

5   Not that we are adequate in ourselves to consider anything as *coming* from ourselves, but our adequacy is from God,

6   who also made us adequate *as* servants of a new covenant, not of the letter, but of the Spirit; for the letter kills, but the Spirit gives life.

7   But if the ministry of death, in letters engraved on stones, came with glory, so that the sons of Israel could not look intently at the face of Moses because of the glory of his face, fading *as* it was,

8   how shall the ministry of the Spirit fail to be even more with glory?

9   For if the ministry of condemnation has glory, much more does the ministry of righteousness abound in glory.

10   For indeed what had glory, in this case has no glory on account of the glory that surpasses *it*.

11   For if that which fades away *was* with glory, much more that which remains *is* in glory.

12   Having therefore such a hope, we use great boldness in *our* speech,

13   and *are* not as Moses, *who* used to put a veil over his face that the sons of Israel might not look intently at the end of what was fading away.

14   But their minds were hardened; for until this very day at the reading of the old covenant the same veil remains unlifted, because it is removed in Christ.

15   But to this day whenever Moses is read, a veil lies over their heart;

16   but whenever a man turns to the Lord, the veil is taken away.

17   Now the Lord is the Spirit; and where the Spirit of the Lord is, *there* is liberty.

18   But we all, with unveiled face beholding as in a mirror the glory of the Lord, are being transformed into the same image from glory to glory, just as from the Lord, the Spirit.

4. An honest ministry

4 Therefore, since we have this ministry, as we received mercy, we do not lose heart,

2   but we have renounced the things hidden because of shame, not walking in craftiness or adulterating the word of God, but by the manifestation of truth commending ourselves to every man's conscience in the sight of God.

3   And even if our gospel is veiled, it is veiled to those who are perishing,

4   in whose case the god of this world has blinded the minds of the unbelieving, that they might not see the light of the gospel of the glory of Christ, who is the image of God.

5   For we do not preach ourselves but Christ Jesus as Lord, and ourselves as your bond-servants for Jesus' sake.

6   For God, who said, "Light shall shine out of darkness," is the One who has shone in our hearts to give the light of the knowledge of the glory of God in the face of Christ.

5. A tried ministry

7   But we have this treasure in earthen vessels, that the surpassing greatness of the power may be of God and not from ourselves;

8   *we are* afflicted in every way, but not crushed; perplexed, but not despairing;

9   persecuted, but not forsaken; struck down, but not destroyed;

10   always carrying about in the body the dying of Jesus, that the life of Jesus also may be manifested in our body.

11   For we who live are constantly being delivered over to death for Jesus' sake, that the life of Jesus also may be manifested in our mortal flesh.

12   So death works in us, but life in you.

13   But having the same spirit of faith, according to what is written, "I BELIEVED, THEREFORE I SPOKE," we also believe, therefore also we speak;

14   knowing that He who raised the Lord Jesus will raise us also with Jesus and will present us with you.

15   For all things *are* for your sakes, that the grace which is spreading to more and more people may cause the giving of thanks to abound to the glory of God.

Cross-references (left margin):

3:4
Eph 3:12
3:5
2 Cor 2:16;
1 Cor 15:10
3:6
Heb 8:6,8;
Gal 3:10;
John 6:63
3:7
Ex 34:29-35

3:9
v. 7;
Rom 1:17;
3:21

3:12
2 Cor 7:4;
Eph 6:19
3:13
v. 7; Ex 34:33
3:14
Rom 11:7;
Acts 13:15;
v. 6
3:16
Rom 11:23
3:17
1 Cor 15:45;
Is 61:1,2;
John 8:32
3:18
1 Cor 13:12;
2 Cor 4:4,6;
Rom 8:29

4:1
2 Cor 3:6;
1 Cor 7:25
4:2
2 Cor 2:17

4:3
2 Cor 2:12;
3:14;
1 Cor 1:18
4:4
John 12:31;
Col 1:15;
John 1:18
4:5
1 Cor 1:13,
23; 9:19
4:6
Gen 1:3;
2 Pet 1:19

4:7
2 Cor 5:1;
1 Cor 2:5
4:8
2 Cor 7:5;
6:12
4:9
John 15:20;
Heb 13:5;
Ps 37:24
4:10
Gal 6:17;
Rom 8:17
4:11
Rom 8:36
4:12
2 Cor 13:9
4:13
Ps 116:10
4:14
1 Thess 4:14

16   Therefore we do not lose heart, but though our outer man is decaying, yet our inner man is being renewed day by day.

17   For momentary, light affliction is producing for us an eternal weight of glory far beyond all comparison,

18   while we look not at the things which are seen, but at the things which are not seen; for the things which are seen are temporal, but the things which are not seen are eternal.

6. *A courageous ministry*

5 For we know that if the earthly tent which is our house is torn down, we have a building from God, a house not made with hands, eternal in the heavens.

2   For indeed in this *house* we groan, longing to be clothed with our dwelling from heaven;

3   inasmuch as we, having put it on, shall not be found naked.

4   For indeed while we are in this tent, we groan, being burdened, because we do not want to be unclothed, but to be clothed, in order that what is mortal may be swallowed up by life.

5   Now He who prepared us for this very purpose is God, who gave to us the Spirit as a pledge.

6   Therefore, being always of good courage, and knowing that while we are at home in the body we are absent from the Lord—

7   for we walk by faith, not by sight—

8   we are of good courage, I say, and prefer rather to be absent from the body and to be at home with the Lord.

9   Therefore also we have as our ambition, whether at home or absent, to be pleasing to Him.

10   For we must all appear before the judgment seat of Christ, that each one may be recompensed for his deeds in the body, according to what he has done, whether good or bad.

7. *A dedicated and reconciling ministry*

11   Therefore knowing the fear of the Lord, we persuade men, but we are made manifest to God; and I hope that we are made manifest also in your consciences.

12   We are not again commending ourselves to you but *are* giving you an occasion to be proud of us, that you may have *an answer* for those who take pride in appearance, and not in heart.

13   For if we are beside ourselves, it is for God; if we are of sound mind, it is for you.

14   For the love of Christ controls us, having concluded this, that one died for all, therefore all died;

15   and He died for all, that they who live should no longer live for themselves, but for Him who died and rose again on their behalf.

16   Therefore from now on we recognize no man according to the flesh; even though we have known Christ according to the flesh, yet now we know *Him thus* no longer.

17   Therefore if any man is in Christ, *he is* a new creature; the old things passed away; behold, new things have come.

18   Now all *these* things are from God, who reconciled us to Himself through Christ, and gave us the ministry of reconciliation,

19   namely, that God was in Christ reconciling the world to Himself, not

---

Cross-references (right margin):

4:16 Rom 7:22; Col 3:10
4:17 Rom 8:18; 1 Pet 1:6
4:18 Rom 8:24; Heb 11:1
5:1 2 Pet 1:13,14
5:2 Rom 8:23; v. 4
5:4 1 Cor 15:53, 54
5:5 Rom 8:23; 2 Cor 1:22
5:6 Heb 11:13,14
5:7 1 Cor 13:12
5:8 Phil 1:23
*5:10 Rom 14:10; Eph 6:8
5:11 Heb 10:31; Jude 23; 2 Cor 4:2
5:12 2 Cor 3:1; 1:14
5:13 2 Cor 11:1, 16,17
5:14 Acts 18:5; Rom 5:15; Gal 2:20
5:15 Rom 14:7-9
5:16 2 Cor 11:18; Phil 3:4; John 8:15
5:17 Rom 16:7; Gal 5:6; Rev 21:4,5
*5:18 Col 1:20; Rom 5:10

5:3 Paul speaks here of the body as an *earthly tent* (v. 1), which is struck down at death; in its place the believer awaits the spiritual house, *eternal in the heavens,* which God has prepared for him (v. 1). It is Paul's deep desire to be clothed with the heavenly dwelling and thus escape the "nakedness" of the bodiless state at death. Notwithstanding his deep anxiety (v. 4), he knows that God will do all things well, for He has given the Spirit as pledge and security that man's mortality will be swallowed up by God's life.
5:10 There is a judgment appointed for believers, which takes place at the coming of the Lord (see also 1 Cor. 4:5; 2 Tim. 4:8; Rev. 22:12). The works of all believers will be reviewed. Note that: (1) all believers must appear (see also Rom. 14:12); (2) each must render an account for himself

(Rom. 14:12); (3) both good deeds and bad must be reviewed; (4) rewards will be given according to what one has done (Rev. 22:12); and (5) some will receive no reward but will only be saved as by fire (1 Cor. 3:12–15).
5:18 Several times the New Testament says that we are *reconciled* to God: (1) through the death of His Son (Rom. 5:10; Col. 1:22); and (2) through the blood of His cross (Eph. 2:16; Col. 1:20). Both in this Corinthian passage and in Romans 5, Paul uses reconciliation and justification as synonymous terms. Man cannot reconcile himself to God but must be reconciled through Christ whose work is appropriated by faith. Those who are reconciled have peace with God and access to Him as His children (Eph. 2:16–18).

counting their trespasses against them, and He has committed to us the word of reconciliation.

20 Therefore, we are ambassadors for Christ, as though God were entreating through us; we beg you on behalf of Christ, be reconciled to God.

21 He made Him who knew no sin *to be* sin on our behalf, that we might become the righteousness of God in Him.

6 And working together *with Him*, we also urge you not to receive the grace of God in vain—

2 for He says,

"AT THE ACCEPTABLE TIME I LISTENED TO YOU,
AND ON THE DAY OF SALVATION I HELPED YOU";

behold, now is "THE ACCEPTABLE TIME," behold, now is "THE DAY OF SALVATION"—

3 giving no cause for offense in anything, in order that the ministry be not discredited,

4 but in everything commending ourselves as servants of God, in much endurance, in afflictions, in hardships, in distresses,

5 in beatings, in imprisonments, in tumults, in labors, in sleeplessness, in hunger,

6 in purity, in knowledge, in patience, in kindness, in the Holy Spirit, in genuine love,

7 in the word of truth, in the power of God; by the weapons of righteousness for the right hand and the left,

8 by glory and dishonor, by evil report and good report; *regarded* as deceivers and yet true;

9 as unknown yet well-known, as dying yet behold, we live; as punished yet not put to death,

10 as sorrowful yet always rejoicing, as poor yet making many rich, as having nothing yet possessing all things.

8. *An exhorting ministry*

a. *A call for sympathy*

11 Our mouth has spoken freely to you, O Corinthians, our heart is opened wide.

12 You are not restrained by us, but you are restrained in your own affections.

13 Now in a like exchange—I speak as to children—open wide *to us* also.

b. *A command to separation*

14 Do not be bound together with unbelievers; for what partnership have righteousness and lawlessness, or what fellowship has light with darkness?

15 Or what harmony has Christ with Belial, or what has a believer in common with an unbeliever?

16 Or what agreement has the temple of God with idols? For we are the temple of the living God; just as God said,

"I WILL DWELL IN THEM AND WALK AMONG THEM;
AND I WILL BE THEIR GOD, AND THEY SHALL BE MY PEOPLE.

17 "Therefore, COME OUT FROM THEIR MIDST AND BE SEPARATE," says the Lord.

Marginal references:

5:20 2 Cor 3:6; Eph 6:20; 2 Cor 6:1
*5:21 1 Pet 2:22; 1 John 3:5; Gal 3:13
6:1 1 Cor 3:9; 2 Cor 5:20; Heb 12:15
6:2 Is 49:8
6:3 Rom 14:13; 1 Cor 9:12; 10:32
6:5 2 Cor 11:23
*6:7 2 Cor 4:2; 10:4; Eph 6:11,13
6:9 Rom 8:36; 2 Cor 1:8-10; 4:10,11
6:10 Rom 8:32; 1 Cor 3:21
6:11 Ezek 33:22; 2 Cor 7:3; Is 60:5
6:13 1 Cor 4:14
6:14 Deut 7:2,3; 1 Cor 5:9,10; Eph 5:7,11; 1 John 1:6
6:16 1 Cor 3:16; Jer 31:1; Ezek 37:27
*6:17 Is 52:11; Rev 18:4

5:21 See note to 1 Pet. 2:24 on substitution.

6:7 Paul speaks of the *weapons of righteousness for the right hand and the left.* The weapon for offense, the sword, was carried in the right hand; that for defense, the shield, in the left hand. These, then, are weapons for offense and defense (see Paul's description of the Christian's armor in Eph. 6:11,13–17).

6:17 Separation from unbelievers and from the world is a policy enjoined by Scripture. Yet it has been misinterpreted and misunderstood by some. The believer is stated to be "in the world" but not "of the world". Separation, therefore, does not consist in leaving the world in a physical sense, whether by isolation, death, or monasticism. Christ Himself was "in the world," but He was not "of the world"; He was not defiled by His contacts with the world. Paul here states that believers are not to fellowship in a compromising relationship with unbelievers, for to do so is to be *bound together* (v. 14), or "unequally yoked" (KJV). This principle undoubtedly involves the following applications: (1) a believer should not marry an unbeliever; (2) he should not choose for his intimate companions those who are not believers; and (3) he should not be in cordial fellowship with those who are theologically apostate. (This, of course, does not preclude contacts such as a missionary might have with infidels for the purpose of converting them to God.) This separation is not simply negative; it has its positive aspects also. One is not only to be separated *from* someone or something; he is also to be separated *to* God. This separation to God will often solve many practical problems. If separation is from people who are unbelievers it is also separation from attitudes and activities that belong to the world and to its system. Hence the Bible teaches that believers are to flee from *the lust of the flesh and the lust of the eyes and the boastful pride of life* (1 John 2:15–17). The Christian must stay away from anything that is evil and cling to everything that is good.

"AND DO NOT TOUCH WHAT IS UNCLEAN;
And I will welcome you.
18   "And I will be a father to you,
And you shall be sons and daughters to Me,"
Says the Lord Almighty.

6:18
Hos 1:10;
Is 43:6

7 Therefore, having these promises, beloved, let us cleanse ourselves from all defilement of flesh and spirit, perfecting holiness in the fear of God.

7:1
2 Cor 6:17,18

c. A plea for fellowship

2   Make room for us *in your hearts;* we wronged no one, we corrupted no one, we took advantage of no one.

7:2
2 Cor 6:12,13

3   I do not speak to condemn you; for I have said before that you are in our hearts to die together and to live together.

7:3
2 Cor 6:11,12

4   Great is my confidence in you, great is my boasting on your behalf; I am filled with comfort. I am overflowing with joy in all our affliction.

7:4
2 Cor 1:4,14;
3:12

d. The joy of good news

5   For even when we came into Macedonia our flesh had no rest, but we were afflicted on every side: conflicts without, fears within.

7:5
2 Cor 2:13;
4:8;
Deut 32:25

6   But God, who comforts the depressed, comforted us by the coming of Titus;

7   and not only by his coming, but also by the comfort with which he was comforted in you, as he reported to us your longing, your mourning, your zeal for me; so that I rejoiced even more.

7:6
2 Cor 1:3,4;
v. 13;
2 Cor 2:13

8   For though I caused you sorrow by my letter, I do not regret it; though I did regret it—*for* I see that that letter caused you sorrow, though only for a while—

7:8
2 Cor 2:2,4

9   I now rejoice, not that you were made sorrowful, but that you were made sorrowful to *the point of* repentance; for you were made sorrowful according to *the will of* God, in order that you might not suffer loss in anything through us.

10   For the sorrow that is according to *the will of* God produces a repentance without regret, *leading* to salvation; but the sorrow of the world produces death.

7:10
Acts 11:18

11   For behold what earnestness this very thing, this godly sorrow, has produced in you: what vindication of yourselves, what indignation, what fear, what longing, what zeal, what avenging of wrong! In everything you demonstrated yourselves to be innocent in the matter.

7:11
2 Cor 2:6;
Rom 3:5

12   So although I wrote to you *it was* not for the sake of the offender, nor for the sake of the one offended, but that your earnestness on our behalf might be made known to you in the sight of God.

7:12
v. 8;
2 Cor 2:3,9;
1 Cor 5:1,2

13   For this reason we have been comforted.
And besides our comfort, we rejoiced even much more for the joy of Titus, because his spirit has been refreshed by you all.

7:13
v. 6;
1 Cor 16:18

14   For if in anything I have boasted to him about you, I was not put to shame; but as we spoke all things to you in truth, so also our boasting before Titus proved to be *the* truth.

7:14
vv. 4,6

15   And his affection abounds all the more toward you, as he remembers the obedience of you all, how you received him with fear and trembling.

7:15
2 Cor 2:9;
Phil 2:12

16   I rejoice that in everything I have confidence in you.

7:16
2 Thess 3:4

III. *The collection for the saints (8:1–9:15)*

A. *The Macedonian example*

8 Now, brethren, we *wish to* make known to you the grace of God which has been given in the churches of Macedonia,

*8:1
Acts 16:9

2   that in a great ordeal of affliction their abundance of joy and their deep poverty overflowed in the wealth of their liberality.

8:2
2 Cor 9:11

3   For I testify that according to their ability, and beyond their ability *they gave* of their own accord,

8:3
1 Cor 16:2

8:1   Paul devotes a lengthy section of this letter to the offering he is carrying to the brethren in Jerusalem (8:1–9:15; see also 1 Cor. 16:1–4). His careful plans, the appointment of trusted men to go with him, and the earnestness of his appeal to the Corinthians by referring to the generosity of the churches in Macedonia (v. 3), show that this offering was more than simply a relief mission. It would be, for the Jerusalem Christians, a demonstration of the oneness of the faith and love that united the Gentile and t¹ Jewish churches into the fellowship of the one bod˙ Christ. (Also see note to 1 Cor. 16:2.)

4   begging us with much entreaty for the favor of participation in the support of the saints,

5   and *this,* not as we had expected, but they first gave themselves to the Lord and to us by the will of God.

6   Consequently we urged Titus that as he had previously made a beginning, so he would also complete in you this gracious work as well.

7   But just as you abound in everything, in faith and utterance and knowledge and in all earnestness and in the [2]love we inspired in you, *see* that you abound in this gracious work also.

B. *The example of Jesus*

8   I am not speaking *this* as a command, but as proving through the earnestness of others the sincerity of your love also.

9   For you know the grace of our Lord Jesus Christ, that though He was rich, yet for your sake He became poor, that you through His poverty might become rich.

10   And I give *my* opinion in this matter, for this is to your advantage, who were the first to begin a year ago not only to do *this,* but also to desire *to do it.*

11   But now finish doing it also; that just as *there was* the readiness to desire it, so *there may be* also the completion of it by your ability.

12   For if the readiness is present, it is acceptable according to what *a man* has, not according to what he does not have.

13   For *this* is not for the ease of others *and* for your affliction, but by way of equality—

14   at this present time your abundance *being a supply* for their want, that their abundance also may become *a supply* for your want, that there may be equality;

15   as it is written, "HE WHO *gathered* MUCH DID NOT HAVE TOO MUCH, AND HE WHO *gathered* LITTLE HAD NO LACK."

C. *The coming of Titus and the messengers*

16   But thanks be to God, who puts the same earnestness on your behalf in the heart of Titus.

17   For he not only accepted our appeal, but being himself very earnest, he has gone to you of his own accord.

18   And we have sent along with him the brother whose fame in *the things of* the gospel *has spread* through all the churches;

19   and not only *this,* but he has also been appointed by the churches to travel with us in this gracious work, which is being administered by us for the glory of the Lord Himself, and *to show* our readiness,

20   taking precaution that no one should discredit us in our administration of this generous gift;

21   for we have regard for what is honorable, not only in the sight of the Lord, but also in the sight of men.

22   And we have sent with them our brother, whom we have often tested and found diligent in many things, but now even more diligent, because of *his* great confidence in you.

23   As for Titus, *he is* my partner and fellow worker among you; as for our brethren, *they are* messengers of the churches, a glory to Christ.

24   Therefore openly before the churches show them the proof of your love and of our reason for boasting about you.

D. *Appeal to their liberality*

9:1
2 Cor 8:4
9:2
2 Cor 7:4;
Rom 15:26;
Acts 18:12;
2 Cor 8:10

9   For it is superfluous for me to write to you about this ministry to the saints;
2   for I know your readiness, of which I boast about you to the Macedonians, *namely,* that Achaia has been prepared since last year, and your zeal has stirred up most of them.

3   But I have sent the brethren, that our boasting about you may not be made empty in this case, that, as I was saying, you may be prepared;

4   lest if any Macedonians come with me and find you unprepared, we (not to speak of you) should be put to shame by this confidence.

5   So I thought it necessary to urge the brethren that they would go on ahead

[2]Lit., *love from us in you;* some ancient mss. read *your love for us*

to you and arrange beforehand your previously promised bountiful gift, that the same might be ready as a bountiful gift, and not affected by covetousness.

E. *God's reward of the liberal giver*

6 Now this *I say,* he who sows sparingly shall also reap sparingly; and he who sows bountifully shall also reap bountifully.

7 Let each one *do* just as he has purposed in his heart; not grudgingly or under compulsion; for God loves a cheerful giver.

8 And God is able to make all grace abound to you, that always having all sufficiency in everything, you may have an abundance for every good deed;

9 as it is written,
"HE SCATTERED ABROAD, HE GAVE TO THE POOR,
HIS RIGHTEOUSNESS ABIDES FOREVER."

10 Now He who supplies seed to the sower and bread for food, will supply and multiply your seed for sowing and increase the harvest of your righteousness;

11 you will be enriched in everything for all liberality, which through us is producing thanksgiving to God.

12 For the ministry of this service is not only fully supplying the needs of the saints, but is also overflowing through many thanksgivings to God.

13 Because of the proof given by this ministry they will glorify God for *your* obedience to your confession of the gospel of Christ, and for the liberality of your contribution to them and to all,

14 while they also, by prayer on your behalf, yearn for you because of the surpassing grace of God in you.

15 Thanks be to God for His indescribable gift!

IV. *Paul's personal defense and appeal (10:1–13:10)*

A. *Paul replies to the charge of weakness and cowardice*

10 Now I, Paul, myself urge you by the meekness and gentleness of Christ—I who am meek when face to face with you, but bold toward you when absent!

2 I ask that when I am present I may not be bold with the confidence with which I propose to be courageous against some, who regard us as if we walked according to the flesh.

3 For though we walk in the flesh, we do not war according to the flesh,

4 for the weapons of our warfare are not of the flesh, but divinely powerful for the destruction of fortresses.

5 *We are* destroying speculations and every lofty thing raised up against the knowledge of God, and *we are* taking every thought captive to the obedience of Christ,

6 and we are ready to punish all disobedience, whenever your obedience is complete.

7 You are looking at things as they are outwardly. If anyone is confident in himself that he is Christ's, let him consider this again within himself, that just as he is Christ's, so also are we.

8 For even if I should boast somewhat further about our authority, which the Lord gave for building you up and not for destroying you, I shall not be put to shame,

9 for I do not wish to seem as if I would terrify you by my letters.

10 For they say, "His letters are weighty and strong, but his personal presence is unimpressive, and his speech contemptible."

11 Let such a person consider this, that what we are in word by letters when absent, such persons *we are* also in deed when present.

12 For we are not bold to class or compare ourselves with some of those who commend themselves; but when they measure themselves by themselves, and compare themselves with themselves, they are without understanding.

B. *Paul stays within the limits of God's appointments*

13 But we will not boast beyond *our* measure, but within the measure of the sphere which God apportioned to us as a measure, to reach even as far as you.

14 For we are not overextending ourselves, as if we did not reach to you, for we were the first to come even as far as you in the gospel of Christ;

9:6
Gal 6:7,9
9:7
Deut 15:7,10;
Ex 25:2;
Rom 12:8;
2 Cor 8:12
9:8
Eph 3:20;
Phil 4:19
9:9
Ps 112:9
9:10
Is 55:10;
Hos 10:12
9:11
1 Cor 1:5,11
9:12
2 Cor 8:14
9:13
2 Cor 8:4;
Rom 15:31;
Matt 9:8;
2 Cor 2:12
9:15
2 Cor 2:14;
Rom 5:15,16

10:1
Gal 5:2;
Rom 12:1
10:2
1 Cor 4:21;
2 Cor 13:2,10
10:3
v. 2
10:4
1 Tim 1:18;
2 Tim 2:3;
Acts 7:22;
1 Cor 2:5;
Jer 1:10
10:5
1 Cor 1:19;
Is 2:11,12;
2 Cor 9:13
10:6
2 Cor 2:9
10:7
John 7:24;
1 Cor 1:12;
14:37
10:8
2 Cor 7:4;
13:10
10:10
1 Cor 2:3;
Gal 4:13,14;
1 Cor 1:17
10:12
2 Cor 3:1;
5:12
10:13
v. 15
10:14
2 Cor 2:12

10:15
Rom 15:20;
2 Thess 1:3

15 not boasting beyond *our* measure, *that is,* in other men's labors, but with the hope that as your faith grows, we shall be, within our sphere, enlarged even more by you,

16 so as to preach the gospel even to the regions beyond you, *and* not to boast in what has been accomplished in the sphere of another.

10:17
Jer 9:24;
1 Cor 1:31
10:18
Rom 2:29;
1 Cor 4:5

17 But HE WHO BOASTS, LET HIM BOAST IN THE LORD.

18 For not he who commends himself is approved, but whom the Lord commends.

C. Paul's fear of false teachers

11:1
vv. 16,17,21;
2 Cor 5:13
11:2
Hos 2:19;
Eph 5:26,27;
2 Cor 4:14
11:3
Gen 3:4;
John 8:44
11:4
1 Cor 3:11;
Rom 8:15;
Gal 1:6-8
11:5
2 Cor 12:11;
Gal 2:6
11:6
1 Cor 1:17;
Eph 3:4;
2 Cor 4:2

11 I wish that you would bear with me in a little foolishness; but indeed you are bearing with me.

2 For I am jealous for you with a godly jealousy; for I betrothed you to one husband, that to Christ I might present you *as* a pure virgin.

3 But I am afraid, lest as the serpent deceived Eve by his craftiness, your minds should be led astray from the simplicity and purity *of devotion* to Christ.

4 For if one comes and preaches another Jesus whom we have not preached, or you receive a different spirit which you have not received, or a different gospel which you have not accepted, you bear *this* beautifully.

5 For I consider myself not in the least inferior to the most eminent apostles.

6 But even if I am unskilled in speech, yet I am not *so* in knowledge; in fact, in every way we have made *this* evident to you in all things.

D. Paul's self-support

11:7
2 Cor 12:13;
1 Cor 9:18
11:8
Phil 4:15,18
11:9
2 Cor 12:13,
14

7 Or did I commit a sin in humbling myself that you might be exalted, because I preached the gospel of God to you without charge?

8 I robbed other churches, taking wages *from them* to serve you;

9 and when I was present with you and was in need, I was not a burden to anyone; for when the brethren came from Macedonia, they fully supplied my need, and in everything I kept myself from being a burden to you, and will continue to do so.

11:10
Rom 9:1;
1 Cor 9:15;
Acts 18:12
11:11
2 Cor 12:15
11:12
1 Cor 9:12

10 As the truth of Christ is in me, this boasting of mine will not be stopped in the regions of Achaia.

11 Why? Because I do not love you? God knows *I do!*

12 But what I am doing, I will continue to do, that I may cut off opportunity from those who desire an opportunity to be regarded just as we are in the matter about which they are boasting.

11:13
Gal 1:7;
2 Pet 2:1;
Phil 3:2
11:15
Phil 3:19

13 For such men are false apostles, deceitful workers, disguising themselves as apostles of Christ.

14 And no wonder, for even Satan disguises himself as an angel of light.

15 Therefore it is not surprising if his servants also disguise themselves as servants of righteousness; whose end shall be according to their deeds.

E. Paul's rightful boasting

1. *The necessity for it*

11:16
v. 1

16 Again I say, let no one think me foolish; but if *you do,* receive me even as foolish, that I also may boast a little.

11:17
1 Cor 7:6,12,
25; Acts 9:24,
25
11:18
Phil 3:3,4

17 That which I am speaking, I am not speaking as the Lord would, but as in foolishness, in this confidence of boasting.

18 Since many boast according to the flesh, I will boast also.

19 For you, being *so* wise, bear with the foolish gladly.

20 For you bear with anyone if he enslaves you, if he devours you, if he takes advantage of you, if he exalts himself, if he hits you in the face.

2. *The grounds for it*

11:21
2 Cor 10:10;
Phil 3:4
11:22
Acts 6:1;
Phil 3:5;
Rom 9:4
11:23
1 Cor 15:10;
Acts 16:23;
2 Cor 6:5

21 To *my* shame I *must* say that we have been weak *by comparison.* But in whatever respect anyone *else* is bold (I speak in foolishness), I am just as bold myself.

22 Are they Hebrews? So am I. Are they Israelites? So am I. Are they descendants of Abraham? So am I.

23 Are they servants of Christ? (I speak as if insane) I more so; in far more

labors, in far more imprisonments, beaten times without number, often in danger of death.

24   Five times I received from the Jews thirty-nine *lashes*.

25   Three times I was beaten with rods, once I was stoned, three times I was shipwrecked, a night and a day I have spent in the deep.

26   *I have been* on frequent journeys, in dangers from rivers, dangers from robbers, dangers from *my* countrymen, dangers from the Gentiles, dangers in the city, dangers in the wilderness, dangers on the sea, dangers among false brethren;

27   *I have been* in labor and hardship, through many sleepless nights, in hunger and thirst, often without food, in cold and exposure.

28   Apart from *such* external things, there is the daily pressure upon me *of* concern for all the churches.

29   Who is weak without my being weak? Who is led into sin without my intense concern?

30   If I have to boast, I will boast of what pertains to my weakness.

31   The God and Father of the Lord Jesus, He who is blessed forever, knows that I am not lying.

32   In Damascus the ethnarch under Aretas the king was guarding the city of the Damascenes in order to seize me,

33   and I was let down in a basket through a window in the wall, and *so* escaped his hands.

12   Boasting is necessary, though it is not profitable; but I will go on to visions and revelations of the Lord.

2   I know a man in Christ who fourteen years ago—whether in the body I do not know, or out of the body I do not know, God knows—such a man was caught up to the third heaven.

3   And I know how such a man—whether in the body or apart from the body I do not know, God knows—

4   was caught up into Paradise, and heard inexpressible words, which a man is not permitted to speak.

5   On behalf of such a man will I boast; but on my own behalf I will not boast, except in regard to *my* weaknesses.

6   For if I do wish to boast I shall not be foolish, for I shall be speaking the truth; but I refrain *from this*, so that no one may credit me with more than he sees *in* me or hears from me.

7   And because of the surpassing greatness of the revelations, for this reason, to keep me from exalting myself, there was given me a thorn in the flesh, a messenger of Satan to buffet me—to keep me from exalting myself!

8   Concerning this I entreated the Lord three times that it might depart from me.

9   And He has said to me, "My grace is sufficient for you, for ³power is perfected in weakness." Most gladly, therefore, I will rather boast about my weaknesses, that the power of Christ may dwell in me.

10   Therefore I am well content with weaknesses, with insults, with distresses,

³Later mss. read *My power*

*11:24
Deut 25:3
11:25
Acts 16:22;
14:19
11:26
Acts 9:23;
14:5; 21:31;
Gal 2:4
11:27
1 Thess 2:9;
1 Cor 4:11;
2 Cor 6:5

11:29
1 Cor 9:22

11:30
1 Cor 2:3
11:31
Gal 1:20;
Rom 9:5
11:32
Acts 9:24,25

12:1
Co 11:30;
v. 7;
Gal 1:12; 2:2
*12:2
Rom 16:7;
Eph 4:10;
2 Cor 11:11

12:4
Luke 23:43

12:6
2 Cor 10:8;
11:16

12:8
Matt 26:44

12:9
Phil 4:13;
2 Cor 11:30;
1 Pet 4:14
12:10
Rom 5:3;
2 Cor 6:4;
2 Thess 1:4

11:24 Paul speaks of having been whipped five times by the Jews with *thirty-nine lashes*. This refers to the beating administered in the synagogue to convicted Jewish offenders. This detail shows that Paul submitted himself to the synagogue discipline even after becoming a Christian: he was no less a Jew for having accepted and confessed Jesus of Nazareth as the promised Messiah and Lord.

The limit was forty lashes (Deut. 25:1–3), but in order not to exceed the limit, only thirty-nine were given. According to the *Mishnah* (tractate "Makkoth"), the prisoner's garments were torn off and he was bound by his hands to two pillars, with arms outstretched. The minister of the synagogue administered the punishment with a triple-thonged whip: twenty-six lashes on the back and thirteen on the breast, while passages from the Old Testament were read. "And he that smites, smites with his one hand with all his might."

12:2 The word *heaven* is used in various senses in the Bible. Often it refers to the abode of God, the place from which Christ came and to which He went at His ascension and from which He is coming again. It is also pictured as the place to which the saints go upon death. Of all the facts concerning heaven the following are of particular interest: (1) it is the place of God's throne (Is. 66:1); (2) Christ our Mediator has entered into heaven (Heb. 6:20; 9:12,24); (3) the angels are in heaven (Matt. 18:10; 24:36); (4) the wicked are excluded from heaven (Gal. 5:21; Rev. 22:15); (5) the saints are rewarded in heaven (1 Pet. 1:4); and (6) here believers are to lay up treasure (Matt. 6:20; Luke 12:33).

12:7 We do not know what Paul's thorn in the flesh was. One thing about it is plain enough: Paul regarded it as having come from Satan, yet he recognized God had permitted it to come into his life and intended to use it for His own glory. It was in the midst of the weakness resulting from this affliction that the power of God was able to manifest itself most conspicuously. It always has been so. Christians in every age find God's sustaining power greater than Satan's ability to afflict them and cast them down.

with persecutions, with difficulties, for Christ's sake; for when I am weak, then I am strong.

F. *The marks of a true apostle*

12:11
2 Cor 11:1,5

11   I have become foolish; you yourselves compelled me. Actually I should have been commended by you, for in no respect was I inferior to the most eminent apostles, even though I am a nobody.

12:12
Rom 15:18,19

12   The signs of a true apostle were performed among you with all perseverance, by signs and wonders and miracles.

12:13
1 Cor 9:12,
18; 2 Cor 11:7

13   For in what respect were you treated as inferior to the rest of the churches, except that I myself did not become a burden to you? Forgive me this wrong!

12:14
2 Cor 13:1;
1 Cor 10:24,
33; 4:14,15;
Prov 19:14

14   Here for this third time I am ready to come to you, and I will not be a burden to you; for I do not seek what is yours, but you; for children are not responsible to save up for *their* parents, but parents for *their* children.

12:15
Phil 2:17;
1 Thess 2:8

15   And I will most gladly spend and be expended for your souls. If I love you the more, am I to be loved the less?

16   But be that as it may, I did not burden you myself; nevertheless, crafty fellow that I am, I took you in by deceit.

17   *Certainly* I have not taken advantage of you through any of those whom I have sent to you, have I?

12:18
2 Cor 8:6,16,
18

18   I urged Titus *to go,* and sent the brother with him. Titus did not take any advantage of you, did he? Did we not conduct ourselves in the same spirit *and walk* in the same steps?

G. *The appeal for repentance*

12:19
Rom 9:1;
2 Cor 10:8

19   All this time you have been thinking that we are defending ourselves to you. *Actually,* it is in the sight of God that we have been speaking in Christ; and all for your upbuilding, beloved.

12:20
2 Cor 2:1-4;
1 Cor 1:11;
3:3

20   For I am afraid that perhaps when I come I may find you to be not what I wish and may be found by you to be not what you wish; that perhaps *there may be* strife, jealousy, angry tempers, disputes, slanders, gossip, arrogance, disturbances;

12:21
2 Cor 2:1,4;
13:2; Gal 5:19

21   I am afraid that when I come again my God may humiliate me before you, and I may mourn over many of those who have sinned in the past and not repented of the impurity, immorality and sensuality which they have practiced.

13:1
2 Cor 12:14;
Deut 19:15;
Matt 18:16

13 This is the third time I am coming to you. EVERY FACT IS TO BE CONFIRMED BY THE TESTIMONY OF TWO OR THREE WITNESSES.

2   I have previously said when present the second time, and though now absent I say in advance to those who have sinned in the past and to all the rest as well, that if I come again, I will not spare *anyone,*

13:3
Matt 10:20;
1 Cor 5:4;
2 Cor 9:8;
10:4

3   since you are seeking for proof of the Christ who speaks in me, and who is not weak toward you, but mighty in you.

13:4
Phil 2:7,8;
1 Pet 3:18;
Rom 6:4,8;
v. 9

4   For indeed He was crucified because of weakness, yet He lives because of the power of God. For we also are weak [4]in Him, yet we shall live with Him because of the power of God *directed* toward you.

13:5
John 6:6;
1 Cor 11:28;
9:27

5   Test yourselves *to see* if you are in the faith; examine yourselves! Or do you not recognize this about yourselves, that Jesus Christ is in you—unless indeed you fail the test?

6   But I trust that you will realize that we ourselves do not fail the test.

7   Now we pray to God that you do no wrong; not that we ourselves may appear approved, but that you may do what is right, even though we should appear unapproved.

8   For we can do nothing against the truth, but *only* for the truth.

13:9
2 Cor 11:30;
12:10

9   For we rejoice when we ourselves are weak but you are strong; this we also pray for, that you be made complete.

13:10
2 Cor 2:3;
Titus 1:13;
2 Cor 10:8

10   For this reason I am writing these things while absent, in order that when present I may not use severity, in accordance with the authority which the Lord gave me, for building up and not for tearing down.

[4]Some early mss. read *with Him*

V. *Conclusion (13:11–14)*

A. *Exhortations and greetings*

11 Finally, brethren, rejoice, be made complete, be comforted, be like-minded, live in peace; and the God of love and peace shall be with you.
12 Greet one another with a holy kiss.
13 All the saints greet you.

13:11
Rom 15:33;
Eph 6:23

13:13
Phil 4:22

B. *Benediction*

14 The grace of the Lord Jesus Christ, and the love of God, and the fellowship of the Holy Spirit, be with you all.

INTRODUCTION TO
THE LETTER OF PAUL TO THE
GALATIANS

Authorship and Background: The questions of the date and the destination of this letter of Paul cannot be answered decisively. As to the first, nothing in the letter itself, or in the book of Acts, determines whether Galatians was written before or soon after the Jerusalem Council in A.D. 49, or a few years later, about the same time Paul wrote to Corinth and Rome, A.D. 55-56. The date depends on whether the visit to Jerusalem described in 2:1-10 is to be identified with that mentioned in Acts 11:30, or in Acts 15:1-29. The "so quickly" in 1:6 seems to favor an earlier and not a later date for the letter.

Who were the Galatians? They were personal acquaintances, among whom Paul had worked (4:13-15). If Acts records Paul's ministry to these people, then they were the residents of the Roman province of Galatia (in the cities of Antioch (of Pisidia), Iconium, Lystra, and Derbe) whom Paul visited during his first missionary journey (Acts 13:14-14:23). Most scholars believe that these were the Galatian churches (1:1) to whom Paul wrote; some, however, hold they were residents of northern Galatia, in and near the cities of Pessinus, Ancyra, and Tavium.

The letter was prompted by the inroads made into the churches by the Judaizers, Jewish Christians who insisted that Gentile converts to the Christian faith should submit to the Jewish rite of circumcision and respect certain ritual distinctions between pure and impure foods. They also attacked Paul personally, saying he was not a true apostle, and thus not on the same footing with the original Twelve, whose authority and prestige they claimed. Paul's gospel, in their eyes, was not the true gospel. Apparently their attempts met with considerable success: the inexperienced Galatians, impressed by their arguments and awed by their credentials, succumbed to their demands. Some, submitting themselves to Jewish legalism (4:21), began to observe Jewish religious feasts (4:10,11) and accept circumcision (5:2-6).

Confronted with this grave danger to the spiritual welfare of the Galatian Christians, Paul wrote, warning, expounding, and pleading with them to resist the blandishments of the Judaizers.

Characteristics: The letter to the Galatians may rightly be called the *Magna Charta* of Christian liberty. Against all attempts to shackle Christian freedom with Jewish legalism, Paul stands firm: such an attempt is, in his thinking, nothing less than a complete perversion of the true gospel, a different, alien gospel (1:6-9). Those who follow this false gospel are apart from Christ and His grace (5:4). Paul's great theme is eloquently stated: the free and sovereign grace of God, by which man is justified, is through faith alone, not by works of the law (2:15,16,21). Christ's death meant that the law is not a means of salvation, and in sharing his death believers also die to the law; for were the law operative as a means of salvation, then Christ's death was useless (3:13,14; 2:20,21). Even Abraham was justified by faith, not by works of law (3:6-9); and it was the prophet Habakkuk (Hab. 2:4) who declared that life belongs to him who has been justified through faith (3:11). The law was never a means of justification: Abraham was justified by faith 430 years before the law (3:16-19), and we are his spiritual descendants, sons, and heirs (3:29-4:7). Christ gives us freedom: let us stand fast and not fall under the yoke of slavery (5:1)!

Contents:

I. Introduction (1:1-10)

II. Paul's apostolic authority (1:11-2:21): Paul's apostleship is from God, and his gospel came through a revelation of Jesus Christ. His conversion and Christian ministry show that he is not inferior in authority to the apostles in Jerusalem.

III. Paul's doctrine of justification (3:1-4:31): Abraham's experience (3:6-9,15-18), Christ's death on the cross (3:13,14), God's gift of the Spirit (4:6,7)—all prove that salvation is a gift by grace through faith, not achieved through works of the law. We are no longer slaves, but sons and heirs.

IV. The effect of Christian liberty (5:1-6:10): The freedom to which we are called is not license; it is the freedom of sons and heirs, enabling us to love one another and live lives of self-control and purity, by the power of the Holy Spirit.

V. Conclusion (6:11-18)

THE LETTER OF PAUL TO THE

GALATIANS

I. *Introduction (1:1–10)*

A. *Salutation*

1:1
2 Cor 1:1;
vv. 11,12;
Acts 9:6; 2:24

1 Paul, an apostle (not *sent* from men, nor through the agency of man, but through Jesus Christ, and God the Father, who raised Him from the dead),

2   and all the brethren who are with me, to the churches of Galatia:

1:2
Phil 4:21;
1 Cor 16:1

3   Grace to you and peace from God our Father, and the Lord Jesus Christ,

1:3
Rom 1:7

4   who gave Himself for our sins, that He might deliver us out of this present evil age, according to the will of our God and Father,

1:4
Rom 4:25;
Gal 2:20;
2 Cor 4:4

5   to whom *be* the glory forevermore. Amen.

1:5
Rom 16:27

B. *The occasion of the letter*

*1:6
Gal 5:8;
2 Cor 11:4

6 I am amazed that you are so quickly deserting Him who called you by the grace of Christ, for a different gospel;

1:7
Acts 15:24;
Gal 5:10

7   which is *really* not another; only there are some who are disturbing you, and want to distort the gospel of Christ.

*1:8
2 Cor 11:4,
14; Rom 9:3

8   But even though we, or an angel from heaven, should preach to you a gospel contrary to that which we have preached to you, let him be accursed.

1:9
Rom 16:17

9   As we have said before, so I say again now, if any man is preaching to you a gospel contrary to that which you received, let him be accursed.

1:10
1 Thess 2:4

10   For am I now seeking the favor of men, or of God? Or am I striving to please men? If I were still trying to please men, I would not be a bond-servant of Christ.

II. *Paul's apostolic authority (1:11–2:21)*

A. *Of divine origin*

1:11
1 Cor 15:1

11 For I would have you know, brethren, that the gospel which was preached by me is not according to man.

1:12
vv. 1,16;
Eph 3:3

12   For I neither received it from man, nor was I taught it, but *I received it* through a revelation of Jesus Christ.

1:13
Acts 8:3; 9:21

13   For you have heard of my former manner of life in Judaism, how I used to persecute the church of God beyond measure, and tried to destroy it;

1:14
Acts 22:3;
Col 2:8

14   and I was advancing in Judaism beyond many of my contemporaries among my countrymen, being more extremely zealous for my ancestral traditions.

1:15
Is 49:1,5;
Jer 1:5;
Acts 9:15;
Rom 1:1

15   But when He who had set me apart, *even* from my mother's womb, and called me through His grace, was pleased

1:16
Acts 9:20;
Eph 6:12

16   to reveal His Son in me, that I might preach Him among the Gentiles, I did not immediately consult with flesh and blood,

17   nor did I go up to Jerusalem to those who were apostles before me; but I went away to Arabia, and returned once more to Damascus.

B. *Independent of the apostles*

*1:18
Acts 9:22,23,
26,27

18 Then three years later I went up to Jerusalem to become acquainted with Cephas, and stayed with him fifteen days.

1:6 Paul's feelings are evident. He writes in the white heat of an emotion compounded of sorrow, astonishment, and indignation, as he contemplates the possible defection of his beloved Galatians. His indignation is vividly stated in the anathema he calls down on those who pervert the gospel (1:7–9), and in the surgery he recommends to those who are so eager to practice their doctrine of circumcision (5:12). His astonishment at the attitude of the Galatian converts runs through the whole letter (1:6; 3:1–5; 4:12–16), while his deep love is expressed in tender terms (4:19). Paul's emotion is caused by his conviction that his readers were running the risk of deserting the gospel, defecting from Christ, and falling away from grace (1:6; 4:9; 5:4). This was no trifling question of doctrinal hairsplitting: it was a matter of life and death.

1:8 *Accursed* is from the Greek word *anathema* now in the English language. Traditionally, an anathema was pronounced against an individual by ecclesiastical authority, and it was accompanied by excommunication.

1:18 *Cephas* is the Aramaic form of the Greek name *Peter*,

19   But I did not see any other of the apostles except James, the Lord's brother.

20   (Now in what I am writing to you, I assure you before God that I am not lying.)

21   Then I went into the regions of Syria and Cilicia.

22   And I was *still* unknown by sight to the churches of Judea which were in Christ;

23   but only, they kept hearing, "He who once persecuted us is now preaching the faith which he once tried to destroy."

24   And they were glorifying God because of me.

C. *Accepted by the church*

2 Then after an interval of fourteen years I went up again to Jerusalem with Barnabas, taking Titus along also.

2   And it was because of a revelation that I went up; and I submitted to them the gospel which I preach among the Gentiles, but *I did so* in private to those who were of reputation, for fear that I might be running, or had run, in vain.

3   But not even Titus who was with me, though he was a Greek, was compelled to be circumcised.

4   But *it was* because of the false brethren who had sneaked in to spy out our liberty which we have in Christ Jesus, in order to bring us into bondage.

5   But we did not yield in subjection to them for even an hour, so that the truth of the gospel might remain with you.

6   But from those who were of high reputation (what they were makes no difference to me; God shows no partiality)—well, those who were of reputation contributed nothing to me.

7   But on the contrary, seeing that I had been entrusted with the gospel to the uncircumcised, just as Peter *had been* to the circumcised

8   (for He who effectually worked for Peter in *his* apostleship to the circumcised effectually worked for me also to the Gentiles),

9   and recognizing the grace that had been given to me, James and Cephas and John, who were reputed to be pillars, gave to me and Barnabas the right hand of fellowship, that we *might go* to the Gentiles, and they to the circumcised.

10   *They* only *asked* us to remember the poor—the very thing I also was eager to do.

D. *Demonstrated in conflict with Peter*

11   But when Cephas came to Antioch, I opposed him to his face, because he stood condemned.

12   For prior to the coming of certain men from James, he used to eat with the Gentiles; but when they came, he *began* to withdraw and hold himself aloof, fearing the party of the circumcision.

13   And the rest of the Jews joined him in hypocrisy, with the result that even Barnabas was carried away by their hypocrisy.

14   But when I saw that they were not straightforward about the truth of the gospel, I said to Cephas in the presence of all, "If you, being a Jew, live like the Gentiles and not like the Jews, how *is it that* you compel the Gentiles to live like Jews?

15   "We *are* Jews by nature, and not sinners from among the Gentiles;

16   nevertheless knowing that a man is not justified by the works of the Law but through faith in Christ Jesus, even we have believed in Christ Jesus, that we may be justified by faith in Christ, and not by the works of the Law; since by the works of the Law shall no flesh be justified.

Marginal references:

1:19 Matt 13:55

1:21
Acts 9:30
1:22
1 Thess 2:14;
Rom 16:7

2:1
Acts 15:2

2:2
Acts 15:12;
Gal 1:6;
Phil 2:16

2:3
2 Cor 2:13;
Acts 16:3;
1 Cor 9:21
2:4
Acts 15:1;
2 Cor 11:26
2:5
v. 14; Col 1:5
2:6
Gal 6:3;
Rom 2:11;
2 Cor 12:11

*2:7
1 Thess 2:4;
Acts 13:46

2:9
Rom 12:3;
Gal 1:16

2:10
Acts 11:29,
30; 24:17

*2:11
Acts 11:10

2:12
Acts 11:2,3

2:13
v. 1

2:14
vv. 5,9,11

2:15
Phil 3:4,5;
Matt 9:11
2:16
Acts 13:39;
Rom 1:17;
3:20

---

both of which mean "rock" (cf. John 1:42). The name Cephas is used of the apostle in John 1:42; 1 Cor. 1:12; 3:22; 9:5; 15:5; Gal. 1:18; 2:9,11,14.

2:7 *the gospel to the uncircumcised.* This, entrusted to Paul, and *the gospel to the circumcised* entrusted to Peter are not two different gospels. The gospel is one and the same everywhere: Paul was given a special commission to proclaim it to the Gentiles; Peter to the Jews.

2:11 Paul did not rebuke Peter (Cephas) for entertaining heretical doctrine, but for his failure to practice consistently what he believed. Nowhere did Peter teach that men could

be saved by circumcision (see 2:14), but he withdrew himself from uncircumcised Gentiles because he was pressed to do so by circumcised Hebrew Christians. Presumably he was motivated by a desire to avoid offending prospective Jewish converts. But in this case his policy of expediency amounted to a surrender of basic principle: that salvation is of grace, apart from obedience to the ritual Law of Moses. While Christians should be circumspect and concerned about the consciences of weaker brothers, there are times when conformity to their false scruples involves a betrayal of the gospel. This was one of those times.

2:17
v. 15;
Gal 3:21

2:19
Rom 8:2;
6:14;
2 Cor 5:15;
1 Thess 5:10
2:20
1 Pet 4:2;
Eph 5:2;
Titus 2:14
2:21
Gal 3:21

17 "But if, while seeking to be justified in Christ, we ourselves have also been found sinners, is Christ then a minister of sin? May it never be!

18 "For if I rebuild what I have *once* destroyed, I prove myself to be a transgressor.

19 "For through the Law I died to the Law, that I might live to God.

20 "I have been crucified with Christ; and it is no longer I who live, but Christ lives in me; and the *life* which I now live in the flesh I live by faith in the Son of God, who loved me, and delivered Himself up for me.

21 "I do not nullify the grace of God; for if righteousness *comes* through the Law, then Christ died needlessly."

III. *Paul's doctrine of justification (3:1–4:31)*

A. *The Galatians deceived*

3:1
Gal 1:2; 5:7;
1 Cor 1:23
3:2
Acts 2:38;
Rom 10:16,17
3:3
Gal 4:9;
Heb 7:16
3:4
1 Cor 15:2
3:5
Phil 1:19;
1 Cor 12:10;
Rom 10:17

3 You foolish Galatians, who has bewitched you, before whose eyes Jesus Christ was publicly portrayed *as* crucified?

2 This is the only thing I want to find out from you: did you receive the Spirit by the works of the Law, or by hearing with faith?

3 Are you so foolish? Having begun by the Spirit, are you now being perfected by the flesh?

4 Did you suffer so many things in vain—if indeed it was in vain?

5 Does He then, who provides you with the Spirit and works miracles among you, do it by the works of the Law, or by hearing with faith?

B. *The witness of Abraham*

*3:6
Gen 15:6;
Rom 4:3;
James 2:23
3:7
v. 9
3:8
Gen 12:3;
Acts 3:25
3:9
Rom 4:16;
v. 7

6 Even so Abraham BELIEVED GOD, AND IT WAS RECKONED TO HIM AS RIGHTEOUSNESS.

7 Therefore, be sure that it is those who are of faith who are sons of Abraham.

8 And the Scripture, foreseeing that God would justify the Gentiles by faith, preached the gospel beforehand to Abraham, *saying*, "ALL THE NATIONS SHALL BE BLESSED IN YOU."

9 So then those who are of faith are blessed with Abraham, the believer.

C. *Faith without works*

*3:10
Deut 27:26

*3:11
Gal 2:16;
Hab 2:4;
Heb 10:38
3:12
Lev 18:5;
Rom 10:5
3:13
Gal 4:5;
Acts 5:30;
Deut 21:23
3:14
Rom 4:9;
Joel 2:28;
Acts 2:33

10 For as many as are of the works of the Law are under a curse; for it is written, "CURSED IS EVERYONE WHO DOES NOT ABIDE BY ALL THINGS WRITTEN IN THE BOOK OF THE LAW, TO PERFORM THEM."

11 Now that no one is justified by the Law before God is evident; for, "THE RIGHTEOUS MAN SHALL LIVE BY FAITH."

12 However, the Law is not of faith; on the contrary, "HE WHO PRACTICES THEM SHALL LIVE BY THEM."

13 Christ redeemed us from the curse of the Law, having become a curse for us—for it is written, "CURSED IS EVERYONE WHO HANGS ON A TREE"—

14 in order that in Christ Jesus the blessing of Abraham might come to the Gentiles, so that we might receive the promise of the Spirit through faith.

D. *The Abrahamic covenant*

3:15
Heb 9:17

3:16
Gen 12:3;
13:15;
Acts 3:25

3:17
Ex 12:40;
Rom 4:13

3:18
Rom 4:14;
8:17

15 Brethren, I speak in terms of human relations: even though it is *only* a man's covenant, yet when it has been ratified, no one sets it aside or adds conditions to it.

16 Now the promises were spoken to Abraham and to his seed. He does not say, "And to seeds," as *referring* to many, but *rather* to one, "And to your seed," that is, Christ.

17 What I am saying is this: the Law, which came four hundred and thirty years later, does not invalidate a covenant previously ratified by God, so as to nullify the promise.

18 For if the inheritance is based on law, it is no longer based on a promise; but God has granted it to Abraham by means of a promise.

3:6 See note to Gen. 12:2 on the Abrahamic covenant.
3:10 Man's inability to keep the law of God inevitably brings him under the curse of God, i.e., God's judgment on sin. There is therefore no way for man to be saved by the law, for only through perfect obedience could men be saved

under the system of law. It is through faith, and faith alone, that man is justified before God and attains to life. The believer is redeemed from the curse of the law since Christ, in His crucifixion, became a curse for us.
3:11 See note to Hab. 2:4 on justification by faith alone.

E. The function of the law

19 Why the Law then? It was added because of transgressions, having been ordained through angels by the agency of a mediator, until the seed should come to whom the promise had been made.

20 Now a mediator is not for one *party only*; whereas God is *only* one.

21 Is the Law then contrary to the promises of God? May it never be! For if a law had been given which was able to impart life, then righteousness would indeed have been based on law.

22 But the Scripture has shut up all men under sin, that the promise by faith in Jesus Christ might be given to those who believe.

F. The superiority of faith over law

23 But before faith came, we were kept in custody under the law, being shut up to the faith which was later to be revealed.

24 Therefore the Law has become our tutor *to lead us* to Christ, that we may be justified by faith.

25 But now that faith has come, we are no longer under a tutor.

26 For you are all sons of God through faith in Christ Jesus.

27 For all of you who were baptized into Christ have clothed yourselves with Christ.

28 There is neither Jew nor Greek, there is neither slave nor free man, there is neither male nor female; for you are all one in Christ Jesus.

29 And if you belong to Christ, then you are Abraham's offspring, heirs according to promise.

4 Now I say, as long as the heir is a child, he does not differ at all from a slave although he is owner of everything,

2 but he is under guardians and managers until the date set by the father.

3 So also we, while we were children, were held in bondage under the elemental things of the world.

4 But when the fulness of the time came, God sent forth His Son, born of a woman, born under the Law,

5 in order that He might redeem those who were under the Law, that we might receive the adoption as sons.

6 And because you are sons, God has sent forth the Spirit of His Son into our hearts, crying, "Abba! Father!"

7 Therefore you are no longer a slave, but a son; and if a son, then an heir through God.

G. Appeal against a return to bondage

8 However at that time, when you did not know God, you were slaves to those which by nature are no gods.

9 But now that you have come to know God, or rather to be known by God, how is it that you turn back again to the weak and worthless elemental things, to which you desire to be enslaved all over again?

10 You observe days and months and seasons and years.

11 I fear for you, that perhaps I have labored over you in vain.

12 I beg of you, brethren, become as I *am*, for I also *have become* as you *are*. You have done me no wrong;

13 but you know that it was because of a bodily illness that I preached the gospel to you the first time;

Cross references (right margin):

3:19 Acts 7:53; Deut 5:5
3:20 Heb 8:6; 9:15; 12:24
3:21 Gal 2:17,21
3:22 Rom 3:9-19; 11:32
3:23 Rom 11:32
*3:24 Rom 10:4; 1 Cor 4:15; Gal 2:16
3:26 John 1:12; Rom 8:14
3:27 Rom 6:3; 13:14
3:28 Col 3:11; John 10:16; Eph 2:14,15
3:29 1 Cor 3:23; Gal 4:28
4:3 Col 2:8,20; Heb 5:12
4:4 Eph 1:10; Matt 5:17
*4:5 Eph 1:7; John 1:12; Eph 1:5
4:6 Rom 5:5; 8:15
4:8 Eph 2:12; 1 Thess 4:5; Rom 1:25; 1 Cor 12:2
4:9 1 Cor 8:3; Col 2:20
4:10 Rom 14:5
4:11 1 Thess 3:5
4:12 Gal 6:18
*4:13 1 Cor 2:3

3:24 The law is good and holy, but it cannot save (Rom. 3:20; 7:12–14). It is like the driver of a school bus who transports children to and from school, but is not the teacher of the children. The law performed this function until Christ came. But even so, the law enlightens but does not empower; it reveals what a man ought to do, but it does not give him the ability to do it. Salvation by law would mean salvation by works (an impossibility since Adam's fall), whereas salvation by grace is apart from justifying works of the law.

4:5 *Adoption* (*huiothesia*, placing as a son) is a word used in the New Testament only by Paul, and designates the privilege of sonship (*sons of God*, and *children of God*) that God confers on His people. It is an adoptive sonship that the believer never possessed by natural birth but that springs from the *new birth* through the redemption of Christ. With this new position come the attendant rights and obligations of sonship. Believers are predestined to sonship (Rom. 8:29; Eph. 1:5–11), and while it is theirs now it extends to the transformation of their bodies only at the resurrection. Adopted children: (1) are objects of the Father's love (John 17:23; 1 John 4:7–11); (2) bear His image (Rom. 8:29; 2 Pet. 1:4); (3) are indwelt by His Spirit (4:6); (4) bear His name (1 John 3:1); (5) are dealt with and chastised as sons (Heb. 12:5–11); and (6) are heirs of God and joint heirs with Christ (Rom. 8:17; 1 Pet. 1:4).

14 and that which was a trial to you in my bodily condition you did not despise or loathe, but you received me as an angel of God, as Christ Jesus *Himself.*

15 Where then is that sense of blessing you had? For I bear you witness, that if possible, you would have plucked out your eyes and given them to me.

16 Have I therefore become your enemy by telling you the truth?

17 They eagerly seek you, not commendably, but they wish to shut you out, in order that you may seek them.

18 But it is good always to be eagerly sought in a commendable manner, and not only when I am present with you.

19 My children, with whom I am again in labor until Christ is formed in you—

20 but I could wish to be present with you now and to change my tone, for I am perplexed about you.

21 Tell me, you who want to be under law, do you not listen to the law?

22 For it is written that Abraham had two sons, one by the bondwoman and one by the free woman.

23 But the son by the bondwoman was born according to the flesh, and the son by the free woman through the promise.

24 This is allegorically speaking: for these *women* are two covenants, one *proceeding* from Mount Sinai bearing children who are to be slaves; she is Hagar.

25 Now this Hagar is Mount Sinai in Arabia, and corresponds to the present Jerusalem, for she is in slavery with her children.

26 But the Jerusalem above is free; she is our mother.

27 For it is written,

"REJOICE, BARREN WOMAN WHO DOES NOT BEAR;
BREAK FORTH AND SHOUT, YOU WHO ARE NOT IN LABOR;
FOR MORE ARE THE CHILDREN OF THE DESOLATE
THAN OF THE ONE WHO HAS A HUSBAND."

28 And you brethren, like Isaac, are children of promise.

29 But as at that time he who was born according to the flesh persecuted him *who was born* according to the Spirit, so it is now also.

30 But what does the Scripture say?

"CAST OUT THE BONDWOMAN AND HER SON,
FOR THE SON OF THE BONDWOMAN SHALL NOT BE AN HEIR WITH THE
SON OF THE FREE WOMAN."

31 So then, brethren, we are not children of a bondwoman, but of the free woman.

IV. *The effect of Christian liberty (5:1–6:10)*

A. *Liberty threatened by legalism*

5 It was for freedom that Christ set us free; therefore keep standing firm and do not be subject again to a yoke of slavery.

2 Behold I, Paul, say to you that if you receive circumcision, Christ will be of no benefit to you.

3 And I testify again to every man who receives circumcision, that he is under obligation to keep the whole Law.

4 You have been severed from Christ, you who are seeking to be justified by law; you have fallen from grace.

5 For we through the Spirit, by faith, are waiting for the hope of righteousness.

6 For in Christ Jesus neither circumcision nor uncircumcision means anything, but faith working through love.

7 You were running well; who hindered you from obeying the truth?

4:13 It is not known for sure what Paul's bodily ailment was. No definite conclusion may be drawn from the little Paul says about it here and in 2 Cor. 12:7–10. From Paul's words one may infer that it was chronic, recurring, and painful, repulsive to the spectator, and humiliating to Paul. Malaria, epilepsy, migraine, and ophthalmia are among the ailments most commonly suggested.
5:1 Christian liberty is a consequence of salvation by grace, and is secured to the believer in and through Jesus Christ (4:3–5; Col. 1:13). Liberty is freedom: (1) from the law (Rom. 7:6; 8:2); (2) from the curse of the law (3:13); (3)

from the fear of death (Heb. 2:15); (4) from sin (Rom. 6:7,18); and (5) from the yoke of Old Testament ritual ordinances (4:3; Col. 2:20). But liberty must never be used as a cloak for sin; liberty must not become license. While the believer should resist any threat to his true liberty under the gospel, he must also remember that his very liberty has brought him into total subjection to Christ, whose servant he is and whom he must always obey (Rom. 12:1). Paradoxically the Christian finds his greatest liberty when he is in bondage to Jesus Christ.

8   This persuasion *did* not *come* from Him who calls you.

9   A little leaven leavens the whole lump *of dough.*

10   I have confidence in you in the Lord, that you will adopt no other view; but the one who is disturbing you shall bear his judgment, whoever he is.

11   But I, brethren, if I still preach circumcision, why am I still persecuted? Then the stumbling block of the cross has been abolished.

12   Would that those who are troubling you would even mutilate themselves.

B. *Freedom defined*

13   For you were called to freedom, brethren; only *do* not *turn* your freedom into an opportunity for the flesh, but through love serve one another.

14   For the whole Law is fulfilled in one word, in the *statement,* "YOU SHALL LOVE YOUR NEIGHBOR AS YOURSELF."

15   But if you bite and devour one another, take care lest you be consumed by one another.

C. *Liberty in practice*

16   But I say, walk by the Spirit, and you will not carry out the desire of the flesh.

17   For the flesh sets its desire against the Spirit, and the Spirit against the flesh; for these are in opposition to one another, so that you may not do the things that you please.

18   But if you are led by the Spirit, you are not under the Law.

19   Now the deeds of the flesh are evident, which are: immorality, impurity, sensuality,

20   idolatry, sorcery, enmities, strife, jealousy, outbursts of anger, disputes, dissensions, factions,

21   envying, drunkenness, carousing, and things like these, of which I forewarn you just as I have forewarned you that those who practice such things shall not inherit the kingdom of God.

22   But the fruit of the Spirit is love, joy, peace, patience, kindness, goodness, faithfulness,

23   gentleness, self-control; against such things there is no law.

24   Now those who belong to Christ Jesus have crucified the flesh with its passions and desires.

D. *Exhortations and warnings*

25   If we live by the Spirit, let us also walk by the Spirit.

26   Let us not become boastful, challenging one another, envying one another.

6   Brethren, even if a man is caught in any trespass, you who are spiritual, restore such a one in a spirit of gentleness; *each one* looking to yourself, lest you too be tempted.

2   Bear one another's burdens, and thus fulfill the law of Christ.

3   For if anyone thinks he is something when he is nothing, he deceives himself.

4   But let each one examine his own work, and then he will have *reason for* boasting in regard to himself alone, and not in regard to another.

5   For each one shall bear his own load.

6   And let the one who is taught the word share all good things with him who teaches.

7   Do not be deceived, God is not mocked; for whatever a man sows, this he will also reap.

8   For the one who sows to his own flesh shall from the flesh reap corruption, but the one who sows to the Spirit shall from the Spirit reap eternal life.

9   And let us not lose heart in doing good, for in due time we shall reap if we do not grow weary.

Cross references (right margin):

5:8 Gal 1:6
5:9 1 Cor 5:6
5:10 2 Cor 2:3; Gal 1:7
5:11 Gal 4:29; 6:12; 1 Cor 1:23
5:13 1 Cor 8:9; 1 Pet 2:16; 1 Cor 9:19
5:14 Lev 19:18; Matt 7:12; 22:39; Rom 13:8
5:16 Rom 8:4; vv. 24,25; Eph 2:3
5:17 Rom 7:15-23
5:18 Rom 6:14
*5:19 Eph 5:3; Col 3:5 [handwritten: Virtually all the deeds of the flesh are self-centered.]
5:21 1 Cor 6:9
5:22 Eph 5:9; Col 3:12-15; 1 Cor 13:7
5:24 Rom 6:6
[handwritten: V25 ← The Spirit is one who walks alongside us]
5:25 Rom 8:4
5:26 Phil 2:3
6:2 Rom 15:1; James 2:8
6:3 Rom 12:3; 1 Cor 8:2; 2 Cor 3:5
6:4 1 Cor 11:28; Phil 1:26
6:6 1 Cor 9:11
6:7 1 Cor 6:9; Job 13:9
6:8 Hos 8:7; James 3:18
6:9 1 Cor 15:58; Heb 3:6; Rev 2:10

5:19 Paul uses the plural word *deeds* when speaking of the *deeds of the flesh,* but in v. 22 when he speaks of the *fruit of the Spirit* he uses the singular word *fruit.* Thus it may be said that the redeemed life is an integrated whole or complete life, whereas the unregenerate life is fragmented and at odds with itself. The *fruit of the Spirit* may be likened to a diamond that has many facets. All of the facets together constitute the gem, but each facet helps to reflect the true splendor of the one stone.

6:10
John 9:4;
Titus 3:8;
Eph 2:19

10   So then, while we have opportunity, let us do good to all men, and especially to those who are of the household of the faith.

V. Conclusion (6:11–18)

A. Liberty and the cross

11   See with what large letters I am writing to you with my own hand.

6:12
Matt 23:27,
28; Acts 15:1;
Gal 5:11
6:13
Rom 2:25;
Phil 3:3
6:14
Gal 2:20;
Rom 6:2,6
6:15
2 Cor 5:17

12   Those who desire to make a good showing in the flesh try to compel you to be circumcised, simply that they may not be persecuted for the cross of Christ.

13   For those who [1]are circumcised do not even keep the Law themselves, but they desire to have you circumcised, that they may boast in your flesh.

14   But may it never be that I should boast, except in the cross of our Lord Jesus Christ, through which the world has been crucified to me, and I to the world.

15   For neither is circumcision anything, nor uncircumcision, but a new creation.

16   And those who will walk by this rule, peace and mercy *be* upon them, and upon the Israel of God.

B. The cost of liberty

6:17
2 Cor 1:5

17   From now on let no one cause trouble for me, for I bear on my body the brand-marks of Jesus.

C. The benediction

18   The grace of our Lord Jesus Christ be with your spirit, brethren. Amen.

[1]Some ancient mss. read *have been*

INTRODUCTION TO

THE LETTER OF PAUL TO THE

EPHESIANS

Authorship and Background: The determination of date, place of writing, and readers, presents problems in the letter of Paul to the Ephesians. All three are intimately related, and the answer to one will help answer the others. As to the readers, the problem exists because the oldest and best Greek manuscripts omit the words "at Ephesus" in 1:1. The absence of any personal greetings and, particularly, of specific matters of faith and conduct, make it probable, as many believe, that the letter to the Ephesians was not written to one church, but to several churches, as a general letter. The only person named is Tychicus (6:21,22), who seems to have been the bearer of the letter. He is mentioned also in Col. 4:7,8, in identically the same terms (Eph. 6:22; Col. 4:8). Paul refers to himself only as a prisoner (3:1; 4:1; 6:20).

Various conclusions have been drawn from these data: the most widely held, probably, is that Paul wrote this letter in Rome during his two-year imprisonment (A.D. 59-61), along with his letters to the Philippians and the Colossians, and his letter to Philemon. This letter to the Ephesians was sent to the various churches in the province of Asia, where Paul had worked for three years on his third missionary journey (Acts 19:1-20:1; 20:20). Some believe this was Paul's last letter; others think it was not written by Paul, but by an intimate disciple, who, writing in the apostle's name, composed it as a covering letter for the published collection of Paul's epistles. It was not until the nineteenth century that the Pauline authorship was called into question, despite the substantial evidence for regarding it as the product of the pen of the apostle Paul. Conservative scholars have always accepted it as genuine, however.

Characteristics: Devoid of personal references and greetings, the letter is written in calm, deliberate fashion, free of polemics and reproof, dwelling profoundly on the person of Christ and the church, the household of God, of which Christ is the cornerstone (2:20), and through which the "manifold wisdom" of God is manifest (3:10). The church is the body of Christ, who is its head (4:15,16); and all believers are members of His body (1:23; 4:25; 5:23,30). The relation of Christ to the church is like that of a husband to his wife (5:22-32). To God be glory in the church and in Jesus Christ for ever (3:21)!

Along with the exalted view of the church goes an equally high view of the unity of the faith (4:4-6), the greatness of God's plan of redemption (1:15-23), and His ultimate purpose to sum up all of creation in Christ (1:10). In a concept nowhere else developed in the New Testament, the apostle speaks of "the heavenly places" as the realm of redemption (1:3,20; 2:6; 3:10; 6:12).

Upon such lofty theological affirmations, the apostle bases his practical exhortations to Christians in their daily lives, in relation to each other, to the world, and in the family (4:1-6:20).

Contents:

I. Salutation (1:1,2)

II. Doctrinal affirmations (1:3-3:21): The one divine purpose to which God draws all creation is effected in the redemptive work of Christ, incarnate, resurrected, and glorified; it is manifest in the church, the body of Christ, into which all, Jews and Gentiles, are drawn in unity and peace. This is the revealed mystery of God's redemptive plan.

III. Practical exhortations (4:1-6:20): How Christians are to behave in the fellowship of the church, and in relation to the world. Husbands and wives, parents and children, masters and slaves, all have privileges and responsibilities alike to persevere in their calling.

IV. Conclusion (6:21-24)

THE LETTER OF PAUL TO THE
EPHESIANS

I. *Salutation (1:1,2)*

1 Paul, an apostle of Christ Jesus by the will of God, to the saints who are [1]at Ephesus, and *who are* faithful in Christ Jesus:

2 Grace to you and peace from God our Father and the Lord Jesus Christ.

1:1
2 Cor 1:1;
1 Cor 1:1;
Phil 1:1;
Col 1:1,2
1:2
Rom 1:7

II. *Doctrinal affirmations (1:3–3:21)*

A. *The origin of the church*

3 Blessed *be* the God and Father of our Lord Jesus Christ, who has blessed us with every spiritual blessing in the heavenly *places* in Christ,

4 just as He chose us in Him before the foundation of the world, that we should be holy and blameless before [2]Him. In love

5 He predestined us to adoption as sons through Jesus Christ to Himself, according to the kind intention of His will,

6 to the praise of the glory of His grace, which He freely bestowed on us in the Beloved.

7 In Him we have redemption through His blood, the forgiveness of our trespasses, according to the riches of His grace,

8 which He lavished upon us. In all wisdom and insight

9 He made known to us the mystery of His will, according to His kind intention which He purposed in Him

10 with a view to an administration suitable to the fulness of the times, *that is,* the summing up of all things in Christ, things in the heavens and things upon the earth. In Him

11 also we have obtained an inheritance, having been predestined according to His purpose who works all things after the counsel of His will,

12 to the end that we who were the first to hope in [3]Christ should be to the praise of His glory.

13 In Him, you also, after listening to the message of truth, the gospel of your salvation—having also believed, you were sealed in Him with the Holy Spirit of promise,

14 who is given as a pledge of our inheritance, with a view to the redemption of *God's own* possession, to the praise of His glory.

*1:3
2 Cor 1:3;
Eph 2:6;
3:10; 6:12
*1:4
Eph 5:27;
Col 1:22;
Eph 4:2,15,
16
1:5
Rom 8:29f

1:7
Col 1:14

1:9
Rom 16:25
1:10
Gal 4:4;
Col 1:16,20

1:11
Eph 3:11;
Rom 9:11;
Heb 6:17
1:12
vv. 6,14
*1:13
Col 1:5;
Eph 4:30

1:14
2 Cor 1:22;
Acts 20:32

[1]Some ancient mss. do not contain *at Ephesus* [2]*Him, in love.* [3]I.e., the Messiah

---

1:3 *in the heavenly places.* This phrase (or "heavenlies," Greek *hoi epouranioi*) is used in 1:3,20; 2:6; 3:10; and 6:12 in a sense quite different from its use elsewhere. It is the realm in which Christ now reigns by virtue of His resurrection from the dead (1:20), which He shares with those who through God's grace have been raised with Christ from their transgressions (2:5,6). In this realm believers enjoy every spiritual blessing (1:3), and here the Christian warfare is waged against the spiritual forces of evil (6:12). Here God's manifold wisdom is made known through the church to these spiritual principalities and powers (3:10).
1:4 "Election" is a sovereign outworking of God's power to effect that which is pleasing to Him according to His righteous and holy will. The New Testament uses the term "elect" (*eklektoi*) to include a variety of meanings. Thus every believer is elected or chosen: (1) to good works (2:10); (2) to conformity to the image of Christ (Rom. 8:29); (3) to eternal glory (Rom. 9:23); and (4) to adoption as a son (1:5). But the aspect of election that has given rise to debate relates to salvation itself. It has been argued that if only those who are elected are saved, then the death of Christ was really intended only for them (limited atonement). Others

insist that a "bona fide" offer to *men that all everywhere should repent* (Acts 17:30) involves a divine intention for Christ's atonement to save all mankind (unlimited atonement). Scripture teaches that election is according to God's sovereign purpose (1:11; Rom. 9:11) and that it is according to His foreknowledge (Rom. 8:29; 1 Pet. 1:2). But nowhere does the Bible make explicit what it is in God's foreknowledge that determines His elective choice. At all events, the Scriptures appear to teach clearly enough that men are free agents with moral responsibility, while at the same time God is sovereign and works out all things according to His own good pleasure.
1:13 Believers are saved by Christ and sealed by the Holy Spirit. Scripture states that Christ Himself was sealed as Messiah by God the Father (John 6:27). Paul says that God *also sealed us and gave us the Spirit in our hearts as a pledge* (2 Cor. 1:22). The seal consists of the indwelling Holy Spirit Himself, and this *pledge* is *for the day of redemption* (4:30). Symbolically, this sealing implies: (1) an ownership or title to the believer that is vested in God (2 Tim. 2:19); and (2) the certainty of final salvation or redemption (4:30).

B. Prayer for the Ephesians

15 For this reason I too, having heard of the faith in the Lord Jesus which *exists* among you, and [4]your love for all the saints,

16 do not cease giving thanks for you, while making mention *of you* in my prayers;

17 that the God of our Lord Jesus Christ, the Father of glory, may give to you a spirit of wisdom and of revelation in the knowledge of Him.

18 *I pray that* the eyes of your heart may be enlightened, so that you may know what is the hope of His calling, what are the riches of the glory of His inheritance in the saints,

19 and what is the surpassing greatness of His power toward us who believe. *These are* in accordance with the working of the strength of His might

20 which He brought about in Christ, when He raised Him from the dead, and seated Him at His right hand in the heavenly *places,*

21 far above all rule and authority and power and dominion, and every name that is named, not only in this age, but also in the one to come.

22 And He put all things in subjection under His feet, and gave Him as head over all things to the church,

23 which is His body, the fulness of Him who fills all in all.

C. The building of the church

2 And you were dead in your trespasses and sins,

2 in which you formerly walked according to the course of this world, according to the prince of the power of the air, of the spirit that is now working in the sons of disobedience.

3 Among them we too all formerly lived in the lusts of our flesh, indulging the desires of the flesh and of the mind, and were by nature children of wrath, even as the rest.

4 But God, being rich in mercy, because of His great love with which He loved us,

5 even when we were dead in our transgressions, made us alive together [5]with Christ (by grace you have been saved),

6 and raised us up with Him, and seated us with Him in the heavenly *places,* in Christ Jesus,

7 in order that in the ages to come He might show the surpassing riches of His grace in kindness toward us in Christ Jesus.

8 For by grace you have been saved through faith; and that not of yourselves, *it is* the gift of God;

9 not as a result of works, that no one should boast.

10 For we are His workmanship, created in Christ Jesus for good works, which God prepared beforehand, that we should walk in them.

11 Therefore remember, that formerly you, the Gentiles in the flesh, who are called "Uncircumcision" by the so-called "Circumcision," *which is* performed in the flesh by human hands—

12 *remember* that you were at that time separate from Christ, excluded from the

Cross-references (margin)

1:15 Col 1:4; Eph 3:18
1:16 Rom 1:8,9; Col 1:3,9
1:17 John 20:17; Col 1:9
1:18 Acts 26:18; Eph 4:4
1:19 Col 1:29; Eph 6:10
1:20 Acts 2:24; Heb 1:3
1:21 Phil 2:9,10
*1:22 Matt 28:18; Eph 4:15; 5:23
1:23 Rom 12:5; Col 2:17
2:1 v. 5; John 5:24
2:2 Eph 6:12; 5:6
2:3 Gal 5:16,17; Rom 2:14; 5:10
2:4 Rom 10:12
2:5 vv. 1,8
*2:6 Eph 1:20
2:7 Titus 3:4
*2:8 Gal 2:16; v. 5
2:9 Rom 3:20,28; 2 Tim 1:9
2:10 Eph 4:24; Titus 2:14
2:11 Rom 2:28; Col 2:11
2:12 1 Thess 4:5; Gal 4:8

Saved by faith → & grace (handwritten margin note)

[4]Many ancient mss. do not contain *your love* [5]Some ancient mss. read *in Christ*

1:22 Christ is the Head of His church, which He purchased with His blood (Acts 20:28) and which He has constituted as a spiritual organism (Rom. 12:5; 1 Cor. 10:17; 12:12; Gal. 3:28). Believers are baptized into this one body by the Holy Spirit (1 Cor. 12:13). All members of that body are subject to Him as Head of the body (5:24; Rom. 7:4). Christ protects His church so that the powers of death will not prevail against it (Matt. 16:18).

All true believers, regardless of denominational attachment, belong to this one true church of Christ. Thus there are people who may be members of visible churches who are not members of the true church of Christ. Likewise there may be those who are not members of any visible organization who are true members of the church of Christ. This body of Christ, by its very nature, possesses a spiritual unity that is independent of ecclesiastical organizations.

2:6 Believers are seated with Christ in the heavenly places by virtue of their union with Him. As such, they have a share in His royal status and authority; and through their intercessory prayers and evangelistic witness, Christ's kingdom is advanced. Moreover, they constitute a heavenly commonwealth (Phil. 3:20); and while they are living in the world they are not of it. Spiritually also their life is *hidden with Christ in God* (Col. 3:3).

2:8 Salvation is by grace through *faith* alone (*sola fide*). Saving faith involves: (1) knowledge of the gospel (Rom. 10:14); (2) assent to the gospel—that is, one is intellectually convinced that the gospel message is true (Mark 1:24; James 2:19); and (3) trust or personal appropriation of Christ and His promises. Knowing and assenting to truth, the believer receives the Lord Jesus as his own (John 1:12). It should be noted that (2) is not enough to satisfy the Scriptural definition of faith; (3) is most essential. While believers are saved through faith alone, saving faith is always attested by good works—because it is alive, it always finds expression through those works of righteousness that are its proper fruit. Biblical faith is a belief in the truth simply because God says so.

commonwealth of Israel, and strangers to the covenants of promise, having no hope and without God in the world.

13 But now in Christ Jesus you who formerly were far off have been brought near by the blood of Christ.

14 For He Himself is our peace, who made both *groups into* one, and broke down the barrier of the dividing wall,

15 by abolishing in His flesh the enmity, *which is* the Law of commandments *contained* in ordinances, that in Himself He might make the two into one new man, *thus* establishing peace,

16 and might reconcile them both in one body to God through the cross, by it having put to death the enmity.

17 AND HE CAME AND PREACHED PEACE TO YOU WHO WERE FAR AWAY, AND PEACE TO THOSE WHO WERE NEAR;

18 for through Him we both have our access in one Spirit to the Father.

19 So then you are no longer strangers and aliens, but you are fellow citizens with the saints, and are of God's household,

20 having been built upon the foundation of the apostles and prophets, Christ Jesus Himself being the corner *stone,*

21 in whom the whole building, being fitted together is growing into a holy temple in the Lord;

22 in whom you also are being built together into a dwelling of God in the Spirit.

D. *The function of the church*

3 For this reason I, Paul, the prisoner of Christ Jesus for the sake of you Gentiles—

2 if indeed you have heard of the stewardship of God's grace which was given to me for you;

3 that by revelation there was made known to me the mystery, as I wrote before in brief.

4 And by referring to this, when you read you can understand my insight into the mystery of Christ,

5 which in other generations was not made known to the sons of men, as it has now been revealed to His holy apostles and prophets in the Spirit;

6 *to be specific,* that the Gentiles are fellow heirs and fellow members of the body, and fellow partakers of the promise in Christ Jesus through the gospel,

7 of which I was made a minister, according to the gift of God's grace which was given to me according to the working of His power.

8 To me, the very least of all saints, this grace was given, to preach to the Gentiles the unfathomable riches of Christ,

9 and to bring to light what is the administration of the mystery which for ages has been hidden in God, who created all things;

10 in order that the manifold wisdom of God might now be made known through the church to the rulers and the authorities in the heavenly *places.*

11 *This was* in accordance with the eternal purpose which He carried out in Christ Jesus our Lord,

12 in whom we have boldness and confident access through faith in Him.

13 Therefore I ask you not to lose heart at my tribulations on your behalf, for they are your glory.

14 For this reason, I bow my knees before the Father,

15 from whom every family in heaven and on earth derives its name,

16 that He would grant you, according to the riches of His glory, to be strengthened with power through His Spirit in the inner man;

17 so that Christ may dwell in your hearts through faith; *and* that you, being rooted and grounded in love,

18 may be able to comprehend with all the saints what is the breadth and length and height and depth,

19 and to know the love of Christ which surpasses knowledge, that you may be filled up to all the fulness of God.

20 Now to Him who is able to do exceeding abundantly beyond all that we ask or think, according to the power that works within us,

21 to Him *be* the glory in the church and in Christ Jesus to all generations forever and ever. Amen.

2:13
Acts 2:39;
Col 1:20
2:14
Col 3:15;
1 Cor 12:13
2:15
Col 1:21,22;
Gal 6:15
2:16
Col 1:20,22
2:17
Is 57:19;
Ps 148:14
2:18
Eph 3:12;
1 Cor 12:13;
Col 1:12
2:19
Phil 3:20;
Gal 6:10
2:20
Matt 16:18;
Rev 21:14
2:21
1 Cor 3:16,17

3:1
Acts 23:18;
Eph 4:1
3:2
Col 1:25;
1 Tim 1:4
3:3
Acts 22:17;
Gal 1:12;
Rom 16:25
3:4
1 Cor 4:1
3:5
Rom 16:26
3:6
Gal 3:29;
Eph 2:15,16
3:8
1 Cor 15:9;
Gal 1:16;
Col 1:27
3:9
Col 1:26,27
3:10
1 Pet 1:12;
1 Cor 2:7;
Eph 1:21
3:12
Heb 4:16;
Eph 2:18
3:13
2 Cor 4:1
3:14
Phil 2:10
3:16
Eph 1:18;
Col 1:11;
Rom 7:22
3:17
John 14:23;
Col 1:23
3:18
Eph 1:18;
Job 11:8,9
3:19
Col 2:10;
Eph 1:23
3:20
Rom 16:25
3:21
Rom 11:36

III. *Practical exhortations (4:1–6:20)*

A. *The unity of the church*

4 I, therefore, the prisoner of the Lord, entreat you to walk in a manner worthy of the calling with which you have been called,

2 with all humility and gentleness, with patience, showing forbearance to one another in love,

3 being diligent to preserve the unity of the Spirit in the bond of peace.

4 *There is* one body and one Spirit, just as also you were called in one hope of your calling;

5 one Lord, one faith, one baptism,

6 one God and Father of all who is over all and through all and in all.

7 But to each one of us grace was given according to the measure of Christ's gift.

8 Therefore it says,

"WHEN HE ASCENDED ON HIGH,
HE LED CAPTIVE A HOST OF CAPTIVES,
AND HE GAVE GIFTS TO MEN."

9 (Now this *expression,* "He ascended," what does it mean except that He also had descended into the lower parts of the earth?

10 He who descended is Himself also He who ascended far above all the heavens, that He might fill all things.)

11 And He gave some *as* apostles, and some *as* prophets, and some *as* evangelists, and some *as* pastors and teachers,

12 for the equipping of the saints for the work of service, to the building up of the body of Christ;

13 until we all attain to the unity of the faith, and of the knowledge of the Son of God, to a mature man, to the measure of the stature which belongs to the fulness of Christ.

14 As a result, we are no longer to be children, tossed here and there by waves, and carried about by every wind of doctrine, by the trickery of men, by craftiness in deceitful scheming;

15 but speaking the truth in love, we are to grow up in all *aspects* into Him, who is the head, *even* Christ,

16 from whom the whole body, being fitted and held together by that which every joint supplies, according to the proper working of each individual part, causes the growth of the body for the building up of itself in love.

B. *The moral standards of the church*

17 This I say therefore, and affirm together with the Lord, that you walk no longer just as the Gentiles also walk, in the futility of their mind,

18 being darkened in their understanding, excluded from the life of God, because of the ignorance that is in them, because of the hardness of their heart;

19 and they, having become callous, have given themselves over to sensuality, for the practice of every kind of impurity with greediness.

20 But you did not learn Christ in this way,

21 if indeed you have heard Him and have been taught in Him, just as truth is in Jesus,

22 that, in reference to your former manner of life, you lay aside the old self, which is being corrupted in accordance with the lusts of deceit,

23 and that you be renewed in the spirit of your mind,

24 and put on the new self, which in *the likeness of* God has been created in righteousness and holiness of the truth.

25 Therefore, laying aside falsehood, SPEAK TRUTH, EACH ONE *of you,* WITH HIS NEIGHBOR, for we are members of one another.

26 BE ANGRY, AND *yet* DO NOT SIN; do not let the sun go down on your anger,

27 and do not give the devil an opportunity.

28 Let him who steals steal no longer; but rather let him labor, performing with his own hands what is good, in order that he may have *something* to share with him who has need.

29 Let no unwholesome word proceed from your mouth, but only such *a word*

as is good for edification according to the need *of the moment*, that it may give grace to those who hear.

30   And do not grieve the Holy Spirit of God, by whom you were sealed for the day of redemption.

31   Let all bitterness and wrath and anger and clamor and slander be put away from you, along with all malice.

32   And be kind to one another, tender-hearted, forgiving each other, just as God in Christ also has forgiven [6]you.

5   Therefore be imitators of God, as beloved children;

2   and walk in love, just as Christ also loved [6]you, and gave Himself up for us, an offering and a sacrifice to God as a fragrant aroma.

3   But do not let immorality or any impurity or greed even be named among you, as is proper among saints;

4   and *there must be no* filthiness and silly talk, or coarse jesting, which are not fitting, but rather giving of thanks.

5   For this you know with certainty, that no immoral or impure person or covetous man, who is an idolater, has an inheritance in the kingdom of Christ and God.

6   Let no one deceive you with empty words, for because of these things the wrath of God comes upon the sons of disobedience.

7   Therefore do not be partakers with them;

8   for you were formerly darkness, but now you are light in the Lord; walk as children of light

9   (for the fruit of the light *consists* in all goodness and righteousness and truth),

10   trying to learn what is pleasing to the Lord.

11   And do not participate in the unfruitful deeds of darkness, but instead even expose them;

12   for it is disgraceful even to speak of the things which are done by them in secret.

13   But all things become visible when they are exposed by the light, for everything that becomes visible is light.

14   For this reason it says,
"Awake, sleeper,
And arise from the dead,
And Christ will shine on you."

15   Therefore be careful how you walk, not as unwise men, but as wise,

16   making the most of your time, because the days are evil.

17   So then do not be foolish, but understand what the will of the Lord is.

18   And do not get drunk with wine, for that is dissipation, but be filled with the Spirit,

19   speaking to one another in psalms and hymns and spiritual songs, singing and making melody with your heart to the Lord;

20   always giving thanks for all things in the name of our Lord Jesus Christ to God, even the Father;

C. The Christian household

21   and be subject to one another in the fear of Christ.

22   Wives, *be subject* to your own husbands, as to the Lord.

[6]Some ancient mss. read *us*

Cross references (right margin):

*4:30
1 Thess 5:19;
Rom 8:23
4:31
Col 3:8;
Titus 3:3
4:32
2 Cor 2:10;
Matt 6:14,15

5:1
Luke 6:36
5:2
1 Thess 4:9;
Gal 1:4;
2 Cor 2:15
5:3
Rom 6:13;
Col 3:5;
1 Cor 5:1
5:5
1 Cor 6:9;
Col 3:5

5:6
Jer 29:8;
Rom 1:18

5:8
John 8:12;
Luke 16:8
5:9
Gal 5:22

5:11
1 Cor 5:9;
Rom 6:21
5:12
Rom 1:24

5:14
Is 60:1;
John 5:25

5:16
Col 4:5;
Eph 6:13
5:17
Rom 12:2;
1 Thess 4:3
*5:18
Prov 20:1;
Luke 1:15
5:19
Col 3:16;
Acts 16:25
5:20
Ps 34:1;
Heb 13:15

*5:22
Gen 3:16;
Eph 6:5

4:30 To grieve the Holy Spirit is to go counter to the will of the third person of the Trinity who dwells within us. Since He is holy, loving, true, and peaceable, sins of unholiness, lack of love, untruthfulness, and harshness grieve Him and interrupt fellowship with God. To grieve the Holy Spirit disturbs communion with Christ and results in the loss of the Spirit's fullness and power. Elsewhere we are commanded: *Do not quench the Spirit* (1 Thess. 5:19). Hebrews 10:29 says some have *insulted the Spirit of grace*.
5:18 All believers are sealed by the Holy Spirit when they are regenerated (1:13,14); however, not all believers are filled with the Spirit. Some remain in a carnal state, leading a defeated life (1 Cor. 3:1). (A *permanent* carnal state is evidence of an unsaved condition, according to Rom. 8:6.)

Yet the goal and ideal of the Christian life is always to be filled and controlled by the Spirit. This may be attained by: (1) being cleansed from all known sin—a prerequisite to being Spirit-filled (2 Cor. 7:1; 1 John 1:7–9); (2) surrendering or yielding of self to the full control of God without any reservation (Rom. 6:13; 12:1); (3) believing that God will fill with His Spirit those who confess their sins and surrender themselves to Him (see Rom. 4:20–22); and (4) embracing by faith the fact that they have already been filled by the Spirit and conducting themselves accordingly when these prior conditions have been met. Sin alone can destroy this kind of life in the Spirit.
5:22 See note to Titus 2:4 on duties of wives to husbands and children.

5:23
1 Cor 11:3;
Col 1:18;
Eph 1:23
5:24
Col 3:18
5:25
Col 3:19

5:26
Titus 3:5

*5:27
Col 1:22;
Eph 1:4
5:28
v. 25

5:30
1 Cor 6:15;
Eph 1:23
5:31
Gen 2:24;
Matt 19:5;
1 Cor 6:16
5:32
Col 3:19;
1 Pet 3:6

6:1
Col 3:20
6:2
Deut 5:16

6:4
Col 3:21;
Gen 18:19
6:5
Col 3:22;
1 Tim 6:1;
Phil 2:12;
1 Chr 29:17

6:7
Col 3:23

6:9
Lev 25:43;
John 13:13;
Col 3:25

6:10
1 Cor 16:13;
Eph 1:19
6:11
1 Cor 16:21
6:12
1 Cor 9:25;
Rom 8:38

6:13
2 Cor 10:4;
Eph 5:16
6:14
Is 11:5; 59:17

6:15
Is 52:7

6:16
1 John 5:4

6:17
Is 59:17;
Heb 4:12

23   For the husband is the head of the wife, as Christ also is the head of the church, He Himself *being* the Savior of the body.

24   But as the church is subject to Christ, so also the wives *ought to be* to their husbands in everything.

25   Husbands, love your wives, just as Christ also loved the church and gave Himself up for her;

26   that He might sanctify her, having cleansed her by the washing of water with the word,

27   that He might present to Himself the church in all her glory, having no spot or wrinkle or any such thing; but that she should be holy and blameless.

28   So husbands ought also to love their own wives as their own bodies. He who loves his own wife loves himself;

29   for no one ever hated his own flesh, but nourishes and cherishes it, just as Christ also *does* the church,

30   because we are members of His body.

31   FOR THIS CAUSE A MAN SHALL LEAVE HIS FATHER AND MOTHER, AND SHALL CLEAVE TO HIS WIFE; AND THE TWO SHALL BECOME ONE FLESH.

32   This mystery is great; but I am speaking with reference to Christ and the church.

33   Nevertheless let each individual among you also love his own wife even as himself; and *let* the wife *see to it* that she respect her husband.

6   Children, obey your parents in the Lord, for this is right.

2   HONOR YOUR FATHER AND MOTHER (which is the first commandment with a promise),

3   THAT IT MAY BE WELL WITH YOU, AND THAT YOU MAY LIVE LONG ON THE EARTH.

4   And, fathers, do not provoke your children to anger; but bring them up in the discipline and instruction of the Lord.

5   Slaves, be obedient to those who are your masters according to the flesh, with fear and trembling, in the sincerity of your heart, as to Christ;

6   not by way of eyeservice, as men-pleasers, but as slaves of Christ, doing the will of God from the heart.

7   With good will render service, as to the Lord, and not to men,

8   knowing that whatever good thing each one does, this he will receive back from the Lord, whether slave or free.

9   And, masters, do the same things to them, and give up threatening, knowing that both their Master and yours is in heaven, and there is no partiality with Him.

D. The church's warfare

10   Finally, be strong in the Lord, and in the strength of His might.

11   Put on the full armor of God, that you may be able to stand firm against the schemes of the devil.

12   For our struggle is not against flesh and blood, but against the rulers, against the powers, against the world forces of this darkness, against the spiritual *forces* of wickedness in the heavenly *places*.

13   Therefore, take up the full armor of God, that you may be able to resist in the evil day, and having done everything, to stand firm.

14   Stand firm therefore, HAVING GIRDED YOUR LOINS WITH TRUTH, and HAVING PUT ON THE BREASTPLATE OF RIGHTEOUSNESS,

15   and having shod YOUR FEET WITH THE PREPARATION OF THE GOSPEL OF PEACE;

16   in addition to all, taking up the shield of faith with which you will be able to extinguish all the flaming missiles of the evil *one*.

17   And take THE HELMET OF SALVATION, and the sword of the Spirit, which is the word of God.

5:25   This is the clearest passage in Scripture that sets forth the character of the church as the bride of Christ. Yet the marriage relationship analogy appears elsewhere in Scripture as typical of God and His people. Hosea refers to this principle in a negative way, decrying the spiritual adultery of Israel. Likewise John, in the Revelation, speaks of the New Jerusalem coming down out of heaven like a *bride* adorned for her husband. Christ Himself used the figure of the bridegroom in His teachings (Matt. 9:15; 25:1–13; Luke 5:34,35). Also see note on 1 Cor. 7:2 on the subject of husbands.

18　With all prayer and petition pray at all times in the Spirit, and with this in view, be on the alert with all perseverance and petition for all the saints,

19　and *pray* on my behalf, that utterance may be given to me in the opening of my mouth, to make known with boldness the mystery of the gospel,

20　for which I am an ambassador in chains; that [7]in *proclaiming* it I may speak boldly, as I ought to speak.

IV. *Conclusion (6:21–24)*

21　But that you also may know about my circumstances, how I am doing, Tychicus, the beloved brother and faithful minister in the Lord, will make everything known to you.

22　And I have sent him to you for this very purpose, so that you may know about us, and that he may comfort your hearts.

23　Peace be to the brethren, and love with faith, from God the Father and the Lord Jesus Christ.

24　Grace be with all those who love our Lord Jesus Christ with *a love* incorruptible.

[7]Some ancient mss. read *I may speak it boldly*

6:18
Luke 18:1;
Matt 26:41;
Phil 1:4
6:19
Acts 4:29;
2 Cor 3:12
6:20
2 Cor 5:20;
Phil 1:20

6:21
Acts 20:4

6:23
1 Pet 5:14;
Gal 5:6

INTRODUCTION TO
THE LETTER OF PAUL TO THE
PHILIPPIANS

Authorship and Background: Paul wrote this letter while in prison (1:12-14,17), so that Philippians is grouped with Colossians, Philemon, and Ephesians as a "Prison Letter." The most widely held view is that all four letters were written during the two-year imprisonment in Rome (Acts 28:30), A.D. 59-61. The references to the praetorian guard (1:13) and to Caesar's household (4:22) seem to support Rome as the place of imprisonment. This is not indisputable, however, and some scholars believe that Caesarea, where Paul was in prison for two years (Acts 24:27), was the place of writing; others hold it was Ephesus, although there is no reference to an imprisonment there, unless 1 Cor. 15:32 is taken quite literally. On the whole, Rome seems to fulfill the requirements of the prison epistles better, assuming they were all written in the same place.

The church at Philippi had sent a gift to Paul by Epaphroditus, their messenger (4:18), who fell sick in Rome; the news of his illness had caused considerable alarm in Philippi and made Epaphroditus all the more eager to return home (2:25-30). Paul therefore wrote this letter to his dear friends in Philippi, expressing his gratitude for their love and help.

Characteristics: Paul's ministry in Philippi is one of the most thrilling chapters in all of Christian missions (Acts 16:12-40). He came to this Roman colony in the province of Macedonia in response to a divine call on his second missionary journey (Acts 16:9-10). Years later he returned to Macedonia after leaving Ephesus on his third missionary journey (Acts 20:1), and once again on his way back to Syria (Acts 20:3-6). Of all the churches Paul had founded, none was so near and dear to him as the church at Philippi. The letter to the Philippians breathes an atmosphere of perfect love and mutual confidence; these were friends who had often helped Paul with their gifts (4:15,16) and had not forgotten him now that he was in prison. Love and gratitude are everywhere expressed in the pages of this Christian love letter. Fourteen times in this short letter the words "joy" and "rejoice" occur; this hymn of joy could have been written only by one who had found Christ to be all-sufficient.

There were perils to be watched: enemies of the gospel within (3:2,3,18,19) and without (1:27,28) who must be withstood and defeated. There was the danger of self-seeking and pride, which could lead to harmful divisions (2:2-4; 4:2,3). With deep affection and from a pastor's heart, Paul wrote his beloved Philippians in terms at once simple and direct, yet also overflowing with love and thanksgiving. The strictly theological affirmations receive less proportionate space in this letter than personal and practical matters. Here, however, is the most sublime and profound statement of the meaning of the incarnation (2:5-11). Paul's own philosophy of life is nowhere better expressed than in the words of 1:21: "For to me, to live is Christ, and to die is gain."

Contents:

I. Introduction (1:1-11): Thanksgiving, joy, assurance, love, grace, righteousness, glory—these are the notes sounded by Paul in the overture to this hymn of joy.

II. Paul's personal circumstances (1:12-30): By transforming his incarceration into an opportunity to preach the gospel, God had shown that in all things He works for good with those who are called by Him, a source of joy to Paul.

22   But if *I am* to live *on* in the flesh, this *will mean* fruitful labor for me; and I do not know which to choose.

23   But I am hard-pressed from both *directions,* having the desire to depart and be with Christ, for *that* is very much better;

24   yet to remain on in the flesh is more necessary for your sake.

25   And convinced of this, I know that I shall remain and continue with you all for your progress and joy in the faith,

26   so that your proud confidence in me may abound in Christ Jesus through my coming to you again.

27   Only conduct yourselves in a manner worthy of the gospel of Christ; so that whether I come and see you or remain absent, I may hear of you that you are standing firm in one spirit, with one mind striving together for the faith of the gospel;

28   in no way alarmed by *your* opponents—which is a sign of destruction for them, but of salvation for you, and that *too,* from God.

29   For to you it has been granted for Christ's sake, not only to believe in Him, but also to suffer for His sake,

30   experiencing the same conflict which you saw in me, and now hear *to be* in me.

III. *The Christian life (2:1–18)*

A. *Christ our model*

2 If therefore there is any encouragement in Christ, if there is any consolation of love, if there is any fellowship of the Spirit, if any affection and compassion,

2   make my joy complete by being of the same mind, maintaining the same love, united in spirit, intent on one purpose.

3   Do nothing from selfishness or empty conceit, but with humility of mind let each of you regard one another as more important than himself;

4   do not *merely* look out for your own personal interests, but also for the interests of others.

5   Have this attitude in yourselves which was also in Christ Jesus,

6   who, although He existed in the form of God, did not regard equality with God a thing to be grasped,

7   but ³emptied Himself, taking the form of a bond-servant, *and* being made in the likeness of men.

8   And being found in appearance as a man, He humbled Himself by becoming obedient to the point of death, even death on a cross.

9   Therefore also God highly exalted Him, and bestowed on Him the name which is above every name,

10   that at the name of Jesus EVERY KNEE SHOULD BOW, of those who are in heaven, and on earth, and under the earth,

11   and that every tongue should confess that Jesus Christ is Lord, to the glory of God the Father.

B. *Obligations of Christians*

12   So then, my beloved, just as you have always obeyed, not as in my presence only, but now much more in my absence, work out your salvation with fear and trembling;

³I.e., laid aside His privileges

Cross references (right margin):

1:23
2 Cor 5:8;
2 Tim 4:6

1:26
2 Cor 1:14;
5:12

1:28
2 Thess 1:5;
Rom 8:17
1:29
Matt 5:12;
Acts 14:22
1:30
1 Thess 2:2;
Col 2:1;
Acts 16:19

2:1
2 Cor 13:14;
Col 3:12
2:2
John 3:29;
Rom 12:16;
1 Pet 3:8
2:3
Gal 5:26;
Rom 12:10;
1 Pet 5:5
2:4
Rom 15:1,2
2:5
Matt 11:29;
1 Pet 2:21
2:6
John 1:1;
2 Cor 4:4;
John 5:18
*2:7
John 1:14;
Gal 4:4;
Heb 2:17
2:8
Matt 26:39;
John 10:18;
Heb 5:8
2:9
Acts 2:33;
Heb 2:9;
Eph 1:20,21
2:10
Matt 28:18;
Rom 14:11
2:11
John 13:13;
Acts 2:36
*2:12f
Phil 1:5;
Eph 6:5

2:7 "Kenosis" is the theological name often used in connection with Christ's incarnation. He "emptied Himself" or "stripped Himself" or "divested Himself" of His divine powers and prerogatives as God the Son when He took upon Himself *the form of a bond-servant.* He assumed the human limitations inherent in His becoming a true human being. It was a voluntary, self-imposed limitation. Christ in human form was both God and man—two distinct natures united in one person. Yet Scripture does not make clear the full implications of the kenosis. There are aspects of mystery connected with it that the minds of finite men are not able to fathom. (See also the following Scriptures associated with the kenosis: Matt. 27:46; Mark 13:32; Luke 2:40–52; John 17:4; 2 Cor. 8:9; Heb. 4:15; 5:7,8.)

2:12,13 Paul here stresses both the free agency of man and the absolute sovereignty of God. He urges the Philippians to work out their own salvation as though they were fully responsible and capable of good by their own exertions. In the next breath he adds *for it is God who is at work in you . . . for His good pleasure,* as though the responsibility were all God's. Both man's free agency and God's unlimited sovereignty are firmly stressed, paradoxical though this may be. Actually, however, these two verses may be brought into harmony by recognizing that because God is at work in believers, and God's grace is available, believers are able to achieve the purposes for which God has saved them (cf. Eph. 2:10).

2:13
2 Cor 3:5

2:14
1 Cor 10:10;
Rom 14:1
2:15
Matt 5:45;
Eph 5:1; 5:8
2:16
2 Cor 1:14;
1 Thess 2:19
2:17
2 Tim 4:6;
Rom 15:16;
Col 1:24

13   for it is God who is at work in you, both to will and to work for *His* good pleasure.

14   Do all things without grumbling or disputing;

15   that you may prove yourselves to be blameless and innocent, children of God above reproach in the midst of a crooked and perverse generation, among whom you appear as lights in the world,

16   holding fast the word of life, so that in the day of Christ I may have cause to glory because I did not run in vain nor toil in vain.

17   But even if I am being poured out as a drink offering upon the sacrifice and service of your faith, I rejoice and share my joy with you all.

18   And you too, *I urge you,* rejoice in the same way and share your joy with me.

IV. *The coming of Timothy and Epaphroditus (2:19–30)*

2:19
Rom 16:21

2:20
1 Cor 16:10

2:21
1 Cor 10:24;
13:5
2:22
1 Cor 4:17;
1 Tim 1:2

19   But I hope in the Lord Jesus to send Timothy to you shortly, so that I also may be encouraged when I learn of your condition.

20   For I have no one *else* of kindred spirit who will genuinely be concerned for your welfare.

21   For they all seek after their own interests, not those of Christ Jesus.

22   But you know of his proven worth that he served with me in the furtherance of the gospel like a child *serving* his father.

23   Therefore I hope to send him immediately, as soon as I see how things *go* with me;

2:24
Phil 1:25
2:25
Phil 4:18;
Philem 2

2:26
Phil 1:8

24   and I trust in the Lord that I myself also shall be coming shortly.

25   But I thought it necessary to send to you Epaphroditus, my brother and fellow worker and fellow soldier, who is also your messenger and minister to my need;

26   because he was longing [4]for you all and was distressed because you had heard that he was sick.

27   For indeed he was sick to the point of death, but God had mercy on him, and not on him only but also on me, lest I should have sorrow upon sorrow.

28   Therefore I have sent him all the more eagerly in order that when you see him again you may rejoice and I may be less concerned *about you.*

2:29
1 Cor 16:18;
1 Tim 5:17
2:30
1 Cor 16:17

29   Therefore receive him in the Lord with all joy, and hold men like him in high regard;

30   because he came close to death for the work of Christ, risking his life to complete what was deficient in your service to me.

V. *Exhortation and doctrine (3:1–4:9)*

A. *The example of Paul*

3:1
Phil 4:4

3:2
Gal 5:15;
2 Cor 11:13
3:3
Rom 2:28,29;
Gal 6:14,15

3   Finally, my brethren, rejoice in the Lord. To write the same things *again* is no trouble to me, and it is a safeguard for you.

2   Beware of the dogs, beware of the evil workers, beware of the false circumcision;

3   for we are the *true* circumcision, who worship in the Spirit of God and glory in Christ Jesus and put no confidence in the flesh,

4   although I myself might have confidence even in the flesh. If anyone else has a mind to put confidence in the flesh, I far more:

3:5
Rom 11:1;
2 Cor 11:22
3:6
Acts 22:3;
Rom 10:5;
Luke 1:6
3:7
Matt 13:44;
Luke 14:33
3:8
Eph 4:13;
2 Pet 1:3
3:9
Rom 10:5;
9:30

5   circumcised the eighth day, of the nation of Israel, of the tribe of Benjamin, a Hebrew of Hebrews; as to the Law, a Pharisee;

6   as to zeal, a persecutor of the church; as to the righteousness which is in the Law, found blameless.

7   But whatever things were gain to me, those things I have counted as loss for the sake of Christ.

8   More than that, I count all things to be loss in view of the surpassing value of knowing Christ Jesus my Lord, for whom I have suffered the loss of all things, and count them but rubbish in order that I may gain Christ,

9   and may be found in Him, not having a righteousness of my own derived from *the* Law, but that which is through faith in Christ, the righteousness which *comes* from God on the basis of faith,

[4]Some ancient mss. read *to see you all*

10   that I may know Him, and the power of His resurrection and the fellowship of His sufferings, being conformed to His death;

11   in order that I may attain to the resurrection from the dead.

12   Not that I have already obtained *it*, or have already become perfect, but I press on in order that I may lay hold of that for which also I was laid hold of by Christ Jesus.

13   Brethren, I do not regard myself as having laid hold of *it* yet; but one thing *I do*: forgetting what *lies* behind and reaching forward to what *lies* ahead,

14   I press on toward the goal for the prize of the upward call of God in Christ Jesus.

15   Let us therefore, as many as are perfect, have this attitude; and if in anything you have a different attitude, God will reveal that also to you;

16   however, let us keep living by that same *standard* to which we have attained.

B. *Warning against antinomianism*

17   Brethren, join in following my example, and observe those who walk according to the pattern you have in us.

18   For many walk, of whom I often told you, and now tell you even weeping, *that they are* enemies of the cross of Christ,

19   whose end is destruction, whose god is *their* appetite, and *whose* glory is in their shame, who set their minds on earthly things.

20   For our citizenship is in heaven, from which also we eagerly wait for a Savior, the Lord Jesus Christ;

21   who will transform the body of our humble state into conformity with the body of His glory, by the exertion of the power that He has even to subject all things to Himself.

C. *Exhortation concluded*

4 Therefore, my beloved brethren whom I long *to see*, my joy and crown, so stand firm in the Lord, my beloved.

2   I urge Euodia and I urge Syntyche to live in harmony in the Lord.

3   Indeed, true comrade, I ask you also to help these women who have shared my struggle in *the cause of* the gospel, together with Clement also, and the rest of my fellow workers, whose names are in the book of life.

4   Rejoice in the Lord always; again I will say, rejoice!

5   Let your forbearing *spirit* be known to all men. The Lord is near.

6   Be anxious for nothing, but in everything by prayer and supplication with thanksgiving let your requests be made known to God.

7   And the peace of God, which surpasses all comprehension, shall guard your hearts and your minds in Christ Jesus.

8   Finally, brethren, whatever is true, whatever is honorable, whatever is right, whatever is pure, whatever is lovely, whatever is of good repute, if there is any excellence and if anything worthy of praise, let your mind dwell on these things.

9   The things you have learned and received and heard and seen in me, practice these things; and the God of peace shall be with you.

VI. *Acknowledgment of the Philippian gift (4:10–20)*

10   But I rejoiced in the Lord greatly, that now at last you have revived your concern for me; indeed, you were concerned *before*, but you lacked opportunity.

11   Not that I speak from want; for I have learned to be content in whatever circumstances I am.

12   I know how to get along with humble means, and I also know how to live in

---

3:10
Rom 6:3-5;
8:17
3:11
Acts 26:7
3:12
1 Tim 6:12;
1 Cor 13:10;
Acts 9:5,6
3:13
Luke 9:62;
1 Cor 9:24
3:14
Heb 6:1;
2 Tim 1:9
3:15
1 Cor 2:6;
Gal 5:10
3:16
Rom 12:16;
Gal 6:16

3:17
1 Cor 4:16;
1 Pet 5:3
3:18
Acts 20:31;
Gal 6:14
3:19
2 Cor 11:15;
Rom 16:18;
6:21; 8:5,6
*3:20
Eph 2:19;
Col 3:1;
1 Cor 1:7
3:21
1 Cor 15:43;
Col 3:4;
Eph 1:19

4:1
Phil 1:8;
1 Cor 16:13;
Phil 1:27
4:2
Phil 2:2
4:3
Rom 16:3;
Luke 10:20;
Rev 3:5
4:4
Rom 12:12;
Phil 3:1
4:5
Heb 10:37;
James 5:8,9
*4:6
Matt 6:25;
Eph 6:18
4:7
John 14:27;
Col 3:15;
1 Pet 1:5
4:8
1 Pet 2:12;
1 Thess 5:22
4:9
Phil 3:17;
Rom 15:33

4:11
1 Tim 6:6
4:12
1 Cor 4:11;
2 Cor 11:9

3:20 The true commonwealth or citizenship (*politeuma*) of the believer is in heaven. The world is not the believer's spirtual home, for it is impermanent and dominated by Satan, whereas heaven obeys the rule of God and endures forever. The normal attitude of the believer, who is in this world but not of it, is to look for the coming of the Lord to celebrate His triumph over the powers of evil and perfect His work of redemption. The Christian rejoices in the prospect of living in the glory of Christ's presence, and of enjoying the bliss and delight of heaven's eternal home.

At the same time, one should neither overlook nor underestimate the present and effective lordship of Christ over all things.

4:6 Believers are to pray with thanksgiving for the perfect answer they know God will give them in response to their petitions. Prayerlessness is sure to bring about growing anxiety and a sense of insecurity. To be anxious about nothing excludes everything. To pray about everything excludes nothing. But effective prayer must be accompanied by thanksgiving, which means that we thank God for the answer as soon as we have asked. This kind of prayer brings peace, a peace that passes natural human understanding because it is independent of circumstances and rests on the perfection and love of God Himself.

prosperity; in any and every circumstance I have learned the secret of being filled and going hungry, both of having abundance and suffering need.

13 I can do all things through Him who strengthens me.

14 Nevertheless, you have done well to share *with me* in my affliction.

15 And you yourselves also know, Philippians, that at the first preaching of the gospel, after I departed from Macedonia, no church shared with me in the matter of giving and receiving but you alone;

16 for even in Thessalonica you sent *a gift* more than once for my needs.

17 Not that I seek the gift itself, but I seek for the profit which increases to your account.

18 But I have received everything in full, and have an abundance; I am amply supplied, having received from Epaphroditus what you have sent, a fragrant aroma, an acceptable sacrifice, well-pleasing to God.

19 And my God shall supply all your needs according to His riches in glory in Christ Jesus.

20 Now to our God and Father *be* the glory forever and ever. Amen.

VII. *Conclusion (4:21–23)*

21 Greet every saint in Christ Jesus. The brethren who are with me greet you.
22 All the saints greet you, especially those of Caesar's household.
23 The grace of the Lord Jesus Christ be with your spirit.

4:13
John 15:5;
2 Cor 12:9
4:14
Phil 1:7
4:15
2 Cor 11:8,9
4:16
Acts 17:1;
1 Thess 2:9
4:17
Titus 3:14
4:18
Phil 2:25;
2 Cor 2:14
4:19
Ps 23:1;
2 Cor 9:8;
Eph 1:7
4:20
Gal 1:4;
Rom 11:36

COLOSSIANS

Authorship and Background: In writing to the Colossians, Paul addressed a group he did not know personally (2:1). Colossae was located in the Lycus Valley, in the province of Asia, some one hundred miles east of the capital city of Ephesus; the city was close to Laodicea and Hierapolis, and the three were often associated together (4:13,15,16; 2:1). Colossae had at one time been the most important of the three cities, but it had declined.

Paul was in prison (4:3,18), and the personal references indicate that the letter was written at the same time as the letter to Philemon. These, with Philippians and Ephesians, are the four "Prison Letters" composed in Rome, A.D. 59-61 (cf. the Introductions to Ephesians and Philippians). The same names appear in Colossians and Philemon: Archippus (Col. 4:17; Philem. 2) and Onesimus (Col. 4:9; Philem. 10), Aristarchus, Mark, Epaphras, Luke, and Demas (Col. 4:10,12,14; Philem. 23-24). Timothy is associated with Paul in the writing of Philippians (1:1), Colossians (1:1), and Philemon (1).

Colossians was written to counteract some erroneous and dangerous teaching; doubtless, Paul heard of this from Epaphras, leader of the work in the three cities, who had come to see him (1:7,8; 4:12,13; cf. Philem. 23). This teaching was related to some form of Gnosticism. Formulated in a Jewish framework, it deprived Jesus Christ of His unique status as the Son of God and Savior, and reduced Him to only one, albeit in an exalted place, of a series of created divine beings emanating in a graduated scale from the Godhead, through which creation and God were joined. Paul feared that asceticism, magical rites, and worship of heavenly bodies, all derived from the Gnostic dualism, would reduce Christianity to another religious philosophy, preliminary and inferior to the real "knowledge" of the Gnostic philosophy. The precise form of this Colossian heresy has long since passed away.

Characteristics: Paul met this dangerous heresy by proclaiming the uniqueness and complete sufficiency of Jesus Christ as the only Savior of all: He is the image of the invisible God, God's first-born who existed prior to all creation, and who was the agent in creation, through whom all created things, in heaven and on earth, came into being. He is the source, the controlling power, and the goal of all creation. In Him alone is the whole of the Godhead to be found—not dispersed through a series of divine and semidivine beings. This being so, the Colossians are to reject any system that would belittle the person of Christ, and stand fast in the faith, holding to the hope contained in the gospel. They must reject fanciful teachings having to do with food, drink, festivals, and misplaced asceticism. In Christ they have been raised to newness of life, and in Him all grace and virtues are to be found. Hold fast to Him who is the source of life and spiritual growth!

Contents:

I. Introduction (1:1-14)

II. Christian doctrine (1:15-3:4): Christ in His relation to God, to creation, and to the church. Through His death on the cross He has saved us: give Him full allegiance and reject all human wisdom and fanciful regulations. With Christ, believers have died (2:20) and been raised (3:1).

III. The Christian life (3:5-4:6): Christians are to put to death all earthly passions (3:5) and discard all sins (3:8), and put on in their place the garments of Christian virtues (3:12), and in particular, love, which binds them all together in perfect harmony (3:14). Wives and husbands, children and parents, slaves and masters, are to manifest this new life (3:18-4:1).

IV. Conclusion (4:7-18)

THE LETTER OF PAUL TO THE
COLOSSIANS

I. Introduction (1:1–14)

A. Salutation

1 Paul, an apostle of Jesus Christ by the will of God, and Timothy our brother,
2 to the saints and faithful brethren in Christ *who are* at Colossae: Grace to you and peace from God our Father.

B. Thanksgiving

3 We give thanks to God, the Father of our Lord Jesus Christ, praying always for you,
4 since we heard of your faith in Christ Jesus and the love which you have for all the saints;
5 because of the hope laid up for you in heaven, of which you previously heard in the word of truth, the gospel,
6 which has come to you, just as in all the world also it is constantly bearing fruit and increasing, even as *it has been doing* in you also since the day you heard *of it* and understood the grace of God in truth;
7 just as you learned *it* from Epaphras, our beloved fellow bond-servant, who is a faithful servant of Christ on [1]our behalf,
8 and he also informed us of your love in the Spirit.

C. Apostolic prayer

9 For this reason also, since the day we heard *of it*, we have not ceased to pray for you and to ask that you may be filled with the knowledge of His will in all spiritual wisdom and understanding,
10 so that you may walk in a manner worthy of the Lord, to please *Him* in all respects, bearing fruit in every good work and increasing in the knowledge of God;
11 strengthened with all power, according to His glorious might, for the attaining of all steadfastness and patience; joyously
12 giving thanks to the Father, who has qualified us to share in the inheritance of the saints in light.
13 For He delivered us from the domain of darkness, and transferred us to the kingdom of His beloved Son,
14 in whom we have redemption, the forgiveness of sins.

II. Christian doctrine (1:15–3:4)

A. The person and work of Christ

15 And He is the image of the invisible God, the first-born of all creation.
16 For by Him all things were created, *both* in the heavens and on earth, visible and invisible, whether thrones or dominions or rulers or authorities—all things have been created by Him and for Him.
17 And He is before all things, and in Him all things hold together.
18 He is also head of the body, the church; and He is the beginning, the first-born from the dead; so that He Himself might come to have first place in everything.
19 For it was the *Father's* good pleasure for all the fulness to dwell in Him,

[1]Some later mss. read *your*

	1:1
	Eph 1:1
	1:2
	Rom 1:7
	1:3
	Eph 1:16
	1:4
	Eph 1:15;
	Gal 5:6
	1:5
	1 Thess 5:8;
	1 Pet 1:4
	1:6
	Matt 24:14;
	John 15:16
	*1:7
	Philem 23;
	Col 4:7
	1:8
	Rom 15:30
	1:9
	Eph 1:15-17;
	Rom 12:2
	1:10
	Eph 4:1;
	1 Thess 4:1;
	Rom 1:13
	1:11
	Eph 3:16;
	4:2; Acts 5:41
	1:12
	Eph 5:20;
	1:11
	1:13
	Eph 6:12;
	2 Pet 1:11
	1:15
	2 Cor 4:4;
	Rev 3:14
	1:16
	Heb 1:2;
	Eph 1:20,21;
	Heb 2:10
	1:17
	John 1:1;
	8:58
	1:18
	Eph 1:22,23;
	Rev 1:5
	1:19
	John 1:16

1:7 *Epaphras* is mentioned also in 4:12 and Philem. 23. Like Timothy, he is called a *fellow bond-servant* of Jesus Christ by Paul. (This term comes from the Greek word *doulos*.) Timothy seems to have been an evangelist and perhaps even the founder of the church of Colossae. He was with Paul during part of his first Roman imprisonment and may even have been imprisoned with him as a co-defendant. No higher tribute could be paid him than that expressed in the words of Paul here: *who is a faithful servant of Christ*.

1:20
2 Cor 5:18;
Eph 2:13,14

1:21
Rom 5:10;
Eph 2:3
*1:22
Rom 7:4;
Eph 2:15;
5:27
1:23
Eph 3:17;
Rom 10:18

20   and through Him to reconcile all things to Himself, having made peace through the blood of His cross; through Him, *I say*, whether things on earth or things in heaven.

21   And although you were formerly alienated and hostile in mind, *engaged* in evil deeds,

22   yet He has now reconciled you in His fleshly body through death, in order to present you before Him holy and blameless and beyond reproach—

23   if indeed you continue in the faith firmly established and steadfast, and not moved away from the hope of the gospel that you have heard, which was proclaimed in all creation under heaven, and of which I, Paul, was made a minister.

B. *The ministry of Paul*

24   Now I rejoice in my sufferings for your sake, and in my flesh I do my share on behalf of His body (which is the church) in filling up that which is lacking in Christ's afflictions.

1:25
Eph 3:2

25   Of *this church* I was made a minister according to the stewardship from God bestowed on me for your benefit, that I might fully carry out the *preaching of* the word of God,

1:26
Eph 3:3,4

26   *that is,* the mystery which has been hidden from the *past* ages and generations; but has now been manifested to His saints,

*1:27
2 Cor 2:14;
Rom 9:23;
1 Tim 1:1
1:28
Col 3:16;
1 Cor 2:6,7
1:29
1 Cor 15:10;
Col 2:1;
Eph 1:19

27   to whom God willed to make known what is the riches of the glory of this mystery among the Gentiles, which is Christ in you, the hope of glory.

28   And we proclaim Him, admonishing every man and teaching every man with all wisdom, that we may present every man complete in Christ.

29   And for this purpose also I labor, striving according to His power, which mightily works within me.

C. *Paul's concern for them*

2:1
Col 1:29; 4:12

*2:2
Phil 3:8

2 For I want you to know how great a struggle I have on your behalf, and for those who are at Laodicea, and for all those who have not personally seen my face,

2   that their hearts may be encouraged, having been knit together in love, and *attaining* to all the wealth that comes from the full assurance of understanding, *resulting* in a true knowledge of God's mystery, *that is*, Christ *Himself*,

2:3
Is 45:3;
Rom 11:33
2:5
1 Thess 2:17;
1 Cor 14:40;
1 Pet 5:9
2:6
1 Thess 4:1
2:7
Eph 2:21

3   in whom are hidden all the treasures of wisdom and knowledge.

4   I say this in order that no one may delude you with persuasive argument.

5   For even though I am absent in body, nevertheless I am with you in spirit, rejoicing to see your good discipline and the stability of your faith in Christ.

6   As you therefore have received Christ Jesus the Lord, *so* walk in Him,

7   having been firmly rooted *and now* being built up in Him and established [2]in your faith, just as you were instructed, *and* overflowing with gratitude.

D. *The sufficiency of Christ*

2:8
1 Cor 8:9;
1 Tim 6:20;
Gal 4:3
2:9
John 1:14;
Col 1:19
2:10
Eph 1:21,22
*2:11f
Rom 2:29;
Phil 3:3;
Rom 6:6;
Gal 5:24

8   See to it that no one takes you captive through philosophy and empty deception, according to the tradition of men, according to the elementary principles of the world, rather than according to Christ.

9   For in Him all the fulness of Deity dwells in bodily form,

10   and in Him you have been made complete, and He is the head over all rule and authority;

11   and in Him you were also circumcised with a circumcision made without

[2]Or, *by*

1:22 Holiness is commanded by God (Lev. 20:7) and has been made attainable by Him (Rom. 6:22). It does not imply sinless perfection (1 John 1:8), but a condition wherein the believer is wholly yielded to God's will and set apart for His service. When the believer's conscience is kept clear before God by repentance and self-dedication, then his heart does not condemn him. Two erroneous notions are prevalent in relation to holiness. The first is that the believer *must* sin and the second that he *cannot* sin. The correct view is that the believer *can* sin but he *need not* do so.
1:27 Union with Christ is twofold: (1) it includes all believers who are partakers of the divine nature and are members of His body through faith (Eph. 3:17), a union that is maintained by faith (Eph. 3:17) as we feed on Him (John

6:56) and as His word abides in us (John 15:7); and (2) it involves abiding in Him for the purpose of growth in grace and fruitfulness.
2:2 Christ is God's mystery. But Paul uses the term *mystery* here not in the sense of a continuing secret, but in the sense that that which was hidden has been disclosed; and it is God's intention for us to grasp, as fully as we are capable of grasping, all that He has revealed to us about the person and the work of Jesus Christ.
2:11,12 These verses have assumed major importance in the discussion of infant baptism. Paedobaptists understand them to signify that New Testament water baptism has replaced Old Testament circumcision as the sign and seal of admission into the covenant of grace. Therefore, since God

hands, in the removal of the body of the flesh by the circumcision of Christ;

12   having been buried with Him in baptism, in which you were also raised up with Him through faith in the working of God, who raised Him from the dead.

13   And when you were dead in your transgressions and the uncircumcision of your flesh, He made you alive together with Him, having forgiven us all our transgressions,

14   having canceled out the certificate of debt consisting of decrees against us *and* which was hostile to us; and He has taken it out of the way, having nailed it to the cross.

15   When He had disarmed the rulers and authorities, He made a public display of them, having triumphed over them through Him.

E. *Asceticism and ritual condemned*

16   Therefore let no one act as your judge in regard to food or drink or in respect to a festival or a new moon or a Sabbath day—

17   things which are a *mere* shadow of what is to come; but the substance belongs to Christ.

18   Let no one keep defrauding you of your prize by delighting in self-abasement and the worship of the angels, taking his stand on *visions* he has seen, inflated without cause by his fleshly mind,

19   and not holding fast to the head, from whom the entire body, being supplied and held together by the joints and ligaments, grows with a growth which is from God.

20   If you have died with Christ to the elementary principles of the world, why, as if you were living in the world, do you submit yourself to decrees, such as,

21   "Do not handle, do not taste, do not touch!"

22   (which all *refer to* things destined to perish with the using)—in accordance with the commandments and teachings of men?

23   These are matters which have, to be sure, the appearance of wisdom in self-made religion and self-abasement and severe treatment of the body, *but are* of no value against fleshly indulgence.

F. *The true locus of the Christian life*

3 If then you have been raised up with Christ, keep seeking the things above, where Christ is, seated at the right hand of God.

2   Set your mind on the things above, not on the things that are on earth.

3   For you have died and your life is hidden with Christ in God.

4   When Christ, who is our life, is revealed, then you also will be revealed with Him in glory.

III. *The Christian life (3:5—4:6)*

A. *The transformed walk*

5   Therefore consider the members of your earthly body as dead to immorality, impurity, passion, evil desire, and greed, which amounts to idolatry.

6   For it is on account of these things that the wrath of God will come[3] ,

7   and in them you also once walked, when you were living in them.

8   But now you also, put them all aside: anger, wrath, malice, slander, *and* abusive speech from your mouth.

[3]Some early mss. add *upon the sons of disobedience*

2:12 Rom 6:4,5; Acts 2:24
2:13 Eph 2:1
2:14 Eph 2:15
2:15 Gen 3:15; Is 53:12; Eph 6:12
2:16 Rom 14:3; 14:17; 14:5; Gal 4:10,11
2:17 Heb 8:5
2:18 Phil 3:14; v. 23
2:19 Eph 1:22; 4:16
***2:20** Rom 6:3,5; Gal 4:3,9
2:22 1 Cor 6:13; Is 29:13; Titus 1:14
2:23 Rom 13:14; 1 Tim 4:8
3:1 Ps 110:1; Rom 8:34
3:2 Phil 3:19,20
3:3 Rom 6:2; 2 Cor 5:14
3:4 1 John 3:2; John 14:6
3:5 Rom 6:13; Eph 5:3,5
3:6 Rom 1:18; Eph 5:6
3:7 Eph 2:2
3:8 Eph 4:22,29

ordained circumcision for the infant children of Israel (Gen. 17:12), baptism also is properly applied to the infants of New Testament believers. On the other hand, opponents of this view feel that the connection made here between circumcision and baptism is merely spiritual and should not be pressed to decide who are the proper subjects of baptism. They also take the phrase "buried with Him in baptism" as indicating immersion to be the proper mode of administering the ordinance. Paedobaptists, however, understand this phrase as referring to the spiritual efficacy of baptism (since a believer by faith is united with Christ both in His death and in His resurrection), and as having nothing to do with the mode.

2:20 This passage agrees with the book of Hebrews in teaching that the ceremonial and ritual commandments of the Old Testament dispensation are no longer binding on believers. The Mosaic code, with its minute prescriptions, replete with symbol and type, is referred to as mere *elements* (so translate *stoicheia* here, rather than the rendering *elementary principles*) that were meant for the training of God's people in their immature stage before Christ's coming. But under the new covenant, the laws of blood sacrifice, the dietary prohibition, and so on, are to be followed no longer, since they were only shadows pointing forward to Jesus of Nazareth.

9   Do not lie to one another, since you laid aside the old self with its *evil* practices,

10   and have put on the new self who is being renewed to a true knowledge according to the image of the One who created him

11   —*a renewal* in which there is no *distinction between* Greek and Jew, circumcised and uncircumcised, barbarian, Scythian, slave and freeman, but Christ is all, and in all.

12   And so, as those who have been chosen of God, holy and beloved, put on a heart of compassion, kindness, humility, gentleness and patience;

13   bearing with one another, and forgiving each other, whoever has a complaint against anyone; just as the Lord forgave you, so also should you.

14   And beyond all these things *put on* love, which is the perfect bond of unity.

15   And let the peace of Christ rule in your hearts, to which indeed you were called in one body; and be thankful.

16   Let the word of [4]Christ richly dwell within you, with all wisdom teaching and admonishing one another with psalms *and* hymns *and* spiritual songs, singing with thankfulness in your hearts to God.

17   And whatever you do in word or deed, *do* all in the name of the Lord Jesus, giving thanks through Him to God the Father.

B. *The Christian family*

18   Wives, be subject to your husbands, as is fitting in the Lord.

19   Husbands, love your wives, and do not be embittered against them.

20   Children, be obedient to your parents in all things, for this is well-pleasing to the Lord.

21   Fathers, do not [5]exasperate your children, that they may not lose heart.

22   Slaves, in all things obey those who are your masters on earth, not with external service, as those who *merely* please men, but with sincerity of heart, fearing the Lord.

23   Whatever you do, do your work heartily, as for the Lord rather than for men;

24   knowing that from the Lord you will receive the reward of the inheritance. It is the Lord Christ whom you serve.

25   For he who does wrong will receive the consequences of the wrong which he has done, and that without partiality.

4   Masters, grant to your slaves justice and fairness, knowing that you too have a Master in heaven.

C. *Prayer*

2   Devote yourselves to prayer, keeping alert in it with *an attitude of* thanksgiving;

3   praying at the same time for us as well, that God may open up to us a door for the word, so that we may speak forth the mystery of Christ, for which I have also been imprisoned;

4   in order that I may make it clear in the way I ought to speak.

D. *Conduct*

5   Conduct yourselves with wisdom toward outsiders, making the most of the opportunity.

6   Let your speech always be with grace, seasoned, *as it were*, with salt, so that you may know how you should respond to each person.

IV. *Conclusion (4:7–18)*

A. *Regarding Tychicus and Onesimus*

7   As to all my affairs, Tychicus, *our* beloved brother and faithful servant and fellow bond-servant in the Lord, will bring you information.

8   For I have sent him to you for this very purpose, that you may know *about* our circumstances and that he may encourage your hearts;

---

[4]Some mss. read *the Lord;* others read *God*   [5]Some early mss. read *provoke to anger*

9   and with him Onesimus, *our* faithful and beloved brother, who is one of your *number*. They will inform you about the whole situation here.

B. *Greetings from friends and final instructions*

10   Aristarchus, my fellow prisoner, sends you his greetings; and *also* Barnabas' cousin Mark (about whom you received instructions: if he comes to you, welcome him);

11   and *also* Jesus who is called Justus; these are the only fellow workers for the kingdom of God who are from the circumcision; and they have proved to be an encouragement to me.

12   Epaphras, who is one of your number, a bondslave of Jesus Christ, sends you his greetings, always laboring earnestly for you in his prayers, that you may stand perfect and fully assured in all the will of God.

13   For I bear him witness that he has a deep concern for you and for those who are in Laodicea and Hierapolis.

14   Luke, the beloved physician, sends you his greetings, and *also* Demas.

15   Greet the brethren who are in Laodicea and also [6]Nympha and the church that is in her house.

16   And when this letter is read among you, have it also read in the church of the Laodiceans; and you, for your part read my letter *that is coming* from Laodicea.

17   And say to Archippus, "Take heed to the ministry which you have received in the Lord, that you may fulfill it."

18   I, Paul, write this greeting with my own hand. Remember my imprisonment. Grace be with you.

[6]Or, *Nymphas* (masc.)

4:9
Philem 10

4:10
Acts 19:29;
15:37; 4:36

4:11
Acts 11:2;
Rom 16:3

4:12
Col 1:7;
Rom 15:30;
Phil 3:15

4:13
Col 2:1

4:14
2 Tim 4:10,
11; Philem 24
4:15
Rom 16:5

4:17
Philem 2;
2 Tim 4:5
4:18
1 Cor 16:21;
Heb 13:3;
13:25

INTRODUCTION TO
THE FIRST LETTER OF PAUL TO THE
THESSALONIANS

Authorship and Background: Paul's two letters to the church at Thessalonica are, in the opinion of most scholars, among the earliest he wrote. Although the letters themselves afford no conclusive evidence as to place and time of writing, it would appear from Acts that they were written during the latter part of Paul's stay in Corinth (A.D. 49-51), on his second missionary journey. Paul arrived in Corinth alone (cf. Introduction to 1 Cor.), after his ministry in Thessalonica, Berea, and Athens (Acts 17:1-18:1). It seems that Timothy, at least, had joined Paul earlier in Athens and had been sent to Thessalonica (3:1,2), although Acts does not mention this. In Corinth, then, Timothy and Silas joined Paul (Acts 18:5; 1 Thess. 3:6); upon receipt of news from Thessalonica, Paul wrote the church there, associating both Silas and Timothy with himself in writing the letters (1:1; 2 Thess. 1:1).

Thessalonica was the capital of the Roman province of Macedonia. It was a free city, ruled by its own magistrates, called "politarchs" (city authorities) (Acts 17:6,8). Paul came to Thessalonica from Philippi on his second missionary journey (Acts 17:1-10). Acts speaks of a three-week ministry in the synagogue there (Acts 17:2), but it would seem from Paul's references to the Christians there as Gentiles (1:9; 2:14; cf. also "great number of the God-fearing Greeks" in Acts 17:4) and other references (cf. 2:9; Phil. 4:16; 2 Thess. 3:8), that the synagogue preaching was only the beginning of Paul's ministry in the city. How long he stayed is a matter of conjecture: perhaps for several months. The implacable hatred of the Thessalonian Jews and their persecutions (Acts 17:5) caused him to leave Thessalonica for Berea (Acts 17:10), and then Athens (Acts 17:13-15). It would seem from the reference to Macedonia in Acts 20:1,3 that Paul visited Thessalonica on his return to Jerusalem at the end of his third missionary journey in A.D. 56.

The following Christians from Thessalonica are known by name: Jason (Acts 17:5-9), Aristarchus (Acts 19:29; 20:4; 27:2), Secundus (Acts 20:4), and Gaius (Acts 19:29).

Characteristics: Timothy brought news to Paul about the Thessalonian church. The letter deals with special problems, particularly the second coming of Christ. Paul's love for the Christians at Thessalonica is evident from the personal references to their steadfast faith (1:3-10; 2:14; 3:6-9) and his lament at his inability to return (2:17-20). He shows concern for their spiritual welfare, warning them to order their lives worthy of Christians in relation to the immoral society in which they lived, and in Christian fellowship with one another (4:9-12; 5:5-22). He is especially concerned lest their misunderstanding about the Lord's return lead them to err in deed and doctrine (4:13-5:11).

Contents:

I. Personal matters (1:1-3:13): Paul's joy over their faith and love, well known to other churches; his self-sacrificing ministry among them; his concern for their spiritual welfare, "for now we really live, if you stand firm in the Lord" (3:8).

II. Exhortation and instruction (4:1-5:28): The Christian demands of purity and holiness; the nature of faith and hope for the Lord's return. Salutation and benediction.

THE FIRST LETTER OF PAUL TO THE
THESSALONIANS

I. *Personal matters (1:1–3:13)*

A. *Salutation*

1 Paul and Silvanus and Timothy to the church of the Thessalonians in God the Father and the Lord Jesus Christ: Grace to you and peace.

B. *Thanksgiving for them*

2 We give thanks to God always for all of you, making mention *of you* in our prayers;

3 constantly bearing in mind your work of faith and labor of love and steadfastness of hope in our Lord Jesus Christ in the presence of our God and Father,

4 knowing, brethren beloved by God, *His* choice of you;

5 for our gospel did not come to you in word only, but also in power and in the Holy Spirit and with full conviction; just as you know what kind of men we proved to be among you for your sake.

6 You also became imitators of us and of the Lord, having received the word in much tribulation with the joy of the Holy Spirit,

7 so that you became an example to all the believers in Macedonia and in Achaia.

8 For the word of the Lord has sounded forth from you, not only in Macedonia and Achaia, but also in every place your faith toward God has gone forth, so that we have no need to say anything.

9 For they themselves report about us what kind of a reception we had with you, and how you turned to God from idols to serve a living and true God,

10 and to wait for His Son from heaven, whom He raised from the dead, *that is* Jesus, who delivers us from the wrath to come.

C. *Paul's work among them*

2 For you yourselves know, brethren, that our coming to you was not in vain,

2 but after we had already suffered and been mistreated in Philippi, as you know, we had the boldness in our God to speak to you the gospel of God amid much opposition.

3 For our exhortation does not *come* from error or impurity or by way of deceit;

4 but just as we have been approved by God to be entrusted with the gospel, so we speak, not as pleasing men but God, who examines our hearts.

5 For we never came with flattering speech, as you know, nor with a pretext for greed—God is witness—

6 nor did we seek glory from men, either from you or from others, even though as apostles of Christ we might have asserted our authority.

7 But we proved to be [1]gentle among you, as a nursing *mother* tenderly cares for her own children.

8 Having thus a fond affection for you, we were well-pleased to impart to you not only the gospel of God but also our own lives, because you had become very dear to us.

9 For you recall, brethren, our labor and hardship, *how* working night and day so as not to be a burden to any of you, we proclaimed to you the gospel of God.

[1]Some ancient mss. read *babes*

*1:1
2 Thess 1:1;
2 Cor 1:19;
Acts 16:1;
17:1;
Rom 1:7

1:2
2 Thess 1:3;
Rom 1:8,9
1:3
2 Thess 1:11;
1:3

1:5
2 Thess 2:14;
Col 2:2;
2 Thess 3:7
1:6
1 Cor 4:16;
11:1;
Acts 17:5-10;
13:52

1:8
Rom 10:18;
1:8; 2 Thess
1:4
1:9
1 Cor 12:2;
Gal 4:8
1:10
2 Pet 3:12;
Acts 2:24;
Rom 5:9

2:1
1 Thess 1:5,9
2:2
Acts 16:22;
1 Thess 1:5;
Phil 1:30
2:3
2 Cor 7:2

2:4
2 Cor 2:17;
Gal 2:7; 1:10
2:5
Acts 20:33;
Rom 1:9
2:6
2 Cor 4:5;
1 Cor 9:1,2
2:7
v. 11;
Gal 4:19
2:8
2 Cor 12:15;
1 John 3:16
2:9
Acts 20:34;
2 Thess 3:8;
2 Cor 12:13

1:1 *Silvanus* is the Latinized name of Paul's companion who in Acts is called *Silas* (Acts 15:22–18:5); in the Epistles he is always called Silvanus (2 Cor. 1:19; 1 Thess. 1:1; 2 Thess. 1:1; 1 Pet. 5:12). He was Paul's trusted companion on the second missionary tour.

2:10
1 Thess 1:5;
2 Cor 1:12
10   You are witnesses, and *so is* God, how devoutly and uprightly and blameless-ly we behaved toward you believers;

2:11
1 Cor 4:14;
v. 7
11   just as you know how we *were* exhorting and encouraging and imploring each one of you as a father *would* his own children,

2:12
Eph 4:1;
1 Pet 5:10
12   so that you may walk in a manner worthy of the God who calls you into His own kingdom and glory.

D. *Paul's reception by them*

*2:13
1 Thess 1:2;
Gal 4:14
13   And for this reason we also constantly thank God that when you received from us the word of God's message, you accepted *it* not *as* the word of men, but *for* what it really is, the word of God, which also performs its work in you who believe.

2:14
Acts 17:5;
2 Thess 1:4
14   For you, brethren, became imitators of the churches of God in Christ Jesus that are in Judea, for you also endured the same sufferings at the hands of your own countrymen, even as they *did* from the Jews,

2:15
Acts 2:23;
7:52
15   who both killed the Lord Jesus and the prophets, and drove us out. They are not pleasing to God, but hostile to all men,

2:16
Acts 9:23;
13:45,50ff;
Matt 23:32
16   hindering us from speaking to the Gentiles that they might be saved; with the result that they always fill up the measure of their sins. But wrath has come upon them [2]to the utmost.

E. *Timothy's mission among them*

2:17
1 Cor 5:3;
1 Thess 3:10
17   But we, brethren, having been bereft of you for a short while—in person, not in spirit—were all the more eager with great desire to see your face.

2:18
Rom 15:22;
1:13
18   For we wanted to come to you—I, Paul, more than once—and *yet* Satan thwarted us.

2:19
2 Cor 1:14;
Phil 4:1;
1 Thess 3:13
19   For who is our hope or joy or crown of exultation? Is it not even you, in the presence of our Lord Jesus at His coming?

2:20
2 Cor 1:14
20   For you are our glory and joy.

3:1
v. 5;
Acts 17:15
3 Therefore when we could endure *it* no longer, we thought it best to be left behind at Athens alone;

3:2
2 Cor 1:1;
Col 1:1
2   and we sent Timothy, our brother and God's fellow worker in the gospel of Christ, to strengthen and encourage you as to your faith,

3:3
Acts 9:16;
14:22
3   so that no man may be disturbed by these afflictions; for you yourselves know that we have been destined for this.

3:4
Acts 20:24;
1 Thess 2:14
4   For indeed when we were with you, we *kept* telling you in advance that we were going to suffer affliction; and so it came to pass, as you know.

3:5
1 Cor 11:3;
Gal 2:2
5   For this reason, when I could endure *it* no longer, I also sent to find out about your faith, for fear that the tempter might have tempted you, and our labor should be in vain.

F. *The good news from them*

3:6
Acts 18:5;
1 Thess 1:3
6   But now that Timothy has come to us from you, and has brought us good news of your faith and love, and that you always think kindly of us, longing to see us just as we also long to see you,

3:7
2 Cor 1:4
7   for this reason, brethren, in all our distress and affliction we were comforted about you through your faith;

3:8
Phil 4:1
8   for now we *really* live, if you stand firm in the Lord.

3:9
1 Thess 1:2
9   For what thanks can we render to God for you in return for all the joy with which we rejoice before our God on your account,

3:10
2 Tim 1:3;
2 Cor 13:9
10   as we night and day keep praying most earnestly that we may see your face, and may complete what is lacking in your faith?

G. *Paul's prayer for them*

3:11
2 Thess 3:5
11   Now may our God and Father Himself and Jesus our Lord direct our way to you;

[2]Or, *forever*; or, *altogether*

2:13   See notes to 2 Tim. 3:16 on inspiration and Ps. 119:11 on proof of inspiration. Paul clearly distinguishes between the word of man and the Word of God.

12 and may the Lord cause you to increase and abound in love for one another, and for all men, just as we also *do* for you;

13 so that He may establish your hearts unblamable in holiness before our God and Father at the coming of our Lord Jesus with all His saints.

II. *Exhortation and instruction (4:1–5:28)*

A. *Exhortation to purity*

4 Finally then, brethren, we request and exhort you in the Lord Jesus, that, as you received from us *instruction* as to how you ought to walk and please God (just as you actually do ³walk), that you may excel still more.

2 For you know what commandments we gave you ⁴by *the authority of* the Lord Jesus.

3 For this is the will of God, your sanctification; *that is,* that you abstain from sexual immorality;

4 that each of you know how to possess his own ⁵vessel in sanctification and honor,

5 not in lustful passion, like the Gentiles who do not know God;

6 *and* that no man transgress and defraud his brother in the matter because the Lord is *the* avenger in all these things, just as we also told you before and solemnly warned *you.*

7 For God has not called us for the purpose of impurity, but in sanctification.

8 Consequently, he who rejects *this* is not rejecting man but the God who gives His Holy Spirit to you.

B. *Exhortation to love and labor*

9 Now as to the love of the brethren, you have no need for *anyone* to write to you, for you yourselves are taught by God to love one another;

10 for indeed you do practice it toward all the brethren who are in all Macedonia. But we urge you, brethren, to excel still more,

11 and to make it your ambition to lead a quiet life and attend to your own business and work with your hands, just as we commanded you;

12 so that you may behave properly toward outsiders and not be in any need.

C. *Comfort about the saved who sleep*

13 But we do not want you to be uninformed, brethren, about those who are asleep, that you may not grieve, as do the rest who have no hope.

14 For if we believe that Jesus died and rose again, even so God will bring with Him those who have fallen asleep in Jesus.

15 For this we say to you by the word of the Lord, that we who are alive, and remain until the coming of the Lord, shall not precede those who have fallen asleep.

16 For the Lord Himself will descend from heaven with a shout, with the voice of *the* archangel, and with the trumpet of God; and the dead in Christ shall rise first.

17 Then we who are alive and remain shall be caught up together with them in the clouds to meet the Lord in the air, and thus we shall always be with the Lord.

18 Therefore comfort one another with these words.

D. *The sudden coming of the Lord*

5 Now as to the times and the epochs, brethren, you have no need of anything to be written to you.

---

³Or, *conduct yourselves*   ⁴Lit., *through the Lord*   ⁵I.e., *body; or possibly, wife*

4:3 *sanctification,* see note to 1 Cor. 6:11.
4:9 See note to Rom. 13:9 concerning *love.*
4:15 In this passage, vv. 14–18, Paul deals with what has been termed by some the "rapture" or the "catching away" of the church. Certain truths appear here with great clarity: (1) the *coming of the Lord* (Greek the *parousia*) of v. 15, who will descend from heaven, shall occur; (2) the resurrection of all believers depends on the resurrection of Jesus (v. 14); (3) the dead in Christ will rise prior to other events connected with His coming (v. 16); and (4) those who are then alive and in Christ along with the resurrected dead in Christ shall *be caught up together with them in the clouds to meet the Lord in*

the air (vv. 16,17), indicating that the Lord Himself will remain in the air and call the saints to His side. The event itself will be accompanied by: (1) the cry of command; (2) the archangel's call; and (3) the sound of the trumpet of God. Some interpreters have seen in this account evidence for the removal of the church for a period of time prior to the second advent. Both the pre-tribulationists and the mid-tribulationists so hold.
5:1 Here Paul warns his readers not to set any timetable for the eschatological events he writes about in 4:13–18. In words reminiscent of Christ's teaching (cf. Matt. 24:42–44; Luke 12:39,40), Paul tells the Thessalonians that Christ's

---

Margin references:

3:12
1 Thess 4:1, 10
3:13
1 Cor 1:8;
1 Thess 2:19;
4:17

4:1
Phil 1:27;
1 Thess 2:12;
Col 1:10

*4:3
1 Cor 6:18;
Col 3:5
4:4
1 Cor 7:2;
1 Pet 3:7
4:5
4:6
Col 3:5;
Eph 4:17;
1 Cor 15:34
4:6
1 Cor 6:8;
Heb 13:4
4:7
Lev 11:44;
1 Pet 1:15;
1 Thess 2:3
4:8
Rom 5:5

*4:9
Rom 12:10;
1 Thess 5:1
4:10
1 Thess 1:7;
3:12
4:11
Eph 4:28;
2 Thess 3:10-12
4:12
Rom 13:13

4:13
Eph 2:12
4:14
1 Cor 15:13, 23
*4:15
1 Kin 13:17;
20:35;
1 Cor 15:51, 52
4:16
Matt 24:31;
1 Cor 15:23;
2 Thess 2:1
4:17
1 Cor 15:52;
Acts 1:9;
Rev 11:12;
John 12:26
*5:1
Acts 1:7;
1 Thess 4:9

2 For you yourselves know full well that the day of the Lord will come just like a thief in the night.

3 While they are saying, "Peace and safety!" then destruction will come upon them suddenly like birth pangs upon a woman with child; and they shall not escape.

4 But you, brethren, are not in darkness, that the day should overtake you like a thief;

5 for you are all sons of light and sons of day. We are not of night nor of darkness;

6 so then let us not sleep as others do, but let us be alert and [6]sober.

7 For those who sleep do their sleeping at night, and those who get drunk get drunk at night.

8 But since we are of *the* day, let us be [6]sober, having put on the breastplate of faith and love, and as a helmet, the hope of salvation.

9 For God has not destined us for wrath, but for obtaining salvation through our Lord Jesus Christ,

10 who died for us, that whether we are awake or asleep, we may live together with Him.

11 Therefore encourage one another, and build up one another, just as you also are doing.

E. *Practical exhortations*

12 But we request of you, brethren, that you appreciate those who diligently labor among you, and have charge over you in the Lord and give you instruction,

13 and that you esteem them very highly in love because of their work. Live in peace with one another.

14 And we urge you, brethren, admonish the unruly, encourage the fainthearted, help the weak, be patient with all men.

15 See that no one repays another with evil for evil, but always seek after that which is good for one another and for all men.

16 Rejoice always;

17 pray without ceasing;

18 in everything give thanks; for this is God's will for you in Christ Jesus.

19 Do not quench the Spirit;

20 do not despise prophetic [7]utterances.

21 But examine everything *carefully*; hold fast to that which is good;

22 abstain from every [8]form of evil.

F. *Conclusion*

23 Now may the God of peace Himself sanctify you entirely; and may your spirit and soul and body be preserved complete, without blame at the coming of our Lord Jesus Christ.

24 Faithful is He who calls you, and He also will bring it to pass.

25 Brethren, pray for us[9].

26 Greet all the brethren with a holy kiss.

27 I adjure you by the Lord to have this letter read to all the brethren.

28 The grace of our Lord Jesus Christ be with you.

[6]Or, *self-controlled* [7]Or, *gifts* [8]Or, *appearance* [9]Some mss. add *also*

coming will be totally unexpected, like that of a thief in the night. No one knows the times and seasons of the day of the Lord (cf. Matt. 24:36; Mark 13:32; Acts 1:7), so it is necessary for believers always to be ready (5:6–8; Matt. 24:42; 25:13; Mark 13:33–37; Luke 12:35–38), not in fear, but in hope and confidence, for *God has not destined us for wrath, but for obtaining salvation through our Lord Jesus Christ* (v. 9).
5:19 See note to Eph. 4:30 on grieving the Spirit. Undoubtedly, Paul was not speaking of quenching the Spirit in the same sense that he spoke of grieving the Spirit. Here he was referring to the gifts of the Spirit that in his day included speaking in tongues, prophesying, and miraculous healings. Christians must beware of falling into two extremes, either being overly enthusiastic about such spiritual gifts or cold and indifferent to them. Paul says that we are not to dampen the fire of the Holy Spirit, but rather, in the

employment of these special gifts by the Spirit, we are to use them: (1) for edifying (1 Cor. 14:26); and (2) decently and in order (4:12; 1 Cor. 14:40).
5:23 Theologians disagree as to whether man is trichotomous (consisting of three parts) or dichotomous (consisting of two parts). Paul here speaks of man as possessing *spirit and soul and body*. The Scriptural data are not so plain that an unqualified judgment can be rendered. Apparently the Hebrews looked on man as a unit, neither dichotomous nor trichotomous. The Hebrew writers used the words "flesh," "heart," "soul" (*nephesh*), "spirit" (*ruach*), and so forth, without supposing that man is the sum of these different parts. However, Scripture does insist on the continued real existence of man in a state of consciousness after physical death as evidenced by Luke 16:19ff.; Phil. 1:23; Rev. 7:14–17.

THESSALONIANS

Authorship and Background: 2 Thessalonians was probably written shortly after 1 Thessalonians, although opinions differ both as to the time and the place. It was designed to correct the widespread misunderstanding of Paul's teaching concerning the return of the Lord. The Thessalonians were disregarding what Paul had explicitly taught them in person (2:5,15; 3:6-10), and what he had written in his previous letter (2:15). Apparently a letter had been received by the Thessalonians, ostensibly from the apostle (2:2), which had led them to conclude that the great eschatological drama had already begun; consequently many of them had ceased working, thinking the end of the world to be at hand. They were living in idleness, thus creating an embarrassing situation (3:6,11). Paul wrote this letter to reprimand them sharply (3:6,14,15), and to command them to continue steadfastly in the true teaching, imitating his own example of work while he was with them (2:15; 3:7-10,12). In this way they will be preparing themselves for the return of Jesus.

Characteristics: Less effusive than the first letter, 2 Thessalonians is marked by some severe warnings and commands, reminiscent of the letter to the Galatians. Paul dwells at length on the signs that will precede the day of the Lord, and stresses the fact that the ultimate manifestation of "the man of lawlessness," in a frenzy of apostasy and blasphemy, will occur before the appearing and coming of the Lord Jesus (2:3-12). He sharply reprimands the idlers, and instructs the church to withdraw fellowship from them, albeit in love, not hatred: "Do not regard him as an enemy, but admonish him as a brother" (3:6,14,15).

Contents:

THE SECOND LETTER OF PAUL TO THE

THESSALONIANS

I. *Salutation (1:1,2)*

1:1
1 Thess 1:1;
2 Cor 1:19;
Acts 16:1
1:2
Rom 1:7;
1 Cor 1:3

1 Paul and Silvanus and Timothy to the church of the Thessalonians in God our Father and the Lord Jesus Christ:
2   Grace to you and peace from God the Father and the Lord Jesus Christ.

II. *Personal matters (1:3–12)*

A. *Thanksgiving*

1:3
1 Thess 1:2;
3:12

3   We ought always to give thanks to God for you, brethren, as is *only* fitting, because your faith is greatly enlarged, and the love of each one of you toward one another grows *ever* greater;

1:4
2 Cor 7:14;
1 Thess 1:3;
2:14

4   therefore, we ourselves speak proudly of you among the churches of God for your perseverance and faith in the midst of all your persecutions and afflictions which you endure.

B. *Encouragement to endure*

1:5
Phil 1:28;
1 Thess 2:14
1:6
Col 3:25;
Rev 6:10
1:7
1 Thess 4:16;
Jude 14
*1:8
Gal 4:8;
Rom 2:8
1:9
Phil 3:19;
2 Pet 3:7;
2 Thess 2:8
1:10
John 17:10;
1 Cor 3:13;
1:6

5   *This is* a plain indication of God's righteous judgment so that you may be considered worthy of the kingdom of God, for which indeed you are suffering.
6   For after all it is *only* just for God to repay with affliction those who afflict you,
7   and *to give* relief to you who are afflicted and to us as well when the Lord Jesus shall be revealed from heaven with His mighty angels in flaming fire,
8   dealing out retribution to those who do not know God and to those who do not obey the gospel of our Lord Jesus.
9   And these will pay the penalty of eternal destruction, away from the presence of the Lord and from the glory of His power,
10   when He comes to be glorified in His saints on that day, and to be marveled at among all who have believed—for our testimony to you was believed.

C. *Prayer*

1:11
v. 5; 1 Thess
1:3

11   To this end also we pray for you always that our God may count you worthy of your calling, and fulfill every desire for goodness and the work of faith with power;

1:12
Phil 2:9ff

12   in order that the name of our Lord Jesus may be glorified in you, and you in Him, according to the grace of our God and the Lord Jesus Christ.

III. *The day of the Lord (2:1–17)*

A. *Events preceding the day of the Lord*

2:1
1 Thess
4:15-17;
Mark 13:27
2:2
Eph 5:6;
2 Thess 3:17;
1 Cor 1:8

2 Now we request you, brethren, with regard to the coming of our Lord Jesus Christ, and our gathering together to Him,
2   that you may not be quickly shaken from your composure or be disturbed

---

1:8 The wrath of God may be thought of as the "zeal" with which God maintains His own holiness, honor, and righteousness. Wrath includes the just visitation of penal judgment on those who violate the law of God and thus oppose His holy nature. But this holy displeasure of God on sin is to be understood as a reflex of His deep and abiding love for His creation. Just because God loves His moral universe so deeply, He cannot remain indifferent when He sees it attacked and violated by those who would trample on His moral law. And because He has a love for the fallen race of Adam, God has made the utmost possible sacrifice for man's redemption, in providing a mediator and sin-bearer in Jesus Christ, who bore the penalty of wrath on the cross. God's anger is said to be visited on: (1) unbelief (John 3:36); (2) apostasy (Heb. 10:26,27); (3) idolatry (Deut. 29:18,20,27, 28); (4) all wickedness (Rom. 1:18). This wrath is averted from sinners only through the blood of Christ (Rom. 5:9) by faith (Rom. 3:25). God's justice is perfect and completely beyond man's questioning (Rom. 9:20–23). In a cataclysmic way the wrath of God may be visited on men and nations in time (thus the fall of Nineveh, Jerusalem, Rome, and other empires), or it may be delayed until its culminating phase in the "great day of their wrath" (Rev. 6:17; 11:18; 19:15) at the end of the age.

either by a spirit or a message or a letter as if from us, to the effect that the day of the Lord has come.

3   Let no one in any way deceive you, for *it will not come* unless the [1]apostasy comes first, and the man of lawlessness is revealed, the son of destruction,

4   who opposes and exalts himself above every so-called god or object of worship, so that he takes his seat in the temple of God, displaying himself as being God.

5   Do you not remember that while I was still with you, I was telling you these things?

6   And you know what restrains him now, so that in his time he may be revealed.

7   For the mystery of lawlessness is already at work; only he who now restrains *will do so* until he is taken out of the way.

8   And then that lawless one will be revealed whom the Lord will slay with the breath of His mouth and bring to an end by the appearance of His coming;

9   *that is,* the one whose coming is in accord with the activity of Satan, with all power and signs and false wonders,

10   and with all the deception of wickedness for those who perish, because they did not receive the love of the truth so as to be saved.

11   And for this reason God will send upon them a deluding influence so that they might believe what is false,

12   in order that they all may be judged who did not believe the truth, but took pleasure in wickedness.

B. *Thanksgiving and exhortation*

13   But we should always give thanks to God for you, brethren beloved by the Lord, because God has chosen you [2]from the beginning for salvation through sanctification by the Spirit and faith in the truth.

14   And it was for this He called you through our gospel, that you may gain the glory of our Lord Jesus Christ.

15   So then, brethren, stand firm and hold to the traditions which you were taught, whether by word *of mouth* or by letter from us.

16   Now may our Lord Jesus Christ Himself and God our Father, who has loved us and given us eternal comfort and good hope by grace,

17   comfort and strengthen your hearts in every good work and word.

IV. *Exhortations (3:1–18)*

A. *To pray*

3   Finally, brethren, pray for us that the word of the Lord may spread rapidly and be glorified, just as *it did* also with you;

2   and that we may be delivered from perverse and evil men; for not all have faith.

3   But the Lord is faithful, and He will strengthen and protect you from the evil *one*.

4   And we have confidence in the Lord concerning you, that you are doing and will *continue to* do what we command.

5   And may the Lord direct your hearts into the love of God and into the steadfastness of Christ.

---

[1]Or, *falling away* from the faith   [2]Some ancient mss. read *first fruits*

*2:3
Eph 5:6-8;
Dan 7:25;
8:25; 11:36;
Rev 13:5ff;
John 17:12
2:4
1 Cor 8:5;
Is 14:13,14;
Ezek 28:2

*2:7
Rev 17:5,7

2:8
Dan 7:10;
Rev 19:15
2:9
Matt 24:24;
John 4:48
2:10
1 Cor 1:18

2:11
Rom 1:28;
Matt 24:5;
1 Tim 4:1
2:12
Rom 1:32

2:13
Eph 1:4;
1 Pet 1:2

2:14
1 Pet 5:10

2:15
1 Cor 16:13;
11:2
2:16
1 Thess 3:11;
John 3:16
2:17
1 Thess 3:2;
2 Thess 3:3

3:1
1 Thess 4:1;
5:25; 1:8
3:2
Rom 15:31

3:3
1 Cor 1:9;
1 Thess 5:24;
2 Pet 2:9
3:4
2 Cor 2:3;
Gal 5:10
3:5
1 Chr 29:18

2:3 Certain events must transpire before the second advent of Christ: (1) the gospel shall be preached to all the world for a witness; and (2) the great tribulation will precede the coming of Christ. During the tribulation period the man of lawlessness (sin) will rise to a short-lived supremacy. It will be a time of unparalleled misfortune for the human race and also of completely unrestrained wickedness. Prophetic references to this period include Dan. 7:8ff.; 9:27; Matt. 24:15; Rev. 13:2–10.
2:7 This is a most difficult verse. Scripture does not plainly indicate the identity of the person or influence that is now

restraining the lawlessness of our present age. Some have suggested that it is the Holy Spirit Himself who shall be removed from the world scene during the tribulation, but this is impossible to reconcile with the large number of conversions that will take place during those troubled years. (Apart from the Holy Spirit no man can be converted.) This much is plain, however, that the time will come when the restraint will be taken away, and the "mystery of iniquity," which now operates underhandedly in response to concealed satanic influences, will be plainly unveiled before the eyes of men in all of its hatefulness.

B. *To labor*

3:6
1 Cor 5:4,11;
2 Thess 2:15

6 Now we command you, brethren, in the name of our Lord Jesus Christ, that you keep aloof from every brother who leads an unruly life and not according to the tradition which you received from us.

3:7
1 Thess 1:6

7 For you yourselves know how you ought to follow our example, because we did not act in an undisciplined manner among you,

3:8
1 Thess 2:9;
Acts 18:3;
Eph 4:28

8 nor did we eat anyone's bread without paying for it, but with labor and hardship we *kept* working night and day so that we might not be a burden to any of you;

3:9
1 Cor 9:4ff

9 not because we do not have the right *to this,* but in order to offer ourselves as a model for you, that you might follow our example.

3:10
1 Thess 4:11

10 For even when we were with you, we used to give you this order: if anyone will not work, neither let him eat.

3:11
1 Tim 5:13

11 For we hear that some among you are leading an undisciplined life, doing no work at all, but acting like busybodies.

3:12
1 Thess 4:1,
11; Eph 4:28

12 Now such persons we command and exhort in the Lord Jesus Christ to work in quiet fashion and eat their own bread.

3:13
Gal 6:9

13 But as for you, brethren, do not grow weary of doing good.

3:14
Matt 18:17

14 And if anyone does not obey our instruction in this letter, take special note of that man and do not associate with him, so that he may be put to shame.

3:15
Gal 6:1;
1 Thess 5:14

15 And *yet* do not regard him as an enemy, but admonish him as a brother.

C. *Prayer, salutation, and benediction*

3:16
Rom 15:33;
Ruth 2:4

16 Now may the Lord of peace Himself continually grant you peace in every circumstance. The Lord be with you all!

3:17
1 Cor 16:21

17 I, Paul, write this greeting with my own hand, and this is a distinguishing mark in every letter; this is the way I write.

3:18
Rom 16:20;
1 Thess 5:28

18 The grace of our Lord Jesus Christ be with you all.

INTRODUCTION TO
THE FIRST LETTER OF PAUL TO
TIMOTHY

Authorship and Background: The letters to Timothy and Titus are called "The Pastoral Letters" since they deal with the qualifications and duties of church ministers.

Several factors have led some scholars to question whether the letters as they now stand were written personally by Paul: (1) Paul's travels described in the Pastorals do not fit into the account in Acts, which closes with Paul in prison, in Rome, for two years; the credibility of these travels rests on the assumption that they took place after the two-year imprisonment. This means that Paul was released, and after a period of freedom, rearrested and imprisoned again in Rome, where he eventually suffered martyrdom. (2) There are significant differences in style, vocabulary, and point of view between the Pastorals and the other Pauline letters. (3) The condemned false doctrines seem to belong to a later period. And, (4) the church organization and the attitude toward the various ministries of the church seem also to belong to a later period.

These factors have led to different conclusions: some hold that Paul merely suggested the subject matter and left it to a scribe to develop and transcribe the letters; others believe that the letters contain some genuinely Pauline fragments, but were written after his death by some devoted disciple; and others conclude that the letters were written as late as the second century and preserve no firsthand information of Paul's ministry.

Scholars who accept the letters as Pauline explain the various factors as follows: (1) Paul was released from prison and traveled widely over the Roman empire for two or three years, going perhaps as far west as Spain, before his last imprisonment and martyrdom. (2) The differences in style and vocabulary spring from the differences in circumstances, needs, and purposes of the letters, and/or the greater part played by an amanuensis in their composition. (3) The heresy combatted in the Pastorals was not unknown during Paul's lifetime, being in many respects similar to the errors attacked in the letter to the Colossians. And, (4) nothing in the nature of the organization of the church requires a date after Paul's lifetime.

The arguments against Paul's authorship are largely inferential, of course, and it remains to be proved that Paul was not the author, since his authorship is clearly stated in the three letters (1:1; 2 Tim. 1:1; Titus 1:1).

Here in 1 Timothy, Paul writes from an undetermined location, perhaps in Macedonia (1:3), while on his way to Nicopolis (cf. Titus 3:12). Timothy was in Ephesus (1:3), and Paul repeatedly states his desire and determination to visit Timothy (3:14,15; 4:13), which shows that he was not in prison when he wrote the letter. Timothy had been assigned to a work that had serious problems; and while the apostle had every confidence in him, he felt that Timothy needed guidance and help if he were to succeed in the oversight of the flock.

Characteristics: The letter concerns itself with the church and the qualifications and duties of various church officers. Timothy, who occupied a position of considerable influence and authority in the work in Ephesus, is carefully instructed in how to carry out his duties. Though no title is applied to him (he is called "servant" in 4:6), the tone of the instructions shows that he occupied a place of authority: he is to see that the teaching is true to the gospel (1:3); he is to supervise the worship (2:1,2,8); he is to regulate the apparel and conduct of women (2:9-12); he is to instruct his fellow Christians (4:6), and carry out the prescribed functions of church service (4:13-15); he is to deal with old and young, both men and women (5:1,2); he is told to enroll in the widows' group only those over sixty years of age who cannot otherwise be cared for (5:3-16); and he is to rebuke elders who sin (5:20), and be an example in his personal conduct of purity and holiness in all things (4:12; 5:21,22; 6:11-14).

Contents:

I. Salutation (1:1,2)

II. Instructions for the church and church officers (1:3-3:16): Warnings against false teachers, including Hymenaeus and Alexander; instructions for church life, prayers, apparel, and conduct of women; qualifications of bishops, deacons, and their wives; proper conduct in the church of the living God, the pillar and bulwark of the truth.

III. Instructions to Timothy (4:1-6:21): Warning against heretical teachings; instructions about Timothy's personal conduct; his relationship to the various groups in the church, particularly the widows; instructions to slaves, and to the rich. "Timothy, guard what has been entrusted to you" (6:20).

[handwritten note, top right] v9.-"mystery of the faith": They don't leave to have all the answers. Cf. v. 16

G. The office of deacon

8 Deacons likewise *must be* men of dignity, not double-tongued, or addicted to much wine or fond of sordid gain,

9 *but* holding to the mystery of the faith with a clear conscience.

10 And let these also first be tested; then let them serve as deacons if they are beyond reproach.

11 Women *must* likewise *be* dignified, not malicious gossips, but temperate, faithful in all things.

12 Let deacons be husbands of *only* one wife, *and* good managers of *their* children and their own households.

13 For those who have served well as deacons obtain for themselves a high standing and great confidence in the faith that is in Christ Jesus.

14 I am writing these things to you, hoping to come to you before long;

15 but in case I am delayed, *I write* so that you may know how one ought to conduct himself in the household of God, which is the church of the living God, the pillar and support of the truth.

16 And by common confession great is the mystery of godliness:
> [1]He who was revealed in the flesh,
> Was vindicated in the Spirit,
> Beheld by angels,
> Proclaimed among the nations,
> Believed on in the world,
> Taken up in glory.

III. *Instructions to Timothy (4:1–6:21)*

A. *Of false doctrine*

4 But the Spirit explicitly says that in later times some will fall away from the faith, paying attention to deceitful spirits and doctrines of demons,

2 by means of the hypocrisy of liars seared in their own conscience as with a branding iron,

3 *men* who forbid marriage *and advocate* abstaining from foods, which God has created to be gratefully shared in by those who believe and know the truth. *Cf 1 Cor 8 re food offered to idols.*

4 For everything created by God is good, and nothing is to be rejected, if it is received with gratitude;

5 for it is sanctified by means of the word of God and prayer.

B. *On godly living*

6 In pointing out these things to the brethren, you will be a good servant of Christ Jesus, *constantly* nourished on the words of the faith and of the sound doctrine which you have been following.

7 But have nothing to do with worldly fables fit only for old women. On the other hand, discipline yourself for the purpose of godliness;

8 for bodily discipline is only of little profit, but godliness is profitable for all things, since it holds promise for the present life and *also* for the *life* to come.

9 It is a trustworthy statement deserving full acceptance.

10 For it is for this we labor and strive, because we have fixed our hope on the living God, who is the Savior of all men, especially of believers.

C. *On faithful service*

11 Prescribe and teach these things.

[1]Some later mss. read *God*

Marginal references:
*3:8 Acts 6:3; Titus 2:3
3:9 1 Tim 1:19
*3:11 2 Tim 3:3; Titus 2:3
3:13 Matt 25:21
3:15 Eph 2:21; v. 5; 1 Tim 4:10; Gal 2:9
*3:16 John 1:14; 1 Pet 3:18; Acts 1:9
4:1 John 16:13; 2 Thess 2:3; 2 Tim 3:1; 3:13; Rev 9:20
4:2 Eph 4:19
4:3 1 Cor 7:28; Heb 13:4; Gen 1:29; Rom 14:6
4:4 Rom 14:14
4:6 2 Cor 11:23; 1 Tim 1:10; 2 Tim 3:10
4:7 2 Tim 2:16; Heb 5:14
4:8 1 Tim 6:6; Ps 37:4; Rom 8:28
4:10 1 Cor 4:11; 1 Tim 2:4
4:11 1 Tim 5:7; 6:2

3:8 Two offices, those of *elder* or *overseer* and *deacon* are to be found in the organization of the New Testament church. (See note to Titus 1:5 on the offices of elder or overseer.) The office of deacon was created in Acts 6:1–6. Its purpose was to free the apostles for the business of preaching the Word and for prayer; temporal affairs, such as caring for the poor, being entrusted to the deacons. The qualifications for this office are found both in Acts 6:3 and 1 Tim. 3:8–13. Like elders and overseers, deacons were ordained by the laying on of hands (Acts 6:6). The word *deacon* comes from the Greek *diakonos* and means "ministrant" (one who serves).

3:11 The women referred to here may be the wives of deacons, or deaconesses of the church. There is no way of determining which is meant. Phoebe (Rom. 16:1) is the only deaconess mentioned in the New Testament.

3:16 See notes to John 1:14 on the incarnation, and Phil. 2:7 on the kenosis.

12   Let no one look down on your youthfulness, but *rather* in speech, conduct, love, faith *and* purity, show yourself an example of those who believe.

13   Until I come, give attention to the *public* reading *of Scripture,* to exhortation and teaching.

14   Do not neglect the spiritual gift within you, which was bestowed upon you through prophetic utterance with the laying on of hands by the presbytery.

15   Take pains with these things; be *absorbed* in them, so that your progress may be evident to all.

16   Pay close attention to yourself and to your teaching; persevere in these things; for as you do this you will insure salvation both for yourself and for those who hear you.

D. *On pastoral duties*

1. *Widows*

5 Do not sharply rebuke an older man, but *rather* appeal to *him* as a father, *to* the younger men as brothers,

2   the older women as mothers, *and* the younger women as sisters, in all purity.

3   Honor widows who are widows indeed;

4   but if any widow has children or grandchildren, let them first learn to practice piety in regard to their own family, and to make some return to their parents; for this is acceptable in the sight of God.

5   Now she who is a widow indeed, and who has been left alone has fixed her hope on God, and continues in entreaties and prayers night and day.

6   But she who gives herself to wanton pleasure is dead even while she lives.

7   Prescribe these things as well, so that they may be above reproach.

8   But if anyone does not provide for his own, and especially for those of his household, he has denied the faith, and is worse than an unbeliever.

9   Let a widow be put on the list only if she is not less than sixty years old, *having been* the wife of one man,

10   having a reputation for good works; *and* if she has brought up children, if she has shown hospitality to strangers, if she has washed the saints' feet, if she has assisted those in distress, *and* if she has devoted herself to every good work.

11   But refuse *to put* younger widows *on the list,* for when they feel sensual desires in disregard of Christ, they want to get married,

12   *thus* incurring condemnation, because they have set aside their previous pledge.

13   And at the same time they also learn *to be* idle, as they go around from house to house; and not merely idle, but also gossips and busybodies, talking about things not proper *to mention.*

14   Therefore, I want younger *widows* to get married, bear children, keep house, *and* give the enemy no occasion for reproach;

15   for some have already turned aside to follow Satan.

16   If any woman who is a believer has *dependent* widows, let her assist them, and let not the church be burdened, so that it may assist those who are widows indeed.

2. *Elders*

17   Let the elders who rule well be considered worthy of double honor, especially those who work hard at preaching and teaching.

18   For the Scripture says, "YOU SHALL NOT MUZZLE THE OX WHILE HE IS THRESHING," and "The laborer is worthy of his wages."

19   Do not receive an accusation against an elder except on the basis of two or three witnesses.

20   Those who continue in sin, rebuke in the presence of all, so that the rest also may be fearful *of sinning.*

21   I solemnly charge you in the presence of God and of Christ Jesus and of *His*

Cross references (left margin):

4:12 Titus 2:7; 1 Pet 5:3; 1 Tim 1:14

4:14 2 Tim 1:6; 1 Tim 1:18; 5:22; Acts 6:6

4:16 Acts 20:28; Ezek 33:9

5:1 Lev 19:32

*5:3 vv. 5,16

5:4 Eph 6:1,2

5:5 vv. 3,16; 1 Cor 7:32; Luke 2:37

5:6 James 5:5

5:7 1 Tim 4:11

5:8 Gal 6:10; Titus 1:16

5:10 Acts 16:15; Heb 13:2; Luke 7:44; v. 16

5:13 2 Thess 3:11; Titus 1:11

5:14 1 Cor 7:9; Titus 2:5

5:16 vv. 3,5

5:17 Phil 2:29; Rom 12:8; Acts 28:10

5:18 1 Cor 9:9; Lev 19:13; Deut 24:14, 15; Matt 10:10

5:19 Deut 19:15

5:20 Titus 1:13; Deut 13:11

5:21 1 Tim 6:13; 2 Tim 2:14

5:3 The lengthy section on widows (5:3–16) shows how important a place they occupied in the organization of the early church. Ordinarily widows would be quite helpless unless they received adequate material support from children or grandchildren, so the churches made the necessary provisions for their welfare (cf. the same care provided by the church in Jerusalem, Acts 6:1). It was very important, however, that the churches provide only for those who were really in need and had no other recourse—hence the detailed instructions as to their enrollment in the widows' group.

chosen angels, to maintain these *principles* without bias, doing nothing in a *spirit of partiality*.

22   Do not lay hands upon anyone *too* hastily and thus share *responsibility for* the sins of others; keep yourself free from sin.

23   No longer drink water *exclusively*, but use a little wine for the sake of your stomach and your frequent ailments.

24   The sins of some men are quite evident, going before them to judgment; for others, their *sins* follow after.

25   Likewise also, deeds that are good are quite evident, and those which are otherwise cannot be concealed.

3. *Servants*

6 Let all who are under the yoke as slaves regard their own masters as worthy of all honor so that the name of God and *our* doctrine may not be spoken against.

2   And let those who have believers as their masters not be disrespectful to them because they are brethren, but let them serve them all the more, because those who partake of the benefit are believers and beloved. Teach and preach these *principles*.

E. *Warning against false teachers*

3   If anyone advocates a different doctrine, and does not agree with sound words, those of our Lord Jesus Christ, and with the doctrine conforming to godliness,

4   he is conceited *and* understands nothing; but he has a morbid interest in controversial questions and disputes about words, out of which arise envy, strife, abusive language, evil suspicions,

5   and constant friction between men of depraved mind and deprived of the truth, who suppose that godliness is a means of gain.

6   But godliness *actually* is a means of great gain, when accompanied by contentment.

7   For we have brought nothing into the world, [2]so we cannot take anything out of it either.

8   And if we have food and covering, with these we shall be content.

9   But those who want to get rich fall into temptation and a snare and many foolish and harmful desires which plunge men into ruin and destruction.

10   For the love of money is a root of all sorts of evil, and some by longing for it have wandered away from the faith, and pierced themselves with many a pang.

F. *Exhortation to Timothy*

11   But flee from these things, you man of God; and pursue righteousness, godliness, faith, love, perseverance *and* gentleness.

12   Fight the good fight of faith; take hold of the eternal life to which you were called, and you made the good confession in the presence of many witnesses.

13   I charge you in the presence of God, who gives life to all things, and of Christ Jesus, who testified the good confession before Pontius Pilate,

14   that you keep the commandment without stain or reproach until the appearing of our Lord Jesus Christ,

15   which He will bring about at the proper time—He who is the blessed and only Sovereign, the King of kings and Lord of lords;

16   who alone possesses immortality and dwells in unapproachable light; whom no man has seen or can see. To Him *be* honor and eternal dominion! Amen.

G. *The use of wealth*

17   Instruct those who are rich in this present world not to be conceited or to fix their hope on the uncertainty of riches, but on God, who richly supplies us with all things to enjoy.

[2]Later mss. read *it is clear that*

5:22 Acts 6:6; 2 Tim 1:6; Eph 5:11
5:23 1 Tim 3:8

6:1 Titus 2:9; 1 Pet 2:18; Titus 2:5,8
6:2 Gal 3:28; Philem 16; 1 Tim 4:11

6:3 2 Tim 1:13; Titus 1:1
6:4 1 Cor 8:2; 2 Tim 2:14
6:5 1 Cor 11:16; Titus 1:11; 2 Pet 2:3
6:6 Phil 4:11; Heb 13:5
6:7 Job 1:21
6:8 Heb 13:5
6:9 1 Tim 3:7; 1:19
***6:10** 1 Tim 3:3; James 5:19

6:12 1 Cor 9:25, 26; 1 Tim 1:18; Heb 13:23
6:13 1 Tim 5:21; John 18:37
6:14 Phil 1:6; 2 Thess 2:8
6:15 1 Tim 1:11, 17; Rev 17:14; 19:16
6:16 1 Tim 1:17; John 1:18; Eph 3:21
6:17 Luke 12:20, 21; 1 Tim 4:10; Acts 14:17

6:10 This verse does not teach that there is anything evil in money as such, or in the possession of wealth. But it does teach that the *love of money* is sinful. Men have been known to commit almost any crime for the sake of money. Hence, as Paul states, *the love of money is a root of all sorts of evil*. In vv. 17,18 Christians are charged to trust in God and not in riches, but they are also admonished to be rich in good works.

6:18
1 Tim 5:10;
Rom 12:8,13

18 *Instruct them* to do good, to be rich in good works, to be generous and ready to share,

19 storing up for themselves the treasure of a good foundation for the future, so that they may take hold of that which is life indeed.

H. *Final charge and benediction*

6:20
2 Tim 1:14;
2:16

20 O Timothy, guard what has been entrusted to you, avoiding worldly *and* empty chatter *and* the opposing arguments of what is falsely called "knowledge"—

21 which some have professed and thus gone astray from the faith.

Grace be with you.

INTRODUCTION TO

THE SECOND LETTER OF PAUL TO

TIMOTHY

Authorship and Background: See the Introduction to 1 Timothy. Paul wrote to Timothy as a prisoner (1:8,16; 2:9) in Rome (1:17), with no hope of release (4:6-8). Sensing that the end was near (4:6-8), and deserted by friends and companions (4:10,11), he longed for Christian companionship. Thus he wrote Timothy, who was, presumably, in Ephesus (Onesiphorus was from Ephesus, 1:16-18; 4:19b; so were Prisca and Aquila, 4:19a; cf. 1 Tim. 1:3). Lonely as Paul must have been in a human sense, he was not alone in his prison cell. With him were the saints and martyrs of all ages who suffered similar imprisonment and pain and who could also say, "I know whom I have believed."

It would seem that 2 Timothy, then, was written after 1 Timothy and Titus; and on the basis of this order of the letters, Paul's travels described in the Pastorals may be set forth as follows: after a visit to Crete, with Titus, whom he left there (Titus 1:5), Paul went to Ephesus (1 Tim. 1:3). Leaving Timothy there, he went on to Miletus (4:20), and then on to Troas, where he left his "books" and "parchments" (4:13). From there he went to Macedonia (1 Tim. 1:3), where he probably wrote 1 Timothy and Titus. He then proceeded to Nicopolis, where he intended to spend the winter (Titus 3:12). He was arrested there and taken to Rome (1:16,17), where he wrote 2 Timothy and soon thereafter died a martyr's death. According to tradition, he died on the Ostian Way, west of the capital, during the reign of Nero.

Characteristics: The letter is intensely personal, and subdued in tone. Sensing that the end of his life is near, the apostle writes with some pathos of his condition, bereft of friends (1:15; 4:10). Luke alone is with him (4:11). Paul longs to see his friend Timothy (4:9), and asks that he bring Mark with him (4:11); winter is coming (4:21), so he asks for his cloak, as well as his books and parchments (4:13). He remembers his past persecutions and sufferings (3:10,11), speaks bitterly of the failure of friends to stand by him in his first trial (4:16), and warns Timothy against men like Hymenaeus and Philetus (2:17,18), and Alexander the coppersmith (4:14,15).

His pastor's heart is burdened for the welfare of his beloved converts and the dangers they run from false teachings (2:14-19; 3:1-9; 4:3,4). At the same time he counsels Timothy to keep aflame the gift of God that is in him (1:6), not to fear persecution and suffering (1:8; 2:3-7), to stay with the sound doctrine he has been taught (1:13,14; 2:15,22-26; 3:14-17), and to preach the message with conviction and power (4:1-5).

In the midst of suffering and betrayals, persecution and bereavements, he knows the One whom he has believed (1:12; 2:11-13), and who will reward him with the crown of righteousness on that day (4:8). The letter ends on a note of triumph: "The Lord will deliver me from every evil deed, and will bring me safely to His heavenly kingdom; to Him be the glory forever and ever" (4:18).

Contents:

I. Salutation (1:1,2)

II. Appeal and exhortation to Timothy (1:3-2:13): Courage, willingness to suffer hardship, steadfastness, are the marks of the true minister; God's Word is not fettered, His grace is sufficient; therefore, "be strong in the grace that is in Christ Jesus" (2:1).

III. Sound doctrine, right conduct, and false teaching (2:14-4:8): False teaching must be opposed, as well as senseless controversies; in a spirit of kindness the Lord's servant must correct such people; he is to follow the apostle's own example of suffering and steadfastness, and faithfully fulfill his ministry.

IV. Conclusion (4:9-22): Bereft of friends, but upheld by his Lord, the apostle calmly awaits the end, knowing that his times are all in God's hands. Greetings and benediction.

THE SECOND LETTER OF PAUL TO

TIMOTHY

I. *Salutation (1:1,2)*

1 Paul, an apostle of Christ Jesus by the will of God, according to the promise of life in Christ Jesus,
2 to Timothy, my beloved son: Grace, mercy *and* peace from God the Father and Christ Jesus our Lord.

II. *Appeal and exhortation to Timothy (1:3–2:13)*

3 I thank God, whom I serve with a clear conscience the way my forefathers did, as I constantly remember you in my prayers night and day,
4 longing to see you, even as I recall your tears, so that I may be filled with joy.
5 For I am mindful of the sincere faith within you, which first dwelt in your grandmother Lois and your mother Eunice, and I am sure that *it is* in you as well.
6 And for this reason I remind you to kindle afresh the gift of God which is in you through the laying on of my hands.
7 For God has not given us a spirit of timidity, but of power and love and discipline.
8 Therefore do not be ashamed of the testimony of our Lord, or of me His prisoner; but join with *me* in suffering for the gospel according to the power of God,
9 who has saved us, and called us with a holy calling, not according to our works, but according to His own purpose and grace which was granted us in Christ Jesus from all eternity,
10 but now has been revealed by the appearing of our Savior Christ Jesus, who abolished death, and brought life and immortality to light through the gospel,
11 for which I was appointed a preacher and an apostle and a teacher.
12 For this reason I also suffer these things, but I am not ashamed; for I know whom I have believed and I am convinced that He is able to guard what I have entrusted to Him until that day.
13 Retain the standard of sound words which you have heard from me, in the faith and love which are in Christ Jesus.
14 Guard, through the Holy Spirit who dwells in us, the treasure which has been entrusted to *you.*
15 You are aware of the fact that all who are in Asia turned away from me, among whom are Phygelus and Hermogenes.
16 The Lord grant mercy to the house of Onesiphorus for he often refreshed me, and was not ashamed of my chains;
17 but when he was in Rome, he eagerly searched for me, and found me—
18 the Lord grant to him to find mercy from the Lord on that day—and you know very well what services he rendered at Ephesus.

2 You therefore, my son, be strong in the grace that is in Christ Jesus.
2 And the things which you have heard from me in the presence of many witnesses, these entrust to faithful men, who will be able to teach others also.
3 Suffer hardship with *me*, as a good soldier of Christ Jesus.
4 No soldier in active service entangles himself in the affairs of everyday life, so that he may please the one who enlisted him as a soldier.
5 And also if anyone competes as an athlete, he does not win the prize unless he competes according to the rules.

1:1
2 Cor 1:1;
Eph 3:6;
Titus 1:2
1:2
1 Tim 1:2

1:3
Rom 1:8,9;
1 Thess 1:2,
21;
Acts 20:37
1:4
2 Tim 4:9
*1:5
1 Tim 1:5;
Acts 16:1
1:6
1 Tim 4:14
1:7
Rom 8:15;
John 14:27
1:8
Rom 1:16;
Eph 3:1;
2 Tim 2:3,9;
4:5
1:9
Heb 3:1;
Rom 16:25
1:10
Eph 1:9;
1 Cor 15:54
1:11
1 Tim 2:7
1:12
Titus 3:8;
1 Tim 6:20
1:13
Titus 1:9;
Rom 2:20;
1 Tim 1:14
1:14
Rom 8:9,11
*1:15
Acts 19:10;
2 Tim 4:10,
11,16
1:16
2 Tim 4:19

1:18
2 Thess 1:10;
Heb 6:10
2:1
2 Tim 1:2;
Eph 6:10
2:2
2 Tim 1:13;
1 Tim 6:12;
1:18; 1:12
2:3
1 Tim 1:18
2:4
2 Pet 2:20
2:5
1 Cor 9:25

1:5 History does not afford us much information relative to Lois and Eunice, the grandmother and mother of Timothy. But Paul states that Timothy's faith is due in part to the influence of these godly women. Paul shows that faith can be communicated and that family religion is not to be sneered at. A godly home and background are a great blessing.

1:15 This is the only place where *Phygelus* and *Hermogenes* are mentioned. We know little concerning them, but their reputation is imperishably established in the Biblical record occasioned by the disgrace attending their defection from the apostle. They are distinguished from the faithful Onesiphorus, who was a devout believer.

"Character is what you are in the dark"—D.L. Moody

6   The hard-working farmer ought to be the first to receive his share of the crops.

7   Consider what I say, for the Lord will give you understanding in everything.

8   Remember Jesus Christ, risen from the dead, descendant of David, according to my gospel,

9   for which I suffer hardship even to imprisonment as a criminal; but the word of God is not imprisoned.

10   For this reason I endure all things for the sake of those who are chosen, that they also may obtain the salvation which is in Christ Jesus *and* with *it* eternal glory.

11   It is a trustworthy statement:
For if we died with Him, we shall also live with Him;

12   If we endure, we shall also reign with Him;
If we deny Him, He also will deny us;

13   If we are faithless, He remains faithful; for He cannot deny Himself.

III. *Sound doctrine, right conduct, and false teaching* (2:14–4:8)

A. *Personal counsel to Timothy*

14   Remind *them* of these things, and solemnly charge *them* in the presence of God not to wrangle about words, which is useless, *and leads* to the ruin of the hearers.

15   Be diligent to present yourself approved to God as a workman who does not need to be ashamed, handling accurately the word of truth.

16   But avoid worldly *and* empty chatter, for it will lead to further ungodliness,

17   and their talk will spread like ¹gangrene. Among them are Hymenaeus and Philetus,

18   *men* who have gone astray from the truth saying that the resurrection has already taken place, and thus they upset the faith of some.

19   Nevertheless, the firm foundation of God stands, having this seal, "The Lord knows those who are His," and, "Let everyone who names the name of the Lord abstain from wickedness."

20   Now in a large house there are not only gold and silver vessels, but also vessels of wood and of earthenware, and some to honor and some to dishonor.

21   Therefore, if a man cleanses himself from these *things*, he will be a vessel for honor, sanctified, useful to the Master, prepared for every good work.

22   Now flee from youthful lusts, and pursue righteousness, faith, love *and* peace, with those who call on the Lord from a pure heart.

23   But refuse foolish and ignorant speculations, knowing that they produce quarrels.

24   And the Lord's bond-servant must not be quarrelsome, but be kind to all, able to teach, patient when wronged,

25   with gentleness correcting those who are in opposition, if perhaps God may grant them repentance leading to the knowledge of the truth,

26   and they may come to their senses *and escape* from the snare of the devil, having been held captive by him to do his will.

¹Or, *cancer*

---

*2:8
Acts 2:24;
Matt 1:1;
Rom 2:16
2:9
Acts 9:16;
Phil 1:7;
Acts 28:31
2:10
Eph 3:13;
2 Cor 1:6

2:12
1 Pet 4:13;
Matt 10:33
2:13
Rom 3:3;
Num 23:19

2:14
1 Tim 5:21;
6:4

2:15
James 1:12

2:16
1 Tim 4:7
2:17
1 Tim 1:20

*2:18
1 Cor 15:12

2:19
Is 28:16,17;
1 Tim 3:15;
John 10:14;
1 Cor 1:2
2:20
Rom 9:21

2:21
Is 52:11;
2 Tim 3:17
2:22
1 Tim 6:11;
1:14; 1:5
2:23
1 Tim 6:4;
Titus 3:9
2:24
1 Tim 3:3;
Titus 1:7;
1 Tim 3:2
2:25
Gal 6:1;
1 Pet 3:15
2:26
1 Tim 3:7

2:8 See note to Luke 24:46.
2:18 Several kinds of error are distinguished in Scripture. Since all believers are imperfect and know only in part, it is impossible for any one individual to grasp all the truth or to be free from all error. There is an error that springs from honest ignorance (Acts 19:1–6). As an illustration of this, the Christian church has long been divided on questions such as baptism and church government. Obviously someone must be embracing error. Well-intentioned believers, however, willingly forsake their error when they are properly instructed, and they are not guilty of intentional sin, even though their error may be a grave one. But Paul is not speaking of the error of ignorance here. Rather he is denouncing those who by their peculiar views relative to the resurrection are upsetting *the faith of some*. It is possible that Paul does not mean to suggest here the idea of apostasy, which is something entirely different from errors of igno-

rance, or even of peculiar doctrinal views that, while incorrect, do not necessarily separate one from the household of faith. The Greek word for "apostasy" occurs in Acts 21:21 and 2 Thess. 2:3,4. To be an apostate is to enter into unbelief and to dissolve any union one might have had with God in Jesus Christ. The normal mark of a genuine apostate is his denial that Christ is very God or his repudiation of Christ's atoning work on the cross (Phil. 3:18; 2 Pet. 2:1; 1 John 4:1–3). Biblical descriptions of apostates may be found in 2 Pet. 2:1–19 and in the book of Jude. They should be dealt with in a forthright fashion (Rom. 16:17,18; 2 Tim. 3:9; 2 John 10). Apostates may be discovered when their doctrines are examined in the light of Scripture (1 John 4:1). There has always been apostasy in the church, but the end of this age will be characterized by widespread departure from the faith (3:1–13).

[handwritten top margin: V5- How do we recognize counterfeit spirituality? By holding fast to the scripture.]

B. *The coming of apostasy*

3 But realize this, that in the last days difficult times will come.

2 For men will be lovers of self, lovers of money, boastful, arrogant, revilers, disobedient to parents, ungrateful, unholy,

3 unloving, irreconcilable, malicious gossips, without self-control, brutal, haters of good,

4 treacherous, reckless, conceited, lovers of pleasure rather than lovers of God;

5 holding to a form of godliness, although they have denied its power; and avoid such men as these.

6 For among them are those who enter into households and captivate weak women weighed down with sins, led on by various impulses,

7 always learning and never able to come to the knowledge of the truth.

8 And just as Jannes and Jambres opposed Moses, so these *men* also oppose the truth, men of depraved mind, rejected as regards the faith.

9 But they will not make further progress; for their folly will be obvious to all, as also that of those *two* came to be.

C. *The defense of the faith*

[handwritten: Confidence that God will keep his promises, so you can bet your life on it]
[handwritten: — lifestyle]

10 But you followed my teaching, conduct, purpose, faith, patience, love, perseverance,

[handwritten right margin: Paul is fortifying Timothy for the storms he would face.]

11 persecutions, *and* sufferings, such as happened to me at Antioch, at Iconium *and* at Lystra; what persecutions I endured, and out of them all the Lord delivered me!

12 And indeed, all who desire to live godly in Christ Jesus will be persecuted.

13 But evil men and impostors will proceed *from bad* to worse, deceiving and being deceived.

14 You, however, continue in the things you have learned and become convinced of, knowing from whom you have learned *them*;

15 and that from childhood you have known the sacred writings which are able to give you the wisdom that leads to salvation through faith which is in Christ Jesus.

16 [2]All Scripture is inspired by God and profitable for teaching, for reproof, for correction, for training in righteousness;

17 that the man of God may be adequate, equipped for every good work.

D. *The charge to preach sound doctrine*

4 I solemnly charge *you* in the presence of God and of Christ Jesus, who is to judge the living and the dead, and by His appearing and His kingdom:

2 preach the word; be ready in season *and* out of season; reprove, rebuke, exhort, with great patience and instruction.

3 For the time will come when they will not endure sound doctrine; but *wanting* to have their ears tickled, they will accumulate for themselves teachers in accordance to their own desires;

4 and will turn away their ears from the truth, and will turn aside to myths.

5 But you, be sober in all things, endure hardship, do the work of an evangelist, fulfill your ministry.

[handwritten right margin: ✳ be ready when or not you feel]
[handwritten: V5 inspired.]

[2]Or possibly, *Every Scripture inspired by God is also profitable*

3:8 According to Jewish traditions Jannes and Jambres were the names of the Egyptian magicians who opposed Moses (Ex. 7:11; 9:11). The names are found in ancient Jewish writings (perhaps as early as the first century A.D.), and in Christian apocryphal works.

3:16 Jesus Christ is the Word of God incarnate. The Bible is the written Word of God. Paul here states that the written Word of God is *God-breathed* (Greek *theopneustos*), from which expression and from other Scripture is derived the concept of the inspiration of the Bible. Historically, the church has always agreed that the Bible is the inspired Word of God. But it has not always been in agreement as to what inspiration actually consists of. Some have assumed that inspiration came via mechanical dictation, in which the writers were simply secretaries who merely recorded what they were told to write down. In this view, Scripture is verbally inspired and inerrant. Another view, which avoids mechanical dictation, holds to verbal inspiration and insists on an inerrant Scripture but allows for the freedom of the writer to use his own style and manner while preserved from error through the superintending power of the Holy Spirit. Both views usually limit inerrancy to the original manuscripts (the autographa), recognizing that errors have crept into present-day manuscripts since God has not guaranteed infallibility in transmission. These views of inspiration are based on what are believed to be Biblically taught doctrines of inspiration derived from Scripture itself. Still others accept the Bible as inspired but do not regard its uniqueness as extending to freedom from error in all matters of science and history. Those who hold this view do not believe that the existence of minor historical and scientific error, or minor alterations of any kind, damages the essential message of the Scriptures or destroys Christian faith.

Cross-references (margin):
- 3:1 — 1 Tim 4:1
- 3:2 — 2 Pet 2:3; Rom 1:30
- 3:3 — Rom 1:31; Titus 1:8
- 3:4 — 2 Pet 2:10; Phil 3:19
- 3:5 — 2 Thess 3:6
- 3:6 — Titus 1:11
- 3:7 — 2 Tim 2:25
- *3:8 — Ex 7:11; Acts 13:8; 1 Tim 6:5
- 3:9 — Ex 7:12
- 3:10 — 1 Tim 4:6; Phil 2:22
- 3:11 — Acts 13:45; 14:2,19
- 3:12 — Ps 34:19; Matt 16:24; 1 Thess 3:3
- 3:13 — 2 Tim 2:16; Titus 3:3
- 3:14 — 2 Tim 1:13
- 3:15 — 2 Tim 1:5; John 5:39
- *3:16 — Rom 15:4; 2 Pet 1:20,21
- 3:17 — 1 Tim 6:11; 2 Tim 2:21
- 4:1 — 1 Tim 5:21; Acts 10:42
- 4:2 — 1 Tim 5:20; Titus 1:13; 1 Tim 4:13
- 4:3 — 2 Tim 3:1,6; 1 Tim 1:10
- 4:5 — Acts 21:8

[handwritten bottom margin: V5- Stability is to be the hallmark of the Christian in an unbalanced and often insane world.]

6   For I am already being poured out as a drink offering, and the time of my departure has come.

7   I have fought the good fight, I have finished the course, I have kept the faith;

8   in the future there is laid up for me the crown of righteousness, which the Lord, the righteous Judge, will award to me on that day; and not only to me, but also to all who have loved His appearing.

IV. *Conclusion (4:9–22)*

9   Make every effort to come to me soon;

10   for Demas, having loved this present world, has deserted me and gone to Thessalonica; Crescens *has gone* to Galatia, Titus to Dalmatia.

11   Only Luke is with me. Pick up Mark and bring him with you, for he is useful to me for service.

12   But Tychicus I have sent to Ephesus.

13   When you come bring the cloak which I left at Troas with Carpus, and the books, especially the parchments.

14   Alexander the coppersmith did me much harm; the Lord will repay him according to his deeds.

15   Be on guard against him yourself, for he vigorously opposed our teaching.

16   At my first defense no one supported me, but all deserted me; may it not be counted against them.

17   But the Lord stood with me, and strengthened me, in order that through me the proclamation might be fully accomplished, and that all the Gentiles might hear; and I was delivered out of the lion's mouth.

18   The Lord will deliver me from every evil deed, and will bring me safely to His heavenly kingdom; to Him *be* the glory forever and ever. Amen.

19   Greet Prisca and Aquila, and the household of Onesiphorus.

20   Erastus remained at Corinth, but Trophimus I left sick at Miletus.

21   Make every effort to come before winter. Eubulus greets you, also Pudens and Linus and Claudia and all the brethren.

22   The Lord be with your spirit. Grace be with you.

4:8 The Scripture inculcates in believers an attitude of eager expectancy toward the second advent of Christ. Implicit in this attitude is the purpose: (1) to love His coming (4:8); (2) to look or wait for His coming (1 Cor. 1:7; Phil. 3:20; 1 Thess. 1:10; Titus 2:13); (3) to be ready for His coming (Matt. 24:44; Luke 12:40); (4) to be patient until His coming (James 5:7,8); and (5) to pray for His coming (Rev. 22:20).

4:19 *Prisca* (called Priscilla in Acts) was the wife of Aquila. Both fled from Rome when Claudius (A.D. 52) expelled the Jews. They went from Rome to Ephesus and returned to Rome later. Here (4:19) they are in Ephesus once again. Both were faithful followers of Christ and warm friends of the apostle Paul.

4:20 *Erastus.* This name is also mentioned in Acts 19:22

and Romans 16:23. It is not known whether these are the same or different people, but the Erastus of Acts could be the same as the one in this verse. *Trophimus,* see note to Acts 21:29 for information on this Gentile Christian.

4:21 *Eubulus.* Nothing is known of this character other than that he was a leading member of the Christian church in Rome who sent greetings to Timothy by the hand of Paul. *Pudens,* a Christian at Rome who sent greetings to Timothy. Beyond this fact nothing more is known about him. *Linus,* a Roman Christian who has been identified with one of the first bishops of Rome having the same name. *Claudia,* a Christian in Rome and friend of Paul who was sometimes thought to be the mother of Linus. She may have become the wife of Pudens.

INTRODUCTION TO

THE LETTER OF PAUL TO

TITUS

Authorship and Background: See the Introduction to 2 Timothy. The letter to Titus was probably written from Macedonia; Titus himself was on the island of Crete (1:5). Paul was on his way to Nicopolis, in Achaia, on the Adriatic Sea (3:12). Apparently he was arrested in Nicopolis and sent on to Rome.

There was much that needed to be done in Crete about the matters of church organization (1:5), false teaching (1:10,11,14-16), and immoral conduct. Paul quotes with approval what Epiminedes the Cretan poet of the sixth century B.C. had written of his fellow countrymen (1:12). All classes in the church needed instruction in Christian living (2:1-10); they are to respect authorities (3:1) and live at peace with all men (3:2). Controversies and senseless debates are to be avoided (3:9); dissenters who persist in their factiousness are to be banished (3:10,11); and all are to do good deeds, in order to discharge their Christian responsibilities (3:14).

The few personal references in the letter (1:5; 3:12-15) afford no sure indication of the exact time and place of writing. Tychicus may soon be sent to Crete (3:12). In 2 Tim. 4:12 it is said he was sent to Ephesus. (See other references to Tychicus in Eph. 6:21; Col. 4:7,8). Artemas (3:12) and Zenas the lawyer (3:13) are not mentioned elsewhere in the New Testament; and Apollos (3:13) is probably the same as the one who appears in Acts (18:24-28) and 1 Corinthians.

Titus himself does not appear by name in the book of Acts, and what information there is about him appears in Paul's letters.

Characteristics: This letter is much like 1 Timothy in its emphasis on church order and sound doctrine. Titus is charged with considerable responsibility on the island of Crete, with the authority to appoint elders in the various churches on the island (1:5), rebuke insubordinates (1:13; 3:10), teach sound doctrine (2:1), exhort and reprove with all authority (2:15; 3:8), and in general exercise spiritual and ecclesiastical oversight over the churches. "Let no one disregard you" (2:15) is the author's advice to him.

Contents:

I. Salutation (1:1-4)

II. Church organization (1:5-16): Qualifications of elders or bishops; the need to silence troublemakers and oppose false teaching.

III. The Christian life (2:1-3:11): Instructions to old and young, men and women alike, and to slaves. God's people should be zealous for good deeds, and must respect constituted authorities. Senseless and futile controversies should be avoided, and the factious individual should be rebuked.

IV. Personal matters and benediction (3:12-15)

THE LETTER OF PAUL TO
TITUS

I. Salutation (1:1–4)

1:1
Rom 1:1;
2 Cor 1:1;
1 Tim 2:4;
6:3
2 Tim 1:1;
Rom 16:25
1:3
2 Tim 1:10;
1 Thess 2:4
1:4
2 Cor 2:13;
Eph 1:2;
1 Tim 1:2

1 Paul, a bond-servant of God, and an apostle of Jesus Christ, for the faith of those chosen of God and the knowledge of the truth which is according to godliness,

2 in the hope of eternal life, which God, who cannot lie, promised long ages ago,

3 but at the proper time manifested, *even* His word, in the proclamation with which I was entrusted according to the commandment of God our Savior;

4 to Titus, my true child in a common faith: Grace and peace from God the Father and Christ Jesus our Savior.

II. Church organization (1:5–16)

A. Qualifications for elders

*1:5
Acts 27:7;
14:23; 11:30
1:6
1 Tim 3:2-4
1:7
1 Cor 4:1;
Eph 5:18
1:8
1 Tim 3:2;
2 Tim 3:3
1:9
1 Tim 1:19;
1:10

5 For this reason I left you in Crete, that you might set in order what remains, and appoint elders in every city as I directed you,

6 *namely*, if any man be above reproach, the husband of one wife, having children who believe, not accused of dissipation or rebellion.

7 For the overseer must be above reproach as God's steward, not self-willed, not quick-tempered, not addicted to wine, not pugnacious, not fond of sordid gain,

8 but hospitable, loving what is good, sensible, just, devout, self-controlled,

9 holding fast the faithful word which is in accordance with the teaching, that he may be able both to exhort in sound doctrine and to refute those who contradict.

B. Exposé of false teachers

1:10
1 Tim 1:6;
Acts 11:2
1:11
2 Tim 3:6;
1 Tim 6:5
1:12
Acts 17:28
1:13
2 Cor 13:10;
Titus 2:2
1:14
1 Tim 1:4;
Is 29:13
1:15
Luke 11:39,
41;
Rom 14:23
1:16
1 John 2:4;
2 Tim 3:5,8

10 For there are many rebellious men, empty talkers and deceivers, especially those of the circumcision,

11 who must be silenced because they are upsetting whole families, teaching things they should not *teach*, for the sake of sordid gain.

12 One of themselves, a prophet of their own, said, "Cretans are always liars, evil beasts, lazy gluttons."

13 This testimony is true. For this cause reprove them severely that they may be sound in the faith,

14 not paying attention to Jewish myths and commandments of men who turn away from the truth.

15 To the pure, all things are pure; but to those who are defiled and unbelieving, nothing is pure, but both their mind and their conscience are defiled.

16 They profess to know God, but by *their* deeds they deny *Him*, being detestable and disobedient, and worthless for any good deed.

1:5 The terms for *bishop* (Greek *episkopos*, "overseer") and *elder* (Greek *presbuteros*) are used interchangeably in the New Testament. Paul so uses the terms in 1:5,7. The New Testament churches undoubtedly were governed by a plural eldership; there is no record of a single bishop or elder in a New Testament church, although there are some references to single individuals, such as Diotrephes of 3 John 9, who seemed to have a controlling authority over the local church. The qualifications for the office of elder are carefully laid down in Scripture (1:5–9; 1 Tim. 3:1–7). Of paramount importance is the call of the Holy Spirit or the divine appointment (Acts 20:28), but the divine call was to be ratified by the church and acknowledged by the laying on of hands by the other elders (1:5; Acts 14:23). The functions of the office included: (1) rulership (1 Tim. 5:17); (2) preaching the gospel and preserving God's people from error (1:9); and (3) watch-care of the flock as a shepherd over sheep (Acts 20:28; 1 Pet. 5:2). The divine appointment was understood to include the divine endowment, with the necessary gifts for the discharge of the functions of the office (1 Cor. 12:28; Eph. 4:11).

III. *The Christian life (2:1–3:11)*

A. *Among Christians*

2 But as for you, speak the things which are fitting for sound doctrine.
2 Older men are to be temperate, dignified, sensible, sound in faith, in love, in perseverance.

3 Older women likewise are to be reverent in their behavior, not malicious gossips, nor enslaved to much wine, teaching what is good,

4 that they may encourage the young women to love their husbands, to love their children,

5 *to be* sensible, pure, workers at home, kind, being subject to their own husbands, that the word of God may not be dishonored.

6 Likewise urge the young men to be sensible;

7 in all things show yourself to be an example of good deeds, *with* purity in doctrine, dignified,

8 sound *in* speech which is beyond reproach, in order that the opponent may be put to shame, having nothing bad to say about us.

9 *Urge* bondslaves to be subject to their own masters in everything, to be well-pleasing, not argumentative,

10 not pilfering, but showing all good faith that they may adorn the doctrine of God our Savior in every respect.

B. *In the light of the blessed hope*

11 For the grace of God has appeared, bringing salvation to all men,

12 instructing us to deny ungodliness and worldly desires and to live sensibly, righteously and godly in the present age,

13 looking for the blessed hope and the appearing of the glory of our great God and Savior, Christ Jesus;

14 who gave Himself for us, that He might redeem us from every lawless deed and purify for Himself a people for His own possession, zealous for good deeds.

15 These things speak and exhort and reprove with all authority. Let no one disregard you.

C. *Faith and works*

3 Remind them to be subject to rulers, to authorities, to be obedient, to be ready for every good deed,

2 to malign no one, to be uncontentious, gentle, showing every consideration for all men.

3 For we also once were foolish ourselves, disobedient, deceived, enslaved to various lusts and pleasures, spending our life in malice and envy, hateful, hating one another.

4 But when the kindness of God our Savior and *His* love for mankind appeared,

5 He saved us, not on the basis of deeds which we have done in righteousness, but according to His mercy, by the washing of regeneration and renewing by the Holy Spirit,

6 whom He poured out upon us richly through Jesus Christ our Savior,

7 that being justified by His grace we might be made heirs according to *the* hope of eternal life.

8 This is a trustworthy statement; and concerning these things I want you to speak confidently, so that those who have believed God may be careful to engage in good deeds. These things are good and profitable for men.

Marginal references:

2:1 / Titus 1:9
2:2 / Titus 1:13
2:3 / 1 Tim 3:8
2:5 / 1 Cor 14:34; Eph 5:22; 1 Tim 6:1
2:7 / 1 Tim 4:12
2:8 / 1 Tim 6:3
2:9 / Eph 6:5
2:10 / Matt 5:16
2:11 / Rom 5:15; 1 Tim 2:4
2:12 / Titus 3:3; 2 Tim 3:12
*2:13 / 2 Thess 2:8; 2 Pet 1:1
2:14 / 1 Tim 2:6; Heb 9:14; Ex 19:5; Eph 2:10
3:1 / Rom 13:1; 2 Tim 2:21
3:2 / Eph 4:31; 2 Tim 2:24,25
3:3 / 1 Cor 6:11; 1 Pet 4:3
3:4 / Titus 2:11; 1 Tim 2:3
3:5 / Rom 3:20; Eph 5:26; Rom 12:2
3:6 / Rom 5:5
3:7 / Rom 3:24; 8:17,24
3:8 / 1 Tim 1:15; Titus 2:14

2:4 The New Testament teaches that the duties of wives to their husbands are: (1) to love them (2:4); (2) to live with them until death separates them (Rom. 7:2,3); (3) to be submissive to them (2:5; 1 Cor. 14:34); (4) to respect them (Eph. 5:33); and (5) to fulfill their marital duty (1 Cor. 7:3–5).

2:13 The *blessed hope* of the Christian is the second advent of Jesus Christ. The Greek word *epiphaneia* was used by heathen authors to refer to the theophanies or appearances of their pagan gods. In the Bible it is used with reference to

the incarnation of Christ, the first "epiphany" (2 Tim. 1:10). But in the present passage it can only refer to the second coming of Christ (1 Tim. 6:14; 2 Tim. 4:1,8), the second "epiphany." But the term *blessed hope* connotes more than simply the coming of Christ. It includes also all the events related to the end of the age, as described in different parts of the New Testament. To limit the *blessed hope* to the rapture of the church can hardly be justified from its Scriptural usage.

3:9
1 Tim 1:4;
2 Tim 2:14
*3:10
Rom 16:17

9 But shun foolish controversies and genealogies and strife and disputes about the Law; for they are unprofitable and worthless.

10 Reject a factious man after a first and second warning,

11 knowing that such a man is perverted and is sinning, being self-condemned.

IV. *Personal matters and benediction (3:12–15)*

3:12
Acts 20:4;
2 Tim 4:9,10
3:13
Acts 18:24

12 When I send Artemas or Tychicus to you, make every effort to come to me at Nicopolis, for I have decided to spend the winter there.

13 Diligently help Zenas the lawyer and Apollos on their way so that nothing is lacking for them.

3:14
v. 8

14 And let our *people* also learn to engage in good deeds to meet pressing needs, that they may not be unfruitful.

3:15
Col 4:18

15 All who are with me greet you. Greet those who love us in *the* faith. Grace be with you all.

3:10 *Factious* is the translation of the Greek *hairetikos* (from which Greek word the English word "heretic" is derived). The word itself describes a man who refuses to abide by generally accepted teaching, and holds stubbornly to different ideas. In 2 Pet. 2:1 the author condemns those who bring in *destructive heresies* (Greek *haireseis*). Paul's instruction on how to deal with the *factious* man implies that such a person has departed from the faith. Therefore: *reject a factious man* (cf. note to 2 Tim. 2:18).

INTRODUCTION TO
THE LETTER OF PAUL TO
PHILEMON

Authorship and Background: Along with Colossians, Philippians, and Ephesians, the letter to Philemon is classified as one of the "Prison Letters" (cf. vv. 9,10,13), written from Rome, A.D. 59-61 (cf. Introduction to Colossians). Onesimus, a slave, had fled from his master Philemon to Rome, where he was converted through Paul's ministry. Paul wanted the slave to return to his master Philemon and sent the letter along, perhaps by Tychicus, who was to accompany Onesimus (Col. 4:7-9).

It should be noted that the letter is addressed not only to Philemon, the master of Onesimus, but also to Apphia (probably Philemon's wife), and Archippus, a fellow minister of the gospel. Some have conjectured that Archippus was the son of Philemon and Apphia. The church that met in Philemon's home is also included among the recipients, so that the letter is not strictly a private communication (notice the plurals "you" in verse 3, "your" and "you" in verse 22, and "your" in verse 25).

The letter itself does not indicate where Philemon lived. From Col. 4:9 it appears that Onesimus ("who is one of your number") was from Colossae; in Col. 4:17, however, Paul instructs the Colossians to give a message to Archippus (cf. Philem. 2), which would be strange if Archippus, a church leader, were in Colossae. That he may have lived in Laodicea is possible, since the injunction to remind Archippus of his ministry comes with greetings to Laodicea and instructions concerning the letter to the Laodiceans (Col. 4:15,16).

There is the possibility, held by some, that the recipients of Philemon were in Laodicea, not Colossae. In any case, the three cities, Colossae, Laodicea, and Hierapolis, were quite close to each other, with Epaphras described as having worked in all three (Col. 4:12,13).

Paul had never visited Colossae (Col. 2:1), so that he must have met Philemon elsewhere, perhaps in Ephesus, the capital of the province of Asia. It seems certain, from Paul's allusive remark in Philem. 19, that Philemon was converted under his ministry. In returning Onesimus to his master, Paul promised to pay whatever Onesimus owed Philemon (vv. 18,19), the implication being that the slave had stolen some money or property when he ran away. As he sent Onesimus back home, Paul expressed the hope of being able to see his friends shortly (v. 22).

Characteristics: Of all Paul's letters, Philemon is the most personal in tone: artless, unpretentious, and direct, Paul writes his friend to receive Onesimus back, no longer merely as a slave, but above all as a brother in Christ (vv. 16,17). Now that he was a believer, Onesimus was really useful (v. 11)—a pun on the name Onesimus, which means "useful." Paul does not plead for Philemon to free the slave, but there is more than a broad hint to that effect in vv. 16,17, "no longer as a slave, but more than a slave . . . accept him as you would me." In verse 21, "I know that you will do even more than what I say" implies the same; perhaps it also implies that Philemon should be kind enough to return Onesimus to Paul so that he might continue to help the apostle (vv. 13,14).

In this brief letter, the shortest of all Paul's surviving correspondence, are to be seen the best qualities of the apostle Paul, ambassador in bonds.

Introduction to Philemon

Contents:

THE LETTER OF PAUL TO
PHILEMON

I. *Salutation (1–3)*

1 Paul, a prisoner of Christ Jesus, and Timothy our brother, to Philemon our beloved *brother* and fellow worker,

2   and to Apphia our sister, and to Archippus our fellow soldier, and to the church in your house:

3   Grace to you and peace from God our Father and the Lord Jesus Christ.

II. *Paul's love for Philemon (4–7)*

4   I thank my God always, making mention of you in my prayers,

5   because I hear of your love, and of the faith which you have toward the Lord Jesus, and toward all the saints;

6   *and I pray* that the fellowship of your faith may become effective [1]through the knowledge of every good thing which is in [2]you for Christ's sake.

7   For I have come to have much joy and comfort in your love, because the hearts of the saints have been refreshed through you, brother.

III. *Appeal for Onesimus (8–22)*

8   Therefore, though I have enough confidence in Christ to order you *to do* that which is proper,

9   yet for love's sake I rather appeal *to you*—since I am such a person as Paul, the aged, and now also a prisoner of Christ Jesus—

10   I appeal to you for my child, whom I have begotten in my imprisonment, [3]Onesimus,   *see note pg 1535*

11   who formerly was useless to you, but now is useful both to you and to me.

12   And I have sent him back to you in person, that is, *sending* my very heart,

13   whom I wished to keep with me, that in your behalf he might minister to me in my imprisonment for the gospel;

14   but without your consent I did not want to do anything, that your goodness should not be as it were by compulsion, but of your own free will.

15   For perhaps he was for this reason parted *from you* for a while, that you should have him back forever,

16   no longer as a slave, but more than a slave, a beloved brother, especially to me, but how much more to you, both in the flesh and in the Lord.

17   If then you regard me a partner, accept him as *you would* me.

18   But if he has wronged you in any way, or owes you anything, charge that to my account;

19   I, Paul, am writing this with my own hand, I will repay it (lest I should mention to you that you owe to me even your own self as well).

20   Yes, brother, let me benefit from you in the Lord; refresh my heart in Christ.

21   Having confidence in your obedience, I write to you, since I know that you will do even more than what I say.

22   And at the same time also prepare me a lodging; for I hope that through your prayers I shall be given to you.

IV. *Greetings and benediction (23–25)*

23   Epaphras, my fellow prisoner in Christ Jesus, greets you,

24   *as do* Mark, Aristarchus, Demas, Luke, my fellow workers.

[1]Or, *in*   [2]Some ancient mss. read *us*   [3]I.e., *useful*

---

2 Philemon's house was a church that had true religion. But the testimony of this house did not affect Onesimus, who remained unconverted until after his contact with Paul.

23 *Epaphras*, see note to Col. 1:7.
24 *Aristarchus*, a native of Thessalonica and follower of the apostle Paul. He may have voluntarily participated in Paul's

---

25
2 Tim 4:22

25 The grace of the Lord Jesus Christ be with your spirit. [4]

[4]Some ancient mss. add *Amen*

bonds, and tradition has it that he was martyred in Rome under Nero. *Demas*, of whom Paul speaks in 2 Timothy 4:10 as having deserted him because he *loved this present world*. Whether his defection was temporary or final is not known, although tradition has it that he was an apostate from the true faith. After leaving Paul he went to Thessalonica, probably his home.

INTRODUCTION TO
THE LETTER TO THE
HEBREWS

Authorship and Background: There is no sure indication of author, place of writing, date, and recipients of Hebrews. It seems almost certain that Paul was not the author; Luke, Apollos, or Barnabas are those most often suggested (if, in fact, the author's name appears in the New Testament). The title "To the Hebrews" is not original with the book but is a deduction from the general nature of the writing. Even its classification as a letter is not altogether irrefutable: the author called his writing a brief "word of exhortation" (13:22); though there are personal greetings at the close (13:22-24), there are none at the beginning; and the whole reads more like a written sermon, or homily, than a letter as such.

The closing greetings afford no sure indication of the destination of the writing: "Those from Italy" in 13:24 is not explicit as to whether the people so named were in or out of Italy.

The author was personally acquainted with his readers (6:9-12; 10:32-34; 13:7), and expressed his hope to return to them (13:19-23). Timothy was a mutual friend (13:23). He and his readers seem to have been second-generation believers, having received the gospel from those who had heard the Lord Jesus (2:3).

Various dates have been suggested for Hebrews, ranging from before A.D. 70 to the last decade of the first century A.D.

The occasion that gave rise to this "word of exhortation" (13:22) was the danger brought about by persecution, which, while it had not yet reached the point of martyrdom (12:4), was severe (10:32-34). The readers seem to have been Jewish Christians who were in danger of abandoning their faith and lapsing back into Judaism; thus they were running the risk of apostasy, although the author felt that they had not yet reached this disastrous state of affairs (6:9-12). So he exhorts them to hold fast to their confession in Christ as Savior and Lord (4:14; 10:23).

Characteristics: This stirring challenge constitutes the earliest literary apology, or defense, of the Christian faith. The sufficiency and finality of Christ, and the consequent superiority of the Christian faith over Judaism, are developed in an orderly and impressive way, and in a dignified, stately, and eloquent literary style. The argument appears to use Neoplatonic philosophic terms, which contrast the real, which is heavenly and eternal, with the apparent, which is earthly and temporary. In all respects Christ is superior: He is superior to the prophets, to angels, and to Moses, Joshua, and the Aaronic priesthood; His covenant is superior, His sacrifices and promises better.

Frequent homiletical devices lend support to the opinion that the major part of the writing was a sermon (cf. 5:11; 6:3; 9:5b; 11:32; 13:22). There are frequent exhortations (2:1; 3:1,2; 4:11,14; 10:19-25,35; 12:1,2,12,13; 13:13-15) and sharp warnings (2:2-4; 3:6,12,13; 3:16-4:1; 6:4-6; 10:26-31; 12:15-17,25). The real humanity of the person of Christ is here emphasized as in no other book in the New Testament (2:9,10; 2:14-18; 4:15; 5:7-9; 12:3; 13:12).

The great roll call of the heroes of the faith (11:1-40) and the challenging exhortation that follows (12:1,2) have served Christians of all times and ages. On the bedrock truth of the all-sufficiency of Jesus Christ, "the same yesterday and today, yes and forever" (13:8), Christians of every clime and age have staked their faith and lives.

Contents:

I. Introduction: Christ the final revelation of God (1:1-3)

II. Christ—better than the angels (1:4-2:18): Christ is the Son, angels are ministering spirits;

therefore the warning: believers cannot escape if they neglect so great a salvation. In His complete identification with mankind, whom He came to save, Jesus as high priest makes expiation for the sins of the people.

III. Christ—better than Moses and Joshua (3:1-4:13): Moses was a servant in God's house, Christ is Son; therefore the warning: do not fall away from the living God, but hold fast in faith. Joshua did not give God's people the promised rest, but Christ offers it; let us therefore strive to enter that rest.

IV. Christ—better than the Aaronic priesthood (4:14-7:28): Through weakness and suffering, Christ is fit to be the perfect representative, the perfect priest. The levitical priesthood could not effect perfection; therefore a new high priest, in the likeness of Melchizedek, holds His priesthood permanently. Beware of the danger of apostasy!

V. Christ—His better covenant (8:1-10:18): The new covenant is based on better promises, and is sealed, not with the blood of animals, but with the blood of Him who offered Himself once for all to put away sin. The old sacrifices were repeated, hence ineffectual; Christ's single sacrifice, once for all, of Himself, has perfected for all time those who are sanctified.

VI. Faith—the better way (10:19-12:29): Like the ancient heroes of faith, believers are to endure, running with patience the course set before them, with eyes fixed on Jesus the beginner and perfecter of their faith.

VII. Conclusion (13:1-25)

HEBREWS

I. *Introduction: Christ the final revelation of God (1:1–3)*

1 God, after He spoke long ago to the fathers in the prophets in many portions and
in many ways,
2 in these last days has spoken to us in *His* Son, whom He appointed heir of all
things, through whom also He made the world.
3 And He is the radiance of His glory and the exact representation of His
nature, and upholds all things by the word of His power. When He had made
purification of sins, He sat down at the right hand of the Majesty on high;

II. *Christ: better than the angels (1:4–2:18)*

A. *Christ the Son of God*

4 having become as much better than the angels, as He has inherited a more
excellent name than they.
5 For to which of the angels did He ever say,
"THOU ART MY SON,
TODAY I HAVE BEGOTTEN THEE"?
And again,
"I WILL BE A FATHER TO HIM,
AND HE SHALL BE A SON TO ME"?
6 And when He again brings the first-born into the world, He says,
"AND LET ALL THE ANGELS OF GOD WORSHIP HIM."
7 And of the angels He says,
"WHO MAKES HIS ANGELS WINDS,
AND HIS MINISTERS A FLAME OF FIRE."
8 But of the Son *He says,*
"THY THRONE, O GOD, IS FOREVER AND EVER,
AND THE RIGHTEOUS SCEPTER IS THE SCEPTER OF [1]HIS KINGDOM.
9 "THOU HAST LOVED RIGHTEOUSNESS AND HATED LAWLESSNESS;
THEREFORE GOD, THY GOD, HATH ANOINTED THEE
WITH THE OIL OF GLADNESS ABOVE THY COMPANIONS."
10 And,
"THOU, LORD, IN THE BEGINNING DIDST LAY THE FOUNDATION OF THE
EARTH,
AND THE HEAVENS ARE THE WORKS OF THY HANDS;
11 THEY WILL PERISH, BUT THOU REMAINEST;
AND THEY ALL WILL BECOME OLD AS A GARMENT,
12 AND AS A MANTLE THOU WILT ROLL THEM UP;
AS A GARMENT THEY WILL ALSO BE CHANGED.
BUT THOU ART THE SAME,
AND THY YEARS WILL NOT COME TO AN END."
13 But to which of the angels has He ever said,
"SIT AT MY RIGHT HAND,
UNTIL I MAKE THINE ENEMIES
A FOOTSTOOL FOR THY FEET"?
14 Are they not all ministering spirits, sent out to render service for the sake of
those who will inherit salvation?

B. *Christ the son of man*

1. *Warning against rejecting God's revelation*

2 For this reason we must pay much closer attention to what we have heard, lest
we drift away *from it.*

1:2
Gal 4:4;
Heb 2:3;
Ps 2:8;
John 1:3;
1 Cor 8:6
1:3
John 1:14;
Col 1:17;
Heb 7:27; 8:1

1:4
Eph 1:21;
Phil 2:9,10
1:5
Ps 2:7

1:6
Heb 10:5;
Deut 32:43
1:7
Ps 104:4

1:8
Ps 45:6,7

1:9
Phil 2:9;
Is 61:1,3

1:10
Ps 102:25

1:11
Is 34:4

1:12
Heb 13:8

1:13
Ps 110:1;
Heb 10:13

1:14
Ps 103:20;
Heb 5:9

[1]Some mss. read *Thy*

*2:2
Heb 1:1;
Acts 7:53;
Heb 10:28,35
2:3
Heb 10:29;
1:1; Luke 1:2
2:4
John 4:48;
1 Cor 12:4;
Eph 1:5

2   For if the word spoken through angels proved unalterable, and every transgression and disobedience received a just recompense,

3   how shall we escape if we neglect so great a salvation? After it was at the first spoken through the Lord, it was confirmed to us by those who heard,

4   God also bearing witness with them, both by signs and wonders and by various miracles and by gifts of the Holy Spirit according to His own will.

2. The kingdom conferred on Christ

2:5
Heb 6:5

5   For He did not subject to angels the world to come, concerning which we are speaking.

2:6
Ps 8:4-6

6   But one has testified somewhere, saying,
   "WHAT IS MAN, THAT THOU REMEMBEREST HIM?
   OR THE SON OF MAN, THAT THOU ART CONCERNED ABOUT HIM?
7   "THOU HAST MADE HIM FOR A LITTLE WHILE LOWER THAN THE ANGELS;
   THOU HAST CROWNED HIM WITH GLORY AND HONOR,
   [2]AND HAST APPOINTED HIM OVER THE WORKS OF THY HANDS;

*2:8
Matt 28:18;
1 Cor 15:27;
15:25

8   THOU HAST PUT ALL THINGS IN SUBJECTION UNDER HIS FEET."
For in subjecting all things to him, He left nothing that is not subject to him. But now we do not yet see all things subjected to him.

*2:9
Phil 2:7-9;
Acts 2:33;
John 3:16;
1 John 2:2

9   But we do see Him who has been made for a little while lower than the angels, namely, Jesus, because of the suffering of death crowned with glory and honor, that by the grace of God He might taste death for everyone.

3. Christ as true man

2:10
Luke 24:46;
Rom 11:36;
Acts 3:15;
5:31;
Luke 13:32
2:11
Heb 10:10;
Acts 17:26;
John 20:17
2:12
Ps 22:22

10   For it was fitting for Him, for whom are all things, and through whom are all things, in bringing many sons to glory, to perfect the author of their salvation through sufferings.

11   For both He who sanctifies and those who are sanctified are all from one Father; for which reason He is not ashamed to call them brethren,

12   saying,
   "I WILL PROCLAIM THY NAME TO MY BRETHREN,
   IN THE MIDST OF THE CONGREGATION I WILL SING THY PRAISE."

2:13
Is 8:17,18;
John 10:29

13   And again,
   "I WILL PUT MY TRUST IN HIM."
And again,
   "BEHOLD, I AND THE CHILDREN WHOM GOD HAS GIVEN ME."

4. Christ as man's true sacrifice

2:14
Matt 16:17;
John 1:14;
1 Cor 15:54-57;
1 John 3:8
2:15
Rom 8:15;
2 Tim 1:7

14   Since then the children share in flesh and blood, He Himself likewise also partook of the same, that through death He might render powerless him who had the power of death, that is, the devil;

15   and might deliver those who through fear of death were subject to slavery all their lives.

16   For assuredly He does not give help to angels, but He gives help to the descendant of Abraham.

*2:17
Phil 2:7;
Heb 4:15;
5:1,2; 1 John
2:2; 4:10

17   Therefore, He had to be made like His brethren in all things, that He might become a merciful and faithful high priest in things pertaining to God, to make propitiation for the sins of the people.

[2]Some ancient mss. do not contain And . . . hands

2:2 *the word spoken through angels.* This refers to the giving of the Law to the Jewish people on Mt. Sinai. Old Testament references to angels at Sinai are found in Deut. 33:2 (LXX, "angels"), and Ps. 68:17. The mediation of angels in the giving of the Law is further referred to in Acts 7:38,53 and Gal. 3:19.
2:8 *in subjecting all things to him.* This is strong language. Christ's sovereignty extends to everything, *nothing . . . is not subject to him.*
2:9 *suffering of death.* This was a divine necessity in accord with the nature of God and the purpose of God to redeem men.
2:17 The term *make propitiation* represents the Greek *hilaskomai,* "to propitiate," "to make atonement." Christ accomplished His redemptive work on Calvary, where He

atoned for the sins of mankind. Three elements are involved in the term "atonement": (1) the idea of *covering*—to put "under the blood" is to cover over, an idea that is emphasized by the Old Testament term *kipper*—"to cover over, or atone for"; (2) the idea of *reconciliation*, by which the broken relationship between sinners and God was restored through the death of Christ; (3) the idea of *substitution*, which requires that someone else actually stand in the sinner's place and bear the penalty due him (Is. 53:5). Old Testament illustrations of atonement are found in Ex. 12:3–14 and Lev. 16. Christ's atonement is founded on the necessity of the shedding of blood for sin (Lev. 17:11; Heb. 9:22). It was a *once* for all sacrifice (9:26). Its benefits are secured to the believer by faith (John 1:12; 3:16; 5:24; 14:6; Eph. 2:8). (See also note to Rom. 3:25.)

18   For since He Himself was tempted in that which He has suffered, He is able to come to the aid of those who are tempted.

2:18
Heb 4:15

III. Christ: better than Moses and Joshua (3:1–4:13)

A. Christ as Lord superior to Moses as servant

3 Therefore, holy brethren, partakers of a heavenly calling, consider Jesus, the Apostle and High Priest of our confession.

3:1
Heb 2:11;
Phil 3:14;
Rom 15:8;
Heb 10:21

2   He was faithful to Him who appointed Him, as Moses also was in all His house.

3   For He has been counted worthy of more glory than Moses, by just so much as the builder of the house has more honor than the house.

3:3
2 Cor 3:7-11

4   For every house is built by someone, but the builder of all things is God.

3:4
Eph 2:10;
Heb 1:2

5   Now Moses was faithful in all His house as a servant, for a testimony of those things which were to be spoken later;

3:5
Num 12:7;
Ex 14:31;
Deut 18:18,
19

6   but Christ *was faithful* as a Son over His house whose house we are, if we hold fast our confidence and the boast of our hope firm until the end.

3:6
Heb 1:2;
1 Cor 3:16;
Rom 5:2;
Col 1:23

B. Christ's rest superior to that of Moses and Joshua

1. Introduction

7   Therefore, just as the Holy Spirit says,
"TODAY IF YOU HEAR HIS VOICE,

3:7
Heb 9:8;
Ps 95:7

8   DO NOT HARDEN YOUR HEARTS AS WHEN THEY PROVOKED ME,
AS IN THE DAY OF TRIAL IN THE WILDERNESS,

9   WHERE YOUR FATHERS TRIED *Me* BY TESTING *Me*,
AND SAW MY WORKS FOR FORTY YEARS.

3:9
Acts 7:36

10   "THEREFORE I WAS ANGRY WITH THIS GENERATION,
AND SAID, 'THEY ALWAYS GO ASTRAY IN THEIR HEART;
AND THEY DID NOT KNOW MY WAYS';

11   AS I SWORE IN MY WRATH,
'THEY SHALL NOT ENTER MY REST.' "

3:11
Heb 4:3,5

2. The necessity of persevering faith to enter Christ's rest

12   Take care, brethren, lest there should be in any one of you an evil, unbelieving heart, in falling away from the living God.

3:12
Heb 12:25;
9:14

13   But encourage one another day after day, as long as it is *still* called "Today," lest any one of you be hardened by the deceitfulness of sin.

3:13
Heb 10:24,
25; Eph 4:22

14   For we have become partakers of Christ, if we hold fast the beginning of our assurance firm until the end;

3:14
v. 6

15   while it is said,
"TODAY IF YOU HEAR HIS VOICE,
DO NOT HARDEN YOUR HEARTS, AS WHEN THEY PROVOKED ME."

3:15
v. 7

16   For who provoked *Him* when they had heard? Indeed, did not all those who came out of Egypt *led* by Moses?

3:16
Num 14:2

17   And with whom was He angry for forty years? Was it not with those who sinned, whose bodies fell in the wilderness?

3:17
Num 14:29;
Ps 106:26

18   And to whom did He swear that they should not enter His rest, but to those who were disobedient?

3:18
Num 14:23;
Heb 4:6

19   And *so* we see that they were not able to enter because of unbelief.

3:19
John 3:36

3. Warning against missing Christ's rest as typified by Canaan rest

4 Therefore, let us fear lest, while a promise remains of entering His rest, any one of you should seem to have come short of it.

4:1
Heb 12:15
*4:2
1 Thess 2:13

2   For indeed we have had good news preached to us, just as they also; but the

---

4:2 "Gospel" comes from the Greek word *euaggelion* meaning *good news, tidings, word*. Among the descriptive phrases occurring in the New Testament are: (1) *the gospel of peace* (Eph. 6:15); (2) *the gospel of Christ* (1 Cor. 9:12); (3) *the gospel of the grace of God* (Acts 20:24); (4) *the gospel of the kingdom* (Matt. 24:14); and (5) *an eternal gospel* (Rev. 14:6). Some have argued for different gospels on the basis of these various titles. It appears, however, that such distinctions are quite forced and unwarrantable, especially in view of the solemn curse of Gal. 1:8. People in all ages have been saved by the gospel, either through a faith that looks forward to the sacrifice of Christ or by one that looks back on it. Paul plainly declares that Abraham was saved by the gospel (Gal. 3:8). The heart of the gospel is that the incarnate Son of God

word they heard did not profit them, because it was not united by faith in those who heard.

3 ³For we who have believed enter that rest, just as He has said,

"AS I SWORE IN MY WRATH,
THEY SHALL NOT ENTER MY REST,"

although His works were finished from the foundation of the world.

4 For He has thus said somewhere concerning the seventh *day*, "AND GOD RESTED ON THE SEVENTH DAY FROM ALL HIS WORKS";

5 and again in this *passage*, "THEY SHALL NOT ENTER MY REST."

6 Since therefore it remains for some to enter it, and those who formerly had good news preached to them failed to enter because of disobedience,

7 He again fixes a certain day, "Today," saying through David after so long a time just as has been said before,

"TODAY IF YOU HEAR HIS VOICE,
DO NOT HARDEN YOUR HEARTS."

8 For if Joshua had given them rest, He would not have spoken of another day after that.

9 There remains therefore a Sabbath rest for the people of God.

10 For the one who has entered His rest has himself also rested from his works, as God did from His.

11 Let us therefore be diligent to enter that rest, lest anyone fall through *following* the same example of disobedience.

12 For the word of God is living and active and sharper than any two-edged sword, and piercing as far as the division of soul and spirit, of both joints and marrow, and able to judge the thoughts and intentions of the heart.

13 And there is no creature hidden from His sight, but all things are open and laid bare to the eyes of Him with whom we have to do.

IV. *Christ: better than the Aaronic priesthood*
(4:14–7:28)

A. *Christ the way of approach to God*

14 Since then we have a great high priest who has passed through the heavens, Jesus the Son of God, let us hold fast our confession.

15 For we do not have a high priest who cannot sympathize with our weaknesses, but one who has been tempted in all things as *we are, yet* without sin.

16 Let us therefore draw near with confidence to the throne of grace, that we may receive mercy and may find grace to help in time of need.

B. *Christ, God's appointed high priest*

5 For every high priest taken from among men is appointed on behalf of men in things pertaining to God, in order to offer both gifts and sacrifices for sins;

2 he can deal gently with the ignorant and misguided, since he himself also is beset with weakness;

3 and because of it he is obligated to offer *sacrifices* for sins, as for the people, so also for himself.

4 And no one takes the honor to himself, but *receives it* when he is called by God, even as Aaron was.

5 So also Christ did not glorify Himself so as to become a high priest, but He who said to Him,

"THOU ART MY SON,
TODAY I HAVE BEGOTTEN THEE";

6 just as He says also in another *passage*,

³Some ancient mss. read *Therefore*

---

has died and risen again for man's justification.
4:15 Sinlessness involves two elements. The first concerns the inward part of man or the motivation that governs his actions. The second has to do with the outward acts of man. Sinlessness implies that both one's inward motives and overt acts are perfect in God's sight. It is actual conformity to the good and the holy. That Jesus our Savior was sinless

is the united testimony of the Bible. We have: (1) the warrant of Jesus' own words (John 8:46; see also John 8:29; 17:19); (2) the testimony of others (Matt. 27:4,19; Luke 23:41; John 18:38); and (3) the testimony of the apostles (2 Cor. 5:21; Heb. 4:15; 7:26,27; 1 Pet. 2:21,22; 1 John 3:5).

"THOU ART A PRIEST FOREVER
ACCORDING TO THE ORDER OF MELCHIZEDEK."

7   In the days of His flesh, He offered up both prayers and supplications with
loud crying and tears to the One able to save Him from death, and He was heard
because of His piety.

8   Although He was a Son, He learned obedience from the things which He
suffered.

9   And having been made perfect, He became to all those who obey Him the
source of eternal salvation,

10   being designated by God as a high priest according to the order of Melchizedek.

C. Exhortation to lay hold of Christ and His redemption

1. The immature reproved

11   Concerning [4]him we have much to say, and it is hard to explain, since you
have become dull of hearing.

12   For though by this time you ought to be teachers, you have need again for
someone to teach you the elementary principles of the oracles of God, and you have
come to need milk and not solid food.

13   For everyone who partakes only of milk is not accustomed to the word of
righteousness, for he is a babe.

14   But solid food is for the mature, who because of practice have their senses
trained to discern good and evil.

2. A warning advanced

6 Therefore leaving the elementary teaching about the Christ, let us press on to
maturity, not laying again a foundation of repentance from dead works and of
faith toward God,

2   of instruction about washings, and laying on of hands, and the resurrection
of the dead, and eternal judgment.

3   And this we shall do, if God permits.

4   For in the case of those who have once been enlightened and have tasted of
the heavenly gift and have been made partakers of the Holy Spirit,

5   and have tasted the good word of God and the powers of the age to come,

6   and then have fallen away, it is impossible to renew them again to repentance, since they again crucify to themselves the Son of God, and put Him to open
shame.

7   For ground that drinks the rain which often falls upon it and brings forth
vegetation useful to those for whose sake it is also tilled, receives a blessing from
God;

8   but if it yields thorns and thistles, it is worthless and close to being cursed,
and it ends up being burned.

3. True believers encouraged

9   But, beloved, we are convinced of better things concerning you, and things
that accompany salvation, though we are speaking in this way.

10   For God is not unjust so as to forget your work and the love which you have
shown toward His name, in having ministered and in still ministering to the saints.

11   And we desire that each one of you show the same diligence so as to realize
the full assurance of hope until the end,

[4]Or, Him; or, this

Cross references (right margin):

5:7 Matt 26:39, 53; 27:46; Mark 14:36; 15:34
5:8 Heb 3:6; Phil 2:8
5:9 Heb 2:10
*5:10 vv. 5,6
5:12 Gal 4:3; Heb 6:1; Acts 7:38; 1 Cor 3:2
5:13 1 Cor 3:1
5:14 Is 7:15
6:1 Phil 3:12-14; Heb 5:12; 9:14
6:2 Acts 19:3,4; 6:6; 17:31,32
6:3 Acts 18:21
*6:4ff Heb 10:26, 32; Eph 2:8; Gal 3:2,5
6:5 Heb 2:5
6:6 Heb 10:26-29
6:7 Ps 65:10
6:8 Gen 3:17,18
6:10 Matt 10:42; 25:40; 2 Thess 1:6, 7; 1 Thess 1:3; Rom 15:25
6:11 Heb 3:6,14; Col 2:2

5:10 See notes to Gen. 14:18 and Ps. 110:1.

6:4–6 For two thousand years Christians have disagreed
about the answer to the question: Can a man who has truly
been converted lose his salvation? Arminians (followers of
Jacobus Arminius, a Dutch theologian who opposed the
views of strict Calvinism) believe he can, and Calvinists
believe he cannot. Arminians believe that vv. 4,5 contain a
description of a truly regenerate man who subsequently falls
away. Calvinists hold that the person described was not
actually born again but was only on the threshold of salvation. This much is clear: v. 4 plainly teaches that if a person

does fall away after enjoying such knowledge, experience,
and privilege, then it is impossible to restore him again to
repentance. Whichever view we adopt of the apostate man
prior to his apostasy, the outcome is virtually the same.
That is to say, if a man openly rejects Jesus Christ, he is, in
either view, to be regarded as an unregenerate, unsaved
man, even though he had formerly appeared to human
observers to be converted. The Arminian would say that he
had lost his salvation, the Calvinist that he had never had it;
but the result is identical.

6:12
Heb 10:36
12   that you may not be sluggish, but imitators of those who through faith and patience inherit the promises.

4. God's covenant promise unchanging

6:13
Gen 22:16,17;
Luke 1:73
13   For when God made the promise to Abraham, since He could swear by no one greater, He swore by Himself,

14   saying, "I WILL SURELY BLESS YOU, AND I WILL SURELY MULTIPLY YOU."

15   And thus, having patiently waited, he obtained the promise.

6:16
Gal 3:15;
Ex 22:11
*6:17
Heb 11:9;
Ps 110:4
16   For men swear by one greater *than themselves*, and with them an oath *given* as confirmation is an end of every dispute.

17   In the same way God, desiring even more to show to the heirs of the promise the unchangeableness of His purpose, interposed with an oath,

6:18
Titus 1:2;
Heb 7:19
18   in order that by two unchangeable things, in which it is impossible for God to lie, we may have strong encouragement, we who have fled for refuge in laying hold of the hope set before us.

6:19
Lev 16:2;
Heb 9:7
6:20
Heb 4:14; 5:6
19   This hope we have as an anchor of the soul, a *hope* both sure and steadfast and one which enters within the veil,

20   where Jesus has entered as a forerunner for us, having become a high priest forever according to the order of Melchizedek.

D. Christ's Melchizedek priesthood surpasses the Levitical

1. The priority of the Melchizedek priesthood

7:1
Gen 14:18-20
7 For this Melchizedek, king of Salem, priest of the Most High God, who met Abraham as he was returning from the slaughter of the kings and blessed him,

2   to whom also Abraham apportioned a tenth part of all *the spoils*, was first of all, by the translation *of his name*, king of righteousness, and then also king of Salem, which is king of peace.

*7:3
vv. 6,28
3   Without father, without mother, without genealogy, having neither beginning of days nor end of life, but made like the Son of God, he abides a priest perpetually.

7:4
Gen 14:20
4   Now observe how great this man was to whom Abraham, the patriarch, gave a tenth of the choicest spoils.

7:5
Num 18:21,
26
5   And those indeed of the sons of Levi who receive the priest's office have commandment in the Law to collect a tenth from the people, that is, from their brethren, although these are descended from Abraham.

7:6
Gen 14:19;
Rom 4:13
6   But the one whose genealogy is not traced from them collected a tenth from Abraham, and blessed the one who had the promises.

7   But without any dispute the lesser is blessed by the greater.

7:8
Heb 5:6; 6:20
8   And in this case mortal men receive tithes, but in that case one *receives them*, of whom it is witnessed that he lives on.

9   And, so to speak, through Abraham even Levi, who received tithes, paid tithes,

10   for he was still in the loins of his father when Melchizedek met him.

2. The transitory priesthood of Aaron versus the eternal priesthood of Christ

7:11
vv. 18,19;
Heb 8:7;
10:1; v. 17
11   Now if perfection was through the Levitical priesthood (for on the basis of it the people received the Law), what further need *was there* for another priest to arise according to the order of Melchizedek, and not be designated according to the order of Aaron?

7:13
vv. 14,11
7:14
Is 11:1;
Matt 1:3;
Luke 3:33;
Rom 1:3;
Rev 5:5
12   For when the priesthood is changed, of necessity there takes place a change of law also.

13   For the one concerning whom these things are spoken belongs to another tribe, from which no one has officiated at the altar.

14   For it is evident that our Lord was descended from Judah, a tribe with reference to which Moses spoke nothing concerning priests.

6:17 God is immutable or unchangeable. The counsel of the Trinity (Father, Son, and Holy Spirit) stands sure from eternity to eternity. This divine immutability is the basis of the believer's faith and hope. Thus, whatever God has promised He will perform. Scripture here indicates that God has given two evidences on which we can build our faith: (1) His immutable promise; and (2) His immutable

oath that He swore by Himself.
7:3 *without father, without mother.* This means that there was no record of Melchizedek's parents: he appears in the narrative without any account of his father or mother (Gen. 14:18–20). In like manner, *neither beginning of days nor end of life* does not mean that he experienced neither birth nor death, but simply that the Scriptures do not record them.

15   And this is clearer still, if another priest arises according to the likeness of Melchizedek,

16   who has become *such* not on the basis of a law of physical requirement, but according to the power of an indestructible life.

7:16
Heb 9:10,14

17   For it is witnessed *of Him*,
> "THOU ART A PRIEST FOREVER
> ACCORDING TO THE ORDER OF MELCHIZEDEK."

7:17
Ps 110:4;
Heb 5:6;
6:20; v.21

18   For, on the one hand, there is a setting aside of a former commandment because of its weakness and uselessness

7:18
Rom 8:3;
Gal 4:9

19   (for the Law made nothing perfect), and on the other hand there is a bringing in of a better hope, through which we draw near to God.

7:19
Acts 13:39;
Rom 3:20;
Gal 2:16;
Heb 9:9;
6:18; 8:6;
4:16

3. *The superior efficacy of Christ's priesthood*

20   And inasmuch as *it was* not without an oath

21   (for they indeed became priests without an oath, but He with an oath through the One who said to Him,
> "THE LORD HAS SWORN
> AND WILL NOT CHANGE HIS MIND,
> 'THOU ART A PRIEST FOREVER' ");

*7:21
Ps 110:4

22   so much the more also Jesus has become the guarantee of a better covenant.

7:22
Heb 8:6;
9:15; 12:24

23   And the *former* priests, on the one hand, existed in greater numbers, because they were prevented by death from continuing,

24   but He, on the other hand, because He abides forever, holds His priesthood permanently.

7:24
v. 28

25   Hence, also, He is able to save forever those who draw near to God through Him, since He always lives to make intercession for them.

7:25
v. 19;
Rom 8:34;
Heb 9:24

26   For it was fitting that we should have such a high priest, holy, innocent, undefiled, separated from sinners and exalted above the heavens;

7:26
Heb 4:15; 8:1

27   who does not need daily, like those high priests, to offer up sacrifices, first for His own sins, and then for the *sins* of the people, because this He did once for all when He offered up Himself.

7:27
Heb 5:1,3;
9:12;
Eph 5:2;
Heb 9:14,28

28   For the Law appoints men as high priests who are weak, but the word of the oath, which came after the Law, *appoints* a Son, made perfect forever.

7:28
Heb 5:2; 1:2;
2:10

V. Christ: His better covenant (8:1–10:18)

A. The old and the new covenants

1. *The new covenant better than the old*

8 Now the main point in what has been said *is this*: we have such a high priest, who has taken His seat at the right hand of the throne of the Majesty in the heavens,

8:1
Heb 2:17; 1:3

2   a minister in the sanctuary, and in the true tabernacle, which the Lord pitched, not man.

8:2
Heb 9:11,24

3   For every high priest is appointed to offer both gifts and sacrifices; hence it is necessary that this *high priest* also have something to offer.

8:3
Heb 5:1; 9:14

4   Now if He were on earth, He would not be a priest at all, since there are those who offer the gifts according to the Law;

8:4
Heb 5:1

5   who serve a copy and shadow of the heavenly things, just as Moses was warned *by God* when he was about to erect the tabernacle; for, "SEE," He says, "THAT YOU MAKE all things ACCORDING TO THE PATTERN WHICH WAS SHOWN YOU ON THE MOUNTAIN."

8:5
Col 2:17;
Heb 9:23;
10:1;
Ex 25:40;
Heb 11:7;
12:25

6   But now He has obtained a more excellent ministry, by as much as He is also the mediator of a better covenant, which has been enacted on better promises.

8:6
1 Tim 2:5;
Heb 7:22

7   For if that first *covenant* had been faultless, there would have been no occasion sought for a second.

8:7
Heb 7:11,18

2. *The new covenant based on superior promises*

8   For finding fault with them, He says,

*8:8
Jer 31:31-34

7:21 *The LORD . . . will not change His mind.* The new covenant is neither provisional nor temporary. It is permanent and it is effective. The purposes of God will be fulfilled, whereby men will be brought into fellowship with God and their sins forgiven.

8:8 The new covenant is superior to the old covenant. Under the old covenant the believer could repose his faith only in symbols and types of Christ, and the law was a standard placed before him for his guidance. But under the new covenant the believer puts his trust in the actual person

"BEHOLD, DAYS ARE COMING, SAYS THE LORD,
WHEN I WILL EFFECT A NEW COVENANT
WITH THE HOUSE OF ISRAEL AND WITH THE HOUSE OF JUDAH;

8:9
Ex 19:5,6

9 NOT LIKE THE COVENANT WHICH I MADE WITH THEIR FATHERS
ON THE DAY WHEN I TOOK THEM BY THE HAND
TO LEAD THEM OUT OF THE LAND OF EGYPT;
FOR THEY DID NOT CONTINUE IN MY COVENANT,
AND I DID NOT CARE FOR THEM, SAYS THE LORD.

8:10
Heb 10:16;
2 Cor 3:3;
Zech 8:8

10 "FOR THIS IS THE COVENANT THAT I WILL MAKE WITH THE HOUSE OF
ISRAEL
AFTER THOSE DAYS, SAYS THE LORD:
I WILL PUT MY LAWS INTO THEIR MINDS,
AND I WILL WRITE THEM UPON THEIR HEARTS.
AND I WILL BE THEIR GOD,
AND THEY SHALL BE MY PEOPLE.

8:11
Is 54:13;
John 6:45;
1 John 2:27

11 "AND THEY SHALL NOT TEACH EVERYONE HIS FELLOW CITIZEN,
AND EVERYONE HIS BROTHER, SAYING, 'KNOW THE LORD,'
FOR ALL SHALL KNOW ME,
FROM THE LEAST TO THE GREATEST OF THEM.

8:12
Heb 10:17

12 "FOR I WILL BE MERCIFUL TO THEIR INIQUITIES,
AND I WILL REMEMBER THEIR SINS NO MORE."

8:13
2 Cor 5:17

13 When He said, "A new *covenant*," He has made the first obsolete. But whatever is becoming obsolete and growing old is ready to disappear.

B. *Old and new covenant sacrifices compared*

1. *The temporary Levitical sacrifices*

9:1
Ex 25:8

9 Now even the first *covenant* had regulations of divine worship and the earthly sanctuary.

*9:2
Ex 25:8,9;
23-39

2 For there was a tabernacle prepared, the outer one, in which *were* the lampstand and the table and the sacred bread; this is called the holy place.

9:3
Ex 26:31-33

3 And behind the second veil, there was a tabernacle which is called the Holy of Holies,

9:4
Ex 30:1-5;
25:10ff;
16:32,33;
Num 17:10
9:5
Ex 25:17ff

4 having a golden altar of incense and the ark of the covenant covered on all sides with gold, in which *was* a golden jar holding the manna, and Aaron's rod which budded, and the tables of the covenant.

5 And above it *were* the cherubim of glory overshadowing the mercy seat; but of these things we cannot now speak in detail.

9:6
Num 28:3

6 Now when these things have been thus prepared, the priests are continually entering the outer tabernacle, performing the divine worship,

9:7
Lev 16:11ff;
Ex 30:10;
Heb 5:2,3

7 but into the second only the high priest *enters*, once a year, not without *taking* blood, which he offers for himself and for the sins of the people committed in ignorance.

9:8
Heb 10:19,
20; John 14:6

8 The Holy Spirit *is* signifying this, that the way into the holy place has not yet been disclosed, while the outer tabernacle is still standing,

9:9
Heb 11:19;
5:1; Gal 3:21

9 which *is* a symbol for the present time. Accordingly both gifts and sacrifices are offered which cannot make the worshiper perfect in conscience,

9:10
Lev 11:2ff;
Col 2:16;
Heb 7:16

10 since they *relate* only to food and drink and various washings, regulations for the body imposed until a time of reformation.

2. *The eternal heavenly sacrifice of Christ*

*9:11ff
Heb 2:17;
10:1; 8:2

11 But when Christ appeared *as* a high priest of the good things [5]to come, *He*

[5]Some ancient mss. read *that have come*

---

of the Lord Jesus Himself and in His deed of atonement already accomplished on Calvary; moreover, the law is now implanted in his heart by the indwelling Holy Spirit Himself, who permanently abides within him. In the Old Testament period Israel fell into a legalistic perversion of God's gracious law, attempting to use it as a means of self-justification and merit-earning. And yet, according to God's own intention, even in Old Testament times, salvation was not obtained by observing the law; it was then, as now, given by the grace of God. The new covenant is based on a better sacrifice: the once-for-all offering up of Christ Himself on

the altar. By this sacrifice our sins are not simply covered, but actually cleansed away (9:26). The single condition for securing the benefits of the new covenant is faith in Christ and total submission to His lordship (see Gal. 3:13–29).
9:2 See note to Ex. 25:9 on the tabernacle.
9:11-15 Christ has become our priest as well as our prophet and king. The function of the Hebrew high priest was to minister at the altar, a function that he shared with his fellow priests. But he alone was permitted to enter into the Holy of Holies, and only on the Day of Atonement. Even then he could not enter without presenting a blood

entered through the greater and more perfect tabernacle, not made with hands, that is to say, not of this creation;

12 and not through the blood of goats and calves, but through His own blood, He entered the holy place once for all, having obtained eternal redemption.

13 For if the blood of goats and bulls and the ashes of a heifer sprinkling those who have been defiled, sanctify for the cleansing of the flesh,

14 how much more will the blood of Christ, who through the eternal Spirit offered Himself without blemish to God, cleanse your conscience from dead works to serve the living God?

3. *The new covenant fulfilled in Christ's death*

a. *The covenant validated by the death of the testator*

15 And for this reason He is the mediator of a new covenant, in order that since a death has taken place for the redemption of the transgressions that were *committed* under the first covenant, those who have been called may receive the promise of the eternal inheritance.

16 For where a covenant is, there must of necessity be the death of the one who made it.

17 For a covenant is valid *only* when men are dead, [6]for it is never in force while the one who made it lives.

18 Therefore even the first *covenant* was not inaugurated without blood.

19 For when every commandment had been spoken by Moses to all the people according to the Law, he took the blood of the calves and the goats, with water and scarlet wool and hyssop, and sprinkled both the book itself and all the people,

20 saying, "THIS IS THE BLOOD OF THE COVENANT WHICH GOD COMMANDED YOU."

21 And in the same way he sprinkled both the tabernacle and all the vessels of the ministry with the blood.

22 And according to the Law, *one may* almost *say*, all things are cleansed with blood, and without shedding of blood there is no forgiveness.

b. *Christ the sufficient offering for sin*

23 Therefore it was necessary for the copies of the things in the heavens to be cleansed with these, but the heavenly things themselves with better sacrifices than these.

24 For Christ did not enter a holy place made with hands, a *mere* copy of the true one, but into heaven itself, now to appear in the presence of God for us;

25 nor was it that He should offer Himself often, as the high priest enters the holy place year by year with blood not his own.

26 Otherwise, He would have needed to suffer often since the foundation of the world; but now once at the consummation of the ages He has been manifested to put away sin by the sacrifice of Himself.

27 And inasmuch as it is appointed for men to die once and after this *comes* judgment,

28 so Christ also, having been offered once to bear the sins of many, shall appear a second time for salvation without *reference to* sin, to those who eagerly await Him.

---

[6]Some ancient mss. read *for is it then . . . lives?*

Marginal references:

9:12 Heb 7:27; 10:4
9:13 Num 19:9,17, 18
9:14 1 John 1:7; 1 Pet 3:18; Titus 2:14
9:15 1 Tim 2:5; Heb 3:1; 7:22
9:17 Gal 3:15
9:18 Ex 24:6
9:19 Ex 24:65ff; Lev 14:4,7
9:20 Ex 24:8; Matt 26:28
9:21 Lev 8:15
*9:22 Lev 17:11
9:23 Heb 8:5
9:24 Heb 6:20; 8:2; 7:25; 1 John 2:1
9:25 v. 7; Heb 10:19
9:26 Heb 4:3; 7:27; 1:2
9:27 Gen 3:19; 2 Cor 5:10
*9:28 Rom 6:10; 1 Pet 2:24; Titus 2:13

---

sacrifice first for himself and then for the sins of the people. Salvation is impossible apart from the priestly work of Christ. Hebrews teaches that as our priest, Christ serves as intermediary between man and God; He has once for all ministered at the altar with His own blood to make an efficacious atonement for the sins of men. Believers today still approach God through the one and only valid priest, Jesus Christ.

9:22 The blood of Christ shed on Calvary is the vital principle behind the atonement. God's forgiveness is possible only through Christ's sacrifice. Undoubtedly the writer here is referring to Christ's own words, *this is My blood of the covenant, which is poured . . . for forgiveness of sins* (Matt. 26:28).

9:28 The second advent of Christ is inextricably linked to the eternal purposes of God. His coming foreshadows: (1) the completion of the salvation of believers (9:28; 1 Pet. 1:5); (2) His reign as absolute sovereign in heaven and earth (Rev. 11:15); (3) the destruction of the power and reign of death (1 Cor. 15:25,26); (4) His being glorified in His saints and marveled at by all who have believed (2 Thess. 1:10); (5) His bringing to light those things that are hidden in darkness (1 Cor. 4:5); and (6) His final judgment of the living and the dead (John 5:22; 2 Tim. 4:1; Jude 15; Rev. 20:11–13). The dead saints will rise first (1 Thess. 4:16), and living saints will be caught up together with them in the clouds (1 Thess. 4:17). The man of sin will be destroyed at Christ's coming (2 Thess. 2:8).

4. *The superiority and finality of the new covenant*

a. *Christ the once-for-all sacrifice*

10 For the Law, since it has *only* a shadow of the good things to come *and* not the very form of things, [7]can never by the same sacrifices year by year, which they offer continually, make perfect those who draw near.

2   Otherwise, would they not have ceased to be offered, because the worshipers, having once been cleansed, would no longer have had consciousness of sins?

3   But in those *sacrifices* there is a reminder of sins year by year.

4   For it is impossible for the blood of bulls and goats to take away sins.

5   Therefore, when He comes into the world, He says,
"SACRIFICE AND OFFERING THOU HAST NOT DESIRED,
BUT A BODY THOU HAST PREPARED FOR ME;

6   IN WHOLE BURNT OFFERINGS AND *sacrifices* FOR SIN THOU HAST TAKEN
NO PLEASURE.

7   "THEN I SAID, 'BEHOLD, I HAVE COME
(IN THE ROLL OF THE BOOK IT IS WRITTEN OF ME)
TO DO THY WILL, O GOD.'"

8   After saying above, "SACRIFICES AND OFFERINGS AND WHOLE BURNT OFFERINGS AND *sacrifices* FOR SIN THOU HAST NOT DESIRED, NOR HAST THOU TAKEN PLEASURE *in them*" (which are offered according to the Law),

9   then He said, "BEHOLD, I HAVE COME TO DO THY WILL." He takes away the first in order to establish the second.

10   By this will we have been sanctified through the offering of the body of Jesus Christ once for all.

b. *The evidence of His finished work*

11   And every priest stands daily ministering and offering time after time the same sacrifices, which can never take away sins;

12   but He, having offered one sacrifice for sins for all time, SAT DOWN AT THE RIGHT HAND OF GOD,

13   waiting from that time onward UNTIL HIS ENEMIES BE MADE A FOOTSTOOL FOR HIS FEET.

14   For by one offering He has perfected for all time those who are sanctified.

15   And the Holy Spirit also bears witness to us; for after saying,

16   "THIS IS THE COVENANT THAT I WILL MAKE WITH THEM
AFTER THOSE DAYS, SAYS THE LORD:
I WILL PUT MY LAWS UPON THEIR HEART,
AND UPON THEIR MIND I WILL WRITE THEM,"

He then says,

17   "AND THEIR SINS AND THEIR LAWLESS DEEDS
I WILL REMEMBER NO MORE."

18   Now where there is forgiveness of these things, there is no longer *any* offering for sin.

VI. *Faith: the better way (10:19–12:29)*

A. *Exhortation to hold firm*

1. *Our access to God the ground of our hope*

19   Since therefore, brethren, we have confidence to enter the holy place by the blood of Jesus,

20   by a new and living way which He inaugurated for us through the veil, that is, His flesh,

21   and since *we have* a great priest over the house of God,

22   let us draw near with a sincere heart in full assurance of faith, having our

---

Marginal references:

10:1 Heb 9:9,11, 23
10:3 Heb 9:7
10:4 Mic 6:6,7
10:5 Ps 40:6-8; Heb 1:6; 1 Pet 2:24
10:7 Jer 36:2
10:8 vv. 5,6; Mark 12:33
10:9 v. 7
10:10 John 17:19; Heb 7:27; 1 Pet 2:24
10:11 Heb 5:1; v. 4
*10:12 Heb 1:3
10:13 Ps 110:1; Heb 1:13
10:14 v. 1
10:15 Heb 3:7
10:16 Jer 31:33,34
10:17 Heb 8:12
10:19 Eph 2:18; Heb 9:8,12
10:20 Heb 9:8,3
10:21 Heb 2:17; 1 Tim 3:15
10:22 Heb 4:16; Eph 3:12;

---

[7]Some ancient mss. read *they can*

10:12 Here and in 1:3 the expression *sat down* is used of the finished work of Christ. In the tabernacle and in the temple the priests performed their functions standing. The high priest who entered the Holy of Holies once a year also stood. The work of the Aaronic priesthood was an unfinished work. But when Christ accomplished His work of redemption, *He sat down at the right hand of the Majesty on high* (1:3) or *at the right hand of God* (10:12), signifying a perfect and completed work.

hearts sprinkled *clean* from an evil conscience and our bodies washed with pure water.

23   Let us hold fast the confession of our hope without wavering, for He who promised is faithful;

24   and let us consider how to stimulate one another to love and good deeds,

25   not forsaking our own assembling together, as is the habit of some, but encouraging *one another*; and all the more, as you see the day drawing near.

2. *The judgment for failure to hold firm*

26   For if we go on sinning willfully after receiving the knowledge of the truth, there no longer remains a sacrifice for sins,

27   but a certain terrifying expectation of judgment, and THE FURY OF A FIRE WHICH WILL CONSUME THE ADVERSARIES.

28   Anyone who has set aside the Law of Moses dies without mercy on *the testimony of* two or three witnesses.

29   How much severer punishment do you think he will deserve who has trampled under foot the Son of God, and has regarded as unclean the blood of the covenant by which he was sanctified, and has insulted the Spirit of grace?

30   For we know Him who said, "VENGEANCE IS MINE, I WILL REPAY." And again, "THE LORD WILL JUDGE HIS PEOPLE."

31   It is a terrifying thing to fall into the hands of the living God.

3. *Future reward for those who endure*

32   But remember the former days, when, after being enlightened, you endured a great conflict of sufferings,

33   partly, by being made a public spectacle through reproaches and tribulations, and partly by becoming sharers with those who were so treated.

34   For you showed sympathy to the prisoners, and accepted joyfully the seizure of your property, knowing that you have for yourselves a better possession and an abiding one.

35   Therefore, do not throw away your confidence, which has a great reward.

36   For you have need of endurance, so that when you have done the will of God, you may receive what was promised.

37   FOR YET IN A VERY LITTLE WHILE,
HE WHO IS COMING WILL COME, AND WILL NOT DELAY.

38   BUT MY RIGHTEOUS ONE SHALL LIVE BY FAITH;
AND IF HE SHRINKS BACK, MY SOUL HAS NO PLEASURE IN HIM.

39   But we are not of those who shrink back to destruction, but of those who have faith to the preserving of the soul.

B. *Definition and illustration of faith*

1. *Faith defined*

11   Now faith is the assurance of *things* hoped for, the conviction of things not seen.

2   For by it the men of old gained approval.

3   By faith we understand that the worlds were prepared by the word of God, so that what is seen was not made out of things which are visible.

2. *Faith of the early patriarchs*

4   By faith Abel offered to God a better sacrifice than Cain, through which he obtained the testimony that he was righteous, God testifying about his gifts, and through faith, though he is dead, he still speaks.

5   By faith Enoch was taken up so that he should not see death; AND HE WAS NOT FOUND BECAUSE GOD TOOK HIM UP; for he obtained the witness that before his being taken up he was pleasing to God.

6   And without faith it is impossible to please *Him*, for he who comes to God must believe that He is, and *that* He is a rewarder of those who seek Him.

7   By faith Noah, being warned *by God* about things not yet seen, in reverence prepared an ark for the salvation of his household, by which he condemned the world, and became an heir of the righteousness which is according to faith.

Heb 9:14;
Ezek 36:25

10:23
Heb 4:14;
1 Cor 1:9
10:24
10:25
Acts 2:42;
Heb 3:13;
Phil 4:5

10:26
Num 15:30;
2 Pet 2:20
10:27
Heb 9:27;
Is 26:11
10:28
Deut 17:2-6;
Heb 2:2
10:29
Heb 2:3; 6:6;
13:20;
Eph 4:30;
Heb 6:4
10:30
Deut 32:35,
36;
Rom 12:19

10:32
Heb 6:4;
Phil 1:29,30
10:33
1 Cor 4:9;
1 Thess 2:14
10:34
Heb 9:15

10:35
Heb 2:2
10:36
Luke 21:19;
Col 3:24
10:37
Hab 2:3,4;
Luke 18:8
10:38
Rom 1:17;
Gal 3:11
10:39
2 Pet 2:20;
Acts 16:30

*11:1
Rom 8:24;
2 Cor 4:18;
5:7
11:2
vv. 4,39
11:3
Gen 1:1;
John 1:3;
Heb 6:5

11:4
Gen 4:4,10;
1 John 3:12;
Heb 12:24
*11:5
Gen 5:21-24

11:6
Heb 7:19

11:7
Gen 6:13-22

11:1 For a definition of faith see note to Eph. 2:8.   **11:5** See note to Gen. 5:24 on translation of Enoch.

3. *The faith of Abraham and his children*

8 By faith Abraham, when he was called, obeyed by going out to a place which he was to receive for an inheritance; and he went out, not knowing where he was going.

9 By faith he lived as an alien in the land of promise, as in a foreign *land*, dwelling in tents with Isaac and Jacob, fellow heirs of the same promise;

10 for he was looking for the city which has foundations, whose architect and builder is God.

11 By faith even Sarah herself received ability to conceive, even beyond the proper time of life, since she considered Him faithful who had promised;

12 therefore, also, there was born of one man, and him as good as dead at that, *as many descendants* AS THE STARS OF HEAVEN IN NUMBER, AND INNUMERABLE AS THE SAND WHICH IS BY THE SEASHORE.

13 All these died in faith, without receiving the promises, but having seen them and having welcomed them from a distance, and having confessed that they were strangers and exiles on the earth.

14 For those who say such things make it clear that they are seeking a country of their own.

15 And indeed if they had been thinking of that *country* from which they went out, they would have had opportunity to return.

16 But as it is, they desire a better *country*, that is a heavenly one. Therefore God is not ashamed to be called their God; for He has prepared a city for them.

17 By faith Abraham, when he was tested, offered up Isaac; and he who had received the promises was offering up his only begotten *son*;

18 *it was he* to whom it was said, "IN ISAAC YOUR DESCENDANTS SHALL BE CALLED."

19 He considered that God is able to raise *men* even from the dead; from which he also received him back as a type.

20 By faith Isaac blessed Jacob and Esau, even regarding things to come.

21 By faith Jacob, as he was dying, blessed each of the sons of Joseph, and worshiped, *leaning* on the top of his staff.

22 By faith Joseph, when he was dying, made mention of the exodus of the sons of Israel, and gave orders concerning his bones.

4. *The faith of Moses the deliverer*

23 By faith Moses, when he was born, was hidden for three months by his parents, because they saw he was a beautiful child; and they were not afraid of the king's edict.

24 By faith Moses, when he had grown up, refused to be called the son of Pharaoh's daughter;

25 choosing rather to endure ill-treatment with the people of God, than to enjoy the passing pleasures of sin;

26 considering the reproach of Christ greater riches than the treasures of Egypt; for he was looking to the reward.

27 By faith he left Egypt, not fearing the wrath of the king; for he endured, as seeing Him who is unseen.

28 By faith he kept the Passover and the sprinkling of the blood, so that he who destroyed the first-born might not touch them.

5. *The faith of the Israelites and Rahab*

29 By faith they passed through the Red Sea as though *they were passing* through dry land; and the Egyptians, when they attempted it, were drowned.

30 By faith the walls of Jericho fell down, after they had been encircled for seven days.

31 By faith Rahab the harlot did not perish along with those who were disobedient, after she had welcomed the spies in peace.

6. *The faith of the judges and prophets*

32 And what more shall I say? For time will fail me if I tell of Gideon, Barak, Samson, Jephthah, of David and Samuel and the prophets,

---

11:32 From v. 32 to v. 35 the writer describes the glorious deliverances that came to those who trusted God. But from the middle of v. 35 the tone changes as the writer mentions other multitudes who also had faith in God but who were

33   who by faith conquered kingdoms, performed *acts of* righteousness, obtained promises, shut the mouths of lions,

34   quenched the power of fire, escaped the edge of the sword, from weakness were made strong, became mighty in war, put foreign armies to flight.

35   Women received *back* their dead by resurrection; and others were tortured, not accepting their release, in order that they might obtain a better resurrection;

36   and others experienced mockings and scourgings, yes, also chains and imprisonment.

37   They were stoned, they were sawn in two, [8]they were tempted, they were put to death with the sword; they went about in sheepskins, in goatskins, being destitute, afflicted, ill-treated

38   (*men* of whom the world was not worthy), wandering in deserts and mountains and caves and holes in the ground.

39   And all these, having gained approval through their faith, did not receive what was promised,

40   because God had provided something better for us, so that apart from us they should not be made perfect.

C. Faith and the believer

1. Christ our example

12 Therefore, since we have so great a cloud of witnesses surrounding us, let us also lay aside every encumbrance, and the sin which so easily entangles us, and let us run with endurance the race that is set before us,

2   fixing our eyes on Jesus, the author and perfecter of faith, who for the joy set before Him endured the cross, despising the shame, and has sat down at the right hand of the throne of God.

2. Chastening for spiritual development

3   For consider Him who has endured such hostility by sinners against Himself, so that you may not grow weary and lose heart.

4   You have not yet resisted to the point of shedding blood in your striving against sin;

5   and you have forgotten the exhortation which is addressed to you as sons,
"MY SON, DO NOT REGARD LIGHTLY THE DISCIPLINE OF THE LORD,
NOR FAINT WHEN YOU ARE REPROVED BY HIM;

6   FOR THOSE WHOM THE LORD LOVES HE DISCIPLINES,
AND HE SCOURGES EVERY SON WHOM HE RECEIVES."

7   It is for discipline that you endure; God deals with you as with sons; for what son is there whom *his* father does not discipline?

8   But if you are without discipline, of which all have become partakers, then you are illegitimate children and not sons.

9   Furthermore, we had earthly fathers to discipline us, and we respected them; shall we not much rather be subject to the Father of spirits, and live?

10   For they disciplined us for a short time as seemed best to them, but He *disciplines us* for *our* good, that we may share His holiness.

11   All discipline for the moment seems not to be joyful, but sorrowful; yet to those who have been trained by it, afterwards it yields the peaceful fruit of righteousness.

3. Exhortation to endurance

12   Therefore, strengthen the hands that are weak and the knees that are feeble,

13   and make straight paths for your feet, so that *the limb* which is lame may not be put out of joint, but rather be healed.

14   Pursue peace with all men, and the sanctification without which no one will see the Lord.

[8]Some mss. do not contain *they were tempted*

11:33
2 Sam 7:11;
Judg 14:5;
1 Sam 17:34;
Dan 6:22
11:34
2 Kin 20:7;
Judg 15:8
11:35
1 Kin 17:22;
Acts 22:25
11:36
Jer 20:2
11:37
1 Kin 21:13;
Acts 7:58;
2 Kin 1:8
11:38
1 Kin 18:4

11:40
Heb 5:9

*12:1
1 Cor 9:24;
Heb 10:36

12:2
Phil 2:8,9;
Heb 1:3,13;
1 Pet 3:22

12:3
Matt 10:24;
Gal 6:9
12:4
Heb 10:32-34;
1 Cor 10:13
12:5
Prov 3:11,12

12:6
Ps 94:12;
James 1:12
12:7
Deut 8:5

12:8
1 Pet 5:9

12:9
Luke 18:2;
Num 16:22;
Is 38:16
12:10
2 Pet 1:4
12:11
1 Pet 1:6;
James 3:17,18

12:12
Is 35:3
12:13
Prov 4:26;
Gal 6:1
12:14
Rom 14:19;
6:22;
Matt 5:8

---

not delivered. While faith in God is essential to the believer's life, it is not the determining factor by which deliverance from difficult circumstances may be secured. The determining factor is the will of God. Therefore, in days past, among people of like faith, some were delivered and others found their deliverance in suffering and martyrdom. **12:1** See note to Rom. 14:8 on the Christian walk.

12:15
Gal 5:4;
Deut 29:18;
Heb 3:12
*12:16
Gen 25:33
12:17
Gen 27:30-40

15   See to it that no one comes short of the grace of God; that no root of bitterness springing up causes trouble, and by it many be defiled;

16   that *there be* no immoral or godless person like Esau, who sold his own birthright for a *single* meal.

17   For you know that even afterwards, when he desired to inherit the blessing, he was rejected, for he found no place for repentance, though he sought for it with tears.

4. *Final warning against apostasy*

12:18
Ex 19:12-22;
Deut 4:11
12:19
Ex 20:19;
Deut 5:5
12:20
Ex 19:12,13

12:21
Ex 19:16

18   For you have not come to *a mountain* that may be touched and to a blazing fire, and to darkness and gloom and whirlwind,

19   and to the blast of a trumpet and the sound of words which *sound was such that* those who heard begged that no further word should be spoken to them.

20   For they could not bear the command, "IF EVEN A BEAST TOUCHES THE MOUNTAIN, IT WILL BE STONED."

21   And so terrible was the sight, *that* Moses said, "I AM FULL OF FEAR and trembling."

12:22
Phil 3:20;
Gal 4:26
12:23
Luke 10:20;
Phil 3:12

12:24
1 Tim 2:5;
Gen 4:10;
Heb 11:4
12:25
Heb 2:2,3;
8:5; 11:7

12:26
Ex 19:18;
Hag 2:6
12:27
1 Cor 7:31;
2 Pet 3:10

12:28
Dan 2:44;
Heb 13:15

12:29
Deut 4:24

22   But you have come to Mount Zion and to the city of the living God, the heavenly Jerusalem, and to myriads of angels,

23   to the general assembly and church of the first-born who are enrolled in heaven, and to God, the Judge of all, and to the spirits of righteous men made perfect,

24   and to Jesus, the mediator of a new covenant, and to the sprinkled blood, which speaks better than *the blood* of Abel.

25   See to it that you do not refuse Him who is speaking. For if those did not escape when they refused him who warned *them* on earth, much less *shall* we *escape* who turn away from Him who *warns* from heaven.

26   And His voice shook the earth then, but now He has promised, saying, "YET ONCE MORE I WILL SHAKE NOT ONLY THE EARTH, BUT ALSO THE HEAVEN."

27   And this *expression*, "Yet once more," denotes the removing of those things which can be shaken, as of created things, in order that those things which cannot be shaken may remain.

28   Therefore, since we receive a kingdom which cannot be shaken, let us show gratitude, by which we may offer to God an acceptable service with reverence and awe;

29   for our God is a consuming fire.

VII. *Conclusion (13:1–25)*

A. *Exhortations and warnings*

1. *General Christian obligations*

13:1
Rom 12:10;
1 Thess 4:9;
1 Pet 1:22
13:2
1 Pet 4:9;
Gen 18:3
13:3
Matt 25:36;
Col 4:18
*13:4
1 Cor 6:9;
Rev 22:15
*13:5
Phil 4:11;
Deut 31:6,8;
Josh 1:5

13 Let love of the brethren continue.
2   Do not neglect to show hospitality to strangers, for by this some have entertained angels without knowing it.

3   Remember the prisoners, as though in prison with them, and those who are ill-treated, since you yourselves also are in the body.

4   *Let* marriage *be held* in honor among all, and let the *marriage* bed *be* undefiled; for fornicators and adulterers God will judge.

5   Let your character be free from the love of money, being content with what you have; for He Himself has said, "I WILL NEVER DESERT YOU, NOR WILL I EVER FORSAKE YOU,"

6   so that we confidently say,
"THE LORD IS MY HELPER, I WILL NOT BE AFRAID.
WHAT SHALL MAN DO TO ME?"

2. *Warning against apostasy*

13:7
v. 17;
Heb 6:12
13:8
Heb 1:12

7   Remember those who led you, who spoke the word of God to you; and considering the result of their conduct, imitate their faith.

8   Jesus Christ *is* the same yesterday and today, *yes* and forever.

12:16 See note to Gen. 25:25 on Esau.   **13:5** See note to 1 Tim. 6:10.
13:4 See note to 1 Cor. 7:25 on marriage.

22   But prove yourselves doers of the word, and not merely hearers who delude themselves.

23   For if anyone is a hearer of the word and not a doer, he is like a man who looks at his natural face in a mirror;

24   for *once* he has looked at himself and gone away, he has immediately forgotten what kind of person he was.

25   But one who looks intently at the perfect law, the *law* of liberty, and abides by it, not having become a forgetful hearer but an effectual doer, this man shall be blessed in what he does.

26   If anyone thinks himself to be religious, and yet does not bridle his tongue but deceives his *own* heart, this man's religion is worthless.

27   This is pure and undefiled religion in the sight of *our* God and Father, to visit orphans and widows in their distress, *and* to keep oneself unstained by the world.

III. *True faith (2:1–3:12)*

A. *Evidenced by impartiality*

2 My brethren, do not hold your faith in our glorious Lord Jesus Christ with *an attitude of* personal favoritism.

2   For if a man comes into your assembly with a gold ring and dressed in fine clothes, and there also comes in a poor man in dirty clothes,

3   and you pay special attention to the one who is wearing the fine clothes, and say, "You sit here in a good place," and you say to the poor man, "You stand over there, or sit down by my footstool,"

4   have you not made distinctions among yourselves, and become judges with evil motives?

5   Listen, my beloved brethren: did not God choose the poor of this world *to be* rich in faith and heirs of the kingdom which He promised to those who love Him?

6   But you have dishonored the poor man. Is it not the rich who oppress you and personally drag you into court?

7   Do they not blaspheme the fair name by which you have been called?

8   If, however, you are fulfilling the royal law, according to the Scripture, "YOU SHALL LOVE YOUR NEIGHBOR AS YOURSELF," you are doing well.

9   But if you show partiality, you are committing sin *and* are convicted by the law as transgressors.

10   For whoever keeps the whole law and yet stumbles in one *point*, he has become guilty of all.

11   For He who said, "DO NOT COMMIT ADULTERY," also said, "DO NOT COMMIT MURDER." Now if you do not commit adultery, but do commit murder, you have become a transgressor of the law.

12   So speak and so act, as those who are to be judged by *the* law of liberty.

13   For judgment *will be* merciless to one who has shown no mercy; mercy triumphs over judgment.

B. *Evidenced by works*

14   What use is it, my brethren, if a man says he has faith, but he has no works? Can that faith save him?

15   If a brother or sister is without clothing and in need of daily food,

16   and one of you says to them, "Go in peace, be warmed and be filled," and yet you do not give them what is necessary for *their* body, what use is that?

17   Even so faith, if it has no works, is dead, *being* by itself.

18   But someone may *well* say, "You have faith, and I have works; show me your faith without the works, and I will show you my faith by my works."

2:1 *personal favoritism.* All are one in Christ; there is neither Jew nor Gentile, bond nor free, male nor female. Position, power, wealth, race, or color distinctions find no support in Scripture. Those who allow for such distinctions are guilty of sin.
2:10 Scripture differentiates between quantitative and qualitative sins. Here James shows that one sin, be it large or small, makes a man a sinner and brings him under the condemnation of the whole law. Thus, while one may distinguish between greater and lesser sinners (quantitative), both *are* sinners (qualitative).

2:14 James presents here the reverse side of the coin of faith. In effect, he argues strongly against the idea that a man can be saved by a faith that does not radically transform his life and conduct. Thus he makes plain the truth that there can be no true faith if there are no evidences to prove that faith. He does not argue that we are saved by works, but that works demonstrate the existence of genuine faith. This is consistent with Paul's teaching that the believer is *a new creature* (2 Cor. 5:17), and as such will manifest a new kind of character and behavior that will reflect the life of the Lord Jesus.

Marginal references: 1:22 Matt 7:21; Rom 2:13; 1 John 3:7 1:23 Luke 6:47; 1 Cor 13:12 1:25 2 Cor 3:18; James 2:12; John 13:17 1:26 Ps 34:13; 1 Pet 1:10 1:27 Matt 25:36; Rom 12:2; 1 John 5:18 *2:1 Prov 24:23; Matt 22:16; 1 Cor 2:8 2:2 v. 3 2:3 v. 2 2:4 John 7:24 2:5 1 Cor 1:26-28; Luke 12:21; James 1:12 2:6 1 Cor 11:22; Acts 8:3 2:8 Lev 19:18; Matt 22:39 *2:10 Matt 5:19; Gal 3:10 2:11 Ex 20:13,14; Deut 5:17,18 2:12 James 1:25 2:13 Matt 5:7; 18:32-35 *2:14 Matt 7:26; James 1:22ff 2:15 Luke 3:11 2:16 1 John 3:17,18 2:18 James 3:13

2:19
Deut 6:4;
Matt 8:29;
Luke 4:34
2:20
v. 17
2:21
Gen 22:9
2:22
Heb 11:17
2:23
Gen 15:6;
Rom 4:3;
2 Chr 20:7;
Is 41:8
2:25
Josh 2:1ff;
Heb 11:31
2:26
v. 20

19   You believe that [2]God is one. You do well; the demons also believe, and shudder.

20   But are you willing to recognize, you foolish fellow, that faith without works is useless?

21   Was not Abraham our father justified by works, when he offered up Isaac his son on the altar?

22   You see that faith was working with his works, and as a result of the works, faith was perfected;

23   and the Scripture was fulfilled which says, "AND ABRAHAM BELIEVED GOD, AND IT WAS RECKONED TO HIM AS RIGHTEOUSNESS," and he was called the friend of God.

24   You see that a man is justified by works, and not by faith alone.

25   And in the same way was not Rahab the harlot also justified by works, when she received the messengers and sent them out by another way?

26   For just as the body without the spirit is dead, so also faith without works is dead.

C. Evidenced by words

3:1
Matt 23:8;
Luke 6:37
3:2
1 Kin 8:46;
1 Pet 3:10;
Matt 12:37;
James 1:26
3:3
Ps 32:9

3 Let not many of you become teachers, my brethren, knowing that as such we shall incur a stricter judgment.

2   For we all stumble in many ways. If anyone does not stumble in what he says, he is a perfect man, able to bridle the whole body as well.

3   Now if we put the bits into the horses' mouths so that they may obey us, we direct their entire body as well.

4   Behold, the ships also, though they are so great and are driven by strong winds, are still directed by a very small rudder, wherever the inclination of the pilot desires.

3:5
Prov 12:18;
Ps 12:3
3:6
Prov 16:27;
Matt 15:11,
18,19

5   So also the tongue is a small part of the body, and yet it boasts of great things. Behold, how great a forest is set aflame by such a small fire!

6   And the tongue is a fire, the very world of iniquity; the tongue is set among our members as that which defiles the entire body, and sets on fire the course of our life, and is set on fire by hell.

7   For every species of beasts and birds, of reptiles and creatures of the sea, is tamed, and has been tamed by the human race.

3:8
Ps 140:3;
Rom 3:13
3:9
Gen 1:26

8   But no one can tame the tongue; it is a restless evil and full of deadly poison.

9   With it we bless our Lord and Father; and with it we curse men, who have been made in the likeness of God;

10   from the same mouth come both blessing and cursing. My brethren, these things ought not to be this way.

11   Does a fountain send out from the same opening both fresh and bitter water?

3:12
Matt 7:16

12   Can a fig tree, my brethren, produce olives, or a vine produce figs? Neither can salt water produce fresh.

IV. True wisdom (3:13–5:18)

A. True versus false wisdom

3:13
Gal 6:4;
James 2:18
3:14
Rom 2:8;
v. 16;
1 Tim 2:4;
James 5:19
3:15
James 1:17;
1 Tim 4:1
3:16
Gal 5:20
3:17
1 Cor 2:6;
Rom 12:9;
1 Pet 1:22
3:18
Prov 11:18;
Is 32:17

13   Who among you is wise and understanding? Let him show by his good behavior his deeds in the gentleness of wisdom.

14   But if you have bitter jealousy and selfish ambition in your heart, do not be arrogant and so lie against the truth.

15   This wisdom is not that which comes down from above, but is earthly, natural, demonic.

16   For where jealousy and selfish ambition exist, there is disorder and every evil thing.

17   But the wisdom from above is first pure, then peaceable, gentle, reasonable, full of mercy and good fruits, unwavering, without hypocrisy.

18   And the seed whose fruit is righteousness is sown in peace by those who make peace.

[2]Or, there is one God

B. *Worldly friendship*

4 What is the source of quarrels and conflicts among you? Is not the source your pleasures that wage war in your members?

2 You lust and do not have; *so* you commit murder. And you are envious and cannot obtain; *so* you fight and quarrel. You do not have because you do not ask.

3 You ask and do not receive, because you ask with wrong motives, so that you may spend *it* on your pleasures.

4 You adulteresses, do you not know that friendship with the world is hostility toward God? Therefore whoever wishes to be a friend of the world makes himself an enemy of God.

5 Or do you think that the Scripture speaks to no purpose: "³He jealously desires the Spirit which He has made to dwell in us"?

6 But He gives a greater grace. Therefore *it* says, "GOD IS OPPOSED TO THE PROUD, BUT GIVES GRACE TO THE HUMBLE."

7 Submit therefore to God. Resist the devil and he will flee from you.

8 Draw near to God and He will draw near to you. Cleanse your hands, you sinners; and purify your hearts, you double-minded.

9 Be miserable and mourn and weep; let your laughter be turned into mourning, and your joy to gloom.

10 Humble yourselves in the presence of the Lord, and He will exalt you.

C. *Slander*

11 Do not speak against one another, brethren. He who speaks against a brother, or judges his brother, speaks against the law, and judges the law; but if you judge the law, you are not a doer of the law, but a judge *of it.*

12 There is *only* one Lawgiver and Judge, the One who is able to save and to destroy; but who are you who judge your neighbor?

D. *False confidence*

13 Come now, you who say, "Today or tomorrow, we shall go to such and such a city, and spend a year there and engage in business and make a profit."

14 Yet you do not know what your life will be like tomorrow. You are *just* a vapor that appears for a little while and then vanishes away.

15 Instead, *you ought* to say, "If the Lord wills, we shall live and also do this or that."

16 But as it is, you boast in your arrogance; all such boasting is evil.

17 Therefore, to one who knows *the* right thing to do, and does not do it, to him it is sin.

E. *The end of the oppressor*

5 Come now, you rich, weep and howl for your miseries which are coming upon you.

2 Your riches have rotted and your garments have become moth-eaten.

3 Your gold and your silver have rusted; and their rust will be a witness against you and will consume your flesh like fire. It is in the last days that you have stored up your treasure!

4 Behold, the pay of the laborers who mowed your fields, *and* which has been withheld by you, cries out *against you*; and the outcry of those who did the harvesting has reached the ears of the Lord of Sabaoth.

5 You have lived luxuriously on the earth and led a life of wanton pleasure; you have fattened your hearts in a day of slaughter.

6 You have condemned and put to death the righteous *man;* he does not resist you.

F. *The patience of the saints*

7 Be patient, therefore, brethren, until the coming of the Lord. Behold, the farmer waits for the precious produce of the soil, being patient about it, until it gets the early and late rains.

8 You too be patient; strengthen your hearts, for the coming of the Lord is at hand.

³Or, *The Spirit which He has made to dwell in us jealously desires us*

Marginal references:

4:1 Titus 3:9; Rom 7:23
4:3 Ps 18:41; 1 John 3:22; 5:14
4:4 James 1:27; 1 John 2:15; John 15:19
4:5 Gen 6:5; Num 11:29
4:6 Ps 138:6; Prov 3:34
4:7 1 Pet 5:6-9
4:8 2 Chr 15:2; Is 1:16; James 1:8
4:9 Luke 6:25
4:10 Matt 23:12
4:11 1 Pet 2:1
4:12 Matt 10:28; Rom 14:4
4:13 Prov 27:1
4:14 Job 7:7; Ps 102:3
4:15 Acts 18:21
4:16 1 Cor 5:6
4:17 Luke 12:47; John 9:41
5:1 Luke 6:24
5:2 Job 13:28; Matt 6:20
5:3 vv. 7, 8
5:4 Lev 19:13; Deut 24:15; Rom 9:29
5:5 Amos 6:1; Jer 12:3; 25:34
5:7 Deut 11:14; Jer 5:24
5:8 1 Pet 4:7

5:9
James 4:11,
12;
Matt 24:33
5:10
Matt 5:12
5:11
Matt 5:10;
Job 1:21,22;
42:10;
Num 14:18

5:12
Matt 5:34-37

5:13
v. 10;
Ps 50:15;
Col 3:16
5:14
Mark 6:13

5:16
Matt 3:6;
1 Pet 2:24;
John 9:31

5:17
Acts 14:15;
1 Kin 17:1;
Luke 4:25
5:18
1 Kin 18:42,
45

*5:19
Matt 18:15

5:20
Rom 11:14;
1 Pet 4:8

9 Do not complain, brethren, against one another, that you yourselves may not be judged; behold, the Judge is standing right at the door.

10 As an example, brethren, of suffering and patience, take the prophets who spoke in the name of the Lord.

11 Behold, we count those blessed who endured. You have heard of the endurance of Job and have seen the outcome of the Lord's dealings, that the Lord is full of compassion and *is* merciful.

G. *The avoidance of oaths*

12 But above all, my brethren, do not swear, either by heaven or by earth or with any other oath; but let your yes be yes, and your no, no; so that you may not fall under judgment.

H. *Prayer for the sick and confession of sins*

13 Is anyone among you suffering? Let him pray. Is anyone cheerful? Let him sing praises.

14 Is anyone among you sick? Let him call for the elders of the church, and let them pray over him, anointing him with oil in the name of the Lord;

15 and the prayer offered in faith will 4restore the one who is sick, and the Lord will raise him up, and if he has committed sins, they will be forgiven him.

16 Therefore, confess your sins to one another, and pray for one another, so that you may be healed. The effective prayer of a righteous man can accomplish much.

17 Elijah was a man with a nature like ours, and he prayed earnestly that it might not rain; and it did not rain on the earth for three years and six months.

18 And he prayed again, and the sky poured rain, and the earth produced its fruit.

V. *Conclusion (5:19,20)*

19 My brethren, if any among you strays from the truth, and one turns him back,

20 let him know that he who turns a sinner from the error of his way will save his soul from death, and will cover a multitude of sins.

4Or, *save*

5:15 God does, on occasion, heal the sick directly, apart from the skill of medical science. The evidences confirm this fact beyond question. James assures us that this healing may be granted in response to the prayer of faith. This makes it plain that believers may be able to pray the prayer of faith and should seek to do so. But it is not always possible to know whether it is the will of God to heal or not. So the believer must always pray, "If it be Thy will." Believers are admonished to pray for healing, but they also are to seek the will of God (1 John 5:14). (See also Paul's experience of praying earnestly for a healing that was not

granted, 2 Cor. 12:7-19.)
5:19 James is not speaking here of one who has departed from theological truth or Christian belief, but of one who has departed from the practice of the faith in his daily life and conduct. A concern for one's bodily infirmities (v. 14) and prayer for deliverance is no more important than prayer for, and deliverance of, a brother who has a need for spiritual help. To aid in bringing back anyone to the right path is a necessary work for all believers, and in so doing they will *save his soul from death.*

INTRODUCTION TO

THE FIRST LETTER OF

PETER

Authorship and Background: "Peter, an apostle of Jesus Christ" (1:1) was the simple and unpretentious way in which the author introduced himself to his readers; he addressed the elders as "your fellow elder and witness of the sufferings of Christ" (5:1). He wrote from "Babylon" (5:13), which was probably a pseudonym for Rome (as in Rev. 14:8; 18:2,10,21). His scribe was Silvanus (5:12), probably the same as Silas in the book of Acts (chs. 15-18), who was called Silvanus in Paul's epistles (2 Cor. 1:19; 1 Thess. 1:1; 2 Thess. 1:1). With him was Mark, whom he designated "my son" (5:13), probably the John Mark of the book of Acts and Paul's epistles (Acts 12:25; 13:4-13; 15:37-39; Col. 4:10; 2 Tim. 4:11; Philem. 24).

Peter wrote to Christians who lived in the Roman provinces of Pontus, Galatia, Cappadocia, Asia, and Bithynia (1:1), in the northern part of Asia Minor. It may be that he named the provinces in the order that conformed to the route the messenger would follow in taking the letter to the churches.

The letter reflects a time of suffering and trial; the readers have already undergone some persecution and further trials await them (1:6; 3:9,13-17; 4:1,2,12-19; 5:9,10). What was the nature of this "fiery ordeal" (4:12)? There is no record of widespread persecution of Christians by the Roman government before the time of Domitian, toward the end of the first century; and Nero's persecution in the sixties was confined to Rome and did not extend to the provinces. The sufferings referred to in this letter, therefore, were those that frequently arose as Christians lived their faith in a pagan and hostile society. The governing authorities are not blamed; on the contrary, the readers are exhorted to be subject to them, and to honor the emperor himself (2:13).

Since Peter died in A.D. 64 (or 67), this letter was probably written in the early sixties of the first century.

The readers are called "aliens, scattered throughout" (1:1; cf. James 1:1), by which is meant that they, like Israel of old, were dispersed throughout the world. Most of them were probably Gentiles, not Jews, as seen from the references to their former way of life (1:14,18; 2:9,10; 4:3,4).

Characteristics: The writer calls his letter a brief message of exhortation and testimony (5:12). This "epistle of grace and hope," as one modern writer calls it, is notable for its gentle tone of admonition and exhortation, which comes from a pastor who does not lord it over his flock but sets an example to them (5:2,3). He exhorts (cf. 2:11; 5:1,12) them to a life of purity and spirituality, abstaining from malice, envy, slander (2:1), and other carnal passions of heathen living (1:14; 2:11; 4:2,3). They are God's chosen people, a royal priesthood, a holy nation, whose high calling it is to proclaim God's great deeds (2:9). They are to use their Christian freedom to live as befits God's servants (2:16), showing sympathy, love (1:22; 4:8), humility (5:1-6), hospitality (4:9), and finally, they are to be "harmonious, sympathetic, brotherly, kindhearted, and humble in spirit" (3:8). In suffering they are to follow Christ's example (2:20-25; 3:17,18; 4:1,12-19); the "living hope" that is theirs is ground for their indestructible confidence in God (1:3,21). In all their afflictions and sufferings they are to trust in God, "because He cares for you" (5:6,7).

No other New Testament book so reflects the real nature and effect of God's love in Christ as this short epistle.

Contents:

THE FIRST LETTER OF
PETER

I. *Salutation (1:1,2)*

1 Peter, an apostle of Jesus Christ, to those who reside as aliens, scattered throughout Pontus, Galatia, Cappadocia, Asia, and Bithynia, who are chosen
2 according to the foreknowledge of God the Father, by the sanctifying work of the Spirit, that you may obey Jesus Christ and be sprinkled with His blood: May grace and peace be yours in fullest measure.

1:1
2 Pet 2:1;
Acts 2:5,9
*1:2
2 Thess 2:13;
Heb 10:22;
2 Pet 1:2

II. *The blessings of the redeemed (1:3–2:10)*

A. *The risen Christ*

3 Blessed be the God and Father of our Lord Jesus Christ, who according to His great mercy has caused us to be born again to a living hope through the resurrection of Jesus Christ from the dead,
4 to *obtain* an inheritance *which is* imperishable and undefiled and will not fade away, reserved in heaven for you,
5 who are protected by the power of God through faith for a salvation ready to be revealed in the last time.
6 In this you greatly rejoice, even though now for a little while, if necessary, you have been distressed by various trials,
7 that the proof of your faith, *being* more precious than gold which is perishable, even though tested by fire, may be found to result in praise and glory and honor at the revelation of Jesus Christ;
8 and though you have not seen Him, you love Him, and though you do not see Him now, but believe in Him, you greatly rejoice with joy inexpressible and full of glory,
9 obtaining as the outcome of your faith the salvation of [1]your souls.

1:3
2 Cor 1:3;
James 1:18;
1 Cor 15:20
1:4
Col 3:24
1:5
John 10:28
1:6
Rom 5:2;
1 Pet 5:10;
James 1:2
1:7
James 1:3;
Ps 66:10;
Rom 2:7
1:8
1 John 4:20;
John 20:29
1:9
Rom 6:22

B. *The witness of the prophets*

10 As to this salvation, the prophets who prophesied of the grace that *would come* to you made careful search and inquiry,
11 seeking to know what person or time the Spirit of Christ within them was indicating as He predicted the sufferings of Christ and the glories to follow.
12 It was revealed to them that they were not serving themselves, but you, in these things which now have been announced to you through those who preached the gospel to you by the Holy Spirit sent from heaven—things into which angels long to look.

1:10
Matt 13:17;
26:24
1:11
2 Pet 1:21;
Is ch. 53
1:12
Dan 9:24;
Eph 3:10

C. *Exhortation to a holy life*

13 Therefore, gird your minds for action, keep sober *in spirit*, fix your hope completely on the grace to be brought to you at the revelation of Jesus Christ.
14 As obedient children, do not be conformed to the former lusts *which were yours* in your ignorance,

1:13
Eph 6:14;
1 Thess 5:6
1:14
Rom 12:2;
Eph 4:18

[1]Some ancient mss. do not contain *your*

1:2 Foreknowledge may be defined as that attribute of God by which all things are known by Him from the beginning. Thus, God knew from eternity who would be converted. The problem is to relate *foreknowledge* to the doctrine of *election*. (See note on Eph. 1:4 on election and foreknowledge.)

Following the Old Testament pattern, the blood was not only shed but it was also sprinkled and applied to the altar or whatever was to be cleansed. This sprinkling, then, signi-

fied that believers had received the benefit of the sacrifice of their innocent substitute. The sprinkled blood of Christ assures New Testament believers of four benefits: (1) that they are justified (Rom. 5:9); (2) that they have the seal of God's covenant promises to them (of which the Lord's Supper is also a sign—Luke 22:20); (3) that they are cleansed from all sin (1 John 1:7); and (4) that they are admitted into the citizenship of heaven (Heb. 10:19).

15 but like the Holy One who called you, be holy yourselves also in all *your* behavior;

16 because it is written, "YOU SHALL BE HOLY, FOR I AM HOLY."

17 And if you address as Father the One who impartially judges according to each man's work, conduct yourselves in fear during the time of your stay *upon earth*;

18 knowing that you were not redeemed with perishable things like silver or gold from your futile way of life inherited from your forefathers,

19 but with precious blood, as of a lamb unblemished and spotless, *the blood* of Christ.

20 For He was foreknown before the foundation of the world, but has appeared in these last times for the sake of you

21 who through Him are believers in God, who raised Him from the dead and gave Him glory, so that your faith and hope are in God.

22 Since you have in obedience to the truth purified your souls for a sincere love of the brethren, fervently love one another from [2]the heart,

23 for you have been born again not of seed which is perishable but imperishable, *that is*, through the living and abiding word of God.

24 For,

"ALL FLESH IS LIKE GRASS,
AND ALL ITS GLORY LIKE THE FLOWER OF GRASS.
THE GRASS WITHERS,
AND THE FLOWER FALLS OFF,

25 BUT THE WORD OF THE LORD ABIDES FOREVER."
And this is the word which was preached to you.

2 Therefore, putting aside all malice and all guile and hypocrisy and envy and all slander,

2 like newborn babes, long for the pure milk of the word, that by it you may grow in respect to salvation,

3 if you have tasted the kindness of the Lord.

D. *Christ our cornerstone*

4 And coming to Him as to a living stone, rejected by men, but choice and precious in the sight of God,

5 you also, as living stones, are being built up as a spiritual house for a holy priesthood, to offer up spiritual sacrifices acceptable to God through Jesus Christ.

6 For *this* is contained in Scripture:

"BEHOLD I LAY IN ZION A CHOICE STONE, A PRECIOUS CORNER *stone*,
AND HE WHO BELIEVES IN HIM SHALL NOT BE DISAPPOINTED."

7 This precious value, then, is for you who believe. But for those who disbelieve,

"THE STONE WHICH THE BUILDERS REJECTED,
THIS BECAME THE VERY CORNER *stone*,"

8 and,

"A STONE OF STUMBLING AND A ROCK OF OFFENSE";
for they stumble because they are disobedient to the word, and to this *doom* they were also appointed.

9 But you are A CHOSEN RACE, A royal PRIESTHOOD, A HOLY NATION, A PEOPLE

Marginal references:

1:15 2 Cor 7:1
1:16 Lev 11:44
1:17 Deut 10:17; Heb 12:28
*1:18 1 Cor 6:20; Ezek 20:18
1:19 Ex 12:5
1:20 Eph 1:4; Heb 9:26
1:22 James 4:8; Heb 13:1
*1:23 John 3:3; 1:13; Heb 4:12
1:24 Is 40:6-9; James 1:10,11
1:25 John 1:1
2:1 Eph 4:22; James 1:21; 4:11; Rom 10:17 [handwritten: V2-Cf Rom 10:17]
2:2 Mark 10:15; 1 Cor 3:2
2:3 Heb 6:5; Titus 3:4
2:4 v. 7
*2:5 Heb 13:15; Phil 4:18
2:6 Is 28:16; Eph 2:20
2:7 Ps 118:22; Matt 21:42
2:8 Is 8:14; 1 Cor 1:23; Rom 9:22
2:9 Deut 10:15; Acts 26:18

[2]Some mss. read *a clean heart*

1:18 The word here translated *redeemed* (lutroō) signifies "to buy back from bondage." (This verb is rendered *redeem* also in Luke 24:21, and the noun *apolutrōsis* is translated "redemption.") The need for redemption arises from the sinner's bondage to sin and Satan (John 8:34; Rom. 6:17, 23). Redemption itself comes from God and is of free grace. It is made possible by Jesus Christ the Redeemer (1 Cor. 1:30; Gal. 3:13; 4:4,5; Eph. 1:7; Titus 2:14) on the basis of His shed blood. Redemption is both past and future. The price has been paid forever and believers are now redeemed, but they wait in hope for the final fulfillment of that which is already theirs by faith (Rom. 8:23). The redeemed, who once belonged to Satan, now belong to God (1 Cor. 6:20). Their chief end in life is to glorify the One who redeemed them (2:9).
1:23 See note to John 3:3 on the new birth.

2:5 Every believer, being united with Christ Himself by faith, is constituted a priest before the Lord. (See also 2:9; Rev. 1:6.) In the Old Testament era, believers required a priest to mediate between them and God through his services at the altar. There was also a high priest who mediated for them in the Holy of Holies. But Christ has now become the believer's high priest (Heb. 4:14; 5:10; 7:27; 9:11). Immediate access to God is possible through Him without any intermediary. The only priesthood of continuing validity spoken of in the New Testament is this priesthood of all believers, both laity and clergy. Never is the term "priest" (*hiereus*) applied to an apostle or ordained elder in the church, except as he partakes of this universal priesthood. A recovery of this New Testament truth furnished one of the great liberating impulses of the Reformation, from the time of Luther on.

FOR *God's* OWN POSSESSION, that you may proclaim the excellencies of Him who has called you out of darkness into His marvelous light;

10   for you once were NOT A PEOPLE, but now you are THE PEOPLE OF GOD; you had NOT RECEIVED MERCY, but now you have RECEIVED MERCY.

III. *The duties of believers (2:11–4:11)*

A. *The Christian and unbelievers*

11   Beloved, I urge you as aliens and strangers to abstain from fleshly lusts, which wage war against the soul.

12   Keep your behavior excellent among the Gentiles, so that in the thing in which they slander you as evildoers, they may on account of your good deeds, as they observe *them,* glorify God in the day of [3]visitation.

B. *The Christian and the state*

13   Submit yourselves for the Lord's sake to every human institution, whether to a king as the one in authority,

14   or to governors as sent by him for the punishment of evildoers and the praise of those who do right.

15   For such is the will of God that by doing right you may silence the ignorance of foolish men.

16   *Act* as free men, and do not use your freedom as a covering for evil, but *use it* as bondslaves of God.

17   Honor all men; love the brotherhood, fear God, honor the king.

C. *The servant and his master*

18   Servants, be submissive to your masters with all respect, not only to those who are good and gentle, but also to those who are unreasonable.

19   For this *finds* favor, if for the sake of conscience toward God a man bears up under sorrows when suffering unjustly.

20   For what credit is there if, when you sin and are harshly treated, you endure it with patience? But if when you do what is right and suffer *for it* you patiently endure it, this *finds* favor with God.

D. *Christ our great example*

21   For you have been called for this purpose, since Christ also suffered for you, leaving you an example for you to follow in His steps,

22   WHO COMMITTED NO SIN, NOR WAS ANY DECEIT FOUND IN HIS MOUTH;

23   and while being reviled, He did not revile in return; while suffering, He uttered no threats, but kept entrusting *Himself* to Him who judges righteously;

24   and He Himself bore our sins in His body on the cross, that we might die to sin and live to righteousness; for by His wounds you were healed.

25   For you were continually straying like sheep, but now you have returned to the Shepherd and Guardian of your souls.

---

[3]I.e., Christ's coming again in judgment

2:10 Hos 1:9,10
2:11 Rom 12:1; Ps 39:12; Gal 5:16; James 4:1
2:12 Phil 2:15; 1 Pet 3:16; Matt 5:16
2:13 Rom 13:1
2:14 Rom 13:4,3
2:15 1 Pet 3:17; Titus 2:8
2:16 Gal 5:1; 1 Cor 7:22
*****2:17** Rom 12:10; Heb 13:1
2:18 Eph 6:5
2:19 Rom 13:5
2:20 1 Pet 3:17
2:21 Matt 16:24; Acts 14:22
2:22 Is 53:9
2:23 Is 53:7; Heb 12:3; Luke 23:46
*****2:24** Heb 9:28
2:25 Rom 6:2; Is 53:5 Is 53:6; 1 Pet 5:4

2:17 The concept of the brotherhood of man must be understood within the limitations imposed by Scripture. There is a sense in which all men are brothers, in that they are descended from Adam as their common ancestor. But the Scripture nowhere speaks of this brotherhood (for Mal. 2:10 is spoken only to Jews within the covenant bond). It does speak, however, of a brotherhood that springs from the new birth and the adoption of sons. By this new spiritual relationship believers are not only connected with God through Christ, but also with each other as children and heirs of God (Gal. 3:26; 1 John 3:2). Only those who have a Christian faith in the Lord are accounted as children of God in the Biblical sense, and because of this they are brothers to all who trust in the same Lord.

2:24 Christ died as a vicarious sacrifice for sin. Three assumptions govern this doctrine: (1) the sinner lies under the wrath of God and is therefore lost and undone (Rom. 1:18; 3:19; 6:23); (2) by the grace of God, provision was made for Christ to offer Himself as a sin-bearer (Is. 53:6; 2 Cor. 5:21); and (3) God was willing to accept the atonement of Christ so that the sinner himself secures the benefits of forgiveness, peace, and fellowship with God (Rom. 5:1, 6,8,10). In the Old Testament the blood sacrifices had to be repeated because they could not take away sin forever. When offered by faith, however, these sacrifices looked toward the future death of Christ and drew in advance on the merit of His atonement. Since His death there is no need for further sacrifice in a holy communion that claims to repeat the sacrifice of Calvary (Heb. 9:11–15; 10:4).

E. *The husband and the wife*

3:1
Eph 5:22;
1 Cor 7:16

3 In the same way, you wives, be submissive to your own husbands so that even if any *of them* are disobedient to the word, they may be won without a word by the behavior of their wives,

2   as they observe your chaste and respectful behavior.

*3:3
1 Tim 2:9;
Is 3:18-23

3   And let not your adornment be *merely* external—braiding the hair, and wearing gold jewelry, or putting on dresses;

3:4
Rom 7:22

4   but *let it be* the hidden person of the heart, with the imperishable quality of a gentle and quiet spirit, which is precious in the sight of God.

3:5
1 Tim 5:5

5   For in this way in former times the holy women also, who hoped in God, used to adorn themselves, being submissive to their own husbands.

3:6
Gen 18:12

6   Thus Sarah obeyed Abraham, calling him lord, and you have become her children if you do what is right without being frightened by any fear.

3:7
Eph 5:25;
1 Thess 4:4;
Matt 5:23ff

7   You husbands likewise, live with *your wives* in an understanding way, as with a weaker vessel, since she is a woman; and grant her honor as a fellow heir of the grace of life, so that your prayers may not be hindered.

F. *Christian conduct in review*

3:8
Phil 2:3;
1 Pet 5:5

8   To sum up, let all be harmonious, sympathetic, brotherly, kindhearted, and humble in spirit;

3:9
Rom 12:17;
Heb 6:14

9   not returning evil for evil, or insult for insult, but giving a blessing instead; for you were called for the very purpose that you might inherit a blessing.

3:10
Ps 34:12-16;
James 1:26;
1 Pet 2:1,22

10   For,

"LET HIM WHO MEANS TO LOVE LIFE AND SEE GOOD DAYS
    REFRAIN HIS TONGUE FROM EVIL AND HIS LIPS FROM SPEAKING GUILE.

11   "AND LET HIM TURN AWAY FROM EVIL AND DO GOOD;
    LET HIM SEEK PEACE AND PURSUE IT.

12   "FOR THE EYES OF THE LORD ARE UPON THE RIGHTEOUS,
    AND HIS EARS ATTEND TO THEIR PRAYER,
    BUT THE FACE OF THE LORD IS AGAINST THOSE WHO DO EVIL."

G. *The Christian and persecution*

3:13
Prov 16:7

13   And who is there to harm you if you prove zealous for what is good?

3:14
1 Pet 2:19ff;
Is 8:12,13

14   But even if you should suffer for the sake of righteousness, *you are* blessed. AND DO NOT FEAR THEIR INTIMIDATION, AND DO NOT BE TROUBLED,

3:15
Col 4:6;
1 Pet 1:3;
1:17

15   but [4]sanctify Christ as Lord in your hearts, always *being* ready to make a defense to everyone who asks you to give an account for the hope that is in you, yet with gentleness and reverence;

3:16
Heb 13:18;
1 Pet 2:12,15

16   and keep a good conscience so that in the thing in which you are slandered, those who revile your good behavior in Christ may be put to shame.

3:17
1 Pet 2:20,15

17   For it is better, if God should will it so, that you suffer for doing what is right rather than for doing what is wrong.

3:18
1 Pet 2:21;
2 Cor 13:4;
Eph 3:12;
1 Pet 4:1,6
*3:19
1 Pet 4:6

18   For Christ also died for sins once for all, *the* just for *the* unjust, in order that He might bring us to God, having been put to death in the flesh, but made alive in the spirit;

19   in which also He went and made proclamation to the spirits *now* in prison,

3:20
Gen 6:3,5;
Heb 11:7;
Gen 8:18
*3:21
Titus 3:5;

20   who once were disobedient, when the patience of God kept waiting in the days of Noah, during the construction of the ark, in which a few, that is, eight persons, were brought safely through *the* water.

21   And corresponding to that, baptism now saves you—not the removal of dirt

[4]I.e., set apart

3:3 Scripture does not prohibit the wearing of adornments and jewelry as such, for that interpretation of this verse would also require a prohibition of wearing *outer clothing* of any sort, since this is the true meaning of the word here translated *dresses*. What is meant here is that the true adornment of the Christian, whether a man or a woman, consists in the spiritual qualities of a gentle and peaceable character. It may be fairly inferred also that a certain modesty and circumspection in dress should characterize Christian women. But what is chiefly emphasized is the inward attitude of the heart and a modesty in external appearance and manner. Doubtless we may assume that anyone who has *crucified the flesh with its passions and desires* (Gal. 5:24) will

avoid any mode of dress that is designed to draw undue attention to one's own person. (See also 1 Tim. 2:9.)
3:19 This verse has been much disputed. Some have interpreted it to mean that Christ, between His crucifixion and resurrection, preached to the lost in Hades (see note to Luke 10:15) so that they might have a second chance. This explanation, however, runs counter to other Scriptures that are quite explicit in precluding the possibility of a second chance (e.g., Luke 16:26; Heb. 9:27). Others interpret this verse by referring to v. 20 and take it to mean that Christ was in Noah by the Holy Spirit when He preached to the doomed race of antediluvians.
3:21 See note to Matt. 28:19a on baptism.

from the flesh, but an appeal to God for a good conscience—through the resurrection of Jesus Christ,

22   who is at the right hand of God, having gone into heaven, after angels and authorities and powers had been subjected to Him.

H. *Exhortation to duty*

4 Therefore, since Christ has [5]suffered in the flesh, arm yourselves also with the same purpose, because he who has suffered in the flesh has ceased from sin,
2   so as to live the rest of the time in the flesh no longer for the lusts of men, but for the will of God.
3   For the time already past is sufficient *for you* to have carried out the desire of the Gentiles, having pursued a course of sensuality, lusts, drunkenness, carousals, drinking parties and abominable idolatries.
4   And in *all* this, they are surprised that you do not run with *them* into the same excess of dissipation, and they malign *you*;
5   but they shall give account to Him who is ready to judge the living and the dead.
6   For the gospel has for this purpose been preached even to those who are dead, that though they are judged in the flesh as men, they may live in the spirit according to *the will of* God.
7   The end of all things is at hand; therefore, be of sound judgment and sober *spirit* for the purpose of prayer.
8   Above all, keep fervent in your love for one another, because love covers a multitude of sins.
9   Be hospitable to one another without complaint.
10   As each one has received a *special* gift, employ it in serving one another, as good stewards of the manifold grace of God.
11   Whoever speaks, *let him speak*, as it were, the utterances of God; whoever serves, *let him do so* as by the strength which God supplies; so that in all things God may be glorified through Jesus Christ, to whom belongs the glory and dominion forever and ever. Amen.

IV. *Constancy in trial (4:12–5:11)*

A. *Exhortation to steadfastness*

12   Beloved, do not be surprised at the fiery ordeal among you, which comes upon you for your testing, as though some strange thing were happening to you;
13   but to the degree that you share the sufferings of Christ, keep on rejoicing; so that also at the revelation of His glory, you may rejoice with exultation.
14   If you are reviled for the name of Christ, you are blessed, because the Spirit of glory and of God rests upon you.
15   By no means let any of you suffer as a murderer, or thief, or evildoer, or a troublesome meddler;
16   but if *anyone suffers* as a Christian, let him not feel ashamed, but in that name let him glorify God.
17   For *it is* time for judgment to begin with the household of God; and if *it begins* with us first, what *will be* the outcome for those who do not obey the gospel of God?
18   AND IF IT IS WITH DIFFICULTY THAT THE RIGHTEOUS IS SAVED, WHAT WILL BECOME OF THE GODLESS MAN AND THE SINNER?
19   Therefore, let those also who suffer according to the will of God entrust their souls to a faithful Creator in doing what is right.

B. *Exhortation to faithfulness*

5 Therefore, I exhort the elders among you, as *your* fellow elder and witness of the sufferings of Christ, and a partaker also of the glory that is to be revealed,
2   shepherd the flock of God among you, exercising oversight not under compulsion, but voluntarily, according to *the will of* God; and not for sordid gain, but with eagerness;

[5]I.e., suffered death

5:1   See note to Titus 1:5 for information on the office of elder.

Marginal references

Heb 9:14;
1 Pet 1:3

3:22
Rom 8:34,38

4:1
1 Pet 3:18;
Gal 5:24
4:2
Gal 2:20;
Rom 6:11
4:3
Eph 4:17

4:4
1 Pet 3:16

4:5
Acts 10:42;
2 Tim 4:1
4:6
1 Pet 3:19

4:7
Rom 13:11;
1 Pet 1:13
4:8
Heb 13:1;
1 Cor 13:7
4:9
Heb 13:2;
2 Cor 9:7
4:10
Rom 12:6,7;
1 Cor 4:1
4:11
Eph 6:10;
5:20;
1 Tim 6:16

4:12
1 Pet 1:6,7

4:13
Phil 3:10;
Rom 8:17
4:14
Matt 5:11

4:15
1 Thess 4:11

4:16
Acts 5:41

4:17
Jer 25:29;
Mal 3:5

4:18
Prov 11:31;
Luke 23:31
4:19
2 Tim 1:12

*5:1
Luke 24:48;
1 Pet 1:5,7;
Rev 1:9
5:2
John 21:16;
1 Cor 9:17;
1 Tim 3:3,8;
Titus 1:7

5:3
Ezek 34:4;
Phil 3:17
*5:4
Heb 13:20;
2 Tim 4:8
5:5
James 4:6;
Is 57:15

5:6
James 4:10

5:7
Ps 37:5;
Matt 6:25;
Heb 13:5
5:8
Luke 21:34;
Job 1:7
5:9
James 4:7;
Col 2:5;
Acts 14:22
5:10
Heb 13:21;
2 Thess 2:17

5:12
2 Cor 1:19;
Heb 13:22

5:13
Acts 12:12

5:14
Rom 16:16;
Eph 6:23

3 nor yet as lording it over those allotted to your charge, but proving to be examples to the flock.

4 And when the Chief Shepherd appears, you will receive the unfading crown of glory.

5 You younger men, likewise, be subject to your elders; and all of you, clothe yourselves with humility toward one another, for GOD IS OPPOSED TO THE PROUD, BUT GIVES GRACE TO THE HUMBLE.

6 Humble yourselves, therefore, under the mighty hand of God, that He may exalt you at the proper time,

7 casting all your anxiety upon Him, because He cares for you.

8 Be of sober *spirit*, be on the alert. Your adversary, the devil, prowls about like a roaring lion, seeking someone to devour.

9 But resist him, firm in *your* faith, knowing that the same experiences of suffering are being accomplished by your brethren who are in the world.

10 And after you have suffered for a little while, the God of all grace, who called you to His eternal glory in Christ, will Himself perfect, confirm, strengthen *and* establish you.

11 To Him *be* dominion forever and ever. Amen.

V. *Conclusion and benediction (5:12–14)*

12 Through Silvanus, our faithful brother (for so I regard *him*), I have written to you briefly, exhorting and testifying that this is the true grace of God. Stand firm in it!

13 [6]She who is in Babylon, chosen together with you, sends you greetings, and *so does* my son, Mark.

14 Greet one another with a kiss of love.

Peace be to you all who are in Christ.

[6]Some mss. read *The church which*

5:4 See note to John 10:11 on Christ, the good shepherd.

INTRODUCTION TO
THE SECOND LETTER OF
PETER

Authorship and Background: The author identifies himself as Simon Peter, "bond-servant and apostle of Jesus Christ" (1:1). He speaks of his imminent death, in conformance with Christ's statement (1:13-15), which is probably a reference to John 21:18,19. He also refers to the transfiguration of Christ "on the holy mountain" (1:16-18). He speaks of a previous letter (3:1), and of the letters of Paul (3:15,16).

The earliest references to this letter, in the writings of Origen, Eusebius, and Jerome, show that there were some who doubted the apostolic authorship of the letter, while others accepted it as apostolic. Eusebius, for example, did not say that the letter was spurious, but at the same time he was not prepared to grant it equal footing with other books of the canon about which he had no question. Nor did Origen say that it was spurious, only that its authenticity was disputed. In the present time, many scholars believe that the letter is pseudonymous, written in the name of the apostle by an unknown Christian leader toward the middle of the second century. They base their position mainly on the difference in style and quality of the Greek from 1 Peter, the description of the heresy being combatted, the reference to Paul's letters as Scriptures, and the time element implied in 3:4. Those who accept the apostolic authorship point to a similarity in the two letters in the use of certain words and phrases, the emphatic autobiographical references, and similarity in teaching. The date of the letter depends, of course, on one's opinion of the authorship. Assuming Petrine authorship, as conservatives have always done, it was written shortly after 1 Peter.

The readers are not identified, but are addressed in general terms (1:1,2). If the previous letter referred to in 3:1 is 1 Peter, then the readers are the same as those addressed in 1 Peter 1:1,2.

Characteristics: The letter is a "reminder" (1:12; 3:1) of the truth of the gospel, against the pernicious attacks of false teachers who were bringing in destructive heresies. Like Israel's false prophets, these false teachers were corrupt and immoral (2:2,3,10), indulging in revelries and carousals (2:13,14), licentious, and defiled by the world and its passions (2:17-22). In their teaching they were scoffing at the belief in the Lord's return (3:3-10). The author, however, reminds his readers that the Lord will keep his promise (3:10-13); therefore, they are warned to keep themselves spotless and blameless (3:14), and to grow in the grace and knowledge of our Lord and Savior Jesus Christ (3:18). God will punish the wicked (2:1,3,9,10,12,17), even as He did the rebellious angels (2:4), the world of Noah's day (2:5), and Sodom and Gomorrah (2:6). He delays His punishment in order that men may repent; but the day will come when He will destroy the whole universe, and then there will be the new heavens and a new earth, in which righteousness dwells (3:8-13).

Contents:

I. Salutation (1:1,2)

II. True knowledge (1:3-21): True knowledge is to know God, by which believers receive divine power that enables them to forsake sin and confirm their call and election. The Christian faith is not based on man-made myths, but on the personal witness of those who saw the glory and majesty of Christ.

III. False teachers (2:1-22): By their immoral lives and false teaching they deny the Master who redeemed them; indulging in lust and defiling passions, they promise freedom, but are themselves slaves. Their punishment is sure.

IV. **The second advent of Christ (3:1-18):** The delay in the coming of the day of the Lord is because of God's forbearance, who wishes all men to repent. The day will come, with punishment for the ungodly and the destruction of the physical universe; but He has promised a new heaven and a new earth. Live in the light of this truth!

THE SECOND LETTER OF
PETER

I. *Salutation (1:1,2)*

1 [1]Simon Peter, a bond-servant and apostle of Jesus Christ, to those who have received a faith of the same kind as ours, by the righteousness of our God and Savior, Jesus Christ:

2 Grace and peace be multiplied to you in the knowledge of God and of Jesus our Lord;

II. *True knowledge (1:3–21)*

A. *The growth of true knowledge*

3 seeing that His divine power has granted to us everything pertaining to life and godliness, through the true knowledge of Him who called us by His own glory and excellence.

4 For by these He has granted to us His precious and magnificent promises, in order that by them you might become partakers of *the* divine nature, having escaped the corruption that is in the world by lust.

5 Now for this very reason also, applying all diligence, in your faith supply moral excellence, and in *your* moral excellence, knowledge;

6 and in *your* knowledge, self-control, and in *your* self-control, perseverance, and in *your* perseverance, godliness;

7 and in *your* godliness, brotherly kindness, and in *your* brotherly kindness, love.

8 For if these *qualities* are yours and are increasing, they render you neither useless nor unfruitful in the true knowledge of our Lord Jesus Christ.

9 For he who lacks these *qualities* is blind *or* short-sighted, having forgotten *his* purification from his former sins.

10 Therefore, brethren, be all the more diligent to make certain about His calling and choosing you; for as long as you practice these things, you will never stumble;

11 for in this way the entrance into the eternal kingdom of our Lord and Savior Jesus Christ will be abundantly supplied to you.

B. *The ground of true knowledge*

12 Therefore, I shall always be ready to remind you of these things, even though you *already* know *them*, and have been established in the truth which is present with *you*.

13 And I consider it right, as long as I am in this *earthly* dwelling, to stir you up by way of reminder,

14 knowing that the laying aside of my *earthly* dwelling is imminent, as also our Lord Jesus Christ has made clear to me.

15 And I will also be diligent that at any time after my departure you may be able to call these things to mind.

16 For we did not follow cleverly devised tales when we made known to you the power and coming of our Lord Jesus Christ, but we were eyewitnesses of His majesty.

17 For when He received honor and glory from God the Father, such an utterance as this was made to Him by the Majestic Glory, "This is My beloved Son with whom I am well-pleased"—

18 and we ourselves heard this utterance made from heaven when we were with Him on the holy mountain.

19 And *so* we have the prophetic word *made* more sure, to which you do well to

[1]Most early mss. read *Simeon*

1:1
Rom 1:1;
1 Pet 1:1;
Rom 1:12;
3:21-26;
Titus 2:13
1:2
1 Pet 1:2;
vv. 3,8

1:3
1 Pet 1:5;
1 Thess 2:12

1:4
2 Cor 7:1;
Eph 4:24;
1 John 3:2;
2 Pet 2:18-20
1:5
2 Pet 3:18;
Col 2:3
1:6
Acts 24:26;
Luke 21:19;
v. 3
1:7
1 Thess 3:12
1:8
John 15:2;
Titus 3:14
1:9
1 John 2:11;
Eph 5:26;
1 John 1:7

1:12
1 John 2:21

1:13
2 Cor 5:1

1:14
2 Tim 4:6;
John 21:18,19

1:16
1 Tim 1:4;
Matt 17:1;
Mark 9:2
1:17
Matt 3:17;
Luke 9:35

1:18
Matt 17:6
1:19
1 Pet 1:10,11;
Ps 119:105;
Rev 22:16

pay attention as to a lamp shining in a dark place, until the day dawns and the morning star arises in your hearts.

20 But know this first of all, that no prophecy of Scripture is *a matter* of one's own interpretation,

21 for no prophecy was ever made by an act of human will, but men moved by the Holy Spirit spoke from God.

III. *False teachers (2:1–22)*

A. *The inroads of error*

2 But false prophets also arose among the people, just as there will also be false teachers among you, who will secretly introduce destructive heresies, even denying the Master who bought them, bringing swift destruction upon themselves.

2 And many will follow their sensuality, and because of them the way of the truth will be maligned;

3 and in *their* greed they will exploit you with false words; their judgment from long ago is not idle, and their destruction is not asleep.

B. *Punishment of error*

4 For if God did not spare angels when they sinned, but cast them into hell and committed them to pits of darkness, reserved for judgment;

5 and did not spare the ancient world, but preserved Noah, a preacher of righteousness, with seven others, when He brought a flood upon the world of the ungodly;

6 and if He condemned the cities of Sodom and Gomorrah to destruction by reducing *them* to ashes, having made them an example to those who would live ungodly thereafter;

7 and if He rescued righteous Lot, oppressed by the sensual conduct of unprincipled men

8 (for by what he saw and heard *that* righteous man, while living among them, felt *his* righteous soul tormented day after day with *their* lawless deeds),

9 *then* the Lord knows how to rescue the godly from temptation, and to keep the unrighteous under punishment for the day of judgment,

C. *Character and conduct of deceivers*

10 and especially those who indulge the flesh in *its* corrupt desires and despise authority. Daring, self-willed, they do not tremble when they revile angelic majesties,

11 whereas angels who are greater in might and power do not bring a reviling judgment against them before the Lord.

12 But these, like unreasoning animals, born as creatures of instinct to be captured and killed, reviling where they have no knowledge, will in the destruction of those creatures also be destroyed,

13 suffering wrong as the wages of doing wrong. They count it a pleasure to revel in the daytime. They are stains and blemishes, reveling in their [2]deceptions, as they carouse with you,

14 having eyes full of adultery and that never cease from sin, enticing unstable souls, having a heart trained in greed, accursed children;

15 forsaking the right way they have gone astray, having followed the way of Balaam, the *son* of Beor, who loved the wages of unrighteousness,

16 but he received a rebuke for his own transgression; *for* a dumb donkey, speaking with a voice of a man, restrained the madness of the prophet.

D. *Evil consequences of their deception*

17 These are springs without water, and mists driven by a storm, for whom the black darkness has been reserved.

[2]Some ancient mss. read *love feasts*, (cf. Jude 12)

1:20,21 See note to 2 Tim. 3:16 on inspiration. Also read v. 19.
2:1 See note to 2 Tim. 2:18 on false doctrine and false teachers.
2:15 The way of Balaam is the way of compromise. Balaam

used his prophetic gift for personal gain. He sought to serve God and self-interest at the same time. False teachers like him will inevitably meet with divine condemnation. (See also notes to Num. 22:19; Jude 11; Rev. 2:14.)

Cross references (left margin):

*1:20f
Rom 12:6

1:21
2 Tim 3:16;
1 Pet 1:11;
Acts 1:16

*2:1
1 Tim 4:1;
Jude 18;
1 Cor 6:20

2:3
1 Tim 6:5;
2 Cor 2:17;
Deut 32:35

2:4
Jude 6;
John 8:44;
Rev 20:1,2
2:5
Gen 7:1;
Heb 11:7;
1 Pet 3:20
2:6
Gen 19:24;
Jude 7;
Num 26:10
2:7
Gen 19:16;
2 Pet 3:17

2:9
1 Cor 10:13;
Jude 6

2:10
2 Pet 3:3;
Jude 8;
Titus 1:7

2:11
Jude 9

2:12
Jude 10

2:13
Rom 13:13;
Jude 12;
1 Cor 11:20,
21
2:14
v. 18;
Jude 11; v. 3;
Eph 2:3
*2:15
Num 22:5,7;
Jude 11
2:16
Num 22:21,
23,28,30,31

2:17
Jude 12,13

18   For speaking out arrogant *words* of vanity they entice by fleshly desires, by sensuality, those who barely escape from the ones who live in error,

19   promising them freedom while they themselves are slaves of corruption; for by what a man is overcome, by this he is enslaved.

20   For if after they have escaped the defilements of the world by the knowledge of the Lord and Savior Jesus Christ, they are again entangled in them and are overcome, the last state has become worse for them than the first.

21   For it would be better for them not to have known the way of righteousness, than having known it, to turn away from the holy commandment delivered to them.

22   It has happened to them according to the true proverb, "A DOG RETURNS TO ITS OWN VOMIT," and, "A sow, after washing, *returns* to wallowing in the mire."

IV. *The second advent of Christ (3:1–18)*

A. *The promise of His coming*

3 This is now, beloved, the second letter I am writing to you in which I am stirring up your sincere mind by way of reminder,

2   that you should remember the words spoken beforehand by the holy prophets and the commandment of the Lord and Savior *spoken* by your apostles.

3   Know this first of all, that in the last days mockers will come with *their* mocking, following after their own lusts,

4   and saying, "Where is the promise of His coming? For *ever* since the fathers fell asleep, all continues just as it was from the beginning of creation."

5   For when they maintain this, it escapes their notice that by the word of God *the* heavens existed long ago and *the* earth was formed out of water and by water,

6   through which the world at that time was destroyed, being flooded with water.

7   But the present heavens and earth by His word are being reserved for fire, kept for the day of judgment and destruction of ungodly men.

B. *The time and circumstances*

8   But do not let this one *fact* escape your notice, beloved, that with the Lord one day is as a thousand years, and a thousand years as one day.

9   The Lord is not slow about His promise, as some count slowness, but is patient toward you, not wishing for any to perish but for all to come to repentance.

10   But the day of the Lord will come like a thief, in which the heavens will pass away with a roar and the elements will be destroyed with intense heat, and the earth and its works will be ³burned up.

11   Since all these things are to be destroyed in this way, what sort of people ought you to be in holy conduct and godliness,

12   looking for and hastening the coming of the day of God, on account of which the heavens will be destroyed by burning, and the elements will melt with intense heat!

13   But according to His promise we are looking for new heavens and a new earth, in which righteousness dwells.

C. *The concluding exhortation*

14   Therefore, beloved, since you look for these things, be diligent to be found by Him in peace, spotless and blameless,

15   and regard the patience of our Lord *to be* salvation; just as also our beloved brother Paul, according to the wisdom given him, wrote to you,

16   as also in all *his* letters, speaking in them of these things, in which are some

³Some ancient mss. read *discovered*

Marginal references

2:18
Jude 16

*2:19f
John 8:34;
Rom 6:16
2:20
Matt 12:45;
Luke 11:26;
2 Pet 1:2

2:21
Heb 6:4ff;
2 Pet 3:2;
Jude 3
2:22
Prov 26:11

3:3
1 Tim 4:1;
Jude 18;
2 Pet 2:10
3:4
Is 5:9;
Jer 17:15;
Ezek 18;
Matt 24:48;
Acts 7:60;
Matt 10:6
3:5
Gen 1:6,9;
Heb 11:3;
Ps 24:2;
Col 1:17
3:6
Gen 7:21,22
3:7
v. 10; 2 Thess
1:7;
1 Cor 3:13
3:8
Ps 90:4
3:9
Heb 10:37;
Is 30:18;
1 Pet 3:20;
Rom 2:4
*3:10
Matt 24:43;
1 Thess 5:2;
Matt 24:35;
Rev 21:1
3:12
1 Cor 1:7;
Titus 2:13;
Ps 50:3;
Is 34:4; v. 10
3:13
Is 65:17;
66:22;
Rev 21:1
3:14
2 Pet 1:10;
1 Cor 15:58;
Phil 2:15
3:15
v. 9;
1 Cor 3:10;
Eph 3:3
3:16
v. 14;

Notes

2:19,20 See note to Heb. 6:4–6.
3:10 *the day of the Lord*. This phrase appears also in Acts 2:20; 1 Cor. 5:5; 1 Thess. 5:2,4; 2 Thess. 2:2. Here, as is usual in the New Testament, the reference is to the second advent of Christ. Concerning that advent, three deductions may be drawn from this Scripture and others related to it: (1) Christ's coming is certain: He will arrive in God's own time, not at a time predictable by man (Mark 13:32; John 14:3); (2) His coming will be sudden, i.e., unexpected and without warning (1 Thess. 5:1–3); and (3) it will be a day of solemn judgment (Acts 17:31). Here in 3:10 it is interesting to note that *the day of the Lord* is spoken of in relation to the dissolution of the material universe. It is this usage that, when coordinated with other eschatological passages in the New Testament, has led some to conclude that *the day of the Lord* is a period of time with at least a thousand years between its beginning and its ending.

Heb 5:11;
2 Pet 2:14;
v. 2
3:17
1 Cor 10:12;
2 Pet 2:18;
Rev 2:5

things hard to understand, which the untaught and unstable distort, as *they do* also the rest of the Scriptures, to their own destruction.

17   You therefore, beloved, knowing this beforehand, be on your guard lest, being carried away by the error of unprincipled men, you fall from your own steadfastness,

18   but grow in the grace and knowledge of our Lord and Savior Jesus Christ. To Him *be* the glory, both now and to the day of eternity. Amen.

INTRODUCTION TO
THE FIRST LETTER OF
JOHN

Authorship and Background: This general letter does not bear the author's name, nor does it identify its readers. From earliest times it was attributed to the apostle John, and no other author has been suggested. The author writes as an eyewitness of the person and ministry of Jesus (1:1-3), in words strongly reminiscent of the Gospel of John (1:14; 19:35; 21:24). The tone of the letter, and especially his references to his readers as "little children" (2:1,12,28; 3:7,18; 4:4; 5:21), imply that he is an old man.

Perhaps the author knew some of his readers, but the absence of personal references makes it likely that this was a general letter, addressed to Christians at large. Besides "children," the writer also calls them "brethren" (3:13) and "beloved" (2:7; 3:2,21; 4:1,7,11). His tone is warm and intimate, as he writes to them with obvious love and concern. Calmly and deliberately he recalls the fundamentals of the Christian faith, and assures them of the reality of their salvation, "that you may know that you have eternal life" (5:13).

He also wrote to warn his readers against a dangerous philosophy that would rob the Christian faith of its distinctive message concerning Jesus Christ. Based on the Greek moral distinction between matter and spirit, Gnostic philosophy regarded matter as inherently evil; for this reason one could not speak of a true incarnation of the Word of God, but only of an apparent one. The Son of God did not really become flesh but only seemed to do so—therefore the name "Docetism" (from Greek *dokeō*, "to seem"). Others affirmed that the divine Christ had come upon the human Jesus at baptism and left Him at the cross, since it was impossible that the divine Son of God should suffer and die.

On both counts, therefore, the Christian faith that the man Jesus was also the Christ, the Son of God, was effectively denied. The writer denounced these "antichrists" who denied the Son and, consequently, the Father as well (2:18-23); they were false prophets, for they did not confess that Jesus had come in the flesh (4:1-3). Jesus Christ is He who came with the water and the blood (5:6-8). Both the real humanity and the real deity of Jesus Christ are emphasized (2:22; 4:2,15; 5:1,5).

The letter is usually dated around A.D. 90, written perhaps from Ephesus.

Characteristics: The book dwells on the great themes of the Christian faith and message in a way that recalls the Gospel of John. The writer contrasts light and darkness (1:6,7; 2:8-11); love of the world versus love of God (2:15-17); the children of God and the children of the devil (3:4-10); love and hatred (3:11-18; 4:7-12,16-21); and the Spirit of God and the spirit of antichrist (4:1-3). He speaks of the forgiveness of sins (1:8-2:2; 2:12), of fellowship (1:3,4), eternal life (2:25; 5:11-13,20), and the Holy Spirit (2:27; 4:12,13). Against the destructive Gnostic teaching that what is done in the flesh cannot affect the spirit, the author stresses the need for obedience and purity of life (1:10; 2:15-17; 3:4-10; 5:18). The sum and substance may be thus summarized: we should "believe in the name of His Son Jesus Christ, and love one another, just as He commanded us" (3:23).

Contents:

III. Assurance and abiding in love (3:1-4:21): We are God's children; the power of sin is broken; love, the royal rule of life, is from God, who manifested His love for us by sending His Son as the expiation for our sins. "We love, because He first loved us" (4:19).

IV. Faith and certainty (5:1-12): To love God and keep His commandments is the whole duty of man. Faith that Jesus is the Son of God brings victory; in Him alone is true life.

V. Conclusion (5:13-21): We know: that God hears us when we ask according to His will; that the Son of God keeps God's children from the power of sin and evil; that we are of God; that the Son of God has come and brought us knowledge of the true God. Worship Him and abjure all idols!

Authorship and Background: This general letter does not bear the author's name; nor does it identify its readers. From earliest times it was attributed to the apostle John, and no other author has been suggested. The author writes as an eyewitness of the person and ministry of Jesus (1:1-3), is wholly reminiscent of the Gospel of John (1:14; 18:35; 21:24). The tone of the letter, and especially his reference to his readers as "little children" (2:1,12,28; 3:7,18; 4:4; 5:21), imply that he is an old man.

Perhaps the author knew some of his readers, but the absence of personal references makes it likely that this was a general letter, addressed to Christians at large. Besides "children," the writer also calls them "brethren" (3:13) and "beloved" (2:7; 3:2,21; 4:1,7,11). His tone is warm and intimate, as he writes to them with obvious love and concern. Calmly and deliberately he recalls the fundamentals of the Christian faith, and assures them of the reality of their salvation, "that you may know that you have eternal life" (5:13).

He also wrote to warn his readers against a dangerous philosophy that would rob the Christian faith of its distinctive message concerning Jesus Christ. Based on the Greek moral disjunction between matter and spirit, Gnostic philosophy regarded matter as inherently evil; for this reason one could not speak of a true incarnation of the Word of God, but only of an appearance. The Son of God did not really become flesh, but only seemed to do so—therefore the name "Docetism" (from Greek dokeo, "to seem"). Others affirmed that the divine Christ had come upon the human Jesus at baptism and left Him at the cross, since it was impossible that the divine Son of God should suffer and die.

On both counts, therefore, the Christian faith that the man Jesus was also the Christ, the Son of God, was effectively denied. The writer denounced these "antichrists" who denied the Son and, consequently, the Father as well (2:18-23); they were false prophets, for they did not confess that Jesus had come in the flesh (4:1-3). Jesus Christ is He who came with the water and the blood (5:6-8). Both the real humanity and the real deity of Jesus Christ are emphasized (2:22; 4:2,15).

The letter is usually dated around A.D. 90, written perhaps from Ephesus.

Characteristics: The book dwells on the great themes of the Christian faith and message in a way that recalls the Gospel of John. The writer contrasts light and darkness (1:5ff.; 2:8-11); love of the world versus love of God (2:15-17); the children of God and the children of the devil (3:4-10); love and hatred (3:11-18; 4:7-12,16-21), and the Spirit of God and the spirit of antichrist (4:1-6). He speaks of the forgiveness of sins (1:8-2:2; 2:12), of fellowship (1:3,7), eternal life (2:25; 5:11-13,20), and the Holy Spirit (2:27; 4:13). Against the derivative Gnostic teaching that what is done in the flesh cannot affect the spirit, the author stresses the need for obedience and purity of life (1:10; 2:15-17; 3:4-10; 5:18). The sum and substance may be thus summarized: we should "believe in the name of His Son Jesus Christ, and love one another, just as He commanded us" (3:23).

Contents:

I. Introduction (1:1-4): The apostolic witness and authority asserted. The purpose of this letter.

II. Assurance and walking in the light (1:5-2:29): Light and darkness; sin and forgiveness; confession and profession; love for the world and love of God; the false teachings of antichrists and the truth of the Spirit.

THE FIRST LETTER OF
JOHN

I. Introduction (1:1–4)

1 What was from the beginning, what we have heard, what we have seen with our eyes, what we beheld and our hands handled, concerning the Word of Life—
2 and the life was manifested, and we have seen and bear witness and proclaim to you the eternal life, which was with the Father and was manifested to us—
3 what we have seen and heard we proclaim to you also, that you also may have fellowship with us; and indeed our fellowship is with the Father, and with His Son Jesus Christ.
4 And these things we write, so that our joy may be made complete.

II. Assurance and walking in the light (1:5–2:29)

A. The test of righteousness

5 And this is the message we have heard from Him and announce to you, that God is light, and in Him there is no darkness at all.
6 If we say that we have fellowship with Him and *yet* walk in the darkness, we lie and do not practice the truth;
7 but if we walk in the light as He Himself is in the light, we have fellowship with one another, and the blood of Jesus His Son cleanses us from all sin.
8 If we say that we have no sin, we are deceiving ourselves, and the truth is not in us.
9 If we confess our sins, He is faithful and righteous to forgive us our sins and to cleanse us from all unrighteousness.
10 If we say that we have not sinned, we make Him a liar, and His word is not in us.

2 My little children, I am writing these things to you that you may not sin. And if anyone sins, we have an [1]Advocate with the Father, Jesus Christ the righteous;
2 and He Himself is the propitiation for our sins; and not for ours only, but also for *those of* the whole world.
3 And by this we know that we have come to know Him, if we keep His commandments.
4 The one who says, "I have come to know Him," and does not keep His commandments, is a liar, and the truth is not in him;
5 but whoever keeps His word, in him the love of God has truly been perfected. By this we know that we are in Him:
6 the one who says he abides in Him ought himself to walk in the same manner as He walked.

B. The test of love

7 Beloved, I am not writing a new commandment to you, but an old commandment which you have had from the beginning; the old commandment is the word which you have heard.
8 On the other hand, I am writing a new commandment to you, which is true

1Gr., *Paracletos*, one called alongside to help

1:1
John 1:1,14;
2 Pet 1:16;
John 20:27
1:2
John 1:1-4;
Rom 16:26;
John 21:24
1:3
Acts 4:20;
1 Cor 1:9
1:4
1 John 2:1;
John 3:29

1:5
1 John 3:11
1:6
2 Cor 6:14;
John 8:55;
3:21
1:7
Heb 9:14;
1 Pet 1:19;
Rev 1:5
1:8
Job 15:14;
Prov 20:9;
James 3:2;
1 John 2:4
*1:9
Ps 51:2
1:10
1 John 5:10;
2:14
*2:1
Rom 8:34;
Heb 7:25
2:2
Rom 3:25;
John 1:29

2:5
John 14:23;
1 John 4:12,
13
2:6
John 15:4;
1 Pet 2:21

2:7
1 John 3:2;
2 John 5;
1 John 3:11
2:8
Eph 5:8;
1 Thess 5:5;
John 1:9

in Him and in you, because the darkness is passing away, and the true light is already shining.

9   The one who says he is in the light and *yet* hates his brother is in the darkness until now.

10   The one who loves his brother abides in the light and there is no cause for stumbling in him.

11   But the one who hates his brother is in the darkness and walks in the darkness, and does not know where he is going because the darkness has blinded his eyes.

12   I am writing to you, little children, because your sins are forgiven you for His name's sake.

13   I am writing to you, fathers, because you know Him who has been from the beginning. I am writing to you, young men, because you have overcome the evil one. I have written to you, children, because you know the Father.

14   I have written to you, fathers, because you know Him who has been from the beginning. I have written to you, young men, because you are strong, and the word of God abides in you, and you have overcome the evil one.

15   Do not love the world, nor the things in the world. If anyone loves the world, the love of the Father is not in him.

16   For all that is in the world, the lust of the flesh and the lust of the eyes and the boastful pride of life, is not from the Father, but is from the world.

17   And the world is passing away, and *also* its lusts; but the one who does the will of God abides forever.

C. *The test of true belief*

18   Children, it is the last hour; and just as you heard that antichrist is coming, even now many antichrists have arisen; from this we know that it is the last hour.

19   They went out from us, but they were not *really* of us; for if they had been of us, they would have remained with us; but *they went out*, in order that it might be shown that they all are not of us.

20   But you have an anointing from the Holy One, and you all know.

21   I have not written to you because you do not know the truth, but because you do know it, and because no lie is of the truth.

22   Who is the liar but the one who denies that Jesus is the Christ? This is the antichrist, the one who denies the Father and the Son.

23   Whoever denies the Son does not have the Father; the one who confesses the Son has the Father also.

24   As for you, let that abide in you which you heard from the beginning. If what you heard from the beginning abides in you, you also will abide in the Son and in the Father.

25   And this is the promise which He Himself made to us: eternal life.

26   These things I have written to you concerning those who are trying to deceive you.

27   And as for you, the anointing which you received from Him abides in you, and you have no need for anyone to teach you; but as His anointing teaches you about all things, and is true and is not a lie, and just as it has taught you, you abide in Him.

28   And now, little children, abide in Him, so that when He appears, we may have confidence and not shrink away from Him in shame at His coming.

29   If you know that He is righteous, you know that everyone also who practices righteousness is born of Him.

III. *Assurance and abiding in love (3:1–4:21)*

A. *Obedience in action*

3   See how great a love the Father has bestowed upon us, that we should be called children of God; and *such* we are. For this reason the world does not know us, because it did not know Him.

2   Beloved, now we are children of God, and it has not appeared as yet what we

---

Cross references (margin)

2:9
2 Pet 1:9

2:10
1 John 3:14;
v. 11
John 12:35

2:12
Luke 24:47

2:13
1 John 1:1;
v. 14

2:14
1 John 1:1;
Eph 6:10;
John 5:38

2:15
Rom 12:2;
Matt 6:24;
James 4:4

2:16
Rom 13:14;
Prov 27:20;
James 4:16

2:17
1 Cor 7:31

*2:18
1 Pet 4:7;
1 John 4:1,3

2:19
Acts 20:30;
Matt 24:24;
1 Cor 11:19

2:20
2 Cor 1:21;
Acts 3:14;
John 14:26

2:21
2 Pet 1:12;
1 John 3:19

2:23
John 14:7

2:24
2 John 6;
John 14:23

2:25
John 17:3
2:26
2 John 7

2:27
John 14:26,17

2:28
1 John 3:2;
21; 4:17;
Mark 8:38;
1 Thess 2:19
2:29
1 John 3:7,9;
4:7

3:1
John 1:12;
16:3
3:2
Rom 8:15;
2 Cor 4:17;

Handwritten margin notes

V11 – Hate is v. 11 like a blinder 2:11

V12- God wants to forgive

v. 15 e.g. survivor ch 2:15 to life rather than guilt news get in reserves 2:16 boast

See I Cor 12:3 Test of a true spirit

✗

2:18 Scripture distinguishes *that antichrist* from *antichrists* and the *spirit of antichrist*. Here John speaks of those who are not *that antichrist* but who make common cause with him and whose malign spirit they emulate. Denying the cardinal truths of the gospel, they are called *antichrists*. (See also note to 4:3 for further discussion on antichrists.)

shall be. We know that, when He appears, we shall be like Him, because we shall see Him just as He is.

3　And everyone who has this hope *fixed* on Him purifies himself, just as He is pure.

4　Everyone who practices sin also practices lawlessness; and sin is lawlessness.

5　And you know that He appeared in order to take away sins; and in Him there is no sin.

6　No one who abides in Him sins; no one who sins has seen Him or knows Him.

7　Little children, let no one deceive you; the one who practices righteousness is righteous, just as He is righteous;

8　the one who practices sin is of the devil; for the devil has sinned from the beginning. The Son of God appeared for this purpose, that He might destroy the works of the devil.

9　No one who is born of God practices sin, because His seed abides in him; and he cannot sin, because he is born of God.

10　By this the children of God and the children of the devil are obvious: anyone who does not practice righteousness is not of God, nor the one who does not love his brother.

B. *Love in action*

11　For this is the message which you have heard from the beginning, that we should love one another;

12　not as Cain, *who* was of the evil one, and slew his brother. And for what reason did he slay him? Because his deeds were evil, and his brother's were righteous.

13　Do not marvel, brethren, if the world hates you.

14　We know that we have passed out of death into life, because we love the brethren. He who does not love abides in death.

15　Everyone who hates his brother is a murderer; and you know that no murderer has eternal life abiding in him.

16　We know love by this, that He laid down His life for us; and we ought to lay down our lives for the brethren.

17　But whoever has the world's goods, and beholds his brother in need and closes his heart against him, how does the love of God abide in him?

18　Little children, let us not love with word or with tongue, but in deed and truth.

19　We shall know by this that we are of the truth, and shall assure our heart before Him,

20　in whatever our heart condemns us; for God is greater than our heart, and knows all things.

21　Beloved, if our heart does not condemn us, we have confidence before God;

22　and whatever we ask we receive from Him, because we keep His commandments and do the things that are pleasing in His sight.

23　And this is His commandment, that we believe in the name of His Son Jesus Christ, and love one another, just as He commanded us.

24　And the one who keeps His commandments abides in Him, and He in him. And we know by this that He abides in us, by the Spirit whom He has given us.

C. *Faith in action*

4　Beloved, do not believe every spirit, but test the spirits to see whether they are from God; because many false prophets have gone out into the world.

2　By this you know the Spirit of God: every spirit that confesses that Jesus Christ has come in the flesh is from God;

3　and every spirit that does not confess Jesus is not from God; and this is the

Cross references

Rom 8:29;
2 Pet 1:4;
2 Cor 3:18

3:4
Rom 4:15;
1 John 5:17
3:5
Is 53:5,6;
2 Cor 5:21

*3:7
1 John 2:1,
26,29
3:8
John 8:44;
16:11;
Heb 2:14
*3:9
1 John 5:18;
1 Pet 1:23
3:10
1 John 2:29

3:11
1 John 1:5;
John 13:34,
35; 2 John 5

3:13
John 15:18
3:14
John 5:24;
1 John 2:9,11
3:15
Matt 5:21,22;
John 8:44;
Gal 5:20,21
3:16
John 3:16;
13:1; 15:13
3:17
Deut 15:7;
1 John 4:20
3:18
Rom 12:9;
James 1:22
3:19
1 John 2:21
3:20
1 Cor 4:4

3:21
1 John 5:14
3:22
Matt 7:7;
21:22; 1 John
2:3
3:23
1 John 2:8
3:24
Rom 8:9;
1 John 4:13

4:1
Matt 24:4;
2 Pet 2:1;
1 John 2:18
4:2
1 Cor 12:3;
1 John 2:23
*4:3
2 John 7;

3:7 The claim to righteousness is most firmly established by the life the believer lives. This Scripture might be paraphrased, "He who performs righteousness is a righteous person." This is analogous to James's teaching that faith without works is dead (James 2:20–26).
3:9 This verse has been taken by some to mean that believers cannot sin. But 1:9 already reveals that believers do sin, and it outlines the method by which cleansing may be obtained. From the Greek tenses used here the verse refers to the practice of sin and might well be paraphrased, "Whoever is born of God does not make sin the *practice* of his life," as our text implies. So while believers do sin, it is not their common custom nor are they confirmed in the direction of sin, for their nature is no longer the old, sinful nature, but one given by God. The thought is expressed further in 5:18: a child of God does not live a life of sin because the Son of God keeps him.
4:3 References to "antichrist(s)" in 2:18,22; 4:3; 2 John 7

spirit of the antichrist, of which you have heard that it is coming, and now it is already in the world.

4 You are from God, little children, and have overcome them; because greater is He who is in you than he who is in the world.

5 They are from the world; therefore they speak as from the world, and the world listens to them.

6 We are from God; he who knows God listens to us; he who is not from God does not listen to us. By this we know the spirit of truth and the spirit of error.

D. The source of love

7 Beloved, let us love one another, for love is from God; and everyone who loves is born of God and knows God.

8 The one who does not love does not know God, for God is love.

9 By this the love of God was manifested in us, that God has sent His only begotten Son into the world so that we might live through Him.

10 In this is love, not that we loved God, but that He loved us and sent His Son to be the propitiation for our sins.

11 Beloved, if God so loved us, we also ought to love one another.

12 No one has beheld God at any time; if we love one another, God abides in us, and His love is perfected in us.

13 By this we know that we abide in Him and He in us, because He has given us of His Spirit.

14 And we have beheld and bear witness that the Father has sent the Son to be the Savior of the world.

15 Whoever confesses that Jesus is the Son of God, God abides in him, and he in God.

16 And we have come to know and have believed the love which God has for us. God is love, and the one who abides in love abides in God, and God abides in him.

17 By this, love is perfected with us, that we may have confidence in the day of judgment; because as He is, so also are we in this world.

18 There is no fear in love; but perfect love casts out fear, because fear involves punishment, and the one who fears is not perfected in love.

19 We love, because He first loved us.

20 If someone says, "I love God," and hates his brother, he is a liar; for the one who does not love his brother whom he has seen, cannot love God whom he has not seen.

21 And this commandment we have from Him, that the one who loves God should love his brother also.

IV. Faith and certainty (5:1–12)

A. Victory through faith

5 Whoever believes that Jesus is the 2Christ is born of God; and whoever loves the Father loves the child born of Him.

2 By this we know that we love the children of God, when we love God and observe His commandments.

3 For this is the love of God, that we keep His commandments; and His commandments are not burdensome.

4 For whatever is born of God overcomes the world; and this is the victory that has overcome the world—our faith.

5 And who is the one who overcomes the world, but he who believes that Jesus is the Son of God?

B. Faith through the Son

6 This is the one who came by water and blood, Jesus Christ; not with the water only, but with the water and with the blood.

2I.e., Messiah

---

make it clear that their fundamental error was the denial of the reality of the incarnation. Some of them (cf. 2:18,19) had belonged to the Christian fellowship, but had forsaken it on account of their heresy. Their repudiation of the reality of the incarnation of the Son involved also a repudiation of the Father: to deny the Son is to deny the Father (2:22,23). It would appear, then, that their denial of the foundational belief of the gospel was a direct result of Gnostic teaching (cf. Introduction to 1 John). See also note to 1 John 2:18.
5:6 Jesus Christ came with the water and the blood. This is

7   And it is the Spirit who bears witness, because the Spirit is the truth.

8   For there are three that bear witness, [3]the Spirit and the water and the blood; and the three are in agreement.

9   If we receive the witness of men, the witness of God is greater; for the witness of God is this, that He has borne witness concerning His Son.

10   The one who believes in the Son of God has the witness in himself; the one who does not believe God has made Him a liar, because he has not believed in the witness that God has borne concerning His Son.

11   And the witness is this, that God has given us eternal life, and this life is in His Son.

12   He who has the Son has the life; he who does not have the Son of God does not have the life.

V. Conclusion (5:13–21)

13   These things I have written to you who believe in the name of the Son of God, in order that you may know that you have eternal life.

14   And this is the confidence which we have before Him, that, if we ask anything according to His will, He hears us.

15   And if we know that He hears us *in* whatever we ask, we know that we have the requests which we have asked from Him.

16   If anyone sees his brother committing a sin not *leading* to death, he shall ask and *God* will for him give life to those who commit sin not *leading* to death. There is a sin *leading* to death; I do not say that he should make request for this.

17   All unrighteousness is sin, and there is a sin not *leading* to death.

18   We know that no one who is born of God sins; but He who was born of God keeps him and the evil one does not touch him.

19   We know that we are of God, and the whole world lies in *the power of* the evil one.

20   And we know that the Son of God has come, and has given us understanding, in order that we might know Him who is true, and we are in Him who is true, in His Son Jesus Christ. This is the true God and eternal life.

21   Little children, guard yourselves from idols.

[3]A few late mss. read *in heaven, the Father, the Word, and the Holy Spirit, and these three are one. And there are three that bear witness on earth, the Spirit*

5:7	John 15:26
5:8	Matt 18:16
5:9	John 8:17,18; Matt 3:16,17
5:10	Rom 8:16; Gal 4:6; John 3:33
5:11	1 John 2:25; John 1:4
5:12	John 3:36
5:13	John 20:31; 1 John 1:1,2
5:14	1 John 3:21, 22; Matt 7:7
5:16	James 5:15; Heb 6:4,6
5:17	1 John 3:4
*5:18	1 John 3:9; John 14:30
5:19	1 John 4:6; Gal 1:4
5:20	Luke 24:45; John 17:3; Rev 3:7
*5:21	1 Cor 10:14

commonly interpreted to refer to the water of His baptism and the blood of His death, of which the Christian sacraments (ordinances) of baptism and the Lord's Supper are signs and symbols. In the context of this letter both emphasize the reality of the incarnation of Christ, whose saving ministry began in the waters of Jordan and was consummated on Calvary's cross.

5:18 *no one who is born of God sins.* The intention of here would be better understood by translating this verse, "anyone born of God does not keep on sinning."
5:21 Idolatry was present everywhere, thus it was necessary for John to warn against this peril, and also to make it clear that there was need for effort on the part of those to whom he was writing. See also note to Ex. 20:3 on idolatry.

INTRODUCTION TO
THE SECOND LETTER OF
JOHN

Authorship and Background: The writer of this short letter called himself "the elder" (v. 1; also 3 John v. 1). Similarity in style and content argues strongly for common authorship of all three epistles, and the majority of scholars believe that the same man wrote all three, whether he was John the apostle, another John known as "the elder," or some other unnamed person. The time and place of writing of all three would be the same, perhaps around A.D. 90 in the city of Ephesus.

The letter was addressed to "the chosen lady and her children" (v. 1); some believe this referred to a woman, "the elect Kyria," and her children. But from the reference to "some of your children" (4), the greetings from "the children of your chosen sister" (13), and the whole tone of the letter it seems conclusive that a church was addressed, not a family.

The elder wrote to emphasize the primacy of love in the Christian fellowship: to love means to obey God, and to obey is to love one another (5,6). He also warned his readers against the heresy of those who denied the incarnation of the Son of God (7): such deceivers were the antichrist, claiming that theirs was a "superior" teaching, above the orthodox Christian message (9). Such false teachers should not even be received at home, for to entertain them meant to share in their wicked work (10,11).

Characteristics: This short letter gives us an insight into church life in the latter part of the first century, as responsible leaders do their best to counteract the ruinous effects of false teaching. False doctrine dilutes the Christian witness, and its effects are felt in the lives of the believers. Orthodox Christian theology is not simply a matter of theory: it is the very basis of the Christian message and mission. The elder's love of the truth and his concern for the spiritual welfare of his readers leads him to write this brief note to a church whose members are in real peril of abandoning the truth as it is in Jesus.

Contents:

I. Salutation (1-3)

II. Counsel and warnings (4-11): The primacy of love in the Christian life; the reality of the incarnation of the Son of God. Take care that you are not deceived by false teachings and lose what you have worked for; shun all who carry strange doctrine.

III. Conclusion (12,13)

THE SECOND LETTER OF

JOHN

I. Salutation (1–3)

1 The elder to the chosen lady and her children, whom I love in truth; and not only I, but also all who know the truth,

2 for the sake of the truth which abides in us and will be with us forever:

3 Grace, mercy *and* peace will be with us, from God the Father and from Jesus Christ, the Son of the Father, in truth and love.

II. Counsel and warnings (4–11)

4 I was very glad to find *some* of your children walking in truth, just as we have received commandment *to do* from the Father.

5 And now I ask you, lady, not as writing to you a new commandment, but the one which we have had from the beginning, that we love one another.

6 And this is love, that we walk according to His commandments. This is the commandment, just as you have heard from the beginning, that you should walk in it.

7 For many deceivers have gone out into the world, those who do not acknowledge Jesus Christ *as* coming in the flesh. This is the deceiver and the antichrist.

8 Watch yourselves, that you might not lose what we have accomplished, but that you may receive a full reward.

9 Anyone who goes too far and does not abide in the teaching of Christ, does not have God; the one who abides in the teaching, he has both the Father and the Son.

10 If anyone comes to you and does not bring this teaching, do not receive him into *your* house, and do not give him a greeting;

11 for the one who gives him a greeting participates in his evil deeds.

III. Conclusion (12,13)

12 Having many things to write to you, I do not want to *do so* with paper and ink; but I hope to come to you and speak face to face, that your joy may be made full.

13 The children of your chosen sister greet you.

1
3 John 1;
1 John 3:18;
John 8:32
2
2 Pet 1:12;
1 John 1:8
3
1 Tim 1:2

4
3 John 3,4

5
1 John 2:7;
3:11
6
1 John 2:5;
2:24

7
1 John 4:1-3;
2:22

8
Mark 13:9;
1 Cor 3:8;
Heb 10:32
9
1 John 2:23

10
Rom 16:17

11
1 Tim 5:22

12
3 John 13,14;
1 John 1:4

13
v. 1

INTRODUCTION TO
THE THIRD LETTER OF
JOHN

Authorship and Background: This letter was also written by "the elder," the author of 2 John. It is a genuinely personal letter: all the second person pronouns are singular. It is addressed to Gaius, obviously a leader in a church; his position, however, is not specified. It may be that the previous letter written to the church, mentioned in verse 9, was 2 John. If so, the two letters were written to the same place, one to the church and the other to Gaius. It is impossible to determine whether this Gaius may be identified with any of the others with the same name in the New Testament (Acts 19:29; 20:4; Rom. 16:23; 1 Cor. 1:14).

The letter was written to solve problems relating to traveling Christian teachers, or prophets, whose ministry included several churches. Those who taught the true doctrine were to be entertained and helped in their travels. But Diotrephes, presumably the local leader, refused to receive these men, rejected the elder's authority, and expelled the members of the church who welcomed the messengers. Therefore, the elder wrote his good friend Gaius, urging him to help these itinerant preachers. Demetrius (v. 12) may have taken the letter to Gaius, or he may have been a member of the church to which Gaius belonged.

Characteristics: The letter exhibits a degree of authority as the elder attacks Diotrephes's lack of cooperation. More may have been involved than the clash of two strong personalities: it is quite possible (especially if 2 John was written to this same church) that the elder feels that theological and doctrinal issues are also at stake (see 2 John 10,11). In any case, the elder promises to visit the church and deal personally with the matter (10,14).

Contents:

I. Salutation (1-4)

II. Encouragement for Gaius (5-8): The elder's messengers had testified to Gaius's help, for which the author thanks and commends him.

III. Reproof for Diotrephes (9,10): Ambitious Diotrephes was rebelling against the elder's leadership, refusing the elders messengers, and expelling church members who disagreed with him. In a personal visit the elder will deal with him.

IV. Commendation for Demetrius (11,12)

V. Conclusion (13-15)

THE THIRD LETTER OF
JOHN

I. *Salutation (1–4)*

1 The elder to the beloved Gaius, whom I love in truth.
2 Beloved, I pray that in all respects you may prosper and be in good health, just as your soul prospers.
3 For I was very glad when brethren came and bore witness to your truth, *that is*, how you are walking in truth.
4 I have no greater joy than this, to hear of my children walking in the truth.

1
2 John 1

3
2 John 4;
vv. 5,10
4
1 Cor 4:15;
Philem 10

II. *Encouragement for Gaius (5–8)*

5 Beloved, you are acting faithfully in whatever you accomplish for the brethren, and especially *when they are* strangers;
6 and they bear witness to your love before the church; and you will do well to send them on their way in a manner worthy of God.
7 For they went out for the sake of the Name, accepting nothing from the Gentiles.
8 Therefore we ought to support such men, that we may be fellow workers with the truth.

5
Rom 12:13;
Heb 13:2
6
Acts 15:3;
Titus 3:13
7
Acts 5:41;
20:33,35

III. *Reproof for Diotrephes (9,10)*

9 I wrote something to the church; but Diotrephes, who loves to be first among them, does not accept what we say.
10 For this reason, if I come, I will call attention to his deeds which he does, unjustly accusing us with wicked words; and not satisfied with this, neither does he himself receive the brethren, and he forbids those who desire *to do so*, and puts *them* out of the church.

9
2 John 9
10
2 John 12;
v. 5;
John 9:34

IV. *Commendation for Demetrius (11,12)*

11 Beloved, do not imitate what is evil, but what is good. The one who does good is of God; the one who does evil has not seen God.
12 Demetrius has received a *good* testimony from everyone, and from the truth itself; and we also bear witness, and you know that our witness is true.

11
Ps 37:27;
1 John 2:29;
3:6,9
12
1 Tim 3:7;
John 21:24

V. *Conclusion (13–15)*

13 I had many things to write to you, but I am not willing to write *them* to you with pen and ink;
14 but I hope to see you shortly, and we shall speak face to face. Peace *be* to you. The friends greet you. Greet the friends by name.

13
2 John 12
14
1 Pet 5:14

INTRODUCTION TO

THE LETTER OF

JUDE

Authorship and Background: The writer identifies himself as "Jude, a bond-servant of Jesus Christ, and brother of James" (v. 1). This has been taken by conservatives to mean the brother of Jesus (cf. Matt. 13:55; Mark 6:3); others think the author was another Jude, otherwise unknown; another opinion is that the letter is pseudonymous, written in the name of Jude, brother of Jesus.

This short letter did not gain immediate acceptance, and as late as the fourth century Eusebius of Caesarea reported that there were those who disputed its apostolic authorship. Nearly all of the contents of this letter are reproduced in 2 Peter, Jude having been written earlier. Some date this letter in the sixties of the first century, others around A.D. 150.

The readers are not identified. The letter was addressed to no particular locality, but to Christians in general (1). The author had intended to write about "our common salvation," but news of the destructive heresy that was being taught led him to write to them about this matter (3,4).

False teachers had appeared, imbued with Gnostic philosophy, who perverted the grace of God into licentiousness and denied the lordship of Christ (4). They were defiling the flesh, rejecting authority, and reviling spiritual powers (8). These worldly people, devoid of the Spirit, were causing divisions in the church (19) with their flagrant immoralities and passions (10-13,16). By denying that sins of the flesh could affect the welfare of the soul, they practiced and taught immoral behavior; it was urgently necessary that they be exposed and their evil teachings condemned.

Characteristics: The author condemns the heretics in no uncertain terms, using the strongest words in describing them (4,8,10,16,18,19). He predicts their punishment and destruction (11-13), and urges his readers to continue growing in the faith and to keep themselves in the love of God and the mercy of Jesus Christ (20,21), helping those who had been led astray by the false teachers (22,23).

In warning his readers against the danger of apostasy, the author reminds them of God's judgment on the faithless Israelites who were destroyed after having been freed from Egypt (5); of the fate of rebellious angels (6); and the destruction of the cities of Sodom and Gomorrah (7). Cain, Balaam, and Korah are other Scriptural examples of the punishment meted out to the disobedient (11).

In verse 9 the author refers to the nonbiblical writing, "The Assumption of Moses," a Jewish work of the first century A.D., in citing the archangel Michael's dispute with the devil over the body of Moses; and in verses 14,15 he quotes another nonbiblical writing, 1 Enoch, concerning the prophecy of "Enoch, in the seventh generation from Adam" about the ultimate punishment of all the ungodly. It was especially this use of 1 Enoch that caused problems in the early church: some felt that 1 Enoch was an inspired writing since it was quoted in a canonical book; others felt that since 1 Enoch was noncanonical, the letter of Jude was not inspired, a view not shared by the Christian church.

Finally, the author calls to mind the predictions of the apostles as to what would happen "in the last time" (17-19). "Keep the faith!" is his urgent counsel.

Contents:

I. Introduction (1-4): Author, readers, and reason for the letter—the work of heretics, who had insinuated themselves into the Christian fellowship.

II. Character and doom of false teachers (5-16): The examples of the faithless Israelites, the rebel angels, Sodom and Gomorrah; Cain, Balaam, and Korah; the case of the archangel Michael; and the prophecy of Enoch. These false teachers were doomed, and for them "the black darkness has been reserved forever" (13).

III. Admonition to hold the true faith (17-23): In faithfulness, prayer, the love of God, and the mercy of Christ, you will remain true to the faith.

IV. Benediction (24,25)

THE LETTER OF
JUDE

I. Introduction (1–4)

1
Acts 1:13;
1 Pet 1:5
2
1 Pet 1:2;
2 Pet 1:2
3
Titus 1:4;
1 Tim 6:12
4
Gal 2:4;
2 Pet 2:1;
Rom 9:22;
2 Pet 2:1

1 Jude, a bond-servant of Jesus Christ, and brother of James, to those who are the called, beloved in God the Father, and kept for Jesus Christ:

2 May mercy and peace and love be multiplied to you.

3 Beloved, while I was making every effort to write you about our common salvation, I felt the necessity to write to you appealing that you contend earnestly for the faith which was once for all delivered to the saints.

4 For certain persons have crept in unnoticed, those who were long beforehand marked out for this condemnation, ungodly persons who turn the grace of our God into licentiousness and deny our only Master and Lord, Jesus Christ.

II. Character and doom of false teachers (5–16)

5
Num 14:29;
Ps 106:26

*6
John 8:44;
2 Pet 2:4;
Rev 20:10

7
2 Pet 2:6;
Gen 19:24

8
2 Pet 2:10
*9
Dan 10:13;
Zech 3:2
10
2 Pet 2:12;
Phil 3:19
*11
Gen 4:3-8;
1 John 3:12;
Num 22:7;
2 Pet 2:15;
Num 16:1-3,
31-35
12
2 Pet 2:13;
1 Cor 11:20ff;
Eph 4:14;
Matt 15:13
13
Is 57:20;
Phil 3:19;
2 Pet 2:17
*14
Gen 5:18;
Deut 33:2;
Dan 7:10

5 Now I desire to remind you, though you know all things once for all, that ¹the Lord, after saving a people out of the land of Egypt, subsequently destroyed those who did not believe.

6 And angels who did not keep their own domain, but abandoned their proper abode, He has kept in eternal bonds under darkness for the judgment of the great day.

7 Just as Sodom and Gomorrah and the cities around them, since they in the same way as these indulged in gross immorality and went after strange flesh, are exhibited as an example, in undergoing the punishment of eternal fire.

8 Yet in the same manner these men, also by dreaming, defile the flesh, and reject authority, and revile angelic majesties.

9 But Michael the archangel, when he disputed with the devil and argued about the body of Moses, did not dare pronounce against him a railing judgment, but said, "The Lord rebuke you."

10 But these men revile the things which they do not understand; and the things which they know by instinct, like unreasoning animals, by these things they are destroyed.

11 Woe to them! For they have gone the way of Cain, and for pay they have rushed headlong into the error of Balaam, and perished in the rebellion of Korah.

12 These men are those who are hidden reefs in your love feasts when they feast with you without fear, caring for themselves; clouds without water, carried along by winds; autumn trees without fruit, doubly dead, uprooted;

13 wild waves of the sea, casting up their own shame like foam; wandering stars, for whom the black darkness has been reserved forever.

14 And about these also Enoch, *in* the seventh *generation* from Adam, prophesied, saying, "Behold, the Lord came with many thousands of His holy ones,

¹Some ancient mss. read *Jesus*

---

6 The fact that these angels are spoken of as *fallen* obviously implies that at one time they were not fallen but enjoyed a heavenly status before God. They departed from righteousness, were expelled from heaven, and were consigned to the lower regions, or *Tartarus* (2 Pet. 2:4) to await their final punishment at the last judgment. At that time these angels will be cast with Satan into the lake of fire (Matt. 25:41; Rev. 20:7-15).
9 This controversy over the body of Moses is narrated in the Jewish apocryphal book, "The Assumption of Moses." According to accounts from some of the early church fathers, the devil tried to claim the body of Moses on two counts: (1) he, the devil, was the lord of matter, to which the angel replied that God is lord of all since He created all matter; and (2) Moses was a murderer, and therefore his body belonged to the devil. At this accusation the angel

replied, "*The Lord rebuke you*" (cf. Zech. 3:2), at which the devil fled.
11 *error of Balaam*. This is to be understood in the light of *the way of Balaam* mentioned in 2 Pet. 2:15. In both instances the element of greed and desire for personal gain is involved. It should, however, be distinguished from *the teaching of Balaam* (Rev. 2:14).
14 The noncanonical book of Enoch (parts of which are to be dated around the beginning of the Christian era) contains the following: "And behold! He cometh with ten thousands of His holy ones to execute judgment upon all, and to destroy all the ungodly: And to convict all flesh of all the works of their ungodliness which they have ungodly committed, and of all the hard things which ungodly sinners have spoken against Him." The phrase, *the seventh generation from Adam*, is from Enoch 60:8.

15   to execute judgment upon all, and to convict all the ungodly of all their ungodly deeds which they have done in an ungodly way, and of all the harsh things which ungodly sinners have spoken against Him."

16   These are grumblers, finding fault, following after their *own* lusts; they speak arrogantly, flattering people for the sake of *gaining an* advantage.

III. *Admonition to hold the true faith (17–23)*

17   But you, beloved, ought to remember the words that were spoken beforehand by the apostles of our Lord Jesus Christ,

18   that they were saying to you, "In the last time there shall be mockers, following after their own ungodly lusts."

19   These are the ones who cause divisions, worldly-minded, devoid of the Spirit.

20   But you, beloved, building yourselves up on your most holy faith; praying in the Holy Spirit;

21   keep yourselves in the love of God, waiting anxiously for the mercy of our Lord Jesus Christ to eternal life.

22   And have mercy on some, who are doubting;

23   save others, snatching them out of the fire; and on some have mercy with fear, hating even the garment polluted by the flesh.

IV. *Benediction (24,25)*

24   Now to Him who is able to keep you from stumbling, and to make you stand in the presence of His glory blameless with great joy,

25   to the only God our Savior, through Jesus Christ our Lord, *be* glory, majesty, dominion and authority, before all time and now and forever. Amen.

Cross references (right column):

15
2 Pet 2:6ff;
1 Tim 1:9

16
2 Pet 2:18

17
2 Pet 3:2

18
1 Tim 4:1;
2 Pet 2:1
19
1 Cor 2:14,
15;
James 3:15
20
Col 2:7;
Eph 6:18
21
Titus 2:13;
2 Pet 3:12

23
Amos 4:11;
Zech 3:2-5

24
Rom 16:25;
Eph 3:20;
Col 1:22
25
1 Tim 1:17;
Rom 11:36

Handwritten note:

v 24 – So often the
response to gods
glory is to fall
on our faces
in submission

INTRODUCTION TO

THE

REVELATION TO JOHN

Authorship and Background: The author's name is John (1:1,4,9; 22:8), and he calls himself a servant of Christ and brother of the suffering Christians to whom he writes (1:1,9). He is in exile on the island of Patmos, off the west coast of Asia Minor, because of his steadfast witness to Jesus Christ (1:9). He writes of things he heard and saw in a revelation granted him by Jesus Christ (1:1,2,19; 22:8).

He is classified as a prophet (22:9; cf. also 10:11), and his book is a prophecy (1:3; 22:7). Nowhere does he indicate that he is an apostle, and in 21:14 he refers to the "twelve apostles of the Lamb" without specifying whether or not he belonged to the group. Traditionally this John has been identified with John the apostle, son of Zebedee, from the earliest references to the book in the second century.

Although some date it earlier, before the destruction of Jerusalem in A.D. 70, the majority of scholars date the book in the latter years of the reign of the emperor Domitian (A.D. 81-96), around the year A.D. 95.

The letter was written because of the persecution begun by the emperor against Christians, who were unwilling to engage in emperor worship. Calling himself "August," "Savior," "Lord," and even "God," the emperor had statues built throughout the empire, and required citizens to offer sacrifices, as evidence of their allegiance to him. Christians, for whom there was only one God, and one Lord (1 Cor. 8:6), refused to participate in this idolatry, and consequently suffered persecution in the form of arrest, loss of possessions, economic boycott, and in many cases, death.

To these persecuted and harried Christians in the churches of the Roman province of Asia, John addresses this strange and wonderful book, stressing the lordship of Christ, the overruling sovereignty of God, and His eventual, final victory over the forces of sin and evil.

Characteristics: John describes the book as "the revelation of Jesus Christ, which God gave Him to show to His bond-servants what must shortly take place" (1:1); this Jesus did by sending His angel to him (1:1; 22:16). This book is a prophecy (1:3; 22:7,10,18,19), and is consciously written as inspired (1:10; 4:2; 17:3; 21:10); dire consequences are threatened against any who would either add to, or subtract from, the words of the book (22:18,19). The author writes of things "which are, and the things which shall take place after these things" (1:19); the latter involves the near advent of Jesus Christ, who promises, "I am coming quickly" (3:11; 22:7,12,20), to which the Spirit and the Bride answer, "Come!" (22:17). These future events are to take place soon (1:1; 22:6); the time is near (1:3; 22:10).

The book is a "revelation" (or apocalypse) (1:1). As such it employs symbols and figures common to apocalyptic literature: supernatural events, unearthly creatures, metaphors, pseudonyms, and numbers. Perhaps not even the original readers of the book understood the precise meaning of all these strange symbols and metaphors; among modern commentators there is no agreement as to what they all mean.

There are four main schemes of interpretation of the book: (1) the preterit—everything has already been fulfilled; (2) the historical—the predictions are in the process of fulfillment; (3) the futurist—all predictions are in the future; and (4) the spiritual—the events described are only symbols of spiritual realities and struggles, without any literal or historical application.

Whatever may be one's approach to and interpretation of this book, two things should be kept in mind: (1) The practical purpose of the book was to strengthen the courage and faith of those early Christians; it was written primarily for them, and was meant to convey to them a message of hope and victory. And, (2) the author clearly and repeatedly stated that the time of these events was quite near (1:1,3; 3:11; 22:6,7,10,12,20). The author anticipated that what he wrote about was to happen soon, either the whole series of events (if the coming of Christ and the end of the world are coincident), or else the first in the series of events (if the coming of Christ is to precede by a considerable length of time the final judgment and the new heaven and new earth). The fact that Christ has not yet returned does not destroy the sense of imminence.

The various interpretations of the thousand years in 20:1-10 have given rise to different eschatological schemes, usually known as premillennial, postmillennial, and amillennial.

The literary development of the book follows a scheme of events in which the number seven often recurs: there are seven spirits of God (1:4; 4:5; 5:6); seven lampstands and seven stars (1:12-20); seven churches to which letters are sent (2:1-3:22); a book sealed with seven seals (5:1), opened one after the other (6:1-17; 8:1); seven angels who blow seven trumpets (8:2-9:21; 11:15-19); seven thunders (10:3,4); seven angels with seven bowls (15:1,5-8; 16:1-21); seven kings (17:10). The number three also occurs: three woes (9:12; 11:14), three angels (14:6-9), three unclean spirits (16:13). The number twelve and its multiples are also used: twenty-four elders on thrones (4:4,10-11); one hundred and forty-four thousand sealed, twelve thousand from each of the twelve tribes (7:4-8); the city with twelve gates and twelve foundations (21:10-21); the tree of life with twelve fruits (22:2). The most famous of all numbers, of course, is six hundred and sixty-six, the number of the beast (13:18).

There are symbolic and allegorical names: the Nicolaitans (2:6,15), Jezebel (2:20-23), Abaddon, Apollyon (9:11), Sodom and Egypt (11:8), Har-Magedon (Armageddon) (16:16), Babylon (17:5; 18:1-24), Gog and Magog (20:8).

It is the person of Christ, however, who dominates the book. He is both the Lamb, "as if slain" (5:6), and the warrior who goes forth to conquer and rule, whose name is The Word of God (19:11-16).

Contents:

I. Introduction (1:1-20): The author's commission to write; his vision of the resurrected and glorified Christ.

II. The messages to the seven churches (2:1-3:22): Churches in the province of Asia: Ephesus, Smyrna, Pergamum, Thyatira, Sardis, Philadelphia, and Laodicea. "Behold, I stand at the door and knock . . . He who has an ear, let him hear what the Spirit says to the churches" (3:20-22).

III. The things that shall be (4:1-22:5):
　(1) The heavenly worship (4:1-11): God on His throne; four living creatures and twenty-four elders offer continuous worship to God.
　(2) Prelude to the seven seals (5:1-14): the scroll opened and the Lamb adored.
　(3) The vision of the seven seals (6:1-8:6): Interlude between the sixth and seventh seals (7:1-17).
　(4) The seven trumpets (8:7-11:19): Interlude between the sixth and seventh trumpet; the prophet eats the little scroll in the angel's hand; he measures the temple of God; the two witnesses, their death, resurrection, and ascension into heaven.
　(5) The seven mystic figures (12:1-14:20)
　(6) The seven bowls of wrath (15:1-16:21)
　(7) The judgment of Babylon (17:1-19:10)
　(8) The defeat of the beast and the false prophet (19:11-21)
　(9) The binding of Satan (20:1-3)
　(10) The millennial reign of Christ (20:4-6)

    (11) The loosing of Satan (20:7-10)
    (12) The great white throne judgment (20:11-15)
    (13) The new heaven and the new earth (21:1-8)
    (14) The new Jerusalem (21:9-22:5)

IV. **Epilogue (22:6-21): The message authenticated, with warnings against any alteration; promise of reward and punishment, "'Yes, I am coming quickly.' Amen. Come, Lord Jesus." (22:20)**

THE

REVELATION TO JOHN

(The Apocalypse)

I. Introduction (1:1–20)

A. The source of the revelation

1 The Revelation of Jesus Christ, which God gave Him to show to His bond-servants, the things which must shortly take place; and He sent and communicated *it* by His angel to His bond-servant John,

2 who bore witness to the word of God and to the testimony of Jesus Christ, *even* to all that he saw.

3 Blessed is he who reads and those who hear the words of the prophecy, and heed the things which are written in it; for the time is near.

B. The salutation

4 John to the seven churches that are in Asia: Grace to you and peace, from Him who is and who was and who is to come; and from the seven Spirits who are before His throne;

5 and from Jesus Christ, the faithful witness, the first-born of the dead, and the ruler of the kings of the earth. To Him who loves us, and released us from our sins by His blood,

6 and He has made us *to be* a kingdom, priests to His God and Father; to Him *be* the glory and the dominion forever and ever. Amen.

7 BEHOLD, HE IS COMING WITH THE CLOUDS, and every eye will see Him, even those who pierced Him; and all the tribes of the earth will mourn over Him. Even so. Amen.

8 "I am the Alpha and the Omega," says the Lord God, "who is and who was and who is to come, the Almighty."

C. The voice and the vision

9 I, John, your brother and fellow partaker in the tribulation and kingdom and perseverance *which are* in Jesus, was on the island called Patmos, because of the word of God and the testimony of Jesus.

10 I was ¹in the Spirit on the Lord's day, and I heard behind me a loud voice like *the sound* of a trumpet,

11 saying, "Write in a book what you see, and send *it* to the seven churches: to

¹Or, *in spirit*

*1:1
John 12:49;
Rev 22:16

1:2
1 Cor 1:6;
Rev 12:17
1:3
Luke 11:28;
Rev 22:10

1:4
John 1:1;
Rev 3:1; 4:5

1:5
Rev 3:14;
Col 1:18;
Ps 89:27;
Rev 17:14;
John 13:34;
Heb 9:14
1:6
1 Pet 2:5;
Rev 5:10;
Rom 11:36
1:7
Zech 12:10
1:8
Rev 21:6;
4:8; 16:7

1:9
Phil 4:14;
2 Tim 2:12

1:10
Rev 4:1,2

*1:11
vv. 8,17

1:1 *Revelation* is not the same as *inspiration. Revelation* means that disclosure of divine truth that is immediately given to holy men by the Holy Spirit. Some of the information in the Bible resulted from the investigation of the Biblical writer himself (Luke 1:1–4). Some Scripture was undoubtedly copied from official records (as is implied by some statements in the Old Testament historical books—2 Kin. 1:18; 8:23; 10:34; 2 Chr. 25:26; 27:7). Some Scripture has come from sources no longer to be identified but which may have included oral tradition (e.g., the events of the first eleven chapters of Genesis). Nevertheless, conservative tradition has always held that the writers, in using information derived from possibly fallible records and oral tradition, were preserved from error by the superintending power of the Holy Spirit. (The doctrine of inspiration does not involve the infallibility of the scribes who later made copies of the originals; yet while minor scribal errors may have crept into the text by transmission, there are no major doctrinal issues at stake in those few places.) Others hold that there are incidental errors in the original manuscripts. **1:11** The messages to the seven churches refer to: (1)

actual, historical churches in existence in Asia Minor at the time John wrote; (2) conditions that existed not only in these churches but also in other churches of that time; and (3) conditions that have arisen in the church of Jesus Christ in subsequent ages. A large and influential school of interpretation understands these seven churches as representing also seven successive epochs of the history of the Christian church as a whole between apostolic times and the end of the church age. As this scheme of interpretation has been worked out, however, it produces some remarkable incongruities, such as identifying the heroic period of the Protestant Reformation with Sardis and its unhappy state of being more dead than alive (3:1). It is therefore questionable whether these messages ought to be applied to particular periods in the history of the Christian church. And yet, in the opinion of many, at the end of the age there will be an intensifying of the evils described in the messages to the seven churches and in particular the lukewarmness and empty self-conceit found in the Laodicean church (3:14–19).

Ephesus and to Smyrna and to Pergamum and to Thyatira and to Sardis and to Philadelphia and to Laodicea."

1:12
Ex 25:27;
Zech 4:2

12   And I turned to see the voice that was speaking with me. And having turned I saw seven golden lampstands;

1:13
Ezek 1:26;
Dan 7:13;
10:5

13   and in the middle of the lampstands one like ²a son of man, clothed in a robe reaching to the feet, and girded across His breast with a golden girdle.

1:14
Dan 7:9;
10:6;
Rev 19:12

14   And His head and His hair were white like white wool, like snow; and His eyes were like a flame of fire;

1:15
Dan 10:6;
Ezek 43:2

15   and His feet *were* like burnished bronze, when it has been caused to glow in a furnace, and His voice *was* like the sound of many waters.

1:16
Rev 2:1; 3:1;
Heb 4:12;
Rev 2:12,16

16   And in His right hand He held seven stars; and out of His mouth came a sharp two-edged sword; and His face was like the sun shining in its strength.

1:17
Ezek 1:28;
Dan 8:18;
10:10; Is 41:4

17   And when I saw Him, I fell at His feet as a dead man. And He laid His right hand upon me, saying, "Do not be afraid; I am the first and the last,

1:18
Rom 6:9;
Rev 4:9; 20:1

18   and the living One; and I was dead, and behold, I am alive forevermore, and I have the keys of death and of Hades.

1:20
Zech 4:2

19   "Write therefore the things which you have seen, and the things which are, and the things which shall take place after these things.

20   "As for the mystery of the seven stars which you saw in My right hand, and the seven golden lampstands: the seven stars are the angels of the seven churches, and the seven lampstands are the seven churches.

II. *The messages to the seven churches (2:1–3:22)*

A. *The message to Ephesus*

2:1
Rev 1:16;
1:13

2   "To the angel of the church in Ephesus write:
The One who holds the seven stars in His right hand, the One who walks among the seven golden lampstands, says this:

2:2
Rev 3:1,8;
1 John 4:1;
2 Cor 11:13

2   'I know your deeds and your toil and perseverance, and that you cannot endure evil men, and you put to the test those who call themselves apostles, and they are not, and you found them *to be* false;

2:3
John 15:21

3   and you have perseverance and have endured for My name's sake, and have not grown weary.

2:4
Matt 24:12
2:5
vv. 16,22,2;
Rev 1:20

4   'But I have *this* against you, that you have left your first love.

5   'Remember therefore from where you have fallen, and repent and do the deeds you did at first; or else I am coming to you, and will remove your lampstand out of its place—unless you repent.

*2:6
v. 15

6   'Yet this you do have, that you hate the deeds of the Nicolaitans, which I also hate.

2:7
Matt 11:15;
Rev 3:6,13;
22:2,14;
Gen 2:9

7   'He who has an ear, let him hear what the Spirit says to the churches. To him who overcomes, I will grant to eat of the tree of life, which is in the Paradise of God.'

B. *The message to Smyrna*

2:8
Rev 1:11,17,
18

8   "And to the angel of the church in Smyrna write:
The first and the last, who was dead, and has come to life, says this:

2:9
Rev 1:9;
James 2:5;
Rev 3:9

9   'I know your tribulation and your poverty (but you are rich), and the blasphemy by those who say they are Jews and are not, but are a synagogue of Satan.

2:10
Rev 3:10;
Dan 1:12

10   'Do not fear what you are about to suffer. Behold, the devil is about to cast some of you into prison, that you may be tested, and you will have tribulation ten days. Be faithful until death, and I will give you the crown of life.

2:11
Rev 20:14;
21:8

11   'He who has an ear, let him hear what the Spirit says to the churches. He who overcomes shall not be hurt by the second death.'

C. *The message to Pergamum*

2:12
Rev 1:11,16

12   "And to the angel of the church in Pergamum write:
The One who has the sharp two-edged sword says this:

---

²Or, *the Son of Man*

2:6 The Nicolaitans were apparently a heretical sect whose doctrines were repudiated by the church at Ephesus but who were tolerated by the church at Pergamum (2:15). They were likely antinomians (see note to Rom. 6:1) who abused Christian liberty under the guise of adherence to the doctrine of grace. Irenaeus, Clement, and Tertullian wrote of their indulgence in vice, adultery, eating of things offered to idols, and of their love of carnal pleasure. They also seem to have embraced errors about the person of Jesus Christ.

13 'I know where you dwell, where Satan's throne is; and you hold fast My name, and did not deny My faith, even in the days of Antipas, My witness, My faithful one, who was killed among you, where Satan dwells.

14 'But I have a few things against you, because you have there some who hold the teaching of Balaam, who kept teaching Balak to put a stumbling block before the sons of Israel, to eat things sacrificed to idols, and to commit *acts of* immorality.

15 'Thus you also have some who in the same way hold the teaching of the Nicolaitans.

16 'Repent therefore; or else I am coming to you quickly, and I will make war against them with the sword of My mouth.

17 'He who has an ear, let him hear what the Spirit says to the churches. To him who overcomes, to him I will give *some* of the hidden manna, and I will give him a white stone, and a new name written on the stone which no one knows but he who receives it.'

D. *The message to Thyatira*

18 "And to the angel of the church in Thyatira write:
The Son of God, who has eyes like a flame of fire, and His feet are like burnished bronze, says this:

19 'I know your deeds, and your love and faith and service and perseverance, and that your deeds of late are greater than at first.

20 'But I have *this* against you, that you tolerate the woman Jezebel, who calls herself a prophetess, and she teaches and leads My bond-servants astray, so that they commit *acts of* immorality and eat things sacrificed to idols.

21 'And I gave her time to repent; and she does not want to repent of her immorality.

22 'Behold, I will cast her upon a bed *of sickness*, and those who commit adultery with her into great tribulation, unless they repent of [3]her deeds.

23 'And I will kill her children with pestilence; and all the churches will know that I am He who searches the minds and hearts; and I will give to each one of you according to your deeds.

24 'But I say to you, the rest who are in Thyatira, who do not hold this teaching, who have not known the deep things of Satan, as they call them—I place no other burden on you.

25 'Nevertheless what you have, hold fast until I come.

26 'And he who overcomes, and he who keeps My deeds until the end, TO HIM I WILL GIVE AUTHORITY OVER THE NATIONS;

27 AND HE SHALL RULE THEM WITH A ROD OF IRON, AS THE VESSELS OF THE POTTER ARE BROKEN TO PIECES, as I also have received *authority* from My Father;

28 and I will give him the morning star.

29 'He who has an ear, let him hear what the Spirit says to the churches.'

E. *The message to Sardis*

3 "And to the angel of the church in Sardis write:
He who has the seven Spirits of God, and the seven stars, says this: 'I know your deeds, that you have a name that you are alive, but you are dead.

2 'Wake up, and strengthen the things that remain, which were about to die; for I have not found your deeds completed in the sight of My God.

3 'Remember therefore what you have received and heard; and keep *it*, and repent. If therefore you will not wake up, I will come like a thief, and you will not know at what hour I will come upon you.

4 'But you have a few people in Sardis who have not soiled their garments; and they will walk with Me in white; for they are worthy.

[3]Some mss. read *their*

2:14 *the teaching of Balaam.* This should be distinguished from *the way of Balaam* (2 Pet. 2:15) and *the error of Balaam* (Jude 11). Balaam taught King Balak to subvert Israel by inviting them to worship his idols and to unite in marriage or ritual prostitution with his people (Num. 31:15,16). Believers in all ages have been lost to the true faith when intermarriage with unbelievers has caused them to turn away from God to false human teachings. This sort of compromise inevitably leads to spiritual declension.

2:20 The teachings of *Jezebel* in Thyatira were the same as those of Balaam (v. 14): *commit acts of immorality and eat things sacrificed to idols.* In both instances it seems clear that the compound sin was that of idolatry and immorality. The two went together, for in many of the religions of that time, sexual indulgence was part of cult worship. It cannot be decided for certain whether Jezebel was the real name of the woman in question or simply a title for her, with obvious connotations (cf. 1 Kin. 16:31; 2 Kin. 9:22).

Cross-references (margin):

2:13 Rev 14:12; v. 9

*2:14 Num 24:14; 2 Pet 2:15; Jude 11; 1 Cor 8:9; 10:19,20; 6:13
2:15 v. 6
2:16 2 Thess 2:8; Rev 1:16
2:17 John 6:49,50; Is 62:2; Rev 19:12

2:18 Rev 1:11,14,15
2:19 v. 2
*2:20 1 Kin 16:31; 21:25; 2 Kin 9:7; Acts 15:20
2:21 Rom 2:4; Rev 9:20
2:22 Rev 17:2; 18:9
2:23 Jer 11:20; Acts 1:24; Rom 8:27; Ps 62:12
2:24 Acts 15:28

2:26 Heb 3:6; Ps 2:8;
Rev 3:21
2:27 Rev 12:5; Is 30:14; Jer 19:11
2:28 Rev 22:16

3:1 Rev 1:4,16; 2:2; 1 Tim 5:6

3:3 1 Thess 5:2, 6; 2 Pet 3:10

3:4 Acts 1:15; Jude 23; Rev 6:11; 7:9,13

3:5
Matt 10:32

5 'He who overcomes shall thus be clothed in white garments; and I will not erase his name from the book of life, and I will confess his name before My Father, and before His angels.

3:6
Rev 2:7

6 'He who has an ear, let him hear what the Spirit says to the churches.'

F. The message to Philadelphia

3:7
Acts 3:14;
1 John 5:20;
Is 22:22

7 "And to the angel of the church in Philadelphia write:

He who is holy, who is true, who has the key of David, who opens and no one will shut, and who shuts and no one opens, says this:

3:8
Acts 14:27;
Rev 2:13

8 'I know your 4deeds. Behold, I have put before you an open door which no one can shut, because you have a little power, and have kept My word, and have not denied My name.

3:9
Rev 2:9;
Is 49:23; 43:4

9 'Behold, I will cause *those* of the synagogue of Satan, who say that they are Jews, and are not, but lie—behold, I will make them to come and bow down at your feet, and to know that I have loved you.

3:10
2 Pet 2:9;
Rev 16:14;
6:10; 17:8

10 'Because you have kept the word of My perseverance, I also will keep you from the hour of testing, that *hour* which is about to come upon the whole world, to test those who dwell upon the earth.

3:11
Rev 22:7,12,
20; 2:25,10

11 'I am coming quickly; hold fast what you have, in order that no one take your crown.

3:12
Gal 2:9;
Rev 22:4;
21:2

12 'He who overcomes, I will make him a pillar in the temple of My God, and he will not go out from it anymore; and I will write upon him the name of My God, and the name of the city of My God, the new Jerusalem, which comes down out of heaven from My God, and My new name.

3:13
v. 6

13 'He who has an ear, let him hear what the Spirit says to the churches.'

G. The message to Laodicea

3:14
Is 65:16

14 "And to the angel of the church in Laodicea write:

The Amen, the faithful and true Witness, the 5Beginning of the creation of God, says this:

3:15
v. 1

15 'I know your deeds, that you are neither cold nor hot; I would that you were cold or hot.

16 'So because you are lukewarm, and neither hot nor cold, I will spit you out of My mouth.

3:17
Hos 12:8;
Zech 11:5;
1 Cor 4:8

17 'Because you say, "I am rich, and have become wealthy, and have need of nothing," and you do not know that you are wretched and miserable and poor and blind and naked,

3:18
Is 55:1;
Matt 13:44;
Rev 7:13

18 I advise you to buy from Me gold refined by fire, that you may become rich, and white garments, that you may clothe yourself, and *that* the shame of your nakedness may not be revealed; and eye salve to anoint your eyes, that you may see.

3:19
Prov 3:11;
Heb 12:5,6;
Rev 2:5

19 'Those whom I love, I reprove and discipline; be zealous therefore, and repent.

3:20
Matt 24:33;
Luke 12:36;
John 14:23

20 'Behold, I stand at the door and knock; if anyone hears My voice and opens the door, I will come in to him, and will dine with him, and he with Me.

3:21
Rev 2:7;
Matt 19:28;
Rev 5:5

21 'He who overcomes, I will grant to him to sit down with Me on My throne, as I also overcame and sat down with My Father on His throne.

3:22
Rev 2:7

22 'He who has an ear, let him hear what the Spirit says to the churches.' "

III. The things that shall be (4:1–22:5)

A. The heavenly worship

4:1
Rev 1:10;
11:12; 1:19

4 After these things I looked, and behold, a door *standing* open in heaven, and the first voice which I had heard, like *the sound* of a trumpet speaking with me, said, "Come up here, and I will show you what must take place after these things."

4:2
Rev 1:10;
Is 6:1;
Ezek 1:26-28;
Dan 7:9

2 Immediately I was 6in the Spirit; and behold, a throne was standing in heaven, and One sitting on the throne.

3 And He who was sitting *was* like a jasper stone and a sardius in appearance; and *there was* a rainbow around the throne, like an emerald in appearance.

4:4
Rev 11:16;
3:4,5

4 And around the throne *were* twenty-four thrones; and upon the thrones *I saw* twenty-four elders sitting, clothed in white garments, and golden crowns on their heads.

4Or, *deeds (behold . . . shut), that you*   5I.e., *origin or source*   6Or, *in spirit*

5 And from the throne proceed flashes of lightning and sounds and peals of thunder. And *there were* seven lamps of fire burning before the throne, which are the seven Spirits of God;

6 and before the throne *there was*, as it were, a sea of glass like crystal; and in the center and around the throne, four living creatures full of eyes in front and behind.

7 And the first creature *was* like a lion, and the second creature like a calf, and the third creature had a face like that of a man, and the fourth creature *was* like a flying eagle.

8 And the four living creatures, each one of them having six wings, are full of eyes around and within; and day and night they do not cease to say,

    "HOLY, HOLY, HOLY, *is* THE LORD GOD, THE ALMIGHTY, who was and
        who is and who is to come."

9 And when the living creatures give glory and honor and thanks to Him who sits on the throne, to Him who lives forever and ever,

10 the twenty-four elders will fall down before Him who sits on the throne, and will worship Him who lives forever and ever, and will cast their crowns before the throne, saying,

11   "Worthy art Thou, our Lord and our God, to receive glory and honor and
        power; for Thou didst create all things, and because of Thy will they
        existed, and were created."

B. *Prelude to the seven seals:*
the scroll opened and the Lamb adored

5 And I saw in the right hand of Him who sat on the throne a book written inside and on the back, sealed up with seven seals.

2 And I saw a strong angel proclaiming with a loud voice, "Who is worthy to open the book and to break its seals?"

3 And no one in heaven, or on the earth, or under the earth, was able to open the book, or to look into it.

4 And I *began* to weep greatly, because no one was found worthy to open the book, or to look into it;

5 and one of the elders *said to me, "Stop weeping; behold, the Lion that is from the tribe of Judah, the Root of David, has overcome so as to open the book and its seven seals."

6 And I saw [7]between the throne (with the four living creatures) and the elders a Lamb standing, as if slain, having seven horns and seven eyes, which are the seven Spirits of God, sent out into all the earth.

7 And He came, and He took *it* out of the right hand of Him who sat on the throne.

8 And when He had taken the book, the four living creatures and the twenty-four elders fell down before the Lamb, having each one a harp, and golden bowls full of incense, which are the prayers of the saints.

9 And they *sang a new song, saying,

    "Worthy art Thou to take the book, and to break its seals; for Thou wast
        slain, and didst purchase for God with Thy blood *men* from every tribe
        and tongue and people and nation.

10   "And Thou has made them *to be* a kingdom and priests to our God; and
        they will reign upon the earth."

11 And I looked, and I heard the voice of many angels around the throne and the living creatures and the elders; and the number of them was myriads of myriads, and thousands of thousands,

12 saying with a loud voice,

    "Worthy is the Lamb that was slain to receive power and riches and
        wisdom and might and honor and glory and blessing."

13 And every created thing which is in heaven and on the earth and under the earth and on the sea, and all things in them, I heard saying,

    "To Him who sits on the throne, and to the Lamb, *be* blessing and honor
        and glory and dominion forever and ever."

---

[7]Lit., *in the middle of the throne and of the four living creatures, and in the middle of the elders*

5:5 *Root of David*, i.e., the Messiah.

Cross-references (margin):

4:5 Rev 8:5; 16:18; 1:4; Zech 4:2
4:6 Rev 15:2; Ezek 1:5
4:7 Ezek 1:10; 10:14
4:8 Is 6:2,3; Rev 1:8,4
4:9 Ps 47:8; Rev 10:6; 15:7
4:10 Rev 5:8,14; vv. 2,9,4
4:11 Rev 5:12; Gen 1:1; Eph 3:9; Rev 10:6
5:1 vv. 7:13; Ezek 2:9,10; Is 29:11; Dan 12:4
5:2 Rev 10:1
*5:5 Gen 49:9; Heb 7:14; Is 11:1,10; Rom 15:12; Rev 22:16
5:6 Rev 4:6; Is 53:7;
5:7 Rev 13:8; Zech 3:9; 4:10; Rev 4:5
v. 1
5:8 Rev 14:2; Ps 141:2
5:9 Ps 40:3; Rev 4:11; 1 Cor 6:20; Heb 9:12
5:10 Ex 19:6; Is 61:6
5:11 Dan 7:10; Heb 12:22
5:12 Rev 4:11
5:13 Phil 2:10; v. 3; 1 Tim 6:16; Rev 1:6; 6:16; 7:10

*5:14
Rev 19:4;
4:9,10

14   And the four living creatures kept saying, "Amen." And the elders fell down and worshiped.

C. The vision of the seven seals

1. The first seal: the white horse

6:1
Rev 5:5-7,1;
14:2; 19:6
6:2
Zech 6:3;
Rev 19:11;
Zech 6:11;
Rev 14:14

6 And I saw when the Lamb broke one of the seven seals, and I heard one of the four living creatures saying as with a voice of thunder, "Come."
2   And I looked, and behold, a white horse, and he who sat on it had a bow; and a crown was given to him; and he went out conquering, and to conquer.

2. The second seal: the red horse

6:3
Rev 4:7

6:4
Zech 6:2

3   And when He broke the second seal, I heard the second living creature saying, "Come."
4   And another, a red horse, went out; and to him who sat on it, it was granted to take peace from the earth, and that men should slay one another; and a great sword was given to him.

3. The third seal: the black horse

6:5
Rev 4:7;
Zech 6:2

*6:6
Rev 4:6,7;
9:4

5   And when He broke the third seal, I heard the third living creature saying, "Come." And I looked, and behold, a black horse; and he who sat on it had a pair of scales in his hand.
6   And I heard as it were a voice in the center of the four living creatures saying, "A [8]quart of wheat for a [9]denarius, and three quarts of barley for a denarius; and do not harm the oil and the wine."

4. The fourth seal: the pale horse

6:7
Rev 4:7

6:8
Zech 6:3;
Hos 13:14;
Ezek 5:12

7   And when He broke the fourth seal, I heard the voice of the fourth living creature saying, "Come."
8   And I looked, and behold, an ashen horse; and he who sat on it had the name Death; and Hades was following with him. And authority was given to them over a fourth of the earth, to kill with sword and with famine and with pestilence and by the wild beasts of the earth.

5. The fifth seal: the martyrs

6:9
Rev 14:18;
16:7; 20:4;
1:9; 12:17
6:10
Zech 1:12;
Ps 79:5;
Rev 3:7; 19:2
6:11
Rev 3:5; 7:9;
14:13;
Heb 11:40

9   And when He broke the fifth seal, I saw underneath the altar the souls of those who had been slain because of the word of God, and because of the testimony which they had maintained;
10   and they cried out with a loud voice, saying, "How long, O Lord, holy and true, wilt Thou refrain from judging and avenging our blood on those who dwell on the earth?"
11   And there was given to each of them a white robe; and they were told that they should rest for a little while longer, until the number of their fellow servants and their brethren who were to be killed even as they had been, should be completed also.

6. The sixth seal: signs in the heavens

6:12
Rev 16:18;
Matt 24:29;
Joel 2:31;
Acts 2:20
6:13
Rev 8:10;
9:1; Is 34:4
6:14
Is 34:4;
Jer 3:23;
4:24;
Rev 16:10
6:15
Is 2:10,19

12   And I looked when He broke the sixth seal, and there was a great earthquake; and the sun became black as sackcloth made of hair, and the whole moon became like blood;
13   and the stars of the sky fell to the earth, as a fig tree casts its unripe figs when shaken by a great wind.
14   And the sky was split apart like a scroll when it is rolled up; and every mountain and island were moved out of their places.
15   And the kings of the earth and the great men and the [10]commanders and the rich and the strong and every slave and free man, hid themselves in the caves and among the rocks of the mountains;

[8]Gr., choenix; i.e., a dry measure almost equal to a quart   [9]The denarius was equivalent to one day's wage   [10]I.e., chiliarchs, in command of one thousand troops

---

5:14   The elders bowed in silent worship.
6:6   The prices quoted for a quart of wheat and three quarts of barley indicate the scarcity of these staples. This means famine, and the little available is sold at a very high price. A denarius was a day's wage.

16   and they *said to the mountains and to the rocks, "Fall on us and hide us from the presence of Him who sits on the throne, and from the wrath of the Lamb;

17   for the great day of their wrath has come; and who is able to stand?"

7. Interlude

a. The sealing of God's servants

7 After this I saw four angels standing at the four corners of the earth, holding back the four winds of the earth, so that no wind should blow on the earth or on the sea or on any tree.

2   And I saw another angel ascending from the rising of the sun, having the seal of the living God; and he cried out with a loud voice to the four angels to whom it was granted to harm the earth and the sea,

3   saying, "Do not harm the earth or the sea or the trees, until we have sealed the bond-servants of our God on their foreheads."

4   And I heard the number of those who were sealed, one hundred and forty-four thousand sealed from every tribe of the sons of Israel:

5   from the tribe of Judah, twelve thousand *were* sealed, from the tribe of Reuben twelve thousand, from the tribe of Gad twelve thousand,

6   from the tribe of Asher twelve thousand, from the tribe of Naphtali twelve thousand, from the tribe of Manasseh twelve thousand,

7   from the tribe of Simeon twelve thousand, from the tribe of Levi twelve thousand, from the tribe of Issachar twelve thousand,

8   from the tribe of Zebulun twelve thousand, from the tribe of Joseph twelve thousand, from the tribe of Benjamin, twelve thousand *were* sealed.

b. The white-robed tribulation saints

9   After these things I looked, and behold, a great multitude, which no one could count, from every nation and *all* tribes and peoples and tongues, standing before the throne and before the Lamb, clothed in white robes, and palm branches *were* in their hands;

10   and they cry out with a loud voice, saying,

"Salvation to our God who sits on the throne, and to the Lamb."

11   And all the angels were standing around the throne and *around* the elders and the four living creatures; and they fell on their faces before the throne and worshiped God,

12   saying,

"Amen, blessing and glory and wisdom and thanksgiving and honor and power and might, *be* to our God forever and ever. Amen."

13   And one of the elders answered, saying to me, "These who are clothed in the white robes, who are they, and from where have they come?"

14   And I said to him, "My lord, you know." And he said to me, "These are the ones who come out of the great tribulation, and they have washed their robes and made them white in the blood of the Lamb.

15   "For this reason, they are before the throne of God; and they serve Him day and night in His temple; and He who sits on the throne shall spread His tabernacle over them.

16   "They shall hunger no more, neither thirst anymore; neither shall the sun beat down on them, nor any heat;

17   for the Lamb in the center of the throne shall be their shepherd, and shall

---

6:16
Hos 10:8;
Luke 23:30;
Rev 9:6
6:17
Zeph 1:14;
Rev 16:14;
Ps 76:7

7:1
Rev 9:4

7:3
Rev 6:6;
Ezek 9:4;
Rev 22:4
*7:4ff
Rev 9:16;
14:1

7:9
Rom 11:25;
Rev 5:9; 3:5,
18; 4:4; 6:11

7:10
Ps 3:8;
Rev 12:10;
19:1; 5:13
7:11
Rev 4:6

7:12
Rev 5:12-14

7:13
v. 9

*7:14
Matt 24:21;
Zech 3:3-5;
Heb 9:14;
1 John 1:7
7:15
Is 4:5,6;
Rev 21:3

7:16
Is 49:10;
Ps 121:5,6;
Rev 21:4

7:4-8 The tribe of Dan is not mentioned here among the twelve tribes. The tribe of Manasseh is substituted in its place, although Ephraim, the brother of Manasseh (both of whom were sons of Joseph and grandsons of Jacob), is not mentioned either. It is very difficult to account for these two omissions, especially since Ephraim was historically one of the most important of the tribes. The *one hundred and forty-four thousand* is hardly to be thought of as an exact number of converted Jews; some have taken it to imply that it represents the complete number of Jews who are the children of Abraham by faith, foreknown and chosen by God, who will turn to Christ during the closing days of the present age. The same number, *one hundred forty-four thousand*, occurs also in 14:1,3.

7:14 The *great tribulation* is marked off in Scripture as part of the closing years of our present age just prior to the return of Jesus Christ. Varying degrees of tribulation will come upon believers in all periods in church history, but the great tribulation is defined (Matt. 24:21) as a time of unprecedented trial and affliction. According to many interpreters, during this time the people of God will be cruelly mistreated and many will have to seal their testimony with the blood of martyrdom. Some interpreters take 13:1–5 to refer to this period of intense persecution and suffering, consisting of three and one-half years just prior to the second advent of Christ. During that period Satan will give power to the *beast coming up out of the sea* (13:1) and God will visit His wrath on men in the judgment of the seven bowls described in chapter 16. See also note to Matt. 24:3.

7:17
Ps 23:1;
John 10:11,
14; Is 25:8

guide them to springs of the water of life; and God shall wipe every tear from their eyes."

8. The seventh seal: making ready the seven trumpets

8:1
Rev 6:1

8 And when He broke the seventh seal, there was silence in heaven for about half an hour.

8:2
1 Cor 15:52;
1 Thess 4:16

2   And I saw the seven angels who stand before God; and seven trumpets were given to them.

8:3
Rev 7:2; 5:8;
Ex 30:1;
Rev 6:9

3   And another angel came and stood at the altar, holding a golden censer; and much incense was given to him, that he might add it to the prayers of all the saints upon the golden altar which was before the throne.

8:4
Ps 141:2

4   And the smoke of the incense, with the prayers of the saints, went up before God out of the angel's hand.

8:5
Lev 16:12;
Rev 4:5; 6:12

5   And the angel took the censer; and he filled it with the fire of the altar and threw it to the earth; and there followed peals of thunder and sounds and flashes of lightning and an earthquake.

8:6
v. 2

6   And the seven angels who had the seven trumpets prepared themselves to sound them.

D. The seven trumpets

1. The first trumpet: hail, fire, and blood

8:7
Ezek 38:22;
Rev 9:4

7   And the first sounded, and there came hail and fire, mixed with blood, and they were thrown to the earth; and a third of the earth was burned up, and a third of the trees were burned up, and all the green grass was burned up.

2. The second trumpet: the sea becomes blood

8:8
Jer 51:25;
Rev 16:3

8   And the second angel sounded, and *something* like a great mountain burning with fire was thrown into the sea; and a third of the sea became blood;

9   and a third of the creatures, which were in the sea and had life, died; and a third of the ships were destroyed.

3. The third trumpet: the falling star

8:10
Is 14:12;
Rev 9:1; 16:4

10   And the third angel sounded, and a great star fell from heaven, burning like a torch, and it fell on a third of the rivers and on the springs of waters;

8:11
Jer 9:15;
23:15

11   and the name of the star is called Wormwood; and a third of the waters became wormwood; and many men died from the waters, because they were made bitter.

4. The fourth trumpet: the darkening of the sun, moon, and stars

8:12
Rev 6:12,13

12   And the fourth angel sounded, and a third of the sun and a third of the moon and a third of the stars were smitten, so that a third of them might be darkened and the day might not shine for a third of it, and the night in the same way.

8:13
Rev 14:6;
19:17; 9:12;
11:14

13   And I looked, and I heard an eagle flying in midheaven, saying with a loud voice, "Woe, woe, woe, to those who dwell on the earth, because of the remaining blasts of the trumpet of the three angels who are about to sound!"

5. The fifth trumpet: the opening of the bottomless pit

9:1
Rev 8:10;
Luke 8:31;
Rev 17:8;
20:1
9:2
Gen 19:28;
Ex 19:18;
Joel 2:2,10

9 And the fifth angel sounded, and I saw a star from heaven which had fallen to the earth; and the key of the bottomless pit was given to him.

2   And he opened the bottomless pit; and smoke went up out of the pit, like the smoke of a great furnace; and the sun and the air were darkened by the smoke of the pit.

9:3
Ex 10:12-15;
v. 10

3   And out of the smoke came forth locusts upon the earth; and power was given them, as the scorpions of the earth have power.

9:4
Rev 6:6; 8:7;
7:2,3

4   And they were told that they should not hurt the grass of the earth, nor any green thing, nor any tree, but only the men who do not have the seal of God on their foreheads.

9:5
vv. 10,3

5   And they were not permitted to kill anyone, but to torment for five months; and their torment was like the torment of a scorpion when it stings a man.

9:6
Job 3:21;
Jer 8:3;
Rev 6:16

6   And in those days men will seek death and will not find it; and they will long to die and death flees from them.

9:7
Joel 2:4;
Nah 3:17;
Dan 7:8

7   And the appearance of the locusts was like horses prepared for battle; and on

their heads, as it were, crowns like gold, and their faces were like the faces of men.

8   And they had hair like the hair of women, and their teeth were like *the teeth* of lions.

9   And they had breastplates like breastplates of iron; and the sound of their wings was like the sound of chariots, of many horses rushing to battle.

10   And they have tails like scorpions, and stings; and in their tails is their power to hurt men for five months.

11   They have as king over them, the angel of the abyss; his name in Hebrew is [11]Abaddon, and in the Greek he has the name Apollyon.

12   The first woe is past; behold, two woes are still coming after these things.

6. *The sixth trumpet: the four angels released*

13   And the sixth angel sounded, and I heard a voice from the [12]four horns of the golden altar which is before God,

14   one saying to the sixth angel who had the trumpet, "Release the four angels who are bound at the great river Euphrates."

15   And the four angels, who had been prepared for the hour and day and month and year, were released, so that they might kill a third of mankind.

16   And the number of the armies of the horsemen was two hundred million; I heard the number of them.

17   And this is how I saw in the vision the horses and those who sat on them: *the riders* had breastplates *the color* of fire and of hyacinth and of brimstone; and the heads of the horses are like the heads of lions; and out of their mouths proceed fire and smoke and brimstone.

18   A third of mankind was killed by these three plagues, by the fire and the smoke and the brimstone, which proceeded out of their mouths.

19   For the power of the horses is in their mouths and in their tails; for their tails are like serpents and have heads; and with them they do harm.

20   And the rest of mankind, who were not killed by these plagues, did not repent of the works of their hands, so as not to worship demons, and the idols of gold and of silver and of brass and of stone and of wood, which can neither see nor hear nor walk;

21   and they did not repent of their murders nor of their sorceries nor of their immorality nor of their thefts.

7. *The second interlude*

a. *John eats the scroll*

10   And I saw another strong angel coming down out of heaven, clothed with a cloud; and the rainbow was upon his head, and his face was like the sun, and his feet like pillars of fire;

2   and he had in his hand a little book which was open. And he placed his right foot on the sea and his left on the land;

3   and he cried out with a loud voice, as when a lion roars; and when he had cried out, the seven peals of thunder uttered their voices.

4   And when the seven peals of thunder had spoken, I was about to write; and I heard a voice from heaven saying, "Seal up the things which the seven peals of thunder have spoken, and do not write them."

5   And the angel whom I saw standing on the sea and on the land lifted up his right hand to heaven,

6   and swore by Him who lives forever and ever, WHO CREATED HEAVEN AND THE THINGS IN IT, AND THE EARTH AND THE THINGS IN IT, AND THE SEA AND THE THINGS IN IT, that there shall be delay no longer,

7   but in the days of the voice of the seventh angel, when he is about to sound, then the mystery of God is finished, as He preached to His servants the prophets.

8   And the voice which I heard from heaven, *I heard* again speaking with me, and saying, "Go, take the book which is open in the hand of the angel who stands on the sea and on the land."

9   And I went to the angel, telling him to give me the little book. And he *said

---

Marginal references (right column):

9:8 Joel 1:6
9:9 Joel 2:5
9:10 vv. 5,19
9:11 Eph 2:2; v. 1
9:12 Rev 8:13
9:13 Ex 30:1-3; Rev 8:3
9:14 Rev 16:12
9:15 v. 18
9:16 Rev 5:11; 7:4
9:17 v. 18; Rev 11:5
9:18 vv. 15,17
9:20 Deut 31:29; 1 Cor 10:20; Ps 115:4; 135:15; Dan 5:23
*9:21 Rev 2:21; 18:23; 17:2,5
10:1 Rev 5:2; Matt 17:2; Rev 1:16,15
10:3 Is 31:4; Rev 4:5
10:4 Dan 8:26; 12:4,9; Rev 22:10
10:5 Ex 6:8; Dan 12:7
10:6 Rev 4:11; 14:7; 16:17
10:7 Rev 11:15; Rom 16:25
10:8 v. 4
10:9 Jer 15:16; Ezek 2:8

---

[11]I.e., destruction   [12]Some ancient mss. do not contain *four*

9:21 One of the characteristic marks of the end of the age is the continued impenitence of the unconverted. Despite the fearful judgments that fall on men and the warning con-veyed by these judgments, they persist in their sins and in their refusal to repent.

to me, "Take it, and eat it; and it will make your stomach bitter, but in your mouth it will be sweet as honey."

10:10
Ezek 3:3

10   And I took the little book out of the angel's hand and ate it, and it was in my mouth sweet as honey; and when I had eaten it, my stomach was made bitter.

10:11
Rev 11:1;
Ezek 37:4,9

11   And they *said to me, "You must prophesy again concerning many peoples and nations and tongues and kings."

b. *The two witnesses*

11:1
Ezek 40:3;
Rev 21:15

11 And there was given me a measuring rod like a staff; and someone said, "Rise and measure the temple of God, and the altar, and those who worship in it.

11:2
Ezek 40:17;
Luke 21:24;
Rev 13:5

2   "And leave out the court which is outside the temple, and do not measure it, for it has been given to the nations; and they will tread under foot the holy city for forty-two months.

*11:3
Rev 19:10;
12:6

3   "And I will grant *authority* to my two witnesses, and they will prophesy for twelve hundred and sixty days, clothed in sackcloth."

11:4
Ps 52:8;
Jer 11:16;
Zech 4:3;
Matt 11:14

4   These are the two olive trees and the two lampstands that stand before the Lord of the earth.

11:5
2 Kin 1:10;
Jer 5:14;
Num 16:29

5   And if anyone desires to harm them, fire proceeds out of their mouth and devours their enemies; and if anyone would desire to harm them, in this manner he must be killed.

11:6
1 Kin 17:1;
Ex 7:17,19

6   These have the power to shut up the sky, in order that rain may not fall during the days of their prophesying; and they have power over the waters to turn them into blood, and to smite the earth with every plague, as often as they desire.

11:7
Rev 13:1;
9:1,2;
Dan 7:21

7   And when they have finished their testimony, the beast that comes up out of the abyss will make war with them, and overcome them and kill them.

11:8
Rev 14:8;
Is 1:9;
Heb 13:12

8   And their dead [13]bodies *will lie* in the street of the great city which [14]mystically is called Sodom and Egypt, where also their Lord was crucified.

9   And those from the peoples and tribes and tongues and nations *will* look at their dead [13]bodies for three and a half days, and will not permit their dead bodies to be laid in a tomb.

11:10
Rev 3:10;
Esth 9:19,22

10   And those who dwell on the earth *will* rejoice over them and make merry; and they will send gifts to one another, because these two prophets tormented those who dwell on the earth.

11:11
Ezek 37:5,9,
10,14

11   And after the three and a half days the breath of life from God came into them, and they stood on their feet; and great fear fell upon those who were beholding them.

11:12
Rev 4:1;
2 Kin 2:11;
Acts 1:9

12   And they heard a loud voice from heaven saying to them, "Come up here." And they went up into heaven in the cloud, and their enemies beheld them.

11:13
Rev 6:12;
14:7; 16:11

13   And in that hour there was a great earthquake, and a tenth of the city fell; and seven thousand people were killed in the earthquake, and the rest were terrified and gave glory to the God of heaven.

11:14
Rev 9:12

14   The second woe is past; behold, the third woe is coming quickly.

8. *The seventh trumpet: the consummation*

*11:15
Rev 10:7;
16:17; 19:1;
12:10;
Dan 2:44;
7:14,27

15   And the seventh angel sounded; and there arose loud voices in heaven, saying,

"The kingdom of the world has become *the kingdom* of our Lord, and of His [15]Christ; and He will reign forever and ever."

11:16
Rev 4:4; 5:8

16   And the twenty-four elders, who sit on their thrones before God, fell on their faces and worshiped God,

11:17
Rev 1:8; 19:6

17   saying,

"We give Thee thanks, O Lord God, the Almighty, who art and who wast, because Thou hast taken Thy great power and hast begun to reign.

11:18
Ps 2:1;
Dan 7:9,10;
Rev 10:7;
19:5

18   "And the nations were enraged, and Thy wrath came, and the time *came* for

[13]Some ancient mss. read *body*   [14]Lit., *spiritually*   [15]I.e., Messiah

---

11:3 The two witnesses who prophesy for *twelve hundred and sixty days* (or forty-two months, or three and a half years) are described in terms identified with Elijah and Moses. It was Elijah who for three and a half years shut the heavens so that it did not rain (cf. Luke 4:25; James 5:17), while Moses was given power to turn the waters into blood, as well as to call down the other plagues on the Egyptians. The two are paired in Mal. 4:4,5 and appeared at the transfiguration of Christ (Mark 9:4 and parallels).

11:15 Here is the fulfillment of *the mystery of God*, as promised in 10:7, namely, the proclamation of the joint kingship of God and Christ. *The kingdom of the world* is the sovereignty, or ruling power, over the world, and the loud voices in heaven proclaim the fact that the kingship over the world has become our Lord's and His Christ's *and He will reign forever and ever*. The words are reminiscent of the resurrected Christ saying to His disciples, *All authority has been given to Me in heaven and on earth* (Matt. 28:18).

the dead to be judged, and *the time* to give their reward to Thy bond-servants the prophets and to the saints and to those who fear Thy name, the small and the great, and to destroy those who destroy the earth."

19   And the temple of God which is in heaven was opened; and the ark of His covenant appeared in His temple, and there were flashes of lightning and sounds and peals of thunder and an earthquake and a great hailstorm.

E. *The seven mystic figures*

1. *The woman with child*

12 And a great sign appeared in heaven: a woman clothed with the sun, and the moon under her feet, and on her head a crown of twelve stars;

2   and she was with child; and she *cried out, being in labor and in pain to give birth.

2. *The dragon*

3   And another sign appeared in heaven: and behold, a great red dragon having seven heads and ten horns, and on his heads *were* seven diadems.

4   And his tail *swept away a third of the stars of heaven, and threw them to the earth. And the dragon stood before the woman who was about to give birth, so that when she gave birth he might devour her child.

3. *The male child*

5   And she gave birth to a son, a male *child*, who is to rule all the nations with a rod of iron; and her child was caught up to God and to His throne.

6   And the woman fled into the wilderness where she *had a place prepared by God, so that there she might be nourished for one thousand two hundred and sixty days.

4. *The angel Michael*

7   And there was war in heaven, Michael and his angels waging war with the dragon. And the dragon and his angels waged war,

8   and they were not strong enough, and there was no longer a place found for them in heaven.

9   And the great dragon was thrown down, the serpent of old who is called the devil and Satan, who deceives the whole world; he was thrown down to the earth, and his angels were thrown down with him.

10   And I heard a loud voice in heaven, saying,

"**N**ow the salvation, and the power, and the kingdom of our God and the authority of His Christ have come, for the accuser of our brethren has been thrown down, who accuses them before our God day and night.

11   "And they overcame him because of the blood of the Lamb and because of the word of their testimony, and they did not love their life even to death.

12   "For this reason, rejoice, O heavens and you who dwell in them. Woe to the earth and the sea, because the devil has come down to you, having great wrath, knowing that he has *only* a short time."

13   And when the dragon saw that he was thrown down to the earth, he persecuted the woman who gave birth to the male *child*.

14   And the two wings of the great eagle were given to the woman, in order that she might fly into the wilderness to her place, where she *was nourished for a time and times and half a time, from the presence of the serpent.

15   And the serpent poured water like a river out of his mouth after the woman, so that he might cause her to be swept away with the flood.

16   And the earth helped the woman, and the earth opened its mouth and drank up the river which the dragon poured out of his mouth.

17   And the dragon was enraged with the woman, and went off to make war with the rest of her offspring, who keep the commandments of God and hold to the testimony of Jesus.

Cross-references (margin):
11:19 Rev 15:5,8; 8:5; 16:21
12:2 Is 66:7; Gal 4:19
12:3 Rev 13:1; Dan 7:7; Rev 19:12
12:4 Rev 8:7,12; Dan 8:10
12:5 Ps 2:9; Rev 2:27; 2 Cor 12:2
12:6 Rev 11:3
12:7 Dan 10:13; Rev 20:2
*12:9 Gen 3:1,4; Rev 20:2,3,8,10; John 12:31
12:10 Rev 11:15; Job 1:9-11; Zech 3:1
12:11 Rom 16:20; Luke 14:26
12:12 Ps 96:11; Is 49:13; Rev 18:20; 8:13; 10:6
12:13 vv. 3,5
12:14 Ex 19:4; Dan 7:25; 12:7
12:15 Is 59:19
12:17 Gen 3:15; Rev 11:7; 14:12; 1:2,9

12:9   The exact time when Satan is thrown down to earth out of heaven is not stated here. No more can be inferred than that in the struggle between God and Satan the latter will become a defeated foe whose end is sure through the victory of Christ (John 12:31).

5. The beast from the sea

13 And he stood on the sand of the seashore.

And I saw a beast coming up out of the sea, having ten horns and seven heads, and on his horns *were* ten diadems, and on his heads *were* blasphemous names.

2   And the beast which I saw was like a leopard, and his feet were *like those* of a bear, and his mouth like the mouth of a lion. And the dragon gave him his power and his throne and great authority.

3   And *I saw* one of his heads as if it had been slain, and his fatal wound was healed. And the whole earth was amazed *and followed* after the beast;

4   and they worshiped the dragon, because he gave his authority to the beast; and they worshiped the beast, saying, "Who is like the beast, and who is able to wage war with him?"

5   And there was given to him a mouth speaking arrogant words and blasphemies; and authority to act for forty-two months was given to him.

6   And he opened his mouth in blasphemies against God, to blaspheme His name and His tabernacle, *that is,* those who dwell in heaven.

7   And it was given to him to make war with the saints and to overcome them; and authority over every tribe and people and tongue and nation was given to him.

8   And all who dwell on the earth will worship him, *everyone* whose name has not been [16]written from the foundation of the world in the book of life of the Lamb who has been slain.

9   If anyone has an ear, let him hear.

10   If anyone [17]*is destined* for captivity, to captivity he goes; if anyone kills with the sword, with the sword he must be killed. Here is the perseverance and the faith of the saints.

6. The beast from the earth

11   And I saw another beast coming up out of the earth; and he had two horns like a lamb, and he spoke as a dragon.

12   And he exercises all the authority of the first beast in his presence. And he makes the earth and those who dwell in it to worship the first beast, whose fatal wound was healed.

13   And he performs great signs, so that he even makes fire come down out of heaven to the earth in the presence of men.

14   And he deceives those who dwell on the earth because of the signs which it was given him to perform in the presence of the beast, telling those who dwell on the earth to make an image to the beast who *had the wound of the sword and has come to life.

15   And there was given to him to give breath to the image of the beast, that the image of the beast might even [18]speak and cause as many as do not worship the image of the beast to be killed.

16   And he causes all, the small and the great, and the rich and the poor, and the free men and the slaves, to be given a mark on their right hand, or on their forehead,

17   and *he provides* that no one should be able to buy or to sell, except the one who has the mark, *either* the name of the beast or the number of his name.

18   Here is wisdom. Let him who has understanding calculate the number of the beast, for the number is that of a man; and his number is [19]six hundred and sixty-six.

7. The Lamb on Mount Zion

14 And I looked, and behold, the Lamb *was* standing on Mount Zion, and with Him one hundred and forty-four thousand, having His name and the name of His Father written on their foreheads.

2   And I heard a voice from heaven, like the sound of many waters and like the sound of loud thunder, and the voice which I heard *was* like *the sound* of harpists playing on their harps.

[16]Or, *written in the book . . . slain from the foundation of the world*   [17]Or, *leads into captivity*   [18]Some ancient mss. read *speak, and he will cause*   [19]Some mss. read 616

13:13 *he performs great signs.* The signs include *makes fire come down out of heaven,* which is reminiscent of Elijah (1 Kin. 18:38; 2 Kin. 1:10). Jesus Christ told His disciples they would work great signs and miracles, but He also warned them against false prophets who would do the same (Mark 13:22). Here that warning is fulfilled.

Cross references (margin):

13:1 — Dan 7:1-6; Rev 17:3
13:2 — Rev 16:10
13:3 — Rev 17:8
13:4 — Rev 18:18
13:5 — Dan 7:8,11, 25; Rev 11:2
13:6 — Rev 12:12
13:7 — Dan 7:21; Rev 11:7; 5:9
13:8 — Phil 4:3; Rev 3:5; 17:8; 5:6
13:9 — Mark 4:23; Rev 2:7
13:10 — Is 33:1; Matt 26:52; Rev 14:12
13:11 — Rev 11:7
13:12 — vv. 4,14; Rev 14:9,11; v. 3
*13:13 — Matt 24:24; Rev 16:14; 1 Kin 18:38; Rev 20:9
13:14 — Rev 12:9; 2 Thess 2:9, 10
13:15 — Dan 3:5; Rev 16:2
13:16 — Rev 11:18; 19:5,18; 14:9
13:17 — Rev 14:9,11; 15:2
13:18 — Rev 17:9; 15:2; 21:17
14:1 — Rev 5:6; Ps 2:6; Rev 3:12; 7:3
14:2 — Rev 1:15; 5:8

3   And they *sang a new song before the throne and before the four living creatures and the elders; and no one could learn the song except the one hundred and forty-four thousand who had been purchased from the earth.

4   These are the ones who have not been defiled with women, for they [20] have kept themselves chaste. These *are* the ones who follow the Lamb wherever He goes. These have been purchased from among men as first fruits to God and to the Lamb.

5   And no lie was found in their mouth; they are blameless.

8. *Interlude: the angelic messages*

6   And I saw another angel flying in midheaven, having an eternal gospel to preach to those who live on the earth, and to every nation and tribe and tongue and people;

7   and he said with a loud voice, "Fear God, and give Him glory, because the hour of His judgment has come; and worship Him who made the heaven and the earth and sea and springs of waters."

8   And another angel, a second one, followed, saying, "Fallen, fallen is Babylon the great, she who has made all the nations drink of the wine of the passion of her immorality."

9   And another angel, a third one, followed them, saying with a loud voice, "If anyone worships the beast and his image, and receives a mark on his forehead or upon his hand,

10   he also will drink of the wine of the wrath of God, which is mixed in full strength in the cup of His anger; and he will be tormented with fire and brimstone in the presence of the holy angels and in the presence of the Lamb.

11   "And the smoke of their torment goes up forever and ever; and they have no rest day and night, those who worship the beast and his image, and whoever receives the mark of his name."

12   Here is the perseverance of the saints who keep the commandments of God and their faith in Jesus.

13   And I heard a voice from heaven, saying, "Write, 'Blessed are the dead who die in the Lord from now on!'" "Yes," says the Spirit, "that they may rest from their labors, for their deeds follow with them."

14   And I looked, and behold, a white cloud, and sitting on the cloud *was* one like [21]a son of man, having a golden crown on His head, and a sharp sickle in His hand.

15   And another angel came out of the temple, crying out with a loud voice to Him who sat on the cloud, "Put in your sickle and reap, because the hour to reap has come, because the harvest of the earth is ripe."

16   And He who sat on the cloud swung His sickle over the earth; and the earth was reaped.

17   And another angel came out of the temple which is in heaven, and he also had a sharp sickle.

18   And another angel, the one who has power over fire, came out from the altar; and he called with a loud voice to him who had the sharp sickle, saying, "Put in your sharp sickle, and gather the clusters from the vine of the earth, because her grapes are ripe."

19   And the angel swung his sickle to the earth, and gathered *the clusters from* the vine of the earth, and threw them into the great wine press of the wrath of God.

20   And the wine press was trodden outside the city, and blood came out from the wine press, up to the horses' bridles, for a distance of [22]two hundred miles.

[20]Lit., *are chaste men*   [21]Or, *the Son of Man*   [22]Lit., *sixteen hundred stadia*. A stadion was about six hundred feet.

Cross references (right margin):

14:3 Rev 5:9; v. 1

14:4 2 Cor 11:2; Rev 3:4; 5:9; James 1:18

14:5 Ps 32:2; Zeph 3:13; Eph 5:27

14:6 Rev 8:13; 3:10; 5:9

14:7 Rev 15:4; 11:13; 4:11; 8:10

*14:8 Is 21:9; Jer 51:8; Rev 18:2; 17:5; 18:10

14:9 Rev 13:14-16

14:10 Is 51:17; Jer 25:15; Rev 18:6; 20:10; 19:20

14:11 Is 34:10; Rev 19:3; 4:8; 13:17

14:12 Rev 13:10; 12:17

14:13 Rev 20:6; 1 Cor 15:18; 1 Thess 4:16

14:14 Dan 7:13; Rev 1:13; 6:2

14:15 Joel 3:13; Jer 51:33; Rev 13:12

14:18 Rev 16:8; Joel 3:13

14:19 Rev 19:15

14:20 Is 63:3; Heb 13:12; Rev 11:8

14:8 Read in this connection 16:17–21 and 17:1–18:24 for further details on Babylon. The positive identification of Babylon in the Revelation with any known city or power is virtually impossible. Many different views have been proposed and sustained with learned argument, only to meet with equally learned dissent. Some have identified it with Babylon of the Old Testament. Some have insisted it is Jerusalem. Some have thought it to be an ecclesiastical rather than a geographical symbol. In this view the Reformers thought it to be the Roman papacy while later writers have held it to be an apostate Christendom at the end of the age. Perhaps the strongest argument favors the identifica-

tion of Babylon with Rome, the capital of Italy, where the emperor ruled over the civilized world of that time. In 17:4,5 the woman arrayed in purple and scarlet is named *Babylon the great,* and in 17:18 she is *the great city, which reigns over the kings of the earth.* In 16:17–21 John sees Babylon's impending destruction. In chapter 18 John sees it as fallen. It is apparent that Babylon, whatever its final identification, sheds the blood of Christians who remain faithful, seduces the peoples under her control, and shares the "wealth of her sensuality" with the merchants of the earth who shall suffer with her. At last *will Babylon . . . be thrown down . . . and will not be found any longer* (18:21).

F. *The seven bowls of wrath*

1. *Preliminary vision in heaven*

15:1
Rev 12:1,3;
16:1;
Lev 26:21;
Rev 14:10

15 And I saw another sign in heaven, great and marvelous, seven angels who had seven plagues, *which are* the last, because in them the wrath of God is finished.

15:2
Rev 4:6;
13:14,15; 5:8

2   And I saw, as it were, a sea of glass mixed with fire, and those who had come off victorious from the beast and from his image and from the number of his name, standing on the sea of glass, holding harps of God.

15:3
Deut 32:3,4;
Ps 111:2;
145:17;
Hos 14:9

3   And they *sang the song of Moses the bond-servant of God and the song of the Lamb, saying,

"**G**reat and marvelous are Thy works,
O Lord God, the Almighty;
Righteous and true are Thy ways,
Thou King of the [23]nations.

15:4
Jer 10:7;
Is 66:23

4   "Who will not fear, O Lord, and glorify Thy name?
For Thou alone art holy;
For ALL THE NATIONS WILL COME AND WORSHIP BEFORE THEE,
For Thy righteous acts have been revealed."

15:5
Rev 11:19;
Num 1:50

5   After these things I looked, and the temple of the tabernacle of testimony in heaven was opened,

15:6
Rev 14:15;
v. 1; Rev 1:13

6   and the seven angels who had the seven plagues came out of the temple, clothed in [24]linen, clean *and* bright, and girded around their breasts with golden girdles.

15:7
Rev 4:6,9;
10:6

7   And one of the four living creatures gave to the seven angels seven golden bowls full of the wrath of God, who lives forever and ever.

15:8
Ex 40:34;
1 Kin 8:10;
Is 6:4

8   And the temple was filled with smoke from the glory of God and from His power; and no one was able to enter the temple until the seven plagues of the seven angels were finished.

16:1
Rev 15:1

16 And I heard a loud voice from the temple, saying to the seven angels, "Go and pour out the seven bowls of the wrath of God into the earth."

2. *The first bowl: sores on men*

16:2
Rev 8:7;
Ex 9:9-11;
Rev 13:15-17

2   And the first *angel* went and poured out his bowl into the earth; and it became a loathsome and malignant sore upon the men who had the mark of the beast and who worshiped his image.

3. *The second bowl: the sea becomes like blood*

16:3
Rev 8:8,9;
Ex 17:17-21

3   And the second *angel* poured out his bowl into the sea, and it became blood like *that* of a dead man; and every living [25]thing in the sea died.

4. *The third bowl: rivers and fountains become blood*

16:4
Rev 8:10;
Ex 7:17-21

4   And the third *angel* poured out his bowl into the rivers and the springs of waters; and [26]they became blood.

16:5
Rev 15:3;
11:17; 15:4

5   And I heard the angel of the waters saying, "Righteous art Thou, who art and who wast, O Holy One, because Thou didst judge these things;

16:6
Rev 17:6;
18:24;
Is 49:26

6   for they poured out the blood of saints and prophets, and Thou hast given them blood to drink. They deserve it."

16:7
Rev 6:9;
14:18; 15:3;
19:2

7   And I heard the altar saying, "Yes, O Lord God, the Almighty, true and righteous are Thy judgments."

5. *The fourth bowl: fierce heat of the sun*

16:8
Rev 8:12;
14:18

8   And the fourth *angel* poured out his bowl upon the sun; and it was given to it to scorch men with fire.

16:9
Rev 2:21;
11:13

9   And men were scorched with fierce heat; and they blasphemed the name of God who has the power over these plagues; and they did not repent, so as to give Him glory.

---

[23]Some ancient mss. read *ages* [24]Some mss. read *stone* [25]Lit., *soul*. Some ancient mss. read *thing, the things in the sea.*
[26]Some ancient mss. read *it became*

6. The fifth bowl: darkness

10 And the fifth *angel* poured out his bowl upon the throne of the beast; and his kingdom became darkened; and they gnawed their tongues because of pain,

11 and they blasphemed the God of heaven because of their pains and their sores; and they did not repent of their deeds.

7. The sixth bowl: the foul spirits prepare for Armageddon

12 And the sixth *angel* poured out his bowl upon the great river, the Euphrates; and its water was dried up, that the way might be prepared for the kings from the east.

13 And I saw *coming* out of the mouth of the dragon and out of the mouth of the beast and out of the mouth of the false prophet, three unclean spirits like frogs;

14 for they are spirits of demons, performing signs, which go out to the kings of the whole world, to gather them together for the war of the great day of God, the Almighty.

15 ("Behold, I am coming like a thief. Blessed is the one who stays awake and keeps his garments, lest he walk about naked and men see his shame.")

16 And they gathered them together to the place which in Hebrew is called [27]HarMagedon.

8. The seventh bowl: the earthquake

17 And the seventh *angel* poured out his bowl upon the air; and a loud voice came out of the temple from the throne, saying, "It is done."

18 And there were flashes of lightning and sounds and peals of thunder; and there was a great earthquake, such as there had not been since man came to be upon the earth, so great an earthquake *was it, and* so mighty.

19 And the great city was split into three parts, and the cities of the nations fell. And Babylon the great was remembered before God, to give her the cup of the wine of His fierce wrath.

20 And every island fled away, and the mountains were not found.

21 And huge hailstones, about [28]one hundred pounds each, *came down from heaven upon men; and men blasphemed God because of the plague of the hail, because its plague *was extremely severe.

G. *The judgment of Babylon*

1. The great harlot

17 And one of the seven angels who had the seven bowls came and spoke with me, saying, "Come here, I shall show you the judgment of the great harlot who sits on many waters,

2 with whom the kings of the earth committed *acts of* immorality, and those who dwell on the earth were made drunk with the wine of her immorality."

3 And he carried me away [29]in the Spirit into a wilderness; and I saw a woman sitting on a scarlet beast, full of blasphemous names, having seven heads and ten horns.

4 And the woman was clothed in purple and scarlet, and adorned with gold and precious stones and pearls, having in her hand a gold cup full of abominations and of the unclean things of her immorality,

5 and upon her forehead a name *was* written, a mystery, "BABYLON THE GREAT, THE MOTHER OF HARLOTS AND OF THE ABOMINATIONS OF THE EARTH."

6 And I saw the woman drunk with the blood of the saints, and with the blood of the witnesses of Jesus. And when I saw her, I wondered greatly.

2. The mystery of the harlot and the beast explained

7 And the angel said to me, "Why do you wonder? I shall tell you the mystery

---

16:10 Rev 13:2; 9:2; 11:10
16:11 vv. 9,21; Rev 11:13; 2:21
16:12 Rev 9:14; Is 41:2
16:13 Rev 12:3; 13:1; 19:20
16:14 1 Tim 4:1; Rev 13:13; 3:10; 17:14
16:15 1 Thess 5:2; 2 Cor 5:3
*16:16 Rev 19:19; 9:11; 2 Kin 23:29, 30
16:17 Eph 2:2; Rev 11:15; 14:15; 21:6
16:18 Rev 4:5; 6:12; Dan 12:1
16:19 Rev 17:18; 14:8; 18:5; 14:10
16:20 Rev 6:14
16:21 Rev 11:19; Ex 9:23

17:1 Rev 21:9; 16:19; 19:2; Jer 51:13
17:2 Rev 18:3; 14:8
17:3 Rev 12:3,6,14
17:4 Jer 51:7; Rev 18:16; 18:6
17:5 2 Thess 2:7; Rev 14:8; 16:19; 18:9
17:6 Rev 18:24; 13:15; 12:11
17:7 vv. 5,3,9

---

[27]Some authorities read *Armageddon*   [28]Lit., *the weight of a talent*   [29]Or, *in spirit*

16:16 Har-Magedon (Armageddon) is the name chosen by John to describe the final battle at the end of the age when the forces of good and evil clash. Evil will be defeated and destroyed. God will triumph. *Amillennialists* hold this to be the beginning of the end of history, for Christ will deliver the kingdom to His Father. *Premillennialists* hold that Christ's triumph in this battle at His second advent opens the period of his thousand-year reign on earth. (Read also 16:12–16 in this connection.) (See note to 2 Chr. 35:22 for location of Har-Magedon.)

of the woman and of the beast that carries her, which has the seven heads and the ten horns.

8 "The beast that you saw was and is not, and is about to come up out of the abyss and [30]to go to destruction. And those who dwell on the earth will wonder, whose name has not been written in the book of life from the foundation of the world, when they see the beast, that he was and is not and will come.

9 "Here is the mind which has wisdom. The seven heads are seven mountains on which the woman sits,

10 and they are seven kings; five have fallen, one is, the other has not yet come; and when he comes, he must remain a little while.

11 "And the beast which was and is not, is himself also an eighth, and is *one* of the seven, and he goes to destruction.

12 "And the ten horns which you saw are ten kings, who have not yet received a kingdom, but they receive authority as kings with the beast for one hour.

13 "These have one purpose and they give their power and authority to the beast.

14 "These will wage war against the Lamb, and the Lamb will overcome them, because He is Lord of lords and King of kings, and those who are with Him *are the* called and chosen and faithful."

15 And he *said to me, "The waters which you saw where the harlot sits, are peoples and multitudes and nations and tongues.

16 "And the ten horns which you saw, and the beast, these will hate the harlot and will make her desolate and naked, and will eat her flesh and will burn her up with fire.

17 "For God has put it in their hearts to execute His purpose by having a common purpose, and by giving their kingdom to the beast, until the words of God should be fulfilled.

18 "And the woman whom you saw is the great city, which reigns over the kings of the earth."

3. The doom of Babylon announced

18 After these things I saw another angel coming down from heaven, having great authority, and the earth was illumined with his glory.

2 And he cried out with a mighty voice, saying, "Fallen, fallen is Babylon the great! And she has become a dwelling place of demons and a prison of every unclean spirit, and a prison of every unclean and hateful bird.

3 "For all the nations [31]have drunk of the wine of the passion of her immorality, and the kings of the earth have committed *acts of* immorality with her, and the merchants of the earth have become rich by the wealth of her sensuality."

4. The call to come out of Babylon

4 And I heard another voice from heaven, saying, "Come out of her, my people, that you may not participate in her sins and that you may not receive of her plagues;

5 for her sins have piled up as high as heaven, and God has remembered her iniquities.

6 "Pay her back even as she has paid, and give back *to her* double according to her deeds; in the cup which she has mixed, mix twice as much for her.

7 "To the degree that she glorified herself and lived sensuously, to the same degree give her torment and mourning; for she says in her heart, 'I SIT *as* A QUEEN AND I AM NOT A WIDOW, and will never see mourning.'

8 "For this reason in one day her plagues will come, pestilence and mourning and famine, and she will be burned up with fire; for the Lord God who judges her is strong.

5. The lament of the world over Babylon

9 "And the kings of the earth, who committed *acts of* immorality and lived sensuously with her, will weep and lament over her when they see the smoke of her burning,

10 standing at a distance because of the fear of her torment, saying, 'Woe, woe, the great city, Babylon, the strong city! For in one hour your judgment has come.'

17:8 Rev 11:7; 13:10; 3:10; 13:3,8
17:9 Rev 13:18
17:11 v. 8
17:12 Dan 7:20; Rev 13:1; 18:10,17,19
17:13 v. 17
17:14 Rev 16:14; 1 Tim 6:15; Rev 19:16; Matt 22:14
17:15 Is 8:7; Rev 5:9; 13:7
17:16 Rev 18:17,19; Ezek 16:37, 39; Rev 19:18
18:8
17:17 2 Thess 2:11; Rev 10:7
17:18 Rev 16:19

18:1 Rev 17:1; 10:1; Ezek 43:2
18:2 Rev 14:8; Is 13:21,22; Jer 50:39
18:3 Rev 14:8; Jer 25:15,27

18:4 Is 48:20; Jer 50:8; 2 Cor 6:17
18:5 Jer 51:9; Rev 16:19
18:6 Ps 137:8; Jer 50:15; Rev 14:10; 16:19
18:7 Ezek 28:2-8; Is 47:7,8; Zeph 2:15
18:8 Is 47:9; Rev 17:16; Jer 50:34; Rev 11:17

18:9 Rev 17:2; Jer 50:46; v. 18; Rev 19:3
18:10 vv. 15,17,16, 19

---

[30]Some ancient mss. read *he goes*   [31]Many ancient mss. read *have fallen by*

11 "And the merchants of the earth weep and mourn over her, because no one buys their cargoes any more;

12 cargoes of gold and silver and precious stones and pearls and fine linen and purple and silk and scarlet, and every *kind of* citron wood and every article of ivory and every article *made* from very costly wood and bronze and iron and marble,

13 and cinnamon and spice and incense and perfume and frankincense and wine and olive oil and fine flour and wheat and cattle and sheep, and *cargoes* of horses and chariots and slaves and human lives.

14 "And the fruit you long for has gone from you, and all things that were luxurious and splendid have passed away from you and *men* will no longer find them.

15 "The merchants of these things, who became rich from her, will stand at a distance because of the fear of her torment, weeping and mourning,

16 saying, 'Woe, woe, the great city, she who was clothed in fine linen and purple and scarlet, and adorned with gold and precious stones and pearls;

17 for in one hour such great wealth has been laid waste!' And every shipmaster and every passenger and sailor, and as many as make their living by the sea, stood at a distance,

18 and were crying out as they saw the smoke of her burning, saying, 'What *city* is like the great city?'

19 "And they threw dust on their heads and were crying out, weeping and mourning, saying, 'Woe, woe, the great city, in which all who had ships at sea became rich by her wealth, for in one hour she has been laid waste!'

6. *Heaven's rejoicing over Babylon's fall*

20 "Rejoice over her, O heaven, and you saints and apostles and prophets, because God has pronounced judgment for you against her."

7. *Babylon's doom symbolically portrayed*

21 And a strong angel took up a stone like a great millstone and threw it into the sea, saying, "Thus will Babylon, the great city, be thrown down with violence, and will not be found any longer.

22 "And the sound of harpists and musicians and flute-players and trumpeters will not be heard in you any longer; and no craftsman of any craft will be found in you any longer; and the sound of a mill will not be heard in you any longer;

23 and the light of a lamp will not shine in you any longer; and the voice of the bridegroom and bride will not be heard in you any longer; for your merchants were the great men of the earth, because all the nations were deceived by your sorcery.

24 "And in her was found the blood of prophets and of saints and of all who have been slain on the earth."

8. *Praise to God for judgment: the marriage supper of the Lamb*

19 After these things I heard, as it were, a loud voice of a great multitude in heaven, saying,

"Hallelujah! Salvation and glory and power belong to our God;

2 BECAUSE HIS JUDGMENTS ARE TRUE AND RIGHTEOUS; for He has judged the great harlot who was corrupting the earth with her immorality, and HE HAS AVENGED THE BLOOD OF HIS BOND-SERVANTS ON HER."

3 And a second time they said, "Hallelujah! HER SMOKE RISES UP FOREVER AND EVER."

4 And the twenty-four elders and the four living creatures fell down and worshiped God who sits on the throne saying, "Amen. Hallelujah!"

5 And a voice came from the throne, saying,

"Give praise to our God, all you His bond-servants, you who fear Him, the small and the great."

6 And I heard, as it were, the voice of a great multitude and as the sound of many waters and as the sound of mighty peals of thunder, saying,

"Hallelujah! For the Lord our God, the Almighty, reigns.

7 "Let us rejoice and be glad and give the glory to Him, for the marriage of the Lamb has come and His bride has made herself ready."

19:7 The marriage supper of the Lamb apparently precedes the second advent of Christ, since it is referred to first. In attendance at the supper are the *saints*, by which is meant the saved of all ages, i.e., those who were redeemed before and after Calvary and who have been declared righteous in Jesus Christ.

Cross references (margin):

18:11 v. 3; Ezek 27:27
18:12 Rev 17:4
18:13 Ezek 27:13
18:15 Ezek 27:36, 31
18:16 Rev 17:4
18:17 Rev 17:16; Is 23:14; Ezek 27:29
18:18 Ezek 27:30; Rev 13:4
18:19 Josh 7:6; Job 2:12; Ezek 27:30
18:20 Is 44:23; Jer 51:48; Rev 19:2
18:21 Jer 51:63; Rev 12:8
18:22 Is 24:8; Ezek 26:13; Jer 25:10
18:23 Jer 25:10; 7:34; 16:9; Is 23:8; Nah 3:4
18:24 Rev 17:6; Jer 51:49
19:1 Rev 11:15; 4:11; 7:10,12; 12:10
19:2 Deut 32:43; Rev 6:10
19:3 Is 34:10; Rev 14:11
19:4 Rev 4:4,6; 5:14
19:5 Ps 134:1; Rev 11:18; 20:12
19:6 Rev 11:15,17; 14:2
*19:7 Matt 22:2; 25:10; 2 Cor 11:2; Eph 5:32; Rev 21:2,9

19:8
Rev 15:4

19:9
v. 10;
Rev 1:19;
Luke 14:15;
Rev 21:5
19:10
Rev 22:8;
Acts 10:26;
Rev 22:9;
12:17

19:11
Rev 15:5;
6:2; 3:14;
Is 11:4
19:12
Rev 1:14;
6:2; 2:17
19:13
Is 63:2,3;
John 1:1
19:14
v. 8
19:15
Is 11:4;
2 Thess 2:8;
Ps 2:9;
Rev 2:27;
14:19,20
19:16
Dan 2:47;
Rev 17:14
19:17
Rev 8:13;
Ezek 39:17
19:18
Ezek 39:18-20;
Rev 11:18

19:19
Rev 11:7;
16:14,16
19:20
Rev 16:13;
13:12ff;
Dan 7:11;
Rev 20:10;
14:10; 21:8
19:21
vv. 11,19,15,
17

20:1
Rev 10:1;
1:18; 9:1
*20:2
2 Pet 2:4;
Jude 6;
Rev 12:9

8   And it was given to her to clothe herself in fine linen, bright *and* clean; for the fine linen is the righteous acts of the saints.

9   And he *said to me, "Write, 'Blessed are those who are invited to the marriage supper of the Lamb.' " And he *said to me, "These are true words of God."

10   And I fell at his feet to worship him. And he *said to me, "Do not do that; I am a fellow servant of yours and your brethren who hold the testimony of Jesus; worship God. For the testimony of Jesus is the spirit of prophecy."

H. *The defeat of the beast and the false prophet*

11   And I saw heaven opened; and behold, a white horse, and He who sat upon it *is* called Faithful and True; and in righteousness He judges and wages war.

12   And His eyes *are* a flame of fire, and upon His head *are* many diadems; and He has a name written *upon Him* which no one knows except Himself.

13   And *He is* clothed with a robe dipped in blood; and His name is called The Word of God.

14   And the armies which are in heaven, clothed in fine linen, white *and* clean, were following Him on white horses.

15   And from His mouth comes a sharp sword, so that with it He may smite the nations; and He will rule them with a rod of iron; and He treads the wine press of the fierce wrath of God, the Almighty.

16   And on His robe and on His thigh He has a name written, "KING OF KINGS, AND LORD OF LORDS."

17   And I saw an angel standing in the sun; and he cried out with a loud voice, saying to all the birds which fly in midheaven, "Come, assemble for the great supper of God;

18   in order that you may eat the flesh of kings and the flesh of ³²commanders and the flesh of mighty men and the flesh of horses and of those who sit on them and the flesh of all men, both free men and slaves, and small and great."

19   And I saw the beast and the kings of the earth and their armies, assembled to make war against Him who sat upon the horse, and against His army.

20   And the beast was seized, and with him the false prophet who performed the signs in his presence, by which he deceived those who had received the mark of the beast and those who worshiped his image; these two were thrown alive into the lake of fire which burns with brimstone.

21   And the rest were killed with the sword which came from the mouth of Him who sat upon the horse, and all the birds were filled with their flesh.

I. *The binding of Satan*

20   And I saw an angel coming down from heaven, having the key of the abyss and a great chain in his hand.

2   And he laid hold of the dragon, the serpent of old, who is the devil and Satan, and bound him for a thousand years,

---

³²I.e., chiliarchs, in command of one thousand troops

20:2 There are three general views of the millennium that find favor today: (1) The *postmillennialist* holds that the millennium is a period of world history in which the reign of Christ has been established through His church, which is destined to conquer the world with the gospel, and at the end of this golden age Christ will personally return to earth and inaugurate a new heaven and a new earth. (2) The *amillennialist* denies that there will ever be a literal earth-rule of a thousand years, either before or after Christ's return. By some the *thousand* years are taken to be simply symbolic of eternity (although v. 5 poses a serious problem for this view), and the only reign spoken of in this passage is an eternal heavenly reign. Christ's return to earth will simply usher in a "new heaven and a new earth," and His only eschatological rule will be celestial, not in this world. By others the one thousand years of Christ's reign are taken to be the period between the first and second comings of Christ. (3) The *premillennialist* looks for the return of Christ to earth at the beginning of a literal, thousand-year reign on the earth, when "the earth will be full of the knowledge of the Lord as the waters cover the sea" and all the nations of mankind will be completely subservient to the Lord Jesus.

At the end of this period Satan will be released again in order to stir up the secretly rebellious portion of mankind to a final open revolt against God (vv. 7–9). After a second "Armageddon," the new heavens and the new earth will be ushered in.

Postmillennialism does not enjoy the favor it once did in Augustine's time and in the optimistic period of 1880–1910, for subsequent global conflicts have dimmed that optimism. As for *amillennialism*, it divests 20:2,7 of real significance and also the numerous Old Testament passages that speak of the ultimate regathering of the nation Israel to Palestine and a time of peace and prosperity for that nation. The issues at stake are not ones that should divide Christians, since all three groups bow to the authority of Scripture, nor does a saving faith make mandatory the adoption of one view as against the others. It should perhaps be added that there is still another school of thought that does not regard any of these general views seriously, but looks upon Revelation as portraying an enduring spiritual struggle between the forces of good and evil in which the heavenly kingdom of God will finally triumph. To these interpreters none of the historical or geographical details have anything more

3   and threw him into the abyss, and shut *it* and sealed *it* over him, so that he should not deceive the nations any longer, until the thousand years were completed; after these things he must be released for a short time.

20:3
Dan 6:17;
Rev 12:9

J. *The millennial reign of Christ*

4   And I saw thrones, and they sat upon them, and judgment was given to them. And I *saw* the souls of those who had been beheaded because of the testimony of Jesus and because of the word of God, and those who had not worshiped the beast or his image, and had not received the mark upon their forehead and upon their hand; and they came to life and reigned with Christ for a thousand years.

20:4
Dan 7:9,22,
27; Rev 6:9;
13:12,15,16

5   The rest of the dead did not come to life until the thousand years were completed. This is the first resurrection.

*20:5
Luke 14:14;
Phil 3:11;
1 Thess 4:16

6   Blessed and holy is the one who has a part in the first resurrection; over these the second death has no power, but they will be priests of God and of Christ and will reign with Him for a thousand years.

20:6
Rev 14:13;
2:11; 21:8;
1:6

K. *The loosing of Satan*

7   And when the thousand years are completed, Satan will be released from his prison,

20:7
v. 2

8   and will come out to deceive the nations which are in the four corners of the earth, Gog and Magog, to gather them together for the war; the number of them is like the sand of the seashore.

20:8
Ezek 38:2;
39:1;
Rev 16:14;
Heb 11:12

9   And they came up on the broad plain of the earth and surrounded the camp of the saints and the beloved city, and fire came down from heaven and devoured them.

20:9
Ezek 38:9,22;
39:6

10   And the devil who deceived them was thrown into the lake of fire and brimstone, where the beast and the false prophet are also; and they will be tormented day and night forever and ever.

*20:10
vv. 3,8

L. *The great white throne judgment*

11   And I saw a great white throne and Him who sat upon it, from whose presence earth and heaven fled away, and no place was found for them.

*20:11f
Rev 4:2;
21:1;
Dan 2:35;
Rev 12:8

12   And I saw the dead, the great and the small, standing before the throne, and books were opened; and another book was opened, which is *the book* of life; and the dead were judged from the things which were written in the books, according to their deeds.

20:12
Matt 16:27;
Rev 2:3;
22:12

13   And the sea gave up the dead which were in it, and death and Hades gave up the dead which were in them; and they were judged, every one *of them* according to their deeds.

20:13
Rev 6:8;
Is 26:19;
Rev 2:23

14   And death and Hades were thrown into the lake of fire. This is the second death, the lake of fire.

20:14
1 Cor 15:26;
Rev 6:8

---

than symbolic significance.

20:5 Here John speaks of *the first resurrection.* From this, many understand that the Scriptures teach us that there will be two resurrections at the end of the present age. The first is the resurrection of the righteous dead. Over them the second death has no power. Those who are so resurrected reign with Christ for a thousand years. After this comes the second resurrection. This distinction lends support to the *premillennial* view. Others hold that the first resurrection referred to here is for a single group of people, the martyrs of v. 4. These share Christ's reign for a thousand years. A general resurrection of the other dead follows.

20:10 Scripture does not answer every question that men raise about the person and work of Satan. His existence and malign influence cannot be denied, however, without denying the Biblical evidences. Apparently Satan was one of God's holy angels who fell through sin and whose ultimate destiny is *the lake of fire.* Many hold that the serpent of Gen. 3:1 was Satan. Jesus was tempted by the devil (Matt. 4:1; Luke 4:2). Paul speaks of him as *the prince of the power of the air* (Eph. 2:2). Christ calls him *the ruler of this world* (John 12:31). Here in chapter 20 John speaks of Satan as *bound for a thousand years* (v. 2), and then *released from his prison* (v. 7), and then *thrown into the lake of fire and brimstone* (v. 10).

Some have challenged the Scriptural teaching of the eternal punishment of the wicked dead. They teach either a universalism in which all are ultimately saved, or annihilationism in which the wicked dead cease to exist in any form whatever. Yet the doctrine of eternal, conscious punishment is well established in Scripture. Compare the use of the following terms: (1) eternal fire (Matt. 25:41); (2) unquenchable fire (Mark 9:48); (3) the lake that burns with fire and brimstone (21:8); and (4) the fact that the same terms are used in the Greek both for the eternal existence and sovereignty of God as are used for endless death or separation from God. In each case the phrase is *eis tous aiōnas tōn aiōnōn,* "unto the ages of ages" (cf. 1:18; 11:15; 14:11; 20:10).

20:11,12 The last judgment will take place, so many believe, at the end of the thousand years when the resurrected wicked dead shall be judged at the great white throne of Jesus Christ. Many see in this passage a reference to three books, the book of life and two other books, which are thought to be the book of memory and the book of works. The absence of the names of the wicked dead from the book of life is reason for the sentence that is pronounced on them. They are cast into the lake of fire. There is no appeal from His sentence. The fact that the works of the wicked are judged, indicates there are degrees of punishment for these malefactors (Luke 12:47,48).

15 And if anyone's name was not found written in the book of life, he was thrown into the lake of fire.

M. *The new heaven and the new earth*

21 And I saw a new heaven and a new earth; for the first heaven and the first earth passed away, and there is no longer *any* sea.
2 And I saw the holy city, new Jerusalem, coming down out of heaven from God, made ready as a bride adorned for her husband.
3 And I heard a loud voice from the throne, saying, "Behold, the tabernacle of God is among men, and He shall dwell among them, and they shall be His people, and God Himself shall be among them,[33]
4 and He shall wipe away every tear from their eyes; and there shall no longer be *any* death; there shall no longer be *any* mourning, or crying, or pain; the first things have passed away."
5 And He who sits on the throne said, "Behold, I am making all things new." And He *said, "Write, for these words are faithful and true."
6 And He said to me, "It is done. I am the Alpha and the Omega, the beginning and the end. I will give to the one who thirsts from the spring of the water of life without cost.
7 "He who overcomes shall inherit these things, and I will be his God and he will be My son.   *Ie, all the unrepentant ones*
8 "But for the cowardly and unbelieving and abominable and murderers and immoral persons and sorcerers and idolaters and all liars, their part *will be* in the lake that burns with fire and brimstone, which is the second death."

N. *The new Jerusalem*

1. *The city*

9 And one of the seven angels who had the seven bowls full of the seven last plagues, came and spoke with me, saying, "Come here, I shall show you the bride, the wife of the Lamb."
10 And he carried me away [34]in the Spirit to a great and high mountain, and showed me the holy city, Jerusalem, coming down out of heaven from God,
11 having the glory of God. Her brilliance was like a very costly stone, as a stone of crystal-clear jasper.
12 It had a great and high wall, with twelve gates, and at the gates twelve angels; and names *were* written on them, which are *those* of the twelve tribes of the sons of Israel.
13 *There were* three gates on the east and three gates on the north and three gates on the south and three gates on the west.
14 And the wall of the city had twelve foundation stones, and on them *were* the twelve names of the twelve apostles of the Lamb.

2. *Its measurements*

15 And the one who spoke with me had a gold measuring rod to measure the city, and its gates and its wall.
16 And the city is laid out as a square, and its length is as great as the width; and he measured the city with the rod, [35]fifteen hundred miles; its length and width and height are equal.
17 And he measured its wall, [36]seventy-two yards, *according to* human measurements, which are *also* angelic *measurements*.
18 And the material of the wall was jasper; and the city was pure gold, like clear glass.
19 The foundation stones of the city wall were adorned with every kind of precious stone. The first foundation stone was jasper; the second, sapphire; the third, chalcedony; the fourth, emerald;

[33]Some ancient mss. add, and be *their God*   [34]Or, *in spirit*   [35]Lit., *twelve thousand stadia;* a stadion was about 600 ft.   [36]Lit., *one hundred forty-four cubits*

21:2 The new Jerusalem is the future abode of the people of God and becomes their eternal habitation after the judgment of the great white throne (Rev. 20:11ff.). There is to be *a new heaven and a new earth* (21:1); the Holy City will come down out of heaven from God. Its boundaries and its furniture and inhabitants are all described. That the description is written in poetic and symbolic language is obvious, but the new Jerusalem inhabitants may rest assured that its beauty and glory will far transcend their fondest imagination.

Margin references: 21:1 Is 65:17; 2 Pet 3:13; Rev 20:11 *21:2 Heb 11:10; 12:22; Rev 3:12 21:3 Ezek 37:27; 2 Cor 6:16; Rev 7:15 21:4 Rev 7:17; 1 Cor 15:26; Rev 20:14; Is 35:10; 65:19 21:5 Rev 4:9; 20:11; Is 43:19; Rev 19:9 21:6 Rev 16:17; 1:8; 22:13; John 4:10 21:7 Rev 2:7; v. 3 21:8 Heb 12:14; Rev 22:15; 19:20; 2:11 21:9 Rev 15:1,6,7; 20:14ff 21:10 Rev 1:10; Ezek 40:2; Rev 17:3 21:11 Rev 15:8; 22:5; 4:6 21:12 Ezek 48:31-34 21:14 Matt 16:18; Eph 2:20 21:15 Rev 11:1 21:18 vv. 11,19,21; Rev 4:6 21:19 Is 54:11,12; vv. 11,18; Rev 4:3

20 the fifth, sardonyx; the sixth, sardius; the seventh, chrysolite; the eighth, beryl; the ninth, topaz; the tenth, chrysoprase; the eleventh, jacinth; the twelfth, amethyst.

21 And the twelve gates were twelve pearls; each one of the gates was a single pearl. And the street of the city was pure gold, like transparent glass.

3. Its light

22 And I saw no temple in it, for the Lord God, the Almighty, and the Lamb, are its temple.

23 And the city has no need of the sun or of the moon to shine upon it, for the glory of God has illumined it, and its lamp *is* the Lamb.

24 And the nations shall walk by its light, and the kings of the earth shall bring their glory into it.

25 And in the daytime (for there shall be no night there) its gates shall never be closed;

26 and they shall bring the glory and the honor of the nations into it;

27 and nothing unclean and no one who practices abomination and lying, shall ever come into it, but only those whose names are written in the Lamb's book of life.

4. Its blessings

22 And he showed me a river of the water of life, clear as crystal, coming from the throne of God and of [37]the Lamb,

2 in the middle of its street. And on either side of the river was the tree of life, bearing twelve [38]*kinds of* fruit, yielding its fruit every month; and the leaves of the tree were for the healing of the nations.

3 And there shall no longer be any curse; and the throne of God and of the Lamb shall be in it, and His bond-servants shall serve Him;

4 and they shall see His face, and His name *shall be* on their foreheads.

5 And there shall no longer be *any* night; and they shall not have need of the light of a lamp nor the light of the sun, because the Lord God shall illumine them; and they shall reign forever and ever.

IV. *Epilogue (22:6–21)*

A. *Testimony to the truth of the revelation*

6 And he said to me, "These words are faithful and true"; and the Lord, the God of the spirits of the prophets, sent His angel to show to His bond-servants the things which must shortly take place.

7 "And behold, I am coming quickly. Blessed is he who heeds the words of the prophecy of this book."

8 And I, John, am the one who heard and saw these things. And when I heard and saw, I fell down to worship at the feet of the angel who showed me these things.

9 And he *said to me, "Do not do that; I am a fellow servant of yours and of your brethren the prophets and of those who heed the words of this book; worship God."

B. *The distinction drawn*

10 And he *said to me, "Do not seal up the words of the prophecy of this book, for the time is near.

11 "Let the one who does wrong, still do wrong; and let the one who is filthy, still be filthy; and let the one who is righteous, still practice righteousness; and let the one who is holy, still keep himself holy."

12 "Behold, I am coming quickly, and My reward *is* with Me, to render to every man according to what he has done.

---

[37]Or, *the Lamb. In the middle of its street, and on either side of the river, was*   [38]Or, *crops of fruit*

22:11 *Let the one who does wrong, still do wrong, and let the one who is filthy, still be filthy.* This phrase points up plainly the truth that the final condition of the wicked is one of hopelessness. There is no evidence here of universal salvation for all people. Rather, the door is shut forever, and

those who remain outside shall never find entrance. But this dark picture must be weighed against the gracious and all-embracing invitation of v. 17, which opens the doors of heaven to all who heed the voice of God and receive Jesus Christ as their sin-bearer and savior.

Margin references:

21:20 Rev 4:3

21:21 vv. 15,25,18

21:22 John 4:21,23; Rev 1:8; 5:6
21:23 Is 24:23; 60:19,20; Rev 22:5
21:24 Is 60:3,5
21:25 Is 60:11; Zech 14:7; Rev 22:5
21:27 Is 52:1; Joel 3:17; Rev 22:14; 3:5

22:1 Ezek 47:1; Zech 14:8; Rev 4:6
22:2 Gen 2:9; Rev 2:7;
22:3 Ezek 47:12
22:3 Zech 14:11; Rev 7:15
22:4 Matt 5:8; Rev 14:1
22:5 Rev 21:25,23; Dan 7:27

22:6 Rev 1:1; 19:19; 21:5
22:7 Rev 3:11; 1:3
22:8 Rev 1:1; 19:10
22:9 Rev 19:10; 1:1; vv. 10, 18,19; Rev 21:2

22:10 Dan 8:26; Rev 1:3
*22:11 Dan 12:10; Ezek 3:27
22:12 Is 40:10; Jer 17:10; Rev 2:23

22:13
Rev 1:8,17;
21:6

13 "I am the Alpha and the Omega, the first and the last, the beginning and the end."

14 Blessed are those who wash their robes, that they may have the right to the tree of life, and may enter by the gates into the city.

22:15
Gal 5:19ff;
Col 3:6;
Phil 3:2

15 Outside are the dogs and the sorcerers and the immoral persons and the murderers and the idolaters, and everyone who loves and practices lying.

C. *The invitation given*

22:16
Rev 1:1; 5:5;
Zech 6:12;
2 Pet 1:19;
Rev 2:28
22:17
Rev 2:7;
21:2; Is 55:1;
Rev 21:6
22:18
Deut 4:2;
Prov 30:6;
Rev 15:6;
16:21

16 "I, Jesus, have sent My angel to testify to you these things for the churches. I am the root and the offspring of David, the bright morning star."

17 And the Spirit and the bride say, "Come." And let the one who hears say, "Come." And let the one who is thirsty come; let the one who wishes take the water of life without cost.

18 I testify to everyone who hears the words of the prophecy of this book: if anyone adds to them, God shall add to him the plagues which are written in this book;

19 and if anyone takes away from the words of the book of this prophecy, God shall take away his part from the tree of life and from the holy city, which are written in this book.

*22:20
Rev 1:2;
2 Tim 4:8;
Rom 16:20;
2 Thess 3:18

20 He who testifies to these things says, "Yes, I am coming quickly." Amen. Come, Lord Jesus.

D. *The benediction*

21 The grace of the Lord Jesus be with [39]all. Amen.

[39]Some ancient mss. read *the saints*

22:20 The Bible opens with man in the Garden of Eden in happiness and contentment. It ends with man in the new Jerusalem, where he is again happy and contented. It is fitting that John should close the book of the Revelation with a prayer in which he breathes out his fervent hope that paradise restored will come about quickly.

INDEX TO THE
Annotations

INDEX TO THE ANNOTATIONS

Concordance

NEW AMERICAN STANDARD BIBLE

The New American Standard
CONCORDANCE
to the Old and New Testaments

This is a collection of the principal **proper nouns** and **key words** in Scripture. The following format is used: Descriptive phrases and references are listed under each **proper noun.** If the descriptive phrases are numbered, this indicates different individuals or identities. **Key words** are immediately followed by explanatory words or synonyms. Under each **key word** examples are listed with text and reference. The **key word** is abbreviated in the text to its first letter, e.g., "abide" is "a". Variants add suffixes, e.g., "abides" appears as "**a-s**" and "abiding" appears as "**a-ing**".

A

AARON
brother of Moses	Ex 4:14
spokesman for Moses	
	Ex 4:28;7:1-2
as priest	Ex 28:1;29:44
rod of	Num 17:8; Heb 9:4
critical of Moses	Num 12:1
death	Deut 10:6

ABADDON
1 region of dead	
	Job 26:6; Prov 15:11
2 angel of bottomless pit	Rev 9:11

ABANDON leave
LORD has a-ed us	Judg 6:13
not a His people	1 Sam 12:22
a the remnant	2 Kin 21:14
not a my soul to	Ps 16:10
not a His people	Ps 94:14
a-ed My inheritance	Jer 12:7
a my soul to Hades	Acts 2:27

ABASE humble
man will be a-d	Is 2:11
lofty will be a-d	Is 10:33
a the haughtiness	Is 13:11
a-d before all	Mal 2:9

ABATED decreased
water was a	Gen 8:8
his vigor a	Deut 34:7

ABBA father
A! Father	Mark 14:36
we cry out, A!	Rom 8:15

ABED-NEGO
Hebrew name Azariah	
friend of Daniel	Dan 1:6,7
faithful to God	Dan 3:16,17
cast into furnace	Dan 3:20

ABEL
son of Adam	Gen 4:2
shepherd	Gen 4:2
favored by God	Gen 4:4
slain by Cain	Gen 4:8
called righteous	Matt 23:35

ABHOR despise, detest
associates a me	Job 19:19
greatly a-red Israel	Ps 78:59
nations will a him	Prov 24:24
To the One a-red	Is 49:7
A what is evil	Rom 12:9

ABIB
early name of first month of	
Hebrew calendar	Ex 34:18
month of Passover and	
Unleavened Bread	Deut 16:1

ABIDE remain, stay
LORD a-s forever	Ps 9:7
a in Thy tent	Ps 15:1
a in the shadow	Ps 91:1
wrath of God a-s	John 3:36
a in My word	John 8:31
If you a in Me	John 15:7
a in My love	John 15:9
now a faith	1 Cor 13:13
word...LORD a-s	1 Pet 1:25
love of God a	1 John 3:17
God a-s in us	1 John 4:12

ABIGAIL
1 wife of Nabal	1 Sam 25:3
kind to David	1 Sam 25:18ff
wife of David	1 Sam 25:42
2 daughter of Nahash	
	2 Sam 17:25

ABIHU
son of Aaron	Ex 6:23
priest	Ex 28:1
disobeyed by God	Lev 10:1
judged by God	Lev 10:2

ABIJAH
1 son of Samuel	1 Sam 8:2
2 son of Jeroboam	1 Kin 14:1
3 son of Becher	1 Chr 7:8
4 line of Eleazar	1 Chr 24:10
5 king of Judah	2 Chr 12:16
6 Hezekiah's mother	2 Chr 29:1
7 priest	Neh 10:7;12:4

ABILITY power, strength
According to their a	Ezra 2:69
a for serving	Dan 1:4

ABIMELECH
1 king of Gerar	Gen 20:1-18
2 king of Gerar	Gen 26:1ff
3 king of Shechem	Judg 9:1ff
4 priest	1 Chr 18:16
5 Psalm title	Ps 34

ABIRAM
opposed Moses	Num 16:1ff
judged by God	Num 16:25ff

ABISHAI
brother of Joab	1 Sam 26:6
warrior of David	1 Chr 18:12
aided Abner's assassination	
	2 Sam 3:30

ABLE qualified
a to conceive	Heb 11:11
a to judge	1 Kin 3:9
a from these stones	Matt 3:9
I am a to do	Matt 9:28
Him who is a	Matt 10:28
a to separate us	Rom 8:39
what you are a	1 Cor 10:13
a to comprehend	Eph 3:18
be a to teach	2 Tim 2:2
a to save Him	Heb 5:7
One who is a	James 4:12
a to open	Rev 5:3

ABNER
Saul's commander	1 Sam 17:55
loyal to David	2 Sam 3:12ff
killed by Joab	2 Sam 3:27
mourned by David	2 Sam 3:32

ABODE habitation
a of righteousness	Jer 31:23
Our a with him	John 14:23
their proper a	Jude 6

ABOLISH
not come to a	Matt 5:17
a-ing in His flesh	Eph 2:15
who a-ed death	2 Tim 1:10

ABOMINABLE detestable
committed a deeds	Ps 14:1
your beauty a	Ezek 16:25
a idolatries	1 Pet 4:3

unbelieving and a | Rev 21:8

ABOMINATION hated things

a to the Egyptians | Ex 8:26
a into your house | Deut 7:26
seen their a-s | Deut 29:17
a to the LORD | Prov 3:32
all their a-s | Ezek 33:29
a of desolation | Matt 24:15
a-s of the earth | Rev 17:5

ABOUND excel, plentiful

faithful man will a | Prov 28:20
May your peace a | Dan 4:1
a in hope | Rom 15:13
a-ing in the work | 1 Cor 15:58
affection a-s | 2 Cor 7:15
all grace a | 2 Cor 9:8

ABOVE over

exalted a the heavens | Ps 57:5
disciple is not a | Matt 10:24
I am from a | John 8:23
a every name | Phil 2:9
exalts himself a | 2 Thess 2:4
gift is from a | James 1:17

ABRAHAM

covenant | Gen 17:1-8
promise of Isaac | Gen 17:19
asked the Lord | Gen 18:22ff
offers Isaac | Gen 22:9,10
death | Gen 25:8
righteousness of | Rom 4:3-9

ABRAHAM'S BOSOM

rabbinic terminology for Paradise
| Luke 16:22

ABRAM

called of God | Gen 12:1-3
rescued Lot | Gen 14:14-16
covenant with God | Gen 15:18
name changed | Gen 17:5

ABSALOM

son of David | 2 Sam 13:1
his revolt | 2 Sam 15:1-2
popular | 2 Sam 15:6
slain by Joab | 2 Sam 18:15

ABSENT being away

we are a one from | Gen 31:49
a in body | 1 Cor 5:3
a from the Lord | 2 Cor 5:6
a from the body | 2 Cor 5:8

ABSTAIN refrain from

a from wine | Num 6:3
a-ing from foods | 1 Tim 4:3
a from wickedness | 2 Tim 2:19
a from fleshly lusts | 1 Pet 2:11

ABUNDANCE plenty, surplus

seven years of a | Gen 41:34
a of all things | Deut 28:47
a of Thy house | Ps 36:8
a of peace | Ps 72:7
a of counselors | Prov 24:6
he who loves a | Eccl 5:10
delight yourself in a | Is 55:2
one has an a | Luke 12:15
the a of grace | Rom 5:17

ABUNDANT enough, plenteous

come...find a water | 2 Chr 32:4
a righteousness | Job 37:23
a in lovingkindness | Ps 86:5
comfort is a | 2 Cor 1:5

ABUNDANTLY

they may breed a | Gen 8:17
Populate the earth a | Gen 9:7
will prosper you a | Deut 30:9
drip upon man a | Job 36:28

ABUSE (n) insulting speech

hurling a at Him | Matt 27:39
was hurling a | Luke 23:39

ABUSE (v) hurt, molest

a-d her all night | Judg 19:25
uncircumcised...me
| 1 Chr 10:4

ABUSIVE filthy, vulgar

a speech from your | Col 3:8
strife, a language | 1 Tim 6:4

ABYSS deep, depth

depart into the a | Luke 8:31
descend into the a | Rom 10:7
angel of the a | Rev 9:11
key of the a | Rev 20:1

ACCEPT receive

a the work of | Deut 33:11
a good from God | Job 2:10
the LORD a-ed Job | Job 42:9
a-ed no chastening | Jer 2:30
hear the word and a | Mark 4:20
God has a-ed him | Rom 14:3
a one another | Rom 15:7

ACCEPTABLE pleasing

my heart Be a | Ps 19:14
sacrifice, a to God | Rom 12:1
a to the saints | Rom 15:31
now is the a time | 2 Cor 6:2
to God an a service | Heb 12:28
sacrifices a to God | 1 Pet 2:5

ACCESS approach, entry

grant you free a | Zech 3:7
our a in one Spirit | Eph 2:18

ACCOMPANY attach to, follow

who a my lord | 1 Sam 25:27
a-ied the king | 2 Sam 19:40
a-ied by trumpets | 2 Chr 5:13
that a salvation | Heb 6:9

ACCOMPLISH perform, realize

a-ed deliverance | 1 Sam 11:13
shall a my desire | 1 Kin 5:9
God...a-es all things | Ps 57:2
has a-ed His wrath | Lam 4:11
a-ed redemption | Luke 1:68
a His work | John 4:34
I am a-ing a work | Acts 13:41
when sin is a-ed | James 1:15
man can a much | James 5:16

ACCORD agreement, union

one a to fight | Josh 9:2
voices...with one a | Acts 4:24
one a in Solomon's | Acts 5:12
multitudes with one a | Acts 8:6

one a they came | Acts 12:20

ACCORDING

a to your word | Gen 30:34
Moses did; a to all | Ex 40:16
a to our sins | Ps 103:10
a to his deeds | Matt 16:27
a to the revelation | Rom 16:25
heirs a to promise | Gal 3:29
a to His riches | Phil 4:19

ACCOUNT (n) reckoning

the a of the heavens | Gen 2:4
On whose a has this | Jon 1:8
settled a-s with | Matt 25:19
who will give an a | Heb 13:17

ACCOUNT (v) reckon

do not a this sin | Num 12:11
I am a-ed wicked | Job 9:29
Thou hast taken a of | Ps 56:8
are a-ed as nothing | Dan 4:35

ACCURATELY correctly

teaching a...things | Acts 18:25
handling a...word | 2 Tim 2:15

ACCURSED damned

camp of Israel a | Josh 6:18
be thought a | Is 65:20
Depart...a ones | Matt 25:41
let him be a | Gal 1:8
in greed, a children | 2 Pet 2:14

ACCUSATION charge of wrong

wrote an a against | Ezra 4:6
find a ground of a | Dan 6:4
What a do you | John 18:29
a against my nation | Acts 28:19
Do not receive an a | 1 Tim 5:19

ACCUSE testify against

a-d his brother | Deut 19:18
a-s you in judgment | Is 54:17
He was being a-d | Matt 27:12
a-ing...vehemently | Luke 23:10
a you before the | John 5:45
alternately a-ing | Rom 2:15
not a-d of dissipation | Titus 1:6
unjustly a-ing us | 3 John 10

ACCUSER complainant

they act as my a-s | Ps 109:4
instructing his a-s | Acts 23:30
when the a-s stood | Acts 25:18
a of our brethren | Rev 12:10

ACHAIA

province of Greece
| Acts 18:12; Rom 15:26;
| 1 Cor 16:15

ACHAN

stole from Jericho | Josh 7:1
executed by people | Josh 7:25

ACKNOWLEDGE confess

I a-d my sin | Ps 32:5
all your ways a Him | Prov 3:6
Pharisees a them all | Acts 23:8
see fit to a God | Rom 1:28

ACQUAINTED become familiar

a with all my ways | Ps 139:3

a with grief   Is 53:3

ACQUAINTANCE *friend*

a-s are...estranged   Job 19:13
dread to my a-s   Ps 31:11
removed my a-s far   Ps 88:8
relatives and a-s   Luke 2:44
And all His a-s   Luke 23:49

ACQUIRE *get, purchase*

a property in it   Gen 34:10
have a-d Ruth   Ruth 4:10
a wise counsel   Prov 1:5
You have a-d riches   Ezek 28:4
Do not a gold   Matt 10:9

ACQUIT *declare innocent*

not a me of my guilt   Job 10:14
A me of hidden *faults*   Ps 19:12
You will not be a-ted   Jer 49:12

ACT (n) *deed, work*

a detestable a   Lev 20:13
mighty a-s as Thine   Deut 3:24
every abominable a   Deut 12:31
the a-s of Solomon   1 Kin 11:41
over the rebellious a   Mic 7:18

ACT (v) *behave*

they refuse to a   Prov 21:7
I a-ed ignorantly   1 Tim 1:13
So speak and so a   James 2:12
are a-ing faithfully   3 John 5

ACTION *behavior, work*

a-s are weighed   1 Sam 2:3
a-s of a...harlot   Ezek 16:30
plan or a should be   Acts 5:38
gird your minds for a   1 Pet 1:13

ADAM

1 *first man*   Gen 2:20
   fall of man   Gen 3:6,7
   type of Christ   Rom 5:14
   compared to Jesus   1 Cor 15:22
2 *site in Jordan Valley*   Josh 3:16

ADAR

twelfth month of Hebrew calendar   Ezra 6:15
Purim observed   Esth 3:7; 9:19ff

ADD

a to your yoke   1 Kin 12:11
a-ing to the wrath   Neh 13:18
not a to His words   Prov 30:6
if anyone a-s to them   Rev 22:18

ADJURE *charge solemnly*

many times...I a   1 Kin 22:16
I a you, O daughters   Song 3:5
I a you by Jesus   Acts 19:13

ADMINISTRATION

a of the province   Dan 3:12
healings, helps, a-s   1 Cor 12:28
in our a of this   2 Cor 8:20
a of the mystery   Eph 3:9

ADMONISH *warn*

prophets...had a-ed   Neh 9:26
How shall I a you   Lam 2:13
not cease to a each   Acts 20:31
able also to a one   Rom 15:14

a-ing one another   Col 3:16
a the unruly   1 Thess 5:14
a him as a brother   2 Thess 3:15

ADONIJAH

1 *son of David*   2 Sam 3:4
   aspired to throne   1 Kin 1:5ff
   pardoned   1 Kin 1:52ff
   executed   1 Kin 2:25
2 *Levite*   2 Chr 17:8
3 *of the restoration*   Neh 10:16

ADOPTION *acceptance*

spirit of a as sons   Rom 8:15
to whom belongs...a   Rom 9:4
receive the a as sons   Gal 4:5
predestined us to a   Eph 1:5

ADORN *array, clothe*

A yourself with   Job 40:10
as a bride a-s herself   Is 61:10
a-ed with beautiful   Luke 21:5
women to a   1 Tim 2:9
a the doctrine of God   Titus 2:10
a-ed with gold   Rev 17:4
as a bride a-ed   Rev 21:2

ADULTERER

a and the adulteress   Lev 20:10
eye of the a waits   Job 24:15
associate with a-s   Ps 50:18
a-s, nor effeminate   1 Cor 6:9
a-s God will judge   Heb 13:4

ADULTERESS

a shall surely be   Lev 20:10
a who flatters with   Prov 2:16
mouth of an a   Prov 22:14
You a wife, who   Ezek 16:32
they are a-es   Ezek 23:45
shall be called an a   Rom 7:3

ADULTERY

shall not commit a   Ex 20:14
man who commits a   Lev 20:10
a-ies of faithless   Jer 3:8
worn out by a-ies   Ezek 23:43
committed a with her   Matt 5:28
woman commits a   Matt 5:32
Do not commit a   Luke 18:20
eyes full of a   2 Pet 2:14

ADVANCE *ahead, beyond*

old, a-d in age   Gen 24:1
a-d *in years*   1 Sam 17:12
have told you in a   Matt 24:25
both a-d in years   Luke 1:7
a-ing in Judaism   Gal 1:14

ADVANTAGE *benefit, profit*

lead surely to a   Prov 21:5
What a does man   Eccl 1:3
Wisdom has the a   Eccl 10:10
a that I go away   John 16:7
what a has the Jew   Rom 3:1
no a be taken of us   2 Cor 2:11
sake of *gaining an a*   Jude 16

ADVERSARY *foe, opponent*

an a to your a-ies   Ex 23:22
an a to Solomon   1 Kin 11:14
Lest my a-ies rejoice   Ps 13:4
a-ies and my enemies   Ps 27:2

redeemed...from the a   Ps 78:42
crush his a-ies   Ps 89:23
there are many a-ies   1 Cor 16:9
consume the a-ies   Heb 10:27
Your a, the devil   1 Pet 5:8

ADVERSITY *distress, misfortune*

death and a   Deut 30:15
not accept a   Job 2:10
relief from...a   Ps 94:13
falls into a   Prov 13:17
A pursues sinners   Prov 13:21

ADVICE *counsel*

forsook the a   1 Kin 12:13
a of the young   2 Chr 10:14
a of the cunning   Job 5:13
they took his a   Acts 5:40
have followed my a   Acts 27:21

ADVISER *counselor*

with his a Ahuzzath   Gen 26:26
Pharaoh's wisest a-s   Is 19:11

ADVOCATE *defender, witness*

my a is on high   Job 16:19
A with the Father   1 John 2:1

AFFECTION *devotion, love*

set His a to love   Deut 10:15
in your own a-s   2 Cor 6:12
a of Christ Jesus   Phil 1:8
fond a for you   1 Thess 2:8

AFFLICT (v) *oppress, trouble*

a with hard labor   Ex 1:11
not a any widow   Ex 22:22
Egyptians...a-ed us   Deut 26:6
bind him to a him   Judg 16:5
the wicked a them   2 Sam 7:10
They a-ed his feet   Ps 105:18
He was a-ed   Is 63:9
will a you no longer   Nah 1:12
were sick or a-ed   Acts 5:16
are a-ed in every   2 Cor 4:8
those who a you   2 Thess 1:6
a-ed, ill-treated   Heb 11:37

AFFLICTED (n) *troubled*

save an a people   2 Sam 22:28
to catch the a   Ps 10:9
justice to the a   Ps 82:3
LORD supports the a   Ps 147:6
days of the a   Prov 15:15
O a one   Is 54:11
good news to the a   Is 61:1

AFFLICTION *oppression*

my a and the toil   Gen 31:42
the land of my a   Gen 41:52
the bread of a   Deut 16:3
LORD saw the a   2 Kin 14:26
Thou didst see the a   Neh 9:9
afflicted in their a   Job 36:15
Look upon my a   Ps 25:18
a severe a   Eccl 6:2
a or persecution   Mark 4:17
healed of her a   Mark 5:29
a-s await me   Acts 20:23
out of much a   2 Cor 2:4
great ordeal of a   2 Cor 8:2
to suffer a   1 Thess 3:4

AFRAID *dreading, fearful*

a because...naked	Gen 3:10
a to look at God	Ex 3:6
a and fainthearted	Deut 20:8
Whoever is a	Judg 7:3
a of the terror	Ps 91:5
not a of the snow	Prov 31:21
a to swear	Eccl 9:2
a of man who dies	Is 51:12
a to take Mary	Matt 1:20
were a of Him	Mark 11:18
Do not be a, Mary	Luke 1:30
a of those who kill	Luke 12:4
a of the people	Luke 22:2
a, lest as the serpent	2 Cor 11:3
Do not be a	Rev 1:17

AGABUS

prophet	Acts 11:28;21:10

AGE *period, year*

David reached old a	1 Chr 23:1
a should speak	Job 32:7
either in this a	Matt 12:32
the end of the a	Matt 13:40
sons of this a are	Luke 16:8
in the a-s to come	Eph 2:7
hidden...past a-s	Col 1:26
in the present a	Titus 2:12

AGED *old*

Wisdom is...a men	Job 12:12
a are among us	Job 15:10
refined, a wine	Is 25:6
Paul, the a	Philem 9

AGONY *anguish*

a has seized me	2 Sam 1:9
A like...childbirth	Jer 50:43
in a in this flame	Luke 16:24
in a He was praying	Luke 22:44
the a of death	Acts 2:24

AGREE *consent*

if two of you a	Matt 18:19
did you not a	Matt 20:13
Jews had already a-d	John 9:22
have a-d together	Acts 5:9
words...Prophets a	Acts 15:15
a with sound words	1 Tim 6:3

AGREEMENT *accord*

an a in writing	Neh 9:38
Saul was in hearty a	Acts 8:1
a has the temple	2 Cor 6:16
three are in a	1 John 5:8

AGRIPPA

1 *Herod Agrippa I*
   see **HEROD**
2 *Herod Agrippa II*
   see **HEROD**

AHAB

1 *king of Israel*	1 Kin 16:28
son of Omri	1 Kin 16:29
married Jezebel	1 Kin 16:31
idolater	1 Kin 16:33
2 *false prophet*	Jer 29:21,22

AHASUERUS

1 *Persian king, Xerxes I*
   Ezra 4:6; Book of Esther
2 *father of Darius the Mede*

	Dan 9:1

AHAZ

1 *son of Jotham*	2 Kin 15:38
king of Judah	2 Kin 16:2
2 *line of Jonathan*	1 Chr 8:35

AHIJAH / AHIAH

1 *prophet of Shiloh*	1 Kin 14:2
2 *of Issachar*	1 Kin 15:27
3 *son of Jerahmeel*	1 Chr 2:25
4 *the Pelonite*	1 Chr 11:36
5 *under Nehemiah*	Neh 10:26

AHIMELECH

1 *high priest*   1 Sam 22:16
   gave bread and sword to David
                        1 Sam 21:1-9
2 *Hittite*   1 Sam 26:6,7

AHITHOPHEL

counselor of David
   2 Sam 15:12; 1 Chr 27:33

AI

place near Bethel	Gen 12:8
defeat of Israelites	Josh 7:5
captured	Josh 8:23, 29

AIJALON

1 *city of refuge*	Josh 10:12
Levitical city	Josh 21:24
2 *valley*	Josh 19:42
3 *Zebulunite town*	Judg 12:12

AIR *breeze, sky*

no a can come	Job 41:16
They pant for a	Jer 14:6
birds of the a	Matt 6:26
not beating the a	1 Cor 9:26
speaking into the a	1 Cor 14:9
power of the a	Eph 2:2
the Lord in the a	1 Thess 4:17

ALABASTER *whitish stone*

stones, and a	1 Chr 29:2
pillars of a	Song 5:15
brought an a vial	Luke 7:37

ALARM (n) *danger, warning*

when you blow an a	Num 10:5
The a of war	Jer 4:19
shout of a at noon	Jer 20:16
a on My...mountain	Joel 2:1

ALARM (v) *frighten, warn*

he is not a-ed	Job 40:23
interpretation a you	Dan 4:19
thoughts a-ed him	Dan 5:6
being much a-ed	Acts 10:4
in no way a-ed by	Phil 1:28

ALERT (n) *watch*

be on the a	Matt 24:42
be a and sober	1 Thess 5:6

ALERT (v) *be watchful*

keeping a in it	Col 4:2
let us be a	1 Thess 5:6

ALEXANDER

1 *son of Simon of Cyrene*
                        Mark 15:21
2 *of priestly family* Acts 4:6
3 *Ephesian Jew*   Acts 19:33
4 *apostate teacher*   1 Tim 1:20

5 *enemy of Paul*   2 Tim 4:14

ALEXANDRIAN

1 *of Alexandria*	Acts 6:9
2 *ship*	Acts 27:6;28:11
3 *Apollos*	Acts 18:24

ALIEN *foreigner, stranger*

love for the a	Deut 10:19
give it to the a	Deut 14:21
Our houses to a-s	Lam 5:2
a-s in a foreign land	Acts 7:6
no longer...a-s	Eph 2:19
he lived as an a	Heb 11:9
I urge you as a-s	1 Pet 2:11

ALIENATE *estrange*

Lest I be a-d	Jer 6:8
a this choice *portion*	Ezek 48:14
were formerly a-d	Col 1:21

ALIVE

Is your father still a	Gen 43:7
down a to Sheol	Num 16:33
go down a to Sheol	Ps 55:15
may keep a a heifer	Is 7:21
when He was...a	Matt 27:63
heard...He was a	Mark 16:11
presented Himself a	Acts 1:3
yet the spirit is a	Rom 8:10
all shall be made a	1 Cor 15:22
made us a together	Eph 2:5
a in the spirit	1 Pet 3:18
I am a forevermore	Rev 1:18

ALLEGIANCE *loyalty*

pledged a to King	1 Chr 29:24
he pledged his a	Ezek 17:18

ALLIANCE *agreement*

formed a marriage a	1 Kin 3:1
after an a is made	Dan 11:23

ALLIED *joined*

a...by marriage	2 Chr 18:1
throne of...a	Ps 94:20

ALLOT *apportion, divide*

only a it to Israel	Josh 13:6
a Him a portion	Is 53:12
a-ted to each...faith	Rom 12:3

ALLOTMENT *portion*

an a from Pharaoh	Gen 47:22
as a perpetual a	Num 18:19
Jacob is the a	Deut 32:9
set apart the...a	Ezek 48:20

ALLOW *permit*

not a the destroyer	Ex 12:23
whether his body a-s	Lev 15:3
a Thy Holy One	Ps 16:10
Nor a Thy Holy One	Acts 2:27
not be a-ed to live	Acts 22:22
a you to be tempted	1 Cor 10:13
not a a woman	1 Tim 2:12

ALMIGHTY *all-powerful*

I am God A	Gen 17:1
vision of the A	Num 24:4
A has afflicted me	Ruth 1:21
limits of the A	Job 11:7
A was yet with me	Job 29:5
destruction from...A	Joel 1:15

Lord God, the **A**	Rev 4:8
the **A**, reigns	Rev 19:6

ALMOND

a and plane trees	Gen 30:37
shaped like **a** *blossoms*	Ex 37:19
and it bore ripe **a-s**	Num 17:8

ALMS *charity*

therefore you give **a**	Matt 6:2
a may be in secret	Matt 6:4
a to the *Jewish*	Acts 10:2
bring **a** to my nation	Acts 24:17

ALONE

So He let him **a**	Ex 4:26
Leave me **a**, for my	Job 7:16
not live on bread **a**	Matt 4:4
He was praying **a**	Luke 9:18
I am not **a** *in it*	John 8:16
receiving but you **a**	Phil 4:15
and not by faith **a**	James 2:24

ALOUD *joyful, piercing*

crying **a** as she	2 Sam 13:19
read **a** from the book	Neh 13:1
I will cry **a**	Ps 77:1
Sing **a** with gladness	Jer 31:7
The king called **a**	Dan 5:7
began to weep **a**	Acts 20:37

ALPHA

first letter of Gr. alphabet	Rev 1:8
title of Jesus Christ	Rev 21:6
expresses eternalness of God	
	Rev 22:13

ALTAR *place of sacrifice*

offerings on the **a**	Gen 8:20
Moses built an **a**	Ex 17:15
fire on the **a**	Lev 6:9
Gideon built an **a**	Judg 6:24
erect an **a** to	2 Sam 24:18
go to the **a** of God	Ps 43:4
a-s may become waste	Ezek 6:6
offering at the **a**	Matt 5:23
a that sanctifies	Matt 23:19
golden **a** of incense	Heb 9:4
we have an **a**	Heb 13:10
horns of the golden **a**	Rev 9:13

ALWAYS *ever, forever*

fear the LORD...**a**	Deut 14:23
He will not **a** strive	Ps 103:9
fear of the LORD **a**	Prov 23:17
a loses his temper	Prov 29:11
will I **a** be angry	Is 57:16
I am with you **a**	Matt 28:20
poor you **a** have	Mark 14:7
Rejoice in the Lord **a**	Phil 4:4
a be with...Lord	1 Thess 4:17
I shall **a** be ready	2 Pet 1:12

AMALEKITES

descendants of Esau	Gen 36:12
tribe in Negev and Sinai	
Ex 17:8,9; Num 14:25; 1 Sam	
15:7; 1 Chr 4:43	

AMASA

1 *son of Abigail*	1 Chr 2:17
Absalom's commander	
	2 Sam 17:25
pardoned	2 Sam 19:13

2 *an Ephraimite*	2 Chr 28:12

AMAZED *astonished, astounded*

are **a** at His rebuke	Job 26:11
a at His teaching	Mark 1:22
heard Him were **a**	Luke 2:47
were **a** and marveled	Acts 2:7
whole earth was **a**	Rev 13:3

AMAZEMENT *astonishment*

a came upon them	Luke 4:36
with wonder and **a**	Acts 3:10

AMAZIAH

1 *king of Judah*	2 Kin 12:21
son of Joash	2 Kin 14:1
2 *a Simeonite*	1 Chr 4:34
3 *son of Hilkiah*	1 Chr 6:45
4 *a priest of Bethel*	Amos 7:10

AMBASSADOR *envoy*

a-s of peace weep	Is 33:7
a-s for Christ	2 Cor 5:20
an **a** in chains	Eph 6:20

AMBITION *design, intention*

out of selfish **a**	Phil 1:17
a to lead a quiet	1 Thess 4:11
jealousy...selfish **a**	James 3:14

AMBUSH (n) *cover, hiding place*

a for the city	Josh 8:2
rise from *your* **a**	Josh 8:7
Israel set men in **a**	Judg 20:29
a...behind them	2 Chr 13:13
Place men in **a**	Jer 51:12

AMBUSH (v) *lie in wait*

going to **a** the city	Josh 8:4
a the innocent	Prov 1:11
a their own lives	Prov 1:18

AMEN *so be it*

people shall say, **A**	Deut 27:16
the LORD forever! **A**	Ps 89:52
glory forever...**A**	Phil 4:20
the **A**, the faithful	Rev 3:14
A, Come, Lord Jesus	Rev 22:20

AMMONITES

tribes E of Jordan	Gen 19:38
defeated Israel	Judg 3:13
hired Arameans	2 Sam 10:6
fought against Judah	2 Kin 24:2

AMNON

1 *eldest son of David*	2 Sam 3:2
raped his sister	2 Sam 13:2ff
ordered killed	2 Sam 13:28
2 *line of Judah*	1 Chr 4:20

AMON

1 *Ahab's governor*	1 Kin 22:26
2 *king of Judah*	2 Kin 21:18-26
3 *of the Nethinims*	Neh 7:59
4 *Egyptian deity*	Jer 46:25

AMORITES

tribe on both sides of Jordan	
Gen 15:16; Ex 34:11; Deut	
1:27; Judg 11:23; Amos 2:9	

AMOS

prophet to Israel	Book of Amos

AMOUNT *measure*

daily **a** of bricks	Ex 5:19
a of your valuation	Lev 27:23
large **a** of bronze	1 Chr 18:8

AMRAM

1 *father of Moses*	
Ex 6:18-20; 1 Chr 23:13	
2 *son of Bani*	Ezra 10:34

ANAK / ANAKIM

pre-Israelite tribe of Palestine	
	Num 13:22-33
giants	Deut 2:10; Josh 14:15

ANANIAS

1 *deceived Jerusalem church*	
	Acts 5:1-5
2 *Damascus Christian*	
	Acts 9:10,17
3 *high priest*	Acts 23:2

ANCESTORS *forefathers*

blessings of my **a**	Gen 49:26
the **a** have set	Deut 19:14
iniquities of their **a**	Jer 11:10

ANCHOR

they weighed **a**	Acts 27:13
they cast four **a-s**	Acts 27:29
an **a** of the soul	Heb 6:19

ANCIENT *aged, old*

of the **a** mountains	Deut 33:15
the records are **a**	1 Chr 4:22
keep to the **a** path	Job 22:15
O **a** doors	Ps 24:9
A of Days	Dan 7:9
the **a-s** were told	Matt 5:21
from **a** generations	Acts 15:21
not spare the **a** world	2 Pet 2:5

ANDREW

fisherman	Matt 4:18
brother of Peter	Matt 4:18
receives Jesus	John 1:40-42
apostle	Luke 6:14

ANGEL *divine messenger*

send His **a** before	Gen 24:7
a-s...were ascending	Gen 28:12
an **a** to Jerusalem	1 Chr 21:15
bread of **a-s**	Ps 78:25
Praise Him, all His **a-s**	Ps 148:2
a of His presence	Is 63:9
a who was speaking	Zech 4:4
give His **a-s** charge	Matt 4:6
a Gabriel was sent	Luke 1:26
they are like **a-s**	Luke 20:36
two **a-s** in white	John 20:12
like the face of an **a**	Acts 6:15
as an **a** of light	2 Cor 11:14
worship of the **a-s**	Col 2:18
entertained **a-s**	Heb 13:2
God did not spare **a-s**	2 Pet 2:4
a of the church	Rev 2:1

ANGEL OF THE LORD

a called to Abraham	Gen 22:15
a took his stand	Num 22:22
I have seen the **a**	Judg 6:22
a said to Elijah	2 Kin 1:3
a destroying	1 Chr 21:12

a encamps around those　Ps 34:7
a admonished Joshua　Zech 3:6
a commanded him　Matt 1:24
a appeared to Joseph　Matt 2:13
a...opened the gates　Acts 5:19

ANGER *indignation, wrath*

My a will be kindled　Ex 22:24
Moses' a burned　Ex 32:19
from His burning a　Deut 13:17
a with their idols　1 Kin 16:13
a kills the simple　Job 5:2
not turn back His a　Job 9:13
not rebuke me in Thine a　Ps 6:1
a is but for a moment　Ps 30:5
He who is slow to a　Prov 14:29
a man *given* to a　Prov 22:24
a of the LORD　Is 5:25
sun go down...a　Eph 4:26
put...aside: a　Col 3:8
slow to a　James 1:19

ANGRY *enraged, indignant*

Why are you a　Gen 4:6
king became very a　Esth 1:12
lest He become a　Ps 2:12
a man stirs up strife　Prov 29:22
a beyond measure　Is 64:9
and a no more　Ezek 16:42
a with his brother　Matt 5:22
Be a...do not sin　Eph 4:26
a with this generation　Heb 3:10

ANGUISH *distress, pain*

writhed in great a　Esth 4:4
My heart is in a　Ps 55:4
land of distress and a　Is 30:6
A has seized us　Jer 6:24
and a of heart　2 Cor 2:4

ANIMAL *beast, creature*

from man to a-s　Gen 6:7
lies with an a　Ex 22:19
the fat of the a　Lev 7:25
wild a-s of the field　Jer 27:6
a blemished a　Mal 1:14
four-footed a-s　Acts 10:12
like unreasoning a-s　2 Pet 2:12

ANNA

prophetess　　　　　Luke 2:36

ANNAS

high priest
　　　　Luke 3:2; John 18:13ff

ANNIHILATE *destroy*

to a all the Jews　Esth 3:13
My enemy a-d them　Lam 2:22
to destroy and a　Dan 11:44
let it be a-d　Zech 11:9

ANNOUNCE *proclaim*

Who a-s peace　Is 52:7
I shall a My words　Jer 18:2
a-ing to...disciples　John 20:18
a-d...the Righteous　Acts 7:52

ANNUL *dismiss, make void*

he shall a her vow　Num 30:8
husband has a-led　Num 30:12
not a Thy covenant　Jer 14:21
a-s one of the least　Matt 5:19

ANOINT (v) *sprinkle oil upon*

a them and ordain　Ex 28:41
a Aaron and his sons　Ex 30:30
LORD a-ed you king
　　　　　　　　1 Sam 15:17
a-ed my head with oil　Ps 23:5
a the most holy *place*　Dan 9:24
has a-ed My body　Mark 14:8
did not a My head　Luke 7:46
and a-ed my eyes　John 9:11
a-ed...feet of Jesus　John 12:3
a-ed Him...Holy Spirit
　　　　　　　　Acts 10:38
a-ing him with oil　James 5:14

ANOINTED (adj) *consecrated*

if the a priest sins　Lev 4:3
not touch My a　1 Chr 16:22
a cherub who　Ezek 28:14
the two a ones　Zech 4:14

ANOINTED (n) *consecrated one*

walk before My a　1 Sam 2:35
he is the LORD's a　1 Sam 24:10
against His A　Ps 2:2

ANOINTING (adj) *consecration*

spices for the a oil　Ex 25:6
shall be a holy a oil　Ex 30:31
for the LORD's a oil　Lev 10:7

ANOINTING (n) *consecration*

a shall qualify them　Ex 40:15
a from the Holy　1 John 2:20
His a teaches you　1 John 2:27

ANSWER (n) *response*

consider what a I　1 Chr 21:12
the king sent an a　Ezra 4:17
Who gives a right a　Prov 24:26
amazed at...His a-s　Luke 2:47

ANSWER (v) *respond*

anyone who will a you　Job 5:1
The LORD a-ed me　Ps 118:5
king a-ed and said　Dan 2:8
Jesus a-ing said　Matt 3:15
who a-s back to God　Rom 9:20

ANT *insect*

to the a, O sluggard　Prov 6:6
a-s are not a strong　Prov 30:25

ANTELOPE *animal*

Like an a in a net　Is 51:20

ANTICHRIST *foe of Christ*

a-s have arisen　1 John 2:18
This is the a　1 John 2:22
the *spirit* of the a　1 John 4:3
deceiver and the a　2 John 7

ANTIOCH

1 *city in Syria*　Acts 6:5;11:19,26
2 *city in Galatia*
　　　　　Acts 13:14; 14:19

ANTIPAS

1 *Pergamum martyr*　Rev 2:13
2 *Herod Antipas*
　　see **HEROD**

ANXIETY *sorrow*

a because of my sin　Ps 38:18

There is a by the sea　Jer 49:23
casting all your a　1 Pet 5:7

ANXIOUS *concern, worry*

and become a for us　1 Sam 9:5
not be a in...drought　Jer 17:8
my spirit is a to　Dan 2:3
not be a for your life　Matt 6:25
not be a for tomorrow　Matt 6:34
be a beforehand　Mark 13:11
a can add a *single*　Luke 12:25
Be a for nothing　Phil 4:6

APART *separate*

So they set a Kedesh　Josh 20:7
tear their fetters a　Ps 2:3
a from your Father　Matt 10:29
a from Him nothing　John 1:3
a from Me you can　John 15:5
faith a from works　Rom 3:28

APOLLOS

Alexandrian Jew　Acts 18:24
taught at Ephesus　Acts 18:24
taught at Corinth　1 Cor 3:4,6

APOSTASY *faithlessness*

a-ies are numerous　Jer 5:6
Turned away in...a　Jer 8:5
I will heal their a　Hos 14:4
unless the a comes　2 Thess 2:3

APOSTLE *sent with authority*

the twelve a-s　Matt 10:2
named as a-s　Luke 6:13
called *as* an a　Rom 1:1
an a of Gentiles　Rom 11:13
fit to be called an a　1 Cor 15:9
men are false a-s　2 Cor 11:13
He gave some *as* a-s　Eph 4:11
Jesus, the A and　Heb 3:1
a-s of the Lamb　Rev 21:14

APOSTLESHIP *office of apostle*

received grace and a　Rom 1:5
seal of my a　1 Cor 9:2
Peter in *his* a to　Gal 2:8

APPAREL *clothing, garment*

of gold on your a　2 Sam 1:24
majestic in His a　Is 63:1
men...in dazzling a　Luke 24:4
put on his royal a　Acts 12:21

APPEAL *ask, entreat*

standing and a-ing　Acts 16:9
I a to Caesar　Acts 25:11
Paul a-ed to be held　Acts 25:21
a-ed to...Emperor　Acts 25:25
a to *him* as a father　1 Tim 5:1
love's sake I...a　Philem 9

APPEAR *become visible*

LORD a-ed to Abram　Gen 12:7
glory of the LORD a-ed　Ex 16:10
a-ed on the wings　2 Sam 22:11
and a-ed to many　Matt 27:53
first a-ed to Mary　Mark 16:9
who, a-ing in glory　Luke 9:31
a-ed to them tongues　Acts 2:3
we must all a before　2 Cor 5:10
a-ing of the glory　Titus 2:13
shall a a second time　Heb 9:28

Chief Shepherd **a-s** 1 Pet 5:4
not **a-ed** as yet 1 John 3:2

APPEARANCE *countenance*

handsome in...**a** Gen 39:6
the **a** of the angel Judg 13:6
at the outward **a** 1 Sam 16:7
a is blacker than soot Lam 4:8
lapis lazuli in **a** Ezek 1:26
they neglect their **a** Matt 6:16
judge according to **a** John 7:24
a of His coming 2 Thess 2:8
a of the locusts Rev 9:7

APPEASE *moderate, mollify*

I will **a** him Gen 32:20
wise man will **a** it Prov 16:14
have **a-d** My wrath Zech 6:8

APPETITE *desire, hunger*

our **a** is gone Num 11:6
a of the young lions Job 38:39
man of *great* **a** Prov 23:2
a is not satisfied Eccl 6:7
enlarged his **a** like Hab 2:5
whose god is *their* **a** Phil 3:19

APPLE *fruit*

as the **a** of the eye Ps 17:8
Like **a-s** of gold Prov 25:11
Refresh me with **a-s** Song 2:5
touches the **a** of His Zech 2:8

APPOINT *assign, commission*

shall **a** *as a penalty* Ex 21:23
I will **a** over you Lev 26:16
who **a-ed** Moses 1 Sam 12:6
to **a** their relatives 1 Chr 15:16
a magistrates and Ezra 7:25
there is a harvest **a-ed** Hos 6:11
a-ed elders for them Acts 14:23
a-ed a preacher and 1 Tim 2:7
For the Law **a-s** men Heb 7:28

APPORTION *distribute*

a the inheritance Num 34:29
a this land Josh 13:7
He **a-s** our fields Mic 2:4

APPROPRIATE *suitable*

blessing **a** to him Gen 49:28
eat at the **a** time Eccl 10:17
a to repentance Acts 26:20

APPROVAL *consent*

loved the **a** of men John 12:43
give hearty **a** to Rom 1:32
men of old gained **a** Heb 11:2

APPROVE *accept, attest*

the Lord does not **a** Lam 3:36
too pure to **a** evil Hab 1:13
standing by **a-ing** Acts 22:20
and **a-d** by men Rom 14:18
present yourself **a-d** 2 Tim 2:15

AQUILA

a native of Pontus Acts 18:2
Corinthian Christian Acts 18:18
co-worker with Paul Rom 16:3

ARAB

1 *town in Judah* Josh 15:52
2 *ethnic identity*
1 Kin 10:15; Neh 2:19;

Is 13:20

ARABAH

1 *desert steppe*
Is 35:1,6; Jer 52:7
2 *Jordan rift valley*
Deut 1:1; Josh 3:17
3 *Dead Sea*
Josh 3:16; 2 Kin 14:25

ARABIA

land SE of Israel / Judah
Is 21:13; Ezek 30:5;
Gal 1:17;4:25

ARAM

1 *son of Shem* Gen 10:22,23
2 *line of Asher* 1 Chr 7:34
3 *ancestor of Jesus, shortened to Ram*
Ruth 4:19; Matt 1:3;
Luke 3:33
4 *Syria and N Mesopotamia*
Num 23:7; 1 Kin 11:25;
2 Kin 13:19; Is 7:8

ARAMAIC

Semitic language
2 Kin 18:26; Ezra 4:7;
Is 36:11; Dan 2:4

ARAMEANS

tribes of Aram
2 Sam 8:5; 1 Kin 20:20;
2 Kin 24:2

ARARAT

kingdom and mountain range in Armenia
Gen 8:4; 2 Kin 19:37;
Jer 51:27

ARAUNAH

Jebusite owner of threshing floor on Mt. Moriah 2 Sam 24:16,18
David purchases threshing floor for altar and later temple
2 Sam 24:23,24
also **Ornan**

ARCHANGEL

voice of *the* **a** 1 Thess 4:16
But Michael the **a** Jude 9

ARCHELAUS *see* HEROD

ARCHER *bowman*

the **a-s** hit him 1 Sam 31:3
a-s shot King Josiah
2 Chr 35:23
a-s equipped with bows Ps 78:9
an **a** who wounds Prov 26:10

ARCHIPPUS

Colossian Christian Col 4:17
co-worker with Paul Philem 2

AREOPAGUS

hill and council in Athens
Acts 17:19,22

ARGUE *dispute, question*

I will **a** my ways Job 13:15
hastily to **a** *your case* Prov 25:8
Pharisees...**a** with Mark 8:11

scribes **a-ing** with Mark 9:14
a-ing with the...*Jews* Acts 9:29

ARGUMENT *disagreement*

Please hear my **a** Job 13:6
mouth are no **a-s** Ps 38:14
a arose among them Luke 9:46

ARIEL

1 *a Moabite*
2 Sam 23:20; 1 Chr 11:22
2 *applied to Jerusalem* Is 29:1ff
3 *sent by Ezra* Ezra 8:16

ARISE *rise, stand*

A, walk about the Gen 13:17
Abraham **arose** early Gen 19:27
will **a** and play Deut 31:16
you have **a-n** early 1 Sam 29:10
arose and tore his robe Job 1:20
when God **a-s** Job 31:14
A, O LORD; save me Ps 3:7
Though war **a** Ps 27:3
A, my darling Song 2:13
a-n *anyone* greater Matt 11:11
false prophets will **a** Matt 24:11
arose from the dead Acts 10:41
A, and be baptized Acts 22:16
a from the dead Eph 5:14
arose loud voices Rev 11:15

ARISTARCHUS

Thessalonian Christian
Acts 20:4; Acts 27:2
co-worker with Paul
Col 4:10; Philem 24

ARK *chest, vessel*

a of gopher wood Gen 6:14
into the **a** to Noah Gen 7:9
a of acacia wood Ex 37:1
a of the covenant Josh 4:7
Noah entered the **a** Matt 24:38
a of His covenant Rev 11:19

ARM (n) *part of body*

the everlasting **a-s** Deut 33:27
a without strength Job 26:2
a-s of the wicked Ps 37:17
His holy **a** have gained Ps 98:1
a seal on your **a** Song 8:6
be carried in the **a-s** Is 60:4
took...in His **a-s** Mark 10:16
with an uplifted **a** Acts 13:17

ARM (v) *mobilize*

A men from among Num 31:3
a-ed for battle Num 32:29
a-ed with iron 2 Sam 23:7
a yourselves also 1 Pet 4:1

ARMAGEDDON

see HAR-MAGEDON

ARMED (adj) *mobilized*

the **a** men went Josh 6:13
their **a** camps 1 Sam 28:1
So the **a** men left 2 Chr 28:14
like an **a** man Prov 6:11

ARMOR *protective device*

a joint of the **a** 1 Kin 22:34
strip off his outer **a** Job 41:13
all his **a** on which Luke 11:22

ARMY

put on...a of light	Rom 13:12
full a of God	Eph 6:11

ARMY *host, war*

not go out with the a	Deut 24:5
like the a of God	1 Chr 12:22
a ready for battle	2 Chr 26:11
officers of the a	Neh 2:9
forth with our a-ies	Ps 60:10
exceedingly great a	Ezek 37:10
a-ies...in heaven	Rev 19:14
and against His a	Rev 19:19

ARNON

river and border	Num 21:13
valley in Moab	Deut 2:24

AROMA *odor*

the soothing a	Gen 8:21
his a has not changed	Jer 48:11
through us...sweet a	2 Cor 2:14
a from life to life	2 Cor 2:16
as a fragrant a	Eph 5:2

AROUSE *raise, stir*

A Thyself to help me	Ps 59:4
a-s for you the spirits	Is 14:9
a-d one from the north	Is 41:25
He will a *His* zeal	Is 42:13
LORD has a-d the spirit	Jer 51:11
Jews a-d the devout	Acts 13:50

ARRANGE *set in order*

a what belongs on it	Ex 40:4
shall a the pieces	Lev 1:8
he a-d the wood	1 Kin 18:33
thus he had a-d it	Acts 20:13

ARRAY (n) *arrangement, order*

went up in martial a	Ex 13:18
in battle a	Josh 4:12
Worship...in holy a	1 Chr 16:29
holy a, from the womb	Ps 110:3

ARRAY (v) *adorn, clothe*

Israel a-ed for battle	Judg 20:20
let them a the man	Esth 6:9
A yourselves before	Job 33:5
God so a-s the grass	Matt 6:30
a-ed Him in a purple	John 19:2

ARREST *restrain*

he a-ed Jeremiah	Jer 37:13
Herod had John a-ed	Matt 14:3
and clubs to a Me	Matt 26:55
proceeded to a Peter	Acts 12:3

ARROGANCE *pride*

your a has come	2 Kin 19:28
Pride and a and	Prov 8:13
a of the proud	Is 13:11
a, pride, and fury	Is 16:6
a of your heart	Jer 49:16
you boast in your a	James 4:16

ARROGANT *proud*

a men have risen up	Ps 86:14
But a fool is a	Prov 14:16
a toward the LORD	Jer 48:26
Knowledge makes a	1 Cor 8:1
boastful, a, revilers	2 Tim 3:2
speaking...a *words*	2 Pet 2:18

ARROW *dart, missile*

shot an a past him	1 Sam 20:36
a-s of the Almighty	Job 6:4
a cannot make him	Job 41:28
make ready their a	Ps 11:2
broke the flaming a-s	Ps 76:3
sword and a sharp a	Prov 25:18
tongue is a deadly a	Jer 9:8
target for the a	Lam 3:12
deadly a-s of famine	Ezek 5:16

ART *craft*

with their secret a-s	Ex 7:22
the perfumers' a	2 Chr 16:14

ARTAXERXES

Persian king

	Ezra 4:7,8;7:1,12;
	Neh 2:1;5:14

ARTEMIS

Greek goddess	Acts 19:24ff

ARTICLE *object, vessel*

a-s of silver	Gen 24:53
any wooden a	Lev 11:32
of every precious a	Hos 13:15
every a of ivory	Rev 18:12

ASA

1 *king of Judah*

	1 Kin 15:8-24; 2 Chr 14:8-15

2 *a Levite*

	1 Chr 9:16

ASCEND *go up*

a into the hill	Ps 24:3
If I a to heaven	Ps 139:8
Who has a-ed into	Prov 30:4
breath of man a-s	Eccl 3:21
has a-ed into heaven	John 3:13
Son of Man a-ing	John 6:62
a-ed to the Father	John 20:17
who a-ed far above	Eph 4:10

ASCENT *hill, rise*

by the a of Heres	Judg 8:13
a of the...Olives	2 Sam 15:30
Song of A-s	Ps 120-134

ASCRIBE *attribute*

have a-d to David	1 Sam 18:8
A to the LORD	1 Chr 16:28
a righteousness to	Job 36:3

ASH

but dust and a-es	Gen 18:27
from the a heap	1 Sam 2:8
a-es on her head	2 Sam 13:19
a-es were poured	1 Kin 13:5
proverbs of a-es	Job 13:12
repent in dust and a-es	Job 42:6
garland instead of a-es	Is 61:3
roll in a-es	Jer 6:26
sackcloth and a-es	Luke 10:13
a-es of a heifer	Heb 9:13

ASHAMED *embarrassed*

naked and were not a	Gen 2:25
Let me never be a	Ps 71:1
a of Me...My words	Mark 8:38
a when He comes	Luke 9:26
not a of the gospel	Rom 1:16
a of the testimony	2 Tim 1:8

God is not a	Heb 11:16
let him not feel a	1 Pet 4:16

ASHDOD

Philistine city

	Josh 15:47; 1 Sam 5:1,6;
	Amos 1:8

ASHER

1 *eighth son of Jacob*

	Gen 35:26;49:20

2 *tribe of Israel*

	Num 1:41;13:13; Rev 7:6

3 *town in hill country*   Josh 17:7

ASHERAH

Canaanite goddess and symbol

	Deut 16:21; Judg 6:25

Asherim *(pl)*

	1 Kin 14:15; Mic 5:14

Asheroth *(pl)*

	Judg 3:7; 2 Chr 19:3

ASHKELON

Philistine city

	Judg 1:18; 2 Sam 1:20;
	Jer 47:5; Zeph 2:4

ASHTORETH

1 *Near Eastern goddess*

	1 Kin 11:5,33; 2 Kin 23:13

Ashtaroth *(pl)*

	Judg 2:13; 1 Sam 7:4;31:10

2 *town of Bashan in E Manasseh*

	Deut 1:4; Josh 13:12

ASIA

Roman province of Asia Minor

	Acts 6:9; Rom 16:5; Rev 1:4

ASK *appeal, beg, inquire*

whatever you a	Ruth 3:11
Two things I a-ed	Prov 30:7
A a sign for yourself	Is 7:11
a for the ancient paths	Jer 6:16
A rain from the LORD	Zech 10:1
Give to him who a-s	Matt 5:42
A, and it shall be	Matt 7:7
a...believing	Matt 21:22
pray and a, believe	Mark 11:24
Jews a for signs	1 Cor 1:22
let him a of God	James 1:5

ASLEEP *death, rest*

sound a...exhausted	Judg 4:21
they fall a	Ps 90:5
not died, but is a	Matt 9:24
in the stern, a	Mark 4:38
Lazarus...fallen a	John 11:11
said this, he fell a	Acts 7:60
fallen a in Jesus	1 Thess 4:14

ASSAIL *attack*

will you a a man	Ps 62:3
Whoever a-s you	Is 54:15
storm was a-ing *us*	Acts 27:20

ASSEMBLE *gather*

a all the congregation	Lev 8:3
A the people to Me	Deut 4:10
David a-d all Israel	1 Chr 13:5
peoples may be a-d	Is 43:9
A...on the mountains	Amos 3:9
I will...a all of you	Mic 2:12

ASSEMBLY (cont.)

whole city **a-d** to — Acts 13:44
a-d to make war — Rev 19:19

ASSEMBLY *congregation*

holy **a** on the seventh — Ex 12:16
the people of the **a** — Lev 16:33
a before the rock — Num 20:10
Or calls an **a** — Job 11:10
a of the righteous — Ps 1:5
hate the **a** of evildoers — Ps 26:5
proclaim a solemn **a** — Joel 2:15
I delight in...**a-ies** — Amos 5:21
the **a** was divided — Acts 23:7
general **a** and church — Heb 12:23
comes into your **a** — James 2:2

ASSOCIATE (n) *colleague*

All my **a-s** abhor me — Job 19:19
high priest and...**a-s** — Acts 5:21

ASSOCIATE (v) *identify with*

shall they **a** with — 1 Kin 11:2
a with adulterers — Ps 50:18
not **a** with a man — Prov 22:24
dared to **a** with them — Acts 5:13
but **a** with the lowly — Rom 12:16
not **a** with him — 2 Thess 3:14

ASSURANCE *confirmation*

no one has **a** of life — Job 24:22
a of understanding — Col 2:2
full **a** of hope — Heb 6:11
full **a** of faith — Heb 10:22
a of *things* hoped for — Heb 11:1

ASSURE *confirm*

kingdom will be **a-d** — Dan 4:26
I **a** you before God — Gal 1:20
shall **a** our heart — 1 John 3:19

ASSYRIA

kingdom name from Asshur
Gen 10:22; 1 Chr 1:17
empire in upper Mesopotamia
2 Kin 19:17; Is 19:24; Jer 2:36

ASTONISHED *amazed*

will be **a** and hiss — 1 Kin 9:8
a at His teaching — Matt 22:33
listeners were **a** — Mark 6:2
were utterly **a** — Mark 7:37
they were all **a** — Luke 1:63

ASTOUNDED *astonished*

prophets will be **a** — Jer 4:9
a at the vision — Dan 8:27
were completely **a** — Mark 5:24

ASTRAY *erring, wandering*

a like a lost sheep — Ps 119:176
leading *them* **a** — Is 9:16
like sheep have gone **a** — Is 53:6
led My people **a** — Jer 23:32
lead the elect **a** — Mark 13:22
a from the faith — 1 Tim 6:21
go **a** in their heart — Heb 3:10
My bond-servants **a** — Rev 2:20

ATHALIAH

1 *wicked*
    daughter of Ahab — 2 Kin 11:1
    wife of Jehoram — 2 Chr 21:6
2 *a Benjamite* — 1 Chr 8:26
3 *returned exile* — Ezra 8:7

ATHENS

leading Greek city — Acts 17:15ff

ATONEMENT *expiation*

by which **a** was made — Ex 29:33
shall make **a** for him — Lev 4:35
a before the LORD — Lev 14:31
how can I make **a** — 2 Sam 21:3
make **a** for iniquity — Dan 9:24

ATONEMENT, DAY OF

see **DAY OF ATONEMENT**

ATTACK (n) *assault*

at the first **a** — 2 Sam 17:9
king ready for the **a** — Job 15:24
joined in the **a** — Acts 24:9

ATTACK (v) *assault, fall upon*

lest he come and **a** — Gen 32:11
adversary who **a-s** — Num 10:9
and **a-ed** the camp — Judg 8:11
a the Philistines — 1 Sam 23:2
it **a-ed** the plant — Jon 4:7
no man will **a** you — Acts 18:10

ATTAIN *acquire*

I cannot **a** to it — Ps 139:6
woman **a-s** honor — Prov 11:16
worthy to **a** to that — Luke 20:35
a-ed righteousness — Rom 9:30
a to the resurrection — Phil 3:11

ATTEND *pay attention to*

a to your priesthood — Num 18:7
thousands were **a-ing** — Dan 7:10
who **a** regularly — 1 Cor 9:13
a to...business — 1 Thess 4:11
ears **a** to their prayer — 1 Pet 3:12

ATTENDANT *helper, servant*

the **a** of Moses — Num 11:28
king's **a-s**, who served — Esth 2:2
a-s of...bridegroom — Mark 2:19

ATTENTION *heed, regard*

no **a** to false words — Ex 5:9
gives **a** to the word — Prov 16:20
pays **a** to falsehood — Prov 29:12
they do not pay **a** — Is 5:12
pay **a** to myths — 1 Tim 1:4
a to the...reading — 1 Tim 4:13

ATTIRE *covering, dress*

in his military **a** — 2 Sam 20:8
cupbearers...**a** — 2 Chr 9:4
Him in holy **a** — 2 Chr 20:21

ATTITUDE *frame of mind*

see your father's **a** — Gen 31:5
a of the righteous — Luke 1:17
Have this **a** in — Phil 2:5
have a different **a** — Phil 3:15

AUGUSTUS

name of Caesar Octavianus
Luke 2:1
see **CAESAR**

AUTHOR *source*

a of their salvation — Heb 2:10
a...perfecter of faith — Heb 12:2

AUTHORITY *power, right*

submit...to her **a** — Gen 16:9

put...your **a** on him — Num 27:20
Who gave Him **a** — Job 34:13
a over...day of death — Eccl 8:8
entrust him with your **a** — Is 22:21
as *one* having **a** — Matt 7:29
a on earth to forgive — Matt 9:6
a over unclean spirits — Matt 10:1
All **a**...given to Me — Matt 28:18
Son of Man has **a** — Luke 5:24
no **a** except from God — Rom 13:1
majesty, dominion...**a** — Jude 25
give **a** over...nations — Rev 2:26

AVENGE *revenge*

He will **a** the blood — Deut 32:43
the LORD **a** me — 1 Sam 24:12
Shall I not **a** Myself — Jer 5:9
I will **a** their blood — Joel 3:21
a-ing our blood — Rev 6:10

AVENGER *revenger*

The blood **a** himself — Num 35:19
lest the **a** of blood — Deut 19:6
a of their *evil* deeds — Ps 99:8
God, an **a** who brings — Rom 13:4
Lord is *the* **a** — 1 Thess 4:6

AVOID *refuse*

A it, do not pass by — Prov 4:15
a-ing...empty chatter — 1 Tim 6:20

AWAIT *wait*

afflictions **a** me — Acts 20:23
a-ing...the revelation — 1 Cor 1:7
who eagerly **a** Him — Heb 9:28

AWAKE *be attentive, watch*

awoke from his sleep — Gen 28:16
A, a, Deborah — Judg 5:12
Thy likeness when I **a** — Ps 17:15
dream when one **a-s** — Ps 73:20
arouse or **a-n** *my* love — Song 2:7
He **a-ns** My ear — Is 50:4
A, a, put on strength — Is 51:9
A, a, drunkards...weep — Joel 1:5
that I may **a** him — John 11:11
hour for you to **a-n** — Rom 13:11

AWARE *know, understand*

the lad was not **a** — 1 Sam 20:39
Will you not be **a** — Is 43:19
But Jesus, **a** of *this* — Matt 12:15
I was **a** that power — Luke 8:46

AWE *fear, reverence*

stand in **a** of Him — Ps 33:8
in **a** of Thy words — Ps 119:161
in **a** of My name — Mal 2:5
feeling a sense of **a** — Acts 2:43

AWESOME *fearful*

How **a** is this place — Gen 28:17
angel of God, very **a** — Judg 13:6
great and **a** God — Neh 1:5
God is **a** majesty — Job 37:22
As **a** as an army — Song 6:4
a day of the LORD — Joel 2:31

AXE *cutting tool*

his **a**, and his hoe — 1 Sam 13:20
hammer nor **a** — 1 Kin 6:7
a head fell into — 2 Kin 6:5

a is already laid   Luke 3:9

AZARIAH

1 *ancestor of Samuel*   1 Chr 6:36
2 *official of Solomon*   1 Kin 4:2
3 *son of Nathan*   1 Kin 4:5
4 *prophet*   2 Chr 15:1-8
5 *two sons of king Jehoshaphat*
       2 Chr 21:2
6 *king of Judah, also* **Uzziah**
   2 Kin 15:1; 2 Chr 26:1
7 *high priest*   1 Chr 6:10
8 *family of Merari*   2 Chr 29:12
9 *son of Hilkiah*   1 Chr 6:13,14
10 *original name of Abed-nego*
       Dan 1:7
*the name of twelve other
  individuals in the OT*

B

BAAL

1 *Canaanite god(s)*
  Num 22:41; Judg 6:25; 1 Kin
       18:40
2 *line of Reuben*   1 Chr 5:5
3 *personal name*   1 Chr 8:30
4 *place name*   1 Chr 4:33

BAAL-HANAN

1 *king of Edom*   Gen 36:38
2 *servant of David*   1 Chr 27:28

BAAL-HAZOR

mountain in central Palestine
       2 Sam 13:23

BAAL-HERMON

part of Mt. Hermon
    Judg 3:3; 1 Chr 5:23

BAAL-ZEBUB

god of Ekron   2 Kin 1:2,16
see also **BEELZEBUL**

BAASHA

king of Israel   1 Kin 15:16,32

BABEL *a city*

founded by Nimrod
    Gen 10:10;11:9
later called Babylon

BABES *infants*

From the mouth of...**b**   Ps 8:2
abundance to their **b**   Ps 17:14
woe...who nurse **b**   Matt 24:19
as to **b** in Christ   1 Cor 3:1
like newborn **b**   1 Pet 2:2

BABY *infant*

b leaped...her womb   Luke 1:41
b wrapped in cloths   Luke 2:12
b as He lay   Luke 2:16

BABYLON *city*

1 *on the Euphrates*
  2 Kin 17:24; Jer 20:4; Ezek
    29:18; Dan 4:29
2 *symbolic of godlessness*
    Rev 14:8;17:5

BACK *part of body*

you shall see My **b**   Ex 33:23

turned his **b** to leave   1 Sam 10:9
law behind their **b-s**   Neh 9:26
my sins behind Thy **b**   Is 38:17

BAD *evil, wrong*

b report of the land   Num 13:32
basket had very **b** figs   Jer 24:2
if your eye is **b**   Matt 6:23
b tree bears **b** fruit   Matt 7:18
B company corrupts
       1 Cor 15:33

BAG *sack*

fill their **b-s**   Gen 42:25
in the shepherd's **b**   1 Sam 17:40
silver in two **b-s**   2 Kin 5:23
carrying *his* **b** of seed   Ps 126:6
b of...weights   Mic 6:11
b for *your* journey   Matt 10:10
Carry no purse, no **b**   Luke 10:4

BAGGAGE *bags, supplies*

stayed with the **b**   1 Sam 25:13
prepare...yourself **b**   Ezek 12:3

BAKE *cook*

b-d unleavened bread   Gen 19:3
b-d food for Pharaoh   Gen 40:17
they **b-d** the dough   Ex 12:39
B what you will **b**   Ex 16:23
grain offering **b-d**   Lev 2:4
b twelve cakes   Lev 24:5
taste of cakes **b-d**   Num 11:8
fire to **b** bread   Is 44:15

BAKER *cook*

b for the king   Gen 40:1
cooks and **b-s**   1 Sam 8:13
from the **b-s'** street   Jer 37:21
oven heated by the **b**   Hos 7:4

BALAAM

diviner
  Num 22:5-31;23:5; Josh 13:22;
       Rev 2:14

BALAK

king of Moab
    Num 22:4; Mic 6:5

BALANCE *scale*

shall have just **b-s**   Lev 19:36
b-s...with my iniquity   Job 6:2
False **b** is an   Prov 11:1
mountains in a **b**   Is 40:12

BALD *hairless*

if...head becomes **b**   Lev 13:41
every head is **b**   Jer 48:37
head was made **b**   Ezek 29:18

BALDHEAD *hairless*

mocked him...you **b**   2 Kin 2:23

BALM *aromatic ointment*

b and myrrh   Gen 37:25
a present, a little **b**   Gen 43:11
no **b** in Gilead   Jer 8:22
Gilead and obtain **b**   Jer 46:11
Bring **b** for her pain   Jer 51:8
honey, oil, and **b**   Ezek 27:17

BALSAM *aromatic gum*

tops of the **b** trees   2 Sam 5:24

like a bed of **b**   Song 5:13

BAN *set apart to God*

city...under the **b**   Josh 6:17
destroy...under the **b**   Josh 7:12
who violated the **b**   1 Chr 2:7
consign Jacob to the **b**   Is 43:28

BAND *bond or group*

b-s *shall be* of silver   Ex 27:10
skillfully woven **b**   Ex 28:8
saw a marauding **b**   2 Kin 13:21
b of destroying angels   Ps 78:49
b-s of the yoke   Is 58:6

BANISH *exile*

b-ed one may not   2 Sam 14:14
assemble the **b-ed**   Is 11:12
gaiety...is **b-ed**   Is 24:11
where I shall **b** them   Ezek 4:13

BANK *slope*

b of the Nile   Gen 41:3
reeds by the **b**   Ex 2:3
b of the river   Ezek 47:7
herd rushed down...**b**
       Luke 8:33

BANNER *flag, standard*

set up our **b-s**   Ps 20:5
b to those who fear   Ps 60:4
b over me is love   Song 2:4
as an army with **b-s**   Song 6:4

BANQUET *dinner, feast*

b lasting seven days   Esth 1:5
brought me to *his* **b**   Song 2:4
lavish **b** for all   Is 25:6
place of honor at **b-s**   Matt 23:6
Herod...gave a **b**   Mark 6:21

BAPTISM *symbolic washing*

Sadducees coming...**b**   Matt 3:7
b of repentance   Mark 1:4
b with which I am   Mark 10:38
with the **b** of John   Luke 7:29
a **b** to undergo   Luke 12:50
through **b** into death   Rom 6:4
one faith, one **b**   Eph 4:5
buried with Him in **b**   Col 2:12

BAPTIZE *symbolic washing*

b...Holy Spirit   Matt 3:11
tax-gatherers...**b-d**   Luke 3:12
Jesus also was **b-d**   Luke 3:21
sent me to **b** in water   John 1:33
b-ing more disciples   John 4:1
b-d with the Holy   Acts 1:5
each of you be **b-d**   Acts 2:38
he arose and was **b-d**   Acts 9:18
household...been **b-d**   Acts 16:15
John **b-d** with the   Acts 19:4
b-d into Christ Jesus   Rom 6:3
b-d into Moses   1 Cor 10:2
b-d into one body   1 Cor 12:13
b-d for the dead   1 Cor 15:29

BAR *metal or block*

b-s of your yoke   Lev 26:13
a **b** of gold   Josh 7:21
like **b-s** of iron   Job 40:18
earth with its **b-s**   Jon 2:6

BARABBAS

robber	Matt 27:16; Luke 23:18
released by Pilate	Matt 27:26

BARAK

Deborah's commander	Judg 4:6

BARBARIAN non-Hellenic

obligation...to b-s	Rom 1:14
who speaks a b	1 Cor 14:11
b, Scythian, slave	Col 3:11

BARE (adj) barren, uncovered

to cover their b flesh	Ex 28:42
he went to a b hill	Num 23:3
strips the forests b	Ps 29:9
were naked and b	Ezek 16:7

BARE (v) expose, uncover

foundations...laid b	Ps 18:15
b-d His holy arm	Is 52:10
foundation is laid b	Ezek 13:14
open and laid b	Heb 4:13

BAREFOOT without sandals

priests walk b	Job 12:19
gone naked and b	Is 20:3

BAR-JESUS

magician	Acts 13:6
also Elymas	

BARLEY grain

land of wheat and b	Deut 8:8
beginning...b harvest	Ruth 1:22
stinkweed instead...b	Job 31:40
has five b loaves	John 6:9

BARN farm building

b-s are torn down	Joel 1:17
seed still in the b	Hag 2:19
wheat into the b	Matt 3:12
nor gather into b-s	Matt 6:26
tear down my b-s	Luke 12:18

BARNABAS

Cyprian by birth	Acts 4:36
introduced Paul	Acts 9:27
co-worker with Paul	Acts 13:2,7
separated from Paul	Acts 15:39

BARREN childless, sterile

Sarai was b	Gen 11:30
but Rachel was b	Gen 29:31
wrongs the b woman	Job 24:21
Shout...O b one	Is 54:1
Blessed are the b	Luke 23:29

BARSABBAS

1 Apostolic candidate, also called Joseph and Justus	Acts 1:23
2 colleague of Paul, also called Judas	Acts 15:22

BARTHOLOMEW

apostle	Matt 10:3; Luke 6:14; Acts 1:13

BARTIMAEUS

healed by Jesus	Mark 10:46

BARUCH

1 scribe	Jer 36:26;43:6
2 priest	Neh 3:20
3 a Judean	Neh 11:5

BASE dishonorable

a b thought	Deut 15:9
b things of...world	1 Cor 1:28

BASEMATH

1 Esau's wife	Gen 26:34
2 daughter of Solomon	1 Kin 4:15

BASHAN

land E of Jordan	Num 21:33; Josh 13:11; Is 2:13

BASIN bowl, vessel

blood...in the b	Ex 12:22
b-s...of pure gold	1 Chr 28:17
a sacrificial b	Zech 9:15
water into the b	John 13:5

BASKET container

got him a wicker b	Ex 2:3
b among the reeds	Ex 2:3
b of summer fruit	Amos 8:1
seven large b-s full	Mark 8:8
twelve b-s full	Luke 9:17
let down in a b	2 Cor 11:33

BATH measure of capacity

two thousand b-s	1 Kin 7:26
100 b-s of oil	Ezra 7:22
only one b of wine	Is 5:10
a tenth of a b from	Ezek 45:14

BATHE wash

wash his clothes and b	Lev 15:5
b his body in water	Num 19:7
saw a woman b-ing	2 Sam 11:2
B-d in milk	Song 5:12

BATHSHEBA

wife of Uriah	2 Sam 11:3
taken by David	2 Sam 11:4
wife of David	2 Sam 11:27
mother of Solomon	2 Sam 12:24

BATTLE (n) conflict, war

b is the LORD's	1 Sam 17:47
b is...God's	2 Chr 20:15
scents the b from afar	Job 39:25
with strength for b	Ps 18:39
noise of b is in	Jer 50:22
another king in b	Luke 14:31
horses prepared for b	Rev 9:7

BATTLE (v) fight

b against the sons	Judg 20:14
drew near to b	1 Sam 7:10
about to go to b	1 Chr 12:19
nations...to b	Zech 14:2

BEACH coast

multitude...on the b	Matt 13:2
Jesus stood on the b	John 21:4
down on the b	Acts 21:5

BEAM log

like a weaver's b	2 Sam 21:19
one was felling a b	2 Kin 6:5
b-s, the thresholds	2 Chr 3:7
b-s of His...chambers	Ps 104:3

BEAR (n) animal

b came and took	1 Sam 17:34
b robbed of...cubs	Prov 17:12
the b will graze	Is 11:7
resembling a b	Dan 7:5

BEAR (v) sustain

too great to b	Gen 4:13
bore you on eagles'	Ex 19:4
not b false witness	Ex 20:16
LORD...b-s our burden	Ps 68:19
b their iniquities	Is 53:11
b the penalty	Ezek 23:49
she will b a Son	Matt 1:21
John bore witness	John 1:15
If I alone b witness	John 5:31
it b-s much fruit	John 12:24
you will b witness	John 15:27
b-ing His own cross	John 19:17
b fruit for God	Rom 7:4
Spirit...b-s witness	Rom 8:16
b the image of	1 Cor 15:49
B...another's burdens	Gal 6:2
b the sins of many	Heb 9:28
bore our sins	1 Pet 2:24

BEARD whiskers

infection...on the b	Lev 13:29
seized him by...b	1 Sam 17:35
shaved...their b-s	2 Sam 10:4
until your b-s grow	1 Chr 19:5

BEARER carrier

the b-s of the ark	2 Sam 6:13
strength of...b-s	Neh 4:10
b of good news	Is 40:9

BEAST animal, creature

God formed every b	Gen 2:19
Noah and all the b-s	Gen 8:1
eliminate harmful b-s	Lev 26:6
b-s of the field	Lev 26:22
But now ask the b-s	Job 12:7
b of the forest	Ps 50:10
b also had four heads	Dan 7:6
they worshiped the b	Rev 13:4
mark of the b	Rev 16:2

BEAT hit, strike

b-ing a Hebrew	Ex 2:11
b out what she	Ruth 2:17
b-ing tambourines	Ps 68:25
B your plowshares	Joel 3:10
b Him with their	Matt 26:67
b-ing His head with	Mark 15:19
b-ing his breast	Luke 18:13
b-en us in public	Acts 16:37
stopped b-ing Paul	Acts 21:32
b-en with rods	2 Cor 11:25

BEAUTIFUL lovely, pleasing

daughters...were b	Gen 6:2
Rachel was b	Gen 29:17
foliage of b trees	Lev 23:40
Most b among women	Song 1:8
Branch...will be b	Is 4:2
Your b sheep	Jer 13:20
enter the B Land	Dan 11:41
How b are the feet	Rom 10:15

BEAUTIFUL GATE

see GATES OF JERUSALEM

BEAUTY

Your b...is slain	2 Sam 1:19

behold the **b** of the LORD
                                    Ps 27:4
Zion...perfection of **b**   Ps 50:2
b is vain   Prov 31:30
see the King in His **b**   Is 33:17

BED *pallet*

My **b** will comfort me   Job 7:13
make my **b** swim   Ps 6:6
remember...on my **b**   Ps 63:6
in **b** with a fever   Matt 8:14
take up your **b**   Matt 9:6
lamp...under a **b**   Mark 4:21

BEDROOM *sleeping area*

and into your **b**   Ex 8:3
you speak in your **b**   2 Kin 6:12
his nurse in the **b**   2 Chr 22:11

BEELZEBUL

N.T. prince of the demons
                    Matt 12:27; Luke 11:15
see also **BAAL-ZEBUB**

BEERSHEBA

well / town in Negev
                    Gen 21:31; Judg 20:1
home of Abraham   Gen 22:19
home of Isaac   Gen 26:23

BEFOREHAND *prior*

do not be anxious **b**   Mark 13:11
anointed My body **b**   Mark 14:8
God announced **b**   Acts 3:18
prepared **b** for glory   Rom 9:23

BEG *appeal, ask*

children wander...**b**   Ps 109:10
b-s during...harvest   Prov 20:4
b You to look at   Luke 9:38
I am ashamed to **b**   Luke 16:3
who used to sit and **b** John 9:8
b-ging them to leave   Acts 16:39

BEGET *bring into being, sire*

Rock who **begot**   Deut 32:18
whom you shall **b**   2 Kin 20:18
begotten the...dew   Job 38:28
I have **begotten** Thee   Ps 2:7
who **b**-s a wise son   Prov 23:24
have **begotten** Thee   Acts 13:33

BEGINNING *origin, starting*

In the **b** God created   Gen 1:1
from **b** to end   1 Sam 3:12
b was insignificant   Job 8:7
fear of the LORD...**b**   Ps 111:10
The **b** of the gospel   Mark 1:1
In the **b** was the Word John 1:1
This **b** of *His* signs   John 2:11
He is the **b**   Col 1:18
the **b** and the end   Rev 21:6

BEGOTTEN (adj) *born one*

b from the Father   John 1:14
the only **b** God   John 1:18
gave His only **b** Son   John 3:16
only **b** Son of God   John 3:18
offering...only **b**   Heb 11:17
sent His only **b** Son   1 John 4:9

BEHALF *sake of*

atonement on his **b**   Lev 5:6
the Father on your **b**   John 16:26

I ask on their **b**   John 17:9
one man to die on **b**   John 18:14
be sin on our **b**   2 Cor 5:21

BEHAVE *act*

David **b**-d himself   1 Sam 18:30
b-ing as a madman   1 Sam 21:14
b properly as in   Rom 13:13
blamelessly we **b**-d   1 Thess 2:10

BEHAVIOR *conduct*

instruction in wise **b**   Prov 1:3
reverent in their **b**   Titus 2:3
holy...in all *your* **b**   1 Pet 1:15
the **b** of their wives   1 Pet 3:1

BEHEADED *cut off*

killed him and **b** him   2 Sam 4:7
John **b** in the prison   Matt 14:10
John, whom I **b**   Mark 6:16
b because of the   Rev 20:4

BEHEMOTH

hippopotamus   Job 40:15

BEHOLD *look, see*

upright will **b** His face   Ps 11:7
b the works of the LORD Ps 46:8
we **beheld** His glory   John 1:14
b the Son of Man   John 6:62
may **b** My glory   John 17:24
b-ing as in a mirror   2 Cor 3:18
No one has **beheld**   1 John 4:12
B, I stand at the door   Rev 3:20

BEING *existence, life*

man became a living **b**   Gen 2:7
a...**b** coming up   1 Sam 28:13
wisdom in the...**b**   Job 38:36
truth in the...**b**   Ps 51:6
four living **b**-s   Ezek 1:5
resembled a...**b**   Dan 10:16

BEL

Babylonian god, related to Baal
                              Jer 50:2;51:44

BELA

1 *king of Edom*   Gen 36:32
2 *son of Benjamin*
                    Gen 46:21; 1 Chr 8:1
3 *a Rubenite*   1 Chr 5:8
4 *city of the plain near the Dead
   Sea*   Gen 14:2,8
also **ZOAR**

BELIEVE *have faith, trust*

he **b**-d in the LORD   Gen 15:6
did not **b** in God   Ps 78:22
naive **b**-s everything   Prov 14:15
you **b** that I am able   Matt 9:28
ask in prayer, **b**-ing   Matt 21:22
repent and **b**   Mark 1:15
they **b**-d...Scripture   John 2:22
whoever **b**-s in Him   John 3:16
will you **b** My words   John 5:47
who **b**-s has eternal   John 6:47
men will **b** in Him   John 11:48
b in the light   John 12:36
not see, and *yet* **b**-d   John 20:29
b-d were of one heart   Acts 4:32
B in the Lord Jesus   Acts 16:31
Abraham **b**-d God   Rom 4:3

how shall they **b**   Rom 10:14
love...**b**-s all   1 Cor 13:7
whom I have **b**-d   2 Tim 1:12
comes to God must **b**   Heb 11:6
demons also **b**   James 2:19
do not **b** every spirit   1 John 4:1

BELIEVERS *faithful ones*

all the circumcised **b**   Acts 10:45
example to all the **b**   1 Thess 1:7
toward you **b**   1 Thess 2:10

BELL

a **b**...a pomegranate   Ex 39:26
b-s of the horses   Zech 14:20

BELLY *stomach*

On your **b**...you go   Gen 3:14
crawls on its **b**   Lev 11:42
b of the sea monster   Matt 12:40

BELOVED *dearly loved*

b of the LORD dwell   Deut 33:12
gives to His **b** *even*   Ps 127:2
b is like a gazelle   Song 2:9
This is My **b** Son   Matt 3:17
your upbuilding, **b**   2 Cor 12:19
stand firm...my **b**   Phil 4:1
faithful and **b** brother   Col 4:9
Luke, the **b** physician   Col 4:14
slave, a **b** brother   Philem 16
This is My **b** Son   2 Pet 1:17
the called, **b** in God   Jude 1

BELSHAZZAR

ruler of Babylon   Dan 5:1;7:1

BELT *waistband*

the **b** of the strong   Job 12:21
leather **b** about his   Matt 3:4
no money in their **b**   Mark 6:8
Paul's **b** and bound   Acts 21:11

BELTESHAZZAR

Daniel's Babylonian name
                    Dan 1:7;2:26;5:12;10:1

BENAIAH

1 *son of Jehoiada*   2 Sam 8:18
   captain of David   2 Sam 23:23
2 *Levitical singer* 1 Chr 15:18,20
3 *a priest*   1 Chr 15:24;16:5
*the name of nine other individuals
   in the OT*

BENEFIT *blessing, profit*

no return for the **b**   2 Chr 32:25
forget none of His **b**-s   Ps 103:2
His **b**-s toward me   Ps 116:12
the **b** of circumcision   Rom 3:1

BEN-HADAD

1 *Ben-hadad I*   1 Kin 15:18-21
2 *Ben-hadad II*   1 Kin 20,22
3 *Ben-hadad III*
                    2 Kin 8:7-15;13:22

BEN-HINNOM, VALLEY OF

see **HINNOM VALLEY**

BENJAMIN

1 *son of Jacob*   Gen 35:18
2 *tribe*   Num 2:22
3 *of clan of Jediael*   1 Chr 7:10
4 *of the restoration*   Neh 3:23

BENJAMIN GATE see GATES OF JERUSALEM

BEREA
city in Macedonia visited by Paul
Acts 17:10,13

BEREAVE *deprive, make sad*
be **b-d** of you both   Gen 27:45
b...of your children   Lev 26:22
I will **b** them   Jer 15:7
longer **b** your nation   Ezek 36:14

BERNICE
daughter of Herod Agrippa I
Acts 25:13,23

BERODACH-BALADAN
king of Babylon   2 Kin 20:12
also **Merodach-Baladan**

BESEECH *ask earnestly*
LORD, I **b** Thee   Ps 116:4
do save, we **b** Thee   Ps 118:25
leper came...**b-ing**   Mark 1:40
b the Lord of the   Luke 10:2

BESIEGE *assail, surround*
When you **b** a city   Deut 20:19
enemies **b** them   2 Chr 6:28
was **b-ing** Jerusalem   Jer 32:2
b-d...with bitterness   Lam 3:5

BESTOWED *granted*
b...royal majesty   1 Chr 29:25
that the Spirit was **b**   Acts 8:18
which He freely **b**   Eph 1:6
b on Him the name   Phil 2:9
Every good thing **b**   James 1:17
love the Father has **b**   1 John 3:1

BETHANY
1 *E of Jerusalem*   Matt 21:17
home of Mary, Martha and
Lazarus   John 11:1,18
2 *where John baptized*   John 1:28

BETHEL
town in Benjamin   Gen 12:8
N of Jerusalem   Josh 8:17

BETHESDA
pool in Jerusalem   John 5:2

BETH-HORON
1 *famous battle site*
pass NW of Jerusalem
Josh 10:10,11
2 *two towns at both ends of*
mountain pass   Josh 16:3,5

BETHLEHEM
1 *town S of Jerusalem* Gen 35:19
home of Ruth and Boaz
Ruth 4:11
birthplace of Jesus   Matt 2:1
2 *Zebulunite village*   Josh 19:15

BETH-PEOR
Moabite city   Deut 4:46;34:6

BETHPHAGE
village on the Mount of Olives
Matt 21:1; Mark 11:1

BETHSAIDA
village on Sea of Galilee
Mark 8:22; Luke 9:10
home of Philip, Andrew and
Peter   John 1:44

BETH-SHAN / BETH-SHEAN
city at junction of Jezreel and
Jordan valleys
Josh 17:11; 1 Kin 4:12;
1 Chr 7:29

BETH-SHEMESH
1 *city of Judah*   Josh 15:10
2 *Issachar border city*   Josh 19:22
3 *city of Naphtali*   Josh 19:38

BETRAY *break faith, disloyal*
do not **b** the fugitive   Is 16:3
wine **b-s** the haughty   Hab 2:5
how to **b** Him   Mark 14:11
one...will **b** Me   Mark 14:18
Judas, are you **b-ing** Luke 22:48

BETROTH *promise to wed*
You shall **b** a wife   Deut 28:30
I will **b** you to Me   Hos 2:19
Mary had been **b-ed**   Matt 1:18
I **b-ed** you to one   2 Cor 11:2

BEWARE *be careful, watch*
B of practicing   Matt 6:1
B of the scribes   Mark 12:38
B of the leaven   Luke 12:1
b...false circumcision   Phil 3:2

BEYOND *over and above*
it was **b** measure   Gen 41:49
remove...**b** Babylon   Acts 7:43
tempted **b** what   1 Cor 10:13
b their ability   2 Cor 8:3
b all that we ask   Eph 3:20
and **b** reproach   Col 1:22

BEZALEL
1 *architect of tabernacle*
Ex 31:1ff
2 *Israelite*   Ezra 10:30

BEZER
1 *son of Zophah*   1 Chr 7:37
2 *city of refuge*   Josh 20:8

BIG *large*
on the **b** toes   Ex 29:20
Pharaoh...a **b** noise   Jer 46:17
gave a **b** reception   Luke 5:29

BILDAD
one of Job's friends
Job 2:11;18:1;42:9

BILHAH
1 *Rachel's servant*   Gen 29:29
Jacob's concubine   Gen 30:3,4
2 *Simeonite town*   1 Chr 4:29

BIND *fasten, secure*
bound his son Isaac   Gen 22:9
were **b-ing** sheaves   Gen 37:7
b them as a sign   Deut 6:8
b-s up their wounds   Ps 147:3
B up the testimony   Is 8:16
b up the brokenhearted Is 61:1

shall **b** on earth   Matt 16:19
and **bound** Him   John 18:12
bound...a thousand   Rev 20:2

BIRD *fowl*
let **b-s** fly above   Gen 1:20
eat any clean **b**   Deut 14:20
b-s of the heavens   Ps 8:8
Flee *as* a **b** to   Ps 11:1
snare of a **b** catcher   Hos 9:8
b-s...*have* nests   Luke 9:58

BIRTH *act of being born*
A time to give **b**   Eccl 3:2
You gave me **b**   Jer 2:27
b of Jesus Christ   Matt 1:18
rejoice at his **b**   Luke 1:14
a man blind from **b**   John 9:1
in pain to give **b**   Rev 12:2

BIRTHDAY *day of birth*
was Pharaoh's **b**   Gen 40:20
Herod's **b** came   Matt 14:6
his **b**...banquet   Mark 6:21

BIRTHRIGHT *first-born rights*
First sell me your **b**   Gen 25:31
He took away my **b**   Gen 27:36
sold his own **b**   Heb 12:16

BITE
serpent **bit** any man   Num 21:9
it **b-s** like a serpent   Prov 23:32
if you **b**...one another   Gal 5:15

BITHYNIA
territory on the Bosporus in Asia
Minor   Acts 16:7; 1 Pet 1:1

BITTER *painful, unpleasant*
b with hard labor   Ex 1:14
waters of Marah...**b**   Ex 15:23
b speech *as* their arrow Ps 64:3
substitute **b** for sweet   Is 5:20
Strong drink is **b**   Is 24:9
fresh and **b** *water*   James 3:11

BITTERNESS *unpleasantness*
in the **b** of my soul   Job 10:1
because of the **b**   Is 38:15
full of cursing and **b**   Rom 3:14
all **b**...be put away   Eph 4:31
no root of **b**   Heb 12:15

BLACK *dark*
sky grew **b** with   1 Kin 18:45
darkness and **b** gloom   Job 3:5
I am **b** but lovely   Song 1:5
behold, a **b** horse   Rev 6:5
sun became **b**   Rev 6:12

BLAME *fault, responsibility*
let me bear the **b**   Gen 43:9
bear the **b**...forever   Gen 44:32

BLAMELESS *faultless*
show Thyself **b**   2 Sam 22:26
just *and* **b** man is a   Job 12:4
His way is **b**   Ps 18:30
b will inherit good   Prov 28:10
a **b** conscience   Acts 24:16
holy and **b** before Him   Eph 1:4
in the Law, found **b**   Phil 3:6
spotless and **b**   2 Pet 3:14

b with great joy   Jude 24

BLASPHEME *curse*

enemies...to **b**   2 Sam 12:14
name is continually **b-d**   Is 52:5
This *fellow* **b-s**   Matt 9:3
b-s...Holy Spirit   Mark 3:29
force them to **b**   Acts 26:11
name of God is **b-d**   Rom 2:24
taught not to **b**   1 Tim 1:20
b-d the God of   Rev 16:11

BLASPHEMY *cursing, profanity*

b against the Spirit   Matt 12:31
b-ies they utter   Mark 3:28
You...heard the **b**   Mark 14:64
man...speaks **b-ies**   Luke 5:21
stone You...for **b**   John 10:33
words and **b-ies**   Rev 13:5

BLAST *burst*

the **b** of Thy nostrils   Ex 15:8
b with the ram's horn   Josh 6:5
a trumpet **b** of war   Jer 49:2

BLAZING *burning*

LORD...a **b** fire   Ex 3:2
furnace of **b** fire   Dan 3:6
and to a **b** fire   Heb 12:18

BLEMISH *imperfection, spot*

there is no **b** in you   Song 4:7
six lambs without **b**   Ezek 46:4
Himself without **b**   Heb 9:14
stains and **b-es**   2 Pet 2:13

BLESS (v) *bestow favor or praise*

God **b-ed** the...day   Gen 2:3
I will greatly **b** you   Gen 22:17
LORD **b-ed** the sabbath   Ex 20:11
and **b** Thine inheritance   Ps 28:9
LORD will **b** His people   Ps 29:11
B the LORD   Ps 103:2
generous will be **b-ed**   Prov 22:9
who **b-es** his friend   Prov 27:14
rise up and **b** her   Prov 31:28
b-ed of My Father   Matt 25:34
He **b-ed** *the food*   Mark 6:41
b...who curse you   Luke 6:28
while He was **b-ing**   Luke 24:51
you are **b-ed** if you   John 13:17
b...who persecute   Rom 12:14
we **b** *our* Lord   James 3:9

BLESSED (adj) *favored, happy*

b be God Most High   Gen 14:20
B are you, O Israel   Deut 33:29
B be the name of   Job 1:21
How **b** is the man   Ps 127:5
b...who finds wisdom   Prov 3:13
nations will call you **b**   Mal 3:12
B are the poor in   Matt 5:3
B are the gentle   Matt 5:5
B *is* the...kingdom   Mark 11:10
B among women *are*   Luke 1:42
more **b** to give   Acts 20:35
looking for...**b** hope   Titus 2:13

BLESSING (n) *God's favor*

you shall be a **b**   Gen 12:2
taken away your **b**   Gen 27:35
a **b** and a curse   Deut 11:26
curse into a **b**   Neh 13:2

b of the LORD be upon   Ps 129:8
showers of **b**   Ezek 34:26
pour out for you a **b**   Mal 3:10
fulness of the **b**   Rom 15:29
cup of **b** which we   1 Cor 10:16
inherit a **b**   1 Pet 3:9
honor and glory and **b**   Rev 5:12

BLIND (adj) *sightless*

misleads a **b** *person*   Deut 27:18
To open **b** eyes   Is 42:7
b...guides a **b** man   Matt 15:14
b beggar *named*   Mark 10:46
b man was sitting   Luke 18:35
I was **b**, now I see   John 9:25

BLIND (n) *without sight*

block before the **b**   Lev 19:14
I was eyes to the **b**   Job 29:15
the **b** receive sight   Matt 11:5
a guide to the **b**   Rom 2:19

BLIND (v) *make sightless*

b-s the clear-sighted   Ex 23:8
bribe to **b** my eyes   1 Sam 12:3
has **b-ed** the minds   2 Cor 4:4
darkness has **b-ed**   1 John 2:11

BLINDNESS *sightlessness*

madness and with **b**   Deut 28:28
struck them with **b**   2 Kin 6:18
every horse...with **b**   Zech 12:4

BLOOD

Whoever sheds man's **b**   Gen 9:6
bridegroom of **b**   Ex 4:25
b shall be a sign   Ex 12:13
not eat...any **b**   Lev 3:17
land is filled with **b**   Ezek 9:9
b did not reveal   Matt 16:17
covenant in My **b**   Luke 22:20
sweat...drops of **b**   Luke 22:44
drinks My **b** abides   John 6:56
Field of **B**   Acts 1:19
the moon into **b**   Acts 2:20
justified by His **b**   Rom 5:9
sharing in the **b**   1 Cor 10:16
redemption...His **b**   Eph 1:7
cleansed with **b**   Heb 9:22
b, as of a lamb   1 Pet 1:19
the sea became **b**   Rev 8:8
b of the saints   Rev 17:6

BLOODGUILTINESS

no **b** on his account   Ex 22:2
b is upon them   Lev 20:11
b shall be forgiven   Deut 21:8
Deliver me from **b**   Ps 51:14

BLOODSHED *killing, murder*

abhors the man of **b**   Ps 5:6
Men of **b** hate   Prov 29:10
the **b** of Jerusalem   Is 4:4
give you over to **b**   Ezek 35:6
b follows **b**   Hos 4:2

BLOSSOM *bloom*

the almond tree **b-s**   Eccl 12:5
Israel will **b** and sprout   Is 27:6
arrogance has **b-ed**   Ezek 7:10
fig tree should not **b**   Hab 3:17

BLOT *erase*

I will **b** out man   Gen 6:7
b me...from Thy book   Ex 32:32
b out their name   Deut 9:14
sin be **b-ted** out   Neh 4:5
b out all my iniquities   Ps 51:9
works...be **b-ted** out   Ezek 6:6

BLOW *forcible stroke*

gave Jesus a **b**   John 18:22
give Him **b-s**   John 19:3
inflicted many **b-s**   Acts 16:23

BLUE *color*

tent of **b** and purple   Ex 26:36
ephod all of **b**   Ex 28:31
royal robes of **b**   Esth 8:15

BOANERGES

name of James and John
                                Mark 3:17

BOAST (n) *bragging*

soul shall make its **b**   Ps 34:2
the **b** of our hope   Heb 3:6

BOAST (v) *brag, glory*

B no more so   1 Sam 2:3
b in the LORD   Ps 34:2
who **b-s** of his gifts   Prov 25:14
not **b** about tomorrow   Prov 27:1
let not a rich man **b**   Jer 9:23
b in God   Rom 2:17
who **b** in the Law   Rom 2:23
b...my weaknesses   2 Cor 12:9
it **b-s** of great things   James 3:5

BOASTFUL *proud*

b shall not stand   Ps 5:5
insolent, arrogant, **b**   Rom 1:30
b pride of life   1 John 2:16

BOASTING *bragging*

Where is your **b**   Judg 9:38
Where then is **b**   Rom 3:27
our **b** about you   2 Cor 9:3
all such **b** is evil   James 4:16

BOAT *watercraft*

slip by like reed **b-s**   Job 9:26
left the **b** and their   Matt 4:22
Peter got out of...**b**   Matt 14:29
filled both of the **b-s**   Luke 5:7
disciples into the **b**   John 6:22

BOAZ

1 *husband of Ruth*   Ruth 4:13
grandfather of David
                                Ruth 4:17ff
2 *temple pillar*   2 Chr 3:17

BODY *corpse, flesh*

b cleaves to the earth   Ps 44:25
lamp of the **b**   Matt 6:22
perfume upon My **b**   Matt 26:12
this is My **b**   Mark 14:22
did not find His **b**   Luke 24:23
b of sin...done away   Rom 6:6
redemption of our **b**   Rom 8:23
present your **b-ies**   Rom 12:1
b-ies are members   1 Cor 6:15
b is a temple   1 Cor 6:19
you are Christ's **b**   1 Cor 12:27

b to be burned 1 Cor 13:3
absent from the **b** 2 Cor 5:8
one **b** and one Spirit Eph 4:4
building up of the **b** Eph 4:12
wives as…own **b-ies** Eph 5:28
transform the **b** Phil 3:21
b be preserved 1 Thess 5:23
bore…sins in His **b** 1 Pet 2:24

BODYGUARD *guard, protector*

captain of the **b** put Gen 40:4
you my **b** for life 1 Sam 28:2

BOIL (n) *sore, swelling*

when…has a **b** Lev 13:18
b-s of Egypt Deut 28:27
smote Job with sore **b-s** Job 2:7

BOIL (v) *cook, heat*

not **b** a kid in its Ex 34:26
we **b-ed** my son 2 Kin 6:29
fire causes water to **b** Is 64:2
b the guilt offering Ezek 46:20

BOISTEROUS *clamorous, loud*

woman of folly is **b** Prov 9:13
of noise, You **b** town Is 22:2
will drink, *and* be **b** Zech 9:15

BOLD *brave, fearless*

wicked man…**b** face Prov 21:29
righteous are **b** as Prov 28:1
I may not be **b** 2 Cor 10:2

BOLDNESS *confidence*

word of God with **b** Acts 4:31
b and…access Eph 3:12
with **b** the mystery Eph 6:19

BOND *band, restraint*

neither **b** nor free 2 Kin 14:26
b of the covenant Ezek 20:37
with **b-s** of love Hos 11:4
in the **b** of peace Eph 4:3
eternal **b-s** under Jude 6

BONDAGE *servitude, slavery*

Israel sighed…**b** Ex 2:23
the **b** of iniquity Acts 8:23
sold into **b** to sin Rom 7:14

BOND-SERVANT *servant, slave*

b-s of…Most High Acts 16:17
Paul, a **b** of Christ Rom 1:1
ourselves as your **b-s** 2 Cor 4:5
b…be quarrelsome 2 Tim 2:24
b of God…apostle Titus 1:1
His **b-s**…serve Him Rev 22:3

BONDSLAVE *servant, slave*

state of His **b** Luke 1:48
a **b** of Jesus Christ Col 4:12
Urge **b-s** to be subject Titus 2:9
use it as **b-s** of God 1 Pet 2:16

BONE

now **b** of my **b-s** Gen 2:23
the **b-s** of Joseph Josh 24:32
my **b-s** are dismayed Ps 6:2
rottenness in his **b-s** Prov 12:4
tongue breaks the **b** Prov 25:15
can these **b-s** live Ezek 37:3
dead men's **b-s** Matt 23:27
Not a **b**…be broken John 19:36

BOOK *scroll*

in a **b** as a memorial Ex 17:14
blot me…from Thy **b** Ex 32:32
found the **b** of the 2 Kin 22:8
seal up the **b** Dan 12:4
not contain the **b-s** John 21:25
names are in the **b** Phil 4:3
worthy to open the **b** Rev 5:2
Lamb's **b** of life Rev 21:27

BOOK OF LIFE

*God's book with names of
righteous*
Ps 69:28; Phil 4:3;
Rev 13:8;17:8;20:15

BOOTHS *shelters*

b for his livestock Gen 33:17
live in **b** for seven Lev 23:42
in **b** during the feast Neh 8:14

BOOTHS, FEAST OF

see FEASTS

BOOTY *loot, plunder*

b that remained Num 31:32
Swift is the **b** Is 8:1
divide the **b** with Is 53:12
have his *own* life as **b** Jer 38:2

BORDER *boundary*

enlarge your **b-s** Ex 34:24
b of…city of refuge Num 35:26
the Jordan as *a* **b** Deut 3:17
God extends your **b** Deut 12:20
peace in your **b-s** Ps 147:14

BORN *brought into life*

man is **b** for trouble Job 5:7
mountains were **b** Ps 90:2
child will be **b** to us Is 9:6
land be **b** in one day Is 66:8
b King of the Jews Matt 2:2
those **b** of women Luke 7:28
b not of blood John 1:13
unless one is **b** again John 3:3
b of the Spirit John 3:6
to one untimely **b** 1 Cor 15:8
b…to a living hope 1 Pet 1:3
loves is **b** of God 1 John 4:7

BORROW *use temporarily*

if a man **b-s** *anything* Ex 22:14
you shall not **b** Deut 28:12
b-s and does not pay Ps 37:21
wants to **b** from you Matt 5:42

BOSOM *breast*

iniquity in my **b** Job 31:33
take fire in his **b** Prov 6:27
to Abraham's **b** Luke 16:22
the **b** of the Father John 1:18

BOTHER *pester*

conscience **b-ed** 1 Sam 24:5
you **b** the woman Matt 26:10
worried and **b-ed** Luke 10:41
this widow **b-s** me Luke 18:5

BOTTOMLESS *without bottom*

key of the **b** pit Rev 9:1
he opened the **b** pit Rev 9:2

BOUGH *branch*

Joseph is a fruitful **b** Gen 49:22
b-s of leafy trees Lev 23:40
cedars…with its **b-s** Ps 80:10
nested in its **b-s** Ezek 31:6

BOUND (adj) *fastened, tied*

Foolishness is **b** up Prov 22:15
cast **b** into the…fire Dan 3:24
A wife is **b** as long 1 Cor 7:39

BOUND (n) *boundary, limit*

utmost **b** of…hills Gen 49:26
set **b-s** for the people Ex 19:12
b-s…the mountain Ex 19:23

BOUNDARY *border, limit*

b-ies of the peoples Deut 32:8
b of light and Job 26:10
the **b-ies** of the earth Ps 74:17
set for the sea its **b** Prov 8:29
the **b** of the widow Prov 15:25

BOUNTY *generous gift*

to his royal **b** 1 Kin 10:13
crowned…with Thy **b** Ps 65:11
over the **b** of the LORD Jer 31:12

BOW (n) *rainbow*

set My **b** in the cloud Gen 9:13

BOW (n) *shooting device*

his **b** remained firm Gen 49:24
a **b** of bronze 2 Sam 22:35
not trust in my **b** Ps 44:6
b-s are shattered Jer 51:56

BOW (v) *bend, worship*

nations to **b** down to Gen 27:29
Israel **b-ed** *in* Gen 47:31
to Him you shall **b** 2 Kin 17:36
My soul is **b-ed** down Ps 57:6
B Thy heavens, O LORD
Ps 144:5
nations will **b** down Zeph 2:11
He **b-ed** His head John 19:30
every knee shall **b** Rom 14:11

BOWELS *entrails, innards*

a disease of your **b** 2 Chr 21:15
smote him in his **b** 2 Chr 21:18
b gushed out Acts 1:18

BOWL *dish, jug*

golden **b** is crushed Eccl 12:6
from sacrificial **b-s** Amos 6:6
dips with Me in…**b** Mark 14:20
b-s full of the wrath Rev 15:7

BOX *container*

b with the golden 1 Sam 6:11
sashes, perfume **b-es** Is 3:20
Judas had the…**b** John 13:29

BOX *type of tree*

b tree and the cypress Is 41:19

BOY *child, lad*

she left the **b** Gen 21:15
let the **b-s** live Ex 1:17
b will lead them Is 11:6
Traded a **b** for a harlot Joel 3:3
b was cured at once Matt 17:18

BRACELETS *armlets*

two **b** for her wrists	Gen 24:22
armlets and **b**	Num 31:50
earrings, **b**, veils	Is 3:19

BRAMBLE *briar*

trees said to the **b**	Judg 9:14
fire...from the **b**	Judg 9:15

BRANCH *bough*

David a righteous **B**	Jer 23:5
b-es *fit* for scepters	Ezek 19:11
beautiful **b-es** and	Ezek 31:3
birds...in its **b-es**	Luke 13:19
b-es of the palm	John 12:13
b...not bear fruit	John 15:2
you are the **b-es**	John 15:5
be holy, the **b-es**	Rom 11:16

BREACH *break*

For every **b** of trust	Ex 22:9
LORD had made a **b**	Judg 21:15
closed up the **b**	1 Kin 11:27
that no **b** remained	Neh 6:1
Heal its **b-es**	Ps 60:2

BREAD *food*

eat unleavened **b**	Ex 12:20
rain **b** from heaven	Ex 16:4
He will bless your **b**	Ex 23:25
b of the Presence	Ex 25:30
not live by **b** alone	Deut 8:3
ravens brought...**b**	1 Kin 17:6
b of heaven	Ps 105:40
satisfy...with **b**	Ps 132:15
b *eaten* in secret	Prov 9:17
eat the **b** of idleness	Prov 31:27
Cast your **b**...waters	Eccl 11:1
not live on **b** alone	Matt 4:4
Give us...daily **b**	Matt 6:11
gives you the true **b**	John 6:32
I am the **b** of life	John 6:35

BREAK *divide, shatter*

b down your pride	Lev 26:19
never **b** My covenant	Judg 2:1
broke the pitchers	Judg 7:20
soft tongue **b-s** the	Prov 25:15
reed He will not **b**	Is 42:3
I broke your yoke	Jer 2:20
B...fallow ground	Hos 10:12
waves were **b-ing**	Mark 4:37
she broke the vial	Mark 14:3
their nets *began* to **b**	Luke 5:6
b-ing the Sabbath	John 5:18
did not **b** His legs	John 19:33
your **b-ing** the Law	Rom 2:23

BREAST *bosom*

orphan from the **b**	Job 24:9
upon my mother's **b-s**	Ps 22:9
b-s are like...fawns	Song 7:3
b-s...never nursed	Luke 23:29
reclining on Jesus' **b**	John 13:23
girded across His **b**	Rev 1:13

BREASTPIECE *breast covering*

a **b** and an ephod	Ex 28:4
make a **b** of judgment	Ex 28:15
they bound the **b**	Ex 39:21

BREASTPLATE *breast armor*

righteousness like a **b**	Is 59:17

b of faith and love	1 Thess 5:8
like **b-s** of iron	Rev 9:9

BREATH *air, spirit, wind*

the **b** of life	Gen 2:7
days are *but* a **b**	Job 7:16
man is a mere **b**	Ps 39:11
b came into them	Ezek 37:10
give **b** to the image	Rev 13:15

BREATHE *inhale and exhale*

Abraham **b-d** his last	Gen 25:8
such as **b** out violence	Ps 27:12
garden **b**...*fragrance*	Song 4:16
b on these slain	Ezek 37:9
He **b-d** His last	Mark 15:39
He **b-d** on them	John 20:22

BRETHREN *brothers*

beating...his **b**	Ex 2:11
b from all the nations	Is 66:20
His **b** Will return	Mic 5:3
b, why do you injure	Acts 7:26
sinning against...**b**	1 Cor 8:12
dangers...false **b**	2 Cor 11:26
Peace be to the **b**	Eph 6:23
faithful **b** in Christ	Col 1:2
the love of the **b**	1 Thess 4:9
b...not grow weary	2 Thess 3:13
my **b**, do not swear	James 5:12
our lives for the **b**	1 John 3:16
accuser of our **b**	Rev 12:10

BRIAR *thistle, thorn*

b-s and thorns will come	Is 5:6
land will be **b-s**	Is 7:24
grapes from a **b** bush	Luke 6:44

BRIBE *illegal gift*

b blinds...clear-sighted	Ex 23:8
nor take a **b**	Deut 10:17
who hates **b-s** will	Prov 15:27
b corrupts the heart	Eccl 7:7
Everyone loves a **b**	Is 1:23

BRICK *clay block*

they used **b** for stone	Gen 11:3
straw to make **b** as	Ex 5:7
deliver...quota of **b-s**	Ex 5:18
burning incense on **b-s**	Is 65:3

BRIDE *newlywed*

as a **b** adorns herself	Is 61:10
the voice of the **b**	Jer 7:34
b out of her *bridal*	Joel 2:16
He who has the **b**	John 3:29
b...of the Lamb	Rev 21:9

BRIDEGROOM *newlywed*

a **b** of blood to me	Ex 4:25
As a **b** decks himself	Is 61:10
voice of the **b**	Jer 7:34
attendants of the **b**	Matt 9:15
out to meet the **b**	Matt 25:1

BRIDLE (n) *head harness*

My **b** in your lips	2 Kin 19:28
a **b** for the donkey	Prov 26:3
up to the horses' **b-s**	Rev 14:20

BRIDLE (v) *control*

not **b** his tongue	James 1:26
man, able to **b**	James 3:2

BRIGHT *shining*

b in the skies	Job 37:21
night is as **b** as	Ps 139:12
B eyes gladden	Prov 15:30
b cloud...them	Matt 17:5
b light...flashed	Acts 22:6
the **b** morning star	Rev 22:16

BRIMSTONE *sulfur*

b and fire from	Gen 19:24
b and burning wind	Ps 11:6
rained fire and **b**	Luke 17:29
tormented with...**b**	Rev 14:10
lake of fire and **b**	Rev 20:10

BRING *carry, lead*

shall **b** forth children	Gen 3:16
Cain brought...offering	Gen 4:3
b two of every *kind*	Gen 6:19
B the ark of God	1 Sam 14:18
Kings will **b** gifts	Ps 68:29
B water for the thirsty	Is 21:14
B the whole tithe	Mal 3:10
b-ing...a paralytic	Matt 9:2
not...to **b** peace	Matt 10:34
brought forth a son	Luke 1:57
I **b** you good news	Luke 2:10
Law **b-s** about wrath	Rom 4:15
b-ing salvation	Titus 2:11

BROAD *wide*

into a **b** place	2 Sam 22:20
land was **b** and	1 Chr 4:40
the sea, great and **b**	Ps 104:25
dark in **b** daylight	Amos 8:9
way is **b** that leads to	Matt 7:13

BROKEN *crushed, separated*

My spirit is **b**	Job 17:1
A **b** and contrite heart	Ps 51:17
they have **b** Thy law	Ps 119:126
deeps were **b** up	Prov 3:20
silver cord is **b**	Eccl 12:6
bind up the **b**	Ezek 34:16
Scripture...be **b**	John 10:35
Not a bone...**b**	John 19:36
Branches were **b** off	Rom 11:19

BROKENHEARTED *grieving*

LORD is near to the **b**	Ps 34:18
He heals the **b**	Ps 147:3
sent me to bind...**b**	Is 61:1

BRONZE *metal*

implements of **b**	Gen 4:22
made a **b** serpent	Num 21:9
bend a bow of **b**	2 Sam 22:35
as walls of **b**	Jer 1:18
third kingdom of **b**	Dan 2:39
costly wood and **b**	Rev 18:12

BROOD *group, offspring*

b of sinful men	Num 32:14
You **b** of vipers	Matt 3:7
hen *gathers* her **b**	Luke 13:34

BROOK *stream, wadi*

stones from the **b**	1 Sam 17:40
by the **b** Cherith	1 Kin 17:5
deer pants for...**b-s**	Ps 42:1
wisdom...bubbling **b**	Prov 18:4

BROTHER *male relative*

Am I my b-'s	Gen 4:9
b-s were jealous	Gen 37:11
b-s may redeem	Lev 25:48
b-s to dwell together	Ps 133:1
b is born for	Prov 17:17
closer than a b	Prov 18:24
b-s of a poor man	Prov 19:7
reconciled to your b	Matt 5:24
b will deliver up b	Matt 10:21
behold, His...b-s	Matt 12:46
not forgive his b	Matt 18:35
My b and sister	Mark 3:35
b of yours was dead	Luke 15:32
left...wife or b-s	Luke 18:29
not even His b-s	John 7:5
b shall rise again	John 11:23
b goes to law with b	1 Cor 6:6
my b to stumble	1 Cor 8:13
yet hates his b	1 John 2:9

BROTHERHOOD

the covenant of b	Amos 1:9
love the b, fear god	1 Pet 2:17

BRUISE (n) *wound*

for wound, b for b	Ex 21:25
Only b-s, welts, and raw	Is 1:6
the b He has inflicted	Is 30:26

BRUISE (v) *batter, crush*

b him on the heel	Gen 3:15
b-s me with a tempest	Job 9:17

BRUTAL *fierce, vicious*

hand of b men	Ezek 21:31
b, haters of good	2 Tim 3:3

BUD *blossom, a sprout*

flax was in b	Ex 9:31
put forth b-s	Num 17:8
the b blossoms	Is 18:5

BUFFET *beat*

I b my body	1 Cor 9:27
Satan to b me	2 Cor 12:7

BUILD *construct, form*

Noah built an altar	Gen 8:20
let us b...a city	Gen 11:4
b for Me a house	1 Chr 17:12
b-ing...house of God	2 Chr 3:3
built high places	2 Chr 33:19
has built up Zion	Ps 102:16
Unless the LORD b-s	Ps 127:1
a time to b up	Eccl 3:3
built his house upon	Matt 7:24
I will b My church	Matt 16:18
able to b *you* up	Acts 20:32
being built together	Eph 2:22
stones...being built	1 Pet 2:5

BUILDER *fashioner, maker*

Solomon's b-s	1 Kin 5:18
b-s had laid the	Ezra 3:10
the b-s rejected	Matt 21:42
as a wise master b	1 Cor 3:10
architect and b is	Heb 11:10

BUILDING *structure*

reconstructing this b	Ezra 5:4
b that *was* in front	Ezek 41:12
what wonderful b-s	Mark 13:1

you are...God's b	1 Cor 3:9
have a b from God	2 Cor 5:1
whole b, being fitted	Eph 2:21

BULB *part of plant*

a b and a flower	Ex 25:33
b-s and their branches	Ex 25:36

BULL *animal*

b of the sin offering	Lev 4:20
b without blemish	Ezek 45:18
blood of b-s and	Heb 10:4

BULRUSH *marsh plant*

b in a single day	Is 9:14
b-es by the Nile	Is 19:7
palm branch or b	Is 19:15

BUNDLE *package*

b...*was* in his sack	Gen 42:35
the b of the living	1 Sam 25:29
in b-s to burn	Matt 13:30

BURDEN (n) *load, weight*

b-s of the Egyptians	Ex 6:6
the b of the people	Num 11:17
I am a b to myself	Job 7:20
who daily bears our b	Ps 68:19
b-s hard to bear	Luke 11:46
Bear one another's b-s	Gal 6:2

BURDEN (v) *weigh down*

b-ed Me with your sins	Is 43:24
were b-ed excessively	2 Cor 1:8
not b you myself	2 Cor 12:16
the church be b-ed	1 Tim 5:16

BURIAL *interment*

give me a b site	Gen 23:4
even have a *proper* b	Eccl 6:3
to prepare Me for b	Matt 26:12
b custom of the Jews	John 19:40

BURN (v) *consume, kindle*

Jacob's anger b-ed	Gen 30:2
bush was b-ing	Ex 3:2
Thine anger b against	Ex 32:11
Moses' anger b-ed	Ex 32:19
did not b any cities	Josh 11:13
jealousy b like fire	Ps 79:5
to b their sons	Jer 7:31
not to b the scroll	Jer 36:25
will b up the chaff	Luke 3:17
b-ed in their desire	Rom 1:27
my body to be b-ed	1 Cor 13:3
works will be b-ed	2 Pet 3:10
lake of fire...b-s	Rev 19:20

BURNING (adj)

Thy b anger	Ex 15:7
shall bewail the b	Lev 10:6
b lips and a wicked	Prov 26:23
b heat of famine	Lam 5:10
b anger of the LORD	Zeph 2:2

BURNISHED *polished*

gleamed like b bronze	Ezek 1:7
feet...like b bronze	Rev 1:15

BURNT OFFERINGS

see OFFERINGS

BURST *break*

great deep b open	Gen 7:11

wine will b the skins	Luke 5:37
b his fetters	Luke 8:29
he b open	Acts 1:18

BURY *place in earth*

b-ied at...old age	Gen 15:15
that I may b my dead	Gen 23:4
b-ied the bones of	Josh 24:32
go and b my father	Matt 8:21
dead to b their own	Matt 8:22
devout...b-ied Stephen	Acts 8:2
that He was b-ied	1 Cor 15:4
b-ied...in baptism	Col 2:12

BUSH *shrub*

boy under...the b-es	Gen 21:15
the b was burning	Ex 3:2
who dwelt in the b	Deut 33:16
like a b in the desert	Jer 17:6

BUSINESS *occupation, work*

until I...told my b	Gen 24:33
carry on the *king's* b	Esth 3:9
another to his b	Matt 22:5
attend to your...b	1 Thess 4:11
engage in b	James 4:13

BUSYBODIES *meddlers*

no work...like b	2 Thess 3:11
gossips and b	1 Tim 5:13

BUTTER

steps...bathed in b	Job 29:6
smoother than b	Ps 55:21
milk produces b	Prov 30:33

BUYER *purchaser*

Bad, bad, says the b	Prov 20:14
the b like the seller	Is 24:2
Let not the b rejoice	Ezek 7:12

BYSTANDERS *onlookers*

b...said to Peter	Matt 26:73
the b heard it	Mark 15:35

BYWORD *contemptible*

b among all peoples	1 Kin 9:7
a proverb and a b	2 Chr 7:20
He has made me a b	Job 17:6
b among the nations	Ps 44:14

C

CAESAR

1 *Roman emperor*
    Matt 22:17,21; Mark 12:14;
    John 19:12
2 *Augustus*   Luke 2:1
3 *Tiberius* Luke 3:1; John 19:12
4 *Claudius* Acts 11:28;17:7;18:2
5 *Nero*
    Acts 25:12;26:32; Phil 4:22

CAESAREA

Roman coastal city
    Acts 8:40;10:1;21:16;25:4

CAESAREA PHILIPPI

city at base of Mt. Hermon
    Matt 16:13; Mark 8:27

CAIAPHAS

high priest
    Matt 26:57; Luke 3:2;
    John 11:49ff; Acts 4:6

CAIN

son of Adam	Gen 4:1
tiller of the ground	Gen 4:2
killed his brother	Gen 4:8
marked by sign	Gen 4:15

CAKE *type of bread*

and make bread c-s	Gen 18:6
took one unleavened c	Lev 8:26
make me a...c	1 Kin 17:13

CALAMITY *adversity, trouble*

day of my c	2 Sam 22:19
sorry over the c	1 Chr 21:15
palate discern c-ies	Job 6:30
c from God is	Job 31:23
stumble in *time of* c	Prov 24:16
beginning to work c	Jer 25:29
relents concerning c	Jon 4:2

CALCULATE *count*

shall c from the year	Lev 25:50
c the cost	Luke 14:28
c the...beast	Rev 13:18

CALEB

1 *aide to Moses*	Num 13:30
son of Jephunneh	Num 32:12
received Hebron	Josh 14:13
2 *son of Hezron*	1 Chr 2:18

CALF *animal*

tender and choice c	Gen 18:7
into a molten c	Ex 32:4
c and the young lion	Is 11:6
skip about like c-ves	Mal 4:2
bring the fattened c	Luke 15:23
blood of...c-ves	Heb 9:12

CALL *address, summon, name*

God c-ed the light day	Gen 1:5
c upon the name	Gen 4:26
c-s up the dead	Deut 18:11
LORD was c-ing...boy	1 Sam 3:8
c-ed fine gold my trust	Job 31:24
c upon the LORD	Ps 18:3
those who c evil good	Is 5:20
c His name Immanuel	Is 7:14
You shall c Me	Jer 3:19
who is c-ed Christ	Matt 1:16
to c the righteous	Matt 9:13
c-s his own sheep	John 10:3
c Me Teacher and	John 13:13
God has not c-ed	1 Thess 4:7
c-s...a prophetess	Rev 2:20

CALLING *summoning*

the c of assemblies	Is 1:13
the c of God	Rom 11:29
For consider your c	1 Cor 1:26
with a holy c	2 Tim 1:9
His c and choosing	2 Pet 1:10

CALM *still*

be c, have no fear	Is 7:4
sea may become c	Jon 1:11
it became perfectly c	Matt 8:26
you ought to keep c	Acts 19:36

CAMEL *animal*

dismounted...the c	Gen 24:64
his wives upon c-s	Gen 31:17

a garment of c-'s hair	Matt 3:4
c...eye of a needle	Matt 19:24
clothed with c-'s hair	Mark 1:6

CAMP (n) *lodging area*

This is God's c	Gen 32:2
people out of the c	Ex 19:17
outside the c seven	Num 31:19
pitch c-s, and place	Ezek 4:2
the c of the saints	Rev 20:9

CAMP (v) *settle*

you shall c in front	Ex 14:2
they shall also c	Num 1:50
Israel c-ed at Gilgal	Josh 5:10
I will c against you	Is 29:3
c around My house	Zech 9:8

CANA

Galilean town	John 2:1,11;4:46

CANAAN

1 *son of Ham*	Gen 9:18,25
2 *Syro-Palestine*	
	Gen 13:12;42:5; Ex 16:35; Ps 105:11
3 *language (Hebrew)*	Is 19:18
see also **HEBREW**	
see also **JUDEAN**	

CANAL *water way*

c-s will emit a stench	Is 19:6
rivers *and* wide c-s	Is 33:21
the Nile c-s dry	Ezek 30:12
in front of the c	Dan 8:3

CAPERNAUM

city on Sea of Galilee	
	Matt 4:13; Luke 4:23; John 6:24,59

CAPHTOR

Crete	
	Deut 2:23; Jer 47:4; Amos 9:7
see also **CRETE**	

CAPITAL *top part of column*

height of the other c	1 Kin 7:16
c on the top of each	2 Chr 3:15
c-s...were on top	2 Chr 4:12

CAPITAL *city*

Susa the c	Esth 2:3

CAPPADOCIA

province in Asia Minor	
	Acts 2:9; 1 Pet 1:1

CAPTAIN *leader*

c of the bodyguard	Gen 39:1
the c-s of hundreds	Num 31:14
c of the host of	Josh 5:14
the c of the ship	Acts 27:11

CAPTIVE *prisoner*

first-born of the c	Ex 12:29
slain and the c-s	Deut 32:42
restores his c people	Ps 14:7
hast led c *Thy* c-s	Ps 68:18
release to the c-s	Luke 4:18
every thought c	2 Cor 10:5
having been held c	2 Tim 2:26

CAPTIVITY *imprisonment*

restore you from c	Deut 30:3

land of their c	2 Chr 6:37
had come from the c	Ezra 8:35
had survived the c	Neh 1:2
destined for c	Rev 13:10

CAPTURE *seize, take*

they c-d and looted	Gen 34:29
c-d all his cities	Deut 2:34
Can anyone c him	Job 40:24
it c-s nothing at all	Amos 3:5

CARAVAN *expedition*

a c of Ishmaelites	Gen 37:25
The c-s of Tema	Job 6:19
O c-s of Dedanites	Is 21:13

CARCASS *corpse*

down upon the c-es	Gen 15:11
one who touches...c	Lev 11:39
c-es shall be food	Deut 28:26
c of the lion	Judg 14:8
c-es of their...idols	Jer 16:18

CARE (n) *concern*

into the c of...sons	Gen 30:35
put him in my c	Gen 42:37
friends and receive c	Acts 27:3
c for one another	1 Cor 12:25

CARE (v) *have concern for*

He c-d for him	Deut 32:10
No one c-s for...soul	Ps 142:4
c for My sheep	Ezek 34:12
and took c of him	Luke 10:34
take c of the church	1 Tim 3:5
he c-s for you	1 Pet 5:7

CAREFUL *watchful, on guard*

I not be c to speak	Num 23:12
c to observe all	Deut 6:25
you shall be c to do	Deut 8:1
be c not to drink	Judg 13:4
be c how you walk	Eph 5:15

CARELESS *thoughtless*

a fool is...c	Prov 14:16
food, and c ease	Ezek 16:49
that every c word	Matt 12:36

CARGO *merchandise*

and they threw the c	Jon 1:5
to unload its c	Acts 21:3
no one buys...c-es	Rev 18:11

CARMEL

1 *range of hills*	
	1 Kin 18:42; 2 Kin 4:25; Jer 46:18
2 *town in Judah*	
	1 Sam 15:12;25:5,40

CARPENTER *craftsman*

c-s and stonemasons	2 Sam 5:11
to the masons and c-s	Ezra 3:7
this the c-'s son	Matt 13:55
c, the son of Mary	Mark 6:3

CARRY *bear*

LORD...c-ied you	Deut 1:31
c an ephod before	1 Sam 2:28
Spirit...will c you	1 Kin 18:12
c them in His bosom	Is 40:11
our sorrows He c-ied	Is 53:4
c-ied away...diseases	Matt 8:17

C no purse, no bag   Luke 10:4
the cross to c   Luke 23:26
c out the desire of   Gal 5:16

CART *wagon*

So Moses took the c-s   Num 7:6
the cows to the c   1 Sam 6:7
sin as if with c ropes   Is 5:18
his c and his horses   Is 28:28

CARVE (v) *cut, fashion*

he c-d all the walls   1 Kin 6:29
who c a resting place   Is 22:16
c-d with cherubim   Ezek 41:18
its maker has c-d it   Hab 2:18

CARVED (adj) *cut, etched*

with c engravings   1 Kin 6:29
c image of the idol   2 Chr 33:7
abdomen is c ivory   Song 5:14

CAST *throw*

one who c-s a spell   Deut 18:11
Joshua c lots for   Josh 18:10
c Thy law behind   Neh 9:26
c *lots* for the orphans   Job 6:27
c My words behind   Ps 50:17
Do not c me away   Ps 51:11
c you out of My sight   Jer 7:15
c-ing...insult   Mark 15:32
will c out demons   Mark 16:17
c Him out of...city   Luke 4:29
c fire upon...earth   Luke 12:49
clothing they c lots   John 19:24
c-ing all your anxiety   1 Pet 5:7
but c them into hell   2 Pet 2:4
c their crowns before   Rev 4:10

CATCH *seize, trap*

shall c his wife   Judg 21:21
to c the afflicted   Ps 10:9
c...with her eyelids   Prov 6:25
C the foxes for us   Song 2:15
caught in My snare   Ezek 12:13
will be c-ing men   Luke 5:10
unable to c Him   Luke 20:26
caught in adultery   John 8:3
who c-es the wise   1 Cor 3:19
if a man is caught   Gal 6:1
child was caught up   Rev 12:5

CATTLE *domestic animals*

c and creeping things   Gen 1:24
the first-born of c   Ex 12:29
defect from the c   Lev 22:19
c on a thousand hills   Ps 50:10
no c in the stalls   Hab 3:17

CAUSE (n) *purpose, reason*

the c of the just   Ex 23:8
to death without a c   1 Sam 19:5
place my c before God   Job 5:8
hate me without a c   Ps 69:4
wounds without c   Prov 23:29
c a man shall leave   Matt 19:5
hated...without a c   John 15:25

CAUSE (v) *make*

I c My name to be   Ex 20:24
c Israel to inherit   Deut 1:38
has c-d His name   Ezra 6:12
c His face to shine   Ps 67:1
speech c you to sin   Eccl 5:6

who c dissensions   Rom 16:17
was c-ing the growth   1 Cor 3:6

CAVE *shelter*

buried him in the c   Gen 25:9
escaped to the c   1 Sam 22:1
by fifties in a c   1 Kin 18:4
mountains and c-s   Heb 11:38
hid...in the c-s   Rev 6:15

CEASE *stop*

you shall c *from labor*   Ex 23:12
poor will never c   Deut 15:11
He makes wars to c   Ps 46:9
C...consideration   Prov 23:4
make this proverb c   Ezek 12:23
c-d to kiss My feet   Luke 7:45
tongues, they will c   1 Cor 13:8
pray without c-ing   1 Thess 5:17

CEDAR *tree, wood*

with the c wood   Lev 14:6
c-s beside the waters   Num 24:6
all the c-s of Lebanon   Is 2:13
the height of c-s   Amos 2:9

CELEBRATE *rejoice*

may c a feast to Me   Ex 5:1
you shall c it in   Lev 23:41
C the Passover   2 Kin 23:21
all Israel were c-ing   1 Chr 13:8
to c *the* feast   2 Chr 30:23

CENSER *incense container*

c-s for yourselves   Num 16:6
his c in his hand   Ezek 8:11
holding a golden c   Rev 8:3
angel took the c   Rev 8:5

CENSUS *population roll*

c of...congregation   Num 1:2
number of the c   1 Chr 21:5
c which...David   2 Chr 2:17
the first c taken   Luke 2:2
in the days of the c   Acts 5:37

CENT *money*

paid up the last c   Matt 5:26
sparrows...for a c   Matt 10:29
amount to a c   Mark 12:42

CENTURION *captain*

Jesus said to the c   Matt 8:13
summoning the c   Mark 15:44
soldiers and c-s   Acts 21:32
gave orders to the c   Acts 24:23

CEPHAS

apostle Peter
          John 1:42; 1 Cor 1:12;15:5;
                                 Gal 2:11

CERTAINTY *sureness*

know with c that   Josh 23:13
c of the words   Prov 22:21
you know with c   Eph 5:5

CERTIFICATE *permit, record*

a c of divorce   Deut 24:1
a c of divorce   Matt 5:31
c of debt   Col 2:14

CHAFF *husk*

consumes them as c   Ex 15:7

c which the wind drives   Ps 1:4
make the hills like c   Is 41:15
c from the summer   Dan 2:35
burn up the c   Matt 3:12

CHAIN *band*

bound...bronze c-s   Judg 16:21
he drew c-s of gold   1 Kin 6:21
whose hands are c-s   Eccl 7:26
was bound with c-s   Luke 8:29
c-s fell off his hands   Acts 12:7
great c in his hand   Rev 20:1

CHALDEA

S Babylonia
          Jer 50:10;51:24; Ezek 23:15

CHALDEANS

inhabitants of Chaldea
          Gen 11:28; 2 Kin 24:2; Job
          1:17; Jer 24:5; Dan 5:11;
                                 Hab 1:6

CHAMBER *room*

entered his c   Gen 43:30
in his cool roof c   Judg 3:20
c-s of the storehouse   Neh 10:38
bridegroom...his c   Ps 19:5
to the c-s of death   Prov 7:27
out of her *bridal* c   Joel 2:16
c-s in the heavens   Amos 9:6

CHAMPION *fighter*

c, the Philistine   1 Sam 17:23
a Savior and a C   Is 19:20
like a dread c   Jer 20:11

CHANGE (n) *alteration*

gave c-s of garments   Gen 45:22
had a c of heart   Ex 14:5
two c-s of clothes   2 Kin 5:23
Until my c comes   Job 14:14
a c of law   Heb 7:12

CHANGE (v) *alter, transform*

and c-d my wages   Gen 31:7
He c-s a wilderness   Ps 107:35
c-d their glory   Jer 2:11
Ethiopian c his skin   Jer 13:23
He who c-s the times   Dan 2:21
LORD c-d His mind   Amos 7:6
I, the LORD, do not c   Mal 3:6
shall all be c-d   1 Cor 15:51

CHANNEL *furrow*

Who has cleft a c   Job 38:25
c-s of water appeared   Ps 18:15
heart is *like* c-s   Prov 21:1
sent out its c-s   Ezek 31:4

CHANT *sing*

David c-ed...this   2 Sam 1:17
Jeremiah c-ed a   2 Chr 35:25
daughters...shall c   Ezek 32:16

CHARACTER

and proven c, hope   Rom 5:4
Let your c be free   Heb 13:5

CHARGE (n) *responsibility*

under Joseph's c   Gen 39:23
keep the c of the LORD   Lev 8:35
c of his household   Matt 24:45
allotted to your c   1 Pet 5:3

CHARGE (n) *accusation*

far from a false **c**	Ex 23:7
bring **c-s** against	Acts 19:38
c against God's elect	Rom 8:33

CHARGE (n) *cost*

gospel without **c**	1 Cor 9:18

CHARGE (v) *command*

Abimelech **c-d** all	Gen 26:11
I **c-d** your judges	Deut 1:16
Moses **c-d** us with a	Deut 33:4
I solemnly **c** you	1 Tim 5:21

CHARGE (v) *exact a price*

not **c** him interest	Ex 22:25
c that to my account	Philem 18

CHARIOT *wagon*

Joseph prepared...**c**	Gen 46:29
appeared a **c** of fire	2 Kin 2:11
Some *boast* in **c-s**	Ps 20:7
c-s of God are myriads	Ps 68:17
Thy **c-s** of salvation	Hab 3:8
I will cut off the **c**	Zech 9:10
and sitting in his **c**	Acts 8:28

CHARIOTEERS *warriors*

David killed 700 **c**	2 Sam 10:18
7,000 **c** and 40,000	1 Chr 19:18
with horses and **c**	Ezek 39:20

CHARITY *alms*

give that...as **c**	Luke 11:41
and give to **c**	Luke 12:33
deeds of...**c**	Acts 9:36

CHARM *beauty*

A bribe is a **c**	Prov 17:8
C is deceitful	Prov 31:30
with *all* your **c-s**	Song 7:6

CHASE *drive, pursue*

Egyptians **c-d** after	Ex 14:9
will **c** your enemies	Lev 26:7
one **c** a thousand	Deut 32:30
c-ing...Philistines	1 Sam 17:53
be **c-d** like chaff	Is 17:13

CHASTE *pure*

c...behavior	1 Pet 3:2
kept themselves **c**	Rev 14:4

CHASTEN *discipline*

Man is also **c-ed**	Job 33:19
Nor **c** me in Thy wrath	Ps 6:1
c-ed every morning	Ps 73:14
who **c-s** the nations	Ps 94:10

CHASTISE *punish*

Thou hast **c-d** me	Jer 31:18
I will **c** all of them	Hos 5:2

CHATTER *babbling*

worldly...empty **c**	1 Tim 6:20
avoid...empty **c**	2 Tim 2:16

CHEAT *deceive*

your father has **c-ed**	Gen 31:7
c with...scales	Amos 8:5

CHEBAR

river in Babylonia

	Ezek 3:15; 10:15

CHEDORLAOMER

king of Elam   Gen 14:9,17

CHEEK *part of face*

slapped me on the **c**	Job 16:10
Your **c-s** are lovely	Song 1:10
tears are on her **c-s**	Lam 1:2
hits you on the **c**	Luke 6:29

CHEERFUL

countenance and be **c**	Job 9:27
joyful heart...a **c**	Prov 15:13
c heart...feast	Prov 15:15
God loves a **c** giver	2 Cor 9:7
Is anyone **c**	James 5:13

CHEMOSH

god of Moab

	Judg 11:24; 1 Kin 11:7;
	Jer 48:13

CHERETHITES

1 tribe on Philistine plain

	1 Sam 30:14; Ezek 25:16;
	Zeph 2:5

2 David's bodyguards

	2 Sam 8:18;15:18; 1 Kin 1:38;
	1 Chr 18:17

CHERISH *love*

or the wife you **c**	Deut 13:6
the wife he **c-es**	Deut 28:54
men **c** themselves	Acts 24:15
c-es it, just as Christ	Eph 5:29

CHERUB *celestial being*

He rode on a **c**	2 Sam 22:11
one **c**...ten cubits	1 Kin 6:26
c stretched out his	Ezek 10:7

CHERUBIM *plural of cherub*

He stationed the **c**	Gen 3:24
c had *their* wings	Ex 37:9
enthroned *above*...**c**	2 Sam 6:2
c appeared to have	Ezek 10:8

CHEST *box*

the priest took a **c**	2 Kin 12:9
money in the **c**	2 Kin 12:10
levies...into the **c**	2 Chr 24:10

CHEW *eat*

which **c** the cud	Lev 11:4
before it was **c-ed**	Num 11:33

CHIEF *head, prominent*

c-s of the sons of	Gen 36:15
the **c-s** of Edom	Gen 36:43
of the thirty **c** men	2 Sam 23:13
c of the magicians	Dan 4:9
C Shepherd appears	1 Pet 5:4

CHILD

c grew...weaned	Gen 21:8
Train up a **c** in	Prov 22:6
discipline from the **c**	Prov 23:13
c will be born to us	Is 9:6
with **c** by the Holy	Matt 1:18
take the **C** and His	Matt 2:13
He called a **c** to	Matt 18:2
saying, **C**, arise	Luke 8:54
a woman with **c**	1 Thess 5:3

CHILDBIRTH

multiply...pain in **c**	Gen 3:16
as of a woman in **c**	Ps 48:6
pains of **c** come	Hos 13:13
suffers the pains of **c**	Rom 8:22

CHILDLESS

I am **c**, and the heir	Gen 15:2
They shall die **c**	Lev 20:20
c among women	1 Sam 15:33
and died **c**	Luke 20:29

CHILDREN

pain...bring forth **c**	Gen 3:16
Are these all the **c**	1 Sam 16:11
compassion on *his* **c**	Ps 103:13
c are a gift	Ps 127:3
c rise up and bless	Prov 31:28
c were dashed to	Nah 3:10
slew all the male **c**	Matt 2:16
stones to raise up **c**	Matt 3:9
c...against parents	Matt 10:21
and become like **c**	Matt 18:3
bringing **c** to Him	Mark 10:13
if **c**, heirs	Rom 8:17
C, obey your parents	Eph 6:1
My little **c**	1 John 2:1
kill her **c** with	Rev 2:23

CHINNERETH / CHINNEROTH

1 lake   Num 34:11; Josh 12:3
    also **Sea of Galilee**
    also **Lake of Gennesaret**
    also **Sea of Tiberius**

2 city of Naphtali

	Deut 3:17; Josh 19:35

3 plain near Galilee

	Josh 11:2; 1 Kin 15:20

CHISLEV

ninth month of Hebrew calendar

	Neh 1:1; Zech 7:1

CHOICE *option* or *best*

Saul, a **c**...*man*	1 Sam 9:2
c men of Israel	2 Sam 10:9
And eat its **c** fruits	Song 4:16
God made a **c** among	Acts 15:7
God's gracious **c**	Rom 11:5
His **c** of you	1 Thess 1:4

CHOIR *chorus*

c proceeded to the	Neh 12:38
two **c-s** took their	Neh 12:40

CHOKE *stifle*

riches **c** the word	Matt 13:22
began to **c** him	Matt 18:28
thorns...**c-d** it	Mark 4:7
c-d with worries	Luke 8:14

CHOOSE *select, take*

C men for us	Ex 17:9
whom the LORD **c-s**	Num 16:7
C wise...discerning	Deut 1:13
He **c-s** our inheritance	Ps 47:4
refuse evil and **c** good	Is 7:15
not God **c** the poor	James 2:5

CHOP *cut*

who **c-s** your wood	Deut 29:11
c-ped down...altars	2 Chr 34:7

C down the tree   Dan 4:14

CHOSE *selected*

Lot **c** for himself   Gen 13:11
God has **c-n** you   Deut 7:6
I **c** David to be   1 Kin 8:16
when I **c** Israel   Ezek 20:5
c twelve of them   Luke 6:13
has **c-n** the weak   1 Cor 1:27
He **c** us in Him   Eph 1:4

CHOSEN *elected, selected*

Moses His **c** one   Ps 106:23
My **c** *one in whom*   Is 42:1
Israel My **c** *one*   Is 45:4
c ones shall inherit   Is 65:9
My Son, *My* **C** One   Luke 9:35
c of God, holy and   Col 3:12
of *His* **c** angels   1 Tim 5:21
you are a **c** race   1 Pet 2:9

CHRIST *Messiah*

birth of Jesus **C** was   Matt 1:18
C should suffer and   Luke 24:46
both Lord and **C**   Acts 2:36
fellow heirs with **C**   Rom 8:17
are one body in **C**   Rom 12:5
preach **C** crucified   1 Cor 1:23
judgment seat of **C**   2 Cor 5:10
ambassadors for **C**   2 Cor 5:20
faith in **C** Jesus   Gal 2:16
as sons through Jesus **C**   Eph 1:5
to live is **C**   Phil 1:21
C, who is our life   Col 3:4
dead in **C** shall   1 Thess 4:16
coming of...**C**   2 Thess 2:1
C...high priest   Heb 9:11
Advocate...Jesus **C**   1 John 2:1
with **C** for a thousand   Rev 20:4

CHRISTIAN *follower of Christ*

first called **C-s** in   Acts 11:26
me to become a **C**   Acts 26:28
suffers as a **C**   1 Pet 4:16

CHRONICLES *book of register*

1 *of kings of Israel*
   1 Kin 14:19;15:31;
   2 Kin 14:28;15:26
2 *of kings of Judah*
   1 Kin 14:29;15:23;
   2 Kin 15:36;24:5
3 *of kings of Media / Persia*
   Esth 10:2

CHURCH *a called out assembly*

I will build my **c**   Matt 16:18
tell it to the **c**   Matt 18:17
shepherd the **c**   Acts 20:28
c-es of the Gentiles   Rom 16:4
together as a **c**   1 Cor 11:18
woman...speak in **c**   1 Cor 14:35
to the **c-es** of Judea   Gal 1:22
Christ...head of the **c**   Eph 5:23
persecutor of the **c**   Phil 3:6
c of the living God   1 Tim 3:15
Spirit says to the **c-es**   Rev 2:11

CILICIA

region in SE Asia Minor
   Acts 15:41;21:39;27:5

CINNAMON *spice*

and of fragrant **c**   Ex 30:23
myrrh, aloes and **c**   Prov 7:17
and **c** and spice   Rev 18:13

CIRCLE *area*

sleeping inside...**c**   1 Sam 26:7
He has inscribed a **c**   Job 26:10
did not sit in the **c**   Jer 15:17

CIRCUIT *course*

on **c** to Bethel   1 Sam 7:16
its **c** to the other end   Ps 19:6

CIRCULATE *spread*

proclamation was **c-d**   Ex 36:6
LORD's people **c-ing**   1 Sam 2:24
to **c** a proclamation   2 Chr 30:5

CIRCUMCISE *be pure or cut off*

every male...be **c-d**   Gen 17:10
Abraham **c-d** his son   Gen 21:4
C then your heart   Deut 10:16
God will **c**...heart   Deut 30:6
C yourselves...LORD   Jer 4:4
came to **c** the child   Luke 1:59
c-d the eighth day   Phil 3:5

CIRCUMCISION *act of purity*

because of the **c**   Ex 4:26
c is...of the heart   Rom 2:29
if you receive **c**   Gal 5:2
if I still preach **c**   Gal 5:11
we are the *true* **c**   Phil 3:3
c made without hands   Col 2:11
those of the **c**   Titus 1:10

CIRCUMSTANCE *condition*

spoken in right **c-s**   Prov 25:11
may know...my **c-s**   Eph 6:21
peace in every **c**   2 Thess 3:16
of humble **c-s**   James 1:9

CISTERN *reservoir*

a **c** collecting water   Lev 11:36
water from your...**c**   Prov 5:15
wheel at the **c** is   Eccl 12:6
prophet from the **c**   Jer 38:10

CITADEL *fortress*

c of the king's   1 Kin 16:18
in the **c** of Susa   Dan 8:2
c-s of Jerusalem   Amos 2:5
Proclaim on the **c-s**   Amos 3:9
tramples on our **c-s**   Mic 5:5

CITIES OF REFUGE

1 *Kedesh in Naphtali*   Josh 20:7
2 *Shechem in Ephraim*   Josh 20:7
3 *Hebron (Kiriath-arba)*
   Josh 20:7
4 *Bezer in Reuben*   Josh 20:8
5 *Ramoth-gilead in Gad*
   Josh 20:8
6 *Golan in Manasseh*   Josh 20:8

CITIZEN *resident*

your fellow **c-s**   Ezek 33:2
fellow **c-s** who talk   Ezek 33:30
c-s hated him   Luke 19:14
c of no insignificant   Acts 21:39
fellow **c-s** with the   Eph 2:19

CITY

Build...a **c**   Gen 11:4
burned...their **c-ies**   Num 31:10
die in my own **c**   2 Sam 19:37
glad the **c** of God   Ps 46:4
LORD guards the **c**   Ps 127:1
the **C** of Destruction   Is 19:18
the **C** of Truth   Zech 8:3
a **c** called Nazareth   Matt 2:23
into the holy **c**   Matt 4:5
the **c** was stirred   Matt 21:10
c, shake off the dust   Luke 9:5
He has prepared a **c**   Heb 11:16
I saw the holy **c**   Rev 21:2

CLAIM *demand*

Let darkness...**c** it   Job 3:5
Do not **c** honor in   Prov 25:6
c-ing to be someone   Acts 8:9

CLAN *family, tribe*

c of the household   Judg 9:1
and by your **c-s**   1 Sam 10:19
among...**c-s** of Judah   Mic 5:2
I will make the **c-s**   Zech 12:6

CLAP *applaud*

c-ped their hands   2 Kin 11:12
c-s his hands among   Job 34:37
rivers **c** their hands   Ps 98:8
trees...will **c**   Is 55:12

CLAUDIA

Roman Christian   2 Tim 4:21

CLAUDIUS

Roman Emperor   Acts 11:28;18:2
see **CAESAR**

CLAUDIUS LYSIAS

Roman tribune   Acts 23:26

CLAY

dwell in houses of **c**   Job 4:19
Father, We are the **c**   Is 64:8
c in the potter's hand   Jer 18:6
the **c** to his eyes   John 9:6

CLEAN *cleansed, washed*

animals that are not **c**   Gen 7:2
eat in a **c** place   Lev 10:14
pronounce him **c**   Lev 13:28
Create in me a **c** heart   Ps 51:10
make yourselves **c**   Is 1:16
You can make me **c**   Matt 8:2
things are **c** for you   Luke 11:41
c because of the word   John 15:3

CLEANSE *purify, wash*

To **c** the house then   Lev 14:49
c the house of the   2 Chr 29:15
I have **c-d** my heart   Prov 20:9
I am willing; be **c-d**   Matt 11:5
the lepers are **c-d**   Matt 11:5
not eat unless they **c**   Mark 7:4
let us **c** ourselves   2 Cor 7:1
C...you sinners   James 4:8
blood...**c-s** us   1 John 1:7

CLEAR *make free or plain*

c away many nations   Deut 7:1
C the way for the LORD   Is 40:3
c His threshing floor   Matt 3:12

CLEAVE *cling, divide*

Christ had made c	2 Pet 1:14
river...c as crystal	Rev 22:1

CLEAVE *cling, divide*

shall c to his wife	Gen 2:24
tongue c-s to my jaws	Ps 22:15
c to Thy testimonies	Ps 119:31
c the earth with rivers	Hab 3:9
shall c to his wife	Eph 5:31

CLEFT *crevice*

in the c of the rock	Judg 15:8
the c-s of the cliffs	Is 2:21
who live in the c-s	Obad 3

CLEOPAS

disciple of Christ	Luke 24:18

CLEVER *smart*

c in their own sight	Is 5:21
cleverness of the c	1 Cor 1:19

CLIFF *crag*

nest is set in the c	Num 24:21
On the c he dwells	Job 39:28
c-s are a refuge	Ps 104:18

CLIMB *ascend*

I will c the palm tree	Song 7:8
the one who c-s	Jer 48:44
c-ed...a sycamore	Luke 19:4
c-s up...other way	John 10:1

CLING *cleave*

and c to Him	Deut 13:4
c to the LORD	Josh 23:8
My soul c-s to Thee	Ps 63:8
Stop c-ing to Me	John 20:17
c to what is good	Rom 12:9

CLOAK *coat, mantle*

Give me the c	Ruth 3:15
neither bread nor c	Is 3:7
fringe of His c	Matt 9:20
Wrap your c around	Acts 12:8

CLOSE *shut, stop*

and the LORD c-d	Gen 7:16
floodgates...were c-d	Gen 8:2
earth c-d over them	Num 16:33
have c-d their eyes	Acts 28:27
every mouth...c-d	Rom 3:19
c-s his heart	1 John 3:17

CLOTH *fabric*

spread over it a c	Num 4:6
is wrapped in a c	1 Sam 21:9
with embroidered c	Ezek 16:10
in the linen c	Mark 15:46

CLOTHE *array, dress*

C me with skin	Job 10:11
meadows are c-d with	Ps 65:13
O Zion; C yourself	Is 52:1
naked...you c-d Me	Matt 25:36
are splendidly c-d	Luke 7:25
c-d with power	Luke 24:49
c...with humility	1 Pet 5:5
c-d in the white robes	Rev 7:13

CLOTHES *garments*

c of her captivity	Deut 21:13
your c have not worn	Deut 29:5
and worn-out c on	Josh 9:5

and changed his c	2 Sam 12:20
without wedding c	Matt 22:12
And tearing his c	Mark 14:63

CLOTHING *clothes, raiment*

reduce...her c	Ex 21:10
c did not wear out	Deut 8:4
purple are their c	Jer 10:9
and the body than c	Matt 6:25
in sheep's c	Matt 7:15
His c became white	Luke 9:29
sister is without c	James 2:15

CLOUD *mist*

set My bow in the c	Gen 9:13
in a pillar of c	Ex 13:21
c where God was	Ex 20:21
c covered...mountain	Ex 24:15
c for a covering	Ps 105:39
voice came out...c	Mark 9:7
Son...coming in c-s	Mark 13:26
in a c with power	Luke 21:27
and a c received Him	Acts 1:9

CLUB *weapon*

went...with a c	2 Sam 23:21
C-s are...as stubble	Job 41:29
Like a c and a	Prov 25:18
with swords and c-s	Matt 26:47

CLUSTER *collection*

c-s produced ripe	Gen 40:10
c-s of raisins	1 Sam 25:18
breasts are...c-s	Song 7:7
gather the c-s	Rev 14:18

COAL *charcoal*

breath kindles c-s	Job 41:21
man walk on hot c-s	Prov 6:28
burning c in his hand	Is 6:6
heap burning c-s	Rom 12:20

COAST

c of the Great Sea	Josh 9:1
along the c of Asia	Acts 27:2

COASTLAND

inhabitants of this c	Is 20:6
to the c-s of Kittim	Jer 2:10
c-s shake at the	Ezek 26:15
c-s of the nations	Zeph 2:11

COAT *cloak*

opening...c of mail	Ex 28:32
with his c torn	2 Sam 15:32
have your c also	Matt 5:40

COBRA *snake*

deadly poison of c-s	Deut 32:33
To the venom of c-s	Job 20:14
tread upon the...c	Ps 91:13

COCK *bird*

The strutting c	Prov 30:31
before a c crows	Matt 26:34
c shall not crow	John 13:38

COFFIN *bier*

in a c in Egypt	Gen 50:26
and touched the c	Luke 7:14

COHORT *military unit*

the whole Roman c	Matt 27:27
called the Italian c	Acts 10:1

of the Augustan c	Acts 27:1

COIN *money*

Show Me the c	Matt 22:19
woman...loses one c	Luke 15:8
He poured out...c-s	John 2:15

COLD *cool*

covering against the c	Job 24:7
Like the c of snow	Prov 25:13
cup of c water	Matt 10:42
love will grow c	Matt 24:12
neither c nor hot	Rev 3:15

COLLAPSE *fall*

grass c-s into the flame	Is 5:24
pathways will c	Ezek 38:20
ancient hills c-d	Hab 3:6

COLLEAGUES *co-workers*

the rest of his c	Ezra 4:7
and your c	Ezra 6:6

COLLECT *exact, take*

c-ed his strength	Gen 48:2
cistern c-ing water	Lev 11:36
c captives like sand	Hab 1:9
C no more than	Luke 3:13
c-ed a tenth from	Heb 7:6

COLLECTION *acquisition*

let your c of idols	Is 57:13
no c-s be made	1 Cor 16:2

COLOSSAE

city in Asia Minor	Col 1:2

COLT *foal*

camels and their c-s	Gen 32:15
Even on a c	Zech 9:9
and a c with her	Matt 21:2
on a donkey's c	John 12:15

COLUMN *pillar, text*

in a c of smoke	Judg 20:40
and marble c-s	Esth 1:6
read three...c-s	Jer 36:23

COME

C, let us build	Gen 11:4
C, let us worship	Ps 95:6
All came from...dust	Eccl 3:20
your king is c-ing	Zech 9:9
Thy kingdom c	Matt 6:10
C to Me, all who	Matt 11:28
children to c to Me	Mark 10:14
not c...temptation	Mark 14:38
Son of Man c-ing	Luke 21:27
Father...hour has c	John 17:1
His judgment has c	Rev 14:7
I am c-ing quickly	Rev 22:20

COMFORT (n) *consolation*

mourning without c	Job 30:28
c in my affliction	Ps 119:50
he will give you c	Prov 29:17
c of the Holy Spirit	Acts 9:31
and God of all c	2 Cor 1:3
your c and salvation	2 Cor 1:6

COMFORT (v) *console, cheer*

relatives came to c	1 Chr 7:22
Thy rod...they c me	Ps 23:4
I, am He who c-s you	Is 51:12

COMFORTER

To c all who mourn Is 61:2
he is being c-ed Luke 16:25
c one another 1 Thess 4:18

COMFORTER *consoler*

Sorry c-s are you all Job 16:2
c-s, but I found none Ps 69:20
She has no c Lam 1:9
Where will I seek c-s Nah 3:7

COMING (n) *arrival*

Joseph's c at noon Gen 43:25
the day of His c Mal 3:2
be the sign of Your c Matt 24:3
c of the Son of Man Matt 24:37
Christ's at His c 1 Cor 15:23
c of the Lord is James 5:8
the promise of His c 2 Pet 3:4

COMMAND (n) *order*

the c of the LORD Lev 24:12
disobeyed the c 1 Kin 13:21
to the king's c 2 Chr 35:10
no c of the Lord 1 Cor 7:25
could not bear the c Heb 12:20

COMMAND (v) *declare, order*

I c-ed you not to eat Gen 3:11
may c his children Gen 18:19
speak all that I c you Ex 7:2
bring all that I c Deut 12:11
the angel...c-ed Matt 1:24
c that these stones Matt 4:3
c-s even the winds Luke 8:25
c-ing the jailer Acts 16:23

COMMANDER *captain, general*

the c-s of Israel Judg 5:9
c of Saul's army 2 Sam 2:8
his chariot c-s 1 Kin 9:22
and Joab was the c 1 Chr 27:34
c for the peoples Is 55:4
the C of the host Dan 8:11
and the flesh of c-s Rev 19:18

COMMANDMENT *instruction*

and keep My c-s Ex 20:6
the Ten C-s Ex 34:28
and keep His c-s Josh 22:5
c of the LORD is pure Ps 19:8
the c of your father Prov 6:20
which is the great c Matt 22:36
A new c I give John 13:34
will keep My c-s John 14:15
I have kept...c-s John 15:10
not writing a new c 1 John 2:7
keep the c-s of God Rev 14:12

COMMEND *praise, present*

So I c-ed pleasure Eccl 8:15
I c you to God Acts 20:32
food will not c us 1 Cor 8:8
to c ourselves again 2 Cor 3:1

COMMISSION *appoint*

c him in their sight Num 27:19
He c-ed Joshua Deut 31:23
king has c-ed me 1 Sam 21:2
c it against the people Is 10:6

COMMISSIONERS *supervisors*

and over them three c Dan 6:2
Then the c and satraps Dan 6:4

COMMIT *entrust, practice*

c-ted to Joseph's Gen 39:22
shall not c adultery Ex 20:14
have c-ted incest Lev 20:12
I c my spirit Ps 31:5
C your way to the LORD Ps 37:5
weary...c-ting iniquity Jer 9:5
Do not c adultery Luke 18:20
I c My spirit Luke 23:46
everyone who c-s sin John 8:34
who c-ted no sin 1 Pet 2:22

COMMON *ordinary, shared*

anyone of...c people Lev 4:27
place of the c people Jer 26:23
iron...with c clay Dan 2:41
had all things in c Acts 2:44
about our c salvation Jude 3

COMMONWEALTH *nation*

from the c of Israel Eph 2:12

COMMOTION *disturbance*

the noise of this c 1 Sam 4:14
great c out of the Jer 10:22
Why make a c and Mark 5:39

COMPANION *comrade, friend*

are you striking your c Ex 2:13
brought thirty c-s Judg 14:11
And a c of ostriches Job 30:29
c of fools will suffer Prov 13:20
your c and your wife Mal 2:14
Paul and his c-s Acts 13:13

COMPANY *assembly, group*

into three c-ies Judg 9:43
c of the godless Job 15:34
c will stone them Ezek 23:47
Bad c corrupts 1 Cor 15:33

COMPARE *contrast, like*

none to c with Thee Ps 40:5
to what shall I c Matt 11:16
c the kingdom of Luke 13:20
be c-d with the glory Rom 8:18

COMPASS

outlines it with a c Is 44:13
four points of the c Dan 11:4

COMPASSION *concern, love*

God...grant you c Gen 43:14
whom I will show c Ex 33:19
in Thy great c Neh 9:19
have c on the poor Ps 72:13
have c on Zion Ps 102:13
His c-s never fail Lam 3:22
He felt c for them Matt 9:36
his father...felt c Luke 15:20
put on a heart of c Col 3:12
Lord is full of c James 5:11

COMPASSIONATE *loving*

your God is a c God Deut 4:31
c, Slow to anger Neh 9:17
He is gracious and c Joel 2:13
a gracious and c God Jon 4:2

COMPEL *force, press*

Egyptians c-led the Ex 1:13
c *them* to come in Luke 14:23
c...to be circumcised Gal 6:12

COMPETE *strive*

can you c with horses Jer 12:5
everyone who c-s 1 Cor 9:25
c-s as an athlete 2 Tim 2:5

COMPLAIN *murmur*

c-ed to Abimelech Gen 21:25
c in the bitterness Job 7:11
I will c and murmur Ps 55:17
Do not c, brethren James 5:9

COMPLAINT *grumbling*

c-s of...Israel Num 14:27
couch will ease my c Job 7:13
today my c is rebellion Job 23:2
hospitable...without c 1 Pet 4:9

COMPLETE (adj) *full, total*

a sabbath of c rest Ex 35:2
be seven c sabbaths Lev 23:15
not...a c destruction Jer 5:10
you have been made c Col 2:10
be perfect and c James 1:4
joy may be made c 1 John 1:4

COMPLETE (v) *finish, fulfill*

God c-d His work Gen 2:2
C the week of this Gen 29:27
C your work quota Ex 5:13
your days are c 2 Sam 7:12
house...was c-d 2 Chr 8:16
thousand years are c-d Rev 20:7

COMPOSE *write*

c words against you Job 16:4
have c-d songs for Amos 6:5
The first account I c-d Acts 1:1

COMPOSE *make calm*

c-d and quieted my Ps 131:2
I c *my* soul Is 38:13

COMPREHEND *understand*

which we cannot c Job 37:5
speech...no one c-s Is 33:19
and they did not c Luke 18:34
darkness did not c John 1:5

COMPULSION *coercion*

under c...let them go Ex 6:1
as it were by c Philem 14
not under c, but 1 Pet 5:2

CONCEAL *cover, hide*

man c-s knowledge Prov 12:23
They do not *even* c it Is 3:9
Do not c *it* but Jer 50:2
was c-ed from them Luke 9:45

CONCEIT *pride*

selfishness or empty c Phil 2:3
he is c-ed 1 Tim 6:4
c-ed, lovers of 2 Tim 3:4

CONCEIVE *become pregnant*

Sarah c-d and bore a Gen 21:2
c-d all this people Num 11:12
sin my mother c-d me Ps 51:5
she c-d and gave birth Is 8:3
when lust has c-d James 1:15

CONCERN *have care*

master does not c Gen 39:8
the LORD was c-ed Ex 4:31

CONCUBINE *secondary wife*

Thou art c-ed about	Job 7:17
c-ed about the poor	John 12:6
is married is c-ed	1 Cor 7:33
not c-ed about oxen	1 Cor 9:9

CONCUBINE *secondary wife*

Ephraim...took a c	Judg 19:1
Now Saul had a c	2 Sam 3:7
king left ten c-s	2 Sam 15:16
three hundred c-s	1 Kin 11:3
in charge of the c-s	Esth 2:14

CONDEMN *discredit, judge*

c-ing the wicked	1 Kin 8:32
my mouth will c me	Job 9:20
he who c-s Me	Is 50:9
will c Him to death	Mark 10:33
do not c, and you	Luke 6:37
you c yourself	Rom 2:1
he stood c-ed	Gal 2:11
our heart c-s us	1 John 3:20

CONDEMNATION *judgment*

receive greater c	Mark 12:40
same sentence of c	Luke 23:40
Their c is just	Rom 3:8
no c...in Christ	Rom 8:1
c upon themselves	Rom 13:2
c...by the devil	1 Tim 3:6

CONDITION *state, stipulation*

with you on this c	1 Sam 11:2
c-s were good in	2 Chr 12:12
c in which...called	1 Cor 7:20
or adds c-s to it	Gal 3:15

CONDUCT (n) *behavior*

queen's c...known	Esth 1:17
turn...from his c	Job 33:17
who are upright in c	Ps 37:14
sensual c of...men	2 Pet 2:7
holy c and godliness	2 Pet 3:11

CONDUCT (v) *behave*

c-s himself arrogantly	Job 15:25
c...same spirit	2 Cor 12:18
C...with wisdom	Col 4:5
c yourselves in fear	1 Pet 1:17

CONDUIT *channel*

c of the upper pool	2 Kin 18:17
at the end of the c	Is 7:3

CONFESS *acknowledge*

that he shall c	Lev 5:5
c-ing the sins of	Neh 1:6
c my transgressions	Ps 32:5
c Me before men	Matt 10:32
c-ing their sins	Mark 1:5
c with your mouth	Rom 10:9
If we c our sins	1 John 1:9
I will c his name	Rev 3:5

CONFESSION *admission*

praying and making c	Ezra 10:1
your c of the gospel	2 Cor 9:13
testified the good c	1 Tim 6:13
the c of our hope	Heb 10:23

CONFIDENCE *boldness, trust*

What is this c	2 Kin 18:19
they lost their c	Neh 6:16
LORD will be your c	Prov 3:26
proud c is this	2 Cor 1:12

c in me may abound	Phil 1:26
no c in the flesh	Phil 3:3

CONFINE *imprison, limit*

who were c-d in jail	Gen 40:5
he does not c it	Ex 21:29
be c-d in prison	Is 24:22
c-d in the court	Jer 33:1

CONFINEMENT *imprisonment*

c in his master's	Gen 40:7
he put me in c	Gen 41:10

CONFIRM *establish, strengthen*

LORD c His word	1 Sam 1:23
c Thine inheritance	Ps 68:9
c the work of our	Ps 90:17
C-ing the word of His	Is 44:26
c-ed...by the signs	Mark 16:20
who shall also c you	1 Cor 1:8

CONFIRMATION *verification*

and c of the gospel	Phil 1:7
an oath given as c	Heb 6:16

CONFLICT *contention*

one of great c	Dan 10:1
in c with the LORD	Jer 50:24
experiencing...c	Phil 1:30
source of...c-s	James 4:1

CONFORMED *being like*

c...image of His Son	Rom 8:29
not be c to...world	Rom 12:2
being c to His death	Phil 3:10

CONFOUND *confuse*

LORD c-ed them	Josh 10:10
c their strategy	Is 19:3
c-ing the Jews	Acts 9:22

CONFRONT *challenge, face*

snares of death c-ed	2 Sam 22:6
Days of affliction c	Job 30:27
Arise, O LORD, c him	Ps 17:13
the elders c-ed Him	Luke 20:1

CONFUSE *perplex*

c their language	Gen 11:7
Send...and c them	Ps 144:6
They are c-d by wine	Is 28:7

CONFUSION *disorder*

into great c	Deut 7:23
Jerusalem was in c	Acts 21:31
not a God of c	1 Cor 14:33

CONGREGATION *assembly*

all the c of Israel	Ex 12:3
c shall stone him	Num 15:35
strife of the c	Num 27:14
Bless God in the c-s	Ps 68:26
c of the godly ones	Ps 149:1
the c of the disciples	Acts 6:2
In the midst of the c	Heb 2:12

CONJURER *magician*

magician, c or	Dan 2:10
wise men and the c-s	Dan 5:15

CONQUER *be victorious*

c-ed all the country	Gen 14:7
but could not c it	Is 7:1
c through Him	Rom 8:37
out c-ing, and to c	Rev 6:2

CONSCIENCE *moral obligation*

David's c bothered	1 Sam 24:5
always a blameless c	Acts 24:16
also for c' sake	Rom 13:5
their c being weak is	1 Cor 8:7
faith with a clear c	1 Tim 3:9
seared in their own c	1 Tim 4:2
keep a good c	1 Pet 3:16

CONSECRATE (v) *sanctify*

sons of Israel c	Ex 28:38
garments shall be c-d	Ex 29:21
c it and all its	Ex 40:9
C yourselves	Lev 11:44
c the fiftieth year	Lev 25:10
c-s his house as holy	Lev 27:14
he shall c his head	Num 6:11
C yourselves	Josh 3:5
have c-d this house	1 Kin 9:3

CONSECRATED (adj) *sanctified*

touch any c thing	Lev 12:4
c people...LORD	Deut 26:19
there is c bread	1 Sam 21:4
c ones were purer	Lam 4:7
ate the c bread	Matt 12:4

CONSENT *agree*

Do not listen or c	1 Kin 20:8
entice you, Do not c	Prov 1:10
If you c and obey	Is 1:19
c-s to live with him	1 Cor 7:12

CONSIDER *observe, think*

were c-ed unclean	Neh 7:64
C my groaning	Ps 5:1
he who c-s the helpless	Ps 41:1
We are c-ed as sheep	Ps 44:22
day of adversity c	Eccl 7:14
c the work of His hands	Is 5:12
C the ravens, for	Luke 12:24
c your calling	1 Cor 1:26
He c-ed me faithful	1 Tim 1:12
c how to stimulate	Heb 10:24
c-ed...God is able	Heb 11:19

CONSIST *composed of*

reverence for Me c-s	Is 29:13
life c of his	Luke 12:15
does not c in words	1 Cor 4:20
c-ing of decrees	Col 2:14

CONSOLATION *comfort*

c-s of God too small	Job 15:11
Thy c-s delight my	Ps 94:19
is any c of love	Phil 2:1

CONSOLE *soothe*

Esau is c-ing himself	Gen 27:42
servants to c him	2 Sam 10:2
c-d...comforted	Job 42:11
c them concerning	John 11:19

CONSPIRACY *plot, scheme*

the c was strong	2 Sam 15:12
found c in Hoshea	2 Kin 17:4
from the c-ies of man	Ps 31:20

CONSPIRE *plot against*

have c-d against me	1 Sam 22:8
c-d against my	2 Kin 10:9
c together against	Ps 83:3
Amos...c-d against	Amos 7:10

CONSTELLATION *stars*

a **c** in its season Job 38:32
c-s Will not flash Is 13:10

CONSTRUCT *build*

c a sanctuary for Me Ex 25:8
c siegeworks Deut 20:20

CONSTRUCTION *structure*

c of the sanctuary Ex 36:3
it has been under **c** Ezra 5:16
the **c** of the ark 1 Pet 3:20

CONSULT *confer*

c-ed with the elders 1 Kin 12:6
C the mediums Is 8:19
Without **c-ing** Me Is 30:2
people **c** their wooden Hos 4:12
not...**c** with flesh Gal 1:16

CONSUME *destroy, devour*

c-d...purchase price Gen 31:35
the bush was not **c-d** Ex 3:2
c-d the burnt offering Lev 9:24
great fire will **c** us Deut 5:25
c the cedars Judg 9:15
Thou dost **c** as a moth Ps 39:11
c-d by Thine anger Ps 90:7
c-s his own flesh Eccl 4:5
fire **c-ing** the stubble Joel 2:5
Zeal...will **c** John 2:17
c your flesh like fire James 5:3

CONSUMING (adj) *destroying*

glory...like a **c** fire Ex 24:17
the flame of a **c** fire Is 29:6
our God is a **c** fire Heb 12:29

CONTAIN *hold*

cannot **c** Thee 1 Kin 8:27
c the burnt offering 2 Chr 7:7
c-ing twenty...gallons John 2:6
not **c** the books John 21:25
is **c-ed** in Scripture 1 Pet 2:6

CONTEMPT *scorn*

He pours **c** on nobles Job 12:21
With pride and **c** Ps 31:18
treating Him with **c** Luke 23:11
your brother with **c** Rom 14:10

CONTEND *strive*

c with him in battle Deut 2:24
c-ed...vigorously Judg 8:1
c with the Almighty Job 40:2
not **c**...without cause Prov 3:30
Who will **c** with me Is 50:8
I will not **c** forever Is 57:16
he **c-ed** with God Hos 12:3
c...for the faith Jude 3

CONTENT *satisfied*

Nor will he be **c** Prov 6:35
c with your wages Luke 3:14
c with weaknesses 2 Cor 12:10
have learned to be **c** Phil 4:11
c with what you have Heb 13:5

CONTENTION *strife*

object of **c** to our Ps 80:6
puts an end to **c-s** Prov 18:18
the **c-s** of a wife Prov 19:13
Strife exists and **c** Hab 1:3

CONTENTIOUS *quarrelsome*

a **c**...woman Prov 21:19
with a **c** woman Prov 25:24
inclined to be **c** 1 Cor 11:16

CONTINUE *persevere, persist*

My covenant may **c** Mal 2:4
c in the grace of Acts 13:43
Are we to **c** in sin Rom 6:1
you **c** in the faith Col 1:23
love of the brethren **c** Heb 13:1

CONTRARY *against*

c to the command Num 24:13
for the wind was **c** Matt 14:24
grafted **c** to nature Rom 11:24
c to the teaching Rom 16:17
a gospel **c** to that Gal 1:8
c to sound teaching 1 Tim 1:10

CONTRIBUTE *give*

Josiah **c-d** to the 2 Chr 35:7
c yearly one third Neh 10:32
c-ing to their support Luke 8:3
c-ing to...the saints Rom 12:13

CONTRIBUTION *gift, offering*

to raise a **c** for Me Ex 25:2
as a **c** to the LORD Lev 7:14
c-s, the first fruits Neh 12:44
a **c** for the poor Rom 15:26
liberality of your **c** 2 Cor 9:13

CONTRITE *sorrowful*

broken and a **c** heart Ps 51:17
humble and **c** of spirit Is 66:2

CONTROL (n) *order, rule*

people were out of **c** Ex 32:25
was it not under...**c** Acts 5:4
children under **c** 1 Tim 3:4

CONTROL (v) *rule, subdue*

he **c-led** himself and Gen 43:31
Joseph could not **c** Gen 45:1
Haman **c-led** himself Esth 5:10

CONTROVERSY *dispute*

wise man has a **c** Prov 29:9
LORD has a **c** with the Jer 25:31
shun foolish **c-ies** Titus 3:9

CONVERSE *discuss*

they were **c-ing** Luke 24:15
Stoic...were **c-ing** Acts 17:18
and **c** with him Acts 24:26

CONVERSION *change*

c of the Gentiles Acts 15:3

CONVERTED *changed*

sinners will be **c** Ps 51:13
unless you are **c** Matt 18:3
perceive...and be **c** John 12:40

CONVICT *condemn, judge*

one of you **c-s** Me John 8:46
c...concerning sin John 16:8
he is **c-ed** by all 1 Cor 14:24
to **c** all the ungodly Jude 15

CONVINCED *persuaded*

c that John was a Luke 20:6
c that neither death Rom 8:38

CONVOCATION *conclave*

sabbath...a holy **c** Lev 23:3
shall have a holy **c** Num 29:7

c in the Lord Jesus Rom 14:14
c of better things Heb 6:9

CONVULSION *paroxysm*

threw him into a **c** Mark 9:20
a **c** with foaming Luke 9:39

COOK *prepare food*

Jacob had **c-ed** stew Gen 25:29
you shall **c** and eat Deut 16:7

COOL *cold*

in the **c** of the day Gen 3:8
in his **c** roof chamber Judg 3:20
who has a **c** spirit Prov 17:27

COPPER *metal*

you can dig **c** Deut 8:9
not acquire...**c** Matt 10:9
widow...**c** coins Luke 21:2

COPY *facsimile*

c of this law on a Deut 17:18
c of...law of Moses Josh 8:32
c of the edict Esth 8:13
mere **c** of the true Heb 9:24

CORBAN *offering*

C (that is...) Mark 7:11

CORD *band, rope*

c-s of Sheol 2 Sam 22:6
c-s of affliction Job 36:8
c-s of death Ps 18:4
silver **c** is broken Eccl 12:6
the **c-s** of falsehood Is 5:18
a scourge of **c-s** John 2:15

CORINTH

city in Greece Acts 18:1
N.T. church site 1 Cor 1:1,2

CORNELIUS

centurion, believer Acts 10:1ff

CORNER *angle, intersection*

the chief **c** *stone* Ps 118:22
lurks by every **c** Prov 7:12
on the street **c-s** Matt 6:5
the chief **c** *stone* Mark 12:10
four **c-s** of the earth Rev 7:1

CORNER GATE

see GATES OF JERUSALEM

CORNERSTONE *support stone*

who laid its **c** Job 38:6
the **c** of her tribes Is 19:13
costly **c** *for* the Is 28:16
From them...the **c** Zech 10:4

CORPSE *dead body*

made unclean by a **c** Lev 22:4
Their **c-s** will rise Is 26:19
a mass of **c-s** Nah 3:3
boy...like a **c** Mark 9:26

CORRECT *reprove*

c him with the rod 2 Sam 7:14
He who **c-s** a scoffer Prov 9:7
C your son, and he Prov 29:17

CORRECTION

C me, O LORD | Jer 10:24
gentleness c-ing | 2 Tim 2:25

CORRECTION *improvement*

Whether for c, or | Job 37:13
refused to take c | Jer 5:3
for reproof, for c | 2 Tim 3:16

CORRUPT (adj) *evil, rotten*

the earth was c | Gen 6:11
detestable and c | Job 15:16
They are c | Ps 14:1
all of them, are c | Jer 6:28

CORRUPT (v) *make evil*

a bribe c-s the heart | Eccl 7:7
c-ed your wisdom | Ezek 28:17
have c-ed the covenant | Mal 2:8
Bad company c-s | 1 Cor 15:33
harlot who was c-ing | Rev 19:2

CORRUPTION *decay, evil*

their c is in them | Lev 22:25
no negligence or c | Dan 6:4
from the flesh reap c | Gal 6:8
c that is in the world | 2 Pet 1:4
slaves of c | 2 Pet 2:19

COSMETICS *beautifying aids*

provided her with...c | Esth 2:9
the c for the women | Esth 2:12

COST *expense, price*

c of their lives | Num 16:38
let the c be paid | Ezra 6:4
calculate the c | Luke 14:28
water...without c | Rev 22:6

COSTLY *expensive*

redemption...is c | Ps 49:8
gold, silver, c stones | Dan 11:38
vial of...c perfume | Mark 14:3
pearls or c garments | 1 Tim 2:9

COUCH *bed, pallet*

he went up to my c | Gen 49:4
falling on the c | Esth 7:8
dissolve my c with my | Ps 6:6
sprawl on their c-es | Amos 6:4

COUNCIL *assembly*

not enter into their c | Gen 49:6
the c of the holy ones | Ps 89:7
the c of My people | Ezek 13:9
to their c *chamber* | Luke 22:66
conferred with his c | Acts 25:12

COUNCIL

Sanhedrin | Matt 26:59
Jewish governing body
   Mark 15:1,43; Luke 23:50

COUNSEL (n) *advice, opinion*

I shall give you c | Ex 18:19
Take c and speak up | Judg 19:30
To Him belong c | Job 12:13
not walk in the c | Ps 1:1
Listen to c and | Prov 19:20
chief priests took c | John 12:10
the c of His will | Eph 1:11

COUNSEL (v) *advise*

he c-ed rebellion | Deut 13:5
I c that all Israel | 2 Sam 17:11

How do you c *me* | 1 Kin 12:6
c you with My eye | Ps 32:8

COUNSELOR *adviser*

the king and his c-s | Ezra 7:15
c-s walk barefoot | Job 12:17
abundance of c-s | Prov 11:14
Wonderful C, Mighty | Is 9:6
who became His c | Rom 11:34

COUNT *consider, number*

c the stars, if you | Gen 15:5
could not be c-ed | 1 Kin 8:5
If I should c them | Ps 139:18
my prayer be c-ed | Ps 141:2
was c-ed among us | Acts 1:17
I c all...loss | Phil 3:8
as some c slowness | 2 Pet 3:9

COUNTENANCE *appearance*

why has your c fallen | Gen 4:6
LORD lift up His c | Num 6:26
light of Thy c | Ps 4:6
an angry c | Prov 25:23

COUNTRY *land, region*

Go forth from your c | Gen 12:1
up into the hill c | Deut 1:24
go out into the hill c | Song 7:11
them from the c-ies | Ezek 34:13
they are seeking a c | Heb 11:14

COUNTRYMAN

not hate...fellow c | Lev 19:17
among your c-men | Deut 17:15
a man and his c | Deut 25:11
my fellow c-men and
   Rom 11:14

COURAGE *heart, valor*

he lost c | 2 Sam 4:1
and do not lose c | 2 Chr 15:7
let your heart take c | Ps 27:14
with justice and c | Mic 3:8
Take c, My son | Matt 9:2
Take c, it is I | Matt 14:27
c; I have overcome | John 16:33
we are of good c | 2 Cor 5:8

COURAGEOUS *brave*

Be strong and c | Deut 31:6
be strong and very c | Josh 1:7
I purpose to be c | 2 Cor 10:2

COURIER *messenger*

c-s went throughout | 2 Chr 30:6
letters...by c-s | Esth 3:13
One c runs to meet | Jer 51:31

COURSE *area, extent, way*

strong man to run his c | Ps 19:5
on its circular c-s | Eccl 1:6
I have finished the c | 2 Tim 4:7
the c of *our* life | James 3:6

COURT *area, hall, tribunal*

c of the tabernacle | Ex 27:9
c of the harem | Esth 2:11
a day in Thy c-s | Ps 84:10
c of the LORD's house | Jer 26:2
c of the guardhouse | Jer 39:15
then you have law c-s | 1 Cor 6:4
drag you into c | James 2:6

COURTYARD *compound*

a well in his c | 2 Sam 17:18
c of the high priest | Matt 26:58
Peter...in the c | Mark 14:66

COVENANT *agreement*

establish My c | Gen 6:18
for a sign of a c | Gen 9:13
for an everlasting c | Gen 17:13
ark of the c | Num 10:33
My c of peace | Num 25:12
book of the c | 2 Kin 23:2
Remember His c | 1 Chr 16:15
who keep His c | Ps 103:18
I will make a new c | Jer 31:31
forsake the holy c | Dan 11:30
a c with Assyria | Hos 12:1
the blood of My c | Zech 9:11
cup...is the new c | Luke 22:20
c which God made | Acts 3:25
this is My c with | Rom 11:27
servants of a new c | 2 Cor 3:6
strangers to the c-s | Eph 2:12
guarantee...better c | Heb 7:22
blood of the...c | Heb 13:20
ark of His c | Rev 11:19

COVER (n)

c of porpoise skin | Num 4:14
the c of a couch | Amos 3:12

COVER (v) *hide, protest*

and c up his blood | Gen 37:26
basket and c-ed it | Ex 2:3
Whose sin is c-ed | Ps 32:1
He will c you with | Ps 91:4
love c-s all | Prov 10:12
not c My face | Is 50:6
c-ed...with sackcloth | Jon 3:6
to the hills, C us | Luke 23:30
c a multitude of sins | James 5:20
love c-s a multitude | 1 Pet 4:8

COVERING *canopy*

made...loin c-s | Gen 3:7
spread a cloud for a c | Ps 105:39
she makes c-s for | Prov 31:22
sackcloth their c | Is 50:3
given to her for a c | 1 Cor 11:15
freedom as a c | 1 Pet 2:16

COVET *crave, desire*

not c your neighbor's | Ex 20:17
You shall not c | Deut 5:21
I c-ed them and took | Josh 7:21
They c fields and then | Mic 2:2
c-ed no one's silver | Acts 20:33

COVETOUS *desirous*

the c and swindlers | 1 Cor 5:10
c, nor drunkards | 1 Cor 6:10

COW *animal*

came up seven c-s | Gen 41:2
c calves and does not | Job 21:10
c and the bear will | Is 11:7
you c-s of Bashan | Amos 4:1

CRAFTINESS *shrewdness*

the wise in their c | 1 Cor 3:19
not walking in c | 2 Cor 4:2
by c in deceitful | Eph 4:14

CRAFTSMAN *artisan*

the hands of the c — Deut 27:15
all the **c-men** and — 2 Kin 24:14
idol, a **c** casts it — Is 40:19
business to…**c-men** — Acts 19:24
c of any craft will — Rev 18:22

CRAG *protrusion, rock*

sharp **c** on the one — 1 Sam 14:4
Upon the rocky **c** — Job 39:28
clefts of the **c-s** — Is 57:5

CRAVE *covet, desire*

day long he is **c-ing** — Prov 21:26
fig *which* I **c** — Mic 7:1
generation **c-s** for — Matt 12:39
should not **c** evil — 1 Cor 10:6

CRAWLING *creeping*

venom of **c** things — Deut 32:24
beasts and the **c** — Acts 11:6
and **c** creatures — Rom 1:23

CREATE *form, make*

c-d the heavens — Gen 1:1
c-d man in His — Gen 1:27
C in me a clean — Ps 51:10
C-ing the praise of — Is 57:19
c new heavens — Is 65:17
one God **c-d** us — Mal 2:10
c-d…for good works — Eph 2:10
c-d in righteousness — Eph 4:24
Thou didst **c** all — Rev 4:11

CREATION

beginning of **c** — Mark 10:6
preach…to all **c** — Mark 16:15
whole **c** groans — Rom 8:22
beginning of **c** — 2 Pet 3:4

CREATOR *Maker*

Remember…your **C** — Eccl 12:1
The **C** of Israel — Is 43:15
rather than the **C** — Rom 1:25
to a faithful **C** — 1 Pet 4:19

CREATURE *created being*

every living **c** that — Gen 1:21
winged **c** will make — Eccl 10:20
and crawling **c-s** — Rom 1:23
in Christ…new **c** — 2 Cor 5:17
as **c-s** of instinct — 2 Pet 2:12

CREDITOR *lender*

not to act as a **c** to — Ex 22:25
every **c** shall release — Deut 15:2
Let the **c** seize all — Ps 109:11
My **c-s** did I sell you — Is 50:1

CREEP *crawl*

everything that **c-s** — Gen 1:25
that **c** on the earth — Ezek 38:20

CREEPING *crawling*

cattle and **c** things — Gen 1:24
c things and fish — 1 Kin 4:33
c locust has eaten — Joel 1:4
c locust strips and — Nah 3:16

CRETANS

inhabitants of Crete
— Acts 2:11; Titus 1:12

CRETE

Mediterranean island
— Acts 27:7,21; Titus 1:5
see also **CAPHTOR**

CRIME *vice*

be a lustful **c** — Job 31:11
committed no **c** — Dan 6:22
full of bloody **c-s** — Ezek 7:23
not of such **c-s** — Acts 25:18

CRIMINAL *lawbreaker*

crucified…the **c-s** — Luke 23:33
imprisonment as a **c** — 2 Tim 2:9

CRIMSON *deep red*

purple, **c** and violet — 2 Chr 2:7
like **c**…be like wool — Is 1:18

CRIPPLED *lame*

a son **c** in his feet — 2 Sam 4:4
enter life **c** or lame — Matt 18:8
bring…**c** and blind — Luke 14:21

CRISPUS

Corinthian Christian
— Acts 18:8; 1 Cor 1:14

CROOKED *evil, twisted*

and **c** generation — Deut 32:5
to their **c** ways — Ps 125:5
What is **c** cannot be — Eccl 1:15
make **c** the straight — Acts 13:10
c and perverse — Phil 2:15

CROP *yield of produce*

old things from the **c** — Lev 25:22
c-s to the grasshopper — Ps 78:46
c began to sprout — Amos 7:1
share of the **c-s** — 2 Tim 2:6

CROSS (n) *execution device*

take his **c** and — Matt 10:38
down from the **c** — Matt 27:40
take up his **c** — Mark 15:21
take up his **c** daily — Luke 9:23
standing by the **c** — John 19:25
hanging Him on a **c** — Acts 5:30
c of Christ should — 1 Cor 1:17
word of the **c** is — 1 Cor 1:18
boast, except in the **c** — Gal 6:14
even death on a **c** — Phil 2:8
enemies of the **c** — Phil 3:18
blood of His **c** — Col 1:20
endured the **c** — Heb 12:2

CROSS (v) *pass over*

you **c** the Jordan — Deut 12:10
c-ed opposite Jericho — Josh 3:16
kept **c-ing** the ford — 2 Sam 19:18
Jesus had **c-ed** over — Mark 5:21
c-ing over to — Acts 21:2

CROUCH *bow, stoop*

sin is **c-ing** at the — Gen 4:7
Beneath Him **c** the — Job 9:13
Nothing…but to **c** — Is 10:4

CROWD *multitude*

because of the **c** — Mark 2:4
c of tax-gatherers — Luke 5:29
they stirred up the **c** — Acts 17:8

CROWN (n) *royal emblem* or *top*

on the **c** of the head — Gen 49:26
the **c** of their king — 2 Sam 12:30
he set the royal **c** — Esth 2:17
wife is the **c** of — Prov 12:4
gray head is a **c** — Prov 16:31
c of the drunkards — Is 28:3
a **c** of thorns — Matt 27:29
receive the **c** of life — James 1:12
c-s before the throne — Rev 4:10
golden **c** on His head — Rev 14:14

CROWN (v) *to place crown on*

c him with glory — Ps 8:5
Who **c-s** you with — Ps 103:4
head **c-s** you like — Song 7:5
c-ed him with glory — Heb 2:7

CRUCIFY *to execute on a cross*

scourge and **c** Him — Matt 20:19
Let Him be **c-ied** — Matt 27:22
Jesus…been **c-ied** — Matt 28:5
c your King — John 19:15
Paul was not **c-ied** — 1 Cor 1:13
preach Christ **c-ied** — 1 Cor 1:23
not have **c-ied** the — 1 Cor 2:8
c-ied with Christ — Gal 2:20
world…**c-ied** to me — Gal 6:14
their Lord was **c-ied** — Rev 11:8

CRUEL *fierce, harsh*

their…**c** bondage — Ex 6:9
c man does…harm — Prov 11:17
compassion…is **c** — Prov 12:10
c and have no mercy — Jer 6:23
people has become **c** — Lam 4:3

CRUMBS *morsels*

dogs feed on the **c** — Matt 15:27
on the chldren's **c** — Mark 7:28

CRUSH *demolish, destroy*

a foot may **c** them — Job 39:15
saves…**c-ed** in spirit — Ps 34:18
lying tongue…**c-es** — Prov 26:28
by **c-ing** My people — Is 3:15
c-ed for our iniquities — Is 53:5
LORD was pleased To **c** — Is 53:10
who **c** the needy — Amos 4:1
c Satan under…feet — Rom 16:20

CRY (n) *scream, sob*

great and bitter **c** — Gen 27:34
the **c** of triumph — Ex 32:18
c has come to Me — 1 Sam 9:16
Hear my **c**, O God — Ps 61:1
the **c** of Jerusalem — Jer 14:2
Jesus uttered a…**c** — Mark 15:37

CRY (v)

do not **c** for help — Job 36:13
c aloud in the night — Lam 2:19
His elect, who **c** — Luke 18:7
stones will **c** out — Luke 19:40
Jesus stood and **c-ied** — John 7:37

CRYSTAL *glass*

awesome gleam of **c** — Ezek 1:22
sea of glass like **c** — Rev 4:6
water…clear as **c** — Rev 22:1

CUB *whelp, young*

robbed of her **c-s** — 2 Sam 17:8

CUBIT

She reared her **c-s** — Ezek 19:2
lioness, and lion's **c** — Nah 2:11

CUBIT *linear measure*

ark three hundred **c-s** — Gen 6:15
length was nine **c-s** — Deut 3:11
gallows fifty **c-s** high — Esth 5:14
the altar by **c-s** — Ezek 43:13
add a *single* **c** to — Matt 6:27

CUD *previously swallowed food*

chews the **c** — Lev 11:3
not chew **c**, it is — Lev 11:7
chews the **c** — Deut 14:6

CULT *religious ritual*

be a **c** prostitute — Deut 23:17
male **c** prostitutes — 1 Kin 14:24
male **c** prostitutes — 2 Kin 23:7

CULTIVATE *till*

no man to **c** the — Gen 2:5
Eden to **c** it — Gen 2:15
and **c** vineyards — Deut 28:39
servants shall **c** — 2 Sam 9:10
and **c** faithfulness — Ps 37:3

CUMMIN *plant for seasoning*

driven over **c** — Is 28:27
mint and dill and **c** — Matt 23:23

CUNNING *crafty*

he is very **c** — 1 Sam 23:22
advice of the **c** — Job 5:13
harlot and **c** of heart — Prov 7:10

CUP *container*

into Pharaoh's **c** — Gen 40:11
My **c** overflows — Ps 23:5
the **c** of salvation — Ps 116:13
a **c** of consolation — Jer 16:7
c of cold water — Matt 10:42
let this **c** pass — Matt 26:39
washing of **c-s** and — Mark 7:4
gives you a **c** of — Mark 9:41
c...new covenant — Luke 22:20
c of blessing — 1 Cor 10:16
eat...drink the **c** — 1 Cor 11:26
c full of abominations — Rev 17:4

CUPBEARER *royal official*

c spoke to Pharaoh — Gen 41:9
his **c-s**, and his — 1 Kin 10:5
c-s and their attire — 2 Chr 9:4
c to the king — Neh 1:11

CURDS *butter, cheese*

he took **c** and milk — Gen 18:8
she brought him **c** — Judg 5:25
with honey and **c** — Job 20:17

CURE *heal*

c him of his leprosy — 2 Kin 5:3
c you of your wound — Hos 5:13
they could not **c** him — Matt 17:16
that...time He **c-d** — Luke 7:21

CURSE (n) *condemning oath*

upon myself a **c** — Gen 27:12
c on Mount Ebal — Deut 11:29
c to My chosen ones — Is 65:15
they will become a **c** — Jer 44:12
will be no more **c** — Zech 14:11
become a **c** for us — Gal 3:13

CURSE (v) *verbally condemn*

who **c-s** you I will **c** — Gen 12:3
You shall not **c** God — Ex 22:28
not **c** a deaf man — Lev 19:14
c-d the...anointed — 2 Sam 19:21
c-d the day of his *birth* — Job 3:1
began to **c** and — Mark 14:71
bless and **c** not — Rom 12:14
with it we **c** men — James 3:9

CURSED (adj) *under a curse*

C is the ground — Gen 3:17
C be Canaan — Gen 9:25
C is the man who — Deut 27:15
C...who trusts — Jer 17:5
C...who hangs — Gal 3:13

CURTAIN *covering, drape*

on the edge of the **c** — Ex 26:4
heaven like a *tent* **c** — Ps 104:2
c-s of your dwellings — Is 54:2
c-s of the land of — Hab 3:7

CUSH

1 *area of W Asia* — Gen 2:13
2 *patriarch* — Gen 10:6,8
3 *region S of Egypt*
— 2 Kin 19:9; Is 20:3
4 *a Benjamite* — Ps 7:title

CUSTODY *prison, protection*

they put him in **c** — Num 15:34
into the **c** of Hegai — Esth 2:3
John...taken into **c** — Matt 4:12
holding Jesus in **c** — Luke 22:63

CUSTOM *manner or tax*

it became a **c** in — Judg 11:39
not pay tribute, **c** — Ezra 4:13
c, He entered the — Luke 4:16
burial **c** of the Jews — John 19:40
c-s...not lawful — Acts 16:21
c-s of our fathers — Acts 28:17
whom tax *is due*; **c** — Rom 13:7

CUT *destroy, divide*

did not **c** the birds — Gen 15:10
c off from the earth — Ex 9:15
c down their Asherim — Ex 34:13
LORD **c** off...lips — Ps 12:3
tongue will be **c** — Prov 10:31
C off your hair and — Jer 7:29
were **c**-ting branches — Matt 21:8
and **c** off his ear — Matt 26:51
were **c** to the quick — Acts 7:54
you...will be **c** off — Rom 11:22

CYMBAL *musical instrument*

castanets and **c-s** — 2 Sam 6:5
loud-sounding **c-s** — 1 Chr 15:16
with loud **c-s** — Ps 150:5
or a clanging **c** — 1 Cor 13:1

CYPRESS *tree*

cedar and **c** timber — 1 Kin 5:10
c and algum timber — 2 Chr 2:8
Our rafters, **c-es** — Song 1:17
Wail, O **c**, for the — Zech 11:2

CYPRUS

Mediterranean island
— Is 23:1; Acts 11:19;15:39;21:16
see also **KITTIM**

CYRENE

NW African port
— Mark 15:21; Luke 23:26;
Acts 2:10;11:20

CYRUS

king of Persia
— 2 Chr 36:22; Is 45:1
decreed to rebuild Temple
— Ezra 1:1;5:13

D

DAGON

god of Philistines
— Judg 16:23; 1 Sam 5:4;
1 Chr 10:10

DAMAGE (n) *destruction*

any **d** may be found — 2 Kin 12:5
the **d-s** of the house — 2 Kin 12:6
d and great loss — Acts 27:10
incurred this **d** and — Acts 27:21

DAMAGE (v) *destroy, hurt*

it will **d** the revenue — Ezra 4:13
and **d-ing** to kings — Ezra 4:15
enemy has **d-d** — Ps 74:3
Lest anyone **d** it — Is 27:3

DAMASCUS

city of Aram (Syria)
— Gen 14:15; 2 Kin 5:12;
Acts 9:3,27;26:20

DAN

1 *son of Jacob* — Gen 30:6;49:16
2 *tribal area*
— Josh 19:40; Judg 18:2
3 *city in N Palestine* — Josh 19:47

DANCE (n) *rhythmic movement*

timbrels...with **d-ing** — Ex 15:20
they sing in the **d-s** — 1 Sam 29:5
shall rejoice in the **d** — Jer 31:13
music and **d-ing** — Luke 15:25

DANCE (v) *move rhythmically*

from those who **d-d** — Judg 21:23
David was **d-ing** — 2 Sam 6:14
and a time to **d** — Eccl 3:4
Herodias **d-d** before — Matt 14:6

DANGER *peril*

not only is there **d** — Acts 19:27
often in **d** of death — 2 Cor 11:23
d-s from...Gentiles — 2 Cor 11:26

DANIEL

1 *son of David and Abigail*
— 1 Chr 3:1
2 *priest* — Ezra 8:2
3 *prophet* — Ezek 14:14; Dan 1:6
also **BELTESHAZZAR**

DARE *presume, risk*

who **d-s** rouse him up — Gen 49:9
who would **d** to risk — Jer 30:21
d from that day — Matt 22:46
did not **d** pronounce — Jude 9

DARIUS

1 *Darius the Mede* — Dan 5:31
2 *Darius I* — Ezra 4:5; Hag 1:1
3 *Darius II* — Neh 12:22

DARK *dim, shadow*

not in **d** sayings   Num 12:8
d places of the land   Ps 74:20
live in a **d** land   Is 9:2
it was still a   John 20:1
shining in a **d** place   2 Pet 1:19

DARKEN *obscure*

the land was **d**-ed   Ex 10:15
this that **d**-s counsel   Job 38:2
the stars are **d**-ed   Eccl 12:2
sun will be **d**-ed   Mark 13:24
their eyes be **d**-ed   Rom 11:10

DARKNESS *gloom, shadow*

blind...gropes in **d**   Deut 28:29
are silenced in **d**   1 Sam 2:9
illumines my **d**   2 Sam 22:29
that stalks in **d**   Ps 91:6
those who dwelt in **d**   Ps 107:10
as light excels in **d**   Eccl 2:13
people who walk in **d**   Is 9:2
light will rise in **d**   Is 58:10
into the outer **d**   Matt 22:13
those who sit in **d**   Luke 1:79
men loved the **d**   John 3:19
turn from **d** to light   Acts 26:18
has light with **d**   2 Cor 6:14
unfruitful deeds of **d**   Eph 5:11
in Him there is no **d**   1 John 1:5
brother is in the **d**   1 John 2:9

DARLING *love*

you are, my **d**   Song 1:15
Arise, my **d**   Song 2:13
my **d**, My dove   Song 5:2

DATHAN

rebelled against Moses
                                Num 16:12; Ps 106:17

DAUGHTER

d-s were born to them   Gen 6:1
if a man sells his **d**   Ex 21:7
inheritance to his **d**   Num 27:8
Kings' **d**-s are among   Ps 45:9
d-s of song   Eccl 12:4
destruction of the **d**   Is 23:4
the **d** of my people   Jer 9:1
D rises up against   Mic 7:6
mother against **d**   Luke 12:53

DAUGHTER-IN-LAW

said to his **d** Tamar   Gen 38:11
nakedness of your **d**   Lev 18:15
said to Ruth her **d**   Ruth 2:22
D against her   Mic 7:6

DAVID

anointed   1 Sam 16:13
killed Goliath   1 Sam 17:50
fled from Saul   1 Sam 19:18
spared Saul   1 Sam 26:9
king of Judah and Israel
                                2 Sam 2:4;5:3
covenant with God   2 Sam 7:8
death   1 Kin 2:10

DAWN (n) *daylight*

at the approach of **d**   Judg 19:25
caused the **d** to know   Job 38:12
rise before **d** and   Ps 119:147
wings of the **d**   Ps 139:9

As the **d** is spread   Joel 2:2

DAWN (v) *become light*

the day began to **d**   Judg 19:26
when morning **d**-s   Ps 46:5
a light **d**-ed   Matt 4:16
d toward the first   Matt 28:1
until the day **d**-s   2 Pet 1:19

DAY *light*

God called the light **d**   Gen 1:5
come on a festive **d**   1 Sam 25:8
d...LORD has made   Ps 118:24
what a **d** may bring   Prov 27:1
d-s of your youth   Eccl 12:1
a **d** of reckoning   Is 2:12
d of the LORD is near   Is 13:6
has despised the **d**   Zech 4:10
the **d** of His coming   Mal 3:2
Give us this **d**   Matt 6:11
raise...the last **d**   John 6:39
judge...the last **d**   John 12:48
the **d** of salvation   2 Cor 6:2
perfect it until the **d**   Phil 1:6
d of the Lord   1 Thess 5:2
d is as a thousand   2 Pet 3:8
tormented **d**...night   Rev 20:10

DAY OF ATONEMENT

month is the **d**   Lev 23:27
for it is a **d**   Lev 23:28

DAZZLING *blinding, bright*

My beloved is **d**   Song 5:10
Like **d** heat   Is 18:4
near...in **d** apparel   Luke 24:4

DEACONS *officer, server*

overseers and **d**   Phil 1:1
D likewise *must be*   1 Tim 3:8
let them serve as **d**   1 Tim 3:10
Let **d** be husbands   1 Tim 3:12
served well as **d**   1 Tim 3:13

DEAD *without life*

you are a **d** man   Gen 20:3
near to a **d** person   Num 6:6
dealt with the **d**   Ruth 1:8
forgotten as a **d** man   Ps 31:12
d do not praise   Ps 115:17
better than a **d** lion   Eccl 9:4
Your **d** will live   Is 26:19
not weep for the **d**   Jer 22:10
rising from the **d**   Mark 9:10
d shall hear the   John 5:25
resurrection of the **d**   Acts 23:6
d in your trespasses   Eph 2:1
first-born from the **d**   Col 1:18
living and the **d**   2 Tim 4:1
repentance...**d** works   Heb 6:1
to those who are **d**   1 Pet 4:6
I was **d**...I am alive   Rev 1:18
Hades gave up the **d**   Rev 20:13

DEAF *without hearing*

makes *him* dumb or **d**   Ex 4:11
not curse a **d** man   Lev 19:14
Like a **d** cobra   Ps 58:4
the **d** shall hear   Is 29:18
and *the* **d** hear   Matt 11:5
the **d** to hear   Mark 7:37
d and dumb spirit   Mark 9:25

DEAL *allot, barter, treat*

let us **d** wisely   Ex 1:10
have you **d**-t with us   Ex 14:11
nor **d** falsely   Lev 19:11
d-t with mediums   2 Kin 21:6
who **d** treacherously   Ps 25:3
has **d**-t bountifully   Ps 116:7
who **d** faithfully   Prov 12:22
Everyone **d**-s falsely   Jer 6:13
when I have **d**-t   Ezek 20:44
has **d**-t with me   Luke 1:25

DEALINGS *actions, relations*

no **d** with anyone   Judg 18:7
no **d** with Samaritans   John 4:9
of the Lord's **d**   James 5:11

DEAR *beloved*

Is Ephraim My **d** son   Jer 31:20
my life...as **d** to   Acts 20:24
had become very **d**   1 Thess 2:8

DEATH *cessation of life*

d of the upright   Num 23:10
d encompassed me   2 Sam 22:5
d for his own sin   2 Chr 25:4
D rather than my pains   Job 7:15
no mention of Thee in **d**   Ps 6:5
cords of **d** encompassed   Ps 18:4
the shadow of **d**   Ps 23:4
escapes from **d**   Ps 68:20
doomed to **d**   Ps 102:20
d of His godly ones   Ps 116:15
who hate me love **d**   Prov 8:36
love is as strong as **d**   Song 8:6
He will swallow up **d**   Is 25:8
D cannot praise Thee   Is 38:18
no pleasure in the **d**   Ezek 18:32
d is better to me   Jon 4:3
let him be put to **d**   Matt 15:4
shall not taste **d**   Matt 16:28
to the point of **d**   Mark 14:34
passed out of **d**   John 5:24
he shall never see **d**   John 8:51
sickness is not unto **d**   John 11:4
the agony of **d**   Acts 2:24
d by hanging Him   Acts 10:39
d reigned from Adam   Rom 5:14
wages of sin is **d**   Rom 6:23
the law of sin and of **d**   Rom 8:2
proclaim...Lord's **d**   1 Cor 11:26
d, where...victory   1 Cor 15:55
even **d** on a cross   Phil 2:8
He might taste **d**   Heb 2:9
it brings forth **d**   James 1:15
passed out of **d**   1 John 3:14
Be faithful until **d**   Rev 2:10
had the name **D**   Rev 6:8
second **d**...no power   Rev 20:6

DEBATE *dispute*

d-d...themselves   Mark 1:27
dissension and **d**   Acts 15:2
had been much **d**   Acts 15:7

DEBORAH

1 *nurse of Rebekah*   Gen 35:8
2 *prophetess, judge*   Judg 4:4ff

DEBT *obligation*

and pay your **d**   2 Kin 4:7
exaction of every **d**   Neh 10:31

sureties for **d-s** Prov 22:26
forgive us our **d-s** Matt 6:12

DEBTOR *borrower*

restores to the **d** Ezek 18:7
forgiven our **d-s** Matt 6:12
had two **d-s** Luke 7:41
his master's **d-s** Luke 16:5

DECAY *corruption*

own eyes see his **d** Job 21:20
Holy One to...**d** Acts 2:27
did not undergo **d** Acts 13:37

DECEASED *dead*

wife of the **d** shall Deut 25:5
the widow of the **d** Ruth 4:5
the name of the **d** Ruth 4:10
the sister of the **d** John 11:39

DECEIT *falsehood, deception*

full of curses and **d** Ps 10:7
in whose spirit...no **d** Ps 32:2
your tongue frames **d** Ps 50:19
D is in the heart Prov 12:20
he lays up **d** Prov 26:24
Offspring of **d** Is 57:4
houses are full of **d** Jer 5:27
house of Israel...**d** Hos 11:12
d, sensuality, envy Mark 7:22
full of envy...**d** Rom 1:29
the lusts of **d** Eph 4:22
nor was any **d** found 1 Pet 2:22

DECEITFUL *false*

From a **d** tongue Ps 120:2
the wicked are **d** Prov 12:5
d are the kisses of Prov 27:6
Charm is **d** and Prov 31:30
The heart is more **d** Jer 17:9
false apostles, **d** 2 Cor 11:13

DECEIVE *cheat, mislead*

have you **d-d** me Gen 29:25
Jacob **d-d** Laban Gen 31:20
d-s his companion Lev 6:2
both stolen and **d-d** Josh 7:11
Do not **d** me 2 Kin 4:28
who **d-s** his neighbor Prov 26:19
Do not **d** yourselves Jer 37:9
your heart had **d-d** you Obad 3
they keep **d-ing** Rom 3:13
Let no one **d** you Eph 5:6
d-ing and being **d-d** 2 Tim 3:13

DECEIVER *liar*

as a **d** in his sight Gen 27:12
as **d-s** and yet true 2 Cor 6:8
d and the antichrist 2 John 7

DECEPTION *falsehood*

their mind prepares **d** Job 15:35
the hills are a **d** Jer 3:23
last **d** will be worse Matt 27:64
philosophy and empty **d** Col 2:8
reveling in their **d-s** 2 Pet 2:13

DECEPTIVE *misleading*

wicked...**d** wages Prov 11:18
Do not trust in **d** words Jer 7:4
d *stream* With water Jer 15:18

DECISION *judgment, resolution*

d is from the LORD Prov 16:33

in the valley of **d** Joel 3:14
My **d** is to gather Zeph 3:8
majority reached a **d** Acts 27:12

DECLARE *explain, proclaim*

Moses **d-d** to...sons Lev 23:44
d to Him the number Job 31:37
d Thy faithfulness Ps 30:9
mouth...**d** Thy praise Ps 51:15
d Thy lovingkindness Ps 92:2
Who has **d-d** *this* Is 41:26
d-s the LORD Amos 4:11
He will **d** all things John 4:25
d-d the Son of God Rom 1:4

DECLINE *decrease*

for the shadow to **d** 2 Kin 20:10
our days have **d-d** Ps 90:9
for the day **d-s** Jer 6:4

DECREASE *abate, subside*

the water **d-d** steadily Gen 8:5
not let their cattle **d** Ps 107:38
increase...I must **d** John 3:30

DECREE (n) *judgment, order*

issued a **d** to rebuild Ezra 5:13
and **d** of the king Esth 2:8
devises mischief by **d** Ps 94:20
only one **d** for you Dan 2:9
delivering the **d-s** Acts 16:4
to the **d-s** of Caesar Acts 17:7

DECREE (v) *decide, determine*

been **d-d** against her Esth 2:1
will also **d** a thing Job 22:28
And rulers **d** justice Prov 8:15
Seventy weeks...**d-d** Dan 9:24

DEDICATE *consecrate, devote*

D yourselves today Ex 32:29
I wholly **d** the silver Judg 17:3
d-d by...David 1 Kin 7:51
David...**d-d** these 1 Chr 18:11
d-d part...the spoil 1 Chr 26:27
d-ing it to Him 2 Chr 2:4

DEDICATION *consecration*

the **d** of the altar 2 Chr 7:9
celebrated the **d** of Ezra 6:16
d of the wall Neh 12:27
d of the image Dan 3:2
assembled for the **d** Dan 3:3

DEDICATION, FEAST OF
see FEASTS

DEED *action or document*

What is this **d** Gen 44:15
for our evil **d-s** Ezra 9:13
blot out...loyal **d-s** Neh 13:14
abominable **d-s** Ps 14:1
I...sealed the **d** Jer 32:10
prophet mighty in **d** Luke 24:19
their **d-s** were evil John 3:19
d-s of the flesh are Gal 5:19
for every good **d** Titus 3:1
I know your **d-s** Rev 2:2

DEEP (adj) *far ranging*

d sleep falls on men Job 4:13
Thy judgments are...**d** Ps 36:6
casts into a **d** sleep Prov 19:15
into **d** darkness Jer 13:16

the well is **d** John 4:11

DEEP (n) *abyss, depth*

fountains of the...**d** Gen 7:11
the **d** lying beneath Deut 33:13
surface of the **d** is Job 38:30
D calls to **d** Ps 42:7
d also trembled Ps 77:16
His wonders in the **d** Ps 107:24
the springs of the **d** Prov 8:28

DEER *animal*

besides **d**, gazelles 1 Kin 4:23
d pants for the water Ps 42:1
lame will leap like a **d** Is 35:6

DEFEAT *conquer, overthrow*

d-ed...and pursued Gen 14:15
able to **d** them Num 22:6
sons of Israel **d-ed** Josh 12:7
d the Arameans 2 Kin 13:17
d-ed the Philistines 1 Chr 18:1
d-ed the entire army Jer 37:10

DEFECT (n) *blemish, spot*

No one who has a **d** Lev 21:18
one ram without a **d** Num 6:14
if it has any **d** Deut 15:21
no **d** in him 2 Sam 14:25
in whom was no **d** Dan 1:4

DEFECT (v) *rebel, disobey*

d to his master 1 Chr 12:19
many **d-ed** to him 2 Chr 15:9
you have deeply **d-ed** Is 31:6

DEFEND *protect*

LORD of hosts will **d** Zech 9:15
d-ed him and took Acts 7:24
or else **d-ing** them Rom 2:15
are **d-ing** ourselves 2 Cor 12:19

DEFENSE *protection*

d-s are **d-s** of clay Job 13:12
the **d** of my life Ps 27:1
Thou hast been a **d** Is 25:4
the **d**...of the gospel Phil 1:7

DEFILE *pollute, profane*

astray...**d-s** herself Num 5:29
d-d the high places 2 Kin 23:8
d-d the priesthood Neh 13:29
d-d Thy holy temple Ps 79:1
your hands are **d-d** Is 59:3
those **d** the man Matt 15:18
is what **d-s** the man Mark 7:20
conscience...is **d-d** 1 Cor 8:7
d-s the entire body James 3:6

DEFILEMENT *filth*

her *interest*, for **d** Ezek 22:3
from all **d** of flesh 2 Cor 7:1

DEFRAUD *deprive, wrong*

whom have I **d-ed** 1 Sam 12:3
To **d** a man Lam 3:36
Do not **d** Mark 10:19
no one keep **d-ing** Col 2:18

DEITY *God, gods*

of strange **d-ies** Acts 17:18
fulness of **D** dwells Col 2:9

DELAY *hinder, linger, stall*

Do not **d** me Gen 24:56

Moses **d**-ed to come   Ex 32:1
shall not **d** to pay   Deut 23:21
bridegroom...**d**-ing   Matt 25:5
Do not **d** to come   Acts 9:38
now why do you **d**   Acts 22:16
in case I am **d**-ed   1 Tim 3:15

DELICACIES *fancy foods*

eat of their **d**   Ps 141:4
Do not desire his **d**   Prov 23:3
Those who ate **d**   Lam 4:5

DELIGHT (n) *pleasure*

I have no **d** in you   2 Sam 15:26
Will he take **d**   Job 27:10
his **d** is in the law   Ps 1:2
commandments...**d**   Ps 119:143
my **d** in the sons of   Prov 8:31
a just weight is His **d**   Prov 11:1
the **d** of kings   Prov 16:13
I took great **d**   Song 2:3
call the sabbath a **d**   Is 58:13
My **d** is in her   Is 62:4

DELIGHT (v) *desire*

LORD **d**-ed over you   Deut 28:63
d in...offerings   1 Sam 15:22
d to revere Thy name   Neh 1:11
d in the Almighty   Job 22:26
D yourself in the LORD   Ps 37:4
not **d** in sacrifice   Ps 51:16
Who **d** in doing evil   Prov 2:14
d in my ways   Prov 23:26
takes no **d** in fools   Eccl 5:4
I **d** in loyalty   Hos 6:6
d-s...unchanging love   Mic 7:18
d-ing...self-abasement   Col 2:18

DELIGHTFUL *pleasant*

d is a timely word   Prov 15:23
to find **d** words   Eccl 12:10
and how **d** you are   Song 7:6
Is he a **d** child   Jer 31:20

DELILAH

Philistine woman   Judg 16:4
enticed Samson   Judg 16:6-20

DELIVER *give, rescue, save*

come down to **d** them   Ex 3:8
d the manslayer   Num 35:25
My...power has **d**-ed   Judg 7:2
can this one **d**   1 Sam 10:27
He will **d** you   Job 5:19
d-ed my soul from   Ps 56:13
none who can **d**   Is 43:13
mind on **d**-ing Daniel   Dan 6:14
d us from evil   Matt 6:13
d Him up to you   Matt 26:15
d-ed over to death   2 Cor 4:11
The Lord will **d** me   2 Tim 4:18
d-ed to the saints   Jude 3

DELIVERANCE *salvation*

by a great **d**   Gen 45:7
given this great **d**   Judg 15:8
with songs of **d**   Ps 32:7
a God of **d**-s   Ps 68:20
d through...prayers   Phil 1:19

DELIVERER *savior*

the LORD raised up a **d**   Judg 3:9
give them **d**-s   Neh 9:27

my fortress and my **d**   Ps 18:2
d-s...ascend Mount   Obad 21
D...come from Zion   Rom 11:26

DELUDE *lead astray*

they have **d**-d you   Is 47:10
no one may **d** you   Col 2:4
who **d** themselves   James 1:22

DEMAND *order, require*

husband may **d** of him   Ex 21:22
but I **d** one thing   2 Sam 3:13
captors **d**-ed of us   Ps 137:3
do not **d** it back   Luke 6:30
d-ing of Him a sign   Luke 11:16

DEMETRIUS

1 *Ephesian smith*   Acts 19:24,38
2 *a Christian*   3 John 12

DEMOLISH *destroy*

d all...high places   Num 33:52
he **d**-ed its stones   2 Kin 23:15
to **d** its strongholds   Is 23:11

DEMON *devil*

sacrificed to **d**-s   Deut 32:17
daughters to the **d**-s   Ps 106:37
after the **d** was cast   Matt 9:33
sacrifice to **d**-s   1 Cor 10:20
d-s also believe   James 2:19
not to worship **d**-s   Rev 9:20

DEMONIACS *possessed ones*

d, epileptics   Matt 4:24
the *incident* of the **d**   Matt 8:33

DEMON-POSSESSED

many who were **d**   Matt 8:16
a dumb man, **d**   Matt 9:32
to the **d** man   Mark 5:16
sayings of one **d**   John 10:21

DEMONSTRATE *show*

God **d**-s His own love   Rom 5:8
to **d** His wrath   Rom 9:22
d-d yourselves to be   2 Cor 7:11
d His...patience   1 Tim 1:16

DEMONSTRATION *a showing*

for the **d**, *I say*   Rom 3:26
in **d** of the Spirit   1 Cor 2:4

DEN *abode*

remains in its **d**   Job 37:8
From the **d**-s of lions   Song 4:8
the viper's **d**   Is 11:8
cast into the lions' **d**   Dan 6:7
it a robbers' **d**   Mark 11:17

DENARIUS

Roman silver coin   Matt 20:2,9
a day's wage   Luke 20:24
Denarii (*pl*)   John 6:7;12:5

DENOUNCE *accuse, slander*

And come, **d** Israel   Num 23:7
the LORD has not **d**-d   Num 23:8
let us **d** him   Jer 20:10

DENY *conceal, refuse*

Sarah **d**-ied it   Gen 18:15
lest you **d** your God   Josh 24:27
not **d**-ied the words   Job 6:10
and **d**-ing the LORD   Is 59:13

whoever shall **d** Me   Matt 10:33
has **d**-ied the faith   1 Tim 5:8
deeds they **d** Him   Titus 1:16
us to **d** ungodliness   Titus 2:12
d-ies the Son   1 John 2:23

DEPART *leave*

scepter shall not **d**   Gen 49:10
sword...never **d**   2 Sam 12:10
to **d** from evil is   Job 28:28
His spirit **d**-s   Ps 146:4
his folly will not **d**   Prov 22:22
turned aside and **d**-ed   Jer 5:23
I never knew you; **d**   Matt 7:23
d from Me, all you   Luke 13:27
D from your country   Acts 7:3
d and be with Christ   Phil 1:23

DEPARTURE *death or leaving*

after their **d** from   Ex 16:1
speaking of His **d**   Luke 9:31
time of my **d** has   2 Tim 4:6
any time after my **d**   2 Pet 1:15

DEPEND *rely, rest*

d-ed on the weapons   Is 22:8
you did not **d** on Him   Is 22:11
d the whole Law   Matt 22:40

DEPORTATION *exile*

after the **d** to   Matt 1:12
to the **d** to Babylon   Matt 1:17

DEPORTED *exiled*

d...to Babylon   Ezra 5:12
d...entire population   Amos 1:6

DEPOSE *release*

d you from your office   Is 22:19
d-d from his royal   Dan 5:20

DEPOSIT (n) *security*

in regard to a **d**   Lev 6:2
d which was entrusted   Lev 6:4

DEPOSIT (v) *place, put*

d them in the tent   Num 17:4
d *it* in your town   Deut 14:28
d...in the temple   Ezra 5:15
had **d**-ed the scroll   Jer 36:20

DEPRAVED *degenerate*

over to a **d** mind   Rom 1:28
men of **d** mind   2 Tim 3:8

DEPRIVE *take away*

d the needy of justice   Is 10:2
d-d of...my years   Is 38:10
d-ing one another   1 Cor 7:5
d-d of the truth   1 Tim 6:5

DEPTH *abyss, deep*

d-s boil like a pot   Job 41:31
hand are the **d**-s   Ps 95:4
went down to the **d**-s   Ps 107:26
sins Into the **d**-s   Mic 7:19
drowned in the **d**   Matt 18:6
it had no **d** of soil   Mark 4:5
nor height, nor **d**   Rom 8:39
the **d** of the riches   Rom 11:33
even the **d**-s of God   1 Cor 2:10

DEPUTY *proconsul*

he was the only **d**   1 Kin 4:19

Solomon's...**d-ies**   1 Kin 5:16
a **d** was king   1 Kin 22:47

DERISION *laughingstock*

d among...enemies   Ex 32:25
d to those around us   Ps 44:13
reproach and **d** all   Jer 20:8
d to the rest of the   Ezek 36:4

DESCEND *go down*

angels of God...**d-ing** Gen 28:12
His glory will not **d**   Ps 49:17
breath of...**d-s**   Eccl 3:21
shall **d** to Hades   Matt 11:23
Spirit **d-ing**...dove   John 1:32
d into the abyss   Rom 10:7
who **d-ed**...ascended   Eph 4:10

DESCENDANT *seed, offering*

your **d-s** I will give   Gen 12:7
will raise up your **d**   2 Sam 7:12
His **d-s** shall endure   Ps 89:36
So shall your **d-s** be   Rom 4:18
to the **d** of Abraham   Heb 2:16

DESCENT *hill or heritage*

of Median **d**   Dan 9:1
the **d** of the Mount   Luke 19:37
were of high-priestly **d**   Acts 4:6

DESCRIBE *explain*

you shall **d** the land   Josh 18:6
man, **d** the temple   Ezek 43:10
who had seen it **d-d**   Mark 5:16

DESECRATE *defile*

d the sanctuary   Dan 11:31
tried to **d** the temple   Acts 24:6

DESERT (n) *wilderness*

d plains of Jericho   Josh 5:10
grieved Him in the **d**   Ps 78:40
better to live in a **d**   Prov 21:19
in the **d** a highway   Is 40:3
Rivers in the **d**   Is 43:19
like a bush in the **d**   Jer 17:6
he lived in the **d-s**   Luke 1:80

DESERT (v) *abandon, forsake*

d-ed to the king   2 Kin 25:11
who had **d-ed** them   Acts 15:38
so quickly **d-ing** Him   Gal 1:6
but all **d-ed** me   2 Tim 4:16
I will never **d** you   Heb 13:5

DESERTERS *changers of loyalty*

d who had deserted   2 Kin 25:11
d who had gone over   Jer 39:9

DESERVE *earn, merit*

with him as he **d-ed**   Judg 9:16
done this **d-s** to die   2 Sam 12:5
He is **d-ing** of death   Matt 26:66
receiving what we **d**   Luke 23:41

DESIGN *creation, plan*

d-s for work in gold   Ex 31:4
makers of **d-s**   Ex 35:35
execute any **d** which   2 Chr 2:14
All their deadly **d-s**   Jer 18:23

DESIGNATE *appoint*

if he **d-s** her for   Ex 21:9
one whom I **d** to   1 Sam 16:3

were **d-d** by name   1 Chr 16:41
being **d-d** by God   Heb 5:10

DESIRABLE *attractive*

the tree was **d**   Gen 3:6
d in your eyes   1 Kin 20:6
more **d** than gold   Ps 19:10
What is **d** in a man   Prov 19:22
every kind of **d** object   Nah 2:9

DESIRE (n) *appetite, craving*

d...for your husband   Gen 3:16
poor from *their* **d**   Job 31:16
the **d-s** of your heart   Ps 37:4
d of the wicked will   Ps 112:10
d of the righteous   Prov 10:24
d of your eyes   Ezek 24:16
great man speaks the **d**   Mic 7:3
d and my prayer   Rom 10:1
d-s of the flesh   Eph 2:3
d to depart and be   Phil 1:23
evil **d**, and greed   Col 3:5

DESIRE (v) *crave, wish*

your heart **d-s**   Deut 14:26
as much as you **d**   1 Sam 2:16
I **d** to argue with God   Job 13:3
Thou dost **d** truth   Ps 51:6
not **d** his delicacies   Prov 23:3
all that my eyes **d-d**   Eccl 2:10
righteous men **d-d**   Matt 13:17
d the greater gifts   1 Cor 12:31
d...a good showing   Gal 6:12
d a better *country*   Heb 11:16

DESOLATE *lonely, waste*

your sanctuaries **d**   Lev 26:31
sons of the **d** one   Is 54:1
high places will be **d**   Ezek 6:6
d wilderness behind   Joel 2:3
loaves in a **d** place   Matt 15:33
homestead be made **d**   Acts 1:20
children of the **d**   Gal 4:27

DESOLATION *ruin, waste*

a **d** and a curse   2 Kin 22:19
a heap forever, a **d**   Josh 8:28
D is left in the city   Is 24:12
d-s of many generations   Is 61:4
and everlasting **d**   Ezek 35:9
the abomination of **d**   Dan 11:31
day of...**d**   Zeph 1:15
her **d** is at hand   Luke 21:20

DESPAIR (n) *grief*

words of one in **d**   Job 6:26
my soul is in **d**   Ps 42:6
Why are you in **d**   Ps 43:5

DESPAIR (v) *grieve*

Saul then will **d**   1 Sam 27:1
I...**d-ed** of all   Eccl 2:20
we **d-ed** even of life   2 Cor 1:8
but not **d-ing**   2 Cor 4:8

DESPISE *reject, scorn*

d-d his birthright   Gen 25:34
those who **d** Me   1 Sam 2:30
d-d...in her heart   2 Sam 6:16
not **d** the discipline   Job 5:17
hate and **d** falsehood   Ps 119:163
Fools **d** wisdom and   Prov 1:7
wisdom...is **d-d**   Eccl 9:16

has **d-d** the day of   Zech 4:10
have we **d-d** Thy name   Mal 1:6
not **d** one of these   Matt 18:10
hold to one, and **d**   Luke 16:13
do you **d**...church   1 Cor 11:22

DESPOIL *injure, lay waste*

d-ed all the cities   2 Chr 14:14
the wicked who **d** me   Ps 17:9
plundered and **d-ed**   Is 42:22

DESTINE *appoint*

is **d-d** for the sword   Job 15:22
d you for the sword   Is 65:12
things **d-d** to perish   Col 2:22
not **d-d** us for wrath   1 Thess 5:9

DESTITUTE *deprived, in need*

prayer of the **d**   Ps 102:17
the land is **d**   Ezek 32:15
being **d**, afflicted   Heb 11:37

DESTROY *abolish, ruin, waste*

to **d** all flesh   Gen 6:17
lest I **d** you   1 Sam 15:6
wouldst Thou **d** me   Job 10:8
seek my life to **d** it   Ps 40:14
the wicked, He will **d**   Ps 145:20
that which **d-s** kings   Prov 31:3
one sinner **d-s** much   Eccl 9:18
stronghold is **d-ed**   Is 23:14
shepherds...are **d-ing**   Jer 23:1
He will **d** mighty men   Dan 8:24
moth and rust **d**   Matt 6:19
who is able to **d**   Matt 10:28
You come to **d** us   Mark 1:24
seeking...to **d** Him   Mark 11:18
d the temple and   Mark 15:29
flood...**d-ed** them   Luke 17:27
D this temple, and   John 2:19
not for **d-ing** you   2 Cor 10:8
to save and to **d**   James 4:12
heavens will be **d-ed**   2 Pet 3:12
d the works of the   1 John 3:8

DESTROYER *devastator*

d of our country   Judg 16:24
of the **d-s** prosper   Job 12:6
d comes upon him   Job 15:21
d-s and devastators   Is 49:17
I shall set apart **d-s**   Jer 22:7

DESTRUCTION *calamity, ruin*

the **d** of my kindred   Esth 8:6
God apportion **d**   Job 21:17
Your tongue devises **d**   Ps 52:2
Pride *goes* before **d**   Prov 16:18
foolish son is **d** to   Prov 19:13
called the City of **D**   Is 19:18
d of the daughter of   Lam 2:11
broad that leads to **d**   Matt 7:13
whose end is **d**   Phil 3:19
d will come   1 Thess 5:3
penalty of eternal **d**   2 Thess 1:9
bringing swift **d** upon   2 Pet 2:1

DETERMINE *decide*

to **d** whether he laid   Ex 22:8
his days are **d-d**   Job 14:5
d-d *their* appointed   Acts 17:26
but rather **d** this   Rom 14:13
d-d to know nothing   1 Cor 2:2

DETEST *despise, loathe*

carcasses you shall **d** Lev 11:11
not **d** an Egyptian Deut 23:7
I **d** his citadels Amos 6:8

DETESTABLE *abominable*

not eat any **d** thing Deut 14:3
who is **d** and corrupt Job 15:16
swine's flesh, **d** Is 66:17
their **d** idols Jer 16:18
remove all its **d** Ezek 11:18
d...sight of God Luke 16:15

DEVASTATE *destroy, lay waste*

d-d the nations 2 Kin 19:17
Until cities are **d-d** Is 6:11
the LORD...**d-s** it Is 24:1
my tents are **d-d** Jer 4:20
d...pride of Egypt Ezek 32:12

DEVASTATION *destruction*

d of the afflicted Ps 12:5
Nor **d** or destruction Is 60:18
raise up the former **d-s** Is 61:4
d in their citadels Amos 3:10

DEVICE *plan, scheme*

By their own **d-s** Ps 5:10
not promote his *evil* **d** Ps 140:8
a man of evil **d-s** Prov 14:17
in their **d-s** you walk Mic 6:16

DEVIL *demon, Satan*

tempted by the **d** Matt 4:1
one of you is a **d** John 6:70
you son of the **d** Acts 13:10
firm against...the **d** Eph 6:11
render powerless...**d** Heb 2:14
serpent...the **d** Rev 12:9
d...into the lake Rev 20:10

DEVISE *design, scheme, plot*

d-d against the Jews Esth 9:25
d-ing a vain thing Ps 2:1
d-s mischief by decree Ps 94:20
d-s evil continually Prov 6:14
man who **d-s** evil Prov 12:2
He **d-s** wicked schemes Is 32:7
do not **d** evil in Zech 7:10
d futile things Acts 4:25

DEVOTE *commit, dedicate*

shall **d** to the LORD Ex 13:12
d...to the law 2 Chr 31:4
d-ing...to prayer Acts 1:14
d-d to one another Rom 12:10
D yourselves to prayer Col 4:2

DEVOTED *set apart (to God)*

d to destruction Lev 27:28
Every **d** thing in Num 18:14
d to destruction 1 Sam 15:21
d thing in Israel Ezek 44:29

DEVOTION *consecration*

his deeds of **d** 2 Chr 32:32
excessive *to books* Eccl 12:12
the **d** of your youth Jer 2:2

DEVOUR *consume, swallow*

wild beast **d-ed** him Gen 37:20
the sword **d** forever 2 Sam 2:26
is **d-ed** by disease Job 18:13

fire from...**d-ed** Ps 18:8
love all words that **d** Ps 52:4
To **d** the afflicted Prov 30:14
has **d-ed** your prophets Jer 2:30
caterpillar was **d-ing** Amos 4:9
d widows' houses Mark 12:40
bite...**d** one another Gal 5:15

DEVOUT *God-fearing*

d men are taken away Is 57:1
was righteous and **d** Luke 2:25
d men, from every Acts 2:5
the **d** women Acts 13:50

DEW *drops of moisture*

God give...the **d** Gen 27:28
d fell on the camp Num 11:9
d on the fleece only Judg 6:37
on him as the **d** 2 Sam 17:12
neither **d** nor rain 1 Kin 17:1
the **d** of Hermon Ps 133:3
skies drip with **d** Prov 3:20
Like a cloud of **d** Is 18:4
drenched with the **d** Dan 4:15
sky has withheld its **d** Hag 1:10

DIALECT *language*

in the Hebrew **d** Acts 21:40
the Hebrew **d** Acts 22:2

DIAMOND *jewel*

a sapphire and a **d** Ex 28:18
With a **d** point Jer 17:1

DICTATION *spoken words*

at the **d** of Jeremiah Jer 36:4
written at the **d** of Jer 36:27
book at Jeremiah's **d** Jer 45:1

DIE *decease, expire*

you shall surely **d** Gen 2:17
not eat...which **d-s** Deut 14:21
Where you **d**, I will **d** Ruth 1:17
Curse God and **d** Job 2:9
even wise men **d** Ps 49:10
fools **d** for lack of Prov 10:21
and the fool alike **d** Eccl 2:16
soul who sins will **d** Ezek 18:4
to **d** with You Matt 26:35
child has not **d-d** Mark 5:39
live even if he **d-s** John 11:25
grain of wheat...**d-s** John 12:24
she fell sick and **d-d** Acts 9:37
d-d for the ungodly Rom 5:6
we who **d-d** to sin Rom 6:2
for whom Christ **d-d** Rom 14:15
I **d** daily 1 Cor 15:31
I **d-d** to the Law Gal 2:19
to **d** is gain Phil 1:21
Jesus **d-d** and rose 1 Thess 4:14
to **d** once and after Heb 9:27
these **d-d** in faith Heb 11:13
who **d** in the Lord Rev 14:13

DIFFICULT *hard*

too **d** for the LORD Gen 18:14
test Solomon with **d** 2 Chr 9:1
anything too **d** for Me Jer 32:27
speech or **d** language Ezek 3:5
solving of **d** problems Dan 5:12
last days **d** times 2 Tim 3:1

DIG *excavate, till*

opens a pit, or **d-s** Ex 21:33
you can **d** copper Deut 8:9
they **d** into houses Job 24:16
He has **dug** a pit Ps 7:15
dug through the wall Ezek 8:8
dug a wine press Matt 21:33
until I **d** around it Luke 13:8

DIGNITY *majesty*

Preeminent in **d** Gen 49:3
What honor or **d** has Esth 6:3
all godliness and **d** 1 Tim 2:2
must be men of **d** 1 Tim 3:8

DILIGENCE *effort*

carried out with all **d** Ezra 6:12
Watch...with all **d** Prov 4:23
lagging behind in **d** Rom 12:11
show the same **d** Heb 6:11

DILIGENT *persistent*

hand of the **d** makes Prov 10:4
plans of the **d** lead Prov 21:5
d to present 2 Tim 2:15
d to enter that rest Heb 4:11
I will also be **d** 2 Pet 1:15

DIM *cloudy, dark*

eye was not **d** Deut 34:7
eyesight...to grow **d** 1 Sam 3:2
d because of grief Job 17:7
windows grow **d** Eccl 12:3

DIMINISH *dwindle, reduce*

you shall **d** its price Lev 25:16
d their inheritance Num 26:54
are **d-ed** and bowed Ps 107:39

DINAH

daughter of *Jacob* Gen 34:1,3
raped by Shechem Gen 34:2,5

DINE *eat*

men are to **d** with Gen 43:16
to **d** with a ruler Prov 23:1
came and were **d-ing** Matt 9:10

DINNER *meal*

I have prepared...**d** Matt 22:4
because of...**d** guests Mark 6:26
was giving a big **d** Luke 14:16

DIP *plunge*

d-ped the tunic in Gen 37:31
priest shall **d** his Lev 4:6
d your piece of bread Ruth 2:14
d-ped...seven times 2 Kin 5:14
d-ped...with Me Matt 26:23
who **d-s** with Me Mark 14:20
robe **d-ped** in blood Rev 19:13

DIRECT *arrange, guide, order*

LORD **d-s** his steps Prov 16:9
d your heart in the Prov 23:19
has **d-ed** the Spirit Is 40:13
walks to **d** his steps Jer 10:23
I **d-ed** the churches 1 Cor 16:1
d their entire body James 3:3

DIRECTION *path or order*

which turned every **d** Gen 3:24
And it changes **d** Job 37:12
d of the daughter Jer 4:11

of their four **d-s**   Ezek 1:17

DIRGE *lament*

for you as a **d**   Amos 5:1
we sang a **d**   Luke 7:32

DISAPPEAR *vanish*

For the faithful **d**   Ps 12:1
When the grass **d-s**   Prov 27:25
old is ready to **d**   Heb 8:13

DISAPPOINT *frustrate*

and were not **d-ed**   Ps 22:5
hope does not **d**   Rom 5:5

DISASTER *calamity*

d was close to them   Judg 20:34
d on this people   Jer 6:19
because of all its **d-s**   Jer 19:8
In the day of their **d**   Obad 13

DISBELIEVE *doubt*

Jews who **d-d** stirred   Acts 14:2
for those who **d**   1 Pet 2:7

DISCERN *understand, recognize*

would **d**...future   Deut 32:29
king to **d** good   2 Sam 14:17
not **d** its appearance   Job 4:16
d-ed...the youths   Prov 7:7
O fools, **d** wisdom   Prov 8:5
d the...sky   Matt 16:3

DISCERNMENT *judgment*

blessed be your **d**   1 Sam 25:33
asked for yourself **d**   1 Kin 3:11
not a people of **d**   Is 27:11
knowledge and all **d**   Phil 1:9

DISCHARGE *emission*

a **d** from his body   Lev 15:2
leper or who has a **d**   Lev 22:4
everyone having a **d**   Num 5:2
d, or who is a leper   2 Sam 3:29
the **d** of your blood   Ezek 32:6

DISCIPLE *student, learner*

to listen as a **d**   Is 50:4
His twelve **d-s**   Matt 10:1
d is not above his   Matt 10:24
d-s rebuked them   Matt 19:13
d-s left Him...fled   Matt 26:56
make **d-s** of all   Matt 28:19
Your **d-s** do not fast   Mark 2:18
Passover...My **d-s**   Mark 14:14
gaze on His **d-s**   Luke 6:20
he cannot be My **d**   Luke 14:26
d-s believed in Him   John 2:11
His **d-s** withdrew   John 6:66
wash the **d-s** feet   John 13:5
d whom He loved   John 19:26
d-s were first called   Acts 11:26

DISCIPLINE (n) *chastisement*

the **d** of the LORD   Deut 11:2
d of the Almighty   Job 5:17
The rod of **d**   Prov 22:15
to see your good **d**   Col 2:5
d...of little profit   1 Tim 4:8

DISCIPLINE (v) *chastise*

as a man **d-s** his son   Deut 8:5
d-d you with whips   1 Kin 12:11
D your son while   Prov 19:18

d-d by the Lord   1 Cor 11:32
father does not **d**   Heb 12:7

DISCLOSE *reveal*

without **d-ing** it to   1 Sam 20:2
Esther had **d-d** what   Esth 8:1
will **d** Myself to him   John 14:21
d the motives of   1 Cor 4:5
secrets...are **d-d**   1 Cor 14:25

DISCOURAGE *dishearten*

d-ing the sons of   Num 32:7
people of the land **d-d**   Ezra 4:4
d-d with the work   Neh 6:9

DISCOVER *find, uncover*

strength was not **d-ed**   Judg 16:9
d the depths of God   Job 11:7
man may not **d**   Eccl 7:14
shamed...he is **d-ed**   Jer 2:26

DISCRETION *understanding*

LORD give you **d**   1 Chr 22:12
sound wisdom and **d**   Prov 3:21
woman who lacks **d**   Prov 11:22
Daniel replied with **d**   Dan 2:14

DISCUSS *converse, reason*

d matters of justice   Jer 12:1
d among themselves   Matt 16:7
What were you **d-ing**   Mark 9:33
d-ed together what   Luke 6:11

DISEASE *sickness*

none of the **d-s** on you   Ex 15:26
harmful **d-s** of Egypt   Deut 7:15
d-d in his feet   2 Chr 16:12
d-d...not healed   Ezek 34:4
heals all your **d-s**   Ps 103:3
various **d-s** and pains   Matt 4:24
power...to heal **d-s**   Luke 9:1

DISGRACE *reproach, shame*

a **d** to us   Gen 34:14
nakedness, it is a **d**   Lev 20:17
sin is a **d** to   Prov 14:34
not **d** the throne   Jer 14:21
and bear your **d**   Ezek 16:52

DISGRACEFUL *shameful*

d thing in Israel   Gen 34:7
shameful and **d** son   Prov 19:26
d for a woman to   1 Cor 11:6

DISGUISE *pretend*

d-d his sanity   1 Sam 21:13
Arise now, and **d**   1 Kin 14:2
king of Israel **d-d**   1 Kin 22:30
he **d-s** his face   Job 24:15
d-ing...as apostles   2 Cor 11:13

DISH *bowl, plate*

prepare a savory **d**   Gen 27:7
was one silver **d**   Num 7:43
as one wipes a **d**   2 Kin 21:13
30 gold **d-es**   Ezra 1:9

DISHEARTENED *discouraged*

not be **d** or crushed   Is 42:4
you **d** the righteous   Ezek 13:22

DISHONEST *untruthful*

those who hate **d** gain   Ex 18:21
order to get **d** gain   Ezek 22:27

cheat with **d** scales   Amos 8:5

DISHONOR (n) *disgrace, shame*

to see the king's **d**   Ezra 4:14
Fill their faces with **d**   Ps 83:16
man conceals **d**   Prov 12:16

DISHONOR (v) *disgrace, shame*

who **d-s** his father   Deut 27:16
be ashamed and **d-ed**   Ps 35:4
and you **d** Me   John 8:49
bodies might be **d-ed**   Rom 1:24
do you **d** God   Rom 2:23

DISMAY *be troubled, fear*

d-ed at his presence   Gen 45:3
not tremble or be **d-ed**   Josh 1:9
d-ed and...afraid   1 Sam 17:11
lest I **d** you   Jer 1:17
are **d-ed** and caught   Jer 8:9
mighty men...be **d-ed**   Obad 9

DISMISS *release, send away*

d-ed the people   Josh 24:28
Solomon **d-ed**   1 Kin 2:27
priest did not **d** *any*   2 Chr 23:8
he **d-ed** the assembly   Acts 19:41

DISOBEDIENCE *rebellion*

the one man's **d**   Rom 5:19
in the sons of **d**   Eph 2:2
d received a just   Heb 2:2
same example of **d**   Heb 4:11

DISOBEDIENT *rebellious*

d and rebelled   Neh 9:26
hardened and **d**   Acts 19:9
d to parents   Rom 1:30
d...obstinate people   Rom 10:21

DISPERSE *spread*

d them in Jacob   Gen 49:7
d-d...the peoples   Esth 3:8
d them among the   Ezek 20:23
who are **d-d** abroad   James 1:1

DISPLAY *declare, show*

to **d** her beauty   Esth 1:11
d-ed Thy splendor   Ps 8:1
d their sin like   Is 3:9
works of God...**d-ed**   John 9:3

DISPLEASE *annoy, trouble*

if it is **d-ing** to you   Num 22:34
d-ing in the sight   1 Sam 8:6
may not **d** the lords   1 Sam 29:7
d-ing in His sight   Is 59:15
it greatly **d-d** Jonah   Jon 4:1

DISPOSSESS *remove*

d-ed the Amorites   Num 21:32
Esau **d-ed** them   Deut 2:12
He will assuredly **d**   Josh 3:10
d-ing the nations   Acts 7:45

DISPUTE (n) *controversy*

When they have a **d**   Ex 18:16
bring the **d-s** to God   Ex 18:19
d in your courts   Deut 17:8
a great **d** among   Acts 28:29

DISPUTE (v) *contend, debate*

wished to **d** with Him   Job 9:3
with Israel he will **d**   Mic 6:2

DISSENSION *division*

great **d** and debate — Acts 15:2
d between the — Acts 23:7
those who cause **d-s** — Rom 16:17
without wrath and **d** — 1 Tim 2:8

without...**d-ing** — Phil 2:14
He **d-d** with the devil — Jude 9

DISSIPATION *intemperance*

weighted...with **d** — Luke 21:34
wine, for that is **d** — Eph 5:18
not accused of **d** — Titus 1:6

DISSOLVE *melt*

dost **d** me in a storm — Job 30:22
I **d** my couch with — Ps 6:6
d-d in tears — Is 15:3
And the hills **d** — Nah 1:5

DISTANCE *far away*

sister stood at a **d** — Ex 2:4
some **d** from the — Judg 18:22
following...at a **d** — Matt 26:58
welcomed...from a **d** — Heb 11:13

DISTINCTION *difference*

the LORD makes a **d** — Ex 11:7
d between the holy — Lev 10:10
have made no **d** — Ezek 22:26
He made no **d** — Acts 15:9
for there is no **d** — Rom 3:22
d-s among yourselves — James 2:4

DISTINGUISH (v) *discern*

I **d** between good — 2 Sam 19:35
not **d** the sound — Ezra 3:13
d...the righteous — Mal 3:18
d-ing of spirits — 1 Cor 12:10

DISTINGUISHING (adj)

became your **d** mark — Ezek 27:7
this is a **d** mark — 2 Thess 3:17

DISTORT *pervert*

who **d-s** the justice — Deut 27:19
my garment is **d-ed** — Job 30:18
they **d** my words — Ps 56:5
d the gospel of Christ — Gal 1:7

DISTRESS *adversity, trouble*

day of my **d** — Gen 35:3
When you are in **d** — Deut 4:30
deliver me...**d** — 1 Sam 26:24
I am in great **d** — 2 Sam 24:14
cry to Thee in our **d** — 2 Chr 20:9
refuge in the day of **d** — Jer 16:19
I am in **d** — Lam 1:20
d upon the land — Luke 21:23
d for every soul — Rom 2:9
assisted those in **d** — 1 Tim 5:10
widows in their **d** — James 1:27

DISTRIBUTE *apportion*

d-d by lot in Shiloh — Josh 19:51
to **d** their kinsmen — Neh 13:13
d it to the poor — Luke 18:22
d-ing to each one — 1 Cor 12:11

DISTRICT *area, province*

the **d** of Jerusalem — Neh 3:12
d around the Jordan — Matt 3:5
d of Galilee — Mark 1:28
the **d-s** of Libya — Acts 2:10

DISTURB *annoy, bother*

Why...**d-ed** me — 1 Sam 28:15
no one **d** his bones — 2 Kin 23:18
d them and destroy — Esth 9:24
being greatly **d-ed** — Acts 4:2
one who is **d-ing** you — Gal 5:10

DISTURBANCE *turmoil*

to cause a **d** in it — Neh 4:8
hear of wars and **d-s** — Luke 21:9
d among the soldiers — Acts 12:18
arrogance, **d-s** — 2 Cor 12:20

DIVIDE *apportion, separate*

that **d-s** the hoof — Deut 14:6
D the living child — 1 Kin 3:25
d my garments among — Ps 22:18
He will **d** the booty — Is 53:12
d-d up His garments — Matt 27:35
d-d his wealth — Luke 15:12

DIVINATION *witchcraft*

nor practice **d** or — Lev 19:26
witchcraft, used **d** — 2 Chr 33:6
false vision, **d** — Jer 14:14
falsehood and lying **d** — Ezek 13:6
a spirit of **d** met us — Acts 16:16

DIVINE (adj) *pertaining to deity*

in whom...**d** spirit — Gen 41:38
I see a **d** being — 1 Sam 28:13
D Nature...gold — Acts 17:29
power and **d** nature — Rom 1:20
is the **d** response — Rom 11:4

DIVINE (v) *practice divination*

d-d that the LORD — Gen 30:27
they **d** lies for you — Ezek 21:29
d-ing lies for them — Ezek 22:28
prophets **d** for money — Mic 3:11

DIVINER *seer*

called for the...**d-s** — 1 Sam 6:2
The **d** and the elder — Is 3:2
your **d-s** deceive you — Jer 29:8
d-s will be embarrassed — Mic 3:7
d-s see lying visions — Zech 10:2

DIVISION *dissension, segment*

d between My people — Ex 8:23
divided..into **d-s** — 1 Chr 23:6
d in the multitude — John 7:43
no **d-s** among you — 1 Cor 1:10
d of soul and spirit — Heb 4:12

DIVORCE (n) *separation*

a certificate of **d** — Deut 24:1
given her a writ of **d** — Jer 3:8
For I hate **d** — Mal 2:16

DIVORCE (v) *separate*

he cannot **d** her — Deut 22:19
husband **d-s** his wife — Jer 3:1
man to **d** his wife — Matt 19:3
Whoever **d-s** his — Mark 10:11

DIVORCED (adj) *separated*

woman **d** from her — Lev 21:7
or of a **d** woman — Num 30:9
marries a **d** woman — Matt 5:32
marries...who is **d** — Luke 16:18

DOCTRINE *teaching*

Teaching as **d-s** the — Matt 15:9

every wind of **d** — Eph 4:14
to teach strange **d-s** — 1 Tim 1:3
to exhort in sound **d** — Titus 1:9

DOCUMENT *manuscript*

the **d** which you sent — Ezra 4:18
And on the sealed **d** — Neh 9:38
Darius signed the **d** — Dan 6:9

DOER *workman*

recompenses the...**d** — Ps 31:23
d-s of the Law will — Rom 2:13
d-s of the word — James 1:22
not a **d** of the law — James 4:11

DOG *animal, scavenger*

Am I a **d** — 1 Sam 17:43
d-s have surrounded — Ps 22:16
they howl like a **d** — Ps 59:6
live **d** is better than — Eccl 9:4
Beware of the **d-s** — Phil 3:2
d-s and the sorcerers — Rev 22:15

DOMAIN *estate*

give You all this **d** — Luke 4:6
the **d** of darkness — Col 1:13
keep their own **d** — Jude 6

DOMINION *authority, rule*

Thine is the **d** — 1 Chr 29:11
places of His **d** — Ps 103:22
d will be from sea — Zech 9:10
and power and **d** — Eph 1:21
thrones or **d-s** or — Col 1:16
glory and the **d** forever — Rev 1:6

DONKEY *ass*

a wild **d** of a man — Gen 16:12
Balaam...to the **d** — Num 22:29
the foal of a **d** — Zech 9:9
you will find a **d** — Matt 21:2
and mounted on a **d** — Matt 21:5
a dumb **d**, speaking — 2 Pet 2:16

DOOR *entrance, opening*

crouching at the **d** — Gen 4:7
set the **d** of the ark — Gen 6:16
Uriah slept at the **d** — 2 Sam 11:9
over the **d** of my lips — Ps 141:3
d turns on its — Prov 26:14
each had a double **d** — Ezek 41:23
shut your **d**, pray — Matt 6:6
I am the **d** — John 10:9
right at the **d** — James 5:9
before you an open **d** — Rev 3:8
I stand at the **d** — Rev 3:20

DOORKEEPER *guard*

d-s have gathered — 2 Kin 22:4
the Levites, the **d-s** — 2 Chr 34:9
eunuchs who were **d-s** — Esth 6:2
commanded the **d** — Mark 13:34
To him the **d** opens — John 10:3

DOORPOST

put it on the two **d-s** — Ex 12:7
write them on the **d-s** — Deut 6:9
on the seat by the **d** — 1 Sam 1:9
Waiting at my **d-s** — Prov 8:34

DOORWAY *entrance, opening*

the **d** of the tent — Judg 4:20
d-s and doorposts — 1 Kin 7:5
at my neighbor's **d** — Job 31:9

chamber with its **d**   Ezek 40:38

DORCAS

Tabitha, a Joppa Christian
   Acts 9:36-43

DOUBT (n) *unbelief*

life shall hang in **d**   Deut 28:66
why do **d-s** arise   Luke 24:38

DOUBT (v) *disbelieve*

why did you **d**   Matt 14:31
not **d** in his heart   Mark 11:23
d-s is condemned   Rom 14:23
who **d-s** is like the   James 1:6

DOUGH *flour mixture*

people took their **d**   Ex 12:34
the first of your **d**   Num 15:20
took **d**, kneaded *it*   2 Sam 13:8
knead **d** to make cakes   Jer 7:18

DOVE *bird*

he sent out a **d**   Gen 8:8
had wings like a **d**   Ps 55:6
eyes are *like* **d-s**   Song 1:15
descending as a **d**   Matt 3:16
descending as a **d**   John 1:32
selling the **d-s**   John 2:16

DOWNFALL *collapse*

became the **d** of   2 Chr 28:23
noise of their **d**   Jer 49:21

DOWNPOUR *rain*

the **d** and the rain   Job 37:6
d of waters swept   Hab 3:10

DOWRY *bequest*

must pay a **d** for her   Ex 22:16
to the **d** for virgins   Ex 22:17
d to his daughter   1 Kin 9:16

DRACHMA

Greek silver coin
   Neh 7:70-72; Matt 17:24

DRAG *draw, pull*

grasshopper **d-s**   Eccl 12:5
D them off like sheep   Jer 12:3
the dogs to **d** off   Jer 15:3
Paul and **d-ged**   Acts 14:19
d you into court   James 2:6

DRAGON *monster, serpent*

d who *lives* in the sea   Is 27:1
Who pierced the **d**   Is 51:9
d stood before the   Rev 12:4
he laid hold of the **d**   Rev 20:2

DRAIN *empty*

blood is to be **d-ed**   Lev 1:15
he **d-ed** the dew   Judg 6:38
must **d** *and* drink down   Ps 75:8
drink it and **d** it   Ezek 23:34

DRAW *haul, pull*

out to **d** water   Gen 24:13
drew him out of the   Ex 2:10
but are **d-n** away   Deut 30:17
He **d-s** up the drops   Job 36:27
d near to my soul   Ps 69:18
They are **d-ing** back   Jer 46:5
redemption is **d-ing**   Luke 21:28
d all men to Myself   John 12:32

D near to God   James 4:8

DRAWERS *servants*

wood and **d** of water   Josh 9:21

DREAD (n) *fear*

in **d**...of Israel   Ex 1:12
in **d** night and day   Deut 28:66
d of the Jews   Esth 8:17
they are in great **d**   Ps 14:5
d comes like a storm   Prov 1:27

DREAD (v) *fear*

what I **d** befalls me   Job 3:25
Whom shall I **d**   Ps 27:1
whose two kings you **d**   Is 7:16
are **d-ed** and feared   Hab 1:7

DREAM (n) *vision*

had a **d**, and behold   Gen 28:12
man was relating a **d**   Judg 7:13
flies away like a **d**   Job 20:8
like a **d**, a vision   Is 29:7
visions and **d-s**   Dan 1:17
to Joseph in a **d**   Matt 2:13

DREAM (v) *see a vision*

asleep and **d-ed**   Gen 41:5
like those who **d**   Ps 126:1
when a hungry man **d-s**   Is 29:8
Your old men will **d**   Joel 2:28

DREAMER *visionary*

Here comes this **d**   Gen 37:19
If a prophet or a **d**   Deut 13:1
your diviners, your **d-s**   Jer 27:9

DRENCH *soak, wet*

d you with my tears   Is 16:9
head is **d-ed** with dew   Song 5:2
d-ed with the dew   Dan 4:33

DRESS (n) *clothing*

have taken off my **d**   Song 5:3
d was of fine linen   Ezek 16:3
or putting on **d-es**   1 Pet 3:3

DRESS (v) *array, clothe*

d-ed in his military   2 Sam 20:8
D-ed as a harlot   Prov 7:10
you **d** in scarlet   Jer 4:30
d-ed Him...purple   Mark 15:17

DRINK (n) *refreshment*

gave the lad a **d**   Gen 21:19
or wine, or strong **d**   Deut 14:26
to desire strong **d**   Prov 31:4
thirsty...gave Me a **d**   Matt 25:35
My blood is true **d**   John 6:55
thirsty, give him a **d**   Rom 12:20

DRINK (v)

he **drank** of the wine   Gen 9:21
Do not **d** wine   Lev 10:9
d from the brook   1 Kin 17:6
they all **drank** from   Mark 14:23
after **d-ing** old *wine*   Luke 5:39
who eats and **d-s**   1 Cor 11:29
ground that **d-s** the   Heb 6:7

DRIP *drop*

clouds...They **d**   Job 36:28
lips...**d** honey   Song 4:11
d-ped with myrrh   Song 5:5

D down, O heavens   Is 45:8

DRIVE *chase, defeat*

Thou hast **d-n** me   Gen 4:14
and **drove** them away   Ex 2:17
angel...**d-ing** *them* on   Ps 35:5
d hard all your workers   Is 58:3
drove *them* all out   John 2:15
to **d** the ship   Acts 27:39

DROP (n) *drip*

the **d-s** of water   Job 36:27
a **d** from a bucket   Is 40:15
like **d-s** of blood   Luke 22:44

DROP (v) *fall*

olives shall **d** off   Deut 28:40
his bonds **d-ped**   Judg 15:14
d off his unripe grape   Job 15:33
d-ped their wings   Ezek 1:24

DROSS *metallic waste*

of the earth *like* **d**   Ps 119:119
Take away the **d**   Prov 25:4
silver has become **d**   Is 1:22
Israel has become **d**   Ezek 22:18

DROUGHT *dryness*

Like heat in **d**   Is 25:5
in regard to the **d**   Jer 14:1
I called for a **d**   Hag 1:11

DROWNED *suffocated*

d in the Red Sea   Ex 15:4
he be **d** in the depth   Matt 18:6
were **d** in the sea   Mark 5:13

DRUNK *intoxicated*

arrows **d** with blood   Deut 32:42
d, but not with wine   Is 29:9
made...**d** in My wrath   Is 63:6
not get **d** with wine   Eph 5:18
I saw the woman **d**   Rev 17:6

DRUNKARD *intoxicated person*

a glutton and a **d**   Deut 21:20
song of the **d-s**   Ps 69:12
Awake, **d-s**, and weep   Joel 1:5
a reviler, or a **d**   1 Cor 5:11

DRUNKEN *intoxicated*

stagger like a **d** man   Job 12:25
become like a **d** man   Jer 23:9

DRUNKENNESS *intoxicated*

and not for **d**   Eccl 10:17
weighted down...**d**   Luke 21:34
in carousing and **d**   Rom 13:13
envying, **d**, carousing   Gal 5:21

DRY (adj) *parched, scorched*

let the **d** land appear   Gen 1:9
In a **d** and weary land   Ps 63:1
Better is a **d** morsel   Prov 17:1
O **d** bones, hear   Ezek 37:4

DRY (v) *scorch, wither*

My strength is **dried**   Ps 22:15
d up...streams   Ps 74:15
I **d** up the sea   Is 50:2
new wine **dries** up   Joel 1:10
dries up...rivers   Nah 1:4

DUE (adj) *proper, right*

In **d** time their foot   Deut 32:35

food in **d** season	Ps 104:27
d penalty of their	Rom 1:27

DUE (n) *what is owed*

as *their* **d** forever	Lev 7:34
be the priests' **d**	Deut 18:3
Indeed it is Thy **d**	Jer 10:7

DULL *heavy, stupid*

eyes are **d** from wine	Gen 49:12
Their ears **d**	Is 6:10
people...become **d**	Matt 13:15
become **d** of hearing	Heb 5:11

DUMB *silent*

who makes *him* **d**	Ex 4:11
I was **d** and silent	Ps 39:2
behold, a **d** man	Matt 9:32
and the **d** to speak	Mark 7:37
astray to the **d** idols	1 Cor 12:2

DUNG *waste*

sweeps away **d**	1 Kin 14:10
dove's **d** for five	2 Kin 6:25
give you cow's **d**	Ezek 4:15
their flesh like **d**	Zeph 1:17

DUNGEON *prison*

put me into the **d**	Gen 40:15
captive...in the **d**	Ex 12:29
prisoners from the **d**	Is 42:7
Jeremiah...into the **d**	Jer 37:16

DUST *dirt, earth*

God formed man of **d**	Gen 2:7
And **d** shall you eat	Gen 3:14
the poor from the **d**	1 Sam 2:8
repent in **d** and ashes	Job 42:6
d before the wind	Ps 18:42
Will the **d** praise Thee	Ps 30:9
You who lie in the **d**	Is 26:19
shake off the **d** of	Matt 10:14
the **d** of your city	Luke 10:11
d on their heads	Rev 18:19

DUTY *responsibility*

perform your **d**	Gen 38:8
charged with any **d**	Deut 24:5
the **d** of a husband's	Deut 25:7
his **d** to his wife	1 Cor 7:3

DWELL *abide, live*

father of those who **d**	Gen 4:20
Behold, I am **d**-ing	1 Chr 17:1
No evil **d**-s with Thee	Ps 5:4
d on Thy holy hill	Ps 15:1
I will **d** in the house	Ps 23:6
d among the wise	Prov 15:31
have **d**-t in Jerusalem	Jer 35:11
flesh, and **d**-t among	John 1:14
of God **d**-s in you	1 Cor 3:16
Christ may **d** in your	Eph 3:17
mind **d** on these things	Phil 4:8

DWELLING *habitation*

earth shall be your **d**	Gen 27:39
name there for His **d**	Deut 12:5
place for Thy **d**	1 Kin 8:13
into the eternal **d**-s	Luke 16:9
might find a **d** place	Acts 7:46

DYED *colored*

rams' skins **d** red	Ex 25:5
A spoil of **d** work	Judg 5:30

E

EAGLE *bird*

bore you on **e-s'** wings	Ex 19:4
the **e** swoops down	Deut 28:49
swifter than **e-s**	2 Sam 1:23
with wings like **e-s**	Is 40:31
the face of an **e**	Ezek 1:10
was like a flying **e**	Rev 4:7

EAR *hearing*

heard with our **e-s**	2 Sam 7:22
the **e** test words	Job 12:11
And His **e-s** are *open*	Ps 34:15
and incline your **e**	Ps 45:10
He whose **e** listens	Prov 15:31
e of the wise seeks	Prov 18:15
e has not been open	Is 48:8
let your **e** receive	Jer 9:20
He who has **e-s** to	Matt 11:15
and cut off his **e**	Matt 26:51
fingers into his **e-s**	Mark 7:33
if the **e** should say	1 Cor 12:16
their **e-s** tickled	2 Tim 4:3
He who has an **e**	Rev 2:7

EARLY *beforetime, soon*

they arose **e** and	Gen 26:31
Let us rise **e**	Song 7:12
dew which goes away **e**	Hos 6:4
e on the first day	Mark 16:2
at the tomb **e**	Luke 24:22
the **e** and late rains	James 5:7

EARNINGS *gain, wages*

her **e** she plants	Prov 31:16
the **e** of a harlot	Mic 1:7

EARRING *ornament*

brought...**e-s**	Ex 35:22
e-s and necklaces	Num 31:50
Like an **e** of gold	Prov 25:12
her **e-s** and jewelry	Hos 2:13

EARTH *land, world*

God created the...**e**	Gen 1:1
Judge of all the **e**	Gen 18:25
the **e** is the LORD's	Ex 9:29
way of all the **e**	Josh 23:14
His stand on the **e**	Job 19:25
foundation of the **e**	Job 38:4
saints...in the **e**	Ps 16:3
the shields of the **e**	Ps 47:9
give birth to the **e**	Ps 90:2
He established the **e**	Ps 104:5
wisdom founded...**e**	Prov 3:19
the **e** remains forever	Eccl 1:4
made the **e** tremble	Is 14:16
the vault of the **e**	Is 40:22
the ends of the **e**	Is 45:22
the **e** is My footstool	Is 66:1
e shone with His	Ezek 43:2
make the **e** dark	Amos 8:9
e will be devoured	Zeph 3:8
shall inherit the **e**	Matt 5:5
you shall bind on **e**	Matt 16:19
on **e** peace among	Luke 2:14
glorified...on the **e**	John 17:4
man is from the **e**	1 Cor 15:47
heavens and a new **e**	2 Pet 3:13
e and heaven fled	Rev 20:11

EARTHENWARE *pottery*

bird in an **e** vessel	Lev 14:5
holy water in an **e**	Num 5:17
shatter them like **e**	Ps 2:9
buy a potter's **e** jar	Jer 19:1
vessels of...**e**	2 Tim 2:20

EARTHQUAKE *temblor*

LORD *was* not...**e**	1 Kin 19:11
punished with...**e**	Is 29:6
be famines and **e-s**	Matt 24:7
will be great **e-s**	Luke 21:11
there was a great **e**	Rev 6:12
killed in the **e**	Rev 11:13

EARTHY *mortal*

man is...**e**	1 Cor 15:47
those who are **e**	1 Cor 15:48

EASE *free from difficulty, pain*

He who is at **e**	Job 12:5
at **e** and satisfied	Job 21:23
women who are at **e**	Is 32:9
Woe to those...at **e**	Amos 6:1
nations who are at **e**	Zech 1:15

EAST *direction of compass*

spread out...to the **e**	Gen 28:14
directed an **e** wind	Ex 10:13
sons of the **e** were	Judg 7:12
men of the **e**	Job 1:3
With the **e** wind Thou	Ps 48:7
offspring from the **e**	Is 43:5
faces toward the **e**	Ezek 8:16
Jerusalem on the **e**	Zech 14:4
saw His star in the **e**	Matt 2:2
lightning...the **e**	Matt 24:27
kings from the **e**	Rev 16:12

EAST GATE

see **GATES OF JERUSALEM**

EASY *without difficulty*

knowledge is **e** to him	Prov 14:6
My yoke is **e**, and	Matt 11:30

EAT *consume, dine, feast*

shall not **e** from it	Gen 3:17
they **ate** every plant	Ex 10:15
not **e**...blood	Lev 19:26
that we may **e** him	2 Kin 6:28
e and be satisfied	Ps 22:26
not **e** the bread of	Prov 31:27
will **e** curds and honey	Is 7:15
words...I **ate** them	Jer 15:16
e this scroll	Ezek 3:1
e-ing grass like cattle	Dan 4:33
what you shall **e**	Matt 6:25
e with unwashed	Matt 15:20
Take, **e**; this is My	Matt 26:26
sinners and **e-s** with	Luke 15:2
e...at My table	Luke 22:30
He took it and **ate**	Luke 24:43
e the flesh of...Son	John 6:53
Peter, kill and **e**	Acts 10:13
kingdom...not **e**-ing	Rom 14:17
ate...spiritual food	1 Cor 10:3
e-s...judgment	1 Cor 11:29

EBAL

1 son of Shobal	Gen 36:23
2 son of Joktan	1 Chr 1:22
also Obal	Gen 10:28
3 *mountain near Shechem*	
	Deut 11:29

EBENEZER
a memorial stone   1 Sam 7:12

EBER
1 *line of Shem*   Gen 10:21-24
  progenitor of Jocktanide Arabs
                              Gen 10:25-30
  progenitor of Hebrews
                              Gen 11:16ff
2 *a Gadite*   1 Chr 5:13
3 *son of Elpaal*   1 Chr 8:12
4 *son of Shashak*   1 Chr 8:22
5 *priest*   Neh 12:20
  see also **HEBER**

EDEN
1 *garden of God*
                Gen 2:15; Is 51:3
2 *city area*
        2 Kin 19:12; Ezek 27:23
3 *son of Joah*   2 Chr 29:12

EDICT *decree*
the king's **e-s**   Ezra 8:36
a royal **e** be issued   Esth 1:19
king's command and **e** Esth 9:1
afraid of the king's **e** Heb 11:23

EDIFICATION *building up*
his good, to his **e**   Rom 15:2
speaks to men for **e**   1 Cor 14:3
all things...for **e**   1 Cor 14:26

EDIFY *build up*
but love **e-ies**   1 Cor 8:1
not all things **e**   1 Cor 10:23
man is not **e-ied**   1 Cor 14:17

EDOM
1 *name of Esau*   Gen 25:30
2 *Edomites*   Num 20:18,20
3 *region or country*
        Gen 32:3; Judg 11:17
  see also **SEIR**

EDUCATED *taught*
be **e** three years   Dan 1:5
Moses was **e** in all   Acts 7:22
e under Gamaliel   Acts 22:3

EFFEMINATE *womanlike*
e, nor homosexuals   1 Cor 6:9

EGG
in the white of an **e** Job 6:6
gathers abandoned **e-s** Is 10:14
hatch adders' **e-s** and Is 59:5
is asked for an **e**   Luke 11:12

EGLON
1 *town in Judah*
        Josh 10:34-37;15:39
2 *Moabite king*   Judg 3:12-30

EGYPT
country in NE Africa
                Gen 12:10;37:25
source of food   Gen 42:1,2
on the Nile   Ex 4:19;7:5
conflict with Moses Ex 7:8ff
scene of Passover   Ex 12:1-36

EHUD
1 *left-handed Benjamite judge of
  Israel*   Judg 3:15,21
2 *son of Bilhan*   1 Chr 7:10
3 *progenitor of clan* 1 Chr 8:6

EKRON
Philistine city
        Josh 13:3; 1 Sam 5:10;
                        Jer 25:20

ELAH
1 *Edomite*   Gen 36:41
2 *valley SW of Jerusalem*
                        1 Sam 17:2
3 *father of Shimei*   1 Kin 4:18
4 *king of Israel*   1 Kin 16:8-10
5 *father of Hoshea*   2 Kin 15:30
6 *son of Caleb*   1 Chr 4:15
7 *son of Uzzi*   1 Chr 9:8

ELAM
1 *son of Shem*   Gen 10:22
2 *son of Shashak*   1 Chr 8:24
3 *Korahite Levite*   1 Chr 26:3
4 *head of restoration family*
        Ezra 2:7; Neh 7:12
5 *head of restoration family*
        Ezra 2:31; Neh 7:34
6 *chief of people*   Neh 10:14
7 *priest*   Neh 12:42
8 *region E of Babylonia*
        Is 21:2; Dan 8:2

ELATH / ELOTH *city*
at Gulf of Aqabah   2 Kin 14:22
near Ezion-geber

EL-BETHEL
altar   Gen 35:7

ELDER *aged, older*
words of her **e** son Gen 27:42
the **e-s** of Israel Ex 17:6
sits among the **e-s** Prov 31:23
Assemble the **e-s**   Joel 2:16
tradition of the **e-s** Matt 15:2
chief priests and **e-s** Matt 27:12
scribes...**e-s** came Mark 11:27
Council of **e-s** of Luke 22:66
e-s of the church Acts 20:17
I saw twenty-four **e-s** Rev 4:4

ELEAZAR
1 *son of Aaron*   Ex 6:23
  high priest   Num 20:25-28
2 *son of Abinadab*   1 Sam 7:1
3 *son of Dodo*   2 Sam 23:9
4 *a Levite*   1 Chr 23:22
5 *son of Phinehas*   Ezra 8:33
6 *son of Parosh*   Ezra 10:18-25
7 *priest*   Neh 12:27
8 *ancestor of Jesus* Matt 1:15

ELECT *chosen*
sake of the **e**   Matt 24:22
to lead the **e** astray Mark 13:22
justice for His **e** Luke 18:7
against God's **e**   Rom 8:33

ELEMENTARY *basic*
e principles of the Col 2:8
e principles of the Heb 5:12

e teaching about the Heb 6:1

ELEMENTS *physical matter*
e will be destroyed 2 Pet 3:10
the **e** will melt with 2 Pet 3:12

ELI
high priest
        1 Sam 1:9;2:12;3:6;4:18

ELIAKIM
1 *son of Hilkiah*
                2 Kin 18:18;19:2
2 *son of Josiah*   2 Kin 23:34
3 *priest*   Neh 12:41
4 *ancestor of Jesus* Matt 1:13
5 *ancestor of Jesus* Luke 3:30,31

ELIEZER
1 *Abraham's servant* Gen 15:2
2 *son of Moses*   1 Chr 23:15
3 *son of Becher*   1 Chr 7:8
4 *priest*   1 Chr 15:24
5 *son of Zichri*   1 Chr 27:16
6 *a prophet*   2 Chr 20:37
7 *served under Ezra* Ezra 8:16
8 *son of Jeshua*   Ezra 10:18
9 *Levite*   Ezra 10:10,23
10 *son Harim*   Ezra 10:10,31
11 *ancestor of Jesus* Luke 3:29

ELIHU
1 *son of Tohu*   1 Sam 1:1
2 *Manassite captain* 1 Chr 12:20
3 *temple gatekeeper* 1 Chr 26:1
4 *officer of Judah*   1 Chr 27:18
5 *one of Job's friends* Job 32:17

ELIJAH
1 *prophet*   1 Kin 17:1
  aided by widow   1 Kin 17:8ff
  revived child   1 Kin 17:23
  defeats prophets   1 Kin 18:20ff
  flees Jezebel   1 Kin 19:4-8
  chooses Elisha   1 Kin 19:19-21
  taken up   2 Kin 2:1-11
2 *Benjamite*   1 Chr 8:27
3 *son of Harim*   Ezra 10:21
4 *son of Elam*   Ezra 10:26

ELIMINATE *remove*
e harmful beasts   Lev 26:6
I am going to **e**   Jer 16:9
stomach, and is **e-d** Mark 7:19

ELIPHAZ
1 *son of Esau*   Gen 36:4
2 *one of Job's friends*
        Job 2:11;4:1;42:7,9

ELISHA
prophet   2 Kin 6:12
called   1 Kin 19:19-21
Elijah's successor   2 Kin 2:1ff
miracle of oil   2 Kin 4:1-7
revived chld   2 Kin 4:8-37
death   2 Kin 13:20

ELIZABETH
mother of John the Baptist
        Luke 1:7,13,41,57

ELOQUENT *persuasive*
I have never been **e** Ex 4:10

Apollos...an **e** man   Acts 18:24

ELUL

sixth month of Hebrew calendar
  Neh 6:15

ELYMAS

magician   Acts 13:8
also **Bar-Jesus**

EMBALM *preserve*

to **e** his father   Gen 50:2
he was **e-ed** and   Gen 50:26

EMBARRASSED *ashamed*

e to lift up my face   Ezra 9:6
e at the gardens   Is 1:29
diviners will be **e**   Mic 3:7

EMBITTERED *resentful*

the people were **e**   1 Sam 30:6
e them against the   Acts 14:2

EMBRACE *clasp, hug*

Esau ran...and **e-d**   Gen 33:4
e...a foreigner   Prov 5:20
A time to **e**   Eccl 3:5
ran and **e-d** him   Luke 15:20

EMBROIDERED *woven*

spoil of dyed work **e**   Judg 5:30
be led...in **e** work   Ps 45:14
silk, and **e** cloth   Ezek 16:13
purple, **e** work   Ezek 27:16

EMERALD *precious stone*

ruby, topaz and **e**   Ex 28:17
throne, like an **e**   Rev 4:3

EMINENT *renowned*

nor anything **e**   Ezek 7:11
the most **e** apostles   2 Cor 11:5
inferior to...**e**   2 Cor 12:11

EMISSION *issuance*

man has a seminal **e**   Lev 15:16
nocturnal **e**   Deut 23:10

EMMAUS

village by Jerusalem   Luke 24:13

EMPOWERED *authorized*

e him to eat from   Eccl 5:19
God has not **e** him   Eccl 6:2

EMPTY (adj) *containing nothing*

Now the pit was **e**   Gen 37:24
did not return **e**   2 Sam 1:22
sent widows away **e**   Job 22:9
deceive you with **e**   Eph 5:6
avoid...**e** chatter   2 Tim 2:16

EMPTY (v) *remove contents*

e-ing their sacks   Gen 42:35
they **e** the house   Lev 14:36
I **e-ied** them out as   Ps 18:42
therefore **e** their net   Hab 1:17
e the golden *oil*   Zech 4:12
but **e-ied** Himself   Phil 2:7

ENCAMP *abide, lodge*

the tabernacle **e-s**   Num 1:51
and **e-ed** together   Josh 11:5
a host **e** against me   Ps 27:3
angel of the LORD **e-s**   Ps 34:7

ENCIRCLE *go around*

entirely **e-ing** the sea   2 Chr 4:3
he **e-d** the Ophel   2 Chr 33:14
cords...have **e-d** me   Ps 119:61
Who **e** yourselves with   Is 50:11

ENCOMPASS *surround*

waves of death **e**   2 Sam 22:5
e-ing the walls of   1 Kin 6:5
e-ed...with bitterness   Lam 3:5
Water **e-ed** me to the   Jon 2:5

ENCOURAGE *strengthen*

charge Joshua and **e**   Deut 3:28
e-d him in God   1 Sam 23:16
e them in the work   Ezra 6:22
Paul was **e-ing** them   Acts 27:33
e one another   1 Thess 5:11
e the young women   Titus 2:4

ENCOURAGEMENT *support*

I arose to be an **e**   Dan 11:1
God who gives...**e**   Rom 15:5
is any **e** in Christ   Phil 2:1
we may have strong **e**   Heb 6:18

END (n) *extremity, goal, result*

e of all flesh has   Gen 6:13
one **e** of the heavens   Deut 4:32
from beginning to **e**   1 Sam 3:12
what is my **e**   Job 6:11
very **e-s** of the earth   Ps 2:8
wicked come to an **e**   Ps 7:9
e is the way of death   Prov 14:12
no **e** to all his labor   Eccl 4:8
summer is **e-ed**   Jer 8:20
The **e** is coming   Ezek 7:2
who endures to...**e**   Matt 24:13
to the **e** of the age   Matt 28:20
kingdom...no **e**   Luke 1:33
He loved...to the **e**   John 13:1
Christ...**e** of the law   Rom 10:4
beginning and the **e**   Rev 21:6

END (v) *complete, stop*

border **e-ed** at the sea   Josh 15:4
words of Job are **e-ed**   Job 31:40
days there were **e-ed**   Acts 21:5
it **e-s** up being burned   Heb 6:8

ENDLESS *limitless*

writing...is **e**   Eccl 12:12
and **e** genealogies   1 Tim 1:4

ENDOW *provide a gift*

God has **e-ed** me   Gen 30:20
e-ed with discretion   2 Chr 2:12
to **e** those who love   Prov 8:21
e-ed with salvation   Zech 9:9

ENDURANCE *patience*

in much **e**, in   2 Cor 6:4
you have need of **e**   Heb 10:36
let us run with **e**   Heb 12:1
of the **e** of Job   James 5:11

ENDURE *persevere*

will be able to **e**   Ex 18:23
that I should **e**   Job 6:11
while the sun **e-s**   Ps 72:5
May his name **e**   Ps 72:17
and your name will **e**   Is 66:22
Can your heart **e**   Ezek 22:14

the one who has **e-d**   Matt 10:22
who **e-s** to the end   Mark 13:13
e-s all things   1 Cor 13:7
discipline that you **e**   Heb 12:7
blessed who **e-d**   James 5:11

ENEMY *foe*

delivered your **e-ies**   Gen 14:20
Thine **e-ies** perish   Judg 5:31
a man finds his **e**   1 Sam 24:19
consider me Thine **e**   Job 13:24
make the **e**...cease   Ps 8:2
presence of my **e-ies**   Ps 23:5
e has persecuted my   Ps 143:3
If your **e** is hungry   Prov 25:21
kisses of an **e**   Prov 27:6
love your **e-ies**, and   Matt 5:44
e of all righteousness   Acts 13:10
e is hungry, feed   Rom 12:20
e...be abolished   1 Cor 15:26
an **e** of God   James 4:4

ENGAGE *be involved, betroth*

virgin who is not **e-d**   Ex 22:16
the girl who is **e-d**   Deut 22:25
e-d in their work   1 Chr 9:33
e-d to...Joseph   Luke 1:27
to **e** in good deeds   Titus 3:8

ENGEDI

spring and town near Dead Sea
  1 Sam 23:29;24:1; Song 1:14

ENGRAVE *inscribe*

shall **e** the two stones   Ex 28:11
e-d on the tablets   Ex 32:16
e an inscription   Zech 3:9
letters **e-d** on stones   2 Cor 3:7

ENGRAVINGS *carvings*

like the **e** of a seal   Ex 28:36
the **e** of a signet   Ex 39:30
carved **e** of cherubim
  1 Kin 6:29

ENGULF *overwhelm, swallow*

water...to **e** them   Deut 11:4
sea **e-ed** their enemies   Ps 78:53
She has been **e-ed**   Jer 51:42
great deep **e-ed** me   Jon 2:5

ENLARGE *extend, increase*

May God **e** Japheth   Gen 9:27
Thou wilt **e** my heart   Ps 119:32
Sheol has **e-d** its   Is 5:14
He **e-s** his appetite   Hab 2:5

ENLIGHTEN *illumine*

e-ing the eyes   Ps 19:8
eyes...may be **e-d**   Eph 1:18
who have...been **e-d**   Heb 6:4

ENMITY *hostility*

e Between you and   Gen 3:15
had everlasting **e**   Ezek 35:5
at **e** with each other   Luke 23:12
sorcery, **e-ies**, strife   Gal 5:20
abolishing...the **e**   Eph 2:15

ENOCH

1 *son of Cain*   Gen 4:17
2 *city*   Gen 4:17
3 *Methuselah's father*   Gen 5:22
  walked with God   Gen 5:24

ENRAGE *anger*

e-d and curse their	Is 8:21
jealousy **e-s** a man	Prov 6:34
he became very **e-d**	Matt 2:16
dragon was **e-d** with	Rev 12:17

ENRICH *make wealthy*

king will **e** the	1 Sam 17:25
Thou dost greatly **e**	Ps 65:9
You **e-ed** the kings	Ezek 27:33

ENROLLED *recorded*

were **e** by genealogy	1 Chr 7:9
people to be **e** by	Neh 7:5
e in heaven	Heb 12:23

ENSLAVE *subjugate*

you have been **e-d**	Is 14:3
e-d and mistreated	Acts 7:6
if he **e-s** you	2 Cor 11:20
e-d to various lusts	Titus 3:3

ENSNARE *catch*

An evil man is **e-d**	Prov 12:13
e him who adjudicates	Is 29:21

ENTANGLE *ensnare*

camel **e-ing** her ways	Jer 2:23
No soldier...**e-s**	2 Tim 2:4
sin which...**e-s** us	Heb 12:1

ENTER *go in*

you shall **e** the ark	Gen 6:18
He **e-s** into judgment	Job 22:4
E His gates with	Ps 100:4
E the rock and hide	Is 2:10
He **e-s** into peace	Is 57:2
Spirit **e-ed** me and	Ezek 2:2
not **e** the kingdom	Matt 5:20
E by the narrow gate	Matt 7:13
to **e** life crippled	Matt 18:8
afraid as they **e-ed**	Luke 9:34
e into the kingdom	John 3:5
not **e** by the door	John 10:1
shall not **e** My rest	Heb 3:11

ENTHRONED *exalt, make king*

e *above* the cherubim	2 Sam 6:2
LORD who is **e** *above*	1 Chr 13:6
e upon the praises of	Ps 22:3
who sits **e** from of old	Ps 55:19
Who is **e** on high	Ps 113:5

ENTICE *deceive, seduce*

E your husband	Judg 14:15
Who will **e** Ahab	2 Chr 18:19
if sinners **e** you	Prov 1:10
e-d by his own lust	James 1:14
e-ing unstable souls	2 Pet 2:14

ENTRAILS *inner organs*

fat that covers the **e**	Ex 29:13
e and the lobe	Lev 8:16
also washed the **e**	Lev 9:14

ENTRANCE *doorway*

cloud...at the **e**	Ex 33:10
mark well the **e** of	Ezek 44:5
stone against the **e**	Matt 27:60
e into the eternal	2 Pet 1:11

ENTREAT *appeal, ask*

E the LORD that he	Ex 8:8
Moses **e-ed** the LORD	Ex 32:11

Please **e** the LORD	1 Kin 13:6
gain if we **e** Him	Job 21:15
centurion...**e-ing** Him	Matt 8:5
demons *began* to **e**	Matt 8:31
they were **e-ing** Him	Luke 8:31
I **e-ed** the Lord	2 Cor 12:8
e you to walk in a	Eph 4:1

ENTRUST *assign, commit*

security **e-ed** *to him*	Lev 6:2
He **e-ed** the vineyard	Song 8:11
to whom they **e-ed**	Luke 12:48
not **e-ing** Himself to	John 2:24

ENVIOUS *covetous*

e of the arrogant	Ps 73:3
not be **e** of evil men	Prov 24:1
is your eye **e**	Matt 20:15
And you are **e**	James 4:2

ENVIRONS *outskirts, suburbs*

the **e** of Jerusalem	Jer 32:44
devour all his **e**	Jer 50:32
Bethlehem...its **e**	Matt 2:16

ENVOY *agent, messenger*

e-s of the rulers	2 Chr 32:31
faithful **e** *brings*	Prov 13:17
sent your **e-s** a great	Is 57:9
his **e-s** to Egypt	Ezek 17:15

ENVY (n) *jealousy*

full of **e**, murder	Rom 1:29
preaching...from **e**	Phil 1:15
out of which arise **e**	1 Tim 6:4
life in malice and **e**	Titus 3:3
e and all slander	1 Pet 2:1

ENVY (v) *be discontent, jealous*

Philistines **e-ied** him	Gen 26:14
e a man of violence	Prov 3:31
not let your heart **e**	Prov 23:17
e-ing one another	Gal 5:26

EPAPHRAS

Colossian Christian	Col 1:7; 4:12
colleague of Paul	Philem 23

EPAPHRODITUS

Philippian Christian	Phil 2:25
colleague of Paul	Phil 4:18

EPHAH

1 *bushel, measure of capacity*
     Lev 5:11; Num 5:15
2 *son of Midian*
     Gen 25:4; 1 Chr 1:33
3 *Caleb's concubine* 1 Chr 2:46
4 *son of Jahdai*   1 Chr 2:47

EPHESUS

city of Asia Minor
     Acts 18:19; 1 Cor 16:8;
     Rev 1:11; 2:1

EPHOD

1 *priestly garment*
     Ex 28:6; 1 Sam 23:9;
     2 Sam 6:14
2 *father of Hanniel* Num 34:23

EPHRAIM

1 *son of Joseph* Gen 41:52; 48:17
2 *tribe*   Josh 16:5; Judg 7:24
3 *northern kingdom*

     Is 7:2-17; Hos 4:17; 9:3-17
4 *city* 2 Sam 13:23; John 11:54

EPHRAIM GATE

see **GATES OF JERUSALEM**

EPHRATH(AH)

1 *Bethlehem*
     Gen 35:19; 48:7; Ruth 4:11;
     Mic 5:2
2 *wife of Caleb* 1 Chr 2:19,50
3 *territory*   Ps 132:6

EPHRON

1 *a Hittite* Gen 23:8; 50:13
2 *mountain ridge* Josh 15:9
3 *city*   2 Chr 13:19

EPICUREAN

a Greek philosophy Acts 17:18

EPOCHS *ages, seasons*

the times and the **e**	Dan 2:21
to know times or **e**	Acts 1:7

EQUAL *same*

shall eat **e** portions	Deut 18:8
a man my **e**	Ps 55:13
That I should be *his* **e**	Is 40:25
have made them **e**	Matt 20:12
Himself **e** with God	John 5:18

EQUIP *furnish, provide*

e-ped for war	Josh 4:13
e-ped for...work	2 Tim 3:17
e you in every good	Heb 13:21

EQUIPMENT *implements*

the **e** for the service	Ex 39:40
e for his chariots	1 Sam 8:12
e of a foolish	Zech 11:15

EQUITY *equality, fairness*

eyes look with **e**	Ps 17:2
hast established **e**	Ps 99:4
justice and **e**	Prov 1:3
e *and* every good	Prov 2:9

ERASTUS

Corinthian Christian
     Acts 19:22; Rom 16:23;
     2 Tim 4:20

ERROR *mistake, sin*

can discern *his* **e-s**	Ps 19:12
like an **e** which goes	Eccl 10:5
e against the LORD	Is 32:6
e of unprincipled	2 Pet 3:17
the spirit of **e**	1 John 4:6
rushed...into the **e**	Jude 11

ESARHADDON

Assyrian king
     2 Kin 19:37; Ezra 4:2; Is 37:38

ESAU

son of Isaac	Gen 25:25
twin of Jacob	Gen 25:26
skillful hunter	Gen 25:27
sold birthright	Gen 25:34
despised Jacob	Gen 27:41
reconciled with Jacob	Gen 33:4

ESCAPE (n) *deliverance, refuge*

there will be no **e**	Job 11:20

is no **e** for me   Ps 142:4
Let there be no **e**   Jer 50:29
provide...**e**   1 Cor 10:13

ESCAPE (v) *elude*

slave who has **e-d**   Deut 23:15
let no one **e** *or*   2 Kin 9:15
Our soul has **e-d**   Ps 124:7
tells lies will not **e**   Prov 19:5
how shall we **e**   Is 20:6
nothing at all **e-s**   Joel 2:3
had not **e-d** notice   Luke 8:47
how shall we **e** if   Heb 2:3
it **e-s** their notice   2 Pet 3:5

ESTABLISH *confirm, found*

I will **e** My covenant   Gen 17:19
how God **e-es** them   Job 37:15
dost **e** the mountains   Ps 65:6
my ways may be **e-ed**   Ps 119:5
e-ed in lovingkindness   Is 16:5
to **e** the heavens   Is 51:16
we **e** the Law   Rom 3:31
may **e** your hearts   1 Thess 3:13
e-ed in the truth   2 Pet 1:12

ESTATE *domain* or *standard*

restore your...**e**   Job 8:6
us in our low **e**   Ps 136:23
squandered his **e**   Luke 15:13

ESTEEM (n) *honor*

man of high **e**   Dan 10:11
held them in high **e**   Acts 5:13

ESTEEM (v) *have high regard*

I **e** right all *Thy*   Ps 119:128
e-ed Him stricken   Is 53:4
e-ed among men   Luke 16:15
e them...in love   1 Thess 5:13

ESTHER

Hadassah, Hebrew name
  cousin of Mordecai   Esth 2:7
  Persian queen   Esth 2:16-18

ESTRANGED *separated*

completely **e** from me   Job 19:13
e from my brothers   Ps 69:8

ETERNAL *everlasting*

e God is a dwelling   Deut 33:27
E Father, Prince of   Is 9:6
An **e** decree   Jer 5:22
cast into the **e** fire   Matt 18:8
guilty of an **e** sin   Mark 3:29
to inherit **e** life   Luke 10:25
He may give **e** life   John 17:2
gift of God is **e** life   Rom 6:23
e weight of glory   2 Cor 4:17
with the **e** purpose   Eph 3:11
Now to the King **e**   1 Tim 1:17
source of **e** salvation   Heb 5:9
through the **e** Spirit   Heb 9:14
kept us in **e** bonds   Jude 6
an **e** gospel to preach   Rev 14:6

ETERNITY *perpetuity*

set **e** in their heart   Eccl 3:11
from **e** I am He   Is 43:13
Jesus from all **e**   2 Tim 1:9
to the day of **e**   2 Pet 3:18

ETHIOPIA

NE African country
  Esth 1:1; Ps 68:31; Nah 3:9;
      Zeph 3:10

EUNICE

mother of Timothy   2 Tim 1:5

EUNUCH *chamberlain official*

seven **e-s** who served   Esth 1:10
Neither let the **e** say   Is 56:3
children, and *the* **e-s**   Jer 41:16
made **e-s** by men   Matt 19:12
an Ethiopian **e**   Acts 8:27

EUPHRATES

river of Mesopotamia
  Gen 2:14; Jer 13:5;46:10;
      Rev 9:14;16:12

EVANGELIST *proclaimer*

house of Philip the **e**   Acts 21:8
and some *as* **e-s**   Eph 4:11
do the work of an **e**   2 Tim 4:5

EVE

first woman   Gen 2:22
wife of Adam   Gen 2:23
deceived by serpent   Gen 3:1-7
named by Adam   Gen 3:20

EVENING *dusk, darkness*

cloud...from **e**   Num 9:21
eats food before **e**   1 Sam 14:24
as the **e** offering   Ps 141:2
not be idle in the **e**   Eccl 11:6
when **e** had come   Matt 8:16

EVENT *happening*

the **e-s** of the war   2 Sam 11:18
e become sin to the   1 Kin 13:34
recorded these **e-s**   Esth 9:20
time for every **e**   Eccl 3:1

EVERLASTING *eternal*

e covenant between   Gen 9:16
the LORD, the **E** God   Gen 21:33
are the **e** arms   Deut 33:27
e to **e**, Thou art God   Ps 90:2
lovingkindness is **e**   Ps 106:1
From **e** I was   Prov 8:23
The **E** God, the LORD   Is 40:28
e name which will   Is 56:5
LORD for an **e** light   Is 60:20
loved you with an **e**   Jer 31:3

EVIDENCE *facts, testimony*

the **e** of witnesses   Num 35:30
on the **e** of two   Deut 19:15
not able to give **e**   Ezra 2:59
and giving **e**   Acts 17:3

EVIDENT *obvious, plain*

the tares became **e**   Matt 13:26
for God made it **e**   Rom 1:19
work will become **e**   1 Cor 3:13
Law before God is **e**   Gal 3:11
it is **e** that our Lord   Heb 7:14

EVIL *bad, wicked, wrong*

man's heart is **e**   Gen 8:21
keep...from every **e**   Deut 23:9
discern good and **e**   2 Sam 14:17
rebellious and **e** city   Ezra 4:12

I fear no **e**   Ps 23:4
repay me **e** for good   Ps 35:12
turn away from **e**   Prov 3:7
run rapidly to **e**   Prov 6:18
returns **e** for good   Prov 17:13
taken away from **e**   Is 57:1
committed two **e-s**   Jer 2:13
deliver us from **e**   Matt 6:13
what **e** has He   Matt 27:23
If you then, being   Luke 11:13
who does **e** hates the   John 3:20
Never...**e** for **e**   Rom 12:17
love of money is...**e**   1 Tim 6:10
tongue...restless **e**   James 3:8

EVILDOER *wicked one*

LORD repay the **e**   2 Sam 3:39
e-s will be cut off   Ps 37:9
e listens to wicked   Prov 17:4
Offspring of **e-s**   Is 1:4
is godless and an **e**   Is 9:17
depart...you **e-s**   Luke 13:27
punishment of **e-s**   1 Pet 2:14

EVIL-MERODACH

king of Babylon
    2 Kin 25:27; Jer 52:31

EWE *female sheep*

seven **e** lambs   Gen 21:28
e lamb without   Lev 14:10
poor man's **e** lamb   2 Sam 12:4
e-s with suckling   Ps 78:71
like a flock of **e-s**   Song 6:6

EXACT (adj) *certain, correct*

e amount of money   Esth 4:7
e meaning of all this   Dan 7:16
know the **e** truth   Luke 1:4
a more **e** knowledge   Acts 24:22

EXACT (v) *collect*

let him **e** a fifth   Gen 41:34
he shall not **e** it   Deut 15:2
He **e-ed** the silver   2 Kin 23:25
You are **e-ing** usury   Neh 5:7
e a tribute of grain   Amos 5:11

EXALT *extol, honor, lift*

He is highly **e-ed**   Ex 15:1
e-ed be God   2 Sam 22:47
He is **e-ed** in power   Job 37:23
let us **e** His name   Ps 34:3
e-ed far above all gods   Ps 97:9
city is **e-ed**   Prov 11:11
my God; I will **e** Thee   Is 25:1
E that which is low   Ezek 21:26
humbles...be **e-ed**   Matt 23:12
e-ed to...right hand   Acts 2:33
be **e-ed** in my body   Phil 1:20
He will **e** you   James 4:10

EXAMINE *investigate, search*

Thou dost **e** him every   Job 7:18
E me, O LORD, and try   Ps 26:2
e my heart's *attitude*   Jer 12:3
e-ing the Scriptures   Acts 17:11
e-d by scourging   Acts 22:24
a man **e** himself   1 Cor 11:28

EXAMPLE *model, pattern*

the **e** of his father   2 Chr 17:3
I gave you an **e**   John 13:15

e of those who | 1 Tim 4:12
e of disobedience | Heb 4:11
be e-s to the flock | 1 Pet 5:3
made them an e | 2 Pet 2:6

EXCEL *be superior*

e in...wickedness | Jer 5:28
wisdom e-s folly | Eccl 2:13
you may e...more | 1 Thess 4:1

EXCELLENCE *perfection*

greatness of Thine e | Ex 15:7
are a woman of e | Ruth 3:11
if there is any e | Phil 4:8
proclaim the e-ies of | 1 Pet 2:9

EXCELLENT *outstanding*

e wife is the crown | Prov 12:4
E speech is not | Prov 17:7
He has done e things | Is 12:5
e governor Felix | Acts 23:26
a still more e way | 1 Cor 12:31
a more e name | Heb 1:4

EXCESS *too much*

he...had no e | Ex 16:18
are in e among them | Num 3:48
same e of dissipation | 1 Pet 4:4

EXCHANGE *trade, transfer*

shall e it for money | Deut 14:25
they e-d their glory | Ps 106:20
shall not sell or e | Ezek 48:14
e-d the truth of God | Rom 1:25

EXCLUDE *refuse to admit*

e-d from...assembly | Ezra 10:8
e-d all foreigners | Neh 13:3
e you for My name's | Is 66:5
e-d from the life of | Eph 4:18

EXCUSE *justification*

began to make e-s | Luke 14:18
no e for their sin | John 15:22
they are without e | Rom 1:20

EXECUTE *carry out*

e-d the justice of | Deut 33:21
He has e-d judgment | Ps 9:16
e vengeance on the | Ps 149:7
Lord will e His word | Rom 9:28
e judgment upon all | Jude 15

EXERCISE *perform*

man has e-d authority | Eccl 8:9
e-s lovingkindness | Jer 9:24
e authority over | Matt 20:25
e-s self-control in all | 1 Cor 9:25

EXHAUSTED *used up, wearied*

sound asleep and e | Judg 4:21
too e to follow | 1 Sam 30:21
of flour was not e | 1 Kin 17:16
Their strength is e | Jer 51:30

EXHORT *admonish, urge*

and kept on e-ing | Acts 2:40
e, with...patience | 2 Tim 4:2
e in sound doctrine | Titus 1:9
e and reprove | Titus 2:15
e-ing and testifying | 1 Pet 5:12

EXHORTATION *urging*

with many other e-s | Luke 3:18

given them much e | Acts 20:2
who exhorts, in his e | Rom 12:8
this word of e | Heb 13:22

EXILE *banishment or capture*

Israel away into e | 2 Kin 17:6
people of the e were | Ezra 4:1
captivity of the e-s | Neh 7:6
into e from Jerusalem | Esth 2:6
e will soon be set free | Is 51:14
Israel went into e | Ezek 39:23

EXIST *be, live, occur*

they had never e-ed | Obad 16
Strife e-s and | Hab 1:3
live and move and e | Acts 17:28
authority...which e | Rom 13:1

EXODUS *departure*

e of...Israel | Heb 11:22

EXPANSE *firmament, vastness*

e of the heavens | Gen 1:20
e of the waters | Job 37:10
in His mighty e | Ps 150:1
from above the e | Ezek 1:25

EXPECT *await*

never e-ed to see | Gen 48:11
e-ed good, then evil | Job 30:26
which we did not e | Is 64:3
lend, e-ing nothing | Luke 6:35

EXPECTATION *anticipation*

your e is false | Job 41:9
e of the wicked | Prov 10:28
to my earnest e | Phil 1:20
e of judgment | Heb 10:27

EXPECTED *awaited*

Are You the E One | Matt 11:3
Are You the E One | Luke 7:20

EXPERIENCE *undergo*

all who had not e-d | Judg 3:1
Thy people e hardship | Ps 60:3
e-s Thy judgments | Is 26:9
e-d mockings and | Heb 11:36

EXPERT *very skillful*

an e in warfare | 2 Sam 17:8
be like an e warrior | Jer 50:9
an e in all customs | Acts 26:3

EXPLAIN *make clear*

no one who could e | Gen 41:24
he did not e to her | 2 Chr 9:2
e its interpretation | Dan 5:7
E the parable to us | Matt 15:15
e-ing the Scriptures | Luke 24:32
e-ed to him the way | Acts 18:26

EXPOSE *disclose, reveal*

shame...be e-d | Is 47:3
He will e your sins | Lam 4:22
deeds should be e-d | John 3:20
would e their infants | Acts 7:19
are e-d by the light | Eph 5:13

EXTEND *enlarge, stretch out*

God e-s...border | Deut 12:20
e-ed lovingkindness | Ezra 7:28
e-s her hand to the | Prov 31:20
I e peace to her | Is 66:12

boundary shall e | Ezek 47:17

EXTENT *amount or degree*

the e of my days | Ps 39:4
e that you did it to | Matt 25:40
such an e that Jesus | Mark 1:45

EXTERMINATE *destroy*

planned to e us | 2 Sam 21:5
He will e its sinners | Is 13:9

EXTERNAL *outward*

not with e service | Col 3:22
adornment be...e | 1 Pet 3:3

EXTINGUISH *put out*

they will e my coal | 2 Sam 14:7
not e the lamp of | 2 Sam 21:17
my days are e-ed | Job 17:1
when I e you | Ezek 32:7
e all the flaming | Eph 6:16

EXTOL *praise*

God, and I will e Him | Ex 15:2
I will e Thee, O Lord | Ps 30:1
I will e Thee, my God | Ps 145:1
We will e your love | Song 1:4

EXTORTION *stealing*

practicing...e | Jer 22:17
practiced e, robbed | Ezek 18:18

EXTRAORDINARY *exceptional*

will bring e plagues | Deut 28:59
His e work | Is 28:21
insight, and e wisdom | Dan 5:14
e miracles by | Acts 19:11
showed us e kindness | Acts 28:2

EXULT *rejoice*

heart e-s in the Lord | 1 Sam 2:1
Let the field e | 1 Chr 16:32
e-ed when evil befell | Job 31:29
let them e before God | Ps 68:3
I will e in the Lord | Hab 3:18
e in our tribulations | Rom 5:3

EXULTATION *jubilation*

e like the nations | Hos 9:1
joy or crown of e | 1 Thess 2:19
may rejoice with e | 1 Pet 4:13

EYE *sight*

e-s are dull from | Gen 49:12
e for e, tooth for | Ex 21:24
be as e-s for us | Num 10:31
his e was not dim | Deut 34:7
right in his own e-s | Judg 17:6
open his e-s that he | 2 Kin 6:17
e-s of the Lord | 2 Chr 16:9
was e-s to the blind | Job 29:15
e-s...look to Thee | Ps 145:15
Haughty e-s, a lying | Prov 6:17
e...mocks a father | Prov 30:17
e is not satisfied | Eccl 1:8
To open blind e-s | Is 42:7
e-s will bitterly weep | Jer 13:17
have e-s to see but | Ezek 12:2
Thine e-s...too pure | Hab 1:13
e for an e, and a | Matt 5:38
e...you to stumble | Matt 18:9
lamp...is your e | Luke 11:34
the clay to his e-s | John 9:6
which e has not seen | 1 Cor 2:9

EYEWITNESSES

e-s of your heart may Eph 1:18
e-s full of adultery 2 Pet 2:14
the lust of the e-s 1 John 2:16
God, who has e-s like Rev 2:18
His e-s are a flame Rev 19:12

EYEWITNESSES observers

e...of the word Luke 1:2
e of His majesty 2 Pet 1:16

EZEKIEL

Hebrew prophet Ezek 1:1
called by God Ezek 1:1,3
spoke to Israel Ezek 14:1ff
taken captive Ezek 33:21
spoke to false prophets
　　　　　　　Ezek 34:2ff
spoke to nations Ezek 35:2ff
restored temple Ezek 40:1ff

EZION-GEBER

on gulf of Aqabah
　　　　　1 Kin 9:26;22:48
near Elath / Eloth
　　　　　Deut 2:8; 2 Chr 8:17

EZRA

priest Ezra 7:1-5
scribe Ezra 7:6
sent by king Ezra 7:14,21
brought exiles Ezra 8:1-14
Nehemiah's colleague Neh 8:2-6

F

FACE countenance

sweat of your f You Gen 3:19
Abram fell on his f Gen 17:3
speak to Moses f to f Ex 33:11
skin of his f shone Ex 34:30
make His f shine Num 6:25
hide Thy f from me Ps 13:1
Who seek Thy f Ps 24:6
His f to shine upon us Ps 67:1
f of Thine anointed Ps 84:9
makes a cheerful f Prov 15:13
set My f against you Jer 44:11
had the f of an eagle Ezek 1:10
Each...had four f-s Ezek 10:21
fast...wash your f Matt 6:17
they spat in His f Matt 26:67
like the f of an angel Acts 6:15
natural f in a mirror James 1:23
His f was like the sun Rev 1:16

FACT truth

f may be confirmed Matt 18:16
are undeniable f-s Acts 19:36
f is to be confirmed 2 Cor 13:1

FACTIONS divisions

be f among you 1 Cor 11:19
dissensions, f Gal 5:20

FADE wither

it f-s, and withers Ps 90:6
people...f away Is 24:4
rich man...will f James 1:11
will not f away 1 Pet 1:4

FAIL be spent or fall short

He will not f you Deut 4:31
none of his words f 1 Sam 3:19

no man's heart f 1 Sam 17:32
not one word...f-ed 1 Kin 8:56
my strength f-s me Ps 38:10
the olive should f Hab 3:17
faith may not f Luke 22:32
Love never f-s 1 Cor 13:8

FAINT languish, swoon

has made my heart f Job 23:16
soul f-ed within Ps 107:5
grow f before Me Is 57:16
I was f-ing away Jon 2:7
men f-ing from fear Luke 21:26
f when...reproved Heb 12:5

FAINTHEARTED weak

Do not be f Deut 20:3
encourage the f 1 Thess 5:14

FAIR HAVENS

harbor in Crete Acts 27:8

FAITH believe, trust

because you broke f Deut 32:51
Will you have f Job 39:12
Who keeps f forever Ps 146:6
will live by his f Hab 2:4
Jesus seeing their f Matt 9:2
f as a mustard seed Matt 17:20
Your f has saved you Luke 7:50
Increase our f Luke 17:5
your f may not fail Luke 22:32
man full of f Acts 6:5
of f to the Gentiles Acts 14:27
sanctified by f in Me Acts 26:18
justified by f Rom 5:1
f...from hearing Rom 10:17
if I have all f 1 Cor 13:2
your f also is vain 1 Cor 15:14
we walk by f 2 Cor 5:7
live by f in the Son Gal 2:20
saved through f Eph 2:8
one Lord, one f Eph 4:5
joy in the f Phil 1:25
stability of your f Col 2:5
breastplate of f 1 Thess 5:8
for not all have f 2 Thess 3:2
fall away from the f 1 Tim 4:1
conduct, love, f 1 Tim 4:12
they upset the f 2 Tim 2:18
sound in the f Titus 1:13
showing all good f Titus 2:10
full assurance of f Heb 10:22
By f Enoch was taken Heb 11:5
perfecter of f Heb 12:2
ask in f James 1:6
prayer offered in f James 5:15
power of God...f 1 Pet 1:5
the f of the saints Rev 13:10

FAITHFUL loyal, trustworthy

the f God, who keeps Deut 7:9
raise...a f priest 1 Sam 2:35
heart f before Thee Neh 9:8
LORD preserves the f Ps 31:23
commandments...f Ps 119:86
f witness will not lie Prov 14:5
the LORD who is f Is 49:7
Well done...f Matt 25:23
God is f 1 Cor 1:9
F is He who calls 1 Thess 5:24
He considered me f 1 Tim 1:12

entrust to f men 2 Tim 2:2
souls to a f Creator 1 Pet 4:19
He is f... to forgive 1 John 1:9
Be f until death Rev 2:10
called F and True Rev 19:11

FAITHFULNESS loyalty

kindness and f Gen 47:29
A God of f Deut 32:4
make known Thy f Ps 89:1
f to all generations Ps 100:5
and mercy and f Matt 23:23
nullify the f of God Rom 3:3
kindness, goodness, f Gal 5:22

FAITHLESS unbelieving

what f Israel did Jer 3:6
O f daughter Jer 31:22
Their heart is f Hos 10:2
If we are f 2 Tim 2:13

FALL descend or fail

deep sleep to f upon Gen 2:21
devices let them f Ps 5:10
I am ready to f Ps 38:17
dread...had f-en Ps 105:38
wicked will f Prov 11:5
a righteous man f-s Prov 24:16
whether a tree f-s Eccl 11:3
Assyrian will f Is 31:8
Babylon has f-en Jer 51:8
f down and worship Dan 3:5
will f into a pit Matt 15:14
f-ing on his knees Mark 1:40
all may f...I will Mark 14:29
appointed for the f Luke 2:34
watching Satan f Luke 10:18
house divided...f-s Luke 11:17
f-ing headlong Acts 1:18
sinned and f short Rom 3:23
have f-en asleep 1 Cor 15:6
f-en from grace Gal 5:4
rich f into temptation 1 Tim 6:9
rocks, F on us Rev 6:16

FALLOW unproductive

rest and lie f Ex 23:11
f ground of the poor Prov 13:23

FALSE deceitful, dishonest

not bear a f report Ex 23:1
I hate every f way Ps 119:104
But a f witness Prov 12:17
f witness will not go Prov 19:5
f scale is not good Prov 20:23
F and foolish visions Lam 2:14
And tell f dreams Zech 10:2
not bear f witness Matt 19:18
f Christs and f Matt 24:24
men are f apostles 2 Cor 11:13
the f circumcision Phil 3:2
and the f prophet Rev 20:10

FALSEHOOD deception

lifted up his soul to f Ps 24:4
delight in f Ps 62:4
I hate and despise f Ps 119:163
Bread obtained by f Prov 20:17
trusted in f Jer 13:25
prophesying f in My Jer 14:14
laying aside f Eph 4:25

FAME greatness

heard of Thy f	Num 14:15
Joshua, and his f	Josh 6:27
the f of Solomon	1 Kin 10:1
heard My f	Is 66:19
f in *the things of*	2 Cor 8:18

FAMILY household, relatives

f-ies from the ark	Gen 8:19
all the f-ies of	Gen 12:3
f may redeem him	Lev 25:49
f-ies of the Levites	Num 3:20
my f is the least	Judg 6:15
f-ies like a flock	Ps 107:41
God of all the f-ies	Jer 31:1
f-ies of the earth	Amos 3:2
every f in heaven	Eph 3:15
upsetting whole f-ies	Titus 1:11

FAMINE shortage of food

a f in the land	Gen 12:10
seven years of f	Gen 41:27
If there is f	2 Chr 6:28
In f He will redeem	Job 5:20
keep them alive in f	Ps 33:19
f and pestilence	Jer 14:12
f and wild beasts	Ezek 5:17
f-s and earthquakes	Matt 24:7
plagues and f-s	Luke 21:11
Now a f came	Acts 7:11
mourning and f	Rev 18:8

FAMISHED hungry, parched

for I am f	Gen 25:30
strength is f	Job 18:12
honorable men are f	Is 5:13

FAMOUS well-known

f in Bethlehem	Ruth 4:11
men of valor, f men	1 Chr 5:24

FAR distant

f from a false charge	Ex 23:7
come from a f country	Josh 9:6
Be not f from me	Ps 22:11
f above all gods	Ps 97:9
As f as the east	Ps 103:12
LORD is f from the	Prov 15:29
a God f off	Jer 23:23
heart is f away from	Matt 15:8
f from the kingdom	Mark 12:34
glory f beyond all	2 Cor 4:17
f above all rule	Eph 1:21

FARM agricultural land

consume the f land	Amos 7:4
one to his own f	Matt 22:5
or f-s, for My sake	Mark 10:29

FARMER husbandman

Does the f plow	Is 28:24
will be your f-s	Is 61:5
f-s...put to shame	Jer 14:4
the f to mourning	Amos 5:16

FASHION create, form

f-ed into a woman	Gen 2:22
f us in the womb	Job 31:15
He who f-s the hearts	Ps 33:15
f a graven image	Is 44:9
I am f-ing calamity	Jer 18:11

FAST (n) food abstinence

Proclaim a f	1 Kin 21:9
you call this a f	Is 58:5
Consecrate a f	Joel 1:14
f was already over	Acts 27:9

FAST (v) abstain from food

and David f-ed	2 Sam 12:16
maidens also will f	Esth 4:16
you f for contention	Is 58:4
had f-ed forty days	Matt 4:2
whenever you f	Matt 6:16
disciples do not f	Mark 2:18
I f twice a week	Luke 18:12
had f-ed and prayed	Acts 13:3

FASTING food abstinence

times of f	Esth 9:31
weak from f	Ps 109:24
to be seen f by men	Matt 6:16
by prayer and f	Matt 17:21
Pharisees were f	Mark 2:18

FAT animal fat or obese

f of the land	Gen 45:18
shall not eat any f	Lev 7:23
Go, eat of the f	Neh 8:10
their body is f	Ps 73:4
Good news puts f	Prov 15:30

FATE destiny

appalled at his f	Job 18:20
one f befalls them	Eccl 2:14
f for the righteous	Eccl 9:2
one f for all men	Eccl 9:3

FATHER God or parent

leave his f...mother	Gen 2:24
f of a multitude	Gen 17:4
Honor your f	Ex 20:12
who strikes his f	Ex 21:15
iniquity of the f-s	Deut 5:9
Is not He your F	Deut 32:6
your f-'s instruction	Prov 1:8
son makes a f glad	Prov 10:1
Eternal F, Prince of	Is 9:6
all have one f	Mal 2:10
F who sees in secret	Matt 6:4
Our F who art in	Matt 6:9
does the will of My F	Matt 7:21
in My F-'s kingdom	Matt 26:29
in the glory of His F	Mark 8:38
be in my F-'s *house*	Luke 2:49
F, hallowed be Thy	Luke 11:2
F, forgive them	Luke 23:34
begotten from the F	John 1:14
my F-'s house a	John 2:16
F...bears witness	John 8:18
the f of lies	John 8:44
I and the F are one	John 10:30
In my F-'s house are	John 14:2
F is the vinedresser	John 15:1
ask the F for	John 16:23
I ascend to My F	John 20:17
one God and F of all	Eph 4:6

FATHER-IN-LAW

she sent to her f	Gen 38:25
returned to Jethro his f	Ex 4:18
his f, the girl's	Judg 19:4
f of Caiaphas	John 18:13

FATHERLESS orphan

father of the f	Ps 68:5
He supports the f	Ps 146:9
fields of the f	Prov 23:10
f and the widow	Ezek 22:7

FATLING young lamb or kid

sacrificed...a f	2 Sam 6:13
f-s...in abundance	1 Kin 1:19
f-s of Bashan	Ezek 39:18

FATNESS abundance

f of the earth	Gen 27:28
Shall I leave my f	Judg 9:9
satisfied as with...f	Ps 63:5
eye bulges from f	Ps 73:7

FAULT error, offense

found no f in him	1 Sam 29:3
let no one find f	Hos 4:4
does He still find f	Rom 9:19
grumblers, finding f	Jude 16

FAVOR kind regard

Noah found f	Gen 6:8
I will grant...f	Ex 3:21
show no f to them	Deut 7:2
Why have I found f	Ruth 2:10
surround him with f	Ps 5:12
show f to Thy land	Ps 85:1
obtains f...LORD	Prov 8:35
f is like a cloud	Prov 16:15
found f with God	Luke 1:30
in f with God and	Luke 2:52
seeking the f of men	Gal 1:10

FEAR (n) awe, dread, reverence

no f of God in	Gen 20:11
f of the LORD is clean	Ps 19:9
f...is the beginning	Ps 111:10
afraid of sudden f	Prov 3:25
f...prolongs life	Prov 10:27
f of man brings a	Prov 29:25
they cried out for f	Matt 14:26
guards shook for f	Matt 28:4
men fainting for f	Luke 21:26
for f of the Jews	John 7:13
no f of God before	Rom 3:18
in weakness and in f	1 Cor 2:3
knowing the f of the	2 Cor 5:11
with f and trembling	Eph 6:5
through f of death	Heb 2:15
love casts out f	1 John 4:18

FEAR (v) be afraid, revere

the midwives f-ed God	Ex 1:21
Moses said...Do not f	Ex 14:13
may learn to f Me	Deut 4:10
not f other gods	2 Kin 17:37
I f no evil	Ps 23:4
Whom shall I f	Ps 27:1
not f evil tidings	Ps 112:7
who f-s the LORD	Prov 31:30
Rather, f God	Eccl 5:7
Take courage, f not	Is 35:4
Do not f, for I am	Is 41:10
shall f and tremble	Jer 33:9
do not f them	Matt 10:26
f-ed the multitude	Matt 21:46
who did not f God	Luke 18:2
slavery leading to f	Rom 8:15
I f for you	Gal 4:11

let us f lest	Heb 4:1

FEARFUL *terrifying*

it is a f thing	Ex 34:10
were f and amazed	Luke 8:25
may be f *of sinning*	1 Tim 5:20

FEAST *celebration*

a f to the LORD	Ex 12:14
godless jesters at a f	Ps 35:16
hate...appointed f-s	Is 1:14
and cheerful f-s	Zech 8:19
refuse of your f-s	Mal 2:3
a wedding f	Matt 22:2
seeking Him at the f	John 7:11
celebrate the f	1 Cor 5:8
f with you without	Jude 12

FEASTS

1 **Feast of Booths**
   Lev 23:24; Deut 16:16; 2 Chr
   8:13
   also **Feast of Ingathering**
2 **Feast of Dedication**
   John 10:22
3 **Feast of Harvest**   Ex 23:16
   also **Feast of Weeks**
   also **Feast of Pentecost**
4 **Feast of Ingathering**
   Ex 23:16
   also **Feast of Booths**
5 **Feast of Passover**
   Ex 34:25; Luke 2:41
6 **Feast of Unleavened Bread**
   Ex 23:15; Luke 22:1
7 **Feast of Weeks**
   Ex 34:22; Deut 16:10,16
   also **Feast of Harvest**
   also **Feast of Pentecost**
8 **Feast of Pentecost**
   Acts 2:1; 20:16; 1 Cor 16:8
   also **Feast of Harvest**
   also **Feast of Weeks**

FEEBLE *weak*

when the flock was f	Gen 30:42
What are these f Jews	Neh 4:2
strengthen the f	Is 35:3
knees that are f	Heb 12:12

FEED *eat, supply*

fed you with manna	Deut 8:3
f him sparingly	1 Kin 22:27
F me with the food	Prov 30:8
He f-s on ashes	Is 44:20
f you on knowledge	Jer 3:15
He fed me this scroll	Ezek 3:2
I will f My flock	Ezek 34:15
dogs f on the	Matt 15:27
hungry, and f You	Matt 25:37
fed...the *crumbs*	Luke 16:21
enemy is hungry, f	Rom 12:20

FEEL *sense, touch*

I may f you, my son	Gen 27:21
Isaac...**felt** him and	Gen 27:22
Let me f the pillars	Judg 16:26
He **felt** compassion	Matt 9:36
she **felt**...was healed	Mark 5:29
Jesus **felt** a love for	Mark 10:21
f-ing a sense of awe	Acts 2:43
f sensual desires	1 Tim 5:11

FELIX

Roman procurator
   Acts 23:26;24:25;25:14

FELL *collapse, come upon*

wall f down flat	Josh 6:20
fire of the LORD f	1 Kin 18:38
the lot f on Jonah	Jon 1:7
seeds f beside the	Matt 13:4
He f asleep	Luke 8:23
he f to the ground	Acts 9:4
Holy Spirit f upon	Acts 10:44
star f from heaven	Rev 8:10

FELLOW *companion*

oil of joy above Thy f-s	Ps 45:7
your f exiles	Ezek 11:15
beat his f slaves	Matt 24:49
f heirs with Christ	Rom 8:17
f citizens with the	Eph 2:19
Gentiles are f heirs	Eph 3:6
brother and f worker	Phil 2:25
f worker in the	1 Thes 3:2
I am a f servant of	Rev 22:9

FELLOWSHIP *companionship*

had sweet f together	Ps 55:14
f...Holy Spirit	2 Cor 13:14
right hand of f	Gal 2:9
f of His sufferings	Phil 3:10
f is with the Father	1 John 1:3
f with one another	1 John 1:7

FEMALE *girl, woman*

and f He created	Gen 1:27
a f slave	Ex 21:7
f from the flock	Lev 5:6
likeness of male or f	Deut 4:16
neither male nor f	Gal 3:28

FERTILE *productive*

a f land	Neh 9:25
the f valley	Is 28:4
in f soil	Ezek 17:5

FERVENT *ardent*

being f in spirit	Acts 18:25
f in spirit, serving	Rom 12:11
keep f in your love	1 Pet 4:8

FESTIVAL *celebration*

celebrate a great f	Neh 8:12
I reject your f-s	Amos 5:21
turn your f-s into	Amos 8:10
during the f, lest	Matt 26:5

FESTUS, PORCIUS

Roman procurator of Judea
   Acts 24:27; 25:14,23; 26:25

FETTERS *chains*

your feet put in f	2 Sam 3:34
they are bound in f	Job 36:8
tear their f apart	Ps 2:3
with f of iron	Ps 149:8
he would burst his f	Luke 8:29

FEVER *inflammation*

bones burn with f	Job 30:30
in bed with a f	Matt 8:14
from a high f	Luke 4:38
He rebuked the f	Luke 4:39
the f left him	John 4:52

FIELD *productive land*

hail struck...the f	Ex 9:25
let me go to the f	Ruth 2:2
glean in another f	Ruth 2:8
f of the sluggard	Prov 24:30
Zion...plowed *as* a f	Jer 26:18
the lilies of the f	Matt 6:28
the f is the world	Matt 13:38
shepherds...in the f-s	Luke 2:8
Two men...in the f	Luke 17:36
f-s...white for	John 4:35
F of Blood	Acts 1:19

FIERCE *violent*

anger, for it is f	Gen 49:7
Wrath is f	Prov 27:4
see a f people	Is 33:19
a f gale of wind	Mark 4:37
scorched with f heat	Rev 16:9
f wrath of God	Rev 19:15

FIERCENESS *intensity*

f of His anger	Josh 7:26
the f of battle	Is 42:25

FIERY *burning*

LORD sent f serpents	Num 21:6
with f heat	Deut 28:22
His arrows f shafts	Ps 7:13
f ordeal among you	1 Pet 4:12

FIG *fruit*

they sewed f leaves	Gen 3:7
But the f tree said	Judg 9:11
a piece of cake	1 Sam 30:12
nor f-s from thistles	Matt 7:16
the f tree withered	Matt 21:19
f-s from thorns	Luke 6:44
under the f tree	John 1:48
Can a f tree	James 3:12

FIGHT *struggle*

Hebrews were f-ing	Ex 2:13
LORD will f for you	Ex 14:14
fought for Israel	Josh 10:14
stars **fought** from	Judg 5:20
and f our battles	1 Sam 8:20
f for your brothers	Neh 4:14
f-ing against God	Acts 5:39
fought the good f	2 Tim 4:7
so you f and quarrel	James 4:2

FIGURATIVE *metaphorical*

in f language	John 16:25

FIGURE *shape, type*

f-s resembling four	Ezek 1:5
f...of a man	Ezek 1:26
using a f of speech	John 16:29

FILIGREE *ornamental work*

f *settings* of gold	Ex 28:13
cords on the two f	Ex 28:25

FILL (n) *satisfaction*

eat your f	Lev 25:19
They drink their f	Ps 36:8
drink our f of love	Prov 7:18
its f of their blood	Jer 46:10

FILL (v) *make full*

and f the earth	Gen 1:28
f-ed with violence	Gen 6:11

Can you f his skin	Job 41:7
was f-ing with smoke	Is 6:4
I am f-ed with power	Mic 3:8
hall was f-ed	Matt 22:10
God of hope f you	Rom 15:13

FILTHY *offensive*

are full of f vomit	Is 28:8
like a f garment	Is 64:6
clothed...f garments	Zech 3:3
let the one who is f	Rev 22:11

FILTHINESS *disgustingly foul*

not washed...his f	Prov 30:12
your f is lewdness	Ezek 24:13
no f and silly talk	Eph 5:4
putting aside all f	James 1:21

FIND *discover, uncover*

not **found** a helper	Gen 2:20
But Noah **found** favor	Gen 6:8
sin will f you out	Num 32:23
that you may f rest	Ruth 1:9
he who f-s me f-s life	Prov 8:35
who f-s a wife f-s	Prov 18:22
f gladness and joy	Is 35:10
few...who f it	Matt 7:14
has **found** his life	Matt 10:39
f rest for your souls	Matt 11:29
f-ing one pearl	Matt 13:46
a colt tied	Mark 11:2
found...sleeping	Mark 14:40
seek, and you shall f	Luke 11:9
found the Messiah	John 1:41
was **found** worthy	Rev 5:4

FINGER *part of hand*

the f of God	Ex 8:19
dip his f in the blood	Lev 4:6
six f-s on each	2 Sam 21:20
twenty-four f-s and	1 Chr 20:6
tip of his f in water	Luke 16:24
with His f wrote	John 8:6
Reach here your f	John 20:27

FINISH *complete*

Moses f-ed the work	Ex 40:33
Solomon f-ed the	2 Chr 7:11
It is f-ed	John 19:30
I may f my course	Acts 20:24
f doing it also	2 Cor 8:11
wrath of God is f-ed	Rev 15:1

FINS *part of fish*

that have f and scales	Lev 11:9
anything that has f	Deut 14:9

FIR *tree, wood*

instruments...of f	2 Sam 6:5
He plants a f	Is 44:14

FIRE *burning or flame*

the f and the knife	Gen 22:6
bush...burning with f	Ex 3:2
pillar of f by night	Ex 13:21
offered strange f	Num 3:4
f of the LORD fell	1 Kin 18:38
a chariot of f	2 Kin 2:11
jealousy burn like f	Ps 79:5
Israel will become a f	Is 10:17
Is not My word like f	Jer 23:29
the Holy Spirit and f	Matt 3:11
with unquenchable f	Matt 3:12

tongues as of f	Acts 2:3
lake that burns with f	Rev 21:8

FIREBRAND *burning wood*

who throws **F-s**	Prov 26:18
you were like a f	Amos 4:11

FIREPAN *used in worship*

a f full of coals	Lev 16:12
the f-s of pure gold	2 Chr 4:22

FIRM *establish, steadfast*

his bow remained f	Gen 49:24
stood f on dry ground	Josh 3:17
making my footsteps f	Ps 40:2
He made f the skies	Prov 8:28
stand f in the faith	1 Cor 16:13
f foundation of God	2 Tim 2:19
hope f until the end	Heb 3:6

FIRST *number*

f fruits of your labors	Ex 23:16
f of all your produce	Prov 3:9
seek f His kingdom	Matt 6:33
f take the log out	Matt 7:5
f will be last	Matt 19:30
f called Christians	Acts 11:26
to the Jew f	Rom 2:10
f fruits of the Spirit	Rom 8:23
He f loved us	1 John 4:19
I am the f and the	Rev 1:17
left your f love	Rev 2:4
f things have passed	Rev 21:4

FIRST-BORN *oldest*

Sidon, his f	Gen 10:15
the f bore a son	Gen 19:37
I am Esau your f	Gen 27:19
LORD killed every f	Ex 13:15
birth to her f son	Luke 2:7
church of the f	Heb 12:23
f of the dead	Rev 1:5

FIRST GATE

see **GATES OF JERUSALEM**

FISH

rule over the f	Gen 1:26
Their f stink	Is 50:2
a great f to swallow	Jon 1:17
loaves and two f	Matt 14:17
snake instead of a f	Luke 11:11
net *full* of f	John 21:8

FISH GATE

see **GATES OF JERUSALEM**

FISHERMEN *fishers*

f will lament	Is 19:8
for they were f	Matt 4:18
the f had gotten out	Luke 5:2

FISHERS *fishermen*

make you f of men	Matt 4:19
become f of men	Mark 1:17

FIT *be suitable, worthy*

f to remove His	Matt 3:11
f for the kingdom	Luke 9:62
f to be...apostle	1 Cor 15:9
body, being f-ted	Eph 4:16
f-ting in the Lord	Col 3:18

FIX *make firm, secure*

I will f your boundary	Ex 23:31

f-ed her hope on God	1 Tim 5:5
f-ing...eyes on Jesus	Heb 12:2
f your hope	1 Pet 1:13

FIXED *established*

the f festivals	1 Chr 23:31
f order of the moon	Jer 31:35
is a great chasm f	Luke 16:26

FLAME *fire*

ascended in the f	Judg 13:20
f...the wicked	Ps 106:18
f of the LORD	Song 8:6
his Holy One a f	Is 10:17
crackling of a f	Joel 2:5
f of a burning thorn	Acts 7:30
eyes *are* a f of fire	Rev 19:12

FLAMING *burning*

the f sword	Gen 3:24
f fire by night	Is 4:5
eyes were like f	Dan 10:6
angels in a f fire	2 Thess 1:7

FLASH *reflect, sparkle*

why do your eyes f	Job 15:12
lightning was f-ing	Ezek 1:13
Polished to f like	Ezek 21:10
He who f-es forth	Amos 5:9
light suddenly f-ed	Acts 22:6

FLASK *utensil*

take this f of oil	2 Kin 9:1
took oil in f-s	Matt 25:4

FLATTER

Nor f *any* man	Job 32:21
f with their tongue	Ps 5:9
adulterous who f-s	Prov 2:16
who f-s his neighbor	Prov 29:5

FLAX *plant*

the f was in bud	Ex 9:31
looks for wool and f	Prov 31:13
made from combed f	Is 19:9

FLEE *escape, run away*

arise, f to Haran	Gen 27:43
F *as* a bird	Ps 11:1
f from Thy presence	Ps 139:7
rulers have **fled**	Is 22:3
f to Egypt	Matt 2:13
left Him and **fled**	Matt 26:56
fled from the tomb	Mark 16:8
f from idolatry	1 Cor 10:14
f from youthful lusts	2 Tim 2:22
and heaven **fled**	Rev 20:11

FLEECE *wool*

put a f of wool	Judg 6:37
dry only on the f	Judg 6:39
warmed with the f	Job 31:20

FLEET *group of ships*

Solomon...built a f	1 Kin 9:26
sent...with the f	1 Kin 9:27

FLESH *body, meat*

f of my f	Gen 2:23
shall become one f	Gen 2:24
from my f I shall see	Job 19:26
heart and my f sing	Ps 84:2
All f is grass	Is 40:6
the f is weak	Matt 26:41

spirit...not have f   Luke 24:39
the Word became f   John 1:14
born of the f is f   John 3:6
who eats My f   John 6:56
children of the f   Rom 9:8
thorn in the f   2 Cor 12:7
desires of the f   Eph 2:3
polluted by the f   Jude 23
filled with their f   Rev 19:21

FLESHLY *carnal*
not in f wisdom   2 Cor 1:12
His f body   Col 1:22
abstain from f lusts   1 Pet 2:11

FLIES *insects*
sent...swarms of f   Ps 78:45
swarm of f *And* gnats   Ps 105:31
Dead f make a   Eccl 10:1

FLIGHT *departure*
F will perish from   Amos 2:14
f may not be in   Matt 24:20
foreign armies to f   Heb 11:34

FLINT *stone*
Zipporah took a f   Ex 4:25
f into a fountain   Ps 114:8
hoofs...seem like f   Is 5:28
emery harder than f   Ezek 3:9
hearts *like* f   Zech 7:12

FLOCK *goats, sheep*
a keeper of f-s   Gen 4:2
water their father's f   Ex 2:16
Thy people like a f   Ps 77:20
He will tend His f   Is 40:11
scattered My f   Jer 23:2
over their f by night   Luke 2:8
shall become one f   John 10:16
f of God among you   1 Pet 5:2

FLOOD *overflowing of water*
I am bringing the f   Gen 6:17
f came upon the earth   Gen 7:10
end...with a f   Dan 9:26
the f-s came   Matt 7:25
f...destroyed   Luke 17:27

FLOOR *ground, level*
threshing f of Atad   Gen 50:11
go down to the...f   Ruth 3:3
the f...with gold   1 Kin 6:30
f-s...full of grain   Joel 2:24
His threshing f   Matt 3:12
fell...from the third f   Acts 20:9

FLOUR *ground grain*
measures of fine f   Gen 18:6
only a handful of f   1 Kin 17:12
f...not exhausted   1 Kin 17:16

FLOURISH *blossom, thrive*
may the righteous f   Ps 72:7
who did iniquity f-ed   Ps 92:7
your bones shall f   Is 66:14
make the dry tree f   Ezek 17:24

FLOW *pour forth*
river f-ed out of Eden   Gen 2:10
f-ing with milk and   Ex 3:8
eyelids f with water   Jer 9:18
hills will f with milk   Joel 3:18
f of her blood   Mark 5:29

f...living waters   John 7:38

FLOWER *blossom*
As a f of the field   Ps 103:15
f-s have *already*   Song 2:12
to the fading f   Is 28:1
glory like the f   1 Pet 1:24

FLUTE *musical instrument*
tambourine, f, and   1 Sam 10:5
playing on f-s   1 Kin 1:40
the f or on the harp   1 Cor 14:7
musicians...f-players   Rev 18:22

FLY *soar*
let birds f above   Gen 1:20
a raven, and it **flew**   Gen 8:7
As sparks f upward   Job 5:7
f-ies away like a dream   Job 20:8
glory will f away   Hos 9:11
heard an eagle f-ing   Rev 8:13
the birds which f   Rev 19:17

FOAL *colt*
ties *his* f to the vine   Gen 49:11
f of a wild donkey   Job 11:12
f of a beast of burden   Matt 21:5

FODDER *animal food*
give his donkey f   Gen 42:27
eat salted f   Is 30:24

FOE *enemy*
before your f-s   1 Chr 21:12
A f and an enemy   Esth 7:6
iniquity of my f-s   Ps 49:5
the evil to my f-s   Ps 54:5
avenge...His f-s   Jer 46:10

FOLD *animal pen*
goats out of your f-s   Ps 50:9
the peaceful f-s   Jer 25:37
cut off from the f   Hab 3:17
not of this f   John 10:16

FOLLOW *imitate, pursue*
not f other gods   Deut 6:14
turn back from f-ing   Ruth 1:16
f the LORD your God
                          1 Sam 12:14
who f...wickedness   Ps 119:150
bloodshed f-s   Hos 4:2
He said to them, F   Matt 4:19
left...and f-ed   Matt 4:20
his cross, and f Me   Matt 16:24
multitude was f-ing   Mark 5:24
allowed no one to f   Mark 5:37
and they f Me   John 10:27
Peter...f-ing Jesus   John 18:15
f-ing after...lusts   Jude 16
ones who f the Lamb   Rev 14:4

FOLLOWERS *disciples*
His f...*began* asking   Mark 4:10

FOLLY *foolishness*
this act of f   Judg 19:23
The naive inherit f   Prov 14:18
of fools spouts f   Prov 15:2
F is joy to him   Prov 15:21
devising of f is sin   Prov 24:9

FOOD *bread, meat*
shall be f for you   Gen 1:29

tree was good for f   Gen 3:6
in giving them f   Ruth 1:6
tears have my f   Ps 42:3
it is deceptive f   Prov 23:3
his f was locusts   Matt 3:4
life more than f   Matt 6:25
f is to do the will   John 4:34
My flesh is true f   John 6:55
milk...not solid f   1 Cor 3:2

FOOL *unwise person*
The f has said in his   Ps 14:1
F-s despise wisdom   Prov 1:7
too high for a f   Prov 24:7
f multiplies words   Eccl 10:14
The prophet is a f   Hos 9:7
shall say, You f   Matt 5:22
f-s and blind men   Matt 23:17
wise, they became f-s   Rom 1:22
f-s for Christ's sake   1 Cor 4:10

FOOLISH *silly, unwise*
O f and unwise   Deut 32:6
a f son is a grief   Prov 10:1
False and f *visions*   Lam 2:14
Woe to the f   Ezek 13:3
f took their lamps   Matt 25:3
O f men and slow   Luke 24:25
let him become f   1 Cor 3:18
You f Galatians   Gal 3:1
do not be f   Eph 5:17

FOOLISHNESS *folly*
folly of fools is f   Prov 14:24
mouth is speaking f   Is 9:17
f of God is wiser   1 Cor 1:25
is f before God   1 Cor 3:19

FOOT *part of body*
she lay at his feet   Ruth 3:14
six toes on each f   2 Sam 21:20
pierced...my feet   Ps 22:16
the f of pride   Ps 36:11
lamp to my feet   Ps 119:105
their **feet** run to evil   Prov 1:16
signals with his **feet**   Prov 6:13
beautiful...your **feet**   Song 7:1
feet of the afflicted   Is 26:6
feet...polished bronze   Dan 10:6
dust of your **feet**   Matt 10:14
Bind...hand and f   Matt 22:13
f causes you to   Mark 9:45
kissing His **feet**   Luke 7:38
anointed the **feet**   John 12:3
the disciples' **feet**   John 13:5
beautiful...the **feet**   Rom 10:15
Satan under...**feet**   Rom 16:20
worship at the **feet**   Rev 22:8

FOOTSTEPS *path*
make His f into a way   Ps 85:13
f of thine anointed   Ps 89:51
my f in Thy word   Ps 119:133

FOOTSTOOL *foot support*
the f of our God   1 Chr 28:2
worship at His f   Ps 99:5
Thine enemies a f   Ps 110:1
the earth is My f   Is 66:1
sit down by my f   James 2:3

FORBEARANCE *restraint*
By f...be persuaded   Prov 25:15

in the f of God   Rom 3:25
showing f to one   Eph 4:2

FORBID *prohibit*

if her father should f   Num 30:5
f-ding to pay taxes   Luke 23:2
do not f to speak   1 Cor 14:39
men who f marriage   1 Tim 4:3
he **f-s** those who   3 John 10

FORCE (n) *power, strength*

with a heavy f   Num 20:20
captains of the **f-s**   2 Kin 25:23
use f against you   Neh 13:21
commanders of the **f-s**   Jer 43:5
with f and with   Ezek 34:4

FORCE (v) *compel*

are **f-d** into bondage   Neh 5:5
man **f-d** to labor   Job 7:1
f you to go one mile   Matt 5:41
not take...by f   Luke 3:14
f them to blaspheme   Acts 26:11
f-d to appeal to   Acts 28:19

FORCED LABOR *work as tax*

Canaanites to f   Josh 17:13
was over the f   2 Sam 20:24
will be put to f   Prov 12:24

FORCED LABORERS

Solomon levied f   1 Kin 5:13
Solomon raised as f   2 Chr 8:8
men will become f   Is 31:8

FORD *shallow place*

the f of the Jabbok   Gen 32:22
the **f-s** of the Jordan   Judg 12:5
f-s...been seized   Jer 51:32

FOREFATHER *ancestor*

iniquity of their **f-s**   Lev 26:40
Your first f sinned   Is 43:27
I swore to your **f-s**   Jer 11:5
Abraham, our f   Rom 4:1
the way my **f-s** did   2 Tim 1:3

FOREHEAD *brow*

on his bald f   Lev 13:42
stone...into his f   1 Sam 17:49
put a mark on the **f-s**   Ezek 9:4
seal of God on their **f-s**   Rev 9:4
upon her f a name   Rev 17:5

FOREIGN *alien, strange*

Put away the f gods   Gen 35:2
sojourner in a f land   Ex 2:22
sell her to a f people   Ex 21:8
drank f waters   2 Kin 19:24
married f women   Ezra 10:2
f armies to flight   Heb 11:34

FOREIGNER *alien, stranger*

no f is to eat of it   Ex 12:43
sell it to a f   Deut 14:21
charge...a f   Deut 23:20
since I am a f   Ruth 2:10
a f in their sight   Job 19:15
f-s entered his gate   Obad 11

FOREKNEW *know beforehand*

whom He f, He also   Rom 8:29
people whom he f   Rom 11:2
He was **foreknown**   1 Pet 1:20

FOREKNOWLEDGE

plan and f of God   Acts 2:23
f of God the Father   1 Pet 1:2

FOREMOST *first*

f commandment   Matt 22:38
among whom I am f   1 Tim 1:15

FORERUNNER *goes before*

Jesus...as a f for   Heb 6:20

FORESKIN

the flesh of your f   Gen 17:11
cut off her son's f   Ex 4:25
a hundred **f-s**   1 Sam 18:25
the **f-s** of your heart   Jer 4:4

FOREST *woods*

f devoured more   2 Sam 18:8
the f of Lebanon   1 Kin 7:2
f will sing for joy   1 Chr 16:33
every beast of the f   Ps 50:10
the glory of his f   Is 10:18
beasts in the f, Come   Is 56:9
a f is set aflame   James 3:5

FORETOLD *predicted*

the Holy Spirit f   Acts 1:16
just as Isaiah f   Rom 9:29

FOREVER *always, eternal*

eat, and live f   Gen 3:22
not strive with man f   Gen 6:3
throne shall be...f   1 Chr 17:14
the LORD abides f   Ps 9:7
LORD sits as King f   Ps 29:10
glorify Thy name f   Ps 86:12
riches are not f   Prov 27:24
One Who lives f   Is 57:15
Christ is to remain f   John 12:34
He...with you f   John 14:16
He is able to save f   Heb 7:25
Son, made perfect f   Heb 7:28
they shall reign f   Rev 22:5

FORFEIT *lose*

possessions..**f-ed**   Ezra 10:8
f-s his own life   Prov 20:2
f my head to the king   Dan 1:10
and **f-s** his soul   Matt 16:26

FORGET *forsake, neglect*

God has made me f   Gen 41:51
lest you f the LORD   Deut 6:12
f-got the God who   Deut 32:18
God **f-s**...iniquity   Job 11:6
nations who f God   Ps 9:17
needy...be **f-gotten**   Ps 9:18
Do not f the afflicted   Ps 10:12
they **f-got** His deeds   Ps 78:11
do not f my teaching   Prov 3:1
you will f the shame   Is 54:4
My people f My name   Jer 23:27
f-ing what *lies* behind   Phil 3:13
f your work and   Heb 6:10

FORGIVE *pardon*

f the transgression   Gen 50:17
f their sin   Ex 32:32
f our sins   Ps 79:9
not f their iniquity   Jer 18:23
f us our debts   Matt 6:12
authority...to f sins   Matt 9:6

f-gave him the debt   Matt 18:27
can f sins but God   Mark 2:7
he who is **f-n** little   Luke 7:47
Father, f them   Luke 23:34
whom you f   2 Cor 2:10
f-ing each other   Eph 4:32
f-n us all our   Col 2:13
righteous to f us   1 John 1:9

FORGIVENESS *pardon*

a God of f   Neh 9:17
there is f with Thee   Ps 130:4
poured out...for f   Matt 26:28
repentance for f   Luke 24:47
receives f of sins   Acts 10:43
f of our trespasses   Eph 1:7
the f of sins   Col 1:14
there is no f   Heb 9:22

FORK *instrument*

a three-pronged f   1 Sam 2:13
His winnowing f   Matt 3:12

FORM (n) *appearance, shape*

beautiful of f and   Gen 29:17
the f of the LORD   Num 12:8
image in the f   Deut 4:23
like the f of a man   Is 44:13
in a different f   Mark 16:12
bodily f like a dove   Luke 3:22
f of corruptible man   Rom 1:23
existed in the f of God   Phil 2:6

FORM (v) *fashion, shape*

f-ed man of dust   Gen 2:7
f-ed the dry land   Ps 95:5
f my inward parts   Ps 139:13
One **f-ing** light   Is 45:7
who **f-s** mountains   Amos 4:13
f-s the spirit of man   Zech 12:1
plot was **f-ed** against   Acts 20:3
Christ is **f-ed** in you   Gal 4:19

FORMATION *rank*

in f against   1 Chr 19:17
battle f in the   2 Chr 14:10

FORMLESS *without form*

earth was f and void   Gen 1:2
behold, *it was* f   Jer 4:23

FORNICATION

f-s, thefts, false   Matt 15:19
were not born of f   John 8:41
strangled and from f   Acts 15:29

FORNICATORS

neither f, nor   1 Cor 6:9
f...God will judge   Heb 13:4

FORSAKE

Then he **f-sook** God   Deut 32:15
not fail you or f you   Josh 1:5
f-sook the law of the   2 Chr 12:1
f Him, He will f you   2 Chr 15:2
God has not **f-n** us   Ezra 9:9
why hast Thou **f-n** me   Ps 22:1
not f your mother's   Prov 1:8
wicked f his way   Is 55:7
Your sons have **f-n** Me   Jer 5:7
f the idols of Egypt   Ezek 20:8
hast Thou **f-n** Me   Matt 27:46
persecuted...not **f-n**   2 Cor 4:9

f-ing...assembling   Heb 10:25
nor will I ever **f** you   Heb 13:5

FORTIFICATIONS *stronghold*

the unassailable **f**   Is 25:12
your **f** are fig trees   Nah 3:12

FORTIFIED *walled*

live in the **f** cities   Num 32:17
f with high walls   Deut 3:5
strike every **f** city   2 Kin 3:19
f cities into   Is 37:26

FORTRESS *stronghold*

God is my strong **f**   2 Sam 22:33
my rock and my **f**   Ps 18:2
My refuge and my **f**   Ps 91:2
wealth is his **f**   Prov 10:15
f-es will be destroyed   Hos 10:14

FORTUNE *one's lot*

and the **f-s** of Israel   Jer 33:7
f-s of My people   Hos 6:11
restore their **f**   Zeph 2:7

FORTY *number*

f days nd **f** nights   Gen 7:4
flood...for **f** days   Gen 7:17
ate the manna **f** years   Ex 16:35
with the LORD **f** days   Ex 34:28
fasted **f** days and **f**   Matt 4:2
f days being tempted   Mark 1:13

FOUL *putrid, rotten*

Nile will become **f**   Ex 7:18
My wounds grow **f**   Ps 38:5
f with your feet   Ezek 34:19

FOUNDATION *establishment*

f-s of heaven were   2 Sam 22:8
I laid the **f** of the   Job 38:4
the **f** of His throne   Ps 97:2
the earth upon its **f-s**   Ps 104:5
an everlasting **f**   Prov 10:25
cornerstone *for* the **f**   Is 28:16
a **f** upon the rock   Luke 6:48
the firm **f** of God   2 Tim 2:19
didst lay the **f**   Heb 1:10
a **f** of repentance   Heb 6:1

FOUNDATION GATE

see **GATES OF JERUSALEM**

FOUNDED *established*

the day it was **f**   Ex 9:18
f it upon the seas   Ps 24:2
by wisdom **f** the earth   Prov 3:19
f His vaulted dome   Amos 9:6
f upon the rock   Matt 7:25

FOUNTAIN *spring, well*

f-s of the great deep   Gen 7:11
is the **f** of life   Ps 36:9
The **f** of wisdom   Prov 18:4
f of living waters   Jer 2:13

FOUNTAIN GATE

see **GATES OF JERUSALEM**

FOWL *bird*

and fattened **f**   1 Kin 4:23
things and winged **f**   Ps 148:10

FOX *small animal*

three hundred **f-es**   Judg 15:4

f-es that are ruining   Song 2:15
like **f-es** among ruins   Ezek 13:4
The **f-es** have holes   Matt 8:20
Go and tell that **f**   Luke 13:32

FRAGMENTS *pieces*

forth His ice as **f**   Ps 147:17
Gather up the...**f**   John 6:12
twelve baskets with **f**   John 6:13

FRAGRANCE *pleasant aroma*

oils have a pleasing **f**   Song 1:3
given forth *their* **f**   Song 2:13
f like *the* cedars   Hos 14:6
we are a **f** of Christ   2 Cor 2:15

FRAME *structure*

f-s of the tabernacle   Num 3:36
with *artistic* **f-s**   1 Kin 6:4
He...knows our **f**   Ps 103:14
My **f** was not hidden   Ps 139:15

FRANKINCENSE *spice*

spices with pure **f**   Ex 30:34
f and the spices   1 Chr 9:29
trees of **f**   Song 4:14
gold and **f** and myrrh   Matt 2:11

FREE *at liberty*

she is not to go **f**   Ex 21:7
be **f** from the oath   Josh 2:20
let the oppressed go **f**   Is 58:6
shall make you **f**   John 8:32
who has died is **f-d**   Rom 6:7
the **f** gift of God   Rom 6:23
f from the law   Rom 8:2
Christ set us **f**   Gal 5:1
whether slave or **f**   Eph 6:8

FREEDOM *liberty*

proclaim...**f** to   Is 61:1
f of the glory   Rom 8:21
you were called to **f**   Gal 5:13
do not use your **f** as   1 Pet 2:16

FREEWILL OFFERINGS

see **OFFERINGS**

FRESH *new, recently prepared*

found a **f** jawbone   Judg 15:15
anointed with **f** oil   Ps 92:10
f water from your   Prov 5:15
new wine into **f**   Mark 2:22
f and bitter *water*   James 3:11

FRIEND *companion, comrade*

man speaks to his **f**   Ex 33:11
f-s are my scoffers   Job 16:20
loved ones and my **f-s**   Ps 38:11
my familiar **f**   Ps 55:13
A **f** loves at all   Prov 17:17
Wealth adds...**f-s**   Prov 19:4
who blesses his **f**   Prov 27:14
confidence in a **f**   Mic 7:5
f of tax-gatherers   Matt 11:19
F, your sins are   Luke 5:20
f of the bridegroom   John 3:29
his life for his **f-s**   John 15:13
You are My **f-s**, if   John 15:14

FRIENDSHIP

the **f** of God   Job 29:4
f with the world   James 4:4

FRIGHTEN *terrify*

to **f** *them* away   Deut 28:26
Thou dost **f** me   Job 7:14
I was **f-ed** and fell   Dan 8:17
Him and were **f-ed**   Mark 6:50
wars, do not be **f-ed**   Mark 13:7

FRINGE *edge*

the **f-s** of His ways   Job 26:14
touched the **f** of His   Matt 9:20

FROGS

smite...with **f**   Ex 8:2
f which destroyed   Ps 78:45
land swarmed with **f**   Ps 105:30
unclean spirits like **f**   Rev 16:13

FRONTALS *prayer bands*

they shall be as **f**   Deut 6:8
f on your forehead   Deut 11:18
see also **PHYLACTERIES**

FROST *freezing*

and the **f** by night   Gen 31:40
fine as the **f**   Ex 16:14
sycamore trees with **f**   Ps 78:47

FRUIT *growth, produce*

f trees bearing **f**   Gen 1:11
she took from its **f**   Gen 3:6
the **f** of the womb   Gen 30:2
offering of first **f-s**   Lev 2:12
its **f** in its season   Ps 1:3
yield **f** in old age   Ps 92:14
eat its choice **f-s**   Song 4:16
eaten the **f** of lies   Hos 10:13
know...by their **f-s**   Matt 7:16
bad tree bears bad **f**   Matt 7:17
f for eternal life   John 4:36
the **f** of the Spirit   Gal 5:22
f in every good work   Col 1:10

FRUITFUL *productive*

be **f** and multiply   Gen 9:7
were **f** and increased   Ex 1:7
gather a **f** harvest   Ps 107:37
into the **f** land   Jer 2:7
f labor for me   Phil 1:22

FRUSTRATE *conteract*

to **f** their cousel   Ezra 4:5
He **f-s** the plotting   Job 5:12
plans are **f-d**   Prov 15:22

FUEL *that which burns*

people are like **f**   Is 9:19
You will be **f**   Ezek 21:32

FUGITIVE *one who flees*

do not betray the **f**   Is 16:3
Meet the **f** with bread   Is 21:14
gather the **f-s**   Jer 49:5

FULFILL *complete*

to **f** the word   2 Chr 36:21
May the LORD **f** all   Ps 20:5
f-ing His word   Ps 148:8
to **f** the visions   Dan 11:14
the prophet was **f-ed**   Matt 2:17
to abolish, but to **f**   Matt 5:17
The time is **f-ed**   Mark 1:15
f-ed in the kingdom   Luke 22:16
Scripture...be **f-ed**   John 13:18

FULFILLMENT (continued)

husband f his duty — 1 Cor 7:3
f the law of Christ — Gal 6:2
f your ministry — 2 Tim 4:5

FULFILLMENT *completion*

the f of every vision — Ezek 12:23
f of what had been — Luke 1:45
f of *the* law — Rom 13:10

FULL *complete, whole*

I went out f — Ruth 1:21
The earth is f of — Ps 33:5
until the f day — Prov 4:18
twelve f baskets — Matt 14:20
f of dead...bones — Matt 23:27
f of the Holy Spirit — Luke 4:1
also is f of light — Luke 11:34
f of grace and truth — John 1:14
f of the Spirit — Acts 6:3
f armor of God — Eph 6:11
f of compassion — James 5:11

FULLER *one who bleaches cloth*

of the f-s' field — 2 Kin 18:17
like f-s' soap — Mal 3:2

FULNESS *completeness*

Thy presence is f of — Ps 16:11
His f we...received — John 1:16
the f of the Gentiles — Rom 11:25
f of the time came — Gal 4:4
all the f of God — Eph 3:19
f to dwell in Him — Col 1:19
the f of Deity dwells — Col 2:9

FURIOUS *angry*

Pharaoh was f — Gen 41:10
became f and very — Neh 4:1
king became...f — Dan 2:12

FURNACE *oven*

As silver tried in a f — Ps 12:6
the f of affliction — Is 48:10
into the midst of a f — Dan 3:6
cast them into the f — Matt 13:42
to glow in a f — Rev 1:15

FURNISH *supply*

f-ed with silver bands — Ex 38:17
shall f him liberally — Deut 15:14
f-ing every kind — Ps 144:13
upper room f-ed — Mark 14:15

FURROWS *trench*

its f weep together — Job 31:38
dost water its f — Ps 65:10
weeds in the f — Hos 10:4

FURY *anger*

brother's f subsides — Gen 27:44
terrify them in His f — Ps 2:5
plucked up in f — Ezek 19:12
the f of a fire — Heb 10:27

FUTILE *useless, vain*

go after f things — 1 Sam 12:21
devise f things — Acts 4:25
f in...speculations — Rom 1:21

FUTURE *that which is ahead*

discern their f — Deut 32:29
no f for the evil — Prov 24:20
is hope for your f — Jer 31:17
foundation for the f — 1 Tim 6:19

G

GABRIEL

angel of high rank
Dan 8:16;9:21; Luke 1:19,26

GAD

1 *son of Jacob* — Gen 30:11;35:26
2 *tribe of* — Num 1:25;2:14
3 *valley* — 2 Sam 24:5
4 *seer, prophet* — 2 Sam 24:11,18

GAIETY *cheerfulness*

g...is banished — Is 24:11
an end to all her g — Hos 2:11

GAIN (n) *profit, increase*

hate dishonest g — Ex 18:21
Ill-gotten g-s do not — Prov 10:2
who rejects unjust g — Is 33:15
greedy for g — Jer 6:13
to die is g — Phil 1:21
fond of sordid g — 1 Tim 3:8

GAIN (v) *acquire*

they might g insight — Neh 8:13
have g-ed the victory — Ps 98:1
he will g knowledge — Prov 19:25
will g ascendancy — Dan 11:5
g-s the whole world — Matt 16:26
that I may g Christ — Phil 3:8
may g the glory — 2 Thess 2:14

GAIUS

1 *Macedonian* — Acts 19:29
2 *companion of Paul* — Acts 20:4
3 *Corinthian believer* — 1 Cor 1:14
4 *addressee of 3 John* — 3 John 1

GALATIA

Roman province in Asia Minor
1 Cor 16:1; 2 Tim 4:10

GALE *storm*

dust before a g — Is 17:13
a fierce g of wind — Mark 4:37

GALILEE

1 *district in N Palestine*
Josh 21:32; 1 Kin 9:11;
Matt 2:22; Acts 10:37
2 *Sea of* — Matt 4:18; Mark 7:31
also **Sea of Chinnereth**
also **Lake of Gennesaret**
also **Sea of Tiberias**

GALL *bitter herb, bitterness*

gave me g for my food — Ps 69:21
drink...with g — Matt 27:34
the g of bitterness — Acts 8:23

GALLIO

governor of Achaia — Acts 18:12,17

GALLOWS *for hanging*

Have a g...made — Esth 5:14
hanged...on the g — Esth 7:10
his sons...on the g — Esth 9:25

GAMALIEL

1 *head of tribe* — Num 2:20;7:54
2 *Pharisee* — Acts 5:34;22:3

GARDEN *planted area*

God walking in the g — Gen 3:8

from the g of Eden — Gen 3:23
Make my g breathe — Song 4:16
plant g-s, and eat — Jer 29:5
tabernacle like a g — Lam 2:6
in the g with Him — John 18:26
the g a new tomb — John 19:41

GARLAND *ornament*

a g instead of ashes — Is 61:3
brought...g-s to the — Acts 14:13

GARMENT *clothing, dress*

God made g-s of skin — Gen 3:21
caught him by his g — Gen 39:12
in g-s of fine linen — Gen 41:42
holy g-s for Aaron — Ex 28:2
divide my g-s among — Ps 22:18
on g-s of vengeance — Is 59:17
g-s of glowing colors — Is 63:1
g of camel's hair — Matt 3:4
g as white as snow — Matt 28:3
I just touch His g-s — Mark 5:28
spread their g-s — Mark 11:8
dividing up His g-s — Luke 23:34
put his outer g on — John 21:7
become old as a g — Heb 1:11
clothed in white g-s — Rev 3:5

GARRISON *defense*

g of the Philistines — 1 Sam 13:4
the g...trembled — 1 Sam 14:15
set g-s in the land — 2 Chr 17:2

GATE *entry way*

is the g of heaven — Gen 28:17
oppressed in the g — Job 5:4
g-s with thanksgiving — Ps 100:4
enter the g-s of Sheol — Is 38:10
justice in the g — Amos 5:15
Enter...narrow g — Matt 7:13
g-s of Hades shall — Matt 16:18
did not open the g — Acts 12:14

GATEKEEPERS *guards*

g for the camp — 1 Chr 9:18
divisions of the g — 1 Chr 26:12
The sons of the g — Ezra 2:42
g, and the singers — Neh 10:39

GATES OF JERUSALEM

alternate names in italics
1 **Beautiful Gate** — Acts 3:10
East Gate
2 **Benjamin Gate**
Jer 20:2; Zech 14:10
Sheep Gate
Inspection Gate
3 **Corner Gate**
2 Kin 14:13; 2 Chr 26:9
4 **East Gate**
Neh 3:29; Ezek 10:19;44:1
Beautiful Gate
5 **Ephraim Gate**
2 Kin 14:13; Neh 8:16
Middle Gate
Old Gate
6 **First Gate** — Zech 14:10
7 **Fish Gate**
2 Chr 33:14; Neh 3:3
8 **Foundation Gate** — 2 Chr 23:5
Gate of Sur
9 **Fountain Gate**
Neh 2:14;12:37

"gate between two walls"
    2 Kin 25:4; Jer 39:4
10 **Guard, Gate of the**
                Neh 12:39
  Inspection Gate
11 **Horse Gate**
    2 Chr 23:15; Neh 3:28
12 **Inspection Gate**   Neh 3:31
  Gate of the Guard
  Benjamin Gate
13 **Middle Gate**   Jer 39:3
  Ephraim Gate
14 **Old Gate**   Neh 3:6;12:39
  Ephraim Gate
15 **Refuse Gate** Neh 2:13;12:31
16 **Sheep Gate**   Neh 3:1
  Benjamin Gate
17 **Sur, Gate of**   2 Kin 11:6
  Foundation Gate
18 **Valley Gate**
      2 Chr 26:9; Neh 3:13
19 **Water Gate**
        Neh 3:26;8:1,3,16

GATEWAY *entrance*

the **g** of the court   Ex 40:8
the **g** of the peoples Ezek 26:2

GATH

Philistine city
    Josh 11:22; 1 Sam 17:23;
                 1 Chr 20:8

GATHER *assemble, collect*

g-ed to his people   Gen 25:8
g stubble for straw   Ex 5:12
He **g**-s the waters   Ps 33:7
G My godly ones   Ps 50:5
g all nations and   Is 66:18
hen **g**-s her chicks Matt 23:37
elders...were **g**-ed Matt 26:3
g...His elect   Mark 13:27
G up the leftover   John 6:12

GAZA

Philistine city
  Gen 10:19; Judg 16:1; Jer 47:5

GAZE (n) *view, glance*

Turn Thy **g** away from Ps 39:13
let your **g** be fixed   Prov 4:25
I lifted my **g** and   Dan 8:3
turning His **g** on His Luke 6:20

GAZE (v) *look, stare*

man...**g**-ing at her Gen 24:21
and **g** after Moses   Ex 33:8
eye **g**-s on their   Job 17:2
LORD **g**-d upon the Ps 102:19
g-ing...into the sky Acts 1:10

GAZELLE *animal*

swift as the **g**-s   1 Chr 12:8
a **g** Or a young stag Song 2:17
like a hunted **g**   Is 13:14

GEDERAH

1 *town of Judah*   Josh 15:36
2 *town of Benjamin* 1 Chr 12:4

GEHAZI

servant of Elisha
    2 Kin 4:12;5:20;8:4

GENEALOGY *family record*

found the book of...**g** Neh 7:5
g of Jesus Christ   Matt 1:1
and endless **g**-ies   1 Tim 1:4
whose **g** is not traced Heb 7:6

GENERATION *age, period*

this evil **g**   Deut 1:35
the righteous **g**   Ps 14:5
faithfulness to all **g**-s Ps 100:5
salvation to all **g**-s   Is 51:8
this **g** seek for a sign Mark 8:12
g-s...not made known Eph 3:5
and perverse **g**   Phil 2:15

GENEROUS *bountiful*

g will be blessed   Prov 22:9
because I am **g**   Matt 20:15
g...ready to share   1 Tim 6:18

GENNESARET

1 *lake*   Luke 5:1
  also **Sea of Chinnereth**
  also **Sea of Galilee**
  also **Sea of Tiberius**
2 *land or district*
      Matt 14:34; Mark 6:53

GENTILES *foreigners, non-Jews*

Galilee of the **G**   Matt 4:15
deliver...to the **G** Matt 20:19
revelation to the **G** Luke 2:32
Why did the **G** rage Acts 4:25
salvation...to the **G** Rom 11:11
preach...among the **G** Gal 1:16

GENTLE *compassionate, mild*

g answer turns away Prov 15:1
I was like a **g** lamb Jer 11:19
Blessed are the **g**   Matt 5:5
G, and mounted on Matt 21:5
a **g** and quiet spirit 1 Pet 3:4

GENTLENESS *kindness*

and a spirit of **g**   1 Cor 4:21
and **g** of Christ   2 Cor 10:1
g, self-control   Gal 5:23
humility and **g**, with Eph 4:2

GERAR

Philistine city Gen 20:2;26:6

GERIZIM

mountain near Shechem
       Deut 11:29; Josh 8:33

GERSHOM

1 *son of Moses*   Ex 2:22;18:3
2 *son of Levi*   1 Chr 6:16,43
3 *line of Phinehas*   Ezra 8:2

GERSHON

son of Levi Gen 46:11; Ex 6:16

GETHSEMANE

garden on Mount of Olives
    Matt 26:36; Mark 14:32

GEZER

Canaanite city of Ephraim
      Josh 10:33; 1 Kin 9:17

GHOST *spirit*

resort to idols and **g**-s Is 19:3

saying, It is a **g** Matt 14:26
it was a **g**   Mark 6:49

GIANT

were born to the **g** 2 Sam 21:22
from the **g**-s   1 Chr 20:6

GIBEAH

1 *village in Judah* Josh 15:57
2 *in Ephraim*   Josh 24:33
3 *town of Benjamin*
  1 Sam 10:26;13:2; 2 Sam 23:29

GIBEON

town in Benjamin
    Josh 9:3,17; 1 Kin 3:5;
             1 Chr 8:29

GIDEON

son of Joash   Judg 6:11, 36
judge   Judg 8:4-21

GIFT *present*

the sacred **g**-s   Num 18:32
children are a **g**   Ps 127:3
to Him **g**-s   Matt 2:11
g of the Holy Spirit Acts 2:38
impart...spiritual **g** Rom 1:11
g of God is eternal Rom 6:23
desire...greater **g**-s 1 Cor 12:31
perfect **g** is from James 1:17

GIHON

1 *river of Eden*   Gen 2:13
2 *Jerusalem spring* 2 Chr 32:30

GILBOA

mountain   2 Sam 1:6
where Saul died 2 Sam 21:12

GILEAD

1 *son of Machir*   Num 36:1
2 *descendant of Gad* 1 Chr 5:14
3 *father of Jephthah* Judg 11:1
4 *land E of Jordan* Num 32:29
5 *mountain*   Judg 7:3
6 *city*   Hos 6:8

GILGAL

1 *in Arabah*   Deut 11:30
2 *encampment in Jordan Valley*
    Josh 5:9; 1 Sam 7:16
  near Jericho Josh 5:8,10
3 *in N Judah*   Josh 15:7
4 *in Galilee*   Josh 12:23
5 *village near Bethel* 2 Kin 2:1

GIRD *bind*

g him with the...band Ex 29:5
g up your loins like Job 38:3
g-ed me with gladness Ps 30:11
g-s herself with Prov 31:17
g-ed...with truth Eph 6:14
g your minds for 1 Pet 1:13
g-ed across His breast Rev 1:13

GIRDLE *belt, waistband*

man with a leather **g** 2 Kin 1:8
binds...with a **g** Job 12:18
with a golden **g**   Rev 1:13

GIRGASHITE(S)

Canaanite tribe
    Gen 10:16; Deut 7:1;
    Josh 24:11; Neh 9:8

GIRL *maiden*

the g and consult	Gen 24:57
sold a g for wine	Joel 3:3
boys and g-s playing	Zech 8:5
the g has not died	Matt 9:24

GIVE *bestow, yield*

g light on the earth	Gen 1:17
g-n you every plant	Gen 1:29
gave me from...tree	Gen 3:12
in the land...God g-s	Ex 20:12
I will g you rest	Ex 33:14
g him to the LORD	1 Sam 1:11
G ear to my prayer	Ps 17:1
gave me vinegar	Ps 69:21
G me neither poverty	Prov 30:8
a son will be g-n	Is 9:6
gave birth to a Son	Matt 1:25
G us this day	Matt 6:11
g-ing thanks, He	Matt 15:36
g you the keys	Matt 16:19
authority...been g-n	Matt 28:18
what shall a man g	Mark 8:37
body which is g-n	Luke 22:19
gave His only...Son	John 3:16
not as the world g-s	John 14:27
gave up His spirit	John 19:30
what I do have I g	Acts 3:6
g-n among men	Acts 4:12
more blessed to g	Acts 20:35
was g-n me a thorn	2 Cor 12:7
always g-ing thanks	Eph 5:20
who gave Himself	1 Tim 2:6
g-s a greater grace	James 4:6
g-n us eternal life	1 John 5:11
to be g-n a mark	Rev 13:16

GLAD *pleased*

g in his heart	Ex 4:14
joy and a g heart	Deut 28:47
righteous see...are g	Job 22:19
Be g in the LORD	Ps 32:11
g when they said	Ps 122:1
son makes a father g	Prov 10:1
Rejoice, and be g	Matt 5:12
Be g in that day	Luke 6:23
who bring g tidings	Rom 10:15

GLADNESS *joy*

celebrate...with g	Neh 12:27
g...for the Jews	Esth 8:17
Serve the LORD with g	Ps 100:2
g and sincerity of	Acts 2:46
With the oil of g	Heb 1:9

GLASS *crystal*

or g cannot equal	Job 28:17
sea of g like crystal	Rev 4:6

GLEAM *brilliance*

awesome g of crystal	Ezek 1:22
g of a Tarshish stone	Ezek 10:9
g of polished bronze	Dan 10:6

GLEAN *gather, pick*

Nor shall you g	Lev 19:10
Do not go to g	Ruth 2:8
she g-ed in the field	Ruth 2:17
they g the vineyard	Job 24:6
g-ing ears of grain	Is 17:5

GLOOM *darkness*

cloud and thick g	Deut 4:11
The land of utter g	Job 10:22
darkness and g and	Heb 12:18
and your joy to g	James 4:9

GLORIFY *honor, worship*

g Thy name forever	Ps 86:12
Let the LORD be g-ied	Is 66:5
g your Father	Matt 5:16
shepherds...g-ing	Luke 2:20
Jesus...not yet g-ied	John 7:39
Father, g Thy name	John 12:28
God is g-ied in Him	John 13:31
were all g-ing God	Acts 4:21
Gentiles to g God	Rom 15:9
g God in your body	1 Cor 6:20
did not g Himself	Heb 5:5

GLORIOUS *exalted, great*

g name be blessed	Neh 9:5
G things are spoken	Ps 87:3
resting place will be g	Is 11:10
the law great and g	Is 42:21
g gospel of...God	1 Tim 1:11

GLORY (n) *honor, splendor*

show me Thy g	Ex 33:18
while My g is passing	Ex 33:22
Tell of His g	1 Chr 16:24
King of g may come	Ps 24:7
exchanged their g	Ps 106:20
earth is full of His g	Is 6:3
their g into shame	Hos 4:7
Solomon in all his g	Matt 6:29
g of the Lord shone	Luke 2:9
G...in the highest	Luke 2:14
He comes in His g	Luke 9:26
do not seek My g	John 8:50
short of the g of God	Rom 3:23
all to the g of God	1 Cor 10:31
eternal weight of g	2 Cor 4:17
body of His g	Phil 3:21
crowned Him with g	Heb 2:7
unfading crown of g	1 Pet 5:4

GLORY (v) *exalt*

and g in thy praise	1 Chr 16:35
G in His holy name	Ps 105:3
in Him they will g	Jer 4:2
I...have cause to g	Phil 2:16

GLUTTON *excessive eater*

g...come to poverty	Prov 23:21
a companion of g-s	Prov 28:7
evil beasts, lazy g-s	Titus 1:12

GNASH *grind*

They g-ed at me	Ps 35:16
He will g his teeth	Ps 112:10
They hiss and g	Lam 2:16
g-ing their teeth	Acts 7:54

GNAT *insect*

dust...became g-s	Ex 8:17
swarm of flies...g-s	Ps 105:31
strain out a g and	Matt 23:24

GO *move, proceed*

Let My people g	Ex 7:16
God who g-es before	Deut 1:30
where you g, I will g	Ruth 1:16
the way he should g	Prov 22:6

g one mile, g...two	Matt 5:41
G into all...world	Mark 16:15
I g to prepare a	John 14:2
night is almost gone	Rom 13:12

GOADS *inducements*

wise men are like g	Eccl 12:11
kick against the g	Acts 26:14

GOAL *end, object*

press on toward the g	Phil 3:14
g...is love	1 Tim 1:5

GOAT *animal*

curtains of g-s' hair	Ex 26:7
g for a sin offering	Num 15:27
quilt of g-s' hair	1 Sam 19:13
g had a...horn	Dan 8:5
shaggy g represents	Dan 8:21
sheep from the g-s	Matt 25:32
blood of g-s...bulls	Heb 9:13

GOD *Deity, Eternal One*

In the beginning G	Gen 1:1
G formed man of dust	Gen 2:7
G sent him out	Gen 3:23
G gave to Abraham	Gen 28:4
tablets were G-'s work	Ex 32:16
G is my...fortress	2 Sam 22:33
G of my salvation	Ps 18:46
In G...put my trust	Ps 56:4
Search me, O G	Ps 139:23
word of G is tested	Prov 30:5
servant of the living G	Dan 6:20
I am G and not man	Hos 11:9
Will a man rob G	Mal 3:8
G descending...dove	Matt 3:16
they shall see G	Matt 5:8
What...G has joined	Matt 19:6
kingdom of G is at	Mark 1:15
My G, why hast	Mark 15:34
You the Son of G	Luke 22:70
the Word was G	John 1:1
No man has seen G	John 1:18
the Lamb of G	John 1:29
G so loved the world	John 3:16
G is spirit	John 4:24
voice of...Son of G	John 5:25
obey G rather than	Acts 5:29
judgment of G	Rom 2:2
bear fruit for G	Rom 7:4
we are children of G	Rom 8:16
are a temple of G	1 Cor 3:16
full armor of G	Eph 6:11
one G...one mediator	1 Tim 2:5
is inspired by G	2 Tim 3:16
word of G is...sharper	Heb 4:12
impossible...G to lie	Heb 6:18
G is love	1 John 4:8
great supper of G	Rev 19:17

GODDESS *female deity*

Ashtoreth the g of	1 Kin 11:5
great g Artemis	Acts 19:27
blasphemers of...g	Acts 19:37

GODLESS *pagan, without God*

hope of the g will	Job 8:13
joy of...g momentary	Job 20:5
g man destroys his	Prov 11:9
hands of g men	Acts 2:23
become of the g	1 Pet 4:18

GODLINESS *holiness*

in all **g** and dignity	1 Tim 2:2
the mystery of **g**	1 Tim 3:16
g is profitable	1 Tim 4:8
to a form of **g**	2 Tim 3:5
g, brotherly kindness	2 Pet 1:7

GODLY *holy*

keeps...His **g** ones	1 Sam 2:9
g man ceases to be	Ps 12:1
not forsake His **g** ones	Ps 37:28
and **g** sincerity	2 Cor 1:12
to live **g** in Christ	2 Tim 3:12
rescue the **g** from	2 Pet 2:9

GOD(S) *false deity, idols*

no other **g-s** before Me	Ex 20:3
New **g-s** were chosen	Judg 5:8
cast their **g-s** into	Is 37:19
bowed...to other **g-s**	Jer 22:9
no other **g** who is	Dan 3:29
The voice of a **g**	Acts 12:22
g-s...become like	Acts 14:11
the **g** of this world	2 Cor 4:4

GOD, SON OF

see **SON OF GOD**

GOG

1 *a Reubenite*	1 Chr 5:4
2 *prince of Meshech and Tubal*	
	Ezek 38:2
3 *symbol of godless nations*	
	Rev 20:8

see also **MAGOG**

GOLAN

city of refuge	Josh 21:27
a Levitical city	1 Chr 6:71

GOLD *precious metal*

g of that land is good	Gen 2:12
mercy seat of pure **g**	Ex 25:17
Almighty...be your **g**	Job 22:25
more desirable than **g**	Ps 19:10
refine them like **g**	Mal 3:3
to Him gifts of **g**	Matt 2:11
Do not acquire **g**	Matt 10:9
Divine nature...**g**	Acts 17:29
coveted no...**g**	Acts 20:33
city was pure **g**	Rev 21:18

GOLDSMITH *gold craftsman*

g-s and...merchants	Neh 3:32
g, and he makes it	Is 46:6

GOLGOTHA

site of Crucifixion	
	Matt 27:33; Mark 15:22;
	John 19:17

GOLIATH

Philistine giant	
	1 Sam 17:4,23; 21:9;
	1 Chr 20:5

GOMER

1 *son of Japheth*	Gen 10:2
2 *group of people*	Ezek 38:6
3 *wife of Hosea*	Hos 1:3

GOMORRAH

city of Jordan plain	
	Gen 10:19; 14:10;19:24

probably S of Dead Sea

	Is 13:19; 2 Pet 2:6

GOOD *complete, right*

God saw that it was **g**	Gen 1:18
knowledge of **g** and	Gen 2:9
Proclaim **g** tidings	1 Chr 16:23
Do not withhold **g**	Prov 3:27
joyful heart is **g**	Prov 17:22
planted in **g** soil	Ezek 17:8
feed in...**g** pasture	Ezek 34:18
Seek **g** and not evil	Amos 5:14
how to give **g** gifts	Matt 7:11
Well done, **g** and	Matt 25:23
sown on the **g** soil	Mark 4:20
Salt is **g**	Mark 9:50
No one is **g** except	Luke 18:19
I am the **g** shepherd	John 10:11
men of **g** reputation	Acts 6:3
perseverance in...**g**	Rom 2:7
nothing **g**...in me	Rom 7:18
work together for **g**	Rom 8:28
overcome evil...**g**	Rom 12:21
is of **g** repute	Phil 4:8
g hope by grace	2 Thess 2:16
Fight the **g** fight	1 Tim 6:12
tasted the **g** word	Heb 6:5

GOODNESS *excellence, value*

My **g** pass before you	Ex 33:19
Surely **g**...will follow	Ps 23:6
How great is Thy **g**	Ps 31:19
kindness, **g**	Gal 5:22
every desire for **g**	2 Thess 1:11

GOODS *possessions, supplies*

the **g** for yourself	Gen 14:21
have acquired...**g**	Ezek 38:12

GORE *stab*

if an ox **g-s** a man	Ex 21:28
g the Arameans	1 Kin 22:11

GOSHEN

1 *district of Egypt in Nile Delta*	
	Gen 45:10; 47:6,27
2 *S Judah region*	Josh 10:41
3 *town in Judah*	Josh 15:51

GOSPEL *good news*

proclaiming the **g** of	Matt 4:23
preach the **g** to all	Mark 16:15
not ashamed of the **g**	Rom 1:16
if our **g** is veiled	2 Cor 4:3
or a different **g**	2 Cor 11:4
distort the **g** of Christ	Gal 1:7
g of your salvation	Eph 1:13
g of peace	Eph 6:15
defense of the **g**	Phil 1:16
the hope of the **g**	Col 1:23
eternal **g** to preach	Rev 14:6

GOSSIP *babbler*

associate with a **g**	Prov 20:19
malice; *they are* **g-s**	Rom 1:29
g-s and busybodies	1 Tim 5:13

GOVERN *rule*

light to **g** the day	Gen 1:16
light to **g** the night	Gen 1:16
when the judges **g-ed**	Ruth 1:1

GOVERNMENT *authority, rule*

g...on His shoulders	Is 9:6
be no end to...*His* **g**	Is 9:7

GOVERNOR *ruler*

not offer it to your **g**	Mal 1:8
brought before **g-s**	Matt 10:18
g was quite amazed	Matt 27:14
Pilate was **g** of Judea	Luke 3:1
g over Egypt	Acts 7:10

GRACE *benevolence, favor*

G is poured upon Thy	Ps 45:2
g to the afflicted	Prov 3:34
g of God was upon	Luke 2:40
full of **g** and truth	John 1:14
g abounded...more	Rom 5:20
g of our Lord Jesus	Rom 16:20
My **g** is sufficient	2 Cor 12:9
by **g** you have been	Eph 2:8
justified by His **g**	Titus 3:7
to the throne of **g**	Heb 4:16
g to the humble	James 4:6

GRACIOUS *kind*

God be **g** to you	Gen 43:29
g to whom I will be	Ex 33:19
a **g** and...God	Neh 9:31
Be **g** to me, O LORD	Ps 6:2
and **g**, Slow to anger	Ps 86:15
g to a poor man	Prov 19:17
be **g** to...remnant	Amos 5:15

GRAFT *insert, join*

I might be **g-ed** in	Rom 11:19
God is able to **g**	Rom 11:23
g-ed into their own	Rom 11:24

GRAIN

Joseph stored up **g**	Gen 41:49
glean among the...**g**	Ruth 2:2
g...for your enemies	Is 62:8
then the mature **g**	Mark 4:28
g of wheat falls	John 12:24

GRAIN OFFERING

see **OFFERINGS**

GRANDCHILDREN

G are the crown of	Prov 17:6
widow has...or **g**	1 Tim 5:4

GRANDDAUGHTER

g-s, and all his	Gen 46:7
g of Omri king of	2 Kin 8:26

GRANDSON

g might fear the LORD	Deut 6:2
sons and thirty **g-s**	Judg 12:14
master's **g** shall eat	2 Sam 9:10

GRANT *give, provide*

g this people favor	Ex 3:21
hast **g-ed** me life	Job 10:12
g us Thy salvation	Ps 85:7
G that we may sit	Mark 10:37
He **g-ed** sight to	Luke 7:21
Father has **g-ed** Me	Luke 22:29
g repentance to	Acts 5:31
g-ing...deliverance	Acts 7:25

GRAPE *fruit*

nor eat...dried **g-s**	Num 6:3
of **g-s** you drank	Deut 32:14

GRASP

when the g harvest is	Is 24:13
G-s are not gathered	Matt 7:16
g-s from a briar	Luke 6:44

GRASP *hold, seize*

hands g the spindle	Prov 31:19
He who g-s the bow	Amos 2:15
a thing to be g-ed	Phil 2:6

GRASS *vegetation*

g springs out	2 Sam 23:4
his days are like g	Ps 103:15
dry g collapses into	Is 5:24
g withers, the flower	Is 40:7
was given g to eat	Dan 5:21
if God so arrays...g	Matt 6:30
All flesh is like g	1 Pet 1:24
not hurt the g	Rev 9:4

GRASSHOPPER *insect*

the g in its kinds	Lev 11:22
we became like g-s	Num 13:33
inhabitants are like g-s	Is 40:22

GRATITUDE *thankfulness*

overflowing with g	Col 2:7
is received with g	1 Tim 4:4
let us show g	Heb 12:28

GRAVE *sepulchre, tomb*

pillar of Rachel's g	Gen 35:20
throat is an open g	Ps 5:9
I will open your g-s	Ezek 37:12
I will prepare your g	Nah 1:14
made the g secure	Matt 27:66

GRAVEN *sculptured*

make...a g image	Deut 4:23
ashamed who serve g	Ps 97:7
praise to g images	Is 42:8

GRAY *color*

g hair...in sorrow	Gen 42:38
with the man of g	Deut 32:25
Both the g-haired	Job 15:10
when I am old and g	Ps 71:18
g head is a crown	Prov 16:31

GRAZE *feed*

cattle...g-ing in	1 Chr 27:29
wolf...shall g	Is 65:25
he will g on Carmel	Jer 50:19

GREAT *big, excellent, grand*

made...two g lights	Gen 1:16
make you a g nation	Gen 12:2
lovingkindness is g	Ps 57:10
your iniquity is g	Jer 30:15
g day of the LORD	Zeph 1:14
rejoiced...with g joy	Matt 2:10
woman...faith is g	Matt 15:28
good news of a g joy	Luke 2:10
reward is g in	Luke 6:23
because of His g love	Eph 2:4
so g a salvation	Heb 2:3
we have a g...priest	Heb 4:14
so g a cloud of	Heb 12:1
g supper of God	Rev 19:17
a g white throne	Rev 20:11

GREATEST *most important*

who is the g among	Luke 22:26
g of these is love	1 Cor 13:13
least to the g	Heb 8:11

GREATNESS *magnitude*

Thine...is the g	1 Chr 29:11
g...lovingkindness	Neh 13:22
g of Thy compassion	Ps 51:1
the g of His strength	Is 63:1
amazed at the g of	Luke 9:43
surpassing g of His	Eph 1:19

GREECE

country in SE Europe

	Dan 8:21; 10:20;11:2;
	Zech 9:13; Acts 20:2

GREED *excessive desire*

caught by their...g	Prov 11:6
every form of g	Luke 12:15
wickedness, g, evil	Rom 1:29
a pretext for g	1 Thess 2:5
a heart trained in g	2 Pet 2:14

GREEDY *craving*

had g desires	Num 11:4
g man curses	Ps 10:3
Everyone is g for	Jer 6:13

GREEKS

people of Greece

	Joel 3:6; Acts 16:1,3;
	Rom 1:16; 1 Cor 12:13

GREEN *fertile, fruitful*

every g plant for	Gen 1:30
lie down in g pastures	Ps 23:2
dry up the g tree	Ezek 17:24
nor any g thing	Rev 9:4

GREET *hail, welcome*

g no one on the way	Luke 10:4
G one another with	1 Pet 5:14

GRIEF *heartache, sorrow*

weeps because of g	Ps 119:28
foolish son is a g	Prov 17:25
acquainted with g	Is 53:3
our g-s He Himself	Is 53:4
joy and not with g	Heb 13:17

GRIEVE *distress, sorrow*

was g-d in His heart	Gen 6:6
Do not be g-d	Neh 8:10
g-d Him in the desert	Ps 78:40
g-d His Holy Spirit	Is 63:10
g-d at their hardness	Mark 3:5
Peter was g-d	John 21:17
not g the Holy Spirit	Eph 4:30

GRIND *crush, press*

my wife g for another	Job 31:10
g-ing...the poor	Is 3:15
millstones and g meal	Is 47:2
women...be g-ing	Matt 24:41
and g-s his teeth	Mark 9:18

GROAN *cry, moan*

From the city men g	Job 24:12
man rules, people g	Prov 29:2
wounded will g	Jer 51:52
whole creation g-s	Rom 8:22

GROANING *crying*

God heard their g	Ex 2:24
O LORD, Consider my g	Ps 5:1
g of the prisoner	Ps 79:11
g-s of a wounded	Ezek 30:24

GROPE *move about blindly*

you shall g at noon	Deut 28:29
They g in darkness	Job 12:25
g like...blind men	Is 59:10
g for Him and find	Acts 17:27

GROUND *earth, land, soil*

man of dust from...g	Gen 2:7
Cursed is the g	Gen 3:17
crossed on dry g	Josh 3:17
a spirit from the g	Is 29:4
talent in the g	Matt 25:25
finger wrote on the g	John 8:6
standing is holy g	Acts 7:33
g that drinks the rain	Heb 6:7

GROUNDED *established*

hope...is firmly g	2 Cor 1:7
rooted and g in love	Eph 3:17

GROW *develop, increase*

Moses had g-n up	Ex 2:11
You are g-n fat	Deut 32:15
my spirit g-s faint	Ps 77:3
youths g weary	Is 40:30
sun and moon g dark	Joel 3:15
lilies of the field g	Matt 6:28
love will g cold	Matt 24:12
Child continued to g	Luke 2:40
grew strong in faith	Rom 4:20
as your faith g-s	2 Cor 10:15
not weary of	2 Thess 3:13
g in the grace	2 Pet 3:18

GROWTH *increase*

new g is seen	Prov 27:25
God who causes the g	1 Cor 3:7

GRUDGE *hostile feeling*

Esau bore a g	Gen 27:41
nor bear any g	Lev 19:18
Herodias had a g	Mark 6:19

GRUMBLE *complain*

they g-d against Moses	Ex 17:3
the congregation g	Num 14:36
g-d in their tents	Ps 106:25
scribes began to g	Luke 15:2
g among yourselves	John 6:43

GRUMBLING *complaint*

for He hears your g-s	Ex 16:7
g-s against Me	Num 17:10
Do all...without g	Phil 2:14

GUARD (n) *keeper*

dost set a g over me	Job 7:12
be a g for them	Ezek 38:7
g-s shook for fear	Matt 28:4
Him away under g	Mark 14:44

GUARD (v) *keep watch*

g the way to the tree	Gen 3:24
g-ed the threshold	2 Kin 12:9
G-ing...justice	Prov 2:8
Discretion will g you	Prov 2:11
soldier...was g-ing	Acts 28:16
shall g your hearts	Phil 4:7
g...from idols	1 John 5:21

GUARDHOUSE *prison*

the court of the g	Jer 37:21

the court of the **g** Jer 38:28

GUARDIAN overseer

g-s of *the children* 2 Kin 10:1
under **g-s** and Gal 4:2
G of your souls 1 Pet 2:25

GUEST visitor

Herod and his...**g-s** Mark 6:22
Where...My **g** room Mark 14:14
to the invited **g-s** Luke 14:7
g of a...sinner Luke 19:7

GUIDANCE counsel

no **g**, the people fall Prov 11:14
make war by wise **g** Prov 20:18

GUIDE (n) advisor, director

The righteous is a **g** Prov 12:26
Woe to...blind **g-s** Matt 23:16
You blind **g-s**, who Matt 23:24
are a **g** to the blind Rom 2:19

GUIDE (v) direct, lead

LORD alone **g-d** him Deut 32:12
He **g-s** me in the paths Ps 23:3
g us until death Ps 48:14
my mind was **g-ing** *me* Eccl 2:3
blind...**g-s** a blind Matt 15:14
g you into...truth John 16:13
unless someone **g-s** Acts 8:31

GUILE deceit

in whom is no **g** John 1:47
all malice and all **g** 1 Pet 2:1
lips from speaking **g** 1 Pet 3:10

GUILT offence

be free from **g** Num 5:31
according to his **g** Deut 25:2
charge me with a **g** 2 Sam 3:8
our **g** has grown Ezra 9:6
land is full of **g** Jer 51:5
must bear their **g** Hos 10:2
I find no **g** in Him John 18:38

GUILT OFFERING
see OFFERINGS

GUILTY charged or condemned

he sins and becomes **g** Lev 6:4
murderer...**g** of Num 35:31
as one who is **g** 2 Sam 14:13
g by the blood Ezek 22:4
g of an eternal sin Mark 3:29
has become **g** of all James 2:10

GUSHED burst, flowed

so that waters **g** out Ps 78:20
the rock...water **g** Is 48:21
all his bowels **g** out Acts 1:18

H

HABAKKUK

prophet Hab 1:1;3:1

HABITATION abode, dwelling

from Thy holy **h** Deut 26:15
a rock of **h** Ps 71:3
h-s of violence Ps 74:20
live in a peaceful **h** Is 32:18
holy and glorious **h** Is 63:15
laid waste his **h** Jer 10:25

a **h** of shepherds Jer 33:12

HABOR

river in Mesopotamia
2 Kin 17:6;18:11; 1 Chr 5:26

HADAD

1 *son of Ishmael*
Gen 25:15; 1 Chr 1:30
2 *king of Edom, son of Bedad*
Gen 36:35,36; 1 Chr 1:46,47
3 *a king of Edom*
Gen 36:39; 1 Chr 1:50,51
4 *Edomite prince* 1 Kin 11:14ff

HADASSAH

Esther's Hebrew name Esth 2:7

HADES hell, place of dead

shall descend to **H** Matt 11:23
in **H** he lifted up Luke 16:23
abandoned to **H** Rev 1:18

HAGAR

Sarah's handmaiden Gen 16:1
Abraham's slave wife Gen 16:3
mother of Ishmael Gen 16:15

HAGGAI

prophet Ezra 5:1; Hag 1:1

HAGGITH

David's wife 2 Sam 3:4
mother of Adonijah 1 Kin 1:11

HAIL (n) pieces of ice

rained **h** on the land Ex 9:23
storehouses of the **h** Job 38:22
gave them **h** for rain Ps 105:32
plague of the **h** Rev 16:21

HAIL (v) greeting

H, Rabbi Matt 26:49
H, King of...Jews Matt 27:29

HAILSTONES pieces of ice

who died from the **h** Josh 10:11
H and coals of fire Ps 18:13
you, O **h**, will fall Ezek 13:11
h...one hundred Rev 16:21

HAIR

gray **h**...to Sheol Gen 42:38
locks of his **h** and Judg 16:14
h...bristled Job 4:15
h...like pure wool Dan 7:9
garment of camel's **h** Matt 3:4
make one **h** white Matt 5:36
h-s...all numbered Matt 10:30
His feet with her **h** John 11:2
not with braided **h** 1 Tim 2:9

HALL corridor

h of pillars 1 Kin 7:6
h of judgment 1 Kin 7:7
wedding **h** was Matt 22:10

HALLELUJAH praise Yahweh

H! Salvation and Rev 19:1
H! Her smoke rises Rev 19:3
Amen. **H** Rev 19:4
H! For the Lord our Rev 19:6

HALLOWED consecrated, holy

H be Thy name Matt 6:9

HAM

1 *son of Noah* Gen 5:32;9:18
2 *city* Gen 14:5
3 *poetic name for Egypt*
Ps 105:27;106:22

HAMAN

Persian prime minister
son of Hammedatha Esth 3:1

HAMATH

city in Aram 2 Kin 23:33;25:21

HAMMER mallet, tool

and seized a **h** Judg 4:21
neither **h** nor axe 1 Kin 6:7
smash with...**h-s** Ps 74:6
like a **h** which Jer 23:29

HAMON-GOG

valley where army of Gog is
defeated Ezek 39:11,15

HANANIAH

1 *son of Zerubbabel* 1 Chr 3:19
2 *son of Shishak* 1 Chr 8:24
3 *musician* 1 Chr 25:4,23
4 *in Uzziah's army* 2 Chr 26:11
5 *repaired wall* Neh 3:30
6 *overseer of palace* Neh 7:2
7 *false prophet* Jer 28:15
8 *Shadrach* Dan 1:6,7
name of six other individuals

HAND part of body

cover you with My **h** Ex 33:22
for tooth, **h** for **h** Deut 19:21
sling was in his **h** 1 Sam 17:40
They pierced my **h-s** Ps 22:16
buries his **h** Prov 19:24
the hollow of His **h** Is 40:12
clay in the potter's **h** Jer 18:6
not let your left **h** Matt 6:3
laying His **h-s** upon Mark 10:16
the right **h** of God Mark 16:19
into the **h-s** of men Luke 9:44
into Thy **h-s** I Luke 23:46
reach here your **h** John 20:27
not made with **h-s** 2 Cor 5:1
lifting up holy **h-s** 1 Tim 2:8
h-s of...God Heb 10:31

HANDMAID servant, slave

save the son of Thy **h** Ps 86:16
the son of Thy **h** Ps 116:16
her **h-s** are moaning Nah 2:7

HANDSOME attractive

a choice and **h** man 1 Sam 9:2
ruddy, with a **h** 1 Sam 17:42

HANG attach, suspend

h you on a tree Gen 40:19
h up the veil Ex 40:8
h-ed is accursed of Deut 21:23
h-ing in an oak 2 Sam 18:10
they **h-ed** Haman Esth 7:10
he...**h-ed** himself Matt 27:5
millstone were **hung** Luke 17:2
h-ing Him on a cross Acts 5:30
who **h-s** on a tree Gal 3:13

HANNAH

mother of Samuel 1 Sam 2:21

HAPPINESS *joy*

give **h** to his wife	Deut 24:5
eat your bread in **h**	Eccl 9:7
I have forgotten **h**	Lam 3:17

HAPPY *blessed, joyful*

Leah said, **H** am I	Gen 30:13
h...man whom God	Job 5:17
h...who keeps the	Prov 29:18

HARAN

1 *brother of Abraham*	Gen 11:27
father of Lot	Gen 11:31
2 *Gershonite Levite*	1 Chr 23:9
3 *Mesopotamian city*	
	Gen 11:32;27:43

HARD *difficult, firm*

bitter with **h** labor	Ex 1:14
case that is too **h**	Deut 1:17
made our yoke **h**	2 Chr 10:4
Water becomes **h**	Job 38:30
h for a rich man	Matt 19:23
h it is to enter	Mark 10:24
worked **h** all night	Luke 5:5

HARDEN *make hard, callous*

h Pharaoh's heart	Ex 7:3
dust **h-s** into a mass	Job 38:38
who **h-s** *his* neck	Prov 29:1
h-s whom He	Rom 9:18
minds were **h-ed**	2 Cor 3:14
Do not **h** your hearts	Heb 3:15

HARDNESS *callousness*

give them **h** of heart	Lam 3:65
Because of your **h**	Matt 19:8
grieved at their **h**	Mark 3:5
unbelief and **h** of	Mark 16:14

HARDSHIP *difficulty*

H after **h** is with me	Job 10:17
people experience **h**	Ps 60:3
afflictions, in **h-s**	2 Cor 6:4
our labor and **h**	1 Thess 2:9
Suffer **h** with *me*	2 Tim 2:3

HAREM *royal wives' quarters*

best place in the **h**	Esth 2:9
the court of the **h**	Esth 2:11
from the **h** to the	Esth 2:13
to the second **h**	Esth 2:14

HARLOT *prostitute*

thought she *was* a **h**	Gen 38:15
the hire of a **h**	Deut 23:18
h whose name was	Josh 2:1
Dressed as a **h**	Prov 7:10
city has become a **h**	Is 1:21
also played the **h**	Ezek 16:26
Traded a boy for a **h**	Joel 3:3
to a **h** is one body	1 Cor 6:16
Mother of **H-s**	Rev 17:5

HARLOTRY *prostitution*

with child by **h**	Gen 38:24
profaned by **h**	Lev 21:7
uncovered her **h-ies**	Ezek 23:18
children of **h**	Hos 1:2
spirit of **h**	Hos 5:4

HARM (n) *evil, hurt*

pillar to me, for **h**	Gen 31:52

h to this people	Ex 5:22
keep *me* from **h**	1 Chr 4:10
Do not devise **h**	Prov 3:29
great **h** to yourselves	Jer 44:7
the fire without **h**	Dan 3:25
did me much **h**	2 Tim 4:14

HARM (v) *damage, hurt*

David seeks to **h**	1 Sam 24:9
planning to **h** me	Neh 6:2
have not **h-ed** me	Dan 6:22
in order to **h** you	Acts 18:10
is there to **h** you	1 Pet 3:13

HAR-MAGEDON

hill of Megiddo	Rev 16:16
see also **MEGIDDO**	

HARMONY *agreement*

what **h** has Christ	2 Cor 6:15
live in **h** in the	Phil 4:2

HARP *musical instrument*

my **h** is turned to	Job 30:31
praises...with a **h**	Ps 33:2
Awake, **h** and lyre	Ps 57:8
gaiety of the **h** ceases	Is 24:8
having each one a **h**	Rev 5:8
holding **h-s** of God	Rev 15:2

HARSH *difficult, hard*

man was **h** and evil	1 Sam 25:3
h word stirs up anger	Prov 15:1
A **h** vision	Is 21:2
under **h** servitude	Lam 1:3

HARVEST *reap and gather*

Seedtime and **h**	Gen 8:22
fruits of the wheat **h**	Ex 34:22
you reap your **h**	Deut 24:19
he who sleeps in **h**	Prov 10:5
snow...time of **h**	Prov 25:13
like rain in **h**	Prov 26:1
the gladness of **h**	Is 9:3
time of **h** will come	Jer 51:33
Lord of the **h**	Matt 9:38
h is the end of the	Matt 13:39
fields...white for **h**	John 4:35
h of the earth is	Rev 14:15

HARVEST, FEAST OF

see FEASTS

HASHUM

1 *family of exiles*	Ezra 2:19
2 *was with Ezra*	Neh 8:4

HASTEN *accelerate*

h-ed after deceit	Job 31:5
H to me, O God	Ps 70:5
they **h** to shed blood	Prov 1:16
bird **h-s** to the snare	Prov 7:23
eye **h-s** after wealth	Prov 28:22
h-ing...day of God	2 Pet 3:12

HATE *despise, loathe*

you **h** discipline	Ps 50:17
who **h** the LORD	Ps 81:15
I **h** every false way	Ps 119:104
fools **h** knowlege	Prov 1:22
spares his rod **h-s**	Prov 13:24
a time to **h**	Eccl 3:8
H evil, love good	Amos 5:15
For I **h** divorce	Mal 2:16

good to those who **h**	Luke 6:27
you will be **h-d**	Luke 21:17
he who **h-s** his life	John 12:25
the very thing I **h**	Rom 7:15
Esau I **h-d**	Rom 9:13
h-ing one another	Titus 3:3
yet **h-s** his brother	1 John 2:9

HATERS *those who hate*

slanderers, **h** of God	Rom 1:30
brutal, **h** of good	2 Tim 3:3

HATRED *hate, ill will*

h for my love	Ps 109:5
H stirs up strife	Prov 10:12
who conceals **h** has	Prov 10:18

HAUGHTY *proud*

nor my eyes **h**	Ps 131:1
H eyes, a lying	Prov 6:17
h spirit before	Prov 16:18
Proud, **H**, Scoffer	Prov 21:24
wine betrays the **h**	Hab 2:5
do not be **h** in mind	Rom 12:16

HAVEN *harbor, shelter*

be a **h** for ships	Gen 49:13
to their desired **h**	Ps 107:30

HAVILAH

1 *second son of Cush*	Gen 10:7
2 *son of Joktan*	
	Gen 10:29; 1 Chr 1:23
3 *region encompassed by one of*	
Eden's rivers	Gen 2:11
4 *area in W Arabia*	Gen 25:18

HAWK *bird*

sea gull, and the **h**	Deut 14:15
h-s shall be gathered	Is 34:15

HAZAEL

anointed by Elijah	1 Kin 19:15
killed Ben Hadad	2 Kin 8:15
Aramaic king	2 Kin 8:15;9:14
defeated Israel	2 Kin 10:32

HAZOR

1 *Canaanite city in N Palestine*	
	Josh 11:11
2 *town of the Negev*	Josh 15:23
3 *Benjamite city*	Neh 11:33
4 *desert kingdom*	Jer 49:33

HEAD *chief* or *part of body*

bruise you on the **h**	Gen 3:15
anointed my **h** with oil	Ps 23:5
h a garland of grace	Prov 4:9
gray **h** is a crown	Prov 16:31
coals on his **h**	Prov 25:22
h was made bald	Ezek 29:18
had four **h-s**	Dan 7:6
an oath by your **h**	Matt 5:36
nowhere to lay His **h**	Matt 8:20
h of John the Baptist	Matt 14:8
not a hair of your **h**	Luke 21:18
crown...on His **h**	John 19:2
God is the **h** of	1 Cor 11:3
husband is the **h**	Eph 5:23

HEADLONG *headfirst*

He rushes **h** at Him	Job 15:26
falling **h**, he burst	Acts 1:18
h into the error	Jude 11

HEAL *make well, restore*

will h their land	2 Chr 7:14
h-s the brokenhearted	Ps 147:3
a time to h	Eccl 3:3
H me, O LORD	Jer 17:14
will h their apostasy	Hos 14:4
h-ed all who were	Matt 8:16
H *the sick, raise*	Matt 10:8
h him on…Sabbath	Mark 3:2
Physician, h yourself	Luke 4:23
you may be h-ed	James 5:16
fatal wound was h-ed	Rev 13:3

HEALING *health, wholeness*

be h to your body	Prov 3:8
h to the bones	Prov 16:24
sorrow is beyond h	Jer 8:18
There is no h for	Jer 46:11
their leaves for h	Ezek 47:12
h every kind of	Matt 4:23
gifts of h	1 Cor 12:9
h of the nations	Rev 22:2

HEALTH *soundness, wholeness*

no h in my bones	Ps 38:3
restore you to h	Jer 30:17
and be in good h	3 John 2

HEAP (n) *mound, pile*

stones and made a h	Gen 31:46
waters stood…like a h	Ex 15:8
made a refuse h	Ezra 6:11
needy from the ash h	Ps 113:7
Jerusalem a h of ruins	Jer 9:11
altars are…h-s	Hos 12:11

HEAP (v) *pile up, place*

h misfortunes on	Deut 32:23
will h burning coals	Prov 25:22
H on the wood	Ezek 24:10
h up rubble to	Hab 1:10

HEAR *listen*

h-d the sound of	Gen 3:10
God h-d their groaning	Ex 2:24
H, O Israel	Deut 6:4
h the wisdom of	1 Kin 4:34
h Thou in heaven	1 Kin 8:30
Will God h his cry	Job 27:9
who dost h prayer	Ps 65:2
h Thy lovingkindness	Ps 143:8
poor h-s no rebuke	Prov 13:8
deaf shall h words	Is 29:18
bones, h the word	Ezek 37:4
ears to h, let him h	Matt 11:15
h of wars and	Mark 13:7
he who h-s My word	John 5:24
does not h sinners	John 9:31
sheep h My voice	John 10:27
we h-d of your faith	Col 1:4
anyone h-s My voice	Rev 3:20

HEARING *listening*

in the LORD's h	1 Sam 8:21
in the h of a fool	Prov 23:9
fulfilled in your h	Luke 4:21
I will give you a h	Acts 23:35
become dull of h	Heb 5:11

HEART *mind or seat of emotions*

intent of man's h is	Gen 8:21
I will harden his h	Ex 4:21
great searchings of h	Judg 5:16
LORD looks at the h	1 Sam 16:7
fool has said in his h	Ps 14:1
meditation of my h	Ps 19:14
My h is like wax	Ps 22:14
in me a clean h	Ps 51:10
and a contrite h	Ps 51:17
Thy word…in my h	Ps 119:11
Deceit is in the h	Prov 12:20
A joyful h is good	Prov 17:22
to a troubled h	Prov 25:20
bribe corrupts the h	Eccl 7:7
a new h and a new	Ezek 18:31
uncircumcised in h	Ezek 44:7
are the pure in h	Matt 5:8
adultery…in his h	Matt 5:28
and humble in h	Matt 11:29
h is far…from Me	Matt 15:8
pondering…in her h	Luke 2:19
pierced to the h	Acts 2:37
cleansing their h-s	Acts 15:9
who searches the h-s	Rom 8:27
tablets of human h-s	2 Cor 3:3
not lose h in doing	Gal 6:9
melody with your h	Eph 5:19
intentions of the h	Heb 4:12
deceives his *own* h	James 1:26

HEAT *hotness, warmth*

the h of the day	Gen 18:1
and h consume	Job 24:19
hidden from its h	Ps 19:6
a shade from the h	Is 25:4
burning h of famine	Lam 5:10
scorching h of the	Matt 20:12
with intense h	2 Pet 3:10
scorched with fierce h	Rev 16:9

HEAVE OFFERING
see OFFERINGS

HEAVEN *place of God or sky*

God created the h-s	Gen 1:1
rain bread from h	Ex 16:4
shut up the h-s	Deut 11:17
thunder in the h-s	1 Sam 2:10
fire came…from h	2 Kin 1:14
make windows in h	2 Kin 7:2
walks…vault of h	Job 22:14
I consider Thy h-s	Ps 8:3
h and earth praise	Ps 69:34
fixed patterns of h	Jer 33:25
lights in the h-s	Ezek 32:8
open…windows of h	Mal 3:10
kingdom of h is at	Matt 3:2
voice out of the h-s	Matt 3:17
reward in h is great	Matt 5:12
Father who art in h	Matt 6:9
shall be loosed in h	Matt 16:19
great signs from h	Luke 21:11
Him go into h	Acts 1:11
no…name under h	Acts 4:12
up to the third h	2 Cor 12:2
citizenship is in h	Phil 3:20
there was war in h	Rev 12:7
new h and a new	Rev 21:1

HEAVENLY *related to God*

h Father is perfect	Matt 5:48
h Father knows that	Matt 6:32
h host praising God	Luke 2:13
I tell you h things	John 3:12
Him in the h *places*	Eph 2:6
partakers of a h	Heb 3:1
shadow of the h	Heb 8:5

HEAVY *burdensome, hard to lift*

Moses' hands were h	Ex 17:12
servitude was h on	Neh 5:18
h drinkers of wine	Prov 23:20
A stone is h	Prov 27:3
Jerusalem a h stone	Zech 12:3
eyes were very h	Mark 14:40

HEBER

1 *son of Beriah*	Gen 46:17
2 *husband of Jael*	Judg 4:17
3 *son of Mered*	1 Chr 4:18
4 *son of Elpaal*	1 Chr 8:17
see also EBER	

HEBREW(S)

1 *people*	
	Gen 14:13; Ex 1:15;9:13; Jon 1:9
2 *language*	
	John 19:17; Acts 22:2;26:14
see also JUDEAN	
see also CANAAN	

HEBRON

1 *site of Sarah's death*	Gen 23:2
visited by spies	Num 13:22
destroyed	Josh 10:37
city of refuge	Josh 20:7
residence of David	2 Sam 2:1
2 *son of Kohath*	Ex 6:18
3 *son of Mareshah*	1 Chr 2:42

HEDGE *border or protection*

Thou not made a h	Job 1:10
as a h of thorns	Prov 15:19
along the h-s, and	Luke 14:23

HEEL *back of foot*

bruise him on the h	Gen 3:15
on to Esau's h	Gen 25:26
his h against Me	John 13:18

HEIFER *young cow*

unblemished red h	Num 19:2
plowed with my h	Judg 14:18
Egypt is a pretty h	Jer 46:20
Like a stubborn h	Hos 4:16

HEIGHT *elevation, heaven, sky*

in the h of heaven	Job 22:12
from His holy h	Ps 102:19
Praise Him in the h-s	Ps 148:1
As the heavens for h	Prov 25:3
ascend above the h-s	Is 14:14
nor h, nor depth	Rom 8:39

HEIR *person who inherits*

in my house is my h	Gen 15:3
has no h-s	Jer 49:1
h-s also, h-s of God	Rom 8:17
an h through God	Gal 4:7
h-s of the kingdom	James 2:5

HELIOPOLIS

ancient Egyptian city	Jer 43:13
also ON	

HELL *place of dead*

go into the fiery **h**	Matt 5:22
soul and body in **h**	Matt 10:28
to be cast into **h**	Mark 9:47
set on fire by **h**	James 3:6
cast them into **h**	2 Pet 2:4

see also **HADES** and **SHEOL**

HELLENISTIC JEWS

Greek speaking Jews

        Acts 6:1;9:29

HELMET *headpiece*

bronze **h** on his	1 Sam 17:5
h of salvation	Is 59:17
take the **h** of	Eph 6:17

HELP (n) *assistance, relief*

h is not within me	Job 6:13
He is our **h** and our	Ps 33:20
present **h** in trouble	Ps 46:1
I cried for **h**	Jon 2:2
gifts of…**h-s**	1 Cor 12:28

HELP (v) *aid, assist*

h-ing the Hebrew	Ex 1:16
the LORD **h-ed** David	2 Sam 8:6
whence shall my **h**	Ps 121:1
I will **h** you	Is 41:13
Lord, **h** me	Matt 15:25
h my unbelief	Mark 9:24
must **h** the weak	Acts 20:35
Spirit also **h-s** our	Rom 8:26
earth **h-ed** the	Rev 12:16

HELPER *one who assists*

h of the orphan	Ps 10:14
be Thou my **h**	Ps 30:10
Behold, God is my **h**	Ps 54:4
give you another **H**	John 14:16
H, the Holy Spirit	John 14:26

HELPLESS *weak*

the **h** has hope	Job 5:16
who considers the **h**	Ps 41:1
while we were still **h**	Rom 5:6

HEMAN

1 *sage of Solomon*	1 Kin 4:31
2 *line of Samuel*	1 Chr 15:19

HEMORRHAGE *bleeding*

suffering from a **h**	Matt 9:20
a **h** for twelve years	Mark 5:25
her **h** stopped	Luke 8:44

HEN *fowl*

h gathers her	Matt 23:37
as a **h** *gathers* her	Luke 13:34

HEPHZIBAH

Manasseh's mother	2 Kin 21:1
Hezekiah's wife	2 Kin 21:3

HERB *dried plant*

bread and bitter **h-s**	Ex 12:8
fade like the green **h**	Ps 37:2
h-s of…mountains	Prov 27:25
sweet-scented **h-s**	Song 5:13

HERD *cattle, flock*

first-born of your **h**	Deut 12:6
h, or flock taste a	Jon 3:7
h of many swine	Matt 8:30

HERDSMEN *keepers of flocks*

h of Abram's livestock	Gen 13:7
between my **h** and	Gen 13:8
the **h** ran away	Matt 8:33

HERITAGE *what is inherited*

the **h** decreed to him	Job 20:29
my **h** is beautiful	Ps 16:6
their land as a **h**	Ps 136:21
inherit the desolate **h-s**	Is 49:8
you who pillage My **h**	Jer 50:11

HERMES

1 *Greek god*	Acts 14:12
2 *Roman Christian*	Rom 16:14

HERMOGENES

Asian Christian who failed to
support Paul   2 Tim 1:15

HERMON

mountain region in N Palestine
     Josh 11:17; Ps 42:6;133:3
N boundary of Promised Land
           Deut 3:8

HEROD

1 **Herod the Great**
   king of Judea   Matt 2:1
   ruled during Jesus' birth
            Matt 2:1ff

2 **Herod Archelaus**
   son of Herod the Great
            Matt 2:22

3 **Herod Antipas**
   son of Herod the Great
            Matt 14:1
   tetrarch of Galilee   Luke 3:1
   ruled at time of Jesus' ministry
      Luke 13:31;23:7,8,11
   executed John the Baptist
     Matt 14:10; Mark 6:27

4 **Herod Philip I**
   brother of Herod Antipas
   son of Herod the Great
            Mark 6:17

5 **Herod Philip II**
   son of Herod the Great
            Luke 3:1

6 **Herod Agrippa I**
   grandson of Herod the Great
            Acts 12:1
   ruler of Judea and Samaria
   persecuted the early church
           Acts 12:2-23

7 **Herod Agrippa II**
   son of Agrippa I   Acts 25:13
   tetrarch of N Palestine
   heard Paul's testimony
      Acts 25:23ff;26:1ff

HERODIANS

influential Jews favoring Herod
     Matt 22:16; Mark 3:6

HERODIAS

wife of Herod Antipas
     Matt 14:3; Mark 6:17
requested head of John the Baptist
     Matt 14:8; Mark 6:24

HETH

1 *son of Canaan*   Gen 10:15

2 *Hebrew eponym for Hittites*
           Gen 23:10

HEW *chop, cut*

h down their Asherim	Deut 7:5
H-n cisterns, vineyards	
	Neh 9:25
h-n out in the rock	Mark 15:46

HEZEKIAH

king of Judah	2 Kin 18:1
reformer	2 Kin 18:4
warrior	2 Kin 18:7,8
builder	2 Kin 20:20

HIDE *conceal, cover*

man and his wife **hid**	Gen 3:8
I **h** from Abraham	Gen 18:17
Moses **hid** his face	Ex 3:6
h me in Sheol	Job 14:13
h-ing my iniquity	Job 31:33
H me in the shadow	Ps 17:8
Do not **h** Thy face	Ps 27:9
wrongs are not **h-den**	Ps 69:5
sees evil *and* **h-s**	Prov 27:12
hid your talent	Matt 25:25
nothing is **h-den**	Mark 4:22
Jesus **hid** Himself	John 8:59
h us from…Him	Rev 6:16

HIDDEN (adj) *concealed*

Acquit me of **h** *faults*	Ps 19:12
h wealth of secret	Is 45:3
h snares for my feet	Jer 18:22
profound and **h**	Dan 2:22
some of the **h** manna	Rev 2:17

HIDING PLACE

Clouds are a **h**	Job 22:14
He lurks in a **h**	Ps 10:9
Thou art my **h**	Ps 32:7
uncovered his **h-s**	Jer 49:10

HIERAPOLIS

city in Asia Minor   Col 4:13

HIGH *elevated* or *heavenly*

it is still **h** day	Gen 29:7
the **h** places of Baal	Num 22:41
h above all nations	Deut 26:19
h as the heavens	Job 11:8
my advocate is on **h**	Job 16:19
set him *securely* on **h**	Ps 91:14
or **h** as heaven	Is 7:11
to a very **h** mountain	Matt 4:8
the **h** priest	Matt 26:57
Son of the Most **H**	Mark 5:7
from a **h** fever	Luke 4:38
He ascended on **h**	Eph 4:8

HIGH PLACE

worship place of God or idols
     Num 22:41; 1 Sam 9:12-14

HIGH PRIEST

first in hierarchy	Ex 27:21
under Aaron	Ex 28:1,2
enters Holy of Holies	
	Ex 28:29,30; Heb 9:7
head of Sanhedrin	
	Matt 26:57; Acts 5:21
Jesus as High Priest	
	Heb 3:1;5:5-9

HIGHWAY *road*

along the king's **h** Num 20:17
h from Egypt to Is 19:23
the **H** of Holiness Is 35:8
a **h** for our God Is 40:3
Go out into the **h-s** Luke 14:23

HILKIAH

1 *father of Eliakim* 2 Kin 18:18
2 *high priest* 2 Kin 22:4-14
3 *Merarite Levite* 1 Chr 6:45
4 *son of Hosah* 1 Chr 26:11
5 *was with Ezra* Neh 8:4
6 *returned from exile* Neh 12:7

HILL *mountain*

the everlasting **h-s** Gen 49:26
the **h** of God 1 Sam 10:5
dwell on Thy holy **h** Ps 15:1
to Thy holy **h** Ps 43:3
cattle...thousand **h-s** Ps 50:10
h-s, Fall on us Hos 10:8
city set on a **h** Matt 5:14
h...brought low Luke 3:5
the brow of the **h** Luke 4:29
h-s, Cover us Luke 23:30

HINDER *delay, impede, restrain*

h meditation before Job 15:4
do not **h** them Matt 19:14
do not **h** them Luke 18:16
h-ed you from obeying Gal 5:7
prayers...not be **h-ed** 1 Pet 3:7

HINNOM

1 *valley SW of Jerusalem*
Josh 15:8; Neh 11:30
2 *person for whom valley named*
2 Kin 23:10; Jer 7:31

HIP *part of body*

the sinew of the **h** Gen 32:32
curves of your **h-s** are Song 7:1
h joints went slack Dan 5:6

HIRAM / HURAM

1 *king of Tyre*
1 Kin 5:1ff; 2 Chr 2:3,11
2 *skilled craftsman*
1 Kin 7:14; 2 Chr 4:11

HIRE (n) *wages*

it came for its **h** Ex 22:15
the **h** of a harlot Deut 23:18

HIRE (v) *engage for labor*

h...for bread 1 Sam 2:5
and **h-d** the Arameans
2 Sam 10:6
to **h**...chariots 1 Chr 19:6
he who **h-s** a fool Prov 26:10
to **h** laborers for Matt 20:1

HIRED (adj) *employed*

as a **h** man, as if Lev 25:40
oppress a **h** servant Deut 24:14
as one of your **h** Luke 15:19

HIRELING *employee*

h...not a shepherd John 10:12
because he is a **h** John 10:13

HISS *to show dislike*

h him from his place Job 27:23

object of...**h-ing** Jer 18:16
They **h** and shake Lam 2:15
h *And* wave his hand Zeph 2:15

HITTITES

1 *people in Palestine in
patriarchal age*
Gen 15:20;49:29
2 *inhabitants of Aram during
Israelite monarchy*
2 Kin 7:6; 2 Chr 8:7

HIVITES

*people dispossessed by the
Israelites*
Ex 23:28; Josh 3:10;
2 Sam 24:7

HOGLAH

daughter of Zelophehad
Num 26:33;27:1; Josh 17:3

HOLD *grasp, retain*

Moses **held** his hand Ex 17:11
h fast to Him Deut 11:22
h fast...evil purpose Ps 64:5
heart **h** fast my words Prov 4:4
Take **h** of instruction Prov 4:13
h to one and despise Matt 6:24
h to the tradition Mark 7:8
h fast the word 1 Cor 15:2
h-ing to the mystery 1 Tim 3:9
h of the eternal 1 Tim 6:12
He **held** seven stars Rev 1:16

HOLE *opening*

the **h** of the cobra Is 11:8
a **h** in the wall Ezek 8:7
a purse with **h-s** Hag 1:6
foxes have **h-s** Matt 8:20

HOLIDAY *period of leisure*

a feast and a **h** Esth 8:17
a **h** for rejoicing Esth 9:19
mourning into a **h** Esth 9:22

HOLINESS *sacredness*

majestic in **h** Ex 15:11
H befits Thy house Ps 93:5
the Highway of **H** Is 35:8
unblamable in **h** 1 Thess 3:13
we may share His **h** Heb 12:10

HOLLOW *empty space*

the **h** of a sling 1 Sam 25:29
in the **h** of His hand Is 40:12

HOLY *sacred, sanctified*

standing is **h** ground Ex 3:5
sabbath...keep it **h** Ex 20:8
you are a **h** people Deut 7:6
ten thousand **h** ones Deut 33:2
h like the LORD 1 Sam 2:2
Worship...**h** array 1 Chr 16:29
His **h** dwelling 2 Chr 30:27
Jerusalem, the **h** city Neh 11:1
Zion, My **h** mountain Ps 2:6
to His **h** land Ps 78:54
bless His **h** name Ps 145:21
H, H, H, is the LORD Is 6:3
the **H** One of Israel Is 30:15
what is **h** to dogs Matt 7:6

righteous and **h** man Mark 6:20
the **H** One of God Luke 4:34
in the **h** Scriptures Rom 1:2
and **h** sacrifice Rom 12:1
with a **h** kiss Rom 16:16
h both in body 1 Cor 7:34
lifting up **h** hands 1 Tim 2:8
with a **h** calling 2 Tim 1:9
I saw the **h** city Rev 21:2

HOLY OF HOLIES

*most holy place in the Tabernacle /
Temple* Ex 26:33,34; 2 Chr 3:8

HOLY SPIRIT

Third Person of the Godhead
Matt 28:19; 2 Cor 13:14
Helper John 14:16,26
Giver of gifts
Rom 12:6-8; 1 Cor 12:8-11
fruit of the Spirit Gal 5:22

HOMAGE *act of reverence*

my people shall do **h** Gen 41:40
did **h** to the LORD 1 Chr 29:20
and paid **h** to Haman Esth 3:2
did **h** to Daniel Dan 2:46

HOME *place of dwelling*

free at **h** one year Deut 24:5
God makes a **h** Ps 68:6
man is not at **h** Prov 7:19
to his eternal **h** Eccl 12:5
Go **h** to your people Mark 5:19
let him eat at **h** 1 Cor 11:34
at **h** in the body 2 Cor 5:6
at **h** with the Lord 2 Cor 5:8

HOMER *measure of capacity*

a **h** of barley Lev 27:16
a **h** of seed Is 5:10
from a **h** of wheat Ezek 45:13

HOMESTEAD *family dwelling*

h forlorn and forsaken Is 27:10
guards his own **h** Luke 11:21
h be made desolate Acts 1:20

HOMOSEXUALS

effeminate, nor **h** 1 Cor 6:9
immoral men and **h** 1 Tim 1:10

HONEST *respectable, truthful*

we are **h** men Gen 42:11
painful are **h** words Job 6:25
an **h** and good heart Luke 8:15

HONEY *sweetness*

with milk and **h** Ex 3:8
swarm of bees and **h** Judg 14:8
is sweeter than **h** Judg 14:18
sweet as **h** in my Ezek 3:3
locusts and wild **h** Matt 3:4

HONEYCOMB *honey storage*

drippings of the **h** Ps 19:10
Pleasant words...a **h** Prov 16:24

HONOR (n) *glory, great respect*

both riches and **h** 1 Kin 3:13
stripped my **h** from Job 19:9
wise will inherit **h** Prov 3:35
is not without **h** Matt 13:57
glory and **h** and Rom 2:10

marriage *be held* in **h**   Heb 13:4
blessing and **h** and   Rev 5:13

HONOR (v) *show respect*

H your father   Ex 20:12
h the aged   Lev 19:32
who **h** Me I will **h**   1 Sam 2:30
am **h**-ed in the sight   Is 49:5
A son **h**-s *his* father   Mal 1:6
may be **h**-ed by men   Matt 6:2
h-s Me with...lips   Matt 15:8
does not **h** the Son   John 5:23
fear God, **h** the king   1 Pet 2:17

HONORABLE *respectable*

the elder and **h** man   Is 9:15
one vessel for **h** use   Rom 9:21
whatever is **h**   Phil 4:8

HOOF *part of animal foot*

which divide the **h**   Lev 11:4
with horns and **h**-s   Ps 69:31
h-s of beasts shall   Ezek 32:13
tear off their **h**-s   Zech 11:16

HOOK *fastener*

into pruning **h**-s   Is 2:4
My **h** in your nose   Is 37:29
h-s into your jaws   Ezek 38:4

HOPE (n) *expectation*

Where now is my **h**   Job 17:15
h of the afflicted   Ps 9:18
My **h** is in Thee   Ps 39:7
Thou art my **h**   Ps 71:5
while there is **h**   Prov 19:18
the **h** of Israel   Jer 17:13
our **h** has perished   Ezek 37:11
on trial for the **h**   Acts 23:6
h does not disappoint   Rom 5:5
rejoicing in **h**   Rom 12:12
may the God of **h**   Rom 15:13
ought to plow in **h**   1 Cor 9:10
now abide faith, **h**   1 Cor 13:13
h of righteousness   Gal 5:5
the **h** of His calling   Eph 1:18
the **h** of the gospel   Col 1:23
the **h** of glory   Col 1:27
the **h** of salvation   1 Thess 5:8
h of eternal life   Titus 3:7
to a living **h**   1 Pet 1:3
h that is in you   1 Pet 3:15

HOPE (v) *expect with confidence*

I will **h** in Him   Job 13:15
For I **h** in Thee   Ps 38:15
We **h** for justice   Is 59:11
are **h**-ing for light   Jer 13:16
Gentiles will **h**   Matt 12:21
h-s all things   1 Cor 13:7
first to **h** in Christ   Eph 1:12
I **h** in the Lord Jesus   Phil 2:19
of *things* **h**-d for   Heb 11:1
I **h** to come to you   2 John 12

HOPHNI

son of Eli   1 Sam 1:3;4:11

HOPHRA

see **PHARAOH**

HOR

mountain   Num 20:22,23

place of Aaron's death
   Num 20:28; Deut 32:50

HORDE *throng*

against Babylon A **h**   Jer 50:9
h-s of grasshoppers   Nah 3:17

HOREB

another name for Mount Sinai
   Ex 3:1; Deut 4:10; Ps 106:19

HORITES

*inhabitants of Mount Seir in
Edom*   Gen 14:6;36:29

HORN

caught...by his **h**-s   Gen 22:13
h-s of the altar   Ex 29:12
you shall sound a **h**   Lev 25:9
with the ram's **h**   Josh 6:5
h of my salvation   2 Sam 22:3
the **h**, flute, lyre   Dan 3:5
it had ten **h**-s   Dan 7:7

HORROR *terror*

h overwhelms me   Is 21:4
object of **h**   Jer 49:13
clothed with **h**   Ezek 7:27
cup of **h**   Ezek 23:33

HORSE *animal*

bites the **h**-'s heels   Gen 49:17
h-s and chariots of   2 Kin 6:17
A **h** is a false hope   Ps 33:17
whip is for the **h**   Prov 26:3
slaves *riding* on **h**-s   Eccl 10:7
behold, a black **h**   Rev 6:5

HORSE GATE

see **GATES OF JERUSALEM**

HORSEMEN *cavalry, horse rider*

Pharaoh, his **h** and   Ex 14:9
chariots and **h**   1 Kin 10:26
h riding on   Ezek 23:12
H charging, Swords   Nah 3:3
armies of the **h**   Rev 9:16

HOSANNA *acclamation of praise*

H to the Son of   Matt 21:9
H in the highest   Mark 11:10
H! Blessed is He   John 12:13

HOSEA

prophet   Hos 1:1,2

HOSHEA

1 *name of Joshua*   Num 13:8,16
2 *king of Israel*
   2 Kin 15:30;17:6
3 *Ephraim's officer*   1 Chr 27:20
4 *signer of covenant*   Neh 10:23

HOSPITABLE *friendly*

h, able to teach   1 Tim 3:2
h, loving what is   Titus 1:8
h to one another   1 Pet 4:9

HOSPITALITY *open to guests*

practicing **h**   Rom 12:13
show **h** to strangers   Heb 13:2

HOST *army, multitude*

all the **h** of heaven   Deut 4:19
captain...LORD's **h**   Josh 5:15

LORD of **h**-s, He is   Ps 24:10
of the heavenly **h**   Luke 2:13

HOSTILE *antagonistic*

h to...Jesus   Acts 26:9
set on the flesh is **h**   Rom 8:7
h to all men   1 Thess 2:15

HOT *very warm, violent*

when the sun grew **h**   Ex 16:21
and **h** displeasure   Deut 9:19
My heart was **h** within   Ps 39:3
man walk on **h** coals   Prov 6:28
neither cold nor **h**   Rev 3:15

HOUR *time*

healed that *very* **h**   Matt 8:13
watch...for one **h**   Matt 26:40
the **h** is at hand   Matt 26:45
ninth **h** Jesus cried   Mark 15:34
save Me from this **h**   John 12:27
the **h** has come   John 17:1
the **h** of testing   Rev 3:10

HOUSE *home or temple*

born in my **h** is my   Gen 15:3
passed over the **h**-s   Ex 12:27
the **h** of slavery   Ex 20:2
consecrates his **h**   Lev 27:14
as for me and my **h**   Josh 24:15
Set your **h** in order   2 Kin 20:1
h of God forsaken   Neh 13:11
h like the spider's   Job 27:18
Holiness befits Thy **h**   Ps 93:5
LORD builds the **h**   Ps 127:1
Wisdom...built her **h**   Prov 9:1
in My **h** of prayer   Is 56:7
O **h** of Israel   Jer 18:6
his **h** upon the rock   Matt 7:24
My **h**...a **h** of   Matt 21:13
devour widow's **h**-s   Mark 12:40
left **h** or wife or   Luke 18:29
In My Father's **h**   John 14:2
h not made...hands   2 Cor 5:1
h for a holy   1 Pet 2:5

HOUSE OF GOD / LORD

see **TEMPLE**

HOUSE OF THE LORD

see **TABERNACLE**

HOUSEHOLD *family, home*

herds and a great **h**   Gen 26:14
stole the **h** idols   Gen 31:19
each one with his **h**   Ex 1:1
to the ways of her **h**   Prov 31:27
like a head of a **h**   Matt 13:52
are of God's **h**   Eph 2:19
manages his own **h**   1 Tim 3:4
in the **h** of God   1 Tim 3:15

HOUSETOP *roof*

As grass on the **h**-s   2 Kin 19:26
lonely bird on a **h**   Ps 102:7
upon the **h**-s   Matt 10:27
Peter went...the **h**   Acts 10:9

HULDAH

a Hebrew prophetess
   2 Kin 22:14; 2 Chr 34:22

HUMAN *mankind, person*

the life of any **h**   Lev 24:17

HUMBLE

guilt of **h** blood	Prov 28:17
they had **h** form	Ezek 1:5
tablets of **h** hearts	2 Cor 3:3

HUMBLE (adj) *gentle, modest*

Moses was very **h**	Num 12:3
h will inherit	Ps 37:11
with the **h** is wisdom	Prov 11:2
H, and mounted on	Zech 9:9
gentle and **h** in	Matt 11:29
along with **h** means	Phil 4:12
grace to the **h**	James 4:6

HUMBLE (v) *modest*

refuse to **h** yourself	Ex 10:3
He might **h** you	Deut 8:2
h...and pray	2 Chr 7:14
h-s...as this child	Matt 18:4
H yourselves	1 Pet 5:6

HUMILIATE *embarrass*

h-d who seek my hurt	Ps 71:24
Neither feel **h-d**	Is 54:4
His opponents...**h-d**	Luke 13:17

HUMILIATION *embarrassment*

h has overwhelmed me	Ps 44:15
go away together in **h**	Is 45:16
let our **h** cover us	Jer 3:25
In **h** His judgment	Acts 8:33

HUMILITY *self-abasement*

before honor...**h**	Prov 15:33
with **h** of mind	Phil 2:3
clothe...with **h**	1 Pet 5:5

HUNDRED *number* or *many*

Adam had lived one **h**	Gen 5:3
h of you will chase	Lev 26:8
captains of **h-s**	Num 31:14
h pieces of money	Josh 24:32
went out by **h-s**	2 Sam 18:4
in companies of **h-s**	Mark 6:40

HUNGER (n) *craving, starvation*

in **h**, in thirst	Deut 28:48
lions...suffer **h**	Ps 34:10
man will suffer **h**	Prov 19:15
h is not satisfied	Is 29:8
faint because of **h**	Lam 2:19
sleeplessness, in **h**	2 Cor 6:5

HUNGER (v) *crave, need food*

the righteous to **h**	Prov 10:3
are those who **h**	Matt 5:6
to Me shall not **h**	John 6:35
They shall **h** no more	Rev 7:16

HUNGRY *empty, needing food*

let you be **h**	Deut 8:3
people are **h** and	2 Sam 17:29
h soul He has filled	Ps 107:9
If your enemy is **h**	Prov 25:21
when a **h** man dreams	Is 29:8
He then became **h**	Matt 4:2
disciples became **h**	Matt 12:1
For I was **h**	Matt 25:35
if your enemy is **h**	Rom 12:20

HUNT *pursue, seek*

to **h** for game	Gen 27:5
h-s a partridge	1 Sam 26:20
evil **h** the violent	Ps 140:11
H-ed me down like	Lam 3:52

| companions **h-ed** for | Mark 1:36 |

HUNTER *seeker of game*

| Nimrod a mighty **h** | Gen 10:9 |
| became a skillful **h** | Gen 25:27 |

HUR

1 *helped Moses and Aaron*
         Ex 17:12;24:14
2 *Bezalel's grandfather* Ex 31:2
3 *king of Midian* Num 31:8
4 *father of Rephaiah* Neh 3:9

HURAM

a Benjamite 1 Chr 8:5
see also **HIRAM / HURAM**

HURT (n) *damage, harm, wound*

Who delight in my **h**	Ps 70:2
hoarded...to his **h**	Eccl 5:13
your brother is **h**	Rom 14:15

HURT (v) *cause pain, wound*

not allow him to **h**	Gen 31:7
may be **h** by them	Eccl 10:9
will not **h** or destroy	Is 11:9
their power to **h** men	Rev 9:10

HUSBAND *family head, spouse*

desire...your **h**	Gen 3:16
honor to their **h-s**	Esth 1:20
crown of her **h**	Prov 12:4
is loved by *her* **h**	Hos 3:1
divorces her **h** and	Mark 10:12
have had five **h-s**	John 4:18
if her **h** dies	Rom 7:2
have her own **h**	1 Cor 7:2
unbelieving **h** is	1 Cor 7:14
h is the head of	Eph 5:23
H-s, love your wives	Eph 5:25
h-s of...one wife	1 Tim 3:12
adorned for her **h**	Rev 21:2

HUSHAI

servant of David
         2 Sam 15:32; 16:17

HYMENAEUS

heretical teacher at Ephesus
         1 Tim 1:20; 2 Tim 2:17

HYMN *song of praise*

h-s of thanksgiving	Neh 12:46
after singing a **h**	Matt 26:30
singing **h-s** of praise	Acts 16:25
psalms and **h-s** and	Eph 5:19

HYPOCRISY *pretense*

full of **h** and	Matt 23:28
love be without **h**	Rom 12:9
without **h**	James 3:17

HYPOCRITE *a pretender*

as the **h-s** do	Matt 6:2
and Pharisees, **h-s**	Matt 23:13
You **h**, first take	Luke 6:42

HYSSOP *fragrant plant*

bunch of **h** and dip it	Ex 12:22
scarlet string and **h**	Lev 14:4
Purify me with **h**	Ps 51:7
upon *a branch of* **h**	John 19:29

I

I AM

related to name of God in Hebrew
I WHO I	Ex 3:14
I has sent me	Ex 3:14
I the LORD	Ex 6:2
I the LORD your God	Lev 19:3
I the first	Is 44:6
I the Son of God	Matt 27:43
Jesus said, I	Mark 14:62
believe that I *He*	John 8:24
will know that I *He*	John 8:28
before Abraham...I	John 8:58
believe that I *He*	John 13:19
I the Alpha and	Rev 1:8
I the first and	Rev 1:17

ICE *frost*

turbid because of i	Job 6:16
womb has come...i	Job 38:29
casts forth His i	Ps 147:17

ICHABOD

1 *son of Phinehas* 1 Sam 4:19,20
  grandson of Eli 1 Sam 14:3
2 *name commemorates departed*
  glory from Israel
         1 Sam 4:21,22

ICONIUM

city of Asia Minor
  Acts 14:1,19; 16:2; 2 Tim 3:11

IDLE *unemployed, uninvolved*

i man will suffer	Prov 19:15
been standing here i	Matt 20:6
this i babbler	Acts 17:18

IDOL *false deity, image*

not make...an i	Ex 20:4
Do not turn to i-s	Lev 19:4
who makes an i or	Deut 27:15
the gods...are i-s	Ps 96:5
who blesses an i	Is 66:3
abstain from...i-s	Acts 15:20
guard...from i-s	1 John 5:21

IDOLATOR *idol worshiper*

covetous, or an i	1 Cor 5:11
do not be i-s	1 Cor 10:7
sorcerers and i-s	Rev 21:8

IDOLATRY *idol worship*

flee from i	1 Cor 10:14
i, sorcery, enmities	Gal 5:20
and abominable i-ies	1 Pet 4:3

IGNORANCE *lack of knowledge*

you worship in i	Acts 17:23
i that is in them	Eph 4:18
silence the i of	1 Pet 2:15

IGNORANT *without knowledge*

I was senseless and i	Ps 73:22
not i of his schemes	2 Cor 2:11
and i speculations	2 Tim 2:23

ILL *unhealthy, sick*

woman who is i	Lev 15:33
became mortally i	Is 38:1
lunatic, and is...i	Matt 17:15
healed many...i	Mark 1:34

ILLEGITIMATE *bastard*
No one of i birth	Deut 23:2
borne i children	Hos 5:7
you are i children	Heb 12:8

ILLNESS *infirmity, sickness*
sick with the i	2 Kin 13:14
after his i and	Is 38:9
because of a bodily i	Gal 4:13

ILLUMINE *light up*
God i-s my darkness	Ps 18:28
fire to i by night	Ps 105:39
glory of God has i-d	Rev 21:23
God shall i them	Rev 22:5

IMAGE *copy, likeness*
make man in Our i	Gen 1:26
i of God He made	Gen 9:6
burn their graven i-s	Deut 7:5
worshiped a molten i	Ps 106:19
made an i of gold	Dan 3:1
i and glory of God	1 Cor 11:7
i of the invisible	Col 1:15
the i of the beast	Rev 13:15

IMITATORS *followers*
be i of me	1 Cor 4:16
be i of God	Eph 5:1
i of the churches	1 Thess 2:14

IMMANUEL
1 *son born to a virgin*	Is 7:14
a sign to King Ahaz	Is 8:8
2 *title of Jesus*	Matt 1:23

IMMORAL *lewd, unchaste*
with i people	1 Cor 5:9
the i man sins	1 Cor 6:18
i men...liars	1 Tim 1:10
i or godless person	Heb 12:16
and i persons	Rev 21:8

IMMORALITY *immoral acts*
no i in your midst	Lev 20:14
except for i	Matt 19:9
Flee i	1 Cor 6:18
abstain from...i	1 Thess 4:3
the wine of her i	Rev 17:2

IMMORTALITY *everlasting life*
must put on i	1 Cor 15:53
alone possess i	1 Tim 6:16
life and i to light	2 Tim 1:10

IMPATIENT *restless*
the people became i	Num 21:4
should I not be i	Job 21:4
my soul was i with	Zech 11:8

IMPERISHABLE *indestructable*
wreath, but we an i	1 Cor 9:25
will be raised i	1 Cor 15:52
inheritance...is i	1 Pet 1:4

IMPLEMENTS *tools, utensils*
forger of all i of	Gen 4:22
the i of the oxen	1 Kin 19:21

IMPLORE *ask, beseech*
I i you, give glory	Josh 7:19
i-d him to avert	Esth 8:3
i the compassion of	Job 8:5
I i You by God	Mark 5:7

IMPORTED *brought in*
chariot was i from	1 Kin 10:29
horses were i	2 Chr 1:16

IMPOSE *force upon*
i-d hard labor on us	Deut 26:6
whatever you i on	2 Kin 18:14
you i heavy rent	Amos 5:11
i-d until a time of	Heb 9:10

IMPOSSIBLE *cannot be done*
nothing...will be i	Gen 11:6
With men this is i	Matt 19:26
i for God to lie	Heb 6:18
without faith it is i	Heb 11:6

IMPRISON *jail, restrict*
i-ed him at Riblah	2 Kin 23:33
i his princes at will	Ps 105:22
not i their survivors	Obad 14
I used to i and beat	Acts 22:19

IMPRISONMENT *confinement*
in i-s, in tumults	2 Cor 6:5
Remember my i	Col 4:18
even to i as a	2 Tim 2:9

IMPURE *unclean*
her i discharge	Lev 15:25
eating...with i hands	Mark 7:2
no immoral or i person	Eph 5:5

IMPURITY *uncleanness*
menstrual i for seven	Lev 15:19
i-ies of the sons of	Lev 16:19
the i of the nations	Ezra 6:21
as slaves to i	Rom 6:19
of i with greediness	Eph 4:19

INCENSE *fragrant substance*
burn frangrant i on	Ex 30:7
i as an offering	Lev 2:16
gold pans, full of i	Num 7:86
My altar, to burn i	1 Sam 2:28
i on the high places	2 Kin 14:4
i before the LORD	1 Chr 23:13
golden altar of i	Heb 9:4
the smoke of the i	Rev 8:4

INCEST *illicit sexual relations*
they...committed i	Lev 20:12

INCITE *stir up*
i-d David against	2 Sam 24:1
Jezebel...i-d him	1 Kin 21:25
I will i Egyptians	Is 19:2
who i-s the people	Luke 23:14

INCLINE *bend, lean*
i your hearts to	Josh 24:23
I my heart to Thy	Ps 119:36
i-s toward wickedness	Is 32:6
I Thine ear, O LORD	Is 37:17
have not i-d your ear	Jer 35:15

INCOME *wages*
i of the wicked	Prov 10:16
i with injustice	Prov 16:8
abundance *with its* i	Eccl 5:10

INCORRUPTIBLE *not impure*
glory of the i God	Rom 1:23
Christ with *a love* i	Eph 6:24

INCREASE (n) *multiplication*
the i of your herd	Deut 7:13
the i of your house	1 Sam 2:33
the LORD give you i	Ps 115:14
i of *His* government	Is 9:7

INCREASE (v) *multiply*
If riches i, do not	Ps 62:10
the righteous i	Prov 28:28
i-ing in wisdom	Luke 2:52
i-ng in...knowledge	Col 1:10
Lord cause...to i	1 Thess 3:12

INCURABLE *fatal, without cure*
with an i sickness	2 Chr 21:18
sickliness and i pain	Is 17:11
Your wound is i	Jer 30:12

INDIA
lower Indus valley in S Asia
Esth 1:1;8:9

INDIGNANT *be angry*
i toward His enemies	Is 66:14
the ten became i	Matt 20:24
Jesus...was i	Mark 10:14
i because Jesus had	Luke 13:14

INDIGNATION *anger*
God who has i	Ps 7:11
Pour out Thine i	Ps 69:24
lips are filled with i	Is 30:27
didst fill me with i	Jer 15:17
stand before His i	Nah 1:6

INDWELLS *inhabits*
but sin which i me	Rom 7:17
His Spirit who i you	Rom 8:11

INFANT *child*
carries a nursing i	Num 11:12
an i *who lives*	Is 65:20
tongue of the i	Lam 4:4
the mouth of i-s	Matt 21:16

INFECTION *disease*
an i of leprosy	Lev 13:2
with the scaly i	Lev 13:31
against an i of	Deut 24:8

INFERIOR *lower in status*
I am not i to you	Job 12:3
i against the honorable	Is 3:5
i to...apostles	2 Cor 12:11

INFINITE *unlimited*
His understanding is i	Ps 147:5

INFLICT *strike, impose*
frogs...He had i-ed	Ex 8:12
i all these curses	Deut 30:7
i-s pain, and gives	Job 5:18
i-ed many blows	Acts 16:23

INGATHERING, FEAST OF
see FEASTS

INHABIT *dwell*
no one would i	Job 15:28
She shall be i-ed	Is 44:26
build houses and i	Is 65:21
those i-ing the desert	Jer 9:26
who i the coastlands	Ezek 39:6
but not i them	Zeph 1:13

INHABITANT resident

i-s of the cities	Gen 19:25
cities...without i	Is 6:11
ruins Without i	Jer 4:7
i-s of the seacoast	Zeph 2:5
i-s of Jerusalem	Zech 12:10

INHERIT receive a legacy

shall i it forever	Ex 32:13
humble will i the land	Ps 37:11
wise will i honor	Prov 3:35
The naive i folly	Prov 14:18
gentle...i the earth	Matt 5:5
do to i the earth	Luke 10:25
not i the kingdom	1 Cor 6:9
might i a blessing	1 Pet 3:9
who overcomes shall i	Rev 21:7

INHERITANCE bequest, legacy

Levites for an i	Num 18:24
the LORD is his i	Deut 10:9
the nations as Thine i	Ps 2:8
will He forsake His i	Ps 94:14
man leaves an i	Prov 13:22
I...abandoned My i	Jer 12:7
Thine i a reproach	Joel 2:17
A man and his i	Mic 2:2
the i will be ours	Mark 12:7
we...obtained an i	Eph 1:11
the i of the saints	Col 1:12
i...imperishable	1 Pet 1:4

INIQUITY injustice, wickedness

bear...their i-ies	Lev 16:22
the i of the fathers	Deut 5:9
those who plow i	Job 4:8
O LORD, Pardon my i	Ps 25:11
my i I did not hide	Ps 32:5
blot out all my i-ies	Ps 51:9
sows i will reap	Prov 22:8
weighed down with i	Is 1:4
the workers of i	Is 31:2
die for his own i	Jer 31:30
Repent...so that i	Ezek 18:30
the bondage of i	Acts 8:23
the very world of i	James 3:6
remembered her i-ies	Rev 18:5

INJUNCTION decree

establish the i	Dan 6:8
that no i or statute	Dan 6:15

INJURE harm, wrong

who seek to i me	Ps 38:12
i-d your neighbors	Ezek 22:12
nothing shall i you	Luke 10:19
do you i one another	Acts 7:26

INJURY wound

there is no further i	Ex 21:22
because of my i	Jer 10:19
no i...was found	Dan 6:23

INJUSTICE inequity, unfairness

do no i in judgment	Lev 19:15
A God...without i	Deut 32:4
there i on my tongue	Job 6:30
They devise i-s	Ps 64:6
is no i with God	Rom 9:14

INK writing liquid

I wrote them with i	Jer 36:18
with pen and i	3 John 13

INN lodge for travelers

no room...in the i	Luke 2:7
brought him to...i	Luke 10:34

INNKEEPER traveler's host

gave them to the i	Luke 10:35

INNOCENCE blamelessness

wash my hands in i	Ps 26:6
be incapable of i	Hos 8:5

INNOCENT blameless

do not kill the i	Ex 23:7
the blood of the i	Deut 19:13
i before the LORD	2 Sam 3:28
the i mock them	Job 22:19
that shed i blood	Prov 6:17
and i as doves	Matt 10:16
betraying i blood	Matt 27:4
i of this Man's	Matt 27:24
holy, i, undefiled	Heb 7:26

INQUIRE ask, seek

to i of the LORD	Gen 25:22
I of God, please	Judg 18:5
David i-d of...LORD	1 Sam 23:2
you come to i of Me	Ezek 20:3
i...where the Christ	Matt 2:4
i-d of them the hour	John 4:52

INSANE mad

a demon and is i	John 10:20
I speak as if i	2 Cor 11:23

INSCRIBE carve, write

were i-d in a book	Job 19:23
i it on a scroll	Is 30:8
and i a city on it	Ezek 4:1
i it on tablets	Hab 2:2

INSCRIPTION writing

could not read the i	Dan 5:8
I will engrave an i	Zech 3:9
Pilate wrote an i	John 19:19
i, To An Unknown	Acts 17:23

INSECTS

swarms of i on you	Ex 8:21
all other winged i	Lev 11:23

INSIGHT discernment

a counselor with i	1 Chr 26:14
according to his i	Prov 12:8
i with understanding	Dan 9:22
not gained any i	Mark 6:52
In all wisdom and i	Eph 1:8

INSIGNIFICANT unimportant

was i in Thine eyes	2 Sam 7:19
your beginning was i	Job 8:7
citizen of no i city	Acts 21:39

INSOLENT arrogant

acts with i pride	Prov 21:24
haters of God, i	Rom 1:30

INSPECTION GATE
see GATES OF JERUSALEM

INSPIRED stimulated

the love we i in you	2 Cor 8:7
All Scripture is i	2 Tim 3:16

INSTINCT natural tendency

as creatures of i	2 Pet 2:12

they know by i	Jude 10

INSTRUCT teach

Thy good Spirit to i	Neh 9:20
I will i you	Ps 32:8
the wise is i-ed	Prov 21:11
i-ed out of the Law	Rom 2:18
just as you were i-ed	Col 2:7
may i certain men	1 Tim 1:3

INSTRUCTION teaching

will walk in My i	Ex 16:4
Heed i and be wise	Prov 8:33
Get wisdom and i	Prov 23:23
i-s to His twelve	Matt 11:1
written for our i	Rom 15:4
i of the Lord	Eph 6:4
goal of our i is love	1 Tim 1:5
i about washings	Heb 6:2

INSTRUMENT object, vessel

cut...with sharp i-s	1 Chr 20:3
and i-s of music	2 Chr 5:13
with stringed i-s	Ps 150:4
he is a chosen i	Acts 9:15
i-s of unrighteousness	Rom 6:13

INSULT (n) affront, indignity

i-s of the nations	Ezek 34:29
casting the same i	Matt 27:44
and cast i-s at you	Luke 6:22
evil, or i for i	1 Pet 3:9

INSULT (v) treat with scorn

and do not i her	Ruth 2:15
to i the LORD	2 Chr 32:17
times you have i-ed	Job 19:3
i-ed the Spirit of	Heb 10:29

INTEGRITY honesty

In the i of my heart	Gen 20:5
dealt in truth and i	Judg 9:19
holds fast his i	Job 2:3
He who walks with i	Ps 15:2
have walked in my i	Ps 26:1
The i of the upright	Prov 11:3

INTELLIGENCE mental ability

He deprives of i	Job 12:24
gave them...i	Dan 1:17
Paulus, a man of i	Acts 13:7

INTELLIGENT bright, smart

was i and beautiful	1 Sam 25:3
mind of the i seeks	Prov 15:14
from the wise and i	Matt 11:25

INTEND purpose

Are you i-ing to kill	Ex 2:14
I i to build a house	1 Kin 5:5
i to make My people	Jer 23:27
i-ing to betray Him	John 12:4
i-ing...to take Paul	Acts 20:13

INTENTION aim, goal

the i-s of the heart	1 Chr 29:18
i of your heart	Acts 8:22
kind i of His will	Eph 1:5

INTERCEDE plead, mediate

i-d for the people	Num 21:7
who can i for him	1 Sam 2:25
And i-d for the	Is 53:12
do not i with Me	Jer 7:16

Spirit Himself **i**-s   Rom 8:26

INTERCOURSE *copulation*

not have **i** with	Lev 18:20
not have **i**...animal	Lev 18:23
husband has had **i**	Num 5:20

INTEREST *concern or usury*

not charge him **i**	Ex 22:25
not take usurious **i**	Lev 25:36
i to a foreigner	Deut 23:20
his money at **i**	Ps 15:5
mind on God's **i**-s	Matt 16:23
money...with **i**	Matt 25:27
he has a morbid **i**	1 Tim 6:4

INTERMARRY

And **i** with us	Gen 34:9
shall not **i** with	Deut 7:3
i with the peoples	Ezra 9:14

INTERPRET *explain, translate*

no one who could **i**	Gen 41:8
one who **i**-s omens	Deut 18:10
He **i** the message	Is 28:9
unless he **i**-s	1 Cor 14:5
pray that he may **i**	1 Cor 14:13

INTERPRETATION *explain*

i-s belong to God	Gen 40:8
the deam and its **i**	Judg 7:15
make its **i** known	Dan 5:16
the **i** of tongues	1 Cor 12:10
of one's own **i**	2 Pet 1:20

INTIMATE *close*

my **i** friends have	Job 19:14
i with the upright	Prov 3:32
separates **i** friends	Prov 16:28

INVADE *attack*

king of Assyria **i**-d	2 Kin 17:5
nation had **i**-d my land	Joel 1:6
Assyrian **i**-s our land	Mic 5:5

INVALIDATE *nullify*

i-d the word of God	Matt 15:6
i-ing the word of	Mark 7:13
does not **i** a covenant	Gal 3:17

INVESTIGATE *examine*

the judges shall **i**	Deut 19:18
the plot was **i**-d	Esth 2:23
i, and to seek wisdom	Eccl 7:25
having **i**-d everything	Luke 1:3

INVISIBLE *unseen*

His **i** attributes	Rom 1:20
image of the **i** God	Col 1:15
visible and **i**	Col 1:16
eternal, immortal, **i**	1 Tim 1:17

INVITE *request*

i-d us to impoverish	Judg 14:15
you shall **i** Jesse	1 Sam 16:3
i-d all the king's	2 Sam 13:23
I am **i**-d by her	Esth 5:12
did not **i** Me in	Matt 25:43
i *the* poor	Luke 14:13

IRON *metal*

was an **i** bedstead	Deut 3:11
whose stones are **i**	Deut 8:9
had **i** chariots	Judg 1:19

made the **i** float   2 King 6:6
break them...rod of **i**   Ps 2:9
from the **i** furnace   Jer 11:4
as strong as **i**   Dan 2:40
rule...rod of **i**   Rev 19:15

ISAAC

birth, son of Abraham	Gen 21:3
offered for sacrifice	Gen 22:2
took Rebekah as wife	Gen 24
father of twins	Gen 25:26
blessed Jacob	Gen 27:1-40

ISAIAH

prophet of Judah	Is 1:1
son of Amoz	2 Kin 19:2
called	Is 6:8ff
under four kings	Is 1:1

ISCARIOT

geographical identity of Judas
   Mark 3:19; John 12:4; 13:26

ISH-BOSHETH

son of Saul   2 Sam 2:8;3:8;4:8

ISHMAEL

1 *son of Abraham*
   Gen 16:11;17:18;25:17
2 *son of nethaniah*   2 Kin 25:23
3 *line of Jonathan*
   1 Chr 8:38;9:44
4 *Zebadiah's father*   2 Chr 19:11
5 *son of Jehohanan*   2 Chr 23:1
6 *son of Pashhur*   Ezra 10:22

ISLAND *surrounded by water*

the many **i**-s be glad	Ps 97:1
He lifts up the **i**-s	Is 40:15
i was called Malta	Acts 28:1
every **i** fled away	Rev 16:20

ISOLATE *set apart*

priest shall **i** him	Lev 13:4
i him for seven days	Lev 13:21
fortified city is **i**-d	Is 27:10

ISRAEL

1 *Jacob*
   Gen 32:28-32;35:10;37:3
2 *line of Jacob*   Gen 34:7
   tribal nation
   Ex 1:7;4:22; Num 10:29
3 *united kingdom*
   1 Sam 15:35; 1 Kin 4:1
4 *northern kingdom*
   1 Kin 14:19;15:9; 2 Kin 10:29
5 *under Roman rule*
   Luke 2:32; John 1:49;
   Rom 9:6

ISSACHAR

1 *son of Jacob*   Gen 30:18;49:14
2 *tribe*
   Num 1:29; Josh 21:28; Rev 7:7
3 *Levite*   1 Chr 26:5

ISSUE (n) *outflow, out go*

first **i** of the womb	Num 3:12
offspring and **i**	Is 22:24
like the **i** of horses	Ezek 23:20
concerning this **i**	Acts 15:2

ISSUE (v) *go forth, put forth*

Moses **i**-d a command	Ex 36:6
shall **i** from you	2 Kin 20:18
decree was **i**-d in	Esth 3:15
i-d a proclamation	Dan 5:29

ITALY

S European country
   Acts 18:2;27:1,6; Heb 13:24

ITURAEA

region N of Palestine   Luke 3:1
tetrarchy of Philip

IVORY *elephant tusk*

a great throne of **i**	1 Kin 10:18
silver, **i** and apes	2 Chr 9:21
Out of **i** palaces	Ps 45:8
every article of **i**	Rev 18:12

J

JABAL

son of Lamech   Gen 4:20
father of herders

JABBOK

tributary of Jordan
   Gen 32:22; Num 21:24;
   Josh 12:2; Judg 11:13,22

JABESH-GILEAD

town of Gilead   Judg 21:8ff
E of Jordan River
   1 Sam 11:1,9; 2 Sam 2:4,5

JACINTH *precious stone*

a **j**, an agate	Ex 28:19
the eleventh, **j**	Rev 21:20

JACKALS *wild dogs*

j in their...palaces	Is 13:22
ruins, A haunt of **j**	Jer 9:11
a lament like the **j**	Mic 1:8

JACOB

1 *son of Isaac*   Gen 25:26
   brother of Esau   Gen 25:27
   obtained birthright   Gen 25:33
   fled to Aram   Gen 28:5,6
   marriage   Gen 29:1ff
   wrestled angel   Gen 32:24ff
   name changed   Gen 35:9,10
   went down to Egypt Gen 46:4ff
   death and burial   Gen 49:28ff
2 *father of Joseph*   Matt 1:15,16

JAEL

wife of Heber   Judg 4:17
slayer of Sisera   Judg 4:21
described as blessed   Judg 5:24

JEHAZIEL

1 *Benjamite warrior*   1 Chr 12:4
2 *priest*   1 Chr 16:6
3 *son of Hebron*   1 Chr 23:19
4 *son of Zechariah*   2 Chr 20:14

JAIL *place of confinement*

put him into the **j**	Gen 39:20
in **j** in the house	Jer 37:15
put them in...**j**	Acts 5:18

JAILER *warden*

sight of the chief **j**   Gen 39:21

JORAM

1 *son of Toi*	2 Sam 8:10
2 *son of Ahab*	2 Kin 8:16
king of Israel	2 Kin 8:25
3 *line of Eliezer*	1 Chr 26:25
4 *son of Jehoshaphat*	Matt 1:8
king of Judah	

see also **JEHORAM**

JORDAN

1 *river in Palestine*
     Gen 32:10; Josh 3:17;
Judg 8:4; 2 Kin 5:10; Matt 3:6
2 *valley*   Gen 13:10,11

JOSEPH

1 *son of Jacob*	Gen 30:23,24
sold by brothers	Gen 37:28
put in prison	Gen 40:3
prime minister	Gen 41:41
revealed himself	Gen 45:4
death	Gen 50:26
2 *father of spy*	Num 13:7ff
3 *son of Asaph*	1 Chr 25:9
4 *son of Bani*	Ezra 10:42
5 *son of Shebaniah*	Neh 12:14
6 *husband of Mary*	
Matt 1:18;2:13; Luke 2:16;	
	John 6:42
7 *brother of Jesus*	Matt 13:55
also **Joses**	
8 *brother of James the Less*	
	Matt 27:56
also **Joses**	
9 *of Arimathea*	Matt 27:57ff
in Sanhedrin (Council)	
	Mark 15:43
disciple of Jesus	John 19:38
provided tomb	Matt 27:57
10 *ancestor of Jesus*	Luke 3:24
11 *ancestor of Jesus*	Luke 3:30
12 *surname Barsabbas*	Acts 1:23
13 *Barnabas*	Acts 4:36

JOSES

1 *brother of James the Less*
     Mark 15:40
also **Joseph**
2 *brother of Jesus*   Mark 6:3
also **Joseph**

JOSHUA

1 *Moses' successor*	Deut 31:23
attended Moses	Num 11:28
chosen by God	Num 27:18
encouraged by God	Josh 1:1-9
charged Israel	Josh 23:1ff
death	Josh 24:29
2 *of Beth-shemesh*	1 Sam 6:14
3 *governor*	2 Kin 23:8
4 *high priest*	
Hag 1:1,12; Zech 3:1ff	
also **Jeshua**	

JOSIAH

1 *son of Amon*   2 Kin 21:24
  king of Judah   2 Kin 21:26
  removed false worship
     2 Kin 23:19,24; 2 Chr 34:33
  responded to the Law
     2 Chr 34:15-28
2 *son of Zephaniah*   Zech 6:10

JOTHAM

1 *son of Gideon*	Judg 9:5ff
2 *king of Judah*	2 Kin 15:5
son of Uzziah	2 Chr 27:2
3 *line of Caleb*	1 Chr 2:47

JOURNEY *traveling, trip*

Let us take our *j*	Gen 33:12
day's *j* on the other	Num 11:31
seek...a safe *j*	Ezra 8:21
a bag for *your j*	Matt 10:10
nothing for *your j*	Luke 9:3
Sabbath day's *j* away	Acts 1:12
on frequent *j-s*	2 Cor 11:26

JOURNEYED *traveled*

about as they *j* east	Gen 11:2
Jacob *j* to Succoth	Gen 33:17
the sons of Israel *j*	Num 22:1
j from the river	Ezra 8:31

JOY *delight, happiness*

raise sounds of *j*	1 Chr 15:16
shouted aloud for *j*	Ezra 3:12
see His face with *j*	Job 33:26
Restore to me the *j*	Ps 51:12
j at Thy name	Ps 89:12
godly ones sing for *j*	Ps 132:9
Everlasting *j* will be	Is 61:7
their mourning into *j*	Jer 31:13
with great *j*	Matt 2:10
enter into the *j*	Matt 25:21
j in heaven over one	Luke 15:7
j in the Holy Spirit	Rom 14:17
love, *j*, peace	Gal 5:22
make my *j* complete	Phil 2:2

JOYFUL *feeling gladness*

be altogether *j*	Deut 16:15
j with gladness	Ps 21:6
shall reap with *j*	Ps 126:5
j heart is good	Prov 17:22

JOYFULLY *full of joy, happy*

go *j* with the king	Esth 5:14
Shout *j* to God, all	Ps 66:1
They shout *j* together	Is 52:8
to praise God *j*	Luke 19:37

JUBAL

inventor of lyre and pipe Gen 4:21

JUBILANT *elated*

no...*j* shouting	Is 16:10
Is this your *j city*	Is 23:7
because you are *j*	Jer 50:11
they may become *j*	Jer 51:39

JUBILEE, YEAR OF

return of ancestral possessions
  every fiftieth year
  year of liberty   Lev 25:8ff

JUDAH

1 *son of Jacob*
   Gen 29:35;37:26;44:14;49:8,10
2 *tribe*
   Num 1:27; Judg 1:8; 2 Sam
     2:4; 1 Kin 12:20
3 *border city*   Josh 19:34
4 *S kingdom*
   1 Kin 14:21; 1 Chr 9:1;
     Ps 60:7; Jer 20:4
5 *relative of Kadmiel* Ezra 2:40

6 *urged by Ezra to put away*	
foreign wife	Ezra 10:23
7 *Benjamite*	Neh 11:9
8 *Levite who returned from*	
captivity	Neh 12:8
9 *participant in wall dedication*	
	Neh 12:34
10 *musician*	Neh 12:36

JUDAISM *Jewish way of life*

manner of life in **J**	Gal 1:13
advancing in **J**	Gal 1:14

JUDAS

1 *Iscariot*	Matt 10:4
used by Satan	Luke 22:3
son of Simon	John 6:71
treasurer	John 13:29
betrayed Jesus	John 18:2
2 *Jesus' brother*	
	Matt 13:55; Mark 6:3
3 *apostle*	Luke 6:16; Acts 1:13
4 *Judas of Galilee*	Acts 5:37
5 *of Damascus*	Acts 9:11
6 *Barsabbas*	Acts 15:22,27

JUDE

brother of Jesus
     Matt 13:55; Mark 6:3
brother of James   Jude 1

JUDEA

Roman province in Palestine
  based on earlier Judah
   Matt 2:1; Mark 1:5; Luke 2:4;
     John 11:7

JUDEAN

language (Hebrew)
   2 Kin 18:26,28; Is 36:11, 13
see also **CANAAN**
see also **HEBREW**

JUDGE (n) *leader*

J of all the earth	Gen 18:25
prince or a *j* over us	Ex 2:14
LORD was with the *j*	Judg 2:18
For God Himself is *j*	Ps 50:6
unrighteous *j* said	Luke 18:6
one Lawgiver and **J**	James 4:12

JUDGE (v) *pass judgment*

LORD *j* between you	Gen 16:5
Moses sat to *j* the	Ex 18:13
LORD will *j*...earth	1 Sam 2:10
coming to *j* the earth	Ps 98:9
He will *j* the poor	Is 11:4
not *j* lest you be *j-d*	Matt 7:1
Son...world to *j*	John 3:17
Law...not *j* a man	John 7:51
not come to *j* the	John 12:47
able to *j*...thoughts	Heb 4:12
adulterers God will *j*	Heb 13:4

JUDGMENT *condemnation*

I will execute *j-s*	Ex 12:12
partiality in *j*	Deut 1:17
let *j* be executed	Ezra 7:26
will not stand in the *j*	Ps 1:5
in the day of *j*	Matt 10:15
j, that the light	John 3:19
resurrection of *j*	John 5:29
My *j* is just	John 5:30

Column 1

after this *comes* j — Heb 9:27
incur a stricter j — James 3:1
not fall under j — James 5:12
kept for the day of j — 2 Pet 3:7
j of the great day — Jude 6
to execute j upon all — Jude 15
His j-s are true — Rev 19:2

JUMP *leap*

legs with which to j — Lev 11:21
if a fox should j — Neh 4:3
j-ed up, and came — Mark 10:50

JUNIPER *tree*

slept under a j tree — 1 Kin 19:5
The j, the box tree — Is 60:13
like a j in the — Jer 48:6

JUST *fair, right*

shall have j balances — Lev 19:36
a man be j with God — Job 25:4
Hear a j cause, O LORD — Ps 17:1
He is j and endowed — Zech 9:9
My judgment is j — John 5:30
the j for *the* unjust — 1 Pet 3:18

JUSTICE *fairness, righteousness*

shall not distort j — Deut 16:19
Does God pervert j — Job 8:3
j to the afflicted — Job 36:6
Righteousness and j — Ps 89:14
do not understand j — Prov 28:5
j is turned back — Is 59:14
let j roll down — Amos 5:24
j and mercy and — Matt 23:23
acknowledged...j — Luke 7:29
grant to your slaves j — Col 4:1

JUSTIFICATION *vindication*

because of our j — Rom 4:25
j of life to all men — Rom 5:18

JUSTIFY *declare guiltless*

how...j ourselves — Gen 44:16
they j the righteous — Deut 25:1
he **j-ied** himself — Job 32:2
wishing to j himself — Luke 10:29
these He also **j-ied** — Rom 8:30
God...**j-ies** — Rom 8:33
seeking to be **j-ied** — Gal 2:17

JUSTUS

1 *Joseph, apostolic candidate*
— Acts 1:23
also called Barsabbas
2 *Titus, Corinthian disciple*
— Acts 18:7
3 *Jewish Christian* — Col 4:11

JUTTAH

Levitical city in Judah
— Josh 15:55;21:16

K

KADESH /
KADESH-BARNEA

desert oasis in Negev — Gen 14:7
Israelite encampment
— Num 13:26;33:37

KEDAR

1 *son of Ishmael* — Gen 25:13
2 *tribal descendants* — Is 42:11

Column 2

KEDEMAH

1 *son of Ishmael* — Gen 25:15
2 *tribal descendants* — 1 Chr 1:31

KEDESH

1 *city in S Judah* — Josh 15:23
2 *city of Issachar* — 1 Chr 6:72
3 *city of Naphtali* — Josh 12:22
4 *city of refuge, in Galilee*
— Josh 20:7

KEEP *hold, guide, preserve*

k the way of the LORD
— Gen 18:19
love Me and k My — Ex 20:6
shall k your sabbath — Lev 23:32
LORD bless you, and k
— Num 6:24
to k the Passover — Matt 26:18
if anyone **k-s** My — John 8:51
he will k My word — John 14:23
k-ing faith and a — 1 Tim 1:19
k yourself free from — 1 Tim 5:22

KEEPER *guard, protector*

Am I my brother's k — Gen 4:9
been **k-s** of livestock — Gen 46:32
The LORD is your k — Ps 121:5
I, the LORD, am its k — Is 27:3

KEILAH

1 *town of Judah*
— Josh 15:44; 1 Sam 23:1ff;
— Neh 3:17,18
2 *line of Caleb* — 1 Chr 4:19

KENAZ

1 *Esau's grandson* — Gen 36:10,11
2 *father of Othniel* — Josh 15:17
3 *line of Caleb* — 1 Chr 4:15

KENITE(S)

Canaanite tribe
— Gen 15:19; Num 24:21
tribe of metal-workers
— Judg 4:11; 1 Sam 15:6

KENIZZITE

Canaanite tribe in S Palestine
and Edom
— Gen 15:19; Num 32:12;
— Josh 14:14

KEREN-HAPPUCH

daughter of Job — Job 42:14

KERIOTH

1 *town of Judah* — Josh 15:25
2 *town in Moab*
— Jer 48:41; Amos 2:2

KETURAH

second wife of Abraham
— Gen 25:1,4; 1 Chr 1:32,33

KEY *unlocking tool*

k-s of the kingdom — Matt 16:19
the k of knowledge — Luke 11:52
k-s of death and of — Rev 1:18
k of the bottomless pit — Rev 9:1

KEZIAH

daughter of Job — Job 42:14

Column 3

KID *young goat*

a k from the flock — Gen 38:17
not boil a k...milk — Ex 34:26
prepare a k for you — Judg 13:15
never given me a k — Luke 15:29

KIDNEYS *innards*

two k and the fat — Ex 29:13
remove with the k — Lev 3:15
He splits my k open — Job 16:13

KIDRON

brook and valley between
Jerusalem and Mount of Olives
— 2 Sam 15:23; 2 Kin 23:6;
— 2 Chr 29:16; John 18:1

KILL *take life*

for Cain **k-ed** him — Gen 4:25
k-ed every first-born — Ex 13:15
who **k-s** a man shall — Lev 24:21
LORD **k-s** and makes — 1 Sam 2:6
Am I God, to k — 2 Kin 5:7
anger **k-s** the simple — Job 5:2
he **k-s** the innocent — Ps 10:8
A time to k — Eccl 3:3
unable to k the — Matt 10:28
k-ed, and be raised — Luke 9:22
do you seek to k Me — John 7:19
Arise, Peter, k and — Acts 10:13
the letter **k-s**, but — 2 Cor 3:6
who k their father — 1 Tim 1:9
k a third of mankind — Rev 9:15

KIND (adj) *good, tender*

be k to this people — 2 Chr 10:7
He Himself is k — Luke 6:35
love is k — 1 Cor 13:4
be k to one another — Eph 4:32

KIND (n) *group, variety*

fruit after their k — Gen 1:11
plant all **k-s** of trees — Lev 19:23
all **k-s** of evil — Matt 5:11
k-s of tongues — 1 Cor 12:28
every k of impurity — Eph 4:19

KINDLE *cause to burn*

anger...was **k-d** — Num 11:10
His breath **k-s** coals — Job 41:21
man to k strife — Prov 26:21
all you who k a fire — Is 50:11
k-d a fire in Zion — Lam 4:11

KINDNESS *tenderness*

teaching of k is on — Prov 31:26
to love k, And to — Mic 6:8
with deeds of k — Acts 9:36
k and...of God — Rom 11:22
joy, peace, patience, k — Gal 5:22
compassion, k — Col 3:12
tasted the k of the — 1 Pet 2:3
godliness, brotherly k — 2 Pet 1:7

KINDRED *relative*

her people or her k — Esth 2:10
destruction of my k — Esth 8:6
no one...of k spirit — Phil 2:20

KING *monarch, regent*

the k-'s highway — Num 20:17
no k in Israel — Judg 17:6
appoint a k for us — 1 Sam 8:5

annointed David **k** 2 Sam 5:3
my **K** and my God Ps 5:2
The LORD is **K** forever Ps 10:16
Who is the **k** of glory Ps 24:8
will shatter **k**-s Ps 110:5
By me **k**-s reign Prov 8:15
He will...before **k**-s Prov 22:29
The Creator...your **K** Is 43:15
O **K** of the nations Jer 10:7
born **K** of the Jews Matt 2:2
Are You the **K** of Matt 27:11
your **K** is coming John 12:15
no **k** but Caesar John 19:15
K of **k**-s and Lord 1 Tim 6:15
God, honor the **k** 1 Pet 2:17

KINGDOM *domain, monarchy*

his **k** was Babel Gen 10:10
to Me a **k** of priests Ex 19:6
tear the **k** from 1 Kin 11:11
will establish his **k** 1 Chr 28:7
the **k** is the LORD'S Ps 22:28
Sing to God, O **k**-s Ps 68:32
an everlasting **k** Ps 145:13
k against **k** Is 19:2
k of heaven is at Matt 3:2
showed Him...**k**-s Matt 4:8
Thy **k** come Matt 6:10
sons of the **k** Matt 13:38
keys of the **k** Matt 16:19
in My Father's **k** Matt 26:29
enter the **k** of God Mark 10:24
to give you the **k** Luke 12:32
cannot see the **k** of John 3:3
preaching the **k** Acts 28:31
k of His beloved Son Col 1:13
to His heavenly **k** 2 Tim 4:18
faith conquered **k**-s Heb 11:33
heirs of the **k** James 2:5

KINSMAN *relative*

of my master's **k** Gen 24:48
he took his **k**-men Gen 31:23
a man has no **k** Lev 25:26
Naomi had a **k** of her Ruth 2:1
k-men stand afar off Ps 38:11
Herodion, my **k** Rom 16:11

KIRIATHAIM

1 *Reubenite city*
Num 32:37; Josh 13:19
2 *Levitical city* 1 Chr 6:76

KIRIATH-ARBA

old name of Hebron
Gen 23:2; Josh 14:15;15:13,54;
Judg 1:10
city of Refuge Josh 20:7

KIRIATH-JEARIM

Gibeonite town
Josh 9:17; Judg 18:12;
Jer 26:20
location of ark of covenant
1 Sam 6:21;7:1,2; 2 Chr 1:4

KISH

1 *father of Saul* 1 Sam 9:3;10:21
2 *son of Jeiel* 1 Chr 8:30
3 *son of Mahli* 1 Chr 23:21
4 *son of Abdi* 2 Chr 29:12
5 *a Benjamite* Esth 2:5

KISHON

battle scene Judg 4:7
river Judg 4:13;5:21
priests of Baal slain on its bank
1 Kin 18:40

KISS (n) *expression of affection*

threw a **k** from my Job 31:27
the **k**-es of his mouth Song 1:2
You gave Me no **k** Luke 7:45
betraying...with a **k** Luke 22:48
with a holy **k** Rom 16:16
with a **k** of love 1 Pet 5:14

KISS (v) *expression of affection*

come close and **k** Gen 27:26
let me **k** my father 1 Kin 19:20
I would **k** you Song 8:1
Whomever I...**k** Mark 14:44
not...to **k** my feet Luke 7:45

KITTIM

1 *grandson of Japheth*
Gen 10:4; 1 Chr 1:7
2 *island of Cyprus*
Num 24:24; Jer 2:10;
Dan 11:30

KNEAD *work dough, clay*

took flour, **k**-ed it 1 Sam 28:24
the women **k** dough Jer 7:18

KNEE *part of body*

strengthened feeble **k**-s Job 4:4
k-s began knocking Dan 5:6
every **k** shall bow Rom 14:11
every **k** should bow Phil 2:10

KNEEL *bend, rest on knee*

made the camels **k** Gen 24:11
people **k**-ed to drink Judg 7:6
k before the LORD Ps 95:6
k-ed...before Him Matt 27:29
man ran...**knelt** Mark 10:17
He **knelt** down Luke 22:41

KNIFE *cutting instrument*

k to slay his son Gen 22:10
jaw teeth *like* **k**-ves Prov 30:14
with a scribe's **k** Jer 36:23

KNIT *joined together*

Jonathan was **k** to 1 Sam 18:1
k me together with Job 10:11
his thighs are **k** Job 40:17
His hand they are **k** Lam 1:14
k together in love Col 2:2

KNOCK *smite, strike*

his knees began **k**-ing Dan 5:6
k, and it shall be Matt 7:7
stand outside and **k** Luke 13:25
he **k**-ed at the door Acts 12:13
at the door and **k** Rev 3:20

KNOW *experience, understand*

like one of Us, **k**-ing Gen 3:22
make **k**-n the statutes Ex 18:16
k that my Redeemer Job 19:25
Make me **k** thy ways Ps 25:4
He **k**-s the secrets Ps 44:21
k that I am God Ps 46:10
made **k**-n His salvation Ps 98:2

Try me and **k** my Ps 139:23
Thou **k**-est me Jer 12:3
left hand **k** what Matt 6:3
k...by their fruits Matt 7:20
I never **knew** you Matt 7:23
God **k**-s your hearts Luke 16:15
you shall **k** the truth John 8:32
I **k** My own John 10:14
k-ing that His hour John 13:1
k that I love You John 21:15
and **k** all mysteries 1 Cor 13:2
who **knew** no sin 2 Cor 5:21
k the love of Christ Eph 3:19
value of **k**-ing Christ Phil 3:8
k...I have believed 2 Tim 1:12
k...eternal life 1 John 5:13
I **k** your deeds Rev 2:2

KNOWLEDGE *information*

tree of the **k** of good Gen 2:9
LORD is a God of **k** 1 Sam 2:3
anyone teach God **k** Job 21:22
k is too wonderful Ps 139:6
the beginning of **k** Prov 1:7
fools hate **k** Prov 1:22
Wise...store up **k** Prov 10:14
k increases power Prov 24:5
would He teach **k** Is 28:9
in accordance with **k** Rom 10:2
K makes arrogant 1 Cor 8:1
k, it will be done 1 Cor 13:8
have no **k** of God 1 Cor 15:34
love...surpasses **k** Eph 3:19
treasures of...**k** Col 2:3
grow in...grace and **k** 2 Pet 3:18

KOHATH

son of Levi
Gen 46:11; Num 3:17;
Josh 21:5

KOHATHITES

line of Kohath
Num 3:30;4:34; Josh 21:4

KOR *measure of capacity*

k-s of fine flour 1 Kin 4:22
20,000 **k**-s of barley 2 Chr 2:10
100 **k**-s of wheat Ezra 7:22
a bath from *each* **k** Ezek 45:14

KORAH

1 *son of Esau* Gen 36:5
2 *opposed Moses* Num 16:8,16
3 *son of Hebron* 1 Chr 2:43
4 *a Kohathite* 1 Chr 6:37

L

LABAN

1 *Abraham's kinsman* Gen 24:29
Rachel's father Gen 29:10,11
2 *place in the desert* Deut 1:1

LABOR (n) *work or childbirth*

fruits of your **l**-s Ex 23:16
their **l** to the locust Ps 78:46
bread of painful **l**-s Ps 127:2
return for their **l** Eccl 4:9
like a woman in **l** Is 42:14
in **l** and hardship 2 Cor 11:27
fruitful **l** for me Phil 1:22

faith and l of love   1 Thess 1:3
cried out, being in l   Rev 12:2

LABOR (v) *toil, work*

Six days you shall l   Ex 20:9
l in vain who build   Ps 127:1
for whom am I l-ing   Eccl 4:8
l-ed over you in vain   Gal 4:11

LABORER *workman*

l-s for his vineyard   Matt 20:1
Call the l-s and pay   Matt 20:8
l-s into His harvest   Luke 10:2
l is worthy of his   Luke 10:7

LACHISH

city in Judah
                          Josh 10:3; 2 Kin 14:19;
                          2 Chr 32:9

LACK (n) *deficiency, need*

where there is no l   Judg 18:10
for l of instruction   Prov 5:23
for l of a shepherd   Ezek 34:5
l of self-control   1 Cor 7:5

LACK (v) *be deficient, need*

shall not l anything   Deut 8:9
l-ing in counsel   Deut 32:28
man l-ing sense   Prov 7:7
am I still l-ing   Matt 19:20
One thing you l   Mark 10:21
not l-ing in any gift   1 Cor 1:7
if any...l-s wisdom   James 1:5

LAD *boy*

God heard the l   Gen 21:17
the l is not *with us*   Gen 44:31
the l was dead   2 Kin 4:32
a l here who has five   John 6:9

LADDER *steps*

l...set on the earth   Gen 28:12

LADY *woman*

Thy noble l-ies   Ps 45:9
elder to the chosen l   2 John 1

LAISH

1 *a Benjamite*
                          1 Sam 25:44; 2 Sam 3:15
2 *place in N Palestine later called*
  Dan   Judg 18:27,29

LAKE *pool, water*

standing by the l   Luke 5:1
wind...upon the l   Luke 8:23
into the l, and were   Luke 8:33
into the l of fire   Rev 20:10

LAMB *young sheep*

l for the burnt   Gen 22:7
shall redeem with a l   Ex 34:20
l without defect   Lev 14:10
will...dwell with the l   Is 11:6
l...led to slaughter   Is 53:7
wolf and the l shall   Is 65:25
send you out as l-s   Luke 10:3
Behold, the L of God   John 1:29
Tend My l-s   John 21:15
l before its shearer   Acts 8:32
Worthy is the L   Rev 5:12
blood of the L   Rev 12:11

LAME *crippled, disabled*

was l in both feet   2 Sam 9:13
feet to the l   Job 29:15
Then the l will leap   Is 35:6
the l walk   Matt 11:5
l from his mother's   Acts 14:8

LAMECH

1 *in linage of Cain*   Gen 4:17,18
2 *father of Noah*   Gen 5:28,29

LAMENT (n) *dirge, wail*

this l over Saul   2 Sam 1:17
chanted a l   2 Chr 35:25
I must make a l   Mic 1:8

LAMENT (v) *mourn, wail*

house of Israel l-ed   1 Sam 7:2
her gates will l   Is 3:26
fisherman will l   Is 19:8
And l over you   Ezek 27:32
weep and l over her   Rev 18:9

LAMENTATION *weeping*

great...sorrowful l   Gen 50:10
in Ramah, L *and*   Jer 31:15
your sons into l   Amos 8:10
made loud l over him   Acts 8:2

LAMP *light*

Thou art my l   1 Sam 22:29
l-s of pure gold   2 Chr 4:20
his l goes out   Job 18:6
Thy word is a l   Ps 119:105
commandment is a l   Prov 6:23
l of the body is the   Matt 6:22
l-s are going out   Matt 25:8
l-s in the upper room   Acts 20:8
l shining in a dark   2 Pet 1:19
seven l-s of fire   Rev 4:5

LAMPSTAND *candlestick*

l of pure gold   Ex 25:31
and a chair and a l   2 Kin 4:10
puts it on a l   Luke 8:16
will remove your l   Rev 2:5

LAND *country, earth*

let the dry l appear   Gen 1:9
famine in the l   Gen 12:10
I have given this l   Gen 15:18
out of the l of Egypt   Ex 6:13
l flowing with milk   Deut 6:3
in to possess the l   Josh 1:11
l of their captivity   2 Chr 6:38
will heal their l   2 Chr 7:14
the l of the living   Job 28:13
will inherit the l   Ps 37:11
In a dry and weary l   Ps 63:1
l be born in one day   Is 66:8
again to this l   Jer 24:6
l is filled with blood   Ezek 9:9
smite the l with a   Mal 4:6
darkness...all the l   Matt 27:45
owned a tract of l   Acts 4:37

LANDOWNER *landlord*

slaves of the l   Matt 13:27
kingdom...like a l   Matt 20:1
l who planted a   Matt 21:33

LANGUAGE *speech, word*

according to his l   Gen 10:5

earth used the same l   Gen 11:1
speech or difficult l   Ezek 3:5
in figurative l   John 16:25
speak in his own l   Acts 2:6
many kinds of l-s   1 Cor 14:10

LANGUISH *faint*

l-ed because of the   Gen 47:13
My soul l-es for   Ps 119:81
never l again   Jer 31:12
refresh...who l-es   Jer 31:25

LAODICEA

city in Asia Minor   Col 2:1
location of early church
                          Col 4:15; Rev 1:11; 3:14

LAODICEANS

people of Laodicea   Col 4:16

LAPIS LAZULI *precious stone*

polishing *was* like l   Lam 4:7
like l in appearance   Ezek 1:26
the jasper; The l   Ezek 28:13

LARGE *big, great, huge*

tears in l measure   Ps 80:5
a l upper room   Mark 14:15
a l multitude   Luke 7:11
what l letters   Gal 6:11

LAST *final, utmost*

breathed his l   Gen 25:8
In the l days   Is 2:2
first will be l   Matt 19:30
The l Adam   1 Cor 15:45
at the l trumpet   1 Cor 15:52
in these l days   Heb 1:2
it is the l hour   1 John 2:18
the first and the l   Rev 1:17

LATIN

language of the Roman Empire
one of three languages written on
  Jesus' cross   John 19:20

LATTICE *trellis*

fell through the l   2 Kin 1:2
looked out...my l   Ps 7:6
peering through...l   Song 2:9

LAUGH *be amused, mock*

Why did Sarah l   Gen 18:13
will l at violence   Job 5:22
l at your calamity   Prov 1:26
weep, and a time to l   Eccl 3:4
began l-ing at Him   Matt 9:24

LAUGHINGSTOCK *derision*

l among the peoples   Ps 44:14
was not Israel a l   Jer 48:27
I have become a l   Lam 3:14

LAUGHTER *amusement*

God has made l for   Gen 21:6
Even in the heart   Prov 14:13
Sorrow is better than l   Eccl 7:3

LAVER *wash basin*

make a l of bronze   Ex 30:18
set the l between   Ex 40:7
anoint the l   Ex 40:11

LAW *scripture, statute*

tablets with the l   Ex 24:12

LAWFUL

Moses wrote this l	Deut 31:9
found the...l	2 Kin 22:8
walk in My l	2 Chr 6:16
l...is perfect	Ps 19:7
I delight in Thy l	Ps 119:70
abolish the L or the	Matt 5:17
Our L...not judge	John 7:51
by that l He ought	John 19:7
by a l of faith	Rom 3:27
L brings...wrath	Rom 4:15
not under l	Rom 6:14
Is the L sin	Rom 7:7
the L is holy	Rom 7:12
L...become our tutor	Gal 3:24
thus fulfill the l	Gal 6:2
L...nothing perfect	Heb 7:19

LAWFUL *legal, right*

not l for him to eat	Matt 12:4
Is it l to heal	Matt 12:10
l...man to divorce	Mark 10:2
All things are l	1 Cor 6:12

LAWGIVER *lawmaker*

The Lord is our l	Is 33:22
one L and Judge	James 4:12

LAWLESS *illegal, without law*

l one will be	2 Thess 2:8
are l and rebellious	1 Tim 1:9
from every l deed	Titus 2:14

LAWYER *interpreter of law*

a l, asked Him *a*	Matt 22:35
one of the l-s said	Luke 11:45
Woe to you l-s	Luke 11:52

LAY *place, put*

laid him on the altar	Gen 22:9
l My hand on Egypt	Ex 7:4
laid its cornerstone	Job 38:6
l my glory in the dust	Ps 7:5
he l-s up deceit	Prov 26:24
l up...treasures	Matt 6:20
laid Him in a tomb	Mark 15:46
l-s down His life	John 10:11
I l down My life	John 10:15
have you laid Him	John 11:34
I L in Zion a stone	Rom 9:33
l-ing aside falsehood	Eph 4:25
l-ing hold of...hope	Heb 6:18

LAYMAN *non-ecclesiastic*

l shall not eat *them*	Ex 29:33
married to a l	Lev 22:12
l who comes near	Num 3:10

LAZARUS

1 *beggar*	Luke 16:20-25
2 *brother of Mary and Martha*	
	John 11:1,2,5,11,43

LAZY *idle, slothful*

Because they are l	Ex 5:8
You are l, *very* l	Ex 5:17
You wicked, l slave	Matt 25:26
beasts, l gluttons	Titus 1:12

LEAD (n) *metal*

They sank like l	Ex 15:10
an iron stylus and l	Job 19:24
l is consumed by	Jer 6:29
l in the furnace	Ezek 22:18

LEAD (v) *direct, guide*

God led the people	Ex 13:18
cloud by day to l	Ex 13:21
l-s me beside quiet	Ps 23:2
L me in Thy truth	Ps 25:5
led captive Thy	Ps 68:18
little boy will l	Is 11:6
lamb that is led to	Is 53:7
not l us into	Matt 6:13
l the elect astray	Mark 13:22
led Him...crucify	Mark 15:20
and l-s them out	John 10:3
led by the Spirit	Rom 8:14
Led captive a host	Eph 4:8
that l-s to salvation	2 Tim 3:15

LEADER *director, guide*

Let us appoint a l	Num 14:4
one l of every tribe	Num 34:18
l over My people	1 Kin 14:7
the l as the servant	Luke 22:26
Obey your l-s	Heb 13:17

LEADING (adj) *chief, noted*

gathered l men	Ezra 7:28
number...l women	Acts 17:4
l men of the Jews	Acts 28:17

LEAF *foliage*

sewed fig l-ves	Gen 3:7
sound of a driven l	Lev 26:36
its l does not wither	Ps 1:3
puts forth its l-ves	Matt 24:32

LEAH

wife of Jacob	Gen 29:23,30
mother of Reuben, Simeon, Levi	
and Judah	Gen 29:32-35

LEAN (adj) *thin*

seven l...ugly cows	Gen 41:20
my flesh has grown l	Ps 109:24
and the l sheep	Ezek 34:20

LEAN (v) *incline, rest*

may l against them	Judg 16:26
l...own understanding	Prov 3:5
l on the God of Israel	Is 48:2

LEAP *jump, spring*

l-ing and dancing	2 Sam 6:16
I can l over a wall	Ps 18:29
baby l-ed in her	Luke 1:41
and l *for joy*	Luke 6:23
l-ed up and *began*	Acts 14:10

LEARN *get knowledge*

l to fear the Lord	Deut 31:13
I may l Thy statutes	Ps 119:71
have I l-ed wisdom	Prov 30:3
will they l war	Is 2:4
l from Me	Matt 11:29
l-ed to be content	Phil 4:11
He l-ed obedience	Heb 5:8

LEARNING (n) *knowledge*

increase *his* l	Prov 9:9
l of the Egyptians	Acts 7:22
great l is driving	Acts 26:24

LEAST *insignificant*

l of my master's	2 Kin 18:24
greatest to the l	2 Chr 34:30

l in the kingdom	Matt 5:19
he who is l...is	Matt 11:11
l of the apostles	1 Cor 15:9
very l of all saints	Eph 3:8

LEATHER *animal skin*

man with a l girdle	2 Kin 1:8
a l belt about his	Matt 3:4
and *wore* a l belt	Mark 1:6

LEAVE *abandon, depart, forsake*

shall l his father	Gen 2:24
arise, l this land	Gen 31:13
not l me defenseless	Ps 141:8
kindness and truth l	Prov 3:3
l the ninety-nine	Matt 18:12
Peace I l with you	John 14:27
I am l-ing...world	John 16:28

LEAVEN *yeast*

no l found in your	Ex 12:19
not be baked with l	Lev 6:17
seven days no l shall	Deut 16:4
heaven is like l	Matt 13:33
little l leavens the	1 Cor 5:6

LEAVENED *raised by yeast*

whoever eats what is l	Ex 12:19
with cakes of l bread	Lev 7:13
not eat l bread	Deut 16:3
until it was all l	Matt 13:33

LEBANON

mountain range N of Israel

	Josh 9:1; Judg 3:3; 1 Kin 5:6
showing God's greatness	Ps 29:6
symbol of prosperity	Ps 92:12

LEGAL *lawful*

has a l matter	Ex 24:14
Give me l protection	Luke 18:3

LEGION *division, group*

twelve l-s of angels	Matt 26:53
My name is L	Mark 5:9
man who had...l	Mark 5:15
L; for many demons	Luke 8:30

LEG *part of body*

l-s are pillars of	Song 5:15
Uncover the l	Is 47:2
not break His l-s	John 19:33

LEMUEL

royal author of section of Proverbs

	Prov 31:1,4

LEND *loan*

l-ing them money	Neh 5:10
l-s...on interest	Ezek 18:13
l, expecting nothing	Luke 6:35
l me three loaves	Luke 11:5

LENDER *loaner*

becomes the l-'s slave	Prov 22:7
l like the borrower	Is 24:2

LENGTH

the l of the ark	Gen 6:15
l of days and years	Prov 3:2
breadth and l and	Eph 3:18
l and width...equal	Rev 21:16

LEOPARD *animal*

l will lie down with	Is 11:6

Column 1

Or the l his spots | Jer 13:23
Like a l I will lie | Hos 13:7
beast...was like a l | Rev 13:2

LEPER *one having leprosy*

As for the l | Lev 13:45
King Uzziah...a l | 2 Chr 26:21
a l came to Him | Matt 8:2
cleanse *the* l-s | Matt 10:8
home of Simon the l | Mark 14:3

LEPROSY *infectious disease*

of l on the skin | Lev 13:2
mark of l on a | Lev 14:34
an infection of l | Deut 24:8
cure him of his l | 2 Kin 5:3
his l was cleansed | Matt 8:3

LEPROUS *having leprosy*

hand was l like snow | Ex 4:6
is a l malignancy | Lev 13:51
ten l...met Him | Luke 17:12

LET *allow, permit*

L there be light | Gen 1:3
L My people go | Ex 5:1
L the children alone | Matt 19:14
l this cup pass from | Matt 26:39
L not your heart be | John 14:1

LETTER *epistle or symbol*

a l sent to Solomon | 2 Chr 2:11
smallest l or stroke | Matt 5:18
You are our l | 2 Cor 3:2
l caused you sorrow | 2 Cor 7:8
large l-s I am writing | Gal 6:11

LEVEL *flat, plain*

lead me in a l path | Ps 27:11
path of the righteous l | Is 26:7
stood on a l place | Luke 6:17

LEVI

1 *son of Jacob* | Gen 34:25
2 *tribe* | Num 1:49; Rev 7:7
3 *two ancestors of Jesus*
| Luke 3:24,29
4 *apostle*
| Mark 2:14; Luke 5:27,29

LEVIATHAN

symbolic monster of the deep
Job 3:8; Ps 104:26; Is 27:1

LEVITES

descendants of Levi | Ex 6:19,25
charged with the care of the
sanctuary | Num 1:50; 3:41

LEVY (n) *payment, tax*

the LORD's l | Num 31:38
l fixed by Moses | 2 Chr 24:6

LEVY (v) *impose a tax*

l a tax for the LORD | Num 31:28
l-ied forced laborers | 1 Kin 9:21

LEWDNESS *lascivious, lust*

land...full of l | Lev 19:29
not commit this l | Ezek 16:43
I will uncover her l | Hos 2:10

LIAR *one telling lies*

who...prove me a l | Job 24:25
a poor man than a l | Prov 19:22

Column 2

I shall be a l like | John 8:55
hypocrisy of l-s | 1 Tim 4:2
we make Him a l | 1 John 1:10

LIBATION *see* **OFFERINGS**

LIBERTY *freedom*

I will walk at l | Ps 119:45
proclaim l to captives | Is 61:1
spy out our l | Gal 2:4
the *law* of l | James 1:25

LIBNAH

1 *place in wilderness* | Num 33:21
2 *Canaanite city*
| Josh 10:29; 2 Kin 23:31
a Levitical city | 1 Chr 6:57

LIBYA

country in N Africa
| Ezek 30:5; Acts 2:10

LICK *lap up*

dogs shall l up your | 1 Kin 21:19
his enemies l the dust | Ps 72:9
dogs were...l-ing | Luke 16:21

LIE (n) *false statement*

speak l-s go astray | Ps 58:3
tells l-s will perish | Prov 19:9
prophesy a l to you | Jer 27:10
the father of l-s | John 8:44
truth of God for a l | Rom 1:25
no l is of the truth | 1 John 2:21

LIE (v) *make false statement*

nor l to one another | Lev 19:11
l-d to Him with their | Ps 78:36
l-d about the LORD | Jer 5:12
l to the Holy Spirit | Acts 5:3
not l to one another | Col 3:9
impossible...God to l | Heb 6:18

LIE (v) *recline*

when you l down | Deut 11:19
she **lay** at his feet | Ruth 3:14
Saul **lay** sleeping | 1 Sam 26:7
makes me l down | Ps 23:2
lying in a manger | Luke 2:12

LIFE *living or salvation*

the breath of l | Gen 2:7
l for l | Ex 21:23
l...is in the blood | Lev 17:11
Our l for yours | Josh 2:14
my l is *but* breath | Job 7:7
Who redeems your l | Ps 103:4
the springs of l | Prov 4:23
way of l and...death | Jer 21:8
to everlasting l | Dan 12:2
take my l from me | Jon 4:3
anxious for your l | Matt 6:25
loses his l for My | Matt 16:25
His l a ransom for | Matt 20:28
to inherit eternal l | Mark 10:17
l is more than food | Luke 12:23
but have eternal l | John 3:16
out of death into l | John 5:24
I am the bread of l | John 6:35
lays down his l | John 10:11
resurrection and...l | John 11:25
truth, and the l | John 14:6
lay down his l for | John 15:13

Column 3

walk in newness of l | Rom 6:4
the Spirit gives l | 2 Cor 3:6
Christ, who is our l | Col 3:4
an undisciplined l | 2 Thess 3:11
receive...crown of l | James 1:12
lay down our l-ves | 1 John 3:16
book of l of the lamb | Rev 13:8

LIFEBLOOD

I will require your l | Gen 9:5
poured out their l | Is 63:6
l of the innocent | Jer 2:34

LIFETIME *length of life*

Throughout his l | 2 Chr 34:33
His favor for a l | Ps 30:5
my l of futility | Eccl 7:15
as the l of a tree | Is 65:22

LIFT *exalt, raise*

l up your eyes and | Gen 13:14
l up your staff and | Ex 14:16
l up your voice | Job 38:34
One who l-s my head | Ps 3:3
I Will l up my eyes | Ps 121:1
will not l up sword | Is 2:4
Spirit l-ed me up | Ezek 3:14
Son of Man be l-ed | John 3:14
He was l-ed up | Acts 1:9
l-ing up holy hands | 1 Tim 2:8

LIGHT *brightness, lamp*

Let there be l | Gen 1:3
Israel had l in | Ex 10:23
l of the wicked | Job 18:5
LORD is my l | Ps 27:1
And a l to my path | Ps 119:105
like the l of dawn | Prov 4:18
walk in the l of the | Is 2:5
your l has come | Is 60:1
stars for l by night | Jer 31:35
the l of the world | Matt 5:14
body will be full of l | Matt 6:22
l of revelation to | Luke 2:32
There was the true l | John 1:9
I am the l | John 8:12
while you have...l | John 12:35
l of the gospel | 2 Cor 4:4
walk as children of l | Eph 5:8
Father of l-s | James 1:17
if we walk in the l | 1 John 1:7

LIGHTNING *flash of light in*
sky

thunder and l flashes | Ex 19:16
He spreads His l | Job 36:30
makes l for the rain | Jer 10:13
l...from the east | Matt 24:27
appearance...like l | Matt 28:3

LIKENESS *similarity*

according to Our l | Gen 1:26
an idol, or any l | Ex 20:4
the l of sinful flesh | Rom 8:3
made in the l of men | Phil 2:7

LILY *flower*

The l of the valleys | Song 2:1
blossom like the l | Hos 14:5
l-ies of the field | Matt 6:28

LIMIT *end, extent*

there is no l | 1 Chr 22:16

Column 1

no l to windy words — Job 16:3
set a l for the rain — Job 28:26
no l to the treasure — Nah 2:9

LINE *boundary* or *cord*

draw your *border* l — Num 34:7
ran from...battle l — 1 Sam 4:12
a l into the Nile — Is 19:8
plumb l in the hand — Zech 4:10

LINEN *type of cloth*

makes l garments — Prov 31:24
buy...a l waistband — Jer 13:1
left the l sheet — Mark 14:52
wrapped Him...l — Mark 15:46
saw the l wrappings — John 20:5
clothed in fine l — Rev 19:14

LINTEL *horizontal crosspiece*

blood on the l — Ex 12:23
l *and* five-sided — 1 Kin 6:31

LION *wild animal*

Judah is a l-'s whelp — Gen 49:9
a l or a bear — 1 Sam 17:34
hunt me like a l — Job 10:16
tear my soul like a l — Ps 7:2
are bold as a l — Prov 28:1
cast into the l-s' — Dan 6:16
like a roaring l — 1 Pet 5:8

LIPS *part of mouth*

My l will praise — Ps 63:3
With her flattering l — Prov 7:21
Your l, *my* bride — Song 4:11
a man of unclean l — Is 6:5
honors Me with...l — Matt 15:8

LIQUOR *alcoholic drink*

concerning wine and l — Mic 2:11
drink no wine or l — Luke 1:15

LISTEN *hear, heed*

Pharaoh will not l — Ex 7:4
l to His voice — Deut 4:30
l...commandments — Deut 11:27
scoffer does not l — Prov 13:1
L to your father — Prov 23:22
draw near to l — Eccl 5:1
L to Me, O Jacob — Is 48:12
L...another parable — Matt 21:33
care what you l to — Mark 4:24
l-ing to the word — Luke 5:1
My Son...l to Him — Luke 9:35

LITERATURE *writings*

teach them the l — Dan 1:4
every *branch of* l — Dan 1:17

LITTLE *small quantity*

a l lower than God — Ps 8:5
a l boy will lead — Is 11:6
O men of l faith — Matt 6:30
forgiven l, loves l — Luke 7:47
a l leaven leavens — 1 Cor 5:6
l children, abide — 1 John 2:28

LIVE (v) *reside* or *be alive*

eat, and l forever — Gen 3:22
does not l by bread — Deut 8:3
my Redeemer l-s — Job 19:25
Let my soul l — Ps 119:175
Listen, that you may l — Is 55:3
can these bones l — Ezek 37:3

Column 2

righteous will l by — Hab 2:4
not l on bread alone — Matt 4:4
l even if he dies — John 11:25
because I l — John 14:19
shall l by faith — Rom 1:17
Christ died and l-d — Rom 14:9
no longer I who l — Gal 2:20
to l is Christ — Phil 1:21
worship Him who l-s — Rev 4:10

LIVER *internal organ*

the lobe of the l — Ex 29:13
l of the sin offering — Lev 9:10
pierces through his l — Prov 7:23
he looks at the l — Ezek 21:21

LIVESTOCK *domestic animals*

was very rich in l — Gen 13:2
their l to Joseph — Gen 47:17
l of Egypt died — Ex 9:6
large number of l — Num 32:1

LIVING (adj) *alive*

man became a l being — Gen 2:7
voice of the l god — Deut 5:26
Divide the l child — 1 Kin 3:25
Son of the l God — Matt 16:16
given you l water — John 4:10
I am the l bread — John 6:51
l and holy sacrifice — Rom 12:1
became a l soul — 1 Cor 15:45
temple of the l God — 2 Cor 6:16
word of God is l — Heb 4:12

LIVING (n) *what is alive*

mother of all *the* l — Gen 3:20
land of the l — Job 28:13
that the l may know — Dan 4:17
God...of the l — Matt 22:32
judge the l and the — 1 Pet 4:5

LOAD *burden*

in all their l-s — Num 4:27
I alone bear the l — Deut 1:12
My l is light — Matt 11:30

LOAF *portion of bread*

gave him a l of bread — Jer 37:21
shall ask him for a l — Matt 7:9
five l-ves and two — Matt 14:17

LO-AMMI

second son of Hosea — Hos 1:9

LOAN *something lent*

your neighbor a l — Deut 24:10
rich with l-s — Hab 2:6

LOATHE *despise, destest*

I l-d *that* generation — Ps 95:10
sated man l-s honey — Prov 27:7
I l the arrogance of — Amos 6:8

LOATHSOME *detestable*

l to the Egyptians — Gen 46:34
like l food to me — Job 6:7
l and malignant sore — Rev 16:2

LOCK (n) *tuft of hair*

seven l-s of my hair — Judg 16:13
flowing l-s of...head — Song 7:5
a l of my head — Ezek 8:3

LOCK (v) *secure, shut*

l the door behind — 2 Sam 13:17

Column 3

l-ed quite securely — Acts 5:23
l up...the saints — Acts 26:10

LOCUST *grasshopper*

wind brought the l-s — Ex 10:13
you may eat: the l — Lev 11:22
come in like l-s — Judg 6:5
leap like the l — Job 39:20
l-s have no king — Prov 30:27
like the swarming l — Nah 3:17
food was l-s and wild — Matt 3:4

LOD / LYDDA

town of Benjamin SE of coastal Jaffa
— 1 Chr 8:12; Neh 11:35; Acts 9:32-38

LODGE *dwell, spend the night*

where you l, I will l — Ruth 1:16
drank and l-d there — Judg 19:4
In his neck l-s — Job 41:22
l in the wilderness — Ps 55:7

LODGING (adj) *dwelling*

fodder at the l place — Gen 42:27
about at the l place — Ex 4:24
A wayfarers' l place — Jer 9:2

LOFTINESS *elevated, haughty*

l of man will be — Is 2:11
l of your dwelling — Obad 3

LOFTY *grand, high*

built Thee a l house — 1 Kin 8:13
high and l mountain — Is 57:7

LOG *beam, wood*

he who splits l-s — Eccl 10:9
l out of your own eye — Matt 7:5

LOINS *lower back*

with your l girded — Ex 12:11
Gird up your l — 2 Kin 4:29
l are full of anguish — Is 21:3
having girded your l — Eph 6:14

LOIS

grandmother of Timothy
— 2 Tim 1:5

LONELY *alone, isolated*

I am l and afflicted — Ps 25:16
makes a home for the l — Ps 68:6
How l sits the city — Lam 1:1
to a l place and rest — Mark 6:31

LONG (adj) *extended*

there was a l war — 2 Sam 3;1
L life is in her — Prov 3:16
you make l prayers — Matt 23:14
if a man has l hair — 1 Cor 11:14

LONG (v) *desire, want*

Who l for death — Job 3:21
my soul l-s for Thee — Is 26:9
l-ing to be fed — Luke 16:21
I l to see you — Rom 1:11
angels l to look — 1 Pet 1:12
l for the pure milk — 1 Pet 2:2

LOOK *see, stare*

Do not l behind you — Gen 19:17
afraid to l at God — Ex 3:6
LORD l-s at...heart — 1 Sam 16:7

L upon my affliction Ps 25:18
The sea **l**-ed and fled Ps 114:3
not **l** on the wine Prov 23:31
l eagerly for Him Is 8:17
l to the Holy One Is 17:7
l on Me...pierced Zech 12:10
L at the birds of Matt 6:26
l-ing up...heaven Matt 14:19
plow and **l**-ing back Luke 9:62
l on the fields John 4:35
l on Him...pierced John 19:37
l-ing for the blessed Titus 2:13
l-ing for...heavens 2 Pet 3:13

LOOSE release

l the cords of Orion Job 38:31
hast **l**-d my bonds Ps 116:16
l on earth shall be Matt 16:19
you **l** on earth Matt 18:18

LORD personal name of God
Old Testament
Different Hebrew words are
translated as Lord
Lord (*Yahweh*)
  Gen 4:1; Ex 3:2,15; Ps 23:1;
  Is 40:31; Ezek 11:23
Lord God (*Adonai Yahweh*)
  Gen 15:2; 2 Sam 7:18,19;
  Is 1:24; Ezek 28:6; Hab 3:19
Lord God (*Yahweh Elohim*)
  Gen 2:4; Ps 59:5; 68:18;
  Jer 15:16; Jon 1:9
Lord (*Adonai*)
  Gen 18:27; Ex 4:10; Josh 3:11;
  Ps 68:19; Mic 4:13
Lord God (*Yah Yahweh*) Is 12:2
New Testament
Different Greek words are
translated as Lord
Lord (*Kyrios, refers to either the*
Father or the Son)
  Matt 1:20; John 11:2; Acts
  5:19; 2 Cor 5:6; 1 Thess 4:16
Lord (*Despotes*)
  Luke 2:29; Acts 4:24; Rev
                                6:10
Lord God (*Kyrios Theos, refers*
to either the Father or the Son)
  Luke 1:32; Rev
  1:8;11:17;16:7;18:8
Lord Jesus (*Kyrios Iesous*)
  Mark 16:19; Luke 24:3; Acts
  4:33; 7:59
Lord Jesus Christ (*Kyrios Iesous*
Christos)
  Acts 15:26; Rom 1:7;5:1;
  1 Cor 1:10; Eph 1:2,3;
  1 Thess 5:9; James 2:1

LORD human master, ruler

Hear us, my **l** Gen 23:6
not my **l** be angry Gen 31:35
Moses, my **l** Num 11:28
l-s of...Philistines Judg 16:27
counsel of my **l** Ezra 10:3
l-s of the nations Is 16:8
his **l** commanded Matt 18:25
write to my **l** Acts 25:26

LO-RUHAMAH
daughter of Hosea Hos 1:6,8

LOSE mislay, suffer loss

do not **l** courage 2 Chr 15:7
lost their confidence Neh 6:16
stars **l** their Joel 2:10
his life shall **l** it Matt 10:39
that which was **lost** Matt 18:11
not **l** his reward Mark 9:41
whoever **l**-s his life Luke 9:24

LOSS damage, what is lost

might not suffer **l** Dan 6:2
damage and great **l** Acts 27:10
might not suffer **l** 2 Cor 7:9
all things to be **l** Phil 3:8

LOST (adj) missing, ruined

like a **l** sheep Ps 119:176
have become **l** sheep Jer 50:6
l sheep...of Israel Matt 10:6
the wine is **l** Mark 2:22

LOST (n) without God

I will seek the **l** Ezek 34:16
sent only to the **l** Matt 15:24

LOT
nephew of Abraham
  Gen 12:5;19:15,36

LOT portion or decision process

one **l** for the LORD Lev 16:8
clothing they cast **l**-s Ps 22:18
your **l** with us Prov 1:14
let us cast **l**-s Jon 1:7
tear it, but cast **l**-s John 19:24
l fell to Matthias Acts 1:26

LOUD great, noisy

very **l** trumpet sound Ex 19:16
with a **l** shout Ezra 3:13
Jesus cried...**l** voice Matt 27:50
heard...a **l** voice Rev 1:10

LOVE (n) compassion, devotion

l covers all Prov 10:12
in unchanging **l** Mic 7:18
l will grow cold Matt 24:12
abide in My **l** John 15:10
Greater **l** has no one John 15:13
demonstrates His...**l** Rom 5:8
separate us from...**l** Rom 8:39
l edifies 1 Cor 8:1
l is kind 1 Cor 13:4
Pursue **l** 1 Cor 14:1
l of Christ controls 2 Cor 5:14
through **l** serve one Gal 5:13
fruit...is **l** Gal 5:22
speaking...truth in **l** Eph 4:15
l of money is a root 1 Tim 6:10
for **l** is from God 1 John 4:7
God is **l** 1 John 4:16
l casts out fear 1 John 4:18
have left your first **l** Rev 2:4

LOVE (v)

who **l** Me and keep My Ex 20:6
l your neighbor as Lev 19:18
l the LORD your God Deut 6:5
the LORD **l**-d Israel 1 Kin 10:9
I **l** Thy testimonies Ps 119:119
LORD **l**-s He reproves Prov 3:12
friend **l**-s at all Prov 17:17
Do not **l** sleep Prov 20:13

A time to **l** Eccl 3:8
Hate evil, **l** good Amos 5:15
do not **l** perjury Zech 8:17
l your enemies Matt 5:44
l to stand and pray Matt 6:5
God so **l**-d the world John 3:16
you **l** one another John 13:34
l-s a cheerful giver 2 Cor 9:7
Husbands, **l**...wives Eph 5:25
Do not **l** the world 1 John 2:15
whom I **l**, I reprove Rev 3:19

LOVERS one who desires, loves

l have been crushed Jer 22:20
I called to my **l** Lam 1:19
the hands of your **l** Ezek 16:39
I will go after my **l** Hos 2:5
l of pleasure...**l** of 2 Tim 3:4

LOVINGKINDNESS
compassion

His **l** is upon Israel Ezra 3:11
abundant in **l** and Ps 86:15
sing of the **l** of the Ps 89:1
By **l** and truth Prov 16:6
with everlasting **l** Is 54:8

LOWLAND low hills

country and in the **l** Deut 1:7
the Negev and the **l** Josh 10:40
sycamores in the **l** 2 Chr 1:15
the cities of the **l** Jer 32:44
see also **SHEPHELAH**

LOWLY humble, little

He sets on high...**l** Job 5:11
He regards the **l** Ps 138:6
associate with the **l** Rom 12:16

LOYALTY faithfulness

Is this your **l** 2 Sam 16:17
proclaims his own **l** Prov 20:6
l delight in **l** Hos 6:6

LUKE

associate of Paul
  2 Tim 4:11; Philem 24
author of Luke and Acts
  Luke 1:1; Acts 1:1
physician Col 4:14

LUKEWARM tepid

because you are **l** Rev 3:16

LUST sexual desire

looks...woman to **l** Matt 5:28
from youthful **l**-s 2 Tim 2:22
You **l** and do not James 4:2
l of the eyes 1 John 2:16

LUXURIANT lush, productive

beneath...**l** tree 1 King 14:23
Israel is a **l** vine Hos 10:1

LUXURY extravagance

L is not fitting for Prov 19:10
clothed and live in **l** Luke 7:25

LUZ

l ancient name of Bethel
  Gen 28:19;48:3
2 town in Aram Judg 1:26

LYCAONIA
Roman province in Asia Minor

Acts 14:6

LYDDA *see* **LOD**

LYDIA
1 *seller of purple dyes and goods*
Acts 16:14,40
2 *region on the W coast of Asia*
Minor   Jer 46:9

LYING (adj) *false*
with a l tongue   Ps 109:2
hatred *has* l lips   Prov 10:18
l pen of the scribes   Jer 8:8
and l divination   Ezek 13:6

LYRE *stringed instrument*
play the l and pipe   Gen 4:21
prophesy with l-s   1 Chr 25:1
Awake, harp and l   Ps 57:8

LYSTRA
a Lycaonian town
Acts 14:6;16:1,2

M

MACEDONIA
Roman province   Acts 16:9,12
N Greece   Phil 4:15; 1 Tim 1:3
visited by Paul
Acts 16:10; 2 Cor 2:13

MACHIR
1 *grandson of Joseph*   Josh 17:1
2 *son of Ammiel*   2 Sam 9:4,5

MACHPELAH
cave near Hebron   Gen 23:17,19
Sarah's burial place   Gen 23:19
Abraham buried there   Gen 25:9
burial place of Jacob, Isaac,
Rebekah, and Leah
Gen 49:29ff;50:13

MAD *insane*
makes a wise man m   Eccl 7:7
nations are going m   Jer 51:7

MADMAN *insane person*
behaving as a m   1 Sam 21:14
m who prophesies   Jer 29:26

MADNESS *lunacy*
laughter, It is m   Eccl 2:2
consider...m and folly Eccl 2:12

MAGADAN
village on the Sea of Galilee
Matt 15:39

MAGDALENE
Mary   Matt 27:56,61
from village of Magdala
Mark 15:40,47; John 20:1,18

MAGI
wise men from Persia who visited
Jesus, Mary, and Joseph
Matt 2:1,7,16

MAGIC *sorcery*
practicing m   Acts 8:9
who practiced m   Acts 19:19

MAGICIAN *sorcerer, wizard*
called for...m-s   Gen 41:8
the m-s of Egypt   Ex 7:11
of any m, conjurer or   Dan 2:10
found a certain m   Acts 13:6

MAGISTRATE
appear before the m   Luke 12:58
to the chief m-s   Acts 16:20

MAGNIFY *extol, praise*
name...be m-ied   2 Sam 7:26
Thou dost m him   Job 7:17
O m the LORD with me   Ps 34:3
hast m-ied Thy word   Ps 138:2
Jesus was...m-ied   Acts 19:17
I m my ministry   Rom 11:13

MAGOG
1 *son of Japheth*   1 Chr 1:5
2 *region in Asia Minor or further*
N ruled by Gog
Ezek 38:2;39:6
see also **GOG**

MAHANAIM
city in Trans-Jordan
Josh 13:26,30
city of refuge   Josh 21:38
Levitical city   1 Chr 6:80

MAHER-SHALAL-HASH-BAZ
symbolic name of one of Isaiah's
sons   Is 8:3

MAHLAH
1 *daughter of Zelophehad*
Num 26:33;27:1; Josh 17:3
2 *a Manassite*   1 Chr 7:18

MAHLON
husband of Ruth   Ruth 1:5;4:10

MAID
Hagar, Sarai's m   Gen 16:8
gave my m to my   Gen 30:18
I am Ruth your m   Ruth 3:9
way of a man...a m   Prov 30:19

MAIDENS *young woman*
at the Nile...her m   Ex 2:5
m...tambourines   Ps 68:25

MAIDSERVANT *female slave*
do...to your m   Deut 15:17
give Thy m a son   1 Sam 1:11
let your m speak   2 Sam 14:12
while your m slept   1 Kin 3:20

MAJESTIC *dignified, grand*
Who is like Thee, m   Ex 15:11
with His m voice   Job 37:4
How m is Thy name   Ps 8:1
They are the m ones   Ps 16:3
m is His work   Ps 111:3
by the M Glory   2 Pet 1:17

MAJESTY *grandeur*
Around God is...m   Job 37:22
He is clothed with m   Ps 93:1
The m of our God   Is 35:2
right hand of the M   Heb 1:3
revile angelic m-ies   Jude 8

MAKE *cause, create, do*
Let Us m man in   Gen 1:26
not m for...an idol   Ex 20:4
M me know Thy ways   Ps 25:4
M ready the way of   Matt 3:3
m you fishers of men   Matt 4:19

MAKER *creator*
Where is God my M   Job 35:10
kneel before...our M   Ps 95:6
M of heaven and   Ps 115:15
I, the LORD, am the m   Is 44:24

MAKKEDAH
Canaanite city in Judah
Josh 10:21; 15:41

MALACHI
prophet   Mal 1:1

MALCHUS
servant whose ear was cut off by
Peter   John 18:10

MALE
m and female He   Gen 1:27
lamb...unblemished m   Ex 12:5
likeness of m or   Deut 4:16
slew...m children   Matt 2:16
made...m and female   Matt 19:4
neither m nor female   Gal 3:28

MALICE *evil, mischief*
perceived their m   Matt 22:18
leaven of m and   1 Cor 5:8
wrath, m, slander   Col 3:8
putting aside all m   1 Pet 2:1

MALICIOUS *harmful, spiteful*
to be a m witness   Ex 23:1
m gossips, without   2 Tim 3:3

MALTA
island S of Sicily where Paul was
shipwrecked   Acts 28:1

MAMMON *wealth*
serve God and m   Matt 6:24
m of unrighteousness   Luke 16:9

MAMRE
1 *Abraham's dwelling place near*
Hebron   Gen 13:18
2 *Amorite chieftain*   Gen 14:24

MAN *male*
make m in Our image   Gen 1:26
God formed m of dust   Gen 2:7
Elisha the m of God   2 Kin 5:8
m is born for trouble   Job 5:7
blessed is the m   Ps 1:1
m is a mere breath   Ps 39:11
righteous m hates   Prov 13:5
Will a m rob God   Mal 3:8
light...before men   Matt 5:16
fishers of men   Mark 1:17
Sabbath...for m   Mark 2:27
rich m to enter   Mark 10:25
what is a m profited   Luke 9:25
a m, sent from God   John 1:6
How can a m be born   John 3:4
a...m of Macedonia   Acts 16:9
through one m sin   Rom 5:12
as is common to m   1 Cor 10:13

when I became a m   1 Cor 13:11
m...leave his father   Eph 5:31

MAN, SON OF
see **SON OF MAN**

MANASSEH
1 *son of Joseph*   Gen 41:51;46:20
2 *tribe and area*
     Num 13:11; Josh 17:1
3 *king of Judah*   2 Kin 21:1,11
4 *Pahath-moab's son*   Ezra 10:30
5 *son of Hashum*   Ezra 10:33

MANDRAKES *love fruit*
found **m** in the field   Gen 30:14
m...fragrance   Song 7:13

MANGER *feeding trough*
spend...at your **m**   Job 39:9
the **m** is clean   Prov 14:4
laid Him in a **m**   Luke 2:7

MANIFEST *reveal*
I **m-ed** Thy name   John 17:6
became **m** to those   Rom 10:20
made **m** to God   2 Cor 5:11
m-ed to His saints   Col 1:26

MANIFOLD *many and varied*
the **m** wisdom of God   Eph 3:10
stewards...**m** grace   1 Pet 4:10

MANKIND *the human race*
God...dwell with **m**   2 Chr 6:18
All **m** is stupid   Jer 51:17
Authority over all **m**   John 17:2
His love for **m**   Titus 3:4
kill a third of **m**   Rev 9:15

MANNA *food of the desert*
Israel named it **m**   Ex 16:31
m was like coriander   Num 11:7
m ceased on the day   Josh 5:12
He rained down **m**   Ps 78:24
Our fathers ate the **m**   John 6:31

MANNER *way*
Thy **m** with those   Ps 119:132
spoke in such a **m**   Acts 14:1
m worthy of...saints   Rom 16:2
walk in a **m** worthy   Eph 4:1

MANOAH
father of Samson   Judg 13:2ff

MANSLAYER
for the **m** to flee to   Num 35:6
m might flee there   Deut 4:42
the **m** who kills any   Josh 20:3

MANTLE *cloak, garment*
threw his **m** on him   1 Kin 19:19
the **m** of Elijah   2 Kin 2:13
as a **m** Thou wilt roll   Heb 1:12

MARAH
spring of bitter water   Ex 15:23

MARCH *pace, walk*
m around...seven times   Josh 6:4
m everyone in his path   Joel 2:8

MARDUK
chief Babylonian god   Jer 50:2

MARESHAH
1 *father of Hebron*   1 Chr 2:42
2 *son of Laadah*   1 Chr 4:21
3 *town in Judah*   2 Chr 11:5-8

MARK *sign, spot*
make any tattoo **m-s**   Lev 19:28
m on the foreheads   Ezek 9:4
m on his forehead   Rev 14:9
m of the beast   Rev 19:20

MARK, JOHN
author of Gospel of Mark
accompanied Paul and Barnabas
     Acts 13:5;15:37
cousin of Barnabas   Col 4:10

MARKET *selling or trading place*
was the **m** of nations   Is 23:3
coastlands were...**m**   Ezek 27:15
idle in the **m** place   Matt 20:3
sold in the meat **m**   1 Cor 10:25

MARRIAGE *wedlock*
a **m** alliance with   1 Kin 3:1
nor are given in **m**   Matt 22:30
m *be held* in honor   Heb 13:4
m supper of the Lamb   Rev 19:9

MARRY *join in wedlock*
m-ied foreign wives   Ezra 10:10
m-ies a divorced   Matt 5:32
better not to **m**   Matt 19:10
neither **m**, nor are   Mark 12:25
m-ied woman is bound   Rom 7:2
better to **m** than to   1 Cor 7:9

MARTHA
sister of Lazarus and Mary
     John 11:1,5

MARVEL *be amazed, wonder*
Jesus heard...**m-ed**   Matt 8:10
the multitude **m-ed**   Matt 15:31
Do not **m** that I said   John 3:7
m at the sight   Acts 7:31

MARVELOUS *extraordinary*
and see this **m** sight   Ex 3:3
It is **m** in our eyes   Ps 118:23
into His **m** light   1 Pet 2:9
m are Thy works   Rev 15:3

MARY
1 *mother of Jesus*   Matt 1:16
2 *Mary Magdalene*
     Matt 27:56; Mark 15:40
3 *mother of James and Joseph*
     Matt 27:56; Mark 16:1
4 *sister of Martha and Lazarus*
     John 11:1
5 *mother of Mark*   Acts 12:12
6 *wife of Clopas*   John 19:25
7 *Roman believer*   Rom 16:6

MASTER *lord, ruler*
God of...**m** Abraham   Gen 24:12
m shall pierce his ear   Ex 21:6
can serve two **m-s**   Matt 6:24
death no longer is **m**   Rom 6:9
sin shall not be **m**   Rom 6:14
obedient to...your **m-s**   Eph 6:5
a **M** in heaven   Col 4:1

MATTHEW
tax-gatherer   Matt 9:9;10:3
apostle
     Matt 10:3; Luke 6:15;
     Acts 1:13

MATTHIAS
replaced Judas   Acts 1:23,26

MATURE *full grown* or *stable*
then the **m** grain   Mark 4:28
those who are **m**   1 Cor 2:6
your thinking be **m**   1 Cor 14:20
food is for the **m**   Heb 5:14

MATURITY *ripeness, adulthood*
bring no fruit to **m**   Luke 8:14
let us press on to **m**   Heb 6:1

MEAL *prepared food*
a **m** for enjoyment   Eccl 10:19
not even eat a **m**   Mark 3:20
washed before...**m**   Luke 11:38
m-s together with   Acts 2:46
for a *single* **m**   Heb 12:16

MEAL OFFERING
see **OFFERINGS**

MEANINGLESS *senseless*
with **m** arguments   Is 29:21
not use **m** repetition   Matt 6:7

MEASURE (n) *amount*
a full and just **m**   Deut 25:15
good **m**, pressed   Luke 6:38
to each a **m** of faith   Rom 12:3
m of Christ's gift   Eph 4:7

MEASURE (v) *determine extent*
he stopped **m-ing** *it*   Gen 41:49
m their former work   Is 65:7
he **m-ed** the gate   Ezek 40:13
shall be **m-ed** to you   Mark 4:24
rod to **m** the city   Rev 21:15

MEASURING *standard*
justice the **m** line   Is 28:17
was given me a **m** rod   Rev 11:1

MEAT *flesh, food*
Who will give us **m**   Num 11:4
LORD...you **m**   Num 11:18
you may eat **m**   Deut 12:20
rained **m** upon them   Ps 78:27
from **m** sacrificed   Acts 21:25
good not to eat **m**   Rom 14:21
I will never eat **m**   1 Cor 8:13
m sacrificed...idols   1 Cor 10:28

MEDE(S)
ancient Indo-Europeans of NW
Iran   Dan 5:31;11:1

MEDEBA
Moabite town E of Dead Sea
     Josh 13:9; 1 Chr 19:7

MEDIA
country of the Medes
     Ezra 6:2; Esth 1:18; Is 21:2

MEDIATOR *intermediary*
by the agency of a **m**   Gal 3:19
one **m**...between God   1 Tim 2:5

MEDITATE *ponder*

Isaac went out to **m**	Gen 24:63
His law he **m-s** day	Ps 1:2
M in your heart	Ps 4:4
I **m** on Thee in the	Ps 63:6

MEDITATION *deep reflection*

m...Be acceptable	Ps 19:14
m be pleasing to Him	Ps 104:34
my **m** all the day	Ps 119:97

MEDIUM *summons spirits*

not turn to **m-s** or	Lev 19:31
m...be put to death	Lev 20:27
a **m,** or a spiritist	Deut 18:11
woman who is a **m**	1 Sam 28:7
will resort to...**m-s**	Is 19:3

MEEKNESS *gentleness*

cause of truth and **m**	Ps 45:4
m and...of Christ	2 Cor 10:1

MEET *encounter*

Esau ran to **m** him	Gen 33:4
people out...to **m** God	Ex 19:17
God...will **m** me	Ps 59:10
Prepare to **m**...God	Amos 4:12
to **m** the bridegroom	Matt 25:1
m-s his accusers	Acts 25:16
m...in the air	1 Thess 4:17

MEETING *assembly*

house of **m** for all	Job 30:23
midst of Thy **m** place	Ps 74:4

MEETING, TENT OF

see **TABERNACLE**

MEGIDDO

strategic city between Manasseh and Issachar
Josh 12:21; 2 Kin 9:27
plain in Jezreel Valley
2 Chr 35:22; Zech 12:11
see also **HAR-MAGEDON**

MELCHIZEDEK

1 *king of Salem*	Gen 14:18,19
priest	Ps 110:4
2 *type of undying priesthood*	
Heb 5:6,10;6:20;7:1ff	

MELODY *tune*

lyre...the sound of **m**	Ps 98:5
singing...making **m**	Eph 5:19

MELT *dissolve*

people **m** with fear	Josh 14:8
His voice...earth **m-ed**	Ps 46:6
mountains **m-ed** like	Ps 97:5
As silver is **m-ed**	Ezek 22:22

MEMBER *part of the whole*

m-s of...household	Matt 10:25
m-s one of another	Rom 12:5
if one **m** suffers	1 Cor 12:26
m-s of His body	Eph 5:30

MEMORIAL *commemoration*

this is My **m-name**	Ex 3:15
in a book as a **m**	Ex 17:14
stones...become a **m**	Josh 4:7
ascended as a **m**	Acts 10:4

MEMORY *remembrance*

M of him perishes	Job 18:17
cut off their **m**	Ps 109:15
m of the righteous	Prov 10:7
spoken of in **m** of	Mark 14:9

MEMPHIS

city in Egypt
Is 19:13; Jer 46:19; Ezek 30:13

MENAHEM

king of Israel 2 Kin 15:14,17

MENSTRUAL

m impurity for seven	Lev 15:19
a woman during...**m**	Ezek 18:6

MENSTRUATION

in the days of her **m**	Lev 12:2
like her bed at **m**	Lev 15:26

MEPHIBOSHETH

1 *son of Jonathan*	2 Sam 4:4
also **Merib-baal**	1 Chr 8:34
2 *son of Saul*	2 Sam 21:8

MERAB

Saul's daughter 1 Sam 18:17,19

MERARI

son of Levi Gen 46:11
head of a Levitical family
Ex 6:19; 2 Chr 34:12

MERCHANDISE

and your **m**	Ezek 27:33
a house of **m**	John 2:16

MERCHANT *buyer / seller*

m-s procured *them*	1 Kin 10:28
m of the peoples	Ezek 27:3
A **m,** in whose hands	Hos 12:7
m seeking...pearls	Matt 13:45
m-s of the earth	Rev 18:3

MERCIFUL *compassionate*

God **m** and gracious	Ps 86:15
the LORD is...and **m**	Ps 145:8
The **m** man...good	Prov 11:17
Blessed are the **m**	Matt 5:7
as your Father is **m**	Luke 6:36
m to me, the sinner	Luke 18:13

MERCY *compassion*

Great are Thy **m-ies**	Ps 119:156
in His **m** He redeemed	Is 63:9
m to *the* poor	Dan 4:27
the orphan finds **m**	Hos 14:3
they shall receive **m**	Matt 5:7
tender **m** of our God	Luke 1:78
m on whom I have **m**	Rom 9:15
by the **m-ies** of God	Rom 12:1
God, being rich in **m**	Eph 2:4

MERCY SEAT *covering over ark*

a **m** of pure gold	Ex 25:17
put the **m** on the ark	Ex 26:34
in front of the **m**	Ex 30:6
sprinkle it on the **m**	Lev 16:15
overshadowing the **m**	Heb 9:5

MERIBAH

1 *fountain of Rephidim*	Ex 17:7
2 *fountain of Kadesh-Barnea*	
	Num 27:14

MERODACH-BALADAN

king of Babylon Is 39:1
also **Berodach-Baladan**

MERRY *joyful, lively*

David...making **m**	1 Chr 15:29
wine makes life **m**	Eccl 10:19
eat, drink *and* be **m**	Luke 12:19
m with my friends	Luke 15:29

MESHA

1 *territorial boundary in Arabia*	
	Gen 10:30
2 *Moabite king*	2 Kin 3:4
3 *man of Judah*	1 Chr 2:42
4 *a Benjamite*	1 Chr 8:9

MESHACH

one of three Jews thrown into furnace Dan 3:19ff
also **Mishael** Dan 1:7

MESHECH

1 *son of Japheth*	Gen 10:2
2 *descendants and nation*	
Is 66:19; Ezek 27:13	

MESOPOTAMIA

land of Tigris and Euphrates Rivers
Deut 23:4; Judg 3:8;
1 Chr 19:6; Acts 7:2

MESSAGE *communication*

m from God for you	Judg 3:20
m...with authority	Luke 4:32
m and my preaching	1 Cor 2:4
the **m** of truth	Eph 1:13
m we have heard	1 John 1:5

MESSENGER *one sent*

My **m** whom I send	Is 42:19
m of the LORD of hosts	Mal 2:7
I send My **m** before	Matt 11:10
m-s of the churches	2 Cor 8:23
m of Satan	2 Cor 12:7

MESSIAH

anointed one
Dan 9:25,26; John 1:41;4:25
Greek: Christ

METAL

like glowing **m**	Ezek 1:4
their **m** images	Dan 11:8

METHUSELAH

son of Enoch	Gen 5:21
grandfather of Noah	Gen 5:25ff

MICAH

1 *an Ephraimite*	Judg 17:1
2 *line of Reuben*	1 Chr 5:5
3 *father of Abdon*	2 Chr 34:20
4 *prophet*	Jer 26:18; Mic 1:1
name of several other people	

MICAIAH

1 *prophet*	1 Kin 22:8-26
2 *father of Achbor*	2 Kin 22:12
3 *wife of Rehoboam*	2 Chr 13:2
4 *under Jehoshaphat*	2 Chr 17:7
5 *line of Asaph*	Neh 12:35
6 *under Nehemiah*	Neh 12:41
7 *son of Gemariah*	Jer 36:11

MICHAEL

1 *an archangel*
Dan 10:21;12:1; Jude 9;
Rev 12:7
2 *Jehoshaphat's son*   2 Chr 21:2
prince of Judah
3 *army captain*   1 Chr 12:20
4 *line of Gershom*   1 Chr 6:40
name of seven other people

MICHAL

daughter of Saul   1 Sam 18:20
David's wife   1 Sam 19:11

MIDDLE *midst*

the **m** of the garden   Gen 3:3
sun stopped in the **m** Josh 10:13
m of the lampstands   Rev 1:13

MIDDLE GATE

see GATES OF JERUSALEM

MIDHEAVEN *directly overhead*

eagle flying in **m**   Rev 8:13
angel flying in **m**   Rev 14:6
birds which fly in **m** Rev 19:17

MIDIAN

1 *a son of Abraham*   Gen 25:1,2
2 *land SE of Canaan in desert*
Ex 2:15; Num 31:8; Judg 8:28

MIDIANITES

people of Midian
Gen 37:36; Num 31:2;
Judg 7:7

MIDST *middle, within*

God is in the **m**   Ps 46:5
in the **m** of the fire   Dan 3:25
Holy One in your **m**   Hos 11:9
I am in their **m**   Matt 18:20

MIDWIFE *aids childbirth*

m...tied a scarlet   Gen 38:28
before the **m** can get   Ex 1:19

MIGDOL

1 *Israelite camp near Red Sea*
Ex 14:2; Num 33:7
2 *town in Egypt*   Jer 44:1

MIGHT *strength*

my first-born; My **m**   Gen 49:3
and with all your **m**   Deut 6:5
With Him are...**m**   Job 12:13
Not by **m** nor by   Zech 4:6
strength of His **m**   Eph 1:19

MIGHTY *powerful*

a **m** hunter before   Gen 10:9
m...awesome God   Deut 10:17
m men of valor   1 Chr 12:8
The LORD **m** in battle   Ps 24:8
a **m** king will rule   Is 19:4
m in the Scriptures   Acts 18:24
the **m** hand of God   1 Pet 5:6

MILCAH

1 *daughter of Haran*   Gen 11:29
2 *daughter of Zelophehad*
Num 26:33;27:1; Josh 17:3

MILCOM

god of Ammonites

---

1 Kin 11:5,33; 2 Kin 23:13;
Zeph 1:5
also **Molech**

MILE *distance, measurement*

one **m**, go with him   Matt 5:41
m-s from Jerusalem Luke 24:13

MILETUS

town in Asia Minor
Acts 20:15,17; 2 Tim 4:20

MILK

land flowing with **m**   Ex 3:8
pour me out like **m**   Job 10:10
m produces butter   Prov 30:33
m to drink, not   1 Cor 3:2
pure **m** of the word   1 Pet 2:2

MILL *grinding stones*

sound of the...**m**   Eccl 12:4
at the grinding **m**   Lam 5:13
women...at the **m**   Matt 24:41

MILLO

1 *fort near Shechem*
Beth-millo   Judg 9:6,20
2 *fortress in Jerusalem*
2 Sam 5:9; 1 Kin 9:15,24;
1 Chr 11:8; 2 Chr 32:5

MILLSTONE *grinding stone*

upper **m** in pledge   Deut 24:6
woman threw...**m**   Judg 9:53
m be hung around   Matt 18:6
stone like a great **m**   Rev 18:21

MINA

measure of gold or silver coin
1 Kin 10:17; Ezra 2:69;
Neh 7:71; Luke 19:13ff

MIND *memory, thought*

God tries the...**m**-s   Ps 7:9
Recall it to **m**   Is 46:8
I test the **m**   Jer 17:10
Let his **m** be changed Dan 4:16
He opened...**m**-s   Luke 24:45
with one **m** in the   Acts 2:46
to a depraved **m**   Rom 1:28
m set on the flesh   Rom 8:7
the **m** of Christ   1 Cor 2:16
m-s were hardened   2 Cor 3:14
with humility of **m**   Phil 2:3

MINDFUL *aware*

Lord be **m** of me   Ps 40:17
He is **m** that we are   Ps 103:14
LORD has been **m**   Ps 115:12
m of the...faith   2 Tim 1:5

MINISTER (n) *one who serves*

m-s before the ark   1 Chr 16:4
spoken of *as* **m**-s   Is 61:6
a **m** and a witness   Acts 26:16
a **m** of Christ Jesus   Rom 15:16
is Christ then a **m**   Gal 2:17
I was made a **m**   Eph 3:7
faithful **m** in the   Eph 6:21
His **m**-s a flame of   Heb 1:7
a **m** in the sanctuary Heb 8:2

MINISTER (v) *give help, serve*

to **m** as priest to Me   Ex 28:1

---

the boy **m**-ed to   1 Sam 2:11
not stand to **m**   1 Kin 8:11
to the LORD, To **m**   Is 56:6
angels were **m**-ing   Mark 1:13
follow Him and **m**   Mark 15:41

MINISTRY *service*

He began His **m**   Luke 3:23
to the **m** of the word   Acts 6:4
m of the Spirit   2 Cor 3:8
m of reconciliation   2 Cor 5:18
fulfill your **m**   2 Tim 4:5
a more excellent **m**   Heb 8:6

MIRACLE *supernatural event*

Work a **m**   Ex 7:9
I will perform **m**-s   Ex 34:10
m-s had occurred   Matt 11:21
He could do no **m**   Mark 6:5
perform a **m** in My   Mark 9:39
this **m** of healing   Acts 4:22
works **m**-s among you   Gal 3:5
wonders and...**m**-s   Heb 2:4

MIRE *mud*

cast me into the **m**   Job 30:19
Deliver me from the **m** Ps 69:14
wallowing in the **m**   2 Pet 2:22

MIRIAM

1 *sister of Moses and Aaron*
Ex 15:20; Num 12:4,10;20:1
2 *line of Ezrah*   1 Chr 4:17

MIRROR *image reflector*

see in a **m** dimly   1 Cor 13:12
natural face in a **m**   James 1:23

MISCARRIAGE *aborted fetus*

so that she has a **m**   Ex 21:22
m-s of a woman   Ps 58:8

MISERABLE *bad, unhappy*

loathe this **m** food   Num 21:5
m and chronic   Deut 28:59
Be **m** and mourn   James 4:9
m and poor and blind Rev 3:17

MISERY *sorrow, suffering*

conscious of my **m**   Job 10:15
Destruction and **m**   Rom 3:16

MISFORTUNE *adversity*

M will not come   Jer 5:12
m which He has   Jer 26:13
The day of his **m**   Obad 12

MISHAEL

1 *of family of Kohath*
Ex 6:22; Lev 10:4
2 *associate of Ezra*   Neh 8:4
3 *Daniel's friend*
Dan 1:6,7,11,19;2:17
also **Meshach**

MISLEAD *lead astray*

m-s a blind *person*   Deut 27:18
m-led My people   Ezek 13:10
that no one **m**-s you   Mark 13:5
m-ing our nation   Luke 23:2

MISSILES *what is thrown or shot*

m of the evil *one*   Eph 6:16

MISTREAT *treat badly, wrong*

not m...the stranger	Jer 22:3
slaves...m-ed them	Matt 22:6
pray for...who m	Luke 6:28
mocked and m-ed	Luke 18:32
m and to stone them	Acts 14:5

MISTRESS *woman in charge*

her m was despised	Gen 16:4
m of the house	1 Kin 17:17
the maid like her m	Is 24:2
the m of sorceries	Nah 3:4

MIZPAH / MIZPEH

1	*heap of stones*	Gen 31:49
2	*near Mt. Hermon*	Josh 11:3
3	*village in Judah*	Josh 15:38
4	*Benjamite town*	Josh 18:26
5	*town of Gilead*	Judg 10:17
6	*Moabite town*	1 Sam 22:3

MIZRAIM

1	*son of Ham*	Gen 10:6
	father of nations	Gen 10:13
2	*Heb. for Egypt*	1 Chr 1:8,11

MOAB

1 *son of Lot*   Gen 19:37
2 *country E of the Dead Sea*
  Ex 15:15; Josh 24:9; Ruth 1:2;
  2 Kin 3:7; Ps 60:8; Jer 48:1

MOCK *ridicule, scorn*

lads...m-ed him	2 Kin 2:23
Fools m at sin	Prov 14:9
who m-s the poor	Prov 17:5
soldiers also m-ed	Luke 23:36
God is not m-ed	Gal 6:7

MOCKERY *object of ridicule*

a m of the Egyptians	Ex 10:2
made a m of me	Num 22:29
a m of justice	Prov 19:28
m *and* insinuations	Hab 2:6

MOLECH

god of the Ammonites
          Lev 18:21; 1 Kin 11:7;
          Jer 32:35

also Milcom

MOLTEN *cast metal*

made it into a m calf	Ex 32:4
make...no m gods	Ex 34:17
destroy...m images	Num 33:52
capitals of m bronze	1 Kin 7:16
his m images are	Jer 10:14

MONEY *currency*

take double *the* m	Gen 43:12
not sell her for m	Deut 21:14
time to receive m	2 Kin 5:26
loves m will not be	Eccl 5:10
no m in their belt	Mark 6:8
m in the bank	Luke 19:23
love of m is a root	1 Tim 6:10

MONEYCHANGERS

the tables of the m	Matt 21:12
coins of the m	John 2:15

MONSTER *enormous animal*

created...sea m-s	Gen 1:21
sea, or the sea m	Job 7:12

sea m-s in the waters	Ps 74:13
belly of the sea m	Matt 12:40

MOON

m and...were bowing	Gen 37:9
the m stopped	Josh 10:13
m and stars to rule	Ps 136:9
beautiful as...m	Song 6:10
the m into blood	Joel 2:31
m will not...light	Matt 24:29
signs in...and m	Luke 21:25

MORALS *principles*

Bad...good m	1 Cor 15:33

MORDECAI

1 *returned from exile with*
  Zerubbabel   Ezra 2:2
2 *Esther's cousin*
          Esth 2:7;3:2;9:20;10:3

MORIAH

land / mountain where Abraham
  offered Isaac   Gen 22:2
threshing floor of Araunah
  (Ornan)   2 Sam 24:18
site of Temple   2 Chr 3:1

MORNING *dawn*

was m, a fifth day	Gen 1:23
Rise early in the m	Ex 8:20
the m stars sang	Job 38:7
m or evening sowing	Eccl 11:6
the bright m star	Rev 22:16

MORSEL *piece of bread*

have eaten my m	Job 31:17
Better is a dry m	Prov 17:1
after the m, Satan	John 13:27

MORTAL *what eventually dies*

not trust...In m man	Ps 146:3
life to your m bodies	Rom 8:11
m...immortality	1 Cor 15:53
in our m flesh	2 Cor 4:11

MOSES

birth	Ex 2:1-3
in Pharaoh's care	Ex 2:5-10
killed an Egyptian	Ex 2:11,12
exiled	Ex 2:15
called by God	Ex 3:1-22
opposed Pharaoh	Ex 5:11
crossed Red Sea	Ex 14
Ten Commandments	Ex 20:1-18
saw Canaan	Deut 3:23ff;34:1ff
death	Deut 31:14;34:5

MOTH *insect*

crushed before the m	Job 4:19
The m will eat them	Is 50:9
like a m to Ephraim	Hos 5:12
m and rust destroy	Matt 6:19

MOTHER

leave...and his m	Gen 2:24
m of all *the* living	Gen 3:20
Honor...and your m	Ex 20:12
a grief to his m	Prov 10:1
Contend with your m	Hos 2:2
When His m Mary	Matt 1:18
take...and His m	Matt 2:13
Who is My m	Matt 12:48
Honor your...m	Matt 19:19

Behold, your m	John 19:27

MOTHER-IN-LAW

who lies with his m	Deut 27:23
Orpah kissed her m	Ruth 1:14
m lying sick in bed	Matt 8:14

MOTIVES *attitudes, intentions*

LORD weighs the m	Prov 16:2
disclose the m of	1 Cor 4:5
than from pure m	Phil 1:17
judges with evil m	James 2:4
ask with wrong m	James 4:3

MOUND *bank of earth, hill*

cities...on their m-s	Josh 11:13
throw up a m	2 Kin 19:32
against the seige m-s	Jer 33:4

MOUNT (n) *hill, mountain*

In the m of the LORD	Gen 22:14
Moses on M Sinai	Num 3:1
Israel at M Carmel	1 Kin 18:19
M Zion which He	Ps 78:68
M of Olives...split	Zech 14:4

MOUNT (v) *climb up*

to m his chariot	2 Chr 10:18
m up *with* wings	Is 40:31
My fury will m up	Ezek 38:18
m-ed on a donkey	Zech 9:9
m-ed on a donkey	Matt 21:5

MOUNT OF OLIVES

see OLIVES, MOUNT OF

MOUNT ZION

see ZION, MOUNT

MOUNTAIN

sacrifice on the m	Gen 31:54
from His holy m	Ps 3:4
lift up...to the m-s	Ps 121:1
lovely on the m-s	Is 52:7
eat at the m shrines	Ezek 18:6
m-s will melt	Mic 1:4
the m will move	Zech 14:4
m-s, Fall on us	Luke 23:30
withdrew...to the m	John 6:15
faith...remove m-s	1 Cor 13:2

MOURN *grieve, lament*

m her father and	Deut 21:13
David m-ed...son	2 Sam 13:37
A time to m	Eccl 3:4
earth m-s *and* withers	Is 24:4
comfort all who m	Is 61:2
Blessed...who m	Matt 5:4
shall m and weep	Luke 6:25
Be miserable and m	James 4:9

MOUSE *rodent*

the mole, and the m	Lev 11:29
five golden mice	1 Sam 6:4
mice that ravage	1 Sam 6:5

MOUTH

has made man's m	Ex 4:11
m condemns you	Job 15:6
From the m of infants	Ps 8:2
Let the words of my m	Ps 19:14
fool's m is his ruin	Prov 18:7
your m is lovely	Song 4:3
out of the m of God	Matt 4:4

confess with your **m** Rom 10:9

MOVE *change position, stir*

Spirit of God...**m-ing** Gen 1:2
pillar of cloud **m-d** Ex 14:19
I shall not be **m-d** Ps 10:6
all the hills **m-d** Jer 4:24
m-d with compassion Mark 1:41
He was deeply **m-d** John 11:33
in Him we live...**m** Acts 17:28
m-d by the...Spirit 2 Pet 1:21

MULE *animal*

mounted his **m** 2 Sam 13:29
Absalom...on *his* **m** 2 Sam 18:9
ride on the king's **m** 1 Kin 1:44
war horses and **m-s** Ezek 27:14

MULTIPLY *increase*

Be fruitful and **m** Gen 1:22
the fool **m-ies** words Eccl 10:14
He **m-ies** lies and Hos 12:1
and peace be **m-ied** 2 Pet 1:2

MULTITUDE *crowd, number*

father of a **m** of Gen 17:4
send the **m-s** away Matt 14:15
He summoned the **m** Mark 8:34
Him a great **m** Luke 23:27
cover a **m** of sins James 5:20
love covers a **m** of 1 Pet 4:8

MURDER *premeditated killing*

You shall not **m** Ex 20:13
Whoever commits **m** Matt 5:21
m-ed the prophets Matt 23:31
full of envy, **m** Rom 1:29

MURDERER *killer*

m shall be put to Num 35:30
m from...beginning John 8:44
this man is a **m** Acts 28:4
no **m** has eternal 1 John 3:15

MUSIC *harmony, melody*

instruments of **m** 1 Chr 15:16
m to the LORD 2 Chr 7:6
m upon the lyre Ps 92:3
heard **m** and Luke 15:25

MUSICIAN *skilled in music*

m, a mighty man 1 Sam 16:18
the **m-s** after *them* Ps 68:25
harpists and **m-s** Rev 18:22

MUSTARD *type of plant*

kingdom...like a **m** Matt 13:31
faith as a **m** seed Matt 17:20
It is like a **m** seed Luke 13:19

MUZZLE *gag*

shall not **m** the ox Deut 25:4
guard...as with a **m** Ps 39:1

MYRIADS *countless*

chariots...are **m** Ps 68:17
m of angels Heb 12:22
number...was **m** Rev 5:11

MYRRH *spice*

aromatic gum...**m** Gen 43:11
Dripping with...**m** Song 5:13
frankincense and **m** Matt 2:11
mixture of **m** and John 19:39

MYRTLE *type of plant*

the **m,** and the olive Is 41:19
among the **m** trees Zech 1:11

MYSTERY *hidden truth, secret*

no **m** baffles you Dan 4:9
God's wisdom in a **m** 1 Cor 2:7
know all **m-ies** 1 Cor 13:2
into the **m** of Christ Eph 3:4
the **m** of the gospel Eph 6:19
the **m** of the faith 1 Tim 3:9

MYTHS *fables*

to pay attention to **m** 1 Tim 1:4
will turn aside to **m** 2 Tim 4:4
attention to Jewish **m** Titus 1:14

N

NAAMAH

1 *daughter of Lamech* Gen 4:22
2 *wife of Solomon* 1 Kin 14:21
3 *town in Judah* Josh 15:41

NAAMAN

1 *son, grandson, and great
  grandson of Benjamin*
          Gen 46:21; Num 26:40;
                          1 Chr 8:7
2 *Ben-hadad's commander*
                  2 Kin 5:1ff

NABAL

husband of Abigail 1 Sam 25:3ff
refused to help David

NABOTH

*owner of a vineyard taken by
  Ahab* 1 Kin 21:1-19

NADAB

1 *son of Aaron* Ex 6:23
2 *king of Israel* 1 Kin 14:20
3 *son of Shammai* 1 Chr 2:28
4 *son of Jehiel* 1 Chr 8:29,30

NAHOR

1 *Abram's grandfather*
                  Gen 11:24ff
2 *brother of Abram*
              Gen 11:27;22:23
3 *city in N Mesopotamia*
                  Gen 24:10

NAHUM

1 *prophet* Nah 1:1
2 *ancestor of Christ* Luke 3:25

NAILED (v) *attached*

you **n** to a cross Acts 2:23
n it to the cross Col 2:14

NAILS (n) *finger ends or pins*

and trim her **n** Deut 21:12
fasten it with **n** Jer 10:4
imprint of the **n** John 20:25

NAIVE *simple, not suspicious*

prudence to the **n** Prov 1:4
n believes everything Prov 14:15
the **n** becomes wise Prov 21:11
goes astray or is **n** Ezek 45:20

NAKED *unclothed*

n and...not ashamed Gen 2:25

n I shall return there Job 1:21
n...you clothed Me Matt 25:36

NAKEDNESS *unclothed*

the **n** of his father Gen 9:22
n of...father's sister Lev 18:12
Your **n**...be uncovered Is 47:3
shame of your **n** Rev 3:18

NAME *designation, title*

man gave **n-s** to all Gen 2:20
takes His **n** in vain Ex 20:7
blot out his **n** Deut 29:20
How majestic is Thy **n** Ps 8:1
sing praises to Thy **n** Ps 18:49
good **n**...desired Prov 22:1
LORD, that is My **n** Is 42:8
Hallowed be Thy **n** Matt 6:9
n-s of the twelve Matt 10:2
such child in My **n** Matt 18:5
n-s are recorded Luke 10:20
will come in My **n** Luke 21:8
baptized in the **n** Acts 2:38
of faith in His **n** Acts 3:16
other **n** under heaven Acts 4:12
n-s are in the book Phil 4:3

NAOMI

woman of Bethlehem Ruth 1:1
Ruth's mother-in-law Ruth 1:4,6

NAPHTALI

1 *son of Jacob* Gen 30:8
2 *tribe / district* Num 13:14;
                  1 Chr 2:2; Rev 7:6

NARD *fragrant ointment*

henna with **n** plants Song 4:13
perfume of pure **n** John 12:3

NARROW *limited*

stood in a **n** path Num 22:24
Enter by the **n** gate Matt 7:13
the way is **n** Matt 7:14

NATHAN

1 *a son of David* 2 Sam 5:14;
                          Luke 3:31
2 *prophet* 2 Sam 7:2;12:1ff
3 *son of Attai* 1 Chr 2:36
4 *helped Ezra* Ezra 8:16,17
several other individuals

NATHANAEL

disciple of Jesus John 1:49

NATION *government, people*

make you a great **n** Gen 12:2
priests and a holy **n** Ex 19:6
scatter...the **n-s** Lev 26:33
the **n-s** in an uproar Ps 2:1
n-s...fear the name Ps 102:15
N will not lift up sword Is 2:4
sprinkle many **n-s** Is 52:15
glory among the **n-s** Is 66:19
n...rise against **n** Matt 24:7
n should not perish John 11:50
men, from every **n** Acts 2:5
tongue...people and **n** Rev 5:9

NATIVE *indigenous*

or a **n** of the land Ex 12:19
Or see his **n** land Jer 22:10
the **n-s** showed us Acts 28:2

n-s saw the creature   Acts 28:4

NATURAL normal

died a n death	Ezek 44:31
n man...not accept	1 Cor 2:14
is sown a n body	1 Cor 15:44

NATURE essence

of the same n as you	Acts 14:15
n itself teach you	1 Cor 11:14
We are Jews by n	Gal 2:15
of the divine n	2 Pet 1:4

NAZARENE

1 of Nazareth	John 18:7
2 follower of Jesus	Acts 24:5

NAZARETH

town of Galilee	Matt 2:23
home of Joseph, Mary, and Jesus	
	Luke 4:16; John 1:45

NAZIRITE

1 one consecrated to God
                Num 6:2,19,20
2 religious vow
                Judg 13:5,7; Amos 2:11,12

NEBO

1 Moabite town   Num 32:38
2 mountain where Moses viewed
   promised land
            Deut 32:49; 34:1
3 Babylonian god   Is 46:1
4 town W of Jordan
           Ezra 2:29; Neh 7:33
5 Jew whose sons married foreign
   wives   Ezra 10:43

NEBUCHADNEZZAR

king of Babylon   2 Kin 24:1,10
captured Judah
         1 Chr 6:15; Ezra 2:1

NEBUZARADAN

Babylonian commander
   responsible for destruction of
   Jerusalem and the Temple
         2 Kin 25:8ff; Jer 39:9,10

NECK part of body

you shall break its n	Ex 13:13
yoke on your n	Deut 28:48
stiffened their n-s	Jer 17:23
risked their own n-s	Rom 16:4

NECKLACE neck ornament

n around his neck	Gen 41:42
earrings and n-s	Num 31:50
pride is their n	Ps 73:6

NECO

see PHARAOH

NEED necessity, obligation

sufficient for his n	Deut 15:8
ministered to...n-s	Acts 20:34
n-s of the saints	2 Cor 9:12
supply all your n-s	Phil 4:19

NEEDLE

the eye of a n	Matt 19:24
n than for a rich	Mark 10:25

NEEDY destitute, poor

to your n and poor	Deut 15:11
a father to the n	Job 29:16
n will not always be	Ps 9:18
the LORD hears the n	Ps 69:33
n will lie down in	Is 14:30

NEGEV

S desert region
       Gen 12:9; Judg 1:9; Jer 32:44;
                      Zech 7:7

NEGLECT disregard, ignore

You n-ed the Rock	Deut 32:18
who n-s discipline	Prov 15:32
n so great a salvation	Heb 2:3
n to show hospitality	Heb 13:2
do not n doing good	Heb 13:16

NEHEMIAH

1 Jewish exile
             Ezra 2:2; Neh 7:7
2 son of Azbuk   Neh 3:16
3 son of Hacaliah   Neh 1:1
   rebuilt walls   Neh 3:1ff
   governor of Jerusalem Neh 8:9

NEIGHBOR one living nearby

not covet...n-'s wife	Ex 20:17
shall love your n	Lev 19:18
make your n-s drink	Hab 2:15
love your n, and	Matt 5:43
And who is my n	Luke 10:29
love your n as	Gal 5:14

NEPHEW

and Lot his n	Gen 12:5
Lot, Abram's n	Gen 14:12

NEPHILIM

people of great stature
         Gen 6:4; Num 13:33

NEST

n is set in the cliff	Num 24:21
n among the stars	Obad 4
birds...have n-s	Matt 8:20

NET snare

a n for my steps	Ps 57:6
an antelope in a n	Is 51:20
casting a n into	Matt 4:18
left the n-s and	Mark 1:18
n full of fish	John 21:8

NETHINIM

temple servants   Ezra 7:24

NEW fresh, recent

nothing n under the	Eccl 1:9
Will gain n strength	Is 40:31
a n spirit within	Ezek 11:19
n wine into old	Mark 2:22
A n commandment	John 13:34
he is a n creature	2 Cor 5:17
a n and living way	Heb 10:20
making all things n	Rev 21:5

NEWBORN just born

like n babes, long   1 Pet 2:2

NEWNESS freshness

walk in n of life	Rom 6:4
in n of the Spirit	Rom 7:6

NEWS report, tidings

a day of good n	2 Kin 7:9
Good n puts fat on	Prov 15:30
the n about Jesus	Matt 14:1
n about Him went	Mark 1:28
n of a great joy	Luke 2:10
n of your faith	1 Thess 3:6

NICODEMUS

Pharisee	John 3:1,4,9
in Sanhedrin	John 7:50; 19:39

NICOLAITANS

sect in Ephesian and Pergamum
   church   Rev 2:6,15

NICOLAS

deacon, servant	Acts 6:1-6
proselyte from Antioch	Acts 6:5

NIGHT darkness

darkness He called n	Gen 1:5
pillar of fire by n	Ex 13:21
meditate...day and n	Josh 1:8
make n into day	Job 17:12
The terror by n	Ps 91:5
At n my soul longs	Is 26:9
over their flock by n	Luke 2:8
a thief in the n	1 Thess 5:2
tormented day and n	Rev 20:10

NILE

river of Egypt
        Gen 41:1; Ex 1:22;7:20;
                      Is 23:10

NIMROD

son of Cush	Gen 10:8
a mighty hunter	Gen 10:9
ruler of Shinar	Gen 10:10

NINEVAH

capital of Assyria	2 Kin 19:36
visited by Jonah	Jon 1:1ff

NISAN

first month of the Hebrew
   calendar   Neh 2:1; Esth 3:7

NOAH

1 son of Lamech   Gen 5:28,29
   father of Shem, Ham, Japeth
                    Gen 5:32
   built an ark   Gen 6:14-22
   saved from Flood
        Gen 6:9;7:15;8:1;8:13
   promised by God Gen 9:9-17
2 daughter of Zelophehad
       Num 26:33;27:1;36:11

NO-AMON

Egyptian city of Thebes Nah 3:8

NOBLE lofty, renown ones

king's most n princes	Esth 6:9
speak n things	Prov 8:6
all the n-s of Judah	Jer 39:6

NOBLEMAN of high rank

the house of the n	Job 21:28
A certain n went to	Luke 19:12

NOISE loud sound

You who were full of n Is 22:2

Egypt *is but* a big **n**	Jer 46:17
from heaven a **n**	Acts 2:2

NOMADS *desert wanderers*

n of the desert bow	Ps 72:9

NONSENSE *foolishness*

a fool speaks **n**	Is 32:6
appeared...as **n**	Luke 24:11

NORTH *direction of compass*

stretches out the **n**	Job 26:7
Zion *in* the far **n**	Ps 48:2
king of the **N** will	Dan 11:13
three gates on the **n**	Rev 21:13

NOSE *part of face*

the ring on her **n**	Gen 24:47
n-s...cannot smell	Ps 115:6
My hook in your **n**	Is 37:29

NOSTRILS *nose*

breathed into his **n**	Gen 2:7
breath of His **n**	2 Sam 22:16
breath of God...my **n**	Job 27:3

NOTICE *attention, seen*

take **n** of me	Ruth 2:10
not the log	Matt 7:3
deeds to be **n**-d by	Matt 23:5

NOURISH *feed, sustain*

n-es and cherishes it	Eph 5:29
constantly **n**-ed on	1 Tim 4:6
she might be **n**-ed	Rev 12:6

NULLIFY *annul, make void*

Lord **n**-ies the counsel	Ps 33:10
unbelief will not **n**	Rom 3:3
the promise is **n**-ied	Rom 4:14
n the grace of God	Gal 2:21

NUMBER (n) *group, total*

their **n** according to	Num 29:21
the **n** of the stars	Ps 147:4
increasing in **n** daily	Acts 16:5
his **n** is six hundred	Rev 13:18

NUMBER (v) *count, enumerate*

n...by their armies	Num 1:3
Thou dost **n** my steps	Job 14:16
hairs...all **n**-ed	Matt 10:30

NUN

father of Joshua
Ex 33:11; Num 14:6; Josh 1:1

NURSE (n) *attendant*

Deborah, Rebekah's **n**	Gen 35:8
and call a **n** for you	Ex 2:7
n carries a nursing	Num 11:12
n in the bedroom	2 Kin 11:2

NURSE (v) *suckle an infant*

Sarah...**n** children	Gen 21:7
the child and **n**-d him	Ex 2:9
morning to **n** my son	1 Kin 3:21
who **n** babes in	Mark 13:17
breasts...never **n**	Luke 23:29

O

OAK *type of tree*

by the **o**-s of Mamre	Gen 13:18
the diviners' **o**	Judg 9:37

o-s of righteousness	Is 61:3
strong as the **o**-s	Amos 2:9

OAR *pole used in rowing*

no boat with **o**-s shall	Is 33:21
all who handle...**o**	Ezek 27:29
straining at the **o**-s	Mark 6:48

OATH *declaration, vow*

confirm the **o** which	Deut 9:5
free from the **o**	Josh 2:20
make no **o** at all	Matt 5:34
priests without an **o**	Heb 7:21

OBADIAH

1 *in Ahab's court*	1 Kin 18:3ff
2 *Gadite warrior*	1 Chr 12:8,9
3 *sent to teach*	2 Chr 17:7
4 *Levite, of Merari*	2 Chr 34:12
5 *son of Jehiel*	Ezra 8:9
6 *signer of covenant*	Neh 10:1,5
7 *prophet*	Obad 1

name of five other Old Testament people

OBED

1 *son of Ruth / Boaz*	Ruth 4:17
ancestor of Jesus	Matt 1:5; Luke 3:32
2 *son of Ephlal*	1 Chr 2:37
3 *warrior*	1 Chr 11:26,47
4 *temple gatekeeper*	1 Chr 26:1,7
5 *father of Azariah*	2 Chr 23:1

OBED-EDOM

1 *a Gittite*	2 Sam 6:10-12
2 *temple musician*	1 Chr 15:21
3 *in charge of Temple vessels*	2 Chr 25:24

OBEDIENCE *submission*

the **o** of the peoples	Gen 49:10
pretend **o** to me	2 Sam 22:45
the **o** of the One	Rom 5:19
leading to **o** of faith	Rom 16:26
in **o** to the truth	1 Pet 1:22

OBEDIENT *willing to obey*

we will be **o**	Ex 24:7
o from the heart	Rom 6:17
o to the...death	Phil 2:8
Children, be **o** to	Col 3:20

OBEY *follow commands, orders*

have **o**-ed My voice	Gen 22:18
o My voice and keep	Ex 19:5
o the Lord your God	Deut 27:10
to **o** is better than	1 Sam 15:22
O-ing...His word	Ps 103:20
and the sea **o** Him	Matt 8:27
o God rather than	Acts 5:29
o your parents	Eph 6:1
O your leaders	Heb 13:17
may **o** Jesus Christ	1 Pet 1:2

OBJECT *implement or goal*

struck...an iron **o**	Num 35:16
an **o** of loathing to	Ps 88:8
o like a great sheet	Acts 10:11
god or **o** of worship	2 Thess 2:4

OBLIGATION *duty*

o toward the Lord	Num 32:22

for his daily **o**-s	2 Chr 31:16
under **o**, not to the	Rom 8:12
o to keep the...Law	Gal 5:3

OBSERVE *keep or notice*

surely **o** My sabbaths	Ex 31:13
o all My statutes	Lev 19:37
you may **o** discretion	Prov 5:2
the ant...**O** her ways	Prov 6:6
O how the lilies	Matt 6:28
o-ing the traditions	Mark 7:3
the word...**o** it	Luke 11:28
o days and months	Gal 4:10

OBSTACLE *hindrance*

Remove *every* **o** out of	Is 57:14
an **o** or a stumbling	Rom 14:13

OBSTINATE *stubborn*

you are an **o** people	Ex 33:3
made his heart **o**	Deut 2:30
Israel is...**o**	Ezek 3:7
disobedient and **o**	Rom 10:21

OBTAIN *get possession of*

o children through	Gen 16:2
finds a wife...**o**-s	Prov 18:22
may **o** eternal life	Matt 19:16
o the gift of God	Acts 8:20
o-ed an inheritance	Eph 1:11
for **o**-ing salvation	1 Thess 5:9

OCCUR *happen, take place*

this sign shall **o**	Ex 8:23
will **o** at the final	Dan 8:19
lest a riot **o**	Matt 26:5
predestined to **o**	Acts 4:28

ODED

1 *father of Azariah*	2 Chr 15:1,8
2 *prophet*	2 Chr 28:9

ODIOUS *offensive*

o in Pharaoh's sight	Ex 5:21
o to the Philistines	1 Sam 13:4

OFFEND *insult or violate*

I will not **o** *anymore*	Job 34:31
A brother **o**-ed *is*	Prov 18:19
Pharisees were **o**-ed	Matt 15:12

OFFENSE *anger or transgression*

of my *own* **o**-s	Gen 41:9
they took **o** at Him	Matt 13:57
of the **o** of Adam	Rom 5:14
and a rock of **o**	1 Pet 2:8

OFFER (v) *give, present*

o him...as a burnt	Gen 22:2
O to God a sacrifice	Ps 50:14
my mouth **o**-s praises	Ps 63:5
o both gifts and	Heb 5:1
o-ed Himself	Heb 9:14
prayer **o**-ed in faith	James 5:15
o...spiritual sacrifices	1 Pet 2:5

OFFERING (n) *contribution*

freewill **o** to the Lord	Ex 35:29
o of first fruits	Lev 2:12
your worthless **o**-s	Is 1:13
presenting your **o**	Matt 5:23
any **o** for sin	Heb 10:18

OFFERINGS

1 Burnt Offering

Gen 22:13; Lev 1:17

2 Drink Offering
Phil 2:17; 2 Tim 4:6
also **Libation**
3 Freewill Offering
Ex 35:29; Lev 7:16
4 Grain Offering
Lev 9:4; Josh 22:29
also **Meal Offering**
5 Guilt Offering
Lev 5:6; Num 6:12
6 Heave Offering Ex 29:27,28
7 Libation Offering
Num 6:15,17;28:9,10
also **Drink Offering**
8 Meal Offering
2 Kin 16:15; Ps 40:6
also **Grain Offering**
9 Ordination Offering
Lev 8:28,31
10 Peace Offering
Lev 4:31; Num 6:14
11 Sin Offering
Ex 29:14; Ezek 46:20
12 Thank Offering
2 Chr 33:16; Jer 33:11
13 Votive Offering
Deut 12:26;23:18
14 Wave Offering
Lev 14:12; Num 18:18

OFFICE *function* or *position*
wield the staff of o   Judg 5:14
priests in their o-s   2 Chr 35:2
sitting in the tax o   Luke 5:27
to the o of overseer   1 Tim 3:1

OFFICIAL *one in authority*
o-s in the palace   2 Kin 20:18
o of the synagogue   Luke 8:41

OFFSPRING *descendants*
o in place of Abel   Gen 4:25
bring forth o from   Is 65:9
Being...the o of God   Acts 17:29
you are Abraham's o   Gal 3:29
and the o of David   Rev 22:16

OG
Amorite King
Num 21:33; Deut 3:4;
Josh 12:4

OHOLAH
symbolic for Samaria   Ezek 23:4

OHOLIBAH
symbolic for Jerusalem   Ezek 23:4

OHOLIBAMAH
1 *wife of Esau*   Gen 36:2-25
2 *descendant of Esau*   Gen 36:41

OIL
o for lighting   Ex 25:6
anointed my head...o   Ps 23:5
the o of joy   Ps 45:7
words...softer than o   Ps 55:21
prudent took o in   Matt 25:4
not anoint...with o   Luke 7:46

OINTMENT *salve*
a jar of o   Job 41:31

anointed...with o   John 11:2

OLD *aged, obsolete*
buried at a...o age   Gen 15:15
too o to have a   Ruth 1:12
honor of o men   Prov 20:29
o men will dream   Joel 2:28
wine into o wineskins   Matt 9:17
be born when he is o   John 3:4
o self was crucified   Rom 6:6
o things passed away   2 Cor 5:17
men of o gained   Heb 11:2
serpent of o...devil   Rev 12:9

OLD GATE
see **GATES OF JERUSALEM**

OLIVE *tree* or *fruit*
freshly picked o leaf   Gen 8:11
land of o oil and   Deut 8:8
cherubim of o wood   1 Kin 6:23
children like o plants   Ps 128:3

OLIVES, MOUNT OF
mountain E of Jerusalem
2 Sam 15:30; Zech 14:4;
Matt 24:3; Mark 11:1
place where Jesus prayed
Matt 26:30; Luke 22:39-41

OMEGA
last letter of Gr. alphabet   Rev 1:8
title of Jesus Christ   Rev 21:6
expresses eternalness of God
Rev 22:13

OMEN *foretells a future event*
who interprets o-s   Deut 18:10
took this as an o   1 Kin 20:33

OMER *dry measure*
take an o apiece   Ex 16:16
o is a tenth of an   Ex 16:36

OMRI
1 *king of Israel*   1 Kin 16:22ff
2 *a Benjamite*   1 Chr 7:8
3 *line of Perez*   1 Chr 9:4
4 *son of Michael*   1 Chr 27:18

ON
1 *Egyptian city*
Gen 41:45,50;46:20
also **Heliopolis**
2 *son of Peleth*   Num 16:1

ONE *single unit*
shall become o flesh   Gen 2:24
God, the LORD is o   Deut 6:4
Holy **O** of Israel   Ps 71:22
His chosen o-s   Ps 105:6
Are You the...**O**   Matt 11:3
joy...over o sinner   Luke 15:7
I...Father are o   John 10:30
they may all be o   John 17:21
o body in Christ   Rom 12:5
o died for all   2 Cor 5:14
o Lord, o faith   Eph 4:5
o God...o mediator   1 Tim 2:5
husband of o wife   1 Tim 3:2

ONESIMUS
Christian slave of Philemon
Col 4:9; Philem 10

ONESIPHORUS
Ephesian Christian
2 Tim 1:16;4:19

ONYX *precious stone*
bdellium and the o   Gen 2:12
o, and the jasper   Ezek 28:13

OPEN (adj) *not shut, exposed*
throat is an o grave   Ps 5:9
Better is o rebuke   Prov 27:5
before you an o door   Rev 3:8

OPEN (v) *expose, free, unfasten*
eyes will be o-ed   Gen 3:5
Ezra o-ed the book   Neh 8:5
He o-s their ear   Job 36:10
O Lord, o my lips   Ps 51:15
O my eyes, that I   Ps 119:18
To o blind eyes   Is 42:7
o...windows of heaven   Mal 3:10
knock...shall be o-ed   Matt 7:7
o-ed a door of faith   Acts 14:27
and o-s the door   Rev 3:20
worthy to o the book   Rev 5:2

OPHEL
citadel on S slope of Temple
Mount in Jerusalem
2 Chr 27:3;33:14; Neh 3:27
home of temple servants
(Nethinim)   Neh 3:26;11:21

OPHIR
1 *son of Joktan*   Gen 10:29
2 *gold producing region of SW*
Arabia
1 Kin 10:11; Job 22:24

OPPONENT *adversary*
friends...with your o   Matt 5:25
protection from my o   Luke 18:3

OPPORTUNITY *occasion*
o to betray Him   Matt 26:16
o for your testimony   Luke 21:13
an o for the flesh   Gal 5:13
not give...devil an o   Eph 4:27

OPPOSE *contend, resist*
o the Prince of   Dan 8:25
o-d the ordinance of   Rom 13:2
men also o the truth   2 Tim 3:8
God is o-d to the   James 4:6

OPPOSITION *hostility*
you...know My o   Num 14:34
these are in o   Gal 5:17
gospel...much o   1 Thess 2:2

OPPRESS (v) *trouble, tyrannize*
enslaved and o-ed   Gen 15:13
Egyptians are o-ing   Ex 3:9
not o your neighbor   Lev 19:13
woman o-ed in   1 Sam 1:15
do not o the widow   Zech 7:10
healing all...o-ed   Acts 10:38
the rich who o you   James 2:6

OPPRESSED (n) *afflicted*
stronghold for the o   Ps 9:9
justice for the o   Ps 146:7
let the o go free   Is 58:6
devour...o in secret   Hab 3:14

vengeance for the **o**   Acts 7:24

OPPRESSION *affliction*

Do not trust in **o**   Ps 62:10
o makes a...man mad   Eccl 7:7
and water of **o**   Is 30:20
o of My people   Acts 7:34

OPPRESSOR *one who afflicts*

And crush the **o**   Ps 72:4
a great **o** lacks   Prov 28:16
punish all their **o-s**   Jer 30:20

ORACLE *revelation*

The **o** of Balaam   Num 24:3
o concerning Babylon   Is 13:1
the **o** of the LORD   Jer 23:33
and misleading **o-s**   Lam 2:14
entrusted with the **o-s**   Rom 3:2

ORDAIN *invest, set apart*

anoint...and **o** them   Ex 28:41
o Aaron and his sons   Ex 29:9
o-ed His covenant   Ps 111:19
law as **o-ed** by angels   Acts 7:53

ORDEAL *difficulty, trial*

great **o** of affliction   2 Cor 8:2
at the fiery **o**   1 Pet 4:12

ORDER (n) *arrangement*

Set your house in **o**   2 Kin 20:1
fixed **o** of the moon   Jer 31:35
the **o** of Melchizedek   Heb 5:6

ORDER (v) *command or request*

I will **o** my prayer   Ps 5:3
o-ed him to tell no   Luke 5:14
confidence...to **o** you   Philem 8

ORDINANCE *statute*

o of the Passover   Ex 12:43
they rejected My **o-s**   Lev 26:43
o-s of the heavens   Job 38:33
opposed the **o** of God   Rom 13:2

ORDINATION

Aaron's ram of **o**   Ex 29:26
and the **o** offering   Lev 7:37
period of your **o**   Lev 8:33

ORDINATION OFFERING
see **OFFERINGS**

ORIGIN *beginning, source*

of Jewish **o**   Esth 6:13
o is from antiquity   Is 23:7
Your **o** and your   Ezek 16:3

ORIGINATE *bring into being*

not **o** from woman   1 Cor 11:8
all things **o**...God   1 Cor 11:12

ORION

constellation of stars
   Job 9:9;38:31; Amos 5:8

ORNAMENT *decoration*

put off your **o-s**   Ex 33:5
o of fine gold   Prov 25:12
beauty of His **o-s**   Ezek 7:20

ORNAN

*Jebusite owner of threshing floor
on Mount Moriah*
   1 Chr 21:15,18

*sells threshing floor to David for
altar and temple* 1 Chr 21:25,28
also **Araunah**

ORPAH

daughter-in-law of Naomi
   Ruth 1:4,14

ORPHAN *fatherless child*

not afflict any...**o**   Ex 22:22
justice for the **o**   Deut 10:18
helper of the **o**   Ps 10:14
may plunder the **o-s**   Is 10:2
Leave...**o-s** behind   Jer 49:11
visit **o-s** and widows James 1:27

OSTRICH *bird*

the **o** and the owl   Lev 11:16
a companion of **o-es**   Job 30:29
cruel Like **o-es**   Lam 4:3
mourning like the **o-es**   Mic 1:8

OTHNIEL

son of Kenaz   Josh 15:17
brother or nephew of Caleb
   Judg 1:13;3:11

OUTBURST *sudden release*

great **o** of anger   Deut 29:24
o of anger I hid My   Is 54:8
jealousy, **o-s** of anger   Gal 5:20

OUTCAST *rejected*

the **o-s** of Israel   Ps 147:2
Hide the **o-s**   Is 16:3
called you an **o**   Jer 30:17
o-s from...synagogue John 16:2

OUTCRY *strong cry or protest*

no **o** in our streets   Ps 144:14
o is heard among the   Jer 50:46
a *single* **o** arose   Acts 19:34

OUTSIDER *stranger*

o may not come near   Num 18:4
toward **o-s**   1 Thess 4:12

OUTSTRETCHED *extended*

redeem...with an **o** arm   Ex 6:6
war...with an **o** hand   Jer 21:5

OUTWARD *external*

at the **o** appearance   1 Sam 16:7
is **o** in the flesh   Rom 2:28

OVEN *baking, cooking vessel*

appeared a...**o**   Gen 15:17
make them as a fiery **o**   Ps 21:9

OVERCOME *conquer, master*

a man **o** with wine   Jer 23:9
I have **o** the world   John 16:33
but **o** evil with good   Rom 12:21
have **o** the evil one   1 John 2:13
who **o-s** shall inherit   Rev 21:7

OVERFLOW *flood, inundate*

My cup **o-s**   Ps 23:5
waters shall **o** the   Is 28:17
I am **o-ing** with joy   2 Cor 7:4
o-ing with gratitude   Col 2:7

OVERLAID *decorate, spread*

o...with gold   1 Kin 6:28
vessel **o** with silver   Prov 26:23

o with gold...silver   Hab 2:19

OVERLOOK *ignore or view*

o a transgression   Prov 19:11
widows were...**o-ed**   Acts 6:1

OVERPOWER *subdue*

deceive you and **o** you   Obad 7
Hades shall not **o**   Matt 16:18
attacks him and **o-s** Luke 11:22

OVERSEER *director, leader*

o in the house of   Jer 29:26
the **o-s** and deacons   Phil 1:1
the office of **o**   1 Tim 3:1
o...above reproach   Titus 1:7

OVERSHADOW *engulf, obscure*

Most High...**o** you   Luke 1:35
o-ing the mercy seat   Heb 9:5

OVERSIGHT *supervision*

o of the house of   2 Kin 12:11
having **o** at...gates   Ezek 44:11
exercising **o** not   1 Pet 5:2

OVERWHELM *crush, overcome*

humiliation has **o-ed**   Ps 44:15
darkness will **o** me   Ps 139:11
my spirit was **o-ed**   Ps 142:3
o-ed by...sorrow   2 Cor 2:7

OWE *be indebted*

Pay...what you **o**   Matt 18:28
O nothing to anyone   Rom 13:8
that you **o** to me   Philem 19

OWL *bird*

the **o**, the sea gull   Deut 14:15
o of the waste places   Ps 102:6
houses...full of **o-s**   Is 13:21

OWN (adj) *belonging to*

man in His **o** image   Gen 1:27
led...His **o** people   Ps 78:52
calls his **o** sheep   John 10:3
in his **o** language   Acts 2:6

OWN (n) *belonging to*

He came to His **o**   John 1:11
provide for his **o**   1 Tim 5:8

OWNER *possessor*

restitution to its **o**   Ex 22:12
when the **o**...comes   Matt 21:40
who were **o-s** of land Acts 4:34

OX *bull used as draft animal*

oxen and donkeys   Gen 12:16
servant or his **o**   Ex 20:17
horns of the wild oxen Ps 22:21
An **o** knows its owner   Is 1:3
not muzzle the **o**   1 Tim 5:8

P

PACE *step, stride*

the **p** of the cattle   Gen 33:14
not slow down the **p** 2 Kin 4:24

PACT *agreement*

Sheol we...made a **p**   Is 28:15
p with Sheol shall   Is 28:18

PADDAN-ARAM

NW Mesopotamia   Gen 25:20

PAHATH-MOAB

home of Laban | Gen 28:5
birthplace of most of *Jacob's* sons
| Gen 35:22-26

PAHATH-MOAB

1 *head of Jewish clan* | Ezra 2:6
2 *Jewish clan* | Neh 3:11

PAIN *discomfort, hurt*

multiply Your **p** | Gen 3:16
p-s came upon her | 1 Sam 4:19
rejoice in unsparing **p** | Job 6:10
rest from your **p** | Is 14:3
Your **p** is incurable | Jer 30:15
bring **p** to my soul | Lam 3:51
suffering great **p** | Matt 8:6
no longer be...**p** | Rev 21:4

PAINFUL *hurting*

p are honest words | Job 6:25
the bread of **p** labors | Ps 127:2

PALACE *royal residence*

build...royal **p** | 2 Chr 2:12
to the king's **p** | Esth 2:8
Out of ivory **p-s** | Ps 45:8
A **p** of strangers | Is 25:2
luxury...royal **p-s** | Luke 7:25

PALLET *bed, mat*

they let down the **p** | Mark 2:4
take up your **p** and | Mark 2:9

PALM *type of tree*

the city of **p** trees | Deut 34:3
flourish like the **p** | Ps 92:12
branches of the **p** | John 12:13

PALTI

1 *son of Raphu* | Num 13:9
spy for Israel | Num 13:2
2 *Michal's husband* 1 Sam 25:44

PAMPHYLIA

Roman province in Asia Minor
| Acts 2:10;13:13;14:24

PANGS *sudden pains*

beginning of birth **p** | Mark 13:8
like birth **p** | 1 Thess 5:3

PANIC *fear*

P seized them there | Ps 48:6
P and pitfall have | Lam 3:47
great **p**...will fall | Zech 14:13

PANT *breathe rapidly*

deer **p-s** for the water | Ps 42:1
my soul **p-s** for Thee | Ps 42:1
I will both gasp and **p** | Is 42:14
beasts...**p** for Thee | Joel 1:20

PAPHOS

city on Cyprus | Acts 13:6,13

PAPYRUS *reed plant*

p...without marsh | Job 8:11
Even in **p** vessels | Is 18:2

PARABLE *story for illustration*

speak a **p** to | Ezek 17:2
p of the sower | Matt 13:18
heard His **p-s** | Matt 21:45
p from the fig tree | Mark 13:28
spoke by way of a **p** | Luke 8:4

PARADISE

abode of the righteous dead
| Luke 23:43; 2 Cor 12:4;
| Rev 2:7
see also **ABRAHAM'S BOSOM**

PARALYTIC

said to the **p**—Rise | Matt 9:6
p, carried by four | Mark 2:3

PARAN

wilderness area in Sinai
| Gen 21:21; Num 13:3
place of Israelite wanderings and
encampments | Num 12:16
mountain in Sinai | Deut 33:2

PARDON *forgive, release*

he will not **p** your | Ex 23:21
May the...LORD | 2 Chr 30:18
O LORD, **P** my iniquity Ps 25:11
He will abundantly **p** | Is 55:7
p, and you will be | Luke 6:37

PARENTS *father and mother*

rise up against **p** | Matt 10:21
left house or...**p** | Luke 18:29
evil, disobedient to **p** Rom 1:30
Children, obey your **p** Eph 6:1
disobedient to **p** | 2 Tim 3:2

PART *portion*

God...have no **p** in | 2 Chr 19:7
form my inward **p-s** Ps 139:13
have no **p** with Me | John 13:8
no **p** or portion in | Acts 8:21
prophesy in **p** | 1 Cor 13:9
now I know in **p** | 1 Cor 13:12
tongue is a small **p** | James 3:5

PARTAKERS *participators*

do not be **p** with | Eph 5:7
become **p** of Christ | Heb 3:14
p of the Holy Spirit | Heb 6:4
p of *the* divine nature 2 Pet 1:4

PARTIAL *favoring*

not be **p** to the poor | Lev 19:15
you shall not be **p** | Deut 16:19
now be **p** to no one | Job 32:21
You are not **p** | Matt 22:16

PARTIALITY *favoritism*

show **p** in judgment | Deut 1:17
p is not good | Prov 28:21
God shows no **p** | Gal 2:6

PARTICIPATE *take part*

not **p**...deeds of | Eph 5:11
p-s in his evil deeds 2 John 11
may not **p** in her sins Rev 18:4

PARTNER *comrade*

is a **p** with a thief | Prov 29:24
been **p-s** with them | Matt 23:30
regard me a **p** | Philem 17

PASS *proceed*

LORD will **p** over the | Ex 12:23
My glory is **p-ing** by | Ex 33:22
heaven and earth **p** | Matt 5:18
words shall not **p** | Matt 24:35
this cup **p** from Me | Matt 26:39
p-ed out of death | John 5:24

old things **p-ed** away 2 Cor 5:17
first earth **p-ed** away | Rev 21:1

PASSION *desire, lust*

p is rottenness to | Prov 14:30
over to degrading **p-s** Rom 1:26
flesh with its **p-s** | Gal 5:24
dead to...**p** | Col 3:5
not in lustful **p** | 1 Thess 4:5

PASSOVER

Israel's firstborn protected from the
plague of death prior to the
exodus from Egypt | Ex 12:1-30
Feast commemorating Israelite
exodus and protection from death
| Ex 12:42,43; Lev 23:5;
| Num 9:2,12,14; Matt 26:2,18;
| John 19:14; Acts 12:4
see also **FEASTS**

PASTORS *shepherds of people*

and some *as* **p** | Eph 4:11

PASTURE (n) *grazing fiield*

lie down in green **p-s** | Ps 23:2
sheep of Thy **p** | Ps 79:13

PASTURE (v) *feed, graze*

Moses...**p-ing** the flock | Ex 3:1
They will **p** on it | Zeph 2:7
So I **p-d** the flock | Zech 11:7

PATCH *mending cloth*

p of unshrunk cloth | Matt 9:16
p pulls away from it Mark 2:21

PATH *way*

snake in the **p** | Gen 49:17
the **p** of life | Ps 16:11
a light to my **p** | Ps 119:105
p of the upright is | Prov 15:19
Make His **p-s** straight Matt 3:3

PATHROS

upper Egypt
| Is 11:11; Jer 44:1,15;
| Ezek 29:14;30:14

PATIENCE *endurance*

try the **p** of men | Is 7:13
in **p**, in kindness | 2 Cor 6:6
love, joy, peace, **p** | Gal 5:22
exhort, with great **p** | 2 Tim 4:2
endure it with **p** | 1 Pet 2:20

PATIENT *bearing, enduring*

Love is **p**, love is | 1 Cor 13:4
p when wronged | 2 Tim 2:24
Lord...is **p** toward | 2 Pet 3:9

PATMOS

Aegean island, site of John's exile
| Rev 1:9

PATRIARCH *father of clan*

regarding the **p** David Acts 2:29
the twelve **p-s** | Acts 7:8
Abraham, the **p**, gave Heb 7:4

PATTERN *model, plan*

fixed **p-s** of heaven | Jer 33:25
walk according to...**p** Phil 3:17

PAUL

heritage
Acts 21:39;22:3; Phil 3:5
persecuted believers
Acts 7:58;8:1,3;9:1,2;
1 Cor 15:9
conversion and call Acts 9:1-19
name changed Acts 13:9
Jerusalem council Acts 15:2-6
missionary journeys
Acts 13:1ff;15:36ff;18:23ff
apostolic defense
Acts 11:5ff; Gal 1:13ff
arrest and imprisonment
Acts 21:33;22:24-28:31
defense
Acts 22:1ff;24:10ff; 25:10,11;
26:2ff
final journey to Rome Acts 27,28
see also SAUL

PAULUS, SERGIUS

proconsul of Cyprus Acts 13:7

PAVEMENT *paved road*

on a **p** of stone 2 Kin 16:17
mosaic **p** of porphyry Esth 1:6
place called The **P** John 19:13

PAY *give what is due*

thief...**p** double Ex 22:7
p Thee my vows Ps 66:13
P back what you Matt 18:28
Never **p** back evil Rom 12:17
p the penalty 2 Thess 1:9

PEACE *calmness, tranquility*

grant **p** in the land Lev 26:6
made **p** with David 1 Chr 19:19
Seek **p**, and pursue Ps 34:14
for the **p** of Jerusalem Ps 122:6
all her paths are **p** Prov 3:17
a time for **p** Eccl 3:8
Prince of **P** Is 9:6
p...like a river Is 66:12
have withdrawn My **p** Jer 16:5
not come to bring **p** Matt 10:34
on earth **p** among Luke 2:14
P I leave with you John 14:27
we have **p** with God Rom 5:1
love, joy, **p** Gal 5:22
He Himself is our **p** Eph 2:14
gospel of **p** Eph 6:15
p of God...surpasses Phil 4:7
p through the blood Col 1:20
take **p** from the earth Rev 6:4

PEACEMAKERS

Blessed are the **p** Matt 5:9

PEACE OFFERING

see OFFERINGS

PEARL *precious gem*

wisdom is above...**p-s** Job 28:18
p-s before swine Matt 7:6
one **p** of great value Matt 13:46

PECK-MEASURE *container*

lamp...under the **p** Matt 5:15
not...put under a **p** Mark 4:21

PEKAH

king of Israel 2 Kin 15:25ff

PEKAHIAH

king of Israel 2 Kin 15:22,23

PELEG

son of Eber Gen 10:25
descendant of Shem Gen 11:18

PENALTY *punishment*

you will bear the **p** Ezek 23:49
pay the **p** of eternal 2 Thess 1:9

PENIEL

where Jacob wrestled with God
Gen 32:30
also **Penuel**

PENTECOST

*Jewish feast held 50 days after
Passover*
Acts 20:16; 1 Cor 16:8
coming of the Holy Spirit
Acts 2:1
see also FEASTS

PENUEL

1 *tower destroyed* Judg 8:17
rebuilt 1 Kin 12:25
also **Peniel**
2 *father of Gedor* 1 Chr 4:4
3 *son of Shashak* 1 Chr 8:25

PEOPLE *group, nation*

they are one **p** Gen 11:6
Let My **p** go Ex 5:1
You are an obstinate **p** Ex 33:5
blessed above all **p-s** Deut 7:14
Forgive Thy **p** Israel Deut 21:8
LORD loves His **p** 2 Chr 2:11
p who are called by 2 Chr 7:14
restores His captive **p** Ps 14:7
We are His **p** Ps 100:3
LORD will judge His **p** Ps 135:14
p are unrestrained Prov 29:18
p whom I formed Is 43:21
do **p** say that I am Mark 8:27
they feared the **p** Luke 20:19
should die for the **p** John 11:50
not rejected His **p** Rom 11:2
every tribe and **p** Rev 13:7

PEOR

1 *mountain in Moab* Num 23:28
2 *Moabite deity* Num 25:3

PERCEIVE *be aware, discern*

p-d all the wisdom 1 Kin 10:4
listening, but do not **p** Is 6:9
p-ing in Himself Mark 5:30
p with their heart John 12:40

PERDITION *damnation*

the son of **p** John 17:12

PEREZ

son of Judah Gen 38:29

PERFECT (adj) *flawless*

His work is **p** Deut 32:4
law of the LORD is **p** Ps 19:7
heavenly Father is **p** Matt 5:48
p bond of unity Col 3:14

be **p** and complete James 1:4
p love casts out 1 John 4:18

PERFECTED *completed*

is **p** in weakness 2 Cor 12:9
love is **p** with us 1 John 4:17

PERFORM *carry out*

I will **p** miracles Ex 34:10
p My judgments Lev 18:4
p-s righteous deeds Ps 103:6
p a miracle in My Mark 9:39
John **p-ed** no sign John 10:41
p-ing great wonders Acts 6:8

PERFUME *fragrant oil*

and **p** make the heart Prov 27:9
instead of sweet **p** Is 3:24
p upon My body Matt 26:12
anointed...with **p** Luke 7:46
prepared...**p-s** Luke 23:56

PERGA

city in Asia Minor Acts 13:13

PERGAMUM

city in Asia Minor Rev 1:11
early church Rev 2:12

PERISH *be destroyed*

we **p**, we are dying Num 17:12
weapons...**p-ed** 2 Sam 1:27
if I **p**, I **p** Esth 4:16
hope...will **p** Job 8:13
the wicked will **p** Ps 1:6
rod of his fury will **p** Prov 22:8
our hope has **p-ed** Ezek 37:11
little ones to Matt 18:14
p by the sword Matt 26:52
p, but have eternal John 3:16
for any to **p** 2 Pet 3:9

PERIZZITES

early Canaanite tribe
Gen 34:30; Ex 23:23; Deut 7:1

PERMANENT *lasting*

it is a **p** ordinance Lev 6:18
p right of redemption Lev 25:32
use them as **p** slaves Lev 25:46
p home for the ark 1 Chr 28:2

PERMISSION *consent*

p they had from Cyrus Ezra 3:7
He gave them **p** Mark 5:13
he had given him **p** Acts 21:40

PERMIT *allow*

not **p-ting**...demons Mark 1:34
p the children Mark 10:14
Spirit...did not **p** Acts 16:7
if the Lord **p-s** 1 Cor 16:7

PERPETUAL *lasting*

p incense before the Ex 30:8
as a **p** covenant Ex 31:16
for a **p** priesthood Ex 40:15
may sleep a **p** sleep Jer 51:39

PERSECUTE *afflict, oppress*

Why do you **p** me Job 19:22
has **p-d** my soul Ps 143:3
pray for those who **p** Matt 5:44
p you in this city Matt 10:23

PERSECUTION

why are you **p-ing** Me   Acts 9:4
used to **p** the church   Gal 1:13

PERSECUTION *oppression*

p arises because of   Mark 4:17
p arose against the   Acts 8:1
a **p** against Paul   Acts 13:50
distress, or **p**, or   Rom 8:35

PERSEVERANCE *persistence*

by **p** in doing good   Rom 2:7
tribulation brings...**p**   Rom 5:3
for your **p** and faith   2 Thess 1:4
p of the saints   Rev 14:12

PERSIA

ancient Near Eastern empire
   2 Chr 36:20; Ezra 1:1; Esth
   1:3; Ezek 27:10; Dan 8:20

PERSON *human being*

If a **p** sins   Lev 4:2
hungry **p** unsatisfied   Is 32:6
p be in subjection   Rom 13:1
hidden **p** of the heart   1 Pet 3:4

PERSUADE *convince, prevail on*

a ruler may be **p-d**   Prov 25:15
trying to **p** Jews and   Acts 18:4
p-s men to worship   Acts 18:13
you will **p** me   Acts 26:28

PERSUASIVE *convincing*

p words of wisdom   1 Cor 2:4
delude you with **p**   Col 2:4

PERVERSE *corrupt*

a **p** and crooked   Deut 32:5
A **p** heart shall depart   Ps 101:4
mind will utter **p**   Prov 23:33
and **p** generation   Phil 2:15

PERVERT *distort, misdirect*

not **p** the justice   Ex 23:6
Does God **p** justice   Job 8:3
have **p-ed** their way   Jer 3:21

PESTILENCE *epidemic, plague*

LORD sent a **p**   2 Sam 24:15
sword, famine, and **p**   Jer 27:13
p and mourning and   Rev 18:8

PETER

heritage and occupation
   Matt 4:18; John 1:42,44
called by Jesus
   Matt 1:17; Mark 3:16;
   Luke 5:1ff
names: Cephas, Simon
   Matt 4:18; Mark 3:16; John
   1:42; Acts 15:14
walked on water   Matt 14:28ff
confessed Jesus as Messiah
   Matt 16:16; Luke 9:20
on mount of Transfiguration
   Matt 17:1ff; Mark 9:2ff
denied Jesus
   Matt 26:70; Mark 14:70;
   Luke 22:58
at Pentecost   Acts 2
apostle of Christ
   Gal 2:8; 1 Pet 1:1; 2 Pet 1:1

PETITION *request, supplication*

God...grant your **p**   1 Sam 1:17
p to any god or man   Dan 6:7
p-s...be made   1 Tim 2:1

PHARAOH *title of Egyptian kings*

1 **Pharaoh**, *time of Abraham*
   Gen 12:15ff
2 **Pharaoh**, *time of Joseph*
   Gen 37:36;39:1-50:26
3 **Pharaoh**, *during oppression*
   Ex 1:8-2:23
4 **Pharaoh**, *during the Exodus*
   Ex 5:1-12:41
5 **Pharaoh**, *father of Bithiah*
   1 Chr 4:17
6 **Pharaoh**, *time of David*
   1 Kin 11:14ff
7 **Pharaoh**, *whose daughter
married Solomon*
   1 Kin 3:1;7:8;9:16
8 **Shishak**, *time of Rehoboam*
   1 Kin 14:25,26
9 **So**, *time of Hoshea* 2 Kin 17:4
10 **Tirhakah**, *time of Hezekiah*
   2 Kin 19:9; Is 37:9
11 **Neco**, *slew Josiah*
   2 Kin 23:29,33,34
12 **Hophra**, *subject of prophecy*
   Jer 44:30

PHARISEES

Jewish religious party
   Matt 3:7;23:13; Mark
   2:18;7:3; Luke 11:42;16:14;
   John 3:1;11:47

PHARPAR

river of Damascus   2 Kin 5:12

PHILADELPHIA

city in Asia Minor   Rev 1:11
early church   Rev 3:7

PHILEMON

owner of Onesimus   Philem 1
friend of Paul

PHILIP

1 *Herod Philip I, son of Herod
the Great*   Mark 6:17
see also **HEROD**
2 *Herod Philip II, son of Herod
the Great*   Luke 3:1
see also **HEROD**
3 *Philip the apostle*
   Matt 10:3; Mark 3:18; Luke
   6:14; John 1:43ff; Acts 1:13
4 *Philip the evangelist*
   Acts 6:5;8:5,29;21:8

PHILIPPI

Macedonian city   Acts 16:12;20:6

PHILIPPIANS

people of Philippi   Phil 4:15

PHILISTIA

coastal area of SW Palestine
   Ex 15:14; Ps 60:8; 83:7;
   Joel 3:4

PHILISTINES

people of Philistia

Gen 10:14; Josh 13:2;
Judg 13:1; 1 Sam 4:2

PHINEHAS

1 *grandson of Aaron*
   Num 25:7;31:6; Judg 20:28
2 *son of Eli*   1 Sam 1:3;4:4,11
3 *father of a priest*   Ezra 8:33

PHOEBE

*Cenchrea (Corinth) deaconess
commended by Paul*   Rom 16:1

PHOENICIA

coastal land N of Land of Israel
   Acts 11:19;21:2
visited by Paul   Acts 15:3

PHRYGIA

Asia Minor province   Acts 2:10
visited by Paul   Acts 16:6;18:23

PHYGELUS

Asian Christian, deserted Paul
   2 Tim 1:15

PHYLACTERIES *prayer bands*

as **p** on your forehead   Ex 13:16
they broaden their **p**   Matt 23:5
see also **FRONTALS**

PHYSICIAN

all worthless **p-s**   Job 13:4
healthy who need a **p**   Matt 9:12
P, heal yourself   Luke 4:23
Luke, the beloved **p**   Col 4:14

PIECE *part, portion*

dip your **p** of bread   Ruth 2:14
thirty **p-s** of silver   Matt 27:3
gave Him a **p**...fish   Luke 24:42
woven in one **p**   John 19:23

PIERCE *penetrate*

master shall **p** his ear   Ex 21:6
They **p-d** my hands   Ps 22:16
He was **p-d** through   Is 53:5
whom they have **p-d**   Zech 12:10
sword will **p**...soul   Luke 2:35
p-d His side   John 19:34
p-d to the heart   Acts 2:37

PIETY *reverence*

learn to practice **p**   1 Tim 5:4
because of His **p**   Heb 5:7

PILATE, PONTIUS

Roman governor of Judea
   Matt 27:2; Luke 3:1
presided at Jesus' trial
   Matt 27:11ff; Mark 15:2ff;
   Luke 23:1ff; John 18:28-38
warned by his wife   Matt 27:19
orders Jesus' crucifixion
   Matt 27:24ff; Mark 15:15;
   Luke 23:24,25; John 19:15,16

PILLAR *column or memorial*

became a **p** of salt   Gen 19:26
p of fire by night   Ex 13:21
set up...a **p**   2 Sam 18:18
hewn...her seven **p-s**   Prov 9:1
feet like **p-s** of fire   Rev 10:1

PILOT *steersman*

sailors, and your **p**-s Ezek 27:27
the **p** and...captain Acts 27:11
inclination of the **p** James 3:4

PINION *wing*

p and plumage of Job 39:13
cover you with His **p**-s Ps 91:4

PINNACLE *highest point*

had Him...on the **p** Matt 4:5
p of the temple Luke 4:9

PISGAH

mountain height in Moab
Num 21:20; Josh 13:20

PISHON

river of Eden Gen 2:11

PISIDIA / PISIDIAN

district of Asia Minor
Acts 13:14;14:24

PIT *deep hole, dungeon*

full of tar **p**-s Gen 14:10
Joseph...not in the **p** Gen 37:29
redeems...from the **p** Ps 103:4
harlot is a deep **p** Prov 23:27
silenced me in the **p** Lam 3:53
to **p**-s of darkness 2 Pet 2:4
the bottomless **p** Rev 9:1

PITCH (n) *tar*

inside and out with **p** Gen 6:14
covered it over...**p** Ex 2:3

PITCH (v) *set up*

p-ed his tent in the Gen 31:25
he will **p** the tents Dan 11:45
tabernacle...Lord **p**-ed Heb 8:2

PITCHER *container*

torches inside the **p**-s Judg 7:16
Fill four **p**-s 1 Kin 18:33
carrying a **p** of Mark 14:13

PITHOM

Egyptian storage city built by
Hebrew slaves Ex 1:11

PITY (n) *sympathy*

shall not show **p** Deut 19:21
I will not show **p** Jer 13:14
No eye looked with **p** Ezek 16:5

PITY (v) *have compassion*

she had **p** on him Ex 2:6
eye shall not **p** them Deut 7:16
P me, **p** me, O you Job 19:21
take **p** on us Mark 9:22
most to be **p**-ied 1 Cor 15:19

PLACE *area, space*

waters...into one **p** Gen 1:9
he enters the holy **p** Ex 28:29
God is a dwelling **p** Deut 33:27
a **p** for My people 1 Chr 17:9
earth out of its **p** Job 9:6
Thou art my hiding **p** Ps 32:7
love the **p** of honor Matt 23:6
a **p** called Golgotha Matt 27:33
I go to prepare a **p** John 14:2

PLAGUE *contagious disease*

no **p** will befall you Ex 12:13
Remove Thy **p** from Ps 39:10
p of the hail Rev 16:21
the seven last **p**-s Rev 21:9

PLAIN *flat area*

p in...Shinar Gen 11:2
desert **p**-s of Jericho Josh 4:13
the **p** of Megiddo 2 Chr 35:22
broad **p** of the earth Rev 20:9

PLAN *design, scheme*

tabernacle...its **p** Ex 26:30
P-s formed long ago Is 25:1
follow our own **p**-s Jer 18:12
p and foreknowledge Acts 2:23

PLANT (n) *growth from soil*

every **p** yielding seed Gen 1:29
eat the **p**-s of the Gen 3:18
hail...struck every **p** Ex 9:25
God appointed a **p** Jon 4:6

PLANT (v) *put into soil*

God **p**-ed a garden Gen 2:8
p...trees for food Lev 19:23
shall **p** a vineyard Deut 28:30
A time to **p** Eccl 3:2
her earnings she **p**-s Prov 31:16
p-ed a vineyard Mark 12:1
I **p**-ed, Apollos 1 Cor 3:6

PLATTER *shallow dish*

on a **p** the head of Matt 14:8
his head on a **p** Mark 6:28

PLAY *take part*

who **p** the lyre Gen 4:21
man who can **p** 1 Sam 16:17
p-ed the fool 1 Sam 26:21
P skillfully with a Ps 33:3
nursing child will **p** Is 11:8
not **p** the harlot Hos 3:3
We **p**-ed the flute Matt 11:17

PLEAD *appeal, beseech*

p-ed with the LORD Deut 3:23
man...**p** with God Job 16:21
LORD...**p** their case Prov 22:23
P for the widow Is 1:17
Elijah...**p**-s with God Rom 11:2

PLEASANT *pleasing*

despised the **p** land Ps 106:24
P words are a Prov 16:24
sleep...is **p** Eccl 5:12
Speak to us **p** words Is 30:10

PLEASE *satisfy*

it **p** Thee to bless 2 Sam 7:29
Thou art **p**-d with me Ps 41:11
sacrifices...not **p** Him Hos 9:4
how he may **p** his 1 Cor 7:33
p all men in all 1 Cor 10:33
striving to **p** men Gal 1:10
to walk and...**p** God 1 Thess 4:1
impossible to **p** Heb 11:6

PLEASING *agreeable, gratifying*

tree that is **p** Gen 2:9
meditation be **p** Ps 104:34
not as **p** men but 1 Thess 2:4

p in His sight 1 John 3:22

PLEASURE *gratification*

old, shall I have **p** Gen 18:12
p in His people Ps 149:4
He who loves **p** *will* Prov 21:17
work for *His* good **p** Phil 2:13
lovers of **p** rather 2 Tim 3:4
passing **p**-s of sin Heb 11:25

PLEDGE *promise*

cloak as a **p** Ex 22:26
those who give **p**-s Prov 22:26
the Spirit as a **p** 2 Cor 5:5
p of our inheritance Eph 1:14

PLEIADES

constellation of stars
Job 9:9;38:31;
Amos 5:8

PLENTIFUL *abundant*

shed abroad a **p** rain Ps 68:9
harvest is **p** Matt 9:37

PLOT *plan, scheme*

wicked **p**-s against Ps 37:12
you have **p**-ted *evil* Prov 30:32
Jews **p**-ted together Acts 9:23

PLOW *dig the soil*

not **p** with an ox Deut 22:10
those who **p** iniquity Job 4:8
sluggard does not **p** Prov 20:4
his hand to the **p** Luke 9:62
ought to **p** in hope 1 Cor 9:10

PLOWSHARES *blade of plow*

their swords into **p** Is 2:4
your **p** into swords Joel 3:10

PLUMB LINE *vertical line*

the **p** of emptiness Is 34:11
p In the midst of My Amos 7:8
when they see the **p** Zech 4:10

PLUNDER (n) *booty, loot*

took no **p** in silver Judg 5:19
You will become **p** Hab 2:7
wealth will become **p** Zeph 1:13

PLUNDER (v) *rob*

will **p** the Egyptians Ex 3:22
stouthearted were **p**-ed Ps 76:5
he will **p** his house Matt 12:29

POINT *particular time*

grieved, to the **p** of Matt 26:38
obedient to the **p** of Phil 2:8
to the **p** of shedding Heb 12:4

POISON *lethal substance*

P...under their lips Ps 140:3
given us **p**-ed water Jer 8:14
turned justice into **p** Amos 6:12

POLL TAX *income and head tax*

collect customs or **p** Matt 17:25
give a **p** to Caesar Matt 22:17

POLLUTE *contaminate*

blood **p**-s the land Num 35:33
earth is also **p**-d Is 24:5

POMEGRANATE *fruit*

golden bell and a **p** Ex 28:34

p-s of blue and purple Ex 39:24
juice of my p-s Song 8:2
the fig tree, the p Hag 2:19

PONDER *think deeply*

not p the path of life Prov 5:6
Or p things...past Is 43:18

PONTUS

region in N Asia Minor
Acts 2:9; 1 Pet 1:1
homeland of Aquila Acts 18:2

POOL *pond*

of the upper p 2 Kin 18:17
rock into a p Ps 114:8
land will become a p Is 35:7
in the p of Siloam John 9:7

POOR *impoverished, needy*

p will never cease Deut 15:11
raises the p from the 1 Sam 2:8
lest you become p Prov 20:13
not rob the p Prov 22:22
are the p in spirit Matt 5:3
a p widow came Mark 12:42
p you always have Mark 14:7
sake He became p 2 Cor 8:9
not God choose the p James 2:5

POPULATE *increase number*

P the earth abundantly Gen 9:7
whole earth was p-d Gen 9:19

POPULATION *people*

with all *his* great p Is 16:14
deported an entire p Amos 1:6

PORPOISE SKIN

covering of p-s above Ex 26:14
put sandals of p on Ezek 16:10

PORTICO *porch*

in the p of Solomon John 10:23
one accord in...p Acts 5:12

PORTION *part, share*

gather a day's p Ex 16:4
LORD's p is...people Deut 32:9
double p of...spirit 2 Kin 2:9
The LORD is my p Ps 119:57
joy over their p Is 61:7

POSSESS *control, take*

give...this land to p Gen 15:7
are to p their land Lev 20:24
go in and p the land Deut 1:8
dost p all the nations Ps 82:8
p-ed by Beelzebul Mark 3:22
sell all you p Mark 10:21
p-ed with demons Luke 8:27
do not p silver and Acts 3:6

POSSESSION *ownership*

for an everlasting p Gen 17:8
you shall be My own p Ex 19:5
people for His own p Deut 4:20
full of Thy p-s Ps 104:24
charge of all his p-s Matt 24:47
selling their...p-s Acts 2:45

POSSIBLE *can be done*

all things are p Matt 19:26
p with God Luke 18:27

POSTERITY *descendants*

P will serve Him Ps 22:30
p of the wicked Ps 37:38

POT *container, vessel*

death in the p 2 Kin 4:40
refining p is for Prov 17:3
I see a boiling p Jer 1:13

POTIPHAR

*Egyptian official who purchased
Joseph* Gen 39:1

POTIPHERA

Joseph's father-in-law
Gen 41:45,50;46:20

POTSHERD *piece of pottery*

p to scrape himself Job 2:8
is dried up like a p Ps 22:15

POTTER *one who molds clay*

clay say to the p Is 45:9
and Thou our p Is 64:8
as it pleased the p Jer 18:4
Throw it to the p Zech 11:13

POTTER'S FIELD

*burial place bought with Judas
money* Matt 27:3ff
also called **Field of Blood**

POUR *cause to flow*

p me out like milk Job 10:10
I p out my soul Ps 42:4
P out your heart Ps 62:8
I will p out My Spirit Is 44:3
P out Thy wrath Jer 10:25
p out...a blessing Mal 3:10
p-ed it upon His Matt 26:7
p forth of My Spirit Acts 2:17

POVERTY *destitution, want*

glutton...come to p Prov 23:21
neither p nor riches Prov 30:8
through His p might 2 Cor 8:9

POWER *authority, strength*

to show you My p Ex 9:16
from the p of Sheol Ps 49:15
the p of His works Ps 111:6
p of the tongue Prov 18:21
the p of the sword Jer 18:21
Not by might nor...p Zech 4:6
Thine is...the p Matt 6:13
the right hand of p Mark 14:62
clothed with p from Luke 24:49
you shall receive p Acts 1:8
gospel...p of God Rom 1:16
the p of our Lord 1 Cor 5:4
p of sin is the law 1 Cor 15:56
p of Christ...dwell 2 Cor 12:9
prince of the p of Eph 2:2
p of His resurrection Phil 3:10
timidity, but of p 2 Tim 1:7
by the word of His p Heb 1:3
quenched the p of Heb 11:34
p-s...been subjected 1 Pet 3:22

POWERLESS *without strength*

p before this great 2 Chr 20:12
He might render p Heb 2:14

PRACTICE (n) *custom, habit*

evil of their p-s Ps 28:4
disclosing their p-s Acts 19:18
laid aside...*evil p-s* Col 3:9

PRACTICE (v) *engage in*

keep...statutes and p Lev 20:8
He who p-s deceit Ps 101:7
Who p righteousness Ps 106:3
p-ing hospitality Rom 12:13
learn to p piety 1 Tim 5:4
the one who p-s sin 1 John 3:8

**PRAETORIUM /
PRAETORIAN** *palace*

1 *Pontius Pilate's palace in
Jerusalem*
Matt 27:27; Mark 15:16;
John 18:28,33
2 *Herod's palace at Caesarea*
Acts 23:35
3 *Imperial palace guards in Rome*
Phil 1:13

PRAISE (n) *acclamation, honor*

offering of p Lev 19:24
sing p-s to Him 1 Chr 16:9
songs of p...hymns Neh 12:46
From Thee...my p Ps 22:25
sound His p abroad Ps 66:8
makes Jerusalem a p Is 62:7
his p is not from men Rom 2:29
anything worthy of p Phil 4:8
a sacrifice of p Heb 13:15
Give p to our God Rev 19:5

PRAISE (v) *extol, glorify*

I will p Him Ex 15:2
greatly to be p-d 1 Chr 16:25
Will the dust p Thee Ps 30:9
My lips will p Thee Ps 63:3
heavens will p Thy Ps 89:5
P Him, sun and moon Ps 148:3
P Him with trumpet Ps 150:3
Death cannot p Thee Is 38:18
I p Thee, O Father Matt 11:25
heavenly host p-ing Luke 2:13
disciples began to p Luke 19:37
leaping and p-ing God Acts 3:8

PRAY *ask, worship*

Abraham p-ed to Gen 20:17
For this boy I p-ed 1 Sam 1:27
found *courage* to p 1 Chr 17:25
For to Thee do I p Ps 5:2
P for...Jerusalem Ps 122:6
p to a god who cannot Is 45:20
We earnestly p Jon 1:14
p for...persecute Matt 5:44
by Himself to p Matt 14:23
p and ask, believe Mark 11:24
until I have p-ed Mark 14:32
Lord, teach us to p Luke 11:1
they ought to p Luke 18:1
I have p-ed for you Luke 22:32
p-ed with fasting Acts 14:23
if I p in a tongue 1 Cor 14:14
p without ceasing 1 Thess 5:17
p for one another James 5:16
p-ing in the...Spirit Jude 20

PRAYER

I have heard your **p**	2 Chr 7:12
And my **p** is pure	Job 16:17
LORD receives my **p**	Ps 6:9
Give ear to my **p**	Ps 55:1
p of the righteous	Prov 15:29
joyful in My house of **p**	Is 56:7
ask in **p**, believing	Matt 21:22
you make long **p-s**	Matt 23:14
whole night in **p**	Luke 6:12
My house...of **p**	Luke 19:46
devoting...to **p**	Acts 1:14
offering **p** with joy	Phil 1:4
but in everything by **p**	Phil 4:6
p-s...not be hindered	1 Pet 3:7
p-s of the saints	Rev 5:8

PREACH *exhort, proclaim*

Jesus began to **p**	Matt 4:17
as you go, **p**	Matt 10:7
teach and **p** in their	Matt 11:1
p-ing...repentance	Mark 1:4
p the gospel to all	Mark 16:15
p the kingdom of	Luke 4:43
he **p-ed** Jesus to him	Acts 8:35
p...the good news	Acts 13:32
how shall they **p**	Rom 10:15
we **p** Christ crucified	1 Cor 1:23
He...**p-ed** peace	Eph 2:17
p the word	2 Tim 4:2

PREACHER *one who proclaims*

hear without a **p**	Rom 10:14
appointed a **p** and an	1 Tim 2:7
Noah, a **p** of	2 Pet 2:5

PRECEPTS *commandments*

All His **p** are sure	Ps 111:7
meditate on Thy **p**	Ps 119:15
as doctrines the **p** of	Matt 15:9

PRECIOUS *beloved* or *costly*

P in the sight of	Ps 116:15
like **p** oil upon the	Ps 133:2
more **p** than jewels	Prov 3:15
p things...no profit	Is 44:9
more **p** than gold	1 Pet 1:7
with **p** blood	1 Pet 1:19

PREDESTINED *foreordained*

purpose **p** to occur	Acts 4:28
foreknew, He also **p**	Rom 8:29
God **p** before the ages	1 Cor 2:7
p us to adoption	Eph 1:5
p according to His	Eph 1:11

PREDETERMINED

p plan...of God	Acts 2:23

PREEMINENT *foremost*

P in dignity	Gen 49:3

PREFECTS *Persian officials*

shatter governors...**p**	Jer 51:23
the satraps, the **p**	Dan 3:3

PREGNANT *with child*

womb of...**p** woman	Eccl 11:5
And her womb ever **p**	Jer 20:17
ripped open...**p**	Amos 1:13
Elizabeth...became **p**	Luke 1:24

PREPARATION *readiness*

distracted with...**p-s**	Luke 10:40

Jewish day of **p**	John 19:42
making **p-s**, he fell	Acts 10:10
p of the gospel of	Eph 6:15

PREPARE *make ready*

p a savory dish	Gen 27:4
mind **p-s** deception	Job 15:35
p a table before me	Ps 23:5
P to meet your God	Amos 4:12
will **p** Your way	Matt 11:10
kingdom **p-d** for	Matt 25:34
to **p** Me for burial	Matt 26:12
p-d spices and	Luke 23:56
I go to **p** a place	John 14:2
worlds were **p-d** by	Heb 11:3

PRESENCE *appearance*

My **p** shall go *with*	Ex 33:14
in the **p** of my enemies	Ps 23:5
the light of Thy **p**	Ps 44:3
tremble at Thy **p**	Is 64:2
the **p** of His glory	Jude 24
the **p** of the Lamb	Rev 14:10

PRESENT (n) *gift*

a **p** for his brother	Gen 32:13
sent a **p** to the king	2 Kin 16:8
and a **p** to Hezekiah	Is 39:1

PRESENT (v) *give, offer*

p you with a crown of	Prov 4:9
you **p** the blind for	Mal 1:8
p Him to the Lord	Luke 2:22
p yourselves to God	Rom 6:13
p your bodies a	Rom 12:1
p you before Him holy	Col 1:22

PRESERVE *protect*

no son to **p** my	2 Sam 18:18
P me, O God	Ps 16:1
Do **p** my soul	Ps 86:2
LORD **p-s** the simple	Ps 116:6
p-d ones of Israel	Is 49:6
p the unity of the	Eph 4:3
be **p-d** complete	1 Thess 5:23

PRESS *compel, force*

measure, **p-ed** down	Luke 6:38
I **p** on toward...goal	Phil 3:14

PRETEND *deceive, feign*

p to be a mourner	2 Sam 14:2
p to be another	1 Kin 14:5
p-s to be poor	Prov 13:7
spies who **p-ed** to	Luke 20:20

PREVAIL *exist* or *triumph*

water **p-ed**...increased	Gen 7:18
not by might...man **p**	1 Sam 2:9
Iniquities **p** against me	Ps 65:3
overcome me and **p-ed**	Jer 20:7

PREY *what is hunted*

birds of **p** came	Gen 15:11
lion tearing the **p**	Ezek 22:25
no longer be a **p** to	Ezek 34:28

PRICE *cost, value*

shall increase its **p**	Lev 25:16
their redemption **p**	Num 18:16
p of the pardoning of	Is 27:9
it is the **p** of blood	Matt 27:6
p of his wickedness	Acts 1:18
kept back *some*...**p**	Acts 5:2

bought with a **p**	1 Cor 7:23

PRIDE *exaggerated self-esteem*

P goes before	Prov 16:18
you an everlasting **p**	Is 60:15
p of Israel testifies	Hos 5:5
envy, slander, **p**	Mark 7:22
boastful **p** of life	1 John 2:16

PRIEST *intermediary*

a **p** of God Most	Gen 14:18
a kingdom of **p-s**	Ex 19:6
Aaron's sons, the **p-s**	Lev 1:5
if the anointed **p** sins	Lev 4:3
p...make atonement	Lev 4:31
without a teaching **p**	2 Chr 15:3
Thou art a **p** forever	Ps 110:4
all the chief **p-s**	Matt 2:4
show yourself to the **p**	Matt 8:4
faithful high **p**	Heb 2:17
have a great high **p**	Heb 4:14
Thou art a **p** forever	Heb 5:6

PRIESTHOOD *office of priest*

for a perpetual **p**	Ex 40:15
have defiled the **p**	Neh 13:29
His **p** permanently	Heb 7:24
royal **p**, a holy nation	1 Pet 2:9

PRIME *fully mature period*

die in the **p** of life	1 Sam 2:33
p of life...fleeing	Eccl 11:10

PRINCE *ruler*

Who made you a **p**	Ex 2:14
p-s of the tribes	1 Chr 29:6
contempt upon **p-s**	Ps 107:40
Do not trust in **p-s**	Ps 146:3
Father, **P** of Peace	Is 9:6
p-s will rule justly	Is 32:1
to death the **P** of life	Acts 3:15
p of...the air	Eph 2:2

PRISCA / PRISCILLA

wife of Aquila	Rom 16:3
co-worker with Paul	
Acts 18:2,18,26; 1 Cor 16:19	

PRISON *jail*

Put this man in **p**	1 Kin 22:27
my soul out of **p**	Ps 142:7
beheaded in the **p**	Matt 14:10
I was in **p**, and	Matt 25:36
opened...the **p**	Acts 5:19
spirits *now* in **p**	1 Pet 3:19

PRISONER *one who is confined*

sets the **p-s** free	Ps 146:7
a notorious **p**	Matt 27:16
p of the law of sin	Rom 7:23
Paul, a **p** of Christ	Philem 1

PRIVATE *not public*

reprove him in **p**	Matt 18:15
but *I* did so in **p**	Gal 2:2

PRIZE *reward*

one receives the **p**	1 Cor 9:24
p of the upward call	Phil 3:14

PROCEED *go forth*

p from evil to evil	Jer 9:3
p-s out of the mouth	Matt 4:4
p-s from...Father	John 15:26

PROCLAIM announce, declare

p...name of the LORD	Ex 33:19
P good tidings	1 Chr 16:23
appointed...to p	Neh 6:7
p liberty to captives	Is 61:1
p justice to the	Matt 12:18
he began to p Jesus	Acts 9:20
first to p light	Acts 26:23
faith is being p-ed	Rom 1:8
p...eternal life	1 John 1:2

PROCLAMATION declaration

a p was circulated	Ex 36:6
made p to the spirits	1 Pet 3:19

PROCONSUL Roman governor

the p, Sergius Paulus	Acts 13:7
p-s are available	Acts 19:38

PRODUCE (n) yield of the soil

land will yield its p	Lev 25:19
tithe all the p	Deut 14:22
earth has yielded its p	Ps 67:6
precious p of...soil	James 5:7

PRODUCE (v) bring forth

milk p-s butter	Prov 30:33
cannot p bad fruit	Matt 7:18
they p quarrels	2 Tim 2:23
faith p-s endurance	James 1:3

PROFANE defile, desecrate

p My holy name	Lev 20:3
is p-d by harlotry	Lev 21:7
and p-d My sabbaths	Ezek 22:8
p-d your sanctuaries	Ezek 28:18
to p the covenant	Mal 2:10

PROFESS confess, declare

P-ing to be wise	Rom 1:22
They p to know God	Titus 1:16

PROFIT (n) benefit, gain

labor there is p	Prov 14:23
no p for the charmer	Eccl 10:11
not seeking my...p	1 Cor 10:33
business...make a p	James 4:13

PROFIT (v) reap an advantage

p...my destruction	Job 30:13
what does it p a	Mark 8:36
the flesh p-s nothing	John 6:63
it p-s me nothing	1 Cor 13:3

PROFITABLE useful

not all things are p	1 Cor 6:12
godliness is p	1 Tim 4:8
p for teaching	2 Tim 3:16

PROMINENT well-known

a p member of the	Mark 15:43
of p Greek women	Acts 17:12
p men of the city	Acts 25:23

PROMISE (n) agreement, pledge

p of the Holy Spirit	Acts 2:33
the p made by God	Acts 26:6
the p is nullified	Rom 4:14
children of the p	Rom 9:8
commandment...a p	Eph 6:2
heirs of the p	Heb 6:17
precious...p-s	2 Pet 1:4
the p of His coming	2 Pet 3:4

PROMISED made an agreement

land which He had p	Deut 9:28
p to keep Thy words	Ps 119:57
p long ages ago	Titus 1:2
He who p is faithful	Heb 10:23

PRONOUNCE declare officially

shall p him clean	Lev 13:23
I will p My judgments	Jer 1:16
Pilate p-d sentence	Luke 23:24
God...p-d judgment	Rev 18:20

PROOF evidence

furnished p to all	Acts 17:31
p of your love	2 Cor 8:24
p of the Christ	2 Cor 13:3

PROPER suitable

fulfilled...p time	Luke 1:20
is it p for a woman	1 Cor 11:13
as is p among saints	Eph 5:3

PROPERTY goods or land

acquire p in it	Gen 34:10
p...too great	Gen 36:7
buys a slave as his p	Lev 22:11
who owned much p	Matt 19:22
selling their p and	Acts 2:45
things...common as	Acts 4:32

PROPHECY proclamation

seal up vision and p	Dan 9:24
p...fulfilled	Matt 13:14
have the gift of p	1 Cor 13:2
no p...of human will	2 Pet 1:21
the spirit of p	Rev 19:10

PROPHESY predict, proclaim

to p with lyres	1 Chr 25:1
he never p-ies good	2 Chr 18:7
p-ing...false vision	Jer 14:14
P over these bones	Ezek 37:4
sons and...will p	Joel 2:28
did we...p in Your	Matt 7:22
P to us...Christ	Matt 26:68
speaking...p-ing	Acts 19:6
who p-ies edifies	1 Cor 14:4

PROPHET spokesman for God

Aaron shall be your p	Ex 7:1
a p or a dreamer	Deut 13:1
I will raise up a p	Deut 18:18
p in your place	1 Kin 19:16
summon all...p-s	2 Kin 10:19
vision of...the p	2 Chr 32:32
Woe...foolish p-s	Ezek 13:3
written by the p	Matt 2:5
persecuted the p-s	Matt 5:12
Beware...false p-s	Matt 7:15
He...receives a p	Matt 10:41
the p Jesus	Matt 21:11
false p-s...arise	Mark 13:22
p of the Most High	Luke 1:76
great p has arisen	Luke 7:16
Are you the P	John 1:21
reading Isaiah the p	Acts 8:30
a Jewish false p	Acts 13:6
All are not p-s	1 Cor 12:29
and some as p-s	Eph 4:11
beast and...false p	Rev 20:10

PROPHETESS speaker for God

Miriam the p	Ex 15:20
Deborah, a p	Judg 4:4
there was a p, Anna	Luke 2:36
calls herself a p	Rev 2:20

PROPHETIC predictive

not...p utterances	1 Thess 5:20
p word...sure	2 Pet 1:19

PROPITIATION atonement

a p in His blood	Rom 3:25
p for the sins	Heb 2:17
He himself is the p	1 John 2:2
p for our sins	1 John 4:10

PROSELYTE convert

both Jews and p-s	Acts 2:10
a p from Antioch	Acts 6:5
God-fearing p-s	Acts 13:43

PROSPER flourish, succeed

I will surely p you	Gen 32:12
David was p-ing	1 Sam 18:14
they built and p-ed	2 Chr 14:7
His ways p at all	Ps 10:5
they p who love you	Ps 122:6

PROSPERITY success, wealth

my p has passed away	Job 30:15
soul will abide in p	Ps 25:13
saw the p of the wicked	Ps 73:3
know how to live in p	Phil 4:12

PROSPEROUS successful

exceedingly p	Gen 30:43
make your way p	Josh 1:8
generous man...be p	Prov 11:25

PROSTITUTE harlot

Where...temple p	Gen 38:21
male cult p-s in the	1 Kin 14:24
an adulterer and a p	Is 57:3

PROSTRATE fall down flat

p-d himself before	2 Sam 18:28
man dies and lies p	Job 14:10
falling down, p-d	Matt 18:26

PROTECT guard, shield

The LORD will p him	Ps 41:2
LORD p-s the strangers	Ps 146:9
LORD...p Jerusalem	Is 31:5
He will...p you	2 Thess 3:3
p-ed by the power of	1 Pet 1:5

PROTECTION safe-keeping

p has been removed	Num 14:9
For wisdom is p	Eccl 7:12
p from the storm	Is 4:6
let him rely on My p	Is 27:5

PROUD exaggerated self-esteem

heart becomes p	Deut 8:14
recompense to the p	Ps 94:2
eyes and a p heart	Prov 21:4
daughters of Zion are p	Is 3:16
opposed to the p	James 4:6

PROVE establish, test

you be p-d a liar	Prov 30:6
shall I Myself holy	Ezek 20:41
p to be My disciples	John 15:8
p...the will of God	Rom 12:2
p yourselves doers	James 1:22

PROVERB *adage, short saying*

become...a p	Deut 28:37
spoke 3,000 p-s	1 Kin 4:32
Israel...become a p	1 Kin 9:7
To understand a p	Prov 1:6
quote this p to Me	Luke 4:23
to the true p	2 Pet 2:22

PROVIDE *furnish, supply*

p for Himself...lamb	Gen 22:8
p for...redemption	Lev 25:24
p bread from heaven	Neh 9:15
Who p-s rain for the	Ps 147:8
p...way of escape	1 Cor 10:13
not p for his own	1 Tim 5:8
God had p-d	Heb 11:40

PROVINCE *district or territory*

rulers of the p-s	1 Kin 20:17
holiday for the p-s	Esth 2:18
whole p of Babylon	Dan 2:48
arrived in the p	Acts 25:1

PROVISION *supply, requirement*

bread of their p was	Josh 9:5
bless her p	Ps 132:15
p-s of the law	Matt 23:23
no p for the flesh	Rom 13:14

PROVOKE *evoke, excite*

images to p Me	1 Kin 14:9
who p God are secure	Job 12:6
love...is not p-d	1 Cor 13:4,5
not p your children	Eph 6:4

PROWL *roam in search*

beasts...p about	Ps 104:20
devil, p-s about like	1 Pet 5:8

PRUDENT *careful, wise*

a p man conceals	Prov 12:16
p wife is from the	Prov 19:14
the p took oil in	Matt 25:4
you are p in Christ	1 Cor 4:10

PRUNING *cutting*

spears into p hooks	Is 2:4

PSALMS *sacred songs*

shout...with p	Ps 95:2
P must be fulfilled	Luke 24:44
speaking...in p	Eph 5:19

PUBLIC *open*

of his p appearance	Luke 1:80
beaten us in p	Acts 16:37
refuted...Jews in p	Acts 18:28
made a p display	Col 2:15
made a p spectacle	Heb 10:33

PUL

Tiglath Pileser III, king of Assyria   2 Kin 15:19; 1 Chr 5:26

PUNISH *chastise, penalize*

p them for their sin	Ex 32:34
and are p-ed for it	Prov 22:3
p the world for its	Is 13:11
will p your iniquity	Lam 4:22
p Him and release	Luke 23:16
I p-ed them often	Acts 26:11
p all disobedience	2 Cor 10:6

PUNISHMENT *penalty*

My p is too great	Gen 4:13
p of the sword	Job 19:29
fear involves p	1 John 4:18
the p of eternal fire	Jude 7

PUPIL *part of eye or student*

as the p of His eye	Deut 32:10
p is not above his	Luke 6:40

PURCHASE *buy*

p-d with His...blood	Acts 20:28
p for God with Thy	Rev 5:9

PURE *genuine, undefiled*

mercy seat of p gold	Ex 25:17
be p before his Maker	Job 4:17
My teaching is p	Job 11:4
commandment...is p	Ps 19:8
pleasant words are p	Prov 15:26
As p as the sun	Song 6:10
hair...like p wool	Dan 7:9
Blessed are the p in	Matt 5:8
whatever is p	Phil 4:8
love from a p heart	1 Tim 1:5
p milk of the word	1 Pet 2:2
the city was p gold	Rev 21:18

PURGE *remove*

p...evil from among	Deut 13:5
Many will be p-d	Dan 12:10

PURIFICATION *cleansing*

Jewish custom of p	John 2:6
He...made p of sins	Heb 1:3

PURIFY *make clean*

p-ied these waters	2 Kin 2:21
P me with hyssop	Ps 51:7
p...a people	Titus 2:14
p your hearts	James 4:8
p-ied your souls	1 Pet 1:22

PURIM

Jewish festival   Esth 9:26ff

PURITY *not corrupted*

who loves p of heart	Prov 22:11
love, faith *and* p	1 Tim 4:12
with p in doctrine	Titus 2:7

PURPLE *color*

a veil of blue and p	Ex 26:31
Those reared in p	Lam 4:5
clothed Daniel with p	Dan 5:29
dressed Him...p	Mark 15:17
a seller of p fabrics	Acts 16:14
clothed in p and	Rev 17:4

PURPOSE *intention, reason*

p of shedding blood	Ezek 22:9
rejected God's p	Luke 7:30
for this p I have	Acts 26:16
according to *His* p	Rom 8:28

PURSE *bag, pouch*

gold from the p	Is 46:6
Carry no p, no bag	Luke 10:4
p-s...do not wear	Luke 12:33

PURSUE *chase, follow*

p the manslayer	Deut 19:6
They p my honor	Job 30:15
the enemy p my soul	Ps 7:5

PUT

Seek peace, and p it	Ps 34:14
Adversity p-s	Prov 13:21
p-s righteousness	Prov 21:21
may p strong drink	Is 5:11
p righteousness	2 Tim 2:22
P peace with...men	Heb 12:14

PUT *place*

p enmity Between	Gen 3:15
He p a new song	Ps 40:3
p on the Lord Jesus	Rom 13:14
p on the new self	Eph 4:24
P on the full armor	Eph 6:11

PUT

1 *son of Ham*   Gen 10:6; 1 Chr 1:8

2 *African country*   Jer 46:9; Ezek 27:10;30:5; Nah 3:9

Q

QUAIL *type of bird*

q-s came up and	Ex 16:13
q from the sea	Num 11:31

QUAKE *shake, tremble*

The mountains q-d	Judg 5:5
made the land q	Ps 60:2
The earth q-d	Ps 68:8
q at Thy presence	Is 64:1

QUALITY *character*

test the q of each	1 Cor 3:13
imperishable q of a	1 Pet 3:4

QUANTITY *amount*

large q-ies of cedar	1 Chr 22:4
a great q of fish	Luke 5:6

QUARANTINE *isolate*

shall q the article	Lev 13:50
q the house for	Lev 14:38

QUARREL (n) *altercation*

if men have a q	Ex 21:18
So abandon the q	Prov 17:14
are q-s among you	1 Cor 1:11
the source of q-s	James 4:1

QUARREL (v) *contend, fight*

did not q over it	Gen 26:22
Why do you q with me	Ex 17:2
any fool will q	Prov 20:3
those who q with you	Is 41:12

QUART *measure*

A q of wheat for a	Rev 6:6

QUEEN *female sovereign*

when the q of Sheba	1 Kin 10:1
king saw Esther the q	Esth 5:2
The q of kingdoms	Is 47:5
The Q *of the* South	Matt 12:42
Candace, q of the	Acts 8:27

QUENCH *extinguish*

donkeys q their thirst	Ps 104:11
waters cannot q love	Song 8:7
not q the Spirit	1 Thess 5:19
q-ed...power of fire	Heb 11:34

QUESTION (n) *inquiry, problem*

Was it not just a q	1 Sam 17:29

QUESTION

answered all her **q-s**	2 Chr 9:2
Jesus asked...a **q**	Matt 22:41
in controversial **q-s**	1 Tim 6:4

QUESTION (v) *ask*

q-ed the priests	2 Chr 31:9
Jeremiah and **q-ed**	Jer 38:27
He *began* to **q** them	Mark 9:33
to **q** Him closely on	Luke 11:53
Q those who have	John 18:21

QUICK (adj) *rapid*

is **q**-tempered exalts	Prov 14:29
q to hear, slow to	James 1:19

QUICK (n) *deepest feelings*

cut to the **q** and	Acts 5:33
were cut to the **q**	Acts 7:54

QUIET (adj) *calm, still*

he knew no **q** within	Job 20:20
me beside **q** waters	Ps 23:2
lead a...**q** life	1 Tim 2:2
gentle and **q** spirit	1 Pet 3:4

QUIET (v) *become calm, still*

God, do not remain **q**	Ps 83:1
and **q**-ed my soul	Ps 131:2
will be **q** in His love	Zeph 3:17
Be **q**, and come out	Mark 1:25

QUIRINIUS

Roman governor at time of	
Judean census	Luke 2:2

QUIVER *case for holding arrows*

your **q** and your bow	Gen 27:3
man whose **q** is full	Ps 127:5
hidden Me in His **q**	Is 49:2
q is like an open grave	Jer 5:16
fill the **q-s**	Jer 51:11

QUOTA *portion assigned*

complete your work **q**	Ex 5:13
deliver the **q** of bricks	Ex 5:18

QUOTE *repeat a passage*

who **q-s** proverbs	Ezek 16:44
will **q** this proverb	Luke 4:23

R

RAAMSES / RAMESES

where Joseph settled	Gen 47:11
Egyptian store-city built by	
Hebrew slaves	Ex 1:11
origin of exodus	
	Ex 12:37; Num 33:3,5

RABBI / RABBONI

respectful form of address	
Matt 23:7;26:25; Mark 10:51	
master, teacher	
John 1:49;6:25;11:8;20:16	

RAB-MAG

title of Babylonian official	
	Jer 39:3,13

RAB-SARIS

title of Assyrian official	
2 Kin 18:17; Jer 39:3,13	

RABSHAKEH

title of Assyrian official	
2 Kin 18:17ff; Is 36:2,4,11	

RACA *worthless fool*

shall say...**R**	Matt 5:22

RACE (n) *nation, people*

r has intermingled	Ezra 9:2
mongrel **r** will dwell	Zech 9:6
advantage of our **r**	Acts 7:19
you are a chosen **r**	1 Pet 2:9

RACE (n) *competition of speed*

r is not to...swift	Eccl 9:11
in a **r** all run, but	1 Cor 9:24
r...set before us	Heb 12:1

RACHEL

Jacob's wife	Gen 29:18,28
mother of Joseph and Benjamin	
	Gen 30:25;35:24;46:19

RADIANCE *brightness*

a **r** around Him	Ezek 1:27
His **r** is like	Hab 3:4
r of His glory	Heb 1:3

RADIANT *shining brightly*

looked to Him...were **r**	Ps 34:5
you will see and be **r**	Is 60:5
His garments...**r**	Mark 9:3

RAFTS *boats*

r *to go* by sea	1 Kin 5:9
bring it to you on **r**	2 Chr 2:16

RAGE (n) *violent anger*

Haman was filled...**r**	Esth 3:5
with **r** as they heard	Luke 4:28

RAGE (v) *be very angry*

r-s against the LORD	Prov 19:3
foolish man...**r-s**	Prov 29:9
Why...Gentiles **r**	Acts 4:25

RAHAB

1 *harlot in Jericho*	Josh 2:1
assisted spies	Josh 2:4-7
family spared	
	Josh 2:13,14;6:22,23
ancestor of Jesus	Matt 1:5
example of faith	
	Heb 11:31; James 2:25
2 *symbolic for sea monster*	
	Job 9:13;26:12; Ps 89:10
3 *symbolic for Egypt*	
	Ps 87:4; Is 30:7

RAID (n) *robbery*

a **r** on the land	1 Sam 23:27
a **r** on the camels	Job 1:17

RAID (v) *make a sudden attack*

r *at* their heels	Gen 49:19
Bandits **r** outside	Hos 7:1

RAIN (n)

God had not sent **r**	Gen 2:5
r fell upon the earth	Gen 7:12
I shall give you **r-s**	Lev 26:4
LORD sent...**r**	1 Sam 12:18
no **r** in the land	1 Kin 17:7
the mountain **r-s**	Job 24:8
shed...a plentiful **r**	Ps 68:9
r is over *and* gone	Song 2:11
anger a flooding **r**	Ezek 13:13
r on *the* righteous	Matt 5:45

ground...drinks the **r**	Heb 6:7

RAIN (v) *fall down, pour*

r bread from heaven	Ex 16:4
the LORD **r-ed** hail	Ex 9:23
it **r-ed** fire and	Luke 17:29
not **r**...for three	James 5:17

RAINBOW *colored arc in sky*

appearance of the **r**	Ezek 1:28
a **r** around the throne	Rev 4:3
r was upon his head	Rev 10:1

RAISE *elevate, lift*

will **r** up a prophet	Deut 18:18
LORD **r-d** up judges	Judg 2:16
r-s the poor from	1 Sam 2:8
eyelids are **r-d** *in*	Prov 30:13
r up shepherds over	Jer 23:4
He will **r** us up	Hos 6:2
Heal...**r** *the* dead	Matt 10:8
He will be **r-d** up	Matt 20:19
three days I will **r**	John 2:19
Jesus God **r-d** up	Acts 2:32
r-d a spiritual	1 Cor 15:44
r-d us up with Him	Eph 2:6
God is able to **r** men	Heb 11:19

RAISIN *dried grapes*

clusters of **r-s**	2 Sam 16:1
Sustain me with **r**	Song 2:5
and love **r** cakes	Hos 3:1

RAM *male sheep*

Abraham...took the **r**	Gen 22:13
a **r** without defect	Lev 5:15
the **r** of atonement	Num 5:8
r which had two horns	Dan 8:3

RAMAH

1 *city of Naphtali*	Josh 19:36
2 *town of Asher*	Josh 19:29
3 *town of Benjamin*	
Josh 18:25; Judg 4:5; 19:13	
4 *town in the Negev*	Josh 19:8
5 *town in Gilead*	
2 Kin 8:28,29; 2 Chr 22:5,6	

RAMOTH

1 *city in Gilead*	
	Deut 4:43; Josh 20:8
see **RAMOTH-GILEAD**	
2 *city in the Negev*	1 Sam 30:27
also **Ramah of the Negev**	
3 *Gershonite city*	1 Chr 6:73

RAMOTH-GILEAD

Gadite city E of the Jordan	
	Deut 4:43
city of refuge	Josh 20:8
Ahab killed	1 Kin 22:29-37

RAMPART *bulwark, siege*

and **r-s** for security	Is 26:1
Whose **r** *was* the sea	Nah 3:8
station myself on the **r**	Hab 2:1

RANK *position*

men of **r** are a lie	Ps 62:9
He...has a higher **r**	Josh 1:15
a Man...higher **r**	John 1:30

RANSOM (n) *payment*

give a **r** for himself	Ex 30:12

not take **r** for — Num 35:31
wicked is a **r** for — Prov 21:18
His life a **r** for — Matt 20:28
gave Himself as a **r** — 1 Tim 2:6

RANSOM (v) *redeem*

Thou hast **r-ed** me — Ps 31:5
R me because of my — Ps 69:18
LORD has **r-ed** Jacob — Jer 31:11
I will **r** them from — Hos 13:14

RAVAGE *devastate*

famine will **r** the — Gen 41:30
mice that **r** the land — 1 Sam 6:5
r-ing the church — Acts 8:3

RAVEN *type of bird*

he sent out a **r** — Gen 8:7
young **r-s** which cry — Ps 147:9
Consider the **r-s** — Luke 12:24

RAVENOUS *wildly hungry*

Benjamin is a **r** wolf — Gen 49:27
inwardly are **r** wolves — Matt 7:15

RAVINE *gorge*

settle on the steep **r-s** — Is 7:19
smooth *stones* of the **r** — Is 57:6
Every **r** shall be filled — Luke 3:5

RAVISH *seize and take*

you may **r** them — Judg 19:24
And their wives **r-ed** — Is 13:16
r-ed...women in Zion — Lam 5:11

RAZOR *instrument for shaving*

no **r** shall pass over — Num 6:5
no **r** shall come upon — Judg 13:5
A **r** has never come — Judg 16:17
Like a sharp **r** — Ps 52:2

READ

you shall **r** this — Deut 31:11
r from the scroll — Jer 36:6
who **r-s** it may run — Hab 2:2
r-ing...Isaiah — Acts 8:28
prophets...are **read** — Acts 13:27
Moses is **read** — 2 Cor 3:15
Blessed is he who **r-s** — Rev 1:3

READY *equipped, prepared*

and **r** to forgive — Ps 86:5
Let Thy hand be **r** — Ps 119:173
Make **r** the way — Matt 3:3
you be **r** too — Matt 24:44
be **r** in season — 2 Tim 4:2
r to make a defense — 1 Pet 3:15

REALIZE *achieve or understand*

Desire **r-d** is sweet — Prov 13:19
r-d through Jesus — John 1:17
to **r**...assurance — Heb 6:11

REALM *area, kingdom*

ruler over the **r** of — Dan 4:17
kingdom is not...**r** — John 18:36

REAP *cut, gather*

when you **r**...harvest — Lev 19:9
iniquity will **r** vanity — Prov 22:8
they **r** the whirlwind — Hos 8:7
neither do they **r** — Matt 6:26
neither sow nor **r** — Luke 12:24
sows...another **r-s** — John 4:37

r eternal life — Gal 6:8
your sickle and **r** — Rev 14:15

REAPER *harvester*

after the **r-s** — Ruth 2:3
will overtake the **r** — Amos 9:13
the **r-s** are angels — Matt 13:39

REASON (n) *explanation*

this **r** the Father — John 10:17
this **r** I found mercy — 1 Tim 1:16
For this **r**, rejoice — Rev 12:12

REASON (v) *analyze, argue*

upright would **r** with — Job 23:7
let us **r** together — Is 1:18
Pharisees began to **r** — Luke 5:21
r-ing in...synagogue — Acts 17:17
as a child, **r** as a — 1 Cor 13:11

REBEKAH

wife of Isaac — Gen 24:67;26:8
mother of Esau and Jacob — Gen 25:21ff

REBEL (n) *rebellious one*

Your rulers are **r-s** — Is 1:23
called a **r** from birth — Is 48:8
their princes are **r-s** — Hos 9:15

REBEL (v) *revolt*

not **r** against the — Num 14:9
r-led against...words — Ps 107:11
r-led against Me — Ezek 20:21

REBELLION *insurrection*

he has counseled **r** — Deut 13:5
I know your **r** — Deut 31:27
r is as the sin of — 1 Sam 15:23
my **r** and my sin — Job 13:23
children of **r** — Is 57:4

REBELLIOUS *defiant*

r against the LORD — Deut 9:7
r generation — Ps 78:8
A **r** man seeks only — Prov 17:11
stubborn and **r** heart — Jer 5:23
there are many **r** — Titus 1:10

REBUILD *restore*

r the house of the — Ezra 1:3
let us **r** the wall — Neh 2:17
r the ancient ruins — Is 58:12
r it in three days — Matt 26:61
r the tabernacle — Acts 15:16

REBUKE (n) *reprimand*

amazed at His **r** — Job 26:11
At Thy **r** they fled — Ps 104:7
the poor hears no **r** — Prov 13:8

REBUKE (v) *scold*

r me not in Thy wrath — Ps 38:1
r the arrogant — Ps 119:21
LORD **r** you, Satan — Zech 3:2
r-d the winds — Matt 8:26
Jesus **r-d** him — Matt 17:18
He **r-d** the fever — Luke 4:39
Do not sharply **r** — 1 Tim 5:1
reprove, **r**, exhort — 2 Tim 4:2

RECEIVE *encounter, take*

The LORD **r-s** my prayer — Ps 6:9
r me to glory — Ps 73:24

man **r-s** a bribe — Prov 17:23
freely you **r-d** — Matt 10:8
who **r-s** you, **r-s** Me — Matt 10:40
the blind **r** sight — Matt 11:5
ask...you shall **r** — Matt 21:22
r-d up into heaven — Mark 16:19
This man **r-s** sinners — Luke 15:2
as many as **r-d** Him — John 1:12
r you to Myself — John 14:3
R the Holy Spirit — John 20:22
you shall **r** power — Acts 1:8
to give than to **r** — Acts 20:35
one **r-s** the prize — 1 Cor 9:24
r the crown of life — James 1:12
whatever...ask we **r** — 1 John 3:22
r-d the mark of — Rev 19:20

RECHABITES

line of Jonadab — Jer 35:6
strict life style — Jer 35:1-18

RECKONED *accounted for*

r it to him as — Gen 15:6
r among the nations — Num 23:9
his wage is not **r** — Rom 4:4
r...as righteousness — James 2:23

RECLINE *lean, lie down*

r on beds of ivory — Amos 6:4
r on the grass — Matt 14:19
r *at the table* in — Luke 13:29
r-ing on Jesus' — John 13:23

RECOGNIZE *be aware, know*

he did not **r** him — Gen 27:23
Saul **r-d** David's — 1 Sam 26:17
r that He is near — Matt 24:33
I did not **r** Him — John 1:31

RECOMPENSE (n) *reward*

the **r** of the wicked — Ps 91:8
r to the proud — Ps 94:2
r of God will come — Is 35:4
received a just **r** — Heb 2:2

RECOMPENSE (v) *compensate*

LORD has **r-d** me — 2 Sam 22:25
He will **r** the evil — Ps 54:5
But if you do **r** Me — Joel 3:4

RECONCILE *bring together*

r-d to your brother — Matt 5:24
be **r-d** to God — 2 Cor 5:20
r them both in one — Eph 2:16
r all...to Himself — Col 1:20

RECONCILIATION

now received the **r** — Rom 5:11
the **r** of the world — Rom 11:15
the ministry of **r** — 2 Cor 5:18
the word of **r** — 2 Cor 5:19

RECORD (n) *document, register*

the **r-s** are ancient — 1 Chr 4:22
r-s of the kings — 2 Chr 33:18
discover in...**r** books — Ezra 4:15
I found the...**r** — Neh 7:5

RECORD (v) *register, write*

r-ed their starting — Num 33:2
R the vision — Hab 2:2
are **r-ed** in heaven — Luke 10:20

RECOVER *reclaim, become well*

did you not r them	Judg 11:26
Will I r from this	2 Kin 8:8
and they will r	Mark 16:18

RED *color*

first came forth r	Gen 25:25
water...r as blood	2 Kin 3:22
they are r like crimson	Is 1:18
the sky is r	Matt 16:2
a great r dragon	Rev 12:3

RED SEA

Hebrew: Sea of Reeds Ex 10:19
*body of water between Egypt and
Sinai*
Ex 13:18; Ps 106:9; Jer 49:21

REDEEM *buy back*

I will also r you	Ex 6:6
family may r him	Lev 25:49
wish to r the field	Lev 27:19
I will r *it*	Ruth 4:4
God will r my soul	Ps 49:15
He will r Israel	Ps 130:8
Christ r-ed us	Gal 3:13
He might r those	Gal 4:5

REDEEMER *one who buys back*

left you without a r	Ruth 4:14
know that my R lives	Job 19:25
my rock and my R	Ps 19:14
your R is the Holy	Is 41:14
our Father, Our R	Is 63:16
Their R is strong	Jer 50:34

REDEMPTION *deliverance*

r of the land	Lev 25:24
have my right of r	Ruth 4:6
r of his soul is	Ps 49:8
r is drawing near	Luke 21:28
r...in Christ Jesus	Rom 3:24
r of our body	Rom 8:23
r through His blood	Eph 1:7
in whom we have r	Col 1:14
obtained eternal r	Heb 9:12

REED *tall marsh grass*

set *it* among the r-s	Ex 2:3
bruised r He will	Is 42:3
the r...to beat Him	Matt 27:30
and put it on a r	Matt 27:48

REEL *stagger, sway*

earth r-s to and fro	Is 24:20
r with strong drink	Is 28:7

REFINE *purify*

r-d seven times	Ps 12:6
in order to r	Dan 11:35
R them as silver	Zech 13:9
r them like gold	Mal 3:3
gold r-d by fire	Rev 3:18

REFRAIN *abstain*

not r from spitting	Job 30:10
to r from working	1 Cor 9:6
R his tongue...evil	1 Pet 3:10
r from judging	Rev 6:10

REFRESH *renew, replenish*

you may r yourselves	Gen 18:5
R me with apples	Song 2:5

times of r-ing may	Acts 3:19
r my heart in Christ	Philem 20

REFUGE *protection, shelter*

in whom I take r	2 Sam 22:3
God is our r	Ps 46:1
r in the LORD	Ps 118:8
the r of lies	Is 28:17
r in...distress	Jer 16:19
who have fled for r	Heb 6:18

REFUGE, CITIES OF
see CITIES OF REFUGE

REFUSE (n) *waste*

be made a r heap	Ezra 6:11
corpses lay like r	Is 5:25
its waters toss up r	Is 57:20
sell...r of the wheat	Amos 8:6

REFUSE (v) *decline*

r you his grave	Gen 23:6
r to let My people go	Ex 10:4
his hands r to work	Prov 21:25
they r to know Me	Jer 9:6
r-d to be comforted	Matt 2:18
can r the water	Acts 10:47
not r Him who is	Heb 12:25

REFUSE GATE
see GATES OF JERUSALEM

REFUTE *prove wrong*

R me if you can	Job 33:5
he...r-d the Jews	Acts 18:28
to r those who	Titus 1:9

REGAIN *recover*

r-ed their sight	Matt 20:34
want to r my sight	Mark 10:51
he might r his sight	Acts 9:12

REGARD (n) *respect*

LORD had r for Abel	Gen 4:4
r to the prayer	1 Kin 8:28
have r for his Maker	Is 17:7
r for the humble	Luke 1:48

REGARD (v) *esteem, respect*

If I r wickedness	Ps 66:18
Yet He r-s the lowly	Ps 138:6
who r-s reproof	Prov 15:5
highly r-ed by him	Luke 7:2
you r one another	Phil 2:3
did not r equality	Phil 2:6

REGENERATION *renewal*

r when the Son	Matt 19:28
the washing of r	Titus 3:5

REGION *area*

r of the Jordan	Josh 22:10
the r-s of Galilee	Matt 2:22
to the r of Judea	Mark 10:1
same r...shepherds	Luke 2:8

REGISTER *enroll, record*

r...people of Israel	2 Sam 24:4
to r for the census	Luke 2:3

REHOBOAM

son of Solomon 1 Kin 11:43
king of Judah
1 Kin 12:16ff; 2 Chr 11:1ff

REIGN *rule*

LORD shall r forever	Ex 15:18
Shall Saul r over	1 Sam 11:12
David r-ed over all	2 Sam 8:15
The LORD r-s	Ps 93:1
By me kings r	Prov 8:15
will r righteously	Is 32:1
death r-ed...Adam	Rom 5:14
He must r until	1 Cor 15:25
also r with Him	2 Tim 2:12
He will r forever	Rev 11:15
will r with Him	Rev 20:6

REJECT *decline, refuse*

have r-ed the LORD	Num 11:20
will r you forever	1 Chr 28:9
not r the discipline	Prov 3:11
A fool r-s his	Prov 15:5
have r-ed this word	Is 30:12
He who r-s unjust gain	Is 33:15
r-ed My ordinances	Ezek 20:13
have r-ed knowledge	Hos 4:6
they r-ed the law	Amos 2:4
the builders r-ed	Matt 21:42
who r-s you r-s Me	Luke 10:16
He who r-s Me	John 12:48

REJOICE *be glad*

r before the LORD	Lev 23:40
R, O nations	Deut 32:43
I r in Thy salvation	1 Sam 2:1
let the earth r	1 Chr 16:31
my soul shall r	Ps 35:9
king will r in God	Ps 63:11
Let us r and be glad	Ps 118:24
I r at Thy word	Ps 119:162
R, young man	Eccl 11:9
God will r over you	Is 62:5
r-d exceedingly	Matt 2:10
r at his birth	Luke 1:14
multitude was r-ing	Luke 13:17
you would have r-d	John 14:28
r-ing in hope	Rom 12:12
yet always r-ing	2 Cor 6:10
R in the Lord	Phil 4:4
I r in my sufferings	Col 1:24
r, O heavens	Rev 12:12

REJOICING (n) *delight*

a holiday for r	Esth 9:19
hills gird...with r	Ps 65:12
Jerusalem *for* r	Is 65:18

RELATIONS *sexual intercourse*

r with his wife Eve	Gen 4:1
had no r with a man	Judg 11:39
we may have r with	Judg 19:22
had r with Hannah	1 Sam 1:19

RELATIVE *kinsman*

and to my r-s	Gen 24:4
The man is our r	Ruth 2:20
My r-s have failed	Job 19:14
among his *own* r-s	Mark 6:4
your r Elizabeth has	Luke 1:36

RELEASE (n) *liberation*

a r through the land	Lev 25:10
r for you the King	Mark 15:9
r to the captives	Luke 4:18

RELEASE (v) *set free*

he **r-d** Barabbas	Matt 27:26
wanting to **r** Jesus	Luke 23:20
efforts to **r** Him	John 19:12
you **r-d** from a wife	1 Cor 7:27
r-d us from our sins	Rev 1:5
R the four angels	Rev 9:14

RELENT *yield*

I am tired of **r-ing**	Jer 15:6
r...the calamity	Jer 18:8
whether He will...**r**	Joel 2:14
God may turn and **r**	Jon 3:9

RELIEF *lessening of burden*

r and deliverance	Esth 4:14
my *prayer for* **r**	Lam 3:56
r of the brethren	Acts 11:29

RELIGION *system of belief*

about their own **r**	Acts 25:19
sect of our **r**	Acts 26:5
pure and undefiled **r**	James 1:27

RELIGIOUS *devout, pious*

r in all respects	Acts 17:22
thinks...to be **r**	James 1:26

RELY *depend, trust*

r-ied on the LORD	2 Chr 16:8
who...**r** on horses	Is 31:1
r on his God	Is 50:10
You **r** on your sword	Ezek 33:26
r upon the Law	Rom 2:17

REMAIN *abide, be left*

While the earth **r-s**	Gen 8:22
R...in his place	Ex 16:29
ark...not **r** with us	1 Sam 5:7
r-s yet...youngest	1 Sam 16:11
flee to Egypt, and **r**	Matt 2:13
dove...**r-ed** upon	John 1:32
not **r** in darkness	John 12:46
not **r** on the cross	John 19:31
let her **r** unmarried	1 Cor 7:11
gospel might **r**	Gal 2:5
He **r-s** faithful	2 Tim 2:13

REMEMBER *recall, recollect*

God **r-ed** Noah	Gen 8:1
I will **r** My covenant	Gen 9:15
R the sabbath day	Ex 20:8
not **r** the sins of my	Ps 25:7
R also your Creator	Eccl 12:1
O LORD, **R** me	Jer 15:15
sin I will **r** no more	Jer 31:34
Peter **r-ed** the word	Matt 26:75
R Lot's wife	Luke 17:32
r the words of	Acts 20:35
to **r** the poor	Gal 2:10

REMEMBRANCE *memory*

Thy **r**, O LORD	Ps 135:13
Put Me in **r**	Is 43:26
a book of **r** was	Mal 3:16
do this in **r** of Me	Luke 22:19
in **r** of Me	1 Cor 11:25

REMNANT *remaining part*

preserve for you a **r**	Gen 45:7
prayer for the **r**	2 Kin 19:4
an escaped **r**	Ezra 9:8
A **r** will return	Is 10:21

the **r** of Israel	Jer 6:9
a **r** of the Spirit	Mal 2:15
r that will be saved	Rom 9:27

REMOVE *take away* or *off*

r your sandals	Ex 3:5
r-d all the idols	1 Kin 15:12
He **r-d** the high	2 Kin 18:4
r the heart of stone	Ezek 36:26
not fit to **r** His	Matt 3:11
r this cup from Me	Luke 22:42
R the stone	John 11:39
as to **r** mountains	1 Cor 13:2

REND *tear*

r the heavens	Is 64:1
r their garments	Jer 36:24
r your heart and not	Joel 2:13

RENDER *inflict, repay*

I will **r** vengeance	Deut 32:41
R recompense to the	Ps 94:2
r to Caesar the	Matt 22:21
R to all what is due	Rom 13:7

RENEW *make new, revive*

r a steadfast spirit	Ps 51:10
r-ed like the eagle	Ps 103:5
R our days as of old	Lam 5:21
inner man...**r-ed**	2 Cor 4:16

RENOWN *fame*

men of **r**	Gen 6:4
a people, for **r**	Jer 13:11
shame into...and **r**	Zeph 3:19

REPAIR *restore*

r the house of	1 Chr 26:27
r-ing...foundations	Ezra 4:12
r of the walls	Neh 4:7

REPAY *pay back*

you thus **r** the LORD	Deut 32:6
so God has **repaid**	Judg 1:7
LORD **r** the evildoer	2 Sam 3:39
repaid me evil for	Ps 109:5
r their iniquity	Jer 16:18
He will fully **r**	Jer 51:56
in secret will **r**	Matt 6:4
is Mine, I will **r**	Rom 12:19
no one **r-s**...evil	1 Thess 5:15

REPENT *change mind*

that He should **r**	Num 23:19
r in dust and ashes	Job 42:6
have refused to **r**	Jer 5:3
R, for the kingdom	Matt 3:2
r-ed long ago in	Matt 11:21
r and believe	Mark 1:15
one sinner who **r-s**	Luke 15:7
R,...be baptized	Acts 2:38
all...should **r**	Acts 17:30
r and turn to God	Acts 26:20

REPENTANCE *penitence*

with water for **r**	Matt 3:11
baptism of **r**	Mark 1:4
r for forgiveness	Luke 24:47
appropriate to **r**	Acts 26:20
r without regret	2 Cor 7:10
r from dead works	Heb 6:1
to come to **r**	2 Pet 3:9

REPHAIM

1 *pre-Israelite people of Palestine*
Gen 14:5;15:20
people of large stature
2 *valley near Jerusalem*
Josh 15:8; 2 Sam 23:13

REPHIDIM

Israelite campsite in Sinai
Ex 17:1,8; Num 33:14,15

REPORT *account, statement*

not bear a false **r**	Ex 23:1
r concerning Him	Luke 7:17
has believed our **r**	John 12:38

REPRESENTATION *likeness*

exact **r** of His nature	Heb 1:3

REPRESENTATIVE *substitute*

people's **r** before God	Ex 18:19
the king's **r**	Neh 11:24

REPROACH (n) *dishonor*

taken away my **r**	Gen 30:23
a **r** on all Israel	1 Sam 11:2
I have become a **r**	Ps 31:11
with dishonor...**r**	Prov 18:3
not fear the **r** of	Is 51:7
the **r** of Christ	Heb 11:26

REPROACH (v) *accuse, rebuke*

to **r** the living God	2 Kin 19:4
My heart does not **r**	Job 27:6
foolish man **r-es** Thee	Ps 74:22
enemies have **r-ed** me	Ps 102:8
He...to **r** the cities	Matt 11:20
r-ed them for	Mark 16:14

REPROOF *correction, rebuke*

spurned all my **r**	Prov 1:30
regards **r** is prudent	Prov 15:5
who hates **r** will	Prov 15:10
and **r** give wisdom	Prov 29:15
for teaching, for **r**	2 Tim 3:16

REPROVE *correct, rebuke*

r your neighbor	Lev 19:17
LORD loves He **r-s**	Prov 3:12
Do not **r** a scoffer	Prov 9:8
R the ruthless	Is 1:17
r him in private	Matt 18:15
r, rebuke, exhort	2 Tim 4:2
whom I love, I **r**	Rev 3:19

REPTILE *snake*

and the sand **r**	Lev 11:30
r-s of the earth	Mic 7:17
r-s and creatures	James 3:7

REPUTATION *character*

seven men of good **r**	Acts 6:3
a **r** for good works	1 Tim 5:10

REQUEST *desire, petition*

my people as my **r**	Esth 7:3
the **r** of his lips	Ps 21:2
He gave them their **r**	Ps 106:15
r-s be made known to	Phil 4:6

REQUIRE *demand, insist*

r your lifeblood	Gen 9:5
God **r** from you	Deut 10:12
as each day **r-d**	Ezra 3:4

your soul is **r-d** Luke 12:20
r-d of stewards 1 Cor 4:2

REQUIREMENT *necessity*

r-s of the Lord Luke 1:6
r of the Law Rom 8:4
law of physical **r** Heb 7:16

RESCUE *deliver, redeem*

O Lord, **r** my soul Ps 6:4
R the weak and needy Ps 82:4
He delivers and **r-s** Dan 6:27
r the godly from 2 Pet 2:9

RESERVE *retain, store up*

r-d a blessing for Gen 27:36
darkness...in **r** Job 20:26
lips may **r** knowledge Prov 5:2
r-s wrath for Nah 1:2
r-d in heaven 1 Pet 1:4
r-d for fire 2 Pet 3:7

RESIDE *dwell, live*

stranger who **r-s** Lev 19:34
a son of man **r** in it Jer 49:18
r-d in...Nazareth Matt 2:23
those who **r** as aliens 1 Pet 1:1

RESIST *oppose, withstand*

not **r** him who is Matt 5:39
none...able to **r** Luke 21:15
r-ing the Holy Spirit Acts 7:51
he who **r-s** authority Rom 13:2
R the devil James 4:7

RESPECT (n) *regard*

no **r** for the old Deut 28:50
where is My **r** Mal 1:6
please *Him* in all **r-s** Col 1:10
to your masters...**r** 1 Pet 2:18

RESPECT (v) *esteem*

They will **r** my son Matt 21:37
not fear God nor **r** Luke 18:4
R what is right Rom 12:17
wife...**r** her husband Eph 5:33

RESPOND *answer, reply*

He will **r** to them Is 19:22
r to the heavens Hos 2:21
how you should **r** Col 4:6
Peter **r-ed** to her Acts 5:8

REST (n) *remainder*

r turned and fled Judg 20:45
the **r** of the exiles Ezra 6:16
the **r** of your days Prov 19:20
I will slay the **r** Amos 9:1
to the **r**...parables Luke 8:10

REST (n) *tranquility*

r from our work Gen 5:29
sabbath of solemn **r** Lev 16:31
God gives you **r** Josh 1:13
the weary are at **r** Job 3:17
Return to your **r** Ps 116:7
whole earth is at **r** Is 14:7
there is no **r** Lam 5:5
I will give you **r** Matt 11:28
no **r** for my spirit 2 Cor 2:13
not enter My **r** Heb 3:11
no **r** day and night Rev 14:11

REST (v) *settled, refresh*

the ark **r-ed** upon Gen 8:4
glory...Lord **r-ed** Ex 24:16
Spirit **r-ed** upon Num 11:25
R in the Lord Ps 37:7
Wisdom **r-s** in Prov 14:33
government will **r** on Is 9:6
iniquity **r-ed** on Ezek 32:27
r-ed on the seventh Heb 4:4
r from their labors Rev 14:13

RESTING PLACE

dove found no **r** Gen 8:9
This is My **r** forever Ps 132:14
Do not destroy his **r** Prov 24:15
r will be glorious Is 11:10

RESTITUTION *reparation*

owner...make **r** Ex 21:34
make **r** in full Num 5:7
r for the lamb 2 Sam 12:6

RESTORE *reestablish, replace*

son he had **r-d** to 2 Kin 8:1
they **r-d** Jerusalem Neh 3:8
r His righteousness Job 33:26
He **r-s** my soul Ps 23:3
R to me the joy Ps 51:12
O God, **r** us Ps 80:3
the Lord **r-s** Zion Is 52:8
R us to Thee Lam 5:21
his hand was **r-d** Mark 3:5
r-ing the kingdom Acts 1:6

RESTRAIN *hold back*

the rain...was **r-ed** Gen 8:2
who can **r** Him Job 11:10
He **r-ed** His anger Ps 78:38
who **r-s** his lips Prov 10:19
Wilt Thou **r** Thyself Is 64:12
R your voice from Jer 31:16
r-ed the crowds Acts 14:18

RESULT (n) *consequence, effect*

a **r** of the anguish Is 53:11
not as a **r** of works Eph 2:9
have *its* perfect **r** James 1:4
as a **r** of the works James 2:22

RESULT (v) *follow, happen*

r-ed In reproach Jer 20:8
sin **r-ing** in death Rom 6:16
proved to **r** in death Rom 7:10
r-ing in salvation Rom 10:10

RESURRECTION

who say...no **r** Matt 22:23
r of the righteous Luke 14:14
being sons of the **r** Luke 20:36
r of judgment John 5:29
the **r** and the life John 11:25
r of the dead Acts 24:21
if there is no **r** 1 Cor 15:13
power of His **r** Phil 3:10
hope through the **r** 1 Pet 1:3
This is the first **r** Rev 20:5

RETRIBUTION *punishment*

days of **r** have come Hos 9:7
stumbling block...**r** Rom 11:9
dealing out **r** to 2 Thess 1:8

RETURN *go back* or *repay*

to dust you shall **r** Gen 3:19
r-ed me evil for 1 Sam 25:21
clouds **r** after the Eccl 12:2
a remnant...will **r** Is 10:22
ransomed...will **r** Is 51:11
r-ed to Galilee Luke 4:14
Repent...and **r** Acts 3:19
not **r-ing** evil for 1 Pet 3:9

REUBEN

1 *son of Jacob / Leah* Gen 29:32
2 *tribe* Ex 6:14; Num 1:21

REVEAL *expose, make known*

God had **r-ed** Himself Gen 35:7
He **r-s** mysteries Job 12:22
will **r** his iniquity Job 20:27
do not **r** the secret Prov 25:9
glory...will be **r-ed** Is 40:5
r this mystery Dan 2:47
r them to babes Matt 11:25
blood did not **r** *this* Matt 16:17
Son of Man is **r-ed** Luke 17:30
glory...to be **r-ed** Rom 8:18
r-ed with fire 1 Cor 3:13
to **r** His Son in me Gal 1:16
lawlessness is **r-ed** 2 Thess 2:3
r-ed in the flesh 1 Tim 3:16

REVELATION *divine disclosure*

a **r** to Thy servant 2 Sam 7:27
the **r** ended Dan 7:28
r to the Gentiles Luke 2:32
r of...judgment Rom 2:5
the **r** of the mystery Rom 16:25
awaiting...the **r** 1 Cor 1:7
through a **r** of Jesus Gal 1:12
by **r**...made known Eph 3:3
The **R** of Jesus Rev 1:1

REVENGE *vengeance*

take our **r** on him Jer 20:10
Never take...**r** Rom 12:19

REVERE *adore, venerate*

r My sanctuary Lev 19:30
nations will **r** Thee Is 25:3

REVERENCE *respect, awe*

you do away with **r** Job 15:4
Worship...with **r** Ps 2:11
bow in **r** for Thee Ps 5:7
in **r** prepared an ark Heb 11:7
service with **r** and Heb 12:28

REVILE *use abusive language*

Do you **r** God's high Acts 23:4
are **r-d**, we bless 1 Cor 4:12
r-d for the name of 1 Pet 4:14
r angelic majesties Jude 8

REVIVE *bring back to life*

they **r** the stones Neh 4:2
let your heart **r** Ps 69:32
r us again Ps 85:6
r me in Thy ways Ps 119:37
r-d your concern Phil 4:10

REVOLT *rebellion*

incited **r** within it Ezra 4:15
Speaking...and **r** Is 59:13
stirred up a **r** Acts 21:38

REWARD *prize*

emptiness...his **r**	Job 15:31
r for the righteous	Ps 58:11
The **r** of humility	Prov 22:4
chases after **r-s**	Is 1:23
His **r** is with Him	Is 62:11
your **r** in heaven	Matt 5:12
not lose his **r**	Matt 10:42
looking to the **r**	Heb 11:26
receive a full **r**	2 John 8

RHODA

Christian servant girl	Acts 12:13

RHODES

Mediterranean isle	Acts 21:1

RIB *bone*

took one of his **r-s**	Gen 2:21
r-s *were* in its mouth	Dan 7:5

RICH (adj) *wealthy*

Abram was very **r**	Gen 13:2
LORD makes poor...**r**	1 Sam 2:7
not a **r** man boast	Jer 9:23
woe to you who are **r**	Luke 6:24
a certain **r** man	Luke 16:1
being **r** in mercy	Eph 2:4
r in good works	1 Tim 6:18

RICH (n) *wealthy*

r shall not pay more	Ex 30:15
the **r** above the poor	Job 34:19
r among the people	Ps 45:12
The **r** and the poor	Prov 22:2

RICHES *wealth*

R do not profit	Prov 11:4
who trusts in his **r**	Prov 11:28
neither poverty nor **r**	Prov 30:8
deceitfulness of **r**	Matt 13:22
choked with...**r**	Luke 8:14
abounding in **r**	Rom 10:12
r of His grace	Eph 1:7
r of Christ	Eph 3:8
His **r** in glory	Phil 4:19
uncertainty of **r**	1 Tim 6:17
Your **r** have rotted	James 5:2

RIDDLE *puzzle*

propound a **r**	Judg 14:12
my **r** on the harp	Ps 49:4
wise and their **r-s**	Prov 1:6
propound a **r**	Ezek 17:2

RIGHT (adj) *correct or direction*

r in the sight of	Deut 12:25
r in his own eyes	Judg 17:6
precepts...are **r**	Ps 19:8
r eye makes you	Matt 5:29
what your **r** hand is	Matt 6:3
Sit at My **r** hand	Matt 22:44
the **r** hand of God	Mark 16:19
at the **r** time Christ	Rom 5:6
r hand of fellowship	Gal 2:9
whatever is **r**	Phil 4:8
forsaking the **r** way	2 Pet 2:15

RIGHT (n) *due, prerogative*

her conjugal **r-s**	Ex 21:10
r of redemption	Lev 25:32
r of the first-born	Deut 21:17
the **r-s** of the poor	Prov 29:7

r-s of the afflicted	Prov 31:9
my **r** in the gospel	1 Cor 9:18

RIGHTEOUS (adj) *virtuous*

Noah was a **r** man	Gen 6:9
LORD is the **r** one	Ex 9:27
You are more **r**	1 Sam 24:17
God is a **r** judge	Ps 7:11
A **r** man hates	Prov 13:5
for David a **r** Branch	Jer 23:5
LORD our God is **r**	Dan 9:14
ninety-nine **r**	Luke 15:7
coming of the **R** One	Acts 7:52
r *man* shall live by	Rom 1:17
none **r**, not even one	Rom 3:10
many will be made **r**	Rom 5:19
prayer of a **r** man	James 5:16

RIGHTEOUS (n) *moral one*

assembly of the **r**	Ps 1:5
LORD tests the **r**	Ps 11:5
LORD loves the **r**	Ps 146:8
the paths of the **r**	Prov 2:20
the **r** will flourish	Prov 11:28
joy for the **r**	Prov 21:15
way of the **r** is	Is 26:7
they sell the **r** for	Amos 2:6
sends rain on *the* **r**	Matt 5:45
r into eternal life	Matt 25:46

RIGHTEOUSNESS

reckoned it...as **r**	Gen 15:6
will repay...his **r**	1 Sam 26:23
I put on **r**	Job 29:14
in the paths of **r**	Ps 23:3
judge the world in **r**	Ps 96:13
declare His **r**	Ps 97:6
His **r** endures forever	Ps 111:3
R exalts a nation	Prov 14:34
clouds pour down **r**	Is 45:8
wrapped me with...**r**	Is 61:10
The LORD our **r**	Jer 23:6
to rain **r** on you	Hos 10:12
to fulfill all **r**	Matt 3:15
and thirst for **r**	Matt 5:6
kingdom and His **r**	Matt 6:33
you enemy of all **r**	Acts 13:10
through one act of **r**	Rom 5:18
breastplate of **r**	Eph 6:14
pursue **r**, faith	2 Tim 2:22
the crown of **r**	2 Tim 4:8
peaceful fruit of **r**	Heb 12:11
not achieve the **r**	James 1:20
suffer for...**r**	1 Pet 3:14

RIMMON

1 *a Benjamite*	2 Sam 4:2
2 *Syrian deity*	2 Kin 5:18
3 *town in Simeon*	Josh 19:1,7
4 *city of Zebulun*	Josh 19:13
5 *rock of*	Judg 20:45;21:13

RING *jewelry, ornament*

make four gold **r-s**	Ex 25:26
took his signet **r**	Esth 3:10
As a **r** of gold	Prov 11:22
finger **r-s**, nose **r-s**	Is 3:21

RIOT *tumult, uprising*

lest a **r** occur	Matt 26:5
a **r** was starting	Matt 27:24
accused of a **r**	Acts 19:40

RIPE *fully developed*

old man of **r** age	Gen 35:29
produced **r** grapes	Gen 40:10
the harvest is **r**	Joel 3:13
harvest...is **r**	Rev 14:15

RISE *go up, issue forth*

mist used to **r** from	Gen 2:6
Cain **rose** up against	Gen 4:8
scepter shall **r**	Num 24:17
witnesses **r** up	Ps 35:11
children **r** up	Prov 31:28
nation with **r**	Matt 24:7
r-n, just as He said	Matt 28:6
children will **r** up	Mark 13:12
R and walk	Luke 5:23
R and pray	Luke 22:46
Lord has really **r-n**	Luke 24:34

RIVER

r flowed out of Eden	Gen 2:10
the **r** Euphrates	Josh 1:4
r of Thy delights	Ps 36:8
He changes **r-s** into	Ps 107:33
the **r-s** of Babylon	Ps 137:1
A place of **r-s** and	Is 33:21
r-s in the desert	Is 43:20
peace...like a **r**	Is 66:12
tears...like a **r**	Lam 2:18
baptized...Jordan **R**	Mark 1:5
r-s of living water	John 7:38
r of the water of life	Rev 22:1

RIZPAH

concubine of Saul	2 Sam 3:7

ROAD *path, way*

a lion in the **r**	Prov 26:13
the rough **r-s** smooth	Luke 3:5
garments in the **r**	Luke 19:36
the Lord on the **r**	Acts 9:27

ROAR (n) *loud deep sound*

the sound of the **r**	1 Kin 18:41
young lions' **r**	Zech 11:3
pass away with a **r**	2 Pet 3:10

ROAR (v) *utter a deep sound*

a voice **r-s**	Job 37:4
Let the sea **r**	Ps 96:11
LORD will **r** from	Jer 25:30
a lion **r** in the	Amos 3:4

ROAST *cook*

grain **r-ed** in the fire	Lev 2:14
r-ed the...*animals*	2 Chr 35:13
slothful man...**r**	Prov 12:27

ROB *steal*

bear **r-bed** of her	Prov 17:12
Do not **r** the poor	Prov 22:22
Will a man **r** God	Mal 3:8
do you **r** temples	Rom 2:22
I **r-bed**...churches	2 Cor 11:8

ROBBER *thief*

she lurks as a **r**	Prov 23:28
become a den of **r-s**	Jer 7:11
crucified two **r-s**	Mark 15:27
he fell among **r-s**	Luke 10:30
a thief and a **r**	John 10:1
r-s of temples	Acts 19:37

ROBBERY *theft*

not vainly hope in **r**	Ps 62:10
I hate **r** in the	Is 61:8
they are full of **r**	Matt 23:25
you are full of **r**	Luke 11:39

ROBE *cloak, garment*

cut off...Saul's **r**	1 Sam 24:4
justice was like a **r**	Job 29:14
r of righteousness	Is 61:10
put a scarlet **r** on	Matt 27:28
walk...in long **r-s**	Mark 12:38
wearing a white **r**	Mark 16:5
bring...the best **r**	Luke 15:22
washed their **r-s**	Rev 7:14
a **r** dipped in blood	Rev 19:13

ROCK *stone*

the cleft of the **r**	Ex 33:22
struck the **r** twice	Num 20:11
R of his salvation	Deut 32:15
LORD is my **r**	2 Sam 22:2
engraved in the **r**	Job 19:24
my **r** and my fortress	Ps 18:2
r and my Redeemer	Ps 19:14
set my feet upon a **r**	Ps 40:2
a **r** to stumble over	Is 8:14
an everlasting **R**	Is 26:4
his house upon the **r**	Matt 7:24
upon this **r** I will	Matt 16:18
the **r-s** were split	Matt 27:51
hewn out in the **r**	Mark 15:46
a **r** of offense	Rom 9:33

ROD *staff, stick*

fresh **r-s** of poplar	Gen 30:37
r of Aaron	Num 17:8
break them with a **r**	Ps 2:9
Thy **r** and Thy staff	Ps 23:4
who spares his **r**	Prov 13:24
The **r** of discipline	Prov 22:15
r of My anger	Is 10:5
rule them with a **r**	Rev 19:15

ROLL *move*

sky will be **r-ed** up	Is 34:4
let justice **r** down	Amos 5:24
r-ed away the stone	Matt 28:2
Who will **r** away the	Mark 16:3

ROMANS

citizens of Roman Empire
　　John 11:48; Acts 16:21,37

ROME

Italian city	Acts 2:10
Roman Empire capital	Acts 18:2
Paul held there	Acts 28:14,16

ROOF

brought...to the **r**	Josh 2:6
r...woman bathing	2 Sam 11:2
removed the **r** above	Mark 2:4
r and let him down	Luke 5:19

ROOM *chamber*

the ark with **r-s**	Gen 6:14
go into your inner **r**	Matt 6:6
a large upper **r**	Mark 14:15
no **r** for them in	Luke 2:7
r for the wrath	Rom 12:19

ROOT (n) *source*

the **r** of Jesse	Is 11:10
no **r**, it withered	Mark 4:6
if the **r** be holy	Rom 11:16
of money is a **r**	1 Tim 6:10
no **r** of bitterness	Heb 12:15
the **R** of David	Rev 5:5

ROOT (v) *establish* or *tear out*

r out your Asherim	Mic 5:14
r-ed and grounded in	Eph 3:17

ROPE *cord*

them down by a **r**	Josh 2:15
bound...two new **r-s**	Judg 15:13
he snapped the **r-s**	Judg 16:12
Instead of a belt, a **r**	Is 3:24

ROSE (n) *flower*

I am the **r** of Sharon	Song 2:1

ROSH

1 *son of Benjamin*	Gen 46:21
2 *place of God*	Ezek 38:2,3;39:1

ROT *decay*

their flesh will **r**	Zech 14:12
riches have **r-ted**	James 5:2

ROTTENNESS *decay*

passion is **r** to	Prov 14:30
r to the house of	Hos 5:12

ROUGH *jagged, uneven*

r ground become a	Is 40:4
the **r** places smooth	Is 45:2

ROYAL *kingly*

captured the **r** city	2 Sam 12:26
his **r** bounty	1 Kin 10:13
all the **r** offspring	2 Kin 11:1
put on her **r** robes	Esth 5:1
And a **r** diadem	Is 62:3
roof of the **r** palace	Dan 4:29
a certain **r** official	John 4:46
fulfilling the **r** law	James 2:8
a **r** priesthood	1 Pet 2:9

RUDDY *reddish in complexion*

he was **r**	1 Sam 16:12
a youth, and **r**	1 Sam 17:42
beloved is...and **r**	Song 5:10

RUHAMAH

symbolic for Israel	Hos 2:1

RUIN (n) *destruction*

shall be a **r** forever	Deut 13:16
become a heap of **r-s**	1 Kin 9:8
the perpetual **r-s**	Ps 74:3
Jerusalem in **r-s**	Ps 79:1
r of the poor is	Prov 10:15
fool's mouth is his **r**	Prov 18:7
rebuild its **r-s**	Acts 15:16

RUIN (v) *destroy*

to **r** him without	Job 2:3
the grain is **r-ed**	Joel 1:10
skins will be **r-ed**	Luke 5:37

RULE (n) *authority, government*

to establish his **r**	1 Chr 18:3
against the **r** of	2 Chr 21:8
will walk by this **r**	Gal 6:16

above all **r** and	Eph 1:21
according to the **r-s**	2 Tim 2:5

RULE (v) *govern*

r over the fish	Gen 1:26
Gideon, **R** over us	Judg 8:22
godless men...not **r**	Job 34:30
r-s over the nations	Ps 22:28
The sun to **r** by day	Ps 136:8
By me princes **r**	Prov 8:16
women **r** over them	Is 3:12
r over the Gentiles	Rom 15:12
peace of Christ **r**	Col 3:15
r them with a rod	Rev 2:27

RULER *king, monarch*

Joseph was the **r**	Gen 42:6
nor curse a **r**	Ex 22:28
no chief...or **r**	Prov 6:7
your **r-s** have fled	Is 22:3
Most High God is **r**	Dan 4:32
come forth a **R**	Matt 2:6
r of the demons	Matt 9:34
r-s of the Gentiles	Mark 10:42
the **r** of this world	John 12:31
Who made you a **r**	Acts 7:27
be subject to **r-s**	Titus 3:1

RUMOR *gossip, hearsay*

r will be *added* to **r**	Ezek 7:26
wars and **r-s** of wars	Matt 24:6

RUN *move rapidly*

to **r** his course	Ps 19:5
their feet **r** to evil	Prov 1:16
streams **r-ning** with	Is 30:25
r and not get tired	Is 40:31
rivers to **r** like oil	Ezek 32:14
Peter arose and **ran**	Luke 24:12
disciple **ran** ahead	John 20:4
who **r** in a race	1 Cor 9:24

RUSH *move quickly*

and **r** upon the city	Judg 9:33
r-s headlong at Him	Job 15:26
herd **r-ed** down the	Matt 8:32
horses **r-ing** to battle	Rev 9:9

RUSHES *marshy plant*

Can the **r** grow	Job 8:11
reeds and **r** will rot	Is 19:6

RUST *corrosion*

in which there is **r**	Ezek 24:6
moth and **r** destroy	Matt 6:19
r will be a witness	James 5:3

RUTH

Moabitess	Ruth 1:4
Naomi's daughter-in-law	
	Ruth 1:14ff
married Boaz	Ruth 4:13
in Messianic line	Matt 1:5

RUTHLESS *cruel*

Reprove the **r**	Is 1:17
song of the **r** is	Is 25:5
most **r** of the	Ezek 28:7

S

SABAOTH

Lord of Sabaoth is same as Lord
of Hosts　Rom 9:29; James 5:4

SABBATH

see also **HOST**

SABBATH *day of rest*

Remember the **s** day	Ex 20:8
LORD bless the **s** day	Ex 20:11
keep My **s-s** and	Lev 26:2
Observe the **s** day	Deut 5:12
new moon nor **s**	2 Kin 4:23
call the **s** a delight	Is 58:13
My **s-s** to be a sign	Ezek 20:12
is Lord of the **S**	Matt 12:8
S was made for man	Mark 2:27
on the **S** to do good	Mark 3:4
the cross on the **S**	John 19:31
a **S** day's journey	Acts 1:12
are read every **S**	Acts 13:27
S rest for the people	Heb 4:9

SABBATICAL YEAR

seventh year of rest	Lev 25:5

SABEANS

people of Sheba in SW Arabia
Job 1:15; Is 45:14; Joel 3:8

SACKCLOTH *coarse cloth*

put **s** on his loins	Gen 37:34
gird on **s** and lament	2 Sam 3:31
put on **s** and ashes	Esth 4:1
sewed **s** over my skin	Job 16:15
with fasting, **s**, and	Dan 9:3
sun became black as **s**	Rev 6:12

SACRED *consecrated, holy*

took all the **s** things	2 Kin 12:18
perform **s** services	1 Cor 9:13
known...**s** writings	2 Tim 3:15
table and the **s** bread	Heb 9:2

SACRIFICE (n) *offering of a life*

Jacob offered a **s**	Gen 31:54
a Passover **s** to	Ex 12:27
s-s of righteousness	Ps 4:5
The **s** of the wicked	Prov 15:8
loyalty rather than **s**	Hos 6:6
compassion...not **s**	Matt 9:13
a **s** to the idol	Acts 7:41
a living and holy **s**	Rom 12:1
an acceptable **s**	Phil 4:18
by the **s** of Himself	Heb 9:26
s-s God is pleased	Heb 13:16
offer up spiritual **s-s**	1 Pet 2:5

SACRIFICE (v) *offer a life*

we may **s** to the Lord	Ex 5:3
s on it your burnt	Ex 20:24
when you **s** a sacrifice	Lev 22:29
they **s-d** to the LORD	Judg 2:5
even **s-d** their sons	Ps 106:37
s-ing to the Baals	Hos 11:2
lamb had to be **s-d**	Luke 22:7
they **s** to demons	1 Cor 10:20

SAD *sorrowful, unhappy*

people heard **s** word	Ex 33:4
Why is your face **s**	Neh 2:2
heart is **s**, the	Prov 15:13

SADDUCEES

Jewish religious party
Matt 3:7;16:11,12; Mark
12:18; Acts 5:17;23:6-8

SAFE *free from danger*

houses are **s** from fear	Job 21:9
runs into it and is **s**	Prov 18:10
back **s** and sound	Luke 15:27

SAIL (n) *canvas for wind*

Nor spread out the **s**	Is 33:23
s was...embroidered	Ezek 27:7

SAIL (v) *proceed by boat*

they **s-ed** to Cyprus	Acts 13:4
to **s** past Ephesus	Acts 20:16
set **s** from Crete	Acts 27:21

SAILOR *mariner, seaman*

s-s...knew the sea	1 Kin 9:27
s-s and your pilots	Ezek 27:27
every passenger and **s**	Rev 18:17

SAINTS *ones faithful to God*

s...in the earth	Ps 16:3
the **s** of the Highest	Dan 7:22
s...fallen asleep	Matt 27:52
lock up...**s** in prisons	Acts 26:10
intercedes for the **s**	Rom 8:27
s will judge the	1 Cor 6:2
citizens with the **s**	Eph 2:19
perseverance of the **s**	Rev 14:12

SALAMIS

city on Cyprus	Acts 13:5

SALEM

Jerusalem
Gen 14:18; Ps 76:2; Heb 7:1,2

SALOME

1 *wife of Zebedee*   Mark 15:40
  mother of James and John at
  open tomb   Mark 16:1
2 *daughter of Herodias*
                Matt 14:6ff; Mark 6:22-26

SALT *preservative*

became a pillar of **s**	Gen 19:26
and sowed it with **s**	Judg 9:45
be eaten without **s**	Job 6:6
the **s** of the earth	Matt 5:13
seasoned, ...with **s**	Col 4:6
can **s** water produce	James 3:12

SALT SEA

the Dead Sea
Gen 14:3; Num 34:3;
Deut 3:17; Josh 15:2

SALT, VALLEY OF

S of Dead Sea
2 Sam 8:13; 2 Chr 25:11

SALVATION *deliverance*

For Thy **s** I wait	Gen 49:18
He has become my **s**	Ex 15:2
scorned...his **s**	Deut 32:15
S belongs to the LORD	Ps 3:8
my light and my **s**	Ps 27:1
lift up the cup of **s**	Ps 116:13
My **s** shall be forever	Is 51:6
helmet of **s** on His	Is 59:17
S is from the LORD	Jon 2:9
eyes have seen Thy **s**	Luke 2:30
s in no one else	Acts 4:12
power of God for **s**	Rom 1:16
now is the day of **s**	2 Cor 6:2

take the helmet of **s**	Eph 6:17
work out your **s** with	Phil 2:12
s through our Lord	1 Thess 5:9
that leads to **s**	2 Tim 3:15
who will inherit **s**	Heb 1:14
neglect so great a **s**	Heb 2:3
S to our God who	Rev 7:10

SAMARIA

1 *capital of N kingdom*
    1 Kin 16:24; 2 Chr 18:9
2 *another name for N kingdom*
    1 Kin 13:32; 2 Kin 17:24;
    Hos 8:5; Amos 3:9; Obad 19
3 *region of central hill country*
    John 4:4-7; Acts 8:1ff

SAMOTHRACE

N Aegean island	Acts 16:11

SAMSON

a Hebrew judge	Judg 13:24
weak in character	Judg 14:1ff
slave of passion	Judg 16:1ff
great strength	Judg 16:5,12

SAMUEL

son of Elkanah and Hannah

	1 Sam 1:20
dedicated to God	1 Sam 1:21ff
called by God	1 Sam 3:1-18
judge	1 Sam 7:15-17
opposed monarchy	1 Sam 8:6
anointed Saul	1 Sam 10:1
anointed David	1 Sam 16:12
death	1 Sam 25:1

SANBALLAT

man of Beth-horon	Neh 2:10
against Nehemiah	Neh 6:1ff

SANCTIFICATION *holiness*

resulting in **s**	Rom 6:22
righteousness and **s**	1 Cor 1:30
will of God, your **s**	1 Thess 4:3
s by the Spirit	2 Thess 2:13
s without which no	Heb 12:14

SANCTIFY *set apart to God*

S to Me every	Ex 13:2
the LORD who **s-ies**	Lev 22:32
They will **s** My name	Is 29:23
will **s** the Holy One	Is 29:23
And **s** My sabbaths	Ezek 20:20
S them in the truth	John 17:17
s-ied by the...Spirit	Rom 15:16
husband is **s-ied**	1 Cor 7:14
s Christ as Lord	1 Pet 3:15

SANCTUARY *place of worship*

construct a **s** for Me	Ex 25:8
revere My **s**	Lev 19:30
utensils of the **s**	1 Chr 9:29
into the **s** of God	Ps 73:17
Praise God in His **s**	Ps 150:1
beautify...My **s**	Is 60:13
a minister in the **s**	Heb 8:2

SAND

descendants as the **s**	Gen 32:12
treasures of the **s**	Deut 33:19
built...upon the **s**	Matt 7:26
innumerable as the **s**	Heb 11:12

SANDAL *footwear*

s has not worn out	Deut 29:5
fit to remove His s-s	Matt 3:11
two tunics, or s-s	Matt 10:10

SANHEDRIN

see COUNCIL

SAPPHIRA

wife of Ananias	Acts 5:1-10
struck dead for lying	

SAPPHIRE *precious stone*

a s and a diamond	Ex 28:18
Inlaid with s-s	Song 5:14
foundations...in s-s	Is 54:11

SARAH / SARAI

wife of Abraham	Gen 11:29
barren	Gen 11:30
beautiful	Gen 12:11
gave birth to Isaac	Gen 21:2,3
death	Gen 23:2

SARDIS

city in Asia Minor	Rev 1:11;3:1,4

SARGON

son of Tiglathpileser III	Is 20:1
king of Assyria	

SATAN

Titles:

Abaddon	Rev 9:11
accuser	Ps 109:6; Rev 12:10
adversary	1 Pet 5:8
Apollyon	Rev 9:11
Beelzebul	Matt 10:25; Mark 3:22
Belial	2 Cor 6:15
deceiver of the world	Rev 12:9
devil	Matt 4:1,5;25:41; John 6:70;13:2; Eph 4:27;6:11; 1 Tim 3:6,7; Heb 2:14; 1 Pet 5:8; Rev 2:10;20:2,10
dragon	Rev 12:9
enemy	Matt 13:28,39
evil one	Matt 13:19,38; John 17:15; Eph 6:16; 1 John 2:13,14;5:18,19
father of lies	John 8:44
god of this world	2 Cor 4:4
liar	John 8:44
murderer	John 8:44
prince of the power of the air	Eph 2:2
ruler of the demons	Matt 9:34; Mark 3:22
ruler of this world	John 12:31;14:30;16:11
serpent of old	Rev 12:9

SATISFY *be content*

eat and not be s-ied	Lev 26:26
s-ied their desire	Ps 78:30
steals To s himself	Prov 6:30
hunger is not s-ied	Is 29:8
to s the multitude	Mark 15:15

SATRAPS *Persian officials*

to the king's s	Ezra 8:36
the s, the governors	Esth 8:9
commissioners and s	Dan 6:4

SAUL

1 *son of Kish*

anointed	1 Sam 9:1,2
first king	1 Sam 10:1ff
rejected as king	1 Sam 11:15
jealous of David	1 Sam 15:11ff
death	1 Sam 18:6ff
	1 Sam 31:4ff

2 *apostle, see* PAUL

SAVE *deliver, rescue*

s-d by the LORD	Deut 33:29
S with Thy right hand	Ps 60:5
He will s you	Prov 20:22
Turn to Me, and be s-d	Is 45:22
s you from afar	Jer 30:10
he will s his life	Ezek 18:27
will s His people	Matt 1:21
wishes to s his life	Matt 16:25
Son...has come to s	Matt 18:11
faith has s-d you	Luke 7:50
world should be s-d	John 3:17
Father, s Me from	John 12:27
by which we...be s-d	Acts 4:12
be s-d by His life	Rom 5:10
will s your husband	1 Cor 7:16
Jesus came...to s	1 Tim 1:15
One who is able to s	James 4:12
the righteous is s-d	1 Pet 4:18

SAVIOR *one who saves*

My s, Thou dost	2 Sam 22:3
forgot God their S	Ps 106:21
send them a S and a	Is 19:20
no s besides Me	Is 43:11
righteous God and a S	Is 45:21
S, who is Christ	Luke 2:11
the S of the world	John 4:42
as a Prince and a S	Acts 5:31
S of all men	1 Tim 4:10
appearing of our S	2 Tim 1:10
our great God and S	Titus 2:13
kingdom of our...S	2 Pet 1:11

SAVORY *appetizing*

prepare a s dish for	Gen 27:4
mother made s food	Gen 27:14

SAWS *cutting tool*

set *them* under s	2 Sam 12:31
cut *them* with s	1 Chr 20:3

SAY *pronounce, speak*

God blessed...s-ing	Gen 1:22
not s in your heart	Deut 9:4
to the wicked God s-s	Ps 50:16
Do not s to your	Prov 3:28
s-s the Preacher	Eccl 1:2
He will s, Here I am	Is 58:9
Many will s to Me	Matt 7:22
If we s...no sin	1 John 1:8

SAYINGS *statements*

utter dark s of old	Ps 78:2
s of understanding	Prov 1:2
s of the wise	Prov 24:23
anyone hears my s	John 12:47

SCALE *for measuring weight*

with accurate s-s	Job 31:6
false s is not good	Prov 20:23
been weighed on the s-s	Dan 5:27

with dishonest s-s	Amos 8:5
justify wicked s-s	Mic 6:11
a pair of s-s in his	Rev 6:5

SCAPEGOAT *for removal of sin*

lot for the s fell	Lev 16:10
released the goat...s	Lev 16:26

SCARLET *bright red*

tied a s thread	Gen 38:28
s thread...window	Josh 2:18
lips are like a s	Song 4:3
sins are as s	Is 1:18
put a s robe on Him	Matt 27:28

SCATTER *spread, sprinkle*

s among the nations	Lev 26:33
Brimstone is s-ed on	Job 18:15
storm will s them	Is 41:16
s-ing the sheep of	Jer 23:1
s him like dust	Matt 21:44
sheep...shall be s-ed	Matt 26:31

SCEPTER *symbol of authority*

s shall not depart	Gen 49:10
s...rise from Israel	Num 24:17
A s of uprightness	Ps 45:6
The s of rulers	Is 14:5
s of His kingdom	Heb 1:8

SCHEME *plan, plot*

s...he had devised	Esth 9:25
s brings him down	Job 18:7
carries out wicked s-s	Ps 37:7
ignorant of his s-s	2 Cor 2:11
the s-s of the devil	Eph 6:11

SCOFF *mock, sneer*

s-ed...His prophets	2 Chr 36:16
The Lord s-s at them	Ps 2:4
s at all the nations	Ps 59:8
were s-ing at Him	Luke 16:14

SCOFFER *mocker*

My friends are my s-s	Job 16:20
sit in the seat of s-s	Ps 1:1
He who corrects a s	Prov 9:7
Behold, you s-s	Acts 13:41

SCORCHING *burning*

words are as a s fire	Prov 16:27
s heat or sun strike	Is 49:10
appointed a s east wind	Jon 4:8
s heat of the day	Matt 20:12

SCORN *treat with contempt*

s-ed...his salvation	Deut 32:15
and s-s a mother	Prov 30:17

SCORPION *poisonous spider*

serpents and s-s	Deut 8:15
discipline...with s-s	1 Kin 12:11
tread upon...s-s	Luke 10:19
not give him a s	Luke 11:12
s-s...have power	Rev 9:3

SCOURGE (n) *whip*

the s of the tongue	Job 5:21
arouse a s against	Is 10:26
He made a s of cords	John 2:15

SCOURGE (v) *flog, whip*

s and crucify *Him*	Matt 20:19
having Jesus s-d	Matt 27:26

lawful for you to **s**   Acts 22:25
He **s-s** every son   Heb 12:6

SCRAPE *rub, scratch*

plaster that they **s**   Lev 14:41
s-d the honey into   Judg 14:9
potsherd to **s** himself   Job 2:8

SCREEN *conceal, separate*

s the ark with the veil   Ex 40:3
s-ed off the ark   Ex 40:21

SCRIBE *copier, writer*

and Sheva was **s**   2 Sam 20:25
then the king's **s**   2 Chr 24:11
Ezra the **s** stood   Neh 8:4
lying pen of the **s-s**   Jer 8:8
chief priests and **s-s**   Matt 2:4
and not as the **s-s**   Mark 1:22
Where is the **s**   1 Cor 1:20

SCRIPTURE

understanding...**S-s**   Matt 22:29
S-s...be fulfilled   Mark 14:49
S has been fulfilled   Luke 4:21
You search the **S-s**   John 5:39
S cannot be broken   John 10:35
mighty in the **S-s**   Acts 18:24
what does the **S** say   Rom 4:3
S is inspired by God   2 Tim 3:16

SCROLL *parchment*

these curses on a **s**   Num 5:23
Take a **s** and write   Jer 36:2
eat this **s**, and go   Ezek 3:1
like a **s**...rolled   Rev 6:14

SEA *body of salt water*

waters He called **s-s**   Gen 1:10
s, or the **s** monster   Job 7:12
founded it upon the **s-s**   Ps 24:2
to the **s** in ships   Ps 107:23
the waters cover the **s**   Is 11:9
rebukes the **s** and   Nah 1:4
walking on the **s**   Matt 14:26
s *began* to be stirred   John 6:18
dangers on the **s**   2 Cor 11:26
s of glass like crystal   Rev 4:6

SEA OF GALILEE
see **GALILEE, SEA OF**

SEACOAST *seashore*

remnant of the **s**   Ezek 25:16
inhabitants of the **s**   Zeph 2:5
s will be pastures   Zeph 2:6

SEAL (n) *mark, stamp*

Your **s** and your cord   Gen 38:18
the engravings of a **s**   Ex 28:21
the **s** of perfection   Ezek 28:12
witness has set his **s**   John 3:33
s of God on their   Rev 9:4

SEAL (v) *mark, secure*

s-ed...his seal   1 Kin 21:8
s *it*...king's signet   Esth 8:8
a spring **s-ed** up   Song 4:12
to **s** up vision   Dan 9:24
s up the book until   Dan 12:4

SEARCH *examine, inquire*

LORD **s-es** all hearts   1 Chr 28:9
S me, O God, and   Ps 139:23

LORD, **s** the heart   Jer 17:10
s for the Child   Matt 2:13
You **s** the Scriptures   John 5:39

SEASHORE *sea coast*

sand that is on the **s**   Josh 11:4
the **s** in abundance   1 Kin 4:20
he stood on...**s**   Rev 13:1

SEASON *time of the year*

rains in their **s**   Lev 26:4
grain in its **s**   Job 5:26
its fruit in its **s**   Ps 1:3
in **s** *and* out of **s**   2 Tim 4:2

SEAT (n) *chair, stool*

mercy **s** of pure gold   Ex 25:17
sit in the **s** of scoffers   Ps 1:1
sit in the **s** of gods   Ezek 28:2
s-s in the synagogue   Matt 23:6
before...judgment **s**   Rom 14:10

SEAT (v) *sit*

s-ed at His feet   Luke 10:39
coming, **s-ed**...colt   John 12:15
s-ed at the right hand   Col 3:1

SECRET *what is hidden*

sets *it* up in **s**   Deut 27:15
the **s-s** of wisdom   Job 11:6
the **s-s** of the heart   Ps 44:21
bread *eaten* in **s**   Prov 9:17
A gift in **s** subdues   Prov 21:14
have not spoken in **s**   Is 45:19
alms may be in **s**   Matt 6:4
Father who sees in **s**   Matt 6:4
God will judge the **s-s**   Rom 2:16

SECT *faction, party*

s of the Sadducees   Acts 5:17
s of the Pharisees   Acts 15:5
s of the Nazarenes   Acts 24:5

SECURE *safe, stable*

overthrows the **s**   Job 12:19
be **s** on their land   Ezek 34:27
s in the mountain   Amos 6:1
made the grave **s**   Matt 27:66

SECURITY *certainty, safety*

Israel dwells in **s**   Deut 33:28
in it living in **s**   Judg 18:7
provides them with **s**   Job 24:23
will lie down in **s**   Is 14:30
will dwell in **s**   Zech 14:11

SEDUCE *entice, persuade*

if a man **s-s** a virgin   Ex 22:16
s you from...LORD   Deut 13:10
s-d them to do evil   2 Kin 21:9
lips she **s-s** him   Prov 7:21

SEE *look, perceive*

I have **s-n** God face   Gen 32:30
No eye will **s** me   Job 24:15
s the works of God   Ps 66:5
the blind shall **s**   Is 29:18
s the glory of the LORD   Is 35:2
to **s** but do not **s**   Ezek 12:2
s your good works   Matt 5:16
and the blind **s-ing**   Matt 15:31
s the Son of Man   Matt 16:28
s-ing their faith   Mark 2:5
s-n Thy salvation   Luke 2:30

No man has **s-n** God   John 1:18
you will **s** Me   John 16:16
s in a mirror dimly   1 Cor 13:12
of things not **s-n**   Heb 11:1

SEED *descendant* or *plant*

sow your **s** uselessly   Lev 26:16
establish your **s**   Ps 89:4
O **s** of Abraham   Ps 105:6
s to the sower   Is 55:10
like a mustard **s**   Matt 13:31
went out to sow his **s**   Luke 8:5
s is the word of God   Luke 8:11
s which is perishable   1 Pet 1:23
His **s** abides in him   1 John 3:9

SEEK *pursue, search for*

s the LORD your God   Deut 4:29
pray, and **s** My face   2 Chr 7:14
S peace, and pursue it   Ps 34:14
s me will find me   Prov 8:17
man **s-s** only evil   Prov 17:11
s wisdom and an   Eccl 7:25
I will **s** the lost   Ezek 34:16
time to **s** the LORD   Hos 10:12
S good and not evil   Amos 5:14
s first His kingdom   Matt 6:33
s, and you shall find   Matt 7:7
s for a sign   Mark 8:12
he who **s-s**, finds   Luke 11:10
I do not **s** My glory   John 8:50
s-ing the favor of men   Gal 1:10
s-ing the things above   Col 3:1

SEER *prophet*

prophets...every **s**   2 Kin 17:13
Who say to the **s-s**   Is 30:10
Go, you **s**, flee away   Amos 7:12
s-s will be ashamed   Mic 3:7

SEIR

1 *land of Edom*
   Gen 32:3;36:8,9; Num 24:18;
           Ezek 25:8
2 *mountain range within Edom*
   Gen 14:6; Deut 1:2;2:4
3 *on boundary of Judah*
        Josh 11:17;15:10

SEIZE *grasp, take*

mother shall **s** him   Deut 21:19
Babylon has been **s-d**   Jer 50:46
and **s** her plunder   Ezek 29:19
fields and then **s** *them*   Mic 2:2
seeking...to **s** Him   John 7:30

SELA

rock city in Edom
       Judg 1:36; Is 16:1;42:11
also **Joktheel**   2 Kin 14:7
later known as Petra

SELAH

musical or liturgical sign
   Ps 3:2,4,8;20:3;60:4; Ps 81:7;
            Hab 3:3,9,13

SELEUCIA

port in N Syria   Acts 13:4

SELF-CONTROL

s and the judgment   Acts 24:25
your lack of **s**   1 Cor 7:5

gentleness, s	Gal 5:23
without s, brutal	2 Tim 3:3
in *your* knowledge, s	2 Pet 1:6

SELFISH *self-centered*

| the bread of a s man | Prov 23:6 |
| s ambition in your | James 3:14 |

SELL *barter, trade*

s me your birthright	Gen 25:31
s me food for money	Deut 2:28
s the oil and pay	2 Kin 4:7
sold a girl for wine	Joel 3:3
sold all that he had	Matt 13:46
s-ing their property	Acts 2:45
sold into bondage	Rom 7:14

SELLER *merchant, trader*

| the buyer like the s | Is 24:2 |
| a s of purple | Acts 16:14 |

SENATE

| *Sanhedrin* | Acts 5:21 |
| *see also* **COUNCIL** | |

SEND *convey, dispatch*

s rain on the earth	Gen 7:4
he sent out a raven	Gen 8:7
Whom shall I s	Is 6:8
Lord God has sent Me	Is 48:16
s-s rain on *the*	Matt 5:45
He has sent Me	Luke 4:18
s-ing His own Son	Rom 8:3
not s her husband	1 Cor 7:13
s him...in peace	1 Cor 16:11
God sent forth His Son	Gal 4:4

SENNACHERIB

king of Assyria	
	2 Kin 18:13;19:16,20;
	2 Chr 32:1-22; Is 36:1;37:17

SENSUALITY

deceit, s, envy	Mark 7:22
promiscuity and s	Rom 13:13
themselves over to s	Eph 4:19
the wealth of her s	Rev 18:3

SENTENCE *judgment*

s is by the decree	Dan 4:17
escape the s of hell	Matt 23:33
Pilate pronounced s	Luke 23:24
to the s of death	Luke 24:20

SEPARATE *divide, set apart*

God s-d the light	Gen 1:4
They s with the lip	Ps 22:7
s-s intimate friends	Prov 16:28
let no man s	Matt 19:6
Who shall s us from	Rom 8:35

SEPARATION *division, isolation*

of his s to the LORD	Num 6:6
his s he is holy	Num 6:8
his s was defiled	Num 6:12
have made a s	Is 59:2

SEPHARAD

| *place in Assyria for Jerusalem* | |
| *exiles* | Obad 20 |

SEPHARVAIM

place in Aram; people relocated to	
Samaria	
	2 Kin 17:31;18:34;

| | Is 36:19;37:13 |

SERAPHIM

| *celestial beings* | Is 6:2,6 |

SERGIUS PAULUS

see **PAULUS, SERGIUS**

SERPENT *snake*

s was more crafty	Gen 3:1
they turned into s-s	Ex 7:12
viper and flying s	Is 30:6
be shrewd as s-s	Matt 10:16
will pick up s-s	Mark 16:18
Moses lifted up the s	John 3:14

SERVANT *helper, slave*

s of s-s He shall be	Gen 9:25
Thy s is listening	1 Sam 3:9
to shine upon Thy s	Ps 31:16
s-s of a new covenant	2 Cor 3:6
they s-s of Christ	2 Cor 11:23
s of Christ Jesus	1 Tim 4:6

SERVE *help, work for*

shall s the LORD	Ex 23:25
s Him with...heart	Josh 22:5
s-d as priests	1 Chr 24:2
you shall s strangers	Jer 5:19
God whom we s is	Dan 3:17
s God and mammon	Matt 6:24
If anyone s-s Me	John 12:26
s-ing the Lord	Rom 12:11
through love s one	Gal 5:13

SERVICE *ministry, work*

s of righteous	Is 32:17
spiritual s of worship	Rom 12:1
for the work of s	Eph 4:12
s with reverence	Heb 12:28

SETH

son of Adam	
	Gen 4:25,26;5:3-8; 1 Chr 1:31
line of Jesus	Luke 3:38

SETTLED *arranged* or *inhabited*

Lot s in the cities	Gen 13:12
cloud s over the	Num 9:18
assault shall be s	Deut 21:5
word is s in heaven	Ps 119:89
mountains were s	Prov 8:25
s in the lawful	Acts 19:39

SEVEN *number*

Jacob served s years	Gen 29:20
For s women...one man	Is 4:1
will be s weeks	Dan 9:25
s other spirits more	Matt 12:45
forgive...s times	Matt 18:21
John to the s churches	Rev 1:4
s golden lampstands	Rev 1:12

SEVERE *difficult, hard*

famine was s	Gen 12:10
a very s pestilence	Ex 9:3
s and lasting plagues	Deut 28:59
s judgments against	Ezek 14:21
a s earthquake had	Matt 28:2

SEW *fasten, join*

s-ed fig leaves together	Gen 3:7
s-ed sackcloth over	Job 16:15
a time to s together	Eccl 3:7

| women who s *magic* | Ezek 13:18 |

SEXUAL

| not in s promiscuity | Rom 13:13 |
| from s immorality | 1 Thess 4:3 |

SHACKLES *fetters*

will tear off your s	Nah 1:13
s broken in pieces	Mark 5:4
with chains and s	Luke 8:29

SHADE *protection*

cover him with s	Job 40:22
The LORD is your s	Ps 121:5
lived under its s	Ezek 31:6
over Jonah to be a s	Jon 4:6
nest under its s	Mark 4:32

SHADOW *image of shade*

days...like a s	1 Chr 29:15
the s of Thy wings	Ps 17:8
in the s...Almighty	Ps 91:1
the s-s flee away	Song 2:17
his s might fall on	Acts 5:15
s of the heavenly	Heb 8:5

SHADRACH

Hebrew: Hananiah	Dan 1:7
friend of Daniel	
	Dan 2:49;3:12-30

SHAKE *quiver, tremble*

made all my bones s	Job 4:14
s my head at you	Job 16:4
peace will not be s-n	Is 54:10
s off the dust	Matt 10:14
A reed s-n by the	Matt 11:7
heavens will be s-n	Luke 21:26
he shook the creature	Acts 28:5
voice shook the earth	Heb 12:26

SHALLUM

1 *king of Israel*	2 Kin 15:8-15
2 *Huldah's husband*	2 Kin 22:14
3 *son of Josiah*	1 Chr 3:15
king of Judah	2 Kin 23:31-33
called **Jehoahaz**	2 Kin 23:30
4 *gatekeeper*	1 Chr 9:17
5 *son of Zadok*	1 Chr 6:12
6 *time of Nehemiah*	Neh 3:12
name of nine other men	

SHALMANESER

| *king of Assyria* | 2 Kin 17:3;18:9 |

SHAME *disgrace, dishonor*

wicked be put to s	Ps 31:17
my reproach and my s	Ps 69:19
s to his mother	Prov 29:15
wise men are put to s	Jer 8:9
unjust knows no s	Zeph 3:5
worthy to suffer s	Acts 5:41
glory is in their s	Phil 3:19
put Him to open s	Heb 6:6

SHAMGAR

| *judge of Israel* | Judg 3:31;5:6 |

SHARE (n) *portion*

them take their s	Gen 14:24
s from My offerings	Lev 6:17
give me the s	Luke 15:12
I do my s	Col 1:24

SHARE (v) *partake, participate*

stranger does not s	Prov 14:10
s in the inheritance	Prov 17:2
s it...yourselves	Luke 22:17
s all good things	Gal 6:6
may s His holiness	Heb 12:10
s the sufferings of	1 Pet 4:13

SHARON

coastal plain in central Israel

Is 33:9; 65:10

SHARP *cutting*

their tongue a s sword	Ps 57:4
S...two-edged sword	Prov 5:4
Put in your s sickle	Rev 14:18

SHATTER *break, burst*

s-ed every tree of the	Ex 9:25
the mighty are s-ed	1 Sam 2:4
s them like earthenware	Ps 2:9
s the doors of bronze	Is 45:2
iron crushes and s-s	Dan 2:40

SHAUL

1 *king of Edom*	Gen 36:37,38
2 *son of Simeon*	Gen 46:10
3 *Kohathite Levite*	1 Chr 6:24

SHAVE *cut or scrape*

he shall s his head	Lev 14:9
s off the seven	Judg 16:19
s-d off half of	2 Sam 10:4
will s with a razor	Is 7:20

SHEAF *bundle of grain stalks*

s-ves in the field	Gen 37:7
s of the first fruits	Lev 23:10
among the s-ves	Ruth 2:15

SHEARER *wool cutter*

silent before its s-s	Is 53:7
lamb before its s	Acts 8:32

SHEAR-JASHUB

son of Isaiah Is 7:3
name symbolizes prophecy

SHEBA

1 *son of Raamah*	Gen 10:7
2 *son of Joktan*	Gen 10:28
3 *grandson of Abraham*	Gen 25:3
4 *Simeonite town*	Josh 19:2
5 *a Benjamite*	2 Sam 20:1-7
6 *a Gadite*	1 Chr 5:13
7 *kingdom*	Job 6:19;
	Ps 72:10,15; Jer 6:20
8 *Queen of*	2 Chr 9:1ff

SHEBAT

eleventh month of Hebrew
calendar Zech 1:7

SHECHEM

1 *city in Ehpraim hill country*	
	Gen 12:6;33:18; 1 Chr 7:28
city of refuge	Josh 20:7
2 *son of Hamor*	Gen 34:2
3 *line of Manasseh*	Num 26:31
4 *son of Shemida*	1 Chr 7:19

SHED *pour out*

Whoever s-s man's	Gen 9:6
s streams of water	Ps 119:136

hasten to s blood	Prov 1:16
will not s its light	Is 13:10
bribes to s blood	Ezek 22:12
swift to s blood	Rom 3:15
s-ding of blood	Heb 9:22

SHEEP *animal*

Rachel came with...s	Gen 29:9
not be like s	Num 27:17
the fleece of my s	Job 31:20
s of His pasture	Ps 100:3
All of us like s	Is 53:6
a s that is silent	Is 53:7
will care for My s	Ezek 34:12
lost s of...Israel	Matt 10:6
s from the goats	Matt 25:32
my s which was lost	Luke 15:6
His life for the s	John 10:11
s hear My voice	John 10:27
Tend My s	John 21:17
Shepherd of the s	Heb 13:20

SHEEP GATE

see GATES OF JERUSALEM

SHEEPFOLDS *enclosure*

s for the flocks	2 Chr 32:28
lie down among the s	Ps 68:13
took him from the s	Ps 78:70

SHEEPSKINS *coverings*

they went about in s Heb 11:37

SHEET

hammered out gold s-s	Ex 39:3
s over *his* naked	Mark 14:51
object like a great s	Acts 10:11

SHELTER *cover, refuge*

under the s of my	Gen 19:8
in the s of Thy wings	Ps 61:4
a s to *give* shade	Is 4:6
a s from the storm	Is 32:2
made a s for himself	Jon 4:5

SHEM

son of Noah
Gen 5:32;6:10;9:27;11:11

SHEOL

place of the dead
Gen 37:35; Job 7:9; Ps 49:15;
Prov 15:11; Is 38:10;
Ezek 32:27; Hab 2:5

SHEPHELAH

low hill country
1 Chr 27:28; Obad 19

SHEPHERD (n)

sheep...have no s	Num 27:17
The LORD is my s	Ps 23:1
Like a s He	Is 40:11
s-s after My own heart	Jer 3:15
for lack of a s	Ezek 34:5
raise up a s	Zech 11:16
sheep without a s	Matt 9:36
strike down the s	Matt 26:31
s-s...in the fields	Luke 2:8
I am the good s	John 10:11
the great S	Heb 13:20
the Chief S	1 Pet 5:4

SHEPHERD (v)

s My people	2 Sam 5:2
s My people	Matt 2:6
S My sheep	John 21:16
to s the church	Acts 20:28
s the flock of God	1 Pet 5:2

SHESHBAZZAR

governor of Judah under Cyprus
Ezra 5:14,16

SHIBBOLETH

test word for identification
Judg 12:6

SHIELD *protection*

Abram, I am a s	Gen 15:1
He is a s to all	2 Sam 22:31
My s is with God	Ps 7:10
faithfulness is a s	Ps 91:4
the s of faith	Eph 6:16

SHILOH

1 *Messianic title*	Gen 49:10
2 *town N of Bethel*	Josh 18:1
site of tabernacle	Judg 18:31

SHINAR

Babylonian plain
Gen 10:10; Gen 11:2;
Josh 7:21; Dan 1:2

SHINE *be radiant, glow*

his face **shone**	Ex 34:29
His face s on you	Num 6:25
Thy face to s *upon us*	Ps 80:3
light s before men	Matt 5:16
s-s in the darkness	John 1:5
lamp s-ing in a dark	2 Pet 1:19
light is...s-ing	1 John 2:8

SHIP *boat*

a haven for s-s	Gen 49:13
to the sea in s-s	Ps 107:23
like merchant s-s	Prov 31:14
escape from the s	Acts 27:30

SHISHAK

see PHARAOH

SHOOT *new growth*

s will spring from	Is 11:1
like a tender s	Is 53:2
His s-s will sprout	Hos 14:6

SHORT *lacking*

Is My hand so s	Is 50:2
days shall be cut s	Matt 24:22
s of the grace	Heb 12:15

SHOULDER *part of body*

He bowed his s	Gen 49:15
turned a stubborn s	Neh 9:29
relieved his s	Ps 81:6
government...on His s-s	Is 9:6

SHOUT *cry out loudly*

s with a great s	Josh 6:5
the people s-ed with	Ezra 3:11
s for joy	Ps 35:27
S joyfully to God	Ps 66:1

SHOW *manifest, reveal*

land...I will s you Gen 12:1

s me Thy glory Ex 33:18
s you the secrets Job 11:6
s Thy lovingkindness Ps 17:7
S us the Father John 14:9
God **s-s** no partiality Gal 2:6
s hospitality Heb 13:2
if you **s** partiality James 2:9

SHOWBREAD

tables of **s** 1 Chr 28:16
s is *set*...table 2 Chr 13:11

SHOWER *abundant flow*

roar of a *heavy* **s** 1 Kin 18:41
Like **s-s** that water Ps 72:6
be **s-s** of blessing Ezek 34:26
A **s** is coming Luke 12:54

SHREWD *cunning*

frustrates...the **s** Job 5:12
be **s** as serpents Matt 10:16

SHRINE *object of worship*

built yourself a **s** Ezek 16:24
tear down your **s-s** Ezek 16:39
who made silver **s-s** Acts 19:24

SHULAMMITE

title of young woman Song 6:13

SHUNAMMITE *from Shunem*

1 *David's nurse*
1 Kin 1:3,15;2:17,21,22
2 *hostess of Elisha* 2 Kin 4:12ff

SHUR

wilderness in NW Sinai
Gen 16:7;20:1; Ex 15:22;
1 Sam 15:7

SHUT *close*

wilderness has **s** them Ex 14:3
s the lions' mouths Dan 6:22
s your door, pray Matt 6:6
power to **s** up the sky Rev 11:6

SIBBOLETH

test word for identification
Judg 12:6

SICK *unwell*

strengthen the **s** Ezek 34:16
lying **s** with a fever Mark 1:30
Lazarus was **s** John 11:2
anyone among you **s** James 5:14

SICKLE *cutting tool*

who wields the **s** Jer 50:16
sharp **s** in His hand Rev 14:14
Put in your **s** Rev 14:15

SICKNESS *illness*

remove from you...**s** Deut 7:15
every kind of **s** Matt 4:23
authority over...**s** Matt 10:1
s is not unto death John 11:4

SIDON

1 *son of Canaan*
Gen 10:15; 1 Chr 1:13
2 *Phoenician port*
Gen 10:19; Is 23:4; Ezek 28:22

SIEGE *encirclement*

city came under **s** 2 Kin 24:10

---

their **s** towers Is 23:13
s against Jerusalem Jer 6:6
build a **s** wall Ezek 4:2

SIGHT *perception, vision*

pleasing to the **s** Gen 2:9
acceptable in Thy **s** Ps 19:14
precious in My **s** Is 43:4
blind receive **s** Matt 11:5
three days without **s** Acts 9:9
by faith, not by **s** 2 Cor 5:7

SIGN *indication or wonder*

a **s** for Cain Gen 4:15
s of the covenant Gen 9:12
this shall be the **s** Ex 3:12
blood shall be a **s** Ex 12:13
His **s-s** in Egypt Ps 78:43
Ask a **s** for yourself Is 7:11
an everlasting **s** Is 55:13
a **s** from You Matt 12:38
s of Your coming Matt 24:3
show **s-s** and Mark 13:22
s-s in sun and moon Luke 21:25
beginning of *His* **s-s** John 2:11
s of circumcision Rom 4:11
Jews ask for **s-s** 1 Cor 1:22
tongues are for a **s** 1 Cor 14:22
s-s...false wonders 2 Thess 2:9

SIGNET *seal*

examine...whose **s** Gen 38:25
engravings of a **s** Ex 39:14
s rings of his nobles Dan 6:17

SILAS

co-worker with Paul
Acts 15:22,32,40;16:19,25;
17:4,10,14

also **Silvanus**

SILENCE *quietness*

My soul *waits* in **s** Ps 62:1
war will be **s-d** Jer 50:30
s the ignorance 1 Pet 2:15
s in heaven Rev 8:1

SILENT *quiet*

Lord, do not keep **s** Ps 35:22
A time to be **s** Eccl 3:7
But Jesus kept **s** Matt 26:63
women keep **s** 1 Cor 14:34

SILOAM

1 *tower in Jerusalem* Luke 13:4
2 *water pool in Jerusalem*
John 9:7,11

SILVANUS

see **SILAS**

SILVER *precious metal*

rich in...**s** Gen 13:2
took no plunder in **s** Judg 5:19
as **s** is refined Ps 66:10
in settings of **s** Prov 25:11
s has become dross Is 1:22
The **s** is Mine Hag 2:8
not acquire...**s** Matt 10:9
thirty pieces of **s** Matt 26:15

SIMEON

1 *son of Jacob* Gen 29:33
2 *tribe* Num 1:23; Rev 7:7
3 *devout Jew* Luke 2:25

---

4 *ancestor of Jesus* Luke 3:30
5 *Christian prophet* Acts 13:1
6 *Simon Peter* Acts 15:14

SIMON

1 *apostle* Matt 4:18; Mark 1:16
see also **PETER**
2 *the Zealot*
Matt 10:4; Mark 3:18;
Luke 6:15
3 *brother of Jesus*
Matt 13:55; Mark 6:3
4 *leper* Matt 26:6; Mark 14:3
5 *a Pharisee* Luke 7:40,43
6 *of Cyrene* Matt 27:32
carried Jesus' cross
Mark 15:21; Luke 23:26
7 *father of Judas* John 6:71;13:2
8 *Magus sorcerer* Acts 8:9,13,18
9 *the tanner* Acts 9:43;10:6,32

SIMPLE *innocent or humble*

making wise the **s** Ps 19:7
Lord preserves the **s** Ps 116:6

SIN (n) *transgression*

please forgive my **s** Ex 10:17
atonement for your **s** Ex 32:30
purification from **s** Num 19:9
s will find you out Num 32:23
s of divination 1 Sam 15:23
the **s-s** of my youth Ps 25:7
s my mother conceived Ps 51:5
Fools mock at **s** Prov 14:9
bore the **s** of many Is 53:12
s-s of her prophets Lam 4:13
an eternal **s** Mark 3:29
forgive us our **s-s** Luke 11:4
takes away the **s** John 1:29
wash away your **s-s** Acts 22:16
wages of **s** is death Rom 6:23
died for our **s-s** 1 Cor 15:3
Him who knew no **s** 2 Cor 5:21
pleasures of **s** Heb 11:25
confess your **s-s** James 5:16
a multitude of **s-s** James 5:20
confess our **s-s** 1 John 1:9
s is lawlessness 1 John 3:4

SIN (v) *transgress*

When a leader **s-s** Lev 4:22
s against the Lord 1 Sam 14:34
Job did not **s** Job 1:22
s against Thee Ps 119:11
Father, I have **s-ned**
Luke 15:18
s no more John 8:11
all have **s-ned** Rom 3:23
that you may not **s** 1 John 2:1

SIN

1 *wilderness in Sinai*
Ex 16:1; Num 33:11,12
2 *Egyptian city* Ezek 30:15,16

SIN OFFERING

see **OFFERINGS**

SINAI

1 *mountain*
Ex 19:11; Lev 26:46;
Num 28:6
where Law received

Ex 31:18;34:29
also **Horeb**
2 desert wilderness
Ex 16:1; Ex 19:1;
Num 1:19;9:5

SINCERE *without deceit*

be s and blameless	Phil 1:10
mindful of the s faith	2 Tim 1:5
s love...brethren	1 Pet 1:22

SINEW *strength or tendon*

with bones and s-s	Job 10:11
neck is an iron s	Is 48:4
will put s-s on you	Ezek 37:6

SINFUL *wicked*

a brood of s men	Num 32:14
s generation	Mark 8:38
I am a s man	Luke 5:8
likeness of s flesh	Rom 8:3

SING

s to the LORD	Ex 15:1
s-ing and dancing	1 Sam 18:6
I will s praises	2 Sam 22:50
morning stars **sang**	Job 38:7
S to Him a new song	Ps 33:3
the righteous s-s	Prov 29:6
birds will s	Zeph 2:14
after s-ing a hymn	Mark 14:26
s-ing...thankfulness	Col 3:16
sang a new song	Rev 5:9

SINGERS

these are the s	1 Chr 9:33
male and female s	Eccl 2:8

SINK *descend, fall*

do not let me s	Ps 69:14
so shall Babylon s	Jer 51:64

SINNER *wrongdoer*

He instructs s-s	Ps 25:8
if s-s entice you	Prov 1:10
Adversity...s-s	Prov 13:21
one s destroys much	Eccl 9:18
a friend of...s-s	Matt 11:19
one s who repents	Luke 15:7
merciful to me...s	Luke 18:13
God...not hear s-s	John 9:31
while we were yet s-s	Rom 5:8
came...to save s-s	1 Tim 1:15

SISERA

1 Canaanite warrior   Judg 4:2ff
2 class of Nethinim
Ezra 2:53; Neh 7:55

SISTER

She is my s	Gen 12:19
We have a little s	Song 8:8
a s called Mary	Luke 10:39
commend...our s	Rom 16:1
younger women...s-s	1 Tim 5:2

SIT *recline, rest*

Moses **sat** to judge	Ex 18:13
Nor s in the seat	Ps 1:1
S at My right hand	Ps 110:1
lonely s-s the city	Lam 1:1
who s in darkness	Luke 1:79
dead man **sat** up	Luke 7:15
where the harlot s-s	Rev 17:15

SIVAN

third month of Hebrew calendar
Esth 8:9

SKILL *proficiency*

filled them with s	Ex 35:35
the heavens with s	Ps 136:5
work of s-ed men	Jer 10:9
s-ed in destruction	Ezek 21:31

SKILLFUL *accomplished*

became a s hunter	Gen 25:27
s player on...harp	1 Sam 16:16
praises with a s psalm	Ps 47:7

SKIN *covering*

garments of s	Gen 3:21
s of his face shone	Ex 34:29
Clothe me with s	Job 10:11
My s turns black	Job 30:30
will burst the s-s	Mark 2:22

SKIP *hop, leap*

children s about	Job 21:11
Lebanon s like a calf	Ps 29:6
go forth and s	Mal 4:2

SKULL *bony framework of head*

head, crushing his s	Judg 9:53
the s and the feet	2 Kin 9:35
Place of a S	Matt 27:33

SKY *heavens*

sun stopped in...s	Josh 10:13
the s grew black	1 Kin 18:45
witness in the s	Ps 89:37
s will be rolled up	Is 34:4
for the s is red	Matt 16:2
will appear in the s	Matt 24:30
s was shut up	Luke 4:25
gazing...into the s	Acts 1:10
s was split apart	Rev 6:14

SLANDER (n) *defamation*

spreads s is a fool	Prov 10:18
s-s, gossip	2 Cor 12:20
and s be put away	Eph 4:31

SLANDER (v) *defame*

He does not s	Ps 15:3
Whoever secretly s-s	Ps 101:5
Do not s a slave	Prov 30:10

SLANDERER *defamer*

s separates...friends	Prov 16:28
s-s, haters of God	Rom 1:30

SLAUGHTER (n) *brutal killing*

great s at Gibeon	Josh 10:10
lamb led to the s	Jer 11:19
as a sheep to s	Acts 8:32
in a day of s	James 5:5

SLAUGHTER (v) *kill*

shall s the bull	Ex 29:11
shall s the lamb	Lev 14:25
Who s the children	Is 57:5
s-ed My children	Ezek 16:21

SLAVE *bondservant*

The Hebrew s	Gen 39:17
s at forced labor	Gen 49:15
sold *in* a s sale	Lev 25:42
Is Israel a s	Jer 2:14

S-s rule over us	Lam 5:8
s above his master	Matt 10:24
good and faithful s	Matt 25:21
shall be s of all	Mark 10:44
is the s of sin	John 8:34
neither s nor free	Gal 3:28
as s-s of Christ	Eph 6:6

SLAVERY *servitude*

from the house of s	Ex 13:3
ransomed you from...s	Mic 6:4
received a spirit of s	Rom 8:15
to a yoke of s	Gal 5:1

SLAY *destroy, kill*

knife to s his son	Gen 22:10
s-s the foolish	Job 5:2
Though He s me	Job 13:15
Evil...s the wicked	Ps 34:21
s her with thirst	Hos 2:3
Lamb that was **slain**	Rev 5:12

SLEEP (n) *rest*

caused a deep s	Gen 2:21
Do not love s	Prov 20:13
a spirit of deep s	Is 29:10
s fled from him	Dan 6:18
overcome by s	Acts 20:9

SLEEP (v) *slumber*

why dost Thou s	Ps 44:23
neither slumber nor s	Ps 121:4
who s-s in harvest	Prov 10:5
found them s-ing	Matt 26:43
we shall not all s	1 Cor 15:51

SLOW *not quick*

I am s of speech	Ex 4:10
gracious, S to anger	Ps 103:8
to hear, s to speak	James 1:19
Lord is not s	2 Pet 3:9

SLUGGARD *lazy one*

to the ant, O s	Prov 6:6
the s craves	Prov 13:4
s buries his hand	Prov 26:15

SLUMBER *sleep*

s in their beds	Job 33:15
He...will not s	Ps 121:3
None s-s or sleeps	Is 5:27
Dreamers...love to s	Is 56:10

SMALL *little*

both s and great	2 Kin 25:26
s among the nations	Jer 49:15
day of s things	Zech 4:10
For the gate is s	Matt 7:14
a few s fish	Mark 8:7
he was s in stature	Luke 19:3
tongue is a s part	James 3:5

SMILE *grin*

I s-d on them	Job 29:24
that I may s *again*	Ps 39:13
she s-s at the future	Prov 31:25

SMITE *hit, strike*

s...with frogs	Ex 8:2
smote Job with sore	Job 2:7
sun will not s you	Ps 121:6
righteous s me	Ps 141:5
s the earth	Rev 11:6

SMITH *worker of metal*

a vessel for the **s**	Prov 25:4
created the **s** who	Is 54:16
s-s from Jerusalem	Jer 24:1

SMOKE *mist, vapor*

s...ascended	Gen 19:28
Sinai *was* all in **s**	Ex 19:18
like **s** they vanish	Ps 37:20
temple was filling with **s**	Is 6:4
s rises up forever	Rev 19:3

SMOOTH *no roughness*

I am a **s** man	Gen 27:11
five **s** stones	1 Sam 17:40
Make **s**...a highway	Is 40:3
the rough roads **s**	Luke 3:5
s...flattering speech	Rom 16:18

SMYRNA

city in Asia Minor	Rev 1:11;2:8

SNAKE *serpent*

horned **s** in the path	Gen 49:17
a **s** bites him	Amos 5:19
s instead of a fish	Luke 11:11

SNARE *trap*

gods shall be a **s**	Judg 2:3
s-s of death	2 Sam 22:6
laid a **s** for me	Ps 119:110
his lips are the **s**	Prov 18:7
caught in My **s**	Ezek 12:13
table become a **s**	Rom 11:9
s of the devil	1 Tim 3:7

SNOW *ice flakes*

storehouses of the **s**	Job 38:22
be whiter than **s**	Ps 51:7
He gives **s** like wool	Ps 147:16
Like **s** in summer	Prov 26:1
as white as **s**	Matt 28:3

SOBER *serious, temperate*

words of **s** truth	Acts 26:25
be alert and **s**	1 Thess 5:6
Be of **s** *spirit*	1 Pet 5:8

SODOM

city S of Dead Sea	Gen 10:19
home of Lot	Gen 19:1,4
destroyed by God	Gen 19:24

SODOMITE

one guilty of unnatural sexual practices	1 Kin 22:46

SOFT *kind*

speak to you **s** words	Job 41:3
s tongue breaks the	Prov 25:15

SOIL *earth, ground*

first fruits of your **s**	Ex 23:19
he loved the **s**	2 Chr 26:10
fell into the good **s**	Mark 4:8
produce of the **s**	James 5:7

SOJOURN *visit temporarily*

S in this land	Gen 26:3
stranger **s-s** with you	Ex 12:48
s...land of Moab	Ruth 1:1

SOJOURNER

s in a foreign land	Ex 2:22

are **s-s** before Thee	1 Chr 29:15
oppressed the **s**	Ezek 22:29

SOLDIER *military man*

s-s took Him away	Mark 15:16
s-s also mocked	Luke 23:36
s-s pierced His side	John 19:34
a devout **s**	Acts 10:7
good **s** of Christ	2 Tim 2:3

SOLEMN *deeply earnest, serious*

sabbath of **s** rest	Lev 16:31
have a **s** assembly	Num 29:35
sworn **s** oaths	Ezek 21:23
bound...a **s** oath	Acts 23:14

SOLOMON

1 *son of David*	2 Sam 12:24
king of Israel	1 Kin 1:43
ruled wisely	1 Kin 4:29,34
built the Temple	1 Kin 6:2;9:1
international fame	1 Kin 10:1
ruled foolishly	1 Kin 11:6
death	1 Kin 11:43
2 *Song of Solomon*	
also **Song of Songs**	

SON *male descendant*

the **s-s** of Noah	Gen 9:18
Take...your only **s**	Gen 22:2
O Absalom, my **s**	2 Sam 18:33
to be a **s** to Me	1 Chr 28:6
s-s of God shouted	Job 38:7
Thou art My **S**	Ps 2:7
wise **s** makes a	Prov 10:1
Discipline your **s**	Prov 19:18
bear a **s**...Immanuel	Is 7:14
Egypt I called My **s**	Hos 11:1
she gave birth to a **S**	Matt 1:25
This is My beloved **S**	Matt 3:17
the carpenter's **s**	Matt 13:55
I am the **S** of God	Matt 27:43
S of Man...suffer	Mark 8:31
her first-born **s**	Luke 2:7
If You are the **S**	Luke 4:3
man had two **s-s**	Luke 15:11
only begotten **S**	John 3:16
S also gives life	John 5:21
become **s-s** of light	John 12:36
sending His own **S**	Rom 8:3
image of His **S**	Rom 8:29
not spare His own **S**	Rom 8:32
fellowship with His **S**	1 Cor 1:9
if a **s**, then an heir	Gal 4:7
shall be a **S** to Me	Heb 1:5
abide in the **S**	1 John 2:24
He who has the **S**	1 John 5:12

SON-IN-LAW

the **s** of the Timnite	Judg 15:6
be the king's **s**	1 Sam 18:18
s of Sanballat	Neh 13:28

SON OF GOD

Messianic title indicating deity of Jesus Christ

	Matt 4:3;8:29;16:16;
Mark 1:20;3:11;14:61; Luke	
1:35;	
	John 3:18;11:27; Acts 8:37

SON OF MAN

Messianic title of Jesus Christ

	Matt 8:20;9:6; Mark 2:10;
10:33; Luke 12:10;18:31;	
John 6:27;13:31	

SONG *melody, music*

LORD is my...**s**	Ex 15:2
ministered with **s**	1 Chr 6:32
gives **s-s** in the night	Job 35:10
s-s of deliverance	Ps 32:7
Sing to Him a new **s**	Ps 33:3
A **s** of my beloved	Is 5:1
Praise the LORD in **s**	Is 12:5
not drink wine with **s**	Is 24:9
hymns...spiritual **s-s**	Eph 5:19

SORCERER *witch*

interprets...or a **s**	Deut 18:10
witness against the **s-s**	Mal 3:5
immoral persons...**s-s**	Rev 21:8

SORCERY *witchcraft*

practiced **s**	2 Chr 33:6
idolatry, **s**, enmities	Gal 5:20
deceived by your **s**	Rev 18:23

SORDID *filthy*

fond of **s** gain	1 Tim 3:8
the sake of **s** gain	Titus 1:11
not for **s** gain	1 Pet 5:2

SOREK

valley SW of Jerusalem

	Judg 16:4

SORROW *grief, sadness*

down to Sheol in **s**	Gen 42:38
life is spent with **s**	Ps 31:10
man of **s-s**	Is 53:3
s is beyond healing	Jer 8:18
s...turned to joy	John 16:20
if I cause you **s**	2 Cor 2:2

SOSTHENES

1 *synagogue leader*	Acts 18:17
2 *Corinthian believer*	1 Cor 1:27

SOUL *life, spirit*

her **s** was departing	Gen 35:18
humble your **s-s**	Lev 16:29
poured out my **s**	1 Sam 1:15
not abandon my **s**	Ps 16:10
He restores my **s**	Ps 23:3
my **s** pants for Thee	Ps 42:1
Bless...LORD, O my **s**	Ps 103:1
who is wise wins **s-s**	Prov 11:30
s who sins will die	Ezek 18:4
unable to kill the **s**	Matt 10:28
exchange for his **s**	Matt 16:26
My **s** is...grieved	Matt 26:38
and forfeit his **s**	Mark 8:36
My **s** exalts the Lord	Luke 1:46
your **s** is required	Luke 12:20
one heart and **s**	Acts 4:32
an anchor of the **s**	Heb 6:19
able to save your **s-s**	James 1:21
save his **s** from	James 5:20
war against the **s**	1 Pet 2:11

SOUND (adj) *accurate, stable*

s wisdom...two sides	Job 11:6
I give you **s** teaching	Prov 4:2
the **s** doctrine	1 Tim 4:6

SOUND (n) *noise*

s of Thee in...garden	Gen 3:10
s of war in the camp	Ex 32:17
s of a great army	2 Kin 7:6
s of many waters	Ezek 43:2

SOUND (v) *express*

s His praise abroad	Ps 66:8
s an alarm	Joel 2:1
trumpet will s	1 Cor 15:52

SOUR *distasteful, tart*

eaten s grapes	Jer 31:29
offering...s wine	Luke 23:36

SOURCE *origin*

the s of sapphires	Job 28:6
s of eternal salvation	Heb 5:9
s of quarrels	James 4:1

SOVEREIGNTY *authority*

His s rules over all	Ps 103:19
s from Damascus	Is 17:3
s will be uprooted	Dan 11:4

SOW *plant, spread*

you may s the land	Gen 47:23
s your seed uselessly	Lev 26:16
who s in tears	Ps 126:5
who s-s iniquity will	Prov 22:8
they s the wind	Hos 8:7
birds...do not s	Matt 6:26
s good seed	Matt 13:27
s-ed spiritual things	1 Cor 9:11
whatever a man s-s	Gal 6:7

SOWER *planter*

seed to the s	Is 55:10
s went out to sow	Matt 13:3
s sows the word	Mark 4:14

SPAIN

S European land	Rom 15:24,28

SPARE *save or be lenient*

did not s their soul	Ps 78:50
who s-s his rod	Prov 13:24
No man s-s his brother	Is 9:19
not s His own Son	Rom 8:32
I will not s *anyone*	2 Cor 13:2
God did not s angels	2 Pet 2:4

SPEAK *proclaim, tell*

God spoke to Noah	Gen 8:15
God s-s with man	Deut 5:24
S of all His wonders	1 Chr 16:9
He who s-s falsehood	Ps 101:7
and a time to s	Eccl 3:7
the dumb to s	Mark 7:37
s that...we know	John 3:11
Never did a man s	John 7:46
s with other tongues	Acts 2:4
we s God's wisdom	1 Cor 2:7
If I s with tongues	1 Cor 13:1

SPEAR *weapon*

leaning on his s	2 Sam 1:6
s-s into pruning hooks	Is 2:4
pruning hooks into s-s	Joel 3:10
pierced...with a s	John 19:34

SPECK *particle*

regarded as a s of	Is 40:15
s out of your eye	Matt 7:4

SPEECH *message, word*

I am slow of s	Ex 4:10
His s was smoother	Ps 55:21
in cleverness of s	1 Cor 1:17
I am unskilled in s	2 Cor 11:6

SPELL *incantation*

one who casts a s	Deut 18:11
skillful caster of s-s	Ps 58:5
power of your s-s	Is 47:9

SPICE

s and the oil	Ex 35:28
mix in the s-s	Ezek 24:10
prepared s-s and	Luke 23:56
wrappings with...s-s	John 19:40

SPIES *clandestine persons*

we are not s	Gen 42:31
two men as s	Josh 2:1
David sent out s	1 Sam 26:4
welcomed the s	Heb 11:31

SPIN *make thread*

nor do they s	Matt 6:28
neither toil nor s	Luke 12:27

SPIRIT

S rested upon them	Num 11:26
God sent an evil s	Judg 9:23
My s is broken	Job 17:1
renew a steadfast s	Ps 51:10
my s grows faint	Ps 77:3
a haughty s before	Prov 16:18
the S lifted me up	Ezek 3:14
his s was troubled	Dan 2:1
four s-s of heaven	Zech 6:5
are the poor in s	Matt 5:3
authority over...s-s	Matt 10:1
put My S upon Him	Matt 12:18
blasphemy...the S	Matt 12:31
yielded up *His* s	Matt 27:50
S like a dove	Mark 1:10
s...not have flesh	Luke 24:39
born of...the S	John 3:5
worship in s and	John 4:24
gave up His s	John 19:30
pour forth of My S	Acts 2:17
Jesus, receive my s	Acts 7:59
power of the S	Rom 15:19
taught by the s	1 Cor 2:13
pray with the s	1 Cor 14:15
walk by the S	Gal 5:16
fruit of the S is love	Gal 5:22
one body and one S	Eph 4:4
be filled with the S	Eph 5:18
sword of the S	Eph 6:17
not quench the S	1 Thess 5:19
division of soul and s	Heb 4:12
the s-s *now* in prison	1 Pet 3:19
S who bears witness	1 John 5:7
see also **HOLY SPIRIT**	

SPIRIT OF GOD

the S was moving	Gen 1:2
S came upon him	1 Sam 10:10
a vision by the S	Ezek 11:24
S descending as a	Matt 3:16
being led by the S	Rom 8:14
S dwells in you	1 Cor 3:16
worship in the S	Phil 3:3
see also **HOLY SPIRIT**	

SPIRIT OF THE LORD

S came upon him	Judg 3:10
S departed from	1 Sam 16:14
S gave them rest	Is 63:14
filled with...the S	Mic 3:8
S is upon Me	Luke 4:18
see also **HOLY SPIRIT**	

SPIRITIST *medium*

not turn to...s-s	Lev 19:31
s...be put to death	Lev 20:27
removed...the s-s	2 Kin 23:24

SPIRITUAL *of the spirit*

the Law is s	Rom 7:14
s service of worship	Rom 12:1
raised a s body	1 Cor 15:44
with every s blessing	Eph 1:3
hymns and s songs	Eph 5:19
offer up s sacrifices	1 Pet 2:5

SPIT

began to s at Him	Mark 14:65
and s upon	Luke 18:32
He spat on...ground	John 9:6
I will s you out	Rev 3:16

SPLENDOR *magnificence*

the moon going in s	Job 31:26
displayed Thy s	Ps 8:1
Thy s and Thy majesty	Ps 45:3
clothed with s	Ps 104:1
s covers the heavens	Hab 3:3

SPLIT *divide*

He s the rock	Is 48:21
valleys will be s	Mic 1:4
Mount...will be s	Zech 14:4
sky was s apart	Rev 6:14

SPOIL *booty, pillage*

he divides the s	Gen 49:27
the s of the cities	Deut 2:35
divide the s with	Prov 16:19
widows may be their s	Is 10:2
for s to the nations	Ezek 25:7

SPONGE *absorbent matter*

taking a s, he filled	Matt 27:48
a s with sour wine	Mark 15:36

SPOT *speck*

Or the leopard his s-s	Jer 13:23
no s or wrinkle	Eph 5:27

SPOTLESS *no defects*

unblemished and s	1 Pet 1:19
s and blameless	2 Pet 3:14

SPREAD *stretch out*

He s His wings	Deut 32:11
I s My skirt over	Ezek 16:8
death s to all men	Rom 5:12

SPRING (adj) *period, season*

has been no s rain	Jer 3:3
Like the s rain	Hos 6:3
s crop began to sprout	Amos 7:1

SPRING (n) *water source*

went down to the s	Gen 24:16
twelve s-s of water	Ex 15:27
stop all s-s of water	2 Kin 3:19
s-s of the deep...fixed	Prov 8:28

the s-s of salvation — Is 12:3
s of the water of life — Rev 21:6

SPRING (v) *jump, leap*

S up, O well — Num 21:17
Truth s-s from the — Ps 85:11
s-ing up to eternal — John 4:14

SPRINKLE *scatter*

take its blood and s — Ex 29:16
s some of the blood — Lev 4:6
s *it* seven times — Lev 4:17
s some of the oil — Lev 14:16

SPY *investigate*

Moses sent...to s — Num 13:17
to s out Jericho — Josh 6:25
spied out Bethel — Judg 1:23
s out our liberty — Gal 2:4

SQUARE *area* or *shape*

altar shall be s — Ex 27:1
voice in the s — Prov 1:20
city is...a s — Rev 21:16

STAFF *rod*

s of God in his hand — Ex 4:20
Thy s, they comfort — Ps 23:4
or sandals, or a s — Matt 10:10
a mere s; no bread — Mark 6:8

STAIN *blemish*

s of your iniquity — Jer 2:22
without s...reproach — 1 Tim 6:14

STAND *maintain position*

s before the LORD — Deut 10:8
O sun, s still — Josh 10:12
s before kings — Prov 22:29
word of our God s-s — Is 40:8
will s on the Mount — Zech 14:4
love to s and pray — Matt 6:5
s-ing by the cross — John 19:25
why do you s looking — Acts 1:11
s by your faith — Rom 11:20
s before...judgment — Rom 14:10
s firm in the faith — 1 Cor 16:13
foundation...s-s — 2 Tim 2:19
I s at the door — Rev 3:20

STANDARD *banner* or *rule*

set up their own s-s — Ps 74:4
set up My s — Is 49:22
s of the Law — Acts 22:12
s of sound words — 2 Tim 1:13

STAR *heavenly body*

He made the s-s — Gen 1:16
s shall come forth — Num 24:17
morning s-s sang — Job 38:7
s of the morning — Is 14:12
s-s for light by night — Jer 31:35
His s in the east — Matt 2:2
morning s arises — 2 Pet 1:19
wandering s-s — Jude 13
s fell from heaven — Rev 8:10
the bright morning s — Rev 22:16

STATE *position*

s of expectation — Luke 3:15
of our humble s — Phil 3:21
s has become worse — 2 Pet 2:20

STATEMENT *assertion*

let your s be — Matt 5:37
trap Him in a s — Mark 12:13
catch Him in...s — Luke 20:20
This is a difficult s — John 6:60

STATURE *height*

was growing in s — 1 Sam 2:26
in wisdom and s — Luke 2:52
he was small in s — Luke 19:3
measure of the s — Eph 4:13

STATUTE *law, rule*

My s-s and My laws — Gen 26:5
a perpetual s — Ex 29:9
keep My s-s — Lev 18:5
Teach me Thy s-s — Ps 119:26
not walked in My s-s — Ezek 5:7

STEADFAST *established, firm*

be s and not fear — Job 11:15
renew a s spirit — Ps 51:10
My heart is s — Ps 57:7
s in righteousness — Prov 11:19
be s, immovable — 1 Cor 15:58

STEAL *rob, take*

You shall not s — Ex 20:15
be in want and s — Prov 30:9
thieves break in...s — Matt 6:19
Do not s — Mark 10:19

STEPHANAS

Corinthian Christian
— 1 Cor 1:16;16:15,17

STEPHEN

deacon — Acts 6:5,8
martyred — Acts 7:59;8:2

STEPS *distance* or *movements*

dost number my s — Job 14:16
s...bathed in butter — Job 29:6
His s do not slip — Ps 37:31
s lay hold of Sheol — Prov 5:5
in the s of the faith — Rom 4:12
follow in His s — 1 Pet 2:21

STEWARD *supervisor*

and sensible s — Luke 12:42
s-s of the mysteries — 1 Cor 4:1
above reproach...s — Titus 1:7

STEWARDSHIP *responsibility*

an account of your s — Luke 16:2
a s entrusted to me — 1 Cor 9:17
s of God's grace — Eph 3:2

STIFFEN *make rigid*

s your neck no more — Deut 10:16
do not s your neck — 2 Chr 30:8
have s-ed their necks — Jer 19:15

STILL *motionless* or *quiet*

O sun, stand s — Josh 10:12
the storm to be s — Ps 107:29
Why are we sitting s — Jer 8:14
sea, Hush, be s — Mark 4:39

STIMULATE *excite*

how to s my body — Eccl 2:3
s one another to — Heb 10:24

STING *pain*

where is your s — 1 Cor 15:55

s of death is sin — 1 Cor 15:56

STIR *agitate*

S up Thyself — Ps 35:23
word s-s up anger — Prov 15:1
man s-s up strife — Prov 29:22
s-red up the water — John 5:4

STOCKS *confinement*

put my feet in the s — Job 13:27
Jeremiah from the s — Jer 20:3
their feet in the s — Acts 16:24

STOMACH *part of body*

s will be satisfied — Prov 18:20
s of the fish — Jon 1:17
Food is for the s — 1 Cor 6:13
s was made bitter — Rev 10:10

STONE (n) *rock*

they used brick for s — Gen 11:3
two s tablets — Ex 34:1
do these s-s mean — Josh 4:6
five smooth s-s — 1 Sam 17:40
there was no s seen — 1 Kin 6:18
Water wears...s-s — Job 14:19
foot against a s — Ps 91:12
in Zion a s — Is 28:16
take the heart of s — Ezek 11:19
serving wood and s — Ezek 20:32
foot against a s — Matt 4:6
will give him a s — Matt 7:9
rolled away the s — Matt 28:2
s-s will cry out — Luke 19:40
six s waterpots — John 2:6
first to throw a s — John 8:7
Remove the s — John 11:39
s-s, wood, hay — 1 Cor 3:12
as to a living s — 1 Pet 2:4
A s of stumbling — 1 Pet 2:8

STONE (v) *throw stones*

people will s us — Luke 20:6
seeking to s You — John 11:8
went on s-ing Stephen — Acts 7:59
they s-d Paul — Acts 14:19

STOP *cease*

the sun s-ped — Josh 10:13
And the oil s-ped — 2 Kin 4:6
put a s to sacrifice — Dan 9:27
s weeping for Me — Luke 23:28
s sinning — 1 Cor 15:34

STORE *accumulate*

s up the grain — Gen 41:35
His sin is s-d up — Hos 13:12
place to s my crops — Luke 12:17
s-d up your treasure — James 5:3

STOREHOUSE *storage place*

s-s of the snow — Job 38:22
wind from His s-s — Jer 10:13
tithe into the s — Mal 3:10

STORK *bird*

the s, the heron — Lev 11:19
the s in the sky — Jer 8:7
wings of a s — Zech 5:9

STORM *tempest, whirlwind*

A refuge from the s — Is 25:4
will come like a s — Ezek 38:9
a great s on the sea — Jon 1:4

mists driven by a **s**   2 Pet 2:17

STRAIGHT *direct*
Make Thy way **s**   Ps 5:8
make your paths **s**   Prov 3:6
Make His paths **s**   Matt 3:3
Make **s** the way   John 1:23

STRANGE *foreign*
offered **s** fire   Lev 10:1
no **s** god among you   Ps 81:9
to teach **s** doctrines   1 Tim 1:3
went after **s** flesh   Jude 7

STRANGER *alien, sojourner*
s-s in a land   Gen 15:13
a **s** and a sojourner   Gen 23:4
shall not wrong a **s**   Ex 22:21
a **s** in the earth   Ps 119:19
LORD protects the **s-s**   Ps 146:9
violence to the **s**   Jer 22:3
I was a **s**   Matt 25:35
hospitality to **s-s**   Heb 13:2

STRAW *stalk of grain*
s to make brick   Ex 5:7
s for the horses   1 Kin 4:28
as **s** before the wind   Job 21:18
wood, hay, **s**   1 Cor 3:12

STRAY *wander*
not **s** into her paths   Prov 7:25
no longer **s** from Me   Ezek 14:11
s-s from the truth   James 5:19
s-ing like sheep   1 Pet 2:25

STREAM *current, flow*
planted by **s-s** of water   Ps 1:3
The **s** of God   Ps 65:9
like a rushing **s**   Is 59:19

STREET *road, way*
Wisdom shouts in...**s**   Prov 1:20
race madly in the **s-s**   Nah 2:4
on the **s** corners   Matt 6:5
s of the city...gold   Rev 21:21

STRENGTH *force, power*
no longer yield its **s**   Gen 4:12
The LORD is my **s**   Ex 15:2
was no **s** in him   1 Sam 28:20
My **s** is dried up   Ps 22:15
The LORD is my **s**   Ps 28:7
s in time of trouble   Ps 37:39
God is our refuge...**s**   Ps 46:1
s of my salvation   Ps 140:7
your **s** to women   Prov 31:3
s to the weary   Is 40:29
Strangers devour his **s**   Hos 7:9
with all your **s**   Mark 12:30
s which God supplies   1 Pet 4:11
sun shining in its **s**   Rev 1:16

STRENGTHEN *make strong*
please **s** me   Judg 16:28
David **s-ed** himself   1 Sam 30:6
s-ed weak hands   Job 4:3
s the feeble   Is 35:3
s the sick   Ezek 34:16
s your brothers   Luke 22:32
s-ed in the faith   Acts 16:5
Him who **s-s** me   Phil 4:3
s-ed with all power   Col 1:11

s your hearts   2 Thess 2:17
who has **s-ed** me   1 Tim 1:12

STRETCH *extend*
I will **s** out My hand   Ex 3:20
He **s-es** out the north   Job 26:7
S-ing out heaven   Ps 104:2
I **s-ed** out the heavens   Is 45:12

STRIFE *discord, quarrel*
s between...herdsmen   Gen 13:7
the **s** of tongues   Ps 31:20
Hatred stirs up **s**   Prov 10:12
fool's lips bring **s**   Prov 18:6
of envy, murder, **s**   Rom 1:29
and **s** among you   1 Cor 3:3
enmities, **s**, jealousy   Gal 5:20

STRIKE *hit*
I will **s** the water   Ex 7:17
you shall **s** the rock   Ex 17:6
He who **s-s** a man   Ex 21:12
s the timbrel   Ps 81:2
you **s** your foot   Ps 91:12
S a scoffer   Prov 19:25
He will **s** the earth   Is 11:4
let us **s** at him   Jer 18:18
S the Shepherd   Zech 13:7
s...the shepherd   Matt 26:31

STRIVE *contend, struggle*
not **s** with man forever   Gen 6:3
He will not always **s**   Ps 103:9
and **s-ing** after wind   Eccl 1:14
s together with me   Rom 15:30
s-ing to please men   Gal 1:10
we labor and **s**   1 Tim 4:10
s-ing against sin   Heb 12:4

STRONG *powerful, steadfast*
a very **s** west wind   Ex 10:19
not drink...**s** drink   Lev 10:9
Be **s** and courageous   Deut 31:6
Israel became **s**   Judg 1:28
God is...**s** fortress   2 Sam 22:33
The LORD **s** and mighty   Ps 24:8
s drink a brawler   Prov 20:1
their Redeemer is **s**   Prov 23:11
ants are not a **s** folk   Prov 30:25
love is as **s** as death   Song 8:6
Their Redeemer is **s**   Jer 50:34
grew **s** in faith   Rom 4:20
act like men, be **s**   1 Cor 16:13
be **s** in the Lord   Eph 6:10
weakness...made **s**   Heb 11:34
I saw a **s** angel   Rev 5:2

STRONGHOLD *fortress, refuge*
David lived in the **s**   2 Sam 5:9
s and my refuge   2 Sam 22:3
s for the oppressed   Ps 9:9
For God is my **s**   Ps 59:9
my salvation, My **s**   Ps 62:2
a **s** to the upright   Prov 10:29

STRUGGLE (n) *conflict*
the days of my **s**   Job 14:14
our **s** is not against   Eph 6:12
have shared my **s**   Phil 4:3

STRUGGLE (v) *contend*
children **s-d** together   Gen 25:22
men **s**...each other   Ex 21:22

STUBBLE *short stumps*
gather **s** for straw   Ex 5:12
fire consumes **s**   Is 5:24
give birth to **s**   Is 33:11
house of Esau...**s**   Obad 18

STUBBORN *obstinate*
Pharaoh's heart is **s**   Ex 7:14
you are a **s** people   Deut 9:6
s...generation   Ps 78:8
house of Israel is **s**   Ezek 3:7

STUBBORNNESS *intractable*
I know your...**s**   Deut 31:27
s of their heart   Ps 81:12
s...unrepentant heart   Rom 2:5

STUMBLE *fall, trip*
your foot will not **s**   Prov 3:23
a rock to **s** over   Is 8:14
arrogant one will **s**   Jer 50:32
eye makes you **s**   Matt 5:29
a stone of **s-ing**   Rom 9:33
all **s** in many *ways*   James 3:2

STUMBLING BLOCK *obstacle*
s before the blind   Lev 19:14
s of iniquity   Ezek 44:12
You are a **s** to Me   Matt 16:23
to Jews a **s**   1 Cor 1:23
s of the cross   Gal 5:11

STUMP *part of plant*
s dies in the dry soil   Job 14:8
The holy seed is its **s**   Is 6:13
the **s** with the roots   Dan 4:26

STUPID *foolish, senseless*
s and the senseless   Ps 49:10
I am more **s** than   Prov 30:2
they are altogether **s**   Jer 10:8

STYLUS *marking/writing device*
an iron **s** and lead   Job 19:24
with an iron **s**   Jer 17:1

SUBDUE *conquer, overcome*
fill the earth, and **s**   Gen 1:28
the land was **s-d**   Josh 18:1
us completely **s** them   Ps 74:8
s nations before him   Is 45:1

SUBJECT (adj) *under authority*
s to forced labor   Judg 1:30
demons are **s** to us   Luke 10:17
church is **s** to Christ   Eph 5:24
s to...husbands   Titus 2:5
be **s** to the Father   Heb 12:9

SUBJECT (v)
s him to a slave's   Lev 25:39
creation was **s-ed**   Rom 8:20
them **s** themselves   1 Cor 14:34
all things are **s-ed**   1 Cor 15:28

SUBJECTION *under authority*
kingdom...in **s**   Ezek 17:14
He continued in **s**   Luke 2:51
s to the governing   Rom 13:1
all things in **s**   1 Cor 15:27

SUBMISSIVE *yielding*
Servants, be **s**   1 Pet 2:18
s to...husbands   1 Pet 3:5

SUBMIT *yield to*

Foreigners s to me	Ps 18:44
s yourself to decrees	Col 2:20
S therefore to God	James 4:7

SUBSTITUTE

s shall become holy	Lev 27:10
s darkness for light	Is 5:20
s bitter for sweet	Is 5:20

SUCCESS *accomplishment*

grant me s today	Gen 24:12
hands cannot attain s	Job 5:12
Daniel enjoyed s	Dan 6:28

SUCCESSFUL *having achieved*

make your journey s	Gen 24:40
make Thy servant s	Neh 1:11
make his ways s	Is 48:15

SUCCOTH

1 *Israelite camping place*
Ex 12:37;13:20
2 *Gadite town in Jordan Valley*
Josh 13:27; Ps 60:6

SUDDENLY *abruptly*

lest he come s	Mark 13:36
s...from heaven	Acts 2:2

SUFFER *experience pain*

s the fate of all	Num 16:29
Son of Man must s	Mark 8:31
s and rise again	Luke 24:46
worthy to s shame	Acts 5:41
we s with *Him*	Rom 8:17
creation...s-s	Rom 8:22
if one member s-s	1 Cor 12:26
s-ing for the gospel	2 Tim 1:8
Christ also s-ed	1 Pet 2:21

SUFFERINGS *distress*

s of this present	Rom 8:18
sharers of our s	2 Cor 1:7
fellowship of His s	Phil 3:10
rejoice in my s	Col 1:24
share the s of Christ	1 Pet 4:13

SUFFICIENT *enough*

s for its redemption	Lev 25:26
bread is not s	John 6:7
My grace is s	2 Cor 12:9

SUMMER *season*

fever heat of s	Ps 32:4
Thou hast made s	Ps 74:17
Like snow in s	Prov 26:1
know that s is near	Matt 24:32

SUMMIT *peak, top*

Like the s of Lebanon	Jer 22:6
hide on the s	Amos 9:3

SUMMON *call, gather*

s-ed all Israel	Deut 5:1
s all the prophets	2 Kin 10:19
He s-s the heavens	Ps 50:4
He s-ed the twelve	Matt 6:7

SUN *heavenly body*

when the s grew hot	Ex 16:21
the s stood still	Josh 10:13
chariots of the s	2 Kin 23:11
God is a s	Ps 84:11

s will not smite	Ps 121:6
s to rule by day	Ps 136:8
new under the s	Eccl 1:9
s go down at noon	Amos 8:9
shine forth as the s	Matt 13:43
signs in the s	Luke 21:25
not let the s go down	Eph 4:26
clothed with the s	Rev 12:1

SUNRISE *appearance of sun*

toward the s	Num 3:38
Jordan toward the s	Josh 1:15

SUNSET

Passover...at s	Deut 16:6
dawn and the s shout	Ps 65:8

SUNSHINE

Through s after rain	2 Sam 23:4
dazzling heat in the s	Is 18:4

SUPPER *meal*

made Him a s	John 12:2
eat the Lord's S	1 Cor 11:20
marriage s of the	Rev 19:9
the great s of God	Rev 19:17

SUPPLICATION *petition*

Make s to the LORD	Ex 9:28
s of Thy people	1 Kin 8:52
LORD has heard my s	Ps 6:9
poor man utters s-s	Prov 18:23
seek *Him* by...s-s	Dan 9:3
by prayer and s	Phil 4:6

SUPPLY *provide*

He who s-ies seed	2 Cor 9:10
my God shall s	Phil 4:19
s moral excellence	2 Pet 1:5

SUPPORT (n) *strength*

the LORD was my s	2 Sam 22:19
gave him strong s	1 Chr 11:10
Both supply and s	Is 3:1
worthy of his s	Matt 10:10

SUPPORT (v) *uphold*

Hur s-ed his hands	Ex 17:12
will He s...evildoers	Job 8:20
He s-s the fatherless	Ps 146:9
ought to s such men	3 John 8

SUR

see GATES OF JERUSALEM

SURE *secure, true*

testimony...is s	Ps 19:7
His precepts are s	Ps 111:7
His water will be s	Is 33:16

SURETY *liable, security*

I myself will be s	Gen 43:9
s for Thy servant	Ps 119:122
s for a stranger	Prov 11:15

SURFACE *exterior*

s of the deep	Gen 1:2
ark floated on the s	Gen 7:18
water was on the s	Gen 8:9

SURPASS *excel*

you s in beauty	Ezek 32:19
s-ing riches of His	Eph 2:7
which s-es knowledge	Eph 3:19

SURRENDER *yield*

s me into his hand	1 Sam 23:11
How can I s you	Hos 11:8

SURROUND *encircle*

s him with favor	Ps 5:12
Sheol s-ed me	Ps 18:5
s me with songs	Ps 32:7
witnesses s-ing us	Heb 12:1

SURVIVE *outlive*

your household will s	Jer 38:17
how can we s	Ezek 33:10

SURVIVORS *continued to live*

inheritance for...s	Judg 21:17
out of...Zion s	2 Kin 19:31
left us a few s	Is 1:9
imprison their s	Obad 14

SUSA

a Persian capital city
Neh 1:1; Esth 1:2,5;3:15;9:15

SUSTAIN *provide for*

land could not s	Gen 13:6
LORD s-s the righteous	Ps 37:17
He will s you	Ps 55:22
S...with raisin cakes	Song 2:5

SWALLOW (n) *bird*

the s a nest	Ps 84:3
like a s in *its*	Prov 26:2

SWALLOW (v) *take in*

earth may s us up	Num 16:34
He will s up death	Is 25:8
great fish to s Jonah	Jon 1:17
s-ed up in victory	1 Cor 15:54

SWARM *collect, gather*

Nile will s with frogs	Ex 8:3
which s on the earth	Lev 11:29
land s-ed with frogs	Ps 105:30

SWEAR *take oath, vow*

s by the LORD	Gen 24:3
oath which I swore	Gen 26:3
person s-s thoughtlessly	Lev 5:4
not s falsely	Lev 19:12
sworn by My holiness	Ps 89:35
s by My name	Jer 12:16
who s-s by heaven	Matt 23:22
began to...s	Matt 26:74
brethren do not s	James 5:12

SWEAT *perspiration*

By the s of your face	Gen 3:19
s...like drops of	Luke 22:44

SWEET *fresh, pleasant*

waters became s	Ex 15:25
s psalmist of Israel	2 Sam 23:1
who had s fellowship	Ps 55:14
s are Thy words	Ps 119:103
your sleep will be s	Prov 3:24
Stolen water is s	Prov 9:17
it was s as honey	Ezek 3:3

SWIFT *fast, rapid*

horses and s steeds	1 Kin 4:28
s as the gazelles	1 Chr 12:8
race is not to the s	Eccl 9:11
riding on a s cloud	Is 19:1

s to shed blood   Rom 3:15

SWINDLER *cheater*

cursed be the s	Mal 1:14
a drunkard, or a s	1 Cor 5:11
revilers, nor s-s	1 Cor 6:10

SWINE *pig*

gold in a s-'s snout	Prov 11:22
Who eat s-'s flesh	Is 65:4
your pearls before s	Matt 7:6
Send us into the s	Mark 5:12

SWORD *weapon with blade*

flaming s...turned	Gen 3:24
by your s you shall	Gen 27:40
the s shall bereave	Deut 32:25
A s for the LORD	Judg 7:20
s devour forever	2 Sam 2:26
fell on his s	1 Chr 10:5
tongue a sharp s	Ps 57:4
as a two-edged s	Prov 5:4
teeth are *like* s-s	Prov 30:14
s against nation	Is 2:4
the power of the s	Jer 18:21
abolish...the s	Hos 2:18
s-s into plowshares	Mic 4:3
perish by the s	Matt 26:52
s of the Spirit	Eph 6:17
than any two-edged s	Heb 4:12
s of My mouth	Rev 2:16

SYCAMORE *tree*

olive and s trees	1 Chr 27:28
plentiful as s-s	2 Chr 1:15
grower of s figs	Amos 7:14
climbed up into a s	Luke 19:4

SYCHAR

town in Samaria	John 4:5
also **Shechem**	

SYMPATHY *mutual feeling*

I looked for s	Ps 69:20
s to the prisoners	Heb 10:34

SYNAGOGUE *assembly*

pray in the s-s	Matt 6:5
He went into their s	Matt 12:9
flogged in the s-s	Mark 13:9
chief seats in...s-s	Luke 20:46
outcasts from the s	John 16:2
taught in s-s	John 18:20
reasoning in the s	Acts 17:17
but are a s of Satan	Rev 2:9

SYRIA

NE of Israel
Matt 4:24; Acts 15:23,41;20:3
see also **ARAM**

T

TAANACH

Canaanite royal city
Josh 12:21;21:25; Judg 5:19

TABERNACLE *assembly and
area for sacrificial worship*

*dwelling place of God among the
Israelites* Ex 25:8
construction directed by God
Ex 25:9
contained Ark of the Covenant
Ex 25:10

**phrases used in connection
with the tabernacle:**
house of the LORD
Ex 23:19;34:26; Deut 23:18
tabernacle of the house of God
1 Chr 6:48
tabernacle of the tent of meeting
Ex 39:40;40:6,29
tabernacle or tent of the testimony
Ex 38:21; Num 1:50,53
tent of meeting
Ex 29:32;30:26;
38:30,43;40:2,6,7

TABITHA
see **DORCAS**

TABLE *furniture*

gold t before the LORD	Lev 24:6
Thou doest prepare a t	Ps 23:5
crumbs...master's t	Matt 15:27
t-s...moneychangers	Matt 21:12
dogs under the t	Mark 7:28
drink at My t	Luke 22:30
in order to serve t-s	Acts 6:2
t of the Lord	1 Cor 10:21

TABLET *writing surface*

give you the stone t-s	Ex 24:12
t-s of the testimony	Ex 31:18
the t of their heart	Jer 17:1
t-s of human hearts	2 Cor 3:3

TABOR

1	*mountain*	Judg 4:6,12
2	*city in Zebulun*	1 Chr 6:77
3	*oak in Benjamin*	1 Sam 10:3

TAHPANHES

Egyptian city Jer 2:16
place where Jeremiah escaped
Jer 43:7-9;44:1

TAHPENES

queen of Egypt 1 Kin 11:19,20

TAIL

grasp *it* by its t	Ex 4:4
the foxes t to t	Judg 15:4
cuts off head and t	Is 9:14
t-s like scorpions	Rev 9:10

TAKE *get, grasp*

t...the tree of life	Gen 3:22
T My yoke upon	Matt 11:29
T, eat; this is My	Matt 26:26
t up your pallet	Mark 2:9
t-s away the sin	John 1:29
day that He was t-n	Acts 1:22

TALENT

measure of weight
Ex 38:27; 2 Sam 12:30;
1 Chr 20:2
measure of money
1 Kin 20:39;
Matt 18:24;25:15,25

TALK (n) *conversation, speech*

argue with useless t	Job 15:3
no...silly t	Eph 5:4
their t will spread	2 Tim 2:17

TALK (v) *converse, speak*

God t-ed with him	Gen 17:3
lips t of trouble	Prov 24:2
who t about you	Ezek 33:30
Paul kept on t-ing	Acts 20:9

TALL *high*

cut..its t cedars	2 Kin 19:23
a nation t and smooth	Is 18:2
grew up, became t	Ezek 16:7

TAMAR

1	*Judah's daughter-in-law*	
		Gen 38:6ff
2	*daughter of David*	2 Sam 13:1
3	*daughter of Absalom*	
		2 Sam 14:27
4	*town near the Dead Sea*	
	1 Kin 9:18; Ezek 47:19;48:28	

TAMARISK *tree*

a t tree at Beersheba	Gen 21:33
under the t tree	1 Sam 22:6

TAMBOURINE

accompanied by...t	Is 5:12
gaiety of t-s ceases	Is 24:8

TAMMUZ

Mesopotamian god Ezek 8:14

TARES *weeds*

t...among the wheat	Matt 13:25
gather up the t	Matt 13:30
parable of the t	Matt 13:36

TARSHISH

1	*lineage of Japheth*	Gen 10:4
2	*ships of*	
	1 Kin 10:22;22:48; 2 Chr 9:21;	
		Ps 48:7
3	*line of Benjamin*	1 Chr 7:6-10
4	*Persian official*	Esth 1:14
5	*city*	Is 66:19; Jon 1:3

TARSUS

birthplace of Paul	Acts 21:39
capital of Cilicia	Acts 22:3

TASKMASTERS *overseers*

appointed t over them	Ex 1:11
Pharaoh commanded...t	Ex 5:6

TASTE *test flavor*

As the palate t-s	Job 34:3
O t and see	Ps 34:8
shall not t death	Matt 16:28
t death for everyone	Heb 2:9
t-d...heavenly gift	Heb 6:4

TASTELESS *without taste*

Can something t be	Job 6:6
salt has become t	Matt 5:13

TAUNT *object of ridicule*

a t among all	Deut 28:37
I have become their t	Job 30:9

TAX *charge, tribute*

a t for the LORD	Num 31:28
money for the king's t	Neh 5:4
sitting in the t office	Matt 9:9
pay t-es to Caesar	Luke 20:22
t to whom t *is* due	Rom 13:7

TAX-GATHERER *tax collector*

t-s do the same	Matt 5:46
many **t-s** and sinners	Matt 9:10
Matthew the **t**	Matt 10:3
a friend of **t-s**	Matt 11:19
he was a chief **t**	Luke 19:2

TEACH *instruct*

t you what...to say	Ex 4:12
t them the good way	1 Kin 8:36
Can anyone **t** God	Job 21:22
T me Thy paths	Ps 25:4
T me to do Thy will	Ps 143:10
would He **t** knowledge	Is 28:9
He *began* to **t** them	Matt 5:2
t-ing...in parables	Mark 4:2
Lord, **t** us to pray	Luke 11:1
Spirit will **t** you	Luke 12:12
He will **t** you all	John 14:26
t strange doctrines	1 Tim 1:3
allow a woman to **t**	1 Tim 2:12
she **t-es** and leads	Rev 2:20

TEACHER *instructor*

will behold your **T**	Is 30:20
T, I will follow You	Matt 8:19
not above his **t**	Matt 10:24
why trouble the **T**	Mark 5:35
the **t** of Israel	John 3:10
call Me **T** and Lord	John 13:13
t of the immature	Rom 2:20
as pastors and **t-s**	Eph 4:11
t of the Gentiles	1 Tim 2:7
false **t-s** among you	2 Pet 2:1

TEACHING (n) *instruction*

t drop as the rain	Deut 32:2
your mother's **t**	Prov 1:8
amazed at His **t**	Matt 7:28
My **t** is not Mine	John 7:16
contrary to sound **t**	1 Tim 1:10

TEAR *crying*

have seen your **t-s**	2 Kin 20:5
my **t-s** in Thy bottle	Ps 56:8
sow in **t-s** shall reap	Ps 126:5
drench you with my **t-s**	Is 16:9
eyes a fountain of **t-s**	Jer 9:1
His feet with her **t-s**	Luke 7:38
God...wipe every **t**	Rev 7:17

TEBETH

name of the tenth month in
Hebrew calendar   Esth 2:16

TEL-ABIB

place in Babylonia   Ezek 3:15
Jewish exiles located there

TELL *relate, speak*

not **t** the riddle	Judg 14:14
T of His glory	1 Chr 16:24
t of Thy righteousness	Ps 71:15
t-s lies will perish	Prov 19:9
t you great and mighty	Jer 33:3
See that you **t** no one	Matt 8:4
t you about Me	John 18:34
t you the mystery	Rev 17:7

TEMA

1 *son of Ishmael*	Gen 25:15
2 *town in Arabia*	
	Job 6:19; Is 21:14

TEMPER *anger*

always loses his **t**	Prov 29:11
the ruler's **t** rises	Eccl 10:4

TEMPEST *storm*

bruises me with a **t**	Job 9:17
stormy wind *and* **t**	Ps 55:8
t of destruction	Is 28:2
on the day of **t**	Amos 1:14

TEMPLE *structure for worship*

doorpost of the **t**	1 Sam 1:9
t is not for man	1 Chr 29:1
LORD is in His holy **t**	Ps 11:4
meditate in His **t**	Ps 27:4
t of the LORD	Jer 7:4
pinnacle of the **t**	Matt 4:5
will destroy this **t**	Mark 14:58
veil of the **t**	Luke 23:45
Destroy this **t**, and	John 2:19
you are a **t** of God	1 Cor 3:16
t of the Holy Spirit	1 Cor 6:19
his seat in the **t**	2 Thess 2:4
the Lamb, are its **t**	Rev 21:22

TEMPT *test, try*

And **t-ed** God in the	Ps 106:14
being **t-ed** by Satan	Mark 1:13
lest Satan **t** you	1 Cor 7:5
t-ed beyond what	1 Cor 10:13
Himself does not **t**	James 1:13

TEMPTATION *testing, trial*

not lead us into **t**	Matt 6:13
not enter into **t**	Matt 26:41
time of **t** fall away	Luke 8:13
t has overtaken you	1 Cor 10:13
the godly from **t**	2 Pet 2:9

TEN *number*

T Commandments	Deut 10:4
it had **t** horns	Dan 7:7
has the **t** talents	Matt 25:28

TEND *take care of*

t his father's flock	1 Sam 17:15
He will **t** His flock	Is 40:11
T My lambs	John 21:15
T My sheep	John 21:17

TENDER *gentle, young*

t and choice calf	Gen 18:7
your heart was **t**	2 Kin 22:19
like a **t** shoot	Is 53:2
t mercy of our God	Luke 1:78

TENT *mobile shelter*

Abram moved his **t**	Gen 13:18
man, living in **t-s**	Gen 25:27
your **t-s**, O Israel	1 Kin 12:16
t-s of the destroyers	Job 12:6
dwell in Thy **t** forever	Ps 61:4
grumbled in their **t-s**	Ps 106:25
Like a shepherd's **t**	Is 38:12

TENT OF MEETING

perhaps the same as the
Tabernacle or at certain periods a
separate meeting place
    Ex 33:7; Lev 1:1; Num 7:5;
               Josh 18:1
see also **TABERNACLE**

TENT OF TESTIMONY

see **TABERNACLE**

TERAH

father of Abraham
    Gen 11:24; Num 33:27;
               Luke 3:34

TERAPHIM

household gods, idols
    2 Kin 23:24; Zech 10:2

TERRIBLE *dreadful*

and **t** wilderness	Deut 8:15
t day of the LORD	Mal 4:5
into **t** convulsions	Mark 9:26

TERRIFY *frighten*

t-ied by the sword	1 Chr 21:30
t me by visions	Job 7:14
t them with Thy storm	Ps 83:15
t you by my letters	2 Cor 10:9

TERRITORY *country, land*

smite your whole **t**	Ex 8:2
God enlarges your **t**	Deut 19:8
t of...inheritance	Josh 19:10
will possess the **t**	Obad 19

TERROR *intense fear*

Sounds of **t** are in	Job 15:21
t-s of thick darkness	Job 24:17
t-s of Sheol came	Ps 116:3
meditate on **t**	Is 33:18
t-s and great signs	Luke 21:11

TERTIUS

Paul's scribe   Rom 16:22

TEST (n) *trial*

put God to the **t**	Ps 78:18
put Him to the **t**	Luke 10:25
you fail the **t**	2 Cor 13:5

TEST (v) *try*

God **t-ed** Abraham	Gen 22:1
Why do you **t** the LORD	Ex 17:2
she came to **t** him	1 Kin 10:1
T my mind and my	Ps 26:2
word of God is **t-ed**	Prov 30:5
Spirit...to the **t**	Acts 5:9
fire itself will **t**	1 Cor 3:13
t the spirits to see	1 John 4:1

TESTIFY *give witness*

nor shall you **t**	Ex 23:2
them **t** against him	1 Kin 21:10
I will **t** against you	Ps 50:7
our sins **t** against us	Is 59:12
Jesus Himself **t-ied**	John 4:44

TESTIMONY *witness*

into the ark the **t**	Ex 25:16
two tablets of the **t**	Ex 31:18
t of the LORD is sure	Ps 19:7
t-ies are righteous	Ps 119:144
Bind up the **t**	Is 8:16
t against Jesus	Matt 26:59
t of two men is true	John 8:17
t concerning Christ	1 Cor 1:6
ashamed of the **t**	2 Tim 1:8
This **t** is true	Titus 1:13

TETRARCH
governor of a region
    Matt 14:1; Luke 3:1,19;
    Acts 13:1

THADDAEUS
apostle   Matt 10:3; Mark 3:18

THANK (v) *express gratitude*
my song I shall t Him	Ps 28:7
God, I t Thee	Luke 18:11
I t God always	1 Cor 1:4

THANKS (n) *gratitude*
give t to the LORD	1 Chr 16:7
It is good to give t	Ps 92:1
giving t, He broke	Matt 15:36
a cup and given t	Matt 26:27
But t be to God	Rom 6:17
not cease giving t	Eph 1:16
always to give t	2 Thess 1:3

THANKSGIVING *gratitude*
the sacrifice of t	Lev 7:12
with the voice of t	Ps 26:7
His presence with t	Ps 95:2
supplication with t	Phil 4:6
t and honor and	Rev 7:12

THEBES
Egyptian city
    Jer 46:25; Ezek 30:14-16

THEFT *robbery*
be sold for his t	Ex 22:3
t-s, murders	Mark 7:21

THEOPHILUS
addressee of Luke's gospel and
Acts   Luke 1:3; Acts 1:1

THESSALONICA
Macedonian city
    Acts 27:2; Phil 4:16
visited by Paul   Acts 17:1,11,13

THICKET *underbrush*
ram caught in the t	Gen 22:13
the t of the Jordan	Jer 50:44

THIEF *robber*
that t shall die	Deut 24:7
partner with a t	Prov 29:24
companions of t-ves	Is 1:23
enter...like a t	Joel 2:9
t comes...to steal	John 10:10
a t in the night	1 Thess 5:2

THIGH *part of leg*
hand under my t	Gen 24:2
socket of Jacob's t	Gen 32:25
Thy sword on *Thy* t	Ps 45:3
on His t...a name	Rev 19:16

THIN *lean*
t ears scorched	Gen 41:27
t yellowish hair	Lev 13:30
streams...will t out	Is 19:6

THINK *ponder, reflect*
as he t-s...so he is	Prov 23:7
not t...to abolish	Matt 5:17
not to t more highly	Rom 12:3
t as a child	1 Cor 13:11

t-s he is something	Gal 6:3
beyond all that we...t	Eph 3:20

THIRD *number*
morning, a t day	Gen 1:13
raised...the t day	Matt 16:21
raised on the t day	1 Cor 15:4
to the t heaven	2 Cor 12:2

THIRST (n) *craving, dryness*
for my t...vinegar	Ps 69:21
donkeys quench...t	Ps 104:11
not hunger or t	Is 49:10
in Me shall never t	John 6:35
no more, neither t	Rev 7:16

THIRST (v) *have a craving*
My soul t-s for God	Ps 42:2
Every one who t-s, come	Is 55:1
t for righteousness	Matt 5:6

THIRSTY *lacking water*
satisfied the t soul	Ps 107:9
In a dry and t land	Ezek 19:13
I was t, and you	Matt 25:35
If any man is t	John 7:37
one who is t come	Rev 22:17

THOMAS
apostle
    Matt 10:3; Mark 3:18; Luke
    6:15
doubted Jesus' resurrection
    John 20:24-28

THORN *sharp point*
Both t-s and thistles	Gen 3:18
as t-s in your sides	Num 33:55
as a hedge of t-s	Prov 15:19
lily among the t-s	Song 2:2
have reaped t-s	Jer 12:13
fell among the t-s	Matt 13:7
a crown of t-s	Matt 27:29
a burning t bush	Acts 7:30
t in the flesh	2 Cor 12:7

THOUGHT *concept, idea*
t-s of his heart	Gen 6:5
knows the t-s of man	Ps 94:11
My t-s are not your t-s	Is 55:8
Jesus knowing...t-s	Matt 9:4
heart come evil t-s	Matt 15:19
every t captive	2 Cor 10:5

THREAD *string*
cord of scarlet t	Josh 2:18
lips...a scarlet t	Song 4:3

THREE *number*
Job's t friends	Job 2:11
or t have gathered	Matt 18:20
deny Me t times	Matt 26:34
t days I will raise	John 2:19

THRESH *beat out*
ox while he is t-ing	Deut 25:4
like dust at t-ing	2 Kin 13:7
will t the mountains	Is 41:15
Arise and t	Mic 4:13

THRESHING FLOOR
winnows...at the t	Ruth 3:2
David bought...t	2 Sam 24:24
clear His t	Matt 3:12

THROAT *part of neck*
t is an open grave	Ps 5:9
my t is parched	Ps 69:3
has enlarged its t	Is 5:14
t is an open grave	Rom 3:13

THRONE *seat of sovereign*
sitting on His t	1 Kin 22:19
LORD's t is in heaven	Ps 11:4
Thy t is established	Ps 93:2
it is the t of God	Matt 5:34
sit upon twelve t-s	Matt 19:28
Thy t...is forever	Heb 1:8
to the t of grace	Heb 4:16
a great white t	Rev 20:11

THRUST *cast, push*
He shall t them out	Josh 23:5
t away like thorns	2 Sam 23:6
Nor to t aside	Prov 18:5
LORD has t...down	Jer 46:15

THUMMIM
kept in high priest's breastplate for
determining will of God
    Ex 28:30; Lev 8:8; Deut 33:8;
    Ezra 2:63; Neh 7:65

THUNDER (n)
LORD sent...t	Ex 9:23
But His mighty t	Job 26:14
the hiding place of t	Ps 81:7
be punished with t	Is 29:6
sound of loud t	Rev 14:2

THUNDER (v)
t in the heavens	1 Sam 2:10
you t with a voice	Job 40:9
LORD also t-ed	Ps 18:13

THYATIRA
city in Asia minor
home of Lydia   Acts 16:14
early church   Rev 1:11;2:18,24

TIBERIAS
city on W shore of Sea of Galilee
    John 6:23
Sea of   John 6:1;21:1
also **Sea of Chinnereth**
also **Sea of Galilee**
also **Lake of Gennesaret**

TIBERIUS
Roman emperor   Luke 3:1
see also **CAESAR**

TIDINGS *information, news*
t of His salvation	1 Chr 16:23
not fear evil t	Ps 112:7
bring glad t of good	Rom 10:15

TIGLATH-PILESER
Assyrian king
    2 Kin 15:29;16:7,10
also **Pul**
also **Tilgath-Pilneser**

TIGRIS
Mesopotamian river
    Gen 2:14; Dan 10:4

TILGATH-PILNESER
Assyrian king
    1 Chr 5:6,26; 2 Chr 28:20

TILLER

also **Pul**
also **Tiglath-Pileser**

TILLER *cultivator*

Cain was a t	Gen 4:2
a t of the ground	Zech 13:5

TIMBER *wood*

cedar and cypress t	1 Kin 9:11
whatever t you need	2 Chr 2:16
t of Lebanon	Song 3:9

TIMBREL *musical instrument*

with songs, with t	Gen 31:27
strike the t	Ps 81:2
Praise Him with t	Ps 150:4

TIME *day, period, season*

in t-s of trouble	Ps 9:9
t-s are in Thy hand	Ps 31:15
for a t, t-s, and half	Dan 12:7
t to seek the LORD	Hos 10:12
signs of the t-s	Matt 16:3
My t is at hand	Matt 26:18
deny Me three t-s	Luke 22:61
My t is not yet	John 7:6
not...you to know t-s	Acts 1:7
is the acceptable t	2 Cor 6:2
grace...in t of need	Heb 4:16
for the t is near	Rev 1:3

TIMOTHY

companion of Paul
Acts 17:15;18:5; Phil 1:1; Col
1:1; Heb 13:23

TIRED *weary*

I am t of living	Gen 27:46
run and not get t	Is 40:31

TIRZAH

1 *daughter of Zelophehad*
Num 26:33;27:1;36:11
2 *royal Canaanite city*
1 Kin 14:17; 2 Kin 15:14

TISHBITE

town identity of Elijah
1 Kin 17:1;21:17; 2 Kin 1:3,8

TITHE (n) *tenth*

all the t of the land	Lev 27:30
a t of the t	Num 18:26
the t of your grain	Deut 12:17
t into the storehouse	Mal 3:10;
t-s of all that I get	Luke 18:12
mortal men receive t-s	Heb 7:8

TITHE (v) *pay a tithe*

shall surely t all	Deut 14:22
you t mint and dill	Matt 23:23

TITUS

co-worker with Paul
2 Cor 2:13;8:23; Gal 2:1

TODAY *present time*

t you...be with Me	Luke 23:43
same yesterday and t	Heb 13:8

TOGARMAH

grandson of Japheth
Gen 10:1-3; 1 Chr 1:6

TOIL (n) *labor, work*

the t of our hands	Gen 5:29
t is not *in* vain	1 Cor 15:58

TOIL (v) *work hard*

I have t-ed in vain	Is 49:4
they do not t nor	Matt 6:28

TOMB *grave, sepulchre*

from womb to t	Job 10:19
you have hewn a t	Is 22:16
like whitewashed t-s	Matt 23:27
laid Him in a t	Mark 15:46
Lazarus out of the t	John 12:17
outside the t	John 20:11

TOMORROW *future time*

not boast about t	Prov 27:1
for t we may die	Is 22:13
not be anxious for t	Matt 6:34

TONGUE *speech, talk*

speech and slow of t	Ex 4:10
flatter with their t	Ps 5:9
their t a sharp sword	Ps 57:4
a lying t	Prov 6:17
t of the wise	Prov 12:18
soft t breaks...bone	Prov 25:15
His t is like...fire	Is 30:27
t is a deadly arrow	Jer 9:8
impediment of his t	Mark 7:35
and his t loosed	Luke 1:64
no one...tame the t	James 3:8

TONGUE *language*

speak with new t-s	Mark 16:17
speak with other t-s	Acts 2:4
t-s of men...angels	1 Cor 13:1
if I pray in a t	1 Cor 14:14
every tribe and t	Rev 5:9

TOOL *work instrument*

among your t-s	Deut 23:13
nor any iron t	1 Kin 6:7
iron into a cutting t	Is 44:12

TOOTH

teeth white from	Gen 49:12
eye for eye, t for t	Ex 21:24
and a t for a t	Matt 5:38

TOPAZ *precious stone*

ruby, t, and emerald	Ex 39:10
t of Ethiopia	Job 28:19
the ninth, t	Rev 21:20

TOPHETH

site of Baal worship in Hinnom
Valley 2 Kin 23:10;
Jer 7:31,32;19:6,12,14

TORMENT (n) *pain, torture*

this place of t	Luke 16:28
their t was like	Rev 9:5
the fear of her t	Rev 18:15

TORMENT (v) *annoy, harass*

long will you t me	Job 19:2
t us before the time	Matt 8:29
do not t me	Luke 8:28

TORRENT *flood*

The ancient t	Judg 5:21
t-s of destruction	2 Sam 22:5

t-s of ungodliness	Ps 18:4
like an overflowing t	Is 30:28

TOUCH *feel, handle*

not eat...or t it	Gen 3:3
an angel t-ing him	1 Kin 19:5
evil will not t you	Job 5:19
not t My anointed	Ps 105:15
T nothing unclean	Is 52:11
t the fringe of His	Matt 14:36
not to t a woman	1 Cor 7:1

TOWER *fortress structure*

t whose top *will* reach	Gen 11:4
Count her t-s	Ps 48:12
name...strong t	Prov 18:10
and built a t	Matt 21:33

TOWN *city, village*

many unwalled t-s	Deut 3:5
founds a t with	Hab 2:12
except in his home t	Matt 13:57

TRADE (n) *business, occupation*

abundance of your t	Ezek 28:16
of the same t	Acts 18:3

TRADE (v) *buy or sell*

may t in the land	Gen 42:34
t-d with them	Matt 25:16

TRADERS *merchants*

Midianite t passed	Gen 37:28
king's t procured	2 Chr 1:16
in a city of t	Ezek 17:4
increased your t	Nah 3:16

TRADITION *custom*

sake of your t	Matt 15:3
hold to the t of men	Mark 7:8
hold...to the t-s	1 Cor 11:2
my ancestral t-s	Gal 1:14

TRAIN *guide, instruct*

T up a child	Prov 22:6
will they t for war	Mic 4:3
t-ed to discern good	Heb 5:14
heart t-ed in greed	2 Pet 2:14

TRAMPLE *crush, hurt*

t-s down the waves	Job 9:8
let him t my life	Ps 7:5
didst t the nations	Hab 3:12
Jerusalem...t-d	Luke 21:24

TRANCE *daze, dream*

he fell into a t	Acts 10:10
in a t I saw a vision	Acts 11:5
fell into a t	Acts 22:17

TRANSFIGURED *changed*

He was t before them Matt 17:2

TRANSFORM *change*

t-ed by the renewing	Rom 12:2
t-ed into the same	2 Cor 3:18
who will t the body	Phil 3:21

TRANSGRESS *break, overstep*

you t the covenant	Josh 23:16
rulers also t-ed	Jer 2:8
they t-ed laws	Is 24:5
disciples t the	Matt 15:2

TRANSGRESSION *trespass, sin*

forgives iniquity, t	Ex 34:7
I am pure, without t	Job 33:9
I know my t-s	Ps 51:3
removed our t-s from	Ps 103:12
love covers all t-s	Prov 10:12
pierced...for our t-s	Is 53:5
not forgive your t-s	Matt 6:15
dead in our t-s	Eph 2:5

TRANSGRESSOR *sinner*

teach t-s Thy ways	Ps 51:13
numbered with the t-s	Is 53:12
a t of the law	James 2:11

TRANSLATED

t and read before me	Ezra 4:18
Immanuel...t means	Matt 1:23
Golgotha, which is t	Mark 15:22
Messiah...t means	John 1:41

TRAP (n) *snare*

a snare and a t	Josh 23:13
hidden a t for me	Ps 142:3
table become...a t	Rom 11:9

TRAP (v) *catch*

they might t Him	Matt 22:15
in order to t Him	Mark 12:13

TRAVAIL *intense pain*

t-ed nor given birth	Is 23:4
woman is in t	John 16:21

TRAVEL *journey*

t by day and by night	Ex 13:21
who t on the road	Judg 5:10
Jesus...*began* t-ing	Luke 24:15

TREACHEROUS *traitorous*

I behold the t	Ps 119:158
t will be uprooted	Prov 2:22
way of the t is hard	Prov 13:15

TREAD *walk on*

They t wine presses	Job 24:11
as the potter t-s clay	Is 41:25
t upon serpents	Luke 10:19
t-s the wine press	Rev 19:15

TREASURE (n) *valuable thing*

t-s of the sand	Deut 33:19
the LORD is his t	Is 33:6
opening their t-s	Matt 2:11
for where your t is	Matt 6:21
have t in heaven	Matt 19:21
t in earthen vessels	2 Cor 4:7
stored up your t	James 5:3

TREASURE (v) *value greatly*

I have t-d the words	Job 23:12
Thy word have I t-d	Ps 119:11
t my commandments	Prov 7:1

TREASURY *place of valuables*

t of the LORD	Josh 6:19
paid from the royal t	Ezra 6:4
fill their t-ies	Prov 8:21
into the temple t	Matt 27:6

TREATY *agreement, contract*

Let there be a t	1 Kin 15:19
go, break your t	2 Chr 16:3

TREE *woody plant*

fruit t-s bearing	Gen 1:11
t of life	Gen 2:9
gave me from the t	Gen 3:12
hang him on a t	Deut 21:22
said to the olive t	Judg 9:8
t *firmly* planted	Ps 1:3
she is a t of life	Prov 3:18
Beneath the apple t	Song 8:5
like a t planted by	Jer 17:8
under his fig t	Mic 4:4
good t bears good	Matt 7:17
the fig t withered	Matt 21:19
a sycamore t	Luke 19:4
autumn t-s without	Jude 12
eat of the t of life	Rev 2:7

TREMBLE *shake*

T before Him	1 Chr 16:30
pillars of heaven t	Job 26:11
T, and do not sin	Ps 4:4
make the heavens t	Is 13:13
His soul t-s	Is 15:4
my inward parts t-d	Hab 3:16

TREMBLING (n) *fear, reverence*

rejoice with t	Ps 2:11
eat...with t	Ezek 12:18
with fear and t	Phil 2:12

TRESPASS *fault, sin*

Saul died for his t	1 Chr 10:13
caught in any t	Gal 6:1
dead in your t-es	Eph 2:1

TRIAL *testing*

if we are on t today	Acts 4:9
which was a t to you	Gal 4:14
perseveres under t	James 1:12

TRIBE *common ancestry*

twelve t-s of Israel	Gen 49:28
a man of each t	Num 1:4
t-s of the LORD	Ps 122:4
judging...twelve t-s	Luke 22:30
men from every t	Rev 5:9

TRIBULATION *affliction*

will be a great t	Matt 24:21
world you have t	John 16:33
exult in our t-s	Rom 5:3
my t-s on your behalf	Eph 3:13
out of the great t	Rev 7:14

TRIBUNAL *court*

before Caesar's t	Acts 25:10

TRIBUTE *tax*

sons of Israel sent t	Judg 3:15
impose a...t or toll	Ezra 7:24
exact a t of grain	Amos 5:11

TRIGON *musical instrument*

sound of...lyre, t	Dan 3:5

TRIUMPH *victory*

the righteous t	Prov 28:12
His t in Christ	2 Cor 2:14
mercy t-s over	James 2:13

TROAS

city in Asia Minor	Acts 16:8,11
visited by Paul	
	Acts 20:5; 2 Cor 2:12

TROPHIMUS

companion of Paul	
	Acts 20:4; 2 Tim 4:20
Ephesian Christian	Acts 21:29

TROUBLE (n) *affliction*

forget all my t	Gen 41:51
man is born for t	Job 5:7
Look upon...my t	Ps 25:18
very present help in t	Ps 46:1
remember his t no	Prov 31:7
t is heavy upon him	Eccl 8:6
day has enough t	Matt 6:34

TROUBLE (v) *bother, disturb*

t you in the land	Num 33:55
t-s his own house	Prov 11:29
also t the hearts	Ezek 32:9
Herod...was t-d	Matt 2:3
why t the Teacher	Mark 5:35
your heart be t-d	John 14:1

TROUBLED (adj) *disturbed*

songs to a t heart	Prov 25:20
soul has become t	John 12:27

TRUE *actual, real, reliable*

gets a t reward	Prov 11:18
There was the t light	John 1:9
gives you...t bread	John 6:32
let God be found t	Rom 3:4
signs of a t apostle	2 Cor 12:12
This testimony is t	Titus 1:13
t grace of God	1 Pet 5:12
faithful and t Witness	Rev 3:14

TRUMPET *wind instrument*

t-s of rams' horns	Josh 6:6
t-s...empty pitchers	Judg 7:16
Praise Him with t	Ps 150:3
do not sound a t	Matt 6:2
at the last t	1 Cor 15:52
voice like...a t	Rev 1:10

TRUST (n) *confidence, hope*

whose t a spider's web	Job 8:14
In God...put my t	Ps 56:11
put My t in Him	Heb 2:13

TRUST (v) *commit to*

t in the LORD	Ps 4:5
Than to t in man	Ps 118:8
t-s in his riches	Prov 11:28
not t in a neighbor	Mic 7:5
not t in ourselves	2 Cor 1:9

TRUSTWORTHY *reliable*

who can find a t	Prov 20:6
It is a t statement	1 Tim 3:1

TRUTH *genuineness, honesty*

walk before Me in t	1 Kin 2:4
speaks t in his heart	Ps 15:2
Thy word is t	Ps 119:160
Buy t, and do not	Prov 23:23
judge with t	Zech 8:16
full of grace and t	John 1:14
worship in...t	John 4:24
t shall make you free	John 8:32
the way, and the t	John 14:6
exchanged the t of	Rom 1:25
t of the gospel	Gal 2:5
speaking the t in love	Eph 4:15

the word of t　　　　2 Tim 2:15
the t is not in us　　　1 John 1:8

TUBAL

1 *son of Japheth*　　　Gen 10:2
2 *land ruled by Gog*
　　　　　　　　　Ezek 38:3;39:1

TUBAL-CAIN

son of Zillah　　　　Gen 4:22
inventor of cutting tools

TUMULT *disturbance*

t of the peoples　　　Ps 65:7
A sound of t　　　　Is 13:4
t of waters　　　　Jer 51:16

TUNIC *cloak, garment*

a varicolored t　　　Gen 37:3
the holy linen t　　　Lev 16:4
or even two t-s　　　Matt 10:10

TURBAN *headdress*

a t of fine linen　　　Ex 28:39
justice was like...a t　Job 29:14
Remove the t　　　Ezek 21:26

TURMOIL *tumult*

treasure and t with　Prov 15:16
rest from your...t　　Is 14:3
ill repute, full of t　Ezek 22:5

TURN *change or move*

not t to mediums　　Lev 19:31
leave you *or* t back　Ruth 1:16
T from your evil　　2 Kin 17:13
forget, nor t away　Prov 4:5
T to Me, and be saved　Is 45:22
t-ed to his own way　Is 53:6
t their mourning into　Jer 31:13
t...shame into praise　Zeph 3:19
t from darkness to　Acts 26:18
he who t-s a sinner　James 5:20
t away from evil　　1 Pet 3:11

TURTLEDOVE *bird*

t for a sin offering　Lev 12:6
the voice of the t　　Song 2:12

TUTOR *teacher*

t-s in Christ　　　1 Cor 4:15
Law...become our t　Gal 3:24

TWELVE *number*

t tribes of Israel　　Gen 49:28
summoned His t　　Matt 10:1
t legions of angels　Matt 26:53
when He became t　Luke 2:42
a crown of t stars　Rev 12:1

TWILIGHT *darkness, dusk*

lamb...offer at t　　Ex 29:39
waits for the t　　　Job 24:15
midday as in the t　Is 59:10

TWINKLING *flicker*

in the t of an eye　1 Cor 15:52

TWINS *pair, two*

t in her womb　　　Gen 25:24
T of a gazelle　　　Song 4:5

TWO-EDGED *with two edges*

than any t sword　Heb 4:12
His mouth...t sword　Rev 1:16

TYRE

Phoenician seaport
　　　Josh 19:29; Ezek 27:3;
　　　Matt 15:21; Acts 21:3

U

UGLY *unsightly*

u and gaunt cows　　Gen 41:4
seven lean...u cows　Gen 41:27

UNBELIEF *lack of faith*

wondered at their u　Mark 6:6
help my u　　　　Mark 9:24
continue in their u　Rom 11:23

UNBELIEVER *non-believer*

a place with the u-s　Luke 12:46
wife who is an u　　1 Cor 7:12
ungifted men or u-s　1 Cor 14:23
bound...with u-s　　2 Cor 6:14
worse than an u　　1 Tim 5:8

UNBELIEVING *doubting*

O u generation　　　Mark 9:19
u husband is　　　1 Cor 7:14
blinded the...u　　　2 Cor 4:4
evil, u heart　　　Heb 3:12

UNBLEMISHED *without defect*

shall be an u male　Ex 12:5
u and spotless　　1 Pet 1:19

UNCEASING *continuous*

u complaint in his　Job 33:19
sorrow and u grief　Rom 9:2

UNCHANGEABLENESS

the u of His purpose　Heb 6:17

UNCIRCUMCISED

But an u male　　　Gen 17:14
u heart...humbled　Lev 26:41
the nations are u　Jer 9:26
who is physically u　Rom 2:27
the gospel to the u　Gal 2:7

UNCIRCUMCISION

has become u　　　Rom 2:25
who are called U　Eph 2:11
the u of your flesh　Col 2:13

UNCLEAN *not clean or not holy*

touches any u thing　Lev 5:2
u in their practices　Ps 106:39
man of u lips　　　Is 6:5
authority over u　Matt 10:1
u spirits entered　Mark 5:13
eaten anything...u　Acts 10:14
nothing is in itself　Rom 14:14

UNCONTENTIOUS

gentle, u, free from　1 Tim 3:3
be u, gentle　　　Titus 3:2

UNCOVER *expose*

to u her nakedness　Lev 18:7
u his feet and　　　Ruth 3:4
head u-ed while　1 Cor 11:5

UNDEFILED *uncorrupted*

holy, innocent, u　Heb 7:26
marriage bed *be* u　Heb 13:4
pure and u religion　James 1:27

imperishable and u　1 Pet 1:4

UNDERGARMENTS

u next to his flesh　Lev 6:10
linen u shall be on　Ezek 44:18

UNDERGO *experience*

Holy One to u decay　Ps 16:10
should not u decay　Ps 49:9
did not u decay　　Acts 13:37

UNDERSTAND *comprehend*

u-s every intent　　1 Chr 28:9
To u a proverb　　Prov 1:6
do not u justice　　Prov 28:5
Who can u it　　　Jer 17:9
u that the vision　Dan 8:17
Hear, and u　　　Matt 15:10
to u the Scriptures　Luke 24:45
Why do you not u　John 8:43
none who u-s　　Rom 3:11
things hard to u　2 Pet 3:16

UNDERSTANDING

a wise and u people　Deut 4:6
servant an u heart　1 Kin 3:9
Holy One is u　　Prov 9:10

UNDISCIPLINED

in an u manner　　2 Thess 3:7
leading an u life　2 Thess 3:11

UNDISTURBED *peaceful*

land was u for forty　Judg 8:28
an u habitation　　Is 33:20

UNFADING *lasting*

u crown of glory　1 Pet 5:4

UNFAITHFUL

u to her husband　Num 5:27
very u to the LORD　2 Chr 28:19
u to our God　　　Ezra 10:2

UNFAITHFULNESS *faithless*

u...they committed　Lev 26:40
to Babylon for their u　1 Chr 9:1
the u of the exiles　Ezra 9:4

UNFATHOMABLE

How...u His ways　Rom 11:33
u riches of Christ　Eph 3:8

UNFRUITFUL *not productive*

the land is u　　　2 Kin 2:19
my mind is u　　1 Cor 14:14
u deeds of darkness　Eph 5:11

UNGODLINESS *sinfulness*

torrents of u terrified　Ps 18:4
remove u...Jacob　Rom 11:26
lead to further u　2 Tim 2:16

UNGODLY *sinful, wicked*

who justifies the u　Rom 4:5
Christ died for the u　Rom 5:6
destruction of u men　2 Pet 3:7
their own u lusts　Jude 18

UNHOLY *not holy*

no *longer* consider u　Acts 10:15
for the u and profane　1 Tim 1:9

UNINTENTIONALLY

If a person sins u　Lev 4:2

who kills a person **u** Num 35:15

UNITED *joined, union*

u as one man Judg 20:11
become **u** with *Him* Rom 6:5
love, **u** in spirit Phil 2:2
not **u** by faith Heb 4:2

UNITY *united, union*

dwell together in **u** Ps 133:1
perfected in **u** John 17:23
all attain to the **u** Eph 4:13
perfect bond of **u** Col 3:14

UNJUST *unfair*

u man is abominable Prov 29:27
For God is not **u** Heb 6:10
the just for *the* **u** 1 Pet 3:18

UNKNOWN *not known*

To An **U** God Acts 17:23
as **u** yet well-known 2 Cor 6:9

UNLEAVENED *non-fermented*

and baked **u** bread Gen 19:3
you shall eat **u** bread Ex 12:15
first day of **U** Bread Matt 26:17
you are *in fact* **u** 1 Cor 5:7

**UNLEAVENED BREAD,
FEAST OF** *see* **FEASTS**

UNLOVED *not loved*

that Leah was **u** Gen 29:31
loved and the **u** Deut 21:15
Under an **u** woman Prov 30:23

UNMARRIED *single*

I say to the **u** 1 Cor 7:8
let her remain **u** 1 Cor 7:11

UNPRINCIPLED *unscrupulous*

conduct of **u** men 2 Pet 2:7
error of **u** men 2 Pet 3:17

UNPROFITABLE *without value*

u and worthless Titus 3:9
grief...**u** for you Heb 13:17

UNPUNISHED *not punished*

not leave him **u** Ex 20:7
shall go **u** Ex 21:19
not let him go **u** 1 Kin 2:9

UNQUENCHABLE

burn...with **u** fire Matt 3:12
into the **u** fire Mark 9:43

UNRESTRAINED *uncontrolled*

the people are **u** Prov 29:18
with **u** persecution Is 14:6

UNRIGHTEOUS *evil, wicked*

u man his thoughts Is 55:7
rain on...*the* **u** Matt 5:45
u in a...little thing Luke 16:10
God...is not **u** Rom 3:5
u shall not inherit 1 Cor 6:9
u under punishment 2 Pet 2:9

UNRIGHTEOUSNESS *evil*

have no part in **u** 2 Chr 19:7
no **u** in Him Ps 92:15
not rejoice in **u** 1 Cor 13:6
cleanse us from all **u** 1 John 1:9
All **u** is sin 1 John 5:17

UNRULY *disorderly*

admonish the **u** 1 Thess 5:14
who leads an **u** life 2 Thess 3:6

UNSEARCHABLE *inscrutable*

His greatness is **u** Ps 145:3
u are His judgments Rom 11:33

UNSKILLED *lack of training*

I am **u** in speech Ex 6:12
u in speech, yet I 2 Cor 11:6

UNSTABLE *unreliable*

Her ways are **u** Prov 5:6
u in all his ways James 1:8
enticing **u** souls 2 Pet 2:14

UNWILLING *reluctant*

u to move the ark 2 Sam 6:10
they were **u** to come Matt 22:3
He was **u** to drink Matt 27:34
u to be obedient Acts 7:39

UNWISE *foolish*

foolish and **u** people Deut 32:6
walk, not as **u** men Eph 5:15

UNWORTHY *not deserving*

u of...lovingkindness Gen 32:10
We are **u** slaves Luke 17:10
u of eternal life Acts 13:46

UPRIGHT *honest, just*

the death of the **u** Num 23:10
blameless and **u** man Job 1:8
u will behold His face Ps 11:7
led you in **u** paths Prov 4:11
God made men **u** Eccl 7:29
no **u**...among men Mic 7:2
Stand **u** on your feet Acts 14:10

UPROAR *loud noise*

Why...such an **u** 1 Kin 1:41
nations in an **u** Ps 2:1
there arose a great **u** Acts 23:9

UPROOT *tear out*

He will **u** Israel 1 Kin 14:15
He has **u**-ed my hope Job 19:10
u-ed and be planted Luke 17:6

UR

1 *city in S Mesopotamia*
Gen 11:31; 15:7
original home of Abraham
Gen 11:28; Neh 9:7
2 *father of Eliphal* 1 Chr 11:35

URBANUS

Roman Christian Rom 16:9

URGE *entreat*

Do not **u** me to leave Ruth 1:16
hunger **u**-s him *on* Prov 16:26
I **u** you therefore Rom 12:1

URIAH

1 *husband of Bathsheba*
2 Sam 11:3;12:9
2 *priest under Ezra* Neh 8:4
3 *priest under Ahaz* Is 8:2
also **Urijah** 2 Kin 16:10ff
4 *time of Jeremiah* Jer 26:20

URIM

*kept in high priest's breastplate for
determining the will of God*
Ex 28:30; Lev 8:8; Num 27:21

USE *utilization*

be of **u** to God Job 22:2
for common **u** Ezek 48:15
for honorable **u** Rom 9:21
not make full **u** of 1 Cor 7:31

USEFUL *beneficial*

man be **u** to himself Job 22:2
u to me for service 2 Tim 4:11

USELESS *worthless*

they have become **u** Rom 3:12
without works is **u** James 2:20

USURY *interest*

leave off this **u** Neh 5:10
by interest and **u** Prov 28:8

UTENSILS *vessels*

table also and its **u** Ex 31:8
u of the sanctuary 1 Chr 9:29

UTTER *express*

righteous **u**-s wisdom Ps 37:30
Let my lips **u** praise Ps 119:171
He **u**-s His voice Jer 10:13
u words of...truth Acts 26:25

UTTERANCE *expression*

was giving them **u** Acts 2:4
in faith and **u** 2 Cor 8:7
u may be given Eph 6:19
through prophetic **u** 1 Tim 4:14

UZ

1 *grandson of Shem* Gen 10:23
2 *son of Nahor* Gen 22:21
3 *son of Dishan* Gen 36:28
4 *home of Job* Job 1:1
land of Uz
Jer 25:20; Lam 4:21

V

VAIN *empty or profane*

name of...God in **v** Ex 20:7
devising a **v** thing Ps 2:1
labor in **v** who build Ps 127:1
our preaching is **v** 1 Cor 15:14

VALIANT *brave, strong*

these...**v** warriors Judg 20:46
be a **v** man for me 1 Sam 18:17
even all the **v** men 1 Chr 28:1
He drags off the **v** Job 24:22

VALLEY *ravine*

v of the Jordan Gen 13:10
the **v** of Aijalon Josh 10:12
v of the shadow of Ps 23:4
The lily of the **v**-s Song 2:1
v of the dead bodies Jer 31:40
v...full of bones Ezek 37:1
the **v** of decision Joel 3:14

VALLEY GATE

see **GATES OF JERUSALEM**

VALOR *bravery*

mighty man of **v** 1 Sam 16:18

mighty men of **v** 1 Chr 12:8

VALUE *worth*

you are of more **v** Matt 10:31
one pearl of great **v** Matt 13:46
v of knowing Christ Phil 3:8

VANISH *disappear*

When a cloud **v-es** Job 7:9
sky will **v** like smoke Is 51:6
v-ed from...sight Luke 24:31

VANITY *futility, pride*

will reap **v** Prov 22:8
V of **v-ies**! All is **v** Eccl 1:2
arrogant *words* of **v** 2 Pet 2:18

VAPOR *smoke*

causes the **v-s** to Ps 135:7
Is a fleeting **v** Prov 21:6
You are *just* a **v** James 4:14

VARICOLORED *multicolored*

made him a **v** tunic Gen 37:3

VARIOUS *different*

v diseases and pains Matt 4:24
led on by **v** impulses 2 Tim 3:6
encounter **v** trials James 1:2
distressed by **v** trials 1 Pet 1:6

VASHTI

deposed queen of Ahasuerus
Esth 1:19; 2:4

VAULT *arched cover*

the **v** of heaven Job 22:14
the **v** of the earth Is 40:22

VEGETABLE *plant*

like a **v** garden Deut 11:10
Better...dish of **v-s** Prov 15:17
weak eats **v-s** *only* Rom 14:2

VEGETATION *plant life*

earth brought forth **v** Gen 1:12
ate up all **v** Ps 105:35
wither all their **v** Is 42:15

VEIL *cover, curtain*

a **v** over his face Ex 34:33
v of the sanctuary Lev 4:6
Remove your **v** Is 47:2
v of the temple Matt 27:51
enters within the **v** Heb 6:19

VENGEANCE *revenge*

not take **v** Lev 19:18
V is Mine Deut 32:35
God...executes **v** 2 Sam 22:48
LORD takes **v** on His Nah 1:2
V is Mine, I will Heb 10:30

VESSEL *utensil*

Go, borrow **v-s** 2 Kin 4:3
I am like a broken **v** Ps 31:12
v-s of wrath Rom 9:22
treasure in...**v-s** 2 Cor 4:7
be a **v** for honor 2 Tim 2:21
as with a weaker **v** 1 Pet 3:7
v-s of the potter Rev 2:27

VESTURE *apparel*

v *was* like...snow Dan 7:9

VIAL *small container*

alabaster **v** of Matt 26:7
she broke the **v** Mark 14:3

VICTORIOUS *triumphant*

A **v** warrior Zeph 3:17
v from the beast Rev 15:2

VICTORY *triumph*

LORD brought...**v** 2 Sam 23:10
had given **v** to Aram 2 Kin 5:1
the glory and the **v** 1 Chr 29:11
gained the **v** for Him Ps 98:1
v belongs to...LORD Prov 21:31
He leads justice to **v** Matt 12:20
swallowed up in **v** 1 Cor 15:54
v that has overcome 1 John 5:4

VIGOR *vitality*

nor his **v** abated Deut 34:7
grave in full **v** Job 5:26
his youthful **v** Job 20:11

VILLAGE *small town*

land of unwalled **v-s** Ezek 38:11
Go into the **v** Matt 21:2
entered a certain **v** Luke 10:38

VINDICATE *justify*

will **v** His people Deut 32:36
V the weak Ps 82:3
wisdom is **v-d** by Matt 11:19

VINE *stem of plant*

trees said to the **v** Judg 9:12
every man...his **v** 1 Kin 4:25
like a fruitful **v** Ps 128:3
the **v-s** in blossom Song 2:13
mother was like a **v** Ezek 19:10
Israel is a luxuriant **v** Hos 10:1
The **v** dries up Joel 1:12
fruit of the **v** Matt 26:29
I am the true **v** John 15:1

VINEDRESSER *gardener*

v-s and plowmen 2 Kin 25:12
My Father is the **v** John 15:1

VINEGAR *sour liquid*

he shall drink no **v** Num 6:3
bread in the **v** Ruth 2:14
gave me **v** to drink Ps 69:21
Like **v** to the teeth Prov 10:26

VINE-GROWERS

rented it out to **v** Matt 21:33
and destroy the **v** Mark 12:9

VINEYARD *grapevines*

Noah...planted a **v** Gen 9:20
Nor...glean your **v** Lev 19:10
Hewn cisterns, **v-s** Neh 9:25
shelter in a **v** Is 1:8
ruined My **v** Jer 12:10
laborers for his **v** Matt 20:1
Who plants a **v** 1 Cor 9:7

VIOLATE *assault or break*

shall not **v** his word Num 30:2
do not **v** me 2 Sam 13:12
who **v-d** the ban 1 Chr 2:7
If they **v** My statutes Ps 89:31

VIOLENCE *destructive action*

earth was filled with **v** Gen 6:11
implements of **v** Gen 49:5
such as breathe out **v** Ps 27:12
drink the wine of **v** Prov 4:17
He had done no **v** Is 53:9
not mistreat *or* do **v** Jer 22:3

VIOLENT *destructive*

a **v**, wicked man Ps 37:35
v men attain riches Prov 11:16
a **v**, rushing wind Acts 2:2

VIPER *snake*

v-'s tongue slays him Job 20:16
hand on the **v-'s** den Is 11:8
v and flying serpent Is 30:6
You brood of **v-s** Matt 3:7

VIRGIN *unmarried maiden*

very beautiful, a **v** Gen 24:16
if a man seduces a **v** Ex 22:16
could I gaze at a **v** Job 31:1
the **v** shall rejoice Jer 31:13
v shall be with child Matt 1:23
kept her a **v** Matt 1:25
comparable to ten **v-s** Matt 25:1
v-'s name was Mary Luke 1:27
if a **v** should marry 1 Cor 7:28

VISIBLE *manifest, seen*

He should become **v** Acts 10:40
becomes **v** is light Eph 5:13
things which are **v** Heb 11:3

VISION *dream, foresight*

to Abram in a **v** Gen 15:1
v-s were infrequent 1 Sam 3:1
Where there is no **v** Prov 29:18
prophets find No **v** Lam 2:9
I saw **v-s** of God Ezek 1:1
in a night **v** Dan 2:19
young men...see **v-s** Joel 2:28
Tell the **v** to no one Matt 17:9
young men...see **v-s** Acts 2:17

VISIT *come or go to see*

v-ing the iniquity of Ex 20:5
Thou dost **v** the earth Ps 65:9
you did not **v** Me Matt 25:43
For He has **v-ed** us Luke 1:68
v orphans...widows James 1:27

VOICE *sound, speech*

have obeyed My **v** Gen 22:18
listen to His **v** Deut 4:30
v of singing men 2 Sam 19:35
Thou wilt hear my **v** Ps 5:3
the **v** of my teachers Prov 5:13
v of the turtledove Song 2:12
Give ear...hear my **v** Is 28:23
A **v** is calling Is 40:3
v came from heaven Dan 4:31
v...heard in Ramah Matt 2:18
v...out of the cloud Mark 9:7
v of one crying in Luke 3:4
v of the Son of God John 5:25
v has gone out Rom 10:18
v of *the* archangel 1 Thess 4:16
His **v** shook...earth Heb 12:26
if anyone hears My **v** Rev 3:20
with a **v** of thunder Rev 6:1

VOID *empty, invalid*

was formless and **v**	Gen 1:2
make **v** the counsel	Jer 19:7
faith is made **v**	Rom 4:14
cross...be made **v**	1 Cor 1:17

VOMIT *throw up*

will **v** them up	Job 20:15
returns to its **v**	Prov 26:11
staggers in his **v**	Is 19:14
and it **v-ed** Jonah	Jon 2:10
returns to its own **v**	2 Pet 2:22

VOTIVE *dedicated*

his offering is a **v**	Lev 7:16
choice **v** offerings	Deut 12:11

VOW *solemn promise*

Jacob made a **v**	Gen 28:20
v of a Nazirite	Num 6:2
I shall pay my **v-s**	Ps 22:25
not make false **v-s**	Matt 5:33
he was keeping a **v**	Acts 18:18

VOYAGE *journey*

v was now dangerous	Acts 27:9

VULTURE *bird*

not eat...the **v**	Deut 14:12
the **v-s** will gather	Matt 24:28
the **v-s** be gathered	Luke 17:37

W

WAFER *thin cake of bread*

w-s with honey	Ex 16:31
one unleavened **w**	Num 6:19

WAGE *salary*

God has given...**w-s**	Gen 30:18
w-s of the righteous	Prov 10:16
w is not reckoned	Rom 4:4
the **w-s** of sin	Rom 6:23
worthy of his **w-s**	1 Tim 5:18

WAIL *lament, mourn*

w with a broken spirit	Is 65:14
w, son of man	Ezek 21:12
I must lament and **w**	Mic 1:8
W, O inhabitants of	Zeph 1:11
weeping and **w-ing**	Mark 5:38

WAIT *expect*

For Thee I **w**	Ps 25:5
I **w** for Thy word	Ps 119:81
who **w** for the LORD	Is 40:31
creation **w-s** eagerly	Rom 8:19
w-ing for the hope	Gal 5:5

WALK *follow, go along*

w-ing in the garden	Gen 3:8
W before Me	Gen 17:1
w in My instruction	Ex 16:4
w in My statutes	Lev 26:3
w-ed forty years	Josh 5:6
w before Me in truth	1 Kin 2:4
W about Zion	Ps 48:12
I will **w** at liberty	Ps 119:45
fool **w-s** in darkness	Eccl 2:14
w in the light	Is 2:5
w and not...weary	Is 40:31
w-ed with Me in peace	Mal 2:6
Rise, and **w**	Matt 9:5

w-ed on the water	Matt 14:29
w in newness of life	Rom 6:4
we **w** by faith	2 Cor 5:7
w by the Spirit	Gal 5:16
w in love	Eph 5:2
w as children of light	Eph 5:8
if we **w** in the light	1 John 1:7
w by its light	Rev 21:24

WALL *structure*

living on the **w**	Josh 2:15
So we built the **w**	Neh 4:6
I can leap over a **w**	Ps 18:29
w-s of Jerusalem	Jer 39:8
built a siege **w**	Jer 52:4
you whitewashed **w**	Acts 23:3
w-s of Jericho fell	Heb 11:30
a great and high **w**	Rev 21:12

WANDER *roam*

w in the wilderness	Num 32:13
I would **w** far away	Ps 55:7
w...Thy statutes	Ps 119:118
people **w** like sheep	Zech 10:2
w-ed...the faith	1 Tim 6:10
w-ing stars, for whom	Jude 13

WANDERER *roamer*

a **w** on the earth	Gen 4:12
an exile and a **w**	Is 49:21
w-s among...nations	Hos 9:17

WAR *battle, conflict*

when they see **w**	Ex 13:17
sound of **w** in...camp	Ex 32:17
land...rest from **w**	Josh 11:23
He makes **w-s** to cease	Ps 46:9
the weapons of **w**	Ps 76:3
A time for **w**	Eccl 3:8
will they learn **w**	Is 2:4
w-s...rumors of **w-s**	Matt 24:6
w against the law	Rom 7:23
w in your members	James 4:1
w against the soul	1 Pet 2:11
judges and wages **w**	Rev 19:11

WARS OF THE LORD, BOOK OF

ancient Hebrew literature

	Num 21:14

WARM *heat*

could not keep **w**	1 Kin 1:1
the child became **w**	2 Kin 4:34
can one be **w** *alone*	Eccl 4:11
no one is **w** *enough*	Hag 1:6

WARN *give notice*

w the people	Ex 19:21
not...**w** the wicked	Ezek 33:8
w-ed...in a dream	Matt 2:12
w you whom to fear	Luke 12:5
Moses was **w-ed**	Heb 8:5

WARRIOR *soldier*

The LORD is a **w**	Ex 15:3
O valiant **w**	Judg 6:12
w from his youth	1 Sam 17:33
w-s will flee naked	Amos 2:16

WASH *bathe, clean*

w your feet, and rest	Gen 18:4
w in the Jordan	2 Kin 5:10

w...in innocence	Ps 26:6
W...from my iniquity	Ps 51:2
w-ed off your blood	Ezek 16:9
do not **w** their hands	Matt 15:2
ceremonially **w-ed**	Luke 11:38
w in the pool of	John 9:7
w the disciples' feet	John 13:5
w away your sins	Acts 22:16
w-ed...saints' feet	1 Tim 5:10
w-ed with pure	Heb 10:22
who **w** their robes	Rev 22:14

WASTE (n) *wilderness*

land was laid **w**	Ex 8:24
land into a salt **w**	Ps 107:34
lay **w** the mountains	Is 42:15
laid **w** like a desert	Jer 9:12
altars may become **w**	Ezek 6:6
Egypt...become a **w**	Joel 3:19

WASTE (v) *destroy, use up*

he **w-d** his seed	Gen 38:9
w away the eyes	Lev 26:16
sick man **w-s** away	Is 10:18
perfume been **w-d**	Mark 14:4

WASTE PLACE *barren*

w-s of the wealthy	Is 5:17
Seek Me in a **w**	Is 45:19
like the ancient **w-s**	Ezek 26:20
w-s will be rebuilt	Ezek 36:10

WATCH (n) *guard*

at the morning **w**	Ex 14:24
in the night **w-es**	Ps 63:6
His eyes keep **w**	Ps 66:7
keep **w** with Me	Matt 26:38
w over their flock	Luke 2:8
w over your souls	Heb 13:17

WATCH (v) *observe*

LORD **w** between you	Gen 31:49
dost **w** all my paths	Job 13:27
W over your heart	Prov 4:23
who **w-es** the wind	Eccl 11:4
w...for the LORD	Mic 7:7

WATCHMAN *one who guards*

w keeps awake in vain	Ps 127:1
w-men for...morning	Ps 130:6
W, how far gone is	Is 21:11
I set **w-men** over you	Jer 6:17
Ephraim *was* a **w**	Hos 9:8

WATER (n) *flood, liquid*

moving over...the **w-s**	Gen 1:2
flood of **w** came	Gen 7:6
w-s *were* like a wall	Ex 14:22
w of bitterness	Num 5:18
the clouds dripped **w**	Judg 5:4
W wears away stones	Job 14:19
poured out like **w**	Ps 22:14
beside quiet **w-s**	Ps 23:2
Stolen **w** is sweet	Prov 9:17
bread on the...**w-s**	Eccl 11:1
come to the **w-s**	Is 55:1
fountain of living **w-s**	Jer 2:13
eyes run...with **w**	Lam 1:16
knees...like **w**	Ezek 7:17
baptize you with **w**	Matt 3:11
a cup of cold **w**	Matt 10:42
walked on the **w**	Matt 14:29

no w for My feet	Luke 7:44
one is born of w	John 3:5
given you living w	John 4:10
John baptized with w	Acts 1:5
of w with the word	Eph 5:26
formed out of w	2 Pet 3:5
by w and blood	1 John 5:6
sound of many w-s	Rev 19:6

WATER (v) *make moist*

to w the garden	Gen 2:10
I will w your camels	Gen 24:46
w their father's flock	Ex 2:16
that w the earth	Ps 72:6
Apollos w-ed	1 Cor 3:6

WAVES *billows*

w of death	2 Sam 22:5
tramples down the w	Job 9:8
Thy w have rolled	Ps 42:7
w were breaking	Mark 4:37
wild w of the sea	Jude 13

WAX *paraffin*

My heart is like w	Ps 22:14
Like w before the fire	Mic 1:4

WAY *manner or path*

guard the w	Gen 3:24
all His w-s are just	Deut 32:4
blameless...His w	2 Sam 22:33
from your evil w-s	2 Kin 17:13
joy of His w	Job 8:19
w of the righteous	Ps 1:6
Commit your w to	Ps 37:5
your w-s acknowledge	Prov 3:6
is the w of death	Prov 14:12
Clear the w	Is 40:3
w of the wicked	Jer 12:1
Make ready the w	Matt 3:3
Pray...in this w	Matt 6:9
w is broad that leads	Matt 7:13
teach...w of God	Mark 12:14
into the w of peace	Luke 1:79
I am the w	John 14:6
belonging to the W	Acts 9:2
the w of salvation	Acts 16:17
unfathomable...w-s	Rom 11:33
the w of escape	1 Cor 10:13
new and living w	Heb 10:20
the w of the truth	2 Pet 2:2

WEAK *feeble*

I shall become w	Judg 16:17
Rescue the w	Ps 82:4
but the flesh is w	Matt 26:41
must help the w	Acts 20:35
who is w in faith	Rom 14:1
God...chosen the w	1 Cor 1:27

WEAKNESS *fault*

Spirit...helps our w	Rom 8:26
bear the w-es	Rom 15:1
w of God is stronger	1 Cor 1:25
it is sown in w	1 Cor 15:43
perfected in w	2 Cor 12:9

WEALTH *riches*

power to make w	Deut 8:18
a man of great w	Ruth 2:1
who trust in their w	Ps 49:6
Honor...from you w	Prov 3:9

W adds many friends	Prov 19:4
A w of salvation	Is 33:6
the w of all nations	Hag 2:7
w of their liberality	2 Cor 8:2
rich by her w	Rev 18:19

WEAPON *armament*

girded on his w-s	Deut 1:41
flee from the iron w	Job 20:24
turn back the w-s	Jer 21:4
w-s of righteousness	2 Cor 6:7

WEARY *tired*

the people were w	1 Sam 14:28
the w are at rest	Job 3:17
w with my crying	Ps 69:3
water to a w soul	Prov 25:25
and not become w	Is 40:31
sustain the w one	Is 50:4
all who are w	Matt 11:28
w of doing good	2 Thess 3:13

WEAVE *interlace*

Thou didst w me	Ps 139:13
w the spider's web	Is 59:5
after w-ing a crown	Matt 27:29

WEB *woven work*

loom and the w	Judg 16:14
trust a spider's w	Job 8:14

WEDDING *marriage*

had no w songs	Ps 78:63
day of his w	Song 3:11
come to the w feast	Matt 22:4
a w in Cana	John 2:1

WEEK *period of time*

Complete the w of	Gen 29:27
Seventy w-s	Dan 9:24
first *day* of the w	Matt 28:1
I fast twice a w	Luke 18:12

WEEKS, FEAST OF
see **FEASTS**

WEEP *cry, sorrow*

sought *a place* to w	Gen 43:30
do not mourn or w	Neh 8:9
My eye w-s to God	Job 16:20
widows could not w	Ps 78:64
Let me w bitterly	Is 22:4
w day and night	Jer 9:1
Rachel w-ing for her	Matt 2:18
w-ing and gnashing	Matt 13:42
he...wept bitterly	Matt 26:75
saw the city...wept	Luke 19:41
w for yourselves	Luke 23:28
Jesus wept	John 11:35
why are you w-ing	John 20:13
w with...who w	Rom 12:15

WEIGH *measure out*

actions are w-ed	1 Sam 2:3
LORD w-s the motives	Prov 16:2

WEIGHT *heaviness*

a full and just w	Deut 25:15
w to the wind	Job 28:25
bag of deceptive w-s	Mic 6:11
eternal w of glory	2 Cor 4:17

WELCOME *gladly receive*

no prophet is w	Luke 4:24

multitude w-d Him	Luke 8:40
who fears Him...w	Acts 10:35
she...w-d the spies	Heb 11:31

WELL *water shaft*

sat down by a w	Ex 2:15
w of Bethlehem	1 Chr 11:17
Like...a polluted w	Prov 25:26
A w of fresh water	Song 4:15
Jacob's w was there	John 4:6

WELL-PLEASED *satisfied*

in whom I am w	Matt 3:17
in Thee I am w	Luke 3:22
God was not w	1 Cor 10:5

WEST *direction*

very strong w wind	Ex 10:19
east is from the w	Ps 103:12
gather you from the w	Is 43:5

WHEAT *grain*

days of w harvest	Gen 30:14
first fruits of the w	Ex 34:22
plant w in rows	Is 28:25
gather His w into	Matt 3:12
to sift you like w	Luke 22:31
unless a grain of w	John 12:24

WHEEL *circular disk*

the w...is crushed	Eccl 12:6
w-s like a whirlwind	Is 5:28
one w were within	Ezek 1:16
rattling of the w	Nah 3:2

WHIRLWIND

take...Elijah by a w	2 Kin 2:1
comes on like a w	Prov 1:27
chariots like the w	Jer 4:13
they reap the w	Hos 8:7

WHISPER *talk quietly*

who hate me w	Ps 41:7
w a prayer	Is 26:16
your speech shall w	Is 29:4

WHISTLE *shrill sound*

And will w for it	Is 5:26
LORD will w for the fly	Is 7:18
I will w for them	Zech 10:8

WHITE *color*

teeth w from milk	Gen 49:12
w of an egg	Job 6:6
be as w as snow	Is 1:18
make one hair w	Matt 5:36
clothing *became* w	Luke 9:29
fields...w for harvest	John 4:35
clothed in w robes	Rev 7:9

WHITEWASHED *wall covering*

like w tombs	Matt 23:27
you w wall	Acts 23:3

WHOLE *entire*

water the w surface	Gen 2:6
w earth...populated	Gen 9:19
leavens the w lump	1 Cor 5:6
keeps the w law	James 2:10

WICK *candle thread*

extinguished like a w	Is 43:17
a smoldering w	Matt 12:20

WICKED *evil, ungodly*

condemn the **w**	Deut 25:1
w ones are silenced	1 Sam 2:9
counsel of the **w**	Ps 1:1
the **w** spurned God	Ps 10:13
The **w** strut about	Ps 12:8
devises **w** plans	Prov 6:18
When a **w** man dies	Prov 11:7
no peace for the **w**	Is 48:22
turn from his **w** way	Jon 3:8
taking...some **w** men	Acts 17:5
righteous and the **w**	Acts 24:15

WICKEDNESS *evil*

w of man was great	Gen 6:5
if I regard **w**	Ps 66:18
eat the bread of **w**	Prov 4:17
inclines toward **w**	Is 32:6
w of My people	Jer 7:12
You have plowed **w**	Hos 10:13
repent of this **w**	Acts 8:22
spiritual *forces* of **w**	Eph 6:12

WIDOW *husband dead*

Remain a **w**	Gen 38:11
not afflict any **w**	Ex 22:22
sent **w**-s away empty	Job 22:9
judge for the **w**-s	Ps 68:5
Plead for the **w**	Is 1:17
devour **w**-s' houses	Matt 23:14
w put in more	Mark 12:43
Honor **w**-s	1 Tim 5:3
visit orphans...**w**-s	James 1:27

WIFE *married woman*

cleave to his **w**	Gen 2:24
man and his **w** hid	Gen 3:8
shall not covet...**w**	Ex 20:17
w of your youth	Prov 5:18
An excellent **w**	Prov 31:10
who divorces his **w**	Matt 5:32
Remember Lot's **w**	Luke 17:32
have his own **w**	1 Cor 7:2
head of the **w**	Eph 5:23
husband of one **w**	1 Tim 3:2
w-ves, be submissive	1 Pet 3:1
w of the Lamb	Rev 21:9

WILD *untamed*

w donkey of a man	Gen 16:12
horns of the **w** ox	Num 23:22
locusts and **w** honey	Mark 1:6
being a **w** olive	Rom 11:17

WILDERNESS *barren area*

water in the **w**	Gen 16:7
journey into the **w**	Ex 5:3
to die in the **w**	Ex 14:11
forty years in the **w**	Deut 29:5
pastures of the **w**	Ps 65:12
roadway in the **w**	Is 43:19
Have I been a **w**	Jer 2:31
preaching in the **w**	Matt 3:1
into the **w**...tempted	Matt 4:1
crying in the **w**	Mark 1:3
manna in the **w**	John 6:31

WILL *attitude, purpose*

delight to do Thy **w**	Ps 40:8
Thy **w** be done	Matt 6:10
the **w** of My Father	Matt 7:21
not My **w**, but	Luke 22:42

nor of the **w** of man	John 1:13
who resists His **w**	Rom 9:19
what the **w** of God	Rom 12:2
knowledge of His **w**	Col 1:9
come to do Thy **w**	Heb 10:9
an act of human **w**	2 Pet 1:21

WIN *succeed*

wise **w**-s souls	Prov 11:30
we will **w** him over	Matt 28:14
that I might **w** Jews	1 Cor 9:20
won without a word	1 Pet 3:1

WIND

caused a **w** to pass	Gen 8:1
scorched by...**w**	Gen 41:27
will inherit **w**	Prov 11:29
prophets are *as* **w**	Jer 5:13
they sow the **w**	Hos 8:7
reed shaken by...**w**	Matt 11:7
w and the sea obey	Mark 4:41
He rebuked the **w**	Luke 8:24
violent, rushing **w**	Acts 2:2
every **w** of doctrine	Eph 4:14
driven by strong **w**-s	James 3:4

WINDOW *opening*

enter through the **w**-s	Joel 2:9
open...**w**-s of heaven	Mal 3:10
sitting on the **w** sill	Acts 20:9
basket through a **w**	2 Cor 11:33

WINE *strong drink*

eyes...dull from **w**	Gen 49:12
Do not drink **w**	Lev 10:9
overflow with new **w**	Prov 3:10
W is a mocker	Prov 20:1
love is better than **w**	Song 1:2
new **w** into old	Matt 9:17
gave Him **w** to	Matt 27:34
made the water **w**	John 4:46
full of sweet **w**	Acts 2:13
not get drunk with **w**	Eph 5:18
not addicted to **w**	1 Tim 3:3

WINESKINS *animal skin bag*

these **w**...were new	Josh 9:13
Like new **w**	Job 32:19
wine into fresh **w**	Matt 9:17

WINGS

bore you on eagles' **w**	Ex 19:4
He spread His **w**	Deut 32:11
under whose **w**	Ruth 2:12
under His **w**...refuge	Ps 91:4
with **w** like eagles	Is 40:31
healing in its **w**	Mal 4:2
chicks under her **w**	Matt 23:37

WINK *blink*

w maliciously	Ps 35:19
w-s with his eyes	Prov 6:13

WINNOW *scatter*

king **w**-s the wicked	Prov 20:26
You will **w** them	Is 41:16
His **w**-ing fork	Matt 3:12

WINTER *season*

And summer and **w**	Gen 8:22
the **w** is past	Song 2:11
even spend the **w**	1 Cor 16:6

WIPE *pass over, rub*

GOD will **w** tears	Is 25:8
w-d His feet	John 11:2
sins...**w**-d away	Acts 3:19
w away every tear	Rev 21:4

WISDOM *discernment*

the spirit of **w**	Ex 28:3
w has two sides	Job 11:6
the beginning of **w**	Ps 111:10
Fools despise **w**	Prov 1:7
w to fear Thy name	Mic 6:9
w given to Him	Mark 6:2
kept increasing in **w**	Luke 2:52
made foolish the **w**	1 Cor 1:20
any of you lacks **w**	James 1:5

WISE *judicious, prudent*

not find a **w** man	Job 17:10
making the simple **w**	Ps 19:7
w in your own eyes	Prov 3:7
the words of the **w**	Prov 22:17
He is not a **w** son	Hos 13:13
Who...you is **w**	James 3:13

WITCHCRAFT *magic, sorcery*

who practices **w**	Deut 18:10
practiced **w** and	2 Kin 21:6

WITHER *dry up*

its leaf does not **w**	Ps 1:3
w...like the grass	Ps 37:2
earth mourns *and* **w**-s	Is 24:4
the leaf shall **w**	Jer 8:13
with a **w**-ed hand	Mark 3:1
the fig tree **w**-ed	Mark 11:20

WITNESS (n) *testimony*

This heap is a **w**	Gen 31:48
is **w** between us	Judg 11:10
my **w** is in heaven	Job 16:19
a **w** to the LORD	Is 19:20
w to all the nations	Matt 24:14
He came for a **w**	John 1:7
My **w** is true	John 8:14
you shall be My **w**-es	Acts 1:8
For God is my **w**	Phil 1:8
w of God is greater	1 John 5:9
Christ, the faithful **w**	Rev 1:5

WITNESS (v) *testify*

not bear false **w**	Ex 20:16
w against you today	Deut 4:26
John bore **w**	John 1:32
bear **w** of Me	John 15:26
Spirit...bears **w**	Rom 8:16
three that bear **w**	1 John 5:8

WOLF *animal*

w will dwell with	Is 11:6
the midst of **w**-ves	Matt 10:16
w snatches them	John 10:12

WOMAN *female, lady*

She shall be called **W**	Gen 2:23
w...not wear man's	Deut 22:5
a **w** of excellence	Ruth 3:11
Man...born of **w**	Job 14:1
gracious **w** attains	Prov 11:16
a contentious **w**	Prov 25:24
like a **w** in labor	Is 42:14
looks on a **w** to lust	Matt 5:28
w-en...grinding	Matt 24:41

Blessed among **w-en** Luke 1:42
W, behold, your son John 19:26
not to touch a **w** 1 Cor 7:1
w is the glory of 1 Cor 11:7
w to speak in 1 Cor 14:35
His Son, born of a **w** Gal 4:4
w clothed with...sun Rev 12:1

WOMB

nations...in your **w** Gen 25:23
LORD...closed her **w** 1 Sam 1:5
from **w** to tomb Job 10:19
formed you from the **w** Is 44:2
baby leaped in...**w** Luke 1:41

WONDER *marvel, sign*

consider the **w-s** of Job 37:14
tell of all Thy **w-s** Ps 9:1
His **w-s** in the deep Ps 107:24
w-s in the sky Joel 2:30
were filled with **w** Acts 3:10

WONDERFUL *marvelous*

His **w** deeds 1 Chr 16:12
name will be called **W** Is 9:6

WOOD *cut tree*

ark of gopher **w** Gen 6:14
other gods, **w** and Deut 28:36
children gather **w** Jer 7:18
stones, **w**, hay 1 Cor 3:12

WOOL *cloth or hair*

of **w** and linen Deut 22:11
put a fleece of **w** on Judg 6:37
They will be like **w** Is 1:18
hair...like pure **w** Dan 7:9
white like white **w** Rev 1:14

WORD *message, speech*

to the **w** of Moses Lev 10:7
declare to you the **w** Deut 5:5
Joshua wrote...**w-s** Josh 24:26
proclaim the **w** of 1 Sam 9:27
Thy **w**...confirmed 2 Chr 6:17
no limit to windy **w-s** Job 16:3
w-s of my mouth Ps 19:14
Thy **w** is a lamp Ps 119:105
harsh **w** stirs up Prov 15:1
w of God is tested Prov 30:5
despised the **w** Is 5:24
w-s of a sealed book Is 29:11
speak My **w** in truth Jer 23:28
conceal these **w-s** Dan 12:4
every **w** that proceeds Matt 4:4
these **w-s** of Mine Matt 7:24
sower sows the **w** Mark 4:14
the **W** was God John 1:1
the **W** became flesh John 1:14
w-s of eternal life John 6:68
abide in My **w** John 8:31
glorifying the **w** Acts 13:48
too deep for **w-s** Rom 8:26
hearing by the **w** Rom 10:17
the **w** of the cross 1 Cor 1:18
fulfilled in one **w** Gal 5:14
no unwholesome **w** Eph 4:29
sanctified by...**w** 1 Tim 4:5
the **w** of truth 2 Tim 2:15
the faithful **w** Titus 1:9
w of God is living Heb 4:12
doers of the **w** James 1:22

pure milk of the **w** 1 Pet 2:2
the **W** of Life 1 John 1:1
The **W** of God Rev 19:13

WORK (n) *act, deed, labor*

God completed His **w** Gen 2:2
You shall **w** six days Ex 34:21
His **w** is perfect Deut 32:4
the **w** of His hands Ps 19:1
see the **w-s** of God Ps 66:5
Commit your **w-s** to Prov 16:3
let Him hasten His **w** Is 5:19
His **w** on Mount Zion Is 10:12
see your good **w-s** Matt 5:16
the **w-s** of Christ Matt 11:2
the **w** of the Law Rom 2:15
faith apart from **w-s** Rom 3:28
not...a result of **w-s** Eph 2:9
for the **w** of service Eph 4:12
began a good **w** Phil 1:6
fruit in...good **w** Col 1:10
rich in good **w-s** 1 Tim 6:18
faith without **w-s** James 2:20

WORK (v) *perform, produce*

has **w-ed** with God 1 Sam 14:45
those who **w** iniquity Ps 28:3
Who...**w-s** wonders Ps 72:18
not **w** for the food John 6:27
w together for good Rom 8:28
So death **w-s** in us 2 Cor 4:12
w out your salvation Phil 2:12
anyone will not **w** 2 Thess 3:10

WORKER *laborer*

O **w** of deceit Ps 52:2
w-s of iniquity Prov 10:29
w is worthy of his Matt 10:10
God's fellow **w-s** 1 Cor 3:9
beware...evil **w-s** Phil 3:2
pure, **w-s** at home Titus 2:5

WORKMAN *craftsman*

a skillful **w** Ex 38:23
approved...as a **w** 2 Tim 2:15

WORKMANSHIP *craftsmanship*

we are His **w** Eph 2:10

WORLD *earth, humanity*

foundations of...**w** 2 Sam 22:16
He will judge the **w** Ps 9:8
first dust of the **w** Prov 8:26
the light of the **w** Matt 5:14
the field is the **w** Matt 13:38
Go into all the **w** Mark 16:15
gains the whole **w** Luke 9:25
God so loved the **w** John 3:16
Savior of the **w** John 4:42
w cannot hate you John 7:7
the light of the **w** John 8:12
overcome the **w** John 16:33
have upset the **w** Acts 17:6
sin entered...the **w** Rom 5:12
reconciling the **w** 2 Cor 5:19
unstained by the **w** James 1:27
flood upon the **w** 2 Pet 2:5
Do not love the **w** 1 John 2:15

WORLDLY *earthly*

w fables fit only 1 Tim 4:7
avoid **w**...chatter 2 Tim 2:16

WORM *creeping animal*

But I am a **w** Ps 22:6
w-s are your covering Is 14:11
God appointed a **w** Jon 4:7
their **w** does not die Mark 9:48
he was eaten by **w-s** Acts 12:23

WORMWOOD

1 *a bitter plant* Deut 29:18
2 *used figuratively*
  Prov 5:4; Amos 6:12; Rev 8:11

WORSHIP *bow, revere*

not **w** any other god Ex 34:14
you shall **w** Him Deut 6:13
W the LORD Ps 2:11
earth will **w** Thee Ps 66:4
in vain do they **w** Matt 15:9
w in spirit and truth John 4:24
w in the Spirit Phil 3:3
w Him who lives Rev 4:10
who **w** the beast Rev 14:11

WORTHLESS *useless*

all **w** physicians Job 13:4
w man digs up evil Prov 16:27
your **w** offerings Is 1:13
your faith is **w** 1 Cor 15:17
w for any good Titus 1:16
man's religion is **w** James 1:26

WORTHY *having merit*

sin **w** of death Deut 21:22
w of his support Matt 10:10
is not **w** of Me Matt 10:37
is **w** of his wages Luke 10:7
manner of the **w** Rom 16:2
w of the gospel Phil 1:27
world was not **w** Heb 11:38
W is the Lamb Rev 5:12

WOUND *injury*

My **w** is incurable Job 34:6
binds up their **w-s** Ps 147:3
Your **w** is incurable Jer 30:12
bandaged...his **w-s** Luke 10:34
by His **w-s** you were 1 Pet 2:24
fatal **w** was healed Rev 13:3

WRAPPINGS *cloth coverings*

bound...with **w** John 11:44
linen **w** lying *there* John 20:5

WRATH *anger, indignation*

and in great **w** Deut 29:28
Nor chasten...in Thy **w** Ps 6:1
Pour out Thy **w** Ps 79:6
turns away **w** Prov 15:1
Lest My **w** go forth Jer 4:4
spent My **w** upon Ezek 5:13
from the **w** to come Matt 3:7
w of God abides on John 3:36
w of God will come Rom 3:5
children of **w** Eph 2:3
w of God will come Col 3:6
the **w** of the Lamb Rev 6:16

WRETCHED *miserable*

in to this **w** place Num 20:5
W man that I am Rom 7:24

WRITE *enscribe*

Moses, **W** this in a Ex 17:14

W them on the tablet   Prov 3:3
he **wrote** the dream   Dan 7:1
w a certificate   Mark 10:4
with His finger **wrote**   John 8:6
w...King of the Jews   John 19:21
W in a book   Rev 1:11

WRITINGS *literary work*

not believe his w   John 5:47
known the sacred w   2 Tim 3:15

WRITTEN *enscribed*

w by...God   Ex 31:18
w in the law   2 Chr 23:18
remembrance was w   Mal 3:16
w by the prophet   Matt 2:5
about whom it is w   Matt 11:10
Law w in...hearts   Rom 2:15
name has not been w   Rev 13:8
w in the Lamb's   Rev 21:27

WRONG *do evil, harm*

not w a stranger   Ex 22:21
not w one another   Lev 25:14
I...have done w   2 Sam 24:17
Love does no w   Rom 13:10

WROUGHT *accomplished*

He w wonders   Ps 78:12
been w in God   John 3:21

Y

YAHWEH

see **YHWH** *and* **LORD**

YEAR *period, time*

atonement...every y   Lev 16:34
fiftieth y...jubilee   Lev 25:11
the y of remission   Deut 15:9
crowned the y with   Ps 65:11
length of...y-s   Prov 3:2
favorable y of the LORD   Is 61:2
thirty y-s of age   Luke 3:23
y of the LORD   Luke 4:19
priest *enters*, once a y   Heb 9:7
sacrifices y by y   Heb 10:1
y-s as one day   2 Pet 3:8
reign...thousand y-s   Rev 20:6

YEARLING *one year old*

a y ewe lamb   Lev 14:10
With y calves   Mic 6:6

YEARNS *deeply moved*

my flesh y for Thee   Ps 63:1
My heart y for him   Jer 31:20

YESTERDAY *past*

we are *only* of y   Job 8:9
thousand years...y   Ps 90:4
same y and today   Heb 13:8

YHWH

*Hebrew tetragrammaton for name
of God, probably pronounced
Yahweh*
*Derived from Hebrew verb
meaning "to be"*
Translated usually as LORD
see also **LORD**
*see also introductory material to
NASB*

YIELD *produce*

no longer y its   Gen 4:12
land...y its produce   Lev 25:19
Which y-s its fruit   Ps 1:3
y-ed up *His* spirit   Matt 27:50
not y in subjection   Gal 2:5
y-s the peaceful   Heb 12:11

YOKE *wooden bar*

break his y from   Gen 27:40
iron y on...neck   Deut 28:48
made our y hard   1 Kin 12:4
the y of their burden   Is 9:4
Take My y upon   Matt 11:29
to a y of slavery   Gal 5:1

YOUNG *early age, youth*

he sent y men   Ex 24:5
or two y pigeons   Lev 15:29
glory of y men is   Prov 20:29
y men stumble   Is 40:30
like a y lion   Hos 5:14
finding a y donkey   John 12:14
y men...visions   Acts 2:17
urge the y men   Titus 2:6

YOUTH *young*

evil from his y   Gen 8:21
fresher than in y   Job 33:25
the sins of my y   Ps 25:7
confidence from my y   Ps 71:5
your y is renewed   Ps 103:5
the wife of your y   Prov 5:18
y-s grow weary   Is 40:30
the reproach of my y   Jer 31:19
life from my y up   Acts 26:4

Z

ZACCHEUS

tax collector who followed Jesus
                            Luke 19:2,5,8

ZACHARIAS

father of John the Baptist
                        Luke 1:5,12,18;3:2

ZAREPHATH

scene of miracle by Elijah
                            1 Kin 17:9,10
Phoenician town
                        Obad 20; Luke 4:26

ZEAL *fervor, passion*

kill them in his z   2 Sam 21:2
my z for the LORD   2 Kin 10:16
z has consumed me   Ps 119:139
Thy z for the people   Is 26:11
have a z for God   Rom 10:2
your z for me   2 Cor 7:7

ZEALOT

*member of radical Jewish
    nationalist party*
                        Matt 10:4; Mark 3:18;
                        Luke 6:15; Acts 1:13

ZEALOUS *fervent*

z for the LORD   1 Kin 19:10
all z for the Law   Acts 21:20
z of...gifts   1 Cor 14:12
z for good deeds   Titus 2:14
be z...and repent   Rev 3:19

ZEBEDEE

father of James and John
                            Matt 4:21;27:56;
                        Mark 1:19;10:35; Luke 5:10;
                            John 21:2

ZEBULUN

1 *son of Jacob*   Gen 30:20
2 *tribe*   Num 34:25; Josh 21:34
3 *territory of the tribe, located in
    N Palestine*
                        Josh 19:27; Judg 12:12;
                        Is 9:1; Ezek 48:27

ZECHARIAH

1 *son of Jeiel*   1 Chr 9:35-37
2 *priest with ark*   1 Chr 15:24
3 *son of Isshiah*   1 Chr 24:25
4 *father of Iddo*   1 Chr 27:21
5 *son of Benaiah*   2 Chr 20:14
6 *son of Jehoshaphat*   2 Chr 21:2
7 *son of Jehoida*   2 Chr 24:20
8 *prophet*   2 Chr 26:5
9 *priest under Ezra*   Neh 12:41
10 *minor prophet*   Zech 1:1

ZELOPHEHAD

Manassite, son of Hepher
                            Num 26:33
daughters became his heirs
                        Num 27:1;36:2

ZEPHANIAH

1 *priest*   2 Kin 25:18
2 *Kohathite Levite*   1 Chr 6:36
3 *minor prophet*   Zeph 1:1
4 *father of Josiah*   Zech 6:10

ZERUBBABEL

line of David   1 Chr 3:1-19
helped rebuild temple   Ezra 3:8

ZERUIAH

*mother of Joab, Abishai, and
    Asahel*   2 Sam 2:18
David's half-sister   1 Chr 2:16

ZIKLAG

town in S Judah
                        Josh 15:31; 1 Sam 27:6;
                            1 Chr 12:1

ZILPAH

concubine of Jacob
                        Gen 29:24;30:10;46:18

ZIN

wilderness in Negev
                        Num 13:21; Deut 32:51;
                            Josh 15:1,3

ZION

1 *hill / City of David which is
    Jerusalem*
                        2 Sam 5:7; 1 Chr 11:5
2 *after Temple built, name
    extended to top of hill, Mount
    Zion*   Is 8:18;18:7; Mic 4:7
3 *applied to all of Jerusalem as
    city spreads*
                    2 Kin 19:21; Ps 69:35; Is 1:8
4 *used in the corporate sense for
    the people and land*
                        Ps 97:8;149:2;

Is 3:16;8:14;59:20; Joel 2:23;
Zech 9:9; Rom 9:33; 1 Pet 2:3
5 *used eschatologically for
heavenly Jerusalem*
Is 60:14; Heb 12:22; Rev 14:1

ZIPPORAH

wife of Moses   Ex 2:21;4:25

ZIV

*name of the second month in
Hebrew calendar*   1 Kin 6:1,37

ZOAN

Egyptian delta city
Num 13:22; Ps 78:12; Is 19:11;
Ezek 30:14

ZOAR

*city of the plain near the Dead
Sea*
Gen 13:10;14:2;19:23,30;
Deut 34:3; Jer 48:34
also **Bela**

ZOPHAR

one of Job's friends
Job 2:11;11:1;20:1;42:9

ZUZIM

pre-Israelite tribe in Palestine
Gen 14:5

The Exodus

BASHAN

The Great Sea
(Mediterranean Sea)

Megiddo

Jordan

Joppa

CANAAN

AMMON

Ai
Jericho

Heshbon

Gaza

Salt
Sea

Jahaz

Dibon

Arad

MOAB

Hormah

Kir-moab

Zoar

Iye-abarim

Raamses
Baal-zephon
Zilu

Goshen

Wilderness
of Zin

Oboth
Punon

Succoth
Pithom

Wilderness
of Shur

Kadesh-barnea

Petra

Bitter
Lakes

EDOM

On
(Heliopolis)

Wilderness
of Paran

Noph
(Memphis)

SINAI

Nile

Marah?

Elim?

Wilderness
of Sin

Ezion-geber

Dophkah?

Hazeroth?

Gulf of Suez

Kibroth-hattaavah?

Rephidim

Mt. Sinai

Gulf of Aqaba

MIDIAN

EGYPT

Red Sea

Probable route of Exodus
Trade routes

© 1976 by The Zondervan Corporation

World of the Patriarchs

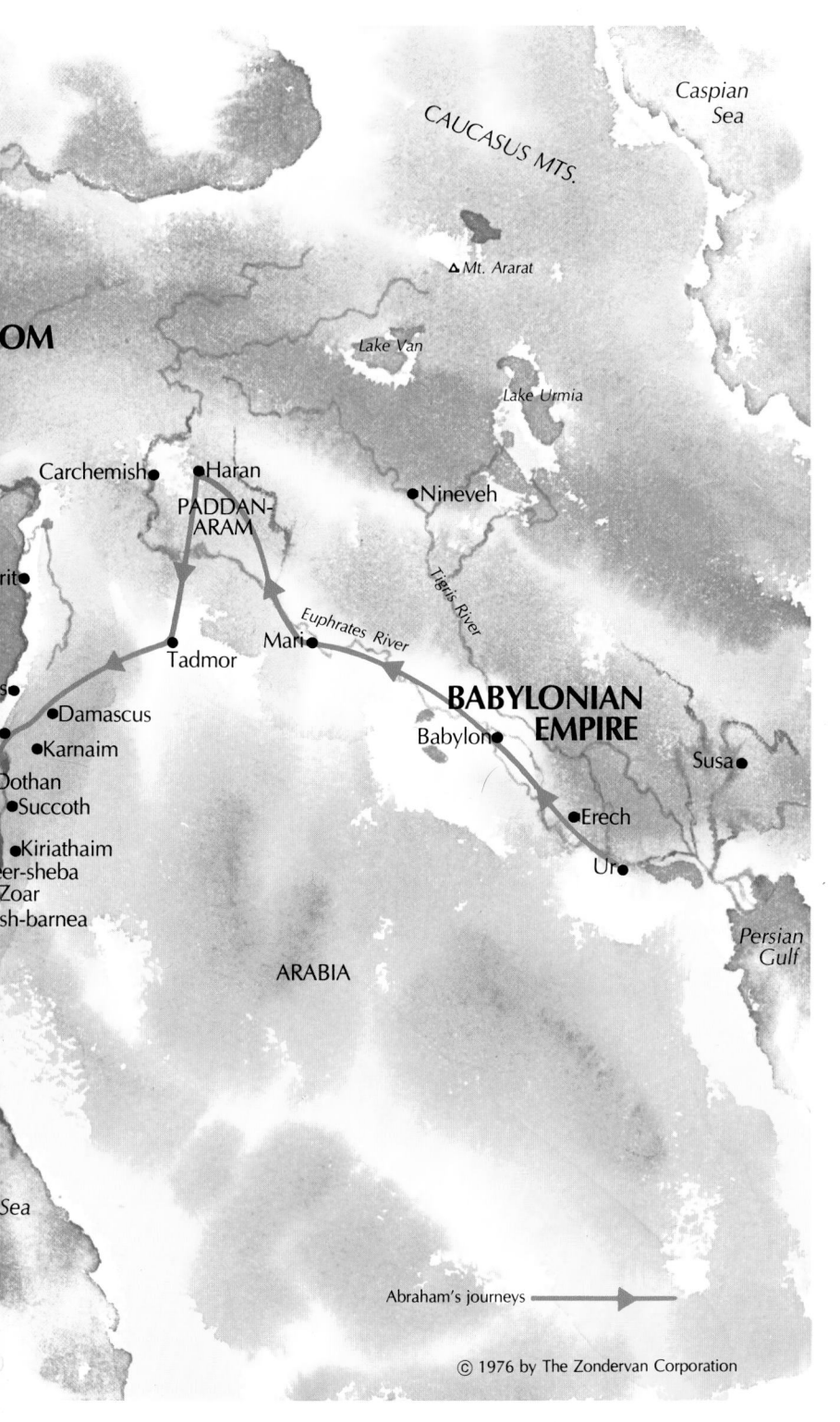

Caspian Sea

CAUCASUS MTS.

△ Mt. Ararat

Lake Van

Lake Urmia

OM

Carchemish●   ●Haran

PADDAN-
ARAM

●Nineveh

rit●

Tigris River

Euphrates River

Mari●

●Tadmor

BABYLONIAN
EMPIRE

●Damascus

s●

●Karnaim

Babylon●

Susa●

Dothan
●Succoth

●Kiriathaim
er-sheba
Zoar
sh-barnea

●Erech

Ur●

Persian
Gulf

ARABIA

Sea

Abraham's journeys ───▶

© 1976 by The Zondervan Corporation

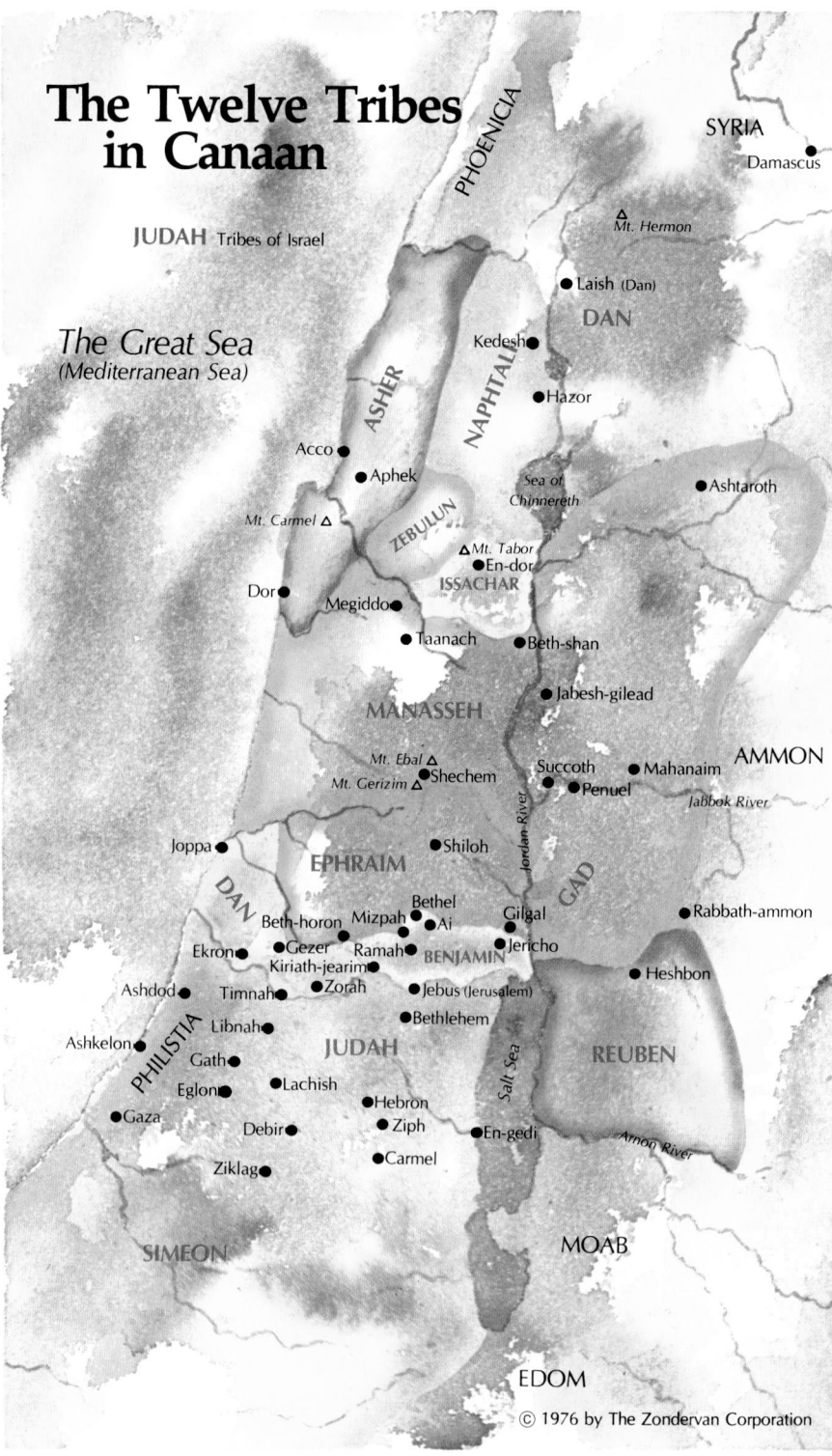

The Twelve Tribes in Canaan

SYRIA

Damascus

JUDAH Tribes of Israel

Mt. Hermon

Laish (Dan)

DAN

The Great Sea
(Mediterranean Sea)

Kedesh

ASHER

NAPHTALI

Hazor

Acco

Aphek

Sea of Chinnereth

Ashtaroth

Mt. Carmel △

ZEBULUN

△ Mt. Tabor
En-dor

ISSACHAR

Dor

Megiddo

Taanach

Beth-shan

Jabesh-gilead

MANASSEH

Mt. Ebal △
Mt. Gerizim △ Shechem

Succoth

Penuel

Mahanaim

AMMON

Jabbok River

Joppa

Shiloh

EPHRAIM

DAN

Bethel

Beth-horon Mizpah Ai

Gilgal

Rabbath-ammon

Ekron Gezer Ramah

Kiriath-jearim

Zorah

BENJAMIN

Jericho

Heshbon

Ashdod Timnah

Jebus (Jerusalem)

Ashkelon

Libnah

Bethlehem

REUBEN

PHILISTIA

Gath

JUDAH

Eglon Lachish

Gaza

Hebron

Debir Ziph

En-gedi

Arnon River

Ziklag

Carmel

Salt Sea

GAD

Jordan River

SIMEON

MOAB

EDON

Haleb

Possible extent of Solomon's empire Euphrates

Tiphsah

HAMATH

KITTIM
(CYPRUS)

Salamis

Hamath

Tadmor

Arvad

Kadesh
Riblah
Zedad
Hazar-enan

The Great Sea
(Mediterranean Sea)

Gebal

PHOENICIA

Berothai

ARAM-
DAMASCUS

Sidon

Damascus

Mt. Hermon

SYRIAN
DESERT

Tyre

Abel Dan
Kedesh

Acco

Hazor

Cabul

Ashtaroth

Dor

Megiddo

Nobah

Taanach

Beth-shan

Edrei
Ramoth-gilead

Mt. Gilboa

Salecah

Shechem

Jordan

Mahanaim
Succoth

AMMON

ISRAEL

Joppa

Gibeah

Rabbath-ammon

Jericho

Ashdod

Jerusalem

Heshbon

Ashkelon

Beth-
shemesh

Medeba

Gaza

PHILISTIA

Hebron

JUDAH

Dead Sea

Aroer

Raphia

Gerar

Ziklag

MOAB

Beer-sheba

Arad

Kir-hareseth

Tamar

EDOM

Bozrah

Kadesh-barnea

Punon

River of Egypt

Sela

The Empire of
David and Solomon

SINAI

Ezion-geber

Jerusalem in David's Time

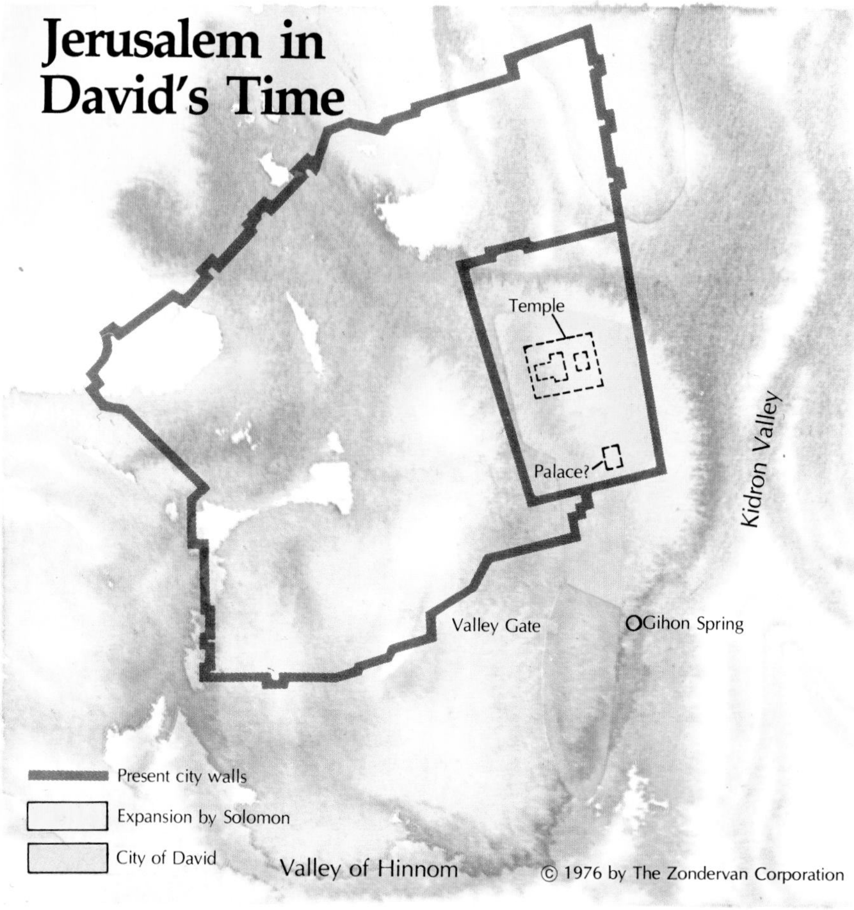

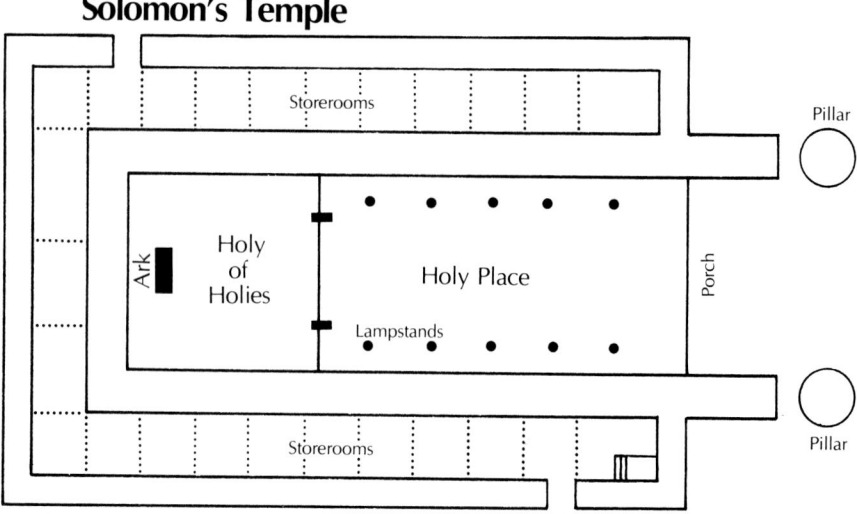

Temple

Palace?

Kidron Valley

Valley Gate

○ Gihon Spring

▬▬▬ Present city walls

Expansion by Solomon

City of David

Valley of Hinnom

© 1976 by The Zondervan Corporation

Solomon's Temple

Storerooms

Pillar

Ark

Holy of Holies

Holy Place

Lampstands

Porch

Storerooms

Pillar

© 1976 by The Zondervan Corporation

Sidon●

Damascus●

SYRIA

PHOENICIA

Tyre●

●Dan

The Great Sea
(Mediterranean Sea)

●Hazor

Acco●

●Ashtaroth

Dor● Megiddo●

Ramoth-gilead●

●Beth-shan

ISRAEL

Samaria●

●Penuel

Shechem●

Jordan River

Rabbath-ammon●

AMMON

Joppa●

●Heshbon

Gezer●

PHILISTIA

●Jerusalem

Ashdod●

Salt Sea

Ashkelon●

●Hebron

●Dibon

JUDAH

Gaza●

●Arad

Raphia●

●Beer-sheba

MOAB

●Kir-moab

Tamar●

EDOM

●Kadesh-barnea

●Bozrah

The Divided Kingdom

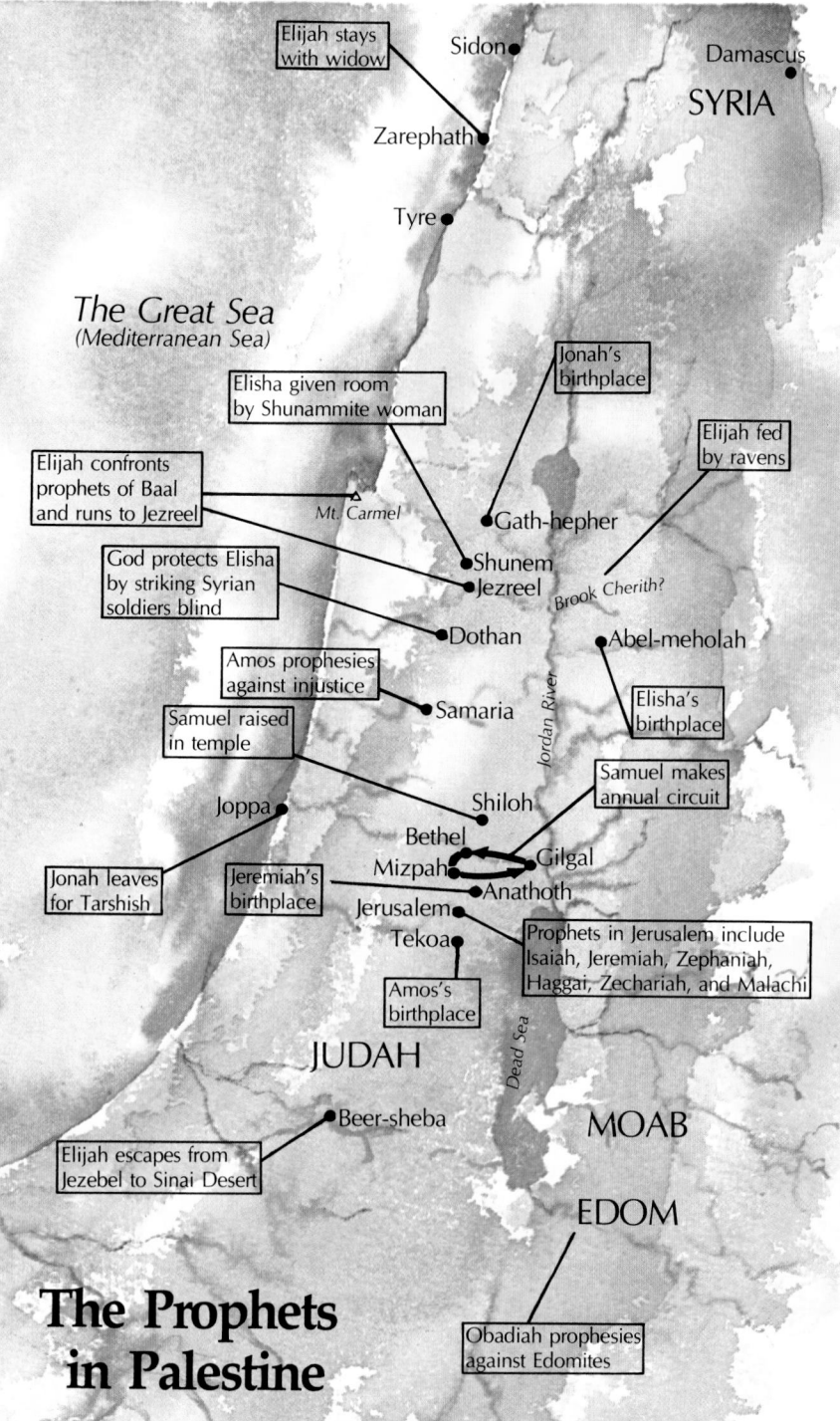

Elijah stays with widow

Sidon

Damascus

SYRIA

Zarephath

Tyre

The Great Sea
(Mediterranean Sea)

Jonah's birthplace

Elisha given room by Shunammite woman

Elijah fed by ravens

Elijah confronts prophets of Baal and runs to Jezreel

Mt. Carmel

Gath-hepher

God protects Elisha by striking Syrian soldiers blind

Shunem

Jezreel

Brook Cherith?

Dothan

Abel-meholah

Amos prophesies against injustice

Samaria

Elisha's birthplace

Jordan River

Samuel raised in temple

Shiloh

Samuel makes annual circuit

Joppa

Bethel

Gilgal

Jonah leaves for Tarshish

Jeremiah's birthplace

Mizpah

Anathoth

Jerusalem

Tekoa

Prophets in Jerusalem include Isaiah, Jeremiah, Zephaniah, Haggai, Zechariah, and Malachi

Amos's birthplace

JUDAH

Dead Sea

Beer-sheba

MOAB

Elijah escapes from Jezebel to Sinai Desert

EDOM

The Prophets in Palestine

Obadiah prophesies against Edomites

© 1976 by The Zondervan Corporation

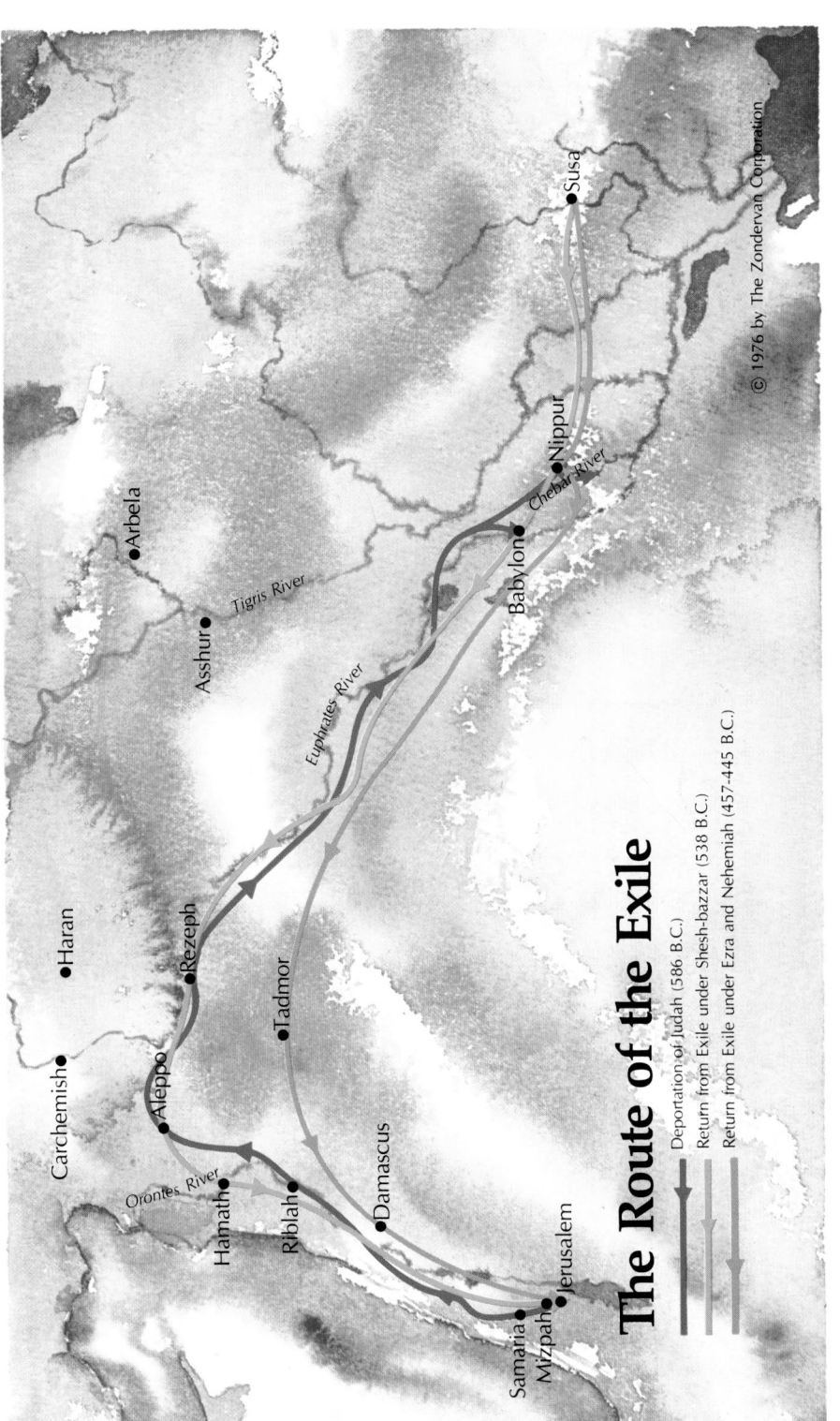

The Route of the Exile

Deportation of Judah (586 B.C.)

Return from Exile under Shesh-bazzar (538 B.C.)

Return from Exile under Ezra and Nehemiah (457-445 B.C.)

Susa

Nippur

Arbela

Chebar River

Babylon

Asshur

Tigris River

Euphrates River

Haran

Rezeph

Tadmor

Carchemish

Aleppo

Damascus

Orontes River

Hamath

Riblah

Jerusalem

Samaria

Mizpah

© 1976 by The Zondervan Corporation

SYRIA

Tyre•

GALILEE

Capernaum• •Bethsaida

•Cana Sea of
Galilee

Mediterranean Sea

Nazareth•

•Nain •Gadara

Caesarea•

SAMARIA

DECAPOLIS

•Sychar

Joppa•

•Arimathea

Jericho•

Jerusalem• •Bethany PEREA

•Bethlehem

JUDEA

•Gaza

Dead
Sea

IDUMEA

Jordan River

Palestine in Jesus' Time

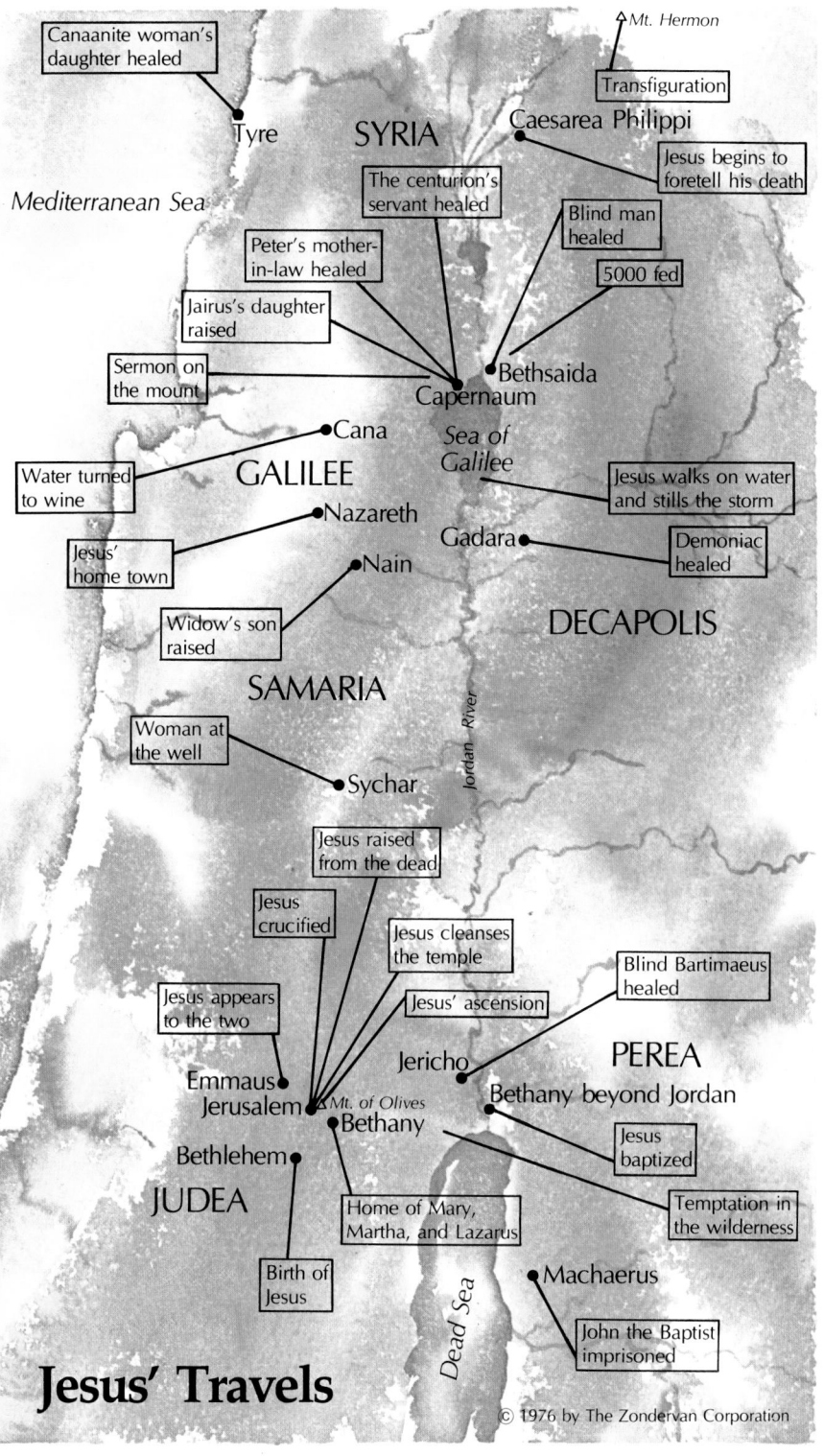

Canaanite woman's daughter healed

Transfiguration

△Mt. Hermon

Tyre

SYRIA

Caesarea Philippi

Mediterranean Sea

Jesus begins to foretell his death

The centurion's servant healed

Blind man healed

Peter's mother-in-law healed

5000 fed

Jairus's daughter raised

Sermon on the mount

●Bethsaida

Capernaum

●Cana

Sea of Galilee

GALILEE

Water turned to wine

Jesus walks on water and stills the storm

●Nazareth

Jesus' home town

Gadara●

Demoniac healed

●Nain

DECAPOLIS

Widow's son raised

SAMARIA

Jordan River

Woman at the well

●Sychar

Jesus raised from the dead

Jesus crucified

Jesus cleanses the temple

Blind Bartimaeus healed

Jesus appears to the two

Jesus' ascension

Jericho

PEREA

Emmaus●

Jerusalem

●

△Mt. of Olives

●Bethany

Bethany beyond Jordan

Jesus baptized

Bethlehem●

Home of Mary, Martha, and Lazarus

Temptation in the wilderness

JUDEA

Birth of Jesus

Dead Sea

●Machaerus

John the Baptist imprisoned

Jesus' Travels

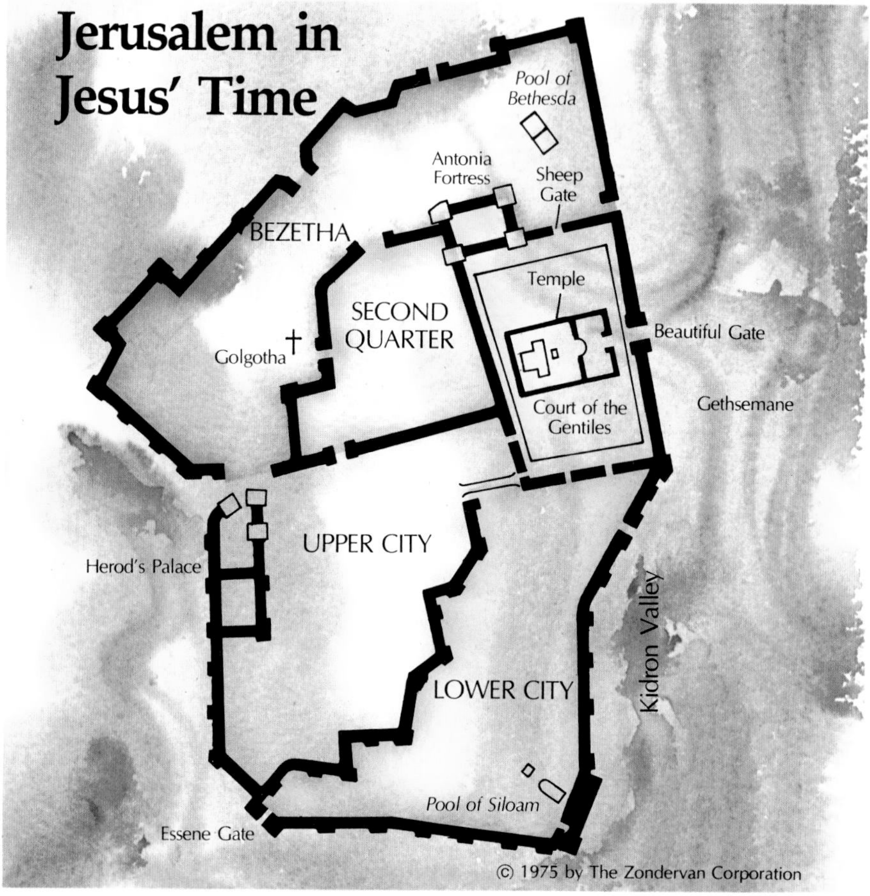

Jerusalem in Jesus' Time

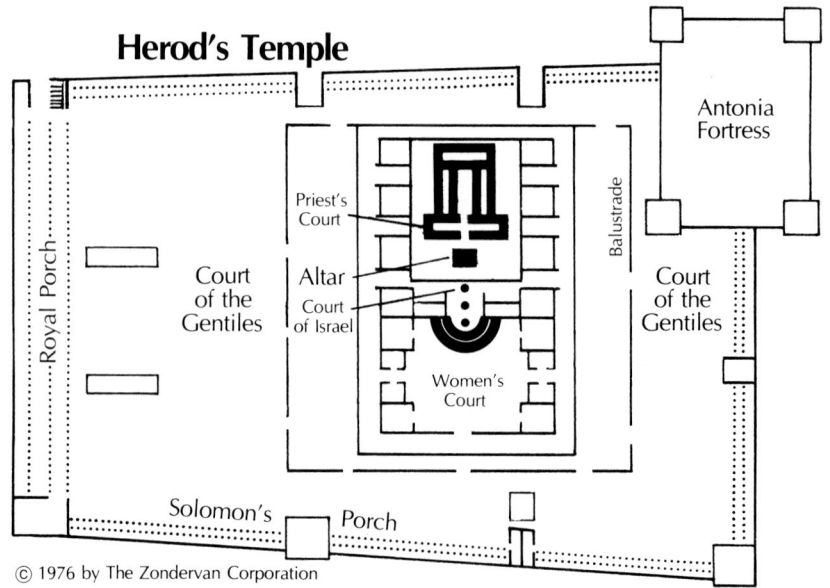

Pool of Bethesda

Antonia Fortress

Sheep Gate

BEZETHA

Temple

SECOND QUARTER

Golgotha

Beautiful Gate

Court of the Gentiles

Gethsemane

UPPER CITY

Herod's Palace

Kidron Valley

LOWER CITY

Pool of Siloam

Essene Gate

© 1975 by The Zondervan Corporation

Herod's Temple

Antonia Fortress

Royal Porch

Court of the Gentiles

Priest's Court

Altar

Court of Israel

Balustrade

Court of the Gentiles

Women's Court

Solomon's Porch

© 1976 by The Zondervan Corporation

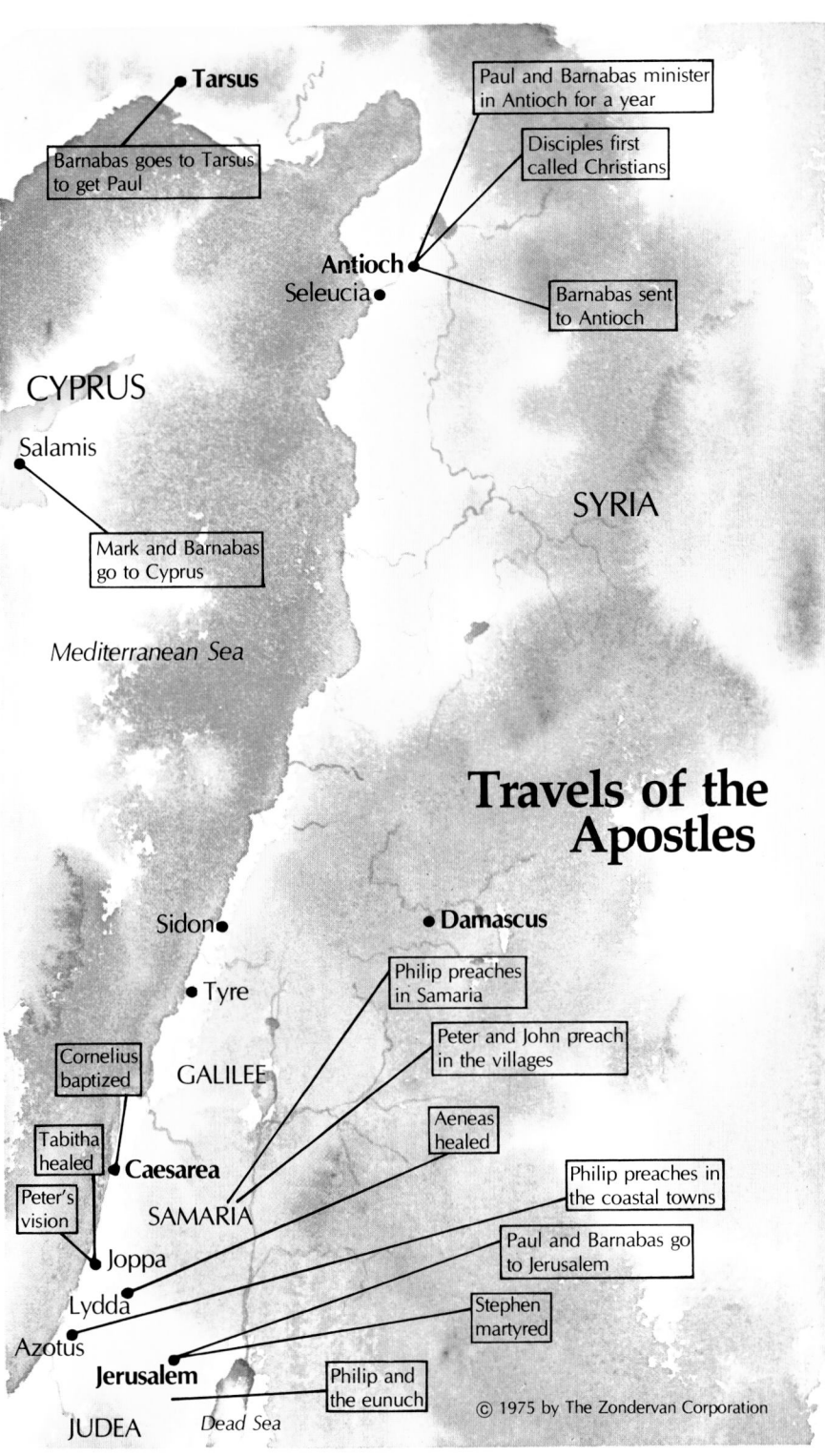

Tarsus

Barnabas goes to Tarsus to get Paul

Paul and Barnabas minister in Antioch for a year

Disciples first called Christians

Antioch
Seleucia

Barnabas sent to Antioch

CYPRUS

Salamis

Mark and Barnabas go to Cyprus

SYRIA

Mediterranean Sea

Travels of the Apostles

Sidon

Damascus

Tyre

Philip preaches in Samaria

Peter and John preach in the villages

Cornelius baptized

GALILEE

Aeneas healed

Tabitha healed

Caesarea

Philip preaches in the coastal towns

Peter's vision

SAMARIA

Paul and Barnabas go to Jerusalem

Joppa

Lydda

Stephen martyred

Azotus

Jerusalem

Philip and the eunuch

© 1975 by The Zondervan Corporation

JUDEA   Dead Sea

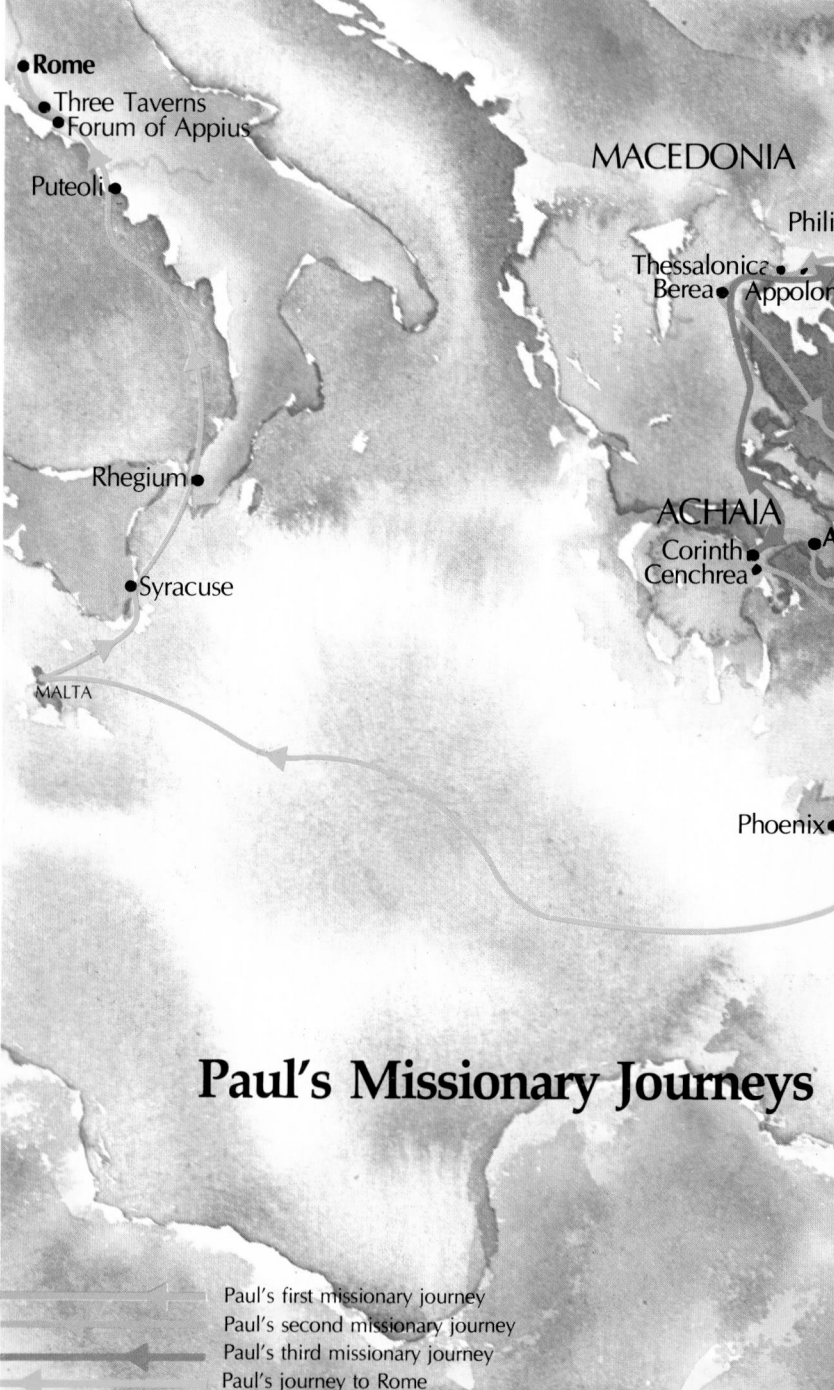

●**Rome**
●Three Taverns
●Forum of Appius

Puteoli●

MACEDONIA

Philipp

Thessalonica● ● ●A
Berea● Appolonia

Rhegium●

ACHAIA
Corinth● ●Ath
Cenchrea●

●Syracuse

MALTA

Phoenix● (

Paul's Missionary Journeys

Paul's first missionary journey
Paul's second missionary journey
Paul's third missionary journey
Paul's journey to Rome

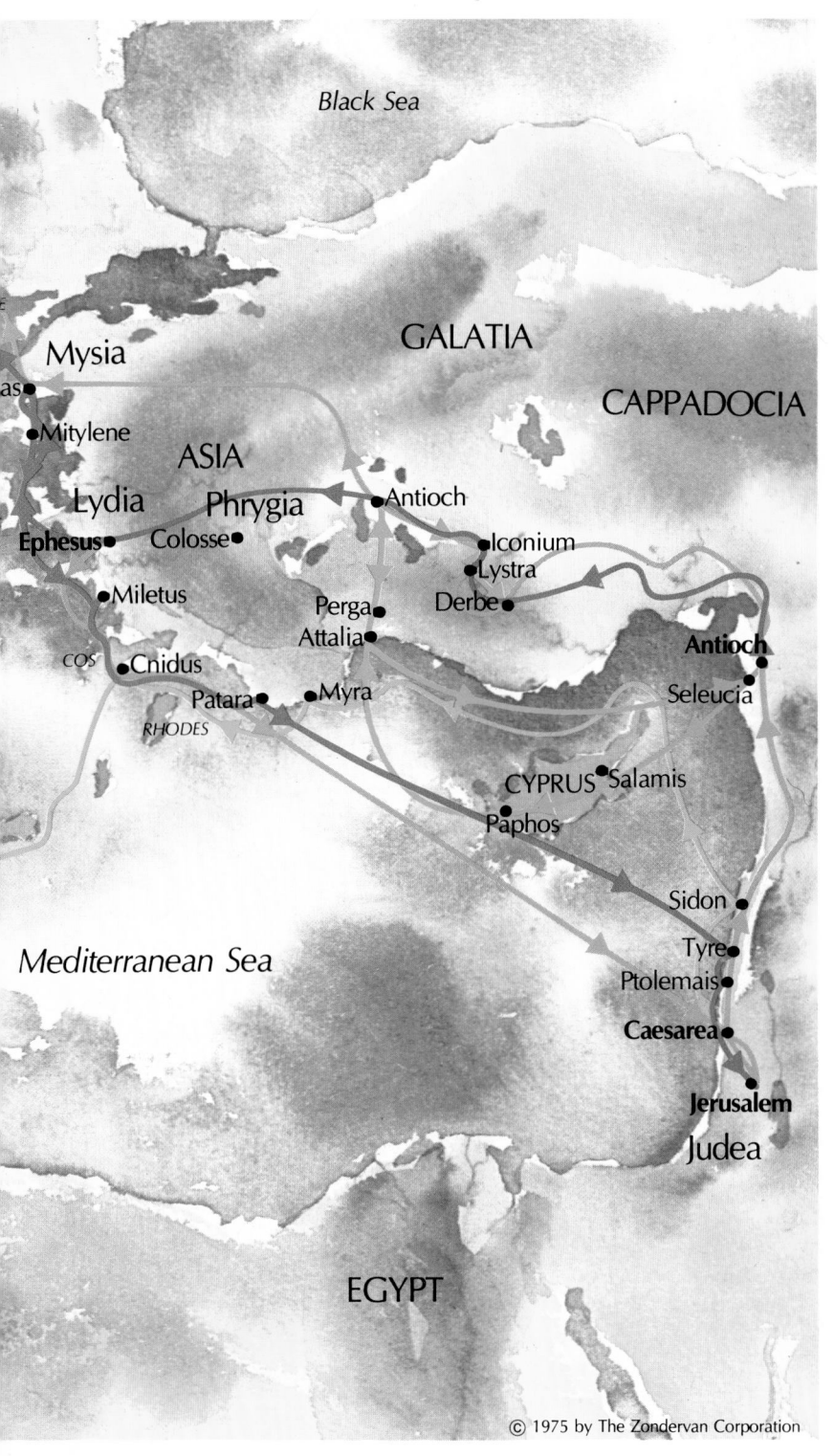

Black Sea

Mysia

as

Mitylene

Lydia

ASIA

Phrygia

GALATIA

CAPPADOCIA

Antioch

Iconium

Lystra

Ephesus

Colosse

Miletus

Derbe

Perga

Attalia

Antioch

Seleucia

COS

Cnidus

Patara

Myra

RHODES

CYPRUS

Salamis

Paphos

Sidon

Tyre

Ptolemais

Caesarea

Jerusalem

Judea

Mediterranean Sea

EGYPT

The Roman Empire

BRITAIN

GERMANY

GAUL

SPAIN

MAURETANIA

Atlantic Ocean

ITALY
Rome

ILLYRICUM

MACEDONIA

ACHAIA

THRACE

DACIA

Black Sea

ARMENIA

CAPPADOCIA

ASIA

Mediterranean Sea

AFRICA

SYRIA

Jerusalem

Alexandria

EGYPT

MESOPOTAMIA

PARTHIA

ARABIA

Red Sea

© 1976 by The Zondervan Corporation

9014

Fresh start	2 Cor 5:17	"He is a new creation..."
Subst. Abuse	1 Cor 6:19	"Your body is the temple of The Holy Spirit
Forgiveness	1 John 1:9	If we confess our sins, he is faithful & just...
Prayer	Rom 8:26	The spirit intercedes w/ sighs ...
Troubles	Jn 16:32-33	In the world you have tribulation
Value	Mt. 6:26	Look at the birds... Your father feeds them
"	Mt 10:29	Are not two sparrows sold for a penny (Lk 12:6)
Burdens	Mt. 11:28	Come unto me, all who labor & are heavily laden
Life	John 7:37	He who believes in me... rivers of living water
Sin	Rom 3:23	For all have sinned, and fall short of the glory...
Jesus	I Tim 2:5	There is one god, and one mediator ...
God's love	John 3:16	For god so loved the world...
Scripture	2 Tim 3:16	All scripture is inspired by God.
Faith	Heb 11:6	He is a rewarder of those who seek Him.
Temptation	I Cor 10:13	God... will not allow you to be tempted...
Pride	I Cor 10:12	Let him who thinks he stands take heed...
Judgment	II Cor 5:10	For we must all appear before the judg. seat...
Eternal Life	Jn. 17:3	This is eternal life, that they may know thee ...
Jesus = God	Jn 5:18	... making himself equal with God.
Falling away	Heb. 6:4-8	for once having tasted of the heavenly gift...
	Heb 10:26	

Lauren Hendrickson
Pat McCabe
Richard Vocks